NEW
WEBSTER'S
DICTIONARY
of the English Language

HANDY SCHOOL AND OFFICE EDITION

elair
PUBLISHING COMPANY INC.

Contents

Guide to the Use of This Dictionary v

New Words xxii

Dictionary of the English Language 1

Metric System 619

Periodic Table of Elements 620

Punctuation 621

Staff

A Guide to the Use of This Dictionary

Introduction

Your dictionary is one of the most comprehensive language tools that you are likely to use. Within its covers is a wealth of information, but that very wealth sometimes makes it difficult to use the book. The purpose of this guide is to introduce you to the means that your dictionary makes available to you for understanding and using language.

To get the most out of the dictionary, you first need to understand what you want from it. To do this, you will have to formulate your questions as clearly as you can. Since you cannot carry on a conversation with a book, the job of asking the right questions and asking for the right information is up to you. This "user's guide" is designed to help you develop skill in asking good questions that can be answered by the NEW WEBSTER'S DICTIONARY OF THE ENGLISH LANGUAGE.

Just so you do not think that all of your success in using this dictionary depends on what you do, let us hasten to add that what this dictionary can offer to you is as important as what you ask of it. For that reason, this "user's guide" will also introduce you to the kinds of information and source material that can be found within a dictionary. This dictionary offers an enormous amount of information, *if* you know how to use it. But its compactness can be a disadvantage until you find the way to unlock its potential and, by so doing, extend your own potential for using the English language.

WHAT IS A DICTIONARY?

In order for you to make full use of the resources in the NEW WEBSTER'S DICTIONARY, you must have some idea of what those resources are. A dictionary can offer you much help with your language, but *you* have to search out that help. The tool called a *dictionary,* like all tools, does nothing for you until you pick it up and use it with some understanding of how it works and what it is designed to do.

First of all, a dictionary is a collection of words. But it is a very special collection, put together with great care. Modern dictionaries are not written by a single scholar tucked away in a dusty room full of books. The people who compile dictionaries are language experts from a large number of fields. Some are historians of language, some are specialists in foreign languages, some are experts in the special vocabularies of medicine, or science, or literature, and so on. A large number of learned men and women contribute to the making of a dictionary, because no one person could possibly know enough about a language to collect and organize more than a small sample of it.

Dictionary users are a varied group, consisting of writers, scientists, students, and readers in all subjects; therefore, a handy, usable dictionary for many people will have to include a wide selection of entries. Linguists have estimated that the English language may include as many as three million separate words—if you counted all the separate compounds and inflected forms. However, the average English-speaking high school graduate understands probably between ten thousand and thirty thousand words.

If a dictionary is a collection of words, it might seem, then, that the best collection would be those ten thousand to thirty thousand most-used words. There are, in fact, pocket-size dictionaries that have about this number of entries. The problem remains, however, that not all speakers of the language use the same words. Also, if we all used exactly the same set of words, and read or wrote the same set of words, there would never be a need to consult a dictionary for definitions. Your vocabulary would be interchangeable with the vocabulary of every other speaker of the language.

Of course, this is impossible. We are all different—in the way we learned language, in our interests, and in our experience and education. Our vocabularies are not the same, and even the most knowledgeable person can discover unfamiliar words whose meanings (and spellings and pronunciations) he does not know.

The dictionary writers must, then, make the very difficult decision of how large a collection of words to include, as well as deciding what words from what disciplines to include. Such decisions are based on studies of how people use language and dictionaries.

The writers (called *editors* or *lexicographers*) of the NEW WEBSTER'S have decided that a collection of about sixty thousand entries (separately listed words) would meet the needs of most people who use a dictionary. They selected enough words to include the basic thirty thousand word vocabularies of most educated adults. To that basic list they added the approximately thirty thousand words that have been shown to be those most often looked for in a hand-sized dictionary.

satisfied. A similar exploration could come from picking a topic or area of interest, making a list of related words, and looking up the same information (definitional and grammatical) for each word. A comparison of your pieces of information should prove to be enlightening.

Next, choose a very common word, one you are sure you know well, such as *door, house,* or *man,* and consult the listing for it in the dictionary. You will probably be impressed with the many different definitions given for such "simple" words.

door, dôr, *n.* An opening or passage into a room, house, or building by which persons enter and leave; a solid barrier that covers the opening of a cabinet, room, or the like, usu. opening and closing by means of hinges or by sliding in a groove; a means of approach or access. —**next door to,** near to. —**out of doors,** out of the house; in the open air.

house, hows, *n. pl.,* **hous•es,** howzʹiz. A building where people live; a habitation, esp. of a single family; a structure used for any purpose, as worship, entertainment, assemblage, eating, storage, keeping animals, or growing plants; an audience; the building in which a legislative body of government meets; *(cap.)* the body itself; a business establishment; *(often cap.)* a family consisting of ancestors and descendants —howz, *v.t.,* **housed, hous•ing.** To put or receive into a house; provide with a house; to give shelter to; harbor; lodge.

man, man, *n. pl.,* **men.** A human being, particularly a male adult; the human species; a male servant; a husband; any human individual; a piece with which a game is played.—*v.t.,* **manned, man•ning.** To supply with men; to assume one's position or station at, on, or in.—*interj. Informal.* An exclamation of surprise or enthusiasm.

GETTING THE MOST OUT OF YOUR DICTIONARY

Getting Acquainted

The resources of your dictionary are so varied that if you would like to get the most out of this language tool, you should spend a few hours becoming acquainted with it. A good way to start is simply to pick a favorite word and locate it in the main listings. Note the pronunciation and other information. Does the listed word suggest other related words that could be consulted? Do the definition or definitions that are given tell you something new about your word? Follow this lead to another word, or perhaps to several more words, until you come to a blind end, or until you feel your curiosity is

After looking at a few words in your exploration, shift your focus to the dictionary itself and its numerous parts. If you prefer the methodical approach, you might start with the table of contents on page 5 and leaf through the sections one by one to the end of the volume. If you prefer the adventurous approach, you might choose to open the volume at any point and thumb through it at random.

Developing the Dictionary Habit

Your dictionary can be helpful to you only if you use it and use it regularly. Keep it at hand where you are most likely to use it, in the room where you study, read, or write. Consult your NEW WEBSTER'S often and learn how to use it quickly and confidently.

(1) Go through the getting-acquainted process discussed in earlier sections.

(2) Learn how to use the guide words that appear at the top of each page. They show the first or last entry on that page and a quick scanning of them will let you flip quickly through the pages to the word you want.

(3) Develop a system for deciding when to look up the definition of an unfamiliar word. Here are some suggestions you may want to use:

(a) Do not feel that you must look up every single unfamiliar word when reading for general information or pleasure.

(b) When reading technical material, look up the unfamiliar word the first time you meet it; it is probably important and might appear again.

(c) When studying a subject or topic, look carefully at the special definitions, derived forms, and synonyms. Such word study will often help tie together ideas and facts on your topic.

(d) When writing, use the dictionary to check spellings and meanings of which you are unsure; but if you can, wait to look up words when you are polishing what you have written for public view. Interruptions may break up the flow of your thought.

Using the Dictionary for Daily Language Growth

After childhood, language is probably best and most easily developed by a process of interested exploration. If you already do crossword puzzles, you probably have much of the curiosity about language that leads to a mature use of it.

Many other ways are open for the person who wants to extend his knowledge and control of his language. One basic fact, however, influences language growth—active use of language in a shared language experience, such as the following:

(1) Writing to others

(2) Reading a book and talking about it with someone

(3) Preparing an oral presentation for a group

(4) Listening to, analyzing, and classifying the language used in the world around you

If you work at them, all of these active language experiences will bring liveliness and precision to your own use of language.

The significant factor in developing your personal control of your language is an open, inquisitive mind. Listen for new, strange, unusual, or particularly fitting words. Make notes, mental or written, on the language you hear. This may become a kind of personal word collection or personal dictionary. Notice variations and differences in the language you and others use.

Keep in mind that your dictionary is a tool, but that you are the user who is in control of it. Language, yours and other people's, is constantly changing. Your dictionary will help you become aware of that change and use it to your advantage.

Why Have a Dictionary?

Most of us buy a dictionary expecting to improve our knowledge of language or at least to avoid making serious language mistakes. We also may have the idea that regular use of a dictionary will bring some improvement in the way we speak and in the way we write. This is quite a bit to ask of any book, but a dictionary like the NEW WEBSTER'S will probably meet these expectations if frequently used.

When you use a dictionary, you seek certain kinds of help. You may look up the meaning of an unfamiliar word, or you may try to determine how a word is pronounced. When you are writing, the dictionary becomes an aid to correct spelling and proper use of words. You may go to the dictionary to try to locate a word that you cannot quite remember but that you know will be perfect for saying what you want to say. The dictionary is a place to go to settle arguments, whether in a word game, a spelling bee, or a more serious language controversy.

A GUIDE TO USING ENTRIES IN THIS DICTIONARY

A brief look through this guide for information on how words appear in your dictionary will help you to use your dictionary more effectively. Consider what you must do to use the dictionary. First you have to spell and find the word or entry about which you want information. Then you will want to determine either the word's pronunciation or its meaning, or both. Finally, you may also want to have certain information about the usage and grammatical status of the entry word.

Answering these initial questions may pose a problem. For example, how do you use the dictionary to find the spelling of a word if you cannot spell it well enough to locate it? What do you do if your pronunciation of English doesn't seem to agree with the pronunciation given after each bold-face main-entry word? How do you choose the correct definition for a word from among the four or five that may be listed?

All of these questions can be dealt with in a systematic manner if you are ready to spend some time learning how to use your dictionary. The sections that follow will attempt to show you how, with a little practice, you can develop skills for answering these and similar questions. The skills that will be covered include four major kinds: (1) locating, and spelling, entries; (2) pronouncing words; (3) locating other information about words; and (4) finding definitions and meanings. Each of these four sections, along with some general aids and discussions of dictionaries, will provide hints for using the dictionary, ways of expanding your knowledge of the language, and examples of things to do with a dictionary that will be of benefit to you in school, at work, and at home.

Spelling and Locating Words

Locating words in a dictionary may seem to be extremely simple or very difficult, depending on the number of times you have looked up words like *phaeton* under *f* or *knurl* as though it were spelled *nurl*.

The problem comes from the occasional differences between the way we pronounce and the way we spell our English sounds. The location problem then becomes one of translating the sounds that you say into letters you can connect into groups to make words, which you then look for in the dictionary's alphabetical arrangement.

All you need are a few uncomplicated rules that will get you started with the most likely spelling of the beginning of a strange word. Once you have that, you can locate the general neighborhood of the entry you are seeking.

From there on you can probably search quickly through a fairly small number of entries to find the word you want.

The first assumption you must make is that by far the greatest part of the English language is *consistent* in its spelling. Furthermore, this consistency is greatest in the initial parts of words where a consonant is usually the first sound and letter to appear. Therefore, your first job in locating a word you cannot spell is to listen to and identify the beginning consonants and vowels.

For example, if you were to hear an actor described as a *mime* (which rhymes with *lime*), you probably could pick out the beginning sequence of sounds with the matching letters *m, i,* and *m* and possibly the final silent *e*. When you pick out those sounds and the letters that represent them, you are using your basic knowledge of the English spelling system. You probably already know that *m* is usually used to spell the sound /m/* at the beginnings of words. There is, perhaps, only one exception, in the word *mnemonics* ("pertaining to the memory") where the initial *m* is not pronounced. In the same way, the /ī/ sound, pronounced as in *lime,* is usually represented by the letter *i*. Possibly these "spelling rules" are something you never learned deliberately, but you may already use them quite automatically.

How does all this help you spell and find words in the dictionary? First, your understanding of the rules of spelling enables you to make some pretty good guesses about spelling from just hearing or sounding out the word you seek. When you have developed your best guess about the word, you can go to the dictionary, look for that word among the entries, and see how close your guess was to being right.

Making guesses of this kind about the spelling of English words will probably require some detailed information about the spelling system. The following set of simple guides to and examples of spelling will give you most of the necessary information.

SPELLING AND LOCATION GUIDES

These are practical rules for figuring out, from the sound of a word, the way it is likely to be spelled. The guides will not give correct spellings in all cases, but they will come close enough to allow you to find most words in the dictionary.

The rules should be applied in the order given until the user is familiar with them. Later, when you are familiar with them, use them in any order that makes sense to you.

All these rules start from the sounds of words and syllables within words. The basic task is as follows: *first,* hear the the word you want to use; *second,*

try to spell the sounds you have heard; *third,* locate the word you have spelled in the dictionary; and *fourth,* try other possible spellings if your first try is not correct. The following are rules for each of these four steps:

Hear the Word you Want to Use

(1) Break the word down into sound syllables if there is more than one syllable in the word.

(2) Syllables in English are generally separated by a brief pause or a cutting off of the air flow somewhere in the vocal chords, the mouth, or at the lips.

(3) Each syllable in English has a single vowel or voice sound in the center of the syllable, as in the examples:

pan	pet	slip	hop	cut
V	V	V	V	V

In this example, V means vowel or voice sound.

(4) Syllables usually have consonant sounds at the beginning and end. Consonants do not appear in the center part of the syllable.

pan	pet	slip	hop	cut
C C	C C	CC C	C C	C C

In this example, C means consonant. There is more about consonants in following paragraphs.

(5) The common pattern for sound syllables in English is shown by the following diagram:

CVC
sat

The beginning sound is a consonant, the middle sound is a vowel, and the ending sound is a consonant. Examples of the CVC syllable pattern are:

pan	pop	rat	gab	dip	
sir	had	tin	dub	rip	
man	kep	nut	con	set	fen

There are thousands of syllables like this in English.

(6) Other common patterns of sound syllables are illustrated in

the following examples:

V	a,o,I	
VC	an, it, on	
VCC	elk, old	
CV	by, me	
CCV	pro, cry	
CCVC	slip, prim, grip	
CCVCC	cramp, glint, plant	
CCCV	stro, scra (only as parts of longer words)	
CCCVC	scrap, strip	

/m/	m	**m**an
/n/	n	**n**ut
/p/	p	**p**ut
/r/	r	**r**at
/s/	s	**s**it
/sh/	sh	**sh**y
/t/	t	**t**op
/th/	th	**th**in
/ᵺ/	th	**th**is
/v/	v	**v**est
/w/	w	**w**in

These vowel and consonant sounds are combined in a great number of ways to make the words we use. A little practice in hearing and naming the CVC, CCV, CCVCC, etc., patterns will make them easily recognizable.

(7) The principal vowel sounds of English are found in the pronunciation guide at the bottom of each right-hand page. Notice that there are many vowel sounds that have more than one spelling. The alternate ways of spelling many vowel and consonant sounds will be shown in the following paragraphs.

Try to Spell the Sounds You Hear

(1) Supply a consonant letter for each consonant sound you have heard in the first syllable of the word you are working with.

(2) Use the guide rule that consonants usually come at the beginning and end of syllables.

(3) The following consonant sounds are spelled in a regular way (with the same letters) most of the time:

sound	letter(s)	example
/b/	b	**b**id
/ch/	ch	**ch**art
/d/	d	**d**og
/f/	f	**f**at
/g/	g	**g**un
/h/	h	**h**am
/j/	j	**j**am
/k/	c, k	**c**atch, **k**ing
/ks/	x	e**x**cuse
/ku/	cu	**cu**te
/kw/	qu	**qu**it
/l/	l	**l**et

(4) Try first to spell those consonant sounds that are regular, appearing in the above list. Write down your trial spellings for the first syllable, if you want to keep track of them.

(5) Try the following additional sounds and variations from the above spellings when they match with sounds you have heard:

sound	letter(s)	example and comments
/b/	bb	*bubble* (in middle of a word of two or more syllables)
/ch/	t	*nature* (begins unaccented syllable)
/ch/	tch	*watchful* (in some words, at end of accented syllable)
/d/	dd	*ladder* (in middle of word of two or more syllables and at the end of a few others, like *add* and *odd*)
/d/	ld	*could, would, solder*
/f/	ff	*effort, differ* (in middle of words of two or more syllables and at end of a few words, like *stuff, cuff, ruff, puff*)
/f/	ft	*soften, often*
/f/	gh	*enough, tough, laugh*

/f/	lf	*half, calf*
/f/	ph	*phonograph* (and in many other words that use Greek root words, such as *sphere, phone, photo, physic, graph*)
/g/	gg	*wiggle, egg*
/g/	gh	*ghost, ghetto, sorghum*, and a few others
/g/	gu	*guard, guise*
/g/	gue	*league, morgue, intrigue.*
/hw/	wh	*what, where, why*
/j/	d	*educate* (always before /ū/)
/j/	dge	*edge* (at ends of words only; becomes *dg* with an added ending, as in *edging*)
/j/	g	*gender, gist*
/k/	ck	*stocking* (and following a short vowel in many words of one syllable, such as *stock*)
/k/	ch	*chlorine* (in a number of terms coming from Greek)
/k/	qu	*physique* (and a few other words)
/k/	lk	*folk, walk, talk*
/l/	ll	*hill* (following short vowels *e,i,o* and *u* at ends of words)
/l/	sl	*island* (and related words)
/m/	mb	*climb, comb, dumb*
/m/	mm	*summer* (between two syllables)
/m/	mn	*hymn* (and a few other words)
/n/	gn	*gnaw, align, reign*
/n/	kn	*knee, knurl*
/n/	nn	*sunny* (always between two syllables, usually a word ending with -*y*, -*ing*, etc.)
/ng/	ng	*bang* (at end of syllable or word)
/p/	pp	*approve, supply* (between two syllables)
/r/	rr	*arrest, marriage* (between two syllables)
/r/	wr	*wrist, awry*
/s/	ss	*fuss* (at endings of words, especially after /a/, /e/, and between two syllables)
/s/	c	*dance* (never at end of a word—usually followed by vowel letters *i* and *e*)
/s/	sc	*science*
/sh/	ci	*racial* (in a number of words with -*cial*, -*cious*, -*cian*, and -*ciate* endings)
/sh/	ch	*machine* (and a few other words of French origin)
/sh/	s	*insure* (usually before /ū/)
/sh/	ssi	*compassion* (usually in words with -*ion* added after -*ss* or -*t* ending or base word with a -*t* changed to -*ss*)
/sh/	ti	*direction* (in -*ation*, -*otion*, -*ction*, -*ution* combinations and -*tial* and -*tiate* combinations)
/t/	ed	*stopped* (only in final position as an added part of a word)
/t/	bt	*doubt, debt, subtle*
/t/	tt	*forgotten* (and before other endings such as -*ed*,

-er, -ing, etc; also after words beginning with *a,* like *attack*)

sound	letter(s)	example and comments
/v/	lv	*calves, halves*
/y/	i	*million* (and other *-ion, -ier,* and *-ian* combinations between two syllables)
/y/	y	*yarn* (at beginning of word or after *w,* as in *lawyer*)
/z/	es	*wolves* (as plural ending on many words)
/z/	s	*rose* (most common spelling—usually at end *-se* or between two single vowels, as in *desert*)
/z/	ss	*dessert* (and in a few other words, like *dissolve, possess*)
/z/	z	*idealize* (commonly in *-ize* combination and at beginnings of words like *zero*)
/z/	zz	*buzz* (and a few other words, like *dazzle* and *fuzzy*)
/zh/	si	*decision* (in *-sion* ending combination)
/zh/	g	*regime*
/zh/	s	*exposure* (in *-sure* endings, except in *azure* and *seizure*)

(6) Other syllables will generally be spelled with groups of consonants (as in the CCVC, CCCVCC patterns).

(7) Try to supply a vowel letter for each vowel sound in the syllables you have heard. The following listing shows the most common ways of spelling each of the vowel sounds. Consult the pronunciation key at the bottom of each right-hand page for further help in working with the pronunciation markings.

Vowel Pronunciation Key

sound	letter(s)	example and comments
/a/	a	*fat* (very few exceptions, such as *plaid*)
/ā/	a	*paper* (usually in accented syllables, often before *-tion* combination or in words with silent final *e,* such as *fate*)
/ā/	ai	*aim* (and a number of other words)
/ā/	ay	*essay* (at endings of words only)
/ā/	ea, ei, eigh, et, ey	*steak, vein, eight, ballet, obey* (other less common spellings of /ā/ sound)
/ā/	a	*fare* (often with final *-e* or in combination with *r,* as in *varied*)
/ā/	e	*where, there* (and in compounds of them)
/ä/	a	*far, palm, mark,* (most common spelling)
/ä/	au, ea	*laugh, heart* (uncommon or rare spellings of /ä/ sound)
/e/	e	*met* (most common spelling)
	ea	*head* (often in combination with *-d,* as in *bread*)

	ie	*friend* (rarely used spelling)
/ē/	e	*me* (most common spelling. often used in combination with silent -e-, as in *here*)
	ea	*repeat* (only used in single-syllable word or the accented syllable of other words)
	ee	*agree* (often at end of words like *tree;* also in a small number of very commonly used words, like *green, need, seen,* and *bleed*)
	y	*partly* ⎫ (less
	ey	*honey* ⎬ commonly
	ei	*ceiling* ⎪ used
	i	*fatigue* ⎭ spellings of /ē/ sound)
/ə(r)/	e(r)	*her* (this sound is also produced by such combinations as -ir, -or, and -ur.)
/i/	i	*pin* (used in almost all places where /i/ sound occurs)
	ie	*mischief* ⎫ (less
	ui	*guilty* ⎬ common
	y	*gyp* ⎪ or rare-
	ei	*foreign* ⎭ ly used spellings of /i/ sound)
/ī/	i	*China, pine* (most common spelling of /ī/ sound, used frequently where final silent -e appears)
	igh	*sight, might, light* (and a few other common words)

	y	*try, unify, by* (commonly at the end of a word)
/ī/	ye	*lye* ⎫ (uncommon
	uy	*buy* ⎬ spelling
	ie	*pie* ⎪ of /ī/,
	ei	*stein* ⎭ sound)
	eye	*eye* (only word with this spelling)
/o/	o	*not, copy* (most common spelling—only a few exceptions)
/o/	a	*swap, squat* (generally used in combinations wa- or qua-, but never at ends of words)
/ō/	o	*note, told* (most common spelling, often used in combination with final silent -e on ends of words)
/ō/	oa	*boat, goal* (a spelling used for a limited number of very common and usually single syllable words)
/ôr/	or	*fort, cordovan, more*
/ôr/	ou	*four, mourn* (uncommon spelling—always used in the middle of words)
/ō/	ow	*blow, show* (usually at endings of words or base forms of words — exceptions include *bowl, toward,* and *owe*)

Sound	Spelling	Example / Notes
/ō/	ough	*dough,* (rarely used spellings of /ō/ or exceptions to other combinations)
	ou	*though*
	oo	*door,*
	au	*chauffeur*
	eau	*plateau*
	ew	*sew*
	oe	*doe*
/oo/	oo	*fool* (most common spelling, usually on accented syllable, occasionally used at ending of word, such as *taboo*)
/oo/	o	*move, do* (used at ending of a few common words or in combination with final silent *-e*)
/oo/	ou	*you,* (much less common or rare spellings of /oo/ sound)
	ue	*true*
	u	*rule*
	ui	*fruit*
/oy/	oi	*oil, coin* (most common spelling for beginning and middle of words)
/oy/	oy	*boy, alloy* (almost always appears at endings of words — exceptions: *boycott, royal,* and compounds)
/ow/	ou	*out, pound* (only spelling commonly used for beginning and middle position in syllables)
/ou/	ow	*now, scow* (usually used for *ou* sound at end of syllables—exceptions are *down, growl,* and in other combinations of *-own,* and *-owl*)
/ə/	u	*shut, tub* (most common spelling)
/ə/	o	*cover, month, ton* (also a limited number of other common words)
/ə/	ou	*young, rough* (an uncommon spelling)
/ə/	oo	*blood, flood* (used only for these words)
/ū/	u	*union, tube* (most common spelling, often used in combinations with final silent *-e*)
/ū/	eu	*eulogy* (and a small number of other words of Greek origin)
/ū/	eu	*new, few* (and a small number of other common words)
/ū/	ieu	*adieu* (used only for a small number of words of French origin
	eau	*beauty* origin)
/ū/	iew	*view* (and in combinations of this word only)
/ū/	iu	*suit, nuisance* (and in combinations of these words)
/ū/	ue	*due, value* (always at the endings of a small number of words)
/û/	u	*bull, hateful* (most common spelling, often appears in combination *-ful*)
/û/	oo	*took, hood, foot* (exceptions are

poor, wool, moor, boor)

| /û/ | ou | tour, courier (and a few other words of French origin) |
| /û/ | o | woman, wolf, bosom (and combinations of these words) |

Note that each vowel letter in an unstressed or unaccented syllable often stands for the *schwa* sound, marked as follows:

/ə/	a	**a**go
/ə/	e	happ**e**n
/ə/	i	foss**i**l
/ə/	o	gall**o**p
/ə/	u	circ**u**s

In addition to the above, the schwa sound (/ə/) can also be spelled by the following less commonly used letters and letter combinations:

sound	*letter(s)*	*examples*
schwa (/ə/)	ai	cert**ai**n
	ea	pag**ea**nt
	eo	dung**eo**n
	eou	gorg**eou**s
	ia	parl**ia**ment
	ie	suffic**ie**nt
	io	reg**io**n
	ou	fam**ou**s
	ue	g**ue**rrilla
	y	eth**y**l

Using the schwa sound in its various forms as a guide to spelling is therefore not too helpful. Here are ways of handling this spelling problem with the help of your dictionary: (1) depend on the more predictable spelling patterns to spell enough of the word for you to find it in the dictionary listing; (2) depend on the fact that many of the schwa sounds come in prefixes at the beginning of words. Learn the common prefixes and their spellings as guides to choosing one of the letters for schwa.

Locating Words in the Dictionary

Once you have decided on a trial spelling of the word you are seeking, you can usually locate it by keeping in mind that all entry words are arranged alphabetically in the dictionary and by using the guide words that appear at the top of each page.

Try Other Spellings If Your First Is Not Correct

See if the spelling you have chosen and found is correct for the meaning of the word you are seeking. Of course you may not know the exact meaning, but you should be able to tell if the definition of the entry you have chosen generally fits the idea of the sentence or context in which you heard or read the word. There are a number of words that have identical sounds but different spellings for different meanings: *cite, site, sight; bare, bear; right, write.*

If your first attempt to spell a word or syllable is not correct, try alternate spellings of the sound or syllable that you have most likely gotten wrong. Try a different vowel, and then perhaps another beginning consonant, and soon your effort will be rewarded.

ENTRIES

I. The Entry Word

The words that make up the vocabulary are printed flush with the left margin of the column and are in boldface type. They are listed in alphabetical order. Guide words at the top of each page indicate the first or last entry on that page and facilitate the location of a particular word. Each entry is fully syllabicated and is followed by its pronunciation, part of speech, inflected form, and definition:

en·due, en·doo′, en·dū′, *v.t.,* **-dued, -du·ing.** To invest or endow with special qualities.

II. Variants

If a word has two or more accepted spellings, the most commonly used spelling is listed first, with the others following in order of preferred use. If the pronunciation of a variant spelling is identical to an entry word, and if both spellings apply to all definitions, then the variant is listed immediately after the entry word in boldface type and is fully syllabicated:

cha·pa·re·jos, cha·pa·ra·jos, chap•ə•rā′hōs, chä•pä•rä′hōs, *n. pl.,* Protective leather breeches worn by horsemen, esp. cowboys. Also **chaps.**

III. Homographs

If words have identical spellings but different backgrounds and meanings, each variation is listed as a separate entry. The preferred or most common meaning is usually entered first.

pump pəmp, *n.* An instrument or machine, consisting of an arrangement of a piston, cylinder, and valves, employed for raising water or other liquid to a higher level, for moving liquids or gases through a pipe or pipeline, or for exhausting or compressing air or other gases.—*v.i.* To work a pump; to move up and down like a pump handle.—*v.t.* To raise with a pump; to free from water or other fluid by a pump, often with *out;* to *pump out* a ship; to inflate with a pump. usu. with *up;* to put artful questions to for the purpose of extracting information; to discharge, eject, drive, or force by means of a pump or as though by a pump. —**pump·a·ble,** *a.* —**pump·er,** *n.*
pump, pəmp, *n.* A woman's shoe, low-cut and without fastenings; a similarly cut type of dress shoe for men.

IV. Subentries

A subentry is a word, usually a grammatical variant of the entry word, that is so linguistically or semantically similar to the entry word that a separate listing does not seem appropriate. Subentries are set in boldface type, syllabicated, and may be followed by a pronunciation, if needed, part of speech, and sometimes a definition. Subentries are preceded by a dash and follow all regular definitions of a word.

flit, flit, *v.i.,* **flit·ted, flit·ting.** To fly or dart; to move quickly and lightly; flutter; to pass rapidly.—*n.* A quick movement. —**flit·ter,** *n.*

V. Special Entries

A. *Abbreviations*
A list of abbreviations used in definitions is located on page xxii of the dictionary. Common abbreviations are listed alphabetically as entries throughout the dictionary. The words represented are indicated in the definition or in a cross-reference to another entry:

DNA, *n.* Deoxynibonucleic acid, a compound found in

B. *Proper Adjectives*
Proper adjectives are alphabetized as entries. The proper nouns from which they are derived are indicated in the definition or, if necessary, defined in a separate entry:

Eng·lish, ing′glish, ing′lish, *a.* Of, pertaining to, or characteristic of England or its inhabitants; of or

C. *Trademarks*
Commonly used trademarks are included in the dictionary. Each trademark is identified as such in its definition:

Dic·ta·phone, dik′tə•fōn, *n. Trademark.* A machine which records verbal dictation for later playback and transcription.

D. *Proper Nouns*
Proper nouns that refer to well-known objects or events are alphabetized as entries:

E·piph·a·ny, i•pif′ə•nē, *n. pl.,* **-nies.** A Christian festival held on January 6 commemorating the manifestation of Jesus Christ to the Magi; *(l.c.)* a manifestation, esp. of a divinity.

VI. Cross References

Semantic relationships between words are indicated by cross references. If two words are identical in meaning, a definition will follow the more common entry and a cross reference will follow the less common entry:

cal·dron, kôl′drən, *n.* Cauldron.

caul·dron, cal·dron, kôl′dron, *n.* A large metal kettle or boiler.

Pronunciation

Pronunciations are given for every entry. A chart explaining pronunciation symbols and sounds and suffix and consonant sounds is included in this Guide. A shortened explanation of pronunciation symbols is printed on the lower margin of each right-hand page and inside each cover.

I. Placement of Pronunciation

The pronunciations follow the entry word. When a word has more than one pronunciation, all pronunciations immediately follow the entry word:

e·phed·rine, i•fed′rin, ef′i•drēn, *n.* A drug used in

The pronunciation for a word may

GUIDE TO THIS DICTIONARY

vary depending on its grammatical functions. A differing pronunciation immediately follows the dash separating the parts of speech and their definitions. The pronunciation is followed by an abbreviation describing its grammatical function:

del·e·gate, del/ə·gāt, *v.t.,* **-gat·ed, -gat·ing.** To send or appoint as a deputy or representative; to assign or entrust (powers or functions) to another.—del/ə·gāt, del/ə·git, *n.* One delegated to act for or represent another; a representative, as at a convention, for a territory, or in certain state legislatures.

II. System of Pronunciation

All pronunciations are in roman type.

op·pro·bri·ous, ə·prō/brē·əs, *a.* Expressing oppro-

Pronunciations begin with a lowercase letter and are followed by a comma. The most common pronunciation is given first:

door·bell, dôr/bel, dōr/bel, *n.* An electric bell, usu. at

III. Syllabication and Stress

Due to different rules, syllabication of the entry and syllabication of pronunciation do not always agree. Syllabication in the pronunciation is indicated by a raised center dot, except between syllables where stress marks are needed. The syllable having the greatest stress is followed by a primary stress mark ('). One-syllable words do not have stress:

Gre·go·ri·an cal·en·dar, gri·gō/rē·ən, gri·gôr/ē·ən, *n.* The calendar now in general use introduced

grey, grā, *n., a., v.i., v.t.* Gray.

IV. Variant Pronunciations

If there is more than one pronunciation for an entry or subentry, the variants follow the entry and are separated by commas:

Don Juan, don wän, don·joo/ən, *n.* A nobleman and

When a plural form, or a different part of speech, or a subentry derived from the entry differs significantly from the entry in pronunciation, the appropriate pronunciation immediately follows the form to which it applies and is separated from it by a comma:

ep·i·thet, ep/i·thet, *n.* A descriptive word or phrase expressing some real or implied quality of a person; a term of abuse. **—ep·i·thet·ic,** ep·i·thet/ik, **ep·i·thet·i·cal,** *a.*

V. Pronunciation of Compounds

Multiword entries are followed by a pronunciation only if one or more of the entry words is not pronounced elsewhere:

oth·er world, *n.* The world of the dead; the world to

flint glass, *n.* A brilliant, heavy glass used esp. for

Hyphenated words are considered as single words and are pronounced:

flea-bit·ten, flē/bit·ən, *a.* Bitten or covered by fleas.

Multiword subentries are not given pronunciations:

grief, grēf, *n.* Emotional pain or distress from an extreme cause, as affliction or bereavement; deep sorrow or sadness; the cause of such sadness. **—to come to grief,** to come to a bad end; to fail.

Other Information About Words

PARTS OF SPEECH

English words are traditionally classified into parts of speech which are determined by their form, meaning, and syntactic function in a sentence. A part of speech is listed for each entry in this dictionary.

I. Abbreviations for Parts of Speech

The part of speech is listed immediately after the pronunciation and is preceded by a comma. Parts of speech are italicized and abbreviated as follows:

n.	noun
v.t.	transitive verb
v.i.	intransitive verb
a.	adjective
adv.	adverb
pron.	pronoun
prep.	preposition
conj.	conjunction
interj.	interjection
art.	article

II. Changing Parts of Speech

If identically spelled words are different parts of speech and their meanings are semantically different, each word and its meaning will be listed as a separate entry.

mine, mīn, *pron.* Possessive of I; belonging to me: *mine* is a brown hat; my; now generally used similarly to **hers, ours, yours, theirs,** as equivalent to **my** followed by a noun and serving either for a nominative or an objective case.
mine, mīn, *n.* A pit or excavation in the earth, from which coal, metallic ores, or other mineral substances are taken by digging; the location, buildings, and

If, however, the definitions for all parts of speech are semantically similar, then all the definitions will appear under a single entry. The definition for each part of speech is then preceded by a dash and the italicized abbreviation of the part of speech which is to be defined:

ghost, gōst, *n.* The soul or spirit of a dead person; a disembodied spirit, esp. one imagined to haunt the living; a specter or apparition; a mere shadow or semblance: the *ghost* of a smile; a distant possibility: a *ghost* of a chance; a spiritual being. *TV.* A duplicate image, usu. faint and slightly displaced from the main image, due to wave reflection. Secondary image, as from a defect in lenses.—*v.t.* Ghostwrite; to appear to or haunt.—*v.i.* Ghostwrite; to go about silently, like a ghost. —**give up the ghost,** to die.

INFLECTIONAL FORMS

All irregular inflected forms of nouns, pronouns, verbs, adjectives, and adverbs are listed immediately after the designated part of speech of an entry. Partial forms of regular and irregular inflections are provided where the base of the word remains unchanged. Inflected forms are preceded by a dash and labeled, where necessary. Labels for inflected forms are abbreviated as follows:

compar.	comparative
nom.	nominative
obj.	objective
pl.	plural
poss.	possessive
pp.	past participle
ppr.	present participle
pres.	present
refl.	reflexive
sing.	singular
subj.	subjunctive
superl.	superlative

I. Declension

A. Nouns

Plurals of nouns that are not formed by adding -s or -es are printed in boldface type and are syllabicated. If more than one plural exists, the preferred is listed first:

cac•tus, kak′təs, *n. pl.,* **-tus•es, -ti,** -tī. Any of several

Nouns that are plural in form but singular in function are so labled.

or•tho•don•tics, ôr′thə•don′tiks, *n. pl. but sing. in constr.* The branch of dentistry which corrects irregu-

B. Pronouns

When necessary, the case, number, and classification for pronouns are listed. The inflected form is then italicized and the label abbreviated:

her, hər, *unstressed* ər, *pron.* The objective case of **she,** as: I love *her.*—*pronominal a.* The possessive case of **she,** used as an attributive: as, *her* face. —**hers,** hərz, *pron.* A possessive case of **she** used, instead of *her* and a noun, as subject, object, or predicate.

II. Conjugation

Irregular constructions of principal parts of verbs are listed following the pronunciation and part-of-speech of the base form.

sing, sing, *v.i.,* **sang** or **sung, sung, sing•ing.** To utter words or sounds with musical inflections of the voice; to perform a vocal composition;

The irregular principal parts of verbs are shortened, where possible, in order to show just the portion of the word that is irregular.

If a verb has additional irregular parts they are listed in the following order: present singular, present plural, past singular, past plural, past participle, present participle:

be, bē, *v.i.,* pres. sing. **am, are, is;** pres. pl. **are;** past sing. **was, were, was;** past pl. **were;** pp. **been;** ppr. **being.** To exist; live; occupy a position; take place.

III. Comparison

Irregular comparative and superlative forms of adjectives and adverbs are preceded by a dash and are shortened, where possible, to show just that portion of the word that is irregular. The comparative form is listed first:

gris•ly, griz′lē, *a.,* **-li•er, -li•est.** Frightful; horrible;

QUALIFYING AND USAGE LABELS

Qualifying and usage labels are used

to give information about or restrict the use of some definitions. These labels introduce the definition to which they apply and are italicized. Labels apply to all definitions which follow until a period or another label intervenes.

I. Qualifying Labels

Qualifying labels refer to capitalization and number. If a label gives information about capitalization, it is italicized and in parentheses. If a label gives information about number, it is italicized only.

Both kinds of labels are abbreviated:

(*cap.*) capital	*pl.* plural
(*l.c.*) lower case	*sing.* singular

pa•pa•cy, pā′pe•sē, *n. pl.,* **-cies.** The office and dignity of the pope; papal authority and jurisdiction; the popedom; the popes collectively; the term of office of a particular pope; *(cap.)* the form of government of the Roman Catholic Church.

II. Usage Labels

The label *Informal* is used in this dictionary to indicate that the entry word is not normally used in formal written or spoken language. The user should exercise care in determining whether the word in question is acceptable for use with the audience for which it is intended.

When a definition and usage of a word are altered by its context, the appropriate word or phrase is indicated:

chap, chap, *v.t.,* **chapped, chap•ping.** To split; crack; make rough, esp. the skin.—*v.i.* To become chapped, as the skin.—*n.* A crack in the skin.
chap, chap. *n. Informal.* A man or a boy; a fellow.

Definitions

All parts of speech of the English language except proper names are included as entries. Each entry word is followed by a definition or by a cross reference except in the case of conjunctions, which are followed by information concerning their use and function, and interjections, which are followed by information concerning the context in which they are used and the mood they convey:

and, and, end, *conj.* A particle or function word joining words and sentences, and expressing the relations of connection or addition.

I. Placement and Style of Definitions

Definitions follow the listing and pronunciation of the entry word with semicolons separating the different meanings. Each new part of speech, multiword subentry, or subentry is introduced with a dash:

change, chānj, *v.t.,* **changed, chang•ing.** To make or become different; to substitute another thing or things for; to shift; to give or get another kind of money for: to *change* a dollar; to give away for a money equivalent of a different kind; to exchange: to *change* places with a person; to place fresh linen on: to *change* a bed or baby.—*v.i.* To suffer change; to be altered; to undergo variation; to be partially or wholly transformed.

II. Order of Definitions

Definitions are listed with the preferred or most common meaning first, followed by the other meanings according to how common their usage.

pant, pant, *v.i.* To breathe quickly or spasmodically; to gasp; to throb or heave rapidly or violently; to yearn or long for.—*v.t.* To breathe or gasp out.—*n.* A quick, short breath; a gasp.

If a word does not have a clear preferred use, the order of definitions is arbitrary:

grit, grit, *n.* Fine, hard grains of sand; a coarsegrained sandstone; firmness of character.—*v.t.,* **grit•ted, grit•ting.** To grate or grind, as the teeth.

Major parts of speech are defined first in an entry. Multiword subentries are then listed and defined. Single word subentries, which are usually grammatical variants of the entry word, are listed in alphabetical order at the end of an entry and are not defined:

grim•y, grī′mē, *a.,* **-i•er, -i•est.** Full of grime; foul; dirty. —**grim•i•ly,** *adv.* —**grim•i•ness,** *n.*

III. Multiword Subentries

Idiomatic and compound expressions in the English language are listed as subentries under the appropriate root word. Multiword subentries are introduced with a dash, printed in bold-faced type, and otherwise treated as entries except that no pronunciation or part of speech is given for them:

grind•stone, grind′ston, *n.* A revolving stone used for grinding or sharpening tools. **—keep one's nose to the grind•stone.** *Informal.* To work diligently and without unnecessary interruptions.

IV. Examples

When examples are used to illustrate the meaning or proper use of a word

they follow the definition to which they apply:

gren•a•dier, gren•′ə•dēr′, *n.* A member of a special regiment, as the *Grenadier* Guards of the British army; originally a soldier trained to use hand grenades.

ABBREVIATIONS

Parts of speech, inflection labels, qualifying labels, and some usage labels are abbreviated in this dictionary. A list of these abbreviations may be found either under the appropriate heading in this Guide, or in the following listing. Standard chemical abbreviations are listed under "Periodic Table of the Elements," which may be found following the dictionary section.

Common Abbreviations

a. or *adj.*	adjective
A.D.	Anno Domini
adv.	adverb
agric.	agriculture
alg.	algebra
anat.	anatomy
art.	article
arch.	architecture
archaeol.	archaeology
arith.	arithmetic
astron.	astronomy
attrib.	attributive, attributively
aux. v.	auxiliary verb
avi.	aviation
bact.	bacteriology
B.C.	Before Christ
b.f.	bold face
biochem.	biochemistry
biol.	biology
bot.	botany
Brit.	British
cap.	capital
caps.	capitals
cent.	century
chem.	chemistry
chem. sym.	chemical symbol
commerc.	commercial
compar.	comparative

conj.	conjunction
conn.	connected
constr.	construction
contr.	contracted, contraction
def.	definite
defs.	definitions
demonst.	demonstrative
deriv.	derivation
ecol.	ecology
econ.	economics
ed.	edition
educ.	education
e.g.	*exempli gratia* (for example)
elect.	electricity
electron.	electronics
embryol.	embryology
Eng.	England
engin.	engineering
entom.	entomology
esp.	especially
etc.	*et cetera* (and so forth)
ethnol.	ethnology
F.	Fahrenheit
fig.	figuratively
fut.	future

genit.	genitive		*p.* or *part.*	participle
geog.	geography		paint.	painting
geol.	geology		paleon.	paleontology
geom.	geometry		pathol.	pathology
gov.	government		perf.	perfect
gram.	grammar		pharm.	pharmacology
hist.	history		philos.	philosophy
hort.	horticulture		photog.	photography
impers.	impersonal		phys.	physical, physics
impf.	imperfect		physiol.	physiology
impv.	imperative		pl.	plural
indef.	indefinite		poet.	poetic
indic.	indicative		polit.	political
inf.	infinitive		poss.	possessive
interj.	interjection		pp.	past participle
interrog.	interrogative		ppr.	present participle
irreg.	irregular, irregularly		*prep.*	preposition
ital.	italics		pres.	present
journ.	journalism		print.	printing
l.c.	lower case		*pron.*	pronoun
ling.	linguistics		psychol.	psychology
liter.	literature, literary		punct.	punctuation
manuf.	manufacturing		rail.	railroad
masc.	masculine		ref.	reference
math.	mathematics		refl.	reflexive
mech.	mechanics		reg.	regular
med.	medical, medicine		rel.	relative
metal.	metallurgy		sculp.	sculpture
meteor.	meteorology		sing.	singular
milit.	military		sociol.	sociology
mineral.	mineralogy		specif.	specific, specifically
mod.	modern		subj.	subjunctive
mus.	music		superl.	superlative
mythol.	mythology		surg.	surgery
n.	noun		syll.	syllable
nat. hist.	natural history		sym.	symbol
nat. sc.	natural science		syn.	synonym
naut.	nautical		techn.	technical
nav.	naval, navy		theatr.	theatrical
navig.	navigation		trig.	trigonometry
neg.	negative		typog.	typography
neut.	neuter		U.S.	United States
nom.	nominative		usu.	usually
north.	northern		*v.*	verb
obj.	objective		var.	variant
ophthalm.	ophthalmology		*vbl. n.*	verbal noun
opt.	optics		veter.	veterinary
orig.	original, originally		*v.i.*	verb intransitive
ornith.	ornithology		W.W.I.	World War One
			W.W.II.	World War Two
			zool.	zoology

New Words

A·C/D·C, ă·sē·dē′sē, *a.* Bisexual.

ac·id rock, *n.* Rock music related to or flowing out of drug-induced experience.

ac·tion paint·ing, *n.* A modern, nonrepresentational style of painting in which paint is often dribbled or smeared to produce a thickly textured surface.

ac·ti·va·tion a·na·ly·sis, *n.* A method of chemical analysis in which a material is bombarded with nuclear particles, producing atoms whose radiations identify the parent elements.

ac·yl, as′*ul*, *n.* A radical obtained from an organic acid by removing the hydroxyl.

ad-mass, ad·mas, *n.* A marketing system which influences large masses of consumers by advertising in the mass-media; a society so influenced.

ad·vance man, *n.* An aide, as for a political candidate or performing artist, who arranges publicity and security in preparation for his employer's personal appearance.

aer·o·bics, ă·rō′biks, *n. pl. but sing. or pl. in constr.* A physical conditioning system which stresses exercises such as swimming, running, walking, which will increase oxygen consumption and improve the functioning of the heart and lungs.

af·firm·a·tive ac·tion plan, *n.* A plan to encourage increased employment of minority group members and women.

A-frame, ā′frăm, *n.* A building with a triangularly-shaped front and rear and a sloping roof reaching nearly to the ground on each side.

ag·gior·na·men·to, *a*·jar·n*a*·men′tō, *n.* [It.] A bringing up to date.

ag·ro·in·dus·tri·al, a·grō·in·dus′trē·al, *a.* Of or relating to that which serves both agriculture and industry.

ai·ki·do, ī·kē′dō, *n.* A Japanese art of self-defense which uses the principle of non-resistance and uses the opponent's own momentum against him or her.

air bag, *n.* A bag designed to inflate automatically in case of an accident to protect riders in an automobile.

air-cush·ion, ār′kush·on, *a.* Of or relating to a vehicle that travels over land or water supported on a cushion of air. Also **air-cush·ioned.**

air door, *n.* A strong temperature-controlled current of air used instead of a solid door.

air taxi, *n.* A small commercial airplane that serves localities not reached by regular airlines.

air time, ār·tīm, *n.* The time that a television or radio station is on the air; any portion of this time.

al den·te, ăl·den′tā, *a.* [It.] Food, esp. pasta, cooked to retain a somewhat firm texture.

AL·GOL, al′gäl, *n.* An algebraic and logical computer language.

A-line, ā′līn, *a.* Referring to a garment with a close-fitting top and flared bottom.

al·pha de·cay, *n.* The decay of an atomic nucleus as it emits an alpha particle.

an·chor·man, ang′kor·man, *n.* The newscaster who coordinates the activities of other broadcasters at a political convention or other complex activity.

an·swer·ing ser·vice, *n.* A commercial service to answer telehone calls for clients.

An·tar·es, an·tar′ēz, *n.* A large reddish star, the brightest star in the constellation Scorpio.

an·ti·anx·i·ety, an·tē·ang·zī′*a*·tē, *a.* Tending to relieve or prevent anxiety: an *antianx* *iety drug.*

an·ti·bus·ing, an·ti·bus´ing, *a.* Opposed to the transport of children to schools outside their neighborhood (generally for the purpose of integration).

an·ti·con·vul·sant, an·ti·kun·vul´sent, *a.* Pertaining to that which can control or prevent convulsions, as in epileptic seizures.

an·ti·de·pres·sant, an·ti· dē·pres´ent, *a.* Pertaining to that which can relieve mental depression. – *n.*

an·ti·establishment, an·tē·e· stab´-lish·ment, *a.* Opposed to the power structure of an established order of society, as of a nation.

an·ti·fun·gal, an·ti·fung´gul, *a.* Pertaining to a substance or procedure effective against fungi; fungicidal: an *antifungal* drug.

an·tique, *v.t.,* **-tiqued, -tiqu·ing.** To shop for or browse among antiques.

an·ti·spas·mod·ic, ant·i·spaz·mäd´ik, *a.* Preventing or relieving spasms or convulsions. – *n.*

ape, āp, *a. Informal.* Wild, crazy: usu. in the phrase *go ape over;* incapable of being restrained.

a·près-ski, a·prä·skē´, *n.* [Fr.] The social activities which take place at a ski lodge after the day's skiing.

ar·e·a code, *n.* A 3-digit number which precedes the 7-digit telephone number in dialing long-distance calls.

art de·co, ärt·dā´kō, *n. (Often cap.)* A popular style in decorative arts of the 1920s and 1930s, using streamlined and natural forms and bold colors and outlines.

as·tro·bi·ol·o·gy, as·trō·bī·ol´o·jē, *n.* The study of life beyond or outside of the earth; also **exobiology.**

at·tri·tion, a·trish´an, *n.* The gradual loss of personnel, as in a labor force or student body, from natural causes (death, retirement, drop out), often without replacement.

au pair girl, ō·pār´girl, *n.* A young woman from abroad who helps with housework in return for room and board and the chance to learn English.

bad-mouth, bad´mouth, *v.t. Informal.* To speak ill of; to severely criticize; to disparage: He's always *bad-mouthing* something.

bag, *n. Informal.* One's specialty; that which one does well or likes to do; one's typical way of life. A small package of a narcotic, as heroin or marijuana.

ba·na·nas, *a. Informal.* Crazy: She drives me *bananas.*

barf, bärf, *v.i. Informal.* To vomit. – *n.*

bar·mitz·vah, bär·mits´va, *v.t. (Often cap.)* To administer the bar mitzvah ceremony.

beau·ti·ful peo·ple, *n.pl. (Often cap.)* People of high society; the rich and/or famous.

be·hav·ior·al sci·en·tist, *n.* A person who specializes in behavioral science.

bells, *n.pl.* Bell bottom pants; pants that flare at the bottom.

be·span·gle, bi·spang´gul *v.t.,* **-gled, -gling.** Spangle. – **be·span·gled,** *a.* Adorned with spangles; glittering with, or as with, spangles.

bi·cul·tur·al, bī·cul´chu·ral, *a.* Of or relating to two different cultures: *bicultural* education. – **bi·cul·tur·al·ism,** *n.*

big bang the·o·ry, *n.* An astronomical theory stating that the universe originated in an explosion of a compressed mass of matter.

bi·lev·el, bī´lev·ul, *n.* A two-story house having the first floor partially below ground level and the entry at ground level.

bin·a·ry no·ta·tion, *n.* A system using only the digits 0 and 1 to express numbers to the base 2: each place represents a power of 2.

bi·o·de·grad·a·ble, bī´ō· di·grā´da·bul, *a.* Capable of being broken down by the action of living organisms into products that will not harm the environment.

bi·o·med·i·cal, bī·ō·me´di·cal, *a.* Of or pertaining to biomedicine.

bi·on·ics, bī·on´iks, *n. pl. but sing. in constr.* A scientific field that applies biological data to the solution of engineering problems.

bi·o·rhy·thm, bī·ō·riTH´am, *n.* A rhythmic biological process which is innately determined, or the determiner of such a process. – **bi·o·rhyth·mic,** bī· ō·riTH´mik, *a.*

black belt, *n.* The rating of an expert in judo, karate, or other self-defense art; the holder of this rating.

black com·e·dy, *n.* A comedy that uses black humor.

black pow·er, *n.* The power of black people, esp. in achieving economic and political rights.

bod·y lang·uage, *n.* Body gestures and

mannerisms used in interpersonal communication.

bod·y shirt, *n.* A woman's top that fits the body closely, covers the torso, and fastens at the crotch.

bod·y stock·ing, *n.* A sheer one-piece garment that fits the body closely and may have sleeves and legs.

brown·ie point, *n. (Often cap.)* A credit earned with a superior, usu. by currying favor.

bump·er stick·er, *n.* A strip of paper with a printed message and an adhesive back, designed for attachment to an automobile bumper.

bus·ing, bus·sing, *n.* Transportation by bus; transportation of children to a school outside their neighborhood, usu. for purposes of integration.

buzz off, *v.i.* To leave immediately; to go away.

cae·si·um, sē′zē·um, *n.* A white soft electropositive metal of the alkali group, used esp. in photoelectric cells. Also **cesium.**

cap·puc·ci·no, käp·u·chē′nō, *n.* [It.] Espresso coffee, served with whipped cream and sometimes with cinnamon.

car·bon dat·ing, *n.* A process which determines the age of an ancient object by measuring the carbon 14 content.

car·di·o·pul·mo·na·ry, kär′dē·ō·pul′ma·ner·ē, *a.* Pertaining to the heart and lungs: *cardiopulmonary* resuscitation.

CB, *n.* Citizens band (radio).

cen·ter·fold, sen′tar·fōld′, *n.* Oversize pages in the center of a magazine, often containing photographs, which are folded to standard page size: the *centerfold* of *Playboy* magazine.

ci·né·ma vé·ri·té, sē·nä·mä′vä·Rē·tä′, *n.* [Fr.] The filming of a motion picture in a candid, realistic style; documentary filming.

cit·i·zens band, *n.* A U.S. radio frequency band set aside for the use of private citizens.

class ac·tion, *n.* Legal action brought by one person or a group of persons on their own behalf and on behalf of all other persons on their own behalf and on behalf of all other persons having a similar interest.

clone, *v.t.,* **cloned, clon·ing.** To grow or culture as a clone; to use a single body cell to grow a genetically identical individual.

clos·ing, *n.* A meeting of the interested parties in a real estate deal to formally transfer title.

cloud nine, *n.* Elation; a feeling of great well being, usu. with *on*: He was on *cloud nine* after the award.

clout, clout, *n.* Influence; the power to affect (usu. political) decisions; pull: people with money and *clout.*

con·sum·er·ism, kon·sö′mer·iz·am, *n.* Promotion of the interests of consumers, esp. in the face of corporate excesses; the theory that increasing consumption is an economic good.

con·ven·i·ence food, *n.* Food that is packaged with quick and easy preparation in mind.

cord·less, kōrd′lis, *a.* Without a cord (said of electrical appliances); battery-powered.

corn row, karn′rō, *v.t.* To divide hair into sections and braid, usu. close to the scalp and in rows.

cost-ef·fec·tive, kast·i·fek′tiv, *a.* Pertaining to a process or transaction in which money spent produces tangible benefits. **cost-ef·fec·tive-ness,** *n.*

crash, *v.i. Informal.* To sleep (for the night); to return to normal after taking drugs.

cre·du·li·ty, kri·dö′li·tē kri·dū′li·tē, *n.* Excessive readiness to believe.

crock, *n. Informal.* Bull; talk which is insincere or designed to mislead or falsely impress listeners: That's a *crock!*

crunch, *n.* The critical point in a developing situation; an economic squeeze.

da·shi·ki, da·shē′kē, *n.* A loose-fitting pullover garment, usu. made of brightly patterned cloth and worn esp. by men.

de·bug, dē·bug′, *v.t.* To remove a concealed listening device from a place or to render such device ineffective.

de·li, del·ly, del′ē, *n.pl.,* **del·is, del·lies.** *Informal.* A delicatessen; a store which sells ready-to-eat food such as salads, sandwich meats, and cheese.

de·mo, dem′ō, *n.pl.,* **-mos.** *Informal.* A demonstration, esp. of a political or protest nature; something used for demonstration.

de·reg·u·late, dē·reg′yu·lāt, *v.t.* To decontrol or remove from regulation. – **de·reg·u·la·tion,** *n.*

dir·ty pool, *n. Informal.* Behavior which is devious, underhanded or unsportsmanlike.

dis·cre·tion·a·ry in·come, *n.* That portion

of income remaining after basic necessities have been paid for.

di·sul·fide, dī·sul′fīd, *n.* A compound in which two atoms of sulfur are combined with a radical.

dog·gie bag, dog·gy bag, *n. Informal.* A bag provided by a restaurant in which patrons can carry home leftover food, esp. meat.

dom·i·no the·o·ry, *n.* The theory that if a certain event occurs, a series of similar events will follow; the political theory that if one country falls under Communist control, neighboring nations will follow suit.

dou·ble bind, *n.* A situation in which a person, esp. a child or dependent, receives conflicting messages from another person, a situation in which there are negative consequences to any course of action.

dove, *n.* One who approaches situations, esp. conflict, with conciliation and compromise.

Down's syn·drome, douns sin′drōm, *n.* A condition of congenital idiocy: the child is born with a broad short skull, slanting eyes, broad hands, and short fingers; mongolism.

dune bug·gy, *n.* A motorized jeep-type vehicle with oversize tires for driving on sand dunes or beaches.

e·go trip, *n. Informal.* That which builds or enhances one's ego.

en·coun·ter group, *n.* A group, usually unstructured, which seeks to develop participants' capacities to express their feelings and to form emotional bonds through largely unrestrained confrontation within the group.

en·dan·gered, en·dān′jėrd, *a.* That which is threatened with extinction, as a species.

eth·no·mu·si·col·o·gy, eth·nō·mū zi·kol′a·je′, *n.* Study of music in relation to the culture that produces it, chiefly that of non-European cultures.

Eu·ro·dol·lar, ūr′o dol′ar, *n.* A U.S. dollar held by parties outside the country, esp. in Europe.

ex·tra·cra·ni·al, ek·stra·krā′nē·al, *a.* Located or occurring outside the cranium.

fan-jet, fan′jet, *n.* A jet engine provided with a fan to draw in extra air which produces added thrust; an airplane powered with this engine.

far-out, fär′out′, *a. Informal.* Extreme; showing a considerable departure from convention or tradition

fast-back, fast′bak, *n.* A passenger car having the back roof sloping toward the rear bumper; such a roof.

fast-food, fast′food, *a.* Pertaining to establishments which specialize in rapid preparation and service of food (sandwiches, chicken, French fries).

Fates, fāts, *n.pl. Gr. and Rom. myth.* The three goddesses, Atropus, Clotho, and Lachesis, who were thought to control men's lives: preceded by *the:* Don't tempt *the Fates.*

fau·ces, fa′sēz, *n.pl. but sing. or pl. in constr. Anat.* The passage from the mouth to the pharynx, between the soft palate and the base of the tongue.

fet·al po·si·tion, *n.* A position similar to that of the fetus in the womb: body curved, legs and arms drawn to the chest, head bent forward: used in some forms of psychic regression.

fi·ber op·tics, *n.pl.* Thin fibers of glass or plastic so bound that they transmit light throughout their transparent flexible length by internal reflection; a bundle of such fibers used in an instrument, as for viewing body cavities.

fiche, fēsh, *n.pl.,* **fiche, fich·es.** A sheet of microfilm with its rows of microimages; micro-fiche.

fish-eye, fish′ī, *a.* Pertaining to that which is, has, or is produced by a wide-angle camera lens that covers a 180 degree angle and produces a circular image with some distortion.

flex-time, fleks- tīm, *n.* A work-scheduling system under which employees can choose their times for starting and finishing work within a certain range.

flight bag, *n.* A bag used esp. for air travel and designed to fit under an airplane seat; a similar lightweight satchel bearing the name of an airline.

flip chart, *n.* A series of large sheets hinged at the top to flip over for viewing.

float·ing dec·i·mal, *n.* A system in which the decimal point is free to move across the display board of an electronic calculator.

flow·er child, *n.* A hippie, referring to their frequent practice of wearing flowers.

FOR·TRAN, far′tran, *n.* A logical and algebraic language used in computer programming.

fox·y, fok´sē, *a.*, **-i·er, -i·est.** *Informal.* Attractive, esp. in a sexy way: that *foxy* lady.

freak out, *v.i. Informal.* To withdraw, as from society or reality, esp. by taking drugs; to hallucinate or have nightmares as a result of drugs; to behave irrationally or in an extreme or unconventional manner under, or as if under, the influence of drugs, –*v.t.* To put under the influence of drugs, esp. psychedelics; to excite intensely; to upset or anger. – **freaked-out,** *a.*

front mon·ey, *n.* Money paid in advance for a promised product or service.

fu·el cell, *n.* A device to continuously and directly convert chemical energy (as from a fuel) into electrical energy.

fun·ny farm, *n. Informal.* A psychiatric hospital; a mental institution.

fu·ture shock, *n.* Psychological and physical distress suffered by people unable to cope with rapid changes in technology and society.

game plan, *n.* The strategy to achieve a goal.

ga·rage sale, *n.* A sale of used household goods (clothing, furniture, tools), usu. held in the seller's garage or yard. Also **yard sale.**

gar·ment bag, *n.* A traveling bag into which garments can be placed on hangers, the bag folded in half and carried by a center handle.

ge·net·ic code, *n.* Molecular arrangements of DNA and RNA which determine the amino acid sequence in proteins and are the biochemical basis of heredity.

go-go, gō´gō, *a.* Relating to a discotheque or the music or dances performed there; active, lively.

grade point, *n.* A number value assigned to each letter grade received in a course and multiplied by the number of credits given for the course.

Gram·my, gram´ē, *n.pl.*, **-mys, -mies.** A trophy awarded for outstanding achievement in the phonograph recording field.

gra·no·la, gra·nō´la, *n.* A mixture of rolled oats or other grains, brown sugar or honey, dried fruits and nuts, used as a health or breakfast food.

Gray Pan·thers, *n.pl.* An organization of militant elderly people; *sing.* a member of this organization.

Green Be·ret, *n.* A member of the U.S. Army's Special Forces.

half·way house, *n.* A center for persons formerly in institutions (as prisoners or mental patients) which aids in their adjustment to private life.

hands-on, hands·on´, *a.* That which provides persons with direct involvement or experience in practical activities.

hang glid·er, *n.* A glider in the form of a large kite from which the rider hangs in a harness. – **hang glid·ing,** *n.*

hard-line, härd´line, *a.* Pertaining to or advocating a firm or severe approach.

haute cui·sine, ōt kwē·zēn´, [Fr.] A refined style of cookery involving elaborate preparation and careful presentation of food.

he·mo·di·al·y·sis, hēmo·dī·al´i·sis, *n.* A process in which blood is removed from the body for purification and then returned.

her·ba·ceous, er·bā´shus, *a.* Like an herb; soft, not woody; of the texture and color of a leaf.

high en·er·gy phy·sics, *n.* A branch of physics that uses particle acceleration to study the properties and interaction of elementary particles.

hip-hug·gers, hip´hug·erz, *n.pl.* Pants that fit closely and rest on the hips.

hit man, *n. Informal.* A man who works for a crime syndicate as its professional assassin.

hy·dro·foil, hī·dro·foil´, *n.* A motorboat which travels a short distance above the water with the aid of metal fins to give it lift.

hype, hīp, *n. Informal.* Something that intends to deceive; exaggerated advertising. – *v.t.,* **hyped, hyp·ing.** – **hyped-up,** *a.*

i·den·ti·ty cri·sis, *n.* An individual's confusion or conflict concerning his or her social role, usu. occurring during adolescence.

im·mu·no·sup·pres·sant, im´yu·nō·su·pres´ant, *n.* A drug that suppresses immune responses of the organism. – **im·mu·no·sup·pres·sion,** *n.*

in·for·ma·tion re·triev·al, *n.* Techniques for storing, recovering, and communicating information, esp. by means of computers.

in-house, in´hous, *a.* Internal; pertaining to that which occurs within an organization or group.

in·ner cit·y, *n.* The central, usu. older and more densely, populated, section of a city. –

in·er·cit·y, *a.*

in·ten·sive care, *n.* Hospital care for gravely ill patients in specially designed facilities with monitoring devices and life-support systems. –*a.*

jaw·bon·ing, *n.* A forceful appeal by the president or chief of state to labor and business leaders for restraint on wages and prices. – **jaw·bone,** *v.t.*, **-boned, -bon·ing.**

Je·sus freak, *n. (Often cap. F)* A member of a group of young fundamentalist Christians, often practicing communal living and street preaching.

kink·y, kingk′ē, *a.*, **-i·er, -i·est.** *Informal.* Appealing to unconventional tastes, esp. as regards sex; strange or outlandish: *kinky* clothes; sexually deviant. – **kink·i·ness,** *n.*

ki·wi fruit, kē′wē frŏt, *n.* The fruit of the Chinese gooseberry. Also **ki·wi berry.**

klutz, klutz, *n.* A clumsy or awkward person. – **klutz·y,** *a.*

knee-jerk, nē′jerk, *a.* Automatic, predictable.

kun·da·li·ni, kûn·da·lē′nē, *n. (Often cap.)* In the discipline of yoga, the life-force that lies at the base of the spine until it is released to cause enlightenment.

kung fu, kung′fö, *n.* A Chinese self-defense or martial art similar to karate.

laid-back, lād bak, *a.* Very relaxed; easygoing: the *laid-back* life in California.

land·mark, *n.* A building or other structure of sufficient historical interest to be set aside for preservation.

L-do·pa, el·dō′pa, *n.* A drug used in the treatment of Parkinson's disease.

LED, el·ē·dē, *n.* A diode that emits light upon application of voltage, used in digital watches and pocket calculators.

lei·sure suit, *n.* An informal suit consisting of a shirt-type jacket and matching pants.

let·ter bomb, *n.* An explosive device mailed in an envelope and designed to explode upon opening.

lib·er·a·tion, *n.* A movement that seeks equal rights for a given group: women's *liberation.*

life-sup·port sys·tem, *n.* A system that provides the necessary items (air, water, waste disposal, etc.) to maintain the life and health of a person in a hostile environment (as outer space).

ma·cho, mä′chō, *a.* Possessing masculine characteristics to a marked degree, esp. a sense of superiority over women; virile.

ma·cro·bi·ot·ic, mak·rŏ·bī·ot′ik, *a.* Pertaining to a restricted diet, containing chiefly whole grains and vegetables undertaken to promote health.

mam·mog·ra·phy, ma·mog′ra·fē, *n.* Breast examination by means of X-ray for early detection of cancer.

ma·ni·cot·ti, man·a·käd′ē, *n.pl.*,

ma·ni·cot·ti [It.] Pasta in the shape of a tube, often stuffed with ricotta cheese and served with a tomato sauce.

mar·tial arts, *n.pl.* Oriental combat arts widely practiced today as sports (as judo, kung fu, karate); sing., one of these arts.

ma·ven, ma·vin, mä′ven, *n.*, An expert; one who is experienced.

mer·cy kill·ing, *n.* Euthanasia.

mer·i·toc·ra·cy, mer·i·tok′ra·se, *n.pl.*, **-cies.** Leadership by those with talent; an educational system that selects and promotes the talented. – **mer·it·o·crat·ic,** mer·it·ŏ·kra′tik, *a.*

mi·cro·dot, mī′kro·dot, *n.* A reproduction of printed material, photographically reduced to a dot for security or ease in transmission.

mi·cro·e·lec·tron·ics, mī·krō·i·lek·t-ron′iks, mi·krŏ·ē·lek·tron′iks, *n.*, A branch of electronics dealing with miniature components and circuits.

mi·cro·sur·ger·y, mī·kro·sur′j·rē, *n.* Extremely delicate manipulation (as by a laser beam) of living tissue or its components.

mi·cro·teach·ing, mī·kro·tē·ching, *n.* A practice teaching technique in which the student teaches a small class for a short period of time and is videotaped for self-viewing and evalution.

mid·dle A·mer·i·ca, *n. (Often cap.)* The middle class in the U.S., esp. the conservative element. – **mid·dle A·mer·i·can,** *a.*

mod, mod, *a. (Often cap.) Informal.* Modern, up-to-date, current; unconventional.

mon·e·tar·ism, mon′i·tar·iz·am, *n.* An economic theory which states that prices vary directly with the amount of money in circulation and its availability while the value of money varies inversely with these factors. – **mon·e·tar·ist,** *a.*

mo·to·cross, mō′ta·kros, *n.* A cross-country motorcycle race.

mo·tor home, *n*. A trailer home; a self-contained home on a bus or truck chassis.

mous·sa·ka, mū'·ä·ka, *n*. A Middle Eastern dish of ground lamb and eggplant, topped with a sauce.

Ms., miz. Used in place of Mrs. or Miss when a woman's marital status is not known or is irrelevant.

mul·ti·lane, mul'ti·lān, *a*. Having many lanes, as for traffic: a *multilane* highway.

mul·ti·me·di·a, mul·ti·mē'·dē·a, *a*. Using or including several media (as print, pictorial, videotape).

mul·ti·na·tion·al, mul·ti·nash'a·nal, *a*. Involving or relating to more than two nations: a *multinational* corporation; involving more than two nationalities: a *multinational* heritage.

my·e·lo·fi·bro·sis, mī·e·lō·fī'brō·sis, *n*. An anemic condition that affects the bone marrow, liver, and spleen. — **my·e·lo·fi·bro·tic,** *a*.

My·lar, mī'lär, *n*. *Trademark*. A polyester film.

na·no·sec·ond, nā'no·sek·and, *n*. One billionth of a second.

Na·tive A·mer·i·can, *n*. An American Indian. — *a*.

na·tur·al food, *n*. Food free from additives (as artificial colorings, flavorings, or preservatives).

ne·ma·toid, nem'a·toid, *a*. Belonging to the phylum of unsegmented, parasitic worms.

new math, new math·e·mat·ics, *n*. An approach to mathematics based on set theory, esp. when taught in elementary and secondary schools.

no-fault, nō'falt, *a*. Pertaining to an insurance plan for motor vehicles under which the victim of an accident is compensated for actual losses but not for claims of pain or suffering by his own insurance company, regardless of who was at fault; pertaining to a divorce law in which neither party is held responsible.

non·a·ligned, non·a·līnd', *a*. Not allied with other countries, esp. not with the Communist or non-Communist blocs: *nonaligned* nations.

non·per·son, non·per'san, *n*. A person regarded as never having existed; one who lacks legal or social status.

nosh, nosh, *n*. A light snack.

nu·die, nöd'ē, nüd'ē, *a*. Featuring nudes (as films or magazines).

nuts and bolts, *n.pl*. The practical working parts of a machine or process, as opposed to theory and speculation. — **nuts-and-bolts,** *a*.

off-track bet·ting, af'trak bet'ing, *n*. Parimutuel betting at places other than the racetrack.

on-cam·er·a, on·kam'ar·a, on·kam'ra, *a*., *adv*. Pertaining to that which is in the range of a movie or T.V. camera.

op-ed page, op'ed, *n*. The page opposite to a newspaper's editorial page, often featuring individual columnists.

o·pen class·room, *n*. A flexible approach to elementary education featuring individualization of activities and open discussion.

o·pen en·roll·ment, *n*. Enrollment of students in public schools other than those in their neighborhood; acceptance in a college or university without meeting formal entrance requirements.

o·pen-heart, ō'pen härt, *a*. Pertaining to or performed on a heart laid open for inspection and treatment, its functions taken over by machines: *open-heart* surgery.

pa·ra·pro·fes·sion·al, par·a·pra·fesh'a·nul, *n*. An aide trained to assist a professional, as a teacher or doctor.

pa·ri·e·tals, pa·rī'i·tals, *n.pl*. Regulations governing visiting privileges for members of the opposite sex in college or university dormitories.

peace·nik, pēs'nik, *n*. One who opposes war; one who participates in organizations, marches, or demonstrations in support of peace and against war.

pet·ro·dol·lars, pe·trō·dol'ers, *n.pl*. The dollars (or other foreign currency) obtained by petroleum exporting countries from their sales abroad.

pill·head, pil'hed, *n*. A person who takes pills, esp. mood-altering drugs, for nonmedical reasons.

plate-tec·ton·ics, plāt·tek·ton'·iks, *n.pl*. *but sing. in constr*. A geological theory that the lithosphere of the earth is divided into plates which float on the mantle and that earthquakes or tremors often occur along the boundaries of these plates.

plea bar·gain·ing, *n*. The process of negotiating an agreement between the de-

fendant and the prosecutor under which the former pleads guilty to a reduced charge.

points, *n.pl.* A percentage of the face value of a loan (as for a mortgage) added on as a service charge.

pole lamp, *n.* A lamp consisting of a pole braced between floor and ceiling to which several light fixtures are attached.

pol·y·un·sat·u·rat·ed, pol·lē·un·sa·tū·rā'·ted, *a.* (Said of a fat or oil) rich in unsaturated bonds. – **pol·y·un·sat·u·rate,** *n.*

poor-mouth, pur'mouTH, *v.i.* To claim poverty as an excuse or defense. – *v.t.* To speak of disparagingly.

po·si·tion pa·per, *n.* A detailed report recommending a particular course of action.

pre·teen, prē'tēn, *a.* Less than 13 years old, esp. between 10 - 13; pertaining to goods produced for preteen children.

pri·or·i·tize, prī'or·i·tīz, *v.t.,* **-tized, -tizing.** To arrange (as in a list or rating system) items, projects, or goals in order of priorty.

pro·mo, prō'mō, *a.* Promotional.

psych-out, sīk'out, *n.* An act or instance of correctly anticipating or analyzing a situation or the motives of another person; an instance of psychological intimidation.

pub·lic tel·e·vi·sion, *n.* Noncommercial television.

pu·er·per·al fe·ver, pū·er'per·al, *n.* A disease that results from infection of the placental site after delivery of the fetus.

pul·sar, pul'sär, *n.* A celestial source of regular radio waves of short interval: thought to be a neutron star.

quark, kwärk, *n.* A hypothetical particle in physics.

qua·sar, kwā'zär, *n.* Quasi-stellar radio source; a distant celestial object that resembles a star and emits radio waves.

rap·id eye move·ment, *n.* Rapid coordinated movements of the eyes associated with certain periods of sleep and dreaming.

red dev·il, *n. Informal.* Secobarbital, a hypnotic and sedative drug, in a red capsule.

reel-to-reel, rēl·to·rēl, *a.* Pertaining to magnetic tape that must be threaded to a take-up reel: a *reel-to-reel* tape recorder.

reg·gae, rā'·gä, *n.* West Indian popular music combining blues elements with a pulsating rhythm.

REM, är·ē·em', *n.* Rapid eye movement.

rep·li·ca·ble, rep'li·ka·bal, *a.* Capable of being replicated.

re·tro-en·gine, re'trō·en·jin, *n.* A spacecraft engine used to reduce speed by producing a thrust in the direction opposite to the motion of the craft.

rhy·thm and blues, *n.* Blues music marked by a strong uncomplicated beat, often with amplified accompaniment.

right on, *interj.* Used to signal agreement or support.

scam, skam, *n.* A deceptive means or instance of obtaining money; a swindle.

scan·ning e·lec·tron mi·cro·scope, *n.* An electron microscope capable of forming a 3-dimensional image of an object on a cathode-ray tube. Also **scan·ning mi·cro·scope.**

scram jet, skram jet, *n.* An airplane engine of the ramjet type which burns fuel in a supersonic airstream to produce thrust after reaching supersonic speed.

self-ac·tu·al·ize, self·ak'·chö·a·līz, *v.i.* To fully realize one's potential.

self-con·cept, self·kon'sept, *n.* One's mental image of oneself.

sem·i-dark·ness, sem·ē·därk'·nis, *n.* Partial darkness.

sem·i-ob·scur·i·ty, sem·ē·ab·skur·i·tē, *n.* Partial obscurity.

sen·si·tiv·i·ty train·ing, *n.* Training in a small interactive group designed to heighten participants' awareness of their own feelings and the feelings of others and to improve interpersonal relations.

she-ass, shē'as, *n.* A female ass.

shrink-wrap, shringk'rap, *v.t.* To package in clear plastic film which is then heat-shrunk to conform to the contours of the object.

si·tu·a·tion com·e·dy, *n.* A television or radio comedy series with the same cast of characters continuing through generally unconnected episodes.

skate-board, skāt'bōrd, skāt'bard, *n.* A board about two feet by six inches mounted on roller-skate wheels and generally ridden in a standing position. – **skate-board·er,** *n.* – **skate-board·ing,** *n.*

skin·ny-dip, skin'ē·dip, *v.i. Informal.* To swim in the nude. – **skin·ny-dip·per,** *n.* – **skin·ny-dip·ping,** *n.*

slam·mer, slam'er, *n. Informal.* Prison or a jail: usu. with *the:* He's in the *slammer* now.

slap shot, *n.* An ice hockey shot made so that the puck is likely to leave the ice.

slop·py joe, slop′ē·jō, *n.* Ground beef in a thick chili sauce, usu. served hot on a bun.

so·di·um·pen·to·bar·bi·tol, sō·dē·um·pen·tō·bär′·bi·tol, *n.* The sodium salt of the barbiturate $C_{11}H_{18}N_2O_3$ used as a sedative and antispasmodic.

sud·den in·fant death syn·drome, *n.* The death of an apparently healthy infant, causes unknown, usu. occurring in the first year of life. Also **crib death.**

swing·er, *n.* A person who is up-to-date and a lively participant in the current fashions; one who is freely sexually active.

tivity by means of mathematical models with a view to determining efficient means of attaining its desired end; the professional which makes such studies. – **sys·tems a·na·lyst,** *a.*

TA, tē·ā, *n.* A teaching assistant, usu. at a university or college.

TA, *n.* Transactional analysis.

tax shel·ter, *n.* An allowance or credit factor which reduces taxes on current earnings for a corporation or an individual investor.

teen·y bop·per, tē′·nē·bop·ər, *n.* A teenager, esp. a girl devoted to current fads in music.

tel·ex, tel′eks, *n.* Teletype communications through automatic exchanges. –*v.t.*

TESL, tē·ē·es·el, *n.* Teaching English as a second language.

tha·lid·o·mide, tha·lid′o·mīd, *n.* A sedative drug which, when used by pregnant mothers, caused malformations in their infants.

theme park, *n.* An amusement park in which the activities, games, and structures relate to a central theme.

third world, *n.* *(Often cap.)* A group of non-aligned nations, esp. in Africa and Asia; the underdeveloped nations of the world; the aggregate of minority groups within a culture.

threads, *n.pl. Informal.* Clothes.

time tri·al, *n.* A competition (as a race) in which participants are individually timed over a set distance.

tish·ri, tish′ri, *n.* The first month in the Jewish calendar (seventh month of the ecclesiastical year).

to·ken·ism, tō′ke·niz·am, *n.* A practice or policy that makes only a small symbolic effort (as towards desegregation).

trade-off, trād′of, *n.* A compromise among desired goals or possibilities when all cannot be achieved simultaneously; yielding one consideration in return for another.

trail bike, *n.* A motorcycle designed to travel cross-country and to be easily transportable on an automobile bumper.

tran·scen·den·tal med·i·ta·tion, *n.* A meditation technique designed to foster spiritual calm and well-being by releasing the mind through use of a mantra.

turn on, *v.t. Informal.* To cause (as a person) to experience intensely, by means of a drug (as marijuana or LSD); to stimulate or pleasurably excite: *The concert really turned him on.* –*v.i.* – **turn-on,** *n.*

un·flap·pa·ble, un·flap′a·bal, *a.* Assured, self-controlled; not easily upset.

u·ni·sex, ū′ni·seks, *n.* Being undistinguishable as to sex. –*a.*

up·tight, up′tīt, *a.* Apprehensive; tense; angry; in financial difficulty; rigidly conventional. – **up·tight·ness,** *n.*

up·ward mo·bil·i·ty, *n.* The ability to rise to a higher socioeconomic level. – **up·ward·ly mo·bile,** *a.*

voice-o·ver, voys′ō·ver, *n.* A disembodied voice used as narration in motion pictures or on T.V.

WASP, Wasp, *n.* A white Anglo-Saxon Protestant; a member of the dominant, privileged class in the U.S. – **Wasp·ish,** *a.* – **Wasp·ish·ness,** *n.*

wa·ter bed, *n.* A bed in which the mattress consists of a large plastic bag containing water.

wind·chill, wind′chil, *n.* The combined effects of a given temperature and wind speed expressed as a still-air temperature having a similar effect. Also **wind-chill fac·tor, wind·chill in·dex.**

wok, wäk, *n.* A pan with a curved bottom used to cook Chinese food.

work·a·hol·ic, wark·a·ha′lik, wark·a·hol′ik, *n.* A person who works compulsively, tending to exclude leisure and family activities.

zip code, ZIP code, *n.* A five-digit number that identifies each postal delivery area in the U.S.

Table of Alphabets

ARABIC   HEBREW   GREEK   RUSSIAN[3]   GERMAN   ROMAN[9]

ARABIC

Letter	Name	Transliteration
ا	alif	'
ب	ba	b
ت	ta	t
ث	sa	th
ج	jim	j
ح	ha	h
خ	kha	kh
د	dal	d
ذ	zal	th
ر	ra	r
ز	za	z
س	sin	s
ش	shin	sh
ص	sad	s
ض	dad	d
ط	ta	t
ظ	za	z
ع	ain	'
غ	ghain	gh
ف	fa	f
ق	qaf	k
ك	kaf	k
ل	lam	l
م	mim	m
ن	nun	n
ه	ha	h
و	waw	w
ى	ya	y

HEBREW

Letter[1]	Name	Transliteration
א	aleph	'
ב	beth	b, v
ג	gimel	g
ד	daleth	d
ה	he	h
ו	vav	v, w
ז	zayin	z
ח	kheth	ḥ
ט	teth	ṭ
י	yod	y, j, i
כ, ך[1]	kaph	k, kh
ל	lamed	l
מ, ם[1]	mem	m
נ, ן[1]	nun	n
ס	samekh	s
ע	ayin	
פ, ף[1]	pe	p, f
צ, ץ[1]	tsadi	ṣ
ק	koph	ḳ
ר	resh	r
שׂ	sin	ś
שׁ	shin	sh
ת	tav	t, th

GREEK

Letter[2]	Name	Transliteration
Α α	alpha	a
Β β	beta	b
Γ γ	gamma	g
Δ δ	delta	d
Ε ε	epsilon	e
Ζ ζ	zeta	z
Η η	eta	ē
Θ θ	theta	th
Ι ι	iota	i
Κ κ	kappa	k
Λ λ	lambda	l
Μ μ	mu	m
Ν ν	nu	n
Ξ ξ	xi	x
Ο ο	omicron	o
Π π	pi	p
Ρ ρ	rho	r, rh
Σ σ, ς[1]	sigma	s
Τ τ	tau	t
Υ υ	upsilon	u, y
Φ φ	phi	ph
Χ χ	chi	kh, ch
Ψ ψ	psi	ps
Ω ω	omega	ō

RUSSIAN[3]

Letter[2]	Transliteration
А а	a
Б б	b
В в	v
Г г	g
Д д	d
Е е	e, ye
Ж ж	zh
З з	z
И и	i
Й й	ĭ, i, y
К к	k
Л л	l
М м	m
Н н	n
О о	o
П п	p
Р р	r
С с	s
Т т	t
У у	u
Ф ф	f
Х х	kh, x
Ц ц	ts, c
Ч ч	ch, č
Ш ш	sh, š
Щ щ	shch, šč
Ъ ъ[4]	''
Ы ы	y, i
Ь ь[5]	'
Э э	e
Ю ю	yu
Я я	ya

GERMAN

Letter[6]	Letter[7]	Transliteration
𝔄 𝔞	Aa	a
𝔄̈ 𝔞̈	Ää	ae
𝔅 𝔟	Bb	b
ℭ 𝔠	Cc	c
𝔇 𝔡	Dd	d
𝔈 𝔢	Ee	e
𝔉 𝔣	Ff	f
𝔊 𝔤	Gg	g
ℌ 𝔥	Hh	h
ℑ 𝔦	Ii	i
𝔍 𝔧	Jj	j
𝔎 𝔨	Kk	k
𝔏 𝔩	Ll	l
𝔐 𝔪	Mm	m
𝔑 𝔫	Nn	n
𝔒 𝔬	Oo	o
𝔒̈ 𝔬̈	Öö	oe
𝔓 𝔭	Pp	p
𝔔 𝔮	Qq	q
ℜ 𝔯	Rr	r
𝔖 ſ, 𝔰[8]	Ss	s
	–ß	ss
𝔗 𝔱	Tt	t
𝔘 𝔲	Uu	u
𝔘̈ 𝔲̈	Üü	ue
𝔙 𝔳	Vv	v
𝔚 𝔴	Ww	w
𝔛 𝔵	Xx	x
𝔜 𝔶	Yy	y
𝔷 𝔷	Zz	z

ROMAN[9]

Letter[2]
A a
B b
C c
D d
E e
F f
G g
H h
I i
J j
K k
L l
M m
N n
O o
P p
Q q
R r
S s
T t
U u
V v
W w
X x
Y y
Z z

1. The alternative form is used only at the end of a word.   2. Upper- and lower-case.   3. Sometimes called Cyrillic. Each Slavic language (see World Families of Languages, page xiv) uses a different modified form of the Cyrillic alphabet.   4. A sign used to indicate the palatalization of a preceding consonant.   5. A sign used to indicate the nonpalatalization of a preceding consonant.   6. German Fraktur, upper- and lower-case.   7. Latin equivalent, upper- and lower-case.   8. The alternative form is used only at the end of a syllable.   9. Scandinavian (North Germanic) languages use the Roman alphabet with the following additional characters: Danish, Å å, Æ æ, Ø ø; Icelandic, Æ æ, Ð ð, Ö ö, Þ þ; Norwegian, Å å, Æ æ, Ø ø; Swedish, Ä ä, Å å, Ö ö.

A

A, a, ā, *n.* The first letter of the English alphabet and of nearly every alphabet in the world.

a, ā, *a, indef. art.* Used before words beginning with consonant sounds, [*an* is used before vowel sounds]. Used before nouns in the singular; before collectives which imply a number of persons or things: *a* dozen, *a* few; before a proper name used as a type of character: *a* Napoleon; with distributive measures: *a* mile *a* minute, *a* hundred *a* year.

A, ā, *n.* A symbol marking the first in order or quality of a series.

A-1, ā/wən/, *a.* Superior; first-class.

aard•vark, ärd/värk, *n.* A large South African four-footed, burrowing, toothless mammal. It has strong claws, an extensible tongue, large ears and tail, and feeds principally on ants and termites.

AB, ā/bē/, *n.* One of the major blood types.

A.B. Abbr. for Bachelor of Arts, a college-level degree.

a•back, ə•bak/, *adv.* Backward; catching the wind against the forward side so as to urge a sailing vessel backward. —**taken aback,** taken by surprise.

ab•a•cus, ab/ə•kəs, ə•bak/əs, *n. pl.,* **ab•a•cus•es,** **ab•a•ci,** ab/ə•sī. A counting frame holding beads on rods, widely used by Orientals for making mathematical calculations.

a•baft, ə•baft/, ə•bäft/, *adv., prep.* On or toward the stern, aft, or hinder part of a ship.

ab•a•lo•ne, ab•ə•lō/nē, *n.* A marine mollusk, a species of ear shell which furnishes lightly colored mother-of-pearl.

a•ban•don, ə•ban/dən, *v.t.* To give up wholly; yield completely; surrender without restraint; forsake or desert; to banish; to bail out of an aircraft; give in to personal feelings.—*n.* a letting oneself go freely. —**a•ban•doned,** *a.* —**a•ban•don•er,** *n.* —**a•ban•don•ment,** *n.*

a•base, ə•bās/, *v.t.,* **a•based, a•bas•ing.** To reduce or lower, as in rank; humble; degrade. —**a•base•ment,** *n.*

a•bash, ə•bash/, *v.t.* To confuse; make ashamed. —**a•bash•ment,** *n.*

a•bate, ə•bāt/, *v.t.,* **a•bat•ed, a•bat•ing.** To bring down; reduce in amount; diminish; curtail; also, to deduct or subtract; omit. *Law.* To put down or suppress, as a nuisance; suspend or extinguish, as an action; annul, as a writ.—*v.i.* To go down; decrease; subside. *Law.* To fail; become void. —**a•bat•a•ble,** *a.* —**a•bate•ment,** *n.* —**a•bat•er,** *n.*

ab•at•toir, ab•ə•twär/, *n.* A slaughterhouse.

ab•ba•cy, ab/ə•sē, *n.* The office, dignity, rights, and privileges of an abbot; the jurisdiction of an abbot or abbey. —**ab•ba•tial,** ə•bā/shəl, *a.*

ab•bey, ab/ē, *n. pl.,* **ab•beys.** A monastery governed by an abbot or a convent governed by an abbess; a society of persons of either sex, secluded from the world, and devoted to religion; the buildings so occupied. —**ab•bess,** *n. fem.* —**ab•bot,** *n.*

ab•bre•vi•a•tion, ə•brē•vē•ā/shən, *n.* Reduction in length; abridgment; reduced or shortened form, esp., part of a word or phrase used as a symbol for the whole. —**ab•bre•vi•ate,** ə•brē/vē•āt, *v.t.,* —**at•ed,** **at•ing.** —**ab•bre•vi•a•tor,** *n.*

ABC, ā•bē•sē/, *n. pl.,* **ABC's, ABCs.** *Usu. pl.* The alphabet. The beginnings of any subject, practice, or field of knowledge.

ab•di•cate, ab/də•kāt, *v.t.,* **-cat•ed, -cat•ing.** To give up, renounce, lay down, relinquish, or withdraw from in a voluntary, public, or formal manner, as a throne, duties, etc.; vacate; surrender; resign; reject; disinher-

it.—*v.i.* To renounce or give up power voluntarily. —**ab•di•ca•tion,** ab•də•kā/shən, *n.*

ab•do•men, ab•də•mən, ab•dō/mən, *n.* That part of the human body which lies between the chest and the hips; the rearmost of the three parts of a perfect insect. —**ab•dom•i•nal,** ab•dom/ə•nəl, *a.* —**ab•dom•i•nal•ly,** *adv.*

ab•duct, ab•dəkt/, *v.t.* To take away secretly and by force; to draw away from the main axis of the body or from a part of the body. —**ab•duc•tion,** ab•dək/shən, *n.* —**ab•duc•tor,** *n.*

a•beam, ə•bēm/, *adv.* In the direction of the beams or sides, that is, at right angles to the length or keel of a ship.

a•bed, ə•bed/, *adv.* In bed; gone to bed; on the bed; restricted to bed.

ab•er•rance, ab•er/əns, *n.* A straying away; deviation from what is regular or normal; condition of aberration; deviation of a curve from its circle of curvature. Also **ab•er•ran•cy.**

ab•er•rant, ab•er/ənt, ə•ber/ənt, *a.* Straying from the usual or normal method or course of action; not being truthful or proper; exceptional or abnormal.—*n.* One who deviates from the accepted social behavior pattern of the group. —**ab•er•rant•ly,** *adv.*

ab•er•ra•tion, ab•ə•rā/shən, *n.* Deviation from the right course, or from a standard or usual action; abnormal action or state; apparent displacement of a heavenly body. —**ab•er•ra•tion•al,** *a.*

a•bet, ə•bet/, *v.t.,* **a•bet•ted, a•bet•ting.** To encourage by aid or approval, referring to evil actions; incite; support; encourage; back up. —**a•bet•ment,** *n.* —**a•bet•tor, a•bet•ter,** *n.*

a•bey•ance, ə•bā/əns, *n.* A state of expectation or waiting: to hold in *abeyance.*

ab•hor, ab•hôr/, ab•hor/, *v.t.,* **ab•horred, ab•hor•ring.** To hate or loathe; shrink from with horror. —**ab•hor•rence,** *n.* —**ab•hor•rer,** *n.*

ab•hor•rent, ab•hôr/ənt, ab•hor/ənt, *a.* Hateful; utterly repugnant. —**ab•hor•rent•ly,** *adv.*

a•bide, ə•bīd/, *v.i.,* **a•bode** or **a•bi•ded, a•bid•ing.** To take up one's abode; to reside.—*v.t.* To be prepared for; to await; be able to endure or sustain; remain firm under; to tolerate. —**abide by,** to adhere to; to maintain; to remain faithful to; to remain satisfied with. —**a•bid•ance,** *n.*

a•bid•ing, ə•bī/ding, *a.* Continuing; permanent; steadfast: an *abiding* faith. —**a•bid•ing•ly,** *adv.*

a•bil•i•ty, ə•bil/ə•tē, *n. pl.,* **-ties.** The state or condition of being able; aptitude; competence; capability; power to do something, whether physical, mental, legal, etc. *Usu. pl.* Talents, or acquired proficiencies; powers of the mind.

ab•ject, ab/jekt, ab•jekt/, *a.* Sunk to a low condition or value; worthless, mean; low, groveling. —**ab•jec•tion,** ab•jek/shən, *n.* A low state; meanness of spirit; abjectness; abasement. —**ab•ject•ly,** *adv.* —**ab•ject•ness,** *n.*

ab•jure, ab•jûr/, *v.t.,* **ab•jured, ab•jur•ing.** To renounce upon oath; forswear; to reject or withdraw from; abandon, as allegiance or errors; to recant or retract; to relinquish. —**ab•ju•ra•tion,** ab•jə•rā/shən, *n.* —**ab•jur•er,** *n.*

ab•late, ab•lāt/, *v.t.,* **ab•lat•ed, ab•lat•ing.** To dissipate by cutting, melting, wearing away, etc.—*v.i.* To be ablated; to be cut or melted and withdrawn at a high temperature; to carry away heat generated by air friction.

ab•la•tion, ab•lā/shən, *n.* The act of taking away;

---

a- hat, fāte, fāre, fäther; **e-** met, mē; **i-** pin, pīne; **o-** not, nōte, ôrb, moove (move), boy, pownd;
u- cūbe, bŭll, tûk (took); **ch-** chin; **th-** thick, ŧhen; **zh-** vizhon (vision); ə- əgo, takən, pencəl, lemən, bərd (bird).

removal, esp. by surgery; the melting of the nose cone of a space vehicle as it reenters the atmosphere; a process of wearing or melting away. **—ab·la·tive,** ab/lə·tiv, a.

a·blaze, ə·blāz/, a. In a blaze; in a state of excitement, anger, or desire; on fire; full of bright color.

a·ble, ā/bəl, a. Having the power, means, skill, or qualification; sufficient; competent; qualified; clever; having strong or unusual powers of mind; gifted; vigorous; active. **—a·bly,** adv.

a·ble-bod·ied, ā/bəl-bod/ēd, a. Having a strong body; having enough strength for work; skilled in seamanship.

a·bloom, ə·bloom/, a., adv. In a blooming state.

ab·lu·tion, ə·bloo/shən, n. The act of washing; cleansing or purification by a liquid, usually water; specifically, a washing of the body as a part of religious rites. **—ab·lu·tion·ar·y,** a.

ab·ne·gate, ab/nə·gāt/, v.t., -gat·ed, -gat·ing. To deny; to renounce; to surrender.

ab·nor·mal, ab·nôr/məl, a. Not conforming to rule; deviating from a type or standard; irregular; unnatural. **—ab·nor·mal·ly,** adv. **—ab·nor·mal·i·ty,** ab·nôr·mal/ə·tē, n. pl., -ties.

a·board, ə·bōrd/, ə·bôrd/, adv. On board; alongside; within a ship, plane, or other passenger vehicle.—prep. On board; into: to go aboard a ship. **—all a·board!** A call for passengers to board a vehicle.

a·bode, ə·bōd/, n. Place of residence; home; a place where a person abides.

a·bol·ish, ə·bol/ish, v.t. To do away with; to nullify; to destroy; to make void; to annul; to put out of existence; to put an end to, as laws, customs, or conditions of existence. **—a·bol·ish·a·ble,** a. **—a·bol·ish·er,** n. **—a·bol·ish·ment,** n. **—ab·o·li·tion,** ab·ə·lish/ən, n.

ab·o·li·tion·ism, ab·ə·lish/ə·niz·əm, n. The principles or policies which foster abolition.

ab·o·li·tion·ist, ab·ə·lish/ən·ist, n. A person who favors the abolition of something, applied especially to those in the 19th century who favored the end of slavery in the United States.

A-bomb, n. The atomic bomb.

a·bom·i·na·ble, ə·bom/ə·nə·bəl, a. Deserving or liable to be disliked; detestable; loathsome; odious in the utmost degree. **—a·bom·i·na·bly,** adv.

a·bom·i·nate, ə·bom/ə·nāt, v.t., -nat·ed, -nat·ing. To hate; to abhor; to detest; to loathe. **—a·bom·i·na·tion,** ə·bom·ə·nā/shən, n.

ab·o·rig·i·ne, ab·ə·rij/ə·nē, n. One of the first inhabitants of a country; pl. the original animals and flowers of a region. **—ab·o·rig·i·nal,** ab·ə·rij/ə·nəl, a., n.

a·bort, ə·bôrt/, v.t. To cut short a procedure with an aircraft or space vehicle.—v.i. To miscarry in giving birth; give birth prematurely; appear in an undeveloped state.

a·bor·tion, ə·bôr/shən, n. The act of miscarrying, or producing young prematurely; the product of premature birth.

a·bor·tion·ist, ə·bôr/shə·nist, n. One who induces abortions.

a·bor·tive, ə·bôr/tiv, a. Brought forth in an immature state; rudimentary; imperfectly formed or developed; failed or gone awry; not brought to completion.

a·bound, ə·bownd/, v.i. To have or possess in great quantity; to be filled to capacity; be fully supplied.

a·bout, ə·bowt/, prep. Around; on the outside or surface of; in a circle surrounding; near to in place, time, size, number, quantity, etc.; near to in action; on the point of, or ready; concerned in; engaged in; concerning; relating to; respecting; in control of.—adv. Around the outside; in a circle; near to in number, time, place, quality, or degree.

a·bout-face, ə·bowt/fās, ə·bowt·fās/, n. A complete reversal of opinion or direction; a command to reverse the direction of march.—v.i. To change one's position

so as to face the opposite direction; to reverse one's opinion completely.

a·bove, ə·bəv/, prep. In or to a higher place than; superior to in any respect; too high for; more in number, quantity, or degree than.—adv. In or to a higher place; overhead; before, in rank or order, especially in a book or writing.—n. Heaven; the aforesaid.—a. Preceding; foregoing. **—above all,** before everything else; before every other consideration.

a·bove·board, ə·bəv/bôrd, ə·bəv/bôrd, adv. Within sight; without tricks, dishonesty, or disguise.

ab·ra·ca·dab·ra, ab·rə·kə·dab/rə, n. A word of Eastern origin used in incantations; any charm supposedly used as a magic formula or spell.

a·brade, ə·brād/, v.t., a·brad·ed, a·brad·ing. To rub or wear down, through friction; to erode; to irritate.

a·bra·sion, ə·brā/zhən, n. The act of abrading, wearing, or rubbing off; an injury of the skin by abrading of the outer layer; any scraped area.

a·bra·sive, ə·brā/siv, ə·brā/ziv, a. Serving to abrade.—n. A substance used in grinding or polishing.

a·breast, ə·brest/, adv., a. Side by side: to march four abreast; up to a level or standard: to keep abreast of science; equal in progress.

a·bridge, ə·brij/, v.t., a·bridged, a·bridg·ing. To make shorter while keeping the important contents; to shorten by using fewer words; to condense; to diminish; **—a·bridg·er,** n. **—a·bridg·a·ble, a·bridge·a·ble,** a. **—a·bridg·ment, a·bridge·ment,** n.

a·broad, ə·brôd/, adv. At large; without being contained in narrow limits; in circulation; about; out of doors; beyond or out of the walls of a house or other enclosure; beyond the boundaries of a country; in foreign countries.

ab·ro·gate, ab/rə·gāt, v.t., -gat·ed, -gat·ing. To repeal; to make void; to annul by an authoritative act. **—ab·ro·ga·tion,** ab·rə·gā/shən, n.

ab·rupt, ə·brəpt/, a. Steep; craggy (of rocks, precipices, etc.); sudden; brusque; without notice to prepare the mind for the event; disconnected; having sudden transitions.

ab·scess, ab/ses, n. A collection of pus in the tissue of a body organ or part. **—ab·scessed,** a.

ab·scis·sa, ab·sis/ə, n. pl., -sas, -sae, -sē. Any part of the diameter of a conic section, as an ellipse, intercepted between the vertex and a line at right angles to the axis.

ab·scis·sion, ab·sizh/ən, ab·sish/ən, n. The act of cutting off; severance; removal.

ab·scond, ab·skond/, v.i. To run away, often with stolen valuables, in order to avoid a legal process.

ab·sence, ab/səns, n. The state of being absent; the state of being at a distance in place; the state of being wanting; lack.

ab·sent, ab/sənt, a. Not present; away; lacking; non-existent. **—ab·sent/,** v.t. To keep away intentionally.

ab·sen·tee, ab·sən·tē/, n. One who is absent.

ab·sen·tee·ism, ab·sən·tē/iz·əm, n. A high rate of absence where regular attendance is expected.

ab·sent-mind·ed, ab/sənt·mīn/did, a. Forgetful; preoccupied.

ab·sent with·out leave, a. In the armed forces, gone or absent from one's place of duty without permission but without the intention of deserting.

ab·sinthe, ab/sinth, n. A popular French liqueur consisting of brandy flavored with wormwood.

ab·so·lute, ab/sə·loot, a. Free from restriction or limitation; unconditional; unqualified; perfect; thorough; positive; independent; despotic: an absolute monarchy; viewed independently; not comparative or relative; ultimate. **—ab·so·lute·ly,** adv.

ab·so·lute pitch, n. The exact position of a tone in a standard scale in terms of vibrations per second. The ability to recognize the pitch of a tone, or to sing a particular note without having heard it.

ab·so·lu·tion, ab·sə·loo/shən, n. The act of absolving, or the state of being absolved; forgiveness; remission, as of sin; a form of prayer for pardon.

ab·so·lut·ism, ab′sə·loo·tiz·əm, *n.* The principle or the use of complete power in government; the doctrine of an absolute being; the quality of certainty; positivism. **—ab·so·lut·ist**, *n.*

ab·solve, ab·zolv′, ab·solv′, *v.t.,* **ab·solved, ab·solv·ing.** To set free or release from some duty, obligation, or responsibility; to liberate from the consequences or penalties arising from actions; acquit; to forgive or grant remission of sins (with *from*). **—ab·solv·a·ble,** *a.* **—ab·solv·er,** *n.*

ab·sorb, ab·sôrb′, ab·zôrb′, *v.t.* To drink in; suck up; swallow up; to take up or engage the complete attention or energies; to assimilate. **—ab·sorb·a·bil·i·ty**, *n.* **—ab·sorb·a·ble,** *a.* **—ab·sorb·en·cy,** *n.* **—ab·sorb·ent,** *a.* **—ab·sorp·tion,** ab·sôrp′shən, *n.* **—ab·sorp·tive,** ab·sôrp′tiv, *a.* **—ab·sorp·tiv·i·ty,** ab·sôrp·tiv′ə·tē, *n.*

ab·sorb·ing, ab·sôr′bing, *a.* Very interesting.

ab·stain, ab·stān′, *v.i.* To keep from doing something. **—ab·sten·tion**, ab·sten′shən, *n.* **—ab·sti·nence**, ab′stə·nəns, *n.* **—ab·sti·nent**, ab′stə·nənt, *a.*

ab·ste·mi·ous, ab·stē′mē·əs, *a.* Temperate in use of food and strong drinks; very moderate and plain; very sparing.

ab·stract, ab·strakt′, *v.t.* To reduce to a short statement of the most important ideas; to take away; to remove; to withdraw; to take away mentally; consider separately. **—ab′strakt,** ab·strakt′, *a.* Thought of in itself; not concrete; considered apart from any particular object; hard to understand; based on theory; not practical or applied.**—***n.* A summary; a brief statement of facts. **—ab·strac·tion**, ab·strak′shən, *n.* **—ab·strac·tive,** ab·strak′tiv, *a.*

ab·stract·ed, *a.* Absorbed in thought. **—ab·stract·ed·ly,** *adv.*

ab·struse, ab·stroos′, *a.* Very hard to understand.

ab·surd, ab·sərd′, ab·zərd′, *a.* Ridiculous; nonsensical; unsound; illogical; contradictory; untrue. **—ab·surd·i·ty,** *n. pl.,* **-ties.** **—ab·surd·ly,** *adv.*

a·bun·dance, ə·bən′dəns, *n.* Fullness; a great quantity; wealth.

a·bun·dant, ə·bən′dənt, *a.* Plentiful; ample; rich in supply; sufficient; abounding; overflowing. **—a·bun·dant·ly,** *adv.*

a·buse, ə·būz′, *v.t.,* **a·bused, a·bus·ing.** To misuse; to put to a bad use; to do wrong to; injure; dishonor; to cheat. **—ə·būs′,** *n.* Improper treatment; improper use; misuse; a corrupt practice or custom: the *abuses* of government; injury; insulting language. **—a·bus·er,** ə·bū′zər, *n.*

a·bu·sive, ə·bū′siv, *a.* Insulting. **—a·bu·sive·ly,** *adv.* **—a·bu·sive·ness,** *n.*

a·but, ə·bət′, *v.t.,* **a·but·ted, a·but·ting.** To join at a border or boundary.**—***v.i.* to form a point or line of contact, used with *on, upon, against:* Their home *abuts against* the beach.

a·but·ment, ə·bət′mənt, *n.* A part that joins; junction; the solid part of a pier or wall that supports or holds up a bridge, arch or building.

a·bysm, ə·biz′əm, *n.* Abyss.

a·bys·mal, ə·biz′məl, *n.* Of an abyss; too great to be measured.

a·byss, ə·bis′, *n.* A bottomless opening; anything profound or measureless; hell.

a·ca·cia, ə·kā′shə, *n.* Any of the ornamental trees and shrubs of a genus that belongs to the legume family.

ac·a·deme, ak·ə·dēm′, *n.* Any place for instruction; an academy; environment of an institution of higher learning.

ac·a·dem·ic, ak·ə·dem′ik, *a.* Having to do with higher education; relating to liberal or classical studies, rather than vocational; theoretical; having no

practical value; learned, but lacking in practical application of knowledge; conforming to rules or traditions; conventional.**—***n.* A student or faculty member of a college or university. **—ac·a·dem·i·cal·ly,** *adv.*

ac·a·dem·i·cal, ak·ə·dem′ə·kəl, *n.* A member of an academy; *pl.* the costume proper to the officers and students of a school or college.

ac·a·dem·ic free·dom, *n.* Freedom to teach or study a subject without fear of being interfered with by any official.

a·cad·e·mi·cian, ə·kad·ə·mish′ən, ak·ə·də·mish′ən, *n.* One who belongs to a society set up to promote interest in arts, sciences, etc.

a·cad·e·my, ə·kad′ə·mē, *n. pl.,* **-mies.** A school at a level between a college and an elementary school; a college or school that teaches military subjects; an association for the promotion of literature, science, or art.

a·can·thus, ə·kan′thəs, *n. pl.,* **-thus·es, -thi,** -thī. A plant of the Mediterranean region having large spiny leaves.

a cap·pel·la, ä·kə·pel′ə, *a.* In the style of chapel music; singing without instrumental accompaniment.

ac·cede, ak·sēd′, *v.i.,* **ac·ced·ed, ac·ced·ing.** To agree or assent to terms proposed by another; to give approval; to become a party to by agreeing to terms; to join or be added; to succeed to.

ac·cel·er·ate, ak·sel′ə·rāt, *v.i., v.t.,* **-at·ed, -at·ing.** To move or cause to move faster; hasten; add to the velocity of; bring about or help to bring about more speedily. **—ac·cel·er·a·tive,** ak·sel′ə·rā·tiv, ak·sel′ər·ə·tiv, *a.*

ac·cel·er·a·tion, ak·sel·ə·rā′shən, *n.* The act of accelerating or state of being accelerated; increase in speed; rate of velocity increase.

ac·cel·er·a·tor, ak·sel′ə·rā·tər, *n.* One who or that which accelerates; a device for opening or closing the throttle in an automobile; any device that increases the speed of charged particles.

ac·cent, ak′sent, *n.* A special effort in speech utterance making one syllable stand out more than others, as by a change of pitch or by stress of voice; stress; a mark indicating stress or some other distinction in pronunciation or value; stress in verse, music, etc.; the spoken language that marks a certain group or locality; *mus.* stress given to particular notes. **—ak′sent,** ak·sent′, *v.t.* To pronounce with an accent or stress; mark with an accent; accentuate; emphasize.

ac·cen·tu·al, ak·sen′choo·əl, *a.* Pertaining to accent; rhythmical.

ac·cen·tu·ate, ak·sen′choo·āt, *v.t.,* **-at·ed, -at·ing.** To mark with an accent; emphasize; to make a part of more prominent or pronounced; accent. **—ac·cen·tu·a·tion,** ak·sen·choo·ā′shən, *n.*

ac·cept, ak·sept′, *v.t.* To take (something offered); receive; accede, or assent to; to respond to in a positive way; to receive formally, as into a college or club; understand; to acknowledge and agree to pay, as a check or draft; to assume responsibility for.**—***v.i.* To accept a gift, proposal, invitation, suggestion, etc. **—ac·cept·ance,** *n.* **—ac·cept·er, ac·cep·tor,** *n.*

ac·cept·a·ble, ak·sep′tə·bəl, *a.* Capable or worthy of being accepted; satisfactory; suitable; meeting minimum requirements; merely adequate. **—ac·cept·a·bil·i·ty,** ak·sep·tə·bil′ə·tē, *n.* **—ac·cept·a·bly,** *adv.*

ac·cept·ed, ak·sep′tid, *a.* Commonly approved.

ac·cess, ak′ses, *n.* A means or way of approach; admittance; the state of being approachable; passage allowing communication.

ac·ces·si·ble, ak·ses′ə·bəl, *a.* Able to be attained or approached; easy of access; open to the influence of. **—ac·ces·si·bil·i·ty,** ak·ses·ə·bil′ə·tē, *n.*

ac·ces·sion, ak·sesh′ən, *n.* The act of acceding;

---

a- hat, fāte, fāre, fäther; **e-** met, mē; **i-** pin, pīne; **o-** not, nōte, ôrb, moove (move), boy, pownd; **u-** cūbe, bûll, tûk (took); **ch-** chin; **th-** thick, ŧhen; **zh-** vizhon (vision); **ə-** əgo, takən, pencəl, lemən, bərd (bird).

attainment to an office, right or dignity; addition or increase; something added; addition to property by growth or improvement; an agreement between states or acceptance of a treaty.

ac•ces•so•ry, ak•ses′ə•rē, *a.* Contributing; aiding in producing some effect, or acting in subordination to the principal agent; contributing to a general effect; belonging to something else; accompanying.—*n. pl.,* **-ries.** One who aids or allows a crime; that which belongs to something else, as its principal; that which contributes to the effect of something more important; an accompaniment. —**ac•ces•so•ri•ly,** *adv.* —**ac•ces•so•ri•ness,** *n.*

ac•ci•dent, ak′si•dənt, *n.* Chance or what happens by chance; an event that happens when quite unlooked for; an unforeseen injury to a person; unexpected happening; casualty; mishap; a property or quality of a thing which is not essential.

ac•ci•den•tal, ak•si•den′təl, *a.* Happening by chance or accident; unexpected; casual; fortuitous; nonessential; not necessarily belonging;—*n.* a note or tone which does not occur in the scale of the key in which the piece is composed. —**ac•ci•den•tal•ly,** *adv.*

ac•claim, ə•klām′, *v.t.* To applaud; to acknowledge; to announce; to declare or salute by acclamation.—*n.* A shout of joy; loud applause; approval.

ac•cla•ma•tion, ak•lə•mā′shən, *n.* A shout of applause made by a crowd, indicating joy, hearty assent, approbation, or good wishes; act of acclaiming; an oral vote, often unanimous, showing acceptance. —**ac•clam•a•to•ry,** ə•klam′ə•tôr•ē, *a.*

ac•cli•mate, ak′lə•māt, ə•klī′mit, *v.t., v.i.,* **-mat•ed, -mat•ing.** To adapt or become adapted to a foreign or unfamiliar environment or climate. —**ac•cli•ma•tion,** ak•lə•mā′shən, *n.*

ac•cli•ma•tize, ə•klī′mə•tīz, *v.t., v.i.,* **-tized, -tiz•ing.** To acclimate. —**ac•cli•ma•ti•za•tion,** ə•klī•mə•tə•zā′shən, *n.*

ac•cliv•i•ty, ə•kliv′i•tē, *n. pl.,* **-ties.** An upward slope; an ascent.

ac•co•lade, ak•ə•lād′, ak•ə•läd′, *n.* A tap on the shoulder with the flat of a sword, given in conferring knighthood; any honor, award or commendable notice; words of praise.

ac•com•mo•date, ə•kom′ə•dāt, *v.t.,* **-dat•ed, -dat•ing.** To make suitable, correspondent, or consistent; to fit; adapt; conform; adjust; reconcile; to supply or furnish with required conveniences; to do a favor for; oblige; to have or make room for.—*v.i.* To act conformably; agree.

ac•com•mo•da•tive, ə•kom′ə•dā•tiv, *a.* Disposed to accommodate.

ac•com•mo•dat•ing, ə•kom′ə•dā•ting, *a.* Obliging; yielding to the desires of others.

ac•com•mo•da•tion, ə•kom•ə•dā′shən, *n.* The act of accommodating; adjustment; adaptation; adjustment of differences; reconciliation; anything which supplies a want, as in respect of ease, refreshment, and the like; a convenience; a loan of money; willingness to help others. *Usu. pl.* lodgings.

ac•com•pa•ni•ment, ə•kum′pə•ni•mənt, ə•kump′ni•mənt, *n.* Something incidental or subordinate to the principal thing. The supporting part or parts performed by instruments accompanying a voice, or several voices, or a principal instrument.

ac•com•pa•nist, ə•kum′pə•nist, ə•kump′nist, *n.* The performer in music who plays or sings the accompaniment.

ac•com•pa•ny, ə•kum′pə•nē, *v.t.,* **-nied, -ny•ing.** To go with or attend as a companion or associate; to go together; to be associated or connected with; to play a subordinate musical part to.

ac•com•plice, ə•kom′plis, *n.* A helper or confederate, especially in a crime; a partner or partaker in guilt, usually a subordinate.

ac•com•plish, ə•kom′plish, *v.t.* To complete; to finish entirely; to execute; to carry out; to fulfill or bring

to pass. —**ac•com•plish•a•ble,** *a.* —**ac•com•plish•ment,** *n.*

ac•com•plished, ə•kom′plisht, *a.* Done, completed; skilled, proficient; having many social graces.

ac•cord, ə•kôrd′, *n.* Agreement; harmony of minds: beliefs in *accord;* just correspondence of things; concord; harmony of sound; a formal act of agreement between governments: the Geneva *accords* of 1954. —*v.t.* To grant; to give; to concede: as, to *accord* due praise.—*v.i.* To be in correspondence or harmony. —**of one's own accord,** voluntarily.

ac•cord•ance, ə•kôr′dəns, *n.* The state of being in harmony or agreement.

ac•cord•ing, ə•kôr′ding, *a.* Agreeing; agreeable; in harmony. —**ac•cord•ing•ly,** *adv.*

ac•cord•ing to, agreeable to; in accordance with; as, *according* to what he says.

ac•cor•di•on, ə•kôr′dē•ən, *n.* A portable, keyed, bellowslike wind instrument sounded by means of metallic reeds.—*a.* Having folds like the bellows of an accordion. —**ac•cor•di•on•ist,** *n.*

ac•cost, ə•kôst′, ə•kost′, *v.t.* To approach and speak first to.

ac•couche•ment, ə•koosh′mənt, *n.* Confinement; childbirth.

ac•count, ə•kownt′, *v.t.* To consider; to credit or impute to.—*v.i.* To render an account or statement of particulars: used with *to* or *for;* to furnish an explanation: with *for.*—*n.* A reckoning, enumeration, or computation; a list of debits and credits, or charges; a statement of things bought or sold, of payments, services, etc.; an explanatory statement of particulars, facts, or events; narrative; relation; description; reason or consideration; ground: on all *accounts;* profit; advantage: to turn to *account;* regard; behalf; sake: trouble incurred on one's *account.*

ac•count•a•ble, ə•kown′tə•bəl, *a.* Responsible for a trust. —**ac•count•a•bil•i•ty,** *n.* —**ac•count•a•bly,** *adv.*

ac•count•an•cy, ə•kown′tən•sē, *n.* The keeping or inspecting of accounts.

ac•count•ant, ə•kown′tənt, *n.* One who makes the keeping or examination of accounts his profession.

ac•count•ing, ə•kown′ting, *n.* The theory and system of setting up, keeping, and auditing accounts.

ac•cred•it, ə•kred′it, *v.t.* To attribute to; give credit to; to certify as coming up to a set standard (an educational institute); to believe (a story); to confer authority on; to send with credentials, as an envoy.

ac•cre•tion, ə•krē′shən, *n.* Growth in size or extent; increase by natural growth or by gradual external addition; adhesion or gradual addition of new matter or parts; a whole which results from such growth and accumulation; also, something adhering or gradually added; an accession. —**ac•cre•tive,** *a.*

ac•cru•al, ə•kroo′əl, *n.* Act or process of accruing; accretion; something accrued.

ac•crue, ə•kroo′, *v.i.,* **ac•crued, ac•cru•ing.** To result as a natural growth or addition.

ac•cu•mu•late, ə•kū′myə•lāt, *v.t.,* **-lat•ed, -lat•ing.** To heap or pile up.—*v.i.* To grow to be extensive in number or quantity; to increase greatly.

ac•cu•mu•la•tion, ə•kū•myə•lā′shən, *n.* A collecting or being heaped up; that which has accumulated.

ac•cu•mu•la•tive, ə•kū′myə•lā•tiv, *a.* Causing an accumulation; cumulative.

ac•cu•mu•la•tor, ə•kū′myə•lā•tər, *n.* One who or that which accumulates; *Brit.* a storage cell or battery.

ac•cu•ra•cy, ak′yər•ə•sē, *n.* The condition or quality of being accurate; correctness.

ac•cu•rate, ak′yər•it, *a.* Free from error or defect; exact; precise. —**ac•cu•rate•ly,** *adv.* —**ac•cu•rate•ness,** *n.*

ac•curs•ed, ac•curst, ə•kər′sid, ə•kərst′, *a.* Lying under a curse. —**ac•curs•ed•ly,** *adv.*

ac•cu•sa•tive, ə•kū′zə•tiv, *a.* The objective case; word used as direct object of a verb or preposition.

ac·cuse, ə·kūz′, *v.t.,* **ac·cused, ac·cus·ing.** To charge with a crime, offense, or fault (with *of*): to *accuse* him *of* lying; to blame.—*v.i.* To make an accusation. **—ac·cu·sa·tion,** ak·yə·zā′shən, *n.* **—ac·cu·sa·to·ry,** ə·kū′zə·tôr·ē, ə·kū′zə·tōr·ē, *a.* **—ac·cus·er,** *n.* **—ac·cus·ing·ly,** *adv.*

ac·cused, ə·kūzd′, *n.* One charged with a crime.

ac·cus·tom, ə·kəs′təm, *v.t.* To familiarize by use or habit; to habituate.

ac·cus·tomed, ə·kəs′təmd, *a.* Customary; habitual; usual.

ace, ās, *n.* A unit; a single spot on a card or die, or the card or face of a die so marked; an expert; a champion; a point won by a single stroke; a combat pilot who has shot down at least five enemy planes.—*a.* Excellent; expert.

a·cer·bi·ty, ə·sər′bi·tē, *n.* Sourness, with roughness or bitterness of taste; harshness or severity of temper.

ac·e·tate, as′ə·tāt, *n.* A salt or ester of acetic acid.

a·ce·tic, ə·sē′tik, ə·set′ik, *a.* Having the properties of vinegar; sour.

a·ce·tic ac·id, *n.* An acid found in vinegar that is colorless and very sour.

a·cet·i·fy, ə·set′ə·fī, *v.t.,* **-fied, -fy·ing.** To convert into acid or vinegar.—*v.i.* To become acid. **—a·cet·i·fi·ca·tion,** ə·set·ə·fə·kā′shən, *n.*

ac·e·tone, as′ə·tōn, *n.* A colorless, flammable liquid used as a solvent for paints and varnishes.

a·cet·y·lene, ə·set′ə·lēn, ə·set′ə·lin, *n.* A flammable gas, HC–CH, made with calcium carbide and water: used as a fuel in welding and in organic synthesis.

ache, āk, *n.* Pain, especially a continued dull pain.—*v.i.,* **ached, ach·ing.** To suffer from such a pain.

a·chieve, ə·chēv′, *v.t.,* **a·chieved, a·chiev·ing.** To accomplish; to carry on to a successful close; to attain, as by effort. **—a·chiev·a·ble,** *a.* **—a·chiev·er,** *n.* **—a·chieve·ment,** *n.*

A·chil·les′ heel, ə·kil′ēz, *n.* The single point of weakness in a person or thing.

ach·ro·mat·ic, ak·rə·mat′ik, *a.* Transmitting light without decomposing it into its primary colors.

ac·id, as′id, *a.* Sour, sharp, or biting to the taste; not sweet; not alkaline; sour, sharp, or biting in disposition or manner.—*n.* a compound containing hydrogen as an essential constituent and which possesses a sour taste, changes blue vegetable colors to red, and combines with bases to form salts. A sour substance. *Informal.* the hallucinogenic drug LSD.

ac·id head, *n. Informal.* One who takes LSD for its hallucinogenic effect.

a·cid·ic, ə·sid′ik, *a.* Forming or containing acid.

a·cid·i·fy, ə·sid′ə·fī, *v.i., v.t.,* **-fied, -fy·ing.** To make acid; to convert into an acid; to turn sour. **—a·cid·i·fi·ca·tion,** ə·sid·ə·fə·kā′shən, *n.* **—a·cid·i·fi·er,** ə·sid′ə·fī·ər, *n.*

a·cid·i·ty, ə·sid′ə·tē, *n.* The quality of being acid or sour; sourness; tartness.

ac·i·do·sis, as·i·dō′sis, *n.* Abnormally high acidity of the blood and body tissues.

ac·id test, *n.* A crucial or conclusive test.

a·cid·u·late, ə·sij′ə·lāt, ə·sid′yə·lāt, *v.t.,* **-lat·ed, -lat·ing.** To make slightly acid. **—a·cid·u·la·tion,** ə·sid·yə·lā′shən, *n.*

a·cid·u·lous, ə·sij′ə·ləs, ə·sid′yə·ləs, *a.* Slightly sour in manner or taste; sharp; caustic.

ac·knowl·edge, ak·nol′ij, *v.t.,* **-edged, -edg·ing.** To own or recognize by avowal or by some act; to express thanks or appreciation for; to show gratitude for; to assent to the truth or claims of; to admit to be; to own or confess to; to avow receiving. **—ac·knowl·edge·a·ble,** *a.* **—ac·knowl·edg·er,** *n.* **—ac·knowl·edg·ment, ac·knowl·edge·ment,** *n.*

ac·me, ak′mē, *n.* The top or highest point; summit.

ac·ne, ak′nē, *n.* An inflammatory disease of the skin, arising from the obstruction of the sebaceous glands, and causing pimples on the face.

ac·o·lyte, ak′ə·līt, *n.* An attendant; one of a minor order of clergy, who assists during service; an altar boy; a follower.

ac·o·nite, ak′ə·nīt, *n.* Any plant of a genus which includes monkshood and wolfsbane.

a·corn, ā′kôrn, ā′korn, *n.* The nut, or fruit, of an oak.

a·cous·tic, ə·koo′stik, *a.* Pertaining to the sense or organs of hearing, or to the science of acoustics. Also **a·cous·ti·cal. —a·cous·ti·cal·ly,** *adv.*

a·cous·tics, ə·koo′stiks, *n.* The scientific study of sound; the properties determining audibility or fidelity of sound in an auditorium, etc.

ac·quaint, ə·kwānt′, *v.t.* To make to know; to make aware of; to apprise; to make familiar; to bring into social contact; inform: usually followed by *with:* acquaint a person *with* facts. **—be acquainted with,** to know, but not intimately.

ac·quaint·ance, ə·kwān′təns, *n.* A state of being acquainted, or of having more or less intimate knowledge; personal knowledge; familiarity, followed by *with;* a person known to one, but not intimately. **—ac·quaint·ance·ship,** *n.*

ac·qui·esce, ak·wē·es′, *v.i.,* **-esced, -esc·ing.** To assent or agree quietly or passively. **—ac·qui·es·cence,** *n.* **—ac·qui·es·cent,** *a.*

ac·quire, ə·kwīr′, *v.t.,* **ac·quired, ac·quir·ing.** To get or gain as one's own; to gain for oneself through one's own action. **—ac·quir·er,** *n.* **—ac·quir·a·ble,** *a.* **—ac·quire·ment,** *n.* **—ac·qui·si·tion,** ak·wə·zish′ən, *n.* **—ac·quis·i·tive,** ə·kwiz′ə·tiv, *a.* **—ac·quis·i·tive·ly,** *adv.* **—ac·quis·i·tive·ness,** *n.*

ac·quit, ə·kwit′, *v.t.,* **ac·quit·ted, ac·quit·ting.** To release or discharge from an obligation or the like; to settle; to conduct (oneself). **—ac·quit·tal,** *n.*

a·cre, ā′kər, *n.* A unit of land measure, 160 square rods or 43,560 square feet. *Pl.* lands; estate.

a·cre·age, ā′kər·ij, *n.* The number of acres in a piece of land; acres taken collectively.

ac·rid, ak′rid, *a.* Sharp or biting to the taste or smell; bitter; caustic. **—a·crid·i·ty,** ə·krid′ə·tē, *n.*

ac·ri·mo·ni·ous, ak·rə·mō′nē·əs, *a.* Bitter; caustic; stinging.

ac·ri·mo·ny, ak′rə·mō·nē, *n.* Sharpness of temper; bitterness of expression.

ac·ro·bat, ak′rə·bat, *n.* One who practices vaulting, tumbling, somersaults, trapeze and trampoline gymnastics, etc. **—ac·ro·bat·ic,** ak·rə·bat′ik, *a.*

ac·ro·bat·ics, ak·rə·bat′iks, *n. pl., sing.* or *pl.* in *constr.* The activities of an acrobat; gymnastics.

ac·ro·nym, ak′rə·nim, *n.* A word formed from the initial syllables or letters of other words, as *radar* from *'radio detecting and ranging';*

ac·ro·pho·bi·a, ak·rə·fō′bē·ə, *n.* A great fear of high places.

a·crop·o·lis, ə·krop′ə·lis, *n.* The highest, fortified part of an ancient Greek city.

a·cross, ə·krôs′, ə·kros′, *adv.* From side to side: on or at the other side; intersecting; passing over at any angle; crosswise.—*prep.*

a·cros·tic, ə·krô′stik, ə·kros′tik, *n.* A word puzzle in which the first, last, or other letters of the lines taken in order form a word or phrase. **—a·cros·ti·cal·ly,** *adv.*

a·cryl·ic, ə·kril′ik, *a.* Referring to a group of man-made fibers (for clothing), transparent plastics, paint bases, and solid sheet plastics used in the manufacture of many toys, building products, etc.

ac·ry·lo·ni·trile, ak·rə·lō·nī′tril, ak·rə·lō·nī′trēl, *n.* A colorless, volatile, combustible liquid mainly used in the polymerization of acrylic fibers, synthetic rubber, and plastics.

---

a- hat, fāte, fāre, fäther; **e-** met, mē; **i-** pin, pīne; **o-** not, nōte, ôrb, moove (move), boy, pownd; **u-** cūbe, bŭll, tŭk (took); **ch-** chin; **th-** thick, then; **zh-** vizhon (vision); **ə-** ego, takən, pencəl, lemən, bərd (bird).

act, akt, *v.i.* To exert power; to produce effects; to be in action or motion; to carry into effect a purpose; to behave; to perform, as an actor;—*v.t.* To transact; to do or perform; to represent as real; to perform on or as on the stage; to play; to feign or counterfeit. —**act as,** to serve as; perform the duties or function of. —**act on,** to obey or act in accordance with; to affect. —**act up,** to behave badly.—*n.* That which is done, a deed; the exertion of power; the effect of which power exerted is the cause; division of a play or opera; a decree, edict, or law, especially one proceeding from a legislative body. —**caught in the act,** discovered during a hidden action. —**get into the act,** to join an activity. —**put on an act,** to pretend.

ACTH, *n.* A pituitary hormone that stimulates the cortex of the adrenal glands.

act·ing, ak′ting, *a.* Temporarily doing the job or duties of another person.

ac·tin·ic, ak·tin′ik, *a.* Pertaining to rays, esp. to the chemical rays of the sun; dealing with, or relating to, actinism.

ac·ti·nide se·ries, ak′tə·nīd, *n.* A group of radioactive elements which contains the elements from actinium to lawrencium.

ac·tin·ism, ak′tə·niz·əm, *n.* The property of the sun's rays which produces chemical effects.

ac·tin·i·um, ak·tin′ē·əm, *n.* A radioactive element discovered in pitchblende.

ac·ti·nom·e·ter, ak·tə·nom′ə·tər, *n.* An instrument for measuring the intensity of the sun's actinic rays.

ac·ti·non, ak′tə·non, *n.* A radioactive, gaseous, inert element, which exists for only a few seconds.

ac·ti·no·zo·an, ak·tə·nə·zō′ən, *n.* Anthozoan.

ac·tion, ak′shən, *n.* The state of being active, as opposed to *rest;* activity; an act or thing done; the performance of a function; a deed; exertion; a battle or engagement; the mechanism of a machine or instrument; agency; operation; procedure; impulse; the series of events forming a drama or work of fiction; gesture; a lawsuit.

ac·tion·a·ble, ak′shə·nə·bəl, *a.* Furnishing ground for a lawsuit. —**ac·tion·a·bly,** *adv.*

ac·ti·vate, ak′tə·vāt, *v.t.,* **-vat·ed, -vat·ing.** To make active; to organize; to render radioactive; to speed up a reaction by applying a catalyst; to render a constituted unit active by sending members to it.—*v.i.* To become active. —**ac·ti·va·tion,** ak·tə·və·vā′shən, *n.* —**ac·ti·va·tor,** *n.*

ac·tive, ak′tiv, *a.* Having the power or property of acting; having power to exert influence; producing results; effective; performing actions quickly; quick; nimble; brisk; agile; engaged constantly in action; accompanied or characterized by action: *active* demand for goods; actually proceeding: *active* warfare; denoting a verb form or voice in which the subject performs the action ('broke' in 'He broke the glass.'); participating: an *active* member; vigorous. —**ac·tive·ly,** *adv.* —**ac·tive·ness,** *n.*

ac·tive du·ty, *n.* Regular full-time duty with a branch of the military service.

ac·tiv·ism, ak′tə·viz·əm, *n.* The belief in or practice of, vigorous action. —**ac·tiv·ist,** *n., a.*

ac·tiv·i·ty, ak·tiv′i·tē, *n. pl.,* **-ties.** The state of being active; active force; liveliness. A natural or normal process; a specific action.

act of God, *n.* An occurrence which no one can predict or prevent, such as a tornado or earthquake.

ac·tor, ak′tər, *n.* One who acts or performs; one who acts in a play, motion picture, or other dramatic performance.

ac·tress ak′tris, *n.* A female actor.

Acts, or **Acts of the A·pos·tles,** *n.* The fifth book of the New Testament, credited to Luke and recounting the origin of the Christian church.

ac·tu·al, ak′choo·əl, *a.* Acting or existing truly and objectively; real; now existing; present; current. —**ac·tu·al·ly,** *adv.*

ac·tu·al·i·ty, ak·choo·al′i·tē, *n. pl.,* **-ties.** The state of being actual; that which is real or actual.

ac·tu·al·ize, ak′choo·ə·līz, *v.t.,* **-ized, -iz·ing.** To make actual; to realize. —**ac·tu·al·i·za·tion,** ak·choo·əl·ə·zā′shən, *n.*

ac·tu·ar·y, ak′choo·er·ē, *n. pl.,* **-ies.** One who computes insurance and annuity premiums, risks, and dividends. —**ac·tu·ar·i·al,** ak·choo·âr′ē·əl, *a.*

ac·tu·ate, ak′choo·āt, *v.t.,* **-at·ed, -at·ing.** To put into action; to move or incite to action; —**ac·tu·a·tion,** ak·choo·ā′shən, *n.* —**ac·tu·a·tor,** *n.*

a·cu·i·ty, ə·kyoo′ə·tē, *n.* Sharpness; acuteness.

a·cu·men, ə·kyoo′mən, ak′yə·mən, *n.* Quickness of perception; keenness of insight.

ac·u·punc·ture, ak′yoo·pungk·chər, *n.* First used by the Chinese, the practice of puncturing the body with needles to help cure disease or relieve pain.

a·cute, ə·kyoot′, *a.* Ending in a sharp point; intellectually sharp; perceiving minute distinctions; sensitive to slight impressions: *acute* hearing; keen; crucial; sharp: said of sound; shrill; less than a right angle. —**a·cute·ly,** *adv.* —**a·cute·ness,** *n.*

ad, ad, *n. Informal.* Advertisement.

ad·age, ad′ij, *n.* A proverb; an old saying.

a·da·gio, ə·dä′jō, ə·dä′zhē·ō, *a., adv.* Slowly, and with grace.—*n.* A slow movement in music or ballet.

Ad·am, ad′əm, *n.* The name of the first man: Gen. ii. 7.

ad·a·mant, ad′ə·mənt, ad′ə·mant, *n.* Any substance of impenetrable hardness.—*a.* Completely set and unchanging in opinion or ideas. —**ad·a·mant·ly,** *adv.*

ad·a·man·tine, ad·ə·man′tin, ad·ə·man′tēn, *a.* Made of or resembling adamant; impenetrable.

Ad·am's ap·ple, *n.* The prominence on the fore part of the throat of the thyroid cartilage.

a·dapt, ə·dapt′, *v.t.* To make suitable; to make fit; to adjust to a set of conditions. —**a·dapt·er,** *n.*

a·dapt·a·ble, ə·dap′tə·bəl, *a.* Capable of being adapted; able to adjust oneself to different conditions. —**a·dapt·a·bil·i·ty,** ə·dap·tə·bil′ə·tē, *n.*

ad·ap·ta·tion, ad·əp·tā′shən, *n.* The act of adapting or making suitable; adjustment; the state of being suitable or fit; that which is adapted.

a·dap·tive, ə·dap′tiv, *a.* Tending to adapt. —**a·dap·tive·ly,** *adv.*

add, ad, *v.t.* To put together to make a larger number; to join or unite; to put into one sum; to annex; say further.—*v.i.* To be or serve as an addition; perform the arithmetical operation of addition. —**add·a·ble, add·i·ble,** *a.*

ad·dend, ad′end, *n.* A number or quantity which is added to another quantity.

ad·den·dum, ə·den′dəm, *n. pl.,* **ad·den·da,** ə·den′də. An addition; an appendix; something which is added.

ad·der, ad′ər, *n.* A poisonous snake found in Europe; a harmless snake of America.

ad·dict, ə·dikt′, *v.t.* To habituate; surrender (oneself) to an undesirable habit, esp. to the use of narcotic drugs. —ad′ikt, *n.* One who is addicted to a practice or a habit, esp. to narcotics. —**ad·dic·tion,** ə·dik′shən, *n.*

ad·dict·ed, ə·dik′tid, *a.* Habitually or slavishly practicing.

ad·dic·tive, ə·dik′tiv, *a.* Causing addiction or characterized by addiction.

ad·di·tion, ə·dish′ən, *n.* The act or process of adding; the branch of arithmetic which treats of adding numbers; an increase; something added; a room, wing, etc. added to a building, or adjacent land added to real estate already owned. —**ad·di·tion·al,** *a.* —**ad·di·tion·al·ly,** *adv.*

ad·di·tive, ad′ə·tiv, *a.* Additional; helping to increase; showing or relating to addition; cumulative.—*n.* A substance added in small amounts to another.

ad·dle, ad′əl, *a.* Confused; disoriented. Rotten, putrid.—*v.t.* To confuse.—*v.i.* To become confused; to spoil.

ad·dle·brained, ad′əl·brānd, *a.* Muddled; confused; witless. Also **ad·dle·head·ed, ad·dle·pat·ed.**

ad·dress, ə·dres′, *v.t.* To direct or aim (words); to apply to by words or writings; to speak to; to direct in writing; to write an address on. —ə·dres′, ad′res, *n.* A communication in speech or writing from one person to another; the act of speaking to another person; name and number of the place where a person may be reached, esp. when written, as on an envelope. **—to ad·dress one·self to,** to speak to; apply oneself to a task.

ad·dress·ee, ad·re·sē′, ə·dre·sē′, *n.* One who is addressed; one to whom a letter is addressed.

ad·duce, ə·doos′, ə·dūs′, *v.t.* To cite; to offer as authority or evidence.

ad·duct, ə·dəkt′, *v.t.* To draw (one's limb) toward the body's main axis. **—ad·duc·tion,** ə·dək′shən, *n.* **—ad·duc·tive,** ə·dək′tiv, *a.*

ad·e·noid, ad′ə·noid, *n. Usu. pl.* An enlarged mass of lymphoid tissue in the upper pharynx, hindering nasal breathing. —*a.* Of glands or adenoids. Also **ad·e· noi·dal.**

a·dept, ad′ept, ə·dept′, *n.* One fully skilled; a trained expert; a person with unusual mental or spiritual powers.—*a.* Well-skilled; proficient. **—a·dept·ly,** *adv.* **—a·dept·ness,** *n.*

ad·e·qua·cy, ad′ə·kwə·sē, *n.* The state of being adequate; sufficiency for a particular purpose.

ad·e·quate, ad′ə·kwit, *a.* Suitable; enough; barely suitable or sufficient. **—ad·e·quate·ly,** *adv.*

ad·here, ad·hēr′, *v.i.,* **-hered, -her·ing.** To cling; to become closely joined or united; to be attached or devoted (to).

ad·her·ence, ad·hēr′əns, *n.* The quality or state of adhering; fidelity.

ad·her·ent, ad·hēr′ənt, *a.* Adhering; clinging; attached.—*n.* One who adheres; a follower or partisan.

ad·he·sion, ad·hē′zhən, *n.* The act or state of adhering; a sticking together; steady attachment of the mind or feelings; assent; concurrence.

ad·he·sive, ad·hē′siv, *a.* Sticky; gummy; tenacious. —*n.* an adhesive substance, as mucilage or glue. **—ad·he·sive·ly,** *adv.* **—ad·he·sive·ness,** *n.*

ad·he·sive tape, *n.* Tape with a gummy substance on one side.

ad hoc, ad hok′, *a., adv.* For a particular purpose or limited time without wider application.

ad ho·mi·nem, ad hō′mi·nem, *a.* Appealing to a person's prejudices and personal feelings rather than his intellect.

ad·i·a·bat·ic, ad·ē·ə·bat′ik, ā·dē·ə·bat′ik, *a.* Of physical changes without gain or loss of heat.

a·dieu, ə·doo′, ə·dū′, *interj.* Farewell; good-by.

ad in·fi·ni·tum, ad in·fə·nī′təm, *a.* Endless.

a·di·os, ä·dē·ōs′, ad·ē·ōs′, *interj.* Adieu; good-by; farewell.

ad·i·pose, ad′ə·pōs, *a.* Fatty.—*n.* Animal fat.

ad·ja·cen·cy, ə·jā′sən·sē, *n. pl.,* **-cies.** The state of being adjacent; adjoining or alongside.

ad·ja·cent, ə·jā′sənt, *a.* Lying near or close; adjoining. **—ad·ja·cent·ly,** *adv.*

ad·jec·tive, aj′ik·tiv, *n.* A word used with a noun to express a quality of the thing named, or to specify something as distinct from something else.—*a.* Of or functioning as an adjective. **—ad·jec·ti·val,** aj·ik·tī′vəl, *a.*

ad·join, ə·joyn′, *v.t.* To be adjacent to; to annex.—*v.i.* To be in contact; to be next to. **—ad·join·ing,** *a.*

ad·journ, ə·jərn′, *v.t.* To put off until a later period; to postpone until a future meeting.—*v.i.* To end a meeting.

ad·journ·ment, ə·jərn′mənt, *n.* The act of adjourning; the period during which a public body is adjourned.

ad·judge, ə·jəj′, *v.t.,* **ad·judged, ad·judg·ing.** To declare or pronounce formally by law; to award judicially; to sentence or condemn; to settle; to rule upon.

ad·ju·di·cate, ə·joo′də·kāt, *v.t.,* **-cat·ed, -cat·ing.** To adjudge.—*v.i.* To give a judicial decision. **—ad·ju· di·ca·tion,** ə·joo·də·kā′shən, *n.* **—ad·ju·di·ca·tor,** *n.*

ad·junct, aj′əngkt, *n.* Something added to another thing but not essential to it; a subordinate colleague; a word or phrase which modifies another word or phrase and is not an essential element in its sentence. **—ad·junc·tive,** ə·jəngk′tiv, *a.*

ad·jure, ə·jûr′, *v.t.,* **ad·jured, ad·jur·ing.** To charge, bind, command earnestly and solemnly, as with an oath. **—ad·ju·ra·tion,** ə·jû·rā′shən, *n.* **—ad·ju·ra· to·ry,** *a.* **—ad·jur·er,** *n.*

ad·just, ə·jəst′, *v.t.* To fix; to put in order; to regulate; to settle or bring to a satisfactory state; to make correspondent.—*v.i.* To conform oneself; to adapt. **—ad·just·a·ble,** *a.,* **—ad·just·er, ad·just·or,** *n.,* **—ad·just·ment,** *n.*

ad·ju·tan·cy, aj′ə·tən·sē, *n.* The rank or office of an adjutant.

ad·ju·tant, aj′ə·tənt, *n.* An officer who assists a commanding officer by communicating orders, writing messages, etc; an assistant. **—ad·ju·tan·cy,** aj′ə·tən·sē, *n.*

ad·ju·tant gen·er·al, *n. pl.,* **ad·ju·tants gen·er·al.** The chief administrative officer of a division or larger unit.

ad lib, ad lib′, ad′lib′, *n.* Something ad-libbed. **—ad· lib,** ad′lib′, *a.* Improvised; spoken without preparation.—*v.t., v.i.* To improvise.

ad·man, ad′man, ad′mən, *n. pl.,* **ad·men.** *Informal.* One who writes, designs, or sells advertisements.

ad·min·is·ter, ad·min′i·stər, *v.t.* To manage or conduct as chief agent or official; to direct or superintend; to give, or supply; to dispense or distribute; to tender, as an oath; to manage an estate.—*v.i.* To contribute assistance; to bring aid or supplies: with *to.*

ad·min·is·trate, ad·min′i·strāt, *v.t.* To administer.

ad·min·is·tra·tion, ad·min·i·strā′shən, *n.* Management; government of public affairs; the executive functions of government and business; the persons, collectively, who are entrusted with such functions, and their period of being in office; the executive. **—ad·min·is·tra·tive,** ad·min′i·strāt·iv, ad·min′i· strə·tiv, *a.* **—ad·min·is·tra·tor,** ad·min′i·strā·tər, *n.*

ad·mi·ral, ad′mi·rəl, *n.* Commander in chief of a fleet; highest rank of naval officer.

ad·mi·ral·ty, ad′mi·rəl·tē, *n. pl.,* **-ties.** Jurisdiction of an admiral; court concerned with maritime problems.

ad·mire, əd·mīr′, *v.t.,* **ad·mired, ad·mir·ing.** To regard with esteem or to look up to. **—ad·mi·ra·ble,** ad′mə·rə·bəl, *adj.,* *n.* **—ad·mi·ra·bly,** *adv.* **—ad·mi· ra·tion,** ad·mə·rā′shən, *n.* **—ad·mi·rer,** əd·mī′rər, *n.* **—ad·mir·ing·ly,** əd·mī′ring·lē, *adv.*

ad·mis·si·ble, ad·mis′ə·bəl, *a.* Capable of being admitted, allowed. **—ad·mis·si·bil·i·ty,** ad·mis·ə· bil′ə·tē, *n.*

ad·mis·sion, ad·mish′ən, *n.* The act of admitting; power or permission to enter; a fee charged for entrance; entrance; access; power to approach; a point or statement admitted; acknowledgment; confession of a charge, error, or crime.

ad·mit, ad·mit′, *v.t.,* **ad·mit·ted, ad·mit·ting.** To allow to enter; to grant entrance to; to give right of entrance to; to grant in argument; to accept as true; to be capable (of); to acknowledge; to confess.—*v.i.* To give allowance; to grant opportunity; to permit; with *of.*

ad·mit·ted·ly, ad·mit′əd·lē, *adv.* By acknowledgment or concession.

ad·mit·tance, ad·mit′əns, *n.* The act of admitting;

permission or right to enter; entrance.

ad·mix, ad·miks′, *v.t.* To mingle with something else; to blend.

ad·mix·ture, ad·miks′chər, *n.* The act of mixing; mixture; any ingredient added to a mixture.

ad·mon·ish, ad·mon′ish, *v.t.* To warn or notify of a fault; to reprove with mildness; to advise or exhort; to recall or urge to duty. —**ad·mon·ish·er**, *n.* —**ad·mo·ni·tion**, ad·mə·nish′ən, *n.* —**ad·mon·i·to·ry**, əd·mon′ə·tôr·ē, ad·mon′ə·tôr·ē, *a.*

a·do, ə·doo′, *n.* Bustle; fuss.

a·do·be, ə·dō′bē, *n.* A sun-dried brick, or the clay used in making this type of brick; a house, wall, etc., that is made of sun-dried brick.

ad·o·les·cence, ad·ə·les′əns, *n.* The state of growing from childhood to adulthood; youth, or the period from childhood to full maturity.

ad·o·les·cent, ad·ə·les′ənt, *a.* Growing up; characteristic of adolescence; advancing from childhood to manhood or womanhood.—*n.* One who is in adolescence.

A·don·is, ə·don′is, *n.* A beautiful youth of Greek mythology; any very handsome young man.

a·dopt, ə·dopt′, *v.t.* To take another's child as one's own, esp. legally; to accept by choice or approval, as policies, etc. —**a·dopt·a·ble**, *a.* —**a·dopt·er**, *n.* —**a·dop·tion**, *n.* —**a·dop·tive**, *a.*

a·dore, ə·dôr′, *v.t.*, **a·dored**, **a·dor·ing**. To worship; to regard with the utmost devotion, love, and respect. —**a·dor·a·ble**, *a.* —**ad·o·ra·tion**, ad·ə·rā′shən, *n.* —**a·dor·ing·ly**, *adv.*

a·dorn, ə·dôrn′, *v.t.* To decorate; to add to the attractiveness of by dress or ornaments. —**a·dorn·ment**, *n.*

ad·re·nal, ə·drē′nəl, *a.* On or near the kidney; pertaining to the adrenal glands.—*n.* An adrenal gland.

ad·re·nal gland, *n.* A small endocrine gland attached to the kidney.

a·dren·a·line, ə·dren′ə·lin, ə·dren′ə·lēn, *n.* Epinephrine, a hormone secreted by the adrenal glands. —**A·dren·a·lin**, ə·dren′ə·lin, *n. Trademark.* A drug used as a heart stimulant, muscle relaxant, etc.

a·drift, ə·drift′, *a.* or *adv.* Floating at random; moving without direction.

a·droit, ə·droyt′, *a.* Nimble in the use of the hands or, figuratively, the mind. —**a·droit·ly**, *adv.* —**a·droit·ness**, *n.*

ad·sorb, ad·sôrb′, ad·zôrb′, *v.t.* To collect, as gases, dissolved substances, or liquids, in a thin layer on a surface. —**ad·sor·bent**, *a.* —**ad·sorp·tion**, *n.*

ad·u·la·tion, aj·ə·lā′shən, *n.* Servile flattery; praise in excess or in the highest degree.

ad·u·late, aj′ə·lāt, *v.t.*, **-lat·ed**, **-lat·ing**. To praise highly or even excessively. —**ad·u·la·tor**, *n.* —**ad·u·la·to·ry**, aj′ə·lə·tôr·ē, *a.*

a·dult, ə·dəlt′, ad′əlt, *a.* Grownup; full-grown; mature: suitable for an adult.—*n.* A person who is full-grown or of legal age; a full-grown animal or plant. —**a·dult·hood**, *n.*

a·dul·ter·ate, ə·del′tə·rāt, *v.t.*, **-at·ed**, **-at·ing**. To debase or lower in quality by mixing in foreign materials. —**a·dul·ter·ant**, *n.*, *a.* —**a·dul·ter·a·tion**, ə·del·tə·rā′shən, *n.* —**a·dul·ter·a·tor**, *n.*

a·dul·ter·y, ə·del′tə·rē, *n.* Voluntary sexual intercourse by a married person with one who is not his or her spouse.

a·dul·ter·er, ə·del′tər·ər, *n.* A man guilty of adultery. —**a·dul·ter·ess**, *n. fem.* —**a·dul·ter·ous**, *a.*

ad·um·brate, ad·əm′brāt, ad′əm·brāt, *v.t.*, **-brat·ed**, **-brat·ing**. Shade or obscure partially; to vaguely foreshadow. —**ad·um·bra·tion**, ad·əm·brā′shən, *n.*

ad va·lo·rem, ad və·lōr′əm, ad və·lôr′əm. According to value.

ad·vance, ad·vans′, ad·väns′, *v.t.*, **ad·vanced**, **ad·vanc·ing**. To bring forward; to move further in front; to promote; to raise to a higher rank; to forward or further; to encourage the progress of; to hasten or place earlier in time; to enhance (price); to accelerate

the growth of; to offer or propose; to bring to view or notice; to allege; to supply beforehand; to furnish on credit.—*v.i.* To move forward; to proceed; to make progress; to rise in rank.—*a.* Placed before; ahead of time.—*n.* A moving forward; gradual progression; improvement; advancement; rise in price; a giving beforehand, especially money; *pl.* Personal approaches in order to gain something. —**in ad·vance**, in front, before; beforehand.

ad·vanced, ad·vanst′, ad·vänst′, *a.* Being in advance; progressive. —**ad·vance·ment**, *n.*

ad·van·tage, ad·van′tij, *n.* A favorable factor or circumstance; a benefit.—*v.t.*, **-taged**, **-tag·ing**. To bring advantage to; help. —**to ad·van·tage**, so as to bring about a desired result.

ad·van·ta·geous, ad·vən·tā′jes, *a.* Profitable. —**ad·van·ta·geous·ly**, *adv.*

ad·vent, ad′vent, *n.* Coming or arrival; (*sometimes cap.*), the birth of Christ; (*cap.*) a season (including four Sundays) preceding Christmas.

Ad·vent·ism, ad′ven·tiz·əm, *n.* The belief that the second coming of Christ is near at hand. —**Ad·vent·ist**, ad′ven·tist, ad·ven′tist, *n.*

ad·ven·ti·tious, ad·vən·tish′əs, *a.* Coming from without; foreign.

ad·ven·tive, ad·ven′tiv, *a.* Not indigenous, as exotic plants or animals; extraneous.

ad·ven·ture, ad·ven′chər, *n.* An exciting experience; a bold and dangerous undertaking of uncertain outcome; a commercial speculation.—*v.t.*, **-tured**, **-tur·ing**. To risk or hazard. —**ad·ven·tur·er**, *n.* —**ad·ven·tur·ess**, *n. fem.* —**ad·ven·tur·ous**, *a.* —**ad·ven·tur·ous·ly**, *adv.* —**ad·ven·tur·ous·ness**, *n.*

ad·ven·ture·some, ad·ven′chər·səm, *a.* Daring.

ad·verb, ad′vərb, *n.* A word which limits or extends the meaning of a verb, adjective, or other adverb with reference to time, place, manner, etc. —**ad·ver·bi·al**, ad·vər′bē·əl.

ad·ver·sar·y, ad′vər·ser·ē, *n. pl.*, **-ies.** An enemy; a foe; an antagonist.

ad·verse, ad′vərs, ad·vərs′, *a.* Acting in a contrary direction; opposing; hostile; unfortunate; unprosperous. —**ad·verse·ly**, ad·vərs′lē, *adv.* **ad·verse·ness**, *n.*

ad·ver·si·ty, ad·vər′sə·tē, *n. pl.*, **-ties.** A condition of distress or suffering; stroke of misfortune.

ad·vert, ad·vert′, *v.i.* To turn the attention (to); to refer (to). —**ad·vert·ence**, *n.* —**ad·vert·ent**, *n.*

ad·ver·tise, ad′vər·tiz, ad·vər·tiz′, *v.t.*, **-tised**, **-tis·ing**. To inform or give notice; to call attention to; to make public, especially by printed or broadcast notice; make known the desirability of in order to sell.—*v.i.* To bring to public attention by means of advertising —**ad·ver·tis·er**, *n.*

ad·ver·tise·ment, ad·vər·tiz′mənt, ad·vər′tis·mənt, *n.* A notice or message, especially a paid notice, printed in a newspaper or magazine or broadcast by radio or television.

ad·ver·tis·ing, ad′vər·ti·zing, *n.* The business concerned with planning, writing, designing, and scheduling advertisements; advertisements.

ad·vice, ad·vis′, *n.* An opinion offered as worthy to be followed; counsel; suggestion; information; notice.

ad·vise, ad·viz′, *v.t.*, **ad·vised**, **ad·vis·ing**. To give advice to; to counsel; to give information to; to inform; to give notice to.—*v.i.* To take counsel. —**ad·vis·a·bil·i·ty**, ad·vi·zə·bil′ə·tē, *n.* —**ad·vis·a·ble**, *a.* —**ad·vis·a·bly**, *adv.* —**ad·vis·er**, **ad·vi·sor**, *n.*

ad·vised, ad·vizd′, *a.* Cautious; carefully considered.

ad·vis·ed·ly, ad·vi′zəd·lē, *adv.* With deliberation; with careful thought beforehand.

ad·vise·ment, ad·viz′mənt, *n.* Careful consideration; advice.

ad·vi·so·ry, ad·vi′zə·rē, *a.* Having power to advise. —*n.* A bulletin that gives information, esp. about the weather.

ad·vo·ca·cy, ad′və·kə·sē, *n. pl.*, **-cies.** The act of advocating; an asking or pleading for; support.

ad•vo•cate, ad/və•kit, ad/və•kāt, *n.* One who pleads the cause of another in a court of law; a pleader in favor of something. —ad/və•kāt, *v.t.,* **-cat•ed, -cat•ing.** To plead in favor of; to recommend publicly. —ad•vo•ca•tion, ad•və•kā/shən, *n.*

adz, adze, adz, *n.* A tool like an ax, with the cutting edge at right angles to the handle, used in trimming wood.

ae•gis, ē/jis, *n. Gr. mythol.* The shield of Zeus, also part of the armor of Athena; a protecting power or influence.

ae•on, ē/ən, ē/on, *n.* An indefinite or interminable period of time. Also **eon.**

aer•ate, ār/āt, ā/ə•rāt, *v.t.,* **-at•ed, -at•ing.** To expose (something) to the effects of air; to combine with air; to supply, as the blood, with oxygen; oxygenate. —aer•a•tion, *n.* —aer•a•tor, *n.*

aer•i•al, ār/ē•əl, ā•er/ē•əl, *a.* Belonging to or like the air; inhabiting the air; pertaining to aircraft; unsubstantial; visionary; lofty; growing in the air, such as certain roots.—ār/ē•əl, *n.* Antenna. —aer•i•al•ly, *adv.*

aer•i•al•ist, ār/ē•ə•list, *n.* An acrobat who performs on a high wire, trapeze, etc., usually in a circus.

aer•ie, ār/ē, ēr/ē, *n.* The nest of a bird of prey; any elevated house or dwelling; eyrie.

aer•i•fy, ār/ə•fī, *v.t.* To infuse air into; to change into vapor. —aer•i•fi•ca•tion, ār•ə•fə•kā/shən, *n.*

aer•o-, ār/ō, A combining form that means: Pertaining to the air, aircraft, or the flying of aircraft.

aer•obe, ār/ōb, *n.* A microorganism whose existence requires oxygen. —aer•o•bic, ār/o/bik, *a.*

aer•o•dy•nam•ics, ār•ō•dī•nam/iks, *n. pl. sing. or pl. in constr.* That branch of dynamics which pertains to the motion of air and other gaseous fluids. —aer•o•dy•nam•ic, *a.*

aer•o•me•chan•ics, ār•ō•mə•kan/iks, *n. pl., sing. or pl. in constr.* The study of air and other gases in motion or equilibrium, or of solid bodies in motion in gases. —aer•o•me•chan•ic, aer•o•me•chan•i•cal, *a.*

aer•o•naut•ics, ār•ə•nô/tiks, ār•ə•not/iks, *n. pl. but sing. in constr.* The science, art, or business of designing, manufacturing, and operating aircraft. —aer•o•naut•ic, *a.* Also **aer•o•nau•ti•cal.**

aer•o•plane, ār/ə•plān, *n. Brit.* airplane.

aer•o•sol, ār/ə•sôl, ār/ə•sol, *n.* A suspension of fine particles, solid or liquid, in a gas producing a smoke or fog. A liquid under pressure with an inert gas in a metal container, producing a fine spray when released.

aer•o•sol bomb, *n.* A small container having a device to release an aerosol.

aer•o•space, ār/ō•spās, *n.* The atmosphere of the earth and the space immediately beyond it; the science and industry involving the study, design, and production of ballistic missiles, earth satellites and the like.

aes•thete, es/thēt, *n.* One devoted to, or pretending devotion to beauty.

aes•thet•ic, es•thet/ik, *a.* Pertaining to the study of taste or beauty; pertaining to the sense of the beautiful; esthetic. —aes•thet•i•cal•ly, *adv.*

aes•thet•ics, es•thet/iks, *n. pl., sing. or pl. in constr.* The theory of the fine arts and the philosophy of the mind and emotions in relation to it; the philosophy of beauty; esthetics.

a•far, ə•fär/, *adv.* At or from a distance.

a•feard, a•feared, ə•fērd/, *a. Brit. and southern U.S.* Frightened; afraid.

af•fa•ble, af/ə•bəl, *a.* Open and easy in conversation without reserve; courteous; gracious; mild. —af•fa•bil•i•ty, af•ə•bil/ə•tē, *n.* —af•fa•bly, *adv.*

af•fair, ə•fār/, *n.* Business of any kind; that which is done, or is to be done; a happening or social gathering; a romance, usually illicit; *pl.* public or monetary concern.

af•fect, ə•fekt/, *v.t.* To act upon; to produce an effect upon; to influence; to excite the feelings (of); make a show of; to pretend. —af•fect•ing, *a.* —af•fect•ing•ly, *adv.*

af•fec•tive, ə•fek/tiv, *a.* Showing affection.

af•fect, af/ekt, *n.* Emotion or feeling; an emotion with accompanying physical movements.

af•fec•ta•tion, af•ek•tā/shən, *n.* Pretending to be or show what is praiseworthy or uncommon; artificial appearance or show.

af•fect•ed, ə•fek/tid, *a.* Given to affectation; pretending to possess what is not natural or real; moved with feeling; deeply touched; acted upon, as by disease. —af•fect•ed•ly, *adv.* —af•fect•ed•ness, *n.*

af•fec•tion, ə•fek/shən, *n.* The state of having one's feelings affected in some way; sentiment; a fond feeling for another; devotion; love.

af•fec•tion•ate, ə•fek/shə•nit, *a.* Having affection; tender. —af•fec•tion•ate•ly, *adv.* —af•fec•tion•ate•ness, *n.*

af•fer•ent, af/ər•ənt, *a.* Leading inward toward a center point, as certain nerves and veins.

af•fi•ance, ə•fī/əns, *v.t.,* **-anced, -anc•ing.** To betroth; to bind by promise of marriage.

af•fi•da•vit, af•i•dā/vit, *n.* A written declaration, sworn to or confirmed before an authorized magistrate.

af•fil•i•ate, ə•fil/ē•āt, *v.t.,* **-at•ed, -at•ing.** To bring into relationship, as by adoption or formal membership; in an institution, to make formal connections with.—*v.i.* To associate oneself. —ə•fil/ē•ət, *n.* An affiliated person, group, or company. —af•fil•i•a•tion, ə•fil•ē•ā/shən, *n.*

af•fin•i•ty, ə•fin/ə•tē, *n. pl.,* **-ties.** The relation by marriage; relation in general, as of languages or sounds; similarity in kind; a natural attraction; the receiver of such an attraction.

af•firm, ə•fərm/, *v.t.* To assert positively; to aver; to confirm or ratify.—*v.i.* To make a legal affirmation. —af•firm•a•ble, *a.* —af•firm•a•bly, *adv.* —af•fir•ma•tion, af•ər•mā/shən, *n.*

af•firm•a•tive, ə•fer/mə•tiv, *n.* A word or phrase expressing assent. —**the affirmative,** that side of a debated question which maintains the truth of the argument.—*a.* Affirming or asserting. —af•firm•a•tive•ly, *adv.*

af•fix, ə•fiks/, *v.t.* To add at the end; append, as one's signature; to fasten or stick, as one thing to another. —af/iks *n.* A prefix or suffix; infix; in language, a part added to the base form of a word to change or strengthen its meaning; anything added on.

af•fla•tus, ə•flā/təs, *n.* Creative or divine inspiration.

af•flict, ə•flikt/, *v.t.* To give pain to the body or mind; to torment; to distress. —af•flict•er, *n.* —af•flic•tion, ə•flik/shən, *n.*

af•flu•ence, af/loo•əns, af•loo/əns, *n.* A flowing to an abundant supply; wealth. —af•flu•ent, *a.* —af•flu•ent•ly, *adv.*

af•ford, ə•fōrd/, ə•fôrd/, *v.t.* To be able to bear the expense of; to give forth; to yield, supply, or produce; to grant or confer; to spare.

af•fray, ə•frā/, *n.* A public fight; brawl.

af•front, ə•frənt/, *v.t.* To offend by an open show of disrespect; to insult; to confront defiantly.—*n.* An open show of disrespect; an insult.

af•ghan, af/gən, af/gan, *n.* A blanket or covering of knitted or crocheted wool.

a•fi•cio•na•do, ə•fish•ə•nä/dō, *n.* An enthusiastic devotee or follower.

a•field, ə•fēld/, *adv.* To the field; in the field; away from home; astray; outside of one's experience or knowledge.

---

a·fire, ə·fīr′, *a., adv.* On fire.

a·flame, ə·flām′, *a., adv.* Flaming.

a·float, ə·flōt′, *a., adv.* Floating; at sea; flooded; drifting; in circulation, as a rumor.

a·foot, ə·fût, *a., adv.* On foot; walking; in progress, as a plan or plot.

a·fore, ə·fōr′, ə·fôr′, *adv., prep., conj. Informal.* Before.

a·fore·men·tioned, ə·fōr′men·shənd, ə·fôr′men·shənd, *a.* Referring to something occurring earlier.

a·fore·said, ə·fōr′sed, ə·fôr′sed, *a.* Mentioned previously.

a·fore·thought, ə·fōr′thôt, ə·fôr′thôt, *a.* Thought of beforehand; premeditated.

a·foul, ə·foul′, *a., adv.* Fouled, tangled. —**afoul of,** In or into conflict or entanglement with: to run *afoul of* the law.

a·fraid, ə·frād′, *a.* Fearful. *Informal.* Inclined to think: to soften an otherwise unpleasant remark: I'm *afraid* you'll have to wait.

a·fresh, ə·fresh′, *adv.* Anew; again.

Af·ro, af′rō, *n.* A hair style, full and unstraightened, worn by a man or a woman.

Af·ro-, af′rō. A combining form, meaning African: *Afro-Asian, Afro-American.*

Af·ro-A·mer·i·can, af·rō-ə·mer′i·kən, *a.* Relating to Americans of African descent.

aft, aft, äft, *a., adv.* At, near, or toward the stern of a ship or aircraft.

af·ter, af′tər, äf′tər, *a.* Later in time; subsequent.— *conj.* Following the time that: *After* she cooks, they eat.—*adv.* Later in time; afterward; behind.—*prep.* Behind in place; later in time; in pursuit of; in search of; in imitation of: *after* a model; according to; in proportion to: *after* our desserts; below in rank or excellence; next to; concerning: inquire *after;* for: named *after* her mother.

af·ter·birth, af′tər·bərth, äf′tər·bərth, *n.* The placenta and fetal membranes which are expelled from the uterus after birth.

af·ter·burn·er, af′tər·bər·nər, äf′tər·bər·nər, *n.* A device which increases the thrust of a jet engine by injecting extra fuel into the exhaust.

af·ter·deck, af′tər·dek, äf′tər·dek, *n.* The section of a deck that is abaft the middle of a ship.

af·ter·ef·fect, af′tər·ə·fekt, äf′tər·ə·fekt, *n.* A delayed effect.

af·ter·glow, af′tər·glō, äf′tər·glō, *n.* A glow seen occasionally in the western sky above the highest clouds in deepening twilight; pleasing recollection of a former experience.

af·ter·im·age, af′tər·im·ij, äf′tər·im·ij, *n.* An image which remains after the stimulus disappears.

af·ter·life, af′tər·līf, äf′tər·līf, *n.* Life following death.

af·ter·math, af′tər·math, äf′tər·math, *n.* Consequence, result.

af·ter·most, af′tər·mōst, äf′tər·mōst, *a.* Hindmost; farthest astern.

af·ter·noon, af′tər·noon, äf′tər·noon, *n.* The part of the day between noon and evening.

af·ter·taste, af′tər·tāst, äf′tər·tāst, *n.* A taste which stays in the mouth after eating or drinking.

af·ter·thought, af′tər·thôt, äf′tər·thôt, *n.* A thought occurring too late after the time of the decision or action to which it refers.

af·ter·ward, af·ter·wards, af′tər·wərd, äf′tər·wərd; af′tər·wərdz, äf′tər·wərdz, *adv.* Later.

a·gain, ə·gen′, ə·gān′, *adv.* A second time; once more; on another occasion; on the other hand; moreover; besides; further; in return; back to the original condition, place, or position; in answer; in addition.

a·gainst, ə·genst′, ə·gānst′, *prep.* Opposite in place, often preceded by *over;* in opposition to; counter to; contrary to; adverse or hostile to: *against* the law or opinion; toward or upon; in contact with; resting upon: to lean *against* the wall.

a·gape, ə·gāp′, ə·gap′, *a., adv.* Having the mouth open, as with surprise or expectation.

a·gar, ä′gär, äg′ər, *n.* A gelatinous product from certain seaweeds, used in the cultivation of bacteria. Also, **agar-agar.**

ag·ate, ag′it, *n.* A mineral consisting of bands or layers of various colors blended together; a size of type, about 5½ point; a playing marble made of or resembling agate.

a·ga·ve, ə·gä′vē, ə·gä′vē, *n.* Any plant of the American (chiefly Mexican) amaryllis family: as the century plant.

age, āj, *n.* The time during which an individual has lived; the latter part of life; the state of being old; old people collectively; life expectancy; legal maturity, or the age when certain rights are granted: to be under *age; informal,* a long or protracted period; as, not to have been there in an *age.* A historical period; an epoch having a particular character: an *age* of expansion; the people who live in a particular period or generation: *ages* yet unborn. *v.i.,* **aged, ag·ing** or **age·ing.** To grow old.—*v.t.* To give the character of age or the signs of age to.

a·ged, ā′jid, ājd, *a.* Very old; pertaining to old age (*a′jid*). Of the age of (*ajd*).

age·less, āj′lis, *a.* Never becoming old or outdated.

age·long, āj′lông′, āj′long′, *a.* Lasting for a long time.

a·gen·cy, ā′jən·sē, *n. pl.,* **-cies.** The state of being in action; means; the office or business of an agent or factor; an organization or company that offers its services; a governmental division.

a·gen·da, ə·jen′də, *n. pl. but sing. in constr.* Memoranda; list or program of things to be done or acted upon.

a·gent, ā′jənt, *n.* One who or that which acts; an active power or cause; a body or substance that causes a certain action to begin; a person entrusted with the business of another. —**a·gen·tial,** ā·jen′shəl, *a.*

a·gent pro·vo·ca·teur, ä·zhon′prō·vō·ka·tər′, *n.* pl., **a·gents pro·vo·ca·teurs.** A secret agent employed to incite people to illegal words or deeds.

age-old, āj′ōld′, *a.* Existing for ages.

ag·er·a·tum, aj·ə·rā′təm, *n.* One of the plants of the aster family with small, dense, blue or white flowerheads.

ag·glom·er·ate, ə·glom′ə·rāt, *v.t.,* **-at·ed, -at·ing.** To collect into a mass.—*v.i.* To cluster together. —ə·glom′ər·it, ə·glom′ə·rāt, *n.* An agglomerate mass.—*a.* Massed together. —**ag·glom·er·a·tion,** ə·glom·ə·rā′shən, *n.* —**ag·glom·er·a·tive,** ə·glom′ə·rā·tiv, ə·glom′ər·ə·tiv, *a.*

ag·glu·ti·nate, ə·gloot′ən·āt, *v.t., v.i.,* **-nat·ed, -nat·ing.** Cause to adhere, as with glue; to combine; to attach. —ə·gloo′tə·nit, ə·gloo′tə·nāt, *a.* United as by glue; joined.

ag·glu·ti·na·tion, ə·gloot·ə·nā′shən, *n.* An agglutinating; adhesion of parts; word formation in which the component elements retain an independence of meaning and form. —**ag·glu·ti·na·tive,** ə·gloo′tə·nā′tiv, ə·gloo′tə·nə·tiv, *a.*

ag·gran·dize, ə·gran′dīz, əg′grən·dīz, *v.t.,* **-dized, -diz·ing.** To make greater in power, wealth, or honor; to extend; to enlarge; to inflate in size, power, or appearance. —**ag·gran·dize·ment,** ə·gran′dīz·mənt, *n.* —**ag·gran·diz·er,** *n.*

ag·gra·vate, ag′rə·vāt, *v.t.,* **-vat·ed, -vat·ing.** To make worse or more severe; *Informal.* to provoke, to irritate. —**ag·gra·vat·ing·ly,** *adv.* —**ag·gra·va·tion,** ag·rə·vā′shən, *n.*

ag·gre·gate, ag′rə·gāt, *v.t.,* **-gat·ed, -gat·ing.** To bring together; to collect; to amount to; to form a sum of. —ag′rə·git, ag′rə·gāt, *n.* A mass of fine stone, gravel, etc., used in making concrete; a mass of particulars; a whole or total. —ag′rə·git, ag′rə·gāt, *a.* Formed into a mass or sum; total. —**in the**

ag·gre·gate, taken altogether; as a whole. **—ag·gre· gate·ly,** ag/rə·git·lē, adv. **—ag·gre·ga·tion,** ag·rə· gā/shən, n. **—ag·gre·ga·tive,** ag/rə·gā·tiv, a.

ag·gres·sion, ə·gresh/ən, n. The first attack or act of hostility; the first act leading to a war or controversy; habitual offensive action.

ag·gress, ə·gres/, v.i. To commit aggression. **—ag· gress·ive,** ə·gres/iv, a. **—ag·gress·ive·ly,** adv. **—ag·gress·ive·ness,** n. **—ag·gress·or,** n.

ag·grieve, ə·grēv/, v.t., **ag·grieved, ag·griev·ing.** To give pain or sorrow to; to oppress or injure in one's rights.

a·ghast, ə·gast/, ə·gäst/, a. Struck with sudden fright or horror.

ag·ile, aj/əl, a. Nimble; spry; quick and light in movement; alert, active. **—ag·ile·ly,** adv.

a·gil·i·ty, ə·jil/i·tē, n. Nimbleness; briskness; activity; intellectual acuity.

ag·i·tate, aj/i·tāt, v.t., **-tat·ed, -tat·ing.** To move or force into violent irregular action; to shake or move briskly; to discuss; debate; arouse public attention to, as by speeches, pamphlets, etc.—v.i. To engage in agitation. **—ag·i·tat·ed·ly,** adv. **—ag·i·ta·tion,** aj·i· tā/shən, n. **—ag·i·ta·tor,** aj/i·tā·tər, n.

a·gleam, ə·glēm/, a. Gleaming; bright, shiny.

a·glow, ə·glō/, a. In a glow; glowing.

ag·no·men, ag·nō/mən, n. pl. **ag·nom·i·na,** ag· nom/ə·nə. An additional name or epithet conferred on a person; a nickname.

ag·nos·tic, ag·nos/tik, n. A person who disclaims any knowledge of God or of the origin of the universe. —a. Referring to the agnostics or their doctrines. **—ag·nos·ti·cism,** ag·nos/ti·siz·əm, n.

a·go, ə·gō/, a., adv. Past; gone: a year ago.

a·gog, ə·gog/, a., adv. Highly excited by eagerness, anticipation, or curiosity.

a·gon·ic, ā·gon/ik, a. Not forming an angle.

ag·o·nize, ag/ə·nīz, v.i., **-nized, -niz·ing.** To be in extreme pain; put forth excessive effort; strain.—v.t. To distress with extreme pain; to torture.

ag·o·ny, ag/ə·nē, n. pl., **-nies.** Extreme bodily or mental pain; intense suffering; anguish; torment; struggle that precedes death.

ag·o·ra·pho·bi·a, ag·ər·ə·fō/bē·ə, n. Fear of open spaces.

a·gou·ti, ə·goo/tē, n. A tropical American rodent somewhat like the guinea pig.

a·grar·i·an, ə·grār/ē·ən, a. Relating to lands, or the division of lands; rural; pertaining to farmers or their interests.—n. One in favor of an equal division of farm lands or income. **—a·grar·i·an·ism,** n.

a·gree, ə·grē/, v.i., **a·greed, a·gree·ing.** To harmonize in opinion; to live in concord; to come to an understanding; to arrive at a settlement; to be consistent; to tally; to match; to correspond; to suit or be acceptable (with): Food agrees with a person. To correspond in number, case, gender, or person. **—a· gree·a·bil·i·ty,** ə·grē·ə·bil/ə·tē, n.

a·gree·a·ble, a. Suitable; pleasing; willing to agree. **—a·gree·a·ble·ness,** n. **—a·gree·a·bly,** adv.

a·greed, ə·grēd/, a. In agreement; settled by contract or common consent.

a·gree·ment, ə·grē/mənt, n. A contract; the state of agreeing or being agreed; harmony; conformity; union of opinions or sentiments; bargain; compact; correspondence, as in gender, case, or number.

ag·ri·cul·ture, ag/rə·kəl·chər, n. The cultivation of the ground; the raising of crops and livestock; farming; agronomy. **—ag·ri·cul·tur·al,** ag·rə·kəl/chə·rəl, a. **—ag·ri·cul·tur·ist,** ag·ri·kul/chər·ist, n.

a·gron·o·my, ə·gron/ə·mē, n. Agriculture; management of farms; science of crop production. **—ag·ro· nom·ic, ag·ro·nom·i·cal,** ag·rə·nom/ik, ag·rə· nom/i·kəl, a. **—a·gron·o·mist,** ə·gron/ə·mist, n.

a·ground, ə·grownd/, a., adv. On the ground; run ashore; stranded.

a·gue, ā/gū, n. An intermittent malarial fever with periodic chills; an attack of shivering; a chill. **—a·gu· ish,** a.

ah, ä, interj. An exclamation of pain, surprise, contempt, joy, etc.

a·ha, ä·hä/, interj. An exclamation of triumph, contempt, surprise, etc.

a·head, ə·hed/, adv. In or to the front; in advance; before; upward in position; further on.

a·hem, ə·hem/, interj. A sound made in the throat to call attention, express doubt or serve as a warning.

a·hoy, ə·hoy/, interj. A word used chiefly at sea in hailing.

aid, ād, v.t. To come to the support or relief of; to help. n. Support; assistance; help given to another person or group; money or goods given out by an official or government; an assistant.

aide, ād, n. An assistant to a superior; subordinate; aide-de-camp.

aide-de-camp, ād/də·kamp/, n. pl., **aides-de-camp,** ādz/də·kamp/. An officer who is assistant and secretary to a higher officer.

ai·grette, ā/gret, ā·gret/, n. The small white egret or heron of Europe; a tuft of feathers used as a head ornament, in millinery, etc.

ail, āl, v.t. To affect with pain or uneasiness; to trouble: What ails her?—v.i. To be in pain, ill health, or trouble. **—ail·ing,** a.

ail·ment, āl/mənt, n. Disease.

ai·lan·thus, ā·lan/thəs, n. An Asiatic tree with illscented green flowers.

ai·ler·on, ā/lə·ron, n. A movable control surface set into or near the trailing edge of an airplane wing.

aim, ām, v.i. To direct a missile toward an object; to direct the mind or attention; to make an attempt; to endeavor (at). v.t. To level an object or remark (at); to intend (to): We aim to finish today. n. The pointing or directing of a missile; the target or object aimed at the mark; a purpose; scheme. **—aim·less,** a.

ain't, ānt. Informal form for: is not; are not; has not; have not, am not. The use of ain't is considered acceptable in some varieties of informal spoken and written English, but is rarely acceptable in formal English.

air, ār, n. A mixture of gases surrounding the earth, consisting primarily of nitrogen and oxygen; the atmosphere we breathe; air in motion. a tune; melody; appearance or manner of a person or thing: an air of importance. **—airs,** n. pl. An affected manner: to put on airs.—v.t. To expose to the air; to let air into; to ventilate: to air a room; to state publicly: to air one's views. **—air·less,** a.

air base, n. The base of operations for military aircraft: in a restricted sense, only the physical installation.

air blad·der, n. A sac filled with air in most fish, and responsible for their buoyancy.

air·borne, ār/bôrn, ār/bōrn, a. Transported by aircraft; moving through or by air.

air brake, n. A mechanical brake operated by compressed air which acts on a piston.

air·brush, ār/brəsh, n. A device attached to a compressed-air hose, for the spraying of paint.

air·burst, ār/bərst, n. An explosion in the air of a bomb, shell, or the like.

air cham·ber, n. Any cavity or compartment filled with air.

air coach, n. The cheaper class of passenger transportation offered by certain airlines.

air-con·di·tion, ār/kən·dish·ən, v.t. To regulate the quality, temperature, etc. of air indoors. **—air-con·di· tioned,** a.

---

air con·di·tion·er, *n.* A ventilating device used esp. for cooling purposes.

air con·di·tion·ing, *n.* The regulating of temperature, humidity, and purity of air in a room or building.

air-cooled, ãr/koold, *a.* Cooled by air, as an automobile engine.

air·craft, ãr/kraft, ãr/kräft, *n. pl.,* **air·craft.** Any machine or craft designed for floating in or flying through the air.

air·craft car·ri·er, *n.* A ship designed as a base for naval airplanes.

air·drome, ãr/drōm, *n.* An airport; aerodrome.

air·drop, ãr/drop, *v.t.,* **-dropped, -drop·ping.** To release persons or equipment from an aircraft in flight. —*n.* An instance of airdropping.

Aire·dale, ãr/dāl, *n.* A large, heavy terrier with a rough brown or tan coat which is black or grizzled over the back; a smaller or miniature of the same type.

air·field, ãr/fēld, *n.* A landing field for airplanes; an airport.

air·foil, ãr/foyl, *n.* Wing, rudder, or any aircraft surface designed to control an airplane by displacing a moving airstream.

air force, *n.* The organization of personnel, equipment, and installations for carrying out military operations in the air; (*cap.*) a numbered or named air force.

air·frame, ãr/frām, *n.* The structural parts of an airplane without the engines.

air gun, *n.* A firearm operated by compressed air; a hand tool operated by compressed air.

air hole, *n.* A natural outlet in the ice covering a pond or river, used by certain water animals such as seals for breathing; an air pocket.

air·ing, ãr/ing, *n.* An exposure to air; a short walk or drive out of doors; the speaking or writing of an idea or plan in order to bring it to public notice.

air lane, *n.* A particular route through the air traversed by aircraft; airway.

air·lift, ãr/lift, *n.* A supply line operated by aircraft. —*v.t.* To transport by air, esp. to a beleaguered place or situation.

air·line, ãr/līn, *n.* A commercial system of aerial transportation; the company owning or operating such a system.

air·lin·er, ãr/līnər, *n.* A commercial transport airplane used by an airline.

air lock, *n.* An airtight area at the entrance of a pressure chamber for the purpose of regulation.

air·mail, air-mail, ãr/māl, *n.* Mail service by airplane; mail so sent.—*v.t.* To send by airmail.—*a.* Relating to airmail.

air·man, ãr/mən, *n. pl.,* **-men.** A civilian aviator; an enlisted member of the Air Force.

air-mind·ed, ãr/mīn·did, *a.* Interested in air travel or things aeronautic.

air·plane, ãr/plān, *n.* A power-driven aircraft supported by the reaction of air flowing over a wing.

air pock·et, *n.* A strong, vertical current of air which causes an aircraft suddenly to rise or drop.

air·port, ãr/pōrt, ãr/pôrt, *n.* An airfield on land or water for the landing, take-off, and servicing of aircraft.

air pow·er, *n.* A nation's command of the air considered as an element of its military strength, esp. the probable command as measured by the number of military aircraft it possesses.

air pres·sure, *n.* Atmospheric pressure.

air pump, *n.* A machine for compressing air, or withdrawing air from a vessel.

air raid, *n.* An attack by enemy aircraft.

air ri·fle, *n.* A rifle that fires by compressed air.

air sac, *n.* A sac containing air; one of certain air-filled cavities in birds, fish, etc.

air·ship, ãr/ship, *n.* An aircraft lighter than air, propelled by an engine or engines; a dirigible.

air·sick·ness, ãr/sik·nis, *n.* A sickness sometimes affecting persons aboard an aircraft in flight, marked

esp. by nausea and dizziness. —**air·sick,** ãr/sik, *a.*

air·space, ãr/spās, *n.* Space in the air esp. such space between flying aircraft; the space above a nation, considered to be under the control of that nation.

air·speed, ãr/spēd, *n.* The speed of an aircraft relative to the surrounding air rather than relative to the ground.

air·strip, ãr/strip, *n.* A flat or cleared surface for airplanes. to take off and land.

air·tight, ãr/tīt, *a.* Not permitting air to pass through; hermetically sealed; leaving no opening for attack or challenge: an *airtight* alibi.

air-to-air, ãr/too·ãr/, ãr/tə·ãr/, *adv.* Between or among aircraft in flight.—*a.* Used or occurring between or among aircraft in the air: an *air-to-air* missile.

air·wave, ãr/wāv, *n. usually pl.* The medium by which radio and television broadcasts are transmitted.

air·way, ãr/wā, *n.* A route for air traffic; a passage for air currents.

air·wor·thy, ãr/wər·thē, *a.* Well adapted or safe for service in the air. —**air·wor·thi·ness,** *n.*

air·y, âr/ē, *a.,* **-i·er, -i·est.** Like air: unsubstantial; exposed to air; gay and sprightly; light in movement; lively. —**air·i·ness,** *n.* —**air·i·ly,** ãr/ə·lē, *adv.*

aisle, īl, *n.* An open passage between objects such as seats in a theater. —**aisled,** *a.*

a·jar, ə·jär/, *a., adv.* Partly opened: said of a door.

a·kim·bo, ə·kim/bō, *a., adv.* With the elbow pointing outwards and the hand resting on the hip: said of the arm.

a·kin, ə·kin/, *a.* Showing a closeness of type or similarity; related by blood; having some of the same properties.

à la, ä/lä, ä/lə, *prep.* According to or in the mode, manner, or style of.

al·a·bas·ter, al/ə·bas·tər, *n.* A hard, white or tinted, translucent, marblelike mineral. —**al·a·bas·trine,** al·ə·bas/trin, *a.*

à la carte, ä lə kärt/, al ə·kärt/, *Fr.* ä lä kärt/, *a.* With a stated price for each dish.

a la mode, al·ə·mōd/, *adv.* In style; served with ice cream: pie *a la mode.*

a·lac·ri·ty, ə·lak/rə·tē, *n.* Cheerful willingness; briskness.

a·larm, ə·lärm/, *n.* A sound to awaken persons or warn them of danger; a device designed to make such a sound; a startled response to a noise or event; apprehension.—*v.t.* To give notice of danger to; to disturb with terror.—**a·larm·ing,** *a.* **a·larm·ing·ly,** *adv.*

a·larm clock, *n.* A clock equipped with a bell or buzzer that can be set to sound at a desired time, as to awaken a sleeper.

a·larm·ist, ə·lär/mist, *n.* One who excites alarm; one who is prone to take alarm with no sufficient reason. —**a·larm·ism,** *n.*

a·las, ə·las/, ə·läs/, *interj.* An exclamation of sorrow, pity, dread, etc.

a·late, ā/lāt, *a.* Having wings or winglike parts. Also **a·lat·ed,** ā/lā·təd.

al·ba·core, al/bə·kōr, al/bə·kôr, *n.* A long-finned, edible ocean fish related to the tuna.

al·ba·tross, al/bə·trôs, al/bə·tros, *n.* A large web-footed sea bird.

al·be·it, ôl·bē/it, *conj.* Although; even though; even if.

al·bi·no, al·bī/nō, *n. pl.* **-nos.** A person or animal with pale, milky complexion, light hair and pink eyes due to a lack of pigmentation or color. —**al·bin·ic,** al·bin/ik, *a.* —**al·bi·nism,** al/bə·niz·əm, *n.*

Al·bi·on, al/bē·ən, *n.* An old name for England.

al·bum, al/bəm, *n.* A book, originally blank, for photographs, memorabilia, etc.; one or more phonograph records or recorded tapes contained in one jacket; the container itself.

al·bu·men, al·byoo/mən, *n.* The white, or clear viscous part of an egg; nourishing matter surrounding the embryo in a seed.

al·bu·min, al·byoo′mən, *n.* A member of a class of proteins which are water-soluble, and are found in the juices and tissues of animals and vegetables. —**al·bu·mi·nous,** *a.*

al·che·my, al′kə·mē, *n.* Medieval chemistry, an art which sought in particular to change common metals into gold; any magical power or process of change. —**al·che·mist,** al′kə·mist, *n.*

al·co·hol, al′kə·hôl, al′kə·hol, *n.* The intoxicating ingredient of liquors formed by fermentation; any alcoholic liquor; any of a class of chemical compounds derived from hydrocarbons by replacing one or more of the hydrogen atoms with an equal number of hydroxyl radicals.

al·co·hol·ic, al·kə·hô′lik, al·kə·hol′ik, *a.* Pertaining to alcohol, or partaking of its qualities.—*n.* One who suffers from alcoholism.

al·co·hol·ism, al′kə·hô·liz·əm, al′kə·ho·liz·əm *n.* The disease or condition of those who habitually drink alcohol immoderately, or are addicted to alcohol.

al·cove, al′kōv, *n.* A wide and deep recess in a room; any natural recess.

al·der, ôl′dər, *n.* Any of several shrubs or small trees bearing catkins, usually growing in moist, cool regions.

al·der·man, ôl′dər·mən, *n. pl.,* -**men.** One of a body of elected municipal officers, ranking below the mayor varying according to locality. —**al·der·man·ic,** al·dər·man′ik, *a.*

ale, āl, *n.* A liquor made by fermentation of malt, flavored with hops.

al·le·a·to·ry, ā′lē·ə·tōr·ē, ā′lē·ə·tôr·ē, *a.* Relating to chance or contingency.

a·lee, ə·lē′, *adv.* On the lee side; on the side away from the wind.

a·lert, ə·lərt′, *a.* Active in vigilance; nimble; lively; bright.—*n.* A warning of immediate danger; the time during which an alert is in effect. —*v.t.* To declare the possibility of danger to; to warn. —**a·lert·ness,** *n.*

ale·wife, āl′wīf, *n. pl.,* -**wives.** A small N. American fish resembling the shad and herring.

al·ex·an·drine, al·ig·zan′drin, al·ig·zan′drēn, *n. (Sometimes cap.)* a kind of verse usually having six iambic feet with a caesura after the third foot.

al·fal·fa, al·fal′fə, *n.* A common U.S. plant of the bean family, widely grown as food for horses and cattle.

al·fres·co, al·fres′kō, *a.* In the open air; out of doors.—*adv.*

al·ga, al′gə, *n. pl.,* **al·gae,** al′jē. Any of various saltwater and fresh-water plants without stems, roots, or leaves, including pond scums, kelps and some seaweeds.

al·ge·bra, al′jə·brə, *n.* That branch of mathematics used to show in which signs are arithmetical operations, and letters are used to represent numbers and quantities. —**al·ge·bra·ic,** al·jə·brā′ik, *a.* —**al·ge·bra·ic·al,** *a.* —**al·ge·bra·ic·al·ly,** *adv.*

Al·gon·qui·an, al·gong′kē·ən, al·gong′kwē·ən, *a.* Belonging to part of a group of North American Indian tribes formerly extending from Labrador and the northern half of the U.S. eastern coast westward to the Rocky Mountains, who shared some common features of their languages and customs. —*n.* A person belonging to an Algonquian tribe.

al·go·ri·thm, al′gō·ri̇th·əm, *n.* A number of rules, which are to be followed for solving a problem.

a·li·as, ā′lē·əs, *adv.* Otherwise known by the name of: John Smith *alias* Thomas Jones, —*n. pl.,* **a·li·as·es,** ā′lē·ə·siz. An adopted or false name.

al·i·bi, al′ə·bī, *n.* The argument or information which shows that a person accused of a crime or act was in another place at the time of its happening. *Informal.*

Any evidence of innocence; excuse. —*v.i. Informal.* To provide an excuse.

al·ien, āl′yən, ā′lē·ən, *a.* Not belonging to a country, land or government; living in a foreign country without possessing the rights and privileges of citizenship; foreign; different in nature, often followed by *to* or *from.* —*n.* A foreigner; one born in or belonging to another country; one who is not a citizen or entitled to the privileges of a citizen of a country. —**al·ien·a·ble,** **al·ien·a·bil·i·ty,** *n.*

al·ien·ate, āl′yə·nāt, ā′lē·ə·nāt, *v.t.,* -**at·ed, -at·ing.** To cause to be withdrawn, as affection; to estrange, followed by *from;* —**al·ien·a·tor, al·ien·a·tion,** *n.*

al·ien·ist, āl′yə·nist, ā′lē·ə·nist, *n.* One who studies or practices the psychiatric treatment of mental diseases. —**al·ien·ism,** *n.*

a·li·form, al′ə·fôrm, ā′lə·fôrm, *a.* Wing-shaped or winglike.

a·light, ə·līt′, *v.i.,* **a·light·ed** or **a·lit, a·light·ing.** To get down or descend, as from horseback or an airplane; to settle as a bird on a tree; to happen upon; followed by *on.*

a·light, ə·līt′, *a., adv.* Lighted, illuminated.

a·lign, ə·līn′, *v.t.* To form in line, as objects or persons.—*v.i.* To join with or ally oneself, as to a party or a cause. Also **a·line.**

a·lign·ment, a·line·ment, *n.* The line of adjustment; the act of aligning oneself to a party or a cause.

a·like, ə·līk′, *a.* Having a similar appearance; without difference.—*adv.* In the same manner, form or degree; equally; resembling exactly; in common: All have erred *alike.*

al·i·ment, al′ə·mənt, *n.* That which nourishes; food.—al′ə·ment, *v.t.* To nourish. —**al·i·men·tal,** al·ə·men′təl, *a.* —**al·i·men·tal·ly,** *adv.* —**al·i·men·ta·tion,** al·ə·mən·tā′shən, *n.*

al·i·men·ta·ry, al·ə·men′tə·rē, *a.* Having to do with food; nourishing.

al·i·men·ta·ry ca·nal, *n.* The body passage from the mouth to the anus through which food passes; digestive tract.

al·i·mo·ny, al′ə·mō·nē, *n.* Money paid by one spouse for the support of the other spouse who is divorced or legally separated.

al·i·quant, al′ə·kwənt, *a.* Applied to a number which does not divide into another number without a remainder: 7 is an *aliquant* part of 20.

al·i·quot, al′ə·kwət, *a.* Applied to a number which can be divided into another without a remainder: 7 is an *aliquot* part of 21.

a·live, ə·līv′, *a.* Having life; living; not dead; in a state of action; aware; existent in operation: to keep an agitation *alive;* full of alacrity; sprightly: *alive* with excitement; sensitive to: *alive* to the beauties of nature.

al·ka·li, al′kə·lī, *n. pl.,* -**lies,** or -**lis.** A hydroxide of sodium, potassium, lithium, rubidium, caesium, and ammonium, which neutralizes acids to form salts and turns red litmus paper blue; any of various other more or less active bases, as calcium hydroxide.

al·ka·line, al′kə·lin, al·kə′līn, *a.* Of or like an alkali. —**al·ka·lin·i·ty,** al·kə·lin′ə·tē, *n.*

al·ka·lize, al′kə·līz, *v.t.,* -**lized, -liz·ing.** To make alkaline. —**al·ka·li·za·tion,** al·kə·lə·zā′shən, *n.*

al·ka·loid, al′kə·loyd, *n.* Any of a class of drugs such as morphine, quinine, aconitine, caffeine, etc., that contain nitrogen. —**al·ka·loi·dal,** al·kə·loy′dəl, *a.*

all, ôl, *a.* Every one of; the whole number or quantity of; belonging to the: *all* the men; during the whole: *all* day, *all* night. —*n.* The whole number; the entire thing; the total.—**above all,** firstly.—**at all,** in the least degree; to the least extent; under any circumstances. —**in all,** everything reckoned or taken into account. —*adv.* Wholly; completely; entirely; altogether: *all*

---

a- hat, fāte, fāre, fäther; **e-** met, mē; **i-** pin, pīne; **o-** not, nōte, ôrb, moove (move), boy, pownd; **u-** cūbe, bŭll, tûk (took); **ch-** chin; **th-** thick, ŧhen; **zh-** vizhon (vision); **ə-** əgo, takən, pencəl, lemən, bərd (bird).

alone.—**all but**, nearly; almost; not quite.—**all one**, the same thing in effect; quite the same.

Al·lah, al′ə, ä′lə, *n.* The Arabic name of the Supreme Being.

all-A·mer·i·can, ôl ə-mer′i·kən, *a.* Made up exclusively of Americans; wholly within the United States; chosen as the best in the U.S., esp. in some sport.—*n.* The player selected for an all-American team.

all-a·round, ôl′ə-round, *a.* Capable of doing things well in different fields; versatile.

al·lay, ə·lā′, *v.t.*, **al·layed**, **al·lay·ing**. To make quiet; to pacify or appease; to lessen; to relieve. —**al·lay·er**, *n.*

all clear, *n.* The signal that an air raid or other danger is over.

al·le·ga·tion, al·ə·gā′shən, *n.* The act of alleging; assertion without proof; assertion to be proved or disproved.

al·lege, ə·lej′, *v.t.*, **al·leged**, **al·leg·ing**. To assert, especially without proof; to pronounce with positiveness; to produce, as an argument, plea, or excuse. —**al·lege·a·ble**, *a.*

al·leged, ə·lejd′, *a.* Declared to be true; supposed. —**al·leg·ed·ly**, *adv.*

al·le·giance, ə·lē′jəns, *n.* The obligation of loyalty of a subject or citizen to his sovereign or government; fidelity; devotion.

al·le·go·ry, al′ə·gôr·ē, *n. pl.*, **-ries.** A figurative story or discourse, in which the principal subject is depicted by another subject resembling it; a symbolic representation; a narrative in which abstract ideas are personified; —**al·le·gor·ic**, al·ə·gôr′ik, **al·e·gor′ik**, *a.* —**al·le·gor·i·cal**, al·ə·gôr′ə·kəl, al·ə·gor′ə·kəl, *a.* —**al·le·gor·i·cal·ly**, al·ə·gôr′ik·le, al·ə·gor′ik·le, *adv.* —**al·le·gor·ist**, *n.*

al·le·gret·to, al·ə·gret′ō, *a., adv. Mus.* Fairly quick; less quick than allegro.

al·le·gro, ə·lā′grō, ə·leg′rō, *a., adv. Mus.* Brisk; rapid.

al·ler·gen, al′ər·jən, *n.* Any substance that induces allergy.

al·ler·gy, al′ər·jē, *n. pl.*, **-gies.** Excess sensitivity producing a bodily reaction to certain substances, as pollen, dust, etc.

al·ler·gic, ə·lər′jik, *a.* Pertaining to or affected with allergy.

al·ler·gist, al′ər·jist, *n.* A medical specialist in allergies.

al·le·vi·ate, ə·lē′vē·āt, *v.t.*, **-at·ed**, **-at·ing**. To make easier to be endured (sorrow, pain, distress). —**al·le·vi·a·tion**, ə·lē·vē·ā′shən, *n.* —**al·le·vi·a·tor**, *n.* —**al·le·vi·a·tive**, *a.* —**al·le·vi·a·to·ry**, *a.*

al·ley, al′ē, *n. pl.*, **al·leys**. A narrow passageway between rows of houses or buildings; a long narrow enclosure with a wood floor for bowling.

al·ley·way, al′ē·wā, *n.* An alley.

All Fools′ Day, *n.* The first day of April; April Fool's Day.

all fours, *n.* All four limbs of an animal or person. —**on all fours**, (of a person) on the hands and knees.

All·hal·lows, ôl·hal′ōz, *n.* All Saints′ Day; Hallowe'en.

al·li·ance, ə·lī′əns, *n.* The relation between families, contracted by marriage; a union between nations, contracted by treaty, etc.; any union of interests; a compact or treaty; the persons or parties allied.

al·lied, ə·līd′, al′īd, *a.* United by agreement or other ties; associated; joined; connected; related.

al·li·ga·tor, al′ə·gā·tər, *n.* Either of two large reptiles found in SE U.S. and China, differing from the true crocodiles in having a shorter and flatter head; leather fashioned from its hide.

al·li·ga·tor pear, *n.* The fruit of the avocado.

al·lit·er·ate, ə·lit′ə·rat, *v.i.*, **-at·ed**, **-at·ing**. To have the same initial letter or sound; also, to use alliteration. —**al·lit·er·a·tive**, ə·lit′ə·rā·tiv, ə·lit′ər·ə·tiv, *a.* —**al·lit·er·a·tive·ly**, *adv.* —**al·lit·er·a·tive·ness**, *n.*

al·lit·er·a·tion, ə·lit·ə·rā′shən, *n.* Constant or frequent repetition of the same initial letter or sound, as in verse.

al·lo·cate, al′ə·kāt, *v.t.*, **-cat·ed**, **-cat·ing**. To assign or allot, as resources or supplies of scarce materials and services; to apportion or distribute, as shares in a corporation. —**al·lo·ca·tion**, al·ə·ka′shən, *n.*

al·lop·a·thy, ə·lop′ə·thē, *n.* The method of treating disease by the use of agents producing effects different from those of the disease treated. —**al·lo·path·ic**, al·o·path′ik, *a.* —**al·lo·path·i·cal·ly**, *adv.* —**al·lo·path**, al′ə·path, *n.*

al·lop·a·thist, ə·lop′ə·thist, *n.* One who practices allopathy.

al·lo·phone, al′ə·fōn, *n.* Any speech sound that is a variant of the same phoneme and which does not mark a difference in meaning.

al·lot, ə·lot′, *v.t.*, **al·lot·ted**, **al·lot·ting**. To pass out in parts or portions among a group of persons; to divide; to assign; to set apart. —**al·lot·ment**, *n.* —**al·lot·ta·ble**, *a.*

al·lot·ro·py, ə·lot′rə·pē, *n.* The property of certain chemical elements, as carbon, sulfur, and phosphorus, which have two or more distinct forms. Also **al·lot·ro·pism**, a·lo′trə·piz·əm.

al·lo·trope, al′ə·trōp, *n.* One of two or more distinct forms of an element. —**al·lo·trop·ic**, al·ə·trop′ik, *a.* —**al·lo·trop·i·cal·ly**, *adv.*

all-out, ôl′out′, *a.* Complete; total.

al·low, ə·low′, *v.t.* To grant, give, or make over; to assign; to admit; to acknowledge; to deduct; to set apart; to grant permission to; —*v.i.* To make provision, followed by *for.* —**al·low·a·ble**, *a.* —**al·low·a·bly**, *adv.*

al·low·ed·ly, *adv.* Admittedly.

al·low·ance, ə·low′əns, *n.* Permission; a quantity granted, esp. money; a deduction; tolerance. —*v.t.*, **-anced**, **-anc·ing**. To put on an allowance.

al·loy, al′oy, ə·loy′, *n.* A substance composed of two or more chemical elements of which at least one is metal. —*v.t.* To reduce the purity of (a metal) by mixing with it a portion of less valuable metal; to reduce, or impair by mixture.

all right, Correct; satisfactory; acceptable; agreeable; safe; well; certainly; yes; okay.

all-round, ôl′round, *a.* Complete; knowledgeable in many fields.

All Saints′ Day, *n.* A church festival held on November 1 in honor of the saints.

all·spice, ôl′spīs, *n.* A spice of a mildly pungent taste, the fruit of a West Indian tree, so called from being regarded as combining many different flavors; pimento.

al·lude, ə·lood′, *v.i.*, **al·lud·ed**, **al·lud·ing**. To refer to something not directly mentioned; to hint at by remote suggestions, followed by *to.*

al·lure, ə·lūr′, *v.t.*, **al·lured**, **al·lur·ing**. To tempt by the offer of some good, real or imagined; to draw or try to draw by some proposed pleasure or advantage; to entice, decoy, tempt, charm, attract.—*n.* Charm; appeal.—**al·lure·ment**, *n.* —**al·lur·er**, *n.*—**al·lur·ing**, *a.* —**al·lur·ing·ly**, *adv.*

al·lu·sion, ə·loo′zhən, *n.* A hint; the act of alluding; a reference to something not explicitly mentioned; an indirect or incidental suggestion; an implied reference; a hint. —**al·lu·sive**, ə·loo′siv, *a.* —**al·lu·sive·ly**, *adv.* —**al·lu·sive·ness**, *n.*

al·lu·vi·al, ə·loo′vē·əl, *n.* Soil deposited by running water. —*a.* Of or pertaining to alluvium.

al·lu·vi·um, ə·loo′·vē·əm, *n. pl.*, **-vi·ums**, **-vi·a**, -vē·ə. A deposit of sand, mud, etc., formed by flowing water.

al·ly, ə·lī′, *v.t.*, **al·lied**, **al·ly·ing**. To unite by marriage, treaty, league, or confederacy; to connect by formal agreement; to bind together or connect.—*v.i.* To form an alliance.

al·ly, al′ī, a·lī′, *n. pl.*, **al·lies**. A prince or state united to another by treaty or league: a confederate; supporter; auxiliary; helper; one who helps another achieve a particular goal; a nation joined with another nation or other nations for the purpose of prosecuting a war against a common enemy, esp. a member of the coalition that fought against Germany in either World War I or World War II.

al·ma ma·ter, äl′mə mä′tər, al′mə mä′tər, al′mə mä′tər, *n.* A school, college, or university where one has been educated.

al·ma·nac, ôl′mə·nak′, *n.* A yearly publication, including a calendar of days, weeks, and months, with the times of the rising of the sun and moon, changes of the moon, eclipses, holidays, etc., for a certain year or years; a yearly publication containing various statistical information.

al·might·y, ôl·mī′tē, *a.* Possessing all power; all-powerful; being of unlimited might.—**the Al·might·y,** God.

al·mond, ä′mənd, am′ənd, *n.* The nutlike stone or kernel of the fruit of the almond tree of warm regions; the tree itself; something almond-shaped.

al·most, ôl′mōst, ôl·mōst′, *adv.* Nearly; for the most part.

aims, ämz, *n. pl.,* **alms.** Anything given freely to relieve the poor; a charitable dole; charity.—**alms·giv·er,** ämz′giv·ər, *n.* —**alms·giv·ing,** *n.*

alms·house, ämz′hows, *n.* A house for the poor, maintained by charity at the public expense.

al·ni·co, al′ni·kō, *n.* A strong permanent-magnet alloy of aluminum, iron, nickel, and other elements.

al·oe, al′ō, *n.* Any plant of a genus of the lily family, chiefly African, various species of which yield a laxative drug; the century plant; American aloe.

a·loft, ə·lôft′, ə·lôft′, *adv.* On high; in the air; high above the ground; on the higher sails or masts.

a·lo·ha, ə·lō′ə, ä·lō′hä, *interj.* A Hawaiian expression of greeting or farewell.—*n.* A greeting.

a·lone, ə·lōn′, *a.* Apart from others; unaccompanied or unaided; solitary; to the exclusion of all others or all else. —*adv.* Only; exclusively; solely; merely; without help. —**a·lone·ness,** *n.*

a·long, ə·lông′, *adv.* By the length; lengthwise; in line with the length: stretched *along*; in line or with progressive motion; onward: walk *along*; in company; together: followed by *with*; from one to another; on hand.—*prep.* By the length of; in a longitudinal direction over or near; in accord with; during.

a·long·shore, ə·lông′shōr, ə·long′shōr, *adv.* By the shore or coast; lengthwise and near the shore.

a·long·side, ə·lông·sīd′, *adv.* Along or by the side; close to the side; beside each other: to lie *alongside.* —*prep.* Beside; by the side of; parallel to.

a·loof, ə·loof′, *adv.* At a distance; intentionally apart from others: to stand, hold, or keep *aloof.*—*a.* Uninvolved; reserved.—**a·loof·ly,** *adv.* —**a·loof·ness,** *n.*

a·loud, ə·lowd′, *adv.* In an audible tone; not whispered; by means of the speaking voice.

al·pen·stock, al′pən·stok, *n.* A strong stick pointed at the end with iron, used in mountain climbing.

al·pha, al′fə, *n.* The first letter in the Greek alphabet; the first or beginning.

al·pha·bet, al′fə·bet, *n.* The letters of a written language arranged in the customary order; any series of elementary signs or symbols used for a similar purpose; hence, first elements; simplest skills or learnings.—**al·pha·bet·ic,** al·fə·bet′ik, *a.* —**al·pha·bet·i·cal,** *a.* —**al·pha·bet·i·cal·ly,** *adv.* —**al·pha·bet·i·za·tion,** al·fə·bet·ə·zā′shən, *n.* —**al·pha·bet·ize,** *v.t.,* **-ized, -iz·ing.**

al·pha·nu·mer·ic, al·fə·noo·mer′ik, al·fə·nū·mer′ik, *a. Computer,* consisting of both numbers and letters: an *alphanumeric* set of characters.

al·pha par·ti·cle, *n.* a subatomic particle, having an atomic weight of 4 and a positive charge equal to 2 electronic charges, which is given off from the nuclei of certain atoms during radioactive disintegration.

al·pha ray, *n.* A stream of alpha particles.

al·read·y, ôl·red′ē, *adv.* Before the present time; before some specified time; previously; so soon.

al·so, ôl′sō, *adv.* In like manner; likewise; as well; in addition; too.

also-ran, ôl′sō·ran, *n.* A person or any contestant who fails to achieve success, used esp. in reference to the loser of an election, horse race, or other contest.

al·tar, ôl′tər, *n.* A raised structure on which sacrifices were offered to a deity or ancestor, or on which incense was burned; a table in a church for the celebration of the Eucharist.

al·tar boy, *n.* One who assists the principal celebrant in a religious ceremony; an acolyte.

al·tar·piece, ôl′tər·pēs, *n.* A painting or piece of sculpture placed behind or above an altar in a church for the purpose of decoration.

al·ter, ôl′tər, *v.t.* To change; to make over or different; to make some change in; to modify; to vary in some degree, without an entire change.—*v.i.* To become, in some respects, different; to vary; to change, as one's personality. —**al·ter·a·bil·i·ty,** al·tər·ə·bil′ə·tē, *n.* —**al·ter·a·ble,** *a.* —**al·ter·a·ble·ness,** *n.* —**al·ter·a·bly,** *adv.* —**al·ter·ant,** *n.* —**al·ter·a·tion,** ä′shən, *n.* —**al·ter·a·tive,** *a.*

al·ter·ca·tion, ôl·tər·kā′shən, al·tər·kā′shən, *n.* Vigorous exchange of words; heated argument or dispute; a wrangle; a fight.

al·ter e·go, *n.* Close friend; second self; an exact substitute.

al·ter·nate, ôl′tər·nāt, al′tər·nāt, *v.t.,* **-nat·ed, -nat·ing.** To perform by turns; cause to take turns; interchange successively, one with another. —*v.i.* To succeed by turns; take turns; change about by turns between points, states, actions. ôl′tər·nit, al′tər·nit, *n.* Something that alternates; an official substitute, as at a political convention. ôl′tər·nit, al′tər·nit, *a.* Forming or having an alternating series; succeeding by turns; recurring as one of an alternating series; appearing in turn or as every other; of leaves, as placed singly and at different heights on the axis, first on one side and then on the other, or at definite angular distances from one another. —**al·ter·nate·ly,** *adv.* —**al·ter·na·tion,** ôl·tər·nā′shən, *n.*

al·ter·nat·ing cur·rent, *n.* a current that reverses direction in cycles.

al·ter·na·tive, ôl·tər′nə·tiv, al·tər′nə·tiv, *n.* A choice between two things, so that if one is taken the other must be left; a possibility of one of two things, so that if one thing is false the other must be true.

—**al·ter·na·tive·ly,** *adv.* —**al·ter·na·tive·ness,** *n.*

al·ter·na·tor, ôl′tər·nā·tər, al′tər·nā·tər, *n.* An electric generator used in the production of alternating current.

al·though, ôl·thō′, *conj.* Even though; even granting all this; supposed that; admit all that.

al·tim·e·ter, al·tim′i·tər, al′tə·mē·tər, *n.* An instrument for measuring distance or height above the earth or above sea level.

al·tim·e·try, al·tim′i·trē, *n.* The science of ascertaining altitudes.

al·ti·pla·no, al·tə·plä′nō, *n.* A high plateau.

al·ti·tude, al′ti·tood, al′ti·tūd, *n.* Height; amount of space to a point above from one below; measure of elevation; a high location or area.

al·to, al′tō, *n.* Contralto; the deepest voice among women and boys, and the highest among men, a special voice above the tenor; a singer in this voice; in a family of musical instruments, the second highest instrument.

---

a- hat, fāte, fāre, fäther; e- met, mē; i- pin, pine; o- not, nōte, ôrb, moove (move), boy, pownd; u- cūbe, bûll, tûk (took); ch- chin; th- thick, ŧhen; zh- vizhon (vision); ə- əgo, takən, pencəl, lemən, bərd (bird).

al·to·cu·mu·lus, al·tō·kŭ′myə·ləs, *n.* A cloud, a form of cumulus of great altitude, appearing in fleecy clumps or globular masses variously grouped.

al·to·geth·er, ôl′tə·geth·ər, *adv.* Wholly; entirely; completely; quite.—*n.* A whole.—**in the al·to·geth·er**, *informal.* in the nude.

al·to·re·lie·vo, al′tō·ri·lē′vō, *n.* High relief; sculpture in which the figures stand out prominently from the background; sculpture in high relief.

al·to·stra·tus, al·tō·strā′təs, *n.* A comparatively high sheetlike cloud that is similar to the cirrostratus, and located from 8,000 to 20,000 feet.

al·tru·ism, al′troo·iz·əm, *n.* Devotion to others or to humanity. —**al·tru·is·tic**, al·troo·is′tik, *a.*

al·lu·mi·na, ə·loo′mə·nə, *n.* The natural or synthetic oxide of aluminum, the most abundant of the earth's elements.

a·lu·mi·nif·er·ous, ə·loo·mə·nif′ər·əs, *a.* Containing alumina or aluminum.

a·lu·mi·nous, ə·loo′mə·nəs, *a.* Pertaining to or containing alumina.

a·lu·mi·num, ə·loo′mə·num, *n.* An oxidation-resistant white metal with a bluish tinge, and a luster somewhat resembling, but far inferior to, that of silver. See Periodic Table of Elements. Also, *Chiefly Brit.*, **al·u·min·i·um**, al·yoo·min′ē·əm.

a·lum·na, ə·ləm′nə, *n. pl.*, **-nae**, -nē. A female graduate of an educational institution.

a·lum·nus, ə·ləm′nəs, *n. pl.*, **-ni**, -nī. A graduate of a college or university.

al·ve·o·lar, al·vē′ə·lər, *a.* Spoken with the tongue near or touching the alveolar ridge.

al·ve·o·lus, al·vē′ə·ləs, *n. pl.*, **-o·li**, -ə·lī. A cell, pit, or small cavity, as in a honeycomb or in a fossil; the socket of a tooth; a terminal air sac deep within the lungs.

al·ways, ôl′wiz, ôl′wāz, *adv.* Perpetually; uninterruptedly; forever; continually: *always* the same; as often as occasion recurs: *always* late; if necessary.

a.m. Before 12:00 noon and after 12:00 midnight.

am, am. The first person singular of the present indicative of the verb *to be*.

a·mal·gam, ə·mal′gəm, *n.* An alloy of mercury with another metal or metals; *fig.* a mixture or combination. —**a·mal·gam·a·ble**, *a.*

a·mal·gam·ate, ə·mal′gə·māt, *v.t.*, **-at·ed, -at·ing.** To form into an amalgam; combine; unite.—*v.i.* To form an amalgam; blend; coalesce.

a·mal·gam·a·tion, ə·mal·gə·mā′shən, *n.* The act of amalgamating, or the resulting state; combination; union; fusion; extraction of the precious metals from their ores by treatment with mercury; the merging of two or more corporations.

a·man·u·en·sis, ə·man·yoo·en′sis, *n. pl.*, **-ses**, -sēz. A person whose job is to write what another person says, or to copy what has been written by another; secretary.

am·a·ryl·lis, am·ə·ril′is, *n.* The belladonna lily, with large, lilylike, normally rose-colored flowers; any of several related plants.

a·mass, ə·mas′, *v.t.* To collect into a heap; to gather a great quantity or number of; to accumulate. —**a·mass·ment**, *n.*

am·a·teur, am′ə·chər, am′ə·tər, am′ə·tûr, am′ə·tyûr, *n.* One who studies and practices any art or occupation for the enjoyment of it, instead of professionally or for gain; a devotee.—*a.* Of or being an amateur; lacking the talent or polish of a professional.

am·a·teur·ism, *n.* The practice or character of an amateur.

am·a·teur·ish, am·ə·chûr′ish, am·ə·tûr′ish, am·ə·tyûr′ish, *a.* Of or being an amateur; suggestive of an amateur, as lacking the skill or finish of a professional. —**am·a·teur·ish·ly**, *adv.* —**am·a·teur·ish·ness**, *n.*

am·a·tive, am′ə·tiv, *a.* Full of love; inclined to love; amorous. —**am·a·tive·ness**, *n.*

am·a·to·ry, am′ə·tôr·ē, *a.* Pertaining to or produc-

ing love; expressive of love, as verses or sighs.

a·maze, ə·māz′, *v.t.*, **a·mazed, a·maz·ing.** To surprise; to confound with sudden surprise or wonder; to confuse utterly; to astound; to astonish; to bewilder. —**a·maz·ed·ly**, ə·mā′zid·lē, *adv.* —**a·maz·ed·ness**, ə·mā′zid·nis, *n.* —**a·maze·ment**, *n.*

a·maz·ing, ə·mā′zing, *a.* Very wonderful; exciting astonishment: *amazing* grace. —**a·maz·ing·ly**, *adv.*

Am·a·zon, am′ə·zon, am′ə·zən, *n.* One of a race of female warriors in Greek legend, supposed to dwell near the Black Sea. (*Often l.c.*) A very tall, strong woman.

Am·a·zo·ni·an, am·ə·zō′nē·ən, *a.* Of like, or befitting an Amazon, female warrior of Greek mythology; warlike; aggressive; referring to the Amazon river.

am·bas·sa·dor, am·bas′ə·dər, *n.* A minister of the highest rank employed by one country at the court of another to carry out his country's affairs; a messenger; intermediary; authorized envoy; official representative: the *ambassador* to France. —**am·bas·sa·do·ri·al**, am·bas·ə·dôr′ē·əl, *a.*

am·ber, am′bər, *n.* A hard, pale-yellow, and sometimes reddish or brownish fossil resin of extinct pine trees, used for ornamental pieces; the pale yellow to brownish color of amber.

am·ber·gris, am′bər·grēs, am′bər·gris, *n.* A solid, waxy, ash-colored substance used in making perfumes; a secretion, probably from the sperm whale.

am·bi·dex·trous, am·bi·dek′strəs, *a.* Able to use both hands with equal ease; double-dealing; versatile.

am·bi·ance, am·bi·ence, am′bē·əns, *n.* The surrounding mood, atmosphere, or environment.

am·bi·ent, am′bē·ənt, *a.* Surrounding; encompassing on all sides.

am·big·u·ous, am·big′ū·əs, *a.* Doubtful or uncertain; likely to be interpreted two ways; equivocal; indefinite. —**am·big·u·ous·ly**, *adv.* —**am·big·u·ous·ness**, *n.*

am·bi·gu·i·ty, am·bə·gū′ə·tē, *n.* The state or quality of being ambiguous or obscure; doubtfulness or uncertainty, particularly of meaning.

am·bit, am′bit, *n.* Compass or circuit; circumference; scope; sphere; bounds; range; extent; limits.

am·bi·tion, am·bish′ən, *n.* A desire for honor, power, fame, or whatever confers distinction; aspiration toward an object; desire to distinguish oneself among others; determination to progress in one's business or other career.

am·bi·tious, am·bish′əs, *a.* Possessing ambition, followed by *of* or *after*; showy; pretentious: an *ambitious* ornament; requiring unusual effort: an *ambitious* undertaking. —**am·bi·tious·ly**, *adv.* —**am·bi·tious·ness**, *n.*

am·biv·a·lence, am·biv′ə·lens, *n.* The state of having contradictory feelings about a particular person, object, or action. —**am·biv·a·lent**, *a.*

am·ble, am′bəl, *v.i.*, **am·bled, am·bling.** To move easily and gently at an unhurried pace; to move by lifting both legs on each side alternately: said of horses, etc. —*n.* Easy motion; gentle pace; the pace of a horse or like animal when ambling. —**am·bler**, *n.*

am·bro·sia, am·brō′zhə, *n.* The fabled food of the ancient Greek gods, which gave immortality to those who ate it; anything very pleasing to the taste or smell. —**am·bro·sial**, *a.* —**am·bro·sial·ly**, *adv.*

am·bu·lance, am′byə·ləns, *n.* A vehicle equipped for conveying the injured and sick.

am·bu·la·to·ry, am′byə·lə·tôr·ē, *a.* Having the power to walk; adapted for walking; not stationary: an *ambulatory* court; movable. —*n.* Any sheltered part of a building intended for walking, a cloister.

am·bu·lant, am′byə·lənt, *a.* Moving from place to place.

am·bu·late, am′byə·lāt, *v.i.*, **-lat·ed, -lat·ing.** To walk; move about.

am·bus·cade. am′bə·skād, *n.* An ambush; —*v.i.*, *vt.*, **-cad·ed, -cad·ing.** To ambush.

am·bush, am′bûsh, *n.* Troops or other persons concealed to attack by surprise; the position or station of the attacking force, or the force itself. —*v.t.* To station troops, etc., for an ambush; conceal in or as in ambush; also, to attack from ambush; waylay. **am·bush·er,** *n.* —**am·bush·ment,** *n.*

a·me·ba, *n.* Amoeba.

a·mel·io·rate, ə·mēl′yə·rāt, *v.t.,* -**rat·ed,** -**rat·ing.** To make better; to improve. —*v.i.* To grow better. —**a·mel·io·ra·ble,** *a.* —**a·mel·io·ra·tion,** ə·mēl′yə·rā′shən, *n.* —**a·mel·ior·a·tive,** ə·mēl′yə·rā·tiv, *a.* —**a·mel·io·ra·tor,** *n.*

a·men, ä·men′, ä·men′, *adv., interj.* Verily; a solemn expression of agreement; be it so, as after a prayer. —*n.* An utterance or use of amen.

a·me·na·ble, ə·mē′nə·bəl, ə·men′ə·bəl, *a.* Accountable; responsible; ready to yield to advice; —**a·me·na·bil·i·ty,** ə·mē·nə·bil′ə·tē, *n.* —**a·me·na·ble·ness,** *n.* —**a·me·na·bly,** *adv.*

a·mend, ə·mend′, *v.t.* To make better, or change for the better; to alter a bill, motion, etc., by formal procedure or vote; to correct.—*v.i.* To become better, as by improving conduct. —**a·mend·a·ble,** *a.* —**a·mend·er,** *n.*

a·mend·ment, ə·mend′mənt, *n.* The act of changing for the better; improvement; (*cap.*) any of the additions to the U.S. Constitution.

a·mends, ə·mendz′, *n. pl.* Compensation for a loss or injury: to make *amends.*

a·men·i·ty, ə·men′ə·tē, ə·mē′nə·tē, *n.* The quality of being pleasant or agreeable. *pl.* Agreeable manners or acts; civilities.

a·merce, ə·mərs′, *v.t.,* **a·merced, a·merc·ing.** To punish by a penalty or arbitrary fine, the amount; to punish by deprivation of any kind; —**a·merce·a·ble,** *a.* —**a·merce·ment,** *n.* —**a·merc·er,** *n.*

A·mer·i·can, ə·mer′ə·kən, *a.* Of or pertaining to either continent of America; often, of or pertaining to the U.S.; A native or inhabitant of America esp. a citizen of the U.S.

A·mer·i·ca·na, ə·mer·ə·kan′·ə, ə·mer·ə·kä′nə, *n. pl.* Books, papers, etc., relating to America, esp. to its history.

A·mer·i·can Eng·lish, *n.* The English language as used in the U. S.

A·mer·i·can In·di·an, *n.* Any of the aboriginal peoples inhabiting N. and S. America, excluding the Eskimo.

A·mer·i·can·ism, ə·mer′ə·kə·niz·əm, *n.* An American trait or usage; a word or idiom originating in America; loyalty to policies and traditions of the U.S.

A·mer·i·can plan, *n.* A way of operating a hotel according to which a fixed charge per day covers rooms and meals.

Am·er·ind, am′ə·rind, *n.* An American Indian or Eskimo. —**Am·er·in·di·an,** am·ə·rin′dē·ən, *a., n.*

am·e·thyst, am′ə·thist, *n.* A violet-blue or purple variety of quartz which is made into various articles of jewelry. —**am·e·thys·tine,** am·ə·this′tin, am·ə·this′tēn, *a.*

a·mi·a·ble, ā′mē·ə·bəl, *a.* Having a kindly and attractive manner or way of acting; pleasing; friendly; good-natured. —**a·mi·a·bil·i·ty,** ā·mē·ə·bil′ə·tē, *n.* —**a·mi·a·ble·ness,** *n.* —**a·mi·a·bly,** *adv.*

am·i·ca·ble, am′ə·kə·bəl, *a.* Friendly; peaceable. —**am·i·ca·bil·i·ty,** am·i·kə·bil′i·tē, *n.* —**am·i·ca·ble·ness,** *n.* —**am·i·ca·bly,** *adv.*

am·ice, am′is, *n.* A piece of fine linen, like a cape, worn by priests during Mass.

a·mid, ə·mid′, *prep.* In the midst or middle of; among. Also **amidst.**

am·ide, am′id, am′id, *n.* Any chemical compound derived from ammonia by replacing acid or acyl groups for the atoms of hydrogen.

a·mid·ships, ə·mid′ships, *adv.* In or toward the middle of a ship or aircraft. Also **a·mid·ship.**

a·midst, ə·midst′, *prep.* Amid.

a·mi·go, ə·mē′gō, ä·mē′gō, *n.* A friend.

a·mine, ə·mēn′, am′in, *n.* Any of the derivative compounds of ammonia in which the hydrogen atoms are replaced by one or more organic hydrocarbon radicals. Also **amin.**

a·mi·no ac·id, ə·mē′nō, am′ə·nō, *n.* Any of a group of complex organic compounds which form the basic building blocks of proteins.

a·mir, ə·mēr′, *n.* In Arab countries, a commander or ruler; a chieftain.

A·mish, ä′mish, am′ish, *a.* Pertaining to Jakob Ammann, a Swiss Mennonite of the 17th century, or to his followers or their sect.—*n. pl.* The Amish Mennonites.

a·miss, ə·mis′, *adv., a.* In a faulty manner; improperly.

am·i·to·sis, am·ə·tō′sis, *n.* The direct method of cell division. —**am·i·tot·ic,** am·ə·tot′ik, *a.* —**am·i·tot·i·cal·ly,** am·ə·tot′ik·lē, *adv.*

am·i·ty, am′ə·tē, *n.* Friendship; harmony, especially between nations.

am·me·ter, am′mē·tər, *n.* An instrument which measures electric currents in amperes.

am·mo·nia, ə·mōn′yə, ə·mō′nē·ə, *n.* A colorless, pungent, suffocating gas, a compound of nitrogen and hydrogen.

am·mon·ic, ə·mon′ik, ə·mō′nik, *a.* Pertaining to ammonia.

am·mo·ni·ac, ə·mō′nē·ak, *n.* A mixture of gum and resin used especially in medicine.

am·mo·ni·um, ə·mō′nē·əm, *n.* A radical, which acts as a metal in compounds formed from ammonia.

am·mo·ni·um chlo·ride, *n.* A volatile, crystalline powder, used chiefly in dry cells and in medicine.

am·mo·ni·um hy·drox·ide, *n.* A compound occurring only in the solution made of ammonia gas and water.

am·mu·ni·tion, am·yə·nish′ən, *n.* Objects used to inflict damage to game or an actual enemy; cartridges, shells, or other projectiles for guns; anything used as a defense.

am·ne·sia, am·nē′zhə, *n.* Partial or complete loss of memory. —**am·ne·sic,** am·nē′sik, am·nē′zik, *a.* —**am·nes·tic,** am·nes′tik, *a.*

am·nes·ty, am′nəs·tē, *n. pl.,* -**ties.** An act of forgiving; forgetting of offenses; a pardon of the offenses of subjects against the government. —*v.t.,* -**tied,** -**ty·ing.** To pardon.

am·ni·on, am′nē·ən, *n. pl.,* **am·ni·ons, am·ni·a,** am′nē·ə. The innermost membrane surrounding a fetus. —**am·ni·on·ic,** am·nē·on′ik, **am·ni·ot·ic,** am·nē·ot′ic, *a.*

a·moe·ba, ə·mē′bə, *n. pl.,* **a·moe·bae,** ə·mē′bē, **a·moe·bas.** A one-celled protozoan of indefinite shape. —**a·moe·bic,** ə·mē′bik, *a.*

a·moe·boid, ə·me′boyd, *a.* Like an amoeba. Also **a·me·ba.**

a·mok, ə·mək′, ə·mok′, *n., a., adv.* Amuck.

a·mong, ə·məng′, *prep.* In or into the midst of; in or into the number of; by the combined action of.

a·mongst, ə·məngst′, *prep.* Among.

a·mor·al, ā·môr′əl, ā·mor′əl, *a.* Lacking moral responsibility; unable to make moral distinctions.

am·o·rous, am′ər·əs, *a.* Having a tendency to love, or to sexual enjoyment; loving; fond; pertaining to love; indicating love. —**am·o·rous·ly,** *adv.* —**am·o·rous·ness,** *n.*

a·mor·phism, ə·môr′fiz·əm, *n.* A formless condition.

a·mor·phous, ə·môr′fəs, *a.* Formless; having no definite form; of irregular shape; not having the regular forms exhibited by the crystals of minerals; not crystallized.

---

a- hat, fāte, fāre, fäther; **e-** met, mē; **i-** pin, pīne; **o-** not, nōte, ôrb, moove (move), boy, pownd; **u-** cūbe, bůll, tûk (took); **ch-** chin; **th-** thick, ŧhen; **zh-** vizhon (vision); ə- əgo, takən, pencəl, lemən, bərd (bird).

am·or·tize, am′ər·tīz, ə·môr′tiz, *v.t.*, **-tized, -tiz·ing.** To pay off a debt, by means of regular payments. **—am·or·ti·za·tion**, am·ər·tə·zā′shən, *n.*

a·mount, ə·mownt′, *n.* The total of two or more sums or quantities; the sum; the effect, substance, or result; money, as principal plus the interest earned. *—v.i.* To total by an accumulation of particulars; to come in the aggregate or whole; to result in; to be tantamount (to).

a·mour, ə·mûr′, *n.* A love affair, usually illicit.

am·per·age, am·pər′ij, am·pēr′ij, *n.* The strength of an electric current measured in amperes.

am·pere, am′pēr, am·pēr′, *n.* The unit of electric current; the current produced by one volt acting through a resistance of one ohm.

am·per·sand, am′pər·sand, *n.* The character &, symbol for *and.*

am·phet·a·mine, am·fet′ə·mēn, am·fet′ə·min, *n.* A drug used in the treatment of colds, depression, etc.

Am·phib·i·a, am·fib′ē·a, *n. pl.* The class of vertebrates, including the frogs, newts, and salamanders, having gills, living in water in larval form, and developing into lung-breathing adults.

am·phib·i·an, am·fib′ē·ən, *a.* Belonging to the class *Amphibia.—n.* An amphibian animal; an amphibious plant; seaplane.

am·phib·i·ous, am·fib′ē·əs, *a.* Able to live on land or water; able to function on land or water: an *amphibious* craft, referring to an assault landing on a shore by combined land and naval forces.

am·phi·the·a·ter, am′fə·thē·ə·tər, *n.* An oval structure with an open central area surrounded by rows of seats; arena; anything, as a natural hollow among hills, resembling an amphitheater. **—am·phi·the·at·ric**, am·fə·thē·at′rik. **—am·phi·the·at·ri·cal**, am·fə·thē·at′ri·kəl, *a.* **—am·phi·the·at·ri·cal·ly**, *adv.*

am·pho·ra, am′fə·rə, *n. pl.*, **-rae**, -rē, **am·pho·ras.** A tall, narrow vessel with two handles, used by the ancient Greeks and Romans.

am·ple, am′pəl, *a.*, **am·pler, am·plest.** Large in dimensions; of great size or extent; wide; spacious; full enough for some purpose; abundant. **—am·ple·ness**, *n.* **—am·ply**, *adv.*

am·pli·fy, am′plə·fi, *v.t.*, **-fied, -fy·ing.** To make larger, more ample; to increase; to explain in greater detail; to increase the strength of electrical impulses. *—v.i.* To elaborate, often followed by *on.* **—am·pli·fi·ca·tion**, am·plə·fə·kā′shən, *n.*

am·pli·fi·er, am′plə·fi·ər, *n.* That which amplifies; a device for increasing the strength of electric impulses, esp. using vacuum tubes or transistors.

am·pli·tude, am′plə·tood, am′plə·tūd, *n.* Largeness of dimensions; abundance; extent of surface or space; greatness; *phys.* the extent of a vibration on each side of the mean position; *electron.* the greatest value of an alternating wave during one oscillation.

am·pli·tude mod·u·la·tion, a system of radio transmission in which the amplitude of the carrier wave is modulated (contrasted with frequency modulation).

am·pul, am′pool, am′pūl, *n.* A small, bulb-shaped, tightly sealed vessel which holds a solution for hypodermic injection. Also **ampoule, ampule.**

am·pu·tate, am′pū·tāt, *v.t.*, **-tat·ed, -tat·ing.** To cut off, as a limb or other member, by a surgical operation. **—am·pu·ta·tion**, am·pū·tā′shən, *n.*

am·pu·tee, am·pū·tē′, *n.* A person who has had one or more limbs, or parts of limbs, amputated.

Am·trak, am′trak, *n.* A national corporation that operates railroad passenger service on nearly all U.S. rail lines, between cities.

a·muck, ə·mək′, *adv.* In a furious, reckless frenzy. **—run a·muck**, to go beserk; to act in a frenzied manner.

am·u·let, am′yə·lit, *n.* Something worn or carried as a charm or preservative against evil.

a·muse, ə·mūz′, *v.t.*, **a·mused, a·mus·ing.** To entertain or occupy pleasantly, as with humor; to divert. **—a·mus·a·ble**, *a.* **—a·mus·ing**, *a.* **—a·mus·ing·ly**, *adv.*

a·muse·ment, ə·mūz′mənt, *n.* The act of amusing, or state of being amused; that which amuses; entertainment; sport; pastime.

a·muse·ment park, *n.* A park with various recreational facilities, such as roller coasters, ferris wheels, etc.

am·yl·ase, am′ə·lās, *n.* Any of the enzymes that convert starch into sugar, esp. in saliva.

an, ən, an, *a., indef. art.* A word used before nouns in the singular number to denote an individual as one among more belonging to the same class, and not marking singleness like *one*, nor pointing to something known and definite like *the*. The form *a* is used before consonants (including the sound of *u* as in *unit*); *an* is used before words beginning with a vowel sound, or sometimes before *h*, usu. silent, when the accent falls on any syllable except the first: *an inn, an historian, an heir.*

An·a·bap·tist, an·ə·bap′tist, *n.* A member of any of various Protestant sects which oppose infant baptism and require the baptism of adults.

a·nach·ro·nism, ə·nak′rə·niz·əm, *n.* Any error which implies the misplacing, usually earlier, of persons or events in time; anything foreign to or out of keeping with a particular time. **—a·nach·ro·nis·tik**, ə·nak·rə·nis′tik, *a.* **—a·nach·ro·nis·ti·cal·ly**, *adv.* **—a·nach·ro·nous**, ə·nak′rə·nəs, *a.*

an·a·con·da, an·ə·kon′də, *n.* A very large nonpoisonous snake which crushes its prey within its coils; any large boa snake.

a·nae·mi·a, ə·nē′mē·ə, *n.* Anemia. **—a·nae·mic**, *adj.*

an·aer·obe, an·âr′ōb, an′ə·rōb, *n.* A microscopic organism that lives without air or free oxygen. **—an·aer·o·bic**, an·âr·ō′bik, an·ə·rō′bik, *a.*

an·aes·the·sia, an·is·thē′zhə, *n.* Anesthesia.

an·aes·thet·ic, an·is·thet′ik, *a., n.* Anesthetic.

an·a·gram, an′ə·gram, *n.* A word or phrase formed by transposing the letters of another word or phrase, as live-evil; **anagrams**, a game in which the objective is the formation of new words through the transposition of letters. **—an·a·gram·mat·ic**, an·ə·grə·mat′ik, *a.* **—an·a·gram·mat·i·cal**, *a.*

a·na·gram·ma·tize, an·ə·gram′ə·tīz, *v.t.*, **-tized, -tiz·ing.** To transpose, as the letters of a word, so as to form an anagram.

a·nal, ā′nal, *a.* Having to do with or located near the anus.

an·a·lects, an′ə·lekts, *n. pl.* Extracts or small pieces of writing selected from different authors and combined. Also **an·a·lec·ta**, an·ə·lek′tə.

an·al·ge·si·a, an·əl·jē′zē·ə, an·əl·jē′sē·ə. *n.* Absence of feeling pain while retaining consciousness.

an·al·ge·sic, an·əl·jē′zik, an·əl·jē′sik, *a.* Of or producing analgesia. *—n.* A drug or other remedy to remove pain.

an·a·log, an′ə·lôg, an′ə·log, *n.* Something having similarity with something else; something similar. **—an·a·log·i·cal**, an·ə·loj′ə·kəl, *a.* **—an·a·log·i·cal·ly**, an·ə·loj′ik·lē, *adv.*

a·nal·o·gize, ə·nal′ə·jīz, *v.t., v.i.*, **-gized, -giz·ing.** To explain or reason by analogy.

an·a·log com·put·er, *n.* A computer which calculates by using physical analogs, such as quantities of electrical resistance, of the variables of a given problem and provides solutions in a graphic representation, such as an oscilloscope pattern.

an·a·logue com·put·er, *n.* See **analog computer.**

a·nal·o·gy, ə·nal′o·jē, *n. pl.*, **-gies.** An agreement or likeness between things in some circumstances or effects but not others; parallelism; likeness. *Biol.* Correspondence in *function* or appearance, but not in structure and origin. **—a·nal·o·gous**, ə·nal′ə·gəs, *a.*

a·nal·y·sis, ə·nal′i·sis, *n. pl.*, **-ses**, -sēz. The study of a complex or compound object to discover and identify its parts: opposed to *synthesis;* a consideration of anything in its separate parts and their relation to each other; a statement of this; the process of subjecting to chemical tests to determine ingredients; psychoanalysis.

an•a•lyst, an′ə•list, *n.* One who analyzes; psychoanalyst. —**an•a•lyt•ic,** an•ə•lit′ik, *a.*

an•a•lyt•ics, an•ə•lit′iks, *n. pl. but sing. in constr.* The branch of logic concerned with analysis.

an•a•lyze, an′ə•līz, *v.t.,* **-lyzed, -lyz•ing.** To resolve into its important parts; to determine the essential features of; to study critically; psychoanalyze. **an•a•lyz•a•ble,** *a.* —**an•a•ly•za•tion,** an•ə•lə•zā′shən, *n.* —**an•a•lyz•er,** *n.*

an•a•pest, an•a•paest, an′ə•pest, *n.* A poetical foot made up of three syllables, the first two short or unaccented, the last long or accented; a line of verse in this style. —**an•a•pes•tic, an•a•paes•tic,** an•ə•pes′tik, *a.*

an•ar•chism, an′ər•kiz•əm, *n.* The doctrine of doing without formal government and of free action for the individual, land and other resources being common property; the practice or support of anarchistic principles; lawlessness.

an•ar•chist, an′ər•kist, *n.* One who advocates or promotes anarchism, especially by overthrowing the established order. —**an•ar•chis•tic,** an•ər•kis′tik, *a.*

an•ar•chy, an′ər•kē, *n.* Lack of government; a state of society when there is no law or supreme power; uncontrolled political confusion and disorder. —**an•ar•chic,** an•ar′kik, *a.* —**an•ar•chi•cal,** *a.*

a•nath•e•ma, ə•nath′ə•mə, *n. pl.,* **-mas.** A person or object that is hated or avoided; a curse or condemnation pronounced with religious authority, and accompanied by excommunication; curse.

a•nath•e•ma•tize, ə•nath′ə•mə•tīz, *v.t.,* **-ized, -iz•ing.** To pronounce an anathema against; to ban; to curse.—*v.i.* To pronounce anathemas; to curse. —**a•nath•e•mat•iz•a•tion,** ə•nath•ə•mə•tə•zā′shən.

a•nat•o•mize, ə•nat′ə•mīz, *v.t.,* **-mized, -miz•ing.** To cut up or dissect for the purpose of displaying or examining the structure of. To expose minutely; to analyze: to *anatomize* an argument. —**a•nat•o•mi•za•tion,** ə•nat•ə•mə•zā′shən, *n.*

a•nat•o•my, ə•nat′ə•mē, *n. pl.,* **-mies.** The art or practice of anatomizing of the internal structure of organized bodies; physique; structure; the act of dissecting something to examine it in detail, analysis. —**an•a•tom•ic,** an•ə•tom′ik, *a.* —**an•a•tom•i•cal,** an•ə•tom′ə•kəl, *a.* —**an•a•tom•i•cal•ly,** an•ə•tom′ik•lē, *adv.* —**a•nat•o•mist,** ə•nat′ə•mist, *n.*

an•ces•tor, an′ses•tər, *n.* One from whom a person descends; forefather; a forerunner of a more recent species or group. —**an•ces•tral,** an•ses′trəl, *a.*

an•ces•tress, an′ses•tris, *n.* A female ancestor.

an•ces•try, an′ses•trē, *n. pl.,* **-tries.** A series of ancestors; lineage; honorable descent.

an•chor, ang′kər, *n.* An iron implement which holds a ship or boat at rest in shallow water by means of hooks or flukes which dig into the bottom; something serving a purpose to that of a ship's anchor; that which gives stability or security; *v.t.* To hold, as a ship, at rest by lowering the anchor; to fix in a stable condition. —*v.i.* To cast anchor; to become anchored. **at an•chor,** floating attached to an anchor; anchored.

an•chor•age, ang′kər•ij, *n.* An anchoring; or being anchored; place to anchor; money charged for anchoring a ship.

an•cho•ress, ang′kər•is, *n.* A female anchoret.

an•cho•rite, ang′kə•rīt, *n.* A hermit; a recluse; one who retires from society to devote himself to religious duties. Also **an•cho•ret,** ang′kə•rit, ang′kə•ret. —**an•cho•rit•ic,** ang•kə•rit′ik.

an•cho•vy, an′chō•vē, an′chə•vē, an•chō′vē, *n. pl.,* **-vies.** A very small fish of the herring family, used for food.

an•cien ré•gime, än•syan′•rā•zhēm′, *n.* The old or earlier government, esp. the political and social system of France before the Revolution of 1789.

an•cient, ān′shənt, *a.* Relating to the historical period from the earliest times to the fall of Rome in 476 A.D.; having happened or existed in times long past; associated with the times of long ago; having lasted from a remote period; of great age; old. *n.* A very old person; **the ancients,** the people of ancient Greece, Rome, etc.; the authors of ancient times. —**an•cient•ly,** *adv.* —**an•cient•ness,** *n.*

an•cil•lar•y, an′sə•ler•ē, *a.* Giving help or assistance; auxiliary; subordinate.

and, and, ənd, *conj.* A particle or function word joining words and sentences, and expressing the relations of connection or addition.

an•dan•te, an•dan′tē, än•dän′tā, *a., adv.* With a moderate, even, slow movement.

and•i•ron, and′ī•ərn, *n.* One of a pair of iron bars used to support pieces of wood for burning in a fireplace.

and or , both or either.

an•dro•gen, an′drə•jən, *n.* A substance which promotes the development of secondary male sex characteristics.

an•drog•y•nous, an•droj′ə•nəs, *a.* Being at the same time both male and female; hermaphroditical; having staminate and pistillate flowers in the same cluster. Also **an•drog•y•nal,** an•droj′ə•nəl, —**an•drog•y•ny,** an•droj′ə•nē, *n.*

an•dros•ter•one, an•dros′tə•rōn, *n.* A male sex hormone.

an•ec•dote, an′ik•dōt, *n.* A short story or description of an interesting, entertaining, often biographical incident.

an•ec•dot•age, an′ik•dō•tij, *n.* The garrulity of dotage, or old age; anecdotes. —**an•ec•do•tal,** an•ik•dō′təl, *a.* —**an•ec•dot•ic,** an•ik•dot′ik, *a.* —**an•ec•dot•i•cal,** an•ik•dot′ə•kəl, *a.* **an•ec•dot•ist,** an′ik•dō•tist, *n.*

a•ne•mi•a, ə•nē′mē•ə, *n.* A lack of hemoglobin or red corpuscles, resulting in a lack of energy and vitality. —**a•ne•mic,** *a.*

an•e•mom•e•ter, an•ə•mom′ə•tər, *n.* An instrument for measuring force and velocity of the wind.

an•e•mom•e•try, an•ə•mom′i•trē, *n.* The process of determining the pressure or force of the wind by an anemometer.

a•nem•o•ne, ə•nem′ə•nē, *n.* A spring flower with slender stem and delicate whitish blossoms; any plant of the same genus having larger, colorful flowers without petals.

an•er•oid, an′ə•royd, *a.* Not using fluid.

an•er•oid ba•rom•e•ter, *n.* A barometer which records the pressure of the atmosphere on a circular metallic box that is completely empty, tightly sealed, and having a slightly elastic top.

an•es•the•sia, an•is•thē′zhə, *n.* A decreased or lost sense of feeling, esp. of pain, caused by drugs, disease, hypnotism, etc.

an•es•thet•ic, an•is•thet′ik, *a.* Of or belonging to anesthesia; causing anesthesia. —*n.* A substance causing anesthesia as chloroform or ether. —**an•es•thet•i•cal•ly,** an•is•thet′ik•lē, *adv.*

an•es•the•tist, ə•nes′thə•tist, *n.* A person trained to give anesthetics.

an•es•the•tize, ə•nes′thə•tiz, *v.t.,* **-tized, -tiz•ing.** To render insensible to the feeling of pain.

an•eu•rysm, an•eu•rism, an′yə•riz•əm, *n.* A bulge or swelling in an artery, due to the pressure of the blood acting on a part weakened by disease or injury.

---

a- hat, fāte, fāre, fäther; **e-** met, mē; **i-** pin, pīne; **o-** not, nōte, ôrb, moove (move), boy, pownd; **u-** cūbe, bůll, tůk (took); **ch-** chin; **th-** thick, ŧhen; **zh-** vizhon (vision); **ə-** əgo, takən, pencəl, lemən, bərd (bird).

—an·eu·rys·mal, an·eu·ris·mal, an·yə·riz/məl, *a.*

a·new, ə·noo/, ə·nū/, *adv.* Again; once more; in a new form; afresh.

an·ga·ry, ang/gə·rē, *n.* The right of a person or nation at war to seize or destroy property of neutrals, without having to pay for this property.

an·gel, ān/jəl, *n.* A messenger, esp. of God; one of a class of spiritual beings, attendants of God, ordinarily represented in human form with wings; A spirit, good or bad; a person of heavenly virtues or charms; *Informal.* a financial backer of a play, etc. —**an·gel·ic,** an·jel/ik, *a.* **an·gel·i·cal,** an·jel/ə·kəl, **an·gel·i·cal·ly,** an·jel/ik·lē, *adv.*

an·gel·i·ca, an·jel/ə·kə, *n.* A plant of the carrot family, grown for its use in flavoring and in medicine.

An·ge·lus, an/jə·lus, *n. Rom. Cath. Ch.* A solemn devotion in memory of the Incarnation; the bell tolled to indicate the time when the Angelus is to be recited.

an·ger, ang/gər, *n.* A strong, antagonistic feeling, often brought about by a real or supposed injury to oneself or others; passion; ire; wrath. —*v.t.* To excite to anger. —*v.i.* To become roused with anger.

an·gi·na, an·jī/nə, *n.* Any disease of the throat with inflammation and a tendency to choke as quinsy, croup, mumps, etc.

an·gi·na pec·to·ris, an·jī/nə pek/tə·ris, *n.* A disease marked by acute pain in the chest, with sense of suffocation, caused by lack of oxygen in the heart muscles.

an·gi·o·sperm, an/jē·ə·spərm, *n.* A plant which has its seed enclosed in a seed vessel. —**an·gi·o·sper·mous,** *a.*

an·gle, ang/gəl, *n.* A space within two or more sides diverging from a common point or line; the figure formed; the amount of divergence of two lines, measured in degrees. *v.t.,* **an·gled, an·gling.** To move or bend in angles. *v.i.* To fish with hook and line; to seek (*for*) by any artful means of catching or obtaining; to slant in a particular direction. —**an·gled,** ang/gəld, *a.*

an·gle i·ron, *n.* A bar of iron in the form of an angle, used in iron constructions.

an·gler, ang/glər, *n.* One who angles; a fisherman with hook and line; a fish which is said to attract small fish, its prey, by the movement of filaments attached to its head and mouth.

an·gle·worm, ang/gəl·wərm, *n.* An earthworm.

An·gli·can, ang/gli·kən, *a.* English; pertaining to the Church of England. —*n.* A member of the Anglican Communion. —**An·gli·can·ism,** *n.*

An·gli·can Com·mu·nion, the Church of England and related churches sometimes including the Episcopal churches of the United States and Canada.

An·gli·cism, ang/gli·siz·əm, *n.* The quality or characteristics of being English; an English idiom in another language; a Briticism.

An·gli·cize, ang/gli·sīz, *v.t.,* **-cized, -ciz·ing.** To make English; to change to the English idiom or to English analogies, esp. a borrowed foreign word. Also **An·gli·fy.** —**An·gli·ci·za·tion,** ang·glə·sə·zā/shən, *n.*

an·gling, ang/gling, *n.* The act or sport of fishing with a rod and line; rod fishing.

Anglo-French, ang·glō·french/, *n.* The French language of England from the Norman Conquest (1066) until the end of the medieval period.

An·glo·ma·ni·a, ang·glo·mā/nē·a, *n.* A too great fondness of or imitation of English institutions and customs by a foreigner.

An·glo-Nor·man, ang·glō·nôr/mən, *n.* One of the Normans who lived in England after the Conquest (1066), their descendants, or their language.

An·glo·phile, ang/glə·fīl, *n.* One who loves a person who admires or sympathizes with England or its customs, institutions, etc.

An·glo·phobe, ang/glə·fōb, *n.* One who is hostile toward anything English.

An·glo-Sax·on, ang/glō·sak/sən, *n.* A member of the nation formed by the Angles, Saxons, and other early Teutonic settlers in Britain, or one of their descendants; one belonging to the English race; the language of the Anglo-Saxons, or Old English; plain language.

an·go·ra, ang·gôr/ə, an·gôr/ə, *n.* A light cloth, made from the wool or long silky hair of the Angora goat, a native animal of Asia Minor.

An·go·ra cat, *n.* A long-haired variety of the domestic cat, orig. from Angora.

an·gos·tu·ra bark, ang·gə·stūr/ə, ang·gə·styūr/ə, *n.* The bitter aromatic bark of a South American tree, used in flavorings and medicine.

An·gos·tu·ra bit·ters, *n. Trademark.* A bitter tonic prepared from angostura bark.

an·gry, ang/grē, *a.* Feeling resentment; provoked; showing anger; caused by anger; raging. —**an·gri·ly,** *adv.* —**an·gri·ness,** *n.*

Angst, angst, *n.* Anguish; dread.

ang·strom u·nit, ang/strəm, *n.* One tenth of a millimicron or one hundred-millionth of a centimeter; a unit used to measure wave lengths, as of light.

an·guish, ang/gwish, *n.* Extreme pain or distress, either of body or mind. *v.t.* To cause acute distress.— *v.i.* To become roused with anger.

an·gu·lar, ang/gyə·lər, *a.* Having an angle or angles; having corners; pointed; measured by an angle; bony. —**an·gu·lar·i·ty,** *n.* —**an·gu·lar·ly,** *adv.* —**an·gu·lar·ness,** *n.*

an·hy·dride, an·hī/drīd, an·hī/drid, *n.* One of a class of oxygen compounds derived from other compounds by removing water.

an·hy·drous, an·hī/drəs, *a.* Without water, especially water of crystallization.

an·i·line, an/ə·lin, an/ə·līn, *n.* A colorless, poisonous compound used in making dyes obtained from coal tar and especially nitrobenzene.

an·i·mad·vert, an·ə·mad·vərt/, *v.i.* To make criticisms, especially adverse criticisms (on or upon); to censure. —**an·i·mad·ver·sion,** *n.*

an·i·mal, an/ə·məl, *n.* A living being not a plant. Unlike plants most animals can move voluntarily but cannot make their own food. An inferior being, as opposed to man; beast; brute.—*a.* Relating to animals; pertaining to the physical part of a person: *animal* passions.

an·i·mal·cule, an·ə·mal/kūl, *n.* A tiny animal, especially one that is invisible to the naked eye. —**an·i·mal·cu·lar,** *a.*

an·i·mal hus·band·ry, *n.* That branch of agriculture pertaining to the care·and breeding of domestic animals.

an·i·mal·ism, an/ə·mə·liz·əm, *n.* The characteristics of being an animal; a theory that man is without a spiritual nature. —**an·i·mal·ist,** *n.*

an·i·mal·i·ty, an·ə·mal/ə·tē, *n.* The state of being an animal; the animal nature in man.

an·i·mal·ize, an/ə·mə·līz, *v.t.,* **-ized, -iz·ing.** To make like an animal; brutalize.

an·i·mal mag·net·ism, *n.* Any force or power in certain individuals said to give them the ability to induce hypnosis; allure for persons of the opposite sex because of one's physical characteristics.

an·i·mal spir·its, *n. pl.* Vigor, exuberance.

an·i·mate, an/ə·māt, *v.t.,* **-mat·ed, -mat·ing.** To make alive; to give life, spirit, or liveliness to; to cause to act; to stimulate or incite. —an/i·mit, *a.* Alive; possessing animal life. —**an·i·ma·tion,** an·ə·mā/shən, *n.*

an·i·mated, an/ə·ma·tid, *a.* Lively; vigorous.

an·i·mat·ing, an/ə·māt·ing, *a.* Giving life; enlivening; rousing. —**an·i·mat·ing·ly,** *adv.*

an·i·mat·ed car·toon, *n.* A motion picture formed by a series of drawings suggesting motion, when filmed, by the slight changes made from one drawing to the next.

a·ni·ma·to, ä·nē·mä/tō, *adv. Mus.* In an animated,

lively, or vigorous manner.

an·i·mism, an′ə·miz·əm, *n.* The attribution of spirit or soul to inanimate things, such as trees, rocks, etc. —**an·i·mist,** *n.* —**an·i·mis·tic,** an·ə·mis′tik, *a.*

an·i·mos·i·ty, an·ē·mos′i·tē, *n.* Bitter feeling; hatred.

an·i·mus, an′ə·məs, *n.* Intention; purpose; especially, hostile spirit; deep-seated ill will.

an·i·on, an′ī·ən, *n.* A negatively charged ion which collects at the positive pole in electrolysis.

an·ise, an′is, *n.* An annual plant of the carrot family, whose seeds have an aromatic smell.

an·i·seed, an′i·sēd, *n.* The seed of the anise, used in flavoring.

an·i·sette, an·i·set′, an·i·zet′, *n.* A liqueur flavored with anise.

an·kle, ang′kəl, *n.* The joint which connects the foot with the leg; the region of this joint.

an·kle·bone, ang′kəl·bōn, *n.* The talus.

an·klet, ang′klit, *n.* An ornament or protection for the ankle; a sock that comes just above the ankle.

an·ky·lose, ang′kə·lōs, *v.t.,* **-losed, -los·ing.** To affect with ankylosis.—*v.i.* To become ankylosed.

an·ky·lo·sis, ang·kə·lō′sis, *n.* Stiffness of a joint, due to disease or surgery; abnormal growing together of bones forming a joint. —**an·ky·lot·ic,** ang·kə·lot′ik, *a.*

an·nal·ist, an′əl·ist, *n.* A writer of annals. —**an·nal·is·tic,** an·ə·lis′tik, *a.*

an·nals, an′əlz, *n. pl.* A history of events in chronological order, year by year; historical records or history.

an·neal, ə·nēl′, *v.t.* To heat, as glass or iron vessels, in an oven or furnace, and then cool slowly, to make it less brittle; to temper; to toughen.

an·ne·lid, an′ə·lid, *n.* One of a phylum of segmented worms, including the earthworms and leeches. Also **an·nel·i·dan,** ə·nel′ə·dən, *a.*

an·nex, ə·neks′, *v.t.* To unite, as a smaller thing to a greater; to incorporate; to attach; to connect, especially as a consequence. *n.* Something annexed; an addition to a building. —**an·nex·a·tion,** an·ek·sa′shən, *n.* —**an·nex·a·tion·ist,** an·ek·sā′shən·ist, *n.*

an·ni·hi·late, ə·nī′ə·lāt, *v.t.,* **-lat·ed, -lat·ing.** To reduce to nothing; to destroy the existence of; to annul; to cancel. —**an·ni·hi·la·tion,** ə·nī·ə·lā′shən, *n.* —**an·ni·hi·la·tor,** *n.*

an·ni·ver·sa·ry, an·ə·vėr′sə·rē, *a.* Returning each year at a stated time; annual; yearly.—*n. pl.,* **-ries.** A stated day on which some event is annually celebrated; the celebration.

an·no Dom·i·ni, an′ō dom′ə·nī, an′ō dom′ə·nē. In the year of the Lord, *i.e.,* of the Christian era. Abbr. *A.D.*

an·no·tate, an′ō·tāt, *v.t.,* **-tat·ed, -tat·ing.** To comment upon; to make remarks on by written notes.—*v.i.* To act as an annotator; to make annotations or notes (with *on*). —**an·no·ta·tion,** an·ə·tā′shən, *n.* —**an·no·ta·tor,** *n.*

an·nounce, ə·nowns′, *v.t.,* **an·nounced, an·nounc·ing.** To give official or public notice of; proclaim; to make known or evident; make known the appearance or arrival of. —**an·nounce·ment,** *n.*

an·nounc·er, ə·nown′sər, *n.* One who announces, esp. a person who introduces programs, etc. on television and radio.

an·noy, ə·noy′, *v.t.* To bother, torment or disturb; to vex, to harm; molest. —**an·noy·ance,** *n.* —**an·noy·er,** *n.* —**an·noy·ing,** *a.*

an·nu·al, an′ū·əl, *a.* Returning every year; lasting one year; performed in a year; reckoned by the year. —*n.* A plant that lives one year or season; an annual publication. —**an·nu·al·ly,** *adv.*

an·nu·i·ty, ə·noo′ə·tē, ə·nū′ə·tē, *n.* A yearly payment of money which a person receives; the right to receive or the obligation to make such payments.

an·nu·i·tant, *n.* One receiving an annuity.

an·nul, ə·nəl′, *v.t.,* **an·nulled, an·nul·ling.** To make void; to abolish; cancel.

an·nul·ment, ə·nəl′mənt, *n.* An annulling; a court decree stating that a marriage no longer exists.

an·nu·lar, an′yə·lər, *a.* Having the form of a ring; pertaining to a ring. —**an·nu·lar·i·ty,** an·yə·lar′ə·tē, *n.* —**an·nu·lar·ly,** *adv.*

an·nu·lar e·clipse, *n.* A solar eclipse in which an outer ring of the sun is not covered by the moon.

an·nu·late, an′yə·lāt, an′yə·lit, *a.* Furnished with rings; having bands.

an·nu·let, an′yə·lit, *n.* A little ring; a ring around a pillar or column.

an·nu·lus, an′yə·ləs, *n. pl.,* **-li, -lī, -lus·es.** A ringlike structure, band, or space.

an·nun·ci·a·tion, ə·nən·sē·ā′shən, ə·nən·shē·ā′shən, *n.* Announcement; (*Cap.*) the news brought by the angel to Mary of the Incarnation of Christ; the church festival in memory of this announcement, falling on March 25.

an·nun·ci·ate, ə·nən′sē·āt, ə·nən′shē·āt, *v.t.,* **-at·ed, -at·ing.** To announce. —**an·nun·ci·a·tor,** *n.*

an·ode, an′ōd, *n.* The positive pole or electrode in a battery, vacuum tube, etc.: opposed to *cathode.* —**an·od·ic,** an·od′ik, *a.*

an·o·dyne, an′ə·dīn, *n.* Any medicine which relieves pain.—*a.* Decreasing pain; relieving.

a·noint, ə·noynt′, *v.t.* To pour oil upon; to smear or rub with oil; to consecrate by the use of oil. —**a·noint·er,** *n.* —**a·noint·ment,** *n.*

a·nom·a·ly, ə·nom′ə·lē, *n.* Departure from the common rule; something abnormal; irregularity. —**a·nom·a·lism,** *n.* —**a·nom·a·lous,** *a.* —**a·nom·a·lous·ly,** *adv.* —**a·nom·a·lous·ness,** *n.*

an·o·mie, an·o·my, an′ə·mē, *n.* A state of society or of a person in which social and behavioral norms are weak or nonexistent.

an·o·nym, an′ə·nim, *n.* An assumed name; a person who remains anonymous.

a·non·y·mous, ə·non′ə·məs, *a.* Having no name; without any name acknowledged as that of author, contributor, etc; lacking individuality. —**an·o·nym·i·ty,** an·ə·nim′ə·tē, *n.* —**a·non·y·mous·ly,** *adv.* —**a·non·y·mous·ness,** *n.*

a·noph·e·les, ə·nof′ə·lēz, *n.* A mosquito which can transmit malaria to man.

an·oth·er, ə·nəth′ər, *a.* Not the same; different; being one more, in addition to a former number; any other. —*pron.* One more; a different one: He took one path, I took *another.* A similar or identical one: He is a baker, and his uncle is *another.*

an·ox·i·a, an·ok′sē·ə, ə·nok′sē·ə, *n.* Not enough oxygen in the body tissues.

An·schluss, än′shlůs, *n. German.* Joining; union.

an·ser·ine, an′sər·īn, an′sər·in, *a.* Relating to or resembling a goose; foolish, silly.

an·swer, an′sər, än′sər, *v.t.* To speak or write in return to; to reply to; to say or do in reply; to act in compliance with, or in fulfillment of; to render account to or for; to be adequate to; to serve; to suit.—*v.i.* To reply; to speak or write by way of return; to respond to some call; to be suitable. *n.* A reply; a response; that which is said, written, or done in return or retaliation to a call, question, argument, etc.; the result of a mathematical operation; a solution; a reply to a charge; a defense. —**an·swer for,** to be accountable for; to guarantee. —**an·swer to,** to be known by; to correspond to.

an·swer·a·ble, *a.* Capable of being answered; responsible. —**an·swer·a·ble·ness,** *n.* —**an·swer·a·**

---

bly, *adv.*

ant, ant, *n.* A small insect usually living in a colony.

ant·ac·id, ant·as′id, *n.* An alkali, or a remedy for acidity in the stomach.

an·tag·o·nist, an·tag′ə·nist, *n.* One who fights, physically or verbally, with another; an opponent; a muscle that counteracts another muscle.

an·tag·o·nism, an·tag′ə·niz·əm, *n.* Character of being antagonistic; an opposing force. —**an·tag·o·nis·tic,** an·tag·ə·nis′tik, *a.* —**an·tag·o·nis·ti·cal·ly,** an·tag·ə·nis′ti·kəl·ē, *adv.*

an·tag·o·nize, an·tag′ə·niz, *v.t.,* -**nized,** -**niz·ing.** To act in opposition; to cause to become hostile.—*v.i.* To make antagonistic; to provoke harsh feelings.

ant·arc·tic, ant·ärk′tik, ant·är′tik, *a. Often cap.* Relating to the southern pole or to the region near it.

ant·arc·tic cir·cle, *Often cap. A and C.* An imaginary line circling the earth parallel to the equator, at about 23½° N. of the South Pole.

ant bear, *n.* A kind of large anteater of S. America; an aardvark.

an·te, an′tē, *n.* In poker, a stake put into the pool or pot by each player before being dealt cards. A payment; a share of the expenses.—*v.i., v.t.,* **an·ted,** **an·te·ing.**

ant·eat·er, ant′ē·tər, *n.* Any of several mammals which feed on ants and other insects by means of a long, sticky tongue.

an·te·bel·lum, an·ti·bel′əm, *a.* Before the war, often meaning the U.S. Civil War.

an·te·ced·ence, an·ti·sēd′əns, *n.* Precedence; priority; going before in time.

an·te·ced·ent, an·tə·sē′dənt, *n.* One who or that which goes before in time or place; the noun to which a relative or other pronoun refers; an ancestor; the first term of a mathematical ratio; *pl.* the earlier events of a man's life; ancestors.—*a.* Going before.

an·te·cede, an·tə·sēd′, *v.t.,* -**ced·ed,** -**ced·ing.** To go before in time. —**an·te·ce·dent·ly,** *adv.*

an·te·cham·ber, an′tə·chām·bər, *n.* A room leading to another room; anteroom.

an·te·choir, an′ti·kwir, *n.* A space, more or less enclosed, in front of the choir of a church.

an·te·date, an′ti·dāt, *v.t.,* -**dat·ed,** -**dat·ing.** To date before the beforehand; to give an earlier date than the real one to; to precede.—*n.* A prior date.

an·te·di·lu·vi·an, an·ti·də·loo′vē·ən, *a.* Before the flood; very old. —*n.* One who lived before the flood.

an·te·lope, an′tə·lōp, *n. pl.,* -**lopes,** -**lope.** One of many species of swift, cud-chewing mammals resembling the deer, having hollow, unbranched horns that do not fall off; leather from the hide of this animal.

an·te me·rid·i·em, an·tē·mə·rid′ē·əm, *n.* Before noon: used to mark the hour. Abbreviated A.M., as, 10 *A.M.* (or *a.m.).*

an·ten·na, an·ten′ə, *n. pl.,* -**nae,** -nē, -**nas.** One of the paired hornlike sense organs that stick out from the head in insects, crustacea, etc.; a feeler. *Radio, TV.* The device through which electromagnetic waves are transmitted and intercepted.

an·te·pe·nult, an·ti·pē′nəlt, an·ti·pi·nəlt′, *n.* The second syllable from the last syllable in a word, as the *hap* in *unhappily.* —**an·te·pe·nul·ti·mate,** an·ti·pi·nəl′tə·mət, *a.*

an·te·ri·or, an·tēr′ē·ər, *a.* Before in time; prior; earlier; before in place; in front.

an·te·room, an′ti·room, an′ti·rūm, *n.* A small room leading into a larger one; an adjoining waiting room.

an·them, an′thəm, *n.* A piece of sacred music set to words taken from the Bible; a song of praise, gladness, or patriotism: the national *anthem.*

an·ther, an′thər, *n.* The part of the stamen of a plant containing the pollen.

an·ther·id·i·um, an·thə·rid′ē·əm, *n. pl.,* -**i·a,** -ē·ə. The male reproductive organ in ferns, mosses, etc., containing male reproductive cells.

an·thol·o·gy, an·thol′ə·jē, *n. pl.,* -**gies.** A collection of literary selections or passages, usu. about a single theme.

an·thol·o·gist, *n.* One who compiles an anthology.

an·thol·o·gize, an·thol′ə·jīz, *v.i.,* -**gized,** -**giz·ing.** To compile an anthology.—*v.t.* To put into an anthology.

an·tho·zo·an, an·thə·zō′ən, *n.* A class of marine animals, including corals and sea anemones.

an·thra·cene, an′thrə·sēn, *n.* A colorless, crystalline hydrocarbon obtained from coal tar, used for making dyes.

an·thra·cite, an′thrə·sīt, *n.* Coal which burns without smoke, with a weak or no flame, and with intense heat; hard coal. —**an·thra·cit·ic,** an·thrə·sit′ik, *a.*

an·thrax, an′thraks, *n. pl.,* **an·thra·ces,** an′thrə·sēz. A malignant infectious disease of cattle, sheep, etc., which may be transmitted to man.

an·thro·po·cen·tric, an·thrə·pō·sen′trik, *a.* Regarding man as the central fact of the universe.

an·thro·po·gen·e·sis, an·thrə·pō·jen′ə·sis, *n.* The study of the genesis or development of man.

an·thro·poid, an′thrə·poyd, *a.* Resembling man.—*n.* Any of the larger apes.

an·thro·pol·o·gy, an·thrə·pol′ə·jē, *n.* The science of human beings, including the study of human origins, physical and cultural development, social conditions, etc. —**an·thro·po·log·ic,** an·thrə·pə·loj′ik, *a.* —**an·thro·po·log·i·cal,** an·thrə·pə·loj′ē·kəl, *a.* —**an·thro·pol·o·gist.** *n.*

an·thro·pom·e·try, an·thrə·pom′ə·trē, *n.* The comparative measurement and study of the human body. —**an·thro·po·met·ric,** an·thrə·pə·met′rik, *a.*

an·thro·po·mor·phic, an·thrə·pə·môr′fik, *a.* Ascribing human form or attributes to beings or things not human, esp. to a deity. —**an·thro·po·mor·phi·cal·ly,** *adv.* —**an·thro·po·mor·phize,** *v.t.,* -**phized,** -**phiz·ing.** —**an·thro·po·mor·phism,** *n.* —**an·thro·po·mor·phist,** *n.*

an·ti-, an′ti, an′tē, an′tī, *prefix.* Against; opposed to: *anti*clerical; used against: *anti*aircraft.

an·ti, an′tī, an′tē, *n. pl.,* **an·tis,** an′tīz, an′tēz. *Informal.* One who is opposed to some course, measure or policy.

an·ti·air·craft, an·tē·âr′kraft, an·tī·âr′kraft, *a.* Used for defense against airborne aircraft, esp. guns or missiles.

an·ti·bi·o·sis, an·tē·bī·ō′sis, an·tī·bī·ō′sis, *n.* A relationship between two organisms which is harmful to one, as parasitism.

an·ti·bi·ot·ic, an·ti·bī·ot′ik, an·ti·bē·ot′ik, *n.* Any of a group of chemical compounds produced by fungi and other microorganisms which, in diluted solution, inhibit or destroy bacteria.

an·ti·bod·y, an′ti·bod·ē, an′tē·bod·ē, *n. pl.,* -**bod·ies.** Any of various substances existing in the blood or developed in immunization which counteract bacteria and their toxins.

an·tic, an′tik, *a.* Odd; fanciful; grotesque; clown; usually an absurd gesture; a caper; a playful trick.

an·ti·christ, an′ti·krist, *n.* An opponent of Christ; a false Christ. *Cap.* A great antagonist who will be conquered at Christ's second coming.

an·tic·i·pate, an·tis′ə·pāt, *v.t.,* -**pat·ed,** -**pat·ing.** To look forward to; to expect; to be before in doing something; to prevent by prior action; to hinder; to realize beforehand; to foretaste or foresee. —**an·tic·i·pant,** *a.* —**an·tic·i·pa·tion,** an·tis·ə·pā′shən, *n.* —**an·tic·i·pa·tive,** an·tis′ə·pā·tiv, an·tis′ə·pe·tiv, *a.* —**an·tic·i·pa·tor,** *n.* —**an·tic·i·pa·to·ry,** an·tis′ə·pə·tôr·ē, *a.*

an·ti·cler·i·cal, an·ti·kler′i·kəl, an·ti·kler′ə·kəl, *a.* Opposed to the influence of the church and clergy in public affairs. —**an·ti·cler·i·cal·ism,** *n.*

an·ti·cli·max, an·ti·klī′maks, *n.* A written or spoken passage in which the ideas first increase in force, and then end in something less important and striking; an abrupt, sometimes ridiculous descent from the important to the trivial. —**an·ti·cli·mac·tic,** an·ti·klī· mak/tik, *a.*

an·ti·cli·nal, an·ti·klī/nəl, *a.* Inclining downward on both sides from a median line or axis, as an upward fold of rock strata; pertaining to such a fold. —**an·ti· cline,** an/ti·klīn, *n.*

an·ti·cy·clone, an·ti·sī/klōn, *n.* Region of high barometric pressure with winds rotating outward from its center.

an·ti·dote, an/ti·dōt, *n.* A medicine or remedy to counteract the effects of poison; anything that prevents or counteracts evil. —**an·ti·dot·al,** an·ti· dot/əl, *a.*

an·ti·fed·er·al·ist, an·ti·fed/ər·ə·list, an·ti· fed/rə·list, *n.* One who is opposed to federalism. (*Cap.*) *U.S. Hist.* An opponent of the adoption in 1787–1788 of the U.S. Constitution. —**an·ti·fed·er·al,** *a.* —**an·ti·fed·er·al·ism,** *n.*

an·ti·freeze, an/ti·frēz, *n.* A liquid having a low freezing point: used in the radiator of an internal-combustion engine to prevent freezing of the cooling system during cold weather.

an·ti·gen, an/tə·jən, *n.* A substance that when introduced into blood or tissue causes the body to form antibodies.

an·ti·he·ro, an/ti·hēr·ō, *n.* A hero in literature or drama who does not possess the usual qualities of a hero, such as courage or righteousness.

an·ti·his·ta·mine, an·ti·his/tə·mēn, an·ti·his/tə· min, *n.* Any of a number of compounds that work against histamine in the body, used mainly for the treatment of allergies and colds.

an·ti·knock, an/ti·nok, *n.* A substance added to an internal-combustion engine fuel that lowers or gets rid of the noise of early ignition while the engine is running.

an·ti·log·a·rithm, an·ti·lôg/ə·rith·əm, an·ti· log/ə·rith·əm, *n.* The number that corresponds to a logarithm.

an·ti·ma·cas·sar, an·ti·mə·kas/ər, *n.* A cloth covering to protect the back and arms of chairs from being soiled.

an·ti·mag·net·ic, an·ti·mag·net/ik, *a.* Made of metals that are resistant to magnetism: an *antimagnetic* precision instrument.

an·ti·mat·ter, an·ti·mat/ər, *n.* Matter that is made up of antiparticles.

an·ti·mis·sile, an·ti·mis/əl, *a.* Designed for defense against enemy missiles.

an·ti·mis·sile mis·sile, *n.* An explosive missile launched to intercept and destroy an enemy missile in flight.

an·ti·mo·ny, an/ti·mō·nē, *n.* A metallic element, brittle, lustrous, and white in color, used chiefly in alloys and (in compounds) in medicine and pigments.

an·ti·neu·tri·no, an·ti·noo·trē/nō, an·ti·nyoo· trē/nō, *n.* The antiparticle of the neutrino, having no electric charge.

an·ti·neu·tron, an·ti·noo/tron, an·ti·nyoo/tron, *n.* The antiparticle of the neutron, having no electric charge.

an·ti·par·ti·cle, an·ti·pär/tə·kəl, *n. Phys.* A subatomic particle which is found in radioactive decay and has a charge and magnetic moment opposite to its corresponding particle.

an·ti·pas·to, an·ti·pas/tō, än·tē·päs/tō, *n.* An appetizer course, usu. of fish, meat, olives, etc.

an·ti·pa·thy, an·tip/ə·thē, *n. pl.,* **-thies.** Natural instinctive dislike; the feeling of dislike or opposition. —**an·ti·pa·thet·ic,** an·ti·pə·thet/ik, *a.*

an·ti·per·son·nel, an·ti·pər·sə·nel/, *a.* Designed or used to kill or wound people rather than to destroy objects: *antipersonnel* bombs.

an·ti·phon, an/tə·fon, *n.* The answer of one choir or one. portion of a congregation to another when an anthem or psalm is sung alternately. —**an·tiph·o·nal,** an·tif/ə·nəl, *n.*

an·ti·pode, an/ti·pōd, *n.* Anything exactly opposite to something else.

an·tip·o·des, an·tip/ə·dēz, *n. pl.* The area on the exact opposite side of the earth; those on the opposite side of the globe; anything opposite or opposed to another.—**an·tip·o·dal,** an·tip/ə·dəl, *a.*

an·ti·pov·er·ty, an·ti·pov/ər·tē, *a.* Designed to relieve poverty: used esp. of a program or organization in economically depressed areas.

an·ti·pro·ton, an·ti·prō/ton, *n. Phys.* The antiparticle of the proton.

an·ti·py·ret·ic, an·ti·pī·ret/ik, *n. Med.* A remedy against fever.

an·ti·quar·i·an, an·ti·kwâr/ē·ən, *a.* Pertaining to antiquaries or to antiquity; relating to rare books.—*n.* An antiquary. —**an·ti·quar·i·an·ism,** *n.*

an·ti·quar·y, an/tə·kwer·ē, *n. pl.,* **-ies.** One devoted to the study of ancient times.

an·ti·quate, an/tə·kwāt, *v.t.,* **-quat·ed, -quat·ing.** To make outdated by substituting something new; to make (something) appear to be an antique.

an·ti·quat·ed, an/ti·kwā·tid, *a.* Old-fashioned; obsolete; behind the times.

an·tique, an·tēk/, *a.* Having existed in ancient times; ancient: an *antique* statue; having the characteristics of an earlier day.—*n.* Anything very old, usually 100 yrs.; a term applied to the relics or objects of ancient art.—*v.t.,* **-tiqued, an·tiq·uing.** To cause something to appear as if an antique; to emboss, as paper or fabric. —**an·tique·ly,** *adv.* —**an·tique·ness,** *n.*

an·tiq·ui·ty, an·tik/wə·tē, *n. pl.,* **-ties.** The quality of being ancient; great age; ancient times; former ages, esp. prior to the Middle Ages; the people of ancient times; *pl.* the remains, institutions, customs, etc., belonging to ancient nations.

an·ti·Sem·i·tism, an·ti·sem/i·tiz·əm, *n.* Hostility or discrimination against Jews.

an·ti·sep·sis, an·ti·sep/sis, *n.* The slowing down of the growth of or destruction of microorganisms; prevention of sepsis.

an·ti·sep·tic, an·ti·sep/tik, *a.* Pertaining to or causing antisepsis; lacking germs; especially clean; stark, uninteresting, or lacking feeling.—*n.* Something that slows down the growth of microorganisms.

an·ti·se·rum, an/ti·sēr·əm, *n.* A serum from the blood of an animal, used to provide immunity against a certain disease.

an·ti·slav·er·y, an·ti·slā/və·rē, *a.* Against slavery. —*n.* Resistance to slavery.

an·ti·so·cial, an·ti·sō/shəl, an·tī·sō/shəl, *a.* Opposed to social contact; opposed to social order, or to the principles on which society is constituted; hostile toward other people; antagonistic.

an·ti·tank, an·ti·tangk/, *a.* Designed or used against a tank or other armored vehicle.

an·tith·e·sis, an·tith/ə·sis, *n. pl.,* **-ses,** -sēz. Opposition; contrast; a figure by which contraries are opposed to contraries; a contrast or opposition of words or sentiments.

an·ti·thet·i·cal, an·ti·thet/ə·kəl, *a.* Opposed.

an·ti·tox·in, an·ti·tok/sin, *n.* A substance formed in the body, capable of counteracting a specific poison; the antibody formed by immunization with a given toxin: used in treating certain infectious diseases or in producing immunity against them. —**an·ti·tox·ic,** *a.*

an·ti·trust, an·ti·trəst/, *a.* Referring to governmental or legal rules against monopoly by large business combinations.

an·ti·ven·in, an·ti·ven/in, *n.* An antitoxin produced in the blood by repeated injections of venom, as of

---

a- hat, fāte, fāre, fäther; **e-** met, mē; **i-** pin, pine; **o-** not, nōte, ôrb, moove (move), boy, pownd; **u-** cūbe, bůll, tûk (took); **ch-** chin, **th-** thick, ŧhen; **zh-** vizhon (vision); **ə-** əgo, takən, pencəl, lemən, bərd (bird).

snakes; also, the serum obtained from such blood.

an·ti·viv·i·sec·tion·ist, an·ti·viv·i·sek/shən·ist, *n.* One who is opposed to scientific experimentation on living animals.

ant·ler, ant/lər, *n.* A bonelike horn of a deer; a branch of this horn.

ant·lered, ant/lərd, *a.* Having antlers.

an·to·nym, an/tə·nim, *n.* A word that is opposite in meaning to another: the opposite of a *synonym.*

an·trum, an/trəm, *n. pl.,* **an·tra,** an/trə. *Anat.* Cavity in a hollow organ; a sinus.

a·nus, ā/nəs, *n.* The opening at the lower end of the digestive canal.

an·vil, an/vil, *n.* An iron or steel block with a smooth face on which metals are hammered and shaped. *Anat.* The incus, a small bone of the ear.

anx·i·e·ty, ang·zī/ə·tē, *n. pl.,* **-ties.** Pain or uneasiness of mind about some event in the future; concern; care.

anx·ious, angk/shəs, ang/shəs, *a.* Full of anxiety or uneasiness. **—anx·ious·ness,** *n.*

an·y, en/ē, *a.* One; a or an; some; few or many: *any* money, *any* eggs; every: *Any* child knows that.—*pron.* Any person or persons; any individual, instance, or number (of several or more possible); also, any quantity or part.—*adv.* In any degree; to any extent; at all.

an·y·bod·y, en/ē·bəd·ē, en/ē·bod·ē, *pron.* Any person; anyone; anyone of importance: Everybody who is *anybody* was present.—*n. pl.,* **an·y·bod·ies.**

an·y·how, en/ē·how, *adv.* In any way whatever; in any case; at all events; carelessly.

an·y·more, en/ē·mōr/, *adv.* Now; contemporaneously; at this time: They don't live here *anymore.*

an·y·one, en/ē·wən, *pron.* Any person; anybody.

an·y·place, en/ē·plās, *adv.* In or to any place.

an·y·thing, en/ē·thing, *n., pron.* Any thing; a thing of any kind; something, no matter what.—*adv.* At all; to any degree: Is soccer *anything* like football?

an·y·way, en/ē·wā, *adv.* In any way; anyhow; to any extent.

an·y·where, en/ē·hwer, *adv.* In, at, or to any place; at all; to any degree or extent.

an·y·wise, en/ē·wīz, *adv.* In any way, respect, or degree; at all.

a·or·ta, ā·ôr/tə, *n. pl.,* **-tas, -tae,** -tē. The main artery that runs from the left ventricle of the heart, and carries blood to all parts of the body except the lungs. **—a·or·tal,** *a.* **—a·or·tic,** *a.*

a·pace, ə·pās/, *adv.* With a quick pace; fast.

a·pache, ə·pash/, ə·päsh/, *n.* A French street gangster.

a·part, ə·pärt/, *adv.* Separately; distinct or away from others; at some distance. Into pieces—*a.* Not together; separated: a world *apart.* **—apart from,** aside from; besides.

a·part·heid, ə·pärt/hāt, ə·pärt/hīt, *n.* The governmental policy of separation of the racial groups and discrimination against nonwhites, as practiced in the Republic of South Africa.

a·part·ment, ə·pärt/mənt, *n.* A room or rooms where people live.

a·part·ment build·ing, *n.* A building divided into apartments. Also **a·part·ment house.**

ap·a·thy, ap/ə·thē, *n. pl.,* **-thies.** Lack of feeling or excitement; indifference. **—ap·a·thet·ic,** ap·ə·thet/ik, *a.* **—ap·a·thet·i·cal·ly,** ap·ə·thet/ik·lē, *adv.*

ape, āp, *n.* One of a family of tailless primates, esp. a gorilla or chimpanzee; a monkey; one who imitates.—*v.t.,* **aped, ap·ing.** To imitate; to mimic.

ap·ish, ā/pish, *a.* Having the qualities of an ape; inclined to imitate superiors. **—ap·ish·ly,** *adv.* **—ap·ish·ness,** *n.*

a·per·ri·tif, ä·per·ə·tēf/, ə·per·i·tēf/, *n.* An alcoholic liquor taken before a meal to stimulate the appetite.

ap·er·ture, ap/ər·chər, *n.* An opening; a hole, entrance, gap, etc.; the opening in the front of a camera through which light rays pass when a picture is taken.

a·pex, ā/peks, *n. pl.,* **a·pex·es, a·pi·ces,** ap/i·sēz, ā/pi·sēz. The tip, highest point, or climax of anything. **—ap·i·cal,** ap/i·kəl, ā/pi·kəl, *a.*

a·pha·sia, ə·fā/zhə, *n.* Partial or total loss of the ability to speak, usually resulting from damage to brain tissue.

a·phe·li·on, ə·fē/lē·ən, *n. pl.,* **-li·a,** -lē·ə. That point of a planet's or comet's orbit which is most distant from the sun: opposed to *perihelion.*

a·phid, ā/fid, af/id, *n.* Any of a family of sucking insects that damage plants; a plant louse.

a·phis, ā/fis, af/is, *n. pl.,* **a·phi·des,** af/i·dēz. A plant louse.

aph·o·rism, af/ə·riz·əm, *n.* A brief sentence containing some important truth; a maxim.

aph·o·rist, af/ə·rist, *n.* A writer of aphorisms. **—aph·o·ris·tic,** af·ə·ris/tik, *a.*

aph·ro·dis·i·ac, af·rə·diz/ē·ak, *a.* Exciting sexual desire.—*n.* Food or a medicine exciting sexual desire.

Aph·ro·di·te, af·rə·dī/tē, *n.* The Greek goddess of love and beauty, identified by the Romans with Venus.

a·pi·an, ā/pē·ən, *a.* Of or concerning bees.

a·pi·ar·i·an, ā·pē·âr/ē·ən, *a.* Relating to bees.—*n.* A beekeeper; an apiarist.

a·pi·a·rist, ā/pē·ə·rist, *n.* One who keeps bees.

a·pi·ar·y, ā/pē·er·ē, *n. pl.,* **-ies.** A place where bees are kept for their honey.

a·pi·cul·ture, ā/pi·kəl·chər, *n.* The raising of bees; beekeeping, esp. for commercial purposes. **—a·pi·cul·tur·al,** *a.*

a·pi·cul·tur·ist, ā·pi·kəl/chə·rist, *n.* A beekeeper.

a·piece, ə·pēs/, *adv.* To each, as the share of each: Two dollars *apiece* was their reward. Each by itself; by the individual.

a·plomb, ə·plom/, ə·pləm/, *n.* Self-confidence; assurance; poise.

a·poc·a·lypse, ə·pok/ə·lips, *n.* A revelation; (*cap.*) the book of the Revelation, the last book of the New Testament. **—a·poc·a·lyp·tic,** ə·pok·ə·lip/tik, *a.*

a·poc·o·pe, ə·pok/ə·pē, *n.* Omission of the last letter or syllable of a word, as *th'* for *the.*

A·poc·ry·pha, ə·pok/rə·fə, *n.* Fourteen books, not considered canonical, which are included in the Old Testament only in the Vulgate and Septuagint versions; (*l.c.*) any writings of doubtful origin or authenticity. **—a·poc·ry·phal,** *a.*

ap·o·gee, ap/ə·jē, *n.* The point in the orbit of the moon, or artificial earth satellite which is at the greatest distance from the earth; the highest point; climax.

a·po·lit·i·cal, ā·pə·lit/i·kəl, *a.* Having no interest in politics.

a·pol·o·get·ics, ə·pol·ə·jet/iks, *n. pl. but sing. in constr.* The branch of theology by which Christians defend their faith.

a·pol·o·gist, ə·pol/ə·jist, *n.* One who defends a person or a cause.

a·pol·o·gize, ə·pol/ə·jīz, *v.i.,* **-gized, -giz·ing.** To make an apology. **—a·pol·o·giz·er,** *n.*

a·pol·o·gy, ə·pol/ə·jē, *n. pl.,* **-gies.** An expression of regret for something wrong that one has done; a poor substitute. **—a·pol·o·get·ic,** ə·pol·ə·jet/ik, *a.* **—a·pol·o·get·i·cal,** *a.*

ap·o·plec·tic, ap·ə·plek/tik, *a.* Pertaining to or consisting in apoplexy; predisposed to apoplexy. Also **ap·o·plec·ti·cal,** ap·ə·plek/ti·kəl. —*n.* A person affected with apoplexy.

ap·o·plex·y, ap/ə·plek·sē, *n.* Sudden loss of feeling and ability to move about, caused by a clot in a brain blood vessel or by the breaking of such a vessel; a stroke.

a·port, ə·pôrt/, *adv.,* *a.* To port; to the left.

a·pos·ta·sy, ə·pos/tə·sē, *n. pl.,* **-sies.** A desertion of one's faith, principles, or party.

a·pos·tate, ə·pos/tāt, ə·pos/tit, *n.* One who has forsaken his faith, principles, or party.—*a.* False; traitorous.

a·pos·ta·tize, ə·pos/tə·tīz, *v.i.,* **-tized, -tiz·ing.** To commit apostasy; to abandon principles, religious faith, or party.

a pos·te·ri·o·ri, ä·pos·tĕr·ē·ô′ī, ä·pos·tĕr·ē· ōr′ī, *a., adv.* Reasoning from facts to principles; from effect to cause; inductive: opposed to *a priori.*

a·pos·tle, ə·pos′əl, *n.* One of the Twelve Disciples of Christ, chosen to preach the gospel; a missionary in the early Christian Church; a high ecclesiastical office in some sects; a member of the Mormon 12-man administration. —**a·pos·tle·ship,** *n.*

A·pos·tles' Creed, *n.* A traditional Christian creed originally attributed to the Twelve Apostles.

a·pos·to·late, ə·pos′tə·lit, ə·pos′tə·lāt, *n.* The dignity, mission, or office of an apostle.

ap·os·tol·ic, ap·ə·stol′ik, *a.* Of or relating to an apostle, esp. the Twelve Apostles. Also **ap·os·tol·i· cal.**

a·pos·tro·phe, ə·pos′trə·fē, *n.* The sign (') which indicates the omission of a letter or letters from a word, as in *don't,* the possessive in nouns, or the plural of numerals or letters, as in *the three R's.*

a·poth·e·car·ies' meas·ure, ə·poth′ə·ker·ēz, *n.* The system of units used in the U.S. in mixing and selling liquid drugs.

a·poth·e·car·ies' weight, *n.* A system of weights used in drugs.

a·poth·e·car·y, ə·poth′ə·ker·ē, *n. pl.,* **-ies.** A druggist.

ap·o·thegm, ap·o·phthegm, ap′ə·them, *n.* A short, pithy, and instructive saying; a maxim. —**ap·o· theg·mat·ic,** ap·ə·theg·mat′ik, —**ap·o·theg·mat·i· cal,** ap·ə·theg·mat′i·kəl, *a.*

a·poth·e·o·sis, ə·poth·ē·ō′sis, ap·ə·thē′ə·sis, *n. pl.,* **-ses.** The placing or ranking of a person among the gods; the glorification of a person.

a·poth·e·o·size, ə·poth′ē·ə·sīz, ap·ə·thē′ə·sīz, *v.t.,* **-sized, -siz·ing.** To exalt to the dignity of a god.

ap·pall, ap·pal, ə·pôl, *v.t.,* **ap·palled, ap·pal·ling.** To fill with overpowering fear; to dismay. —**ap·pall· ing,** *a.* —**ap·pall·ing·ly,** *adv.*

ap·pa·rat·us, ap·ə·rat′əs, ap·ə·rā′təs, *n. pl.,* **ap· pa·rat·us, ap·pa·rat·us·es.** A device or tool for a specific purpose; things provided as means to some end; the organization of a group or movement, often political and conspiratorial; a group of organs having the same function: digestive *apparatus.*

ap·par·el, ə·par′əl, *n.* Clothing; dress. —*v.t.,* **-eled, -el·ing.** To dress or clothe; to cover.

ap·par·ent, ə·par′ənt, ə·pār′ənt, *a.* Evident; appearing to the eye or to the judgment; seeming, rather than real; obvious; plain.

ap·pa·ri·tion, ap·ə·rish′ən, *n.* The act of appearing, a ghost. —**ap·pa·ri·tion·al,** *a.*

ap·peal, ə·pēl′, *v.i.* To call, as for aid, mercy, sympathy, and the like; to refer to another person or authority for a decision or vindication; to be interesting to: The story *appealed* to him. To refer to a higher judge or court for a final settlement.—*v.t.* To refer (a case) to a superior judge or court—*n.* A call for sympathy, mercy, aid, and the like; the referral of a case or suit to a superior court; a challenge; a reference to another for proof or decision. —**ap·peal·a·ble,** *a.* —**ap·peal· er,** *n.* —**ap·peal·ing·ly,** *adv.*

ap·pear, ə·pēr′, *v.i.* To come in sight; to become visible to the eye; to stand in the presence of one; to be obvious; to perform publicly; to be clear or made clear by evidence; to seem; to look like.

ap·pear·ance, *n.* The act of appearing or coming into sight; a coming into the presence of a person; an apparition; external show; build and carriage; figure.

ap·pease, ə·pēz′, *v.t.,* **ap·peased, ap·peas·ing.** To seek peace by yielding to the terms of (an enemy); to satisfy. —**ap·pease·ment,** *n.* —**ap·peas·a·ble,** *a.*—**ap·peas·er,** *n.*

ap·pel·lant, ə·pel′ənt, *n.* One who appeals.

ap·pel·late, ə·pel′it, *a.* Having to do with a legal appeal; having the authority to hear and decide appeals from the decisions of a lower court.

ap·pel·la·tion, ap·ə·lā′shən, *n.* The word by which a thing or person is known; name, title; the act of naming.

ap·pel·la·tive, ə·pel′ə·tiv, *a.* Referring to a common noun; name-giving or marking out.—*n.* An appellation; a descriptive name; a common noun.

ap·pend, ə·pend′, *v.t.* To add to a thing; to attach.

ap·pend·age, ə·pen′dij, *n.* Something attached.

ap·pend·ant, ə·pen′dənt, *a.* Hanging to; attached.

ap·pen·dec·to·my, ap·ən·dek′tə·mē, *n.* Removal of the appendix.

ap·pen·di·ci·tis, ə·pen·də·sī′tis, *n.* Inflammation of the appendix, a small hollow part attached. to the cecum in man and some animals.

ap·pen·dix, ə·pen′diks, *n. pl.,* **ap·pen·dix·es, ap· pen·di·ces,** ə·pen′di·sēz. Something added to a book relating, but not essential, to the main work; the vermiform appendix.

ap·per·cep·tion, ap·ər·sep′shən, *n.* Perception; apprehension; conscious perception; a voluntary mental activity accompanied by self-consciousness. —**ap·per·cep·tive,** *a.*

ap·per·tain, ap′ər·tān, *v.i.* To belong or pertain: with *to.*

ap·pe·tite, ap′ə·tīt, *n.* A desire for food and drink; eagerness or longing.

ap·pe·tiz·er, ap′ə·tī·zər, *n.* A food or drink served before a meal to excite the appetite.

ap·pe·tiz·ing, ap′ə·tī·zing, *a.* Exciting the appetite; tempting to the appetite.

ap·plaud, ə·plôd′, *v.t.* To show approval by clapping the hands; to praise highly.—*v.i.* To give praise; to give approval.

ap·plause, ə·plôz′, *n.* Approval shown by clapping the hands or shouting.

ap·ple, ap′əl, *n.* A fleshy, red or yellow fruit of the apple tree; the tree itself; also, any of various exotic fruits or trees having some resemblance to the apple, as the pineapple, etc.

ap·ple·jack, ap′əl·jak, *n.* Brandy made from apple cider.

ap·pie-pie or·der, ap′əl·pī, *a.* Perfect or excellent condition or order.

ap·pli·ance, ə·plī′əns, *n.* A device, esp. an electrical device that does some household task, such as a toaster, a blender, or a refrigerator.

ap·pli·ca·ble, ap′li·kə·bəl, ə·plik′ə·bəl, *a.* Capable of being applied; fit to be applied; relevant. —**ap·pli· ca·bil·i·ty,** ap·li·kə·bil′ə·tē, —**ap·pli·ca·ble·ness,** *n.* —**ap·pli·ca·bly,** *adv.*

ap·pli·cant, ap′li·kənt, *n.* One who applies.

ap·pli·ca·tion, ap·li·kā′shən, *n.* The act of applying or putting to use; the thing applied; the act of requesting; close study; attention; the testing of something theoretical by applying it in practice; a form asking for admission, employment, etc.

ap·pli·ca·tive, ap′li·kā·tiv, ə·plik′ə·tiv, *a.* Having an application; pertaining to that which may be applied. Also **ap·pli·ca·to·ry.**

ap·pli·ca·tor, ap′li·kā·tər, *n.* Any device for applying medicine, cosmetics, chemicals, etc.

ap·plied, ə·plīd′, *a.* Put to practical or actual use: *applied* science.

ap·pli·qué, ap·li·kā′, *a.* Applied; formed with ornamentation of one material sewed to another.—*n.* Work done in this way.—*v.t.,* **-quéd, -qué·ing.** To sew an appliqué to (a background); to apply as in appliqué work.

ap·ply, ə·plī′, *v.t.,* **ap·plied, ap·ply·ing.** To put or place on another thing; to use or employ; to put, refer,

---

or use as suitable; to study hard: *apply* oneself to the task.—*v.i.* To suit; to agree; to make a request. **—ap•pli•er,** *n.*

ap•point, ə•poynt′, *v.t.* To assign to a particular use, task, or office; designate; to equip or provide with: a well-*appointed* office. **—ap•point•a•ble,** *a.* **—ap•point•er,** *n.*

ap•point•ee, ə•poyn•tē′, *n.* A person appointed; legal appointment.

ap•poin•tive, ə•poyn′tiv, *a.* Filled by appointment: an *appointive* position.

ap•point•ment, ə•poynt′mənt, *n.* The act of appointing; ordainment; designation to office; engagement for a meeting; *usu. pl.,* equipment.

ap•por•tion, ə•pôr′shən, *v.t.* To divide according to a definite rule; to distribute in proper shares; to allot. **—ap•por•tion•ment,** *n.*

ap•pose, ə•pōz′, *v.t.,* **ap•posed, ap•pos•ing.** To put one thing next to another.

ap•po•site, ap′ə•zit, *a.* Suitable; fit; appropriate.

ap•po•si•tion, ap•ə•zish′ən, *n.* The act of adding one thing to another; the placing of two nouns next to each other in a sentence, both of which refer to the same object or person: *Churchill, the Prime Minister,* was there. **—ap•po•si•tion•al,** *a.*

ap•pos•i•tive, ə•poz′ə•tiv, *a.* In apposition. —*n.* A word in apposition.

ap•praise, ə•prāz′, *v.t.,* **ap•praised, ap•prais•ing.** To set a price upon; to estimate the value of. **—ap•prais•er,** *n.*

ap•prais•al, ə•prā′zəl, *n.* An evaluation; an official price.

ap•pre•ci•a•ble, ə•prē′shē•ə•bəl, ə•prē′shə•bəl, *a.* Capable of being appreciated or estimated; sufficiently great to be capable of estimation or of being measured. **—ap•pre•ci•a•bly,** *adv.*

ap•pre•ci•ate, ə•prē′shē•āt, *v.t.,* **-at•ed, -at•ing.** To be grateful for; to regard highly; to value properly; to set a just price on.—*v.i.* To rise in value; to become of more value.

ap•pre•ci•a•tion, ə•prē•shē•ā′shən, *n.* The act of appreciating; the act of valuing; an increase in value; gratitude; awareness of value.

ap•pre•ci•a•tive, ə•prē′shə•tiv, ə•prē′shē•ā•tiv, *a.* Showing appreciation. Also **ap•pre•ci•a•to•ry.**

ap•pre•hend, ap•ri•hend′, *v.t.* To arrest; to understand; to expect with fear.—*v.i.* To understand. **—ap•pre•hen•si•ble,** ap•rə•hen′sə•bəl, *a.* **—ap•pre•hen•si•bil•i•ty,** ap•rə•hen•sə•bil′ə•tē, *n.*

ap•pre•hen•sion, ap•ri•hen′shən, *n.* A feeling of fear; seizure or arrest; understanding; opinion.

ap•pre•hen•sive, ap•ri•hen′siv, *a.* Fearful: *apprehensive* of evil, *apprehensive* for our lives. **—ap•pre•hen•sive•ly,** *adv.* **—ap•pre•hen•sive•ness,** *n.*

ap•pren•tice, ə•pren′tis, *n.* A person bound by legal contract to an expert to learn some art, trade, or profession in return for instruction; a beginner in any subject. —*v.t.,* **-ticed, -tic•ing.** To become or accept as an apprentice. **—ap•pren•tice•ship,** *n.*

ap•prise, ap•prize, ə•prīz′, *v.t.,* **ap•prised** or **ap•prized, ap•pri•sing** or **ap•pri•zing.** To inform.

ap•proach, ə•prōch′, *v.i.* To come or go near.—*v.t.* To come or draw near to; to come near to, so as to be compared with; to approximate; to make a proposition to; to set about. —*n.* The act of drawing near an object; a way to come near something; in golf, a shot that comes near the green. **—ap•proach•a•bil•i•ty,** ə•prō•chə•bil′ə•tē, *n.* **—ap•proach•a•ble,** *a.*

ap•pro•ba•tion, ap•rə•bā′shən, *n.* The act of approving.

ap•pro•ba•tive, ap′rə•bā•tiv, *a.* Approving. Also **ap•pro•ba•to•ry,** ə•prō′bə•tôr•e.

ap•pro•pri•ate, ə•prō′prē•āt, *v.t.,* **-at•ed, -at•ing.** To take for oneself; to claim or use by an exclusive right; to set apart for a particular purpose; to provide (funds or money), esp. by an act of Congress.—ə•prō′prē•it, *a.* Set apart for a particular use or person; belonging

to; suitable; fit; proper. **—ap•pro•pri•ate•ly,** *adv.* **—ap•pro•pri•ate•ness,** *n.* **—ap•pro•pri•a•tor,** *n.*

ap•pro•pri•a•tion, ə•prō•prē•ā′shən, *n.* The act of appropriating; anything set apart; official permission to spend funds; the money so approved. **—ap•pro•pri•a•tive,** ə•prō′prē•ā•tiv, ə•prō′prē•ə•tiv, *a.*

ap•prov•al, ə•proo′vəl, *n.* The act of approving; official permission.

ap•prove, ə•proov′, *v.t.,* **ap•proved, ap•prov•ing.** To admit the excellence of; to think or judge well of; to find to be satisfactory; to give official permission to.—*v.i.* To be pleased; to think or judge well (of). **—ap•prov•a•ble,** *a.* **—ap•prov•er,** *n.* **—ap•prov•ing•ly,** *adv.*

ap•prox•i•mate, ə•prok′sə•mit, *a.* Being near in state, place, or amount; nearly equal or like. —ə•prok′sə•māt, *v.t.* To come or bring near; to estimate; to cause to approach (in amount, state, or degree).—*v.i.* To come near; to approach. **—ap•prox•i•mate•ly,** *adv.* **—ap•prox•i•ma•tion,** ə•prok•sə•mā′shən, *n.*

ap•pur•te•nance, ə•pər′tə•nəns, *n.* Something of less importance which is added to something else; *pl.* necessary equipment. **—ap•pur•te•nant,** *a.*

ap•ri•cot, ap′rə•kot, ā′prə•kot, *n.* A roundish fruit that tastes like the peach or plum; the tree; a pinkish-yellow or light orange color.

A•pril, ā′prəl, *n.* The fourth month of the year, containing 30 days.

A•pril fool, *n.* The butt of a practical joke on April 1.

a pri•o•ri, ā•prī•ôr′ī, ä•prē•ôr′ē, *a., adv.* Reasoning from cause to effect; or from a general proposition to a particular case; analytic; deductive; applied to knowledge independent of or prior to all experience.

a•pron, ā′prən, *n.* A garment worn over the front part of the body to protect the clothes underneath or adorn a costume; any shielding piece or part; a paved area at an airport where airplanes take on and discharge passengers; the part of a stage in front of the proscenium arch.

ap•ro•pos, ap•rə•pō′, *a., adv.* Opportune; suitable; pertinent.

ap•ro•pos of, *prep.* With relation to, concerning, pertaining to.

apse, aps, *n.* A projecting part of a building, especially the vaulted, semicircular eastern end of a church.

apt, apt, *a.* Fit; suitable; pertinent; quick to learn; having a tendency; liable; inclined. **—apt•ly,** *adv.* **—apt•ness,** *n.*

ap•ter•ous, ap′tər•əs, *a.* Wingless.

ap•ti•tude, ap′ti•tood, ap′ti•tūd, *n.* Natural ability; tendency; fitness; suitableness; readiness in learning.

aq•ua, ak′wə, ä′kwə, *n. pl.,* **aq•uas, aq•uae,** ak′wē, ä′kwē. Water.—*a.* Bluish-green.

a•qua•cul•ture, ak′wə•kəl•chər, *n.* The farming underwater of plants and animals.

aq•ua for•tis, ak′wə fôr′təs, *n.* Nitric acid.

Aq•ua•lung, ak′wə•ləng, *n. Trademark.* A device to permit breathing under water, consisting of a watertight face mask and cylinders of compressed air.

aq•ua•ma•rine, ak•wə•mə•rēn′, ä•kwə•mə•rēn′, *n.* The finest beryl, so-called from its bluish-green tint; also the bluish-green color.

aq•ua•naut, ak′wə•nôt, *n.* A diver who stays underwater for long periods of time to test living and working conditions in an underwater environment.

aq•ua•plane, ak′wə•plān, *n.* A board on which a person stands as it is pulled over the water by a speedboat.—*v.i.,* **-planed, -plan•ing.** To ride an aquaplane.

aq•ua re•gi•a, ak′wə•rē′jē•ə, *n.* A mixture of nitric acid and hydrochloric acid which dissolves gold or platinum.

a•quar•i•um, ə•kwār′ē•əm, *n. pl.,* **-i•ums, -i•a,** -ē•ə. A glass tank, or the like, in which water plants and animals are kept; a place containing a collection of such tanks for public exhibition.

a•quat•ic, ə•kwat′ik, ə•kwot′ik, *a.* Pertaining to water; living in water. —*n.* A plant which grows in water; *pl.,* sports practiced on or in water.

aq·ua·tint, ak/wə·tint, ä/kwə·tint, *n.* A method of etching on copper by which a water-color effect is produced; the etching so produced.

aq·ua vi·tae, ak/wə vī/tē, *n.* Alcohol; a strong liquor, as brandy or whiskey.

aq·ue·duct, ak/wə·dəkt, *n.* A pipe or channel for carrying water from one place to another; a structure for carrying water for the supply of a town.

a·que·ous, ā/kwē·əs, ak/wē·əs, *a.* Of, like, or containing water; watery.

a·que·ous hu·mor, *n.* The watery fluid which fills the part of the eye between the lens and the cornea.

aq·ui·line, ak/wə·līn, ak/wə·lin, *a.* Of or like the eagle; like an eagle's beak; curving; hooked.

Ar·ab, ar/əb, *n.* A native of Arabia, or a member of a Semitic people now widespread in Asia and Africa, and formerly in southern Europe; a horse of an originally Arabian breed noted for its speed and grace. —**A·ra·bi·an,** ə·rā/bē·ən, *a.*

ar·a·besque, ar·ə·besk/, *n.* Decoration in which flowers, foliage, fruits, geometrical figures, etc., are combined in an intricate pattern. A ballet position in which the artist, standing on one leg, extends the body and one arm forward while the other arm and leg reach backward.

Ar·a·bic, ar/ə·bik, *a.* Belonging to or derived from Arabia or the Arabians.—*n.* The Semitic language of the Arabs.

Ar·a·bic nu·mer·als, *n.* The figures 1, 2, 3, 4, 5, 6, 7, 8, 9, and 0.

ar·a·ble, ar/ə·bəl, *a.* Fit for plowing. —**ar·a·bil·i·ty,** ar·ə·bil/ə·tē, *n.*

a·rach·nid, ə·rak/nid, *n.* Any member of a class of wingless anthropods with jointed bodies, including spiders, mites, and scorpions. —**a·rach·ni·dan,** *adj., n.*

Ar·a·ma·ic, ar·ə·mā/ik, *n.* A group of dialects, belonging to the Semitic family, including the dialect spoken in Palestine at the time of Christ.

ar·ba·lest, ar·ba·list, är/bə·list, *n.* A kind of powerful crossbow used during the Middle Ages. —**ar·ba·lest·er,** *n.*

ar·bi·ter, är/bi·tər, *n.* A person chosen to settle differences; one whose power of deciding and governing is final or absolute. —**ar·bi·tral,** *a.*

ar·bit·ra·ment, är·bit/rə·mənt, *n.* Determination by an arbiter; decision; settlement.

ar·bi·trar·y, är/bi·trer·ē, *a.* Exercised according to one's will, opinion, prejudice, etc.; decided by an arbiter rather than by law; tyrannical. —**ar·bi·trar·i·ly,** ar·bi·trār/ə·lē, *adv.* —**ar·bi·trar·i·ness,** *n.*

ar·bi·trate, är/bi·trāt, *v.i.* -trat·ed, -trat·ing. To act as an arbiter; to hear and decide in a dispute.—*v.t.* To hear and decide on; determine. —**ar·bi·tra·ble,** ar/bə·trə·bəl, *a.* —**ar·bi·tra·tor,** *n.*

ar·bi·tra·tion, är·bi·trā/shən, *n.* The hearing and determination of a cause between parties in a disagreement or labor dispute, by a person or persons chosen by the parties.

ar·bor, är/bər, *n.* A tree- or vine-shaded place often framed by a latticework entwined with climbing shrubs or vines.

Ar·bor Day, *n.* A day publicly appointed in individual States of the U.S. for the planting of trees.

ar·bo·re·al, är·bôr/ē·əl, *a.* Of or like trees; living in or among trees.

ar·bo·res·cent, är·bə·res/ənt, *a.* Treelike; forming branches.

ar·bo·re·tum, är·bə·rē/təm, *n. pl.,* **-tums, -ta,** -tə. A botanical garden for scientific, educational, or decorative purposes.

ar·bor·vi·tae, är/bər·vī/tē, *n.* A common name of

certain evergreen trees of the pine family.

ar·bu·tus, är·bū/təs, *n.* An evergreen tree or shrub of the heath family, with bright red berries; a plant, the trailing arbutus, with fragrant pink flowers.

arc, ärk, *n.* Something bow-shaped, as a rainbow; an architectural arch; any part of a circle or other curved line; the apparent course of a heavenly body either above or below the horizon; the luminous bridge formed by the passage of an electric current across a gap between two conductors.—*v.i.,* **arced** or **arcked,** **arc·ing** or **arck·ing.** To form an electric arc.

ar·cade, är·kād/, *n.* A series of arches supported on pillars; a covered passageway, sometimes lined with shops; an arched building or passageway in a building.

Ar·ca·di·a, är·kā/dē·ə, *n.* Any region (real or ideal) characterized by pastoral simplicity, innocence, and contentment. —**Ar·ca·di·an,** *a.*

ar·cane, är·kān/, *a.* Hidden; secret.

arch, ärch, *n.* A structure made of separate wedge-shaped pieces, arranged on a curved line, that keep their position by mutual pressure; a covering, or structure, of a bow shape; a doorway with a curved head; a vault.—*v.t.* To furnish, cover, or span with an arch; also, to curve like an arch.—*v.i.* To form an arch.

arch, ärch, *a.* Cunning, sly; mischievously saucy; roguish; most important; chief. —**arch·ly,** *adv.* —**arch·ness,** *n.*

arch-, *prefix.* Chief; principal.

ar·chae·ol·o·gy, ar·che·ol·o·gy, är·kē·ol/ə·jē, *n.* The science which investigates remote, especially prehistoric, peoples by digging up and studying the remains of their cities, monuments, pottery, etc. —**ar·chae·o·log·i·cal, ar·che·o·log·i·cal,** är·kē·ə·loj/ə·kəl, *a.* —**ar·chae·ol·o·gist, ar·che·ol·o·gist,** *n.*

Ar·chae·o·zo·ic, Ar·che·o·zo·ic, är·kē·ə·zō/·ik, *a.* Pertaining to the earliest era of geological history.

ar·cha·ic, är·kā/ik, *a.* Old-fashioned; not commonly used during the present time, as words.

ar·cha·ism, är/kē·iz·əm, är/kā·iz·əm, *n.* A word or idiom no longer in general use; antiquity of style or use. —**ar·cha·ist,** *n.* —**ar·cha·is·tic,** *a.*

arch·an·gel, ärk/ān·jəl, *n.* An angel of the highest rank. —**arch·an·gel·ic,** ärk·an·jel/ik, *a.*

arch·bish·op, ärch/bish/əp, *n.* A bishop who has the supervision of other bishops.

arch·bish·op·ric, ärch·bish/əp·rik, *n.* The jurisdiction, office, or see of an archbishop.

arch·dea·con, ärch·dē/kən, *n.* In England, a high church official, next in rank below a bishop.

arch·di·o·cese, ärch·dī/ə·sis, ärch·dī/ə·sēs, *n.* The diocese of an archbishop. —**arch·di·oc·e·san,** ärch·dī·os/ə·sən, *a.*

arch·du·cal, ärch·doo/kəl, ärch·dū/kəl, *a.* Pertaining to an archduke or archduchy.

arch·duch·ess, ärch·dəch/is, *n.* The wife or widow of an archduke; a woman who has a rank equal to that of an archduke.

arch·duch·y, ärch·dəch/ē, *n. pl.,* **-duch·ies.** The territory of an archduke or archduchess.

arch·duke, ärch·dook/, ärch·dūk/. *n.* A prince belonging to the imperial family of the former Austrian empire; any ruling prince.

arch·en·e·my, ärch·en/ə·mē, *n. pl.,* **-mies.** A principal enemy; Satan.

arch·er, är/chər, *n.* One who uses, or is skilled in the use of, the bow and arrow; a bowman.

ar·cher·y, är/chə·rē, *n.* The practice, art, or skill of shooting with a bow and arrow; the equipment used by the archer.

ar·che·type, är/ki·tīp, *n.* A model or first form; the original pattern from which a thing is made, or to which it corresponds. —**ar·che·typ·al,** *a.* —**ar·che·**

---

a- hat, fāte, fāre, fäther; e- met, mē; i- pin, pīne; o- not, nōte, ôrb, moove (move), boy, pownd; u- cūbe, bŭll, tûk (took); ch- chin; th- thick, ŧhen; zh- vizhon (vision); ə- əgo, takən, pencəl, lemən, bərd (bird).

typ·i·cal, är·ki·tip/i·kəl.

arch·fiend, ärch/fēnd/,˝ n. A chief fiend; with *the,* Satan.

ar·chi·e·pis·co·pate, är·kē·ə·pis/kə·pit, är·kē· ə·pis/kə·pāt, n. Archbishopric. —**ar·chi·e·pis·co· pal,** a.

ar·chi·pel·a·go, är·kə·pel/ə·gō, n. pl., **-goes, -gos.** A sea with many islands; a group of many islands.

ar·chi·tect, är/ki·tekt, n. One whose occupation is to design buildings, and superintend their erection; a designer or creator.

ar·chi·tec·ton·ic, är·ki·tek·ton/ik, a. Resembling architecture in structure or design; constructive.

ar·chi·tec·ton·ics, är·ki·tek·ton/iks, n. pl. but sing. in constr. The science of architecture.

ar·chi·tec·ture, är/ki·tek·chər, n. The art or science of building, including design, construction, and often decorations; the character or style of building: the *architecture* of Rome; a building or buildings; the structure of anything. —**ar·chi·tec·tur·al,** är·ki· tek/chər·əl, a.

ar·chi·trave, är/ki·trāv, n. The lowest part of the structure that rests on top of a column; also, a band of moldings about a door or other opening.

ar·chive, är/kīv, n. Documents or public records of a family, corporation, nation, etc.; the location of such records. —**ar·chi·val,** är·kī/vəl, a.

ar·chi·vist, är/kə·vist, n. A keeper of records.

ar·chon, är/kon, n. A chief magistrate of ancient Athens.

arch·priest, ärch/prēst/, n. Chief priest; dean of a cathedral chapter.

arch·way, ärch/wā, n. A passage under an arch.

arc lamp, n. A form of lamp employing an electric arc. Also **arc light.**

arc·tic, ärk/tik, a. (Often cap.) Surrounding or lying near the North Pole; of, or like the arctic region; cold, frigid.—**the Arc·tic,** the region within the Arctic Circle.

arc·tic, ärk/tik, n. A waterproof rubber or plastic overshoe reaching to or above the ankle.

arc·tic cir·cle, n. (Often cap.) An imaginary circle parallel to the equator and located about 23¹/₂° south of the North Pole.

ar·dent, är/dənt, a. Passionate; zealous; fervent; burning; hot; glowing. —**ar·dent·ly,** adv.

ar·dor, är/dər, n. Warmth of the passions and affections; eagerness; intensity; zeal; burning heat.

ar·du·ous, är/joo·əs, a. Difficult; strenuous: requiring great effort; energetic; vigorous; hard to climb; steep. —**ar·du·ous·ly,** adv. —**ar·du·ous·ness,** n.

are, är. The present tense plural and the second person singular of the verb *to be.*

are, är, n. A unit of measure for area, equivalent to 100 square meters or 119.6 square yards.

ar·e·a, är/ē·ə, n. Any plane surface within boundaries, as the floor of a hall, etc.; a geographical region; a space reserved for a particular function; an areaway; a yard; a surface, as given in square inches, feet, yards, etc.; field of study or inquiry; range; scope. —**ar·e·al,** a.

ar·e·a·way, är/ē·ə·wā, n. A sunken space for air and light in front of a basement door or window; a passageway.

a·re·na, ə·rē/nə, n. The enclosed space in the central part of the Roman amphitheater; the scene or theater of a contest, show, or game.

aren't, ärnt, är/ənt. Are not.

a·re·o·la, ə·rē/ə·lə, n. pl., **a·re·o·lae,** ə·rē/ə·lē, **a·re·o·las.** The colored circle surrounding a nipple, pustule, etc.

ar·gent, är/jənt, n. Archaic or Poetic. Silver.—a. Resembling silver; made of silver.

ar·gen·tine, är/jən·tēn, är/jən·tīn, a. Silvery.

ar·gil, är/jil, n. Clay or potter's earth.

ar·gon, är/gon, n. A colorless, odorless, inert gas used in electric bulbs and electron tubes.

Ar·go·naut, är/gə·nôt, n. One of the persons who, in

the Greek legend, sailed with Jason in the ship Argo in quest of the Golden Fleece.

ar·go·sy, är/gə·sē, n. pl., **-sies.** A large merchant ship, especially if richly laden; a fleet of ships.

ar·got, är/gō, är/gət, n. The jargon of thieves; the jargon or specialized vocabulary of any class or group; slang. —**ar·got·ic,** är·got/ik, a.

ar·gue, är/gū, v.i., **ar·gued, ar·gu·ing.** To offer reasons for or against; to debate; to dispute.—v.t. To debate or discuss; to prove; show; to cause to be inferred: conduct which *argued* suspicion; to convince through argument. —**ar·gu·a·ble,** a. —**ar·gu· er,** n.

ar·gu·ment, är/gyə·mənt, n. A verbal dispute; the subject of a discourse or writing; a summary of a book or section of a book; a reason offered for or against something; a debate or discussion; a process of reasoning.

ar·gu·men·ta·tion, är·gyə·mən·tā/shən, n. The act of arguing; discussion.

ar·gu·men·ta·tive, är·gyə·men/tə·tiv, a. Consisting of argument; controversial; fond of arguing; disputations.

ar·gyle, ar·gyll, är/gīl, n. (Often cap.) A pattern of different-colored diamonds on a single-colored background used in knitting; a sock knit in that pattern.

a·ri·a, ä/rē·ə, är/ē·ə, n. A song; a tune; a melody for a single voice and accompaniment, as in an opera.

ar·id, ar/id, a. Dry; parched with heat; unimaginative; lifeless. —**a·rid·i·ty,** ə·rid/i·tē, n.

a·right, ə·rīt/, adv. Correctly; rightly.

a·rise, ə·rīz/, v.i., **a·rose, a·ris·en, a·ris·ing.** To move to a higher place; to come up, to come into view; to appear; to leave a sitting or lying position; to begin; to start into action; to rise.

ar·is·toc·ra·cy, ar·i·stok/rə·sē, n. pl., **-cies.** Government by the nobility or a privileged upper class; a country so governed; the nobility or upper class; any group that is superior because of intelligence, culture, wealth, etc. —**a·ris·to·crat,** ə·ris/tə·krat, ar/is·tə· krat, n. —**a·ris·to·crat·ic,** ə·ris·tə·krat/ik, a.

a·rith·me·tic, ə·rith/mə·tik, n. The science of numbers or the art of computation by figures or numerals. —**ar·ith·met/ik,** a. Pertaining to arithmetic. Also **ar· ith·met·i·cal. —ar·ith·met·i·cal·ly,** ar·ith·met/ik·lē, adv. —**ar·ith·me·ti·cian,** ə·rith/mə·tish·ən, ar·ith· mə·tish/ən, n.

ar·ith·met·ic mean, n. A quantity formed by adding the values of a group or set of numbers together and dividing the total by the number of members of that group or set.

ar·ith·met·ic pro·gres·sion, n. A series of numbers showing increase or decrease by a constant quantity, as 2, 4, 6, 8, etc.

ark, ärk, n. In the Bible: the wooden chest that held the Hebrew sacred tablets of the law; a place of safety; the ship of Noah; a scow.

arm, ärm, n. The limb of the human body which extends from the shoulder to the hand; a forelimb; anything that sticks out from a main body, as a branch of a tree; a narrow inlet of waters from the sea; a support, as part of a chair.

arm, ärm, n. A weapon; a branch of the military service; pl., weapons; war; the military profession; insignia used by governments or in heraldry.—v.t. To furnish with weapons; provide with whatever will add strength or security; fortify.—v.i. To provide oneself with arms. —**arm·er,** n.

ar·ma·da, är·mä/də, är·mā/də, n. A fleet of armed ships.

ar·ma·dil·lo, är·mə·dil/ō, n. pl., **-los.** A burrowing mammal found in warm regions of N. and S. America, covered with a hard bony shell divided into small separate plates.

Ar·ma·ged·don, är·mə·ged/ən, n. The scene of the final conflict of nations, Rev. xvi. 16; any great and final conflict.

ar·ma·ment, är′mə·mənt, *n.* A nation's military forces equipped for war; a land force or a naval force; armor and combat equipment; preparation for combat.

ar·ma·ture, är′mə·chər, *n.* A piece of iron connecting two poles of a magnet; the part of a generator made up mainly of coils or wire around a core of iron.

arm·chair, ärm′châr, *n.* A chair with arms to support the elbows and arms.

armed forc·es, *n. pl.* The combined military forces of a nation.

arm·ful, ärm′fûl, *n. pl.,* **-fuls.** As much as one or both arms can hold; that which is so held.

arm·hole, ärm′hōl, *n.* An opening for the arm in an article of clothing.

ar·mi·stice, är′mə·stis, *n.* A stopping of military operations by agreement among the warring parties; truce.

Ar·mi·stice Day, *n.* Veterans Day.

arm·let, ärm′lit, *n.* A little arm, as of the sea; an ornamental band for the upper arm.

ar·moire, ärm·wär′, *n.* A large cupboard, closet, or wardrobe.

ar·mor, är′mər, *n.* Defensive arms; any covering worn to protect the body in battle, sports, etc.; the steel covering that protects an airplane, tank, or warship.

ar·mored, är′mərd, *a.* Protected by armor. Of a military force, provided with tanks and other armored equipment.

ar·mor·er, är′mər·ər, *n.* A maker or manufacturer of armor or arms, or one who keeps them in repair.

ar·mor·y, är′mər·ē, *n. pl.,* **-ies.** A place to store arms; a place where military reserves are trained; a factory for making arms.

arm·pit, ärm′pit, *n.* The hollow under the shoulder or upper arm.

ar·my, är′mē, *n. pl.,* **ar·mies.** A large organization of armed men trained for military duty especially on land; the total military land forces of a nation; any large, organized group of people; a vast number.

ar·ni·ca, är′nə·kə, *n.* Any of several composite perennial herbs; a preparation of the dried flower heads used to treat wounds and bruises.

a·ro·ma, ə·rō′mə, *n.* An agreeable odor; fragrance; a distinctive characteristic.

ar·o·mat·ic, ar·ə·mat′ik, *a.* Giving out an aroma; fragrant. Also **ar·o·mat·i·cal.—***n.* A plant, drug, or medicine which yields a fragrant smell.

a·round, ə·rownd′, *adv.* In a circle; in circumference; on every side: A dense mist lay *around. Informal.* Here and there: to travel *around;* somewhere about or near: to wait *around* for; in the opposite direction: to turn *around.—prep.* In a direction that turns about; so as to encircle or encompass; on all sides of. *Informal.* Here and there in: to roam *around* the country; somewhere in or near: to stay *around* the house.

a·rouse, ə·rowz′, *v.t.,* **a·roused, a·rous·ing.** To excite into action; to put in motion; to rouse; to awaken. *—v.i.* To become aroused.—**a·rous·al,** *n.*

ar·peg·gi·o, är·pej′ē·ō, är·pej′ō, *n. pl.,* **-os.** The sounding of notes of a chord in rapid succession; a chord done in arpeggio.

ar·raign, ə·rān′, *v.t.* To call to a court of justice to answer a legal charge; to call in question; to accuse or charge. **—ar·raign·ment,** *n.*

ar·range, ə·rānj′, *v.t.,* **ar·ranged, ar·rang·ing.** To put in proper order; to dispose or set out; to adjust; to settle; to come to an agreement; to prepare; to adapt, as a musical score.—*v.i.* To make plans; to come to an agreement. **—ar·rang·er,** *n.*

ar·range·ment, ə·rānj′mənt, *n.* An arranging; that which is arranged. *Usu. pl.* Preparations.

ar·rant, ar′ənt, *a.* Thoroughgoing; notorious. **—ar·rant·ly,** *adv.*

ar·ras, ar′əs, *n.* Tapestry; a wall hanging.

ar·ray, ə·rā′, *n.* A collection of men or things in regular order; raiment; dress.—*v.t.* To arrange in order; to marshal; to adorn or dress.

ar·rear, ə·rēr′, *n. Usu. pl.* The state of being behind in completing one's debts; unpaid debts or unfinished work.

ar·rest, ə·rest′, *v.t.* To check; to stop; to seize by legal authority; to seize and fix (attention).—*n.* The act of arresting; seizure. **—ar·rest·er, ar·res·tor,** *n.*

ar·ri·val, ə·rī′vəl, *n.* The act of arriving; the person or thing which arrives.

ar·rive, ə·rīv′, *v.i.,* **ar·rived, ar·riv·ing.** To come to a certain place or point; to get to a destination; to attain a certain result followed by *at:* to *arrive at* an answer; to attain success; to finally occur.

ar·ro·gant, ar′ə·gənt, *a.* Making unreasonable claims on account of one's rank, power, worth; presumptuous; haughty; overbearing. **—ar·ro·gance,** *n.* **—ar·ro·gant·ly,** *adv.*

ar·ro·gate, ar′ə·gāt, *v.t.,* **-gat·ed, -gat·ing.** To claim or demand without right or presumptuously. **—ar·ro·ga·tion,** ar·ə·gā′shən, *n.*

ar·row, ar′ō, *n.* A long slender shaft with a sharp, pointed head, used for shooting from a bow; a mark similar in form to show direction; anything resembling an arrow.

ar·row·head, ar′ō·hed, *n.* The head or tip of an arrow.

ar·row·root, ar′ō·root, *n.* A tropical American plant whose roots yield a nutritious starch used in food preparations; the starch itself.

ar·roy·o, ə·roy′ō, *n. pl.,* **-os.** *Southwestern U.S.* A stream; also, the dry bed of a stream; a gully.

ar·se·nal, är′sə·nəl, *n.* A place for storing arms; a government building where military equipment is manufactured or stored.

ar·se·nate, är′sə·nāt, är′sə·nit, *n.* A salt of arsenic acid.

ar·se·nic, är′sə·nik, *n.* A usually brittle, grayish-white element which forms poisonous compounds used in medicine and industry. Symbol As.

ar·son, är′sən, *n.* The crime of intentionally burning property. **—ar·son·ist,** *n.*

art, ärt, *n.* The creation of meaningful or beautiful objects through skill and imagination; the objects so created; any of the fine arts, especially painting, drawing, or sculpture; the fine arts collectively; the profession or craft of an artist; a branch of learning; a system of rules or methods; knowledge or skill which depends more on special practice than general principles; artfulness; cunning. *Pl.* Liberal arts.

art, ärt. *Archaic, poet.* Second person sing., present tense, of *be:* used with *thou.*

ar·te·ri·al, är·tēr′ē·əl, *a.* Of or like an artery; having with the oxygen-rich blood in the arteries; bright red.

ar·te·ri·o·scle·ro·sis, är·tēr·ē·ō·sklə·rō′sis, *n.* A hardening of the arterial walls, hindering blood circulation.

ar·ter·y, är′tə·rē, *n. pl.,* **-ies.** One of a system of tubes which convey the blood from the heart to all parts of the body; a main channel, as for transportation.

ar·te·sian well, är·tē′zhən, *n.* A well which reaches water that is under enough pressure to rise to the surface without the need for pumping.

art·ful, ärt′fəl, *a.* Sly; devious; crafty; skillful; ingenious. **—art·ful·ly,** *adv.* **—art·ful·ness,** *n.*

ar·thri·tis, är·thrī′tis, *n.* Any inflammation of the joints. **—ar·thrit·ic,** är·thrit′ik, *a.*

ar·thro·pod, är′thrə·pod, *n.* Any of a group of invertebrates with jointed bodies and jointed limbs, including insects, spiders, and crabs. **—ar·throp·o·dal,** är·throp′ə·dəl, **ar·throp·o·dous,** är·throp′ə·dəs, *a.*

---

a- hat, fāte, fâre, fäther; **e-** met, mē; **i-** pin, pīne; **o-** not, nōte, ôrb, moove (move), boy, pownd; **u-** cūbe, bûll, tûk (took); **ch-** chin; **th-** thick, ŧhen; **zh-** vizhon (vision); ə- əgo, takən, pencəl, lemən, bərd (bird).

ar·ti·choke, är/ti·chōk, *n.* A thistlelike plant grown for its flower head, used as a cooked vegetable; Jerusalem artichoke.

ar·ti·cle, är/ti·kəl, *n.* A single item, or particular; a provision of a contract or treaty; a prose contribution to a newspaper, magazine, or other periodical; a particular substance; a part of speech used before nouns to limit or define their application: in English, *a* or *an*, and *the*.

ar·tic·u·lar, är·tik/yə·lər, *a.* Having to do with joints or to a joint.

ar·tic·u·late, är·tik/yə·lit, *a.* Jointed; having segments; pronounced distinctly; expressed clearly; distinct; able to speak with ease or effectiveness. —är·tik/yə·lāt, *v.t.,* **-lat·ed, -lat·ing.** To joint; to unite by means of a joint; to pronounce distinctly or speak clearly.—*v.i.* To utter articulate sounds; to speak distinctly. **—ar·tic·u·late·ly,** *adv.* **—ar·tic·u·late·ness,** *n.* **—ar·tic·u·la·tor,** *n.*

ar·tic·u·la·tion, är·tik·yə·lā/shən, *n.* Way of speaking; enunciation; act or manner of articulating; a joining of the bones; a joint.

ar·tic·u·la·to·ry, är·tik/yə·lə·tōr·ē, är·tik/yə·lə·tôr·ē, *a.* Of or concerned with articulation.

ar·ti·fact, ar·te·fact, är/tə·fakt, *n.* Any man-made object, esp. a simple ornament or tool; an artificial product.

ar·ti·fice, är/tə·fis, *n.* Ingenious contrivance; a clever trick; stratagem; guile.

ar·tif·i·cer, är·tif/ə·sər, *n.* A skillful or artistic worker; a maker or contriver; a mechanic.

ar·ti·fi·cial, är·tə·fish/əl, *a.* Made by human art or labor; made in imitation of something natural; affected. **—ar·ti·fi·ci·al·i·ty,** är·tə·fish·ē·al/ə·tē, *n. pl.,* **-ties. —ar·ti·fi·cial·ly,** *adv.* **—ar·ti·fi·cial·ness,** *n.*

ar·ti·fi·cial res·pi·ra·tion, *n.* The rhythmic forcing of air into and out of the lungs of a person whose breathing has ceased.

ar·til·ler·y, är·til/ə·rē, *n.* Guns of large size; mounted guns; cannon; the science of the use of large guns; a branch of an army using such guns. **—ar·til·ler·ist,** *n.* **—ar·til·ler·y·man,** *n.*

ar·ti·san, är/tə·zən, *n.* A craftsman; a mechanic.

art·ist, är/tist, *n.* One skilled in the arts; one skilled in any of the fine arts; a person whose work shows artistic qualities; a craftsman.

ar·tiste, är·tēst/, *n.* Any very skillful performer, especially an entertainer.

ar·tis·tic, är·tis/tik, *a.* Of art or artists; satisfying the aesthetic standards of art; showing taste or sensitivity. **—ar·tis·ti·cal·ly,** *adv.*

art·ist·ry, är/tə·strē, *n.* High quality of workmanship; artistic ability.

art·less, ärt·lis, *a.* Lacking in art or skill; natural; simple. **—art·less·ly,** *adv.* **—art·less·ness,** *n.*

art·y, är/tē, *a.,* **-i·er, -i·est.** Imitative of art, esp. garish, crude, or showy. **—ar·ti·ness,** *n.*

Ar·y·an, är/ē·an, är/yən, *n.* A descendant of speakers of early Indo-European languages. In Nazi ideology, a non-Jewish Caucasian of Nordic extraction.

as, az, *adv.* To such a degree or extent: the antecedent in the correlation *as . . . as* (*as* good as gold); for example.—*conj.* The consequent in the correlations *as . . . as, so . . . as,* etc., noting degree, extent, etc. (as good *as* gold), or in the correlations *so as, such as,* noting purpose or result: listen so *as* to hear; during the time that; while; because; though.—*prep.* Like; in the role or capacity of: He works *as* a salesman. —*pron.* A fact that: He studies hard, *as* his grades show; that, which, who: He hits the same way *as* I do. **—as yet,** until now; so far. **—as if,** as it would be if; also **as though.** **—as it were,** so to speak.

as·bes·tos, as·bes·tus, as·bes/təs, az·bes/təs, *n.* A fibrous, silicate mineral having fine, elastic filaments, which will not burn; fireproof cloth, paper, etc., made from asbestos.

as·cend, ə·send/, *v.i.* To climb or go upward; slope upward; go toward the source or beginning; go back in time.—*v.t.* To climb; mount. **—as·cend·ance,** *n.* **—as·cend·ence,** *n.* **—as·cend·an·cy, as·cend·en·cy,** *n.* **—as·cend·a·ble, as·cend·i·ble,** *a.*

as·cend·ant, as·cend·ent, ə·sen/dənt, *a.* Ascending; rising, esp. above the horizon; superior; dominant.—*n.* A position of controlling influence; the zodiac sign above the horizon at a given time.

as·cen·sion, ə·sen/shən, *n.* The act of ascending; (*cap.*) the bodily rising of Christ from earth to heaven. **—as·cen·sion·al,** *a.*

as·cent, ə·sent/, *n.* The act of rising; upward motion; rise in rank; an upward slope.

as·cer·tain, as·ər·tān/, *v.t.* To find out by trial or examination; to determine with certainty. **—as·cer·tain·a·ble,** *a.* **—as·cer·tain·ment,** *n.*

as·cet·ic, ə·set/ik, *n.* One who practices unusual or extreme self-denial, austerity, or devotion, especially for religious reasons.—*a.* Very self-denying; austere; rigorous. Also **as·cet·i·cal. —as·cet·i·cism,** *n.*

a·scor·bic ac·id, ə·skôr/bik, *n.* Vitamin C.

as·cot, as/kət, *n.* A wide neck scarf that is looped and knotted under the chin.

as·cribe, ə·skrīb/, *v.t.,* **as·cribed, as·crib·ing.** To attribute, as to a cause; to assign, as a quality or attribute. **—as·crib·a·ble,** *a.* **—as·crip·tion,** ə·skrip/shən, *n.*

a·sep·sis, ā·sep/sis, ə·sep/sis, *n.* Absence of microorganisms; prevention of infection.

a·sep·tic, ā·sep/tik, ə·sep/tik, *a.* Free from germs causing disease.

a·sex·u·al, ā·sek/shoo·əl, *a.* Not sexual; having no distinctive sex organs; without the union of males and females. **—a·sex·u·al·i·ty,** ā·sek·shoo·al/ə·tē, *n.* **—a·sex·u·al·ly,** *adv.*

ash, ash, *n.* (Often pl.) What remains of a completely burned material; a dust or powdery substance.

ash, ash, *n.* Tree grown widely for its tough, elastic timber; the timber.

a·shamed, ə·shāmd/, *a.* Feeling shame; exhibiting shame; deterred by fearing shame. **—a·sham·ed·ly,** *adv.*

ash·en, ash/ən, *a.* Of or made from the ash tree.

ash·en, ash/ən, *a.* Of or like ashes; pale; gray.

ash·lar, ash·ler, ash/lər, *n.* Squared building stone; a facing made of squared stones on the front of buildings; hewn stone for such facing.

a·shore, ə·shôr/, *adv., a.* On the shore; to the shore.

Ash Wed·nes·day, *n.* The first day of Lent.

ash·y, ash/ē, *a.,* **-i·er, -i·est.** Like ashes; pale, as ashes.

a·side, ə·sīd/, *adv.* On or to one side; apart; out of one's thoughts or regard: to lay cares *aside;* in reserve; in a separate place.—*n.* The lines of an actor heard by the audience but supposedly not by the other actors. **—a·side from,** *prep.* Besides; excluding.

as·i·nine, as/ə·nīn, *a.* Like an ass; stupid; obstinate; silly.

ask, ask, äsk, *v.t.* To request; to seek to get by words; to petition (with *of*); to require; to demand; to question; to inquire about; to seek to be informed about; to invite.—*v.i.* To make a request or petition (with *for*); to inquire (often followed by *after*). **—ask·er,** *n.*

a·skance, ə·skans/, *adv.* Sideways; with suspicion. Also **a·skant,** ə·skant/.

a·skew, ə·skū/, *adv., a.* In an oblique or skew position; obliquely; awry.

a·slant, ə·slant/, ə·slänt/, *adv.* At a slant; obliquely. —*prep.* Slantingly across; athwart.—*a.* Slanting.

a·sleep, ə·slēp, *a.,* *adv.* In or into a state of sleep; in a dormant state; sleeping; numb; dead.

a·slope, ə·slōp/, *a., adv.* Sloping; diagonally.

a·so·cial, ā·sō/shəl, *a.* Withdrawn; avoiding the company of others; selfish.

asp, asp, *n.* A deadly species of viper, esp. the Egyptian cobra; a species of viper found on the continent of Europe.

as•par•a•gus, ə•spar′ə•gəs, *n.* A yearly herb of the lily family grown for its edible young shoots; the shoots of this plant.

as•pect, as′pekt, *n.* Look; view; appearance to the eye or the mind; countenance; mien; air: a severe *aspect;* one side of a subject or object; view commanded; feature; prospect; outlook: a house with a southern *aspect;* any configuration of the planets.

as•pen, as′pən, *n.* A poplar whose leaves tremble in the slightest breeze.

as•per•i•ty, as•per′ə•tē, *n. pl.,* **-ties.** Roughness or harshness to the touch, taste, hearing, or feelings.

as•perse, ə•spərs′, *v.t.,* **as•persed, as•pers•ing.** To slander.

as•per•sion, ə•spər′zhən, ə•spər′shən, *n.* The spread of false and damaging reports; calumny; defamation, or a defamatory statement.

as•phalt, as′fôlt, as′falt, *n.* A black or brown substance which melts easily and has a strong pitchy odor; a mixture of asphalt and sand or other substances, used for pavements, floors, etc. **—as•phal•tic,** as•fôl′tik, as•fal′tik, *a.*

as•pho•del, as′fə•del, *n.* Any of various plants of the lily family, with white or yellow flowers.

as•phyx•ia, as•fik′sē•ə, *n.* Lack of oxygen or an excess of carbon dioxide in the blood, resulting in fainting or suffocation.

as•phyx•i•ate, as•fik′sē•āt, *v.t.,* **-at•ed, -at•ing.** To cause asphyxia in; suffocate.—*v.i.* To become asphyxiated. **—as•phyx•i•a•tion,** as•fik•sē•ā′shən, *n.*

as•pic, as′pik, *n.* A meat, fish, or tomato jelly.

as•pi•dis•tra, as•pə•dis′trə, *n.* An herb of the lily family, with large, glossy leaves.

as•pir•ant, as′pər•ənt, ə•spīr′ənt, *n.* One who aspires.—*a.* Aspiring.

as•pi•rate, as′pə•rāt, *v.t.,* **-rat•ed, -rat•ing.** To pronounce with a breathing outward, as the letter *h* in the word *horse;* to remove fluid from the lungs. —as′pər•ət, *n.* A sound made with outward breathing.

as•pi•ra•tion, as•pə•rā′shən, *n.* An aspirated sound; the act of aspiring; an ardent desire; the use of an aspirator.

as•pi•ra•tor, as′pə•rā•tər, *n.* A device that uses suction to remove fluids or gases from the body.

as•pire, ə•spīr′, *v.i.,* **as•pired, as•pir•ing.** To desire with eagerness; to aim at something elevated; to ascend. **—as•pir•er,** *n.*

as•pi•rin, as′pər•in, as′prin, *n.* A white crystalline derivative of salicylic acid used to relieve pain and reduce fever.

ass, as, *n.* A four-footed animal of the horse family, used as a beast of burden; a donkey; a dull, stupid fellow; a dolt.

as•sail, ə•sāl′, *v.t.* To fall upon with intent to harm; to set upon; assault; attack with arguments. **—as•sail•a•ble,** *a.* **—as•sail•ant,** *n.*

as•sas•sin, ə•sas′in, *n.* One who kills, esp. for money or because of fanatical beliefs; a murderer, esp. of a high-ranking political figure.

as•sas•si•nate, ə•sas′ə•nāt, *v.t.,* **-nat•ed, -nat•ing.** To kill by surprise or secret assault; to destroy treacherously. **—as•sas•si•na•tion,** ə•sas•ə•nā′shən, *n.* **—as•sas•si•na•tor,** *n.*

as•sault, ə•sôlt, *n.* An attack or violent onset, physical or verbal; a threat or attempt to injure a person; a sudden, strong attack on a fortified defense.—*v.t.* To make an assault.

as•say, ə•sā′, ə•sā′, *n.* Analysis of an alloy or ore to determine how much gold, silver, etc., is in it; the material to be analyzed; the results of the analysis; any trial or examination. —ə•sā′, *v.t.* To make an assay of.—*v.i.* To have a measurable content of precious metal as shown by an assay. **—as•say•er,** ə•sā′ər, *n.*

as•sem•blage, ə•sem′blij, *n.* The act of assembling;

a collection or gathering.

as•sem•ble, ə•sem′bəl, *v.t.,* **-bled, -bling.** To bring or call together; to convene; to fit together, as pieces of mechanism.—*v.i.* To come together; to congregate. **—as•sem•bler,** *n.*

as•sem•bly, ə•sem′blē, *n. pl.,* **-blies.** A collection of human beings in the same place, usually for the same purpose; the legislative body in various states. The fitting together of intricate machinery; a collection of machine parts; a signal for troops to form ranks.

as•sem•bly line, *n.* Production line along which operations are performed until the final product is completed.

as•sem•bly•man, ə•sem′blē•mən, *n. pl.,* **-men.** Member of a legislative assembly.

as•sent, ə•sent′, *n.* Consent; concurrence; agreement to a proposal;—*v.i.* To express agreement; to concur. **—as•sent•er,** *n.*

as•sert, ə•sərt′, *v.t.* To vindicate a claim or title to; to affirm positively; to aver; **—assert oneself,** to come forward and assume one's rights, claims, etc. **—as•ser•tion,** *n.* **—as•sert•er, as•sert•or,** *n.*

as•ser•tive, ə•sər′tiv, *a.* Positive; affirming confidently; peremptory. **—as•ser•tive•ly,** *adv.* **—as•ser•tive•ness,** *n.*

as•sess, ə•ses′, *v.t.* To set a certain sum, as a tax or fine, upon; to evaluate, as property, for taxation; to determine the amount of, as of damages. **—as•sess•a•ble,** *a.* **—as•sess•ment,** *n.* **—as•ses•sor,** *n.*

as•set, as′et, *n.* An item having value; a property; *pl.,* property available for the payment of a person's debts; a balance sheet showing property owned.

as•sev•er•ate, ə•sev′ə•rāt, *v.t.,* **-at•ed, -at•ing.** To affirm positively or with. **—as•sev•er•a•tion,** ə•sev•ə•rā′shən, *n.*

as•si•du•i•ty, as•ə•doo′ə•tē, as•ə•dū′ə•tē, *n. pl.,* **-ties.** The quality of being assiduous; constant application to any business.

as•sid•u•ous, ə•sij′oo•əs, *a.* Constant in application; devoted; diligent; unremitting. **—as•sid•u•ous•ly,** *adv.* **—as•sid•u•ous•ness,** *n.*

as•sign, ə•sīn′, *v.t.* To mark out as a portion allotted; to apportion; to fix or specify; to appoint; to refer or attribute; to transfer or make over to another.—*n.* An assignee. **—as•sign•a•bil•i•ty,** ə•sī•nə•bil′ə•tē, *n.* **—as•sign•a•ble,** *a.* **—as•sign•a•bly,** *adv.*

as•sig•na•tion, as•ig•nā′shən, *n.* An appointment for meeting: chiefly of illicit love meetings; an allotting; a legal assignment.

as•sign•ee, ə•sī•nē′, as•ə•nē′, *n.* A person to whom a legal assignment is made.

as•sign•ment, ə•sīn′mənt, *n.* An assigning; something assigned; a position or task to which one is appointed; the legal transfer of some property, right, claim, etc.

as•sim•i•late, ə•sim′ə•lāt, *v.t.,* **-lat•ed, -lat•ing.** To make alike; to cause to resemble; to absorb food into the system of a plant or animal; to liken or compare. —*v.i.* To become similar; to become incorporated with the body.**—as•sim•i•la•bil•i•ty,**ə•sim•ə•lə•bil′ə•tē,*n.* **—as•sim•i•la•ble,** *a.* **—as•sim•i•la•tion,** ə•sim•ə•lā′shən, *n.* **—as•sim•i•la•tive,** ə•sim′ə•lā•tiv, ə•sim′ə•lə•tiv, *a.* **—as•sim•i•la•tor,** *n.* **—as•sim•i•la•to•ry,** ə•sim′ə•lə•tôr•ē.

as•sist, ə•sist′, *v.i.* To give aid.—*v.t.* To aid; help; be associated with as assistant.—*n.* An act of assisting, as in making a goal in hockey or an out in baseball. **—as•sist•ance,** *n.*

as•sis•tant, ə•sis′tənt, *a.* Assisting; auxiliary.—*n.* A helper; an aid; an auxiliary.

as•size, ə•sīz′, *n.* (*Usu. pl.*) The sessions of court in English counties. An ordinance; an assessment.

as•so•ci•ate, ə•sō′shē•āt, ə•sō′sē•āt, *v.t.,* **-at•ed, -at•ing.** To adopt as a partner, companion, or the like;

---

a- hat, fâte, fāre, fäther; **e-** met, mē; **i-** pin, pīne; **o-** not, nōte, ôrb, moove (move), boy, pownd; **u-** cūbe, bûll, tûk (took); **ch-** chin; **th-** thick, +hen; **zh-** vizhon (vision); **ə-** əgo, takən, pencəl, lemən, bərd (bird).

to join intimately (things together); to connect mentally (ideas or feelings); to unite; to combine.—*v.i.* To unite in company; to join in a confederacy with others. —ə·sō′/shē·it, ə·sō′/sē·it, *a.* Joined in interest, object, office, etc.; combined; having subordinate rank or privileges.—*n.* A companion; an ally; a partner; a member with only partial privileges; an idea or feeling connected with another. —**as·so·ci·a·tion,** ə·sō·sē· ā′/shən, ə·sō·shē·ā′/shən, *n.* —**as·so·ci·a·tion·al,** *a.* —**as·so·ci·a·tive,** ə·sō′/shē·ā·tiv, ə·sō′/sē·ā·tiv, *a.*

as·so·ci·a·tion foot·ball, *n.* Soccer.

as·so·nance, as′/ə·nəns, *n.* Resemblance of sounds; an imperfect rhyme using the same vowel sound with different consonants following: lame, rain. —**as·so· nant,** *a.*

as·sort, ə·sôrt′, *v.t.* To separate and distribute into sorts, classes, or kinds; to furnish with a suitable variety; to adapt or suit.—*v.i.* To agree; to associate.

as·sort·ed, ə·sôr′/tid, *a.* Made up of various types; fitted or matched.

as·sort·ment, ə·sôrt′/mənt, *n.* A mixed collection of things.

as·suage, ə·swāj′, *v.t.*, **as·suaged, as·suag·ing.** To lessen pain or grief; to moderate; to appease passion or tumult. —**as·suage·ment,** *n.*

as·sume, ə·soom′, *v.t.*, **as·sumed, as·sum·ing.** To take upon oneself; to undertake; to appear in; to appropriate; to usurp; to take for granted; suppose; to pretend to possess; to put on.

as·sum·ing, ə·soo′/ming, *a.* Putting on airs of superiority; presumptuous.

as·sump·tion, ə·səmp′/shən, *n.* The act of assuming; thing assumed; arrogance; presumption; (*cap.*) a church festival celebrated August 15 in honor of the ascent to heaven of the Virgin Mary's body after death. —**as·sump·tive,** ə·sump′/tiv, *a.*

as·sur·ance, ə·shûr′/əns, *n.* The act of assuring; a pledge furnishing ground of full confidence; certain expectation; self-confidence; excess of boldness; impudence.

as·sure, ə·shûr′, *v.t.*, **as·sured, as·sur·ing.** To make (a person) sure or certain; to convince; to declare solemnly to; to ensure; to secure; insure. —**as·sur·er,** *n.*

as·sured, ə·shûrd′, *a.* Certain; bold to excess; confident; having life or goods insured (in this sense often a noun, sing. or pl.). —**as·sur·ed·ly,** *adv.* —**as·sur· ed·ness,** *n.*

as·ter, as′/tər, *n.* A large group of plants, with ray or tubular flowers, which somewhat resemble stars.

as·ter·isk, as′/tə·risk, *n.* A figure resembling a star (*), used in printing and writing, to indicate a footnote, omission, etc.—*v.t.* To note with an asterisk; to star.

a·stern, ə·stərn′, *adv.* At, or toward the stern of a ship; behind a ship; backward.

as·ter·oid, as′/tə·royd, *n.* One of the small planets that revolve about the sun mainly between the orbits of Mars and Jupiter; a starfish. Also **as·ter·oi·dal,** as·tə·roy′/dəl.

asth·ma, az′/mə, as′/mə, *n.* A chronic disorder of respiration, marked by difficulty in breathing.

asth·mat·ic, az·mat′/ik, as·mat′/ik, *a.* Pertaining to asthma.—*n.* A person troubled with asthma.

a·stig·ma·tism, ə·stig′/mə·tiz·əm, *n.* A defect of the eye or of a lens whereby rays of light from an external point fail to come to a sharp focus, thus giving rise to imperfect vision or images. —**as·tig·mat·ic,** as·tig· mat′/ik, *a.*

a·stir, ə·stər′, *adv., a.* Stirring; moving.

as·ton·ish, ə·ston′/ish, *v.t.* To impress with wonder or surprise; to amaze. —**as·ton·ish·ing,** *a.* —**as·ton· ish·ing·ly,** *adv.* —**as·ton·ish·ment,** *n.*

as·tound, ə·stownd′, *v.t.* To astonish; to shock; to amaze. —**as·tound·ing,** *a.*

a·strad·dle, ə·strad′/əl, *adv, a.* Astride.

as·tra·khan, as′/trə·kən, as′/trə·kan, *n.* Closely curled fur of young lambs from Astrakhan; a rough

cloth resembling it. Also **as·tra·chan.**

as·tral, as′/trəl, *a.* Starry.

a·stray, ə·strā′, *adv., a.* Having strayed; off the correct path; into error.

a·stride, ə·strīd′, *a., adv.* With one leg on each side.—*prep.* Above with a leg on either side of.

as·trin·gent, ə·strin′/jənt, *a.* Stern; severe; terse. Styptic; contracting the organic tissues of the body, and thereby checking bleeding.—*n.* An astringent substance, such as alum, etc. —**as·trin·gen·cy,** *n.*

as·tro·dome, as′/trə·dōm, *n.* An enclosed, climate-controlled arena for sporting events and other entertainment.

as·tro·labe, as′/trə·lāb, *n.* An instrument formerly used for taking the altitude of the sun or stars at sea.

as·trol·o·gy, ə·strol′/ə·jē, *n.* A supposed science which is concerned with the effect and influence of celestial bodies on human affairs. —**as·trol·o·ger,** *n.* —**as·tro·log·ic,** as·trə·loj′/ik, *a.* Also **as·tro·log·i· cal.** —**as·tro·log·i·cal·ly,** as·trə·loj′/ik·lē, *adv.*

as·tro·naut, as′/trə·nôt, *n.* A person who rides in a space vehicle; a traveler in interplanetary space.

as·tro·nau·tics, as·trə·nô′/tiks, *n. pl., but sing. in constr.* The science, skill, or activity of space travel. —**as·tro·nau·tic, as·tro·nau·ti·cal,** *a.* —**as·tro· nau·ti·cal·ly,** *adv.*

as·tro·nom·ic, as·trə·nom′/ik, *a.* Pertaining to astronomy. Enormous; exceedingly large. Also **as·tro· nom·i·cal.** —**as·tro·nom·i·cal·ly,** as·trə·nom′/ik·lē, *adv.*

as·tron·o·my, ə·stron′/ə·mē, *n.* The science that deals with the location, sizes, motions, and constitution of celestial bodies. —**as·tron·o·mer,** *n.*

as·tro·phys·ics, as·trō·fiz′/iks, *n. pl. but sing. in constr.* A branch of astronomy that treats of the chemical and physical properties of celestial bodies. —**as·tro·phys·i·cist,** as·trō·fiz′/ə·sist, *n.*

as·tute, ə·stoot′, ə·stūt′, *a.* Shrewd; sagacious; keen. —**as·tute·ly,** *adv.* —**as·tute·ness,** *n.*

a·sun·der, ə·sən′/dər, *adv., a.* Apart; into parts or pieces; separately.

a·sy·lum, ə·sī′/ləm, *n.* A sanctuary or place of refuge; any place of retreat and security; an institution which cares for the insane, the blind, the poor, etc.

a·sym·me·try, ā·sim′/ə·trē, *n.* Lack of symmetry. —**a·sym·met·ric,** ā·sə·met′/rik, **a·sym·met·ri·cal,** ā·sə·met′/rə·kəl, *a.* —**a·sym·met·ri·cal·ly,** *adv.*

at, at, *prep.* Showing position, state or location: in time (*at* first); in space (*at* home, *at* church); in occupation (*at* work, *at* prayer); in degree or condition (*at* best, *at* the worst); in effect (*at* the sight); in relation (*at* your command); in value (*at* a dollar a head); also, direction toward (fire *at* the target).—**at large,** at liberty; unconfined; also, generally; as a whole (the country *at large*).

at·a·vism, at′/ə·viz·əm, *n.* The resemblance of offspring to a remote ancestor; reversion to the original type. —**at·a·vist,** *n.* —**at·a·vis·tic,** at·ə·vis′/tik, *a.*

a·tax·i·a, ə·tak′/sē·ə, *n.* Irregularity in bodily functions; inability to coordinate voluntary muscular movements. —**a·tax·ic,** *a.*

at·el·ier, at′/əl·yā, *n.* A workshop; an artist's studio.

a·the·ism, ā′/thē·iz·əm, *n.* The disbelief in the existence of a God. —**a·the·ist,** *n.* —**a·the·is·tic,** ā·the· is′/tik, **a·the·is·ti·cal,** *a.* —**a·the·is·ti·cal·ly,** *adv.*

ath·er·o·scle·ro·sis, ath·ə·rō·sklə·rō′/sis, *n.* A disease in which an artery is dangerously narrowed by fatty deposits in the inner walls.

a·thirst, ə·thərst′, *a.* Thirsty; eager or longing (for).

ath·lete, ath′/lēt, *n.* One trained to exercises or games of agility and strength.

ath·lete's foot, *n.* Ringworm of the feet, a contagious disease caused by a fungus.

ath·let·ic, ath·let′/ik, *a.* Pertaining to athletes or such exercises as are practiced by athletes; strong; robust; active; vigorous.

ath·let·ics, ath·let′/iks, *n. pl., sing. or pl. in constr.*

Athletic exercises; sports such as tennis, rowing, boxing, etc. —**ath•let•i•cism**, ath•let′ə•siz•əm, *n.*.

at-home, at•hōm′, *n.* An informal reception of visitors at one's home.

a•thwart, ə•thwôrt′, *prep.* Across; from side to side of; across the line of a ship's course; in opposition to.—*adv.* In an opposing manner; perversely; across the course of.

a•tilt, ə•tilt′, *a.,adv.* At a tilt; tilted.

at•las, at′ləs, *n. pl.*, **at•las•es.** A collection of maps in a volume; a volume of tables illustrating some subject.

at•mos•phere, at′mə•sfēr, *n.* The whole mass of gases surrounding the earth or any heavenly body; the air; the air in a particular place; a unit of pressure equal to 14.69 pounds per square inch; general feeling, aura, environment. —**at•mos•pher•ic**, at•mə•sfēr′ik, *a.* —**at•mos•pher•i•cal**, *a.* —**at•mos•pher•i•cal•ly**, at•mə•sfēr′ik•lē, *adv.*

at•mos•pher•ics, at•mə•sfēr′iks, *n. pl.* Radio static; inflated statements, as by a government spokesman; double talk.

at•oll, at′ôl, at′ol, ə•tôl′, *n.* A ring-shaped coral island, surrounding or partly surrounding a central lagoon.

at•om, at′əm, *n.* The smallest particle of an element which can enter into a chemical combination without being changed or destroyed; a minute quantity. —**a•tom•ic**, ə•tom′ik, *a.* —**a•tom•i•cal**, *a.* —**a•tom•i•cal•ly**, ə•tom′ik•lē, *adv.*

a•tom•ic bomb, *n.* A bomb whose explosive power comes from the splitting of nuclei of atoms (plutonium, uranium) by bombardment with neutrons to release atomic energy. Also **at•om bomb, A-bomb.**

a•tom•ic clock, *n.* A very precise timing instrument that depends on the vibration frequency of atoms or molecules of certain substances.

a•tom•ic en•er•gy, *n.* Energy obtained from changes within the nucleus of an atom, as by controlled fission or fusion.

a•tom•ic num•ber, *n.* An integer that expresses the positive charge of the nucleus; the number of electrons outside the nucleus of a neutral atom and the number of protons in the nucleus.

a•tom•ic pile, *n.* A nuclear reactor.

a•tom•ic the•o•ry, *n.* The theory that all matter is composed of atoms; any of the theories of the structure of the atom.

a•tom•ic weight, *n.* The mass of an atom of any element according to a standard of comparison, hydrogen being assigned the atomic weight 1.

at•om•ize, at′ə•mīz, *v.t.*, **-ized, -iz•ing.** To reduce to atoms; to reduce to small particles or a spray.

at•om•iz•er, at′ə•mīz•ər, *n.* An apparatus for reducing a liquid into spray.

a•tom smash•er, *n.* Cyclotron.

a•to•nal•i•ty, ā•tō•nal′ə•tē, *n.* Absence of tonality; a system of tonality in which the tones and chords are not related to a central keynote. —**a•to•nal**, ā•tō′nəl, *a.* —**a•to•nal•ly**, *adv.*

a•tone, ə•tōn′, *v.i.*, **a•toned, a•ton•ing.** To make amends for sin or wrongdoing.

a•tone•ment, ə•tōn′ment, *n.* The act of atoning; amends; reconciliation. *Usu. cap.* The reconciliation of God with man through Christ. —**a•ton•er**, *n.*

a•top, ə•top′, *adv.* On or at the top.—*prep.* On the top of.

a•tri•um, ā′trē•əm, *n. pl.*, **a•tri•a**, ā′trē•ə, **a•tri•ums.** The entrance hall and usually the most splendid apartment of an ancient Roman house; a central open area at the core of a house; an auricle of the heart.

a•tro•cious, ə•trō′shəs, *a.* Extremely wicked, criminal, or cruel. *Informal.* Very bad; abominable. —**a•tro•cious•ly**, *adv.* —**a•tro•cious•ness**, *n.*

a•troc•i•ty, ə•tros′ə•tē, *n. pl.*, **-ties.** The state or quality of being atrocious; an atrocious deed.

at•ro•phy, at′rə•fē, *n. pl.*, **-phies.** A wasting away or shriveling up of the body or of an organ or part; degeneration.—*v.t.*, **-phied, -phy•ing.** To affect with atrophy.—*v.i.* To undergo atrophy. —**a•troph•ic**, ə•trof′ik, *a.*

at•ro•pine, at′rə•pēn, *n.* A very poisonous drug obtained from the deadly nightshade, used esp. to dilate the pupil of the eye and to ease spasms. Also **at•ro•pin**, at′rə•pin.

at•tach, ə•tach′, *v.t.* To cause to stick to; to fasten; to connect; to join as an adjunct; to assign or appoint; to attribute; to affix; to bind by affection; to seize by lawful authority.—*v.i.* To be attached or connected. —**at•tach•a•ble**, *a.* —**at•tach•ment**, *n.*

at•ta•ché, at•ə•shā′, *n.* One attached to an embassy or legation of his country in a foreign nation.

at•ta•ché case, *n.* A lightweight suitcase for carrying business papers.

at•tack, ə•tak′, *v.t.* To assault; to criticize severely; to assail; to undertake vigorously; to seize, as a disease. —*v.i.* To make an attack.—*n.* A falling on, with force or violence; an assault.

at•tain, ə•tān′, *v.t.* To reach by effort; to achieve; acquire, gain; reach.—*v.i.* To succeed in reaching (to). —**at•tain•a•ble**, *a.* —**at•tain•a•bil•i•ty**, ə•tān•ə•bil′ə•tē, *n.* —**at•tain•a•ble•ness**, *n.* —**at•tain•ment**, *n.*

at•tain•der, ə•tān′dər, *n.* The taking away of a person's property and civil rights when he is sentenced for a serious crime.

at•taint, ə•tānt′, *v.t.* To affect with attainder, to disgrace.—*n.*

at•tar, at′ər, *n.* A perfume from the petals of flowers, ɔ. roses.

at•tempt, ə•tempt′, *v.t.* To make an effort; to endeavor; to undertake; to try; to attack: to *attempt* someone's life.—*n.* An endeavor; an effort to accomplish something; an attack. —**at•tempt•a•ble**, *a.*

at•tend, ə•tend′, *v.t.* To accompany as a companion or servant; to be present at (church, a concert, etc.); to accompany as a result; to pay attention; to minister to; to apply oneself (to).—*v.i.* To pay regard or heed; to be present.

at•tend•ance, ə•ten′dəns, *n.* The act of attending; the persons, or number of persons, attending.

at•tend•ant, ə•ten′dənt, *a.* Accompanying; being present; immediately following.—*n.* One who accompanies another; an usher; a servant; a follower; one who is present; that which accompanies.

at•ten•tion, ə•ten′shən, *n.* The act of attending; the focusing of the mind upon something; heedfulness; care; military position of readiness, or the command to assume this position; *pl.*, acts of devotion of a suitor.

at•ten•tive, ə•ten′tiv, *a.* Paying attention; heedful; courteous; polite.

at•ten•u•ate, ə•ten′yoo•āt, *v.t.*, **-at•ed, -at•ing.** To make thin; make slender; reduce in density; to weaken; lower; reduce.—*v.i.* To become thin, slight, or weak. —**at•ten•u•a•tion**, ə•ten•yoo•ā′shən, *n.*

at•test, ə•test′, *v.t.* To bear witness to; to certify; to affirm to be true or genuine; to declare the truth of.—*v.i.* To bear witness (to). —**at•tes•ta•tion**, at•ə•stā′shən, *n.*

at•tic, at′ik, *n.* A space or room beneath the roof of a building; a garret.

at•tire, ə•tīr′, *v.t.*, **at•tired, at•tir•ing.** To dress; array; adorn.—*n.* Clothing; garb.

at•ti•tude, at′ə•tood, at′ə•tūd, *n.* Posture or position of a person; manner, emotion, or actions toward an object or person.

at•ti•tu•di•nize, at•ə•too′də•nīz, at•ə•tū′də•nīz, *v.i.*, **-nized, -niz•ing.** To assume affected attitudes, postures.

---

a- hat, fāte, fāre, fäther; e- met, mē; i- pin, pīne; o- not, nōte, ôrb, moove (move), boy, pownd; u- cūbe, bůll, tůk (took); ch- chin; th- thick, ŧhen; zh- vizhon (vision); ə- əgo, takən, pencəl, lemən, bərd (bird).

at·tor·ney, ə·tėr′nē, *n. pl.,* **-neys.** A legal agent who represents a client in legal affairs; a lawyer. —**at·tor·ney·ship,** *n.*

at·tor·ney at law, *n.* Lawyer.

at·tor·ney gen·er·al, *n.* The chief legal officer of a nation or state.

at·tract, ə·trakt′, *v.t.* To draw toward, either in a physical or mental sense; to cause to draw near by some influence; to invite; to entice; to win.—*v.i.* To exert the power of attraction. —**at·tract·a·ble,** *a.* —**at·trac·tive,** *a.* —**at·tract·or,** *n.*

at·trac·tion, ə·trak′shən, *n.* An attracting; a force by which all particles of matter are drawn toward each other; allurement; charm.

at·tri·bute, ə·trib′yūt, *v.t.,* **-but·ed, -but·ing.** To state or consider as belonging to; to ascribe; to impute. —*at′rə·būt, n.* Any property or characteristic that can be ascribed to a person or thing; a symbol of office or character added to any figure. —**at·tri·but·a·ble,** ə·trib′yə·tə·bəl, *a.* —**at·tri·bu·tion,** at·rə·bū′shən, *n.*

at·trib·u·tive, ə·trib′yə·tiv, *a.* Pertaining to or expressing an attribute; coming before the noun it qualifies.—*n.* A noun or adjective which modifies a noun immediately following: a *university* graduate.

at·tri·tion, ə·trish′ən, *n.* A wearing down or away by friction or by abuse, harassment, etc.; weakening.

at·tune, ə·tūn′, ə·toon′, *v.t.,* **at·tuned, at·tun·ing.** To tune; to bring into harmony or agreement.

a·typ·i·cal, ā·tip′ə·kəl, *a.* Not typical; irregular; abnormal. Also **a·typ·ic.** —**a·typ·i·cal·ly,** ā·tip′ik·lē, *adv.*

au·burn, ô′bėrn, *a., n.* Reddish-brown.

au cou·rant, ō·koo·rôn′, *a.* Up-to-date; aware of current happenings.

auc·tion, ôk′shən, *n.* A public sale of property to the highest bidder;—*v.t.* To sell by auction.

auc·tion·eer, ôk·shə·nēr′, *n.* One whose business it is to sell things by auction.

au·da·cious, ô·dā′shəs, *a.* Daring; bold; insolent; shameless. —**au·da·cious·ness,** *n.* —**au·dac·i·ty,** ô·das′ə·tē, *n.*

au·di·ble, ô′də·bəl, *a.* Capable of being heard. —**au·di·bil·i·ty,** ô·də·bil′ə·tē, *n.* —**au·di·ble·ness,** *n.* —**au·di·bly,** *adv.*

au·di·ence, ô′dē·əns, *n.* The act of listening; a hearing; opportunity of being heard; an assembly of hearers; formal interview with a high official; the people reached by a magazine, television show, etc.

au·di·o, ô′dē·ō, *a.* Relating to audible sound waves. —*n.* The sound portion of a television production.

au·di·o fre·quen·cy, ô·dē·ō frē′kwən·sē, *a.* Pertaining to audible frequencies of sound waves, from about 20 to 20,000 cycles per second.

au·di·o·vis·u·al, ô·dē·ō·vizh′oo·əl, *a.* Pertaining to moving pictures, charts, phonographs, etc., used as teaching aids.

au·dit, ô′dit, *n.* An official examination of accounts; a final statement or adjusting of accounts.—*v.t.* To make audit of; to enroll in a course of study without earning credit.

au·di·tion, ô·dish′ən, *n.* The act of hearing; a hearing; a trial performance to evaluate abilities.—*v.t., v.i.* To give an audition.

au·di·tor, ô′də·tər, *n.* A hearer; a listener; a person appointed to audit accounts; one who attends a class but who does not participate for credit.

au·di·to·ri·um, ô·də·tôr′ē·əm, *n.* In an opera house, public hall, etc., the space allotted to the audience; a building, hall, or large room used for public gatherings.

au·di·to·ry, ô′də·tôr·ē, *a.* Relating to hearing or to the organs of hearing.

au·ger, ô′gər, *n.* A tool for boring holes in wood, soil, etc.

aught, ôt, *n.* A zero.

aught, ôt, *adv.* In any respect; at all.—*n.* Anything.

aug·ment, ôg·ment′, *v.t.* To increase; to enlarge.

—*v.i.* To increase; to grow larger. —**aug·ment·a·ble,** *a.* —**aug·ment·er,** *n.* —**aug·men·ta·tion,** ôg′men·tā′shən, *n.* —**aug·ment·a·tive,** ôg·men′tə·tiv, *a.*

au grat·in, ō·grät′ən, ō·grat′ən, *a.* Cooked with grated cheese or crumbs.

au·gur, ô′gər, *n.* An ancient Roman priest who foretold future events by omens; a soothsayer; a prophet. —*v.i.* To conjecture, as from omens; to bode.—*v.t.* To conjecture; to predict; to forebode.

au·gu·ry, ô′gyə·rē, *n. pl.,* **-ries.** The art or practice of divination.

au·gust, ô·gəst′, *a.* Majestic. —**au·gust·ly,** *adv.* —**au·gust·ness,** *n.*

Au·gust, ô′gəst, *n.* The eighth month of the year, containing thirty-one days.

auk, ôk, *n.* Any of several short-winged, web-footed, diving sea birds of the upper Northern Hemisphere.

auld lang syne, ôld′lang′zīn′, *n.* Old times, esp. as fondly remembered.

au na·tu·rel, ō nä·tû·rel′, *a.* In a natural state; nude; plainly cooked.

aunt, änt, ant, *n.* A sister of one's father or mother; an uncle's wife.

aunt·y, aunt·ie, än′tē, an′tē, *n.* Familiar diminutive of **aunt.**

au·ra, ô′rə, *n. pl.,* **au·ras, au·rae,** ô′rē. A subtle influence or quality emanating from or surrounding a person or object; an exhalation.

au·ral, ô′rəl, *a.* Relating to the ear or hearing. —**au·ral·ly,** *adv.*

au·re·ate, ô′rē·it, *a.* Golden; brilliant.

au·re·ole, ô′rē·ōl, *n.* An illumination surrounding a holy person; a halo; a corona. Also **au·re·o·la,** ô·rē′ə·lə.

Au·re·o·my·cin, ô·rē·ō·mī′sin, *n. Trademark.* An antibiotic effective against certain diseases.

au re·voir, ō·rə·vwär′, *interj.* Goodby for now; farewell until we meet again.

au·ri·cle, ô′rə·kəl, *n.* The external ear; either of the two cavities in the heart which receive blood from the veins.

au·ric·u·lar, ô·rik′yə·lər, *a.* Pertaining to the ear or the sense of hearing, or to an auricle; shaped like the ear.

au·rif·er·ous, ô·rif′ər·əs, *a.* Yielding gold; containing gold.

au·ro·ra, ô·rôr′ə, ə·rôr′ə, *n.* The occasional emission of bands or streamers of light from the upper atmosphere seen esp. in the polar night sky. —**au·ro·ral,** *a.*

au·ro·ra aus·tral·is, ô·strä′lis, *n.* The aurora of the Southern Hemisphere.

au·ro·ra bor·e·al·is, bôr·ē·al′əs, *n.* The aurora of the Northern Hemisphere; the northern lights.

aus·cul·tate, ô′skəl·tāt, *v.t.,* **-tat·ed, -tat·ing.** To examine the internal organs by listening, as with a stethoscope. —**aus·cul·ta·tion,** ô·skəl·tā′shən, *n.*

aus·pice, ô′spis, *n. pl.,* **aus·pic·es,** ôs′pə·sēz, An augury from birds; an omen. *Usu. pl.* Support; protection; favorable influence.

aus·pi·cious, ô·spish′əs, *a.* Having omens of success; propitious; favorable; prosperous. —**aus·pi·cious·ly,** *adv.* —**aus·pi·cious·ness,** *n.*

aus·tere, ô·stēr′, *a.* Harsh; tart; sour; severe; severely simple; rigorous; stern. —**aus·ter·i·ty,** ô·ster′ə·tē, *n. pl.,* **-ties.**

aus·tral, ô′strəl, *a.* Southern.

Aus·tral·ian bal·lot, ô·strä′lyən, *n.* A ballot containing the names of all the candidates marked in seclusion by qualified voters.

au·then·tic, ô·then′tik, *a.* Reliable; being what it says it is; genuine; authoritative.

au·then·ti·cate, ô·then′tə·kāt, *v.t.,* **-cat·ed, -cat·ing.** To render or prove authentic; to give authority to by proof, attestation, etc.; to determine as genuine. —**au·then·ti·ca·tion,** ô·then·tə·kā′shən, *n.* —**au·then·tic·i·ty,** ô·then·tis′ə·tē, *n.* —**au·then·ti·ca·tor,**

n.

au•thor, ô′thər, *n.* The originator or creator of anything; the original writer of a literary work; an author's writings collectively.—*v.t.* To write or create (something).

au•thor•i•tar•i•an, ə•thôr•i•tãr′ē•ən, ə•thor•i•tãr′ē•ən, *a.* Favoring submission to authority as opposed to individual freedom.—*n.* **—au•thor•i•tar•i•an•ism,** *n.*

au•thor•i•ta•tive, ə•thôr′i•tā•tiv, ə•thor′i•tā•tiv, *a.* Having authority; proceeding from proper authority; peremptory; dictatorial. **—au•thor•i•ta•tive•ness,** *n.*

au•thor•i•ty, ə•thôr′ə•tē, ə•thor′ə•tē, *n. pl.,* **-ties.** Power or right to command or act; dominion; *pl.,* persons exercising power, esp. government officials; a reference source or expert in a field; a ruling; proof; credibility; assurance.

au•thor•ize, ô′thə•rīz, *v.t.,* **-ized, -iz•ing.** To give authority, or legal power to; to warrant; to sanction. empower. **—au•thor•i•za•tion,** ô•thər•ə•zā′shən, *n.* **—au•thor•iz•er,** *n.*

au•thor•ship, ô•thər•ship, *n.* The occupation of an author; the source from which a work comes.

au•to, ô′tō, *n. Informal.* Automobile.

au•to•bi•og•ra•phy, ô•tə•bi•og′rə•fē, ô•tə•bē•og′rə•fē, *n. pl.,* **-phies.** Biography or memoirs of a person's life written by himself. **—au•to•bi•og•ra•pher,** *n.* **—au•to•bi•o•graph•ic,** ô•tə•bi•ə•graf′ik, *a.* **—au•to•bi•o•graph•i•cal,** *a.* **—au•to•bi•o•graph•i•cal•ly,** *adv.*

au•toc•ra•cy, ô•tok′rə•sē, *n. pl.,* **-cies.** Supreme power held by a single person; the government or power of an absolute monarch; dictatorship.

au•to•crat, ô′tə•krat, *n.* An absolute ruler; one who assumes unlimited authority in any relation. **—au•to•crat•ic,** ô•tə•krat′ik, **au•to•crat•i•cal,** *a.* **—au•to•crat•i•cal•ly,** *adv.*

au•to•da•fé, ô•tō•də•fā′, ow•tō•də•fā′, *n. pl.,* **au•tos-da-fé,** ô•tōz•də•fā′, ow•tōz•də•fā′. A public ceremony, formerly held by the courts of the Inquisition at the execution of heretics condemned to the stake.

au•to•graph, ô′tə•graf, ô′tə•gräf, *n.* A person's own handwriting; an original manuscript or signature.—*v.t.* To write in one's own hand; to write one's signature on.

au•to•mat, ô′tə•mat, *n.* A restaurant having automatic compartments for serving articles of food to customers when they drop coins into a slot.

au•to•mat•ic, ô•tə•mat′ik, *a.* Predominantly or completely involuntary or reflexive; self-regulating, as machinery; acting independently of will, as certain muscular actions. In firearms, using the recoil force to eject the used cartridge shell, insert a new cartridge, and fire it.—*n.* An automatic firearm, or machine.

au•to•mat•ic gun, *n.* A rifle, pistol, or other firearm that after the first shot fires others in rapid succession.

au•to•mat•ic pi•lot, *n.* An electronic mechanism that automatically holds an aircraft to its course and maintains stability.

au•to•ma•tion, ô•tə•mā′shən, *n.* The technique of making an industrial machine, a production line, etc., operate more automatically, as through a succession of self-regulating machines.

au•to•mate, ô′tə•mat, *v.t., v.i.,* **-mat•ed, -mat•ing.** To control by automation; to convert to automation.

au•tom•a•tism, ô•tom′ə•tiz•əm, *n.* Automatic action; the functioning of the body, or of bodily organs or processes, either without external stimuli or without conscious will.

au•tom•a•ton, ô•tom′ə•ton, ô•tom′ə•tən, *n. pl.,* **-tons, -ta,** -tə. A self-acting machine; a mechanical contrivance which imitates the motions of living beings; a robot; a person who acts mechanically.

au•to•mo•bile, ô′tə•mə•bēl, ô•tə•mə•bēl′, ô•tə•

mō′bēl, *n.* A four-wheeled vehicle, esp. a car for passengers, carrying its own propelling mechanism, usu. an internal-combustion engine; a car. **—au•to•mo•bil•ist,** *n.*

au•to•mo•tive, ô•tə•mō′tiv, *a.* Self-moving or self-propelled; of automobiles.

au•to•nom•ic, ô•tə•nom′ik, *a.* Autonomous; relating to the autonomic nervous system. **—au•to•nom•i•cal•ly,** *adv.*

au•to•nom•ic ner•vous sys•tem, *n.* That part of the nervous system which innervates the blood vessels, heart, viscera, smooth muscles, and glands, and regulates involuntary actions.

au•ton•o•mous, ô•ton′ə•məs, *a.* Self-governing; independent; *biol.,* existing as an independent organism; *bot.,* spontaneous movements. **—au•ton•o•mous•ly,** *adv.*

au•ton•o•my, ô•ton′ə•mē, *n. pl.,* **-mies.** The condition of being autonomous; self-government, or the right of self-government; independence; a self-governing community. **—au•ton•o•mist,** *n.*

au•top•sy, ô′top•sē, ô′təp•sē, *n.* A post-mortem examination of a body, to determine the cause of death.

au•to•sug•ges•tion, ô•tō•səg•jes′chən, *n.* Suggestion by the mind to itself of ideas that produce actual or physical effects.

au•tumn, ô•təm, *n.* The third season of the year, or the season between summer and winter; a time of maturity or decline. **—au•tum•nal,** ô•təm′nəl, *a.*

au•tum•nal e•qui•nox, *n.* See **e•qui•nox.**

aux•il•ia•ry, ôg•zil′yər•ē, ôg•zil′ər•ē, *a.* Helping; subsidiary; supplementary; serving in reserve.—*n. pl.,* **-ries.** A helper or aid; a confederate; a group which is subordinate to another organization; *usu. pl.,* a foreign force helping a nation at war; a verb, as *have, will, be, may, do,* etc., which indicates tense, person, voice, and mood, and is used with participial forms of main verbs.

a•vail, ə•vāl′, *v.t.* To assist or profit; to benefit.—*v.i.* To be of use, benefit, or advantage.—*n.* Effective use in reaching one's goal: Arguing with her was to no *avail.*

a•vail•a•bil•i•ty, ə•vāl•ə•bil′i•tē, *n.* The state of being available; validity.

a•vail•able, ə•val′ə•bəl, *a.* Capable of being used; accessible; valid. **—a•vail•a•ble•ness,** *n.* **—a•vail•a•bly,** *adv.*

av•a•lanche, av′ə•lanch, av′ə•länch, *n.* A vast body of snow, ice, rock, or earth sliding down a mountain or over a precipice; something like an avalanche.—*v.i.,* **-lanched, -lanch•ing.** To slide or fall down in, or as in, an avalanche.

a•vant-garde, ə•vänt•gärd′, ə•vant•gärd′, *n.* The people with the newest ideas in any field, esp. artists or writers.—*a.* Belonging or pertaining to the avant-garde.

av•a•rice, av′ə•ris, *n.* A great desire to gain and possess wealth; covetousness. **—av•a•ri•cious,** av•ə•rish′əs, *a.* **—av•a•ri•cious•ly,** *adv.* **—av•a•ri•cious•ness,** *n.*

a•vast, ə•vast′, ə•väst′, *interj. Naut.* The order to stop, hold, cease, or stay.

av•a•tar, av′ə•tär, *n.* The incarnation of the Hindu deities; any incarnation.

a•ve, ä′vā, ä′vē, *interj.* Hail! Farewell!

A•ve Ma•ri•a, ä′vā mə•rē′ə, *n.* Title of the Latin version of the Hail Mary, a prayer to the Virgin used in the Roman Catholic Church.

a•venge, ə•venj′, *v.t.,* **a•venged, a•veng•ing.** To get even with by inflicting pain or evil on the wrongdoer; to deal punishment for (injury done).—*v.i.* To take vengeance. **—a•veng•er,** *n.*

av•e•nue, av′ə•noo, av′ə•nū, *n.* A passage; a way or opening for entrance; a wide, straight roadway or street; an alley or walk planted on each side with trees;

---

a- hat, fâte, fâre, fäther; **e-** met, mē; **i-** pin, pīne; **o-** not, nōte, ôrb, moove (move), boy, pownd;
u- cūbe, bůll, tûk (took); **ch-** chin; **th-** thick, ᵺen; **zh-** vizhon (vision); **ə-** ə̇go, takən, pencəl, lemən, bərd (bird).

means of access or attainment.

a·ver, ə·vər′, *v.t.* **a·verred, a·ver·ring.** To affirm with confidence; to assert; to verify or justify (a plea). **—a·ver·ment,** *n.*

av·er·age, av′rij, av′ə·rij, *n.* An arithmetic mean; a ratio of successful tries to total tries: batting *average;* a typical example of a group, class, etc.—*v.t.,* **-aged, -ag·ing.** To find the average of; to reduce to a mean sum or quantity; to have as an average or mean as.—*v.i.* To purchase or sell securities to maintain a more favorable average price for all one's holdings; amount on an average to.—*a.* Exhibiting a mean proportion; forming an average; typical; ordinary.

a·verse, ə·vərs′, *a.* Turned away from; opposed; unwilling; followed by *to.* **—a·verse·ly,** *adv.* **—a·verse·ness,** *n.*

a·ver·sion, ə·vər′zhən, *n.* Opposition or repugnance; antipathy; the cause of antipathy; disinclination; averting.

a·vert, ə·vert, *v.t.* To turn or to cause to turn off or away (the eyes, calamity, etc.); to prevent.

a·vi·ar·y, ā′vē·er·ē, *n. pl.,* **-ies.** A building or enclosure for live birds. **—a·vi·a·rist,** ā′vē·ə·rist, ā′vē·er·ist, *n.*

a·vi·a·tion, ā·vē·ā′shən, av·ē·ā′shən, *n.* The operation, design, or manufacture of airplanes.

a·vi·a·tor, ā′vē·ā·tər, *n.* One who engages in aviation; a pilot.

av·id, av′id, *a.* Eager; enthusiastic; greedy. **—a·vid·i·ty,** ə·vid′ə·tē, *n.* **—av·id·ly,** *adv.*

a·vi·on·ics, ā·vē·on′iks, av·ē·on′iks, *n. pl.* The application of electronic and electrical devices to airplanes, missiles, and spacecraft.

av·o·ca·do, av·ə·kä′dō, äv·ə·kä′dō, *n. pl.,* **-dos.** The edible, dark green or purple fruit of a small tree of tropical America and the West Indies; the avocado tree.

av·o·ca·tion, av·ə·kā′shən, *n.* A chosen spare-time occupation or hobby; a person's regular job or occupation.

a·void, ə·voyd′, *v.t.* To shun; to keep away from; to make void. **—a·void·a·ble,** *a.* **—a·void·ance,** *n.*

av·oir·du·pois, av·ər·də·poyz′, *n.* The ordinary system of weights in the U.S., in which 1 lb. contains 16 oz.

a·vouch, ə·vowch′, *v.t.* To affirm openly; to avow; to vouch for; to admit; to guarantee; to acknowledge.

a·vow, ə·vow′, *v.t.* To declare openly; to acknowledge; to confess; to own. **—a·vow·er,** *n.*

a·vow·al, ə·vow′əl, *n.* An avowing.

a·vowed, ə·vowd′, *a.* Open; declared; acknowledged.

a·vun·cu·lar, ə·vəng′kyə·lər, *a.* Pertaining to or like an uncle.

a·wait, ə·wāt′, *v.t.* To wait for; to look for or expect; to be in store for; to be ready for.—*v.i.*

a·wake, ə·wāk′, *a.* Not sleeping; alert.—*v.t.,* **a·woke, a·waked, a·wak·ing.** To rouse from sleep; arouse. —*v.i.* To become awake or alert.

a·wak·en, ə·wā′kən, *v.i., v.t.* To awake. **—a·wak·en·ing,** *n.*

a·ward, ə·wôrd′, *v.t.* To adjudge; to assign or decide judicially; to give as due; to give as a prize.—*n.* Judgment; decision; a prize. **—a·ward·a·ble,** *a.* **—a·ward·er,** *n.*

a·ware, ə·wār, *a.* Cognizant; informed; conscious: followed by *of.* **—a·ware·ness,** *n.*

a·wash, ə·wosh′, ə·wôsh′, *a., adv.* Even with, or just covered by water; washed over; washed about.

a·way, ə·wā′, *adv.* At a distance; apart; in another place; to a distance; without hesitation: Fire *away!;* out of one's keeping: give money *away;* out of existence: The sound faded *away;* on and on, continuously: He kept working *away.*—*a.* Not present at a place;

afar; on an opponent's grounds; not at home: an *away* game.

awe, ô, *n.* Dread or fear mingled with reverence; reverential fear.—*v.t.,* **awed, aw·ing.** To strike withawe; to deter by fear, reverence, or respect.

a·weigh, ə·wā′, *a.* Raised just clear of the bottom: said of an anchor.

awe·some, ô′səm, *a.* Inspiring awe; expressive of awe. **—awe·some·ly,** *adv.* **—awe·some·ness,** *n.*

awe·strick·en, ô′strik·ən, *a.* Impressed with awe. Also **awe·struck,** ô′strək.

aw·ful, ô′fəl, *a.* Dreadful; unpleasant; ugly; objectionable; inspiring with awe; filling with dread.

aw·ful·ly, ô′fəl·lē, *adv.* In an awful manner. *Informal.* Terribly; excessively; extremely. **—aw·ful·ness,** *n.*

a·while, ə·hwīl′, ə·wīl′, *adv.* For some time.

awk·ward, ôk′wərd, *a.* Lacking dexterity in the use of the hands or of instruments; bungling; clumsy; inconvenient; uncouth; unmanageable; hazardous; embarrassing. **—awk·ward·ly,** *adv.* **—awk·ward·ness,** *n.*

awl, ôl, *n.* A pointed instrument for piercing small holes in leather, wood, etc.

awn, ôn, *n.* The bristle of corn or grass, or any similar bristlelike part. **—awned,** *a.* **—awn·less,** *a.*

awn·ing, ô′ning, *n.* A canvas-covered frame or similar structure that shelters a window, deck, or the like from sun and rain.

AWOL, A.W.O.L., ā′wôl, *n., a., adv.* (*Sometimes l.c.*). *Informal.* Absent without leave.

a·wry, ə·rī′, *a., adv.* Turned or twisted toward one side; crooked.

ax, axe, aks, *n. pl.,* **ax·es.** An instrument with a bladed head attached to a handle, used for chopping, hewing, etc.—*v.t.,* **axed, ax·ing.** To cut, shape, or dress with an ax. *Informal.* To discharge; to fire; to remove. **—get the ax,** *informal,* to be removed from office or employment.

ax·i·al, ak′sē·əl, *a.* Pertaining to, forming, or located along an axis. **—ax·i·al·ly,** *adv.*

ax·i·ol·o·gy, ak′sē·ol′ə·jē, *n.* The study of values and value judgments.

ax·i·om, ak′sē·əm, *n.* A self-evident truth or proposition; an established or universally received principle. **—ax·i·o·mat·ic,** ak·sē·ə·mat′ik, *a.* **—ax·i·o·mat·i·cal,** *a.* **—ax·i·o·mat·i·cal·ly,** *adv.*

ax·is, ak′sis, *n. pl.,* **ax·es,** ak′sēz. A straight line, real or imaginary, that passes through a body and about which the body may, or actually does, revolve; a hypothetical line in reference to which a plane or solid figure is symmetrical; a reference line in a graph; a partnership or alliance, as between several nations.

ax·le, ak′səl, *n.* The bar, shaft, or the like, on which a wheel or wheels rotate; an axletree.

ax·le·tree, ak′səl·trē, *n.* A bar fixed crosswise with a rounded spindle at each end upon which a wheel rotates.

ay, aye, ā, *adv. Poet.* Ever; always.

aye, ay, ī, *interj.* Yes; yea.—*n.* An affirmative vote.

a·zal·ea, ə·zā′lyə, *n.* Any of certain flowering plants of the heath family, many of which are grown for their profuse, showy blooms.

az·i·muth, az′ə·məth, *n.* In air navigation, the angular distance in the horizontal plane measured clockwise from true north to a certain course. In celestial navigation, the angle at the zenith measured clockwise from true north to the vertical circle passing through the body. **—az·i·muth·al,** az·ə·məth′əl, *a.*

a·zo·ic, ə·zō′ik, ā·zō′ik, *a.* Pertaining to the period of geologic time before the first appearance of life on earth.

az·ure, azh′ər, ā′zhər, *a.* Sky blue.—*n.* The blue color of the sky; the name of several blue pigments; the sky.

B

B, b, bē, *n.* The second letter and the first consonant in the English alphabet.

baa, bä, ba, *n.* Bleating of a sheep.—*v.i.,* **baaed, baa·ing.**

bab·bitt, bab′it, *n.* Babbitt metal.

Bab·bitt met·al, *n.* An alloy of copper, tin, and antimony used for lining bearings.

bab·ble, bab′əl, *v.i.,* **-bled, -bling.** To utter words imperfectly or indistinctly; to make a continuous murmuring sound; to prate; to tell secrets.—*v.t.* To prattle; to blurt out.—*n.* Idle talk; senseless prattle; murmur, as of a stream.—**bab·bler,** *n.*

babe, bāb, *n.* An infant; a childlike or inexperienced person. *Informal.* A girl or woman.

ba·bel, bā′bəl, bab′əl, *n.* A scene of noise and confusion; a confusion of sounds. Also **Ba·bel.**

ba·boon, ba·boon′, *n.* Any of certain primates of Africa and Asia, having long muzzles like a dog.

ba·bush·ka, bə·bûsh′kə, bə·boosh′kə, *n.* A woman's headpiece made by folding a kerchief into a triangle.

ba·by, bā′bē, *n. pl.,* **ba·bies.** A very young child; an infant; a newborn animal; the youngest or smallest member of a family or group; one who acts in a childish manner. *Informal.* One's sweetheart; a woman or girl; a person or thing.—*a.*—*v.t.,* **ba·bied, ba·by·ing.** To care for carefully; to pamper.—**ba·by·hood,** *n.* —**ba·by·ish,** *a.*

ba·by-sit, bā′bē-sit, *v.i.,* **-sat, -sit·ting.** To take care of young children while the parents are away. —**ba·by-sit·ter,** *n.*

bac·ca·lau·re·ate, bak·ə·lôr′ē·ət, *n.* The degree of Bachelor of Arts; sermon addressed to a graduating class at commencement.

bac·ca·rat, bä′kə·rä, bak′ə·rä, *n.* A game of cards in which players bet against a banker.

bac·cha·nal, bä·kə·näl′, bak′ə·nəl, *a.* Characterized by intemperate drinking; riotous; noisy. Also **bac·cha·na·li·an,** bak·ə·nä′lē·ən, bak·ə·näl′yən.—*n.* A drunken feast or reveler.

Bac·cha·na·li·a, bak·ə·nä′lē·ə, bak·ə·näl′yə, *n. pl., sing. or pl. in constr.* A drunken orgy.

bac·chant, bak′ənt, *n.* A bacchanal.

bac·chan·te, bə·kan′tē, bə·kant′, bak′ənt, *n.* A female bacchanal.

bach, bach, *v.i. Informal.* To live by oneself as does a bachelor: *to bach it.*

bach·e·lor, bach′ə·lər, bach′lər, *n.* A man who is not married; one who has the first and lowest degree at a college or university. —**bach·e·lor·hood, bach·e·lor·ship,** *n.*

bac·il·lar·y, bas′ə·ler·ē, *a.* Relating to bacilli; rod-shaped.

ba·cil·lus, bə·sil′əs, *n. pl.,* **ba·cil·li,** bə·sil′ī. Any rod-shaped bacterium; a bacterium, esp. a pathogenic one.

back, bak, *n.* The rear part of the trunk; the region of the spine; the hinder part of the body in man and the upper in other animals; that which is behind or furthest from the face or front; the rear; the part which is least used or not used: the *back* of the hand; the part of a garment covering the back; a player positioned behind the front line in some games.—*v.i.* To move or go back; to move in a reverse direction.—*v.t.* To furnish with a back or backing; to support; to strengthen by aid; to wager in favor of; to endorse; to mount (a horse); to move backwards.—*a.* Belonging to the back; lying in the rear; remote; in a backward direction; overdue; originating at an earlier time: *back*

issues of a newspaper.—*adv.* To or toward the rear or the past; in restraint or hindrance; toward times or things past; again; in return; by reverse movement; in withdrawal. —**be·hind one's back,** in secret, or when one is absent. —**(in) back of,** behind. —**back down,** to give up; withdraw; abandon. —**back off,** to retreat. —**back out (of),** to abandon an undertaking; to break a promise. —**back up,** to move backward; to support; to cause a delay or form a bottleneck.

back·bite, bak′bīt, *v.t., v.i.,* **-bit, -bit·ten** or *informal* **-bit, -bit·ing.** To slander someone behind his back. —**back·bit·er,** *n.*

back·board, bak′bōrd, bak′bôrd, *n. Basketball.* The board to which the basket is attached.

back·bone, bak′bōn, *n.* The spine; the vertebral column; something resembling a backbone; the sturdiest part of something; decisive character; fortitude.

back·drop, bak′drop, *n.* A curtain serving as the background of a stage setting; the setting for an event.

back·er, bak′ər, *n.* One who supports another, esp. financially; one who bets on a contestant.

back·field, bak′fēld, *n.* In football, the players or positions behind the front line.

back·fire, bak′fīr, *n.* A premature explosion in the cylinder of an internal-combustion engine; an action that achieves an unexpected result opposite to its intended purpose.—*v.i.,* **-fired, -fir·ing.**

back·gam·mon, bak′gam·ən, bak·gam′ən, *n.* A game played by two persons upon a board with pieces, dice boxes, and dice; a victory in this game.

back·ground, bak′grownd, *n.* The part of a picture represented as farthest from the spectator; the ground behind another object or representation; the combination of happenings or conditions which existed previous to an event or phenomenon.—*n.* The set of influences and environmental development affecting an individual's personality; music or sound effects played during a play, movie, radio program, etc. —**in the background,** out of view.

back·hand, bak′hand, *n.* The hand turned backward in making a stroke, as in tennis; handwriting in which the upward slope of the letters is to the left.—*adv.* By means of a backhand.—*a.* Backhanded.

back·hand·ed, bak′han·dəd, *a.* With the back of the hand: a *backhanded* blow; marked by a backward slope, as handwriting; awkward; indirect; equivocal; insincere: a *backhanded* compliment.

back·ing, bak′ing, *n.* The back part of a thing; something behind anything to support or strengthen it; support of any kind; supporters collectively.

back·lash, bak′lash, *n.* Any sudden or violent reaction, esp. against some innovation seen as threatening one's traditional way of life; a tangle in fishing line which is wound around a casting reel.

back·log, bak′lôg, bak′log, *n.* An accumulated volume of stock, work, etc., awaiting processing or held in reserve; a large log located at the back of a hearth fire.

back or·der, *n.* An order set aside to be completed or filled in the future because goods are temporarily unavailable. —**back·or·der,** *v.*

back seat, *n.* An inferior position; the rear seat.

back·side, bak′sid, *n.* The back part of anything; the posterior or rump.

back·slide, bak′slīd, *v.i.,* **-slid; -slid** or **-slid·den; -slid·ing.** To slide back; to turn away from religion or morality. —**back·slid·er,** *n.*

back·spin, bak′spin, *n.* A reverse rotation on an object moving forward, as a ball.

---

a- hat, fāte, fāre, fäther; **e-** met, mē; **i-** pin, pīne; **o-** not, nōte, ôrb, moove (move), boy, pownd; **u-** cūbe, bûll, tûk (took); **ch-** chin; **th-** thick, ŧhen; **zh-** vizhon (vision); **ə-** əgo, takən, pencəl, lemən, bərd (bird).

back·stage, bak/stāj/, *adv.* In the dressing rooms; at the rear area of the stage.—*a.* Pertaining to the backstage area.

back·stairs, bak/stārz/, *a.* Indirect; underhand; secret: as *backstairs* gossip.

back·stay, bak/stā, *n.* A long rope or stay, extending from the top of a mast backward to the side of a ship.

back·stop, bak/stop, *n.* A barrier located behind a playing area to keep the ball from rolling away, as a wire screen.

back·stretch, bak/strech, *n.* That part of a race track furthest across the infield from the grandstand.

back·stroke, bak/strōk, *n.* A backhanded stroke; a swimming stroke executed on the back.

back talk, *n.* An impudent or disrespectful reply.

back·track, bak/trak, *v.i.* To retrace one's steps; to withdraw from a position, etc.

back·up, bak/əp, *n.* An item kept available to replace another item if it fails to perform satisfactorily; cessation of movement due to an obstacle.—*a.* Pertaining to a person or object available as a replacement: as, a *backup* crew for a space mission.

back·ward, bak/wərd, *adv.* Toward the back, rear, or past; with the back foremost; in the reverse of the usual or right way; retrogressively. Also **back·wards.** —*a.* Directed toward the back or the past; in reverse; returning; behind in time or progress; late; dull; retarded; reluctant; bashful.

back·ward·ness, bak/wərd·nis, *n.* Slow retardation.

back·wash, bak/wosh, bak/wôsh, *n.* The water thrown back by a boat's motor, oars, or the like; the results of an event.

back·wa·ter, bak/wô·tər, bak/wot·ər, *n.* Water turned or held back, as by a dam; ebbtide; backwash; a place which is isolated, stagnant, or backward.

back·woods, bak/wůdz, *n. pl., sing. or pl. in constr.* Woody districts which are unsettled or sparsely settled; a culturally unadvanced area. —**back·woods·man,** *n.*

ba·con, bā/kən, *n.* The back and sides of a hog salted, dried, and usu. smoked.

bac·ter·i·a, bak·tēr/ē·ə, *n. pl.* of **bac·ter·i·um.** Any of numerous widely distributed microscopic organisms having round, spiral, or rod-shaped bodies, which bring about fermentation and putrefaction, produce disease, etc. —**bac·te·ri·al,** *a.*—**bac·te·ri·al·ly,** *adv.*

bac·te·ri·cide, bak·tēr/ə·sīd, *n.* Anything capable of destroying bacteria. —**bac·te·ri·ci·dal,** bak·tēr·ə·sī/dəl, *a.*

bac·te·ri·ol·o·gy, bak·tēr·ē·ol/ə·jē, *n.* The branch of biology or medicine concerned with bacteria. —**bac·te·ri·ol·o·gist,** *n.* —**bac·te·ri·o·log·i·cal,** bak·tēr·ē·ə·loj/ə·kəl, *a.*

bac·te·ri·o·phage, bak·tēr/ē·ə·fāj, *n.* A bactericidal virus normally found in sewage or body products.

bac·te·ri·um, bak·tēr/ē·əm, *n. sing.* of **bac·ter·i·a.**

bad, bad, *a.,* **worse, worst.** The opposite of good; not coming up to a certain standard; wicked; immoral; debasing; ill; unwholesome or rotten; defective or insufficient; unfortunate; incompetent; disagreeable; worthless; severe; unsound.—*n.* That which is bad; the state of being bad.—**go to the bad,** to fall into bad company, bad ways, etc.

bad blood, *n.* Continued bad feelings between or among persons.

badge, baj, *n.* A mark, sign, token, etc., worn to indicate occupation, rank, membership, an award, etc.; a token; a symbol.—*v.t.,* **badged, badg·ing.** To mark or distinguish with a badge.

badg·er, baj/ər, *n.* Any of various burrowing mammals of Europe and North America; the fur of a badger.—*v.t.* To harass; torment; pester.

bad·i·nage, bad·ə·näzh/, bad/ə·nəj, *n.* Playful discourse; banter.

bad·land, bad/land,*n. pl.,* **-lands.** *Usu. pl.* A highly eroded, inhospitable area with little vegetation and many intricate rock formations.

bad·ly, bad/lē, *adv.* In a bad manner. *Informal.* Very much; greatly.

bad·min·ton, bad/min·tən, *n.* An outdoor game played with shuttlecocks, light rackets, and a high net.

Bae·de·ker, bā/də·kər, *n.* A guidebook.

baf·fle, baf/əl, *v.t.,* **-fled, -fling.** To elude; to foil, bewilder, or perplex; to frustrate; to thwart.—*n.* A plate or screen that regulates flow of a gas, liquid, etc. —**baf·fler,** *n.* —**baf·fling,** *a.*

bag, bag, *n.* A receptacle of leather, cloth, paper, etc., capable of being closed at the mouth; a sack; a pouch; a valise; a purse or moneybag; the contents of a bag; a sportsman's take of game, etc.; something resembling a bag; an animal sac; an udder; in baseball, a base. *Informal.* An unpleasant, often untidy female.—*v.i.,* **bagged, bag·ging.** To swell or bulge; hang loosely. —*v.t.* To cause to swell or bulge; put into a bag; kill or catch, as in hunting.

ba·gasse, bə·gas/, *n.* Sugarcane or sugar beets in a dry, crushed state after the juice has been extracted.

bag·a·telle, bag·ə·tel/, *n.* A trifle; a game similar to billiards.

ba·gel, bā/gəl, *n.* A leavened hard roll, glazed, and shaped like a doughnut.

bag·gage, bag/əj, *n.* Luggage; things required for a journey; the equipment of an army that is carried.

bag·gy, bag/ē, *a.,* **-gi·er, -gi·est.** Having the appearance of a bag; loose; puffy, as eyes.

bag·man, bag/mən, *n. pl.,* **-men.** A person who collects or distributes bribes or payoff money.

bagn·io, ban/yō, bän/yō, *n. pl.,* **-ios.** A house of prostitution; a brothel.

bag·pipe, bag/pīp, *n. Often pl.* A reed musical instrument consisting of a leather bag and pipes, played esp. in Scotland. —**bag·pip·er,** *n.*

ba·guette, ba·get/, *n.* A narrow, rectangularly cut gem.

bail, bāl, *v.t.* To empty (a boat) of water with a bucket or other utensil, usually used with *out.*—*v.i.* To free of water; to parachute from an airplane or other vehicle, used with *out.*

bail, bāl, *n.* The person or persons who procure the release of a prisoner by becoming surety for his appearance in court; an amount guaranteed for a prisoner's release.—*v.t.* To free from arrest by giving bail. —**bail·a·ble,** *a.*

bail, bāl, *n.* The hoop-shaped handle of a kettle or pail; any hoop-shaped support.

bail·iff, bā/lif, *n.* A sheriff's deputy; a court officer who has custody of a prisoner in court, and who also acts as a messenger or usher. *Chiefly Brit.* The overseer of an estate; the chief magistrate of certain districts.

bail·i·wick, bā/li·wik, *n.* The district in which a bailiff has jurisdiction; a person's area of influence or authority.

bails·man, bālz/mən, *n. pl.,* **-men.** One who gives bail for another.

bait, bāt, *n.* Any substance used as a lure to catch fish or other animals; an allurement; enticement.—*v.t.* To furnish with bait; to lure; to use dogs to provoke a bull or a bear; to annoy; to persecute.

baize, bāz, *n.* A thick woolen fabric with a nap, used as a billiard table cover.

bake, bāk, *v.t.,* **baked, bak·ing.** To cook (food) by dry heat as in an oven; harden bricks, pottery, etc., by heat.—*v.i.* To bake bread, etc.; to become baked.

Ba·ke·lite, bā/kə·līt, bāk/līt, *n. Trademark.* A hard, non-inflammable synthetic material having many uses.

bak·er, bā/kər, *n.* One whose occupation is to bake food; a small portable oven.

bak·er's doz·en, *n.* Thirteen.

bak·er·y, bā/kə·rē, *n. pl.,* **-ies.** A place for baking bread and cakes; a store which sells baked products. Also **bake·shop.**

bak·ing pow·der, *n.* A mixture of baking soda and an acid substance, used as a leavening agent.

bak·ing so·da, *n.* Sodium bicarbonate.

bak·sheesh or **bak·shish,** bak'shēsh, *n.* In Turkey, India, etc., a tip, a gift, or alms; a bribe.

bal·a·lai·ka, bal·ə·lī'kə, *n.* A Russian musical instrument like a guitar.

bal·ance, bal'əns, *n.* An instrument for weighing, typically a bar swaying on a central support according to the weights borne in scales suspended at the ends: hence, power to decide as by a balance; authoritative control; a balance wheel; a condition in which the weights in a balance are equal; a state of equilibrium or equipoise; harmonious arrangement, esp. in design; mental stability; composure; something used to produce equilibrium; an act of balancing; comparison as to weight, amount, etc.; estimate; the excess of either side, debit or credit, of an account over the other; the remainder; equality between the totals of the two sides of an account; a balancing movement in dancing.—*v.t.,* **-anced, -anc·ing.** To weigh in or as in a balance; ponder over; compare as to relative weight, value, importance, etc.; bring to or hold in equilibrium; poise; adjust evenly; to be proportionate to; offset; reckon up, adjust, or settle, as accounts.—*v.i.* To be in equilibrium; be even; sway; waver. —**bal·ance·a·ble,** *a.* —**bal·anc·er,** *n.*

bal·ance of pow·er, *n.* An equilibrium of power among nations so that one nation or a coalition cannot endanger the sovereignty of any other.

bal·ance of trade, *n.* The difference in value between the exports and the imports of a country.

bal·ance sheet, *n.* An itemized statement showing the financial condition of a corporation as of a specific date.

bal·ance wheel, *n.* A wheel in a watch which regulates its motion.

bal·brig·gan, bal·brig'ən, *n.* A knitted cotton fabric used esp. for underwear and hosiery.

bal·co·ny, bal'kə·nē, *n. pl.,* **-nies.** A platform projecting from the upper wall of a building, with a railing around it; a projecting gallery in the interior of a building, as of a theater.

bald, bôld, *a.* Having no hair on the head; lacking the natural or usual covering; unadorned; unconcealed; marked with white. —**bald·ly,** *adv.*—**bald·ness,** *n.*

bald ea·gle, *n.* The white-headed eagle of North America.

bal·der·dash, bôl'dər·dash, *n.* Senseless talk; nonsense.

bald·head, bôld'hed, *n.* A person bald on the head; a member of a certain breed of domestic widgeons. Also **bald·pate.**

bal·dric, bôl'drik, *n.* A broad belt, stretching from the shoulder diagonally across the body, either as an ornament or to support a sword or horn.

bale, bāl, *n.* A bundle of goods usually bound with cord or wire.—*v.t.,* **baled, bal·ing.** To make into a bale.

ba·leen, bə·lēn', *n.* Whalebone.

bale·ful, bāl'fəl, *a.* Destructive; foreboding; portending evil. —**bale·ful·ly,** *adv.*

balk, bôk, *n.* A miss, slip, or failure; an illegal motion of a baseball pitcher, as if to pitch; a check or hindrance; a large beam or timber; a ridge between furrows.—*v.t.* To miss; to hinder, thwart, or foil.—*v.i.* To stop short and stubbornly refuse to go on. —**balk·er,** *n.*

bal·kan·ize, bôl'kə·nīz, *v.t.,* **-ized, -iz·ing.** *(Often cap.)* To partition, as an area, into various small, often hostile units. —**bal·kan·i·za·tion,** bôl·kə·nə·zā'shən, *n.*

balk·y, bô'kē, *a.,* **-i·er, -i·est.** Apt to balk, as a horse or mule.

ball, bôl, *n.* A spherical body; a sphere; a globe; a round or roundish body, often inflated, for use in various games; such a ball in play or action; a baseball pitched too high or too low or not over the plate, and not struck at by the batter; a game played with a ball, esp. baseball; any rounded mass; any rounded part of a thing that sticks out, esp. the palm; the earth.—*v.t.* To form or make into a ball. —**get the ball roll·ing,** *informal,* to initiate activity.—**have a ball,** to enjoy oneself greatly. —**on the ball,** *informal,* alert; able; knowledgeable. —**play ball,** to start or resume a ball game, *informal,* to cooperate.—**to ball up,** to ruin by blundering; to confuse.

ball, bôl, *n.* A large, formal gathering for dancing.

bal·lad, bal'əd, *n.* Any light, simple song, esp. one of sentimental character, having two or more stanzas sung to the same melody; a narrative poem, of popular origin, composed in short stanzas.

bal·lade, bə·läd', ba·läd', *n.* A type of fixed verse form; a romantic, dramatic, or epic musical composition, esp. for piano.

bal·lad·ry, bal'ə·drē, *n.* Ballad poetry.

ball-and-sock·et joint, bôl'ən·sok'it, *n.* A joint which allows, within limits, rotary movement in every direction.

bal·last, bal'əst, *n.* Heavy matter, as stone, sand, or iron carried in the bottom of a ship or car of a balloon to steady it; gravel or crushed stone beneath the crossties on a railroad in order to make it firm and solid; that which confers stability on a person.—*v.t.* To place ballast in or on; to steady.

ball bear·ing, *n.* A bearing in which the shaft turns upon a number of steel balls running in a track; any of the steel balls so used.

bal·le·ri·na, bal·ə·rē'nə, *n.* A female ballet dancer.

bal·let, ba·lā', bal'ā, *n.* An elaborate dance in which usually a story is told by gesture, accompanied by dancing, scenery, etc.; the dancers.

bal·lis·tic mis·sile, *n.* Any missile controlled in the upward part of its trajectory, but becoming a free-falling body in its descent.

bal·lis·tics, bə·lis'tiks, *n. pl., but sing. in constr.* The study of the behavior of missiles or projectiles in flight. —**bal·lis·tic,** *a.* —**bal·lis·ti·cian,** bal·əs·tish'ən, *n.*

bal·loon, bə·loon', *n.* A large airtight bag filled with a gas lighter than air causing it to rise and float in the atmosphere, and often fitted with a basket for carrying passengers or scientific equipment. A small, inflatable rubber bag used as a toy.—*v.t.* To fill with air or inflate.—*v.i.* To go aloft in a balloon; to expand; to grow rapidly.

bal·lot, bal'ət, *n.* A paper, slip, etc., used to cast a vote in a secret election; action or system of voting by marking a ballot or using a voting machine; the whole number of votes cast or recorded; the right to vote. —*v.t.* To vote on by ballot.—*v.i.,* **-lot·ed, -lot·ing.**

bal·lot box, *n.* The container for voters' ballots.

ball·point pen, bôl'poynt, *n.* A pen with a tiny steel ball as a writing point, inked by rotating against a cartridge of ink. Also **ball-point pen.**

ball·room, bôl'room, *n.* A large room for balls or dancing.

bal·ly·hoo, bal'ē·hoo, *n. Informal.* Blatant advertising or publicity; clamor or outcry, —*v.i., v.t.,* **-hooed, -hoo·ing.** *Informal.* To use or advertise by ballyhoo.

balm, bôm, *n.* Any of various oily, fragrant, sticky substances, often of medicinal value, seeping from certain plants; a plant or tree yielding such a substance; any of various aromatic plants resembling mint; an aromatic or fragrant ointment; anything that heals or soothes.

balm of Gil·e·ad, *n.* A fragrant ointment gotten from a small Asian evergreen tree; the balsam poplar; the balsam fir.

balm·y, bä'mē, *a.,* **-i·er, -i·est.** Aromatic; fragrant; healing; soothing. *Informal.* Silly, crazy, or foolish.

—**balm·i·ly,** *adv.* —**balm·i·ness,** *n.*

ba·lo·ney, bə·lō′nē, *n. Informal.* Nonsense; bologna sausage. Also **bo·lo·ney.**

bal·sa, bôl′sə, bäl′sə, *n.* A tree of tropical America, which has a very light wood used esp. for toys and rafts; a raft made of balsa wood; the wood.

bal·sam, bôl′səm, *n.* Any of various fragrant drippings from certain trees; balm; an oleoresin; a plant or tree yielding a balsam including the balsam poplar and balsam fir of North America; a common garden plant; any aromatic ointment; any healing or soothing agent. —**bal·sam·ic,** bôl·səm′ik, *a.*

bal·us·ter, bal′ə·stər, *n.* A small pillar supporting the rail of a balustrade.

bal·us·trade, bal′ə·strād, *n.* A row of balusters, joined by a rail.

bam·bi·no, bam·bē′nō, *n. pl.,* **-ni,** -nē, **-nos.** A child or baby; an image of the infant Jesus.

bam·boo, bam·boo′, *n.* A woody tropical plant of the grass family; the hollow, jointed stem of this plant, used for building, for furniture, and for fishing poles.

bam·boo·zle, bam·boo′zəl, *v.t.,* **-zled, -zling.** *Informal.* To impose upon; to hoax; to humbug; to perplex. —**bam·boo·zler,** *n.*

ban, ban, *v.t.,* **banned, ban·ning.** To prohibit; interdict; bar.—*n.* An authoritative prohibition or interdiction; censure; prohibition, as by public opinion; a sentence of outlawry.

ba·nal, bān′əl, bə·nal′, bə·näl′, ban′əl, *a.* Hackneyed, commonplace, or trite. —**ba·nal·i·ty,** bə·nal′ə·tē, *n.*

ba·nan·a, bə·nan′ə, *n.* A herbaceous plant extensively cultivated in tropical countries for its long, pulpy, usu. yellow fruit; the fruit of this plant.

band, band, *n.* A company or group of persons united by some common bond; a troop; a gang; a body of instrumental musicians, esp. one using wind and percussion instruments only.—*v.t.* To unite in a band.

band, band, *n.* A fetier or similar fastening; a narrow strip or ribbon-shaped ligature, tie, or connection; a division of a long-playing record; a fillet; a border or strip on an article of dress; the linen ornament about the neck of a clergyman. In radio broadcasting, a range of frequencies within two definite limits.—*v.t.* To tie up with a band; to mark with a band.

band·age, ban′dij, *n.* A strip of cloth or gauze used in dressing and binding up wounds, etc.—*v.t.,* **-aged, -ag·ing.** To dress, as a wound; apply a bandage to.

Band·aid, band′ād, *n. Trademark.* A small bandage with adhesive, used to protect small cuts and other minor injuries.

ban·dan·a, ban·dan·na, ban·dan′ə, *n.* A large, colorfully printed kerchief.

ban·deau, ban·dō′, ban′dō, *n. pl.,* **-deaux,** -dōz′, -dōz. A band worn about the head; a fillet; a brassiere.

ban·de·role, ban·de·rol, ban′də·rōl, *n.* A little flag or streamer.

ban·dit, ban′dit, *n. pl.,* **-dits, -dit·ti,** -dit′ē. An outlaw; a robber; a highwayman. —**ban·dit·ry,** *n.*

band·mas·ter, band′mas·tər, band′mä·stər, *n.* Conductor of a musical band.

ban·do·leer, ban·do·lier, ban·də·lēr′, *n.* A shoulder belt carrying cartridges.

band saw, *n.* A power saw consisting of a flexible toothed belt of steel revolving on pulleys.

band shell, *n.* A bandstand with a concave rear wall to improve the sound for the audience.

bands·man, bandz′mən, *n. pl.,* **-men.** A player in a band.

band·stand, band′stand, *n.* A usually roofed platform for musical bands.

band·wag·on, band′wag·ən, *n.* A wagon carrying a musical band in a parade. *Informal.* A party, candidate, or cause which appears destined for assured success: He jumped on the party *bandwagon.*

ban·dy, ban′dē, *v.t.,* **-died, -dy·ing.** To bat back and **forth,** as a ball in play; to toss from one to another; to

exchange (words, compliments).—*a.* Bent; bowed: said of a person's legs.

ban·dy-leg·ged, ban′dē·leg·id, ban′dē·legd, *a.* Having bandy legs; bowlegged.

bane, bān, *n.* Any cause of mischief or destruction; ruin; curse; deadly poison.

bane·ful, bān′fəl, *a.* Destructive; pernicious. —**bane·ful·ness,** *n.*

bang, bang, *v.t.* To beat noisily, as with a club; thump; cudgel; beat or handle roughly; bring a sudden loud noise from, as in slamming a door.—*v.i.* To resound with or produce a loud noise; to thump violently.—*n.* A loud, sudden sound; a heavy blow; a sudden spurt of energy. *Informal.* A thrill.—*adv.* With a bang; suddenly and loudly; abruptly.

bang, bang, *n. Usu. pl.* A fringe of hair cut straight across the forehead.—*v.t.* To cut short and straight across.

ban·gle, bang′gəl, *n.* An ornamental bracelet or anklet.

ban·ish, ban′ish, *v.t.* To condemn to leave a country; to exile; to drive away; to expel. —**ban·ish·er,** *n.* —**ban·ish·ment,** *n.*

ban·is·ter, ban·nis·ter, ban′ə·stər, *n.* A baluster; an upright in a stair rail; a handrail.

ban·jo, ban′jō, *n.* A musical instrument having five or six strings, a body like a tambourine, and a neck like a guitar.

bank, bangk, *n.* A mound or heap of earth; a mass of clouds or fog; any steep acclivity; the rising ground in the sea; a shoal; lateral tilt of an airplane.—*v.t.* To border with or like a bank; embank; to raise in a bank; heap (*up*); to cover (a fire) with ashes, so that it will burn long and slowly; to rebound (a billiard ball) off a cushion; to make an upward lateral slope in a curve of a road; to incline (an airplane) laterally, usually when making a turn.—*v.i.* To rise in or form banks; to bank an airplane.

bank, bangk, *n.* An establishment for the deposit, custody, sending, lending, and issue of money; the office in which these transactions are conducted; the funds of a gaming establishment; a fund in certain card games; a place where reserve supplies are kept. —*v.i.* To bank; to operate a bank; do business with a bank. —**bank on,** *informal,* to rely on; be sure of. —**bank·a·ble,** *a.*

bank, bangk, *n.* A bench, platform, or table; a tier or row of objects; a row of keys as on an organ or typewriter; part of a headline.

bank·book, bangk′bûk, *n.* Passbook.

bank·er, bang′kər, *n.* One engaged in the business of banking; player who keeps the bank in a gambling game.

bank·ing, bangk′ing, *n.* The business or profession of a banker.

bank note, *n.* A promissory note issued by a bank and payable on demand, serving as currency.

bank·roll, bangk′rōl, *n.* All the money that one possesses.—*v.t. Informal.* To finance.

bank·rupt, bangk′rəpt, *n.* A business or a person who is adjudged insolvent by a court, and whose property is administered for and divided among his creditors; one who is destitute or hopelessly in debt.—*a.* Legally adjudged unable to pay one's debts; insolvent.—*v.t.* To make bankrupt. —**bank·rupt·cy,** *n. pl.,* **-cies.**

ban·ner, ban′ər, *n.* A piece of cloth with a design or words on it, attached by one side to the upper part of a pole or staff; a flag; type running the width of the page.—*a.* Leading; foremost.

ban·nis·ter, ban′i·stər, *n.* Banister.

banns, banz, *n. pl.* An announcement of a proposed marriage, made in a church or other prescribed place.

ban·quet, bang′kwit, *n.* An elegant feast; a formal dinner followed by speeches.—*v.t.* To treat with a banquet.—*v.i.* To feast. —**ban·quet·er,** *n.*

ban·quette, bang·ket′, *n.* A platform or bank running along the inside of a parapet; *esp. South.,* a sidewalk;

a long upholstered bench.

ban·shee, ban/shē, *n.* In Gaelic folklore, a female spirit whose wailing foretells a death in the family.

ban·tam, ban/təm, *n.* A tiny domestic fowl of any or varied breeds; a small person of quarrelsome nature.

ban·tam·weight, ban/təm-wāt, *n.* A boxer who weighs between 113 and 118 lbs.

ban·ter, ban/tər, *n.* Humorous and good-natured raillery; joking.—*v.t.* To address humorous banter to.—*v.i.* To speak teasingly. **—ban·ter·er,** *n.* **—ban·ter·ing·ly,** *adv.*

ban·yan, ban·ian, ban/yen, *n.* An Indian fig tree remarkable for its horizontal branches sending down shoots which take root and form secondary trunks.

ban·zai, bän·zī/, bän/zī, *interj.* A Japanese cheer, battle cry, greeting, etc. It means "(May you live) ten thousand years!"

ba·o·bab, bā/ō-bab, bä/ō-bab, *n.* A large African tree with a very thick trunk, bearing a pulpy fruit.

bap·tism, bap/tiz-əm, *n.* A sacramental or ritual ceremony signifying purification and initiation into a Christian church, usu. accomplished by immersion in or sprinkling of water; any experience which initiates or sanctifies. **—bap·tis·mal,** bap·tiz/məl, *a.*

bap·tist, bap/tist, *n.* One who baptizes; (*cap.*) a member of a Christian denomination which maintains that baptism, usually implying immersion, can be administered only upon a personal profession of Christian faith.—*a.* (*cap.*) Of or pertaining to Baptists.

bap·tis·ter·y, bap/tis-trē, bap/tis-tə-rē, *n. pl.,* **-ies.** A building or part of a church in which baptism is administered.

bap·tize, bap-tīz/, bap/tīz, *v.t., v.i.,* **-tized, -ti·zing.** To administer baptism to; to purify; to dedicate; to christen.

bar, bär, *n.* A relatively long and evenly-shaped piece of some solid substance; esp. such a piece of wood or metal used as a guard or obstruction; any barrier or obstruction; a bank of sand, etc., in water; a railing enclosing the space occupied by counsel in a court of justice; the legal profession; the place in court where prisoners are stationed; any tribunal; a counter or a place where liquor is served to customers; a band or stripe. *Mus.* A vertical line marking off a measure on the staff; also, the measure. The metal part of a horse's bit.—*v.t.,* **barred, bar·ring.** To provide, fasten, or obstruct with a bar or bars; shut in or out by bars; to block; hinder; debar; exclude; to mark with bars, stripes, or bands.—*prep.* Barring; except: *bar* none.

barb, bärb, *n.* A beard-like growth or part; a point projecting backward from a main point, as of a fishhook or an arrowhead; a sharply critical remark.—*v.t.* To furnish with a barb or barbs.

bar·bar·i·an, bär-bâr/ē-ən, *n.* A person, esp. a foreigner, who belongs to a primitive civilization; an uncivilized person; a cruel, savage man.—*a.*

bar·bar·ic, bär-bar/ik, *a.* Pertaining to a barbarian; uncivilized; savage; ornate; bizarre.

bar·ba·rism, bär/bə-riz-əm, *n.* An uncivilized state; rudeness of manners; an act of barbarity; any form of speech contrary to accepted standards.

bar·bar·i·ty, bär-bar/i-tē, *n. pl.,* **-ties.** The state of being barbarous; a barbarous act; barbaric taste or style.

bar·ba·rize, bär/bə-rīz, *v.t.,* **-ized, -iz·ing.** To make or become barbarous, as language. **—bar·bar·i·za·tion,** bär·bə-rə-zā/shən, *n.*

bar·ba·rous, bär/bə-rəs, *a.* Unacquainted with arts and civilization; rude and ignorant; barbaric; cruel; fierce; (of language) filled with barbarisms.

Bar·ba·ry ape, bär/bə-rē, *n.* A tailless, easily-tamed monkey of Gibraltar and northern Africa.

bar·be·cue, bär/bə-kū, *n.* A social gathering where meats are roasted or broiled over an open fire; a lamb, pig, or other large animal cooked in this fashion; a metal grill, wooden framework, etc. for such cooking. **—***v.t.,* **-cued, -cu·ing.** To broil or roast (food) outdoors over an open fire; to prepare in a well-seasoned sauce.

barbed, bärbd, *a.* Furnished with a barb or barbs, as a fishhook; sharp; piercing.

barbed wire, *n.* Fence wire having sharp points at short intervals. Also **barb·wire,** bärb/wīr.

bar·ber, bär/bər, *n.* One whose occupation is to shave beards or to cut and dress hair.—*v.t.* To shave or trim and dress the hair and beard of (men).

bar·ber·ry, bär/ber-ē, bär/bə-rē, *n. pl.,* **-ries.** A shrub bearing small red berries; the berry.

bar·ber·shop, bär/bər-shop, *n.* The place where a barber does his work of cutting hair, etc.

bar·bi·tal, bär/bi-tal, bär/bi-tôl, *n.* A drug containing barbituric acid, used as a hypnotic and sedative.

bar·bi·tu·rate, bär-bich/ə-rāt, bär-bich/ər-it, bär-bə-tyûr/āt, bär-bə-tyûr/it, *n.* A derivative of barbituric acid, esp. one used as a sedative or hypnotic.

bar·bi·tur·ic ac·id, bär-bə-tyûr/ik, bär-bə-tûr/ik, *n.* A substance that is the basis for many sedative and hypnotic drugs.

bar·ca·role, bar·ca·rolle, bär/kə-rōl, *n.* A Venetian gondolier's song with a rowing rhythm; music imitating such a song.

bard, bärd, *n.* An ancient Celtic poet and singer; a poet. **—bard·ic,** *a.*

bare, bâr, *a.,***bar·er, bar·est.** Naked; without covering; laid to open view; detected; plain; unadorned; unfurnished; empty; just enough; mere; threadbare.—*v.t.* To make naked; to reveal; to uncover. **—bare·ness,** *n.*

bare·back, bâr/bak, *a., adv.* On the bare back of a horse or other animal.

bare·faced, bâr/fāst, *a.* Having the face uncovered; undisguised; shameless; impudent; audacious. **—bare·fac·ed·ly,** *adv.* **—bare·fac·ed·ness,** *n.*

bare·foot, bâr/fût, *a.* Without shoes or stockings. **—***adv.* Also **bare·foot·ed.**

bare·hand·ed, bâr/han/did, *a.* Without gloves; without a tool, weapon, etc.

bare·head·ed, bâr/hed/id, *a., adv.* Without covering on the head.

bare·ly, bâr/lē, *adv.* Only just; scarcely; hardly; nakedly; plainly; openly.

bar·gain, bär/gin, *n.* An agreement between persons to trade or exchange; a good trade or exchange: He made a *bargain;* the thing purchased or stipulated for; something bought or sold at a low price.—*v.i.* To make a bargain; to discuss terms and try to get good ones; to negotiate; to dicker.—*v.t.* To sell or dispose of by bargaining. **—bar·gain·er,** *n.*

barge, bärj, *n.* A comparatively large, usually flat-bottomed boat used for transporting freight; a large boat used for pleasure excursions, pageants, etc.; a large motorboat or rowboat for the use of a naval flag officer.—*v.t.,* **barged, barg·ing.** To transport by barge.—*v.i.* To move slowly and clumsily. *Informal.* To intrude rudely or awkwardly.

bar·i·tone, bar/ə-tōn, *n.* A male voice or voice part with a range between the bass and the tenor; a person with a voice of this quality; a deep-toned brass instrument.

bar·i·um, bâr/ē-əm, bar/ē-əm, *n.* A soft, whitish metallic element occurring in combination.

bar·ium sul·fate, *n.* An insoluble compound used in medicine, as a pigment, and as a substance impenetrable to x-rays.

bark, bärk, *v.i.* To emit the short, sharp cry of a dog, or a similar sound; to speak in a curt, loud, or snapping tone.—*n.* The short, sharp sound of a dog.

bark, bärk, *n.* The tough covering of the outside stems, branches, and roots of plants, esp. trees.—*v.t.* To strip

---

a- hat, fāte, fâre, fäther; e- met, mē; i- pin, pīne; o- not, nōte, ôrb, moove (move), boy, pownd; u- cūbe, bûll, tûk (took); ch- chin; th- thick, ŧhen; zh- vizhon (vision); ə- ago, takən, pencəl, lemən, bərd (bird).

off the bark of; remove a circle of bark from; scrape or rub off the skin from; to treat with an infusion of bark; tan.

bark, bärk, *n.* A ship with its mizzenmast rigged fore-and-aft and its other masts square-rigged.

bar·keep·er, bär′kē·pər, *n.* A bar owner or manager; a bartender. Also **bar·keep.**

bar·ken·tine, bar·kan·tine, bär′kən·tēn, *n.* A three-masted vessel with the foremast square-rigged and the mainmast and mizzenmast fore-and-aft rigged.

bark·er, bär′kər, *n.* One that barks; a person stationed before a carnival, sideshow, etc., to persuade passers-by to enter.

bar·ley, bär′lē, *n. pl.,* **-leys.** A widely distributed cereal plant; its grain or seed, used as food and in the making of beer, ale, and whiskey.

Bar·ley·corn, John, bär′lē·kôrn, *n.* A humorous personification of liquor, esp. malt liquor.

barm, bärm, *n.* Yeast formed on malt liquors during fermentation.

bar·maid, bär′mād, *n.* A female bartender.

bar·man, bär′mən, *n. pl.,* **-men.** Bartender.

bar mitz·vah, bär mits′və, *n.* A Jewish boy reaching his thirteenth birthday, the age of adult religious duties and responsibilities; the ceremony recognizing the boy as a bar mitzvah.

barm·y, bär′mē, *a.,* **-i·er, -i·est.** Full of barm. *Informal.* Silly, crazy.

barn, bärn, *n.* A building for storing grain, hay, etc., and often also for housing farm animals or equipment.

bar·na·cle, bär′nə·kəl, *n.* Any of certain crustaceans which attach themselves to ship's bottoms, rocks, etc.

barn dance, *n.* A dance often in a barn, and usually featuring square dances.

barn·storm, bärn′stôrm, *v.i., v.t.* To tour (rural districts) making speeches, acting plays, demonstrating stunt flying, etc. **—barn·storm·er,** *n.* **—barn·storm·ing,** *a., n.*

barn·yard, bärn′yärd, *n.* Yard adjoining a barn.—*a.*

bar·o·graph, bar′ə·graf, bar′ə·gräf, *n.* An automatically recording barometer.

ba·rom·et·er, bə·rom′ə·tər, *n.* An instrument for measuring atmospheric pressure, used to measure elevations, indicate probable weather changes, etc.; something which registers changes. **—bar·o·met·ric,** bar·ə·met′rik, *a.* **—bar·o·met·ric·al,** bar·ə·met′rə·kəl, *a.*

bar·on, bar′ən, *n.* In Great Britain, one who holds the lowest rank in the peerage; a nobleman of varying ranks in other countries; in the U.S., a man of great power in a commercial field. **—ba·ro·ni·al,** bə·rō′nē·əl, *a.*

bar·on·age, bar′ə·nij, *n.* The whole body of barons or peers; the nobility; the rank or title of a baron.

bar·on·ess, bar′ə·nis, *n.* A baron's wife or widow; a holder of the title in her own right.

bar·on·et, bar′ə·nit, bar·ə·net′, *n.* One who possesses a hereditary rank next below a baron but superior to a knight. **—bar·on·et·age,** *n.* **—bar·on·et·cy,** *n.*

bar·o·ny, bar′ə·nē, *n. pl.,* **-nies.** The rank, title, or lands of a baron.

ba·roque, bə·rōk′, *a.* Pertaining to a style of art and architecture common in Europe in the 17th century; ornate; complex and bizarre; grotesque; irregular.

barque, bärk, *n.* Bark (vessel).

bar·quen·tine, bär′kən·tēn, *n.* Barkentine.

bar·rack, bar′ək, *n. Usu. pl.* A building or group of buildings for lodging soldiers; a large, plain building or buildings.—*v.t.* To lodge in barracks.

bar·ra·cu·da, bar·ə·koo′də, *n. pl.,* **-da, -das.** A large, voracious fish of tropical seas.

bar·rage, bə·räzh′, bə·räj′, *n.* A barrier of artillery fire to prevent the enemy from advancing and enable troops behind it to operate more safely; an overwhelming assault, as of words.—*v.t., v.i.,* **-raged,**

-rag·ing. To subject to a barrage.

bar·ra·try, bar′ə·trē, *n. pl.,* **-tries.** The practice of persistently inciting lawsuits; any willful, illegal act by a shipmaster or crew to the injury of the owners or insurers. **—bar·ra·tor,** *n.* **—bar·ra·trous,** *a.*

barred, bärd, *a.* Having bars; having stripes or bands; prohibited.

bar·rel, bar′əl, *n.* A wooden vessel, approximately cylindrical, with slightly bulging sides made of staves hooped together, and with flat, parallel ends; the quantity which such a vessel can hold; any vessel similar in form; the firing tube of a gun.—*v.t.,* **-reled** or **-relled, -rel·ing** or **-rel·ling.** To put in a barrel.—*v.i. Informal.* To move fast.

bar·rel or·gan, *n.* A hand organ.

bar·ren, bar′ən, *a.* Incapable of producing offspring; unfruitful; sterile; unproductive; unprofitable; uninteresting.—*n.* A barren tract of land. **—bar·ren·ly,** *adv.* **—bar·ren·ness,** *n.*

bar·rette, bə·ret′, *n.* A clasp for holding a woman's hair up or back.

bar·ri·cade, bar′ə·kād, bar·ə·kād′, *n.* A rough, hastily built barrier for defense; any barrier or obstruction.—*v.t.,* **-cad·ed, -cad·ing.** To block off or defend with a barricade.

bar·ri·er, bar′ē·ər, *n.* A fence, a railing, or any obstruction natural or manmade; something that separates or keeps apart.

bar·ring, bär′ing, *prep.* Excluding from consideration; excepting.

bar·ri·o, bär′ē·ō, *n. pl.,* **-os.** In the U.S., a section of a city in which Puerto Rican and other Spanish-speaking people live.

bar·ris·ter, bar′ə·stər, *n. Brit.* A lawyer allowed to plead in any court.

bar·room, bär′room, bär′rŭm, *n.* A room where alcoholic drinks are served at a bar; a bar; a tavern.

bar·row, bar′ō, *n.* A flat, rectangular frame with projecting shafts at each end for handles, used for carrying a load; a wheelbarrow; the load carried on a barrow.

bar·row, bar′ō, *n.* A mound of earth or stones built over a grave.

bar sin·is·ter, *n.* A heraldic insignia supposedly denoting illegitimacy.

bar·ten·der, bär′ten·dər, *n.* One who serves alcoholic beverages at a bar.

bar·ter, bär′tər, *v.i.* To trade by exchanging items or commodities, rather than by the use of money.—*v.t.* To exchange one commodity for another; to trade. —*n.* Exchange. **—bar·ter·er,** *n.*

ba·sal, bā′səl, bā′zəl, *a.* Of or at a base; fundamental. **—bas·al·ly,** *adv.*

ba·sal me·tab·o·lism, *n.* The amount of energy required by a person to maintain minimum vital functions.

ba·salt, bə·sôlt′, bas′ôlt, bā′sôlt, *n.* Any of various heavy, dark-colored, basic rocks of volcanic origin.

bas·cule bridge, bas′kūl, *n.* A kind of drawbridge in which each end counter balances the other, like a seesaw.

base, bās, *n.* The bottom of anything, considered as its support; a fundamental principle; the principal element or ingredient of anything; the stem of a word; a starting point; any of the four corners of a baseball diamond; the lowest member of a wall, monument, or the like; that part of a column on which the shaft rests; the part of an organ nearest its point of attachment; the point of attachment; the side of a geometric figure on which it is supposed to stand; or the number on which some numerical system depends; a line used as a starting point in surveying; a fortified or protected place from which military operations proceed or supplies are obtained; a compound which reacts with an acid to form a salt;—*v.t.,* **based, bas·ing.** To make or form a base for; establish.—**off base,** *informal,* mistaken; not in contact with a base, as a runner.

base, bās, *a.,* **bas·er, bas·est.** Morally low; mean; selfish; cowardly; befitting an inferior person; abject; menial; coarse in quality; not classical or refined, as language; of little comparative value; debased or counterfeit, as coin.

base·ball, bās′bôl, *n.* A game played with bat and ball by two teams of nine players each on a diamond with four bases; the hard, round ball used in the game.

base·board, bās′bôrd, bās′bôrd, *n.* A strip of board skirting the base of a wall, next to the floor; any board that forms a base.

base·born, bās′bôrn, *a.* Of low or humble birth; of base origin; illegitimate.

base hit, *n.* A hit in baseball which enables the batter to reach base safely without an error and without forcing out another base runner.

base·less, bās′lis, *a.* Groundless: a *baseless* rumor.

base line, *n.* Any line or specified quantity used as a point of reference; the path between bases which base runners must stay within.

base·ment, bās′mənt, *n.* A story of a building wholly or partly below ground; the lowest division of the wall of a building.

base run·ner, *n.* A baseball player of the team at bat that is on base.

bash, bash, *v.t. Informal.* To beat violently; to knock out of shape.—*n. Informal.* A powerful blow; a lively, lavish party.

bash·ful, bash′fəl, *a.* Modest to excess; diffident; shy; self-conscious. **—bash·ful·ly,** *adv.* **—bash·ful·ness,** *n.*

ba·sic, bā′sik, *a.* Of, pertaining to, or forming a base; fundamental. *Chem.* Pertaining to, of the nature of, or containing a base; alkaline. **—ba·si·cal·ly,** *adv.*

Ba·sic Eng·lish, *n.* A copyrighted system of English speech with a vocabulary reduced to 850 essential words.

ba·sil, baz′əl, bā′zəl, *n.* An aromatic plant of the mint family used for flavoring foods.

ba·sil·i·ca, bə·sil′ə·kə, *n.* An ancient Roman building of oblong shape with a broad nave and two side aisles divided by columns; a structure in this style or design, used as a Christian church.

bas·i·lisk, bas′ə·lisk, baz′ə·lisk, *n.* A fabled reptile said by the ancients to kill by its breath or look; a tropical American lizard with an erectile crest along the back.

ba·sin, bā′sən, *n.* A round, wide, shallow vessel used for holding liquids; the amount held by such a vessel; any reservoir for water, natural or artificial; the whole tract of country drained by a river and its tributaries.

ba·sis, bā′sis, *n. pl.,* **ba·ses,** bā′sēz. The bottom or base of anything; a foundation or support; a groundwork or fundamental principle; the principal constituent or ingredient.

bask, bask, bäsk, *v.i.* To lie in and enjoy warmth; to enjoy a friendly atmosphere.

bas·ket, bas′kit, bäs′kit, *n.* A container made of straw, rushes, thin strips of wood, or other flexible material; any object similar in shape or for the same purpose; the contents of such a vessel.

bas·ket·ball, bas′kit·bôl, bäs′kit·bôl, *n.* A game played between two teams of five players, the object being to throw the ball into raised basketlike goals at opposite ends of the court; the inflated ball used in this game.

bas·ket·ry, bas′kə·trē, *n.* The procedure or craft of basket making.

bas·re·lief, bä·ri·lēf′, bas·ri·lēf′, *n.* A sculpture in low relief; a mode of sculpturing figures on a flat surface.

bass, bās, *n.* The lowest part in the harmony of a musical composition, vocal or instrumental; the lowest male voice; a person with such a voice; a deep-toned musical instrument: a *bass* fiddle.—*a.* Low; deep; grave.

bass, bas, *n. pl.,* **bass, bass·es.** A variety of North American fish; the European perch.

bass, bas,*n.* The American linden or basswood tree.

bass horn, bās, *n.* A tuba.

bas·si·net, bas·ə·net′, *n.* A basket with a hood over one end, used as an infant's bed.

bas·so, bas′ō, bäs′ō, *n. pl.,* **bas·sos.** A singer of bass parts.

bas·soon, ba·soon′, bə·soon′, *n.* The bass among woodwind instruments.

bass·wood, bas′wûd, *n.* A linden; the wood of such a tree.

bast, bast, *n.* The inner bark of trees; phloem; rope or matting of this.

bas·tard, bas′tərd, *n.* A child born out of wedlock; what is false or inferior in quality. *Informal.* A low, cruel person.—*a.* Born out of wedlock; not genuine; not of the first or usual order or character. **—bas·tard·ize,** *v.t.,* **-ized, -iz·ing. —bas·tard·ly,** *a.* **—bas·tard·y,** *n.*

baste, bāst, *v.t.,* **bast·ed, bast·ing.** To sew with long stitches, and usually to keep parts together temporarily.

baste, bāst, *v.t.,* **bast·ed, bast·ing.** To drip fat, etc. upon meat while cooking.

bas·tille, ba·stēl′, *n.* Any tower, prison, or fortification; (*cap.*) an old fortress in Paris used as a prison.

bas·ti·on, bas′chən, bas′tē·ən, *n.* A fortified location; a stronghold. **—bas·ti·oned,** *a.*

bat, bat, *n.* A mammal possessing a pair of leathery wings for flying.

bat, bat, *n.* A heavy stick or club; a piece of wood used in hitting the ball in baseball and similar games. —*v.i.,* **bat·ted, bat·ing.** To take one's turn at bat. **—bat·ter,** *n.*

bat, bat, *v.t.,* **—bat·ted, bat·ting.** To wink or blink the eyes. **—not bat an eye,** *informal,* to remain calm without change of expression despite sudden surprise or danger.

batch, bach, Any quantity of a thing made at once; a number of articles similar to each other.—*v.t., v.i.* To prepare by the batch.

bate, bāt, *v.t.,* **bat·ed, bat·ing.** To abate or reduce: *bate* one's breath.

bath, bath, bäth, *n. pl.,* **baths.** A dipping of the body in water or other liquid for cleansing; water for this purpose; bathtub; a room with equipment for bathing; *often pl.,* a building containing rooms arranged for bathing.

bathe, bāth, *v.t.,* **bathed, bath·ing.** To wash or moisten with any liquid; to go for a swim.—*v.i.* To take a bath; to be in water or in other liquid; to be immersed or surrounded as if with water. **—bath·er,** *n.*

bath·robe, bath′rōb, bäth′rōb, *n.* A long, loose garment for wear in going to and from a bath, and as leisure wear in the home.

bath·y·scaphe, bath·y·scaph, bath′ə·skaf, *n.* A deep-sea device for exploring that will submerge to great depths.

bath·y·sphere, bath′ə·sfēr, *n.* A diving sphere used for observation of deep-sea life.

ba·tik, bə·tēk′, bat′ik, *n.* A process of printing designs on a fabric by covering with melted wax the portions forming the pattern, and not to be dyed; fabric so decorated.

ba·tiste, bə·tēst′, ba·tēst′, *n.* A fine, sheer fabric of natural or synthetic fibers.

bat·on, bə·ton′, ba·ton′, *n.* A staff or club, esp. as a mark of authority; the wand used by a conductor for beating time; the stick used by a band's drum major.

bat·tal·ion, bə·tal′yən, *n.* An army or Marine unit

---

consisting of a headquarters and two or more companies or batteries; any large group or force: a *battalion* of ants.

bat·ten, bat′ən, *n.* A long piece of wood used for flooring or as a support; a plank.—*v.t.* To fasten with battens.

bat·ter, bat′ər, *v.t.* To beat with continuous blows; to wear out, by long service.—*v.i.* To make attacks, as by a battering ram or artillery.

bat·ter, bat′ər, *n.* A mixture of several ingredients, beaten together with some liquid into a paste, and used in baking.

bat·ter·ing ram, bat′ər·ing, *n.* An ancient engine of war used to beat down the walls of besieged places.

bat·ter·y, bat′ə·rē, *n. pl.,* **-ies.** The act of beating or battering; an unlawful beating, wounding, or touching another person; two or more pieces of artillery used together; an artillery unit, like a company of infantry; a dry cell; a device for storing electricity; in baseball, the pitcher and catcher together; any group or series of related things, as a group of tests.

bat·ting, bat′ing, *n.* Cotton wool in rolls used as stuffing or lining.

bat·tle, bat′əl, *n.* A fight between opposing armies; a combat, conflict, or struggle.—*v.i.,* **-tled, -tling.** To join in battle; to struggle; to strive or exert oneself.—*v.t.* To struggle against.

bat·tle cry, *n.* A cry or shout of troops rushing into or engaged in battle.

bat·tle·field, bat′əl·fēld, *n.* The field or scene of a land battle.

bat·tle·ment, bat′əl·mənt, *n.* A wall at the top of a castle, with notches that defenders could shoot through.

bat·ty, bat′ē, *a.,* **-ti·er, -ti·est.** *Informal.* Insane; odd.

bau·ble, bô′bəl, *n.* Something showy without real value; a trifle.

baulk, bôk′, *n.* Balk.

baux·ite, bôk′sīt, bō′zīt, *n.* A mineral consisting essentially of a hydrated aluminum oxide, used as a source of alum and aluminum.

bawd, bôd, *n.* A person who keeps a house of prostitution.

bawd·y, bô′dē, *a.,* **-i·er, -i·est.** Obscene; suggestive.

bawl, bôl, *v.i.* To cry out with a loud sound; to weep loudly, as a child.—*v.t.*—*n.* A vehement cry; a period of loud weeping. —**bawl out,** *informal,* to scold angrily. —**bawl·er,** *n.*

bay, bā, *n.* A bay window; a wing of a building; a section on a ship or in an airplane: a bomb *bay.*

bay, bā, *n.* A wide inlet of a sea or lake; a gulf.

bay, bā, *n.* A horse of reddish-brown color; the color of a bay horse.

bay, bā, *n.* The laurel tree or sweet bay; any of various related trees or shrubs.

bay, bā, *n.* The bark of a dog, esp. a howl; the situation of being cornered and forced to fight.—*v.i.* To bark with a deep sound.—*v.t.* To bark at; to hold at bay.

bay·o·net, bā′ə·nit, bā′ə·net, bā·ə·net′, *n.* A short sword or dagger that may be fixed upon the muzzle of a rifle.—*v.t.,* **-net·ed, -net·ing.** To stab with a bayonet.

bay·ou, bī′oo, bī′ō, *n.* An inlet or outlet of a lake, river, etc.

bay win·dow, *n.* A window of an alcove which extends beyond a wall.

ba·zaar, bə·zär′, *n.* In the Orient, a market of small shops or stalls in a narrow street; a sale of various articles for charity.

ba·zoo·ka, bə·zoo′kə, *n.* A portable rocket gun which shoots armor-piercing projectiles.

be, bē, *v.i.,* pres. sing. **am, are, is;** pres. pl. **are;** past sing. **was, were, was;** past pl. **were;** pp. **been;** ppr. **being.** To exist; live; occupy a position; take place; remain as before: he *is* no more; it was not to *be;* think what might have *been;* the wedding *was* last week; let it *be.* A link connecting a subject with predicative or qualifying words or serving to form infinitive and participial phrases: you *are* late; he *is* much to blame; *is* he here? he *is* (here); do *be* still; *be* it so; try to *be* just; the art of *being* agreeable. *Auxiliary.* Used to form a continuous present tense: I *am* waiting, or to form the passive voice: the date *was* fixed; it must *be* done; also used with an infinitive to express future time: They *are* to start later.

beach, bēch, *n.* That part of the shore of the sea, or of a large river or a lake, which is washed by the tide or waves.—*v.t., v.i.* To run or haul up a vessel on the beach.

beach·comb·er, bēch′kō·mər, *n.* One who earns a living by collecting wreckage along ocean beaches; a long wave that rolls in from the ocean onto the beach.

beach·head, bēch′hed, *n.* A seashore area taken and held by the attacking force in an amphibious invasion.

bea·con, bē′kən, *n.* Any signal that serves to guide, as a fire, a lighthouse, a radio beacon, etc.; a movable or stationary apparatus that sends out beams to guide ships or aircraft; a beacon transmitter or a beacon station.—*v.t.* To light up by a beacon; to signal.

bead, bēd, *n.* One of the small, perforated, usually round objects threaded on a string to form a rosary to keep count of prayers; a similar object used with others for ornament, as in a necklace; a small globule or drop, as of liquid; a small projecting piece of metal near the muzzle of a firearm, serving as a sight.—*v.t.* To furnish with beads. —**bead·ed,** *a.* —**bead·like,** *a.*

bead·y, bē′dē, *a.,* **-i·er, -i·est.** Consisting of or containing beads; beadlike; small, round, and bright.

beak, bēk, *n.* The bill of a bird; anything in some way resembling a bird's bill. *Informal.* Someone's nose. —**beaked,** bēkt, *a.*

beak·er, bē′kər, *n.* A large drinking vessel with a wide mouth; an open-mouthed vessel of glass, etc., often with a lip for pouring, used chiefly in scientific experiments.

beam, bēm, *n.* A straight, heavy piece of timber, iron, or the like for support, esp. a horizontal timber; the part of a scale which supports the weighing tray(s); the width of a vessel; a ray of light; a constant radio signal. —**on the beam,** *informal.* Correct; alert; on the right track.—*v.t.* To give forth in the form of rays or beams.—*v.i.* To shine; to smile enthusiastically.

bean, bēn, *n.* Any of several kinds of edible seeds of the legume family, contained in a pod; any plant producing them, as the common bean. *Informal.* The top of the head; the mind.—*v.t. Informal.* To strike on the head, esp. with a pitched ball.

bear, bâr, *n. pl.,* **bears, bear.** Any of several mammals having massive bodies, long shaggy hair, short limbs, and very small tails; a rough, gruff, or surly person; person who sells stocks in the market, hoping that prices will fall.

bear, bâr, *v.t.,* **bore, borne** or **born, bear·ing.** To hold up or support; carry or bring; press against or push back; undergo, without giving way; endure pain or loss; stand, as annoyance; meet or accept expense; have a name, aspect, marks, traces, or the like; wield or exercise influence; deport or conduct oneself; bring forth or produce fruit.—*v.i.* To suffer or endure; hold, or remain firm under pressure, often with *up;* be patient, followed by *with;* press or use force, with *down, on,* or *against;* have an effect, reference, or bearing, followed by *on;* tend in course or direction; move or go; be situated: The land *bore* due west from the ship.—**bear down,** to exert pressure; apply oneself diligently; to strive.—**bear in mind,** to remember; to take into account.—**bear out,** to give support to a person or thing; to uphold.—**bear up,** to be firm; to keep one's spirits and physical strength.—**bear with,** to tolerate. —**bear·a·ble,** *a.* —**bear·a·bly,** *adv.* —**bear·er,** *n.*

beard, bērd, *n.* The hair that grows on the chin, lips, and nearby parts of the face of male adults; anything resembling this; a hairy, bristly, or threadlike appendage of various kinds.—*v.t.* To take by the beard; to challenge boldly. **—beard•ed,** a. **—beard•less,** a.

bear•ing, bãr′ing, n. The act of a person or thing that bears; a product of bearing; usu. pl., a part in which a shaft moves; the horizontal direction of an object or point.

bear•ish, bãr′ish, a. Resembling a bear; rude.

bear•skin, bãr′skin, n. The skin of a bear.

beast, bēst, n. Any four-footed animal, as distinguished from birds, insects, fishes, and man; a brutal man; a filthy, disgusting person. **—beast•li•ness,** n. **—beast•ly,** a., **-li•er, -li•est.**

beat, bēt, v.t., **beat, beat•en, beat•ing.** To strike repeatedly; stir with vigor; overcome in a battle, contest; be too difficult for; baffle; fatigue utterly; to flutter, as wings.—n. A rhythmical blow; musical emphasis; an area patrolled by a policeman. **—beat a•bout,** to search by various means or ways. **—beat a re•treat,** to give a signal to retreat; to retreat or withdraw. **—beat a•round the bush,** informal, to evade telling the truth or bad news by talking around a subject. **—beat back,** to compel to return. **—beat down,** to lay flat; to lessen the price or value of; to depress or crush. **—beat off,** to repel or drive back. **—beat out,** to extend by hammering. **—beat up,** to attack suddenly and viciously. **—beat time,** to regulate tempo in music by the motion of the hand or the sound of a metronome. **—beat•en,** a. **—beat•er,** n.

beat gen•er•a•tion, n. A term applied to the young bohemian nonconformists of the early 1950's.

be•a•tif•ic, bē•ə•tif′ik, a. Blessing or making happy.

be•at•i•fy, bē•at′ə•fī, v.t., **-fied, -fy•ing.** To make happy; declare by public decree that a person is to be revered as "blessed," and is entitled to public religious honor. **—be•at•i•fi•ca•tion,** bē•at•ə•fə•kā′shən, n.

be•at•i•tude, bē•at′ə•tood, bē•at′ə•tūd, n. Blessedness; the highest consummate bliss.

beat•nik, bēt′nik, n. Informal. A person who disregards ordinary social conventions of behavior and dress.

beau, bō, n. pl., **beaus, beaux,** bōz. A fop; a dandy; a male sweetheart or lover.

beau geste, bō•zhest′, n. pl., **beaux gestes,** bō•zhest′. A graceful or magnanimous gesture, often only for appearance's sake.

beau•te•ous, bū′tē•əs, a. Possessing beauty; beautiful. **—beau•te•ous•ly,** adv.

beau•ti•cian, bū•tish′ən, n. One who works in or manages a beauty shop.

beau•ti•fy, bū′tə•fī, v.t., **-fied, -fy•ing.** To make beautiful; to adorn.—v.i. to grow beautiful. **—beau•ti•fi•ca•tion,** bū•tə•fə•kā′shən, n. **—beau•ti•fi•er,** n.

beau•ty, bū′tē, n. pl., **-ties.** Those qualities that give pleasure to the aesthetic sense; any quality that delights the eye, ear, or mind; loveliness; elegance; grace; a particular grace or charm; a beautiful person or thing, especially a beautiful woman. **—beau•ti•ful,** bū′tə•fəl, a. **—beau•ti•ful•ly,** adv.

beau•ty shop, n. An establishment where a woman may receive a hairdress, manicure, and other beauty treatments. Also **beau•ty par•lor, beau•ty sa•lon.**

beaux-arts, bō•zär′, n. pl. The fine arts.

bea•ver, bē′vər, n. An amphibious rodent with soft brown fur and a broad flat tail, noted for its skill in damming streams; beaver fur; a high silk hat.

bea•ver, bē′vər, n. The face-guard of a helmet; a visor.

be•bop, bē′bop, n. Jazz style characterized by dissonance, complex rhythms, and bravura performance.

be•calm, bē•käm′, v.t. To render calm or quiet; to keep from motion for want of wind, as a ship.

be•cause, bē•kôz′, bē•kəz′, conj. For the reason that; since. **—because of,** on account of; as a result of.

beck, bek, n. A beckoning gesture. **—at one's beck and**

call, ever ready; subject to one's slightest wish.

beck•on, bek′ən, v.i. To signal or summon by a motion of the hand or head; to lure.—v.t. To beckon to.—n. A summoning gesture.

be•cloud, bē•klowd′, v.t. To obscure.

be•come, bi•kəm′, v.i., **be•came, be•come, be•com•ing.** To come, change, or grow to be.—v.t. To be suitable to; to befit; to grace: The dress becomes her. **—be•come of,** to be the fate or condition of.

be•com•ing, bi•kəm′ing, a. Suitable; appropriate; pleasing; attractive. **—be•com•ing•ly,** adv.

bed, bed, n. A piece of furniture on which to sleep or rest; any place where one sleeps or rests; a mattress; a bedstead; the use of a bed; the bed as the place of sex relations; something resembling a bed; a plot of ground in which plants are grown; a layer or stratum; the ground at the bottom of a body of water; the flat base or foundation on which anything rests.—v.t. **bed•ded, bed•ding.** To provide with a bed; to put to bed; plant in a bed; lay flat, or in a layer; to take to bed; embed, as in a substance.—v.i. To go to bed; form a compact layer; stratify.

be•daub, bē•dôb′, v.t. To daub over; to ornament to excess.

be•daz•zle, bi•daz′əl, v.t., **-zled, -zling.** To blind; impress, or confuse by dazzling. **—be•daz•zle•ment,** n.

bed•bug, bed′bəg, n. A small, bloodsucking insect that infests houses and esp. beds.

bed•clothes, bed′klōz, bed′klōᵺz, n. pl. Blankets, sheets, coverlets, etc., for beds.

bed•ding, bed′ing, n. Bedclothes; material used as a bed for animals; a foundation; the lowest layer; placement of rocks in strata.

be•deck, bi•dek′, v.t. To deck out; adorn.

be•dev•il, bi•dev′əl, v.t., **-iled, -il•ing.** To treat in a devilish way; torment; to possess as with a devil; bewitch; to confound; muddle; spoil. **—be•dev•il•ment,** n.

be•dew, bi•doo′, bi•dū′, v.t. To wet with or as if with dew.

bed•fast, bed′fast, bed′fäst, a. Bedridden.

bed•fel•low, bed′fel•ō, n. A sharer of one's bed; companion; associate.

be•dim, bi•dim′, v.t., **-dimmed, -dim•ming.** To make dim; obscure.

bed•lam, bed′ləm, n. Wild uproar and confusion; an insane asylum.

Bed•ou•in, Bed•u•in, bed′oo•in, bed′win, n. pl., **-in, -ins.** A nomadic Arab; a nomad; wanderer.

bed•pan, bed′pan, n. A pan used as a toilet by bedridden persons.

be•drag•gle, bi•drag′əl, v.t., **-gled, -gling.** To soil or soak, as by dragging through mud.

bed•rid•den, bed′rid•ən, a. Confined to bed, esp. for a long time. Also **bed•rid.**

bed•rock, bed′rok, n. Solid rock beneath the looser earth at the surface; the lowest level or bottom; foundation; basis.

bed•room, bed′room, bed′rûm, n. A sleeping room.

bed•room sub•urb, n. A suburb with little or no industry, and populated mainly by the families of men who commute daily to jobs in the city.

bed•side, bed′sīd, n. The side of a bed, esp. a sick person's bed.

bed•sore, bed′sōr, bed′sôr, n. A sore liable to occur on bedridden persons where the body presses constantly against the bed.

bed•spread, bed′spred, n. An outer bedcover, usually decorative.

bed•spring, bed′spring, n. A spring for the support of the mattress on a bed.

bed•stead, bed′sted, bed′stid, n. A framework to support a bed.

---

a- hat, fāte, fãre, fäther; e- met, mē; i- pin, pīne; o- not, nōte, ôrb, moove (move), boy, pownd; u- cūbe, bûll, tûk (took); ch- chin; th- thick, ᵺen; zh- vizhon (vision); ə- əgo, takən, pencəl, lemən, bərd (bird).

bed·time, bed′tīm, *n*. The time to go to bed; the usual hour of retiring to rest.

bee, bē, *n*. Any of various insects that produce honey and wax, and form highly organized colonies; any of various similar insects; *chiefly U.S.*, a social gathering for joint work or amusement: a husking *bee*.—**a bee in one's bon·net,** a preoccupation or obsession with something.

bee·bread, bē′bred, *n*. A bitter brownish substance, consisting of pollen, or pollen and honey, stored up by bees as food.

beech, bēch, *n*. A tree of temperate regions, having a smooth gray bark, and bearing small edible triangular nuts; its wood.

beef, bēf, *n. pl.,* **beefs, beeves,** bēvz. An adult bovine animal, whether a steer, bull, or cow; the flesh of such an animal used as food. *Informal.* Muscle; brawn; a complaint or grievance.—*v.i. Informal.* To complain; protest.—**beef up,** *Informal.* To strengthen; reinforce.

beef·eat·er, bēf′ē·tər, *n*. A yeoman of the royal guard of England.

beef·steak, bēf′stāk, *n*. A steak or slice of beef for broiling.

beef·y, bē′fē, *a.,* **-i·er, -i·est.** Fleshy; brawny; solid; heavy.

bee·hive, bē′hīv, *n*. A hive serving as a home for bees; any busy, crowded location.

bee·line, bē′līn, *n*. The direct line or shortest distance between two places.—**make a bee·line for,** hurry directly to.

beer, bēr, *n*. An alcoholic beverage usually made by fermentation from malted barley flavored with hops. Any of various beverages made from roots, etc.

beer·y, bēr′ē, *a.,* **-i·er, -i·est.** Of or like beer; affected by beer.

beest·ings, bē′stingz, *n. pl., but sing. in constr.* The first milk given by a mammal, esp. a cow, after giving birth.

bees·wax, bēz′waks, *n*. The wax secreted by bees from which they construct their honeycomb.—*v.t.* To treat with beeswax.

beet, bēt, *n*. Any of various biennial plants including the common red beet, which has a thick, fleshy edible root, and the sugar beet which has a thick white root; the roots of either of these plants.

bee·tle, bē′təl, *n*. Any insect of an order having a pair of hard outer wings protecting an inner pair when at rest; popularly, any insect resembling a beetle.

bee·tle, bē′təl, *n*. A heavy hammering instrument, usually of wood, used to drive wedges, etc.; a mallet for mashing or pounding.

bee·tle, bēt′əl, *v.i.,* **-tled, -tling.** To be prominent; to overhang; to jut.—*a.*

bee·tle-browed, bē′təl-browd, *a*. Having prominent brows; frowning; sullen.

be·fall, bi·fôl′, *v.t., v.i.,* **be·fell, be·fall·en, be·fall·ing.** To happen (to); to occur (to).

be·fit, bi·fit′, *v.t.,* **be·fit·ted, be·fit·ting.** To be fitting for; to be appropriate for; to suit. —**be·fit·ting,** *a.*

be·fog, bi·fog′, bi·fôg′, *v.t.,* **be·fogged, be·fog·ging.** To obscure in fog; hence, to confuse; to becloud.

be·fore, bi·fōr′, bi·fôr′, *adv*. In front; ahead; previously; earlier or sooner.—*prep*. In front of; ahead of; previous to; earlier than; in precedence of, as in order or rank; in preference to; rather than; in the presence or sight of.—*conj*. Previous to the time when: *Before* we leave, let's have some coffee; rather than.

be·fore·hand, bi·fōr′hand, bi·fôr′hand, *adv*. In advance; at a time prior to.

be·foul, bi·fowl′, *v.t.* To make foul; sully.

be·friend, bi·frend′, *v.t.* To act as a friend to; to make friends with; to assist.

be·fud·dle, bi·fəd′əl, *v.t.,* **-dled, -dling.** To render stupid with or as if with liquor; to confuse.

beg, beg, *v.t.,* **begged, beg·ging.** To ask for charity; to ask for earnestly (alms); to ask for earnestly or humbly; to beseech.—*v.i.* To ask alms or charity; to

beseech; to live by asking alms.—**beg off,** to avoid some duty, engagement, etc., through pleading.—**beg the ques·tion,** to take for granted the very issue being discussed.—**go beg·ging,** to remain unused or unsold.

be·get, bi·get′, *v.t.,* **be·got, be·got·ten** or **be·got, be·get·ting.** To procreate, as a father or sire; to cause to exist; to generate.—**be·get·ter,** *n.*

beg·gar, beg′ər, *n*. One who lives by begging; a mendicant; a penniless person; a wretch or rogue.—*v.t.* To reduce to begging; impoverish; to exhaust the resources of: to *beggar* description. —**beg·gar·dom, beg·gar·hood,** *n.*

beg·gar·ly, beg′ər·lē, *a*. Like or befitting a beggar; wretchedly poor.

be·gin, bi·gin′, *v.i.,* **be·gan, be·gun, be·gin·ning.** To take the first step; to commence; to come or bring into being; to originate.—*v.t.* To do the first act of; to enter on; to commence.

be·gin·ner, bi·gin′ər, *n*. A person who begins, esp. a novice in some trade, art, etc.; a founder.

be·gin·ning, bi·gin′ing, *n*. The first cause; origin; commencement; the first part. *Pl.* Origin; initial stage.

be·go·ni·a, bi·gōn′yə, bi·gō′nē·ə, *n*. A tropical plant with handsome, often varicolored leaves and waxy flowers.

be·grime, bi·grīm′, *v.t.,* **be·grimed, be·grim·ing.** To dirty; to make grimy.

be·grudge, bi·grəj′, *v.t.,* **be·grudged, be·grudg·ing.** To be reluctant to give or allow (something); to resent (someone's) possession of.—**be·grudg·ing·ly,** *adv.*

be·guile, bi·gīl′, *v.t.,* **be·guiled, be·guil·ing.** To practice guile upon; to deceive; to cheat; to charm; to amuse; to while away (time). —**be·guil·er,** *n.*

be·half, bi·haf′, bi·häf′, *n*. Interest; support; defense; often in such phrases as in or on *behalf* of, in or on one's *behalf.*

be·have, bi·hāv′, *v.t.,* **be·haved, be·hav·ing.** To conduct (oneself) properly.—*v.i.* To act in a certain manner; to act properly or suitably.

be·hav·ior, bi·hāv′yər, *n*. Manner of behaving; conduct; deportment.

be·hav·ior·ism, bi·hāv′yə·riz·əm, *n*. A theory that objective facts of behavior of both man and animals are the sole proper subject matter of scientific psychology. —**be·hav·ior·ist, be·hav·ior·is·tic,** *a.*

be·head, bi·hed′, *v.t.* To cut off the head of; decapitate.

be·he·moth, bi·hē′məth, bē′ə·məth, *n*. A huge animal mentioned in the Bible; anything huge or monstrous.

be·hest, bi·hest′, *n*. A command; an urgent request.

be·hind, bi·hīnd′, *prep*. At the back of; in support of; toward the back or far side of; remaining after; later in time than; in an inferior position to; hidden by.—*adv*. At the back; in or toward the rear; farther back; out of sight; backward; slow; late.—*n. Informal.* The buttocks.

be·hind·hand, bi·hīnd′hand, *adv., a*. In arrears; backward; slow; late.

be·hold, bi·hōld′, *v.t.,* **be·held, be·hold·ing.** To observe; to see. —*Interj.* Look! See! —**be·hold·er,** *n.*

be·hold·en, bi·hōl′dən, *a*. Indebted.

be·hoove, bi·hoov′, *v.t.,* **be·hooved, be·hoov·ing.** To be appropriate or necessary for: It *behooves* us to visit her.

beige, bāzh, *n*. The light brownish-gray color of unbleached, undyed wool.

be·ing, bē′ing, *n*. Existence; essence; life; a person; a creature.

be·la·bor, bi·lā′bər, *v.t.* To beat soundly; to argue at unnecessary length.

be·lat·ed, bi·lā′təd, *a*. Late; too late. —**be·lat·ed·ly,** *adv.* —**be·lat·ed·ness,** *n.*

be·lay, bi·lā′, *v.t.,* **be·layed, be·lay·ing.** To fasten, as a rope, by winding around a pin or the like. *Informal.* To stop or hold.

belch, belch, *v.t.* To throw out with violence, as from the stomach through the mouth, or from a deep hollow place; to cast forth.—*v.i.* To eject wind noisily from the stomach; to issue out in a violent spasm.—*n.* A belching.

be·lea·guer, bi·lē′gər, *v.t.* To besiege; to surround with an army so as to preclude escape; to blockade; to harass.

bel·fry, bel′frē, *n. pl.*, **-fries.** A bell tower; that part of a steeple or other structure in which a bell is hung.

be·lie, bi·lī′, *v.t.*, **be·lied, be·ly·ing.** To report falsely; to misrepresent; to prove mistaken; to slander.

be·lief, bi·lēf′. An acceptance of the truth or reality of something without certain proof; the thing believed; trust; confidence; religious faith.

be·lieve, bi·lēv′, *v.i.*, **be·lieved, be·liev·ing.** To accept the truth or reality of; to have confidence (*in*); trust; have religious faith.—*v.t.* To have belief in; credit the veracity of; think; suppose. **—be·liev·a·ble,** *a.* **—be·liev·er,** *n.*

be·lit·tle, bi·lit′əl, *v.t.*, **-tled, -tling.** To make little or less important; speak slightingly of; depreciate; disparage.

bell, bel, *n.* A hollow metallic object, generally cup-shaped, which gives forth a ringing sound when struck; the sound of a bell; anything in the form of a bell, as certain flowers or the lower end of some musical instruments; the stroke of a bell every half hour for a four-hour period on shipboard.—*v.t.* To put a bell on.—*v.i.* To take the shape of a bell.

bel·la·don·na, bel·ə·don′ə, *n.* A poisonous plant with reddish flowers and black berries whose root and leaves yield atropine.

bell·boy, bel′boy, *n.* In a hotel, an employee who serves guests by carrying luggage, running errands, etc.

belle, bel, *n.* A beautiful woman or girl; a popular beauty.

belles let·tres, bel·let′rə, *n. pl.* Aesthetic rather than practical or informational literature: poetry, drama, etc.

bell·hop, bel′hop, *n.* A bellboy.

bel·li·cose, bel′ə·kōs, *a.* Inclined to war; warlike; pugnacious. **—bel·li·cos·i·ty,** bel·ə·kos′ə·tē, *n.*

bel·lig·er·ence, bə·lij′ər·əns, *n.* The act of carrying on war; warfare; warlike nature.

bel·lig·er·en·cy, bə·lij′ər·ən·sē, *n.* The state of being involved in a war as a legally recognized belligerent; belligerence.

bel·lig·er·ent, bə·lij′ər·ənt, *a.* Warlike; bellicose; pertaining to or engaged in warfare.—*n.* A nation or person engaged in war; a combatant. **—bel·lig·er·ent·ly,** *adv.*

bel·low, bel′ō, *v.i.*, *v.t.* To make the loud, deep, hollow sound of a bull; roar; shout.—*n.* The act or sound of bellowing.

bel·lows, bel′ōz, bel′əs, *n. pl.*, *sing. or pl. in constr.* An instrument which by expansion and contraction of an air chamber can produce a strong current of air, as for blowing a fire or sounding a musical instrument; the folding part of a camera; the lungs.

bell·weth·er, bel′weth·ər, *n.* A ram which leads the flock, with a bell on his neck; one who takes the lead.

bel·ly, bel′ē, *n. pl.*, **-lies.** That part of the human body which contains the stomach and intestines; the abdomen; any bulging surface; the corresponding part of other animals; the section of a bulging muscle which is fleshy; the bulging part of anything, or the cavity inside.—*v.t.*, *v.i.*, **-lied, -ly·ing.** To swell; bulge.

bel·ly·ache, bel′ē·āk, *n.* Pain in the belly.—*v.i.*, **-ached, -ach·ing.** *Informal.* To complain; grumble.

bel·ly·but·ton, bel′ē·bet·ən, *n. Informal.* Navel.

be·long, bi·lông′, bi·long′, *v.i.* To have a proper place; to be suitable; **—belong to,** to be a part,

member, or property of.

be·long·ings, bē·lông′ingz, *n. pl.* Possessions.

be·loved, bi·lev′əd, bi·levd′, *a.* Greatly loved.—*n.* One who is greatly loved.

be·low, bi·lō′, *prep.* Lower; beneath; inferior in rank or degree; unworthy of.—*adv.* In a lower place; on a lower level; downstairs; beneath; on the earth, as opposed to the heavens; in hell; further down on a page or in a book.

belt, belt, *n.* A band, often of leather, worn around the waist to support clothing, a weapon, etc.; anything resembling a belt; a strip; a band; a continuous band for transmitting power or conveying foods; an area having a distinctive feature; a zone. *Informal.* A blow or whack.—*v.t.* To surround as with a belt; to fasten with a belt; to strike with a belt; to strike. **—be·low the belt,** unfairly. **—belt·ed,** *a.*

belt·way, belt′wā, *n.* An express highway that bypasses a city or congested area by going around it.

be·lu·ga, bə·loo′gə, *n.* A white sturgeon of the Black and Caspian seas; a dolphin of arctic waters, white when adult.

be·mire, bi·mīr′, *v.t.*, **be·mired, be·mir·ing.** To soil with mud; to sink in mud.

be·moan, bi·mōn′, *v.t.* To mourn for; to express sorrow for.—*v.i.* To mourn.

be·muse, bi·mūz′, *v.t.*, **be·mused, be·mus·ing.** To confuse or stupefy; bewilder; cause to muse. **—be·mused,** *a.*

bench, bench, *n.* A long seat of wood, marble, etc.; the seat on which judges sit in court; the office or dignity of a judge; a court of justice; the body of persons sitting as judges; a seat occupied by persons in their official capacity; the work table of a carpenter or other mechanic; a raised, level tract of land; the substitute players on a team.—*v.t.* To furnish with benches; to seat on a bench; to remove a player from a game.

bench mark, *n.* A mark cut into some durable material, as stone, to serve as a reference in topographical surveys, etc.; any point of reference.

bench war·rant, *n.* A warrant issued by a presiding judge or a court against a person charged with some offense.

bend, bend, *v.t.*, **bent, bend·ing.** To render curved or angular; flex; crook; cause to bow or yield; turn in a particular direction; incline; direct the mind or efforts; to fasten (a sail, rope, etc.).—*v.i.* To become curved, crooked, or bent; bow in submission or reverence; submit; turn in a particular direction; direct one's energies.—*n.* A bending, or a bent condition; a bent thing; a curve; a crook; a knot by which a rope is fastened to another rope or to something else.

bend·er, ben′dər, *n.* One who or that which bends. *Informal.* A drinking spree.

bends, bendz, *n. pl. Informal.* Caisson disease.

be·neath, bi·nēth′, *adv.* In or to a lower place; below; underneath.—*prep.* Under; on the underside of; lower than in rank, dignity, or excellence; subject to the dictates of; unworthy of.

ben·e·dict, ben′i·dikt, *n.* A newly married man, especially one who has long been a bachelor.

ben·e·dic·tion, ben·ə·dik′shən, *n.* The act of invoking divine blessings at the end of a church service; a blessing uttered in favor of any person or thing. **—ben·e·dic·to·ry,** *a.*

ben·e·fac·tion, ben·ə·fak′shən, *n.* A benefit.

ben·e·fac·tor, ben′ə·fak·tər, *n.* One who confers a benefit; a kindly helper; one who confers a benefit to a charitable or religious institution. **—ben·e·fac·tress,** *n. fem.*

be·nef·ic, bə·nef′ik, *a.* Doing good.

ben·e·fice, ben′ə·fis, *n.* A church post or position, appointment to which includes an endowment of property or income.—*v.t.*, **-ficed, -fic·ing.** To appoint to a benefice.

be·nef·i·cent, bə·nef′ə·sənt, *a.* Performing, or causing to be done, acts of kindness; doing good. —**be·nef·i·cence**, *n.*

ben·e·fi·cial, ben·ə·fish′əl, *a.* Conferring benefit; advantageous; helpful. —**ben·e·fi·cial·ly**, *adv.*

ben·e·fi·ci·ar·y, ben·ə·fish′ē·er·ē, ben·ə·fish′ə·rē, *n. pl.*, **-ar·ies.** One named to receive the property, benefits, or grants provided by insurance, a trust fund, etc.; one who holds a benefice.

ben·e·fit, ben′ə·fit, *n.* A kindness or favor; anything that is for the good of a person or thing; advantage or profit; a theatrical performance or other public entertainment given to raise money for a special cause; payment, as by an insurance company, in time of sickness, old age, etc.—*v.t.* To do good to; of benefit to.—*v.i.* To derive benefit.

ben·e·fit of cler·gy, *n.* Clerical privilege of trial before an ecclesiastical court rather than a civil one; the sanction of the church.

be·nev·o·lence, bə·nev′ə·ləns, *n.* The disposition to do good; good will; kindness; charitableness; an act of kindness. —**be·nev·o·lent**, *a.* —**be·nev·o·lent·ly**, *adv.*

be·night·ed, bi·nī′tid, *a.* Overtaken by night; ignorant; unenlightened.

be·nign, bi·nīn′, *a.* Of a kind disposition; gracious; favorable; salutary; mild; not malignant. —**be·nig·ni·ty**, bi·nig′ni·tē, *n. pl.*, **-ties.** —**be·nign·ly**, *adv.*

be·nig·nant, bi·nig′nənt, *a.* Kind; gracious; favorable; benign. —**be·nig·nan·cy**, *n. pl.*, **-cies.**

ben·i·son, ben′ə·zən, ben′ə·sən, *n.* A blessing; a benediction.

ben·ny, ben′ē, *n. pl.*, **-nies.** *Informal.* A pill of Benzedrine or some similar stimulant.

bent, bent, *a.* Deviated from a straight, even, or level condition; resolved or determined, followed by *on.*—*n.* An inclination or natural tendency; capacity of endurance; a being curved.

bent, bent, *n.* A stiff, wiry grass that grows on waste ground or sandy shores.

be·numb, bi·nəm′, *v.t.* To make numb; to stupefy; to deaden.

Ben·ze·drine, ben′zə·drēn, *n. Trademark.* A drug used to stimulate the central nervous system, etc.; amphetamine.

ben·zene, ben′zēn, ben·zēn′, *n.* A clear, colorless, aromatic liquid extracted from coal tar, used as a solvent and in organic synthesis. Also **ben·zol.**

ben·zine, ben′zēn, ben·zēn′, *n.* A colorless, volatile liquid consisting of a mixture of hydrocarbons derived from petroleum, used as a solvent, cleaner, or motor fuel.

ben·zo·ate, ben′zō·āt, *n.* A salt or ester of benzoic acid.

ben·zo·ic ac·id, ben·zō′ik, *n.* A crystalline compound occurring naturally, as in benzoin, or synthesized, and used as a preservative, germicide, etc.

ben·zo·in, ben′zōyn, ben′zō·in, *n.* A resin from a tree of Sumatra or Java, used in medicine and as a perfume; a compound used as an antiseptic.

ben·zol, ben′zōl, ben′zôl, *n.* Benzene; impure or crude benzene.

be·queath, bi·kwēth′, bi·kwēth′, *v.t.* To give or leave by will; to hand down.

be·quest, bi·kwest′, *n.* The act of bequeathing; something left by will; a legacy.

be·rate, bi·rāt′, *v.t.*, **be·rat·ed, be·rat·ing.** To chide vehemently; to admonish; to scold.

ber·ceuse, ber·sûz′, *n.* A lullaby.

be·reave, bi·rēv′, *v.t.*, **be·reaved** or **be·reft, be·reav·ing.** To deprive of someone loved or something that is prized, usually followed by *of.* —**be·reave·ment,** *n.*

be·ret, bə·rā′, ber′ā, *n.* A soft, visorless, cloth cap with a broad, flat crown.

berg, berg, *n.* An iceberg.

ber·ga·mot, ·bər′gə·mot, *n.* A citrus fruit, the rind of which yields a fragrant oil; a perfume from the fruit; any of various mints.

ber·i·ber·i, ber′ē·ber′ē, *n.* A disease of the nerves caused by lack of vitamin B_1, characterized by loss of muscular power, emaciation, and exhaustion.

berke·li·um, bərk′lē·əm, *n.* Synthetic radioactive element first produced by helium-ion bombardment of americium.

Berk·shire, bərk′shēr, bərk′shər, *n.* A breed of black and white hogs of medium size.

berm, bərm, *n.* A narrow shelf, path or ledge at the edge of a road.

Ber·mu·das, bər·mū′dəz, *n.* Shorts extending to just above the knee, worn by men and women. Also **Ber·mu·da shorts.**

ber·ret·ta, bə·ret′ə, *n.* Biretta.

ber·ry, ber′ē, *n. pl.*, **-ries.** A succulent or pulpy fruit, containing many seeds, and usually small, such as the strawberry; certain dried seeds as grain, coffee; a simple fruit, as the grape or tomato, with the seeds in a juicy pulp.—*v.i.*, **-ried, -ry·ing.** To produce berries; to pick berries.

ber·serk, bər·sərk′, bər·zərk′, *a.* Violent; frenzied; in an uncontrolled rage.—*adv.* Into a violent frenzy: to go *berserk.*

berth, bərth, *n.* Searoom for a vessel; a space allowed for convenience or safety: to give one a wide *berth.* A station for a vessel at anchor or at a wharf; a sleeping place or bunk in a ship, railroad car, etc.; a position or job; a post of employment on vessels.—*v.t.* To place (a boat) in, or assign to, a berth; provide with a berth or berths.—*v.i.* To have or occupy a berth.

ber·tha, bər′thə, *n.* A collar worn by women about the shoulders, as at the top of a low-necked dress.

ber·yl, ber′əl, *n.* A mineral, a silicate of aluminum and beryllium, occurring in various colors, esp. green, and including the emerald and aquamarine.

be·ryl·li·um, bə·ril′ē·əm, *n.* A hard, steel-gray, bivalent, light metallic element always occuring in combination. Sym. Be.

be·seech, bi·sēch′, *v.t.*, **be·sought** or **be·seeched, be·seech·ing.** To beg eagerly for; entreat; implore. —**be·seech·ing·ly**, *adv.*

be·set, bi·set′, *v.t.*, **be·set, be·set·ting.** To set or stud with something; to surround; hem in; besiege; attack on all sides; assail.

be·set·ting, bi·set′ing, *a.* Habitually attacking: a *besetting* sin.

be·side, bi·sīd′, *prep.* At the side of; in comparison with; in addition to; near to; apart from; not connected with.—**be·side one·self**, out of one's wits or senses.

be·sides, bi·sīdz′, *adv.* Along the side of; moreover; over and above; not included in what has been mentioned.—*prep.* Over and above; separate or distinct from; in addition to.

be·siege, bi·sēj′, *v.t.*, **be·sieged, be·sieg·ing.** To lay seige to; to crowd around; to overwhelm with gifts, requests, etc. —**be·sieg·er**, *n.*

be·smear, bi·smir′, *v.t.* To smear all over; to soil.

be·smirch, bi·smərch′, *v.t.* To sully; to tarnish.

bes·om, bē′zəm, *n.* A broom; a brush of twigs for sweeping.

be·sot, bi·sot′, *v.t.*, **be·sot·ted, be·sot·ting.** To make mentally dull, as with drink; to stupefy. —**be·sot·ted,** *a.*

be·spat·ter, bi·spat′ər, *v.t.* To soil by spattering; slander.

be·speak, bi·spēk′, *v.t.*, **be·spoke, be·spoke** or **be·spok·en, be·speak·ing.** To order or engage against a future time; to indicate by outward appearance: action that *bespoke* a kind heart.

best, best, *a., superlative of* **good.** Having good qualities in the highest degree; possessing the highest advantages; largest; most.—*adv.* In the highest degree; in the most desirable way; most excellently.—*n.* Highest possible state of excellence; all that one can do, or show in oneself.—*v.t.* To defeat; to outdo.—**at best,** in the most favorable light.—**make the best of,** to use to the best advantage; to do with as well as one can.

bes·tial, bes′chəl, best′yəl, *a.* Having the qualities of a beast; brutal; brutish. —**bes·tial·ly,** *adv.* —**bes·ti·al·i·ty,** bes·chē·al′ə·tē, bes·tē·al′ə·tē, *n. pl.,* **-ties.**

be·stir, bi·stər′, *v.t.,* **be·stirred, be·stir·ring.** To rouse to action: *Bestir* yourself!

best man, *n.* The right-hand man or chief attendant of the bridegroom at a wedding.

be·stow, bi·stō′, *v.t.* To stow away; to lodge; to give; to confer (on or upon). —**be·stow·al,** *n.*

be·strew, bi·stroo′, *v.t.* To scatter over; to strew.

be·stride, bi·strīd′, *v.t.,* **be·strode, be·strid·den, be·strid·ing.** To stride over; to stand or sit on with the legs on either side.

best sel·ler, *n.* Any item, esp. a book, which sells extremely well.

bet, bet, *n.* A wager; that which is staked on the result of any uncertain question or event; the terms of the bet; the stake. *v.t., v.i.,* **bet** or **bet·ted, bet·ting.** To stake in wagering; to wager.

be·ta, bā′tə, bē′tə, *n.* The second letter of the Greek alphabet; the second of any series.

be·take, bi·tāk′, *v.t.,* **be·took, be·tak·en, be·tak·ing.** To go; take (oneself).

be·ta par·ti·cle, *n.* An electron.

be·ta rays, *n.* Stream of high speed electrons or positrons occurring in radioactive disintegration.

be·ta·tron, bā′tə·tron, bē′tə·tron, *n.* A device for the high-speed acceleration of electrons to form a beam of beta rays.

be·tel, bē′təl, *n.* An East Indian pepper plant, the leaves of which are chewed in Southeast Asia.

be·tel palm, *n.* The palm of southeastern Asia, that bears the betel nut.

bête noire, bāt·nwär′, *n. pl.,* **bêtes noires,** bāt·nwär′. Something dreaded or loathed; a bugaboo.

beth·el, beth′əl, *n.* A hallowed spot; a church or chapel for seamen.

be·tide, bi·tīd′, *v.t.,* **be·tid·ed, be·tid·ing.** To happen to.—*v.i.* To happen.

be·to·ken, bi·tō′kən, *v.t.* To be or serve as a token of; to foreshow.

be·tray, bi·trā′, *v.t.* To deliver to an enemy by treachery; to seduce and abandon; to cheat or mislead; to disclose; to reveal inadvertently. —**be·tray·al,** *n.* —**be·tray·er,** *n.*

be·troth, bi·trōth′, bi·trôth′, *v.t.* To agree to marry; to affiance.

be·troth·al, bi·trō′thəl′, bi·trô′thəl, *n.* The act of betrothing; engagement. Also **be·troth·ment.**

be·trothed, bi·trōthd′, bi·trôtht′, *n.* A person promised in marriage.

bet·ter, bet′ər, *a., comparative of* **good.** Having good qualities in a greater degree than another; superior in excellence; of a higher quality; preferable; improved in health.—*adv. comparative of* **well.** In a more excellent manner; in a higher degree; more.—*n.* Something or someone of greater excellence; advantage; *usu. pl.,* one's superiors.—*v.t.* To make better; to improve; to surpass;—*v.i.* To become better.—**be better off,** be in improved circumstances.

bet·ter·ment, bet′ər·mənt, *n.* A making better; improvement; value added to property from public improvements.

bet·tor, bet·ter, bet′ər, *n.* One who bets.

be·tween, bi·twēn′, *prep.* In the space or time separating two points, objects, etc.; intermediate to in degree, amount, etc.; connecting; involving both of; by joint action or possession of.—*adv.* In the intervening space, time, position, or relation.

be·twixt, bi·twikst′, *prep., adv.* Between.

bev·el, bev′əl, *n.* The inclination of one surface to another when not 90°; an instrument for drawing or measuring angles—*a.* Slanting; oblique.—*v.t.,* **-eled, -el·ing.** To cut to a bevel.—*v.i.* To slant.

bev·er·age, bev′ər·ij, bev′rij, *n.* Drink; any liquid used for drinking.

bev·y, bev′ē, *n. pl.,* **-ies.** A flock of birds; a group, esp. of women.

be·wail, bi·wāl′, *v.t., v.i.* To lament; mourn.

be·ware, bi·wār′, *v.i.* To be wary or cautious (of).—*v.t.* To be on guard against; look out for.

be·wil·der, bi·wil′dər, *v.t.* To lead into complete perplexity; to puzzle; to confuse. —**be·wil·der·ing·ly,** *adv.* —**be·wil·der·ment,** *n.*

be·witch, bi·wich′, *v.t.* To cast a charm or spell over; to fascinate; attract irresistibly. —**be·witch·er,** *n.* —**be·witch·er·y,** *n.* —**be·witch·ing,** *a.* —**be·witch·ing·ly,** *adv.* —**be·witch·ment,** *n.*

bey, bā, *n.* A governor of a Turkish district.

be·yond, bi·yond′, *adv.* Farther away.—*prep.* On or to the farther side of; farther away than; later than; out of reach of; above or surpassing; more than; in addition to.—*n.* Heaven; the hereafter: the great *beyond.*

be·zique, bə·zēk′, *n.* A card game somewhat like pinochle.

bi·an·nu·al, bī·an′ū·əl, *a.* Having a frequency of twice a year.

bi·as, bī′əs, *n.* An oblique line across a fabric: cut on the *bias;* an inclination of the mind; a bent; prejudice. —*a.* Oblique; diagonal; running diagonally to the texture of a fabric.—*adv.* Obliquely.—*v.t.,* **bi·ased** or **bi·assed, bi·as·ing** or **bi·as·sing.** To give a bias to; to prejudice.

bi·ax·i·al, bī·ak′sē·əl, *a.* Having two axes, as a crystal. —**bi·ax·i·al·ly,** *adv.*

bib, bib, *n.* A cloth worn under the chin by a child, esp. while eating, to protect the clothing; the upper part of an apron or overalls.

bi·be·lot, bib′lō, *Fr.* bē·blō′, *n. pl.,* **-lots.** Any small object of curiosity, beauty, or rarity.

Bi·ble, bī′bəl, *n.* The collection of sacred writings of the Christian religion, comprising the Old and New Testaments; the Old Testament in the form received by the Jews ("Hebrew Bible"); (*often cap.*) the sacred writings of any religion; (*l.c.*) any book accepted as an authority.

Bi·ble belt, *n.* An area of southern and midwestern U.S. where fundamentalist interpretation of the Bible prevails.

Bib·li·cal, bib′li·kəl, *a. (Sometimes l.c.)* Of or contained in the Bible; in accordance with the Bible. —**Bib·li·cal·ly,** *adv.*

bib·li·og·ra·phy, bib·lē·og′rə·fē, *n. pl.,* **-phies.** A study of the authorship, editions, dates, etc., of books or manuscripts; a list of books, articles, etc., about a subject or person; a list of a certain author's works. —**bib·li·og·ra·pher,** *n.* —**bib·li·o·graph·ic,** bib·lē·ə·graf′ik, *a.*

bib·li·o·ma·ni·a, bib·lē·ə·mā′nē·ə, bib·lē·ə·mān′yə, *n.* Book-madness; a rage for possessing books. —**bib·li·o·ma·ni·ac,** *n.*

bib·li·o·phile, bib′lē·ə·fīl, bib′lē·ə·fil, *n.* A lover of books.

bib·u·lous, bib′yə·ləs, *a.* Fond of drinking intoxicants.

bi·cam·er·al, bī·kam′ər·əl, *a.* Consisting of two legislative chambers or branches.

bi·car·bo·nate, bī·kär′bə·nit, bī·kär′bə·nāt, *n.* A carbonate in which one half of the hydrogen of the carbonic acid is replaced by a metal.

bi·car·bo·nate of so·da, *n.* Sodium bicarbonate.

bi·cen·te·nar·y, bī·sen·ten′ə·rē, bī·sen′tə·ner·ē, *a., n. pl.,* **-nar·ies.** Bicentennial.

bi·cen·ten·ni·al, bī·sen·ten′ē·əl, *n.* A two-

---

hundredth anniversary.—*a.* Relating to a two-hundred-year period; recurring every two hundred years.

bi·ceps, bī′seps, *n. pl.* A muscle having two heads or origins; the name of two muscles, one of the upper arm, the other of the thigh.

bi·chlo·ride, bī·klōr′īd, bī·klôr·īd, *n.* A compound in which two atoms of chlorine are combined with another element or radical; bichloride of mercury.

bick·er, bik′ər, *v.i.* To quarrel; to wrangle; to quiver; to flicker.—*n.* A quarrel; a petty dispute.

bi·con·cave, bī·kon′kāv, bī·kon·kāv′, *a.* Hollow or concave on both sides.

bi·con·vex, bī·kon′veks, bī·kon·veks′, *a.* Convex on both sides, as a lens.

bi·cus·pid, bī·kəs′pid, *a.* Having two cusps or points, as certain teeth.—*n.* A premolar tooth. —**bi·cus·pi·dal, bi·cus·pi·date,** *a.*

bi·cy·cle, bī′si·kəl, *n.* A vehicle having a metal frame with two wheels, one in front of the other, and a seat, handlebars, and pedals.—*v.i.,* **-cled, -cling.** To ride a bicycle. —**bi·cy·cler, bi·cy·clist,** *n.*

bid, bid, *v.t.,* **bid** or **bade, bid, bid·den, bid·ding.** To ask, request, or command; to order; to summon; to say to or utter; to offer (a price); to declare what one will make or win in a card game.—*v.i.* To make a bid.—*n.* An offer of a price; an act of bidding. *Informal.* An invitation; an effort to achieve some goal. *Cards.* An announcement of a certain number of points or tricks one will achieve; the amount of a bid. —**bid·da·ble,** *a.* **bid·der,** *n.*

bid·dy, bid′ē, *n. pl.,* **-dies.** A hen.

bide, bīd, *v.i.,* **bid·ed, bid·ing.** To dwell; to abide.—*v.t. Archaic.* To endure; to suffer; to bear. —**bide one's time,** to wait for the best or first opportunity.

bi·en·ni·al, bī·en′ē·əl, *a.* Happening once in two years; lasting for two years.—*n.* A biennial event; a plant that produces flowers and fruit, and dies in its second year. —**bi·en·ni·al·ly,** *adv.*

bier, bēr, *n.* A framework on which a corpse or coffin is laid; the coffin and framework.

biff, bif, *v.t. Informal.* To hit, whack.—*n. Informal.* A blow; whack.

bi·fid, bī′fid, *a.* Cleft; forked.

bi·fo·cal, bī·fō′kəl, *a.* Having two foci. —**bi·fo·cals,** *n. pl.* Eyeglasses with bifocal lenses.

bi·fo·cal lens, *n.* A lens with two parts: one for near and one for distant vision.

bi·fur·cate, bī′fər·kāt, bī·fər′kāt, *v.t., v.i.,* **-cat·ed, -cat·ing.** To divide into two branches.—*a.* Forked; divided into two branches. —**bi·fur·ca·tion,** bī·fər·kā′shən, *n.*

big, big, *a.,* **big·ger, big·gest.** Having size; great; filled; important; large; bulky; pregnant; generous; pompous; proud; loud; full; grown up.—*adv.* Boastfully: as, to talk *big.*—**go o·ver big,** to attain popularity; to be successful.

big·a·my, big′ə·mē, *n. pl.,* **-mies.** The crime of marrying another person when one's legal spouse is still alive. —**big·a·mist,** *n.* —**big·a·mous,** *a.*

Big Dipper, *n.* The constellation Ursa Major.

big game, *n.* The larger wild animals and fish prized as trophies by sportsmen.

big-heart·ed, big′här·tid, *a.* Kind; compassionate; generous.

big·horn, big′hôrn, *n.* A large, wild, grayish-brown sheep with curving horns, found in the western mountains of N. America.

bight, bīt, *n.* A bend; an angle; the loop or bent part of a rope; the part of a rope between the ends; a bend or curve in a sea or river; a bay formed by such a bend.

big·no·ni·a, big·nō′nē·ə, *n.* Any of various vines, including species much cultivated for their showy, trumpet-shaped flowers.

big·ot, big′ət, *n.* A person obstinately and unreasonably wedded to a particular opinion, party, religion, etc., and bitterly intolerant of those who believe differ-

ently. —**big·ot·ed,** *a.* —**big·ot·ed·ly,** *adv.* —**big·ot·ry,** *n. pl.,* **-ries.**

big shot, *n. Informal.* An important, successful, or influential person. Also **big·wig, big wheel.**

big top, *n.* The principal tent of a circus.

bi·jou, bē′zhoo, bē·zhoo′, *n. pl.,* **bi·joux,** bē′zhooz, bē·zhooz′. A jewel; something small and choice.

bi·ju·gous, bī′joo·gəs, bī′jū·gəs, *a.* Having two pairs of leaflets. Also **bi·ju·gate,** bī′joo·gāt, bī′joo·git.

bike, bīk, *n., v.i. Informal.* Bicycle.

bi·ki·ni, bi·kē′nē, *n.* A woman's very scanty two-piece bathing suit.

bi·la·bi·al, bī·lā′bē·əl, *a.* Referring to a speech sound produced when the lips are close or touching, as in the sounds of *b, p, m,* and *w;* having two lips.—*n.* A speech sound so produced.

bi·la·bi·ate, bī·lā′bē·āt, bī·lā′bē·it, *a.* Having two lips, as a mint corolla.

bi·lat·er·al, bī·lat′ər·əl, *a.* Pertaining to or having two sides; two-sided; of a contract, mutually binding. —**bi·lat·er·al·ly,** *adv.*

bil·ber·ry, bil′ber·ē, *n. pl.,* **-ries.** The edible fruit, whortleberry, of a shrub; the shrub itself.

bile, bīl, *n.* A bitter, viscid, yellow or greenish alkaline liquid secreted by the liver and aiding in digestion; ill humor; anger.

bilge, bilj, *n.* The protuberant part of a cask; the lowest part of a ship's hull or hold. *Informal.* Nonsense; drivel; bilge water.

bilge wa·ter, *n.* A water which enters a ship and lies upon her bilge or bottom.

bil·i·ar·y, bil′ē·er·ē, *a.* Pertaining to or carrying bile.

bi·lin·gual, bī·ling′gwəl, *a.* Containing, or expressed in, two different languages; capable of speaking two languages.

bil·ious, bil′yəs, *a.* Suffering from or caused by disorder of the liver or bile; pertaining to bile; choleric, peevish, or testy.

bilk, bilk, *v.t.* To defraud, cheat, elude, avoid payment of. —*n.* A fraud; a hoax. —**bilk·er,** *n.*

bill, bil, *n.* A statement of particulars; an itemized list; a written or printed public notice or advertisement, as a handbill, placard, or poster; an account of money due or claimed, for goods supplied or services rendered; a bank note or other like piece of paper money; *informal,* $100. A bill of exchange; a draft of a proposed statute, presented to a legislature for adoption; a written statement, usually of complaint, presented to a court; a theater program or entertainment.—*v.t.* To enter in a bill; charge in a bill; to announce by bill; to post bills in or on; to list on a theatrical program.

bill, bil, *n.* The horny sheath enveloping the jaws of a bird; a similar structure in other animals, as the turtle; a beak.—*v.i.* Of birds, to join bills.

bill, bil, *n.* A bill-hook.

bil·la·bong, bil′ə·bong, *n.* A branch of a river flowing away from the main stream.

bill·board, bil′bōrd, bil′bôrd, *n.* A board, fence, or other construction on which large, printed advertisements are affixed.

bil·let, bil′it, *n.* Nonmilitary quarters for a soldier; a directive to provide such quarters.—*v.t.* To quarter or place in lodgings, as soldiers in private houses.

bil·let, bil′it, *n.* A thick stick of wood, esp. one for fuel; a bar or slab of iron or steel, esp. when obtained from an ingot by forging, etc.

bil·let-doux, bil·ē·doo′, *n. pl.,* **bil·lets-doux,** bil·ē·dooz′. A love note or short love letter.

bill·fold, bil′fōld, *n.* A wallet.

bill·hook, bil′hûk, *n.* An instrument with a blade curving inward at the tip, for pruning or cutting.

bil·liards, bil′yərdz, *n. pl., sing. or pl. in constr.* A game played on a long, rectangular, cloth-covered table, without pockets, with three ivory balls: scores are made by the use of a cue to cause one ball to strike the other two.

bil·lings·gate, bil′ingz·gāt, *n.* Profane or abusive

language; ribaldry.

bil·lion, bil'yən, *n.* A thousand millions in the U.S., Great Britain, and France; a million millions in Germany. **—bil·lionth,** *a., n.*

bil·lion·aire, bil·yə·nâr', *n.* The owner of a billion dollars, francs, pounds, etc.

bill of ex·change, *n.* An order in writing to pay a certain sum in money to a specified person or to his order.

bill of fare, *n.* A list of the dishes served at a meal, as at a restaurant; menu.

bill of health, *n.* An official certificate as to the health of a ship's company at the time of her clearing any port.—**clean bill of health,** *Informal.* A good report; a declaration of qualifications or suitability.

bill of lad·ing, *n.* A written receipt given by a carrier for goods delivered to the carrier for transportation.

bill of rights, *n.* A formal statement of the fundamental rights of the people of a nation; (*cap.*) the first ten amendments to the Constitution of the United States.

bill of sale, *n.* A written statement stating the transfer of property.

bil·low, bil'ō, *n.* A great wave or surge of the sea; a wavelike mass, as of flame. **—bil·low·y,** *a.,* **-i·er, -i·est.** *—v.i.* To swell; to rise and roll in large waves or surges.

bil·ly goat, *n.* A male goat.

bi·met·al·ism, bī·met'əl·iz·əm, *n.* That system of currency which recognizes coins of two metals, as silver and gold, as legal tender. **—bi·met·al·list,** *n.* **—bi·me·tal·lic,** bī·mə·tal'ik, *a.*

bi·month·ly, bī·mənth'lē, *a., adv.* Occurring every two months; twice a month.—*n. pl.,* **-lies.** A bimonthly publication.

bin, bin, *n.* A box or enclosed place used as a storage place for any commodity.

bi·na·ry, bī'nə·rē, *a.* Consisting of two; paired; double.—*n. pl.,* **-ries.** A combination of two things; a binary star.

bi·na·ry star, *n.* A pair of stars revolving about a common center of gravity.

bi·na·ry sys·tem, *n. Computer.* A numeration system with base 2 (contrasted with our common system of base 10) used in digital computers.

bi·nate, bī'nāt, *a. Bot.* Being double or in couples; growing in pairs.

bin·au·ral, bin·nôr'əl, bin·ôr'əl, *a.* Having two ears; for both ears; stereophonic.

bind, bīnd, *v.t.,* **bound, bind·ing.** To tie with a cord; to fasten or encircle, as with a band; to put a ligature or bandage on; to put in bonds; to confine or restrain; to make cohere; to engage by a vow, law, duty, or other tie; to form a border on; to sew together and cover (a book); to place under legal obligation; to indenture (a person) as an apprentice; to constipate.—*v.i.* To be obligatory; to have binding force; to tie up; to exercise a restraining force; to grow hard or stiff (of soil); to jam.—*n.* That which binds.

bind·er, bīnd'ər, *n.* A person or thing that binds; one whose occupation is to bind books; a machine that binds sheaves; a cover for holding together loose sheets of paper.

bind·er·y, bīn'də·rē, bīn'drē, *n. pl.,* **-er·ies.** A place where books are bound.

bind·ing, bīn'ding, *n.* The act of one who binds; anything which binds; the cover of a book; something that secures the edges of cloth; a set of ski fastenings used to secure the boot onto the ski.—*a.* Serving to bind; having power to hold to some agreement, pledge, etc.; obligatory.

binge, binj, *n. Informal.* A spree.

bin·go, bing'gō, *n.* A game similar to lotto, often played simultaneously by large groups.

bin·na·cle, bin'ə·kəl, *n.* A case on the deck of a

vessel, near the helm, containing the compass.

bi·noc·u·lar, bə·nok'yə·lər, bī·nok'yə·lər, *a.* Pertaining to or employing both eyes.—*n. Usu. pl.* A binocular optical instrument, as a field glass.

bi·no·mi·al, bī·nō'mē·əl, *a.* Consisting of or pertaining to two terms connected by the sign + or −.

bio·chem·is·try, bī·ō·kem'is·trē, *n.* The science that studies the chemical processes of plant and animal life. **—bio·chem·i·cal,** *a.* **—bio·chem·ist,** *n.*

bi·o·e·col·o·gy, bī·ō·ē·kol'ə·jē, *n.* Ecology dealing with the interaction of plants and animals with their environment.

bi·o·en·gi·neer·ing, bī·ō·en·jə·nēr'ing, *n.* Engineering principles applied to the processes and products of biology.

bi·o·gen·e·sis, bī·ō·jen'ə·sis, *n.* The doctrine that living organisms can be produced only by other living organisms. **—bio·ge·net·ic,** bī·ō·jə·net'ik, *a.*

bi·og·ra·phy, bī·og'rə·fē, bē·og'rə·fē, *n. pl.,* **-phies.** The history of the life and character of another person; biographical writings as a department of literature. **—bi·og·ra·pher,** *n.* **—bi·o·graph·ic,** bī·ə·graf'ik, **bi·o·graph·i·cal,** bī·ə·graf'i·kəl, *a.* **—bi·o·graph·i·cal·ly,** *adv.*

bi·o·log·i·cal clock, *n.* A combination of internal functions in living organisms which commands the rhythmic cycles of diverse involuntary activities.

bi·o·log·i·cal con·trol, *n.* Attack on pests and parasites by interfering with their relationship to their environment, as by the introduction of their natural enemies.

bi·o·log·i·cal war·fare, *n.* Warfare using bacteria or viruses or other products against men, domestic imals, or food plants.

bi·ol·o·gy, bī·ol'ə·jē, *n.* The science which deals with life, with vital processes, and with the morphology, physiology, origin, development, and distribution of plants and animals. **—bi·o·log·i·cal,** bī·ə·loj'i·kəl, *a.* Also **bi·o·log·ic.** **—bi·ol·o·gist,** *n.*

bi·o·met·rics, bī·ō·met'riks, *n. pl., sing. in const.* The branch of biological science concerned with quantitative statistics.

bi·om·e·try, bī·om'ə·trē, *n.* The measurement of life; the calculation of the probable duration of human life. Also **bi·o·met·rics.**

bi·o·nom·ics, bī·ə·nom'iks, *n. pl., sing. or pl. in constr.* Ecology.

bi·o·phys·ics, bī·ō·fiz'iks, *n. pl., sing. or pl. in constr.* The study of living things using the methods and principles of physics. **—bi·o·phys·i·cal,** *a.* **—bi·o·phys·i·cist,** *n.*

bi·op·sy, bī'op·sē, *n. pl.,* **-sies.** The examination of tissue from a living subject.

bi·o·sphere, bī'ə·sfēr, *n.* The earth, water, and region of the atmosphere that supports plant and animal life.

bi·o·tin, bī'ə·tin, *n.* A crystalline growth vitamin, of the vitamin B complex.

bi·par·ti·san, bī·pär'tə·zən, *a.* Of or representing two parties, esp. the Democratic and Republican parties.

bi·par·tite, bī·pär'tīt, *a.* Having two parts; *bot.,* divided into two parts nearly to the base, as a leaf. **—bi·par·ti·tion,** bī·pär·tish'ən, *n.*

bi·ped, bī'ped, *n.* An animal having two feet, as man. **—bi·ped·al,** *a.*

bi·plane, bī'plān, *n.* An early type of airplane with two wings, one above the other.

bi·po·lar, bī·pō'lər, *a.* Having two poles; pertaining to or found at both poles; having two diametrically opposed views or natures. **—bi·po·lar·i·ty,** bī·pō·lar'ə·tē, *n.*

birch, bərch, *n.* A graceful tree having small leaves, and a smooth, multi-layered, whitish bark; its hard wood, often used for furniture; a birch rod used for whipping.—**birch·en,** *a.*

bird, bərd, *n.* Any of a class of warm-blooded vertebrates having a body more or less covered with feathers, and the forelimbs modified to form wings; a game bird; a shuttlecock; a clay pigeon.

bird·bath, bərd′bath, bərd′bäth, *n.* An ornamental basin placed outdoors to be filled with water in which birds may bathe.

bird·brain, bərd′brān, *n. Informal.* A scatterbrain. —**bird·brained,** *a.*

bird·call, bərd′kôl, *n.* The call of a bird; an instrument or sound imitating the call.

bird dog, *n.* Any of several breeds of dogs, used in hunting and fetching birds.

bird·ie, bər′dē, *n.* In golf, a score of one stroke under par on a hole; a small bird.

bird·lime, bərd′līm, *n.* A viscous substance smeared on twigs to catch small birds.

bird·man, bərd′man, bərd′mən, *n. pl.,* **-men.** An ornithologist. *Informal.* An aviator.

bird of par·a·dise, *n.* A tropical bird noted for magnificent plumage.

bird of pas·sage, *n.* A migratory bird. *Informal.* A migratory or footloose person.

bird of prey, *n.* A predatory bird, such as the eagle, hawk, vulture, etc.

bird's-eye, bərdz′ī, *a.* Seen comprehensively, as by a bird flying above: a *bird's-eye* view; general; having markings or spots resembling birds' eyes.

bi·ret·ta, bə·ret′ə, *n.* A stiff, square cap with three (or four) upright projecting pieces worn by Roman Catholic ecclesiastics. Also **bir·ret·ta.**

birl, bərl, *v.t.* To rotate a floating log by treading; to whirl; to pour; to ply with drink.

birth, bərth, *n.* The act of being born; the occasion of coming into life; the act of bringing forth; parturition; lineage; noble lineage; natural inheritance; that which is born; origin; beginning.

birth cer·ti·fi·cate, *n.* An official copy of the record of one's birth.

birth con·trol, *n.* The prevention or the regulation of conception through the use of drugs or devices.

birth·day, bərth′dā, *n.* The day on which any person is born, or the anniversary of the day; day or time of origin.

birth·mark, bərth′märk, *n.* Some congenital mark on a person's body.

birth·place, bərth′plās, *n.* The place of one's birth; place of origin.

birth rate, *n.* The ratio of the number of births in a given time to the total population or esp. to each thousand of population.

birth·right, bərth′rīt, *n.* Any right to which a person is entitled by birth.

birth·stone, bərth′stōn, *n.* A precious or semiprecious stone associated with a certain month or sign of the zodiac.

bis·cuit, bis′kit, *n.* Bread baked in small pieces from dough leavened with soda, yeast, or baking powder; *Brit.,* a cracker; a light brown color; pottery baked once but not glazed.

bi·sect, bī·sekt′, bī′sekt, *v.t.* To divide into two parts; esp. into two equal parts, as a line, etc.; to intersect. —*v.i.* To fork, as in a road. —**bi·sec·tion,** bī·sek′shən, *n.* —**bi·sec·tor,** *n.*

bi·sex·u·al, bī·sek′shoo·əl, *a.* Of both. sexes; hermaphrodite; responsive sexually to either sex.

bish·op, bish′əp, *n.* A prelate who generally has the spiritual direction and government of a diocese; a chess piece which moves only diagonally.

bish·op·ric, bish′əp·rik, *n.* The office, rank, or diocese of a bishop.

bis·muth, biz′məth, *n.* A brittle, reddish-white metallic element, having compounds used in medicine.

bi·son, bī′sən, bī′zən, *n.* Either of two bovine mammals, the European bison and the American bison or

buffalo, the latter having short, rounded horns, and on the shoulders a large fleshy hump.

bisque, bisk, *n.* A thick, rich soup made of shellfish or game stewed long and slowly; any smooth, creamy soup; a kind of ice cream containing powdered macaroons.

bis·ter, bis·tre, bis′tər, *n.* A dark-brown pigment, often used in drawing, which is prepared from the soot of wood; also, the color of this. —**bis·tered, bis·tred,** *a.*

bis·tro, bis′trō, *Fr.* bē·strō′, *n. pl.,* **bis·tros,** bis′trōz, *Fr.* bē·strō′. A small bar, restaurant, or night club.

bi·sul·fide, bī·səl′fīd, bī·səl′fid, *n.* A disulfide.

bit, bit, *n.* A piece bitten off; a small piece or quantity of anything. *Informal.* A short time; multiples of 12¹/₂ cents: two *bits*, twenty-five cents; a small part or routine in a play or movie.

bit, bit, *n.* The biting, cutting, or penetrating part of various tools; the movable boring or drilling part used in a carpenter's brace, a drilling machine, or the like; the part of a key which enters the lock; the metallic mouthpiece of a bridle; anything that curbs or restrains.—*v.t.,* **bit·ted, bit·ting.** To put a bit in the mouth of; bridle; curb; restrain.

bit, bit, *n.* A unit of information in a computer language using two characters.

bitch, bich, *n.* The female of the dog, or of other, esp. canine, animals: sometimes applied abusively to a woman.—*v.i. Informal.* To complain.

bite, bīt, *v.t.,* **bit, bit·ten** or **bit, bit·ing.** To cut, break, penetrate, or seize with the teeth; to cause a sharp or smarting pain in; to pinch or nip; to blast or blight; to grip or catch into or on; to corrode or eat into.—*v.i.* To have a habit of biting; to seize a bait with the mouth; to grip or hold onto; to be tricked or cheated.—*n.* The seizure of anything by the teeth or with the mouth; a morsel of food; a snack; a wound made by the mouth; catch or hold of one object on another.—**bite the dust,** *informal.* To die; to fail; to meet defeat.

bit·ing, bī′ting, *a.* Sharp; cutting; caustic; sarcastic. —**bit·ing·ly,** *adv.*

bit·stock, bit′stok, *n.* A brace for a bit.

bitt, bit, *n. Naut.* A piece of wood or frame secured to the deck, on which to make fast the mooring lines. —*v.t.* To secure a ship's cables to, as a bitt.

bit·ter, bit′ər, *a.* Having the harsh taste characteristic of quinine, etc.; painful to the mind or body; unpleasant to accept; distressful; expressing intense grief; stinging; causing pain or smart, as cold; harsh or cutting, as words; cruel; characterized by intense animosity.—*n.* That which is bitter; bitterness.—*v.t., v.i.* To make or become bitter. —**bit·ter·ish,** *a.* —**bit·ter·ly,** *adv.* —**bit·ter·ness,** *n.*

bit·tern, bit′ərn, *n.* A name given to several wading birds of the heron family, known for their characteristic booming cry.

bit·ter·root, bit′ər·root, bit′ər·rût, *n.* A plant having fleshy roots and handsome pink flowers, growing in the mountains of Idaho, Montana, etc.

bit·ters, bit′ərz, *n. pl.* A liquid, usually alcoholic, impregnated with a bitter plant product.

bit·ter·sweet, bit′ər·swēt, bit′ər·swēt′, *n.* A climbing plant with scarlet berries; a climbing plant with orange capsules opening to expose red-coated seeds.—bit′ər·swēt′, *a.* Both bitter and sweet at the same time.

bi·tu·men, bi·too′mən, bi·tū′mən, *n.* Any of various mineral substances of a resinous nature and highly inflammable, as asphalt, naphtha, petroleum, etc., containing mainly hydrocarbons. —**bi·tu·mi·nous,** *a.*

bi·tu·mi·nous coal, *n.* An impure coal containing volatile hydrocarbons, which burns with a smoky flame; soft coal.

bi·va·lent, bī·vā′lənt, biv′ə·lənt, *a.* Having a valence of two. —**bi·va·lence,** *n.*

bi·valve, bī′valv, *n.* A mollusk having a shell consisting of two parts joined by an elastic hinge, as the oyster, clam, mussel, etc.—*a.* Having two valves. Also **bi·val·vu·lar,** biv/val/vyə·lər.

biv·ou·ac, biv/wak, biv/oo·ak, *n.* A temporary encampment of soldiers in the open, with little or no shelter; any similar encampment.—*v.i.,* **-acked, -ack·ing.** To encamp in bivouac.

bi·week·ly, bī·wēk/lē, *a.* Occurring every two weeks; occurring twice a week; semiweekly.—*n. pl.,* **-lies.** A publication issued biweekly.—*adv.*

bi·year·ly, bī·yēr/lē, *a.* Occurring once in two years; biennial; biannual.—*adv.*

bi·zarre, bi·zär/, *a.* Strikingly singular; odd; fantastic; grotesque. **—bi·zarre·ly,** *adv.* **—bi·zarre·ness,** *n.*

blab, blab, *v.t.* **—blabbed, blab·bing.** To utter in a thoughtless manner what ought to be kept secret; to let out (secrets).—*v.i.* To talk incoherently or excessively; to prattle.—*n.* Idle chatter; one who blabs; a telltale. **—blab·ber, blab·ber·mouth,** *n.*

black, blak, *a.* Of the darkest possible color; absorbing all light, or incapable of reflecting it; of an extremely dark color; dark-skinned; Negro; soiled or stained; dismal or gloomy; boding ill; sullen and forbidding; evil or wicked; calamitous or disastrous; malignant; indicating blame or disgrace; clad in black.—*n.* The darkest color, opposite of white; a black dye or pigment; black attire; mourning; something black, as soot; a Negro.—*v.t.* To make black; put a black color on; clean and polish (shoes, etc.) with blacking; blacken.—*v.i.* To become black. **—to black out,** to darken completely; to delete; to suffer a temporary loss of vision or consciousness; to extinguish all lights.

black·a·moor, blak/ə·mûr, *n.* A Negro; a dark-skinned human being.

black-and-blue, blak·ən·bloo/, *a.* Of a dark, livid color, as of bruised skin.

black and white, *n.* Writing or print; artwork rendered in black and white.

black art, *n.* Black magic.

black·ball, blak/bôl, *n.* A vote against an applicant or candidate.—*v.t.* To vote against; ostracize.

black bass, *n.* An American freshwater game fish.

black bear, *n.* A large, common, North American bear.

black·ber·ry, blak/ber·ē, blak/bə·rē, *n. pl.,* **-ries.** The juicy, edible fruit, black or very dark purple when ripe, of certain bushes and vines; the plant.

black·bird, blak/bərd, *n.* A European bird of the thrush family, the male having black plumage and a yellow bill; any of several North American birds.

black·board, blak/bōrd, blak/bôrd, *n.* A dark, smooth hard surface, as of slate, etc., for writing or drawing on with chalk or crayons.

black·bod·y, blak/bod/ē, *n.* A hypothetical body or surface that completely absorbs without reflection all radiant energy falling upon it.

black·cap, blak/kap, *n.* A European bird of the warbler family, with a black tufted crown; a chickadee; a species of raspberry having black fruit, native to North America; black raspberry.

Black Death, *n.* The bubonic plague, which was epidemic in Europe and Asia during the fourteenth century.

black·en, blak/ən, *v.t.* To make black; to polish with blacking; to defame; to slander.—*v.i.* To become black or dark.

black eye, *n.* An eye with a black or blackish-brown iris; an eye with the surrounding flesh or skin discolored by a blow or bruise. *Informal.* A bad reputation; dishonor.

black-eyed Su·san, blak/īd soo/zən, *n.* Any of several plants having yellow flowers or heads with a dark center.

black flag, *n.* The flag formerly flown by pirates bearing the mark of a white skull and crossbones on black background.

black grouse, *n.* European and Asian gamebird, the plumage of which is black on the male and spotted on the female.

black·guard, blag/ärd, blag/ərd, *n.* A scoundrel; a rogue.—*v.t.* To revile in low or scurrilous language.

Black Hand, *n.* A lawless European society; in the U.S., a secret society engaged in blackmail, extortion, terrorism, etc.

black·head, blak/hed, *n.* A skin blemish consisting of a blackish fatty secretion at the root of a hair; any of several birds having a black head, as the scaup; a malignant, infectious disease of turkeys, peacocks, etc.

black-heart·ed, blak/här·tid, *a.* Evil.

black hole, *n.* The supposed final stage of existence of certain stars, in which the star has collapsed to such an extremely small, dense mass that not even light can escape its gravitational field.

black hu·mor, *n.* A type of fictional writing which contains grotesquely, absurdly, or morbidly humorous plots and descriptions.

black·ing, blak/ing, *n.* A preparation used to color an object black.

black·jack, blak/jak, *n.* The flag of a pirate; a small leather-covered club weighted at the head; a card game.—*v.t.* To coerce; to strike with a blackjack.

black lead, *n.* Graphite.

black let·ter, *n.* Heavy-faced ornate type characteristic of or resembling early printed books.—*a.* Printed in black letter.

black light, *n.* A type of spotlight utilizing invisible ultraviolet or infrared light; an ultraviolet or infrared light.

black·list, blak/list, *n.* An unfavorable list, as of persons to be censured, companies to be boycotted, job-seekers to be refused employment, etc.—*v.t.* To place on a blacklist.

black·ly, blak/lē, *adv.* Darkly; gloomily; wickedly.

black mag·ic, *n.* Witchcraft; evil magic.

black·mail, blak/māl, *n.* Extortion of money or equivalent from a person by threats of public accusation, exposure, or censure; any extorted payment.—*v.t.* To extort money from in this way.

Black Ma·ri·a, blak mə·rī/ə, *n. Informal.* A police patrol wagon.

black mark, *n.* A mark of censure, punishment, failure, etc.

black mar·ket, *n.* Trade in violation of official prices or quantities.

Black Mus·lims, *n.* Popular name for a black American sect which believes in the Islamic religion, black racial superiority, and the segregation of blacks and whites. Its members prefer to be called **Ministers of Islam.**

black·out, blak/owt, *n.* A period of darkness, usu. as an air raid precaution; the extinguishing of stage lights to end a scene or play; censorship; a temporary loss of vision or consciousness, such as an aviator experiences from a sudden dive.

black sheep, *n.* A person viewed as a disgrace or embarrassment by the other members of his family or group.

black·smith, blak/smith, *n.* One who works in iron and makes iron utensils; a person who shoes horses.

black·snake, blak/snāk, *n.* Any of various snakes of a black or very dark color, including two nonvenomous snakes in the U.S.; a heavy whip of braided rawhide or leather.

black·thorn, blak/thôrn, *n.* A much-branched, thorny European shrub bearing small, plumlike fruits. Also **sloe.** A walking stick made from the stem of this shrub.

black tie, *n.* Men's semiformal evening attire; a tuxedo, worn with a black bow tie.

---

black·top, blak′top, *n.* A bituminous material, as asphalt, for paving roads, etc.

black wal·nut, *n.* The edible, oily nut of a tree of eastern North America; the tree; its hard, dark-brown wood used in furniture.

black wid·ow spi·der, *n.* The female of an American spider with a poisonous bite, and so named because of its glossy black body and habit of devouring its mate.

blad·der, blad′ər, *n.* A stretchable, membranous sac which stores and secretes urine from the kidneys; any similar sac or receptacle. **—blad·der·y,** *a.*

blad·der·wort, blad′ər·wərt, *n.* Any of various herbs, some of which float free in water by means of small bladders on the leaves, and others root in mud.

blade, blād, *n.* The leaf of a grass plant or cereal; the broad part of a leaf; a thin, flat part of something, as of an oar; the cutting part of a weapon or tool; a sword; a swordsman; a dashing or rakish fellow; the bottom running edge of ice skates; the front flat part of the tongue.

blain, blān, *n.* A pustule; a blister.

blame, blām, *v.t.,* **blamed, blam·ing.** To place the responsibility on, as a person or thing; to express disapproval of; to find fault with.—*n.* An expression of censure; reproach; that which is deserving of censure. **—be to blame,** deserve blame. **—blam·a·ble, blame·a·ble,** *a.* **—blame·ful,** *a.* **—blame·less,** *a.* **—blame·less·ly,** *adv.* **—blame·less·ness,** *n.*

blame·wor·thy, blām′wər·thē, *a.* Deserving blame. **—blame·wor·thi·ness,** *n.*

blanch, blanch, blänch, *v.t.* To make white, esp. by removing the color; bleach; whiten; to make pale, as with sickness, fear, cold, etc.; to remove skins from by dipping in hot water.—*v.i.* To become white; turn pale.

blanc-mange, blə·mänj′, *n.* A whitish, jellylike dessert composed of milk, egg-white, and flavoring thickened with cornstarch, gelatine, etc.

bland, bland, *a.* Smooth, suave, or agreeable; soft, gentle, or balmy; mild. **—bland·ly,** *adv.* **—bland·ness,** *n.*

blan·dish, blan′dish, *v.t.* To coax with flattery; cajole.—*v.i.* To use flattery. **—blan·dish·er,** *n.* **—blan·dish·ment,** *n. Usu. pl.*

blank, blangk, *a.* White or pale; of paper, etc., left white, or free from marks; not filled out, as a check; empty; without contents; void or bare; lacking some usual feature; void of interest, showing no attention or emotion, as a person's look; disconcerted; complete, utter: *blank* stupidity.—*n.* Something left blank, or not written on; a form with spaces to be filled in; any of these spaces; any vacant space; a void; anything insignificant; a piece of metal prepared to be formed into a coin, key, etc.—*v.t.* To make blank or void; keep an opponent from scoring. **—blank·ly,** *adv.* **—blank·ness,** *n.*

blank check, *n.* A bank check, signed but with the amount not specified; carte blanche; authority without limitation.

blan·ket, blang′kit, *n.* A large piece of soft, loosely woven, usu. wool fabric, used to cover people or animals; anything like a blanket, esp. a covering layer.—*v.t.* To cover with or as with a blanket; to obscure; to apply to uniformly; to hinder; to interfere with.—*a.* Covering a wide range of things, or everything: a *blanket* indictment.

blank verse, *n.* Unrhymed verse, esp. in iambic pentameter.

blare, blâr, *v.i., v.t.,* **blared, blar·ing.** To sound loudly, like a trumpet; to proclaim noisily; utter brazenly.—*n.* A loud, brazen sound; bright glare of color.

blar·ney, blär′nē, *n.* Gross flattery; smooth, deceitful talk.—*v.t.* To flatter; to humbug with talk.

bla·sé, blä·zā′, blä′zā, *a.* Satiated with enjoyment; exhausted by overindulgence; bored.

blas·pheme, blas·fēm′, blas′fēm, *v.t., v.i.,* **-phemed, -phem·ing.** To speak impiously or contemptuously of

God or sacred things; to speak evil of; calumniate.—*v.i.* To utter impious or abusive words. **—blas·phem·er,** blas·fē′mər, *n.* **—blas·phem·ous,** blas′fə·məs, *a.* **—blas·phem·y,** blas′fə·mē, *n. pl.,* **-phem·ies.**

blast, blast, bläst, *n.* A blowing or gust of wind; a forcible stream of air, steam, etc.; the blowing of a trumpet, etc.; the sound produced by this; any pernicious influence; a blight; the act of rending rock, etc., by an explosive; the charge of explosive used for this.—*v.i.* To cause to shrivel or wither; blight; destroy; rend, as rock, by an explosive. **—at full blast,** in full operation. **—to blast off,** to take off, as a rocket.

blast·ed, blas′tid, blä′stid, *a.* Withered; blighted; damned; cursed.

blast fur·nace, *n.* A furnace in which ores are smelted by the aid of a blast of air.

blast-off, blast′ôf, blast′of, *n.* Take-off, esp. of a rocket.

blas·tu·la, blas′chə·lə, *n. pl.,* **-las** or **-lae,** -lē. The stage of an embryo in which a single layer of cells encloses a fluid-filled cavity.

blat, blat, *v.i.,* **blat·ted, blat·ting.** *Informal.* To bleat, as a sheep.—*v.t. Informal.* To utter loudly and indiscreetly; blurt out.

bla·tant, blā′tənt, *a.* Clamorous; loud-mouthed; brazenly obvious: a *blatant* lie. **—bla·tan·cy,** *n.* **bla·tant·ly,** *adv.*

blath·er·skite, blath′ər·skīt, *n.* A blustering or babbling person; babble.

blaze, blāz, *n.* The stream of light and heat from any object when burning; a flame; brilliance; a sudden outburst; a violent display.—*v.i.* To burn brightly; to shine; to display bright colors; to burn with anger, excitement, etc.

blaze, blāz, *n.* A white spot on the face of a horse, cow, etc.; a mark made on a tree, as by removing a piece of the bark.—*v.t.,* **blazed, blaz·ing.** To mark, as a tree, with a blaze; indicate, as a trail, by blazes.

bla·zer, blā′zər, *n.* A bright-colored jacket.

bleach, blēch, *v.t.* To make white or whiter, as by exposure to sunlight or by chemical agents.—*v.i.* To become white.—*n.* The act of bleaching; any agent used for bleaching.

bleach·er, blē′chər, *n.* One who or that which bleaches; *pl.,* unroofed, low-priced, outdoor seats for spectators.

bleak, blēk, *a.* Exposed to cold and winds; desolate; dreary; cold; chill. **—bleak·ly,** *adv.* **—bleak·ness,** *n.*

blear, blēr, *a.* Dim, as from tears; misty; indistinct; —*v.t.* To make dim or blurred. **—blear·y-eyed,** *a.*

blear·y, blēr′ē, *a.,* **-i·er, -i·est.** Blurred; dim. **—blear·i·ness,** *n.*

bleat, blēt, *v.t.* To utter the cry of a sheep or a similar cry; to whine.—*n.* The act or sound of bleating.

bleed, blēd, *v.i.,* **bled, bleed·ing.** To lose blood; to be drained of blood; to let sap or other moisture flow from itself; to trickle or flow; to feel pity, grief, or anguish; to pay out money or have it extorted.—*v.t.* To take blood from; to exude, as sap, juice, etc.; to extort money from.

bleed·er, blē′dər, *n.* A person predisposed to bleeding; hemophiliac.

bleed·ing heart, *n.* A garden plant with racemes of red, heart-shaped flowers.

blem·ish, blem′ish, *v.t.* To mar; to sully; to tarnish. —*n.* A defect of the skin; a blot or stain.

blench, blench, *v.i.* To shrink back or flinch, as in fear.

blend, blend, *v.t.,* **blend·ed** or **blent, blend·ing.** To mix; combine so that the things mixed cannot be distinguished; mix in order to produce a uniform product.—*v.i.* To become mixed; unite in a uniform or harmonious whole; pass or shade imperceptibly, as colors into one another.—*n.* A mixing or a mixture. **—blend·er,** *n.*

bless, bles, *v.t.,* **bless·ed** or **blest, bles·sing.** To invoke the divine favor on; to express a wish for the good fortune of; to bestow happiness or good things upon; to make and pronounce holy; to praise; to esteem or account happy.

bless·ed, bles′id, blest, *a.* Favored with blessings; enjoying spiritual blessings and the favor of God; fraught with or imparting blessings; holy. **—bless·ed·ly,** *adv.* **—bless·ed·ness,** *n.*

bless·ing, bles′ing, *n.* The act of one who blesses; a prayer or solemn wish imploring happiness upon another; a benediction; the act of pronouncing a benediction; any good thing falling to one's lot; a mercy.

blight, blīt, *n.* Some disease that destroys plants, arrests their growth, etc.; any insect or fungus which infects or destroys plants; any malignant influence. *—v.t.* To cause to wither or decay; to frustrate; to ruin.*—v.i.* To injure as blight does.

blimp, blimp, *n.* A small, nonrigid dirigible.

blind, blīnd, *a.* Not having sight; not having the faculty of discernment; not based on reason or evidence; not easily discernible; navigating by instruments, without visibility: *blind* flying; without openings for admitting light; closed at one end: a *blind* alley.*—v.t.* To make unable to see; to rob of ability to reason or judge; to dazzle; to obscure.*—n.* Something to hinder sight or keep out light; a place to hide oneself from view; a false identity or activity to conceal or deceive. **—blind·ing,** *a.* **—blind·ing·ly,** *adv.* **—blind·ly,** *adv.* **—blind·ness,** *n.*

blind date, *n.* A date between two persons of opposite sex who have not previously met.

blind·er, blīn′dər, *n.* One that blinds; a blinker on a horse's bridle.

blind·fold, blīnd′fōld, *v.t.* To cover the eyes of; to hoodwink.*—a.* With the eyes covered; reckless.*—n.* A cloth or other covering, placed over the eyes.

blind·man's buff, blīnd′manz, *n.* A group game in which one person is blindfolded and tries to catch and identify another.

blind spot, *n.* The point in the retina that is insensitive to light; a subject about which one is ignorant or biased; an area where radio signals are poorly received.

blink, blingk, *v.i.* To wink, esp. rapidly and repeatedly; look with winking eyes; glance with dim vision; to look evasively; to shine unsteadily; twinkle.*—v.t.* To cause to blink; to shut the eyes to; evade.*—n.* The act of blinking; a glimpse.**—on the blink,** *Informal.* Not in proper working condition.

blink·er, bling′kər, *n.* One who blinks; a leather flap to prevent a horse from seeing sideways or backward. Also **blind·er.** A light that flashes as a warning or signal.

blintze, blintz, blints, *n.* A kind of pancake, usually with a filling of fruit or cheese.

biip, blip, *n.* A spot of light on a radar scope, or the like.

bliss, blis, *n.* The highest degree of happiness; blessedness; felicity. **—bliss·ful,** *a.* **—bliss·ful·ly,** *adv.* **—bliss·ful·ness,** *n.*

blis·ter, blis′tər, *n.* A thin vesicle on the skin, containing watery matter or serum, as from an injury; a pustule; a similar swelling on the surface of plants, paint, etc.*—v.t.* To raise a blister or blisters on; to reprimand harshly.*—v.i.* To become blistered. **—blis·ter·y,** *a.*

blithe, blīth, blīth, *a.* Gay; merry; joyous. **—blithe·ly,** *adv.*

blithe·some, blīth′səm, blīth′səm, *a.* Full of blitheness. **—blithe·some·ly,** *adv.*

blitz, blits, *n.* Any all-out effort.*—v.t.* To attack by blitz.

blitz·krieg, blits′krēg, *n.* A technique of warfare consisting of a violent, massive, surprise attack by tanks, aircraft, etc. Also **blitz.**

bliz·zard, bliz′ərd, *n.* A violent snowstorm with strong winds and intense cold.

bloat, blōt, *v.t.* To cause to swell with air or water; to cause to swell with conceit.*—v.i.* To become swollen or puffed up.

blob, blob, *n.* A small globe of liquid; a bubble; a thing of undefined shape.

bloc, blok, *n.* An association of groups, nations, legislators, etc., united to further their joint interests: the farm *bloc* in Congress.

block, blok, *n.* A solid mass of wood, stone, or the like, usually with one or more plane faces; a hollow building unit; a cubical toy for children to build with; a solid mass of wood, a platform, etc., on which meat is chopped, goods are auctioned, etc.; a mold on which something is shaped: a hat *block;* an object, with a design cut on the surface, used for printing; a block and tackle.*—n.* A connected mass of buildings; a portion of a city bordered by four neighboring streets; the length of one side of this; a quantity or section taken as a unit: a *block* of tickets; a section of railroad track controlled by signals.*—v.t.* To shape into blocks or with a block; to strengthen with blocks. **—to block out** or **in,** to outline; plan roughly. **—block·er,** *n.*

block, blok, *n.* An obstacle or hindrance; a stoppage, as of traffic; obstruction of a nerve, blood vessel, etc.; stopping an opponent's play, as in football; a cessation of thought or memory, caused by emotional stress.*—v.t.* To hinder passage; to obstruct; to oppose or interfere successfully, as in football or boxing.*—v.i.* To obstruct an opponent's actions.**—block out,** to obscure from view. **—block·age,** *n.* **—block·er,** *n.*

block·ade, blo·kād′, *n.* The blocking of entry to and exit from a harbor, line of coast, etc., by hostile ships or troops; a blockading force; any obstruction of passage.*—v.t.,* **-ad·ed, -ad·ing.** To subject to a blockade; to obstruct. **—block·ad·er,** *n.*

block and tack·le, *n.* A set of pulleys and rope used for lifting or hauling heavy objects.

block·bust·er, blok′bəs·tər, *n. Informal.* A very large aerial demolition bomb; something overwhelmingly effective.

block·head, blok′hed, *n.* A stupid fellow.

block·house, blok′hows, *n.* Formerly a small, fortified building made of logs or timber, having loopholes for musketry; any reinforced building used for protection against enemy troops.

block·ish, blok′ish, *a.* Like a block; stupid; dull. **—block·ish·ly,** *adv.*

block let·ter, *n.* A letter or type face without serifs.

block·y, blok′ē, *a.* Similar to a block; stocky, chunky; marked by blocks or patches of unequally distributed light and shade.

blond, blonde, blond, *a.* Of a fair color of hair or complexion.*—n.* A person with blond hair (*blonde* is the feminine form).

blood, blud, *n.* The fluid that circulates in the vascular system of the vertebrates, in humans, having a red color; the vital fluid as shed from a wound; gore; bloodshed or murder; juice or sap, as of plants; the physical nature; temper or state of mind; birth, parentage, kinship, or breed, esp. good breed; lineage; royal lineage; family, race; offspring; a spirited or dashing fellow.

blood bank, *n.* An institution for storing and processing blood or blood plasma; blood or plasma so stored.

blood bath, *n.* Wholesale killing; a massacre.

blood broth·er, *n.* Brother by birth; one tied to another by strong bonds of friendship.

blood count, *n.* Determination of the number and proportion of red and white cells in a specific volume of blood.

blood·curd·ling, blud′kərd·ling, *a.* Frightening; terrifying.

blood·ed, blud′id, *a.* Of good blood or breed, as thoroughbred horses or cattle.

---

blood group, *n.* One of several classifications into which human blood can be divided, based on the presence or absence of specific antigens.

blood·hound, bləd′hownd, *n.* One of a breed 'of medium to large powerful dogs with a very acute sense of smell. *Informal.* A relentless pursuer.

blood·less, bləd′lis, *a.* Without blood; drained of blood; dead; without shedding blood; without spirit; cruel. **—blood·less·ly,** *adv.* **—blood·less·ness,** *n.*

blood·let·ting, bləd′let·ing, *n.* The act of opening a vein, as a remedial measure; bloodshed.

blood mon·ey, *n.* Money paid to procure or to compensate for the killing of a person.

blood poi·son·ing, *n.* A diseased condition of the blood due to toxic matter or microorganisms.

blood pres·sure, *n.* The pressure of the blood against the inner walls of the blood vessels, varying with exertion, strength of the heart, age, or health.

blood re·la·tion, *n.* One related by birth; a kinsman. Also **blood rel·a·tive.**

blood·shed, bləd′shed, *n.* The shedding of blood; slaughter. Also **blood·shed·ding.**

blood·shot, bləd′shot, *a.* Red and inflamed or tinged with blood: said of the eye.

blood·stained, bləd′stānd, *a.* Stained with blood; guilty of killing.

blood·stone, bləd′stōn, *n.* A greenish kind of quartz with small blood-like spots of red jasper scattered through it.

blood·suck·er, bləd′sək·ər, *n.* Any animal that sucks blood, as a leech, a fly, etc.; a hard niggardly man; an extortioner.

blood·thirst·y, bləd′thər′stē, *a.* Sadistic; anxious to shed blood; murderous. **—blood·thirst·i·ly,** *adv.*

blood type, *n.* Blood group.

blood ves·sel, *n.* Any of the vessels of the body, including arteries, veins, and capillaries, through which the blood circulates.

blood·y, bləd′ē, *a.,* **-i·er, -i·est.** Of, like, or composed of blood; stained with blood; bleeding; blood-red; seeking or involving bloodshed; bloodthirsty; cruel. *Brit. Informal.* Cursed.—*v.t.,* **-ied, -y·ing.** To stain with blood. **—blood·i·ly,** *adv.* **—blood·i·ness,** *n.*

bloom, bloom, *n.* A blossom; the flower of a plant; the act or state of blossoming; fullness of life and vigor; a flourishing condition; a glow of health or beauty; the powdery coating upon certain fruits.—*v.i.* To produce blossoms; to flower; to glow with health; flourish.—*v.t.* To impart a bloom or radiance to.

bloom·ers, bloo′mərz, *n. pl.* Loose trousers gathered at the knee, formerly worn by women for physical training; undergarments of similar style.

bloom·ing, bloo′ming, *a.* Blossoming; flourishing. **—bloom·ing·ly,** *adv.*

bloop·er, bloo′pər, *n. Informal.* An embarrassing blunder; a weak fly ball falling between the infield and outfield.

blos·som, blos′əm, *n.* A flower, esp. of a plant yielding fruit; a state or period of flowering.—*v.i.* To put forth flowers; to bloom; to flourish.

blot, blot, *n.* A spot or stain, as of ink; a blemish; a stain upon reputation.—*v.t.,* **blot·ted, blot·ting.** To stain, as with ink; to detract from a person's reputation; dry with blotting paper or the like.—*v.i.* To make blots; to become blotted.—**blot out,** to hide; obscure; to obliterate.

blotch, bloch, *n.* An inflamed eruption or discolored patch on the skin; any large irregular spot or blot.—*v.t.* To cover or mark with blotches. **—blotch·y,** *a.*

blot·ter, blot′ər, *n.* A piece of blotting paper; a book in which sales, arrests, etc., are recorded as they take place.

blot·ting pa·per, *n.* A porous, unsized paper, used to absorb excess ink.

blouse, blows, blowz, *n.* A woman's loose, lightweight garment extending to the waist or below; the jacket of the U.S. Army service uniform; a garment resembling a smock.

blow, blō, *v.i.,* **blew, blown, blow·ing.** To make or form a current of air, as with the mouth; to move, as wind or air; to pant; to puff; to give out sound by being blown, as a horn; to burst. *Informal.* To boast; to depart from a place.—*v.t.* To drive a current of air upon; to drive by a current of air; to sound by the breath, as a horn; to form or swell by injecting air into; to put out of breath; to shatter by explosives; to melt (a fuse). *Informal.* To squander (money, etc.).—*n.* A gale of wind; a blast of air; the breathing or spouting of a whale; the act of producing a stream of air.—**blow in,** *informal,* appear unexpectedly.—**blow out,** to burst; to extinguish by blowing; to melt, as a fuse.—**blow over,** to subside; to pass without bad result.—**blow up,** to fill with air; to explode; to enlarge (a photograph); to arise or become stronger. *Informal.* To become very angry. **—blow·er,** *n.*

blow, blō, *n.* A stroke with the hand or fist, or a weapon; a knock; a sudden attack, calamity, or shock.

blow·fly, blō′flī, *n. pl.,* **-flies.** Any of various two-winged flies which deposit their eggs on meat or in wounds.

blow·gun, blō′gən, *n.* A long pipe or tube through which darts or pellets are blown.

blow·hole, blō′hōl, *n.* Either of two nasal openings at the top of the head in whales; any hole for the passage or escape of air.

blown, blōn, *a.* Carried by the wind; inflated; put out of breath; exhausted; tainted; unsavory; shaped with a blowtube.

blow·out, blō′owt, *n.* A rupture of an automobile tire; a sudden or violent escape of air, steam, or the like; the melting of an electric fuse. *Informal.* A lavish social event.

blow·pipe, blō′pīp, *n.* A tube through which a stream of air or gas is forced into a flame to direct and increase its heating action; a blowgun.

blow·torch, blō′tôrch, *n.* A small torch which gives an extremely hot flame, used for soldering and the like.

blow·up, blō′əp, *n.* An explosion. *Informal.* An outburst of anger; an enlarged photograph.

blow·y, blō′ē, *a.* Windy.

blowz·y, blow′zē, *a.* Redfaced; stout; coarse-looking; untidy.

blub·ber, bləb′ər, *n.* The fat of whales and other large sea mammals; the act of sobbing uncontrollably.—*v.i.* To sob noisily.—*v.t.* To utter while sobbing. **—blub·ber·y,** *a.*

bludg·eon, blej′ən, *n.* A short, heavy club with one end thicker than the other.—*v.t.* To beat; to coerce.

blue, bloo, *a.,* **blu·er, blu·est.** Of a color like or that of the clear sky in daylight; azure; cerulean; livid; low in spirits; dismal. *Informal.* Risqué; indecent.—*n.* The hue between green and violet in the spectrum; azure; a blue dye or pigment; bluing; something blue; as the sky or the sea.—**out of the blue,** totally unexpected. —*v.t.,* **blued, blu·ing.** To make blue; tinge with bluing. **—blue·ness,** *n.*

Blue·beard, bloo′bērd, *n.* Person in medieval tale; (*l.c.*) a wife-murderer.

blue·bell, bloo′bel, *n.* Any of various plants with blue, bell-shaped flowers.

blue·ber·ry, bloo′ber·ē, *n. pl.,* **-ries,** The edible, bluish berry of various shrubs; any of these shrubs.

blue·bird, bloo′bərd, *n.* A small N. American songbird whose prevailing color is blue.

blue blood, *n.* A person of aristocratic family. **—blue-blood·ed,** *a.*

blue·bon·net, bloo′bon·it, *n.* An annual plant of the pea family, having blue flowers.

blue book, *n.* A register of socially prominent persons.

blue·bot·tle, bloo′bot·əl, *n.* The cornflower; any of several species of large blowflies with a blue abdomen.

blue chip, *n.* A blue poker chip of highest value; a

thing of superior quality or reputation.

blue·coat, bloo′kōt, *n.* A policeman.

blue·col·lar, bloo′kol′ər, *a.* Referring to the wage-earning class who wear work clothes as distinguished from dress shirts.

blue·fish, bloo′fish, *n.* Any of certain American food fishes, common on the Atlantic coast.

blue·grass, bloo′gras, *n.* A name of several grasses, especially a grass of Kentucky.

blue·gum, bloo′gəm, *n.* A eucalyptus tree.

blue·jack·et, bloo′jak·it, *n.* A sailor.

blue jay, *n.* A North American bird, the crest and back of which are blue.

blue jeans, *n.* Pants of blue denim.

blue laws, *n. pl.* Severe or puritanic laws, especially those forbidding any entertainment or business on the Sabbath.

blue·nose, bloo′nōz, *n.* One who advocates a rigorous moral code.

blue note, *n.* A deliberately flatted note, characteristic of jazz and blues music.

blue-pen·cil, bloo′pen′səl, *v.t.* To alter or cancel with a pencil that makes a blue mark, as in editing a manuscript.

blue·print, bloo′print, *n.* A photographic print consisting of white lines on a blue ground, used for copying architect's plans, drawings, etc.; a detailed plan.

blue rib·bon, *n.* A piece of blue ribbon signifying the highest award, as first prize.

blues, blooz, *n. pl.* A style of jazz developed from a song of melancholy character and slow tempo written in characteristic key; a passing spell of mental depression.

blue·stock·ing, bloo′stok·ing, *n.* A woman having literary or intellectual tastes.

blue streak, *n.* An exceedingly fast-moving body; a rapid flow of speech.

blu·et, bloo′it, *n.* Any of various plants with blue flowers.

bluff, bləf, *a.* Presenting a nearly perpendicular front, as a cliff; rough and hearty, plain and frank.—*n.* A steep bank or cliff.

bluff, bləf, *n.* A bold pretense of strong resources for the purpose of daunting or deceiving or testing an opponent; one who bluffs.—*v.t., v.i.* To mislead or daunt by putting on a bold pretense.

blu·ing, bloo′ing, *n.* A chemical used in laundering to offset the yellow tinge of linen or cotton.

blun·der, blən′dər, *v.t.* To do clumsily and wrong; bungle; to blurt out.—*v.i.* To move or act blindly and clumsily; to make a stupid mistake.—*n.* A stupid mistake.—**blun·der·er,** *n.* —**blun·der·ing·ly,** *adv.*

blun·der·buss, blən′dər·bəs, *n.* An obsolete short gun with a large bore and funnel-shaped muzzle.

blunt, blənt, *a.* Having a thick edge or point, as an instrument; dull; dull in understanding; abrupt; plain; unceremonious. —**blunt·ly,** *adv.* —**blunt·ness,** *n.* —*v.t., v.i.* To make or become blunt.

blur, blər, *v.t., v.i.* **blurred, blur·ring.** To obscure as by smearing with ink; stain; obscure by making confused in form or outline; render indistinct.—*v.i.* To become blurred.—*n.* A smudge or smear; a blurred condition; something lacking distinct outlines.—**blur·ry,** *a.*

blurb, blərb, *n.* A praising announcement or advertisement, as on a book jacket.

blurt, blərt, *v.t.* To utter suddenly or unthinkingly, with *out.*

blush, bləsh, *v.i.* To redden in the face, as from shame, confusion, or modesty; to feel embarrassment; to flush; to exhibit a red color.—*n.* The reddening of the face through confusion, shame, or the like; a rosy tint. —**at first blush,** at first consideration. —**blush·ful,** *a.* —**blush·ing·ly,** *adv.*

blus·ter, bləs′tər, *v.i.* To roar as wind; to be loud, noisy, or swaggering; to make loud, empty threats. —*v.t.* To utter or effect in a blustering manner, with *out.*—*n.* A violent blast of wind; noisy talk; boisterousness.—**blus·ter·er,** *n.* —**blus·ter·ing·ly,** *adv.* —**blus·ter·ous, blus·ter·y,** *a.*

bo·a, bō′ə, *n.* Any of various large, nonvenomous tropical serpents with powerful coils for crushing prey, as **bo·a con·stric·tor,** a common tropical American species. A long feather or fur scarf worn by women.

boar, bōr, bôr, *n.* The uncastrated male of swine, wild or tame; the wild boar.

board, bōrd, bôrd, *n.* A piece of timber sawed thin; a flat slab or surface used for a specific purpose: a black*board* or ironing *board;* a pasteboard; a table, esp. on which to serve food; daily meals provided for pay; a body of persons directing some activity; border or edge. *Pl.* The stage of a theater.—*v.t.* To cover with boards; furnish with food, or with food and lodging, esp. for pay; to come up alongside of (a ship); go on board of (a ship, train, etc.).—*v.i.* To be supplied with food and sometimes lodging, in another's house at a fixed price. —**by the board,** overboard. —**on board,** aboard a ship, plane, etc.

board·er, bōr′dər, *n.* One who boards; esp., one who has his meals, or both meals and lodging, in the house of another for pay.

board foot, *n.* A unit of measure equal to a board one foot square and one inch thick (144 cubic inches).

board·ing house, bōr′ding·hows, bôr′ding·hows, *n.* A house where meals, or meals and lodging, are furnished for pay.

board·ing school, *n.* A school in which pupils are boarded and lodged.

board meas·ure, *n.* A system of cubic measure in which the unit is the board foot.

board·walk, bōrd′wôk, *n.* A promenade of boards along a beach.

boast, bōst, *v.i.* To speak in praise of oneself or one's belongings, followed by *of;* to brag; to exult; to bluster.—*v.t.* To speak of with pride, vanity, or exultation; to take pride in possessing.—*n.* A boastful statement; the cause of boasting. —**boast·er,** *n.* —**boast·ful,** *a.* —**boast·ful·ness,** *n.* —**boast·ing·ly,** *adv.*

boat, bōt, *n.* A small open vessel moved by oars, engine, etc.; any waterborne vessel; a dish shaped like a boat.—*v.t., v.i.* To put in or go by boat. —**in the same boat,** in the same situation. —**miss the boat,** to lose one's opportunity.

boat·house, bōt′hows, *n.* A house or shed, usu. along the water, for sheltering boats.

boat·man, bōt′mən, *n. pl.,* **-men.** A man who manages or works on boats.

boat·swain, bō′sən, bōt′swān, *n.* A ship's officer in charge of the hull, rigging, anchors, cables, etc. Also **bosun.**

bob, bob, *n.* The weight at the end of a pendulum, plumb line, etc.; a short jerking action or motion; A short haircut; a float for a fishing line; shortened tail of a horse.—*v.t.,* **bobbed, bob·bing.** To move up and down; to cut (the hair) short.—*v.i.* To move up and down irregularly; to curtsy; to fish with a bob.

bob·bin, bob′in, *n.* A reel or spool upon which yarn or thread is wound.

bob·ble, bob′əl, *v.i.,* **-bled, -bling.** To blunder.—*n.* An error; in sports, a misplay.

bob·by pin, bob′ē, *n.* A flat, metal hair pin which clasps and holds the hair in place.

bob·by socks, bob·by sox, *n. pl. Informal.* Short socks worn esp. by young girls. —**bob·by·sox·er,** bob′ē·sok·sər, *n.*

bob·cat, bob′kat, *n.* A common N. Amer. wildcat; the lynx.

---

a- hat, fāte, fāre, fäther; e- met, mē; i- pin, pīne; o- not, nōte, ôrb, moove (move), boy, pownd; u- cūbe, bůll, tûk (took); ch- chin; th- thick, ŧhen; zh- vizhon (vision); ə- əgo, takən, pencəl, lemən, bərd (bird).

bob·o·link, bob′ə·lingk, *n.* An American migratory songbird.

bob·sled, bob′sled, *n.* Two short sleds coupled in tandem, used in racing; a sled formed of two short sleds coupled in tandem; either one of the sleds thus coupled.—*v.i.* To ride on a bobsled.

bob·tail, bob′tāl, *n.* A naturally short tail or one that is docked; an animal having such a tail.—*a.* Cut short.—*v.t.* To cut or dock the tail of.

bob·white, bob·hwīt′, *n.* The common N. American quail with mottled reddish-brown, black, and white plumage.

bock beer, bok, *n.* A strong, dark beer, commonly drunk in the spring. Also **bock.**

bode, bōd, *v.t.,* **bod·ed, bod·ing.** To portend.—*v.i.* To promise good or ill.

bode, bōd, past tense of **bide.**

bod·ice, bod′is, *n.* A woman's laced outer garment covering the waist and bust.

bod·i·ly, bod′ə·lē, *adv.* Entirely; completely; in person.—*a.* Referring to the body; corporeal.

bod·kin, bod′kin, *n.* A small pointed instrument for piercing holes in cloth, etc.; a blunt needlelike instrument for drawing tape, etc., through a hem or the like; a long hairpin.

bod·y, bod′ē, *n.* The material substance of man or any animal; a dead organism; a mass; a complete portion of matter. *Informal.* A person. The main part of a human or animal; the torso; the main portion: the *body* of a document; a group of persons as an entity: the student *body;* consistency; substance; fullness in flavor.—*v.t.,* **bod·ied, bod·y·ing.** To embody; to give physical reality.—**bod·ied,** *a.*

bod·y·guard, bod′ē·gärd, *n.* The guard who protects or defends one's person.

bod·y pol·i·tic, *n.* A people forming a political body under an organized government.

bog, bog, bôg, *n.* A place of wet, spongy ground; a quagmire; a marsh.—**bog·gy,** *a.*—*v.t., v.i.,* **bogged, bog·ging.** To sink or stick in or as in a bog, often followed by *down.*

bo·gey, bo·gie, bō′gē, *n.* In golf, one stroke over par on a hole.—*v.t.*

bog·gle, bog′əl, *v.i.,* **-gled, -gling.** To doubt; to hesitate; to waver; to shrink; to shilly-shally.—*v.t.* To amaze; to shock; to bungle.—**bog·gler,** *n.*

bo·gus, bō′gəs, *a.* Counterfeit.

bo·gy, bo·gey, bog·ie, bō′gē, bû′gē, *n.* A hobgoblin; any object of dread.

bo·he·mi·an, bō·hē′mē·ən, *n.* A person, esp. an artist or writer, who leads an unconventional life.—*a.*

boil, boyl, *n.* A painful suppurating inflammatory sore forming a central core.

boil, boyl, *v.i.* To bubble up and emit vapor, as a liquid under the action of heat; to reach a boiling point; to undergo treatment in liquid so heated; to move in agitation; seethe; be violently agitated or incensed.—*v.t.* To cause (liquid) to boil; to cook or treat in a boiling liquid; to separate (salt, sugar, etc.) in solution by means of boiling off the liquid.—*n.* The act or state of boiling. —**boil down,** to reduce the amount by boiling; condense.—**boil o·ver,** to overflow while boiling; to let loose a simmering rage or passion.

boil·er, boyl′ər, *n.* A vessel in which anything is boiled in great quantities; a strong metallic vessel in which steam is generated for driving engines or other purposes.

boil·ing point, *n.* The degree of heat at which a liquid boils.

bois·ter·ous, boy′stər·əs, boy′strəs, *a.* Uproarious; rowdy; exuberant; tumultuous; violent; rough.—**bois·ter·ous·ly,** *adv.*—**bois·ter·ous·ness,** *n.*

bo·la, bō′lə, *n.* A weapon consisting of a cord with weighted balls fastened at the ends. Also **bo·las,** bō′ləs.

bold, bōld, *a.* Daring; intrepid; fearless; exhibiting courage; executed with courage; rude; forward; impudent; striking to the eye; markedly conspicuous; steep; abrupt. —**bold·ly,** *adv.* —**bold·ness,** *n.*

bold·face, bōld′fās, *n.* Thick-lined type used for emphasis and conspicuousness.

bole, bōl, *n.* The body or stem of a tree.

bo·le·ro, bə·lār′o, bō·lār′ō, *n. pl.,* **-ros.** A lively Spanish dance, or the music for it; a short jacket.

boll, bōl, *n.* The pod or capsule as of flax or cotton.

bol·lix, bol′iks, *v.t.* To bungle.

boll wee·vil, *n.* A weevil, the larva of which feeds on cotton bolls.

boll·worm, bōl′wərm, *n.* A larva that eats bolls of cotton, ears of corn, etc.

bo·lo, bō′lō, *n.* A large, heavy knife with a single edge, resembling a machete.

bo·lo·gna, bə·lō′nē, bə·lō′nə, bə·lōn′yə, *n.* A large sausage made of beef, veal, and pork. Also **bo·lo·gna sau·sage.**

bo·lo·ney, bə·lō′nē, *n.* See **baloney.**

bol·ster, bōl′stər, *n.* A long pillow used on a bed or couch; a pad or cushion.—*v.t.* To furnish or support with a bolster; to support, generally followed by *up:* as, to *bolster up* one's courage. —**bol·ster·er,** *n.*

bolt, bōlt, *n.* An arrow; a thunderbolt; a stroke of lightning; a stout metallic pin with a head on one end and a screw thread for a nut on the other; a movable bar for fastening a door, or the like; portion of a lock which is acted upon by a key; a sudden withdrawal from a cause, movement, meeting, etc.; a roll of fabric.—*v.t.* To fasten with a bolt; to swallow hurriedly; to utter impulsively; to roll into bolts; to sieve, as flour; to withdraw suddenly, as from a political party.—*v.i.* To shoot forth suddenly; to break away from.—*adv.* Like a bolt; suddenly; as straight as a bolt: seated *bolt* upright. —**a bolt from the blue,** a sudden, wholly unanticipated event. —**bolt·er,** *n.*

bomb, bom, *n.* A hollow projectile filled with a bursting charge, and exploded by means of a fuse, by impact, or otherwise; a shell; a sudden, unexpected event. *Informal.* A failure.—*v.t.* To drop bombs upon.—*v.i. Informal.* To fail miserably.

bom·bard, bom·bärd′, *v.t.* To attack with bombs; to fire shells at or into; to shell; to assail relentlessly. —**bom·bard·ment,** *n.*

bom·bar·dier, bom·bər·dēr′, *n.* A crew member on a bomber plane who aims and releases aerial bombs.

bom·bast, bom′bast, *n.* High-sounding words; inflated or boastful language; fustian. —**bom·bas·tic,** bom·bas′tik, *a.* —**bom·bas·ti·cal·ly,** *adv.*

bomb·er, bom′ər, *n.* A plane or person that drops bombs.

bomb·proof, bom′proof, *a.* Secure against the force of bombs.

bomb·shell, bom′shel, *n.* A bomb; an unexpected happening or sensation.

bomb·sight, bom′sīt, *n.* A device which enables a bombardier to aim bombs.

bo·na fide, bō′nə fīd′, bō·nə fī′dē, *a.* With good faith; without fraud; genuine.

bo·nan·za, bə·nan′zə, bō·nan′zə, *n.* A rich mass of ore, as found in mining; any rich source of profit.

bon·bon, bon′bon, *n.* A sweetmeat or sugarplum; a piece of confectionery.

bond, bond, *n.* Anything that binds, confines, or holds together; a link or tie; an adhesive, cement, or glue; an obligation imposing moral duty; a legal instrument, under seal; an interest-bearing certificate issued by a government or corporation promising payment of principal at a certain time; the state of goods stored in a warehouse until taxes are paid on them; a bondsman.—*v.t.* To bind or join firmly together; to put under a legal bond.

bond·age, bon′dij, *n.* Slavery or involuntary servitude; subjection to some dominating power or influence.

bond·ed, bon′did, *a.* Secured by bonds; placed in bond, as goods.

bond·man, bond/mən, *n. pl.,* **bond·men.** Serf; a man bound to service without wages. **—bond·wom·an,** *n. fem.*

bonds·man, bondz/mən, *n. pl.,* **bonds·men.** One who assumes responsibility for another by posting a bond.

bone, bōn, *n.* The hard, porous material which forms the skeletons of vertebrate animals; a separate part of the skeleton; various hard animal substances resembling bone, such as ivory, etc.—*v.t.,* **boned, bon·ing.** To remove the bones from.—*v.i. Informal.* To study intensively (usu. with *up*).

bones, *n. pl.* The complete skeleton of a body. *U.S. Informal.* Dice.

bone·head, bōn/hed, *n. Informal.* A stupid person.

bon·er, bō/nər, *n. Informal.* A mistake; a silly blunder.

bon·fire, bon/fīr, *n.* Any outdoor fire, as to burn rubbish or to celebrate.

bon·go, bong/gō, *n. pl.,* **-gos, -goes.** One of a pair of small, connected drums, played by the hands.

bon·ho·mie, bon/ə·mē, bon·ə·mē/, *n.* Good nature; unaffected affability.

bon·net, bon/it, *n.* A headdress formerly worn generally by women, usu. tied under the chin with strings or ribbons; an American Indian's feather headdress; any of various sheltering devices over ventilators, valve chambers, etc.

bon·ny, bon·nie, bon/ē, *a.* Handsome; fair; pretty; healthy; fine.

bo·nus, bō/nəs, *n. pl.,* **bo·nus·es.** A sum given or paid over and above what is required.

bon voy·age, bon voy·äzh/, *n.* A good trip: used as a goodbye or farewell.

bon·y, bō/nē, *a.,* **-i·er, -i·est.** Pertaining to, consisting of, or resembling bone; having prominent bones.

boo, boo, *interj., n.* An exclamation of contempt, dislike, etc., or to frighten.—*v.i., v.t.,* **booed, boo·ing.** To cry "boo" (at); hoot.

boob, boob, *n.* A stupid person; dunce.

boo-boo, boo-boo, *n. Informal.* Blunder.

boo·by, boo/bē, *n. pl.,* **-bies.** A dunce; the person with the worst score in certain games; any of the small gannets of tropical regions.

boo·by trap, *n.* An explosive camouflaged in such a way as to appear harmless; any trap laid for the unwary person.

boo·dle, boo/dəl, *n. Informal.* Goods fraudulently obtained; gain made by cheating or bribery; crowd of people.

boo·hoo, boo·hoo/, *interj., n.* Noisy weeping.—*v.i.,* **-hooed, -hoo·ing.** To weep noisily.

book, bûk, *n.* A written or printed work of some length, esp. on sheets fastened or bound together; a volume; *(cap.)* the Bible; a libretto; a major division of a literary work; a record of bets; any collection of sheets bound together; a trick at cards, or a number of tricks forming a set.—*v.t.* To enter in a book or list; record; to engage (a place, passage, etc.); to enter a lecturer, etc. for an engagement; to enter on a police register the official charge against (a suspect).—*v.i.* To make a reservation. **—book·bind·er,** *n.*

book·case, bûk/kās, *n.* An upright case with shelves for holding books.

book·end, bûk/end, *n.* A support, often ornamental, for placing at the end of a row of books in order to keep the volumes upright.

book·ie, bûk/ē, *n. Informal.* In horse-racing, a bookmaker.

book·ish, bûk/ish, *a.* Given to reading or study; more acquainted with books than with the real world. **—book·ish·ness,** *n.*

book·keep·ing, bûk/kē·ping, *n.* The art of recording transactions by keeping accounts in a book or books. **—book·keep·er,** *n.*

book·let, bûk/lit, *n.* A little book.

book·mak·er, bûk/mā·kər, *n.* A printer or binder of books; a person who accepts bets on horse racing and other sports events.

book·mark, bûk/märk, *n.* A ribbon, etc., inserted in a book to mark a place.

book·mo·bile, bûk/mə·bēl, *n.* A truck or trailer used as a traveling library.

book·plate, bûk/plāt, *n.* An identifying label bearing the owner's name or crest or some other device, for pasting in a book.

book re·view, *n.* A critical analysis or examination of a recently published book.

book·sell·er, bûk/sel·ər, *n.* One whose business is to sell books. **—book·sell·ing,** *n.*

book·stall, bûk/stôll, *n.* A stand where books (usu. second-hand) are sold.

book·worm, bûk/wərm, *n.* A person who is dedicated to books and scholarship. An insect larva which feeds on books.

boom, boom, *n.* A long pole or spar used to extend the foot of certain sails or to project from the mast of a derrick; a chain, cable or a series of timbers, serving to confine floating timber, etc. **—lower the boom.** *Informal.* To punish; to discipline.

boom, boom, *n.* A deep hollow noise, as the roar of waves or the sound of distant guns; a time of sudden increase in prices, wages, and general prosperity; a vigorous growth or pushing.—*v.i.* To make a deep, prolonged, resonant sound; to move with a resounding rush; to develop rapidly.—*v.t.* To give forth with a booming sound; to promote strongly.

boo·me·rang, boo/mə·rang, *n.* A bent or curved piece of hard wood used by the native Australians, which can be so thrown as to return to the thrower; a statement, plan, etc. which recoils on the originator. —*v.i.* To recoil in this way.

boon, boon, *n.* A great benefit; a blessing.

boon·dog·gle, boon/dog·əl, *n.* Any wasteful or unnecessary labor.

boor, bûr, *n.* A countryman; a peasant; one who is rude or insensitive in manners. **—boor·ish,** *a.* **—boor·ish·ness,** *n.*

boost, boost, *v.t.* To lift by shoving up from behind; push up; to advance or aid.—*n.* A push from behind. **—boost·er,** *n.*

boot, boot, *n.* A sheath of leather, rubber, or plastic material to cover the foot and leg; a shoe that reaches above the ankle; a sharp kick; a recruit taking basic training in the armed services; in sports, an error. *Informal.* Abrupt dismissal.—*v.t.* To put boots on; to kick; in sports, to make an error. *Informal.* To dismiss or discharge.

boot, boot, *n.* Profit; advantage.**—to boot,** in addition to; into the bargain.

boot·black, boot/blak, *n.* One whose business is to shine boots or shoes.

boot·ee, boo·tē/, boo/tē, *n.* A baby's knitted sock; a half-boot for women.

booth, booth, *n.* A covered stall at a trade show, exposition, polling place, etc.; a seating compartment in a restaurant.

boot·jack, boot/jak, *n.* A v-shaped instrument for drawing off boots.

boot·leg, boot/leg, *n.* Merchandise, esp. liquor, that is manufactured, transported, or sold illegally.—*v.t.,* **-legged, -leg·ging.** To circumvent legal prohibition.—*v.i.* To practice bootlegging.—*a.* Illegal. **—boot·leg·ger,** *n.*

boot·less, boot/ləs, *a.* Without profit; useless. **—boot·less·ly,** *adv.* **—boot·less·ness,** *n.*

boot·lick, boot/lik, *v.t., v.i.* To be servile; to toady. **—boot·lick·er,** *n.*

boo·ty, boo/tē, *n. pl.,* **-ties.** Spoils taken from an

---

a- hat, fāte, fāre, fäther; **e-** met, mē; **i-** pin, pīne; **o-** not, nōte, ôrb, moove (move), boy, pownd; **u-** cūbe, bûll, tûk (took); **ch-** chin; **th-** thick, ŧhen; **zh-** vizhon (vision); **ə-** ego, takən, pencəl, lemən, bərd (bird).

enemy in war; plunder; any prize or gain.

booze, booz, *n.* Any alcoholic drink; a drinking spree. —*v.t., v.i.* To drink excessively. **—booz•er,** *n.* **—booz•y,** *a.,* **-i•er, -i•est.**

bop, bop, *n.* Bebop.

bo•rax, bōr′aks, bōr′əks, bôr′aks, *n.* A white crystalline salt, used as an antiseptic, cleansing agent, etc.

bor•der, bôr′dər, *n.* The outer part or edge of anything, as of a garment, country, etc.; margin; decorative margin; boundary; frontier. —*v.i.* To have the edge or boundary adjoining; to be adjacent; to come near: with *on* or *upon.*—*v.t.* To make a border to; to form a border to; to be next to. **—bor•dered,** *a.*

bor•der•land, bôr′dər•land, *n.* Land forming a border; debatable or undefined area.

bor•der•line, bôr′dər•līn, *a.* Located near a boundary line; of uncertain classification.

bore, bōr, bôr, *v.t.,* **bored, bor•ing.** To pierce with or as if by a rotary cutting tool; to construct by hollowing out, such as a tunnel or mine; to cut a hole to an exact diameter; to force an opening.—*v.i.* To make a hole by piercing; to admit of being drilled; to force a passage.

bore, bōr, bôr, *v.t.,* **bored, bor•ing.** To weary by tedious repetition, by dullness, etc.—*n.* A dull, tiresome person or thing; a hole made by or as by boring; the cylindrical cavity of a tube, as a gun barrel; the internal diameter of a tube. **—bor•er,** *n.*

bore, bōr, bôr, *n.* A high, abrupt tide which rushes inland with great violence.

bo•re•al, bōr′ē•əl, bôr′ē•əl, *a.* Northern.

bore•dom, bōr′dəm, bôr′dəm, *n.* The state of being bored.

bo•ric, bōr′ik, bôr′ik, *a.* Pertaining to or containing boron.

bo•ric ac•id, *n.* A white crystalline acid, used as a weak antiseptic.

born, bôrn, *a.* Brought into being by birth; possessing characteristics from birth: a *born* poet.

borne, bôrn, bôrn, pp. of **bear,** to carry.

bo•ron, bōr′on, bôr′on, *n.* A metalloid element found in nature only in combination, as borax, boric acid, etc.

bor•ough, bər′ō, *n.* An incorporated municipality smaller than a city; one of the five administrative divisions of the city of New York. *Brit.* An urban community incorporated by royal charter; a constituency represented by a member of Parliament.

bor•row, bor′ō, bôr′ō, *v.t.* To obtain, with the intention of returning same or an equivalent; to adopt from another source for one's own use; to derive; appropriate; in subtraction, to regroup by sets of ten the components of the minuend. **—bor•row•er,** *n.*

bosh, bosh, *n. Informal.* Nonsense.

bos•om, bûz′əm, boo′zəm, *n.* The breast of a human being, esp. a woman; the part of a garment which covers the breast; the breast as the seat of thought or emotion; a hollow interior, an inmost recess, etc.; familiar inner circle.—*v.t.* To take to the bosom; embrace; to conceal.—*a.* Of or worn on the bosom; intimate or confidential.

boss, bôs, bos, *n.* A foreman or superintendent; a manager or employer; one who exerts authority; a politician who controls his party.—*v.t.* To be master of or over; control; manage; to domineer.—*v.i.* To act as a boss.

boss, bôs, bos, *n.* A protuberant part; a raised circular projection; a raised ornamentation, as a decorative knob or stud on a shield. *Arch.* An ornamental projecting block or rounded mass.—*v.t.* To furnish or ornament with bosses; emboss.

boss•ism, bô′siz•əm, bos′iz•əm, *n.* Control by bosses, esp. political bosses.

boss•y, bô′sē, bos′ē, *a.,* **-i•er, -i•est.** *Informal.* Given to acting like a boss; domineering. **—boss•i•ness,** *n.*

bo•sun, bō′sən, *n.* A boatswain. Also **bos′n, bo′s′n, bo′sun.**

bot•a•ny, bot′ə•nē, *n.* A division of biology which treats of the plant kingdom, dealing with the structure of plants, their distribution, their history, etc.; the plant life of a particular region; a botanical study. **—bo•tan•ic,** bə•tan′ik, **—bo•tan•i•cal,** *a.* **—bo•tan•i•cal•ly,** bə•tan′ik•lē, *adv.* **—bot•a•nist,** bot′ə•nist, *n.*

botch, boch, *n.* A swelling on the skin; a clumsy patch; poorly done work.—*v.t.* To patch in a clumsy manner; to perform in a bungling manner. **—botch•y,** *a.,* **-i•er, -i•est.**

both, bōth, *a.* Two considered together.—*conj.* Equally; alike.—*pron.* The two considered together.

both•er, both′ər, *n.* The state of annoyance; worry; trouble; something that bothers; someone who vexes; inconvenience; fuss.—*v.t.* To annoy; irk; confuse or puzzle.—*v.i.* To cause annoyance or trouble; to trouble oneself.

both•er•some, both′ər•səm, *a.* Causing bother; troublesome; annoying; vexing.

bot•tle, bot′əl, *n.* A vessel with a neck or mouth that may be closed with a stopper, for holding liquids; contents of such a vessel; **—the bottle,** strong drink; bottled formula for infants.—*v.t.,* **-tled, -tling.** To put into bottles; to store or shut within, usu. with *up.* **—bot•tle•ful,** *n.* **—bot•tler,** *n.*

bot•tle•neck, bot′əl•nek, *n.* A narrowed area, esp. in a flow of traffic; a block to progress.—*v.i.* To slow or bring to a standstill, as traffic.

bot•tom, bot′əm, *n.* The lowest part; the foot, base, or foundation; the underlying ground, as beneath water. The buttocks; the seat of a chair; the part of a ship below the wales; origin; basis; stamina. *Usu. pl.* Low land adjacent to a river; sediment.—*a.* Lowest; undermost; fundamental.—*v.t.* To furnish with a bottom; to base or found (*on* or *upon*); to fathom.—*v.i.* To be based; rest; to reach the bottom. **—bot•tom•less,** *a.*

bot•u•lism, boch′ə•liz•əm, *n.* A form of poisoning produced by eating spoiled food, due to a toxin.

bou•doir, boo′dwär, bû′dwär, *n.* A lady's retiring room or private sitting room.

bouf•fant, boo•fänt′, *a.* Puffed out; full, as sleeves or hairdo.—*n.*

bough, bow, *n.* A branch of a tree, esp. one of the larger or main branches.

bought, bôt, past and past participle of **buy.**

bought•en, bôt′ən, *a. Dial.* Bought, esp. as opposed to **home-made.**

bouil•lon, bûl′yon, bûl′yən, *n.* A clear, thin broth.

boul•der, bōl′dər, *n.* A large rock rounded by the action of weather and water.

boul•e•vard, bûl′ə•värd, boo′lə•värd, *n.* A broad, handsome avenue of a city.

bounce, bowns, *v.i.,* **bounced, bounc•ing.** To strike a surface and rebound; move with a springing step; spring back suddenly. *Informal.* Of a bank check, to be returned as worthless.—*v.t.* To cause to spring back. *Informal.* To dismiss from employment; to eject by force.—*n.* A bound or rebound; the capacity to spring; a sudden leap; verve, vivacity; resilience. **—bounc•er,** *n.*

bounc•ing, bown′sing, *a.* Big; stout, strong, or vigorous.

bound, bownd, *n. Usu. pl.* That which defines or circumscribes; boundary; limit; area near or within a boundary.—*v.i.* To adjoin; abut.—*v.t.* To set bounds or limits; to act as a boundary; to name the boundaries of.

bound, bownd, *v.i.* To leap; to move forward by leaps; to rebound; to spring.—*v.t.* To cause to bound.—*n.* A leap; spring; rebound.

bound, bownd, *a.* Secured by a band; tied; in bonds; contained within a cover; under obligation, legally or morally; destined or sure; determined or resolved.

bound, bownd, *a.* Ready to go; having set out: He is *bound* for Chicago.

bound•a•ry, bown′də•rē, bown′drē, *n. pl.,* **-ries.** Something that indicates bounds or limits; a limiting line or bound.

bound·less, bownd′lis, *a.* Without bounds; vast; infinite. **—bound·less·ness,** *n.*

boun·te·ous, bown′tē·əs, *a.* Inclined to give freely; generous; abundant; plentiful. **—boun·te·ous·ness,** *n.*

boun·ti·ful, bown′tə·fəl, *a.* **—**Bounteous.

boun·ty, bown′tē, *n. pl.,* **-ties.** Generosity; munificence; a benevolent gift; a premium or reward.

bou·quet, bō·kā′, boo·kā′, *n.* A nosegay; a bunch of flowers fastened together; a distinct aroma, as of fine wines.

bour·bon, bər′bən, *n.* A whiskey made from malt, corn, and rye.

bour·geois, bûr′zhwä′, bûr′zhwä, *n. pl.,* **-geois.** A member of the middle class.—*a.* Middle-class; common; lacking refinement or elegance.

bour·geoi·sie, bûr·zhwä·zē′, *n. pl.,* **-sie.** The bourgeois class; a member of that class.

bourse, bûrs, *n.* A stock exchange, as that of Paris.

bout, bowt, *n.* A time of anything; as much as is performed at one time; a set-to; a contest.

bou·tique, boo·tēk′, *n.* A small retail shop.

bou·ton·niere, boo·tə·nyär′, *n.* A buttonhole flower or bouquet.

bo·vine, bō′vīn, bō′vin, *a.* Oxlike; stolid; dull.—*n.* A bovine animal.

bow, bō, *n.* A bend or curve; something curved or arc-shaped, as a rain*bow;* saddle*bow;* a strip of flexible wood bent by a string stretched between its ends, used for shooting arrows; a bowman or archer; an implement with horsehairs stretched upon it, for playing a violin; a single stroke of such an implement; a knot made by looping and tying ribbon or string for decoration.—*v.t.* To bend or curve; to play a stringed instrument with a bow.—*v.i.* To be curved.

bow, bow, *n.* The forward part of a ship.

bow, bow, *v.i.* To bend or stoop, as in respect or worship.—*v.t.* To cause to bend; incline; an inclination of the head or body as in respect, submission, or assent. **—bow out,** to withdraw. **—bow and scrape,** to be overly polite. **—bow to fate,** to submit to the inevitable. **—make a bow,** to stand for recognition. **—take a bow,** to be presented publicly for the first time.

bow·el, bow′əl, bowl, *n. Usu. pl.* Part of the intestines; the interior part of anything: the *bowels* of the earth. —*v.t.* **bow·eled, bow·el·ing.** To take out the bowels of; to eviscerate.

bow·er, bow′ər, *n.* A shady recess; a retreat.—*v.t.* To shelter in or as in a bower.

bow·ie knife, boo′ē, bō′ē, *n. pl.,* **bow·ie knives.** A heavy sheath knife having a long single-edged blade.

bow·ing, bō′ing, *n.* The act of playing a stringed instrument.

bow·knot, bō′not, *n.* A decorative looped slipknot, with two loops and two ends.

bowl, bōl, *n.* A vessel of greater width than depth, usually hemispherical or nearly so; the contents of a bowl; a toilet receptacle; any bowl-shaped formation or structure.

bowl, bōl, *n.* One of the balls used in playing ninepins, tenpins, or lawn bowling; a delivery of the ball in bowling.—*v.i.* To play at bowling.—*v.t.* Knock or strike (*over* or *down*) as by the ball in bowling. **—bowl o·ver,** to greatly surprise.

bow·leg, bō′leg, *n.* Outward curvature of the legs; a leg so curved. **—bow·leg·ged,** bō′legd, bō′leg·id, *a.*

bowl·er, bō′lər, *n.* One who bowls; *chiefly Brit.,* a derby hat.

bow·line, bō′lin, bō′līn, *n.* A knot used to make a loop that cannot slip.

bowl·ing, bō′ling, *n.* A game in which heavy balls are rolled down a lawn or an indoor alley at a set of pins; ninepins; tenpins.

bowl·ing al·ley, *n.* A long narrow lane used for bowling; or the building.

bowl·ing green, *n.* A smooth, closely mowed lawn used for bowling.

bow·man, bō′mən, *n. pl.,* **bow·men.** An archer; a soldier armed with a bow.

bow·man, bow′mən, *n. pl.,* **bow·men.** The oarsman who sits nearest the bow of a boat.

bow saw, bō′ sô, *n.* A saw with a light bow-shaped frame.

bow·string, bō′string, *n.* The string of a bow for use in archery or music.

bow tie, bō, *n.* A short necktie tied with a bow at the collar.

box, boks, *n.* A case or receptacle in many forms and sizes; a chest; the quantity contained in a box; a compartment, as a seating compartment in a theater; a small shelter: a sentry *box;* a space in a newspaper, etc., set off as by enclosing lines.—*v.t.* To enclose, as in a box; to confine. **—box·ful,** *n. pl.,* **box·fuls.**

box, boks, *n.* An evergreen shrub or small tree for ornamental borders.

box, boks, *v.t.* To strike with the fist or hand.—*v.i.* To fight with the fists; to be in a boxing match.

box·car, boks′kär, *n.* An enclosed and covered freight car.

box·er, bok′sər, *n.* One who boxes; a prizefighter.

box·ing, bok′sing, *n.* Fist fighting with or without padded gloves, practiced as a sport.

box·ing glove, *n.* A large padded glove used for boxing.

box of·fice, *n.* In a theater, etc., the office in which tickets are sold.

box score, *n.* The play-by-play record of a game of baseball, basketball, etc.

box seat, *n.* A seat in a box of an auditorium.

box spring, *n.* A bedspring encased in padded upholstery.

box stall, *n.* A stall used as an enclosure for a large animal such as a horse.

boy, boy, *n.* A male child from birth to the age of puberty; a man lacking maturity or judgment; an associate or friend: to go out with the *boys.* **—boy·hood,** boy′hûd, *n.* **—boy·ish,** boy′ish, *a.* **—boy·ish·ly,** *adv.* **—boy·ish·ness,** *n.*

boy·cott, boy′kot, *v.t.* To combine in refusing to work for, or deal with, in order to intimidate or force to act.—*n.* A refusal to buy, deal with, etc.

boy·friend, boy′frend, *n. Informal.* A male companion of a girl or woman.

boy scout, *n.* A member of an organization of boys (Boy Scouts).

boy·sen·ber·ry, boy′zən·ber·ē, *n. pl.,* **-ries.** A large edible berry with a flavor resembling raspberry.

bra, brä, *n. Informal.* A brassiere.

brace, brās, *n.* Something that holds parts together or in place, as a clasp or clamp. *Pl.* An appliance for supporting a weak back, etc.; anything that imparts rigidity or steadiness.—*v.t.,* **braced, brac·ing.** To fasten, or strengthen with or as with a brace; increase the tension of; give firmness to; bring to greater vigor, etc., often used with *up.*—*v.i.* To acquire vigor; rouse one's strength or energy.

brace·let, brās′lit, *n.* An ornamental band or circlet for the wrist or arm. *Informal.* A handcuff. **—brace·let·ed,** *a.*

brac·er, brā′sər, *n.* One who or that which braces; a tonic or stimulating drink.

bra·ces, brā′səz, *n. pl.* Connecting wires attached to teeth to correct irregularities.

brac·ing, brā′sing, *n.* A brace, or braces collectively. —*a.* Stimulating; invigorating.

brack·en, brak′ən, *n.* A large fern.

brack·et, brak′it, *n.* A projection from the face of a

wall, to support a statue, pier, etc.; any projecting support, as for a shelf, or for a fixture for gas or electricity; one of two marks, [ ], used in writing or printing to enclose parenthetic matter.—*v.t.* To support with a bracket; enclose in brackets.

brack·ish, brak′ish, *a.* Slightly salt, as water; unpleasant. —**brack·ish·ness**, *n.*

brad, brad, *n.* A thin wire nail with a small deep head.—*v.t.*, **brad·ded, brad·ding.** To attach with brads.

brag, brag, *v.i.*, **bragged, brag·ging.** To boast.—*v.t.* To boast about: He *bragged* that he was first to finish.—*n.* A boast or boasting; a vaunt; the thing boasted of.

brag·gart, brag′ərt, *n.* A.boaster.—*a.* Boastful.

braid, brād, *v.t.* To weave or intertwine, as hair or thread, by forming three or more strands into one; to plait.—*n.* A narrow textile band formed by plaiting or weaving; a plait or plaited tress of hair. —**braid·er**, *n.*

braid·ing, brād′ing, *n.* Braid, or trimming made of braid.

braille, brāl, *n.* A system of writing or printing for the blind, in which combinations of raised dots represent letters.

brain, brān, *n.* The soft mass of grayish and whitish nerve tissue that fills the cranium of humans and other vertebrates, which governs or coordinates mental and physical motions; *sometimes pl.*, intellectual power. In many invertebrates, a part of the nervous system more or less corresponding to the brain of vertebrates. A mechanical device that serves to perform functions of the human brain for command, guidance, or computation: the *brain* of a guided missile.—*v.t.* To dash out the brains of; to strike or beat severely about the head.

brain·child, brān′chīld, *n.* An original creation or design of one's imagination.

brain drain, *n.* A deficiency of professional help caused by the emigration of such workers to more profitable employment abroad.

brain·less, brān′les, *a.* Having no judgment; stupid.

brain·pow·er, brān′pow·ər, *n.* Mental capacity, esp. in the sense of superior, collective ability.

brain·storm, brān′stôrm, *n.* A sudden inspiration, esp. one which leads to creativity.

brain·storm·ing, brān′stôr·ming, *n.* *Informal.* A group technique for stimulating creative thinking.

brain trust, *n.* A group of experts who act as consultants to high public officials.

brain·wash·ing, brān′wosh·ing, brān′wô·shing, *n.* Indoctrination by psychological manipulation to undermine or change political beliefs.—*v.t.*, **brain·wash.**

brain wave, *n.* An electric impulse given off by tissuesof the brain. *Informal.* A brainstorm; inspiration.

brain·y, brā′nē, *a.*, **-i·er, -i·est.** Having brains; intellectual.

braise, brāz, *v.t.*, **braised, brais·ing.** To brown (meat) in a small amount of fat, then simmer gently in its own juice or a little added liquid in a covered skillet.

brake, brāk, *n.* A mechanical device which slows down or stops the motion of a wheel or vehicle by means of friction.—*v.t.*, **braked, brak·ing.**

brake, brāk, *n.* A place overgrown with bushes or shrubs; a thicket.

brake·man, brāk′mən, *n. pl.*, **-men.** A man who operates brakes, as on a railroad.

bram·ble, bram′bəl, *n.* A prickly trailing shrub of the rose family growing in hedges and bearing a black berry; the berry. —**bram·bly**, *a.*

bran, bran, *n.* The outer coat of wheat, rye, or other grain, separated from the flour by grinding.

branch, branch, brănch, *n.* A limb or offshoot; an extension; a subdivision or department.—*a.* Forming a branch; of or pertaining to a branch.—*v.t.* To put forth branches; spread in branches; issue or diverge as a branch from a main stem (with *from, out, off,* etc.) —**branch·ed**, *a.*

branch of·fice, *n.* Another office of the same business or industry located in areas away from the parent firm.

brand, brand, *n.* An instrument used to brand cattle: as, a *branding* iron; a mark made by a branding iron; a trademark; a class of goods made by a certain manufacturer; a stigma.—*v.t.* To burn or impress a mark upon with a hot iron, or to distinguish by a similar mark; to stigmatize as infamous; to mark permanently. —**brand·er**, brand′ər, *n.*

bran·dish, bran′dish, *v.t.* To shake or wave (a weapon, etc.) threateningly; flourish.—*n.* A wave or flourish.

brand-new, brand′noo′, brand′nū′, *a.* Quite new; unused.

bran·dy, bran′dē, *n. pl.*, **bran·dies.** An alcoholic liquor distilled from wine, or from the fermented juice of the grape, apple, peach, etc.—*v.t.*, **bran·died, bran·dy·ing.** To mix, flavor, or preserve with brandy. —**bran·died**, *a.*

brash, brash, *a.* Hasty; rash; impudent.

bra·sier, brā′zhər, *n.* Brazier.

brass, bras, bräs, *n.* A durable, soft yellow alloy, containing copper and zinc; a brass musical instrument, or such instruments collectively in a band or orchestra. *Informal.* Impudence; military officers, esp. those of high rank; officials or other people of authority.—*a.* Made of brass; brazen; brass-colored.

brass band, *n.* A band which uses only brass instruments.

bras·se·rie, bras·ə·rē′, *n. pl.*, **-ries.** A restaurant serving simple fare.

brass hat, *n.* *Informal.* An officer of high rank in the armed forces; a person in authority.

bras·siere, brə·zēr′, *n.* An undergarment worn by women to support the breasts.

brass knuck·les, *n.* A weapon fashioned of a metal strip with four holes, worn over the knuckles.

brass tacks, *n.* *Informal.* Fundamental facts of a situation: to get down to *brass tacks.*

brass·y, bras′ē, *a.*, **-i·er, -i·est.** Impudent; harsh.

brat, brat, *n.* An annoying, spoiled, or ill-mannered child. —**brat·tish, brat·ty**, *a.*

bra·va·do, brə·vä′dō, *n.* Swaggering defiance; a bold show of indifference.

brave, brāv, *a.* Courageous; bold; daring; intrepid; high-spirited; fearless.—*v.t.*, **braved, brav·ing.** To meet, with courage, or without being moved; to defy; to dare.—*n.* A brave, or daring person; a North American Indian warrior. —**brave·ness**, *n.* —**brav·er·y**, *n. pl.*, **-ies.**

bra·vo, brä′vō, brä·vō′, *interj.* Fine! Excellent! Well done!—*n. pl.*, **bra·vos**, brä′vōz, brä·voz′. A cry of "bravo!"

bra·vu·ra, brə·vyû′rə, *n.* Display of daring; show of brilliant performance; dash. *Mus.* A florid passage or piece, requiring great skill and spirit in the performer. —*a. Mus.* Spirited; dashing.

brawl, brôl, *v.i.* To quarrel or fight noisily; to be loud.—*n.* A noisy quarrel; an uproar. *Informal.* A loud and usually drunken party. —**brawl·er**, *n.*

brawn, brôn, *n.* Firm, well-developed muscular tissue; muscular strength. —**brawn·i·ness**, *n.* —**brawn·y**, *a.*, **-i·er, -i·est.**

bray, brā, *v.i.* To utter a harsh cry: said especially of the donkey.—*v.t.* To utter with a loud harsh sound, sometimes with *out.*—*n.* The harsh sound of mules and donkeys.

bra·zen, brā′zən, *a.* Made of brass; extremely strong; pertaining to brass; proceeding from brass; impudent.—*v.t.* To behave with insolence: *brazen* it out.

bra·zier, brā′zhər, *n.* An open pan for burning wood or coal used for heating a room; a similar pan used for cooking food in which a grill holds the food above the embers. Also **bra·sier**.

breach, brēch, *n.* The act of breaking; a break or rupture; a gap; violation, as of the peace, of faith, or trust.—*v.t.* To make a breach or opening in; to break (a contract or law).

breach of prom·ise, *n.* Violation of one's solemnly given word of honor, especially of an engagement to marry.

bread, bred, *n.* A food made of flour or meal, milk or water, etc., mixed into a dough or batter, with or without yeast, and baked; food; livelihood.—*v.t.* To cover or dress with bread crumbs before final cooking.

bread and but·ter, *n.* Bread spread with butter: wholesome food, representing the material essentials of life; sustaining source of business profit.

bread·fruit, bred'froot, *n.* A large, round starchy fruit yielded by a tree of islands in the South Pacific, used for food; the tree bearing this fruit.

bread line, *n.* A line of needy persons waiting to receive bread and sometimes other food for free.

breadth, bredth, bretth, *n.* The measure of a flat surface from side to side; the measure or extent of any plane surface from side to side; width; liberality; wide intellectual grasp.

breadth·ways, bredth'wāz, *adv.* In the direction of the breadth. Also **breadth·wise.**

bread·win·ner, bred'win·ər, *n.* One in the family who works to support the family and himself or herself.

break, brāk, *v.t.,* **broke, bro·ken, break·ing.** To divide into parts by a blow or pull; shatter; crush; violate: to *break* a contract; dissolve or annul: often with *off;* crack; bruise or abrade; to interrupt or destroy the continuity or uniformity of: to *break* step; discontinue abruptly; discover the key to a cipher system; make one's way out of: as *break* jail; to better or exceed: *break* a record; to make known in speech or writing: to *break* the news; ruin financially or make bankrupt; impair or weaken in strength, spirit, force, or effect; to show the faulty logic of: *break* an alibi; tame; accustom to a method or procedure, often with *in;* to train away from a habit or practice, with *of. Elect.* To make a circuit incomplete and so stop the flow of current.—*v.i.* To become broken; burst; fall apart; crack; burst open, as a boil; to become inoperative due to damage or excessive wear; change suddenly or abruptly, as in sound, movement, or direction; free oneself or escape suddenly, often with *away;* force a way, often with *in* or *through;* to dawn, as day; give way or fail under strain, often with *down;* become bankrupt; become detached, often with *off;* to sever relations, used with *with.*—*n.* A breaking, or shattering; a gap; an interruption of continuity; a stoppage; a severance of relations; an abrupt or marked change, as in sound or direction; a breaking forth or away, as from restraint; a sudden emergence; dawn (of day); opportunity; luck, good or bad; a short time of rest from work; the making of a circuit incomplete and the discontinuance of the current. —**break down,** to collapse; to make inoperative; to separate into component parts; to analyze. —**break e·ven,** to operate an enterprise or business with balancing profit and loss. —**break in,** to teach (beginners) in a new job or sport; to ease the stiffness of (a new article); to enter, using force. —**break out,** to have a skin eruption indicating a specific disease; to release from an inhibition. —**break·a·ble,** *a.*

break·age, brā'kij, *n.* The act of breaking; a break; damage or loss by breaking; allowance made for this.

break·a·way, brāk'ə·wä, *n.* A breaking away; a start, as of competitors in a contest.

break·down, brāk'down, *n.* A breaking down; a collapse; an analysis, as of a total.

break·er, brā'kər, *n.* One who or that which breaks; a wave that breaks into foam; a device for opening an electric circuit.

break-e·ven point, brāk'ē·vən, *n.* The level of a business at which its income equals expenses.

break·fast, brek'fəst, *n.* The first meal of the day; a morning meal.—*v.i.* To take breakfast.—*v.t.* To supply with breakfast.

break·ing point, brāk'ing, *n.* The point of stress at which a material or a person gives way.

break·neck, brāk'nek, *a.* Endangering the neck or life; very dangerous: *breakneck* speed.

break·out, brāk'owt, *n.* A forceful breaking from restraint, sometimes an escape; public evidence of group feelings or activity.

break·through, brāk'throo, *n.* A sudden advance in the solution of a problem or discovery of a new technique; the penetration of a barrier or defensive line.

break·up, brāk'əp, *n.* A disruption; a separation of a mass into parts.

break·wa·ter, brāk'wô'tər, brāk'wot·ər, *n.* Any structure serving to break the force of waves and protect a harbor or anything exposed to the waves.

breast, brest, *n.* Either of the two soft structures on the chest in females, containing the milk-secreting organs; the front of the chest in either sex; the bosom; the chest.—*v.t.* To face; advance against. —**to make a clean breast of,** to make full confession of.

breast·bone, brest'bōn, *n.* The bone of the breast; the sternum.

breast·plate, brest'plāt, *n.* A piece of armor for the breast.

breast stroke, *n.* A swimming stroke in which the swimmer moves the arms together toward and then away from the chest, while doing a frog kick.

breath, breth, *n.* The air inhaled and exhaled in respiration; respiration; power of breathing freely: out of *breath;* pause or respite; a single respiration; an instant; something generated by breathing, as the condensed moisture seen on a cold day; a light current of air; a hint. —**un·der one's breath,** in a low voice or a whisper. —**to save one's breath,** refrain from useless debate. —**breath·less,** *a.* —**breath·less·ness,** *n.*

breathe, brēth, *v.i.,* **breathed, breath·ing.** Inhale and exhale air, or respire; live or exist; take a rest; emit audible breath or sound; blow lightly, as air.—*v.t.* Inhale and exhale in respiration; inject by breathing, or infuse; whisper; allow to rest, as to recover breath; put out of breath; blow into or cause to sound by the breath. —**breathe free·ly,** to be free from worry. —**not breathe a word or syl·la·ble,** to keep a secret.

breath·er, brē'thər, *n.* One who breathes; a pause for breath: She took a *breather.*

breath·ing, brē'thing, *n.* The act of one that breathes; a pause for breath; an *h*-sound.—*a.* Alive.

breath·tak·ing, breth'tā·king, *a.* Causing extreme pleasure, awe, excitement; thrilling. —**breath·tak·ing·ly,** *adv.*

breath·y, breth'ē, *a.,* **breath·i·er, breath·i·est.** Characterized by a conspicuous use of the breath.

breech, brēch, *n.* The lower rear part of the body; the buttocks; the hinder part of anything; the large, thick end of a gun.—*v.t.* To fit or furnish with a breech.

breech birth, *n.* Breech delivery.

breech de·liv·er·y, *n.* Delivery of a fetus when the breech (buttocks) or the feet appear first in the birth canal.

breech·es, brich'iz, *n. pl.* Short trousers fitting snugly just below the knees.

breech·load·er, brēch'lō·dər, *n.* Any gun that is loaded at the breech end.

breed, brēd, *v.t.* **bred, breed·ing.** To produce (offspring); to raise, as cattle; to get by the mating of parents: They *breed* white rats for the laboratory; to improve or develop (wanted characteristics) through selective mating (of animals) or controlled pollination (of plants); to cause: War *breeds* destruction; to be the

---

a- hat, fāte, fāre, fäther; e- met, mē; i- pin, pīne; o- not, nōte, ôrb, moove (move), boy, pownd;
u- cūbe, bull, tûk (took); ch- chin; th- thick, then; zh- vizhon (vision); ə- əgo, takən, pencəl, lemən, bərd (bird).

native place of: Swamps *breed* mosquitoes; to bring up, rear or train.—*v.i.* To reproduce: Some animals *breed* several times a year; to grow; develop; to originate: Homosexuality *breeds* in prisons.—*n.* Lineage; strain; kind or sort in a general sense. —**breed·er,** *n.*

breed·ing, brē'ding, *n.* Nurture or training; manners, esp. good manners.

breeze, brēz, *n.* A wind, generally a light or not very strong wind. *Informal.* An easy task.—*v.i.* To blow a breeze; to move in a carefree manner: as, *breeze* in or out.—*v.t.* To hurry or move something.

breeze·way, brēz'wā, *n.* A roofed passageway with open sides joining two buildings.

breez·y, brēz'ē, *a.,* **-i·er, -i·est.** Fanned with gentle breezes; brisk, fresh; informal. —**breez·i·ness,** *n.*

breth·ren, breth'ren, *n.* Plural of **broth·er;** now usually denoting spiritual brotherhood.

breve, brēv, brev, *n.* A writ, as one issued by a court of law; a mark (˘) placed over a vowel to show that it is short.

bre·vet, bra·vet', brev'it, *n.* A patent conferring a privilege or rank; esp., a commission promoting a military officer to a higher rank without increase of pay.—*v.t.,* **-vet·ted, -vet·ting.**

bre·vi·a·ry, brē'vē·er·ē, brev'ē·er·ē, *n. pl.,* **-ries.** A summary; a book of daily offices of the Roman Catholic Church, to be read by those in major orders; any similar books used in other churches.

brev·i·ty, brev'a·tē, *n.* The state of being brief; shortness; conciseness.

brew, broo, *v.t.* To prepare beer, or similar liquor from malt or other materials, by boiling and fermentation; to mix; to prepare a hot beverage, as tea or coffee, by steeping a solid in boiling water; to plot.—*v.i.* To perform the business of brewing or making beer; to be mixing, forming, or collecting: a storm *brews.*—*n.* That which is brewed; a mixture of uncommon ingredients: a witch's *brew.* —**brew·er,** *n.*

brew·er·y, broo'a·rē, brŭ'rē, *n. pl.,* **-ies.** An establishment for brewing malt liquors.

bri·ar, brī'er, *n.* A plant having a thorny stem; a tree whose root wood is used to make tobacco pipes; a pipe made from this root wood. —**bri·ar·y,** *a.*

bribe, brīb, *n.* A price, reward, gift or favor bestowed or promised with a view to corrupt judgment or conduct.—*v.t.,* **bribed, brib·ing.** To gain over by a bribe.—*v.i.* To give a bribe to a person. —**brib·a·ble,** *a.*

brib·er·y, brī'ba·rē, *n. pl.,* **-ies.**

bric-a-brac, brik'a·brak, *n.* Knickknacks.

brick, brik, *n.* A block of clay, usually rectangular, hardened by drying or by burning in a kiln, and used for building, paving, etc.; such blocks collectively: a house of *brick;* the material used in making bricks; blocks used for building which are made from another material: a concrete *brick;* block-shaped objects: a *brick* of ice cream.—*v.t.* To lay or build with brick.

brick·lay·er, brik'lā·er, *n.* One whose occupation is to build with bricks. —**brick·lay·ing,** *n.*

brick red, *n.* A yellowish or brownish red.

brick·work, brik'werk, *n.* Masonry consisting of bricks.

brick·yard, brik'yärd, *n.* A place where bricks are made, stocked, or sold.

brid·al wreath, brī'dal, *n.* A shrub, bearing long sprays of small white flowers, much cultivated for ornament.

bride, brīd, *n.* A woman newly married, or on the eve of being married. —**brid·al,** *a.*

bride·groom, brīd'groom, *n.* A man newly married, or just about to be married.

brides·maid, brīdz'mād, *n.* A woman or girl who attends the bride at a wedding.

bridge, brij, *n.* A structure spanning a river, chasm, road, or the like, and affording passage; any structure or part similar in form or use; a link between two activities, subjects, periods of time, etc.; a mounting

for artificial teeth, fastened to adjoining teeth. A raised platform on a ship, for the officers or pilot.—*v.t.* To make a bridge over; span. —**to burn one's bridges (behind one),** to sever all possible ways of turning back.

bridge, brij, *n.* A card game for four players, derived from whist.

bridge·work, brij'werk, *n.* The fitting in of artificial teeth with bridges.

bri·dle, brī'dal, *n.* The part of the harness of a horse, etc., about the head, used to restrain and guide the animal; anything that restrains or curbs.—*v.t.,* **bri·dled, bri·dling.** To put a bridle on; to restrain.—*v.i.* To hold the head up and backward; to toss the head.

bri·dle path, *n.* A path for riding horseback.

brief, brēf, *a.* Short; fleeting; concise. —*n.* A short writing or statement; a summary; an outline following certain rules to cover all points on one side of a controversy; an official letter. A case at law; a writ calling one to whom it is issued to follow certain action.—*v.t.* To summarize or make a written abstract; to instruct: to *brief* an airplane crew. *Law.* To furnish a memorandum, concisely stated, of (a client's case). —**brief·ly,** *adv.*

brief case, *n.* A flat, rectangular case for carrying business papers.

brief·ing, brē'fing, *n.* Instruction concerning procedures and particulars.

briefs, brēfs, *n.* Very short, snug underpants for men or women.

bri·er, brī'er, *n.* A prickly plant or shrub; a mass of these plants.

brig, brig, *n.* The prison on a warship. *Informal.* Guardhouse.

brig, brig, *n.* A two-masted vessel, square-rigged on both masts.

bri·gade, bri·gād', *n.* A large body of troops, esp. a unit of organization in an army, commonly consisting of two or more regiments; any group organized for a special purpose: a fire *brigade.*

brig·a·dier, brig·a·dēr', *n.* An officer in command of a brigade; a brigadier general.

brig·a·dier gen·er·al, *n.* An officer in command of a brigade or engaged in other duties, in the U.S. ranking next below a major-general.

brig·an·tine, brig'an·tēn, brig'an·tīn, *n.* A square-rigged, two-masted vessel which differs from a brig in not having a square mainsail.

bright, brīt, *a.* Radiating or reflecting light; shining; brilliant, as color; splendid; quick-witted or intelligent, as a person; characterized by happiness or gladness. —**bright·ly,** *adv.* —**bright·ness,** *n.*

bright·en, *v.t.* To make bright or brighter.—*v.i.* To grow bright or more bright.

bril·liance, bril'yans, *n.* Great brightness; luster; striking achievement; ability. —**bril·lian·cy,** *n.* —**bril·liant,** *a.*

brim, brim, *n.* The upper edge of anything hollow, as a cup; a projecting edge, border, or rim, as of a hat.— *v.t.,* **brimmed, brim·ming.** To fill to the brim, or top.— *v.i.* To be full to the brim; to be full to overflowing. —**brim o·ver,** to be so full as to overflow.

brim·stone, brim'stōn, *n.* Sulfur.

brine, brīn, *n.* Water saturated with salt, like the water of the ocean; salt water.—*v.t.* To steep in brine. —**brin·y,** *a.*

bring, bring, *v.t.,* **brought, bring·ing.** To bear from a distant to a nearer place, or to a person; to fetch; to carry; to accompany; to change in state or condition: *bring* to nought; to persuade: *bring* to reason, to terms. —**bring a·bout,** to cause to happen. —**bring down,** to cause to come down; to humiliate; to shoot, as game. —**bring forth,** to produce; to beget; to cause. —**bring for·ward,** to present for consideration: to *bring forward* proposals. —**bring in,** to introduce; to supply; to yield, as profit or income. —**bring off,** to have success: He *brought off* the performance well.

—**bring on,** to cause to begin: to *bring on* an attack; to originate: to *bring on* a headache. —**bring out,** to emphasize; to reveal; to introduce, as a new model car. —**bring to light,** to reveal. —**bring to mind,** to recall. —**bring to pass,** to cause to happen. —**bring up,** to feed, and tend; to rear; to introduce to notice: *to bring up* a subject.

brink, bringk, *n.* The edge, margin, or border of a steep place; a situation extremely close to danger or success: the *brink* of war.

bri•oche, brē′ōsh, brē′osh, *n.* A small breakfast roll.

bri•quette, bri•quet, bri•ket′, *n.* A molded block of compacted charcoal for fuel; a similar block of some other combustible.—*v.t.,* **bri•quet•ted, bri•quet•ting.**

brisk, brisk, *a.* Quick and active; lively; of liquors, effervescing; bracing; sharp in demeanor.—*v.t.* To make brisk.—*v.i.* To become brisk. —**brisk•ly,** *adv.* —**brisk•ness,** *n.*

bris•ket, bris′kit, *n.* The breast of an animal, or the part of the breast lying next to the ribs.

bris•tle, bris′əl, *n.* One of the short, stiff, coarse hairs of certain animals, esp. hogs, used extensively in making brushes, etc.; any similar short, stiff hair or hairlike appendage.—*v.i.,* **bris•tled, bris•tling.** To stand or rise stiffly, like bristles; to erect the bristles, as an irritated animal (sometimes with *up,* and often *fig.,* of persons); be rough; to be visibly roused or stirred (*with*); to assume a self-assertive disposition.—*v.t.* To erect like bristles; to furnish with bristles; to rouse or disturb. —**bris•tly,** bris′lē, *a.*

Bri•tan•ni•a, bri•tan′ē•ə, bri•tan′yə, *n.* The ancient Roman name for Great Britain; Great Britain; the United Kingdom.

britch•es, brich′iz, *n. pl. Informal.* Trousers; breeches.

Brit•ish, brit′ish, *a.* Of or pertaining to Great Britain, the British Commonwealth, or its inhabitants.—*n.* The British people; the ancient British tongue; British English.

Brit•ish•er, brit′i•shər, *n.* A British native.

Brit•ish ther•mal u•nit (BTU), *n.* The heat necessary to raise the temperature of one pound of water one degree Fahrenheit at or near its point of maximum density.

Brit•on, brit′ən, *n.* One of the Celtic people who in early times occupied the southern part of Britain; a native or inhabitant of Great Britain, or of the British Empire, esp. an Englishman.

brit•tle, brit′əl, *a.* Hard, but breaking readily, as glass; fragile; dry, sharp: a *brittle* tone; shallow, cold: a *brittle* personality.

brit•tle, brit′əl, *n.* A caramelized-sugar candy, usually containing nuts.

broach, brōch, *n.* A spit for roasting meat; any of various tools or drills for boring or widening holes; a reamer; a brooch.—*v.t.* To mention or suggest a subject for the first time; pierce with a spit; tap a cask; expand a hole; shape a stone with a broach.—*v.i.* To rise above the surface from below.

broad, brôd, *a.* Wide; large; of great range: *broad* principles; not limited or narrow: *broad* views; liberal; main or general: the *broad* outlines of a subject; unrestricted or full: *broad* daylight; plain: a *broad* hint; blunt; bold.—*n.* The broad part of anything: the *broad* of the hand. *Informal.* A woman.

broad•cast, brôd′kast, brôd′käst, *v.t.,* **-cast** or **-cast•ed, -cast•ing.** To send out by radio or television; scatter over an area; to spread widely.—*v.i.* To send out in a radio or television program; to scatter something; to talk or act on a radio or television program; to assume the cost of a radio or television program.—*n.* An audio and visual image sent by radio or television; a radio or television program.

broad•cloth, brôd′klôth, brôd′kloth, *n.* A wool or

worsted fabric closely woven in a plain or twill pattern having a sheen; any closely woven fabric, having a smooth surface.

broad jump, *n.* In track and field athletics, a jump for distance. Also **long jump.**

broad-mind•ed, brôd′mīn′did, *a.* Free from prejudice; liberal; tolerant.

broad•side, brôd′sīd, *n.* All the guns on one side of a ship; any comprehensive attack.—*adv.* With the side turned toward something: One car struck the other *broadside.*

Broad•way, brôd′wā, *n.* Street in New York City, known as the heart of the commercial or legitimate theater in the U.S.

bro•cade, brō•kād′, *n.* Material woven in an elaborate pattern, esp. having an over-all, raised design.—*v.t.,* **-cad•ed, -cad•ing.** To weave with a design or figure.

broc•co•li, brok′ə•lē, *n.* A variety of cabbage with edible green florets and stalks.

bro•chure, brō•shûr′, *n.* A pamphlet.

brogue, brōg, *n.* A heavy shoe.

brogue, brōg, *n.* An Irish accent in the pronunciation of English.

broil, broyl, *v.t.* To cook by putting close to a fire; grill; make very hot.—*v.i.* To be exposed to great heat; burn as with impatience.—*n.* Something broiled.

broil•er, broy′lər, *n.* A device for broiling meat, etc.; a fowl for broiling.

broke, brōk, *a. Informal.* Without money; in bankruptcy.

bro•ken, brō′kən, *a.* In pieces; uneven or irregular; fragmentary or incomplete; changing direction abruptly, as a line; imperfectly spoken, as language; ruined; weakened in strength or spirit; tamed.

bro•ken-down, brō′kən•down′, *a.* Shattered or collapsed; ruined.

bro•ken-heart•ed, brō′kən•här′tid, *a.* Crushed by grief or despair.

bro•ker, brō′kər, *n.* One who buys and sells stocks, bonds, or other property, on commission; a pawnbroker.

bro•ker•age, brō′kər•ij, *n.* The business, service, or commission of a broker.

bro•mide, brō′mīd, brō′mid, *n.* Any of various compounds of bromine that are used in medicine as sedatives and hypnotics.

bro•mine, brō′mēn, *n.* A dark reddish corrosive and toxic element obtained from sea water and used for the manufacture of gasoline anti-knock compounds. See Periodic Table of Elements.

bronc, brongk, *n.* Bronco.

bron•chi, brong′ki, *n. pl.,* **bron•chus.**

bron•chi•al tubes, brong′kē•əl, *n.* The bronchi.

bron•chi•tis, brong•ki′tis, *n.* An inflammation of the lining membrane of the bronchial tubes; inflammation of the bronchia and lungs.

bron•chus, brong′kəs, *n. pl.,* **-chi,** -kī. Either of the two main branches of the windpipe.

bron•co, brong′kō, *n. pl.,* **-cos.** A partly-broken horse or mustang of the western U.S. Also **bronc.**

bron•to•saur, bron′tə•sôr, *n.* A very large plant-eating dinosaur that once lived in North America.

bronze, bronz, *n.* An alloy of copper and tin; something made of bronze; a lustrous brown color.—*v.t.,* **bronzed, bronz•ing.** To give the appearance or color of bronze to; make brown, as by exposure to the sun.—*v.i.* To take on a bronze color.

Bronze Age, *n.* The age in the history of mankind between the Stone and Iron Ages, marked by the use of bronze tools.

brooch, brōch, brooch, *n.* An ornamental pin or clasp.

brood, brood, *n.* A family of young birds; a family's children; breed or kind.—*a.* For breeding.—*v.i.* To sit as a bird over eggs to be hatched; rest fixedly; think

---

a- hat, fāte, fāre, fäther; **e-** met, mē; **i-** pin, pīne; **o-** not, nōte, ôrb, moove (move), boy, pownd; **u-** cūbe, bûll, tûk (took); **ch-** chin; **th-** thick, ŧhen; **zh-** vizhon (vision); **ə-** əgo, takən, pencəl, lemən, bərd (bird).

about for a long time, with *on* or *over.—v.t.* To sit as a bird over (eggs or young); incubate.

brook, brŭk, *n.* A small stream of water.

broom, broom, brûm, *n.* Any of the shrubby plants common in western Europe, which grows uncultivated and has long, slender branches and yellow flowers. A sweeping tool having a brush of straw attached to a stick or handle, originally made with twigs of the broom plant.—*v.t.* To sweep, as with a broom.

broom·stick, broom'stik, *n.* The handle of a broom.

broth, brôth, broth, *n.* The juice from boiled meat, fish, vegetables; thin soup.

broth·el, broth'əl, broth'əl, *n.* A house of prostitution.

broth·er, brəth'ər, *n. pl.,* **broth·ers, breth·ren.** A son of the same parents or parent; a male member of the same tribe, nationality, fraternal order, or profession; a male member of a religious order; a monk; a male black American.—*a.* Being a brother; related by brotherhood.—*v.t.* To treat or address as a brother; admit to or join in brotherhood.

broth·er·hood, brəth'ər·hûd, *n.* The state of being a brother; a group of men of the same class, profession, or occupation; a fraternal or trade organization.

broth·er-in-law, brəth'ər·in·lô, *n. pl.,* **broth·ers-in-law.** The brother of one's husband or wife; a sister's husband.

brow, brow, *n.* The forehead ridge over the eye; eyebrow; forehead; edge.

brow·beat, brow'bēt, *v.t.,* **-beat, -beat·en, -beat·ing.** To frighten by cruel looks or words; bully.

brown, brown, *a.* Of a dark or dusky color.—*n.* A dark color between red and yellow, and resulting from a mixture of red, black, and yellow.—*v.i., v.t.* To become or cause to become brown, as by painting, sunning, scorching.

brown·ie, brow'nē, *n.* A merry, elfin creature in Scottish folklore; a small, square cake or cookie, usually chocolate, containing nuts; (*cap.*) a junior girl scout, aged 7 to 10.

brown·out, brown'owt, *n.* A loss or reduction of electric power.

brown·stone, brown'stōn, *n.* A reddish-brown sandstone; a building with a brownstone front.

brown su·gar, *n.* Unrefined or partially refined sugar.

browse, browz, *v.t.,* **browsed, brows·ing.** Of cattle, deer, to eat, as tender shoots of shrubs and trees; graze.—*v.i.* To leisurely inspect.

bru·in, broo'in, *n.* A bear.

bruise, brooz, *v.t.,* **bruised, bruis·ing.** To injure by a blow or by pressure without cutting; to discolor the skin, as a result of a blow; to batter or dent; to crush to injure the feelings.—*v.i.* To become bruised.—*n.* An injury or discoloration of the skin due to bruising.

bruis·er, broo'zər, *n. Informal.* A big, heavily-built man.

brunch, brənch, *n.* A meal that combines breakfast with lunch.

bru·net, broo·net', *a.* Dark or brownish; brown or black-haired.—*n.* A person having dark complexion, hair, and eyes.

brunt, brənt, *n.* The shock or force of an attack; chief stress, force, or violence.

brush, brəsh, *n.* An instrument consisting of bristles or hair, set in a handle and used for removing dirt or dust, polishing, smoothing, applying moisture or paint, etc.; something resembling or suggesting this, as the bushy tail of the fox; a piece of carbon or copper in a dynamo or motor, which touches the commutator and connects it with the outside circuit; a brushing, or an application of a brush; a short, brisk fight.—*v.t.* To pass a brush over; polish or improve by using a brush, with *up;* wet or paint lightly with a brush, with *over;* strike or graze lightly, as in passing.—*v.i.* To use a brush; refresh one's knowledge of some subject, with *up;* pass over or touch against something lightly like a brush; move quickly or in haste. —**brush off,** *Informal.*

To reject rudely.

brush, brəsh, *n.* A dense growth of bushes; a remote, partly wooded area.

brush-off, brəsh'ôf, brəsh'of, *n. Informal.* Snub; a quick, firm dismissal.

brusque, brusk, brəsk, *a.* Abrupt in manner; blunt; rude.

Brus·sels sprouts, brəs'əlz sprowts, *n. pl.* A kind of cabbage that bears along its stalk tiny cabbagelike heads, eaten as a vegetable.

bru·tal, broo'təl, *a.* Like or resembling brutes; irrational; rude, or unrefined; inhuman, savage, or cruel; gross or sensual.

bru·tal·i·ty, broo·tal'ə·tē, *n.* A savage act.

bru·tal·ize, broo'tə·līz, *v.t.,* **-ized, -iz·ing.** To make brutal; to treat in a brutal manner.—*v.i.* To become brutal. —**bru·tal·i·za·tion,** broo·tə·lə·zā'shən, *n.*

brute, broot, *a.* Having no reason or understanding: *brute* beasts; pertaining to qualities or actions characteristic of animals as distinguished from humans; crude; savage; merely physical; lacking life and soul. —*n.* A brute creature, animal rather than human; the animal nature in humans; a person resembling an animal in some quality, as cruelty or sensuality.

brut·ish, broo'tish, *a.* Of or like brutes; savage; coarse.

bub·ble, bəb'əl, *n.* A thin film of liquid inflated with air or gas; a small globule of air or gas in a liquid in a solid substance; anything lacking substance, or reality; the act, process, or sound of bubbling; a globular shelter; a dome.—*v.i.,* **-bled, -bling.** To gurgle; form bubbles; to rise in bubbles; to arise or issue like bubbles; be in a state of animation.—*v.t.* To cause to bubble; to form bubbles in, as liquids.

bub·ble gum, *n.* A thick chewing gum which can be blown into bubbles.

bub·bler, bəb'lər, *n.* A drinking fountain which causes water to spout upward.

bu·bon·ic plague, bŭ·bon'ik, boo·bon'ik, *n.* An epidemic disease caused by infection from rodents and fleas and characterized by the formation of inflammatory swelling of lymphatic glands, esp. in the groin and armpits.

buc·ca·neer, bək·ə·nēr', *n.* A pirate.

buck, bək, *n.* A male deer, goat, antelope, rabbit, or hare; a dashing fellow; a male person.—*v.i.* Of a horse, to leap with arched back and land with stiffened forelegs. *Informal.* To resist obstinately; of a vehicle, to move jerkily.—*v.t.* To throw by bucking. —**buck up,** to be encouraged.

buck, bək, *n. Informal.* An American dollar.

buck, bək, *n.* An article or counter used in poker to keep track of the deal.—**to pass the buck,** *Informal.* To pass a burden, as responsibility or blame, to another.

buck·a·roo, buck·e·roo, bək·ə·roo', *n.* A cowboy.

buck·board, bək'bōrd, bək'bôrd, *n.* A four-wheeled carriage in which a long flexible board or frame is fastened to the axle without springs.

buck·et, bək'it, *n.* A cylindrical container for scooping up or holding liquids or solids; pail; the amount a bucket will hold.—*v.t.,* **-et·ed, -et·ing.** To lift or carry in buckets.

buck·et seat, *n.* A single low seat, with a slightly rounded back, used in automobiles and airplanes.

buck·eye, bək'ī, *n.* A tree or shrub related to the horse chestnut.

buck·le, bək'əl, *n.* A clasp with a tongue and catch, used for fastening together two loose ends of a belt or strap; a clasplike ornament used to adorn garments, handbags, shoes.—*v.t.,* **-led, -ling.** To fasten with a buckle, with *up;* to join together.—*v.i.* To warp or curl due to heat or weight. —**buck·le down,** to apply oneself vigorously.

buck·ram, bək'rəm, *n.* A coarse linen or cotton fabric stiffened with glue or gum, used for bookbinding.

buck·saw, bək'sô, *n.* A saw set across an upright frame, used with both hands in cutting wood.

buck•shot, bək′shot, *n.* A large leaden pellet used to kill game.

buck•skin, bək′skin, *n.* The skin of a buck or deer; a strong, soft leather, yellowish or grayish in color, now often sheepskin; *pl.,* breeches or other clothing made of buckskin.

buck•tooth, bək′tooth, *n. pl.,* **-teeth,** -tēth. A front tooth that sticks out. **—buck′toothed,** *a.*

buck•wheat, bək′hwēt, bək′wēt, *n.* A plant grown for its triangular seeds, used as a food for animals, and made into a dark flour used for making pancakes; the seeds; the flour.

bu•col•ic, bū-kol′ik, *a.* Of or pertaining to shepherds; rustic; countrified.

bud, bəd, *n.* An undeveloped plant stem or branch; a leaf or flower not yet opened; any undeveloped state; a taste bud.—*v.i.,* **bud•ded, bud•ding.** To produce buds, as a plant; to begin to grow or develop.—*v.t.* To cause to bud; to produce by means of buds.

Bud•dha, bŭd′ə, boo′də, *n.* "The Enlightened One," a title applied esp. to the founder of Buddhism.

Bud•dhism, bŭd′iz-əm, boo′diz-əm, *n.* The religious system founded by Buddha, practiced in much of Asia. **—Bud•dhist,** *n.*

bud•dy, bud•die, bəd′ē, *n. pl.,* **-dies.** A comrade or pal.

budge, bəj, *v.i.* To move slightly; stir.

budg•et, bəj′it, *n.* A financial statement of estimated income and expenditures; a plan for financing operations, based on such a statement.—*v.t.* To provide for in a budget; confine to a budget; plan the utilization of: Students must learn to *budget* their time.—*v.i.* To plan a budget; to limit expenditures, as: We're *budgeting* in order to buy a house. **—budg•et•ar•y,** *a.*

buff, bəf, *n.* A kind of thick leather, having a fuzzy surface, and used for making belts or pouches; the color of leather, a light brown. *Informal.* The bare skin; a well-informed enthusiast.—*a.* Made of buff leather; of the color buff.—*v.t.* To impart to (something) a fuzzy surface like that of buff leather; to polish with a buff; to make buff in color.

buff, bəf, *n.* A fan: a football *buff.*

buf•fa•lo, bəf′ə-lō, *n. pl.,* **-loes, -los.** A cud-chewing mammal of the ox family somewhat larger than the common ox; bison; water buffalo; Cape buffalo.—*v.t.,* **-loed, -lo•ing.** *Informal.* To render completely helpless.

buff•er, bəf′ər, *n.* Anything serving to deaden or sustain a shock; a substance added to neutralize both acids and bases in solution.—*v.t.* To shield or cushion.

buf•fet, bəf′it, *n.* A blow, as with the fist.—*v.t.,* **-fet•ed, -fet•ing.** To strike as with the fist; beat; batter.—*v.i.* To deal blows; fight; struggle.

buf•fet, bə-fā′, bŭ-fā′, *n.* A cabinet for holding china, silverware, and table linen; a counter at which lunch or refreshments are served in restaurants; informal meal served on a buffet or table.

buf•foon, bə-foon′, *n.* A clown; one given to coarse or undignified joking. **—buf•foon•er•y,** *n. pl.,* **-ies. —buf•foon•ish,** *a.*

bug, bəg, *n.* Any insect with a piercing, sucking mouth part; any of various insects; bedbug. *Informal.* A failing in a machine or the like; a disease-causing microbe, as a germ or virus; a person with an avid or obsessive interest: a motorcycle *bug;* a tiny microphone, concealed so as to secretly record conversations.—*v.t.,* **bugged, bug•ging.** *Informal.* To plant a hidden device on or within, as a phone; to pester.—*v.i.* To stare: Her eyes *bugged* at the news.

bug•a•boo, bəg′ə-boo, *n.* An imaginary object of fright.

bug•gy, bəg′ē, *a.,* **-gi•er, -gi•est.** Infested with bugs. *Informal.* Crazy; ludicrous.

bug•gy, bəg′ē, *n. pl.,* **-gies.** A light one-horse carriage; a baby carriage. *Informal.* An old or run-down car.

bu•gle, bū′gəl, *n.* A brass or copper wind instrument, like a trumpet, but having no keys or valves.—*v.i.,* **-gled, -gling.** To sound a bugle.—*v.t.* To call by bugle. **—bu•gler,** *n.*

build, bild, *v.t.,* **built, build•ing.** To construct or erect by putting materials together; to make; to establish by gradual means.—*v.i.* To erect a dwelling or other building; to progress toward a goal.—*n.* Style or manner of construction; physique. **—build•er,** *n.*

build•ing, bil′ding, *n.* A structure, usually with a roof and four walls, intended as a working or dwelling place; the business of construction.

build•up, bild′əp, *n.* An accumulation of materials for a future need; an effort to enhance the image of a person or thing.

built-in, bilt′in′, *a.* Permanently attached to a larger structure: The kitchen has a *built-in* dishwasher. Having inherent or natural characteristics: Her gentle manner displayed *built-in* sensitivity.

built-up, bilt′əp′, *a.* Made of various layers fastened together; densely covered with dwelling units.

bulb, bəlb, *n.* An underground leaf bud, capable of developing into new plants, sending down roots from its base, and producing a stem from its center, as the onion, lily, or hyacinth; a plant developing from a bulb; any bulge at the end of a stalk or long and slender body, as in the tube of a thermometer; the round part of an electric light.—*v.i.* To stick out. **—bul•ba•ceous,** bəl-bā′shəs, *a.*

bul•bar, bəl′bər, bəl′bär, *a.* Having to do with a bulb, esp. the medulla oblongata.

bul•bous, bəl′bəs, *a.* Having or having to do with bulbs or a bulb; swelling out.

bulge, bəlj, *n.* A swelling; a hump.—*v.t.,* **bulged, bulg•ing.** To make swell out.—*v.i.* To swell out. **—bulg•y,** *a.*

bulk, bəlk, *n.* A large mass; main body or greater part; volume.—*v.i.* To be of great volume or size; to expand.—*v.t.* To cause to expand or bulge. **—in bulk,** not in separate packages: sugar *in bulk.*

bulk•head, bəlk′hed, *n.* One of the upright partitions dividing a ship into water-tight compartments to prevent sinking; a resisting partition or wall.

bulk•y, bəl′kē, *a.,* **-i•er, -i•est.** Large; clumsy. **—bulk•i•ly,** *adv.* **—bulk•i•ness,** *n.*

bull, bŭl, *n.* The male of domestic beef cattle; the male of various other animals, as the elephant, whale, etc.; one who buys stocks, expecting that prices will rise. *Informal.* A policeman; foolish or nonsensical talk.—*v.t.* To endeavor to raise the price of (stocks) in the stock exchange. To push or force (one's way).

bull, bŭl, *n. Informal.* Bragging talk; a gross exaggeration.—*a.* A male of large size; increasing: a *bull* market.

bull•dog, bŭl′dôg, bŭl′dog, *n.* A medium-sized, short-haired, muscular variety of dog, with a large head and prominent lower jaw.—*v.t.* To force to the ground, as a steer, by seizing his horns and twisting his neck.

bull•doze, bŭl′dōz, *v.t.,* **-dozed, -doz•ing.** To clear off an area by pushing with a bulldozer. *Informal.* To bully.

bull•doz•er, bŭl′dō-zər, *n.* A powerful tracked machine with a blunt blade at the front end, used for moving earth; one who bulldozes.

bul•let, bŭl′it, *n.* A projectile generally of lead to be shot from rifles or pistols; a small ball.

bul•le•tin, bŭl′ə-tən, *n.* A brief statement concerning current matters of public interest, issued by an authoritative source.

bul•let•proof, bŭl′it-proof, *a.* Made so that a bullet cannot penetrate.

bull•fight, bŭl′fīt, *n.* A combat between men and a bull

---

a- hat, fāte, fâre, fäther; e- met, mē; i- pin, pīne; o- not, nōte, ôrb, moove (move), boy, pownd; u- cūbe, bŭll, tŭk (took); ch- chin; th- thick, ᵺen; zh- vizhon (vision); ə- əgo, takən, pencəl, lemən, bərd (bird).

or bulls in an arena. —**bull·fight·er,** *n.* —**bull·fight· ing,** *n.*

bull·finch, bûl′finch, *n.* A European bird, with a short, stout bill, valued as a cage bird.

bull·frog, bûl′frog, bûl′frôg, *n.* A large frog with a loud bass voice.

bull·head·ed, bûl′hed′id, *a.* Headstrong; stubborn.

bull·horn, bûl′hôrn, *n.* An electric megaphone.

bul·lion, bûl′yən, *n.* Gold or silver in the mass; a cordlike trimming used to ornament uniforms, etc.

bull·ock, bûl′ək, *n.* An ox or castrated bull; a steer.

bull·pen, bûl′pen, *n.* A pen for bulls. *Informal.* An enclosure in which prisoners are temporarily confined; in baseball, a place for pitchers and catchers to warm up.

bull ring, *n.* A circular arena for bullfights.

bull's-eye, bûlz′ī, *n.* The center of a target, or a shot that hits it; a remark or action which is especially relevant.

bull·whip, bûl′hwip, bûl′wip, *n.* A whip with a long plaited lash of rawhide and a short handle.

bul·ly, bûl′ē, *n. pl.,* **-lies.** A quarrelsome, overbearing person who bothers others weaker than himself.—*a.* Good; excellent: *Bully* for you!—*v.t.,* **-lied, -ly·ing.** To threaten.—*v.i.* To be arrogant.

bul·rush, bûl′rəsh, *n.* Any of various large rushes that grow in marshy places; papyrus, used to make paper in ancient times.

bul·wark, bûl′wərk, *n.* A wall against injury or danger; any moral or spiritual strength which fosters support: *Freedom of speech is a bulwark against oppression; a person of strong support: The older son was a real bulwark in that family.*—*v.t.* To shelter, or protect.

bum, bəm, *n.* A loafer; a drunk; a person who earns or sponges enough to eke out a living and spends most of his time at a sport: a ski *bum.*—*v.i.* To live off others; to live idly; to travel without expense to oneself, by begging or stealing food and lodging.—*v.t. Informal.* To appropriate, as an item, with no intention of repayment.—*a.,* **bum·mer, bum·mest.** *Informal.* Of poor quality; in poor physical condition: a *bum* leg. —**on the bum.** *Informal.* Out of order; living like a tramp. —**bum's rush.** *Informal.* Coerced expulsion, as a disorderly customer from a tavern.

bum·ble·bee, bəm′bəl·bē, *n.* A large, hairy, social bee.

bum·mer, bəm′ər, *n. Informal.* A very bad experience.

bump, bəmp, *v.t.* To strike heavily against; to dislocate, followed by *off.*—*v.i.* To knock heavily into something: often with *into* or *against. Informal.* To dance by thrusting forward the pelvis: as, to *bump* and grind.— *n.* A sudden heavy blow. A sudden rise on a surface: a *bump* in a road. —**bump in·to,** *Informal.* To meet by chance. —**bump off,** to kill; murder.

bump·er, bəm′pər, *n.* A device for absorbing shock in a collision, especially a bar across the end of an automobile; one that bumps;—*a.* Unusually plentiful: a *bumper* crop.

bump·kin, bəmp′kin, *n.* An awkward, clumsy rustic.

bump·tious, bəmp′shəs, *a.* Offensively self-assertive. —**bump·tious·ness,** *n.*

bump·y, bəm′pē, *a.,* **-i·er, -i·est.** Having bumps; causing bumps or jolts: a *bumpy road;* characterized by bumps or the like: *bumpy weather.* —**bump·i·ly,** *adv.* —**bump·i·ness,** *n.*

bun, bən, *n.* A kind of cake or bread-roll, variously shaped; a bun-shaped knot of hair.

bunch, bənch, *n.* A cluster of things growing or held together; a collected mass. *Informal.* An assemblage of people.—*v.i.* To form a bunch.—*v.t.* To form into a bunch; gather into groups.—**bunch·y,** *a.,* **-i·er, -i·est.**

bun·co, bəng′kō, *n.* Bunko.

bun·combe, bəng′kəm, *n.* Bunkum.

bun·dle, bən′dəl, *n.* A number of things tied or fastened together; a package or parcel; a collection of traits or qualities considered together, as: He is a *bundle* of inconsistencies. *Informal.* A large amount of

money.—*v.t.,* **-dled, -dling.** To tie together or bind into a roll or bundle, usually with *up;* to wrap warmly, with *off;* to send away unceremoniously.

bun·ga·low, bəng′gə·lō, *n.* A small house with one story.

bun·gle, bəng′gəl, *n.* A clumsy or unskillful performance or piece of work; a blunder.—*v.t.,* **-gled, -gling.** To do, make, or mend clumsily; botch.—*v.i.* To work or act clumsily or unskillfully. —**bun·gler,** *n.*

bun·ion, bən′yən, *n.* A knob on the side of the ball of the big toe resulting from chronic inflammation of the bursa.

bunk, bəngk, *n.* A frame serving for a bed, as in a ship or a dormitory, often one of two or more arranged one above another.—*v.i. Informal.* To occupy a bunk; to sleep, esp. in rough quarters.

bunk, bəngk, *n. Informal.* Claptrap; mere pretense.— *v.t. Informal.* To delude.

bunk·er, bəng′kər, *n.* A large bin for coal, or fuel oil, esp. on board ship; a fortification or trench, usually in a battle zone.

bunk·house, bəngk′hows, *n.* A roughly constructed building with quarters for workers.

bun·ko, bun·co, bəng′kō, *n. Informal.* A swindle.— *v.t.* To cheat or swindle.

bun·kum, bun·combe, bəng′kəm, *n.* Insincere talk.

bun·ny, bən′ē, *n. pl.,* **-nies.** A young rabbit.

bunt, bənt, *v.t., v.i.* To strike with the head or horns, as a goat does; in baseball, to allow a pitch to strike the bat without swinging it, so that the ball rolls only a short distance.—*n.* The act of bunting a baseball; a bunted baseball.

bun·ting, bən′ting, *n.* A lightweight woolen or cotton fabric used for flags and decorations; a ship's flags; a type of hooded sleeping bag for babies.

bu·oy, boo′ē, boy, *n.* An upright float fixed in a certain place to indicate the position of a rock or other object beneath the water, or to mark a channel or the like; life buoy.—*v.t.* To mark with a buoy or buoys; keep afloat; encourage.

buoy·an·cy, boy′ən·sē, boo′yən·sē, *n.* The power to float or rise in a fluid; relative lightness; the upward pressure exerted upon a body by the fluid in which it is immersed, which is equivalent to the weight of the fluid which the body displaces; cheerfulness. —**buoy·ant,** *a.* —**buoy·ant·ly,** *adv.*

bur, bər, *n.* Burr.

bur·ble, bər′bəl, *n.* A gentle, bubbling flow; a bubbling speech pattern.

bur·den, bər′dən, *n.* A load; a responsibility; something borne with labor or difficulty; a heavy lot or fate; a load considered as a measure of quantity; the carrying of loads: a beast of *burden.*—*v.t.* To load; place a load on; oppress.

bur·den·some, bər′dən·səm, *a.* Heavy or hard to bear; oppressive.

bur·dock, bər′dok, *n.* A coarse weed with burrs which stick to the clothing.

bu·reau, byûr′ō, *n. pl.,* **bu·reaus, bu·reaux,** byûr′ōz. A chest of drawers for clothing; a dresser; a commercial agency for transacting business, giving out and exchanging information, etc.; a department of government, or a specialized administrative unit for the transaction of public business.

bu·reauc·ra·cy, byûr·rok′rə·sē, *n. pl.,* **-cies.** Government by bureaus; a body of officials administering government bureaus; excessive red tape and inflexibility. —**bu·reau·crat,** byûr′ə·krat, *n.* —**bu·reau· crat·ic,** byûr·ə·krat′ik, *a.*

bu·rette, byû·ret′, *n.* A graduated glass tube, used for measuring small quantities of liquid.

burg, bərg, *n. Informal.* A town or city.

bur·geon, bər′jən, *n.* A bud or sprout.—*v.i.* To bud.— *v.t.* To put forth, as buds.

burg·er, bər′gər, *n. Informal.* A hamburger.

bur·gess, bər′jis, *n.* Citizen of a borough; a representative in the colonial legislature of Maryland and Virginia.

bur·glar, bər/glər, n. One guilty of burglary.

bur·glar·ize, bər/glə·rīz, v.t., **-ized, -iz·ing.** To commit burglary upon.—v.i. To commit a burglary; to rob.

bur·gla·ry, bər/glə·rē, n. pl., **-ries.** The crime of breaking into the house of another with criminal intent to steal something.

bur·gle, bər/gəl, v.i., v.t., **-gled, -gling.** Informal. To burglarize.

bur·i·al, ber/ē·əl, n. The act or ceremony of burying a deceased person.

bur·lap, bər/lap, n. A coarse plain-woven fabric of flax, jute or hemp, used for sacking or wrappings.

bur·lesque, bər·lesk/, n. A literary composition that treats a lofty subject in a ridiculous way; caricature; an entertainment with skits, bawdy humor, and striptease acts; a ludicrous or debasing caricature of any kind. —a. Exciting laughter; comical.—v.t., **bur·lesqued, bur·les·quing.** To imitate grotesquely; caricature.— v.i. To use burlesque. —**bur·les·quer,** n.

bur·ly, bər/lē, a., **-li·er, -li·est.** Great in bodily size; bulky; lusty; forceful; abrupt. —**bur·li·ly,** adv. —**bur·li·ness,** n.

burn, bərn, v.i., **burned** or **burnt, burn·ing.** To be on fire; contain fire; be fierce or vehement; be inflamed with passion, desire, etc.; be or become very hot; feel excess of heat; be affected with a sensation of heat; to give light; glow like fire; undergo destruction, injury, or change from exposure to fire or heat; become charred, singed, scorched, etc.; become tanned; suffer death by fire; undergo combustion; oxidize.—v.t. To consume or destroy by fire; set on fire; put to death by fire; keep alight; inflame with passion, desire, etc.; expose to the action of fire or heat; make by means of fire; injure or change by fire or heat; char, singe, scorch, etc.; change the color of by fire or heat; wound or hurt by contact with fire or with something very hot; cauterize; brand with a hot iron; produce an effect or a sensation like that of fire or heat on something; cause to undergo combustion; oxidize.— n. An injury or wound caused by burning; a mark made by burning; a sunburn; a firing of a rocket. —**burn·a·ble,** a. —**burn·ing,** a.

burn·er, bər/nər, n. A device on a stove or lamp from which the flame comes.

bur·nish, bər/nish, n. Gloss; brightness; luster.—v.t. To shine or buff; to refine; to make smooth.—v.i. To grow bright; to become glossy. —**bur·nish·er,** bər/nish·ər, n.

bur·noose, bur·nous, bər·noos/, bər/noos, n. A hooded mantle or cloak worn by Arabs.

burn·sides, bərn/sīdz, n. pl. Side-whiskers and a mustache, the chin being clean-shaven.

burnt, bərnt, a. Affected by, scorched, or darkened as by burning; relating to colors of earth pigments: burnt umber; relating to colors of deep hue: burnt orange.

burp, bərp, n. Informal. A noisy emission of gas from stomach to mouth; belch.—v.i., v.t. To belch.

burr, bur, bər, n. A rough or prickly seed-vessel, as of the chestnut; a plant bearing such burrs, as the burdock; something that sticks like a burr; something producing a choking sensation in the throat; a rough edge on any object; a dentist's drill; a guttural or rough pronunciation of the letter r characteristic of the speech of Scotland; a whirring noise.—v.i., **burred, bur·ring.** To speak with a burr; to make a whirring sound.—v.t. To pronounce, as the letter r, with a burr. To form into a rough edge; to remove burrs from.

bur·ro, bər/ō, bûr/ō, n. pl., **-ros.** A small donkey, used as a pack animal.

bur·row, bər/ō, n. A hole in the ground made by an animal, as a rabbit or a fox, for refuge and habitation. —v.i. To make a burrow for habitation; work a way into or under something; hide oneself.—v.t. To make a

burrow or burrows in; construct by burrowing. —**bur·row·er,** n.

bur·sa, bər/sə, n. pl., **-sae,** -sē. A sac to ease motion, as between a tendon and a bone. —**bur·sal,** a.

bur·sar, bər/sər, bər/sär, n. A treasurer, esp. of a college. —**bur·sa·ri·al,** bər·sär/ē·əl, a.

bur·sa·ry, bər/sə·rē, n. pl., **-ries.** A treasury, esp. of a college.

bur·si·tis, bər·sī/tis, n. Inflammation of a bursa.

burst, bərst, v.i., **burst, burst·ing.** To break or be broken suddenly; explode; fly open suddenly; be extremely full, as if ready to break open; break or give way, or be on the verge of giving way, from violent pain or emotion; make a sudden display of activity or emotion; issue forth suddenly and forcibly from confinement; become visible, audible or evident suddenly and clearly.—v.t. To cause to burst; break suddenly and violently; shatter.—n. The act or result of bursting; a sudden display of feeling or energy; an outburst; continuous fire from an automatic weapon. —**burst·er,** n.

bur·y, ber/ē, v.t., **bur·ied, bur·y·ing.** To deposit in a grave or tomb, as a dead body; inter; cover up; cover over so as to conceal or forget: They buried their differences.

bur·y·ing ground, A graveyard; a cemetery.

bus, bəs, n. pl., **bus·es, bus·ses.** A motor-driven vehicle for public transportation. Informal. An automobile.—v.t., **bused** or **bussed, bus·ing** or **buss·ing.** To transport by bus.—v.i. To go by bus; to work as a busboy.

bus·boy, bəs/boy, n. An employee in a restaurant who clears and sets tables.

bus·by, bəz/bē, n. pl., **-bies.** A tall fur hat worn by hussars, artillerymen, and engineers in the British army in full-dress uniform.

bush, bûsh, n. A low shrub with many branches; a small clump of shrubs; thicket; undergrowth; a fox's tail; uncleared country sparsely populated, as in Australia; the country as opposed to the towns.—v.t. To cover with bushes; protect with bushes.—v.i. To become bushy; branch or spread like a bush.

bush, bûsh, v.t. To line with a bush or bushing.—n. Bushing.

bushed, bûsht, a. Informal. Exhausted; worn out. Australian. Lost.

bush·el, bûsh/əl, n. A dry measure containing 4 pecks, equivalent to 2,150.42 cubic inches; a vessel of this capacity. Informal. An indefinitely large quantity.

bu·shi·do, boo/shē·dō, n. The code of moral principles which the knights and warriors of feudal Japan followed.

bush·ing, bûsh/ing, n. A lining for a hole; a tube or cylinder mounted in an opening, used to reduce the opening's size.

bush league, n. Informal. A professional sports league of a minor rank. —**bush lea·guer,** n.

bush·man, bûsh/mən, n. pl., **-men.** Australian. A woodsman; a settler in the bush; (cap.) an aborigine living near the Cape of Good Hope, Africa.

bush·mas·ter, bûsh/mas·tər, bûsh/mäs·tər, n. A viper of tropical America, the largest New World snake.

bush·rang·er, bûsh/rān·jər, n. One who lives in the woods; in Australia, a criminal.

bush·whack, bûsh/hwak, bûsh/wak, v.i. To hack one's way through dense underbrush; to fight as a partisan.—v.t. To attack from ambush. —**bush·whack·er,** n. —**bush·whack·ing,** n.

bush·y, bûsh/ē, a., **-i·er, -i·est.** Full of bushes; shaggy. —**bush·i·ness,** n.

bus·i·ly, biz/ə·lē, adv. In a busy manner.

busi·ness, biz/nis, biz/niz, n. Commercial activity engaged in as means of livelihood; a trade, profession,

---

a- hat, fāte, fāre, fäther; **e-** met, mē; **i-** pin, pīne; **o-** not, nōte, ôrb, moove (move), boy, pownd; **u-** cūbe, bûll, tûk (took); **ch-** chin; **th-** thick, then; **zh-** vizhon (vision); **ə-** əgo, takən, pencəl, lemən, bərd (bird).

line, or occupation; a particular field of endeavor; a role or function extended over a considerable period of time; a task, assignment or chore extended over a limited period of time; something felt to be one's own affair, personal concern, responsibility or duty; activities of a person, partnership or corporation involved in commerce, manufacturing, or performing a service; a profit-seeking commercial or industrial enterprise; a firm, factory, or store; a building or locale where commercial or industrial work takes place. The gestures and movements used by actors to help create atmosphere and interpret a part.

busi·ness·like, biz′nis·līk, a. Suitable for business or trade; methodical; systematic.

busi·ness·man, biz′nis·man, n. pl., -men. A man who is active in industry or commerce. —**busi·ness·wom·an,** n. pl., busi·ness·wom·en.

bus·kin, bəs′kin, n. A half-boot, reaching halfway to the knee; the cothurnus of ancient Greek and Roman tragic actors, sometimes taken as a symbol of tragedy. —**bus·kined,** a.

buss, bəs, n. A hearty kiss.—v.t. To kiss.

bust, bəst, n. The chest or breast; the bosom; a sculpture of the human head, shoulders, and breast.

bust, bəst, v.t. Informal. To burst; to cause financial ruin to; to discipline or break, as an animal; to strike suddenly; to arrest; to lower in grade or rank.—v.i. To burst; to lack funds.—n. A failure; a spree; an arrest.

bus·tard, bəs′tərd, n. Any of various Old World birds related to both the cranes and the plovers.

bus·tle, bəs′əl, v.i., -tled, -tling. To move or act with a great show of energy; to hasten.—v.t. To cause to bustle; force, drive, etc., by bustling.—n. Activity with noise. —**bus·tler,** n. —**bus·tling,** a.

bus·tle, bəs′əl, n. A pad or wire framework worn about 1880 beneath the skirt of a woman's dress, expanding and supporting it.

bus·y, biz′ē, a., -i·er, -i·est. Actively or attentively engaged; closely occupied; employed or in use; having much business; in constant motion or activity; full of or indicating activity or business; carried on energetically; meddlesome; prying; having too many designs or colors.—v.t., **bus·ied, bus·y·ing.** To be occupied.

bus·y·bod·y, biz′ē·bod·ē, n. pl., -ies. A prying person who concerns himself with the affairs of others.

but, bət, conj. Except or save: as, right but for one thing, or, anywhere but in America; unless; except that, often used with that, as: Nothing would do but that I should come in; on the contrary; nevertheless: as, famous but humble; without the circumstance that, as: It never rains but it pours; otherwise: as, I cannot but hope. That: as, no question but he will win; that . . . not: as, not so fine a student but she could improve; were it not that, as: I would come in but that it is impossible. Unless, as: But he be dead he will hear you. Than, as: He no sooner left but he returned. Only or merely, as: He is but a boy. Informal. Very; exceedingly: as, to leave but fast.—pron. But who; but that: as, No one but has his troubles.—prep. With the exception of: No one replied but me. Except; save; as: She talked of nothing but her new home.—n. An objection, as: He must go; no ifs or buts about it.

bu·ta·di·ene, bū·tə·dī′ĕn, n. A flammable colorless hydrocarbon gas that polymerizes readily, used chiefly in making synthetic rubber.

bu·tane, bū′tān, bū·tān′, n. A colorless flammable hydrocarbon gas obtained from petroleum or natural gas, used principally for making a butadiene and as a fuel.

butch·er, bûch′ər, n. One who slaughters animals, or dresses their flesh, for food or for market; one who deals in meat; formerly, a candy and fruit seller on a train. One guilty of killing indiscriminately or brutally; Informal. An unskillful or bungling worker.—v.t. To slaughter, as animals, or dress, as meat, for market; to murder indiscriminately or brutally; to treat bungling-

ly, or spoil by bad work. —**butch·er·er,** n.

butch·er·bird, bûch′ər·bərd, n. Any of various shrikes.

butch·er's-broom, bûch′ərz·broom, n. A stiff, spiny shrub, belonging to the lily family.

butch·er·y, bûch′ə·rē, n. pl., -ies. A slaughterhouse or butcher's shop; the trade or business of a butcher; the act of butchering animals for food; brutal slaughter; carnage.

but·ler, bət′lər, n. A manservant having charge of the wines and liquors in a household; the head male servant of a household. —**but·ler·ship,** n.

butt, bət, n. A target for archery practice; an erection on which this is placed; a mound or embankment to receive shots fired in rifle or gunnery practice or experiments; pl., a range for archery, rifle, or gunnery practice. An object of ridicule, scorn, or abuse.

butt, bət, n. The end or extremity of anything, esp. the thicker, larger, or blunt end, as of a rifle, fishing rod, whip handle, arrow, etc. Also **butt end.** An unused stub, as of a cigar; the trunk of a tree, esp. just above the root; the base of a leaf-stalk. Informal. A buttock or the buttocks; the thicker or hinder part of a hide or skin; the thick leather made from this.

butt, bət, v.i. To join at the end; abut; be contiguous; fit together end to end; to strike or push with head first; to pitch forward; to jut or project.—v.t. To strike or push with the head or horns.—n. A thrust or push with the head or horns.

butt, bət, n. A large cask, esp. for wine or ale; a measure of capacity equivalent to 108 imperial gallons; any cask or barrel.

butte, būt, n. Western U.S., Canada. A conspicuous isolated hill or mountain rising abruptly.

but·ter, bət′ər, n. The fatty portion of milk, separating as a soft whitish or yellowish solid when milk or cream is agitated or churned, and processed for the table or cookery; a soft, edible spread: peanut butter, apple butter.—v.t. Informal. To spread with butter; put butter on or in. —**but·ter up,** to flatter with the intent of gaining special considerations; wheedle.

but·ter bean, n. A lima bean, especially in southern U.S.; a wax bean.

but·ter·cup, bət′ər·kəp, n. Any plant of the genus, typically with yellow cup-shaped flowers.

but·ter·fat, bət′ər·fat, n. The fatty component of milk extracted to make butter.

but·ter·fin·gered, bət′ər·fing·gerd, a. Apt to let things slip or fall through the fingers; careless; clumsy. —**but·ter·fin·gers,** n.

but·ter·fish, bət′ər·fish, n. Any of various fishes with a smooth, slippery coating.

but·ter·fly, bət′ər·flī, n. pl., -flies. Any of a group of insects, characterized by club-shaped antennae, a slender body with broad wings, often beautifully colored and patterned; anything that resembles a butterfly; a showily dressed, trifling or giddy person.

but·ter·milk, bət′ər·milk, n. The sour liquid remaining after butter has been churned from milk.

but·ter·nut, bət′ər·nət, n. The American walnut; the edible nut of this tree; its wood, used in cabinetmaking.

but·ter·scotch, bət′ər·skoch, n. A hard candy deriving its flavor primarily from butter and brown sugar.—a. Having the flavor of this mixture.

but·ter·y, bət′ə·rē, n. pl., -ies. Chiefly Brit. A room in which wines and liquors are kept; a pantry.

but·ter·y, bət′ə·rē, a. Of the nature of or resembling butter in consistency or appearance; containing or covered with butter; given to gross flattery.

but·tock, bət′ək, n. Either of the two fleshy protuberances forming the lower and back part of the human trunk; pl., the rump.

but·ton, but′ən, n. A knob or disk with holes for sewing or attaching to a garment, used generally for securing one part to another by passing through a buttonhole or a loop; any of various objects of similar shape or function, as the knob fixed to the point of a fencing foil, or the knob or disk pressed to ring an electric bell; a bud or other protuberant part of a plant; a young or undeveloped mushroom.—*v.t.* To fasten with a button or buttons; to furnish with a button or buttons.—*v.i.* To be capable of being buttoned, as: His coat *buttons* in front.

but·ton·hole, bət'ən·hōl, *n.* The hole, loop, or slit through which a button is passed and fastened.—*v.t.,* **-holed, -hol·ing.** To sew with the buttonhole stitch; to insert buttonholes in; to seize by the buttonhole and detain in conversation. —**but·ton·hol·er,** *n.*

but·ton·wood, bət'ən·wûd, *n.* A tall, massive plane tree, yielding a useful timber. Also **but·ton·ball.**

but·tress, bət'ris, *n.* A structure built against or projecting from a wall or building for the purpose of giving it stability; something resembling such a structure in use or appearance; a prop or support.—*v.t.* To support by a buttress; to prop up; to uphold or strengthen (a person, an argument, etc.).

bu·ty·ric, bū·tir'ik, *a.* Of or pertaining to butyric acid.

bu·ty·ric ac·id, *n.* A fatty acid found in butter in glyceride form, obtained by oxidation of butyl alcohol and used as a basic material for manufacturing flavorings and some plastics.

bux·om, buk'səm, *a.* Amply proportioned, esp. full-bosomed, said of a woman. —**bux·om·ly,** *adv.* —**bux·om·ness,** *n.*

buy, bī, *v.t.,* **bought, buy·ing.** To acquire possession of, esp. by paying money; purchase; hire; bribe. *Informal.* To accept (a statement) as true; accept (a plan, proposition) as agreeable, as: I will *buy* that suggestion.—*v.i.* To make a purchase or purchases.—*n.* Something bought or to be bought. —**buy·a·ble,** *a.*

buy·er, bī'ər, *n.* One who buys; a purchaser; the head of a department in a retail store.

buzz, buz, *v.i.* To make a continuous humming sound such as that of bees; make an indistinct murmuring sound, as a number of people talking together; to move about busily.—*v.t.* To utter or express in a murmur or whisper; spread with busy talk; to cause to buzz; to call or signal with a buzzer; to fly, as a plane, quickly over an area at a very low altitude. *Informal.* To telephone.—*n.* A continuous humming sound such as that of bees; a confused humming sound, as of a number of people busily engaged in conversation; the sound of bustling activity; a state of activity or excitement; a report or rumor. *Informal.* A phone call.

buz·zard, bəz'ərd, *n.* Any of various sluggish, heavily-built birds of the hawk family; the turkey buzzard.

buzz bomb, *n.* An aerial projectile launched mainly against England by the Germans during World War II.

buzz·er, bəz'ər, *n.* One who or that which buzzes; a device, esp. an electrical one, for making a buzzing noise as a signal.

buzz saw, *n.* A small circular power saw, named for the sound it makes.

by, bī, *prep.* Beside or near; in the direction of: as, east *by* south; not later than: *by* six o'clock; through the means of, or efficacy of; begot or born of; with the witness of; according to: to learn *by* rote; in relation to; to the amount or extent of; separately with: two *by* two; combined with in multiplication or measuring relative dimensions: four feet *by* six feet.—*adv.* Near, or at hand: close *by;* past, in place or time: days gone *by;* aside or away: to put or lay a thing *by.*—*a.* Situated to one side or in an out-of-the-way place; secondary to the main point.

bye, bī, *n.* Something aside from the main course or consideration; a sportsman in a tournament who is without an opponent.

by·e·lec·tion, bī'i·lĕk·shən, *n. Brit., Canadian.* A special local election to replace a Member of Parliament or Member of the Legislative Assembly.

by·gone, bī'gôn, bī'gon, *a.* Past; former; departed; out of date.—*n. pl.* That which is past.

by·law, bī'lô, *n.* A standing rule of an organized group, created for the regulation of its internal organization and the governing of its members.

by·line, bī'līn, *n.* The author's name printed with a news story, column, or feature article in a newspaper or magazine.

by·pass, bī'pas, bī'päs, *n.* A detour; a secondary route or passage which avoids congested or obstructed areas.—*v.t.* To take a secondary route around; to avoid, as an obstacle; to ignore or sidestep.

by·path, bī'path, bī'päth, *n.* A path, road, street, or way which is secondary to a main road or street; a lesser, private, or obscure way. Also **by-street.**

by·play, bī'plā, *n.* Action or speech carried on aside while the main action proceeds, esp. on the stage; something apart from the main purpose.

by·prod·uct, bī'prod·əkt, *n.* A secondary product; something obtained in addition to the principal product or material; a minor consequence.

by·road, bī'rōd, *n.* A side road; a road other than the main or usual road.

by·stand·er, bī'stan·dər, *n.* An onlooker or spectator; one present but taking no part in what is going on.

byte, bit, *n.* A sequence of binary digits operated upon as a unit and almost always shorter than a word.

by·way, bī'wā, *n.* A by-road.

by·word, bī'wərd, *n.* A proverb or proverbial saying; a person or thing that becomes proverbial as a type; an object of derision or contempt; a nickname.

---

a- hat, fāte, fāre, fäther; **e-** met, mē; **i-** pin, pīne; **o-** not, nōte, ôrb, moove (move), boy, pownd; **u-** cūbe, bûll, tûk (took); **ch-** chin; **th-** thick, then; **zh-** vizhon (vision); **ə-** əgo, takən, pencəl, lemən, bərd (bird).

C

C, c, sē, *n.* The third letter in the English alphabet.

cab, kab, *n.* A passenger automobile available for public hire, usually equipped with a meter which registers the fare; a taxicab; a horse-drawn vehicle, such as the hansom; in a truck or locomotive, the roofed compartment for the driver.

ca·bal, kə·bal′, *n.* A number of persons secretly united in some intrigue.—*v.i.,* **ca·balled, ca·ball·ing.** To form a cabal; to intrigue.

cab·a·la, kab′ə·lə, kə·bä′lə, *n.* A system of esoteric theosophy which was developed among Jewish rabbis during the 6th century A.D.; any occult or secret doctrine or science. Also **cab·ba·la, kab·a·la, kab·ba·la.** —**cab·a·lism,** kab′ə·liz·əm, *n.* —**cab·a·list,** kab′ə·list, *n.* —**cab·a·lis·tic,** kab·ə·lis′tik, *a.*

ca·bal·le·ro, kab·əl·yär′ō, *n. pl.,* **-ros.** A Spanish gentleman; in southwestern U.S., a horseman; an escort.

ca·ba·na, kə·ban′ə, kə·bä′nə, *n.* A cabin or very small house, as at a summer resort; a bathhouse, on a beach or beside a swimming pool.

cab·a·ret, kab·ə·rā′, kab′ə·ret, *n.* A restaurant providing entertainment; a floor show provided by the restaurant or night club.

cab·bage, kab′ij, *n.* Any of various cultivated varieties of the plant, esp. one with short stem and leaves formed into a compact, edible head, but including also such plants as the cauliflower, Brussels sprouts, kale, etc.; the head of the ordinary cabbage; any of various similar plants.—*v.i.,* **-baged, -bag·ing.** To form a head like a cabbage.

cab·bage palm, *n.* Any palm having an edible leaf bud.

cab·by, kab′ē, *n. pl.,* **-bies.** *Informal.* Cab driver.

ca·ber, kā′bər, *n.* A pole or young tree trunk, esp. one used for tossing as a trial of strength in the Highland exercise or game, "tossing the caber."

cab·in, kab′in, *n.* A small rude house; a hut; any small room or enclosed space; a temporary room or cell; a room in a plane or ship for officers or passengers.—*v.t.* To confine in a limited space.—*v.i.* To live in a cabin.

cab·in boy, *n.* A boy employed to wait on officers and passengers of a ship.

cab·i·net, kab′ə·nit, *n.* A piece of furniture consisting of a chest or box, with drawers and doors; a cupboard with shelves and doors. (*Often cap.*) The collective body of ministers who direct the government of a nation or country.—*a.* Relating to a political cabinet.

cab·i·net·mak·er, kab′ə·nit·mā·kər, *n.* A man whose occupation is making furniture. —**cab·i·net·mak·ing,** *n.*

cab·i·net·work, kab′ə·nit·wərk, *n.* Woodwork of fine quality, such as in furniture construction or shelving.

ca·ble, kā′bəl, *n.* A thick, strong rope of hemp; a thick wire rope; the rope or chain used to hold a vessel at anchor or for supporting the roadway of a suspension bridge; an electrical conductor composed of a number of separately insulated wires twisted together; an electrical line under water for dispatching telegraph messages; a cablegram.—*v.t.,* **ca·bled, ca·bling.** To furnish with a cable; fasten with or as with a cable; to transmit by underwater telegraph cable.—*v.i.* To send a message by underwater telegraph cable.

ca·ble car, *n.* A car used to transport passengers on a cable railroad or cableway.

ca·ble·gram, kā′bəl·gram, *n.* A telegram sent overseas by underwater cable.

cab·o·chon, kab′ə·shon, *Fr.* ka·bô·shôn′, *n.* A precious stone of convex rounded form which has been polished but not cut into facets.

ca·boo·dle, kə·boo′dəl, *n. Informal.* The whole lot, pack, or crowd.

ca·boose, kə·boos′, *n.* The last car of a freight train, used chiefly by the crew.

cab·ri·o·let, kab·rē·ə·lā′, *n.* A light, hooded, one-horse carriage with two wheels and a single seat; a cab; a type of automobile somewhat like a convertible, with a folding top.

cab·stand, kab′stand, *n.* A place where taxicabs wait for public hire.

ca·ca·o, kə·kā′ō, kə·kä′ō, *n.* A small evergreen tree native of tropical America, grown for its seeds, which are used in making cocoa and chocolate; the seeds of this tree.

cach·a·lot, kash′ə·lot, kash′ə·lō, *n.* The sperm whale.

cache, kash, *n.* A hiding place, esp. one in the ground, for hiding a store of provisions; the provisions or other items so hidden.—*v.t.,* **cached, cach·ing.** To put in a cache; conceal or hide away.

ca·chet, ka·shā′, kash′ā, *n.* A seal, as on a letter; characteristic mark conveying prestige; a message or design on an envelope.

ca·cique, kə·sēk′, *n.* A native Indian chief of Mexico or the West Indies.

cack·le, kak′əl, *v.i.,* **-led, -ling.** To utter a shrill noisy cry; to laugh with a broken noise, like the cackling of a goose.—*n.* The shrill cry of a goose. —**cack·ler,** *n.*

ca·coph·o·ny, kə·kof′ə·nē, *n. pl.,* **-nies.** Harsh sound; an inharmonious combination of sounds.

cac·tus, kak′təs, *n. pl.,* **-tus·es, -ti,** -tī. Any of several fleshy-stemmed plants, usu. leafless and spiny, with showy flowers, growing chiefly in hot and dry regions.

cad, kad, *n.* An ungentlemanly person. —**cad·dish,** *a.*

ca·dav·er, kə·dav′ər, *n.* A dead body, esp. of a human being used for dissection. —**ca·dav·er·ous,** *a.*

cad·die, cad·dy, kad′ē, *n.* A person who carries golf clubs for a golfer. —*v.i.,* **-died, -dy·ing.** To serve as a caddy.

cad·dis fly, kad′is, *n. pl.,* **cad·dis flies.** Any of various mothlike insects with four membranous wings.

cad·dy, kad′ē, *n. pl.,* **-dies.** A small box for keeping small items.

ca·dence, kād′əns, *n.* A rhythmic succession of words in oratory or poetry; the beat of a rhythmical movement; the modulation of the voice in reading.

ca·den·za, kə·den′zə, *n.* A flourish or elaborate passage for exhibiting a soloist's musical skill.

ca·det, kə·det′, *n.* A student in training for the rank of an officer; a junior male member of a noble family.

cadge, kaj, *v.t.,* **cadged, cadg·ing.** To obtain, at another's expense.

cad·mi·um, kad′mē·əm, *n.* A white, ductile metallic element resembling tin in appearance.

ca·dre, kad′rē, *n.* A specially trained group of key personnel who can capably train or lead others.

ca·du·ce·us, kə·doo′sē·əs, *n. pl.,* **-ce·i,** -sē·ī. The emblem of the medical profession and the insignia of the U.S. Army Medical Corps.

Cae·sar, sē′zər, *n.* The title of the emperor of Rome from Augustus to Hadrian; any emperor or despot.

Cae·sar·e·an sec·tion, si·zār′ē·ən, *n.* The surgical delivery of a child through the wall of the abdomen.

cae·su·ra, si·zhûr′ə, siz·yûr′ə, *n. pl.,* **-ras, -rae,** -rē. A pause or division in a verse.

ca·fe, ca·fé, ka·fā′, kə·fā′, *n.* A coffeehouse; a restaurant; a barroom, tavern, or night club; coffee.

caf·e·te·ri·a, kaf·ə·tēr′ē·ə, *n.* A restaurant in which the customers wait on themselves.

caf·feine, ka·fēn′, kaf′ēn, kaf′ē·in, *n.* A slightly bitter stimulant found in coffee, tea, and cola drinks.

caf·tan, kaf'tən, käf·tän', n. A long, flowing garment with full-length sleeves, cinched at the waist by a girdle, worn in Near East countries.

cage, käj, n. A boxlike enclosure of wires or bars for confining birds or other animals; a prison or place of confinement; a lockup. —v.t., **caged, cag·ing.** To confine or lock up, as in a cage.

cai·man, cay·man, kā'mən, n. Any of several crocodilians, similar to alligators, found in Central and South America.

cairn, kärn, n. A heap of stones, set up as a monument, tombstone, or landmark.

cais·son, kā'sən, kā'son, n. A watertight chamber used in underwater construction; an ammunition chest; a vehicle for carrying ammunition.

cais·son dis·ease, n. A severe sickness caused by an increase of nitrogen bubbles in the bloodstream of divers who surface too quickly, marked by pains in the chest and joints, convulsions, and eventually physical collapse.

cai·tiff, kā'tif, n. A wretched or miserable person; a base or vile person.

ca·jole, kə·jōl', v.t., **ca·joled, ca·jol·ing.** To persuade by deliberate flattery; coax; to deceive by false promises. —**ca·jol·er·y,** n. pl., **-ies.** —**ca·jol·ing·ly,** adv.

Ca·jun, kā'jən, n. One of the Louisiana descendants of the Acadian French; a person of mixed white, Indian, and Negro ancestry in southwest Alabama and adjoining sections of Mississippi.

cake, kāk, n. A sweet food, prepared by baking batter into a definite form, sometimes coated with an icing; a pancake; a shaped patty or mass of fish or meat; a shaped or molded mass: a cake of soap. —v.t., **caked, cak·ing.** To form into a compact mass. —v.i. To become formed into a cake, crust, or compact mass.

cake·walk, kāk'wôk, n. Formerly, a promenade or march of American Negro origin in which a cake was awarded as a prize.

cal·a·bash, kal'ə·bash, n. Any of various gourds; bottle gourd.

cal·a·boose, kal'ə·boos, n. Informal. A jail.

cal·a·mine, kal'ə·mīn, kal'ə·min n. A water-insoluble powder, used in lotions and ointments.

ca·lam·i·ty, kə·lam'ə·tē, n. pl., **-ties.** Any great misfortune or cause of misery; a disaster accompanied with extensive evils; misfortune; mishap. —**ca·lam·i·tous,** a.

cal·cic, kal'sik, a. Containing calcium.

cal·ci·fy, kal'sə·fī, v.t., v.i., **-fied, -fy·ing.** To change into a stony condition by the secretion of calcium salts. —**cal·ci·fi·ca·tion,** kal·sə·fə·kā'shən, n.

cal·ci·mine, kal'sə·mīn, n. A white or lightly tinted wash made of whiting, glue, and water, for use on walls and ceilings.

cal·cite, kal'sīt, n. Calcium carbonate, found in various mineral forms, such as limestone, marble, and chalk.

cal·ci·um, kal'sē·əm, n. An alkaline earth element used in the manufacture of metals and alloys, found naturally only in compounds like limestone or chalk. It is an essential element of bones and teeth.

cal·ci·um car·bon·ate, A colorless or gray powder found naturally in limestone, marble, and chalk, used in making lime and cement.

cal·cu·la·ble, kal'kyə·lə·bəl, a. Able to be calculated. —**cal·cu·la·bil·i·ty,** kal·kyə·lə·bil'ə·tē, n.

cal·cu·late, kal'kyə·lāt, v.t., **-lat·ed, -lat·ing.** To find out by mathematical methods; compute; to estimate by common-sense judgment, as distinguished from mathematical methods; to plan in advance or think out; to adapt or fit for a purpose. —**cal·cu·la·tion,** kal·kyə·lā'shən, n.

cal·cu·lat·ed, kal'kyə·lā·tid, a. Found out by mathe-

matical processes; carefully estimated; deliberate.

cal·cu·lat·ing, kal'kyə·lā·ting, a. Able to calculate; given to forethought and careful analysis; selfishly and coldly scheming.

cal·cu·la·tor, kal'kyə·lā·tər, n. One who calculates; a machine which does mathematical computations.

cal·cu·lus, kal'kyə·ləs, n. pl., **-li,** -lī, **-lus·es.** The study of variations of functions, using a specialized set of algebraic symbols and a systematic method of computation.

cal·dron, kôl'drən, n. Cauldron.

cal·en·dar, kal'ən·dər, n. A register of the year, in which the months, weeks, and days are set down in order; a list; a catalogue; a register. —v.t. To enter in a calendar.

cal·ends, kal·ends, kal'əndz, n. pl. The first day of the month in the Roman calendar.

calf, kaf, käf, n. pl., **calves,** kavz, kävz. The young of the cow or certain other animals, as the elephant, seal, whale; calfskin leather.

calf, kaf, käf, n. pl., **calves,** kavz, kävz. The fleshy back part of the human leg below the knee.

calf·skin, kaf'skin, käf'skin, n. The skin or hide of a calf, or leather made from it.

cal·i·ber, cal·i·bre, kal'ə·bər, n. The diameter of a gun barrel or bullet; degree of worth or quality.

cal·i·brate, kal'ə·brāt, v.t., **-brat·ed, -brat·ing.** To measure the caliber of; to determine the range of. —**cal·i·bra·tion,** kal·ə·brā'shən, n.

cal·i·co, kal'ə·kō, n. pl., **-coes, -cos.** A cotton cloth printed with a pattern on one side. —a. Made of or resembling printed cotton cloth; a horse or other animal marked with patches of different colors.

cal·i·per, cal·li·per, kal'ə·pər, n. An instrument, having two legs, used to measure the thickness of objects or distances between surfaces.

ca·liph, ca·lif, kā'lif, kal'if, n. A Muslim religious and civil leader. —**cal·iph·ate, cal·if·ate,** kāl'ə·fāt, kai'ə·fit, n.

cal·is·then·ics, kal·is·then'iks, n. The art or practice of taking exercise for health, strength, or grace of movement.

call, kôl, v.t. To utter in a loud voice; to command or request to come; to get in touch with by telephone; to attract or lure; to demand payment; to name; summon to an office or duty; halt: call a game because of rain. —v.i. To speak loudly, as to attract attention; to telephone; shout; cry. —n. The act of calling; a shout or cry; a communication by telephone; a musical signal; a short visit; a stop for business or commercial reasons; a vocation. —**call for,** demand; send for. —**call off,** cancel; read out, as a list of names. —**call up,** to telephone; to summon to the armed forces.

call·boy, kal'boi, n. A boy whose duty it is to call actors on to the stage at the proper moment; a bellboy.

call girl, n. A prostitute.

cal·lig·ra·pher, kə·lig'rə·fər, n. One who does beautiful handwriting; a fine penman; a transcriber of manuscripts.

cal·lig·ra·phy, kə·lig'rə·fē, n. Beautiful handwriting; fine penmanship.

call·ing, kô'ling, n. A vocation; profession; trade; usual occupation or employment; persons following any profession; an impelling inner force; a summons; a convening, as of Congress.

call·ing card, n. A small card, printed or engraved, used to give notice of a visit.

cal·li·o·pe, kə·lī'ə·pē, kal'ē·ōp, n. A musical organlike instrument made up of a series of steam whistles played by keys.

call num·ber, n. A combination of letters and numbers assigned to a library book, indicating the shelf location.

---

a- hat, fāte, fāre, fäther; e- met, mē; i- pin, pīne; o- not, nōte, ôrb, moove (move), boy, pownd;
u- cūbe, bůll, tůk (took); ch- chin; th- thick, ŧhen; zh- vizhon (vision); ə- əgo, takən, pencəl, lemən, bərd (bird).

cal·lous, kal′əs, *a.* Hard, as skin; hardened in mind or feelings; unfeeling. —*v.t., v.i.* To make or become thickened or hardened. —**cal·loused,** kal′əst, *a.*

cal·low, kal′ō, *a.* Lacking maturity or judgment; very young; unsophisticated; inexperienced.

cal·lus, kal′əs, *n. pl.,* **cal·lus·es.** A hardened or thickened portion of the skin; a new growth of matter at the ends of a fractured bone, serving to unite them. —*v.t., v.i.* To form, or cause to form, a callus.

calm, käm, *n.* Freedom from motion or disturbance; stillness; absence of wind. —*a.* Without motion; still; not windy; undisturbed; tranquil; free from excitement or passion. —*v.i.* To relax. —*v.t.* To quiet.

ca·lor·ic, kə·lôr′ik, kə·lor′ik, *a.* Of or having to do with heat or calories.

cal·o·rie, kal′ə·rē, *n. pl.,* **-ries.** A unit for measuring heat; a unit of food measurement.

cal·o·rif·ic, kal·ə·rif′ik, *a.* Capable of producing heat.

cal·u·met, kal′yə·met, kal·yə·met′, *n.* An American Indian ceremonial peace pipe.

cal·um·ny, kal′əm·nē, *n. pl.,* **-nies.** A malicious false statement tending to defame; slander. —**ca·lum·ni·ate,**kə·ləm′nē·āt, *v.t.,* **-at·ed, -at·ing.** —**ca·lum·ni·a·tion,** kə·ləm·nē·ā′shən, *n.*

Cal·va·ry, kal′və·rē, *n.* The place where Christ was crucified; a sculpture of the Crucifixion, erected in open air or in a church or chapel; an experience of acute mental agony.

calve, kav, käv, *v.t., v.i.,* **calved, calv·ing.** To give birth to a calf.

ca·lyp·so, kə·lip′sō, *n. pl.,* **ca·lyp·sos.** A type of music of the West Indies marked by improvised lyrics.

ca·lyx, kā′liks, kal′iks, *n. pl.,* **ca·lyx·es, cal·y·ces,** kal′ə·sēz, kā′lə·sēz. The outside, usu. green part of a flower; the sepals.

cam, kam, *n.* A device for converting regular rotary motion into irregular rotary or reciprocating motion, commonly an oval or heart-shaped piece, or eccentric disc, fastened on and revolving with a shaft, and engaging with other mechanisms.

ca·ma·ra·de·rie, kä·mə·rä′də·rē, *n.* Comradeship; friendly fellowship.

cam·ber, kam′bər, *v.t., v.i.* To arch slightly; bend or curve upward in the middle. —*n.* A slight upward bend or curve.

cam·bi·um, kam′bē·əm, *n.* The soft layer of tissue between the bark and the wood in the roots and stems of trees and shrubs.

cam·bric, kām′brik, *n.* A fine, thin linen or cotton fabric.

came, kām, *v., past* of **come.**

cam·el, kam′əl, *n.* Either of two large cud-chewing, four-footed animals: the dromedary, with one hump, and the Bactrian camel with two humps.

ca·mel·lia, kə·mēl′yə, kə·mēl′lē·ə, *n.* A plant, native to Asia, with glossy evergreen leaves and white, red, or pink roselike flowers.

cam·el's hair, *n.* The hair of the camel, used for cloth of a tan color; the cloth made of camel's hair.

cam·e·o, kam′ē·ō, *n.* A precious stone carved so there is a raised design on a flat background.

cam·er·a, kam′ər·ə, kam′rə, *n.* A device for making photographs by exposing light-sensitive film; the part of a television system that changes an image into an electrical signal; a judge's private rooms.

cam·er·a·man, kam′ər·ə·man, kam′rə·man, *n.* A person who operates a still, motion-picture, or television camera.

cam·i·sole, kam′ə·sōl, *n.* A sleeveless underbodice.

cam·o·mile, cham·o·mile, kam′ə·mīl, *n.* An herb with strongly scented foliage and flowers that are used in medicine.

cam·ou·flage, kam′ə·fläzh, *n.* The act of disguising or concealing military troops or equipment; the material used for such a disguise; a disguise or plan used as a false front. —*v.t.,* **-flaged, -flag·ing.** To disguise or conceal. —*v.i.* To practice camouflage; wear a disguise.

camp, kamp, *n.* A place where a group of people live for a short time; a temporary shelter used while fishing, hunting, etc.; a recreation area for group living, usually in the country: a summer *camp* for children; a town, usually temporary, in a mining or lumbering area; a place where a military group lives; a group of persons who defend a theory or idea: a political *camp.* —*v.i.* To set up a camp; stay in a camp; take up temporary quarters; live temporarily in a tent or in rough shelters for recreation, often with *out.*

camp, kamp, *n.* Something outlandish or distastefully extravagant that can be enjoyed for its artistic style.

cam·paign, kam·pān′, *n.* The military operations of an army in the field during one season; any organized activity to achieve a political or social goal. —*v.i.* To serve in or go on a campaign. —**cam·paign·er,** *n.*

cam·pa·ni·le, kam·pə·nē′lē, *n. pl.,* **-les, -li, -lī.** A clock or bell tower.

camp·er, kam′pər, *n.* A person who lives in a tent, or lodge, or outdoors in a vacation area; a boy or girl who attends summer camp; a person who takes part in a work-camp program or a camp meeting; a recreational vehicle used for sleeping and eating.

camp·fire, kamp′fīr, *n.* A fire in a camp for warmth or cooking; a social gathering or reunion of soldiers or scouts.

cam·phor, kam′fər, *n.* A whitish, aromatic crystalline substance, from a tree of the laurel family, used in medicine, and as an irritant and stimulant.

cam·pus, kam′pəs, *n. pl.,* **cam·pus·es.** The grounds of an American college or other school.

camp·y, kam′pē, *a.,* **-i·er, -i·est.** Appealing to, or having the characteristics of camp; amusingly affected or theatrical, esp. when applied to trivia.

cam·shaft, kam′shaft, kam′shäft, *n.* The shaft on which a cam is mounted.

can, kan, *aux. v.,* **could.** To know how to; to have the ability, power, right, qualifications or means to. *Informal.* To be permitted.

can, kan, *n.* A vessel for holding or carrying liquids; an airtight container of tin or other metal for preserving food and drink. —*v.t.,* **canned, can·ning.** To put or preserve in a can or jar. *Informal.* To dismiss or fire.

ca·nal, kə·nal′, *n.* A waterway, dug for the passage of boats or ships; a tube or duct in the body. —*v.t.,* **ca·naled, ca·nal·ing** or **ca·nalled, ca·nal·ling.** To make a canal through; furnish with a canal or canals.

can·a·pé, kan·ə·pē′, kan′ə·pā, *n.* A thin, small piece of toast, bread, or a cracker covered with fish, meat, cheese, or other seasoned preparation.

ca·nard, kə·närd′, *n.* A false or made-up story; a hoax.

ca·nar·y, kə·när′ē, *n.* A small singing bird often kept as a pet.

ca·nas·ta, kə·nas′tə, *n.* A card game which originated in Argentina.

can·can, kan′kan, *n.* A dance performed by women entertainers, marked by high kicking.

can·cel, kan′səl, *v.t.,* **-celed, -cel·ing** or **-celled, -cel·ling.** To destroy the validity of; to annul; to call off; to deface, mark, or perforate, to show it may not be used again; to eliminate by striking out a factor common to both terms of a fraction or from both sides of an equation. —*v.i.* To counterbalance; to compensate for one another; to neutralize each other's strength.

can·cel·la·tion, kan·sə·lā′shən, *n.* The act of canceling, making void, or invalidating; the marks made on something when an item is canceled.

can·cer, kan′sər, *n.* A malignant growth or tumor; an evil that is like a malignant sore.

can·de·la·brum, kan·də·lä′brəm, *n. pl.,* **-bra,** -brə, **-brums.** A branched, ornamental candlestick.

can·did, kan′did, *a.* Frank; outspoken; open and sincere.

can·di·da·cy, kan′də·də·sē, *n. pl.,* **-cies.** A candidate.

can·di·date, kan′də·dāt, kan′də·dit, *n.* One who is proposed for an appointment, office, or honor.

can·died, kan′dēd, *a.* Preserved; cooked in sugar; glazed.

can·dle, kan′dəl, *n.* A stick of tallow or wax enclosing a wick, which is burned to give light. —*v.t.,* **-dled, -dling.** To examine eggs for freshness by holding between the eye and a lighted candle or any bright light.

can·dle·light, kan′dəl·līt, *n.* The light of a candle.

can·dle·pow·er, kan′dəl·pow·ər, *n.* The light-giving power of a standard candle: used as a unit of measurement of light.

can·dle·stick, kan′dəl·stik, *n.* A holder for a candle.

can·dor, kan′dər, *n.* Quality of being open, frank, or straightforward.

can·dy, kan′dē, *n. pl.,* **-dies.** A sweet made by boiling sugar syrup.—*v.t.,* **can·died, can·dy·ing.** To coat, preserve, or saturate with sugar syrup. —*v.i.* To become coated with or crystallized into sugar.

can·dy strip·er, *n. Informal.* A young female volunteer aide at a hospital.

cane, kān, *n.* The stem of some palms and grasses; a walking stick.—*v.t.,* **caned, can·ing.** To beat with a cane or walking stick; to furnish or build with cane, as chairs.

cane sug·ar, *n.* Sugar obtained from the sugar cane; sucrose.

ca·nine, kā′nīn, *a.* Of or like a dog.—*n.* A dog; any of the four teeth next to the incisors.

can·is·ter, kan′i·stər, *n.* A small box of tin, plastic, or the like, for tea, coffee, or other dry materials.

can·ker, kang′kər, *n.* An open sore.—*v.t.* To infect with canker. —*v.i.* To grow corrupt; to be infected with canker. —**can·ker·ous,** kang′kər·əs, *a.*

can·ker sore, *n.* An open sore of the lips or lining of the mouth.

can·na·bis, kan′ə·bis, *n.* The tops and leaves of Indian hemp used as a narcotic or intoxicant; marihuana; marijuana.

canned, kand, *a.* Preserved in a can or jar; recorded or taped.

can·nel coal, kan′əl kōl, *n.* A glistening, bituminous coal that burns with a bright flame like a candle.

can·ner, kan′ər, *n.* One who cans meat, fish or fruit, for preservation.

can·ner·y, kan′ə·rē, *n. pl.,* **-ies.** A plant for canning or preserving meat, fish, or fruit.

can·ni·bal, kan′ə·bal, *n.* A human being who eats human flesh; any animal that eats its own kind. —**can·ni·bal·ism,** *n.*

can·ni·bal·ize, kan′ə·bə·līz, *v.t.,* **-ized, -iz·ing.** To remove parts from one unit for use in the completion or repair of another unit.

can·non, kan′ən, *n. pl.,* **can·nons,** or, esp. collectively, **can·non.** A mounted gun for firing explosive shells.—*v.i.* To discharge cannon.

can·non ball, *n.* A round missile or solid projectile shot from a cannon.

can·not, ka·not′, kə·not′, *aux. v.* A common form of can not.

can·ny, kan′ē, *a.,* **-ni·er, -ni·est.** Knowing; shrewd; astute; skilled or expert; frugal or thrifty. —**can·ni·ly,** *adv.* —**can·ni·ness,** *n.*

ca·noe, kə·noo′, *n.* A slender, open boat, propelled by paddles.—*v.i.,* **ca·noed, ca·noe·ing.** To paddle a canoe; to travel by canoe.—*v.t.* To carry in a canoe. —**ca·noe·ist,** *n.*

can·on, kan′ən, *n.* A rule or law enacted by a church council; a fundamental principle; a standard or criterion; the books of the Bible, Holy Scripture, recognized by the Christian church; that part of the mass between the Sanctus and the Lord's Prayer; a composition in which the different participants begin the same melody one after another at regular intervals, at the same or at a different pitch.

can·on, kan′ən, *n.* A clergyman attached to a cathedral or collegiate church.

ca·non·i·cal, kə·non′ə·kəl, *a.* Relating to or conforming to a canon or canons.

can·on·ize, kan′ə·nīz, *v.t.,* **-ized, -iz·ing.** To place in the catalogue of the saints; to glorify. —**ca·non·i·za·tion,** kan·ə·nə·zā′shən, *n.*

can·on law, *n.* The body of laws made by a church for its own direction.

can·o·py, kan′ə·pē, *n. pl.,* **-pies.** An overhanging protection or shelter; the transparent cover over the pilot's seat in an airplane.—*v.t.,* **-pied, -py·ing.** To cover with, or as with, a canopy.

cant, kant, *n.* Insincere talk; whining or singsong speech of beggars; the unusual speech forms of special groups, or professions.

cant, kant, *n.* A slanting or tilted position; a sudden pitch or toss; slanting.—*v.t.* To bevel; to give a slanting surface to; turn over; to throw with a sudden jerk.—*v.i.* To take or have an inclined position; tilt; turn.

can't, kant, känt. Contraction of **cannot.**

can·ta·loup, can·ta·loupe, can·ta·lope, kan′-tə·lōp, *n.* A variety of muskmelon, having a sweet, orange-colored flesh.

can·tan·ker·ous, kan·tang′kər·əs, *a.* Ill-natured; cross.

can·ta·ta, kən·tä′tə, *n.* A choral composition, such as an oratorio, or lyric drama.

can·teen, kan·tēn′, *n.* A store or location for the sale of food or drink; a small container for carrying water or other liquids; a place for recreation or eating in a place of business.

can·ter, kan′tər, *n.* A horse's gait, easier and slower than a gallop.—*v.i.* To ride on a horse at a canter.—*v.t.* To cause to go, as a horse, at a moderate gallop.

can·ti·cle, kan′ti·kəl, *n.* A song, esp. an unmetrical hymn for chanting in a church service.

can·ti·lev·er, kan′tə·lev·ər, *n.* A beam or member projecting beyond a single support at one end.

can·to, kan′tō, *n. pl.,* **can·tos.** A part or division of a long poem.

can·ton, kan′tən, kan′ton, kan·ton′, *n.* One of the states of Switzerland.

can·tor, kan′tər, kan′tôr, *n.* The synagogue official who helps lead the liturgy, singing, or chants the solo parts.

can·vas, kan′vəs, *n.* A closely woven, heavy cloth of hemp, flax, or cotton, used for artwork, tents, and sails.

can·vass, kan′vəs, *v.t.* To discuss or examine carefully; to ask for opinions, votes, or subscriptions.—*v.i.* To go about engaging in discussion or debate.—*n.* The act of canvassing; an investigation by inquiry; a soliciting of votes, orders, etc. —**can·vass·er,** *n.*

can·yon, kan′yən, *n.* A narrow valley with steep sides, formed by erosion.

caou·tchouc, koo′chŏŏk, kow·chook′, *n.* Natural rubber.

cap, kap, *n.* A brimless covering for the head; the topmost part; a small, tight-fitting lid.—*v.t.,* **capped, cap·ping.** To put a cap on; to cover with a cap.

ca·pa·bil·i·ty, kā·pə·bil′ə·tē, *n. pl.,* **-ties.** The quality of being capable; capacity; ability.

ca·pa·ble, kā′pə·bəl, *a.* Having power, skill, ability; able; competent; fit; qualified. —**ca·pa·bly,** *adv.*

ca·pa·cious, kə·pā′shəs, *a.* Capable of containing much; large; wide; spacious.

ca·pac·i·tate, kə·pas′ə·tāt, *v.t.,* **-tat·ed, -tat·ing.** To make capable; to enable; to qualify.

ca·pac·i·ty, kə·pas′ə·tē, *n. pl.,* **-ties.** The power of

---

a- hat, fāte, fāre, fäther; **e-** met, mē; **i-** pin, pīne; **o-** not, nōte, ôrb, moove (move), boy, pownd; **u-** cūbe, bŭll, tûk (took); **ch-** chin; **th-** thick, then; **zh-** vizhon (vision); **ə-** əgo, takən, pencəl, lemən, bərd (bird).

receiving or containing; the power of containing a certain quantity exactly; cubic contents; the power of receiving ideas or knowledge; ability; legal qualification; character: to act in the *capacity* of a friend; maximum possible output.

cape, kāp, *n.* A piece of land jutting into the sea or a lake; a headland.

cape, kāp, *n.* A sleeveless garment fitting closely around the neck and falling loosely from the shoulders.

ca·per, kā′pər, *n.* A frolicsome leap or spring; a prank or wild escapade.—*v.i.* To leap or skip playfully.

ca·per, kā′pər, *n.* A shrub of Mediterranean regions, or its flower bud, which is pickled and used as a seasoning.

ca·pi·as, kā′pē·as, kap′ē·as, *n.* A judicial writ ordering an officer to take a person into custody.

cap·il·lar·i·ty, kap·ə·lar′ə·tē, *n.* The attraction and repulsion of molecules on the surface of a liquid in contact with a solid which results in the rise (**capillary attraction**) or fall (**capillary repulsion**) of a liquid when in narrow tubes or fibers, or in the wetting of a solid by a liquid, as in blotting action.

cap·il·lar·y, kap′ə·ler·ē, *a.* Like a hair; very slender; having a very small bore; pertaining to or occurring in a tube of fine bore.—*n. pl.,* **-lar·ies.** One of the minute blood vessels between the ends of the arteries and the beginnings of the veins.

cap·il·lar·y ac·tion, *n.* Capillarity.

cap·i·tal, kap′ə·təl, *a.* Pertaining to the head or top; involving the loss of life; fatal or serious, as an error; referring to large size letters used at the beginning of a sentence, or as the first letter of a proper name; principal; first-rate; referring to financial capital.—*n.* A capital letter; the city or town which is the official seat of government in a country or state; any form of wealth employed for the production of more wealth; the wealth thus employed by a business or industrial enterprise; an excess of assets over liabilities.

cap·i·tal, kap′ə·təl, *n.* The head, or uppermost part, of a column or pillar.

cap·i·tal·ism, kap′ə·tə·liz·əm, *n.* Possession of capital; a system under which the production and distribution of goods and services are privately managed; free enterprise. —**cap·i·tal·is·tic,** kap·ə·tə·lis′tik, *a.*

cap·i·tal·ist, kap′ə·tə·list, *n.* One who has capital, esp. a person who has extensive wealth employed in business enterprises.

cap·i·tal·ize, kap′ə·tə·līz, *v.t.,* **-ized, -iz·ing.** To write or print in capital letters, or with an initial capital; to convert into or use as capital; furnish with capital; convert into an equivalent capital; to fix the capital of a corporation at a certain sum; to use to one's advantage, with *on.* —**cap·i·tal·i·za·tion,** kap·ə·tə·lə·zā′shən, *n.*

cap·i·tal·ly, kap′ə·tə·lē, *adv.* In an excellent, commendable way.

cap·i·tal pun·ish·ment, *n.* The death penalty for a convicted criminal.

cap·i·tal ship, *n.* A battleship; a large warship.

cap·i·ta·tion, kap·ə·tā′shən, *n.* A tax, fee, or payment fixed on a per capita basis.

Cap·i·tol, kap′ə·təl, *n.* In the U.S., the edifice occupied by Congress at Washington, D.C. *Often l.c.* A statehouse.

ca·pit·u·late, kə·pich′ə·lāt, *v.t.,* **-lat·ed, -lat·ing.** To yield or acquiesce; to surrender, esp. by stated terms. —**ca·pit·u·la·tion,** kə·pich·ə·lā′shən, *n.* —**ca·pit·u·la·tor,** *n.*

ca·pon, kā′pon, kā′pən, *n.* A male chicken or rooster with its reproductive organs removed for the purpose of improving the flesh for eating.

ca·pote, kə·pōt′, *n.* A long cloak with a hood; a close-fitting, caplike bonnet worn by women and children.

ca·pric·ci·o, kə·prē′chē·ō, *It.* kä·prēt′chō, *n.* A ca-

price; a whim; a musical piece which is free and fanciful in form.

ca·price, kə·prēs′, *n.* A sudden change of mind without apparent motive; a whim; susceptibility to varying or freakish impulses; a capriccio. —**ca·pri·cious,** kə·prish′əs, *a.* —**ca·pri·cious·ly,** *adv.* —**ca·pri·cious·ness,** *n.*

cap·ri·ole, kap′rē·ōl, *n.* A caper or leap; an in-place leap given by a horse in an exhibition.—*v.i.,* **-oled, -ol·ing.** To execute a capriole.

cap·size, kap′sīz, kap·sīz′, *v.i., v.t.,* **-sized, -siz·ing.** To upset or overturn, as a boat.

cap·stan, kap′stən, *n.* A device having a vertical axis, turned by a bar or lever, usually for raising weights.

cap·stone, kap′stōn, *n.* The top stone of a structure.

cap·sule, kap′səl, *n.* A small case, envelope, or covering; a gelatinous case enclosing a dose of medicine; a membranous sac; a dry fruit or seed vessel. A detachable part of an airplane, rocket, etc., containing people, animals, instruments, etc.—*a.* Very brief; summarized. —**cap·su·lar,** kap′sə·ler, *a.*

cap·tain, kap′tən, *n.* One who has authority over others; a chief; a leader; an army officer ranking next above a lieutenant; a navy officer ranking next above a commander; the commander of a ship, airplane, etc.; one who leads a team in sports.—*v.t.* To lead or command. —**cap·tain·cy,** *n.* —**cap·tain·ship,** *n.*

cap·tion, kap′shən, *n.* A heading or title, as of a chapter or article; description accompanying a picture, photograph, or illustration.—*v.t.* To write or provide a caption for.

cap·tious, kap′shəs, *a.* Apt to notice unimportant faults; faultfinding. —**cap·tious·ness,** *n.*

cap·ti·vate, kap′tə·vāt, *v.t.,* **-vat·ed, -vat·ing.** To capture as by beauty or excellence; charm. —**cap·ti·vat·ing·ly,** *adv.* —**cap·ti·va·tion,** kap·tə·vā′shən, *n.* —**cap·ti·va·tor,** kap′tə·vā·tər, *n.*

cap·tive, kap′tiv, *a.* Made or held prisoner, as in war; kept in confinement.—*n.* A prisoner. —**cap·tiv·i·ty,** kap·tiv′ə·tē, *n. pl.,* **-ties.**

cap·tive au·di·ence. A group of persons forced by circumstance to see an advertisement, hear a speech, etc.

cap·tor, kap′tər, *n.* One who captures.

cap·ture, kap′chər, *n.* The act of taking as by force or stratagem; that which is so taken.—*v.t.,* **-tured, -tur·ing.** To take by force or stratagem; seize. —**cap·tur·er,** *n.*

car, kär, *n.* An automobile; a vehicle running on rails; the part of a balloon, elevator, or the like, for carrying passengers; a wheeled vehicle. *Poet.* A chariot.

car·a·cole, kar′ə·kōl, *n.* A half turn executed by a trained saddle horse.—*v.i.,* **-coled, -col·ing.** To execute caracoles; wheel; prance.

car·a·cul, kar′ə·kəl, *n.* The flat, loose, curly fur of very young Asiatic or Russian sheep.

ca·rafe, kə·raf′, kə·räf′, *n.* A glass water bottle or decanter.

car·a·mel, kar′ə·məl, kar′ə·mel, *n.* Burnt sugar, used for coloring and flavoring food; a kind of chewy candy.

car·a·pace, kar′ə·pās, *n.* The hard, bony shell or shield on the back of a turtle, lobster, horseshoe crab, armadillo, etc.

car·at, kar′ət, *n.* A standard unit, 200 milligrams, for weighing precious stones.

car·a·van, kar′ə·van, *n.* A company of travelers who journey together through hostile territory; a group of vehicles or pack of animals traveling in a file; a large, closed vehicle used for transporting traveling exhibitions.

car·a·van·sa·ry, kar·ə·van′sə·rē, *n. pl.,* **-ries.** In the Near East, an inn, usually enclosing a large courtyard; any inn or hostelry.

car·a·vel, kar′ə·vel, *n.* A small, fast ship formerly used by the Spanish and Portuguese. Also **car·vel,** kär′vel.

car·a·way, kar/ə·wā, *n.* A biennial plant, the seeds of which are used to flavor various foods.

car·bide, kär/bīd, kär/bid, *n.* A compound of carbon with a more electropositive element, esp. calcium carbide.

car·bine, kär/bīn, kär/bēn, *n.* A light, short rifle or musket for cavalry troops; a lightweight automatic military rifle. Also **car·a·bine,** kar/ə·bīn.

car·bo·hy·drate, kär·bō·hī/drāt, *n.* A chemical compound made of carbon, hydrogen, and oxygen, including sugars, starch, and cellulose.

car·bo·lat·ed, kär/bə·lā·tid, *a.* Containing carbolic acid.

car·bol·ic ac·id, kär·bol/ik as/id, *n.* Phenol.

car·bon, kär/bən, *n.* A very common nonmetallic element which occurs in a pure state as the diamond and as graphite, and in an impure state as charcoal; a rod or plate composed in part of carbon; a piece of carbon paper; a carbon copy.

car·bon 14, *n.* Radioactive carbon, used especially in the dating of geological and archaeological material.

car·bo·na·ceous, kär·bə·nā/shəs, *a.* Pertaining to or yielding carbon.

car·bo·nate, kär/bə·nāt, kär/bə·nit, *n.* A salt of carbonic acid.—**car·bo·na·tion,** kär·bə·nā/shən, *n.*

car·bon di·ox·ide, *n.* A heavy, colorless, odorless, noncombustible gas present in the atmosphere.

car·bon·if·er·ous, kär·bə·nif/ər·əs, *a.* Coalbearing, pertaining to .—*n. (Cap.)* A geological period of the Paleozoic era, marked by great forests which produced coal beds.

car·bon·ize, kär/bə·nīz, *v.t.,* **-ized, -iz·ing.** To convert into carbon, as by partial combustion; cover with carbon; combine with carbon. —**car·bon·i·za·tion,** kär·bə·nə·zā/shən, *n.*

car·bon mon·ox·ide, *n.* A colorless, odorless, very poisonous gas, formed when carbon burns with an insufficient supply of air.

car·bon pa·per, *n.* Paper coated with carbon, etc., inserted between two sheets of paper for making a copy of what is written on the upper sheet.

car·bon tet·ra·chlo·ride, *n.* A colorless, nonflammable liquid, used as a refrigerant, cleaning fluid, etc.

Car·bo·run·dum, kär·bə·ran/dəm, *n. Trademark.* A very hard, abrasive compound, made of carbon and silicon.

car·boy, kär/boy, *n.* A large, strong, glass bottle, protected by an outside covering, used to contain acids.

car·bun·cle, kär/bəng·kəl, *n.* A painful, local, inflamed swelling under the skin; a red garnet cut without facets. —**car·bun·cled,** *a.* —**car·bun·cu·lar,** kär·bəng/kyū·lər, *a.*

car·bu·re·tor, kär/bə·rā·tər, kär/bū·ret·ər, *n.* A device which mixes vaporized fuel with air in order to provide explosive power for an internal-combustion engine.

car·ca·jou, kär/kə·joo, kär/kə·zhoo, *n.* The wolverine.

car·cass, car·case, kär/kəs, *n.* The dead body of an animal or (now only in contempt) of a human being; a living body, now chiefly in contempt or ridicule; an unfinished framework or skeleton.

car·cin·o·gen, kär·sin/ə·jən, *n.* A substance that produces cancer. —**car·cin·o·gen·ic,** kär·sin·ə·jen/ik, *a.*

car·ci·no·ma, kär·sə·nō/mə, *n. pl.,* **-mas, -ma·ta,** -mə·tə. A cancer.

card, kärd, *n.* A piece of stiff paper or thin pasteboard, usually rectangular; one of a set of pieces of card or cardboard printed with marks or figures used in playing various games. *Pl.* A game played with such a set; cardplaying. *Informal.* A peculiar or amusing person. —*v.t.* To provide with a card; to fasten on a card; to list

on a card.—**in the cards,** likely to occur.

card, kärd, *n.* A wire-toothed brush or some similar implement.—*v.t.* To comb or open wool, flax, or hemp with a card. —**card·er,** *n.*

car·da·mom, kär/də·məm, *n.* The aromatic seed of various plants of the ginger family, employed in medicine and as seasoning; the plant.

card·board, kärd/bôrd, kärd/bōrd, *n.* A stiff, moderately thick pasteboard used to make cards, boxes, etc.

car·di·ac, kär/dē·ak, *a.* Pertaining to the heart; pertaining to the upper part of the stomach.—*n.* A person with a heart disease; a medicine which excites action in the heart.

car·di·gan, kär/də·gən, *n.* A close-fitting, collarless, knitted, woolen jacket.

car·di·nal, kär/də·nəl, *n.* A prince of the Roman Catholic Church, next in rank to the Pope; a North American finch, the male bird having brilliant red plumage.—*a.* Chief; principal; vivid red color.

car·di·nal num·ber, *n.* The number *one, two,* or *three,* etc., as distinct from the ordinal number *first, second,* or *third,* etc.; a numeral indicating the number of units, but not the order of arrangement.

car·di·o·graph, kär/dē·ə·graf, *n.* An instrument tracing and recording the action of the heart. —**car·di·og·ra·phy,** kär·dē·og/rə·fē, *n.*

card·sharp, kärd/shärp, *n.* One who cheats at cards, esp. as a livelihood.

care, kâr, *v.i.,* **cared, car·ing.** To be concerned; have thought or regard; to be inclined to.—*n.* Grief; anxiety; concern; serious attention; caution; watchful oversight; charge; an object of concern or attention. —**care for,** to provide for; look after; to have a liking or affection for; to want; wish.

ca·reen, kə·rēn/, *v.t.* To bring, as a ship, to lie on one side; to repair or clean, as a boat, in this position.—*v.i.* To incline to one side; to teeter from side to side; lurch.

ca·reer, kə·rēr/, *n.* A person's profession; one's life's work; a swift and steady course; full speed; progress. —*v.i.* To move or run very rapidly.—*a.* Making one's occupation a serious lifework: a *career* horticulturist.

care·free, kâr/frē, *a.* Free of care; without anxiety; happy-go-lucky.

care·ful, kâr/fəl, *a.* Prudent and cautious; painstaking in execution. —**care·ful·ly,** *adv.* —**care·ful·ness,** *n.*

care·less, kâr/lis, *a.* Showing no care; being heedless; lacking in attention; inaccurate; lacking in consideration. —**care·less·ly,** *adv.* —**care·less·ness,** *n.*

ca·ress, kə·res/, *n.* An act of endearment; an expression of affection by touch, such as a kiss or a pat.—*v.t.* To show affection with caresses or patting, or fondling. —**ca·ress·ing·ly,** *adv.*

car·et, kar/ət, *n.* A mark (ʌ) placed in written or printed matter to show where something must be inserted.

care·tak·er, kâr/tā·kər, *n.* One who takes care of a building, etc.; a custodian.

care·worn, kâr/wôrn, kâr/wōrn, *a.* Showing marks of care or anxiety; drained by fatigue due to prolonged overwork.

car·fare, kär/fâr, *n.* Fare charged a passenger on a public vehicle, such as a bus.

car·go, kär/gō, *n. pl.,* **-goes** or **-gos.** The goods loaded on a ship or vehicle; load.

car·hop, kär/hop, *n.* An employee who carries food to customers in their cars at drive-in restaurants.

car·i·bou, kar/ə·boo, *n. pl.,* **-bous** or **-bou.** A North American reindeer.

car·i·ca·ture, kar/i·kə·chûr, kar/ə·kə·chər, *n.* A picture or description in which peculiarities or defects of a person or thing are ridiculously exaggerated; the art or act of producing caricatures; an absurdly incompetent imitation.—*v.t.,* **-tured, -tur·ing.** To make a caricature of. —**car·i·ca·tur·ist,** *n.*

---

a- hat, fāte, fâre, fäther; e- met, mē; i- pin, pīne; o- not, nōte, ôrb, moove (move), boy, pownd; u- cūbe, bũll, tûk (took); ch- chin; th- thick, ŧhen; zh- vizhon (vision); ə- əgo, takən, pencəl, lemən, bərd (bird).

car·ies, kãr′ēz, kâr′ē·ēz, *n.* Decay of bone, teeth, or plant tissue.

car·il·lon, kar′ə·lon, kar′ə·lən, *n.* A set of bells arranged for playing melodies; a melody played on such bells; an organ stop imitating bells. —*v.i.,* **-lonned, -lon·ning.** —**car·il·lon·neur,** kar·ə·lə·nər′, *n.*

car·load, kãr′lōd, *n.* The load carried in a car, esp. a freight car.

car·mine, kãr′min, kãr′mīn, *n.* The pure coloring matter or principle of cochineal; a red or crimson pigment made from cochineal.—*a.* Red; crimson.

car·nage, kãr′nij, *n.* Slaughter; massacre.

car·nal, kãr′nəl, *a.* Pertaining to the body, not spiritual; fleshly; sensual. —**car·nal·i·ty,** kãr·nal′ə·tē, *n.* —**car·nal·ly,** *adv.*

car·na·tion, kãr·nā′shən, *n.* Flesh-color; pink; sometimes, red; any of numerous plants with fragrant flowers of various colors.—*a.* Carnation-colored.

car·nel·ian, kãr·nēl′yən, *n.* A variety of red chalcedony, used for jewelry.

car·ni·val, kãr′nə·vəl, *n.* The season immediately preceding Lent, observed with merrymaking and revelry; a large, usually public merrymaking; a travelling show with amusements such as side-shows and rides; an entertainment.

car·ni·vore, kãr′nə·vōr, kãr′nə·vôr, *n.* A flesh-eating animal or plant, esp. an order of mammals, including the cats, dogs, and others.

car·niv·o·rous, kãr·niv′ər·əs, *a.* Flesh-eating; pertaining to the carnivores which are mammals. —**car·niv·o·rous·ly,** *adv.* —**car·niv·o·rous·ness,** *n.*

car·ol, kar′əl, *n.* A song, esp. of joy; a Christmas song.—*v.i., v.t.,* **-oled, -ol·ing.** To sing in joy or festivity, as Christmas carols. —**car·ol·er,** *n.*

car·om, kar′əm, *n.* A shot in billiards in which the ball struck with the cue is made to hit two balls in succession. A movement, as of a ball, striking and rebounding.—*v.i.* To make a carom; to strike, esp. obliquely, and rebound.

ca·rot·id, kə·rot′id, *a.* Of or pertaining to the two great arteries, one on either side of the neck, which convey the blood from the aorta to the head and brain.—*n.* One of these arteries.

ca·rous·al, kə·row′zəl, *n.* A noisy, drunken revel.

ca·rouse, kə·rowz′, *n.* A drinking bout; a carousal. —*v.i.,* **ca·roused, ca·rous·ing.** To go on a drinking spree; to drink heavily and often. —**ca·rous·er,** *n.*

car·ou·sel, car·rou·sel, kar·ə·sel′, kar·ə·zel′, *n.* A merry-go-round; a medieval tournament in which the horsemen performed in skillful turns.

carp, kãrp, *n. pl.,* **carp, carps.** A soft-finned, edible, fresh-water fish, found in China, Europe, and America; any similar fish, such as minnows and goldfish.

carp, kãrp, *v.i.* To complain or find fault, particularly without reason.—**carp·ing,** *a.*

car·pal, kãr′pəl, *n.* A bone of the carpus.—*a.* Pertaining to the carpus.

car·pel, kãr′pəl, *n.* A simple pistil, or a single member of a compound pistil: regarded as a modified leaf. —**car·pel·lar·y,** kãr·pə·ler′ē, *a.*

car·pen·ter, kãr′pən·tər, *n.* One who builds or works with wood. —**car·pen·try,** kãr′pən·trē, *n.*

car·pet, kãr′pit, *n.* A thick fabric used for covering floors, stairs; a covering resembling a carpet.—*v.t.* To cover with a carpet.—**be on the carpet,** to be criticized.

car·pet·bag·ger, kãr′pit·bag·ər, *n.* A Northerner who sought political or commercial advantages in the South, following the Civil War.

car·pet·ing, kãr′pit·ing, *n.* Cloth for carpets; carpets.

car·port, kãr′pôrt, kãr′pōrt, *n.* A shelter for motor vehicles with a roof and open sides, usually attached to the house.

car·pus, kãr′pəs, *n. pl.,* **-pi, -pī.** The wrist; the wrist bones.

car·riage, kar′ij, *n.* The act of carrying; conveyance; commercial transportation, or its cost; a wheeled vehicle for conveying persons, esp. one drawn by horses; a wheeled support, as for a cannon; a part, as of a machine, designed for carrying something; manner of holding the head and limbs; bearing or mien.

car·ri·er, kar′ē·ər, *n.* One who or that which carries; a person or an association of persons that undertakes to transport goods or people for hire; a person who is immune to a disease which he can transmit to others.

car·ri·er pi·geon, *n.* A homing pigeon; a pigeon with large wattles.

car·ri·ole, kar′ē·ōl, *n.* Cariole.

car·ri·on, kar′ē·ən, *n.* Dead and rotting flesh.—*a.* Referring to carrion; feeding on carrion.

car·rot, kar′ət, *n.* A plant having a long, edible, orange-colored root, used as a vegetable.

car·rot·y, kar′ə·tē, *a.* Like a carrot in color; red-haired.

car·ry, kar′ē, *v.t.,* **-ried, -ry·ing.** To bear, convey, or transport an object; to drive, drag, or fetch; to sway by emotion, usu. with *away;* to capture; to transfer from one spot to another; to channel the course of; to have on one's person; to possess as a characteristic; to bear, as oneself, in a specified manner. To bear the weight of; to sing relatively on pitch; to stock merchandise; to extend or continue in time or space or degree; to win a victory; appear in print; to keep on one's ledgers. *Southern U.S.* To escort.—*v.i.* To act as carrier; to be able to cover or reach a certain distance; to gain victory or acceptance.—*n. pl.,* **-ries.** A carrying; a portage; range, as of a gun; the distance covered. *Football.* A single offensive running play.—**carry off,** to cause to die; to win, as an award; to succeed despite obstacles; brazen out; to abduct.—**carry on,** to do, manage, or conduct; to keep going; to continue after stopping. *Informal.* To behave wildly or foolishly.—**carry out,** to do; accomplish; complete.—**carry over,** to retain beyond the usual time; to postpone; to transfer a bookkeeping amount to the following column, page, or book.—**carry through,** to complete; to support to the end.

car·ry·all, kar′ē·ôl, *n.* A light, covered, four-wheeled one-horse carriage.

car·ry-o·ver, kar′ē·ō·vər, *n.* A part left over; a bookkeeping sum carried forward.

car·sick·ness, kãr′sik·nis, *n.* Nausea caused by riding in a car.—**car·sick,** *a.*

cart, kãrt, *n.* A two-wheeled vehicle for the conveyance of heavy goods; a light, two-wheeled vehicle used for pleasure or business; any small vehicle moved by hand.—*v.t., v.i.* To drive, use, or carry in a cart. —**car·ter,** *n.*

cart·age, kãr′tij, *n.* The act or the cost of carting.

carte blanche, kãrt′blänsh′, *n.* Complete authority to make decisions.

car·tel, kãr·tel′, kãr′təl, *n.* An organization, often international, which seeks monopolistic control of a market; an agreement between warring states, usually providing for the exchange of prisoners; a combination of political groups uniting in a common cause.

car·ti·lage, kãr′tə·lij, *n.* An elastic tissue composing most of the skeleton in embryos and young vertebrates; a part made of this tissue: knee *cartilage.*

car·ti·lag·i·nous, kãr·tə·laj′ə·nəs, *a.* Resembling a cartilage; gristly; having a skeletal cartilage only, and not true bones.

car·tog·ra·phy, kãr·tog′rə·fē, *n.* The making of maps or charts. —**car·tog·ra·pher,** *n.* —**car·to·graph·ic,** kãr·tə·graf′ik, *a.*

car·ton, kãr′tən, *n.* A box made of thin pasteboard.

car·toon, kãr·toon′, *n.* A caricature, often satirical, representing important events in politics or important public figures; the comic strips; a design drawn as a study for a fresco, mosaic, etc., to be painted in the same size; animated cartoon.—*v.t., v.i.* To draw cartoons. —**car·toon·ist,** *n.*

car•tridge, kär′trij, *n.* A tube of pasteboard or metal for holding a charge of powder, a bullet, or the shot for a firearm; a roll of unexposed film for a camera; a small removable container in a record player holding the mechanism and needle; cassette.

cart•wheel, kärt′hwēl, kärt′wēl, *n.* Wheel of a cart; a sideways somersault.

carve, kärv, *v.t.,* **carved, carv•ing.** To cut, as some solid material, in order to produce a decorative design; to make or shape by cutting; to hew or slash; to cut into small pieces or slices.—*v.i.* To make a carving; to cut up meat. —**carv•er,** *n.*

car•vel, kär′vəl, *n.* Caravel.

carv•ing, kär′ving, *n.* A branch of sculpture usually limited to works in wood or ivory; the device or figure carved.

car•y•at•id, kar•ē•at′id, *n. pl.,* **-ids, -i•des,** -ə•dēz. A statue of a woman serving to support entablatures.

ca•sa•ba, cas•sa•ba, kə•sä′bə, *n.* A sweet, edible, winter melon with a yellow, netted skin. Also **ca•sa•ba me•lon.**

Cas•a•no•va, kaz•ə•nō′və, kas•ə•nō′və, *n.* An unscrupulous lover of many women; a Don Juan.

cas•cade, kas•kād′, *n.* A small waterfall over a precipice or other drop; something resembling a waterfall. —*v.i.,* **-cad•ed, -cad•ing.** To fall in or form a cascade.

case, kās, *n.* An instance; example; an instance of disease or injury, or the patient exhibiting it. *Informal.* A peculiar or unusual person. The actual facts or state of things; a situation, condition, or plight; a state of things involving a question for discussion; a suit or action at law; the presentation of facts or evidence; a set of arguments or reasons to support something; a question, or moral problem; one of the forms of a noun, pronoun, or adjective, that expresses its relation to other words; a particular relation of this kind.—**in any case,** in any event; anyhow.—**in case,** in the event that.—**in no case,** under no circumstances.

case, kās, *n.* A receptacle or box for containing or enclosing something; a sheath, or outer covering; a quantity contained in a box; the enclosing frame of a door, window, or stairs; a set. *Print.* A tray divided into compartments for holding type.—*v.′* **.** **cased, cas•ing.** To put or enclose in a case; encase. *Informal.* To survey, esp. in preparation for an intended robbery.

case•hard•en, kās′här•dən, *v.t.* To harden (steel or an alloy) on the surface only; to render callous or unfeeling.

ca•sein, kā′sēn, kā′sē•in, *n.* A white protein found in milk, and which is the basic ingredient of cheese.

case knife, *n.* A long knife kept in a case or sheath; a large table knife.

case•mate, kās′māt, *n.* A vault in a rampart, or an armored enclosure in a warship, with embrasures for artillery firing. —**case•mat•ed,** *a.*

case•ment, kās′mənt, *n.* A window opening by swinging on hinges; a casing or covering. *Poetic.* Any window. —**case•ment•ed,** *a.*

case•work•er, kās′wər•kər, *n.* An investigator who interviews handicapped or maladjusted persons and needy families to provide aid and guidance. —**case•work,** *n.*

cash, kash, *n.* Money, esp. ready money; money, or an equivalent, as a check, paid at the time of making a purchase.—*v.t.* To give or obtain cash for (a check).—**cash in,** to turn in and receive cash for, as gambling chips. *Informal.* To die.—**cash in on,** *informal:* to make a profit from; to use to advantage.

cash•book, kash′bůk, *n.* A book which records money received and spent.

cash•ew, kash′oo, kə•shoo′, *n.* A tropical American evergreen which bears a small, edible, kidney-shaped nut; the nut.

cash•ier, ka•shēr′, *v.t.* To dismiss or discharge, esp. with ignominy.

cash•ier, ka•shēr′, *n.* One who has charge of or collects money in a bank, restaurant, store, etc.

cash•mere, kash′mēr, *n.* The fine, soft under-wool of a breed of goats of Kashmir and Tibet; a costly kind of shawl made of this wool; a fine, soft, woolen dress fabric.

cash reg•is•ter, *n.* A device, usu. with a money drawer, which records the amount of cash received.

cas•ing, kā′sing, *n.* A protective or confining covering; a supporting frame around a door or window; the outer covering of a pneumatic tire.

ca•si•no, kə•sē′nō, *n. pl.,* **-nos.** A large room or building for amusements, esp. gambling; a card game.

cask, kask, käsk, *n.* A barrel made of staves and hoops for holding liquids; the quantity such a vessel holds.

cas•ket, kas′kit, kä′skit, *n.* A small chest, or box for jewels. *U.S.* A coffin.

cas•sa•ba, kə•sä′bə, *n.* Casaba.

Cas•san•dra, kə•san′drə, *n.* One who utters unheeded prophesies of disaster.

cas•sa•va, kə•sä′və, *n.* A tropical American shrub; the nutritious starch from its root, the source of tapioca.

cas•se•role, kas′ə•rōl, *n.* A stewpan; a dish, esp. a covered baking dish, in which food is cooked and served; the food prepared in such a utensil.

cas•sette, kə•set′, ka•set′, *n.* A type of tape cartridge; a plate or film holder of a camera.

cas•si•no, kə•sē′nō, *n.* Casino.

cas•sock, kas′ək, *n.* A long, close-fitting, usually black garment worn by clergymen, choir singers, etc. —**cas•socked,** *a.*

cas•so•war•y, kas′ə•wer′ē, *n. pl.,* **-war•ies.** Any of several large, three-toed, flightless birds of Australasian regions, resembling the ostrich but smaller.

cast, kast, käst, *v.t.,* **cast, cast•ing.** To throw; fling or hurl, often used with *away, off, out;* direct, as the eye or glance; throw out, down, off, aside, forth, up, or away; part with; shed or drop; deposit, as a vote; allot the parts of, as a play, to the actors; assign (a part) to an actor; form, as molten metal, into a particular shape by pouring into a mold; to calculate; add; let go or let loose, as a vessel, from a mooring, with *loose* or *off.*—*v.i.* To throw, as with a fishing line, dice, etc.; receive form in a mold; calculate or add; consider; scheme; look about one mentally, usually with *about;* turn; tack.—*n.* The act of casting; that which is cast; the actors to whom the parts in a play are assigned; casting or founding; quantity of metal cast at one time; something shaped in a mold; a casting; a reproduction made in a mold; form or appearance; sort, kind, or style; bent or tendency; a permanent twist or turn; a warp; a slight tinge of some color.

cas•ta•net, kas•tə•net′, *n.* One of a pair of small concave pieces of ivory or hard wood, fastened to the thumb and clicked with the middle finger in certain Spanish dances.

cast•a•way, kast′ə•wā, *n.* A shipwrecked person; an outcast.—*a.* Thrown away; abandoned.

caste, kast, käst, *n.* One of the hereditary social classes into which the Hindus are divided; any rigid or exclusive social class; a social system having such classes.

cas•tel•lat•ed, kas′tə•lā•tid, *a.* Furnished with turrets and battlements.

cast•er, kas′tər, kä′stər, *n.* One who or that which casts; a small wheel on a piece of furniture for ease of movement; a small cruet or bottle for holding condiments; a stand for such bottles.

cas•ti•gate, kas′tə•gāt, *v.t.,* **-gat•ed, -gat•ing.** To censure or punish; criticize severely. —**cas•ti•ga•tion,** kas•tə•gā′shən, *n.* —**cas•ti•ga•tor,** *n.*

cast•ing, kas′ting, kä′sting, *n.* The act of one who

---

a- hat, fāte, fāre, fäther; e- met, mē; i- pin, pīne; o- not, nōte, ôrb, moove (move), boy, pownd; u- cūbe, bůll, tůk (took); ch- chin; th- thick, ŧhen; zh- vizhon (vision); ə- əgo, takən, pencəl, leмən, bərd (bird).

casts; something cast or formed in a mold.

cast i·ron, *n.* A hard, brittle, impure form of iron obtained by casting.—**cast-iron,** *a.* Made of cast iron; inflexible or unyielding; strong; rugged.

cas·tle, kas′əl, kä′səl, *n.* A building, or series of connected buildings, fortified for defense against an enemy; a fortified residence; a large and stately residence. *Chess.* Rook.—*v.t.,* **-tled, -tling.** *Chess.* To move (the king) two squares toward either rook and place that rook on the square passed over by the king.—*v.i.* To castle or be castled. —**cas·tled,** *a.*

cas·tle in the air, *n.* A fanciful scheme; daydream.

cast-off, kast′ôf, kast′of, käst′ôf, käst′of, *a.* Thrown away; discarded.—*n.* Something discarded.

cas·tor, kas′tər, *n.* A beaver hat, or some similar hat; a substance with a strong penetrating smell, secreted by special glands of the beaver, and used in medicine and perfumery.

cas·tor-oil plant, kas′tər-oyl, *n.* A tall plant, native in India, yielding the castor bean and castor oil.

cas·trate, kas′trāt, *v.t.,* **-trat·ed, -trat·ing.** To deprive of the testicles; to geld; to spay; to emasculate; to expurgate. —**cas·trat·er,** *n.* —**cas·tra·tion,** ka·strā′shən, *n.*

cas·u·al, kazh′û·əl, *a.* Happening by chance; accidental; fortuitous; occurring irregularly; occasional; uncertain; indefinite; without plan or method; careless; offhand; concerned with what is occasional and not regular: a *casual* laborer.—*n.* A soldier who for the time being is separated from his unit; a casual laborer; one who receives occasional public aid. —**cas·u·al·ly,** *adv.* —**cas·u·al·ness,** *n.*

cas·u·al·ty, kazh′û·əl·tē, *n. pl.,* **-ties.** Chance or accident; an unfortunate accident, esp. one involving bodily injury or death; a soldier or sailor lost through any cause.

cas·u·ist, kazh′û·ist, *n.* One who studies cases of conscience or conduct; an overly clever reasoner upon such matters. —**cas·u·is·tic,** kazh·û·is′tik, *a.* —**cas·u·ist·ry,** *n. pl.,* **-ries.**

cat, kat, *n.* A small, tame mammal, valued as a pet and for killing mice and rats; the fur of this cat; any other member of the cat family, including lions, tigers, leopards, etc.; something like a cat; a gossiping or spiteful woman; the ship's tackle used to raise the anchor to the cathead; a catfish. *Informal.* A Caterpillar tractor; a jazz musician or fan.—*v.t.,* **cat·ted, cat·ting.** To raise, as an anchor, to the cathead of a ship; to flag. *Informal.* A person, a fellow. —**let the cat out of the bag,** to disclose a secret, usually inadvertently.

cat·a·clysm, kat′ə·kliz·əm, *n.* A sudden and violent change in the earth's surface, as a flood or earthquake; any violent upheaval. —**cat·a·clys·mal,** kat·ə·kliz′məl, *a.*

cat·a·comb, kat′ə·kōm, *n.* Usu. *pl.* An underground burial place, esp. one with galleries having dug-out tombs in the walls.

cat·a·falque, kat′ə·falk, kat′ə·fôlk, *n.* A raised structure on which the coffin of a dead person lies.

cat·a·lep·sy, kat′ə·lep·sē, *n.* A loss of consciousness and will by a kind of fit marked with rigidity of the muscles. —**cat·a·lep·tic,** kat·ə·lep′tik, *a., n.*

cat·a·log, cat·a·logue, kat′ə·lôg, kat′ə·log, *n.* A list or register, esp. a list arranged in alphabetical or other methodical order; a systematic arrangement of listed items giving descriptive details; a book or pamphlet containing such a list; the material in such a list. —*v.t., v.i.* **-loged, -log·ing,** or **-logued, -logu·ing.** To make or enter into a catalog. —**cat·a·log·er,** cat·a·log·ist, *n.*

ca·tal·pa, kə·tal′pə, *n.* A tree of Asia and North America with heart-shaped leaves, showy flowers, and long pods.

ca·tal·y·sis, kə·tal′ə·sis, *n. pl.,* **-ses,** -sēz. The causing or accelerating of a chemical change by the addition of an agent which is not permanently affected by the reaction. —**cat·a·lyt·ic,** kat·a·lit′ik, *a.*

cat·a·lyst, kat′ə·list, *n.* In catalysis, the substance which causes the chemical change.

cat·a·lyze, kat′ə·līz, *v.t.,* **-lyzed, -lyz·ing.** To act upon by catalysis.

cat·a·ma·ran, kat·ə·mə·ran′, *n.* A narrow float or sailing raft made of several logs or pieces of wood lashed together; any craft with twin parallel hulls.

cat·a·mount, kat′ə·mownt, *n.* A wildcat, such as the cougar or lynx.

cat·a·pult, kat′ə·pəlt, kat′ə·pûlt, *n.* An ancient weapon for hurling missiles; a device for launching an airplane from the deck of a ship.—*v.t.* To shoot from, or as if from, a catapult.—*v.i.* To be catapulted.

cat·a·ract, kat′ə·rakt, *n.* A great fall of water; a waterfall; any furious downpour of water; a disease of the eye consisting of opacity of the crystalline lens or its capsule, which impairs or destroys vision.

ca·tarrh, kə·tär′, *n.* Inflammation of a mucous membrane, esp. of the respiratory tract, causing a discharge of mucus.

ca·tas·tro·phe, kə·tas′trə·fē, *n.* A widespread, disastrous event; any overwhelming misfortune or failure; a sudden violent disturbance, esp. of the earth's surface. —**cat·as·troph·ic,** kat·as·trof′ik, *a.*

cat·bird, kat′bərd, *n.* A black-capped, dark gray American songbird, with a catlike cry.

cat·boat, kat′bōt, *n.* A small sailboat, usually with a single mast set well forward and one large sail extended by a boom.

cat·call, kat′kôl, *n.* A shrill, mewing call or whistle indicating scorn.—*v.t., v.i.* To utter or deride with catcalls.

catch, kach, *v.t.,* **caught, catch·ing.** To capture, seize, or take captive, esp. after pursuit; snare; come upon suddenly; grasp or snatch; to grip or entangle; grab; overtake (something) in motion, or be in time to reach; hold; to hit. To incur: to *catch* the mumps; be affected by: the leaves *caught* fire; take; get; apprehend; captivate; grasp (the senses, etc.). *Informal.* See (a film, concert, etc.).—*v.i.* To become gripped or entangled; to take hold; become fastened; become lighted; burn. *Baseball.* To play the catcher's position.—*n.* The act of catching; anything that catches, as a device for fastening something; that which is caught. *Informal.* A good person to marry; a game in which a ball is thrown from one player to another; a grasp of a batted or thrown ball before it touches ground; a trick or hidden condition in a contract, etc.—*a.* Arousing interest or attention; tricky or deceptive.—**catch on,** *Informal.* To understand; to become widely accepted or popular. —**catch one's breath,** to stop breathing suddenly, as in fear; to rest.—**catch up,** to reach or overtake; to pick up suddenly; snatch; to regain lost ground; to heckle; to find in error; to engross.

catch·all, kach′ôl, *n.* A bag, basket, or other receptacle for odds and ends.

catch·er, kach′ər, *n.* One who or that which catches. *Baseball.* The player who squats behind home base to catch the pitched ball.

catch·ing, kach′ing, *a.* Infectious; attractive.

catch·up, kach′əp, kech′əp, *n.* Ketchup.

catch·word, kach′wərd, *n.* An often repeated word or phrase, as a political or advertising slogan; a word at the head of a page or column which identifies the first or last item on the page.

catch·y, kach′ē, *a.,* **-i·er, -i·est.** Attractive and easily recalled; tricky or deceptive.

cat·e·chism, kat′ə·kiz·əm, *n.* a book containing a summary of the principles of a religious creed, esp. in the form of questions and answers; a similar book of instruction in other subjects; a series of formal questions put to candidates. —**cat·e·chis·mal,** kat·ə·kiz′məl, *a.*

cat·e·chize, kat′ə·kīz, *v.t.,* **-chized, -chiz·ing.** To instruct orally by means of questions and answers, esp. in Christian doctrine; to question searchingly. Also **cat·e·chise.** —**cat·e·chi·za·tion,** kat·ə·ki·

zā-shen, *n.* —cat·e·chist, *n.* —cat·e·chiz·er, *n.*

cat·e·chu·men, kat·ə·kū′mən, *n.* A person who is receiving instruction in basic elements, esp. those of Christianity.

cat·e·gor·i·cal, kat·ə·gôr′ə·kəl, kat·ə·gor′ə·kəl, *a.* Positive; unqualified or unconditional; pertaining to a category. —cat·e·gor·i·cal·ly, *adv.*

cat·e·go·ry, kat′ə·gô·rē, kat′ə·gôr·ē, *n. pl.,* -ries. Any general or comprehensive division in classification; a class; group. —cat·e·gor·ize, kat′ə·gə·rīz, *v.t.,* -ized, -iz·ing.

ca·ter, kā′tər, *v.i.* To provide what is desired for use, pleasure, or entertainment; give special attention. —*v.t.* To provide food and provisions for: to *cater* a dinner.

ca·ter·er, kā′tər·ər, *n.* One who caters; a provider of food and provisions for a party, etc.

cat·er·pil·lar, kat′ər·pil·ər, *n.* The wormlike larva of a butterfly or moth or similar larva of other insects. (*Cap.*) Trademark. A tractor which has the wheels mounted inside an endless metal belt on each side.

cat·er·waul, kat′ər·wôl, *v.i.* To utter noisy, disagreeable cries, like a cat during mating season; to screech.—*n.*

cat·fish, kat′fish, *n. pl.,* -fish, -fish·es. A scaleless fish with a large head and long feelers around the mouth.

cat·gut, kat′gət, *n.* A tough cord made from the intestines of sheep or other animals, used for violin strings, tennis rackets, etc.

ca·thar·sis, kə·thär′sis, *n. pl.,* -ses, -sēz. Purgation; emotional release provided by an artistic or theatrical experience.

ca·thar·tic, kə·thär′tik, *a.* Purgative.—*n.* A purgative.

ca·the·dral, kə·thē′dral, *n.* The official church of a bishop; any large or important church.—*a.* Relating to a bishop's throne; like a cathedral; authoritative.

cath·e·ter, kath′ə·tər, *n.* A hollow tube inserted into the body to drain away fluids.

cath·ode, kath′ōd, *n.* The negative terminal of an electroplating cell; the positive terminal of a storage battery, from which positively charged electric current leaves.

cath·ode ray, *n.* A stream of electrons from cathode to anode in a vacuum tube.

cath·ode-ray tube, *n.* A type of vacuum tube which utilizes a stream of cathode rays projected onto a fluorescent screen, such as a television picture tube.

cath·o·lic, kath′ə·lik, kath′lik, *a.* Universal in extent; general; broad-minded; liberal; pertaining to the whole Christian church. (*Cap.*) Pertaining to the Roman Catholic Church.—*n.* (*Cap.*) A member of a Catholic church, esp. of the Roman Catholic Church. —cath·o·lic·i·ty, kath·ə·lis′ə·tē, *n.* —ca·thol·i·cize, kə·thol′ə·sīz, *v.t., v.i.,* -cized, -ciz·ing.

Ca·thol·i·cism, kə·thol′ə·siz·əm, *n.* The faith, system and practice of a Catholic church, esp. the Roman Catholic Church. (*L.c.*) The state of being catholic or universal.

cat·i·on, kat′ī·on, *n.* An electropositive ion.

cat·kin, kat′kin, *n.* The spikelike scaly blossom of the willow, birch, or hazel, resembling a cat's tail.

cat·mint, kat′mint, *n.* Catnip.

cat·nap, kat′nap, *n.* A short nap or doze.—*v.i.,* -napped, -nap·ping. To doze.

cat·nip, kat′nip, *n.* A mint plant of which cats are fond; catmint.

cat-o'-nine-tails, kat·ə·nīn′tālz, *n.* A whip of nine knotted cords on a handle.

cat's-paw, cats-paw, kats′pô, *n.* A person used by another as a tool or dupe; a light breeze which ruffles a small surface of water during a calm.

cat·sup, kat′sup, kech′up, *n.* Ketchup.

cat·tail, kat′tāl, *n.* A tall, reedlike marsh plant with flowers in long, dense cylindrical spikes; a catkin.

cat·tle, kat′əl, *n.* Domesticated, four-legged bovine animals, including cows, bulls, and steers; livestock in general.

cat·tle·man, kat′əl·mən, *n. pl.,* -men. One who rears or tends cattle.

cat·ty, kat′ē, *a.,* cat·ti·er, cat·ti·est. Spiteful; like a cat. —cat·ti·ly, *adv.* —cat·ti·ness, *n.*

cat·ty-cor·ner, cat·ty-cor·nered, kat′ē·kôr·nər, kat′ē·kôr·nərd, *a., adv.* Diagonal, diagonally. Also **kit·ty-cor·ner, kit·ty-cor·nered, cat·er-cor·ner, cat·er-cor·nered.**

cat·walk, kat′wôk, *n.* Any very narrow place for walking.

Cau·ca·sian, kô·kā′zhən, kô·kā′shən, *a.* Of or pertaining to the Caucasus region or mountain range; pertaining to the so-called white race.—*n.* A native of the Caucasus; a member of the Caucasian race.

cau·cus, kô′kəs, *n. pl.,* -cus·es. In the U.S., a meeting of a group of members of a political party to nominate candidates, elect delegates to a convention, etc.—*v.i.,* -cused, -cus·ing. To hold or meet in a caucus.

cau·dal, kôd′əl, *a.* Of, at, or near the tail; taillike.

cau·date, kô′dāt, *a.* Having a tail or taillike part. Also **cau·dat·ed.**

cau·dle, kôd′əl, *n.* A warm drink made of wine or ale to which eggs, gruel, or bread are sometimes added, given esp. to sick persons.

caul, kôl, *n.* A membrane sometimes surrounding the head of a child when born.

caul·dron, cal·dron, kôl′dron, *n.* A large metal kettle or boiler.

cau·li·flow·er, kô′lē·flow·ər, *n.* A plant related to the cabbage family with a compact, fleshy head of white flowers.

cau·li·flow·er ear, *n.* An external ear which has become scarred and bent through injury from boxing punches.

caulk, calk, kôk, *v.t.* To fill the seams of, as a ship or boat, with oakum or other substance to make watertight; fill or close the seams or crevices of, as a tank, window, boiler, etc. —caulk·er, *n.* Also calk·er.

caus·al, kô′zəl, *a.* Relating to a cause or causes; expressing a cause or causes; causative. —caus·al·ly, *adv.*

cau·sal·i·ty, kô·zal′ə·tē, *n. pl.,* -ties. The state of being causal; the fact of acting as a cause; the power of a cause, in producing its effect; the principle that every effect implies the presence of a cause.

cause, kôz, *n.* That which produces an effect; that which brings about a change; that from which anything proceeds; reason or motive; sufficient reason; good grounds; an ideal or movement which an individual or a party upholds and works for; case; matter; affair; subject under discussion; a suit or action in court; lawsuit.—*v.t.,* caused, caus·ing. To be the cause of; to effect; to bring about. —cau·sa·tion, kô·zā′shən, *n.* —caus·a·tive, kô′zə·tiv, *a.* —cause·less, *a.* —caus·er, *n.*

cause cé·lè·bre, kôz′sə·leb′rə, *Fr.* kōz sä·leb′rə, *n.* A legal case or other controversy that attracts attention or becomes famous.

cause·way, kôz′wā, *n.* A road or path raised above the ground by stones, earth, timber, to be a passage over marshy ground; a raised and paved roadway. —*v.t.* To provide a causeway for; to pave, as a road.

caus·tic, kô′stik, *a.* Capable of burning, corroding, or destroying animal tissue; severely critical or sarcastic.—*n.* A caustic substance. —caus·ti·cal·ly, *adv.*

caus·tic so·da, *n.* Sodium hydroxide.

cau·ter·ize, kô′tə·rīz, *v.t.,* -ized, -iz·ing. To burn with fire, a hot iron, or with caustics to avoid infection. —cau·ter·i·za·tion, kô·tə·rə·zā′shən, *n.*

cau·ter·y, kô′tə·rē, *n. pl.,* -ies. A cauterizing; the instrument or chemical agent used in cauterizing.

---

a- hat, fāte, fāre, fäther; **e-** met, mē; **i-** pin, pīne; **o-** not, nōte, ôrb, moove (move), boy, pownd; **u-** cūbe, bůll, tûk (took); **ch-** chin; **th-** thick, then; **zh-** vizhon (vision); **ə-** əgo, takən, pencəl, lemən, bərd (bird).

cau·tion, kô′shən, *n.* A cautious behavior; a measure taken for security; a warning. *Informal.* A person or thing that astonishes.—*v.t., v.i.* Warn; to urge to be careful. —**cau·tion·ar·y,** *a.*

cau·tious, kô′shəs, *a.* Having caution; prudent; wary; careful.

cav·al·cade, kav·əl·kād′, kav′əl·kād, *n.* A procession of persons on horseback or in carriages; a parade.

cav·a·lier, kav·ə·lēr′, *n.* A knight; a courtly gentleman; a man escorting a woman.—*a.* Offhand; free and easy; haughty; disdainful. —**cav·a·lier·ly,** *adv.*

cav·al·ry, kav′əl·rē, *n. pl.,* **-ries.** Mounted soldiers; that part of a military force whose troops once served on horseback, and more recently in armored vehicles. —**cav·al·ry·man,** *n. pl.,* **-men.**

cave, kāv, *n.* A hollow in the earth, or in a hill or mountain.—*v.t.,* **caved, cav·ing.** To hollow out.—*v.i.* To fall in.—**cave in,** to fall in or cause to fall in; smash. *Informal.* Submit; collapse.

ca·ve·at, kā′vē·at, *n.* A legal notice to a judicial officer to not do anything further until the notifier is given a hearing; a warning or caution.

cave-in, kāv′in, *n.* A caving in; the location where something has fallen in.

cave man, *n.* A name given to the earliest races of prehistoric man which dwelt in natural caves. *Informal.* A rough, crude man.

cav·ern, kav′ərn, *n.* A large cave. —**cav·ern·ous,** *a.*

cav·i·ar, cav·i·are, kav′ē·är, kä′vē·är, *n.* Salted eggs of the sturgeon, prepared as a food.

cav·il, kav′əl, *v.i.,* **-iled, -il·ing.** To raise trivial objections; to find fault without good reason, with *at* or *about.*—*v.t.* To oppose by finding trivial faults.—*n.* A trivial objection. —**cav·il·er,** *n.*

cav·i·ty, kav′ə·tē, *n. pl.,* **-ties.** A hollow place; a hollow; a void; a hollow part of the human body.

ca·vort, kə·vôrt′, *v.i. Informal.* To prance or caper about.

caw, kô, *v.i.* To cry like a crow, rook, or raven.—*n.* The cry of the rook or crow.

cay, kā, *n.* An islet; a range or reef of sand or coral; key.

cay·enne, kī·en′, kā·en′, *n.* A hot, biting condiment composed of the ground pods and seeds of hot peppers; red pepper.

cay·man, kā′mən, *n. pl.,* **-mans.** Any of several tropical American crocodilians similar to the alligator.

cay·use, kī·ūs′, *n.* A small horse; an Indian pony.

cease, sēs, *v.i.,* **ceased, ceas·ing.** To stop; to leave off; to desist; to come to an end.—*v.t.* To put a stop to; put an end to; desist from.—*n.* End; cessation. —**cease·less,** *a.*

cease-fire, sēs′fīr, *n.* A truce; an armistice; an order to stop firing.

ce·cum, cae·cum, se′kəm, *n. pl.,* **-ca, -kə.** A sac or cavity with an opening only at one end, esp. the one of the large intestine. —**ce·cal, cae·cal,** *a.*

ce·dar, sē′dər, *n.* Any of a genus of Old World evergreen trees; any of various junipers, as the red cedar, an American tree with a fragrant reddish wood; any of various other evergreen trees; any of various tropical trees; the durable and fragrant wood of any such tree.

ce·dar wax·wing, *n.* A North American bird with chiefly light brown plumage.

cede, sēd, *v.t.,* **ced·ed, ced·ing.** To yield or formally resign and surrender to another.

ce·dil·la, si·dil′ə, *n.* A mark placed under *c* before *a, o,* or *u,* as in *façade,* to show that it has the sound of *s.*

ceil·ing, sē′ling, *n.* The overhead inner lining of a room; the maximum altitude an aircraft can reach under certain conditions; a topmost limit, esp. one set on wages or prices.

cel·an·dine, sel′ən·dīn, *n.* A yellow-flowered biennial herb of the poppy family; a yellow-flowered perennial crowfoot.

cel·e·brant, sel′ə·brənt, *n.* One who celebrates, esp. the officiating priest in the celebration of the Eucharist.

cel·e·brate, sel′ə·brāt, *v.t.,* **-brat·ed, -brat·ing.** To perform with appropriate ceremonies; solemnize; commemorate an event with ceremonies; to extol; make known publicly.—*v.i.* To perform (a religious ceremony); to observe or commemorate with ceremonies. —**cel·e·bra·tion,** sel·ə·brā′shən, *n.* —**cel·e·bra·tor,** *n.*

cel·e·brat·ed, sel′ə·brā·tid, *a.* Famous; renowned; well-known.

ce·leb·ri·ty, sə·leb′rə·tē, *n. pl.,* **-ties.** A famous person; fame; renown.

ce·ler·i·ty, sə·ler′ə·tē, *n.* Swiftness; speed.

cel·er·y, sel′ə·rē, *n.* A biennial herb grown as a vegetable, whose stalks are eaten raw or cooked.

ce·les·tial, sə·les′chəl, *a.* Of or pertaining to the sky or visible heaven; heavenly; divine.—*n.* An inhabitant of heaven.

ce·li·ac, coe·li·ac, sē′lē·ak, *a.* Pertaining to the cavity of the abdomen.

cel·i·ba·cy, sel′ə·bə·sē, *n.* The state of being unmarried; abstention from sexual intercourse. —**cel·i·bate,** sel′ə·bit, sel′ə·bāt, *n.*

cell, sel, *n.* A small room in a prison, monastery, etc.; a cave or hermitage; any small, hollow place; a small group of people making up a single basic unit within a larger organization: a Communist *cell;* the basic unit of all living things, made up of a nucleus and cytoplasmic material, surrounded by a membrane in animals and a cell wall in plants; a device which generates electricity, made up of electrodes in contact with an electrolyte, forming the whole or part of a voltaic battery.

cel·lar, sel′ər, *n.* A room in a house or other building, either wholly or partly underground, used for storage purposes; basement; basement for or stock of wines; the lowest rank.

cel·lo, 'cel·lo, chel′ō, *n. pl.,* **-los.** Shortened form of violoncello, a large stringed instrument tuned an octave lower than a viola, and played while held between the performer's knees. —**cel·list, 'cel·list,** *n.*

cel·lo·phane, sel′ə·fān, *n.* A strong, transparent, flexible film, made of treated cellulose, used for protective wrapping.

cel·lu·lar, sel′yə·lər, *a.* Referring to or characterized by having cells.

cel·lule, sel′ūl, *n.* A little cell.

Cel·lu·loid, sel′yə·loyd, *n. Trademark.* A highly inflammable, solid substance consisting essentially of soluble guncotton and camphor.—*a. (L.c.)* Referring to the movie industry.

cel·lu·lose, sel′yə·lōs, *n.* A carbohydrate, the main part of the cell walls of plants, forming an essential part of wood, cotton, hemp, paper, etc.

Celt, kelt, selt, *n.* One of a distinct group of early Indo-European peoples, including the Bretons, Welsh, Scottish Highlanders, Cornish, and the Irish. Also **Kelt.**

Celt·ic, kel′tik, sel′tik, *n.* The language or group of dialects spoken by the Celts.—*a.* Pertaining to the Celts, or to their language.

ce·ment, si·ment′, *n.* A fine gray powder, mainly alumina, lime, iron oxide, and silica burned together, then pulverized, which forms a hard mass when mixed with water, used to make sidewalks, streets, walls, etc.; any sticky substance which makes things stick tightly together after drying; anything that joins or unites.—*v.t.* To unite by cement; to overspread with cement; to unite firmly or closely.—*v.i.* To become cemented; to unite and cohere.

cem·e·ter·y, sem′ə·ter·ē, *n. pl.,* **-ies.** A place for burying the dead; a graveyard.

ce·no·bite, sē′nə·bīt, sen′ə·bīt, *n.* One of a religious order living in a convent or community. —**ce·no·bit·ic,** sē·nə·bit′ik, sen·ə·bit′ik, *a.*

cen·o·taph, sen′ə·taf, sen′ə·täf, *n.* A monument erected to one who is buried elsewhere.

Ce·no·zo·ic, sē·nə·zō′ik, sen·ə·zō′ik, a. Pertaining to the most recent geological era, following the Mesozoic.

cen·ser, sen′sər, n. A vase in which incense is burned, esp. in a religious ceremony.

cen·sor, sen′sər, n. An official who examines books, plays, and prohibits or suppresses them if deemed objectionable on moral, political, military, or other grounds; one who censures; one given to faultfinding.—a. Pertaining to a censor.—v.t. To examine, as a censor does. **—cen·so·ri·al,** sen·sō′rē·əl, sen·sô′rē·əl. **—cen·sor·ship,** n.

cen·so·ri·ous, sen·sōr′ē·əs, sen·sôr′ē·əs, a. Severely critical; faultfinding. **—cen·so·ri·ous·ly,** adv. **—cen·so·ri·ous·ness,** n.

cen·sure, sen′shər, n. A criticizing; a hostile criticism.—v.t., **cen·sured, cen·sur·ing.** Criticize; find fault with.—v.i. To give criticism or blame. **—cen·sur·er,** n. **—cen·sur·a·ble,** a. **—cen·sur·a·bly,** adv.

cen·sus, sen′səs, n. pl., **cen·sus·es.** In modern times, an official count of inhabitants, with details of age, sex, or interests; in ancient Rome, the registration of citizens and their property, for purposes of taxation.—v.t., **cen·sused, cen·sus·ing.** To take a census of.

cent, sent, n. A coin equal to the hundredth part of a monetary unit, esp. of the dollar.

cen·tare, sen′tər, n. Centiare.

cen·taur, sen′tôr, n. A fabulous being, half man and half horse.

cen·te·nar·i·an, sen·tə·nər′ē·ən, n. A person 100 years old or over.

cen·te·na·ry, sen′tə·ner·ē, sen·ten′ə·rē, n. pl., **-nar·ies.** The period or age of 100 years.

cen·ten·ni·al, sen·ten′ē·əl, a. Marking the end of a 100-year period.—n. A hundredth anniversary or its commemoration.

cen·ter, Brit. **cen·tre,** sen′tər, n. A point, equally distant from all points of a circle. A point, pivot, or axis around which something rotates or revolves; the core; the middle section of anything; the nucleus of an object or idea; a place in which an interest, activity, or purpose is centered.—v.t. To place in or on a center; collect at a center, mark the center of; adjust an object or part, so that it is in a central or normal position.—v.i. To be at or come to a center; concentrate.

cen·ter·board, sen′tər·bōrd, sen′tər·bord, n. A wooden or metal slab that can be lowered through the bottom of a sailboat, in order to increase the draft and prevent drifting.

cen·ter field, n. Baseball. Roughly, the center one-third of the outfield.

cen·ter of grav·i·ty, n. That point on a body, freely acted upon by the earth's gravity, about which the body is in equilibrium in all positions.

cen·ter of mass, n. Phys. The point on a body which behaves as if all the mass of the body were concentrated there.

cen·ter·piece, sen′tər·pēs, n. An ornament placed in the middle or center of something, as of a table.

cen·ti·are, sen′tē·ār, sen′tē·är, n. A surface measure equal to one-hundredth of an are, or one square meter.

cen·ti·grade, sen′tə·grād, a. A temperature scale, which is divided into 100 degrees from the freezing point of water, or 0°, to the boiling point of water, or 100°; abbreviated C. Also **Cel·si·us.**

cen·ti·gram, sen′tə·gram, n. A unit of weight equal to one-hundredth of a gram, or 0.1543 grain.

cen·ti·li·ter, sen′tə·lē·tər, n. A unit of capacity equal to one-hundredth of a liter.

cen·ti·me·ter, sen′tə·mē·tər, n. A measure of length, the hundredth part of a meter; slightly more than 0.39 of an inch.

cen·tral, sen′trəl, a. Forming the center; in, at, or near the center; in a middle position between extremes.

cen·tral·ize, sen′trə·līz, v.t. **-ized, -iz·ing.** To draw to a center; to bring under one control.

cen·trif·u·gal, sen·trif′ū·gəl, sen·trif′ə·gəl, a. Tending to move away from the center; acting by or depending on centrifugal force.—n. A centrifuge.

cen·trif·u·gal force, n. A force which tends to pull objects outward from a center of rotation.

cen·tri·fuge, sen′trə·fūj, n. A machine which uses centrifugal force.

cen·trip·e·tal, sen·trip′ə·təl, a. Tending or progressing toward a center; pertaining to centripetal force.

cen·trip·e·tal force, n. A force which tends to pull objects toward a center.

cen·tu·ri·on, sen·tû′rē·ən, n. In ancient Rome, a military officer who commanded a company of infantry consisting of a hundred men.

cen·tu·ry, sen′chə·rē, n. pl., **cen·tu·ries.** Anything consisting of a hundred in number; a period of a hundred years; a subdivision or company in the ancient Roman army consisting of 100 men.

ce·ram·ic, sə·ram′ik, a. Referring to pottery, earthenware, porcelain, or similar products made of fired clay.

ce·ram·ics, sə·ram′iks, n. The art of shaping and baking clay articles, as pottery, earthenware, porcelain.

ce·re·al, sēr′ē·əl, n. Any grass which produces a starchy, edible grain, as wheat, oats, barley, rice, rye, or corn; the grain itself; a breakfast food processed from such a grain.

cer·e·bel·lum, ser·ə·bel′əm, n. A large section of the brain, coordinating center for voluntary movements, equilibrium and posture, adjacent to and underlying the cerebrum.

cer·e·bral, ser′ə·brəl, sə·rē′brəl, a. Referring to the cerebrum or brain.

cer·e·bral hem·i·sphere, n. Either of the two convoluted halves into which the cerebrum is divided.

cer·e·bral pal·sy, n. Paralysis, due to brain damage prior to birth or during delivery, and marked by a lack of muscular coordination, spasms, and difficulties in speech.

cer·e·brum, ser′ə·brəm, sə·rē′brəm, n. The main, anterior part of the brain, divided into halves, or cerebral hemispheres, and, in man, considered the center of conscious and voluntary processes.

cer·e·mo·ni·al, ser·ə·mō′nē·əl, n. A system of rites; ceremonies or formalities to be observed on some particular occasion.—a. Relating to ceremonies; ritual. **cer·e·mo·ni·al·ism,** n. **cer·e·mo·ni·al·ly,** adv. **—cer·e·mo·ni·al·ness,** n.

cer·e·mo·ni·ous, ser·ə·mō′nē·əs, a. Full of ceremony and formalities.

cer·e·mo·ny, ser′ə·mō·nē, n. pl., **-nies.** Formal rite or observance.

ce·rise, sə·rēs′, sə·rez′, n., a. Cherry-red.

ce·ri·um, sēr′ē·əm, n. A ductile, metallic element of the rare-earth series. **—ce·ric,** sēr′ik, ser′ik, a.

cer·tain, sər′tən, a. Sure; undoubtedly true; unfailing; free from doubt; not specifically named.—pron., pl. in constr. An indefinite number: Certain of the zoo animals were born in captivity. **—cer·tain·ly,** adv. Without doubt or question.

cer·tain·ty, n. pl., **-ties.** A fact or truth certainly established.

cer·tif·i·cate, sər·tif′ə·kit, n. A written testimony to the truth of certain facts; a kind of license.—sər·tif′ə·kāt, v.t. To give a certificate to, as one who has passed an examination.

cer·ti·fi·ca·tion, sər·tə·fə·kā′shən, n. The act of certifying.

---

cer·ti·fied pub·lic ac·count·ant, *n.* A public accountant who meets the state requirements for proficiency in the profession, and is granted a certificate. Also **CPA.**

cer·ti·fy, sər/tə·fī, *v.t., v.i.,* **-fied, -fy·ing.** To testify to in writing; to make known or establish as a fact. **—cer·ti·fi·a·ble,** sər·tə·fī/ə·bəl, *a.* **—cer·ti·fi·a·bly,** *adv.* **—cer·ti·fi·er,** *n.*

cer·ti·tude, sər/tə·tood, sər/tə·tūd, *n.* Certainty; state of feeling certain.

ce·ru·le·an, sə·roo/lē·ən, *a.* Sky-colored; azure; blue.

cer·vi·cal, sər/və·kəl, *a. Anat.* Belonging to the neck; pertaining to the narrow lower part of the uterus.

cer·vix, sər/viks, *n. pl.,* **cer·vix·es, cer·vi·ces,** sər·vī/sēz, sər/vi·sēz. The neck; the back of the neck; any necklike part, esp. the narrow lower part of the uterus.

ces·sa·tion, se·sā/shən, *n.* A ceasing; a stop.

ces·sion, sesh/ən, *n.* A giving up; surrender; handing over.

cess·pool, ses/pool, *n.* A pit for collecting drainage or sewage. *Fig.* Any place of moral corruption.

ce·ta·cean, si·tā/shən, *n.* A marine mammal of the order that includes whales, dolphins, and porpoises. **—ce·ta·ceous,** si·tā/shəs, *a.*

chafe, chāf, *v.t.,* **chafed, chaf·ing.** To stimulate to warmth by rubbing; to anger; to excite violent action in; to fret and wear by rubbing. **—v.i.** To be excited or heated; to rage; to fret; to rage or boil, as the sea; to be fretted and worn by rubbing.

chaf·er, chā/fər, *n.* A beetle destructive to plants.

chaff, chaf, chäf, *n.* The husks of grain separated by thrashing, sifting, or winnowing.

chaff, chaf, chäf, *v.t., v.i.* To tease; to banter; to jest.**—***n.* Banter; good-natured teasing. **—chaf·fer,** *n.*

chaf·fer, chaf/ər, *v.i.* To bargain or haggle.**—v.t.** To bandy (words); to haggle for.**—***n.* A bargaining or haggling over price. **—chaff·er·er,** *n.*

cha·grin, shə·grin/, *n.* A feeling of vexation, disappointment, or humiliation.**—v.t.,** **cha·grined, cha·grin·ing.** To mortify.

chain, chān, *n.* A series of links joined together. *Fig.* That which binds, restrains, confines; a bond; a fetter; bondage; a series of things linked together: a *chain* of causes; a group of similar places of business under one management: a hotel *chain.* **—v.t.** To unite firmly.

chain gang, *n.* A group of convicts chained together while working outdoors.

chain let·ter, *n.* A letter sent to a number of persons who are asked to send copies to other persons for some supposed advantage.

chain re·ac·tion, *n.* Any series of events each of which is caused by one before. A reaction between particles which is started artificially by added energy, and continues by sustaining itself. **—chain·re·act,** *v.i.*

chain saw, *n.* A power saw with teeth on a continuous band or chain.

chain store, *n.* One of a group of stores owned and operated by one owner or company.

chair, chār, *n.* A seat with a back, and often arms, for one person; a seat of office or authority, or the office itself; the person occupying the seat or office, esp. the chairman of a meeting.**—v.t.** To place or seat in a chair; install in a chair of office; to preside over, as a meeting.

chair·man, chār/mən, *n. pl.,* **chair·men,** chār/men. The presiding officer of a company, committee or public meeting; the administrative head of a department in a university or college; one whose business is to carry a sedan chair.**—v.t.,** **-maned** or **-manned, -man·ing** or **-man·ning.** To preside as chairman of a group, meeting or committee.

chair·man·ship, chār/mən·ship, *n.* The office of a chairman or presiding officer of a meeting.

chair·per·son, chār/pər·sən, *n.* A person who presides at a meeting.

chair·wom·an, chār/wŭm·ən, *n. pl.,* **-wom·en,** -wi·mən. A woman who presides at a meeting.

chaise, shāz, *n.* A light, one-horse open carriage, two-wheeled and for two persons.

chaise longue, shāz lông/, *n. pl.,* **chaise longues, chais·es longues.** A kind of reclining chair with an elongated seat.

chal·et, sha·lā/, shal/ā, *n.* A Swiss house with wide eaves.

chal·ice, chal/is, *n.* A drinking cup used in the celebration of the Lord's Supper.

chalk, chôk, *n.* A soft limestone made of tiny shells; a prepared piece of marking chalk; a mark made with chalk.**—v.t.** Whiten or make pale with chalk; to mark, write, or draw with chalk.**—v.i.** To become powdery, as a painted surface exposed to weather. **—chalk·y,** *a.*

chal·lenge, chal/ənj, *n.* A demand for an explanation or justification; a dare.**—v.t.,** **chal·lenged, chal·leng·ing.** To call to a contest; to summon to fight, or to a duel; to demand as a right; to object to; to take exception to; to call in question.

cham·ber, chām/bər, *n.* A room, usually private; a bedroom; a judge's consultation room; an enclosed space or compartment; a compartment in the cartridge or a revolver.**—v.t.** To shut up in, or as in, a chamber.

cham·ber·maid, chām/bər·mād, *n.* A person who takes care of bedrooms, making the beds and cleaning.

cham·ber mu·sic, *n.* Music suited for a small room; music for a trio, quartet, etc.

cham·ber of com·merce, *n.* An organization of businessmen and merchants who meet to promote commercial and industrial interests in their area.

cha·me·le·on, kə·mē/lē·ən, kə·mēl/yən, *n.* Any lizard with the ability to change color to match surroundings.**—a.** Fickle; changeable.

cham·ois, sham/ē, *n. pl.,* **cham·ois,** sham/ēz. A type of goatlike antelope; a kind of soft leather made from the skin of the chamois.

champ, champ, *v.t.* To crush with the teeth and chew vigorously or noisily; bite upon repeatedly, esp. impatiently.

champ, *n.* A champion.

cham·pagne, sham·pān/, *n.* An effervescent wine, usually white; a pale yellow.

cham·pi·on, cham/pē·ən, *n.* One who fights for a cause; one who wins first place. **—cham·pi·on·ship,** *n.*

chance, chans, chäns, *n.* An event occurring without apparent cause or control; luck; a risk.**—v.i.** To happen.**—v.t.** To risk.

chance·ful, chans/fəl, *a.* Hazardous.

chan·cel·lor, chan/sə·lər, chan/slər, *n.* A high-ranking administrative person.

chanc·y, chan/sē, chän/sē, *a.,* **chanc·i·er, chanc·i·est.** Dependent on chance; uncertain; risky.

chan·de·lier, shan·də·lēr/, *n.* A branched lighting fixture hung from the ceiling.

change, chānj, *v.t.,* **changed, chang·ing.** To make or become different; to substitute another thing or things for; to shift; to give or get another kind of money for: to *change* a dollar; to give away for a money equivalent of a different kind; to exchange: to *change* places with a person; to get fresh linen on: to *change* a bed or baby.**—v.i.** To suffer change; to be altered; to undergo variation; to be partially or wholly transformed.

change·a·ble, chān/jə·bəl, *a.* Liable to change; subject to alteration; fickle; inconsistent; unstable.

change·ful, chānj/fəl, *a.* Inconstant; fickle.

change of heart, *n.* A changed opinion.

change of life, *n.* Menopause.

chan·nel, chan/əl, *n.* The bed of a stream or waterway; the part of a waterway which is navigable; a broadcasting band (a range of wave lengths).

chant, chant, chänt, *v.t.* To sing.**—n.** A short, repetitive melody.

chan·ti·cleer, chan/tə·klēr, *n.* A rooster.

cha·os, kā/os, *n.* Great confusion; complete disorder; infinite space or formless matter before the universe existed.

cha·ot·ic, kā·ot/ik, *a.* In utter confusion or disorder.

chap, chap, *v.t.,* **chapped, chap·ping.** To split; crack; make rough, esp. the skin.—*v.i.* To become chapped, as the skin.—*n.* A crack in the skin.

chap, chap, *n. Informal.* A man or a boy; a fellow.

cha·pa·re·jos, cha·pa·ra·jos, chap·ə·rā/hōs, chä·pä·rä/hōs, *n. pl.* Protective leather breeches worn by horsemen, esp. cowboys. Also **chaps.**

chap·ar·ral, chap·ə·ral/, *n.* A close growth of low evergreen oaks; any dense thicket.

cha·peau, sha·po/, *Fr.* shä·pō/, *n. pl.,* **-peaux,** -pōz/, *Fr.* -pō/. A hat.

chap·el, chap/əl, *n.* A building for Christian worship, not as large as a church; room or building for worship.

chap·e·ron, chap·er·one, shap/ə·rōn, *n.* A person who supervises a party.

chap·fall·en, chap/fô·lən, *a.* Having the lower jaw depressed, from exhaustion, humiliation, or dejection.

chap·lain, chap/lin, *n.* A clergyman who performs divine service in a chapel.

chap·let, chap/lit, *n.* A wreath for the head; a string of beads; a string of beads for counting prayers.

chaps, chaps, shaps, *n.* Widely-flared leather leggings worn by cowboys as extra protection when riding through brush and thorns.

chap·ter, chap·tər, *n.* A division of a book; an important division in a series of events, often marked by a significant event or a turning point; a local branch of a college fraternity, sorority, or other society or organization; the council of a bishop, attached to a collegiate or cathedral church, and presided over by a dean; the meeting of certain religious orders and societies.

char, chär, *v.t.,* **charred, char·ring.** To burn or reduce to charcoal; to burn slightly; scorch.—*v.i.* To become charred.—*n.* Charcoal; a charred substance.

char·ac·ter, kar/ik·tər, *n.* A significant mark made by cutting, stamping, or drawing; a symbol as used in writing or printing, esp. one employed in recording speech, as a letter of the alphabet; writing or printing, or a style of writing or printing; the system of symbols employed in writing a particular language; a symbol representing information in coded form for use in a computer; a distinguishing mark or feature; a characteristic; the aggregate of characteristics or distinguishing features of a thing; peculiar quality; moral constitution; strongly developed moral quality; reputation; good repute; an account of the qualities or peculiarities of a person or thing; status or capacity; a person considered as exhibiting certain qualities; one of the persons represented in a drama or novel, a part or role. *Informal.* A person of marked peculiarities. —*v.t.* To portray; describe.

char·ac·ter·is·tic, kar·ik·tər·is/tik, *a.* Showing the character or peculiar quality of.—*n.* A distinguishing feature or quality. —**char·ac·ter·is·ti·cal·ly,** *adv.*

char·ac·ter·ize, kar/ik·tər·īz, *v.t.,* **-ized, -iz·ing.** To portray; describe the character or peculiar quality of. —**char·ac·ter·i·za·tion,** kar·ik·tər·ə·zā/shən, *n.* —**char·ac·ter·iz·er,** *n.*

cha·rade, shə·rād/, *n.* A word or phrase depicted, usually by pantomime, in a guessing game; *pl.,* the parlor game in which words or phrases are acted out.

char·coal, chär/kōl, *n.* The end product of burning animal or vegetable matter until the lighter materials are burned off as smoke; partly-burned material used as fuel.

char·coal grill, *n.* A grill for outdoor use employing charcoal as fuel.

chard, chärd, *n.* A vegetable with thick stalks and large, tender green leaves.

charge, chärj, *v.t.,* **charged, char·ging.** To load or fill up to the required amount; impose a task or responsibility on; accuse formally; to register a debt; to impose or ask a price; defer payment until a bill is sent by the creditor; to attack violently.—*v.i.* To demand a payment; to require payment for a service; to make a *charge,* as to attack.—*n.* A full load or burden; a quantity of explosive powder to be detonated at one time; a duty or responsibility entrusted to one; the care, safekeeping, and support of another; a command or official instruction; an accusation or indictment; the expense or cost of something; a sum or fixed price; a record of debit: a *charge* account; an accumulation or store of force; an impetuous onset or attack. *Informal.* A feeling of amusement.

charge ac·count, *n.* A credit arrangement whereby a customer may make immediate purchases and delay payment to the creditor until a later specified date.

char·gé d'af·faires, shär·zhä/ də·fār/, shär/zhä də·fār/, *n. pl.,* **char·gés d'af·faires,** shär·zhäz də·fär. A government official left in charge of diplomatic business during the temporary absence of the ambassador or minister.

charg·er, chär/jər, *n.* A horse for riding in battles; a war horse; a device for charging storage batteries.

char·i·ot, char/ē·ət, *n.* A two-wheeled, horse-drawn vehicle used by the ancients in war, racing, and processions. —**char·i·ot·eer,** char·ē·ə·tēr/, *n.*

cha·ris·ma, kə·riz/mə, *n.* A personal quality of individuals who have special powers of leadership and can inspire devotion and support.

char·i·ta·ble, char/ə·tə·bəl, *a.* Full of good will or tenderness; generous in giving aid to needy persons; referring to gifts or relief to the poor. —**char·i·ta·ble·ness,** *n.* —**char·i·ta·bly,** *adv.*

char·i·ty, char/ə·tē, *n. pl.,* **-ties.** Love for one's fellowmen; leniency in judging others or their actions; the private or public relief of the poor; a charitable act or work.

cha·riv·a·ri, shə·riv·ə·rē/, shiv·ə·rē/, shiv/ə·rē, *n.* A concert of noises made with kettles, pans, or horns, to a newly married couple. Also **chiv·a·ree, shiv·a·ree.**

char·la·tan, shär/lə·tən, *n.* One who pretends to have more knowledge or skill than he has; a quack. —**char·la·tan·ism,** *n.* —**char·la·tan·ry,** *n.*

char·ley horse, chär/lē, *n.* Cramping pain in the muscle of an arm or leg.

charm, chärm, *n.* A saying believed to have magic powers; a trinket worn on a bracelet or watch-chain; the ability to please and attract.—*v.t.* To fascinate; to enchant; to bewitch.—*v.i.* To be pleasing; to act as a charm or spell.

charm·er, chär/mər, *n.* One who charms, enchants, or attracts.

char·nel, chär/nəl, *n.* A place, sometimes under or near a church, where bodies or the bones of the dead are deposited.

chart, chärt, *n.* A graph or table on which information is shown in an organized visual form; a marine map, indicating the coasts, islands, rocks, and soundings. —*v.t.* To delineate, as on a chart; to map out; to plan.

char·ter, chär/tər, *n.* Any deed or instrument drawn up granting powers, rights, and privileges; privilege; immunity; exemption.—*v.t.* To hire, as a ship, by charter or contract; to establish; to grant; to privilege.

char·treuse, shär·trooz/, *n.* An aromatic liqueur, green, yellow, or white; a clear, light green color with a yellowish tinge.

char·wom·an, chär/wûm·ən, *n.* A woman employed by the day to do odd jobs about a house.

char·y, chär/ē, *a.,* **-i·er, -i·est.** Careful; cautious; frugal; sparing.

chase, chās, *v.t.,* **chased, chas·ing.** To pursue with

---

intent to capture; to pursue in order to seize or overtake.—*v.i.* To hunt; follow in pursuit.—*n.* The act of chasing; pursuit; an object of pursuit, as a hunted animal; a body of persons pursuing game.

chase, chās, *v.t.,* **chased, chas·ing.** To ornament, as metal, by engraving or embossing.

chas·er, chā'ser, *n.* One who or that which chases metal; one who pursues. *Informal.* A mild beverage, as water, taken after a drink of liquor.

chasm, kaz'əm, *n.* A gaping or yawning opening in the earth; a wide difference of views or outlook.

chas·sis, chas'ē, shas'ē, *n.* The framework which supports the body of an automobile; the frame and working parts.

chaste, chāst, *a.* Not having indulged in premarital or extramarital sexual intercourse; virtuous; free from impurity in thought and language; not gaudy. —**chaste·ly,** *adv.*

chas·ten, chā'sən, *v.t.* To punish for purposes of moral improvement; to restrain, moderate, or temper; make chaste in style; to remove excessive ornamentation.

chas·tise, chas·tīz', *v.t.,* **-tised, -tis·ing.** Punish by physical means. —**chas·tise·ment,** chas'tīz·mənt, chas·tīz'mənt, *n.* —**chas·tis·er,** *n.*

chas·ti·ty, chas'tə·tē, *n.* The quality of being chaste; pure.

chat, chat, *v.i.,* **chat·ted, chat·ting.** To talk casually or in a familiar manner.—*n.* Friendly conversation.

cha·teau, shä·tō', *n. pl.,* **cha·teaux,** shä·tōz'. A French castle; a country estate.

chat·e·laine, shat'ə·lān, *n.* The mistress of a castle.

chat·tel, chat'əl, *n.* Any article of personal property except land and buildings.

chat·ter, chat'ər, *v.i.* To utter a succession of quick, speech-like sounds; to talk rapidly; to make a rapid clicking noise by striking together; to vibrate in cutting.—*v.t.* To utter rapidly or idly; to cause to chatter. —*n.* The act or sound of chattering; idle conversation.

chat·ter·box, chat'ər·boks, *n.* One who chatters or talks incessantly.

chat·ty, chat'ē, *a.,* **-ti·er, -ti·est.** Given to chat or familiar talk; conversational. —**chat·ti·ly,** *adv.* —**chat·ti·ness,** *n.*

chauf·feur, shō'fər, shō·fər', *n.* One who is hired to drive an automobile.—*v.i.* To hold a position as chauffeur.—*v.t.* To drive, as an automobile used for transportation of another person.

chau·vin·ist, shō'vən·ist, *n.* Anyone possessed by an absurdly exaggerated enthusiasm for a cause, country, sex, etc. —**chau·vin·ism,** shō'vin·iz·əm, *n.* —**chau·vin·is·tic,** *a.*

cheap, chēp, *a.* Priced low; inferior; stingy.—*adv.* At a low price; in a cheap way or manner.—**cheap·ly,** *adv.* —**cheap·ness,** *n.*

cheap·en, chē'pən, *v.t.* To make cheap; lower the price of; lower the value of.

cheap·skate, chēp'skāt, *n. Informal.* A stingy person; a person who avoids paying his share of expenses.

cheat, chēt, *v.t.* To deceive; to trick.—*v.i.* To act dishonestly. *Informal.* To be unfaithful to one's mate. —*n.* A deception; a person who cheats; the fraudulent obtaining of someone else's property.

check, chek, *n.* The act of suddenly stopping; an examination or control to evaluate objects or material; a measure to prevent errors or dishonesty; a written order for money drawn on a bank; a bill for food or beverages in a restaurant; a mark put against names or items on going over a list; a ticket for articles or baggage that has been checked; a pattern on cloth resembling the squares of a chessboard; a small crack in paint; a halt by a hockey player in the progress of an opposing player.—*v.t.* To stop the motion of; to restrain; to investigate; to examine for correctness; to leave or accept, as an item, temporarily in a checkroom; to deliver, as baggage, for shipment; to designate with a check mark to indicate an item has been looked over; to decorate with a pattern of squares. —*v.i.* To agree detail for detail; to give up the privilege of starting the betting in a round; to place an opponent's king under direct attack; to halt the progress of a hockey player carrying the puck.—*interj.* A warning that an opponent's king in chess is in danger; all right; I understand. —**check out,** to test for being ready to use; to itemize, charge, and wrap a customer's purchases; to settle one's hotel or motel bill; to sign out, as library books.

check·book, chek'bûk, *n.* A book containing blank bank checks.

check·er, chek'ər, *n.* A small red or black circular piece made of plastic or wood used by the players in a checkers game; one of the divisions of a pattern that consists of squares; a person that checks; *pl. but sing. in constr.,* a game played by two people, each moving his twelve men on a checkerboard.—*v.t.* To mark with little squares, like a chessboard.

check·er·board, chek'ər·bôrd, chek'ər·bôrd, *n.* A board with sixty-four squares of two alternating colors on which checkers or chess are played.

check·ing ac·count, *n.* A bank account established by a depositor for the specified purpose of drawing checks against it.

check·list, chek'list, *n.* A list of names for purpose of comparison, verification or identification: a *checklist* of the birds of a region.

check·mate, chek'māt, *n.* The position of a king in chess when he is in check and cannot release himself, which brings the game to a close; the act of putting the king in this position; defeat.—*v.t.,* **-mat·ed, -mat·ing.** To put in check.

check·out, chek'owt, *n.* A test of readiness for use.

check·point, chek'poynt, *n.* A place where traffic is stopped for inspection and clearance; a known location used by a flier to determine his position.

check·room, chek'room, chek'rûm, *n.* A room where clothing, luggage, or packages are left for safekeeping for a limited time.

check·up, chek'əp, *n.* An examination or test; a physical examination.

ched·dar, ched'ər, *n.* A firm-textured cheese varying in taste from sharp to mild, and in color from dark yellow to white. Also **Ched·dar cheese.**

cheek, chēk, *n.* Either side of the face below the eye and above the mouth; either of two parts forming matching sides of anything. *Informal.* Impudence; a buttock.

cheek·bone, chēk'bōn, *n.* Bony prominence below the eye.

cheek·y, chē'kē, *a.,* **-i·er, -i·est.** *Informal.* Bold; impudent; insolent. —**cheek·i·ly,** *adv.* —**cheek·i·ness,** *n.*

cheer, chēr, *n.* Gladness of feeling or spirits; something which promotes good spirits; food or drink; a shout of acclamation.—*v.t.* To gladden; to encourage, comfort, or make hopeful; to express confidence or approval of with shouts or chants, often with *on.*—*v.i.* To grow cheerful or joyous, often used with *up;* to utter a cheer.

cheer·ful, chēr'fəl, *a.* Having good spirits; willing. —**cheer·ful·ly,** *adv.* —**cheer·ful·ness,** *n.*

cheer·lead·er, chēr'lē·dər, *n.* A person who leads cheers and yells at sporting events and school rallies.

cheer·less, chēr'lis, *a.* Without joy; gloomy. —**cheer·less·ly,** *adv.* —**cheer·less·ness,** *n.*

cheer·y, chēr'ē, *a.,* **-i·er, -i·est.** Showing cheerfulness or good spirits. —**cheer·i·ly,** *adv.* —**cheer·i·ness,** *n.*

cheese, chēz, *n.* The pressed curd of milk prepared in many varieties as food; a mass or cake of this substance.

cheese·burg·er, chēz'bər·gər, *n.* A hamburger with a slice of cheese melted on top of the meat.

cheese·cake, chēz'kāk, *n.* A rich cake- or pie-shaped, custardlike dessert containing cottage and/or cream cheese, sugar, and eggs.

cheese·cloth, chēz′klôth, chēz′kloth, *n.* A light cotton fabric of open texture.

chees·y, chē′zē, *a.,* **-i·er, -i·est.** Of or like cheese. *Informal.* Of poor quality; cheap. **—chees·i·ness,** *n.*

chee·tah, chē′tə, *n.* A cat of southern Asia and Africa that resembles the leopard, and is the fastest animal alive.

chef, shef, *n.* A chief cook of a kitchen; a cook.

chem·i·cal, kem′i·kəl, *n.* A substance produced by or used in a chemical process.—*a.* Of, pertaining to, or concerned with the science or processes of chemistry. **—chem·i·cal·ly,** *adv.*

chem·i·cal en·gi·neer·ing, *n.* Industrial applications of chemistry.

chem·i·cal war·fare, *n.* Warfare using asphyxiating, poisonous, and corrosive gases and oil flames.

che·mise, shə·mēz′, *n.* A woman's loose-fitting, shirtlike undergarment; a short slip.

chem·ist, kem′ist, *n.* One versed in chemistry.

chem·is·try, kem′is·trē, *n.* The scientific study of the composition and interaction of compounds and elements.

chem·o·ther·a·py, kem·ō·ther′ə·pē, *n.* The treatment of disease with chemicals.

che·nille, shə·nēl′, *n.* A fuzzy cord or yarn used in embroidery or fringes; a fabric made with such yarn.

cheque, chek, *n.* Brit. Check.

cher·ish, cher′ish, *v.t.* To hold dear; to treat with tenderness and affection.

che·root, shə·root′, *n.* A cigar which has both ends cut off square.

cher·ry, cher′ē, *n. pl.,* **-ries.** A small round fruit, usually red, with a hard smooth pit; the tree itself; the wood.—*a.* Bright red or cerise in color.

cher·ub, cher′əb, *n. pl.,* **cher·ubs, cher·u·bim,** cher′yə·bim. A winged childlike figure regarded as a guardian of a sacred place and a servant of God; a person having an innocent face, generally chubby and rosy. **—che·ru·bic,** chə·roo′bik, *a.*

cher·vil, chər′vil, *n.* A garden or pot herb of the parsley family.

chess, ches, *n.* A game in which each of two players uses 16 pieces to move offensively and defensively across a checkerboard of 64 squares, with the object of immobilizing the opponent's king, in a maneuver called checkmate. **—chess·man,** *n. pl.,* **-men.**

chest, chest, *n.* That part of the body enclosed by the ribs and breastbone, extending from neck to abdomen; the thorax; a box-like container with a lid, for storing or shipping articles of value.

chest·nut, ches′nət, *n.* The edible nut of a tree of the beech family; the tree itself or its timber; a reddish-brown color. *Informal.* An old joke.

chest·y, ches′tē, *a.,* **-i·er, -i·est.** *Informal.* Having a large chest; puffed up or self-important.

chev·ron, shev′rən, *n.* A V-shaped insignia worn on the sleeve of a military or police uniform to indicate rank.

chew, choo, *v.t.* To crush or grind with the teeth; masticate.—*v.i.* To perform the act of crushing or grinding with the teeth. *Informal.* To use tobacco for chewing. —*n.* The act of chewing; that which is chewed; a portion of tobacco, for chewing. **—chew·er,** *n.*

chew·ing gum, *n.* A preparation of chicle or similar gum, sweetened and flavored, for chewing.

chi·a·ro·scu·ro, kē·är·ə·skyūr′ō, *n.* A painting, sketch, or woodcut using only light and shade; an artist's way of using light and shade. **—chi·a·ro·scu·rist,** *n.*

chic, shēk, shik, *n.* Fashion know-how.—*a.* Smart; sophisticated; exceptionally stylish.

chi·can·er·y, shi·kā′nə·rē, *n. pl.,* **-ies.** Trickery or deception to gain an advantage.

Chi·ca·no, chi·kä′nō, *n.* An American of Mexican descent; a Mexican-American.

chi·chi, shē′shē, *a.* Stylish in a showy way.

chick, chik, *n.* A young chicken; a young bird; a baby. *Informal.* A young woman.

chick·a·dee, chik′ə·dē, *n.* A small North American bird with black, white, and gray feathers, without a crest.

chic·ken, chik′ən, *n.* The common barnyard fowl, and its young; the meat of this fowl; a coward.—*a.* Having no more courage than a chicken; made of or with chicken; sticking to the rules to the point of being petty.

chic·ken·heart·ed, chik′ən·här′tid, *a.* *Informal.* Cowardly; fearful.

chick·en pox, *n.* An acute, contagious, eruptive disease generally appearing in children.

chic·le, chik′əl, *n.* Elastic gum from the sapodilla tree, usual base of chewing gum.

chic·o·ry, chik′ə·rē, *n. pl.,* **-ries.** A perennial, blue-flowered herb with leaves used in salads, and its root used for mixing with coffee or as a coffee substitute.

chide, chīd, *v.t.* **chid·ed** or **chid, chid·ed** or **chid·den, chid·ing.** To scold; to rebuke.—*v.i.* To scold; to find fault.

chief, chēf, *a.* Highest in office, authority, or rank; most important; at the head; leading.—*n.* The person highest in authority; the head or leader. **—chief·ly,** *adv.*

Chief Ex·ec·u·tive, *n.* The President of the United States.

chief jus·tice, *n.* The presiding judge of a court.

Chief Jus·tice of the U.S., *n.* The judge who presides over the U.S. Supreme Court.

chief of state, *n.* The formal head of a country.

chief·tain, chēf′tən, *n.* A leader or commander, esp. of guerrilla forces; a chief, as of an Amer. Indian tribe.

chif·fon, shi·fon′, shif′on, *n.* Any bit of feminine finery; a soft, very thin, transparent fabric.—*a.* Of, like, or made of chiffon; pertaining to a light frothy texture, as in foods containing whipped egg whites.

chif·fo·nier, shif·ə·nēr′, *n.* A cabinet with drawers; a case of drawers, high in proportion to its width.

chi·gnon, shēn′yon, shēn·yən′, *n.* A large roll of hair worn at the back of the head.

chil·blain, chil′blān, *n.* An inflamed sore produced by cold.—*v.t.* To produce chilblains on.

child, chīld, *n. pl.,* **chil·dren,** chil′drən. A son or a daughter, esp. of an age between infancy and youth; a very young person of either sex; one of crude or immature knowledge, experience, judgment, or attainments.

child·bear·ing, chīld′bār·ing, *n.* The act of producing or bringing forth children; parturition.

child·birth, chīld′bərth, *n.* The act of bringing forth a child.

child·hood, chīld′hůd, *n.* The state of being a child; the time in which a person is classed as a child.

child·ish, chīl′dish, *a.* Of or belonging to a child or to childhood; like a child; trifling; silly; weak. **—child·ish·ly,** *adv.*

child·like, chīld′līk, *a.* Resembling a child or that which belongs to children.

chil·i, chil·li, chil·e, chil′ē, *n. pl.,* **chil·ies, chil·lies, chil·es.** A Spanish-American dish of beans and meat flavored with chili powder; hot pepper.

chil·i con car·ne, chil′ē kən kär′nē, *n.* A variation of a Mexican dish popular in the U.S., consisting of ground meat, chopped peppers, chili powder, and kidney beans.

chill, chil, *n.* Coldness, esp. a moderate but penetrating coldness, as in the air; a sensation of cold.—*v.i.* To become cold; be seized with a chill.—*v.t.* To affect with

---

cold; make chilly.—*a.* Cold; tending to cause shivering; affected by cold; shivering with cold. —**chill·ing·ly,** *adv.*

chill·y, chil′ē, *a.,* **-i·er, -i·est.** Producing a sensation of cold; so cold as to cause shivering; feeling cold; sensitive to cold. —**chill·i·ly,** *adv.* —**chill·i·ness,** *n.*

chime, chīm, *n.* The sound of bells or musical instruments; a set of bells, tuned to a musical scale.

chime, chīm, *v.i.* To sound in rhythm or harmony; to agree; to suit; to express agreement, often with *in* with: to *chime in with* one's personal opinions.—*v.t.* To cause to sound as a set of bells. —**chim·er,** *n.*

chi·me·ra, chi·mae·ra, ki·mēr′ə, kī·mēr′ə, *n.* (*Cap.* or *l.c.*) An unreal creature of the imagination; a phantom.

chi·mer·ic, ki·mer′ik, ki·mēr′ik, kī·mer′ik, kī·mēr′ik, *a.* Unreal; imaginary; wildly fanciful. Also **chi·mer·i·cal.** —**chi·mer·i·cal·ly,** *adv.* —**chi·mer·i·cal·ness,** *n.*

chim·ney, chim′nē, *n.* A construction having a passage for the smoke of a fire or furnace to escape to the open air; a tall glass to surround the flame of a lamp; any chimney-like structure.

chim·ney sweep, *n.* One whose occupation is to clean chimneys of soot.

chim·pan·zee, chim·pan·zē′, chim·pan′zē, *n.* An anthropoid ape of equatorial Africa, smaller and less ferocious than the gorilla. Also **chimp.**

chin, chin, *n.* The lower extremity of the face, below the mouth; the point of the under jaw.—*v.t.,* **chinned, chin·ning.** To bring up to the chin; to bring one's chin up to a horizontal bar. *Informal.* To talk.

chi·na, chī′nə, *n.* A kind of earthenware made in China, or in imitation of that made there; porcelain.

chin·chil·la, chin·chil′ə, *n.* A rodent of the South American continent, which produces a fine pearly-gray fur; the fur of the chinchilla.

chink, chingk, *n.* A cleft, rent, or fissure of greater length than breadth.—*v.t.* To cause to open or part and form a fissure; to make chinks in; to fill up chinks in.—*v.i.* To crack; to open.

chi·no, chē′no, *n. pl.,* **-nos.** A fabric of heavy cotton twill, usu. used in military uniforms; *pl.,* slacks or trousers made of this fabric.

chi·noi·se·rie, shēn·woz·ə·rē′, shēn·woz′ə·rē, *n.* A form of ornamentation characterized by intricate patterns; an object decorated with this ornamentation.

chintz·y, chint′sē, *a.,* **-i·er, -i·est.** Cheap; stingy.

chip, chip, *v.t.,* **chipped, chip·ping.** To cut away in small pieces with a tool.—*v.i.* To break off in small pieces.—*n.* A small, thin piece cut or broken off.

chip in, chip, *v.t. Informal.* To give money or help for a common purpose.

chip·munk, chip′mungk, *n.* A small ground squirrel.

chipped beef, *n.* Smoked dried beef, sliced very thin and often served in a cream sauce.

chip·per, chip′ər, *a.* Cheerful; sprightly.

chips, chipz, *n. pl.* British french fries.

chi·rog·ra·pher, kī·rog′rə·fər, *n.* A person who studies handwriting; one who exercises or studies the art of writing.

chi·rog·ra·phy, kī·rog′rə·fē, *n.* Handwriting.

chi·rop·o·dist, ki·rop′ə·dist, kī·rop′ə·dist, *n.* One who treats ailments and irregularities of the feet; podiatrist. —**chi·rop·o·dy,** *n.*

chi·ro·prac·tic, kī′rə·prak·tik, *n.* Treatment of diseases by stretching or bending the spine.

chi·ro·prac·tor, kī′rə·prak·tər, *n.* One who practices chiropractic.

chirp, chərp, *v.i.* To make short, sharp sounds.—*n.* A short, shrill sound made by birds and insects.

chis·el, chiz′əl, *n.* A cutting tool with a sharp edge at the end of a strong blade, for shaping wood, stone, or metal.—*v.t.,* **-eled, -elled, -el·ing, -el·ling.** To cut or shape with a chisel. *Informal.* To cheat.—*v.i.* To work with a chisel.

chis·el·er, chis·el·ler, *n.* One who chisels, as a stone carver; one who cheats.

chit, chit, *n.* A short note or memo, esp. proof that a small amount of money is owed.

chit, chit, *n.* A young person, esp. a girl: used in contempt.

chit·chat, chit′chat, *n.* Friendly, informal talk.—*v.i.* To carry on a friendly conversation.

chi·tin, kī′tin, *n.* The substance covering the wings of insects. —**chi·tin·ous,** kī′tin·əs, *a.*

chit·ter·ling, chit·ling, chit·lin, chit′ər·ling, chit′lən, *n. pl.,* **chit·ter·lings, chit·lings, chit·lins.** Part of the small intestines of pigs, fried for food; generally used in the plural.

chiv·al·ry, shiv′əl·rē, *n. pl.,* **-ries.** The qualities of bravery, honor, and courtesy of knights. —**chiv·al·ric,** *a.* —**chiv·al·rous,** *a.* —**chiv·al·rous·ly,** *adv.* —**chiv·al·rous·ness,** *n.*

chive, chīv, *n.* A plant whose leaves are used to season cooking.

chlo·rine, klōr′ēn, klôr′ēn, *n.* A chemical element used for cleaning and disinfecting.

chlo·ro·form, klōr′ə·fôrm, klôr′ə·fôrm, *n.* A sweetish smelling liquid used as an anesthetic.

chlo·ro·phyll, chlo·ro·phyl, klōr′ə·fil, klôr′ə·fil, *n.* The green coloring matter in plants that makes food for the plant when in sunlight.

chock, chok, *n.* A block or wedge preventing movement.

chock-full, chok′fûl′, *a.* As full as possible; crammed.

choc·o·late, chôk′lit, chok′lit, *n.* Ground cocoa seeds mixed with sugar; a beverage made by dissolving chocolate in boiling water or milk; a candy made of chocolate or dipped in chocolate.—*a.* Made of chocolate.

choice, choys, *n.* The act of choosing; selection; the best part of anything.—*a.* Carefully selected. —**choice·ly,** *adv.* —**choice·ness,** *n.*

choir, kwir, *n.* A group of singers, esp. in a church. —*v.t., v.i.* To sing together.

choir·boy, kwīr′boy, *n.* A boy member of a church choir.

choke, chōk′, *v.t.,* **choked, chok·ing.** To stop the breath of, by squeezing the windpipe; to strangle.—*v.i.* To suffer strangling; to be clogged.—*n.* The act or sound of choking; the valve that cuts off the air to a gasoline engine.

chok·er, chō′kər, *n.* A high, close-fitting collar; a tight necklace.

chol·er, kol′ər, *n.* Anger; irritable disposition.

chol·er·a, kol′ər·ə, *n.* A painful disease of the stomach and intestines.

chol·er·ic, kol′ər·ik, kə·ler′ik, *a.* Quick-tempered.

cho·les·te·rol, kə·les′tə·rol, kə·les′tə·rōl, kə·les′tə·rôl, *n.* A fatty substance found in animal tissue, thought to be what clogs blood vessels.

choose, chooz, *v.t.,* **chose, cho·sen, choos·ing.** To select from a number, or in preference to another or others; to pick out.—*v.i.* To make a choice.

choos·y, choo′zē, *a.,* **-i·er, -i·est.** Hard to please.

chop, chop, *v.t.,* **chopped, chop·ping.** To cut with a quick, heavy blow.—*v.i.* To take away the power or amount of, used with *down;* move suddenly or violently.—*n.* A cutting blow; a slice of mutton, veal, or pork, usually one containing a rib.

chop·per, chop′ər, *n.* A short ax with a large blade. *Informal.* A helicopter.

chop·pi·ness, chop′ē·nes, *n.* Being not regular in shape or style, as broken waves.

chop·py, chop′ē, *a.,* **-pi·er, -pi·est.** Shifting suddenly or irregularly; moving in short, broken waves.

chop·sticks, chop′stiks, *n.* A pair of small sticks used by many Orientals to eat with.

chop su·ey, chop′soo′ē, *n.* A mixed dish consisting of fowl or other meat cut into bits with vegetables and seasoning, in a gravy or sauce.

cho·ral, kōr′əl, *a.* Of or sung by a chorus or a choir.—*n.* A chorale. —**cho·ral·ly,** *adv.*

cho•rale, kə•ral′, kō•ral′, *n.* A hymn, esp. a simple sacred tune.

chord, kôrd, *n.* A combination of three or more tones sounded simultaneously. —**chord•al**, *a.*

chord, kôrd, *n.* A string of a musical instrument; a feeling or emotion; the part of a straight line between two of its intersections with a curve.

chore, chôr, chōr, *n.* A task; a small odd job; a difficult or unpleasant task.

cho•re•a, kô•rē′ə, kō•rē′ə, *n.* St. Vitus' dance; convulsive motions of the limbs.

cho•re•og•ra•phy, kōr•ē•og′rə•fē, *n.* The art of designing and arranging ballet and other dance compositions; ballet dancing. —**cho•re•og•ra•pher**, *n.* —**cho•re•o•graph•ic**, kōr•ē•ə•graf′ik, *a.*

cho•ric, kōr′ik, *a.* Of or for a chorus.

chor•is•ter, kor′i•stər, *n.* A singer in a choir; esp. a male singer in a church choir; a choir boy; a choir leader.

chor•tle, chôr′təl, *v.i.*, **-tled**, **-tling**. To chuckle or utter with glee.

cho•rus, kōr′əs, *n. pl.*, **-rus•es**. A song in which the company joins the singer, or the singing of the company with the singer; a dancing and singing ensemble of girls, men, or both in a show; a union of voices in general; a composition in parts sung by many voices; the whole body of vocalists other than soloists.—*v.t.*, *v.i.*, **-rused**, **-rus•ing**. To sing in chorus; to speak in concert.

chos•en, chō′zən, *a.* Selected from a number; preferred.

chow, *n.* A Chinese breed of dog, of medium size with a thick coat of brown, black, or red hair. *Informal.* Food. Also **chow chow**.

chow•der, chow′dər, *n.* A kind of thick soup or stew made of clams or fish with potatoes, onions, etc.

chow mein, chow•mān′, *n.* A stew usually served over fried noodles and consisting of pieces of meat and a variety of vegetables.

chrism, kriz′əm, *n.* A consecrated oil used by certain churches in the rites of baptism, confirmation, etc.

Christ, krīst, *n.* The name given to Jesus of Nazareth by the Christian world as the one fulfilling the prophecy in the Old Testament of a Messiah.

chris•ten, kris′ən, *v.t.* To receive into the Christian church by baptism; baptize; give a name to at baptism; name and dedicate. *Informal.* Use for the first time. —**chris•ten•ing**, kris′ə•ning, kris′ning, *n.*

Chris•ten•dom, kris′ən•dəm, *n.* Christian lands; all Christians.

Chris•tian, kris′chən, *n.* One who believes in the religion of Christ and whose behavior exemplifies His teachings; one who belongs to a Christian church.—*a.* Pertaining to or believing in Christ or Christianity. *Informal.* Humane; decent; respectable.

Chris•ti•an•i•ty, kris•chē•an′ə•tē, *n. pl.*, **-ties**. The religion of Christians; the doctrines taught by Christ; Christian practice or character; Christendom.

Chris•tian•ize, kris′chə•nīz, *v.t.*, **-ized**, **-iz•ing**. To convert to Christianity.

Chris•tian name, *n.* A baptismal or first name.

Chris•tian Sci•ence, *n.* A religion and system of healing, founded about 1866 by Mary Baker Eddy. —**Chris•tian Sci•en•tist**, *n.*

Christ•like, krīst′līk, *a.* Of or like Christ; showing the spirit of Christ.

Christ•mas, kris′məs, *n.* The 25th day of December, annually celebrated in memory of the birth of Christ.

Christ•mas•tide, kris′məs•tīd, *n.* The season of Christmas.

Christ•mas tree, *n.* An evergreen or artificial tree or facsimile, decorated for Christmas.

chro•mate, krō′māt, *n.* A salt of chromic acid.

chro•mat•ic, krō•mat′ik, *a.* Of color or colors. *Mus.*

Involving or progressing by semitones, and not by the regular intervals of the diatonic scale. —**chro•mat•i•cal•ly**, *adv.*

chro•mat•ics, krō•mat′iks, *n.* The science of colors.

chro•ma•tic scale, *n. Mus.* A scale made up of thirteen successive semitones.

chro•ma•tin, krō′mə•tin, *n.* The easily stained part of a chromosome which is believed to carry the genes.

chrome, krōm, *n.* Chromium, esp. as the source of various pigments; something plated with chromium, esp. certain parts of an automobile.

chro•mic, krō′mik, *a.* Of or containing chromium.

chro•mic ac•id, *n.* An acid, known in the form of salts and in solution.

chro•mi•um, krō′mē•əm, *n.* A lustrous, hard, metallic element, resistant to corrosion, and widely used for making alloys and pigments.

chro•mo, krō′mō, *n. pl.*, **-mos**. A chromolithograph.

chro•mo•lith•o•graph, krō•mō•lith′ə•graf, krō•mō•lith′ə•gräf, *n.* A picture printed in colors by means of the lithographic process. —**chro•mo•li•thog•ra•pher**, krō•mō•li•thog′rə•fər, *n.* —**chro•mo•lith•o•graph•ic**, *a.*

chro•mo•some, krō′mə•sōm, *n.* One of the rod- or thread-shaped bodies containing chromatin which carry the genes and are present in all the cell nuclei of plants and animals.

chro•mo•sphere, krō′mə•sfēr, *n.* A reddish, gaseous layer surrounding the sun above the photosphere.

chron•ic, kron′ik, *a.* Long-lasting or recurring frequently; of a disease of long duration or repeated occurrences; constant. —**chron•i•cal•ly**, *adv.*

chron•i•cle, kron′i•kəl, *n.* A detailed record of facts or events set down in the order of occurrence.—*v.t.*, **-cled**, **-cling**. To record in a chronicle or in the style of a chronicle. —**chron•i•cler**, *n.*

chron•o•log•i•cal, kron•ə•loj′ə•kəl, *a.* Containing an account of events in the order of time; according to the order of time. —**chron•o•log•i•cal•ly**, *adv.*

chro•nol•o•gy, krə•nol′ə•jē, *n. pl.*, **-gies**. The science of ascertaining the proper sequence of historical events; an arrangement according to time sequence; a reference work organized according to the time sequence of past events. —**chro•nol•o•gist**, **chro•nol•o•ger**.

chro•nom•e•ter, krə•nom′ə•tər, *n.* Any instrument that measures time, esp. a highly precise timepiece. —**chron•o•met•ric**, kron•ə•met′rik, *a.*

chrys•a•lis, kris′ə•lis, *n. pl.*, **-lis•es, chry•sal•i•des**, kri•sal′ə•dēz. The encased form assumed by butterflies, moths, and other insects before they arrive at their final state; a pupa; anything uncompleted or developing.

chry•san•the•mum, kri•san′thə•məm, *n.* Any of several composite plants known for their showy autumnal flowers; the flower of such a plant.

chrys•o•lite, kris′ə•līt, *n.* A semiprecious stone, varying from yellow to green; olivine.

chub, chəb, *n. pl.*, **chubs** or, esp. collectively, **chub**. A common fish of Europe, related to the carp; any of various American fishes.

chub•by, chəb′ē, *a.*, **-bi•er**, **-bi•est**. Round and fat; plump. —**chub•bi•ness**, *n.*

chuck, chək, *v.t.* To strike, or give an affectionate tap; to throw; toss. *Informal.* To quit.

chuck, chək, *n.* Cut of beef between the neck and the shoulder; a clamp, block, or the like, as on a lathe, for holding a boring tool, or a piece of work while it is being shaped.

chuck•full, chək′fûl′, *a.* Chock-full.

chuck•le, chək′əl, *v.i.*, **-led**, **-ling**. To laugh in an easy manner, with satisfaction; to cluck, as a fowl.—*n.* A quiet laugh.

chuck wag•on, *n.* A wagon that carries food and

---

a- hat, fāte, fāre, fäther; **e-** met, mē; **i-** pin, pīne; **o-** not, nōte, ôrb, moove (move), boy, pownd; **u-** cūbe, bûll, tûk (took); **ch-** chin; **th-** thick, then; **zh-** vizhon (vision); **ə-** əgo, takən, pencəl, lemən, bərd (bird).

cooking equipment.

chug, chəg, *n.* A short, dull, coughlike noise.—*v.i.* To make such a sound.

chuk·ker, chuk·kar, chək′ər, chə·kär′, *n.* One of the periods of play in polo.

chum, chəm, *n.* A close companion; a bosom friend; a roommate.—*v.i.* To be someone's chum.

chum·my, chəm′ē, *a.,* **-mi·er, -mi·est.** *Informal.* Friendly; intimate. —**chum·mi·ly,** *adv.*

chump, chəmp, *n.* A short, thick, heavy piece of wood. *Informal.* A blockhead; dolt.

chunk, chəngk, *n.* A thick mass or lump. *Informal.* A thick-set, strong person or beast. —**chunk·y,** *a.,* **-i·er, -i·est.**

church, chərch, *n.* An edifice for public, esp. Christian, worship; the worship or religious service; Christians collectively; a group of Christians professing the same creed; a denomination; a congregation; the ecclesiastical organization; the clerical order or profession.—*a.* Of a church. —**church·li·ness,** *n.* **church·ly,** *a.*

church·go·er, chərch′gō·ər, *n.* One who goes to church, esp. habitually or frequently. —**church·go·ing,** *n., a.*

church·man, chərch′mən, *n. pl.,* **-men.** A clergyman; an adherent of the church.

Church of Eng·land, *n.* The national church of England, as established by law.

church·war·den, chərch′wôr·dən, *n.* A lay officer in an Anglican church whose duties include the management of the church property and legal representation of the parish. *Informal.* A clay tobacco-pipe with a very long stem.

church·yard, chərch′yärd, *n.* The yard adjoining a church, often used as a graveyard.

churl, chərl, *n.* A rustic; a peasant; a rude, surly man.

churl·ish, chər′lish, *a.* Rude; surly.

churn, chərn, *n.* A vessel in which cream or milk is shaken in order to separate the fatty parts to make butter.—*v.t.* To stir or agitate (milk or cream) in order to make into butter; to make, as butter, in a churn; to agitate with violence.—*v.i.* To move in an agitated manner; to work a churn.

churr, chər, *n.* A whirring noise made by some birds and insects.—*v.i.* To make this sound.

chute, shoot, *n.* A steep descent, as in a river; a rapid; an inclined channel, trough, or shaft, for sliding or dropping things to a lower level; a steep slope for tobogganing. *Informal.* A parachute.

chut·ney, chət′nē, *n.* An East Indian relish made of citrus fruit, raisins, and spices. Also **chut·nee.**

chutz·pah, hûts′pə, *n. Informal.* Gall; impudence.

chyme, kīm, *n.* The semiliquid mass into which food is converted by gastric secretion during digestion.

ci·bo·ri·um, si·bôr′ē·əm, si·bôr′ē·əm, *n. pl.,* **-ri·a.** A permanent canopy placed over an altar; a vessel for the consecrated bread or wafers of the Eucharist.

ci·ca·da, si·kā′də, *n. pl.,* **-das, -dae, -dē.** A large winged insect, the male of which can produce a shrill noise.

cic·a·trix, sik′ə·triks, *n. pl.,* **-tri·ces, -trī′sēz.** A scar. *Bot.* A scar left on the branch by a fallen leaf.

cic·a·trize, sik′ə·trīz, *v.t., v.i.,* **-trized, -triz·ing.** To heal by forming a scar.

cic·e·ro·ne, sis·ə·rō′nē, *Ital.* chē·chä·rō′nä, *n.* A guide for tourists.

ci·der, sī′dər, *n.* A drink prepared from apple juice; apple juice used to make vinegar.

ci·gar, si·gär′, *n.* A small, tight roll of tobacco leaves prepared for smoking.

cig·a·rette, cig·a·ret, sig·ə·ret′, sig′ə·ret, *n.* A roll of finely cut tobacco for smoking, enclosed in thin paper.

cil·i·a, sil′ē·ə, *n. pl.* of **cil·i·um.** Eyelashes; small, generally microscopic, hairlike processes, esp. those growing out from animal membranes.

cil·i·ar·y, sil′ē·er·ē, *a.* Of or like cilia.

cil·i·ate, sil′ē·it, *n.* Any of a class of one-celled animals, covered or partly covered with cilia.

cinch, sinch, *n.* A strong girth for a saddle or pack horse. *Informal.* A firm hold or grip on anything; something sure or easy.—*v.t.* To gird with a cinch; bind firmly. *Informal.* To seize on or make sure of.

cin·cho·na, sin·kō′nə, *n.* Any of the trees or shrubs of a genus native in the Andes, cultivated for their bark, which yields quinine.

cinc·ture, singk′chər, *n.* A belt; girdle; that which rings; enclosure.

cin·der, sin′dər, *n.* A burned-out piece of coal, wood, etc. (*often pl.*); *pl.,* any residue of combustion; ashes.

cin·e·ma, sin′ə·mə, *n. pl.,* **-mas.** A motion-picture theater; a motion picture; with the, motion pictures collectively. —**cin·e·mat·ic,** sin·ə·mat′ik, *a.*

cin·e·mat·o·graph, sin·ə·mat′ə·graf, *n.* An apparatus for projecting motion pictures on a screen; the camera for taking motion pictures.—*v.t.* To reproduce by a cinematograph. —**cin·e·ma·tog·ra·pher,** sin·ə·mə·tog′rə·fər, *n.* —**cin·e·ma·tog·ra·phy,** sin·ə·mə·tog′rə·fē, *n.*

cin·e·rar·i·um, sin·ə·rār′ē·əm, *n. pl.,* **-i·a.** A place for depositing the ashes of the dead after cremation.

cin·na·bar, sin′ə·bär, *n.* Red mercuric sulfide, the chief ore of mercury; red mercuric sulfide, when used as a pigment; the color vermilion.

cin·na·mon, sin′ə·mən, *n.* Inner bark of a tree of the laurel family, native to tropical Asia, used as a spice or in medicine; the spice; the tree having this bark; a reddish brown.

cinque·foil, singk′foyl, *n. Arch.* An ornament resembling five leaves about a common center; the name of various plants of the rose family, having leaves with five lobes.

ci·on, sī′ən, *n.* Scion; a cutting.

ci·pher, sī·fər, *n.* The numerical character 0, or nothing; any Arabic numeral; some unimportant person or thing; a monogram; a kind of secret writing which follows a prearranged system; a communication written in code; a key to a code.—*v.i.* To use figures; to practice arithmetic.—*v.t.* To figure mathematically; to write in secret characters.

cir·ca, sər′kə, *adv., prep.* About; used esp. in giving approximate dates: *circa* 1550.

cir·ca·di·an, sər·kə·dē′ən, *a.* Having to do with cycles of biological rhythm that recur every day.

cir·cle, sər′kəl, *n.* A plane figure formed by a single curved line, every point of which is equally distant from a point within it; the line bounding such a figure; a thing in circular form, as a ring, halo, or diadem; a tier of seats in a theater or the like; a ring; a cycle; a series or process which returns to its starting point and may repeat the entire cycle; a sphere of influence; a coterie; a group having a common tie; a round body; an orb; the orbit of a heavenly body.—*v.t., v.i.,* **-cled, -cling.** To enclose in or move in a circle; surround; revolve. —**cir·cler,** *n.*

cir·clet, sər′klit, *n.* A little circle; a ring; a circular ornament, esp. one for the head.

cir·cuit, sər′kit, *n.* The act of going or moving around; a round; a periodical journey from place to place to perform certain duties, as of judges or ministers; the persons making such a journey; the route followed or district covered by such a journey; the line bounding any space; the distance around a space; the space enclosed; the complete path of an electric current; a theater chain in which productions are shown in turn; a league.—*v.t., v.i.* To make a circuit of; go in a circuit.

cir·cu·i·tous, sər·kū′ə·təs, *a.* Roundabout; not direct. —**cir·cu·i·tous·ly,** *adv.* —**cir·cu·i·tous·ness,** *n.*

cir·cuit rid·er, *n.* A traveling minister, who preaches at churches along a circuit.

cir·cu·lar, sər′kyə·lər, *a.* In the form of a circle; round; passing over or forming a circle, circuit, or round; roundabout; indirect; pertaining to a circle. —*n.* A letter, notice, or advertisement printed for general distribution. —**cir·cu·lar·i·ty,** sər·kyə·lar′ə·

tē, n.

cir·cu·lar·ize, sər/kyə·lə·rīz, v.t., -ized, -iz·ing. To send circulars to; to make circular or into a circular. —**cir·cu·lar·i·za·tion,** sər·kyə·lə·rə·zā/shən, n.

cir·cu·la·tion, sər·kyə·lā/shən, n. The act of moving or flowing in a course leading back to the starting point; the continuous movement of blood from the heart to the arteries and veins and back to the heart; the act of passing from place to place or from person to person; the extent and amount of distribution of periodicals; coins, notes, and bills in use as money; number of books and other library materials in use. —**cir·cu·late,** sər/kyə·lāt, v.i., v.t., -lat·ed, -lat·ing. —**cir·cu·la·tive,** sər/kyə·lā·tiv, a. —**cir·cu·la·tor,** sər/kyə·lā·tor, n.—**cir·cu·la·to·ry,** sər/kyə·lə·tôr·e, a.

cir·cum·am·bi·ent, sər·kəm·am/bē·ənt, a. Surrounding; encompassing.

cir·cum·cise, sər/kəm·siz, v.t., -cised, -cis·ing. To cut off the foreskin of the penis in males, or the clitoris in females. —**cir·cum·cis·er,** n. —**cir·cum·ci·sion,** sər·kəm·sizh/ən, n.

cir·cum·fer·ence, sər·kəm/fər·əns, n. The line that bounds a circle or other figures and objects; periphery; the distance around. —**cir·cum·fer·en·tial,** sər·kəm·fə·ren/shəl, a.

cir·cum·flex, sər/kəm·fleks, n. A mark, ∧ or ⌃ or ∼, to indicate some pronunciation.—a. Of, having, or pronounced with a circumflex; winding or bending around.

cir·cum·flu·ent, sər·kəm/floo·ənt, a. Flowing around; encompassing.

cir·cum·fuse, sər·kəm·fūz/, v.t., -fused, -fus·ing. To pour around; diffuse; to surround; suffuse. —**cir·cum·fu·sion,** n.

cir·cum·lo·cu·tion, sər·kəm·lō·kū/shən, n. The use of more words than necessary to express an idea. —**cir·cum·lo·cu·to·ry,** sər·kəm·lok/yə·tôr·e, a.

cir·cum·nav·i·gate, sər·kəm·nav/ə·gāt, v.t., -gat·ed, -gat·ing. To sail around. —**cir·cum·nav·i·ga·tion,** sər·kəm·nav·ə·gā/shən, n. —**cir·cum·nav·i·ga·tor,** n.

cir·cum·scribe, sər/kəm·skrib, v.t., -scribed, -scrib·ing. To draw a line around; encircle or surround; enclose within bounds; limit or confine; mark off or define. Geom. To draw a figure around (another figure) so as to touch as many points as possible without intersecting; to enclose another figure in this manner. —**cir·cum·scrib·er,** n. —**cir·cum·scrip·tion,** sər·kəm·skrip/shən, n. —**cir·cum·scrip·tive,** a.

cir·cum·spect, sər/kəm·spekt, a. Wary; prudent; cautious.

cir·cum·stance, sər/kəm·stans, n. A condition which accompanies, determines, or modifies a fact or event; a matter of secondary importance; a particular or detail; an incident or occurrence; usu. pl., the existing condition or state of affairs; pl., the financial condition of a person.

cir·cum·stan·tial, sər·kəm·stan/shəl, a. Based on other than absolute evidence; pertaining to conditions of material welfare; of the nature of a circumstance; secondary; incidental; giving circumstances; detailed; particular. —**cir·cum·stan·ti·al·i·ty,** sər·kəm·stan·shē·al/ə·tē, n.

cir·cum·stan·ti·ate, sər·kəm·stan/shē·āt, v.t., -at·ed, -at·ing. To confirm by circumstances; to describe in full detail. —**cir·cum·stan·ti·a·tion,** sər·kəm·stan·shē·ā/shən, n.

cir·cum·vent, sər·kəm·vent/, v.t. To avoid, as defeat, by cunning; to outwit; to trick into a trap; to go around; to gain advantage over by artfulness, etc. —**cir·cum·ven·tion,** n. —**cir·cum·ven·tive,** a. —**cir·cum·ven·tor,** n.

cir·cus, sər/kəs, n. pl., -cus·es. A traveling show of acrobats, clowns, wild animals, etc.; a performance of such a show; an area, often tented, for such a show; in ancient Rome, a circular or oval arena surrounded by tiers of seats; or public entertainment held in such. Informal. Someone or something hilariously funny.

cir·rho·sis, si·rō/sis, n. A disease marked by excessive formation of connective tissue in the liver. —**cir·rhot·ic,** si·rot/ik, a.

cir·rus, sir/əs, n. pl., cir·ri, sir/ī. A thin fleecy cloud at very high altitudes, consisting of minute ice crystals.

cis·tern, sis/tərn, n. A reservoir or receptacle for holding water; a space containing lymph; a sac.

cit·a·del, sit/ə·dəl, sit/ə·del, n. A fortress or stronghold, esp. one commanding a city; a refuge.

cite, sīt, v.t., cit·ed, cit·ing. To call upon officially to appear in court; to summon or rouse to action; to quote, as a passage, author, or book; to refer to in support or confirmation; mention in a report, as for courageous conduct. —**ci·ta·tion,** si·tā/shən, n.

cith·a·ra, sith/ə·rə, n. An ancient Greek stringed instrument resembling the lyre.

cit·i·zen, sit/ə·zən, n. A native or naturalized member of a state or nation; an inhabitant of a city or town; a civilian. —**cit·i·zen·ship,** n.

cit·i·zen·ry, sit/ə·zən·rē, n. pl., -ries. Citizens as a group.

cit·rate, sit/rāt, n. A salt of citric acid.

cit·ric, sit/rik, a. Derived from lemons, citrons, etc.

cit·ric a·cid, n. The acid derived from lemons and similar fruits or obtained synthetically, used for flavoring, medicine, etc.

cit·ron, sit/rən, n. A pale yellow, thick-skinned fruit resembling the lemon, but larger and less acid; the tree this fruit grows on; the candied rind of the fruit, used esp. in fruitcake.

cit·ron·el·la, sit·rə·nel/ə, n. A fragrant grass of southern Asia, the source of an oil used in making insect repellent, liniment, perfume, and soap.

cit·rus, sit/rəs, n. pl., cit·rus, cit·rus·es. The genus of trees and shrubs bearing grapefruit, lemons, oranges, and similar fruit.

cit·rus, sit/rəs, cit·rous, sit/rəs, a. Pertaining to this genus, or esp. its fruits.

cit·tern, sit/ərn, n. An instrument somewhat resembling a lute, popular in the Renaissance. Also **cith·er, cith·ern,** sith/ər, sith/ərn.

cit·y, sit/ē, n. pl., cit·ies. A large and important population center. U.S. An incorporated town usually governed by a mayor and aldermen; the inhabitants of a city collectively.—a. Pertaining to a city.

cit·y hall, n. A building containing offices for those who work for the city government; the city government.

cit·y man·ag·er, n. A skilled administrator appointed by the city council to manage a city's government.

cit·y-state, sit/ē·stāt, n. An autonomous city and its dependent territories.

civ·et, siv/it, n. A strong-smelling substance taken from a gland of the civet cats, used in perfumery; a civet cat or its fur.

civ·et cat, n. Any of several meat-eating mammals native to Africa and southern Asia.

civ·ic, siv/ik, a. Pertaining to a city, a citizen, or citizenship.

civ·ics, siv/iks, n. The science of the rights and duties of citizens, and of civic affairs.

civ·il, siv/əl, a. Relating to the community, or to the policy and government of a state; pertaining to or happening among citizens; not ecclesiastical or military; pertaining to individual rights of citizens, esp. to legal proceedings in defense of such rights; civilized; courteous; polite. —**civ·il·ly,** adv.

civ·il dis·o·be·di·ence, n. Noncompliance with certain civil laws, esp. by means of passive resistance

---

a- hat, fāte, fāre, fäther; **e-** met, mē; **i-** pin, pīne; **o-** not, nōte, ôrb, moove (move), boy, pownd; **u-** cūbe, bŭll, tŭk (took); **ch-** chin; **th-** thick, ŧhen; **zh-** vizhon (vision); **ə-** əgo, takən, pencəl, lemən, bərd (bird).

for the purpose of protesting and publicizing some injustice, inequality, etc.

civ·il en·gi·neer, *n.* An engineer skilled in the design, construction, and maintenance of bridges, roads, and related public works. **—civ·il en·gi·neer·ing,** *n.*

ci·vil·ian, si·vil′yən, *n.* One not in military life.—*a.* Relating to civilians.

ci·vil·i·ty, sə·vil′ə·tē, *n. pl.,* **-ties.** Politeness, or an act of politeness; courtesy.

civ·i·li·za·tion, siv·ə·lə·zā′shən, *n.* The state of human society marked by an advanced stage of social development; the people who have reached this state; comforts made possible by such a state; the act of civilizing or becoming civilized; the culture of a definite period: Roman *civilization.*

civ·i·lize, siv′ə·līz, *v.t.,* **-lized, -liz·ing.** To bring out of a savage state; introduce order and civic organization among; to refine and enlighten.

civ·il law, *n.* That division of law dealing with the interpretation and preservation of private and civil rights.

civ·il lib·er·ties, *n. pl.* Those political guarantees a person is legally free to practice without government interference.

civ·il rights, *n. pl.* (*Often cap.*) Rights to which an individual is lawfully entitled by virtue of his citizenship, esp. those rights safeguarded by the 13th and 14th Amendments to the Constitution.

civ·il serv·ice, *n.* The branches of the public service that are not military, naval, legislative, or judicial. **—civ·il serv·ant,** *n.*

civ·il war, *n.* A war between the people of the same state or country.

clab·ber, klab′ər, *n.* Milk which has turned sour and thick.—*v.i.* Of milk, to become thick in souring.

clack, klak, *v.i.* To make a sudden sharp noise; to rattle; to prattle or chatter.—*v.t.* To cause to make a sharp, short sound; to blab.—*n.* A sharp, abrupt sound; prattle.

clad, klad, *a.* Clothed; decked; adorned.

claim, klām, *v.t.* To ask or seek to obtain by virtue of authority or right; assert a right to; demand as due; require; maintain.—*n.* A demand of a right; an assertion which is open to challenge; a right to demand; a just title to anything; the thing claimed, as a piece of public land staked out. **—claim·a·ble,** *a.* **—claim·ant, claim·er,** *n.*

clair·voy·ance, klār·voy′əns, *n.* A power by which a person discerns objects concealed from sight; intuitive knowledge. **—clair·voy·ant,** *a.*

clam, klam, *n.* Any of certain edible bivalvular shellfish. *Informal.* A closemouthed person.—*v.i.,* **clammed, clam·ming.** To dig for clams.

clam·bake, klam′bāk, *n.* A picnic at which clams are baked. *Informal.* A raucous gathering, esp. a political rally.

clam·ber, klam′bər, *v.i., v.t.* To climb, using both feet and hands; climb with difficulty.—*n.* A clambering.

clam·my, klam′ē, *a.,* **-mi·er, -mi·est.** Soft and damp; cool and moist. **—clam·mi·ly,** *adv.* **—clam·mi·ness,** *n.*

clam·or, klam′ər, *n.* A loud outcry; a forceful complaint or urgent demand; any loud and continued noise; a din.—*v.t.* To utter in a loud voice; to prevail upon by clamor.—*v.i.* To make a clamor. **—clam·or·ous,** *a.*

clamp, klamp, *n.* A device that can hold objects together; a vise.—*v.t.* To fasten with clamps; to fix a clamp on.—**clamp down,** *Informal.* To become more strict.

clan, klan, *n.* A number of families or households claiming descent from a common ancestor; any group of related persons. **—clan·nish,** *a.*

clan·des·tine, klan·des′tin, *a.* Secret; private.

clang, klang, *n.* A loud, ringing, metallic sound.—*v.i., v.t.* To make or cause to sound with a clang.

clang·or, klang′ər, klang′gər, *n.* A clang, or a series of clangs; a din.—*v.i.* To clang. **—clang·or·ous,** *a.*

clank, klangk, *n.* A sharp, metallic sound.—*v.t., v.i.* To sound or make to sound with a clank.

clans·man, klanz′mən, *n. pl.,* **-men.** A member of a clan.

clap, klap, *v.t.,* **clapped** or **clapt, clap·ping.** To strike (two objects) against each other; strike (the palms of one's hands) together to produce a sharp sound, as in applauding; to administer a light, friendly slap to; to put or place hastily.—*v.i.* To make a sharp, percussive sound; to applaud.—*n.* A loud, percussive noise; the sound made by striking one's hands together, as applause; an unexpected blow; a light, friendly slap.

clap·board, klab′ərd, klap′bōrd, klap′bôrd, *n.* A long, thin board, thicker along one edge than along the other, used in covering the outer walls of buildings.—*v.t.* To cover with clapboards.

clap·per, klap′ər, *n.* One that claps; the tongue of a bell.

clap·trap, klap′trap, *n.* Pretentiousness or bombastic nonsense; any flashy or hollow display; insincerity, artifice.—*a.* Showy and shoddy.

claque, klak, *n.* A group paid to applaud a performance; a company of sycophants.

clar·et, klar′it, *n.* A general name for dry red table wines, esp. those from the Bordeaux wine district of France; a deep, purplish-red color.—*a.* Purplish-red.

clar·i·fy, klar′ə·fī, *v.t.,* **-fied, -fy·ing.** To make clear or explain; to purify.—*v.i.* To become clear. **—clar·i·fi·er,** *n.* **—clar·i·fi·ca·tion,** klar·ə·fə·kā′shən, *n.*

clar·i·net, klar·ə·net′, *n.* A single-reed woodwind instrument in the shape of a cylindrical tube with a flaring end. **—clar·i·net·ist, clar·i·net·tist,** *n.*

clar·i·on, klar′ē·ən, *n.* A small trumpet with clear, shrill tones; a clear, shrill sound.—*a.* Clear, shrill, and loud.

clar·i·ty, klar′ə·tē, *n.* The state of being clear.

clash, klash, *v.i.* To collide, making a loud, harsh noise; come into conflict; disagree.—*v.t.* To strike with a resounding collision.—*n.* A harsh, frequently metallic sound, as of a collision; a collision; a conflict; strong disagreement.

clasp, klasp, *n.* A device for holding things or parts of a thing together; a grasp; a close embrace.—*v.t.* To fasten together with a clasp; to encircle with the arms and hold tightly; to embrace; to seize firmly with the hand. **—clasp·er,** *n.*

class, klas, klās, *n.* Any division of society according to status; caste; social rank, esp. high rank; a number of pupils in a school, ranked together or graduated in the same year; the assembly of such a body; group of students taught together; a meeting of such a group. *Informal.* Excellence or style. Any division of persons or things according to rank or grade, or a system of such divisions; a kind or sort; a zoological or botanical group ranking below a phylum, and above an order. —*v.t., v.i.* To arrange in or be placed in classes. **—class·a·ble,** *a.*

clas·sic, klas′ik, *a.* Of the highest class or rank; serving as a standard; pertaining to, in the style of, or characteristic of Greek and Roman antiquity, esp. with reference to literature and art; classical; balanced, simple, restrained; of literary or historical renown.—*n.* An author or a literary production of the first rank; something regarded as a nearly perfect example or model; *pl.,* the literature of ancient Greece and Rome.

clas·si·cal, klas′ə·kəl, *a.* Classic; marked by classicism; pertaining to the ancient classics; pertaining to serious music, esp. that in the tradition of the great European composers like Bach, Mozart, etc. **—clas·si·cal·ly,** *adv.*

clas·si·cism, klas′ə·siz·əm, *n.* The principles of classic literature or art, or adherence to them; the classical style in literature or art, characterized by balance, simplicity, restraint, etc.; a classical idiom or form; classical scholarship or learning. Also **clas·si·**

cal·ism, klas′ə·kə·liz·əm, *n.* —**clas·si·cist,** klas′ə·sist, *n.*

clas·si·fied, klas′ə·fīd, *a.* Arranged in classes; of certain government and military documents, withheld from general circulation. *Informal.* Confidential.

clas·si·fied ad, *n.* Want ad.

clas·si·fy, klas′ə·fī, *v.t.,* **-fied, -fy·ing.** To arrange in a class or classes; to arrange according to some pattern or system; to restrict the circulation of (a document). —**clas·si·fi·er,** *n.* —**clas·si·fi·ca·tion,** klas·ə·fə·kā′shən, *n.*

class·mate, klas′māt, kläs′māt, *n.* A member of the same class in school or college.

class·room, klas′room, klas′rŭm, *n.* A room in which classes are held.

class·y, klas′ē, *a.,* **-i·er, -i·est.** *Informal.* Of high class, rank, or grade; stylish; fine.

clat·ter, klat′ər, *v.i.* To make rattling sounds; move or go with such a sound; to prattle or chatter noisily.—*v.t.* To cause to clatter.—*n.* A rapid succession of abrupt, sharp, rattling sounds; noisy chatter.

clause, klôz, *n.* A word group containing both a subject and its predicate; a distinct part of a contract, will, agreement, or the like; a condition; proviso. —**claus·al,** *a.*

claus·tro·pho·bi·a, klôs·trə·fō′bē·ə, *n.* A morbid fear of closed-in spaces.

clav·i·chord, klav′ə·kôrd, *n.* An early stringed musical instrument with a keyboard.

clav·i·cle, klav′ə·kəl, *n.* Either of two slender bones that connect the shoulderbone with the breastbone; the collarbone.

cla·vier, klə·vēr′, klav′ē·ər, *n.* Any musical instrument with a keyboard, as a harpsichord or pianoforte.

claw, klô, *n.* The sharp hooked nail of a mammal, bird, or other animal; the whole foot of an animal with hooked nails; the pincers of lobsters, scorpions, etc.; anything shaped like the claw of an animal.—*v.t., v.i.* To tear, scratch, pull, dig, or seize with or as with claws or nails.

clay, clā, *n.* A natural earthy material, plastic when wet, used chiefly for making bricks or pottery; earth or mud; the human body. —**clay·ey,** *a.*

clay·more, klā′mōr, klā′môr, *n.* A double-edged broadsword once used by the Scottish Highlanders.

clay pig·eon, *n.* A saucer of baked clay or other material to be thrown into the air by a trap as a target.

clean, klēn, *a.* Free from foreign matter; pure; free from dirt or filth; unsoiled or unstained; free from defilement; innocent; neatly made or proportioned; shapely; clever; free from obstructions; complete or perfect; regarding atomic weapons, having little or no fallout.—*v.t.* To make clean; with *off,* to remove in the process of cleaning.—*v.i.* To perform or undergo cleaning.—*adv.* In a clean manner; cleanly; wholly; completely.—**clean out,** to clear of trash; to empty (a place) of contents. *Informal.* To leave without money. —**clean up,** to clean completely. *Informal.* To make a large profit.

clean-cut, klēn′kət′, *n.* Clear-cut; distinctly outlined; well-cut; shapely; of a well-defined or well-constituted character; wholesome; neat in appearance.

clean·er, klē′nər, *n.* One who cleans, esp. one whose business is cleaning; an apparatus that cleans; a preparation for cleaning; *pl.,* a plant for dry cleaning.

clean·ly, klen′lē, *a.,* **-li·er, -li·est.** Neat; carefully avoiding filth.—klēn′lē, *adv. In a clean manner.* —**clean·li·ness,** *n.*

cleanse, klenz, *v.t.,* **cleansed, cleans·ing.** To make clean; to purify. —**cleans·er,** *n.*

clean·up, klēn′əp, *n.* An act or instance of cleaning; reform. *Informal.* A large profit; a killing.

clear, klēr, *a.* Bright or shining; transparent; of a pure, even color; easily seen, heard, or understood; distinct;

evident; plain; discerning distinctly; convinced; free from guilt or blame; innocent; free from obstructions; open; unentangled or disengaged; free; free from debt; without deduction; without limitation; sheer. —*v.t.* To make clear; free from darkness, indistinctness, uncertainty, obstruction, obligation, or liability; free from guilt; pass without collision; leap over without touching; to obtain or give clearance for; gain; pass, as checks, through a clearing house; remove so as to leave something clear, used with *away.*—*v.i.* To become clear; with *away,* pass away or disappear; settle balances, as in a clearing house; to obtain clearance.—*adv.* In a clear manner; clearly; entirely. Also **clear·ly.** —*n.* A clear or unobstructed space. —**clear·ness,** *n.*

clear·ance, klēr′əns, *n.* The act of clearing; a clear space between two objects; sale of goods at lowered prices; formal permission to use classified information.

clear-cut, klēr′kət′, *a.* Cut or formed with clearly defined outlines; distinctly defined.

clear head·ed, klēr′hed′id, *a.* Having a clear head or understanding.

clear·ing, klēr′ing, *n.* The act of one who clears; a tract of land cleared of wood or cultivation.

clear·ing·house, klēr′ing·hows, *n.* An institution through which the claims of banks against one another are settled.

clear-sight·ed, klēr′sī′tid, *a.* Seeing with clearness; having good judgment.

cleat, klēt, *n.* A piece of wood or iron used in a ship to fasten ropes upon; a piece of iron, leather, or rubber worn on a shoe to provide traction; a piece of wood or metal fastened to anything for support.—*v.t.* To strengthen with a cleat or cleats.

cleav·age, klē′vij, *n.* The act of cleaving or splitting; the manner in which rocks or mineral substances regularly split; space between a woman's breasts.

cleave, klēv, *v.t.,* **cleft, cleaved, clove; cleft, cleaved, clov·en; cleav·ing.** To part by or as by a cutting blow; split; to penetrate or pass through; to make by cutting.—*v.i.* To part or split; to penetrate or pass, used with *through;* to adhere; cling; be faithful (to).

cleav·er, klē′vər, *n.* Onethat cleaves; a butcher's instrument for cutting meat into joints or pieces.

clef, klef, *n.* A character in music, placed at the beginning of a staff, to indicate the pitch of its notes.

cleft, kleft, *n.* A space or opening made by splitting; a crack; a crevice.—*a.* Partially split; having deep fissures.

clem·en·cy, klem′ən·sē, *n.* Mildness of temper; disposition to forgive; mercy; leniency; mildness of the weather. —**clem·ent,** *a.*

clench, klench, *v.t.* To clinch, as a nail; close, as the hands or teeth, tightly; grasp firmly, or grip.—*n.* The act of clenching; tight hold; grip.

clere·sto·ry, clear-sto·ry, klēr′stōr·ē, klēr′stôr·ē, *n. pl.,* **-ries.** An outside wall of a building, esp. a church, rising above an adjoining roof and having a series of windows which admit daylight to the interior; any similar construction.

cler·gy, klər′jē, *n. pl.,* **-gies.** The body of men ordained to the service of God in the Christian church; ministers, pastors, and priests.

cler·gy·man, klər′jē·mən, *n. pl.,* **-men.** One who is a member of the clergy.

cler·ic, klėr′ik, *a.* Pertaining to the clergy; clerical.—*n.* Clergyman.

cler·i·cal, klėr′i·kəl, *a.* Of the clergy or a clergyman; upholding the power or influence of the clergy; pertaining to a clerk or office worker.—*n.* A cleric.

cler·i·cal·ism, klėr′ə·kə·liz·əm, *n.* Clerical power or influence, esp. in politics. —**cler·i·cal·ist,** *n.*

clerk, klərk, *n.* A person who performs general duties

in an office or who keeps records and accounts; a salesperson; minor official who keeps records and performs routine assignments for a court or legislature; a cleric.—*v.i.* To act or serve as a clerk.

clev·er, klĕv′ər, *a.* Intelligent; quick-witted; physically dexterous; ingenious. **—clev·er·ly,** *adv.* **—clev·er·ness,** *n.*

clev·is, klĕv′is, *n. pl.* **-is·es.** A piece of metal, usually U-shaped, with a pin or bolt passing through holds at the two ends.

clew, kloo, *n.* A ball of thread; clue.—*v.t.* To coil into a ball.

cli·ché, klē-shā′, *n.* A word, phrase, or idea weakened from overuse.

click, klik, *n.* A slight, sharp sound, as of the cocking of a pistol; any of a class of sounds produced by withdrawing the tongue from a part of the mouth; some clicking mechanism.—*v.i.* To make a small sharp sound. *Informal.* To succeed; to get along well together.—*v.t.* To cause to make a clicking sound.

cli·ent, klī′ənt, *n.* One who resorts to another, esp. a lawyer, for professional services; a customer.

cli·en·tele, klī-ən-tel′, *n.* A body of clients; one's clients collectively.

cliff, klif, *n.* A precipice; a steep rock; a headland.

cliff·hang·er, klif′hang-ər, *n.* A contest in which the outcome remains uncertain to the last moments; an adventure serial.

cli·mac·ter·ic, klī-mak′tər-ik, klī-mak-tər′ik, *n.* A critical period in life, esp. the menopause or corresponding period in the male.

cli·mate, klī′mit, *n.* The kind of weather a region has, including temperature, wind, moisture, etc.; the prevailing temper of some group or period; milieu. **—cli·mat·ic,** klī-mat′ik, **cli·mat·i·cal,** *a.*

cli·max, klī′maks, *n.* In a play or novel, the highest point of suspense, conflict, or tension when the plot takes a major turn; the highest point of anything; the culmination; acme; an orgasm.—*v.i., v.t.* To bring or come to a climax. **—cli·mac·tic,** klī-mak′tik.

climb, klīm, *v.i.* To mount; to rise slowly by continued effort; to rise in status, rank, etc.; to ascend by twining, as a vine; to slope upward.—*v.t.* To ascend by using the hands or feet.—*n.* A climbing; an ascent by climbing; a place to be climbed. **—climb down,** to descend, esp. with the hands and feet. **—climb·a·ble,** *a.* **—climb·er,** *n.*

clinch, klinch, *v.t.* To secure, as a driven nail, by beating down the point; to fasten together thus; fix or confirm decisively.—*v.i.* To grapple, as in boxing. *Informal.* To embrace, as lovers.—*n.* A clinching or act of clinching; a grappling, as in boxing. *Informal.* A close embrace.

clinch·er, klin′chər, *n.* A person or thing that clinches. *Informal.* Something decisive; a conclusive factor in an issue or debate.

cling, kling, *v.i.,* **clung, cling·ing.** To stick closely; to hold fast, esp. by winding round or embracing. **—cling·ing·ly,** *adv.* **—cling·er,** *n.*

clin·ic, klin′ik, *n.* The examination and treatment of patients in the presence of medical students; a place for the examination and treatment of nonresident patients, as in a hospital.

clin·i·cal, klin′i·kəl, *a.* Pertaining to a clinic; based on examination in a clinic; dealing with the study of patients as opposed to laboratory experiment; objective. **—clin·i·cal·ly,** *adv.*

clink, klingk, *v.i.* To give out a small, sharp, ringing sound.—*v.t.* Cause to clink.—*n.* A small, sharp, ringing sound.

clink, klingk, *n. Informal.* A prison.

clink·er, kling′kər, *n.* A very hard brick; a mass of residue fused together, as in the burning of coal.

clip, klip, *v.t.,* **clipped, clip·ping.** To cut, or cut off or out, as with shears; trim by cutting; shear; to cut short; curtail, as syllables of words; to fasten with or as with a clip. *Informal.* To cheat or overcharge; to hit sharp-

ly.—*v.i.* To cut; to move swiftly.—*n.* An act of clipping; anything clipped off. *Informal.* A smart blow; a rapid motion.

clip, klip, *n.* A device for gripping and holding tightly; a metal clasp, as for letters or papers.—*v.t.* **clipped, clip·ping.** To fasten with or as with a clip.

clip·per, klip′ər, *n.* An instrument used for cutting; a sailing vessel built and rigged for speed.

clip·ping, klip′ing, *n.* A piece clipped off or out, as from a newspaper.

clique, klēk, klik, *n.* An exclusive set of persons. **—cliqu·ey, cliqu·y, cliqu·ish,** *a.*

clit·o·ris, klit′ər-is, klī′tər-is, *n.* A small erectile organ of female mammals, located at the upper part of the vulva.

clo·a·ca, klō-ā′kə, *n. pl.,* **-cae,** -sē. A cavity in birds, reptiles, many fish, and lower mammals, into which the intestinal, urinary, and reproductive tracts all open. **—clo·a·cal,** *a.*

cloak, klōk, *n.* A loose outer garment worn over other clothes; a thing which conceals; a disguise.—*v.t.* To cover with a cloak; to disguise.

clob·ber, klob′ər, *v.t. Informal.* To beat up; to defeat overwhelmingly.

cloche, klōsh, *n.* A woman's hat, close-fitted to the face.

clock, klok, *n.* Any of several devices that measure and indicate the time.—*v.t.* To time or test with a stopwatch.

clock·wise, klok′wīz, *adv., a.* In the direction of rotation of the hands of a clock.

clock·work, klok′wərk, *n.* The machinery of a clock; a mechanism producing regularity of movement similar to that of a clock; precision.

clod, klod, *n.* A lump or mass in general; a lump of earth, soil, etc.; a dull, gross, stupid person. **—clod·dish,** *a.* **—clod·dy,** *a.*

clog, klog, *v.t.,* **clogged, clog·ging.** To impede the movements of; to encumber or hamper; to choke up; to obstruct so as to hinder passage through.—*v.i.* To become filled; to dance with clogs.—*n.* An encumbrance that hinders motion or renders it difficult; a sort of shoe with a wooden sole; a dance in which such shoes are worn.

clois·ter, kloy′stər, *n.* A covered walk running round the walls of monastic or collegiate buildings; a place of religious retirement; a monastery; a convent.—*v.t.* To confine in a cloister; to shut up in retirement from the world. **—clois·tral,** *a.*

close, klōz, *v.t.,* **closed, clos·ing.** To bring together the parts of; to shut; make fast; to end; to fill or stop up; to consolidate: often followed by *up.*—*v.i.* To come together; to unite; to end; to become closed. To engage in close encounter (with); to come to an agreement (with).—*n.* An arriving at a conclusion; the conclusion.

close, klōs, *a.,* **clos·er, clos·est.** Closed; shut in or enclosed; without opening; confined or narrow; lacking fresh air; heavy or oppressive, as the air; strictly guarded; secluded; hidden; practicing secrecy; reticent; stingy; scarce, as money; having the parts near together; compact; near, or near together; intimate or confidential; fitting tightly; strict or minute; nearly even or equal, as a contest; uttered with a relatively contracted opening of the oral cavity.—*adv.* Tightly; in strict confinement. **—close·ly,** *adv.* **—close·ness,** *n.*

closed shop, *n.* A place of business in which only labor union members can work.

close·fist·ed, klōs′fis′tid, *a.* Stingy.

close-mouthed, klōs′mouthd′, klōs′mouthd, *a.* Reticent; uncommunicative.

clos·et, kloz′it, *n.* A private room, usu. of small size, for retirement, counsel, or devotions; a small room for storage of clothing, provisions, etc.; a water closet or toilet.—*v.t.,* **-et·ed, -et·ing.** To shut up in a private place for intensive work or secret talk.—*a.* Private; theoretical.

close-up, klōs'əp, *n.* A picture taken at close range or with a telescopic lens; a close view.

clo·sure, klō'zhər, *n.* The act of closing; an end; that which closes; cloture.

clot, klot, *n.* A coagulated mass of soft or fluid matter, as of blood or cream.—*v.i., v.t.,* **clot·ted, clot·ting.** To coagulate or form into clots.

cloth, klôth, kloth, *n. pl.,* **cloths.** Any fabric of wool, hair, cotton, flax, hemp, or man-made filaments, formed by weaving; a tablecloth; canvas used to make or reinforce a sail.

clothe, klōth, *v.t.,* **clothed** or **clad, cloth·ing.** To cover with garments; to dress; to furnish with clothes; to cover as if by clothing; to furnish; equip.

clothes, klōz, klōthz, *n. pl.* Garments worn by human beings; apparel; bedclothes.

clothes·horse, klōz'hôrs, klōthz'hôrs, *n.* A frame to hang clothes on. *Informal.* A person who is excessively interested in clothes.

clothes·line, klōz'līn, klōthz'līn, *n.* A strong line of rope, plastic cord, or wire on which clothes are hung to dry.

clothes·pin, klōz'pin', klōthz'pin, *n.* A spring clamp, or forked piece of plastic or wood, used to fasten articles on a line to dry.

clothes tree, *n.* An upright stand on which to hang clothes.

cloth·ier, klōth'yər, *n.* A maker or retailer of cloth or of clothes.

cloth·ing, klō'thing, *n.* Garments collectively; clothes.

clo·ture, klō'chər, *n.* Termination of a debate usually by calling for a vote. Also **clo·sure.**

cloud, klowd, *n.* A visible collection of particles of water or ice hanging in the air, usually at a considerable elevation; any similar mass, as of smoke or flying dust; a dim or obscure area; a throng or multitude; anything that darkens or threatens, as with gloom or trouble.—*v.t.* To cover with or as with clouds; obscure or darken; to make indistinct; render gloomy; place under a cloud, as of suspicion or disgrace; to variegate with ill-defined patches of another color.—*v.i.* To grow cloudy.

cloud·burst, klowd'bərst, *n.* A sudden, violent downpour of rain.

cloud·y, klow'dē, *a.,* **-i·er, -i·est.** Of the nature of a cloud; resembling clouds; overcast with clouds; not clear or transparent; having cloudlike markings; obscure or indistinct; darkened by gloom or trouble. —**cloud·i·ly,** *adv.* —**cloud·i·ness,** *n.*

clout, klowt, *n. Informal.* A hard blow, struck usually with the fist; influence, esp. clandestine, based on one's power, connections, etc.—*v.t. Informal.* To strike forcefully, esp. with the hand.

clove, klōv, *n.* The dried flower bud of a tropical evergreen tree used whole or ground as a very aromatic spice; the tree yielding cloves.

clove, klōv, *n.* One of the small bulbs formed in the axils of the scales of a mother bulb, as in garlic.

clo·ven, klō'vən, *a.* Divided; cleft; split.

clo·ver, klō'vər, *n.* An herb bearing three-lobed leaves and roundish heads or oblong spikes of small flowers, widely grown for fodder.

clo·ver·leaf, klō'vər·lēf, *n.* A road plan laid out in the form of a four-leaf clover.

clown, klown, *n.* A performer in a circus or play usually in ridiculous dress and makeup; an awkward man of coarse manners.—*v.i.* To act like a clown. —**clown·ish,** *a.*

cloy, kloy, *v.t.* To gratify to excess so as to cause loathing; to surfeit.—*v.i.* To cause surfeit. —**cloy·ing·ly,** *adv.*

club, kləb, *n.* A stick or piece of wood with one end thicker than the other; a club with a heavy head for driving a golf ball; playing card with a figure resembling a 3-leaf clover; *pl.,* the suit so marked.—*v.t.* To beat with a club. A select number of persons in the habit of meeting for some common purpose; a clubhouse; a nightclub.—*v.i.,* **clubbed, club·bing.** To form a club.

club·foot, kləb'fût, *n. pl.,* **-feet.** A short misshapen foot that is a birth defect. —**club·foot·ed,** *a.*

club·house, kləb'hows, *n.* A house or building occupied by a club.

cluck, klək, *v.t.* To utter the cry of a hen calling young chicks; to make a similar sound.—*v.i.* To call by clucking.—*n.* A sound uttered by a hen.

clue, kloo, *n.* Information that contributes to the solution of a problem or mystery.

clump, kləmp, *n.* A shapeless mass; a lump; a cluster; a dull, heavy gait.—*v.i.* To walk in a clumsy, lumbering manner; to form a clump. —**clump·y,** *a.*

clum·sy, kləm'zē, *a.,* **-si·er, -si·est.** Awkward; ungainly; badly constructed; tactless; unskillfully performed. —**clum·si·ly,** *adv.* —**clum·si·ness,** *n.*

clus·ter, kləs'tər, *n.* A number of things, as fruits, growing naturally together; a bunch; a group.—*v.i.* To grow or be assembled in clusters.—*v.t.* To collect into or produce a cluster.

clutch, kləch, *v.t.* To seize, clasp, or grip with the hand; to hold tightly.—*v.i.* To seek to seize and hold, with *at.*—*n.* A grasping; a paw, talon, or grasping hand; *usu. pl.,* merciless power or mastery. A device for connecting shafts with each other or with wheels, so that they may be disconnected at will; the lever or control that operates this device. *Informal.* A crucial situation or moment.

clutch, kləch, *n.* The eggs laid by a bird at one time; a brood of chickens.

clut·ter, klət'ər, *n.* Confused noise; bustle; confusion; litter.—*v.t.* To put in a clutter.—*v.i.* To make a bustle or disturbance.

coach, kōch, *n.* A large, enclosed carriage, often a public passenger vehicle; a class of airline travel less costly than first class; a railroad passenger-car; a bus; a private tutor who prepares a candidate for an examination; one who instructs others in preparation for an athletic contest.—*v.t.* To give instruction or advice to.—*v.i.* To act as a coach; study with or be instructed by a coach.

coach·man, kōch'mən, *n. pl.,* **-men.** A man employed to drive a coach.

co·ag·u·late, kō·ag'yə·lāt, *v.t., v.i.,* **-lat·ed, -lat·ing.** To change from a fluid into a thickened substance; to curdle, congeal, or clot. —**co·ag·u·la·tion,** kō·ag·yə·lā'shən, *n.*

coal, kōl, *n.* A black or dark-brown mineral formed from decayed vegetable matter under great pressure, burned for its heat; a piece of this substance; a glowing, hot fragment.—*v.t.* To provide with coal.—*v.i.* To take in coal for fuel.

co·a·lesce, kō·ə·les', *v.i.,* **-lesced, -les·cing.** To unite by growth into one body; to fuse; combine; blend. —**co·a·les·cence,** *n.* —**co·a·les·cent,** *a.*

coal gas, *n.* The gas formed by burning coal; a gas used for illuminating and heating, produced by distilling bituminous coal.

co·a·li·tion, kō·ə·lish'ən, *n.* Union into one body or mass; voluntary union for a common object or cause; an alliance.

coal oil, *n.* Kerosene; petroleum.

coal tar, *n.* A thick, black, viscid liquid which is formed during the distillation of bituminous coal, and which upon further distillation yields products such as benzene, phenol, dyes, etc.

coarse, kōrs, kôrs, *a.,* **coars·er, coars·est.** Of ordinary or inferior quality; common; base; lacking in fineness of texture or elegance of form; rough; crude; vulgar; gross; unrefined. —**coars·en,** *v.t., v.i.*

---

a- hat, fāte, fāre, fäther; **e-** met, mē; **i-** pin, pīne; **o-** not, nōte, ôrb, moove (move), boy, pownd;
u- cūbe, bůll, tûk (took); **ch-** chin; **th-** thick, then; **zh-** vizhon (vision); **ə-** əgo, takən, pencəl, lemən, bərd (bird).

—coarse•ly, adv.

coast, kōst, n. The margin of the land next to the sea; the seashore, or the region adjoining it; a slope down which one may slide on a sled. (Cap., with the.) The part of the U.S. bordering on the Pacific Ocean. —v.i. To slide on a sled down a slope; descend a hill without propelling power; to advance without added effort. —v.t. To sail along the shoreline of.

coast•er, kō′stər, n. One who or that which coasts; a vessel engaged in coastwise trade; a sled used in coasting; a small tray placed under an object to protect a surface.

coast guard, n. A military or naval force employed along a coast to protect lives, prevent smuggling, break up ice floes, etc.

coast•line, kōst′līn, n. The shoreline; the land and water along the shoreline.

coat, kōt, n. A warm outer garment with sleeves; a layer of one substance covering another; a coating; the external covering: as fur, hair, or wool of an animal. —v.t. To cover with a coat.

coat•ing, kō′ting, n. Any substance spread over for cover or protection; cloth for coats.

coat of arms, n. An escutcheon or shield of arms; a drawing of an escutcheon.

coat of mail, n. Defensive armor consisting of a network of iron or steel rings.

co•au•thor, kō-ô′thər, n. A joint author.—v.t. To write with someone else.

coax, kōks, v.t. To persuade by words or actions; to wheedle; to maneuver by adroit handling. —coax•ing•ly, kōk′sing•lē, adv.

cob, kob, n. A corncob; a short-legged horse; a male swan.

co•balt, kō′bôlt, n. A silver-white, magnetic, metallic element that is tough, lustrous, and ductile, found in and with various ores such as iron and nickel. Usage includes preparation of alloys and compounds, the silicates of which yield blue coloring for ceramics, inks, and paints.

co•balt blue, n. A blue to green pigment compounded essentially of cobalt oxide and alumina; a deep blue color.

co•balt 60, n. A heavy radioactive isotope of cobalt, used as a source of gamma rays, esp. in radiotherapy.

cob•ble, kob′əl, v.t., -bled, -bling. To make or repair, as shoes. —cob•bler,n.

cob•ble, kob′əl, n. Cobblestone.—v.t., -bled, -bling. To pave with cobblestones.

cob•ble•stone, kob′əl•stōn, n. A rounded stone formerly used in paving.

COBOL, Cobol, kō′bōl, kō′bôl, n. A computer language, using common English words.

co•bra, kō′brə, n. Any of several venomous hooded snakes of Asia and Africa; the skin as used for leather.

cob•web, kob′web, n. The web spun by a spider; any single thread formed by a spider; the thread or web which an insect larva spins; anything resembling a cobweb. —cob•webbed, a. —cob•web•by, a.

co•ca, kō′kə, n. A shrub, native to the Andes and grown for its dried leaves, chewed for their stimulant properties and which yield cocaine and other alkaloids.

co•caine, kō•kān′, kō′kān, n. A bitter crystalline alkaloid, obtained from coca leaves, used in medicine as a local anesthetic and as a narcotic.

coc•cyx, kok′siks, n. pl., coc•cy•ges, kok•sī′jēz. A small triangular bone at the base of the spine. —coc•cyg•e•al, kok•sij′ē•əl, a.

coch•le•a, kok′lē•ə, n. A spiral structure in the internal ear that contains the auditory nerve endings.

cock, kok, n. The male of the domestic fowl; the male of any bird; a figure or representation of a cock; a weathercock; a leader; a faucet, tap, or valve; in a firearm, the hammer; the position into which the hammer of a firearm is brought before firing.—v.t. To raise the hammer of a firearm; to turn or tilt upward.

cock•ade, kok•ād′, n. A small knot of ribbon worn as a badge on the hat.

cock•a•too, kok′ə•too, n. pl., -toos. Any of the crested parrots of the East Indies or Australia.

cock•crow, kok′krō, n. The time at which cocks crow; early morning.

cock•er span•iel, kok′ər, n. One of a breed of small spaniels trained for use in hunting or kept as pets.

cock•eyed, kok′īd, a. Crosseyed. Informal. Completely wrong; drunk.

cock•fight, kok′fīt, n. A fight between gamecocks which have been fitted with steel spurs. —cock•fight•ing, n.

cock•le, kok′əl, n. Any edible saltwater bivalve mollusk.

cock•le•bur, kok′əl•bər, n. Any of a genus of coarse weeds with spiny burs; the burdock.

cock•le•shell, kok′əl•shel, n. The shell of the cockle, or one of its valves.

cock•ney, kok′nē, n. pl., -neys. (Often cap.) A native of the East End of London; the dialect of that district. —a. Of or pertaining to cockneys or their dialect.

cock•pit, kok′pit, n. In small airplanes, an enclosed space containing a seat for a pilot or passenger; a pit or enclosed place for cockfights.

cock•roach, kok′rōch, n. Any of a family of usu. nocturnal insects that infest kitchens and pantries.

cocks•comb, koks′kōm, n. The comb of a cock; a garden plant with red or yellow flowers.

cock•sure, kok′shūr′, a. Perfectly sure or certain; over-confident.

cock•tail, kok′tāl, n. Any of various drinks containing such alcoholic beverages as gin, whiskey, or brandy mixed with other liquors or juices; an appetizer.

cock•y, kok′ē, a., -i•er, -i•est. Informal. Pertly self-assertive; conceited. —cock•i•ly, adv. —cock•i•ness, n.

co•coa, kō′kō, n. The roasted, husked, and ground seeds of the cacao; a hot beverage made from this powder.

co•co•nut, co•coa•nut, kō′kə•nət, n. The large, hard-shelled nut of the coconut palm, with a white, edible meat, and containing a milky liquid.

co•co•nut palm, n. A tall, slender tropical tree with an edible fruit.

co•coon, kə•koon′, n. The silky tissue or envelope which the larvae of many insects spin as a covering for themselves while they are in an undeveloped state.

cod, kod, n. pl., cod, cods. A large food fish, found in the colder regions of the North Atlantic Ocean; also cod•fish.

C.O.D., c.o.d., abbr. for collect on delivery. Payment at the time delivery is made to the purchaser.

cod•dle, kod′əl, v.t., -dled, -dling. To pamper; to cook slowly and gently: to coddle an egg.

code, kōd, n. Any system or collection of rules and regulations; a system of signals for communication; a system of arbitrarily chosen words; a cipher; numbers, letters or combinations of both used to represent or identify a thing in a storage system; a set of symbols which represent information in a form that can be used by a computer.

code, kōd, v.t., cod•ed, cod•ing. To arrange in a code.

co•deine, kō′dēn, n. A white, crystalline, slightly bitter alkaloid, obtained from opium, used in medicine to deaden pain and to cause sleep.

codg•er, kod′jər, n. Informal. Curious old character.

cod•i•cil, kod′ə•səl, n. A supplement to a will, containing some change to the will.

cod•i•fy, kod′ə•fī, kō′də•fī, v.t., -fied, -fy•ing. To reduce to a code or digest, as laws. —cod•i•fi•ca•tion, kod•ə•fə•kā′shən, n.

cod-liv•er oil, kod′liv•ər, n. A pale yellow oil extracted mainly from cod livers, used chiefly in medicine as a source of vitamins A and D.

co•ed, kō′ed′, n. A female student in a coeducational institution, as a college or university. —co•ed, co•

ed, *a.*

co·ed·u·ca·tion, kō·ej·û·kā′shən, *n.* Education of persons of both sexes in the same classes of an institution.

co·ef·fi·cient, kō·ə·fish′ənt, *n.* A factor of an algebraic term that multiplies the other terms: in the term 3*x*, 3 and *x* are *coefficients* of each other.

coe·len·ter·ate, si·len′tə·rāt, si·len′tə·rit, *n.* Any of a large group of saltwater animals that have a single internal cavity, such as jellyfish and the corals.

co·e·qual, kō·ē′kwəl, *a.* Equal in rank.—*n.* One that is equal in rank.

co·erce, kō·ərs′, *v.t.,* **co·erced, co·er·cing.** To restrain by force, as by law or authority; to repress; to compel to compliance. —**co·er·ci·ble,** *a.* —**co·er·cion,** kō·ər′shən, *n.* —**co·er·cive,** kō·ər′siv, *a.*

co·ex·ist, kō·ig·zist′, *v.i.* To exist at the same time with another. —**co·ex·ist·ence,** *n.* —**co·ex·ist·ent,** *a.*

cof·fee, kô′fē, kof′ē, *n.* A hot or chilled drink made from roasted and ground coffee beans, the seeds of certain evergreen plants or trees of tropical regions; these seeds; a cup of coffee; the color of coffee containing cream.

cof·fee·house, kô′fē·hows, kof′ē·hows, *n.* A restaurant which serves different kinds of coffee and light refreshments.

cof·fee·pot, kô′fē·pot, kof′ē·pot, *n.* An appliance for making or serving coffee.

cof·fee shop, *n.* A small restaurant, which serves snacks and light meals.

cof·fee ta·ble, *n.* A low table usu. placed in front of a living room sofa, for serving refreshments.

cof·fee tree, *n.* Any tree which yields coffee beans.

cof·fer, kô′fər, kof′ər, *n.* A box or chest, esp. a safe for valuables. *Pl.* A treasury; funds.—*v.t.* To deposit or lay up in a coffer or chest.

cof·fin, kô′fin, kof′in, *n.* The box in which a dead human body is buried in a vault.

cog, kog, kôg, *n.* A tooth or projection on a wheel, that transmits motion to or receives motion from a corresponding tooth or part; a cogwheel; an unimportant person or part in a large organization.

co·gent, kō′jənt, *a.* Compelling or persuading by means of a clear, forcible presentation of facts and arguments; pertinent; convincing. —**co·gen·cy,** *n.* —**co·gent·ly,** *adv.*

cog·i·tate, koj′ə·tāt, *v.i.,* **-tat·ed, -tat·ing.** To think deeply; to ponder.—*v.t.* To think about. —**cog·i·ta·ble,** *a.*—**cog·i·ta·tion,** koj·ə·tā′shən, *n.* —**cog·i·ta·tive,** *a.*

cog·nac, kōn′yak, kon′yak, *n.* A French brandy, so called from the town of the same name.

cog·nate, kog′nāt, *a.* Related by birth; of the same family, as words, roots, languages; having affinity of any kind.—*n.* Anything related to another by origin or nature.

cog·ni·tion, kog·nish′ən, *n.* The act or fact of coming to know or of knowing; knowledge. —**cog·ni·tive,** kog′nə·tiv, *a.*

cog·ni·zance, kog′nə·zəns, *n.* Knowledge or notice; observation; judicial knowledge; the right to try and to determine causes.

cog·ni·zant, kog′nə·zənt, *a.* Acquainted with (followed by *of*).

cog·wheel, kog′hwēl, kog′wēl, *n.* A wheel with teeth; a gear wheel.

co·hab·it, kō·hab′it, *v.i.* To dwell or live together as husband and wife without being married. —**co·hab·i·ta·tion,** kō·hab·ə·tā′shən, *n.*

co·here, kō·hēr′, *v.i.,* **co·hered, co·her·ing.** To stick together; to be logically consistent.

co·her·ent, kō·hēr′ənt, *a.* Sticking together; having an agreement or harmony of parts, as of a pattern; logical; consistent: a *coherent* argument, a *coherent*

speaker. —**co·her·ence,** *n.* Also **co·her·en·cy.** —**co·her·ent·ly,** *adv.*

co·he·sion, kō·hē′zhən, *n.* The act or state of cohering or sticking together.—**co·he·sive,** kō·hē′siv, *a.* —**co·he·sive·ly,** *adv.* —**co·he·sive·ness,** *n.*

co·hort, kō′hôrt, *n.* A companion.

coif, koyf, *n.* Any of various types of close-fitting hoodlike caps.—*v.t.* To cover or dress with or as with a coif; to dress, as hair.

coif·feur, kwä·fer′, *n.* A hairdresser.

coif·fure, kwä·fyûr′, *n.* A headdress; a style of hair arrangement.—*v.t.,* **-fured, -fur·ing.** To arrange or dress the hair.

coil, koyl, *n.* A ring or series of rings or spirals into which a rope, chain, or flexible body is wound; an induction coil.—*v.t.* To gather into a series of rings or spirals.—*v.i.* To form rings or coils.

coin, koyn, *n.* A piece of metal converted into money by impressing some stamp on it; money.—*v.t.* To make into money by stamping; to make or invent: to *coin* an expression.

coin·age, koy′nij, *n.* The act or process of coining money; money coined; the act of inventing, producing; what is invented, as a word.

co·in·cide, kō·in·sīd′, *v.i.,* **-cid·ed, -cid·ing.** To have the same place in space or time; to correspond exactly in nature or character; to agree in opinion.

co·in·ci·dence, kō·in′sə·dəns, *n.* Exact correspondence, esp. a striking occurrence of two or more events at one time.

co·in·ci·dent, kō·in′sə·dənt, *a.* Occupying the same place or position; happening at the same time; in exact agreement.

co·in·ci·den·tal, kō·in·sə·den′təl, *a.* Involving coincidence; happening or existing simultaneously. —**co·in·ci·den·tal·ly,** *adv.* —**co·in·ci·dent·ly,** *adv.*

co·i·tion, kō·ish′ən, *n.* Sexual intercourse.

co·i·tus, kō′ə·təs, *n.* Sexual intercourse.—**co·i·tal,** *a.*

coke, kōk, *n.* A fuel with a high carbon content obtained by heating coal to drive off its gases.—*v.t., v.i.,* **coked, cok·ing.** To convert into coke.

co·la, kō′lə, *n.* Any of several carbonated soft drinks made from the extracts of kola nut seeds and coca plant leaves.

col·an·der, kəl′ən·dər, kol′ən·dər, *n.* A vessel with a bottom perforated with little holes, used for straining liquids; a strainer.

cold, kōld, *a.* Having a relatively low temperature; chilly; frigid; deficient in passion, emotion, enthusiasm, or ardor; indifferent; lacking sensual desire; not affectionate, cordial, or friendly; failing to excite feeling or interest; of coloring, inclining to blue or gray, rather than red or yellow. —**cold·ness,** *n.*

cold, kōld, *n.* The relative absence of heat; a condition of low temperature; the sensation produced by loss of heat from the body; chill; a viral infection of the upper respiratory passages, marked by catarrh, hoarseness, and coughing.

cold-blood·ed, kōld′bləd′id, *a.* Having cold blood; referring to animals, as fishes and reptiles, whose blood temperature changes with the temperature of the surroundings; lacking in emotion; unsympathetic; cruel.

cold cream, *n.* A heavy, oily cream used for cleansing and lubricating the skin.

cold cuts, *n. pl.* Various sliced cold meats and cheeses.

cold feet, *n. Informal.* Loss of courage or confidence.

cold shoul·der, *n. Informal.* An open show of coldness.

cold sore, *n.* A blister or blisters around the mouth, often accompanying a cold.

cold war, *n.* Intense diplomatic and economic rivalry for national advantage which does not reach the point

---

a- hat, fāte, fåre, fäther; **e-** met, mē; **i-** pin, pīne; **o-** not, nōte, ôrb, moove (move), boy, pownd; **u-** cūbe, bûll, tûk (took); **ch-** chin; **th-** thick, ŧhen; **zh-** vizhon (vision); **ə-** əgo, takən, pencəl, lemən, bərd (bird).

of actual military operations.

cold wave, *n.* A rapid fall in temperature which affects a wide area.

cole, kōl, *n.* Any of several plants that are related to the cabbage. Also **cole•wort.**

cole•slaw, kōl/slô, *n.* A salad made of raw, sliced cabbage leaves.

col•ic, kol/ik, *n.* A painful spasm of the intestines, esp. of the colon. —**col•ick•y,** kol/i•kē, *a.*

col•i•se•um, kol•ə•sē/əm, *n.* A large stadium or amphitheater housing sports events, fairs, exhibitions, or conventions.

co•li•tis, kə•li/tis, *n.* Inflammation of the colon.

col•lab•o•rate, kə•lab/ə•rāt, *v.i.,* -rat•ed, -rat•ing. To work together with others; cooperate with the enemy of one's country. —**col•lab•o•ra•tion,** kə•lab•ə•rā/shən, *n.* —**col•lab•o•ra•tion•ism,** *n.* —**col•lab•o•ra•tion•ist,** *n.* —**col•lab•o•ra•tor,** *n.*

col•lage, kə•läzh/, *n.* An art form in which bits of newspapers, magazines, drawings, etc., are pasted onto a background.

col•lapse, kə•laps/, *v.i.,* col•lapsed, col•laps•ing. To break down, to fall in or cave in suddenly; to come to nothing.—*v.t.* To cause to collapse.—*n.* A falling inward; a complete failure; a breakdown. —**col•lap•si•ble,** *a.*

col•lar, kol/ər, *n.* That part of a shirt or coat worn around the neck; anything worn around the neck; a band around an animal's neck.—*v.t.* To seize by the collar; to put a collar on.

col•lar•bone, kol/ər•bōn, *n.* The clavicle.

col•late, kol/āt, kə•lāt/, kō/lāt, *v.t.,* -lat•ed, -lat•ing. To bring together and compare; to gather and arrange in order, as the sheets of a book for binding. —**col•la•tion,** *n.* —**col•la•tor,** *n.*

col•lat•er•al, kə•lat/ər•əl, *a.* Secondary; side by side; parallel; auxiliary; subsidiary; descending in a different line from the same ancestor; guaranteed by property.—*n.* Property pledged as a guarantee of payment.

col•league, kol/ēg, *n.* A partner or associate in the same employment or profession.

col•lect, kol/ekt, *n.* A short prayer.

col•lect, kə•lekt/, *v.t.* To gather into one body or place; to take or regain possession of; to receive or to obtain payment of.—*v.i.* To gather; to assemble; to accumulate.—*a.* To be paid by the receiver: a collect call.—*adv.* So that the receiver pays: call collect. —**col•lect•i•ble,** col•lect•a•ble, *a.* —**col•lect•i•bil•i•ty,** col•lect•a•bil•ity, *n.* —**col•lect•or,** *n.*

col•lect•ed, kə•lek/tid, *a.* Gathered together; self-possessed.

col•lec•tion, kə•lek/shən, *n.* The act of collecting; that which is collected, as stamps, paintings, and other objects of interest; that which is collected for a charitable, or other purpose.

col•lec•tive, kə•lek/tiv, *a.* Formed by collection; combined; pertaining to a group of individuals taken together; of nouns, expressing in singular form a group of individual objects or persons, as herd, jury, clergy. —**col•lec•tive•ly,** *adv.*

col•lec•tive bar•gain•ing, *n.* Bargaining about wages, work time, and other benefits, by employees collectively with their employers.

col•lec•tiv•i•ty, *n.* A collective body; an aggregate.

col•lec•tiv•ism, kə•lek/tə•viz•əm, *n.* A theory that the land and means of production and distribution should belong to the people collectively. Also **col•lec•tiv•i•ty,** *n.* —**col•lec•tiv•ize,** *v.t.,* -ized, -iz•ing. —**col•lec•tiv•i•za•tion,** *n.*

col•lege, kol/ij, *n.* A school of higher learning leading to the bachelor's degree; a subdivision of a university: the college of engineering; a school for specialized instruction: a business college; buildings that house a college. —**col•le•gi•al,** kə•lē/jē•əl, *a.*

col•le•gian, kə•lē/jən, kə•lē/jē•ən, *n.* A college student.

col•le•giate, kə•lē/jit, kə•lē/jē•it, *a.* Of or pertaining to a college or college students.

col•lide, kə•līd/, *v.i.,* -lid•ed, -lid•ing. To strike or dash against each other; to meet in opposition or antagonism. —**col•li•sion,** *n.*

col•li•mate, kol/ə•māt, *v.t.,* -mat•ed, -mat•ing. To bring into line; adjust the line of sight of. —**col•li•ma•tion,** *n.*

col•lo•cate, kol/ə•kāt, *v.t.,* -cat•ed, -cat•ing. To put or place in the proper order. —**col•lo•ca•tion,** kol•ə•kā/shən, *n.*

col•loid, kol/oyd, *n.* A liquid mixture of gas containing very fine dispersed particles of liquid or solid.

col•lo•qui•al, kə•lō/kwē•əl, *a.* Peculiar to the language of conversation; pertaining to conversation. —**col•lo•qui•al•ly,** *adv.*

col•lo•qui•al•ism, kə•lō/kwē•ə•liz•əm, *n.* A word or phrase peculiar to the language of common conversation.

col•lo•quy, kol/ə•kwē, *n. pl.,* -quies. A conversation or dialog; a conference. —**col•lo•quist,** *n.*

col•lu•sion, kə•loo/zhən, *n.* Secret agreement for deceit or fraud. —**col•lu•sive,** *a.*

co•logne, kə•lōn/, *n.* A scented toilet water.

co•lon, kō/lən, *n. pl.,* co•lons, co•la, kō/lə. The part of the large intestine which extends from the cecum to the rectum.

co•lon, kō/lən, *n.* A punctuation mark (:) used to begin a list or series, introduce a speech, separate the hour from the minute in time expressions, and after a formal salutation.

colo•nel, kėr/nəl, *n.* A commissioned officer ranking above a lieutenant colonel and below a brigadier general.

co•lo•ni•al, kə•lō/nē•əl, *a.* Of or pertaining to a colony or colonies; esp. pertaining to the thirteen British colonies which became the United States of America, or to their period.—*n.* An inhabitant of a colony.

co•lo•ni•al•ism, kə•lō/nē•ə•liz•əm, *n.* The colonial system. —**co•lo•ni•al•ist,** *a., n.*

col•o•nist, kol/o•nist, *n.* An inhabitant of or settler in a colony.

col•on•nade, kol•ə•nād/, *n.* A series of columns placed at regular intervals and usually supporting a roof.

col•o•ny, kol/ə•nē, *n. pl.,* -nies. A group of people moved from their mother country to a remote province or country, and remaining subjects of the parent state; the country colonized; any group of people with common or similar language, interests, or occupations, living in close association: an artist colony. —**col•o•nize,** *v.t.,* -nized, -niz•ing. —**col•o•niz•er,** *n.* —**col•o•ni•za•tion,** kol•ə•nə•zā/shən, *n.*

col•or, kəl/ər, *n.* The visual property of an object apart from its form, dependent upon a response to light, including the attributes of hue, brightness, and saturation; any hue or tint as distinguished from white, black, or gray; pigment, paint, or dye; a true-to-life effect created by specific treatment of the special features of a particular place or time: local color. Usu. pl. A flag or standard borne in an army or fleet; general character or nature: as, to show one's true colors.—*v.t.* To tinge; to paint; to stain; to distort; misrepresent; change.—*v.i.* To blush; to become different in color. —**col•or•er,** *n.* —**col•or•less,** *a.*

col•or•a•tion, kəl•ə•rā/shən, *n.* Coloring; the tints of an object.

col•or-blind, kəl/ər•blīnd, *a.* Unable to accurately distinguish colors. —**col•or-blind•ness,** *n.*

col•or•cast, kəl/ər•kast, *n.* A broadcast of a television program in color.—*v.t., v.i.* To televise in color.

col•ored, kəl/ərd, *a.* Having color; slanted: a point of view colored by circumstances.

col•or•fast, kəl/ər•fast, *a.* Keeping its original shade of color: a colorfast fabric.

col•or•ful, kəl/ər•fəl, *a.* Having a lot of color; richly picturesque: a *colorful* historical period.

col·or·ing, kol'ər·ing, *n.* The art of putting color on; the color put on; something used to give color, as a dye; appearance with regard to color, as of a complexion.

co·los·sal, kə·los'əl, *a.* Very large.

co·los·sus, kə·los'əs, *n. pl.,* **co·los·si,** kə·los'ī, **co·los·sus·es.** A statue of a gigantic size; any object of gigantic size.

colt, kōlt, *n.* A young male horse; a young donkey or mule; young person or novice.

colt·ish, kōl'tish, *a.* Frisky; playful.

col·um·bine, kol'əm·bīn, *n.* A plant of the crowfoot family with showy, variously-colored flowers.

col·umn, kol'əm, *n.* A pillar, esp. a decorative or supporting member; any column-like object formation: the spinal *column;* a vertical row of lines of type: a newspaper *column;* an article in a periodical written by a special editor; a group of soldiers, ships, or vehicles, usu. arranged in single file. **—co·lum·nar,** kə·ləm'nər, *a.* **—col·umned,** kol'əmd, *a.*

col·um·nist, kol'əm·nist, kol'əm·ist, *n.* The editor or writer of a special column in a newspaper.

co·ma, kō'mə, *n. pl.,* **co·mas.** A state of prolonged unconsciousness caused by disease or serious injury; stupor. **—co·ma·tose,** kō'mə·tōs, *a.*

comb, kōm, *n.* A toothed instrument of bone, metal, plastic, or rubber, for arranging the hair, or for keeping it in place; any comblike object; the fleshy growth on the head of the domestic fowl.—*v.t.* To dress the hair, with or as with a comb; to search thoroughly.

com·bat, kəm·bat', *v.t.,* **-bat·ed, -bat·ing** or **-bat·ted, -bat·ting.** To fight; oppose.—*v.i.* To fight; to do battle. —kom'bat, kəm'bat, *n.* A battle or skirmish in war; a struggle; a conflict.

com·bat·ant, kəm·bat'ənt, kom'bə·tənt, *a.* Combating; fighting; disposed to combat.

com·ba·tive, kəm·bat'iv, kom'bə·tiv, *a.* Eager to fight.

comb·er, kōm'ər, *n.* One who combs; a big wave.

com·bi·na·tion, kom'bə·nā'shən, *n.* The act of combining; a number of things combined, or something formed by combining; the set or series of numbers or letters used in setting the mechanism of a certain type of lock. **—com·bi·na·tion·al,** *a.* **—com·bi·na·tive,** kom'bə·nā·tiv, kəm·bī'nə·tiv, *a.*

com·bine, kəm·bīn', *v.t.,* **-bined, -bin·ing.** To join into a close union; unite.—*v.i.* To enter into chemical union.—kom'bīn, *n.* A group united for purposes of controlling something; a harvesting machine which automatically cuts and threshes grain. **—com·bin·a·ble,** *a.* **—com·bin·er,** *n.*

com·bin·ing form, *n.* A word element used for combining with other words or word elements, as 'Anglo-,' in 'Anglophile.'

com·bo, kom'bō, *n. pl.,* **com·bos.** A small group of musicians who play jazz or music for dancing.

com·bus·ti·ble, kəm·bəs'tə·bəl, *a.* Capable of catching fire and burning; flammable; fiery; hot-tempered.—*n.* A substance that can readily catch fire and burn. **—com·bus·ti·bil·i·ty,** kəm·bəs·tə·bil'ə·tē, *n.*

com·bus·tion, kəm·bəs'chən, *n.* The act or process of burning; the action of fire on burnable things; violent excitement; tumult. **—com·bus·tive,** *a.*

come, kəm, *v.i.,* **came, come, coming.** To move toward something; approach; to be of similar quality; arrive at through a changed condition: The water *came* to a boil. To appear as a result of: This *comes* of carelessness. To move toward in the sense of achievement: to *come* up the hard way. To extend or reach: The dress *comes* to her knees. To turn out to be: to *come* loose, to *come* to life. To occur to the mind: The name *came* to him in a flash. To occur: No good will *come* of this. To originate: He *comes* from England. To enter a specified state or condition: to *come* into use. To be classified or part of: to *come* under my jurisdiction. To be obtainable: To *come* in two colors. *Informal:* to reach an orgasm; to assume a role: to *come* as the haughty queen.—*impv.* To call attention or remonstrate: *Come,* that will do! **—come across,** meet or find by chance. **—come along,** show progress. **—come back,** return to a former position. **—come down with,** fall ill with. **—come in,** to enter; to be among winners in a race; receive: *come in* for criticism. **—come into,** get possession of: she will *come into* a fortune at 21. **—come off,** to be successful. **—come on,** to start: The storm *came on* suddenly. **—come out,** to appear after being obscured or kept secret. **—come over,** change one's mind; have an effect on: a strange feeling *came over* me. **—come round,** recover; slowly see another's views. **—come to,** amount to: The bill *came to* six dollars; regain consciousness: He *came to* after an hour. **—come through,** survive a bad experience; perform as hoped: We know you will *come through.* **—come up,** be spoken of; suggest or supply something: *come up* with a good idea.

come·back, kəm'bak, *n. Informal.* A successful attempt to regain one's lost skill or public acceptance; a recovery of strength or health; a clever response.

co·me·di·an, kə·mē'dē·ən, *n.* An actor in comedy; a writer of comedy; a professional entertainer who amuses by means of jokes and comic behavior; any amusing or comical person. **—co·me·di·enne,** kə·mē·dē·en', *n. fem.*

come·down, kəm'down, *n. Informal.* An unexpected or humiliating descent from dignity, importance, or prosperity.

com·e·dy, kom'ə·dē, *n. pl.,* **-dies.** A dramatic composition of light and humorous character; the comic element of drama, of literature generally, or of life.

come·ly, kəm'lē, *a.* Handsome; graceful. **—come·li·ness,** *n.*

come-on, kəm'on, kəm'ôn, *n. Informal.* Anything intended to lure another.

com·er, kəm'ər, *n.* One who comes: All *comers* are welcome. *Informal.* One who shows promise of future achievement.

com·et, kom'it, *n.* One of the heavenly bodies, orbiting the sun in eccentric paths, each of which is a small, dense nucleus surrounded by a large mass of gases and dust, called the coma, that extends into a long tail.

come·up·pance, kəm·əp'əns, *n. Informal.* A deserved punishment or reprimand.

com·fort, kəm'fərt, *v.t.* To bring out of depression; to soothe when in grief or trouble; to cheer.—*n.* Relief in affliction; consolation; a person or thing that affords consolation.

com·fort·a·ble, kəmf't·bəl, kəm'fər·tə·bəl, *a.* Being in comfort; giving comfort. **—com·fort·a·bly,** *adv.*

com·fort·er, kəm'fər·tər, *n.* One who or that which comforts; a woolen scarf for wrapping round the neck in cold weather; a light, warm bedcover.

com·fy, kəm'fē, *a.,* **-fi·er, -fi·est.** *Informal.* Comfortable.

com·ic, kom'ik, *a.* Of, or pertaining to the comedy; humorous; laughable.—*n.* A comic actor or performer; a comic paper or periodical. **—com·i·cal,** *a.*

com·ic strip, *n.* A series of narrative cartoons appearing in sequence, usually in a newspaper.

com·ing, kəm'ing, *n.* Approach; arrival.—*a.* Next: the *coming* spring; soon to be famous.

com·i·ty, kom'ə·tē, *n. pl.,* **-ties.** Courtesy; civility.

com·ma, kom'ə, *n. pl.,* **com·mas,** A punctuation mark (,) used to indicate small interruptions in thought or grammatical construction within a sentence.

com·mand, kə·mand', kə·mänd', *v.t.* To direct with

authority; have or exercise power or authority over; to demand; to overlook by reason of location; to have charge of a military or naval unit.—*v.i.* To issue orders; to have or exercise power or authority; to overlook a region.—*n.* Authority; an order; troops, district, or region under a commander; mastery; ability to control; an outlook over.—*a.* Done in answer to an order: a *command* performance.

com·man·dant, kom·ən·dant′, kom·ən·dänt′, *n.* The commanding officer of a place or military body.

com·man·deer, kom·ən·dēr′, *v.t.* To order or force into active military service; to seize private property, for military or other public use.

com·mand·er, kə·man′dər, *n.* One authorized to command; one who commands an army or army unit; a naval officer below a captain and above a lieutenant commander. —**com·mand·er·ship,** *n.*

com·mand·er in chief, *n. pl.,* **com·mand·ers in chief.** One who has supreme command of the armed forces of a nation; one who commands part of an army.

com·mand·ing of·fi·cer, *n.* The commissioned officer in charge who is in command of an organization or base.

com·mand·ment, kə·mand′mənt, kə·mänd′mənt, *n.* A command or mandate; a divine command: one of the Ten Commandments.

com·man·do, kə·man′dō, *n. pl.,* **-dos, -does.** A military force that carries out surprise raids into enemy territory; a member of such a force.

com·mem·o·rate, kə·mem′ə·rāt, *v.t.,* **-rat·ed, -rat·ing.** To honor the memory of with a celebration. —**com·mem·o·ra·ble,** kə·mem′ə·rə·bəl, *a.* —**com·mem·o·ra·tion,** kə·mem·ə·rā′shən, *n.* —**com·mem·o·ra·tive,** kə·mem′ə·rā·tiv, *a.* —**com·mem·o·ra·to·ry,** kə·mem′ər·ə·tôr·ē, *a.*

com·mence, kə·mens′, *v.i., v.t.,* **-menced, -menc·ing.** To begin; start.

com·mence·ment, kə·mens′mənt, *n.* The act of commencing; the ceremony of graduation where diplomas or degrees are conferred; day when this ceremony takes place.

com·mend, kə·mend′, *v.t.* To praise; recommend; to call for attention: This subject *commends* itself to our attention.—*v.i.* To approve; to praise. —**com·mend·a·ble,** *a.* —**com·mend·a·bly,** *adv.*

com·men·da·tion, kə·men·dā′shən, *n.* Praise. —**com·mend·a·to·ry,** kə·men′də·tôr·ē, *a.*

com·men·su·rate, kə·men′sər·it, kə·men′shər·it, *a.* In the right proportion; of equal size; adequate. —**com·men·su·rate·ly,** *adv.* —**com·men·su·ra·tion,** kə·men·sə·rā′shən, *n.*

com·ment, kom′ent, *v.i.* To make remarks or observations.—*v.t.* To remark upon.—*n.* An expression of opinion, an observation, or a criticism; a note that explains.

com·men·tar·y, kom′ən·ter·ē, *n. pl.,* **-ies.** A series of comments; anything meant to explain a comment.

com·men·ta·tor, kom′ən·tā·tər, *n.* A person who writes a commentary; one who reports news, weather, or sports on radio or television.

com·merce, kom′ərs, *n.* Exchange of goods, esp. between different countries; trade; business.

com·mer·cial, kə·mər′shəl, *n.* An advertisement made over radio or television.—*a.* Having to do with commerce or trade; made for mass consumption: *commercial* products. —**com·mer·cial·ism,** *n.* —**com·mer·cial·ize,** *v.t.,* **-ized, -iz·ing.** —**com·mer·cial·i·za·tion,** kə·mər·shə·lə·zā′shən, *n.*

com·mie, kom′ē, *n. Informal.* A communist.

com·mis·er·ate, kə·miz′ə·rāt, *v.t.,* **-at·ed, -at·ing.** To feel sorrow or pain through sympathy; to pity. —**com·mis·er·a·tion,** kə·miz·ə·rā′shən, *n.* —**com·mis·er·a·tive,** *a.*

com·mis·sar, kom′ə·sär, kom·ə·sär′, *n.* A Communist party official formerly in charge of a government department in Russia.

com·mis·sar·y, kom′ə·ser·ē, *n. pl.,* **-ies.** A store for equipment, provisions, or food operated for military, lumber camp, mining personnel, etc.; food supplies in general.

com·mis·sion, kə·mish′ən, *n.* An official paper granting some authority to act; the position or rank of an officer in the army or navy; a group authorized to act; the condition of having special authority to act; the condition of anything in active service or use: as, to be in or out of *commission;* a sum or percentage allowed to the agent in a commercial transaction for his or her services.—*v.t.* To authorize; delegate; to put in commission; to give a commission or order for. —**com·mis·sioned,** *a.*

com·mis·sion·er, kə·mish′ə·nər, *n.* A person who has a commission or warrant from proper authority to perform some office or execute some business.

com·mit, kə·mit′, *v.t.,* **-mit·ted, -mit·ting.** To give in trust or charge; consign for safekeeping; to consign to a mental institution or prison; to do; to perpetrate, as a crime, error, or folly; to bind by pledge.

com·mit·ment, kə·mit′mənt, *n.* The act of committing, or the state of being committed; the act of taking financial responsibilities.

com·mit·tee, kə·mit′ē, *n.* A person or a group of persons appointed to investigate, report, or act in special cases. —**com·mit·tee·man,** *n.* —**com·mit·tee·wo·man,** *n.*

com·mode, kə·mōd′, *n.* A low cabinet or chest of drawers; a toilet.

com·mo·di·ous, kə·mō′dē·əs, *a.* Roomy and convenient.

com·mod·i·ty, kə·mod′ə·tē, *n. pl.,* **-ties.** Something that is of use or is valuable; an article of trade or commerce.

com·mo·dore, kom′ə·dōr, kom′ə·dôr, *n.* A commissioned officer in the U.S. Navy ranking under a rear admiral.

com·mon, kom′ən, *a.* Familiar or usual; ordinary; of or pertaining to a community at large: *common* language; belonging to or equally shared by two or more individuals: *common* property; joint or united: a *common* front; widespread or general: *common* knowledge; simple in nature: *common* courtesy; vulgar: His clothes were tasteless and *common;* second rate or inferior in quality: The cabinets were made of the most *common* wood; lacking in status: a *common* foot soldier.—*n.* A piece of land used by all community members.—**in common,** in joint possession.

com·mon·al·ty, kom′ən·al·tē, *n. pl.,* **-ties.** The general body or mass, as of mankind.

com·mon car·ri·er, *n.* An individual or a corporation whose business is the transportation of goods or passengers, as a railroad or a bus company.

com·mon law, *n.* The unwritten law based on usage and custom, as distinct from statute law.

com·mon-law mar·riage, *n.* A marriage in which a man and a woman simply agree to live together without going through any ceremony.

com·mon mar·ket, *n.* A customs union. *(Cap.)* Association formed in 1958 by Belgium, France, Italy, Luxembourg, the Netherlands, and West Germany which is officially known as the European Economic Community.

com·mon·place, kom′ən·plās, *n.* A common or customary subject of remark; something taken for granted.—*a.* Ordinary.

com·mons, kom′ənz, *n. pl.* The common people; food served for a large group; a dining hall.

com·mon sense, *n.* Sound practical judgment.

com·mon touch, *n.* The personal quality of appeal to the common people.

com·mon·weal, kom′ən·wēl, *n.* The welfare of the public.

com·mon·wealth, kom′ən·welth, *n.* The people of a nation, state, or other political unit; a nation or state where the people rule. *Informal.* A state of the U.S.

com•mo•tion, kə•mō′shən, *n.* Disturbance; excitement.

com•mu•nal, kom′yə•nəl, kə•mū′nəl, *a.* Relating to a commune or a community; owned in common. **—com•mu•nal•i•ty,** kom•ū•nal′ə•tē, *n.*

com•mune, kə•mūn′, *v.i.,* **-muned, -mun•ing.** To converse; to talk together familiarly.

com•mune, kom′ūn, *n.* A community; a small rural community organized as a collective unit; a unit of government believing in revolutionary or communist principles.

com•mu•ni•cant, kə•mū′nə•kənt, *n.* One who communicates; one who partakes, or is entitled to partake, of the Eucharist. **—a.**

com•mu•ni•cate, kə•mū′nə•kāt, *v.t.,* **-cat•ed, -cat•ing.** To give to another; transmit, as a disease; make known; to administer the Eucharist to.—*v.i.* To have interchange of thoughts. **—com•mu•ni•ca•ble,** kə•mū′nə•kə•bəl, *a.* **—com•mu•ni•ca•tive,** kə•mū′nə•kā•tiv, *a.*

com•mu•ni•ca•tion, kə•mū•nə•kā′shən, *n.* The act or fact of communicating; a document or message imparting views or information.

com•mu•ni•ca•tions, kə•mū•nə•kā′shənz, *n. pl. but sing. in constr.* A system of facilities used for communicating messages or orders; the technology or industry of transmitting messages by means of a system of electrical or electronic facilities; the combined study of effective communication in all forms, including speech and writing, and graphic and dramatic arts.

com•mun•ion, kə•mū′nyən, *n.* The act of sharing, or holding in common; a spiritual interchange of ideas or feelings, usu. between man and nature or the supernatural. (*Often cap.*) The celebration of the Lord's Supper; the Eucharist.

com•mu•ni•qué, kə•mū•nə•kā′, kə•mū′nə•kā, *n.* An official communication.

com•mun•ism, kom′yə•niz•əm, *n.* A theory or system of social organization based on the holding of property in common, actual ownership being in the hands of the community as a whole or the state; communalism.

com•mun•ist, kom′yə•nist, *n.* An advocate of communism. (Cap.) Member of a party that works for the establishment of communism.

com•mu•ni•ty, kə•mū′nə•tē, *n. pl.,* **-ties.** A number of individuals associated together by the fact of residence in the same locality, or of subjection to the same laws and regulations, or having common ties or interests; the body of people of a place; the public; common character.

com•mu•ni•ty prop•er•ty, *n.* Any property jointly owned by husband and wife.

com•mu•nize, kom′yə•nīz, *v.t.,* **-nized, -niz•ing.** To transfer individual ownership of (property) to community ownership.

com•mu•ta•tion, kom•yə•tā′shən, *n.* Exchange; substitution; repeated travel between home and work.

com•mu•ta•tor, kom′yə•tā•tər, *n.* A device for reversing the direction of a current.

com•mute, kə•mūt′, *v.t.,* **-mut•ed, -mut•ing.** To exchange for another or something else; interchange. *Elect.* To alter or direct (a current) by a commutator.—*v.i.* To make substitution; serve as a substitute; travel daily from the suburbs to the city to work. **—com•mut•a•ble,** *a.*

com•mut•er, kə•mū′tər, *n.* One who travels to and from work.

com•pact, kom′pakt, *n.* An agreement; a small case, usu. carried in a woman's purse with a mirror and face powder and sometimes rouge; an economically-operated small model of a standard-sized automobile.

com•pact, kəm•pakt′, kom′pakt, *a.* Having the parts

or particles close; solid; dense; not diffuse; not verbose; concise; composed.—*v.t.,* To thrust, drive, or press closely together; to consolidate; to unite or connect firmly, as in a system.

com•pan•ion, kəm•pan′yən, *n.* One who accompanies another; an associate; a person employed to afford company or assistance to another; a mate or match for a thing.—*v.t.*

com•pan•ion•a•ble, kəm•pan′yən•ə•bəl, *a.* Sociable.

com•pan•ion•ship, kəm•pan′yən•ship, *n.* Association as companions; a body of companions.

com•pa•ny, kəm′pə•nē, *n. pl.,* **-nies.** A number of individuals assembled or associated together; a guest or guests; society collectively, esp. a number of persons united or incorporated for joint action; companionship; an association for carrying on a commercial enterprise; a military unit commanded by a captain, made up of three platoons; a group of performers.— **keep com•pa•ny,** to associate with or be friendly with.—**part com•pa•ny,** to discontinue friendship or an association.

com•pa•ra•ble, kom′pə•rə•bəl, *a.* Capable of being compared. **—com•pa•ra•bil•i•ty,** *n.*

com•par•a•tive, kəm•par′ə•tiv, *a.* Estimated by comparison; involving comparison as a method of study; expressing a degree of comparison greater than the positive: a *comparative* adjective.—*n.* the form of an adjective or adverb that shows this degree, such as *faster* or *more beautiful.*

com•pare, kəm•pār′, *v.t.,* **-pared, -par•ing.** To examine and note the similarities and differences of (two or more things, ideas, or people); to form the comparative degree of adjectives and adverbs.—*v.i.* To contrast one thing with another.—*n.* Comparison, as: His craftsmanship is beyond *compare.*

com•par•i•son, kəm•par′ə•sən, *n.* The act of examining in order to discover how one thing compares to another; the change of an adjective or adverb to show degrees.

com•part•ment, kəm•pärt′mənt, *n.* A separate part of a general design, as a building, railroad car, picture, or plan.—*v.t.* To partition. **—com•part•men•tal,** *a.* **—com•part•ment•ed,** *a.* **—com•part•men•tal•ize,** kəm•pärt•men′tə•līz, *v.t.* **-ized, -iz•ing.**

com•pass, kəm′pəs, *n.* An instrument for determining directions, which is a freely pivoting magnetized needle or bar which points to the magnetic north; an instrument for drawing circles, etc., and measuring distances, made of two movable legs hinged at one end; space within some limits; boundary or circumference; range of a voice or musical instrument.—*v.t.* To enclose; to grasp, as with the mind; obtain, as: He was unable to *compass* his ambitions.

com•pas•sion, kəm•pash′ən, *n.* A sympathetic emotion created by the misfortunes of another, accompanied by a desire to help; mercy. **—com•pas•sion•ate,** kəm•pash′ə•nit, *a.*

com•pat•i•ble, kəm•pat′ə•bəl, *a.* Capable of existing together in harmony; congenial; agreeable. **—com•pat•i•bly,** *adv.* **—com•pat•i•bil•i•ty,** kəm•pat•ə•bil′ə•tē, *n.*

com•pa•tri•ot, kəm•pā′trē•ət, *n.* A fellow countryman or countrywoman.

com•peer, kəm•pēr′, kom′pēr, *n.* An equal; a companion.

com•pel, kəm•pel′, *v.t.,* **-pelled, -pel•ling.** To drive or urge with force; to oblige or necessitate.

com•pen•di•ous, kəm•pen′dē•əs, *a.* Succinct; concise. **—com•pen•di•um,** kəm•pen′dē•əm, *n. pl.,* **-di•ums, -di•a,** -dē•ə. A brief treatment or summary of a larger work or body of knowledge; an abridgment.

com•pen•sate, kom′pən•sāt, *v.t.,* **-sat•ed, -sat•ing.** To counterbalance or offset; make up for; to pay

---

a- hat, fāte, fâre, fäther; **e-** met, mē; **i-** pin, pīne; **o-** not, nōte, ôrb, moove (move), boy, pownd; **u-** cūbe, bůll, tůk (took); **ch-** chin; **th-** thick, ŧhen; **zh-** vizhon (vision); **ə-** əgo, takən, pencəl, lemən, bərd (bird).

for.—*v.i.* Make amends. —**com·pen·sa·tive**, kəm·pen/sə·tiv, *a.* —**com·pen·sa·tor**, *n.* —**com·pen·sa·to·ry**, kəm·pen/sə·tôr/ē, *a.*

com·pen·sa·tion, kom·pən·sā/shən, *n.* The act of compensating; that which supplies the place of something else or makes good a deficiency.

com·pete, kom·pēt/, *v.i.,* -**pet·ed**, -**pet·ing**. Engage in a contest; vie. —**com·pet·i·tor**, kəm·pet/ə·tər, *n.*

com·pe·tence, kom/pə·təns, *n.* State of being competent; adequacy. Also **com·pe·ten·cy**.

com·pe·tent, kom/pə·tənt, *a.* Answering all requirements; suitable.

com·pe·ti·tion, kom·pə·tish/ən, *n.* The act of competing; rivalry; a trial of skill proposed as a test of superiority or comparative fitness.

com·pet·i·tive, kəm·pet/ə·tiv, *a.* Relating to competition: *competitive* prices.

com·pile, kəm·pīl/, *v.t.,* -**piled**, -**pil·ing**. To put (various materials) into a volume; to draw together. —**com·pi·la·tion**, kom·pə·lā/shən, *n.*

com·pla·cence, kəm·plā/səns, *n.* A feeling of quiet pleasure based on self-satisfaction. Also **com·pla·cen·cy**. —**com·pla·cent**, *a.*

com·plain, kəm·plān/, *v.i.* To express grief, pain, uneasiness, or resentment; to make a charge, followed by *of.*

com·plain·ant, kəm·plā/nənt, *n.* One who makes a complaint. *Law.* One who prosecutes by complaint; a plaintiff.

com·plaint, kəm·plānt/, *n.* Expression of grief, regret, pain, censure, or resentment; a finding fault; an ailment; accusation; the first complaint made by a plaintiff in a civil court.

com·plai·sance, kəm·plā/səns, *n.* Desire to please; disposition to oblige.—**com·plai·sant**, kəm·plā/sənt, *a.*

com·plect·ed, kəm·plek/tid, *a. Informal.* Complexioned: dark-*complected.*

com·ple·ment, kom/plə·mənt, *n.* That which completes or makes perfect; full quantity or amount; full number of officers and men needed to man a ship; quantity that makes up a whole when added to another part.—kom/plə·ment, *v.t.* To complete. —**com·ple·men·tal**, *a.* —**com·ple·men·ta·ry**, *a.*

com·plete, kəm·plēt/, *a.* Having no lack; perfect; thorough; finished; ended.—*v.t.,* -**plet·ed**, -**plet·ing**. To make whole or entire; to finish. —**com·plet·a·ble**, *a.*

com·ple·tion, kəm·plē/shən, *n.* Act of completing; state of being complete; accomplishment.

com·plex, kəm·pleks/, kom/pleks, *a.* Characterized by an involved combination of parts; complicated; intricate. —kom/pleks, *n.* A structural whole made of interconnected parts: a school *complex;* an industrial *complex. Informal.* A fixed idea; an obsessive notion.

com·plex·ion, kəm·plek/shən, *n.* The color or hue of the skin, particularly of the face; the general appearance of anything. —**com·plex·ioned**, *a.*

com·plex·i·ty, kəm·plek/sə·tē, *n. pl.,* -**ties**. Intricacy; something complex.

com·pli·ance, kəm·plī/əns, *n.* The act of complying with a demand or an order. Also **com·pli·an·cy**. —**com·pli·ant**, *a.*

com·pli·cate, kom/plə·kāt, *v.t.,* -**cat·ed**, -**cat·ing**. To make complex, or involved.—*v.i.* To become intricate. —**com·pli·cat·ed**, kom/plə·kā/tid, *a.* —**com·pli·ca·tion**, kom·plə·kā/shən, *n.*

com·plic·i·ty, kəm·plis/ə·tē, *n. pl.,* -**ties**. The state of being an accomplice; partnership in crime.

com·pli·ment, kom/plə·mənt, *n.* An expression of admiration; *pl.,* good wishes; praise. —kom/plə·ment, *v.t.* To pay a compliment to.

com·pli·men·ta·ry, kom·plə·men/tə·rē, kom·plə·men/trē, *a.* Intended to express a compliment; free. —**com·pli·men·ta·ri·ly**, *adv.*

com·ply, kəm·plī/, *v.t.,* -**plied**, -**ply·ing**. To fulfill; execute.—*v.i.* To act in accordance with wishes, requests, or requirements; to yield; conform.

com·po·nent, kəm·pō/nənt, *n.* An essential part.—*a.* Constituting; entering into as a part.

com·port, kəm·pōrt/, kəm·pôrt/, *v.t.* To bear or conduct (oneself); behave.—*v.i.* To agree with; suit.

com·port·ment, kəm·pōrt/mənt, kəm·pôrt/mənt, *n.* Behavior; demeanor.

com·pose, kəm·pōz/, *v.t.,* -**posed**, -**pos·ing**. To form by uniting two or more things; to form; to write, as an author; to calm; to set type in printing.—*v.i.* To practice literary, musical, or artistic composition.

com·posed, kəm·pōzd/, *a.* Calm; quiet.

com·pos·er, kəm·pō/zər, *n.* One who writes an original work, esp. one who composes musical pieces.

com·pos·ite, kəm·poz/it, *a.* Made up of various parts or elements; compound; belonging to the largest vegetable family of plants, in which tiny florets are massed into flowerlike heads, as in the daisy.—*n.* Something compound; a composite plant.

com·po·si·tion, kom·pə·zish/ən, *n.* The act or manner of writing prose, verse, a musical, or other artistic work; a short essay written as a school exercise; the act of combining parts to form a whole; the manner in which such parts are combined; a compound or composite substance; the setting up of type for printing.

com·post, kom/pōst, *n.* A mixture of various substances, as dung or dead leaves, for fertilizing land.—*v.t.* To treat with or make into compost.

com·po·sure, kəm·pō/zhər, *n.* A settled state of mind; calmness.

com·pote, kom/pōt, *n.* Fruit, stewed or preserved in syrup and served as dessert.

com·pound, kəm·pownd/, kom/pownd, *v.t.* To combine; construct; to heighten by adding something new.—*v.i.* To make a bargain; compromise; settle a debt by compromise. —kom/pownd, kəm·pownd/, *a.* Composed of two or more parts; involving two or more actions or functions; composite. —kom/pownd, *n.* Something formed by compounding or combining parts.

com·pound, kom/pownd, *n.* A large area enclosed by a wall or fence, esp. one for prisoners of war.

com·pound frac·ture, *n.* A fracture in which a bone is broken and sticks through the skin surface.

com·pound in·ter·est, *n.* That interest computed from the principal plus its accrued interest.

com·pound word, *n.* A word made up of two or more words which retain their separate form and signification.

com·pre·hend, kom·pri·hend/, *v.t.* To understand; to include by implication or signification; to include. —**com·pre·hend·i·ble**, *a.*

com·pre·hen·si·ble, kom·pri·hen/sə·bəl, *a.* Capable of being understood; intelligible. —**com·pre·hen·si·bil·i·ty**, kom·pri·hen·sə·bil/ə·tē, *n.* —**com·pre·hen·si·bly**, *adv.*

com·pre·hen·sion, kom·pri·hen/shən, *n.* The act of comprehending, including, or embracing; capacity of the mind to understand.

com·pre·hen·sive, kom·pri·hen/siv, *a.* Wide in scope; having the power to comprehend or understand.

com·press, kəm·pres/, *v.t.* To press together; to form into a solid mass; condense. —kom/pres, *n.* A soft pad of cloth for applying pressure, cold, heat, or medicine. —**com·pressed**, *a.* —**com·press·i·ble**, *a.* —**com·press·i·bil·i·ty**, kəm·pres·ə·bil/ə·tē, *n.*

com·pres·sion, kəm·presh/ən, *n.* The act of compressing or the state of being compressed.

com·pres·sor, kəm·pres/ər, *n.* A machine that reduces the volume of gases and increases their pressure so they can be used in refrigeration or for driving an engine.

com·prise, kəm·prīz/, *v.t.,* -**prised**, -**pris·ing**. To include; be made up of: The United States *comprises* fifty states; to form; to make up: Twenty-six characters *comprise* our alphabet.

com·pro·mise, kom′prə·mīz, *n.* A settlement of differences by mutual concessions; anything resulting from compromise; a compromising or endangering, as of reputation.—*v.t.,* **-mised, -mis·ing.** To settle by a compromise; endanger, as to reputation; involve unfavorably—*v.i.* To make a compromise.

comp·trol·ler, kən·trō′lər, *n.* A controller; an officer who examines expenditures and checks finances of a company.

com·pul·sion, kəm·pəl′shən, *n.* The act of compelling or the state of being compelled; a strong, irresistible impulse to carry out an act.

com·pul·sive, kəm·pəl′siv, *a.* Compulsory; dictated by irresistible psychological urges.

com·pul·so·ry, kəm·pəl′sə·rē, *a.* Compelling; enforced; mandatory.

com·punc·tion, kəm·pəngk′shən, *n.* Regret for wrongdoing; a questioning of the rightness of one's actions; a qualm.

com·pute, kəm·pūt′, *v.t.,* **-put·ed, -put·ing.** To calculate; to estimate.—*v.i.* To reckon by means of a computer or data processing machine. **—com·put·a·ble,** *a.* **—com·pu·ta·tion,** kom·pyə·tā′shən, *n.*

com·put·er, kəm·pū′tər, *n.* An electronic machine which solves problems and does complicated calculations by processing data according to programmed instructions and then prints, shows, or retains the outcome of these processes; a calculator.

com·put·er·ize, kəm·pū′tə·rīz, *v.t.,* **-ized, -iz·ing.** To execute, regulate, or store with a computer; to furnish with computers. **—com·put·er·i·za·tion,** kəm·pū·tər·ə·zā′shən, *n.*

com·rade, kom′rad, *n.* A companion in work, interests, or activities; a fellow soldier or other fighting man; a fellow party member. **—com·rade·ship,** *n.*

com·sat, kom′sat, *n.* Any of several man-made satellites that relay ground communication signals.

con, kon, *adv.* Against.

con, kon, *v.t.,* **conned, con·ning.** *Informal.* To trick; to persuade.—*a.* Deceiving: a *con* game.

con, kon, *n.* *Informal.* A convict.

con·cave, kon·kāv′, kon′kāv, *a.* Hollow and curved or rounded, as the inner surface of a spherical body; incurved. **—kon′kāv, kong·kāv,** *n.* A concave surface or line.

con·ceal, kən·sēl′, *v.t.* To hide; to cover or keep from sight; to keep close or secret. **—con·ceal·a·ble,** *a.* **—con·ceal·ment,** *n.*

con·cede, kən·sēd′, *v.t.,* **-ced·ed, -ced·ing.** To admit as true, just, or proper; to grant as a privilege; to acknowledge, as an opponent's victory, before an official decision has been made.—*v.i.* To make concession; to grant a request or petition; to yield.

con·ceit, kən·sēt′, *n.* An exaggerated opinion of one's own worth or importance; a thought; an idea; favorable opinion; a fancy or whim; witty thought or expression; a fanciful metaphor.

con·ceit·ed, kən·sē′tid, *a.* Vain.

con·ceive, kən·sēv′, *v.t.,* **-ceived, -ceiv·ing.** To become pregnant with; form a notion or idea of; imagine; to experience or entertain, as a feeling.—*v.i.* To become pregnant; to form an idea of; think. **—con·ceiv·a·ble,** *a.* **—con·ceiv·a·bly,** *adv.*

con·cen·trate, kon′sən·trāt, *v.t.,* **-tra·ted, -trat·ing.** To cause to come together to one spot or point; to direct toward one object, as all one's attention; to reduce to a state of great strength and purity.—*v.i.* To approach or meet in a common point or center.—*n.* Something that has been concentrated. **—con·cen·tra·tive,** *a.* **—con·cen·tra·tor,** *n.*

con·cen·tra·tion, kon·sən·trā′shən, *n.* Exclusive attention to one object; close mental application; something concentrated.

con·cen·tra·tion camp, *n.* A camp with barracks

and fence, patrolled by the military, used for the detention and punishment of people.

con·cen·tric, kən·sen′trik, *a.* Having a common center, as circles or spheres; center. Also **con·cen·tri·cal. —con·cen·tric·i·ty,** kon·sen·tris′ə·tē, *n.*

con·cept, kon′sept, *n.* That which is conceived in the mind; a general notion or idea. **—con·cep·tu·al,** kən·sep′choo·əl, *a.*

con·cep·tion, kən·sep′shən, *n.* The act of conceiving, or the state of being conceived; the inception of life; beginning; that which is conceived; the embryo or fetus; a notion or idea; a concept; a design or plan. **—con·cep·tive,** *a.*

con·cep·tu·al·ize, kən·sep′choo·ə·līz, *v.t.,* **-ized, -iz·ing.** To form into a concept.—*v.i.* To think in concepts. **—con·cep·tu·al·i·za·tion,** kən·sep·choo·ə·lə·zā′shən, *n.*

con·cern, kən·sern′, *v.t.* Be of interest or importance to; to interest, or involve: to *concern* oneself *with* a matter, to be *concerned in* a transaction; to disquiet or trouble: He was *concerned* about my health.—*n.* Interest; solicitude or anxiety; a matter that engages one's attention, interest, or care; a commercial or manufacturing firm or establishment. **—con·cerned,** *a.*

con·cern·ing, kən·sər′ning, *prep.* Relating to; regarding; about.

con·cert, kon′sərt, *n.* A musical performance in which several singers, an orchestra, a ballet group, etc., take part; accord or harmony.

con·cert·ed, kən·sər′tid, *a.* Contrived or arranged by agreement; done in concert.

con·cer·ti·na, kon·sər·tē′nə, *n.* A small, portable, bellows-like musical instrument.

con·cert·mas·ter, kon′sərt·mas·tər, *n.* The first violinist of an orchestra.

con·cer·to, kən·cher′tō, *n. pl.,* **-tos, -ti,** -tē. A musical composition for one principal instrument, with accompaniments for a full orchestra.

con·ces·sion, kən·sesh′ən, *n.* The act of conceding or yielding, as a point or fact in an argument; that which is conceded; a right, or franchise to perform some service, or to sell, such as cigarettes or food at a ball game.

con·ces·sion·aire, kən·sesh·ə·nār′, *n.* One to whom a concession has been granted.

conch, kongk, konch, *n. pl.,* **conchs,** kongks, **conches,** kon′chiz. A shellfish, or its shell.

con·cil·i·ate, kən·sil′ē·āt, *v.t.,* **-at·ed, -at·ing.** To overcome, as distrust or hostility, by soothing or pacifying means; placate; reconcile. **—con·cil·i·a·tion,** kən·sil·ē·ā′shən, *n.* **—con·cil·i·a·to·ry,** kən·sil′ē·ə·tôr·ē, *a.*

con·cise, kən·sīs′, *a.* Expressing much in few words; brief and comprehensive; succinct; terse. **—con·cise·ness,** *n.* **—con·cise·ly,** *adv.*

con·clave, kon′klāv, kong′klāv, *n.* A meeting of individuals with special power or influence; a secret assembly.

con·clude, kən·klood′, *v.t.,* **-clud·ed, -clud·ing.** To arrive at a decision by reasoning; deduce; settle or arrange finally; to end.—*v.i.* To resolve; to end.

con·clu·sion, kən·kloo′zhən, *n.* The end or close; the final part; a result, or outcome; a deduction or inference; final decision.

con·clu·sive, kən·kloo′siv, *a.* Serving to settle or decide a question; convincing.

con·coct, kon·kokt′, kən·kokt′, *v.t.* To devise; to plot, as a scheme; to mix by combining different ingredients, as in cooking.

con·coc·tion, kən·kok′shən, *n.* The act of mixing ingredients; the thing concocted.

con·com·i·tant, kon·kom′ə·tənt, kən·kom′ə·tənt, *a.* Accompanying; concurrent.—*n.* An accompaniment; an accessory. **—con·com·i·tance,** *n.*

---

a- hat, fāte, fâre, fäther; **e-** met, mē; **i-** pin, pīne; **o-** not, nōte, ôrb, moove (move), boy, pownd; **u-** cūbe, bûll, tûk (took); **ch-** chin; **th-** thick, ŧhen; **zh-** vizhon (vision); **ə-** əgo, takən, pencəl, lemən, bərd (bird).

con·cord, kon′kôrd, kong′kôrd, *n.* Agreement between persons; accord; peace; harmony; grammatical agreement.

con·cord·ance, kon·kôr′dəns, kən·kôr′dəns, *n.* An alphabetical list of the main words in a work; agreement; harmony. **—con·cord·ant,** *a.*

con·course, kon′kōrs, kon′kôrs, kong′kōrs, kong′kôrs, *n.* A moving, flowing, or running together; a crowd; a street, road or other broad thoroughfare; grounds used for racing or other athletic sports; an open space where people congregate, as in a railroad terminal.

con·crete, kon′krēt, kon·krēt′, *a.* Not abstract; specific. United in a coagulated, condensed, or solid state; made of concrete; constituting an actual thing or instance.—*n.* An artificial stonelike material used for pavement and foundations, made by mixing cement, sand, and broken stones with water; a concrete idea or term; a concrete object or thing. **—kon′krēt′,** *v.t.,* **-cret·ed, -cret·ing.** To render solid; unite or combine, as qualities or attributes; to make concrete, as an idea; cover with concrete.

con·cre·tion, kon·krē′shən, *n.* The act or process of concreting; a solid mass formed by the clinging together of particles, or cohesion. **—con·cre·tive,** *a.*

con·cu·bine, kong′kū·bīn, kon′kū·bīn, *n.* A woman who cohabits with a man without being legally married to him; a mistress; a secondary wife among certain peoples.

con·cur, kən·kər′, *v.i.,* **-curred, -cur·ring.** To agree: to *concur* with a person in an opinion; to coincide or take place simultaneously. **—con·cur·rence,** *n.* **—con·cur·rent,** *a.*

con·cus·sion, kən·kəsh′ən, *n.* The act of shaking or shocking, as by a blow; shock occasioned by the impact of a collision; injury to the brain or spine, from a blow or fall. **—con·cus·sive,** kən·kəs′iv, *a.*

con·demn, kən·dem′, *v.t.* Express strong disapproval of; to pronounce to be guilty; doom; to adjudge to be unfit for use or service, as a ship; declare subject to use for a public purpose, under the right of eminent domain. **—con·dem·na·ble,** kən·dem′nə·bəl, *a.* **—con·dem·na·tion,** kon·dem·nā′shən, kon·dəm·nā′shən, *n.* **—con·dem·na·to·ry,** kən·dem′nə·tôr·ē, *a.*

con·dense, kən·dens′, *v.t.,* **-densed, -dens·ing.** To make more dense or compact; to reduce the volume of; to compress or abridge: as, to *condense* a magazine article; to reduce, as a gas or vapor, to the condition of a solid or liquid.—*v.i.* To become less dense. **—con·den·sa·ble,** *a.* **—con·densed,** *a.* **—con·den·sa·tion,** kon·den·sā′shən, *n.*

con·dens·er, kən·den′sər, *n.* An apparatus for condensing vapor to a liquid or solid form; a device for accumulating and holding a charge of electricity; a capacitor.

con·de·scend, kon·di·send′, *v.i.* To come down for a short time to the level of someone considered inferior; to assume or behave in a patronizing manner. **—con·de·scend·ing,** *a.* **—con·de·scen·sion,** kon·di·sen′shən, *n.*

con·di·ment, kon′də·mənt, *n.* Something used to season food; relish.

con·di·tion, kən·dish′ən, *n.* State in which someone or something is; a circumstance necessary for something to happen; *pl.,* circumstances that bear on a situation; state of health; good health; social position; quality or character; a characteristic.—*v.t.* To form or be a condition of; determine, limit, or restrict, as a condition; stipulate; to subject to particular conditions or circumstances; to test, as a commodity; to ascertain its condition; to put in fit or proper state.—*v.i.* To make conditions. **—con·di·tion·al,** *a.* **—con·di·tion·er,** *n.*

con·di·tioned, kən·dish′ənd, *a.* Having a nature or disposition as specified, trained to a certain response.

con·dole, kən·dōl′, *v.i.,* **-doled, -dol·ing.** To express sympathy to one in grief or misfortune. **—con·do·la·to·ry,** *a.* **—con·do·ler,** *n.*

con·do·lence, kən·dō′ləns, *n.* Expression of sympathy with another's grief.

con·dom, kon′dəm, kən′dəm, *n.* A thin sheath, often of rubber, worn over the penis during coitus to prevent conception and venereal infection.

con·do·min·i·um, kon·də·min′ē·əm, *n.* A residential building consisting of multiple units, each under individual ownership; one residential unit in such a building.

con·done, kən·dōn′, *v.i.,* **-doned, -don·ing.** To pardon; to overlook (an offense). **—con·do·na·tion,** kon·dō·nā′shən, *n.*

con·dor, kon′dər, *n.* A large American vulture.

con·duce, kən·doos′, kən·dūs′, *v.i.,* **-duced, -duc·ing.** To contribute to a result.

con·du·cive, kən·doo′siv, kən·dū′siv, *a.* Promoting, or furthering; tending to advance or bring about (with *to*).

con·duct, kən·dəkt′, *v.t.* To lead or guide; escort; manage; to direct as leader: to *conduct* an orchestra; to behave, as oneself; to serve as a medium for transmitting heat or electricity.—kon′dəkt, *n.* Personal behavior; direction. **—con·duct·i·bil·i·ty,** kən·dək·tə·bil′ə·tē, *n.* **—con·duct·i·ble,** *a.*

con·duct·ance, kən·dək′təns, *n.* Power of a conductor to transmit a current.

con·duc·tion, kən·dək′shən, *n.* A conducting, as of water through a pipe; transmission through a conductor.

con·duc·tiv·i·ty, kon·dək·tiv′ə·tē, *n. pl.,* **-ties.** Power of conducting heat, electricity, or sound.

con·duc·tor, kən·dək′tər, *n.* One who conducts; a leader; a guide; the director of an orchestra or chorus; the official in charge of a railroad train, or other public vehicle; a substance capable of transmitting heat, electricity, or sound.

con·duit, kon′doo·it, *n.* A pipe, tube, or other channel for the conveyance of fluids; a tube or pipe for protecting electric wires or cables.

cone, kōn, *n.* A solid figure that rises from a circular base and tapers upward to a point; a surface generated by a moving straight line, one point of which is fixed, which constantly touches a fixed curve; anything cone-shaped: an ice-cream *cone;* the multiple fruit of the pine or fir.

Con·es·to·ga wag·on, kon′i·stō′gə, *n.* A large, broad-wheeled, covered wagon used during the western migration of American pioneers.

co·ney, kō′nē, kən′ē, *n.* Cony.

con·fab, kon′fab, *n. Informal.* Discussion; conversation.—*v.i.* **-fabbed, -fab·bing.**

con·fab·u·late, kən·fab′yə·lāt, *v.i.,* **-lat·ed, -lat·ing.** To chat. **—con·fab·u·la·tion,** kən·fab·yə·lā′shən, *n.*

con·fec·tion, kən·fek′shən, *n.* A sweet candy or preserve. **—con·fec·tion·a·ry,** *a.*

con·fec·tion·er, kən·fek′shə·nər, *n.* One who makes or sells candies, and sometimes ice cream and cakes.

con·fec·tion·er·y, kən·fek′shə·ner·ē, *n. pl.,* **-ies.** A candy shop; confections or sweetmeats collectively; the work or business of a confectioner.

con·fed·er·a·cy, kən·fed′ər·ə·sē, *n. pl.,* **-cies.** A league or alliance of persons, parties, or states for the purpose of acting on mutual goals; a combination of persons for unlawful purposes; a conspiracy.—**the Con·fed·er·a·cy,** *n. U.S. hist.* The southern states which seceded from the Union in 1860–1861.

con·fed·er·ate, kən·fed′ər·it, *a.* United in a league or alliance, or a conspiracy. (*Cap.*) *U.S. hist.* Pertaining to the southern states which seceded from the Union in 1860–61 and formed a separate government.—*n.* One united with others; an ally. —kən·fed′ə·rāt, *v.t., v.i.,* **-at·ed, -at·ing.** To unite.

con·fed·er·a·tion, kən·fed·ə·rā′shən, *n.* A league or alliance; a body of confederates, esp. of states more or less permanently united for common purposes.

con·fer, kən·fėr′, *v.t.*, **-ferred**, **-fer·ring**. To give or bestow (with *on* or *upon*).—*v.i.* To consult together on some special subject. —**con·fer·ral**, *n.*

con·fer·ee, kon·fə·rē′, *n.* One on whom something is conferred.

con·fer·ence, kon′fėr·əns, *n.* A meeting for consultation, discussion, or instruction between individuals or groups; an association or league of schools, teams, or other groups. —**con·fer·en·tial**, kon·fə·ren′shəl, *a.*

con·fess, kən·fes′, *v.t.* To admit or acknowledge, as a crime, or something that is against one's interest or reputation; to own to; to declare belief in; to admit. —**con·fess·ed·ly**, *adv.*

con·fes·sion, kən·fesh′ən, *n.* The act of confessing; that which is confessed; a disclosing of sins or faults to a priest.

con·fes·sion·al, kən·fesh′ə·nəl, *n.* A compartment or cell in which a priest sits to hear confessions.

con·fes·sor, kən·fes′ėr, *n.* One who confesses; a priest who hears confessions.

con·fet·ti, kən·fet′ē, *n. pl., but sing. in constr.* Narrow streamers or bits of colored paper thrown at weddings, parties, parades, etc.

con·fi·dant, kon·fi·dant′, kon·fi·dänt′, kon′fi·dant, kon′fi·dänt, *n.* One to whom secrets are confided; a confidential friend. —**con·fi·dante**, *n. fem.*

con·fide, kən·fīd′, *v.i.*, **-fid·ed, -fid·ing.** To show trust by imparting secrets.—*v.t.* To entrust.

con·fi·dence, kon′fə·dəns, *n.* Full belief in the trustworthiness or reliability of a person or thing; self-reliance; a confidential communication. —**con·fi·dent**, *a.*

con·fi·den·tial, kon·fə·den′shəl, *a.* Intended to be treated as private, or kept in confidence; secret; entrusted with secrets or with private affairs.

con·fid·ing, kən·fī′ding, *a.* Trusting.

con·fig·u·ra·tion, kən·fig·yə·rā′shən, *n.* External form; conformation. —**con·fig·u·ra·tion·al**, *a.*

con·fine, kon′fīn, *n. Usu. pl.* Border; frontier; limit. —kən·fīn′, *v.t.*, **-fined, -fin·ing.** To limit or restrain; enclose within bounds; to imprison.

con·fined, kən·fīnd′, *a.* Restricted to quarters; being in childbirth. —**con·fine·ment**, kən·fīn′mənt, *n.*

con·firm, kən·fėrm′, *v.t.* To make firm or more firm; to strengthen; to settle or establish; to make certain; to assure; to verify; to strengthen in resolution; to admit to full membership in a church. —**con·firm·a·ble**, *a.* —**con·fir·ma·tion**, kon·fėr·mā′shən, *n.* —**con·fir·ma·tive**, *a.* —**con·fir·ma·to·ry**, *a.*

con·firmed, kən·fėrmd′, *a.* Fixed; settled; settled in certain habits. —**con·firm·ed·ly**, *adv.* —**con·firm·ed·ness**, *n.*

con·fis·cate, kon′fi·skāt, kən·fis′kāt, *v.t.*, **-cat·ed, -cat·ing.** To seize as forfeited to the public treasury; to seize by or as if by authority; to appropriate summarily. —**con·fis·ca·tion**, *n.* —**con·fis·ca·tor**, *n.* —**con·fis·ca·to·ry**, kən·fis′kə·tōr′ē, kən·fis·kə·tôr′ē, *a.*

con·fla·gra·tion, kon·flə·grā′shən, *n.* A great fire.

con·flict, kon′flikt, *n.* A fight, struggle, or combat; a controversy or quarrel; active opposition—kən·flikt′, *v.i.* To meet in opposition or hostility; to struggle; to disagree; clash. —**con·flict·ing, con·flic·tive**, *a.* —**con·flic·tion**, *n.*

con·flu·ence, kon′floo·əns, *n.* A flowing together, as of two rivers; a flowing together of people or things; a crowd. —**con·flu·ent**, *a.*

con·flux, kon′fləks, *n.* A confluence.

con·form, kən·fôrm′, *v.t.* To make of the same form or character; to make like; to bring into harmony; to adapt.—*v.i.* To act in compliance, esp. with conventional behavior; to correspond. —**con·form·ist**, *n.* —**con·form·ism**, *n.*

con·form·a·ble, kən·fôr′mə·bəl, *a.* Corresponding in form; similar; harmonious; suited; submissive. —**con·form·a·bly**, *adv.*

con·form·ance, kən·fôr′məns, *n.* Conformity.

con·for·ma·tion, kon·fėr·mā′shən, *n.* The act or process of conforming, as in adaptation; a symmetrical arrangement of parts; correspondence with a model; structure, shape, or contours.

con·form·i·ty, kən·fôr′mə·tē, *n. pl.*, **-ties.** Correspondence in form or manner; agreement; congruity; harmony; accordance; behavior that agrees with accepted or conventional standards; submission.

con·found, kon·fownd′, kən·fownd′, *v.t.* To confuse; bewilder; to mistake (one) for another; to contradict; to increase the confusion of; to perplex; to astound.

con·found·ed, kon·fown′did, *a. Informal.* Damned; detestable: used as a mild oath. —**con·found·ed·ly**, *adv.*

con·front, kən·frənt′, *v.t.* To stand facing; to face; to meet in hostility; to oppose; to set face to face; to bring together. —**con·fron·ta·tion**, kon·frən·tā′shən, *n.*

con·fuse, kən·fūz′, *v.t.*, **-fused, -fus·ing.** To mix up; to throw together indiscriminately; to confound; to bewilder; to embarrass; to disconcert; to mistake (one thing for another). —**con·fus·ed·ly**, *adv.* —**con·fus·ed·ness**, *n.*

con·fu·sion, kən·fū′zhən, *n.* A state in which things are confused; disorder; bewilderment; embarrassment; distraction; disconcertment.

con·fute, kən·fūt′, *v.t.*, **-fut·ed, -fut·ing.** To prove, as an argument or statement, to be false; to prove (a person) wrong; overcome with argument; to confound; bring to naught. —**con·fu·ta·tion**, kon·fū·tā′shən, *n.*

con·ga, kong′gə, *n. pl.*, **-gas.** A Cuban dance in which the dancers form a winding line.

con·geal, kən·jēl′, *v.t., v.i.* To freeze; to coagulate; to check the flow of. —**con·geal·ment**, *n.*

con·gen·ial, kən·jēn′yəl, *a.* Compatible in spirit; sympathetic; agreeable; existing together sociably and harmoniously. —**con·ge·ni·al·i·ty**, kən·jē·nē·al′ə·tē, *n.* —**con·gen·ial·ly**, *adv.*

con·gen·i·tal, kən·jen′ə·təl, *a.* Existing in an individual from birth.

con·ger, kong′gėr, *n.* A large marine eel used for food along the coasts of Europe. Also **con·ger eel.**

con·ge·ries, kon·jėr′ēz, *n. sing. or pl. in constr.* An aggregate; a heap.

con·gest, kən·jest′, *v.t.* To heap together; to collect in undue quantity; to cause an excess of blood in the vessels of, as an organ or part.—*v.i.* To collect together in undue quantity. —**con·ges·tion**, *n.* —**con·ges·tive**, *a.*

con·glom·er·ate, kən·glom′ėr·it, *a.* Gathered into a rounded mass; made up of heterogeneous material cemented together loosely.—*n.* Anything composed of heterogeneous elements; a rock consisting of pebbles, etc., embedded in a finer cementing material; a large corporation or trust having distinct companies or subsidiaries.—kən·glom′ə·rāt, *v.t., v.i.*, **-at·ed, -at·ing.** To gather into a ball or rounded mass. —**con·glom·er·a·tion**, kən·glom·ə·rā′shən, *n.*

con·go snake, *n.* A snakelike amphibian of the southeastern U.S., having small forelimbs. Also **Congo eel.**

con·grat·u·late, kən·grach′ə·lāt, *v.t.*, **-lat·ed, -lat·ing.** To express pleasure on some piece of good fortune happening to, as another party. —**con·grat·u·la·tor**, *n.* —**con·grat·u·la·to·ry**, kən·grach′ə·lə·tōr′ē, kən·grach′ə·lə·tôr′ē, *a.* —**con·grat·u·la·tion**, kən·grach·ə·lā′shən, *n., usu. pl.*

con·gre·gate, kong′grə·gāt, *v.t.*, **-gat·ed, -gat·ing.** To bring together in a crowd or mass; assemble.—*v.i.*

To flock together; gather.—*a.* Assembled.

con·gre·ga·tion, kong·grə·gā′shən, *n.* The act of congregating; an assemblage; a body of persons assembled for religious worship; a particular assemblage of worshipers.

con·gre·ga·tion·al, kong·grə·gā′shə·nəl, *a.* Pertaining to a congregation. (*Cap.*) Referring to a form of church government.

con·gress, kong′gris, *n.* A formal meeting of representatives for the discussion of some matter of common interest; the national legislative body of a nation, esp. of a republic. (*Cap.*) The national legislative body of the U.S., consisting of the Senate and the House of Representatives; this body as it exists for the two years during which the representatives hold their seats: the 69th *Congress.* —**con·gres·sion·al, Con·gres·sion·al**, kən·gresh′ə·nəl, *a.*

con·gress·man, kong′gris·mən, *n. pl.*, -**men.** (Often *cap.*) A member of the U.S. Congress, esp. of the House of Representatives. —**con·gress·wom·an**, kong′gris·wûm·ən, *n. pl.*, -**wom·en.** (Often *cap.*)

con·gru·ent, kong′groo·ənt, *a.* Agreeing; corresponding. *Geom.* Exactly coinciding. —**con·gru·ent·ly**, *adv.* —**con·gru·ence**, *n.* —**con·gru·en·cy**, *pl.*, -**cies.**

con·gru·ous, kong′groo·əs, *a.* Agreeing or harmonious in character; consonant; appropriate or fitting. *Geom.* Exactly coinciding. —**con·gru·ous·ly**, *adv.* —**con·gru·ous·ness**, *n.* —**con·gru·i·ty**, kən·groō′ə·tē, kən·groo′ə·tē, *n. pl.*, -**ties.**

con·ic, kon′ik, *a.* Having the form of, relating to, or looking like a cone. —**con·i·cal**, *a.*

co·ni·fer, kon′ə·fər, kō′nə·fər, *n.* Any of a group of trees and shrubs including the pine, fir, spruce, and other cone-bearing trees.

con·jec·ture, kən·jek′chər, *n.* A guess or inference based on the probability of a fact, or on slight evidence.—*v.t.*, -**tured, -tur·ing.** To surmise; guess.—*v.i.* To form conjectures. —**con·jec·tur·al**, *a.*

con·join, kən·joyn′, *v.t., v.i.* To join together; to unite.

con·joint, kən·joynt′, *a.* Joined together; united; joint. —**con·joint·ly**, *adv.*

con·ju·gal, kon′jə·gəl, *a.* Of, pertaining to, or of the nature of marriage. —**con·ju·gal·ly**, *adv.*

con·ju·gate, kon′jə·gāt, *v.t.*, -**gat·ed, -gat·ing.** To inflect (a verb) according to voices, moods, tenses, numbers, and persons in a prescribed order.—*v.i. Biol.* To unite, as two sex cells or gametes.—kon′jə·git, *n.* One of a group of words having a common derivation.—kon′jə·git, *a.* Joined together; coupled. —**con·ju·ga·tion**, kon·jə·gā′shən, *n.* —**con·ju·ga·tive**, *a.*

con·junc·tion, kən·jəngk′shən, *n.* Union; connection; association; that position of a planet in which it is in a line with the earth or another planet and the sun; any one of a group of words serving to unite words, sentences, or clauses of a sentence.

con·junc·tive, kən·jəngk′tiv, *a.* Uniting; serving to connect; of or like a conjunction; uniting, as such conjunctive adverbs as *moreover, yet.*

con·ju·ra·tion, kon·jû·rā′shən, *n.* The act of conjuring; adjuration; an incantation; a spell.

con·jure, kon′jər, kən·jûr′, *v.t.*, -**jured, -jur·ing.** To summon in a solemn manner; to adjure. To affect or effect by magic or enchantment; to call up or bring into existence, usu. with *up.*—kon′jər, *v.i.* To practice the arts of a sorcerer; to use magic. —**con·jur·er, con·jur·or**, *n.*

conk, kongk, *v.i.*, To hit on the head.—**conk out.** *Informal.* To become weak or unconscious; to break down, as a motor.

con man, *n. Informal.* A confidence man; a swindler.

con·nect, kə·nekt′, *v.t.* To bind or fasten together; link; to establish communication between; to bring into relation.—*v.i.* To become connected; join or unite; of trains, buses, etc., to arrive at a time when passengers may transfer to another train, bus, etc.

—**con·nec·tor, con·nect·er**, *n.*

con·nec·tion, kə·nek′shən, *n.* The act of connecting, or the state of being connected; junction; union; logical sequence of words or ideas; context; anything that connects; a bond or tie; a relative; a body of persons connected; the meeting of means of conveyance for transfer of passengers without delay; *usu. pl.*, friends or associates with influence.

con·nec·tive, kə·nek′tiv, *n.* Anything that connects; a word used to connect words, phrases, clauses, and sentences, as a conjunction.—*a.*

con·nip·tion, kə·nip′shən, *n. Informal.* A fit of hysterics or rage.

con·nive, kə·nīv′, *v.i.*, -**nived, -niv·ing.** To feign ignorance of or tacitly encourage wrongdoing; cooperate secretly. —**con·niv·ance**, kə·nī′vəns, *n.*

con·nois·seur, kon·ə·sər′, *n.* One competent to pass critical judgments in an art or in matters of taste.

con·note, kə·nōt′, *v.t.*, -**not·ed, -not·ing.** To denote secondarily; suggest in addition to the primary meaning; imply. —**con·no·ta·tion**, kon·ə·tā′shən, *n.* —**con·no·ta·tive**, *a.*

con·nu·bi·al, kə·noo′bē·əl, kə·nū′bē·əl, *a.* Referring to marriage. —**con·nu·bi·al·ly**, *adv.*

con·quer, kong′kər, *v.t.* To acquire by force of arms; win in war; gain or obtain by effort; surmount.—*v.i.* To be victorious. —**con·quer·a·ble**, *a.* —**con·quer·or**, *n.*

con·quest, kon′kwest, kong′kwest, *n.* The act of conquering; that which is conquered; captivation of a person's favor or affections; the person so captivated.

con·quis·ta·dor, kon·kwis′tə·dôr, *Sp.* kōng·kēs·tä·thôr′, *n. pl.* -**dors**, *Sp.* -**dor·es**, -thôr′äs. A conqueror; esp. the Spanish conquerors of Mexico and Peru in the 16th century.

con·san·guin·e·ous, kon·sang·gwin′ē·əs, *a.* Of the same blood; related, as having had the same ancestor. —**con·san·guin·i·ty**, *n.*

con·science, kon′shəns, *n.* The faculty which decides upon the moral quality of one's actions and motives.

con·sci·en·tious, kon·shē·en′shəs, *a.* Governed by a strict regard to the dictates of conscience; painstaking; careful. —**con·sci·en·tious·ly**, *adv.* —**con·sci·en·tious·ness**, *n.*

con·sci·en·tious ob·jec·tor, *n.* One who objects, on moral or religious grounds, to military service or the bearing of arms.

con·scious, kon′shəs, *a.* Inwardly aware of one's own existence, emotions, and thoughts, or of external objects and conditions; mentally alert; aware of what one is doing; known to oneself; intentional; conscious. —**con·scious·ly**, *adv.* —**con·scious·ness**, *n.*

con·script, kon′skript, *n.* A draftee.—*a.* Enrolled; drafted.—kən·skript′, *v.t.* To draft; to enroll by compulsion for military service. —**con·scrip·tion**, kən·skrip′shən, *n.*

con·se·crate, kon′sə·krāt, *v.t.*, -**crat·ed, -crat·ing.** To make or declare to be sacred with certain ceremonies or rites; to appropriate to sacred uses; to canonize; to dedicate with solemnity; to render venerable; to make respected; to hallow. —**con·se·cra·tive**, *a.* —**con·se·cra·tor**, *n., a.* —**con·se·cra·tion**, kon·sə·krā′shən, *n.*

con·sec·u·tive, kən·sek′yə·tiv, *a.* Following one another in uninterrupted intervals; successive; marked by logical sequence. —**con·sec·u·tive·ly**, *adv.*

con·sen·sus, kən·sen′səs, *n.* A general agreement; majority of opinion.

con·sent, kən·sent′, *v.i.* To agree; to yield, as to persuasion; to comply—*n.* Voluntary approval; permission; acquiescence; accord; agreement. —**con·sent·er**, *n.*

con·se·quence, kon′sə·kwens, kon′sə·kwəns, *n.* The effect which follows any cause; result; outcome; deduction; conclusion from premises; importance.

con·se·quent, kon′sə·kwent, kon′sə·kwənt, *a.* Fol-

lowing as an effect; resulting; following as a logical conclusion; logically consistent.—*n.* An effect or result; anything that follows upon something else. —**con·se·quent·ly,** *adv.*

con·se·quen·tial, kon·sə·kwen′shəl, *a.* Following as an effect; resultant; of consequence; self-important; pompous. —**con·se·quen·ti·al·i·ty,** kon·sə·kwen·she·al′ə·tē, *n.* —**con·se·quen·tial·ly,** *adv.*

con·ser·va·tion, kon·sər·vā′shən, *n.* The act of conserving; official supervision of rivers, forests, and other natural resources; a district under such supervision. —**con·ser·va·tion·al,** *a.* —**con·ser·va·tion·ist,** *n.*

con·ser·va·tion of en·er·gy, *n.* The principle that the total energy of a closed system, such as the universe, is constant.

con·serv·a·tive, kən·sər′və·tiv, *a.* Tending to preserve; inclined to keep existing institutions and customs; opposed to radical changes; moderate; cautious.—*n.* A conservative person. —**con·serv·a·tism,** *n.* —**con·serv·a·tive·ly,** *adv.*

con·serv·a·to·ry, kən·sər′və·tôr·ē, *n. pl.,* **-ries.** A greenhouse, usually glass-enclosed, for the displaying and growing of plants; a place or school for instruction in one of the arts, esp. music.—*a.* Preservative.

con·serve, kən·sərv′, *v.t.,* **-served, -serv·ing.** To keep in a safe or sound state; preserve from loss, decay, waste, or injury; to preserve, as fruit, with sugar.—kon′sərv, kən·sərv′, *n. Often pl.* A jam consisting of several fruits cooked together with sugar. —**con·serv·a·ble,** *a.* —**con·serv·er,** *n.*

con·sid·er, kən·sid′ər, *v.t.* To think about with care; to ponder; to study; to respect; to take into account; to judge to be.—*v.i.* To think seriously; to reflect.

con·sid·er·a·ble, kən·sid′ər·ə·bəl, *a.* Worthy of consideration; important; fairly large or great.—*n. Informal.* Much; a great deal. —**con·sid·er·a·bly,** *adv.*

con·sid·er·ate, kən·sid′ər·it, *a.* Given to sober reflection; prudent; mindful of others' feelings.

con·sid·er·a·tion, kən·sid·ə·rā′shən, *n.* The act of considering; thought or reflection; something taken into account; a recompense; a compensation; thoughtful or sympathetic regard; thoughtfulness for others; esteem; importance.

con·sid·er·ing, kən·sid′ər·ing, *prep.* Taking into account; in view of.—*adv. Informal.* Taking all into account.

con·sign, kən·sin′, *v.t.* To give or hand over; to transfer or deliver; to entrust, as goods, to an agent for safekeeping or sale; to set apart; assign. —**con·sign·er, con·sign·or,** *n.* —**con·sign·ment,** *n.*

con·sign·ee, kon·si·nē′, *n.* One that goods are delivered to.

con·sist, kən·sist′, *v.i.* To be comprised or contained (with *in*); to be composed or to be made up (with *of*); to be compatible or harmonious (with *with*).

con·sist·en·cy, kən·sis′tən·sē, *n. pl.,* **-cies.** Coherence; firmness; degree of density or viscosity; agreement; congruity; a keeping to or an agreeing with one's principles, previous statements, etc. Also **con·sist·ence.**

con·sist·ent, kən·sis′tənt, *a.* Agreeing; compatible; not self-contradictory; in harmony with one's previous statements, behavior, etc. —**con·sist·ent·ly,** *adv.*

con·sis·to·ry, kən·sis′tə·rē, *n. pl.,* **-ries.** A council, esp. any of various ecclesiastical councils or tribunals; the place where it meets.

con·so·la·tion, kon·sə·lā′shən, *n.* A comfort; solace; one who or that which offers consolation; a contest between those persons or teams eliminated before the final competition. —**con·sol·a·to·ry,** kən·sol′ə·tôr·ē, *a.*

con·sole, kən·sōl′, *v.t.,* **-soled, -sol·ing.** To comfort; to solace. —**con·sol·a·ble,** *a.*

con·sole, kon′sōl, *n.* Any bracket or bracketlike support; desklike structure containing the keyboards of an organ; a cabinet, standing on the floor, which holds a radio, TV, tape deck, or phonograph.

con·sole ta·ble, *n.* A table, with consolelike legs, which fits against a wall.

con·sol·i·date, kən·sol′ə·dāt, *v.t.,* **-dat·ed, -dat·ing.** To make solid or compact; to bring together into one close mass or body; to unite; combine. *Milit.* To regroup for strength after action.—*v.i.* To grow firm and hard; to unite and become solid. —**con·sol·i·da·tion,** kən·sol·ə·dā′shən, *n.*

con·som·mé, kon·sə·mā′, *n.* A strong, clear soup made by boiling meat long and slowly.

con·so·nant, kon′sə·nənt, *a.* Corresponding in sound; harmonious; in agreement; accordant to; consonantal.—*n.* One of the speech sounds produced by partial closure of the breath canal; a letter representing such a sound. —**con·so·nance,** *n.* —**con·so·nant·ly,** *adv.*

con·so·nan·tal, kon·sə·nan′təl, *a.* Pertaining to a consonant or its sound.

con·sort, kon′sôrt, *n.* An intimate associate, particularly a wife or husband; any vessel accompanying another.—kən·sôrt′, *v.t.* To associate; sound in harmony.—*v.i.* To associate; to agree or harmonize.

con·sor·ti·um, kən·sôr′shē·əm, *n. pl.,* **-ti·a,** -shē·ə. A combination of financial institutions for some venture requiring large sources of capital.

con·spic·u·ous, kən·spik′ū·əs, *a.* Easy to be seen; clearly visible; readily attracting the attention; noteworthy. —**con·spic·u·ous·ly,** *adv.* —**con·spic·u·ous·ness,** *n.*

con·spire, kən·spir′, *v.i.,* **-spired, -spir·ing.** To agree together, esp. secretly, to do something reprehensible or illegal; plot; to act in combination.—*v.t.* To plot. —**con·spir·a·cy,** kən·spir′ə·sē, *n. pl.,* **-cies.** —**con·spir·a·tor,** kən·spir′ə·tər, *n.* —**con·spir·a·to·ri·al,** kən·spir·ə·tôr′ē·əl, *a.* —**con·spir·er,** *n.* —**con·spir·ing·ly,** *adv.*

con·sta·ble, kon′stə·bəl, kən′stə·bəl, *n.* Any of various officials who keep the peace and perform minor judicial duties. —**con·sta·ble·ship,** *n.*

con·stab·u·lar·y, kən·stab′yə·ler·ē, *n. pl.,* **-ies.** The constables of a district; a police force organized on a military basis.—*a.*

con·stant, kon′stənt, *a.* Standing firm in mind or purpose; invariable or unchanging; uniform; always present; continuing without pause; steadfast; faithful.—*n.* Something constant, invariable, or unchanging. *Math.* A quantity assumed to be invariable throughout a given discussion. —**con·stan·cy,** *n.*

con·stant·ly, kon′stənt·lē, *adv.* Incessantly; very often; unchangingly.

con·stel·la·tion, kon·stə·lā′shən, *n.* Any of various groups of fixed stars; a division of the heavens occupied by such a group; any brilliant assemblage.

con·ster·na·tion, kon·stər·nā′shən, *n.* Dismayed astonishment; paralyzing fear.

con·sti·pa·tion, kon·stə·pā′shən, *n.* A condition of the bowels marked by irregular or difficult evacuation. —**con·sti·pate,** kon′stə·pāt, *v.t.*

con·stit·u·en·cy, kən·stich′oo·ən·sē, *n. pl.,* **-cies.** The body of voters, or, loosely, of residents, in a district represented by an elective officer; the district itself.

con·stit·u·ent, kən·stich′oo·ənt, *a.* Constituting; empowered to appoint or elect a representative; having power to frame or alter a political constitution; serving to make up a thing; component.—*n.* That which constitutes as a part, or an essential part; one who elects or appoints another as his representative.

con·sti·tute, kon′stə·toot, kon′stə·tūt, *v.t.* To compose; form; to appoint or elect; to set up or establish;

---

a- hat, fāte, fāre, fäther; **e-** met, mē; **i-** pin, pīne; **o-** not, nōte, ôrb, moove (move), boy, pownd; **u-** cūbe, bůll, tůk (took); **ch-** chin; **th-** thick, then; **zh-** vizhon (vision); **ə-** ego, taken, pencəl, lemən, bərd (bird).

give legal form to.

con·sti·tu·tion, kon·stə·too′shən, kon·stə·tū′shən, n. The act of constituting; a making or appointing; make-up or composition; esp. the physical character of the body as to strength or health; the system of fundamental principles according to which a nation, state, corporation, or the like is governed, or the document embodying these principles: as, the *Constitution* of the U.S.

con·sti·tu·tion·al, kon·stə·too′shə·nəl, kon·stə·tū′shə·nəl, a. Belonging to or inherent in the constitution of a person or thing; affecting the bodily constitution; pertaining to or in accordance with the constitution of a state, corporation, etc.—n. A walk or other exercise taken for the benefit of health. **—con·sti·tu·tion·al·i·ty,** kon·stə·too·shən·al′ə·tē, n. **—con·sti·tu·tion·al·ly,** adv.

con·strain, kən·strān′, v.t. To force, compel, or oblige; to confine forcibly, as by bonds; to repress or restrain. **—con·strain·a·ble,** a. **—con·strained,** a.

con·straint, kən·strānt′, n. Compulsion; confinement or restriction; repression; unnatural restraint in manner.

con·strict, kən·strikt′, v.t. To draw together as by an encircling pressure; compress; cramp. **—con·stric·tive,** a. **—con·stric·tion,** n.

con·stric·tor, kən·strik′tər, n. One who or that which constricts; a snake that crushes its prey in its coils.

con·struct, kən·strəkt′, v.t. To form by putting together parts; build. *Geom.* To draw, as a figure, so as to fulfill given conditions.—kon′strəkt, n. Something constructed. **—con·struc·tor, con·struc·ter,** n.

con·struc·tion, kən·strək′shən, n. The act or art of constructing; the way in which a thing is constructed; a building; the arrangement of words in a sentence according to accepted usages; syntactical connection; explanation or interpretation. **—con·struc·tion·al,** a.

con·struc·tive, kən·strək′tiv, a. Constructing, or tending to construct; structural; inferential; intended to be helpful; building up. **—con·struc·tive·ly,** adv. **—con·struc·tive·ness,** n.

con·strue, kən·stroo′, v.t., **-strued, -stru·ing.** To arrange words syntactically; to analyze the grammatical construction of, as a sentence; to translate, esp. orally; to interpret, as a law; put one's own interpretation on; to deduce by interpretation; infer.—v.i. To admit of grammatical analysis; infer; deduce. **—con·stru·a·ble,** a. **—con·stru·er,** n.

con·sul, kon′səl, n. An agent residing in a foreign city to care for the commercial and other interests there of citizens of his own country. **—con·su·lar,** a. **—con·sul·ship,** n.

con·su·late, kon′sə·lit, n. The office, term of office, authority, or place of business of a consul.

con·sult, kən·səlt′, v.i. To seek the advice of another; to take counsel together; to deliberate in common. —v.t. To ask the advice of; to seek the opinion of; have regard for; take into consideration. **—con·sul·ta·tion,** kon·səl·tā′shən, n.

con·sult·ant, kən·səl′tənt, n. One who consults; one who offers business, professional, or expert advice for a fee.

con·sume, kən·soom′, v.t., **-sumed, -sum·ing.** To destroy, as by decomposition or burning; to expend; use up; waste.—v.i. To be consumed. **—con·sum·a·ble,** a., n.

con·sum·er, kən·soo′mər, n. One who or that which consumes; the buyer or user of commodities and services.

con·sum·mate, kon′sə·māt, v.t., **-mat·ed, -mat·ing.** To bring to completion; fulfill; to complete (a marriage) by sexual intercourse.—kən·səm′it, a. Complete or perfect; of the highest quality. **—con·sum·mate·ly,** adv. **—con·sum·ma·tion,** kon·sə·mā′shən, n.

con·sump·tion, kən·səmp′shən, n. The act of consuming, or the state of being consumed; destruction;

decay; tuberculosis; progressive wasting of the body.

con·sump·tive, kən·səmp′tiv, a. Tending to consume; destructive; wasteful; pertaining to or of the nature of tuberculosis; disposed to or affected with tuberculosis.—n. One who suffers from tuberculosis.

con·tact, kon′takt, n. A state or condition of touching; connection; a junction of two electrical conductors through which current flows; a carrier of contagion; one who provides access to an advantageous opportunity.—v.t. To bring into contact. *Informal.* To get in touch with.—v.i. To be in contact.

con·tact lens, n. A small prescription plastic lens to correct vision, which is applied directly to the surface of the cornea.

con·ta·gion, kən·tā′jən, n. The communication of disease by contact; a disease so communicated; the medium by which a contagious disease is transmitted; pestilential influence; the communication of any influence from one to another. **—con·ta·gious,** a. **—con·ta·gious·ness,** n.

con·tain, kən·tān′, v.t. To have within itself; hold within fixed limits; to be capable of holding; to be equal to; comprise; include; to keep within proper bounds; restrain; to be divisible by, esp. without a remainder. **—con·tain·a·ble,** a.

con·tain·er, kən·tā′nər, n. Carton, case, or other containing structure.

con·tain·ment, kən·tān′mənt, n. The prevention of a hostile power from territorial or ideological expansion.

con·tam·i·nate, kən·tam′ə·nāt, v.t., **-nat·ed, -nat·ing.** To render impure by contact; defile; pollute. **—con·tam·i·nant,** n. **—con·tam·i·na·tion,** kən·tam·ə·nā′shən, n. **—con·tam·i·na·tive,** a. **—con·tam·i·na·tor,** n.

con·tem·plate, kon′təm·plāt, v.t., **-plat·ed, -plat·ing.** To look at with continued attention; observe thoughtfully; to consider thoroughly and deliberately; to intend; expect.—v.i. To muse; meditate. **—con·tem·pla·tion,** kon·təm·plā′shən, n. **—con·tem·pla·tive,** kən·tem′plə·tiv, kon′təm·plā·tiv, a.

con·tem·po·ra·ne·ous, kən·tem·pə·rā′nē·əs, a. Belonging within the same time period; contemporary.

con·tem·po·rar·y, kən·tem′pə·rer·ē, a. Existing or occurring at the same time; belonging to the same age or date.—n. pl., **-rar·ies.** One who or that which is contemporary.

con·tempt, kən·tempt′, n. The feeling of one who regards something as mean, vile, or worthless; disdain; scorn; the state of being despised; dishonor; disgrace; disobedience to, or open disrespect for, the rules or orders of a court or legislature.

con·tempt·i·ble, kən·temp′tə·bəl, a. Worthy of contempt. **—con·tempt·i·bly,** adv.

con·temp·tu·ous, kən·temp′choo·əs, a. Expressing contempt; scornful. **—con·temp·tu·ous·ly,** adv.

con·tend, kən·tend′, v.i. To struggle in opposition; to strive in rivalry; to assert rigorously.—v.i. To assert; maintain as true. **—con·tend·er,** n.

con·tent, kən·tent′, a. Having the desires limited by what one has; satisfied; easy in mind; willing or resigned.—v.t. To make content; to make easy in any situation; to please. **—con·tent·ment,** n.

con·tent, kon′tent, n. Usu. pl. That which is contained, as in a cask or book; the substance or purport, as of a document; power of containing; capacity; amount contained; volume.

con·tent·ed, kən·ten′tid, a. Satisfied; easy in mind; **—con·tent·ed·ly,** adv. **—con·tent·ed·ness,** n.

con·ten·tion, kən·ten′shən, n. The act of contending; strife; a quarrel; a striving in rivalry; competition; a dispute; a point contended for in controversy.

con·ten·tious, kən·ten′shəs, a. Given to or causing contention; argumentative. **—con·ten·tious·ly,** adv. **—con·ten·tious·ness,** n.

con·ter·mi·nous, kən·tər′mə·nəs, a. Having a common boundary; bordering; meeting at the ends; having the same boundaries; coextensive. Also **co·ter·mi·nous.**

con·test, kən·test´, *v.t.* To call in question; argue against; dispute; to struggle for.—*v.i.* To contend; compete. —**con·test·a·ble,** *a.* —**con·test·er,** *n.*— kon´test, *n.* A struggle for victory, or superiority; struggle in arms; dispute; debate. —**con·test·a·ble,** *a.* —**con·test·ant,** *n.* —**con·test·er,** *n.*

con·text, kon´tekst, *n.* The parts which precede or follow a word, sentence, or passage, and affect its meaning.

con·tig·u·ous, kən·tig´ū·əs, *a.* Situated so as to touch or almost touch; close together; adjoining. —**con·ti·gu·i·ty,** kon·tə·gū´ə·tē, *n. pl.,* **-ties.** —**con·tig·u·ous·ly,** *adv.* —**con·tig·u·ous·ness,** *n.*

con·ti·nence, kon´tə·nəns, *n.* Self-restraint, esp. in regard to sexual passion; chastity. Also **con·ti·nen·cy.** —**con·ti·nent,** *a.* —**con·ti·nent·ly,** *adv.*

con·ti·nent, kon´tə·nənt, *n.* A continuous tract of land; the mainland; one of the seven main land masses of the globe: Europe, Asia, Africa, North America, South America, Australia, and Antarctica.—**the Con·ti·nent,** the mainland of Europe.

con·ti·nen·tal, kon·tə·nen´təl, *n. Usually cap.* An inhabitant of the mainland of Europe. (*Cap.*) A soldier of the American army in the Revolutionary War. (*L.c.*) A piece of paper money issued during the American Revolution.—*a.* Of, or of the nature of a continent; (*usually cap.*) of or pertaining to the mainland of Europe; (*cap.*) of or pertaining to the American colonies during and immediately after the Revolutionary War.

con·tin·gent, kən·tin´jənt, *a.* Happening by chance or without known cause; accidental; liable to happen or not; uncertain; possible; dependent for existence on something not yet certain.—*n.* Something contingent; a share to be furnished; a quota; any one of the representative groups composing an assemblage. —**con·tin·gen·cy,** *n. pl.,* **-cies.** —**con·tin·gent·ly,** *adv.*

con·tin·u·al, kən·tin´ū·əl, *a.* Going on without stopping; reoccurring frequently. —**con·tin·u·al·ly,** *adv.*

con·tin·u·ance, kən·tin´ū·əns, *n.* Continuation; postponement, as of a trial or suit, to a future date.

con·tin·ue, kən·tin´ū, *v.t.,* **-ued, -u·ing.** Prolong; to cause to last or endure; maintain or retain, as in a position; persist, as in an action; to carry on from the point of interruption; to postpone, as a legal proceeding.—*v.i.* To go forward; keep on; to go on after interruption; to last or endure; to remain in a place, state, or capacity. —**con·tin·u·a·tion,** kən·tin·ū·ā´shən, *n.* —**con·tin·u·er,** *n.*

con·ti·nu·i·ty, kon·tə·noo´ə·tē, kon·tə·nū´ə·tē, *n. pl.,* **-ties.** The state or quality of being continuous; a continuous or connected whole; a scenario or other dramatic script which gives the action in detail.

con·tin·u·ous, kən·tin´ū·əs, *a.* Holding together without break or interruption; connected; unbroken. —**con·tin·u·ous·ly,** *adv.*

con·tin·u·um, kən·tin´ū·əm, *n. pl.,* **-u·a,** -ū·ə. That which is continuous and homogeneous.

con·tort, kən·tôrt´, *v.t.* To twist, as the body; to bend out of shape; distort. —**con·tor·tion,** *n.* —**con·tor·tive,** *a.*

con·tor·tion·ist, kən·tôr´shə·nist, *n.* One who performs gymnastic feats involving contorted postures.

con·tour, kon´tûr, *n.* The outline of a figure or body. —*v.t.* to mark with lines showing the contour of.—*a.* Plowing the land along its natural ridges in order to reduce erosion; showing topographical features by means of altitude lines.

con·tra·band, kon´trə·band, *n.* Illegal, or prohibited traffic; smuggling; goods imported or exported con-

trary to law or proclamation.—*a.* Prohibited by law; forbidden; authorized.

con·tra·cep·tive, kon·trə·sep´tiv, *a.* Deliberately preventing impregnation.—*n.* A contraceptive agent or device. —**con·tra·cep·tion,** *n.*

con·tract, kən·trakt´, kon´trakt, *v.t.* To draw together or into a smaller compass; to reduce in size or duration; condense; to acquire, as vicious habits or debts; to shorten (a word) by combining or omitting a letter or syllable; to make or settle by contract.—*v.i.* To be drawn together; to shrink; to make a mutual agreement. —kon´trakt, *n.* An agreement between two or more persons; a formal covenant of marriage. *Law.* An enforceable pact. —**con·tract·ed,** *a.* —**con·tract·i·ble,** *a.* —**con·trac·tu·al,** kən·trak´choo·əl, *a.*

con·tract bridge, *n.* A variety of bridge in which only the number of tricks named in the final bid can count toward game.

con·trac·tion, kən·trak´shən, *n.* The act of contracting; the state of being contracted; something contracted; a shortened form: 'aren't' is a *contraction* of 'are not'. —**con·trac·tive,** —**con·trac·tile,** *a.*

con·trac·tor, kon´trak·tər, kən·trak´tər, *n.* One who or that which contracts; one who contracts to furnish supplies or perform work at a certain price, esp. for the construction of buildings.

con·tra·dict, kon·trə·dikt´, *v.t.* To assert not to be so, or to assert to be contrary to what has been asserted; to deny; to be directly contrary to; to be logically inconsistent with. —**con·tra·dict·a·ble,** *a.* —**con·tra·dic·tion,** *n.* —**con·tra·dic·to·ry,** *a.*

con·tra·dis·tinc·tion, kon·trə·di·stingk´shən, *n.* Distinction by opposite qualities.

con·trail, kon´trāl, *n.* The vapor trail left by a plane, rocket, or missile.

con·tral·to, kən·tral´tō, *n. pl.,* **-tos** or **-ti,** -tē. The lowest female voice or voice-part; a singer with a contralto voice.—*a.* Referring to a contralto.

con·trap·tion, kən·trap´shən, *n. Informal.* A contrivance; a device; a gadget.

con·tra·pun·tal, kon·trə·pən´təl, *a. Mus.* Pertaining to or according to the rules of counterpoint.

con·tra·ri·wise, kon´trer·ē·wīz, *adv.* On the contrary; in the opposite way; perversely.

con·tra·ry, kon´trer·ē, *a.* Opposite in nature or character; completely different; antagonistic; opposite in direction or position; unfavorable.—*n. pl.,* **-ries.** That which is contrary or opposite.—kən·trär´e, *a.* Stubborn; perverse. —**con·tra·ri·ly,** *adv.* —**con·tra·ri·ness,** *n.* —**on** or **to the contrary,** in opposition to what has been stated.

con·trast, kən·trast´, *v.t.* To compare by observing differences; place in immediate relation in order to heighten an effect by emphasizing differences; set off.—*v.i.* To form a contrast.—kon´trast, *n.* The act of contrasting; a striking unlikeness; something or someone strikingly different. —**con·trast·a·ble,** *a.* —**con·trast·ing·ly,** *adv.*

con·tra·vene, kon·trə·vēn´, *v.t.,* **-vened, -ven·ing.** To come or be in conflict with; to obstruct; to violate; to transgress. —**con·tra·ven·er,** *n.* —**con·tra·ven·tion,** kon·trə·ven´shən, *n.*

con·trib·ute, kən·trib´ūt, *v.t.,* **-ut·ed, -ut·ing.** To give in common with others or for a common purpose; to pay as a share; to submit for publication.—*v.i.* To make a contribution; to have a share in any act or effect, with *to.* —**con·trib·ut·a·ble,** *a.* —**con·trib·u·tor,** *n.* —**con·trib·u·tor·y,** *a.*

con·tri·bu·tion, kon·trə·bū´shən, *n.* The act of contributing; something contributed, esp. an article for a periodical; an impost or levy. —**con·trib·u·tive,** kən·trib´yə·tiv, *a.*

con·trite, kən·trīt´, kon´trīt, *a.* Broken in spirit by a sense of guilt; penitent; proceeding from remorse.

---

a- hat, fāte, fāre, fäther; **e-** met, mē; **i-** pin, pīne; **o-** not, nōte, ôrb, moove (move), boy, pownd; **u-** cūbe, bůll, tûk (took); **ch-** chin; **th-** thick, ᵵhen; **zh-** vizhon (vision); **ə-** əgo, takən, pencəl, lemən, bərd (bird).

—con·trite·ly, adv. —con·trite·ness, n. —con·tri·tion, kən·trish/ən, n.

con·trive, kən·trīv/, v.t., -trived, -triv·ing. To plan with ingenuity; devise; invent; manage to do something.—v.i. To plan; plot; scheme. —con·triv·ance, n.

con·trived, kən·trīvd/, a. Affected; simulated; artificial.

con·trol, kən·trōl/, v.t., -trolled, -trol·ling. To check or regulate; to exercise restraint over; dominate; curb.—n. The act or power of controlling; regulation; domination; restraint; something that serves to control; a standard of comparison in scientific experimentation; a device that regulates a machine. Often pl. A set of such devices. —con·trol·la·ble, a.

con·trol·ler, kən·trō/lər, n. One employed to check income and expenditures; a comptroller; a person or device that controls. —con·trol·ler·ship, n.

con·tro·ver·sy, kon/trə·vər·sē, n. pl., -sies. Dispute, debate, or contention; disputation concerning a matter of opinion; a quarrel. —con·tro·ver·sial, kon·trə·vər/shəl, a. —con·tro·ver·sial·ly, adv.

con·tro·vert, kon/trə·vərt, kon·trə·vərt/, v.t. To dispute; deny; debate; discuss.

con·tu·me·ly, kon/tū·mə·lē, kon/tū·mə·lē, n. pl., -lies. Haughtiness and contempt in language or behavior; insolence; an insult.

con·tuse, kən·tooz/, kən·tūz/, v.t., -tused, -tus·ing. To bruise. —con·tu·sion, kən·too/zhən, kən·tū/zhən, n.

co·nun·drum, kə·nən/drəm, n. A riddle the answer to which involves a play on words; anything that puzzles.

con·va·lesce, kon·və·les/, v.i., -lesced, -les·cing. To grow better after sickness.

con·va·les·cence, kon·və·les/əns, n. The gradual recovery of health and strength after being ill; the time during which one convalesces. —con·va·les·cent, a., n.

con·vec·tion, kən·vek/shən, n. Circulation of heat caused by the movement of currents in a fluid or gas of uneven temperature due to the variation of its density; the act of conveying.

con·vene, kən·vēn/, v.i., -vened, -ven·ing. To come together; to assemble.—v.t. To cause to assemble; to summon judicially. —con·ven·er, n.

con·ven·ience, kən·vēn/yəns, n. The quality of being convenient; adaptiveness for easy use; a situation or a time convenient for one; a convenient appliance, utensil, etc.

con·ven·ient, kən·vēn/yənt, a. Agreeable to the needs or purpose; easily done; in satisfactory nearness. —con·ven·ient·ly, adv.

con·vent, con/vent, n. A community of persons, esp. nuns, devoted to religious life; the building or buildings occupied by such a community.

con·ven·tion, kən·ven/shən, n. A meeting or assembly; a formal assembly for action on particular matters; the delegates to such an assembly; an agreement, compact, or contract; general agreement or consent; a rule, method, or practice established by general consent or accepted usage.

con·ven·tion·al, kən·ven/shə·nəl, a. Established by general consent or accepted usage; traditional; not original; in accordance with accepted models; stylized. —con·ven·tion·al·ism, n. —con·ven·tion·al·ist, n. —con·ven·tion·al·i·ty, kən·ven·shə·nal/ə·tē, n. pl., -ties.

con·ven·tion·al·ize, kən·ven/shə·nə·līz, v.t., -ized, -iz·ing. To render conventional; to render in a conventional way.

con·verge, kən·vərj/, v.i., -verged, -verg·ing. To tend to meet in a point; to tend to a common result.—v.t. To cause to converge. —con·ver·gence, con·ver·gen·cy, n. —con·ver·gent, a.

con·ver·sant, kən·vər/sənt, kon/vər·sənt, a. Knowledgeable or experienced (usu. followed by with).

con·ver·sa·tion, kon·vər·sā/shən, n. Informal oral communication; association or intimate acquaintance. —con·ver·sa·tion·al, a.

con·ver·sa·tion·al·ist, kon·vər·sā/shə·nə·list, n. One who excels in or enjoys good conversation.

con·verse, kən·vərs/, v.i., -versed, -vers·ing. To exchange informal verbal communication.—kon/vərs, n. A conversation.

con·verse, kən·vərs/, kon/vərs, a. Turned about or reversed in order; opposed; contrary.—kon/vərs, n. A thing which is the opposite or contrary of another; something reversed. —con·verse·ly, kən·vərs/lē, adv.

con·ver·sion, kən·vər/zhən, kən·vər/shən, n. The act or state of converting.

con·vert, kən·vərt/, v.t. To effect a change from one condition to another; to exchange for an equivalent; to alter from an original use; to appropriate wrongfully to one's own use; to cause a change from one belief, allegiance, or esp. religion, to another; to change chemically.—v.i. To become converted; to score the point after touchdown in football.—kon/vərt, n. One who is converted, esp. from one set of beliefs to another.

con·vert·er, con·vert·or, kən·vər/tər, n. One who or that which converts; a vessel in which pig iron is converted into steel; a device for changing the form of electrical energy, as from direct to alternating current.

con·vert·i·ble, kən·vər/tə·bəl, a. Capable of being converted.—n. An automobile having a top which may be lowered. —con·vert·i·bil·i·ty, kən·vər·tə·bil/ə·tē, n. —con·vert·i·bly, adv.

con·vex, kon/veks, kən·veks/, a. Denoting a surface that is curved or rounded outward.—kon/veks, n. A convex part. —con·vex·ly, kon·veks/lē, adv. —con·vex·i·ty, kən·vek/sə·tē, n.

con·vey, kən·vā/, v.t. To carry or transport; to transmit; hand over; to communicate; express; to transfer rights, real estate, or other property from one person to another. —con·vey·a·ble, a.

con·vey·ance, kən·vā/əns, n. The act of conveying; the means by which anything is conveyed, esp. a vehicle; the transferring of property from one person to another.

con·vey·er, con·vey·or, kən·vā/ər, n. A person or thing that conveys; a mechanical contrivance for transporting material, such as a belt, rollers, etc.

con·vict, kən·vikt/, v.t. To prove or declare guilty, esp. after trial.—kon/vikt, n. One who has been convicted; a convicted person serving a prison term.

con·vic·tion, kən·vik/shən, n. The act of convicting, or the state of being convicted; the act of convincing, or the state of being convinced; settled persuasion; a fixed or firm belief. —con·vic·tion·al, a.

con·vince, kən·vins/, v.t., -vinced, -vinc·ing. To persuade or satisfy by evidence, argument, or proof. —con·vinc·er, n. —con·vinc·i·ble, a.

con·vinc·ing, kən·vins/ing, a. That convinces; believable. —con·vinc·ing·ly, adv.

con·viv·i·al, kən·viv/ē·əl, a. Relating to a feast or entertainment; fond of feasting and good fellowship; jovial. —con·viv·i·al·i·ty, n. —con·viv·i·al·ly, adv.

con·vo·ca·tion, kon·və·kā/shən, n. The act of convoking; a number of persons met in answer to a summons; an assembly. —con·vo·ca·tion·al, a.

con·voke, kən·vōk/, v.t., -voked, -vok·ing. To call together; to summon to meet. —con·vok·er, n.

con·vo·lute, kon/və·loot, v.t., -lut·ed, -lut·ing. To coil up.—a. Rolled up together, or one part over another. —con·vo·lute·ly, adv.

con·vo·lu·tion, kon·və·loo/shən, n. A rolling or coiling together; rolled up or coiled condition; a whorl; a sinuosity, esp. one of the sinuous folds or ridges of the surface of the brain.

con·voy, kon/voy, kən·voy/, v.t. To accompany or escort, now usually for protection.—kon/voy, n. The act of convoying; the protection afforded by an escort;

an escort, esp. for protection, as an armed force or warship; a formation of ships, etc., traveling together.

con·vulse, kən·vəls′, *v.t.,* **-vulsed, -vuls·ing.** To shake violently; affect with irregular spasms; to cause to laugh violently.

con·vul·sion, kən·vəl′shən, *n.* Violent agitation; commotion. *Often pl.* A violent and involuntary spasmodic contraction of the muscles; spasm; a violent fit of laughter. **—con·vul·sive,** *a.* **—con·vul·sive·ly,** *adv.*

co·ny, kō′nē, kən′ē, *n.* A kind of rabbit; its fur.

coo, koo, *v.i.,* **cooed, coo·ing.** To utter the soft, murmuring sound characteristic of pigeons or doves; to murmur or talk fondly or amorously.—*v.t.* To utter by cooing.—*n.* A cooing sound. **—coo·ing·ly,** *adv.*

cook, kûk, *v.i.* To prepare food by the action of heat; to undergo cooking.—*v.t.* To prepare (food) by the action of heat; subject (anything) to the action of heat. *Informal.* To concoct or invent falsely, often with *up.*—*n.* One who cooks; a chef.

cook·book, kûk′bûk, *n.* A book containing recipes and instructions for cooking.

cook·e·ry, kûk′ə·rē, *n. pl.,* **-ries.** The art or practice of cooking; a place for cooking.

cook·ie, cook·y, kûk′ē, *n. pl.,* **cook·ies.** A small, flat, sweet cake.

cook·out, kûk′owt, *n. Informal.* A meal cooked outdoors.

cool, kool, *a.* Moderately cold; neither warm nor very cold; not excited by passion; calm; unmoved; deficient in enthusiasm; calmly audacious or impudent; producing a cool impression. *Informal.* Without exaggeration or qualification: a *cool* thousand dollars; excellent.—*v.t., v.i.* To make or become cool.—*n.* That which is cool; the cool part, place, or time; composure. **—cool·ish,** *a.* **—cool·ly,** *adv.* **—cool·ness,** *n.*

cool·ant, koo′lənt, *n.* A cooling agent, usually fluid or gas.

cool·er, koo′lər, *n.* That which cools or makes cool; a vessel or apparatus for cooling liquids. *Informal.* A jail.

coo·lie, coo·ly, koo′lē, *n. pl.,* **coo·lies.** Formerly among Europeans in India and China, an unskilled native laborer.

coon, koon, *n. Informal.* A raccoon.

coop, koop, kûp, *n.* An enclosure, cage, or pen for poultry; any narrow confining thing or place. *Informal.* A prison.—*v.t.* To place in or as in a coop; confine narrowly: often with *up.*

co-op, kō′op, kō·op′, *n.* A cooperative.

coop·er, koo′pər, kûp′ər, *n.* One who makes or repairs barrels, casks, etc—*v.t.* To make or repair (casks and barrels).—*v.i.* To work as a cooper.

coop·er·age, koo′pər·ij, kûp′ər·ij, *n.* The work or shop of a cooper.

co·op·er·ate, kō·op′ə·rāt, *v.i.,* **-at·ed, -at·ing.** To work or act together.

co·op·er·a·tion, kō·op·ə·rā′shən, *n.* The act of cooperating; united effort; the combination of persons for purposes of production, purchase, or distribution for their joint benefit.

co·op·er·a·tive, kō·op′ə·rā·tiv, kō·op′ər·ə·tiv, *a.* Cooperating; of or pertaining to cooperation; pertaining to economic cooperation. —*n.* A business organization established on a basis of economic cooperation. **—co·op·er·a·tive·ly,** *adv.*

co-opt, kō·opt′, *v.t.* To elect into a body by the votes of the existing members; preempt; esp. to preempt or neutralize a group by means of infiltration, bribery, cajolery, etc. **—co·op·ta·tion,** kō·op·tā′shən, *n.*

co·or·di·nate, kō·ôr′də·nit, kō·ôr′də·nāt, *a.* Of the same order or degree; equal in rank or importance; involving coordinate parts; referring to coordinates. —kō·ôr′də·nāt, *v.t.,* **-nat·ed, -nat·ing.** To class in the same order, rank, or division; to arrange in proper relative position; combine in harmonious relation or action.—*v.i.* To become coordinate; act in harmonious combination.—*n.* One who or that which is equal in rank or importance; an equal; a number, or one of a set of numbers, which locates a point in space in relation to a line, or a system of lines. **—co·or·di·nate·ly,** *adv.* **—co·or·di·na·tor,** *n.* **—co·or·di·nation,** kō·ôr·də·nā′shən, *n.*

coot, koot, *n.* Any of various widely distributed swimming and diving birds. *Informal.* A stupid or foolish person, often with *old.*

coot·ie, koo′tē, *n. Informal.* A louse.

cop, kop, *v.t.,* **copped, cop·ping.** *Informal.* To catch; to steal.—*n. Informal.* A policeman.**—cop out,** *Informal,* to evade or shrink from a difficult decision, an action, a fact, etc.

co·pa·cet·ic, co·pe·set·ic, kō·pə·set′ik, *a. Informal.* Entirely satisfactory.

co·part·ner, kō·pärt′nər, kō′pärt·nər, *n.* A partner with others; associate. **—co·part·ner·ship,** *n.*

cope, kōp, *n.* A cloak or cape worn by ecclesiastics in processions and on other occasions; any cloaklike or canopylike covering.—*v.t.,* **coped, cop·ing.** To furnish with or as with a cope.

cope, kōp, *v.i.,* **coped, cop·ing.** To strive or contend on equal terms (with); to deal with successfully.

cope·stone, kōp′stōn, *n.* The top stone of a building; the finishing touch.

cop·i·er, kop′ē·ər, *n.* One who copies; a machine that makes copies.

co·pi·lot, kō′pī·lət, *n.* The assistant or second pilot of an aircraft.

cop·ing, kō′ping, *n.* The uppermost course of a wall or the like, usually made sloping so as to carry off water.

cop·ing saw, *n.* A narrow saw in a U-shaped frame, for cutting curved pieces.

co·pi·ous, kō′pē·əs, *a.* Having or yielding an abundant supply, as of matter or words; abundant; plentiful. **—co·pi·ous·ly,** *adv.* **—co·pi·ous·ness,** *n.*

cop-out, kop′owt, *n. Informal.* An evading or shrinking from a difficult decision, action, etc.

cop·per, kop′ər, *n.* A malleable, ductile, reddishbrown metallic element used for electric wiring, for alloys such as brass or bronze, and for electroplating; a copper coin; a vessel made of copper.—*a.* Referring to copper; copper-colored.—*v.t.* To cover with copper. **—cop·per·y,** *a.*

cop·per·head, kop′ər·hed, *n.* A poisonous snake of the U.S., having a copper-colored head.

cop·per·plate, kop′ər·plāt, *n.* A plate of copper on which something is engraved or etched for printing; a print from such a plate; engraving or printing of this kind.

cop·pice, kop′is, *n.* Copse.

cop·ra, kop′rə, *n.* The dried kernel or meat of the coconut.

copse, kops, *n.* A wood of small trees; a growth of underwood or brush wood.

cop·u·la, kop′yə·lə, *n. pl.,* **-las, -lae,** -lē. Something that connects; a linking verb, esp. a form of the verb *be.* **—cop·u·lar,** *a.*

cop·u·late, kop′yə·lāt, *v.i.,* **-lat·ed, -lat·ing.** To have sexual intercourse. **—cop·u·la·tion,** kop·yə·lā′shən, *n.*

cop·u·la·tive, kop′yə·lā·tiv, *a.* Serving to unite or couple; connecting, as a *copulative* conjunction like *and,* or a *copulative* verb like *be;* pertaining to copulation.—*n.* A copulative word. **—cop·u·la·tive·ly,** *adv.*

cop·y, kop′ē, *n. pl.,* **cop·ies.** A transcript, reproduction, or imitation of an original; one of the various examples or specimens of the same book, engraving, or the like; that which is to be reproduced or imitated; written material to be set in type.—*v.t.,* **cop·ied, cop·y·ing.** To make a copy of; transcribe; reproduce; to

---

a- hat, fāte, fâre, fäther; **e-** met, mē; **i-** pin, pīne; **o-** not, nōte, ôrb, moove (move), boy, pownd; **u-** cūbe, bûll, tûk (took); **ch-** chin; **th-** thick, ᵺen; **zh-** vizhon (vision); **ə-** əgo, takən, pencəl, lemən, bərd (bird).

follow as a model; imitate.—*v.i.* To make a copy.

cop•y•book, kop′ē•bŭk, *n.* A book with handwriting models to be copied.—*a.* Commonplace; trite.

cop•y•cat, kop′ē•kat, *n.* An imitator.

co•py desk, *n.* The desk in a newspaper office at which copy is edited.

cop•y•ist, kop′ē•ist, *n.* A copier; a transcriber of documents.

cop•y•right, kop′ē•rīt, *n.* An author's exclusive right of property to his work for a certain time.—*a.* Relating to, or protected by the law of copyright.—*v.t.* To secure by copyright, as a book.

co•quet, kō•ket′, *v.i.,* **-quet•ted, -quet•ting.** To trifle in love; flirt. —**co•quet•ry,** kō′kə•trē, kō•ke′trē, *n. pl.,* **-ries.**

co•quette, kō•ket′, *n.* A woman who tries to gain the admiration and affections of men for mere self-gratification; a flirt. —**co•quet•tish,** *a.* —**co•quet•tish•ly,** *adv.*

cor•a•cle, kôr′ə•kəl, kor′ə•kəl, *n.* A small boat made by covering a wicker frame with leather, horsehide, etc.

cor•al, kôr′əl, kor′əl, *n.* The hard, limy, red, white, or black skeleton of any of various marine invertebrate animals; such skeletons collectively, as forming reefs or islands; an animal of this kind; color, usu. a deep pink.—*a.* Composed of coral; deep-pink; red.

cor•al reef, *n.* An extensive reef built mainly by the gradual deposit of coral.

cor•al snake, *n.* Any of various small, poisonous snakes of tropical New World areas, having brilliant bands of red, black, yellow, or white.

cor•bel, kôr′bəl, *n.* A projection from the vertical face of a wall to support a weight.

cord, kôrd, *n.* A string or small rope composed of several strands twisted or woven together; anything which binds or restrains; a flexible insulated electrical cable with a plug at one or both ends; a rib on the surface of cloth; a ribbed fabric, esp. corduroy; *pl.,* corduroy breeches or trousers. A measure of cut wood equal to 128 cubic feet; a cordlike structure: the spinal *cord.*—*v.t.* To bind with cords; to stack up, as wood, in cords. —**cord•ed,** *a.*

cord•age, kôr′dij, *n.* Cords or ropes collectively, esp. in a ship's rigging; quantity of wood measured in cords.

cor•date, kôr′dāt, *a.* Heart-shaped. —**cor•date•ly,** *adv.*

cor•dial, kôr′jəl, *a.* Coming from the heart; courteous; warm; refreshing; invigorating.—*n.* Something that strengthens, invigorates, or stimulates; a liqueur. —**cor•dial•i•ty,** kôr•jal′ə•tē, kôr•jē•al′ə•tē, *n.* —**cor•dial•ness,** *n.* —**cor•dial•ly,** *adv.*

cor•dil•le•ra, kôr•dil•yâr′ə, kôr•dil′ər•ə, *n.* A ridge or chain of mountains.

cord•ite, kôr′dīt, *n.* A gunpowder composed mainly of nitroglycerin and guncotton.

cor•don, kôr′dən, *n.* A cord, braid, or ribbon worn for ornament or as a badge of honor; a line of sentinels, military posts, or the like, enclosing or guarding a particular place.

cor•do•van, kôr′də•vən, *a.* Designating a kind of fine leather.

cor•du•roy, kôr′də•roy, kôr•də•roy′, *n.* A thick cotton fabric corded or ribbed on the surface; *pl.,* trousers or breeches made of this; *sing.,* a corduroy road.—*a.* Made of corduroy; resembling corduroy; constructed of logs laid together transversely: a *corduroy* road.

cord•wood, kôrd′wŭd, *n.* Wood stacked in cords; logs cut into lengths of approximately four feet.

core, kōr, kôr, *n.* The central part of a fleshy fruit, containing the seeds; the innermost or most essential part of anything; the piece of iron or the like, forming the central portion of an electromagnet or induction-coil.—*v.t.,* **cored, cor•ing.** To remove the core, as of fruit.

co•re•spond•ent, kō•ri•spon′dənt, *n.* A person accused of adultery with the wife or husband being sued for divorce.

co•ri•an•der, kôr•ē•an′dər, kōr•ē•an′dər, *n.* An annual plant of the carrot family, with seeds that are aromatic and flavorful and are used in certain liqueurs, and in cookery.

Co•rin•thi•an, kə•rin′thē•ən, *a.* Referring to Corinth; ornate; luxurious; licentious; pertaining to the most elaborate Greek order of architecture, distinguished by a capital adorned with rows of acanthus leaves.

cork, kôrk, *n.* The outer bark of a species of oak, used for making stoppers for bottles, insulation, or floats; the tree itself; something made of cork; a stopper for a bottle; an outer tissue of bark on woody plants.—*v.t.* To stop with or as with a cork, often with *up;* to blacken with burnt cork.

cor•ker, kôr′kər, *n. Informal.* Something that closes a discussion; something excellent or astonishing.

cork•screw, kôrk′skroo, *n.* An instrument used to draw corks from bottles.—*a.* Helical or spiral.—*v.t., v.i.* To move or twist in a spiral course.

corm, kôrm, *n.* A fleshy, bulblike, subterranean stem.

corn, kôrn, *n.* A tall cereal plant of the grass family, widely grown for its edible kernels borne on ears; Indian corn; a small, hard seed or fruit, esp. of a cereal plant; collectively, the seeds of cereal plants, or the plants themselves, used for food; in the U.S., maize or Indian corn; something corny.—*v.t.* To preserve and season with salt in grains; put in brine, as meat. —**corned,** *a.*

corn, kôrn, *n.* A horny thickening of the skin, esp. on a toe.

corn bread, *n.* Bread made of corn meal.

corn•cob, kôrn′kob, *n.* The long, hard interior of an ear of corn which bears the grains or kernels; a tobacco pipe with a bowl made of this cob.

cor•ne•a, kôr′nē•ə, *n.* The transparent part of the external coat of the eye, covering the iris and the pupil. —**cor•ne•al,** *a.*

cor•ner, kôr′nər, *n.* The meeting place of two converging lines or surfaces; an angle; a projecting angle, esp. the place where two streets meet; the space between two converging lines or surfaces near their intersection; any narrow, secluded, or secret place; a region; a piece to protect the corner of anything; a monopoly of the available supply of a stock or commodity, for the purpose of raising the price; an awkward or inextricable position.—*a.* At a corner; for a corner.—*v.t.* To place in or drive into a corner; to force into an awkward or inextricable position; to obtain a corner on (a stock, etc.).—*v.i.* To meet in, or be situated on or at, a corner; to turn a corner.

cor•ner•stone, kôr′nər•stōn, *n.* A stone which lies at the corner of two walls, and serves to unite them; something of fundamental importance to a belief or an ideology.

cor•net, kôr•net′, *n.* A brass wind instrument related to the trumpet; a little cone of paper twisted at the end, used for enclosing candy, etc. —**cor•net•ist, cor•net•tist,** *n.*

corn•flow•er, kôrn′flow•ər, *n.* Any of several plants growing in grainfields with blue, purple, pink, or white flowers.

cor•nice, kôr′nis, *n.* A horizontal molded projection which crowns or finishes a wall or building.

corn meal, *n.* Coarsely-ground meal made of corn. —**corn•meal,** kôrn′mēl, *a.*

corn pone, *n.* Corn bread, esp. of a plain or simple kind popular in southern U.S.

corn•starch, kôrn′stärch, *n.* A starch, or a starchy flour made from corn, used for thickening puddings and gravies.

cor•nu•co•pi•a, kôr•nə•kō′pe•ə, *n.* A horn overflowing with flowers and fruit, symbolizing plenty; a horn-shaped receptacle or ornament.

corn•y, kôr′nē, *a.,* **-i•er, -i•est.** Of, or abounding in corn. *Informal.* Sentimental or unsophisticated; trite; banal.

co•rol•la, kə•rol′ə, *n.* The part of a flower inside the calyx, and composed of one or more petals.

cor•ol•lar•y, kôr′ə•ler•ē, kor′ə•ler•ē, *n. pl.,* -ies. An inference; a natural consequence or result.

co•ro•na, kə•rō′nə, *n. pl.,* -nas, -nae, -nē. A white or colored circle of light seen round the sun or moon; a luminous envelope outside of the sun's chromosphere, observable during eclipses; the crown, as of the head or a tooth; a crownlike appendage, esp. one on the inner side of a corolla; a luminous discharge at the surface of an electrical conductor.

cor•o•nar•y, kôr′ə•ner•ē, kor′ə•ner•ē, *a.* Of or like a crown; referring to either or both of the two arteries supplying blood to the heart muscle.—*n.* Coronary thrombosis.

cor•o•nar•y throm•bo•sis, *n.* Clotting of blood in one of the arteries of the heart.

cor•o•na•tion, kôr•ə•nā′shən, kor•ə•nā′shən, *n.* The act or ceremony of investing with a crown; the crowning of a sovereign.

cor•o•ner, kôr′ə•nər, kor′ə•nər, *n.* A local officer who investigates, by inquest before a jury (cor•o•ner's ju•ry) any death not clearly due to natural causes. —cor•o•ner•ship, *n.*

cor•o•net, kôr′ə•net′, kor′ə•nit, *n.* A crown representing a dignity inferior to that of the sovereign; a crownlike headdress or ornament for the head. —cor•o•net•ed, *a.*

cor•po•ral, kôr•pər•əl, *a.* Of or pertaining to the human body: *corporal* punishment.

cor•po•ral, kôr′pər•əl, *n.* The noncommissioned officer of a company of soldiers, next below a sergeant.

cor•po•rate, kôr′pər•it, *a.* United in one body; forming a corporation; incorporated; pertaining to a corporation. —cor•po•rate•ly, *adv.* —cor•po•ra•tive, kôr′pə•rā′tiv, kôr′pər•ə•tiv, *a.*

cor•po•ra•tion, kôr•pə•rā′shən, *n.* A number of persons under authority of law, that operate as a single person in business according to a charter. —cor•po•rat•ism, kôr′pə•rə•tiz•əm, *n.*

cor•po•re•al, kôr•pōr′ē•əl, kôr•pôr′ē•əl, *a.* Relating to the physical body; bodily; tangible. —cor•po•re•al•i•ty, kôr•pôr•ē•al′ə•tē, *n.* —cor•po•re•al•ness, *n.*

corps, kōr, kôrz, *n. pl.,* corps, kōrz. An organized military body: *Corps* of Engineers; a unit made up of two divisions; a group of people acting together.

corpse, kôrps, *n.* A dead body, usually of a human being.

corps•man, kōr′mən, kôr′man, *n. pl,* corps•men. An enlisted man in the U.S. Navy who assists a medical officer.

cor•pu•lent, kôr′pyə•lənt, *a.* Portly; stout; fat. —cor•pu•lence, cor•pu•len•cy, *n.*

cor•pus, kôr′pəs, *n. pl.,* -po•ra, -pə•rə. A body of works or collection of laws or writings of a single class; the essential part of something; the body of a man or animal, especially a dead body.

cor•pus•cle, kôr′pə•səl, *n.* A small particle that makes up the blood of many animals; any tiny particle. Also cor•pus•cule. —cor•pus•cu•lar, kôr•pəs′kyə•lər, *a.*

cor•pus de•lic•ti, kôr′pəs də•lik′tī, *n.* The element of a criminal case which proves that a crime was committed; a body.

cor•ral, kə•ral′, *n.* A pen for horses and cattle. —*v.t.,* -ralled, -ral•ling. To confine in, or as in a corral; to seize or capture.

cor•rect, kə•rekt′, *v.t.* To set right; to point out or mark the errors in; punish; to adjust in order to make reach a standard.—*a.* Proper; free from error; accurate. —cor•rect•a•ble, cor•rect•i•ble, *a.* —cor•rect•ness, *n.* —cor•rec•tor, *n.*

cor•rec•tion, kə•rek′shən, *n.* The act of correcting, or the state of being corrected; an alteration; punishment. —cor•rec•tion•al, *a.*

cor•rec•tive, kə•rek′tiv, *a.* Tending to correct; remedial: *corrective* physical exercises.—*n.*

cor•re•late, kor′ə•lāt, kor′ə•lāt, *v.t., v.i.,* -lat•ed, -lat•ing. To have a mutual relation.—*v.t.* To place in or bring into mutual relation.—*a.* Mutually related.—*n.* Either of two related things, esp. when one implies the other.

cor•re•la•tion, kôr•ə•lā′shən, kor•ə•lā′shən, *n.* Mutual relation of two or more things or parts; the act of correlating.

cor•rel•a•tive, kə•rel′ə•tiv, *a.* Having a correlation; used together in grammar and indicating a relationship, as *either* and *or.*—*n.* Either of two things that correlate.

cor•re•spond, kôr•ə•spond′, kor•ə•spond′, *v.i.* To be in agreement; to be similar or analogous; to exchange letters. —cor•re•spond•ing, *a.* —cor•re•spond•ing•ly, *adv.*

cor•re•spond•ence, kôr•ə•spon′dəns, kor•ə•spon′dəns, *n.* Communication by means of letters; the act or fact of corresponding; conformity; letters between correspondents.

cor•re•spond•ent, kôr•ə•spon′dənt, kor•ə•spon′dənt, *a.* Corresponding.—*n.* One who communicates by letters; one who contributes to a newspaper, esp. one employed to report news regularly from a distant place; something that corresponds to something else.

cor•ri•dor, kôr′ə•dər, kôr′ə•dôr, kor′ə•dər, *n.* A gallery or passage connecting parts of a building; a passage into which several apartments open; a heavily populated area that includes major cities and their suburbs.

cor•ri•gi•ble, kôr′ə•jə•bəl, kor′ə•jə•bəl, *a.* Capable of being corrected. —cor•ri•gi•bil•i•ty, kor•ə•jə•bil′ə•tē, *n.* —cor•ri•gi•bly, *adv.*

cor•rob•o•rate, kə•rob′ə•rāt, *v.t.,* -rat•ed, -rat•ing. To confirm; to authenticate. —cor•rob•o•ra•tion, kə•rob•ə•rā′shən, *n.* —cor•rob•o•ra•tive, *a.* —cor•rob•o•ra•to•ry, *a.*

cor•rode, kə•rōd′, *v.t.,* -rod•ed, -rod•ing. *a.* To eat away or wear away by degrees. —cor•rod•i•ble, *a.*

cor•ro•sion, kə•rō′zhən, *n.* The action of wearing away by degrees; a product of such wearing away, esp. rust.

cor•ro•sive, kə•rō′siv, *a.* Able to corrode; irritating. —*n.* A substance that corrodes.

cor•ru•gate, kôr′ə•gāt, kor′ə•gāt, *v.t., v.i.,* -gat•ed, -gat•ing. To wrinkle or bend into folds. —cor•ru•ga•tion, kôr•ə•gā′shən, *n.*

cor•rupt, kə•rəpt′, *v.t., v.i.* To contaminate; to weaken morally; pervert; deprave; bribe.—*a.* Corrupted. —cor•rupt•er, *n.* —cor•rup•ti•ble, *a.* —cor•rup•ti•bil•i•ty, kə•rəp•tə•bil′ə•tē, *n.* —cor•rupt•ly, *adv.* —cor•rupt•ness, *n.*

cor•rup•tion, kə•rəp′shən, *n.* The act of corrupting, or the state of being corrupt; depravity; corrupt or dishonest proceedings; bribery.

cor•sage, kôr•säzh′, *n.* A bouquet to be worn by a woman.

cor•sair, kôr′sār, *n.* A pirate; a ship used by pirates.

cor•set, kôr′sit, *n.* A shaped, close-fitting undergarment extending above and below the waistline, worn to shape and support the body. —cor•set•ed, *a.*

cor•tex, kôr′teks, *n. pl.,* cor•ti•ces, kôr•tə•sēz. The outermost layer of the brain, kidney or the adrenal glands; tree bark.

cor•ti•cal, kôr′tə•kəl, *a.* Having to do with cortex; having to do with the brain cortex.

cor•ti•sone, kôr′tə•sōn, kôr′tə•zōn, *n.* A hormone that is secreted by the cortex of the adrenal glands; the similar synthetic hormone.

---

a- hat, fāte, fāre, fäther; e- met, mē; i- pin, pīne; o- not, nōte, ôrb, moove (move), boy, pownd; u- cūbe, bůll, tûk (took); ch- chin; th- thick, ŧhen; zh- vizhon (vision); ə- əgo, takən, pencəl, lemən, bərd (bird).

co·run·dum, kə·rən′dəm, *n.* A very hard mineral that exists as sapphire and ruby; a grinding agent.

co·sig·na·to·ry, kō·sig′nə·tôr·ē, kō·sig′nə·tôr·ē, *n. pl.,* **-ries.** One who is joint signer of a promissory note, a treaty, or other agreement.

cos·met·ic, koz·met′ik, *a.* Beautifying; done to improve a condition, such as plastic surgery.—*n.* Any preparation that helps to beautify and improve the skin and hair.

cos·mic, koz′mik, *a.* Of or pertaining to the cosmos; immeasurably large. **—cos·mi·cal·ly,** *adv.*

cos·mic dust, *n.* Matter in fine particles existing in or falling from space.

cos·mic rays, *n.* Electromagnetic rays of extremely high frequency and energy that originate in outer space and bombard the atoms of the earth's atmosphere.

cos·mog·o·ny, koz·mog′ə·nē, *n. pl.,* **-nies.** The origin or creation of the world or universe; a theory of this creation. **—cos·mo·gon·ic,** koz·mə·gon′ik, *a.* **—cos·mog·o·nist,** *n.*

cos·mog·ra·phy, koz·mog′rə·fē, *n. pl.,* **-phies.** The science which describes and maps the heavens and the earth. **—cos·mog·ra·pher,** *n.* **—cos·mo·graph·ic,** kos·mə·graf′ik, *a.*

cos·mol·o·gy, koz·mol′ə·jē, *n. pl.,* **-gies.** The general science or theory of the cosmos or material universe. **—cos·mo·log·ic,** koz·mə·loj′ik, *a.* **—cos·mo·log·i·cal,** *a.* **—cos·mol·o·gist,** *n.*

cos·mo·naut, koz′mə·nôt, *n.* An astronaut, esp. of the Soviet Union.

cos·mo·pol·i·tan, koz·mə·pol′ə·tən, *a.* Belonging to all parts of the world; feeling at home everywhere in the world.—*n.* A person who has cosmopolitan tastes. **—cos·mo·pol·i·tan·ism,** *n.*

cos·mop·o·lite, koz·mop′ə·līt, *n.* One at home in all parts of the world.

cos·mos, koz′məs, koz′mōs, *n.* The universe thought of as a system of order and harmony; a system of order and harmony; a plant with flowers of several colors that blooms in the fall.

cost, kôst, kost, *n.* The price paid or charged for something; loss or penalty, for a thing suffered; *pl.,* expenses as the result of a legal suit.—*v.t., v.i.,* **cost** or **cost·ed, cost·ing.** To require an expenditure; to determine the cost of production.—**at all costs** or **at any cost,** no matter what expense is necessary.

cost·ly, kôst′lē, kost′lē, *a.,* **-li·er, -li·est.** Costing much; lavish or extravagant; entailing great sacrifice. **—cost·li·ness,** *n.*

cost of liv·ing, *n.* The average cost of consumer goods and services on the national level.

cost-plus, kôst′pləs, kost′pləs′, *a.* Billed according to the cost of production plus an additional fee or percentage as an agreed rate of profit: a *cost-plus* contract.

cos·tume, kos′toom, kos′tūm, *n.* The style of dress, including ornaments and hair styles; dress belonging to another period or place, as worn on the stage or at balls. **—kos·toom′, kos·tūm′,** *v.t.,* **-tumed, -tum·ing.** To furnish with a costume.

cos·tum·er, kos·too′mər, kos·tū′mər, *n.* One who makes or deals in costumes.

co·sy, kō′zē, *a.,* **-si·er, -si·est.** Cozy.

cot, kot, *n.* A light, portable bed.

co·te·rie, kō′tə·rē, *n.* A set or circle of friends who meet to share interests; a clique.

co·ter·mi·nous, kō·ter′mə·nəs, *a.* Conterminous.

co·til·lion, co·til·lon, kō·til′yən, kə·til′yən, *n.* A formal dance at which debutantes are presented socially.

cot·tage, kot′ij, *n.* A small dwelling; a small country residence; one of several detached houses forming an institution, as a resort or a hospital.

cot·tage cheese, *n.* A kind of soft white cheese made of skim-milk curds.

cot·ter pin, kot′ər, *n.* A metal strip used as a fastener on bolts and nuts.

cot·ton, kot′ən, *n.* The soft, white, downy fibers attached to the seeds of plants used in making thread or fabric; a plant yielding cotton; these plants collectively, making a commercial crop; cloth or thread made of cotton fibers.—*a.* Made of cotton.—*v.i. Informal.* Get along well with someone. **—cot·ton·y,** *a.*

cot·ton gin, *n.* A machine for separating cotton seeds from cotton fibers.

cot·ton·mouth, kot′ən·mowth, *n.* Water moccasin.

cot·ton·seed, kot′ən·sēd, *n.* The seed of the cotton plant, yielding **cot·ton·seed oil,** used as a substitute for olive oil and in cooking.

cot·ton·tail, kot′ən·tāl, *n.* The common North American rabbit.

cot·ton·wood, kot′ən·wûd, *n.* Any of several American species of poplar with cottonlike tufts on the seeds.

couch, kowch, *n.* An upholstered piece of living room furniture seating at least two persons and long enough to lie down on.—*v.t.* To cause to lie down; to put into words.—*v.i.* To lie down.

cough, kôf, kof, *n.* Pushing air from the lungs marked by sudden loud noise; an illness characterized by such a condition.—*v.i.* To expel air from the lungs with noise and effort.—*v.t.* To expel from the lungs.

could, kûd. The past form of **can.**

could·n't, kûd′ənt. Contraction of **could not.**

cou·lée, koo′lē, *n. Western U.S.* A deep ravine or gulch; a stream of lava.

coun·cil, kown′səl, *n.* An assembly called together or voted into being for consultation, deliberation, and advice; a federation of organizations; the governing body of such a federation; a local chapter of a parent organization. **—coun·cil·or,** *n.* **—coun·cil·man,** *n.* **—coun·cil·or·ship,** *n.*

coun·sel, kown′səl, *n.* Advice; consultation or deliberation about future actions; deliberate purpose; secret opinions or purposes; a lawyer engaged in a court trial or appointed as an adviser.—*v.t.,* **-seled,-sel·ing.** To advise or give deliberate opinion; warn, or instruct; to recommend.

coun·sel·ing, kown′sə·ling, *n.* The act or process of giving professionally competent advice; the use of psychological methods in professional guidance of an individual.

coun·se·lor, kown′sə·lər, *n.* An adviser; a lawyer; a supervisor at a summer camp for children. **—coun·se·lor·ship,** *n.*

count, kownt, *n.* A rank and accompanying title in the order of nobility.

count, kownt, *v.t.* To number; to reach a total; to name (numerals) in order; to check by numbering in the sense of inventory; to consider or regard; estimate to be.—*v.i.* To indicate numbers in order by groups; to be of value.—*n.* The act of counting; a number that represents the result of counting; a charge in an indictment; a referee's call of ten seconds after a boxer has been knocked down. **—count·a·ble,** *a.*

count·down, kownt′down, *n.* The count by seconds prior to some event from some number down to zero.

coun·te·nance, kown′tə·nəns, *n.* The face; appearance or expression of the face. Goodwill; support.—*v.t.,* **-nanced, -nanc·ing.** To allow; to favor; to support; to abet. **—coun·te·nanc·er,** *n.*

count·er, kown′tər, *n.* A table or board on which money is counted, business is transacted, or goods are laid for examination; in a restaurant, a flat serving area with seating facilities on one side; in a kitchen, a long working space.

count·er, kown′tər, *n.* One who counts; an apparatus for keeping count of something.

coun·ter, kown′tər, *adv., a.* In the opposite; contrary. —*v.t.* To go counter to; oppose; to meet or answer a move or blow by another in return.—*v.i.* To make an opposing move.—*n.* That which is counter, opposite, or contrary to something else.

coun·ter·act, kown′tər·akt′, *v.t.* To act in opposition to; to oppose; withstand. **—coun·ter·ac·tion,** *n.* **—coun·ter·ac·tive,** *a.*

coun·ter·at·tack, kown′tər·ə·tak, *n.* An attack in response to another attack.—*v.t., v.i.* To attack in response.

coun·ter·bal·ance, kown·tər·bal′əns, *v.t.,* **-anced, -anc·ing.** To serve as a balance to; to act against with equal power or effect.—*n.*

coun·ter·charge, kown′tər·chärj, *v.t.,* **-charged, -char·ging.** Make an accusation against (one's accuser).—*n.*

coun·ter·claim, kown′tər·klām, *n.* A claim set up against another claim.—*v.i., v.t.* To make a counterclaim. **—coun·ter·claim·ant,** *n.*

coun·ter·clock·wise, kown·tər·klok′wīz, *adv., a.* In a direction opposite to that in which the hands of a clock rotate; from right to left.

coun·ter·cul·ture, *n.* A non-violent underground movement; a dissentive minority view of values existing in the culture at large.

coun·ter·es·pi·o·nage, kown·tər·es′pē·ə·näzh, kown·tər·es′pē·ə·nij, *n.* The measures taken by a nation through its intelligence agency to detect and defeat enemy espionage.

coun·ter·feit, kown′tər·fit, *a.* Made to imitate, and pass for, something else; not genuine; forged.—*n.* An imitation; a forgery.—*v.t.* To imitate with intent to defraud; to forge; to assume the appearance of.—*v.i.* To make counterfeit things; to pretend. **—coun·ter·feit·er,** *n.*

coun·ter·in·tel·li·gence, kown·tər·in·tel′ə·jəns, *n.* The activity of an intelligence agent or agency in combating sabotage or other activity by enemy intelligence.

coun·ter·mand, kown′tər·mand, kown′tər·mänd, *v.t.* To revoke, as a former command; to order or direct in opposition to an order before given, thereby annuling it.

coun·ter·meas·ure, kown′tər·mezh·ər, *n.* An action intended as a retaliation against another measure.

coun·ter·of·fen·sive, kown·tər·ə·fen′siv, *n.* A major military action undertaken to combat an attacking enemy force.

coun·ter·pane, kown′tər·pān, *n.* A bedcover; a quilt.

coun·ter·part, kown′tər·pärt, *n.* A copy; a thing which fits together, completes, or complements another.

coun·ter·point, kown′tər·poynt, *n.* A melody or voice part added to another as accompaniment; the art of adding one or more melodies to a given melody according to fixed rules; the art of polyphonic or concerted composition.

coun·ter·poise, kown′tər·poyz, *n.* A counterbalancing weight; any equal and opposing power or force; the state of being in equilibrium.—*v.t.,* **-poised, -pois·ing.** To balance by an opposing weight.

coun·ter·rev·o·lu·tion, kown′tər·rev·ə·loo′shən, *n.* A revolution opposed to a former one.

coun·ter·sign, kown′tər·sīn, *n.* A signature added to another signature, as for authentication.—*v.t.* Add one's signature to (something already signed by another) by way of authentication; ratify. **—coun·ter·sig·na·ture,** kown·tər·sig′nə·chər, *n.*

coun·ter·sink, kown′tər·singk, *v.t.,* **-sank** or **-sunk, -sink·ing.** To put a hole in (timber or other materials) so as to receive the head of a bolt or screw and make it flush with the surface; to sink the head of a screw below the level of the surface.—*n.* A drill or brace bit for countersinking; the cavity made by countersinking.

coun·ter·spy, kown′tər·spī, *n. pl.,* **-spies.** One who spies against the espionage activities of an enemy country.

coun·ter·weight, kown′tər·wāt, *n.* A weight that counterbalances.

coun·tess, kown′tis, *n.* The wife or widow of a count in the nobility of Europe; a woman having the rank of a count or earl in her own right.

count·less, kownt′lis, *a.* Incapable of being counted; innumerable.

coun·tri·fied, kən′tri·fīd, *a.* As things are in the country; rustic.

coun·try, kən′trē, *n. pl.,* **-tries.** A land, with reference to character or features; the territory of a nation; a state distinct in name, race, and language; rural districts, as opposed to cities or towns; the people of a district, state, or nation.—*a.* Like the country; rural.

coun·try club, *n.* A club in the country or a suburban area, with facilities for such sports as golf, tennis, and swimming.

coun·try·man, kən′trē·mən, *n. pl.,* **-men.** A native or inhabitant of a particular region; a man of one's own country. **—coun·try·wo·man,** *n. fem.*

coun·try·side, kən′trē·sīd, *n.* A particular section of a country; the land adjacent to, but outside, the corporate limits of a city or town.

coun·ty, kown′tē, *n. pl.,* **-ties.** *U.S.* The largest geographic division for administrative purposes within a state; the people that live in a county.

coun·ty seat, *n.* The town or city in which county government is centered.

coup, koo, *n. pl.,* **coups,** kooz. A stroke or blow; a sudden, highly successful stroke or move.

coupé, coupe, koo·pā′, koop, *n.* An enclosed two-door automobile.

ᴄ up·le, kəp′əl, *n.* A combination of two; a man and a woman united by marriage or betrothal, or associated as partners in a dance or the like. *Informal.* A few.—*v.t.,* **-led, -ling.** To fasten or link together in pairs; to join or connect; to unite in matrimony or sexual union; to join or associate by means of a coupler.—*v.i.* To form in a pair; to copulate.

coup·ler, kəp′lər, *n.* One who or that which couples or links together.

coup·ling, kəp′ling, *n.* The bringing or joining together; sexual union; anything that couples.

cou·pon, koo′pon, kū′pon, *n.* One of a series of tickets or forms which gives the holder something of value when presented to the issuer; a statement that can be cut off a bond, and presented for payment of interest.

cour·age, kər′ij, *n.* That quality of mind which enables a person to encounter danger and difficulties with firmness, or without fear; bravery. **—cou·ra·geous,** kə·rā′jəs, *a.*

cour·i·er, kûr′ē·ər, kər′ē·ər, *n.* A messenger, carrying urgent news or reports.

course, kōrs, kôrs, *n.* The path or route along which anything moves; progress onward or through a succession of stages; customary manner of procedure; a particular manner of proceeding; a systematized or prescribed series, as of studies, lectures, medical treatments; a part of a meal served at one time; the point of the compass toward which a ship sails.—**of course,** in the common manner of proceeding: hence, naturally; obviously.—*v.t.,* **coursed, cours·ing.** To chase; to hunt game with hounds.

cours·er, kôr′sər, *n.* A very fast horse.

court, kōrt, kôrt, *n.* An open area, usually enclosed; a courtyard; the place of residence of a king or sovereign prince; the collective body of persons who compose the retinue or council of a sovereign; a hall, chamber, or place where justice is administered; any judicial body, civil or military; space prepared for playing such games as basketball or tennis.—*v.t., v.i.* To win over by attention and flattery; to seek the affections or love of; to solicit for marriage; to seek: as, to *court* applause.

cour·te·ous, kər/tē·əs, *a.* Polite, considerate of others. —**cour·te·ous·ly,** *adv.*

cour·te·sy, kər/tə·sē, *n. pl.,* **-sies.** Politeness of manners combined with kindness; a favor or indulgence, as contradistinguished from right.

court·house, kōrt/hows, kôrt/hows, *n.* A building in which established courts are held. *U.S.* The county seat.

cour·ti·er, kōr/tē·ər, kôr/tē·ər, *n.* One who attends or frequents the court of a sovereign; one who courts or flatters another to obtain favor.

court·ly, kōrt/lē, kôrt/lē, *a.,* **-li·er, -li·est.** Refined and dignified; polite; courteous.—*adv.* In a courtly manner. —**court·li·ness,** *n.*

court-mar·tial, kōrt/mär·shəl, kôrt/mär·shəl, *n. pl.,* **courts-mar·tial.** A court of military personnel, for the trial of military offenses; a trial by court-martial.—*v.t.,* **-mar·tialed, -mar·tial·ing.**

court·room, kōrt/room, kôrt/rûm, *n.* A room housing a court of law, in which trials are held.

court·ship, kōrt/ship, kôrt/ship, *n.* The act of courting or soliciting favor; period of time during which such wooing takes place.

court·yard, kōrt/yärd, kôrt/yärd, *n.* A court or enclosure around a house or next to it.

cous·in, kəz/ən, *n.* The son or daughter of an uncle or aunt; any distant or remote relative. —**cous·in·hood,** *n.* —**cous·in·ly,** *adv.*

cou·tu·rier, koo·tû·rē·ā, *n.* A person who designs, makes, and sells fashionable women's clothes.

cove, kōv, *n.* A sheltered nook; a small sheltered bay or creek; a cave or cavern.

cov·e·nant, kəv/ə·nənt, *n.* An agreement between two or more persons to do or refrain from doing some act; a contract; in the Bible, the agreements of God with man.—*v.t.* To agree according to a covenant. —**cov·e·nan·ter, cov·e·nan·tor,** *n.*

cov·er, kəv/ər, *v.t.* To put something over or upon as for protection or concealment; to serve as a covering for; occupy the surface of; hide from view; to aim directly at, as with a pistol; to act as reporter or photographer of or at, as occurrences or performances, as for a newspaper.—*v.i.* To provide or serve as a covering; start in place of someone who is absent.—*n.*

cov·er, kəv/ər, *n.* That which covers, as the lid of a vessel; protection or concealment; funds to cover liability or secure against risk of loss. —**cov·ered,** *a.* —**cov·er·less,** *a.*

cov·er·age, kəv/ər·ij, *n.* A provision for something by agreement or contract; that which is so covered; the sending and receiving areas of radio or television stations; the number of readers in an area served by a publication; the writing, publishing, or broadcasting of news; protection against a specific risk or risks.

cov·er·all, kəv/ər·ôl, *n.* A loose, one-piece, outer work garment worn to protect other clothing. Also **cov·er·alls.**

cov·er charge, *n.* A predetermined charge added to the bill at night clubs or restaurants to pay for entertainment.

cov·ered wag·on, *n.* A large wagon with high, curved hoops covered by a canvas top, used to transport pioneers westward during the 19th century.

cov·er·ing, kəv/ər·ing, *n.* Something placed over or around a thing to conceal, shield, or provide warmth; the act of one who covers.

cov·er·let, kəv/ər·lit, *n.* A bedspread; a covering.

cov·ert, kəv/ərt, kō/vərt, *a.* Covered; sheltered; secret. *Fig.* Concealed. *Law.* Under protection of a husband.—*n.* —**cov·ert·ly,** *adv.* —**cov·ert·ness,** *n.*

cov·er-up, kəv/ər·əp, *n.* Whatever is done to conceal wrongdoing. —**cov·er up,** *v.i.*

cov·et, kəv/it, *v.t.* To wish for, esp. eagerly; desire wrongfully.—*v.i.* —**cov·et·a·ble,** *a.* —**cov·et·er,** *n.*

cov·et·ous, kəv/ə·təs, *a.* Eager to possess that to which one has no right. —**cov·et·ous·ly,** *adv.* —**cov·et·ous·ness,** *n.*

cov·ey, kəv/ē, *n.* A small flock of quail or similar birds. *Fig.* A company; a group.

cow, kow, *n. pl.,* **cows** (*archaic,* **kine,** kīn.) The female of a bovine animal, esp. of the domestic species; the female of various other large animals, as the elephant.—*v.t.* Intimidate; overawe.

cow·ard, kow/ərd, *n.* One who lacks courage to meet danger or difficulty.—*a.* —**cow·ard·ly,** *a., adv.* —**cow·ard·li·ness,** *n.*

cow·ard·ice, kow/ər·dis, *n.* Lack of courage.

cow·boy, kow/boy, *n.* A man who looks after cattle on a large ranch and does this work on horseback; a man who possesses the skills of a cowboy, esp. those associated with the rodeo.

cow col·lege, *n. Informal.* A small agricultural college situated in a rural area.

cow·er, kow/ər, *v.i.* To stoop or sink downward, as from fear. —**cow·er·ing·ly,** *adv.*

cow·hide, kow/hīd, *n.* The hide or skin of a cow, made or to be made into leather.—*v.t.,* **-hid·ed, -hid·ing.** To whip with a cowhide lash.

cowl, kowl, *n.* A hooded garment worn by monks; the hood of this garment; a hood-shaped covering for a chimney or ventilating shaft, to increase the draft.—*v.t.* To cover with a cowl. —**cowled,** *a.*

cow·lick, kow/lik, *n.* A tuft of hair growing in a wayward direction and turned up, often over the forehead.

cowl·ing, kow/ling, *n.* A metal covering for an engine. *Aeron.* The removable housing for an aircraft component, used for the purpose of protecting, streamlining, or regulating the flow of cooling air.

cow·man, kow/man, *n. pl.,* **-men.** *Western U.S.* An owner of cattle; a cowboy.

co-work·er, kō·wər/kər, kō/wər·kər, *n.* One who works with another; a co-operator.

cow·poke, kow/pōk, *n. Western Informal.* A cowhand; a cowboy.

cow·pox, kow/poks, *n.* A disease which appears on the teats of the cow in the form of vesicles or blisters; the fluid or virus contained therein is capable of immunizing man against smallpox.

cow·ry, cow·rie, kow/rē, *n. pl.,* **-ries.** A shell of any of various mollusks, used as money in parts of Africa or Asia.

cox·swain, kok/sən, kok/swān, *n.* The steersman of a boat.

coy, koy, *a.* Shy; modest; bashful. —**coy·ly,** *adv.* —**coy·ness,** *n.*

coy·o·te, ki·ō/tē, ki/ōt, *n.* The American prairie wolf noted for its howling at night. *Informal.* A contemptible person.

coz·en, kəz/ən, *v.t.* To cheat; to deceive.—*v.i.* —**coz·en·age,** *n.* —**coz·en·er,** *n.*

co·zy, kō/zē, *a.,* **-zi·er, -zi·est.** Snug; comfortable.—*n. pl.,* **-zies.** A padded covering for a teapot. —**co·zi·ly,** *adv.* —**co·zi·ness,** *n.*

crab, krab, *n.* A crustacean with a short, broad, more or less flattened body, the abdomen or so-called tail being small and folded under the thorax; any of various other crustaceans resembling the true crab; an ill-tempered or crabbed person.—*v.i.,* **crabbed, crab·bing.** To catch crabs; to act like a crab in crawling backward or sideways. —**crab·by, crab·bed,** krab/id, *a.* Ill-tempered; sour; peevish. —**crab·bed·ly,** *adv.* —**crab·bed·ness,** *n.*

crab, krab, *v.i.,* **crabbed, crab·bing.** *Informal.* To find fault; grumble.

crab ap·ple, *n.* A small, sour, wild apple.

crab grass, *n.* An annual grass often found as a weedy pest in lawns.

crack, krak, *v.t.* To break, or burst; to break partially; to utter with smartness: to *crack* a joke; to snap; to cause to make a sharp sudden noise like a whip, to break open, into, or through, as a safe or a secret code.—*v.i.*

To break with a sharp sound; to burst; to open in chinks; to be fractured without quite separating into different parts; to give out a loud or sharp, sudden sound; to fall or give way, as or as if under strain.—*n.* A chink or fissure; a burst of sound; flaw; blemish.—*a. Informal.* First-rate; excellent: a *crack* regiment.

crack•down, krak′down, *n.* The sudden and severe enforcement of existing regulations.

crack•er, krak′ər, *n.* A thin, crisp biscuit; a small kind of firework which explodes with a sharp noise.

crack•ing, krak′ing, *n.* The act of one who or that which cracks.

crack•le, krak′əl, *v.i.,* **-led, -ling.** To make slight, sharp noises, as the tiny explosive sounds of burning wood; to be vibrant or sparkling: Her conversation *crackles* with enthusiasm; to change by cracking or forming tiny surface cracks: Paint, improperly applied, may *crackle.*—*n.* The act of crackling; fine cracks in the surface of porcelain glaze. —**crack•led,** *a.*

crack-up, krak′əp, *n.* A collision. *Informal.* Loss or breakdown of a person's health.

cra•dle, krā′dəl, *n.* A little bed or cot for an infant, usually constructed for a rocking or swinging motion; the place where anything is nurtured during its early existence.—*v.t., v.i.,* **-dled, -dling.** To rock in a cradle; put in a cradle.

craft, kraft, kräft, *n.* Skill; dexterity; an occupation or employment requiring skills; trade; members of a trade; a vessel or vessels, such as ships; guile.

crafts•man, krafts′mən, kräfts′mən, *n. pl.,* **-men.** An artisan; a mechanic. —**crafts•man•ship,** *n.*

craft•y, kraf′tē, kräf′tē, *a.,* **-i•er, -i•est.** Cunning; sly. —**craft•i•ly,** *adv.* —**craft•i•ness,** *n.*

crag, krag, *n.* A steep, rugged rock. —**crag•ged,** krag′id, *a.* —**crag•gy,** krag′ē, *a.* —**crag•gi•ness,** *n.*

cram, kram, *v.t.,* **crammed, cram•ming.** To force or stuff hastily or carelessly, frequently used with *down* or *into:* to *cram* all one's belongings *into* a small suitcase; to prepare, as oneself or another person, by filling the mind with information, as in hurried studying for an examination.—*v.i.* To eat greedily; to memorize facts. —**cram•mer,** *n.*

cramp, kramp, *n.* A small metal bar that holds things together; a clamp.—*v.t.* To fasten or hold with a cramp; to confine narrowly; to restrict.

cramp, kramp, *n.* An involuntary, spasmodic, painful contraction of a muscle or muscles, as from a slight strain or sudden chill; a sudden, violent abdominal pain; *pl.,* continuing abdominal pain.—*v.t.*

cran•ber•ry, kran′ber•ē, kran′bə•rē, *n. pl.,* **-ries.** The red, acid fruit or berry of a type of plant, used in making sauce, jelly, etc.; the plant itself.

crane, krān, *n.* Any of a group of large wading birds with very long legs and neck; a device for moving heavy weights, having two motions, one a direct lift and the other a horizontal movement.—*v.t., v.i.,* **craned, cran•ing.** To stretch (the neck) as a crane does; to hoist, lower, or move by or as by a crane.

cra•ni•um, krā′nē•əm, *n. pl.,* **-ni•ums, -ni•a,** -nē•ə. That part of the skull which encloses the brain. —**cra•ni•al,** krā′nē•əl, *a.* —**cra•ni•ate,** krā′nē•it, krā′nē•āt, *a.* —**cra•ni•al•ly,** *adv.*

crank, krangk, *n.* A device for conveying motion, consisting in its simplest form of an arm or handle secured at right angles to a shaft, which receives or imparts the motion. *Informal.* A bad-tempered person; a person with impracticable notions; an eccentric notion or whim.—*v.t.* To move with a crank.

crank•case, krangk′kās, *n.* In an internal-combustion engine, the case which encloses the crankshaft, connecting rods, and allied parts.

crank•shaft, krangk′shaft, krangk′shäft, *n.* A shaft receiving motion from, or imparting motion to a crank.

crank•y, krang′kē, *a.,* **-i•er, -i•est.** Ill-tempered;

cross; grouchy. —**crank•i•ly,** *adv.* —**crank•i•ness,** *n.*

cran•ny, kran′ē, *n. pl.,* **-nies.** A small, narrow opening, or chink, as in a wall or other substance.—*v.i.* —**cran•nied,** *a.*

crap, krap, *n.* Craps. *Informal.* Nonsense; misleading statements.

craps, kraps, *n.* A game of chance using two dice.

crash, krash, *v.t.* To shatter; to force or drive in, through, or out with violence and noise.—*v.i.* To land in an abnormal manner.—*n.* A breaking or falling to pieces with loud noise; the shock of collision and breaking; a sudden and violent falling to ruin; a sudden, loud noise, as of something dashed to pieces; an act of crashing.—*a.* Of or pertaining to hasty, intensive effort: a *crash* program to rebuild.

crash hel•met, *n.* A sturdy helmet worn for protection by pilots and others.

crash-land, krash′land′, *v.t., v.i.* To land (an airplane in an emergency) where normal procedures are impossible, causing damage to the craft.

crass, kras, *a.* Gross; coarse; dense. —**crass•ly,** *adv.* —**crass•ness,** *n.*

crate, krāt, *n.* Any openwork casing, as a box made of slats for packing and transporting commodities.—*v.t.,* **crat•ed, crat•ing.**

cra•ter, krā′tər, *n.* A hole, pit, or depression in the ground caused by an explosion, volcanic action, or other natural happenings. —**cra•ter•al,** *a.* —**cra•tered,** *a.*

cra•vat, krə•vat′, *n.* A man's scarf; a necktie.

crave, krāv, *v.t.,* **craved, crav•ing.** To ask for with earnestness; to long for.—*v.i.* To beg, ask; to long or hanker eagerly, followed by *for.* —**crav•er,** *n.* —**crav•ing,** *n.* Vehement or earnest desire; a longing. —**crav•ing•ly,** *adv.*

cra•ven, krā′vən, *a.* Cowardly.—*n.* A coward. —**cra•ven•ly,** *adv.*

craw, krô, *n.* An enlargement of the gullet in front of the stomach of fowls; the stomach of an animal.

craw•fish, krô′fish, *n.* Crayfish.—*v.i.* To back out or retreat from a position or undertaking.

crawl, krôl, *v.i.* To move slowly on the hands and knees; of plants or vines, to spread by extending tendrils; to creep along the ground, as, a snake crawls; to move or walk slowly.—*n.* The act of crawling; slow, creeping motion, a swimming stroke performed in a face-down position from which the swimmer uses an alternate overarm stroke. —**crawl•y,** *a.* —**crawl•ing•ly,** *adv.*

crawl•er, krô′lər, *n.* A creeper; a reptile; a worm used as fish bait.

crawl space, *n.* An open area in a building which provides for ventilation, maintenance, and storage.

cray•fish, krā′fish, *n. pl.,* **-fish•es, -fish.** A crustacean closely related to the lobsters, but smaller.

cray•on, krā′on, krā′ən, *n.* A pencil of colored chalk or wax used for drawing; a drawing made with crayons.—*v.t.*

craze, krāz, *v.t.,* **crazed, craz•ing.** To crackle; make insane.—*v.i.* To become insane; to develop tiny cracks.—*n.* A popular rage; fad; a minute crack in the glaze of pottery.

cra•zy, krā′zē, *a.,* **-zi•er, -zi•est.** *Informal.* Insane; eccentric; very infatuated, usu. followed by *about.* —**cra•zi•ly,** *adv.* —**cra•zi•ness,** *n.*

crazy bone, *n.* The elbow; the funny bone.

creak, krēk, *v.i.* To make a sharp, harsh, grating sound.—*v.t.*—*n.* A sharp, harsh, grating sound. —**creak•i•ly,** *adv.* —**creak•i•ness,** *n.,* —**creak•y,** *a.,* **-i•er, -i•est.**

cream, krēm, *n.* The fatty part of milk, which rises to the surface when the liquid is allowed to stand; something resembling this substance, as a confection; an emulsified cosmetic; a yellowish white color.

---

a- hat, fāte, fāre, fäther; **e-** met, mē; **i-** pin, pīne; **o-** not, nōte, ôrb, moove (move), boy, pownd; **u-** cūbe, bûll, tûk (took); **ch-** chin; **th-** thick, ŧhen; **zh-** vizhon (vision); **ə-** əgo, takən, pencəl, lemən, bərd (bird).

Fig. The best part of anything.—*v.t.* To coat with a cosmetic cream; to allow (milk) to form cream; take the cream or best part of.—*v.i.* To form cream: hence, to foam. —**cream·i·ly,** *adv.* —**cream·i·ness,** *n.* —**cream·y,** *a.,* **-i·er, -i·est.**

cream cheese, *n.* Any of various soft, rich, unripened cheeses made with cream.

cream·er, krē/mər, *n.* A small jug or pitcher for holding cream.

cream·er·y, krē/mə·rē, *n. pl.,* **-ies.** An establishment engaged in the production of butter and cheese; a place for the sale of milk and its products.

crease, krēs, *n.* A line or mark made by folding or doubling anything: hence, a similar mark, however produced.—*v.t., v.i.,* **creased, creas·ing.** —**creas·y,** krē/sē, *a.,* **-i·er, -i·est.**

cre·ate, krē·āt/, *v.t., v.i.,* **cre·at·ed, cre·at·ing.** To bring into being; produce; specif. to evolve from one's own thought or imagination.

cre·a·tion, krē·ā/shən, *n.* The act of creating or producing; especially, the act of bringing the world into existence; the production of that which is original, or imaginative. —**cre·a·tion·al,** *a.*

cre·a·tive, krē·ā/tiv, *a.* Having the power to create, or exerting the act of creating. —**cre·a·tiv·i·ty,** krē·ā·tiv/ə·tē, *n.*

cre·a·tor, krē·ā/tər, *n.* One who or that which creates. (*Cap.*) The Maker of all things.

crea·ture, krē/chər, *n.* Any created thing; an animate being; an animal, distinct from man; a human being or person; a result or product.

crea·ture com·forts, *n. pl.* Those things, as food, clothing, and shelter, which minister to bodily comfort.

cre·dence, krēd/əns, *n.* Reliance on evidence; belief or credit, the communion table, on which the bread and wine are placed.

cre·den·tial, kri·den/shəl, *n.* A title or claim to confidence or credit.—*a. Pl.* Testimonials or documents giving a person belief or authority.

cre·den·za, kri·den/zə, *n.* A sideboard.

cred·i·ble, kred/ə·bəl, *a.* Capable of being believed. —**cred·i·bil·i·ty,** kred·ə·bil/ə·tē, *n.* —**cred·i·bly,** *adv.*

cred·it, kred/it, *v.t.* To believe; to sell or lend on the basis of future payment; to give credit for.—*n.* Approval or honor given for some quality or action; good name; reputation for commercial solvency or stability; the selling of goods or lending of money on the basis of future payment; the time extended for payment for goods or services sold on trust; recorded acknowledgment of the work of a student in a particular course of study. —**cred·it·a·ble,** kred/ə·tə·bəl, *a.* —**cred·it·a·bil·i·ty,** kred·ə·tə·bil/ə·tē, *n.* —**cred·it·a·bly,** kred/ə·tə·blē, *adv.*

cred·it card, *n.* A small card establishing the right of its holder to credit on certain purchases, as meals, lodging, gasoline, or merchandise.

cred·i·tor, kred/i·tər, *n.* One who gives goods or money on credit; one to whom money is due.

cre·do, krē/dō, krā/dō, *n. pl.,* **-dos.** Any creed or formula of belief.

cred·u·lous, krej/ə·ləs, *a.* Apt to believe without good evidence; easily deceived; stemming from gullibility or credulity.

creed, krēd, *n.* Any formula of religious belief, as of a particular denomination; any system of belief or of opinion.

creek, krēk, krik, *n.* A small stream.

creel, krēl, *n.* A basket used to carry fish.

creep, krēp, *v.i.,* **crept, creep·ing.** To move along the ground; to move on hands and knees, as a child; to move slowly, or stealthily.—*n.* The act of creeping. *Informal.* An odd or obnoxious person.—**the creeps,** *informal,* a feeling of repulsion or fear: generally used as the object of *give.* —**creep·y,** krē/pē, *a.,* **-i·er, -i·est.** —**creep·i·ness,** *n.*

creep·er, krē/pər, *n.* One who or that which creeps; a plant which grows along the land by sending or shooting out stems.

cre·mate, krē/māt, *v.t.,* **-mat·ed, -mat·ing.** To burn, esp. to reduce a corpse to ashes. —**cre·ma·tion,** kri·mā/shən, *n.* —**cre·ma·ter,** *n.*

cre·ma·to·ry, krē/mə·tôr·ē, *n.* A furnace for cremating dead bodies or other matter. Also, **cre·ma·to·ri·um,** krē·mə·tôr/ē·əm. *n.*

Cre·ole, krē/ōl, *n.* Orig., in the West Indies and Spanish America, one born in the region but of European, usually Spanish, ancestry; similarly, in Louisiana and elsewhere, a person born in the region but of French ancestry.—*a. (L.c.)* Bred or growing in a country, but of foreign origin, as, an animal or plant.

cre·o·sote, krē/ə·sōt, *n.* An oily liquid with a powerful odor, distilled from wood tar, and used to preserve wood.

crêpe, krāp, krep, *n.* A thin, light fabric of silk, cotton, or other fiber, with a finely crinkled or ridged surface; a very thin French pancake.

crepe, *v.t.,* **creped, crep·ing.** To cover with crepe; to frizzle or curl.

crepe pa·per, *n.* A decorative paper, wrinkled to resemble crepe fabric.

cre·pus·cu·lar, kri·pəs/kyə·lər, *a.* Referring to twilight; flying or active at twilight.

cres·cen·do, krə·shen/dō, krə·sen/dō, *a.* Gradually increasing in force or loudness.—*n. pl.,* **-dos.**

cres·cent, kres/ənt, *n.* The crescent moon; any crescent-shaped object, as a croissant.—*a.*

cress, kres, *n.* A type of plant used as a salad.

crest, krest, *n.* The head or top of anything; the summit of a hill, etc.; the highest or best of the kind, a ridge or ridgelike formation.—*v.t.* To furnish with a crest; to serve as a crest for; crown or top; to reach, as the crest or summit of.—*v.i.* To form or rise into a crest, as a wave. —**crest·ed,** *a.* —**crest·less,** *a.*

crest·fall·en, krest/fô·lən, *a.* Dejected; discouraged.

cre·ta·ceous, kri·tā/shəs, *a.* Composed of or having the qualities of chalk.

cre·tin·ism, krē/tən·iz·əm, *n.* A chronic disease marked by retardation and physical deformity, caused by a low production of thyroid secretion.

cre·tonne, kri·ton/, krē/ton, *n.* A cotton cloth with various textures of surface printed with pictorial and other patterns.

cre·vasse, krə·vas/, *n.* A fissure or rent: generally applied to a fissure across a glacier.

crev·ice, krev/is, *n.* A crack; a cranny.

crew, kroo, *n.* A body of persons engaged upon a particular work; a gang or crowd, usu. a derogatory term.

crew cut, *n.* A haircut in which the hair is cropped close to the scalp.

crew·el, kroo/əl, *n.* A kind of fine worsted or thread of silk or wool; the embroidery made of this floss or yarn.

crib, krib, *n.* A child's bed with high, usu. slatted sides; a framework enclosure such as a stall or pen in which cattle are stabled; any cramped habitation; a petty theft. *Informal.* A device, such as a list of correct answers, employed by students for cheating.—*v.t.,* **cribbed, crib·bing.**—*v.i.* —**crib·ber,** *n.*

crib·bage, krib/ij, *n.* A game of cards, for two, three, or four players, a characteristic feature of which is the crib, which is composed of the players' discards.

crick, krik, *n.* A painful muscle spasm, esp. of the neck or back.—*v.t.*

crick·et, krik/it, *n.* An insect noted for the chirping or creaking sound produced by the male.

crick·et, krik/it, *n.* A popular outdoor game, played esp. in England, honorable behavior.

cri·er, krī/ər, *n.* An official, as of a court or a town, who makes public announcements; a hawker.

crime, krīm, *n.* An act or omission, esp. one of a grave nature, punishable by law as forbidden by statute or injurious to the public welfare; serious violation of human law; serious wrongdoing; sin.

crim·i·nal, krim′ə·nəl, *a.* Guilty of a crime; involving a crime.—*n.* A person guilty of crime. **—crim·i·nal·i·ty,** krim·ə·nal′ə·tē, *n.* **—crim·i·nal·ly,** *adv.*

crim·i·nal law, *n.* Any of the legal enactments dealing with crimes and their punishment.

crim·i·nol·o·gy, krim·ə·nol′ə·jē, *n.* The scientific study of crime and criminals. **—crim·i·nol·o·gist,** *n.*

crimp, krimp, *v.t.,* To flute or make ridges on; to press (the ends of something) together; to hinder. **—***n.* **—crimp·y,** *a.,* **-i·er, -i·est.**

crim·son, krim′zən, *n.* A deep red.—*a.* Deep-red.

cringe, krinj, *v.i.,* **cringed, cring·ing.** To shrink, from fear; cower; fawn.—*n.*

crin·kle, kring′kəl, *v.i., v.t.,* **-kled, -kling.** To wrinkle or ripple; to make slight, sharp sounds; to rustle.—*n.* **—crin·kly,** *a.,* **-kli·er, -kli·est.**

crip·ple, krip′əl, *n.* A partially disabled or lame person or animal.—*a.* Lame; inferior.—*v.t.,* **-pled, -pling.**

cri·sis, krī′sis, *n. pl.,* **cri·ses,** krī′sēz. The point of time when an affair has reached its height, and must soon terminate or suffer a material change; turning point.

crisp, krisp, *a.* Brittle; fresh; brisk; sparkling.—*v.t.* To make or become crisp. **—crisp·er,** *n.* **—crisp·ness,** *n.* **—crisp·y,** *a.,* **-i·er, -i·est.**

criss·cross, kris′krôs, kris′kros, *n.* A crossing or intersection.—*a.* Crossed.—*adv.* In a crisscross manner; crosswise.—*v.t., v.i.* To mark with or form crossing lines.

cri·te·ri·on, krī·tēr′ē·ən, *n. pl.,* **-ri·a,** -rē·ə, **-ri·ons.** A standard of judging by which a correct judgment may be made.

crit·ic, krit′ik, *n.* A person skilled in judging the merit of anything by certain standards or criteria; a reviewer; one who judges with severity.

crit·i·cal, krit′i·kəl, *a.* Relating to criticism; inclined to find fault or to judge with severity; pertaining to any crisis; important, as to consequences; dangerous; hazardous. **—crit·i·cal·ly,** *adv.* **—crit·i·cal·ness,** *n.*

crit·i·cism, krit′ə·siz·əm, *n.* The art of judging the merit of any performance; a critical judgment.

crit·i·cize, krit′ə·sīz, *v.i.,* **-cized, -ciz·ing.** To judge critically; to pick out faults.—*v.t.* **—crit·i·ciz·a·ble,** *a.*

cri·tique, kri·tēk′, *n.* A written estimate of the merits of a performance; a criticism.

crit·ter, krit′ər, *n. U.S.* Creature.

croak, krōk, *v.i.* To make a low, hoarse noise in the throat, as a frog; to speak with a low, hollow voice; to grumble. *Informal.* To die.—*v.t.*—*n.* The low, harsh sound uttered by a frog, or a like sound. **—croak·y,** *a.,* **-i·er, -i·est.**

croak·er, krō′kər, *n.* Someone or something which croaks; a habitual complainer.

cro·chet, krō·shā′, *n.* A kind of knitting done with a needle having at one end a small hook for drawing the thread or yarn into place; the work or fabric made.— *v.t., v.i.,* **-cheted,** -shād, **-chet·ing,** -shā′ing. **—cro·chet·er,** *n.*

crock, krok, *n.* An earthen vessel.

crock·er·y, krok′ə·rē, *n.* Earthenware.

croc·o·dile, krok′ə·dīl, *n.* Any of the large, thick-skinned, lizard-like reptiles inhabiting the waters of tropical Africa, Asia, Australia, and America; the skin of these reptiles.

cro·cus, krō′kəs, *n. pl.,* **-cus·es, -ci,** -sī. Any of the small bulbous plants grown for their showy, solitary flowers, which commonly appear before the leaves in early spring.

crois·sant, *Fr.* krwä·sän′, *n.* A crescent-shaped roll of bread dough.

Cro-Mag·non, krō·mag′nən, krō·man′yən, *a.* Referring to a group of tall, erect, prehistoric people who lived in southwestern Europe and used bone and stone implements.—*n.*

crone, krōn, *n.* A contemptuous term for an old woman.

cro·ny, krō′nē, *n. pl.,* **-nies.** A close friend; a follower.

crook, krůk, *n.* A hook; the hooked part of anything; the act of crooking or bending. *Informal.* A swindler, or thief.—*v.t., v.i.*

crook·ed, krůk′id, *a.* Bent; deformed; dishonest.

croon, kroon, *v.t., v.i.* To utter a low murmuring sound; sing softly and monotonously.—*n.* A low humming or singing. **—croon·er,** *n.*

crop, krop, *n.* The cultivated produce of the ground, as grain or fruit; the yield of some other product in a season; the stock or handle of a whip; a short riding whip with a loop instead of a lash; a cutting off, as of the hair; a mark produced by clipping the ears, as of an animal. A special pouchlike swelling or the gullet of many birds, in which the food undergoes partial preparation for digestion, or a similar organ in other animals; the craw.—*v.t.,* **cropped, crop·ping.** To cut off or remove (the head or top) of a plant; to cut off the ends of a part of; cut short; clip (the ears or hair of); cut closely (the margins of a book); to remove by or as by cutting; to cause to bear a crop or crops.—*v.i.* To appear incidentally or unexpectedly, usually with *up* or *out.*

crop·per, krop′ər, *n.* One who raises a crop, esp. on shares.**—come a cropper,** to fall heavily, as from a horse, or to undergo a disastrous failure or collapse.

cro·quet, krō·kā′, *n.* A lawn game played by knocking wooden balls through a set of wickets by means of mallets.

cro·quette, krō·ket′, *n.* A mixture of minced meat or fish formed into a ball, and fried in deep fat.

cross, krôs, kros, *n.* Two pieces of timber, or of other material, placed across each other, either in form of +, T, or ×, variously modified; (*cap.*) that on which Christ suffered: the symbol of the Christian religion; the religion itself; an ornament in the form of a cross; any figure or sign in the form of a cross, or formed by two lines crossing each other, such as the mark made instead of a signature by those who cannot write; anything that thwarts, obstructs, or perplexes; misfortune, or opposition; a mixing of breeds; a hybrid.—*a.* Passing from side to side; adverse; snappish; peevish; ill-humored.—*v.t.* To draw or run (a line) across; to make the sign of the cross upon; to pass from side to side of; obstruct; to contradict; to clash with; to mix the breed of.—*v.i.*—*adv.* Not parallel; crosswise. **cross one's path,** to come upon unexpectedly. **—cross·ly,** *adv.*

cross·bar, krôs′bär, kros′bär, *n.* A transverse bar, line, or stripe; a horizontal bar used for exercises in a gymnasium.

cross·bones, krôs′bōnz, kros′bōnz, *n. pl.* A symbol of death, consisting of two human thigh or arm bones placed crosswise, generally in conjunction with a skull; the design of the flag of pirate ships.

cross·bow, krôs′bō, kros′bō, *n.* A medieval weapon formed by placing a bow transversely on a stock from which stones or arrows were released.

cross·bred, krôs′bred, kros′bred, *a.* Applied to an animal produced from a male and female of different breeds.**—cross·breed,** krôs′brēd, kros′brēd, *v.t., v.i.* **—cross·breed·ing,** *n.*

cross-coun·try, krôs′kən·trē, kros′kən·trē, *a.* Directed across fields or open country.

cross·cut, krôs′kət, kros′kət, *n.* Something that cuts across.—*a.*—*v.t.,* **-cut, -cut·ting.**

cross-ex·am·ine, krôs′ig·zam′in, kros′ig·zam′in, *v.t.,* **-ined, -in·ing.** To examine (a witness) anew, to test the validity of previous testimony.

cross-fer·ti·li·za·tion, krôs′fər·tə·lə·zā′shən, kros′fər·tə·lə·zā′·shən, *n.* The fertilization of the ovules of one plant by the pollen of another.

---

a- hat, fāte, fāre, fäther; **e-** met, mē; **i-** pin, pīne; **o-** not, nōte, ôrb, moove (move), boy, pownd; **u-** cūbe, bůll, tûk (took); **ch-** chin; **th-** thick, ŧhen; **zh-** vizhon (vision); **ə-** əgo, takən, pencəl, lemən, bərd (bird).

—cross·fer·ti·lize, krôs′fər′tə·līz, *v.t.,* **-lized, -liz·ing.**

cross·hatch, krôs′hach, kros′hach, *v.t.* To shade with two series of parallel lines crossing each other.

cross·ing, krôs′ing, kros′ing, *n.* Any place where things cross; place where something may be crossed, esp. a road or railroad; act of going across.

cross-pol·li·na·tion, krôs′pol·ə·nā′shən, *n.* Cross-fertilization. **—cross-pol·li·nate,** krôs′pol′ə·nāt, *v.t.*

cross-pur·pose, krôs′pər′pəs, *n.* A contrary purpose; a misunderstanding.

cross-ref·er·ence, krôs′ref′ər·əns, *n.* A reference from one part of a book, list, or card file to another. **—cross-re·fer,** krôs′rə·fər′, *v.t., v.i.* **-ferred, -fer·ring.**

cross·road, krôs′rōd, kros′rōd, *n.* A road that crosses another; *pl.,* the place where one road intersects another; the point at which a fateful decision must be made.

cross sec·tion, *n.* The cutting of any body at right angles to its length; a sample showing all aspects.

cross-stitch, krôs′stich, kros′stich, *n.* A kind of stitching employing pairs of diagonal stitches.

cross·tie, krôs′tī, kros′tī, *n.* A tie placed transversely to form a foundation or support, as under a railroad track.

cross·walk, krôs′wôk, kros′wôk, *n.* A specially marked pedestrian lane, as across a street or highway.

cross·wise, krôs′wīz, kros′wīz, *a., adv.* Across. Also **cross·ways.**

cross·word puz·zle, krôs′wərd, kros′wərd, *n.* A puzzle in which words corresponding to given meanings are to be supplied and fitted into a particular figure divided into spaces.

crotch, kroch, *n.* A fork or forking; the part of the human body or of trousers where the legs are joined.

crotch·et·y, kroch′ə·tē, *a.* Grouchy; odd. **—crotch·et·i·ness,** *n.*

crouch, krowch, *v.i.* To bend or stoop low; to lie close to the ground, as an animal.—*v.t.* To bend, esp. in humility or fear.

croup, kroop, *n.* An inflammation of the respiratory passages characterized by highly labored breathing and a hoarse, rasping cough. **—croup·y,** *a.*

croup, kroop, *n.* The highest part of the hindquarters or rump of a four-legged animal.

crou·pi·er, kroo′pē·ər, *Fr.* kroo·pyä′, *n.* An employee of a gambling establishment who supervises a gaming table, accepting bets and paying off wagers.

crou·ton, kroo′ton, kroo·ton′, *n.* A small piece of fried or toasted bread used as a garnish for salads and soups.

crow, krō, *n.* Any of a genus of birds with lustrous black plumage and a characteristic harsh cry or caw; a crowbar.—*n.* The cry of a rooster or cock; an exultant or exuberant human cry.—*v.i.* To make the sound or cry of a cock; to gloat.

crow·bar, krō′bär, *n.* A bar of iron or steel with a bent and sometimes forked end, used as a lever.

crowd, krowd, *n.* A number of persons or things collected or closely pressed together; an audience; a throng.—*v.i.* To press forward; throng; swarm.—*v.t.* To push or shove; fill full or to excess. *Informal.* To urge or annoy by urging.

crown, krown, *n.* A decorative covering for the head, worn as a symbol of sovereignty; (*cap.*) with *the,* the sovereign as head of the state; (*l.c.*) an exalting or chief attribute: Any of various coins, orig. one bearing the representation of a crown; something having the form of a crown; the top or highest part of anything; that part of a tooth that sticks up past the gum; an artificial substitute for that part of a tooth; the highest or most perfect state of anything.—*v.t.* To place a crown or garland upon the head of; specif. to invest with a regal crown, or with regal dignity and power; to cover the top of a tooth with a false crown. *Informal.* To hit on the head.

crown prince, *n.* The heir apparent of a monarch.

crown prin·cess, *n.* The wife of a crown prince; a female heir apparent.

crow's-foot, krōz′fŏt, *n. pl.,* **-feet.** *Usu. pl.* A wrinkle at the outer corner of the eye.

crow's-nest, krōz′nest, *n.* A lookout box, secured near the top of a mast.

cru·cial, kroo′shəl, *a.* Critical; decisive, cross-shaped. **—cru·ci·al·i·ty,** kroo·shē·al′ə·tē, *n.* **—cru·cial·ly,** *adv.*

cru·ci·ble, kroo′sə·bəl, *n.* A vessel of clay, porcelain, or the like, in which metals can be melted or heated; a severe test.

cru·ci·fix, kroo′sə·fiks, *n.* An image of Jesus Christ crucified on the cross; the cross as a symbol of Christianity.

cru·ci·fix·ion, kroo·sə·fik′shən, *n.* The act of crucifying; (*cap.*) the putting to death of Christ upon the cross. A picture or representation of this; severe persecution, pain, or suffering.

cru·ci·form, kroo′sə·fôrm, *a.* Cross-shaped.

cru·ci·fy, kroo′sə·fī, *v.t.,* **-fied, -fy·ing.** To put to death by nailing or fastening to a cross; to treat extremely harshly.

crude, krood, *a.,* **crud·er, crud·est.** Being in a raw or unprepared state, as manufacturing materials; underdeveloped or imperfect, as ideas or opinions; lacking in culture, tact, or the like, as persons, or their behavior or speech. **—crude·ly,** *adv.* **—crude·ness,** *n.* **—cru·di·ty,** kroo′də·tē, *n. pl.,* **-ties.**

cru·el, kroo′əl, *a.* Without pity, or kindness; causing pain, grief, or distress; inhuman; tormenting; **—cru·el·ly,** *adv.* **—cru·el·ness,** *n.* **—cru·el·ty,** kroo′əl·tē, *n.*

cru·et, kroo′et, *n.* A glass bottle, esp. one for holding vinegar or oil for the table.

cruise, krooz, *v.i., v.t.,* **cruised, cruis·ing.** To sail from place to place, as for pleasure; to move around without a special reason, but available for duty or service, as police cars, or taxis; to operate, as an airplane, at less than maximum speed.—*n.*

cruis·er, kroo′zər, *n.* Something that cruises, esp. an armed warship faster and smaller than a battleship; a small, powered pleasure boat; ship; an armed vessel or warship; a squad car used for police patrol.

crumb, krəm, *n.* A small particle of bread or cake that breaks or falls off; a small particle or portion of anything. *Informal.* A useless or despicable person.— *v.t.* To break into crumbs; to prepare with bread crumbs.

crum·ble, krəm′bəl, *v.t., v.i.,* **-bled, -bling.** To break into crumbs; reduce to small fragments.—*n.* Something crumbling or crumbled. **—crum·bly,** *a.,* **-bli·er, -bli·est. —crum·bli·ness,** *n.* **—crum·blings,** *n. pl.*

crum·my, krəm′ē, *a.,* **-mi·er, -mi·est.** *Informal.* Disgusting; cheap; worthless.

crum·pet, krəm′pit, *n.* A soft cake resembling a muffin.

crum·ple, krəm′pəl, *v.t.,* **-pled, -pling.** To make crooked; bend together; rumple.—*v.i.* To become crumpled; shrivel. **—crum·pler,** *n.* **—crum·ply,** *a.,* **-pli·er, -pli·est.**

crunch, krənch, *v.t., v.i.,* To crush with the teeth; to crush or grind noisily.—*n.* The act or sound of crunching. **—crunch·y,** krən′chē, *a.,* **-i·er, -i·est.**

cru·sade, kroo·sād′, *n. (Often cap.)* Any of the military expeditions undertaken by the Christians of Europe in the 11th, 12th, and 13th centuries for the recovery of the Holy Land from the Moslems; any aggressive movement for the defense or advancement of an idea or cause, or against a public evil.—*v.i.,* **-sad·ed, -sad·ing.** To go on a crusade. **—cru·sad·er,** *n.*

crush, krəsh, *v.t., v.i.,* To squeeze or batter out of shape; to crumple; to press or squeeze forcibly or violently; overpower.—*n.* The act of crushing, or the state of being crushed. *Informal.* An intense infatuation, usu. short-lived. **—crush·er,** *n.* **—crush·ing,** *a.* **—crush·ing·ly,** *adv.*

crust, krəst, *n.* The hard outer portion of a loaf of bread or pie; any more or less hard external covering or coating.—*v.t., v.i.* To cover with or form a crust. —**crus•tal,** *a.*

crus•ta•cean, krə•stā′shən, *a.* Belonging to a class of chiefly aquatic animals, including the lobsters, shrimps, crabs, barnacles, and wood lice, commonly having the body covered with a hard shell or crust.—*n.*

crust•y, krəs′tē, *a.,* **-i•er, -i•est.** Of the nature of or resembling a crust; surly in manner or speech. —**crust•i•ly,** *adv.* —**crust•i•ness,** *n.*

crutch, krəch, *n.* A staff, usually with a crosspiece at one end, to assist a lame or infirm person in walking; a forked support or part; that which is used as an expedient when needed resources are inadequate.—*v.t.* To prop or sustain.

crux, krəks, *n. pl.,* **crux•es, cru•ces,** kroo′sēz. A cross; a fundamental point; a perplexing difficulty.

cry, krī, *v.i.,* **cried, cry•ing.** To call loudly; shout; to shed tears.—*v.t.* To shout loudly; call out; sell by shouting.—*n. pl.,* **cries.** The act or sound of crying; a shout; a call of wares for sale, as by a street vender; an opinion generally expressed; a political or party catchword; a fit of weeping; the characteristic call of an animal.—**cry wolf,** to give a false alarm. —**cry•ing,** *a.*

cry•ba•by, krī′bā•bē, *n. pl.,* **-bies.** A person who cries or complains often.

cry•o•gen•ics, krī•ō•jen′iks, *n. pl., sing. in constr.* The branch of physics that deals with very low temperatures. —**cry•o•gen•ic,** *a.*

cry•o•sur•ger•y, krī•ō•sər′jər•ē, *n.* Surgery using extreme cold to destroy or remove diseased tissue.

crypt, kript, *n.* An underground chamber or vault, esp. one used as a burial place. —**crypt•al,** *a.*

crypt•a•nal•y•sis, krip•tə•nal′ə•sis, *n.* The study and solution of secret, written codes.

cryp•tic, krip′tik, *a.* Hidden; secret. —**cryp•ti•cal.** —**cryp•ti•cal•ly,** *adv.*

cryp•to•gram, krip′tə•gram, *n.* A piece of writing in secret characters.

cryp•to•graph, krip′tə•graf, *n.* A system of secret writing. —**cryp•tog•ra•phy,** krip•tog′rə•fē, *n.* —**cryp•to•graph•ic,** krip•tə•graf′ik, *a.* —**cryp•tog•ra•pher,** krip•tog′rə•fər, *n.*

crys•tal, kris′təl, *n.* A clear, transparent mineral resembling ice; anything made of or resembling such a substance; glass of a high degree of brilliance; the glass cover over the face of a watch.—*a.* Made of crystal; like crystal; transparent.

crys•tal gaz•ing, *n.* A steady staring at a crystal or glass ball in order to predict the future; predicting the future without the necessary facts. —**crys•tal gaz•er,** kris′təl gā′zər, *n.*

crys•tal•line, kris′tə•lin, kris′tə•līn, *a.* Resembling crystal; pure; clear; transparent.

crys•tal•lize, kris′tə•līz, *v.t.,* **-lized, -liz•ing.** To form into crystals; *fig.,* to give definite or concrete form to. —*v.i.* To form crystals. —**crys•tal•ized,** *a.* —**crys•tal•liz•er,** *n.* —**crys•tal•liz•a•ble,** *a.* —**crys•tal•li•za•tion,** kris•tə•lə•zā′shən, *n.*

cub, kəb, *n.* The young of certain animals, as the fox or bear; an awkward youth; an inexperienced newspaper reporter.

cub•by, kəb′ē, *n. pl.,* **-bies.** A snug, confined place.

cub•by•hole, kəb′ē•hōl, *n.* A very small, snug room or place.

cube, kūb, *n. Geom.* A solid bounded by six equal squares, the angle between any two adjacent faces being a right angle. *Math.* The third power of a quantity: as, the *cube* of 4 is 4 × 4 × 4, or 64.—*v.t.,* **cubed, cub•ing.** To measure the cubic contents of; to raise to the third power; find the cube of.—**cube root,** *n.* A quantity of which a given quantity is the cube: as, for the given quantity 64, 4 is the *cube* root.

cu•bic, kū′bik, *a.* Having the form of a cube; of three dimensions; solid, or pertaining to solid content; being of the third power or degree. —**cu•bi•cal,** *a.*

cubic measure, the measurement of volume in cubic units; a system of such units.

cu•bi•cle, kū′bi•kəl, *n.* Any small space or compartment partitioned off.

cub•ism, kū′biz•əm, *n.* A phase of modern art developed in Paris in the early 20th century.

cu•bit, kū′bit, *n.* An ancient linear unit based on the length of the forearm.

cub scout, *n.* A member of that division of the Boy Scouts of America including boys 8 to 11 years of age.

cuck•old, kək′əld, *n.* The husband of an unfaithful wife.—*v.t.* To make a cuckold of. —**cuck•old•ry,** *n.*

cuck•oo, kûk′oo, *n. pl.,* **-oos.** A common European migratory bird, noted for its characteristic call; the call of the cuckoo; a fool.—*v.i., v.t.,* **-ooed, -oo•ing.** —*a. Informal.* Foolish; crazy.

cuck•oo clock, *n.* A clock which announces the hours by a sound like the call of the cuckoo.

cu•cum•ber, kū′kəm•bər, *n.* A creeping plant, yielding a long, fleshy fruit commonly eaten green in a salad and when young used for pickling; the fruit of this plant.

cud, kəd, *n.* Food passed up from the first stomach of a cud-chewing animal into its mouth in order to be chewed again; a portion of tobacco held in the mouth and chewed.

cud•dle, kəd′əl, *v.t.,* **-dled, -dling.** To hug tenderly; fondle.—*v.i.* To lie close and snug; nestle. —**cud•dle•some,** kəd′əl•səm, *a.* —**cud•dly,** *a.,* **-dli•er, -dli•est.**

cudg•el, kəj′əl, *n.* A short, thick stick; a club.—*v.t.,* **-eled, -eling.** To beat with a cudgel or thick stick; to beat in general.

cue, kū, *n.* Any sound, word, or action that signals an action; a guiding hint or suggestion.—*v.t.,* **cued, cu•ing.**—**cue in,** to give information to someone.

cue, kū, *n.* A queue of hair; a long line of people; a long, straight, tapering rod tipped with a soft pad, used to strike the ball in billiards and pool.—*v.t.,* **cued, cu•ing.**

cuff, kəf, *n.* A fold or band for a sleeve at the wrist; a turned-up fold at the bottom of trouser legs; a handcuff.—*v.t.*

cuff, kəf, *n.* A blow with the fist.—*v.t.* To strike with the fist.

cui•sine, kwi•zēn′, *n.* A quality, or style of cooking; cookery.

cul-de-sac, kəl′də•sak′, kûl′də•sak′, *n. pl.,* **culs-de-sac.** A sac-like cavity, tube, or the like, open only at one end; a street or other passage closed at one end.

cu•li•nar•y, kū′lə•ner•ē, kəl′ə•ner•ē, *a.* Relating to the kitchen, or to the art of cooking.

cull, kəl, *v.t.* To choose or select; pick; to collect or gather; to gather the choice things or parts from.—*n.* Culling; something picked out and put aside as inferior.

cul•mi•nant, kəl′mə•nənt, *a.* Culminating; at the peak.

cul•mi•nate, kəl′mə•nāt, *v.i.,* **-nat•ed, -nat•ing.** To reach the highest point, as of rank or development; to finish or end. —**cul•mi•na•tion,** kəl•mə•nā′shən, *n.*

cu•lottes, koo•lots′, kū•lots′, *n.* A woman's skirt or dress divided like trousers but cut full so as to appear to be a skirt.

cul•pa•ble, kəl′pə•bəl, *a.* Blamable, immoral: said of persons or their conduct. —**cul•pa•bil•i•ty,** kəl•pə•bil′ə•tē, *n.* —**cul•pa•bly,** *adv.*

cul•prit, kəl′prit, *n.* A person charged legally with a crime; one guilty of an offense or fault; an offender.

cult, kəlt, *n.* A system of religious worship, esp. with reference to its ceremonies; a sect adhering to a common doctrine or leader, esp. when such devotion

---

a- hat, fāte, fāre, fäther; **e-** met, mē; **i-** pin, pīne; **o-** not, nōte, ôrb, moove (move), boy, pownd; **u-** cūbe, bûll, tûk (took); **ch-** chin; **th-** thick, ŧhen; **zh-** vizhon (vision); **ə-** əgo, takən, pencəl, lemən, bərd (bird).

is based on fanatical beliefs; an instance of fixed, almost religious veneration for a person or thing, esp. by a body of admirers. —**cul•tic,** *a.*

cul•ti•vate, kəl′tə•vāt, *v.t.,* **-vat•ed, -vat•ing.** To prepare land for raising a crop; till; to improve the growth of, as a plant, by labor and attention; train; refine; to devote oneself to, as an art, or practice; to seek, to promote or acquire, as an interest, or taste; seek the friendship of. —**cul•ti•va•tion,** kəl•tə•vā′shən, *n.* —**cul•ti•va•ble, cul•ti•vat•a•ble,** *a.*

cul•ti•vat•ed, kəl′tə•vā•tid, *a.* Prepared for cultivation, as land; produced or improved by cultivation, as a plant; improved by education or training; cultured; refined.

cul•ti•va•tor, kəl′tə•vā•tər, *n.* An agricultural implement for loosening earth and destroying weeds.

cul•tur•al, kəl′chə•rəl, *a.* Of or pertaining to culture; educational; refined.

cul•ture, kəl′chər, *n.* The whole behavior and technology of any people that is passed on from generation to generation; the acquired ability of an individual or a people to recognize and appreciate generally accepted esthetic and intellectual excellence; a particular state or stage of civilization: Chinese *culture;* the cultivation of micro-organisms, as bacteria, for scientific study or medicinal use; the product or growth resulting from such cultivation; tillage; the raising of plants or animals, esp. with a view to their improvement.—*v.t.,* **-tured, -tur•ing.** To cultivate; to develop bacteria in a culture.

cul•tured, kəl′chərd, *a.* Cultivated; refined.

cul•vert, kəl′vərt, *n.* A drain, as under a road; a sewer.

cum•ber, kəm′bər, *v.t.* To overload; to retard; to obstruct. —**cum•ber•some,** *a.*

cum•brance, kəm′brəns, *n.* Something that cumbers or encumbers; an encumbrance.

cum lau•de, kûm low′dā, kəm•lô′dē, *a., adv.* With honor: used to designate an academic rank of graduates; above average.

cum•mer•bund, kəm′ər•bənd, *n.* A wide sash wrapped about the waist.

cu•mu•late, kū′mū•lāt, *v.t.,* **-lat•ed, -lat•ing.** To heap up; amass.—kū′mū•lit, kū′mū•lāt, *a.* Heaped up. —**cu•mu•la•tion,** kū•mū•lā′shən, *n.*

cu•mu•la•tive, kū′mū•lā•tiv, kū′mū•lə•tiv, *a.* Increasing by accumulation; pertaining to or characterized by accumulation.

cu•mu•lo•nim•bus, kū•mū•lō•nim′bəs, *n. pl.,* **-bus•es, -bi,** -bī. A thundercloud.

cu•mu•lus, kū′myə•ləs, *n. pl.,* **-li,** -lī. A heap or pile; a cloud with domelike summit or one that is made up of rounded heaps, seen in fair weather. —**cu•mu•lous,** kū′myə•ləs, *a.*

cu•ne•i•form, kū•nē′ə•fôrm, kū′nē•ə•fôrm, *a.* Wedge-shaped.—*n.* Cuneiform letters or writing.

cun•ni•lin•gus, kən•ə•ling′gəs, *n.* Oral stimulation of the female genitalia.

cun•ning, kən′ing, *n.* Skill employed in a crafty manner; craftiness; guile.—*a.* Showing ingenuity; crafty; pleasing or attractive. —**cun•ning•ly,** *adv.* —**cun•ning•ness,** *n.*

cup, kəp, *n.* A small, open vessel, as of porcelain or metal, used esp. to drink from, made either with or without a handle; any cuplike utensil, organ, part, or cavity; the quantity contained in a cup; a state of intoxication.—*v.t.,* **cupped, cup•ping.** To take or place in or as in a cup. —**cupped,** *a.*

cup•board, kəb′ərd, *n.* A closet with shelves for dishes.

cup•cake, kəp′kāk, *n.* A small cake for an individual serving, baked in a cup-shaped compartment of a pan.

cup•ful, kəp′fûl, *n. pl.,* **-fuls.** The amount that a cup holds.

Cu•pid, kū′pid, *n.* The Roman god of love commonly represented as a winged boy with bow and arrows; (*l.c.*) a symbol of love.

cu•pid•i•ty, kū•pid′ə•tē, *n.* An eager desire to possess something; avarice.

cu•po•la, kū′pə•lə, *n.* A vault or dome that is a roof or ceiling; any of various domelike structures.

cur, kər, *n.* A worthless dog; a mean, contemptible person.

cur•a•ble, kûr′ə•bəl, *a.* Able to be cured. —**cur•a•bil•i•ty,** kûr•ə•bil′ə•tē, *n.* —**cur•a•bly,** *adv.*

cu•rate, kûr′it, *n.* A clergyman employed as assistant or deputy of a rector or vicar.

cur•a•tive, kûr′ə•tiv, *a.* Serving to cure or heal; pertaining to curing or remedial treatment.

cu•ra•tor, kū•rā′tər, kûr′ə•tər, *n.* The director of a museum or art gallery; an overseer. —**cu•ra•to•ri•al,** kûr•ə•tôr′ē•əl, *a.* —**cu•ra•tor•ship,** *n.*

curb, kərb, *n.* A restraint; the part of a halter that restrains the horse; an enclosing framework or border; the border, as of stone, at the outer edge of a sidewalk.—*v.t.* To put a curb on, as on a horse; to control as with a curb; check. —**curb•a•ble,** *a.*

curb•ing, kərb′ing, *n.* The material, as stones, forming a curb; a curb, or part of one.

curb•stone, kərb′stōn, *n.* One of the stones, or a range of stones, forming a curb.

curd, kərd, *n.* (*Often pl.*) A substance consisting of casein, obtained from milk by coagulation, used for making cheese or eaten as food; any substance resembling this.—*v.t., v.i.* To turn into curd; coagulate; congeal.

cur•dle, kər′dəl, *v.i.,* **-dled, -dling.** To coagulate; to thicken or change into curd; to congeal; to go bad. —*v.t.* To change into curd.

cure, kûr, *v.t.,* **cured, cur•ing.** Restore to health; relieve or rid of something troublesome or detrimental, as a bad habit; to prepare, as meat or fish, for preservation, by salting or drying; to vulcanize.—*v.i.* To bring about a cure; of meat, to become cured.—*n.* Restoration to health; a means of healing or curing; a remedy; the act or a method of curing meat or fish. —**cur•er,** *n.*

cure-all, kûr′ôl, *n.* A cure for all ills.

cur•few, kər′fū, *n.* A police or military order requiring withdrawal of persons from the streets or closing of businesses at a specified hour; the ringing of a bell at this fixed hour; the time of ringing, the bell itself, or its sound.

cu•ri•a, kûr′ē•ə, *n. pl.,* **-ae,** -ē. (*Often cap.*) The Papal court; the Pope and those about him in Rome engaged in the administration of the Roman Catholic Church. —**cu•ri•al,** *a.*

cu•rie, kûr′ē, kû•rē′, *n.* The official international unit of radioactivity.

cu•ri•o, kûr′ē•ō, *n. pl.,* **-os.** Any article, object of art, or piece of bric-a-brac, etc., valued as a curiosity.

cu•ri•os•i•ty, kûr•ē•os′ə•tē, *n. pl.,* **-ties.** A desire to see what is new or unusual; inquisitiveness; a curious object.

cu•ri•ous, kûr′ē•əs, *a.* Desirous of learning or knowing; often inquisitive or prying; odd.

cu•ri•um, kûr′ē•əm, *n.* A silvery, metallic radioactive element.

curl, kərl, *v.t.* To coil; make undulations in.—*v.i.* To form curls or ringlets, as the hair; to coil.—*n.* A ringlet of hair; anything of a spiral or curved shape; a coil. —**curl•er,** *n.*

curl•i•cue, kər′lə•kū, *n.* A fancy curl or scroll-like twist. Also **curl•y•cue.**

curl•ing, kər′ling, *n.* A game played on ice in which heavy stones are slid toward a target called the tee.

curl•ing i•ron, *n.* A metal instrument, usu. tongs, that curls or waves the hair when the locks are twined around the heated rod. Also **curl•ing i•rons, curl•ing tongs.**

curl•y, kər′lē, *a.,* **-i•er, -i•est.** Curling or tending to curl; having curls, as hair; having a wavy grain: *curly* maple. —**curl•i•ness,** *n.*

cur•rant, kər′ənt, *n.* The small, edible, acid round fruit or berry of certain wild or cultivated shrubs; the shrub itself; any of various similar fruits or shrubs.

cur·ren·cy, kər′ən·sē, *n. pl.,* **-cies.** Circulation, as of coin or paper money; that which is current as a medium of exchange; the money in actual use; general acceptance; prevalence; vogue.

cur·rent, kər′ənt, *a.* Prevalent, generally accepted, or in vogue; of the present time; passing from one to another, as a coin; publicly reported or known: *current* information.—*n.* Flow of a river; that which flows; a body of water or air moving in a certain direction; general course or trend of time or events; movement of electricity; the rate of this flow.

cur·ric·u·lum, kə·rik′yə·ləm, *n. pl.,* **-lums, -la, -lə.** A course of study; all courses offered at a school. **—cur·ric·u·lar,** *a.*

cur·rish, kər′ish, *a.* Like a cur; quarrelsome.

cur·ry, kər′ē, *n. pl.,* **-ries.** An East Indian sauce or relish, containing a mixture of turmeric and other spices, seeds, vegetables, and fruits, eaten with rice or combined with meat, fish, or other food; curry powder; a dish prepared with such a sauce or with curry powder.—*v.t.,* **-ried, -ry·ing.** To prepare food with a curry sauce or with curry powder. **—cur·ried,** *a.*

cur·ry, kər′ē, *v.t.,* **-ried, -ry·ing.** To treat leather after it is tanned; to rub and clean (a horse). **—cur·ri·er,** *n.* **—curry favor,** to seek favor by officiousness.

cur·ry·comb, kər′ē·kōm, *n.* A comb with short teeth for combing and cleaning horses.—*v.t.* To rub down.

curse, kərs, *v.t.,* **cursed** or **curst, curs·ing.** To utter a wish of evil against; to blast; to blight; to torment with great calamities.—*v.i.* To utter imprecations; to use blasphemous or profane language; to swear.—*n.* A malediction; the expression of a wish of evil to another; that which brings evil or severe affliction; torment; condemnation or sentence of divine vengeance on sinners. **—curs·ed·ly,** *adv.* **—curs·ed·ness,** *n.*

cur·sive, kər′siv, *a.* Printed or written with the letters joined one to another.—*n.* A printed or written cursive character. **—cur·sive·ly,** *adv.*

cur·so·ry, kər′sə·rē, *a.* Rapidly done, without noticing details; hasty; superficial. **—cur·so·ri·ly,** *adv.* **—cur·so·ri·ness,** *n.*

curt, kərt, *a.* Short or shortened; brief or terse, as speech or style; abrupt or rudely short, as speech or manner. **—curt·ly,** *adv.* **—curt·ness,** *n.*

cur·tail, kər·tāl′, *v.t.* To cut short; to abridge; to diminish. **—cur·tail·ment,** *n.*

cur·tain, kər′tən, kər′tin, *n.* A movable, hanging piece of material used to screen, conceal, or adorn; anything serving to shut off, cover, or conceal; a hanging drapery separating the auditorium from the stage; —*v.t.* To provide, shut off, conceal, or adorn with or as with a curtain or curtains.

cur·tain call, *n.* The presentation of the cast of a theatrical production in response to the applause of the audience after the performance.

curt·sy, kərt′sē, *n. pl.,* **-sies.** A bow made by women, consisting of a bending of the knees and a lowering of the body.—*v.i.,* **-sied, -sy·ing.** To make a curtsy.

cur·va·ceous, kər·vā′shəs, *a. Informal.* Of a woman, having a shapely figure with pronounced curves.

cur·va·ture, kər′və·chər, *n.* The act of curving; a curved condition; a curve or bend.

curve, kərv, *n.* A continuously bending line without angles; any curved outline; a curving; a line no part of which is straight; a baseball pitched with a spin causing it to veer.—*v.t., v.i.,* **curved, curv·ing.** To bend in a curve; cause to take, or take the course of, a curve.—*a.* Curved. **—curv·ed·ness,** *n.*

cur·vi·lin·e·ar, kər·və·lin′ē·ər, *a.* Having the shape of a curved line; bounded by curved lines. Also **cur·vi·lin·e·al,** kər·və·lin′ē·əl.

cush·ion, kûsh′ən, *n.* A baglike case filled with soft material, used to support the body; anything that resembles this in appearance; a pillow; something

used to counteract any shock or jolt.—*v.t.* To place on or support by a cushion; to furnish with a cushion or cushions; to suppress quietly by ignoring; to soften or decrease the effect or impact of.

cush·y, kûsh′ē, *a.,* **-i·er, -i·est.** *Informal.* Comfortable or easy.

cusp, kəsp, *n.* A point or pointed end; a point of a crescent, esp. of the moon; a point on the crown of a tooth.

cus·pid, kəs′pid, *n.* A canine tooth. **—cus·pi·dal,** kəs′pə·dəl, *a.*

cus·pi·date, kəs′pə·dāt, *a.* Having a cusp or cusps; ending in a cusp or sharp point, as a canine tooth. Also **cus·pi·dat·ed.**

cus·pi·dor, kəs′pə·dôr, *n.* A spittoon.

cuss, kəs, *n. Informal.* A curse; a fellow.—*v.t., v.i. Informal.* To curse.

cuss·ed, kəs′əd, *a. Informal.* Cursed; mean. **—cuss·ed·ly,** *adv.* **—cuss·ed·ness,** *n.*

cus·tard, kəs′tərd, *n.* A mixture of milk, eggs, and sweetening, which is baked, boiled, or frozen.

cus·to·di·an, kə·stō′dē·ən, *n.* One who has the care or custody of anything; a guardian; a caretaker. **—cus·to·di·an·ship,** *n.*

cus·to·dy, kəs′tə·dē, *n. pl.,* **-dies.** A keeping; a guarding; guardianship; the state of being held under guard; imprisonment. **—cus·to·di·al,** kə·stō′dē·əl, *a.*

cus·tom, kəs′təm, *n.* A habitual practice of an individual or group; established usage; convention; a long-established practice which has acquired the force of law; habitual patronage of a business establishment; the customers of a business firm; a toll or duty; *pl.,* duties or tariffs imposed by law on imports or exports. —*a.* Made to order; dealing in things so made or doing work to order.

cus·tom·ar·y, kəs′tə·mer·ē, *a.* According to custom or established usage; usual; habitual; in common practice.—*n. pl.,* **-ies.** A book containing the legal customs and rights of a locality. **—cus·tom·ar·i·ly,** *adv.* **—cus·tom·ar·i·ness,** *n.*

cus·tom·built, kəs′təm·bilt′, *a.* Designed or made to meet an individual customer's specifications.

cus·tom·er, kəs′tə·mər, *n.* One who shops regularly at a particular place. *Informal.* A person with whom one has to deal.

cus·tom·house, kəs′təm·hows, *n.* A government office where customs or duties are collected.

cus·tom·ize, kəs′tə·mīz, *v.t.,* **-ized, -iz·ing.** To design, construct, fit, or alter to an individual's specifications.

cus·tom·made, kəs′təm·mād, *a.* Made to order rather than ready-made.

cut, kət, *v.t.,* **cut, cut·ting.** To separate or divide by an edged instrument; to make an incision in; to put an end to; to sever; to strike sharply, as with a whip; shorten, as by editing; to stop shooting, as a sequence or scene; to stop taping, recording, or broadcasting; to divide a pack of cards at random into two or more parts. To fell, as a tree; to mow or reap, as grass or hay; to remove, as the nails or hair; to fashion by, or as by, cutting or carving; to carve; to grow, as baby teeth out of gums; to wound the feelings of; to affect deeply; to intersect; to cross: One line *cuts* another. *Informal.* To no longer have anything to do with; to quit; to snub or shun; to absent oneself from.—*v.i.* To admit of being cut; to change direction sharply.—*n.* The act of cutting; a wound caused by cutting; a part excised or omitted; a piece of meat cut off; a reduction in price; a passage or course straight across: a short *cut;* the manner or fashion in which anything is cut; style; manner; kind; a passage or channel made by cutting or digging; an engraved block or plate used for printing, or an impression from it; a refusal to recognize an acquaintance; a cutting of the cards in card-

---

a- hat, fāte, fâre, fäther; **e-** met, mē; **i-** pin, pīne; **o-** not, nōte, ôrb, moove (move), boy, pownd; **u-** cūbe, bûll, tûk (took); **ch-** chin; **th-** thick, ŧhen; **zh-** vizhon (vision); **ə-** əgo, takən, pencəl, lemən, bərd (bird).

playing. *Informal.* A share or percentage of a profit. —*a.* That has been cut or incised; watered; diluted; reduced. —**cut back,** to make short by removing the end; to reduce production; to run or move in a different direction. —**cut down,** reduce in size or quantity. —**cut in,** to break into a line, a conversation, etc.; interrupt; to interrupt a dancing couple in order to replace one of them. —**cut off,** to detach by cutting; to stop; shut off; to interrupt; intercept; disinherit. —**cut out,** to remove by cutting; make or shape by cutting; to best, oust, or supplant; to take or leave out. *Informal.* To stop doing; cease; suited for: He's not *cut out* for piano-playing. —**cut up,** to cut into pieces. *Informal.* To hurt or distress; to make jokes, play tricks, etc.; show off. —**cut and dried,** prearranged; all ready; routine; boring.

cu·ta·ne·ous, kū·tā′nē·əs, *a.* Pertaining to the skin.

cut·back, kət′bak, *n.* A reduction in personnel, or in scheduled production; any reduction.

cute, kūt, *a.*, **cut·er, cut·est.** *Informal.* Pleasing or engagingly attractive; clever; shrewd. —**cute·ly,** *adv.* —**cute·ness,** *n.*

cu·ti·cle, kū′ti·kəl, *n.* The non-living skin which frames the nails of fingers and toes.

cut·lass, kət′ləs, *n.* A short, heavy, slightly curved sword.

cut·ler·y, kət′lə·rē, *n.* The business of making, sharpening, repairing, or selling knives and other cutting instruments; such instruments collectively, esp. those for cutting and serving food.

cut·let, kət′lit, *n.* A slice of meat for broiling or frying; a flat croquette of minced chicken, lobster, or the like.

cut·off, kət′ôf, kət′of, *n.* A shorter way, as across a bend.

cut·out, kət′owt, *n.* A device for breaking an electric circuit; a device which permits an internal-combustion engine to exhaust directly into the air; something cut out from something else.

cut-rate, kət′rāt, *a.* Sold or selling below the usual price.

cut·ter, kət′ər, *n.* One who or that which cuts; a launch, belonging to a ship of war; a one-masted vessel rigged like a sloop; a lightly-armed vessel used by the coast guard; a small sleigh.

cut·throat, kət′thrōt, *n.* A murderer.—*a.* Murderous; cruel; ruthless.

cut·ting, kət′ing, *n.* The act of one that cuts; something cut off; a small shoot cut from a plant to start a new plant.—*a.* Pertaining to a cut; piercing; sharp; wounding the feelings; sarcastic. —**cut·ting·ly,** *adv.*

cut·tle, kət′əl, *n.* A cuttlefish.

cut·tle·fish, kət′əl·fish, *n. pl.,* **-fish, -fish·es.** Any of various cephalopods having sucker-bearing arms and calcified internal shells.

cut·up, kət′əp, *n. Informal.* One who clowns or plays pranks.

cut·worm, kət′wərm, *n.* Any of various caterpillars which feed at night by cutting the stems of plants at or near the ground.

cy·an·ic, sī·an′ik, *a.* Blue; pertaining to or containing cyanogen.

cy·a·nide, sī′ə·nīd, sī′ə·nid, *n.* A powerful poison.

cy·a·no·sis, sī·ə·nō′sis, *n.* Blueness or lividness of the skin, as from imperfectly oxygenated blood.

cy·ber·na·tion, sī·bər·nā′shən, *n.* Automation.

cy·ber·net·ics, sī·bər·net′iks, *n.* The comparative study of the communication system formed by the human nervous system, and similar systems in complex electronic devices. —**cy·ber·net·ic,** *a.*

cyc·la·men, sik′lə·mən, sik′lə·men, *n.* A genus of plants of the primrose family, with very handsome flowers.

cy·cle, sī′kəl, *n.* A round of years or a recurring period of time, in which certain events repeat themselves; any long period of years; an age; any complete course or series; a bicycle, tricycle, or the like.—*v.i.,* **cy·cled, cy·cling.** To move or revolve in cycles; pass through cycles; to ride a bicycle.

cy·clic, sī′klik, sik′lik, *a.* Of or pertaining to a cycle or cycles; revolving or recurring in cycles; arranged in a ring. Also **cy·cli·cal.** —**cy·cli·cal·ly,** *adv.*

cy·clist, sī′klist, *n.* One who rides a bicycle.

cy·clom·e·ter, sī·klom′ə·tər, *n.* A device for recording the revolutions of a wheel, esp. to register distance traveled.

cy·clone, sī′klōn, *n.* A system of winds rotating around a calm center, and advancing at a rate of about 20 or 30 miles an hour; any violent windstorm or tornado.

cy·clo·ram·a, sī·klə·ram′ə, sī·klə·rä′mə, *n.* A picture of a landscape or a battle, on the wall of a cylindrical room. —**cy·clo·ram·ic,** *a.*

cy·clo·tron, sī′klə·tron, sik′lə·tron, *n.* An accelerator which whirls charged particles at very high speeds in a strong magnetic field.

cyg·net, sig′nit, *n.* A young swan.

cyl·in·der, sil′in·dər, *n.* A solid figure having curved sides and enclosed by two parallel circular bases; any cylinderlike object or part, whether solid or hollow; the rotating part of a revolver, which contains the chambers for the cartridges; the chamber in an engine in which the working fluid acts upon the piston. —**cy·lin·dric,** si·lin′drik, *a.* —**cy·lin·dri·cal,** si·lin′drik·əl.

cym·bal, sim′bəl, *n.* A musical instrument, circular like a dish, made of brass or bronze, two of which are struck glancingly together, producing a sharp, ringing sound. —**cym·bal·ist,** *n.*

cyn·ic, sin′ik, *n.* A faultfinder; one who disbelieves in the goodness of human motives.—*a.* Of or pertaining to cynical acts or feelings. —**cyn·i·cism,** sin′i·siz·əm, *n.*

cyn·i·cal, sin′i·kəl, *a.* Like a cynic; sneering; sarcastic. —**cyn·i·cal·ly,** *adv.*

cy·no·sure, sī′nə·shûr, sin′ə·shûr, *n.* Anything that strongly attracts attention; something that guides.

cy·pher, sī′fər, *n.* Cipher.

cy·press, sī′prəs, *n.* Any of a genus of mostly evergreen trees of the pine family with dark, scalelike leaves, hard wood, and symmetrical growth; any of various related trees; the wood of any of these trees.

cyst, sist, *n.* A bladder or sac; an abnormal sac containing fluid. —**cys·tic,** *a.*

cys·tic fi·bro·sis, *n.* A hereditary disease appearing in childhood, involving the pancreas and lungs.

cy·tol·o·gy, sī·tol′ə·jē, *n.* The scientific study of the structure, functions, and life cycle of cells. —**cy·tol·o·gist,** *n.*

czar, zär, *n.* An emperor or king; title of the former emperors of Russia; an autocrat. Also **tsar, tzar.**

czar·e·vitch, zär′ə·vich, *n.* In earlier use, any son of the emperor of Russia; later, the eldest son.

cza·ri·na, zä·rē′nə, *n.* A czar's wife; a Russian empress.

D

D, d, dē, *n.* In the English alphabet, the fourth letter; the Roman numeral for 500. *Mus.* The second note of the natural scale of C.

dab, dab, *v.t.,* **dabbed, dab·bing.** To strike quickly but lightly with the hand or with some soft or moist substance; to apply lightly; pat; tap.—*n.* A quick but light blow; a small mass of anything soft or moist; a little bit. —**dab·ber,** *n.*

dab·ble, dab′əl, *v.t.,* **-bled, -bling.** To moisten; to spatter.—*v.i.* To play in water, as with the hands; to splash; to engage in anything in a superficial manner. —**dab·bler,** *n.*

Da·cron, dā′kron, dak′ron, *n. Trademark.* A synthetic fiber having resilience and resistance to wrinkling.

dac·tyl, dak′təl, dak′til, *n.* A poetical foot of three syllables, the first long and the others short. —**dac·tyl·ic,** dak·til′ik, *a., n.*

dad, dad, *n. Informal.* Father. Also **dad·dy,** dad′ē, *pl.,* **dad·dies.**

dad·dy-long-legs, dad′ē·lông′legz, dad′ē·long′legz, *n. pl.* Any of various long-legged animals, esp. one resembling the spider.

dae·mon, dē′mən, *n.* See **demon.**

daf·fo·dil, daf′ə·dil, *n.* A species of plant with single or double yellow flowers.

daf·fy, daf′ē, *a.,* **daf·fi·er, daf·fi·est.** *Informal.* Silly; weak-minded.

daft, daft, däft, *a.* Silly or foolish; crazy.

dag·ger, dag′ər, *n.* A weapon with a short, sharp-pointed blade, used for stabbing; a mark of reference in printing, †.

da·guerre·o·type, də·ger′ə·tīp, də·ger′ē·ə·tīp, *n.* An early photographic method using silver-coated metallic plates; a picture made by this process.

dahl·ia, dal′yə, däl′yə, *n.* Any plant of an asterlike genus widely cultivated for its showy, variously colored flowers.

dai·ly, dā′lē, *a.* Of, pertaining to, occurring, or issued each successive day or, sometimes, each successive weekday.—*n. pl.,* **-lies.** A newspaper published each weekday.—*adv.* Every day; day by day.

dain·ty, dān′tē, *a.,* **-ti·er, -ti·est.** Delicately beautiful; delicious, as food; particular; overly particular; fastidious.—*n. pl.,* **-ties.** A delicacy. —**dain·ti·ly,** *adv.* —**dain·ti·ness,** *n.*

dai·qui·ri, dī′kə·rē, dak′ə·rē, *n. pl.,* **-ris.** A cocktail made of rum, lime juice, and sugar.

dair·y, dâr′ē, *n. pl.,* **dair·ies.** A place, as a room or building, where milk and cream are kept and processed; a shop where milk, butter, cheese, etc., are sold; the business of producing milk and milk products; a farm for producing milk, butter, etc.

dair·y·man, dâr′ē·mən, *n. pl.,* **-men.** An owner, manager, or an employee of a dairy.

da·is, dā′is, dī′is, dās, *n.* A raised platform in a hall for a throne, speaker's desk, or table for prominent persons.

dai·sy, dā′zē, *n. pl.,* **-sies.** An often cultivated composite plant having flowers with a yellow disk and white or pink rays.

dale, dāl, *n.* Vale or valley.

dal·ly, dal′ē, *v.i.,* **-lied, -ly·ing.** To amuse oneself with idle play; to trifle; to linger; to waste time; to flirt; philander. —**dal·li·ance,** *n.*

dam, dam, *n.* A barrier to obstruct the flow of a liquid; masonry, built across a stream; water confined by a dam; any dam-like barrier.—*v.t.,* **dammed, dam·ming.** To furnish with a dam; obstruct or confine with a dam; to stop up or shut up.

dam, dam, *n.* A female parent: used now only of quadrupeds, unless in contempt.

dam·age, dam′ij, *n.* Any injury or harm to person, property, character, etc.; *usu. pl.,* the estimated money equivalent for detriment or injury sustained. *Informal.* Charge or expense.—*v.t.,* **-aged, -ag·ing.** To injure; to impair; to lessen the soundness or value of.—*v.i.* To become injured or impaired. —**dam·age·a·ble,** *a.*

dam·a·scene, dam′ə·sēn, dam·ə·sēn′, *v.t.,* **-scened, -scen·ing.** To ornament or form wavy designs, as on metal, by inlaying with gold or other precious metals, or by etching.—*a.* Of or having to do with damascening.—*n.* Work or patterns produced by damascening.

dam·ask, dam′əsk, *a.* Of, from, or named for the city of Damascus; pink or rose-colored; made of damask. —*n.* Damask steel; a fabric of silk, linen, cotton, or wool, with a woven, often elaborate pattern; a pink or rose color.—*v.t.* To make damask steel.

dam·ask steel, *n.* A kind of steel used in making sword blades, originally made in Damascus, Syria.

dame, dām, *n.* An elderly woman; a matron. *Informal.* A woman. (*Cap.*) The legal title given to the wife of a knight or baronet; the title given to a woman upon whom a dignity corresponding to that of a knight has been conferred.

damn, dam, *v.t.* To condemn or censure; to bring condemnation upon; to condemn to hell; to use the word *damn* when swearing or cursing.—*v.i.* To curse. —*n.* Uttering *damn* as a curse; the smallest, most worthless bit.—*adv., a.* Damned.—*interj.* An oath expressing anger or frustration.

dam·na·ble, dam′nə·bəl, *a.* Worthy of damnation; detestable; outrageous. —**dam·na·ble·ness,** *n.* —**dam·na·bly,** *adv.*

dam·na·tion, dam·nā′shən, *n.* The act of damning or the state of being damned; a cause of being damned; eternal punishment, or condemnation to it; an oath or curse.—*interj.* Damn.

damned, damd, *a.* Condemned, esp. to eternal punishment; accursed: often used as an expletive or intensive.—*adv. Informal.* Very.

damp, damp, *a.* Moderately wet; moist; humid.—*n.* Moist air; humidity; moisture; a noxious exhalation issuing from the earth; discouragement; check.—*v.t.* To dampen; moisten; to stifle or suffocate; deaden; check.

damp·en, dam′pən, *v.t.* To make damp; moisten; to dull or deaden; depress.—*v.i.* To become damp.

damp·er, dam′pər, *n.* One who or that which damps or depresses; a plate sliding across a flue of a furnace to check or regulate the draft of air; a device in a piano which checks the vibration of the strings.

dam·sel, dam′zəl, *n.* A maiden; a girl.

dam·son, dam′zən, *n.* A small dark-blue or purple plum; the tree bearing this fruit.

dance, dans, däns, *v.i.,* **danced, danc·ing.** Move with the feet or body rhythmically, esp. to music; take part in a dance; to leap, skip, as from excitement; move nimbly; to bob up and down.—*v.t.* To cause to dance; to perform a dance.—*n.* Movement in rhythm, esp. to music; an act or round of dancing; any of the many kinds of dancing steps; any leaping, springing, or similar movement; a piece of music for dancing; a social gathering for dancing; a ball. —**dan·cer,** *n.*

dan·de·li·on, dan′də·lī·ən, *n.* A common composite plant with deeply toothed leaves and golden-yellow flowers.

dan·der, dan′dər, *n.* Anger or temper. —**get one's**

---

dander up, become angry.

dan·dle, dan′dəl, *v.t.,* **-dled, -dling.** To move lightly on the knees or in one's arms, as an infant; to fondle, amuse; to pet.

dan·druff, dan′drəf, *n.* A scurf which forms on the scalp.

dan·dy, dan′dē, *n. pl.,* **-dies.** A man conspicuous for careful elegance of dress; a fop. *Informal.* Something very fine.—*a.,* **-di·er, -di·est.** Foppish; first-rate. —**dan·dy·ism,** *n.*

dan·ger, dān′jər, *n.* Exposure to ruin, injury, loss, or other evil; peril; risk; a cause of peril or risk.

dan·ger·ous, dān′jər·əs, *a.* Attended with danger; perilous. —**dan·ger·ous·ly,** *adv.* —**dan·ger·ous·ness,** *n.*

dan·gle, dang′gəl, *v.i.,* **-gled, -gling.** To hang loose, shaking, or waving; to hang and swing; to hang about or be dependent on.—*v.t.* To cause to dangle. —**dan·gler,** *n.*

dank, dangk, *a.* Disagreeably damp; moist; humid. —**dank·ly,** *adv.* —**dank·ness,** *n.*

dan·seuse, dän·sûz′, *n. pl.,* **-seus·es,** -sûz′əz. A professional female dancer, esp. a ballet dancer.

dap·per, dap′ər, *a.* Neat; trim; small and active.

dap·ple, dap′əl, *n.* Spots or small blotches of coloring; an animal with a mottled skin or coat.—*a.* Spotted.—*v.t., v.i.,* **-pled, -pling.** To mark or become marked with spots. —**dap·pled,** *a.*

dare, dār, *v.i.,* **dared** or (*archaic*) **durst, dared, daring.** To have the necessary courage or boldness for something.—*v.t.* To have courage for; venture on; to expose oneself to; meet defiantly; to challenge.—*n.* An act of daring; a challenge.

dare·dev·il, dār′dev·əl, *n.* One who is recklessly daring.

dar·ing, dār′ing, *n.* Adventurous courage; boldness. —*a.* —**dar·ing·ly,** *adv.*

dark, därk, *a.* Devoid of or deficient in light; dim; approaching black in hue; not fair: a *dark* complexion; evil; wicked; cheerless; dismal; sad; sullen; frowning; obscure; difficult to interpret; hidden or secret; unenlightened.—*n.* Darkness; night; nightfall; a dark place; a dark color; obscurity; secrecy; ignorance. —**dark·ish,** *a.* —**dark·ly,** *adv.* —**dark·ness,** *n.*

Dark Ag·es, *n. pl.* The early Middle Ages, from app. 500 to app. 1100 A.D.

dark·en, därk′ən, *v.i., v.t.* To make or become dark.

dark horse, *n.* A competitor about whom nothing certain is known or who unexpectedly comes to the front.

dark lan·tern, *n.* A hand lantern whose light can be obscured by an opaque slide or cover at the opening.

dark·ling, därk′ling, *a., adv.* In the dark.

dark·room, därk′room, därk′rûm, *n.* A room used for developing photographs.

dar·ling, där′ling, *n.* A person very dear to another; one much beloved.—*a.* Very dear; dearly loved. —**dar·ling·ly,** *adv.* —**dar·ling·ness,** *n.*

darn, därn, *v.t., v.i.* To mend or sew with rows of stitches run from side to side.—*n.* An act of darning; a darned place. —**darn·er,** *n.*

darn, därn, *n., a., adv., interj.* Damn.

dart, därt, *n.* A long, slender, pointed weapon thrown by the hand or otherwise; the stinger of an insect; a tapering seam made to adjust the fit of a garment; a sudden swift movement.—*v.t.* To throw or thrust suddenly and rapidly; emit.—*v.i.* To move swiftly, like a dart.

dart·er, där′tər, *n.* One who or that which darts; any of the small fresh-water fishes of the perch family in America which dart quickly when disturbed.

Dar·win·ism, där′win·iz·əm, *n.* The doctrine, taught by Darwin, of the origin and modifications of species by means of the natural selection of those best adapted to survive. —**Dar·win·ist,** *n.*

dash, dash, *v.t.* To strike violently, esp. so as to break to pieces; to throw violently; to splash; to adulterate or dilute; to mix; to ruin or frustrate; to depress or dispirit; abash; to write hastily, with *off.*—*v.i.* To strike with violence; to rush.—*n.* A violent blow or stroke; a check or discouragement; the splashing of liquid; a small quantity of anything; a tinge; a hasty stroke, as of a pen; a horizontal line of varying length used in writing and printing as a mark of punctuation, as to note an abrupt break in a sentence, or to begin and to end a parenthetic clause, as an indication of omission of letters, etc.; the long sound in Morse code; a rush; a sprint or short race; spirited action; vigor in style; an ostentatious display; a dashboard.

dash·board, dash′bōrd, dash′bôrd, *n.* The instrument panel of an automobile or airplane; a board or panel on the front of a vehicle to intercept mud, water, or snow.

dash·ing, dash′ing, *a.* Impetuous; spirited; showy; brilliant.

das·tard, das′tərd, *n.* A coward; one who furtively does base acts.—*a.* Cowardly. —**das·tard·li·ness,** *n.* —**das·tard·ly,** *a.*

da·ta, dā′tə, dat′ə, dä′tə, *pl.* of datum.

da·ta proc·ess·ing, *n.* The processing of information by computing machines.

date, dāt, *n.* The oblong, fleshy, one-seeded fruit of a species of palm; the tree bearing this fruit. Also **date palm.**

date, dāt, *n.* The time when any event happened, or when anything is to be done; a statement of time; period of time. *Informal.* An appointment; a person of the opposite sex with whom one has an appointment for a social engagement.—*v.t.,* **dat·ed, dat·ing.** To write down the date on; to append the date to; to note or fix the time or era of. *Informal.* To have a meeting, or regular meetings, with a person of the opposite sex.—*v.i.* To reckon time; to begin at a certain date. *Informal.* To go out with members of the opposite sex. —**dat·a·ble,** *a.* —**dat·er,** *n.*

date·less, dāt′lis, *a.* Having no date; undated; so old as to be beyond date; having no fixed limit; eternal.

date line, *n.* A theoretical line coinciding with the meridian of 180° from Greenwich, the regions on either side of which are counted as differing by one day in their calendar dates.

date·line, dāt′līn, *n.* A line in a letter, newspaper article, or the like, giving the date and often the place of origin.

da·tive, dā′tiv, *a.* Pertaining to the indirect object of a verb.—*n.* The dative case; a word in the dative case.

da·tum, dā′təm, dat′əm, dä′təm, *n. pl.,* **da·ta.** *Usu. pl.* Some fact or condition granted to be used for further research or reasoning.

daub, dôb, *v.t., v.i.* To smear with mud, plaster, etc.; to soil; to besmear; to paint coarsely.—*n.* The act of daubing or anything daubed; coarse painting. —**daub·er,** *n.*

daugh·ter, dô′tər, *n.* In relation to her real or adopted parents, a female child; a female descendant; a female person having a spiritual relationship similar to the physical one of child to parent.—*a.* —**daugh·ter·ly,** *a.*

daugh·ter-in-law, dô′tər·in·lô, *n. pl.,* **daughters-in-law.** A son's wife.

daunt, dônt, dänt, *v.t.* To intimidate; to dishearten.

daunt·less, dônt′lis, dänt′lis, *a.* Bold; not discouraged; fearless. —**daunt·less·ly,** *adv.* —**daunt·less·ness,** *n.*

dau·phin, dô′fin, *Fr.* dō·fan′, *n. pl.,* **-phins,** *Fr.* dō·fan′. (*Often cap.*) Prior to the revolution of 1830, the eldest son of the king of France.

dav·en·port, dav′ən·pôrt, dav′ən·pôrt, *n.* A kind of large sofa or divan, often one convertible into a bed.

dav·it, dav′it, dā′vit, *n.* Either of the two cranelike devices projecting over the side or stern of a vessel, used for suspending or lowering and hoisting boats, anchors, etc.

Da·vy Jones, dā′vē jōnz. *n.* The sailor's devil.

Da·vy Jones's lock·er, *n.* The ocean's bottom,

esp. as the grave of all who perish at sea.

daw, dô, *n.* A jackdaw.

daw·dle, dô′dəl, *v.i., v.t.,* **-dled, -dling.** To waste time; to trifle; to loiter. **—daw·dler,** *n.*

dawn, dôn, *v.i.* To grow light; to begin to develop or appear; to begin to be realized or understood.—*n.* The first appearance of light in the morning; beginning; rise.

day, dā, *n.* The time between sunrise and sunset; the interval represented by one rotation of the earth on its axis; a similar interval of some heavenly body; daylight; the portion of a day allotted to labor; a day assigned to a particular purpose or observance; contest or combat; a period of power or influence. *Usu. pl.* A particular time or period. *Often pl.* A period of life or activity.

day·break, dā′brāk, *n.* The dawn or first appearance of light in the morning.

day·dream, dā′drēm, *n.* A reverie; a visionary fancy indulged in when awake.—*v.i.* To have reveries. **—day·dream·er,** *n.*

day la·bor·er, *n.* One who works by the day, as an unskilled laborer.

day·light, dā′līt, *n.* The light of day; openness or publicity; daytime; daybreak.

day·light-sav·ing time, dā′līt-sā′ving, *n.* Time usually one hour later than standard time, to provide extra evening daylight.

day nurs·er·y, *n.* A nursery for the care of small children during the day.

Day of A·tone·ment, *n.* Yom Kippur.

day school, *n.* A school held in the daytime, esp. a private school for students who live at home.

day·time, dā′tīm, *n.* The time of daylight.

daze, dāz, *v.t.,* **dazed, daz·ing.** To stun or stupefy; bewilder; dazzle.—*n.* The state of being dazed. **—daz·ed·ly,** *adv.*

daz·zle, daz′əl, *v.t.,* **-zled, -zling.** To overpower or dim, as the vision, by intense light; to overcome by brilliancy or display of any kind.—*v.i.* To be overpowered by light; to excite admiration.—*n.* The act or fact of dazzling; bewildering brightness. **—daz·zler,** *n.* **—daz·zling·ly,** *adv.*

D-day, dē′dā, *n.* A day planned for launching an operation, usually unannounced.

DDT, *n.* A powerful insecticide.

dea·con, dē′kən, *n.* A lay church official or subordinate minister; a member of the clerical order below a priest. **—dea·con·ry,** *n.* **—dea·con·ship,** *n.*

dea·con·ess, dē′kə·nis, *n.* A female deacon; in certain Protestant churches, one of an order of women who care for the sick and poor.

dead, ded, *a.* Deprived or devoid of life; not alive; inanimate; numb; resembling death; insensitive; unfeeling; barren; no longer in operation; dreary; unexciting; lacking its characteristic quality: a *dead* tennis ball, *dead* beer, etc.; commercially unproductive; not in use; perfectly still or motionless; precise; exact; sure or unerring; complete; absolute. *Informal.* Completely exhausted. *Sports.* Out of play. —*adv.* To the last degree; completely; directly; precisely. —*n.* The time of greatest stillness, darkness, gloom, etc. **—the dead,** those who are dead.

dead·beat, ded′bēt, *n. Informal.* One who avoids paying for what he gets; a sponger; an idler.

dead cen·ter, *n.* Either of two positions of the crank in a reciprocating engine in which the connecting rod has no power to turn the crank.

dead·en, ded′ən, *v.t.* To weaken in sensitivity, intensity, vitality, or animation; benumb; dull; make soundproof.—*v.i.* To become dead. **—dead·en·er,** *n.*

dead-end, ded′end′, *a.* Closed at one end; leading nowhere.

dead end, *n.* A cul-de-sac; an impasse.

dead let·ter, *n.* A law which has lost its force; a letter which the post office is unable to deliver or to return to the sender.

dead·line, ded′līn, *n.* A line or limit that must not be crossed; the latest possible time for doing something.

dead·lock, ded′lok, *n.* A standstill resulting from equal opposing forces.—*v.t., v.i.* To bring to or come to a deadlock.

dead·ly, ded′lē, *a.,* **-li·er, -li·est.** Causing or likely to cause death; fatal; implacable; enervating; causing spiritual death; resembling death; excessive. *Informal.* Unbearably dull.—*adv.* Deathly. *Informal.* Very. **—dead·li·ness,** *n.*

dead pan, *n. Informal.* A face completely without expression. **—dead-pan,** *a., adv., v.i.*

dead reck·on·ing, *n.* The calculation of a vessel's position by studying the course followed, the distance covered, and the known or expected drift.

dead·wood, ded′wûd, *n.* Dead branches or trees; something useless.

deaf, def, *a.* Lacking the sense of hearing, either wholly or in part; not willing to listen; inattentive; unheeding. **—deaf·ly,** *adv.* **—deaf·ness,** *n.*

deaf·en, def′ən, *v.t.* To make deaf; to stun with loud noise; to soundproof; to drown a sound by a louder sound. **—deaf·en·ing·ly,** *adv.*

deaf-mute, def′mūt, def·mūt′, *n.* A person who is both deaf and dumb.

deal, dēl, *n.* A quantity; amount; the distribution to the players of the cards used in a game; a player's turn to distribute the cards; the cards distributed; a hand. *Informal.* A business transaction; a bargain or arrangement for mutual advantage.—*v.t.,* **dealt,** delt, **deal·ing.** To distribute among a number of recipients; to give to one as his share or portion; to administer or deliver.—*v.i.* To distribute the cards required in a game; to treat; trade or do business: to *deal* with a firm, to *deal* in an article; occupy oneself or itself, with *in* or *with;* to take action; to conduct oneself in a specified way. **—deal·er,** *n.*

deal, dēl, *n.* A board or plank, esp. of fir or pine; such boards collectively.

deal·ing, dē′ling, *n. Usu. pl.* Intercourse, as of friendship or business.

dean, dēn, *n.* An administrative officer of a college or university, under the president, or heading the faculty of a division or college; head of the chapter of a collegiate church or cathedral; a senior member of any body. **—dean·ship,** *n.*

dear, dēr, *a.* Beloved; regarded with esteem or affection; precious; high-priced.—*n.* One who is dear. —*adv.* Dearly; fondly; at great cost.—*interj.* An exclamation of surprise, distress, etc. **—dear·ly,** *adv.* **—dear·ness,** *n.*

dearth, dərth, *n.* Scarcity; lack; famine.

death, deth, *n.* The act or fact of dying; the state of being dead; any end like dying; extinction; bloodshed or murder; a cause of death; (*often cap.*) the annihilating power personified, usually as a skeleton. **—death·less,** *a.* **—death·ly,** *a., adv.*

death·blow, deth′blō, *n.* A blow causing death; anything which ends something.

death house, *n.* A place where condemned prisoners are held, awaiting execution.

death rate, *n.* The ratio between the number of deaths and a total population.

death's-head, deths′hed, *n.* A human skull, esp. as a symbol of mortality.

death·trap, deth′trap, *n.* A structure or situation involving imminent risk of death.

death war·rant, *n.* An official order for execution; something that ends all hope.

death·watch, deth′woch, deth′wôch, *n.* A watch beside anyone dying or dead; a guard over a prisoner

---

a- hat, fāte, fâre, fàther; **e-** met, mē; **i-** pin, pīne; **o-** not, nōte, ôrb, moove (move), boy, pownd; **u-** cūbe, bûll, tûk (took); **ch-** chin; **th-** thick, ŧhen; **zh-** vizhon (vision); ə- əgo, takən, pencəl, lemən, bərd (bird).

before execution.

de·ba·cle, dā·bä′kəl, dā·bak′əl, də·bä′kəl, *n.* A calamitous breakdown, rout, or collapse; a sudden breaking up of ice in a river; a sudden outbreak of water.

de·bar, di·bär′, *v.t.,* **de·barred, de·bar·ring.** To bar; to preclude; to prohibit. —**de·bar·ment,** *n.*

de·bark, di·bärk′, *v.t., v.i.* To land from a ship or aircraft; to disembark. —**de·bar·ka·tion,** dē·bär·kā′shən, *n.*

de·base, di·bās′, *v.t.,* **de·based, de·bas·ing.** To lower in quality; to degrade; to abase. —**de·base·ment,** *n.* —**de·bas·er,** *n.*

de·bate, di·bāt′, *v.i., v.t.,* **de·bat·ed, de·bat·ing.** To engage in discussion, esp. in a public meeting; to discuss reasons for and against; to deliberate.—*n.* Argument; discussion; a discussion, esp. of public question in an assembly. —**de·bat·a·ble,** *a.* —**de·bat·er,** *n.*

de·bauch, di·bôch′, *v.t.* To corrupt by sensuality or intemperance; to corrupt; deprave.—*v.i.* To indulge in a debauch.—*n.* A period of excessive indulgence in sensual pleasures. —**de·bauch·er,** *n.* —**de·bauch·ment,** *n.* —**de·bauch·er·y,** *n. pl.,* **-ies.**

deb·au·chee, deb·ô′chē, deb·ô·shē′, *n.* One addicted to excessive indulgence in sensual pleasures.

de·ben·ture, di·ben′chər, *n.* A certificate of indebtedness.

de·bil·i·tate, di·bil′ə·tāt, *v.t.,* **-tat·ed, -tat·ing.** To weaken; to enfeeble. —**de·bil·i·ta·tion,** de·bil·ə·tā′shən, *n.*

de·bil·i·ty, di·bil′ə·tē, *n. pl.,* **-ties.** General bodily weakness; feebleness.

deb·it, deb′it, *n.* That which is entered in an account as a debt; the left-hand side of an account, where debts are recorded.—*v.t.* To charge with a debt; to enter on the debit side of an account.

deb·o·nair, deb·ə·nâr′, *a.* Carefree; courteous; pleasant; cheerful. Also **deb·o·naire, deb·on·naire.**

de·bris, də·brē′, dā′brē, *n.* Rubbish; fragments; ruins; a mass of stones, fragmented rocks, etc.

debt, det, *n.* That which one person is bound to pay to or perform for another; an obligation.

debt·or, det′ər, *n.* A person in debt.

de·bunk, di·bəngk′, *v.t. Informal.* To expose the sham, errors, sentimentality, or the like, in something. —**de·bunk·er,** *n.*

de·but, dé·but, dā·bū′, di·bū′, dā′bū, deb′ū, *n.* A first appearance in society or before the public; the start of a career or profession.

deb·u·tante, déb·u·tante, deb′yû·tänt, deb′yû·tant, *n.* A young woman making a debut, esp. into society.

de·cade, dek′ād, *n.* A period of ten years; a group consisting of ten.

dec·a·dent, dek′ə·dənt, di·kād′ənt, *a.* Deteriorating; being in a state of decline or decay.—*n.* One who is decadent. —**dec·a·dence,** *n.* —**dec·a·dent·ly,** *adv.*

dec·a·gon, dek′ə·gon, *n.* A plane figure having ten sides.

dec·a·gram, dek′ə·gram, *n.* A unit of metric measure that equals ten grams.

dec·a·he·dron, dek·ə·hē′drən, *n. pl.,* **-drons, -dra.** A solid figure having ten faces.

de·cal, dē′kal, di·kal′, *n.* The process of transferring a design or picture from a specially prepared paper to the surface of wood, glass, etc.; the picture or design transferred. Also **de·cal·co·ma·ni·a**, di·kal·kə·mā′nē·ə, di·kal·kə·mān′yə.

Dec·a·logue, Dec·a·log, dek′ə·lôg, dek′ə·log, *n.* The Ten Commandments.

de·camp, di·kamp′, *v.i.* To break camp; to depart suddenly or secretly. —**de·camp·ment,** *n.*

de·cant, di·kant′, *v.t.* To pour off gently, as liquor, without disturbing the sediment.

de·cant·er, di·kan′tər, *n.* A vessel used for decanting; a vessel from which wine, brandy, or other beverages are served.

de·cap·i·tate, di·kap′ə·tāt, *v.t.,* **-tat·ed, -tat·ing.** To behead. —**de·cap·i·ta·tion,** di·kap·ə·tā′shən, *n.*

dec·a·pod, dek′ə·pod, *n.* Any of an order of ten-footed crustaceans, or of ten-armed cephalopods.—*a.* Having ten feet or legs.

de·cath·lon, di·kath′lon, *n.* An athletic contest comprising ten different exercises or events.

de·cay, di·kā′, dē·kā′, *v.i.* To fall away from a state of excellence or prosperity; deteriorate; to become decomposed; rot.—*v.t.* To cause to decay.—*n.* The process of decaying, or the resulting state; radioactive decay.

de·cease, di·sēs′, *n.* Death.—*v.i.* To die. —**de·ceased,** di·sēst′, *a., n.*

de·ceit, di·sēt′, *n.* The act or practice of deceiving; deception; fraud; cheating; an act or device intended to deceive. —**de·ceit·ful,** *a.* —**de·ceit·ful·ly,** *adv.* —**de·ceit·ful·ness,** *n.*

de·ceive, di·sēv′, *v.t.,* **de·ceived, de·ceiv·ing.** To cause to believe what is false or disbelieve what is true; mislead; delude.—*v.i.* To practice deceit. —**de·ceiv·er,** *n.* —**de·ceiv·ing·ly,** *adv.* —**de·ceiv·a·ble,** *a.*

de·cel·er·ate, dē·sel′ə·rāt, *v.t.,* **-at·ed, -at·ing.** To decrease the velocity of.—*v.i.* To decrease in velocity. —**de·cel·er·a·tion,** dē·sel·ər·ā′shən, *n.*

De·cem·ber, di·sem′bər, *n.* The twelfth and last month of the year, having 31 days.

de·cen·cy, dē′sən·sē, *n. pl.,* **-cies.** The state or quality of being decent; propriety in behavior; decorum; modesty; *pl.,* the standards of decent living and proper conduct.

de·cen·ni·al, di·sen′ē·əl, *a.* For ten years; happening every ten years. —**de·cen·ni·al·ly,** *adv.*

de·cent, dē′sənt, *a.* Having a character that gains general approval; suitable, as to words, behavior, etc.; decorous; modest; tasteful; respectable. —**de·cent·ly,** *adv.*

de·cen·tral·ize, dē·sen′trə·līz, *v.t.,* **-ized, -iz·ing.** To distribute or disperse into smaller parts what has been centralized. —**de·cen·tral·i·za·tion,** dē·sen·trə·lə·zā′shən, *n.*

de·cep·tion, di·sep′shən, *n.* The act of deceiving or state of being deceived; that which deceives; delusion; fraud. —**de·cep·tive,** *a.* —**de·cep·tive·ly,** *adv.* —**de·cep·tive·ness,** *n.*

dec·i·bel, des′ə·bəl, *n.* A measure of the relative intensities of sounds.

de·cide, di·sīd′, *v.t.,* **de·cid·ed, de·cid·ing.** To settle, finally or authoritatively; to conclude; resolve; to bring (someone) to a decision.—*v.i.* To give or make a decision. —**de·cid·a·ble,** *a.*

de·cid·ed, di·sī′dəd, *a.* Resolute; determined; definite; unquestionable. —**de·cid·ed·ly,** *adv.* —**de·cid·ed·ness,** *n.*

de·cid·u·ous, di·sij′oo·əs, *a.* Falling off or shed at a particular season or stage of growth, as leaves, horns, or teeth; shedding the leaves annually. —**de·cid·u·ous·ly,** *adv.*

dec·i·mal, des′ə·məl, *a.* Of or pertaining to tens; numbered or proceeding by tens;—*n.* A decimal fraction.

dec·i·mal frac·tion, *n.* A fraction with a denominator of 10, or a power of 10.

dec·i·mal point, *n.* A period used before a decimal fraction.

dec·i·mal sys·tem, *n.* A system of weights, measures, etc., based on multiples of ten.

dec·i·mate, des′ə·māt, *v.t.,* **-mat·ed, -mat·ing.** To destroy a great number of, esp. every tenth man. —**dec·i·ma·tion,** des·ə·mā′shən, *n.*

de·ci·pher, di·sī′fər, *v.t.* To explain (what is written in ciphers) by using a key; decode; to discern the meaning of words which are poorly written, obscure, foreign, etc. —**de·ci·pher·a·ble,** *a.*

de·ci·sion, di·sizh′ən, *n.* The act of deciding a question or issue; final judgment or opinion; a statement of a conclusion, as of a court; unwavering firmness.

de·ci·sive, di·sī′siv, a. Final; unquestionable; making up one's mind quickly and firmly. —**de·ci·sive·ly**, adv. —**de·ci·sive·ness**, n.

deck, dek, v.t. To clothe; array; adorn.—n. A flooring extending from side to side of a ship; any platform or part resembling this; a pack of playing cards.

deck hand, n. A seaman who does menial tasks, esp. on a ship's deck.

deck·le edge, dek′əl, n. A rough edge of untrimmed or handmade paper.

de·claim, di·klām′, v.i. To make a formal speech or oration; to inveigh against; to recite in public; to exhibit elocutionary skill; to speak or write for oratorical effect.—v.t. To utter rhetorically. —**dec·la·ma·tion**, dek·lə·mā′shən, n. —**de·clam·a·tor·y**, di·klam′ə·tôr·ē, a.

de·clare, di·klār′, v.t., **de·clared**, **de·clar·ing**. To proclaim; to announce officially; to state emphatically; to affirm; to manifest or reveal; to make a full statement of taxable income, goods etc.; in bridge, to announce trump.—v.i. To make a declaration or decision. —**de·clar·a·tive**, **de·clar·a·to·ry**, a. —**de·clar·er**, n. —**dec·la·ra·tion**, dek·lə·rā′shən, n.

de·clas·si·fy, dē·klas′ə·fī, v.t., **-fied**, **-fy·ing**. To remove security classification from, as secret information.

de·clen·sion, di·klen′shən, n. The act or fact of sloping downward; a sinking down; deterioration; decline; deviation from a standard; the formation of the cases of a noun, pronoun, or adjective by adding inflectional endings.

dec·li·na·tion, dek·lə·nā′shən, n. The act of moving, sloping, or bending down; deterioration; a polite refusal; the distance of a heavenly body from the celestial equator; the variation of the magnetic needle from true north.

de·cline, di·klīn′, v.i., **de·clined**, **de·clin·ing**. To lean or slope downward; to sink to a lower level; to diminish in strength, value, etc.; decay; to courteously refuse.—v.t. To cause to bend downward; to refuse. Gram. To inflect through case and number.—n. A downward slope; a gradual loss, as in value, strength, etc.; deterioration; an ending or last part. —**de·clin·a·ble**, a.

de·cliv·i·ty, di·kliv′ə·tē, n. pl., **-ties**. Slope or inclination downward.

de·code, dē·kōd′, v.t., **de·cod·ed**, **de·cod·ing**. To translate, as a coded message, into ordinary language. —**de·cod·er**, n.

dé·colle·tage, dā·kol·täzh′, n. A very low-cut neckline of a garment; a garment with such a neckline. —**dé·colle·té**, dā·kol·tā′, a.

de·com·pose, dē·kəm·pōz′, v.t., v.i., **-posed**, **-pos·ing**. To separate into constituent parts; decay or rot. —**de·com·po·si·tion**, dē·kom·pə·zish′ən, n.

de·com·press, dē·kəm·pres′, v.t. To release from pressure as in an air lock. —**de·com·pres·sion**, n.

de·con·tam·i·nate, dē·kən·tam′ə·nāt, v.t., **-nat·ed**, **-nat·ing**. To purify; to free from contamination. —**de·con·tam·i·na·tion**, n.

de·con·trol, dē·kən·trōl′, v.t., **-trolled**, **-trol·ling**. To remove from control.—n. The removal of controls.

de·cor, dé·cor, dā·kôr′, dā′kôr, n. Style of decoration; theatrical scenery.

dec·o·rate, dek′ə·rāt, v.t., **-rat·ed**, **-rat·ing**. To furnish with something becoming or ornamental; to paint or paper a home, office, or other interior; embellish; to confer distinction upon with a badge, medal, etc. —**dec·o·ra·tion**, dek·ə·rā′shən, n. —**dec·o·ra·tive**, dek′ər·ə·tiv, dek′ə·rā·tiv, a. —**dec·o·ra·tive·ly**, adv. —**dec·o·ra·tor**, n.

dec·o·rous, dek′ər·əs, di·kôr′əs, a. Well-behaved; becoming; seemly; proper. —**dec·o·rous·ly**, adv.

de·co·rum, di·kōr′əm, di·kôr′əm, n. Propriety of speech, appearance, or behavior; seemliness; decency.

de·coy, di·koy′, dē′koy, n. A fowl, or the likeness of one, employed to lead other fowl into a trap or within range of gunshot; a thing or person intended to lead into a snare. —di·koy′, v.t. To lead into a snare; to entrap by deception.

de·crease, di·krēs′, v.i., v.t., **de·creased**, **de·creas·ing**. To grow or make less. —dē′krēs, di·krēs′, n. The process of growing less; the amount by which a thing is lessened. —**de·creas·ing·ly**, adv.

de·cree, di·krē′, n. An edict promulgated by civil or other authority; an authoritative decision.—v.t. **de·creed**, **de·cree·ing**. To ordain or decide authoritatively.—v.i. To issue a decree.

de·crep·it, di·krep′it, a. Broken down or weakened by long use or old age. —**de·crep·i·tude**, n. —**de·crep·it·ly**, adv.

de·cre·scen·do, dē·kri·shen′dō, dā·kri·shen′dō, a. Mus. Gradually decreasing in force or loudness.—n. pl., **-dos**.

de·cry, di·krī′, v.t., **de·cried**, **de·cry·ing**. Censure; disparage; depreciate, as coins. —**de·cri·al**, n.

ded·i·cate, ded′ə·kāt, v.t., **-cat·ed**, **-cat·ing**. To set apart for a sacred purpose; to appropriate to any person or purpose; often refl., to give wholly or earnestly up to. To inscribe or address (a book, etc.) to a patron or friend as a mark of esteem. —**ded·i·ca·to·ry**, ded′ə·kə·tôr·ē, **ded·i·ca·tive**, a. —**ded·i·ca·tion**, ded·ə·kā′shən, n.

de·duce, di·doos′, di·dūs′, v.t., **de·duced**, **de·duc·ing**. To derive, as a conclusion, from something known or assumed; infer; to trace the course of. —**de·duc·i·ble**, a.

de·duct, di·dəkt′, v.t. To subtract or to take away. —**de·duct·i·ble**, a.

de·duc·tion, di·dək′shən, n. The act of subtracting; that which is deducted; abatement; the method of, or conclusion from, deducing from premises. —**de·duc·tive**, a. —**de·duc·tive·ly**, adv.

deed, dēd, n. That which is done; an act; an exploit; achievement; a written agreement, esp. one conveying real estate to a purchaser or donee.—v.t. To transfer by deed.

deem, dēm, v.t., v.i. To think; judge; believe.

deep, dēp, a. Situated far down from the surface; in depth; extending to or coming from a depth; difficult to understand; lying below the surface; not superficial; grave; heartfelt; intense or extreme; low in pitch; profound; shrewd or artful; with the mind preoccupied: deep in thought.—adv. To or at a considerable or specified depth; far on in time.—n. The sea or ocean; any depth in space or time; the part of greatest intensity. —**deep·ly**, adv. —**deep·ness**, n.

deep·en, dē′pən, v.t., v.i. To make or become deeper.

deep-root·ed, dēp′roo′tid, dēp′rūt′id, a. Deeply rooted; firmly established.

deep-seat·ed, dēp′sē′tid, a. Situated far beneath the surface; deeply rooted.

deer, dēr, n. pl., **deer**. A ruminant animal of a family including moose, elk, and esp. smaller species. The males usually have deciduous horns or antlers.

deer·skin, dēr′skin, n. The hide of a deer; leather made from this.—a.

de·es·ca·late, dē·es′kə·lāt, v.t., v.i., **-lat·ed**, **-lat·ing**. To reduce in intensity or quantity, esp. arms. —**de·es·ca·la·tion**, dē·es·kə·lā′shən, n.

de·face, di·fās′, v.t., **de·faced**, **de·fac·ing**. To mar the face of; to disfigure; to erase. —**de·face·ment**, n. —**de·fac·er**, n.

de fac·to, dē·fak′tō, a., adv. In fact; actually existing, whether lawfully or not.

de·fame, di·fām′, v.t., **de·famed**, **de·fam·ing**. To slander; to calumniate; to libel. —**def·a·ma·tion,** def·ə·mā′shən, dē·fə·mā′shən, n. —**de·fam·a·to·ry,** di·fam′ə·tôr·ē, n. —**de·fam·er,** n.

de·fault, di·fôlt′, n. Failure to appear; neglect; failure to meet financial obligations; failure to perform an obligatory act; failure to compete in or finish a scheduled contest.—v.t., v.i. To fail to act, appear, pay, etc.; to fail to play or complete an athletic contest; to forfeit by default. —**de·fault·er,** n.

de·feat, di·fēt′, n. An overthrow; loss of battle; setback; frustration; disappointment.—v.t. To overcome; win a victory over; to frustrate; to disappoint; to render null and void.

de·feat·ism, di·fē′tiz·əm, n. Expectation of or resignation to defeat. —**de·feat·ist,** n.

def·e·cate, def′ə·kāt, v.t., -cat·ed, -cat·ing. v.i. To void excrement from the bowels. —**def·e·ca·tion,** def·ə·kā′shən, n.

de·fect, dē′fekt, di·fekt′, n. A fault; an imperfection; that which is lacking for completeness; fault; failing. —di·fekt′, v.i. To desert one party, country, etc., for another.

de·fec·tion, di·fek′shən, n. The act of defecting; a falling away; apostasy. —**de·fec·tor,** n.

de·fec·tive, di·fek′tiv, a. Wanting in anything necessary; imperfect; faulty; marked by a subnormal condition, either mental or physical; lacking some of the usual forms of declension or conjugation.—n. One who is physically or mentally deficient. —**de·fec·tive·ly,** adv. —**de·fec·tive·ness,** n.

de·fend, di·fend′, v.t. To protect against any attack or injury; to vindicate, uphold, or support; to contest (a lawsuit); to act as lawyer for.—v.i. To make a defense. —**de·fend·er,** n.

de·fend·ant, di·fen′dənt, n. One against whom a charge is made in a lawsuit.

de·fense, de·fence, di·fens′, dē′fens, n. Resistance against attack; protection; the practice of defending oneself, as in fencing or boxing; something that defends; the defending of a cause by speech or argument; a speech or argument in vindication; the denial or pleading of the defendant in answer to the claim against him; a defendant and his legal agents; the team or players trying to thwart the attack of the opposing team. —**de·fense·less,** a. —**de·fense·less·ly,** adv. —**de·fense·less·ness,** n. —**de·fen·si·ble,** a. —**de·fen·si·bil·i·ty,** di·fen·sə·bil′ə·tē, n. —**de·fen·si·bly,** adv.

de·fen·sive, di·fen′siv, a. Carried on in resisting attack; of or relating to defense.—n. An attitude or position of defense; something that defends. —**de·fen·sive·ly,** adv.

de·fer, di·fər′, v.t., v.i., **de·ferred, de·fer·ring.** To delay; to postpone. —**de·fer·ment,** n.

de·fer, di·fər′, v.i., **de·ferred, de·fer·ring.** To yield to another's opinion; to submit courteously (to).

def·er·ence, def′ər·əns, n. A yielding in opinion or judgment of another; respect; courteous consideration. —**def·er·en·tial,** def·ə·ren′shəl, a. —**def·er·en·tial·ly,** adv.

de·fi·ance, di·fī′əns, n. The act of defying; a challenge to meet in combat or contest; a bold resistance to authority or to any opposing force; open disregard. —**de·fi·ant,** a. —**de·fi·ant·ly,** adv.

de·fi·cient, di·fish′ənt, a. Lacking some characteristic necessary to completeness, or having an insufficient measure of it; defective; lacking. —**de·fi·cien·cy,** di·fish′ən·sē, n. pl., -cies. —**de·fi·cient·ly,** adv.

def·i·cit, def′ə·sit, Brit. di·fis′it, n. A falling short; the amount by which a sum of money falls short of the required amount.

de·file, di·fīl′, v.t., **de·filed, de·fil·ing.** To soil or sully; to make ceremonially unclean; to corrupt; to violate. —**de·file·ment,** n. —**de·fil·er,** n.

de·file, di·fīl′, dē′fīl, v.i., **de·filed, de·fil·ing.** To march off in a line.—n. A narrow passage; a long pass, as between hills.

de·fine, di·fīn′, v.t., **de·fined, de·fin·ing.** To state the meaning or significance, as of a word or phrase; to explain the nature of; to determine the boundaries of; fix; specify distinctly. —**de·fin·er,** n. —**de·fin·a·ble,** a. —**de·fin·a·bly,** adv.

def·i·nite, def′ə·nit, a. Clearly defined; not vague; precise; having fixed limits; positive; certain; specifying precisely: the definite article. —**def·i·nite·ly,** adv. —**def·i·nite·ness,** n.

def·i·ni·tion, def·ə·nish′ən, n. The act of defining; a precise description of a word or thing by its properties; an explanation; the power of making a thing sharp and clear, esp. a lens; the sharpness or accuracy of an image, a sound, etc.

de·fin·i·tive, di·fin′ə·tiv, a. Conclusive; final; serving to fix or specify definitely. —**de·fin·i·tive·ly,** adv.

de·flate, di·flāt′, v.t., **de·flat·ed, de·flat·ing.** To release gas or air from; to lower or reduce; to reduce spending, or the available currency, so that prices come down.—v.i. To become deflated. —**de·fla·tion,** n. —**de·fla·tion·ary,** a.

de·flect, di·flekt′, v.i., v.t. To turn aside; to deviate or cause to deviate from a true course or straight line; to swerve. —**de·flec·tion,** n. —**de·flec·tive,** a. —**de·flec·tor,** n.

de·flow·er, di·flow′ər, v.t. To deprive of virginity; ravish; strip of flowers; rob of beauty, freshness, etc.

de·fo·li·ate, dē·fō′lē·āt, v.t., -at·ed, -at·ing. To strip prematurely of leaves.

de·for·est, dē·fôr′ist, dē·for′ist, v.t. To divest of trees. —**de·for·est·a·tion,** dē·fôr·əs·tā′shən, n.

de·form, di·fôrm′, v.t. To mar the form of; to disfigure; to render ugly; to transform.—v.i. To become deformed. —**de·for·ma·tion,** dē·fôr·mā′shən, def·ər·mā′shən, n. —**de·formed,** a.

de·form·i·ty, di·fôr′mə·tē, n. pl., -ties. The state of being deformed; some misshapen part of the body; distortion; irregularity; ugliness.

de·fraud, di·frôd′, v.t. To deprive of some right or property by fraud; cheat.

de·fray, di·frā′, v.t. To pay (expenses, costs, etc.). —**de·fray·al, de·fray·ment,** n. —**de·fray·a·ble,** a.

de·frost, di·frôst′, di·frost′, v.t. To remove frost or ice from.—v.i. To thaw. —**de·frost·er,** n.

deft, deft, a. Dexterous; clever; apt. —**deft·ly,** adv. —**deft·ness,** n.

de·funct, di·fəngkt′, a. Dead; extinct.

de·fy, di·fī′, v.t., **de·fied, de·fy·ing.** To challenge (someone); dare; resist boldly; brave. —**de·fi·er,** n.

de·gen·er·ate, di·jen′ə·rāt, v.i., -at·ed, -at·ing. To decline in physical, mental, or moral qualities; deteriorate. —di·jen′ər·it, n. One who has regressed in character to an evil, perverted, or morbid condition. —di·jen′ər·it, a. Declined physically, mentally, or morally from the normal standard base; mean; perverted; degraded. —**de·gen·er·ate·ly,** adv. —**de·gen·er·a·cy, de·gen·er·a·tion,** di·jen·ə·rā′shən, n. —**de·gen·er·a·tive,** a.

de·grade, di·grād′, di·grād′, v.t., **de·grad·ed, de·grad·ing.** To reduce to a lower rank or degree; deprive of office, rank, etc.; to lower in quality or moral character; debase; deprave; to wear down by erosion. —**deg·ra·da·tion,** deg·rə·dā′shən, n. —**de·grad·ed,** a. —**de·grad·ing,** a.

de·gree, di·grē′, n. A step or stage in a process, scale, order, etc.; rank or station; relative extent, measure, or scope; unit for measuring angles or arcs, the 360th part of the circumference of a circle; a unit for measuring temperature; a legal measure of the gravity of a crime; an academic title awarded by institutions of learning upon completion of a course of study, or as an honor; one of the three forms used in the comparison of an adjective or adverb; the highest exponent, or sum of the exponents, in certain algebraic terms or equations; a step in a line of genealogical descent; a space or line of the musical staff; an interval between notes of the scale. —**by degrees,** in easy stages; gradually. —**to a degree,** to an extent; somewhat.

de·his·cence, di·his′əns, *n.* The splitting open, as of the seed capsules of a plant. —**de·his·cent,** *a.*

de·hy·drate, dē·hī′drāt, *v.t.,* **-drat·ed, -drat·ing.** To remove water from (a substance or mixture); to remove moisture from.—*v.i.* To lose water or moisture. —**de·hy·dra·tion,** dē·hī·drā′shən, *n.*

de·i·fy, dē′ə·fī, *v.t.,* **-fied, -fy·ing.** To make a god of; to treat as an object of supreme regard. —**de·i·fi·ca·tion,** dē·ə·fə·kā′shən, *n.* —**de·i·fi·er,** *n.*

deign, dān, *v.i.* To consider something befitting; condescend.—*v.t.* To condescend to give or grant.

de·ist, dē′ist, *n.* One whose religion is based on reason rather than revelation, or esp. one who believes in a God who created the universe but takes no part in its operations. —**de·ism,** dē′iz·əm, *n.* —**de·is·tic,** dē·is′tik, *a.* —**de·is·ti·cal,** dē·is′tə·kəl, *a.*

de·i·ty, dē′ə·tē, *n. pl.,* **-ties.** Divine nature; godhood; a god or goddess. —**the Deity,** God.

de·ject·ed, di·jek′tid, *a.* Downcast; depressed; sad; sorrowful. —**de·jec·ted·ly,** *adv.* —**de·jec·tion,** di·jek′shən, *n.*

de ju·re, dē jûr′ē, *Lat.* According to law.

de·lay, di·lā′, *v.t.* To prolong the time of doing or proceeding with; to put off; to defer; to retard; to make late; detain.—*v.i.* To linger; procrastinate.—*n.* Act of delaying; condition of being delayed. —**de·lay·er,** *n.*

de·lec·ta·ble, di·lek′tə·bəl, *a.* Delightful; highly pleasing, esp. to the taste. —**de·lec·ta·ble·ness,** *n.* —**de·lec·ta·bly,** *adv.* —**de·lec·ta·tion,** dē·lek·tā′shən, *n.*

del·e·gate, del′ə·gāt, *v.t.,* **-gat·ed, -gat·ing.** To send or appoint as a deputy or representative; to assign or entrust (powers or functions) to another. —del′ə·gāt, del′ə·git, *n.* One delegated to act for or represent another; a representative, as at a convention, for a territory, or in certain state legislatures.

del·e·ga·tion, del·ə·gā′shən, *n.* The act of delegating, or the fact of being delegated; a body of delegates.

de·lete, di·lēt′, *v.t.,* **de·let·ed, de·let·ing.** To blot out; to erase; to strike out (written or printed matter). —**de·le·tion,** *n.*

del·e·te·ri·ous, del·ə·tēr′ē·əs, *a.* Injurious; pernicious; harmful.

de·lib·er·ate, di·lib′ə·rāt, *v.t.,* **-at·ed, -at·ing.** To weigh in the mind; consider.—*v.i.* To think carefully or attentively; to confer formally; hold formal discussion, as with reference to proposed measures. —di·lib′ər·it, *a.* Carefully weighed or considered; studied; intentional; careful or slow in deciding; leisurely; slow. —**de·lib·er·ate·ly,** *adv.* —**de·lib·er·ate·ness,** *n.* —**de·lib·er·a·tion,** *n.* —**de·lib·er·a·tive,** *a.* —**de·lib·er·a·tor,** *n.*

del·i·ca·cy, del′ə·kə·sē, *n. pl.,* **-cies.** Exquisite quality or character; a food delightful to the palate; fineness; softness; subtle quality; fineness of feeling; sensitiveness; the quality of requiring great care or tact; decorum; consideration for the feelings of others; frailty; bodily weakness.

del·i·cate, del′ə·kit, *a.* Fine in texture; susceptible to sickness; fragile; soft or slight; mild; subtle; exquisite in perception or feeling; exquisite in action, as an instrument; requiring great care or tact; decorous; considerate; dainty or choice, as food; fastidious. —**del·i·cate·ly,** *adv.* —**del·i·cate·ness,** *n.*

del·i·ca·tes·sen, del·ə·kə·tes′ən, *n.* A store which sells prepared foods such as cooked meats, sausages, cheese, salads, etc.; *usu. construed as pl.,* the foods.

de·li·cious, di·lish′əs, *a.* Highly pleasing to the taste or smell; delightful. —**de·li·cious·ly,** *adv.* —**de·li·cious·ness,** *n.*

de·light, di·līt′, *v.t.* To provide great pleasure.—*v.i.* To have great pleasure.—*n.* Great pleasure; joy; that which gives great pleasure. —**de·light·ed,** *a.* —**de·light·ed·ly,** *adv.*

de·light·ful, di·līt′fəl, *a.* Highly pleasing; charming. —**de·light·ful·ly,** *adv.* —**de·light·ful·ness,** *n.*

de·lim·it, di·lim′it, *v.t.* To fix the limits of; define. —**de·lim·i·ta·tion,** *n.*

de·lin·e·ate, di·lin′ē·āt, *v.t.,* **-at·ed, -at·ing.** To describe the form of; sketch or design; to depict verbally. —**de·lin·e·a·tion,** di·lin·ē·ā′shən, *n.* —**de·lin·e·a·tor,** *n.*

de·lin·quent, di·ling′kwənt, *a.* Failing in or neglectful of a duty or obligation; guilty of a misdeed or offense.—*n.* One who is delinquent, esp. a juvenile delinquent. —**de·lin·quen·cy,** *n. pl.,* **-cies.**

de·lir·i·um, di·lēr′ē·əm, *n. pl.,* **-i·ums, -i·a,** -e·ə. Temporary disorder of the mental faculties, as in fevers and intoxication, characterized by restlessness, excitement, irrationality, and hallucinations. A state of violent excitement or rapture. —**de·lir·i·ous,** *a.* —**de·lir·i·ous·ly,** *adv.*

de·liv·er, di·liv′ər, *v.t.* To carry and turn over to the intended recipients; to give forth in words, utter, or pronounce; to discharge; to throw; to set free; to save; to aid in the process of giving birth to; of oneself, to disburden of thoughts or opinions.—*v.i.* To make delivery. —**de·liv·er·a·ble,** *a.* —**de·liv·er·er,** *n.*

de·liv·er·ance, di·liv′ər·əns, *n.* The act of delivering or condition of being delivered, as from captivity or danger; a usu. formal opinion or decision.

de·liv·er·y, di·liv′ə·rē, *n. pl.,* **-ies.** The act of delivering mail or goods; oratorical style; the act or manner of giving, throwing, etc.; a rescuing or liberation; a yielding, handing over; parturition; thing delivered.

dell, del, *n.* A deep natural hollow, often with wooded slopes; a small valley.

de·louse, dē·lows′, *v.t.,* **de·loused, de·lous·ing.** To free from lice.

del·phin·i·um, del·fin′ē·əm, *n.* The larkspur.

del·ta, del′tə, *n.* The fourth letter of the Greek alphabet (Δ, δ); a typically triangular tract of alluvial land between diverging branches of the mouth of a river.

del·toid, del′toyd, *n.* A large triangular-shaped muscle covering the joint of the shoulder.—*a.* Triangular.

de·lude, di·lood′, *v.t.,* **de·lud·ed, de·lud·ing.** To lead from truth or into error; to mislead; to beguile. —**de·lud·er,** *n.* —**de·lu·sive, de·lu·so·ry,** *a.* —**de·lu·sive·ly,** *adv.*

del·uge, del′ūj, *n.* A great flood or rainfall; anything that overwhelms, as a great calamity. —**the Deluge,** *n. Bible.* The great flood in the days of Noah.—*v.t.,* **-uged, -ug·ing.** To overflow; to inundate; to overwhelm.

de·lu·sion, di·loo′zhən, *n.* The act of deluding; the state of being deluded; false impression or belief; a false, fixed belief held in the presence of evidence normally sufficient to destroy it.

de·luxe, de luxe, də·lûks′, də·ləks′, *a., adv.* Of superior quality or elegance.

delve, delv, *v.i.,* **delved, delv·ing.** To carry on laborious research for information.

dem·a·gogue, dem·a·gog, dem′ə·gôg, dem′ə·gog, *n.* A person who makes use of popular emotions and prejudices for personal power. —**dem·a·gogu·er·y,** *n.* —**dem·a·gog·ic, dem·a·gog·i·cal,** *a.*

de·mand, di·mand′, di·mänd′, *v.t.* To ask for with authority, or to claim as a right; to summon, as to court; to call for or require as proper or necessary; to ask to be told.—*v.i.* To make a demand.—*n.* The act of demanding; an authoritative request or claim; a legal claim; call or desire, as for a commodity; requirement; an inquiry; that which is demanded; the desire to buy coupled with the power to buy. —**de·mand·er,** *n.*

de·mar·ca·tion, dē·mär·kā′shən, *n.* The act of

---

marking off the limits of anything; separation; distinction. Also **de·mar·ka·tion.**

de·mean, di·mēn′, v.t. Of oneself, to conduct or behave.

de·mean, di·mēn′, v.t. To lower in dignity or standing; degrade; humiliate.

de·mean·or, di·mēn′ər, n. Way of acting; behavior; hearing.

de·ment·ed, di·men′tid, a. Mad; insane.

de·men·tia, di·men′shə, di·men′shē·ə, n. Loss or major impairment of mental powers.

de·mer·it, di·mer′it, n. A fault; defect; a mark against a person for misconduct or deficiency.

dem·i·god, dem′i·god, n. A person whose qualities approach the divine; a minor or lesser god.

dem·i·john, dem′i·jon, n. A narrow-necked bottle, often enclosed in wickerwork.

de·mise, di·miz′, n. The death of a person; decease; termination of operation or existence; the transfer of sovereignty, or of the rights of an estate.—v.t. **de·mised,** **de·mis·ing.** To transfer, as an estate; to bequeath; to grant by will.—v.i. To pass by will or inheritance.

dem·i·tasse, dem′i·tas, n. A small cup for serving coffee after dinner; the contents of such a cup.

de·mo·bi·lize, dē·mō′bə·liz, v.t., **-lized, -liz·ing.** Of troops, to disband. —**de·mo·bi·li·za·tion,** dē·mō·bəl·ə·zā′shən, n.

de·moc·ra·cy, di·mok′rə·sē, n. pl., **-cies.** Government by the people; a form of government in which the supreme power is vested in the people and exercised by them or their elected agents; a state having such a form of government; a state of society characterized by equality of rights and privileges.

dem·o·crat, dem′ə·krat, n. An advocate of democracy; one who adheres to the principles of political or social equality. (Cap.) U.S. politics. A member of the Democratic Party.

dem·o·crat·ic, dem·ə·krat′ik, a. Pertaining to or of the nature of democracy; advocating democracy, or the principle of political or social equality for all. (Cap.) U.S. politics. Of or pertaining to the Democratic Party. —**dem·o·crat·i·cal·ly,** adv.

Dem·o·crat·ic Party, n. One of the two main political parties in the U.S.

de·moc·ra·tize, di·mok′rə·tiz, v.t., v.i., **-tized, -tiz·ing.** To make or become democratic. —**de·moc·ra·ti·za·tion,** di·mok·rə·tə·zā′shən, n.

de·mog·ra·phy, di·mog′rə·fē, n. The science of statistics on populations. —**de·mog·ra·pher,** n. —**dem·o·graph·ic,** dem·ə·graf′ik, a.

de·mol·ish, di·mol′ish, v.t. To pull down; to raze; to destroy. —**dem·o·li·tion,** dem·ə·lish′ən, dē·mə·lish′ən, n.

de·mon, dē′mən, n. An evil spirit; a devil; an atrociously wicked or cruel person; an evil passion or influence; a person of great energy; a guiding spirit; daemon. —**de·mon·ic,** di·mon′ik, a.

de·mon·e·tize, dē·mon′ə·tiz, dē·mən′ə·tiz, v.t., **-tized, -tiz·ing.** To deprive of standard value, as money. —**de·mon·e·ti·za·tion,** dē·mon·ə·tə·zā′shən, n.

de·mo·ni·ac, di·mō′nē·ak, a. Of demons; demonic; fiendish; raging; frantic. Also **de·mo·ni·a·cal,** dē·mə·ni·ə·kəl.—n. One seemingly possessed by a demon; a lunatic.

de·mon·ol·o·gy, dē′mə·nol′ə·jē, n. The study of demons; the study of politics in the Kremlin. —**de·mon·ol·o·gist,** n.

dem·on·strate, dem′ən·strāt, v.t., **-strat·ed, -strat·ing.** To show clearly; to explain or describe by experiments, etc.; to show or prove by reasoning; to exhibit, esp. something for sale.—v.i. To show; to congregate, march, picket, etc., to publicize or support a cause; to make a display of military strength. —**de·mon·stra·ble,** di·mon′strə·bəl, a. —**de·mon·stra·bly,** adv. —**dem·on·stra·tion,** dem·ən·strā′shən, n.

de·mon·stra·tive, də·mon′strə·tiv, a. Serving to demonstrate; outwardly expressive of feelings; clearly indicating that to which it refers: a demonstrative adjective or pronoun.—n. A word that clearly indicates an object. —**de·mon·stra·tive·ly,** adv. —**de·mon·stra·tive·ness,** n. —**dem·on·stra·tor,** n.

de·mor·al·ize, di·môr′ə·liz, di·mor′ə·liz, v.t., **-ized, -iz·ing.** To deprive of spirit, courage, discipline, or the like; reduce to a state of disorder; to corrupt the morals of. —**de·mor·al·i·za·tion,** di·môr·ə·lə·zā′shən, n. —**de·mor·al·iz·er,** n.

de·mote, di·mōt′, v.t., **de·mot·ed, de·mot·ing.** To reduce to lower rank. —**de·mo·tion,** n.

de·mur, di·mər′, v.i., **de·murred, de·mur·ring.** To object, esp. because of scruples.—n. Objection. —**de·mur·ral, de·mur·rer,** n.

de·mure, di·mūr′, a., **de·mur·er, de·mur·est.** Sedate; decorous; affectedly prim. —**de·mure·ly,** adv. —**de·mure·ness,** n.

de·mur·rage, di·mər′ij, n. Detention of a freight train, truck, ship, etc., beyond a specified time; a charge for such detention.

den, den, n. A cave or subterranean recess; a hiding place or lair; any squalid place; a wooded hollow; a quiet retreat; a small, cozy room.

de·nat·u·ral·ize, dē·nach′ər·ə·liz, v.t., **-ized, -iz·ing.** To render unnatural; to deprive of citizenship. —**de·nat·u·ral·i·za·tion,** dē·nach·ər·əl·ə·zā′shən, n.

de·na·ture, dē·nā′chər, v.t., **-tured, -tur·ing.** To change the nature of; to render unfit for human consumption, without impairing usefulness for other purposes, as alcohol.

den·drite, den′drit, n. A hairlike, branching process of a neuron which conducts impulses toward the nerve cell body.

de·ni·al, di·ni′əl, n. The act of denying.

de·ni·er, di·ni′ər, n. One who denies.

den·im, den′əm, n. A heavy, twilled cotton fabric used for overalls, etc.

den·i·zen, den′ə·zən, n. An inhabitant; one who frequents a place; a foreign person or thing adapted to a new place or condition.—v.t. To make (one) a denizen of; to naturalize.

de·nom·i·nate, di·nom′ə·nāt, v.t., **-nat·ed, -nat·ing.** To give a name to; name.

de·nom·i·na·tion, di·nom·ə·nā′shən, n. A name for a class of things; a collection or society, esp. a religious sect; one of the grades or degrees in a series of designations: money of small denomination. —**de·nom·i·na·tion·al,** a. —**de·nom·i·na·tion·al·ism,** n.

de·nom·i·na·tive, di·nom′ə·nā·tiv, di·nom′ə·nə·tiv, a. Conferring a distinctive name; appellative; formed from a substantive or an adjective, as a denominative verb.—n. A denominative word.

de·nom·i·na·tor, di·nom′ə·nā·tər, n. That term of a fraction, usually written under the line, which shows the number of equal parts into which the unit is divided.

de·note, di·nōt′, v.t., **de·not·ed, de·not·ing.** To stand as a symbol for; to indicate; to be a name for; designate; to mean, esp. to mean in a literal sense, without implication or connotation. —**de·no·ta·tion,** dē·nō·tā′shən, n.

de·noue·ment, dā·noo·män′, n. The final disentangling of the intricacies of a plot, as of a drama or novel; the final outcome.

de·nounce, di·nowns′, v.t., **de·nounced, de·noun·cing.** To condemn openly; assail with censure; to announce threateningly; to make formal accusation against; accuse; of treaties, etc., to give formal notice of the termination of. —**de·nounce·ment,** n. —**de·nun·ci·a·tion,** di·nən·sē·ā′shən, n. —**de·nun·ci·a·to·ry,** di·nən′sē·ə·tôr·ē, a.

dense, dens, a., **den·ser, den·sest.** Closely compacted together; compact; obtuse or stupid. —**dense·ly,** adv. —**dense·ness,** n.

den·si·ty, den′si·tē, n. pl., **-ties.** The state or quality of being dense; compactness; thickness; stupidity; the amount of matter per unit of volume.

dent, dent, *n.* A hollow or depression, as from a blow.—*v.t.* To make a dent in.—*v.i.* To become indented.

den•tal, den′təl, *a.* Of or pertaining to the teeth; of or pertaining to dentistry; of speech sounds, formed by placing the tip of the tongue against or near the upper front teeth.—*n.* A dental sound.

den•tal floss, *n.* A soft thread used to clean between teeth.

den•tate, den′tāt, *a.* Toothed; notched.

den•ti•frice, den′tə•fris, *n.* A powder, paste, or liquid for cleaning the teeth.

den•tin, den′tən, den′tin, *n.* The hard, calcareous tissue composing the greater part of the tooth. Also **den•tine,** den′tēn.

den•tist, den′tist, *n.* A doctor who practices dentistry.

den•tist•ry, den′ti•strē, *n.* That profession which deals with the diagnosis, prevention, and treatment of any disease affecting the teeth and their related structures.

den•ti•tion, den•tish′ən, *n.* Teething; the tooth system, including number, kind, and arrangement.

den•ture, den′chər, *n.* A set of teeth, or esp. of artificial teeth.

de•nude, di•nood′, di•nūd′, *v.t.,* **de•nud•ed, de•nud•ing.** To make bare; to strip; to lay (rock, etc.) bare by an erosive process. —**den•u•da•tion,** den•yû•dā′shən, dē•nû•dā′shən, *n.*

de•nun•ci•ate, di•nən′sē•āt, *v.t., v.i.,* **-at•ed, -at•ing.** To denounce. —**de•nun•ci•a•tion,** di•nən•sē•ā′shən, *n.* —**de•nun•ci•a•to•ry,** *a.*

de•ny, di•nī′, *v.t.,* **de•nied, de•ny•ing.** To declare not to be true; to refuse to believe; reject as erroneous; to refuse to recognize; disavow. —**deny oneself,** to exercise self-denial.

de•o•dor•ant, dē•ō′dər•ənt, *n.* An agent for destroying odors.—*a.* —**de•o•dor•ize,** *v.t.,* **-ized, -iz•ing.**

de•ox•y•ri•bo•nu•cle•ic ac•id, dē•ok•si•rī′bō•noo•klē′ik as′id. See **DNA.**

de•part, di•pärt′, *v.i.* To go or move away; to leave or desist, as from a practice; to forsake; to die.—*v.t.* To leave; to go away from.

de•part•ed, di•pär′tid, *a.* Gone; dead. —**the de•part•ed,** *n.* The dead person or persons.

de•part•ment, di•pärt′mənt, *n.* A division of a complex whole or organized system; one of the separate branches of a governmental organization; one of the sections of a retail store. —**de•part•men•tal,** di•pärt•men′təl, dē′pärt•men′təl, *a.*

de•par•ture, di•pär′chər, *n.* The act of departing; a going away; a divergence or deviation.

de•pend, di•pend′, *v.i.* To be controlled or conditioned (*on* or *upon*); to trust, or rely for support (*on* or *upon*). —**de•pend•ence, de•pend•ance,** *n.*

de•pend•a•ble, di•pen′də•bəl, *a.* Reliable; trustworthy. —**de•pend•a•bly,** *adv.* —**de•pend•a•bil•i•ty,** *n.*

de•pend•en•cy, de•pend•an•cy, di•pen′dən•sē, *n. pl.,* **-cies.** Dependence; a dependent thing or person; a territory separate from the state to which it belongs, but subject to its rule.

de•pend•ent, de•pend•ant, di•pen′dənt, *n.* One who is sustained by another, or who relies on another for support or favor.—*a.* Hanging down; controlled or conditioned by something else; relying on another for support; not used in isolation: a *dependent* clause.

de•pict, di•pikt′, *v.t.* To paint; to portray; to represent in words; to describe. —**de•pic•tion,** *n.*

de•pil•a•to•ry, di•pil′ə•tôr•ē, *n. pl.,* **-ries.** A cosmetic to remove superfluous hairs.—*a.* Having the power to remove hair.

de•plete, di•plēt′, *v.t.,* **de•plet•ed, de•plet•ing.** To decrease; reduce; exhaust; empty. —**de•ple•tion,** *n.*

de•plor•a•ble, di•plôr′ə•bəl, *a.* Lamentable; miserable; pitiable. —**de•plor•a•bly,** *adv.*

de•plore, di•plôr′, *v.t.,* **de•plored, de•plor•ing.** To feel or express deep grief for; to lament.

de•ploy, di•ploy′, *v.t., v.i.* To spread out, as troops, so as to form an extended front; arrange in formation. —**de•ploy•ment,** *n.*

de•po•nent, di•pō′nənt, *a.* Denoting a verb with a passive voice form, but active in meaning.—*n.* A deponent verb; one who gives written testimony under oath.

de•pop•u•late, dē•pop′yû•lāt, *v.t.,* **-lat•ed, -lat•ing.** To deprive of inhabitants. —**de•pop•u•la•tion,** dē•pop•yə•lā′shən, *n.*

de•port, di•pôrt′, di•pōrt′, *v.t.* To eject from a country under compulsory edict; to carry away; to conduct or behave, followed by *oneself.* —**de•por•ta•tion,** dē•pōr•tā′shən, dē•pôr•tā′shən, *n.*

de•port•ment, di•pôrt′mənt, *n.* Manner of acting; behavior; demeanor.

de•pose, di•pōz′, *v.t.,* **de•posed, de•pos•ing.** To remove from a throne or other high office; to testify under oath.—*v.i.* To give testimony under oath. —**de•pos•a•ble,** *a.*

de•pos•it, di•poz′it, *v.t.* To place or set down with care; to lay down or precipitate by natural processes; to entrust for safekeeping; to put down, as a pledge or partial payment.—*v.i.* To be put down, or precipitated. —*n.* That which is laid down; any matter laid down by natural processes; sediment; mineral masses, as oil or coal; anything entrusted to the care of another; a sum of money lodged in a bank; a pledge; a thing given as security or for part payment. —**de•pos•i•tor,** *n.*

dep•o•si•tion, dep•ə•zish′ən, dē•pə•zish′ən, *n.* A deposing; the process of depositing; a deposit; testimony under oath; such testimony, taken down in writing.

de•pos•i•to•ry, di•poz′ə•tôr•ē, di•poz′ə•tôr•ē, *n.* A place where or person to whom anything is entrusted for safekeeping.

de•pot, dē′pō, dep′ō, *n.* A railroad station; a depository; a warehouse, esp. for military supplies; a station; a station where recruits are received and drilled.

de•prave, di•prāv′, *v.t.,* **de•praved, de•prav•ing.** To make bad or worse; to vitiate; to corrupt; to pervert. —**de•praved,** *a.* —**de•prav•i•ty,** di•prav′ə•tē, *n. pl.,* **-ties.**

dep•re•cate, dep′rə•kāt, *v.t.,* **-cat•ed, -cat•ing.** To plead earnestly against; to express strong disapproval of. —**dep•re•cat•ing•ly,** *adv.* —**dep•re•ca•tion,** dep•rə•kā′shən, *n.*

dep•re•ca•to•ry, dep′rə•kə•tôr′ē, dep′rə•kə•tôr′ē, *a.* Expressing deprecation; apologetic.

de•pre•ci•ate, di•prē′shē•āt, *v.t.,* **-at•ed, -at•ing.** To bring down the price or value of; to cause to be less valuable; to represent as of little value; belittle; disparage; undervalue.—*v.i.* To fall in value. —**de•pre•ci•a•tion,** di•prē•shē•ā′shən, *n.* —**de•pre•ci•a•to•ry,** *a.* —**de•pre•ci•a•tor,** *n.*

dep•re•date, dep′rə•dāt, *v.t.,* **-dat•ed, -dat•ing.** To plunder; pillage; spoil. —**dep•re•da•tion,** dep•rə•dā′shən, *n.*

de•press, di•pres′, *v.t.* To press down; to lower; to render dull or languid; to make sad; to lower in value.

de•pres•sant, di•pres′ənt, *a.* Decreasing the vital activities.—*n.* A depressant substance; a sedative.

de•pressed, di•prest′, *a.* Dejected; dispirited; pressed down; lowered; suffering economic adversity. *Bot., zool.* Flattened in shape.

de•pres•sion, di•presh′ən, *n.* A low place or surface; the state of being depressed or act of depressing; low spirits; gloominess; a period of severely subnormal economic activity.

de·prive, di·prīv′, *v.t.,* **de·prived, de·priv·ing.** To divest of something; to keep from acquiring, doing, or using something. **—dep·ri·va·tion,** dep·rə·vā′shən, *n.*

depth, depth, *n.* The quality of being deep; measure or distance downward, inward, or backward; deepness; abstruseness; profundity of thought or feeling; intensity or richness; lowness of pitch; *often pl.,* the most remote, most central, most intense, or deepest part of something.

depth charge or **bomb,** *n.* A bomb which is dropped or thrown into the water and explodes at a predetermined depth.

dep·u·ta·tion, dep·yə·tā′shən, *n.* The act of deputing; the person or persons appointed to transact business for another.

de·pute, di·pūt′, *v.t.,* **de·put·ed, de·put·ing.** To appoint, as a substitute or agent, to act for another; to transfer authority to another.

dep·u·tize, dep′yə·tīz, *v.t.,* **-tized, -tiz·ing.** To appoint as deputy; depute.

dep·u·ty, dep′yə·tē, *n. pl.,* **-ties.** A person appointed to act for another or others; an authorized representative; a representative in certain legislative bodies.—*a.* Acting as deputy. **—dep·u·ty·ship,** *n.*

de·rail, dē·rāl′, *v.i.* Of a train, to run off the rails.—*v.t.* To cause to run off the rails. **—de·rail·ment,** *n.*

de·range, di·rānj′, *v.t.,* **de·ranged, de·rang·ing.** To disturb the arrangement or order of; to unsettle the reason of; make insane. **—de·ranged,** *a.* **—de·range·ment,** *n.*

Der·by, dûr′bē, *Brit.* där′bē, *n. pl.,* **Der·bies.** An annual horse race in England; any of several other annual horse races: the Kentucky *Derby; (l.c.)* a contest open to all; a stiff felt hat with rounded crown and narrow brim.

der·e·lict, der′ə·likt, *a.* Left or abandoned; neglectful of duty; delinquent.—*n.* One guilty of neglect of duty; a worthless or deserted person; a vessel abandoned at sea. **—der·e·lic·tion,** der·ə·lik′shən, *n.*

de·ride, di·rīd′, *v.t.,* **de·rid·ed, de·rid·ing.** To laugh at in contempt; mock; ridicule.

de·ri·sion, di·rizh′ən, *n.* The act of deriding, the object of deriding, or the state of being derided.

de·ri·sive, di·rī′siv, *a.* Mocking; ridiculing. **—de·ri·sive·ly,** *adv.* **—de·ri·so·ry,** *a.*

der·i·va·tion, der·ə·vā′shən, *n.* The act of deriving, or the fact of being derived; source or root; the tracing of the origin of a word; a statement or theory of such origin.

de·riv·a·tive, di·riv′ə·tiv, *a.* Derived; not original. —*n.* Something derived; a word derived from another word or from a root, stem, or the like; a compound obtained from a specified substance.

de·rive, di·rīv′, *v.t.,* **de·rived, de·riv·ing.** To draw or obtain from a source or origin; to take, as a word, from a particular source; to obtain, as one substance or compound, from another. To trace from a source or origin, as a custom or word; to obtain by reasoning; deduce.—*v.i.* To originate. **—de·riv·a·ble,** *a.*

der·ma, dûr′mə, *n.* The true skin, beneath the epidermis; the skin in general. **—der·mal,** *a.*

der·ma·tol·o·gy, dûr·mə·tol′ə·jē, *n.* The science of the skin and its diseases. **—der·ma·to·log·i·cal,** *a.* **—der·ma·tol·o·gist,** *n.*

der·mis, dûr′mis, *n.* Derma.

der·o·gate, der′ə·gāt, *v.t.,* **-gat·ed, -gat·ing.** To lessen the worth of; to disparage.—*v.i.* To detract; to lessen by taking away a part, used with *from.* **—der·o·ga·tion,** der·ə·gā′shən, *n.*

de·rog·a·to·ry, di·rog′ə·tōr′ē, *a.* Detracting; disparaging; stating a low estimation of. **—de·rog·a·to·ri·ly,** di·rog·ə·tōr′ə·lē, *adv.*

der·rick, der′ik, *n.* An apparatus for hoisting heavy weights, usually consisting of a boom with a tackle rigged at the end; a tower-like framework built over an oil well or deep drilling hole.

der·rin·ger, der′in·jər, *n.* A short-barreled pistol of large caliber.

der·vish, dûr′vish, *n.* A member of certain Muslim religious orders.

des·cant, des′kant, *n.* A melody or counterpoint accompanying a simple musical theme and usually written above it; in part-music, the soprano. **—des·cant′,** dis·kant′, *v.i.* To sing or play a melody in harmony with the chief melody; discourse at length.

de·scend, di·send′, *v.i.* To move from a higher to a lower place; to slope downward; to arrive in a multitude; to proceed from a source or origin; to pass from one heir to another; to move from the general to the particular, or the significant to the insignificant; to move toward the horizon; to lower or degrade oneself; to stoop.—*v.t.* To walk, move, or pass downward. **—de·scend·a·ble,** *a.*

de·scend·ant, di·sen′dənt, *n.* An individual proceeding from an ancestor in any degree; an offspring.

de·scend·ent, de·scend·ant, di·sen′dənt, *a.* Descending.

de·scent, di·sent′, *n.* The act of passing from a higher to a lower place; declivity; decline; ancestry; lineage; means of descending; a lowering of oneself.

de·scribe, di·skrīb′, *v.t.,* **de·scribed, de·scrib·ing.** To portray orally or in writing; to delineate or trace the form. **—de·scrib·a·ble,** *a.* **—de·scrib·er,** *n.*

de·scrip·tion, di·skrip′shən, *n.* The act of describing; delineation; sort or variety. **—de·scrip·tive,** *a.* **—de·scrip·tive·ly,** *adv.* **—de·scrip·tive·ness,** *n.*

de·scry, di·skrī′, *v.t.,* **de·scried, de·scry·ing.** To espy; see or behold from a distance.

des·e·crate, des′ə·krāt, *v.t.,* **-crat·ed, -crat·ing.** To divert from a sacred to a profane purpose; to profane. **—des·e·cra·tion,** des·ə·krā′shən, *n.*

de·seg·re·gate, dē·seg′rə·gāt, *v.t.,* **-gat·ed, -gat·ing.** To abolish racial segregation in.—*v.i.* **—de·seg·re·ga·tion,** dē·seg·rə·gā′shən, *n.*

des·ert, dez′ərt, *n.* A wilderness; a vast sandy or rocky expanse, almost destitute of moisture and vegetation; a region devoid of something: a spiritual *desert.*—*a.* Uncultivated and uninhabited; arid; barren.

de·sert, di·zərt′, *v.t.* To abandon or forsake; depart from; to leave in violation of duty.—*v.i.* To forsake one's duty; of military personnel, to leave the service without permission and without intention to return. **—de·sert·er,** *n.*

de·sert, di·zərt′, *n. Usu. pl.* Reward or punishment merited: He received his just *deserts.*

de·ser·tion, di·zər′shən, *n.* The act of deserting, esp. in violation of duty or obligation; the state of being deserted.

de·serve, di·zərv′, *v.t.,* **de·served, de·serv·ing.** To merit; to be worthy of, as reward or punishment, praise or censure.—*v.i.* To be deserving of. **—de·serv·ed·ly,** *adv.*

de·serv·ing, di·zər′ving, *a.* Worthy of reward or praise; meritorious.

des·ha·bille, dez·ə·bēl′, *n.* Dishabille.

des·ic·cate, des′ə·kāt, *v.t.,* **-cat·ed, -cat·ing.** To dry thoroughly; to preserve (foods, etc.) by drying.—*v.i.* To become dry. **—des·ic·ca·tion,** des·ə·kā′shən, *n.* **—des·ic·ca·tive,** *a.*

de·sid·er·a·tum, di·sid·ər·ā′təm, *n. pl.,* **-ta,** -tə. That which is desirable or needed.

de·sign, di·zīn′, *v.t.* To prepare the preliminary sketch or the plans for; to form in the mind; contrive; plan; contemplate; to intend.—*v.i.* To make drawings, preliminary sketches or plans; to have intentions or purposes.—*n.* An outline, sketch, or plan, as of a work of art, an edifice, or a machine; the combination of details or features, as of a picture, building or bridge; a piece of artistic work; the art of designing; intention; a plan; a scheme; a hostile plan or crafty intention; the object of a plan.

des·ig·nate, dez′ig·nāt, *v.t.,* **-nat·ed, -nat·ing.** To point out; indicate; specify; to name or entitle; to nominate for a duty or office; appoint. —dez′ig·nit, dez′ig·nāt, a. Nominated or appointed, but not yet installed. —**des·ig·na·tion**, dez·ig·nā′shən, n. —**des·ig·na·tive**, a. —**des·ig·na·tor**, n.

de·sign·ed·ly, dē·zīn′əd·lē, adv. Intentionally.

de·sign·er, di·zī′nər, n. One who designs; a contriver; a schemer or intriguer.

de·sign·ing, di·zī′ning, a. Scheming; artful.—n. The art of making designs.

de·sire, di·zīr′, v.t., **de·sired, de·sir·ing.** To wish or long for; crave sexually; want; to ask for, or request. —v.i. To have or feel a desire.—n. The fact or state of desiring; a longing or craving; a wish; sexual craving; lust; an expressed wish; a request; something or someone desired. —**de·sir·a·ble**, a. —**de·sir·a·bil·i·ty**, di·zī·rə·bil′ə·tē, n. —**de·sir·a·bly**, adv. —**de·sir·ous**, a.

de·sist, di·zist′, di·sist′, v.i. To cease; discontinue.

desk, desk, n. A table or similar piece of furniture, with a usu. level surface for reading, writing, or drawing, and often with drawers and compartments; a pulpit; a department of an organization; a stand or counter.

des·o·late, des′ə·lāt, v.t., -**lat·ed, -lat·ing.** To make unfit for habitation; lay waste; to deprive of inhabitants; to render disconsolate; to forsake. —des′ə·lit, a. Dreary; barren; devastated; deserted; lonely; miserable. —**des·o·late·ly**, adv. —**des·o·la·tion**, des·ə·lā′shən, n.

des·ox·y·ri·bo·nu·cle·ic ac·id, des·ok′si·rī·bō·noo·klē′ik as′id, n. DNA.

de·spair, di·spâr′, v.i. To give up all hope or be without hope (with of).—n. Hopelessness; that which causes despair. —**de·spair·ing**, a. —**de·spair·ing·ly**, adv.

des·per·a·do, des·pə·rä′dō, des·pə·rā′dō, n. pl., -**does, -dos.** A fearless, reckless criminal.

des·per·ate, des′pər·it, a. Without hope; reduced to extremity and reckless of consequences; frantic; irretrievable; past cure; excessive; intense. —**des·per·ate·ly**, adv. —**des·per·ate·ness**, n. —**des·per·a·tion**, des·pə·rā′shən, n.

des·pi·ca·ble, des′pi·kə·bəl, di·spik′ə·bəl, a. Deserving of being despised; contemptible. —**des·pi·ca·bly**, adv.

de·spise, di·spīz′, v.t., **de·spised, de·spis·ing.** To have the lowest opinion of; scorn.

de·spite, di·spīt′, n. Extreme malice; contemptuous hate; an act of spite or contempt.—prep. In spite of.

de·spoil, di·spoyl′, v.t. To take from by force; to rob. —**de·spoil·er**, n. —**de·spo·li·a·tion**, di·spō·lē·ā′shən, n.

de·spond, di·spond′, v.i. To lose heart, courage, or hope; become depressed. —**de·spond·en·cy**, n. —**de·spond·ence**, n. —**de·spond·ent**, a. —**de·spond·ent·ly**, adv.

des·pot, des′pət, des′pot, n. An absolute ruler; autocrat; tyrant. —**des·pot·ic**, di·spot′ik, a. —**des·pot·i·cal·ly**, adv.

des·pot·ism, des′pə·tiz·əm, n. The exercise of absolute authority; tyranny; an absolute or autocratic form of government.

des·sert, di·zərt′, n. A dish served at the end of a meal, such as ice cream, pastry, or fruit.

des·ti·na·tion, des·tə·nā′shən, n. The predetermined end of a journey or voyage; the purpose for which anything is intended.

des·tine, des′tin, v.t., -**tined, -tin·ing.** To ordain beforehand; to set aside; design; intend. —**destined for**, foreordained, intended, or bound for.

des·ti·ny, des′tə·nē, n. pl., -**nies.** That which is predetermined to happen; fate; one's lot or fortune.

des·ti·tute, des′ti·toot, des′ti·tūt, a. Not having; lacking (with of); not possessing the necessities of life; in abject poverty. —**des·ti·tu·tion**, des·ti·

de·stroy, di·stroy′, v.t. To knock to pieces; to ruin; to annihilate; to put an end to; to kill; to ravage; to make ineffective or neutral.

de·stroy·er, di·stroy′ər, n. One who or that which destroys; a small, swift class of naval vessel, intended for the destruction of torpedo craft and for escort duty.

de·struc·tion, di·strək′shən, n. The act of destroying; the state of being destroyed; demolition; ruin; cause or means of destroying. —**de·struct·i·ble**, a. —**de·struct·i·bil·i·ty**, di·strək·tə·bil′ə·tē, n.

de·struc·tive, di·strək′tiv, a. Causing destruction; having a tendency to destroy; tearing down; not helpful. —**de·struc·tive·ly**, adv. —**de·struc·tive·ness**, n.

des·ue·tude, des′wi·tood, des′wi·tūd, n. Disuse.

des·ul·to·ry, des′əl·tōr·ē, des′əl·tôr·ē, a. Passing from one thing to another without order or natural connection; rambling; aimless. —**des·ul·to·ri·ly**, adv.

de·tach, di·tach′, v.t. To unfasten and separate; disengage; disunite. Milit. To send away on a special mission. —**de·tach·a·ble**, a.

de·tached, di·tacht′, a. Separated or disengaged; unattached; impartial.

de·tach·ment, di·tach′mənt, n. Separation; a state of aloofness; impartiality; a number of troops separated for special service.

de·tail, di·tāl′, v.t. To relate in particulars; to enumerate. Milit. To appoint to a particular duty. —di·tāl′, dē′tāl, n. An item; a particular; the treatment of particulars; a minor or secondary element of a painting, building, etc. Milit. A small detachment on special duty. —**in detail**, item by item. —**de·tailed**, di·tāld′, dē′tāld, a.

de·tain, di·tān′, v.t. To keep or restrain from proceeding; to hinder; to hold in custody. —**de·tain·ment**, n. —**de·tain·er**, n.

de·tect, di·tekt′, v.t. To discover or catch in the performance of some act; to find out; discover the existence of. Radio. To subject to the action of a detector. —**de·tect·a·ble, de·tect·i·ble**, a. —**de·tec·tion**, n.

de·tec·tive, di·tek′tiv, n. A police official or private individual whose function is to detect and investigate crimes, gather evidence, etc.—a. Pertaining to detection or detectives.

de·tec·tor, di·tek′tər, n. One who or that which detects; a device which rectifies the alternating currents in a radio receiver.

dé·tente, dā·tänt′, n. pl., **dé·tentes.** A thaw in tension, as between two countries; a lessening of hostility.

de·ten·tion, di·ten′shən, n. The act of detaining, or the state of being detained; confinement.

de·ter, di·tər′, v.t., **de·terred, de·ter·ring.** To discourage or intimidate and thereby prevent from acting or proceeding.

de·ter·gent, di·tər′jənt, a. Cleansing.—n. A cleansing agent.

de·te·ri·o·rate, di·tēr′ē·ə·rāt, v.i., v.t., -**rat·ed, -rat·ing.** To grow or make worse; depreciate. —**de·te·ri·o·ra·tion**, di·tēr·ē·ə·rā′shən, n.

de·ter·mi·na·ble, di·tər′mə·nə·bəl, a. Capable of being determined.

de·ter·mi·nant, di·tər′mə·nənt, n. That which determines.

de·ter·mi·nate, di·tər′mə·nit, a. Limited; fixed; definite; established; positive; fixed in purpose; resolute.

de·ter·mi·na·tion, di·tər·mə·nā′shən, n. The act of deciding; firm resolution; resoluteness; the act of establishing or verifying something after careful examination; conclusion; decision; the fixing of the position, amount, etc., of anything; an inclination or proceeding toward a particular end. —**de·ter·mi·na·**

---

tive, di·tėr'mə·nā·tiv, di·tėr'mə·nə·tiv, *a., n.*

de·ter·mine, di·tėr'min, *v.t.* **-mined, -min·ing.** To settle, fix, establish; to settle conclusively, ultimately, or beforehand; to set bounds or limits to; to give a bent or direction to; to cause to come to a conclusion or resolution; to ascertain; to regulate; to influence. *Law.* To bring to an end.—*v.i.* To resolve; to decide. **—de·ter·min·er,** *n.*

de·ter·mined, di·tėr'mind, *a.* Firm; resolute. **—de·ter·mined·ly,** *adv.*

de·ter·min·ism, di·tėr'mə·niz·əm, *n.* The doctrine that all existences and happenings, including human behavior, are the inevitable outcome of preceding conditions. **—de·ter·min·ist,** *n., a.*

de·ter·rent, di·tėr'ənt, *a.* Deterring; restraining.—*n.* Something that deters; known military strength, weaponry or retaliatory capacity sufficient to restrain a potential aggressor. **—de·ter·rence,** *n.*

de·test, di·test', *v.t.* To abhor; hate extremely. **—de·test·a·ble,** *a.* **—de·test·a·bly,** *adv.*

de·tes·ta·tion, dē·te·stā'shən, *n.* Extreme hatred; a person or thing loathed.

de·throne, dē·thrōn', *v.t.* **de·throned, de·thron·ing.** To remove from a throne; depose. **—de·throne·ment,** *n.*

det·o·nate, det'ə·nāt, *v.i., v.t.* **-nat·ed, -nat·ing.** To explode suddenly and violently. **—det·o·na·tion,** de·tə·nā'shən, *n.* **—det·o·na·tor,** *n.*

de·tour, dē'tûr, di·tûr', *n.* The use of an alternate road when a more direct road is impassable; a roundabout way.—*v.i., v.t.* To make or cause to make a detour.

de·tract, di·trakt', *v.t.* To divert or distract; take away.—*v.i.* To take away a part; lessen (with *from*). **—de·trac·tion,** di·trak'shən, *n.* **—de·trac·tor,** *n.*

det·ri·ment, de'trə·ment, *n.* Loss, damage, or injury; that which causes loss, damage, or injury. **—det·ri·men·tal,** de·trə·men'təl, *a.* **—det·ri·men·tal·ly,** *adv.*

de·tri·tus, di·trī'təs, *n.* Rock fragments or other material worn away from a mass.

deuce, doos, dūs, *n.* In card games or dice, two; a card, or the side of a die, having two spots. *Tennis.* A tie score at 40 points each in a game.

deuce, doos, dūs, *n. Informal.* The devil: used in mild imprecations.

deu·te·ri·um, doo·tēr'ē·əm, dū·tēr'ē·əm, *n.* A nonradioactive isotope of hydrogen that has twice the mass of ordinary hydrogen. Also **heav·y hy·dro·gen.**

de·val·u·ate, dē·val'ū·āt, *v.t.,* **-at·ed, -at·ing.** To reduce the value of. **—de·val·u·a·tion,** dē·val·ū·ā'shən, *n.*

dev·as·tate, dev'ə·stāt, *v.t.,* **-tat·ed, -tat·ing.** To lay waste; ravage; desolate. *Informal.* To overwhelm; crush. **—dev·as·ta·tion,** dev·ə·stā'shən, *n.* **—dev·as·ta·ting,** *a.*

de·vel·op, di·vel'əp, *v.t.* To gradually acquire; to bring about growth or enlargement; to cause to become active; to unfold gradually; to disclose or show all the ramifications of; to alter or elaborate on, as a musical theme. *Photog.* To bring out the latent image on a sensitized surface by the action of chemical agents;—*v.i.* To advance from one stage to another; evolve; to increase capabilities and become more mature; to be disclosed; to become manifest. **—de·vel·op·ment,** *n.*

de·vel·op·er, di·vel'ə·pər, *n.* One who or that which develops; a chemical used to develop photographs; an individual who invests in and develops real estate.

de·vi·ate, dē'vē·āt, *v.i.,* **-at·ed, -at·ing.** To turn aside or wander from the common or right way, course, or line; to diverge.—*v.t.* To cause to deviate. —dē'vē·it, *n.* A person differing markedly from the standards of his group. Also **de·vi·ant.** **—de·vi·a·tion,** dē·vē·ā'shən, *n.*

de·vice, di·vīs', *n.* That which is formed by design or invented for a specific use; a scheme, contrivance, machine; an ornamental design; an emblematic de-

sign, such as a family or institutional crest; motto; *usu. pl.,* desire or inclination: He would be an artist, if left to his own *devices.*

dev·il, dev'əl, *n.* An evil spirit or being; demon; (*sometimes cap.*) Satan; a very wicked person; a dashing, somewhat reckless, mischievous, very clever, or energetic person; an unfortunate, wretched person; a printer's errand boy.—*interj.* An exclamation of anger, annoyance, etc. (with *the*). —*v.t.,* **-iled, -il·ling.** To season food highly. *Informal.* To tease or pester. **—dev·il·ment,** *n.* **—dev·il·try,** *n. pl.,* **-tries. —dev·il·ry,** *n.*

dev·il·ish, dev'əl·ish, *a.* Having qualities of the devil; daring; diabolical; mischievous; excessive; extreme. —*adv.* **—dev·il·ish·ly,** *adv.* **—dev·il·ish·ness,** *n.*

dev·il·may·care, dev'əl·mā·kâr', *a.* Reckless; happy-go-lucky; jaunty.

dev·il's ad·vo·cate, *n.* One who defends an opposing or worse position in order to stimulate argument.

de·vi·ous, dē'vē·əs, *a.* Circuitous or indirect; rambling; going astray; deceptive. **—de·vi·ous·ly,** *adv.* **—de·vi·ous·ness,** *n.*

de·vise, di·vīz', *v.t.,* **de·vised, de·vis·ing.** To invent, contrive; to plan; to scheme; to give or bequeath, esp. real estate, by will.—*v.i.* To form a scheme. —*n. Law.* the act of bequeathing real property by will; the will itself; a share of an estate bequeathed. **—de·vis·a·ble,** *a.* **—de·vis·al,** *n.* **—de·vi·see,** di·vī·zē', *n.* **—de·vi·sor,** di·vī'zər, *n.*

de·void, di·voyd', *a.* Void (of).

de·volve, di·volv', *v.t.,* **de·volved, de·volv·ing.** To transfer or delegate, as a duty or responsibility, to another; to pass on; to hand down.—*v.i.* To be transferred or handed down. **—dev·o·lu·tion,** *n.*

de·vote, di·vōt', *v.t.,* **de·vot·ed, de·vot·ing.** To give (one's complete attention) or to apply (one's time) zealously to some activity, pursuit, or cause; to dedicate; to consecrate.

de·vot·ed, di·vō'tid, *a.* Loyal; faithful; dedicated. **—de·vot·ed·ly,** *adv.*

dev·o·tee, dev·ə·tē', *n.* One who is wholly devoted, as to a religion or mentor.

de·vo·tion, di·vō'shən, *n.* The act of devoting, or the state of being devoted; dedication; consecration; zealousness in religious observance; deep attachment; loyalty; faithfulness. *Usually pl.* An act of worship or prayer. **—de·vo·tion·al,** *a., n.*

de·vour, di·vowr', *v.t.* To eat up voraciously; to consume wantonly; to destroy or waste; swallow up or engulf; take in greedily with the senses or intellect; to absorb wholly. **—de·vour·er,** *n.* **—de·vour·ing·ly,** *adv.*

de·vout, di·vowt', *a.* Expressing religious devotion or piety; warmly devoted; sincere; earnest. **—de·vout·ly,** *adv.* **—de·vout·ness,** *n.*

dew, doo, dū, *n.* The moisture which is deposited in small drops, especially during the night, on the surfaces of bodies when they have become colder than the surrounding atmosphere; something resembling, or fresh as dew.—*v.t.* To wet with dew; moisten.

dew·ber·ry, doo'ber·ē, dū'ber·ē, *n. pl.,* **-ries.** The fruit of any of several species of trailing blackberries; the plant bearing such fruit.

dew·drop, doo'drop, *n.* A drop of dew.

dew·lap, doo'lap, dū'lap, *n.* The fold of skin that hangs from the throat of oxen, cows, etc.

dew point, *n.* The temperature at which dew forms or vapor condenses.

dew·y, doo'ē, dū'ē, *a.,* **-i·er, -i·est.** Of dew; like dew; moist with or as with dew; refreshing like dew. **—dew·i·ness,** *n.*

dew·y-eyed, doo'ē·īd, dū'ē·īd, *a.* Showing youthful innocence and idealism; naïve.

dex·ter·ous, dek'strəs, dek'stər·əs, *a.* Having skill with the hands, or with the body; deft; nimble; mentally adroit; clever. Also **dex·trous. —dex·ter·i·ty,** dek·ster'ə·tē, *n.* **—dex·ter·ous·ly,** *adv.*

dex·trose, dek′strōs, *n.* A sugar found in many plants, a form of glucose.

di·a·be·tes, dī·ə·bē′tis, dī·ə·bē′tēz, *n.* A disease. **di·a·be·tes mel·li·tus,** mə·lī′təs, marked by excessive sugar in the blood. **—di·a·bet·ic,** dī·ə·bet′ik, dī·ə·bē′tik, *a., n.*

di·a·bol·ic, dī·ə·bol′ik, *a.* Devilish; pertaining to the devil; infernal; impious; atrocious. Also **di·a·bol·i·cal.** **—di·a·bol·i·cal·ly,** *adv.*

di·a·crit·ic, dī·ə·krit′ik, *a.* Diacritical.—*n.* A diacritical mark.

di·a·crit·i·cal, dī·ə·krit′ə·kəl, *a.* Distinctive; distinguishing. **—di·a·crit·i·cal·ly,** *adv.*

di·a·crit·i·cal mark, *n.* A symbol put adjacent to a letter, to distinguish it from another, to give it a particular phonetic value, etc.

di·a·dem, dī′ə·dem, *n.* A crown.

di·ag·nose, dī′əg·nōs, dī′əg·nōz, *v.t.,* **-nosed, -nos·ing.** To ascertain the cause, as of a disease, by studying symptoms; to determine the nature or cause, as of a malfunction or problem, by means of examination and analysis. **—di·ag·no·sis,** dī·əg·nō′sis, *n. pl.,* **-ses,** -sēz. **—di·ag·nos·tic,** dī·əg·nos′tik, *a.* **—di·ag·nos·ti·cian,** dī·əg·nos·tish′ən, *n.*

di·ag·o·nal, dī·ag′ə·nəl, *a.* Extending from one angle to the opposite, or one corner to the opposite, esp. in a quadrilateral figure; lying in an oblique direction.—*n.* A diagonal line; anything running diagonally. **—di·ag·o·nal·ly,** *adv.*

di·a·gram, dī′ə·gram, *n.* A figure, drawing, outline, plan, etc., of a geometrical figure, an area, or the structure or operation of something.—*v.t.,* **-gramed, -gram·ing** or **-grammed, -gram·ming.** To describe or represent by a diagram. **—di·a·gram·mat·ic,** dī·ə·grə·mat′ik, *a.* Also **di·a·gram·mat·i·cal.**

di·al, dī′əl, dīl, *n.* The face of a watch, clock, or other timekeeper, such as a sundial; any usually circular plate or face with graduations on which a pointer moves to indicate a measurement; a rotating disk for electrical connection and/or regulation of a device. —*v.t.,* **di·aled, di·al·ing.** To indicate with a dial; to regulate by turning a dial; to call by means of a dial telephone.

di·a·lect, dī′ə·lekt, *n.* A form of a language prevailing in a particular district and marked by peculiarities of vocabulary or pronunciation; one of a number of languages regarded as a family; a form of language characteristic of a particular profession or trade. **—di·a·lec·tal,** dī·ə·lek′təl, *a.*

di·a·lec·tic, dī·ə·lek′tik, *a.* Pertaining to logical argumentation; dialectal. Also **di·a·lec·ti·cal.**—*n.* The art or practice of logical discussion; *often pl.,* logic or a branch of it. **—di·a·lec·ti·cian,** dī·ə·lek·tish′ən, *n.*

di·a·logue, dī′ə·lôg, dī′ə·log, *n.* A conversation between two or more persons; a conversation in theatrical performances; a composition in which two or more persons are represented as conversing.

di·am·e·ter, dī·am′ə·tər, *n.* A straight line passing from one side to the other through the center of a circle or other curvilinear figure; the length of such a line.

di·a·met·ric, dī·ə·met′rik, *a.* Of or having to do with diameter; directly opposed: *diametric* views. Also, **di·a·met·ri·cal.** **—di·a·met·ri·cal·ly,** *adv.*

dia·mond, dī′ə·mənd, dī′mənd, *n.* A naturally crystallized, nearly pure carbon, important to industry because it is the hardest substance known; a clear, flawless piece of this stone, valued as a precious gem; a four-sided figure with the sides equal or nearly so, and having two ootuse and two acute angles; a lozenge; a red, lozenge-shaped mark on a playing card, or a card so marked; *pl.,* the suit of cards so marked; a type of small size, 4½ point. *Baseball.* The infield or entire playing field.—*a.* Resembling or made of diamonds.—*v.t.* To ornament with, or as if, with diamonds.

dia·per, dī′ə·pər, dī′pər, *n.* A soft, absorbent cloth used as a breechcloth for infants too young to be toilet-trained.—*v.t.* To put a diaper on.

di·aph·a·nous, dī·af′ə·nəs, *a.* Transparent or translucent, as filmy fabric; ethereal.

di·a·phragm, dī′ə·fram, *n.* A partition or septum; a plate with a circular hole, used in cameras and optical instruments; a vibrating disk in a telephone; the partition separating the chest cavity from the abdominal cavity in mammals; a device placed over the uterine cervix for contraception.—*v.t.* To furnish or act upon with a diaphragm.

di·ar·rhe·a, dī·ə·rē·ə, *n.* Abnormally frequent and fluid evacuation of the bowels. Also **di·ar·rhoe·a.**

di·a·ry, dī′ə·rē, *n. pl.,* **-ries.** A daily record, esp. of the writer's own experiences or observations; a book for keeping such a record. **—di·a·rist,** *n.*

di·as·to·le, dī·as′tə·lē, *n.* The normal rhythmical dilatation of the heart, esp. that of the ventricles, after each contraction; the lengthening of a syllable regularly short. **—di·as·tol·ic,** dī·ə·stol′ik, *a.*

di·a·ther·mic, dī·ə·thər′mik, *a.* Transmitting radiant heat; relating to diathermy.

di·a·ther·my, dī′ə·thər·mē, *n.* The generation of heat in tissues by electric current, esp. for surgical purposes.

di·a·tom, dī′ə·təm, dī′ə·tom, *n.* Any of numerous microscopic, one-celled marine or fresh-water algae, whose walls contain silica.

di·a·ton·ic, dī·ə·ton′ik, *a. Mus.* Pertaining to the chords and intervals of the standard major or minor scales.

di·a·tribe, dī′ə·trīb, *n.* An abusive, bitter harangue.

dib·ble, dib′əl, *n.* A pointed instrument used to make holes for planting seeds or bulbs.—*v.t.,* **-bled, -bling.** To plant or dig with a dibble.

dice, dīs, *n. pl., sing.* **die.** Small cubes whose sides are marked with different numbers of spots from one to six, used in games; the game played; any small cubes. —*v.i.,* **-diced, dicing.** To play at dice.—*v.t.* To cut into small cubes. **—no dice,** *Informal.* No; any refusal; in vain.

di·chot·o·my, dī·kot′ə·mē, *n. pl.,* **-mies.** Division into two parts; a mode of branching by constant bifurcation. **—di·chot·o·mous,** *a.* **—di·cho·tom·ic,** dī·kə·tom′ik, *a.*

dick·ens, dik′ənz, *interj.* Devil: Where the *dickens* is my hat?

dick·er, dik′ər, *v.i.* To bargain; to haggle.—*v.t.* To trade with haggling.—*n.* A bargain.

dick·ey, dick·y, dick·ie, dik′ē, *n. pl.,* **dick·eys, dick·ies.** A detachable shirt front, esp. for men's formal dress.

Dic·ta·phone, dik′tə·fōn, *n. Trademark.* A machine which records verbal dictation for later playback and transcription.

dic·tate, dik′tāt, dik·tāt′, *v.t.,* **-tat·ed, -tat·ing.** To deliver or enounce with authority; give orders; to utter or read aloud for a person or a machine to record. —*v.i.* To say aloud, as in giving dictation; to give orders. —dik′tāt, *n.* An order delivered; a command; a rule or precept. **—dic·ta·tion,** dik·tā′shən, *n.*

dic·ta·tor, dik′tā·tər, dik·tā′tər, *n.* A person exercising absolute authority, esp. in government; one who dictates. **—dic·ta·tor·ship,** *n.*

dic·ta·to·ri·al, dik·tə·tôr′ē·əl, *a.* Of or pertaining to a dictator; imperious; overbearing. **—dic·ta·to·ri·al·ly,** *adv.*

dic·tion, dik′shən, *n.* A person's selection of words in speaking or writing; one's manner of voicing sounds in speaking; enunciation.

dic·tion·ar·y, dik′shə·ner·ē, *n. pl.,* **-ar·ies.** A book containing alphabetically arranged words of a language or branch of knowledge, along with explanations of their meanings and other information; a lexicon.

dic·tum, dik'təm, *n. pl.,* **-tums, -ta,** -tə. An authoritative utterance or pronouncement; a saying or maxim.

did, did, *v.t.* Past tense of do.

di·dac·tic, dī·dak'tik, *a.* Intended to instruct; tending to lecture; pedantic. Also **di·dac·ti·cal.** —**di·dac·ti·cal·ly,** *adv.*

did·dle, did'əl, *v.t.,* **-dled, -dling.** *Informal.* To cheat. —*v.i. Informal.* To dawdle.

did·n't, did'ənt. Contraction of did not.

die, dī, *v.i.,* **died, dy·ing.** To cease to live. To cease to exist; come to an end. To become extinct, with *off* or *out;* to pass gradually away or fade away; lose force, strength, or active qualities, often with *away, down,* or *out;* to cease to function; stop; to suffer pain or mental anguish. *Informal.* To desire greatly; to faint; to fail; to lose virginal life.

die, dī, *n. pl.,* **dice.** One of a set of dice.—*n. pl.,* **dies.** Any of various hard, metal devices for cutting, stamping, or shaping material.—*v.t.,* **died, die·ing.** To shape with a die. —**the die is cast.** The decision, or course of action, is irrevocable.

di·e·cious, dī·ē'shəs, *a.* Dioccious.

die-hard, dī'härd, *n.* One who resists to the last.—*a.* Obstinate; stubbornly conservative. Also **die·hard.**

di·e·lec·tric, dī·ə·lek'trik, *n.* A nonconducting or insulating material.—*a.*

di·er·e·sis, dī·er'ə·sis, *n. pl.,* **-ses,** -sēz. Separation of one syllable into two; a mark which signifies such a division, as the umlaut in *naïve,* usu. used to separate the pronunciation of two adjacent vowels. Also **di·aer·e·sis.**

die·sel en·gine, dē'zəl, *n. (Sometimes cap.)* A type of internal-combustion engine in which the fuel oil is ignited in the cylinder by the high temperature of compressed air.

die·sink·er, dī'sing·kər, *n.* An engraver of dies for coins, etc. —**die·sink·ing,** *n.*

di·et, dī'it, *n.* A person or an animal's regular food and drink; food and drink chosen for health reasons, and esp. to lose weight.—*v.i.* To eat according to a diet. —**di·et·er,** *n.*

di·et, dī'it, *n.* An assembly of dignitaries or delegates; session; *(often cap.)* the legislative or administrative assemblies of certain countries.

di·e·tar·y, dī'i·ter·ē, *a.* Pertaining to diet or the rules of diet.—*n. pl.,* **-tar·ies.**

di·e·tet·ic, dī·i·tet'ik, *a.* Pertaining to diet. Also **di·e·tet·i·cal.** —**di·e·tet·i·cal·ly,** *adv.*

di·e·tet·ics, dī·i·tet'iks, *n. pl.* The science of planning and regulating feeding according to nutritional principles.

di·e·ti·cian, dī·i·tish'ən, *n.* One skilled in dietetics; one who arranges diets.

dif·fer, dif'ər, *v.i.* To be unlike, dissimilar, or various (often with *from*); to disagree.

dif·fer·ence, dif'ər·əns, dif'rəns, *n.* The state of being different; an instance of dissimilarity; a point in which things differ; a distinguishing characteristic; distinction; an important effect on a state of affairs, used with *make:* it *makes a difference;* a disagreement in opinion; a dispute; the degree or amount by which one thing differs from another; the remainder in subtraction.—*v.t.,* **-enced, -enc·ing.** To make different.

dif·fer·ent, dif'ər·ənt, dif'rənt, *a.* Of various natures; unlike; dissimilar; separate; various; unusual; novel. —**dif·fer·ent·ly,** *adv.*

dif·fer·en·tial, dif·ə·ren'shəl, *a.* Of or pertaining to difference or diversity; showing a difference; distinguishing; distinctive; pertaining to distinguishing characteristics.—*n.* A differential duty or rate; the difference involved; a differential gear which allows for the difference in speed of two driving wheels. —**dif·fer·en·tial·ly,** *adv.*

dif·fer·en·ti·ate, dif·ə·ren'shē·āt, *v.t.,* **-at·ed, -at·ing.** To distinguish; alter; make different by modification, as a biological species; to obtain the differential of.—*v.i.* To become different or specialized; to discriminate. —**dif·fer·en·ti·a·tion,** dif·ə·ren·shē·ā'shən, *n.*

dif·fi·cult, dif'ə·kəlt, *a.* Hard to make, do, or perform; hard to understand; hard to please; stubborn. —**dif·fi·cult·ly,** *adv.*

dif·fi·cul·ty, dif'ə·kəl·tē, *n. pl.,* **-ties.** The state or quality of being difficult; that which is hard to do; obstacle; perplexity; *usu. pl.,* trouble, esp. financial. A problem; an objection; a controversy; a quarrel.

dif·fi·dence, dif'i·dəns, *n.* Lack of self-confidence; modest reserve. —**dif·fi·dent,** *a.* —**dif·fi·dent·ly,** *adv.*

dif·fuse, di·fūz', *v.t.,* **-fused, -fus·ing.** To pour out and cause to spread, as a fluid; to distribute; disseminate; to spread by or subject to.—*v.i.* To become diffused.—di·fūs', *a.* Widely spread; lacking conciseness; verbose. —**dif·fuse·ly,** di·fūs'lē, *adv.* —**dif·fuse·ness,** *n.* —**dif·fu·sion,** di·fū'zhen, *n.* —**dif·fu·sive·ly,** *adv.* —**dif·fu·sive·ness,** *n.*

dig, dig, *v.t.,* **dug, dig·ging.** To break up, turn, or remove, as with a spade or other sharp instrument; to excavate; to form by digging; to raise from the earth by digging; to jab, thrust, or drive. *Informal.* To understand; to like.—*v.i.* To work with a spade or other similar instrument; to work one's way by or as by digging; to search through. *Informal.* To study hard; plod.—*n. Informal.* A sharp poke; an unkind remark; the site of an archaeological excavation. —**dig in,** to excavate trenches; to entrench oneself; to begin to apply oneself vigorously. Also **dig into.**

di·gest, di·jest', dī·jest', *v.t.* To convert, as food or drink, in the alimentary canal into a form absorbable by the body tissues; to assimilate mentally; to order for being conveniently consulted or studied; classify; summarize; to soften, decompose, or prepare, as with heat, moisture, or chemicals; endure.—*v.i.* To undergo digestion; to digest food or drink.—dī'jest, *n.* A systematic compilation, as of literary or scientific material, frequently abridged or summarized. —**di·gest·er,** *n.* —**di·gest·i·ble,** *a.* —**di·gest·i·bil·i·ty,** *n.* —**di·ges·tion,** *n.* —**di·ges·tive,** *a.*

dig·ger, dig'ər, *n.* One who or that which digs; an implement or machine for digging.

dig·gings, dig'ingz, *n. pl.* An area of excavation, esp. a mining area.

dig·it, dij'it, *n.* A finger or a toe; any positive integer under 10, usu. including 0.

dig·it·al, dij'i·təl, *a.* Of or pertaining to digits.—*n.* A key of the organ, piano, etc.

dig·it·al com·put·er, *n.* A computer in which information is represented in numbers, esp. simple numbers in a binary system.

dig·i·tal·is, dij·i·tal'is, dij·i·tā'lis, *n.* Any of several herbs like the foxglove, used esp. as a powerful heart stimulant.

dig·ni·fied, dig'nə·fīd, *a.* Invested with dignity; noble; stately.

dig·ni·fy, dig'nə·fī, *v.t.,* **-fied, -fy·ing.** To invest with dignity; to elevate; to honor; to give a prestigious name to.

dig·ni·tary, dig'nə·ter·ē, *n. pl.,* **-tar·ies.** One who holds high rank or office.

dig·ni·ty, dig'nə·tē, *n. pl.,* **-ties.** Formal or restrained deportment; self-respect; majesty or stateliness; the quality of being worthy of esteem; comparative importance or excellence; rank; an elevated position, title, or rank; a dignitary; dignitaries collectively.

di·graph, dī'graf, dī'gräf, *n.* A union of two letters representing a single sound, as *ea* in *head.*

di·gress, di·gres', dī·gres', *v.i.* To depart or wander from the main subject of a discourse, or narration. —**di·gres·sion,** di·gresh'ən, dī·gresh'ən, *n.* —**di·gres·sive,** *a.* —**di·gres·sive·ly,** *adv.*

di·he·dral, dī·hē'drəl, *n.* A figure formed by two

intersecting planes. —a. Having or formed by a dihedral; of an airplane, having wings that make a dihedral, esp. when not horizontal.

dike, dīk, n. An embankment constructed to restrain flood waters; an artificially created waterway, as a ditch; a bank of debris that results from excavating; a raised causeway. *Informal.* A lesbian.—v.t., **diked, dik∙ing.** To surround with a dike; to drain by ditching.

di∙lap∙i∙dat∙ed, di∙lap'ə∙dā'tid, a. In a run-down condition; reduced to decay. —**di∙lap∙i∙da∙tion,** di∙lap∙ə∙dā'shən, n.

dil∙a∙ta∙tion, dil∙ə∙tā'shən, dī∙lə∙tā'shən, n. Dilation.

di∙late, di∙lāt', dī∙lāt', dī'lāt, v.t., **-lat∙ed, -lat∙ing.** To expand or swell out; to distend.—v.i. To expand, swell, or extend in all directions; to discourse at length. —**di∙lat∙a∙bil∙i∙ty,** di∙lā∙tə∙bil'ə∙tē, n. —**di∙lat∙a∙ble,** a., adv. —**di∙la∙tion,** n.

dil∙a∙to∙ry, dil'ə∙tōr'ē, dil'ə∙tôr∙ē, a. Marked with or given to delay; slow; tardy; making delay. —**dil∙a∙to∙ri∙ly,** adv.

di∙lem∙ma, di∙lem'ə, n. A predicament; an insoluble problem.

dil∙et∙tan∙te, dil'i∙tant, dil∙i∙tän'tā, n. pl., **-ti,** -tē, **-tes.** A person who pursues an art or science merely for amusement; a dabbler.—a. Of or pertaining to dilettantes.

dil∙i∙gence, dil'i∙jəns, n. Steady application; constant effort; industry; care. —**dil∙i∙gent,** dil'i∙jənt, a. —**dil∙i∙gent∙ly,** adv.

dill, dil, n. An herb with aromatic seeds and foliage used for flavoring; a dill pickle.

dill pick∙le, n. A dill-flavored, pickled cucumber.

dil∙ly∙dal∙ly, dil'ē∙dal∙ē, dil∙ē∙dal'ē, v.i., **-lied, -ly∙ing.** To loiter; to delay; to trifle.

di∙lute, di∙loot', dī∙loot', v.t., **-lut∙ed, -lut∙ing.** To make liquid or more liquid, esp. by mixing with water; to weaken by an admixture.—a. Diluted; reduced in strength by intermixture. —**di∙lute∙ness,** n. —**di∙lu∙tion,** n.

dim, dim, a., **dim∙mer, dim∙mest.** Somewhat dark; not clearly seen, heard, understood; obscure; not seeing, hearing, or understanding clearly.—v.t., v.i., **dimmed, dim∙ming.** To render or become dim. —**dim∙ly,** adv. —**dim∙ness,** n.

dime, dīm, n. A partly silver coin of the United States and Canada equal to ten cents.

dime nov∙el, n. A cheap, sensational, or melodramatic paperback novel.

di∙men∙sion, di∙men'shən, n. Magnitude in length, breadth, thickness, or time. *Usu. pl.*, measure, size, or range. —**di∙men∙sion∙less,** a. —**di∙men∙sion∙al,** a.

dime store, n. A five-and-ten.

di∙min∙ish, di∙min'ish, v.t. To cause to be or appear less or smaller by any means; to impair, degrade, or belittle.—v.i. To decrease. —**di∙min∙ish∙a∙ble,** a.

di∙min∙u∙en∙do, di∙min∙ū∙en'dō, a., adv. Mus. Gradually diminishing in loudness; decrescendo.—n. pl., **-dos.** Mus. A gradual decrease in loudness; a passage marked by such a decrease.

dim∙i∙nu∙tion, dim∙ə∙noo'shən, dim∙ə∙nū'shən, n. The act, or process of diminishing; lessening; reduction.

di∙min∙u∙tive, di∙min'ū∙tiv, a. Small; tiny; signifying smallness or endearment.—n. A diminutive thing or person; a diminutive word or affix. —**di∙min∙u∙tive∙ly,** adv. —**di∙min∙u∙tive∙ness,** n.

dim∙mer, dim'ər, n. One who or that which dims; a device for gradual variation in the illumination of an electric light.

dim-out, dim'owt, n. The process or the result of restricting or concealing night lighting, esp. as a defense against air raids.

dim∙ple, dim'pəl, n. A small, natural depression in the cheek or other part of the human body; a slight depression on any surface.—v.i. **-pled, -pling.** To form or show dimples.—v.t. To mark with dimples.

dim∙wit, dim'wit, n. *Informal.* A stupid or obtuse person. —**dim-wit∙ted,** a.

din, din, n. Noise; particularly loud, confused sound that is continued.—v.t., **dinned, din∙ning.** To assail with loud noise; to press with constant repetition.—v.i. To make a din.

dine, dīn, v.i., **dined, din∙ing.** To eat the chief meal of the day; to take dinner; to have any meal.

din∙er, dī'nər, n. One who dines; a railroad dining car; a restaurant.

di∙nette, dī∙net', n. A small dining area off the kitchen or pantry.

ding, ding, v.i. To sound as a bell when struck; to ring, esp. continuously; to talk continuously.—v.t. To force by repetition, to ring.—adv., n. A word imitative of the sound of a bell.

ding-dong, ding'dông, ding'dong, n. The sound of bells, or any similar sound; monotonous repetition.

din∙ghy, ding'ē, n. pl., **-ghies.** Any of various kinds of small rowboats or sailboats. Also **din∙gey, din∙gy.**

din∙gy, din'jē, a., **-gi∙er, -gi∙est.** Of a dirty white or dusky color; soiled; sullied; dusky. —**din∙gi∙ness,** n.

din∙ing car, dī'ning, n. A railroad car in which meals are served to passengers.

din∙ing room, dī'ning, n. A room to dine in; a place for public dining.

dink∙y, ding'kē, a., **-i∙er, -i∙est.** *Informal.* Small; insignificant.

din∙ner, din'ər, n. The chief meal of the day; a formal meal in honor of a person or an event.

di∙no∙saur, dī'nə∙sôr, n. Any of a group of extinct reptiles, including the largest known land animals.

dint, dint, n. Means; force; a dent.—v.t. To dent.

di∙o∙cese, dī'ə∙sēs, dī'ə∙sis, n. The circuit or extent of a bishop's jurisdiction.

di∙oc∙e∙san, dī∙os'ə∙sən, a. Pertaining to a diocese.—n. A bishop in charge of a diocese.

di∙o∙ram∙a, dī∙ə∙ram'ə, dī∙ə∙rä'mə, n. A painted scene in three dimensions, viewed through an aperture; an exhibit with modeled figures against a painted background.

dip, dip, v.t., **dipped, dip∙ping.** To plunge temporarily into a liquid; to obtain or take up by bailing or ladling; to lower and raise again; to baptize, dye, or disinfect by immersion; to make, as a candle, by repeatedly dipping a wick into melted tallow.—v.i. To plunge into water or other liquid and emerge quickly; to plunge the hand or a dipper down into or below a surface, esp. to withdraw something; to sink or drop down suddenly; to incline or slope downward; to decrease slightly and usu. temporarily; to drop suddenly, then rise again.—**dip into,** to read cursorily; glance at.—n. The act of dipping; a plunge into water, as for a brief swim; a lowering momentarily; a sinking down; a short downward plunge, as of an airplane; a quantity taken up by dipping; a candle made by dipping; a liquid or sauce into which something is dipped; a slight or temporary decrease; a downward inclination; the degree of such an inclination; a hollow or depression. *Informal.* A pickpocket.

diph∙the∙ri∙a, dif∙thēr'ē∙ə, dip∙thēr'ē∙ə, n. An epidemic inflammatory disease of the air passages, characterized by the formation of false membranes which hinder breathing.

diph∙thong, dif'thông, dif'thong, dip'thông, dip'thong, n. A continuous monosyllabic speech sound made by gliding from the sound of one vowel into the sound of another, as oy in toy.

di∙plo∙ma, di∙plō'mə, n. A document signed by competent authority, conferring some power, privilege, or honor, as that given to graduates of colleges and

---

a- hat, fāte, fāre, fäther; e- met, mē; i- pin, pīne; o- not, nōte, ôrb, moove (move), boy, pownd;
u- cūbe, bŭll, tŭk (took); ch- chin; th- thick, ŧhen; zh- vizhon (vision); ə- əgo, takən, pencəl, lemən, bərd (bird).

universities upon completion of graduation requirements.

di·plo·ma·cy, di·plō′mə·sē, *n. pl.,* **-cies.** The science or art of conducting negotiations between nations; the forms of international negotiations; skill in managing negotiations; tact.

dip·lo·mat, dip′lə·mat, *n.* A person representing his government in negotiations with other nations and international organizations; a tactful person. **—dip·lo·mat·ic,** dip·lə·mat′ik, *a.* **—dip·lo·mat·i·cal·ly,** *adv.*

dip·per, dip′ər, *n.* One who or that which dips; a cup or vessel provided with a handle and used to dip liquids. *(Cap.)* The Big Dipper or Little Dipper.

dip·so·ma·ni·a, dip·sə·mā′nē·ə, *n.* An irresistible craving for intoxicating drink. **—dip·so·ma·ni·ac,** *n.*

dip·stick, dip′stik, *n.* A marked rod for measuring oil in the crankcase of an automobile.

dire, dir, *a.,* **dir·er, dir·est.** Dreadful; horrible. **—dire·ly,** *adv.* **—dire·ness,** *n.*

di·rect, di·rekt′, dī·rekt′, *a.* The shortest, nearest, least complicated way; without obstacles or intermediaries; immediate; straightforward, candid, or clear; in an unbroken line of descent; absolute or exact.—*v.t.* To guide; to control, manage, or govern; to command; to address (words, etc.) to someone; to point the way; to project toward a specific place.—*v.i.* To act as a guide; to give commands or orders; to conduct (an orchestra, etc.); to supervise production of a play, film, etc.—*adv.* In a straight line or straightforward manner. **—di·rect·ness,** *n.*

di·rect cur·rent, *n.* A current flowing continuously in one direction in a circuit.

di·rec·tion, di·rek′shən, dī·rek′shən, *n.* The course or line along which anything moves or is directed; the region toward which something is directed, as north; management; an order; *usu. pl.,* instructions about where to go, what to do, etc.; the act of directing an orchestra or a theatrical production; a trend of thought or action.

di·rec·tion·al, di·rek′shə·nəl, dī·rek′shə·nəl, *a.* Indicating direction in space; adapted for indicating the direction of signals received; adapted for transmitting signals in a certain direction.

di·rec·tive, di·rek′tiv, dī·rek′tiv, *a.* Having the power of directing.—*n.* An instruction or direction.

di·rect·ly, di·rekt′lē, dī·rekt′lē, *adv.* In a straight line; immediately; without delay.

di·rec·tor, di·rek′tər, dī·rek′tər, *n.* One who or that which directs; one of a body appointed to direct the affairs of a company; a person who directs a production for stage, film, TV, or radio. **—di·rec·to·ri·al,** di·rek·tôr′ə·əl, *a.* **—di·rec·tor·ship,** *n.*

di·rec·to·rate, di·rek′tər·it, dī·rek′tər·it, *n.* The office of a director; a body of directors.

di·rec·to·ry, di·rek′tə·rē, dī·rek′tə·rē, *n. pl.,* **-ries.** A book containing an alphabetical list, as of the names and addresses of people, businesses, etc.; a book of regulations; a directorate.—*a.* Serving to direct.

di·rect pri·ma·ry, *n.* A preliminary election in which members of a party select their candidates by a direct vote.

di·rect tax, *n.* A tax on income, property, etc., paid directly by the taxpayer.

dirge, dərj, *n.* A funeral hymn; a musical composition expressing sorrow.

dirk, dərk, *n.* A dagger.—*v.t.* To stab with a dirk.

dirt, dərt, *n.* Any foul or filthy substance, as excrement, mud, mire, dust; loose soil or earth; mean or petty action, thought, or speech; obscenity; earth from which a valuable metal is separated.

dirt·y, dər′tē, *a.,* **-i·er, -i·est.** Foul; nasty; filthy; impure; mean; underhand; dull; clouded; causing much radioactive fallout; sleety, rainy, or sloppy, as weather.—*v.t.,* **-dirt·ied, dirt·y·ing.** To make dirty; to soil. **—dirt·i·ly,** *adv.* **—dirt·i·ness,** *n.*

dis·a·ble, dis·ā′bəl, *v.t.,* **-bled, -bling.** To deprive of

strength or power, physical or mental; to incapacitate; cripple; deprive of legal qualifications. **—dis·a·bil·i·ty,** dis·ə·bil′i·tē, *n. pl.,* **-ties.** **—dis·a·ble·ment,** *n.*

dis·a·buse, dis·ə·būz′, *v.t.,* **-bused, -bus·ing.** To free from mistaken notions; undeceive.

dis·ad·van·tage, dis·ad·van′tij, dis·ad·vän′tij, *n.* Absence or deprivation of advantage; that which prevents success or renders it difficult; drawback; handicap; loss; injury.—*v.t.* To subject to a disadvantage. **—dis·ad·van·ta·geous,** dis·ad·van·tā′jəs, *a.* **—dis·ad·van·ta·geous·ly,** *adv.*

dis·af·fect, dis·ə·fekt′, *v.t.* To make discontented, or disloyal, or unfriendly. **—dis·af·fec·tion,** *n.*

dis·af·fect·ed, dis·ə·fek′tid, *a.* Alienated; estranged; unfriendly.

dis·a·gree, dis·ə·grē′, *v.i.,* **-greed, -gree·ing.** To differ; to fail to agree, as facts; to vary in opinion; to quarrel.

dis·a·gree·a·ble, dis·ə·grē′ə·bəl, *a.* Unpleasant; bad-tempered; quarrelsome.—*n.* **—dis·a·gree·a·ble·ness,** *n.* **—dis·a·gree·a·bly,** *adv.*

dis·a·gree·ment, dis·ə·grē′mənt, *n.* Lack of agreement; difference of opinion; difference; unlikeness; a dispute or quarrel.

dis·al·low, dis·ə·low′, *v.t.* To refuse to allow; refuse to admit the truth or validity of; reject. **—dis·al·low·ance,** *n.*

dis·ap·pear, dis·ə·pēr′, *v.i.* To vanish from sight; to cease to be or exist. **—dis·ap·pear·ance,** *n.*

dis·ap·point, dis·ə·poynt′, *v.t.* To fall short of fulfilling the hopes or expectations of; to hinder the fulfillment of, as of hopes; to frustrate. **—dis·ap·point·ment,** *n.*

dis·ap·pro·ba·tion, dis·ap·rə·bā′shən, *n.* Disapproval.

dis·ap·prove, dis·ə·proov′, *v.t.,* **-proved, -prov·ing.** To censure; condemn; refuse to approve.—*v.i.* To express or feel disapproval, often with *of.* **—dis·ap·prov·al,** *n.* **—dis·ap·prov·ing·ly,** *adv.*

dis·arm, dis·ärm′, *v.t.* To take the arms or weapons from; to reduce or abolish military forces, equipment, etc.; to render harmless; to turn suspicion or hostility into friendliness.—*v.i.* To lay down arms; to disband armed forces; to limit armaments and forces to peace-time proportions.

dis·ar·ma·ment, dis·är′mə·mənt, *n.* The act of disarming; the reduction or elimination of a military establishment.

dis·ar·range, dis·ə·rānj′, *v.t.,* **-ranged, -rang·ing.** To put out of order; unsettle the arrangement of. **—dis·ar·range·ment,** *n.*

dis·ar·ray, dis·ə·rā′, *v.t.* To throw into disorder; to undress.—*n.* Disorder; confusion; disordered dress.

dis·as·sem·ble, dis·ə·sem′bəl, *v.t.* To take apart.

dis·as·ter, di·zas′tər, dī·zäs′tər, *n.* Any unfortunate event, esp. a great misfortune causing widespread damage or suffering; calamity. **—dis·as·trous,** *a.* **—dis·as·trous·ly,** *adv.*

dis·a·vow, dis·ə·vow′, *v.t.* To deny cognizance of or a responsibility for; disown; reject. **—dis·a·vow·al,** *n.*

dis·band, dis·band′, *v.t.* To break up an organization; to dismiss from military service; to disperse.—*v.i.* To become disbanded. **—dis·band·ment,** *n.*

dis·bar, dis·bär′, *v.t.,* **-barred, -bar·ring.** To expel officially from the legal profession.

dis·be·lieve, dis·bi·lēv′, *v.t., v.i.,* **-lieved, -liev·ing.** To withhold belief or refuse to believe; reject. **—dis·be·lief,** *n.* **—dis·be·liev·er,** *n.*

dis·burse, dis·bərs′, *v.t.,* **-bursed, -burs·ing.** To pay out as money; to expend. **—dis·burse·ment,** *n.* **—dis·burs·er,** *n.*

disc, disk, *n., v.t.* Disk.

dis·card, dis·kärd′, *v.t.* To cast aside as no longer usable; in a card game, to throw from one's hand. **—dis**/kärd, *n.* The act of discarding; that which is cast aside; cards which are discarded.

dis·cern, di·sərn′, di·zərn′, *v.t.* To perceive as being

different; to discriminate, as by the eye or intellect.
—*v.i.* To see or understand differences. —**dis·cern·er,**
n. —**dis·cern·i·ble,** *a.* —**dis·cern·i·bly,** *adv.*
dis·cern·ing, di·sėr′ning, di·zėr′ning, *a.* Discrimi-
nating; penetrating; shrewd. —**dis·cern·ing·ly,** *adv.*
dis·cern·ment, di·sėrn′mənt, di·zėrn′mənt, *n.*
Acuteness of judgment; insight; shrewdness; act of
discerning.
dis·charge, dis·chärj′, *v.t.,* **-charged, -charg·ing.** To
relieve of a charge or load; to relieve or free of
anything; to dismiss from service or employment; to
set free from custody; to rid of a charge of electricity;
to unload, as a cargo; to fire or shoot, as a gun; to
pour forth, as water; to pay a debt; to fulfill a duty; to
set aside or annul, as an order of a court.—*v.i.* To
discharge a burden or load; to throw off a burden; to
deliver a charge or load; to emit contents; to fire, as a
gun. —dis′chärj, dis·chärj′, *n.* The act of discharging
a ship or a gun; ejection; emission; something discharged; a relieving or fulfilling of an obligation; the
payment of a debt; the performance of a duty; release
or dismissal from office, employment, or military duty;
annulment, as of a court order; acquittal; release from
custody; a sending away; a certificate of release; the
equalization of the difference of potential between two
electrical terminals. —**dis·charge·a·ble,** *a.* —**dis·
char·ger,** *n.*
dis·ci·ple, di·sī′pəl, *n.* A follower of a particular
teacher or school of thought; one of the twelve chosen
apostles of Jesus Christ. —**dis·ci·ple·ship,** *n.*
dis·ci·pli·nar·i·an, dis·ə·plə·nãr′ē·ən, *n.* One who
disciplines or advocates strict maintenance of discipline.—*a.* Disciplinary.
dis·ci·pline, dis′ə·plin, *n.* A state of order maintained by training and control; a particular system of
regulations for conduct; systematic training, esp. of
the mind or character; drill; punishment; chastisement; the effect of training, esp. order, efficiency, or
obedience; a branch of instruction or learning; the
methods or rules employed in regulating the conduct
of the members of a church.—*v.t.,* **-plined, -plin·ing.**
To bring to a state of order and obedience; to correct;
to chastise; to drill. —**dis·ci·pli·nar·y,** *a.*
disc jock·ey, *n.* See **disk jockey.**
dis·claim, dis·klām′, *v.t.* To deny responsibility for or
approval of; disown; disavow; to relinquish all claim
to.—*v.i.* Law. To relinquish a claim.
dis·claim·er, dis·klā′mər, *n.* A person who disclaims; an act of disclaiming; a means, such as a
written statement, of disclaiming.
dis·close, dis·klōz′, *v.t.,* **-closed, -clos·ing.** To allow
to be seen; to bring to light; to make known; reveal;
tell. —**dis·clos·er,** *n.* —**dis·clo·sure,** dis·klō′zhər, *n.*
dis·coid, dis′koyd, *a.* Having the form of a disk; flat
and circular.
dis·col·or, dis·kəl′ər, *v.t.* To alter or mar the color of;
stain.—*v.i.* To become discolored. —**dis·col·or·a·
tion,** dis·kəl·ə·rā′shən, *n.*
dis·com·fit, dis·kəm′fit, *v.t.* To rout, defeat, or scatter in flight; to foil or frustrate the plans of; to confound; disconcert; embarrass. —**dis·com·fi·ture,** *n.*
dis·com·fort, dis·kəm′fərt, *n.* Minor pain, or uneasiness.—*v.t.* To disturb the peace or happiness of; to
make uneasy; to pain slightly.
dis·com·mode, dis·kə·mōd′, *v.t.,* **-mod·ed, -mod·
ing.** To inconvenience; to disturb.
dis·com·pose, dis·kəm·pōz′, *v.t.,* **-posed, -pos·ing.**
To disorder; to disturb the self-possession of; to
agitate or vex. —**dis·com·po·sure,** *n.*
dis·con·cert, dis·kən·sėrt′, *v.t.* To throw into disorder or confusion; to undo; to frustrate; to disturb the
self-possession of. —**dis·con·cert·ing,** *a.* —**dis·con·
cert·ed,** *a.*
dis·con·nect, dis·kə·nekt′, *v.t.* To separate or sever

the connection between; to disunite; to detach.
—**dis·con·nec·tion,** dis·kə·nek′shən, *n.* —**dis·con·
nect·ed,** *a.* —**dis·con·nect·ed·ness,** *n.*
dis·con·so·late, dis·kon′sə·lit, *a.* Hopelessly dejected; gloomy. —**dis·con·so·late·ly,** *adv.*
dis·con·tent, dis·kən·tent′, *n.* Lack of contentment;
uneasiness; dissatisfaction. Also **dis·con·tent·
ment.**—*a.* Uneasy; dissatisfied.—*v.t.* To make dissatisfied. —**dis·con·tent·ed,** *a.* —**dis·con·tent·ed·ly,** *adv.*
dis·con·tin·ue, dis·kən·tin′ū, *v.t.,* **-ued, -u·ing.** To
continue no longer; to cease from; to stop; to put an
end to; to abandon or terminate some legal action.
—*v.i.* To cease. —**dis·con·tin·u·ance,** *n.* —**dis·con·
tin·u·a·tion,** dis·kən·tin·ū·ā′shən, *n.*
dis·con·tin·u·ous, dis·kən·tin′ū·əs, *a.* Not continuous; discrete; interrupted. —**dis·con·ti·nu·i·ty,**
dis·kon·tə·noo′ə·tē, dis·kon·tə·nū′ə·tē, *n.*
dis·cord, dis′kôrd, *n.* Lack of concord; disagreement;
contention. *Mus.* A union of sounds disagreeable to
the ear; dissonance.—dis·kôrd′, *v.i.* To disagree; to be
out of harmony. —**dis·cord·ance,** dis·kôr′dəns, *n.*
—**dis·cor·dan·cy,** dis·kôr′dən·sē, —**dis·cord·ant·
ly,** *adv.*
dis·co·thèque, dis·kō·tek′, *n.* Nightclub where the
patrons dance to recorded music.
dis·count, dis′kownt, *n.* Any deduction from the customary price of goods or from a bill; an interest
deduction made in advance on a note; the act of
discounting.—dis′kownt, dis·kownt′, *v.t.* To lend or
advance a sum of money, deducting the interest from
the principal; to deduct a portion of a bill; to offer for
sale at a lower than customary price; to estimate or
take into account beforehand; to leave out of account
or disregard; to make an allowance for; to anticipate
and thereby lessen the effect of.—*v.i.* To give or make
discounts.
dis·cour·age, dis·kėr′ij, *v.t.,* **-aged, -ag·ing.** To dishearten; to deprive of self-confidence; to attempt to
repress or prevent by disapproving; to dissuade, usu.
with *from.* —**dis·cour·age·ment,** *n.* —**dis·cour·ag·
ing,** *a.*
dis·course, dis′kōrs, dis′kôrs, *n.* Conversation or
speech; a formal, systematic written or oral examination of a subject.—*v.i.,* **-coursed, -cours·ing.** To converse or talk; to speak or write formally.
dis·cour·te·ous, dis·kėr′tē·əs, *a.* Uncivil; rude.
—**dis·cour·te·ous·ly,** *adv.* —**dis·cour·te·ous·ness,**
n. —**dis·cour·te·sy,** *n. pl.,* **-sies.**
dis·cov·er, dis·kəv′ər, *v.t.* To see, detect, or come
upon, esp. for the first time. —**dis·cov·er·a·ble,** *a.*
—**dis·cov·er·er,** *n.*
dis·cov·er·y, dis·kəv′ə·rē, *n. pl.,* **-ies.** The act of
discovering; that which is discovered.
dis·cred·it, dis·kred′it, *n.* Some degree of disgrace
or reproach; disrepute; loss of belief, trust, or confidence; disbelief; something that injures reputation.
—*v.t.* To withhold belief, credit, or confidence in; to
bring into disgrace or disrepute; to give no credence
to. —**dis·cred·it·a·ble,** *a.* —**dis·cred·it·a·bly,** *adv.*
dis·creet, dis·krēt′, *a.* Prudent in conduct; circum-
spect; cautious. —**dis·creet·ly,** *adv.*
dis·crep·an·cy, dis·krep′ən·sē, *n. pl.,* **-cies.** A difference or inconsistency between facts, testimony, or
theories; disagreement; divergence.
dis·crete, dis·krēt′, *a.* Separate or distinct from others; consisting of individual parts.
dis·cre·tion, dis·kresh′ən, *n.* The quality of being
discreet; circumspection; individual freedom of decision or choice. —**dis·cre·tion·ar·y,** *a.*
dis·crim·i·nate, dis·krim′ə·nāt, *v.t.,* **-nat·ed, -nat·
ing.** To make or constitute a distinction in or between;
differentiate; to note as different.—*v.i.* To make a
distinction, as in favor of or against a person or thing,
esp. to make a distinction between persons on the

a- hat, fāte, fãre, fäther; **e-** met, mē; **i-** pin, pīne; **o-** not, nōte, ôrb, moove (move), boy, pownd;
u- cūbe, bûll, tûk (took); **ch-** chin; **th-** thick, ŧhen; **zh-** vizhon (vision); **ə-** əgo, takən, pencəl, lemən, bėrd (bird).

basis of race, sex, or religion rather than individual merit; distinguish accurately; perceive subtle distinctions.—dis•crim′ə•nit, a. Marked by discrimination; making subtle distinctions. —dis•crim•i•nate•ly, adv. —dis•crim•i•nat•ing, a. —dis•crim•i•na•tion, dis•krim•ə•nā′shən, n. —dis•crim•i•na•tive, a. —dis•crim•i•na•to•ry, dis•krim′ə•nə•tôr•ē, adv. —dis•crim•i•na•tor, n.

dis•cur•sive, dis•kər′siv, a. Passing rapidly from one subject to another; desultory; rambling; marked by analytical reasoning. —dis•cur•sive•ly, adv. —dis•cur•sive•ness, n.

dis•cus, dis′kəs, n. pl., -cus•es. A circular plate of stone or metal for throwing to a distance as an athletic event.

dis•cuss, dis•kəs′, v.t. To treat as the subject of conversation or writing; to examine by argument or reason; to talk over informally. —dis•cuss•i•ble, a. —dis•cus•sion, dis•kəsh′ən, n.

dis•dain, dis•dān′, v.t. To regard as unworthy; to scorn; to reject with contempt.—n. An attitude of superiority; haughtiness; scorn. —dis•dain•ful, a. —dis•dain•ful•ly, adv.

dis•ease, di•zēz′, n. A sickness of a living thing, esp. a sickness with particular symptoms; any disordered or unwholesome state of mind, public affairs, etc. —v.t., -eased, -eas•ing. To make ill; corrupt. —dis•eased, a.

dis•em•bark, dis•em•bärk′, v.t., v.i. To put or go ashore from a ship; land; unload. —dis•em•bar•ka•tion, dis•em•bar•kā′shən, —dis•em•bark•ment, n.

dis•em•bod•y, dis•em•bod′ē, v.t., -bod•ied, -bod•y•ing. To divest from the body. —dis•em•bod•i•ment, n.

dis•em•bow•el, dis•em•bow′əl, v.t., -eled, -el•ing. To deprive of or rip out the bowels. —dis•em•bow•el•ment, n.

dis•en•chant, dis•en•chant′, dis•en•chänt′, v.t. To free from fascination or delusion; to disillusion. —dis•en•chant•ment, n.

dis•en•cum•ber, dis•en•kəm′bər, v.t. To free from encumbrance.

dis•en•fran•chise, dis•en•fran′chīz, v.t., -chised, -chis•ing. Disfranchise.

dis•en•gage, dis•en•gāj′, v.t., -gaged, -gag•ing. To set free from attachment, occupation, obligation, etc. —v.i. To remove oneself; to become unattached. —dis•en•gage•ment, n.

dis•en•tan•gle, dis•en•tang′gəl, v.t., -gled, -gling. To free from entanglements; unravel; extricate. —dis•en•tan•gle•ment, n.

dis•es•tab•lish, dis•e•stab′lish, v.t. To end established status; of a church, to deprive of exclusive government support. —dis•es•tab•lish•ment, n.

dis•fa•vor, dis•fā′vər, n. The state of being unacceptable, disliked, or opposed; disapproval.—v.t. To withdraw or withhold favor, friendship, or support from.

dis•fig•ure, dis•fig′yər, v.t., -ured, -ur•ing. To spoil in appearance; to mar or make unsightly. —dis•fig•ure•ment, n.

dis•fran•chise, dis•fran′chīz, v.t., -chised, -chis•ing. To deprive of the rights and privileges of a free citizen; to deprive of any franchise, esp. of the right of voting. —dis•fran•chise•ment, n.

dis•gorge, dis•gôrj′, v.t., -gorged, -gorg•ing. To vomit; to discharge violently; to empty or pour out the contents of; to give up unwillingly.—v.i. To discharge contents.

dis•grace, dis•grās′, n. A state of being out of favor; a state of dishonor, shame, or infamy; ignominy; that which causes shame or dishonor.—v.t., -graced, -grac•ing. To put out of favor; to bring shame or reproach on.

dis•grace•ful, a. Entailing disgrace; shameful; dishonorable. —dis•grace•ful•ly, adv. —dis•grace•ful•ness, n.

dis•grun•tle, dis•grən′təl, v.t., -tled, -tling. To dis-please; to put in a bad mood. —dis•grun•tled, a.

dis•guise, dis•gīz′, v.t., -guised, -guis•ing. To alter the ordinary appearance of; to hide or mask a true identity of; to conceal or obscure by false representation.—n. That which disguises; anything serving to conceal or mask identity, character, or manner. —dis•guis•er, n.

dis•gust, dis•gəst′, n. Distaste; nausea; aversion; loathing.—v.t. To cause to feel disgust. —dis•gust•ed, a. —dis•gust•ing, a.

dish, dish, n. A broad open vessel made of various materials, used esp. for serving food; loosely, any plate, bowl, cup, etc., employed in serving food; any particular kind of food; the quantity accommodated by a dish; something shaped like a dish. Informal. An attractive woman.—v.t. To put into a dish; to serve in a dish; to make concave in the center.

dis•ha•bille, dis•ə•bēl′, n. A state of partial undress or of loose or negligent dress; garments worn in this state. Also des•ha•bille, dez•ə•bēl′.

dis•har•mo•ny, dis•här′mə•nē, n. pl., -nies. Discord; lack of harmony.

dis•heart•en, dis•här′tən, v.t. To discourage; dispirit. —dis•heart•en•ing, a.

di•shev•eled, di•shev′əld, a. Disarranged; rumpled; having unkempt hair or an untidy appearance.

dis•hon•est, dis•on′ist, a. Not honest. —dis•hon•est•ly, adv. —dis•hon•es•ty, n. pl., -ties.

dis•hon•or, dis•on′ər, n. Loss of honor; disgrace; shame; anything that disgraces; nonpayment of a note, bill, etc., when due.—v.t. To disgrace; to bring shame on; to refuse or decline to pay, as a bill of exchange.

dis•hon•or•a•ble, dis•on′ər•ə•bəl, a. Shameful; disgraceful; bringing shame; unprincipled. —dis•hon•or•a•bly, adv.

dis•il•lu•sion, dis•ə•loo′zhən, v.t. To free from illusion.—n. Disenchantment. —dis•il•lu•sion•ment, n.

dis•in•cline, dis•in•klīn′, v.t., v.i., -clined, -clin•ing. To make or be unwilling. —dis•in•cli•na•tion, dis•in•klə•nā′shən, n.

dis•in•fect, dis•in•fekt′, v.t. To cleanse of disease germs; sterilize. —dis•in•fect•ant, n., a. —dis•in•fec•tion, dis•in•fek′shən, n.

dis•in•her•it, dis•in•her′it, v.t. To deprive of an inheritance; to dispossess of natural or customary rights or privileges. —dis•in•her•i•tance, n.

dis•in•te•grate, dis•in′tə•grāt, v.t., -grat•ed, -grat•ing. To reduce to powder or fragments; to destroy the cohesion or unity of.—v.i. To break into component particles or parts; to sustain a change in nuclear composition. —dis•in•te•gra•tion, dis•in•tə•grā′shən, n. —dis•in•te•gra•tor, n.

dis•in•ter, dis•in•tər′, v.t., -terred, -ter•ring. To take out of a grave or out of the earth; to bring from obscurity into view. —dis•in•ter•ment, n.

dis•in•ter•est, dis•in′tər•ist, n. Absence of interest; indifference.

dis•in•ter•es•ted, dis•in′tər•es•tid, a. Free from considerations of personal interest or advantage; not influenced by selfish motives. Informal. Not interested. —dis•in•ter•est•ed•ly, adv.

dis•join, dis•joyn′, v.t. To separate; detach.—v.i. To be separated.

dis•joint, dis•joynt′, v.t. To separate at the joints; to put out of joint; to dislocate; to derange; to render incoherent.—v.i. To become dislocated. —dis•joint•ed, a. —dis•joint•ed•ness, n. —dis•joint•ed•ly, adv.

dis•junc•tion, dis•jəngk′shən, n. The act of disjoining, or the state of being disjoined; disunion; separation.

disk, disc, disk, n. Any thin, flat, circular plate or object; a phonograph record; any of various roundish, flat structures or parts; a discus; any round, flat surface. —disk•like, disc•like, a.

disk jock•ey, n. Informal. A person who conducts a radio program consisting mainly of recorded music.

dis·like, dis·līk′, *n.* A feeling of not liking; distaste; antipathy.—*v.t.*, **-liked, -lik·ing.** To feel dislike toward. —**dis·lik·a·ble**, *a.*

dis·lo·cate, dis′lō·kāt, *v.t.*, **-cat·ed, -cat·ing.** To move out of place; displace; disrupt the established order of. —**dis·lo·ca·tion**, dis·lō·kā′shen, *n.*

dis·lodge, dis·loj′, *v.t.*, **-lodged, -lodg·ing.** To remove or force from the fixed position or place occupied.—*v.i.* To go from a lodging place.

dis·loy·al, dis·loy′el, *a.* Not loyal; faithless; treacherous. —**dis·loy·al·ly**, *adv.* —**dis·loy·al·ty**, *n. pl.*, **-ties.**

dis·mal, diz′mel, *a.* Dark; gloomy; depressing; melancholy; depressed. —**dis·mal·ly**, *adv.*

dis·man·tle, dis·man′tel, *v.t.*, **-tled, -tling.** To strip of furniture, equipment, fortifications, and the like; to disassemble; take apart.

dis·may, dis·mā′, *v.t.* To deprive of courage or resolution; to discourage; daunt; distress.—*n.* Loss of courage together with consternation; distress.

dis·mem·ber, dis·mem′ber, *v.t.* To separate the members of; to mutilate; to sever and distribute the parts of. —**dis·mem·ber·ment**, *n.*

dis·miss, dis·mis′, *v.t.* To send away; to permit to depart; to remove from office, service, or employment; to disregard; to deal with quickly; to reject as unworthy of notice. —**dis·mis·sal**, *n.*

dis·mount, dis·mownt′, *v.i.* To get off or alight, as from a horse.—*v.t.* To knock, throw, or pull from a mounted position; unhorse; to remove from a mounting or setting; disassemble.

dis·o·be·di·ence, dis·e·bē′dē·ens, *n.* Neglect or refusal to obey. —**dis·o·be·di·ent**, *a.* —**dis·o·be·di·ent·ly**, *adv.*

dis·o·bey, dis·e·bā′, *v.t., v.i.* To neglect or refuse to obey. —**dis·o·bey·er**, *n.*

dis·or·der, dis·ôr′der, *n.* Lack of order; irregularity; confusion; tumult; disturbance of the peace; sickness; derangement.—*v.t.* To disrupt the order of; to throw into confusion; to produce sickness or indisposition in. —**dis·or·dered**, *a.*

dis·or·der·ly, dis·ôr′der·lē, *a.* Marked by disorder; confused; unmethodical; irregular; tumultuous; unruly; violating laws governing order and morality.—*adv.* In an unorderly manner. —**dis·or·der·li·ness**, *n.*

dis·or·gan·ize, dis·ôr′ge·nīz, *v.t.*, **-ized, -iz·ing.** To throw into confusion or disorder. —**dis·or·gan·i·za·tion**, dis·ôr·ge·ni·zā·shen, *n.*

dis·o·ri·ent, dis·ôr′ē·ent, dis·ōr′ē·ent, *v.t.* To cause to lose one's bearings; to confuse. —**dis·o·ri·en·ta·tion**, dis·ôr·e·en·tā′shen, *n.*

dis·own, dis·ōn′, *v.t.* To refuse to acknowledge as one's own; to disclaim; repudiate.

dis·par·age, di·spar′ij, *v.t.*, **-aged, -ag·ing.** To bring reproach or discredit upon; to speak of slightingly; depreciate; belittle. —**dis·par·age·ment**, *n.* —**dis·par·ag·ing·ly**, *adv.*

dis·pa·rate, dis′per·it, di·spar′it, *a.* Essentially different; dissimilar; unlike. —**dis·pa·rate·ly**, *adv.* —**dis·pa·rate·ness**, *n.*

dis·par·i·ty, di·spar′e·tē, *n. pl.*, **-ties.** Inequality; difference; dissimilarity; unlikeness.

dis·pas·sion, dis·pash′en, *n.* Freedom from passion; the state or quality of being unexcitable or impartial. —**dis·pas·sion·ate·ness**, *n.* —**dis·pas·sion·ate**, *a.* —**dis·pas·sion·ate·ly**, *adv.*

dis·patch, di·spach′, *v.t.* To send or send away, implying haste; to put to death; to perform or execute speedily; to finish.—*n.* The act of putting to death; speedy and efficient performance; haste; a message sent or to be sent with haste; a news story transmitted by a reporter or a news service; an organization or a means for the fast and efficient sending of messages or goods.

dis·patch·er, *n.* One who dispatches, esp. one who

routes or schedules planes, trains, buses, trucks, or taxicabs.

dis·pel, dis·pel′, *v.t.*, **-pelled, -pel·ling.** To scatter or drive away by force.

dis·pen·sa·ble, dis·pen′se·bel, *a.* That may be done without. —**dis·pen·sa·bil·i·ty**, dis·pen·se·bil′e·tē, *n.*

dis·pen·sa·ry, dis·pen′se·rē, *n. pl.*, **-ries.** A place in which medicines are given away free or for a small charge.

dis·pen·sa·tion, dis·pen·sā′shen, *n.* The act of distributing; following a specific plan; official permission to disregard a rule.

dis·pense, dis·pens′, *v.t.*, **-pensed, -pens·ing.** To give out or distribute; to excuse.

dis·perse, dis·pers′, *v.t.*, **-persed, -pers·ing.** To scatter; send or drive off in various directions.

dis·place, dis·plās′, *v.t.*, **-placed, -plac·ing.** To remove something from its usual place or position.

dis·play, dis·plā′, *v.t.* To show something as to attract attention to it.

dis·please, dis·plēz′, *v.t.* **-pleased, -pleas·ing.** To annoy, to make angry, usually in a slight degree.—*v.i.* To slightly anger or annoy; to produce displeasure.

dis·pleas·ure, dis·plezh′er, *n.* The feeling of one who is annoyed.

dis·port, dis·pōrt′, dis·pôrt′, *v.t..* To act in a sportive way; to act gaily.

dis·pos·a·ble, di·spō′ze·bel, *a.* Subject to being thrown out; available for free use.

dis·pose, dis·pōz′, *v.t.*, **-posed, -pos·ing.** To put in a certain order or position; to get rid of as necessary.

dis·po·si·tion, dis·pe·zish′en, *n.* A person's way of acting toward others or thinking about things.

dis·pro·por·tion, dis·pre·pōr′shen, dis·pre·pôr′shen, *n.* Lack of equality between one thing and another.—*v.t.* To make or cause to be unbalanced or unequal; adequate. —**dis·pro·por·tion·ate·ness**, *n.*

dis·prove, dis·proov′, *v.t.*, **-proved, -prov·ing.** To prove to be false.

dis·pute, dis·pūt′, *v.i.*, **-puted, -put·ing.** To argue or fight over. —**dis·put·a·ble**, dis·pū′te·bel, dis·pyū′te·bel, *a.*

dis·qual·i·fy, dis·kwol′e·fī, *v.t.*, **-fied, -fy·ing.** To make unable to do something because of a violation of a rule. —**dis·qual·i·fi·ca·tion**, dis·kwol·e·fe·kā′shen, *n.*

dis·qui·et, dis·kwī′et, *n.* Uneasiness.—*v.t.* To make uneasy or to disturb.

dis·re·gard, dis·ri·gärd′, *n.* Lack of attention.—*v.t.* Pay no attention to or take no notice of.

dis·re·pair, dis·ri·pâr′, *n.* Bad condition.

dis·rep·u·ta·ble, dis·rep′ū·te·bel, *a.* Not respectable.—*n.* Loss of reputation.

dis·re·spect, dis·ri·spekt′, *n.* Lack of respect or discourtesy.—*v.t.* To treat rudely. —**dis·re·spect·ful**, *a.*

dis·re·spect·a·ble, *a.* Unworthy of respect.

dis·robe, dis·rōb′, *v.t., v.i.*, **-robed, -robing.** To undress.

dis·rupt, dis·rept′, *v.t.* To throw into disorder or upset.

dis·rup·tion, dis·rep′shen, *n.* The act of breaking up; a disrupted or disordered condition.

dis·rup·tive, dis·rep′tiv, *a.* Causing disruption. —**dis·rup·tive·ly**, *adv.* —**dis·rup·tive·ness**, *n.* —**dis·rupt·er**, *n.*

dis·sat·is·fac·tion, dis·sat·is·fak′shen, *n.* A feeling of discontent; a lack of satisfaction.

dis·sat·is·fac·to·ry, dis·sat·is·fak′te·rē, *a.* Displeasing.

dis·sat·is·fy, dis·sat′is·fī, *v.t.*, **-fied, -fy·ing.** To fail to satisfy; to displease.

dis·sect, di·sekt′, dī·sekt′, *v.t.* To divide, separate, or

---

cut apart, esp. an animal body or plant for scientific investigation. **—dis·sect·ed,** a. **—dis·sec·tion,** n.

dis·sem·blance, di·sem/blens, n. Lack of resemblance or likeness.

dis·sem·ble, di·sem/bel, v.t., **-bled, -bling.** To disguise or hide (one's true feelings or motives).—v.i. To try to appear other than one's natural self. **—dis· sem·bler,** n.

dis·sem·i·nate, di·sem/e·nāt, v.t., **-nat·ed, -nat· ing.** To spread or scatter, as seeds, especially information or knowledge; to broadcast. **—dis·sem·i·na· tion,** di·sem·e·nā/shen, n. **—dis·sem·i·na·tive,** a. **—dis·sem·i·na·tor,** n.

dis·sent, di·sent/, v.i. To disagree in opinion; to think in a different manner.—n. Difference of opinion; disagreement. **—dis·sent·ing,** a. **—dis·sen·sion,** di· sen/shen, n. **—dis·sen·tious,** di·sen/shes, a.

dis·sent·er, n. One who differs in opinion.

dis·ser·tate, dis/er·tāt, v.i., **-ta·ted, -tat·ing.** To present in formal writing or speech; writing or speech on a topic. **—dis·ser·ta·tion,** dis·er·tā/shen, n. **—dis· ser·ta·tor,** n.

dis·serve, dis·serv/, v.t., **-served, -serv·ing.** To do an injury to someone or something.

dis·serv·ice, dis·ser/vis, n. An injury.

dis·si·dence, dis/e·dens, n. Disagreement.

dis·si·dent, dis/e·dent, a. Dissenting; disagreeing with an opinion or group.—n. One who dissents from others; a dissenter.

dis·sim·i·lar, di·sim/e·ler, a. Unlike; different. **—dis·sim·i·lar·i·ty,** di·sim·e·lar/e·tē, n. **—dis·sim· i·lar·ly,** adv.

dis·sim·i·late, di·sim/e·lāt, v.t., v.i., **-at·ed, -at·ing.** To make or become unlike. **—dis·sim·i·la·tion,** n. **—dis·sim·i·la·tive, dis·sim·i·la·to·ry,** a.

dis·si·mil·i·tude, dis·i·mil/e·tood, dis·i·mil/e·tūd, n. Unlikeness; difference; a point of difference.

dis·sim·u·late, di·sim/ye·lāt, v.t., **-lat·ed, -lat·ing.** To disguise or conceal.—v.i. To dissemble. **—dis· sim·u·la·tion,** n. **—dis·sim·u·la·tive,** a. **—dis·sim· u·la·tor,** n.

dis·si·pate, dis/e·pāt, v.t., **-pat·ed, -pat·ing.** To scatter; disperse; dispel.—v.i. To become scattered or dispersed.

dis·si·pat·ed, dis/e·pā·tid, a. Indulging in excessive pleasure. **—dis·si·pat·ed·ly,** adv. **—dis·si·pat·ed· ness,** n. **—dis·si·pa·tive,** a. **—dis·si·pa·tor,** n.

dis·si·pa·tion, dis·e·pā/shen, n. The act of dissipating.

dis·so·ci·ate, di·sō/shē·āt, v.t., **-at·ed, -at·ing.** Disunite; separate.—v.i. To withdraw from association; to undergo dissociation. **—dis·so·ci·a·tive,** a.

dis·so·ci·a·tion, di·sō·sē·ā/shen, di·sō·shē· ā/shen, n. The act of dissociating.

dis·so·lute, dis/e·loot, a. Loose in behavior and morals. **—dis·so·lute·ly,** adv.

dis·so·lu·tion, dis·e·loo/shen, n. A breaking up, a loosening.

dis·solve, di·zolv/, v.t., **-solved, -solv·ing.** To melt; break up; terminate.—v.i. To slowly disappear.—n. A simultaneous fading out of one scene, on a motion picture or TV screen, while fading in another. **—dis· solv·er,** n. **—dis·solv·a·ble,** a.

dis·so·nance, dis/e·nens, n. A mixture of harsh sounds.

dis·so·nant, dis/e·nent, a. Unpleasant to the ear. **—dis·so·nant·ly,** adv.

dis·suade, di·swād/, v.t., **-suad·ed, -suad·ing.** To persuade not to do something. **—dis·suad·er,** n. **—dis·sua·sion,** di·swā/zhen, n. **—dis·sua·sive,** a.

dis·taff, dis/taf, n. A split stick used to hold wool for spinning.—a. Female.

dis·tal, dis/tel, a. Distant; of the farthest end.

dis·tance, dis/tens, n. The space or length between two points or objects; remoteness. —v.t., **-tanced, -tan·cing.** To place with space between objects or points.

dis·tant, dis/tent, a. Separate or removed; far away; cold in personality. **—dis·tant·ly,** adv.

dis·taste, dis·tāst/, n. Dislike. **—dis·taste·ful,** a. **—dis·taste·ful·ly,** adv. **—dis·taste·ful·ness,** n.

dis·tem·per, dis·tem/per, n. Ill humor; a disease of animals.—v.t. To sicken the body or the mind.

dis·tend, dis·tend/, v.t. To stretch or swell out.—v.i. To become swollen or inflated. **—dis·ten·sion, dis· ten·tion,** n.

dis·till, Brit. **dis·til,** dis·til/, v.t., **-tilled, -till·ing.** To purify or refine a liquid by heating the liquid until it becomes steam and then catching the cooled drops. **—dis·till·a·ble,** a. **—dis·tilled,** a. **—dis·til·la·tion,** dis·te·lā/shen, n.

dis·til·late, dis/ti·lit, dis/ti·lāt, di·stil/it, n. The liquid formed from the cooled drops in distillation.

dis·till·er, di·stil/er, n. A person who distills.

dis·till·er·y, di·stil/e·rē, n. pl., **dis·till·er·ies.** The building where distilling is done.

dis·tinct, dis·stingkt/, a. Not alike; separate; well-defined. **—dis·tinct·ly,** adv. **—dis·tinct·ness,** n.

dis·tinc·tion, di·stingk/shen, n. Something which is shown to be different; mark or sign of honor.

dis·tinc·tive, di·stingk/tiv, a. Indicating difference.

dis·tin·guish, di·sting/gwish, v.t. To set apart as different or separate; to recognize as different; to find or show the difference.

dis·tin·guish·a·ble, di·sting/gwish·e·bel, a. Having a difference.

dis·tin·guished, di·sting/gwisht, a. Famous; well-known.

dis·tort, dis·tôrt/, v.t. To twist out of natural or regular shape or to change the true meaning. **—dis·tor·tion,** n. **—dis·tor·tion·al,** a.

dis·tort·ed, dis·tôr/tid, a. Twisted.

dis·tract, dis·trakt/, v.t. To draw away attention from one thing to another; to confuse. **—dis·tract·ing·ly,** adv.

dis·tract·ed, di·strak/tid, a. Confused. **—dis·tract· ed·ly,** adv.

dis·trac·tion, di·strak/shen, n. Someone or something which draws away attention, sometimes to something more pleasant. **—dis·trac·tive,** a.

dis·trait, di·strā/, Absent-minded; inattentive because of a distraction.

dis·traught, di·trôt/, a. Distracted; disturbed mentally.

dis·tress, dis·tres/, n. Extreme pain in mind or body. —v.t. To cause pain or make miserable. **—dis·tress· ful,** a. **—dis·tress·ful·ly,** adv. **—dis·tress·ful·ness,** n. **—dis·tress·ing,** a. **—dis·tress·ing·ly,** adv.

dis·tress, dis·tres/, a. Pertaining to merchandise sold at a loss, as, a distress sale.

dis·trib·ute, dis·trib/yût, v.t., **-ut·ed, -ut·ing.** To divide or give out in shares; to arrange in proper places. **—dis·trib·ut·a·ble,** a. **—dis·tri·bu·tion,** dis·tre· bū/shen, n. **—dis·trib·u·tor,** n.

dis·trict, dis/trikt, n. A portion of a country, state, or city serving as a unit for schools, political representation, etc.—v.t. To divide a region or locality into districts.

dis·trict at·tor·ney, n. The prosecuting officer of a judicial district.

dis·trust, dis·trest/, v.t. To doubt.—n. Doubt or suspicion. **—dis·trust·ful,** a. **—dis·trust·ful·ly,** adv. **—dis· trust·ful·ness,** n.

dis·turb, dis·terb/, v.t. To destroy the peace, quiet, or rest of; to interfere. **—dis·turb·ance,** di·ster/bens, n.

dis·turbed, di·sterbd/, a. Showing signs of mental or emotional interest.

dis·un·ion, dis·ūn/yen, n. Separation; disagreement.

dis·u·nite, dis·yû·nīt/, v.t., **-nit·ed, -nit·ing.** To separate.; to become separated.—v.i. **dis·u·ni·ty,** dis· ū/ne·tē, n. pl., **dis·u·ni·ties.** A lack of unity.

dis·use, dis·ūs/, n. Lack of use or exercise; to stop using.—dis·ūz/, v.t. **-used, -us·ing.**

ditch, dich, n. A trench or long, narrow place dug in the earth.—*v.t.* To dig a ditch in; to get rid of or abandon. —*v.i.* To dig a ditch. —**ditch·er**, *n.*

dith·er, dith′ər, *n.* Trembling; quivering; a condition of excitement or confusion.—*v.i.* To act hesitantly, irresolutely, or in a disturbed or excited manner.

dit·to, dit′ō, *n. pl.*, **-tos**. The aforesaid; the same: a term used in accounts, lists, or the like to avoid repetition; also *ditto mark. Informal.* A duplicate or copy.—*adv.* As already stated.—*v.t.*, **-toed, -to·ing.**

dit·ty, dit′ē, *n. pl.*, **-ties**. A song; a little poem to be sung.

di·u·ret·ic, dī·yû·ret′ik, *a.* Having the power to increase the amount of urine discharged.—*n.* A medicine that increases the secretion of urine.

di·ur·nal, dī·ər′nəl, *a.* Of the daylight hours; happening every day. —**di·ur·nal·ly,** *adv.*

di·van, di·van′, di·vän′, dī′van, *n.* A long, cushioned seat, often without arms or a back; a sofa or couch.

dive, dīv, *v.i.*, **dived** or **dove, dived, div·ing.** To plunge head-first into water; to submerge, as a submarine or skin diver; to penetrate suddenly into anything, as with the hand; to enter deeply into anything, as a hobby or discussion; of an airplane, to plunge downward.—*n.* An act of diving. *Informal.* A disreputable place for drinking and gambling. —**div·er**, *n.*

dive bomb·er, *n.* An airplane that drops its bombs while in a steep dive. —**dive-bomb**, *v.t.*, *v.i.*

di·verge, di·vərj′, dī·vərj′, *v.i.*, **-verged, -verg·ing.** To tend or proceed from a common point in different directions; to differ or vary.—*v.t.* To turn aside or turn away. —**di·ver·gence**, di·vər′jəns, *n.* —**di·ver·gen·cy**, di·vər′jən·sē, *n.* —**di·ver·gent**, *a.*

di·vers, dī′vərz, *a.* Various.

di·verse, di·vərs′, dī·vərs′, *a.* Different; unlike. —**di·ver·si·fi·ca·tion**, di·vər·sə·fə·kā′shən, *n.* —**di·ver·si·fy**, di·vər′sə·fī, *v.t.*, **-fied, -fy·ing.** —**di·ver·si·fied**, *a.*

di·ver·sion, di·vər′zhən, dī·vər′shən, *n.* The act of diverting or turning aside from any course; that which diverts the mind from care, business, or study; play; pastime. —**di·ver·sion·ar·y**, *a.*

di·ver·si·ty, di·vər′si·tē, *n.* The state of being diverse; difference.

di·vert, di·vərt′, *v.t.* To turn off from any course; to turn aside: to *divert* a stream or traffic; to entertain.

di·vide, di·vīd′, *v.t.*, **-vid·ed, -vid·ing.** To part or separate into pieces; to classify; to keep apart, as by a partition; to make partition of among a number; to disunite in opinion or interest.—*v.i.* To become separated; to fork, as a road; to do mathematical division.

div·i·dend, div′ə·dend, *n.* A sum or a number to be divided; something extra or beyond the expected; the proportion of profit or gain made by a corporation which is divided among the stockholders.

di·vine, di·vīn′, *a.* Pertaining to God; holy; excellent in the highest degree; relating to divinity or theology. *Informal.* Very delightful; wonderful.—*v.t.*, **di·vined, di·vin·ing.** To foretell; to predict.

div·ing bell, *n.* An apparatus, originally bell-shaped, in which persons can descend into the water and remain for a length of time.

di·vin·ing rod, di·vī′ning, *n.* A forked stick, usu. of hazel, which is believed useful for indicating the presence of water or metal deposits. Also **dows·ing rod.**

di·vin·i·ty, di·vin′ə·tē, *n. pl.*, **-ties**. The state of being divine; deity; sacredness; theology. (*Cap.*) God; Deity.

di·vis·i·ble, di·viz′ə·bəl, *a.* Capable of division; separable. —**di·vis·i·bly**, *adv.*

di·vi·sion, di·vizh′ən, *n.* The act of dividing or separating into parts; separation; something that separates or traces the boundaries of; distributing or apportioning; a part separated from the whole, as a segment or section; discord.

di·vi·sive, di·vī′siv, *a.* Serving or tending to divide; causing dissention or strife.

di·vi·sor, di·vī′zər, *n.* The number by which the dividend is divided.

di·vorce, di·vōrs′, di·vôrs′, *n.* A legal dissolution of the marriage relation; a complete separation of any kind.—*v.t.*, **-vorced, -vorc·ing.** To separate by divorce; to separate; cut off.

di·vor·cé, di·vōr′sā, *n.* A divorced man.

di·vor·cee, di·vor·cée, di·vōr·sē′, di·vōr·sā′, *n.* A divorced woman.

di·vulge, di·velj′, *v.t.*, **di·vulged, di·vulg·ing.** To tell or make known, as what was before private or secret; to reveal. —**di·vul·gence**, *n.*

Dix·ie, dik′sē, *n.* The southern states of the U.S., esp. the states comprising the Confederacy during the Civil War.

diz·zy, diz′ē, *a.*, **-zi·er, -zi·est.** Having a sensation of whirling with instability or proneness to fall; giddy; mentally confused or dazed; causing giddiness: a *dizzy* height; caused or characterized by giddiness. *Informal.* Silly.—*v.t.*, **-zied, -zy·ing.** To make dizzy or giddy; to confuse. —**diz·zi·ly**, *adv.* —**diz·zi·ness**, *n.*

DNA, *n.* Deoxynibonucleic acid, a compound found in chromosomes, subdivisions of which are believed to be the genes.

do, doo, *v.t.*, **did, done, do·ing.** To perform, as an act; to complete or accomplish: He *did* the work; to exert: I *did* my utmost; to be the cause of: to *do* good, to *do* harm; to give or render: as, to *do* justice; to deal with, in the manner appropriate to the act: to *do* dishes, to *do* one's hair; to cover or traverse: to *do* a hundred miles an hour; to suffice, it will *do* me for the present; to remain a period of time: to *do* a second term in office; to change the language of: They are *doing* Cervantes' novel in musical form.—*v.i.* To fare: The patient is *doing* as well as expected; to suffice for the purpose: This will *do;* to take place: What's *doing* at the club?—*aux. v.* In interrogative, negative, or inverted construction, *do* is used for idiomatic word order and has no special meaning: *Do* you know where you are going? We *do* not wish to go there. *Do* expresses emphasis in such constructions as: I *do* work. *Do* is used in elliptical constructions, as: *Did* you go? I *did.*—**do away with**, to put an end to: to *do away with* unnecessary tasks.—**do by**, to treat: He *does* well *by* his children. —**do or die**, to make a very great effort —**do out of**, to cheat or swindle: The peddler *did* him *out* of five dollars.—**do over**, to repeat; to redecorate: to *do* the dining room *over.*—**do without**, to dispense with: to *do without* a car.—**have to do with**, to have a connection or an association with: What does that *have to do with* the problem? —**make do**, to get along despite inadequacy: as, to *make* old clothes *do.*

do, dō, *n. pl.*, **dos**. The name given to the first of the syllables used in solmization; the first or key note of the diatonic scale.

do·a·ble, doo′ə·bəl, *a.* Capable of being done or executed.

doc·ile, dos′əl, *a.* Easily managed; teachable.

dock, dok, *v.t.* To deprive of something.

dock, dok, *n.* An enclosure artificially formed on the side of a harbor or the bank of a river for reception of ships; a wharf; a waterway together with surrounding piers and wharves; a shipping or loading platform for any type of vehicle, such as trucks or freight trains. —*v.t.*, *v.i.* To bring or come into dock.

dock, dok, *v.t.* To join and couple together two or more objects orbiting in outer space. —**dock·ing**, *n.*

dock·yard, dok′yärd, *n.* A yard containing naval stores and facilities for building or repairing ships.

doc·tor, dok′tər, *n.* A person duly licensed to practice medicine; a physician, dentist, or veterinarian; one who has received the degree of this name from a university, being *doctor* of laws, philosophy, etc.—*v.t.* To serve as physician to; to treat with remedies; patch up; to falsify.—*v.i.*

doc·tor·al, dok/tər·əl, *a.* Relating to the degree of a doctor.

doc·tor·ate, dok/tər·it, *n.* The university degree of doctor.

doc·trine, dok/trin, *n.* That which is taught; a body or system of teachings relating to a particular subject; a particular principle taught or advocated; a tenet or dogma. —**doc·tri·nal,** dok/trə·nəl, *a.*

doc·u·ment, dok/yə·mənt, *n.* A written or printed paper furnishing information or evidence; a legal or official paper.—*v.t.* To support by documentary evidence; to furnish with documents, evidence, or the like.

doc·u·men·ta·ry, dok·yə·men/tə·rē, *a.* Derived from documents.—*n. pl.,* **-ries.** A dramatic or instructive presentation prepared for motion pictures or TV. —**doc·u·men·ta·ri·ly,** *adv.*

doc·u·men·ta·tion, dok·yə·men·tā/shən, *n.* The use of documentary evidence; a furnishing with authentic documents.

dod·der, dod/ər, *v.i.* To tremble or shake, as from old age. —**dod·dered,** *a.*

dodge, doj, *v.i.,* **dodged, dodg·ing.** To move back and forth or to and fro; move aside or change position suddenly, as to avoid a blow or to get behind something; to use evasive methods.—*v.t.* To elude by evasive methods.—*n.* An act of dodging; a springing aside; a shifty trick. —**dodg·er,** *n.*

do·do, dō/dō, *n. pl.,* **-dos, -does.** A clumsy, flightless, extinct bird. *Informal.* One who is slow-witted.

doe, dō, *n. pl.,* **does, doe.** The female of the deer, goat, antelope, and rabbit.

do·er, doo/ər, *n.* One who performs what is required, as opposed to a mere talker or theorizer.

doe·skin, dō/skin, *n.* The skin of a doe.

doesn't, dez/ənt. Contraction of does not.

doff, dôf, dof, *v.t.* To take off, as clothing.

dog, dôg, dog, *n.* A tame, meat-eating, four-footed animal; any animal belonging to the same family which includes the wolves, jackals and foxes; the male of such an animal; a despicable person.—*v.t.,* **dogged, dog·ging.** To follow or track like a dog, esp. with hostile intent; to hound.—*adv.* Completely or extremely, usu. used in combination: *dog-tired.*—**go to the dogs,** to go to ruin.

dog-eared, dôg/ērd, *a.* Having the corners of pages turned down from careless handling.

dog-eat-dog, dôg/ēt·dôg/, dog/ēt·dog/, *a.* Characterized by ruthless competition.

dog·fight, dôg/fit, dog/fit, *n.* A fight between dogs. *Informal.* Close combat between fighter airplanes.

dog·ged, dô/gid, dog/id, *a.* Tenacious; obstinate. —**dog·ged·ly,** *adv.* —**dog·ged·ness,** *n.*

dog·gone, dôg/gôn, dog/gon/, *interj.* or *v.t.,* **-goned, -gon·ing.** *Informal.* Damn! Darn! —**dog·goned,** *a.*

dog·house, dôg/hows, dog/hows, *n.* A dog's small house or shelter.—**in the doghouse,** *Informal.* In disfavor.

dog·ma, dôg/mə, dog/mə, *n. pl.,* **-mas, -ma·ta, -mə·tə.** A settled opinion or belief; a tenet, as of a religious faith.

dog·mat·ic, dôg·mat/ik, dog·mat/ik, *a.* Pertaining to dogma; asserting opinions authoritatively or peremptorily; positive; overbearing. Also **dog·mat·i·cal.** —**dog·mat·i·cal·ly,** *adv.*

dog·ma·tism, dôg/mə·tiz·əm, dog/mə·tiz·əm, *n.* Authoritative or overbearing assertion of opinion or belief. —**dog·ma·tist,** *n.*

dog·ma·tize, dôg/mə·tiz, dog/mə·tiz, *v.i.,* **-tized, -tiz·ing.** To express oneself in a dogmatic way.

do-good·er, doo·gûd/ər, *n.* A zealous but impractical humanitarian or social activist.

dog tag, *n.* A disk fastened to a dog's collar giving the animal's identifying license number; one of the pair of

identification tags worn by a member of the armed forces.

dog·wood, dog/wûd, *n.* A tree or shrub that bears small flowers with white or pink bracts like petals.

doi·ly, doy/lē, *n. pl.,* **-lies.** A small, ornamental cloth mat.

do·ing, doo/ing, *n.* A performance; personal effort; *pl.,* social activities; events; deeds.

do-it-your·self, doo/it·yər·self/, *a.* Pertaining to supplies and materials manufactured and marketed esp. for the use of hobbyists or amateurs. —**do-it-your·self·er,** *n.*

dol·drums, dōl/drəmz, dol/drəmz, *n. pl..* The parts of the ocean near the equator that abound in calms, squalls, and light baffling winds; low spirits; a period of inactivity.

dole, dōl, *n.* That which is dealt out or distributed; that which is given in charity.—*v.t.,* **doled, dol·ing.**

dole·ful, dōl/fəl, *a.* Full of or causing grief; mournful; melancholy.

doll, dol, *n.* A toy representing a child or other human being. *Informal.* A man or woman who is considered attractive by the opposite sex.

dol·lar, dol/ər, *n.* The monetary unit of the U.S.; the corresponding unit, coin, or note in Canada and several other countries or territories.

doll·y, dol/ē, *n. pl.,* **-lies.** A child's name for a doll; a low platform on rollers or wheels, used for transporting heavy objects.—*v.t.,* **dol·lied, dol·ly·ing.** To transport on or handle with a dolly.

dol·or·ous, dol/ər·əs, dō/lər·əs, *a.* Sorrowful; expressing pain or grief.

dol·phin, dol/fin, dôl/fin, *n.* Any of various cetaceans, some of which are commonly called porpoises.

dolt, dōlt, *n.* A dull, stupid person. —**dolt·ish,** *a.*

do·main, dō·mān/, *n.* Absolute ownership of property; property so owned; a realm; a field of action, influence, or thought.

dome, dōm, *n.* A large hemispherical or approximately hemispherical roof; a cupola, anything shaped like a cupola.—*v.t., v.i.,* **domed, dom·ing.**

do·mes·tic, də·mes/tik, *a.* Of or pertaining to the home or the household; of or pertaining to one's own or a particular country; belonging, existing, or produced within a country: *domestic* trade; of an animal, living with humans: tame.—*n.* A hired or household servant; *pl.,* home manufactures or goods. —**do·mes·ti·cal·ly,** *adv.*

do·mes·ti·cate, də·mes/tə·kāt, *v.t.,* **-cat·ed, -cat·ing.** To convert to domestic uses; to tame, as an animal. —**do·mes·ti·ca·ble,** *a.* —**do·mes·ti·ca·tion,** də·mes·tə·kā/shən, *n.*

do·mes·tic·i·ty, dō·me·stis/ə·tē, *n. pl.,* **-ties.** The state of being domestic; *pl.,* domestic affairs.

dom·i·cile, dom/i·sil, dom/i·səl, *n.* A place of residence; a house or home.—*v.t.,* **-ciled, -cil·ing.** To set up in a domicile.

dom·i·nance, dom/ə·nəns, *n.* Rule; authority. Also, **dom·i·nan·cy.**

dom·i·nant, dom/ə·nənt, *a.* Ruling; prevailing; governing; predominant.

dom·i·nate, dom/ə·nāt, *v.t.,* **-nat·ed, -nat·ing.** To have power or sway over; to govern; to triumph over; to overlook from a greater height.—*v.i.* To predominate; to occupy a higher position. —**dom·i·na·tion,** dom·ə·nā/shən, *n.* —**dom·i·na·tor,** *n.*

dom·i·neer, dom·ə·nēr/, *v.i.* To rule arbitrarily or with insolence.—*v.t.* —**dom·i·neer·ing,** *a.*

do·min·ion, də·min/yən, *n.* The power or right of governing and controlling; rule; control; lands or domains subject to sovereignty or control; a territory under its own form of government: the *Dominion* of Canada.

dom·i·no, dom/ə·nō, *n. pl.,* **-noes.** A masquerade dress, consisting of a loose cloak and usu. a half mask; *pl.,* a game played with twenty-eight flat blocks, dotted, as on dice, with a certain number of points.

don, don, *v.t.,* **donned, don·ning.** To put on; to dress in; to assume.

do·nate, dō′nāt, dō·nāt′, *v.t.,* **-nat·ed, -nat·ing.** To make a gift of.—*v.i.* To contribute. **—do·na·tor,** *n.*

do·na·tion, dō·nā′shən, *n.* The act of giving or bestowing; a grant; a gift.

done, dən, *a.* Executed; completed; finished.

do·nee, dō·nē′, *n.* The recipient of a gift.

Don Juan, don wän, don·joo′ən, *n.* A nobleman and seducer of Spanish legend; a seducer; a rake.

don·key, dong′kē, dəng′kē, *n. pl.,* **-keys.** An ass; a stupid or obstinate person.

do·nor, dō′nər, *n.* One who gives or donates; one who gives blood for transfusion, or organs or tissue for transplant.

do-noth·ing, doo′nəth·ing, *n.* One who does nothing; an idler.—*a.*

don't, dōnt. Contraction of do not.—*n.* An instruction not to do something.

doo·dad, doo′dad, *n. Informal.* Any trifling ornament; a gadget.

doo·dle, doo′dəl, *n. Informal.* An aimless design or scribble.—*v.i., v.t.,* **-dled, -dling.** To sketch or scribble while the mind is preoccupied.

doom, doom, *n.* A judgment; passing of sentence; the final judgment; fate; fortune, generally evil; ruin; destruction.—*v.t.* To condemn to punishment; to pronounce sentence on; to decree.

dooms·day, doomz′dā, *n.* The day of the Last Judgment, as the end of the world; any day of sentence or condemnation.

door, dōr, *n.* An opening or passage into a room, house, or building by which persons enter and leave; a solid barrier that covers the opening of a cabinet, room, or the like, usu. opening and closing by means of hinges or by sliding in a groove; a means of approach or access.—**next door to,** near to.—**out of doors,** out of the house; in the open air.

door·bell, dōr′bel, dōr′bel, *n.* An electric bell, usu. at the side of a door.

door·jamb, dōr′jam, dōr′jam, *n.* The vertical sides of a door frame which support the lintel.

door·knob, dōr′nob, dōr′nob, *n.* The knob or handle on a door, for opening.

door·mat, dōr′mat, dōr′mat, *n.* A small rug or pad at a door for cleaning shoes before entering. *Informal.* A person who submits to ill-treatment without protest.

door·step, dōr′step, dōr′step, *n.* A step at a door.

door·way, dōr′wā, dōr′wā, *n.* The opening into a room or house that is closed by a door.

dope, dōp, *n.* Any thick liquid or pasty preparation, as a sauce, lubricant, etc. *Informal.* Opium used for smoking; any addictive drug; information or data; a person under the influence of, or addicted to, the use of drugs; an unintelligent person.—*v.t.,* **doped, dop·ing.** To affect with stupefying or stimulating drugs. —*v.i. Informal.* To use stimulating drugs.

dop·ey, dop·y, dō′pē, *a.,* **-i·er, -i·est.** *Informal.* Affected by or as by dope; dull-witted; slow. **—dop·i·ness,** *n.*

dorm, dôrm, *n. Informal.* Dormitory.

dor·mant, dôr′mənt, *a.* Sleeping; lying asleep or as if asleep; inactive as in sleep. **—dor·man·cy,** dôr′mən·sē, *n.*

dor·mer, dôr′mər, *n.* A vertical window in a section that sticks out from a sloping roof. Also **dor·mer win·dow. —dor·mered,** *a.*

dor·mi·to·ry, dôr′mə·tōr·ē, dôr′mə·tōr·ē, *n. pl.,* **-ties.** A sleeping room, esp. a large room containing a number of beds; a residence hall with rooms for sleeping. Also **dorm.**

dor·sal, dôr′səl, *a.* Of or having to do with the back of the body; *dorsal* fins.

dor·y, dôr′ē, dōr′ē, *n. pl.,* **dor·ies.** A small boat with a

dos·age, dō′sij, *n.* The administration of medicine in doses; the amount of medicine to be administered.

dose, dōs, *n.* A quantity of medicine prescribed to be taken at one time; a quantity of anything unpleasant that must be taken or endured.—*v.t.,* **dosed, dos·ing.** To give as a dose; to give a dose to.

dos·si·er, dos′ē·ā, dô·syā′, *n.* A collection of documents or papers containing detailed information about a person or subject.

dot, dot, *n.* A small point or spot made with a pen or other pointed instrument; a speck, used in marking a writing; a precise point in time.—*v.t.,* **dot·ted, dot·ting.** To mark with dots.—*v.i.* To make dots or spots.

dot·age, dō′tij, *n.* Feebleness or imbecility, particularly in old age; foolish affection.

dot·ard, dō′tərd, *n.* One whose intellect is impaired by age; a senile.

dote, dōt, *v.i.,* **dot·ed, dot·ing.** To love to excess or extravagance; to have the intellect impaired by age, so that the mind wanders or wavers; to be in a state of senile silliness. **—dot·er,** *n.* **—dot·ing·ly,** dō′ting·lē, *adv.*

dot·ty, dot′e, *a.,* **ti·er, -ti·est.** *Informal.* Slightly mad or eccentric.

dou·ble, dəb′əl, *a.* Twofold in form, size, amount, or extent; paired; twice as great, heavy, or strong; twofold in character, meaning, or conduct; ambiguous; deceitful; hypocritical; insincere; something double or twice as much; a fold; one who looks very much like another; an apparition; a sudden turning back on a course; an actor who takes the place of another; a two-base hit in baseball.—*v.t.,* **-bled, -bling.** To make double or twice as great in number, size, value, or strength; to bend or fold one part into another.—*v.i.* To become double or twice as much; turn back on a course; to hit a two-base hit in baseball.—**double up,** to share one's quarters with another; to laugh uproariously, bending over with mirth. **—doub·ly,** *adv.*

dou·ble-breast·ed, dəb′əl-bres′tid, *a.* Referring to a coat or vest with an overlapping front, having a double row of buttons and a single row of buttonholes.

dou·ble-cross, dəb′əl-krôs, dəb′əl-kros, *n.* A betrayal of a person; an act of treachery or perfidy. **—dəb′əl-krôs′, dəb′əl-kros,** *v.t.*

dou·ble date, *n.* A date arranged by two couples. **—dou·ble-date,** *v.i.,* **-dat·ed, -dat·ing.**

dou·ble-deal·ing, dəb′əl-dē′ling, *n.* Duplicity.—*a.* Given to duplicity; deceitful. **—dou·ble-deal·er,** *n.*

dou·ble-deck·er, dəb′əl-dek′ər, *n.* A bus or a ship with a lower and upper floor of seats; a sandwich with two layers of filling in three slices of bread.

dou·ble-faced, dəb′əl-fāst, *a.* Deceitful; hypocritical; showing two sides or faces.

dou·ble fea·ture, *n.* Two movies shown on one program.

dou·ble-head·er, dəb′əl-hed′ər, *n.* Two games played in a row, seen for the price of one.

dou·ble-joint·ed, dəb′əl-joyn′tid, *a.* Having joints that allow great freedom of motion.

dou·ble play, *n.* A play in baseball in which two base runners are put out.

dou·ble stand·ard, *n.* A code that discriminates between two groups, esp. the moral standard which applies more stringent rules to women than to men.

dou·ble-take, dəb′əl-tāk, *n.* A delayed second look or reaction showing surprise to what at first appeared unsurprising.

dou·ble-time, dəb′əl-tim, *n.* Double-quick time or step; a rate of pay twice that of the regular wage scale.—*v.t.,* **-timed, -tim·ing.**

doubt, dowt, *v.i.* To waver or fluctuate in opinion; to be uncertain respecting the truth or fact; to be undeter-

---

a- hat, fāte, fāre, fäther; e- met, mē; i- pin, pīne; o- not, nōte, ôrb, moove (move), boy, pownd; u- cūbe, bůll, tůk (took); ch- chin; th- thick, <del>t</del>hen; zh- vizhon (vision); ə- əgo, takən, pencəl, lemən, bərd (bird).

mined.—*v.t.* To hold questionable; hesitate to believe.
—*n.* Uncertainty; indecision.

doubt•ful, dowt′fəl, *a.* Entertaining doubt; undetermined; not clear in its meaning; questionable.

doubt•less, dowt′lis, *adv., a.* Without doubt or question.

douche, doosh, *n.* A jet of water or the like applied to a particular cavity of the body for hygienic or medicinal purposes; the application of such a jet; an instrument for administering it.—*v.t., v.i.,* **douched, douch•ing.** To apply a douche to, or take a douche.

dough, dō, *n.* A pasty mixture; a mass composed of flour or meal moistened and kneaded but not baked; *Informal.* Money.

dough•nut, dō′nət, *n.* A small, roundish cake, usually with a hole in the center and deep-fat fried.

dough•ty, dow′tē, *a.,* **-ti•er, -ti•est.** Brave; valiant. —**dough•ti•ly,** *adv.* —**dough•ti•ness,** *n.*

dour, dûr, dow′ər, *a.* Sullen; gloomy; stern. —**dour•ly,** *adv.* —**dour•ness,** *n.*

douse, dows, *v.t.,* **doused, dous•ing.** To plunge into water; to immerse. *Informal.* To put out or extinguish.

dove, dəv, *n.* Any bird of the pigeon family, a symbolic messenger of peace, usu. depicted carrying an olive branch; (*cap.*) the Holy Ghost.

dove, dōv, past tense of **dive.**

dove•cote, dəv′kōt, dəv′kot, *n.* A small birdhouse, esp. for pigeons.

dove•tail, dəv′tāl, *n.* A projection at the end of a piece of metal, wood, etc., designed to interlock and form a joint with a corresponding opening at the end of another piece; the joint thus formed.—*v.t., v.i.* To join by a dovetail; to fit together exactly or harmoniously.

dow•a•ger, dow′ə•jər, *n.* A widow who has property or a title inherited from her deceased husband. *Informal.* An elderly woman of dignified bearing.

dow•dy, dow′dē, *a.,* **-di•er, -di•est.** Shabby, not stylish; frumpish. —*n.* —**dow•di•ness,** *n.*

dow•el, dow′əl, *n.* A wooden or iron pin used to join together two pieces of any substance.—*v.t.,* **-eled, -el•ing, -elled, -ell•ing.** To fasten with dowels.

dow•er, dow′ər, *n.* That with which one is endowed; that part of her dead husband's real estate which a widow is endowed with for life.—*v.t.* To endow; furnish with a dower.

down, down, *adv.* From higher to lower; in a descending direction or order, as from the top, head, or beginning; from an earlier to a later time or person; below the horizon; as a deposit: fifty dollars *down*; in writing: to jot *down;* to a depressed or prostrate position; into or in a lower position or condition; to or at a low point, degree, rate, or pitch; in due position or state: to settle *down* to work.—*prep.* In a descending direction on, over, or along.—*a.* Downward; downcast; dejected; behind an opponent by a specified amount.—*n.* A downward movement; a descent; a reverse of fortune; in football, one of the offensive team's four chances to advance the football ten yards.—*v.t.* To put, throw, knock, or lie down; to swallow.—**down on,** *Informal.* Unsympathetic or hostile to.—**down with.** (Let us) abolish or destroy (something).

down, down, *n.* The fine, soft plumage of birds under the outer feathers, esp. on the breasts of waterfowl; any fine feathery or hairy substance. —**down•i•ness,** *n.* —**down•y,** *a.*

down•cast, down′kăst, down′kast, *a.* Cast downward; in low spirits; dejected.

down•fall, down′fôl, *n.* A sudden descent from power, honor, or the like; ruin; a fall, esp. one that is heavy or sudden, of rain or snow. —**down•fall•en,** *a.*

down•grade, down′grād, *n.* A gradually descending slope.—*v.t.,* **-grad•ed, -grad•ing.** To reduce in salary, status, etc.—*a., adv.* Downward.

down•heart•ed, down′här′tid, *a.* Dejected; discouraged.

down•hill, down′hil, *n.* A slope.—*adv.* Downward.—*a.*

Descending; worse.

down•pour, down′pôr, down′pōr, *n.* An especially heavy, usually sudden, rain.

down•right, down′rīt, *adv.* Completely; thoroughly. —*a.* Thorough; utter; plain; straightforward.

down•stairs, down′stärz′, *n. pl. but sing. in constr.* The lower floor or floors of a building.—*adv.* Down the stairs; to or on a lower floor.—*a.* On a lower floor.

down•stream, down′strēm′, *adv.* In the direction of the current of a river or stream.

down-to-earth, down′tə•ərth′, *a.* Realistic; practical; without affectation.

down•town, down′town′, *n.* The business center of a city or town.—*a., adv.*

down•trod•den, down′trod-ən, *a.* Oppressed; trampled.

down•ward, down′wərd, *adv.* From a higher place to a lower; in a descending course. Also **down•wards.** —**down•ward•ly,** *a.*

down•wind, down′wind′, *a., adv.* In the same direction the wind is blowing.

dow•ry, dow′rē, *n. pl.,* **-ries.** The money, goods, or estate which a woman brings to her husband in marriage; a natural talent. Also **dower.**

dox•ol•o•gy, dok•sol′ə•jē, *n.* An expression of praise to God, esp. a hymn in church.

doze, dōz, *v.i.,* **dozed, doz•ing.** To sleep lightly; to be or half asleep.—*n.* A light sleep; a nap. —**doz•er,** *n.*

doz•en, dəz′ən, *n. pl.,* **doz•ens;** after a numeral, **doz•en.** A group of twelve.—*a.* —**doz•enth,** *a.*

drab, drab, *n.* Any of various cloths of a dull color, esp. brown or gray; the color of drab.—*a.,* **drab•ber, drab•best.** Dull, cheerless, or monotonous; dull brown or gray. —**drab•ly,** *adv.* —**drab•ness,** *n.*

drab, drab, *n.* A slattern; a whore.

draft, draft, dräft, *n.* The act of pulling or drawing loads; a pull or haul; the act of inhaling; that which is inhaled; the drawing of a liquid from its receptacle, as of ale from a cask; the act of drinking; the amount taken in one drink; a current of air in an enclosed space; a device for regulating a current of air, as in a fireplace; the selecting of persons for some special purpose, esp. compulsory military service; those selected; a written order drawn by one person or bank on another for the payment of money; a drawing, sketch, or design, as a construction plan; a first or preliminary form of any writing.—*a.* Suited for pulling heavy loads; drawn from a cask: *draft* beer.—*v.t.* To draw or pull; take by draft; draw up in preliminary form.—**on draft,** of beer, ready to be drawn from a cask. —**draft•er,** *n.*

draft dodg•er, *n.* One who evades or tries to evade compulsory service in the armed forces.

draft•ee, draf•tē′, dräf•tē′, *n.* One who is drafted, as for military service.

drafts•man, drafts′mən, dräfts′mən, *n. pl.,* **-men.** One employed in making mechanical drawings, as of machines and structures; one who draws up documents. —**drafts•man•ship,** *n.*

draft•y, draf′tē, dräf′tē, *a.,* **-i•er, -i•est.** Characterized by or allowing air currents to enter: a *drafty* room. —**draft•i•ly,** *adv.*

drag, drag, *v.t.,* **dragged, drag•ging.** To pull heavily or slowly along; haul; trail; to protract or pass tediously, often with *out* or *on*.—*v.i.* To be drawn or hauled; move heavily or with effort; lag behind; fish or search with a drag; to proceed laboriously or drably.—*n.* Something used by or for dragging, as a dragnet or a dredge; a heavy harrow; anything that retards progress; the act of dragging. *Informal.* A boring thing or person; transvestite clothing; influence; pull; a draw on a cigarette, etc. —**drag•ging•ly,** *adv.*

drag•gle, drag′əl, *v.t., v.i.* To make or become soiled or wet by dragging through mud, water, etc.; to straggle.

drag•net, drag′net, *n.* A net drawn along the bottom of water or along the ground to catch something; any system for catching a person, esp. a fugitive criminal.

drag·on, drag′ən, *n.* A mythical, monstrous animal resembling a winged snake or crocodile; a fierce or violent person; a very strict and vigilant person, esp. a chaperon.

drag·on·fly, drag′ən·flī, *n. pl.,* **-flies.** Any of various large, harmless insects with long, slender bodies and gauzy wings, which feed on flies, mosquitoes, etc.

drag race, *n. Informal.* A short race between two or more cars to see which one accelerates fastest.

drain, drān, *v.t.* To draw off gradually, as a liquid; to draw off or take away completely; to make empty or dry by drawing off liquid; to deprive of possessions or resources by gradual withdrawal; to exhaust.—*v.i.* To flow off gradually; become empty or dry by gradual flowing away of liquid.—*n.* The act of draining or drawing off; a gradual or continuous outflow, expenditure, or depletion; that which causes such outflow; that by which anything is drained, as a pipe or conduit. —**drain·a·ble,** *a.* —**drain·er,** *n.*

drain·age, drā′nij, *n.* The act or process of draining; a system of drains, artificial or natural; that which is drained off; sewage.

drain·age ba·sin, *n.* A usu. large area whose waters drain into a major river and its tributaries.

drain·pipe, drān′pīp, *n.* A pipe used for draining.

drake, drāk, *n.* A male duck.

dram, dram, *n.* An apothecaries' weight equal to one eighth of an ounce; in avoirdupois weight, one sixteenth of an ounce; any small amount.

dra·ma, drä′mə, dram′ə, *n.* A composition presenting in dialogue a story of life or character, esp. one intended to be acted on the stage; a play; the branch of literature having such compositions as its subject; any series of events having dramatic interest and leading up to a climax. —**dra·mat·ic,** drə·mat′ik, *a.* —**dra·mat·i·cal·ly,** *adv.*

dra·mat·ics, drə·mat′iks, *n. pl.* Amateur theatrical productions; excessive emotional behavior; *sing.* or *pl. in constr.,* the art of producing or acting plays.

dram·a·tist, dram′ə·tist, drä′mə·tist, *n.* A playwright.

dram·a·tize, dram′ə·tīz, drä′mə·tīz, *v.t.,* **-tized, -tiz·ing.** To compose in the form of a drama.—*v.i.* To express in a dramatic way. —**dram·a·ti·za·tion,** dram·ə·ti·zā′shən, *n.*

drape, drāp, *v.t.,* **draped, drap·ing.** To cover or hang with some fabric in graceful folds.—*v.i.* To hang or fall in folds.—*n.* A curtain or drapery; the manner in which cloth hangs.

drap·er, drā′pər, *n.* One who drapes; *esp. Brit.,* a dealer in cloth or dry goods.

dra·per·y, drā′pə·rē, *n. pl.,* **-per·ies.** Fabric coverings, hangings, or clothing disposed in loose, graceful folds; the draping or disposing of fabrics in graceful folds.

dras·tic, dras′tik, *a.* Acting with strength or violence; severe. —**drast·i·cal·ly,** *adv.*

draught, draft, dräft, *v., n.* Esp. Brit. for **draft.**—*n. pl. but sing. in use, Brit.,* the game of checkers.

draw, drô, *v.t.,* **drew, drawn, draw·ing.** To pull, haul, or drag; to lead or take along; to obtain or remove; to extract; to eviscerate; to draw forth; to make by extracting the essence; to steep, esp. tea; to attract; to take in as by sucking or inhaling; to deduce or infer; to derive, acquire, or obtain; to drain; to sketch in lines or words; depict; delineate; to shut; to fill up; to select or acquire by chance; to make or manufacture by stretching or hammering, as wire or dies; to wrinkle or shrink by contraction; to accumulate or gain; to withdraw, as money from a bank; to draft (a check); to formulate; to specify in legal form; to leave, as a contest, undecided; to tie; of a ship, to need (a certain amount of water) to float.—*v.i.* To exert a pulling,

moving, or attracting force; to move, go, or pass gradually; to take out a sword, pistol, or similar instrument for action; to produce or have a draft of air, as a pipe or flue; to effect drainage; to leave a contest undecided; to settle in water, as a boat; to levy or call for money or supplies; to make demands, as for money due or on deposit; to shrink; to wrinkle or pucker up; to practice the art of drawing; sketch.—*n.* The act, process, or result of drawing; a lot or chance picked at random; a tie or undecided contest; a basin or valley, into or through which water drains; something which attracts attention or patronage. —**draw out,** to persuade to speak freely; to prolong; to remove, as money. —**draw up,** to arrange into position; to come or bring to a standstill; to come alongside; to write out in proper or legal form; to stand erect.

draw·back, drô′bak, *n.* That which detracts from success, progress, etc.; a disadvantage; hindrance; a refund on money paid.

draw·bridge, drô′brij, *n.* A bridge which can be wholly or partly raised, lowered, or moved aside.

draw·er, drô′ər, *n.* One who draws; one who draws an order, draft, or bill of exchange. —drôr. A sliding storage compartment in a piece of furniture that may be pulled out and pushed back.

draw·ers, drôrz, *n. pl.* Underpants.

draw·ing, drô′ing, *n.* The act of a person or thing that draws; that which is drawn; a sketch or design; a lottery.

draw·ing card, *n.* One who or that which attracts patronage or attention.

draw·ing room, *n. U.S.* A private room in a railway passenger car; a room in a house for receiving company.

drawl, drôl, *v.t., v.i.* To utter or pronounce in a slow manner by prolongation of the vowels.—*n.*

drawn, drôn, *v.* Past participle of **draw.**

drawn, drôn, *a.* Haggard; taut or tense.

dread, dred, *v.t.* To anticipate with terror or apprehension.—*n.* Apprehension; person or thing inspiring apprehension; awe.—*a.* Dreaded; dreadful.

dread·ful, dred′fəl, *a.* Causing dread; terrible; awe-inspiring. *Informal.* Shocking; disgusting; very bad. —**dread·ful·ly,** *adv.*

dream, drēm, *n.* A succession of images or ideas present in the mind during sleep; the sleeping state in which this occurs; a reverie; an aim or hope; sometimes, a wild or vain fancy; something of beauty or charm associated with dreams rather than with reality.—*v.i.,* **dreamed** or **dreamt, dream·ing.** To have a dream or dreams; to conceive as possible.—*v.t.* To see or imagine in, or as in a dream; to spend or waste (time) in dreaming. —**dream up.** *Informal.* To conceive or concoct, esp. something very ingenious or impractical. —**dream·er,** *n.* —**dream·ful·ly,** *adv.* —**dream·like,** *a.*

dream·y, drē′mē, *a.,* **-i·er, -i·est.** Full of dreams; impractical; visionary; causing dreams; soothing; like a dream; vague; blurry. *Informal.* Wonderful.

drear·y, drēr′ē, *a.,* **-i·er, -i·est.** Dismal; gloomy; oppressively monotonous. —**drear·i·ly,** *adv.* —**drear·i·ness,** *n.*

dredge, drej, *n.* A contrivance for gathering objects or material from the bed of a river, lake, or harbor, by dragging along the bottom; an apparatus with a net used esp. for gathering fish, etc.—*v.t.,* **dredged, dredg·ing.** To clear, deepen, or gather with a dredge. —*v.i.* To use a dredge. —**dredg·er,** *n.*

dreg, dreg, *n. Usu. pl.* The sediment of liquors; grounds; any waste or worthless residue. *Sing.* Any small quantity; a drop. —**dreg·gy,** *a.*

drench, drench, *v.t.* To soak; to saturate.—*n.* A thorough soaking; something that drenches; a solution for soaking.

---

a- hat, fāte, fāre, fäther; **e-** met, mē; **i-** pin, pīne; **o-** not, nōte, ôrb, moove (move), boy, pownd; **u-** cūbe, bůll, tûk (took); **ch-** chin; **th-** thick, ŧhen; **zh-** vizhon (vision); **ə-** əgo, takən, pencəl, lemən, bərd (bird).

dress, dres, *v.t.,* **dressed** or **drest, dres·sing.** To put clothes upon; to trim; to clean or prepare by a special process; bring into line, as troops; to apply bandages or medications to.—*v.i.* To come into line, as troops; to put on or wear clothing, esp. formal clothes.—*n.* Clothing; apparel; the outer garment of girls and women consisting of skirt and blouse, usu. in one piece; a frock; formal clothes; a certain aspect or appearance.—*a.* Of or for a dress; of or requiring formal dress. **—dress down,** to scold; rebuke. **—dress up,** to put on a good suit or dress, etc.; put on formal clothes.

dress·er, dres'ər, *n.* A bureau or chest of drawers for clothing, often with a mirror.

dress·er, dres'ər, *n.* One who helps another dress; a valet; one who dresses in a distinctive manner: a fancy *dresser.*

dress·ing, dres'ing, *n.* The act of one who or that which dresses; that with which something is dressed, as bandages for a wound; a mixture for stuffing fowl; a sauce added to a dish: salad *dressing.*

dress·ing gown, *n.* A loose gown or robe worn at home.

dress·ing room, *n.* A room used while dressing, esp. backstage in a theater or in a clothing store.

dress·mak·er, dres'māk·ər, *n.* A person whose occupation is making or altering women's clothing to order.

dress re·hears·al, *n.* A play rehearsal, complete with costumes, makeup, scenery, props, and lighting.

dress shirt, *n.* A man's shirt for semiformal or formal evening wear.

dress·y, dres'ē, *a.,* **-i·er, -i·est.** *Informal.* Elaborate or rather formal in attire; chic.

drib·ble, drib'əl, *v.i.,* **-bled, -bling.** To fall or flow in drops or small quantities; trickle.—*v.t. Sports.* To move along by a rapid succession of short kicks, bounces, or pushes.—*n.* A dripping; a small, trickling stream; a drop; a small quantity of anything. *Sports.* The act of dribbling. **—drib·bler,** *n.*

drib·let, drib'lit, *n.* One of a number of small pieces or parts. Also **drib·blet.**

dried, drīd, *v.* Past tense and past participle of **dry.**

dri·er, dry·er, drī'ər, *n.* One who or that which dries; a mechanical contrivance or apparatus for removing moisture.

drift, drift, *n.* The act of moving or driving something along by, or as by, a current of air, water, or similar force; something heaped or piled into masses by currents, as snow or sand; the direction of thought; tenor; the direction or rate of movement of a current of water, air, etc.; the current; flow; the deviation of aircraft from a set course due to winds; a horizontal passage in a mine; a deposit of sand, clay, gravel, and boulders carried by a glacier or glacial water.—*v.i.* To move or be driven in a current; to be heaped up, as by water or by the wind; to move along aimlessly, carelessly, or effortlessly; be without goals or direction. —*v.t.* To cause to drift. **—drift·age,** *n.* **—drift·er,** *n.*

drift·wood, drift'wûd, *n.* Wood floating on, or cast ashore by, the water.

drill, dril, *v.t., v.i.* To pierce or bore with a drill, as a hole; to pierce or bore a hole in; to instruct and exercise in military tactics and the use of arms; to discipline; to teach by repetition.—*n.* A tool or machine for drilling holes; instruction by constant repetition; any strict, methodical training. **—drill·er,** *n.*

drill, dril, *n.* A small furrow made in the soil, in which to sow seeds; a machine for sowing seeds in rows.—*v.t.* To sow or raise in drills, as seed or crops.

drill·ing, dril'ing, *n.* A stout twilled cotton or linen fabric used for linings, pockets, overalls, or summer clothing. Also **drill.**

drill·mas·ter, dril'mas·tər, dril'mä·stər, *n.* One who gives practical instruction in military tactics and the use of arms; one who trains in fundamentals.

dri·ly, drī'lē, *adv.* Dryly.

drink, dringk, *v.i.,* **drank, drunk, drink·ing.** To swallow water or other liquid; to imbibe alcoholic liquors, esp. habitually or to excess; to drink in honor of or homage to (used with *to*).—*v.t.* To swallow; imbibe; to absorb (liquid or moisture); to take in eagerly through the senses or mind.—*n.* Any liquid which is swallowed; a beverage; alcoholic liquor; drinking alcoholic liquor to excess. *Informal.* A body of water. **—drink·a·ble,** *a.* **—drink·er,** *n.*

drip, drip, *v.t., v.i.,* **dripped** or **dript, drip·ping.** To fall or cause to fall in drops.—*n.* The falling of a liquid in drops; the liquid; the sound of the falling; a cornice or other device for shedding rainwater. *Informal.* Someone very dull, insipid, or disagreeable. **—drip·py,** *a.*

drip-dry, drip'drī', drip'drī, *v.i.,* **-dried, -dry·ing.** Of a fabric article, to dry wrinkle-free, or nearly so, when hung up dripping wet.—*v.t., a.*

drip·ping, drip'ing, *n.* Usu. pl. The fat which falls from meat in roasting; anything that drips.—*a.* Very wet.

drive, drīv, *v.t.,* **drove, driv·en, driv·ing.** To push or propel onward; force along; to cause or force (someone) to some act or condition: despair *drove* him to drink; guide the movement of; convey in a vehicle; to keep going, as machinery; propel; impel or urge; compel to work or overwork; to carry through vigorously, as business or a bargain; to propel or hit hard, as a ball; to penetrate by force, or produce by such penetration: *drive* a well; to provide the power for.—*v.i.* To move along, esp. rapidly; to strike or propel a ball, etc. with force; to drive a vehicle, esp. an automobile.—*n.* The act of driving; a road to drive on; a trip in a vehicle, esp. an automobile; energy; aggressiveness; any strong motivating force; an organized effort; the propelling of a ball, etc.; the propelling mechanism of an automobile, etc.; a usu. large-scale military attack; a compelling need, force, or pressure; a gathering and guiding, esp. of logs or animals; the things guided. **—drive at,** to mean or intend.

drive-in, drīv'in, *n.* A theater, restaurant, bank, or other business that caters to customers who remain in their automobiles while being served.—*a.*

driv·el, driv'əl, *v.i., v.t.,* **-eled, -el·ing.** To let saliva flow from the mouth; slaver; to talk childishly or idiotically; utter silly nonsense.—*n.* **—driv·el·er,** *n.*

driv·er, drī'vər, *n.* One who or that which drives; a wooden-headed golf club for driving from the tee; a part that transmits motion, as in a machine; one who works the people under him very hard.

drive·way, drīv'wā, *n.* A road, esp. a private drive, leading from a public road to a building.

driz·zle, driz'əl, *v.i.,* **-zled, -zling.** To rain in small drops.—*v.t.* To shed in small particles.—*n.* A small or fine rain. **—driz·zly,** *a.*

droll, drōl, *a.* Comical; humorously odd. **—droll·er·y,** *n. pl.,* **-er·ies.**

drom·e·dar·y, drom'ə·der·ē, drəm'ə·der·ē, *n. pl.,* **-dar·ies.** An unusually swift camel, esp. a one-humped Arabian camel.

drone, drōn, *n.* The male honeybee; a humming or low sound.—*v.i.,* **droned, dron·ing.** To make a low, heavy, dull sound; to hum; to talk in a dull monotonous tone.

drool, drool, *v.i.* To water at the mouth; to show effusive pleasure; gloat.—*v.t.—n.* Senseless talk; drivel.

droop, droop, *v.i.* To sink or hang down; to languish from grief or other cause; to fail or sink.—*n.* A drooping. **—droop·ing·ly,** *adv.* **—droop·y,** *a.,* **droop·i·er, droop·i·est.**

drop, drop, *n.* A small quantity of liquid which falls or is produced in a more or less spherical mass; a liquid globule; a very small quantity of liquid; a minute quantity of anything; *usu. pl.,* liquid medicine given in drops; something like or likened to a drop, as a lozenge; a fall or descent; the distance or depth to which anything drops; that which drops or is used for dropping.—*v.i.,* **dropped** or **dropt, drop·ping.** To fall in globules or small portions, as a liquid; drip; have an abrupt descent; fall wounded, dead, or exhausted; to quit or withdraw; to come to an end; cease; to decrease or decline; to pass into some condition.—*v.t.* To let fall in small portions; distill; shed, as tears; to let fall or cause to fall like a drop; allow to sink or cause to sink to a lower position; of animals, give birth to; to utter casually or incidentally, as a hint; send, as a note, in a casual or offhand manner; lose or part with, as money; bring to the ground by a blow or shot; set down, as from a ship or vehicle; omit, as a letter or syllable, in pronouncing or writing; to lower or cast down, as the eyes; to decrease, as in value; to dismiss, as an employee. —**drop in** or **by,** to visit casually or unexpectedly. —**drop off,** to decrease; to take to and let out of a certain place; to fall asleep; to die. —**drop out,** to withdraw, as from membership or from school.

drop kick, *n.* A kick given a football as it hits the ground after being dropped.

drop·let, drop/lit, *n.* A tiny drop.

drop-off, drop/ôf, *n.* A very steep descent; a decline.

drop·out, drop/owt, *n.* A withdrawal; a person who discontinues his formal education prior to graduation, as from high school or college.

drop·per, drop/ər, *n.* One who or that which drops; a tube of glass or similar material with a flexible rubber bulb at one end, for drawing a liquid and expelling it in drops.

drop·sy, drop/sē, *n.* Edema.

dross, drôs, dros, *n.* The refuse or impurities on the surface of melted metal; waste matter.

drought, drowt, *n.* Dry weather; a long period of dry weather that affects crops; thirst; scarcity. Also **drouth,** drowth. —**drought·y,** *a.,* **-i·er, -i·est.**

drove, drōv, *v.* Past tense of **drive.**

drove, drōv, *n.* A number of animals, as oxen, sheep, or swine, driven in a body; a crowd of people in motion. —**dro·ver,** *n.*

drown, drown, *v.t.* To deprive of life by immersion in water or other fluid; to overflow, overwhelm.—*v.i.* To die by suffocation in a liquid.

drowse, drowz, *v.i.,* **drowsed, drows·ing.** To be listless, sleepy, or half asleep.—*v.t.* To make listless or sleepy; to pass (time) in drowsing.—*n.* A condition of drowsing or of being half asleep. —**drow·si·ly,** *adv.* —**drow·si·ness,** *n.* —**drow·sy,** *a.,* **-si·er, -si·est.**

drub, drəb, *v.t.,* **drubbed, drub·bing.** To beat with a stick; defeat in a game, fight, etc.—*n.* A blow with a stick. —**drub·bing,** *n.*

drudge, drəj, *v.i.,* **drudged, drudg·ing.** To work hard; to labor in menial work.—*n.* One who labors hard in servile employment; a slave. —**drudg·er·y,** *n. pl.,* **-er·ies.** —**drudg·ing·ly,** *adv.*

drug, drəg, *n.* Any medicinal substance for internal or external use; often, a habit-forming medicinal substance; a narcotic; an overabundant commodity.—*v.t.,* **drugged, drug·ging.** To administer (usu. harmful) drugs to; to put a harmful drug in (food, drink, etc.); to stupefy, poison, or alter consciousness with a drug or drugs.

drug·gist, drəg/ist, *n.* A pharmacist.

drug·store, drəg/stôr, drəg/stōr, *n.* A place of retail business where prescriptions are filled, and drugs and miscellaneous merchandise are sold.

dru·id, droo/id, *n. Often cap.* One of an order of priests or ministers of religion among the ancient Celts of Gaul, Britain, and Ireland.

drum, drəm, *n.* A musical instrument consisting of a hollow body covered at one or both ends with a tightly stretched membrane, or head; the sound produced by this instrument when struck or beaten, or any noise suggestive of it; something resembling a drum in shape or structure or in the noise it produces; the tympanic membrane or middle ear.—*v.i.,* **drummed, drum·ming.** To beat or play on a drum; to tap or strike rhythmically or continuously.—*v.t.* To perform or summon by drumming; to drive or force by persistent repetition. —**drum out,** to expel dishonorably. —**drum up,** to stir or work up (esp. business) by soliciting, advertising, etc.

drum ma·jor, *n.* The chief or first drummer of a regiment; the marching leader of a band or drum corps.

drum·mer, drəm/ər, *n.* One who beats a drum. *Informal.* A traveling salesman.

drum·stick, drəm/stik, *n.* A stick for beating a drum; the lower joint of the leg of a dressed fowl.

drunk, drəngk, *a.* Intoxicated with strong drink; overwhelmed or dominated by some feeling or emotion, as if by alcohol.—*n.* A bout or spell of drinking to intoxication; a drunken person.

drunk·ard, drəng/kərd, *n.* An inebriate.

drunk·en, drəng/kən, *a.* Intoxicated; drunk; unsteady. —**drunk·en·ly,** *adv.* —**drunk·en·ness,** *n.*

dry, drī, *a.,* **dri·er, dri·est.** Free from moisture; not wet or damp; lacking rain or humidity; not underwater; depleted of liquid; not yielding milk; free from tears; drained or evaporated; thirsty; causing thirst; eaten or served without butter or the like: *dry* toast; free from sweetness: a *dry* wine; characterized by or favoring prohibition of the manufacture and sale of alcoholic liquors; of or pertaining to nonliquid substances or commodities: *dry* measure; stated in a straight-faced, pithy manner: *dry* humor; uninteresting: a *dry* topic. —*v.t., v.i.* **dried, dry·ing.** To make or become dry. —**dry up,** to become totally dry; to cease to be productive; to cease to be. *Informal.* To stop talking. —**dry·ly,** *adv.* —**dry·ness,** *n.*

dry·ad, drī/əd, drī/ad, *n. pl.,* **-ads, -a·des,** -ə-dēz. In classical mythology, a woodland nymph.

dry cell, *n.* A voltaic cell whose liquid contents have been made more or less solid by means of absorbent material. Also **dry bat·ter·y.**

dry-clean, drī/klēn, *v.t.* To clean (textiles) with solvents other than water. —**dry clean·er,** klē/nər, *n.* —**dry clean·ing,** klē/ning, *n.*

dry dock, *n.* A basinlike structure from which the water can be removed after the entrance of a ship, used during cleaning, construction, or repairs. —**dry·dock,** *v.t.*

dry·er, dry·est, drī/ər, drī/ist. Variants of **dri·er, dri·est.**

drygoods, *n. pl.* Textile fabrics as distinguished from groceries, hardware, etc.

Dry Ice, *n. Trademark.* Solidified carbon dioxide, usually in the shape of blocks, used as a refrigerant.

dry meas·ure, *n.* System of units of capacity used to measure dry commodities. *U.S.* Two pints make one quart, eight quarts make one peck, four pecks make one bushel of 2150.42 cubic inches.

dry rot, *n.* A decay of seasoned timber causing it to become brittle and to crumble to a dry powder; any concealed or unsuspected inward decay. —**dry-rot,** *v.t., v.i.*

dry run, *n.* A trial run or rehearsal; a military practice without live ammunition.

du·al, doo/əl, dū /əl, *a.* Of or indicating two; twofold; double; having two different natures. —**du·al·i·ty,** doo·al/ə·tē, dū·al/ə·tē, *n.*

du·al·ism, doo/ə·liz·əm, dū/ə·liz·əm, *n.* A twofold division; the theory that the universe is composed of two distinct, and usu. opposed principles, such as good and evil, matter and spirit, etc. —**du·al·ist,** *n.* —**du·al·is·tic,** doo·ə·lis/tik, *a.* —**du·al·i·ty,** doo·al/ə·tē, *n.*

dub, dəb, *v.t.,* **dubbed, dub·bing.** To strike lightly with a sword in the ceremony of conferring knighthood; to invest with any dignity or title; to style, name, or call by a descriptive nickname.

---

a- hat, fāte, fâre, fäther; **e-** met, mē; **i-** pin, pīne; **o-** not, nōte, ôrb, moove (move), boy, pownd; **u-** cūbe, bůll, tûk (took); **ch-** chin; **th-** thick, ŧhen; **zh-** vizhon (vision); **ə-** əgo, takən, pencəl, lemən, bərd (bird).

dub, dəb, *v.t.,* **dubbed, dub·bing.** To equip, as a film, with a new sound track; used with *in,* to add (music, dialogue, or other sounds) to a film, radio, or television tape recording; to transfer (recorded material) to a new record or tape.—*n.* Any sounds added to a sound track. —**dub·ber,** *n.*

du·bi·ous, doo′be·əs, dū′bē·əs, *a.* Doubtful; of questionable ethics or taste. —**du·bi·e·ty,** doo·bī′e·tē, *n.* —**du·bi·ous·ly,** *adv.* —**du·bi·ous·ness,** *n.*

du·cal, doo′kəl, dū′kəl, *a.* Referring to a duke. —**du·cal·ly,** *adv.*

du·cat, dək′ət, *n.* A gold coin formerly common to several European states. *Informal.* A ticket.

duch·ess, dəch′is, *n.* The wife or widow of a duke; a woman who has the sovereignty of a duchy.

duch·y, dəch′ē, *n. pl.,* **duch·ies.** The territory controlled or governed by a duke or duchess; a dukedom.

duck, dək, *n.* Any of numerous species of waterfowl that have a small body, a short neck, broad, flat bill, short legs, and a waddling gait; the flesh of the bird used as food. *Informal.* A person; fellow.

duck, dək, *v.t.* To plunge under water for a brief period of time; to bow; to stoop or nod in order to escape a blow; to evade a responsibility.—*v.i.* To plunge or dip into water briefly; to drop the head suddenly; to bow; to evade a disagreeable task.—*n.* The act or result of ducking.

duck, dək, *n.* A type of coarse, tightly-woven cloth resembling canvas.

duck·bill, dək′bil, *n.* The platypus.

duck·ling, dək′ling, *n.* A young duck.

duck soup, *n. Informal.* Something very easy to do.

duck·y, dək′ē, *a.,* **-i·er, -i·est.** *Informal.* Delightful; darling.

duct, dəkt, *n.* Any pipe, tube, canal, or conduit by which fluid or other substances are conducted or conveyed; such a tube carrying bodily secretions. —**duct·less,** *a.*

duc·tile, dək′til, *a.* Capable of being hammered out thin, as certain metals; malleable. —**duc·til·i·ty,** dək·til′ə·tē, *n.*

dud, dəd, *n. Informal.* A shell or bomb that fails to explode; a person, thing, or undertaking that fails.

dude, dood, dūd, *n.* A man whose appearance shows excessive care and delicacy; a dandy. *Informal.* A city-bred person, esp. an Easterner who spends a vacation on a ranch; a person; a cool person.

duds, dədz, *n. pl. Informal.* Clothes.

due, doo, dū, *a.* Owed or payable as an obligation or debt, esp. payable at once because the required date has been reached; owed or owing because of a moral or natural right; rightful, proper, or fitting; adequate or sufficient; expected or scheduled to be ready, arrive, or be present.—*n.* That which is due or owed; *pl.,* a charge or fee paid at regular intervals, as for the privilege of membership in a club.—*adv.* Directly or straight. —**due to,** caused by.

du·el, doo′əl, dū′əl, *n.* A prearranged combat between two persons, fought with deadly weapons according to an accepted code of procedure, esp. to settle a private quarrel; any contest between two persons or parties.—*v.i.,* **du·eled, du·el·ing.** —**du·el·ist,** *n.*

du·en·na, doo·en′ə, dū·en′ə, *n.* In Spanish and Portuguese families, an older woman appointed to serve as chaperon to the young ladies; a governess.

du·et, doo·et′, dū·et′, *n.* Music for two voices or instruments.

duf·fel bag, dəf′əl, *n.* A large canvas bag, cylindrical in shape when packed, used by campers, hunters, and members of the armed forces for carrying personal items.

duff·er, dəf′ər, *n.* A stupid, ineffectual, or clumsy person; a person who is inept at a particular sport or game.

dug, dəg, *v.* Past tense and past participle of **dig.**

dug, dəg, *n.* The pap or nipple of a female mammal.

dug·out, dəg′owt, *n.* A boat made by hollowing out a large log; an underground shelter for troops in trenches; a shelter at the side of a baseball field containing the players' bench.

duke, dook, dūk, *n.* A nobleman of the highest rank after a prince. *Informal, pl.* Fists or hands. —**duke·dom,** *n.*

dul·cet, dəl′sit, *a.* Sweet to the ear; melodious.

dull, dəl, *a.* Deficient in understanding or intelligence; stupid; unfeeling; not intense or acute; drowsy or heavy; listless or spiritless; uninteresting; not sharp, as a knife; not bright, as color, light, or sound; lusterless; dim; muffled.—*v.t., v.i.* To make or become dull. —**dull·ard,** *n.* —**dull·ish,** *a.* —**dull·ness, dul·ness,** *n.* —**dul·ly,** *adv.*

du·ly, doo′lē, dū′lē, *adv.* In a due manner; properly or fittingly; punctually.

dumb, dəm, *a. Informal.* Slow-witted; mute; without the power of speech; silent. —**dumb·ly,** *adv.* —**dumb·ness,** *n.*

dumb·bell, dəm′bel, *n. Usu. pl.* A weight used for exercising, consisting of two iron or wooden balls with a short bar between them for grasping. *Informal.* A stupid person.

dumb show, *n.* Gestures without words; pantomime.

dumb·struck, dəm′strək, *a.* Temporarily without speech, because of astonishment or confusion.

dumb·wait·er, dəm′wā·tər, *n.* A small elevator, for conveying food or other small articles, from floor to floor in a building.

dum·dum, dəm′dəm, *n.* A soft-nosed bullet which expands on striking.

dum·found, dəm·fownd′, dəm′fownd, *v.t.* To strike dumb with amazement; to astound. Also **dumb·found.**

dum·my, dəm′ē, *n. pl.,* **-mies.** The exposed hand in bridge which is played by the declarer along with his own hand; the player whose hand is exposed; a copy or sham object doing service for a real one; a figure on which merchants display clothing; one who is unable to speak; one who is usually silent. *Informal.* One who is stupid.—*a.* Sham; fictitious; counterfeit; artificial; seeming to act for oneself while really acting for another.

dump, dəmp, *v.t.* To throw down in a mass; fling down or drop heavily; to empty out by tilting or overturning; to get rid of suddenly and irresponsibly; to put goods on the market in large quantities at a low price.—*v.i.* To plunge; cast off refuse.—*n.* A mass of material, as rubbish, dumped or thrown down, or a place where it is deposited; a place for storing ammunition or other military supplies. *Informal.* A dilapidated or slovenly place. —**dump·er,** *n.*

dump·ling, dəmp′ling, *n.* A rounded mass of boiled or steamed dough often served with stewed meat; a kind of pudding consisting of a wrapping of dough enclosing an apple or other fruit, and boiled or baked.

dumps, dəmps, *n. pl. Informal.* A dull, gloomy state of mind.

dump truck, *n.* A truck with a special kind of body that can be tilted back to unload the contents through a rear opening.

dump·y, dəm′pē, *a.,* **-i·er, -i·est.** Squat; sulky; dilapidated. —**dump·i·ness,** *n.*

dun, dən, *v.t.,* **dunned, dun·ning.** To call on continually for payment of a debt; importune.—*n.* A demand for such payment; one who duns.

dun, dən, *a.* Of a grayish-brown or dull brown color. —*n.* A dull, grayish-brown color; a dun-colored horse.

dunce, dəns, *n.* An ignoramus; a person too stupid to learn; a dullard.

dune, doon, dūn, *n.* A hill or ridge of sand formed by wind, often near oceans or in deserts.

dung, dəng, *n.* The excrement of animals.—*v.t.* To manure with dung. —**dung·y,** *a.*

dun·ga·ree, dəng·gə·rē′, *n.* A coarse, durable cotton, generally blue, used for work clothes. *Pl.* Such clothing made of this cotton twill; blue jeans.

dyspeptic

dun·geon, dən·jən, *n.* A strong, close prison or cell, generally underground.

dung·hill, dəng′hil, *n.* A heap of dung; a vile place, thing, or situation.

dunk, dəngk, *v.t.* To dip into a liquid before eating; to dip or temporarily submerge into a liquid.—*v.i.* To dip. —**dunk·er,** *n.*

dun·nage, dən′ij, *n.* Baggage; mats, braces, blocks, etc., to protect cargo in a ship, truck, etc.

du·o, doo′ō, dū′ō, *n.* A pair. *Mus.* A duet.

du·o·dec·i·mal, doo·ə·des′ə·məl, dū·ə·des′ə·məl, *a.* Proceeding in computation by twelves; of or referring to 12 or twelfths.—*n.* One part of 12 equal parts; a number in a numbering system with base 12.

du·o·de·num, doo·ə·dē′nəm, doo·od′ə·nəm, dū·ə·dē′nəm, dū·od′ə·nəm, *n. pl.,* -**na.** The first portion of the small intestine, just below the stomach. —**du·o·de·nal,** *a.*

dupe, doop, dūp, *n.* A person who is easily cheated, or one easily led astray by his credulity.—*v.t.,* **duped, dup·ing.** To deceive; trick.

du·plex, doo′pleks, dū′pleks, *a.* Double; twofold.—*n.* Anything that is double or twofold. An apartment of rooms on two floors. Also **du·plex a·part·ment.**

du·pli·cate, doo′plə·kāt, dū′plə·kāt, *v.t.* -**cat·ed,** -**cat·ing.** To double; make twofold; to copy exactly. —doo′plə·kit, dū′plə·kit, *a.* Double; consisting of or existing in two corresponding parts of examples; exactly like or corresponding to something else.—*n.* One of two things exactly alike; a copy exactly like an original. —**in du·pli·cate,** in two copies, exactly alike. —**du·pli·ca·tion,** doo·plə·kā′shən, dūp·lə·kā′shən, *n.* —**du·pli·ca·tor,** *n.*

du·plic·i·ty, doo·plis′ə·tē, dū·plis′ə·tē, *n. pl.,* -**ties.** The practice of speaking or acting in two ways in relation to the same matter with intent to deceive; double-dealing.

du·ra·ble, dûr′ə·bəl, *a.* Lasting or enduring. —**du·ra·bil·i·ty,** dûr·ə·bil′ə·tē, *n.* —**dur·a·bly,** *adv.*

dur·ance, dûr′əns, *n.* Imprisonment.

du·ra·tion, dû·rā′shən, *n.* Continuance in time; the time during which anything lasts.

du·ress, dû·res′, dyû·res′, *n.* Coercion; imprisonment.

dur·ing, dûr′ing, *prep.* Throughout the course or existence of; at a point in.

dusk, dəsk, *a.* Dark; tending to darkness; dusky.—*n.* The darker stage of twilight; moderate darkness; shade; gloom.—*v.i., v.t.* To make or become dark or dim. —**dusk·i·ly,** *adv.* —**dusk·i·ness,** *n.* —**dusk·y,** *a.,* -**i·er,** -**i·est.**

dust, dəst, *n.* Earth or other matter in fine, dry particles; any finely powdered substance; a cloud of finely powdered earth or other matter in the air; confusion or turmoil; a low or humble condition; anything worthless; gold dust. *Informal.* Money.—*v.t., v.i.* To free from dust; to sprinkle with dust or powder; sprinkle as dust.

dust bowl, *n.* An area, such as south central U.S., that is subject to frequent dust storms and drought.

dust·er, dəs′tər, *n.* One who or that which dusts; anything, as a cloth or a machine, for removing dust; a long, light overgarment to protect the clothing from dust.

dust jack·et, *n.* A removable paper cover for a book, used to protect the binding.

dust·pan, dəst′pan, *n.* A utensil into which dust is swept for the purpose of removal.

dust storm, *n.* A wind storm which raises dense masses of dust into the air, occurring during a drought in areas of arable land.

dust·y, dəs′tē, *a.,* -**i·er,** -**i·est.** Filled or covered with dust; clouded with or as with dust; of the nature of dust; powdery. —**dust·i·ly,** *adv.* —**dust·i·ness,** *n.*

Dutch, dəch, *a.* Pertaining to the people, language, or culture of the Netherlands.—*n.*—**in Dutch.** *Informal.* In disgrace or trouble.

Dutch treat, *n.* A meal or entertainment for which each person pays his own expenses.

Dutch un·cle, *n. Informal.* A person who bluntly and sternly criticizes or admonishes someone else.

du·ti·a·ble, doo′tē·ə·bəl, dū′tē·ə·bəl, *a.* Subject to the imposition of duty or customs.

du·ti·ful, doo′ti·fəl, dū′ti·fəl, *a.* Performing the duties or obligations required by law or propriety; obedient. —**du·ti·ful·ly,** *adv.* —**du·ti·ful·ness,** *n.*

du·ty, doo′tē, dū′tē, *n. pl.,* -**ties.** That which a person is bound by any natural, moral, or legal obligation to do or perform; an act of obedience or respect, esp. respectful conduct toward one's parents or elders; a tax, esp. an import tax. —**off duty,** not at work. —**on duty,** at work.

dwarf, dwôrf, *n.* A human being, animal, or plant, much smaller than the ordinary stature or size; a mythical being, usually small and ugly, credited with magical powers.—*a.* Unusually small; stunted.—*v.t.* To render dwarf or dwarfish; to render insignificant in extent or character.—*v.i.* To become dwarfed or smaller. —**dwarf·ish,** *a.*

dwell, dwel, *v.i.,* **dwelt** or **dwelled, dwell·ing.** To abide as a permanent resident; to reside; linger or pause in thought or action; put stress (on).

dwell·ing, dwel′ing, *n.* A place of residence or abode; a house.

dwin·dle, dwin′dəl, *v.t., v.i.,* -**dled,** -**dling.** To diminish gradually; to shrink; to waste away.

dye, dī, *n.* Color or hue; a coloring material or matter. —*v.t.,* **dyed, dye·ing.** To color (cloth, hair, etc.), esp. by soaking in a liquid containing coloring matter. —**dye·ing,** *n.*

dyed-in-the-wool, dīd′in·thə·wûl′, *a. Informal.* Confirmed; complete and unqualified.

dye·stuff, dī′stəf, *n.* Coloring matter used in dyeing.

dy·ing, dī′ing, *a.* Ceasing to exist; nearing death; pertaining to or associated with death; fading away. —*n.* Death.

dyke, dīk, *n., v.t.* Dike.

dy·nam·ic, dī·nam′ik, *a.* Of or pertaining to force not in equilibrium, or to force in any state; active; forceful, or effective.—*n.* Dynamics; motive force. —**dy·nam·i·cal,** *a.* —**dy·nam·i·cal·ly,** *adv.* —**dy·na·mism,** dī′nə·miz·əm, *n.*

dy·nam·ics, dī·nam′iks, *n.* The study of the motion of bodies and of the effects of forces in producing motion.

dy·na·mite, dī′nə·mīt, *n.* An explosive consisting of nitroglycerin in an absorbent substance.—*v.t.* To shatter with dynamite.

dy·na·mo, dī′nə·mō, *n. pl.,* -**mos.** Dynamoelectric machine. *Informal.* A very forceful or energetic person.

dy·na·mo·e·lec·tric, dī·nə·mō·ə·lek′trik, *a.* Pertaining to the conversion of mechanical energy into electric energy, or vice versa.

dy·nas·ty, dī′nə·stē, *n. pl.,* -**ties.** A succession of rulers of the same line or family, who govern a particular country; the period during which they rule. —**dy·nas·tic,** dī·nas′tik, *a.*

dyne, dīn, *n.* That force which, acting on a mass of one gram, gives it an acceleration of one centimeter per second per second.

dys·en·ter·y, dis′ən·ter·ē, *n.* An infectious disease characterized by inflammation of the bowels, with diarrhea. *Informal.* Diarrhea.

dys·func·tion, dis·fəngk′shən, *n.* Abnormal or impaired functioning.

dys·pep·sia, dis·pep′shə, dis·pep′sē·ə, *n.* Impaired digestion; indigestion.

dys·pep·tic, dis·pep′tik, *a.* Pertaining to or suffering from dyspepsia; peevish; gloomy. Also **dys·pep·**

---

a- hat, fāte, fāre, fäther; **e-** met, mē; **i-** pin, pīne; **o-** not, nōte, ôrb, moove (move), boy, pownd; **u-** cūbe, bûll, tûk (took); **ch-** chin; **th-** thick, ŧhen; **zh-** vizhon (vision); **ə-** ego, taken, pencəl, lemən, bərd (bird).

ti·cal. —*n.* A person with dyspepsia. —**dys·pep·ti·cal·ly,** *adv.*

dys·tro·phy, dis′trə·fē, *n.* Faulty nutrition; any of several neuromuscular ailments marked by degeneration or weakness of muscle.

E

E, e, ē, *n.* The second vowel and the fifth letter of the English alphabet. (*Cap.*) *Mus.* the third tone in the natural scale of C.

each, ēch, *a.* Every one of any number separately considered or treated; every one of two or more considered individually: *Each* child carried his lunch to school.—*pron.* Each one: *Each* struggled with the job.—*adv.* To, for, or from each; apiece: They received one apple *each.*

each oth·er, *pron.* Each the other: They struck *each other;* one another: They struck at *each other.*

ea·ger, ē′gər, *a.* Characterized by enthusiastic, keen, or impatient feelings, interests, or desires; marked by great earnestness or diligence. —**ea·ger·ly,** *adv.* —**ea·ger·ness,** *n.*

ea·ger bea·ver, *n. Informal.* An overly zealous or diligent individual.

ea·gle, ē′gəl, *n.* Any of a family of large, very strong birds of prey, characterized by a hooked beak, sharp talons, and great powers of flight and vision; a representation of such a bird, often used as an emblem; a former U.S. gold coin worth ten dollars; in golf, two strokes below par for any hole.

ea·gle eye, *n.* Unusually keen visual power; the ability to watch or observe carefully. —**ea·gle-eyed,** *a.*

ea·glet, ē′glit, *n.* A young eagle.

ear, ēr, *n.* The organ of hearing which, in humans and higher animals, is composed of the external ear, the middle ear, and the internal ear; the external ear alone; the sense of hearing; the power to distinguish sounds, esp. acute perception of the differences of musical tone and pitch; attention; a favorable hearing; a projecting part from the side of anything, as the handle of a pitcher. —**eared,** ērd, *a.* —**be all ears,** to give one's full attention. —**fall on deaf ears,** to go unheeded or be ignored. —**up to the ears,** deeply involved; almost fully immersed.

ear, ēr, *n.* A spike or head of corn or other grain; that part of cereal plants which contains the flowers and seeds.—*v.i.* To form ears, as corn.

ear·ache, ēr′āk, *n.* Pain in the ear.

ear·drum, ēr′drəm, *n.* The tympanic membrane which separates the middle ear from the external ear.

earl, ərl, *n.* A nobleman, the third in rank, being directly below a marquis, and above a viscount. —**earl·dom,** *n.*

ear lobe, *n.* The soft, pendent part of the human ear or the ear of certain fowls. Also **ear·lap.**

ear·ly, ər′lē, *adv.,* -**li·er,** -**li·est.** In or during the first part of some division of time, or of some course or series; far back in time; before the usual or appointed time.—*a.* —**ear·li·ness,** *n.*

ear·ly bird, *n. Informal.* A person who arises or arrives early.

ear·mark, ēr′märk, *n.* A mark on the ear for distinguishing ownership of sheep, pigs, or cattle; any mark for distinction or identification.—*v.t.* To distinguish by putting an earmark on; to set apart for a specific purpose.

ear·muff, ēr′məf, *n. Often pl.* One of a pair of adjustable coverings for protecting the ears in cold weather.

earn, ərn, *v.t.* To gain by labor or service rendered; to gain as a due return or profit; to get as one's desert or due; deserve. —**earn·er,** *n.*

ear·nest, ər′nist, *a.* Serious in intention; sincerely zealous; of serious importance, or demanding serious attention. —**in ear·nest,** seriously; having, or with, a serious purpose. —**ear·nest·ly,** *adv.* —**ear·nest·ness,** *n.*

ear·nest, ər′nist, *n.* Something given as a pledge and security for the whole, or as a token of more to come.

earn·ings, ər′ningz, *n. pl.* That which is earned; wages; profit.

ear·phone, ēr′fōn, *n.* A device, worn over or in the ear, in which electrical energy is converted into sound waves.

ear·ring, ēr′ring, ēr′ing, *n.* An ornament worn on or hanging from the lobe of the ear.

ear·shot, ēr′shot, *n.* Range of hearing.

earth, ərth, *n.* (*Often cap.*) The planet on which we live, third in order from the sun; the abode of mortal man; the realm of mundane affairs; the surface of this planet; soil or dirt; dry land; the ground; the lair of any burrowing animal.—*v.t.* To drive into hiding, as an animal; to heap up or mound with soil for protection. —*v.i.* To hide in the ground; to burrow.

earth·bound, ərth′bownd, *a.* Firmly fixed in or to the earth; unimaginative; pedestrian.

earth·en, ər′thən, *a.* Made of earth; composed of baked clay.

earth·en·ware, ər′thən·wer, *n.* Pottery, dishes, etc., made of coarse baked clay.

earth·ly, ərth′lē, *a.,* -**li·er,** -**li·est.** Pertaining to the earth or this world; worldly; possible; conceivable.

earth·quake, ərth′kwāk, *n.* A trembling or undulation of a part of the earth's crust, due to volcanic activity, or other disturbances.

earth sci·ence, *n.* Any science dealing with the earth or any part or aspect of it, as geology, geography, oceanography.

earth·ward, ərth′wərd, *adv.* Toward the earth. Also **earth·wards.**—*a.*

earth·work, ərth′wurk, *n.* A fortification constructed of earth.

earth·worm, ərth′wərm, *n.* Any of the segmented worms found in the earth, esp. one which is often used as bait by anglers; angleworm.

earth·y, ər′thē, *a.,* -**i·er,** -**i·est.** Composed of earth or soil; like earth or having some of its properties; crude or unrefined; natural or down-to-earth. —**earth·i·ness,** *n.*

ear·wax, ēr′waks, *n.* A yellowish waxlike secretion from certain glands in the external auditory canal.

ease, ēz, *n.* Freedom from labor, physical pain, disturbance, excitement, or annoyance; repose; freedom from constraint, formality, or unnatural arrangement; unaffectedness.—*v.t.,* **eased, eas·ing.** Relieve; to give rest to; to move with care; to render less difficult.—*v.i.* To lessen tension, severity, pain, pressure, etc.: usu. with *up* or *off.* —**at ease,** of soldiers, free to assume a relaxed stance; comfortable; relaxed.

ea·sel, ē′zəl, *n.* A frame in the form of a tripod, for supporting an artist's canvas, or the like.

ease·ment, ēz′mənt, *n.* Convenience; accommodation; the right to use another's property.

eas·i·ly, ē′zə·lē, *adv.* In an easy manner; beyond question. —**eas·i·ness,** *n.*

east, ēst, *n.* One of the four cardinal points of the compass, directly opposite west; the direction of the sunrise; (*cap.*) areas lying east of a definite or implied point; the Orient.—*a.* —*adv.* In an easterly direction; eastward; in the east.

East·er, ē′stər, *n.* An annual Christian festival in commemoration of the resurrection of Jesus Christ, observed on the first Sunday after the full moon that occurs on or next after March 21.

east·er·ly, ē′stər·lē, *a., adv.* Toward or from the east.

east·ern, ē′stərn, *a.* Lying toward or situated in the east; coming from the east, as a wind; (*often cap.*) of or pertaining to the east; (*usu. cap.*) oriental. —**East·ern·er,** *n.* —**east·ern·most,** *a.*

East·ern Hem·i·sphere, *n.* The half of the earth east of the Atlantic Ocean, comprising the land masses of Africa, Asia, Australia, and Europe.

east·ward, ēst′wərd, *adv.* Toward the east. Also **east·wards.**—*a.*

eas·y, ē′zē, *a.,* **-i·er, -i·est.** Having or characterized by ease; comfortable; free from anxiety or care; not difficult; not hard to obtain; compliant; lenient; free from formality or embarrassment; smooth or flowing; gentle.—*adv. Informal.* With little effort; easily. —**on easy street,** financially secure; well-to-do.

eas·y·go·ing, ē′zē·gō′ing, *a.* Calm, relaxed.

eas·y mark, *n. Informal.* One who can easily be victimized, cheated, or fooled.

eat, ēt, *v.t.,* **ate, eat·en, eat·ing.** To take into the mouth, chew, and swallow for nourishment; to consume or destroy as if by eating (usu. with *up* or *away*); wear or waste away.—*v.i.* To consume food; take a meal. —**eats,** *n. pl. Informal:* Food.—**be eating someone,** to trouble a person. —**eat one's words,** to be forced to retract one's statements. —**eat·a·ble,** *a., n.* —**eat·er,** *n.*

eau de co·logne, ō·də kə·lōn′, *n.* A perfumed toilet water.

eaves, ēvz, *n. pl.* The overhanging lower edge of a roof.

eaves·drop, ēvz′drop, *v.i.,* **-dropped, -drop·ping.** To listen clandestinely to a private conversation. —**eaves·drop·per,** *n.*

ebb, eb, *n.* The return of tidewater toward the sea; a decline; decay.—*v.i.* To recede; decay; decline.

eb·on·y, eb′ə·nē, *n. pl.,* **-ies.** A hard, black, heavy wood from tropical trees, used for cabinet work, the black keys of pianos, etc.; the tree yielding this wood. —*a.* Made of ebony; like ebony; black; dark. Also, *poetic,* **eb·on,** *a., n.*

e·bul·lience, i·bəl′yəns, *n.* A boiling over; overflow; exuberance; exhilaration. —**e·bul·lient,** *a.* —**e·bul·li·tion,** eb·ə·lish′ən, *n.*

ec·cen·tric, ik·sen′trik, ek·sen′trik, *a.* Deviating from the usual practice; odd; not situated in the center; not moving in a circle or circular orbit; not having the same center; off center.—*n.* An eccentric person or thing. —**ec·cen·tri·cal·ly,** *adv.*

ec·cen·tric·i·ty, ek·sən·tris′ə·tē, *n.pl.,*-**ties.** Behavior that deviates from the usual; oddity; whimsicality.

ec·cle·si·as·tic, i·klē·zē·as′tik, *a.* Pertaining to the church or the clergy. Also **ec·cle·si·as·ti·cal.**—*n.* A clergyman. —**ec·cle·si·as·ti·cal·ly,** *adv.*

ech·e·lon, esh′ə·lon, *n.* Level of command; degree of rank or authority; a steplike pattern of troops, planes, etc.—*v.t., v.i.* To form in echelon.

e·chi·no·derm, i·kī′nə·dərm, ek′ə·nō·dərm, *n.* Any of a phylum of marine animals with radial bodies and spiny shells, including the starfish and sea urchin.

ech·o, ek′ō, *n. pl.,* **ech·oes.** A repetition of sound, produced by the reflection of sound waves; the sound so produced; any repetition or close imitation of the ideas or opinions of another; one who imitates another; a sympathetic response.—*v.t.,* **ech·oed, ech·o·**

ing. To sound again; send or repeat back sound; to repeat (words, opinions, behavior, etc.) in imitation. —*v.i.* To sound again; be repeated. —**ech·o·er,** *n.*

e·cho·ic, e·kō′ik, *a.* Imitating some sound.

e·clair, ā·klār′, i·klār′, *n.* An oblong pastry puff, filled with custard, whipped cream, or ice cream.

ec·lec·tic, i·klek′tik, *a.* Choosing what seems best from the doctrines, works, or styles of others; composed of such selections.—*n.* One who follows an eclectic method. —**ec·lec·ti·cal·ly,** *adv.* —**ec·lec·ti·cism,** ek·lek′tə·siz·əm, *n.*

e·clipse, i·klips′, *n.* The interception or obscuration of the light of the sun, moon, or other heavenly body, by the intervention of another heavenly body either between it and the eye or between it and the source of its illumination; any obscuration or overshadowing. —*v.t.,* **e·clipsed, e·clips·ing.** To cause to suffer eclipse; to obscure; darken; to obscure the importance, beauty, fame, etc. of; render dim by comparison; surpass; overshadow.

e·clip·tic, i·klip′tik, *a.* Pertaining to an eclipse; pertaining to the ecliptic.—*n.* The great circle formed by the intersection of the plane of the earth's orbit with the celestial sphere; the apparent annual path of the sun in the heavens.

e·col·o·gy, i·kol′ə·jē, *n.* The branch of biology that studies the relationships between organisms and their total environment; bionomics. —**ec·o·log·ic,** ek·ə·loj′ik, **ec·o·log·i·cal,** ek·ə·loj′ə·kəl, *a.* —**e·col·o·gist,** *n.*

e·co·nom·ic, ē·kə·nom′ik, ek·ə·nom′ik, *a.* Of or relating to economics; pertaining to the management of the income, expenses, resources, etc., of a community, nation, or individual; pertaining to financial matters; thrifty; utilitarian.

e·co·nom·i·cal, ē·kə·nom′i·kəl, ek·ə·nom′i·kəl, *a.* Frugal; avoiding waste; pertaining to economics.

e·co·nom·ics, ē·kə·nom′iks, ek·ə·nom′iks, *n. pl. but sing. in constr.* The science treating of the production, distribution, and consumption of wealth, or the material welfare of mankind; economic matters.

e·con·o·mist, i·kon′ə·mist, *n.* One who is expert in economics; one who is careful and frugal.

e·con·o·mize, i·kon′ə·mīz, *v.t.,* **-mized, -miz·ing.** To manage frugally or to best advantage.—*v.i.* Manage thriftily; cut down expenses. —**e·con·o·miz·er,** *n.*

e·con·o·my, i·kon′ə·mē, *n. pl.,* **-mies.** Thrifty management; frugality in the expenditure or consumption of money or materials; a saving; the management of the resources of a country, with regard to its productivity: the national *economy;* the disposition or regulation of the parts or functions of any complex whole; a judicious or sparing use of anything.

ec·o·sys·tem, ek′ō·sis·təm, *n.* The basic ecological unit, a community of living organisms interacting with their inanimate environment.

ec·ru, ek′roo, ā′kroo, *a.* Pale yellowish brown or beige in color.—*n.*

ec·sta·sy, ek′stə·sē, *n. pl.,* **-sies.** A state of intense, overpowering emotion; a state of exultation or mental rapture induced by beauty, music, or artistic creations; rapturous delight; a trance.

ec·stat·ic, ek·stat′ik, *a.* Of, like, or expressing ecstasy; rapturous; transported. Also **ec·stat·i·cal.**—*n.* One subject to ecstasies; *pl.,* fits of ecstasy.

ec·to·morph, ek′tə·môrf, *n.* A type of body structure, characterized by linearity and leanness. —**ec·to·mor·phic,** ek·tə·môr′fik, *a.*

ec·to·plasm, ek′tə·plaz·əm, *n.* The outer portion of the cytoplasm in a cell; the supposed emanation from the body of a spiritualist medium during a trance.

ec·u·men·i·cal, ek·yū·men′i·kəl, *a.* General; universal; of or representing the whole Christian Church; fostering worldwide Christian unity or cooperation.

---

a- hat, fāte, fāre, fäther; **e-** met, mē; **i-** pin, pīne; **o-** not, nōte, ôrb, moove (move), boy, pownd; **u-** cūbe, bůll, tůk (took); **ch-** chin; **th-** thick, then; **zh-** vizhon (vision); **ə-** ago, takən, pencəl, leman, bərd (bird).

Also **ec·u·men·ic.** —**ec·u·men·i·cal·ly,** *adv.* —**ec·u·men·ism,** ek/ū·mə·niz·əm, *n.*

ec·ze·ma, ek/sə·mə, eg/zə·mə, eg·zē/mə, *n.* An inflammatory disease of the skin attended with itching and the exudation of serous matter.

ed·dy, ed/ē, *n. pl.,* **-dies.** A current of air or water turning round in a direction contrary to the main stream, esp. a current moving circularly; a small whirlpool; any substance moving in a similar manner. —*v.i.,* **-died, -dy·ing.** To move circularly, or in eddies. —*v.t.* To cause to move in an eddy.

e·de·ma, i·dē/mə, *n. pl.,* **-ma·ta,** -mə·tə. A swelling due to excessive accumulation of fluid in a cavity or connective tissue.

E·den, ēd/ən, *n.* The garden in which Adam and Eve first lived; a paradise.

e·den·tate, ē·den/tāt, *a.* Toothless; belonging to an order of mammals, including the sloths, armadillos, and South American anteaters, in which the incisors and canines, or all the teeth, are lacking.—*n.* An edentate mammal.

edge, ej, *n.* The thin, sharp side of the blade of a cutting instrument or weapon; the sharpness proper to a blade; sharpness or keenness; fitness for action or operation; the line in which two surfaces of a solid object meet; a border or margin; the brink or verge. *Informal.* Advantage or superiority.—*v.t.,* **edged, edg·ing.** To put an edge on; to move edgeways; move or force gradually or by imperceptible degrees.—*v.i.* To move edgeways; advance slowly upon. —**on edge,** eager or impatient; in a state of acute and uncomfortable sensibility. —**edged,** *a.*

edge·wise, ej/wiz, *adv.* With the edge directed forward; in the direction of the edge; sideways. Also **edge·ways.**

edg·ing, ej/ing, *n.* A border or trimming.

edg·y, ej/ē, *a.,* **edg·i·er, edg·i·est.** Sharp-edged; irritable or nervous. —**edg·i·ness,** *n.*

ed·i·ble, ed/ə·bəl, *a.* Fit to be eaten as food; eatable. —*n. Usu. pl.* Anything fit or meant to eat.

e·dict, ē/dikt, *n.* An order issued by a ruler as a law requiring obedience; a decree.

ed·i·fice, ed/ə·fis, *n.* A building, esp. a large and impressive one.

ed·i·fy, ed/ə·fī, *v.t.,* **-fied, -fy·ing.** To instruct and improve in knowledge; improve morally; benefit spiritually. —**ed·i·fi·ca·tion,** ed/ə·fə·kā/shən, *n.* —**ed·i·fy·ing,** *a.*

ed·it, ed/it, *v.t.* To prepare or revise (literary matter) for publication; supervise the publication of (a newspaper, magazine, or other printed matter).

e·di·tion, i·dish/ən, *n.* The form in which a literary work is published; the whole number of copies of a book or newspaper, printed from one set of type and issued at one time.

ed·i·tor, ed/i·tər, *n.* One who edits; a writer of editorials. —**ed·i·tor·ship,** *n.*

ed·i·to·ri·al, ed·ə·tôr/ē·əl, *a.* Pertaining to editors. —*n.* An article, as in a newspaper, written by the editor or under his direction, and setting forth the position or opinion of the publication upon some subject; a statement of opinion broadcast by a radio or television station. —**ed·i·to·ri·al·ly,** *adv.*

ed·i·to·ri·al·ize, ed·i·tôr/ē·əl·īz, ed·i·tō/rē·əl·īz, *v.i.,* **-ized, -iz·ing.** To set forth one's opinions in, or as if in, an editorial; to express personal opinion in a supposedly factual report.

ed·u·cate, ej/û·kāt, ej/ə·kāt, *v.t.,* **-cat·ed, -cat·ing.** To advance the mental, aesthetic, physical, or moral development of, esp. by teaching or schooling; to send to school; to teach. —**ed·u·ca·ble,** ej/ə·kə·bəl, *a.* —**ed·u·cat·ed,** . —**ed·u·ca·tive,** *a.* —**ed·u·ca·tor,** *n.*

ed·u·ca·tion, ej·û·kā/shən, ej·ə·kā/shən, *n.* The process of educating, teaching, or training; a part of or a stage in this training; the learning or development which results from this process of training; the aca-

demic discipline dealing with teaching and learning methods in the schools. —**ed·u·ca·tion·al,** *a.*

e·duce, i·doos/, i·dūs/, *v.t.,* **-duced, -duc·ing.** To bring or draw out; to deduce. —**e·duc·i·ble,** *a.* —**e·duc·tion,** i·duk/shən, *n.*

eel, ēl, *n. pl.,* **eels,** eel. A fish characterized by its slimy serpent-like elongated body. —**eel·like,** *a.* —**eel·y,** *a.*

e'en, ēn, *adv. Poetic.* Even.

e'er, âr, *adv. Poetic.* Ever.

ee·rie, ēr/ē, *a.,* **ee·ri·er, ee·ri·est.** Frightening; suggesting supernatural influence or potential danger; strange. Also **ee·ry.** —**ee·ri·ly,** *adv.* —**ee·ri·ness,** *n.*

ef·face, i·fās/, *v.t.,* **-faced, -fac·ing.** To rub out or obliterate; to render inconspicuous. —**ef·face·ment,** *n.* —**ef·fac·er,** *n.*

ef·fect, i·fekt/, *n.* That which is produced by some agency or cause; a result; a consequence; power to produce results; purport; meaning; a mental impression produced; a combination, as of form, color, light, and shade, producing a particular mental impression. *Pl.* Goods; personal estate; property.—*v.t.* To bring about; accomplish; fulfill; produce or make. —**for effect,** for show; to impress or influence others. —**in effect,** in result or consequence; in operation; in reality; virtually. —**take effect,** to begin to act; become operative.

ef·fec·tive, i·fek/tiv, *a.* Serving to effect the purpose; producing the intended or expected result; in force or operation; fit for duty; striking; impressive.—*n.* A soldier or sailor equipped and available for military duty. —**ef·fec·tive·ly,** *adv.* —**ef·fec·tive·ness,** *n.*

ef·fec·tu·al, i·fek/choo·al, *a.* Producing, or capable of producing, an intended effect; legally valid or binding. —**ef·fec·tu·al·i·ty,** i·fek·chū·al/ə·tē, *n.*

ef·fec·tu·ate, i·fek/choo·āt, *v.t.,* **-at·ed, -at·ing.** To bring about; accomplish; cause.

ef·fem·i·nate, i·fem/ə·nit, *a.* Having qualities unsuitable to a man; womanish. —**ef·fem·i·na·cy,** *n. pl.,* **-cies.** —**ef·fem·i·nate·ly,** *adv.*

ef·fer·vesce, ef·ər·ves/, *v.i.,* **-vesced, -vesc·ing.** To bubble, hiss, and froth; to show liveliness or exhilaration. —**ef·fer·ves·cence,** *n.* —**ef·fer·ves·cent,** *a.*

ef·fete, e/fēt, i·fēt/, *a.* Lacking vitality; exhausted; incapable of bearing young.

ef·fi·ca·cious, ef·ə·kā/shəs, *a.* Effectual; producing the effect intended or desired.

ef·fi·ca·cy, ef/ə·kə·sē, *n. pl.,* **-cies.** Power to produce effects; effectiveness.

ef·fi·cien·cy, i·fish/ən·sē, *n. pl.,* **-cies.** Competence for one's duties; power of producing intended effect in relation to cost in time, money, and energy.

ef·fi·cient, i·fish/ənt, *a.* Acting or functioning competently; able to be used with satisfaction and economy; competent; causing desired effects. —**ef·fi·cient·ly,** *adv.*

ef·fi·gy, ef/i·jē, *n. pl.,* **-gies.** A representation or image of something, esp. a sculptured likeness of a person; a stuffed figure representing an obnoxious person.

ef·flo·resce, ef·lô·res/, *v.i.,* **-resced, -resc·ing.** To burst into bloom, as a flower; to change from crystals to powder through evaporation of water; become covered with a powdery crust; to flower; reach full or ripe development. —**ef·flo·res·cence,** *n.* —**ef·flo·res·cent,** *a.*

ef·flu·ent, ef/loo·ant, *a.* Flowing out.—*n.* That which flows out; an outflow of water from industrial sewage, a lake, etc. Also **ef·flu·ence.**

ef·flu·vi·um, i·floo/vē·əm, *n. pl.,* **-vi·a,** -vē·ə, **-vi·ums.** An invisible emanation or exhalation, esp. a fetid or putrid one. —**ef·flu·vi·al,** *a.*

ef·fort, ef/ərt, *n.* An exertion of strength or power, whether physical or mental; something produced by conscious mental or physical exertion; endeavor. —**ef·fort·less,** *a.* —**ef·fort·less·ly,** *adv.* —**ef·fort·less·ness,** *n.*

ef·fron·ter·y, i·frən/tə·rē, *n. pl.,* **-ter·ies.** Audacious impudence or boldness; shamelessness.

ef·ful·gent, i·ful'jənt, a. Radiant; shining brilliantly. —**ef·ful·gence,** n.

ef·fuse, i·fūz', v.t., **-fused, -fus·ing.** To pour out, as a fluid; to flow.—v.i. —i·fūs', a. Spilling out.

ef·fu·sion, i·fū'zhən, n. A pouring out; unrestrained expression.

ef·fu·sive, i·fū'siv, a. Showing overflowing kindness or cordiality; without reserve. —**ef·fu·sive·ly,** adv. —**ef·fu·sive·ness,** n.

e·gal·i·tar·i·an, i·gal·ə·târ'ē·ən, a. Pertaining to or believing in equality, esp. social, political, or economic equality.—n. One who believes in equality. —**e·gal·i·tar·i·an·ism,** n.

egg, eg, n. The roundish reproductive body in a shell or membrane, consisting of the ovum or female reproductive cell together with its appendages; the body of this sort produced by birds, esp. by the domestic hen; anything resembling a hen's egg.—v.t. To prepare (food) with eggs. Informal. To pelt with eggs. —**lay an egg,** to fail in any endeavor.

egg, eg, v.t. To incite, urge, or provoke, usu. followed by on.

egg·head, eg'hed, n. Informal. An intellectual.

egg·nog, eg'nog, n. A drink of eggs beaten up with sugar, milk, nutmeg, and sometimes alcoholic liquor.

egg·plant, eg'plant, eg'plänt, n. A plant with purplish, eggshaped fruit which is served as a vegetable.

egg·shell, eg'shel, n. The shell or calcareous covering of an egg; a pale yellow color.—a. Fragile and thin; colored pale yellow.

e·go, ē'gō, eg'ō, n. pl., **e·gos.** The individual self as a thinking, feeling, acting entity conscious of its distinction from other selves and objects external to itself; the conscious mind. Informal. Egotism, vanity, or self-esteem.

e·go·cen·tric, ē·gō·sen'trik, eg·ō·sen'trik, a. Having or regarding self as the center of all things.

e·go·ism, ē'gō·iz·əm, eg'ō·iz·əm, n. Habit or doctrine of valuing everything only in reference to one's personal interest; self-centeredness; egotism. —**e·go·ist,** n. —**e·go·is·tic,** ē·gō·is'tik, eg·ō·is'tik, a.

e·go·tism, ē'gō·tiz·əm, eg'ō·tiz·əm, n. Excessive reference to oneself; self-centeredness; selfishness; conceit; vanity. —**e·go·tist,** n. —**e·go·tis·tic,** ē·gō·tis'tik, eg·ō·tis'tik, **e·go·tis·ti·cal,** a.

e·gre·gious, i·grē'jəs, a. Flagrant; outrageous; conspicuously bad. —**e·gre·gious·ly,** adv.

e·gress, ē'gres, n. The act of going or issuing out; the right to depart; a way or a means of departing; an exit.

e·gret, ē'grit, eg'rit, n. Any of those species of herons which have long, white, flowing plumes during their breeding period; a plume of an egret; aigrette.

ei·der·down, ī'dər·down, n. Down or soft feathers from the breast of the female eider; duck; a pillow, quilt, etc., stuffed with eiderdown.

eight, āt, a. One more than seven in number.—n. A cardinal number between seven and nine, or a symbol representing it. —**eighth,** ātth, a., n.

eight·ball, āt'bôl, n. A black pool ball marked with the number eight. —**behind the eightball,** in a baffling or disadvantageous position.

eight·een, ā'tēn', n. A cardinal number, eight plus ten; the symbol representing this sum; a set of 18 persons or things.—a. —**eight·eenth,** a, n.

eight·fold, āt'fōld, a. Eight times the number or quantity; composed of eight parts.—adv.

eight·y, ā'tē, n. pl., **eight·ies.** A cardinal number, eight times ten; fourscore; a symbol for this number; a set of 80 persons or things.—a. —**eight·i·eth,** a., n.

ei·ther, ē'thər, ī'thər, a., pron. One or the other; each of two.—conj. A disjunctive conjunction always used as correlative to and preceding or: either the one or the other.—adv. Too; also; likewise.

e·jac·u·late, i·jak'yə·lāt, v.t., **-lat·ed, -lat·ing.** To exclaim; to utter suddenly and briefly; to eject swiftly from a living body, esp. to eject at orgasm.—v.i. To eject semen. —**e·jac·u·la·tion,** i·jak·yə·lā'shən, n. —**e·jac·u·la·to·ry,** a.

e·ject, i·jekt', v.t. To throw out; to expel; to turn out. —**e·jec·tion,** i·jek'shən, n. —**e·ject·ment,** n. —**e·jec·tor,** n.

eke, ēk, v.t., **eked, ek·ing.** To increase; lengthen. —**eke out,** to supplement to make up for deficiencies; to make last by economy; to make (a living) laboriously, precariously or meagerly.

el, el, n. Informal. Elevated train.

e·lab·o·rate, i·lab'ə·rāt, v.t., **-rat·ed, -rat·ing.** To work out or complete with great detail; to produce with labor.—v.i. To give more detailed treatment. —i·lab'er·it, a. Wrought with labor; executed with exactness; marked by great detail or complexity. —**e·lab·o·rate·ly,** adv. —**e·lab·o·rate·ness,** n. —**e·lab·o·ra·tion,** i·lab·ə·rā'shən, n.

é·lan, ā·län', n. Dash; impetuous ardor.

e·lapse, i·laps', v.i., **-lapsed, -laps·ing.** To slip or glide away; to pass away silently: said of time.

e·las·tic, i·las'tik, a. Of solids, capable of spontaneously recovering original shape, size, and form after being altered by some force such as stretching, bending, or pressure; capable of easy adjustment to circumstances; adaptable; flexible; capable of recovering spirits or rebounding; buoyant; bouncy. —**e·las·ti·cal·ly,** adv. —**e·las·tic·i·ty,** i·las·tis'ə·tē, n. —n. A flexible or stretchable fabric endowed with elasticity by the interweaving of rubber threads; cords, strings, or bands made of rubber.

e·late, i·lāt', v.t., **e·lat·ed, e·lat·ing.** To put in high spirits; to make proud; to make happy. —**e·lat·ed,** a. —**e·la·tion,** n.

el·bow, el'bō, n. The outer part of the bend or joint of the arm; the angle at this joint when bent; the portion of a sleeve that covers this joint; something bent like the elbow.—v.t. To push with, or as with, the elbow; jostle.—v.i.

el·bow grease, n. Informal. Energetic labor, esp. physical.

el·bow·room, el'bō·room, el'bō·rûm, n. Room to extend the elbows; ample room.

el·der, el'dər, n. Any tree or shrub of the honeysuckle family with white flowers and purple berrylike drupes.

eld·er, el'dər, a. Having lived a longer time; prior in origin; senior in rank; pertaining to earlier times; older; senior.—n. One who is older than another or others; an ancestor; a person of great influence in a tribal community; a lay official in Presbyterian churches; a Mormon priest. —**eld·er·ship,** n.

el·der·ly, el'dər·lē, a. Somewhat old; advanced beyond middle age; quite old. —**eld·er·li·ness,** n.

eld·est, el'dist, a. Oldest; most advanced in age.

e·lect, i·lekt', v.t. To select for an office by vote or designation; to choose; to determine in favor of.—v.i. To make a choice.—a. Chosen or elected but not yet invested with office; chosen for eternal life.—n. pl., **e·lect.** One or several chosen or set apart; those esp. favored by God.

e·lec·tion, i·lek'shən, n. The act of electing; liberty to choose or act; predetermination by God for salvation.

e·lec·tion·eer, i·lek·shə·nēr', v.i. To work to obtain the election of a candidate or party.

e·lec·tive, i·lek'tiv, a. Chosen by election; dependent on choice; pertaining to or consisting in choice or right of choosing; exerting the power of choice; optional.—n. In education, an optional course of study.

e·lec·tor, i·lek'tər, n. One who elects or has the right to elect; one of the persons elected, by vote of the people, to the electoral college, designed to elect the President and Vice-President of the U.S. —e·lec·tor·al, a.

e·lec·tor·ate, i·lek′tər·it, n. The whole body of voters or electors.

e·lec·tric, i·lek′trik, a. Pertaining to, consisting of, or containing electric current; producing, conveying, operated, or produced by electricity; stirring; exhilarating. —e·lec·tri·cal, a. —e·lec·tri·cal·ly, adv.

e·lec·tric chair, n. A chair used in prisons for executions by electrocution.

e·lec·tric eye, n. A photoelectric cell.

e·lec·tri·cian, i·lek·trish′ən, ē·lek·trish′ən, n. One who makes, repairs, installs, or operates electric devices or equipment.

e·lec·tric·i·ty, i·lek·tris′ə·tē, ē·lek·tris′ə·tē, n. A fundamental property of matter, related to the movement of subatomic particles which generate energy, usu. utilized in the form of electric currents; such a current or flow of electrons; the science which deals with the causes, nature, and application of electric energy; a state of excitement or anticipation.

e·lec·tri·fy, i·lek′trə·fī, v.t., -fied, -fy·ing. To equip with electricity; to affect by electricity; to give a sudden shock; to thrill. —e·lec·tri·fi·ca·tion, i·lek·trə·fə·kā′shən, n. —e·lec·tri·fi·er, n.

e·lec·tro·car·di·o·graph, i·lek·trō·kär′dē·ə·graf, i·lek·trō·kär′dē·ə·gräf, n. An instrument used in medical diagnosis to detect and record the electrical activity of the heart muscle.

e·lec·tro·cute, i·lek′trə·kūt, v.t., -cut·ed, -cut·ing. To execute or kill by means of an electric current or shock. —e·lec·tro·cu·tion, i·lek·trə·kū′shən, n.

e·lec·trode, i·lek′trōd, n. One of the terminals by which an electric current enters or leaves an electrolytic cell or other electrical device.

e·lec·tro·dy·nam·ics, i·lek·trō·dī·nam′iks, n. pl. but sing. in constr. The study of the interactions of moving electric charges.

e·lec·trol·y·sis, i·lek·trol′ə·sis, ē·lek·trol′ə·sis, n. The decomposition of a chemical compound by an electric current; the destruction of tumors or hair roots by an electric current. —e·lec·tro·lyze, i·lek′trə·līz, v.t., -lyzed, -lyz·ing.

e·lec·tro·lyte, i·lek′trə·līt, n. A substance whose solutions are capable of conducting electric current, esp. a compound that decomposes by electrolysis. —e·lec·tro·lyt·ic, i·lek·trə·lit′ik, a.

e·lec·tro·mag·net, i·lek·trō·mag′nit, n. A magnet consisting of a core, usu. of soft iron, magnetized by an electric current passing through a wire coiled around the core.

e·lec·tro·mag·net·ism, i·lek·trō·mag′nə·tiz·əm, n. The study of the relation between electric currents and magnetism; magnetism caused by electric current. —e·lec·tro·mag·net·ic, i·lek·trō·mag·net′ik, a.

e·lec·tron, i·lek′tron, n. An elementary particle of negative charge found outside the nucleus of an atom.

e·lec·tron·ic mu·sic, i·lek·tron′ik, n. Music in which the sounds are electronically made.

e·lec·tron·ics, i·lek·tron′iks, ē·lek·tron′iks, n. pl. but sing. in constr. The branch of physics that studies the behavior and applies the effects of the flow of electrons in vacuum tubes, gases, and semiconductors. —e·lec·tron·ic, a. —e·lec·tron·i·cal·ly, adv.

e·lec·tron mi·cro·scope, n. An instrument which utilizes an electron beam to obtain magnification and resolution of minute structures.

e·lec·tron tube, n. Any of numerous devices consisting of a sealed glass tube containing a vacuum or a gas at low pressure, in which controlled conduction of electrons occurs; a vacuum tube.

e·lec·tro·plate, i·lek′trə·plāt, v.t., -plat·ed, -plat·ing. To plate or give a coating of silver or other metal by means of electrolysis.—n. Articles coated by the process of electroplating.

e·lec·tro·ther·a·py, i·lek·trō·ther′ə·pē, n. The treatment of disease by the use of brief, non-convulsive electric shocks.

e·lec·trum, i·lek′trəm, n. A pale yellow alloy of gold and silver.

el·ee·mos·y·nar·y, el·ə·mos′ə·ner·ē, el·ē·ə·mos′ə·ner·ē, a. Relating to charity; supported by or dependent on charity.

el·e·gant, el′ə·gənt, a. Tastefully fine or luxurious in dress, manners; gracefully refined, as in tastes, habits, or literary style; characterized by a graceful distinction in form or appearance. Informal. Choice, fine, or pleasingly superior. —el·e·gance, el·e·gan·cy, n. —el·e·gant·ly, adv.

el·e·gy, el′i·jē, n. pl., -gies. A mournful or plaintive poem, or a funeral song. —el·e·gi·ac, el·ə·jī′ak, i·lē′jē·ak, a. —el·e·gist, n. —el·e·gize, el′ə·jīz, v.i., -gized, -giz·ing.

el·e·ment, el′ə·mənt, n. A component part of a whole; one of the substances, usu. earth, water, air, or fire, formerly considered as constituting the material universe; the natural habitat or environment of an animal or person. One of a class of substances that consist solely of atoms of the same atomic number, and none of which can be decomposed by ordinary chemical means. Pl. Weather conditions, esp. severe; the basic principles of an art or science; the bread and wine used in the Eucharist.

el·e·men·tal, el·ə·men′təl, a. Of, or relating to a fundamental constituent; simple; uncompounded; basic; of or suggesting the simple but powerful forces of nature; referring to the chemical elements. —el·e·men·tal·ly, adv.

el·e·men·ta·ry, el·ə·men′tə·rē, el·ə·men′trē, a. Containing or relating to first principles or rudiments; referring to an elementary school; simple or uncompounded; having the characteristics of an element or principal substance; primary; elemental; referring to the elements. —el·e·men·ta·ri·ly, adv.

el·e·men·ta·ry school, n. A school covering the first 6 to 8 years of instruction to children 6 to 12 or 14 years old.

el·e·phant, el′ə·fənt, n. Any of various large, hoofed mammals with the nose drawn into a long, prehensile proboscis or trunk and lower incisor teeth that form tusks of ivory. —el·e·phan·tine, el·ə·fan′tēn, el·ə·fan′tin, a.

el·e·vate, el′ə·vāt, v.t., -vat·ed, -vat·ing. To raise; to raise from a low or deep place to a higher place; to raise to a higher state or station; to improve, refine, or dignify; to raise the spirits of; cheer; elate.

el·e·vat·ed, el′ə·vā·tid, a. Raised up; high; formal; noble; elated.—n. Informal. A usu. urban railway operating chiefly on an elevated structure.

el·e·va·tion, el·ə·vā′shən, n. An elevating; height above sea level; a high or raised place; loftiness of thought, feeling, rank, etc.; a drawing representing the exterior of something as seen from one side.

el·e·va·tor, el′ə·vā·tər, n. One who or that which elevates; a mechanical contrivance for raising passengers or goods from a lower place to a higher one; a hoist; a granary provided with devices for lifting grain.

el·ev·en, i·lev′ən, n. The cardinal number between 10 and 12; a symbol, like 11 or xi, representing it; a set of 11 persons or things.—a. —e·lev·enth, a.

elf, elf, n. pl., elves. A small imaginary being with magical powers, usu. thought to be in human form; a mischievous person. —elf·in, a., n. —elf·ish, a.

e·lic·it, i·lis′it, v.t. To bring or draw out; to bring to light; to evoke.

el·i·gi·ble, el′i·jə·bəl, a. Fit to be chosen for some purpose or duty; worthy of choice; legally qualified to be chosen.—n. A person who is eligible. —el·i·gi·bil·i·ty, el·i·jə·bil′ə·tē, n. —el·i·gi·bly, adv.

e·lim·i·nate, i·lim′ə·nāt, v.t., -nat·ed, -nat·ing. To take out or separate as being neither necessary nor an element of value; to ignore; omit; of an organism, to discharge wastes; to remove (an unknown quantity) by combining two or more algebraic equations. —e·lim·

i·na·tion, i·lim·ə·nā′shən, *n.* **—lim·i·na·tor,** *n.*

e·lite, i·lēt′, ā·lēt′, *n.* Those who are choice or select; the best.—*a.* **—e·lit·ism,** *n.* **—e·lit·ist,** *n.*

e·lix·ir, i·lik′sər, *n.* An aromatic, sweetened alcoholic liquid containing medicinal agents; an alchemic preparation previously thought to be capable of changing base metals into gold, or for prolonging life; the quintessence or absolute embodiment of anything.

E·liz·a·beth·an, i·liz·ə·bē′thən, *a.* Pertaining to Queen Elizabeth I of England (ruled 1558-1603), her period, or its culture.—*n.* A person, esp. a writer, of this period.

elk, elk, *n. pl.,* **elks, elk.** In Europe and Asia, the largest member of the deer family, similar to the moose; in America, the wapiti, a member of the deer family, next in size to the moose.

ell, el, *n.* Something shaped like an L; an extension to a building, at right angles to one end. Also **el.**

e·lipse, i·lips′, *n.* A closed plane curve such that the sum of the distances of one of the points on the curve from two fixed points, called foci, is constant; an oval figure.

el·lip·sis, i·lip′sis, *n. pl.,* **-ses,** -sēz. The omission of words not necessary for understanding; marks (. . . or * * *) indicating omission in writing or printing.

el·lip·ti·cal, i·lip′ti·kəl, *a.* Pertaining to an ellipse; having the form of an ellipse; pertaining to ellipsis. Also **el·lip·tic.** **—el·lip·ti·cal·ly,** *adv.*

elm, elm, *n.* A valuable timber and shade tree found in North America and Europe.

el·o·cu·tion, el·ə·kū′shən, *n.* The art of speaking effectively in public; the manner in which a speech is delivered. **—el·o·cu·tion·ar·y,** *a.* **—el·o·cu·tion·ist,** *n.*

e·lon·gate, i·lông′gāt, i·long′gāt, *v.t.,* **-gat·ed, -gat·ing.** To draw out to greater length; lengthen; extend.—*v.i.*—*a.* Outstretched; protracted; elongated. **—e·lon·gat·ed,** *a.* **—e·lon·ga·tion,** ē·lông·gā′shən, i·lon·gā′shən, *n.*

e·lope, i·lōp′, *v.i.,* **eloped, e·lop·ing.** To run away with a lover, esp. to be married without parental consent; to escape. **—e·lope·ment,** *n.* **—e·lop·er,** *n.*

el·o·quence, el′ə·kwəns, *n.* The action, or art of using language with fluency, force, grace, and aptness; the quality of being very moving or persuasive.

el·o·quent, el′ə·kwənt, *a.* Characterized by eloquence. **—el·o·quent·ly,** *adv.*

else, els, *a.* Other; in addition.—*adv.* Otherwise; if the fact were different.

else·where, els′hwer, els′wer, *adv.* In, at, or to another place.

e·lu·ci·date, i·loo′sə·dāt, *v.t.,* **-dat·ed, -dat·ing.** To make clear or manifest; to explain. **—e·lu·ci·da·tion,** i·loo·sə·dā′shən, *n.* **—e·lu·ci·da·tor,** *n.*

e·lude, i·lood′, *v.t.,* **e·lud·ed, e·lud·ing.** To baffle; escape the comprehension of; to evade or avoid by deceit, or dexterity. **—e·lu·sion,** *n.*

e·lu·sive, i·loo′siv, *a.* Tending to elude. Also **e·lu·so·ry.** **—e·lu·sive·ly,** *adv.* **—e·lu·sive·ness,** *n.*

elves, elvz, *n.* Plural of **elf.**

elv·ish, el′vish, *a.* Pertaining to elves or fairies; mischievous; elfish.

em, em, *n. Print.* The square of any size of type used as the unit of measurement for printed matter.

e·ma·ci·ate, i·mā′shē·āt, *v.i.,* **-at·ed, -at·ing.** To lose flesh gradually.—*v.t.* To cause to lose flesh gradually; to reduce to leanness. **—e·ma·ci·at·ed,** *a.* **—e·ma·ci·a·tion,** i·mā·shē·ā′shən, *n.*

em·a·nate, em′ə·nāt, *v.i.,* **-nat·ed, -nat·ing.** To flow forth; issue.—*v.t.* **—em·a·na·tion,** em·ə·nā′shən, *n.*

e·man·ci·pate, i·man′sə·pāt, *v.t.,* **-pat·ed, -pat·ing.** To restore from bondage to freedom; to free from bondage, restriction, or restraint of any kind. **—e·man·ci·pa·tion,** i·man·sə·pā′shən, *n.* **—e·man·ci·**

pa·tor, *n.*

e·mas·cu·late, i·mas′kyə·lāt, *v.t.,* **-lat·ed, -lat·ing.** To castrate; to deprive of masculine vigor; weaken. —i·mas′kū·lit, i·mas′kū·lāt, *a.* Castrated; effeminate; weakened. **—e·mas·cu·la·tion,** i·mas·kyə·lā′shən, *n.*

em·balm, em·bäm′, *v.t.* Of a dead body, to protect from decay by treating with drugs and chemicals; to preserve from loss or decay. **—em·balm·er,** *n.* **—em·balm·ment,** *n.*

em·bank·ment, em·bangk′mənt, *n.* A mound or bank of earth, stones, etc., used to hold back water, support a roadway, etc.

em·bar·go, em·bär′gō, *n. pl.,* **-goes.** A government order forbidding merchant vessels to enter or leave its ports; any authoritative stoppage of freight or commerce; a restraint or hindrance imposed on anything. —*v.t.,* **-goed, -go·ing.** To put an embargo on.

em·bark, em·bärk′, *v.t.* To put or receive on board a ship; of a person, to involve in an enterprise.—*v.i.* To board a ship, as for a voyage; to engage in an enterprise or a business. **—em·bar·ka·tion,** em·bär·kā′shən, **em·bark·ment,** *n.*

em·bar·rass, em·bar′əs, *v.t.* To cause to feel self-conscious; to confuse, disconcert, or abash; complicate; to beset with financial difficulties.—*v.i.* To feel self-conscious. **—em·bar·rass·ing·ly,** *adv.* **—em·bar·rass·ment,** *n.*

em·bas·sy, em′bə·sē, *n. pl.,* **-sies.** The mission or function of an ambassador; an ambassador together with his staff; the official office and residence of an ambassador.

em·bat·tle, em·bat′əl, *v.t.,* **-tled, -tling.** To arrange in order of battle; to prepare or equip for battle. **—em·bat·tle·ment,** *n.*

em·bed, em·bed′, *v.t.,* **-bed·ded, -bed·ding.** To fix or enclose in a surrounding mass; to lay in or as in a bed.

em·bel·lish, em·bel′ish, *v.t.* To adorn; to decorate; to heighten the attractiveness, as of a story, by adding colorful or imaginary details. **—em·bel·lish·ment,** *n.*

em·ber, em′bər, *n.* A small live coal or glowing piece of wood; *pl.,* the smoldering remains of a fire.

em·bez·zle, em·bez′əl, *v.t.,* **-zled, -zling.** To appropriate fraudulently to one's own use that which is entrusted to one's care, as money, securities, etc. **—em·bez·zle·ment,** *n.* **—em·bez·zler,** *n.*

em·bit·ter, em·bit′ər, *v.t.* To make bitter or more bitter. **—em·bit·ter·ment,** *n.*

em·bla·zon, em·blā′zən, *v.t.* To depict, as an armorial ensign on a shield; to decorate in bright colors; to celebrate; proclaim sensationally. **—em·bla·zon·er,** *n.* **—em·blaz·on·ment,** *n.* **—em·bla·zon·ry,** *n.*

em·blem, em′bləm, *n.* An object, or a representation of it, symbolizing something, as a quality, state, or class of persons; a symbol; a distinctive badge of something, as of a person, family, or nation. **—em·blem·at·ic,** em·blə·mat′ik, **em·blem·at·i·cal,** *a.*

em·bod·y, em·bod′ē, *v.t.,* **-bod·ied, -bod·y·ing.** To lodge in or invest with a body; to provide with a concrete form; to collect into a whole; incorporate. **—em·bod·i·ment,** *n.*

em·bold·en, em·bōl′dən, *v.t.* To give boldness or courage to; to encourage.

em·bo·lism, em′bə·liz·əm, *n.* Blockage of a blood vessel by an embolus.

em·bo·lus, em′bə·ləs, *n. pl.,* **-li,** -lī. An abnormal particle circulating in the bloodstream, as an air bubble or blood clot.

em·bos·om, em·bûz′əm, em·boo′zəm, *v.t.* To enclose; to take into or hold in the bosom; to cherish.

em·boss, em·bôs′, em·bos′, *v.t.* To fashion relief or raised work on; to represent in relief, as a surface design. **—em·boss·ment,** *n.*

em·bou·chure, äm·bû·shûr′, *n. Mus.* The part of a

wind instrument to which the mouth is applied; the shaping of the lips to this mouthpiece.

em·brace, em·brās′, *v.t.,* **-braced, -brac·ing.** To take or clasp in the arms; to hug; to accept, or avail oneself of; to take in or include; to surround or contain.—*v.i.* To hug one another.—*n.* An embracing; a hug.

em·broi·der, em·broy′dər, *v.t.* To adorn, as a fabric, or make, as a design, with ornamental needlework; to embellish, as a tale, with imaginary details.—*v.i.* To do embroidery. —**em·broi·der·y,** *n. pl.,* **-der·ies.**

em·broil, em·broyl′, *v.t.* To mix up or entangle in a quarrel or disturbance; to complicate or confuse. —**em·broil·ment,** *n.*

em·bry·o, em′brē·ō, *n. pl.,* **-bry·os.** A multicellular organism at any stage in development before birth or hatching, esp. the early stages; in human beings, the stages of development until about eight weeks after conception; a young plant within the seed; something in an as yet undeveloped state. —**em·bry·on·ic,** em·brē·on′ik, *a.*

em·bry·ol·o·gy, em·brē·ol′ə·jē, *n.* The study of the development of embryos; the development process itself.

em·cee, em′sē′, *v.i.,* **-ceed, -cee·ing.** To function as the master of ceremonies.—*v.t.*—*n.* The master of ceremonies.

e·mend, i·mend′, *v.t.* To make corrections or changes in (a faulty text, document, etc.); to correct; free from defects.

em·er·ald, em′ər·əld, em′rəld, *n.* A green, transparent variety of beryl used as a gemstone.—*a.* Of a clear, deep green color.

e·merge, i·mərj′, *v.i.,* **-merged, -merg·ing.** To rise out of or come forth; to come into notice; to come into existence through evolution. —**e·mer·gence,** *n.* —**e·mer·gent,** *a.*

e·mer·gen·cy, i·mər′jən·sē, *n. pl.,* **-cies.** A sudden, usu. unexpected, occasion or combination of events calling for immediate action.

e·mer·i·tus, i·mer′ə·təs, *a.* Retired because of age, length of service, or infirmity, but retaining the honorary title of the position: a professor *emeritus.*

em·er·y, em′ə·rē, em′rē, *n.* A mineral substance consisting of a hard, grayish-black variety of corundum, used for grinding and polishing.

e·met·ic, i·met′ik, *a.* Inducing vomiting.

em·i·grant, em′ə·grənt, *n.* One who emigrates.

em·i·grate, em′ə·grāt, *v.i.,* **-grat·ed, -grat·ing.** To quit one country, state, or region and settle in another; to remove from one country or state to another. —**em·i·gra·tion,** em·ə·grā′shən, *n.*

é·mi·gré, em′ə·grā, *n. pl.,* **-grés.** An emigrant; a refugee.

em·i·nence, em′ə·nəns, *n.* A station of distinction due to office, rank, or personal achievements; a person of outstanding attainments; something prominent; a hill.

em·i·nent, em′ə·nənt, *a.* High in office, rank, esteem, etc.; distinguished; noteworthy; high; lofty. —**em·i·nent·ly,** *adv.*

em·i·nent do·main, *n.* The dominion of a government over all the property within the state, by which it can take private property for public use.

em·is·sar·y, em′ə·ser·ē, *n. pl.,* **-sar·ies.** A person sent on a mission; a secret agent or spy.

e·mis·sion, i·mish′ən, *n.* The act or a case of emitting; that which is emitted. —**e·mis·sive,** *a.*

e·mit, i·mit′, *v.t.,* **e·mit·ted, e·mit·ting.** To throw or give out, as light, heat, steam; to utter, as a sound; to circulate; issue. —**e·mit·ter,** *n.*

e·mol·lient, i·mol′yənt, *a.* Softening; soothing. —*n.* A medicine which softens and soothes.

e·mol·u·ment, i·mol′yə·mənt, *n.* The profit arising from office or employment; remuneration.

e·mote, i·mōt′, *v.i.,* **-mot·ed, -mot·ing.** To show emotion; to behave with exaggerated emotion. —**e·mo·tive,** *a.*

e·mo·tion, i·mō′shən, *n.* An affective state of consciousness in which joy, sorrow, fear, hate, or the like is experienced; any of the feelings of joy, sorrow, fear, hate, love, or the like. —**e·mo·tion·al,** *a.* —**e·mo·tion·al·ly,** *adv.*

e·mo·tion·al·ism, i·mō′shə·nə·liz·əm, *n.* The state of being emotional; undue appeal to, display of, or susceptibility to emotion; emotional overindulgence.

em·pan·el, em·pan′əl, *v.t.* Impanel.

em·pa·thize, em′pə·thīz, *v.i.,* **-thized, -thiz·ing.** To feel or regard with empathy.

em·pa·thy, em′pə·thē, *n.* Mental entrance into the feeling or spirit of another person or thing; appreciative perception or understanding. —**em·pa·thet·ic,** em·pə·thet′ik, **em·path·ic,** em·path′ik, *a.*

em·per·or, em′pər·ər, *n.* The highest office or person in an empire.

em·pha·sis, em′fə·sis, *n. pl.,* **-ses,** -sēz. Importance or significance attached to anything; stress of voice on words or syllables.

em·pha·size, em′fə·sīz, *v.t.,* **-sized, -siz·ing.** To give emphasis to; stress.

em·phat·ic, em·fat′ik, *a.* Direct and forceful speech or action. —**em·phat·i·cal·ly,** *adv.*

em·phy·se·ma, em·fi·sē′mə, *n.* A disease of the lungs in which lung tissues lose their elasticity, causing severe breathing problems.

em·pire, em′pīr, *n.* The territory, countries, or peoples governed by an emperor; imperial power and dominion; a powerful enterprise under the exclusive control of a single individual, family, or group.

em·pir·i·cal, em·pēr′i·kəl, *a.* Depending upon experience or observation alone, rather than science and theory. —**em·pir·i·cal·ly,** *adv.*

em·pir·i·cism, em·pēr′i·siz·əm. *n.* The belief that knowledge is derived from experiment or experience alone. —**em·pir·i·cist,** *n.*

em·place·ment, im·plās′mənt, *n.* Position; location; the space or platform for a gun or battery and its accessories.

em·ploy, em·ploy′, *v.t.* To engage the services of; to hire; to keep busy or at work; to make use of. —*n.* A state of being hired for wages; employment. —**em·ploy·a·ble,** *a.*

em·ploy·ee, em·ploy·e, em·ploy′ē, em·ploy·ē′, *n.* One who works for an employer for salary or wages.

em·ploy·er, em·ploy′ər, *n.* One that employs.

em·ploy·ment, em·ploy′mənt, *n.* The state of being employed; occupation; business; that which one undertakes to occupy his time.

em·po·ri·um, em·pōr′ē·əm, em·pôr′ē·əm, *n pl.,* **-ums, -a.** A department store.

em·pow·er, em·pow′ər, *v.t.* To authorize; to license.

em·press, em′pris, *n.* The wife of an emperor; a woman who rules an empire.

emp·ty, emp′tē, *a.,* **-i·er, -i·est.** Containing nothing; not occupied; not inhabited; meaningless; insincere; feeling hunger; unproductive. —*v.t.,* **emp·tied, emp·ty·ing.** To remove the contents from; to discharge. —*v.i.* To become empty. —**emp·ti·ly,** *adv.* —**emp·ti·ness,** *n.*

emp·ty-hand·ed, emp′tē·han′did, *a.* Having or carrying nothing in the hands; without accomplishment.

emp·ty-head·ed, emp′tē·hed′id, *a.* Without thought; flighty.

e·mu, ē′mū, *n.* A flightless Australian bird related to the ostrich.

em·u·late, em′ū·lāt, *v.t.,* **-lat·ed, -lat·ing.** To strive to equal or excel by imitating. —**em·u·la·tion,** em·ū·lā′shən, *n.*

e·mul·si·fy, i·məl′sə·fī, *v.t.,* **-fied, -fy·ing.** To make into an emulsion. —**e·mul·si·fi·ca·tion,** i·məl·sə·fə·kā′shən, *n.* —**e·mul·si·fi·er,** *n.*

e·mul·sion, i·məl′shən, *n.* A mixture of two liquids which are kept in suspension, one within the other. *Photog.* A coating on photographic films sensitive to rays of light. —**e·mul·sive,** *a.*

en, en, *n. Print.* Half of the width of an em.

en·a·ble, en·āʹbəl, *v.t.,* **-bled, -bling.** To give means, ability, or authority; to make easy or possible. **—en·a·bling.**

en·act, en·aktʹ, *v.t.* To make into an act or law; to act the part of or represent.

e·nam·el, i·namʹəl, *n.* A colorful substance used as an ornamental or protective coating for metal, glass, or pottery articles; any of the glossy paints or varnishes; the smooth, hard substance which covers the outside of a tooth. *—v.t.,* **-eled, -el·ing.** To lay enamel on; to paint in enamel.*—v.i.* To practice the use of enamel or the art of enameling. **—e·nam·el·er,** *n.* **—e·nam·el·ware,** *n.*

en·am·or, en·amʹər, *v.t.* To inflame with love: usu. followed by *of* or *with.* **—en·am·ored·ness,** *n.*

en·camp, en·kampʹ, *v.i.* To stay in a camp, to make a camp. *—v.t.* To place in a camp. **—en·camp·ment,** *n.*

en·cap·su·late, en·kapʹsə·lāt, *v.t.,* **-lat·ed, -lat·ing.** To enclose in or as in a capsule; to express in a brief summary. *—v.i.* To become enclosed in a capsule. Also **en·cap·sule.**

en·case, en·kāsʹ, *v.t.,* **-cased, -cas·ing.** To enclose in or as in a case.

en·ceinte, än·santʹ, *a.* Pregnant; with child.

en·ceph·a·li·tis, en·sef·ə·līʹtis, *n.* Inflammation of the brain. **—en·ceph·a·lit·ic,** en·sef·ə·litʹik, *a.*

en·ceph·a·lon, en·sefʹə·lon, *n. pl.,* **-la.** The brain.

en·chant, en·chantʹ, en·chäntʹ, *v.t.* To cast under a spell; bewitch; to delight; to charm. **—en·chant·er,** *n.* **—en·chant·ress,** *n.*

en·chant·ing, en·chanʹting, en·chänʹting, *a.* Charming; delightful; bewitching. **—en·chant·ing·ly,** *adv.*

en·chant·ment, en·chantʹmənt, en·chäntʹmənt, *n.* The act, art, or action of enchanting; the state of being enchanted; that which enchants.

en·chi·la·da, en·chə·läʹdə, *n.* A spicy meat or cheese mixture rolled up in a tortilla, with a chili sauce over it.

en·cir·cle, en·sərʹkəl, *v.t.,* **-cled, -cling.** To form a circle about; surround; to move circularly around. **—en·cir·cle·ment,** *n.*

en·clave, enʹklāv, *n.* A territory surrounded by the territory of another power; an area populated by a minority group.

en·close, en·klōzʹ, *v.t.,* **-closed, -clos·ing.** To surround on all sides; to put in an envelope with a letter or in a package. Also **in·close.**

en·clo·sure, en·klōʹzhər, *n.* The act of enclosing; the state of being enclosed; that which is enclosed. Also **in·clo·sure.**

en·code, en·kōdʹ, *v.t.,* **-cod·ed, -cod·ing.** To convert, as a message, into code; to write.

en·co·mi·ast, en·kōʹmē·ast, *n.* One who authors or delivers an encomium; a eulogist.

en·com·pass, en·kəmʹpəs, *v.t.* To form a circle about; to envelop; to include. **—en·com·pass·ment,** *n.*

en·core, ängʹkôr, än·kôrʹ, *n.* A demand by an audience for an additional number or piece; an additional performance in response to such a demand.

en·coun·ter, en·kownʹtər, *n.* An accidental meeting; a hostile meeting; conflict; a minor battle. *—v.t.* To meet suddenly to engage with in battle; to be faced with. *—v.i.* To meet each other unexpectedly; to meet in hostile fashion.

en·cour·age, en·kərʹij, en·kûrʹij, *v.t.,* **-aged, -ag·ing.** To inspire with courage, confidence, or hope. **—en·cour·ag·ing,** *a.* **—en·cour·ag·ing·ly,** *adv.*

en·croach, en·krōchʹ, *v.i.* To trespass; intrude on the rights or possessions of another. **—en·croach·er,** *n.***—en·croach·ment,** *n.*

en·crust, en·krəstʹ, *v.t.* To cover with a crust. **—en·crus·ta·tion,** en·krəs·tāʹshən, *n.*

en·cum·ber, en·kəmʹbər, *v.t.* To impede or hamper; to burden with debts or duties; to complicate. Also **in·cum·ber. —en·cum·brance,** *n.* That which encumbers; a burden or obstacle. *Law.* A burden or claim on property, as a mortgage.

en·cy·clo·pe·di·a, en·sī·klə·pēʹdē·ə, *n.* A book or set of books containing alphabetic articles on all subjects; a dictionary of things, not words. Also **en·cy·clo·pae·di·a.**

en·cy·clo·pe·dic, en·sī·klə·pēʹdik, *a.* Universal in knowledge and information. Also **en·cy·clo·pe·di·cal, —en·cy·clo·pe·di·cal·ly,** *adv.*

en·cyst, en·sistʹ, *v.t., v.i.* To enclose or become enclosed in a cyst or sac.

end, end, *n.* The extreme point of a line; the conclusion, or last part; death; consequence; result; the ultimate point at which one aims his views; purpose; scope; aim; fragment; extreme limit of something; bounds. **—on end,** resting on one end. **—make both ends meet,** to live within one's income. **—at loose ends,** without work; lack of recreation. **—at wit's end,** puzzled. **—go off the deep end,** lose control of one's emotions. *—v.t.* To put an end to; conclude; terminate. *—v.i.* To come to an end.

en·dan·ger, en·dānʹjər, *v.t.* To put in danger; imperil; to expose to loss or injury. **—en·dan·ger·ment,** *n.*

en·dear, en·dērʹ, *v.t.* To make beloved.

en·dear·ment, en·dērʹmənt, *n.* The act of endearing; *usu. pl.,* action or words showing affection.

en·deav·or, en·devʹər, *n.* A serious effort; a strenuous attempt. *—v.i.* To try; to attempt. *—v.t.* To try to bring about.

en·dem·ic, en·demʹik, *a.* Of a disease, peculiar to a people, locality, or region. Also **en·dem·i·cal. —***n.* A disease to which inhabitants of a particular region are subject. **—en·dem·i·cal·ly,** *adv.*

end·ing, enʹding, *n.* The concluding part.

end·less, endʹlis, *a.* Having no end or conclusion; forming a closed loop. **—end·less·ly,** *adv.* **—end·less·ness,** *n.*

end·most, endʹmōst, *a.* Farthest; most remote.

en·do·crine, enʹdō·krin, enʹdō·krīn, enʹdō·krēn, *a.* Referring to any of the various glands which release certain secretions directly to the blood or lymph. *—n.* An endocrine gland or its internal secretion.

en·do·cri·nol·o·gy, en·dō·kri·nolʹə·jē, en·dō·krī·nolʹə·jē, *n.* The science that deals with the endocrine glands.**—en·do·crin·o·log·ic,** en·dō·krin·ə·lojʹik, **en·do·crin·o·log·i·cal,** *a.* **—en·do·cri·nol·o·gist,** *n.*

en·dog·e·nous, en·dojʹə·nəs, *a.* Developing, or originating from within.

en·dorse, en·dôrsʹ, *v.t.,* **-dorsed, -dors·ing.** To write one's signature on the back (of a check), to obtain the cash or credit represented on the face of the document; to lend support to a candidate or policy. **—en·dor·see,** en·dôr·sēʹ, in·dôr·sēʹ, **en·dor·ser,** *n.*

en·dorse·ment, en·dôrsʹmənt, *n.* The signature of the holder of a check, note, or bill, written on its back; support and approval; a provision added to an insurance contract.

en·do·sperm, enʹdō·spərm, *n.* The part of a seed that contains the supply of food for the germinating embryo.

en·dow, en·dowʹ, *v.t.* To provide with a permanent fund or provision for support; to furnish with any gift, quality, talent. **—en·dow·ment,** *n.* Revenue or property given to any person or place for income; a natural capacity.

end ta·ble, *n.* A small table placed at the end of a couch or next to a chair.

en·due, en·dooʹ, en·dūʹ, *v.t.,* **-dued, -du·ing.** To invest or endow with special qualities.

en·dur·ance, en·dûrʹəns, en·dyûrʹəns, *n.* A bearing

---

a- hat, fāte, fāre, fäther; e- met, mē; i- pin, pīne; o- not, nōte, ôrb, moove (move), boy, pownd; u- cūbe, bŭll, tûk (took); ch- chin; th- thick, ₊hen; zh- vizhon (vision); ə- əgo, takən, pencəl, lemən, bərd (bird).

up under pain or distress without yielding; fortitude.

en·dure, en·dûr′, en·dyûr′, v.t., **-dured, -dur·ing.** To undergo; to suffer without yielding; to bear with patience; to undergo, or experience. —v.i. To last; continue to be; to put up with. **—en·dur·a·ble,** a. **—en·dur·a·bly,** adv.

en·dur·ing, en·dûr′ing, en·dyûr′ing, a. Permanent; lasting. **—en·dur·ing·ly,** adv. **—en·dur·ing·ness,** n.

end·ways, end′wāz, adv. With the end forward or upward. Also **end·wise,** end′wiz.

en·e·ma, en′ə·mə, n. The injection of fluid into the rectum for cleansing or diagnosis; the liquid injected.

en·e·my, en′ə·mē, n. pl., **-mies.** One hostile to another; a foe; an adversary; a hostile military force; that which is harmful.

en·er·get·ic, en·ər·jet′ik, a. Acting with or exhibiting energy; vigorous. Also **en·er·get·i·cal. —en·er·get·i·cal·ly,** adv.

en·er·gize, en′ər·jīz, v.i., **-gized, -giz·ing.** To act with energy or force.—v.t. To give strength or force to; activate. **—en·er·gi·zer,** n.

en·er·gy, en′ər·jē, n. pl., **-gies.** Inherent power; the power of operating, whether exerted or not; power vigorously exerted; strength of expression; the actual or potential ability to do work.

en·er·vate, en′ər·vāt, v.t., **-vat·ed, -vat·ing.** To deprive of nerve, force, or strength; to weaken. —i·nər′vit, a. **—en·er·vat·ed,** a. **—en·er·va·tion,** en·ər·vā′shən, n.

en·fee·ble, en·fē′bəl, v.t., **-bled, -bling.** To weaken; to debilitate. **—en·fee·ble·ment,** n.

en·fi·lade, en·fə·lād′, en′fə·lād, n. A position of troops subjecting them to fire from the flanks along the length of the line; the fire thus directed. —v.t., **-lad·ed, -lad·ing.** To fire in the flank of a troop; to be in position to deliver such fire.

en·fold, en·fōld′, v.t. To wrap in layers; to clasp in the arms.

en·force, en·fōrs′, en·fôrs′, v.t., **-forced, -forc·ing.** To force compliance with laws; to add strength or emphasis to; to compel. n. **—en·force·a·ble,** a. **—en·force·ment,** n. **—en·forc·er,** n.

en·fran·chise, en·fran′chīz, v.t., **-chised, -chis·ing.** To set free from slavery; to grant the right of voting; **—en·fran·chise·ment,** n.

en·gage, en·gāj′, v.t., **-gaged, -gag·ing.** To hire or employ; to bind by a contract; to betroth; to attract; to occupy the attention of; to do battle with; to interlock or mesh, as gears; to touch or interlock, as weapons in fencing. —v.i. To pledge oneself; to undertake to begin combat; to mesh; to be in gear.

en·gaged, en·gājd′, a. Occupied; employed; enlisted; affianced; committed; in combat with; meshed or in gear.

en·gage·ment, en·gāj′mənt, n. Act of engaging; act or state of betrothal; appointment; agreement; occupation; period of employment; conflict between warring factions; act or state of meshing.

en·gag·ing, en·gā′jing, a. Winning; attractive; pleasing. **—en·gag·ing·ly,** adv.

en·gen·der, en·jen′der, v.t. To produce; to cause to exist. —v.i. To be caused or produced.

en·gine, en′jən, n. A machine that uses thermal energy to do work; a locomotive; any mechanical device.

en·gi·neer, en·jə·nēr′, n. One who practices engineering; one who operates a machine or locomotive; a person who skillfully manages a project. —v.t. To perform the duties of an engineer; to maneuver by contrivance.

en·gi·neer·ing, en·jə·nēr′ing, n. The practical application of scientific knowledge; the professional knowledge and work of an engineer.

Eng·lish, ing′glish, a. Of, pertaining to, or characteristic of England or its inhabitants; of or pertaining to the English language. —n. The English language, spoken in the U.S., England, and areas now

or previously controlled by Great Britain; pl. in constr., the English people. A particular style of the English language as used in a given time or area or by an individual; a school subject or course in English composition and literature; an English translation, as of a foreign word; an understandable version of anything obscure or very technical; (sometimes l.c.) a spinning motion imparted to a ball by striking it off-center, or by the manner of releasing it.

Eng·lish horn, n. A woodwind instrument somewhat larger than the oboe and having a pitch a fifth lower.

en·gorge, en·gôrj′, v.t., **-gorged, -gorg·ing.** To swallow greedily; to congest with blood. **—en·gorge·ment,** n.

en·grave, en·grāv′, v.t., **-graved, -grav·ing.** To cut figures or letters into a hard substance; to picture or cut on stone, metal, or wood, for printing purposes; to print from such a surface. **—en·grav·er,** n.

en·grav·ing, en·grā′ving, n. The art of cutting designs or writing into any hard substance; an engraved plate or block; an impression or print taken from an engraved surface.

en·gross, en·grōs′, v.t. To occupy wholly; absorb; to copy in a large, formal manner for preservation; to acquire the whole of in order to control the market; monopolize. **—en·grossed,** a. **—en·gross·er,** n. **—en·gross·ing,** a. **—en·gross·ing·ly,** adv. **—en·gross·ment,** n.

en·gulf, en·gəlf′, v.t. To swallow up; to overwhelm; immerse. **—en·gulf·ment,** n.

en·hance, en·hans′, en·häns′, v.t., **-hanced, -hanc·ing.** To increase, as price, value, beauty, or pleasure. **—en·hance·ment,** n.

e·nig·ma, i·nig′mə, n. Anything or anyone puzzling or inexplicable; a riddle. **—en·ig·mat·ic;** en·ig·mat′ik, ē·nig·mat′ik, **en·ig·mat·i·cal,** a. Perplexing; mysterious. **—en·ig·mat·i·cal·ly,** adv.

en·join, en·joyn′, v.t. To admonish, instruct, or command with authority. **—en·join·er,** n. **—en·join·ment,** n.

en·joy, en·joy′, v.t. To receive pleasure from; to have, possess, and use with satisfaction. **—en·joy·a·ble,** a. **—en·joy·a·ble·ness,** n. **—en·joy·a·bly,** adv. **—en·joy·ment,** n.

en·large, en·lärj′, v.t., **-larged, -larg·ing.** To make larger. —v.i. To speak or write with greater detail. **—en·large·a·ble,** a. **—en·larg·er,** n.

en·large·ment, en·lärj′mənt, n. The act of making larger; the state of being enlarged; a photograph which has been printed larger.

en·light·en, en·līt′ən, v.t. To give insight to; to impart knowledge; to instruct.

en·light·en·ment, en·līt′ən·mənt, n. Act of enlightening; state of being enlightened.

en·list, en·list′, v.t. To join the military; to employ in advancing some interest. —v.i. To enroll in the armed services voluntarily; to enter heartily into a cause. **—en·list·ed,** a. **—en·list·ment,** n.

en·list·ed man, n. A member of the U.S. armed forces who ranks below a commissioned officer or warrant officer.

en·liv·en, en·lī′vən, v.t. To make gay or cheerful. **—en·liv·en·er,** n.

en masse, än mas′, en mas′, adv. As a whole; all together; in a body.

en·mesh, en·mesh′, v.t. To catch in; to entangle.

en·mi·ty, en′mi·tē, n. pl., **-ties.** Hostility; ill will.

en·no·ble, en·nō′bəl, in·ō′bəl, v.t., **-bled, -bling.** To dignify; to elevate in degree, qualities, or excellence. **—en·no·ble·ment,** n. **—en·no·bler,** n.

en·nui, än′wē, n. A feeling of weariness arising from lack of occupation or interest; boredom.

e·nor·mi·ty, i·nôr′mi·tē, n. pl., **-ties.** The state or quality of being outrageous; very wicked; an atrocity.

e·nor·mous, i·nôr′məs, a. Great in size; excessively large; excessively wicked; atrocious. **—e·nor·mous·ly,** adv. **—e·nor·mous·ness,** n.

e·nough, i·nəf′, *a.* Adequate for the want or need; —*n.* An adequate quantity. —*adv.* To a satisfactory degree; sufficiently; tolerably or passably.

en·plane, en·plān′, *v.t., v.i.,* **-planed, -plan·ing.** To go aboard an airplane.

en·rage, en·rāj′, *v.t.,* **-raged, -rag·ing.** To make furious; to exasperate.

en·rap·ture, en·rap′chər, *v.t.,* **-tured, -tur·ing.** To delight beyond measure. —**en·rapt,** *a.*

en·rich, en·rich′, *v.t.* To make rich; to increase meaning; to improve the quality of; —**en·rich·er,** *n.* —**en·rich·ment,** *n.*

en·roll, en·rōl′, *v.t.* To write in a roll or register; to enlist; to record; to wrap. —*v.i.* To cause oneself to be registered.

en·roll·ment, en·rōl′mənt, *n.* The act of enrolling; the number registered. Also **en·rol·ment.**

en route, än root′, en root′, *adv.* On the way; along the way.

en·sconce, en·skons′, *v.t.,* **-sconced, -sconc·ing.** To cover or shelter; to settle comfortably.

en·sem·ble, än·säm′bəl, *n.* All the parts of anything considered as a whole; the complete outfit of a person; a full group of singers, players, or the like.

en·shrine, en·shrīn′, *v.t.,* **-shrined, -shrin·ing.** To place in a shrine; to preserve with care; to cherish.

en·shroud, en·shrowd′, *v.i.* To cover with; to veil or shroud; conceal.

en·sign, en′sīn, en′sən, *n.* A national flag or banner, esp. of an army or ship; a badge, or symbol of office. —en′sən. *Milit.* The lowest commissioned officer in the U. S. Navy.

en·si·lage, en′sə·lij, *n.* A mode of storing green fodder in pits or silos; the fodder thus treated. —*v.t.,* **-laged, -lag·ing.** To store in a silo.

en·slave, en·slāv′, *v.t.,* **-slaved, -slav·ing.** To make a slave of. —**en·slave·ment,** *n.* —**en·slav·er,** *n.*

en·snare, en·snār′, *v.t.,* **-snared, -snar·ing.** To catch in a snare; to trick. Also **in·snare.** —**en·snare·ment,** *n.* —**en·snar·er,** *n.* —**en·snar·ing·ly,** *adv.*

en·sue, en·soo′, *v.i.,* **-sued, -su·ing.** To follow as a consequence. —**en·su·ing,** *a.* —**en·su·ing·ly,** *adv.*

en·sure, en·shûr′, *v.t.,* **-sured, -sur·ing.** To make sure or certain. —**en·sur·er,** *n.*

en·tail, en·tāl′, *v.t.* To limit an inheritance of real property to specified heirs; to impose a burden upon someone; to bring on or involve. —*n.* The act of entailing, or the state of being entailed; the rule of descent settled for an estate; that which is entailed. —**en·tail·er,** *n.* —**en·tail·ment,** *n.*

en·tan·gle, en·tang′gəl, *v.t.,* **-gled, -gling.** To make tangled or snarled; to involve in anything complicated; —**en·tan·gle·ment,** *n.* The act of entangling or state of being entangled; a complication. —**en·tan·gler,** *n.*

en·tente, än·tänt′, *n.* An understanding between two or more nations to follow a common course of action; the parties to such an understanding.

en·ter, en′tər, *v.t.* To come or go into; to pierce; to penetrate; to insert; to begin; to join; to become a member of; to set down in a book or other record; to enroll; to report at the custom house on arrival in port; to place in regular form before a court. —*v.i.* To come in; embark in an affair, business, or profession; to be enrolled in a school; to join a competition. —**to enter into,** to get into the inside or interior of; to penetrate; to engage in; to deal with or treat by way of discussion or argument; to be an ingredient in; to form a constituent part in. —**en·ter·a·ble,** *a.*

en·ter·i·tis, en·tə·rī′tis, *n.* Inflammation of the intestines, esp. the small intestine.

en·ter·prise, en′tər·prīz, *n.* A project attempted; particularly, a bold or hazardous undertaking; adventurous spirit; a firm or business. —**en·ter·pris·ing,** en′tər·prī·zing, *a.* —**en·ter·pris·ing·ly,** *adv.*

en·ter·tain, en·tər·tān′, *v.t.* To treat with hospitality; to amuse; to take into consideration. —*v.i.* To provide diversions, amusements, or entertainment for; to receive company. —**en·ter·tain·er,** *n.*

en·ter·tain·ing, en·tər·tān′ing, *a.* Providing entertainment; amusing; diverting. —**en·ter·tain·ing·ly,** *adv.*

en·ter·tain·ment, en·tər·tān′mənt, *n.* The act of entertaining; the receiving and accommodating of guests; something that serves for amusement, as a dramatic performance.

en·thrall, en·thrôl′, *v.t.,* **-thralled, -thrall·ing.** To charm or to captivate. Also **en·thral.** —**en·thrall·ment,** *n.*

en·throne, en·thrōn′, *v.t.,* **-throned, -thron·ing.** To place on a throne; exalt; revere. —**en·throne·ment,** *n.*

en·thuse, en·thooz′, *v.i., v.t.,* **-thused, -thus·ing.** To arouse enthusiasm.

en·thu·si·asm, en·thoo′zē·az·əm, *n.* A keen and active interest.

en·thu·si·ast, en·thoo′zē·ast, *n.* One full of enthusiasm for something; a person of ardent zeal.

en·thu·si·as·tic, en·thoo·zē·as′tik, *a.* Filled with or characterized by enthusiasm; prone to enthusiasm; ardent; devoted. —**en·thu·si·as·ti·cal·ly,** *adv.*

en·tice, en·tīs′, *v.t.,* **-ticed, -tic·ing.** To attract by exciting hope or desire; lure. —**en·tice·ment,** *n.* —**en·tic·er,** *n.* —**en·tic·ing,** *a.* —**en·tic·ing·ly,** *adv.*

en·tire, en·tīr′, *a.* Whole; having all the parts or elements; full or thorough; not broken, mutilated, or decayed; intact; having an unbroken outline; without notches or indentations, as leaves or shells. —*n.* —**en·tire·ly,** *adv.* —**en·tire·ness,** —**en·tire·ty,** *n. pl.,* **-ties.**

en·ti·tle, en·tī′təl, *v.t.,* **-tled, -tling.** To give a right, or claim; to give a name or title to. —**en·ti·tle·ment,** *n.*

en·ti·ty, en′ti·tē, *n. pl.,* **-ties.** A being or species of being; an existing thing.

en·to·mol·o·gy, en·tə·mol′ə·jē, *n. pl.,* **en·to·mol·o·gies.** That branch of zoology which deals with insects. —**en·to·mo·log·ic,** —**en·to·mo·log·i·cal,** en·tə·mə·loj′i·kəl, *a.* —**en·to·mo·log·i·cal·ly,** *adv.* —**en·to·mol·o·gist,** *n.*

en·tou·rage, än·tû·räzh′, *n.* The group of associates and attendants surrounding an important person.

en·trails, en′trālz, en′trəlz, *n. pl.* The internal parts of animal bodies; the bowels; the insides of anything.

en·train, en·trān′, *v.t.* To put aboard a train. —*v.i.* To board a train. —**en·train·er,** *n.*

en·trance, en′trəns, *n.* The act of entering; the power or liberty of entering; admission; the doorway or passage by which a place may be entered. Also **en·trance·way.**

en·trance, en·trans′, en·träns′, *v.t.,* **-tranced, -tranc·ing.** To fill with delight or wonder; to throw into a trance. —**en·trance·ment,** *n.* —**en·tranc·ing,** *a.* —**en·tranc·ing·ly,** *adv.*

en·trant, en′trənt, *n.* One who enters; one taking part in a contest.

en·trap, en·trap′, *v.t.,* **-trapped, -trap·ping.** To catch as in a trap. —**en·trap·ment,** *n.*

en·treat, en·trēt′, *v.t.* To ask earnestly; to beseech; to plead for. —**en·treat·ing·ly,** *adv.* —**en·treat·ment,** *n.* —**en·treat·y,** *n.*

en·tree, än′trā, *n.* Entry; freedom of access; a way of obtaining access; the main course of a meal.

en·trench, en·trench′, *v.t.* To dig or cut a trench or trenches around; to fortify with a ditch and parapet; to place in a strong position. —*v.i.* To encroach, with *on* or *upon.* —**en·trench·ment,** *n.* Any protection.

en·tre·pre·neur, än·trə·prə·nər′, *n.* The person who organizes, manages, and assumes the risks of a business; a successful businessman. —**en·tre·pre·neur·i·al,** *a.* —**en·tre·pre·neur·ship,** *n.*

---

a- hat, fāte, fāre, fäther; **e-** met, mē; **i-** pin, pīne; **o-** not, nōte, ôrb, moove (move), boy, pownd; **u-** cūbe, bûll, tûk (took); **ch-** chin; **th-** thick, ŧhen; **zh-** vizhon (vision); **ə-** əgo, takən, pencəl, lemən, bərd (bird).

en·tro·py, en′trə·pē, *n.* The degree of uniformity in anything; sameness.

en·trust, en·trəst′, *v.t.* To trust or confide to the care of; to commit with confidence; consign; commit; confide. —**en·trust·ment**, *n.*

en·try, en′trē, *n. pl.,* -**tries.** The act of entering; entrance; a contestant in a contest; the act of recording in a book; an item entered or set down; the act of taking possession of lands.

en·twine, en·twin′, *v.t.,* -**twined,** -**twin·ing.** To twist around or together. —*v.i.* To become twisted or twined.

e·nu·mer·ate, i·noo′mə·rāt, i·nū′mə·rāt, *v.t.;* -**at·ed,** -**at·ing.** To name one by one; to count; to recount. —**e·nu·mer·a·ble,** *a.* —**e·nu·mer·a·tion,** i·noo·mə·rā′shən, *n.* —**e·nu·mer·a·tive,** *a.* —**e·nu·mer·a·tor,** *n.*

e·nun·ci·ate, i·nən′sē·āt, i·nən′shē·āt, *v.t.,* -**at·ed,** -**at·ing.** To pronounce, esp. in a particular manner; to state or declare definitely. —*v.i.* To utter or pronounce words. —**e·nun·ci·a·tion,** i·nən·sē·ā′shən, *n.* —**e·nun·ci·a·tive,** *a.* —**e·nun·ci·a·tor,** *n.*

en·u·re·sis, en·yū·rē′sis, *n.* Incontinence or involuntary urination. —**en·u·ret·ic,** en·yū·ret′ik, *a., n.*

en·vel·op, en·vel′əp, *v.t.,* -**oped,** -**op·ing.** To wrap up or surround entirely; to form a covering about. —**en·vel·op·ment,** *n.*

en·ve·lope, en′və·lōp, än·və·lōp, *n.* A paper cover, usu. sealable for enclosing a letter; anything that is wrapped around or envelops something.

en·vi·a·ble, en′vē·ə·bəl, *a.* Exciting envy; highly desirable. —**en·vi·a·ble·ness,** *n.* —**en·vi·a·bly,** *adv.*

en·vi·ous, en′vē·əs, *a.* Feeling or harboring envy; excited or directed by envy. —**en·vi·ous·ly,** *adv.* —**en·vi·ous·ness,** *n.*

en·vi·ron, en·vī′rən, *v.t.* To surround, encompass, or encircle.

en·vi·ron·ment, en·vī′rən·mənt, *n.* All the physical, social, and cultural factors and conditions influencing the growth and well-being of an organism or group of organisms; the act of surrounding; surroundings. —**en·vi·ron·men·tal,** en·vī·rən·men′təl, *a.* —**en·vi·ron·men·tal·ly,** *adv.*

en·vi·rons, en·vī′rənz, *n. pl.* Surrounding areas; the vicinity.

en·vis·age, en·viz′ij, *v.t.,* -**aged,** -**ag·ing.** To contemplate; to form a mental picture of.

en·vi·sion, en·vizh′ən, *v.t.* To picture in one's mind, esp. a future happening.

en·voy, en′voy, än′voy, *n.* One sent on a mission; a diplomatic agent ranking below an ambassador.

en·vy, en′vē, *n. pl.,* -**vies.** Resentment or jealousy excited by the sight of another's superiority or success. —*v.t.,* -**vied,** -**vy·ing.** To feel envy toward or on account of; to regard with jealousy; to desire earnestly. —**en·vi·er,** *n.* —**en·vy·ing·ly,** *adv.*

en·zyme, en′zim, *n.* A very large class of substances that are produced by living cells and act as catalysts in the metabolism. —**en·zy·mat·ic,** en·zī·mat′ik, en·zi·mat′ik, *a.* —**en·zy·mat·i·cal·ly,** *adv.*

e·on, ae·on, ē′ən, ē′on, *n.* A long, indefinite space of time; an age.

ep·au·let, ep′ə·let, *n.* A shoulder decoration worn by military and naval officers.

é·pée, ā·pā′, *n. Fencing.* A blunt-tipped sword having no cutting edge. —**é·pée·ist,** *n.*

e·phed·rine, i·fed′rin, ef′i·drēn, *n.* A drug used in the treatment of colds, asthma, and hay fever.

e·phem·er·al, i·fem′ər·əl, *a.* Short-lived; existing a short time only. —*n.* Anything fleeting or short-lived. *n.* Also **e·phem·er·al·ness.** —**e·phem·er·al·ly,** *adv.*

ep·ic, ep′ik, *a.* Of, pertaining to, or resembling an epic; heroic; majestic; grandiose; of extraordinary size or extent. Also **ep·i·cal.** —*n.* A long, narrative poem describing extraordinary events; any work of art whose subject or scale resembles an epic.

ep·i·cen·ter, ep′i·sen·tər, *n.* That part of the earth's surface above the source of an earthquake.

ep·i·cure, ep′i·kyûr, *n.* A connoisseur or lover of good food and wines. —**e·pi·cu·re·an,** ep·i·kyū·rē′ən, *a.*

ep·i·dem·ic, ep·ə·dem′ik, *a.* Affecting a great number in a community at the same time, as a contagious disease. —*n.* An occurrence of an epidemic disease; an outbreak of anything which spreads or increases rapidly. —**ep·i·dem·i·cal·ly,** *adv.*

ep·i·der·mis, ep·i·dər′mis, *n.* The outer layer of the skin, covering the true skin; cuticle. **ep·i·der·mal, ep·i·der·mic,** *a.*

ep·i·glot·tis, ep·ə·glot′is, *n.* A thin plate behind the tongue, which covers the glottis like a lid during the act of swallowing and thus prevents food or drink from entering the larynx.

ep·i·gram, ep′i·gram, *n.* A brief, witty, pointed saying; a short poem, usu. satirical. —**ep·i·gram·mat·ic,** ep·ə·grə·mat′ik, **ep·i·gram·mat·i·cal,** *a.* —**ep·i·gram·mat·i·cal·ly,** *adv.* —**ep·i·gram·ma·tist,** ep·ə·gram′ə·tist, *n.*

ep·i·gram·ma·tize, ep·i·gram′ə·tīz, *v.t.,* -**tized,** -**tiz·ing.** To represent or express by or in epigrams. —*v.i.* To make an epigram.

ep·i·lep·sy, ep′ə·lep·sē, *n.* A chronic nervous disease characterized by brief convulsive seizures and loss of consciousness.

ep·i·lep·tic, ep·ə·lep′tik, *a.* Pertaining to, or affected with, epilepsy. —*n.* One affected with epilepsy.

ep·i·logue, ep·i·log, ep′ə·lôg, ep′ə·log, *n.* A section following a piece of literature that ends or explains the preceding expression.

E·piph·a·ny, i·pif′ə·nē, *n. pl.,* -**nies.** A Christian festival held on January 6 commemorating the manifestation of Jesus Christ to the Magi; (*l.c.*) a manifestation, esp. of a divinity.

e·pis·co·pa·cy, i·pis′kə·pə·sē, *n. pl.,* -**cies.** Government of the church by bishops; the order of bishops; the office of a bishop.

e·pis·co·pal, i·pis′kə·pəl, *a.* Pertaining to a bishop; based on or recognizing a governing order of bishops; (*cap.*) used to designate the Anglican Church or some branch of it.

e·pis·co·pa·lian, i·pis·kə·pāl′yən, i·pis·kə·pā′lē·ən, *a.* Referring to the episcopal form of church government; (*cap.*) referring to the Episcopal Church. —*n.* An adherent of the episcopal system; (*cap.*) a member of the Episcopal Church. —**e·pis·co·pa·lian·ism,** *n.*

e·pis·co·pate, i·pis′kə·pit, i·pis′kə·pāt, *n.* A bishopric; the office and dignity of a bishop; the collective body of bishops.

ep·i·sode, ep′i·sōd, *n.* An incident in a series of events; an incident in a piece of writing or an oral account; part of a serial. —**ep·i·sod·ic,** ep·i·sod′ik, **ep·i·sod·i·cal,** *a.* —**ep·i·sod·i·cal·ly,** *adv.*

e·pis·te·mol·o·gy, i·pis·tə·mol′ə·jē, *n.* The theory or study of the origin, nature, methods, and limits of knowledge. —**e·pis·te·mo·log·i·cal,** i·pis·tə·mə·loj′i·kəl, *a.* —**e·pis·te·mol·o·gist,** *n.*

e·pis·tle, i·pis′əl, *n.* A letter, esp. a formal or morally instructive letter. (*Cap.*) One of the apostolic letters of the New Testament.

e·pis·to·lar·y, i·pis′tə·ler·ē, *a.* Of or appropriate for correspondence; contained in letters.

ep·i·taph, ep′i·taf, ep′i·täf, *n.* An inscription on a tomb or a brief composition written to praise someone deceased. —**ep·i·taph·ic,** ep·i·taf′ik, *a.* —**ep·i·taph·ist,** *n.*

ep·i·thet, ep′i·thet, *n.* A descriptive word or phrase expressing some real or implied quality of a person; a term of abuse. —**ep·i·thet·ic,** ep·i·thet′ik, **ep·i·thet·i·cal,** *a.*

e·pit·o·me, i·pit′ə·mē, *n.* A summary or abstract; a compendium; abridgement; a person or thing that typifies the whole.

e·pit·o·mize, i·pit′ə·mīz, *v.t.,* -**mized,** -**miz·ing.** To make a summary of; to abstract; to typify.

ep·och, ep′ək, *Brit.* ē′pok, *n.* A particular period of time as marked by distinctive character, events, or the like; a point of time from which succeeding years are numbered; the beginning of any distinctive period in the history of anything; an interval of geologic time. **—ep·och·al,** *a.*

ep·ox·y, e·pok′sē, *n.* Epoxy resin. **—***a.* Of or referring to a compound containing an oxygen atom united with two carbon atoms that are already joined in some other way.

ep·ox·y res·in, *n.* Any one of a group of resins useful for its toughness, adhesiveness, corrosion and chemical resistance; in finished products, used principally for surface coatings, adhesives, and electrical insulation.

Ep·som salt, ep′səm sôlt, *n.* *Usu. pl.* A compound used in the leather industry, in textiles, and in medicine.

eq·ua·ble, ek′wə·bəl, ē′kwə·bəl, *a.* Marked by uniformity; fair; uniform in action; steady; even. **—eq·ua·bil·i·ty,** ek·wə·bil′ə·tē, **eq·ua·ble·ness,** *n.* **—eq·ua·bly,** *adv.*

e·qual, ē′kwəl, *a.* Alike in quantity, degree, value, or size; of the same rank, ability, or merit; as great as another, followed by *to* or *with;* having adequate power, ability, or means; evenly proportioned or balanced: as an *equal* contest; even or regular, as motion; level. **—***n.* One who or that which is equal. **—***v.t.,* **e·qualed, e·qual·ing.** To be or become equal to; to match; to make or do something equal to. **—e·qual·ly,** *adv.* **—e·qual·ness,** *n.*

e·qual·i·tar·i·an, i·kwol·i·târ′ē·ən, *a.* Referring or holding to the ideal of equality among men. **—***n.* One who believes in equality among men. **—e·qual·i·tar·i·an·ism,** *n.*

e·qual·i·ty, i·kwol′i·tē, *n. pl.,* **-ties.** The state of being equal; likeness in size, number, quantity, value, qualities, or degree.

e·qual·ize, ē′kwəl·īz, *v.t.,* **-ized, -iz·ing.** To make equal. **—e·qual·i·za·tion,** ē·kwəl·ə·zā′shən, *n.* **—e·qual·iz·er,** *n.*

e·qua·nim·i·ty, ē·kwə·nim′i·tē, ek·wə·nim′i·tē, *n.* Evenness of mind or temper; calmness; self-possession.

e·quate, i·kwāt′, *v.t.,* **e·quat·ed, e·quat·ing.** To state the equality of or between; to make equal.

e·qua·tion, i·kwā′zhən, i·kwā′shən, *n.* The act of making equal; an expression of the equality of two quantities, usu. with the sign = between them; of a chemical reaction. **—e·qua·tion·al,** *a.* **—e·qua·tion·al·ly,** *adv.*

e·qua·tor, i·kwā′tər, *n.* That great circle of the earth which divides the earth into the northern and southern hemispheres; a circle dividing the surface of any body or any surface into two parts, usu. equal.

e·qua·to·ri·al, ē·kwə·tôr′ē·əl, ek·wə·tôr′ē·əl, *a.* Of, or near an equator, esp. the equator of the earth; of the regions of the earth's equator. **—e·qua·to·ri·al·ly,** *adv.*

e·ques·tri·an, i·kwes′trē·ən, *a.* Referring to horses or horsemanship; showing a person on horseback; **—***n.* A rider on horseback. **—e·ques·tri·enne,** i·kwes·trē·en′, *n. fem.*

e·qui·dis·tance, ē·kwi·dis′təns, *n.* Equal distance. **—e·qui·dis·tant,** *a.* **—e·qui·dis·tant·ly,** *adv.*

e·qui·lat·er·al, ē·kwə·lat′ər·əl, *a.* Having all the sides equal. **—***n.* A geometric form with all sides equal; a side equal to all others.

e·qui·li·brate, i·kwil′ə·brāt, ē·kwə·li′brāt, *v.t.,* **-brat·ed, -brat·ing.** To balance equally; to keep in equilibrium. **—***v.i.* To balance. **—e·qui·li·bra·tion,** ē·kwə·lə·brā′shən, i·kwil·ə·brā′shən, *n.* **—e·qui·li·bra·tor,** *n.*

e·qui·lib·ri·um, ē·kwə·lib′rē·əm, *n. pl.,* **-ums, -a.** Equal balance between opposing forces; a state of rest due to the balance of counteracting forces; mental balance.

e·quine, ē′kwīn, *a.* Like or resembling a horse. **—***n.* A horse.

e·qui·noc·tial, ē·kwə·nok′shəl, *a.* Of or relating to the equinoxes; equality of day and night. **—***n.* The celestial equator; a severe storm.

e·qui·nox, ē′kwə·noks, *n.* The time when the sun crosses the equator and day and night are of equal length all over the world: the vernal *equinox* is on about March 21, the autumnal *equinox* on about September 23.

e·quip, i·kwip′, *v.t.,* **e·quipped, e·quip·ping.** To provide with everything necessary for an undertaking; to prepare for some duty or service. **—e·quip·per,** *n.*

eq·ui·page, ek′wə·pij, *n.* A carriage with a horse or horses; materials with which a person or thing is equipped; equipment.

e·quip·ment, i·kwip′mənt, *n.* Articles used in equipping; the act of equipping; the knowledge and skill needed to perform a task; furnishings.

e·qui·poise, ē′kwə·poyz, ek′wə·poyz, *n.* Equality of weight or force; equilibrium.

eq·ui·ta·ble, ek′wi·tə·bəl, *a.* Equal in regard to the rights of persons; just; fair; impartial. **—eq·ui·ta·ble·ness,** *n.* **—eq·ui·ta·bly,** *adv.*

eq·ui·ty, ek′wi·tē, *n. pl.,* **-ties.** The quality of being fair or impartial; fairness; that which is fair and just; justice or right; a legal system that includes a rule determining what is equitable and fair, which supplements the defects of common and statute law; the value of a property in excess of all liens and claims against it.

e·quiv·a·lance, i·kwiv′ə·ləns, *n.* The state or fact of being equivalent; equality in value, force, or meaning. Also **e·quiv·a·len·cy.**

e·quiv·a·lent, i·kwiv′ə·lənt, *a.* Equal in value, measure, force, effect, or meaning. **—***n.* That which is equivalent; something equal or corresponding to something. **—e·quiv·a·lent·ly,** *adv.*

e·quiv·o·cal, i·kwiv′ə·kəl, *a.* Being of doubtful meaning; ambiguous; open to double meaning; uncertain; doubtful; questionable. **—e·quiv·o·cal·ly,** *adv.* **—e·quiv·o·cal·ness,** *n.*

e·quiv·o·cate, i·kwiv′ə·kāt, *v.i.,* **-cat·ed, -cat·ing.** To use ambiguous expressions in order to mislead; to quibble. **—e·quiv·o·ca·tor,** *n.* **—e·quiv·o·ca·tion,** i·kwiv·ə·kā′shən, *n.*

e·ra, ē′rə, ir′ə, *n.* A period of time marked by special character or events; a point of time from which later years are numbered; special date, event, or character forming the beginning of an age or period.

e·rad·i·cate, i·rad′i·kāt, *v.t.,* **-cat·ed, -cat·ing.** To destroy thoroughly; eliminate by erasing; pull up by the roots. **—e·rad·i·ca·ble,** *a.* **—e·rad·i·ca·tion,** i·rad·i·kā′shən, **—e·rad·i·ca·tive,** *a.* **—e·rad·i·ca·tor,** *n.*

e·rase, i·rās′, *v.t.,* **e·rased, e·ras·ing.** To rub out, as letters or characters; to obliterate; to eliminate, as recorded material, from magnetic tape or wire. *Informal.* To kill. **—***v.i.* To become erased easily; remove marks from. **—e·ras·a·bil·i·ty,** i·rā·sə·bil′ə·tē, *n.* **—e·ras·a·ble,** *a.*

e·ras·er, i·rā′sər, *n.* One who or something which erases; a piece of rubber or cloth, used to erase writing or other marks.

e·ras·ure, i·rā′shər, *n.* The act of erasing or scratching out; the impression left on a surface after erasing.

ere, âr, *conj., prep. Poet.* Before; sooner than.

e·rect, i·rekt′, *v.t.* To raise and set in an upright position; to build as a building; to set up as an institution; to cause to come into being; to *erect* a social barrier.—*a.* Upright in position or posture; raised upward. —**e·rect·a·ble,** *a.* —**e·rect·er,** *n.* —**e·rec·tive,** *a.* —**e·rect·ly,** *adv.* —**e·rect·ness,** *n.*

e·rec·tile, i·rek′təl, i·rek′til, *a.* Capable of being erected or set upright. —**e·rec·til·i·ty,** i·rek·til′i·tē, ē·rek·til′i·tē, *n.*

e·rec·tion, i·rek′shən, *n.* The act of erecting; the state of being erected; something constructed, as a building or other structure; a rigid state of an organ or part which contains erectile tissue, esp. of the penis or the clitoris.

e·rec·tor, i·rek′tər, *n.* One who or that which erects.

erg, ərg, *n.* The unit of work done by a force of one dyne moving through a distance of one centimeter.

er·go, ər′gō, *adv., conj.* Therefore.

Er·in, er′in, âr′in, *n. Poet.* Ireland.

er·mine, ər′min, *n. pl.,* **-mine, -mines.** A small mammal with a white winter coat and black tail; the white fur itself.

e·rode, i·rōd, *v.t.,* **e·rod·ed, e·rod·ing.** To eat away; to destroy by slow consumption; to form, as a channel, by eating or wearing away; to slowly wear away, as the earth's surface, by the action of wind or water. —*v.i.* To become eroded.

e·rog·e·nous, i·roj′ə·nəs, *a.* Inducing sexual desire; sexually excitable; the body's *erogenous* zones.

e·ro·sion, i·rō′zhən, *n.* The act or operation of eating or wearing away; the wearing away of soil or rock by the influence of water, ice, winds, and other forces of nature.

e·rot·ic, i·rot′ik, *a.* Referring to sexual love; increasing sexual desire; moved by sexual desire. —**e·rot·i·cal·ly,** *adv.*

e·rot·i·cism, i·rot′i·siz·əm, *n.* A sexual quality; use of sexually stimulating ideas in art, literature, and drama; a condition of sexual excitement.

err, ər, âr, *v.i.* To wander; to go astray, esp. in thought; to be wrong; fail morally; blunder; —**err·ing·ly,** *adv.*

er·rand, er′ənd, *n.* A trip to carry a message or to do a job; the purpose of any short trip or journey; a service or favor done for another.

er·rant, er′ənt, *a.* Journeying or traveling; wandering or straying. —**er·rant·ly,** *adv.*

er·rat·ic, i·rat′ik, *a.* Wandering; having no certain course; deviating from the proper or usual conduct or opinion; eccentric; queer. —*n.* A wanderer; an erratic or eccentric person. —**er·rat·i·cal·ly,** *adv.*

er·ra·tum, i·ra′təm, i·rä′təm, *n. pl.,* **-ta.** An error or mistake in writing or printing; *pl.,* a list of mistakes in writing or printing.

er·ro·ne·ous, ə·rō′nē·əs, i·rō′nē·əs, *a.* Wrong; mistaken; false; inaccurate. —**er·ro·ne·ous·ly,** *adv.* —**er·ro·ne·ous·ness,** *n.*

er·ror, er′ər, *n.* A mistake, as in action; an inaccuracy, as in speaking or writing; false belief; wrongdoing; in baseball, a faulty defensive play. —**er·ror·less,** *a.*

er·satz, er′zäts, *a.* Substitute; artificial or synthetic; often inferior.

erst·while, ərst′hwil, *a.* Former. —*adv. Archaic.* A while before; formerly.

er·u·dite, er′û·dit, er′oo·dit, *a.* Learned; scholarly. —**er·u·dite·ly,** *adv.* —**er·u·dite·ness,** *n.*

er·u·di·tion, er·û·dish′ən, er·oo·dish′ən, *n.* Knowledge gained chiefly from books and study; scholarship.

e·rupt, i·rəpt′, *v.i.* To burst forth, as volcanic matter; to eject matter, as a volcanic geyser; to burst forth in a sudden or violent manner; to break out in a rash or blemish; of teeth, to break through the skin of the gums. —*v.t.* To cause to burst forth; to eject; to force through the gums; to break out. —**e·rup·tion,** i·rəp′shən, *n.* —**e·rup·tive,** i·rəp′tiv, *a.* —**e·rup·tive·ly,** *adv.* —**e·rup·tive·ness,** *n.*

es·ca·lade, es·kə·lād′, *n.* A scaling or mounting by means of ladders.—*v.t.,* **-lad·ed, -lad·ing.** To mount, pass, or enter by means of ladders. —**es·ca·lad·er,** *n.*

es·ca·late, es′kə·lāt, *v.t.,* **-lat·ed, -lat·ing.** To in-

crease in scope or intensity; to raise or go up on a moving stairway. —**es·ca·la·tion,** es·kə·lā′shən, *n.*

es·ca·la·tor, es′kə·lā·tər, *n.* A moving staircase.

es·ca·la·tor clause, *n.* A part of a contract which raises or lowers wages or costs to conform with the rise or fall of living costs or expenses.

es·cal·lop, es·kol′əp, es·kal′əp, *n., v.t.* Scallop.

es·ca·pade, es′kə·pād, es·kə·pād′, *n.* An adventurous action; a thoughtless action done without regard for consequences; an escape from confinement.

es·cape, es·kāp′, *v.i.,* **-caped, -cap·ing.** To get away; to avoid capture, punishment, or evil; to go out from a container, as a fluid; to fade away, as from the memory. —*v.t.* To get away from; to *escape* prison; slip out, as a remark; to fail to be noticed or recollected by.—*n.* The act of escaping, or the fact of having escaped; a getting away from confinement or restraint; a relief from reality; leakage; a means of escaping; a fire *escape.* —*a.* Allowing a means of evading obligation; an *escape* clause. —**es·cap·er,** *n.*

es·ca·pee, es·kāp′ē, es·kā·pē′, *n.* One who has escaped, esp. from imprisonment.

es·cape hatch, *n.* An emergency exit.

es·cape rock·et, *n. Aerospace.* A small rocket engine attached to the end of an escape tower of a space capsule, and used for separation of the capsule from the booster in an emergency.

es·cape tow·er, *n. Aerospace.* A trestle tower on top of a space capsule which connects the capsule to the escape rocket during lift-off, protecting the capsule from the heat of the escape rocket.

es·cape ve·loc·i·ty, *n.* The minimum speed which a body must acquire in order to escape the gravitational field of a planet or celestial body.

es·cap·ist, es·skā′pist, *n.* One who seeks escape from unpleasant reality in daydreams and fancies. —*a.* —**es·cap·ism,** *n.*

es·carp·ment, e·skärp′mənt, *n.* A steep slope.

es·chew, es·choo′, *v.t.* To shun; to avoid. —**es·chew·al,** *n.* —**es·chew·er,** *n.*

es·cort, es′kôrt, *n.* A male who accompanies a woman on a date; a body of persons, or a single person, accompanying another or others for protection; military protection, safeguard, or guidance on a journey. —e·skôrt′, *v.t.* To attend or accompany as an escort.

es·cri·toire, es·kri·twär′, *n.* A writing desk.

es·crow, es′kro, e·skrō′, *n.* A deed, bond, money, or property held in custody by a third person, until the fulfillment of some condition. —*v.t.*

es·cutch·eon, e·skech′ən, *n.* A shield, or shield-shaped surface; the protective plate around a keyhole or light switch. —**es·cutch·eoned,** *a.*

Es·ki·mo, es′ki·mō, *n. pl.,* **-mos, -mo.** A people, inhabiting the arctic coasts of America from Greenland to Alaska; the language of this region. —*a.* Of or pertaining to their language.

e·soph·a·gus, oe·soph·a·gus, i·sof′ə·gəs, ē·sof′ə·gəs, *n. pl.,* **-gi, -ji.** The muscular tube that connects the throat to the stomach; the gullet.

es·o·ter·ic, es·ə·târ′ik, *a.* Understood only by those few with special interest or knowledge. —**es·o·ter·i·cal,** *a.* —**es·o·ter·i·cal·ly,** *adv.*

ESP. Extrasensory perception.

es·pal·ier, e·spal′yər, *n.* A framework on which trees are trained to grow in flattened form; a tree or plant thus trained. —*v.t.* To train on or furnish with an espalier.

es·pe·cial, e·spesh′əl, *a.* Of a distinct sort or kind; special; particular; peculiar. —**es·pe·cial·ly,** *adv.* —**es·pe·cial·ness,** *n.*

Es·pe·ran·to, es·pə·rän′tō, es·pə·ran′tō, *n.* An artificial international language based on word roots common to the principal European languages.

es·pi·o·nage, es′pē·ə·näzh, es′pē·ə·nij, *n.* The practice of spying; the use of spies for securing confidential information.

es·pla·nade, es·plə·nād′, es·plə·näd′, *n.* Any open level space, esp. one for public walks or drives.

es·pouse, e·spowz′, *v.t.,* **-poused, -pous·ing.** To embrace or to adopt, as a cause or quarrel; to marry. **—es·pous·er,** *n.*

es·pous·al, es·powz′əl, *n.* An espousing, as of a cause; a betrothal; a wedding.

es·pres·so, e·spres′ō, *n.* Strong coffee brewed by steam forced through powdered coffee beans.

es·prit, e·sprē′, *n.* Spirit; intelligence; wit.

es·prit de corps, e·sprē′ də kôr′, *n.* A sense of union among a group of persons.

es·py, e·spī′, *v.t.,* **-pied, -py·ing.** To see at a distance; to discover.

es·quire, es′kwīr, *n.* (*Cap.*) A title of respect or courtesy placed in abbreviated form after the surname, esp. in a written address: abbr. Esq. (L.c.) A gentleman who escorts a lady in public. **—es·kwīr′,** *v.t.,* **-quired, -quir·ing.** To address as "Esquire"; to escort as an esquire.

es·say, es′ā, e·sā′, *n.* A trial or attempt; a test or experiment; a short, literary piece, written to prove some point or illustrate a particular subject.**—v.t.** To attempt; to try, as an experiment. **—es·say·er,** *n.*

es·say·ist, es′ā·ist, *n.* A writer of essays.

es·sence, es′əns, *n.* That which is the special nature of a thing; intrinsic value; the properties of any plant or drug extracted, refined, or distilled into a condensed form; an extract; a perfume.

es·sen·tial, ə·sen′shəl, *a.* Important; fundamental; basic; absolutely necessary; containing an essence of a plant or drug. **—n.** Something belonging to the essence or nature of a thing; something indispensable; basic; necessary; a chief point. **—es·sen·ti·al·i·ty,** ə·sen·shē·al/i·tē, *n.* **—es·sen·tial·ly,** *adv.* **—es·sen·tial·ness,** *n.*

es·tab·lish, e·stab′lish, *v.t.* To make firm; to install on a permanent basis; to prove; to enact: as, to *establish* law and order; to originate and secure permanently: as, to *establish* a custom; to found: as, to *establish* a business. **—es·tab·lish·er,** *n.*

es·tab·lish·ment, e·stab′lish·mənt, *n.* That which has been established; the act of establishing; the state of being established; the power structure of an established order of society; a public or private institution; a place of business or residence and everything connected with it; a permanent civil or military organization; confirmation. **—the Es·tab·lish·ment,** those members of a society or particular field who form the power structure of that group.

es·tate, e·stāt′, *n.* Property; a large piece of land with a manor house on it; property or possessions; the amount of one's holdings in land and other property; property left at a person's death; a major social group having political power; social status or rank.

es·teem, e·stēm′, *v.t.* To have a high regard for; respect; admire. **—n.** Favorable opinion; high regard.

es·thete, es′thēt, *n.* Aesthete.

es·thet·ic, es·thet′ik, *a.* Aesthetic.

es·ti·ma·ble, es′ti·mə·bəl, *a.* Estimated or valued; worthy of esteem; deserving of good opinion. **—es·ti·ma·ble·ness,** *n.* **—es·ti·ma·bly,** *adv.*

es·ti·mate, es′ti·māt, *v.t.,* **-mat·ed, -mat·ing.** Calculate approximately; to form an opinion of; judge.**—v.i.** To submit figures, as of the cost of work to be done. **—es′ti·mit,** es′ti·māt, *n.* An approximate judgment or calculation; an approximate statement of the charge for certain work to be done; a judgment or opinion, as of the qualities of a person or thing. **—es·ti·ma·tive,** *a.* **—es·ti·ma·tor,** *n.*

es·ti·ma·tion, es·ti·mā′shən, *n.* Judgment or opinion; the act of estimating or appraising; estimate; valuation in respect of excellence or merit; approximate calculation.

es·trange, e·strānj′, *v.t.,* **-tranged, -trang·ing.** To turn away in feeling or affection; to cause to be strange or as a stranger. **—es·trange·ment,** *n.* **—es·tran·ger,** *n.*

es·trus, es′trəs, *n.* The point of highest sexual excitability in the female, during which conception is possible; the period of heat. Also **es·trum, oes·trus.**

es·tu·ar·y, es′chū·er·ē, *n. pl.,* **-ies.** The wide mouth of a river where the tide meets the currents. **—es·tu·ar·i·al,** es·chū·är′ē·əl, *a.*

et cet·er·a, et set′ər·ə, et set′rə, *n.* A number of other things or persons unspecified; *pl.,* extras or additional items.

etch, ech, *v.t.* To cut or corrode with an acid; engrave by the action of an acid so as to form a design or picture; to produce or copy by this method; to draw clearly, as a person's likeness; to impress firmly on the mind.**—v.i.** To practice etching.**—n.** A chemical used for etching. **—etch·er,** *n.*

etch·ing, ech′ing, *n.* The process or art of one who etches; a process for forming a design or drawing on a metal plate from which an ink impression on paper can be taken; the design or picture produced.

e·ter·nal, i·tər′nəl, *a.* Having no beginning or end of existence; everlasting; endless. **—the E·ter·nal,** *n.* An appellation for God. **—e·ter·nal·ly,** *adv.*

e·ter·ni·ty, i·tər′ni·tē, *n. pl.,* **-ties.** The condition or quality of being eternal; being without beginning or end; endless past time or endless future time; the state or condition which begins at death; immortality.

e·ter·nize, i·tər′nīz, *v.t.,* **-nized, -niz·ing.** To make eternal or endless. **—e·ter·ni·za·tion,** i·tər·nə·zā′shən, *n.*

eth·a·nol, eth′ə·nôl, eth′ə·nōl, *n.* Ethyl alcohol.

e·ther, ē′thər, *n.* A highly volatile and inflammable colorless liquid, used mainly as an anesthetic and a solvent; the clear sky; the heavens.

e·the·re·al, i·thēr′ē·əl, *a.* Delicate and airy; heavenly; celestial. **—e·the·re·al·i·ty,** i·thēr·ē·al′i·tē, *n.* **—e·the·re·al·ly,** *adv.* **—e·the·re·al·ness,** *n.*

e·the·re·al·ize, i·thēr′ē·ə·līz, *v.t.,* **-ized, -iz·ing.** To make spiritlike or ethereal. **—e·the·re·al·i·za·tion,** i·thēr·ē·əl·i·zā′shən, *n.*

eth·ic, eth′ik, *a.* Pertaining to morals; ethical.**—n.** A system or philosophy of conduct.

eth·i·cal, eth′i·kəl, *a.* Pertaining to morals or morality; right and wrong in conduct; in agreement with the rules for right conduct or practice; referring to drugs that have been proven by clinical trial and are available by prescription. **—eth·i·cal·ly,** *adv.*

eth·ics, eth′iks, *n. pl. but sing. in constr.* The principles of morality, or the field of study of morals or right conduct.**—n. pl., sing. or pl. in constr.** A particular ethical system.

eth·nic, eth′nik, *a.* Relating to those groups sharing a common language or set of customs; pertaining to such peoples, their origin, characteristics, and classification; belonging to the distinctive cultural traditions of a particular country or people. Also **eth·ni·cal.** **—eth·ni·cal·ly,** *adv.*

eth·nol·o·gy, eth·nol′ə·jē, *n.* A branch of anthropology that deals with the various groups of mankind.

eth·yl, eth′əl, *n.* A univalent hydrocarbon radical. (*Cap.*) Trademark. Tetraethyl lead, or motor fuel to which it has been added as an antiknock compound. **—e·thyl·ic,** ə·thil′ik, *a.*

eth·yl al·co·hol, *n.* Grain alcohol; a colorless, volatile liquid, used as a solvent or in beverages.

eth·yl·ene gly·col, *n. Chem.* Ethylene alcohol, a clear, colorless, syrupy liquid with a sweet taste: used in automobile radiator antifreeze and brake fluid.

e·ti·ol·o·gy, ē·tē·ol′ə·jē, *n.* The study of causation in the fields of pathology, biology, philosophy, and physics. **—e·ti·o·lo·gist,** *n.* **—e·ti·o·log·i·cal,** ē·tē·ə·loj′i·kəl, *a.* **—e·ti·o·log·i·cal·ly,** *adv.*

---

et·i·quette, et′ə·ket, *n.* Requirements for proper social behavior; proper conduct as established in any community or for an occasion; the accepted code of ceremony, as at a court, in official or other formal observances, or in polite society generally.

E·trus·can, i·trus′kən, *a.* Relating to Etruria, an ancient country in west central Italy.—*n.* A native of ancient Etruria. Also **E·tru·ri·an,** i·trŭr′ē·ən.

e·tude, ā′tood, ā′tūd, *n.* A composition intended mainly for the practice of some point of technique; a study.

et·y·mol·o·gy, et·i·mol′ə·jē, *n. pl.,* **-gies.** Explanation of the origin and changes of a particular word; the derivation of a word. —**et·y·mo·log·ic,** et·ə·mə·loj′ik, **et·y·mo·log·i·cal,** *a.* —**et·y·mol·o·gist,** *n.*

eu·ca·lyp·tus, ū·kə·lip′təs, *n. pl.,* **-tus·es,** -tī, -tī. Any member of a genus including many tall, aromatic evergreen trees, native to Australia.

Eu·cha·rist, ū′kə·rist, *n.* The Christian sacrament of the Lord's Supper; the Holy Communion; the consecrated elements of bread and wine; (*l.c.*) thanksgiving. —**Eu·cha·ris·tic,** ū·kə·ris′tik, **Eu·cha·ris·ti·cal,** *a.*

Eu·clid·e·an, Eu·clid·i·an, ū·klid′ē·ən, *a.* Of or pertaining to Euclid, his geometry, or the geometry based on his or similar postulates.

eu·gen·ic, ū·jen′ik, *a.* Pertaining to or bringing about improvement in the type of offspring produced. —**eu·gen·i·cal·ly,** *adv.*

eu·gen·ics, ū·jen′iks, *n. pl. but sing. in constr.* The science of improving the qualities of the human species; the science of bringing about an improved type of offspring of the human species.

eu·lo·gize, ū′lə·jīz, *v.t.,* **-gized, -giz·ing.** To speak or write in praise of another; to praise. —**eu·lo·giz·er,** *n.*

eu·lo·gy, ū′lə·jē, *n. pl.,* **-gies.** Praise; a speech or writing in commendation of a living or dead person. —**eu·lo·gist,** *n.* —**eu·lo·gis·tic,** ū·lə·jis′tik, *a.* —**eu·lo·gis·ti·cal·ly,** ū·lə·jis′tik·lē, *adv.*

eu·nuch, ū′nək, *n.* A castrated male; a male deprived of the testes.

eu·phe·mism, ū′fə·miz·əm, *n.* The substitution of an inoffensive word or phrase for one which may be unpleasant; the term so substituted. —**eu·phe·mist,** *n.* —**eu·phe·mis·tic,** ū·fə·mis′tik, **eu·phe·mis·ti·cal,** *a.* —**eu·phe·mis·ti·cal·ly,** *adv.*

eu·phe·mize, ū′fə·mīz, *v.t.,* **-mized, -miz·ing.** To express by means of a euphemism.

eu·pho·ni·ous, ū·fō′nē·əs, *a.* Agreeable to the ear; characterized by euphony. —**eu·pho·ni·ous·ly,** *adv.* —**eu·pho·ni·ous·ness,** *n.*

eu·pho·ny, ū′fə·nē, *n.* Agreeableness of sound. —**eu·phon·ic,** ū·fon′ik, **eu·phon·i·cal,** *a.* —**eu·phon·i·cal·ly,** *adv.*

eu·pho·ri·a, ū·fō′rē·ə, ū·fôr′ē·ə, *n.* A feeling of well-being; a mood of elation. —**eu·phor·ic,** *a.*

Eur·a·sian, ū·rā′zhən, ū·rā′shən, *a.* Of or pertaining to Europe and Asia taken together; of mixed European and Asiatic descent.—*n.* A person of mixed European and Asiatic descent.

eu·re·ka, ū·rē′kə, *interj.* An expression of triumph at a discovery or supposed discovery.

Eu·ro·pe·an, yūr·ə·pē′ən, *a.* Of or pertaining to Europe, its inhabitants, or its culture.—*n.* A native or inhabitant of Europe; a person of European descent.

Eu·ro·pe·an·ize, yūr·ə·pē′ə·nīze, *v.t.,* **-ized, -iz·ing.** To cause to become European, as in ideas, manners, or characteristics. —**Eu·ro·pe·an·i·za·tion,** yūr·ə·pē·ən·ə·zā′shən, *n.*

Eu·ro·pe·an plan, *n.* A hotel policy of charging a fixed rate for room and service, meals being extra.

Eu·sta·chian tube, ū·stā′shən, ū·stā′kē·ən, *n.* The tube between the middle ear, or tympanum, and the pharynx. Also **au·di·to·ry ca·nal.**

eu·tha·na·sia, ū·thə·nā′zhə, ū·thə·nā′zhē·ə, *n.* A painless putting to death of persons having an incurable disease; an easy death. Also **mer·cy kill·ing.**

e·vac·u·ate, i·vak′yū·āt, *v.t.,* **-at·ed, -at·ing.** To make empty, to expel the contents of; to leave empty; to vacate; to withdraw from or quit; to discharge or eject, as through the excretory passages, esp. from the bowels.—*v.i.* To leave or withdraw from a place, as in an emergency. —**e·vac·u·a·tion,** i·vak·yū·ā′shən, *n.* —**e·vac·u·a·tive,** *a.* —**e·vac·u·a·tor,** *n.*

e·vac·u·ee, i·vak·yū·ē, i·vak·yū·ē′, *n.* One who is removed, for safety or protection, from a disaster area or an area threatened by danger.

e·vade, i·vād′, *v.t.,* **e·vad·ed, e·vad·ing.** To avoid, escape from, or elude in any way; to elude doing; to shun replying directly, as to a question; to escape the grasp or comprehension of; to baffle or foil.—*v.i.* To escape; to avoid a question. —**e·vad·a·ble, e·vad·i·ble,** *a.* —**e·vad·er,** *n.* —**e·vad·ing·ly,** *adv.*

e·val·u·ate, i·val′yū·āt, *v.t.,* **-at·ed, -at·ing.** To determine the value of; to appraise carefully. —**e·val·u·a·tion,** i·val·yū·ā′shən, *n.* —**e·val·u·a·tor,** *n.*

ev·a·nesce, ev·ə·nes′, *v.i.,* **-nesced, -nesc·ing.** To vanish; to disappear slowly.

ev·a·nes·cent, ev·ə·nes′ənt, *a.* Vanishing; fleeting; passing away. —**ev·a·nes·cence,** *n.* —**ev·a·nes·cent·ly,** *adv.*

e·van·gel, i·van′jəl, *n.* The gospel; (*usu. cap.*) one of the gospels.

e·van·gel·i·cal, ē·van·jel′i·kəl, ev·ən·jel′i·kəl, *a.* Of or pertaining to the gospel or the four Gospels; referring to the Protestant churches which hold to the doctrines of salvation and personal conversion; spiritually minded; zealous for practical Christian living; seeking the conversion of sinners.—*n.* An adherent of evangelical doctrines; a member of an evangelical church or party. Also **e·van·gel·ic.** —**e·van·gel·i·cal·ism,** *n.* —**e·van·gel·i·cal·ly,** *adv.* —**e·van·gel·i·cal·ness,** *n.*

e·van·ge·lism, i·van′jə·liz·əm, *n.* The zealous preaching of the gospel; the work of an evangelist; evangelicalism; zeal. —**e·van·ge·lis·tic,** i·van·jə·lis′tik, *a.* —**e·van·ge·lis·ti·cal·ly,** *adv.*

e·van·ge·list, i·van′jə·list, *n.* (*Often cap.*) Any of the gospel writers. (*L.c.*) A preacher of the gospel; an occasional or itinerant preacher; a revivalist; a patriarch in the Mormon Church.

e·van·ge·lize, i·van′jə·līz, *v.t.,* **-lized, -liz·ing.** To instruct in the gospel; to preach the gospel to and convert.—*v.i.* To preach the gospel. —**e·van·ge·li·za·tion,** i·van·jə·lə·zā′shən, *n.* —**e·van·ge·liz·er,** *n.*

e·vap·o·rate, i·vap′ə·rāt, *v.i.,* **-rat·ed, -rat·ing.** To be changed to vapor; to pass off in vapor; disappear.—*v.t.* To cause to evaporate; to cause to disappear. —**e·vap·o·ra·ble,** *a.* —**e·vap·o·ra·tion,** i·vap·ə·rā′shən, *n.* —**e·vap·o·ra·tive,** *a.* —**e·vap·o·ra·tor,** *n.*

e·va·sion, i·vā′zhən, *n.* The act of avoiding or escaping; the means used to avoid; an excuse; the avoiding of an argument or question.

e·va·sive, i·vā′siv, *a.* Avoiding. —**e·va·sive·ly,** *adv.* —**e·va·sive·ness,** *n.*

eve, ēv, *n.* The period just preceding some event: as, on the *eve* of a revolution; the evening.

e·ven, ē′vən, *a.* Level or flat; smooth, as a surface; free from variations; uniform; impartial, or fair, on the same level; leaving no balance of debt on either side; equal in measure or quantity; of a number, divisible by two: opposed to *odd*; without fractional parts, as an *even* mile or an *even* hundred. —*adv.* In an even manner; evenly; just; still; yet; indeed. —*v.t.* To make even; to level; to smooth; to balance, often followed by *up*.—*v.i.* To become even. —**e·ven·ly,** *adv.* —**e·ven·ness,** *n.*

e·ven-hand·ed, ē′vən·han′did, *a.* Impartial; just.

eve·ning, ēv′ning, *n.* The close of the day and the beginning of darkness or night; the time from sunset until darkness.—*a.*

eve·ning dress, *n.* Formal clothes worn for social occasions in the evening.

eve·nings, ēv′ningz, *adv.* In or during the evening on a regular basis.

e•vent, i•vent′, *n.* Anything that happens; the fact of happening; an occurrence, esp. one of some importance. *Sports.* Each of the items in a program. **—at all events, in any event,** whatever happens; in any case. **—in the event,** if.

e•vent•ful, i•vent′fəl, *a.* Full of events or incidents; having important results. **—e•vent•ful•ly,** *adv.* **—e•vent•ful•ness,** *n.*

e•ven•tu•al, i•ven′chů•əl, *a.* Coming later or as a result; final. **—e•ven•tu•al•ly,** *adv.*

e•ven•tu•al•i•ty, i•ven•chů•al′i•tē, *n. pl.,* **-ties.** That which may happen.

e•ven•tu•ate, i•ven′chů•āt, *v.i.,* **-at•ed, -at•ing.** To result, as a consequence; to happen; to come to pass.

ev•er, ev′ər, *adv.* At any time past or future; at all times; always; eternally; constantly; continually.

ev•er•green, ev′ər•grēn, *a.* Always green; of trees or shrubs, having green leaves throughout the year; fresh and vigorous at all times.—*n.* An evergreen plant with needle-shaped leaves, esp. pine, spruce, or fir; *pl.,* evergreen branches used for decoration, esp. at Christmas.

ev•er•last•ing, ev•ər•las′ting, ev•ər•läs′ting, *a.* Lasting forever; eternal.—*n.* Eternity; (*cap.*) God. **—ev•er•last•ing•ly,** *adv.* **—ev•er•last•ing•ness,** *n.*

ev•er•more, ev•ər•mōr′, ev•ər•môr′, *adv.* Always; from this time forward.

e•vert, i•vərt′, *v.t.* To turn outward or inside out. **—e•ver•si•ble,** i•vər′si•bəl, *a.* **—e•ver•sion,** i•vər′zhən, i•vər′shən, *n.*

eve•ry, ev′rē, *a.* Each of a number singly or one by one; all conceivable; total.

eve•ry•bod•y, ev′rē•bod•ē, *pron.* Every person.

eve•ry•day, ev′rē•dā, *a.* Daily; of or for ordinary days; ordinary; commonplace.

eve•ry•one, ev′rē•wən, *pron.* Every person; everybody.

eve•ry•thing, ev′rē•thing, *pron.* Every object or particular of a total; all; something extremely important, as: This news means *everything* to us.

eve•ry•where, ev′rē•hwər, *adv.* In every place.

e•vict, i•vikt′, *v.t.* To expel by force; to expel from property by a legal process. **—e•vic•tion,** *n.* **—e•vic•tor,** *n.*

ev•i•dence, ev′i•dəns, *n.* That which shows or establishes the truth or falsity of something; proof; testimony. **—state's ev•i•dence,** evidence for the prosecution given by an accomplice in a crime. **—in ev•i•dence,** easily seen or noticed.—*v.t.,* **-denced, -denc•ing.** To prove; to show or indicate.

ev•i•dent, ev′i•dənt, *a.* Easily seen or understood; obvious; plain. **—ev•i•dent•ly,** ev′i•dənt•lē, ev•i•dent′lē, *adv.*

ev•i•den•tial, ev•i•den′shəl, *a.* Affording evidence; pertaining to or based on evidence. ev•i•den•tial•ly, *adv.*

e•vil, ē′vəl, *a.* Morally wrong; sinful; wicked; causing trouble or pain; bad; harmful. **—***adv.* In an evil manner; badly; ill. **—***n.* That which is evil; evil quality or conduct; harm; sin; something evil; anything causing injury or harm. **—e•vil•do•er,** *n.* **—e•vil•do•ing,** *n.* **—e•vil•ly,** *adv.* **—e•vil•ness,** *n.*

e•vil-mind•ed, ē′vəl-mīn′did, *a.* Having evil intentions; given to an indecent interpretation of things done or said. **—e•vil-mind•ed•ly,** *adv.* **—e•vil-mind•ed•ness,** *n.*

e•vince, i•vins′, *v.t.,* **e•vinced, e•vinc•ing.** To show; to prove; evident. **—e•vin•ci•ble,** *a.*

e•vis•cer•ate, i•vis′ə•rāt, *v.t.,* **-at•ed, -at•ing.** To disembowel; to remove the important part or parts. **—e•vis•cer•a•tion,** i•vis•ə•rā′shən, *n.*

e•voke, i•vōk′, *v.t.,* **e•voked, e•vok•ing.** To call up, produce, or elicit, as a response, a memory, a feeling, or a supernatural spirit. **—ev•o•ca•tion,** ev•ō-

kā′shən, *n.*

ev•o•lu•tion, ev•ə•loo′shən, *n.* Development; any process of formation or growth; something evolved; a movement of troops or ships; development from a simple to a more complex state; the fact or doctrine of the descent of all living things from a few simple forms of life. **—ev•o•lu•tion•al, ev•o•lu•tion•ar•y,** *a.* **—ev•o•lu•tion•ism,** *n.* **—ev•o•lu•tion•ist,** *n.*

e•volve, i•volv′, *v.t.,* **e•volved, e•volv•ing.** To develop by degrees; to develop to a more highly organized condition.—*v.i.* To come forth gradually into being; develop; to be involved in the process of evolution. **—e•volv•a•ble,** *a.* **—e•volve•ment,** *n.* **—e•volv•er,** *n.*

ewe, ū, *n.* A female sheep, goat, or related animal.

ew•er, ū′ər, *n.* A large pitcher used for pouring water.

ex•ac•er•bate, ig•zas′ər•bāt, *v.t.,* **-bat•ed, -bat•ing.** To increase the intensity of; to irritate or embitter. **—ex•ac•er•ba•tion,** ig•zas•ər•bā′shən, *n.*

ex•act, ig•zakt′, *v.t.* To call for, demand, or require. **—ex•act•a•ble,** *a.* **—ex•ac•tor, ex•act•er,** *n.*

ex•act, ig•zakt′, *a.* Strictly accurate or correct; precise; strict. **—ex•act•ness,** *n.*

ex•act•ing, ig•zak′ting, *a.* Severe in demands or requirements; requiring close attention, as a task. **—ex•act•ing•ly,** *adv.* **—ex•act•ing•ness,** *n.*

ex•act•i•tude, ig•zak′ti•tood, *n.* Exactness.

ex•act•ly, ig•zakt′lē, *adv.* In an exact manner; just or precisely.

ex•ag•ger•ate, ig•zaj′ə•rāt, *v.t.,* **-at•ed, -at•ing.** To magnify; overstate; to increase or enlarge.—*v.i.* To employ exaggeration, as in speech or writing. **—ex•ag•ger•at•ed,** *a.* **—ex•ag•ger•a•tion,** ig•zaj•ə•rā′shən, *n.* **—ex•ag•ger•a•tor,** *n.*

ex•alt, ig•zôlt′, *v.t.* To raise up in rank, honor, power, or quality; to dignify; glorify; ennoble; praise. **—ex•al•ter,** *n.*

ex•al•ta•tion, eg•zôl•tā′shən, *n.* The act of exalting or the state of being exalted.

ex•alt•ed, ig•zôl′tid, *a.* Elevated, as in rank or character. **—ex•alt•ed•ly,** *adv.* **—ex•alt•ed•ness,** *n.*

ex•am, ig•zam′, *n. Informal.* Examination.

ex•am•i•na•tion, ig•zam•ə•nā′shən, *n.* A careful search, inquiry, or inspection; a process for testing qualifications, knowledge, progress, or skills of students or candidates; a particular test; inquiry into facts by testimony or interrogation; a medical inspection for health.

ex•am•ine, ig•zam′in, *v.t.,* **-ined, -in•ing.** To inspect or observe carefully; to question, as a witness. **—ex•am•in•a•ble,** *a.* **—ex•am•i•nant, ex•am•in•er,** *n.* **—ex•am•i•nee,** ig•zam•ə•nē′, *n.*

ex•am•ple, ig•zam′pəl, *n.* A sample; a model; a particular case illustrating a general rule.—*v.t.,* **-pled, -pling.** To present or serve as an example of; exemplify.

ex•as•per•ate, ig•zas′pə•rāt, *v.t.,* **-at•ed, -at•ing.** To irritate extremely; to anger.—*a.* **—ex•as•per•a•tion,** ig•zas•pə•rā′shən, *n.*

ex•ca•vate, eks′kə•vāt, *v.t.,* **-vat•ed, -vat•ing.** To make a hole or cavity in; to expose by digging; unearth. **—ex•ca•va•tion,** *n.* **—ex•ca•va•tor,** *n.*

ex•ceed, ik•sēd′, *v.t.* To pass or go beyond the given limit, measure, or quantity of; to surpass; to excel. **—***v.i.* To excell over others.

ex•ceed•ing, ik•sē′ding, *a.* Great in extent, quantity, degree, or duration; exceptional. **—ex•ceed•ing•ly,** *adv.*

ex•cel, ik•sel′, *v.t.,* **-celled, -cel•ling.** To surpass in good qualities; to outdo.—*v.i.* To surpass others.

ex•cel•lence, ek′sə•ləns, *n.* Superiority; any valuable quality.

ex•cel•len•cy, ek′sə•lən•sē, *n. pl.,* **ex•cel•len•cies.** (*Usu. cap.*) A title of honor given to governors, ambassadors, ministers, and the like.

---

a- hat, fāte, fâre, fäther; **e-** met, mē; **i-** pin, pīne; **o-** not, nōte, ôrb, moove (move), boy, pownd; **u-** cūbe, bůll, tůk (took); **ch-** chin; **th-** thick, then; **zh-** vizhon (vision); **ə-** ego, takən, pencəl, lemən, bərd (bird).

ex·cel·lent, ek′sə·lənt, *a.* Extremely good; choice. **—ex·cel·lent·ly**, *adv.*

ex·cel·si·or, ik·sel′sē·ər, ek·sel′sē·ər, *a.* (*Cap.*) Upward.—*n.* A kind of fine stuffing or packing.

ex·cept, ik·sept′, *v.t.* To take or leave out of any number; to exclude.—*v.i.* To object; to take exception, usu. followed by *to.*—*prep.* With exception of; excepting.—*conj.* Excepting; unless.

ex·cept·ing, ik·sep′ting, *prep.* With exception of; excluding; unless; except.

ex·cep·tion, ik·sep′shən, *n.* The act of excluding; exclusion; the thing or person so excluded; an objection; offense: as, to take *exception* to a remark. **—ex·cep·tion·a·ble**, *a.*

ex·cep·tion·al, ik·sep′shə·nəl, *a.* Out of the ordinary; unusual; remarkable; superior; of a child, intellectually superior or handicapped either physically or mentally and therefore requiring special training.

ex·cerpt, ek·sərpt′, *v.t.* To pick out from a book or other composition for quotation; to select. **—**ek′sərpt, *n.* An extract from a book or writing of any kind.

ex·cess, ek′ses, *n.* A going beyond ordinary limits; an extreme amount or degree; the amount by which one thing exceeds another; intemperance. **—**ek′ses, ik·ses′, *a.* Being more than what is necessary, usual, or specified.

ex·ces·sive, ik·ses′iv, *a.* Exceeding the usual or proper; immoderate; unreasonable. **—ex·ces·sive·ly**, *adv.* **—ex·ces·sive·ness**, *n.*

ex·change, iks·chānj′, *n.* The act of exchanging; the giving up of something for something else; the replacing of one thing by another; a return; the act of giving and receiving evenly; a place for exchanging items; a place where merchants, brokers, or bankers meet to transact business; a central office or station: as, a telephone *exchange.*

ex·change, iks·chānj′, *v.t.*, **-changed, -chang·ing.** To give up (something) for something else; to replace by another or something else; to give to and receive from each other; to interchange.—*v.i.* To make an exchange; to pass or be taken in exchange or as an equivalent. **—ex·change·a·bil·i·ty**, *n.* **ex·change·a·ble**, *a.* **—ex·chan·ger**, *n.*

ex·cheq·uer, eks·chek′ər, *n.* The treasury of a nation or organization.

ex·cise, ek′sīz, ek′sis, ik·sīz′, *n.* A tax on certain items, as spirits or tobacco, levied on their manufacture, sale, or consumption within the country.—**ex·cise tax**, a tax levied for a license to carry on certain trades or to pursue certain sports. —ik·sīz′, *v.t.*, **-cised, -cis·ing.** To impose an excise on. **—ex·cis·a·ble**, *a.*

ex·cise, ek·sīz′, *v.t.*, **-cised, -cis·ing.** To cut out or off; to remove by cutting, as in surgery; to delete. **—ex·cis·a·ble**, *a.* **—**ek·siz′ə·bəl, *a.* **—ex·ci·sion**, ek·sizh′ən, ik·sizh′ən, *n.*

ex·cit·a·ble, ik·sī′tə·bəl, *a.* Easily excited or stirred up. **—ex·cit·a·bil·i·ty**, *n.* **—ex·cit·a·bly**, *adv.*

ex·ci·ta·tion, ek·si·tā′shən, *n.* The act of exciting; condition of being excited.

ex·cite, ik·sīt′, *v.t.*, **-cit·ed, -cit·ing.** To call into action; to stir up the feelings of; to cause to act; to raise to a state of higher energy.

ex·cit·ed, ik·sī′təd, *a.* Emotionally aroused; stimulated; agitated. **—ex·cit·ed·ly**, *adv.* **—ex·cit·ed·ness**, *n.*

ex·cite·ment, ik·sīt′mənt, *n.* The state of being excited; that which excites or arouses; that which moves, stirs, or induces action.

ex·cit·ing, ik·sī′ting, *a.* Producing excitement; thrilling. **—ex·cit·ing·ly**, *adv.*

ex·claim, ik·sklām′, *v.i.* To cry out or say, suddenly and emotionally.—*v.t.* To say with strong emotion.

ex·cla·ma·tion, ek·sklə·mā′shən, *n.* The act of exclaiming.

ex·cla·ma·tion point, *n.* A mark or sign (!) in written or printed matter, used with an interjection or exclamation to indicate forcefulness or surprise. Also

ex·cla·ma·tion mark.

ex·clam·a·to·ry, ik·sklam′ə·tōr·ē, *a.* Expressing exclamation. **—ex·clam·a·to·ri·ly**, *adv.*

ex·clude, ik·sklood′, *v.t.*, **-clud·ed, -clud·ing.** To shut or keep out; prevent entry of; deny consideration. **—ex·clud·a·bil·i·ty**, *n.* **—ex·clud·a·ble, ex·clud·i·ble**, *a.* **—ex·clud·er**, *n.*

ex·clu·sion, ik·skloo′zhən, *n.* The act of excluding or the state of being excluded; that which is excluded.

ex·clu·sive, ik·sloo′siv, *a.* Owned, used, or controlled by one person or group; shutting out others; snobbish; catering to a select group; complete, undivided; incompatible: as, mutually *exclusive* ideas; sole or only.—*n.* A news story released to or obtained by a news organization having the privilege of first usage. **—ex·clu·sive of**, not including or taking into consideration. **—ex·clu·sive·ly**, *adv.* **—ex·clu·sive·ness**, ex·clu·siv·i·ty, eks·kloo·siv′i·tē, *n.*

ex·com·mu·ni·cate, eks·kə·mū′ni·kāt, *v.t.*, **-cat·ed, -cat·ing.** To expel or eject from the church by censure; to expel from any association and deprive of the privileges of membership. —eks·kə·mū′ni·kit, eks·kə·mū′ni·kāt, *n.* One who is excommunicated; one cut off from any privilege.—*a.* Also **ex·com·mu·ni·cant.** **—ex·com·mu·ni·ca·ble**, *a.*

ex·com·mu·ni·ca·tion, eks·kə·mū·ni·kā′shən, *n.* Expulsion from the communion of a church and deprivation of its rights, privileges, and advantages. **—ex·com·mu·ni·ca·tive**, *a.* **—ex·com·mu·ni·ca·to·ry**, *a.*

ex·co·ri·ate, ik·skōr′ē·āt, *v.t.*, **-at·ed, -at·ing.** To abrade the skin; to denounce.

ex·co·ri·a·tion, ik·skōr·ē·ā′shən, *n.* The act of excoriating; abrasion; a verbal whipping.

ex·cre·ment, ek′skrə·mənt, *n.* Refuse matter discharged from the body after digestion. **—ex·cre·men·tal**, ek·skrə·men′təl, *a.*

ex·cres·cence, ik·skres′əns, *n.* Abnormal growth; an outgrowth; an unnatural outgrowth, esp. an abnormal or unsightly outgrowth on an animal or plant; any disfiguring addition.

ex·cres·cent, ik·skres′ənt, *a.* Growing out from something else, esp. abnormally.

ex·cre·ta, ik·skrē′tə, *n. pl.* Excreted matter; the excretions of the body, as sweat or urine. **—ex·cre·tal**, *a.*

ex·crete, ik·skrēt′, *v.t.*, **-cret·ed, -cret·ing.** To eliminate from a body; expel from the blood or tissues, as waste or harmful matters.

ex·cre·tion, ik·skrē′shən, *n.* The act of excreting; the substance excreted, as sweat, urine, or certain plant juices.

ex·cru·ci·ate, ik·skroo′shē·āt, *v.t.*, **-at·ed, -at·ing.** To cause extreme pain to; to torture; to cause extreme mental agony to.

ex·cru·ci·at·ing, ik·skroo′shē·ā·ting, *a.* Extremely painful; torturing; agonizing. **—ex·cru·ci·at·ing·ly**, *adv.* **—ex·cru·ci·a·tion**, *n.*

ex·cul·pate, ek′skəl·pāt, ik·skəl′pāt, *v.t.*, **-pat·ed, -pat·ing.** To clear from a charge of guilt. **—ex·cul·pa·tion**, *n.* **—ex·cul·pa·to·ry**, *a.*

ex·cur·sion, ik·skər′zhən, ik·skər′shən, *n.* A trip made for a particular reason; a trip made at specially reduced fares; a group taking such a trip; digression. —*v.i.* To make an excursion.—*a.* Pertaining to or intended for use on excursions. **—ex·cur·sion·al, ex·cur·sion·ar·y**, *a.* **—ex·cur·sion·ist**, *n.*

ex·cur·sive, ik·skər′siv, *a.* Of speech or thought, rambling; wandering. **—ex·cur·sive·ly**, *adv.* **—ex·cur·sive·ness**, *n.*

ex·cus·a·to·ry, ik·skū′zə·tōr·ē, ik·skū′zə·tōr·ē, *a.* Making excuse; containing excuse or apology.

ex·cuse, ik·skūz′, *v.t.*, **-cused, -cus·ing.** To offer an apology for; seek to remove the blame from; pardon; to release from an obligation or duty; dispense with. **—ex·cus·a·ble**, *a.* **—ex·cus·a·bly**, *adv.* **—ex·cus·er**, *n.*

ex·cuse, ik·skūs′, *n.* The act of excusing; a reason, or an expression of regret for failure to perform; an explanation for an absence. —**ex·cuse·less,** *a.* —**ex·cus·er,** *n.* —**ex·cus·ing·ly,** *adv.*

ex·e·cra·ble, ek′si·krə·bəl, *a.* Hateful; extremely bad. —**ex·e·cra·ble·ness,** *n.* —**ex·e·cra·bly,** *adv.*

ex·e·crate, ek′si·krāt, *v.t.,* crat·ed, -crat·ing. To denounce as evil or detestible; to curse; to abhor. —**ex·e·cra·tive,** *a.* —**ex·e·cra·tor,** *n.*

ex·e·cra·tion, ek·si·krā′shən, *n.* The act of execrating; a curse pronounced.

ex·e·cute, ek′sə·kūt, *v.t.,* -cut·ed, -cut·ing. To carry through to the end; to inflict capital punishment on, esp. with legal sentence; to perform or do skillfully; to put into effect; to administer, transact, or carry through in the manner prescribed by law. —**ex·e·cut·a·ble,** *a.* —**ex·e·cut·er,** *n.*

ex·e·cu·tion, ek·sə·kū′shən, *n.* The act or process of executing; style of performance; technical skill; capital punishment; effective action or use, esp. of weapons.

ex·e·cu·tion·er, ek·sə·kū′shən·ər, *n.* An official who inflicts capital punishment; one who executes.

ex·ec·u·tive, ig·zek′ū·tiv, *a.* Suited for executing or carrying into effect; charged with administration of affairs; made for or used by an executive or executives.—*n.* The executive branch of a government; the person or persons in whom the supreme executive power of a government is vested; any person or body charged with administrative work; a person skilled in such work. —**ex·ec·u·tive·ly,** *adv.*

ex·ec·u·tive coun·cil, *n.* A council charged with supreme executive authority; a council that acts as advisory aide to a government head.

Ex·ec·u·tive Man·sion, *n. (Also l.c.) U.S.* The White House, in Washington, D.C., official residence of the President; the official residence of a governor of one of the states.

ex·ec·u·tive or·der, *n. (Often cap.)* A command having the power of law, issued by the President or other head of state.

ex·ec·u·tive ses·sion, *n.* A legislative session, usu. not open to the public.

ex·ec·u·tor, ig·zek′ū·tēr, *n.* One who executes, carries out, performs, or fulfills. *Law.* A person appointed to carry out the provisions of a will. —**ex·ec·u·tor·ship,** *n.*

ex·e·ge·sis, ek·si·jē′sis, *n. pl.,* **ex·e·ge·ses,** ek·si·jē′sēz. Critical explanation or interpretation, esp. of Scripture.

ex·em·plar, ig·zem′plər, *n.* A model, or pattern to be copied; a person who serves as a model; a specimen or copy.

ex·em·pla·ry, ig·zem′plə·rē, *a.* Serving as a model, pattern, or specimen; worthy of imitation; commendable; such as may serve for a warning; typical. —**ex·em·pla·ri·ly,** *adv.* —**ex·em·pla·ri·ness,** *n.*

ex·em·pli·fy, ig·zem′plə·fī, *v.t.,* -fied, -fy·ing. To show or illustrate by example; to serve as an example or instance of. —**ex·em·pli·fi·a·ble,** *a.* —**ex·em·pli·fi·ca·tion,** *n.*

ex·empt, ig·zempt′, *v.t.* To free or permit to be free from any duty, to which others are subject; to grant immunity to.—*a.* Not included; free.—*n.*

ex·emp·tion, ig·zemp′shən, *n.* The act of exempting; the state of being exempt; immunity. *U.S.* One who or that which is a deduction on an income tax form.

ex·er·cise, ek′sər·sīz, *n.* Bodily activity for training or improvement; a putting into action; something done or performed as practice or training; a performance or ceremony: as, graduation *exercises.*

ex·er·cise, ek′sər·sīz, *v.t.,* -cised, -cis·ing. To put through exercises, practice or exertion, designed to train, develop, or keep in condition; to put into action, practice, or use; to bring to bear; to drill; to occupy the attention of; to worry.—*v.i.* To go through exercise; to take bodily exercise. —**ex·er·cis·er,** *n.* —**ex·er·cis·a·ble,** *a.*

ex·ert, ig·zərt′, *v.t.* To put forth or exercise; to put in action; to bring into active operation, as the mind or the bodily powers; to put forth one's powers.

ex·er·tion, ig·zər′shən, *n.* The act of exerting; an effort; a striving or struggling; trial.

ex·fo·li·ate, eks·fō′lē·āt, *v.i.,* -at·ed, -at·ing. To separate and come off in scales; to grow by producing leaves. —*v.t.* To free from scales; to grow by producing leaves. —**ex·fo·li·a·tion,** *n.*

ex·ha·la·tion, eks·hə·lā′shən, *n.* The act of exhaling; that which is exhaled.

ex·hale, eks·hāl′, *v.i.,* -haled, -hal·ing. To breathe out.—*v.t.* To expel from or let out of the lungs; to emit or give off, as vapor. —**ex·hal·ant,** eks·hā′lənt, *a.*

ex·haust, ig·zäst′, *v.t.* To use up completely; to create a vacuum in; to deprive wholly of useful properties, as soil; to drain of resources, as a person or country; to wear out or fatigue greatly; to draw out all that is essential; to treat or study thoroughly.—*v.i.* To discharge contents: as, an engine which *exhausts* directly into the air. —**ex·haust·er,** *n.* —**ex·haust·i·bil·i·ty,** *n.* —**ex·haust·i·ble,** *a.*

ex·haust·ed, ig·zäs′təd, *a.* Completely spent or drained; greatly fatigued. —**ex·haust·ed·ly,** *adv.*

ex·haus·tion, ig·zäs′chən, *n.* The state of being exhausted; extreme weakness or fatigue. —**ex·haust·ing,** *a.*

ex·haus·tive, ig·zäs′tiv, *a.* Comprehensive; thorough; tending to exhaust or drain, as of resources or strength. —**ex·haus·tive·ly,** *adv.* —**ex·haus·tive·ness,** *n.*

ex·hib·it, ig·zib′it, *v.t.* To expose to view; present for inspection; to place on display; to manifest or reveal. —*v.i.* To make or give an exhibition; present something to public view. —**ex·hib·it·a·ble,** *a.* —**ex·hib·i·tor, ex·hib·i·ter,** *n.* —**ex·hib·i·to·ry,** *a.*

ex·hib·it, ig·zib′it, *n.* An exhibition; that which is exhibited; an object or a collection of objects shown in an exhibition or fair. *Law.* A document or other object exhibited in court as evidence.

ex·hi·bi·tion, ek·sə·bish′ən, *n.* Show; a public display, as of works of art.

ex·hi·bi·tion·ism, ek·sə·bish′ə·niz·əm, *n.* A desire for showing off or for attracting attention to oneself. —**ex·hi·bi·tion·ist,** *n.* —**ex·hi·bi·tion·is·tic,** *a.*

ex·hil·a·rate, ig·zil′ə·rāt, *v.t.,* -rat·ed, -rat·ing. To make cheerful; to stimulate. —**ex·hil·a·rat·ing,** *a.* —**ex·hil·a·ra·tion,** *n.* —**ex·hil·a·ra·tive, ex·hil·a·ra·to·ry,** *a.*

ex·hort, ig·zôrt′, *v.t.* To encourage; to advise or caution.—*v.i.* To use constructive criticism to encourage. —**ex·hor·ta·tive, ex·hor·ta·to·ry,** *a.* —**ex·hort·er,** *n.* —**ex·hort·ing·ly,** *adv.*

ex·hor·ta·tion, eg·zôr·tā′shən, *n.* The act of exhorting; language intended to incite and encourage.

ex·hume, ig·zoom′, ig·zūm′, eks·hūm′, *v.t.,* -humed, -hum·ing. To dig up after having been buried.

ex·i·gen·cy, ek′si·jən·sē, *n. pl.,* **ex·i·gen·cies.** A situation which demands immediate attention; an emergency; *usu. pl.,* urgent necessities.

ex·i·gent, ek′si·jənt, *a.* Urgent; demanding prompt attention; demanding. —**ex·i·gent·ly,** *adv.*

ex·ile, eg′zīl, ek′sīl, *n.* Separation from one's native country, either voluntary or forced; a person thrown out of his country. —*v.t.,* **ex·iled, ex·il·ing.** To banish; to cause to be an exile. —**ex·il·a·ble,** *a.* —**ex·il·er,** *n.*

ex·ist, ig·zist′, *v.i.* To have being or reality; to be; to live; to have life; to occur in certain places or under specific conditions.

ex·ist·ence, ig·zis′təns, *n*. The state of existing; the condition of being; life; living.

ex·ist·ent, ig·zis′tənt, *a*. Having being; having existence.

ex·is·ten·tial, eg·zi·sten′shəl, ek·si·sten′shəl, *a*. Relating to existence.

ex·it, eg′zit, ek′sit, *n*. A passage out of; any departure; the act of quitting the stage; death.—*v.i*. To leave.

ex li·bris, eks lē′bris, *n. pl*., **ex li·bris**. From the library of; a bookplate.

ex·o·dus, ek′sə·dəs, *n*. Departure from a place, esp. by a large number of people; mass migration. (*Cap*.) The migration from Egypt by Moses and the Israelites.

ex of·fi·ci·o, eks ə·fish′ē·ō, *adv., a*. By virtue of official position: as, *ex officio* authority.

ex·og·a·my, ek·sog′ə·mē, *n*. Marriage outside the tribe. —**ex·og·a·mous**, ek·sog′ə·məs, *a*.

ex·og·e·nous, ek·soj′ə·nəs, *a. Bot*. Growing by additions on the outside. —**ex·og·e·nous·ly**, *adv*.

ex·on·er·ate, ig·zon′ə·rāt, *v.t*., **-at·ed, -at·ing**. To clear of a charge or of blame. —**ex·on·er·a·tion**, ig·zon·ə·rā′shən, *n*. —**ex·on·er·a·tive**, *a*.

ex·or·bi·tant, ig·zôr′bə·tənt, *a*. Going beyond the limits of right; excessive; extravagant; enormous. —**ex·or·bi·tance**, *n*. —**ex·or·bi·tant·ly**, *adv*.

ex·or·cise, ex·or·cize, ek′sôr·siz, *v.t*., **-cised, -cis·ing**. To expel or cast out, as an evil spirit; to purify or deliver from the influence of spirits or demons. —**ex·or·cism**, *n*. —**ex·or·cist**, *n*.

ex·o·tic, ig·zot′ik, *a*. Of foreign origin or character; not native; introduced from abroad; unusual in appearance; mysterious; different; strange.—*n*. Anything exotic, as a plant. —**ex·ot·i·cal·ly**, *adv*. —**ex·ot·i·cism**, ig·zot′ə·siz·əm, *n*.

ex·pand, ik·spand′, *v.t*. To spread out or unfold; spread out to view or display; to express in greater detail; to develop, as a statement; to increase in extent, size, or volume; enlarge; make more comprehensive.—*v.i*. To spread out; unfold; to express in fuller form, usu. followed by *on* or *upon*; to increase, as in extent or bulk; become dilated or enlarged. —**ex·pand·er**, *n*.

ex·panse, ik·spans′, *n*. An uninterrupted space, esp. one of considerable extent; a wide extent of anything.

ex·pan·si·ble, ik·span′sə·bəl, *a*. Capable of being expanded. —**ex·pan·si·bil·i·ty**, ik·span·sə·bil′ə·tē, *n*.

ex·pan·sion, ik·span′shən, *n*. The act of expanding or the state of being expanded; increase in size or volume; the amount or degree of expanding; anything spread out; an expanse.

ex·pan·sion·ism, ik·span′shə·niz·əm, *n*. A national policy of expansion, as of territory or currency. —**ex·pan·sion·ist**, *n*.

ex·pan·sive, ik·span′siv, *a*. Tending to expand or capable of expanding; pertaining to or characterized by expansion; expanding over a large area. —**ex·pan·sive·ly**, *adv*. —**ex·pan·sive·ness**, *n*.

ex·pa·ti·ate, ik·spā′shē·āt, *v.i*., **-at·ed, -at·ing**. To enlarge in writing; to be extensive in discussion. —**ex·pa·ti·a·tion**, ik·spā·shē·ā′shən, *n*.

ex·pa·tri·ate, eks·pā′trē·āt, *v.t*., **-at·ed, -at·ing**. To banish, as a person, from his native country; to withdraw, as oneself, from residence in one's native country.—*a*. —iks·pā′trē·it, *n*. An expatriated person. —**ex·pa·tri·a·tion**, iks·pā·trē·ā′shən, *n*.

ex·pect, ik·spekt′, *v.t*. To await or look forward to; to anticipate the occurrence or birth of; to regard as likely to occur; to suppose or surmise.—*v.i*. To be pregnant; to wait. —**ex·pect·a·ble**, *a*. —**ex·pect·a·bly**, *adv*. —**ex·pect·ing·ly**, *adv*.

ex·pect·an·cy, ik·spek′tən·sē, *n. pl*., **-cies**. The act or state of expecting; an object of expectation.

ex·pect·ant, ik·spek′tənt, *a*. Expecting or anticipating; having expectations; pregnant.—*n*. One who waits in expectation. —**ex·pect·ant·ly**, *adv*.

ex·pec·ta·tion, ek·spek·tā′shən, *n*. The act or state

of expecting; something expected.

ex·pec·to·rate, ik·spek′tə·rāt, *v.t*., **-rat·ed, -rat·ing**. To discharge, as phlegm, by coughing and spitting.—*v.i*. To eject matter by coughing and spitting; to spit.

ex·pec·to·ra·tion, ik·spek·tə·rā′shən, *n*. The act of expectorating; the matter expectorated.

ex·pe·di·en·cy, ik·spē′dē·ən·sē, *n*. The seeking of immediate or selfish gain or advantage at the expense of principle.

ex·pe·di·ent, ik·spē′dē·ənt, *a*. Tending to achieve desired results by the most direct, sometimes ruthless, method; proper under the circumstances; acting for expedience.—*n*. Means employed to accomplish an end. —**ex·pe·di·ent·ly**, *adv*.

ex·pe·dite, ek′spə·dīt, *v.t*., **-dit·ed, -dit·ing**. To help the progress of; hasten. —**ex·pe·dit·er**, *n*.

ex·pe·di·tion, ek·spə·dish′ən, *n*. An excursion or voyage made for some specific purpose; the body of persons engaged in such an excursion; promptness in action. —**ex·pe·di·tion·ar·y**, *a*.

ex·pe·di·tious, ek·spə·dish′əs, *a*. Performed with efficiency and speed; quick; hasty. —**ex·pe·di·tious·ly**, *adv*. —**ex·pe·di·tious·ness**, *n*.

ex·pel, ik·spel′, *v.t*., **ex·pelled, ex·pel·ling**. To drive or force out or away; to cut off from membership: to *expel* a student.

ex·pend, ik·spend′, *v.t*. To pay out; use up, as time or energy.

ex·pend·a·ble, ik·spen′də·bəl, *a*. Able to be disposed of without loss; able to be sacrificed, as men, supplies, or equipment. —**ex·pend·a·bil·i·ty**, *n*.

ex·pend·i·ture, ik·spen′də·chər, *n*. The act of expending; that which is expended.

ex·pense, ik·spens′, *n*. Cost or charge; that which is expended; an outlay, esp. of money; a cause or occasion of expenditure. *Pl*. Charges incurred by a person in the execution of his duties. —**at the expense of**, with the sacrifice or loss of.

ex·pen·sive, ik·spen′siv, *a*. Entailing great expense; costly. —**ex·pen·sive·ly**, *adv*. —**ex·pen·sive·ness**, *n*.

ex·pe·ri·ence, ik·spēr′ē·əns, *n*. The process of personally observing or undergoing something; a particular instance of personally undergoing something; the observing, encountering, or undergoing of things generally as they occur; knowledge or practical wisdom gained from what one has observed, encountered, or undergone.—*v.t*., **-enced, -enc·ing**. To have experience of; meet with; undergo; feel; to learn by experience. —**ex·pe·ri·enced**, *a*.

ex·pe·ri·en·tial, ik·spēr·ē·en′shəl, *a*. Pertaining to or derived from experience. —**ex·pe·ri·en·tial·ly**, *adv*.

ex·per·i·ment, ik·sper′ə·mənt, *n*. A test or trial; a controlled project to establish a hypothesis, illustrate a known law or effect, or discover one which is unknown; the conducting of such projects. —ek·sper′ə·ment, *v.i*. To make experiments. —**ex·per·i·men·ta·tion**, ik·sper·ə·men·tā′shən, *n*.

ex·per·i·men·tal, ik·sper·ə·men′təl, *a*. Derived from, or founded on experiment; based on or derived from experience; empirical. —**ex·per·i·men·tal·ism**, *n*. —**ex·per·i·men·tal·ist**, *n*. —**ex·per·i·men·tal·ly**, *adv*.

ex·pert, ik·spərt′, ek′spərt, *a*. Experienced; taught by use or practice; skillful; dexterous; having a skill in operation or performance from practice. —ek′spərt, *n*. A skillful or practiced person; an authority in a particular field. —**ex·pert·ly**, *adv*. —**ex·pert·ness**, *n*.

ex·per·tise, ek·spər·tēz′, *n*. Specialized knowledge.

ex·pi·ate, ek′spē·āt, *v.t*., **-at·ed, -at·ing**. To make up or pay for; to make redress or reparation for. —**ex·pi·a·ble**, *a*. —**ex·pi·a·tion**, ek·spē·ā′shən, *n*. —**ex·pi·a·tor**, *n*. —**ex·pi·a·to·ry**, ek′spē·ə·tôr·ē, *a*.

ex·pi·ra·tion, ek·spə·rā′shən, *n*. The act of breathing out; emission of breath; exhalation. —**ex·pir·a·**

to·ry, ik·spīr′ə·tôr·ē, a.

ex·pire, ik·spīr′, v.t., ex·pired, ex·pir·ing. To breathe out; to exhale.—v.i. To emit breath; to die; to come to an end, as an agreed period of time.

ex·plain, ik·splān′, v.t. To make plain; to clear of obscurity; to make clear or evident; to expound; to give or show the meaning or reason for.—v.i. To give explanations. —ex·plain·a·ble, a. —ex·plain·er, n.

ex·pla·na·tion, ek·splə·nā′shən, n. The act of explaining; a making clear or understandable; the clearing up of a misunderstanding. —ex·plan·a·to·ry, ik·splan′ə·tôr·ē, a. Also ex·plan·a·tive, ik·splan′ə·tiv. —ex·plan·a·to·ri·ly, adv.

ex·ple·tive, ek′splə·tiv, a. Superfluous.—n. An additional word, syllable, or phrase used to fill a vacancy of a sentence; an obscene word or phrase.

ex·pli·ca·ble, ek′spli·kə·bəl, ik·splik′ə·bəl, a. Capable of being explained.

ex·pli·cate, ek′splə·kāt, v.t., -cat·ed, -cat·ing. To interpret clearly and simply the meaning or sense of; to explain. —ex·pli·ca·tion, ek·splə·kā′shən, n. —ex·pli·ca·tive, ek′splə·kā·tiv, ik·splik′ə·tiv, a. —ex·pli·ca·tor, n.

ex·plic·it, ik·splis′it, a. Precise in expression; leaving nothing unclear; thoroughly developed. —ex·plic·it·ly, adv. —ex·plic·it·ness, n.

ex·plode, ik·splōd′, v.i., ex·plod·ed, ex·plod·ing. To blow up; to expand with force and noise because of rapid chemical change, as gunpowder or nitroglycerin; to burst, fly into pieces, or break up violently with a loud report; to burst forth violently or noisily with emotion.—v.t. To cause to break apart or blow up noisily; to detonate; to discredit, disprove, or cause to be rejected, as a belief. —ex·plod·er, n.

ex·ploit, ek′sployt, ik·sployt′, n. A deed that is striking, or notable; a feat or heroic act. —ik·sployt′, v.t. To use for profit; to use selfishly for one's own ends; to promote. —ex·ploit·a·ble, a. —ex·ploi·ta·tion, ek·sploy·tā′shən, n. —ex·ploit·er, n. —ex·ploit·ive, a.

ex·plore, ik·splōr′, ik·splôr′, v.t. To travel or range over an area with the intent of making discovery; to investigate; to scrutinize.—v.i. To engage in systematic investigation. —ex·plo·ra·tion, ek·splə·rā′shən, n. —ex·plor·a·to·ry, a. —ex·plor·er, n.

ex·plo·sion, ik·splō′zhən, n. Exploding; a violent, noisy expansion or bursting; the noise itself; a violent outburst of emotion, as of laughter or anger; a sudden, widespread outcropping or increase: population explosion.

ex·plo·sive, ik·splō′siv, a. Tending or serving to explode; pertaining to, or of the nature of, an explosion.—n. An explosive agent or substance. —ex·plo·sive·ly, adv. —ex·plo·sive·ness, n.

ex·po·nent, ik·spō′nent, ek′spō·nənt, n. One who explains anything; one who stands as a symbol of something. —ex·po·nen·tial, ek·spō·nen′shəl, a. —ex·po·nen·tial·ly, adv.

ex·port, ik·spōrt′, ik·spôrt′, ek′spōrt, ek′spôrt, v.t. To send, as goods, for sale or consumption in foreign countries. —ek′spōrt, ek′spôrt, n. The act of exporting; an item that is exported.—a. —ex·port·a·ble, a. —ex·por·ta·tion, ek·spōr·tā′shən, ek·spôr·tā′shən, n. —ex·port·er, n.

ex·pose, ik·spōz′, v.t., ex·posed, ex·pos·ing. To leave unprotected; to place in danger; to uncover; to display; to exhibit; to lay open to examination; to subject to light or other energy. —ex·pos·er, n.

ex·po·sé, ik·spō·zā′, n. Exposure; revelation of something concealed.

ex·po·si·tion, ek·spə·zish′ən, n. A laying open; a setting out to public view; explanation; a laying open of the sense or meaning of; an exhibition or show. —ex·pos·i·tor, ik·spoz′ə·tər, n. —ex·pos·i·to·ry, ik·spoz′ə·tôr·ē, a.

ex post fac·to, eks′ pōst·fak′tō, a. Formulated after the fact, thereby changing a previous situation.—adv. After the fact.

ex·pos·tu·late, ik·spos′chə·lāt, v.i., -lat·ed, -lat·ing. To reason earnestly with a person on some impropriety of his conduct; to criticize. —ex·pos·tu·la·tion, ik·spos·chə·lā′shən, n. —ex·pos·tu·la·tive, ex·pos·tu·la·to·ry, a.

ex·po·sure, ik·spō′zhər, n. The act of exposing or the state of being exposed; an act of abandoning without shelter or protection; disclosure of something private or secret; a laying open to the action or influence of something; presentation to open view; position with regard to access of sunlight and wind; something exposed to view; the act of exposing light-sensitive photographic film; a section of film or plate so exposed; the time required for light to produce the desired picture.

ex·pound, ik·spownd′, v.t. To explain; to argue the defense of; to clear of obscurity; to interpret. —ex·pound·er, n.

ex·press, ik·spres′, v.t. To declare by words; to make known, esp. one's own opinions or ideas; to press or squeeze out; to send by an especially fast system.—a. Given in direct terms; clearly stated; precise; plain; special or specific; referring to a direct or fast means of transportation, as a train or highway.—n. Transmission of freight that is faster but more expensive than ordinary service; any vehicle or other conveyance sent on a special mission; a train which travels at a high rate of speed; that which is sent by express; a concern engaged in the business of express transportation.—adv. By way of express, as: Ship the goods express. —ex·press·er, n. —ex·press·i·ble, a.

ex·pres·sion, ik·spresh′ən, n. The act of setting forth in words; the manner in which a thing is put into words; a particular word, phrase, or form of words; the quality or ability of expressing emotion; pressing out, as juice from a fruit.

ex·pres·sive, ik·spres′iv, a. Serving to express; full of expression; significant. —ex·pres·sive·ly, adv. —ex·pres·sive·ness, n.

ex·press·ly, ik·spres′lē, adv. In direct terms; plainly.

ex·press·way, ik·spres′wā, n. A highway, usu. with divided lanes and limited access, used for high-speed traffic.

ex·pro·pri·ate, eks·prō′prē·āt, v.t., -at·ed, -at·ing. To take or transfer, as real estate, from the owner, esp. to take for public use by the right of eminent domain; to dispossess of ownership. —ex·pro·pri·a·tor, n. —ex·pro·pri·a·tion, eks·prō·prē·ā′shən, n.

ex·pul·sion, ik·spəl′shən, n. The act of driving out or expelling. —ex·pul·sive, ik·spəl′siv, a.

ex·punge, ik·spənj′, v.t., ex·punged, ex·pung·ing. To blot out. —ex·pung·er, n.

ex·pur·gate, ek′spər·gāt, ik·spər′gāt, v.t., -gat·ed, -gat·ing. To purify by removing objectionable material; to delete or omit. —ex·pur·ga·tion, ek·spər·gā′shən, n. —ex·pur·ga·tor, n.

ex·pur·ga·tory, ik·spər′gə·tôr·e, a. Cleansing; purifying; serving to expurgate. —ex·pur·ga·to·ri·al, a.

ex·qui·site, ek′skwi·zit, ik·skwiz′it, a. Of exceptionally choice quality, as food, wines, laces, or fabrics; of rare excellence; of refinement or elegance; of uncommon beauty; keen, as pleasure or pain; keenly or delicately sensitive or responsive to impressions.—n. A person who is a dandy. —ex·qui·site·ly, adv. —ex·qui·site·ness, n.

ex·tant, ek′stənt, ik·stant′, a. Still existing; in being; not destroyed or lost.

ex·tem·po·ra·ne·ous, ik·stem·pə·rā′nē·əs, a. Performed at the time, without previous thought or study; off-hand; made to meet an immediate need;

improvised. —**ex·tem·po·ra·ne·ous·ly,** adv. —**ex· tem·po·ra·ne·ous·ness,** n.

ex·tem·po·rize, ik·stem′pə·riz, v.i., **-rized, -riz·ing.** To speak without previous thought, study, or preparation.—v.t. To make without forethought; prepare in great haste with the means within one's reach. —**ex· tem·po·ri·za·tion,** ik·stem·pə·rə·za′shən, n. —**ex· tem·po·riz·er,** n.

ex·tend, ik·stend′, v.t. To stretch out in distance, space, or time; to pull out to the full length; to exert to the fullest; to straighten or hold out; to spread out in area; to enlarge in quantity by adulteration; to widen the scope of; offer; give.—v.i. To be or become extended or stretched out; to reach toward a particular point; to increase in length, area, or scope. —**ex· tend·i·bil·i·ty,** n. —**ex·tend·i·ble,** a.

ex·tend·ed, ik·sten′did, a. Stretched out; pulled out; straightened; continued; widespread or extensive. —**ex·tend·ed·ly,** adv. —**ex·tend·ed·ness,** n.

ex·tend·er, ik·sten′dər, n. That which is added to a product to increase the quantity; an adulterant.

ex·ten·si·ble, ik·sten′sə·bəl, a. Capable of being extended. —**ex·ten·si·bil·i·ty,** ik·sten·sə·bil′ə·tē, n.

ex·ten·sion, ik·sten′shən, n. The act of extending; the state of being extended; the thing extended; the range or degree to which a thing may be extended; an added portion; an additional telephone, esp. one operating on the same line as another. —**ex·ten·sion· al,** a.

ex·ten·sive, ik·sten′siv, a. Of great extent; wide; broad; great; comprehensive. —**ex·ten·sive·ly,** adv. —**ex·ten·sive·ness,** n.

ex·tent, ik·stent′, n. The space or degree to which a thing extends; length, area, amount, or scope; an extended space.

ex·ten·u·ate, ik·sten′ū·āt, v.t., **-at·ed, -at·ing.** To weaken the force of; to underestimate; to attach little importance to. —**ex·ten·u·a·tion,** ik·sten·ū·ā′shən, n. —**ex·ten·u·a·tor,** n.

ex·te·ri·or, ik·stēr′ē·ər, a. External; outer; outward; situated beyond the limits of; proper for use on the outside.—n. The outer surface; the outside; the external features. —**ex·te·ri·or·ly,** adv.

ex·ter·mi·nate, ik·stər′mə·nāt, v.t., **-nat·ed, -nat· ing.** To destroy utterly; to eradicate. —**ex·ter·mi·na· tion,** ik·stər·mə·nā′shən, n. **ex·ter·mi·na·tive,** a. —**ex·ter·mi·na·tor,** n. —**ex·ter·mi·na·to·ry,** a.

ex·ter·nal, ik·stər′nəl, a. Of the outside; exterior; belonging to or coming from without; applied or to be applied to the outside of the body.—n. The outside; that which is external; pl., external or outward features or circumstances. —**ex·ter·nal·ly,** adv.

ex·tinct, ik·stingkt′, a. No longer in existence; having died out; extinguished.

ex·tinc·tion, ik·stingk′shən, n. The act of extinguishing; a dying out as of a species.

ex·tin·guish, ik·sting′gwish, v.t. To put out, as fire; to quench, as hopes or passions; to put an end to or wipe out of existence. —**ex·tin·guish·a·ble,** a. —**ex· tin·guish·er,** n. —**ex·tin·guish·ment,** n.

ex·tir·pate, ek′stər·pāt, ik·stər′pāt, v.t., **-pat·ed, -pat·ing.** To pull or pluck up by the roots; to destroy totally. —**ex·tir·pa·tion,** ek·stər·pā′shən, n. —**ex· tir·pa·tive,** a.

ex·tol, ik·stōl′, v.t., **ex·tolled, ex·toll·ing.** To praise; to applaud. Also **ex·toll.** —**ex·tol·ler,** n. —**ex·tol· ling·ly,** adv. —**ex·tol·ment, ex·toll·ment,** n.

ex·tort, ik·stôrt′, v.t. To obtain from a person by force or threat of force, torture, or authority. —**ex·tor·ter,** n. —**ex·tor·tive,** a.

ex·tor·tion, ik·stôr′shən, n. The act of extorting; the act or practice of extorting money from people by any undue or illegal exercise of power; that which is extorted. —**ex·tor·tion·ar·y,** a. —**ex·tor·tion·ate,** a. —**ex·tor·tion·er, ex·tor·tion·ist,** n.

ex·tra, ek′strə, a. More than what is usual, expected, or necessary; additional; larger or better than what is usual.—n. Something additional; an additional cost; something of higher quality.—adv. In excess of the usual amount; beyond the ordinary; unusually; uncommonly.

ex·tract, ik·strakt′, v.t. To pull out by force; to obtain by force from someone; to take or copy out, as a passage from a book; to make excerpts, as from a book. —ek′strakt, n. Something extracted; a passage selected from a book or the like; a concentrated preparation of a substance: almond extract. —**ex· tract·a·ble, ex·tract·i·ble,** a. —**ex·trac·tive,** n. —**ex·trac·tor,** n.

ex·trac·tion, ik·strak′shən, n. The act of extracting or drawing out; the state of being extracted; descent; lineage; something extracted.

ex·tra·cur·ric·u·lar, ek·strə·kə·rik′yə·lər, a. Outside the scope of the curriculum, e.g. other than academic studies, as sports, or school publications.

ex·tra·dite, ek′strə·dit, v.t., **-dit·ed, -dit·ing.** To deliver or give up, as a criminal, to another authority; to obtain the extradition of. —**ex·tra·dit·a·ble,** a.

ex·tra·di·tion, ek·strə·dish′ən, n. Delivery of a criminal or fugitive from justice by one country, state, or other authority to another.

ex·tra·ne·ous, ik·strā′nē·əs, a. Not belonging to a thing; alien; outside of. —**ex·tra·ne·ous·ly,** adv. —**ex·tra·ne·ous·ness,** n.

ex·traor·di·nar·y, ik·strôr′də·ner·ē, ek·strə· ôr′də·ner·ē, a. Beyond an ordinary, common, usual, or customary method; sent for a special purpose. —**ex·traor·di·nar·i·ly,** ik·strôr·də·nār′ə·lē, adv.

ex·trap·o·late, ik·strap′ə·lāt, ek′strə·pə·lāt, v.t., v.i., **-lat·ed, -lat·ing.** To project data or experience, by inferences, into an unknown area. —**ex·trap·o·la· tion,** ek·strap·ə·lā′shən, n.

ex·tra·sen·so·ry, ek·strə·sen′sə·rē, a. Outside of the normal range of the senses.

ex·tra·ter·res·tri·al, ek·strə·tə·res′trē·əl, a. Originating or existing outside the limits of the earth.

ex·tra·ter·ri·to·ri·al, ek·strə·ter·ə·tôr′ē·əl, a. Beyond territorial jurisdiction; beyond the jurisdiction of the country in which one resides. —**ex·tra·ter·ri·to· ri·al·i·ty,** ek·strə·ter·ə·tôr·ē·al′ə·tē, n.

ex·trav·a·gance, ik·strav′ə·gəns, n. Unrestrained excess; an extravagant action or notion; excessive expenditure; an instance of wastefulness. Also **ex· trav·a·gan·cy.**

ex·trav·a·gant, ik·strav′ə·gənt, a. Spending more money than necessary; wasteful. —**ex·trav·a·gant·ly,** adv.

ex·trav·a·gan·za, ik·strav·ə·gan′zə, n. An elaborate musical or dramatic production.

ex·treme, ik·strēm′, a. Utmost in degree; of a character farthest removed from the ordinary; going to great lengths; located at the farthest point from a center; farthest in any direction; final.—n. The highest degree; one of two things as different from each other as possible; an excessive length beyond the ordinary. —**ex·treme·ly,** adv. —**ex·treme·ness,** n.

ex·trem·ist, ik·strē′mist, n. One who goes to extremes. —**ex·trem·ism,** n.

ex·trem·i·ty, ik·strem′ə·tē, n. pl., **-ties.** The extreme point or part of something; moment of danger or approaching death; the utmost. Usu. pl. The end part of a limb, or the limb itself, esp. the human hand or foot.

ex·tri·cate, ek′strə·kāt, v.t., **-cat·ed, -cat·ing.** To free or remove from a difficulty; to disengage; to disentangle. —**ex·tri·ca·ble,** a. —**ex·tri·ca·tion,** ek· strə·kā′shən, n.

ex·trin·sic, ik·strin′sik, a. Acquired or developed; originating from without.

ex·tro·vert, ek′strō·vərt, n. One whose interest and attention is directed primarily toward what is outside the self; one who is outgoing, active, and expressive. —**ex·tro·ver·sion,** ek·strō·vər′zhən, n.

ex·trude, ik·strood′, v.t., **ex·trud·ed, ex·trud·ing.** To thrust out; force or press out; to form, as metal or plastic, by forcing through a die.—*v.i.* To protrude. **—ex·tru·sion,** ik·strooʹzhən, *n.* **—ex·tru·sive,** ek·strooʹsiv, *a.*

ex·u·ber·ance, ig·zooʹbər·əns, *n.* The state or quality of being exuberant; an expression of this in speech or action.

ex·u·ber·ant, ig·zooʹbər·ənt, *a.* Full of joyful enthusiasm; high-spirited; unrestrained; overflowing. **—ex·u·ber·ant·ly,** *adv.*

ex·ude, ig·zoodʹ, ik·soodʹ, *v.i.,* **ex·ud·ed, ex·ud·ing.** To ooze; to seep out gradually, as sweat through the pores.—*v.t.* To discharge; to give off; to express: to *exude* hostility. **—ex·u·da·tion,** ek·sū·dāʹshən, *n.*

ex·ult, ig·zəltʹ, *v.i.* To rejoice in triumph. **—ex·ult·ant,** *a.* **—ex·ult·ant·ly,** *adv.* **—ex·ul·ta·tion,** eg·zəl·tāʹshən, *n.* **—ex·ult·ing·ly,** *adv.*

ex·ur·ban·ite, eks·ərʹbər·nīt, *n.* A former city dweller who has moved to a semi-rural area beyond the suburbs, but who usu. continues to work in the city and retains his urban life style.

eye, ī, *n.* An organ of sight, which, in man and other vertebrates, is normally one of a pair of bodies set in an orbit or socket in the skull; the visible portion of the organ; the iris in reference to its color; sight; power of seeing together with intellectual perception; a look or glance; view; regard; keen interest in: as, an *eye* to one's future; careful watch; surveillance; *often pl.,* opinion or judgment. Anything resembling or suggesting an eye in shape, general appearance, or function, as the bud or shoot of a plant tuber, the hole in a needle; an area of relative calm in the center of a tropical cyclone. **—an eye for an eye,** revenge equivalent to injury. **—catch someone's eye,** attract someone's visual attention. **—see eye to eye,** concur; agree.—*v.t.,* **eyed, ey·ing** or **eye·ing.** To fix the eyes upon; to view; to observe or watch narrowly.

eye·ball, īʹbôl, *n.* The ball or globe of the eye.

eye·brow, īʹbrow, *n.* The arch or ridge forming the upper part of the orbit of the eye, or the fringe of hair growing upon it.

eye·ful, īʹfûl, *n. pl.,* **-fuls.** A complete view of something. *Informal.* An attractive thing, esp. a beautiful woman.

eye·glass, īʹglas, īʹgläs, *n.* A lens worn to assist vision; an eyecup.**—eye·glass·es,** *n. pl.* A device for correcting defective vision or for protecting the eyes, consisting of two lenses set in a frame which holds them in place.

eye·hole, īʹhōl, *n.* The socket or orbit of the eye; a hole to look through; a circular opening.

eye·lash, īʹlash, *n.* One of the hairs that edge the eyelid; the entire fringe of these hairs.

eye·let, īʹlit, *n.* A small hole to receive a lace; a metal ring to line such a hole.

eye·lid, īʹlid, *n.* That portion of movable skin that serves as a cover for the eyeball.

eye-o·pen·er, īʹō·pə·nər, *n.* A surprising experience. *Informal.* An early morning drink of liquor. **—eye-o·pen·ing,** *a.*

eye·piece, īʹpēs, *n.* In an optical instrument, the lens to which the eye is applied.

eye·sight, īʹsit, *n.* The ability to see; vision; view.

eye·sore, īʹsôr, *n.* Something offensive to look at.

eye·strain, īʹstrān, *n.* Discomfort or fatigue of the eyes.

eye·tooth, īʹtooth, *n. pl.,* **-teeth.** An upper canine tooth.

eye·wash, īʹwosh, īʹwôsh, *n.* A lotion to cleanse or treat the eye. *Informal.* Flattery or nonsense.

eye·wit·ness, īʹwit·nis, īʹwitʹnis, *n.* One who sees an act and can give a report of it.—īʹwitʹnis, *v.t.* To witness.—*a.* Of or by an eyewitness.

ey·rie, ey·ry, ārʹē, ērʹē, *n. pl.,* **ey·ries.** Aerie.

F

F, f, ef, *n.* The sixth letter of the English alphabet.

fa·ble, fāʹbəl, *n.* A story or tale, often with animals, designed to convey a moral; a myth. **—fa·bled,** *a.*

fab·ric, fabʹrik, *n.* A woven, felted, or knitted cloth; construction, structure, or framework.

fab·ri·cate, fabʹrə·kāt, *v.t.,* **-cat·ed, -cat·ing.** To build, make, or construct; to form by connecting the parts; to assemble; to make up. **—fab·ri·ca·tion,** fab·rə·kāʹshən, *n.* **—fab·ri·ca·tive,** *a.* **—fab·ri·ca·tor,** *n.*

fab·u·lous, fabʹyə·ləs, fabʹū·ləs, *a.* Remarkably good; wonderful; invented; not real. **—fab·u·lous·ly,** *adv.* **—fab·u·lous·ness,** *n.*

fa·cade, fə·sädʹ, *n. pl.,* **-cades,** -sädz. Face or front view, esp. of a building; artificial or false appearance.

face, fās, *n.* The front part of the head; an expression; a frown; self-respect; all type of one particular style. —*v.t.,* **faced, fac·ing.** To turn the face toward; look toward; to be opposite to; to come face to face with; to confront; to oppose; to smooth the surface of; to line, as a garment; to turn in a certain direction; to overlay with a different material.—*v.i.* To have or turn the face in a given direction.**—face to face,** in one another's actual company; confronting each other, followed by *with.*—**in the face of,** despite; notwithstanding.—**on the face of it,** according to appearances; manifestly.

—**fly in the face of,** to act in open disregard of.—**lose face,** to undergo shame, disrepute, or loss of dignity. —**save face,** to retain one's self-respect or good reputation.—**show one's face,** to appear, esp. briefly. —**to one's face,** in one's immediate presence.

face card, *n.* A jack, queen, or king in a deck of playing cards.

face-lift·ing, fāsʹlif·ting, *n.* Plastic surgery for eliminating signs of aging on the face.

fac·et, fasʹit, *n.* A small, flat surface, esp. on a gem or crystal; a part of a subject.—*v.t.* To cut facets on.

fa·ce·tious, fə·sēʹshəs, *a.* Without serious intent; witty; full of playful humor. **—fa·ce·tious·ly,** *adv.* **—fa·ce·tious·ness,** *n.*

fa·cial, fāʹshəl, *a.* Of the face; for the face.—*n.* A facial massage or beauty treatment. **—fa·cial·ly,** *adv.*

fac·ile, fasʹil, *a.* Easily done, or used; moving, acting, or working with ease; affable or agreeable. **—fac·ile·ly,** *adv.* **—fac·ile·ness,** *n.*

fa·cil·i·tate, fə·silʹə·tāt, *v.t.,* **-tat·ed, -tat·ing.** To make easy or less difficult.

fa·cil·i·ty, fə·silʹə·tē, *n. pl.,* **-ties.** Freedom from difficulty; *often pl.,* something built to serve a particular purpose.

fac·ing, fāʹsing, *n.* A lining at the edge of a garment; *pl.,* the trimmings on a coat or jacket.

---

a- hat, fāte, fāre, fäther; **e-** met, mē; **i-** pin, pīne; **o-** not, nōte, ôrb, moove (move), boy, pownd; **u-** cūbe, bûll, tûk (took); **ch-** chin; **th-** thick, ŧhen; **zh-** vizhon (vision); **ə-** əgo, takən, pencəl, lemən, bərd (bird).

fac·sim·i·le, fak·sim/ə·lē, *n.* An exact copy or likeness.

fact, fakt, *n.* Something that has really happened or is actually the case; the quality of being real and actual; a truth known by actual observation.

fac·tion, fak/shən, *n.* A group within a larger organization, usu. in opposition to the main group. **—fac·tion·al,** fak/shə·nəl, *a.* **—fac·tion·al·ism,** *n.* **fac·tion·al·ly,** *adv.*

fac·ti·tious, fak·tish/əs, *a.* Conforming to a conventional standard. **—fac·ti·tious·ly,** *adv.* **—fac·ti·tious·ness,** *n.*

fac·tor, fak/tər, *n.* A contributing element in bringing about any given result; one of two or more numbers, expressions, or the like, which produce a given product.—*v.t.* To resolve into factors.

fac·to·ry, fak/tə·rē, *n. pl.,* **-ries.** A building or collection of buildings used for the manufacture of goods.

fac·to·tum, fak·tō/təm, *n.* One hired to perform a variety of tasks.

fac·tu·al, fak/choo·əl, *a.* Referring to facts; of the nature of fact; dealing only in fact. **—fac·tu·al·ly,** *adv.*

fac·ul·ty, fak/əl·tē, *n.* A natural or acquired ability; extraordinary talent or skill; any mental or bodily power; the teaching staff of any institution of learning.

fad, fad, *n.* A passing fashion pursued for a time. **—fad·dish,** fad/ish, *a.* **—fad·dism,** *n.* **—fad·dist,** *n.*

fade, fād, *v.i.,* **fad·ed, fad·ing.** To lose brightness or color; to lose freshness; wither; fail gradually in strength or health.—*v.t.* To cause to fade. **—fade in,** to introduce gradually and with increasing strength. **—fade out,** to cause to fade or disappear.

fa·er·ie, fa·er·y, fā/ə·rē, fār/ē, *n. pl.,* **-ies.** The land of the fairies.

fag, fag, *v.t.,* **fagged, fag·ging.** To exhaust, usu. with *out.*—*v.i.* To become weary through work.—*n. Informal.* A man who is a homosexual.

fag·got, fag/ət, *n.* Fagot. *Informal.* A male homosexual.

fag·ot, fag/ət, *n.* A bundle of wood, used for fuel.—*v.t.* To bind or make into a fagot.

Fahr·en·heit, far/ən·hīt, *a.* Of or pertaining to a thermometer with a scale, on which the boiling point of water is 212° above zero of the scale, the freezing point 32° above zero of the scale.

fail, fāl, *v.i.* To fall short; to decline or be diminished; to become weaker; to become extinct; to stop functioning; to be unsuccessful in receiving a passing mark in; to be guilty of omission or neglect; to become bankrupt.—*v.t.* To neglect, omit, or leave undone; to disappoint; to not promote or grade, as a student, as ineligible for promotion.—*n.* Failure; deficiency; want.**—without fail,** without doubt; certainly.

fail·ing, fā/ling, *n.* An imperfection; a weakness; a fault; the act or state of a person or thing that fails.—*prep.* Lacking; without. **—fail·ing·ly,** *adv.*

fail·safe, fāl/sāf, *n.* A safety warning system which reacts automatically to a possible source of failure.

fail·ure, fāl/yər, *n.* The act of failing; the state of having failed; one who is unsuccessful; a weakening of physical powers; a state of bankruptcy.

faint, fānt, *v.i.* To become unconscious for a short time.—*n.* A momentary loss of consciousness.—*a.* Feeble; weak. **—faint·ly,** *adv.* **—faint·ness,** *n.*

faint·heart·ed, fānt/här/tid, *a.* Cowardly. **—faint·heart·ed·ly,** *adv.* **—faint·heart·ed·ness,** *n.*

fair, fār, *a.* Pleasing to the eye; pretty; light in hue; blond; bright, or sunny; honest, open, frank, acceptable, good, promising, as a choice; adequate, as quantity or amount; mediocre.—*adv.* Fairly. **—fair·ness,** *n.*

fair, fār, *n.* An exhibition of various products, often combined with entertainment.

fair·ground, fār/grownd, *n. Usu. pl.* A place set aside for fairs, carnivals, and exhibitions.

fair·ly, *adv.* In an impartial manner; moderately; completely; suitably; legitimately; clearly.

fair·mind·ed, fār/mīn/did, *a.* Reasonable and unbiased. **—fair·mind·ed·ness,** *n.*

fair-trade, fār/trād/, *v.t.,* **-trad·ed, -trad·ing.** To sell a manufacturer's product for no less than a specified price.

fair-weath·er, fār/weth·ər, *a.* Intended for use or carried on in fair weather only; undependable in time of adversity.

fair·y, fār/ē, *n. pl.,* **-ies.** An imaginary being having a small, graceful, human form and superhuman powers; an elf or fay.—*a.* Connected with fairies; coming from fairies; resembling a fairy. Also **fair·y·like.**

fair·y tale, *n.* A tale of magical creatures; an unbelievable story; a lie. Also **fair·y sto·ry.**

faith, fāth, *n.* Confidence; loyalty; belief; belief in God; belief in the teachings of a religion.

faith·ful, fāth/fəl, *a.* Loyal to one's promises and duty; trustworthy; adhering to fact or true to an original.—*n. pl.,* **faith·ful, faith·fuls.** The loyal members of any party or group.

faith·less, fāth/lis, *a.* Not holding to vows or duty; not trustworthy; without religious faith or belief. **—faith·less·ly,** *adv.* **—faith·less·ness,** *n.*

fake, fāk, *v.t.,* **faked, fak·ing.** To prepare or change in order to give a false look to; to simulate. *Informal.* To act by improvising.—*v.i.* To pretend something.—*n.* A counterfeit; a fraud; one who fakes.—*a.* **—fak·er,** *n.*

fal·con, fôl/kən, fal/kən, *n.* Any of various birds of prey having long, pointed wings and a hooked bill.

fal·con·ry, fôl/kən·rē, fal/kən·rē, *n.* The sport of training falcons.

fall, fôl, *v.i.,* **fell, fall·en, fall·ing.** To drop down suddenly; to lose high position; to come as if by descending; to become detached and drop off; to issue forth; to hang down; to sink to a lower level; to decline; to ebb; to slope; to lose animation; to be cast down; to be reduced; to be lowered; to decrease; collapse; to be overthrown; to do wrong or sin; to drop down wounded or dead, esp. to be slain; to come by chance into a particular position; to enter in a mental or physical state: to *fall* in love, to *fall* ill; to come to pass; occur; happen.—*n.* The act of dropping from a higher to a lower place; the descent of rain or snow; the quantity that descends; autumn; a sinking to a lower level; decline or decay; *usu. pl.,* a waterfall. Downward direction; the distance through which anything falls; a falling from an erect position; being thrown on one's back by an opponent in wrestling; a bout at wrestling; surrender or capture; a falling covering or piece of material; a loosely hanging veil; a woman's long hair piece.—*a.* Of autumn. **—fall away,** to decline, decay, or perish; to become lean or emaciated. **—fall back,** to recede; to retreat; to give way. **—fall behind,** to drop back; to fail to pay on time. **—fall down,** to fail; to disappoint. **—fall for,** to be deceived by; to fall in love with. **—fall in,** to sink inward; to take one's proper place in line, as a soldier. **—fall in with,** to come together; to meet; to agree; to conform to. **—fall off,** to drop off; to separate or withdraw; to decrease in number, amount, or intensity; to diminish. **—fall on, fall upon,** to assault; to discover by chance; to become the duty or responsibility of; to have or know; experience: to *fall on* hard times. **—fall out,** to drop out of one's place in line; to disagree or quarrel; to occur or happen. **—fall short,** to fail. **—fall through,** to come to naught; to fail. **—fall to,** to set to work; apply oneself; to begin to eat.

fal·la·cious, fə·lā/shəs, *a.* Misleading, or false. **—fal·la·cious·ly,** *adv.* **—fal·la·cious·ness,** *n.*

fal·la·cy, fal/ə·sē, *n.* Something misleading, or false.

fall·en, fô/lən, *a.* Having dropped; no longer chaste; overthrown; slain.

fall guy, *n.* One who is made to take the blame; scapegoat.

fal·li·ble, fal/ə·bəl, *a.* Liable to fail; mistaken or deceived. **—fal·li·bil·i·ty,** fal·ə·bil/ə·tē, *n.* **—fal·li·bly,** *adv.*

fall·ing star, fô/ling, *n.* A meteor.

Fal·lo·pi·an tube, fə·lō′pē·ən, *n.* (*Sometimes l.c.*) Either of a pair of slender tubes which convey the ova from the ovaries to the uterus.

fall·out, fôl′owt, *n.* Material blown into the atmosphere by a nuclear explosion, and made radioactive by it; the descent of such particles, a by-product of any sort.

fal·low, fal′ō, *n.* Land that has lain unseeded after plowing and harrowing.—*a.* Plowed and left unseeded for a season or more; uncultivated.—*v.t.* To plow and harrow, as land, without seeding. **—fal·low·ness,** *n.*

fal·low, fal′ō, *a.* Of a pale yellowish or brownish color.

false, fôls, *a.,* **fals·er, fals·est.** Untrue, or incorrect; faithless; deceptive; not genuine; counterfeit; used to deceive or mislead; having a resemblance to something that bears the name.—*adv.* In a false manner; incorrectly or wrongly; treacherously or faithlessly. **—false·ly,** *adv.* **—false·ness,** *n.*

false·hood, fôls′hûd, *n.* An untrue statement; a lie.

fal·si·fy, fôl′sə·fī, *v.t.,* **-fied, -fy·ing.** To make false, as by changing, esp. for the purpose of fraud; to represent falsely; to disprove.—*v.i.* To lie. **—fal·si·fi·ca·tion,** fôl·se·fə·kā′shən, *n.* **—fal·si·fi·er,** *n.*

fal·si·ty, fôl′sə·tē, *n.* That which is false; a lie.

fal·ter, fôl′tər, *v.i.* To move unsteadily; to speak hesitatingly; stammer; to waver in action or purpose. —*v.t.* To talk brokenly.—*n.* A faltering; an unsteadiness. **—fal·ter·er,** *n.* **—fal·ter·ing·ly,** *adv.*

fame, fām, *n.* Widespread public renown or recognition.

famed, fāmd, *a.* Much talked of; renowned; celebrated.

fa·mil·ial, fə·mil′yəl, fə·mil′ē·əl, *a.* Referring to or characteristic of the family.

fa·mil·iar, fə·mil′yər, *a.* Well-known; well-acquainted; well-versed; informal; pertaining to a family.—*n.* An intimate friend. **—fa·mil·iar·ly,** *adv.*

fa·mil·i·ar·i·ty, fə·mil·ē·ar′ə·tē, *n. pl.,* **-i·ties.** The state of being familiar; a thorough acquaintance or knowledge of a person or subject; intimacy. *Pl.* Over-friendly actions.

fa·mil·iar·ize, fə·mil′yə·rīz, *v.t.,* **-ized, -iz·ing.** To make oneself familiar or accustomed to. **—fa·mil·iar·i·za·tion,** *n.*

fam·i·ly, fam′ə·lē, fam′lē, *n. pl.,* **-lies.** The unit consisting of parents and their children; descendants of a common progenitor; a clan; noble or distinguished lineage; the group of persons who live in one household and under one head; a class of things sharing certain characteristics and functions.—*a.* Of or pertaining to a family.

family name, *n.* A surname; the last name of an individual.

family tree, *n.* A diagram of a family showing all family members and their relationships. Also **ge·ne·a·log·i·cal tree.**

fam·ine, fam′in, *n.* Widespread scarcity of food; a general shortage of anything.

fam·ish, fam′ish, *v.t., v.i.* To cause to suffer from hunger or thirst.

fam·ished, fam′isht, *a.* Suffering from extreme hunger.

fa·mous, fā′məs, *a.* Widely known; celebrated.

fa·mous·ly, fā′məs·le, *adv.* Ably; excellently; successfully.

fan, fan, *n.* A wedge-shaped or circular hand implement for producing cooling air currents; anything resembling a fan; any of various machines with revolving blades to produce an air current. **—fan·like,** *a.* **—fan·ner,** *n.*

fan, fan, *v.t.,* **fanned, fan·ning.** To move air with a fan; to stir to activity with or as with a fan; to spread out like a fan.—*v.i.* To move or spread as a fan does. *Baseball.* To strike out.

fan, fan, *n.* An enthusiast of any sport or amusement; an admirer.

fa·nat·ic, fə·nat′ik, *n.* Zealot.—*a.* Wildly enthusiastic; marked by extreme, uncritical zeal. Also **fa·nat·i·cal. —fa·nat·i·cal·ly,** *adv.*

fa·nat·i·cism, fə·nat′ə·siz·əm, *n.* Excessive zeal or unreasoning fervor; behavior marked by such zeal or fervor.

fa·nat·i·cize, fə·nat′ə·sīz, *v.t.,* **-cized, -ciz·ing.** To make fanatic.

fan·ci·er, fan′sē·ər, *n.* One having a specialized interest in something: a dog *fancier.*

fan·ci·ful, fan′sə·fəl, *a.* Guided by fancy rather than by reason and experience; whimsical. **—fan·ci·ful·ly,** *adv.* **—fan·ci·ful·ness,** *n.*

fan·cy, fan′sē, *n. pl.,* **-cies.** Imagination, esp. of a capricious type; an idea or opinion with little foundation; a whim; a fondness; taste, as in fashion or art; breeding of animals or plants to develop points of beauty or excellence.—*a.,* **-ci·er, -ci·est.** Ornamental; select or extra fine; bred, as to develop special points of beauty or excellence; based on ideas of the fancy or imagination; depending on the exercise of imagination.—*v.t.,* **-cied, -cy·ing.** To picture; imagine; to believe without being sure or certain; to take a liking to; like. **—fan·ci·ly,** *adv.* **—fan·ci·ness,** *n.*

fan·cy·work, fan′sē·wərk, *n.* Ornamental needlework.

fan·fare, fan′fār, *n.* A flourish of trumpets. *Informal.* Publicity; advertising.

fang, fang, *n.* A long, pointed tooth of an animal; one of the long teeth of a poisonous snake by which venom is injected. **—fanged,** fangd, *a.*

fan·light, fan′līt, *n.* A transom window, usu. semicircular, above a door or larger window.

fan·tas·tic, fan·tas′tik, *a.* Existing in imagination only; whimsical; odd in appearance; incredible; outstanding; irrational. Also **fan·tas·ti·cal,** fan·tas′ti·kəl. **—fan·tas·ti·cal·i·ty,** *n.* **—fan·tas·ti·cal·ly,** *adv.* **—fan·tas·ti·cal·ness,** *n.*

fan·ta·sy, fan′tə·sē, fan′tə·zē, *n. pl.,* **-sies.** A creation of the imagination; whimsical notion; a mental image, esp. when odd; a supposition based on no solid foundation.

far, fär, *adv.,* **far·ther** or **fur·ther, far·thest** or **fur·thest.** At a great distance; remote in space or time; to an advanced degree; greatly or very much; by a great interval; widely; at or to a definite distance, point of progress, or degree, preceded by *as, so, how.*—**by far,** by a great extent; very much.—**far and away,** unquestionably.—**in so far, so far as,** to such an extent.—*a.* Distant or remote in space or time; extending to a great distance; more distant of the two.

far·a·way, fär′ə·wā, *a.* Distant: as, *faraway* places; dreamy: as, a *faraway* look in the eyes.

farce, färs, *n.* A comedy with exaggerated incidents; ridiculous pretense; mere show.—*v.t.,* **farced, farc·ing.** To introduce witty material into a speech, play, or literary composition.

far·ci·cal, fär′sə·kəl, *a.* Belonging to a farce; of the character of a farce. **—far·ci·cal·i·ty,** fär·sə·kal′ə·tē, *n.* **—far·ci·cal·ly,** *adv.*

fare, fār, *v.i.,* **fared, far·ing.** To be in a certain condition, as: We *fare* well; to eat or drink.—*n.* The price paid or charged for transportation; a passenger who pays for public conveyance; food and drink. **—far·er,** *n.*

fare·well, fär·wel′, *interj.* An expression of leave-taking; good-by.—*n.* Good-by; an act of departure. —*a.* Final; parting.

far-fetched, fär′fecht′, *a.* Unbelievable; improbable.

far-flung, fär′fləng′, *a.* Scattered; over a wide range of space or time.

farm, färm, *n.* A tract of land devoted to the production

---

a- hat, fāte, fāre, fäther; **e-** met, mē; **i-** pin, pīne; **o-** not, nōte, ôrb, moove (move), boy, pownd; **u-** cūbe, bûll, tûk (took); **ch-** chin; **th-** thick, ᴛhen; **zh-** vizhon (vision); ə- əgo, takən, pencəl, lemən, bərd (bird).

of crops, livestock, or poultry; a tract of water set aside for cultivating aquatic life. *Baseball.* A minor-league team to train players.—*v.t.* To cultivate, as land; to let the services of someone for hire.—*v.i.* To operate a farm.—**farm out**, to send out work to be taken care of by persons on the outside.

farm·er, färm′mǝr, *n.* One who raises crops or animals; one who operates a farm.

farm·hand, färm′hand, *n.* One who works on a farm, esp. for pay.

farm·house, färm′hows, *n.* A residence on a farm.

farm·ing, färm′ming, *n.* The act or vocation of one who farms; agriculture.

farm·yard, färm′yärd, *n.* An area surrounded by or connected with farm buildings.

far-off, fär′ôf′, fär′of′, *a.* Distant or faraway; remote in space or time.

far-reach·ing, fär′rē′ching, *a.* Having wide influence and great effect. —**far-reach·ing·ly**, *adv.* —**far-reach·ing·ness**, *n.*

far-see·ing, fär′sē′ing, *a.* Showing foresight; able to see things clearly at great distances.

far-sight·ed, fär′sī′tid, *a.* Seeing more clearly at a distance than close at hand; far-seeing; showing good judgment. —**far·sight·ed·ly**, *adv.* —**far·sight·ed·ness**, *n.*

far·ther, fär′thǝr, *a.* More remote; more distant than something else.—*adv.* At or to a greater distance or degree.

far·ther·most, fär′thǝr·mōst, *a.* Farthest.

far·thest, fär′thǝst, *a.* Superlative of **far.** At the greatest distance either in time or place.—*adv.* At or to the greatest distance or degree.

fas·ci·a, fash′ē·ǝ, *n. pl.,* -ci·ae, -shē·ē, -ci·as. A band or fillet; a band or sheath of connective tissue. —**fas·ci·al**, *a.*

fas·ci·cle, fas′ǝ·kǝl, *n.* A small bundle. —**fas·ci·cled,** *a.*

fas·ci·nate, fas′ǝ·nāt, *v.t.,* -nat·ed, -nat·ing. To attract by some powerful or irresistible influence.—*v.i.* To be fascinating. —**fas·ci·nat·ing·ly**, *adv.*

fas·ci·na·tion, fas·ǝ·nā′shǝn, *n.* The act of fascinating.

fas·cism, fash′iz·ǝm, *n.* An autocratic system of government, characterized by strict social and economic control, aggressive nationalistic policies often accompanied by racism, and the crushing of opposition. —**fas·cist**, fash′ist, *n., a.* —**fa·scis·tic**, fǝ·shis′tik, *a.* —**fa·scis·ti·cal·ly**, *adv.*

fash·ion, fash′ǝn, *n.* The make or form of anything; mode or way; the current vogue in dress, style, manners, living, or the arts.—*v.t.* To form; to give shape to.

fash·ion·a·ble, fash′ǝ·nǝ·bǝl, *a.* Conforming to the current fashion or established mode; or of pertaining to the world of fashion.—*n.* —**fash·ion·a·ble·ness**, *n.* —**fash·ion·a·bly**, *adv.*

fash·ion plate, *n.* An outstandingly fashionable person who consistently dresses in the latest style.

fast, fast, fäst, *a.* Swift; rapid; firmly fixed; steadfast; faithful; not changeable; lasting; dissipated; of questionable morals; of a timepiece, ahead of the true time.—*adv.* Swiftly; rapidly; with quick steps or progression; of a timepiece, ahead of the true time; wastefully; with dissipation; tightly; deeply, as: He was *fast* asleep. —**fast·ness,** *n.*

fast, fast, fäst, *v.i.* To go without food voluntarily.—*n.* Abstinence from food; the time of fasting.

fas·ten, fas′ǝn, fä′sǝn, *v.t.* To fix firmly; to make fast; to secure; to join; to attach.—*v.i.* To fix oneself or itself; to become attached. —**fas·ten·er**, *n.* —**fas·ten·ing**, *n.*

fas·tid·i·ous, fa·stid′ē·ǝs, *a.* Hard to please; squeamish; delicate to a fault; over-nice. —**fas·tid·i·ous·ly**, *adv.* —**fas·tid·i·ous·ness**, *n.*

fat, fat, *a.,* fat·ter, fat·test. Fleshy; plump; obese; oily; greasy; producing a large income; rich; fertile; nourishing.—*v.t.,* **fat·ted, fat·ting.** To make fat; to fatten.

—*v.i.* To grow fat.—*n.* The tissues of animals, and sometimes plants, that contain an oily or greasy substance; corpulence; the best or richest part of a thing. —**fat·ly,** *adv.* —**fat·ness,** *n.*

fa·tal, fā′tǝl, *a.* Causing death; determining or critically important. —**fa·tal·ly,** *adv.*

fa·tal·ism, fā′tǝ·liz·ǝm, *n.* The doctrine that all things are predetermined or subject to fate. —**fa·tal·ist,** *n.* —**fa·tal·is·tic,** *a.* —**fa·tal·is·ti·cal·ly,** *adv.*

fa·tal·i·ty, fā·tal′ǝ·tē, fǝ·tal′ǝ·tē, *n. pl.,* -ties. A fixed, unalterable course of things; a calamitous accident; a violent death.

fate, fāt, *n.* Destiny; that which is ordained to happen; one's appointed lot; death, destruction, or ruin.—*v.t.,* **fat·ed, fat·ing.** To predetermine, as by the decree of fate; destine.

fat·ed, fā′tid, *a.* Predetermined by fate.

fate·ful, fāt′fǝl, *a.* Involving momentous consequences; prophetic. —**fate·ful·ly,** *adv.* —**fate·ful·ness,** *n.*

fa·ther, fä′thǝr, *n.* A man who begets a child; a male ancestor; a male parent or guardian; the founder of a family or race; a respectful means of address to an old man; a priest; an originator or founder of something.

fa·ther·hood, fä′thǝr·hûd, *n.* The state of being a father; the character or authority of a father.—*v.t.* To beget as a father; to accept responsibility for. —**fa·ther·li·ness**, *n.* —**fa·ther·ly**, *a., adv.*

fa·ther-in-law, fä′thǝr·in·lô, *n. pl.,* **fa·thers-in-law.** The father of one's husband or wife.

fa·ther·land, fä′thǝr·land, *n.* One's native country; the country of one's fathers or ancestors.

fath·om, fath′ǝm, *n. pl.,* -oms, -om. A measure of length containing six feet, used chiefly for depths. —*v.t.* To try the depth of; to sound; to penetrate or comprehend. —**fath·om·a·ble,** *a.* —**fath·om·less,** *a.*

fa·tigue, fǝ·tēg′, *n.* Weariness from bodily labor or mental exertion; fatigue duty; *pl.,* the rugged and durable clothes worn while on fatigue duty.—*v.t.,* **fa·tigued, fa·tig·uing.** To weary with labor or any bodily or mental exertion.—*v.i.* To tire or wear out.

fat·i·ga·ble, fat′ǝ·gǝ·bǝl, *a.* Easily tired; fatigued. —**fat·i·ga·bil·i·ty,** *n.*

fat·ten, fat′ǝn, *v.t.* To make fat.—*v.i.* To become plump or fleshy. —**fat·ten·er,** *n.*

fat·ty, fat′ē, *a.,* -ti·er, -ti·est. Greasy; containing much fat. —**fat·ti·ness,** *n.* —**fat·tish,** *a.*

fa·tu·i·ty, fǝ·too′ǝ·tē, fǝ·tū′ǝ·tē, *n. pl.,* -ties. A stupid or foolish act or remark.

fat·u·ous, fach′oo·ǝs, *a.* Idiotically silly; foolish. —**fat·u·ous·ly,** *adv.* —**fat·u·ous·ness,** *n.*

fau·cet, fô′sit, *n.* A device with a valve which controls the flow of liquid from a pipe or container; tap.

fault, fôlt, *n.* A defect or imperfection; a flaw; a failing; an error or mistake; a misdeed or transgression; cause for blame. *Geol.* A break in rock formation.—*v.t.* To find fault with; blame. *Geol.* To cause a fault in.—*v.i.* To commit a fault. *Geol.* To undergo a fault.

fault·find·er, fôlt′fīn·dǝr, *n.* One who finds fault. —**fault·find·ing**, *n., a.*

fault·less, fôlt′lis, *a.* Without fault or flaw; perfect. —**fault·less·ly**, *adv.* —**fault·less·ness**, *n.*

fault·y, fôl′tē, *a.,* -i·er, -i·est. Containing faults or defects; having, or marked by, imperfections or failings. —**fault·i·ly**, *adv.* —**fault·i·ness**, *n.*

fau·na, fô′nǝ, *n. pl.,* -nas, -nae, -nē. A collective term for the animals or animal life peculiar to a region, epoch, or environment.

faux pas, fō pä′, *n. pl.,* **faux pas**, fō päz′. Social blunder; a breach of etiquette.

fa·vor, *Brit.* **fa·vour**, fā′vǝr, *n.* Something done or granted out of good will; a kind act; the state of being approved; something bestowed as a token of good will or kind regard; a gift; kindness.—**in favor of**, in support of; on the side of; to the advantage of.—*v.t.* To regard with favor; have a liking for; to show favor to; to deal with gently, spare, or ease; lend support or confirmation to; to resemble. —**fa·vor·ing·ly**, *adv.*

fa·vor·a·ble, *Brit.* **fa·vour·a·ble,** fā/vər·ə·bəl, *a.* Advantageous; approving; winning favor; pleasing. **—fa·vor·a·ble·ness,** *n.* **—fa·vor·a·bly,** *adv.*

fa·vored, fā/vərd, *a.* Regarded or treated with favor; enjoying special favors or advantages; having a particular appearance: as, ill-*favored.* **—fa·vored·ly,** *adv.* **—fa·vored·ness,** *n.*

fa·vor·ite, fā/vər·it, *n.* A person or thing regarded with special favor, preference, or affection; the competitor most likely to win.—*a.* Regarded with particular affection or preference.

fa·vor·it·ism, fā/vər·ə·tiz·əm, *n.* Preferential treatment of one person or group over others having equal claims.

fawn, fôn, *n.* A young deer in its first year; a light, grayish-brown color.—*a.* Of a light, grayish-brown color.—*v.i.* Of a deer, to bring forth a fawn.

fawn, fôn, *v.i.* To seek favor by servile behavior or flattery; to show servile fondness, as a dog.

faze, fāz, *v.t.,* **fazed, faz·ing.** *Informal.* To disturb; discomfit; daunt.

fe·al·ty, fē·əl·tē, *n. pl.,* **-ties.** Faithfulness and loyalty.

fear, fēr, *n.* A painful emotion caused by an expectation of evil, danger, or anxiety; awe and reverence for God; dread.—*v.t.* To feel fear; to be afraid of.—*v.i.* To be afraid.

fear·ful, fēr/fəl, *a.* Afraid; apprehensive; terrible; dreadful; awful; extreme. **—fear·ful·ly,** *adv.* **—fear·ful·ness,** *n.*

fear·less, fēr/lis, *a.* Bold; courageous; intrepid; undaunted. **—fear·less·ly,** *adv.* **—fear·less·ness,** *n.*

fear·some, fēr/səm, *a.* Alarming; frightening. **—fear·some·ly,** *adv.* **—fear·some·ness,** *n.*

fea·si·ble, fē/zə·bəl, *a.* Capable of being accomplished; practicable; likely. **—fea·si·bil·i·ty,** fē·zə·bil/ə·tē, **fea·si·ble·ness,** *n.* **—fea·si·bly,** *adv.*

feast, fēst, *n.* A large meal; something particularly pleasing to the senses or the mind.

feat, fēt, *n.* An act, exploit, or accomplishment, esp. one marked by extraordinary strength, skill, or courage.

feath·er, feth/ər, *n.* One of the outer structures covering the body of a bird; kindred: as birds of a *feather;* something resembling a feather, as a tuft or fringe of hair. *Rowing.* The act of feathering an oar.**—a feather in one's cap,** a mark of distinction; an honor. **—feath·ered,** *a.*—*v.t.* To clothe or cover with feathers; provide with feathers. *Rowing.* To turn, as an oar, to a nearly horizontal position as it returns for the next stroke.—*v.i.* To grow feathers; to be feathery in appearance; move like feathers; to feather an oar or airplane propeller.**—feather one's nest,** to obtain wealth for oneself, either ethically or unethically.

feath·er·bed·ding, feth/ər·bed·ing, *n.* The practice of hiring unnecessary workers to meet union standards and limit the activity or production of each worker.

fea·ture, fē/chər, *n.* Any part of the face; a characteristic part of anything; something offered as a special attraction; a principal movie on a program; a special magazine or newspaper article.—*v.t.,* **-tured, -tur·ing.** To resemble in features; outline; to make a feature of, or give prominence to. **—fea·tured,** *a.*

fea·ture·less, fē/chər·lis, *a.* Uninteresting.

fe·brile, fē/brəl, feb/rəl, *a.* Feverish.

Feb·ru·ar·y, feb/roo·er·ē, feb/ū·er·ē, *n. pl.,* **Feb·ru·ar·ies.** The second month in the year consisting ordinarily of 28 days, or of 29 in leap years.

fe·ces, fē/sēz, *n. pl.* Excrement; dregs; sediment. **—fe·cal,** fē/kəl, *a.*

feck·less, fek/lis, *a.* Weak; impotent; listless; indolent; irresponsible.

fe·cund, fē/kənd, fek/ənd, *a.* Fruitful; prolific; fertile. **—fe·cun·di·ty,** fi·kən/də·tē, *n.*

fe·cun·date, fē/kən·dāt, fek/ən·dāt, *v.t.,* **-dat·ed, -dat·ing.** To impregnate; fertilize. **—fe·cun·da·tion,** *n.*

fed·er·al, fed/ər·əl, *a.* Pertaining to a union of states under a central government distinct from the governments of the individual states: as, the *federal* government of the U.S.; favoring a strong central government in such a union.—*n.* An advocate of federalism.

fed·er·al·ism, fed/ər·əl·iz·əm, *n.* The federal principle of government.

fed·er·al·ist, fed/ər·əl·ist, *n.* An advocate of federalism.

fed·er·al·ize, fed/ər·ə·līz, *v.t.,* **-ized, -iz·ing.** To unite in a federal union; bring under the control of a federal union or government. **—fed·er·al·i·za·tion,** fed·ə·rəl·ə·zā/shən, *n.* **—fed·er·al·ly,** *adv.*

fed·er·ate, fed/ə·rāt, *v.t., v.i.,* **-at·ed, -at·ing.** To unite in a league or federation; to organize on a federal basis.—fed/ər·it, *a.* Federated; allied.

fed·er·a·tion, fed·ə·rā/shən, *n.* The act of federating or uniting in a league. **—fed·er·a·tive,** *a.* **—fed·er·a·tive·ly,** *adv.*

fee, fē, *n.* A payment for professional service, as of a physician; a charge for licenses, registrations, permits; a sum paid for a privilege: as, an admission *fee;* a gratuity or tip. *Law.* Currently, an estate or inheritance in land.

fee·ble, fē/bəl, *a.,* **-bler, -blest.** Physically weak; weak intellectually or morally; lacking in force or effectiveness. **—fee·bly,** *adv.*

fee·ble-mind·ed, fē/bəl·mīn/did, *a.* Deficient in mentality. **—fee·ble-mind·ed·ness,** *n.*

feed, fēd, *v.t.,* **fed, feed·ing.** To give food to; supply th nourishment; to serve as food for; to furnish for consumption; to gratify; to provide with the needed materials for maintenance or operation, as a machine.—*v.i.* To take food or eat, esp. used of livestock; to be nourished or gratified as if by food; to pass successively into a machine for the purpose of being processed or utilized.—*n.* Food, esp. for domestic animals; fodder; an allowance of such food; the act or process of feeding a furnace or other machine; the material, or the amount of it, so fed or supplied; a feeding mechanism. **—feed·er,** *n.*

feed·back, fēd/bak, *n.* The return of energy from the output of a system to the input of the same system.

feel, fēl, *v.t.,* **felt, feel·ing.** To perceive by the touch; to have a sense of; to be affected by; to be conscious, as of pain, pleasure, or disgrace; to experience; to suffer; to examine by touching; to be convinced of, or believe in; to think.—*v.i.* To appear, seem; to perceive oneself to be; to know certainly or without misgiving; to have pity or compassion.—*n.* The act of feeling; intuitive knowledge; sensation or impression on being touched; sense of touch; sensation of feeling something.

feel·er, fē/lər, *n.* One who feels; an organ of touch, as antennae; any device for the purpose of ascertaining the designs, opinions, or sentiments of others.

feel·ing, fē/ling, *a.* Possessing great sensibility.—*n.* The sense of touch; the sensation conveyed by the sense of touch; the act or power of feeling; physical sensation other than that due to sight, hearing, taste, or smell; an emotion; consciousness; opinion; conviction; tenderness of heart; fine sensibility; *pl.,* sensitiveness; collective susceptibilities. **—feel·ing·ly,** *adv.* **—feel·ing·ness,** *n.*

feet, fēt, *n. pl.* of **foot.**

feign, fān, *v.t.* To pretend; to simulate; to invent an excuse; to imitate deceptively, or counterfeit.—*v.i.* To make believe; pretend. **—feigned,** *a.* **—feign·ed·ly,** fā/nid·lē, *adv.* **—feign·er,** *n.* **—feign·ing·ly,** *adv.*

feint, fānt, *n.* A movement made with the object of deceiving; a pretense.—*v.i.* To make a feint.

---

a- hat, fāte, fāre, fäther; e- met, mē; i- pin, pīne; o- not, nōte, ôrb, moove (move), boy, pownd; u- cūbe, bůll, tůk (took); ch- chin; th- thick, ŧhen; zh- vizhon (vision); ə- əgo, takən, pencəl, lemən, bərd (bird).

feist·y, fīstē, *a.*, **-i·er**, **-i·est**. Excited; agitated; petulant; quarrelsome.

fe·lic·i·tate, fə·lis′ə·tāt, *v.t.*, **-tat·ed**, **-tat·ing**. To congratulate; to express joy or pleasure to another at his good fortune. **—fe·lic·i·ta·tion**, fə·lis·ə·tā′shən, *n.*

fe·lic·i·tous, fə·lis′ə·təs, *a.* Extremely appropriate, suitable, or well expressed; of a person, having a special ability for apt expression. **—fe·lic·i·tous·ly**, *adv.* **—fe·lic·i·tous·ness**, *n.*

fe·lic·i·ty, fə·lis′ə·tē, *n. pl.*, **-ties**. The state of being happy; extreme enjoyment; source of happiness; skillfulness.

fe·line, fē′līn, *a.* Belonging to the cat family; like a cat; stealthy.—*n.* **—fe·line·ly**, *adv.* **—fe·lin·i·ty**, fi·lin′i·tē, *n.*

fell, fel, *v.t.* To cause to fall; to hew down; to knock down; to finish a seam by folding one raw edge over the other and then stitching along the folded edge. **—fell·a·ble**, *a.* **—fell·er**, *n.*

fell, fel, *n.* A skin or hide of an animal; a seam sewed down level with the cloth.

fell, fel, *a.* Cruel; barbarous; inhuman; fierce; deadly.

fel·la·ti·o, fə·lā′shē·ō, *n.* Stimulation of the penis by oral means.

fel·low, fel′ō, *n.* A man or boy; companion; associate; an equal in rank, character or qualification; a peer; one of a pair; a graduate student given a grant for further study; a person belonging to one of several learned societies.—*a.*

fel·low·ship, fel′ō·ship, *n.* The condition or relation of being a fellow; community of interest; companionship; communion; friendliness; a body of fellows; a company; a guild or corporation; the position or pay of a fellow of a university; a foundation for the maintenance of such a fellow.

fel·on, fel′ən, *n.* A person who has committed a felony.

fel·o·ny, fel′ə·nē, *n. pl.*, **-nies**. *Law.* Any crime of a more serious nature than a misdemeanor. **—fe·lo·ni·ous**, fə·lō′nē·əs, *a.* **—fe·lo·ni·ous·ly**, *adv.* **—fe·lo·ni·ous·ness**, *n.*

felt, felt, *n.* A fabric made by matting wool, hair, or fur into a compact substance by pressure, moisture, or heat; an article made of felt.—*v.t.* To make into felt. —*v.i.* To become matted, as felt.

fe·male, fē′māl, *n.* An animal of the sex which conceives and gives birth to young; a girl or woman; that portion of a flower called the pistil which receives the pollen or male element.—*a.* Belonging to the sex which gives birth to young or produces eggs; pertaining to or characteristic of this sex; feminine; having to do with any reproductive structure containing the egg which requires fertilization; pistillate; designating a part into which a corresponding part fits.

fem·i·nine, fem′ə·nin, *a.* Pertaining to a woman or the female sex; womanly; lacking in manly characteristics; effeminate. *Gram.* The gender of words which signify females.—*n.* A word of the feminine gender. **—fem·i·nine·ly**, *adv.* **—fem·i·nine·ness**, *n.* **—fem·i·nin·i·ty**, fem·ə·nin′ə·tē, *n.*

fem·i·nism, fem′i·niz·əm, *n.* The doctrine advocating that social and political rights of women be equal to those possessed by men; a movement to acquire such rights. **—fem·i·nist**, *n.* **—fem·i·nis·tic**, fem·i·nis′tik, *a.*

fem·i·nize, fem′i·nīz, *v.t.*, **-nized**, **-niz·ing**. To make feminine or womanish.—*v.i.* To acquire a feminine or effeminate character. **—fem·i·ni·za·tion**, fem·i·ni·zā′shən, *n.*

fe·mur, fē′mər, *n. pl.*, **fe·murs**, **fem·o·ra**, fem′ər·ə. A bone in the leg, extending from the hip to the knee; the thighbone. **—fem·o·ral**, fem′ər·əl, *a.*

fen, fen, *n.* Boggy land; a marsh. **—fen·ny**, fen′ē, *a.*, **-ni·er**, **-ni·est**.

fence, fens, *n.* A barrier enclosing some area, usu. of railings, posts, boards, or wire; the art of fencing; skill in argument and repartee; a receiver of stolen goods; a place dealing in stolen merchandise.—*v.t.*, **fenced**, **fenc·ing**. To enclose with a fence.—*v.i.* To practice fencing; to parry arguments; to equivocate.—**on the fence**, in a neutral or uncommitted position. **—fenc·er**, *n.*

fencing, fen′sing, *n.* The art of using a sword or foil in attack or defense; material used in making fences; that which encloses an area; fences.

fend, fend, *v.t.* To ward off or avert, usu. followed by *off.*—*v.i.* To make defense; to offer resistance; to parry; to manage without assistance; to provide, as a livelihood, used with *for.*

fen·der, fen′dər, *n.* One who or that which fends; the part of a vehicle covering each wheel; a device at the front of a locomotive or street car for pushing aside obstructions; a metal screen or guard before a fireplace.

fe·ral, fēr′əl, *a.* Wild, or existing in a state of nature; pertaining to or characteristic of the wild state; savage.

fer·ment, fər·ment′, *v.t.* To act upon as a ferment; to agitate; excite; inflame; foment.—*v.i.* To undergo fermentation; seethe with agitation or excitement. **—fer·ment·a·ble**, *a.*

fer·ment, fər′ment, *n.* A substance capable of producing fermentation. *Fig.* Agitation; excitement; tumult.

fer·men·ta·tion, fər·men·tā′shən, *n.* The act or process of fermenting; a change brought about by a ferment; agitation or excitement.

fern, fərn, *n.* A seedless, flowerless plant having fronds which bear spores.

fern·er·y, fər′nə·rē, *n. pl.*, **-ies**. A place where ferns are artificially grown.

fe·ro·cious, fə·rō′shəs, *a.* Savage; cruel; brutal. *Informal.* Intense or very great. **—fe·ro·cious·ly**, *adv.* **—fe·ro·cious·ness**, *n.* **—fe·ro·ci·ty**, fə·ros′ə·tē, *n.*

fer·ret, fer′it, *n.* A domesticated polecat bred to hunt rabbits and kill rats; any diligent searcher, as a detective or investigator.—*v.t.* To hunt with ferrets; to drive out of a lurking place; to search out. **—fer·ret·er**, *n.*

Fer·ris wheel, fer′is, *n.* An amusement ride consisting of a large upright wheel rotating about a fixed axis, and having passenger cars suspended around its rim.

fer·ro·con·crete, fer·ō·kon′krēt, fer·ō·kon·krēt′, *n.* Concrete in which steel rods are embedded; reinforced concrete.

fer·ro·mag·net·ic, fer·ō·mag·net′ik, *a. Phys.* Of or pertaining to a magnetic material, esp. a strong, permanent magnet.

fer·ru·gi·nous, fə·roo′jə·nəs, *a.* Containing iron; colored like iron rust.

fer·rule, fer′əl, fer′ool, *n.* A metal ring or cap put around the end of a post or tool handle, for strength or protection.

fer·ry, fer′ē, *v.t.* To carry across a narrow body of water by boat; to deliver, as an airplane, boat, or other craft, under its own power.—*v.i.* To travel by ferry.—*n. pl.*, **fer·ries**. A place where ferry service is provided; the right to operate a ferry or ferry line and to charge a toll; a ferryboat. **—fer·ry·boat**, *n.* **—fer·ry·man**, *n.*

fer·tile, fər′təl, *a.* Producing or able to produce crops in abundance; able to produce offspring; creative or inventive: a *fertile* imagination. **—fer·tile·ly**, *adv.* **—fer·tile·ness**, *n.*

fer·til·i·ty, fər·til′ə·tē, *n.* The state of being fertile; the ability to produce offspring.

fer·ti·li·za·tion, fər·tə·lə·zā′shən, *n.* The act or process of making fertile or productive; the application of a fertilizer; the union of a sperm cell and an ovum. **—fer·ti·li·za·tion·al**, *a.*

fer·ti·lize, fər′tə·līz, *v.t.*, **-ized**, **-iz·ing**. To make fertile; to make fruitful or productive; to enrich. **—fer·ti·liz·a·ble**, *a.*

fer·ti·liz·er, fər′tə·lī·zər, *n.* One who or that which fertilizes; any substance, such as manure or a chemical compound, used to enrich the soil.

fer•vent, fər/vənt, *a.* Earnest; animated; glowing with religious feeling; zealous; intensely warm. **—fer•ven•cy,** fər/vən•sē, *n.* **—fer•vent•ly,** *adv.*

fer•vid, fər/vid, *a.* Impassioned; zealous; very hot; burning. **—fer•vid•ly,** *adv.* **—fer•vid•ness,** *n.*

fer•vor, fər/vər, *n.* Intense feeling; passion; zeal; heat.

fes•ter, fes/tər, *v.i.* To form pus; to decay; to rankle, as a feeling of pique or resentment.—*n.* Act of festering or rankling.

fes•ti•val, fes/tə•vəl, *n.* A time of religious or other celebration; a program of cultural events.—*a.* Pertaining to a feast or festival.

fes•tive, fes/tiv, *a.* Pertaining to or appropriate for a feast; joyous; gay. **—fes•tive•ly,** *adv.* **—fes•tive•ness,** *n.*

fes•tiv•i•ty, fe•stiv/ə•tē, *n.* A joyous time or celebration; social joy or gaiety; *pl.,* the activities or events of a festive occasion.

fes•toon, fe•stoon/, *n.* A garland suspended so as to form hanging loops or curves. *Arch.* An ornamental reproduction of a festoon. Also **fes•toon•er•y,** *pl.,* **-ies.**—*v.t.* To adorn with festoons; to make into festoons; to connect by festoons.

fe•tal, foe•tal, fē/təl, *a.* Pertaining to, or having the character of a fetus.

fetch, fech, *v.t.* To go and bring back; to bring as a price. *Informal.* To attract or captivate; to strike, as a blow or stroke.—*v.i.* To go and bring things.—*n.* The act of fetching. **—fetch•er,** *n.*

fetch•ing, *a.* Charming; captivating. **—fetch•ing•ly,** *adv.*

fete, fête, fāt, *Fr.* fet. *n. pl.,* **fetes,** fāts, *Fr.* fet. A holiday; a large lavish party or entertainment.—*v.t.* To honor with a fete.

fet•id, fet/id, fē/tid, *a.* Having an offensive smell. **—fet•id•ly,** *adv.* **—fet•id•ness,** *n.*

fet•ish, fet•ich, fet/ish, fē/tish, *n.* Any object regarded as having mysterious powers; anything one unquestionably devotes oneself to. *Psychiatry.* Any object or part of the body, not of the generative system, which arouses sexual interest.

fet•ish•ism, fet/ə•shiz•əm, fē/tə•shiz•əm, *n.* Belief in or practice of assigning mysterious powers to an inanimate object; unquestioning devotion to anything. **—fet•ish•ist,** *n.* **—fet•ish•is•tic,** *a.*

fet•lock, fet/lok, *n.* A tuft of hair above and behind a horse's hoof; the joint at this point.

fet•ter, fet/ər, *n.* A chain or shackle for the foot; anything that confines or restrains.—*v.t.* To put fetters on; to bind; to confine; to restrain.

fet•tle, fet/əl, *n.* A state or condition: in fine *fettle.*

fe•tus, foe•tus, fē/təs, *n. pl.,* **fe•tus•es, foe•tus•es.** The young in the womb of an animal in the larger stages of development; an unborn human from after the third month of pregnancy until birth.

feud, fūd, *n.* A state of bitter and continuous mutual hostility, esp. between two families or clans; a quarrel or contention.—*v.i.* To quarrel, fight, or seek revenge. **—feud•ist,** *n.*

feu•dal, fū/dəl, *a.* Of or pertaining to feudalism.

feu•dal•ism, fū/də•liz•əm, *n.* The medieval feudal system; the system of holding lands in return for military and other services.

feu•dal•ist, fūd/ə•list, *n.* A supporter of the feudal system. **—feu•dal•is•tic,** *a.*

feu•dal•i•za•tion, fūd•ə•li•zā/shən, *n.* The act of feudalizing.

feu•dal•ize, fūd/ə•līz, *v.t.,* **-ized, -iz•ing.** To reduce to a feudal tenure; to conform to feudalism.

fe•ver, fē/vər, *n.* An abnormal increase in body temperature; any disease having high temperature as a principal symptom; excitement by anything that strongly affects the passions; contagious zeal.—*v.t.* To put in a fever.

fe•ver blis•ter, *n.* A cold sore.

fe•ver•ish, *a.* Having fever, esp. a slight degree of fever; of, indicating, or pertaining to fever; tending to cause fever. **—fe•ver•ish•ly,** *adv.* **—fe•ver•ish•ness,** *n.*

fe•ver•ous, fē/vər•əs, *a.* Feverish. **—fe•ver•ous•ly,** *adv.*

few, fū, *a.* Being of small number; not many.—*n. sing. but pl. in constr.* A small number; a small amount; a minority.—*pron., pl. in constr.* A small number of individuals or things.—**the few,** the minority.

fey, fā, *a.* Under a spell; of the nature of fairies or sprites; elfin; enchanted.

fi•an•cé, fē•än•sā/, fē•än/sā, *n.* A man engaged to be married.

fi•an•cée, fē•än•sā/, fē•än/sā, *n. fem.* A woman engaged to be married.

fi•as•co, fē•as/kō, *n. pl.,* **-cos, -coes.** A complete and humiliating failure.

fi•at, fī/ət, fī/at, fē/at, *n.* A decree or dictatorial order; sanction by a person in authority.

fiat mon•ey, *n.* Paper currency issued by a government as legal tender, which is not convertible into coin.

fib, fib, *n.* A falsehood, esp. one that is not malicious. —*v.i.* **—fib•ber, fib•ster,** *n.*

fiber, *Brit.* **fi•bre,** fī/bər, *n.* A slender filament; a fine threadlike part of a substance, as of wool, jute, or asbestos; one of the threadlike elements composing the tissue of muscles and nerves; internal strength, or character: women of strong *fiber.* **—fi•bered,** *a.*

fi•ber•board, fī/bər•bōrd, fī/bər•bôrd, *n.* A construction material of wood or other plant fiber compressed into large sheets.

fi•ber•glass, fī/bər•glas, fī/bər•gläs, *n.* Fine and flexible filaments of glass which can be spun into textiles or matted for insulation; spun glass.

fi•bril, fī/brəl, *n.* A small or very fine fiber or filament.

fi•bril•la•tion, fī•brə•lā/shən, fib•rə•lā/shən, *n.* The twitching of certain muscle fibers without coordination or control; erratic and irregular contractions of heart muscle fibers resulting in abnormally rapid heartbeats.

fi•broid, fī/broyd, *a.* Resembling or formed of fibrous tissue.—*n.* A fibroid tumor.

fi•brous, fī/brəs, *a.* Containing, consisting of, or resembling fibers.

fib•u•la, fib/ū•lə, *n. pl.,* **fib•u•las, fib•u•lae,** fib/ū•lē. The outer and smaller of the two bones of the lower leg. **—fib•u•lar,** *a.*

fick•le, fik/əl, *a.* Wavering; inconstant, in affections, opinions or purpose; capricious. **—fick•le•ness,** *n.*

fic•tion, fik/shən, *n.* A creation of the imagination, a falsehood; literature of imagined events in the form of a novel, novella, or short story; the act of inventing or imagining. *Law.* An assumption that something false may be accepted as true. **—fic•tion•al,** *a.* **—fic•tion•al•ly,** *adv.*

fic•ti•tious, fik•tish/əs, *a.* Feigned; not genuine; untrue; of or pertaining to fiction; dealing with imaginary characters and events. **—fic•ti•tious•ly,** *adv.* **—fic•ti•tious•ness,** *n.*

fid•dle, fid/əl, *n.* A violin.—*v.i.* To play on a fiddle or violin.—*v.t.* To play as a tune, on a fiddle or violin. **—fid•dler,** *n.*—*v.i.,* **-dled, -dling.** To fidget nervously with the fingers or hands; to interfere or meddle. **—fid•dler,** *n.*

fid•dle, fid/əl, *n. Naut.* A frame or ledge, used aboard ships, esp. in rough weather, to prevent dishes and other utensils from sliding off a table.

fi•del•i•ty, fi•del/ə•tē, fī•del/ə•tē, *n.* Faithfulness to a person, cause; careful loyalty; exactness in reproduc-

---

a- hat, fāte, fâre, fäther; **e-** met, mē; **i-** pin, pīne; **o-** not, nōte, ôrb, moove (move), boy, pownd;
u- cūbe, bùll, tûk (took); **ch-** chin; **th-** thick, ᵺen; **zh-** vizhon (vision); **ə-** əgo, takən, pencəl, leman, bərd (bird).

tion; adherence to fact or truth; the quality or degree of accuracy in sound reproduction, as of a radio.

fidg·et, fij′it, *v.i.* To make restless, twitchy movements; to have the jitters.—*v.t.* To cause to become restless or agitated.—*n.* Usu. pl. Irregular, uneasy movements due to nervousness or restlessness. (*L.c.*) A nervous, jumpy person. **—fidg·et·y,** *a.,* **-i·er, -i·est.**

fi·du·ci·ar·y, fi·doo′shē·er·ē, fi·dū′shē·er·ē, *a.* Of or indicating a trustee or his office; accepted only because the public has faith in its value—*n. pl.,* **-ar·ies.** One who holds a thing in trust for another; a trustee.

fie, fī, *interj.* An exclamation of contempt, dislike, or disbelief, now usu. used humorously.

fief, fēf, *n.* An estate held on feudal tenure.

field, fēld, *n.* A piece of land suitable for tillage or pasture; cleared land; cultivated ground; a distinct division of a farm; an area having a particular natural resource: as, oil *field*; an area set aside for a particular activity: as, playing *field,* air*field*; the area where military operations are carried out; any large unbroken stretch of something: as, *field* of ice; a sphere of interest or knowledge: as, the *field* of chemistry; an area of operations that is away from the office or headquarters; the ground or blank space on which figures or designs are drawn, as on medals, coins, or flags; the surface of a heraldic shield or escutcheon. *Athletics.* All those entered in an event or contest; the area where such an event takes place; those players, esp. in football, who are in action. *Baseball, cricket.* The team not at bat. *Phys.* The space within which a given force operates; as, magnetic *field;* that area which can be seen through a lens, as of a telescope or other optical instrument.—*v.t.* To respond to satisfactorily, as to a difficult question. *Baseball.* Of a defensive player, to catch or handle, as a batted ball.—*v.i.* To make a successful defensive play in baseball or cricket.—*a.* Of, related to, grown in, or inhabiting the fields; used in the field: as, *field* boots; played in the field.

field ar·til·ler·y, *n.* Mobile artillery which accompanies troops in the field.

field day, *n.* A day of outdoor sports and competition; a day for military field exercises; any occasion or time of unrestricted activity, excitement, or success.

field·er, fēl′dər, *n. Baseball, cricket.* One who fields the ball; a defensive player positioned in the field.

field·er's choice, *n.* An attempt by a fielder to put out a player already on base rather than the batter, even though the play to first base could put out the batter.

field glass, *n.* A binocular telescope for outdoor use. Also **field glass·es.**

field house, *n.* A building connected with an athletic field and providing locker rooms and other facilities; a building which encloses an area used for various indoor sports.

field mar·shal, *n.* An officer of the highest rank in many armies, such as the British and Canadian.

field of force, *n. Phys.* A space in which a given force is effective.

field·work, fēld′wark, *n.* Investigation, exploration, or research performed in the field by geologists, archaeologists, engineers, or surveyors.

fiend, fēnd, *n.* An evil spirit; a demon; a malicious or wicked person; an annoying or mischievous person: as, a *fiendish* child; one with an exaggerated interest in a subject, as in sports; one who overindulges; an addict. **—fiend·ish,** *a.* **—fiend·ish·ly,** *adv.* **—fiend·ish·ness,** *n.*

fierce, fērs, *a.* Savage; ferocious; violently aggressive or hostile in temperament or nature. **—fierce·ly,** *adv.* **—fierce·ness,** *n.*

fier·y, fī′rē, fī′ə·rē, *a.* **-i·er, -i·est.** Characterized by or containing fire; intensely hot; flashing or glowing; inflamed, as a tumor or sore. **—fier·i·ly,** *adv.* **—fier·i·ness,** *n.*

fif·teen, fif·tēn′, *a.* One more than 14 in number.—*n.* The cardinal number between 14 and 16; a symbol representing it; a set of 15 persons or things.

fif·teenth, fif·tēnth′, *a.* Following the fourteenth; being the ordinal of 15; being one of 15 equal parts into which anything is divided.—*n.* One of 15 equal parts; that which follows the fourteenth in a series.

fifth, fifth, *a.* Following the fourth; being the ordinal of five; being one of five equal parts into which anything is divided.—*n.* One of five equal parts; that which follows the fourth in a series; a fifth of a gallon, esp. of spirituous liquor.

fifth col·umn, *n.* Citizens of a country who are in sympathy with its enemies. **—fifth col·umn·ist,** *n.*

fif·ti·eth, fif′tē·ith, *a.* Following the forty-ninth; being the ordinal of 50; being one of 50 equal parts into which anything is divided.—*n.* One of 50 equal parts; that which follows the forty-ninth in a series.

fif·ty, fif′tē, *a.* One more than 49 in number—*n. pl.,* **fif·ties.** The numbers, years between 50 and 60; the cardinal number between 49 and 51; a symbol representing it; a set of 50 persons or things.

fig, fig, *n.* A small, sweet, pear-shaped fruit; the tropical tree that bears such fruit. *Informal.* A contemptibly small amount, as: I do not care a *fig* for him.

fight, fīt, *v.i.* To take part in battle or in single combat; to strive or struggle; to resist or oppose.—*v.t.* To carry on or wage, as a battle; to contend with; to defend against; to oppose or resolve by striving or contending; to win or gain by struggle: as, to *fight* one's way; to manage or maneuver in a fight: as, to *fight* one's ship.—*n.* A contest; a battle; verbal contention or argument; any struggle for victory.

fight·er, fī′tər, *n.* One who or that which fights; a combatant.**—fight it out,** to struggle until a decisive result is attained.

fig·ment, fig′mənt, *n.* An invention; a fiction; something feigned or imagined.

fig·ur·a·tion, fig·yə·rā′shən, *n.* The act of shaping into a particular figure; the resulting figure or shape; the act of representing figuratively; a figurative representation.

fig·ur·a·tive, fig′yər·ə·tiv, *a.* Involving a figure of speech; metaphorical, not literal; abounding in figures of speech; representing by means of a figure, emblem, or likeness, as in a drawing or sculpture; emblematic. **—fig·ur·a·tive·ly,** *adv.* **—fig·ur·a·tive·ness,** *n.*

fig·ure, fig′yər, *n.* The form of anything as expressed by the outline or contour; shape; the human shape or form; a pictorial representation of the human body or an object; appearance or impression made by a person; an emblem or symbol; a number symbol; value or amount stated in numbers; mathematical calculations; a pattern or design; movements in a dance or skating.**—cut a figure,** to appear to advantage or disadvantage.—*v.t.,* **fig·ured, fi·gur·ing.** To compute or calculate numerically; to make a figure or likeness of; to cover or adorn with figures or ornamental designs; to imagine or picture mentally; to represent by a figure of speech; to think about; consider; believe.—*v.i.* To be a prominent personage; to compute; to make a figure.**—figure out,** to solve. **—fig·ure·less,** *a.* **—fig·ur·er,** *n.*

fig·ured, fig′yərd, fig′ūrd, *a.* Formed or shaped; adorned with a pattern or design. *Mus.* Having the accompanying chords indicated.

fig·ure·head, fig′yər·hed, *n.* A person who is nominally the head of a society, company, or group, but has no real authority or responsibility; an ornamental or carved figure placed over the prow of a ship.

fig·ure of speech, *n.* A mode of expression, as a simile or metaphor, where words are used in a nonliteral or unusual sense for special effects.

fig·ur·ine, fig·yə·rēn′, *n.* A small ornamental figure of china, pottery, or metalwork; a statuette.

fil·a·ment, fil′ə·mənt, *n.* A very fine thread or fiber; the threadlike wire enclosed in an electric lamp that is heated to incandescence by the passage of electric current. *Electron.* The direct or indirect heater of the cathode of an electron tube. *Bot.* The part of a stamen, supporting the anther. **—fil·a·men·ta·ry**, *a.* **—fil·a·ment·ed,** *a.* **—fil·a·men·tous,** *a.*

filch, filch, *v.t.* To steal, esp. something of little value; to pilfer. **—filch·er,** *n.*

file, fīl, *n.* A tool having sharp ridges across its surface, for cutting, abrading, and smoothing metal, wood, and other materials.—*v.t.,* **filed, fi·ling.** To rub smooth, reduce, or cut with a file or as with a file.

file, fīl, *n.* A cabinet or a folder, in which papers are arranged or classified for convenient reference; a collection of papers or records systematically arranged; a line of persons or things arranged one behind another; a line of men standing or marching one behind the other in a military formation; one of the vertical rows of squares on a chessboard running directly from player to player.—*v.t.,* **filed, fi·ling.** To place in a file; to arrange, as papers or records, methodically for preservation or reference; to send, as copy or a news story, to a newspaper.—*v.i.* To march or move in file; to register as a candidate.**—on file,** on or in a file for convenient reference.

fi·let, fi·lā′, fil′ā, *n.* A boneless piece of lean meat or fish, sometimes rolled and tied for roasting. Also **fil·let.**—*v.t.* To slice, as meat or fish, into filets. Also **fil·let.**

fi·let mi·gnon, fi·lā′ min·yon′, *Fr.* fē·le mē·nyan′, *n. pl.,* **fi·lets mi·gnons.** A small, boneless, and lean steak, cut from the tenderloin of beef.

fil·i·al, fil′ē·əl, *a.* Pertaining to or assuming the relation of a son or daughter; befitting a child in relation to his parents; of or designating a generation following the parental. **—fil·i·al·ly,** *adv.*

fil·i·bus·ter, fil′ə·bəs·tər, *n.* An effort by a minority group of legislators to defeat or delay legislation by obstructionist tactics, esp. by long speeches.—*v.i.* To defeat or delay legislation by obstructionist tactics. —*v.t.* To block, as legislation, by obstructionist tactics.

fil·i·gree, fil′ə·grē, *n.* Ornamental work of fine wire, esp. jewelers' work of gold or silver in a delicate, lacy design; intricate ornamental openwork; anything very delicate or fanciful.—*a.* Composed of or resembling filigree.—*v.t.,* **-greed, -gree·ing.** To adorn with or form into filigree.—Also **fil·a·gree, fil·la·gree.**

fil·ings, fī′lingz, *n. pl.* Particles, esp. metal, removed by a file.

fill, fil, *v.t.* To make full; put as much as can be held into; complete by inserting written matter, usu. with *in, out,* or *up;* to close or repair, as a hole, crack, or cavity; furnish with an occupant or incumbent; to occupy to the full capacity; to hold or perform the duties of, as an office or position; satisfy, as food does; meet satisfactorily, as requirements; execute, as a business order; make up or compound, as a medical prescription; distend, as the wind does a sail; raise the level of, as an area of ground, with earth and rocks. —*v.i.* To become full; to become distended; to fill a cup or other receptacle.**—fill up,** to make or become completely full.—*n.* A full supply or desired amount: as, one's *fill* of food or sleep; a quantity sufficient to fill something: as, a single *filling* or charge; a mass of earth and stones used to level an area of ground.**—fill the bill,** *informal:* to satisfy the requirements of the case.**—fill one's shoes,** *informal:* to assume another's position and responsibilities.

fill·er, fil′ər, *n.* One who or that which fills; a material used to fill something; a liquid or paste used to stop up cracks or pores, as in preparing a surface for painting; a brief item of copy used to fill a vacant space in a newspaper or magazine.

fil·let, fil′it, *n.* A narrow band of ribbon worn around the head as a decoration; any narrow strip of any-

thing.—*v.t.* To bind or adorn with or as with a fillet.

fill-in, fil′in′, *n.* A person or thing serving as a replacement; a brief review of essential information.

fill·ing, fil′ing, *n.* The act of one who or that which fills; a making or becoming full; that which is put in to fill something.

fill·ing sta·tion, *n.* Gas station.

fil·lip, fil′əp, *v.t.* To flick smartly with the finger by first curling the finger tightly against the thumb, then quickly straightening the finger; to arouse or urge into action.—*n.* The fillip movement; a tap or strike made with a fillip; something which sharply rouses or stimulates.

fil·ly, fil′ē, *n. pl.,* **-lies.** A young female horse. *Informal.* A girl, esp. a spirited one.

film, film, *n.* A thin skin; a thin coating or overlay; a delicate network of fine threads; a haze or blur; transparent; flexible material in strips or sheets covered with an emulsion which is sensitive to light, used in taking photographs or making motion pictures; a motion picture; motion pictures collectively.—*v.t.* To coat or cover with or as with a film; to make a motion picture of.—*v.i.* To become covered by a film; to be suitable for filming; to make a motion picture.

film·strip, film′strip, *n.* A series of individual still pictures on a length of film, to be projected on a screen.

film·y, fil′mē, *a.,* **-i·er, -i·est.** Covered with a film; blurry; hazy; of or like a film; gauzy. **—film·i·ness,** *n.*

fil·ter, fil′tər, *n.* Any contrivance or porous substance, as felt, paper, charcoal, or sand, through which liquid or gas is passed to remove impurities or other matter; an apparatus which regulates or discriminates among sound waves, light waves, electrical currents, etc.—*v.t.* To pass, as air, through a filter in order to strain or purify; to remove by the action of a filter; to act as a filter for.—*v.i.* To pass through or as through a filter.

filth, filth, *n.* Foul matter; disgusting dirt; moral corruption; vulgar language; obscenity. **—filth·i·ness,** *n.* **—filth·y,** fil′thē, *a.,* **-i·er, -i·est.**

fin, fin, *n.* A winglike or paddlelike organ attached to the body of fishes and certain other aquatic animals; anything resembling a fin. *Informal.* A five-dollar bill; the arm or hand.—*v.t.,* **finned, fin·ning.** To remove the fins from.—*v.i.* To move the fins, esp. violently. **—fin·less,** *a.* **—fin·like,** *a.*

fi·na·gle, fi·nā′gəl, *v.t.,* **-gled, -gling.** To acquire through intrigue; to wangle.—*v.i.* To use intrigue or deceit to achieve one's ends. **—fi·na·gler,** *n.*

fi·nal, fīn′əl, *a.* Coming at the end; last in place, order or time; the ultimate; conclusive or decisive; relating to purpose.—*n.* Something final. *Usu. pl.* The last and decisive game, match, or examination, etc.

fi·na·le, fi·nal′ē, fi·nä′lē, *n.* The final section of a musical composition; final scene of a play, etc.; the concluding part; end.

fi·nal·ist, fīn′ə·list, *n.* One who is entitled to take part in a final, decisive trial or round.

fi·nal·i·ty, fi·nal′i·tē, *n. pl.,* **-ties.** The state or fact of being final, concluded, or irrevocable; something that is final, as an act or utterance.

fi·nal·ize, fīn′ə·līz, *v.t.,* **-ized, -iz·ing.** To make final; arrange in final form.

fi·nal·ly, fīn′ə·lē, *adv.* At the final point; in the end; conclusively or decisively.

fi·nance, fi·nans′, fī′nans, *n.* The management of affairs, esp. large sums of money, etc., in government or corporations; *pl.,* income or resources of corporations, governments, or individuals.—*v.t.,* **-nanced, -nanc·ing.** To manage the finances of; provide capital for. **—fi·nan·cial,** fi·nan′shəl, *a.* **—fi·nan·cial·ly,** *adv.*

fin·an·cier, fin·ən·sēr′, fī·nən·sēr′, *n.* One occupied with or skilled in financial affairs or operations.

finch, finch, *n.* Any of numerous small, seed-eating

songbirds, including the buntings, sparrows, goldfinches, and canaries.

find, find, *v.t.,* **found, find·ing.** To come upon by chance: meet with; discover; to ascertain by study or calculation; recover, as something lost; to recover the use of; come to have; arrive at, as a destination; to provide or furnish; to determine after judicial inquiry. —*v.i.* To determine an issue after judicial inquiry; render a verdict.—*n.* An act of finding; something found.—**find one·self,** to discover one's true abilities or vocation.—**find out,** to discover or learn; to detect the true character or identity of.

find·er, fīn/dər, *n.* One who or that which finds.

find·ing, fīn/ding, *n.* Discovery; something found; a decision or verdict after judicial inquiry.

fine, fīn, *a.,* **fin·er, fin·est.** Of very high grade or quality; free from imperfections; choice, excellent; consisting of minute particles; very thin or slender; sharp, as a tool; delicate in texture; highly skilled; polished or refined; clear or bright, as weather; showy or smart; good looking; having a high proportion of pure metal.—*adv. Informal.* Excellently; very well. —**fine·ly,** *adv.* —**fine·ness,** *n.*

fine, fīn, *n.* A payment exacted as punishment.—*v.t.,* **fined, fin·ing.** To require money as part punishment. —**in fine,** in short; finally.

fine art, *n. pl.,* **fine arts.** *Usu. pl.* Art concerned with beauty, esp. painting, drawing, sculpture, architecture.

fin·er·y, fī/nə·rē, *n. pl.,* **-ies.** Fine clothes, jewels, or other ornamentation.

fi·nesse, fi·nes/, *n.* Delicacy of execution; artful management, as of a difficult situation requiring diplomatic handling; strategy; stratagem.—*v.i.,* **fi·nessed, fi·nes·sing.** To make a finesse at cards; use finesse. —*v.t.* To accomplish by finesse.

fin·ger, fing/gər, *n.* Any of the members of the hand, usu. excluding the thumb; the part of a glove made to fit the finger; something resembling a finger in shape or use; the width of a finger; the length of a finger. —*v.t.* To touch with the fingers; handle; to pilfer.—*v.i.* To touch or handle something with the fingers.

fin·ger·bowl, fing/gər·bōl, *n.* A bowl at a dining table to hold water for rinsing the fingers after eating.

fin·ger·ing, fing/gər·ing, *n.* The act of touching lightly or handling.

fin·ger·nail, fing/gər·nāl, *n.* The hard substance at the upper surface of the end of each finger.

fin·ger·print, fing/gər·print, *n.* An impression of the markings of the last joint of the thumb or a finger.—*v.t.* To take the fingerprints of.

fin·i·al, fin/ē·əl, fī/nē·əl, *n.* The ornamental termination of a pinnacle, canopy, gable, piece of furniture.

fin·i·cal, fin/i·kəl, *a.* Finicky; affectedly fastidious. —**fin·i·cal·ly,** *adv.*

fin·ick·y, fin/ə·kē, *a.* Unduly particular; fussy. Also **fin·ick·ing.**

fin·is, fin/is, fī/nis, *n. pl.,* **-is·es.** The end.

fin·ish, fin/ish, *v.t.* To bring to an end; to arrive at the end of; to use up; to perfect; to polish to a high degree; to prepare the surface of. *Informal.* To kill; defeat.—*v.i.* To complete a task; terminate.—*n.* The end; perfection, as of detail, style, manner; that which finishes; the surface quality of paint, a cloth, etc. —**fin·ished,** *a.* —**fin·ish·er,** *n.*

fin·ish·ing school, *n.* A private school which instructs young women in the social graces.

fi·nite, fī/nīt, *a.* Having bounds or limits; not infinite or infinitesimal.—*n.* That which is finite. —**fi·nite·ly,** *adv.* —**fi·nite·ness,** *n.*

fink, fingk, *n. Informal.* A strikebreaker; an informer; an undesirable person.

fir, fer, *n.* Any of several trees of the pine family; their wood.

fire, fīr, *n.* Rapid combustion in which a substance ignites and burns, producing heat, light, and flame; fuel in combustion; a firelike flash or spark; the discharge of firearms; anything that suggests fire; ardor; liveliness; heat; fever; severe criticism; harsh ordeal.—*v.t.* **fired, fir·ing.** To kindle; to add fuel to; to heat, as for baking or drying; to inflame or irritate; to animate; to cause to explode; to discharge, as a gun. *Informal.* To hurl; to discharge from a job.—*v.i.* To take fire; to explode or shoot.—**on fire,** ignited; burning; ardent.—**fir·er,** *n.*

fire·arm, fīr/ärm, *n.* A weapon, usu. small, whose shot is charged by gunpowder.

fire·ball, fīr/bôl, *n.* An incandescent meteor; lightning shaped like a ball; the center of a nuclear explosion. *Informal.* A very energetic person.

fire·brand, fīr/brand, *n.* A piece of burning wood; an agitator.

fire·bug, fīr/bəg, *n. Informal.* A pyromaniac.

fire·crack·er, fīr/krak·ər, *n.* A paper cylinder enclosing an explosive and a fuse.

fire en·gine, *n.* A truck equipped to extinguish fires.

fire es·cape, *n.* A stairway, ladder, etc., enabling the occupants of a building to escape during a fire.

fire ex·tin·guish·er, *n.* A portable device which is used to extinguish fires.

fire·fight·er, fīr/fī·tər, *n.* A person who fights fires; a fireman.

fire·fly, fīr/flī, *n. pl.,* **-flies.** Any winged insect which gives off light, esp. the lightning bug.

fire·man, fīr/mən, *n. pl.,* **-men.** A man who fights fires; a man who tends fires in a furnace or steam engine.

fire·place, fīr/plās, *n.* The lower part of a chimney which opens into a room and in which fuel is burned; a hearth.

fire·plug, fīr/pləg, *n.* A hydrant which provides water for extinguishing fires.

fire·pow·er, fīr/pow·ər, *n.* The volume of projectiles that can be delivered on a specific target.

fire·proof, fīr/proof, *a.* Almost totally resistant to fire; incombustible.—*v.t.* To make fireproof.

fire·side, fīr/sīd, *n.* The side of the fireplace; the hearth; home.

fire·trap, fīr/trap, *n.* A building which is very flammable, or difficult to escape from in case of fire.

fire·wa·ter, fīr/wô·tər, fīr/wot·ər, *n.* Strong alcoholic drink.

fire·wood, fīr/wûd, *n.* Wood for fuel.

fire·works, fīr/wərks, *n. pl.* Firecrackers or other devices for producing brilliant displays of light or loud noise, as on the Fourth of July; a pyrotechnic display.

fir·ing squad, fīr/ing, *n.* A military squad assigned to carry out an execution by shooting; a similar squad assigned to fire a salvo at the burial of a person receiving military honors.

firm, fərm, *n.* A partnership for carrying on a business; a commercial concern.

firm, fərm, *a.* Comparatively solid, stiff, or unyielding under pressure; securely held in place or immovable; fixed; steady; not fluctuating; steadfast; showing resoluteness or determination.—*v.t., v.i.* To make or become firm.—*adv.* Fixedly; resolutely. —**firm·ly,** *adv.* —**firm·ness,** *n.*

fir·ma·ment, fər/mə·mənt, *n.* The expanse of the heavens; sky.

first, fərst, *a.* Being before all others; the ordinal of one. *Mus.* Highest in pitch or most prominent.—*adv.* Before all others or anything else; in the first place; before some other thing or action; in preference to something else; for the first time.—*n.* That which is before all others in time, order, rank, or importance; the beginning; the winning position in a competition.

first aid, *n.* Emergency treatment given to an injured or ill person before regular medical services can be obtained.

first base, *n. Baseball.* The base that is to be reached first by a base runner; the position of the player defending that base.

first-born, fərst/bôrn/, *a.* Of a child; eldest.—*n.* The first-born child.

first class, *n.* The first, best, or highest rank, level, or grade of something, such as accommodations on an airplane, train, or steamship. —**first-class,** *a., adv.*

first-hand, first-hand, fərst′hand′, *a., adv.* From the point of origin; direct.

first la•dy, *n. (Often cap.)* The wife of the U.S. president.

first•ling, fərst′ling, *n.* The first of its kind; the first product or result, esp. the first offspring of an animal.

first•ly, fərst′lē, *adv.* In the first place.

first per•son, *n.* The forms of pronouns and verbs which refer to the speaker or writer, such as *I, we, am.*

first-rate, fərst′rāt′, *a.* Of the first rate or class; excellent; very good.—*adv. Informal.* Excellently; very well.

first ser•geant, *n.* A senior noncommissioned officer, usu. assisting in administration of a company-sized unit.

first-string, fərst′string′, *a.* First-rate; regular, as against substitute.

fis•cal, fis′kəl, *a.* Financial; pertaining to the public treasury or public revenues. —**fis•cal•ly,** *adv.*

fish, fish, *n. pl.,* **fish, fish•es.** A cold-blooded, completely aquatic vertebrate, having an elongated body, often covered with scales and with fins and gills; loosely, any animal resembling a fish or living in water; fish used as food; the constellation, Pisces. *Informal.* A person.—*v.i.* To catch or attempt to catch fish; to seek to obtain something indirectly.—*v.t.* To catch or attempt to catch as fish or the like; to try to catch fish in, as a stream; to draw as by fishing, often followed by *up* or *out.* —**fish•like,** *a.*

fish•er, fish′ər, *n.* A fisherman; a mammal related to the weasel.

fish•er•man, fish′ər•man, *n. pl.,* **-men.** One who fishes, for profit or pleasure; a fishing boat.

fish•er•y, fish′ə•rē, *n. pl.,* **-er•ies.** The occupation or industry of catching fish; a place where such an industry is carried on.

fish•hook, fish′hûk, *n.* A hook, usu. barbed, used for catching fish.

fish•ing, fish′ing, *n.* The catching of fish as an occupation or sport.—*a.*

fish sto•ry, *n. Informal.* An extravagant cr incredible story or tale.

fish•wife, fish′wīf, *n. pl.,* **-wives.** A woman who sells fish; a vulgar, abusive woman.

fish•y, fish′ē, *a.,* **-i•er, -i•est.** Of, like, or full of fish. *Informal.* Dubious.

fis•sile, fis′əl, *a.* Capable of being split; capable of nuclear fission.

fis•sion, fish′ən, *n.* The act of splitting into parts by natural division, or in the process of releasing nuclear energy.

fis•sure, fish′ər, *n.* A cleft; a crack; a narrow opening; a splitting apart.—*v.t., v.i.,* **-sured, sur•ing.** To cleave or make a fissure in.

fist, fist, *n.* The hand closed tightly; a grasp or hold. *Print.* The index sign. *Informal.* The hand or handwriting.

fist•ic, fis′tik, *a.* Of or pertaining to boxing.

fist•i•cuff, fis′tə•kəf, *n.* A cuff or blow with the fists; *pl.,* combat with the fists.

fit, fit, *n.* An attack of a disease marked by loss of consciousness or by convulsions; an uncontrollable attack of any physical or emotional disturbance; an intensive but brief occurrence of something.

fit, fit, *a.,* **fit•ter, fit•test.** Well adapted or suited; worthy; proper or right; qualified; in good physical condition.—*v.t.,* **fit•ted** or **fit, fit•ting.** To suit or be proper for; to be of the right size or shape for; to alter or adjust to a purpose or to the proper size; to put into place exactly; to render qualified; prepare; supply; to furnish.—*v.i.* To be of the right size or shape; to

belong, go with, or be suitable.—*n.* The condition of fitting or being fitted; the manner in which a thing fits; something that fits well. —**fit•ly,** *adv.* —**fit•ness,** *n.* —**fit•ter,** *n.*

fit•ful, fit′fəl, *a.* Occurring in starts and stops; irregular. —**fit•ful•ly,** *adv.* —**fit•ful•ness,** *n.*

fit•ting, fit′ing, *n.* The act of one who or that which fits; the act of trying on clothes for the purpose of alteration; *pl.,* furnishings or fixtures.—*a.* Fit or appropriate; proper. —**fit•ting•ly,** *adv.* —**fit•ting•ness,** *n.*

five, fīv, *a.* One more than four in number.—*n.* The cardinal number between four and six; a symbol representing this number; a set of five persons or things.—**five•fold,** *a.*

five-and-ten, fīv′ən•ten′, *n.* A store selling mainly inexpensive items; a dime store.

fix, fiks, *v.t.* To make fast, firm, or stable; to place or attach permanently; to implant firmly, as principles; to settle definitely; to determine; to direct, as the eyes, steadily; to look at with a steady gaze; to set or make rigid; to repair; to treat to keep from changing or fading; to put in order; adjust; to provide or supply; to prepare, as a meal. *Informal.* To influence an event or decision, esp. by bribery; to castrate or spay, as a pet; to punish or get revenge on.—*v.i.* To become fixed. —*n. Informal.* An inextricable position; a predicament; the position of an aircraft or a ship as determined by bearings taken on two or more known points; an act of predetermining a result, influencing a decision, etc., esp. by bribery or collusion; an injection of a narcotic, esp. heroin. —**fix•a•ble,** *a.* —**fixed,** *a.* —**fix•ed•ly,** fiks′ed•lē, *adv.* —**fix•er,** *n.*

fix•a•tion, fik•sā′shən, *n.* The act of fixing or the state of being fixed; an attaching or arresting of development at an early stage; any morbid preoccupation.

fix•a•tive, fik′sə•tiv, *a.* Making fixed or permanent. —*n.* A fixative substance.

fix•ings, fik′singz, *n. pl. Informal.* Trimmings.

fix•i•ty, fik′sə•tē, *n. pl.,* **-ties.** The state or quality of being fixed; something fixed or stable.

fix•ture, fiks′chər, *n.* Something securely fixed in position; a person or thing long established in the same place or position.

fiz•zle, fiz′əl, *v.i.,* **-zled, -zling.** To make a hissing or sputtering sound. *Informal.* To fail ignominiously.—*n.* A hissing or sputtering sound. *Informal.* A fiasco.

fiz•zy, fiz′ē, *a.,* **-zi•er, -zi•est.** Effervescent; bubbly.

flab•ber•gast, flab′ər•gast, *v.t.* To overcome with surprise; astound.

flab•by, flab′ē, *a.,* **-bi•er, -bi•est.** Hanging loosely or limply; flaccid; lacking firmness; feeble. —**flab•bi•ly,** *adv.* —**flab•bi•ness,** *n.*

flac•cid, flak′sid, fla′səd, *a.* Soft and limp; weak.

flag, flag, *v.i.,* **flagged, flag•ging.** To decline in vigor, interest, or activity; to become limp; droop.

flag, flag, *n.* A piece of cloth of varying size, shape, design, and color, which stands for a country, a club, etc.; something resembling a flag.—*v.t.,* **flagged, flag•ging.** To place a flag or flags over or on; decorate with flags; to signal or warn with or as with a flag.

flag, flag, *n.* Any of various plants with long, sword-shaped leaves, as the purple iris.

flag, flag, *n.* A flagstone.—*v.t.,* **flagged, flag•ging.** To pave with flags.

flag•el•lant, flaj′ə•lənt, flə•jel′ənt, *n.* One who whips, esp. one who whips himself or is whipped by another.

flag•el•late, flaj′ə•lāt, *v.t.,* **-lat•ed, -lat•ing.** To whip; to scourge. —**flag•el•la•tion,** flag•ə•lā′shən, *n.*

flag•ging, flag′ing, *n.* Flagstones collectively; a pavement of flagstones.

fla•gi•tious, flə•jish′əs, *a.* Shamefully vicious; infamous. —**fla•gi•tious•ly,** *adv.*

flag of•fic•er, *n.* An admiral.

---

a- hat, fāte, fāre, fäther; **e-** met, mē; **i-** pin, pīne; **o-** not, nōte, ôrb, moove (move), boy, pownd; **u-** cūbe, bûll, tûk (took); **ch-** chin; **th-** thick, ŧhen; **zh-** vizhon (vision); **ə-** əgo, takən, pencəl, lemən, bərd (bird).

flag·on, flag′ən, *n.* A large bottle for wines or liquors; a vessel, esp. with a handle, spout, and lid, for holding and carrying liquids.

flag·pole, flag′pōl, *n.* The pole or staff on which a flag is displayed. Also **flag·staff.**

flag·rank, *n.* Any naval rank above captain.

fla·grant, flā′grənt, *a.* Notorious or scandalous. —**fla·grant·ly,** *adv.*

flag·ship, flag′ship, *n.* The ship bearing the flag officer and displaying his flag.

flag·stone, flag′stōn, *n.* A flat slab of stone for paving.

flag-wav·ing, flag′wā·ving, *n.* An appeal to patriotism.

flail, flāl, *n.* An instrument for threshing grain by hand.—*v.t.* To strike with or as with a flail; to thrash.

flair, flār, *n.* Natural skill; innate talent; keen perception.

flak, flak, *n.* Anti-aircraft fire.

flake, flāk, *n.* A small, loosely cohering piece or mass, as of falling snow; a scale or a small, flat piece.—*v.i., v.t.,* **flaked, flak·ing.** To fall in, peel off in, cover with, break or form into, or remove in flakes.

flak·y, flā′kē, *a.,* **-i·er, -i·est.** Consisting of, or easily formed into flakes. *Informal.* Foolish; crazy. —**flak·i·ness,** *n.*

flam·boy·ant, flam·boy′ənt, *a.* Showily dashing; florid or ornate; marked by wavy, flamelike lines and curves. —**flam·boy·ance, flam·boy·an·cy,** *n.* —**flam·boy·ant·ly,** *adv.*

flame, flām, *n.* Burning vapor or gas rising from a fire in bright, hot gleams; a single tongue of light from a fire; a blaze; anything suggesting a flame, as in brilliance or color; ardor. *Informal.* A sweetheart.—*v.i.,* **flamed, flam·ing.** To send out a flame; to shine with flamelike brilliance; glow; to become or act excited or enraged. —**flam·ing,** *a.* —**flam·ing·ly,** *adv.*

flame·throw·er, flām′thrō·ər, *n.* A weapon which shoots a stream of flaming liquid.

flam·ma·ble, flam′ə·bəl, *a.* Burnable; easily ignited.

flange, flanj, *n.* A projecting rim, collar, or ridge, intended to strengthen a part, attach it, guide it, etc.—*v.i., v.t.* To form, project like, or furnish with a flange.

flank, flangk, *n.* The side of an animal or person, between the ribs and the hip; a cut of meat or flesh from this part; the side of anything.—*v.t.* To stand or be at the side of; to command or attack the side of; to pass around the flank of.—*v.i.* To hold a position at the side. —**flank·er,** *n.*

flan·nel·ette, flan·nel·et, flan·ə·let′, *n.* A light cotton flannel having a nap on one side.

flap, flap, *v.t.,* **flapped, flap·ping.** To move, as wings, up and down; to cause to swing or sway loosely, esp. with noise. *Informal.* To toss, fold, or shut roughly or noisily; to strike with something broad and flexible. —*v.i.* To swing or sway loosely; to flutter.—*n.* Anything broad and flexible that hangs loose or is attached by one movable end or side; a flapping motion; the noise caused by flapping; a broad flat piece of any material; a control surface of a plane used to increase the lift or drag of the airplane. *Informal.* A state of confusion.

flap·jack, flap′jak, *n.* A griddlecake.

flare, flār, *v.i.,* **flared, flar·ing.** To burn with a sudden or unsteady flame; to spread outward like the side of a bell; to burst in sudden, fierce activity or passion, usu. with *up* or *out.*—*v.t.* To cause to flare; to signal by flares of light.—*n.* An unsteady or swaying flame or light; a sudden burst of flame; a blaze of fire or light used to signal; a sudden burst, as of zeal or temper; glare; a gradual spreading outward in form. —**flar·ing,** *a.*

flare-up, flār′əp, *n.* A sudden bursting into flame; an abrupt outburst of passion, violence, etc.

flash, flash, *n.* A sudden, transitory outburst of flame or light; a gleam; an instant; a sudden brief outburst, as of joy or wit; ostentatious display; a brief initial news report giving a hurried summary.—*a.* Of short duration or sudden origin; showy; gaudy.—*v.i.* To break forth into sudden flame or light, esp. intermittently; to burst suddenly into view; to shine or gleam; to move suddenly or very quickly.—*v.t.* To emit as fire or light, in sudden flashes; to cause to flash; to communicate by or as by flashes; to convey by instantaneous communication, as by telegraph. *Informal.* To display abruptly or ostentatiously. —**flash·er,** *n.*

flash·back, flash′bak, *n.* A technique which shows previous action, thoughts, or events alongside the existing action.

flash lamp, *n.* A device producing a momentary light sufficiently bright for taking photographs. Also **flash bulb.**

flash·light, flash′līt, *n.* A device for giving flashes of light for signaling, as in a lighthouse; a hand-held electric light powered by batteries.

flash·y, flash′ē, *a.,* **-i·er, -i·est.** Sparkling or brilliant, esp. in a superficial way or for the moment; showy; gaudy. —**flash·i·ly,** *adv.* —**flash·i·ness,** *n.*

flask, flask, flåsk, *n.* A type of bottle; a narrow-necked rounded glass vessel; a small, flattened container, as of metal.

flat, flat, *a.* Horizontal and level; even; lying with one surface completely against something; shallow; positive or absolute; without interest; dull; lifeless; tasteless or stale; deflated; having no shine or gloss; having no depth; monotonous; of times, exact; below the natural or true pitch. *Gram.* Derived without change in form.—*adv.* In a flat manner; precisely; totally; below the proper pitch. Also **flat·ly.**—*n.* Something flat; the flat part of anything; a plain. *Informal.* A deflated tire; a suite of rooms on one floor of a building or apartment; a shoal or marsh.—*v.t., v.i.,* **flat·ted, flat·ting.** To make or become flat. —**flat·ness,** *n.*

flat·car, flat′kär, *n.* A railroad freight car with no sides or roof.

flat·foot, flat′fůt, *n.* A condition in which the arch of the foot is flattened; a human foot so formed. *Informal.* A policeman.

flat-foot·ed, flat′fůt·id, *a.* Having flat feet. *Informal.* Plain and forthright; resolute; unprepared.—*adv.* Also **flat-foot·ed·ly,** *adv.* —**flat-foot·ed·ness,** *n.*

flat·ten, flat′ən, *v.t., v.i.* To make or become flat. —**flat·ten·er,** *n.*

flat·ter, flat′ər, *v.t.* To praise excessively and usu. insincerely; to promote one's interests by praising; to make more attractive than what is true.—*v.i.* To practice flattery. —**flat·ter·er,** *n.* —**flat·ter·ing·ly,** *adv.*

flat·ter·y, flat′ə·rē, *n. pl.,* **-ies.** The act of flattering; extravagant, usu. insincere, praise.

flat·u·lent, flach′ə·lənt, *a.* Affected with or causing gas in the alimentary canal; puffy; pompous; inane. —**flat·u·lence, flat·u·len·cy,** *n.* —**flat·u·lent·ly,** *adv.*

flat·ware, flat′wār, *n.* Table utensils, esp. those containing silver; dishes that are flat.

flaunt, flônt, *v.i., v.t.* To make a brazen display; to wave conspicuously.—*n.* The act of flaunting. —**flaunt·er,** *n.* —**flaunt·ing·ly,** *adv.* —**flaunt·y,** *a.,* **-i·er, -i·est.**

flau·tist, flô′tist, flow′tist, *n.* A flutist.

fla·vor, flā′vər, *n.* Taste; the quality of any substance which affects the taste; flavoring; a characteristic quality of something.—*v.t.* To give flavor or some quality to. —**fla·vored,** *a.* —**fla·vor·less,** *a.*

fla·vor·ing, flā′vər·ing, *n.* Any substance used for imparting or heightening flavor; seasoning.

flaw, flô, *n.* Any imperfection; a defect; a fault; a crack or fissure.—*v.t.* To make a flaw in.—*v.i.* To become defective or cracked. —**flaw·less,** *a.*

flax, flaks, *n.* A slender, erect annual plant with blue flowers grown for its fiber; the fiber of this plant used in the manufacture of linen thread.

flax·en, flak′sən, *a.* Made of flax; colored like flax; fair; pale yellow.

flax·seed, flaks′sēd, *n.* Linseed.

flay, flā, v.t. To skin; to strip off the skin or outer layer of, esp. by whipping; to criticize ruthlessly; to cheat; fleece.

flea, flē, n. Any of many small, wingless, blood-sucking insects.

flea-bit·ten, flē′bit·ən, a. Bitten or covered by fleas. *Informal.* Run-down.

flea mar·ket, n. An outdoor market where cheap or secondhand items are for sale.

fleck, flek, n. A spot; a dapple; a little bit.—v.t. To spot; to streak.

flec·tion, flek′shən, n. The act of bending; a curved or bowed part.

fledge, flej, v.i., **fledged, fledg·ing.** Of a young bird, to acquire the feathers necessary for flight.—v.t. To bring up, as a young bird, until able to fly; to furnish with feathers.

fledg·ling, flej′ling, n. A young bird just fledged; an inexperienced person.

flee, flē, v.i., **fled, flee·ing.** To run away; take flight; depart hastily; to move swiftly.—v.t. To run away from, as a place or person.

fleece, flēs, n. The coat of wool that covers a sheep or some similar animal; the wool shorn from a sheep at one time; something resembling a fleece; a soft, deep-piled fabric.—v.t., **fleeced, fleec·ing.** To cut the fleece from; to strip of money or belongings; victimize; swindle. —**fleeced,** a.

fleec·y, flē′sē, a., **-i·er, -i·est.** Covered with, made of, or similar to fleece; fluffy or soft. —**fleec·i·ness,** n.

fleet, flēt, a. Swift; nimble.—v.i. To fly or move swiftly. —**fleet·ly,** adv.

fleet, flēt, n. A unit of armed vessels; any group of ships or boats sailing in company; a group of vehicles owned or operated as a unit.

fleet·ing, flē′ting, a. Passing rapidly; transitory. —**fleet·ing·ly,** adv. —**fleet·ing·ness,** n.

flesh, flesh, n. The soft substance of an animal body, consisting mainly of muscle and fat; such substance considered as food, esp. muscle tissue; meat; the body; man's physical or animal nature; mankind; living creatures in general; kindred or family; the soft, pulpy portion of a fruit or vegetable; the surface of an animal body; a slightly yellowish, pinkish-white color. —v.t. To initiate into battle, bloodshed, or the taste of flesh.

flesh·ly, flesh′lē, a., **-li·er, -li·est.** Of or pertaining to the flesh or body; corporeal; sensual or lustful.

flesh·pots, flesh′pots, n. pl. The comforts and pleasures of high living.

flesh·y, flesh′ē, a., **-i·er, -i·est.** Having much flesh; plump; fat; of or like flesh; pulpy, as a fruit. —**flesh·i·ness,** n.

flex, fleks, v.t., v.i. To bend, as a leg; to contract, as a muscle.

flex·i·ble, flek′sə·bəl, a. Capable of being bent; easily bent or pliant; yielding to persuasion or argument; capable of being adapted or modified. —**flex·i·bil·i·ty,** flek·sə·bil′ə·tē, n. —**flex·i·bly,** adv.

flex·ion, flek′shən, n. Flection.

flex·or, flek′sər, n. A muscle which serves to bend a joint of the body.

flex·ure, flek′shər, n. A flexing or curving; a fold; a bent part or thing.

flib·ber·ti·gib·bet, flib′ər·tē·jib·it, n. A chattering or flighty person, usu. a woman.

flick, flik, n. A sudden light blow or stroke, as with a whip or a finger; the sound thus made; a sharp, quick movement. *Informal.* A motion picture.—v.t. To strike lightly with a whip or finger; to remove with such a stroke; to move with a sudden stroke or jerk.—v.i. To move with a snap jerk or jerks; to flutter.

flick·er, flik′ər, v.i. To burn, shine, or emit light unsteadily; to move in a wavering manner; to quiver or

vibrate; to flutter.—v.t. To make flicker.—n. An act of flickering; a wavering or flashing movement or light; a momentary occurrence. —**flick·er·ing,** a.

fli·er, flī′ər, n. Something that flies; an aviator; one who or that which moves with great speed. *Informal.* A flying leap; a risky financial venture; a handbill or circular.

flight, flīt, n. The act, manner, or power of flying; a trip by an airplane; the distance covered or the course pursued by a flying object; a number of things flying through the air together; swift movement; a soaring above or transcending of ordinary bounds; a series of steps or stairs between two adjacent landings; a fleeing; hasty departure. —**flight·less,** a.

flight·y, flī′tē, a., **-i·er, -i·est.** Moved by sudden and irrational whims; fickle; capricious; light-headed; mildly crazy. —**flight·i·ly,** adv. —**flight·i·ness,** n.

flim·flam, flim′flam, n. *Informal.* A trick or deception; trickery; mere nonsense.—v.t., **-flammed, -flam·ming.** To trick; delude; cheat.

flim·sy, flim′zē, a., **-si·er, -si·est.** Lacking in strength or solidity; light and thin; unconvincing; frail. —**flim·si·ly,** adv. —**flim·si·ness,** n.

flinch, flinch, v.i. To draw back from pain or danger; to wince.—n. The act of flinching. —**flinch·er,** n. —**flinch·ing·ly,** adv.

flin·ders, flin′dərz, n. pl. Fragments; splinters.

fling, fling, v.t., **flung, fling·ing.** To throw, cast off, or hurl, esp. with force; to put or move with impatience, violence, or suddenness; to discard; to throw to the ground; to energetically involve, as oneself, in a project.—v.i. To move with haste or violence; dash; to speak angrily or abusively, usu. followed by *out.* —n. An act of flinging; a period of irresponsible fun or indulgence. *Informal.* An attempt; a lively Scottish dance.

flint, flint, n. A hard fine-grained rock; a piece of this used with a piece of steel to strike a spark or start a fire; something very hard and obdurate.

flint glass, n. A brilliant, heavy glass used esp. for lenses.

flint·y, flin′tē, a., **-i·er, -i·est.** Consisting of flint; very hard; unmerciful; unyielding. —**flint·i·ness,** n.

flip, flip, v.t., **flipped, flip·ping.** To toss into the air, as a coin, with a sudden or snapping movement, esp. to cause to turn over; to flick; to turn over.—v.i. To make a snapping or flicking movement; to strike at something quickly or sharply; to move suddenly or jerkily. *Informal.* To react enthusiastically or violently.—n. An instance or act of flipping; a smart blow or flick; any of a number of sweetened mixed drinks.—a. Impertinent; flippant.

flip-flop, flip′flop, n. The noise or movement of something flapping loosely; a quick change of direction or opinion; a backward handspring.—v.i., **flopped, flop·ping.**

flip·pant, flip′ənt, a. Impertinent; showing undue levity; disrespectful. —**flip·pan·cy,** n. —**flip·pant·ly,** adv.

flip·per, flip′ər, n. A broad, flat limb, as of a seal, adapted for swimming.

flirt, flert, v.i. To play at love; to engage in coquetry; to toy with; to dart; to expose oneself carelessly.—v.t. To throw or move with a jerk; to fling suddenly.—n. Also **flirt·er.**

flir·ta·tion, flər·tā′shən, n. A brief, trifling, amorous adventure; a flirting. —**flir·ta·tious,** a.

flit, flit, v.i., **flit·ted, flit·ting.** To fly or dart; to move quickly and lightly; flutter; to pass rapidly.—n. A quick movement. —**flit·ter,** n.

flitch, flich, n. A salted and cured cut of meat from the side of a hog: a *flitch* of bacon.

float, flōt, v.i. To rest or move gently on the surface of a liquid; to be buoyant; to rest or move in a liquid; to drift; to rest or move in the air; to hover; to move

---

a- hat, fāte, fāre, fäther; **e-** met, mē; **i-** pin, pīne; **o-** not, nōte, ôrb, moove (move), boy, pownd; **u-** cūbe, bûll, tûk (took); **ch-** chin; **th-** thick, ᴛhen; **zh-** vizhon (vision); **ə-** ego, takən, pencəl, lemən, bərd (bird).

gracefully or effortlessly; to move randomly, from one person or thing to another.—*v.t.* To cause to float; to launch, as a company or scheme; to put on the market, as a stock or bond; to cover with water; irrigate.—*n.* Something that floats on a liquid surface or buoys up something on a liquid surface; a raft; a life preserver; a piece of cork on a baited fishline; a platform on wheels carrying a display as a part of a parade; a beverage with a scoop of ice cream floating in it. —**float·a·ble,** *a.*

float·a·tion, flō·tā′shen, *n.* Flotation.

float·er, flō′ter, *n.* One who or that which floats; one who floats about from one place or job to another; a drifter.

float·ing, flō′ting, *a.* Buoyed upon water or liquid; having little or no attachment; abnormally located or movable: a *floating* kidney; in circulation or used, as capital; not funded, as a debt.

floc·cu·lent, flok′ye·lent, *a.* Composed of a mass of loosely joined particles; similar to a tuft of wool. —**floc·cu·lence,** *n.*

flock, flok, *n.* A group of animals of the same kind, esp. sheep or birds, that are assembled, fed, or herded together; a large group of people; a Christian congregation in relation to its pastor.—*v.i.* To gather in flocks.

flock, flok, *n.* A lock or tuft of wool; wool or cotton waste used for stuffing mattresses and cushions; finely powdered wool or cloth.

floe, flō, *n.* A large mass of ice floating on the ocean; a floating section of a mass of ice.

flog, flog, flôg, *v.t.,* **flogged, flog·ging.** To beat or whip; to chastise severely. —**flog·ger,** *n.* —**flog·ging,** *n.*

flood, fled, *n.* A great flow of water; a body of water rising and overflowing the land; the flowing in of the tide; a great outpouring; superabundance. —**the Flood,** the Deluge.—*v.t.* To overflow; to inundate; to supply excessively.—*v.i.* To rise to or flow in a flood. —**flood·er,** *n.*

flood·gate, fled′gāt, *n.* A gate in a canal or a river to control the flow and depth of the water; anything used to control an outflow.

flood·light, fled′līt, *n.* A lamp that projects a bright, broad beam of light; the light.—*v.t.,* **-light·ed** or **-lit, -light·ing.** To illuminate by floodlight.

floor, flôr, flōr, *n.* The part of a building or room upon which one walks; a story of a building; a flat surface or bottom; a level area or platform with a special purpose; the minimum price paid or charged; the part of a legislative hall or the like from which the members speak; the right to speak in parliamentary procedure; the trading area of a stock and commodity exchange. —*v.t.* To furnish with a floor; to strike or push down level with the floor. *Informal.* To confound; overwhelm.

floor·ing, flôr′ing, flōr′ing, *n.* A floor; materials for floors.

floor lead·er, *n.* A legislator who manages the activities of his party on the floor of a federal or state legislature.

floor show, *n.* Singing, dancing, or other entertainment presented at a night club.

floor·walk·er, flôr′wô·ker, flōr′wô·ker, *n.* One who supervises sales personnel and directs customers in a retail store.

floo·zy, floo′zē, *n. pl.,* **-zies.** *Informal.* A slut; prostitute.

flop, flop, *v.i.,* **flopped, flop·ping.** To fall suddenly, heavily, or clumsily; drop or turn with a bump or thud; to flap. *Informal.* To yield or fail.—*v.t.* To drop or throw with a sudden bump or thud; to flap clumsily and heavily, as wings.—*n.* The act or sound of flopping. *Informal.* A failure. —**flop·per,** *n.*

flop·house, flop′hows, *n. Informal.* A cheap rundown rooming house or hotel.

flop·py, flop′ē, *a.,* **-pi·er, -pi·est.** Tending to flop. —**flop·pi·ly,** *adv.* —**flop·pi·ness,** *n.*

flo·ra, flôr′e, *n. pl.,* **-ras, -rae,** -rē. Plants, esp. those indigenous to any district, region, or period.

flo·ral, flô′rel, flō′rel, *a.* Of, pertaining to, or like flowers.

flo·res·cence, flō′res′ens, flō·res′ens, *n.* The act, state, or period of flowering. —**flo·res·cent,** *a.*

flo·ret, flôr′it, flōr′it, *n.* A small flower; a single small flower in the cluster forming the head of a composite plant.

flo·ri·cul·ture, flô′re·kel·cher, flō′re·kel·cher, *n.* The cultivation of flowers. —**flo·ri·cul·tur·al,** *a.* —**flo·ri·cul·tur·ist,** *n.*

flor·id, flôr′id, flōr′id, *a.* Having a flowery, overly ornate style; showy; ruddy; flushed with red. —**flo·rid·i·ty,** flô·rid′e·tē, flō·rid′e·tē, *n.* —**flor·id·ly,** *adv.* —**flor·id·ness,** *n.*

flo·rist, flôr′ist, flōr′ist, *n.* One who cultivates or sells flowers and ornamental plants.

floss, flôs, flos, *n.* Silk or silklike fiber in untwisted filaments; any silky matter; any similar soft thread. Also **floss silk.** —**floss·y,** *a.,* **-i·er, -i·est.**

flo·ta·tion, flō·tā′shen, *n.* The act or state of floating; the launching of a commercial venture or a loan.

flo·til·la, flō·til′e, *n.* A little fleet; a fleet of small vessels.

flot·sam, flot′sem, *n.* Ship's cargo or wreckage found floating on a body of water; a worthless or drifting person or thing.

flounce, flowns, *v.i.,* **flounced, flounc·ing.** To throw the body about, as in floundering or struggling; to go with an angry fling of the body.—*n.* A flouncing movement.

flounce, flowns, *n.* A gathered or pleated strip of fabric used to trim a skirt, dress, etc.—*v.t.,* **flounced, flounc·ing.** To decorate with a flounce or flounces.

floun·der, flown′der, *v.i.* To slip or stumble about; to proceed clumsily or confusedly.—*n.* A stumbling or floundering.

flour, flowr, *n.* The finely ground meal of grain, esp. wheat; the finer part of meal separated by sifting; the fine powder of any substance.—*v.t.* To convert into or cover with flour. —**flour·y,** *a.,* **-i·er, -i·est.**

flour·ish, fler′ish, *v.i.* To be in good health; to thrive; to be at the height of success or development; to add embellishments to handwriting; to make a display; to play a showy passage; to sound a fanfare.—*v.t.* To brandish or wave about; to display ostentatiously; to adorn with decorative work or designs.—*n.* A brandishing or waving; an ostentatious display; an embellishment in writing, or note language. *Mus.* An elaborate passage; a fanfare. —**flour·ish·ing,** *a.*

flout, flowt, *v.t.* To mock or insult; to jeer at; scoff at.—*v.i.* To behave with contempt.—*n.* A mock; an insult. —**flout·er,** *n.*

flow, flō, *v.i.* To move along in a stream; to circulate; to proceed continuously and smoothly; to fall or hang loosely at full length; to stream forth; to gush out; to rise and advance, as the tide; to overflow; be plentiful.—*v.t.* To cause to flow; to cover or flood with some liquid.—*n.* The act of flowing; any continuous movement; an outpouring; the rise of the tide; an overflowing; that which flows; the rate of flowing; the volume of that which flows; a current; stream.

flow·er, flow′er, *n.* The blossom or bloom of a plant; a plant cultivated for its floral beauty; the state of bloom: plants in *flower*; the best or finest part, product, time, etc.; the prime.—*v.i.* To produce flowers; to blossom; to come into full development; to flourish. —*v.t.* To cover or decorate with flowers. —**flow·ered,** *a.* —**flow·er·ing,** *a.*

flow·er·y, flow′er·ē, *a.* Full of flowers; richly embellished with ornate language. —**flow·er·i·ness,** *n.*

flu, floo, *n. Informal.* Influenza.

flub, fleb, *v.t., v.i.,* **flubbed, flub·bing.** *Informal.* To botch; blunder.

fluc·tu·ate, flek′choo·āt, *v.i.,* **-at·ed, -at·ing.** To shift irregularly; to move in waves; to be wavering or unsteady; to oscillate; to vacillate.—*v.t.* To cause to fluctuate. —**fluc·tu·a·tion,** flĕk·choo·ā/shən, *n.*

flue, floo, *n.* Any duct or passage for air, gases, or the like; a flue pipe.

flu·ent, floo/ənt, *a.* Flowing; having words at one's command and uttering them with facility; voluble. —**flu·en·cy,** *n.* —**flu·ent·ly,** *adv.*

fluff, flŭf, *n.* Light, downy particles, as of cotton; a downy mass. Something light and trivial.—*v.t.* To shake or pat until light and fluffy.—*v.i.* To become fluffy. —**fluff·i·ness,** *n.* —**fluff·y,** *a.,* -**i·er,** -**i·est.**

flu·id, floo/id, *a.* Capable of flowing; liquid; gaseous; not fixed or rigid.—*n.* A substance that flows, esp. any liquid or gas. —**flu·id·i·ty,** floo·id/ə·tē, *n.* —**flu·id·ly,** *adv.* —**flu·id·ness,** *n.*

flu·id ounce, *n.* A measure for liquids, equal to one-sixteenth pint in the U.S.

fluke, flook, *n.* The part of an anchor which catches in the ground; a barbed head, of a harpoon, arrow, or the like.

fluke, flook, *n.* An accidental advantage or stroke of luck; an accidentally successful stroke, as in golf or billiards. —**fluk·y,** *a.,* -**i·er,** -**i·est.**

flume, floom, *n.* A deep, narrow passage containing a mountain torrent; an artificial channel or trough for conducting water.

flum·mer·y, flŭm/ə·rē, *n. pl.,* -**mer·ies.** Oatmeal or flour boiled with water until thick; an empty compliment; nonsense.

flunk, flŭngk, *v.i. Informal.* To fail, as a student in a course or examination.—*v.t.* To fail in, as a course; give a failing grade to.—*n.* A flunking; a failure.

flun·ky, flun·key, flŭng/kē, *n. pl.,* -**kies.** A male servant in livery; a servile person.

flu·o·resce, floo·ə·res/, *v.i.,* -**resced, -resc·ing.** To exhibit fluorescence.

flu·o·res·cence, floo·ə·res/əns, *n.* The emission of light by certain substances as the result of absorption of radiations such as an electric discharge or an ultraviolet light. —**flu·o·res·cent,** *a.*

flu·o·res·cent lamp, *n.* An electric lamp containing a tube whose inside walls are coated with a fluorescent substance and which is filled with argon and mercury vapor.

fluor·i·da·tion, flûr·ə·dā/shən, *n.* The addition of a fluoride to drinking water, esp. to decrease tooth decay. —**fluor·i·date,** *v.t.,* -**dat·ed, -dat·ing.**

fluor·o·scope, flûr/ə·skōp, floo/ər·ə·skōp, *n.* An instrument for observing the internal structure of an opaque object, usu. by means of X rays.

flur·ry, flŭr/ē, *n. pl.,* -**ries.** A sudden gust of wind; a sudden, gusty rain or snowfall; sudden agitation, commotion, or bustle.—*v.t.,* -**ried, -ry·ing.** To agitate, confuse, or alarm.

flush, flŭsh, *v.t.* To wash out or purify, as a sewer or toilet, by means of a sudden gush of liquid; to redden; cause to blush; to animate or elate.—*v.i.* To flow with a rush; flow and spread suddenly; to become suffused with color; redden; blush.—*n.* A rushing or over-spreading flow, as of water; a blush; a rosy glow; freshness or vigor; a rush of emotion; elation; a feverish or overheated feeling.

flush, flŭsh, *a.* Even or level, as with a surface, aligned; well supplied, esp. with money; affluent; abundant or plentiful; suffused with a reddish color; blushing; full of vigor.—*v.t.* To make flush or even.—*adv.* Squarely; evenly.

flush, flŭsh, *v.t.* To cause, as birds, to leave protective cover.—*v.i.* To fly out or start up suddenly.

flush, flŭsh, *n.* In poker and certain other card games, a hand all of the same suit.

flus·ter, flŭs/tər, *v.t.* To agitate; to confuse; to befuddle.—*v.i.* To become or behave agitated or confused. —*n.* Agitation; confusion.

flute, floot, *n.* A musical woodwind instrument consisting of a hollow cylindrical tube with a series of fingerholes or keys, played by blowing across a hole near one end; a furrow or groove as ornamentation on a column, in a cloth, etc.—*v.i.,* **flut·ed, flut·ing.** To play on a flute; to produce flutelike sounds.—*v.t.* To utter in flutelike tones; to form flutes in a dress, column, etc. —**flut·ed,** *a.* —**flut·ist,** *n.*

flut·ing, floo/ting, *n.* Material or decorations made with flutes; act of making fluted material.

flut·ter, flŭt/ər, *v.i.* To wave or flap in the wind; to move or flap the wings rapidly; to move with quick vibrations or undulations; to move about with quick, erratic motions; to be agitated or upset; to beat irregularly, as the heart.—*v.t.* To cause to flutter; to agitate or throw into confusion.—*n.* Quick and irregular motion; agitation or confusion. —**flut·ter·er,** *n.* —**flut·ter·ing·ly,** *adv.* —**flut·ter·y,** *a.,* -**i·er,** -**i·est.**

flux, flŭks, *n.* The state of flowing; constant change or movement; a flow or discharge; the inward flow of the tide; an abnormal evacuation of fluid matter from the body.—*v.t., v.i.* To cause to flow; to make fluid; to fuse by melting; to flow.

flux·ion, flŭk/shən, *n.* A flux or flowing.

fly, flī, *n. pl.,* **flies.** Any of numerous insects with one pair of transparent wings, esp. the common housefly; a hook dressed to resemble a fly or other insect, used by anglers.

fly, flī, *v.i.,* **flew, flown, fly·ing.** To move through the air on wings; to move through the air by force of wind or other propulsion; to journey through the air in an aircraft; to pass with swiftness; to move swiftly; to run away; to flee or escape; to burst in pieces; to flutter or wave; to be spent rapidly.—*v.t.* To operate, as an aircraft; to travel over in an aircraft; to transport by aircraft; to flee from; shun.—*n. pl.,* **flies.** A flap of cloth covering a zipper or other fastener, esp. in a pair of men's trousers; a flap making up the door of a tent; a baseball batted high into the air; a flyleaf; a flywheel.

fly·blown, flī/blōn, *a.* Tainted, esp. by the eggs or larvae of flies; seedy.

fly-by-night, flī/bī·nīt, *a.* Not responsible or trustworthy, esp. in financial or business matters; not lasting; ephemeral.

fly·er, flī/ər, *n.* Flier.

fly·ing, flī/ing, *a.* Capable of or suited for flight; moving, floating, or waving in the air; swift, brief and fast; hasty.

fly·ing col·ors, *n. pl.* Success; excellence.

fly·ing jib, *n. Naut.* A sail extended outside of the jib on the extended jib boom.

fly·ing sau·cer, *n.* Any of various unidentified, disk-shaped, airborne objects; an unidentified flying object.

fly·leaf, flī/lēf, *n. pl.,* -**leaves.** A blank page at the beginning or end of a book or pamphlet.

fly·pa·per, flī/pā·pər, *n.* A sticky or poisoned paper for killing flies.

fly·speck, flī/spek, *n.* A speck from the excrement of a fly; a minute spot.—*v.t.* To mark with specks.

fly·wheel, flī/hwēl, flī/wēl, *n.* A heavy wheel used to ensure uniform motion in all working parts of a machine.

FM, F.M. Frequency modulation.

foal, fōl, *n.* A young horse, donkey, etc.; a colt or filly.—*v.t., v.i.* To give birth to, as a foal.

foam, fōm, *n.* The mass of minute bubbles formed on the surface of liquids by fermentation or agitation; froth.—*v.i.* To gather foam; to froth.—*v.t.* To cause to foam. —**foam·i·ness,** *n.* —**foam·y,** *a.,* -**i·er,** -**i·est.**

foam rub·ber, *n.* A spongy rubber, used for pillows, mattresses, etc.

fob, fob, *n.* A short chain or ribbon, usu. decorative, attached to a watch and worn hanging from the pocket in which the watch is carried; the pocket; an ornament at the end of the chain or ribbon.

fob, fob, *v.t.,* **fobbed, fob·bing.** To dispose of by deceit, put off by evasion, or try to pass as genuine: usu. followed by *off.*

fo·cal, fō/kəl, *a.* Of or pertaining to a focus. **—fo·cal·ly,** *adv.*

fo·cal·ize, fō/kə·līz, *v.t.,* **-ized, -iz·ing.** To focus.**—v.i.** To become focused.

fo·cal length, *n.* The distance from the optical center of a lens or mirror to the point where light rays converge. Also **fo·cal dis·tance.**

fo'c's'le, fo'c'sle, fōk/səl, *n.* Forecastle.

fo·cus, fō/kəs, *n. pl.,* **fo·cus·es, fo·ci,** fō/sī. A point at which rays of light, heat, or the like, meet, appear to meet, or would meet after being reflected or refracted by a lens, mirror, etc.; the position of an object, or the adjustment of an optical device, necessary to produce a clear image: in *focus,* out of *focus;* the focal point or the focal length of a lens; a central point, as of attraction, attention, or activity.**—v.t.,** **-cused** or **-cussed, -cus·ing** or **-cus·sing.** To bring into focus, as an image; to concentrate; to adjust to a focus, as a camera lens or the eye.**—v.i.** To become focused. **—fo·cus·er,** *n.*

fod·der, fod/ər, *n.* Coarse feed for cattle and other livestock.

foe, fō, *n.* An enemy.

foe·tus, fē/tus, *n.* Fetus. **—foe·tal,** *a.*

fog, fog, fôg, *n.* Condensed water vapor in the atmosphere near the earth's surface, often interfering with visibility; any hazy, dim, or misty state of the atmosphere; a state of confusion or blurred perception. **—v.t.,** **fogged, fog·ging.** To envelop with or as with fog; to confuse.**—v.i.** To become confused or enveloped with fog.

fog bank, *n.* A mass of fog as seen from a distance.

fog·gy, fog/ē, fôg/ē, *a.,* **-gi·er, -gi·est.** Filled with fog; misty; dim; dull; bewildered. **—fog·gi·ly,** *adv.* **—fog·gi·ness,** *n.*

fog·horn, fog/hôrn, fôg/hôrn, *n.* A loud horn for warning vessels during a fog.

fo·gy, fo·gey, fō/gē, *n. pl.,* **-gies, -geys.** An old-fashioned or extremely conservative person, usu. preceded by *old.* **—fo·gy·ish, fo·gey·ish,** *a.*

foi·ble, foy/bəl, *n.* A trivial or minor fault.

foil, foyl, *n.* Metal hammered or rolled into a very thin sheet; a person or thing that sets off another by contrast; a leaflike arc, space, piece of tracery, etc.**—v.t.** To cover or back with foil; to set off by contrast.

foil, foyl, *v.t.* To prevent from being successful; to frustrate or thwart.

foil, foyl, *n.* A long, flexible sword with a blunt point, for use in fencing.

foist, foyst, *v.t.* To pass off an unworthy person or thing upon another by deception or fraud; to insert secretly or fraudulently.

fold, fōld, *v.t.* To double or bend, as cloth or paper, over upon itself; to shut or bring into a compact form by bending and laying parts together, often with *up;* to bring together or intertwine, as the arms or hands; to clasp or embrace; to enclose or wrap.**—v.i.** To become folded. *Informal.* To collapse or fail.**—n.** A folded part, form, or layer of something; a pleat; a bend or curvative in stratified rock; an act of folding or doubling over; the space between folds.

fold, fōld, *n.* A pen or enclosure for sheep or similar animals; a flock of sheep; a church or its congregation.**—v.t.** To confine in a fold.

fold·er, fōl/dər, *n.* One who or that which folds; a folded printed sheet, as a circular or a timetable; a protective covering, as of folded cardboard, for loose papers, etc.

fol·de·rol, fol/də·rol, *n.* Nonsense; a trifle. Also **fal·de·ral.**

fo·li·a·ceous, fō·lē·ā/shəs, *a.* Leaflike; of or like the leaves of a plant; made of laminated or leaflike plates.

fo·li·age, fō/lē·ij, *n.* Leaves; leaves or leafy growths represented ornamentally.

fo·li·ate, fō/lē·āt, *v.t.,* **-at·ed, -at·ing.** To shape like a leaf; to beat or roll, as gold, into thin sheets or foil.**—v.i.** To put forth leaves; to split into thin leaflike layers.**—**fō/lē·it, fō/lē·āt, *a.* Having or covered with leaves; leaflike.

fo·li·a·tion, fō·lē·ā/shən, *n.* The act of bursting into leaf; the state of being in leaf; the arrangement of the leaves in a bud; the consecutive numbering of the leaves of a book; ornamentation with representations of foliage.

fo·li·o, fō/lē·ō, *n. pl.,* **-os.** A sheet of paper folded once to make two leaves or four pages to each sheet; a volume printed on such sheets, having pages of the largest size; the size of such a volume; one of a collection of leaves, as of a manuscript or book, numbered consecutively on the front side only; the number of a page; a portfolio.**—a.** Pertaining to or having the size of a folio.**—v.t.,** **-oed, -o·ing.** To number consecutively the leaves or pages of.

folk, fōk, *n. pl.,* **folk** or **folks.** People in general; a separate class of people; people as the preservers of culture.**—a.** Originating among or representative of the common people, their customs, legends, music, etc.**—folks,** *n. pl.* One's own family, esp. one's parents.

folk dance, *n.* A dance originated among and transmitted through the common people; music for such a dance.

folk·lore, fōk/lôr, fōk/lōr, *n.* The traditional beliefs, customs, legends, and songs of a people; the study of these traditions. **—folk·lor·ist,** *n.*

folk mu·sic, *n.* Music created by and handed down among the common people.

folk song, *n.* A song originating among and transmitted orally by the common people; a song written in imitation of this type.

folk·sy, fōk/sē, *a.,* **-si·er, -si·est.** *Informal.* Sociable; unpretentious. **—folk·si·ness,** *n.*

folk·ways, fōk/wāz, *n. pl.* Traditional habits and customs informally established and perpetuated within a society.

fol·li·cle, fol/ə·kəl, *n.* A small cavity, sac, or gland. *Bot.* A dry, one-celled seed vessel that grows from a single carpel. **—fol·lic·u·lar,** fə·lik/yə·lər, *a.*

fol·low, fol/ō, *v.t.* To go or come after; move behind in the same direction; to come after in natural sequence or order of time; succeed; come after, as a result to accept the authority of, as a leader; to comply with or obey; to imitate; to go along; to pursue; to accompany; to engage in as a pursuit; to watch the progress or course of; to attend to and comprehend, as an argument.**—v.i.** To go or come after; to come after as a result; to pay attention; to understand.**—n.** The act of following.**—fol·low suit,** to play a card of the same suit as that first played; to follow the example of another.**—fol·low out,** to follow or carry to a conclusion; to execute, as orders.**—fol·low through,** to extend a stroke or motion to its full extent, as in golf or tennis; to pursue an activity or plan to completion.**—fol·low up,** to pursue closely; pursue to a conclusion; increase the effect of by further action.

fol·low·er, fol/ō·ər, *n.* One who or that which follows; one who follows another's beliefs or teachings; an attendant, retainer, or servant.

fol·low·ing, fol/ō·ing, *n.* A body of followers, attendants, or adherents.**—a.** That follows; follow.

fol·ly, fol/ē, *n. pl.,* **-lies.** The state of being foolish; lack of understanding or good judgment; a foolish action, practice, or idea; an absurdity; a costly and foolish undertaking. *Pl.* A musical revue or stage show.

fo·ment, fō·ment/, *v.t.* To promote or encourage discord, rebellion, etc.; to instigate. **—fo·men·ta·tion,** fō·men·tā/shən, *n.* **—fo·ment·er,** *n.*

fond, fond, *a.* Having affection for, usu. followed by *of;* loving or tender; excessively affectionate; doting; cherished.

fon·dle, fon′dəl, *v.t.,* **-dled, -dling.** To caress; to touch lovingly.—*v.i.* To exhibit affection by caressing. **—fon·dler,** *n.* **—fond·ly,** *adv.* **—fond·ness,** *n.*

fon·due, fon·doo′, fon′doo, *n.* A dish composed of melted cheese, eggs, butter, etc.; any of various other melted dishes.

font, font, *Brit.* **fount,** fownt, *n.* A complete assortment of type of one style and size.

font, font, *n.* A receptacle for holy water or baptismal water; a source or origin.

food, food, *n.* A substance taken into and absorbed by an organism to sustain life and enable growth and repair of tissues; more or less solid nutriment, as opposed to drink; a particular kind of nutriment; something for consumption or use.

food·stuff, food′stəf, *n.* A substance suitable for food.

fool, fool, *n.* One who lacks judgment or sense; a silly or stupid person; one who is made to appear ridiculous or stupid; a dupe; a professional jester formerly kept by a person of rank to provide entertainment; a clown.—*v.i.* To act like a fool; jest or play.—*v.t.* To trick or deceive; to waste foolishly, usu. with *away.*—**fool around,** to waste time.

fool·er·y, foo′lə·rē, *n. pl.,* **-er·ies.** Foolish action or conduct.

fool·har·dy, fool′har·dē, *a.* Recklessly bold; rash. **—fool·har·di·ness,** *n.*

fool·ish, foo′lish, *a.* Lacking good sense; silly; resulting from a lack of sense; unwise. **—fool·ish·ly,** *adv.* **—fool·ish·ness,** *n.*

fool·proof, fool′proof, *a.* Infallible; involving no risk or chance of error.

fools·cap, foolz′kap, *n.* A size of paper, approx. 13 × 16 inches.

fool's gold, *n.* Iron or copper pyrites, which are sometimes mistaken for gold.

foot, fut, *n. pl.,* **feet.** The terminal part of the vertebrate leg, on which the body stands and moves; any part similar to or resembling a foot in form, use, or position; a unit of measurement equal to 12 inches; step; pace; the bottom or base of something; something that covers the foot; the major unit of poetic meter consisting of a group of stressed and unstressed syllables; soldiers who march or fight on foot.—*v.i.* To walk or dance, often followed by *it.*—*v.t.* To set foot on; walk or dance on; to add, often with *up. Informal.* To pay, as a bill; to make or attach a foot to.

foot·age, fut′ij, *n.* Length or extent in feet.

foot·ball, fut′bôl, *n.* A game played by opposing teams of eleven men each, on a field 100 yards long with a goal at each end; ball used in this game, inflated and leather-covered; any of various somewhat similar games, such as soccer or rugby.

foot·board, fut′bôrd, fut′bōrd, *n.* A board or small platform on which to support the feet; an upright piece across the foot of a bedstead.

foot-can·dle, fut′kan·dəl, *n.* A unit of illumination equivalent to that produced by a standard candle at a distance of one foot.

foot·ed, fut′id, *a.* Provided with a foot or feet; having a certain number of feet.

foot·fall, fut′fôl, *n.* A footstep; the sound made by a footstep.

foot·hill, fut′hil, *n.* A low hill at the base of a mountain or mountain range.

foot·hold, fut′hōld, *n.* A place where one may tread securely; firm standing; footing; stable position.

foot·ing, fut′ing, *n.* A firm or secure position for the feet; foothold; a secure position or basis; social, economic, or professional standing in relation to others; an adding or the resulting sum.

foot·lights, fut′līts, *n. pl.* A row of lights at the front of a stage; the theater as a profession.

foot·loose, fut′loos, *a.* Free to go about at will; not confined by ties or responsibilities.

foot·note, fut′nōt, *n.* A note at the bottom of a page which documents or supplements the text.—*v.t.,* **-not·ed, -not·ing.** To supply with footnotes.

foot·path, fut′path, *n.* A narrow path for pedestrians only.

foot·print, fut′print, *n.* The impression left by a foot, as in sand or soft earth.

foot sol·dier, *n.* An infantryman.

foot·sore, fut′sôr, fut′sōr, *a.* Having the feet sore or tender, as from much walking.

foot·step, fut′step, *n.* The act of taking a step; the distance traversed by one step; the sound of a step; a footprint; a stair.

foot·stool, fut′stool, *n.* A low stool upon which to rest the foot or feet.

foot·wear, fut′wār, *n.* Protective covering for the feet, as boots, shoes, or slippers.

foot·work, fut′wərk, *n.* Management or control of the feet, as in dancing or boxing.

foo·zle, foo′zəl, *n., v.t., v.i.,* **-zled, -zling.** Fumble; bungle.

fop, fop, *n.* A vain man who is unduly concerned with his dress, appearance, and manners. **—fop·per·y,** *n. pl.,* **-per·ies. —fop·pish,** *a.* **—fop·pish·ly,** *adv.* **—fop·pish·ness,** *n.*

for, fôr, *unstressed,* fər, *prep.* In the interest of or on behalf of; in place of; in return for; in exchange for; in favor of; in honor of; with the purpose of; conducive to; in order to obtain, save, become, keep, etc.; with inclination or sensitivity toward; in proportion to; with the purpose of reaching; intended to belong to or be used with; suited to; in assignment to; appropriate to, such as to allow of, or result in; with regard to; as affecting the circumstances of; as being: to know a thing *for* a fact; by reason of; in spite of: she loved him, *for* all his faults; during; throughout; to the extent of; that (one) should or might: It is time *for* him to leave home. —*conj.* Because; since.

for·age, fôr′ij, for′ij, *n.* Food for horses and cattle; fodder; the act of searching for provisions.—*v.t.,* **-aged, -ag·ing.** To collect forage from; strip of supplies; plunder; to supply with forage.—*v.i.* To wander in search of, or make a raid to capture supplies.

for·as·much as, fôr′əs·mech′, *conj.* In view of the fact that; since.

for·ay, fôr′ā, for′ā, *v.t., v.i.* To ravage; to pillage; to forage.—*n.* A predatory excursion; a raid.

for·bear, fôr′bâr, *v.t.,* **-bore, -borne, -bear·ing.** To refrain or desist from; to keep back; withhold.—*v.i.* To refrain; to be patient; to practice self-control. **—for·bear·ance,** *n.* **—for·bear·ing·ly,** *adv.*

for·bear, fôr′bâr, *n.* Forebear.

for·bid, fər·bid′, fôr·bid′, *v.t.,* **-bade** or **-bad, -bid·den, -bid·ding.** To command against an action; prohibit; to hinder or prevent; to exclude or bar from use. **—for·bid·dance,** *n.* **—for·bid·den,** *a.*

for·bid·ding, fər·bid′ing, fôr·bid′ing, *a.* Grim or disagreeable; threatening; repellent; causing aversion or dislike. **—for·bid·ding·ly,** *adv.* **—for·bid·ding·ness,** *n.*

force, fôrs, fōrs, *n.* Strength or power; strength or power exerted upon an object; physical coercion; violence; power of overcoming resistance; power to influence or control; any body of persons combined for joint action; binding power, as of an agreement; validity; a cause, or potential cause, of change in the state of rest or motion of a body. *Often pl.* A body of armed men.—*v.t.,* **forced, forc·ing.** To compel or oblige; to effect by force; to impose forcibly, followed by *on* or *upon;* to drive or propel against resistance; to overcome the resistance of; compel by force; to obtain by force; extort; to take or enter by force; to break open; to cause, as plants, to grow by artificial means;

to hasten the progress or development of; to press to violent effort or to the utmost; to strain; to use force upon. —**force·a·ble**, a. —**force·less**, a. —**forc·er**, n.

forced, fôrst, fōrst, a. Subjected to force; compulsory; strained, unnatural, or affected.

force·ful, fôrs′fəl, fōrs′fəl, a. Full of force; powerful; vigorous; effective. —**force·ful·ly**, adv. —**force·ful·ness**, n.

for·ceps, fôr′səps, n. An instrument, as pincers or tongs, for seizing and holding objects, as in surgical operations.

for·ci·ble, fôr′sə·bəl, a. Having force; exercising force; powerful; marked by force; effective. —**for·ci·ble·ness**, n. —**for·ci·bly**, adv.

ford, fôrd, fōrd, n. A place in a river or other body of water where it is shallow enough to be passed by wading.—v.t. To pass or cross, as a stream, by wading. —**ford·a·ble**, a.

fore, fôr, fōr, a. Situated at or toward the front; forward; earlier.—n. The forepart; the front.—interj. In golf, a cry of warning to persons who may be in the path of one's hit ball.

fore-and-aft, fôr′ən·aft′, fōr′ən·aft′, a. Situated along the length of a ship; lengthwise.

fore·arm, fôr′ärm, fōr′ärm, n. That part of the arm between the elbow and wrist.

fore·arm, fôr·ärm′, fōr·ärm′, v.t. To arm or prepare for attack beforehand.

fore·bear, for·bear, fôr′bâr, fōr′bâr, n. Usu. pl. Ancestors; forefathers.

fore·bode, for·bode, fôr′bōd′, fōr·bōd′, v.t., -bod·ed, -bod·ing. To foretell; presage; to feel a premonition of evil or misfortune.—v.i. To make predictions. —**fore·bod·er**, n. —**fore·bod·ing**, n., a.

fore·brain, fôr′brān, fōr′brān, n. The anterior division of the brain.

fore·cast, fôr′kast, fōr′kast, v.t., -cast or -cast·ed, -cast·ing. To predict; to make a prediction, as of the weather; to foreshadow; to contrive or plan beforehand.—n. —**fore·cast·er**, n.

fore·close, fôr·klōz′, fōr·klōz′, v.t., -closed, -clos·ing. To deprive of the right to redeem mortgaged property; exclude; hinder or prevent.—v.i. To foreclose a mortgage. —**fore·clo·sure**, n.

fore·fa·ther, fôr′fä·thər, fōr′fä·thər, n. An ancestor.

fore·fin·ger, fôr′fing·gər, fōr′fing·gər, n. The finger next to the thumb; index finger.

fore·foot, fôr′fût, fōr′fût, n. pl., -feet. A front foot of a quadruped or multiped.

fore·front, fôr′frənt, fōr′frənt, n. The foremost part, place, or position.

fore·gath·er, fôr·gath′ər, fōr·gath′ər, v.i. Forgather.

fore·go, fôr·gō′, fōr·gō′, v.t. Forgo.

fore·go, fôr·gō′, fōr·gō′, v.t., v.i., -went, -gone, -go·ing. To go before; to precede. —**fore·go·ing**, fôr·gō′ing, fōr·gō′ing, a. —**fore·gone**, fôr·gôn′, a.

fore·gone con·clu·sion, n. An obvious, inevitable result; a conclusion determined before consideration of evidence.

fore·ground, fôr′grownd, fōr′grownd, n. The part of a scene or picture which is nearest to the observer; the forefront.

fore·hand, fôr′hand, fōr′hand, a. In tennis, etc., making a stroke with the palm facing forward.—n. A forehand stroke.—adv. With a forehand stroke.

fore·hand·ed, fôr·han′did, fōr·han′did, a. Providing for the future; prudent; thrifty; well-to-do. —**fore·hand·ed·ness**, n.

fore·head, fôr′id, for′id, fôr′hed, n. The part of the face above the eyes; the front of anything.

for·eign, fôr′in, for′in, a. Belonging or relating to another country; located outside of one's own country; relating to dealings with other countries; alien; strange; unfamiliar; present or occurring where not normally found; not belonging.

for·eign af·fairs, n. pl. The relations of one country with other countries.

for·eign·er, fôr′in·ər, for′in·ər, n. A person born in or belonging to a foreign country; an alien. —**for·eign·ness**, n.

fore·know, fôr·nō′, fōr·nō′, v.t., -knew, -known, -know·ing. Know beforehand. —**fore·knowl·edge**, fôr′nol·ij, fōr′nol·ij, n.

fore·leg, fôr′leg, fōr′leg, n. One of the front legs, as of an animal or chair.

fore·lock, fôr′lok, fōr′lok, n. A lock of hair growing over the forehead.

fore·man, fôr′mən, fōr′mən, n. pl., -men. A man who supervises others, as in a work crew; the chairman of a jury.

fore·most, fôr′mōst, fōr′most, fôr′məst, a. First in place, rank, order, or time.—adv. In the first place.

fore·noon, fôr′noon, fôr·noon′, n. The morning hours before noon.

fo·ren·sic, fə·ren′sik, a. Pertaining to, connected with, or used in courts of law or public debate.—n. A spoken or written exercise in argumentation, as in a college.

fore·or·dain, fôr·ôr·dān′, fōr·ôr·dān′, v.t. To ordain beforehand; preordain.

fore·quar·ter, fôr′kwôr·tər, fōr′kwôr·tər, n. One of the two halves of the front portion of the body of a lamb, cow, etc.

fore·run, fôr·rən′, fōr·rən′, v.t., -ran, -run, -run·ning. To precede; to be a prediction or omen of; to be a herald of; to forestall.

fore·run·ner, fôr′rən·ər, n. A herald; a harbinger; a sign or omen of something to follow; an ancestor; an antecedent.

fore·see, fôr·sē′, fōr·sē′, v.t., -saw, -seen, -see·ing. To see or know in advance. —**fore·see·a·ble**, a. —**fore·se·er**, n.

fore·shad·ow, fôr·shad′ō, fōr·shad′ō, v.t. To give evidence of beforehand; to prefigure.—n. —**fore·shad·ow·er**, n.

fore·short·en, fôr·shôr′tən, fōr·shôr′tən, v.t. In drawing, to shorten a line, part of an object, etc., to create the illusion of depth; to make shorter.

fore·sight, fôr′sīt, fōr′sīt, n. Provident care for the future; insight; the act or power of foreseeing; foreknowledge. —**fore·sight·ed**, a. —**fore·sight·ed·ness**, n.

fore·skin, fôr′skin, fōr′skin, n. The fold of skin which covers the glans of the penis; the prepuce.

for·est, fôr′ist, for′ist, n. A large tract of land covered with trees and underbrush; the trees.—v.t. To convert into a forest.

fore·stall, fôr·stôl′, fōr·stôl′, v.t. To prevent by action in advance; to deal with in advance.

for·est·a·tion, fôr·is·tā′shən, for·is·tā′shən, n. The act or process of planting a forest.

for·est·er, fôr′i·stər, for′i·stər, n. A person skilled in forestry; one who or that which lives in a forest.

for·est·ry, fôr′i·strē, for′i·strē, n. The science of planting and managing forests; forest land.

fore·taste, fôr′tāst, fōr′tāst, n. Anticipation; enjoyment in advance.—fôr·tāst′, fōr·tāst′, v.t., -tast·ed, -tast·ing. To taste beforehand; anticipate.

fore·tell, fôr·tel′, fōr·tel′, v.t., v.i., -told, -tell·ing. To tell of in advance; to predict; to prophesy. —**fore·tell·er**, n.

fore·thought, fôr′thôt, fōr′thôt, n. A thinking beforehand; provident care; foresight.

for·ev·er, fôr·ev′ər, fər·ev′ər, adv. Eternally; continually.

for·ev·er·more, fôr·ev′ər·môr, fər·ev′ər·môr, adv. For always; forever.

fore·warn, fôr·wôrn′, fōr·wôrn′, v.t. To warn beforehand.

fore·word, fôr′wərd, fōr′wərd, n. A preface; an introduction.

for·feit, fôr′fit, v.t. To lose the right to, by some fault, crime, or neglect.—n. The act of forfeiting; that which is forfeited; a fine; a penalty.—a. Forfeited or subject to be forfeited. —**for·feit·er,** *n.*

for·fei·ture, fôr′fi·chər, *n.* The act of forfeiting; a penalty or fine; that which is forfeited.

for·gath·er, fore·gath·er, fôr·gath′ər, *v.i.* To meet; to convene; to meet accidentally; to associate or be friendly.

forge, fôrj, fōrj, *n.* An apparatus in which metal is heated and softened before shaping; a workshop where metal is heated in such an apparatus; a furnace or industrial plant where metal is melted and refined. —*v.t.,* **forged, forg·ing.** To heat in a forge and form or shape; to form or make in any way; to invent, devise, or produce in order to deceive; to imitate fraudulently, as a signature or work of art.—*v.i.* To commit forgery; to work at a forge; to heat metal. —**forg·er,** *n.*

forge, fôrj, fōrj, *v.i.,* **forged, forg·ing.** To move forward, esp. slowly, or with difficulty.

for·ger·y, fôr′jə·rē, fōr′jə·rē, *n. pl.,* **-ies.** The production of an imitation which is claimed to be genuine, as a coin, work of art, signature, etc.; something produced by forgery.

for·get, fôr·get′, *v.t.,* **-got, -got·ten** or **-got, -get·ting.** To be unable to recall; to omit or neglect to take, mention, think of, etc; to overlook, disregard, or slight.—*v.i.* To fail or be unable to remember. —**for·get·ta·ble,** *a.* —**for·get·ter,** *n.*

for·get·ful, fər·get′fəl, *a.* Apt to forget; heedless or neglectful. —**for·get·ful·ly,** *adv.* —**for·get·ful·ness,** *n.*

for·give, fər·giv′, fôr·giv′, *v.t.,* **-gave, -giv·en, -giv·ing.** To cease to feel resentment against; to grant remission of an offense, debt, fine, or penalty; to pardon.—*v.i.* To grant pardon; show forgiveness. —**for·giv·a·ble,** *a.*

for·give·ness, fər·giv′nəs, fôr·giv′nes, *n.* The act of forgiving; disposition or willingness to forgive. —**for·giv·er,** *n.*

for·giv·ing, fər·giv′ing, fôr·giv′ing, *a.* Disposed to forgive; compassionate.

for·go, fôr·gō′, fōr·gō′, *v.t.,* **-went, -gone, -go·ing.** To do without; give up; renounce; resign. —**for·go·er,** *n.*

fork, fôrk, *n.* A tool, such as an eating utensil, an agricultural implement, etc., having a handle and two or more prongs or tines at one end; the point at which a river or road splits into branches; any one of these branches.—*v.t.* To make fork-shaped; to pierce, raise, pitch, or dig with a fork.—*v.i.* To form a fork; to divide into branches.

forked, fôrkt, fôr′kid, *a.* Having a fork or bifurcation; zigzag, as lightning.

fork·lift, fôrk′lift, *n.* A machine having two long metal fingers for securing and lifting heavy loads. Also **lift truck.**

for·lorn, fôr·lôrn′, *a.* Abandoned; bereft; wretched in feeling, condition, or appearance. —**for·lorn·ly,** *adv.* —**for·lorn·ness,** *n.*

form, fôrm, *n.* Appearance apart from color or material; shape; a body; the structural condition of a thing; a particular character as to spelling and inflection, exhibited by a word; proper shape; good order; the manner of arranging parts for a pleasing or effective result; a prescribed or customary method of doing something; a set order of words; a document with blank spaces to be filled in with particulars; a sample document; a formality or ceremony; a manner or method of doing something; fitness for performing; an image of a shape; something that gives shape, as molds; the essence or intrinsic nature of something; an assemblage of type set in a case to print from.—*v.t.* To give form or shape to; give a particular form to; to mold; to place in order; to construct; to frame in the mind; to develop; make up or compose; to draw up into battle lines or formations.—*v.i.* To assume form; to begin to exist; to assume a particular form.

—**form·er,** *n.*

for·mal, fôr′məl, *a.* In accordance with prescribed or customary forms; done with proper or official forms; rigorously methodical; very regular or symmetrical; marked by ceremony; observant of form; ceremonious, punctilious, or precise; perfunctory; of language: proper, refined, elaborate, or erudite, and usu., punctilious and conservative in grammar, syntax, pronunciation, and diction.—*n.* An occasion, evening gown, etc., of a formal nature. —**for·mal·ly,** *adv.*

for·mal·ism, fôr′mə·liz·əm, *n.* Strict adherence to; of prescribed or customary forms, as in religion or art.

for·mal·i·ty, fôr·mal′ə·tē, *n. pl.,* **-ties.** Accordance with prescribed, customary, or due forms; conventionality; excessive regularity or stiffness; ceremoniousness; an established order or mode of proceeding; something done merely for form's sake; a requirement of custom or etiquette.

for·mal·ize, fôr′mə·līz, *v.t.,* **-ized, -iz·ing.** To give form to; to make formal.—*v.i.* To be formal; act with formality. —**for·mal·i·za·tion,** fôr·mə·lə·zā′shən, *n.*

for·mat, fôr′mat, *n.* The layout and physical appearance of a book, newspaper, or magazine; any general plan or arrangement.

for·ma·tion, fôr·mā′shən, *n.* The act or process of forming, or the state of being formed; the manner in which a thing is formed; structure or arrangement; something formed; a mass or deposit of rock or mineral of a particular composition or origin.

form·a·tive, fôr′mə·tiv, *a.* Forming; shaping; molding; pertaining to formation or development; serving to form words.—*n.* An element of a word, as a prefix or a suffix, added to the base of a word to give it new grammatical form.

for·mer, fôr′mər, *a.* Before; long past; preceding; earlier; first mentioned; having previously been.

for·mer·ly, fôr′mər·lē, *adv.* In time past, either some time ago or a long time ago.

For·mi·ca, fôr·mī′kə, *n. Trademark.* Any of various laminated plastic products used for table tops, counters, wall panels, etc.

for·mi·da·ble, fôr′mi·də·bəl, fôr·mid′ə·bəl, *a.* Exciting fear or awe, due to strength or size; so difficult as to discourage approach, encounter, or undertaking. —**for·mi·da·ble·ness,** *n.* —**for·mi·da·bly,** *adv.*

form·less, fôrm′lis, *a.* Not having any regular or definite shape. —**form·less·ly,** *adv.* —**form·less·ness,** *n.*

for·mu·la, fôr′myə·lə, *n. pl.,* **-las, -lae, -lē.** A prescribed form of words or symbols in which something is stated; a written confession of faith; a formal enunciation of doctrines; a rule, concept, or principle expressed in algebraic symbols; an expression by means of symbols and letters of the constituents of a compound; recipe or prescription.

for·mu·lar·y, fôr′myə·ler·ē, *n. pl.,* **-lar·ies.** A book containing formulas; a formula.—*a.* Pertaining to formulas.

for·mu·late, fôr′myə·lāt, *v.t.,* **-lat·ed, -lat·ing.** To reduce to or express in a formula; to put into a precise and systematic statement. —**for·mu·la·tion,** *n.* —**for·mu·la·tor,** *n.*

for·ni·cate, fôr′nə·kāt, *v.i.,* **-cat·ed, -cat·ing.** To commit fornication. —**for·ni·cat·or,** *n.*

for·ni·ca·tion, fôr·nə·kā′shən, *n.* Voluntary sexual intercourse between two unmarried persons.

for·sake, fôr·sāk′, *v.t.,* **-sook, -sak·en, -sak·ing.** To quit or leave entirely; to desert; to abandon. —**for·sak·en,** *a.* —**for·sak·en·ly,** *adv.*

for·swear, fôr·swār′, *v.t.,* **-swore, -sworn, -swear·ing.** To reject or renounce upon oath; to deny earnestly or upon oath. *Refl.* To swear falsely; to perjure (oneself).—*v.i.* To swear falsely; to commit perjury. Also **fore·swear.** —**for·swear·er,** *n.* —**for·sworn,** *a.*

---

a- hat, fāte, fāre, fäther; **e-** met, mē; **i-** pin, pīne; **o-** not, nōte, ôrb, moove (move), boy, pownd; **u-** cūbe, bŭll, tŭk (took); **ch-** chin; **th-** thick, ŧhen; **zh-** vizhon (vision); **ə-** ego, takən, pencəl, lemən, bərd (bird).

fort, fôrt, fōrt, *n.* A strong or fortified place; a fortress.

forte, fôrt, *n.* A particular talent or faculty of a person; a strong point.

for•te, fôr′tā, *adv. Mus.* Loudly; forcefully.

forth, fôrth, fōrth, *adv.* Onward or forward; out into view.

forth•com•ing, fôrth′kəm′ing, fōrth′kəm′ing, *a.* Soon to appear, arrive, or occur; available.—*n.* A coming forth.

forth•right, fôrth′rīt, fōrth′rīt, *a.* Straightforward; direct; outspoken; frank.—*adv.* Directly forward; immediately. —**forth•right•ness,** *n.*

forth•with, fôrth•with′, fōrth•with′, *adv.* Immediately; without delay; directly.

for•ti•fi•ca•tion, fôr•tə•fə•kā′shən, *n.* The act of fortifying; something which fortifies; the art or science of fortifying; a fortified place; a fort.

for•ti•fy, fôr′tə•fī, *v.t.,* **-fied, -fy•ing.** To add strength to; to surround with fortification or armaments; to reinforce; strengthen morally or mentally; to encourage; to confirm; to enrich food by adding ingredients; to increase the alcoholic content of.—*v.i.* To construct fortifications. —**for•ti•fi•er,** *n.*

for•tis•si•mo, fôr•tis′ə•mō, *a. Mus.* Very loud.—*adv.* Very loudly.

for•ti•tude, fôr′tə•tood, fôr′tə•tūd, *n.* Strength of mind in the face of pain, danger, etc.; resolute endurance.

fort•night, fôrt′nīt, fōrt′nit, *n.* The space of fourteen days; two weeks.

fort•night•ly, fôrt′nīt•lē, *adv.* Once a fortnight; every fortnight.—*a.* Occurring or appearing once a fortnight.—*n. pl.,* **-lies.** A publication appearing every two weeks.

for•tress, fôr′tris, *n.* A fortified place; stronghold.

for•tu•i•tous, fôr•too′ə•təs, fôr•tū′ə•təs, *a.* Accidental; happening by chance; lucky. —**for•tu•i•tous•ly,** *adv.* —**for•tu•i•ty,** *n. pl.,* **-ties.**

for•tu•nate, fôr′chə•nit, *a.* Having good fortune; lucky; bringing good fortune; auspicious. —**for•tu•nate•ly,** *adv.*

for•tune, fôr′chən, *n.* Great wealth; one's total possessions; luck, good or bad; *sometimes pl.,* the good or ill that happens or may happen. (*Often cap.*) Fate or destiny; prosperity or good luck.

for•tune•tell•er, fôr′chən•tel•ər, *n.* One who purports to foretell events in a person's future. —**for•tune•tell•ing,** *n., a.*

for•ty, fôr′tē, *n. pl.,* **-ties.** Four times ten; the cardinal number between 39 and 41; a symbol representing it.—*a.*

for•ty-nin•er, fôr•tē•nī′nər, *n.* A person who migrated to California during 1849 to seek gold.

fo•rum, fôr′əm, fōr′əm, *n. pl.,* **-rums, -ra,** -rə. The marketplace or public place of an ancient Roman city; a court or tribunal; an assembly for the discussion of questions of public interest.

for•ward, fôr′wərd, *adv.* Toward or at a place, point, or time in advance; onward; ahead. Also **for•wards.**—*a.* Situated in the front; directed toward a point in advance; onward; well advanced; precocious; ready or eager; presumptuous or bold; radical or extreme; pertaining to the future. —*n.* A player stationed in advance of others on his team.—*v.t.* To send forward; transmit, as a letter, esp. to a new destination; to help onward; promote or hasten. —**for•ward•er,** *n.* —**for•ward•ly,** *adv.* —**for•ward•ness,** *n.*

for•ward pass, *n.* A football pass down field, to a receiver positioned in the direction of the opponent's goal.

fos•sil, fos′əl, *n.* Any remains of an animal or plant found in the earth's crust or strata. *Informal.* An antiquated person or thing.—*a.* Of the nature of a fossil; extracted from the earth: *fossil* fuels; belonging to a past epoch; antiquated.

fos•sil•ize, fos′ə•līz, *v.t.,* **-ized, -iz•ing.** To change into or as if into a fossil; petrify; render rigidly anti-

quated, as persons or ideas.—*v.i.* To become fossilized. —**fos•sil•i•za•tion,** fos•ə•lə•zā′shən, *n.*

fos•ter, fô′stər, fos′tər, *v.t.,* **-tered, -ter•ing.** To promote the growth of; to bring up; nurture; to cherish. —*a.* Giving or receiving parental care though unrelated by birth or legal ties: a *foster* child, a *foster* parent.

fought, fôt, *v.* Past tense and past participle of **fight.**

foul, fowl, *a.* Noxious or offensive to the senses; covered or clogged with filth; unclean; polluted; stormy or inclement: *foul* weather; obscene or abusive; morally repugnant; vile; unfair or unlawful; pertaining to an act contrary to the rules of a game; outside one of the foul lines; entangled, or involving danger of collision. —In a foul or unfair manner. Also **foul•ly.**—*n.* An act contrary to the rules of a game or sport.—*v.t.* To make dirty, to defile; to soil; to obstruct or choke; to have a collision with; to cause to entangle; to dishonor; to commit a foul or unfair act against; to hit into foul territory.—*v.i.* To commit a foul; to hit a ball foul; to become entangled or clogged.—**fall foul of, fall afoul of, run foul of,** to run against or collide with; to clash or have a conflict with.—**foul up,** *informal.* To bring about confusion or disorder; blunder. —**foul•ness,** *n.*

fou•lard, foo•lärd′, *n.* A soft, lightweight silk, rayon, or cotton cloth, used for scarves, neckties, etc.

found, fownd, *v.* Past tense and past participle of **find.**

found, fownd, *v.t.* To set up or establish; to lay the foundation of; to base or ground, usu. with *on* or *upon.*—*v.i.* To be founded or based, with *on* or *upon.*

found, fownd, *v.t.* To melt, as iron, and pour into a mold; to mold; to cast.

foun•da•tion, fown•dā′shən, *n.* The act of founding or establishing; that on which something is founded; the lowest division of a building or wall; the basis or ground of anything; an endowed institution. —**foun•da•tion•al,** *a.*

found•er, fown′dər, *n.* One who founds or establishes, as a college, business, etc.

found•er, fown′dər, *v.i.* To fill with water and sink; to fall in or sink down; to stumble or go lame, as a horse; to fail utterly.—*v.t.* To cause to sink.

found•er, fown′dər, *n.* One who casts metals in various forms.

found•ling, fownd′ling, *n.* A child found after being abandoned by its parents.

found•ry, fown′drē, *n. pl.,* **-ries.** The art of casting metals; an establishment for casting metals; castings.

fount, fownt, *n.* A fountain; a source.

fount, fownt, *n. Brit. print.* Type font.

foun•tain, fown′tən, *n.* A spring or source of water; the source of a stream; the source of anything; a jet of water, made by mechanical means; a structure for discharging such a jet, often elaborate with basins, sculptures, etc.; a structure for furnishing fresh water for drinking; a soda fountain; a reservoir for ink or other liquids.

foun•tain•head, fown′tən•hed, *n.* The source of a stream; any primary source.

foun•tain pen, *n.* A pen with a reservoir which supplies ink continuously.

four, fôr, fōr, *a.* One more than three in number; twice two.—*n.* The cardinal number between three and five; a symbol representing it.

four•flush•er, fôr′flesh•ər, fōr′flesh•ər, *n. Informal.* One who bluffs; a cheat.

four•fold, fôr′fōld, *a.* Consisting of four parts or units; quadruple.—*adv.*

four-in-hand, fôr′in•hand, fōr′in•hand, *n.* A vehicle drawn by four horses and guided by one driver; a four-horse team; a necktie tied with a slipknot at the collar, with the ends hanging in front.

four-post•er, fôr′pōs′tər, fōr′pō′stər, *n.* A bed having four tall posts at its corners, orig. for the support of a curtain or canopy.

four•score, fôr′skôr, fōr′skōr, *a.* Four times twenty; eighty.

four·some, fôr′səm, fōr′səm, *n.* A game, esp. of golf, between two pairs of partners; the players in such a game; any group numbering four.

four·square, fôr′skwār′, fōr′skwār′, *a.* Square; solid; firm; direct; blunt.—*adv.* Bluntly; frankly.—*n.* A square.

four·teen, fôr·tēn′, fōr·tēn′, *a.* One more than 13 in number; four and ten; twice seven.—*n.* The cardinal number between 13 and 15; a symbol representing it. —**four·teenth,** *a., n.*

fourth, fôrth, fōrth, *a.* Following the third; being the ordinal of four; being one of four equal parts.—*n.* That which follows the third in a series; one of four equal parts. Also **fourth·ly.**

fourth di·men·sion, *n.* A dimension besides those of length, breadth, and depth, esp. time in relativity theory.

fourth es·tate, *n. (Often cap.)* The public press.

Fourth of July, *n.* Independence Day.

fowl, fowl, *n. pl.,* **fowls, fowl.** The domestic cock or hen; any of various other birds used for food, as the turkey or duck; the flesh of a fowl; a bird of any kind.—*v.i.* To hunt wild fowl. —**fowl·er,** fow′lər, *n.*

fox, foks, *n. pl.,* **fox·es, fox.** Any of a group of wild, carnivorous mammals of the dog family having a pointed muzzle, erect ears, and a long, bushy tail; the fur of the fox; a cunning or crafty person.—*v.t.* To outwit or deceive.—*v.i.* To become discolored.

fox·hole, foks′hōl, *n.* A small pit dug in a battle area for individual shelter from enemy fire.

fox·hound, foks′hownd, *n.* One of various breeds of fleet, keen-scented hounds trained to hunt foxes.

fox·tail, foks′tāl, *n.* The tail of a fox; any of various weedy grasses with soft, brushlike spikes of flowers.

fox·y, fok′sē, *a.,* **-i·er, -i·est.** Cunning or crafty; a yellowish or reddish brown; discolored or stained. —**fox·i·ly,** *adv.* —**fox·i·ness,** *n.*

foy·er, foy′ər, foy′ā, *n.* A lobby or anteroom in a public building, as a theater; an entrance hall or vestibule.

fra·cas, frā′kəs, *n. pl.,* **-cas·es.** An uproar; a noisy quarrel; a brawl.

frac·tion, frak′shən, *n.* A part of a unit; one or more of a number of equal parts into which a unit is divided; a part, as distinct from the whole of anything; a very small portion; fragment. —**frac·tion·al,** *a.*

frac·tious, frak′shəs, *a.* Apt to quarrel; cross; peevish; unruly. —**frac·tious·ly,** *adv.*

frac·ture, frak′chər, *n.* The act of breaking, or the state of being broken; the breaking of a bone or cartilage; a break, breach, or split; the texture of a broken surface, as of a mineral.—*v.t.,* **-tured, -tur·ing.** To break or crack.—*v.i.* To undergo fracture.

frag·ile, fraj′əl, *a.* Brittle; easily broken; delicate; frail; flimsy. —**fra·gil·i·ty,** frə·jil′ə·tē, *n.*

frag·ment, frag′mənt, *n.* A part broken off; a detached or incomplete portion of anything; a part of an unfinished whole.—*v.t., v.i.* To break into fragments. —**frag·men·tal,** frag·men′təl, *a.* —**frag·men·tar·i·ness,** frag·men·ter′i·nəs, *n.* —**frag·men·tar·y,** *a.*

frag·men·ta·tion, frag·mən·tā′shən, *n.* A breaking up into fragments; the scattering of the fragments of an exploding shell, bomb, or grenade.

frag·ment·ize, frag′mən·tīz, *v.t., v.i.,* **-ized, -iz·ing.** To fragment.

fra·grance, frā′grəns, *n.* Sweetness of smell; pleasing scent; perfume. —**fra·grant,** *a.* —**fra·grant·ly,** *adv.*

frail, frāl, *a.* Lacking physical strength and robust health; weak; delicate; fragile; not durable; susceptible to temptation. —**frail·ly,** *adv.* —**frail·ness,** *n.*

frail·ty, frāl′tē, *n. pl.,* **-ties.** The condition of being frail; liableness to be tempted; a fault proceeding from weakness of character; a foible.

frame, frām, *n.* A structure for admitting or enclosing something; an enclosing border or case; a framework;

a system, order, or way something is constructed; the body, esp. its skeleton; a device which functions by means of a framework; one exposure on a strip of movie film; a turn at bowling; the triangular form used to set up the balls for a pool game. *Informal.* A frame-up.—*v.t.,* **framed, fram·ing.** To provide with or put into a frame; to surround, as with a frame; to fashion or shape; to adapt to a particular purpose; to construct the frame of; to devise; to conceive; to utter. *Informal.* To contrive fraudulently, as a charge against someone; to incriminate unjustly; to prearrange the result of.—**frame of mind,** mood; mental state. —**fram·er,** *n.*

frame-up, frām′əp, *n. Informal.* An act or plot to produce unjust results, such as the conviction of an innocent person or the predetermination of the outcome of a contest.

frame·work, frām′wərk, *n.* A frame or structure composed of parts fitted together, esp. one designed to support or enclose something; a basic system or structure around which something is built.

franc, frangk, *n.* The monetary unit of France and several other countries.

fran·chise, fran′chīz, *n.* The right to vote; a privilege conferred by a governmental grant, as the right to be a corporation or to provide a public utility; the permission to sell a product, often within a specified territory, granted to a retailer by the manufacturer or by the owner of a business chain; the business so franchised.—*v.t.,* **-chised, -chis·ing.** To invest with a franchise; to enfranchise.

fran·gi·ble, fran′jə·bəl, *a.* Breakable.

frank, frangk, *a.* Open or unrestrained, esp. in speech; candid; outspoken; sincere; undisguised or plainly evident.—*n.* A signature or mark affixed to a letter or package to ensure its transmission free of charge; the letter or package; the privilege of sending articles in such a way.—*v.t.* To mark or send a letter or package free of charge. —**frank·er,** *n.* —**frank·ly,** *adv.* —**frank·ness,** *n.*

Frank·en·stein, frangk′ən·stīn, *n.* One who creates a monster that he cannot control or that brings about his own ruin; the monster itself, or anything which destroys its own creator.

frank·furt·er, frangk′fər·tər, *n.* A small, linked sausage composed of beef, or beef and pork. Also **frank·fort·er, frank·fort, frank·furt.**

frank·in·cense, frang′kin·sens, *n.* An aromatic gum-resin from various Asiatic and African trees.

fran·tic, fran′tik, *a.* Overcome by fear, anxiety, grief, etc.; frenzied. —**fran·ti·cal·ly, fran·tic·ly,** *adv.*

fra·ter·nal, frə·tər′nəl, *a.* Brotherly; pertaining to a society of men. —**fra·ter·nal·ly,** *adv.*

fra·ter·nal twin, *n.* One of twins each originating from separately fertilized ova.

fra·ter·ni·ty, frə·tər′nə·tē, *n. pl.,* **-ties.** The state or relationship of a brother; a body of men associated for their common interest, business, or pleasure; in U.S. high schools and colleges, a society of male students; a group of people gathered for a common purpose.

frat·er·nize, frat′ər·nīz, *v.i.,* **-nized, -niz·ing.** To associate in a brotherly way; to associate intimately with the enemy or with inhabitants of a vanquished land. —**frat·er·niz·er,** *n.*

frat·ri·cide, frat′rə·sīd, *n.* One who murders or kills a brother or sister; the act of murdering a brother or sister. —**frat·ri·cid·al,** *a.*

fraud, frôd, *n.* Deceit or trickery; an instance of such deceit; deception or artifice of any kind; a deceptive or spurious thing; an impostor; humbug.

fraud·u·lent, frô′jə·lənt, *a.* Proceeding from fraud; given to using fraud; deceitful; dishonest. —**fraud·u·lence,** *n.* —**fraud·u·lent·ly,** *adv.*

fraught, frôt, *a.* Filled or laden (*with*).

---

a- hat, fāte, fāre, fäther; **e-** met, mē; **i-** pin, pīne; **o-** not, nōte, ôrb, moove (move), boy, pownd; **u-** cūbe, bull, tûk (took); **ch-** chin; **th-** thick, ŧhen; **zh-** vizhon (vision); **ə-** əgo, takən, pencəl, lemən, bərd (bird).

fray, frā, *v.t.* To cause weakening by rubbing, as threads or fibers; to cause to ravel or tear, esp. at the ends; to irritate.—*v.i.* To become frayed.

fray, frā, *n.* A quarrel; conflict; brawl.

fraz•zle, fraz′əl, *v.i., v.t.,* **-zled, -zling.** To wear to threads; fray; to tire out.—*n.* Condition of being frazzled.

freak, frēk, *n.* An unpredictable or bizarre happening; an abnormal or deformed person or thing; monstrosity; a sudden whim or odd notion.—*a.* Bizarre; grotesque; capricious. Also **freak•ish.** —**freak•ish•ness,** *n.*

freak•y, frē′kē, *a.,* **-i•er, -i•est.** *Informal.* Freakish.

freck•le, frek′əl, *n.* A small brownish spot on the skin.—*v.t., v.i.,* **-led, -ling.** To mark or become marked with freckles. —**freck•led,** *a.* —**freck•ly,** *a.,* **-li•er, -li•est.**

free, frē, *a.,* **fre•er, fre•est.** Not being under physical or moral restraint; exempt from subjection to the will of others; having political, religious, or civil liberty; unconfined; acquitted; used or enjoyed without charge; not obstructed; not bound by a form or rule; outspoken; frank; going beyond due limits in speaking or acting; open to all; abundant; exempt from taxes or restrictions; not occupied; not fixed or attached; generous; liberal; not chemically combined with any other body.—*v.t.* To make free; to release from slavery, confinement, or the like; to let loose; to clear of obstruction; disengage.—*adv.* In a free manner; without charge. —**free•ly,** *adv.*

free•bie, frē′bē, *n. Informal.* Anything given free.

free•boot•er, frē′boo•tər, *n.* A buccaneer or pirate.

free•dom, frē′dəm, *n.* The state of being free; exemption or liberation from confinement or constraint; liberty; independence; political liberty; frankness; outspokenness; unrestrictedness; permission; liberality; ease of movement; free use; improper familiarity.

free-for-all, frē′fər•ôl, *n.* A competition, fight, or debate open to all; a brawl.

free•hand, frē′hand, *a., adv.* Done by hand without assistance by any guiding or measuring instruments.

free•hand•ed, frē′han′did, *a.* Openhanded, liberal.

free-lance, frē′lans, frē′läns, *a.* A writer, artist, etc; roving and independent, and esp. working without long-term commitment to any one employer.—*v.i.* **-lanced, -lanc•ing.**

Free•ma•son, frē′mā•sən, *n.* A member of a widely distributed secret order, having for its object mutual assistance and the promotion of brotherly love among its members. —**Free•ma•son•ry,** *n.*

free on board, *adv., a.* Without charge to the buyer for placing merchandise on board a common carrier.

free-spoken, frē′spō′kən, *a.* Speaking without reserve; outspoken. —**free-spo•ken•ness,** *n.*

free•stone, frē′stōn, *n.* Any stone, esp. limestone or sandstone, which can be easily quarried and worked; a fruit easily freed from its pit.

free-think•er, frē′thing′kər, *n.* A person who forms his opinions without regard for authority or tradition, esp. in matters of religion. —**free-think•ing,** *n., a.*

free trade, *n.* International trade without governmental regulation or custom duties; such trade where tariffs are used only as needed for revenue.

free verse, *n.* Verse which lacks a regular rhythm or metrical pattern.

free•way, frē′wā, *n.* A multiple-lane expressway which bypasses populated areas, and moves traffic without interruption; a toll-free highway.

free•wheel, frē′hwēl′, frē′wēl′, *v.i.* To live freely or irresponsibly.

free will, *n.* The power of voluntary decision; the doctrine that human decisions and actions are not wholly determined by divine will, physical necessity, or causal law.

free-will, frē′wil′, *a.* Voluntary.

freeze, frēz, *v.i.,* **froze, fro•zen, freez•ing.** To be changed from a liquid to a solid state by the loss of heat; to be hardened into ice; to become extremely cold; to become stiff, hard, or chilled with cold; to become filled or covered with ice; to become rigid through fear; to adhere by the formation of ice; to become icy or stiff in manner; to be injured or killed by cold.—*v.t.* To congeal or cause to freeze; to harden into ice; to give the sensation of cold and shivering; to clog or block by ice; to make adhere by ice; to stiffen by freezing; to make rigid or motionless through fear; to injure or kill by cold; to make insensitive by cold; to make aloof or hostile; alienate; to fix wages, rents, or prices at a specific level; to prohibit the liquidation, collection, or use of assets, loans, or funds by law.—*n.* The act of freezing; a weather condition of intense cold.

freeze-dry, frēz′drī, *v.t.,* **-dried, -dry•ing.** To dry in a high vacuum for preservation at room temperature.

freez•er, frē′zər, *n.* One who or that which freezes; a room or refrigerator cabinet used for freezing and keeping perishable foods.

freez•ing point, *n.* The temperature at which a liquid freezes: 0° centigrade or 32° Fahrenheit for water.

freight, frāt, *n.* Transportation of goods by water, air, or land; the price paid for such transportation; the cargo carried; a train of cars for transporting goods: also **freight train.**—*v.t.* To send by or as freight; to load with goods for transportation; to load; burden.

freight•age, frā′tij, *n.* The transportation of goods, or the price paid for this; freight, cargo, or lading.

freight•er, frā′tər, *n.* A ship engaged chiefly in the transportation of goods.

French, french, *a.* Of, pertaining to, or characteristic of France, its inhabitants, its culture, or its language. —*n.* The people or language of France. —**French•man,** *n.*

French fries, *n. pl. (Often l.c.)* Deep-fried strips of potatoes.

French horn, *n.* A musical wind instrument of brass having several curves, and gradually widening from the mouthpiece to a flaring bell at the other end.

French leave, *n.* A secret, informal, hasty, or improper departure.

French toast, *n.* Bread dipped in a batter of milk and eggs and fried.

fre•net•ic, frə•net′ik, *a.* Frenzied; frantic. Also **phre•net•ic.** —**fre•net•i•cal•ly,** *adv.*

fren•zy, fren′zē,n. *pl.,* **-zies.** Violent mental agitation; wild excitement; delirium.—*v.t.,* **-zied, -zy•ing.** To render frantic. —**fren•zied,** *a.*

Fre•on, frē′on, *n. Trademark.* Any of a group of chemicals used as refrigerants and aerosol propellants.

fre•quen•cy, frē′kwən•sē, *n. pl.,* **-cies.** Frequent occurrence. Also **fre•quence.** Rate of occurrence; the number of cycles per second of an alternating electric current.

fre•quen•cy mod•u•la•tion, *n.* A modulation of the frequency of transmitted radio waves, rather than the amplitude; a broadcasting system using this type of modulation.

fre•quent, frē′kwənt, *a.* Happening or appearing often; occurring at short intervals; habitual or recurrent.—fri•kwent′, frē′kwənt, *v.t.* To visit often; be in or at often. —**fre•quent•er,** *n.* —**fre•quent•ly,** *adv.*

fre•quen•ta•tive, fri•kwen′tə•tiv, *a.* Denoting frequent repetition of an action.—*n.* A frequentative verb.

fres•co, fres′kō, *n. pl.,* **-coes, -cos.** A method of painting on plaster that is still moist; a picture or design so painted.—*v.t.,* **-coed, -co•ing.** To paint in fresco.

fresh, fresh, *a.* Of water, not salt; pure; not stale; vigorous; bright; vivid; recently grown or obtained; not smoked, frozen, or preserved; in good condition; not faded or worn; not exhausted; clear; recent; new; cool; refreshing; youthful; healthy; inexperienced; untrained; newly arrived; original; additional; not previously known; of a wind, moderately brisk. *Informal.*

Impudent or saucy.—*n.* A freshet; the fresh or early part.—*adv.* Just recently. —**fresh·ly,** *adv.* —**fresh· ness,** *n.*

fresh·en, fresh′ən, *v.t., v.i.* To make or become fresh. —**fresh·en·er,** *n.*

fresh·et, fresh′it, *n.* A small stream of fresh water; a flood or overflowing, as of a river, due to heavy rains or melted snow.

fresh·man, fresh′mən, *n. pl.,* **-men.** A first-year student in a high school or university; a novice.—*a.*

fresh-wa·ter, fresh′wô·tər, fresh′wot·er, *a.* Pertaining to or living in water that is fresh, or not salt.

fret, fret, *v.i.,* **fret·ted, fret·ting.** To become angry; to worry; to become eaten, worn, or corroded; to gnaw; cause corrosion; to become agitated, as the surface of water.—*v.t.* To irritate; vex; make angry; to gnaw; rub or wear away; to agitate or disturb.—*n.* A state of irritation; vexation or anger. —**fret·ful,** *a.* —**fret·ful·ly,** *adv.*

fret, fret, *n.* A kind of ornament formed of bands or fillets esp. in interlocking rectangular motifs.—*v.t.,* **fret·ted, fret·ting.** To ornament with frets.

fret, fret, *n.* Any of the ridges set across the finger board of certain stringed instruments to guide the fingers in regulating the pitch of notes.—*v.t.,* **fret·ted, fret·ting.** To provide with frets.

fret·work, fret′wərk, *n.* Ornamental work, usu. openwork, consisting of a series or combination of frets.

Freud·i·an, froy′dē·ən, *a.* Of, pertaining to, or in accordance with the psychoanalytic theories and practices of Sigmund Freud.

fri·a·ble, frī′ə·bəl, *a.* Easily crumbled.

fri·ar, frī′er, *n.* A man belonging to any of several religious orders, esp. the mendicant ones.

fri·ar·y, frī′ə·rē, *n. pl.,* **-ar·ies.** A monastery of friars; a brotherhood of friars.

fric·as·see, frik·ə·sē′, *n.* Meat, as chicken or veal, cut up, stewed, and served in a sauce made of its own juices.—*v.t.,* **-seed, -see·ing.** To prepare as a fricassee.

fric·tion, frik′shən, *n.* The rubbing of the surface of one body against that of another; the resistance to motion of surfaces of bodies in contact; clashing as of temperaments or opinions.

fric·tion·al, frik′shə·nəl, *a.* Of, pertaining to, or of the nature of friction; moved, worked, or produced by friction. —**fric·tion·less,** *a.*

Fri·day, frī′dā, frī′dē, *n.* The sixth day of the week; the day following Thursday; a devoted servant or helper.

friend, frend, *n.* One attached to another by affection or regard; an intimate; an acquaintance; a member of the same nation or political group; a patron; (*cap.*) a member of the Society of Friends, the Christian sect called Quakers. —**friend·less,** *a.* —**friend·less·ness,** *n.* —**friend·ship,** *n.*

friend·ly, frend′lē, *a.,* **-li·er, -li·est.** Characteristic of a friend; like a friend; favorably disposed; inclined to approve or support; not hostile.—*adv.* In a friendly manner; like a friend. —**friend·li·ly,** *adv.* —**friend·li· ness,** *n.*

frieze, frēz, *n.* A horizontal strip between an architrave and cornice, usu. sculptured with figures or other ornaments; any decorated or sculptured horizontal band around a room, building, etc.

frieze, frēz, *n.* A coarse woolen cloth having a shaggy nap on one side.

fright, frīt, *n.* Sudden and violent fear; terror. *Informal.* A person or object of a shocking, disagreeable, or ridiculous appearance.

fright·en, frīt′ən, *v.t.* To strike with fright; to scare; to drive away by scaring.—*v.i.* To become afraid. —**fright·en·ing·ly,** *adv.*

fright·ful, frīt′fəl, *a.* Causing fright; terrible; dreadful; horrible or shocking. *Informal.* Awful or dreadful;

extreme. —**fright·ful·ly,** *adv.* —**fright·ful·ness,** *n.*

frig·id, frij′id, *a.* Very cold; devoid of warmth of feeling; chilling; stiff or formal; abnormally averse to sexual intercourse. —**fri·gid·i·ty,** fri·jid′ə·tē, *n.* —**frid·id·ly,** *adv.* —**frig·id·ness,** *n.*

frill, fril, *n.* A strip of cloth or lace, gathered or pleated at one edge and loose at the other, used as trimming on clothing; a ruff or fringe of hair or feathers about the neck of dogs or birds; an affectation; an extravagance or nonessential.—*v.t.* To trim with a frill or form into a frill. —**fril·ly,** *a.,* **-i·er, -i·est.**

fringe, frinj, *n.* A decorative border of bunched or loosely hanging threads or strands; anything resembling a fringe or border; something marginal or supplementary.—*v.t.,* **fringed, fring·ing.** To border with a fringe; to be a fringe for.

fringe ben·e·fit, *n.* Any benefit, such as paid holidays, insurance, or pensions, given an employee in addition to salary or wages; any incidental benefit.

frip·per·y, frip′ə·rē, *n. pl.,* **-per·ies.** Finery in dress, esp. when tawdry or showy; gaudy ornamentation; empty display; ostentation.

frisk, frisk, *v.i.* To dance, leap, skip, or gambol, as in frolic.—*v.t. Informal.* To search for stolen property, concealed weapons, etc., by running one's hands quickly over a person's clothing and pockets; to steal from someone in this way.—*n.* A frolic. *Informal.* The act of searching or frisking.

frisky, fris′kē, *a.,* **-i·er, -i·est.** Lively; playful. —**frisk· i·ly,** *adv.* —**frisk·i·ness,** *n.*

frit·ter, frit′er, *v.t.* To waste (away) little by little; to spend frivolously; to cut or break into small pieces or fragments.—*n.* A fragment.

frit·ter, frit′er, *n.* Batter shaped into a small cake and fried in deep fat or sautéed, sometimes with a filling of fruit or meat.

friv·o·lous, friv′ə·ləs, *a.* Of little importance; trifling; not serious; silly. —**fri·vol·i·ty,** fri·vol′ə·tē, *n. pl.,* **-ties.** —**friv·o·lous·ly,** *adv.*

frizz, friz, *v.t.* To form into tufts or knots; form into small, very tight or kinky curls.—*v.i.* To become frizzed.—*n.* That which is frizzed; a curl. Also **friz.** —**friz·zi·ness,** *n.* —**friz·zy,** *a.,* **-i·er, -i·est.**

friz·zle, friz′əl, *v.t., v.i.,* **-zled, -zling.** To frizz.—*n.* —**friz·zly,** *a.,* **-zli·er, -zli·est.**

fro, frō, *adv.* From; away; back: to and *fro.*

frock, frok, *n.* A woman's dress; a coarse outer garment worn by monks; a loose outer garment; smock. —*v.t.* To clothe in a frock.

frog, frog, frôg, *n.* Any of various tailless amphibians of a web-footed, aquatic genus, having strong hind legs enabling them to leap; a slight hoarseness due to mucus on the vocal cords; a triangular horny substance in the sole of the hoof of a horse or other hoofed animal; a device in the rail of a railroad for connecting one track with another crossing or branching from it; an ornamental fastening for a coat or other garment.—*v.i.,* **frogged, frog·ging.** To search for frogs.

frog·man, frog′man, frog′mən, *n. pl.,* **-men.** A person especially trained and equipped to swim under water, usu. for purposes of exploration and demolition.

frol·ic, frol′ik, *n.* A merry prank; a flight of levity; a scene of gaiety; a merrymaking.—*v.i.,* **-icked, -ick·ing.** To play merry pranks; to play in a light-hearted manner; to romp.

frol·ic·some, frol′ik·səm, *a.* Full of gaiety and mirth; sportive.

from, frəm, from, *prep.* A particle or function word specifying a starting point, source, or origin; a particle expressing removal or separation; a particle expressing discrimination or distinction; a particle indicating cause.

frond, frond, *n.* A large leaf, esp. that of a palm tree; a fern leaf; a leaflike extension of a plant.

front, frənt, *n.* The foremost part or surface of anything; the part or side which is directed forward; the side of a building which has the main entrance; frontage; the foremost line or part of an army; a line of battle; place where active operations are carried on; a movement, usu. political, to achieve a common goal; an eminent person serving as a nominal official of a group or company to give it prestige; bearing or demeanor. *Informal.* An outward appearance of wealth or position assumed to impress others; any person or business which masks or disguises illegal activity; a line which separates dissimilar masses of air.—*a.* Of or pertaining to the front; situated in or at the front.—*v.t.* To have the front toward; face; to meet face to face; confront; defy; oppose; supply with a front; to serve as a front to.—*v.i.* To face; serve as a front.

front·age, frən′tij, *n.* The front of a building or lot; the length of this front; the direction something faces; exposure; land abutting a body of water or a street; land between a building and the street.

fron·tal, frən′təl, *a.* Pertaining to, in, or at the front; pertaining to the forehead. —**fron·tal·ly,** *adv.*

fron·tier, frən·tēr′, *n.* The part of a country that faces or borders another country; that part of a country which forms the border of its settled or inhabited regions; a new or untapped area of knowledge or achievement.—*a.* Of, on, or pertaining to a frontier. —**fron·tiers·man,** frən·tērz′mən, *n. pl.,* **-men.**

fron·tis·piece, frən′tis·pēs, fron′tis·pēs, *n.* An illustration facing the title page of a book; the front of a building; a highly decorated facade; a pediment.

frost, frôst, frost, *n.* A temperature below the freezing point of water; a covering of ice crystals formed from the atmosphere when it cools below the freezing point; frozen vapor; coldness of manner or temperament. *Informal.* A failure.—*v.t.* To cover with frost; to give a frostlike surface to, as glass; to ice, as a cake; to damage or kill by frost. —**frost·ed,** *a.*

frost·bite, frôst′bīt, frost′bīt, *n.* Damage to tissues in any part of the body occasioned by exposure to severe cold.—*v.t.,* **-bit, -bit·ten, -bit·ing.** To damage by severe cold. —**frost·bit·ten,** *a.*

frost·ing, frô′sting, fros′ting, *n.* An edible, sweetened mixture used to cover cakes and other pastries; icing; a lusterless finish, as on metal or glass.

frost·y, frô′stē, fros′tē, *a.,* **-i·er, -i·est.** Producing frost; very cold; lacking warmth of feeling; chilling; consisting of or covered with frost; resembling frost; hoary. —**frost·i·ly,** *adv.* —**frost·i·ness,** *n.*

froth, frôth, froth, *n.* Foam; a foam of saliva; something unsubstantial or trivial, as talk.—*v.t.* To cause to foam; to emit like froth; to cover with froth.—*v.i.* To give off froth. —**froth·i·ness,** *n.* —**froth·y,** *a.,* **-i·er, -i·est.**

frou·frou, froo′froo, *n.* A rustling sound; elaborate ornamentation.

fro·ward, frō′wərd, frō′ərd, *a.* Perverse; ungovernable; refractory; disobedient.

frown, frown, *v.i.* To express displeasure or disapproval by contracting the brow; to scowl.—*v.t.* To show or express by scowling; to express disapproval by a grimace.—*n.* A contraction or wrinkling of the brow; a severe or stern look; a scowl. —**frown·ing·ly,** *adv.*

frow·zy, frow′zē, *a.,* **-zi·er, -zi·est.** Slovenly; unkempt; having a stale, musty odor. Also **frow·sy.**

fro·zen, frō′zən, *a.* Preserved by quick freezing; congealed by cold; covered with ice; obstructed by ice, as pipes; injured or killed by frost; very cold; cold and unfeeling in manner; rendered impossible of liquidation; fixed in price, rate, etc. —**fro·zen·ly,** *adv.* —**fro·zen·ness,** *n.*

fruc·ti·fy, frək′tə·fī, *v.t.,* **-fied, -fy·ing.** To make fruitful; fertilize.—*v.i.* To bear fruit. —**fruc·ti·fi·ca·tion,** frək·tə·fə·kā′shən, *n.*

fru·gal, froo′gəl, *a.* Economical; thrifty; not lavish; costing little. —**fru·gal·i·ty,** froo·gal′ə·tē, *n. pl.,* **-ties.** —**fru·gal·ly,** *adv.*

fruit, froot, *n. pl.,* **fruit** or **fruits.** Any product of vegetable growth useful to men or animals; the matured ovary of a plant with its contents and accessory parts; the pulpy edible substance covering the seeds of various flowering plants and trees; an offspring; result; profit. *Informal.* A male homosexual.—*v.i., v.t.* To bear or bring to bear fruit.

fruit·ful, froot′fəl, *a.* Bearing fruit abundantly; very fertile or productive; productive of results; profitable. —**fruit·ful·ly,** *adv.* —**fruit·ful·ness,** *n.*

fru·i·tion, froo·ish′ən, *n.* Attainment of a goal; accomplishment; enjoyment of something realized; condition of bearing fruit.

fruit·less, froot′lis, *a.* Not bearing fruit; barren; unproductive; ineffectual. —**fruit·less·ly,** *adv.* —**fruit·less·ness,** *n.*

fruit·y, froo′tē, *a.* Having the taste or flavor of fruit. *Informal.* Mentally disturbed or eccentric; homosexual.

frump, frəmp, *n.* A dowdy, cross-tempered, or old-fashioned female. —**frump·ish,** *a.*—**frump·y,** *a.,* **-i·er, -i·est.**

frus·trate, frəs′trāt, *v.t.,* **-trat·ed, -trat·ing.** To disappoint or thwart; defeat; baffle; nullify. —**frus·tra·tion,** frə·strā′shən, *n.*

fry, frī, *v.t., v.i.,* **fried, fry·ing.** To cook in a pan over a fire using fat.—*n.* A social occasion on which fried food is served; a dish of anything fried.

fry, frī, *n.* The young of fishes or of some other animals; adult fish of lesser size; offspring; children.

fry·er, frī′ər, *n.* A young chicken, suitable for frying; one who or that which fries. Also **fri·er.**

fud·dle, fəd′əl, *v.t.,* **-dled, -dling.** To make foolish or stupid by drink; to make tipsy.—*v.i.* To tipple.

fud·dy-dud·dy, fəd′ē-dəd·ē, *n. pl.,* **-dud·dies.** *Informal.* A stuffy, old-fashioned, or fussy person.

fudge, fəj, *v.i.,* **fudged, fudg·ing.** To cheat; to hedge; to welsh.—*v.t.* To evade; to fake; to falsify.—*n.* A soft candy composed of sugar, butter, chocolate, etc; a made-up story; nonsense.

fu·el, fū′əl, *n.* Combustible matter used to maintain fire, as coal, wood, or oil; a means of sustaining or increasing strong feeling.—*v.t.,* **-eled, -el·ing.** To supply with fuel.—*v.i.* To get fuel.

fu·gi·tive, fū′jə·tiv, *a.* Fleeing, or tending to flee; having taken flight; wandering; vagabond; fleeting or transitory; quickly fading; dealing with subjects of temporary interest; occasional.—*n.* A runaway; a refugee. —**fu·gi·tive·ly,** *adv.*

ful·crum, fûl′krəm, fəl′krəm, *n. pl,* **-crums, -cra,** -krə. A prop or support; the support by which a lever is sustained or the point about which a lever turns in lifting a body.

ful·fill, ful·fil, fûl·fil′, *v.t.,* **-filled, -fil·ling.** To accomplish, as a prophecy or promise; to perform; to meet or satisfy, as requirements; to complete. —**ful·fill·ment, ful·fil·ment,** *n.*

full, fûl, *a.* Containing all that can be held; filled; containing a plentiful amount; of the maximum amount, extent, or volume; complete or entire; copious; preoccupied or engrossed; satisfied, as with food; filled or rounded out, as in form; wide, ample, or having ample folds; having ample volume and depth of sound.—*adv.* Exactly, directly, or straight; very or quite.—*n.* Complete measure; utmost extent; highest degree.—*v.t.* To make full by gathering, tucking, or pleating.—*v.i.* Of the moon, to become completely illuminated. —**full·ness,** *n.* —**ful·ly,** *adv.*

full·back, fûl′bak, *n.* A player whose position is far back, the farthest back, from the front line in certain sports; the position.

full-blood·ed, fûl′bləd′id, *a.* Of pure blood; thoroughbred; vigorous.

full-blown, fûl′blōn′, *a.* Fully expanded, as a blossom; mature; completely developed.

full dress, *n.* Formal or ceremonial attire. —**full-dress,** *a.*

full-fledged, fūl′flejd′, *a.* Completely developed; matured; of full status or rank.

full moon, *n.* The moon with its whole disk illuminated.

full-scale, fūl′skāl′, *a.* Equal in size or proportion; using all available resources.

ful•mi•nate, fəl′mə•nāt, *v.i.,* **-nat•ed, -nat•ing.** To explode with a loud noise; detonate; to issue denunciations or invectives.—*v.t.* To cause to explode; to denounce vehemently.—*n.* An unstable, explosive salt. —**ful•mi•na•tion,** fəl•mə•nā′shən, *n.*

ful•some, fūl′səm, fəl′səm, *a.* Offensive, as from excess of praise or insincerity of motive; disgusting. —**ful•some•ly,** *adv.*

fum•ble, fəm′bəl, *v.i.,* **-bled, -bling.** To feel or grope about; to attempt something awkwardly. *Sports.* To drop the ball or fail to handle it properly.—*v.t.* To handle clumsily or ineffectively. *Sports.* To drop awkwardly.—*n.* An act or instance of fumbling. —**fumbler,** *n.*

fume, fūm, *n. Often pl.* Smoke, gas, or vapor, esp. when odorous, stifling, or offensive. An angry or irritable mood.—*v.i.,* **fumed, fum•ing.** To emit fumes; to rise or pass off as fumes; to show irritation or anger.—*v.t.* To treat with fumes. —**fum•ing•ly,** *adv.*

fu•mi•gate, fū′mə•gāt, *v.t.,* **-gat•ed, -gat•ing.** To expose to fumes, esp. for disinfection. —**fu•mi•ga•tion,** fū•mə•gā′shən, *n.* —**fu•mi•ga•tor,** *n.*

fun, fən, *n.* That which is diverting, amusing, or mirthful; recreation; playfulness.—*v.i.,* **funned, fun•ning.** *Informal.* To make fun; joke.—*a.* Full of fun.

func•tion, fəngk′shən, *n.* The normal or proper activity; proper work; purpose; a formal or elaborate social occasion; a quantity whose value is dependent on the value of another quantity.—*v.i.* To perform usual or specified activity; to serve in a particular capacity. —**func•tion•less,** *a.*

func•tion•al, fəngk′shə•nəl, *a.* Of or pertaining to a function or functions; having a particular use; capable of performing its function; useful; adaptable. —**func•tion•al•ly,** *adv.*

func•tion•ar•y, fəngk′shə•ner•ē, *n. pl.,* **-ar•ies.** One who holds an office or trust; an official who has special duties.

fund, fənd, *n.* A store or stock of something, esp. a stock of money. *Pl.* Money in hand; pecuniary resources.—*v.t.* To provide a fund to pay the interest or principal of, as a debt; to convert into a long-term debt; to provide funds for.

fun•da•men•tal, fən•də•men′təl, *a.* Of, pertaining to, or being the foundation of something; essential; elementary; primary.—*n.* A primary principle, rule, or law; something essential. *Phys.* The lowest of the component frequencies of a periodic wave. —**fun•da•men•tal•ly,** *adv.*

fun•da•men•tal•ism, fən•də•men′tə•liz•əm, *n.* A belief that the Bible is to be accepted literally as an infallible document. (*Often cap.*) An early 20th century U.S. Protestant movement stressing this belief. —**fun•da•men•tal•ist,** *n., a.*

fu•ner•al, fū′nər•əl, *n.* The ceremony or procession immediately prior to burying or cremating a dead person; obsequies.—*a.*

fu•ne•re•al, fū•nēr′ē•əl, *a.* Pertaining to a funeral; gloomy; mournful.

fun•gi•cide, fən′jə•sīd, *n.* A chemical which kills fungi. —**fun•gi•cid•al,** fən•ji•sī′dəl, *a.* —**fun•gi•cid•al•ly,** *adv.*

fun•gous, fəng′gəs, *a.* Pertaining to, resembling, or caused by fungi. *Fig.* Springing up or spreading rapidly.

fun•gus, fəng′gəs, *n. pl.,* **-gi, -gus•es.** Any of a group of plants including mushrooms, molds, mildews, and smuts, that have no flowers, leaves, or chlorophyll; a spongy growth.—*a.* Fungous.

fu•nic•u•lar, fū•nik′yə•lər, *a.* Of or run by a rope, cable, or cord.—*n.* Funicular railway.

fu•nic•u•lar rail•way, *n.* A cable railway used for ascending and descending a mountain.

funk, fəngk, *n. Informal.* A coward; a state of extreme fright or dejection.—*v.t.* To fear; to avoid doing or facing.—*v.i.* To draw back because of fear. —**funk•y,** *a.,* **-i•er, -i•est.**

funk•y, fəng′kē, *a.,* **-i•er, -i•est.** *Informal.* Foul-smelling; offensive. *Jazz.* Marked by an earthy quality, with a basis in the blues.

fun•nel, fən′əl, *n.* A utensil, usu. a hollow cone with a slim tube or pipe extending from its narrowest point, used for pouring liquids or powders into containers with narrow openings; anything in the shape of a funnel; any flue or chimney, esp. the smokestacks of steamships.—*v.i.,* **-neled, -nel•ing.** To be shaped like a funnel; to move through or as if through a funnel.—*v.t.* To shape like a funnel; to cause to move through or as if through a funnel: to *funnel* requests through headquarters.

fun•ny, fən′ē, *a.,* **-ni•er, -ni•est.** *Informal.* Amusing; comical; underhanded; involving deceit, or deceitful. —*n. pl.,* **fun•nies.** *Informal.* Comic strip. —**fun•ni•ly,** *adv.* —**fun•i•ness,** *n.*

fun•ny bone, *n.* The part of the elbow which when struck causes a tingling sensation in the arm and hand; the crazy bone.

fur, fər, *n.* The skin of certain animals, as the sable, ermine, and beaver, covered with a fine, soft, thick, hairy coating; the hairy coating on such a skin; such skins as a material for clothing; clothing.—*a.* Of fur. —*v.t.,* **furred, fur•ring.** To line or trim with fur. To coat with matter. *Building.* To apply furring strips to.

fur•bish, fər′bish, *v.t.* To rub or scour to brightness; to polish; to renovate: sometimes with *up.*

fu•ri•ous, fyŭr′ē•əs, *a.* Full of fury, violent anger, or rage; of unrestrained energy or speed: a *furious* pace. —**fu•ri•ous•ly,** *adv.*

furl, fərl, *v.t.* To wrap or roll, as a flag or a sail.—*v.i.* To become furled.—*n.* Something which is furled; the act or process of furling.

fur•long, fər′lông, fər′long, *n.* A measure of length, equal to one-eighth of a mile, 40 rods, or 220 yards.

fur•lough, fər′lō, *n.* Leave or permission given, esp. to a soldier, to be absent from service for a certain time; the period of time granted.—*v.t.* To grant a furlough.

fur•nace, fər′nis, *n.* A structure in which to generate heat, as for melting ores, baking pottery, or heating houses. *Fig.* Any place of extreme heat.

fur•nish, fər′nish, *v.t.* To provide or supply with something necessary, useful, or desired; to equip, as a house or room, with necessary appliances, as furniture.

fur•nish•ings, fər′ni•shingz, *n. pl.* Furniture for a house or room; accessories of men's apparel.

fur•ni•ture, fər′nə•chər, *n.* The movable articles, as tables, chairs, desks, required for use or ornament in a house or office.

fu•ror, fyŭr′ôr, *n.* A general outburst of enthusiasm or excitement; mania for or against something; fury; rage.

fur•ri•er, fər′ē•ər, *n.* A dealer in furs and fur garments; one who makes and repairs fur garments.

fur•ring, fər′ing, *n.* The act of lining or trimming clothing with fur; the fur used; a coating of matter on something; the nailing on of thin strips, as wood or metal, to make a level surface for lathing or plastering; the strips used.

fur•row, fər′ō, *n.* A trench in the earth made by a plow; a groove; a wrinkle in the face.—*v.t.* To make furrows in.—*v.i.* To become furrowed.

fur•ry, fər′ē, *a.,* **-ri•er, -ri•est.** Of or like fur; covered

a- hat, fāte, fâre, fäther; **e-** met, mē; **i-** pin, pīne; **o-** not, nōte, ôrb, moove (move), boy, pownd;
u- cūbe, bŭll, tŭk (took); **ch-** chin; **th-** thick, then; **zh-** vizhon (vision); **ə-** əgo, takən, pencəl, lemən, bərd (bird).

with fur.

fur·ther, fer′ther, *adv.* At or to a more advanced point in time or space; to a greater extent; farther; in addition; moreover.—*a.* Additional; more; more distant or remote; farther.—*v.t.* To help forward; promote; advance.

fur·ther·more, fer′ther·môr, *adv.* Moreover; besides; in addition.

fur·ther·most, fer′ther·mōst, *a.* Most distant or remote.

fur·thest, fer′thist, *a., adv.* Farthest.

fur·tive, fer′tiv, *a.* Taken or done stealthily: *a furtive glance;* surreptitious; sly.

fu·ry, fūr′ē, *n. pl.,* **-ries.** Violent or unrestrained anger; rage; unrestrained energy or speed: to work with *fury;* any avenging spirit.

fuse, fūz, *n.* A safety device in an electric circuit, containing a strip of metal which melts when the current becomes excessive, thus breaking the circuit; a tube, cable, or wick filled with combustible matter, used to ignite an explosive charge.—*v.t.,* **fused, fus·ing.** To furnish with a fuse. Also **fuze.**

fuse, fūz, *v.t.,* **fused, fus·ing.** To blend or unite by melting together; to melt or liquefy.—*v.i.* To melt by heat; to become blended.

fu·see, fū·zē′, *n.* A match with a large head which ignites by friction and is not easily extinguished; the fuse of an explosive device; a signal light or flare used on railroads.

fu·se·lage, fū′se·läzh, fū′ze·läzh, fū′se·lij, *n.* The main structure of an airplane, which contains the crew, passengers, and cargo; body or hull.

fu·si·bil·i·ty, fū·ze·bil′e·tē, *n.* The quality or extent of being fusible.

fu·si·ble, fū′ze·bel, *a.* Capable of being fused or melted.

fu·si·form, fū′ze·fôrm, *a.* Spindle-shaped.

fu·sil·lade, fū′se·lād, fū′se·läd, fū′ze·lād, *n.* A simultaneous discharge of firearms. *Fig.* A general discharge or outpouring of anything.—*v.t.,* **-lad·ed, -lad·ing.** To attack by a fusillade.

fu·sion, fū′zhen, *n.* The act of fusing; the state of being fused; a melting by heat; the uniting of various elements into a whole as if by melting together; something formed by fusing; the coalition of parties or factions; the group resulting from such coalition; the combining of the nuclei of atoms under intense heat to release nuclear energy.

fuss, fes, *n.* An excessive display of anxious activity, esp. over trifles.—*v.i.* To give excess attention to, usu. with *over;* make much ado about trifles or small details.—*v.t.* To bother with trifles.

fuss·y, fes′ē, *a.,* **-i·er, -i·est.** Excessively anxious or particular about trifles or details; elaborately made or trimmed, as clothing. —**fuss·i·ly,** *adv.* —**fuss·i·ness,** *n.*

fus·tian, fes′chen, *n.* A coarse fabric of cotton and linen; a stout twilled fabric of cotton with a pile, as corduroy; an inflated style of speaking or writing; bombast.—*a.* Made of fustian; bombastic.

fus·ty, fes′tē, *a.,* **-ti·er, -ti·est.** Moldy; musty; ill-smelling; clinging to old ideas. —**fus·ti·ly,** *adv.* —**fus·ti·ness,** *n.*

fu·tile, fū′tel, fū′til, *a.* Serving no useful end; of no effect; vain, fruitless, or unsuccessful.

fu·til·i·ty, fū·til′e·tē, *n. pl.,* **-ties.** The quality of being futile, or producing no valuable effect; an act or effort which is futile.

fu·ture, fū′cher, *a.* Of or connected with time to come; any time that is to come.—*n.* Time to come; what will exist or happen in the time to come; a state or condition yet to come, usu. a better or more prosperous time: as, to have a *future* in business; the future tense; a verb in the future tense.

fu·tur·ism, fū′che·riz·em, *n.* A movement in the fine arts during World War I, rejecting traditional forms of expression in order to portray the dynamic movement of a mechanized era; the study of trends and projections of current conditions into the future.

fu·tur·is·tic, fū·cher·is′tik, *a.* Of or having to do with the future, or futurism.

fu·tu·ri·ty, fū·tûr′e·tē, fū·tyûr′e·tē, *n. pl.,* **-ties.** Future time; a future quality, state, condition, or event.

fuze, fūz, *n.* See **fuse.**

fu·zee, fū·zē′, *n.* Fusee.

fuzz, fez, *n.* Loose, light, fibrous matter; a coating of such matter.—*v.i.* To form, or become fuzzy.—*v.t.* To cover with fuzz; make fuzzy.

fuzz·y, fez′ē, *a.,* **-i·er, -i·est.** Covered with fuzz; indistinct; hazy. —**fuzz·i·ly,** *adv.* —**fuzz·i·ness,** *n.*

G

G, g, jē, *n.* The seventh letter of the English alphabet; the graphic representation of this letter; any spoken sound represented by this letter; anything shaped like the letter G. (*Cap.*) *Mus.* The fifth tone of the scale of C major. Also **sol.**

gab, gab, *v.i.,* **gabbed, gab·bing.** To talk idly.—*n. Informal.* Idle talk; chatter. —**gab·ber,** *n.*

gab·ar·dine, gab′er·dēn, gab·er·dēn′, *n.* A closely woven fabric with fine diagonal ribs. Also **gab·er·dine.**

gab·ble, gab′el, *v.i.,* **-bled, -bling.** To talk noisily and rapidly, or without meaning.—*n.* Loud or rapid talk without meaning. —**gab·bler,** *n.*

gab·by, gab′ē, *a.,* **-bi·er, -bi·est.** *Informal.* Full of gab.

ga·ble, gā′bel, *n.* That portion of a building enclosed by the sloping ends, usu. triangular, of a ridged roof; any architectural structure or ornament resembling a gable.—*v.t.,* **-bled, -bling.** To build with a gable or gables.—*v.i.* To be in the form of or end in a gable. —**ga·bled,** *a.*

gad, gad, *n.* A goad.—*v.t.,* **gad·ded, gad·ding.** To goad.

gad, gad, *v.i.,* **gad·ded, gad·ding.** To rove or ramble restlessly, usu. with *about.* —**gad·der,** *n.*

gad·a·bout, gad′e·bowt, *n.* One who wanders out of restless idleness; one who gads.—*a.* Fond of frivolous social activity.

gad·fly, gad′flī, *n. pl.,* **-flies.** A large fly, as the horsefly that annoys or stings domestic animals; a bothersome person who annoys others.

gad·get, gaj′it, *n.* A small contrivance or device; any novel device, interesting object, or trifle.

gaff, gaf, *n.* A strong hook with a handle used for landing large fish; the spar extending the upper edge of a fore-and-aft sail. *Informal.* An ordeal or abuse; something difficult to endure: to stand the *gaff.*—*v.t.* To hook or land with a gaff.

gaffe, gaf, *n.* A stupid mistake; a blunder; a faux pas.

gaf·fer, gaf′er, *n.* An old man.

gag, gag, *v.t.,* **gagged, gag·ging.** To stop up, as the mouth, with something so as to prevent speech or sound; to silence by force or authority; to cause to vomit; to choke or prevent passage through.—*v.i.* To heave with nausea; to choke.—*n.* Something put into the mouth to prevent speech or sound; something which limits free speech. *Informal.* A joke, line, or story intended to produce laughter.

ga·ga, gä′gä, *a. Informal.* Doting; foolish.

gage, gāj, *n.* Something given as a security to ensure the fulfillment of some act; a pledge; something thrown down as a token of challenge to combat.

gage, gāj, *n., v.t.* Gauge.

gai·e·ty, gā′ə·tē, *n. pl.,* **-ties.** The state of being gay or cheerful; merrymaking or festivity; showiness; finery.

gai·ly, gā′lē, *adv.* In a gay manner; cheerfully; brightly or showily.

gain, gān, *v.t.* To obtain or earn as a profit or advantage; win, as in competition; to attain or reach; to win over to one's friendship or purposes, often followed by *over;* to make or acquire an increase of: to *gain* five pounds.—*v.i.* To profit; benefit; to improve; make progress.—*n.* Profit or advantage; an increase or advance; a gaining or winning. *Pl.* Profits. —**gain on** or **upon,** to advance nearer to, as a person or thing pursued.

gain·er, gā′nər, *n.* One who or that which gains.

gain·ful, gān′fəl, *a.* Producing profit or advantage; lucrative.

gain·say, gān′sā, *v.t.,* **-said, -say·ing.** To contradict; to deny; to dispute.

gait, gāt, *n.* A manner of walking or stepping; any one of the paces of a horse, as the walk, canter, or trot.

ga·la, gā′lə, gal′ə, *a.* Festive; suitable for a celebration.—*n.* An occasion of public festivity.

ga·lac·tic, gə·lak′tik, *a. Astron.* Pertaining to a galaxy, or the Milky Way.

gal·ax·y, gal′ək·sē, *n. pl.,* **-ies.** A system of stars held together by gravity and separated from other systems by immense regions of space, as the Milky Way; an assemblage of splendid persons or things.

gale, gāl, *n.* A strong wind, specif. one between 32 and 63 miles per hour; a noisy fit or outburst.

gall, gôl, *n.* Something very bitter or severe; bitterness of spirit; rancor; bile of an animal; impudence.

gall, gôl, *n.* A sore on the skin, esp. of a horse, due to rubbing; something irritating or vexing.—*v.t.* To make sore by rubbing; chafe; annoy or vex: the umpire's decision *galled* the player.—*v.i.* To become chafed.

gall, gôl, *n.* An abnormal vegetable growth on plants caused by certain parasites, insects, bacteria, or fungi.

gal·lant, gal′ənt, gə·lant′, gə·länt′, *a.* Brave, high-spirited, or chivalrous: a *gallant* soldier; polite and attentive to women; splendid or fine; stately: a *gallant* vessel; gay or showy, as in dress.—*n.* A gay, dashing man; a man of dauntless spirit; a man particularly attentive to women; a suitor or lover.

gal·lant·ry, gal′ən·trē, *n. pl.,* **-ries.** Dashing courage; heroic bravery; gallant or courtly attention to women; a polite or chivalrous action or speech; gay or fine appearance.

gall blad·der, *n.* A small membranous sac, shaped like a pear, which receives and stores bile from the liver.

gal·ler·y, gal′ə·rē, *n. pl.,* **-ies.** A long covered walkway: an aquarium *gallery;* an area or room used for public displays and sales, as of art and antiques; a balcony which projects from an interior wall and contains seats for an audience; the uppermost balcony in a theater; the occupants who sit there.

gal·ley, gal′ē, *n.* An early form of seagoing vessel propelled by oars and sometimes by sails; the kitchen of a ship; a long, narrow tray, usu. metal, to hold type which has been set; a galley proof.

gal·ley proof, *n.* A proof taken from type on a galley to permit corrections before the page is printed.

gal·ley slave, *n.* A person condemned to work at the oar on a galley; a drudge; one who is overworked.

gal·li·cism, gal′ə·siz·əm, *n. (Often cap.)* A French idiom used in another language.

gal·li·mau·fry, gal′ə·mô′frē, *n. pl.,* **-fries.** A hodgepodge; a jumbled mixture or medley.

gall·ing, gôl′ing, *a.* Vexing; annoying.

gal·li·vant, gal′ə·vant, *v.i.* To gad or run about; to flirt.

gal·lon, gal′ən, *n.* A unit of measure equal to four quarts. See Measures and Weights table.

gal·lop, gal′əp, *v.i.* To move or run by leaps, as a horse; to ride at a gallop, or at full speed; to go fast.—*v.t.* To cause to gallop, as a horse or other animal; to drive or convey at a gallop.—*n.* The fastest gait of a horse in which all four feet are off the ground simultaneously once during each stride; a run or ride at this gait; a rapid rate of going.

gal·lows, gal′ōz, *n. pl.,* **-lows·es, -lows.** A wooden frame, consisting of a crossbeam on two uprights, on which condemned persons are executed by hanging; any similar structure.

gall·stone, gôl′stōn, *n.* A stonelike mass formed in the gall bladder.

ga·loot, gal·loot, gə·loot′, *n. Informal.* An uncouth or clumsy fellow.

ga·lore, gə·lôr′, gə·lōr′, *adv.* In profusion or abundance.

ga·losh, ga·loshe, gə·losh′, *n. Usu. pl.* An overshoe worn to keep the feet dry.

ga·lumph, gə·ləmf′, *v.i.* To gallop or bump along clumsily.

gal·van·ic, gal·van′ik, *a.* Of, pertaining to, or produced by galvanism; voltaic; shocking or stimulating.

gal·va·nism, galvə·niz·əm, *n.* Electricity produced by chemical action.

gal·va·nize, gal′və·nīz, *v.t.,* **-nized, -niz·ing.** To stimulate by or as by electric current; to coat, as iron, with zinc.

gal·va·nom·e·ter, gal·və·nom′ə·tər, *n.* An instrument for detecting the existence and determining the strength and direction of an electric current.

gam·bit, gam′bit, *n.* The sacrifice of a pawn early in the game, for the purpose of taking up an attacking position; any action, trick, or strategy intended to gain an initial advantage.

gam·ble, gam′bəl, *v.i.,* **-bled, -bling.** To play at any game of chance for stakes; to risk anything of value on something involving chance; to take a risk.—*v.t.* To stake, bet, or wager; to squander by betting, usu. followed by *away.*—*n.* A venture in or as in gambling; any matter or thing involving risk or uncertainty.

gam·bol, gam′bəl, *v.i.* To dance and skip playfully about; to leap; to frolic.—*n.* A frolic; a playful skip or leap.

gam·brel, gam′brəl, *n.* The hock of an animal, esp. a horse.

gam·brel roof, *n.* A roof whose sides have two slopes, the lower one being the steeper.

game, gām, *n.* An amusement or pastime; a diversion in the form of chance, skill, endurance, or a combination of these, pursued according to certain rules: card *games,* a *game* of football; the equipment used in playing games; a particular contest in the process of play; or a specific portion of play within the contest: to see a baseball *game,* to win four *games* in a set of tennis; the state of a contest, indicated by the score, at a particular time: The *game* was two to one; the number of points necessary to win such a contest; a particular manner or quality of play: He plays a strong *game* of golf; a proceeding executed in the manner of a game: to play a waiting *game;* the use of skill and endurance, similar to that employed in a game: the *game* of diplomacy; wild animals which are hunted or

---

a- hat, fāte, fâre, fäther; **e-** met, mē; **i-** pin, pīne; **o-** not, nōte, ôrb, moove (move), boy, pownd;
u- cūbe, bůll, tûk (took); **ch-** chin; **th-** thick, ŧhen; **zh-** vizhon (vision); **ə-** əgo, takən, pencəl, lemən, bərd (bird).

taken for sport or profit; the flesh of wild animals used for food; any object of pursuit or attack.—*a.,* **gam·er, gam·est.** Of or pertaining to animals hunted or taken as game; plucky. *Informal.* Having determination, spirit, or will; lame, as a leg.—*v.i.,* **gamed, gam·ing.** To play, sport, or jest; to play games, esp. games of chance.

game·keep·er, gām′kē·pər, *n.* A person employed to look after the wild animals living on a game preserve, and to prevent illegal hunting or fishing.

games·man·ship, gāmz′mən·ship, *n.* The practice of using questionable but not illegal methods in order to win in a game.

game·some, gām′səm, *a.* Sportive; playful; frolicsome.

game·ster, gām′stər, *n.* A gambler.

gam·ete, gam′ēt, gə·mēt′, *n.* Either of the two reproductive germ cells which unite to form a new organism. —**ga·met·ic,** gə·met′ik, *a.*

game the·o·ry, *n.* A mathematical theory applied in games, business situations, and military problems to determine how to achieve the most accurate results between at least two strategies.

gam·in, gam′in, *Fr.* ga·man′, *n.* A street urchin; a neglected boy.

gam·ing, gā′ming, *n.* Gambling.

gam·ma, gam′ə, *n.* The third letter of the Greek alphabet.

gam·ma glob·u·lin, *n.* A protein separated from blood and containing antibodies: used in inoculation against measles, poliomyelitis, and infectious hepatitis.

gam·ma rays, *n.* Penetrating rays emitted from radioactive material.

gam·mon, gam′ən, *n.* Smoked ham or the lower part from a side of bacon.

gam·ut, gam′ət, *n.* The whole series of recognized musical notes; the whole range or series of anything.

gam·y, gā′mē, *a.,* **-i·er, -i·est.** Having the flavor of game; plucky. —**gam·i·ly,** *adv.* —**gam·i·ness,** *n.*

gan·der, gan′dər, *n.* The male of the goose.

gan·der, gan′dər, *n. Informal.* A look or glance, usu. with *take.*

gang, gang, *n.* A group; a number of young people closely associated socially; a set of persons working together in a squad or shift: a road *gang;* a company of persons working together for antisocial purposes: as, a *gang* of hoodlums; a number of similar tools, machines, or the like: a *gang* of saws.—*v.t.* To arrange or form into a gang; to attack, usu. followed by *up on.*—*v.i.* To arrange or behave as a gang.

gang·land, gang′land, *n.* The organized criminal elements of society; the underworld.

gang·gling, gang′gling, *a.* Awkwardly tall and slender; lank and loosely built.

gan·gli·on, gang′glē·ən, *n. pl.,* **-gli·a,** -glē·ə, **-gli·ons.** Group of nerve cells forming a nerve center.

gan·gly, gang′glē, *a.,* **-gli·er, -gli·est.** Gangling; spindly.

gang·plank, gang′plangk, *n.* A plank or long narrow structure used as a temporary bridge for getting on and off a ship.

gang plow, *n.* A plow with several shares, or several plows in a common frame.

gan·grene, gang′grēn, gang·grēn′, *n.* The dying of tissue, as from interruption of circulation; mortification.—*v.t., v.i.,* **-grened, -gren·ing.** To affect or become affected with gangrene. —**gan·gre·nous,** gang′grə·nəs, *a.*

gang·ster, gang′stər, *n.* One of a gang or syndicate of criminals; a mobster; a racketeer.

gang·way, gang′wā, *n.* A passageway; a passageway on a ship; a gangplank.—*interj.* Move out of the way.

gant·let, gônt′lit, gant′lit, *n.* Gauntlet.

gan·try, gan′trē, *n. pl.,* **-tries.** A framework that is used in displaying signals or supporting cranes; a movable scaffold used in the servicing and launching of rockets.

gaol, jāl, *n. Brit.* Jail.

gap, gap, *n.* A break or opening; a vacant space or interval; a wide divergence; a blank or deficiency in something; a deep, sloping ravine or cleft cutting a mountain ridge.—*v.t.,* **gapped, gap·ping.** To make a gap or opening in.

gape, gāp, gap, *v.i.,* **gaped, gap·ing.** To stare with open mouth; to yawn—*n.* The act of gaping; a yawn; a stare with open mouth.

gar, gär, *n. pl.,* **gar, gars.** Any of various N. Amer. fishes with a long, sharp snout or beak.

ga·rage, gə·razh′, ga·räj′, *n.* A place for sheltering or repairing motor vehicles.—*v.t.,* **ga·raged, ga·rag·ing.** To store or place in a garage.

garb, gärb, *n.* Fashion or mode of dress, esp. when particularly distinctive or characteristic: priestly *garb;* clothing; outward semblance or form.—*v.t.* To dress in a particular garb or manner.

gar·bage, gär·bij, *n.* Refuse; table waste; any worthless, offensive, or inferior matter; worthless goods.

gar·ble, gär′bəl, *v.t.,* **-bled, -bling.** To make unfair or misleading selections from, as from a text or speech; to mutilate so as to misrepresent; distort or jumble. —*n.* The process or act of garbling; something garbled.

gar·den, gär′dən, *n.* A plot of ground for growing vegetables, herbs, fruits, or flowers; a piece of ground or other space, commonly with ornamental plants and trees, used as a place of public resort; a highly cultivated region; a fertile and delightful spot.—*v.i.* To cultivate or tend a garden.—*v.t.* To cultivate, as a garden.—*a.* Referring to or produced in a garden; ordinary, common; hardy.

gar·gan·tu·an, gär·gan′choo·ən, *a.* Gigantic; enormous.

gar·gle, gär′gəl, *v.i.,* **-gled, -gling.** To wash or rinse the mouth or throat with a liquid kept in motion by air expelled from the lungs.—*v.t.* To wash or rinse by gargling.—*n.* Any liquid preparation for washing the mouth and throat.

gar·goyle, gär′goyl, *n.* A projecting spout for conducting rainwater from the gutters of a building, generally carved into a grotesque figure from whose mouth the water gushes.

gar·ish, gâr′ish, gar′ish, *a.* Gaudy; showy; overbright; dazzling.

gar·land, gär′lənd, *n.* A wreath or rope made of leaves, twigs, flowers.—*v.t.* To deck with a garland or garlands.

gar·ment, gär′mənt, *n.* Any article of clothing.—*v.t.* To clothe.

gar·ner, gär′nər, *n.* A storehouse for grain; a store of anything. —*v.t.* To store in a garner; to collect; to acquire.

gar·net, gär′nit, *n.* A hard mineral occurring in a number of varieties; the common deep red transparent variety used as a gem; the red color of this gem.

gar·nish, gär′nish, *v.t.* To decorate: to *garnish* a dish with parsley; to serve with a legal warning or garnishment; to garnishee. —*n.* Decoration; something added to a dish for flavor or decoration.

gar·nish·ee, gär′ni·shē′, *n.* A person served with a garnishment. —*v.t.,* **-eed, -ee·ing.** To attach, as money or property, by garnishment.

gar·nish·ment, gär′nish·mənt, *n.* Decoration; act of garnishing; a warning served on a person to hold, subject to the court's direction, money or property in his possession belonging to a defendant.

gar·ni·ture, gär′ni·chər, *n.* Anything that garnishes or decorates.

gar·ret, gar′it, *n.* That part of a house which is on the uppermost floor, immediately under the roof; a loft.

gar·ri·son, gar′i·sən, *n.* Troops stationed in a fort or fortified place; a fort, military post, or fortified town furnished with troops.—*v.t.* To place a garrison in; to secure or defend by troops.

gar·rote, gə·rot′, gə·rōt′, *n.* A kind of capital punishment by strangulation with an iron collar; the instrument used; strangulation or throttling.—*v.t.,* **-rot·ed, -rot·ing. —gar·rot·er,** *n.*

gar·ru·lous, gar′ə·ləs, gar′yə·ləs, *a.* Very talkative; characterized by rambling speech.

gar·ter, gär′tər, *n.* An elastic band worn around the leg or a supporter on an undergarment that holds up a stocking or sock; a band to hold up a sleeve. (*Cap.*), *Brit.* The blue velvet badge of the Order of the Garter; membership in the same; the order itself.

gar·ter snake, *n.* Any of the various harmless snakes having a brownish or greenish body and three lengthwise stripes, and commonly found in North and Central America.

gas, gas, *n.* A state of matter in which the molecules are free to move in any direction, expand to fill a container in which they are held, and tend to expand indefinitely when not confined; any substance in the form of a gas or any mixture of gases except air; a substance in the form of a gas burned for light or heat; a chemical in the form of a gas that anesthetizes or poisons. *Informal.* Gasoline; empty or longwinded talk.—*v.t.,* **gassed, gas·sing.** To affect or overcome with gas; to supply or treat with gas.—*v.i.* To give off gas. *Informal.* To indulge in empty talk.

gas cham·ber, *n.* A chamber where a convicted prisoner is executed by the use of poisonous gas.

gas·e·ous, gas′ē·əs, gas′yəs, *a.* Of the nature of gas; pertaining to gas; in the form of gas; not solid.

gash, gash, *n.* A deep and long cut.—*v.t.* To make a deep cut in.

gas·i·fy, gas′ə·fī, *v.t.,* **-fied, -fy·ing.** To convert into gas.—*v.i.* To become gas. **—gas·i·fi·ca·tion,** gas·ə·fə·kā′shən, *n.* **—gas·i·fi·er,** *n.*

gas·ket, gas′kit, *n.* One of several lines used to bind a furled sail to a yard; a ring of plaited hemp, tow, rubber, or metal used to make a joint watertight.

gas·light, gas′līt, *n.* Light made by burning gas.

gas·lit, gas′lit, *a.* Lighted by burning gas.

gas mask, *n.* A masklike device which chemically filters the air, worn as protection against poisonous gases used in warfare or certain occupations.

gas·o·line, gas·ə·lēn′, gas′ə·lēn, *n.* A flammable liquid made from petroleum, and used chiefly as fuel for internal-combustion engines in automobiles and trucks.

gasp, gasp, gäsp, *v.i.* To catch the breath, or labor for breath, with open mouth.—*v.t.* To breathe or utter with gasps.—*n.* A short, convulsive effort to breathe; a short, convulsive utterance or breath.

gas·ser, gas′ər, *n.* A well yielding natural gas. *Informal.* Any thing or person that is remarkable.

gas·sy, gas′ē, *a.,* **-si·er, -si·est.** Full of or containing gas; full of empty talk. **—gas·si·ness,** *n.*

gas·tric, gas′trik, *a.* Of or pertaining to the stomach.

gas·tric juice, *n.* An acidic digestive fluid containing enzymes and hydrochloric acid, secreted by glands in the lining of the stomach.

gas·tri·tis, ga·strī′tis, *n.* Chronic inflammation of the stomach.

gas·tro·in·tes·ti·nal, gas·trō·in·tes′tə·nəl, *a.* Relating to or affecting the stomach and intestines.

gas·tron·o·my, ga·stron′ə·mē, *n.* The art of good eating. **—gas·tro·nom·ic,** gas·trə·nom′ik, *a.* **—gas·tro·nom·i·cal,** *a.* **—gas·tro·nom·i·cal·ly,** *adv.*

gas tur·bine, *n.* A turbine engine activated by a stream of hot gases under pressure.

gas·works, gas′wərks, *n. pl., but sing. in constr.* A place where gas is manufactured for heat and light.

gat, gat, *n. Informal.* A gun, pistol, or revolver.

gate, gāt, *n.* A movable structure used to open or close any passageway; any passageway into and out of an enclosure; a structure built about such an opening; a contrivance for regulating the passage of water or steam, as a valve; any natural means of access or entrance; anything providing access: the *gate* to wealth; the number of persons who pay an admission fee at an entrance; the total amount of money received from them.

gate·crash·er, gāt′krash·ər, *n. Informal.* One who attends without an invitation or gains admission without paying. **—gate·crash·ing,** *n.*

gate·house, gāt′hows, *n.* A house at or over a gate, used as quarters by the gatekeeper.

gate·keep·er, gāt′kē·pər, *n.* The person who has charge of a gate.

gate·post, gāt′pōst, *n.* The post on which a gate swings, or the one against which it closes.

gate·way, gāt′wā, *n.* An entrance which is or may be closed with a gate; a means of entry.

gath·er, gath′ər, *v.t.* To bring together; to collect; to congregate; to harvest; to accumulate; to bring together in folds or plaits, as a garment; to acquire or gain, with or without effort: to *gather* strength; to deduce by inference; to conclude; to attract: flowers *gathering* bees; to wrap about or enfold: to *gather* the coat around oneself.—*v.i.* To collect; to become assembled; to congregate; to take origin and grow; to come to a head, as a boil; to become folded or creased, as cloth.—*n.* A plait or fold in cloth; the act or instance of drawing together, collecting, or assembling. **—gath·er one·self to·geth·er,** to collect all one's powers for a strong effort.

gath·er·ing, gath′ər·ing, *n.* A crowd; an assembly.

gauche, gōsh, *a.* Awkward; tactless; clumsy.

gau·cho, gow′chō, *n.* A cowboy of S. America, usu. of mixed Spanish and Indian blood.

gaud, gôd, *n.* A showy ornament.

gaud·y, gô′dē, *a.,* **-i·er, -i·est.** Garish; tawdry; tastelessly or glaringly showy. **—gaud·i·ly,** *adv.* **—gaud·i·ness,** *n.*

gauge, gāj, *n.* A standard of measure, dimension, or capacity; a means of estimating or testing; criterion; any of various tools used for measuring; the distance between the two rails of a railroad; a measure of the caliber of a shotgun.—*v.t.,* **gauged, gaug·ing.** To measure the contents or capacity of; to measure in respect to capability, power, or character; to appraise; to estimate; to make correspond to a standard.

gaunt, gônt, *a.* Emaciated by age, hunger, or illness; haggard; of places and things, desolate.

gaunt·let, gônt′lit, gänt′lit, *n.* A glove with fingers covered with small plates, formerly worn as armor; a glove which covers both the hand and wrist; any type of protective glove, as used in industry. **—take up the gaunt·let,** to accept the challenge. **—throw down the gaunt·let,** to challenge.

gaunt·let, gônt′lit, gänt′lit, *n.* A method of punishment whereby two lines of men bearing weapons strike the victim who must run between the lines. **—run the gaunt·let,** to undergo this punishment; to go through severe criticism, controversy, or illtreatment.

gauss, gows, *n. Phys.* A unit of magnetic induction.

gauze, gôz, *n.* A thin transparent fabric in an open meshlike weave; any woven material resembling this: wire *gauze.* **—gauz·i·ness,** *n.* **—gauz·y,** *a.,* **-i·er, -i·est.**

gav·el, gav′əl, *n.* A small mallet used by a presiding officer to signal for attention or order.

gawk, gôk, *n.* An awkward, oafish person; a fool or simpleton.—*v.i.* To stare idly or stupidly; to gape.

gawk·y, gô′kē, *a.,* **-i·er, -i·est.** Awkward, clumsy, or ungraceful. **—gawk·i·ly,** *adv.* **—gawk·i·ness,** *n.*

gay, gā, *a.* In or showing a joyous, merry mood; cheerfully lively; given to or abounding in social pleasures: a *gay* social event; dissipated; licentious; bright

---

a- hat, fāte, fāre, fäther; e- met, mē; i- pin, pīne; o- not, nōte, ôrb, moove (move), boy, pownd;
u- cūbe, bûll, tûk (took); ch- chin; th- thick, ŧhen; zh- vizhon (vision); ə- əgo, takən, pencəl, lemən, bərd (bird).

or brilliantly colored. *Informal*. Homosexual.

gay·e·ty, gā′ĭ·tē, *n*. Gaiety.

gay·ly, gā′lē, *adv*. Gaily.

gaze, gāz, *v.i.*, **gazed, gaz·ing.** To look steadily, intently, and earnestly.—*n*. A fixed look. **—gaz·er,** *n*.

ga·ze·bo, gə·zē′bō, gə·zā′bō, *n. pl.*, **-bos, -boes.** A structure commanding an extensive view, as a balcony, projecting window, or summerhouse.

ga·zelle, gə·zel′, *n. pl.*, **ga·zelles, ga·zelle.** Any of various small Asian and African antelopes noted for graceful movements and lustrous eyes.

ga·zette, gə·zet′, *n*. A newspaper.

gaz·et·teer, gaz·ə·tēr′, *n*. A geographical dictionary.

gear, gēr, *n*. A mechanism for transmitting or changing motion by interaction of parts, as by toothed wheels; an assembly of parts which serves a specific purpose in a machine; a toothed wheel which engages or meshes with another wheel or part; the connection of a machine part with a motor or shaft; a particular connection governing speed and direction variations: reverse *gear;* apparatus or equipment: fishing *gear*. —*v.t.* To connect by gearing; to put into gear; to provide with gear or equipment; to adjust according to certain conditions: to *gear* instruction to student ability.—*v.i.* To fit exactly; come into or be in gear.

gear·box, gear box, gēr′boks, *n*. A motor vehicle transmission.

gear·ing, gēr′ing, *n*. The parts of a machine by which motion is transmitted or changed; the act of providing with gears.

gear·shift, gēr′shift, *n*. A device by which transmission gears are engaged and disengaged.

gear·wheel, gēr′hwēl, gēr′wēl, *n*. A wheel having teeth or cogs which engage with the teeth of another wheel. Also **cog·wheel.**

gee, jē, *interj*. A word of command to horses, directing them to turn to the right.—*v.i.*, **geed, gee·ing.** To turn to the right.

gee, jē, *interj*. A mild expression of wonder, astonishment, or enthusiasm.

gee·zer, gē′zər, *n. Informal*. An odd character.

Gei·ger count·er, gī′gər, *n*. An instrument for detecting and measuring radioactivity.

gei·sha, gā′shə, *n. pl.*, **-sha, -shas.** A Japanese girl trained to entertain men with dance, song, and conversation.

gel, jel, *n*. A jellylike, colloidal suspension, semisolid in consistency, as gelatin.—*v.i.*, **gelled, gel·ling.** To form a jellylike substance.

gel·a·tin, jel′ə·tin, *n*. A glutinous protein obtained from various animal tissues, used in making various stiff, jellylike food products, and in photography.

ge·lat·i·nous, jə·lat′ə·nəs, *a*. Of, pertaining to, or consisting of gelatin; resembling gelatin.

ge·la·tion, jē·lā′shən, jə·lā′shən, *n*. Solidification by cold; freezing.

geld, geld, *v.t.*, **geld·ed** or **gelt, geld·ing.** To castrate.

geld·ing, gel′ding, *n*. A castrated animal, esp. a horse.

gel·id, jel′id, *a*. Very cold; icy.

gem, jem, *n*. A precious or semiprecious stone, esp. when cut and polished for ornament; a jewel; something or someone likened to a gem because of beauty, perfection, or worth.—*v.t.*, **gemmed, gem·ming.** To adorn with gems.

gem·i·nate, jem′ə·nāt, *v.i., v.t.*, **-nat·ed, -nat·ing.** To become or cause to become doubled. —jem′ə·nit, jem′ə·nāt, *a*. Combined in a pair or pairs; coupled; binate. **—gem·i·nate·ly,** *adv*. **—gem·i·na·tion,** jem·ə·nā′shən, *n*.

gem·ol·o·gy, jem·ol′ə·jē, *n*. Scientific study of gems. **—gem·o·log·i·cal,** jem·ə·loj′ə·kəl, *a*. **—gem·ol·o·gist,** *n*.

gem·stone, jem′stōn, *n*. A precious stone which can be refined by cutting and polishing for use in jewelry.

gen·darme, zhän′därm, *Fr*. zhän·därm′, *n*. One of the armed police of France and some other European countries. *Informal*. Any policeman.

gen·der, jen′dər, *n. Gram*. Any of the classes into which nouns, pronouns, and their modifiers, are distinguished with reference to sex, as masculine, feminine, or neuter; membership in such a class. *Informal*. Sex, male or female.

gene, jēn, *n*. The element of a chromosome which carries and transfers an inherited characteristic from parent to offspring.

ge·ne·al·o·gy, jē·nē·ol′ə·jē, jē·nē·al′ə·jē, *n. pl.*, **-gies.** An account or record which traces the ancestry of a certain individual or family; descent from an ancestor; the study of family history. **—ge·ne·a·log·i·cal,** jē·nē·ə·loj′ə·kəl, *a*. **—ge·ne·al·o·gist,** *n*.

gen·er·al, jen′ər·əl, *a*. Referring to the whole of something; common to many or most, though not universal: a *general* practice; prevalent; usual; not specialized and not limited to a precise application or area: the practice of *general* medicine; considered with reference to main elements or features rather than details or exceptions: a *general* knowledge of a subject; not specific or special: *general* instructions; indefinite or vague; having extended command, or superior or chief rank.—*n*. Any general officer; a U.S. Army or Air Force officer ranking below General of the Army or Air Force and above lieutenant-general; the highest-ranking U.S. Marine Corps officer. **—in gen·er·al,** with respect to the whole class referred to; commonly; usually; considering the whole and disregarding details.

gen·er·al·is·si·mo, jen·ər·ə·lis′ə·mō, *n. pl.*, **-mos.** The supreme commanding officer of all armed forces in certain countries.

gen·er·al·ist, jen′ər·ə·list, *n*. One who is knowledgeable in several different fields.

gen·er·al·i·ty, jen·ə·ral′ə·tē, *n. pl.*, **-ties.** A statement or principle that is undetailed or vague; the state or quality of being general.

gen·er·al·ize, jen′ər·ə·līz, *v.t.*, **-ized, -iz·ing.** To make general; to bring into general use; to give a broad rather than a specific character or application to; to avoid making specific or detailed; to induce or formulate, as a general rule or conclusion, from particular facts or instances.—*v.i.* To infer a general principle; to deal or indulge in generalities. **—gen·e·ral·i·za·tion,** jen·ər·ə·lə·zā′shən, *n*. **—gen·er·al·iz·er,** *n*.

gen·er·al prac·ti·tion·er, *n*. A physician who does not confine his practice to a special field of medicine.

gen·er·al store, *n*. A retail store, selling merchandise of many kinds.

gen·er·ate, jen′ə·rāt, *v.t.*, **-at·ed, -at·ing.** To procreate; to cause to be; bring into existence; produce, as heat or electricity; to be the stimulus for; to create, as a line, figure, or plane, by a moving point, line, or figure. **—gen·er·a·tive,** *a*. **—gen·er·a·tive·ly,** *adv*.

gen·er·a·tion, jen·ə·rā′shən, *n*. A single genealogical succession in natural descent; 30 years; people who are born and living at approximately the same time; such a group of people having approximately the same age, status, ideas, or problems; the act of generating.

gen·er·a·tor, jen′ə·rā·tər, *n*. One who generates; something that generates or produces; an apparatus for producing a gas or vapor; a machine by which mechanical energy is converted into electrical energy.

ge·ner·ic, jə·ner′ik, *a*. Referring to or characteristic of a genus, kind, or class; applicable or referring to all of the individuals forming a group, kind, or class; not registered as a trademark: a *generic* name of a drug. Also **ge·ner·i·cal.** **—ge·ner·i·cal·ly,** *adv*.

gen·er·ous, jen′ər·əs, *a*. Free and unselfish in giving; large, ample, or bountiful, as of size; noble in spirit. **—gen·er·os·i·ty,** jen·ə·ros′ə·tē, *n. pl.*, **-ties.**

gen·e·sis, jen′ə·sis, *n. pl.*, **-ses,** -sēz. Creation; (*cap*.) the first book of the Old Testament.

ge·net·ic, jə·net′ik, *a*. Referring to the science of genetics; pertaining to genes; pertaining to the origins or development of something. **—ge·net·i·cal·ly,** *adv.*

ge·net·ics, jə·net′iks, *n. pl. but sing. in constr.* The science of the hereditary and evolutionary similarities and differences of related organisms. **—ge·net·i·cist,** jə·net′ə·sist, *n.*

gen·ial, jēn′yəl, jē′nē·əl, *a.* Kindly; cordial; cheerful; comfortably warm or mild, as a climate. **—ge·ni·al·i·ty,** jē·nē·al′ə·tē, *n.*

ge·nie, jē′nē, *n. pl.,* **ge·nies, ge·ni·i,** jē′nē·ī. Any spirit, specif. of Islamic mythology.

gen·i·tal, jen′ə·təl, *a.* Referring to reproduction, or to the sexual organs.

gen·i·ta·li·a, jen·ə·tā′lē·ə, jen·ə·tāl′yə, *n. pl.* The genitals.

gen·i·tals, jen′ə·təlz, *n. pl.* The organs of the system of reproduction, esp. the external organs.

gen·ius, jēn′yəs, *n. pl.,* **gen·ius·es.** An unusual natural intellectual capacity as indicated in original and creative activity; a person who has unusual ability and very high intelligence, commonly, one possessing an I.Q. of 140 or above; a natural aptitude for some specific thing: to have a *genius* for finance; a person who has such an aptitude; a person who influences for good or evil the conduct, behavior, or destiny of another or others.

gen·o·cide, jen′ə·sīd, *n.* Deliberate mass murder of a race, people, or minority group. **—gen·o·ci·dal,** jen·ə·sī′dəl, *a.*

gen·re, zhän′rə, *n.* Kind; sort; style; a specific category of artistic or literary accomplishment distinguished by form, technique, and subject matter.

gent, jent, *n. Informal.* Gentleman.

gen·teel, jen·tēl′, *a.* Well-bred; refined; polished or polite; often, affecting politeness or delicacy.

gen·tian, jen′shən, *n.* Any plant of a large genus comprising herbs having blue, yellow, white, or red flowers.

gen·tile, jen′tīl, *a. (Often cap.)* Of or pertaining to any people not Jewish; esp. among Mormons, not Mormon.—*n. (Often cap.)* A person not a Jew; a pagan or heathen; among Mormons, a non-Mormon.

gen·til·i·ty, jen·til′ə·tē, *n. pl.,* **-ties.** Superior refinement or elegance, whether possessed or affected; the condition of being wellborn; people of gentle birth; gentry.

gen·tle, jen′təl, *a.,* **-tler, -tlest.** Kindly or amiable in manner; mild or moderate; not severe, violent, or loud: a *gentle* wind, a *gentle* sound; gradual, as a slope; tame or easily managed, as an animal; of, or characteristic of, good birth or family; wellborn; refined; honorable; courteous or generous: as, *gentle* reader. —*v.t.,* **-tled, -tling.** To make mild or calm; soften; to tame, as a horse. **—gen·tly,** *adv.*

gen·tle·folk, jen′təl·fōk, *n. pl.* Persons of good family and breeding.

gen·tle·man, jen′təl·mən, *n. pl.,* **-men.** A man of good family or good social position; a man of good breeding, politeness, and courtesy. *Often pl.* A polite or formal appellation by which men are addressed.

gen·tle·men's a·gree·ment, *n.* An agreement which rests solely on the honor of the persons involved.

gen·tle·wom·an, jen′təl·wûm·ən, *n. pl.,* **-wom·en.** A woman of good family or good breeding; a woman who serves as personal attendant to a lady of high rank.

gen·try, jen′trē, *n.* Wellborn and well-bred people; in England, the class next below the nobility.

gen·u·flect, jen′ū·flekt, *v.i.* To bend the knee or knees as in worship. **—gen·u·flec·tion,** jen·ū·flek′shən, *n.* **—gen·u·flec·tor,** *n.*

gen·u·ine, jen′ū·in, *a.* Authentic; being truly such, rather than counterfeit or pretended; properly so called; sincere or free from pretense or affectation, as

a person.

ge·nus, jē′nəs, *n. pl.,* **gen·e·ra,** jen′ər·ə, **ge·nus·es.** A kind, class, or sort; a class of a greater extent than a species; a category or class of animals and plants marked by certain common characteristics, usu. comprising several species, and forming a subdivision of a family.

ge·o-, jē′ō. A combining form meaning: the earth.

ge·o·cen·tric, jē·ō·sen′trik, *a.* Measured or seen from the earth's center; having reference to the earth as a center. **—ge·o·cen·tri·cal·ly,** *adv.*

ge·o·chem·is·try, jē·ō·kem′i·strē, *n.* The science dealing with the chemical changes in, and the composition of, the earth's crust. **—ge·o·chem·i·cal,** *a.* **—ge·o·chem·ist,** *n.*

ge·ode, jē′ōd, *n.* A hollow stone frequently lined with crystals; the cavity of this stone.

ge·o·des·ic, jē·ō·des′ik, *a.* Having a curve the same as the curve of the earth.

ge·og·ra·phy, jē·og′rə·fē, *n. pl.,* **-phies.** The science which treats of the surface of the earth, dealing with topography, climate, the oceans, and plant and animal life, and with the political and social characteristics of the various peoples and nations who inhabit the earth; the topographical aspects of the earth or a particular area on the earth: the *geography* of South America; a book on the subject of geography. **—ge·o·gra·pher,** *n.* **—ge·o·graph·ic,** jē·ə·graf′ik, *a.* **—ge·o·graph·i·cal,** *a.* **—ge·o·graph·i·cal·ly,** *adv.*

ge·ol·o·gy, jē·ol′ə·jē, *n. pl.,* **-gies.** The science that deals with the physical history and structure of the earth and the physical changes which it has undergone or is still undergoing, esp. as recorded in rocks or rock formations; the geologic features or structure of a given region of the earth. **—ge·o·log·ic,** jē·ə·loj′ik, *a.* **—ge·o·log·i·cal,** *a.* **—ge·o·log·i·cal·ly,** *adv.* **—ge·ol·o·gist,** *n.*

ge·o·mag·net·ic, jē·ō·mag·net′ik, *a.* Of or referring to the earth's magnetism. **—ge·o·mag·ne·tism,** jē·ō·mag′nə·tiz·əm, *n.*

ge·o·met·ric, jē·ə·met′rik, *a.* Referring to geometry; according to the rules of geometry; characterized by or forming straight lines, triangles, circles, or similar regular forms: a *geometric* design.

ge·om·e·try, jē·om′ə·trē, *n. pl.,* **-tries.** That branch of mathematics which treats of the properties, relationships, and measurement of points, lines, angles, surfaces, and solids; a book or other writing on the subject of geometry.

ge·o·phys·ics, jē·ō·fiz′iks, *n. pl. but sing. in constr.* The science dealing with the relations between the earth's features and the agencies that produce them, including meteorology, oceanography, seismology, volcanology, magnetism, and other related fields. **—ge·o·phys·i·cal,** *a.* **—ge·o·phys·i·cist,** *n.*

ge·o·pol·i·tics, jē·ō·pol′ə·tiks, *n. pl., sing. or pl. in constr.* The study of the influence of geographical factors upon politics. **—ge·o·pol·i·tic,** *a.* **—ge·o·po·lit·i·cal,** jē·ō·pə·lit′ə·kəl, *a.* **—ge·o·po·lit·i·cal·ly,** *adv.*

ge·o·ther·mal, jē·ō·thər′məl, *a.* Of or pertaining to the internal heat of the earth.

ger·bil, jər′bil, *n.* A small, burrowing, gnawing animal related to the mouse, usu. found in the sandy parts of Africa and Asia, and popularized as a pet in the U.S.

ger·i·at·rics, jer·ē·at′riks, *n. pl. but sing. in constr.* The area of medicine which deals with the diseases of old age and the problems and care of aging persons. **—ger·i·at·ric,** *a.* **—ger·i·a·tri·cian,** jer·ē·ə·trish′ən, *n.* **—ger·i·at·rist,** *n.*

germ, jərm, *n.* A disease-producing microorganism; a seed; a bud; the earliest rudiment of a living organism; an embryo in its early stages; something that serves as source or seed: the *germ* of hate.

ger·mane, jər·mān′, *a.* Significantly related; appropriate; relevant; pertinent.

Ger·man mea·sles, jər/mən, *n. pl., sing. or pl. in constr.* An infectious virus disease, less severe than measles.

Ger·man shep·herd, *n.* Any of a breed of shepherd dogs marked by intelligence, and often used for police work and as guides for the blind.

germ cell, *n. Biol.* A cell capable of sexual reproduction; sperm or egg cell.

ger·mi·cide, jər/mi·sĭd, *n.* A substance that destroys germs. —**ger·mi·cid·al,** jər·mi·sĭd/əl, *a.*

ger·mi·nate, jər/mə·nāt, *v.i.,* -**nat·ed,** -**nat·ing.** To begin to develop; to start to grow. *Bot.* To sprout.—*v.t.* To cause to sprout or bud. —**ger·mi·na·tion,** jər·mə· nā/shən, *n.*

germ war·fare, *n.* Biological warfare.

ger·on·tol·o·gy, jer·ən·tŏl/ə·jē, *n.* The scientific study of aging and its problems. —**ger·on·tol·o·gist,** *n.*

ger·ry·man·der, jer/ē·man·dər, *n. U.S. politics.* An arbitrary arrangement of the election districts of a state or county made to give one party an unfair advantage in elections.—*v.t.* To subject to a gerrymander, as a state; *fig.,* to manipulate unfairly.

ger·und, jer/ənd, *n. Gram.* The -*ing* form of a verb used as a noun.

ges·so, jes/ō, *n.* A preparation of plaster of Paris and glue used in sculpture, or as a surface for painting and gilding; a prepared surface made of such a preparation.

ges·tate, jes/tāt, *v.t.,* -**tat·ed,** -**tat·ing.** To carry in the womb during pregnancy; *fig.,* to form and gradually mature, as a project, in the mind. —**ges·ta·tion,** je·stā/shən, *n.*

ges·tic·u·late, je·stik/ū·lāt, *v.i.,* -**lat·ed,** -**lat·ing.** To make or use gestures, esp. in an animated or excited manner.—*v.t.* To express by gestures. —**ges·tic·u· la·tion,** *n.* —**ges·tic·u·la·tive, ges·tic·u·la·to·ry,** *a.* —**ges·tic·u·la·tor,** *n.*

ges·ture, jes/chər, *n.* A motion or action intended to express an idea or feeling, or to enforce an argument or opinion; movement of the body or limbs; an action done as a token: a *gesture* of peace.—*v.t.,* -**tured,** -**tur·ing.** To express by gesture.—*v.i.* To make gestures. —**ges·tur·er,** *n.*

ge·sund·heit, gə·zûnt/hīt, *interj.* An exclamation wishing good health, esp. to someone who just sneezed.

get, get, *v.t.,* **got, got** or **got·ten, get·ting.** To come into possession of or obtain: earn, gain, or win: to *get* an award for scholarship; ascertain by calculation or experiment; to receive; acquire or come to have: They *get* skill through practice; catch or contract, as an illness; receive or suffer; capture. *Informal.* To corner, as in an argument. To influence or achieve power over: to *get* someone to eat; bring into a particular position, situation, or condition: to *get* a fire under control; prepare, as a meal; cause, as a person or thing, to be as specified: as, to *get* one's hair cut. *Informal.* To grasp the meaning of: to *get* the point of a lecture; to perplex or nettle; to kill or to seek vengeance upon.—*v.i.* To succeed in coming, going, or arriving somewhere, usu. followed by *away, in, to, over,* or *through:* to *get* home, to *get through* an ordeal; to bring oneself into a particular condition: to *get* involved; attain or manage, followed by an infinitive: as, to *get to see* him. —**get a·cross.** *Informal.* To make a point or be understood. —**get a·long,** to make progress; proceed; advance; to fare in a specified manner; manage; take care of one's needs; to maintain harmonious relations, or agree, as with a person; to move on in years; grow older. Also **get on.** —**get a·round,** to travel extensively; to have many social contacts; to become widely known by going from one to another, as news. —**get at,** to reach; determine or ascertain: to *get at* the heart of the matter; approach in meaning; intend; to undertake or set oneself to: to *get at* one's chores. —**get a·way,** to escape; to start, as in

a race. —**get a·way with.** *Informal.* To manage to avoid; avoid the consequences of one's behavior. —**get by,** to slip past without notice; to manage to exist or survive despite difficulties. —**get e·ven with.** *Informal.* To be revenged. —**get off.** *Informal.* To escape penalty; to leave from: as, to *get off* the train. —**get on,** to get along; to board or mount, as a train or horse. —**get o·ver.** *Informal.* To recover, as from a condition. —**get up,** to rise from bed; stand up.

get·a·way, get/ə·wā, *n.* An escape; the start, as of a race.

get-to·geth·er, get/tû·geth·ər, *n.* A party or meeting, usu. small and informal.

get-up, get-up, get/əp, *n. Informal.* Style, choice, or arrangement of clothing; one's outfit or costume.

gew·gaw, gū/gô, goo/gô, *n.* A showy trifle; a pretty thing of little worth; a toy; a bauble.—*a.* Showy, but worthless.

gey·ser, gī/zər, gī/sər, *n.* A spring of hot water and steam characterized by periodic eruptions; the water rising from such a spring.

ghast·ly, gast/lē, gäst/lē, *a.,* -**li·er,** -**li·est.** Frightful or dreadful; horrible: a *ghastly* crime; suggestive of the color of a dead person or a ghost: a *ghastly* pallor. —*adv.* —**ghast·li·ness,** *n.*

gher·kin, gər/kin, *n.* A small, spiny cucumber used for pickles; the plant yielding this cucumber; any small cucumber, used for pickling.

ghet·to, get/ō, *n. pl.,* **ghet·tos, ghet·toes.** A city area populated largely by people of a minority group; formerly, in countries of Europe, a section of a city in which Jews were required to live.

ghost, gōst, *n.* The soul or spirit of a dead person; a disembodied spirit, esp. one imagined to haunt the living; a specter or apparition; a mere shadow or semblance: the *ghost* of a smile; a distant possibility: a *ghost* of a chance; a spiritual being. *TV.* A duplicate image, usu. faint and slightly displaced from the main image, due to wave reflection. Secondary image, as from a defect in lenses.—*v.t.* Ghostwrite; to appear to or haunt.—*v.i.* Ghostwrite; to go about silently, like a ghost. —**give up the ghost,** to die.

ghost·ly, gōst/lē, *a.,* -**li·er,** -**li·est.** Resembling, or pertaining to a ghost. —*adv.* —**ghost·li·ness,** *n.*

ghost town, *n.* A formerly flourishing town, now abandoned.

ghost writ·er, *n.* A person who writes material that is to be spoken or published as the work of another. —**ghost·write,** *v.t., v.i.,* -**wrote,** -**writ·ten,** -**writ·ing.**

ghoul, gool, *n.* An evil demon of Oriental stories, supposed to rob graves and feed on corpses; anyone who robs graves or the unburied dead; one who revels in what is revolting.

GI, jē/ī/, *a. Milit.* Of, suited to, or characteristic of an enlisted man of the U.S. armed forces; issued by a U.S. Army supply department; conforming to military regulations.—*n. pl.,* **GI's** or **GIs.** A serviceman of the U.S. armed forces, esp. an enlisted man. Also **G.I.**

gi·ant, jī/ənt, *n.* An imaginary being of human form but superhuman size and strength; a person or thing of unusually great size; one who towers above others or is eminent in endowments, achievements, or importance: an intellectual *giant.*—*a.* Giantlike; of extraordinary size or strength; great or eminent above others.

gib·ber·ish, jib/ər·ish, gib/ər·ish, *n.* Rapid and inarticulate talk; unintelligible language; speech or writing using obscure or excessively technical expressions.

gib·bon, gib/ən, *n.* Any of various tailless apes of the East Indies and southern Asia, that are small, slender, and long-armed.

gibe, jibe, jīb, *v.i.* To utter derisive, sarcastic words; to flout; to jeer.—*v.t.* To taunt; to mock; to deride or sneer at.—*n.* —**gib·er,** *n.* —**gib·ing·ly,** *adv.*

gib·let, jib/lit, *n. Usu. pl.* The heart, liver, gizzard, or some other edible part of a fowl, often separated in cooking.

gid·dy, gid′ē, *a.,* **-di·er, -di·est.** Having a sensation of whirling about; dizzy; inducing dizziness; inconstant; changeable; flighty; frivolous. **—gid·di·ly,** *adv.* **—gid·di·ness,** *n.*

gift, gift, *n.* That which is given or bestowed without charge; a present; a donation; the act, right, or power of giving; a natural quality or endowment; a talent.

gig, gig, *n.* A light, two-wheeled, one-horse carriage. *Naut.* A ship's boat for either rowing or sailing; a long rowboat used chiefly for racing. *Jazz.* A temporary professional engagement.**—***v.t.* To spear with a gig. **—***v.i.* To take fish with a gig.

gi·gan·tic, jī·gan′tik, *a.* Of the size or proportions of a giant; colossal; huge.

gi·gan·tism, jī·gan′tiz·əm, *n. Pathol.* Excessive growth of the body or parts of the body, most often caused by a malfunction of the pituitary gland.

gig·gle, gig′əl, *v.i.* **-gled, -gling.** To laugh in a silly or undignified way, as from nervousness or foolishness; to titter.**—***n.* **—gig·gler,** *n.* **—gig·gly,** *a.,* **-gli·er, -gli·est.**

gig·o·lo, jig′ə·lō, zhig′ə·lō, *n.* A man employed to be a woman's escort or dancing partner.

gild, gild, *v.t.* To overlay with gold; to give a golden hue to; to brighten; *fig.,* to give a falsely attractive appearance to. **—gild the lil·y,** to add ornamentation unnecessarily to an already beautiful object.

gill, gil, *n.* The respiratory organ of fishes and other animals which obtain oxygen from water. *Bot.* The radiating plates on the underside of a mushroom. *Informal.* The flesh under or about a person's chin: green around the *gills.*

gilt, gilt, *a.* Gilded; golden in color.**—***n.* The gold or other material applied in gilding; gilding.

gilt, gilt, *n.* A young female hog.

gilt-edged, gilt′ejd′, *a.* Having the edges gilded, as paper; of the highest order or quality, as securities. Also **gilt-edge.**

gim·crack, jim′krak, *n.* A showy, useless trifle; a trivial knicknack; any worthless article or object.**—***a.*

gim·let, gim′lit, *n.* A small tool for boring holes.

gim·mick, gim′ik, *n.* A crafty device, as one for controlling gambling apparatus; a trick; an ingenious expedient or contrivance.

gimp, gimp, *n. Informal.* A person who limps; a hobbling gait.**—***v.i. Informal.* To limp; hobble.

gin, jin, *n.* A machine for separating cotton from its seeds; a trap or snare for game.**—***v.t.* To clear cotton of seeds with a gin; to catch or snare in a gin, as game.

gin, jin, *n.* A distilled alcoholic liquor made from a mash of rye or other grain and juniper berries.

gin, jin, *n.* Gin rummy.**—***v.t.* To win, as a hand in gin rummy, by having all one's cards in sets.

gin·ger, jin′jer, *n.* The pungent, spicy rhizome of a plant of tropical Asia, used in cooking and medicine; this plant; a light sandy or tawny color. *Informal.* Spiciness or piquancy; spirit or animation.

gin·ger ale, *n.* A non-alcoholic, carbonated drink similar to ginger beer, but containing less ginger extract.

gin·ger beer, *n.* A non-alcoholic effervescing drink flavored with ginger.

gin·ger·bread, jin′jer·bred, *n.* A plain cake flavored with ginger, and usu. sweetened with molasses; showy ornamentation.**—***a.* Showy; gaudy; tawdry.

gin·ger·ly, jin′jer·lē, *adv.* With extreme care or caution; cautiously; warily.**—***a.* Cautious or wary. **—gin·ger·li·ness,** *n.*

gin·ger·snap, jin′jer·snap, *n.* A thin, brittle cookie spiced with ginger and molasses.

gin·ger·y, jin′jə·rē, *a.* Gingerlike; hot; pungent; spicy; tawny in color.

ging·ham, ging′əm, *n.* A cotton fabric woven of dyed yarns, usu. in striped, checked, or plaid patterns.

gin rum·my, *n.* A variation of the card game rummy.

gip, jip, *n., v.t.* Gyp.

Gip·sy, gip·sy, jip′sē, *n. pl.,* **gip·sies.** Gypsy.

gi·raffe, jə·raf′, *Brit.* jə·räf′, *n.* A long-necked, spotted ruminant of Africa, the tallest of existing quadrupeds.

gird, gərd, *v.t.* To bind or encircle with a belt or girdle; to equip, as with a sword, at the belt. *Fig.* To equip oneself for action; to invest or imbue, as with some quality or power. To surround; confine; hem in.

gird·er, gər′dər, *n.* A main horizontal supporting beam in a floor or other structural work.

gir·dle, gər′dəl, *n.* That which girds or encloses; an undergarment for the area of the body below the waist, worn to give support and to improve the lines of the figure; a sash or belt.**—***v.t.,* **-dled, -dling.** To encompass with a belt; to circle.

girl, gərl, *n.* A child or young person of the female sex. *Informal.* A woman; a female servant; a sweetheart. **—girl·hood,** *n.*

girl friend, *n.* A girl a man regards with particular affection; a sweetheart; a female friend.

girl guide, *n.* A member of an organization of girls in Britain or Canada, the Girl Guides, similar to the Girl Scouts.

girl·ish, gər′lish, *a.* Like or pertaining to a girl; befitting a girl.

girl scout, *n.* A member of an organization of girls, aiming to promote in its members good health, good citizenship, and good character.

girth, gərth, *n.* A band passed under the belly of a horse or other pack animal to keep a saddle or pack on its back; the measure around anything.**—***v.t.* To girdle; encircle; to fasten with a girth.

gist, jist, *n.* The substance or core of a matter: to give one the *gist* of an argument in a few words; the essential part.

give, giv, *v.t.,* **gave, giv·en, giv·ing.** To place physically into or within another's grasp; to present as a gift; to donate; to offer; to exchange or trade; to lend; to permit: as, to *give* permission to; to perform; to sacrifice: to *give* one's life; to administer: to *give* first aid; to endow with a quality: to *give* form to a piece of clay; to be the material cause of: Food *gives* nourishment. To commit or relinquish: to *give* oneself totally to one's job; to provide or yield; to impart, transmit, or convey: to *give* someone a cold, or to *give* my regards; to offer as entertainment: to *give* a party. To present as a toast; to assign or hand out; to ascribe; to pledge or promise: to *give* one's word.**—***v.i.* To make gifts; to donate; to yield, as to pressure; to recede; to afford entrance or view.**—***n.* The ability or tendency to yield under pressure; resilience; flexibility. **—give away,** to give as a present; to hand over, as the bride to the bridegroom, at a wedding; to betray; to divulge, as a secret. **—give ground,** to yield; to retreat before force. **—give in,** to yield; to confess oneself defeated. **—give off,** to emit; to send forth, as an odor. **—give out,** to break down; become exhausted, as a supply; to make known; to distribute. **—give up,** to surrender; hand over; to abandon all hope; to devote oneself fully to; to abandon, as a plan, an activity, or a contest. **—give way,** to retreat, to break down; to collapse under stress. **—giv·er,** *n.*

give-and-take, giv′ən·tāk, *n.* The process of making mutual concessions; compromise; a friendly exchange of point of view.

give·a·way, giv′ə·wā, *n.* An accidental disclosure or betrayal; something given free of charge, esp. to promote business or publicity; in television or radio, a program where prizes are given to participants.

giv·en, giv′ən, *a.* Bestowed; conferred; admitted; stated; disposed: as, *given* to arguing; assumed, as a fact.

giv·en name, *n.* First name, as distinguished from

---

a- hat, fāte, fâre, fäther; e- met, mē; i- pin, pīne; o- not, nōte, ôrb, moove (move), boy, pownd; u- cūbe, bůll, tûk (took); ch- chin; th- thick, then; zh- vizhon (vision); ə- əgo, takən, pencəl, lemən, bərd (bird).

the surname; Christian name.

giz·zard, giz′ərd, n. A bird's second stomach; *Informal.* The innards collectively.

gla·cial, glā′shəl, a. Characterized by the presence of glaciers: the *glacial* epoch; due to or associated with the action of ice or glaciers; bitterly cold; coldly unresponsive: a *glacial* manner.

gla·cier, glā′shər, n. A vast accumulation of ice formed from snow, slowly descending from mountains, as valley *glaciers*, or spreading outward from centers, as continental *glaciers*.

glad, glad, a., **glad·der, glad·dest.** Cheerful, joyous, or merry; characterized by or showing cheerfulness, joy, or pleasure: *glad* feelings, looks, smiles, or utterances; causing joy or pleasure: a *glad* occasion, *glad* tidings. —**glad·ly,** adv. —**glad·ness,** n.

glad·den, glad′ən, v.t. To make glad; to cheer.—v.i.

glade, glād, n. An open area in a wood or forest.

glad·i·a·tor, glad′ē·ā·tər, n. In the arenas of ancient Rome, a paid combatant, slave, or captive who, armed, fought to the death. —**glad·i·a·to·ri·al,** glad·ē·ə·tôr′ē·əl, a.

glad·i·o·lus, glad·ē·ō′ləs, n. pl., **-li, -lī, -lus, -lus·es.** Any plant of the iris family, native esp. to South Africa, with erect, swordlike leaves and spikes of brightly-colored flowers. Also **glad·i·o·la.**

glad·some, glad′səm, a. Glad; cheerful or joyous; causing joy.

glam·or·ize, glam·our·ize, glam′ə·rīz, v.t., **-ized, -iz·ing.** To make glamorous; romanticize. —**glam·or·i·za·tion, glam·our·i·za·tion,** glam·ə·rə·zā′shən, n. —**glam·or·iz·er, glam·our·iz·er,** n.

glam·or·ous, glam·our·ous, glam′ər·əs, a. Full of glamor, romantic attraction and excitement, or alluring charm. —**glam·or·ous·ly, glam·our·ous·ly,** adv. —**glam·or·ous·ness, glam·our·ous·ness,** n.

glam·our, glam·or, glam′ər, n. Excitement and allure: the *glamour* of being a film star; fascinating, bewitching, and often illusory charm.

glance, glans, gläns, v.i., **glanced, glanc·ing.** To look quickly or briefly: to *glance* at or over something; to glide off in an oblique direction from an object struck, as a weapon or missile; to dart off or aside; to gleam or flash.—v.t. To shoot or hit obliquely.—n. A quick or brief look; a glancing off, as of an object after striking; a gleam or flash, as of light.

gland, gland, n. An organ by which certain constituents are separated from the blood or lymph for use in the body or for ejection from it.

glan·du·lar, glan′jə·lər, a. Consisting of a gland or glands; pertaining to glands.

glare, glār, v.i., **glared, glar·ing.** To shine with a strong, dazzling light; to be intensely bright in color; to glower; to look with a fierce or piercing stare.—v.t. To express, as hostility, by a frown or glower.—n. A strong, dazzling light; dazzling brilliance of light; shine; showy or dazzling appearance; a fierce or angry look. —**glar·i·ness,** n. —**glar·y,** a., **-i·er, -i·est.**

glar·ing, glār′ing, a. Emitting or reflecting harshly dazzling or bright light; unpleasantly conspicuous; plainly obvious; vulgarly showy; looking with anger or fierceness; staring.

glass, glas, gläs, n. A hard, brittle, transparent, artificial substance formed by fusing sand with an alkali; something made of glass; a mirror; a drinking vessel without a handle; the quantity which such a vessel holds; an optical instrument, such as a lens, spyglass, or telescope; pl., a pair of eyeglasses; spectacles.—a. Made of glass; fitted with glass parts; pertaining to glass.—v.t. To cover with glass.

glass·blow·ing, glas′blō·ing, n. The art of producing fine glassware and glass ornaments by blowing through a long pipe which holds a blob of molten glass at its end. —**glass·blow·er,** n.

glass·ful, glas′fŭl, gläs′fŭl, n. pl., **-fuls.** As much as a drinking glass will hold.

glass·ware, glas′wār, gläs′wār, n. Articles made of glass.

glass·y, glas′ē, glä′sē, a., **-i·er, -i·est.** Resembling glass, as in transparency or smoothness; fixed, unintelligent, or expressionless: a *glassy* stare. —**glass·i·ly,** adv. —**glass·i·ness,** n.

glau·co·ma, glô·kō′mə, glow·kō′mə, n. A disease of the eye characterized by increased internal pressure and progressive loss of vision.

glaze, glāz, v.t., **glazed, glaz·ing.** To furnish or fit with glass, as a window; to cover with a smooth and lustrous coating; give a glassy surface to.—v.i. To become glazed or glassy.—n. Any smooth, glossy surface or coating or a substance for producing it.

gla·zier, glā′zhər, n. One who fits windows and picture frames with glass.

gleam, glēm, n. A beam or flash of light; a ray; a subdued brightness or glow; a small stream of reflected light; a trace: a *gleam* of hope.—v.i. To shine or radiate softly; to glimmer; to appear briefly and clearly.

glean, glēn, v.t. To gather, as scattered grain, from a reaped cornfield; to collect slowly and arduously, as data; to pick up here and there; to discover, as news.—v.i. To pick up anything slowly or by degrees.

glee, glē, n. Joy; merriment; mirth; gaiety; an unaccompanied musical composition consisting of two or more contrasted movements. —**glee·ful,** a.

glee club, n. A group organized for singing songs.

glen, glen, n. A secluded narrow valley; a dale; a depression or space between hills.

glib, glib, a., **glib·ber, glib·best.** Having superficial, smooth words always ready; with sincerity in speech; smooth; slippery. —**glib·ly,** adv. —**glib·ness,** n.

glide, glīd, v.i., **glid·ed, glid·ing.** To move smoothly along, without effort or difficulty; to go quietly, stealthily, or unperceived; slip; steal; to move in the air, esp. at an easy angle downward, guided by air currents, gravity, or momentum already acquired.—v.t. To cause to glide.—n. The act of gliding; a gliding movement, as in dancing.

glim·mer, glim′ər, v.i. To shine faintly; to give a feeble light; to flicker; to appear indistinctly or dimly.—n. A faint and unsteady light; a shimmer; a twinkle; a vague perception; an inkling.

glimpse, glimps, n. A quick, passing view or look; a brief appearance; a slight suggestion or inkling.—v.t., **glimpsed, glimps·ing.** To get a quick view of.—v.i. To look fleetingly or glance, usu. followed by at.

glint, glint, n. A flash; a gleam; sheen or luster; a faint appearance or suggestion.—v.i. To gleam or flash; to dash or dart.—v.t. To cause to flash; to reflect.

glis·san·do, gli·sän′dō, n. pl., **-di, -dē, -dos.** A quick, continuous sliding up or down the scale.

glis·ten, glis′ən, v.i. To shine or glow with a luster, as if wet; to sparkle with reflected light.—n. Glitter; sparkle.

glit·ter, glit′ər, v.i. To shine with a broken and scattered light; to gleam, sparkle, or glisten; to be showy or brilliant.—n. Bright sparkling light; brilliance; luster; splendor; sparkling ornamentation.

gloam·ing, glō′ming, n. The twilight; dusk.

gloat, glōt, v.i. To contemplate with evil satisfaction; to gaze with admiration, eagerness, or desire.

glob, glob, n. A drop of semi-liquid substance; a rounded lump or mass.

glob·al, glō′bəl, a. Spherical; globeshaped; pertaining to the earth; worldwide. —**glob·al·ly,** adv.

globe, glōb, n. The earth, usu. preceded by *the;* a sphere on whose surface is drawn a map of the earth or of the heavens; a spherical solid body; a ball; any of several things somewhat spherical in shape.

globe·trot·ter, glōb′trot·ər, n. One who travels widely over the world. —**globe·trot·ting,** n., a.

glob·u·lar, glob′yə·lər, a. Spherical; composed of globules; world-wide.

glob·ule, glob′ūl, n. A small particle of matter of a spherical form.

glock·en·spiel, glok′ən·spēl, glok′ən·shpēl, *n.* A musical instrument consisting of a series of metal bars, mounted in a frame or support, and struck with hammers.

gloom, gloom, *n.* Obscurity; partial darkness; dejection; a depressing state of affairs; a dismal prospect. —*v.i.* To appear dimly; to look gloomy, sad, or dismal; to frown.—*v.t.* To make gloomy; to fill with gloom or sadness.

gloom·y, gloo′mē, *a.*, **-i·er**, **-i·est**. Involved in gloom; imperfectly illuminated; dark; wearing the aspect of sorrow; dejected; dismal; doleful. —**gloom·i·ly**, *adv.* —**gloom·i·ness**, *n.*

glo·ri·fy, glōr′ə·fī, glōr′ə·fī, *v.t.*, **-fied**, **-fy·ing**. To give or ascribe glory to; to praise; to magnify and honor; to extol; to make glorious; to exalt. —**glo·ri·fi·ca·tion**, glōr·ə·fə·kā′shən, *n.* —**glo·ri·fied**, *a.* —**glo·ri·fi·er**, *n.*

glo·ri·ous, glōr′ē·əs, glōr′ē·əs, *a.* Of exalted excellence and splendor; splendid; noble; illustrious or renowned; celebrated; magnificent or wonderful. —**glo·ri·ous·ly**, *adv.* —**glo·ri·ous·ness**, *n.*

glo·ry, glōr′ē, glōr′ē, *n. pl.*, **-ries**. Praise, honor, or distinction; something assuring fame or praise; thanksgiving expressed in adoration; a state of happiness; the blessings of heaven; summit of worldly achievement; corona.—*v.i.*, **-ried**, **-ry·ing**. To exult with joy; to rejoice; to be boastful; to take pride in.

gloss, glos, *n.* Brightness or luster; a false appearance or representation.—*v.t.* To give gloss or luster to; to give a false appearance to.

glos·sa·ry, glos′ə·rē, glôs′ə·rē, *n. pl.*, **-ries**. A dictionary or vocabulary of the technical, dialectical, or obscure words of a specific field or work.

gloss·y, glôs′ē, glos′ē, *a.*, **-i·er**, **-i·est**. Having a gloss; having a smooth, shining surface. —**gloss·i·ly**, *adv.* —**gloss·i·ness**, *n.*

glot·tis, glot′is, *n. pl.*, **-tis·es**, **-ti·des**, **-tə·dēz**. The opening at the upper part of the windpipe between the vocal chords.

glove, gləv, *n.* A covering for the hand, having a separate sheath for each finger and the thumb; a boxing glove.—*v.t.*, **gloved**, **glov·ing**. To cover with or as with a glove; provide with gloves; to serve as a glove for.

glow, glō, *v.i.* To emit bright light and heat without flame; to be incandescent; to shine like something intensely heated; to be lustrously brilliant; to be hot; to feel an intense heat; to burn or be animated with emotion or passion: to *glow* with excitement.—*n.* The state of glowing; light emitted by a body heated to luminosity; incandescence; brightness of color; vivid redness; a state of bodily heat; warmth of emotion. —**glow·er**, *n.* —**glow·ing**, *a.*

glow·er, glow′ər, *v.i.* To look angrily, with sullen dislike or discontent; scowl.—*n.* A glowering look.

glow·worm, glō′wərm, *n.* Any of various luminous insects or insect larvae.

glu·cose, gloo′kōs, *n.* A sugar which occurs in many plant and animal tissues.

glue, gloo, *n.* A strong adhesive, used for uniting pieces of wood or other materials; any of various other binding preparations.—*v.t.*, **glued**, **glu·ing**. To join or cover with glue.

glum, gləm, *a.*, **glum·mer**, **glum·mest**. Frowning; sullen.

glut, glət, *v.t.*, **glut·ted**, **glut·ting**. To feed or fill to satiety; sate; to indulge to the utmost; to feed or fill to excess; to overstock, as a market.—*v.i.* To eat to satiety.—*n.* The act of glutting, or the state of being glutted; a full or excessive supply; a supply of goods in excess of the demand.

glu·ten, gloo′tən, *n.* The tough, sticky substance which remains when the flour of wheat or other grain is washed with water to remove the starch; the protein in flour and bread.

glu·ti·nous, gloo′tə·nəs, *a.* Sticky.

glut·ton, glət′ən, *n.* One who indulges to excess in eating; one who has an extraordinary capacity for something: a *glutton* for punishment.

glut·ton·ous, glət′ən·əs, *a.* Given to excessive eating; greedy. —**glut·ton·y**, *n.*

glyc·er·in, glis′ər·in, *n.* Glycerol. Also **glyc·er·ine**, glis′ər·in.

glyc·er·ol, glis′ər·ōl, glis′ə·rol, *n.* An odorless, colorless, syrupy, sweet-tasting liquid compound obtained from fats and oils.

G-man, jē′man, *n. pl.*, **G-men**. A nickname for a special agent of the Federal Bureau of Investigation, a division of the U.S. Department of Justice.

gnarl, närl, *n.* A protuberance on the outside of a tree; a knot.—*v.t.* To twist or make twisted. —**gnarled**, närld, *a.* —**gnarl·y**, när′lē, *a.*, **-i·er**, **-i·est**.

gnash, nash, *v.t.* To strike or grind together, as the teeth, esp. in rage or pain; to strike or grind the teeth upon; bite with grinding teeth.—*v.i.* To strike or grind teeth together.

gnat, nat, *n.* Any of various small, biting flies.

gnaw, nô, *v.t.*, **gnawed**, **gnawed** or **gnawn**, **gnaw·ing**. To wear away by persistent biting; to bite persistently; to fret or torment by repeated annoyance.—*v.i.* To bite persistently; to produce pain or worry.

gneiss, nīs, *n.* A metamorphic rock similar to granite.

gnome, nōm, *n.* An imaginary dwarfed and misshapen human being, supposedly inhabiting the subterranean parts of the earth, and guarding mines, esp. those of precious metals.

gnu, noo, nū, *n. pl.*, **gnu**, **gnus**. Any of several large African antelopes with an oxlike head, curved horns, and a long, flowing tail. Also **wil·de·beest**.

go, gō, *v.i.*, **went**, **gone**, **go·ing**. To move, pass along, proceed; to move or pass away or out; depart; to continue, or be habitually, in a particular circumstance: to *go* in rags; to keep or be in motion; act, or function satisfactorily; to pass or elapse, as time; to be admissible or satisfactory: anything *goes;* to be known: to *go* under an alias; to harmonize or be compatible: colors that *go* well together; to turn out or result: How did the match *go?* To pass, as by sale; to come to an end; be consumed; to fail, wear away or out; to die; to be capable of fitting in, or of being divided: a book that will *go* into one's pocket, or a quantity which *goes* into twelve three times; to belong: This book *goes* on the top shelf; to pass, be awarded: First prize *goes* to a dark horse; to be applied: All the money *goes* for medicine; to open into or lead to: Does that door *go* to the kitchen? To pass into a particular condition: to *go* to ruin; become: as, to *go* mad; to happen or occur, followed by *on*, as: What *goes on* here? To put oneself to; as to *go* to great lengths; to be worded, as a phrase, or composed, as a tune, in a certain way: How does that song *go?* To be about to, intending, or destined to do something: It is *going* to rain.—*v.t.* To go or proceed on, along, or through: *going* my way; to go to the extent of, or venture as far as.—*n. pl.*, **goes**. The act of going, as: the come and *go* of the seasons. *Informal.* Energy, spirit, or animation: That horse has lots of *go;* a proceeding, turn of affairs, or state of things; a turn, chance, or attempt at something; something that proves successful: to make a *go* of a venture.—*a.* Ready, esp. of rockets ready for launch: All systems are *go.* —**go a·bout**, to change the course of a vessel by wearing or tacking; to busy oneself with. —**go af·ter**, to try for; pursue; hunt for. —**go at**, to assail; to attack; to set about vigorously. —**go for**, to be taken or valued as; to attempt to obtain; to attack or assail; to prefer. *Informal.* To have an affinity for or be attracted

---

by. **—go in for.** *Informal.* To make one's particular interest or amusement: to *go in for* stamp collecting. **—go off,** explode or burst, as fireworks; to happen or occur. **—go out,** to become outmoded or obsolete; to cease to work or operate, as a light; to take part in social activity; to date; to participate in a strike; to feel compassion: My heart *goes out* to her; to be a contender: to *go out* for the team. **—go o•ver,** to look over; to reexamine; to study again; to rehearse; to switch opinion or allegiance. *Informal.* To prove successful. **—go un•der,** to be submerged or overwhelmed; to succumb; to be ruined, as an enterprise. **—go up,** to rise or ascend; to advance or increase, as costs or values. **—go with,** to accompany; associate with; to socialize with or date; to harmonize with, as colors or styles. **—no go.** *Informal.* Of no use; futile. **—on the go.** *Informal.* Constantly going; busy. **—to go,** unexpired, remaining: 15 minutes *to go;* to be taken out and consumed elsewhere, as restaurant food.

goad, gōd, *n.* A pointed instrument used to urge animals forward; anything that stimulates.—*v.t.* To drive with a goad; to incite, spur, or prod.

go-a•head, gō′ə•hed, *n.* Permission or notice to advance: The contractor received the *go-ahead* to begin building.

goal, gōl, *n.* The point set as the end of a race; an aim or objective; in various games, the area, space, or object into which the players attempt to place the ball or puck; the act of scoring points in this way; the score which is made in this way.—*v.i.*

goal•keep•er, gōl′kē•per, *n.* A player whose function is to guard the goal. Also **goal•ie.**

goat, gōt, *n.* Any of various agile, hollow-horned cud-chewing mammals closely related to the sheep, found native in rocky and mountainous regions of the Old World, and including domesticated forms common throughout the world. **—get one's goat.** *Informal.* To disgust, anger, or annoy a person. **—goat•ish, goat•like,** *a.*

goat•ee, gō•tē′, *n.* A man's small, neat beard that is trimmed to a point and has no side whiskers.

goat•herd, gōt′herd, *n.* One whose occupation is to tend goats.

goat•skin, gōt′skin, *n.* The skin or hide of a goat, or leather made from it.

gob, gob, *n. Informal.* A sailor of the U.S. navy; a mass or lump.

gob•ble, gob′əl, *v.t.,* **-bled, -bling.** To swallow in large pieces; to swallow hastily; to grasp or seize eagerly, often followed by *up.*—*v.i.* To eat hurriedly; to make a noise in the throat, as by a male turkey.—*n.* A noise made in the throat, as that of a male turkey.

gob•ble•dy•gook, gob•ble•de•gook, gob′əl-dē•gûk, *n. Informal.* Pretentious, redundant, and obscure speech or writing; jargon.

gob•bler, gob′ler, *n.* A male turkey.

go-be•tween, gō′bi•twēn, *n.* One who serves as a broker or agent between persons or groups of people; a mediator; an intermediary.

gob•let, gob′lit, *n.* A drinking glass having a stem and a base.

gob•lin, gob′lin, *n.* An evil or mischievous sprite, usu. thought to be extremely ugly.

go-cart, gō′kärt, *n.* A simple framework device with casters or small wheels, designed to teach a small child to walk; a chairlike carriage or stroller for a small child; a handcart.

God, god, *n.* Creator and ruler of the universe; eternal, infinite Spirit; the Supreme Being, almighty and omniscient, worshiped by men; *O.T.,* Jehovah.

god, god, *n.* A person, spirit, or object, worshipped and adored, to whom supernatural powers are attributed; a deity in mythology; an idol; a person possessing supreme authority; a person, as an athlete or other notable, who is publicly admired to a degree approaching worship; a person or thing valued above all.

god•child, god′chīld, *n. pl.,* **-chil•dren.** A child for

whom one has been sponsor at a baptism or at a corresponding ceremony of another faith. **—god•daugh•ter,** god′dô•ter, *n.* **—god•son,** god′sən, *n.*

god•dess, god′is, *n.* A female deity; a woman who is adored; a very beautiful young lady.

god•fa•ther, god′fä•ther, *n.* A man who sponsors at baptism a child not his own progeny; the head of a Mafia clan.

god•head, god′hed, *n.* Godship; deity; divinity; divine nature or essence. **—The God•head,** the Deity; God; the Supreme Being.

god•less, god′lis, *a.* Having or acknowledging no god; impious; ungodly; irreligious; wicked. **—god•less•ness,** *n.*

god•like, god′līk, *a.* Resembling a god or God; divine; of superior excellence.

god•ly, god′lē, *a.,* **-li•er, -li•est.** Pious; revering God and His laws; devout; righteous.—*adv.* Piously; righteously. **—god•li•ness,** *n.*

god•moth•er, god′məth•ər, *n.* A female sponsor of a child at baptism.

god•par•ent, god′per•ent, *n.* A sponsor of a child at its baptism.

god•send, god′send, *n.* An unexpected acquisition or piece of good fortune, almost as if sent by God.

God•speed, god′spēd′, *n.* Success; a prosperous journey, usu. expressed as a wish: to bid a person *Godspeed.*

go-get•ter, gō′get′ər, *n. Informal.* An enterprising, enthusiastic individual; one who is ambitious and aggressive.

gog•gle, gog′əl, *n.* A stare; a wide-eyed look.—*v.i.,* **-gled, -gling.** To stare, esp. wide-eyed or with bulging, protuberant eyeballs; of the eyes, to bulge and stare. —*v.t.* To cause to roll, as the eyes. **—gog•gle-eyed,** gog′əl•id, *a.*

gog•gles, gog′əlz, *n. pl.* Protective spectacles with special lenses, rims, or esp. side shields.

go•ing, gō′ing, *n.* The act of moving away; departure; the condition of the ground or the surface of a road, path, racetrack, or the like in reference to its suitability for walking, driving, or racing; the act of progressing toward a goal in any activity.—*a.* That goes; that moves or functions; functioning or operating successfully: a *going* business; standard, prevailing, or available: the *going* rate of exchange; existing. **—go•ings on, go•ings-on,** activities; conduct, esp. such as evokes criticism.

goi•ter, goi′ter, **goi•tre,** goi′tər, *n.* An enlargement of the thyroid gland, forming a bulge on the side or front part of the neck.

gold, gōld, *n.* A metallic element of deep yellow color, noted for its softness, beauty, and resistance to corrosion; used for coins, jewelry, dentures, and filaments for threads and fabrics; a coin made of gold; money; riches; wealth; a bright yellow color.—*a.* Made of or consisting of gold; colored like gold.

gold-brick, gōld′brik, *n. Informal.* A person who shirks his duties.

gold•en, gōl′dən, *a.* Made or consisting of gold; containing gold; of the color of gold; yellow; bright or shining, like gold; resembling gold in value; most excellent; exceedingly favorable, as an opportunity; flourishing or joyous, as a time or period.

gold•en rule, *n.* A rule stating that one is to behave toward others as one wishes them to behave toward oneself.

gold leaf, *n.* Gold hammered into extremely thin sheets used primarily for gilding.

gold•smith, gōld′smith, *n.* A craftsman who makes, or a dealer who sells, gold objects.

gold stand•ard, *n.* A monetary system in which the value of a national currency is based on gold of prescribed fineness and weight.

golf, golf, gôlf, *n.* A game played with clubs and a small white ball, generally over a large course with strategic obstacles, the object being to drive the ball, with as few strokes as possible, into nine or eighteen holes placed considerable distances apart.—*v.i.*

go·nad, gō′nad, gon′ad, *n.* A male or female reproductive gland that produces gametes, sperm, or ovum; a testis or ovary.

gon·do·la, gon′də·lə, *n.* A long, narrow boat with a high peak at each end and often a small cabin near the middle, used on the Venetian canals, and usu. propelled at the stern by a single oar or pole; a kind of lighter or barge; a railway freight car with low sides and no top.

gon·do·lier, gon·də·lēr′, *n.* A man who rows or poles a gondola.

gone, gôn, gon, *a.* Departed; finished or consumed; over or past: *gone* ages; dead; lost, undone, or hopeless: a *gone* case; weak and faint: a *gone* feeling. —**far gone,** much advanced or deeply involved.

gon·er, gôn′ər, gon′ər, *n. Informal.* A person or thing that is dead, lost, or past recovery.

gong, gông, gong, *n.* A metallic disk which produces a sonorous sound when struck; a saucer-shaped bell sounded by a hammer.

gon·or·rhe·a, gon·or·rhoe·a, gon·ə·rē′ə, *n.* A contagious, inflammatory ailment of the male urethra or the female vagina, accompanied by secretions of mucus and pus. —**gon·or·rhe·al, gon·or·rhoe·al,** *a.*

goo, goo, *n. Informal.* Sticky matter; excessive sentimentality. —**goo·ey,** *a.,* **-i·er, -i·est.**

goo·ber, goo′bər, *n.* A peanut. Also **goo·ber pea.**

good, gûd, *n.* That which is good; advantage, desire, or benefit: to work for the common *good.* *Pl.* Property or possessions, usu. portable or movable: household *goods;* cloth or fabric: curtain *goods.*—*a.,* **bet·ter, best.** Of favorable quality or character: *good* weather, *good* shoes, *good* news; virtuous or morally excellent: *good* works; satisfactory or excellent in degree or kind: *good* food, a *good* book; responsible or trustworthy: a *good* face; right or proper: Do what seems *good* to you. Appropriate or fitting for a particular purpose: a *good* day for a swim; useful, advantageous, or profitable, as an idea or a trade; genuine or legally valid, as money or a title; endurable, used with *for: good* for a lifetime; real or true: He made *good* his threats. Sound or valid: *good* judgment; guaranteed to give or pay, used with *for: good* for a loan; agreeable or pleasant: a *good* time; generous or kind: a *good* deed; sufficient or ample in quantity: *good* measure; full: a *good* day's journey; fairly great: a *good* deal of time; faithful or conforming: a *good* Catholic; competent or skillful: a *good* doctor; clever or adroit: *good* at sports; well-behaved, as a child; well-regarded or honorable: a *good* reputation; pertaining to a noble or respectable class: a *good* family; intimate: a *good* friend. —**as good as,** practically or in effect: *as good.* —**for good,** finally and permanently; forever: to leave a place *for good.* —**good and.** *Informal.* Completely; very: *good and* hot. —**to make good,** to perform; to fulfill; to verify or establish, as an accusation; to make up a deficit; to make up for a defect; to maintain or carry out successfully. —**to the good,** on the side of profit or advantage: He came out five dollars *to the good* in that transaction.

good-by, good-bye, gûd·bī′, *a., interj., n. pl.,* **-bys, -byes.** Farewell.

good-for-nothing, gûd′fer·nəth′ing, *a.* Worthless. —*n.* A worthless person.

Good Fri·day, *n.* Friday before Easter, a holy day of the Christian church, observed as commemorative of Christ's crucifixion.

good-heart·ed, gûd′härt′tid, *a.* Considerate; charitable; kind.

good hu·mor, *n.* A cheerful temper or state of mind.

good·ish, gûd′ish, *a.* Somewhat good; rather big.

good-look·ing, gûd′lûk′ing, *a.* Of pleasing appearance; attractive; handsome.

good·ly, gûd′lē, *a.,* **-li·er, -li·est.** Being pleasing in appearance; of a fine quality; large or considerable: a *goodly* share.

good-na·tured, gûd′nā′chərd, *a.* Naturally mild in temperament.

good·ness, gûd′nis, *n.* The state or quality of being good; virtue or integrity; kindness; the best part of a thing, its essence; a euphemism for God: thank *goodness.*

good-tem·pered, gûd′tem′pərd, *a.* Having an agreeable disposition.

good will, *n.* Friendly disposition; benevolence; favor; cheerful acquiescence; readiness or zeal; the value of a business due to reputation. Also **good·will,** gûd′wil′.

good·y, gûd′ē, *n. pl.,* **-ies.** *Usu. pl. Informal.* Something good to eat or otherwise pleasing.—*interj.* Good: an expression of delight used esp. by children.

goof, goof, *v.i. Informal.* To make an error; blunder; to waste time, often with *off* or *around.*—*v.t. Informal.* To make a mess of; bungle: He *goofed* his chance to be promoted.

goof-off, goof′ôf′, *n. Informal.* An individual who constantly wastes time, neglects his job, or shrinks from responsibility.—*v.t.*

goof·y, goo′fē, *a.,* **-i·er, -i·est.** *Informal.* Foolish; silly; stupid. —**goof·i·ness,** *n.*

goon, goon, *n. Informal.* A stupid, silly, or unattractive person; a hoodlum, esp. one employed to break strikes.

goose, goos, *n. pl.,* **geese.** Any of numerous wild or domesticated, web-footed birds, mostly larger and with a longer neck than the ducks; the female of this bird, as distinguished from the male or gander; the flesh of the goose; a foolish person; a simpleton.

goose·ber·ry, goos′bər·ē, gooz′bər·ē, *n. pl.,* **-ries.** The small, edible, acid, round berry of certain shrubs; the shrub itself.

goose flesh, *n.* A rough condition of the skin, resembling that of a plucked goose, induced by cold or fear. Also **goose bumps, goose pim·ples, goose skin.**

goose step, *n.* A marching step in which the legs are swung high with straight, stiff knees.

gore, gōr, gôr, *n.* Blood that is shed; clotted blood.

gore, gōr, gôr, *n.* A tapering piece of cloth used as a panel in a skirt or sail to provide extra width.—*v.t.* To insert, as a gore.

gore, gōr, gôr, *v.t.,* **gored, gor·ing.** Of a bull, elephant, etc., to pierce with a horn or tusk.

gorge, gôrj, *n.* A narrow ravine, esp. one through which a stream runs.—*v.t.,* **gorged, gorg·ing.** To stuff with food.—*v.i.* To eat greedily.

gor·geous, gôr′jəs, *a.* Splendid in dress, appearance, or coloring. —**gor·geous·ly,** *adv.* —**gor·geous·ness,** *n.*

gor·y, gôr′ē, gōr′ē, *a.,* **-i·er, -i·est.** Bloody; extremely unpleasant: the *gory* details of his trial.

gosh, gosh, *Interj.* A mild oath; an expression of surprise or admiration.

gos·ling, goz′ling, *n.* A young goose.

gos·pel, gos′pəl, *n.* The body of doctrine taught by Christ and the apostles; the story of Christ's life and teachings, esp. as contained in the first four books of the New Testament; (*usu. cap.*) one of these books; (*often cap.*) an extract from one of these four books. Something infallibly true or implicitly believed: His word is taken for *gospel* by the neighborhood children.

gos·sa·mer, gos′ə·mər, *n.* A fine, filmy, cobwebby substance seen on grass and bushes or floating in the air in calm weather, esp. in autumn; any thin, light fabric or other delicate substance.—*a.* Of or like gossamer; thin; light; filmy. —**gos·sa·mer·y,** *a.,* **-i·er, -i·est.**

---

a- hat, fāte, fâre, fäther; e- met, mē; i- pin, pīne; o- not, nōte, ôrb, moove (move), boy, pownd; u- cūbe, bûll, tûk (took); ch- chin; th- thick, ᵺen; zh- vizhon (vision); ə- əgo, takən, pencəl, lemən, bərd (bird).

gos·sip, gos′əp, *n.* Idle talk; rumors; a person given to idle talk or the spreading of reports about others. —*v.t.* To repeat as gossip. —*v.i.* To talk idly, esp. about other people; to go about tattling.

Goth·ic, goth′ik, *a.* Denoting a style of architecture utilizing the pointed arch, buttress, and ribbed vaulting current in western Europe from 1200 to 1500 A.D.

gouge, gowj, *n.* A chisel whose blade is shaped like a scoop, with a concave-convex cross section; the act of gouging; a groove or hole caused by gouging; a swindle. —*v.t.,* **gouged, goug·ing.** To make with or as with a gouge; to dig or force out with or as with a gouge; to cheat or swindle. —**goug·er,** *n.*

gou·lash, goo′läsh, goo′lash, *n.* A stew of beef, veal, and vegetables, with paprika or other seasoning.

gourd, gōrd, gôrd, gûrd, *n.* The fruit of melons, pumpkins, and the like; a pepo; the dried shell of this fruit, used for decoration or as a bottle.

gour·mand, gûr′mənd, *n. pl.,* **-mands.** One who is informed about and enjoys good eating.

gour·met, gûr·mā′, gûr′mā, *n. pl.,* **-mets.** A connoisseur of food and drink; an epicure.

gout, gowt, *n.* A disease caused by defective metabolism and characterized by inflamed joints, esp. in the big toe; a drop or clot, as of blood. —**gout·y,** *a.,* **-i·er, -i·est.**

gov·ern, gəv′ərn, *v.t.* To direct, control, or regulate by authority; to guide or influence; to restrain; check; keep under control. —*v.i.* To exercise authority; to administer the laws; to maintain control. —**gov·ern·a·ble,** *a.*

gov·ern·ess, gəv′ər·nis, *n.* A female teacher hired to instruct and train children in a private household.

gov·ern·ment, gəv′ərn·mənt, gəv′ər·mənt, *n.* The exercise of political authority, direction, and restraint over the actions of the inhabitants of communities, societies, or states; governing organization or body of a nation, state, or community; the system according to which the legislative, executive, and judicial powers are vested and exercised. —**gov·ern·men·tal,** gəv·ərn·men′təl, *a.*

gov·er·nor, gəv′ər·nər, *n.* One who governs; the executive head of a state of the U.S. *Brit.* The official title of the representative of the British Crown serving in a colony or dependency of Great Britain. A contrivance in mills and machinery for maintaining a uniform velocity with a varying resistance; a contrivance in a steam engine which automatically regulates admission of steam to the cylinder. —**gov·er·nor·ship,** *n.*

gown, gown, *n.* A woman's dress, esp. her formal attire; a dressing gown or a nightgown; the official robe worn by members of certain professions. —*v.t.* To put a gown on; to clothe or dress in a gown. —*v.i.* To put on a gown; to wear a gown or robe.

grab, grab, *v.t.,* **grabbed, grab·bing.** To seize suddenly and eagerly; snatch. —*v.i.* To make a grab or snatch. —*n.* The act of grabbing; a sudden, eager grasp or snatch. —**grab·ber,** *n.*

grab bag, *n.* A bag from which a person may draw without examining any of the various articles within.

grace, grās, *n.* Elegance or dignity of form, movement, or expression; beauty, charm, or any pleasing attribute; favor, good will, or kindness; a sense of decency or propriety; a special dispensation or privilege; mercy or pardon; a temporary reprieve. *Law.* A period of time following the due date of a debt during which the debtor is allowed to make payment without penalty. *Theol.* The unmerited love and favor of God; a short prayer before or after meals giving thanks or asking a blessing. (*Usu. cap.*) A title used in addressing a duke, duchess, or bishop, usu. preceded by *your, her,* or *his.* —*v.t.,* **graced, grac·ing.** To lend or add grace to; to adorn; to dignify or honor. —**in the good** or **bad grace·es of,** in the favor or disfavor of. —**with good grace,** willingly or graciously. —**with bad grace,** reluctantly or ungraciously.

grace·ful, grās′fəl, *a.* Marked by or displaying grace

or elegance in form, action, or expression. —**grace·ful·ly,** *adv.* —**grace·ful·ness,** *n.*

grace·less, grās′lis, *a.* Void of grace or pleasing qualities; possessing no sense of propriety.

grace note, *n. Mus.* A note added by way of ornament and written in smaller notation.

gra·cious, grā′shəs, *a.* Characterized by kindness, courtesy, or benevolence; refined; polite in a condescending manner; merciful, used esp. of royalty.

gra·da·tion, grā·dā′shən, *n.* An orderly arrangement or placing, according to relative rank, degree, size, or quality; a succession or change by gradual steps or degrees.

grade, grād, *n.* A degree in any series, rank, or order; relative position or standing, as in quality or seniority; one of the sections of a school system, as divided into the pupils' years of work; a mark rating a pupil's work; a class comprising things of the same quality; the rate of ascent or descent, as of a sloping road; the part of a road which slopes. —*v.t.,* **grad·ed, grad·ing.** To arrange in order according to size, quality, rank, or degree of advancement; to reduce, as a railway line, to such levels or degrees of inclination as may make it suitable for use; to determine the grade of. —*v.i.* Blend; to form or be a grade or series.

grade cross·ing, *n.* A crossing of railroad tracks or highways, or of a railroad track and a highway, on the same level.

grad·er, grā′dər, *n.* One who or that which grades; a pupil of a school grade: *fifth grader.*

grade school, *n.* An elementary school.

gra·di·ent, grā′dē·ənt, *n.* Degree of slope or inclination, as of the ground; the rate of ascent or descent; a slope, incline, or grade; the rate of change of a variable quantity such as temperature or pressure. —*a.* Rising or descending by regular degrees; suited for walking.

grad·u·al, graj′ū·əl, *a.* Proceeding, changing, or moving by degrees or little by little. —**grad·u·al·ly,** *adv.* —**grad·u·al·ness,** *n.*

grad·u·ate, graj′ū·āt, *v.t.,* **-at·ed, -at·ing.** To confer a degree or diploma upon at the close of a course of study; to divide into or mark with degrees, as the scale of a thermometer; to arrange in grades or gradations. —*v.i.* To receive a degree or diploma on completing a course of study; to change gradually. —graj′ū·it, *a.* Of or pertaining to study beyond the bachelor's degree. —graj′ū·it, *n.* One who has received an academic degree or diploma on completing a course of study; a graduated vessel for measuring, as a beaker.

grad·u·a·tion, graj·ū·ā′shən, *n.* The act of graduating or the state of being graduated; the ceremony of conferring degrees or diplomas, as at a college or school; a mark or marks, as on an instrument or a vessel, for indicating degree or quantity; these marks or divisions collectively.

graf·fi·to, grə·fē′tō, *n. pl.,* **-ti, -tē,** *sing.* or *pl.* in *constr.* Inscriptions or drawings scrawled on walls, sidewalks, or the like.

graft, graft, gräft, *n.* A shoot or part of a plant inserted in a groove, slit, or the like in another plant or tree so it will grow there; the plant or tree resulting from such an operation. A portion of living tissue transplanted by surgery from one body or part of a body to another. —*v.t.* To insert part of one plant into another plant; to transplant by surgical grafting. —*v.i.* To insert a graft or grafts; to become grafted.

graft, graft, gräft, *n.* The acquisition of gain or advantage by dishonest, unfair, or illegal means, esp. through the abuse of one's position or influence in politics or business; the gain or advantage acquired. —*v.i.* To practice graft. —*v.t.* To obtain by graft.

gra·ham flour, grā′əm flow′ər, *n.* Wheat flour made from the whole kernel; wholewheat flour.

Grail, grāl, *n.* The Holy Grail.

grain, grān, *n.* A single seed of the cereal grasses; the seeds of these plants in general, as wheat, rye, oats, and corn; the plants themselves; any small, hard particle, as of sand, sugar, or salt; a small amount: not a *grain* of sense; the pattern or direction of the fibers or particles in wood, leather, or stone; natural temperament.—*v.t.* To paint so as to give the appearance of grains or fibers.

grain al·co·hol, *n.* An ethyl alcohol distilled from grains.

grain·y, grā′nē, *a.,* **-i·er, -i·est.** Grainlike or granular; full of grains or grain; resembling the grain of wood. —**grain·i·ness,** *n.*

gram, gram, *n.* A metric unit of weight equivalent to about .035 ounces avoirdupois.

gram·mar, gram′ər, *n.* The study or science of the forms and rules of a language; the forms and syntax of its words; the principles of correct usage; speech or writing in accordance with established grammatical usage: That sentence contains bad *grammar.* —**gram·mar·i·an,** grə·mār′ē·ən, *n.*

gram·mar school, *n.* Elementary school. *Brit.* A secondary school in which the curriculum corresponds generally to that of U.S. high schools.

gram·mat·i·cal, grə·mat′i·kəl, *a.* Of or pertaining to grammar: a *grammatical* error; in accordance with the rules of grammar: That sentence is not *grammatical.* —**gram·mat·i·cal·ly,** *adv.*

gra·na·ry, grā′nə·rē, gran′ə·rē, *n. pl.,* **-ries.** A storehouse for grain; a region where grain is produced in abundance.

grand, grand, *a.* Vast in scope or size; great; illustrious; high in power or dignity; noble; splendid; principal or chief: a *grand* juror.—*n. Informal.* A thousand dollars. —**grand·ly,** *adv.*

grand·child, gran′chīld, *n.* A son's or daughter's child.

grand·daugh·ter, gran′dôt·ər, *n.* A daughter of a son or of a daughter.

grand duke, *n.* The title of a sovereign of certain European states; a Russian czar's son or grandson.

gran·dee, gran·dē′, *n.* A Spanish or Portuguese nobleman of high rank; any man of high rank or social position.

gran·deur, gran′jer, gran′jûr, *n.* The state or quality of being grand; imposing or awesome greatness; majesty; magnificence; exalted rank, dignity, or importance.

grand·fa·ther, grand′fä·thər, *n.* A father's or mother's father; ancestor, forebear.

gran·dil·o·quence, gran·dil′ə·kwəns, *n.* Bombastic or lofty discourse; high-sounding words. —**gran·dil·o·quent,** *a.*

gran·di·ose, gran′dē·ōs, *a.* Impressive; very imposing; aiming at or affecting grandeur. —**gran·di·ose·ly,** *adv.*

grand ju·ry, *n.* A specially impaneled jury numbering 12 to 24 people whose duty it is to hear accusations against offenders, examine evidence of the state, and if just cause exists, to find a bill of indictment.

grand·moth·er, grand′məth·ər, *n.* A father's or mother's mother; a female forebear.

grand op·er·a, *n.* Opera similar in plot and characterization to serious drama, but having the text completely set to music.

grand·par·ent, grand′per·ənt, *n.* A parent of a parent.

grand pi·an·o, *n.* A piano with strings stretched horizontally in a harp-shaped body.

grand·son, grand′sən, *n.* A son of a son or of a daughter.

grand·stand, grand′stand, *n.* An elevated series of seats for spectators at a racecourse or sports stadium.—*v.i.* To perform in a showy manner in order to impress the spectators.

grange, grānj, *n.* A farm, with its buildings. (*Cap.*) One of the local lodges of the farmers' organization called 'The Patrons of Husbandry'; the organization itself. —**grang·er,** *n.*

gran·ite, gran′it, *n.* An igneous rock, one of the most abundant in the earth's crust, composed generally of grains or crystals of quartz, feldspar, and mica. —**gra·nit·ic,** grə·nit′ik, *a.*

gran·ny, gran·nie, gran′ē, *n. pl.,* **-nies.** *Informal.* A grandmother; an old woman; one exhibiting fussiness.

gran·ny knot, *n.* An incorrectly tied square knot which slips and jams easily.

grant, grant, gränt, *v.t.* To give or accord: to *grant* permission; to bestow or confer, as a right; to admit or concede; transfer or convey, as property, esp. by deed or writing.—*n.* The act of granting; that which is granted.

gran·u·lar, gran′yə·lər, *a.* Consisting of or resembling granules or grains. —**gran·u·lar·i·ty,** gran·yə·lär′i·tē, *n.*

gran·u·late, gran′yə·lāt, *v.t.,* **-lat·ed, -lat·ing.** To form into grains or granules; to make rough on the surface.—*v.i.* To collect or be formed into grains; to become granular.

gran·u·la·tion, gran·yə·lā′shən, *n.* The act or condition of granulating; the process of reducing into small grains.

gran·ule, gran′ūl, *n.* A little grain; a small particle.

grape, grāp, *n.* The edible, pulpy, smoothskinned fruit which grows in clusters on vines, and from which wine is made; any vine bearing this fruit; a dark purple color.

grape·fruit, grāp′froot, *n.* An edible, large, round, pale yellow fruit with an acid, flavorful pulp; the tree.

grape sug·ar, *n.* Dextrose.

grape·vine, grāp′vīn, *n.* A vine that bears grapes; an informal method of communicating information from person to person.

graph, graf, gräf, *n.* A diagrammatic representation of a system of connections or relations between at least two things by a number of spots, lines, or bars; a pattern of lines which connect points. *Math.* A curve or pattern representing an equation or function.—*v.t. Math.* To draw or plot, as a curve, from its equation or function; to draw, as a curve, representing an equation or function.

graph·ic, graf′ik, *a.* Accurately or vividly described; lifelike; pertaining to the use of graphs; of or pertaining to writing: *graphic* symbols; of or pertaining to the graphic arts. Also **graph·i·cal.** —**graph·i·cal·ly, graph·ic·ly,** *adv.*

graph·ic arts, *n. pl.* The arts of painting and drawing; the reproduction of those arts, as engraving, lithography, or etching.

graph·ite, graf′īt, *n.* Soft carbon, having an iron-gray color and metallic luster, used in lead pencils, crucibles, and as a lubricant.

graph·ol·o·gy, gra·fol′ə·jē, *n.* The study of handwriting, esp. for analysis of the writer's character. —**graph·ol·o·gist,** *n.*

graph pa·per, *n.* A type of paper with printed ruled lines, forming a grid pattern on which graphs and curves are plotted.

grap·nel, grap′nəl, *n.* An instrument having several hooks or clamps for seizing and holding objects; a small anchor with four or five claws; a grappling iron.

grap·ple, grap′əl, *n.* A grapnel; the act of grappling; a grip or close hold, as in wrestling.—*v.t.,* **-pled, -pling.** To seize, hold, or fasten with or as with a grapple.—*v.i.* To use a grapple; to hold or make fast to something; to seize another, or each other, in a firm grip; to clinch; to contend or struggle, usu. followed by *with.* —**grap·pler,** *n.*

grap·pling i·ron, *n.* Grapnel. Also **grap·pling hook.**

---

grasp, grasp, gräsp, *v.t.* To seize and hold by or as by clasping with the fingers; seize upon; hold firmly; to lay hold of with the mind; comprehend.—*v.i.* To make the motion of seizing; clutch something firmly or eagerly.—*n.* A grasping or gripping; a grip of the hand or of the arms; power of seizing and holding; hold, possession, or mastery; mental hold or ability to understand: a subject beyond one's *grasp.*

grasp·ing, gras/ping, gräs/ping, *a.* That seizes; avaricious or greedy: He is a *grasping* individual.

grass, gras, gräs, *n.* The plants on which grazing animals pasture; any plant of a family characterized by jointed stems, long, narrow leaves, and flower spikelets. *Informal.* Marijuana; lawn. —**grass·y,** *a.,* **-i·er, -i·est.**

grass·hop·per, gras/hop·ər, gräs/hop·ər, *n.* A leaping insect commonly living in grass.

grass·land, gras/land, gräs/land, *n.* Meadow land; permanent pasture.

grass roots, *n. pl., sing. or pl. in constr.* An area comprising the small towns and rural sections of the U.S.; a hypothetical segment of the U.S. population considered representative of qualities of the national character.

grass wid·ow, *n.* A woman who is separated or who lives apart from her husband, by reason of divorce or otherwise. —**grass wid·ow·er,** *n.*

grate, grāt, *n.* A framework of parallel or crossed bars used as a partition, guard, or screen; a frame of metal bars for holding fuel in a fireplace or a furnace; a fireplace.—*v.t.,* **grat·ed, grat·ing.** To fit with a grate.

grate, grāt, *v.t.,* **grat·ed, grat·ing.** To grind into particles; pulverize; to scrape with a harsh, jarring noise; to irritate.—*v.i.* To scrape or rub noisily; to have an irritating effect: The sounds of squeaking chalk *grate* on my nerves.

grate·ful, grāt/fəl, *a.* Appreciative of favors; thankful; pleasing, agreeable or welcome: *grateful* news. —**grate·ful·ly,** *adv.* —**grate·ful·ness,** *n.*

grat·i·fy, grat/i·fī, *v.t.,* **-fied, -fy·ing.** To give pleasure to; to satisfy desires, needs, or appetites; to indulge or humor. —**grat·i·fi·ca·tion,** grat·ə·fə·kā/shən, *n.* —**grat·i·fy·ing,** *a.*

grat·ing, grā/ting, *n.* A grate, or framework of parallel or crossed bars.

grat·ing, grā/ting, *a.* Harsh or jarring, as sound; irritating or unpleasant in effect.

gra·tis, grat/is, grā/tis, *adv.* For nothing; without charge.—*a.* Given or done free of charge.

grat·i·tude, grat/i·tood, grat/i·tūd, *n.* A warm and friendly appreciation of a favor received; thankfulness; gratefulness.

gra·tu·i·tous, grə·too/i·təs, grə·tū/i·təs, *a.* Given without charge; free; not required by the circumstances; unjustified: a *gratuitous* assumption. —**gra·tu·i·tous·ly,** *adv.*

gra·tu·i·ty, grə·too/i·tē, grə·tū/i·tē, *n. pl.,* **-ties.** A free gift; a donation; a tip; anything given without obligation or claim.

grave, grāv, *v.t.,* **graved, grav·en** or **graved, grav·ing.** To carve or cut; to engrave.

grave, grāv, *n.* An excavation in the earth in which a dead body is buried; any place of interment; a tomb.

grave, grāv, *a.,* **grav·er, grav·est.** Solemn; serious; important; momentous; critical or threatening; somber or drab, as color. —**grave·ly,** *adv.* —**grave·ness,** *n.*

grav·el, grav/əl, *n.* Small stones and pebbles loosely mixed; small stones and sand combined.—*v.t.,* **-eled, -el·ing.** To cover with gravel.

grav·el·ly, grav/ə·lē, *a.* Abounding in, consisting of, or resembling gravel; harsh or grating: *gravelly* speech.

grav·en, grā/vən, *a.* Of or denoting that which is deeply impressed or fixed; sculptured or carved: a *graven* image.

grave·stone, grāv/stōn, *n.* A stone placed at a grave as a monument or marker.

grave·yard, grāv/yärd, *n.* A place of burial or interment of the dead; a cemetery.

grav·i·tate, grav/i·tāt, *v.i.,* **-tat·ed, -tat·ing.** To move under the influence of gravitation; to sink downward; to have a tendency toward some attracting influence. —*v.t.* To move by gravitation.

grav·i·ta·tion, grav·i·tā/shən, *n.* The act or process of gravitating. *Phys.* The force by which all masses or bodies are mutually attracted to each other. An attraction toward an object. —**grav·i·ta·tion·al,** *a.*

grav·i·ty, grav/i·tē, *n. pl.,* **-ties.** Solemnity of character or demeanor; seriousness; weightiness; enormity: the *gravity* of an offense. *Phys.* The force which causes bodies to tend toward the center of the earth. Also **grav·i·ta·tion.** —*a.* Of or pertaining to seriousness, solemnity, or weightiness.

gra·vy, grā/vē, *n. pl.,* **-vies.** The juices that drip from meat in cooking; these juices made into a sauce for meat and vegetables.

gray, grey, grā, *a.* Of a color between white and black; dismal or gloomy: a *gray* existence.—*n.* Any neutral color consisting of a black and white mixture. —*v.t.* To make *gray.*—*v.i.* To become *gray.* —**gray·ish, grey·ish,** *a.* —**gray·ly, grey·ly,** *adv.* —**gray·ness, grey·ness,** *n.*

gray·ling, grā/ling, *n.* Any of the freshwater fishes related to the trout, but having a longer and higher pectoral fin.

gray mat·ter, *n.* Nerve tissue, as of the spinal cord and brain. *Informal.* Brains; intelligence.

graze, grāz, *v.i.,* **grazed, graz·ing.** To feed on growing grass, as cattle; to pasture.—*v.t.* To put to feed on pasturage; to put to pasture.

graze, grāz, *v.t.,* **grazed, graz·ing.** To touch against or rub lightly in passing. —*v.i.* To touch or rub something lightly in passing.—*n.* A grazing, touching, or rubbing lightly in passing; a slight abrasion or scratch.

graz·ing, grā/zing, *n.* Pasture land.

grease, grēs, *n.* The melted or rendered fat of animals; fatty or oily matter in general; a thick lubricant.—*v.t.,* **greased, greas·ing.** To smear with grease; to lubricate with grease.

grease paint, *n.* A heavy, oily variety of theatrical make-up used by performers.

greas·y, grē/sē, grē/zē, *a.,* **-i·er, -i·est.** Composed of or containing grease; oily; smeared or soiled with grease; greaselike in appearance; *fig.,* slippery or unsavory. —**greas·i·ly,** *adv.* —**greas·i·ness,** *n.*

great, grāt, *a.* Unusually large in size or number; unusual or considerable in degree; beyond what is ordinary, as in extent, scope, character; of much consequence; important; distinguished, illustrious, or famous; of high rank, official position, or social standing. *Informal.* First-rate, fine, amusing, as: a *great* time.—*n. Usu. pl.* Those who have attained outstanding success, fame, or distinction. —**great·ly,** *adv.* —**great·ness,** *n.*

great-aunt, grāt/ant/, grāt/änt/, *n.* The aunt of either of one's parents. Also **grand·aunt,** grand/ant/, grand/änt/, *n.*

great cir·cle, *n.* A circle on the surface of a sphere, the plane of which passes through the center of the sphere.

great·coat, grāt/kōt, *n. Brit.* An overcoat.

Great Di·vide, *n.* The Rocky Mountains; N. America's continental divide.

great-heart·ed, grāt/här/tid, *a.* Having or showing a brave, noble, or generous heart; magnanimous.

great-un·cle, grāt/eng·kəl, *n.* The uncle of either of one's parents. Also **grand·uncle,** grand/ən·kəl, *n.*

Gre·cian, grē/shən, *a., n.* Greek.

greed, grēd, *n.* Desire for possessing or having more than one needs, esp. money or property; avarice.

greed·y, grē/dē, *a.,* **-i·er, -i·est.** Desirous to have more than needed; avaricious; covetous; having an inordinate desire for food or drink; ravenous; voracious; in general, having eager desire: *greedy* for praise. —**greed·i·ly**, *adv.* —**greed·i·ness**, *n.*

Greek, grēk, *n.* A native or inhabitant of ancient or modern Greece; the language of the people of Greece. *Informal.* Anything unintelligible, as speech or statements: The letter, being in French, was *Greek* to him.—*a.* Of or pertaining to Greece, the Greeks, or their language.

Greek Or·tho·dox, *a.* Of or pertaining to the Orthodox Church of Greece.

green, grēn, *a.* Of the color of growing grass; covered with a growth of grass or foliage; full of life and vigor; not fully developed; unripe or immature; unseasoned, as timber; not dried or cured; not fired, as bricks or pottery; immature in age or judgment; inexperienced. —*n.* A green color.—*n. pl.* Fresh leaves or branches of trees or shrubs, used for decoration; the leaves and stems of plants, as lettuce or spinach, used for food. —**green·ness**, *n.*

green·back, grēn′bak, *n.* Any piece of U.S. paper money, the back of which is printed in green.

green·er·y, grē′nə·rē, *n. pl.*, **-ies**. Green foliage or vegetation.

green·gro·cer, grēn′grō·sər, *n. Brit.* A retailer of vegetables and fruit. —**green·gro·cer·y**, *n. pl.*, **-ies**.

green·horn, grēn′hôrn, *n.* An inexperienced person.

green·house, grēn′hows, *n. pl.*, **-hous·es**. A heated glass building for growing plants.

green·ing, grē′ning, *n.* A variety of apple, the ripe skin of which is green.

green·ish, grē′nish, *a.* Somewhat green; having a green tinge. —**green·ish·ness**, *n.*

green light, *n.* A signal of clearance or freedom to proceed, esp. a traffic signal light. *Informal.* Permission.

green·sward, grēn′swôrd, *n.* Turf green with grass.

green thumb, *n.* Superior ability to cultivate plants, esp. garden flowers.

Green·wich Time, grin′ij, gren′ij, *n.* The mean standard time, determined from the prime meridian time at Greenwich, England, serving as the basis for calculating standard time elsewhere in the world. Also **Green·wich Mean Time**.

greet, grēt, *v.t.* To address with expressions of kind wishes; to meet; to salute; to hail. —**greet·er**, *n.*

greet·ing, grē′ting, *n.* Salutation at meeting; *usu. pl.*, compliment sent by one absent.

gre·gar·i·ous, gri·gār′ē·əs, *a.* Sociable; participating in groups; pertaining to a herd or flock. —**gre·gar·i·ous·ly**, *adv.* —**gre·gar·i·ous·ness**, *n.*

Gre·go·ri·an cal·en·dar, gri·gō′rē·ən, gri·gôr′ē·ən, *n.* The calendar now in general use introduced by Pope Gregory XIII in 1582.

Gre·go·ri·an chant, *n.* A plain song used in Roman Catholic and some other church services.

grem·lin, grem′lin, *n.* A fictitious, ill-tempered elf or sprite, blamed for mechanical difficulties.

gre·nade, gri·nād′, *n.* A small explosive shell thrown by hand or discharged from a rifle.

gren·a·dier, gren·ə·dēr′, *n.* A member of a special regiment, as the *Grenadier* Guards of the British army; originally a soldier trained to use hand grenades.

gren·a·dine, gren·ə·dēn′, gren′ə·dēn, *n.* A thin, open-textured fabric; a sweet red syrup obtained from pomegranates.

grey, grā, *n., a., v.i., v.t.* Gray.

grid, grid, *n.* A grating; a gridiron. *Elect.* A ridged or perforated lead plate used in a storage battery; one of the interior elements of a vacuum tube. *Surv.* Base lines intersecting at right angles.

grid·dle, grid′əl, *n.* A flat, often heavy, rimless frying pan used in cooking hotcakes.

grid·dle·cake, grid′əl·kāk, *n.* A pancake.

grid·i·ron, grid′ī·ərn, *n. Football.* The field of play.

Cookery. A utensil having parallel bars on which food may be broiled; any network or framework resembling this. *Theater.* A structure above the stage of a theater, from which the drop scenes are manipulated.

grief, grēf, *n.* Emotional pain or distress from an extreme cause, as affliction or bereavement; deep sorrow or sadness; the cause of such sadness. —**to come to grief**, to come to a bad end; to fail.

griev·ance, grē′vəns, *n.* A cause of grief, as a wrong or slight, real or imagined.

grieve, grēv, *v.t.*, **grieved**, **griev·ing**. To cause to feel grief; to make sorrowful.—*v.i.* To feel grief; to sorrow; to mourn.

griev·ous, grē′vəs, *a.* Causing grief or sorrow; serious; grave; severe; full of grief; expressing great grief or affliction. —**griev·ous·ly**, *adv.*

grif·fin, **grif·fon**, grif′ən, *n.* A winged creature with the forepart of an eagle and the body of a lion.

grill, gril, *v.t.* To broil on a grate; to mark with a pattern resembling a grill. *Informal.* To interrogate relentlessly.—*n.* A grate for broiling food over heat; a gridiron; grilled food; a restaurant that specializes in grilled food.

grille, **grill**, gril, *n.* A metal lattice or grating; a piece of ornamental ironwork; grillwork.

grim, grim, *a.*, **grim·mer**, **grim·mest**. Of a forbidding or fear-inspiring aspect; fierce; stern; sullen; sour; surly. —**grim·ly**, *adv.* —**grim·ness**, *n.*

grim·ace, gri·mās′, grim′əs, *n.* A facial distortion expressing scorn, pain, disgust, affectation, disapproval, or other emotion; a smirk; a wry face.—*v.i.*, **-aced**, **-ac·ing**. To make grimaces.

grime, grīm, *n.* Dirt; foul matter; soot; dirt deeply ingrained.—*v.t.*, **grimed**, **grim·ing**. To sully or soil deeply; to dirty.

grim·y, grī′mē, *a.*, **-i·er**, **-i·est**. Full of grime; foul; dirty. —**grim·i·ly**, *adv.* —**grim·i·ness**, *n.*

grin, grin, *v.i.*, **grinned**, **grin·ning**. To smile broadly; to draw back the lips so as to show the teeth, as a snarling dog or a person in pain.—*n.* The act of grinning; a broad smile. —**grin·ner**, *n.*

grind, grīnd, *v.t.*, **ground**, **grind·ing**. To reduce to fine particles, as by pounding or crushing; to pulverize; to wear smooth, or sharpen by friction: to *grind* a lens; to rub harshly or gratingly; rub or grate together: *grind* one's teeth; to operate by turning a crank, as a coffee-mill; to oppress or torment; study or learn by close application.—*v.i.* To perform the act or operation of grinding something; to become ground; to rub harshly; grate. *Informal.* To work or study laboriously. —*n.* The act of grinding; a grinding sound; tiresome work. *Informal.* An overly diligent student.

grind·er, grīn′dər, *n.* A person who sharpens tools or finishes rough materials; equipment for grinding; a molar tooth.—*n. pl. Informal.* The teeth.

grind·stone, grīnd′stōn, *n.* A revolving stone used for grinding or sharpening tools. —**keep one's nose to the grind·stone**. *Informal.* To work diligently and without unnecessary interruptions.

grin·go, gring′gō, *n. pl.*, **-gos**. A foreigner in Spain or Spanish America, esp. an Englishman or an American; frequently derogatory.

grip, grip, *n.* The act of grasping; a seizing and holding fast; the strength of one's hand; a special mode of clasping hands, as among members of a secret society; grasp, hold, or control: to lose one's *grip* on a situation; mental or intellectual hold: to have a *grip* of a subject; a handle; a small valise; grippe.—*v.t.*, **gripped**, **grip·ping**. To grasp or seize firmly; hold fast; to take hold on (the mind); hold the interest or attention of; to attach by a grip or clutch.—*v.i.* To take firm hold; hold fast; to take hold on the mind: a story that *grips* the imagination. —**come to grips with**, grapple; firmly deal with; cope.

---

a- hat, fāte, fāre, fäther; **e-** met, mē; **i-** pin, pīne; **o-** not, nōte, ôrb, moove (move), boy, pownd; **u-** cūbe, bûll, tûk (took); **ch-** chin; **th-** thick, ŧhen; **zh-** vizhon (vision); **ə-** əgo, takən, pencəl, lemən, bərd (bird).

gripe, grīp, v.t., **griped, grip·ing.** Informal. To irritate, annoy. To produce pain in the bowels of.—v.i. Informal. Grumble; complain. To suffer pain in the bowels. —n. Informal. A complaint. Usu. pl. An intermittent spasmodic pain in the bowels. —**grip·er,** n.

grippe, grip, n. Influenza.

gris·ly, griz′lē, a., **-li·er, -li·est.** Frightful; horrible; grim. —**gris·li·ness,** n.

grist, grist, n. Grain ground or to be ground in a mill. —**grist for one's mill,** anything that can be turned to one's advantage or profit.

gris·tle, gris′əl, n. Cartilage. —**gris·tly,** gris′lē, a., **-tli·er, -tli·est.**

grit, grit, n. Fine, hard grains of sand; a coarsegrained sandstone; firmness of character.—v.t., **grit·ted, grit·ting.** To grate or grind, as the teeth.

grits, grits, n. pl., sing. or pl. in constr. Coarsely ground grain.

grit·ty, grit′ē, a., **-ti·er, -ti·est.** Consisting of, containing, or resembling grit; sandy. Informal. Courageous. —**grit·ti·ly,** adv. —**grit·ti·ness,** n.

griz·zled, griz′əld, a. Gray.

griz·zly, griz′lē, a., **-zli·er, -zli·est.** Grizzled; gray.—n. pl., **-zlies.** A grizzly bear.

groan, grōn, v.i. To utter a deep inarticulate sound expressive of grief, pain, or disapproval; moan; overburdened.—v.t. To utter or express with groans.—n. A groaning utterance or sound. —**groan·er,** n.

gro·cer, grō′sər, n. A retail merchant selling food and household items.

gro·cer·y, grō′sə·rē, n. pl., **-ies.** A retail store dealing in food and household items; pl., the goods sold by such stores.

grog, grog, n. An alcoholic beverage, usu. rum diluted with water.

grog·gy, grog′ē, a., **-gi·er, -gi·est.** In a state of exhaustion from lack of sleep; dizzy. —**grog·gi·ly,** adv. —**grog·gi·ness,** n.

groin, groyn, n. The fold or hollow on either side of the body where the thigh joins the abdomen; the curved, projecting edge formed by the intersection of two vaults.—v.t. To form or build with groins.

grom·met, grom′it, n. Mech. An eyelet. Naut. A ring of rope, with or without a metal eye, used for securing sails, oars, or the like.

groom, groom, n. A bridegroom; a man or boy who has charge of horses or the stable.—v.t. To make clean and neat; to curry or care for, as a horse; to train, condition, or otherwise prepare for a specific purpose, as for a job, position, or office.

groove, groov, n. A furrow or long hollow, such as is cut by a tool; a narrow channel; the fixed routine of one's life.—v.t., **grooved, groov·ing.** To cut a groove or channel in; to furrow. —**groov·er,** n.

groov·y, groo′vē, a., **-i·er, -i·est.** Informal. Exciting; pleasing; charming.

grope, grōp, v.i., **groped, grop·ing.** To feel one's way; to search perplexedly.—v.t. To search out by feeling one's way: They grope their way toward the exit.

gros·grain, grō′grān, n. A closely woven silk or rayon fabric with heavy transverse threads but little luster, often used for ribbons.

gross, grōs, a. Of or constituting a total without or prior to deductions: gross income; glaring or flagrant: gross mistake; coarse or unrefined; great or enormous; obese; dense; visible to the naked eye.—v.t. To earn without or prior to deductions.—n. A totality prior to deductions.—n. pl., **gross, gross·es.** Twelve dozen; 144 units. —**gross·ly,** adv. —**gross·ness,** n.

gro·tesque, grō·tesk′, a. Ridiculous or unnatural in design, appearance, or nature; bizarre. —**gro·tesque·ly,** adv.

grot·to, grot′ō, n. pl., **-toes, -tos.** A cave, natural recess, or cavity in the earth; an artificially constructed cavern.

grouch, growch, v.i. Informal. To be sulky or morose; show discontent.—n. Informal. A sulky or morose

mood; a morose, irritable person. —**grouch·y,** a., **-i·er, -i·est.** —**grouch·i·ness,** n.

ground, grownd, n. The surface of the earth; the soil. Sometimes pl. Land designated for a particular use: hunting ground; that on which anything may rest, rise, or originate; basis; foundation; support, as for a belief or argument; a cause or motivation for action. Elect. The connection of an electrical conductor to the earth; background. Pl. The land around a building, constituting part of the total property; sediment at the bottom of a liquid; dregs.—v.t. To cause, as an airplane or pilot, to be restricted to the ground. Elect. To connect, as an electrical conductor, to a ground.—v.i. Baseball. To hit a ball on the ground. —**break ground,** to penetrate the soil for the first time; to take the first step in any undertaking. —**gain ground,** to advance; to become more generally accepted or known. —**give ground,** to yield advantage. —**lose ground,** to lose advantage; to decline in popularity or effect. —**stand one's ground,** to stand firm; to refuse to yield.

ground, grownd, v. Past tense and past participle of **grind.**

ground crew, n. Ground technicians responsible for the mechanical maintenance and servicing of aircraft.

ground·er, grown′dər, n. Baseball, soccer, cricket. A ball batted, kicked, or thrown along the ground.

ground floor, n. The floor of a house on a level, or nearly so, with the exterior ground. —**in on the ground floor,** availing oneself of an exceptional opportunity as an early investor.

ground hog, n. A woodchuck.

ground·less, grownd′lis, a. Without sound cause; irrational; baseless; false. —**ground·less·ly,** adv. —**ground·less·ness,** n.

ground·ling, grownd′ling, n. A plant or animal that grows or remains close to the ground; a fish that swims close to the bottom; a person with poor taste, esp. in cultural areas.

ground·nut, grownd′nət, n. The peanut, earth nut, or goober; any of the edible fruits formed underground by such plants.

ground squir·rel, n. Any of several animals allied to the true squirrels, as the chipmunks and gophers, usu. having cheek pouches and living in holes.

ground swell, n. A deep swell or rolling of the sea, occasioned along the shore by a distant storm or gale.

ground wa·ter, n. The source of fresh water beneath the earth's surface, as that supplying wells and springs, made available by the seepage of surface water.

ground·work, grownd′wərk, n. The work which forms the foundation of anything; a basis.

group, groop, n. Any assemblage of persons or things; a number of persons or things ranged or considered together as being related in a scientific, natural, or other way. U.S. Air Force. A unit immediately subordinate to a wing. U.S. Army. A unit comprising two or more battalions.—v.t. To arrange in or form into a group or groups; classify.—v.i. To form a group; be part of a group.

group·ie, groo′pē, n. Informal. A girl who idolizes and slavishly follows after, popular performing groups or stars.

grouse, grows, v.i., **groused, grous·ing.** To grumble; complain.—n. Complaint. —**grous·er,** n.

grove, grōv, n. A cluster of trees, esp. of growing fruit or nut trees.

grov·el, grəv′əl, grov′əl, v.i., **-eled, -el·ing.** To lie or move with the face downward as in abject humility or fear; to humble oneself. —**grov·el·er,** n.

grow, grō, v.i., **grew, grown, grow·ing.** To undergo the process of development, esp. toward maturity; to survive, maintain life, or exist: The plant can grow under severe conditions; be produced by natural processes, as leaves or fruit; arise: Love grows out of friendship; increase or become greater; become gradually attached or united: grow fast to a thing; come to be: *grow* old or rich.—*v.t.* To cause to grow. —**grow up**, spring up; arise; increase in growth; advance toward maturity; increase maturity. —**grow·er**, *n.*

growl, growl, *v.i.* To utter a deep guttural sound of anger or hostility, as a dog or a bear does; to rumble; to murmur or complain angrily; grumble.—*v.t.* To express by growling or grumbling.—*n.* The act or sound of growling; a rumbling; a grumbling or complaining. —**growl·er**, *n.*

grown, grōn, *a.* Advanced in growth; arrived at full growth or maturity: a *grown* man; adult.

grown-up, grōn′əp, *n.* A fully grown person; an adult.

grown-up, grōn′əp, *a.* Suitable or appropriate to an adult; having reached physical or mental maturity.

growth, grōth, *n.* The act, process, or manner of growing; something that has grown: a *growth* of weeds, the *growth* of a legend; an abnormal tissue development, as a tumor.

grub, grəb, *v.t.*, **grubbed**, **grub·bing.** To dig up; uproot.—*v.i.* To dig; to lead a laborious or groveling life; drudge.—*n.* The larva of an insect, esp. of a beetle; a dull, plodding person; a drudge. *Informal.* Food. —**grub·ber**, *n.*

grub·by, grəb′ē, *a.*, **-bi·er**, **-bi·est.** Dirty; slovenly; infested with or affected by grubs or larvae.

grub·stake, grəb′stāk, *n. Informal.* Food, equipment, or money given to a prospector in return for a share of what he may find.—*v.t.*, **-staked**, **-stak·ing.** *Informal.* To provide with a grubstake.

grudge, grəj, *v.t.*, **grudged**, **grudg·ing.** To permit or grant with reluctance; to begrudge.—*v.i.* To be envious; to feel ill will.—*n.* Reluctance felt in giving; ill will from envy or sense of injury. —**grudg·ing·ly**, *adv.*

gru·el, groo′əl, *n.* A light, usu. thin, liquid food or cereal made by boiling meal, esp. oatmeal, in water or milk; any similar substance.

gru·el·ing, groo′ə·ling, groo′ling, *a.* Causing strain; severely testing one's strength or endurance.

grue·some, groo′səm, *a.* Horrible or frightening. —**grue·some·ly**, *adv.*

gruff, grəf, *a.* Surly or stern in manner; harsh or blunt in speech. —**gruff·ly**, *adv.* —**gruff·ness**, *n.*

grum·ble, grəm′bəl, *v.i.*, **-bled**, **-bling.** To express discontent or complaint; to utter in a low voice; to rumble.—*v.t.* To express or utter by grumbling or in complaint.—*n.* A complaint; a discontented murmur; an utterance of complaint. —**grum·bler**, *n.*

grump·y, grəm′pē, *a.*, **-i·er**, **-i·est.** Surly; irritable; gruff. —**grump·i·ly**, *adv.* —**grump·i·ness**, *n.*

grunt, grənt, *v.i.* To utter the deep guttural sound of a hog; to utter a similar sound; to grumble, as in discontent.—*v.t.* To express with a grunt.—*n.* A deep guttural sound, as that uttered by a hog; any similar utterance.

G-string, jē′string, *n.* A narrow loincloth, esp. one worn as part of a stripteaser's or female entertainer's costume.

gua·no, gwä′nō, *n. pl.*, **-nos.** A natural manure composed chiefly of the excrement of sea birds; any similar substance.

guar·an·tee, gar·ən·tē′, *n.* A pledge that stated specifications or obligations will be met, often given for genuineness, quality, or durability; that which is given as security; a guaranty; a guarantor; that person to whom a guaranty is given; something serving as security or collateral to indicate or assure a specified outcome.—*v.t.*, **-teed**, **-tee·ing.** To be or become a guaranty for; to undertake to secure to another, as rights or possessions; engage to uphold or maintain; engage to protect; engage, as to do something; to serve as a warrant or guaranty for.

guar·an·tor, gar′ən·tôr, gar′ən·tər, *n.* One who or that which pledges or guarantees; one who gives or makes a guaranty.

guar·an·ty, gar′ən·tē, *n. pl.*, **-ties.** The act of warranting or providing security; a warranty, pledge, or promise given by way of security; a formal or written assurance by which one person or party undertakes to be responsible for the carrying out of an obligation, or the condition or treatment of merchandise; something that serves as a warrant or security; one who warrants, or gives a formal assurance of being responsible for something.—*v.t.*, **-tied**, **-ty·ing.** To guarantee.

guard, gärd, *v.t.* To keep safe from harm; protect or defend; to watch over; to prevent escape. *Sports.* To hinder the actions of, as an opponent; to protect, as a goal.—*v.i.* To give protection; to keep watch; to take precautions, used with *against:* to *guard against* errors.—*n.* Protection or defense; a posture of defense, as in fencing or boxing; a sentry; a member of a guarding force. *Football.* A player situated on the line of scrimmage, who runs interference for the ball carrier and protects the passer from the onrushing defensive linemen. *Basketball.* On offense, the player who brings the ball upcourt and designates the plays. —**off one's guard**, unprepared; unwary. —**on one's guard**, in a position of readiness; watchful or vigilant; cautious; wary. Also **on guard.**

guard·ed, gär′did, *a.* Cautious: *guarded* behavior. —**guard·ed·ly**, *adv.*

guard·house, gärd′hows, *n.* A house for the accommodation of guards; a building where military prisoners are confined.

guard·i·an, gär′dē·ən, *n.* One who has charge or custody of any person or thing. *Law.* One who is invested by law with care of the person and/or the estate of a minor or a person judged unable to administer his own affairs.—*a.* Protecting.

guards·man, gärdz′mən, *n. pl.*, **-men.** A man who acts as a guard; a member of the National Guard.

gua·va, gwä′və, *n.* Any of various trees or shrubs of tropical or subtropical America, with a fruit used for making jelly or preserves; the fruit.

gu·ber·na·to·ri·al, goo·bər·nə·tôr′ē·əl, gū·bər·nə·tôr′ē·əl, *a.* Pertaining to a governor.

gudg·eon, gəj′ən, *n.* A small European fresh-water fish of the carp family, easily caught, and much used for bait.

guer·ril·la, gue·ril′la, *n.* One of a band of independent soldiers who prey on the enemy by harassment, surprise attack, and short, sharp engagements, often behind the lines.—*a.* Pertaining to guerrillas or their tactics.

guess, ges, *v.t.* To deduce, infer, or surmise (factual information) with little or no real evidence or by chance; to deduce correctly: to *guess* an answer. *Informal.* To think or believe.—*v.i.* To conjecture.—*n.* A conjecture; an estimate; an opinion reached by guessing. —**guess·er**, *n.*

guess·work, ges′wərk, *n.* Mere conjecture; an assumption.

guest, gest, *n.* One who is afforded hospitality or entertainment in another's home or business establishment as a friend, visitor, patron, client, or customer either gratuitously or with payment for accommodations.

guf·faw, gə·fô′, *n.* A loud or sudden burst of laughter.—*v.i.* To burst into a loud or sudden laugh.

guid·ance, gīd′əns, *n.* The act or service of counseling or supervising; a mechanism, system, or built-in device which guides the operation of a machine.

guide, gīd, *v.t.*, **guid·ed**, **guid·ing.** To lead or direct. —*v.i.* To function as a guide.—*n.* A person or thing that guides; guidebook.

guide·book, gīd′būk, *n.* A book for giving travelers or tourists information about the places they intend to visit.

guid·ed mis·sile, *n.* A rocket or other missile whose

course is determined by self-contained instruments or radio signals.

guide·post, gīd'pōst, *n.* A post to which a signboard is attached for directing travelers.

gui·don, gī'dən, *n.* A small flag or streamer carried as a guide by troops.

guild, gild, *n.* In medieval times, an organization of merchants or artisans; an association of men having similar interests or engaged in the same business, often formed for mutual aid.

guild·hall, gild'hôl, *n.* A town hall; a hall for meetings of a guild or corporation.

guile, gīl, *n.* Craft; cunning; artifice; duplicity; deceit. —**guile·ful,** *a.* —**guile·ful·ly,** *adv.* —**guile·less,** *a.* —**guile·less·ly,** *adv.*

guil·lo·tine, gil'ə·tēn, gē'ə·tēn, *n.* An instrument for beheading persons by means of a weighted blade which, when released, slides down between two upright posts.—gil·ə·tēn', *v.t.* **-tined, -tin·ing.**

guilt, gilt, *n.* The fact of having performed a wrong act; wrong conduct or behavior; a feeling of remorse due to personal responsibility, real or imagined, for an offense. —**guilt·less,** *a.* —**guilt·less·ly,** *adv.*

guilt·y, gil'tē, *a.* **-i·er, -i·est.** Having committed a crime or a moral wrong; judged responsible for an offense; often followed by *of: guilty of* a misdemeanor; indicating guilt: a *guilty* look. —**guilt·i·ly,** *adv.* —**guilt·i·ness,** *n.*

guin·ea hen, gin'ē, *n.* The female of the guinea fowl.

guin·ea pig, gin'ē, *n.* A short-eared, short-tailed rodent, usu. white, black, and tawny, much used in biological experiments; any subject of experimentation.

guise, gīz, *n.* Outward appearance; dress; garb; assumed or deceptive appearance; pretense.

gui·tar, gi·tär', *n.* A musical instrument with a long, fretted neck and a violinlike body, played by plucking the strings, usu. six in number, with the fingers or a pick. —**gui·tar·ist,** *n.*

gulch, gəlch, *n.* A deep ravine caused by the action of water; the dry bed of a stream; a gully.

gulf, gəlf, *n.* A portion of an ocean or sea extending into the land; a deep hollow; a chasm or abyss; any wide separation, as in social, educational, or economic level; something that engulfs or swallows up.

gull, gəl, *v.t.* To make a fool of; to mislead by deception; to trick.—*n.* One who is easily cheated.

gull, gəl, *n.* Any of more than 40 species of swimming birds having large wings, slender legs, and webbed feet.

gul·let, gəl'it, *n.* The passage by which food and liquid are taken into the stomach; the esophagus; the throat or something resembling it; a gully or narrow valley.

gul·li·ble, gəl'ə·bəl, *a.* Easily gulled or cheated; credulous. —**gul·li·bil·i·ty,** gəl·ə·bil'ə·tē, *n.* —**gul·li·bly,** *adv.*

gul·ly, gəl'ē, *n. pl.,* **-lies.** A channel or valley worn in the earth by a current of water; a ravine; a ditch; a gutter.—*v.t.,* **-lied, -ly·ing.** To cut or wear into a gully.

gulp, gəlp, *v.t.* To swallow eagerly; to hold back or suppress as if by swallowing.—*v.i.* To gasp, as when swallowing; to gasp, as in suppressing a sob.—*n.* The act of taking a large swallow; the amount taken.

gum, gəm, *n. Often pl.* The fleshy tissue around the teeth.

gum, gəm, *n.* A water-soluble, sticky substance which exudes from certain plants and trees and thickens or hardens when exposed to air; a gum tree; mucilage; glue; the adhesive on a postage stamp; chewing gum.—*v.t.,* **gummed, gum·ming.** To smear or stiffen with gum; to stick together with gum.—*v.i.* To become sticky. —**gum up.** *Informal.* To spoil, bungle, or ruin.

gum ar·a·bic, är'ə·bik, *n.* The gum of various species of acacia, used in medicine, inks, adhesives, and in certain foods as a thickener.

gum·bo, gəm'bō, *n. pl.,* **-bos.** The okra plant, or its edible pods; a soup, thickened with these pods, and often made with other vegetables, meat, chicken, or seafood; a kind of silty, fine soil found in southern and western U.S. which becomes very sticky when wet.

gum·drop, gəm'drop, *n.* A candy of gum arabic, gelatin, or the like, with sugar and flavoring.

gum·my, gəm'ē, *a.,* **-mi·er, -mi·est.** Exuding gum or covered with gum; sticky. —**gum·mi·ness,** *n.*

gump·tion, gəmp'shən, *n. Informal.* Courage; pluckiness; personal initiative; shrewd, practical sense.

gum res·in, *n.* Any of various natural mixtures of gum and resin, obtained from certain plants.

gum·shoe, gəm'shoo, *n.* A shoe made of rubber; a rubber overshoe. *Informal.* A detective.—*v.i.,* **-shoed, shoe·ing.** *Informal.* To walk softly or stealthily.

gum tree, *n.* Any tree that exudes gum, as the eucalyptus, the sour gum, or the sweet gum.

gun, gən, *n.* A weapon, esp. a long cannon or an automatic weapon; any portable firearm, as a rifle; any similar device for projecting something: a cement *gun;* the discharge of a gun, as in a salute or signal. —*v.i.,* **gunned, gun·ning.** To shoot with a gun; hunt with a gun.—*v.t.* To wound or kill with a gun, often followed by *down.*

gun·boat, gən'bōt, *n.* A small, armed vessel of light draft, used for visiting minor ports and patrolling rivers.

gun·fight, gən'fit, *n.* A fight utilizing guns. —**gun· fight·er,** *n.*

gun·fire, gən'fīr, *n.* The firing of a gun or guns.

gun·man, gən'mən, *n. pl.,* **-men.** A man who uses a gun unlawfully.

gun met·al, *n.* Any of various alloys or metallic substances with a dark-gray or blackish color; the color. —**gun-met·al,** gən'met·əl, *a.*

gun·ner, gən'ər, *n.* One who works a gun or cannon; *U.S. Navy, Marine Corps,* a warrant officer connected with or in charge of ordnance; a person who uses a gun for hunting.

gun·ner·y, gən'ə·rē, *n.* The art of firing or managing guns; the science of artillery; collectively, guns.

gun·ny, gən'ē, *n. pl.,* **-nies.** A strong, coarse cloth manufactured of jute and used for making bags and sacks; burlap.

gunny·bag, *n.* A sack, etc, made of gunny. Also **gun·ny sack.**

gun·pow·der, gən'pow·dər, *n.* An explosive mixture of potassium nitrate, sulfur, and charcoal, for use in fireworks, blasting, and sometimes in certain guns.

gun·shot, gən'shot, *n.* The projectile fired from a gun; the shooting of a firearm; the distance to which shot can be thrown so as to be effective.—*a.* Made by the shot of a gun: *gunshot* wounds.

gun·smith, gən'smith, *n.* One whose occupation is the making or repairing of small firearms.

gun·stock, gən'stok, *n.* The wooden support or handle in which the barrel of a gun is fixed.

gun·wale, gun·nel, gən'əl, *n.* The upper edge of a ship's or boat's side.

gup·py, gəp'ē, *n. pl.,* **-pies.** A small, colorful tropical fish, often prized and kept as an aquarium fish.

gur·gle, gər'gəl, *v.i.,* **-gled, -gling.** To run or flow in an irregular, noisy current, as water from a bottle; to flow with a murmuring sound.—*v.t.* To utter in a gurgling manner.—*n.* The sound made by a liquid flowing through a narrow opening.

gu·ru, gû·roo', goo'roo, *n.* In India, esp. among the Hindus, a religious teacher or spiritual guide. *Informal.* Any leader or teacher.

gush, gəsh, *v.i.* To rush forth; flow suddenly or copiously; be extravagantly and effusively sentimental. —*v.t.* To emit suddenly, copiously, or with violence. —*n.* A sudden and violent issue of a fluid; an emission of liquid in a large quantity and with force; an outpour; an effusive display of sentiment. —**gush·ing,** *a.*

gush·er, gəsh'ər, *n.* An oil well that yields oil without being pumped.

gush·y, gəsh'ē, *a.,* **-i·er, -i·est.** Characterized by very effusive talk or behavior; extremely sentimental; excessively enthusiastic. **—gush·i·ness,** *n.*

gus·set, gəs′it, *n.* A usu. triangular piece of cloth inserted in a garment to strengthen or enlarge some part.

gust, gəst, *n.* A violent blast of wind; a sudden rushing of fire, water, sound, or the like; a burst of passion. *—v.i.* To blow in gusts.

gus·ta·to·ry, gəs′tə·tôr·ē, *a.* Of or pertaining to tasting or the sense of taste.

gus·to, gəs′tō, *n.* Keen relish or zest.

gust·y, gəs′tē, *a.,* **-i·er, -i·est.** Characterized by gusts; windy; stormy; subject to outbursts of feeling; tempestuous; blustery. **—gust·i·ly,** *adv.* **—gust·i·ness,** *n.*

gut, gət, *n.* The intestinal canal from the stomach to the anus; an intestine; animal intestine used for making the strings of musical instruments, tennis rackets, and the like; the entrails or bowels. *Pl. Informal.* Pluck or courage; grit.*—v.t.,* **gut·ted, gut·ting.** To remove or take out, as the entrails of; to destroy the inside of.

gut·ter, gət′ər, *n.* A channel at the side or in the middle of a road or street for carrying off water; a channel at the eaves or on the roof of a building for drainage of rain water; any channel, trough, groove, or the like.*—v.t.* To form or cut in, as a channel or groove; to furnish with a gutter.*—v.i.* To form gutters, as water does; to flow in streams; to become channeled and lose molten wax, as a burning candle does.

gut·tur·al, gət′ər·əl, *a.* Of or pertaining to the throat; harsh, rasping, or throaty, as certain vocal sounds.*—n.* A guttural sound, **—gut·tur·al·ly,** *adv.*

guy, gī, *n.* A rope or appliance used to guide, steady, or secure something.*—v.t.* To guide, steady, or secure with a guy.

guy, gī, *n. Informal.* A boy or man; a fellow.*—v.t. Informal.* To jeer at or make fun of; ridicule.

guz·zle, gəz′əl, *v.i., v.t.,* **-zled, -zling.** To drink greedily or excessively. **—guz·zler,** *n.*

gym, jim, *n. Informal.* Gymnasium.

gym·na·si·um, jim·nā′zē·əm, *n. pl.,* **-si·ums, -si·a.** A place or building for athletic exercises or contests; a school for gymnastics.

gym·nast, jim′nast, *n.* One who practices or teaches gymnastic exercises.

gym·nas·tic, jim·nas′tik, *a.* Pertaining to athletic exercises.

gym·nas·tics, jim·nas′tiks, *n. pl.* Athletic exercises, esp. those performed on gymnasium apparatus. *Sing. in constr.* The art of performing certain athletic exercises.

gy·ne·col·o·gy, gy·nae·col·o·gy, gī·nə·kol′ə·jē, jīn·ə·kol′ə·jē, *n.* That aspect of medical science which deals with the functions and diseases peculiar to women, esp. of the organs of reproduction. **—gy·ne·co·log·ic,** gī·nə·kə·loj′ik, jīn·ə·kə·loj′ik, **gy·ne·co·log·i·cal,** *a.* **—gy·ne·col·o·gist, gy·nae·col·o·gist,** *n.*

gyp, jip, *n. Informal.* A swindle; a cheat; a swindler. *—v.t.,* **gypped, gyp·ping.** To swindle or cheat.

gyp·sum, jip′səm, *n.* A mineral used to make plaster of Paris, ornamental material, and fertilizer.

gyp·sy, jip′sē, *n. pl.,* **-sies.** A person who leads a vagrant life; a wanderer. *(Cap.)* One of a nomadic, tawny-skinned, black-haired race of Hindu origin, now found in many parts of the world; the language of these people; Romany.

gy·rate, jī′rāt, jī·rāt′, *v.i.,* **-rat·ed, -rat·ing.** To move in a circle or spiral; revolve round a fixed point or on an axis; rotate; whirl. **—gy·ra·tion,** jī·rā′shən, *n.* **—gy·ra·tor,** *n.*

gy·ro·scope, jī′rə·skōp, *n.* An apparatus consisting of a heavy, swiftly rotating wheel, so mounted that its axis can turn freely in certain or all directions, and which is capable of maintaining the same absolute direction in space in spite of movements of the mountings or surrounding parts, used to maintain equilibrium and determine direction. **—gy·ro·scop·ic,** jī·rə·skop′ik, *a.* **—gy·ro·scop·i·cal·ly,** *adv.*

gyve, jīv, *n. Usu. pl.* A shackle, esp. for the legs; a fetter.*—v.t.,* **gyved, gyv·ing.** To shackle; to chain.

H

H, h, āch, *n. pl.,* **H's, h's.** The eighth letter of the English alphabet.

ha, hä, *interj.* An exclamation denoting surprise, wonder, joy, or other sudden emotion. Also **hah.**

ha·be·as cor·pus, hā′bē·əs kôr′pəs, *n. Law.* A writ, the function of which is to release a person from unlawful detention, by bringing him before a court or judge to decide the legality of his detention.

hab·er·dash·er, hab′ər·dash·ər, *n.* The proprietor of a store which deals in men's furnishings. **—hab·er·dash·er·y,** *n. pl.,* **-ies.**

ha·bil·i·ment, hə·bil′ə·mənt, *n. Usu. pl.* Clothing.

hab·it, hab′it, *n.* A tendency to act constantly in a certain manner; a customary condition, constitution, or characteristic trait. *Biol.* A characteristic form of an animal or plant. A costume indicating rank, membership in a religious order, or a special activity: a riding *habit* or a nun's *habit.*

hab·it·a·ble, hab′i·tə·bəl, *a.* Capable of being inhabited; suitable for a habitation.

hab·i·tat, hab′i·tat, *n.* The natural abode or locality of a plant or animal; a place where someone or something is usu. found.

hab·i·ta·tion, hab·i·tā′shən, *n.* A residence or dwelling; a house or other place in which man or any animal dwells; act of inhabiting.

ha·bit·u·al, hə·bich′û·əl, *a.* Formed or acquired by habit, frequent use, or custom; constantly practiced; customary; regular; as a matter of course. **—ha·bit·u·al·ly,** *adv.* **—ha·bit·u·al·ness,** *n.*

ha·bit·u·ate, hə·bich′û·āt, *v.t.,* **-at·ed, -at·ing.** To accustom; to make familiar by frequent use or practice; to familiarize. **—ha·bit·u·a·tion,** hə·bich·û·ā′shən, *n.*

ha·bit·u·é, hə·bich·û·ā′, hə·bich′û·ā, *n. pl.,* **-és.** A frequenter of any place or type of place.

ha·ci·en·da, hä·sē·en′də, *n. pl.,* **-das.** In Spanish-speaking countries, a landed estate, large farm, stock-raising ranch, or country house; a ranch building.

hack, hak, *v.t.* To make irregular cuts in or upon.*—v.i.* To make rough cuts or notches; to emit short, frequently repeated coughs.*—n.* A short, broken cough.

hack, hak, *n.* A horse for hire; sometimes, an old or worn-out horse; a coach or carriage kept for hire; a hackney. *Informal.* A taxicab. A person who hires himself out for general work, esp. general literary work.—*a.* Of a hired sort; much in use; hackneyed or trite.

hack·le, hak′əl, *n.* A comb for dressing flax or hemp; one of the long, slender feathers on the neck of certain birds; the neck plumage of the domestic cock; a kind of artificial fly for anglers; *usu. pl.,* the hairs or ruff on the back of a dog's neck.—*v.t.,* **-led, -ling.** To comb with a hackle; to cut roughly; to mangle.

hack·ney, hak′nē, *n.* A trotting horse used for riding or to pull a light vehicle; a hired carriage.—*v.t.* To overuse, wear out, or make trite.

hack·neyed, hak′nēd, *a.* Discussed endlessly; overworked, trite, or commonplace.

hack·saw, hak′sô, *n.* A hand saw used for cutting metal, consisting of a narrow, finetoothed blade anchored in a metal frame.

had, had, *v.* Past tense and past participle of **have.**

Ha·des, hā′dēz, *n. Class. mythol.* The subterranean world of departed spirits; the lord of the lower world, Pluto; the abode of the dead; (*l.c.*) hell.

had·n't, had′ənt.Contraction of **had not.**

hae·mo·glo·bin, hē′mə·glō·bən, hem′ə·glō·bən, *n.* Hemoglobin.

hae·mo·phil·i·a, hē·mə·fil′ē·ə, hem·ə·fil′ē·ə, *n.* Hemophilia.

haft, haft, häft, *n.* A handle of an implement or weapon.

hag, hag, *n.* An ugly old woman; a witch; a sorceress.

hag·gard, hag′ərd, *a.* Appearing wasted by want or suffering; having a worn and pale appearance; gaunt; tired. —**hag·gard·ly,** *adv.*

hag·gle, hag′əl, *v.i.,* **-gled, -gling.** To bargain with; to dispute over small points.—*n.* The act or process of haggling. —**hag·gler,** *n.*

hag·i·ol·o·gy, hag·ē·ol′ə·jē, hä·jē·ol′ə·jē, *n. pl.,* **-gies.** Literature dealing with the lives and legends of saints; a list of saints. —**hag·i·ol·o·gist,** *n.*

hag·rid·den, hag′rid·ən, *a.* Tormented; sorely troubled.

hah, hä, *interj.* Ha.

hai·ku, hi′koo, *n. pl.,* **-ku.** A Japanese form of verse having three lines and 17 syllables; a poem in this form.

hail, hāl, *v.t.* To salute or greet; to welcome; to call out to, esp. in order to attract attention.—*n.* A salutation or greeting; the act of hailing; a shout or call to attract attention.—*interj.* A salutation; hello: an exclamation of greeting. —**hail from,** to come from. —**with·in hail·ing dis·tance,** within sound of a loud shout.

hail, hāl, *n.* Small pellets of ice which fall during showers or storms; any showering suggestive of falling hail—*v.i.* To pour down hail; to fall in the manner of hail.—*v.t.* To shower or cast down like hail.

hail·stone, hāl′stōn, *n.* A single pellet of hail.

hail·storm, hāl′stôrm, *n.* A storm having hail.

hair, hār, *n.* One of the fine filaments which grow from the skin of animals and man; the mass of such fibers forming an extra thick covering on parts of the human body, as on the head; such fibers forming the outer protective coat of animals. *Bot.* Such filaments on the epidermis of plants. A slight measure; a fraction: missed by a *hair*.—*a.* Of or with hair; for hair: as, a *hair* spray. —**get in one's hair,** annoy or irritate someone. —**let one's hair down,** to relax. —**with·out turn·ing a hair,** remaining unperturbed.

hair·breadth, hār′bredth, hār′bretth, *n.* A minute distance.—*a.* Very narrow: a *hairbreadth* escape. Also **hair's·breadth, hairs·breadth.**

hair·brush, hār′brəsh, *n.* A brush for dressing and grooming hair.

hair·cut, hār′kət, *n.* The act of trimming or cutting and shaping the hair; the style of the cut.

hair·do, hār′doo, *n. pl.,* **-dos.** Coiffure; any arranged style for a woman's hair; hair so dressed.

hair·dress·er, hār′dres·ər, *n.* One who cuts and styles hair, esp. women's hair.

hair·line, hār′līn, *n.* The beginning of the scalp or the

hair above the brow on a human head; a very slender line, as a stroke in writing or printing.

hair·pin, hār′pin, *n.* A doubled pin of metal or plastic used by women to hold hair in place.—*a.* Sharply curved or U-shaped, as a turn in a road.

hair·rais·ing, hār′rā·zing, *a.* Frightening; terrifying.

hair·split·ter, hār′split·ər, *n.* One who makes excessively fine distinctions. —**hair·split·ting,** *n., a.*

hair·spring, hār′spring, *n.* The fine, often spiral, spring which regulates the action of the balance wheel of a watch or clock.

hair trig·ger, *n.* A trigger of a firearm, so delicately adjusted that the slightest pressure will discharge the weapon. —**hair-trig·ger,** hār′trig·ər, *a.* Responsive to the slightest stimulus; easily activated.

hair·y, hār′ē, *a.,* **-i·er, -i·est.** Covered with hair; having abundant hair; of or similar to hair. —**hair·i·ness,** *n.*

hal·cy·on, hal′sē·ən, *a.* Calm, quiet, and peaceful.

hale, hāl, *v.t.,* **haled, hal·ing.** To compel to comply: *hale* before the magistrate.

hale, hāl, *a.,* **hal·er, hal·est.** Free from disease or bodily infirmity; robust; vigorous.

half, haf, häf, *n. pl.,* **halves,** havz, hävz. One of two equal, or approximately equal parts; one of two equal periods of play in certain games.—*a.* Being one of the two equal or approximately equal parts; being equal to only about half of full measure: *half* speed; partial, incomplete.—*adv.* To the extent or measure of half: a bucket *half*-full of water; in part, partly; to some extent; to a great extent, preceded by *not*: as, *not half* bad.

half-and-half, haf′ənd·haf′, häf′ənd·häf′, *a.* Half one thing and half another; half the thing specified and half not.—*n.* Cream and milk mixed in equal parts; a mixture of two things in equal parts.

half·back, haf′bak, häf′bak, *n. Football.* One of two ball carriers in the offensive backfield, positioned behind the line and usu. on either side of the fullback.

half·baked, haf′bākt′, häf′bākt′, *a.* Insufficiently cooked; incompletely planned; lacking mature judgment. *Informal.* Half-witted.

half·breed, haf′brēd, häf′brēd, *n.* One born of parents of different races, specif. applied to the offspring of an American Indian and a white person.

half broth·er, *n.* A male offspring having one parent in common with another offspring.

half·caste, haf′kast, häf′käst, *n.* A person of mixed parentage, esp. one of mixed European and Hindu parentage.

half cock, *n.* The position of the hammer of a firearm when raised halfway and held by the mechanism so that the trigger will not operate. —**half-cocked,** haf′kokt′, häf′kokt′, *a.* —**go off half-cocked.** *Informal.* To act prematurely; take action without due preparation or forethought.

half dol·lar, *n.* A partly silver U.S. coin worth fifty cents.

half-heart·ed, haf′här′tid, häf′här′tid, *a.* Lacking eagerness or enthusiasm; indifferent. —**half-heart·ed·ly,** *adv.*

half-hour, haf′ow′ər, häf′ow′ər, *n.* The half of an hour; an interval of thirty minutes.

half·life, haf′līf, häf′līf, *n. pl.,* **-lives.** The length of time in which one half of the radioactive atoms present in a substance will decay.

half-mast, haf′mast′, häf′mäst′, *n.* A position halfway or less below the top of a mast, staff, or pole.

half-moon, haf′moon′, häf′moon′, *n.* The moon at the quarters, when half its disk appears illuminated; a crescent-shaped object.

half nel·son, *n.* A hold in which a wrestler standing behind his opponent places one arm under the corresponding arm of the opponent so that the hand grips the nape of the opponent's neck.

half note, *n.* A note equivalent to one half of a whole note.

half sis·ter, *n.* A female offspring having one parent in common with another offspring.

half step, *n.* A semitone.

half·tone, haf′tōn, häf′tōn, *n.* A tone intermediate between the extreme lights and shades of a picture. *Photoengraving.* A process in which gradation of tone is obtained by a system of minute dots; a metal plate made by this process, or a print from it.

half tone, *n.* A semitone.

half-track, haf′trak, häf′trak, *n.* A type of armored military vehicle propelled by caterpillar treads at the rear and conventional wheels at the front.

half-truth, haf′trooth, häf′trooth, *n.* A partially true assertion usu. intended to be deceptive or evasive.

half·way, haf′wā′, häf′wā′, *adv.* Half over the way: to go *halfway* to Rome; to or at half the distance: The rope reaches only *halfway;* to half the full extent: The morning is *halfway* over.—*a.* Midway between two points; going to or covering only half the full extent, or partial: *halfway* measures.

half-wit, haf′wit, häf′wit, *n.* A feebleminded person. —**half·wit·ted,** *a.*

hal·i·but, hal′ə·bət, häl′ə·bət, *n. pl.,* **-but, -buts.** Either of the two largest species of flatfish, both important food fish, sometimes weighing several hundred pounds.

hal·i·to·sis, hal·i·tō′sis, *n.* Condition of having foul or offensive breath.

hall, hôl, *n.* A large room for public assembly; a room at the entrance of a house; a passageway connecting areas of a building; a manor house.

hal·le·lu·jah, hal·ə·loo′ya, *interj.* Praise ye the lord!—*n.* An exclamation of 'hallelujah!'; a song of praise to God. Also **hal·le·lu·iah.**

hall·mark, hôl′märk, *n.* The official stamp attesting that articles in gold and silver meet the legal standard; any mark certifying quality.—*v.t.* To mark with a hallmark.

hal·lo, hal·loo, hə·lō′, hə·loo′, *interj.* An exclamation to invite attention.—*n.* The shout "*halloo.*"—*v.i.* To call "*halloo.*"—*v.t.* To shout to.

hal·low, hal′ō, *v.t.* To consecrate; to honor as sacred. —**hal·lowed,** *a.*

Hal·low·een, hal·ō·ēn′, hol·ō·ēn′, *n.* The evening of Oct. 31, the eve of Allhallows or All Saints' Day, on which celebrants wear disguises and play pranks. Also **Hal·low·e'en.**

hal·lu·ci·nate, hə·loo′sə·nāt, *v.t.,* **-nat·ed, -nat·ing.** To affect with hallucination.

hal·lu·ci·na·tion, hə·loo·sə·nā′shən, *n.* An apparent perception, as by sight or hearing, for which there is no real external cause; the imagined object of an hallucination; a false notion; a delusion. —**hal·lu·ci·na·to·ry,** hə·loo′sə·nə·tô·rē, *a.*

hal·lu·cin·o·gen, hə·loo′sin·ə·jen, *n.* A chemical substance or drug that causes hallucinations. —**hal·lu·cin·o·gen·ic,** hə·loo·sə·nō·jen′ik, *a.*

hall·way, hôl′wā, *n.* A corridor, entrance hall, or passage, as in a building.

ha·lo, hā′lō, *n. pl.,* **-los, -loes.** A disk or circle of light represented about the head of a saint or angel; a circle of light seen around the moon or the sun, due to the refraction produced by ice particles in the atmosphere.

halt, hôlt, *v.i.* To stand in doubt, waver, or hesitate. —**halt·ing,** *a.* —**halt·ing·ly,** *adv.*

halt, hôlt, *n.* A stop: to call a *halt.*—*v.i.* To make a halt or temporary stop, as in marching or traveling.—*v.t.* To cause to halt; to restrain.

hal·ter, hôl′tər, *n.* A rope or strap with a noose or headstall, for leading or tying horses or cattle; a rope with a noose for hanging lawbreakers; death by hanging. A woman's sports top which fastens around the neck and leaves the back and arms exposed.

halve, hav, häv, *v.t.,* **halved, halv·ing.** To divide into halves.

halves, havz, hävz, *n.* Plural of **half.**

hal·yard, hal′yərd, *n.* A rope or tackle for hoisting and lowering sails, yards, or flags.

ham, ham, *n.* The meat of a hog's thigh used for food; the part of the leg behind the knee; *usu. pl.,* the back of the thigh together with the buttocks. *Theatr.* An inferior performer who overacts. *Radio.* A licensed operator of an amateur radio station. —**ham·my,** *a.,* **-mi·er, -mi·est.**

ham·burg·er, ham′bər·gər, *n.* Raw beef chopped or ground; a sandwich consisting of ground beef shaped into a patty, broiled, and placed between halves of a round bun.

ham·let, ham′lit, *n.* A small village; a cluster of houses in the country.

ham·mer, ham′ər, *n.* A tool consisting of a steel head set crosswise on a handle, used for beating metals or driving nails; any of various instruments resembling a hammer in form, action, or use; metal ball attached to a long, flexible handle, used in throwing contests. —*v.t.* To beat or drive with a hammer; to form or build with a hammer; to impress or teach by repetition: to *hammer* a rule into the students' heads; to work out laboriously.—*v.i.* To strike blows with or as with a hammer, esp. repeatedly; to make persistent or laborious attempts.

ham·mer and sick·le, *n.* The Soviet Union's emblem.

ham·mer lock, *n.* A hold in which a wrestler twists his opponent's arm and forces it upward behind the back.

ham·mock, ham′ək, *n.* A kind of hanging bed, consisting of a piece of canvas or netting, suspended from each end by cords and hooks.

ham·per, ham′pər, *v.t.* To impede; to restrain.

ham·per, ham′pər, *n.* A kind of basket used as a case for packing articles, for stowing picnic gear, or for storing laundry.

ham·ster, ham′stər, *n.* A short-tailed, burrowing rodent with large cheek pouches, inhabiting parts of Europe and Asia.

ham·string, ham′string, *n.* In man, any of the tendons behind the knee; in quadrupeds, the great tendon at the back of the hock—*v.t.,* **-strung, -string·ing.** To cut the hamstring or hamstrings of; to cripple, disable, or render powerless.

hand, hand, *n.* The extremity of the arm, consisting of the palm, four fingers, and thumb; the corresponding part of the forelimb in any of the higher vertebrates; a part or share in something: to have a *hand* in a matter; side: on the right *hand;* promise of marriage; a person employed in manual labor; a person considered a source: knowledge obtained at first *hand;* skill or knack at doing something; a turn of play in certain games; applause; style of handwriting; something resembling a hand in shape or function; a measure used in giving the height of horses, equal to four inches. *Cards.* The cards dealt to or held by each player at one time. *Pl.* Possession or power: to put a matter into a person's *hands.*—*a.* Made by, operated by, using, or belonging to the hand.—*v.t.* To grasp, touch, manage, or work with the hands; to lead or conduct with the hand: to *hand* a child across the street; to pass: *Hand* me my hat. —**at hand,** within reach; near by; near in time. —**at the hands of, at the hand of,** through the agency of someone or something. —**by hand,** done with the hands only, without mechanical help. —**from hand to mouth,** with attention to immediate wants only. —**hand and foot,** totally; completely. —**hand in glove,** in very close agreement or connection. —**hand in hand,** holding hands; in union; jointly. —**hand o·ver fist.** *Informal.* Rapidly; in

---

a- hat, fāte, fāre, fäther; **e-** met, mē; **i-** pin, pīne; **o-** not, nōte, ôrb, moove (move), boy, pownd; **u-** cūbe, bůll, tůk (took); **ch-** chin; **th-** thick, ŧhen; **zh-** vizhon (vision); **ə-** ego, takən, pencəl, lemən, bərd (bird).

large quantities. **—hands down,** unquestionably; effortlessly. **—hand to hand,** in close combat; at close quarters. **—in hand,** in immediate possession: cash *in hand;* under control. **—off one's hands,** out of one's charge or care. **—on hand,** in immediate possession; before one for attention; in attendance or present. **—on one's hands,** resting on one as a responsibility. **—out of hand,** beyond control. **—to hand,** within reach; into one's possession. **—to hand down,** to transmit to one's heirs; to formulate and express (the decision of a court). **—to hand over,** to yield possession of. **—to have one's hands full,** having to do all one can possibly do.

hand·bag, hand′bag, *n.* A pocketbook, held in the hand or worn over the shoulder, for carrying small purchases, toilet articles, or money.

hand·ball, hand′bôl, *n.* A game in which a small rubber ball is batted with the hands against a wall; the ball used in this game.

hand·bill, hand′bil, *n.* A printed paper or sheet to be circulated for the purpose of making some public announcement.

hand·book, hand′bûk, *n.* A small book or treatise; a manual.

hand·cuff, hand′kəf, *n. Usu. pl.* A metal bracelet with lock, usu. in pairs chained together.—*v.t.* To put handcuffs on; to fetter.

hand·ed, hand′did, *a.* Having a hand possessed of a specified property, used esp. in compounds: as, right-*handed,* empty-*handed.*

hand·ful, hand′fûl, *n. pl.,* **-fuls.** As much as the hand will contain; a small quantity or number; as much as one can manage. *Informal.* A thing or person difficult to control.

hand·i·cap, han′dē·kap, *n.* A race or other contest in which certain disadvantages or advantages are given to competitors to equalize their chances of winning; the disadvantage or advantage itself; any encumbrance or physical disadvantage.—*v.t.,* **-capped, -cap·ping.** To assign a handicap; to serve as a handicap: Age *handicaps* him. **—hand·i·cap·per,** *n.*

hand·i·craft, han′dē·kraft, han′dē·kräft, *n.* The skill of one's hands; work of an artisan, hobbyist, or tradesman; an object produced by handicraft.

hand·i·ly, han′də·lē, *adv.* In a handy manner. **—hand·i·ness,** *n.*

hand·i·work, han′dē·wərk, *n.* Work done by the hands.

hand·ker·chief, hang′kər·chif, *n.* A hemmed square of cloth carried for personal use or as a decorative accessory.

han·dle, han′dəl, *n.* A part which is intended to be grasped by the hand.—*v.t.,* **-dled, -dling.** To touch, feel, or use the hands on; to manage, direct, or control: to *handle* troops in battle; to deal with or treat in a particular way: to *handle* a person with discretion; to deal or trade in, as in goods.—*v.i.* To respond, perform, or behave in a specific way when handled or controlled: This boat *handles* well. **—fly off the han·dle,** to be angered suddenly and violently. **—han·dler,** *n.*

han·dle·bar, han′dəl·bär, *n. Often pl.* The curved bar in front of the rider on a bicycle or motorcycle by which the vehicle is guided.

hand·made, hand′mād′, *a.* Made by hand (rather than machinery).

hand·maid·en, hand′mād·ən, *n.* A female servant or attendant. Also **hand·maid.**

hand-me-down, hand′mē·down, *n.* A used item of clothing passed from one person to another.

hand·out, hand′owt, *n. Informal.* A portion of food or the like given to a beggar.

hand-pick, hand′pik′, *v.t.* To pick by hand; to select carefully; to choose for a specific purpose. **—hand·picked,** *a.*

hand·rail, hand′rāl, *n.* A railing grasped by the hand for support.

hand·shake, hand′shāk, *n.* The clasping of hands between two people in greeting, agreement, or farewell.

hand·some, han′səm, *a.,* **-som·er, -som·est.** Good-looking; generous: a *handsome* gift. **—hand·some·ly,** *adv.* **—hand·some·ness,** *n.*

hand·spring, hand′spring, *n.* An acrobatic feat in which the body turns a complete circle in the air, touching ground with the hands first, then the feet.

hand-to-hand, hand′tə·hand′, *a.* At close range; in close touch, as fighting.

hand-to-mouth, hand′tə·mowth′, *a.* Providing limited means of support; leading a financially insecure existence; having nothing to spare.

hand·work, hand′wərk, *n.* Work done by the hands, as opposed to work done by machines.

hand·writ·ing, hand′rī·ting, *n.* The style of writing peculiar to each person; writing done by hand.

hand·y, han′dē, *a.,* **-i·er, -i·est.** Convenient; near or easily accessible; skilled in using the hands.

hand·y·man, han′dē·man, *n. pl.,* **-men.** One doing or hired to do odd jobs.

hang, hang, *v.t.,* **hung or hanged** (esp. for capital punishment and suicide), **hang·ing.** To fasten using support from above; to suspend so as to allow free movement; to suspend by the neck, as a method of capital punishment or suicide; to let droop or bend downward: to *hang* one's head in shame; to attach, as paper, to walls; to furnish or decorate with something suspended or attached; to keep a jury from rendering a verdict by refusing to agree with the other jurors. —*v.i.* To be suspended; to swing freely, as on a hinge; to die or be put to death by suspension from a cross or gallows; to bend forward or downward; to lean over; to rest for support, followed by *on* or *upon;* to be dependent or contingent; to remain attentive, as to a person's words; to hold fast, cling or adhere; to remain in doubtful suspense; to remain unsettled or unfinished; to fail to agree, as a jury.—*n.* The way in which a thing hangs. *Informal.* The precise manner or knack of using or doing something: to get the *hang* of a card trick; meaning: to get the *hang* of a subject. **—hang on,** to keep a telephone line open; to cling (to); persist tenaciously; depend on. **—hang out,** to lean out. *Informal.* To spend one's time. **—hang up,** to end a telephone conversation, esp. by putting the receiver back in place; to place on a hook, hanger, etc.; to delay or suspend; hold up. **—let it all hang out,** to reveal everything; to express oneself; to be uninhibited or completely natural.

hang·ar, hang′ər, *n.* A shelter for housing or repairing airplanes.

hang·dog, hang′dôg, hang′dog, *a.* Guilty or shifty in appearance.

hang·er, hang′ər, *n.* Something by which a thing is hung; one who hangs something: a paper-*hanger.*

hang·er-on, hang′ər·on′, hang′ər·ôn′, *n. pl.,* **-ers-on.** A follower; a parasite.

hang·ing, hang′ing, *n.* Execution by suspending by the neck until dead; *usu. pl.,* something that hangs or is hung, as drapery.—*a.* Dangling; suspended.

hang·man, hang′mən, *n. pl.,* **-men.** One whose office is to hang persons condemned to death; a public executioner.

hang·nail, hang′nāl, *n.* A small piece of skin, partly detached, at the base or side of a fingernail.

hang·out, hang′owt, *n. Informal.* A place one visits frequently.

hang·o·ver, hang′ō·vər, *n.* A situation or thing that remains from a former period; the physical discomfort suffered after overindulgence in alcohol.

hang-up, hang′əp, *n.* Delay; difficulty. *Informal.* Obsession; problem.

hank, hangk, *n.* A definite length or weight of thread or yarn; a coil, knot, or loop, as of hair.

hank·er, hang′kər, *v.i.* To long for. **—hank·er·ing.** *n.*

han·som, han′səm, *n.* A low, covered, two-wheeled

vehicle drawn by a horse, the driver being mounted on an elevated seat behind the cab.

Ha·nuk·kah, hä′nə·kə, *n.* The Jewish Festival of Lights, lasting eight days, which commemorates the rededication of the Temple of Jerusalem after its defilement by the Syrians under King Antiochus.

hap·haz·ard, hap′haz·ərd, *n.* Chance or accident. —hap·haz′ərd, *a.* Accidental; determined by chance. **—hap·haz·ard·ly,** *adv.* **—hap·haz·ard·ness,** *n.*

hap·less, hap′lis, *a.* Luckless, unfortunate. **—hap·less·ly,** *adv.*

hap·ly, hap′lē, *adv. Archaic.* By luck or chance; by accident; perhaps.

hap·pen, hap′ən, *v.i.* To occur or take place; to come to pass by chance; have the fortune: I *happened* to see him; to come upon by chance: to *happen* on a clue to a mystery; to be, come, or go by chance: to *happen* along.

hap·pen·ing, hap′ə·ning, *n.* An event; an occurrence or gathering.

hap·pen·stance, hap′ən·stans, *n.* An occurrence caused by chance.

hap·pi·ness, hap′ē·nis, *n.* The state or quality of being content.

hap·py, hap′ē, *a.,* **-pi·er, -pi·est.** Delighted, pleased, or glad; indicative of pleasure or contentment; joyful; fortunate or lucky; skillful or apt. **—hap·pi·ly,** *adv.*

hap·py-go-luck·y, hap′ē·gō·lək′ē, *a.* Trusting cheerfully to luck.

ha·ra·ki·ri, här′ə·kēr′ē, *n.* A traditional Japanese method of suicide, ceremonially performed by slashing the abdomen with a dagger; self-destruction or suicide. Also, *informal,* **ha·ri·ka·ri,** här′ē·kar′ē.

ha·rangue, hə·rang′, *n.* A passionate, vehement, or loud speech; a pompous, didactic, or scolding speech; a tirade.—*v.t.,* **-rangued, -rang·uing.** To address in a harangue.—*v.i.* To deliver a harangue.

har·ass, har′əs, hə·ras′, *v.t.* To annoy by repeated attacks or raids; to harry; to pester. **—har·ass·ment,** *n.*

har·bin·ger, här′bin·jər, *n.* One who or that which precedes and foreshadows a future occurrence; omen; a forerunner or precursor.

har·bor, här′bər, *n.* A protected anchorage near a coast for ships; a port; a place of shelter, haven, or refuge.—*v.t.* To give shelter or refuge to; to entertain within the mind, as thoughts and feelings.

hard, härd, *a.* Solid and firm; difficult to do: a *hard* task; carrying on with energy: a *hard* worker; difficult or troublesome: *hard* to please, *hard* of hearing; difficult to understand, explain, or solve: a *hard* subject; difficult to bear or endure: as, a *hard* life; not easily impressed or moved; harsh or severe in dealing with others: a *hard* master; based on actual facts: *hard* evidence; severe or rigorous: a *hard* bargain; searching: a *hard* look; harsh or unfriendly: *hard* feelings; vigorous or violent: a *hard* rain; of water, containing mineral salts; strong or intoxicating: liquors.—*adv.* So as to be hard, solid, or firm: frozen *hard;* firmly or tightly: to hold *hard* by the wrist; with difficulty: breathing *hard;* harshly or severely: to treat or press *hard;* with great vigor: to work *hard;* earnestly, intently, or searchingly: to look *hard* at a thing or a person; being close or near, as in place, amount, or time: to follow *hard* after a person; with bitter feelings: He took his humiliation *hard.* **—hard of hearing,** somewhat deaf. **—hard up.** *Informal.* Very much in need of something (with *for*); short of cash; poor; broke. **—hard·ness.** *n.*

hard-bit·ten, härd′bit′ən, *a.* Hardened by conflict; tough; unyielding.

hard-boiled, härd′boyld′, *a.* Boiled until hard, as an egg. *Informal.* Hardened by experience; not easily impressed or moved; tough.

hard coal, *n.* Anthracite.

hard-core, härd′kôr′, *a.* Aggressive; unyielding: a *hard-core* criminal.

hard·en, här′dən, *v.t.* To make hard.—*v.i.* To become hard. **—hard·en·er,** *n.*

hard goods, *n.* Merchandise designed to last a relatively long time, as machinery and appliances.

hard-hat, härd′hat, *n. Informal.* A worker in the construction trades who wears a protective helmet.—*a.*

hard-head·ed, härd′hed′id, *a.* Not easily moved or deceived; practical; shrewd; stubborn.

hard-heart·ed, härd′här′tid, *a.* Pitiless; unfeeling.

har·di·hood, här′dē·hûd, *n.* Hardy spirit or character; boldness; daring.

har·di·ness, här′dē·nis, *n.* The quality or state of being hardy.

hard·ly, härd′lē, *adv.* Scarcely; barely; not quite; unlikely; severely; harshly.

hard·pan, härd′pan, *n.* A layer of firm soil underlying soft soil.

hard·ship, härd′ship, *n.* A condition that is hard to bear.

hard·tack, härd′tak, *n.* A type of hard biscuit made without salt, used chiefly as army rations or aboard ships.

hard·top, härd′top, *n.* An automobile with the design of a convertible, but having a rigid roof.

hard·ware, härd′wer, *n.* Metalware or articles, as tools, locks, hinges, cutlery, or utensils; any mechanical, electrical, or electronic computer equipment.

hard·wood, härd′wûd, *n.* The compact wood of such trees as hickory, oak, beech, ash, and cherry; any tree which yields such wood; any broad-leafed tree, distinguished from a conifer or needle-leafed tree.—*a.* Consisting of hardwood.

har·dy, här′dē, *a.,* **-di·er, -di·est.** Able to endure fatigue, hardship, and the like; bold, brave, or daring. **—har·di·ly,** *adv.*

hare, hār, *n. pl.,* **hares, hare.** A small mammal with long ears, a divided upper lip, a short tail, and lengthened hind legs adapted for leaping.

hare·brained, hār′brānd, *a.* Giddy; heedless.

hare·lip, hār′lip, *n.* A congenital division of the upper lip, sometimes extending to the palate; the deformed lip itself. **—hare·lipped,** *a.*

har·em, hār′əm, har′əm, *n.* The area reserved for women in a Muslim family; these women: wives, concubines, and servants.

hark, härk, *v.i.* To listen. **—hark back,** to go back to something prior; revert; retrace one's steps.

har·ken, heark·en, här′kən, *v.i.* To listen; to pay attention; to give heed.

har·le·quin, här′lə·kwin, här′lə·kin, *n. (Cap.)* A comic pantomime character, usu. masked, dressed in parti-colored tights and bearing a wooden sword or magic wand. *(L.c.)* A buffoon.—*a.* Particolored.

har·lot, här′lət, *n.* A woman who is promiscuous; a prostitute. **—har·lot·ry,** *n.*

harm, härm, *n.* Physical or moral injury; hurt; damage. —*v.t.* To injure; to hurt; to damage.

harm·ful, härm′fəl, *a.* Inflicting harm; capable of causing hurt or danger; injurious. **—harm·ful·ly,** *adv.* **—harm·ful·ness,** *n.*

harm·less, härm′lis, *a.* Lacking ability or inclination to injure or harm; innocuous; inoffensive. **—harm·less·ly,** *adv.* **—harm·less·ness,** *n.*

har·mon·ic, här·mon′ik, *a.* Pertaining to or marked by harmony; pertaining to harmonics or overtones. —*n.* The overtone of a fundamental. **—har·mon·i·cal·ly,** *adv.*

har·mon·i·ca, här·mon′i·kə, *n.* A musical instrument having a set of small metallic reeds mounted in a case and played by the breath inhaling and exhaling; a mouth organ.

---

a- hat, fāte, fāre, fäther; **e-** met, mē; **i-** pin, pīne; **o-** not, nōte, ôrb, moove (move), boy, pownd; **u-** cūbe, bûll, tûk (took); **ch-** chin; **th-** thick, then; **zh-** vizhon (vision); **ə-** əgo, takən, pencəl, lemən, bərd (bird).

har·mon·ics, här·mon′iks, *n. pl.*, *sing. or pl. in constr.* The branch of acoustics dealing with musical sounds.

har·mo·ni·ous, här·mō′nē·əs, *a.* Marked by agreement in feeling or action: a *harmonious* decision; forming a pleasingly consistent whole; exhibiting harmony; being in harmony. **—har·mo·ni·ous·ly**, *adv.*

har·mo·nize, här′mə·nīz, *v.i.*, **-nized**, **-niz·ing.** To be in harmony.—*v.t.* To bring into harmony; to set accompanying parts to, as to a melody.

har·mo·ny, här′mə·nē, *n. pl.*, **-nies.** Accord in facts, views, or acts; sympathetic relationship; friendship; inner calm; a pleasing integration of components. The science of musical chords; coincident combination of musical tones.

har·ness, här′nis, *n.* The working gear of a horse or other draft animal, except the ox; any similar combination of straps, bands, or the like.—*v.t.* To put a harness on; attach by a harness, as to a vehicle to be drawn; to bring under conditions for working: to *harness* water power.

harp, härp, *n.* A musical instrument, played by plucking strings which are stretched within a triangular framework.—*v.i.* To play on the harp. *Informal.* To dwell on a subject tiresomely and repeatedly, usu. followed by *on* or *upon.* **—harp·ist**, *n.*

har·poon, här·poon′, *n.* A spear attached to a long cord, used to strike and kill whales and large fish.—*v.t.* To strike or capture with or as with a harpoon.

harp·si·chord, härp′si·kôrd, *n.* A keyboard instrument in general use from the 16th to the 18th century in which the strings are plucked by leather or quill points connected with the keys.

har·py, här′pē, *n. pl.*, **-pies.** A grasping, greedy person; any of several mythological foul monsters having the face of a woman and the body of a bird.

har·ri·dan, har′ə·dən, *n.* A bad-tempered, hateful, or vicious old woman; a hag.

har·row, har′ō, *n.* An agricultural implement, consisting of a row of teeth, spikes, or upright disks protruding downward from a supporting frame, which is drawn across plowed soil to level it and crumble clods or to cover sown seed.—*v.t.* To draw a harrow over; to distress painfully; to torment; to harass.—*v.i.* To be prepared by harrowing, as a field.

har·row·ing, har′ō·ing, *a.* Causing acute mental or emotional distress.

har·ry, har′ē, *v.t.*, **-ried**, **-ry·ing.** To pillage or plunder; to harrass; to torment or worry.

harsh, härsh, *a.* Grating or unpleasant to the senses, the mind, or the esthetic sense; crude; unrefined; acrid; rough; austere; severe; strident. **—harsh·ly**, *adv.* **—harsh·ness**, *n.*

hart, härt, *n. pl.*, **harts, hart.** A stag or male deer when he has passed his fifth year.

har·um-scar·um, har′əm·skar′əm, här′əm·skär′əm, *a.* Irresponsible, harebrained, or reckless.—*n.* A flighty, unsettled person.—*adv.* In a reckless or giddy manner.

har·vest, här′vist, *n.* The act or process of gathering any ripened crop; the time of such reaping and gathering; that which is reaped and gathered in; the product of any labor; gain; result; effect; consequence.—*v.t.* To reap or gather, as corn or fruit; to reap from, as fields; to gain or win by effort.—*v.i.* To gather crops.

har·ves·ter, här′vi·stər, *n.* One who or that which harvests; a mower; a reaper.

har·vest moon, *n.* The full moon at the time of harvest, or about the autumnal equinox.

has, haz, *v.* Third person singular, present indicative, of **have.**

has-been, haz′bin, *n. Informal.* One who has passed the period of his greatest effectiveness, achievement, or popularity.

hash, hash, *n.* Cooked meat which has been chopped up and reheated with potatoes and other vegetables; a revision of old material; a jumble; a mess. *Informal.*

Hashish.—*v.t.* To chop into small pieces; to mince and mix; to talk over. **—hash o·ver**, to discuss, consider, review.

hash·ish, hash·eesh, hash′ēsh, hash′ish, *n.* The flowering tops and leaves of the hemp which are drunk, chewed, or smoked for their narcotic and intoxicating effect; any of certain preparations made from this plant.

has·n't, haz′ənt. Contraction of **has not.**

hasp, hasp, häsp, *n.* A clasp that passes over a staple, to be fastened by a padlock; a metal hook for fastening a door.—*v.t.*

has·sle, has′əl, *n. Informal.* A disagreement or argument; a fight. **—***v.t.*, *v.i.*, **-sled, -sling.** To vex; struggle with.

has·sock, has′ək, *n.* A footstool. A thick clump of grass found in a marsh.

haste, hāst, *n.* Speed; rashness; quickness. **—make haste**, to hasten; to proceed rapidly.

has·ten, hā′sən, *v.i.* To move or act with haste; hurry.—*v.t.* To cause to make haste; urge or impel to greater speed.

hast·y, hā′stē, *a.*, **-i·er**, **-i·est.** Moving or acting with haste; rash; irritable; easily aroused to anger. **—hast·i·ly**, *adv.* **—hast·i·ness**, *n.*

hat, hat, *n.* Any of various head coverings for both men and women.—*v.t.*, **hat·ted, hat·ting.** To provide with a hat. **—come with hat in hand**, to come humbly or respectfully. **—pass the hat**, to collect money contributions, usu. at a meeting. **—take off one's hat to**, to recognize some superior quality or accomplishment in another. **—talk through one's hat**, to speak foolishly or irresponsibly. **—toss one's hat in the ring**, to enter a contest, esp. to become a candidate for political office.

hatch, hach, *n.* An opening in a ship's deck, a floor, or a roof; a hatchway; a cover for such an opening.

hatch, hach, *v.t.* To bring forth, as young, from the egg; to cause young to emerge from (the egg); to produce; devise; contrive secretly: to *hatch* a plot. —*v.i.* To be hatched.—*n.* A brood.

hatch·er·y, hach′ə·rē, *n. pl.*, **-ies.** A place for hatching eggs, esp. fish or poultry eggs.

hatch·et, hach′it, *n.* A small ax with a short handle, used with one hand; a tomahawk. **—bur·y the hatch·et**, to make peace.

hatch·way, hach′wā, *n.* An opening covered by a hatch in a ship's deck for passage of cargo; a hatch; a similar opening in a floor or roof.

hate, hāt, *v.t.*, **hat·ed, hat·ing.** To dislike greatly or intensely; to have a great aversion to; to loathe; to detest.—*v.i.* To experience dislike; to detest.—*n.* Great dislike or aversion; an object of extreme dislike or aversion. **—hat·er**, *n.*

hate·ful, hāt′fəl, *a.* Exciting animosity; odious; detestable; feeling hatred; malevolent. **—hate·ful·ly**, *adv.* **—hate·ful·ness**, *n.*

ha·tred, hā′trid, *n.* Great dislike or aversion; detestation; active antipathy; animosity.

hat·ter, hat′ər, *n.* One who produces, sells, or refurbishes hats, usu. men's hats.

haugh·ty, hô′tē, *a.*, **-ti·er**, **-ti·est.** Proud; disdainful. **—haugh·ti·ly**, *adv.* **—haugh·ti·ness**, *n.*

haul, hôl, *v.t.* To pull or draw with force; to transport, as in a truck or car; to drag; to tug.—*v.i.* To carry freight commercially; to tug; to change the direction in sailing.—*n.* A forceful pulling; that which is caught, taken, or received together: a good *haul* of lobsters; the distance something is carried. **—haul off**, to pull back the arm before striking a blow. **—haul·age**, *n.*

haunch, hônch, hänch, *n.* The hip; the fleshy hindquarter of a man or animal; flank; the upper leg and loin of beef, pork, or other meat animals.

haunt, hônt, hänt, *v.t.* To frequent; to recur frequently to; to be much about; to appear as a ghost.—*v.i.* To be much about a place; to make frequent visits.—*n.* A place one frequents; a favorite resort; a common gathering place.

haunt·ed, hôn′tĕd, hän′tĕd, *a.* Supposedly visited or frequented by ghosts.

haunt·ing, hôn′ting, hän′ting, *a.* Lingering; often remembered; not easily forgotten.

hau·teur, hō·tər′, *n.* Pride; haughtiness; arrogance; a snobbish or spirited manner.

have, hav (*unstressed* hɘv, ɘv), *v.t., pres. sing.* **have, have, have;** *pres. pl.* **have;** *past had;* *past participle* **had;** *present participle* **hav·ing.** To possess; to hold or control; to include or contain; to be in a particular relation to: to *have* a sister, to *have* an acquaintance; to display or show: to *have* the audacity, to *have* compassion; to obtain: to *have* it at all costs, to *have* news of; to be impelled: to *have* to do the work; to experience or suffer from; to take part in or conduct: to *have* an argument; to maintain or hold an opinion; to bring about or cause to be: to *have* him arrested; to invite or extend hospitality to: to *have* overnight guests; to consume: to *have* dinner; to allow: to *have* no argument; to bear or bring forth in childbirth; to place or hold in a particular position: to *have* them cornered.—*aux. v.* Used with a past participle to form a present perfect, past perfect, or future perfect tense: I *have* come. She *had* gone. They will *have* finished. **—have done,** to stop or complete. **—have it out,** to pursue to a final decision. **—have to do with,** to be associated with.

ha·ven, hā′vɘn, *n.* A harbor or port; a place of safety.

have-nots, hav′nots, *n. pl. Sometimes sing.* The underprivileged; persons or countries having few material possessions.

have·n't, hav′ɘnt. Contraction of **have not.**

hav·er·sack, hav′ɘr·sak, *n.* A strong cloth bag with a single strap, worn over the shoulder to carry provisions or supplies.

haves, havz, *n pl. Sometimes sing.* A previleged country or group.

hav·oc, hav′ɘk, *n.* Devastation; wide and general destruction; disorder; confusion. **—play hav·oc with,** to cause confusion in; to ruin.

haw, hô, *interj.* A word of command to horses, usu. directing them to turn to the left.—*v.i., v.t.* To turn to the left.

haw, hô, *v.i.* To falter in speaking; to stammer or hesitate in speech.—*n.* A meaningless utterance marking a hesitation in speech or a search for words.

hawk, hôk, *n.* Any of several daytime birds of prey; one who advocates or strongly supports a war; a jingoist; a swindler.—*v.t.* To hunt game with a hawk; to practice falconry; to fly or hunt in the manner of the hawk. **—hawk·ish,** *a.*

hawk, hôk, *v.t.* To sell, or try to sell, by crying in the streets or calling at people's doors.—*v.i.* To peddle merchandise from place to place. **—hawk·er,** *n.*

hawk, hôk, *v.t.* To cough; to clear the throat.—*n.* A clearing of the throat by coughing.

haw·ser, hô′zɘr, hô′sɘr, *n.* A large, heavy rope used in towing or securing a ship.

hay, hā, *n.* Grass cut and dried for use as fodder; grass mowed or ready for mowing.—*v.t.* To furnish with hay, as horses.—*v.i.* To cut and dry grass for use as fodder.

hay fe·ver, *n.* An allergy to the pollen of various plants, marked by sneezing, inflamed eyes, and other symptoms similar to a cold.

hay·loft, hā′lôft, hā′loft, *n.* A loft in a stable or barn for the storage of hay; haymow.

hay·mak·er, hā′mā·kɘr, *n.* One who or that which makes, dries, or cures hay; a powerful or knockout punch.

hay·mow, hā′mow, *n.* A mass of hay stored in a barn; hayloft.

hay·seed, hā′sēd, *n.* Seed shaken out of hay. *Informal.* A rube; a hick.

hay·stack, hā′stak, *n.* A hay pile outdoors.

hay·wire, hā′wīr, *n.* Wire used to bind bales of hay. **—***a. Informal.* In disorder; broken down; out of control; wild or crazy: to go *haywire.*

haz·ard, haz′ɘrd, *n.* A risk; peril: the *hazards* of war; chance; a chance; any of the various obstacles on a golf course.—*v.t.* To take or run the risk of; to venture or offer, as an opinion. **—haz·ard·ous,** *a.* **—haz·ard·ous·ly,** *adv.* **—haz·ard·ous·ness,** *n.*

haze, hāz, *n.* Mist, smoke, or a dusky vapor in the air; vagueness; mental fog.

haze, hāz, *v.t.,* **hazed, haz·ing.** To annoy; to bully or humiliate, esp. school freshmen or newcomers.

ha·zel, hā′zɘl, *n.* A shrub or small tree native to N. America, Europe, and Asia, producing edible hazel-colored nuts; the nut fruit of this shrub; a light reddish-brown color.—*a.* Of a light reddish-brown color: *hazel* eyes.

ha·zel·nut, hā′zɘl·nɘt, *n.* The edible reddish-brown fruit of the hazel.

ha·zy, hā′zē, *a.,* **-zi·er, -zi·est.** Misty; mentally confused; vague. **—ha·zi·ly,** *adv.* **—ha·zi·ness,** *n.*

H-bomb, āch′bom, *n.* Hydrogen bomb.

he, hē (*unstressed* ē), *pron., sing. nom.* **he,** *poss.* **his,** *obj.* **him;** *intens. and refl.* **himself;** *pl. nom.* **they,** *poss.* **their** or **theirs,** *obj.* **them.** The hon. third pers. sing. masc. pron. representing the male being in question or last mentioned; the man or male; anyone: *He* who betrays his king must die.—*n. pl.,* **hes.** A man or male animal.

head, hed, *n.* The upper part of the human body, joined to the trunk by the neck; the corresponding part of an animal's body; mind or understanding: to have a good *head;* mental aptitude: to have a *head* for mathematics; presence of mind or self-control: to keep one's *head;* a leader or chief: *head* of state; one of a number or group: five dollars a *head;* collectively, a unit for totaling: 10 *head* of cattle; anything resembling a head in form or position: the *head* of a pin; the end of something, as a bed or grave, toward which the head is placed; the top of a page; something at the top of a page, column, or section; froth or foam rising to the top of a liquid, as beer; the side of a coin, bearing a head; the end or part of a machine, implement, or weapon, as a hammer, arrow, golf club, or lathe, which performs its main function, as striking or cutting; the maturating part of an abscess or boil; culmination or crisis: to bring matters to a *head;* the pressure of a confined body, as of steam; the top part of a plant when compact or rounded, as the leaves of lettuce. **—***v.t.* To lead or be at the head of: to *head* a committee; to direct the course of: to *head* one's boat for shore; to get in front of so as to cause to turn back or aside, often used with *off.*—*v.i.* To move or be directed toward a point or in a specified direction: to *head* for the hills; to form or come to a head.—*a.* Pertaining to the head; situated at the head, top, or front: the *head* division of a parade; coming from in front, as a wind; chief; principal. **—get one's head together,** to find oneself; to straighten oneself out; to become sober or rational after being high on intoxicating or hallucinogenic drugs. **—head o·ver heels,** entirely: *head over heels* in love. **—lose one's head,** to lose one's restraint or self-discipline. **—not make head or tail of,** to fail to understand; to find incomprehensible. **—out of one's head,** demented, delirious, or crazy. **—o·ver one's head,** beyond one's comprehension; passing over or ignoring a superior: to go *over* the supervisor's *head* with the problem. **—head·ship,** *n.*

head·ache, hed′āk, *n.* A pain in the head. *Informal.* A source of annoyance or worry.

head·band, hed′band. *n.* A band worn around the head.

head·dress, hed′dres, *n.* An ornamental head cover-

---

ing.

head·er, hed′ər, n. A person or machine that removes the heads from something, as grain from stalks; a headfirst plunge or dive.

head·first, hed′fərst′, adv. With the head in a forward position; rashly; with premature haste. Also **head· fore·most,** hed′fôr′mōst.—a.

head·gear, hed′gēr, n. Any covering or protection for the head; the parts of a harness around an animal's head.

head·hunt·er, hed′hən·tər, n. One who beheads enemies and preserves their heads as trophies. Informal. An employment agent who tries to lure a person from one job and place him in another, for a fee: also **body-snatcher.**

head·ing, hed′ing, n. An object that acts as a front, beginning, or upper part of anything; the title of a chapter or page; a division of a discourse; the direction in which an aircraft is pointing.

head·land, hed′lənd, n. A point of land projecting out over the sea; a promontory.

head·less, hed′lis, a. Without a head; without a leader; without brains.

head·light, hed′līt, n. A brilliant light on the front of a locomotive, automobile, or other vehicle.

head·line, hed′līn, n. A title line over a newspaper article summarizing content.—v.t., **-lined, -lin·ing.** To furnish with a headline; to feature or give top billing to.

head·long, hed′lông, hed′long, adv. Headfirst; rashly; unchecked by caution or forethought; precipitately; without delay.—a. Hasty, impetuous, or precipitate; with the head first.

head·mas·ter, hed′mas′tər, hed′mä′stər, n. Brit. The male principal of an elementary or secondary school. U.S. The male principal of a private school.

head·mis·tress, hed′mis′tris, n. Brit. The female principal of an elementary or secondary school. U.S. The female principal of a private school.

head·most, hed′mōst, a. Most advanced; foremost.

head-on, hed′on′, hed′ôn′, a. Meeting or coming together with the heads or fronts foremost.—adv. With the heads or fronts foremost.

head·piece, hed′pēs, n. A helmet; a hat or other covering for the head; the head; intelligence; a headset.

head·quar·ters, hed′kwôr′tərz, n. pl., sing. or pl. in constr. The office of a commander of a military or political organization; a center of authority or order; the central office of a business.

head·set, hed′set, n. A set of earphones.

head start, n. A given or achieved advantage over others, as a handicap in a competitive event or race.

head·stone, hed′stōn, n. The stone at the head of a grave; the chief stone or cornerstone of a foundation.

head·strong, hed′strông, hed′strong, a. Restive, obstinate, or unmanageable; bent on pursuing one's own way.

head·wait·er, hed′wā′tər, n. One who supervises a public dining room, esp. the work of waiters and other employees serving food and drinks.

head·wa·ters, hed′wô·tərz, hed′wät·ərz, n. pl. The tributaries at the source of a river.

head·way, hed′wā, n. Motion forward or ahead; advance; progress or success in general; headroom.

head·wind, hed′wind, n. A wind directly opposed to a vehicle's course, esp. that of an airplane or ship.

head·y, hed′ē, a., **-i·er, -i·est.** Apt to affect the mental faculties; strongly intoxicating: a heady wine; exciting: heady news of his first promotion; rash or hasty; clever; headstrong. **—head·i·ly,** adv. **—head· i·ness,** n.

heal, hēl, v.t. To make hale, sound, or whole; to cure of a disease or wound and restore to health; to reconcile, as a breach or difference.—v.i. To grow sound; to return to a sound state, sometimes followed by up or over. **—heal·er,** n.

health, helth, n. The sound condition of a living organism; physical or mental vigor; absence of ailments; a wish offered for a person's well-being or happiness, as a toast.

health·ful, helth′fəl, a. Full of health; free from disease; healthy; promoting health; wholesome.

health·y, hel′thē, a., **-i·er, -i·est.** Enjoying or being in good health; conducive to health; wholesome. **—health·i·ly,** adv. **—health·i·ness,** n.

heap, hēp, n. A mass of things lying one on top of another; a pile. Informal. Quantity or number.—v.t. To gather or put in a heap; to cast or bestow in great quantity: to heap blessings upon a person; to load or supply abundantly: to heap a person with benefits; to fill, as a vessel, to overflowing.—v.i. To become heaped.

hear, hēr, v.t., **heard, hear·ing.** To perceive by the ear; to listen; attend; obey; to give legal audience to.—v.i. To possess the faculty of perceiving and realizing sound; to consider, usu. preceded by a negative and followed by of: He wouldn't hear of it. **—hear·er,** n.

hear·ing, hēr′ing, n. The act of perceiving sound; the faculty or sense by which sound is perceived; reach of sound, earshot; audience; an opportunity to be heard. Law. Preliminary investigation of a case to determine its validity; a judicial investigation before a court.

heark·en, här′kən, v.i., v.t. Harken.

hear·say, her′sā, n. Rumor; common talk.

hearse, hers, n. A funeral vehicle for transporting a dead person to the place of burial.

heart, härt, n. The hollow muscular organ of vertebrates that circulates blood throughout the body by means of rhythmic contractions and dilations; the seat of emotion, affection, and passions; core or center part; a figure or an object with rounded sides meeting in an obtuse point at the bottom and curving inward to a cusp at the top; a playing card of a suit marked with such figures in red. **—at heart,** intrinsically. **—change of heart,** reversal of decision. **—eat one's heart out,** to grieve or suffer longing. **—from the heart, from the bot·tom of one's heart,** with sincerity. **—have one's heart in one's mouth,** to be very worried or frightened. **—set one's heart on,** to have an intense desire for something. **—take to heart,** to take seriously.

heart·ache, härt′āk, n. Grief.

heart·break, härt′brāk, n. Overwhelming sorrow or grief. **—heart·break·ing,** a.

heart·brok·en, härt′brō·kən, a. Deeply grieved; in despair.

heart·burn, härt′bern, n. A burning sensation in the thorax and stomach.

heart·en, här′tən, v.t. To encourage.

heart·felt, härt′felt, a. Deeply felt.

hearth, härth, n. The floor of a fireplace, usu. of brick or stone; the fireside; the home.

hearth·stone, härth′stōn, n. The stone forming the hearth.

heart·less, härt′lis, a. Destitute of feeling; cruel. **—heart·less·ly,** adv. **—heart·less·ness,** n.

heart·rend·ing, härt′ren·ding, a. Grievous; overpowering with anguish.

heart·sick, härt′sik, a. Sick at heart; deeply grieved or depressed.

heart·strings, härt′stringz, n. pl. The strongest emotions or feelings.

heart-to-heart, härt′tə·härt′, a. Candid; intimate.

heart·y, här′tē, a., **-i·er, -i·est.** Sincere; warm; cordial; zealous; sound and healthy; substantial or large to satisfaction: a hearty meal. **—heart·i·ly,** adv. **—heart·i·ness,** n.

heat, hēt, n. A quality of being hot; hotness or warmth; a degree of warmth; temperature; depth of feeling; utmost ardor or violence; agitation or stress; period of sexual ardor in female animals: estrus; single effort as in a race.—v.t. To make hot or warm; stimulate emotionally.—v.i. To become emotionally excited.

heat·ed, hē′tid, a. With intensity of feeling.

heat·er, hē′tər, *n.* One who or that which heats.

heath, hēth, *n.* A tract of open, uncultivated wasteland, often overgrown with heather and other shrubs.

hea·then, hē′thən, *n.* A member of a people which does not acknowledge the Jewish, Christian, or Islamic God; a pagan or idolater; an irreligious or unenlightened person.—*a.* Pagan; irreligious or unenlightened.

heave, hēv, *v.t.,* **heaved** or **hove, heav·ing.** To lift with effort or force; to hurl, as something heavy; to utter with effort or pain, as a sigh; to haul, draw, or pull. —*v.i.* To breathe with effort, or pant; to retch; to labor or strive to do something. *Naut.* To haul, pull or push.—*n.* The act of heaving; a lifting or upward movement; a rhythmical rise and fall, as of waves.

heav·en, hev′ən, *n.* The final place where the blessed go after death; the place where the blessed meet God; (*cap.*) God or Providence. Supreme felicity; bliss; a sublime condition; the blue expanse which surrounds the earth, and in which the sun, moon, and stars seem to be set. *Usu. pl.* The sky; the upper regions.

heav·en·ly, hev′ən·lē, *a.* Celestial; beautiful; delightful; very happy; holy; divine; relating to the physical heavens.

heav·en·ward, hev′ən·wərd, *adv. a.* Toward heaven. —**heav·en·wards,** *adv.*

heav·y, hev′ē, *a.,* **-i·er, -i·est.** Of great weight; of great amount: a *heavy* vote; of great force or intensity: *heavy* sleep; being such in an unusual degree: a *heavy* drinker; of more than the usual, average, or specified weight; having much weight in proportion to bulk; grave or serious, as a fault or offense; grievous or distressing; oppressive; depressed with trouble, sorrow, or care: a *heavy* heart; drooping with weariness, as the eyelids; weighted or laden: air *heavy* with moisture; big with young; sober, serious, or somber, as a role. —**heav·i·ly,** *adv.* —**heav·i·ness,** *n.*

heav·y-du·ty, hev′ē·doo′tē, hev′ē·dū′tē, *a.* Constructed to withstand extremely hard usage or great physical stress.

heav·y-hand·ed, hev′ē·han′did, *a.* Harsh; stern; demanding; clumsy.

heav·y-heart·ed, hev′ē·här′tid, *a.* Defeated; melancholy; mournful.

heav·y·weight, hev′ē·wāt, *n.* A boxer, wrestler, or other athlete of the heaviest class, usu. more than 175 pounds; a person considerably above average weight. *Informal.* Anyone of superior intelligence, education, or skill.—*a.*

He·brew, hē′broo, *n.* A member of that branch of the Semites descended from the line of Abraham; an Israelite; a Jew; the language of ancient and now modern Israel.—*a.* —**He·bra·ic,** hi·brā′ik, *a.* —**He·bra·i·cal·ly,** *adv.*

heck·le, hek′əl, *v.t.,* **-led, -ling.** To harass by interrupting, as a public speaker; badger. —**heck·ler,** *n.*

hec·tare, hek′tār, *n.* In the metric system, a unit of land area equal to 100 ares or 2.471 acres.

hec·tic, hek′tik, *a.* Pertaining to undue turmoil; having a fluctuating fever. —**hec·ti·cal·ly,** *adv.*

hec·to·gram, hek′tə·gram, *n.* In the metric system, a unit of mass equal to 100 grams or 3.527 avoirdupois ounces.

hec·to·li·ter, hek′tə·lē·tər, *n.* In the metric system, a unit of capacity equal to 100 liters, equivalent to 1.056 liquid quarts, or 0.908 dry quart.

hec·to·me·ter, hek′tə·mē·tər, *n.* In the metric system, a unit of length equal to 100 meters or 328 feet.

he'd, hēd, *unstressed* ēd. Contraction of **he had** or **he would.**

hedge, hej, *n.* A fence or barrier formed by dense bushes or small trees; any line of shrubbery closely planted; any barrier; a means of protection against a loss, as of a wager, through a counterbalancing ac-

tion; a guarded statement.—*v.t.,* **hedged, hedg·ing.** To enclose; to obstruct; to hem in; to protect against a loss through a counterbalancing action.—*v.i.* To plant or care for a hedge; to avoid a direct statement. —**hedg·er,** *n.*

he·don·ism, hēd′ə·niz·əm *n.* The doctrine that the chief good lies in the pursuit of pleasure; the psychological theory that man's actions are governed by a desire to experience pleasant feelings and avoid pain. —**he·don·ist,** *n.* —**he·do·nis·tic,** hē·də·nis′tik, *a.*

heed, hēd, *v.t.* To listen to with care; to take notice of; to attend to.—*v.i.* To give attention.—*n.* Care; attention; notice: often preceded by *give* or *take.*

hee·haw, hē′hô, *n.* The braying sound made by an ass; rude laughter; a guffaw.—*v.i.* To utter heehaws.

heel, hēl, *v.i.* To incline from a vertical position, as a ship.—*v.t.* To cause to tilt.—*n.* The act of inclining; the hind part of the foot; the hind part of a shoe or stocking; the solid portion attached to the sole at the rear of a shoe or boot; something shaped like a human heel, or that occupies a corresponding position, as the crust of a loaf of bread. *Informal.* A loathsome individual.—*v.t.* To add a heel to; to follow closely; to furnish with something, as money.—*v.i.* To follow closely. —**at one's heels,** close behind. —**down at the heels,** shabby.

heft, heft, *n.* Weight; bulk.—*v.t.* To raise high; to measure the weight of by hoisting.

heft·y, hef′tē, *a.,* **-i·er, -i·est.** Strong; heavy; large in bulk.

he·gem·o·ny, hi·jem′ə·nē, hej′ə·mō·nē, *n. pl.,* **-nies.** Leadership; predominance; preponderance of one state among several. —**heg·e·mon·ic,** hej·ə·mon′ik, *a.*

he·gi·ra, hi·jī′rə, hej′ər·ə, *n.* Any flight, usu. to escape danger. (*Cap.*) The flight of Mohammed from Mecca in 622 A.D.; the Moslem era. Also **he·ji·ra, He·ji·ra.**

heif·er, hef′ər, *n.* A young cow that has not borne a calf.

height, hīt, *n.* The state or condition of being tall; the vertical distance from the lowest level to a given point; altitude or elevation; stature, as applied to living creatures. *Pl.* The highest point: He reached the *heights* of his profession. *Often pl.* Utmost degree in advancement; a place of elevation.

height·en, hīt′ən, *v.t.* To make or raise higher; to increase; to augment; to intensify.—*v.i.* To become great or greater in amount, degree, or extent. —**height·en·er,** *n.*

hei·nous, hā′nəs, *a.* Completely abominable; utterly detestable; thoroughly evil. —**hei·nous·ly,** *adv.* —**hei·nous·ness,** *n.*

heir, âr, *n.* One who inherits or is entitled to inherit.

heir ap·par·ent, *n. pl.,* **heirs ap·par·ent.** An heir who is legally certain to inherit, provided he survives the ancestor.

heir·ess, *n.* A female heir, esp. one inheriting or expected to inherit considerable wealth.

heir·loom, âr′loom, *n.* Any possession transmitted from generation to generation.

heist, hīst, *v.t. Informal.* To burglarize; to rob.—*n. Informal.* A robbery; a theft.

hel·i·cop·ter, hel′ə·kop·tər, *n.* An aircraft sustained in the air by engine-propelled blades rotating on a vertical axis, capable of moving vertically as well as horizontally.

he·li·um, hē′lē·əm, *n.* A gaseous, inert element, nonflammable and lighter than air.

he·lix, hē′liks, *n. pl.,* **hel·i·ces,** hel′i·sēz, **he·lix·es.** A spiral line, as of wire in a coil; something that is spiral.

hell, hel, *n.* The abode of evil and condemned spirits; the place or state of punishment of the wicked after death; any state of torment or misery: a *hell* on earth.

Informal. An extreme condition; as, a *hell* of a mess. —*interj.* An expression of disgust or impatience. —**give some·one hell,** *informal.* To rebuke severely. —**raise hell,** *informal.* To cause a commotion; to object vehemently.

he'll, hĕl, *unstressed* ĕl,hil,il. Contraction of **he will** or **he shall.**

hell-bent, hel′bent, *a. Informal.* Stubbornly determined; going ahead regardless of consequences.

hell·cat, hel′kat, *n.* A shrew or hag.

hel·lion, hel′yən, *n. Informal.* A mischievous person; an unruly troublemaker.

hell·ish, hel′ish, *a.* Pertaining to hell; infernal; malignant; wicked; detestable. —**hell·ish·ly,** *adv.* —**hell·ish·ness,** *n.*

hel·lo, he·lō′, hə·lō′, hel′ō, *interj.* A greeting or an exclamation to attract attention; an exclamation of surprise.—*n. pl.,* **-los.**

helm, helm, *n.* The instruments by which a ship is steered, consisting of a rudder, a tiller, and in large vessels a wheel; in a limited sense, the tiller or wheel; the place of direction, management, or control.—*v.t.* To steer; to guide. —**helm·less,** *a.*

hel·met, hel′mit, *n.* A defensive covering for the head, worn by participants in dangerous sports or by motorcyclists, etc.; head armor composed of metal, leather, or plastic. —**hel·met·ed,** *a.*

helms·man, helmz′mən, *n. pl.,* **-men.** The man who steers a ship.

help, help, *v.t.* To provide assistance to; to contribute aid to; to cooperate with; to relieve; to remedy; to benefit; to promote; to be of use to; to avoid or prevent, usu. with *cannot:* You *can't help* but laugh; to serve; to furnish with; to appropriate for use: *help* myself to.—*v.i.* To be of use; to give aid or assistance: Every little bit *helps.*—*n.* Aid; assistance; remedy; succor; one who gives assistance; a hired servant; collectively, a group of servants.—*interj.* A call for aid. —**help out,** to be of assistance. —**help·er,** *n.*

help·ful, help′fəl, *a.* Beneficial; useful; rendering aid. —**help·ful·ly,** *adv.* —**help·ful·ness,** *n.*

help·ing, hel′ping, *n.* A single serving of food. —**help·ing hand,** assistance.

help·less, help′lis, *a.* Defenseless; weak; affording no help; perplexed or bewildered. —**help·less·ly,** *adv.* —**help·less·ness,** *n.*

help·mate, help′māt, *n.* An assistant; a helper; a husband or wife. Also **help·meet.**

hel·ter-skel·ter, hel′tər-skel′tər, *adv.* In confused haste; in a disordered way or manner.—*n.* Disorder; confusion.—*a.* Marked by confusion; hurried.

hem, hem, *n.* The border of a piece of cloth, made by doubling over the edge and sewing it down; any edge, border, margin.—*v.t.,* **hemmed, hem·ming.** —**hem in,** to enclose and confine.

hem, hem, *interj.* An exclamation, consisting of a sort of half-cough, expressing embarrassment or used to attract attention; ahem.—*v.i.* To make such a sound; to hesitate or stammer in speaking.

he-man, hē′man, *n. pl.,* **he-men.** A man notably muscular and tough.—*a.* Markedly virile.

hem·i·sphere, hem′i·sfēr, *n.* One half of a sphere or globe; half of the terrestrial or of the celestial globe. —**hem·i·spher·ic,** hem·i·sfēr′ik, **hem·i·spher·i·cal,** *a.*

hem·lock, hem′lok, *n.* An evergreen coniferous tree in the pine family; the softwood of this tree; any of various poisonous herbaceous plants, as water-*hemlock* and poison-*hemlock.*

he·mo·glo·bin, hae·mo·glo·bin, hē′mə·glō′bin, hem′ə·glō·bin, *n.* A red pigment in the red blood corpuscles, composed of iron-containing protein matter which carries oxygen.

he·mo·phil·i·a, hae·mo·phil·i·a, hē·mə·fil′ē·ə, hem·ə·fēl′yə, *n.* An inherited defect that leads to excessive bleeding due to deficiency of a coagulant factor in the blood.

hem·or·rhage, hem′ər·ij, hem′rij, *n.* A rapid and heavy flow of blood from a ruptured blood vessel. —*v.i.,* **-rhaged, -rhag·ing.** To bleed heavily. —**hem·or·rhag·ic,** hem·ə·raj′ik, *a.*

hem·or·rhoid, haem·or·rhoid, hem′ə·royd, hem′royd, *n. Usu. pl.* A swelling formed by the dilatation of a blood vessel at the anus. Also **piles.** —**hem·or·rhoi·dal, haem·or·rhoi·dal,** *a.*

hemp, hemp, *n.* A tall annual herb; the female plant, from which hashish and marijuana are produced; the tough fiber of the male plant, from which coarse fabrics and rope are made; any of various plants similar to or yielding hemp fibers: as, sisal *hemp. Informal.* A hangman's rope. —**hemp·en,** *a.*

hem·stitch, hem′stich, *v.t.* To embroider along a line from which threads have been drawn out, gathering the remaining threads so as to form decorative patterns.—*n.*

hen, hen, *n.* The female domestic barnyard fowl; the female of other related birds, the lobster, and some fishes. *Informal.* Any woman, esp. a fussy older woman.

hence, hens, *adv.* From this place; from this time; therefore; thus; consequently.

hence·forth, hens′fôrth′, hens′fōrth, *adv.* From this time forward. Also **hence·for·ward,** hens·fôr′wərd.

hench·man, hench′mən, *n. pl.,* **-men.** A trusted attendant or follower; a close and obedient adherent, esp. one who carries out without scruple the instructions of a leader, usu. for personal gain. —**hench·man·ship,** *n.*

hen·na, hen′ə, *n.* A tropical plant; a dye made from the leaves of this plant and formerly used to tint hair red, now chiefly for dyeing fabrics and leather; the color of henna, a rich brownish red.—*v.t.* To color with henna dye or paste.

hen par·ty, *n. Informal.* A women's social gathering.

hen·peck, hen′pek, *v.t.* To dominate, nag, or persistently annoy, as one's husband.

hep, hep, *a. Informal.* Knowledgeable about the latest ideas, styles, or developments.

hep·a·ti·tis, hep·ə·tī′tis, *n.* Inflammation of the liver.

her, hər, *unstressed* ər, *pron.* The objective case of **she,** as: I love *her.*—*pronominal a.* The possessive case of **she,** used as an attributive: as, *her* face. —**hers,** hərz, *pron.* A possessive case of **she** used, instead of *her* and a noun, as subject, object, or predicate.

her·self, hər·self′, *pron.* A reflexive or emphatic form of the third pers. sing. fem. pron.: She improved *herself.* She *herself* is to blame. A denotation of a usual or customary state: She wasn't *herself* all evening.

her·ald, her′əld, *n.* Formerly an officer or ambassador responsible for carrying messages between leaders, esp. in war; one who proclaims or announces; a bearer of messages; a forerunner.—*v.t.* To introduce or to give tidings of, as by a herald; to proclaim. —**he·ral·dic,** he·ral′dik, *a.*

her·ald·ry, her′əl·drē, *n. pl.,* **-ries.** The science of armorial bearings; heraldic pomp or ceremony.

herb, ərb, hərb, *n.* Any plant with a soft or succulent stem which dies to the root every year; any similar plant, esp. used in medicines, scents, or seasonings. —**her·ba·ceous,** hər·bā′shəs, ər·bā′shəs, *a.*

her·bage, ər′bij, hər′bij, *n.* Herbs collectively; grass and other nonwoody growths.

her·biv·o·rous, hər·biv′ər·əs, *a.* Subsisting on plants.

her·cu·le·an, hər·kū′lē·ən, hər·kyə·lē′ən, *a.* Very great in strength, courage, vigor, or size; very difficult to perform: a *herculean* task.

herd, hərd, *n.* A group of animals, usu. of one kind, traveling, feeding, or kept together; the masses of common people.—*v.t., v.i.* To assemble in a group; to gather together; to care for; to drive. —**herd·er,** *n.*

herds·man, hərdz′mən, *n. pl.,* **-men.** A keeper of a

herd; one who tends or breeds livestock. Also **herd•er.**

here, hĕr, *adv.* In or at this particular place; towards this place, as: *Here* comes Mary; now; at this point, as: We'll stop the lesson *here*; in this life; used emphatically or indicatively, as: John *here* is a lawyer. *Here* is your pen.—*interj.* Present, as in answering a roll call.—*n.* This place; this world; this life.

here•af•ter, hĕr•ăf′tər, hĕr•äf′tər, *adv.* After this in order or time; in time to come; in the world to come.—*n.* Life after death; the future.

he•red•i•tar•y, hə•red′ə•ter•ē, *a.* Inherited; descending from genetic inheritance; transmitted or transmissible in the line of descent by force of law; holding a title or position by inheritance. **—he•red•i•tar•i•ly,** hə•red•ə•tär′ə•lē, *adv.* **—he•red•i•tar•i•ness,** *n.*

he•red•i•ty, hə•red′ə•tē, *n. pl.,* **-ties.** Inheritance; tradition; the transmission of characteristics of parents to offspring.

here•in, hĕr•in′, *adv.* In this; in here; in this case; into here.

here•of, hĕr•əv′, hĕr•ov′, *adv.* Concerning this; of this; about this.

her•e•sy, her′ə•sē, *n. pl.,* **-sies.** A belief opposed to the accepted doctrine of a church; a belief opposed to authoritative opinion in any area of thought.

her•e•tic, her′ə•tik, *n.* One who holds religious opinions contrary to the doctrines of his church; a dissenter from accepted beliefs or dogma of any kind. Also **he•ret•i•cal.—heret•i•cal•ly,** *adv.*

here•to, hĕr•too′, *adv.* To this, as to place, thing, document, or circumstance.

here•to•fore, hĕr′tə•fōr, hĕr′tə•fôr, *adv.* Previously; formerly; up to now.

here•up•on, hĕr′ə•pon, hĕr′ə•pôn, *adv.* Following immediately after this.

here•with, hĕr•with′, hĕr•with′, *adv.* With this; by means of this.

her•it•a•ble, her′ə•tə•bəl, *a.* Capable of being inherited; inheritable. **—her•it•a•bil•i•ty,** her•ə•tə•bil′ə•tē, *n.* **—her•it•a•bly,** *adv.*

her•it•age, her′ə•tij, *n.* A legacy, as a culture or tradition; that which may be inherited through the legal process, as property or land.

her•maph•ro•dite, hər•maf′rə•dīt, *n.* An animal or human being having the sexual characteristics of both male and female.—*a.* Including or being of both sexes. **—her•maph•ro•dit•ic,** hər•maf•rə•dit′ik, *a.* **—her•maph•ro•dit•i•cal•ly,** *adv.* **—her•maph•ro•dit•ism,** *n.*

her•met•ic, hər•met′ik, *a.* Airtight. Also **her•met•i•cal. —her•met•i•cal•ly,** *adv.*

her•mit, hər′mit, *n.* A recluse; any person living in seclusion, esp. religious seclusion.

her•mit•age, hər′mə•tij, *n.* The habitation of a hermit; any secluded habitation.

her•ni•a, hər′nē•ə, *n.* The projection of any internal organ or tissue through an abnormal aperture in the wall which encloses it, usu. in the abdominal area. Also **rup•ture. —her•ni•al,** *a.* **—her•ni•a•tion,** hər•nē•ā′shən, *n.*

he•ro, hĕr′ō, *n. pl.,* **he•roes.** A man of distinguished valor or fortitude; a man admired for his noble deeds or qualities; the principal male character in a poem, story, play, or the like.

he•ro•ic, hi•rō′ik, *a.* Pertaining to heroes; characteristic of or befitting a hero, as conduct; daring. Also **he•ro•i•cal.—n.** Heroic verse; bombast. **—he•ro•i•cal•ly,** *adv.*

her•o•in, her′ō•in, *n.* A morphine derivative, white, odorless, and crystalline, and a dangerously addictive narcotic.

her•o•ine, her′ō•in, *n.* A woman that is heroic; a major female character in a play or story.

her•o•ism, her′ō•iz•əm, *n.* The qualities of a hero or

heroine; heroic conduct.

her•on, her′ən, *n.* Any of the wading birds having long bills, necks, and legs.

her•ring•bone, her′ing•bōn, *n.* A pattern made up of slanting parallel lines in rows, thus resembling the ribs of the herring, often used in textile weaves, embroidery, or masonry.—*a.* Resembling the spine of a herring.—*v.t.,* **-boned, -bon•ing.** To put a herringbone design in or on.—*v.i.* To create a herringbone pattern.

hers, hərz, *pron.* See **her.**

her•self, hər•self′, *pron.* A reflexive or emphatic form of the third pers. sing. fem. pron.: She improved *herself,* she *herself* is to blame; a denotation of a usual or customary state: She wasn't *herself* all evening.

he's, hēz, *unstressed* ēz. Contraction of **he is** or **he has.**

hes•i•tant, hez′ə•tənt, *a.* Hesitating; wanting readiness of speech; lacking certainty. **—hes•i•tan•cy,** hez′ə•tən•sē, *n. pl.,* **-cies.** Also **hes•i•tance. —hes•i•tant•ly,** *adv.*

hes•i•tate, hez′i•tāt, *v.i.,* **-tat•ed, -tat•ing.** To stop or pause; to be reluctant in decision or action; to be doubtful as to fact, principle, or determination; To stammer; to stop in speaking. **—hes•i•tat•er, hes•i•ta•tor,** *n.* **—hes•i•tat•ing•ly,** *adv.*

hes•i•ta•tion, hez•ə•tā′shən, *n.* The act of pausing; a state of indecision; a pause or stammer in speech.

het•er•o•dox, het′ər•ə•doks, *a.* Contrary to established or generally accepted doctrines, standards, or opinions, esp. in theology. **—het•er•o•dox•y,** *n.*

het•er•o•ge•ne•ous, het•ər•ə•jē′nē•əs, *a.* Differing in kind; having dissimilar elements. **—het•er•o•ge•ne•i•ty,** het•ər•ə•jə•nē′ə•tē, **het•er•o•ge•ne•ous•ness,** *n.* **—het•er•o•ge•ne•ous•ly,** *adv.*

het•er•o•sex•u•al, het•ər•ə•sek′shoo•əl, *a.* Of or pertaining to sexual orientation toward the opposite sex; pertaining to different sexes.—*n.* One who is heterosexual. **—het•er•o•sex•u•al•i•ty,** het•ər•ə•sek•shoo•al′ə•tē, *n.*

het up, het′əp′, *a. Informal.* Distraught; excited.

hew, hū, *v.t.,* **hewed, hewed** or **hewn, hew•ing.** To chop; to hack; to cut down or fell, as trees; to shape with cutting blows; to give rough form to.—*v.i.* To deal cutting blows; to conform closely to a prescribed line of conduct. **—hew•er,** *n.*

hex, heks, *v.t.* To jinx; to bewitch; to put under an evil spell.—*n.* A jinx; a magic spell; a witch. **—hex•er,** *n.*

hex•a•gon, hek′sə•gon, *n.* A plane figure having six angles and six sides. **—hex•ag•o•nal,** hek•sag′ə•nəl, *a.* **—hex•ag•o•nal•ly,** *adv.*

hey, hā, *interj.* An exclamation, used to express joy or surprise and to call attention.

hey•day, hey•dey, hā′dā, *n.* A time or period of best condition, strength, or creativity; prime.

hi, hī, *interj.* Hello.

hi•a•tus, hī•ā′təs, *n. pl.,* **hi•a•tus•es** or **hi•a•tus.** An interruption or break in continuity.

hi•ba•chi, hi•bä′chē, *n.* A small cast-iron charcoal stove or brazier used for cooking and heating.

hi•ber•nate, hī′bər•nāt, *v.i.,* **-nat•ed, -nat•ing.** To pass the winter in a suspended, dormant, or torpid condition. **—hi•ber•na•tion,** hī•bər•nā′shən, *n.*

hi•bis•cus, hī•bis′kəs, hi•bis′kəs, *n.* A plant of the mallow family, with large, showy, colored flowers.

hic•cup, hik′əp, *n.* A quick, involuntary intake of breath suddenly checked by closure of the glottis, producing a characteristic sound; *usu. pl.,* an attack of such spasms.—*v.i.,* **-cuped** or **-cupped, -cup•ing** or **-cup•ping.** To make the sound of a hiccup; to be affected with hiccups. Also **hic•cough,** hik′əp.

hick, hik, *n. Informal.* An unsophisticated, usu. country person.—*a.* Pertaining to lack of sophistication.

hid•den, hid′ən, *a.* Concealed; secret; mysterious; obscure. **—hid•den•ness,** *n.*

---

a- hat, fāte, fāre, fäther; **e-** met, mē; **i-** pin, pīne; **o-** not, nōte, ôrb, moove (move), boy, pownd; **u-** cūbe, bǔll, tûk (took); **ch-** chin; **th-** thick, ŧhen; **zh-** vizhon (vision); **ə-** əgo, takən, pencəl, lemən, bərd (bird).

hide, hīd, *v.t.*, **hid, hid·den** or **hid, hid·ing.** To conceal intentionally from sight; to prevent from being observed readily; to conceal from discovery; to obstruct the view of; to keep secret.—*v.i.* To keep out of sight; to conceal oneself. **—hid·er,** *n.*

hide, hīd, *n.* The pelt of an animal, either raw or tanned. *Informal.* The human skin.

hide, hīd, *v.t.*, **hid·ed, hid·ing.** To beat, whip, or thrash; to flog. **—hid·ing,** *n.*

hide·bound, hīd′bownd, *a.* Narrow-minded.

hid·e·ous, hīd′ē·əs, *a.* Extremely ugly; shocking in a moral way; detestable; horrible. **—hid·e·ous·ly,** *adv.* **—hid·e·ous·ness,** *n.*

hide·out, hīd′owt, *a.* A spot used for concealment, esp. as refuge from the authorities.

hie, hī, *v.i.*, **hied, hie·ing** or **hy·ing.** To hasten.—*v.t.* To hurry: used reflexively.

hi·er·ar·chy, hī′ə·rär·kē, *n. pl.,* **-chies.** A ranking of individuals according to their authority or function in a church or government; a logical arrangement of scientific or other items. **—hi·er·ar·chal,** hī·ər·är′kəl, **hi·er·ar·chic, hi·er·ar·chi·cal,** *a.* **—hi·er·ar·chi·cal·ly,** *adv.*

hi·er·o·glyph·ic, hī·ər·ə·glif′ik, hī·rə·glif′ik, · *a.* Pertaining to pictographic inscriptions used in ancient Egyptian records; mysteriously symbolic. Also **hi·er·o·glyph·i·cal.**—*n.* A picture or character representing a word or idea. Also **hi·er·o·glyph,** hī′ər·ə·glif. **—hi·er·o·glyph·i·cal·ly,** *adv.*

hi-fi, hī′fī′, *n.* Equipment used in reproducing sound with high fidelity.—*a.*

high, hī, *a.* Lofty; elevated; tall; situated far above the ground or some other base level; exalted in rank or estimation; lofty: as, *high* resolves; grave: as, *high* treason; principal or main; luxurious: as, *high* living; of great amount, degree, or force: as, a *high* price, *high* speed; expensive; denoted by a high number: as a *high* latitude; advanced to the utmost extent: as, *high* noon; fully advanced: as, *high* time to begin work; haughty; extreme in opinion; merry: as, *high* spirits; acute in pitch, as a note; shrill. *Informal.* Excited with drink.—*adv.* At or to a high point, place, level, rank, amount, or degree.—*n.* A position of height, as: The stocks reached a new *high*; a transmission gear in an automobile enabling rapid speed. **—high and low,** everywhere. **—on high,** at or to a height; above.

high·ball, hī′bôl, *n.* An iced alcoholic drink composed of liquor mixed with a carbonated beverage or water and served in a tall glass.—*v.i. Informal.* Of a train, to move at high or full speed.

high·born, hī′bôrn, *a.* Being of noble birth.

high·boy, hī′boy, *n.* A tall chest of drawers supported on legs.

high·brow, hī′brow, *n. Informal.* An intellectual person or one with intellectual pretensions: sometimes used in a derogatory sense.—*a.* Also **high·browed.** **—high·brow·ism,** *n.*

high·er-up, hī′ər·əp, *n. pl.,* **high·er-ups.** A person of superior rank, importance, or authority in any organization.

high·fa·lu·tin, hī·fə·loo′tən, *a. Informal.* Pompous or bombastic. Also **high·fa·lu·ting, hi·fa·lu·tin, hi·fa·lu·ting.**

high fi·del·i·ty, *n.* The reproduction of sound with minimal distortion of the original signals. Also **hi·fi.**

high-flown, hī′flōn′, *a.* Extravagant or pompous in language or taste; pretentious.

high-grade, hī′grād′, *a.* Of excellent quality.

high-hand·ed, high-hand·ed, hī′han′did, *a.* Oppressive; domineering; arbitrary. **—high-hand·ed·ly,** *adv.* **—high-hand·ed·ness,** *n.*

high-hat, hī′hat′, *a. Informal.* Condescending; arrogant; proud.—*v.t.,* **-hat·ted, -hat·ting.** To snub.

high·land, hī′lənd, *n.* An elevated or mountainous region.—*a.* Pertaining to or characteristic of a lofty, hilly region.

high·light, hī′līt, *n.* An interesting, important, or conspicuous point in an activity, scene, or the like.—*v.t.* To feature; focus one's attention on; to illuminate or give highlights to.

high-mind·ed, hī′mīn′did, *a.* Characterized by lofty principles and feelings; honorable; magnanimous. **—high-mind·ed·ly,** *adv.* **—high-mind·ed·ness,** *n.*

high·ness, hī′nis, *n.* Height; (*cap.*) a form of address for royalty or for others of high rank: used with *His, Her,* or *Your.*

high-pres·sure, hī′presh′ər, *a.* Having, exerting, or involving a pressure much greater than that of the atmosphere. *Informal.* Intense, pressing, and insistent: as, a *high-pressure* salesman.—*v.t.,* **-sured, -sur·ing.** To influence or persuade by aggressive tactics.

high rise, hī′rīz, *n.* A multistoried building, usu. an apartment building. **—high-rise,** *a.*

high school, *n. U.S.* The level of education usu. including grades 9 or 10 through 12. **—high-school,** *a.*

high seas, *n. pl.* The sea or ocean, lying outside the territorial jurisdiction of any nation. **—high-sea,** *a.*

high-spir·it·ed, hī′spir′ə·tid, *a.* Courageous; bold; energetic; elated. **—high-spir·it·ed·ly,** *adv.* **—high-spir·it·ed·ness,** *n.*

high-strung, hī′strəng′, *a.* Nervous or excitable.

high·tail, hī′tāl, *v.i. Informal.* To run away, usu. followed by *it.*

high-ten·sion, hī′ten′shən, *a.* Capable of carrying or operating under high voltage.

high tide, *n.* The tide at its highest level; the time that the tide reaches this point.

high-toned, hī′tōnd′, *a.* High-principled; dignified; excessively stylish.

high·way, hī′wā, *n.* A public road; any principal route, whether on water or land.

high·way·man, hī′wā·mən, *n. pl.,* **-men.** A person who robbed others along a highway.

hi·jack, high·jack, hī′jak, *v.t., v.i.* To rob in transit, as a person; to take by force, as something in transit: to *hijack* an aircraft. **—hi·jack·er,** *n.* **—hi·jack·ing,** *n.*

hike, hīk, *v.i.,* **hiked, hik·ing.** To walk for exercise or pleasure, esp. a long distance.—*v.t. Informal.* To move or raise with a sudden jerk, often with *up*; to increase, as prices, often with *up.*—*n.* A march or constitutional; a walk. *Informal.* An increase or rise. **—hik·er,** *n.*

hi·lar·i·ous, hi·lar′ē·əs, hī·lar′ē·əs, *a.* Very funny; laughter-inducing. **—hi·lar·i·ous·ly,** *adv.* **—hi·lar·i·ous·ness,** *n.* **—hi·lar·i·ty,** hi·lar′ə·tē, hī·lar′ə·tē, *n.*

hill, hil, *n.* A natural elevation of the earth's surface much smaller than a mountain; an artificial heap; a heap of earth packed at the roots of a young plant for support.—*v.t.* To form into a hill or a heap; to surround with hills, as plants. **—hill·y,** *a.,* **-i·er, -i·est.** *a.*

hill·bil·ly, hil′bil·ē, *n. pl.,* **-lies.** *Informal.* A rustic or unsophisticated person originating or residing in a deprived backwoods area, usu. in or from the mountains of the southern U.S.

hill·ock, hil′ək, *n.* A small hill.

hill·side, hil′sīd, *n.* The side or slope of a hill.

hill·top, hil′top, *n.* The top of a hill.

hilt, hilt, *n.* The handle of a sword or dagger; the handle of any weapon or tool.

him, him, *pron.* The objective case of **he.**

him·self, him·self′, *pron.* A form of him. A reflexive or emphatic form of **he,** as: He struck himself. A denotation of his usual state, as: He is not *himself* at all.

hind, hīnd, *n. pl.,* **hinds, hind.** The female of the deer, chiefly the red deer, esp. in and after the third year.

hind, hīnd, *a.,* **hind·er, hind·most** or **hind·er·most.** Pertaining to or situated at the part which follows or is behind; rear.

hin·der, hin′dər, *v.t.* To obstruct or impede; to thwart or stop; to interrupt.—*v.i.* To serve as an obstacle or impediment. **—hind·er·er,** *n.*

hind·er, hīn′dər, *a.* In the rear; at the back.

hind·most, hīnd′mōst, *a.* Farthest behind.

hind·quar·ter, hīnd′kwor·tər, *n.* One of the posterior

quarters when a half carcass of beef or lamb is sectioned; *pl.*, the rump.

hin·drance, hin′drəns, *n.* The act of delaying or thwarting; impediment.

hind·sight, hīnd′sīt, *n.* Perception, understanding, or judgment of an incident after it has happened.

Hin·du, hin′doo, *n.* Any adherent of Hinduism; in general, any native of Hindustan.—*a.* Of or pertaining to the Hindus or Hinduism.

Hin·du·ism, hin′doo·iz·əm, *n.* The religious and social system of the Hindus. Also **Hin·doo·ism.**

hinge, hinj, *n.* The movable joint or device on which a door, gate, or the like turns or moves; a natural joint. Also **hinge joint.**—*v.t.,* **hinged, hing·ing.** To furnish with or attach by a hinge.—*v.i.* To hang or turn on, or as on, a hinge; to depend, usu. followed by *on.*

hint, hint, *n.* A suggestion; something insinuated rather than said; a clue; a small amount of something.—*v.t.* To suggest indirectly.—*v.i.* To allude indirectly: usu. followed by *at.* —**hint·er,** *n.* —**hint·ing·ly,** *adv.*

hin·ter·land, hin′tər·land, *n.* Land lying behind a coastal district; country remote from urban centers; interior or back country.

hip, hip, *n.* The side of the pelvis and upper region of the thigh with their fleshy covering parts; the haunch; the hip joint.

hip, hip, *a. Informal.* Familiar with current trends and happenings.

hipped, hipt, *a. Informal.* Having a mental obsession: as, *hipped* on modern art.

hip·pie, hip′ē, *n.* A young adult, usu. nonconformist in dress and behavior, and characterized esp. by pacifistic, anarchistic, anti-intellectual, or anti-establishment opinions or outlooks.

hip·po, hip′ō, *n. pl.,* **-pos.** *Informal.* Hippopotamus.

hip·po·drome, hip′ə·drōm, *n.* Any area or structure for equestrian and other displays, circuses, and the like.

hip·po·pot·a·mus, hip·ə·pot′ə·məs, *n. pl.,* **-mus·es, -mi,** -mī. A large plant-eating mammal having a thick-skinned, hairless body, short legs, and large head and muzzle.

hire, hīr, *v.t.* To engage the services or labor of in exchange for payment.—*v.i.* To engage oneself for a compensation, often with *out.*—*n.* The price paid or contracted to be paid for the use of something or for personal services or labor; the act of hiring or the fact of being hired. —**hir·er,** *n.*

hire·ling, hīr′ling, *n.* One serving for hire; a mercenary: used in contempt.—*a.* Serving or to be had for hire.

hir·sute, hər′soot, *a.* Hairy; shaggy. —**hir·sute·ness,** *n.*

his, hiz. The possessive case of the personal pronoun **he:** *his* picture.—*pron.* Of or belonging to him: That's *his.*

hiss, his, *v.i.* To make a sound like that of the letter s; to emit a similar sound in disapprobation.—*v.t.* To utter with a hissing sound; to express disapproval by hissing; to silence by uttering a hissing sound, often with *down* or *off.*—*n.* The sound made by propelling the breath between the tongue and upper teeth, as in pronouncing the letter *s,* especially as expressive of disapprobation; any similar sound. —**hiss·er,** *n.*

hist, hist, *interj.* A sibilant exclamation used to attract attention or command silence.

his·ta·mine, his′tə·mēn, his′tə·min, *n.* An amine, found in the tissue of all plants and animals and released during allergic reactions. —**his·ta·min·ic,** his·tə·min′ik, *a.*

his·to·ri·an, hi·stôr′ē·ən, hi·stōr′ē·ən, *n.* A writer of history, an authority in history; one who compiles records or documents for a particular purpose; a chronicler.

his·tor·ic, hi·stôr′ik, hi·stor′ik, *a.* Celebrated in history; memorable; historical.

his·tor·i·cal, hi·stôr′ə·kəl, hi·stor′ə·kəl, *a.* Of or pertaining to history; in accordance with history, esp. as opposed to legend or fiction; using history as a basis: a *historical* novel; noted or celebrated in history: historic. —**his·tor·i·cal·ly,** *adv.* —**his·tor·i·cal·ness,** *n.*

his·to·ry, his′tə·rē, his′trē, *n. pl.,* **-ries.** That branch of knowledge which deals with past events; an account of past events in the life of a nation, community, institution, or the like; the sum total of past happenings; any past filled with unusual or memorable happenings.

his·tri·on·ic, his·trē·on′ik, *a.* Pertaining to actors or to acting; theatrical; affected; melodramatic. Also **his·tri·on·i·cal.** —**his·tri·on·i·cal·ly,** *adv.*

his·tri·on·ics, his·trē·on′iks, *n. pl., sing. or pl. in constr.* Dramatics; affected behavior; an insincere display of emotion.

hit, hit, *v.t.,* **hit, hit·ting.** To deal a blow to; to come against with an impact; to reach with a missile, a weapon, a blow, or the like; to strike with a bat; to drive or propel by a stroke; affect severely: to be badly *hit* in a financial panic. *Informal.* To attain or arrive at: to *hit* shore; to demand, as money, from.—*v.i.* To deal a blow or blows; to strike with a missile or weapon; to come into collision, often with *against, on,* or *upon*; to come to light, with *upon* or *on.*—*n.* An impact, collision, or blow; any shot that reaches its objective; an effective remark or expression; one who or that which is a noted success: His new album is a big *hit*; a stroke of good fortune; a base hit.

hit-and-run, hit′ən·ren, *a.* Designating the driver of a vehicle who fails to stop upon being involved in an accident.

hitch, hich, *v.t.* To fasten temporarily by a knot or hook; to harness or yoke to a vehicle; to jerk or raise up. *Informal.* To hitchhike; to marry.—*v.i.* To move jerkily or haltingly; to become entangled, caught, or hooked; to be linked or yoked; to hitchhike.—*n.* A sudden jerk, tug, or catch; an unexpected hindrance in plans; a device for attaching something temporarily. *Informal.* A period spent in military service; a ride or lift. —**hitch·er,** *n.*

hitch·hike, hich′hīk, *v.i.,* **-hiked, -hik·ing.** To travel by signaling vehicles and obtaining free rides.—*v.t.* —**hitch·hik·er,** *n.*

hith·er, hith′ər, *adv.* To this place; here.—*a.* On this side or in this direction; nearer.

hith·er·to, hith′ər·too, *adv.* To this time; until now.

hive, hīv, *n.* An artificial shelter for a swarm of honeybees; a place swarming with busy occupants; the bees inhabiting a hive; a swarming or teeming multitude. —*v.t.,* **hived, hiv·ing.** To gather into a hive.—*v.i.* To enter a hive, as bees.

hives, hīvz, *n. pl., sing. or pl. in constr.* A skin condition in which there is an eruption of itching wheals over the body.

hoar, hōr, *n.* Hoarfrost; an appearance of age or venerability.

hoar·y, hōr′ē, *a.,* **-i·er, -i·est.** Gray or white as with age; of or pertaining to age or venerability. —**hoar·i·ness,** *n.*

hoard, hôrd, *n.* An accumulation of articles preserved for future use.—*v.t.* To collect and lay up in a hoard. —*v.i.* To collect and form a hoard. —**hoard·er,** *n.* —**hoard·ing,** *n.*

hoar·frost, hôr′frost, *n.* White frost; a coating of ice particles.

hoarse, hôrs, hōrs, *a.* Having a rough or grating voice; sounding husky, harsh, or gruff. —**hoarse·ly,** *adv.* —**hoars·en,** *v.t., v.i.* —**hoarse·ness,** *n.*

hoax, hōks, *n.* Something done for deception or mock-

---

a- hat, fāte, fâre, fäther; **e-** met, mē; **i-** pin, pīne; **o-** not, nōte, ôrb, moove (move), boy, pownd; **u-** cūbe, bûll, tûk (took); **ch-** chin; **th-** thick, *th*en; **zh-** vizhon (vision); **ə-** əgo, takən, pencəl, lemən, bərd (**bird**).

ery; a trick played upon another in sport; a practical joke.—*v.t.* To play a trick upon, for sport or for purposes of deception. —**hoax•er,** *n.*

hob•ble, hob⁄əl, *v.i.,* -**bled, -bling.** To move unsteadily; limp; to proceed irregularly and haltingly, as in action or speech.—*v.t.* To cause to limp; to fasten together the legs of, as a horse or mule, so as to prevent free motion; to embarrass; perplex.—*n.* A limp; a rope or strap used to hobble an animal; a fetter.

hob•by, hob⁄ē, *n. pl.,* -**bies.** An activity carried on outside of a major occupation for mere pleasure or relaxation; avocation.

hob•by-horse, hob⁄ē-hôrs, *n.* A figure of a horse, or a stick with a horse's head, ridden by children.

hob•gob•lin, hob⁄gob⁄lin, *n.* An elf; something causing unreasonable fear.

hob•nail, hob⁄nāl, *n.* A nail with a thick strong head used for the soles of heavy boots and shoes; a decorative type of knob pattern. —**hob•nailed,** *a.*

hob•nob, hob⁄nob, *v.t.,* -**nobbed, -nob•bing.** To be on a familiar basis.

ho•bo, hō⁄bō, *n. pl.,* -**boes, ho•bos.** A wanderer or vagrant; a tramp. —**ho•bo•ism,** *n.*

hock, hok, *n.* The joint in the hind leg of the horse, ox, or similar animal appearing as if bent backward.

hock, hok, *n.* Pawn. *Informal.* Prison.—*v.t. Informal.* To pawn. —**hock•er,** *n.*

hock•ey, hok⁄ē, *n.* A game played on ice in which opposing teams, on skates, use long curved sticks to try to send a small disk, called a puck, into each other's goal. Also **ice hock•ey.** A similar game played on a field with a ball rather than a puck. Also **field hock•ey.**

ho•cus-po•cus, hō⁄kəs-pō⁄kəs, *n.* Sleight of hand; trickery; a nonsense saying used to conjure or to cover up deception.

hod, hod, *n.* A kind of trough for carrying mortar and bricks.

hodge•podge, hoj⁄poj, *n.* A jumble.

hoe, hō, *n.* A long-handled tool with a thin, flat blade, used for breaking up the surface of the ground or removing weeds.—*v.t.,* **hoed, hoe•ing.** To cultivate with a hoe.—*v.i.* To work with a hoe. —**ho•er,** *n.*

hoe•down, hō⁄down, *n.* A dance featuring square and folk dances with hillbilly music.

hog, hôg, hog, *n.* A swine, esp. an adult swine raised for slaughter; a selfish, gluttonous, or filthy person. —*v.t.,* **hogged, hog•ging.** To take more than one's share.

hog•gish, hog⁄ish, hôg⁄ish, *a.* Selfish; gluttonous; filthy. —**hog•gish•ly,** *adv.* —**hog•gish•ness,** *n.*

hogs•head, hôgz⁄hed, hogz⁄hed, *n.* A large cask, esp. a cask containing from 63 to 140 gallons; a liquid measure of 63 gallons or 238.5 liters.

hog•tie, hôg⁄tī, hog⁄tī, *v.t.,* -**tied, -ty•ing.** To tie together the four feet or both hands and feet of; render ineffective.

hog•wash, hôg⁄wôsh, hog⁄wosh, *n.* Refuse or swill given to hogs. *Informal.* Any worthless stuff; senseless, exaggerated talk or writing.

hoi pol•loi, hoy•pə•loy⁄, *n.* The many; the multitude.

hoist, hoyst, *v.t.* To raise or lift, esp. by some mechanical appliance.—*n.* The act or an act of hoisting; a lift; an apparatus for hoisting; an elevator. —**hoist•er,** *n.*

ho•kum, hō⁄kəm, *n.* Material introduced into a speech or drama to promote laughter or sentiment regardless of truth or falsity; nonsense; bunk.

hold, hōld, *v.t.,* **held, hold•ing.** To have or grasp in the hand; to keep in a certain position; to consider or regard, as: I *hold* him in honor; to contain; to keep or to be in possession of; to set aside or reserve; to have or to entertain: as, to *hold* enmity; to stop, restrain, or withhold; to keep fixed, as to a certain line of action; to bind or oblige: as, to *hold* one to his promise; to carry out, as a meeting.—*v.i.* To take or keep a thing in one's grasp; to continue firm; to adhere; to stand, be

valid, or apply; to remain in force or valid—**hold forth,** to speak in public.—**hold off,** to remain aloof; to keep from touching; to delay.—**hold out,** to continue resistance; to endure; to stretch forth; offer.—**hold up,** to support; exhibit; delay; stop. *Informal.* Endure; stay firm; to stop forcibly so as to rob.—**hold wa•ter,** to be logically sound or capable of standing investigation. —**hold with,** to side or concur with.

hold, hōld, *n.* The interior of a ship below the deck.

hol•der, hōl⁄dər, *n.* Something grasped for support; a receptacle for something; a prison or prison cell.

hold•ing, hōl⁄ding, *n.* Tenure of land; *often pl.,* owned property of any kind, but esp. stocks and bonds.

hold•ing com•pa•ny, *n.* A company which owns sufficient stock in one or more other companies to influence or esp. control them.

hold•out, hōld⁄owt, *n.* One who refuses to participate.

hold•o•ver, hōld⁄ō•vər, *n. Informal.* A person who remains in possession or in office beyond the regular term; something which remains behind from a former period.

hold•up, hōld⁄əp, *n. Informal.* A forcible stopping of a person or vehicle for the purpose of robbery.

hole, hōl, *n.* A hollow place in a solid body or mass; a cavity; an excavation; an opening through anything; an aperture or perforation; an orifice; a gap or rent; a fault or flaw; the excavated habitation of an animal; a burrow; a small, dingy, or mean abode; a cell or dungeon. *Informal.* An embarrassing predicament: as, to find oneself in a *hole. Sports.* A small cavity into which a marble, ball, or the like is to be played for a score in various games.—*v.t.,* **holed, hol•ing.** To make a hole or holes; drive, as a golf ball, into a hole; to retire into a hole or hide away (with *up*). —**hole•y,** *a.*

hol•i•day, hol⁄i•dā, *n.* A commemorative day of rest fixed by law or convention; a holy day; *pl.,* a vacation or period of leave.—*a.* Pertaining to a joyous occasion or state of being.—*v.i. Brit.* To take a vacation, usu. with *at* or *in.*

ho•li•ness, hō⁄lē•nis, *n.* The state or character of being holy; (*cap.*) a title of the Pope.

hol•ler, hol⁄ər, *v.i. Informal.* Cry out; shout.—*v.t. Informal.* To cry out.—*n. Informal.* A loud wail or utterance of complaint or pain; a call to one out of normal hearing range; a loud cheer.

hol•low, hol⁄ō, *a.* Having an empty space within; not solid; sunken; sounding as if reverberating from a cavity; deep or low; meaningless; not sincere or faithful; false; deceitful; hungry.—*n.* A depression or excavation below the general level or in the substance of anything; a cavity.—*v.t., v.i.* To make a hollow or cavity in, usu. with *out.* —**hol•low•ly,** *adv.* —**hol•low•ness,** *n.*

hol•ly, hol⁄ē, *n. pl.,* -**lies.** Trees or shrubs having glossy, spiny-toothed leaves and red berries.

hol•ly•hock, hol⁄ē•hok, *n.* A tall, cultivated garden plant of the mallow family, having coarse, wavy-edged leaves and spirelike spikes of showy, variously colored flowers.

hol•mi•um, hōl⁄mē•əm, *n.* A rare metallic element.

hol•o•caust, hol⁄ə•kôst, *n.* Vast or total destruction, usu. by fire; great loss of life and/or property by earthquake, flood, war, or otherwise.

ho•lo•gram, hō⁄lə•gram, hol⁄ə•gram, *n.* A three-dimensional image made by means of a laser beam.

hol•o•graph, hol⁄ə•graf, hol⁄ə•gräf, *n.* A handwritten document, as a will, letter, or deed, which bears the signature of the author.

hol•ster, hōl⁄stər, *n.* A leather case for a pistol, usu. hung on a belt or saddle.

ho•ly, hō⁄lē, *a.,* -**li•er, -li•est.** Consecrated to God; dedicated by religious authority; exalted by dedication to service of the church or of religion; saintly in character; awesome; of divine origin.—*n. pl.,* -**lies.** A consecrated place.

Ho•ly Ghost, *n.* The Spirit of God; third person in the Trinity.

Ho·ly Grail, *n.* The chalice or cup supposed to have been used by Christ at the Last Supper; the object of any arduous quest.

ho·ly or·ders, *n.* Ordination; the clerical status of an ordained minister; the ranks of the Christian clergy.

Ho·ly Spir·it, *n.* Holy Ghost.

Ho·ly Week, *n.* The week preceding Easter.

hom·age, hom′ij, om′ij, *n.* Respect; an action showing respect.

hom·bre, om′brā, om′brē, *n. pl.,* **-bres.** *Informal.* A man.

home, hōm, *n.* A dwelling or abode; a house or apartment that is the fixed residence of a person, a family, or a household; an accustomed or familiar neighborhood; one's native city, region, or country; the dwelling place of an animal; a region where something is native or common; the habitat or seat; an institution for the care of the homeless, sick, infirm, or orphaned; in various games, the point which one tries to reach: *home* plate in baseball; heaven.—*a.* Of or connected with one's home; domestic; being the headquarters: as, the *home* office.—*adv.* To or toward one's home or one's native country; to the point; to the mark aimed at; so as to produce an intended effect: as, to bring a lesson *home* to a person; effectively.—*v.t.,* **homed, hom·ing.** To cause (a guided missile) to proceed toward a target; to furnish with a home.—*v.i.* To go or return home; have residence. —**home in (on),** of guided missiles, to be directed toward a target.—**at home,** in or about one's own familiar territory; at one's ease: as, to make oneself *at home.* —**home·less,** *a.* —**home·less·ness,** *n.*

home·com·ing, hōm′kəm·ing, *n.* A return to one's home; an annual celebration at high schools, colleges, and universities for returning alumni.

home e·co·nom·ics, *n.* The science of homemaking, including the study of nutrition, child care, clothing, budgeting, and the like.

home·ly, hōm′lē, *a.,* **-li·er, -li·est.** Pertaining to home; unpretentious; plain in appearance; unattractive. —**home·li·ness,** *n.*

home·made, hōm′mād′, *a.* Made at home; of simple or crude deisgn.

home plate, *n.* In baseball, the base or marker beside which a batter stands, and to which he returns in order to score.

hom·er, hō′mər, *n. Baseball.* A home run.—*v.i. Baseball.* To hit a home run.

home run, *n. Baseball.* A hit which, unaided by errors, allows the batter to circle the bases and return to home plate, scoring a run.

home·sick, hōm′sik, *a.* Ill or depressed by a longing for home while absent from it. —**home·sick·ness,** *a.*

home·spun, hōm′spən, *a.* Spun or made at home, as yarn or cloth; garments of such origin or character; plain or simple; unpolished or rude.—*n.* Cloth of a plain or simple weave made at home; cloth of similar appearance.

home·stead, hōm′sted, *n.* A home or dwelling, esp. a house with the ground and buildings immediately connected with it; a tract of land, esp. 160 acres, granted by Congress to a settler for development and ownership.—**home·stead·er,** *n.*

home stretch, *n.* The section of a race course between the last curve and the finish; the last part.

home·ward, hōm′wərd, *adv.* Toward home. Also **home·wards.**—*a.* In the direction of home.

home·work, hōm′wərk, *n.* Work to be done at home, esp. that assigned by a teacher to students.

home·y, hom·y, hō′mē, *a.,* **-i·er, -i·est.** Informal, cozy, comfortable, as a home. —**hom·ey·ness, hom·i·ness,** *n.*

hom·i·cide, hom′i·sīd, *a* The killing of one human being by another. —**hom·i·ci·dal,** hom·i·sī′dəl, *a.*

hom·i·let·ics, hom·ə·let′iks, *n. pl. but sing. in constr.* The art of preaching; the branch of practical theology concerned with preparing and delivering sermons. —**hom·i·let·ic,** *a.*

hom·i·ly, hom′ə·lē, *n. pl.,* **-lies.** A religious discourse or sermon; an admonitory discourse on moral or upright behavior.

hom·ing pi·geon, hō′ming, *n.* A pigeon, frequently used for carrying messages, bred and trained to return home from great distances.

hom·i·ny, hom′ə·nē, *n.* Corn hulled and sometimes coarsely ground, prepared for food by being boiled in water or milk.

ho·mo·ge·ne·ous, hō·mə·jē′nē·əs, hom·ə·jē′nē·əs, *a.* Of the same kind or nature; uniform in structure; similar; composed of parts all of the same kind. —**ho·mo·ge·ne·i·ty,** hō·mə·jə·nē′ə·tē, hom·ə·jə·nē′ə·tē, *n.* —**ho·mo·ge·ne·ous·ly,** *adv.* —**ho·mo·ge·ne·ous·ness,** *n.*

ho·mog·e·nize, hə·moj′ə·nīz, *v.t.,* **-nized, -niz·ing.** To make homogeneous.

hom·o·graph, hom′ə·graf, hō′mə·graf, *n.* A word having the same spelling as another, but a different origin, meaning, and sometimes pronunciation: for example, *wound* (injury) and *wound* (coiled).

ho·mol·o·gous, hō·mol′ə·gəs, *a.* Related or similar in structure, nature, position, or value; alike in origin and structure, as the foreleg of a horse and the wing of a bird. —**ho·mol·o·gy,** hō·mol′ə·jē, *n. pl.,* **-gies.**

hom·o·nym, hom′ə·nim, *n.* A word spelled and pronounced like another, but differing in meaning. —**hom·o·nym·ic,** hom·ə·nim′ik, *a.*

hom·o·phone, hom′ə·fōn, hō′mə·fōn, *n.* A word of like sound with another but having different spelling, origin, and meaning: for example, *write* and *right.* —**hom·o·phon·ic,** hom·ə·fon′ik, hō·mə·fon′ik, *a.*

Ho·mo sa·pi·ens, hō′mō sā′pē·ənz, *n.* Modern man; scientific name for any human being.

ho·mo·sex·u·al, hō·mə·sek′shū·əl, *n.* One who is characterized by a sexual interest in a person of the same sex.—*a.* —**ho·mo·sex·u·al·i·ty,** hō·mə·sek·shū·al′i·tē, *n.*

hone, hōn, *n.* A stone used for sharpening instruments.—*v.t.,* **honed, hon·ing.** To sharpen on a hone; to smooth or finish as though with a sharpened edge: as, to *hone* a skill.

hon·est, on′ist, *a.* Without deceit or fraud; honorable in principles, intentions, and actions, as persons; showing uprightness, straightforwardness, or fairness: as, *honest* actions; gained by fair means: as, an *honest* penny; truthful or sincere, as persons, utterances, or feelings; frank, open, or without disguise: as, *honest* opposition; genuine. —**hon·est·ly,** *adv.*

hon·es·ty, on′i·stē, *n. pl.,* **-ties.** The quality or fact of being honest; truthfulness, sincerity, or frankness.

hon·ey, hən′ē, *n. pl.,* **-eys.** A sweet, viscid fluid made by bees from the nectar collected from flowers, and stored in their nests or hives as food; any of various similar products produced by insects or in other ways; *fig.,* sweetness, or something sweet, delicious, or delightful: as, the *honey* of flattery; sweet one, a term of endearment.—*a.* Of or like honey; sweet; dear.—*v.t.,* **-eyed** or **-ied, -ey·ing.** To sweeten with or as with honey; to talk sweetly to; flatter.—*v.i.* To coax with flattery, usu. with *up.*

hon·ey·bee, hən′ē·bē, *n.* A bee that produces and stores honey.

hon·ey·comb, hən′ē·kōm, *n.* A structure of wax containing rows of hexagonal cells formed by bees for the purpose of storing honey and their eggs; something resembling this.—*a.* Having the structure or appearance of a honeycomb.—*v.t.* To pierce with many holes or cavities; to penetrate in all parts: a city *honeycombed* with vice.

---

a- hat, fāte, fāre, fäther; e- met, mē; i- pin, pīne; o- not, nōte, ôrb, moove (move), boy, pownd;
u- cūbe, bûll, tûk (took); ch- chin; th- thick, then; zh- vizhon (vision); ə- əgo, takən, pencəl, lemən, bərd (bird).

hon•ey•moon, hən′ē•moon, *n.* A holiday spent by a newly married couple in traveling or visiting.—*v.i.* To spend or have a honeymoon. —**hon•ey•moon•er,** *n.*

hon•ey•suck•le, hən′ē•sək•əl, *n.* Any of a group of upright or climbing shrubs in the honeysuckle family, some of which are ornamental and cultivated for their fragrant, nectar-filled flowers. —**hon•ey•suck•led,** *a.*

honk, hongk, hôngk, *n.* The cry of a goose; any similar sound, as of an auto horn.—*v.t., v.i.*

honk•y-tonk, hong′kē•tongk, hông′kē•tôngk, *n. Informal.* A cheap, low-class bar or night club; the style of music played in such places, usu. on a piano with a distinctive tinny sound.—*a.*

hon•or, on′ər, *n.* High public esteem, credit, fame, or glory; an exemplary sense of personal moral standards and conduct; a source or cause of credit or distinction: as, to be an *honor* to one's family; chastity or purity in a woman; (*usu. cap.*) a deferential title, as for judges or mayors, preceded by *Your* or *His. Pl.* Courtesies or civilities: as, to do the *honors* in serving as host.—*v.t.* To hold in honor or high respect; to show respect to; to confer honor upon; to accept and pay, as a bill; to carry out or fulfill, as a promise.

hon•or•a•ble, on′ər•ə•bəl, *a.* Worthy of being honored; motivated by principles of honor; conferring honor. —**hon•or•a•bly,** *adv.*

hon•o•rar•i•um, on•ə•râr′ē•əm, *n. pl.,* **-ums, -a.** A payment for services performed for which established practice or propriety discourages charging a fixed fee.

hon•or•ar•y, on′ə•rer•ē, *a.* Bestowed in honor; indicative of honor or distinction; possessing a title or post without performing services or receiving benefit or reward: as, *honorary* services.

hon•or•if•ic, on•ə•rif′ik, *a.* Granting respect or honor; showing respect or deference.—*n.*

hooch, hooch, *n. Informal.* Alcoholic drink, esp. illegal alcoholic drink.

hood, hd, *n.* A soft covering for the head and neck; a cowl; anything that resembles a hood in form or in use; condition, state, or quality, used in combination: as mother*hood,* false*hood,* hardi*hood.*—*v.t.* To cover with a hood. —**hood•ed,** *a.*

hood, hd, *n. Informal.* Hoodlum.

hood•lum, hood′ləm, *n.* A thug or gangster; a young rowdy.

hoo•doo, hoo′doo, *n.* Something which brings misfortune; a jinx.—*v.t.* To bring bad luck to. —**hoo•doo•ism,** *n.*

hood•wink, hood′wingk, *v.t.* To deceive; to cheat. —**hood•wink•er,** *n.*

hoo•ey, hoo′ē, *n. interj. Informal.* Nonsense.

hoof, hf, hoof, *n. pl.,* **hoofs, hooves.** The horny covering protecting the toe or encasing the foot in certain animals; the foot of a hoofed animal, as the horse.—*v.i. Informal.* To travel on foot, usu. with *it;* to dance. —**hoofed,** *a.*

hoof•er, hf′ər, hoo′fər, *n. Informal.* A professional dancer.

hook, hk, *n.* A curved piece of metal or other firm material adapted to catch, hold, cut, or pull something, as a fishhook or sickle; something bent like a hook. *Sports.* A mid-flight change in the direction of a ball hit, as in golf, or thrown, as in baseball and bowling. *Boxing.* A short blow struck from the side. —*v.t.* To fasten or catch hold of and lift or draw, as with a hook. *Informal.* To seize by stealth; pilfer; steal.—*v.i.* To curve or bend like a hook; to become attached or fastened by a hook.—**by hook or by crook,** by any means, fair or foul.—**off the hook,** released from a difficulty, responsibility, or obligation.

hooked, hkt, *a. Informal.* Addicted to the use of habit-forming drugs.

hook•er, hk′ər, *n. Informal.* A prostitute; a generous drink of liquor.

hook•up, hk′əp, *n.* A diagram of a radio or other apparatus, showing the arrangement and connection of the different elements; the apparatus. *Informal.* Any

alliance, cooperation, or relationship, as between persons, factions, or countries.

hoo•li•gan, hoo′li•gən, *n.* A street ruffian or hoodlum.—*a.* —**hoo•li•gan•ism,** *n.*

hoop, hoop, hp, *n.* A circular band used to hold together the staves of a cask, barrel, or the like; a large ring of metal, plastic, or wood for a child to use in play.—*v.t.* To bind or fasten with a hoop or hoops; to encircle. —**hooped, hoop•like,** *a.*

hoop•la, hoop′lä, *n. Informal.* Lively and loud excitement; statements made for the purpose of confusing an issue.

hoo•ray, h•rā′, *interj. v.i., n.* Hurrah.

hoose•gow, hoos•gow, hoos′gow, *n. Informal.* A jail.

hoot, hoot, *v.i.* To cry out or shout, esp. in disapproval or derision; of an owl, to utter its cry; to utter or make a similar sound.—*v.t.* To assail with cries or shouts of disapproval or derision; express in hoots.—*n.* A cry or shout, esp. of disapproval or derision; the cry of an owl; any similar sound, as of a whistle, or horn. *Informal.* The least concern or smallest amount, as: He doesn't give a *hoot.* —**hoot•er,** *n.* —**hoot•ing•ly,** *adv.*

hop, hop, *v.i.,* **hopped, hop•ping.** To leap with a springy movement on one foot; to leap by lifting both or all feet, as a bird or frog. *Informal.* To make a short flight or trip.—*v.t.* To leap over. *Informal.* To climb aboard, as a train or bus.—*n.* An act of hopping. *Informal.* A short trip in a plane; a kind of dance or a dance party.

hop, hop, *n.* A twining plant in the mulberry family, with three- to five-lobed leaves; *pl.,* the dried conelike fruits of the female plant used in brewing and medicine.

hope, hōp, *n.* The belief that one's desires may be attained; the thing hoped for or desired; that which gives hope.—*v.i.,* **hoped, hop•ing.** To have hope with the expectation of attainment: as, to *hope* for the best.—*v.t.* To long for or entertain hope for. —**hop•er,** *n.*

hope•ful, hōp′fəl, *a.* Full of hope; inspiring hope; promising.—*n.* A promising young person. —**hope•ful•ly,** *adv.* —**hope•ful•ness,** *n.*

hope•less, hōp′lis, *a.* Despairing; affording no hope. —**hope•less•ly,** *adv.* —**hope•less•ness,** *n.*

hop•head, hop′hed, *n. Informal.* A person addicted to narcotic drugs.

hop•per, hop′ər, *n.* One who or that which hops; any insect adapted for leaping, such as a grasshopper or leafhopper; a large, funnel-shaped chamber for temporarily storing loose materials, such as grain or coal, which are later dispensed through the bottom.

hop•scotch, hop′skoch, *n.* A children's game in which the player, while hopping on one foot, moves a flat stone or the like according to a diagram traced on the ground.

horde, hôrd, *n.* A mob; a multitude; a gang; a pack, as of animals; a swarm, as of insects.—*v.i.,* **hord•ed, hord•ing.** To live in hordes; to huddle together.

ho•ri•zon, hə•rī′zən, *n.* The line or circle which forms the apparent boundary between earth and sky; *fig.,* the limit or range of perception, knowledge, or the like.

hor•i•zon•tal, hôr′i•zon′təl, hor•i•zon′təl, *a.* Parallel to the plane of the horizon; level.—*n.* A horizontal line, plane, or the like; horizontal position. —**hor•i•zon•tal•ly,** *adv.*

hor•mone, hôr′mōn, *n.* A secretion of an endocrine gland, distributed in the blood stream or in bodily fluids to stimulate its specific functional effect in another part of the body; such a substance produced synthetically. —**hor•mo•nal,** hôr•mō′nəl, *a.*

horn, hôrn, *n.* A hard projecting appendage growing on the heads of certain animals, as cattle, goats, and deer; the material of which such horns are composed; a wind instrument, orig. made of horn, now of brass, esp. the French horn; something similar to a horn, as in shape, position, or use; a device for sounding a warning.—*v.t.* To provide with, shape like or attack with a horn or horns.—**horn in,** *informal*. To meddle; intrude; butt into a conversation, line, etc. —**horned,** *a.* —**horn·like,** *a.* —**horn·y,** *a.,* **-i·er, -i·est.**

hor·net, hôr′nit, *n.* A large, strong, social wasp having an exceptionally severe sting.

horn of plen·ty, *n.* Cornucopia.

horn·swog·gle, hôrn′swog·əl, *v.t.,* **-swog·gled, -swog·gling.** *Informal.* To trick; hoax; dupe; cheat; deceive.

ho·rol·o·gy, hô·rol′ə·jē, hō·rol′ə·jē, *n.* The science of measuring time; the art of constructing machines for measuring time. —**ho·rol·o·ger, ho·rol·o·gist,** *n.*

hor·o·scope, hôr′ə·skōp, hor′ə·skōp, *n.* A pattern or diagram of the heavens· at a given time, used by astrologers to predict future events in the lives of persons, according to the position of the stars at the time of their birth.

hor·ren·dous, hô·ren′dəs, ho·ren′dəs, *a.* Dreadful; terrible; horrible. —**hor·ren·dous·ly,** *adv.*

hor·ri·ble, hôr′ə·bəl, hor′ə·bəl, *a.* Exciting or tending to excite horror; very disagreeable; dreadful; terrible; shocking; hideous. *Informal.* Excessive. —**hor·ri·bly,** *adv.*

hor·rid, hôr′id, hor′id, *a.* Exciting horror; dreadful; hideous; shocking. *Informal.* Very offensive. —**hor·rid·ly,** *adv.* —**hor·rid·ness,** *n.*

hor·ri·fy, hôr′i·fī, hor′i·fī, *v.t.,* **-fied, -fy·ing.** To strike or impress with horror; to appall. —**hor·ri·fi·ca·tion,** hôr·i·fi·kā′shən, *n.*

hor·ror, hôr′ər, hor′ər, *n.* A powerful feeling of fear, dread, abhorrence; that which excites horror. *Pl., Informal.* The blues; delirium tremens.

hors d'oeu·vre, ôr·dərv′, *n. pl.,* **d'oeu·vres.** *Usu. pl.* An appetizer or relish.

horse, hôrs, *n. pl.,* **hors·es, horse.** A large, solid-hoofed four-footed animal, domesticated since prehistoric times, and employed as a beast of draft and burden and for carrying a rider; a trestle. *Informal.* A crib, translation, or other illicit aid to study; heroin. —*v.t.,* **horsed, hors·ing.** To provide with a horse or horses; to set on horseback. *Informal.* To subject to teasing.—*v.i.* To mount a horse; to ride horseback. *Informal.* To frolic, often with *around.*

horse·back, hôrs′bak, *n.* The back of a horse.—*adv.* On horseback.

horse·fly, hôrs′flī, *n. pl.,* **-flies.** A large fly that sucks the blood of horses, cattle, and other animals.

horse·hair, hôrs′her, *n.* The hair of horses, particularly of the mane and tail; cloth or fabric produced from this hair.

horse·laugh, hôrs′laf, hôrs′läf, *n.* A loud, coarse, often scornful laugh.

horse·man, hôrs′mən, *n. pl.,* **-men.** A man on horseback; a person skilled in horseback riding; one who raises, tends, or trains horses. —**horse·man·ship,** *n.* —**horse·wom·an,** *n. pl.,* **-wom·en.**

horse op·er·a, *n. Informal.* A motion picture or television play featuring the adventures of cowboys of the Wild West.

horse·play, hôrs′plā, *n.* Rough or rowdy play or practical jokes; rude pranks.

horse·pow·er, hôrs′pow·ər, *n.* A unit for measuring power or rate of work, as of the engine of an automobile: equiv. to 550 foot-pounds per second.

horse·rad·ish, hôrs′rad·ish, *n.* A tall herb of the mustard family; its hot-tasting white root, used as a condiment.

horse sense, *n. Informal.* Practical good sense.

horse·shoe, hôrs′shoo, hôrsh′shoo, *n.* A metal plate, U-shaped to follow the outline of a horse's hoof to which it is attached for protection from rough surfaces; *pl.,* a form of quoits played by tossing horseshoes over a peg. —**horse·sho·er,** *n.*

horse·whip, hôrs′hwip, *n.* A kind of whip, usu. of

leather, used to control horses.—*v.t.,* **-whipped, -whip·ping.** To lash or flagellate with or as with a horsewhip.

hors·ey, hors·y, hôr′sē, *a.,* **-i·er, -i·est.** Associated with the nature or quality of horses; engrossed with horses, as with their breeding or racing. *Informal.* Appearing gross, crass, or clumsy. —**hors·i·ly,** *adv.* —**hors·i·ness,** *n.*

hor·ta·to·ry, hôr′tə·tōr·ē, hôr′tə·tôr·ē, *a.* Exhorting.

hor·ti·cul·ture, hôr′ti·kəl·chər, *n.* The cultivation of a garden; the science and art of cultivating flowers, herbs, shrubs, fruits, and garden vegetables. —**hor·ti·cul·tur·al,** hôr·ti·kəl′chər·əl, *a.* —**hor·ti·cul·tur·ist,** hôr·ti·kəl′chər·ist, *n.*

ho·san·na, hō·zan′ə, *interj.* An exclamation, used as an acclamation of praise to God or Christ.

hose, hōz, *n. pl.,* **hose.** Stockings; socks.

hose, hōz, *n. pl.,* **hos·es.** A flexible tube for conveying liquids to a desired point: as, a garden *hose.*—*v.t.,* **hosed, hos·ing.** To water, wash, or drench by means of a hose.

ho·sier·y, hō′zhə·rē, *n.* Socks or stockings of any kind.

hos·pice, hos′pis, *n.* A place of refuge for travelers.

hos·pi·ta·ble, hos′pi·tə·bəl, hos·pit′ə·bəl, *a.* Giving or affording a generous welcome and entertainment to guests or strangers. —**hos·pi·ta·bly,** *adv.*

hos·pi·tal, hos′pi·təl, *n.* An institution in which sick or injured persons are given medical, obstetric, psychiatric, or surgical treatment, or nursing care.

hos·pi·tal·i·ty, hos·pi·tal′i·tē, *n. pl.,* **-ties.** The generous reception and gracious entertainment of strangers or guests; the disposition to extend friendly treatment to guests.

hos·pi·tal·i·za·tion, hos·pi·təl·ə·zā′shən, *n.* A hospitalizing; insurance which provides complete or partial coverage of hospital expenses.

hos·pit·tal·ize, hos′pi·tə·līz, *v.t.,* **-ized, -iz·ing.** To place for care or treatment in a hospital.

host, hōst, *n.* One who receives and entertains another at his own house or elsewhere; a landlord of a hostel or an inn; an animal or plant organism upon which a parasite is dependent for its existence.—*v.t.*

host, hōst, *n.* A great number of things or persons; a multitude; armed forces.

host, hōst, *n. (Often cap.)* The altar bread or wafer in the Eucharist.

hos·tage, hos′tij, *n.* A person handed over or held as a pledge for the performance of certain conditions.

hos·tel, hos′təl, *n.* A lodging, supervised by adults, planned for the use of young hikers and bicyclists. —**hos·tel·ry,** *n. pl.,* **-ries.**

host·ess, hō′stis, *n.* A female host; a woman who entertains a guest or guests; a woman employed by a restaurant, resort, airline, etc. to greet, seat, serve, and assist patrons.

hos·tile, hos′til, *a.* Antagonistic; of or pertaining to an enemy or actions characteristic of an enemy; unfriendly.—*n.* A hostile person; an enemy. —**hos·tile·ly,** *adv.*

hos·til·i·ty, hos·til′ə·tē, *n. pl.,* **-ties.** Hostile state, feeling, or action; enmity; antagonism; a hostile act. *Pl.* Acts of warfare; war.

hos·tler, os′lər, hos′lər, *n.* A stableman; groom; one who services a vehicle or machine. Also **os·tler.**

hot, hot, *a.,* **hot·ter, hot·test.** Having or communicating heat, esp. in a high degree; very warm, as weather or climate; having a sensation of great bodily heat; attended with or producing such a sensation, as a blush or fever; having an affect of burning on the tongue, skin, etc., as pepper, mustard, or a blister; peppery; biting; pungent; acrid; having or showing intense feeling; passionate, vehement, or fiery, as persons, temper, or words; inflamed; violent; furious; intense; strong or fresh, as a scent or trail. *Informal.* Excited about; highly enthusiastic for; wild; unrestrained; passionate or very sexy; showing luck or skill; stolen or ill-gotten; uncomfortable or unpleasant.—*adv.* Also **hot·ly.**

hot air, *n. Informal.* Empty, pretentious talk or writing.

hot·bed, hot′bed, *n.* A glass-covered bed of earth heated for growing plants out of season; atmosphere which produces rapid growth or development, esp. of something undesirable.

hot-blood·ed, hot′bled′id, *a.* Excitable.

hot dog, *n.* A cooked frankfurter or sausage, esp. as served in a split roll.

ho·tel, hō·tel′, *n.* A building or establishment that provides living accommodations, food, etc., for transient visitors and sometimes long-term residents.

hot·head, hot′hed, *n.* A rash, impetuous person. —**hot·head·ed,** *a.* —**hot·head·ed·ness,** *n.*

hot·house, hot′hows, *n.* An artificially heated greenhouse for the cultivation of tender plants.—*a.* Pertaining to a plant raised in a greenhouse; tender; overly delicate.

hot line, *n.* An open telephone line between two heads of state for use in emergencies, and esp. to prevent inadvertent war; any telephone line that is, by plan, always answered.

hot plate, *n.* A simple, portable appliance for cooking, heated by gas burners or by electricity.

hot rod, *n. Informal.* A usu. old automobile, stripped of nonessential equipment, with the engine adjusted for greater acceleration and speed.

hot rod·der, *n. Informal.* A driver of a hot rod.

hot seat, *n. Informal.* The electric chair; a difficult situation or an embarrassing position.

hot·shot, hot′shot, *n. Informal.* A successful and important person, as in business; a person displaying skill, as in a game.

hot war, *n. Informal.* Actual war with severe fighting, in contrast to the threats and tensions of cold war.

hot wa·ter, *n. Informal.* Serious difficulty; a condition of distress, usu. preceded by *in.*

hound, hownd, *n.* A dog, now esp. one of various breeds trained to hunt by scent or sight; a mean, despicable fellow; an addict; a hobbyist.—*v.t.* To pursue or drive relentlessly. —**hound·er,** *n.*

hour, owr, ow′ər, *n.* A space of time equal to the 24th part of a mean solar or civil day; 60 minutes; a particular or specific time; any definite time of day; the distance which can be traveled in one hour: as, living an *hour* from the nearest hospital; a regular or customary time: as, the cocktail *hour;* the length of one class period; one unit measure of academic credit.

hour·glass, owr′glas, ow′ər·glas, *n.* A horological device having two bulbous glass vessels joined by a narrow passage through which a quantity of sand or mercury descends within a specific time.—*a.*

hour·ly, owr′lē, ow′ər·lē, *a.* Recurring or performed every hour; frequent; calculated in terms of hour units.—*adv.* At every hour or during each hour; frequently.

house, hows, *n. pl.,* **hous·es,** howz′iz, *a.* A building where people live; a habitation, esp. of a single family; a structure used for any purpose, as worship, entertainment, assemblage, eating, storage, keeping animals, or growing plants; an audience; the building in which a legislative body of government meets; (*cap.*) the body itself; a business establishment; (*often cap.*) a family consisting of ancestors and descendants. —*howz, v.t.,* **housed, hous·ing.** To put or receive into a house; provide with a house; to give shelter to; harbor; lodge.

house·boat, hows′bōt, *n.* A boat fitted for use as a dwelling, esp. one having a flat bottom and a houselike structure built on the deck.

house·bro·ken, hows′brō·kən, *a.* Trained, as dogs or cats, to excrete only in the proper place. —**house·break,** *v.t.,* **-broke, -brok·en, -break·ing.**

house·fly, hows′flī, *n. pl.,* **-flies.** A two-winged insect common in dwellings.

house·hold, hows′hōld, *n.* Those who dwell under the same roof and comprise a family; any group living under the same domestic government; house; family. —*a.* Pertaining to the house and family; domestic.

house·hold·er, hows′hōl·dər, *n.* The head of a household; the owner or occupant of a home.

house·keep·er, hows′kē·pər, *n.* One who maintains a home, in the manner of a housewife; a person employed to care for a home or institution. —**house·keep·ing,** *n.*

house·maid, hows′mād, *n.* A female servant employed in a household to do housework.

House of Com·mons, *n.* The chamber of the legislature in the British and Canadian parliaments whose members are elected by the constituents of the counties and boroughs they represent.

House of Lords, *n.* The nonelective chamber in the British Parliament in which the members are hereditary or appointed peers and peeresses: it is also the final court of appeal for civil and criminal cases.

House of Rep·re·sen·ta·tives, *n.* The larger branch of the U.S. Congress and of most state legislatures, whose members represent election districts determined by population.

house·warm·ing, hows′wôr·ming, *n.* A party to celebrate moving into a new house.

house·wife, hows′wīf, *n. pl.,* **-wives.** A wife, specif. in the capacity of manager of domestic affairs. —**house·wife·ly,** *a., adv.* —**house·wif·er·y,** *n.*

house·work, hows′werk, *n.* The tasks involved in housekeeping, as cooking and cleaning.

hous·ing, how′zing, *n.* The act of one who houses or puts something under shelter; shelter, as in a house; lodging; houses collectively; something serving as a shelter or covering.

hov·el, hav′əl, hov′əl, *n.* An open shed, as a shelter for cattle or tools; a small, mean dwelling; a wretched hut.—*v.t.,* **hov·eled, hov·el·ing.** To shelter or lodge as in a hovel.

hov·er, hav′ər, hov′ər, *v.i.* To hang fluttering in the air, as a bird in suspended flight; to be in doubt, uncertainty, hesitation, or irresolution; to move to and fro near something threateningly or vigilantly.—*n.* An act or state of hovering. —**hov·er·er,** *n.* —**hov·er·ing,** *a.*

how, how, *adv.* In what manner; to what extent; to qualify an adverb or adjective of degree or quantity, as: *How* big? In what condition, state, or plight; for what reason; why, as: *How* could you want this?

how·ev·er, how·ev′ər, *adv.* In whatever manner or degree; in whatever state; notwithstanding; yet; still; but; on the other hand.—*conj.* In whatever manner or degree.

how·itz·er, how′it·sər, *n.* A short-barreled cannon firing a heavy shell at a high angle.

howl, howl, *v.i.* To utter a loud, prolonged, mournful cry, as that of a dog or wolf; to utter or make a similar sound, as the wind or a person in distress; wail.—*v.t.* To utter howls; to drive or force by howls.—*n.* The prolonged, mournful cry of a dog, wolf, man, or other animal; a loud cry or wail, as of pain or rage; a prolonged sound like wailing, as of the wind.

howl·er, how′lər, *n.* One who or that which howls. *Informal.* A comical mistake or blunder, esp. a verbal one.

how·so·ev·er, how·sō·ev′ər, *adv.* In whatever way or manner; to whatever extent or degree.

hoy·den, hoi·den, hoyd′ən, *n.* A boisterous, bold girl; tomboy. —**hoy·den·ish,** *a.*

Hoyle, hoyl, *n.* A book of recognized authority giving the rules for card games and other games.—**ac·cord·ing to Hoyle,** as prescribed by rule; fairly; correctly.

hub, həb, *n.* The central part of a wheel; a center of great importance or activity.

hub·bub, hŏb/əb, *n.* A tumult; uproar.

huck·le·ber·ry, hŏk/əl·ber·ē, *n. pl.,* **-ries.** The dark-blue or black edible berry of any of various shrubs of the heath family; a shrub yielding such a berry.

huck·ster, hŏk/stər, *n.* A peddler, esp. in agricultural produce; a hawker. *Informal.* Someone in the advertising business: usu. derogatory; anyone using especially aggressive or dramatic sales techniques to persuade: as, political *hucksters.*—*v.i.* To deal in small articles or in petty bargains.—*v.t.* To retail or peddle.

hud·dle, hŏd/əl, *v.i.,* **hud·dled, hud·dling.** To crowd together in a group; to hunch one's body together. —*v.t.* To crowd together without order; to hunch together, as one's body, often with *up.*—*n.* A crowd or confused mass. *Football.* A gathering of players behind the line of scrimmage for instructions; a private conference. —**hud·dler,** *n.*

hue, hū, *n.* Color; a shade, tint, or gradation of a color.

hue and cry, *n.* Any public protest or outcry.

huff, hŏf, *n.* A feeling of petulant anger or offended dignity: as, to be in a *huff.*—*v.i.* To puff or pant; to take offense.

huff·y, hŏf/ē, *a.,* **huf·fi·er, huf·fi·est.** Easily offended; touchy; offended or irritated. —**huff·i·ly,** *adv.* —**huff·i·ness,** *n.*

hug, hŏg, *v.t.,* **hugged, hug·ging.** To press or embrace closely with the arms, esp. affectionately; to cherish in the mind; to keep close to.—*v.i.* To embrace.—*n.* A close embrace. —**hug·ger,** *n.*

huge, hūj, *a.,* **hug·er, hug·est.** Having an immense bulk; very large in area; enormous; very great in any respect. —**huge·ly,** *adv.* —**huge·ness,** *n.*

Hu·gue·not, hū/gə·not, *n.* French Protestant of the 16th and 17th centuries.—*a.*

hu·la, hoo/lə, *n.* A traditional Hawaiian dance. Also **hu·la-hu·la,** hoo/lə·hoo/lə.

hulk, hŏlk, *n.* The body of an old ship laid by as unfit for service; something or someone bulky or unwieldy. —*v.i.* To come into view or appear in a massive form, usu. with *up.*

hulk·ing, hŏlk/ing, *a.* Large and clumsy; ungainly.

hull, hŏl, *n.* The husk, shell, or outer covering of a seed or fruit, as in grains.—*v.t.* To remove the hull of.

hull, hŏl, *n.* The frame or body of a ship.

hul·la·ba·loo, hŏl/ə·bə·loo, *n.* Uproar; loud, noisy confusion.

hum, hŏm, *v.i.,* **hummed, hum·ming.** To make a prolonged sound like that of a bee; to utter a similar sustained sound with the lips closed; to sing in this manner; to emit steady, mingled sounds of activity. —*v.t.* To sing or utter with a humming sound and without articulation.—*n.* Any inarticulate, murmuring sound. —**hum·mer,** *n.*

hu·man, hū/mən, *a.* Pertaining to, belonging to, or having the qualities of mankind; having the qualities or attributes of man.—*n.* A human being. —**hu·man·ness,** *n.*

hu·mane, hū·mān/, *a.* Kind; benevolent; tender; merciful; tending to civilize or refine. —**hu·mane·ly,** *adv.* —**hu·mane·ness,** *n.*

hu·man·ism, hū/mə·niz·əm, *n.* Any system or mode of thought or action in which human and secular interests predominate; (*sometimes cap.*) the renewed interest in the literature and ideas of the Renaissance humanists, which often de-emphasized religion.—**hu·man·ist,** *n., a.* —**hu·man·is·tic,** hū·mə·nis/tik, *a.*

hu·man·i·tar·i·an, hū·man·i·tār/ē·ən, *a.* Tending to promote the welfare of mankind; philanthropic.—*n.* One who professes or practices humanitarian doctrines. —**hu·man·i·tar·i·an·ism.**

hu·man·i·ty, hū·man/i·tē, *n. pl.,* **-ties.** Mankind; the quality of being human; the quality of being humane. *Pl.* The fields of learning including the arts, history, literature, and philosophy, excluding the sciences, usu. used with *the.*

hu·man·ize, hū/mə·nīz, *v.t.,* **-ized, -iz·ing.** To render human or humane; to attribute human qualities to. —*v.i.* To become kind, compassionate, or civilized; to become human. —**hu·man·i·za·tion,** hū·mə·nə·zā/shən, *n.* —**hu·man·iz·er,** *n.*

hu·man·kind, hū/mən·kīnd, *n.* Mankind.

hu·man·ly, hū/mən·lē, *adv.* In a human manner; within human understanding or ability; according to feelings or judgments of human beings.

hum·ble, hŏm/bəl, *a.,* **-bler, -blest.** Modest; low in rank or conditions.—*v.t.,* **hum·bled, hum·bling.** To render humble. —**hum·ble·ness,** *n.* —**hum·bler,** *n.* —**hum·bly,** *adv.*

hum·ble pie, *n.* A pie made of deer entrails or organs.—**eat humble pie,** to apologize; humiliate oneself; be forced to admit error.

hum·bug, hŏm/bŏg, *n.* A deluding trick, hoax, fraud, or pretense; an imposter.—*v.t., v.i.,* **-bugged, bug·ging.** To deceive; to trick or delude. —**hum·bug·ger,** *n.* —**hum·bug·ger·y,** *n.*

hum·ding·er, hŏm/ding/ər, *n. Informal.* A person or thing that is remarkable or outstandingly excellent.

hum·drum, hŏm/drəm, *a.* Commonplace; dull; monotonous.—*n.* The quality of being commonplace, routine, or workaday, or something having this quality.

hu·mer·us, hū/mər·əs, *n. pl.,* **-i, -ī.** The long, cylindrical bone of the arm of man, extending from shoulder to elbow. *Zool.* The forelimb correspondingly located in other vertebrates.

hu·mid, hū/mid, *a.* Moist; damp. —**hu·mid·ly,** *adv.*

hu·mid·i·fy, hū·mid/i·fī, *v.t.,* **-fied, -fy·ing.** To make humid. —**hu·mid·i·fi·er,** *n.*

hu·mid·i·ty, hū·mid/i·tē, *n.* The state of being humid; moistness; dampness.—**rel·a·tive hu·mid·i·ty,** the percentage of water vapor in the air compared with that which is required to saturate it at the same temperature.

hu·mi·dor, hū/mi·dôr, *n.* A container in which a suitable humidity is maintained, esp. one for storing cigars or tobacco.

hu·mil·i·ate, hū·mil/ē·āt, *v.t.,* **-at·ed, -at·ing.** To reduce the dignity or pride of; to humble; to disgrace. —**hu·mil·i·at·ing,** *a.* —**hu·mil·i·a·tion,** hū·mil·ē·ā/shən, *n.*

hu·mil·i·ty, hū·mil/i·tē, *n.* The state of being humble.

hum·ming·bird, hŏm/ing·bərd, *n.* A tiny bird characterized by a long, narrow bill, brilliant plumage of the male, and by narrow wings whose rapid vibration creates a humming sound.

hum·mock, hŏm/ək, *n.* A rounded knoll; a protuberance on an ice field; a wooded ridge of land adjacent to a marsh or swamp. Also **ham·mock.** —**hum·mock·y,** *a.,* **-i·er, -i·est.**

hu·mor, hū/mər, ū/mər, *n.* That quality in speech, writing, or action which tends to excite laughter; the capacity for perceiving the amusing or ludicrous; anything, as speech, writing, or action, intended to be comical; disposition or characteristic emotional state; temperament; frame of mind: to be in a good *humor.* —**out of hu·mor,** displeased.—*v.t.* To comply with the humor or inclination of.

hu·mor·ist, hū/mər·ist, ū/mər·ist, *n.* One who possesses a sense of humor; one who uses humor skillfully, as a professional storyteller. —**hu·mor·is·tic,** hū·mə·ris/tik, *a.*

hu·mor·ous, hū/mər·əs, ū/mər·əs, *a.* Comical; amusing. —**hu·mor·ous·ly,** *adv.* —**hu·mor·ous·ness,** *n.*

hump, hŏmp, *n.* A rounded protuberance, esp. on the back; a mound or low hill.—*v.t.* To raise, as the back, in a hump. *Informal.* To exert, as oneself.—*v.i. Infor-*

---

a- hat, fāte, fāre, fäther; **e-** met, mē; **i-** pin, pīne; **o-** not, nōte, ôrb, moove (move), boy, pownd; **u-** cūbe, bŭll, tûk (took); **ch-** chin; **th-** thick, ŧhen; **zh-** vizhon (vision); **ə-** əgo, takən, pencəl, lemən, bərd (bird).

mal. To hurry or exert oneself. —**humped,** *a.* —**hump·y,** *a.,* **-i·er, -i·est.**

hump·back, həmp′bak, *n.* A back with a hump; a large whale; a hunchback. —**hump·backed,** *a.*

hu·mus, hū′məs, *n.* The organic constituent of soil, produced by the partial decomposition of plant and animal matter and essential for plant nutrition.

Hun, hən, *n.* One of an Asiatic race of warlike nomads who overran much of Europe in the 5th century; (*often l.c.*) an uncivilized or barbarous devastator. —**Hun·nish,** *a.* —**Hun·nish·ness,** *n.*

hunch, hənch, *v.t.* To thrust out or up in a hump.—*v.i.* To lunge or push oneself ahead jerkily; to be in a bent posture while sitting or standing.—*n.* A protuberance or hump; a lump or thick piece. *Informal.* A premonition or suspicion.

hunch·back, hənch′bak, *n.* A back deformed by a convex curvature of the spine; one who has such a back. Also **hump·back.** —**hunch·backed,** *a.*

hun·dred, hən′drid, *n. pl.,* **-dred** or **-dreds.** The cardinal number between 99 and 101; a symbol representing it, as *100* or *C;* any collection of 100 units.—*a.* —**hun·dredth,** *n., a.*

hun·dred·weight, hən′drid·wāt, *n. pl.,* **-weights** or **-weight.** A unit of weight equal to 100 pounds in the United States; *Brit.,* a unit equaling 112 pounds.

hun·ger, həng′gər, *n.* An uneasy sensation or weakened physical condition caused by a lack of food; a craving for food; any strong or eager desire.—*v.i.* To feel hunger; to desire eagerly.—*v.t.* To cause hunger in; starve.

hun·gry, həng′grē, *a.,* **-gri·er, -gri·est.** Having a need or craving for food; having a strong desire. —**hun·gri·ly,** *adv.* —**hun·gri·ness,** *n.*

hunk, həngk, *n. Informal.* A large lump or portion; a virile man.

hunt, hənt, *v.t.* To chase or search for, as game, for the purpose of catching or killing; to pursue with force or hostility, often followed by *down;* to search for or seek.—*v.i.* To engage in hunting animals as a sport or to obtain food; make a search or quest, often followed by *for.*—*n.* The act or practice of hunting game; the chase; the act of seeking something; a search; a body of persons associated for the purpose of hunting. —**hunt·er,** *n.* —**hunt·ing,** *n.* —**hunt·ress,** *n.* —**hunts·man,** *n. pl.,* **-men.**

hur·dle, hər′dəl, *n.* An obstacle or barrier, man-made or natural, which must be jumped over or vaulted in certain competitive sports such as track and horse-racing; any barrier or problem to be overcome. —*v.t.,* **hur·dled, hur·dling.** To jump over, as in racing; to overcome or conquer, as a handicap or difficulty. —*v.i.* To leap over a hurdle. —**hur·dler,** *n.*

hur·dy-gur·dy, hər′dē·gər′dē, *n. pl.,* **-gur·dies.** Any of various instruments operated by a hand crank, esp. a barrel organ.

hurl, hərl, *v.t.* To pitch, drive, throw, or fling away forcefully; to utter with vehemence: as, to *hurl* a tirade of abuse.—*v.i.* To throw a missile. *Baseball.* To pitch. —*n.* A forcible or violent throw; a fling. —**hurl·er,** *n.*

hurl·y-burl·y, hər′lē·bər·lē, *n. pl.,* **-burl·ies.** Commotion; tumult; bustle; confusion.—*a.* Noisy; uproarious; tumultuous.

hur·rah, hə·rä′, hə·rô′, *interj.* An exclamation expressive of joy, applause, or encouragement.—*v.i.* To utter a hurrah.—*n.* Commotion; excitement; a joyous or encouraging exclamation. Also **hur·ray,** hə·rā′.

hur·ri·cane, hər′i·kān, hər′i·kən, *n.* A violent, tropical, cyclonic storm with winds greater than 75 miles per hour; anything suggesting such a storm.

hur·ry, hər′ē, *v.t.,* **hur·ried, hur·ry·ing.** To impel to greater speed or haste; to urge to act or proceed hastily; to cause to be performed with great or undue rapidity; to hasten.—*v.i.* To move or act with haste, often followed by *up.*—*n.* The act of hurrying; urgency; bustle; confusion. —**hur·ried,** *a.* —**hur·ried·ly,** *adv.* —**hur·ry·ing·ly,** *adv.*

hurt, hərt, *v.t.,* **hurt, hurt·ing.** To cause physical or mental pain; to harm; to damage.—*v.i.* To feel or cause physical or mental pain to; to cause harm.—*n.* A wound, bruise, or the like; anguish; loss; damage.

hurt·ful, hərt′fəl, *a.* Harmful; injurious. —**hurt·ful·ly,** *adv.*

hur·tle, hər′təl, *v.i.,* **hur·tled, hur·tling.** To move rapidly and sometimes noisily; to rush; to strike forcibly or collide, with *against* or *together.*—*v.t.* To fling or dash violently; to hurl.

hus·band, həz′bənd, *n.* A married man.—*v.t.* To administer or manage with prudence and economy. —**hus·band·less,** *a.*

hus·band·ry, həz′bən·drē, *n.* Agricultural cultivation, production of crops, and the breeding of animals for food, esp. through scientific control and management; frugal and thrifty conservation; household management.

hush, həsh, *v.t.* To still; to silence; to make quiet; to allay or calm, as fears; to suppress or keep concealed, as news, used with *up.*—*v.i.* To be or become silent. —*n.* Stillness; quiet.—*interj.* A word used to enjoin silence.—**hush mon·ey,** a bribe paid to prevent disclosure of facts.

hush-hush, həsh′həsh, *a.* Highly confidential; secret.

husk, həsk, *n.* The external covering of certain fruits or seeds of plants; an outer frame or shell.—*v.t.* To deprive of the husk: as, to *husk* corn. —**husk·er,** *n.*

husk·y, həs′kē, *a.,* **husk·i·er, husk·i·est.** Rough in tone, as the voice; hoarse of voice, as or as if caused by emotion. —**husk·i·ly,** *adv.* —**husk·i·ness,** *n.*

husk·y, həs′kē, *a.,* **husk·i·er, husk·i·est.** Burly; powerful; robust; large in stature.—*n. pl.,* **husk·ies.** One who is large and robust. —**husk·i·ness,** *n.*

hus·sar, hû·zär′, *n.* A member of any of various lightly-armed units maintained in some European armies, often distinguished by showy dress uniforms.

hus·sy, həs′ē, həz′ē, *n. pl.,* **huss·ies.** A disreputable, brazen woman; a pert, saucy wench; minx.

hus·tings, həs′tingz, *n. pl. or sing.* A platform or other place where political speeches are made.

hus·tle, həs′əl, *v.t.,* **-tled, -tling.** To push or shove along; to jostle; to force roughly or hurriedly, as into, out of, or through a place. *Informal.* To hurry; to sell or obtain aggressively or by questionable tactics; to seek clients as a prostitute.—*v.i.* To push or force one's way; proceed or work rapidly or energetically.—*n.* The act of one who hustles. —**hus·tler,** *n.*

hut, hət, *n.* A dwelling, usu. small and simply constructed; shack; cabin.—*v.t.,* **hut·ted, hut·ting.** To place in or furnish with a hut.—*v.i.* To take lodging in huts.

hutch, həch, *n.* A pen or enclosed coop for confining small animals; a cupboard or case with open shelves to display dishes; a chest, box, or compartment for storing things.

huz·zah, huz·za, hə·zä′, *interj.* An expression of appreciation, joy, or approval.

hy·a·cinth, hī′ə·sinth, *n.* Any of various bulbous plants of the lily family characterized by fragrant spikes of bell-shaped flowers; the bulb of this plant.

hy·brid, hī′brid, *n.* The offspring of two animals or plants of different races, varieties and, rarely, species and genera; anything derived from heterogeneous sources or composed of elements of different or incongruous kinds.—*a.* —**hy·brid·ism,** *n.*

hy·brid·ize, hī′bri·dīz, *v.t.,* **-ized, -iz·ing.** To cause to produce hybrids; to cross; interbreed.—*v.i.* To cause the production of hybrids by crossing different varieties or races; to produce hybrids. —**hy·brid·i·za·tion,** hī·brid·i·zā′shən, *n.*

hy·dra, hī′drə, *n. pl.,* **-dras, -drae,** -drē. Any of various fresh-water polyps. (*Cap.* or *l.c.*) *Class. mythol.* A monstrous, nine-headed serpent slain by Hercules. Any persistent problem or evil.

hy·dran·gea, hī·drān′jə, *n.* A shrub cultivated for its clustered pink, white, or blue flowers.

hy·drant, hī′drənt, *n.* An upright pipe with valves and an outlet from which water is drawn and discharged for fighting fires and watering streets.

hy·drate, hī′drāt, *n.* Any of a class of compounds produced when certain substances, as metallic salts, unite with water; a hydroxide.—*v.t., v.i.,* **hy·dra·ted, hy·dra·ting.** To combine chemically with water; to form into a hydrate. —**hy·dra·tion,** hī·drā′shen, *n.* —**hy·dra·tor,** *n.*

hy·drau·lic, hī·drô′lik, *a.* Pertaining to water or other liquid in motion, or to hydraulics; operated by or employing water; operated by means of pressure produced by forcing a liquid, as oil or water, though a narrow opening or pipe; hardening under water, as a cement. —**hy·drau·li·cal·ly,** *adv.*

hy·drau·lics, hī·drô′liks, *n. pl., sing. or pl. in constr.* The science dealing with water or other liquid in motion, its uses in engineering, and the laws governing its action.

hy·dro·car·bon, hī·dre·kär′ben, *n.* Any one of the compounds consisting of hydrogen and carbon only, as benzene or methane.

hy·dro·chlo·ric·ac·id, hī·dre·klôr′ik, *n.* A strong, fuming, highly corrosive acid used in industry, research, and medicine. Also **mu·ri·at·ic acid,** myūr·ē· at′ik.

hy·dro·dy·nam·ics, hī·drō·dī·nam′iks, *n. pl., sing. or pl. in constr.* That branch of science dealing with the application of forces to fluids, especially when producing motion. —**hy·dro·dy·nam·ic,** *a.*

hy·dro·e·lec·tric, hī·drō·i·lek′trik, *a.* Pertaining to the producing of electric current by the energy of moving water.

hy·dro·gen, hī′dre·jen, *n.* A colorless, odorless, flammable gaseous element, the lightest of the known elements. —**hy·drog·e·nous,** hī·droj′e·nes, *a.*

hy·dro·gen bomb, *n.* A bomb that uses the fusion of light nuclei, as hydrogen isotopes, under very high temperature, to produce a powerful explosion. Also **H-bomb.**

hy·dro·gen per·ox·ide, *n.* A colorless, unstable, oily liquid, the aqueous solution of which is used chiefly as a bleaching and oxidizing agent and as a mild antiseptic.

hy·drol·y·sis, hī·drol′i·sis, *n. pl.,* **-ses,** -sēz. Chemical decomposition in which a compound is divided into other compounds by taking up the elements of water.

hy·drom·e·ter, hī·drom′i·ter, *n.* A device for measuring specific gravity of fluids. —**hy·dro·met·ric,** hī· dre·me′trik, **hy·dro·met·ri·cal,** *a.* —**hy·drom·e·try,** *n.*

hy·dro·pho·bi·a, hī·dre·fō′bē·e, *n.* An abnormal fear of water; rabies.

hy·dro·plane, hī′dre·plān, *n.* A kind of motorboat provided with a plane or planes by means of which it can reduce its displacement at high speed or skim along the surface of the water.—*v.i.,* **-planed, -plan·ing.** To move swiftly over the water with the hull above water level; to travel in or operate a hydroplane.

hy·dro·pon·ics, hī·dre·pon′iks, *n. pl. but sing. in constr.* A method of growing plants by rooting them in chemical solutions instead of soil. —**hy·dro·pon·ic,** *a.*

hy·dro·ther·a·py, hī·drō·ther′e·pē, *n.* The scientific treatment of disease by means of water. Also **hy·drop·a·thy,** hī·drop′e·thē. —**hy·dro·ther·a·pist,** *n.*

hy·drous, hī′dres, *a.* Containing water; containing water in some kind of chemical union as in hydrates or in hydroxides.

hy·drox·ide, hī·drok′sīd, *n.* A compound formed by the union of an element or radical with one or more hydroxyl radicals.

hy·drox·yl, hī·drok′sil, *n.* A univalent radical or group containing hydrogen and oxygen, found in hydroxides, organic acids, and alcohols.

hy·dro·zo·an, hī·dre·zō′en, *n.* Any of a class of invertebrate aquatic animals, including the hydras and other polyps and the small jelly fishes.

hy·e·na, hī·ē′ne, *n.* A large, powerful, carnivorous animal of Asia and Africa, feeding chiefly on carrion, and of nocturnal habits, recognized by its piercing cry. Also **hy·ae·na.**

hy·giene, hī′jēn, *n.* The system or practice of principles or rules designed for promotion and maintenance of health and cleanliness. —**hy·gi·en·ic,** hī·ji·en′ik, hī·jē′nik, *a.* —**hy·gi·en·i·cal·ly,** hī·ji·en′ik·lē, hī· jē′nik·lē, *adv.* —**hy·gien·ist,** *n.*

hy·men, hī′men, *n.* A mucous membrane, situated at the entrance of the vagina.

hy·me·ne·al, hī·me·nē′el, *a.* Referring to marriage. —*n.* A wedding song. —**hy·me·ne·al·ly,** *adv.*

hymn, him, *n.* A song or ode in adoration of God or a deity.—*v.t.* To worship or praise in a hymn.—*v.i.* To sing hymns in homage.

hym·nal, him′nel, *n.* A book of hymns compiled for worship services. Also **hymn·book.**

hy·per·bo·la, hī·per′be·le, *n.* A curve formed by the intersection of a plane with two similar right circular cones placed apex to apex.

hy·per·bo·le, hī·per′be·lē, *n.* Deliberate exaggeration used for effect; an extravagant statement not intended to be understood in the literal sense. —**hy·per·bo·lize,** *v.t., v.i.,* **-lized, -liz·ing.**

hy·per·bol·ic, hī·per·bol′ik, *a.* Pertaining to a hyperbola; of, like, or using hyperbole.

hy·per·crit·i·cal, hī·per·krit′i·kel, *a.* Overcritical; excessively exact. —**hy·per·crit·i·cal·ly,** *adv.*

hy·per·sen·si·tive, hī·per·sen′si·tiv, *a.* Excessively sensitive. —**hy·per·sen·si·tive·ness, hy·per·sen·si·tiv·i·ty,** hī·per·sen·se·stiv′e·tē, *n.*

hy·per·ten·sion, hī·per·ten′shen, *n.* A condition characterized by high blood pressure, esp. in the arteries.

hy·per·thy·roid·ism, hī·per·thī′roi·diz·em, *n.* Excessive activity of the thyroid gland causing rapid heartbeat and increased metabolism.

hy·phen, hī′fen, *n.* A short line (-) used to connect the parts of a compound word or the parts of a word divided for any purpose.

hy·phen·ate, hī·fen·āt, *v.t.,* **-at·ed, -at·ing.** To join by a hyphen; write with a hyphen.

hyp·no·sis, hip·nō′sis, *n. pl.,* **-ses,** -sēz. A condition or state, allied to normal sleep, which can be artificially induced and is characterized by marked susceptibility to suggestion, and considerable loss of will power and sensation; hypnotism.

hyp·not·ic, hip·not′ik, *a.* Pertaining to or susceptible to hypnotism; inducing sleep.—*n.* An agent or drug that produces sleep; a sedative; a person under the influence of hypnotism; one subject to hypnotic influence.

hyp·no·tism, hip′ne·tiz·em, *n.* The induction of hypnosis; the science dealing with the induction of hypnosis; hypnosis. —**hyp·no·tist,** *n.*

hyp·no·tize, hip′ne·tīz, *v.t.,* **-tized, -tiz·ing.** To put into a hypnotic state.

hy·po, hī′pō, *n. Informal.* A fixing agent in developing film; a hypodermic syringe or injection.

hy·po·chon·dri·a, hī·pe·kon′drē·e, *n.* A morbid condition, characterized by depressed spirits and fancies of ill health.

hy·po·chon·dri·ac, hī·pe·kon′drē·ak, *n.* A person suffering from or subject to hypochondria.

hy·poc·ri·sy, hī·pok′re·sē, *n. pl.,* **-sies.** The act or practice of simulating or feigning feelings or beliefs. —**hyp·o·crite,** *n.*

hy·po·der·mic, hī·pe·der′mik, *a.* Characterized by the introduction of medical preparations under the skin.

---

a- hat, fāte, fâre, fäther; **e-** met, mē; **i-** pin, pīne; **o-** not, nōte, ôrb, moove (move), boy, pownd; **u-** cūbe, bůll, tůk (took); **ch-** chin; **th-** thick, ŧhen; **zh-** vizhon (vision); **e-** ego, taken, pencel, lemen, berd (bird).

hy·po·der·mic in·jec·tion, *n.* The forceful implanting of fluid by inserting a syringe under the skin.

hy·po·sen·si·tize, hī·pō·sen/sə·tīz, *v.t.,* **-tized, -tiz·ing.** To lessen sensitivity of; reduce the allergic reaction to.

hy·po·ten·sion, hī·pō·ten/shən, *n.* A condition marked by unusually low blood pressure.

hy·pot·e·nuse, hī·pot/ə·noos, hī·pot/ə·nūs, *n.* That side of a right triangle which is opposite the right angle.

hy·poth·e·cate, hī·poth/ə·kāt, hī·poth/ə·kāt, *v.t.,* **-cat·ed, -cat·ing.** To pledge in security for a debt, but without transfer; to mortgage; to theorize.

hy·poth·e·sis, hī·poth/ə·sis, hī·poth/ə·sis, *n. pl.,* **-ses,** -sēz. A proposition put forth as a basis for reasoning; a supposition formulated from proved data

and presented as a temporary explanation of an occurrence. —**hy·poth·e·size,** *v.i.,* **-sized, -siz·ing.**

hy·po·thet·i·cal, hī·pə·thet/i·kəl, *a.* Referring to an idea or a statement unsupported by fact or evidence.

hys·sop, his/əp, *n.* An aromatic herb of the mint family, usu. with blue flowers.

hys·ter·ec·to·my, his·tə·rek/tə·mē, *n. pl.,* **-mies.** The removal of the uterus.

hys·te·ri·a, his·tēr/ē·ə, his·tār/ē·ə, *n.* A psychoneurotic disorder characterized variously by violent emotional outbreaks, irrationality, simulated bodily symptoms due to autosuggestion, and impairment of motor and sensory functions; any emotional frenzy. —**hys·ter·ic,** his·tār/ik, **hys·ter·i·cal,** *a.*

hys·ter·ics, his·tār/iks, *n. pl., sing. or pl. in constr.* A fit of hysteria; an uncontrollable outburst.

I, i, ī, *n.* The ninth letter and the third vowel of the English alphabet.

I, ī, *pron.* The nominative case of the pronoun of the first person singular, by which a speaker or writer denotes himself.

i·amb, ī/am, ī/amb, *n. pl.,* **i·ambs.** *Usu. pl.* In verse, a metrical foot of two syllables, the first short and the last long, or the first unaccented and the last accented, as in *delight.* Also **i·am·bus,** ī·am/bəs, *pl.,* **i·am·bus·es,** i·am·bi, ī·am/bī. —**i·am·bic,** ī·am/bik, *a., n.*

i·at·ric, ī·a/trik, ē·a/trik, *a.* Referring to a physician or to medicine.

i·bid. Abbreviation for **i·bi·dem.**

i·bi·dem, ib/i·dem, i·bī/dem, *adv.* In the same place; in that part of a literary work just mentioned: used in footnotes.

i·bis, ī/bis, *n. pl.,* **i·bis·es, i·bis.** Any of various large wading birds of a family allied to the herons and storks.

ice, īs, *n.* The solid form of water, produced by freezing; the frozen surface of a body of water; cake icing; a dessert made of water and fruit juice, sweetened and frozen. *Informal.* Jewels, esp. diamonds.—*v.t.,* **iced, ic·ing.** To cover with ice; to convert into ice; to freeze. To refrigerate with ice; cool with ice; to cover with icing; frost.—*v.i.* To turn to ice; to freeze.—**break the ice,** to begin something, esp. to initiate conversation. —**on ice,** *Informal.* Set aside, as for safekeeping; having every probability of success.

ice age, *n.* The Pleistocene glacial epoch.

ice·bag, īs/bag, *n.* A waterproof bag for ice.

ice·berg, īs/bərg, *n.* A large floating mass of ice, detached from a glacier.

ice·boat, īs/bōt, *n.* A strong boat that can break a passage through ice.

ice·box, īs/boks, *n.* A chest for ice to cool and preserve food; any refrigerator.

ice·cap, īs/kap, *n.* A permanent cap or covering of ice over an area.

ice-cold, īs/kōld, *a.* Very cold; freezing.

ice cream, *n.* A frozen dessert food made of sweetened cream or milk with various fruits or flavors added.

ice·man, īs/man, *n. pl.,* **-men.** A man who sells and delivers ice.

ice pack, *n.* A large floating mass of ice formed from separate ice sections joined over a period of years; a tub of ice in which a patient is immersed as a form of shock treatment.

ice pick, *n.* An awllike tool for chipping ice.

ice sheet, *n.* A continental glacier.

ice skate, *n.* One of a pair of leather shoes with metal blades which enable the wearer to glide upon ice. —**ice-skate,** īs/skāt, *v.i.,* **-skat·ed, -skat·ing.** To glide along by means of skates upon ice. —**ice skat·er,** *n.*

ich·nol·o·gy, ik·nol/ə·jē, *n.* The study of fossil footmarks of animals. —**ich·no·log·i·cal,** ik·nə·loj/ə·kəl. *a.*

ich·thy·ol·o·gy, ik·thē·ol/ə·jē, *n.* A branch of zoology that studies fishes. —**ich·thy·o·log·i·cal,** ik·thē·ə·loj/i·kəl, *a.* —**ich·thy·ol·o·gist,** *n.*

i·ci·cle, ī/si·kəl, *n.* A hanging mass of ice formed by the freezing of water as it drips.

i·ci·ly, ī/sə·lē, *adv.* In an icy manner.

i·ci·ness, ī/sē·nis, *n.* The state of being icy or very cold.

ic·ing, ī/sing, *n.* A sugary preparation for frosting cakes and other pastries.

i·con, ī·kon, *n.* An image, representation, or picture; a religious image, considered sacred by members of the Eastern Orthodox Church.

i·con·o·clasm, ī·kon/ə·klaz·əm, *n.* The acts, or practices of an iconoclast. —**i·con·o·clas·tic,** ī·kon·ə·klas/tik, *a.*

i·con·o·clast, ī·kon/ə·klast, *n.* One who makes attacks on cherished beliefs or institutions.

i·cy, ī/sē, *a.,* **i·ci·er, i·ci·est.** Pertaining to, composed of, resembling, or abounding in ice; slippery; very cold; freezing; characterized by coldness or aloofness.

id, id, *n.* A part of the psyche, constituting the unconscious, which is the source of instinctual energy.

I'd, īd. Contraction of **I would, I should,** or **I had.**

i·de·a, ī·dē/ə, *n.* A thought, conception, or notion; an impression; a conviction or opinion; a plan of action; vague knowledge; inkling; whim.

i·de·al, ī·dē/əl, ī·dēl/, *a.* Achieving a standard of perfection or excellence; referring to or representing a mental image or conception rather than a material object; visionary.—*n.* A conception or standard of something in its highest perfection; a person or thing conforming to such a standard, and taken as a model for imitation. —**i·de·al·ness,** *n.*

i·de·al·ism, ī·dē/əl·iz·əm, *n.* The tendency to represent things in an ideal form, or as they might be rather than as they are; the cherishing or pursuit of ideals. —**i·de·al·ist,** *n.* —**i·de·al·is·tic,** ī·dē·əl·is/tik, *a.*

i·de·al·ize, ī·dē/ə·liz, *v.t.,* **-ized, -iz·ing.** To represent in an ideal form or character.—*v.i.* To imagine or form an ideal. —**i·de·al·i·za·tion,** ī·dē·ə·lə·zā/

hən, *n.*

i·de·al·ly, ĭ·dē′ə·lē, *adv.* In accordance with imagined perfection; theoretically.

i·dem, ĭ′dem, id′em, *pron., a.* The same as previously given: used to avoid repetition. Abbr. **id.**

i·den·ti·cal, ĭ·den′ti·kəl, i·den′ti·kəl, *a.* The same, or being the same one. —**i·den·ti·cal·ly**, *adv.* —**i·den·ti·cal·ness,** *n.*

i·den·ti·fi·a·ble, ĭ·den′tə·fī·ə·bəl, i·den′tə·fī·ə·bəl, *a.* Capable of being recognized or identified. —**i·den·ti·fi·a·bly**, *adv.*

i·den·ti·fi·ca·tion, ĭ·den·tə·fə·kā′shən, i·den·tə·fə·kā′shən, *n.* The act of identifying; something that identifies a person or thing.

i·den·ti·fy, ĭ·den′tə·fī, i·den′tə·fī, *v.t.,* **-fied, -fy·ing.** To recognize or establish as being a particular person or thing; to attest or prove to be as purported or asserted. —**i·den·ti·fi·er,** *n.*

i·den·ti·ty, ĭ·den′ti·tē, i·den′ti·tē, *n. pl.,* **-ties.** The state or fact of being or remaining the same one; the condition or character that distinguishes a person or a thing; individuality.

i·de·ol·o·gist, ĭ·dē·ol′ə·jist, id·ē·ol′ə·jist, *n.* A supporter of a particular ideology.

i·de·ol·o·gy, ĭ·dē·ol′ə·jē, id·ē·ol′ə·jē, *n. pl.,* **-gies.** A particular system of ideas, esp. on social or political subjects.

ides, īdz, *n. pl., sing. or pl. in constr.* In the ancient Roman calendar the 15th of March, May, July, and October, and the 13th of other months.

id·i·o·cy, id′ē·ə·sē, *n. pl.,* **-cies.** The condition of being an idiot; mental deficiency; senseless folly.

id·i·om, id′ē·əm, *n.* A form of expression peculiar to one language; an expression whose understood meaning is not expressed by the individual words, as *to get along with;* the language peculiar to a people; a variety or form of a language; a dialect; the individual manner of expression characteristic of a certain group, profession, or the like. —**id·i·o·mat·ic**, id·ē·ə·mat′ik, *a.* —**id·i·o·mat·i·cal·ly**, *adv.*

id·i·o·syn·cra·sy, id·ē·ə·sing′krə·sē, *n. pl.,* **-sies.** A personal peculiarity of constitution, temperament, or manner; a quirk. —**id·i·o·syn·crat·ic**, id·ē·ō·sin·krat′ik, *a.* —**id·i·o·syn·crat·i·cal·ly**, *adv.*

id·i·ot, id′ē·ət, *n.* One who suffers from mental retardation in one of its most severe forms, having a mental age of three years or less; an extremely incompetent or foolish person. —**id·i·ot·ic**, id·ē·ot′ik, *a.* —**id·i·ot·i·cal·ly**, *adv.*

i·dle, ī′dəl, *a.,* **i·dler, i·dlest.** Not engaged in any occupation; doing nothing; useless, ineffectual, or fruitless: *idle* rage; trifling or irrelevant: *idle* talk.—*v.i,* **i·dled, i·dling.** To lose or spend time inactively or without being employed.—*v.t.* To spend in idleness, usu. followed by *away;* to run without producing power, as a machine. —**i·dle·ness**, *n.* —**i·dler**, *n.* —**i·dly**, *adv.*

i·dol, ī′dəl, *n.* An image, representation, or symbol of a deity made or consecrated as an object of worship; a false or pagan god; *fig.*, the object of excessive attachment, admiration, or infatuation.

i·dol·a·try, ĭ·dol′ə·trē, *n. pl.,* **-tries.** The worship of idols; excessive admiration or veneration. —**i·dol·a·ter**, ĭ·dol′ə·tər, *n.* —**i·dol·a·trous**, *a.*

i·dol·ize, ī′dəl·īz, *v.t.,* **-ized, -iz·ing.** To worship as an idol; to make an idol of.—*v.i.* To practice worship or extreme devotion. —**i·dol·i·za·tion**, ī·də·li·zā′shən, *n.* —**i·dol·iz·er,** *n.*

i·dyll, i·dyl, ī′dəl, *n.* An elaborately structured short poem or narrative prose work, usu. describing idealized scenes or events from rustic life; a picturesque or charmingly simple scene. —**i·dyl·lic**, ī·dil′ik, *a.* —**i·dyl·lic·al·ly**, *adv.*

if, if, *conj.* In case that; granting or supposing that; on condition that: *If* it doesn't rain, we'll go; even though: an imaginative *if* impractical procedure; whether: She asked *if* I remembered. Used to introduce a wishful sentiment: *If* only it wouldn't rain.

if·fy, if′ē, *a. Informal.* Unresolved or conditional; uncertain.

ig·loo, ig′loo, *n. pl.,* **-loos.** An Eskimo hut, dome-shaped, and built of blocks of hard snow or ice.

ig·ne·ous, ig′nē·əs, *a.* Produced by fire or intense heat within the earth, as rocks of volcanic origin; of fire.

ig·nite, ig·nīt′, *v.t.,* **-nit·ed, -nit·ing.** To set on fire. —*v.i.* To take fire; to begin to burn. —**ig·nit·er**, *n.* —**ig·nit·a·ble, ig·nit·i·ble**, *a.* —**ig·nit·a·bil·i·ty, —ig·nit·i·bil·i·ty**, ig·nīt·ə·bil′i·tē, *n.*

ig·ni·tion, ig·nish′ən, *n.* The act of igniting or the state of being ignited; in an internal-combustion engine, the igniting of the charge in the cylinder; the device which ignites.

ig·no·ble, ig·nō′bəl, *a.* Mean, worthless, dishonorable, or base; of low birth or family. —**ig·no·bil·i·ty**, ig·nō·bil′i·tē, **ig·no·ble·ness**, *n.* —**ig·no·bly**, *adv.*

ig·no·min·y, ig′nə·min·ē, *n. pl.,* **-ies.** Public disgrace; shame; dishonor; infamy. —**ig·no·min·i·ous**, ig·nə·min′ē·əs, *a.* —**ig·no·min·i·ous·ly**, *adv.* —**ig·no·min·i·ous·ness,** *n.*

ig·no·ra·mus, ig·nə·rā′məs, ig·nə·ram′əs, *n.* An ignorant person.

ig·no·rant, ig′nər·ənt, *a.* Lacking in knowledge of either general information or a specific field: *ignorant* of physics; uninformed; untaught; unenlightened. **ig·no·rance,** *n.* —**ig·no·rant·ly**, *adv.*

ig·nore, ig·nor′, ig·nôr′, *v.t.,* **-nored, -nor·ing.** To disregard; to refuse to notice, consider, or recognize.

i·gua·na, i·gwä′nə, *n.* A large lizard found in tropical America.

ilk, ilk, *n.* Family, class, kind, or breed: Jones and his *ilk.*—**of that ilk,** of the same family name.

ill, il, *a.,* **worse, worst.** Sick or indisposed; producing evil or misfortune; calamitous or unfortunate: an *ill* end; hostile; bad or evil; wicked: *ill* repute; not proper; rude or unpolished: *ill* manners; incorrect; not skillful.—**ill at ease**, nervous or not comfortable.

I'll, il. Contraction of **I will** or **I shall.**

ill-ad·vised, il′əd·vīzd′, *a.* Badly informed; resulting from bad counsel or from lack of good counsel. —**ill-ad·vis·ed·ly**, il·əd·vī′zid·lē, *adv.*

ill-bred, il′bred′, *a.* Impolite; vulgar.

il·le·gal, i·lē′gəl, *a.* Contrary to official rules; unlawful; illicit. —**il·le·gal·i·ty**, il·ē·gal′i·tē, *n.* —**il·le·gal·ly**, *adv.*

il·leg·i·ble, i·lej′ə·bəl, *a.* Incapable of being read; poorly written. —**il·leg·i·bil·i·ty**, i·lej·ə·bil′ə·tē, **il·leg·i·ble·ness**, *n.* —**il·leg·i·bly**, *adv.*

il·le·git·i·mate, il·i·jit′ə·mət, *a.* Illegal; unauthorized or unwarranted; born out of wedlock. —**il·le·git·i·ma·cy**, *n. pl.,* **-cies.** —**il·le·git·i·mate·ly**, *adv.*

ill-fat·ed, il′fā′tid, *a.* Doomed; unlucky.

ill-fa·vored, il′fā′vərd, *a.* Ugly; displeasing or offensive.

ill-got·ten, il′got′ən, *a.* Dishonestly acquired.

il·lib·er·al, i·lib′ər·əl, i·lib′rəl, *a.* Of narrow mind or opinions; not generous.

il·lic·it, i·lis′it, *a.* Prohibited; unlawful.

il·lim·it·a·ble, i·lim′i·tə·bəl, *a.* Incapable of being limited.

il·lit·er·ate, i·lit′ər·it, *a.* Unable to read or write; uneducated.—*n.* —**il·lit·er·a·cy**, *n. pl.,* **-cies.**

ill na·ture, n. Evil nature or disposition. —**ill-na·tured**, il′nā′chərd, *a.*

ill·ness, il′nis, *n.* The state or condition of being sick.

il·log·i·cal, i·loj′i·kəl, *a.* Contrary to logic and its rules. —**il·log·ic**, *n.*

ill-starred, il′stärd′, *a.* Unlucky; ill-fated.

---

ill tem·per, *n.* A surly or irritable mood. —**ill-tem·pered,** il/tem/pərd, *a.* —**ill-tem·pered·ly,** *adv.* —**ill-tem·pered·ness,** *n.*

ill-timed, il/tīmd/, *a.* Inopportune.

il·lu·mi·nate, i·loom/i·nāt, *v.t.,* -**nat·ed,** -**nat·ing.** To light up; to enlighten; to make clear; to decorate with lights; to adorn, as a manuscript, with gilded and colored decorations. —**il·lu·mi·nat·ing,** *a.* —**il·lu·mi·na·tor,** i·loom/i·nā·tər, *n.*

il·lu·mi·na·tion, i·loo·mə·nā/shən, *n.* The act of illuminating.

il·lu·mine, i·loo/min, *v.t., v.i.,* -**mined,** -**min·ing.** To illuminate.

ill-use, il/ūz/, *v.t.,* -**used,** -**us·ing.** Treat unjustly or cruelly.—il/ūs/, *n.* Also **ill-us·age,** il/ū/sij.

il·lu·sion, i·loo/zhən, *n.* A false impression or belief; false perception or conception of some object of sense. —**il·lu·sive,** i·loo/siv, *a.* —**il·lu·sive·ly,** *adv.* —**il·lu·sive·ness,** *n.*

il·lu·so·ry, i·loo/sə·rē, *a.* Causing illusion; deceptive. —**il·lu·so·ri·ly,** *adv.* —**il·lu·so·ri·ness,** *n.*

il·lus·trate, il/ə·strāt, i·ləs/trāt, *v.t.,* -**trat·ed,** -**trat·ing.** To make clear; throw light on by examples; to ornament by means of pictures, drawings, diagrams, or the like.—*v.i.* To supply an example.

il·lus·tra·tion, il·ə·strā/shən, *n.* The act of illustrating; a picture or the like which clarifies or decorates. —**il·lus·tra·tive,** i·ləs/tra·tiv, il/ə·strā·tiv, *a.* —**il·lus·tra·tive·ly,** *adv.* —**il·lus·tra·tor,** il/ə·strā·tər, i·ləs/trā·tər, *n.*

il·lus·tri·ous, i·ləs/trē·əs, *a.* Distinguished; esteemed; renowned; accomplished.—**il·lus·tri·ous·ly,** *adv.* —**il·lus·tri·ous·ness,** *n.*

ill will, *n.* Hate; enmity.

I'm, īm. Contraction of **I am.**

im·age, im/ij, *n.* A representation of any person or thing; that which forms a likeness of something else; a mental picture; the composite public impression of a person, organization, or company.—*v.t.,* **im·aged, im·ag·ing.** To represent by an image. —**im·age·a·ble,** *a.* —**im·ag·er,** *n.*

im·age·ry, im/ij·rē, *n. pl.,* -**ries.** Mental images; figurative language. —**im·a·ge·ri·al,** im·ə·jēr/ē·əl, *a.*

im·ag·i·na·ble, i·maj/i·nə·bəl, *a.* Capable of being imagined. —**i·mag·i·na·ble·ness,** *n.* —**i·mag·i·na·bly,** *adv.*

im·ag·i·nar·y, i·maj/i·ner·ē, *a.* Existing only in imagination; not real.—*n. pl.,* -**ies.** —**i·mag·i·nar·i·ly,** *adv.* —**i·mag·i·nar·i·ness,** *n.*.

im·ag·i·na·tion, i·maj·ə·nā/shən, *n.* The action of imagining, or of forming mental images or concepts of what is not actually present to the senses; the power of the mind to reproduce images or concepts stored in the memory under the suggestion of associated images, or of recombining former experiences in the creation of new images. —**i·mag·i·na·tion·al,** *a.*

im·ag·i·na·tive, i·maj/i·nə·tiv, i·maj/i·nā·tiv, *a.* Having powers of imagination pertaining to or concerned with imagination. —**i·mag·i·na·tive·ly,** *adv.* —**i·mag·i·na·tive·ness,** *n.*

im·ag·ine, i·maj/in, *v.t., v.i.,* -**ined,** -**in·ing.** To form a mental image of; conceive; suppose; think.

im·bal·ance, im·bal/əns, *n.* A lack of equilibrium or equality.

im·be·cile, im/bə·sil, im/bə·səl, *n.* One who is mentally deficient; a person having an intelligence quotient between 25 and 50 or a mental age of about seven.—*a.* Mentally feeble; foolish. Also **im·be·cil·ic,** im·bə·sil/ik. —**im·be·cile·ly,** *adv.* —**im·be·cil·i·ty,** im·bə·sil/i·tē, *n.*

im·bed, im·bed/, *v.t.,* -**bed·ded,** -**bed·ding.** Embed.

im·bibe, im·bīb/, *v.t.,* -**bibed,** -**bib·ing.** To drink; to receive into the mind.—*v.i.* To drink; to absorb. —**im·bib·er,** *n.*

im·bro·glio, im·brōl/yō, *n. pl.,* -**glios.** A complicated or difficult situation; a confused misunderstanding.

im·bue, im·bū/, *v.t.,* -**bued,** -**bu·ing.** To soak with

moisture or dye; to inspire or impregnate, as with emotions or opinions.

im·i·ta·ble, im/i·tə·bəl, *a.* Capable of being imitated or copied.

im·i·tate, im/i·tāt, *v.t.,* -**tat·ed,** -**tat·ing.** To follow as an example; to copy; to produce a likeness of. —**im·i·ta·tor,** *n.*

im·i·ta·tion, im·i·tā/shən, *n.* The act of imitating; that which is made or produced as a copy.—*a.* —**im·i·ta·tive,** im/i·tā·tiv, *a.*

im·mac·u·late, i·mak/yə·lit, *a.* Free from stain; spotlessly clean; free from moral impurity; without flaw or error. —**im·mac·u·la·cy, im·mac·u·late·ness,** *n.* —**im·mac·u·late·ly,** *adv.*

im·ma·nent, im/ə·nənt, *a.* Remaining within; indwelling; inherent; of God, pervading the universe. —**im·ma·nence, im·ma·nen·cy,** *n.* —**im·ma·nent·ly,** *adv.*

im·ma·te·ri·al, im·ə·tēr/ē·əl, *a.* Of no essential consequence; unimportant; not consisting of matter. —**im·ma·te·ri·al·ly,** *adv.* —**im·ma·te·ri·al·ness,** *n.* —**im·ma·te·ri·al·i·ty,** im·ə·tēr·ē·al/ə·tē.

im·ma·ture, im·ə·tyûr/, im·ə·chûr/, im·ə·tûr/, *a.* Not mature or ripe; unripe; not brought to a completed state.—*n.* —**im·ma·ture·ly,** *adv.* —**im·ma·ture·ness, im·ma·tu·ri·ty,** *n.*

im·meas·ur·a·ble, i·mezh/ər·ə·bəl, *a.* Incapable of being measured; boundless. —**im·meas·ur·a·ble·ness,** *n.* —**im·meas·ur·a·bly,** *adv.*

im·me·di·a·cy, i·mē/dē·ə·sē, *n. pl.,* -**cies.** The condition or quality of being immediate; immediateness; proximity; *usu. pl.,* that which is immediate or which pertains to the moment.

im·me·di·ate, i·mē/dē·it, *a.* Occurring or done without separation by an interval of space or time; instant; related to the present time; in closest relation. Acting or occurring without a medium, or without an intervening cause, means, or condition; direct. —**im·me·di·ate·ly,** *adv.* —**im·me·di·ate·ness,** *n.*

im·me·mo·ri·al, im·ə·môr/ē·əl, im·ə·mō/rē·əl, *a.* Beyond memory, or record; existing or occurring in the far distant past. —**im·me·mo·ri·al·ly,** *adv.*

im·mense, i·mens/, *a.* Vast; very great; boundless; huge; enormous. —**im·mense·ly,** *adv.* —**im·mense·ness,** *n.* —**im·men·si·ty,** *n.*

im·merge, i·merj/, *v.i.,* -**merged,** -**merg·ing.** To plunge into or under a fluid; to disappear by entering into any medium. —**im·mer·gence,** *n.*

im·merse, i·mers/, *v.t.,* -**mersed,** -**mers·ing,** To plunge into anything that covers or surrounds, as into a fluid; to dip; to engage deeply or involve. —**im·mer·sion,** i·mer/zhən, i·mer/shən, *n.*

im·mi·grant, im/ə·grənt, *n.* One who or that which immigrates, esp. a person who migrates into a country of which he is not a native, for permanent residence.—*a.*

im·mi·grate, im/ə·grāt, *v.i.,* -**grat·ed,** -**grat·ing.** To move into a country of which one is not a native for the purpose of permanent residence.—*v.t.* To send in or cause to enter as immigrants. —**im·mi·gra·tion,** im·ə·grā/shən, *n.* —**im·mi·gra·tor,** *n.*

im·mi·nent, im/i·nənt, *a.* Impending; near at hand. —**im·mi·nence,** *n.*

im·mo·bile, i·mō/bəl, i·mō/bēl, *a.* Immovable; not able to move; fixed. —**im·mo·bil·i·ty,** im·ō·bil/i·tē, *n.* —**im·mo·bi·lize,** i·mō/bə·līz, *v.t.,* -**lized,** -**liz·ing.**

im·mod·er·ate, i·mod/ər·it, *a.* Without restraint; excessive. —**im·mod·er·ate·ly,** *adv.* —**im·mod·er·ate·ness,** *n.*

im·mod·est, i·mod/ist, *a.* Lacking modesty or propriety; boldly assertive. —**im·mod·est·ly,** *adv.* —**im·mod·es·ty,** *n.*

im·mo·late, im/ə·lāt, *v.t.,* -**lat·ed,** -**lat·ing.** To kill, esp. by fire, as a victim offered in sacrifice; to kill or destroy as in war. —**im·mo·la·tion,** im·ə·lā/shən, *n.* —**im·mo·la·tor,** *n.*

im·mor·al, i·môr/əl, *a.* Not moral; not conforming to

accepted patterns of what is considered right and wrong behavior in a culture. —im·mor·al·ist, n. —im·mo·ral·i·ty, im·ə·ral/i·tē, n. pl., -ties. —im·mor·al·ly, adv.

im·mor·tal, i·môr/təl, a. Not mortal; not liable or subject to death; remembered or celebrated through all time. —im·mor·tal·i·ty, im·ôr·tal/i·tē, n. —im·mor·tal·ize, i·môr/təl·īz, v.t., -ized, -iz·ing. —im·mor·tal·ly, adv.

im·mov·a·ble, i·moo/və·bəl, a. Stationary; not subject to change; unalterable; emotionless; impassive. —im·mov·a·bil·i·ty, i·moo·və·bil/ə·tē, n. —im·mov·a·bly, adv.

im·mune, i·mūn/, a. Exempt; free from; not susceptible to a disease, usu. by inoculation.—n.

im·mu·ni·ty, i·mū/ni·tē, n. pl., -ties. Exemption from obligation, service, or duty; the state of being immune from a disease.

im·mu·nize, im/yə·nīz, v.t., -nized, -niz·ing. To render immune or exempt. —im·mu·ni·za·tion, im·yə·nə·zā/shən, n.

im·mu·nol·o·gy, im·yə·nol/ə·jē, n. That branch of medical science which deals with immunity from disease and the production of such immunity.

im·mure, i·myūr/, v.t., -mured, -mur·ing. To enclose or imprison within walls; to confine.

im·mu·ta·ble, i·mū/tə·bəl, a. Unchangeable. —im·mu·ta·bil·i·ty, i·mū·tə·bil/ə·tē, —im·mu·ta·ble·ness, n. —im·mu·ta·bly, adv.

imp, imp, n. A small devil; a mischievous child.

im·pact, im/pakt, n. The striking of one body against another; a collision; the force of a collision or impingement.—im·pakt/, v.t. To drive or press closely or firmly into something. —im·pac·tion, im·pak/shən, n.

im·pact·ed, im·pak/tid, a. Wedged or packed in tightly; of a tooth, so firmly held by the jawbone that it cannot emerge from the gum.

im·pair, im·pâr/, v.t. To make worse; to lessen; to deteriorate. —im·pair·er, n. —im·pair·ment, n.

im·pal·a, im·pal/ə, im·pä/lə, n. pl., -as, -a. An antelope native to Africa noted for its leaping ability.

im·pale, im·pāl/, v.t., -paled, -pal·ing. To fix upon a sharpened stake or the like; pierce. —im·pale·ment, n. —im·pal·er, n.

im·pal·pa·ble, im·pal/pə·bəl, a. Incapable of being distinguished by the touch; not easily grasped by the mind. —im·pal·pa·bil·i·ty, im·pal·pə·bil/ə·tē, n. —im·pal·pa·bly, adv.

im·pan·el, im·pan/əl, v.t., -eled, -el·ing. To enter on a list for jury duty; to select a jury from a panel.

im·part, im·pärt/, v.t. To make known; to give; to bestow a portion of.

im·par·tial, im·pär/shəl, a. Not partial; unprejudiced; just. —im·par·ti·al·i·ty, im·pär·shē·al/i·tē, im·par·tial·ness, n. —im·par·tial·ly, adv.

im·pass·a·ble, im·pas/ə·bəl, im·päs/ə·bəl, a. Incapable of being passed over, through, or along. —im·pass·a·bil·i·ty, im·pas·ə·bil/ə·tē, im·pass·a·ble·ness, n. —im·pass·a·bly, adv.

im·passe, im/pas, im·pas/, n. A position from which there is no escape; a deadlock.

im·pas·si·ble, im·pas/i·bəl, a. Incapable of pain, passion, or suffering; without emotion. —im·pas·si·bil·i·ty, im·pas·ə·bil/ə·tē, im·pas·si·ble·ness, n. —im·pas·si·bly, adv.

im·pas·sion, im·pash/ən, v.t. To move or affect strongly with passion. —im·pas·sioned, im·pash/ənd, a. —im·pas·sioned·ly, adv. —im·pas·sioned·ness, n.

im·pas·sive, im·pas/iv, a. Without emotion; unmoved. —im·pas·sive·ly, adv. —im·pas·sive·ness, im·pas·siv·i·ty, im·pə·siv/ə·tē, n.

im·pa·tient, im·pā/shənt, a. Not patient; eager for change; intolerant, followed by with, of, at, for, under; prompted by, exhibiting or expressing impatience. —im·pa·tience, n. —im·pa·tient·ly, adv.

im·peach, im·pēch/, v.t. To charge with wrongdoing; to accuse, as a public official before a tribunal, of misconduct in office; to challenge the credibility of.—n. —im·peach·a·ble, a. —im·peach·ment, n.

im·pec·ca·ble, im·pek/ə·bəl, a. Faultless; flawless; perfect. —im·pec·ca·bil·i·ty, im·pek·ə·bil/ə·tē, n. —im·pec·ca·bly, adv.

im·pe·cu·ni·ous, im·pə·kū/nē·əs, a. Not having money; without funds; indigent. —im·pe·cu·ni·ous·ly, adv. —im·pe·cu·ni·ous·ness, n.

im·pede, im·pēd/, v.t., -ped·ed, -ped·ing. To obstruct; to hinder.

im·ped·i·ment, im·ped/ə·mənt, n. A hindrance; a handicap, esp. a speech defect.

im·pel, im·pel/, v.t., -pelled, -pel·ling. Drive or urge forward; excite to motion or action.

im·pend, im·pend/, v.i. To be imminent; to be ready to happen. —im·pend·ing, a.

im·pen·e·tra·bil·i·ty, im·pen·i·trə·bil/i·tē, n. The condition of being impenetrable.

im·pen·e·tra·ble, im·pen/ə·trə·bəl, a. Incapable of being penetrated or pierced; impermeable; inaccessible; incomprehensible; inscrutable. —im·pen·e·tra·ble·ness, n. —im·pen·e·tra·bly, adv.

im·pen·i·tent, im·pen/ə·tənt, a. Not repenting of sin.—n. —im·pen·i·tence, n. —im·pen·i·tent·ly, adv.

im·per·a·tive, im·per/ə·tiv, a. Not to be avoided or evaded; urgent and necessary; obligatory. —im·per·a·tive·ly, adv. —im·per·a·tive·ness, n.

im·per·cep·ti·ble, im·pər·sep/tə·bəl, a. Very slight; subtle; not discernible by the senses or the mind. —im·per·cep·ti·bil·i·ty, im·pər·sep·tə·bil/ə·tē, n. —im·per·cep·ti·bly, adv. —im·per·cep·tive, a. —im·per·cep·tive·ness, n.

im·per·fect, im·pər/fikt, a. Not perfect; incomplete; defective; denoting incomplete action or state, esp. in past time. —im·per·fect·ly, adv. —im·per·fect·ness, n.

im·per·fec·tion, im·pər·fek/shən, n. Defectiveness; a defect or fault.

im·pe·ri·al, im·pēr/ē·əl, a. Of or pertaining to an empire, or to an emperor or empress; supreme in authority; of a commanding quality, manner, or aspect; domineering; magnificent. —im·pe·ri·al·ly, adv.

im·pe·ri·al·ism, im·pēr/ē·ə·liz·əm, n. Imperial system of government; advocacy of imperial interests; specif. the policy of extending the rule or authority of an empire or nation over foreign countries either by direct acquisition of territory, or by indirect control of economic and political life; the policy of acquiring and holding colonies and dependencies. —im·pe·ri·al·ist, n., a. —im·pe·ri·al·is·tic, im·pēr·ē·ə·lis/tik, a. —im·pe·ri·al·is·ti·cal·ly, adv.

im·per·il, im·pār/il, v.t., -iled, -il·ing. To endanger. —im·per·il·ment, n.

im·pe·ri·ous, im·pēr/ē·əs, a. Dictatorial; haughty; domineering. —im·pe·ri·ous·ly, adv. —im·pe·ri·ous·ness, n.

im·per·ish·a·ble, im·pār/i·shə·bəl, a. Not subject to decay; indestructible. —im·per·ish·a·bil·i·ty, im·per·i·shə·bil/ə·tē. —im·per·ish·a·ble·ness, n. —im·per·ish·a·bly, adv.

im·per·ma·nent, im·pər/mə·nənt, a. Not enduring; transient. —im·per·ma·nence, im·per·ma·nen·cy, n. —im·per·ma·nent·ly, adv.

im·per·me·a·ble, im·pər/mē·ə·bəl, a. Not permitting the passage of a fluid through the pores or interstices. —im·per·me·a·bil·i·ty, im·pər·mē·ə·bil/ə·tē, im·per·me·a·ble·ness, n. —im·per·me·a·bly, adv.

im·per·son·al, im·pėr′sə·nəl, *a.* Without personal reference or connection; of pronouns, indefinite; of verbs, having the non-personal or nonspecific subject *it* expressed or understood, as: *It* rains. **—im·per·son·al·i·ty**, im·pėr·sə·nal′i·tē, *n. pl.,* **-ties. —im·per·son·al·ly**, *adv.*

im·per·son·ate, im·pėr′sə·nāt, *v.t.,* **-at·ed, -at·ing.** To assume the appearance, mannerisms, and speech of someone. **—im·per·son·a·tion**, im·pėr·sə·nā′shən, *n.* **—im·per·son·a·tor**, *n.*

im·per·ti·nent, im·pėr′tə·nənt, *a.* Rude, intrusive, or presumptuous, as persons or their actions or speech; insolent or saucy; not pertinent or relevant. **—im·per·ti·nence**, *n.* **—im·per·ti·nent·ly**, *adv.*

im·per·turb·a·ble, im·pėr·tėr′bə·bəl, *a.* Not easily agitated; calm. **—im·per·turb·a·bly**, *adv.*

im·per·vi·ous, im·pėr′vē·əs, *a.* Incapable of being passed through, as by a liquid; incapable of being emotionally affected or influenced by argument. **—im·per·vi·ous·ly**, *adv.* **—im·per·vi·ous·ness**, *n.*

im·pe·ti·go, im·pə·tī′gō, *n.* A contagious skin disease.

im·pet·u·ous, im·pech′ū·əs, *a.* Rashly impulsive; hasty. **—im·pet·u·os·i·ty**, im·pe·chū·os′i·tē, *n.* **—im·pet·u·ous·ly**, *adv.* **—im·pet·u·ous·ness**, *n.*

im·pe·tus, im′pi·təs, *n. pl.,* **-tus·es.** The force with which a moving body tends to maintain its velocity and overcome resistance; energy of motion; anything that is an incentive to action; stimulus.

im·pi·e·ty, im·pī′i·tē, *n. pl.,* **-ties.** Lack of reverence for God; lack of respect, as toward parents.

im·pinge, im·pinj′, *v.i.,* **-pinged, -ping·ing.** To strike or dash, used with *on, upon,* or *against;* collide; to encroach or infringe, used with *on* or *upon.* **—im·pinge·ment**, *n.* **—im·ping·er**, *n.*

im·pi·ous, im′pē·əs, *a.* Wanting in reverence, for God; religious observances or symbols; profane; lacking in respect, as for one's parents. **—im·pi·ous·ly**, *adv.* **—im·pi·ous·ness**, *n.*

im·plac·a·ble, im·plak′ə·bəl, im·plā′kə·bəl, *a.* Not to be appeased or pacified; stubborn. **—im·plac·a·bil·i·ty**, im·plak·ə·bil′ə·tē, **im·plac·a·ble·ness**, *n.* **—im·plac·a·bly**, *adv.*

im·plant, im·plant′, *v.t.* To fix firmly in the mind, as truths or principles; to plant or insert deeply or firmly. **—im′plant**, im′plänt, *n.* **—im·plan·ta·tion**, im·plan·tā′shən, *n.* **—im·plant·er**, *n.*

im·plau·si·ble, im·plô′zə·bəl, *a.* Not having the appearance of truth or credibility. **—im·plau·si·bly**, *adv.* **—im·plau·si·bil·i·ty**, im·plô·zə·bil′ə·tē, *n.*

im·ple·ment, im′plə·mənt, *n.* An instrument, tool, or utensil used in manual labors.—im′plə·ment, *v.t.* To fulfill or satisfy the conditions of; to perform; to put into effect; to supplement. **—im·ple·men·tal**, im·plə·men′təl, *a.* **—im·ple·men·ta·tion**, im·plə·men·tā′shən, *n.*

im·pli·cate, im′plə·kāt, *v.t.,* **-cat·ed, -cat·ing.** To involve as being concerned in a matter, affair, or condition.

im·pli·ca·tion, im·plə·kā′shən, *n.* The act of implying, or the state of being implied; something implied; the act of implicating or the resulting condition.

im·plic·it, im·plis′it, *a.* Understood, though not expressed in words; implied; inherent, though not expressed or readily seen; absolute. **—im·plic·it·ly**, *adv.* **—im·plic·it·ness**, *n.*

im·plode, im·plōd′, *v.i., v.t.,* **-plod·ed, -plod·ing.** To burst inward. **—im·plo·sion**, im·plō′zhən, *n.* **—im·plo·sive**, *a., n.*

im·plore, im·plôr′, im·plōr′, *v.t.,* **-plored, -plor·ing.** to pray earnestly; to entreat; to beg.—*v.i.* **—im·plo·ra·tion**, im·plə·rā′shən, *n.*

im·ply, im·plī′, *v.t.,* **-plied, -ply·ing.** To involve or contain as an essential part or as a consequence; to hint; signify.

im·po·lite, im·pə·līt′, *a.* Not polite; rude. **—im·po·lite·ly**, *adv.* **—im·po·lite·ness**, *n.*

im·pol·i·tic, im·pol′i·tik, *a.* Unwise; imprudent; indiscreet; injudicious. **—im·pol·i·tic·ly**, *adv.*

im·pon·der·a·ble, im·pon′dėr·ə·bəl, *a.* That cannot be weighed, measured, or evaluated.—*n.* Anything imponderable. **—im·pon·der·a·bil·i·ty**, im·pon·dėr·ə·bil′ə·tē, **im·pon·der·a·ble·ness**, *n.* **—im·pon·der·a·bly**, *adv.*

im·port, im·pōrt′, im·pôrt′, *v.t.* To bring in, esp. to bring in from a foreign country, as goods or merchandise for sale or use; to mean, signify, or imply; to make known—im′pōrt, im′pôrt, *n.* **—im·port·a·ble**, im·pôr′tə·bəl, *a.* **—im·port·er**, im·pôr′tėr, *n.*

im·por·tance, im·pôr′təns, *n.* Significance, consequence, or moment; notable character; important position or standing; personal or social consequence. **—im·por·tant**, im·pôr′tənt, *a.* **—im·por·tant·ly**, *adv.*

im·por·ta·tion, im·pôr·tā′shən, *n.* The act of importing or bringing in.

im·por·tu·nate, im·pôr′chə·nit, *a.* Urgent or persistent in demands; troublesome. **—im·por·tu·nate·ly**, *adv.*

im·por·tune, im·pôr·tūn′, im·pôr·toon′, im·pôr′chən, *v.t., v.i.,* **-tuned, -tun·ing.** To make urgent or persistent solicitations. **—im·por·tun·er**, *n.*

im·pose, im·pōz′, *v.t.,* **-posed, -pos·ing.** To put or set by or as by authority; to lay on as something to be obeyed or fulfilled; to obtrude or thrust upon others; pass or palm off deceptively; foist.—*v.i.* To take undue advantage of; to pass off something fraudulent. **—im·pos·ter**, *n.* **—im·po·si·tion**, im·pə·zish′ən, *n.*

im·pos·ing, im·pō′zing, *a.* Making an impression on the mind, as by great size, appearance, or dignity. **—im·pos·ing·ly**, *adv.*

im·pos·si·ble, im·pos′ə·bəl, *a.* Not possible; not capable of being or being done. *Informal.* Objectionable or intolerable. **—im·pos·si·bil·i·ty**, im·pos·ə·bil′ə·tē, *n. pl.,* **-ties. —im·pos·si·bly**, *adv.*

im·post, im′pōst, *n.* That which is imposed; a tax, tribute, or duty.

im·pos·tor, im·pos′tėr, *n.* A person who assumes the character or name of another in order to deceive.

im·pos·ture, im·pos′chėr, *n.* The act of an impostor.

im·po·tent, im′pə·tənt, *a.* Entirely lacking strength; specif. in the male, completely powerless to perform sexual intercourse. **—im·po·tence, im·po·ten·cy**, *n.* **—im·po·tent·ly**, *adv.*

im·pound, im·pownd′, *v.t.* To shut up in a pound, as an animal; confine within an enclosure, as: to *impound* water in a reservoir; to seize and retain in custody of the law. **—im·pound·age**, *n.*

im·pov·er·ish, im·pov′ėr·ish, im·pov′rish, *v.t.* To reduce to poverty; to exhaust the strength, richness, or fertility of. **—im·pov·er·ish·ment**, *n.*

im·prac·ti·ca·ble, im·prak′ti·kə·bəl, *a.* Not practicable; unfeasible. **—im·prac·ti·ca·bil·i·ty**, im·prak·ti·kə·bil′i·tē, **im·prac·ti·ca·ble·ness**, *n.* **—im·prac·ti·ca·bly**, *adv.*

im·prac·ti·cal, im·prak′ti·kəl, *a.* Not practical.

im·pre·cate, im′prə·kāt, *v.t.,* **-cat·ed, -cat·ing.** To call down, as a curse, by prayer. **—im·pre·ca·tion**, im·prə·kā′shən, *n.*

im·preg·na·ble, im·preg′nə·bəl, *a.* Not able to be taken by force; not to be moved or shaken. **—im·preg·na·bil·i·ty**, im·preg·nə·bil′i·tē, **im·preg·na·ble·ness**, *n.* **—im·preg·na·bly**, *adv.*

im·preg·nate, im·preg′nāt, *v.t.,* **-nat·ed, -nat·ing.** To make pregnant or with young; to fertilize; to fill or saturate with some substance; to imbue, as with ideas.—im·preg′nit, im·preg′nāt, *a.* **—im·preg·na·tion**, im·preg·nā′shən, *n.* **—im·preg·na·tor**, *n.*

im·pre·sa·ri·o, im·pri·sär′ē·ō, *n. pl.,* **-os.** One who organizes, manages, or conducts a company of operatic or other musical performers; one who arranges or produces entertainment.

im·press, im·pres′, *v.t.* To press into or on something so as to leave a mark; to stamp or imprint; to fix firmly on the mind or memory; to urge; to affect deeply or strongly in mind or feelings; to make an impression on; to influence in opinion.—im′pres, *n.* —**im·press·er**, im·pres′ər, *n.* —**im·press·i·ble**, im·pres′ə·bəl, *a.*

im·press, im·pres′, *v.t.* To press or force into public service; to seize or take for public use.—im′pres, *n.* —**im·press·ment**, im·pres′mənt, *n.*

im·pres·sion, im·presh′ən, *n.* The act of impressing, or the state of being impressed; a mark, indentation, or figure produced by pressure; the effect produced by any agency or influence; a strong effect produced on the intellect, feelings, or conscience.

im·pres·sion, im·presh′ən, *n.* An imitation of a famous person. —**im·pres·sion·ist**, *n.*

im·pres·sion·a·ble, im·presh′ə·nə·bəl, *a.* Sensitive; suggestible; capable of being impressed or influenced. —**im·pres·sion·a·bly**, *adv.*

im·pres·sion·ism, im·presh′ə·niz·əm, *n.* A theory or method; literature, art, and music whose aim is to depict impressions rather than strict objective detail. —**im·pres·sion·ist**, *n.* —**im·pres·sion·is·tic**, im·presh·ə·nis′tik, *a.*

im·pres·sive, im·pres′iv, *a.* Making or tending to make an impression. —**im·pres·sive·ly**, *adv.* —**im·pres·sive·ness**, *n.*

im·pri·ma·tur, im·pri·mä′tər, im·pri·mā′tər, A license, esp. to print or publish.

im·print, im·print′, *v.t.* To mark by pressure; to impress.—im′print, *n.* the name of the printer or publisher of a book, with the place and date of publication. —**im·prin·ter**, im·prin′tər, *n.*

im·pris·on, im·priz′ən, *v.t.* To put into a prison; to incarcerate; to confine; to restrain. —**im·pris·on·ment**, *n.*

im·prob·a·ble, im·prob′ə·bəl, *a.* Not probable; unlikely. —**im·prob·a·bil·i·ty**, im·prob·ə·bil′i·tē, **im·prob·a·ble·ness**, *n.* —**im·prob·a·bly**, *adv.*

im·promp·tu, im·promp′too, im·promp′tū, *a.* Offhand; on the spur of the moment.—*n.*, *adv.*

im·prop·er, im·prop′ər, *a.* Not proper; not suited; indecent; erroneous; not normal. —**im·prop·er·ly**, *adv.* —**im·prop·er·ness**, *n.*

im·pro·pri·e·ty, im·prə·prī′i·tē, *n. pl.*, **-ties.** The quality of being improper; an unsuitable act or expression; incorrect.

im·prove, im·proov′, *v.t.*, **-proved, -prov·ing.** To bring to a more desirable or excellent condition; to better; to make more useful.—*v.i.* To convalesce; to increase in value or excellence. —**im·prov·a·bil·i·ty**, im·proov·ə·bil′ə·tē, *n.* —**im·prov·a·ble**, *a.*

im·prove·ment, im·proov′mənt, *n.* Act of improving; increase in value or excellence; a valuable addition to real property.

im·prov·i·dent, im·prov′i·dənt, *a.* Lacking in foresight. —**im·prov·i·dence**, *n.* —**im·prov·i·dent·ly**, *adv.*

im·prov·i·sa·tion, im·prov·ə·zā′shən, im·prə·vi·zā′shən, The act of improvising; something impromptu, as music or verse. —**im·prov·i·sa·tion·al**, *a.*

im·pro·vise, im′prə·vīz, *v.t.*, **-vised, -vis·ing.** To compose, as music or verse, on the spur of the moment; to extemporize.—*v.i.* To compose, perform, or provide anything extemporaneously. —**im·pro·vi·ser**, *n.*

im·pru·dent, im·prood′ənt, *a.* Not prudent; rash. —**im·pru·dence**, *n.* —**im·pru·dent·ly**, *adv.*

im·pu·dent, im′pū·dənt, *a.* Offensively forward; impertinent. —**im·pu·dence**, *n.* —**im·pu·dent·ly**, *adv.*

im·pugn, im·pūn′, *v.t.* To challenge as false. —**im·pugn·er**, *n.*

im·pulse, im′pəls, *n.* An impelling action of force, driving onward or inducing motion; the effect of an impelling force; the inciting influence of a particular feeling or mental state; a sudden involuntary inclination prompting to action. —**im·pul·sion**, im·pəl′shən, *n.*

im·pul·sive, im·pəl′siv, *a.* Driving onward or inducing motion; tending to act impetuously.

im·pu·ni·ty, im·pū·ni·tē, *n.* Exemption from punishment, injury, suffering, or loss.

im·pure, im·pyūr′, *a.* Containing extraneous matter; foul; not morally pure; corrupt. —**im·pure·ly**, *adv.* —**im·pure·ness**, *n.* —**im·pu·ri·ty**, *n. pl.*, **-ties.**

im·pute, im·pūt′, *v.t.*, **-put·ed, -put·ing.** To attribute to a person; to attribute a fault; blame. —**im·pu·ta·ble**, *a.* —**im·pu·ta·tion**, im·pyū·tā′shən, *n.* —**im·put·a·tive**, *a., adv.* —**im·put·er**, *n.*

in, in, *prep.* A particle or function word expressing inclusion or presence within limits of place, time, or circumstances; an expression of inclusion within or occurrence during the course of a period of time; an indication of situation, action, manner, relation, or respect; an indication of object or purpose; into. —*adv.* In or into some place, position, state, or relationship; on the inside; within.—*a.* That is in; internal; inward; incoming. *Informal.* Up-to-date or socially acceptable or desirable: the *in* thing to do.—*n.* One of those who are in power.

in·a·bil·i·ty, in·ə·bil′ə·tē, *n.* The state of being unable; lack of power, means, or ability.

in·ac·ces·si·ble, in·ak·ses′ə·bəl, *a.* Not accessible; not to be reached, obtained or approached. —**in·ac·ces·si·bil·i·ty**, **in·ac·ces·si·ble·ness**, *n.* —**in·ac·ces·si·bly**, *adv.*

in·ac·cu·rate, in·ak′yər·it, *a.* Not accurate, exact, or correct; containing incorrect statements; not according to truth; erroneous. —**in·ac·cu·rate·ly**, *adv.* —**in·ac·cu·ra·cy**, *n. pl.*, **-cies.**

in·ac·tion, in·ak′shən, *n.* State of being inactive; idleness.

in·ac·tive, in·ak′tiv, *a.* Not active; inert; idle; out of use; indolent; sluggish. *Milit.* Not mobilized. —**in·ac·tive·ly**, *adv.* —**in·ac·tiv·i·ty**, in·ak·tiv′ə·tē, *n.*

in·ad·e·quate, in·ad′ə·kwit, *a.* Not adequate; not equal to the purpose; insufficient; inept. —**in·ad·e·qua·cy**, *n. pl.*, **-cies.** —**in·ad·e·quate·ly**, *adv.*

in·ad·mis·si·ble, in·əd·mis′ə·bəl, *a.* Not admissible; not proper to be admitted, allowed, or received. —**in·ad·mis·si·bly**, *adv.*

in·ad·vert·ent, in·əd·vər′tənt, *a.* Not paying strict attention; failing to notice or observe; heedless; unintentional. —**in·ad·vert·ence**, **in·ad·vert·en·cy**, *n.* —**in·ad·vert·ent·ly**, *adv.*

in·al·ien·a·ble, in·āl′yə·nə·bəl, in·ā′lē·ə·nə·bəl, *a.* Incapable of being taken away or transferred to another. —**in·al·ien·a·bly**, *adv.*

in·am·o·ra·ta, in·am·ə·rä′tə, *n. pl.*, **-tas.** A female lover; a sweetheart.

in·ane, i·nān′, *a.* Empty; foolish; void of meaning.—*n.* —**in·ane·ly**, *adv.* —**in·ane·ness**, *n.* —**in·an·i·ty**, in·an′ə·tē, *n. pl.*, **-ties.**

in·an·i·mate, in·an′ə·mit, *a.* Not animate; destitute of life or animation; without vivacity or briskness; dull; inactive; sluggish.

in·ap·pro·pri·ate, in·ə·prō′prē·it, *a.* Not appropriate; unsuitable; not proper. —**in·ap·pro·pri·ate·ly**, *adv.* —**in·ap·pro·pri·ate·ness**, *n.*

in·apt, in·apt′, *a.* Not apt; unsuitable; inept; unskilled; awkward. —**in·ap·ti·tude**, in·ap′tə·tood, *n.* —**in·apt·ly**, *adv.* —**in·apt·ness**, *n.*

in·ar·tic·u·late, in·är·tik′yə·lit, *a.* Not intelligible; unable to use clear or understandable speech; dumb; unable to use speech to convey ideas; not expressed in speech. —**in·ar·tic·u·late·ly**, *adv.* —**in·ar·tic·u·late·ness**, *n.*

in·as·much as, in·əz·much′, *conj.* Insofar as, or to such a degree as; in view of the fact that; seeing that; since.

in·at·ten·tion, in·ə·ten′shən, *n.* Failure to pay attention; heedlessness. —**in·at·ten·tive,** *a.* —**in·at·ten·tive·ly,** *adv.*

in·au·gu·ral, in·ô′gyə·rəl, *a.* Of an inauguration; relating to or designating a beginning; first.—*n.* A speech at an inauguration; ceremony marking induction into office; inauguration.

in·au·gu·rate, in·ô′gyə·rāt, *v.t.,* **-rat·ed, -rat·ing.** To induct into office with formal ceremonies; install; to make a formal beginning of; to initiate; commence or begin. —**in·au·gu·ra·tion,** in·ô·gyə·rā′shən, *n.*

in·aus·pi·cious, in·ôs·pish′əs, *a.* Ill-omened; unlucky; unfavorable. —**in·aus·pi·cious·ly,** *adv.*

in·board, in′bôrd, *a., adv.* Within the hull or interior, or toward the center, of a ship or boat: as, an *inboard* motor; near the fuselage or center of an airplane.

in·born, in′bôrn′, *a.* Innate; inherent; implanted by nature.

in·bound, in′bownd, *a.* Inward bound.

in·bred, in′bred, *a.* Innate; natural, brought about by inbreeding.

in·breed, in′brēd, in·brēd′, *v.t.,* **-bred, -breed·ing.** To cross or mate closely related individuals. —**in·breed·ing,** *n.*

in·cal·cu·la·ble, in·kal′kyə·lə·bəl, *a.* Beyond calculation; too great to be counted or measured; unpredictable. —**in·cal·cu·la·bly,** *adv.*

in·can·des·cent, in·kən·des′ənt, *a.* Glowing with heat; intensely bright; brilliant. —**in·can·des·cence,** *n.* —**in·can·des·cent·ly,** *adv.*

in·can·ta·tion, in·kan·tā′shən, *n.* The words sung or spoken to raise spirits or perform magical actions; a magical spell, charm, or ceremony.

in·ca·pa·ble, in·kā′pə·bəl, *a.* Not capable; possessing inadequate power or ability for a particular purpose; incompetent: as, an *incapable* assistant; not admitting or susceptible due to type or condition, used only with *of*: as, a gas *incapable* of being reduced to a liquid; unable: as, *incapable* of working hard. *Law.* Unqualified or disqualified; not having the ability, understanding, or other qualification for certain legal matters.—*n.* One physically or mentally unable to act with effect; an inefficient or incompetent person; one mentally defective. —**in·ca·pa·bly,** *adv.*

in·ca·pac·i·tate, in·kə·pas′i·tat, *v.t.,* **-tat·ed, -tat·ing.** To make unable or unfit; to disqualify.

in·ca·pac·i·ty, in·kə·pas′i·tē, *n. pl.,* **-ties.** Lack of capacity, power, or ability; incompetency.

in·car·cer·ate, in·kär′sə·rāt, *v.t.,* **-at·ed, -at·ing.** To imprison; to shut up or enclose. —**in·car·cer·a·tion,** in·kär·sə·rā′shən, *n.*

in·car·nate, in·kär′nāt, *v.t.,* **-nat·ed, -nat·ing.** To invest with a form; to be the embodiment of.—in·kär′nit, in·kär′nāt, *a.*

in·car·na·tion, in·kär·nā′shən, *n.* The state of being incarnate, esp. assumption of human form or nature, as by a divine being; an incarnate being or form; a person or thing representing or exhibiting something, as a quality or idea, in typical form; the personification or embodiment of an idea, quality, spirit, or god.

in·cen·di·a·ry, in·sen′dē·er·ē, *a.* The malicious or criminal setting on fire of buildings or other property; used for setting property on fire: *incendiary* bombs; tending to arouse strife, riot, or rebellion; inflammatory.—*n. pl.,* **-ries.**

in·cense, in′sens, *n.* An aromatic gum or other substance producing a sweet odor when burned; the fragrance from such a substance when burned; any pleasant fragrance.—*v.t.,* **-censed, -cens·ing.** *v.i.* To burn or offer incense.

in·cense, in·sens′, *v.t.,* **-censed, -cens·ing.** To make angry; enrage.

in·cen·tive, in·sen′tiv, *n.* A motive; a stimulus or incitement.

in·cep·tion, in·sep′shən, *n.* Beginning; commencement; origin.

in·ces·sant, in·ses′ənt, *a.* Continuing without interruption; continual. —**in·ces·sant·ly,** *adv.*

in·cest, in′sest, *n.* The act of sexual intercourse or marriage between close blood relations. —**in·ces·tu·ous,** in·ses′chū·əs, *a.* —**in·ces·tu·ous·ly,** *adv.* —**in·ces·tu·ous·ness,** *n.*

inch, inch, *n.* A measure of length, the twelfth part of a foot, or 2.54 centimeters.—*v.t., v.i.* To move slowly by inches or small degrees.

in·cho·ate, in·kō′it, *a.* Just begun; rudimentary; incomplete. —**in·cho·ate·ly,** *adv.* —**in·cho·ate·ness,** *n.*

in·ci·dence, in′si·dəns, *n.* The range of occurrence or influence of a thing or the extent of its effects: the *incidence* of a disease.

in·ci·dent, in′si·dənt, *n.* A distinct occurrence or event; an event or matter of accessory or subordinate character; a seemingly minor occurrence likely to touch off more serious consequences, as in international relations.—*a.* Liable or apt to happen; conjoined or attaching, esp. as subordinate to a principal thing.

in·ci·den·tal, in·si·den′təl, *a.* Occurring or liable to occur in connection with something else; happening in fortuitous or subordinate conjunction with something else; casual or accidental.—*n.* Something incidental; *pl.,* incidental items. —**in·ci·den·tal·ly,** *adv.*

in·cin·er·ate, in·sin′ə·rāt, *v.t., v.i.,* **-at·ed, -at·ing.** To burn or reduce to ashes; cremate. —**in·cin·er·a·tion,** in·sin·ə·rā′shən, *n.*

in·cin·er·a·tor, in·sin′ə·rā′tər, *n.* A furnace or apparatus for incinerating.

in·cip·i·ent, in·sip′ē·ənt, *a.* In the beginning stage; beginning to appear. —**in·cip·i·ent·ly,** *adv.*

in·cise, in·sīz′, *v.t.,* **-cised, -cis·ing.** To cut into; to carve; to engrave.

in·ci·sion, in·sizh′ən, *n.* That which is produced by cutting or incising; a cut, particularly one made in surgery; a gash; a notch; sharpness; keenness.

in·ci·sive, in·sī′siv, *a.* Cutting; sharp; biting; trenchant. —**in·ci·sive·ly,** *adv.* —**in·ci·sive·ness,** *n.*

in·ci·sor, in·sī′zər, *n.* One of the front cutting teeth, located between the canines.

in·cite, in·sīt′, *v.t.,* **-cit·ed, -cit·ing.** To move to action; to stir up. —**in·cite·ment,** *n.* —**in·cit·er,** *n.*

in·clem·ent, in·klem′ənt, *a.* Severe; harsh; unkind; without mercy. —**in·clem·en·cy,** *n.* —**in·clem·ent·ly,** *adv.*

in·cli·na·tion, in·klə·nā′shən, *n.* A disposition more favorable to one thing or person than to another; preference; the state of being inclined; a slanted surface; tendency, esp. of the mind or will. Also **in·clin·ing.**

in·cline, in·klīn′, *v.t.,* **-clined, -clin·ing.** To cause to lean or bend; give a slanting direction or position to; to give a particular tendency to, as to the mind, heart, or will; dispose or influence in mind, will, or habit. —*v.i.* To lean, bend, or slant; to tend in course or character; have a mental tendency; be disposed. —in′klīn, in·klīn′, *n.* A slope or plane. —**in·clined,** *a.* —**in·clin·er,** *n.*

in·clude, in·klood′, *v.t.,* **-clud·ed, -clud·ing.** To hold or put within limits; to place in an aggregate, class, or category; to contain, embrace, or comprise; contain as a subordinate element; involve as a factor. —**in·clud·a·ble, in·clud·i·ble,** *a.* —**in·clu·sion,** *n.*

in·clu·sive, in·kloo′siv, *a.* Comprising, encompassing, comprehensive; including everything concerned; covering the specified limits: from 1960 to 1965 *inclusive.* —**in·clu·sive·ly,** *adv.* —**in·clu·sive·ness,** *n.*

in·cog·ni·to, in·kog′ni·tō, in·kog·nē′tō, *a.* Having a concealed or assumed identity.—*adv.* With the real name or identity concealed.—*n. pl.,* **-tos.**

in·co·her·ent, in·kō·hēr′ənt, *a.* Not coherent; without physical cohesion, unconnected, or loose, as matter; without logical connection, disjointed, or rambling; characterized by such thought or language, as a person. —**in·co·her·ence,** *n.* —**in·co·her·ent·ly,** *adv.*

in·come, in′kəm, *n.* Receipts or benefits, usu. monetary, accruing from labor, business, property, or investments.

in•come tax, *n.* A tax levied on incomes, esp. by a government.

in•com•ing, in/kəm•ing, *a.* Entering; arriving; beginning or taking a new post or position.—*n.* The act of coming in.

in•com•men•su•ra•ble, in•kə•men/shər•ə•bəl, in•kə•men/sər•ə•bəl, *a.* Not commensurable; having no common measure or standard of comparison; utterly disproportionate. *Math.* Having no common measure.—*n.* —**in•com•men•su•ra•bly,** *adv.*

in•com•men•su•rate, in•kə•men/shər•it, in•kə•men/sər•it, *a.* Insufficient; not adequate or of sufficient amount; disproportionate; incommensurable. —**in•com•men•su•rate•ly,** *adv.*

in•com•mo•dious, in•kə•mō/də•əs, *a.* Not roomy; cramped; causing discomfort; inconvenient.

in•com•pa•ra•ble, in•kom/pər•ə•bəl, in•kom/prə•bəl, *a.* Not able to be compared with others because of dissimilar natures or qualities; unequaled. —**in•com•pa•ra•bly,** *adv.*

in•com•pat•i•ble, in•kəm•pat/i•bəl, *a.* Unable to coexist in harmony; discordant; inconsistent.—*n.* —**in•com•pat•i•bil•i•ty,** in•kəm•pat•ə•bil/ə•tē, *n.* —**in•com•pat•i•bly,** *adv.*

in•com•pe•tent, in•kom/pi•tənt, *a.* Lacking adequate strength, power, capacity, means, or qualifications; unable; incapable; inadequate.—*n.* One who is incompetent. —**in•com•pe•tence, in•com•pe•ten•cy,** *n.* —**in•com•pe•tent•ly,** *adv.*

in•com•plete, in•kəm•plēt/, *a.* Not finished; not having all parts or sections; imperfect. —**in•com•plete•ly,** *adv.* —**in•com•plete•ness,** *n.* —**in•com•ple•tion,** *n.*

in•com•pre•hen•si•ble, in•kom•pri•hen/sə•bəl, *a.* Not to be grasped by the mind; not to be understood; unintelligible. —**in•com•pre•hen•si•bly,** *adv.* —**in•com•pre•hen•sion,** *n.*

in•con•ceiv•a•ble, in•kən•sē/və•bəl, *a.* Unimaginable; incredible. —**in•con•ceiv•a•bly,** *adv.*

in•con•clu•sive, in•kən•kloo/siv, *a.* Indeterminate; indefinite; indecisive; not resolving doubtful questions; not producing a final result. —**in•con•clu•sive•ly,** *adv.* —**in•con•clu•sive•ness,** *n.*

in•con•gru•ous, in•kong/grū•əs, *a.* Inharmonious in character; out of place; inappropriate; unbecoming; lacking harmony of parts. —**in•con•gru•ous•ly,** *adv.* —**in•con•gru•ous•ness,** *n.* —**in•con•gru•i•ty,** in•kən•groo/i•tē, *n. pl.,* **-ties.**

in•con•se•quen•tial, in•kon•sə•kwen/shəl, *a.* Of no consequence; trivial; unimportant. —**in•con•se•quen•tial•ly,** *adv.*

in•con•sid•er•a•ble, in•kən•sid/ər•ə•bəl, *a.* Unimportant; small; trivial; insignificant. —**in•con•sid•er•a•bly,** *adv.*

in•con•sid•er•ate, in•kən•sid/ər•it, *a.* Not acting with regard for the feelings of others; thoughtless. —**in•con•sid•er•ate•ly,** *adv.* —**in•con•sid•er•ate•ness,** *n.*

in•con•sis•tent, in•kən•sis/tənt, *a.* Not consistent; lacking agreement; at variance; discrepant; incongruous; lacking harmony between the different parts or elements; self-contradictory; acting at variance with professed principles or former conduct; not consistent in conduct or principles; erratic. —**in•con•sist•ent•ly,** *adv.*

in•con•sol•a•ble, in•kən•sō/lə•bəl, *a.* Incapable of being consoled. —**in•con•sol•a•ble•ness,** *n.* —**in•con•sol•a•bly,** *adv.*

in•con•spic•u•ous, in•kən•spik/yū•əs, *a.* Not readily noticed. —**in•con•spic•u•ous•ly,** *adv.* —**in•con•spic•u•ous•ness,** *n.*

in•con•stant, in•kon/stənt, *a.* Subject to change; unsteady; fickle. —**in•con•stan•cy,** *n.,* **-cies.** —**in•**

in•con•test•a•ble, in•kən•tes/tə•bəl, *a.* Not to be disputed. —**in•con•test•a•bly,** *adv.*

in•con•ti•nent, in•kon/ti•nənt, *a.* Not restraining the passions or appetites, particularly the sexual appetite.—*adv.* —**in•con•ti•nence, in•con•ti•nen•cy,** *n.* —**in•con•ti•nent•ly,** *adv.*

in•con•tro•vert•i•ble, in•kon•trə•vər/ti•bəl, *a.* Not arguable; too clear or certain to admit of dispute or controversy.

in•con•ven•ience, in•kən•vēn/yəns, *n.* The quality of being inconvenient. Also **in•con•ven•ien•cy.**—*v.t.,* **-ienced, -ienc•ing.** To put to inconvenience; to disturb.

in•con•ven•ient, in•kən•vēn/yənt, *a.* Giving trouble or discomfort; wanting due facilities; causing embarrassment; inopportune. —**in•con•ven•ient•ly,** *adv.*

in•cor•po•rate, in•kôr/pə•rāt, *v.t.,* **-rat•ed, -rat•ing.** To form into a legal corporation; to combine into one body or uniform substance; to take in or include as a part, as the body or mass does; to embody or give material form to.—*v.i.* To form a corporation; to unite or combine so as to form one body.—in•kôr/pə•rit, in•kôr/prit, *a.* Constituted as a corporation; combined into one body. Also **in•cor•po•ra•ted.** —**in•cor•po•ra•tion,** in•kôr•pə•rā/shən, *n.* —**in•cor•po•ra•tor,** *n.*

in•cor•po•re•al, in•kôr•pôr/ē•əl, *a.* Not corporeal; immaterial; pertaining to spiritual beings. *Law.* Without material existence, but existing in contemplation of law, as a franchise or a right of way.

in•cor•rect, in•kə•rekt/, *a.* Not correct; not exact; erroneous; not according to fact; improper or unsuitable. —**in•cor•rect•ly,** *adv.*

in•cor•ri•gi•ble, in•kôr/i•jə•bəl, in•kor/i•jə•bəl, *a.* Incapable of being corrected or reformed.—*n.* —**in•cor•ri•gi•bil•i•ty,** in•kôr•i•jə•bil/i•tē, **in•cor•ri•gi•ble•ness,** *n.* —**in•cor•ri•gi•bly,** *adv.*

in•cor•rupt•i•ble, in•kər•rəp/ti•bəl, *a.* Incapable of corruption, decay, or dissolution; inflexibly upright. —*n.* —**in•cor•rupt•i•bil•i•ty,** in•kər•rəp•tə•bil/ə•tē, **in•cor•rupt•i•ble•ness,** *n.* —**in•cor•rup•ti•bly,** *adv.*

in•crease, in•krēs/, *v.i.,* **-creased, -creas•ing.** To become greater; to grow; to multiply by the production of young.—*v.t.* To make greater or larger; to augment in bulk, quantity, amount, or degree; to add to.—in/krēs, *n.* A growing greater or larger; the amount by which anything is augmented. —**in•creas•a•ble,** *a.* —**in•creas•ing•ly,** *adv.*

in•cred•i•ble, in•kred/i•bəl, *a.* Too extraordinary and improbable to be believed. —**in•cred•i•bil•i•ty,** in•kred•ə•bil/i•tē, **in•cred•i•ble•ness,** *n.* —**in•cred•i•bly,** *adv.*

in•cred•u•lous, in•krej/ə•ləs, *a.* Skeptical; expressing or showing disbelief. —**in•cre•du•li•ty,** in•kri•doo/li•tē, in•kri•dū/li•tē, **in•cred•u•lous•ness,** *n.* —**in•cred•u•lous•ly,** *adv.*

in•cre•ment, in/krə•mənt, ing/krə•mənt, *n.* Augmentation or growth; increase; profit. —**in•cre•men•tal,** in•krə•men/təl, *a.*

in•crim•i•nate, in•krim/i•nāt, *v.t.,* **-nat•ed, -nat•ing.** To charge with a crime or fault; to accuse; to implicate in a wrongdoing. —**in•crim•i•na•tion,** in•krim•ə•nā/shən, *n.* —**in•crim•i•na•tor,** *n.* —**in•crim•i•na•to•ry,** in•krim/i•nə•tôr•ē, *a.*

in•crust, in•krəst/, *v.t.* To cover with a crust; to form a crust on the surface of. —**in•crus•ta•tion,** in•krə•stā/shən, *n.*

in•cu•bate, in/kyə•bāt, ing/kyə•bāt, *v.t.,* **-bat•ed, -bat•ing.** To sit upon, as eggs, for the purpose of hatching; hatch by artificial heat, as in an incubator; maintain, as bacterial cultures or embryos, in a controlled environment most suitable for development. —*v.i.* To sit upon eggs; brood; undergo incubation. —**in•cu•ba•tion,** in•kyə•bā/shən, *n.*

---

in·cu·ba·tor, in′kyə-bā-tər, ing′kyə-bā-tər, *n.* An apparatus for hatching eggs by artificial heat; an apparatus for maintaining suitable temperature, humidity, and oxygen for premature babies.

in·cu·bus, in′kyə-bəs, ing′kyə-bəs, *n. pl.*, **-bus·es**, **-bi**, -bī. Nightmare; something that weighs heavily on the mind or feelings.

in·cul·cate, in·kəl′kāt, inĕēkəl·kāt, *v.t.*, **-cat·ed**, **-cat·ing**. To impress by frequent admonitions; to teach and enforce by frequent repetitions. —**in·cul·ca·tion**, in·kəl·kā′shən, *n.* —**in·cul·ca·tor**, *n.*

in·cul·pate, in·kəl′pāt, in′kəl·pāt, *v.t.*, **-pat·ed**, **-pat·ing**. To show to be at fault; to accuse of crime; to impute guilt to; to incriminate. —**in·cul·pa·tion**, in·kəl·pā′shən, *n.*

in·cum·bent, in·kəm′bənt, *a.* Lying or resting upon; resting upon a person, as a duty or obligation to be performed; filling a post or political office.—*n.* A person in possession of a political office, ecclesiastical benefice, or other position. —**in·cum·ben·cy**, *n. pl.*, **-cies**. —**in·cum·bent·ly**, *adv.*

in·cur, in·kər′, *v.t.*, **-curred**, **-cur·ring**. To become responsible for, as some undesirable consequence or inconvenience; become liable to; contract, as a debt.

in·cur·a·ble, in·kyūr′ə-bəl, *a.* Beyond medical help or skill.—*n.* —**in·cur·a·bil·i·ty**, in·kyūr·ə·bil′ə·te, **in·cur·a·ble·ness**, *n.* —**in·cur·a·bly**, *adv.*

in·cur·sion, in·kər′zhən, in·kər′shən, *n.* An invasion of a territory; raid. —**in·cur·sive**, *a.*

in·debt·ed, in·det′id, *a.* In debt; beholden; obliged by something received, for which gratitude is due. —**in·debt·ed·ness**, *n.*

in·de·cent, in·dē′sənt, *a.* Offensive to modesty and good taste; vulgar. —**in·de·cen·cy**, *n. pl.*, **-cies**. —**in·de·cent·ly**, *adv.*

in·de·ci·sion, in·di·sizh′ən, *n.* Want of decision; a wavering of the mind..

in·de·ci·sive, in·di·sī′siv, *a.* Not decisive; unable to make decisions; vacillating. —**in·de·ci·sive·ly**, *adv.* —**in·de·ci·sive·ness**, *n.*

in·deed, in·dēd′, *adv.* In reality; in truth; in fact. —*interj.* An expression of surprise or disbelief.

in·de·fat·i·ga·ble, in·di·fat′ə·gə·bəl, *a.* Tireless; not yielding to fatigue. —**in·de·fat·i·ga·bil·i·ty**, in·di·fat·ə·gə·bil′ə·tē, **in·de·fat·i·ga·ble·ness**, *n.* —**in·de·fat·i·ga·bly**, *adv.*

in·de·fen·si·ble, in·di·fen′sə·bəl, *a.* Incapable of being excused, vindicated, or justified; defended. —**in·de·fen·si·bil·i·ty**, in·di·fen·sə·bil′ə·tē, *n.* —**in·de·fen·si·bly**, *adv.*

in·def·i·nite, in·def′ə·nit, *a.* Without fixed or specified limit; unlimited; not clearly defined; vague; not specifying precisely: the *indefinite* article *a*, or an *indefinite* pronoun, *any, some,* or the like. —**in·def·i·nite·ly**, *adv.* —**in·def·i·nite·ness**, *n.*

in·del·i·ble, in·del′ə·bəl, *a.* Incapable of being obliterated; making marks difficult to efface. —**in·del·i·bil·i·ty**, in·del·ə·bil′ə·tē, **in·del·i·ble·ness**, *n.* —**in·del·i·bly**, *adv.*

in·del·i·cate, in·del′ə·kit, *a.* Lacking modesty or propriety; having no tact. —**in·del·i·ca·cy**, **in·del·i·cate·ness**, *n.* —**in·del·i·cate·ly**, *adv.*

in·dem·ni·fy, in·dem′nə·fī, *v.t.*, **-fied**, **-fy·ing**. To secure against loss, damage, or penalty; to reimburse for expenditures made or damages suffered. —**in·dem·ni·fi·ca·tion**, in·dem·nə·fə·kā′shən, *n.* —**in·dem·ni·fi·er**, *n.*

in·dem·ni·ty, in·dem′nə·tē, *n. pl.*, **-ties**. Security or exemption from damage, loss, injury, or punishment; compensation or equivalent for loss, damage, or injury sustained.

in·dent, in·dent′, *v.t.* To begin, as a line of type, farther in from the margin than the rest of the paragraph; to notch, jag, or cut into points.—*v.i.* To begin a line of type or writing farther in from the margin than other lines; to form or be cut into notches or jags. —in′dent, in·dent′, *n.* The blank space at the begin-

ning of the first line of a paragraph; a notch or indentation; an indenture.

in·dent, in·dent′, *v.t.* To make a dent in.—in′dent, in·dent′, *n.* A dent or depression in the surface of anything, as from a blow.

in·den·ta·tion, in·den·tā′shən, *n.* The act of indenting; a notch or series of notches along an edge; an indention. —**in·dent·ed**, in·den′tid, *a.* —**in·den·tion**, in·den′shən, *n.*

in·den·ture, in·den′chər, *n.* A deed or written contract. *Usu. pl.* A contract by which one person is bound to another under certain conditions and for a specified length of time.—*v.t.*, **-tured**, **-tur·ing**. To bind by indentures.

in·de·pend·ence, in·di·pen′dəns, *n.* Freedom from control of others; the state of being independent. Also **in·de·pend·en·cy**.

in·de·pend·ent, in·di·pen′dənt, *a.* Not dependent; not subject to the control of others; not swayed by bias or influence; self-directing; not committed to a particular political party, esp. in voting. Possessing or constituting a competence.—*n.* One not bound by a political party.—**in·de·pend·ent of**, irrespective of; without regard to. —**in·de·pend·ent·ly**, *adv.*

in·de·scrib·a·ble, in·di·skrī·bə·bəl, *a.* Beyond description. —**in·de·scrib·a·bil·i·ty**, in·di·skrī·bə·bil′ə·tē, **in·de·scrib·a·ble·ness**, *n.* —**in·de·scrib·a·bly**, *adv.*

in·de·struct·i·ble, in·di·strək′tə·bəl, *a.* Incapable of being destroyed. —**in·de·struct·i·bil·i·ty**, in·di·strək·tə·bil′ə·tē, **in·de·struct·i·ble·ness**, *n.* —**in·de·struct·i·bly**, *adv.*

in·de·ter·mi·nate, in·di·ter′mə·nit, *a.* Not settled or fixed; not definite; uncertain; not precise. —**in·de·ter·mi·nate·ly**, *adv.* —**in·de·ter·mi·nate·ness**, **in·de·ter·mi·na·cy**, *n.* —**in·de·ter·mi·na·tion**, in·di·ter·mə·nā′shən, *n.*

in·dex, in′deks, *n. pl.*, **-dex·es**, **-di·ces**, -di·sēz. An alphabetical or classified list, as one placed at the end of a book, for facilitating reference to material within the body of the text; anything used to indicate or point out; the forefinger; something that serves to direct attention to a fact or condition; an indication.—*v.t.* To provide with an index, as a book; enter in an index, as a word; to serve to indicate. —**in·dex·er**, *n.*

in·dex fin·ger, *n.* Forefinger.

In·di·an club, in′dē·ən, *n.* A bottle-shaped wooden club used in gymnastic exercises.

In·di·an corn, in′dē·ən, *n.* Maize; corn.

In·di·an file, *n.* A single line; single file.

In·di·an giv·er, *n. Informal.* One who takes back a gift he has given or expects a gift in return for one. —**In·di·an giv·ing**, *n.*

In·di·an sum·mer, *n.* Unusually temperate weather during the late fall or early winter.

in·di·cate, in′də·kāt, *v.t.*, **-cat·ed**, **-cat·ing**. To point out; to suggest; to show or signify, as a symptom; to imply; to express briefly. —**in·di·ca·tion**, in·də·kā′shən, *n.*

in·dic·a·tive, in·dik′ə·tiv, *a.* Serving to indicate; pointing out; stating something actual, not merely possible, as a method of the verb used in stating or questioning an objective fact.—*n.* A verb in the indicative mood. —**in·dic·a·tive·ly**, *adv.*

in·di·ca·tor, in′də·kā·tər, *n.* One who or that which indicates; a recording instrument of various kinds. —**in·dic·a·to·ry**, in′dik·ə·tôr·ē, in·dik′ə·tôr·ē, *a.*

in·dict, in·dīt′, *v.t.* To accuse or charge with a crime. —**in·dict·a·ble**, *a.* —**in·dict·er**, **in·dict·or**, *n.* —**in·dict·ment**, *n.*

in·dif·fer·ent, in·dif′ər·ənt, *a.* Without interest or concern; not making a difference either way; unbiased. —**in·dif·fer·ence**, in·dif′ər·əns, *n.* —**in·dif·fer·ent·ist**, *n.* —**in·dif·fer·ent·ly**, *adv.*

in·dig·e·nous, in·dij′ə·nəs, *a.* Originating or produced in a country or region; native. —**in·dig·e·nous·ly**, *adv.* —**in·dig·e·nous·ness**, *n.*

in·di·gent, in/di·jənt, *a.* Wanting the means of subsistence; needy; impoverished; poor.—*n.* **—in·di·gence,** in/di·jəns, *n.* **—in·di·gent·ly,** *adv.*

in·di·gest·i·ble, in·di·jes/tə·bəl, *a.* Not digestible. **—in·di·gest·i·bil·i·ty,** in·di·jes·tə·bil/ə·tē, **in·di·gest·i·ble·ness,** *n.*

in·di·ges·tion, in·di·jes/chən, in·dī·jes/chən, *n.* Incapability of or difficulty in digesting food; stomach discomfort caused by this. **—in·di·ges·tive,** *a.*

in·dig·nant, in·dig/nənt, *a.* Exhibiting displeasure or outrage at what seems unjust or unworthy. **—in·dig·nant·ly,** *adv.*

in·dig·na·tion, in·dig·nā/shən, *n.* Displeasure at what seems unworthy or base; anger, mingled with contempt, disgust, or abhorrence.

in·dig·ni·ty, in·dig/ne·tē, *n. pl.,* **-ties.** An act which shows contempt for a person or is humiliating; an insult; an outrage.

in·di·go, in/də·gō/, *n. pl.,* **-gos, -goes.** A deep violet blue; any of several blue dyes synthesized or obtained from plants.

in·di·rect, in·də·rekt/, in·dī·rekt/, *a.* Deviating from a direct course; circuitous; not open and straightforward; underhanded; deceitful. **—in·di·rec·tion,** in·də·rek/shən, *n.* **—in·di·rect·ly,** *adv.* **—in·di·rect·ness,** *n.*

in·di·rect ob·ject, *n.* A word that usu. follows a verb of telling, asking, or giving, and indicates the receptor: Bake *me* a cake.

in·dis·creet, in·di·skrēt/, *a.* Lacking sound judgment or discretion. **—in·dis·creet·ly,** *adv.* **—in·dis·creet·ness,** *n.*

in·dis·crete, in·di·skrēt/, *a.* Not consisting of distinct parts.

in·dis·cre·tion, in·di·skresh/ən, *n.* The condition or quality of being indiscreet.

in·dis·crim·i·nate, in·di·skrim/ə·nit, *a.* Random; without a distinction; lacking perception; confused. **—in·dis·crim·i·nate·ly,** *adv.* **—in·dis·crim·i·nate·ness,** *n.* **—in·dis·crim·i·nat·ing,** *a.* **—in·dis·crim·i·na·tion,** in·di·skrim·ə·nā/shən, *n.*

in·dis·pen·sa·ble, in·di·spen/sə·bəl, *a.* Absolutely necessary. **—in·dis·pen·sa·bil·i·ty,** in·di·spen·sə·bil/ə·tē, **in·dis·pen·sa·ble·ness,** *n.* **—in·dis·pen·sa·bly,** *adv.*

in·dis·pose, in·di·spōz/, *v.t.,* **-posed, -pos·ing.** To make unwilling; to render unfit or ill-suited; to disqualify; to cause to become sick.

in·dis·posed, in·dis·pōzd/, *a.* Mildly ill; unwilling. **—in·dis·po·si·tion,** in·dis·pə·zish/ən, *n.*

in·dis·sol·u·ble, in·di·sol/yə·bəl, *a.* Not capable of being dissolved or decomposed; stable. **—in·dis·sol·u·bil·i·ty,** in·di·sol·yə·bil/ə·tē, **in·dis·sol·u·ble·ness,** *n.* **—in·dis·sol·u·bly,** *adv.*

in·di·um, in/dē·əm, *n.* A rare metallic element, silver-white, malleable, and easily fusible, found in sphalerite and various ores.

in·di·vid·u·al, in·di·vij/ū·əl, *a.* Subsisting as one indivisible entity or distinct being; single; peculiar to or characteristic of a particular person or thing.—*n.* A single person, animal, or thing, as distinct from a group; a particular person. **—in·di·vid·u·al·ly,** *adv.*

in·di·vid·u·al·ism, in·di·vij/ū·əl·iz·əm, *n.* A social theory advocating the liberty, rights, or independent action of the individual; the principle or habit of independent thought or action; individuality. **—in·di·vid·u·al·ist,** *n.* **—in·di·vid·u·al·is·tic,** in·di·vij·ū·ə·lis/tik, *a.* **—in·di·vid·u·al·is·ti·cal·ly,** *adv.*

in·di·vid·u·al·i·ty, in·di·vij·ū·al/ə·tē, *n. pl.,* **-ties.** The condition of having a distinct and separate existence; the sum of the characteristics or traits peculiar to an individual.

in·di·vid·u·al·ize, in·di·vij/ū·ə·līz, *v.t.,* **-ized, -iz·ing.** To mark as an individual; to treat as an individual.

—in·di·vid·u·al·i·za·tion, *n.*

in·doc·tri·nate, in·dok/trə·nāt, *v.t.,* **-nat·ed, -nat·ing.** To instruct in any doctrine. **—in·doc·tri·na·tion,** in·dok·trə·nā/shən, *n.* **—in·doc·tri·na·tor,** *n.*

in·do·lent, in/də·lənt, *a.* Habitually idle; lazy. **—in·do·lence,** *n.* **—in·do·lent·ly,** *adv.*

in·dom·i·ta·ble, in·dom/i·tə·bəl, *a.* Not to be tamed or subdued; unconquerable; unyielding. **—in·dom·i·ta·bil·i·ty,** in·dom·i·tə·bil/ə·tē, **in·dom·i·ta·ble·ness,** *n.* **—in·dom·i·ta·bly,** *adv.*

in·door, in/dôr, in·dôr/, *a.* Occurring, used, or belonging in a house or building; the interior of a house or building.

in·doors, in·dôrz/, *adv.* In or into a house or building.

in·du·bi·ta·ble, in·doo/bə·tə·bəl, in·dū/bə·tə·bəl, *a.* Certain; too obvious to be of doubt; unquestionable. **—in·du·bi·ta·ble·ness, in·du·bi·ta·bil·i·ty,** in·doo·bi·tə·bil/ə·tē, *n.* **—in·du·bi·tab·ly,** *adv.*

in·duce, in·doos/, *v.t.,* **-duced, -duc·ing.** To lead or prevail on by persuasion or argument; to bring on, produce, or cause. **—in·duce·ment,** *n.* **—in·duc·er,** *n.* **—in·duc·i·ble,** *a.*

in·duct, in·dəkt/, *v.t.,* To bring in as a member; to call into military service. **—in·duct·ee,** *n.*

in·duc·tion, in·dək/shən, *n.* The act of inducting; introduction or initiation; installation into office or benefice; the act of causing or bringing about; the act of presenting, as facts or evidence. **—in·duc·tive,** in·dək/tiv, *a.*

in·dulge, in·dəlj/, *v.t.,* **-dulged, -dulg·ing.** To yield or to gratify the wishes or whims of; to humor; to satisfy as a personal inclination.—*v.i.* To indulge oneself; to yield to an inclination or impulse, often followed by *in:* to *indulge* in a sneer.

in·dul·gence, in·dəl/jəns, *n.* The act or practice of indulging; that which is indulged in. **—in·dul·gent,** *a.* **—in·dul·gent·ly,** *adv.*

in·dus·tri·al, in·dəs/trē·əl, *a.* Characteristic of, referring to, or resulting from industry or productive labor; engaged in or connected with industries; pertaining to those who work in industries.—*n. pl.* The stocks and bonds of industrial enterprises. **—in·dus·tri·al·ly,** *adv.* **—in·dus·tri·al·ness,** *n.*

in·dus·tri·al arts, *n. pl. but sing. in constr.* A course of study which trains students in technical skills.

in·dus·tri·al·ism, in·dəs/trē·ə·liz·əm, *n.* An economic system in which industrial interests predominate, as opposed to the interests of agriculture or foreign trade.

in·dus·tri·al·ize, in·dəs/trē·ə·līz, *v.t.,* **-ized, -iz·ing.** To organize large industries in; to introduce the economic system of industrialism into.—*v.i.* To become industrialized. **—in·dus·tri·al·i·za·tion,** in·dəs·trē·ə·lə·zā/shən, *n.* **—in·dus·tri·al·ist,** *n.*

in·dus·tri·al un·ion, *n.* A labor union with membership open to all workers in an industry, regardless of occupation, skill, or craft; a vertical union, as opposed to *craft union.*

in·dus·tri·ous, in·dəs/trē·əs, *a.* Characterized by industry; hardworking. **—in·dus·tri·ous·ly,** *adv.*

in·dus·try, in/dəs·trē, *n. pl.,* **-tries.** Trade or manufacturing in general; specif. that concerned with a particular business: the automobile *industry,* the steel *industry;* diligence in employment; steady attention to work or business.

in·e·bri·ate, in·ē/brē·āt, *v.t.,* **-at·ed, -at·ing.** To make drunk; intoxicate; to excite or confuse.—*in·ē/brē·it,* *n.* A drunkard.—*a.* Drunk. Also **in·e·bri·at·ed.** **—in·e·bri·a·tion,** in·ē·brē·ā/shən, **in·e·bri·e·ty,** in·ē·brī/ə·tē, *n.*

in·ed·u·ca·ble, in·ej/ə·kə·bəl, *a.* Not capable of being educated.

in·ef·fa·ble, in·ef/ə·bəl, *a.* Incapable of being expressed in words; too holy or lofty to be spoken.

—in·ef·fa·bil·i·ty, in·ef·ə·bil/ə·tē, in·ef·fa·ble·ness, n. —in·ef·fa·bly, adv.

in·ef·fec·tive, in·i·fek/tiv, a. Not producing desired or required results; incompetent; inefficient. —in·ef·fec·tive·ly, adv. —in·ef·fec·tive·ness, n.

in·ef·fec·tu·al, in·i·fek/chû·əl, a. Not effectual; unable or unwilling to produce a required result; futile. —in·ef·fec·tu·al·i·ty, in·i·fek·chû·al/ə·tē, in·ef·fec·tu·al·ness, n. —in·ef·fec·tu·al·ly, adv.

in·ef·fi·cient, in·i·fish/ənt, a. Lacking competence; not effecting desired results economically. —in·ef·fi·cien·cy, n. pl., -cies. —in·ef·fi·cient·ly, adv.

in·el·i·gi·ble, in·el/i·jə·bəl, a. Not qualified or fit to be elected or adopted. —in·el·i·gi·bil·i·ty, in·el·i·jə·bil/ə·tē, n. —in·el·i·gi·bly, adv.

in·e·luc·ta·ble, in·i·lək/tə·bəl, a. That cannot be escaped from or avoided; inevitable.

in·ept, in·ept/, i·nept/, a. Not suitable; inappropriate; absurd or foolish; awkward or inefficient. —in·ept·i·tude, in·ep/ti·tood, in·ep/ti·tūd, n. —in·ept·ly, adv. —in·ept·ness, n.

in·e·qual·i·ty, in·i·kwol/ə·tē, n. The state or condition of being unequal; lack of proportion; unevenness; injustice.

in·eq·ui·ta·ble, in·ek/wi·tə·bəl, a. Not equitable; not just or fair.

in·eq·ui·ty, in·ek/wi·tē, n. pl., -ties. Lack of justice; an unfair thing.

in·ert, in·ərt/, a. Having no inherent power of action, motion, or resistance; inactive, inanimate, or without life; of an inactive or sluggish habit or nature. —in·ert·ly, adv. —in·ert·ness, n.

in·er·tia, in·ər/sha, n. Passiveness; inactivity; sluggishness; the property of matter by which it retains its state of rest or of uniform straight-line motion so long as no external cause acts to change that state. —in·er·tial, a.

in·es·cap·a·ble, in·ə·skā/pə·bəl, a. That cannot be escaped; unavoidable.

in·es·ti·ma·ble, in·es/tə·mə·bəl, a. Too valuable, great, or excellent to be rated or fully appreciated; incalculable. —in·es·ti·ma·bly, adv.

in·ev·i·ta·ble, in·ev/ə·tə·bəl, a. Unavoidable; unalterable; certain to happen. —in·ev·i·ta·bil·i·ty, in·ev·i·tə·bil/ə·tē, in·ev·i·ta·ble·ness, n. —in·ev·i·ta·bly, adv.

in·ex·haust·i·ble, in·ig·zôs/tə·bəl, a. Incapable of being exhausted or spent; unfailing; tireless. —in·ex·haust·i·bil·i·ty, in·ig·zos·tə·bil/ə·tē, in·ex·haust·i·ble·ness, n. —in·ex·haust·i·bly, adv.

in·ex·o·ra·ble, in·ek/sər·ə·bəl, a. Unyielding; incapable of being moved by entreaty or prayer. —in·ex·o·ra·bil·i·ty, in·ek·sər·ə·bil/ə·tē, in·ex·o·ra·ble·ness, n. —in·ex·o·ra·bly, adv.

in·ex·pe·ri·ence, in·ik·spēr/ē·əns, n. Want of experience, or of knowledge or skill gained from experience. —in·ex·pe·ri·enced, a.

in·ex·pert, in·eks/pərt, a. Not skilled. —in·ex·pert·ly, adv. —in·ex·pert·ness, n.

in·ex·pi·a·ble, in·eks/pē·ə·bəl, a. Incapable of being atoned for; unpardonable. —in·ex·pi·a·ble·ness, n. —in·ex·pi·a·bly, adv.

in·ex·pli·ca·ble, in·eks/plə·kə·bəl, a. Incapable of being explained. —in·ex·pli·ca·bil·i·ty, in·ek·spli·kə·bil/ə·tē, in·ex·pli·ca·ble·ness, n. —in·ex·pli·ca·bly, adv.

in·ex·press·i·ble, in·ik·spres/ə·bəl, a. Not expressible; not to be uttered; unspeakable; indescribable. —in·ex·press·i·bil·i·ty, in·ek·spres·ə·bil/ə·tē, in·ex·press·i·ble·ness, n. —in·ex·press·i·bly, adv.

in·ex·tin·guish·a·ble, in·ik·sting/gwi·shə·bəl, a. Not to be extinguished or brought to an end. —in·ex·tin·guish·a·bly, adv.

in·ex·tri·ca·ble, in·eks/tri·kə·bəl, a. Incapable of being freed or extricated from; unsolvable; unable to be untangled, undone, or loosed, as a knot. —in·ex·tri·ca·bil·i·ty, in·ek·stri·kə·bil/ə·tē, in·ex·tri·ca·ble·ness, n. —in·ex·tri·ca·bly, adv.

in·fal·li·ble, in·fal/ə·bəl, a. Exempt from liability to error or failure; absolutely trustworthy or certain. —in·fal·li·bil·i·ty, in·fal·i·bil/ə·tē, in·fal·li·ble·ness, n. —in·fal·li·bly, adv.

in·fa·mous, in/fə·məs, a. Notoriously bad; scandalous. —in·fa·mous·ly, adv. —in·fa·mous·ness, n.

in·fa·my, in/fə·mē, n. pl., -mies. Evil or shameful notoriety, or public reproach; infamous character or behavior; an infamous act.

in·fan·cy, in/fən·sē, n. pl., -cies. The state or period of being an infant; the corresponding period in the existence of anything.

in·fant, in/fənt, n. A child during the earliest period of its life; a baby.—a. Being in the earliest period or stage. —in·fant·hood, n. —in·fant·like, a.

in·fan·tile, in/fən·tīl, in/fən·til, a. Of or pertaining to infants; babyish or childish; being in the earliest stage of development. Also in·fan·tine, in/fən·tin, in/fən·tin. —in·fan·til·i·ty, in·fən·til/ə·tē, n.

in·fan·tile pa·ral·y·sis, n. Poliomyelitis.

in·fan·try, in/fən·trē, n. pl., -tries. Troops regularly serving on foot and carrying small arms. —in·fan·try·man, in/fən·trē·mən, n. pl., -men.

in·fat·u·ate, in·fach/û·āt, v.t., -at·ed, -at·ing. To inspire or possess with a foolish, irrational, or blind passion. —in·fat·u·at·ed, a. —in·fat·u·at·ed·ly, adv. —in·fat·u·a·tion, in·fach·û·ā/shən, n.

in·fect, in·fekt/, v.t. Contaminate with disease-producing germs; to imbue with an opinion, attitude, or belief.—a. —in·fect·ed·ness, n. —in·fect·er, in·fec·tor, n.

in·fec·tion, in·fek/shən, n. The penetration of body tissue by disease-producing organisms; a disease or injury resulting from pathogenic organisms; the area affected by the injurious organisms; an epidemic.

in·fec·tious, in·fek/shəs, a. Causing or carrying infection; communicable by infection; tending to spread from one to another, as feelings or actions; contagious; catching. —in·fec·tious·ly, adv. —in·fec·tious·ness, n. —in·fec·tive, a.

in·fer, in·fər/, v.t., -ferred, -fer·ring. To conclude by reasoning; to deduce; to indicate as a conclusion, or imply.—v.i. To draw a conclusion, as by reasoning. —in·fer·a·ble, in·fer·i·ble, in·fer·ri·ble, a. —in·fer·a·bly, adv. —in·fer·ence, in/fər·əns, n. in·fer·rer, n.

in·fe·ri·or, in·fēr/ē·ər, a. Lower in station, rank, degree, or grade, usu. followed by to; lower in place or position; of lower grade or poorer quality.—n. One inferior to another or others. —in·fe·ri·or·i·ty, in·fēr·ē·ôr/ə·tē, n. —in·fe·ri·or·ly, adv.

in·fer·nal, in·fər/nəl, a. Hellish; fiendish; diabolical. Informal. Execrable or outrageous.

in·fer·no, in·fər/nō, n. pl., -nos. An infernal or hell-like region; anything that resembles hell.

in·fest, in·fest/, v.t. To overrun in great numbers or in a troublesome manner; to be numerous in, as anything troublesome. —in·fes·ta·tion, in·fe·stā/shən, n. —in·fest·er, n.

in·fi·del, in/fi·dəl, n. A disbeliever; one who has no religious faith.

in·fi·del·i·ty, in·fə·del/ə·tē, n. pl., -ties. Want of faith or belief; skepticism; unfaithfulness in married persons.

in·field, in/fēld, n. The diamond portion of a baseball playing field marked off by four bases; collectively, the shortstop and three basemen. —in·field·er, n.

in·fight·ing, in/fī·ting, n. Fighting at close quarters, esp. in boxing; a struggle within an organization, as for leadership in a political party. —in·fight·er, n.

in·fil·trate, in/fil/trāt, in/fil·trāt, v.t., -trat·ed, -trat·ing. To join secretly or take a position in, for the purpose of spying or taking control; to cause to pass in by filtering; to filter through; to permeate.—v.i. To pass in or through a substance by filtering; to permeate—n. One who or that which infiltrates. —in·fil·

tra·tion, in·fil·trā'shən, *n.* —**in·fil·tra·tive,** in'fil·trā·tiv, in·fil'tra·tiv, *a.*

in·fi·nite, in'fə·nit, *a.* Without limits; exceedingly great in excellence, degree, and capacity; boundless. —*n.* That which is limitless, absolute, or perfect; a boundless space or extent. —**in·fi·nite·ly,** *adv.* —**in·fi·nite·ness, in·fin·i·tude,** in·fin'ə·tood, in·fin'ə·tūd, *n.*

in·fin·i·tes·i·mal, in·fin·ə·tes'ə·məl, *a.* Infinitely or immeasurably small; less than any assignable quantity.—*n.* —**in·fin·i·tes·i·mal·ly,** *adv.*

in·fin·i·tive, in·fin'ə·tiv, *n.* A verb form which expresses the meaning of the verb without specifying person or number and which may function as a noun, usu. preceded by *to: To err* is human, or as a verb, usu. with auxiliary verbs: They must *be* there.—*a.* Not limited or restricted as to person or number. —**in·fin·i·tive·ly,** *adv.*

in·fin·i·ty, in·fin'ə·tē, *n. pl.,* -ties. The state or quality of being infinite; that which is boundless; an unlimited extent or number; that which can never be completely counted.

in·firm, in·fėrm', *a.* Feeble or weak in body or health; not firm, solid, or strong; not steadfast or resolute. —**in·firm·ly,** *adv.* —**in·firm·ness,** *n.*

in·fir·ma·ry, in·fėr'mə·rē, *n. pl.,* -ries. A small hospital or dispensary for the care of the sick, injured, or infirm.

in·fir·mi·ty, in·fėr'mə·tē, *n. pl.,* -ties. A physical or moral malady; a defect or flaw.

in·flame, in·flām', *v.t.,* -flamed, -flam·ing. To set afire; to excite violent passion, feeling, or emotion in; to rouse, intensify, or increase, as anger; to produce inflammation in.—*v.i.* To burst into flame; to take fire; to become aroused or excited; to become inflamed. —**in·flam·er,** *n.*

in·flam·ma·ble, in·flam'ə·bəl, *a.* Capable of being set on fire; flammable; easily excited to anger. —**in·flam·ma·bil·i·ty,** in·flam·ə·bil'ə·tē, **in·flam·ma·ble·ness,** *n.* —**in·flam·ma·bly,** *adv.*

in·flam·ma·tion, in·flə·mā'shən, *n.* The act of inflaming; a redness and swelling of any part of the body, attended with heat and pain.

in·flam·ma·to·ry, in·flam'ə·tôr·ē, *a.* Tending to inflame or to excite anger, animosity, or disorder; tending to cause inflammation.

in·flate, in·flāt', *v.t.,* -flat·ed, -flat·ing. To distend with air or gas; to distend, swell, or puff out; to dilate; to puff up with pride, self-importance, or satisfaction; to elate; raise above the usual or proper amount or value.—*v.i.* To become inflated. —**in·flat·a·ble,** *a.* —**in·flat·ed,** *a.* —**in·flat·ed·ness,** *n.* —**in·flat·er, in·fla·tor,** *n.*

in·fla·tion, in·flā'shən, *n.* The act of inflating, or the state of being inflated; an expansion of the volume of currency and bank credit, out of proportion to available goods and services, and resulting in a considerable and prolonged rise in prices, wages, and other costs. —**in·fla·tion·ar·y,** *a.* —**in·fla·tion·ism,** *n.* —**in·fla·tion·ist,** *n.*

in·flect, in·flekt', *v.t.* To modulate, as the voice; to vary in form, as a word, to indicate number, case, mood, or tense; decline or conjugate. —**in·flec·tion,** in·flek'shən, *n.* —**in·flec·tion·al,** *a.* —**in·flec·tion·al·ly,** *adv.* —**in·flec·tion·less,** *a.* —**in·flec·tive,** *a.* —**in·flec·tor,** *n.*

in·flex·i·ble, in·flek'sə·bəl, *a.* Incapable of being bent; firm in purpose; immovable; stubborn; unalterable. —**in·flex·i·bil·i·ty,** in·flek·sə·bil'ə·tē, **in·flex·i·ble·ness,** *n.* —**in·flex·i·bly,** *adv.*

in·flict, in·flikt', *v.t.* To cause to bear or suffer from; to bring about; to cause to feel; to impose on, as punishment. —**in·flict·a·ble,** *a.* —**in·flict·er, in·flic·tor,** *n.* —**in·flic·tion,** *n.* —**in·flic·tive,** *a.*

in·flu·ence, in'floo·əns, *n.* Exertion of power; power of affecting others through the use of authority, money, or social position; power of producing effects by invisible means; a person or thing that exerts such force.—*v.t.,* -enced, -enc·ing. To exert influence; to affect by intangible means; to move; impel. —**in·flu·ence·a·ble,** *a.* —**in·flu·enc·er,** *n.* —**in·flu·en·tial,** in·floo·en'shəl, *a.* —**in·flu·en·tial·ly,** *adv.*

in·flu·en·za, in·floo·en'zə, *n.* An acute, infectious, and highly contagious disease affecting the respiratory tract, producing symptoms such as fever, muscular pain, intestinal disorders, and general prostration, and caused by viruses. —**in·flu·en·zal,** *a.* —**in·flu·en·za·like,** *a.*

in·flux, in'fləks, *n.* The act of flowing in.

in·form, in·fôrm', *v.t.* To communicate knowledge to.—*v.i.* To give information.—**inform against,** to communicate incriminating facts about. —**in·formed,** *a.* —**in·for·mer,** *n.*

in·for·mal, in·fôr'məl, *a.* Not in the regular or usual form; unofficial; without ceremony; casual; pertaining to casual but educated conversation, as opposed to *formal* writing or discourse. —**in·for·mal·i·ty,** in·fôr·mal'ə·tē, *n.* —**in·for·mal·ly,** *adv.*

in·form·ant, in·fôr'mənt, *n.* One who supplies information.

in·for·ma·tion, in·fėr·mā'shən, *n.* News or intelligence communicated by word or in writing; facts or data; knowledge derived from reading or instruction, or gathered in any way. —**in·for·ma·tion·al,** *a.* —**in·for·ma·tive,** in·fôr'mə·tiv, *a.* —**in·for·ma·tive·ly,** *adv.* —**in·for·ma·tive·ness,** *n.* —**in·for·ma·to·ry,** in·fôr'mə·tôr·ē, *a.*

in·frac·tion, in·frak'shən, *n.* The act of infringing; violation; breaking.

in·fran·gi·ble, in·fran'jə·bəl, *a.* Unbreakable; not to be violated. —**in·fran·gi·bil·i·ty,** in·fran·jə·bil'ə·tē, **in·fran·gi·ble·ness,** *n.* —**in·fran·gi·bly,** *adv.*

in·fra·red, in·frə·red', *a.* Below the red, as the invisible rays of the spectrum lying outside the red end of the visible spectrum; pertaining to these rays.

in·fra·struc·ture, in'frə·strək·chər, *n.* A foundation; the permanent structure of a military organization.

in·fre·quent, in·frē'kwənt, *a.* Seldom; rare; placed at wide intervals; occasional. —**in·fre·quen·cy,** *n.* —**in·fre·quent·ly,** *adv.*

in·fringe, in·frinj', *v.t.,* -fringed, -fring·ing. To break, as laws or contracts; to violate; to impair or encroach on.—*v.i.* To encroach; followed by *on* or *upon.* —**in·fringe·ment,** *n.* —**in·fring·er,** *n.*

in·fu·ri·ate, in·fyûr'ē·āt, *v.t.,* -at·ed, -at·ing. Render furious; enrage. —**in·fu·ri·at·ing·ly,** *adv.* —**in·fu·ri·a·tion,** in·fyûr·ē·ā'shən, *n.*

in·fuse, in·fūz', *v.t.,* -fused, -fus·ing. To pour into or in; introduce, usu. by pouring; instill; to steep in a liquid without boiling to separate the soluble from the insoluble components. —**in·fus·er,** *n.* —**in·fus·i·bil·i·ty,** in·fū·zə·bil'ə·tē, *n.* —**in·fus·i·ble,** *a.* —**in·fu·sion,** in·fū'zhən, *n.* —**in·fu·sive,** in·fū'siv, *a.*

in·gen·ious, in·jēn'yəs, *a.* Possessed of cleverness, resourcefulness, or inventiveness; clever or original in conception or design. —**in·gen·i·ous·ly,** *adv.* —**in·gen·ious·ness,** *n.*

in·gé·nue, an'zhə·noo, än'zhə·noo, *n. pl.,* -nues, -nooz. An innocent or ingenuous girl, esp. as represented on the stage; an actress who plays such a part.

in·ge·nu·i·ty, in·jə·noo'ə·tē, in·jə·nū'ə·tē, *n.* Inventiveness; cleverness.

in·gen·u·ous, in·jen'ū·əs, *a.* Innocent; artless; naïve; candid; straightforward. —**in·gen·u·ous·ly,** *adv.* —**in·gen·u·ous·ness,** *n.*

in·gest, in·jest', *v.t.* To put or take, as food, into the body. —**in·ges·tion,** in·jes'chən, *n.* —**in·ges·tive,** *a.*

---

a- hat, fāte, fāre, fäther; e- met, mē; i- pin, pīne; o- not, nōte, ôrb, moove (move), boy, pownd; u- cūbe, bûll, tûk (took); ch- chin; th- thick, then; zh- vizhon (vision); ə- əgo, takən, pencəl, lemən, bėrd (bird).

in·glo·ri·ous, in·glôr′ē·əs, *a.* Shameful; ignominious. **—in·glo·ri·ous·ly,** *adv.* **—in·glo·ri·ous·ness,** *n.*

in·got, ing′gət, *n.* A mass of metal molded into a convenient shape.

in·grain, in·grān′, *v.t.* To fix deeply and firmly, as in the character or mind; to infuse: to *ingrain* a habit. Also **en·grain.** **—in·grained,** *a.*

in·grate, in′grāt, *n.* An ungrateful person.

in·gra·ti·ate, in·grā′shē·āt, *v.t.,* **-at·ed, -at·ing.** To deliberately seek the favor or good graces of others, usu. followed by *with.* **—in·gra·ti·at·ing,** *a.* **—in·gra·ti·a·tion,** in·grā·shē·ā′shən, *n.*

in·grat·i·tude, in·grat′i·tood, in·grat′i·tūd, *n.* Want of gratitude; unthankfulness.

in·gre·di·ent, in·grē′dē·ənt, *n.* An element of any mixture; a component part or any compound or combination.

in-group, in′groop, *n.* A group whose members are homogeneous and cohesive to the point of excluding others.

in·grow·ing, in′grō·ing, *a.* Growing within or inward; of a nail, growing into the flesh. **—in·grown,** *a.* **—in·growth,** *n.*

in·gulf, in·gulf′, *v.t.* Engulf.

in·hab·it, in·hab′it, *v.t.* To live or dwell in; to occupy as a place of settled residence; to exist within. **—in·hab·it·a·ble,** *a.* **—in·hab·i·ta·tion,** in·hab·i·tā′shən, *n.* **—in·hab·it·er,** *n.* **—in·hab·it·ed,** *a.*

in·hab·it·ant, in·hab′i·tənt, *n.* One who inhabits; a permanent resident.

in·hal·ant, in·hā′lənt, *a.* Inhaling; used for inhaling. *—n.* An apparatus or a medicine used for inhaling. **—in·ha·la·tion,** in·hə·lā′shən, *n.*

in·ha·la·tor, in·hə·lā·tər, *n.* A device used for aid breathing, or to administer a medicine in vapor form.

in·hale, in·hāl, *v.t., v.i.,* **in·haled, in·hal·ing.** To breathe in.

in·hal·er, in·hā′lər, *n.* An apparatus used in inhaling medicinal vapors; a respirator; one who inhales.

in·here, in·hēr′, *v.i.,* **-hered, -her·ing.** To exist or be fixed in; to belong; to be innate. **—in·her·ence,** *n.* **—in·her·ent,** in·hēr′ənt, in·her′ənt, *a.* **—in·her·ent·ly,** *adv.* **—in·he·sion,** in·hē′zhən, *n.*

in·her·it, in·her′it, *v.t.* To receive or obtain, as property, rights, or duties, from an ancestor or predecessor; derive or acquire, as traits or characteristics, through heredity.*—v.i.* To receive an inheritance. **—in·her·it·a·ble,** in·her′ə·tə·bəl, *a.* **—in·her·i·tor,** *n.*

in·her·it·ance, in·her′ə·təns, *n.* That which is or may be inherited; a legacy; a heritage; property, title, or position derived from one's ancestors or predecessors.

in·hib·it, in·hib′it, *v.t.* To restrain; to hinder; to prohibit. **—in·hib·i·tive, in·hib·i·to·ry,** *a.* **—in·hib·i·ter, in·hib·it·or,** *n.*

in·hi·bi·tion, in·i·bish′ən, in·hi·bish′ən, *n.* The act of inhibiting.

in·hos·pi·ta·ble, in·hos′pi·tə·bəl, in·ho·spit′ə·bəl, *a.* Not hospitable; not friendly or generous to guests; barren or uninviting. **—in·hos·pi·tal·i·ty,** in·hos·pi·tal′ə·tē, *n.*

in·hu·man, in·hū′mən, *a.* Not human; barbarous; brutal; cruel. **—in·hu·man·i·ty,** in·hū·man′ə·tē, *n.*

in·hu·mane, in·hū·mān′, *a.* Lacking in humanity, kindness, or sympathy for the suffering of others; cruel.

in·im·i·cal, i·nim′i·kəl, *a.* Unfriendly; hostile; adverse; harmful: as, an action *inimical* to commerce.

in·im·i·ta·ble, i·nim′i·tə·bəl, *a.* Incapable of being imitated or copied; matchless.

in·iq·ui·ty, i·nik′wi·tē, *n. pl.,* **-ties.** Gross injustice; sin; a wicked act. **—in·iq·ui·tous,** *a.*

in·i·tial, i·nish′əl, *a.* Placed at the beginning; of or pertaining to the beginning.*—n.* The first letter of a word; the first letters in order of a proper name.*—v.t.,* **-tialed, -tial·ing.** To put one's initials on or to. **—i·ni·tial·ly,** *adv.*

in·i·ti·ate, i·nish′ē·āt, *v.t.,* **-at·ed, -at·ing.** To begin or enter upon; to set going; to guide or direct by instruction in rudiments or principles; to introduce or admit into a fraternity, or other organization.*—n.* One who has been initiated. **—in·i·ti·a·tion,** i·nish·ē·ā′shən, *n.* **—in·i·ti·a·tor,** *n.*

in·i·ti·a·tive, i·nish′ē·ə·tiv, i·nish′ə·tiv, *a.* Serving to initiate; initiatory.*—n.* An introductory act or step; power or ability to take the lead or originate action.

in·ject, in·jekt′, *v.t.* To force a fluid into a passage, cavity, or tissue; to introduce something new and different into a situation or subject, as a remark; to interject. **—in·jec·tion,** *n.* **—in·jec·tor,** *n.*

in·ju·di·cious, in·joo·dish′əs, *a.* Acting without sound judgment or discretion; unwise; imprudent.

in·junc·tion, in·jəngk′shən, *n.* The act of ordering or directing; a command, admonition, or precept. *Law.* A writ requiring a person to refrain from doing certain acts. **—in·junc·tive,** *a.*

in·jure, in′jər, *v.t.,* **-jured, -jur·ing.** To do harm to; to hurt or wound; to offend or be unjust to, as another's feelings. **—in·ju·ri·ous,** in·jûr′ē·əs, *a.*

in·ju·ry, in·jə·rē, *n. pl.,* **-ries.** Harm or damage occasioned; a wrong received.

in·jus·tice, in·jəs′tis, *n.* Want of fairness or equity; violation of another's rights; a wrong or unjust act.

ink, ingk, *n.* A colored liquid used for writing, printing, and drawing.*—v.t.* **—ink·y,** *a.,* **-i·er, -i·est.**

ink-blot, ingk′blot, *n.* Blot drawing, used in psychological tests.

ink·ling, ingk′ling, *n.* A hint or whisper; uncertain or incomplete knowledge of.

in·laid, in′lād, *a.* Laid or set in the surface of a thing: an *inlaid* decorative design in wood.

in·land, in′lənd, *a.* Interior; away from the sea. *—in′land,* in′lənd, *adv.* In or toward the interior of a country.*—in′land,* in′lənd, *n.* The interior part of a country.

in-law, in′lô, *n. Informal.* A person connected with one by marriage.

in·lay, in′lā, in·lā′, *v.t.,* **-laid, -lay·ing.** To insert for ornamentation into a surface.*—in′lā,* *n.* An inlaid surface or decoration.

in·let, in′let, in′lit, *n.* A narrow passage or strip of water between islands; a recess in a shore.

in·mate, in′māt, *n.* An occupant of an asylum, prison, or hospital.

in me·mo·ri·am, in mə·môr′ē·əm, *prep., adv.* In memory of.

in·most, in′mōst, *a.* Farthest within; innermost.

inn, in, *n.* A public house for the lodging and entertainment of travelers; a small hotel or restaurant; a tavern.

in·nards, in′ərdz, *n. pl. Informal.* The internal organs or parts of a body, machine, etc.

in·nate, i·nāt′, in′āt, *a.* Inborn; native; inherent.

in·ner, in′ər, *a.* Interior or internal; private or intimate: *inner* feelings.

in·ner·most, in′ər·mōst, *a.* Farthest inward; inmost.*—n.*

in·ner·sole, in′ər·sōl, *n.* The permanently attached lining of a shoe; the removable inner sole of a shoe. Also **in·sole.**

in·ner tube, *n.* A flexible ring-shaped tube, usu. of rubber, inflated by air pressure; used inside the casing of a pneumatic tire.

in·ner·vate, i·nər′vāt, in′ər·vāt, *v.t.,* **-vat·ed, -vat·ing.** To supply with nerves; to communicate nervous energy to. **—in·ner·va·tion,** in·ər·vā′shən, *n.*

in·nerve, i·nərv′, *v.t.,* **-nerved, -nerv·ing.** To supply with nervous energy; invigorate.

in·ning, in′ing, *n.* A division of a baseball game in which each team has the opportunity to score while at bat; a turn or opportunity.

inn·keep·er, in′kē·pər, *n.* One who manages or owns an inn.

in·no·cence, in′ə·səns, *n.* The quality of being innocent.

in•no•cent, in′ə•sənt, *a.* Free from sin, guilt, malice, or guile; free from the guilt of a particular crime or evil action; without worldly knowledge.

in•noc•u•ous, i•nok′ū•əs, *a.* Producing no ill effect; inoffensive; insipid.

in•no•vate, in′ə•vāt, *v.t.,* **-vat•ed, -vat•ing.** To change or alter by introducing something new.—*v.i.* To make changes in anything established, used with *on* or *in:* as, to *innovate on* established customs. **—in•no•va•tion,** in•ə•vā′shən, *n.* **—in•no•va•tive,** *a.* **—in•no•va•tor,** *n.*

in•nu•en•do, in•ū•en′dō, *n. pl.,* **-dos, -does.** An indirect intimation, usu. of a derogatory nature; an insinuation.

in•nu•mer•a•ble, i•nū′mər•ə•bəl, i•noo′mər•ə•bəl, *a.* Countless. Also **in•nu•mer•ous. —in•nu•mer•a•bly,** *adv.*

in•ob•serv•ance, in•əb•zərv′əns, *n.* Failure to observe or heed. **—in•ob•serv•ant,** *a.* **—in•ob•serv•ant•ly,** *adv.*

in•oc•u•lant, i•nok′yə•lənt, *n.* Inoculum.

in•oc•u•late, i•nok′yə•lāt, *v.t.,* **-lat•ed, -lat•ing.** To implant, as virus or bacteria, within a human body to cause a mild disease and thus ensure immunity from that disease.—*v.i.* **—in•oc•u•la•tion,** i•nok•yə•lā′shən, *n.* **—in•oc•u•la•tor,** *n.*

in•oc•u•lum, i•nok′yə•ləm, *n.* The prepared material for injections, usu. composed of bacteria or viruses.

in•of•fen•sive, in•ə•fen′siv, *a.* Giving no offense; harmless.

in•op•er•a•ble, in•op′ər•ə•bəl, *a.* Not practicable or workable.

in•op•er•a•tive, in•op′ər•ə•tiv, in•op′ə•rā•tiv, *a.* Not operative; not working.

in•op•por•tune, in•op•ər•toon′, in•op•ər•tūn′, *a.* Happening at an inconvenient or inappropriate time; unseasonable. **—in•op•por•tu•ni•ty,** *n.*

in•or•di•nate, in•ôr′də•nit, *a.* Excessive.

in•pa•tient, in′pā•shənt, *n.* A patient who is lodged and fed as well as treated in a hospital or the like; opposed to *outpatient.*

in•pour, in•pôr′, in•pōr′, *v.t., v.i.* To cause, as liquid, to flow into a container.

in•put, in′pût, *n.* That which is put in; the amount of power, energy, current, or voltage supplied to a machine or electric circuit; coded information ready for computer processing; the process of feeding information to the computer.—*a.* Referring to data or equipment for input to a computer.—*v.t., v.i.,* **in•put•ted, in•put•ting.** To supply or cause to be supplied, as with data, for processing.

in•quest, in′kwest, *n.* A legal or judicial inquiry, esp. before a jury; a post mortem investigation made by a coroner.

in•qui•e•tude, in•kwī′ə•tood, in•kwī′ə•tūd, *n.* Uneasiness; restlessness.

in•quire, in•kwir′, *v.t.,* **-quired, -quir•ing.** To ask for information about: as, to *inquire* one's name.—*v.i.* To make an investigation or search, with *into;* to seek information by questioning. Also **en•quire.—in•quire af•ter,** to ask about, as one's health. **—in•quir•er,** *n.*

in•quir•y, in′kwə•rē, in•kwī′rē, *n. pl.,* **-ies.** A seeking for truth, information, or knowledge; investigation; research. Also **en•quir•y.**

in•qui•si•tion, in•kwə•zish′ən, *n.* The act of investigating; an inquiry, esp. severe or prolonged. *Law.* An inquest.

in•quis•i•tive, in•kwiz′i•tiv, *a.* Inclined to seek information; eager for learning; given to prying; overly curious.

in•quis•i•tor, in•kwiz′ə•tər, *n.* One who inquires and examines, officially or not.

in•road, in′rōd, *n.* Usu. pl. A harmful encroachment: to make *inroads* on my savings; a sudden raid or invasion.

in•rush, in′rəsh, *n.* An influx; a rushing in.

in•sane, in•sān′, *a.* Not sane or of sound mind; mentally ill; mad; utterly senseless; pertaining to a place where mentally ill persons are confined and treated: an *insane* asylum.

in•san•i•ty, in•san′ə•tē, *n. pl.,* **-ties.** The condition of being insane; extreme folly or an instance of it.

in•sa•tia•ble, in•sā′shə•bəl, in•sā′shē•ə•bəl, *a.* Incapable of being satisfied or appeased. **—in•sa•tia•bil•i•ty,** in•sā•shə•bil′ə•tē, in•sā•shē•ə•bil′ə•tē, *n.* **—in•sa•tia•bly,** *adv.*

in•sa•ti•ate, in•sā′shē•it, *a.* Insatiable.

in•scribe, in•skrib′, *v.t.,* **-scribed, -scrib•ing.** To write down or engrave; to etch, as a name, or dedication, into something durable; to write, as characters, in code. **—in•scrip•tion,** in•skrip′shən, *n.* **—in•scrip•tive,** in•skrip′tiv, *a.*

in•scru•ta•ble, in•skroo′tə•bəl, *a.* Incapable of being searched into and understood; impenetrable. **—in•scru•ta•bil•i•ty,** in•skroo•tə•bil′ə•tē, *n.* **—in•scru•ta•bly,** *adv.*

in•seam, in′sēm, *n.* An inside seam of a piece of clothing or footwear.

in•sect, in′sekt, *n.* One of a class of small arthropods characterized in maturity by a body divided into a head, thorax, and abdomen, by three pairs of legs, and usu. by two pairs of wings; a contemptible person.—*a.* Like an insect.

in•sec•ti•cide, in•sek′tə•sid, *n.* A substance or preparation used for killing insects; the killing of insects. **—in•sec•ti•cid•al,** in•sek•tə•sid′əl, *a.*

in•se•cure, in•sə•kyûr′, *a.* Prone to fear or anxiety; unsafe; precarious. **—in•se•cu•ri•ty,** *n.*

in•sem•i•nate, in•sem′ə•nāt, *v.t.,* **-nat•ed, -nat•ing.** To inject, as seed, into something; implant, as ideas; impregnate, esp. with semen. **—in•sem•i•na•tion,** in•sem•ə•nā′shən, *n.*

in•sen•sate, in•sen′sāt, in•sen′sit, *a.* Lacking feeling.

in•sen•si•ble, in•sen′sə•bəl, *a.* Unconscious; numb to pain; unable to perceive or understand.

in•sen•si•tive, in•sen′si•tiv, *a.* Not sensitive. **—in•sen•si•tiv•i•ty,** in•sen•si•tiv′ə•tē, *n.*

in•sen•ti•ent, in•sen′shē•ənt, in•sen′shənt, *a.* Not sentient; lacking sensation.

in•sep•a•ra•ble, in•sep′ər•ə•bəl, *a.* Incapable of being parted or disjoined.—*n.* **—in•sep•a•ra•bil•i•ty,** in•sep•ər•ə•bil′ə•tē, *n.* **—in•sep•a•ra•bly,** *adv.*

in•sert, in•sərt′, *v.t.* To put or set in; to place in a hole or space, or between parts.—in′sərt, *n.* Something inserted or to be inserted. **—in•sert•er,** *n.*

in•ser•tion, in•sər′shən, *n.* The act of inserting; that which is inserted.

in•set, in•set′, *v.t.,* **-set, -set•ting.** To insert or place in, as material in a garment.—in′set, *n.*

in•shore, in′shôr, in′shōr′, *a., adv.* Near or toward the shore.

in•side, in′sīd′, *n.* An inner side, surface, or part; a favorable position that allows one an advantage; *pl.,* the inner body parts, as the stomach and intestines.—in•sīd′, in′sīd′, *a.* Being on or in the inside; within; internal; known only to a few.—in•sīd′, *adv.* On the inside; within.—in•sīd′, in′sīd, *prep.* Within.—**in•side of,** within.

in•sid•er, in•sī′dər, *n.* A person whose position allows him or her an advantage.

in•sid•i•ous, in•sid′ē•əs, *a.* Seeking or intended to entrap or beguile; stealthily treacherous or deceitful.

in•sight, in′sīt, *n.* The act or power of grasping or intuitively understanding the essence of something; discernment; penetration; perception. **—in•sight•ful,** *a.*

in•sig•ni•a, in•sig′nē•ə, *n. pl.* Badges or distinguishing marks of office, honor, or membership.

in·sig·nif·i·cant, in·sig·nif'ə·kənt, *a.* Having little importance. **—in·sig·nif·i·cance,** *n.*

in·sin·cere, in·sin·sēr', *a.* Not honest in the expression of actual feeling; deceitful. **—in·sin·cer·i·ty,** in·sin·ser'ə·tē, *n. pl.,* **-ties.**

in·sin·u·ate, in·sin'ū·āt, *v.t.,* **-at·ed, -at·ing.** To introduce by concealed or guarded means; to hint or suggest subtly.**—v.i.** To intimate or imply, usu. something unfavorable. **—in·sin·u·at·ing,** *a.* **—in·sin·u·a·tor,** *n.*

in·sin·u·a·tion, in·sin·ū·ā'shən, *n.* An indirect suggestion, esp. a derogatory or unfavorable one; an innuendo.

in·sip·id, in·sip'id, *a.* Tasteless; dull, heavy, or uninteresting. **—in·si·pid·i·ty,** in·si·pid'ə·tē, **in·sip·id·ness,** *n.*

in·sist, in·sist', *v.i.* To demand firmly, with *on* or *upon:* to *insist* on locking the windows; to assert an opinion or resolution emphatically, with *on* or *upon.*—*v.t.* To contend or assert absolutely: to *insist* that the story is untrue; to demand emphatically: I *insist* that you leave. **—in·sist·ence,** in·sis'təns, *n.* **—in·sist·ent,** *a.* **—in·sist·ent·ly, in·sist·ing·ly,** *adv.*

in·so·bri·e·ty, in·sə·brī'ə·tē, *n.* Intemperance; drunkenness.

in·so·cia·ble, in·sō'shə·bəl, *a.* Not sociable; taciturn. **—in·so·cia·bil·i·ty,** in·sō·shə·bil'ə·tē, *n.* **in·so·cia·bly,** *adv.*

in·so·far, in·sə·fär', in·sō·fär', *adv.* To this degree or to such an extent, usu. followed by *as.*

in·sole, in'sōl, *n.* The inner sole of a shoe or boot.

in·so·lent, in'sə·lənt, *a.* Of a person, saucily disrespectful; of language or conduct, rudely overbearing. —*n.* **—in·so·lence,** *n.*

in·sol·u·ble, in·sol'yə·bəl, *a.* Incapable of being dissolved, particularly by a liquid; not to be solved or explained. **—in·sol·u·bil·i·ty,** in·sol·yə·bil'ə·tē, *n.* **—in·sol·u·bly,** *adv.*

in·solv·a·ble, in·sol'və·bəl, *a.* Not to be solved.

in·sol·vent, in·sol'vənt, *a.* Not solvent.—*n.* A person with debts he cannot pay. **—in·sol·ven·cy,** *n.*

in·som·ni·a, in·som'nē·ə, *n.* Inability to sleep, esp. when chronic; sleeplessness. **—in·som·ni·ac,** in·som'nē·ak, *n., a.*

in·so·much, in·sō·much', *adv.* To such a degree; so, usu. followed by *that* or *as.***—in·so·much as,** inasmuch as.

in·spect, in·spekt', *v.t.* To examine or view carefully or closely.

in·spec·tion, in·spek'shən, *n.* The act of inspecting; a critical examination or careful viewing.

in·spec·tor, in·spek'tər, *n.* A person who reviews or examines critically; a police official, ranking below superintendent, in command of several precincts.

in·spi·ra·tion, in·spə·rā'shən, *n.* A prompting, esp. to creative action, that arises within the mind; an illumination; the act of inspiring; state of being inspired; any source or agent of inspiration; breathing. **—in·spi·ra·tion·al,** *a.*

in·spire, in·spīr', *v.t.,* **-spired, -spir·ing.** To arouse thought or feeling; to prompt creative action; stir; animate; to draw into the lungs.—*v.i.* To inhale.

in·spir·it, in·spir'it, *v.i.* To enliven.

in·sta·ble, in·stā'bəl, *a.* Unstable. **—in·sta·bil·i·ty,** in·stə·bil'ə·tē, *n.*

in·stall, in·stôl', *v.t.* To set up or adjust for use or service: to *install* a heating system; to appoint to an office or post, usu. with formal ceremony. **in·stall·er,** *n.*

in·stal·la·tion, in·stə·lā'shən, *n.* Any mechanical device or apparatus set up or adjusted for use; the act of establishing or installing; any military post or camp equipped for official activity.

in·stall·ment, in·stôl'mənt, *n.* Any of the specified parts of a debt or sum due at set intervals over a stated time period; one of a number of parts, as of a story,

issued at fixed intervals; an installation; the act of installing.

in·stance, in'stəns, *n.* An example, esp. one given as an illustration or proof; one event in a series.

in·stant, in'stənt, *a.* Immediate; imminent; current; pressing; urgent. *Informal.* Of foods, readily prepared, usu. by adding water.—*n.* The point of time now present; an infinitesimal or very short space of time. —*adv.* Instantly; at once.

in·stan·ta·ne·ous, in·stən·tā'nē·əs, *a.* Occurring, accomplished, or completed within an imperceptible amount of time; immediate.

in·stant·ly, in'stənt·lē, *adv.* Immediately; at once. —*conj.* As soon as.

in·state, in·stāt', *v.t.,* **-stat·ed, -stat·ing.** To install or place in a particular position or office. **—in·state·ment,** *n.*

in·stead, in·sted', *adv.* In the place; rather than, with *of:* She chose the trip *instead of* the money; in lieu; as an alternative or substitute, with *of.*

in·step, in'step, *n. Anat.* The arched part of the upper side of the human foot; that part of a shoe or stocking which covers the instep.

in·sti·gate, in'stə·gāt, *v.t.,* **-gat·ed, -gat·ing.** To spur on or incite to some action or course. **—in·sti·ga·tion,** in·stə·gā'shən, *n.* **—in·sti·ga·tor,** *n.*

in·still, in·stil', *v.t.,* **in·stilled, in·still·ing.** To introduce drop by drop; to infuse by degrees into the mind. **—in·stil·la·tion,** in·stə·lā'shən, *n.*

in·stinct, in'stingkt, *n.* An innate, automatic impulse, in humans and animals, to satisfy basic biological needs, leading to behavior that is purposeful and directive; a natural aptitude or gift for something.

in·stinc·tive, in·stingk'tiv, *a.* Not learned; spontaneous. Also **in·stinc·tu·al,** in·stingk'chü·əl. **—in·stinc·tive·ly,** *adv.*

in·sti·tute, in'sti·toot, in'sti·tūt, *v.t.,* **-tut·ed, -tut·ing.** To set up or establish; to bring into use or practice.—*n.* A society or organization for carrying on a particular work, as of literary, scientific, or educational character; the building occupied by such a society. **—in·sti·tut·er, in·sti·tu·tor,** *n.*

in·sti·tu·tion, in·stə·too'shən, in·stə·tū'shən, *n.* The act of instituting; establishment; foundation; an established law, custom, practice, or organization. *Informal.* Any familiar practice or object. An organization or establishment instituted for some public, educational, or charitable purpose; the building devoted to its work; a place of confinement: a penal *institution.*

in·sti·tu·tion·al, in·sti·too'shə·nəl, *a.* Pertaining to or of the nature of an institution; characterized by the drabness and conformity associated with large institutions. **—in·sti·tu·tion·al·ism,** in·stə·too'shə·nə·liz·əm, *n.* **—in·sti·tu·tion·al·ize,** in·stə·too'shə·nə·līz, *v.t.,* **-ized, -iz·ing.**

in·struct, in·strəkt', *v.t.* To teach; to educate; to train.

in·struc·tion, in·strək'shən, *n.* The act of instructing or teaching; information; an order, or direction.

in·struc·tive, in·strək'tiv, *a.* Conveying knowledge; serving to enlighten or inform.

in·struc·tor, in·strək'tər, *n.* One who instructs; a teacher; a college teacher who ranks below assistant professor.

in·stru·ment, in'strə·mənt, *n.* A tool, implement, or utensil; a means by which something is performed or effected; any contrivance from which music is produced.—*v.t.* To provide with instruments.

in·stru·men·tal, in·strə·men'təl, *a.* Acting as a means to some end; pertaining to instruments, esp. musical instruments.

in·stru·men·ta·list, in·strə·men'tə·list, *n.* One who plays upon a musical instrument.

in·stru·men·ta·tion, in·strə·men·tā'shən, *n.* The art of arranging music for a number of instruments; execution of music on an instrument.

in·sub·or·di·nate, in·sə·bôr'də·nit, *a.* Not submitting to authority; rebellious.—*n.* **—in·sub·or·di·na·**

tion, in•sə•bôr•də•nā′shən, *n.*

in•sub•stan•tial, in•səb•stan′shəl, *a.* Lacking substance. **—in•sub•stan•ti•al•i•ty,** in•səb•stan•shē•al′ə•tē, *n.*

in•suf•fer•a•ble, in•suf′ər•ə•bəl, *a.* Not to be suffered, borne or endured; intolerable; unendurable. **—in•suf•fer•a•bly,** *adv.*

in•suf•fi•cient, in•sə•fish′ənt, *a.* Not sufficient. **—in•suf•fi•cience, in•suf•fi•cien•cy,** *n.*

in•su•lar, in′sə•lər, in′syə•lər, *a.* Of or pertaining to an island or islands; detached, or standing alone; narrow, provincial, or illiberal. **—in•su•lar•i•ty,** in•sə•lar′ə•tē, *n.*

in•su•late, in′sə•lāt, in•syə•lāt, *v.t.,* **-lat•ed, -lat•ing.** To place in detachment; to isolate; to cover, surround, or separate with nonconducting material to prevent or lessen the passage of electricity, heat, or sound.

in•su•la•tion, in•sə•lā′shən, *n.* The act of insulating, or the resulting state; a nonconducting material.

in•su•la•tor, in′sə•la•tər, *n.* A nonconductor.

in•su•lin, in′sə•lin, in′syə•lin, *n.* A body hormone necessary for the proper metabolism of carbohydrate; a preparation of a synthetic hormone used in the treatment of diabetes.

in•sult, in′səlt, *n.* Any gross affront or indignity offered to another, either by words or action.—in•səlt′, *v.t.* To treat with gross abuse, insolence, or contempt.

in•sup•port•a•ble, in•sə•pôr′tə•bəl, *a.* Not to be supported; unjustifiable.

in•sup•press•i•ble, in•sə•pres′ə•bəl, *a.* Incapable of being suppressed or concealed.

in•sur•ance, in•shûr′əns, *n.* The act of insuring; the act, system, or business of insuring property, life, or person against loss or harm arising from fire, accident, death, etc., in consideration of a payment proportionate to the risk involved; the contract thus made, set forth in a written or printed agreement or policy; the sum paid for insuring anything; the amount for which anything is insured.

in•sure, in•shûr′, *v.t.,* **-sured, -sur•ing.** To guarantee against risk; to secure indemnity to in case of loss; to issue an insurance policy on. **—in•sur•er,** *n.*

in•sured, in•shûrd′, *n.* A person who has insurance against loss of any kind.

in•sur•gent, in•sər′jənt, *a.* Actively revolting against existing government; rebellious.—*n.* **—in•sur•gence, in•sur•gen•cy,** *n.*

in•sur•mount•a•ble, in•sər•mown′tə•bəl, *a.* Incapable of being surmounted, passed over, or overcome.

in•sur•rec•tion, in•sə•rek′shən, *n.* The act of rising in open resistance against established authority; a revolt. **—in•sur•rec•tion•ar•y,** *n., a.*

in•sus•cep•ti•ble, in•sə•sep′tə•bəl, *a.* Not susceptible.

in•tact, in•takt′, *a.* Untouched or unaffected by anything that might harm or impair.

in•take, in′tāk, *n.* The point at which a fluid or gas enters a channel or pipe; the act of taking in; that which is taken in.

in•tan•gi•ble, in•tan′jə•bəl, *a.* Not tangible. **—in•tan•gi•bil•i•ty,** in•tan•jə•bil′ə•tē, **in•tan•gi•ble•ness,** *n.* **—in•tan•gi•bly,** *adv.*

in•te•ger, in′tə•jər, *n.* A whole number; a whole.

in•te•gral, in′tə•grəl, *a.* Whole; entire; complete; belonging to or forming a necessary part of a whole.—*n.* A whole; an entire thing. **—in•te•gral•ly,** *adv.*

in•te•grate, in′tə•grāt, *v.t.,* **-grat•ed, -grat•ing.** To make up or complete as a whole, as parts do; to bring together, as parts, into a whole; to unite; to indicate the total amount or the mean value of; to make available equally to members of all races, religions, or ethnic groups.—*v.i.* To become complete or whole.

in•te•gra•tion, in•tə•grā′shən, *n.* The act of integrating; the act of combining into an integral whole;

harmonization; the act of making equally available, as organizations, services, or places of business, to members of all races, religions, and ethnic groups. **—in•te•gra•tion•ist,** *n.*

in•teg•ri•ty, in•teg′rə•tē, *n.* Unimpaired moral principles; honesty; soundness; the quality of being whole or undivided.

in•tel•lect, in′tə•lekt, *n.* Mental capacity to comprehend ideas and relationships and to exercise judgment; the power to learn and to think.

in•tel•lec•tu•al, in•tə•lek′choo•əl, *a.* Relating to the intellect and the exercise of mental faculties; demanding the employment of one's intelligence; rational; highly intelligent.

in•tel•lec•tu•al•ism, in•tə•lek′choo•ə•liz•əm, *n.* Dedication to intellectual interests. **—in•tel•lec•tu•al•ize,** *v.t.,* **-ized, -iz•ing.**

in•tel•li•gence, in•tel′ə•jəns, *n.* The faculty or ability for comprehending and reasoning with facts, truths, or propositions; intellectual power; knowledge imparted or acquired; secret enemy information; an agency that seeks to secure such information.

in•tel•li•gence quo•tient, *n.* A technique for stating a person's general intelligence.

in•tel•li•gence test, *n.* One or more standardized graded tests, aimed at measuring an individual's general intelligence.

in•tel•li•gent, in•tel′ə•jənt, *a.* Having the faculty of understanding and reasoning; rational; having a good intellect. **—in•tel•li•gent•ly,** *adv.*

in•tel•li•gent•si•a, in•tel•i•jent′sē•ə, *n. pl.* Intellectuals.

in•tel•li•gi•ble, in•tel′ə•jə•bəl, *a.* Capable of being understood. **—in•tel•li•gi•bil•i•ty,** in•tel•ə•jə•bil′ə•tē, *n.* **—in•tel•li•gi•bly,** *adv.*

in•tem•per•ance, in•tem′pər•əns, *n.* Lack of moderation or due restraint; habitual or excessive indulgence in alcoholic liquors. **—in•tem•per•ate,** in•tem′pər•it, *a.*

in•tend, in•tend′, *v.t.* To have in mind as something willed to be done or brought about; to design or mean for a particular purpose.—*v.i.* To have a purpose or design: He may *intend* otherwise. **—in•tend•er,** *n.*

in•tend•ed, in•ten′did, *a.* Intentional or designed: to produce the *intended* effect; prospective, as one's future husband or wife.—*n. Informal.* One who is betrothed.

in•tense, in•tens′, *a.* Existing or occurring in a high degree; having characteristic qualities in a high degree; performed earnestly, or strenuously, as an activity; very great or strong, as sensations or emotions; having or showing great strength of feeling, as a person, the face, language, or the like. **—in•tense•ly,** *adv.* **—in•tense•ness,** *n.*

in•ten•si•fy, in•ten′sə•fī, *v.t.,* **-fied, -fy•ing.** To render intense or more intense.—*v.i.* **—in•ten•si•fi•ca•tion,** in•ten•sə•fə•kā′shən, *n.* **—in•ten•si•fi•er,** *n.*

in•ten•sion, in•ten′shən, *n.* Intensity.

in•ten•si•ty, in•ten′sə•tē, *n. pl.,* **-ties.** The state of being intense.

in•ten•sive, in•ten′siv, *a.* Of, pertaining to, or characterized by intensity. **—in•ten•sive•ly,** *adv.* **—in•ten•sive•ness,** *n.*

in•tent, in•tent′, *a.* Fixed with strained or earnest attention, as the gaze or mind, used with *on* or *upon:* to be *intent on* gain; earnest; having the mind, gaze, or thoughts fixed on some object or with some purpose in view.—*n.* The action of intending; a particular intention or design; meaning or import.—**to all intents and pur•pos•es,** for all practical purposes; practically.

in•ten•tion, in•ten′shən, *n.* The act or fact of intending or proposing; a determination upon some action or result; a purpose or design; *pl.,* purposes with

---

a- hat, fāte, fâre, fäther; **e-** met, mē; **i-** pin, pīne; **o-** not, nōte, ôrb, moove (move), boy, pownd; **u-** cūbe, bůll, tůk (took); **ch-** chin; **th-** thick, ŧhen; **zh-** vizhon (vision); **ə-** əgo, takən, pencəl, lemən, bərd (bird).

respect to a proposal of marriage. The end or object intended. —**in·ten·tion·al,** *a.* —**in·ten·tion·al·ly,** *adv.*

in·ten·tioned, in·ten'shənd, *a.* Having intentions: as, well-*intentioned.*

in·ter, in·tər', *v.t.,* **in·terred, in·ter·ring.** to bury. —**in·ter·ment,** *n.*

in·ter·act, in·tər·akt', *v.i.* To act on each other. —**in·ter·ac·tion,** *n.* —**in·ter·ac·tive,** *a.*

in·ter·breed, in·tər·brēd', *v.t.,* **-bred, -breed·ing.** To breed by crossing one variety of animal or plant with another; crossbreed.—*v.i.*

in·ter·cede, in·tər·sēd', *v.i.,* **-ced·ed, -ced·ing.** To act between parties with a view to reconciling their differences or points of contention; mediate; to plead on behalf of another. —**in·ter·ced·er,** *n.*

in·ter·cept, in·tər·sept', *v.t.* To take or stop while on the way; to interrupt the journey or passage of, as a messenger or letter; to obstruct the progress of. —**in·ter·cep·ter, in·ter·cep·tor,** *n.* —**in·ter·cep·tion,** *n.* —**in·ter·cep·tive,** *a.*

in·ter·ces·sion, in·tər·sesh'ən, *n.* The act of interceding; prayer or petition in behalf of another.

in·ter·change, in·tər·chānj', *v.t., v.i.,* **-changed, -chang·ing.** To change reciprocally; to put each in the place of the other; to transpose; to cause to succeed alternately; to exchange.—in'tər·chānj, *n.* An exchange, alternate succession; an intersection of highways where automobiles can enter or depart without crossing or obstructing the flow of traffic. —**in·ter·change·a·ble,** *a.* —**in·ter·change·a·bil·i·ty,** *n.* —**in·ter·change·a·ble·ness,** *n.* —**in·ter·change·a·bly,** *adv.*

in·ter·col·le·gi·ate, in·tər·kə·lē'jit, in·tər·kə·lē'jē·it, *a.* Between colleges: *intercollegiate* competition. *a.*

in·ter·com, in'tər·kom, *n. Informal.* Intercommunications system.

in·ter·com·mu·ni·cate, in·tər·kə·mū'nə·kāt, *v.i.,* **-cat·ed, -cat·ing.** To communicate mutually. —**in·ter·com·mu·ni·ca·tion,** in·tər·kə·mū·nə·kā'shən, *n.*

in·ter·com·mu·ni·ca·tion sys·tem, *n.* A system of two-way communication consisting of a microphone and loudspeaker at each station.

in·ter·con·nect, in·tər·kə·nekt', *v.t., v.i.* To connect with or between one another. —**in·ter·con·nec·tion,** in·tər·kə·nek'shən, *n.*

in·ter·con·ti·nen·tal, in·tər·kon·tə·nen'təl, *a.* Between continents.

in·ter·course, in'tər·kôrs, in'tər·kōrs, *n.* Reciprocal dealings or communication between persons, groups of persons, or nations; interchange of thought and feeling; sexual union; copulation.

in·ter·cul·tur·al, in·tər·kəl'chər·əl, *a.* Pertaining to or taking place between two or more cultures.

in·ter·cur·rent, in·tər·kər'ənt, *a.* Running between; intervening.

in·ter·de·nom·i·na·tion·al, in·tər·di·nom·ə·nā'shə·nəl, *a.* Occurring between or shared by religious denominations. —**in·ter·de·nom·i·na·tion·al·ism,** *n.*

in·ter·de·part·men·tal, in·tər·də·pärt·men'təl, *a.* Involving or occurring between two or more departments.

in·ter·de·pend·ent, in·tər·di·pen'dənt, *a.* Mutually dependent. —**in·ter·de·pend,** *v.i.* —**in·ter·de·pend·ence,** in·tər·di·pend·en·cy, *n.*

in·ter·dict, in·tər·dikt', *v.t.* To debar, forbid, or prohibit.—*n.* A prohibition. —**in·ter·dic·tion,** *n.*

in·ter·dis·ci·pli·nar·y, in·tər·dis'ə·plə·ner·ē, *a.* Involving more than one area of academic pursuit.

in·ter·est, in'tər·ist, in'trist, *n.* The feeling of attentiveness or curiosity aroused by something; a particular feeling of this kind; the power or quality in something which arouses such feeling; the position of being affected by something; benefit or advantage; regard for one's own profit or advantage; self-interest; *sometimes pl.,* behalf or welfare: to labor in the

interests of peace. A right or title to a share in the ownership of property or a commercial enterprise; a business or cause in which one is involved; money paid for the use of money borrowed.—*v.t.* To induce to participate in an undertaking; to concern, as a person, in something, esp. through its bearing on personal welfare; to involve.

in·ter·est·ed, in'tər·i·stid, *a.* Feeling or showing curiosity, attention, or involvement in something. —**in·ter·est·ed·ly,** *adv.*

in·ter·est·ing, in'tər·i·sting, *a.* That interests; exciting or engaging the attention or curiosity.

in·ter·face, in'tər·fās, *n.* A surface regarded as the common boundary of two bodies or spaces. —**in·ter·fa·cial,** in·tər·fā'shəl, *a.*

in·ter·faith, in'tər·fāth, *a.* Including persons of different religions.

in·ter·fere, in·tər·fēr', *v.i.,* **-fered, -fer·ing.** To come into opposition, with the effect of hampering action; clash or impede; to intervene in another's concerns, esp. without warrant; to meddle. —**in·ter·fer·ence,** *n.* —**in·ter·fer·er,** *n.* —**in·ter·fer·ing·ly,** *adv.*

in·ter·ga·lac·tic, in·tər·gə·lak'tik, *a.* Occurring or located in the vast spaces between the galaxies of the heavens.

in·ter·im, in'tər·im, *n.* An intervening time; the meantime; a temporary arrangement.—*a.* Pertaining to an intervening time period; temporary: an *interim* plan.

in·te·ri·or, in·tēr'ē·ər, *a.* Inner; pertaining to the inside; situated inland: as, the *interior* part of a country; internal or domestic; private or secret; mental; spiritual.—*n.* The inside or internal part; the inner or inward nature or character of anything; the inside of a building or room.

in·te·ri·or dec·o·ra·tion, *n.* The art of designing, decorating, and furnishing interiors of homes, offices, apartments, and other internal areas.

in·ter·ject, in·tər·jekt', *v.t.* To throw between; interrupt; interpose. —**in·ter·jec·tion,** in·tər·jek'shən, *n.* The act of throwing between; an interruption; an interposition; an expression of emotion or passion. —**in·ter·jec·tion·al·ly,** *adv.* —**in·ter·jec·to·ry,** *a.*

in·ter·lay·er, in'tər·lā·ər, *n.* A thickness or layer located between other layers.

in·ter·leaf, in'tər·lēf, *n. pl.,* **-leaves,** lēvz. A sheet of paper, usu. blank, which has been bound or inserted between two regular pages of a book. —**in·ter·leave,** in·tər·lēv', *v.t.,* **-leaved, -leav·ing.**

in·ter·line, in'tər·līn, *v.t.,* **-lined, -lin·ing.** To provide, as a garment, with an inner lining inserted between the ordinary lining and the outer fabric. —**in·ter·lin·ing,** in'tər·lī·ning, in·tər·lī'ning, *n.*

in·ter·link, in·tər·lingk', *v.t.* To link, one with another.—in'tər·lingk, *n.* A connecting link.

in·ter·lock, in·tər·lok', *v.i.* To interlace; to be linked together; to be locked together by a series of connections.—*v.t.* To lock one in another firmly.—in'tər·lok, *n.*

in·ter·lo·cu·tion, in·tər·lō·kū'shən, *n.* Interchange of speech; conversation; a dialogue of colloquy. —**in·ter·loc·u·tor,** in·tər·lok'ū·tər, *n.* —**in·ter·loc·u·to·ry,** in·tər·lok'ū·tōr·ē, in·tər·lok'ū·tôr·ē, *a.*

in·ter·lope, in·tər·lōp', *v.i.,* **-loped, -lop·ing.** To intrude into some region or field of trade without a proper license; to thrust oneself into the domain or affairs of others.

in·ter·lop·er, in'tər·lō·pər, *n.* An intruder; a trespasser.

in·ter·lude, in'tər·lood, *n.* An interval; a temporary pause or lull during some other activity; an intervening episode or period.

in·ter·lu·nar, in·tər·loo'nər, *a.* Pertaining to the moon's monthly period of invisibility between the old moon and the new. Also **in·ter·lu·na·ry.**

in·ter·mar·ry, in·tər·mar'ē, *v.i.,* **-mar·ried, -mar·ry·ing.** To become connected by marriage, as two families, tribes, castes, or religions; to marry within the limits of the family or of near relationship. —**in·ter·mar·riage,** n.

in·ter·me·di·ar·y, in·tər·mē′dē·er·ē, a. Being between; intermediate; acting between persons or parties.—n. pl. **in·ter·me·di·ar·ies.** An intermediate agent or agency; a go-between.

in·ter·me·di·ate, in·tər·mē′dē·it, a. Being, situated, or occurring between two points, stages, or things; acting between others; intervening.—n. —in·tər·mē·dē·āt, v.i., **-at·ed, -at·ing.** To act as an intermediary; to mediate. —**in·ter·me·di·a·tion,** in·tər·mē·dē·ā′shən, n. —**in·ter·me·di·a·tor,** n. —**in·ter·me·di·a·to·ry,** in·tər·mē′dē·ə·tōr′ē, a.

in·ter·mi·na·ble, in·tər′mə·nə·bəl, a. Boundless; unending; wearisomely prolonged.

in·ter·min·gle, in·tər·ming′gəl, v.t., v.i., **-gled, -gling.** To mix together.

in·ter·mis·sion, in·tər·mish′ən, n. The act of intermitting; a temporary pause; a space of time between periods of action or activity; an interval between the acts of a play or other public performance. —**in·ter·mis·sive,** in·tər·mis′iv, a.

in·ter·mit, in·tər·mit′, v.t. **-mit·ted, -mit·ting.** To cause or cease for a time; to stop; to suspend or discontinue.—v.i. —**in·ter·mit·tence,** **in·ter·mit·ten·cy,** n. —**in·ter·mit·tent,** a. —**in·ter·mit·tent·ly,** **in·ter·mit·ting·ly,** adv.

in·ter·mix, in·tər·miks′, v.t., v.i. To mix together; to intermingle. —**in·ter·mix·ture,** n.

in·tern, in′tərn, n. A recent medical graduate acting as assistant in a hospital for the purpose of clinical training. —**in·tern·ship,** n.

in·tern, in·tərn′, v.t., v.i., To confine within a prescribed area, esp. in a war.

in·ter·nal, in·tər′nəl, a. Of or pertaining to the inside or inner part; interior. Anat. Inner. Existing in the mind; subjective. —**in·ter·nal·ly,** adv.

in·ter·nal·ize, in·tər′nə·līz, v.t., **-ized, -iz·ing.** To make internal or subjective; to adopt or incorporate, as cultural patterns or values. —**in·ter·nal·i·za·tion,** in·tər·nə·lə·zā′shən, n.

in·ter·nal med·i·cine, n. Medicine concerned with the diagnosis and treatment of nonsurgical diseases, usu. of adults.

in·ter·na·tion·al, in·tər·nash′ə·nəl, a. Between or among nations; pertaining to the relations between nations: as, international law; affecting or participated in by different nations; having members in several countries, as a group or an organization.—n. —**in·ter·na·tion·al·i·ty,** in·tər·nash·ə·nal′ə·tē, n. —**in·ter·na·tion·al·ly,** adv. —**in·ter·na·tion·al·ize,** in·tər·nash′ə·nə·līz, v.t., **-ized, -iz·ing.** —**in·ter·na·tion·al·i·za·tion,** in·tər·nash·ə·nə·lə·zā′shən, n.

in·ter·na·tion·al·ism, in·tər·nash′ə·nə·liz·əm, n. International character, relations, or control; the principle of cooperation among nations to promote their common good, as contrasted with nationalism, or devotion to the interests of a particular nation.

in·ter·na·tion·al law, n. A set of rules which control the conduct of nations toward each other in peace or war.

in·tern·ee, in·tər·nē′, n. A person who has been interned as a prisoner of war.

in·tern·ist, in′tər·nist, in·tər′nist, n. A physician who treats internal diseases; a specialist in internal medicine.

in·tern·ment, in·tərn′mənt, n. The act of interning, or the state of being interned or confined.

in·tern·ment camp, n. A confinement camp for prisoners of war, enemy aliens, and the like, during wartime.

in·ter·of·fice, in·tər·ô′fis, in·tər·of′is, a. Operating or communicating between offices of a company.

in·ter·pen·e·trate, in·tər·pen′ə·trāt, v.t. To penetrate between the parts of.—v.i. —**in·ter·pen·e·tra·tion,** in·tər·pen·ə·trā′shən, n.

in·ter·plan·e·tar·y, in·tər·plan′ə·ter·ē, a. Situated or existing between the planets, or between the sun and a planet.

in·ter·play, in′tər·plā, n. Reciprocal play, action, or influence; interaction. —in·tər·plā′, v.i. To interact.

in·ter·po·late, in·tər′pə·lāt, v.t., **-lat·ed, -lat·ing.** To alter, as a text, by the insertion of new matter, esp. deceptively or without authorization; to insert, as new or spurious matter; to insert or find intermediate terms in, as a series or sequence.—v.i. To make interpolations. —**in·ter·po·la·tion,** in·tər·pə·lā′shən, n. —**in·ter·po·la·tive,** a. —**in·ter·po·la·tor,** n.

in·ter·pose, in·tər·pōz′, v.t., **-posed, -pos·ing.** To put between; to cause to intervene in place, time, or order; put or bring in an objection or delay; to bring influence or action to bear between parties, or on behalf of a party or person; to put in a remark or statement in the midst of a conversation, discourse, or the like.—v.i. To come between; to mediate. —**in·ter·pos·er,** n. —**in·ter·po·si·tion,** in·tər·pə·zish′ən, n.

in·ter·pret, in·tər′prit, v.t. To set forth the meaning of; to clarify or explain, as oracles, omens, or obscure passages; explain; translate; to construe or understand in a particular way; render or present in a revealing manner; of things, to express, indicate, or reveal.—v.i. To explain; translate. —**in·ter·pret·a·ble,** a. —**in·ter·pret·er,** n. —**in·ter·pre·tive,** a.

in·ter·pre·ta·tion, in·tər·prə·tā′shən, n. The act of interpreting; the meaning ascribed to words or actions as a result of interpreting; an explanation or translation. —**in·ter·pre·ta·tion·al,** a. —**in·ter·pre·ta·tive,** in·tər′prə·tā·tiv, a.

in·ter·ra·cial, in·tər·rā′shəl, a. Regarding or involving persons of different races.

in·ter·re·late, in·tər·ri·lāt′, v.t., v.i., **-lat·ed, -lat·ing.** To bring into or have reciprocal relation.

in·ter·ro·gate, in·ter′ə·gāt, v.t., **-gat·ed, -gat·ing.** To examine by asking questions, esp. officially or in a formal, systematic way.

in·ter·ro·ga·tion, in·ter·ə·gā′shən, n. The act of questioning; a question. —**in·ter·ro·ga·tion·al,** a.

in·ter·ro·ga·tion mark or point, n. Question mark (?) at the end of a sentence, used to indicate a question.

in·ter·rog·a·tive, in·tə·rog′ə·tiv, a. Denoting a question; expressed in the form of a question; inquisitive.—n. A question word, such as who? what? which?

in·ter·ro·ga·tor, in·ter′ə·gā·tər, n. One who asks questions.

in·ter·rupt, in·tə·rəpt′, v.t. To make a break in, as in an otherwise continuous course; to break off or cause to cease, in the midst or course of; hinder the continuation of; to stop, as a person, in the midst of doing or saying something.—v.i. To cause a break or discontinuance; to interrupt action or speech. —**in·ter·rup·tion,** in·tə·rəp′shən, n. —**in·ter·rup·tive,** a.

in·ter·rupt·er, in·ter·rup·tor, in·tə·rəp′tər, n. A person or thing that interrupts; a device for interrupting or periodically making and breaking a circuit.

in·ter·scho·las·tic, in·tər·skə·las′tik, a. Between schools: interscholastic games.

in·ter·sect, in·tər·sekt′, v.t. To cut into or between; to cut or pass across; to divide into parts by crossing or passing through.—v.i. To meet and cross each other.

in·ter·sec·tion, in·tər·sek′shən, n. The act or place of intersecting; a point of crossing: a street or road intersection.

in·ter·space, in′tər·spās, n. A space between things; an intervening space, or interval, of time.—in·tər·spās′, v.t., **-spaced, -spac·ing.**

---

in·ter·sperse, in·tər·spərs′, *v.t.*, **-spersed, -spers·ing**. To scatter or set here and there among other things; to diversify by scattering objects. **—in·ter·sper·sion**, in·tər·spər′zhən.

in·ter·state, in·tər·stāt′, *a.* Between states; between or jointly involving states of the U.S.: *interstate* commerce. A section of the federal interstate highway system.

in·ter·stel·lar, in·tər·stel′ər, *a.* Occurring or situated among the stars.

in·ter·tid·al, in·tər·tīd′əl, *a.* Relating or belonging to that part of the coastal zone between low tide and high tide marks.

in·ter·twine, in·tər·twīn′, *v.t., v.i.*, **-twined, -twin·ing**. To twine, as one with another.—*adv.*

in·ter·ur·ban, in·tər·ər′bən, *a.* Between cities.—*n.* A railway or bus between cities.

in·ter·val, in′tər·vəl, *n.* An intervening period of time; a pause; a gap; a space intervening between things, points, or limits.

in·ter·vene, in·tər·vēn′, *v.i.*, **-vened, -ven·ing**. To come between in action; to intercede or interfere; to come or be between places, times, or events; to occur incidentally so as to modify a result; to enter into an affair between parties as for the purpose of adjusting differences or aiding one party. **—in·ter·ven·er, in·ter·ve·nor**, *n.* **—in·ter·ven·tion**, in·tər·ven′shən, *n.*

in·ter·view, in′tər·vū, *n.* A meeting of persons, as for a conference or evaluation: a job *interview;* a meeting between a representative of the press and a person from whom information is sought for publication; the conversation at such a meeting, or the published report of it.—*v.t.* To have an interview with. **—in·ter·view·er**, *n.*

in·ter·weave, in·tər·wēv′, *v.t., v.i.*, **-wove, -wov·en, -weav·ing**. To weave together; to combine as if by weaving: to *interweave* truth with fiction. **—in·ter·wo·ven**, in·tər·wō′vən, *a.*

in·tes·tate, in·tes′tāt, in·tes′tit, *a.* Without having made a will.—*n.* A person who dies without having made a will.

in·tes·tine, in·tes′tin, *n.* Often *pl.* The lower part of the alimentary canal, extending from the stomach to the anus. See **large in·tes·tine, small in·tes·tine**. **—in·tes·ti·nal**, in·tes′tə·nəl,*a.*

in·ti·mate, in′tə·mit, *a.* Characterized by involving, or arising from close personal connection or experience: an *intimate* friend; very private or closely personal; pertaining to, or maintaining, sexual relations; inmost.—in′tə·māt, *v.t.*, **-mat·ed, -mat·ing**. To make known by hint or indication. **—in·ti·mate·ly**, *adv.* **—in·ti·ma·tion**, in·tə·mā′shən, *n.*

in·tim·i·date, in·tim′ə·dāt, *v.t.*, **-dat·ed, -dat·ing**. To make timid or fill with fear; to force into or deter from an action by inducing fear: to *intimidate* a witness. **—in·tim·i·da·tion**, in·tim·ə·dā′shən, *n.* **—in·tim·i·da·tor**, *n.*

in·ti·tle, in·tīt′əl, *v.t.*, **-tled, -tling**. Entitle.

in·to, in′too, in′tŭ, in′tə, *prep.* A function word expressing motion or direction toward the inner part of a place or thing: going *into* a house; against or to a point or touching: walk *into* a closed door; an indication of insertion: screwing a fuse *into* the socket; an indication of entrance or inclusion: welcomed *into* the community; to the condition, circumstance, relation, or occupation of: fell *into* confusion, went *into* teaching; an indication of an extension of space or time: lasting far *into* the night; an indication of division: Two *into* eight equals four.

in·tol·er·a·ble, in·tol′ər·ə·bəl, *a.* Not able to be tolerated; not able to be endured. **—in·tol·er·a·bly**, *adv.*

in·tol·er·ant, in·tol′ər·ənt, *a.* Refusing to tolerate others' opinions, rights, religious beliefs, etc.; bigoted; prejudiced. **—in·tol·er·ance**, *n.*

in·tomb, in·toom′, *v.t.* Entomb.

in·to·nate, in′tə·nāt, *v.t.*, **-nat·ed, -nat·ing**. To pronounce with a certain tone or modulation; to intone.

in·to·na·tion, in·tə·nā′shən, *n.* The change in pitch of the voice in speaking, often modifying meanings, characterizing dialects, or registering emotional reaction; the manner of producing tones.

in·tone, in·tōn′, *v.t.*, **-toned, -ton·ing**. To utter in a singing voice or tone; chant; recite in monotone.—*v.i.* **—in·ton·er**, *n.*

in·tox·i·cant, in·tok′sə·kənt, *n.* That which intoxicates, as an intoxicating liquor or drug.—*a.* Intoxicating or exciting.

in·tox·i·cate, in·tok′sə·kāt, *v.t.*, **-cat·ed, -cat·ing**. To make drunk, as with alcoholic liquor; to excite the spirits to a very high pitch; to elate to enthusiasm or frenzy. **—in·tox·i·cat·ed**, *a.* **—in·tox·i·cat·ing**, *a.*

in·tox·i·ca·tion, in·tok·sə·kā′shən, *n.* Inebriation; frenzied enthusiasm.

in·trac·ta·ble, in·trak′tə·bəl, *a.* Not tractable; not to be governed or managed. **—in·trac·ta·bil·i·ty**, in·trak·tə·bil′ə·tē, *n.*

in·tra·mu·ral, in·trə·mūr′əl, *a.* Existing within the limits of an institution or community. **—in·tra·mu·ral·ly**, *adv.*

in·tran·si·gent, in·tran′sə·jənt, *a.* Refusing to agree or to come to a settlement; uncompromising; unbending.—*n.* **—in·tran·si·gence, in·tran·si·gen·cy**, *n.*

in·tran·si·tive, in·tran′si·tiv, *a.* Referring to a verb which in itself completes the subject and does not require or take a direct object.

in·tra·state, in·trə·stāt′, *a.* Occurring or carried on within a single state.

in·tra·u·ter·ine, in·trə·ū′tər·in, *a.* Occurring or situated within the uterus.

in·tra·u·ter·ine de·vice, *n.* A means of continuous contraception placed within the uterus, as a plastic coil.

in·tra·ve·nous, in·trə·vē′nəs, *a.* Occurring or introduced within a vein or veins, esp. by means of injection: *intravenous* feeding.

in·trench, in·trench′, *v.t.* Entrench.

in·trep·id, in·trep′id, *a.* Fearless; bold. **—in·tre·pid·i·ty**, in·trə·pid′ə·tē, *n.*

in·tri·cate, in′tri·kit, *a.* Entangled; involved; difficult to unravel; complicated; difficult to understand. **—in·tri·ca·cy**, in′tri·kə·sē, *n. pl.*, **-cies**. **—in·tri·cate·ly**, *adv.* **—in·tri·cate·ness**, *n.*

in·trigue, in·trēg′, *v.t.*, **-trigued, -tri·guing**. To excite the curiosity of; to beguile; to cause to ponder; to bring about by trickery.—*v.i.* To use underhanded methods; to scheme craftily; to carry on a secret love affair. —in·trēg′, in′trēg, *n.* The use of crafty dealings; a plot or scheme; a secret love affair. **—in·tri·guer**, *n.* **—in·tri·guing**, *a.*

in·trin·sic, in·trin′sik, in·trin′zik, *a.* Inherent; essential; innate; belonging to the thing in itself. Also **in·trin·si·cal**. **—in·trin·si·cal·ly**, *adv.*

in·tro·duce, in·trə·doos′, in·trə·dūs′, *v.t.*, **-duced, -duc·ing**. To make acquainted; to present to others; to bring before an audience for the first time; to bring forward for official attention; to lead to a knowledge of, for the first time, followed by *to;* to enthusiasm; to begin, as a topic or speech; to put into. **—in·tro·duc·er**, *n.* **—in·tro·duc·tion**, in·trə·dək′shən, *n.* **—in·tro·duc·to·ry**, in·trə·dək′tə·rē, *a.*

in·tro·spect, in·trə·spekt′, *v.t.* To look into or examine, as one's own feelings or thoughts.—*v.i.* To look within; to practice self-observation **—in·tro·spec·tion**, *n.* **—in·tro·spec·tive**, *a.*

in·tro·ver·sion, in·trə·vər′zhən, in·trə·vər′shən, *n.* The act of introverting; an introverted state; concern and interest directed inward toward oneself. **—in·tro·ver·sive**, *a.*

in·tro·vert, in·trə·vərt′, *v.t.* To direct the mind upon itself. —in′trə·vərt, *n.* A person who is shy or reserved. **—in·tro·vert·ed**, *a.*

in·trude, in·trood′, *v.i.*, **-trud·ed, -trud·ing**. To thrust oneself into any place or company without welcome or invitation; to force oneself upon others; to encroach. —*v.t.* —**in•trud•er,** *n.* —**in•tru•sion,** in•troo′zhən, *n.* —**in•tru•sive,** *a.*

in•trust, in•trəst′, *v.t.* Entrust.

in•tu•it, in•too′it, in•tū′it, *v.t., v.i.* To know by intuition.

in•tu•i•tion, in•too•ish′ən, in•tū•ish′ən, *n.* Knowledge discerned directly by the mind without reasoning or analysis; a truth or revelation arrived at by insight; the power or capacity to perceive truth without apparent reasoning. —**in•tu•i•tion•al,** *a.*

in•tu•i•tive, in•too′i•tiv, in•tū′i•tiv, *a.* Perceived by the mind immediately without the intervention of reasoning.

in•un•date, in′ən•dāt, in•ən′dāt, *v.t.,* -**dat•ed, -dat•ing.** To overflow or flood; to overwhelm with an abundance. —**in•un•da•tion,** in•ən•dā′shən, *n.* —**in•un•da•tor,** *n.*

in•ure, in•yûr, *v.t.,* **in•ured, in•ur•ing.** Become accustomed to something painful or undesirable.

in•vade, in•vād′, *v.t.,* -**vad•ed, -vad•ing.** To enter with armed force for conquest; make a hostile incursion into; to enter as an enemy; to permeate; intrude upon, as privacy or thoughts; encroach, or infringe upon. —*v.i.* —**in•vad•er,** *n.*

in•va•lid, in′və•lid, *n.* A person suffering from ill health or disabling injury; one who is incapacitated by old age or illness. —*a.* Impaired in health; sick or infirm; of or for invalids. —*v.t.* To make an invalid of. —*v.i.* To become an invalid.

in•val•id, in•val′id, *a.* Not valid; having no force, weight, or cogency, as an argument; without legal force, or void, as a contract. —**in•va•lid•i•ty,** in•və•lid′ə•tē, *n.*

in•val•i•date, in•val′ə•dāt, *v.t.,* -**dat•ed, -dat•ing.** To render invalid. —**in•val•i•da•tion,** in•val•ə•dā′shən, *n.* —**in•val•i•da•tor,** *n.*

in•va•lid•ism, in′və•lid•iz•əm, *n.* The condition of prolonged ill health.

in•val•u•a•ble, in•val′ū•ə•bəl, *a.* Of inestimable value; priceless.

in•var•i•a•ble, in•vār′ē•ə•bəl, *a.* Not variable; constant. —**in•var•i•a•bil•i•ty,** in•vār•ē•ə•bil′ə•tē, **in•var•i•a•ble•ness,** *n.*

in•var•i•ant, in•vār′ē•ənt, *a.* Not variant; invariable; constant. —**in•var•i•ance,** *n.*

in•va•sion, in•vā′zhən, *n.* The act of invading. —**in•va•sive,** *a.*

in•vec•tive, in•vek′tiv, *n.* An abusive or violent utterance; a severe, formal censure, either oral or written.

in•veigh, in•vā′, *v.i.* To protest verbally against. —**in•veigh•er,** *n.*

in•vent, in•vent′, *v.t.* To originate; to contrive or construct, as something that did not exist before; to construct by use of imagination. —**in•vent•i•ble, in•vent•a•ble,** *a.* —**in•ven•tor,** *n.*

in•ven•tion, in•ven′shən, *n.* The act of inventing; a contrivance or device which did not before exist; something invented or devised.

in•ven•tive, in•ven′tiv, *a.* Able to invent; quick at invention; imaginative; ingenious. —**in•ven•tive•ness,** *n.*

in•ven•to•ry, in′vən•tôr•ē, *n. pl.,* -**ries.** A list of goods, usu. with a description and valuation; a merchant's list of merchandise on hand, prepared annually; any catalogue or account of particular things. —*v.t.,* -**ried, -ry•ing.**

in•verse, in•vərs′, in′vərs, *a.* Opposite in order or relation; inverted; turned upside down or inside out. —*n.*

in•ver•sion, in•vər′zhən, in•vər′shən, *n.* The act of inverting; a change of order or position so that what was after is now before, and vice versa.

in•vert, in•vərt′, *v.t.* To turn upside down; put in reverse order. —*n.* Any inverted thing; a homosexual.

in•ver•te•brate, in•vər′tə•brit, in•vər′tə•brāt, *a.* Not vertebrate; without a backbone; of or pertaining to animals without a vertebral column; without strength of character. —*n.*

in•vert•ed, in•vər′tid, *a.* Turned to a contrary direction; turned upside down; changed in order.

in•vest, in•vest′, *v.t.* To clothe; to surround; to place in possession of an office, rank, or dignity; to install; to furnish with authority; to give to or endow with a trait or quality; to put, as money or capital, into some type of property, with the purpose of getting a profitable return; to spend or commit in the hope of future benefit. —*v.i.* To make an investment. —**in•ves•tor,** *n.*

in•ves•ti•gate, in•ves′tə•gāt, *v.t.,* -**gat•ed, -gat•ing.** To search into; to research; inquire into and examine with care. —*v.i.* To make an examination or inquiry. —**in•ves•ti•ga•tion,** in•ves•tə•gā′shən, *n.* —**in•ves•ti•ga•tive,** *a.* —**in•ves•ti•ga•tor,** *n.*

in•ves•ti•ture, in•ves′tə•chər, *n.* The act of investing; the act of confirming or bestowing office, authority, rank, or title; that which invests or covers.

in•vest•ment, in•vest′mənt, *n.* That in which money is invested; the act of investing; the laying out of money for profit in the purchase of some type of property; money laid out for profit; investiture, as with office.

in•vet•er•ate, in•vet′ər•it, *a.* Deep-rooted or ingrained.

in•vid•i•ous, in•vid′e•əs, *a.* Causing ill will; offensive; harmful or causing injury.

in•vig•or•ate, in•vig′ə•rāt, *v.t.,* -**at•ed, -at•ing.** To give life and energy to; to strengthen. —**in•vig•or•ant,** in•vig′ər•ənt, *n.* —**in•vig•or•a•tion,** in•vig•ə•rā′shən, *n.* —**in•vig•or•a•tor,** *n.*

in•vin•ci•ble, in•vin′sə•bəl, *a.* Incapable of being conquered; incapable of being overcome; unconquerable. —**in•vin•ci•bil•i•ty,** in•vin•sə•bil′ə•tē, **in•vin•ci•ble•ness,** in•vin′si•bil′i•tē, *n.* —**in•vin•ci•bly,** *adv.*

in•vi•o•la•ble, in•vī′ə•lə•bəl, *a.* Not to be violated. —**in•vi•o•la•bil•i•ty,** in•vi•ə•lə•bil′ə•tē, *n.* —**in•vi•o•la•bly,** *adv.*

in•vi•o•late, in•vī′ə•lit, in•vī′ə•lāt, *a.* Not violated or desecrated; pure.

in•vis•i•ble, in•viz′ə•bəl, *a.* Incapable of being seen; imperceptible; concealed; not open to public knowledge. —*n.* —**in•vis•i•bil•i•ty,** in•viz•ə•bil′ə•tē, *n.* —**in•vis•i•bly,** *adv.*

in•vi•ta•tion, in•vi•tā′shən, *n.* The act of inviting; a request to come to a place; a form of spoken or written words, esp. a formal, printed one, in which such a request is conveyed. —**in•vi•ta•tion•al,** *a.*

in•vite, in•vīt′, *v.t.,* -**vit•ed, -vit•ing.** To ask, as a person, to come to a place or gathering; request politely or formally; give occasion for; to attract or tempt. —in′vīt, *n. Informal.* An invitation. —**in•vit•er,** *n.* —**in•vit•ing,** *a.*

in•vo•ca•tion, in•və•kā′shən, *n.* The act of invoking or addressing in prayer; a prayer said at the opening of a ceremony or service; a calling upon a legal or moral standard or right.

in•voice, in′voys, *n.* A list of items of merchandise shipped or sent to a purchaser with charges and terms; the merchandise or shipment itself; a bill.

in•voke, in•vōk′, *v.t.,* **in•voked, in•vok•ing.** To call upon, as a divine spirit, in prayer; to appeal to, as for aid or protection; to call for earnestly.

in•vol•un•tar•y, in•vol′ən•ter•ē, *a.* Not voluntary; not able to act according to will; independent of will or choice; unintentional; not proceeding from choice; not done willingly; unwillingly; operating independently of will. —**in•vol•un•tar•i•ly,** in•vol′ən•tār•ə•lē, *adv.* —**in•vol•un•tar•i•ness,** *n.*

in•vo•lute, in′və•loot, *a.* Involved; complicated.

in·vo·lu·tion, in·və·loo′shən, n. The act of involving, or the state of being involved; entanglement or complication.

in·volve, in·volv′, v.t., **in·volved, in·volv·ing.** To include as a necessary circumstance or consequence; imply; affect; to include within itself or its scope; to cause to be concerned; to occupy absorbingly; to entangle; to bring into an intricate or complicated form. **—in·volved,** a. **—in·volve·ment,** n. **—in·volv·er,** n.

in·vul·ner·a·ble, in·vəl′nər·ə·bəl, a. Not vulnerable.

in·ward, in′wərd, adv. Near or toward the inside, interior, or center; toward the mind or soul. **in·wards.**—a. Located on the inside or interior; within the body; internal; inner; of the mind or soul; mental; spiritual; proceeding or directed toward the inside. —n. That which is on the inside; an internal part. Pl. internal parts of the body; also *innards.* **—in·ward·ly,** adv. **—in·ward·ness,** n. in′wərd·nis, n.

in·weave, in·wēv′, v.t., **in·wove** or **in·weaved, in·wov·en, in·weav·ing.** To weave together. Also **en·weave.**

in·wrought, in·rôt′, a. Worked into or combined with other things; embellished with decorative ornamentation; worked into or on something, as a design or engraving.

i·o·dine, ī′ə·dīn, ī′ə·din, ī′ə·dēn, n. A nonmetallic element occurring, at ordinary temperatures, as a grayish-black crystalline solid, which changes to a dense violet vapor when heated: used in medicine and photography.

i·on, ī′ən, ī′on, n. An electrified atom or group of atoms, having either a positive or negative charge, which has increased or decreased its number of electrons after electrolysis. **—i·on·ic,** ī·on′ik, a.

i·on·ize, ī′ə·nīz, v.t., **-ized, -iz·ing.** To separate into ions; produce ions in. **—i·on·i·za·tion,** ī·ə·nə·zā′shən, n. **—i·on·iz·er,** n.

i·on·o·sphere, ī·on′ə·sfēr, n. An ionized region of the atmosphere, located beyond the stratosphere.

i·o·ta, ī·ō′tə, n. The ninth letter of the Greek alphabet; a very small quantity; a jot.

IOU, ī·ō·ū′, n. An acknowledgment of a debt, esp. a paper having on it these letters, followed by a sum, and duly signed.

ip·so fac·to, ip′sō fak′tō, adv. Literally, by the fact itself; by the very nature of the act: Such a deed makes one a criminal, *ipso facto.*

IQ, I.Q. Abbr. for intelligence quotient.

i·ras·ci·ble, i·ras′ə·bəl, ī·ras′ə·bəl, a. Quick-tempered; readily aroused to anger; cranky or irritable; characterized or caused by anger. **—i·ras·ci·bil·i·ty,** i·ras·ə·bil′ə·tē, **i·ras·ci·ble·ness,** n. **—i·ras·ci·bly,** adv.

i·rate, ī′rāt, ī·rāt′, a. Angry; incensed; enraged; characterized or caused by anger.

ire, īr, n. Anger.

ir·i·des·cent, ir·ə·des′ənt, a. Giving out or displaying colors like those of the rainbow, as mother-of-pearl. **—ir·i·des·cence,** n.

i·rid·i·um, i·rid′ē·əm, ī·rid′ē·əm, n. A hard but brittle silvery metallic element resembling platinum: one of the heaviest substances known.

i·ris, ī′ris, n. pl., **i·ris·es, ir·i·des,** ir′ə·dēz, ī′rə·dēz. The circular diaphragm forming the colored portion of the eye and containing the pupil in its center; a type of plant having sword-shaped leaves and handsome flowers; the flower itself.

I·rish, ī′rish, a. Of, pertaining to, or characteristic of Ireland or its people.—n. The inhabitants of Ireland and their descendants.

irk, ərk, v.t. To annoy.

irk·some, ərk′səm, a. Tending to annoy.

i·ron, ī′ərn, n. A metallic element, silver-white, malleable and ductile, strongly attracted by magnets, and easily oxidized: widely used in the form of steel for making building materials, machinery, tools, and many other products; anything that is unyielding, strong, or firm; an instrument made of iron; an appliance that, when heated, is used for pressing cloth. Pl. Fetters; chains; handcuffs.—a. Consisting of iron; resembling iron; harsh; rude; severe; capable of great endurance; firm.—v.t. To smooth with an iron; to fetter or handcuff; to furnish or arm with iron.—v.i. To press clothing, etc., with a heated iron. **—i·ron out,** Informal. Smooth out; to remove problems. **—i·ron·er,** n.

I·ron Age, n. The cultural time period after the Bronze Age, distinguished by the use of iron, as in tools and weapons.

i·ron·clad, ī′ərn·klad′, a. Covered or clothed with iron; strict; fixed: an *ironclad* contract.—n. A warship of the 19th century, covered with thick iron plates.

i·ron cur·tain, n. A barrier to information and communication, existing between countries which differ in military, ideological, and political beliefs.

i·ron·hand·ed, ī′ərn·han′did, a. Exerting strict or rigorous control; despotic; severe.

i·ron·heart·ed, ī′ərn·här′tid, a. Informal. Hardhearted; unfeeling; unsympathetic.

i·ron·ic, ī·ron′ik, a. Pertaining to, of the nature of, or characterized by irony. Also **i·ron·i·cal.**

i·ron·ing board, ī′ərn·ing, n. A flat board or similar surface, on which clothes are ironed.

i·ron lung, n. A sealed chamber placed over or around the chest of a patient, acting as a substitute for normal lung action.

i·ron·smith, ī′ərn·smith, n. A worker in iron, as a blacksmith or locksmith.

i·ron·stone, ī′ərn·stōn, n. Iron ore; any rock or mineral which contains iron.

i·ron·ware, ī′ərn·wər′, n. Utensils, tools, and other lightweight articles made from iron; hardware.

i·ron·work, ī′ərn·wərk, n. Any object made of iron; pl., sing. or pl. in constr., a factory where iron is produced. **—i·ron·work·er,** n.

i·ro·ny, ī′rə·nē, n. pl., **-nies.** A figure of speech in which the literal meaning is the opposite of the intended meaning: used in ridicule, contempt, or humor. An outcome opposed to that which one has been led to expect.

ir·ra·di·ate, i·rā′dē·āt, v.t., **-at·ed, -at·ing.** To shed light on; to enlighten; penetrate by rays; heal by radiation; use radiant energy as heat. **—ir·ra·di·a·tion,** i·rā·dē·ā′shən, n. **—ir·ra·di·a·ter,** n.

ir·rad·i·ca·ble, i·rad′ə·kə·bəl, a. Impossible to erase.

ir·ra·tion·al, i·rash′ə·nəl, a. Void of reason; absurd; mentally unstable. **—ir·ra·tion·al·i·ty,** i·rash·ə·nal′ə·tē, n.

ir·re·claim·a·ble, i·ri·klā′mə·bəl, a. Incapable of being reclaimed or reformed.

ir·rec·on·cil·a·ble, i·rek′ən·sī·lə·bəl, i·rek·ən·sī′lə·bəl, a. Not to be reconciled. **—ir·rec·on·cil·a·bil·i·ty,** i·rek·ən·sī·lə·bil′ə·tē, n.

ir·re·cov·er·a·ble, i·ri·kəv·ər·ə·bəl, a. Incapable of being recovered or regained.

ir·re·deem·a·ble, i·ri·dē′mə·bəl, a. Not redeemable; hopeless.

ir·re·duc·i·ble, i·ri·doo′sə·bəl, ir·i·dū′sə·bəl, a. Not reducible.

ir·ref·u·ta·ble, i·ref′ū·tə·bəl, i·ri·fū′tə·bəl, a. Not refutable; incapable of being refuted or disproved.

ir·re·gard·less, ir·i·gärd′lis, a., adv. Nonstandard form of regardless.

ir·reg·u·lar, i·reg′yə·lər, a. Not regular; lacking symmetry; uneven; occurring in no regular time pattern or interval: an *irregular* heartbeat; not in accordance with rules.—n. A damaged manufactured product. **—ir·reg·u·lar·i·ty,** i·reg·yə·lar′ə·tē, n.

ir·rel·e·vant, i·rel′ə·vənt, a. Not applicable or pertinent. **—ir·rel·e·vance, ir·rel·e·van·cy,** n.

ir·re·li·gion, ir·i·lij′ən, n. Lack of religion or contempt for it; impiety. **—ir·re·li·gious,** a.

ir·re·mis·si·ble, ir·i·mis′ə·bəl, *a.* Not remissible; unpardonable.

ir·re·mov·a·ble, ir·i·moo′və·bəl, *a.* Not removable; inflexible; fixed.

ir·rep·a·ra·ble, i·rep′ər·ə·bəl, *a.* Not reparable.

ir·re·place·a·ble, ir·i·plā′sə·bəl, *a.* Not able to be replaced.

ir·re·press·i·ble, ir·i·pres′ə·bəl, *a.* Incapable of being repressed or restrained. —**ir·re·press·i·bil·i·ty,** ir·i·pres·ə·bil′ə·tē, *n.* —**ir·re·press·i·bly,** *adv.*

ir·re·proach·a·ble, ir·i·prō′chə·bəl, *a.* Incapable of being reproached; innocent; faultless; unblemished.

ir·re·sist·i·ble, ir·i·zis′tə·bəl, *a.* Not resistible; incapable of being successfully resisted or opposed; lovable; romantically appealing; tempting. —**ir·re·sist·i·bil·i·ty,** ir·i·zis·tə·bil′ə·tē, *n.*

ir·res·o·lute, i·rez′ə·loot, *a.* Not resolute; not firm or constant in purpose; undecided. —**ir·res·o·lu·tion,** i·rez·ə·loo′shən, *n.*

ir·re·spec·tive, ir·i·spek′tiv, *a.* Having no relation to particular conditions; without regard to certain circumstances; leaving out of account, usu. followed by *of.*

ir·re·spon·si·ble, ir·i·spon′sə·bəl, *a.* Unreliable; incapable of or unqualified for responsibility. —**ir·re·spon·si·bil·i·ty,** ir·i·spon·sə·bil′ə·tē, *n.*

ir·re·spon·sive, ir·i·spon′siv, *a.* Unable or not inclined to respond or react to a stimulus. —**ir·re·spon·sive·ness,** *n.*

ir·re·triev·a·ble, ir·i·trē′və·bəl, *a.* Not retrievable; irrecoverable. —**ir·re·triev·a·bil·i·ty,** ir·i·trē·və·bil′ə·tē, *n.*

ir·rev·er·ence, i·rev′ər·əns, *n.* Lack of reverence or veneration; irreverent conduct, action, or words. —**ir·rev·er·ent,** i·rev′ər·ənt, *a.*

ir·re·vers·i·ble, ir·i·vər′sə·bəl, *a.* Not reversible; incapable of being reversed or altered. —**ir·re·vers·i·bil·i·ty,** ir·ə·vər·sə·bil′ə·tē, *n.* —**ir·re·vers·i·bly,** *adv.*

ir·rev·o·ca·ble, i·rev′ə·kə·bəl, *a.* Not to be recalled or revoked; irreversible. —**ir·rev·o·ca·bil·i·ty,** i·rev·ə·kə·bil′ə·tē, *n.*

ir·ri·gate, ir′ə·gāt, *v.t.,* **-gat·ed, -gat·ing.** To water, as land, by artificial means such as channels, sprinklers, or flooding; to cleanse or flush, as a wound, with a stream or spray of liquid. —**ir·ri·ga·tion,** ir·i·gā′shən, *n.* —**ir·ri·ga·tor,** *n.*

ir·ri·ta·ble, ir′i·tə·bəl, *a.* Capable of being irritated; readily provoked; of a fiery temper. —**ir·ri·ta·bil·i·ty,** ir·i·tə·bil′ə·tē, **ir·ri·ta·ble·ness,** *n.*

ir·ri·tant, ir′i·tənt, *a.* Irritating; causing irritation.—*n.* Anything that irritates.

ir·ri·tate, ir′i·tāt, *v.t.,* **-tat·ed, -tat·ing.** To excite anger in; to provoke; to vex; to cause displeasure to; to inflame; to excite, as a bodily part, to a particular function or action; to cause to exhibit irritation.—*v.i.* —**ir·ri·ta·tion,** ir·i·tā′shən, *n.*

ir·ri·tat·ed, ir′i·tā·tid, *a.* Inflamed; annoyed.

ir·rupt, i·rəpt′, *v.i.* To break in; rush in violently or forcibly.

is, iz, *v.i.* The third person sing., present indicative of the verb **be.**

Is·lam, is′läm, iz′läm, is·ləm′, *n.* The Muslim faith; collectively, the followers of the Muslim faith. —**Is·lam·ic,** is·lam′ik, is·lä′mik, iz·lam′ik, iz·lä′mik, *a.* —**Is·lam·ism,** *n.*

is·land, ī′lənd, *n.* Land surrounded by water; anything resembling an island; a raised pedestrian platform surrounded by traffic.—*v.t.* To cause to become or appear like an island; to isolate; to dot, as with islands.

is·land·er, ī′lən·dər, *n.* An inhabitant of an island.

isle, īl, *n.* An island, esp. a small island.

is·let, ī′lit, *n.* A small island.

ism, iz′əm, *n.* A distinctive doctrine, theory, system, or practice, esp. one that ends in *-ism,* such as *fascism, socialism.*

isn't, iz′ənt. Contraction of **is not.**

i·so·bar, ī′sə·bär′, *n.* A line drawn on a map connecting places at which the barometric pressure is the same. —**i·so·bar·ic,** i·sə·bar′ik, *a.*

i·so·gloss, ī′sə·glôs, ī′sə·glos, *n.* A line on a map that separates areas where there are differences in language.

i·so·late, ī′sə·lāt, is′ə·lāt, *v.t.,* **-lat·ed, -lat·ing.** To place apart; to cause to be alone; to cut off from all contact with others; to insulate; to obtain, as a pure substance, free from all its combinations; to quarantine. —**i·so·la·tion,** ī·sə·lā′shən, is·ə·lā′shən, *n.*

i·so·la·tion·ism, ī·sə·lā′shə·niz·əm, *n.* A doctrine that a nation serves its own welfare best by concentrating upon its own internal affairs, refusing political, military, or economic alliances or entanglements with other nations. —**i·so·la·tion·ist,** *n., a.*

i·so·met·ric, ī·sə·me′trik, *a.* Pertaining to or having equality of measure. Also **i·so·met·ri·cal.**

i·so·met·ric ex·er·cise, *n.* Physical exertion which does not involve motion, muscle tone being achieved by setting one muscle against another muscle or against a fixed object, as pushing against the stomach or a wall with one's hands. Also **i·so·met·rics,** *n. pl. but sing. in constr.*

i·so·met·ric line, *n.* A map line showing temperature and pressure changes while holding volume constant; a line representing a constant value.

i·son·o·my, ī·son′ə·mē, *n.* Equality by law; equal distribution of rights and privileges.

i·sos·ce·les, ī·sos′ə·lēz, *a.* Having two equal sides: an *isosceles* triangle.

i·so·therm, ī′sə·thərm, *n.* A line on a chart or map passing through places having a corresponding temperature at any particular time.

i·so·ton·ic, ī·sə·ton′ik, *a.* Characterized by equal osmotic pressure.

i·so·tope, ī′sə·tōp, *n.* Any of two or more forms of the same element having the same atomic number and nearly the same chemical properties but with different atomic weights. —**i·so·top·ic,** *a.*

Is·rae·li, iz·rā′lē, *a.* Of or pertaining to modern Israel, its culture, or an inhabitant of modern Israel.—*n. pl.,* **Is·rae·lis, Is·rae·li.** A person who lives in, or comes from, modern Israel.

is·su·ance, ish′oo·əns, *n.* The act of issuing.

is·sue, ish′oo, *n.* A going, coming, passing, or flowing out; the process of coming out, distributing, or putting forth; outflow; a place or means of outflow; that which comes out; offspring; descendant or descendants; the ultimate result or consequence of a preceding affair; a point in question; a point at which a matter is ready for decision; a point or matter, the decision of which is of special or public importance; a quantity issued at one time; a discharge of blood, pus, or the like; an incision or ulcer emitting such a discharge.—*v.i.,* **-sued, -su·ing.** To go, pass, or flow out; to come from some source; to come as a result; to be published.—*v.t.* To send out or give forth; to put forth officially; to distribute; to publish. —**at is·sue,** in controversy; in question. —**take is·sue,** to join the controversy; take a contrary view; disagree.

isth·mus, is′məs, *n. pl.,* **isth·mus·es, isth·mi,** is′mī. A narrow strip of land, bordered on both sides by water, connecting two larger bodies of land.

it, it, *pron.* The third person singular neuter pronoun, corresponding to *he* and *she;* a substitute for a neuter noun or a noun representing something possessing sex when sex is not particularized or considered; a reference to some matter expressed or understood, or some thing or abstract idea not definitely conceived; a

---

a- hat, fāte, fâre, fäther; **e-** met, mē; **i-** pin, pīne; **o-** not, nōte, ôrb, moove (move), boy, pownd; **u-** cübe, bůll, tůk (took); **ch-** chin; **th-** thick, then; **zh-** vizhon (vision); **ə-** ego, takən, pencəl, lemən, bərd (bird).

reference to the subject of inquiry or attention, whether impersonal or personal, as: What was *it? It* is I. *It* is they who are at fault. The grammatical subject of a clause of which the logical subject is a phrase or clause regarded as in apposition with *it,* as: *It* is hard to believe that. *It* is believed that he is dead. An impersonal subject which expresses an action or condition without referring to a specific agent, as: *It* snows. An object of indefinite force following certain verbs: as, to foot *it.—n.* The person who, in children's games, performs an action different from that of the other players, as the person who finds the other players in hide and seek; the general trend or state of events, as: How did *it* go for you last year?

I·tal·ian, i·tal′yən, *a.* Of or pertaining to Italy, its people, or their language; characteristic of or conforming to Italian style or custom.

i·tal·ic, i·tal′ik, ĭ·tal′ik, *n. Usu. pl.* A style of printing in which the letters slope to the right, used to indicate emphasis, a foreign word or expression, and titles of books: *esprit de corps, Gulliver's Travels.*

i·tal·i·cize, i·tal′i·sīz, ĭ·tal′i·sīz, *v.t.,* **-cized, -ciz·ing.** To print in italic type.—*v.i.* To use italics. **—i·tal·i·ci·za·tion,** i·tal·i·sə·zā′shən, *n.*

itch, ich, *v.i.* To have an irritation of the skin which causes a desire to scratch the part affected; to cause such an irritation; to have an uneasy desire.—*n.* The sensation of itching; an uneasy desire: an *itch* for travel; a contagious disease caused by the itch mite, which burrows under the skin, usu. preceded by *the.* **—itch·i·ness,** *n.* **—itch·y,** ich′ē, *a.*

i·tem, ī′təm, *n.* A separate article in an enumeration; a single detail of any list; a separate piece of information or news.—*adv.* Likewise; also.

i·tem·ize, ī′tə·mīz, *v.t.,* **-ized, -iz·ing.** To set down by items; specify the items of.

it·er·ate, it′ə·rāt, *v.t.,* **-at·ed, -at·ing.** To utter or repeat, as for a second time. **—it·er·a·tion,** it·ə·rā′shən, *n.* **—it·er·a·tive,** *a.*

i·tin·er·ant, ī·tin′ər·ənt, i·tin′ər·ənt, *a.* Traveling about: an *itinerant* preacher; wandering; strolling.—*n.* A person who travels from place to place.

i·tin·er·ar·y, ī·tin′ə·rer·ē, i·tin′ə·rer·ē, *n. pl.,* **-ies.** A travel route; the plan of a journey.—*a.* Traveling; pertaining to a journey.

i·tin·er·ate, ī·tin′ə·rāt, i·tin′ə·rāt, *v.i.,* **-at·ed, -at·ing.** To travel from place to place, particularly for the purpose of preaching. **—i·tin·er·ant, i·tin·er·a·tion,** ī·tin·ər·ā′shən, *n.*

it'll, it′əl. Contraction of **it will** or **it shall.**

its, its, *pronominal a.* Possessive case of the pronoun *it,* used attributively: The bird called *its* mate.

it's, its. Contraction of **it is** or **it has.**

it·self, it·self′, *pron.* A reflexive or emphatic form of the third pers. sing. neut. pron: The dog saw *itself* in the mirror. A denotation of its usual or customary state: The cat hasn't been *itself* since the accident.

I.U.D., *n.* Intrauterine device.

I've, iv. Contraction of **I have.**

i·vied, ī′vēd, *a.* Covered or overgrown with ivy.

i·vo·ry, ī′və·rē, *n. pl.,* **-ries.** The hard, smooth-textured, creamy-white dentine from the tusks of elephants and walruses; the dentine from the teeth of any animal; a product made from the tusks of these animals; a yellow to creamy-white color. *Pl., Informal.* Piano keys; dice; teeth.—*a.* Made of ivory; of ivory color.

i·vo·ry tow·er, *n.* A place of seclusion; a place to withdraw to from worldly matters.

i·vy, ī′vē, *n. pl.,* **i·vies.** A creeping or climbing plant, with evergreen leaves and aerial rootlets, which is widely grown.

J

J, j, jā, *n.* The tenth letter of the English alphabet.

jab, jab, *v.t.,* **jabbed, jab·bing.** To strike or thrust at, as with something sharp; to punch sharply.—*v.i.—n.* A sharp, direct blow or thrust, as in boxing.

jab·ber, jab′ər, *v.i.* To talk rapidly, indistinctly, or nonsensically; chatter; babble.—*v.t.* To utter rapidly. —*n.* Fast, indistinct talk. **—jab·ber·er,** *n.*

jack, jak, *n.* A fellow or man; a workman, usu. in combination: steeple*jack,* lumber*jack;* (*often cap.*) a sailor; a machine for raising weights short distances; a card picturing a boy or knave; any instrument useful in some task, as a device for turning a roasting spit, often in combination: a boot*jack;* one of the small stones or six-pointed metal pieces used in the game of jacks; *pl. but sing in constr.,* a children's game in which a player simultaneously bounces a small ball and picks up or moves jacks; connecting apparatus used to complete a circuit. *Informal.* Money.—*a.* Denoting the male of a species: a *jack*ass.—*v.t.* To lift or move with or as with a jack, used with *up. Informal.* To raise or increase, used with *up:* to *jack up* prices.

jack·al, jak′əl, *n.* Any of several species of wild dogs of Asia and Africa; one who does debasing or servile work for another.

jack·ass, jak′as, *n.* A male donkey or ass; a foolish or stupid person.

jack·boot, jak′boot, *n.* A heavy military boot reaching up over the knee.

jack·et, jak′it, *n.* A short outer garment; a protective outer covering, as of cloth, paper, metal, or the like: a book *jacket;* an open envelope for documents; the skin of a potato.—*v.t.* To cover or furnish with a jacket. **—jack·et·ed,** *a.*

Jack Frost, *n.* Frost or freezing weather personified.

jack·ham·mer, jak′ham·ər, *n.* A machine tool for drilling rocks, powered by compressed air.

jack-in-the-box, jak′in·thə·boks, *n. pl.,* **jack-in-the-box·es.** A toy box from which a clownlike figure springs when the lid is released.

jack·knife, jak′nīf, *n. pl.,* **jack·knives.** A large, strong pocketknife; a front dive in which the diver bends his body at the waist and touches his hands to his feet, then straightens just before entering the water headfirst.—*v.t.,* **-knifed, -knif·ing.** To use a jackknife.—*v.i.* To bend in the middle like a jackknife: The large truck skidded, *jackknifed,* and overturned.

jack-of-all-trades, jak·əv·ôl′trädz′, *n. pl.,* **jacks-of-all-trades.** A person handy with tools; a person possessing a superficial skill in several trades.

jack-o'-lan·tern, jak′ə·lan·tərn, *n.* A lantern made from a hollowed pumpkin carved to resemble a face.

jack·pot, jak′pot, *n.* In poker, the stakes which accumulate during play until one player opens the betting; the highest prize in any contest involving stakes. **—hit the jack·pot,** *Informal.* To win the biggest prize or reward; to achieve a remarkable success.

jack rab·bit, *n.* A hare, with long ears and hind legs longer than forelegs, native to western N. America.

jac·o·net, jak′ə·net, *n.* A soft, light cotton fabric.

jac·quard, jak′ärd, jə·kärd′, *n.* (*Often cap.*) A fabric having a fancy or figured weave; the weave itself. Also **Jac·quard weave.**

jade, jād, *n.* A hard gemstone, often green in color, and highly regarded as an ornament; an ornament carved from jade; jade green.

jade, jād, *n.* A worthless, uncontrollable, or worn-out horse; a disreputable or bad-tempered woman.—*v.t.* **jad·ed, jad·ing.** To drive severely; to weary or wear out, as by overwork or excessive use.—*v.i.* To become weary; to lose spirit.

jad·ed, jā′did, *a.* Worn-out; fatigued.

jag, jag, *v.t.,* **jagged, jag·ging.** To notch; to cut, tear, or slash into points or teeth like those of a saw.—*n.* A notch or denticulation; a sharp protuberance or indentation. —**jag·ged,** *a.*

jag, jag, *n. Informal.* A condition of intoxication, usu. from liquor; a bout, spree, or binge: a smoking *jag,* a crying *jag.*

jag·uar, jag′wär, *n.* A large, powerful, black-spotted feline of Central and S. America.

jail, jāl, *n.* A prison.—*v.t.* To imprison.

jail·bird, jāl′bərd, *n.* A prisoner or former prisoner, esp. a habitual or frequent lawbreaker.

jail·break, jāl′brāk, *n.* A prison escape achieved through force.

jail·er, jail·or, jā′lər, *n.* One who oversees or has charge of a jail or its inmates.

ja·lop·y, jə·lop′ē, *n. pl.,* **-ies.** *Informal.* An old, decrepit, or unpretentious automobile.

jal·ou·sie, jal′û·sē, zhal·û·zē′, *n.* A window blind with adjustable horizontal louvers which permit ventilation and light but protect from rain and direct sun rays; a window having louvers of glass with a similar function.

jam, jam, *v.t.,* **jammed, jam·ming.** To press or squeeze tightly between bodies or surfaces so that motion is made difficult or impossible; to crush by squeezing; to cause to become wedged or displaced so that it cannot work; to render unworkable by such wedging or displacement; to press, push, or thrust violently; to fill or block up by crowding; to interfere with radio signals by sending out others of approximately the same wavelength.—*v.i.* To become wedged or fixed; to become unworkable by displacement of a part; to press violently.—*n.* The act of jamming or the state of being jammed; the mass of objects so pressed or crowded together; an obstruction. *Informal.* A predicament or an embarrassing involvement. —**jam·mer,** *n.*

jam, jam, *n.* A fruit preserve cooked with sugar and water until thick, used as a spread.

jamb, jam, *n.* The side or vertical piece of an opening in a wall: a door *jamb.*

jam·bo·ree, jam·bə·rē′, *n.* A Boy Scout assembly of national or international scope. *Informal.* A noisy gathering or festivity.

jam ses·sion, *n.* An impromptu performance by musicians, usu. for their own enjoyment.

Jane Doe, *n.* A feminine name used in examples or hypotheses, esp. where the name of the woman involved is not important.

jan·gle, jang′gəl, *v.i.,* **-gled, -gling.** To sound harshly or discordantly; to dispute or speak angrily.—*v.t.* To cause to make harsh, discordant sounds.—*n.* Harsh or discordant sound; a quarrel or dispute. —**jan·gler,** *n.* —**jan·gly,** *a.*

jan·i·tor, jan′i·tər, *n.* A person hired to clean and maintain an office, school, or other building; a caretaker of a building. —**jan·i·to·ri·al,** jan··i·tôr′ē·əl, *a.*

Jan·u·ar·y, jan′ū·er·ē, *n.* The first month of the year, having 31 days.

Jap·a·nese, jap·ə·nēz′, jap·ə·nēs′, *a.* Pertaining to Japan, a country located off the east coast of Asia.—*n. pl.,* **Jap·a·nese.**

Jap·a·nese bee·tle, *n.* A small green and brown beetle which is destructive to grasses and to many crops.

jar, jär, *n.* A broadmouthed vessel of glass or earthenware, usu. cylindrical in shape; the contents of a jar. —**jar·ful,** *n.*

jar, jär, *v.i.,* **jarred, jar·ring.** To give out a harsh or discordant sound; to grate; to have an annoying or unpleasant effect, used with *on;* to jolt or shake from an unexpected contact; to clash; to quarrel or dispute.—*n.* A rattling vibration of sound; a harsh sound; clash of opinions; jolt.

jar·di·niere, jär·də·nēr′, *n.* An ornamental stand or pot for plants and flowers; a garnish made of cooked and diced vegetables for serving with meat.

jar·gon, jär′gən, *n.* The terminology or phraseology used by a particular class, trade, or profession: legal *jargon;* a rude language or dialect, esp. one resulting from a mixture of languages, as pidgin English; a kind of speech abounding in unfamiliar words; unintelligible speech or writing; gibberish.

jas·mine, jas·min, jaz′min, jas′min, *n.* A fragrant-flowered shrub in the olive family; any of various similar plants with scented flowers; the fragrance resembling that of these flowers; a pale, soft-yellow color. Also **jes·sa·mine.**

jaun·dice, jôn′dis, jän′dis, *n.* An abnormal physical condition due to bile pigments in the blood, characterized by yellowness of the skin and sclera of the eye, and by lassitude and loss of appetite; a state of biased views and warped judgment due to bitterness or envy.—*v.t.,* **-diced, -dic·ing.** To affect with jaundice; *fig,* to distort through envy. —**jaun·diced,** jôn′dist, jän′dist, *a.*

jaunt, jônt, jänt, *v.i.* To make a short journey, esp. for pleasure.—*n.*

jaun·ty, jôn′tē, jän′tē, *a.,* **-ti·er, -ti·est.** Having a breezy manner; brisk; perky. —**jaun·ti·ly,** *adv.* —**jaun·ti·ness,** *n.*

Ja·va, jä′və, *n.* A variety of coffee. (*L.c.*) *Informal.* Coffee.—*n.*

jave·lin, jav′lin, jav′ə·lin, *n.* A light spear thrown in ancient warfare and hunting; a spearlike, metal-tipped shaft of wood, used in distance-throwing contests; a distance-throwing contest using a javelin.—*v.t.* To strike or wound with a javelin.

jaw, jô, *n.* One of the two bones which form the framework of the mouth; *often pl.,* the mouth parts collectively; one of two or more mechanical parts which grasp something; *pl.,* the two sides of a narrow pass. *Informal.* Insolent or offensive talk.—*v.i. Informal.* To talk; to gossip; to use abusive language.—*v.t. Informal.* To scold.

jaw·bone, jô′bōn, *n.* A bone of the jaw, esp. the lower jaw or mandible.

jaw·break·er, jô′brā·kər, *n. Informal.* A word that is hard to pronounce; an extremely hard candy.

jay, jā, *n.* Any of numerous noisy birds known for their colorful plumage and marauding instincts; a gabby chatterer.

Jay·cee, jā′sē′, *n.* One who belongs to a junior chamber of commerce.

jay·walk, jā′wôk, *v.i.* To cross a street carelessly and away from a regular crossing place, often amid traffic. —**jay·walk·er,** *n.*

jazz, jaz, *n.* A kind of music, improvised or arranged, and marked by its rhythmic emphasis, syncopation, and harmonic and melodic variations. *Informal.* Liveliness; nonsensical, idle, or empty talk.—*v.i.* To play jazz music; to dance to such music.—*v.t.* To play in the manner of jazz. *Informal.* To accelerate or infuse with liveliness or excitement, usu. with *up.* —**jazz·ist,** *n.* —**jazz·man,** jaz′man, jaz′mən, *n.*

jazz·y, jaz′ē, *a.,* **-i·er, -i·est.** *Informal.* Pertaining to or

---

a- hat, fāte, fâre, fäther; **e-** met, mē; **i-** pin, pīne; **o-** not, nōte, ôrb, moove (move), boy, pownd; **u-** cūbe, bûll, tûk (took); **ch-** chin; **th-** thick, ᵺen; **zh-** vizhon (vision); **ə-** ego, takən, pencəl, lemən, bərd (bird).

reminiscent of jazz music; lively; flashy. —**jazz·i·ly**, *adv.* —**jazz·i·ness**, *n.*

jeal·ous, jel′əs, *a.* Feeling resentment at the success of another; proceeding from envious resentment: *jealous* pride; suspiciously watchful; vigilant in maintaining or guarding something: a nation *jealous* of its liberties; intolerant of unfaithfulness or rivalry: a *jealous* god.

jeal·ous·y, jel′ə·sē, *n. pl.*, -**ies**. Mental uneasiness due to suspicion or fear of rivalry; an instance of jealous feeling.

jean, jēn, *n.* A strong, twilled fabric, usu. cotton. Also **den·im.**—*n. pl.* Casual trousers or slacks made of denim or jean. Also **den·ims.** *Informal.* Slacks.

Jeep, jēp, *n. Trademark.* A small, sturdy, military automobile with four-wheel drive.

jeer, jēr, *v.i.* To say or shout mockingly or derisively; to scoff.—*v.t.* To ridicule.—*n.* A gibe. —**jeer·er**, *n.*

Je·ho·vah, ji·hō′və, *n.* An Old Testament name of the Supreme Being; God.

jell, jel, *v.i.* To assume the consistency of jelly; crystallize; to become definite in shape or form: The project has not begun to *jell* yet.

jel·li·fy, jel′ə·fī, *v.t.*, *v.i.*, -**fied**, -**fy·ing**. To make or turn into jelly.

Jell-O, jel′ō, *n. Trademark.* A gelatin dessert with sugar and fruit flavoring.

jel·ly, jel′ē, *n. pl.*, -**lies**. A soft, gelatinous food product made with boiled fruit juice and sugar; any substance having a similar consistency.—*v.t.*, *v.i.*, -**lied**, -**ly·ing**. —**jel·lied**, jel′ēd, *a.* —**jel·ly·like**, *a.*

jel·ly·bean, jel′ē·bēn, *n.* A bean-shaped, sugar-coated candy with a jellylike center.

jel·ly·fish, jel′ē·fish, *n. pl.*, -**fish**, -**fish·es**. Any of several marine animals of a jellylike substance, esp. those with umbrella-shaped bodies and long tentacles, as the medusa; one who is weakwilled or lacking in stamina.

jen·ny, jen′ē, *n. pl.*, -**nies**. The female of certain animals: *jenny* ass, *jenny* wren; a spinning jenny.

jeop·ar·dy, jep′ər·dē, *n.* Exposure to death, loss, or harm; hazard; danger. —**jeop·ar·dize**, *v.t.*, -**dized**, -**diz·ing**. To expose to loss or injury; to put in danger; to risk. Also **jeop·ard.**

jerk, jərk, *v.t.* To thrust with a sudden effort; to give a sudden pull; to twitch; to throw with a sudden, quick motion.—*v.i.* To make a sudden motion; to give a start; to speak haltingly.—*n.* A short sudden thrust, push, or twitch; a jolt; a sudden spring; a start; a leap or bound. *Informal.* An ineffectual, dumb person. *Pl.* Tremblings, as delirium tremens. —**jerk·er**, *n.* —**jerk·i·ly**, *adv.* —**jerk·i·ness**, *n.* —**jerk·y**, *a.*, -**i·er**, -**i·est**.

jer·kin, jər′kin, *n.* A sleeveless, collarless jacket of hip length with a snug, belted waist.

jer·ry·build, jer′ē·bild, *v.t.*, -**built**, -**build·ing**. To build cheaply and flimsily. —**jer·ry·build·er**, *n.* —**jer·ry·built**, *a.*

jer·sey, jər′zē, *n.* A knitted fabric of wool, nylon, cotton, or silk, usu. soft and elastic; a close-fitting knit dress, shirt, or sweater.

jes·sa·mine, jes′ə·min, *n.* Jasmine.

jest, jest, *n.* A joke; a witty, mocking act or remark; the object of laughter.—*v.i.* To speak or act playfully, amusingly; to trifle; to joke; to jeer. —**in jest**, in the spirit of fun; not in earnest.

jest·er, jes′tər, *n.* One who jests; a person retained in a medieval court to amuse a ruler; a professional fool or buffoon. —**jest·ing**, *a., n.*

Jes·u·it, jezh′oo·it, jez′ū·it, *n.* A member of a Roman Catholic religious order, the Society of Jesus.

Je·sus, jē′zəs, *n.* The founder of Christianity.

jet, jet, *n.* A shooting forth; that which streams forth from a narrow opening, as water, gas, or flame; the nozzle of a pipe or hose through which gas, liquid, or flame gushes; a jet engine; a jet plane.—*v.i.*, **jet·ted**, **jet·ting**. To issue in a jet; to shoot out; to move swiftly; to travel by jet plane or jet propulsion.—*v.t.* To emit; to

spout forth, as water.—*a.* Referring to jet propulsion or jet plane travel.

jet, jet, *n.* A hard black mineral, allied to coal, which, when highly polished, is used for making deep, lustrous black jewelry, ornaments, and buttons.—*a.*

jet en·gine, *n.* An engine, used chiefly in aircraft, which achieves its fast forward propulsion by discharging its oxidized fuel as hot air and gases through one or more rear exhausts.

jet·lin·er, jet′li·nər, *n.* A jet plane used by commercial airlines.

jet plane, *n.* Any airplane propelled by one or more jet engines.

jet·port, jet′pôrt, *n.* An airport used chiefly or exclusively by jet planes.

jet-pro·pelled, jet′prə·peld′, *a.* Moved by the power of a jet engine or rocket engine, as an airplane; moving swiftly and strongly, as if driven by jet power.

jet pro·pul·sion, *n.* Propulsion by means of a jet of gas or fluid; propulsion by means of a jet engine.

jet·sam, jet′səm, *n.* Goods thrown overboard to lighten a vessel in distress, esp. such goods when washed ashore; anything thrown away.

jet set, *n.* A group of wealthy, sophisticated, and socially prominent people who travel by jet from one fashionable resort to another.

jet stream, *n.* A strong, high-speed wind current, moving from west to east around the poles of the earth, in the earth's atmosphere; a trailing stream of fluid or gas exhaust from a rocket or jet engine.

jet·ti·son, jet′ə·sən, *n.* The act of sacrificing the cargo of a ship or aircraft in an emergency to lighten the vessel; abandonment; the goods thrown overboard; jetsam.—*v.t.*

jet·ty, jet′ē, *n. pl.*, -**ties**. A pier of stones sticking out from shore into a body of water to protect a harbor; a wharf; an overhanging part of a building.

Jew, joo, *n.* One whose faith is Judaism; a descendant of the Hebrews.

jew·el, joo′əl, *n.* A costly article of personal adornment, esp. one of gold or gems; a gem or precious stone; a precious stone or substitute used as a watch bearing; a thing or person of great worth or rare excellence; a precious possession.—*v.t.*, -**eled**, -**el·ing**. To adorn with jewels. —**jew·el·ly**, *a.*

jew·el·er, joo′əl·ər, *n.* One who makes, repairs, or deals in jewelry and watches.

jew·el·ry, joo′əl·rē, *n.* Jewels; articles made of gold, silver, precious stones, or similar materials for personal ornament.

Jew·ish, joo′ish, *a.* Of or pertaining to the Jews.—*n. Informal.* Yiddish.

Jew·ry, joo′rē, *n.* Jewish people collectively.

jew's-harp, jews'-harp, jooz′harp, *n.* A small, lyre-shaped musical instrument held between the teeth, and played by plucking a flexible metal tongue.

jib, jib, *n.* The foremost sail of a ship, triangular in shape and extended from the outer end of a jib boom; the projecting arm or boom of a crane.

jibe, jīb, *v.i.*, **jibed**, **jib·ing**. *Informal.* To be in harmony or accord; to agree.

jif·fy, jif′ē, *n. pl.*, -**fies**. *Informal.* A moment; an instant. Also **jiff.**

jig, jig, *n.* A rapid, lively, irregular dance; the music for a jig; a device which guides a mechanical tool or holds the material being worked.—*v.t.*, *v.i.*, **jigged**, **jig·ging**. To dance a jig; to play fast music; move with a jerky motion; to fish with a jig.

jig·ger, jig′ər, *n.* A person or thing that jigs; a kind of potter's wheel; a jig for separating ore; a gadget or mechanical device. *Informal.* Any contrivance, article, or part that one cannot name more precisely. A measure for liquor containing about one and one-half ounces.

jig·ger, jig′ər, *n.* Any of the small red larvae of various mites which fasten themselves to the skin, causing itching and irritation.

jig·gle, jig'əl, *v.t., v.i.,* **-gled, -gling.** To move up and down or back and forth with short, quick jerks.—*n.* A jiggling movement. —**jig·gly,** *a.*

jig·saw, jig'sô, *n.* A narrow saw operated with an up-and-down motion, used for cutting curved or irregular lines.

jig·saw puz·zle, *n.* A puzzle consisting of variously shaped pieces of cardboard, wood, or similar material which form a picture when properly assembled.

jilt, jilt, *v.t.* To discard or cast off, as a fiancé, lover, or sweetheart. —**jilt·er,** *n.*

Jim Crow, jim'krō', *n.* The practice of discrimination against Negroes, as segregation of public places. —**Jim-Crow,** *a.* (*Sometimes l.c.*) —**Jim Crow·ism,** *n.*

jim-dan·dy, jim'dan'dē, *a. Informal.* Excellent, admirable, or superior.

jim·my, jim'ē, *n. pl.,* **-mies.** A short crowbar used by burglars.—*v.t.,* **-mied, -my·ing.** To force open, as a door or window, by means of a jimmy or similar tool.

jin·gle, jing'gəl, *v.i.,* **-gled, -gling.** To make a tinkling sound; to clink; to rhyme or have repetitive rhythm. —*v.t.* To cause to make a tinkling sound.—*n.* A clinking sound; something that jingles; a correspondence of sound in rhymes, as alliteration in poetry; a short catchy tune.

jinx, jingks, *n. Informal.* Something which brings bad luck.—*v.t.* To cause or bring bad luck to.

jit·ney, jit'nē, *n. pl.,* **-neys.** A small bus or automobile which carries passengers.

jit·ter, jit'ər, *v.i.* To behave nervously. —**jit·ters,** *n. pl. Informal.* Excessive nervousness; a feeling of uneasiness or fear. —**jit·ter·y,** jit'ə·rē, *a.*

jit·ter·bug, jit'ər·bug, *n.* A popular dance of the 1940's characterized by quick steps, splits, and twirls; one who does this dance.—*v.i.,* **-bugged, -bug·ging.**

jive, jīv, *n.* Swing or jazz music; the dancing to swing music; jargon used by jazz enthusiasts and musicians; misleading talk.—*v.i.* To dance to this music.—*v.t. Informal.* To tease; to fool or confuse.

job, job, *n.* A piece of work, esp. an individual piece of work done in the routine of one's occupation or trade, or for a fixed price; anything one has to do; a duty; the object worked on; a task which demands unusual exertion; the process involved in accomplishing a task. *Informal.* A criminal deed, as a theft or robbery. —**job·less,** job'lis, *a.*

job, job, *v.i.,* **jobbed, job·bing.** To work at jobs or odd pieces of work; work by the piece; to buy and sell as a broker, middle man, or jobber; to turn public business improperly to private gain.—*v.t.*

job·ber, job'ər, *n.* One who deals in goods or merchandise as a wholesaler; one who does piecework or one who does work by the job.

job·hold·er, job'hōl·dər, *n.* A person working at a steady job.

job lot, *n.* A miscellaneous collection of merchandise sold in a single dealing, usu. at a lower price, to a retailer.

jock, jok, *n.* Jockey; jockstrap. *Informal.* An athlete.

jock·ey, jok'ē, *n. pl.,* **-eys.** One whose profession is to ride horses in horse races. *Informal.* One who drives, pilots, or guides: a car *jockey.*—*v.t.,* **-eyed, -ey·ing.** To ride in a race; to maneuver; to drive or pilot; guide; to cheat; to trick; to deceive; to manipulate.—*v.i.*

jock·strap, jok'strap, *n.* An elastic waist band and groin pouch worn esp. by male athletes for genital protection and support. Also **ath·let·ic sup·port·er.**

jo·cose, jō·kōs', *a.* Given to jokes and jesting. —**jo·cos·i·ty,** jō·kos'ə·tē, *n.*

joc·u·lar, jok'yə·lər, *a.* Joking; witty; humorous; playful. —**joc·u·lar·i·ty,** jok'yə·lar'ə·tē, *n.*

joc·und, jok'ənd, jō'kənd, *a.* Cheerful; gay; merry. —**jo·cun·di·ty,** jō·kən'də·tē, *n.*

jodh·pur, jod'pər, *n.* A riding boot, made esp. for wearing with jodhpurs. Also **jodh·pur boot, jodh·pur shoe.** —**jodh·purs,** *n. pl.* Riding breeches styled wide at the hips, that narrow at the knees and fit tightly to the ankles.

joe, jō, *n. Informal.* A man: He's a great *joe.*

jog, jog, *v.t.,* **jogged, jog·ging.** To push or shake suddenly; to nudge; to arouse by an idea or a reminder; to cause to move with a momentary jerk; to pace at a regular gait.—*v.i.* To move in a jolting or jerky manner; to move at a slow trot; to walk or travel idly or slowly, with little progress, usu. followed by *on* or *along.*—*n.* The act of jogging. —**jog·ger,** *n.*

jog·gle, jog'əl, *v.t.,* **-gled, -gling.** To shake slightly; to give a sudden but slight push; to cause to become unstable by a sudden contact; to unite; to shift a fitting part until it falls in place.—*v.i.* To shake; to totter.

jog trot, *n.* A slow, easy trot, usu. interspersed with periods of brisk walking, used for physical fitness; a slow gait, usu. of a horse.

john, jon, *n. Informal.* A toilet.

John Doe, *n.* A name used in legal procedure to indicate an unnamed person; a name used to denote the average man.

John Han·cock, jon han'kok, *n. Informal.* One's signature.

John Hen·ry, jon hen'rē, *n. Informal.* One's signature.

join, joyn, *v.t., v.i.,* Connect or bring together; to combine; to associate with; to unite with; to become a member of; to unite through marriage.—*n.* A seam or joint. —**join·a·ble,** *a.*

join·er, joy'nər, *n.* One who joins; a carpenter, esp. one who does the woodwork of houses; a member of many clubs and organizations.

joint, joynt, *n.* The place or part at which two separate things are joined or united: building *joint;* the mode of connection of two things; junction; the joining of two or more bones, as in the elbow. *Informal.* A place or establishment of low character or reputation; a marijuana cigarette.—*a.* Shared by two or more: a *joint* savings account; united or combined: *joint* efforts. —*v.t.* To form or unite with a joint or joints; to cut or divide into joints or pieces. —**out of joint,** dislocated, as a shoulderbone; relating to confusion and disorder. —**joint·ed,** *a.* —**joint·ly,** *adv.*

joint res·o·lu·tion, *n.* A resolution approved by both houses of a legislature, which becomes law when signed by the chief executive.

joint re·turn, *n.* A tax report of the income of both husband and wife.

joint stock, *n.* Stock held in common.

joint ten·an·cy, *n.* Common ownership of property by two or more persons.

joist, joyst, *n.* A horizontal timber, running parallel from wall to wall, that supports the boards of a floor or the laths of a ceiling.

joke, jōk, *n.* A thing said or an action performed to evoke laughter; the ridiculous side of something; a matter of small importance; a trifle.—*v.i.,* **joked, jok·ing.** To say or do something funny.—*v.t.* To make fun of; to make merry with; to tease. —**joke·ster,** jōk'stər, *n.* —**jok·ing·ly,** *adv.*

jok·er, jō'kər, *n.* A person who jokes or teases; an extra playing card added to a deck allowing special privileges. *Informal.* An obnoxious individual.

jol·ly, jol'ē, *a.,* **-li·er, -li·est.** Merry; gay; lively; exciting mirth or gaiety.—*v.i.,* **-lied, -ly·ing.** To participate in friendly banter.—*v.t. Informal.* To try to induce a pleasant, agreeable state of mind in.

Jol·ly Rog·er, *n.* A flag used by pirates and marked by a white skull and crossbones on a black background.

jolt, jōlt, *v.t.* To shake as by a sudden rough thrust; shake up roughly; to deliver a blow to; to upset

---

a- hat, fāte, fāre, fäther; **e-** met, mē; **i-** pin, pīne; **o-** not, nōte, ôrb, moove (move), boy, pownd; **u-** cūbe, bůll, tůk (took); **ch-** chin; **th-** thick, ŧhen; **zh-** vizhon (vision); **ə-** əgo, takən, pencəl, lemən, bərd (bird).

suddenly; to interrupt abruptly or roughly.—*v.i.* To move with a shock or jerk.—*n.* A sudden blow, shock, or movement; a sudden upset; the cause of such an upset. —**jolt•er,** *n.* —**jolt•ing•ly,** *adv.* —**jolt•y,** *a.*

jon•quil, jon′kwil, jong′kwil, *n.* A species of narcissus, similar to the daffodil.

josh, josh, *v.t. Informal.* To chaff; banter in a teasing way.—*v.i. Informal.* To join in banter.—*n. Informal.* A good-natured remark, banter, or joke.

jos•tle, jos′əl, *v.t.* **-tled, -tling.** To bump, strike, or push roughly or rudely against; to drive or force, by pushing or shoving.—*v.i.* To bump, collide, or push, as in passing or in a crowd, usu. followed by *against* or *with.* —**jos•tler,** *n.*

jot, jot, *n.* An iota; a point.—*v.t.* **jot•ted, jot•ting.** To write down quickly or hurriedly, as in a diary or memorandum book; to make a memorandum of.

joule, jool, jowl, *n.* Amount of energy or work which is equal to the energy required to exert a force of one newton over a distance of one meter, and equal to 10 million ergs.

jour•nal, jər′nəl, *n.* A diary; an account of daily events, or the book containing such an account; a record of the transactions of an organization or legal body; any periodical or magazine, esp. one published for a specific profession; the part of a shaft or axle that moves on bearings.

jour•nal box, *n.* A metal enclosure which houses a journal and bearing.

jour•nal•ism, jər′nə•liz•əm, *n.* The occupation of conducting a news medium, including publishing, editing, writing, or broadcasting; an academic field concerned with the procedures involved in conducting a news medium.

jour•nal•ist, jər′nə•list, *n.* The conductor of a news medium, as a newspaper editor. —**jour•nal•is•tic,** jər•nə•lis′tik, *a.*

jour•ney, jər′nē, *n.* Travel from one place to another; the distance or time traveled; a trip.—*v.i., v.t.* To travel.

jour•ney•man, jər′nē•mən, *n. pl.,* **-men.** A workman who has completed his apprenticeship.

joust, jowst, jəst, joost, *n.* A fight between mounted knights wearing armor and using lances.—*v.i.* To take part in a joust; tilt.

jo•vi•al, jō′vē•əl, *a.* Gay; merry; good-humored. —**jo•vi•al•i•ty,** jō•vē•al′ə•tē, *n.*

jowl, jowl, jōl, *n.* A jaw, esp. the under jaw; the cheek; a fold of flesh hanging from the jaw, as of a fat person. —**jowled, jowl•y,** *a.*

joy, joy, *n.* Excitement or pleasurable feeling caused by the acquisition or expectation of good; gladness; pleasure; delight; the cause of satisfaction and happiness.—*v.i.* To rejoice; to be glad.

joy•ful, joy′fəl, *a.* Full of joy; glad.

joy•less, joy′lis, *a.* Destitute of joy; giving no pleasure or gladness.

joy•ous, joy′əs, *a.* Gay; joyful.

joy•ride, joy′rīd, *n. Informal.* A pleasure ride in an automobile, esp. when the car is driven recklessly or used without the owner's permission.

ju•bi•lant, joo′bə•lənt, *a.* Rejoicing; exhibiting joy; triumphant. —**ju•bi•lance, ju•bi•lan•cy,** *n.*

ju•bi•la•tion, joo•bə•lā′shən, *n.* A rejoicing; a triumph. —**ju•bi•late,** joo′bə•lāt, *v.i.,* **-lat•ed, -lat•ing.**

ju•bi•lee, joo′bə•lē, joo•bə•lē′, *n.* The celebration of any of certain anniversaries: the 25th silver *jubilee,* or 50th golden *jubilee;* the completion of the 50th year of any continuous course or period; any season or occasion for rejoicing or festivity; rejoicing or jubilation.

Ju•da•ism, joo′dē•iz•əm, *n.* The religion of the Jewish people as prescribed in the Old Testament and in the rabbinical commentaries of the Talmud, characterized by a belief in one God; the traditional, religious, and ethical beliefs and customs of the Jewish people. —**Ju•da•ic,** joo•dā′ik, **Ju•da•i•cal,** *a.*

Ju•das, joo′dəs, *n.* One treacherous enough to betray a friend; one who disguises friendship as friendship.

judge, jəj, *n.* A public officer authorized to hear and determine causes in a court of law; one who gives judgment or passes sentence; an appointed person who pronounces a decision in a dispute or contest, as an arbiter; one qualified to pass a critical judgment. —*v.t.,* **judged, judg•ing.** To hear, critically examine, and decide, as a court case; to try; to pass sentence on, as a person; to decide judicially; to form an opinion or estimate of; to infer, think, or hold an opinion.—*v.i.*

judg•ment, jəj′mənt, *n.* The act of judging, as the act of deciding or passing decision on something; the act or faculty of judging truly, wisely, or skillfully; good sense; discernment; understanding; opinion or notion formed by judging or considering. *Logic.* The act or mental faculty by which man compares ideas and ascertains the relations of terms and propositions; a determination of the mind so formed, producing a proposition when expressed in words. *Law.* The sentence pronounced on a case by the judge or court by which it is tried; the obligation, esp. debt, imposed by a negative court decision; the certificate indicating the verdict of the case and served to the obligor, usu. the debtor. A calamity regarded as sent by God for the punishment of sinners. —**judg•men•tal,** jəj•men′təl, *a.*

ju•di•cial, joo•dish′əl, *a.* Relating to judicial administration; relating to courts of justice or judges; having the tendency to judge, discriminate, or criticize; serving to determine or decide; participating in a judgment.

ju•di•ci•ar•y, joo•dish′ē•er•ē, joo•dish′ə•rē, *a.* Referring to the judgments of law courts, the courts themselves, or judges.—*n.* The governmental branch engaged in judicial concerns; the court system of a country; judges taken collectively.

ju•di•cious, joo•dish′əs, *a.* Relating to the use of good judgment; wise; prudent.

ju•do, joo′dō, *n.* A method of defense similar to jujitsu in its reliance upon body movement and leverage rather than weapons.

jug, jug, *n.* A vessel in various forms for holding liquids, having a handle, often a spout or lip, and sometimes a lid; a pitcher; a deep vessel, usu. earthenware, with a handle and a narrow neck stopped by a cork; the contents of any such vessel. *Informal.* A prison or jail.—*v.t.,* **jugged, jug•ging.** To put into a jug; cook in a jug. *Informal.* To imprison. —**jug•ful,** jug′fûl, *n. pl.,* **-fuls.**

jug•ger•naut, jəg′ər•nôt, *n.* Any overpowering and terrible force; any idea, custom, or loyalty demanding blind devotion or terrible sacrifice.

jug•gle, jəg′əl, *v.t., v.i.,* **-gled, -gling.** To perform feats of manual or bodily dexterity, such as tossing up and keeping in continuous motion a number of balls, plates, or knives; to use trickery.—*v.t.—n.* An act of juggling. —**jug•gler,** jəg′lər, *n.*

jug•u•lar, jəg′yə•lər, joo′gyə•lər, *a.* Of or pertaining to the throat or neck; relating to certain veins in the neck.—*n.* A jugular vein, one of the two large veins of the neck returning blood from the neck, face, and brain to the heart.

juice, joos, *n.* The fluid part of animal substances, fruits, or vegetables, esp. those which can be extracted; natural body fluids: as, digestive *juices;* essential or vital element. *Informal.* Electricity; fuel, esp. gasoline; intoxicating liquor. —**juice•less,** *a.*

juic•er, joo′sər, *n.* An appliance for the extraction of fruit and vegetable juices.

juic•y, joo′sē, *a.* Abounding with juice; succulent; interesting; colorful, esp. when racy or spicy. —**juic•i•ly,** *adv.* —**juic•i•ness,** *n.*

ju•jit•su, joo•jit′soo, *n.* A style of Japanese wrestling in which agility, leverage, and a knowledge of muscular action are utilized to disable the opponent.

juke•box, jook′boks, *n.* An automatic, usu. coin-operated record player, in a brightly illuminated cabinet which permits pushbutton record selection.

ju·lep, jū′lip, *n.* A sweet drink, esp. an alcoholic drink with bourbon, sugar, crushed ice, and mint.

ju·li·enne, joo·lē·en′, *a.* Sliced in long thin strips, as vegetables or other food.—*n.* A clear soup made from meat stock and containing julienne vegetables.

Ju·ly, jῡ·lī′, joo·lī′, *n.* The seventh month of the year, containing 31 days.

jum·ble, jəm′bəl, *v.t.,* **-bled, -bling.** To mix in a confused mass; to throw together without order; to confuse in the mind.—*v.i.* To meet, mix, or unite in a confused manner.—*n.* Confused mixture, mass, or collection.

jum·bo, jəm′bō, *n. pl.,* **-bos.** A big person, animal, or thing.—*a.* Unusually large.

jump, jəmp, *v.i.* To spring clear of the ground or floor by a sudden muscular effort; throw oneself in any direction from the ground; leap; to move or go suddenly; to start, as from nervous excitement; to rise suddenly in amount or price; to be bustling with activity.—*v.t.* To pass over by a leap; leap over; to skip or pass over. *Informal.* To abscond from, or evade by absconding: to *jump* bail; to get on board: *jump* a freight. To spring off or leave: A train *jumps* a track; to pounce on; come down upon violently or suddenly; seize upon by sudden, unexpected action.—*n.* An act of jumping; a leap; a space or obstacle cleared in a leap; a sudden start, as from nervous excitement; a sudden upward or other movement of an inanimate object; a sudden rise in amount or price; an abrupt change of level; an abrupt transition from one point or thing to another, with omission of what intervenes; a brief journey; a sports event featuring competitive jumping. **—jump at,** embrace or accept with eagerness. **—jump·ing,** *a.* **—jump·i·ness,** *n.* **—jump·y,** *a.*

jump·er, jəm′pər, *n.* One who or that which jumps; a kind of loose-fitting jacket; a sleeveless dress esp. one-piece, usu. worn over a blouse.

jump·ing-off place, jəm′ping·of′, *n.* An out-of-the-way or remote place; the farthermost limits.

jump-off, jəmp′ôf, *n.* The onset of a battle or a race.

jump seat, *n.* A movable or folding extra seat, as in a taxicab.

jump suit, *n.* A one-piece uniform worn for parachute jumping; a similarly styled article of clothing.

junc·tion, jəngk′shən, *n.* The act or operation of joining; the state of being joined; the place or point of union; joint; a crossing or merging of two roads.

junc·ture, jəngk′chər, *n.* The line or point at which two bodies are joined; a point of time, esp. one rendered critical or important by a combination of circumstances.

June, joon, *n.* The sixth month of the year, containing 30 days.

June bug, *n.* A large brown beetle, appearing in early summer.

jun·gle, jəng′gəl, *n.* A wild tropical forest of rank vegetation and dense undergrowth; any coarse, rank vegetation; a jumbled mass. *Informal.* An area of merciless competition or struggle for success.

jun·ior, joon′yər, *a.* Younger; applied to distinguish the younger of two persons, usu. father and son, bearing the same name; intended for youth; lower or younger in standing; later in date; of or denoting the third year of a four-year course of study.—*n.* Abbr. **jr., Jr.**

jun·ior col·lege, *n.* A two-year institution of learning following high school and offering a general curriculum.

jun·ior high school, *n.* An intermediary school comprised of the seventh, eighth, and sometimes the ninth grades.

ju·ni·per, joo′nə·pər, *n.* An evergreen tree or shrub, having blue berrylike cones used in medicine and in the flavoring of gin.

junk, jəngk, *n.* Old or discarded material, as metal, paper, or rags; anything that is regarded as worthless or mere trash. *Informal.* A narcotic.—*v.t.* To cast aside; to discard as no longer of use. **—junk·man,** *n.* **—junk·y,** *a.*

junk, jəngk, *n.* A flat-bottomed ship used in China and Japan.

jun·ket, jəng′kit, *n.* A dish made of milk curdled with rennet, sweetened, and flavored; a feast; a picnic; a pleasure excursion.—*v.i.*

junk·ie, jəng′kē, *n. Informal.* One who is addicted to drugs.

jun·ta, hûn′tə, jən′tə, *n.* An administrative council, esp. in Spain and Latin America; an interim government by a committee following a revolution; a group of persons united for a common goal, often for intrigue.

ju·ris·dic·tion, jûr·is·dik′shən, *n.* The right or power of administering law or justice; judicial authority; authority in general; rule; control; the range of judicial authority; the territory over which authority is exercised; a judicial organization; a court, or system of courts, of justice. **—ju·ris·dic·tion·al,** *a.*

ju·ris·pru·dence, jûr·is·prood′əns, *n.* The science of law; the formal principles upon which laws are based; a body of court decisions; a department of law. **—ju·ris·pru·dent,** *a., n.* **—ju·ris·pru·den·tial,** jûr·is·proo·den′shəl, *a.*

ju·rist, jûr′ist, *n.* A lawyer; a judge; one versed in law, esp. civil law; a writer on law.

ju·ror, jûr′ər, *n.* One of a body of persons sworn to deliver a verdict in a legal case; a member of any jury; one who has taken an oath; one who serves on a panel judging a contest.

ju·ry, jûr′ē, *n. pl.,* **-ries.** A certain number of persons selected according to law and sworn to determine facts, and to arrive at a verdict; a committee selected to adjudge prizes, as at a fair, beauty contest, or other public exhibition.

just, jəst, *a.* Acting in accordance with what is right; impartial; fair; merited: *just* reward; proper; legal: *just* debts.—*adv.* Exact in time: *just* now; exactly: *just* as they were; a moment before: She *just* arrived. **—just·ly,** *adv.* **—just·ness,** *n.*

jus·tice, jəs′tis, *n.* Equitableness; impartiality; lawfulness; what is rightly due; governmental judiciary department: the U.S. Department of *Justice;* a judge: *justice* of the U.S. Supreme Court. **—jus·tice·less,** *a.* **—jus·tice·like,** *a.*

jus·tice of the peace, *n.* A local civil officer who may fine or even imprison in certain minor cases, conduct preliminaries in more serious cases, perform marriages, and administer oaths.

jus·ti·fi·ca·tion, jəs·tə·fə·kā′shən, *n.* The act of justifying; the state of being justified; a fact or circumstance that justifies.

jus·ti·fy, jəs′tə·fī, *v.t.,* **-fied, -fy·ing.** To prove to be guiltless or blameless; vindicate; show to be just, right, or warranted; to furnish a reason or excuse for.—*v.i.* **—jus·ti·fi·a·ble,** *a.*

jut, jət, *v.i.,* **jut·ted, jut·ting.** To project beyond the main body.—*n.* That which juts; a projection.

jute, joot, *n.* A fiber obtained from plants native to India and the East Indies, and used in the manufacture of gunny sacks, burlap, and other coarse cloths; the plant itself.

ju·ve·nile, joo′və·nəl, joo′və·nīl, *a.* Young; youthful; immature; pertaining or suited to youth.—*n.* A young person or youth; a children's book.

ju·ve·nile court, *n.* A court exercising jurisdiction in cases concerning children under 18 who are neglected, dependent, or delinquent.

ju·ve·nile de·lin·quen·cy, *n.* The antisocial actions or legal violations of a minor, subject to the jurisdiction of a juvenile court. —**ju•ve•nile de•lin•quent,** *n.*

jux•ta•pose, jək•stə•pōz′, *v.t.,* **-posed, -pos•ing.** To place near or next to; place side by side, often for comparing or contrasting. —**jux•ta•po•si•tion,** jək•stə•pə•zish′ən, *n.*

K

K, k, kā, *n.* The eleventh letter of the English alphabet.

ka•bob, kə•bob′, *n.* Meat cut into cubes and broiled on a skewer with vegetables such as mushrooms, tomatoes, and onions.

kai•ser, kī′zər, *n.* An emperor. (*Cap.*) Title of the Holy Roman Emperors; title of Austrian emperors from 1804 to 1918; title of German rulers from 1871 to 1918.

kale, kail, kāl, *n.* One of several varieties of cabbage, with curled leaves that do not form a head.

ka•lei•do•scope, kə•lī′də•skōp, *n.* An instrument which exhibits, by means of mirror reflection, a variety of beautiful colors and symmetrical forms; a changing or complex design or scene. —**ka•lei•do•scop•ic,** kə•lī•də•skop′ik, **ka•lei•do•scop•i•cal,** *a.*

ka•mi•ka•ze, kä•mi•kä′zē, *n.* A Japanese pilot of World War II who flew a suicidal mission by diving an airplane laden with explosives into an enemy ship or other target.

kan•ga•roo, kang•gə•roo′, *n. pl.,* **-roos, -roo.** Any of certain pouched mammals of Australia, with long powerful hind legs for leaping, small short forelegs, and a long broad tail.

kan•ga•roo court, *n.* An irregular, unofficial court where the law is deliberately misinterpreted or totally disregarded.

ka•o•lin, ka•o•line, kā′ə•lin, *n.* A mineral clay that remains white after firing, used in manufacturing high grade porcelain, paper, cloth, window shades, paint, and soaps.

ka•pok, kā′pok, *n.* The silky mass which covers the seeds of a silk-cotton tree of the East Indies, Africa, and tropical America: used esp. in stuffing pillows, sleeping bags, and for insulation.

ka•put, kə•pût′, *a. Informal.* Done for; dead; not in working order; having no possibility of success.

kar•at, kar′ət, *n.* A measure of the fineness of gold determined by the weight of pure gold in a twenty-fourth part of an alloy; a measure of weight for precious gems.

ka•ra•te, kə•rä′tē, *n.* A method of combat, developed in Japan, in which the hands, feet, knees, and elbows are used to inflict quick, damaging blows on an opponent.

kar•ma, kär′mə, *n.* The quality of a person's actions in one existence which determines his destiny in the next; destiny; fate. —**kar•mic,** *a.*

ka•ty•did, kā′tē•did, *n.* Any of several pale-green, long-horned grasshoppers.

kay•ak, kai•ak, kī′ak, *n.* A canoe of arctic America, made of sealskins stretched around a frame, with an opening in the middle for the occupant.

kay•o, kā′ō, *n. pl.,* **-os.** *Informal.* In boxing, a knockout.—*v.t.*

kedge, kej, *v.t.,* **kedged, kedg•ing.** To move or haul, as a ship, by pulling a rope attached to a dropped anchor.—*v.i.* To put into motion by being kedged.—*n.* A small anchor used in kedging a ship. Also **kedge an•chor.**

keel, kēl, *n.* A longitudinal structure extending along the middle of the bottom of a vessel from stem to stern and supporting the whole frame; a corresponding part in some other structure, as in a dirigible balloon.—*v.t.,* *v.i.* To turn upside down. —**keel o•ver,** to fall bringing the wrong side uppermost; capsize; to fall over or faint suddenly.

keel•haul, kēl′hôl, *v.t.* To punish by hauling under the keel of a ship; to sternly punish or reproach.

keel•son, kel′sən, kēl′sən, *n.* An internal beam laid on the middle of the floor timbers over the keel.

keen, kēn, *a.* So shaped as to cut readily; sharp, piercing, or biting; mentally acute; extremely sensitive in perception; intense; vivid; enthusiastic. *Informal.* Fine; excellent. —**keen•ly,** *adv.* —**keen•ness,** *n.*

keen, kēn, *v.i.* To wail in lamentation over the dead. —*n.* A wailing lament for the dead. —**keen•er,** *n.*

keep, kēp, *v.t.,* **kept, keep•ing.** Possess or have; retain possession of; avoid yielding to others; fulfill, as a promise; support, as a family; care for; maintain; protect; detain; employ; retain; withhold; to stock; save; prevent, usu. with *from;* manage; preserve; to conduct the activities of; to hold in custody; to observe with formalities or rites; to maintain one's position in or on.—*v.i.* To remain or stay; continue or persist; to continue unimpaired or without spoiling. —*n.* The means of subsistence; care; the most secure tower in a medieval castle; a dungeon. —**for keeps,** with complete seriousness; permanently. —**keep up,** to remain even or equal to; to maintain in good condition; to stay informed; persist in; continue without interruption; to cause to stay awake. —**keep•er,** *n.*

keep•ing, kē′ping, *n.* Possession or charge; just proportion; harmony; support or maintenance. —**be in keep•ing with,** accord or harmonize with; be consistent with.

keep•sake, kēp′sāk, *n.* Anything kept as a souvenir or as a remembrance of the giver; a memento.

keg, keg, *n.* A small barrel, usu. having a capacity of 5 to 10 gallons; 100 pounds of nails.

keg•ler, keg′lər, *n. Informal.* A bowler.

kelp, kelp, *n.* Any of various large, coarse, brown seaweeds; the ash of such seaweeds.

ken, ken, *v.t., v.i.* To know or have knowledge of.—*n.* Range of perception or knowledge.

ken•nel, ken′əl, *n.* A shelter for dogs; a doghouse; *often pl.,* a place where dogs are bred or boarded. A pack of dogs.—*v.i.,* **-neled, -nel•ing.** To live in a kennel, as a dog.—*v.t.* To keep or confine in a kennel.

ke•no, kē′nō, *n.* A game of chance, adapted from lotto for gambling purposes.

kept, kept, *v.* The past tense and past participle of **keep.**

ker•a•tin, ker′ə•tin, *n.* An albuminous compound present in horns, hair, and nails.

ker•chief, kər′chif, *n.* A cloth to dress or cover the head or neck; a handkerchief.

ker•mis, ker•mess, kir•mess, kər′mis, *n.* In Belgium, the Netherlands, etc., an annual fair or festival with sports and merrymaking; an entertainment, usu. for charitable purposes.

ker•nel, kər′nəl, *n.* The usu. edible substance contained in the shell of a nut, in a seed, or in the stone of a fruit; a grain of corn or wheat; the main or essential part of a matter; core; gist.

ker•o•sene, ker•o•sine, ker′ə•sēn, ker′ə•sēn′, *n.*

A liquid hydrocarbon distilled from coals, bitumen, or petroleum and extensively used in lamps and stoves; coal oil.

kes·trel, kes′trəl, n. A common small European falcon.

ketch, kech, n. A fore-and-aft rigged vessel with two masts, a large mainmast toward the bow, and a smaller mizzenmast toward the stern but in front of the rudder.

ketch·up, kech′əp, kach′əp, n. A sauce for meat, fish, etc., usu. a thick, seasoned tomato sauce. Also **catch·up, cat·sup**.

ke·tone, kē′tōn, n. Any of a class of organic compounds, as acetone, often used as solvents in industry.

ket·tle, ket′əl, n. A vessel, usu. of metal, for boiling liquids, esp. a teakettle; a pot. —**kettle of fish**, a trying or awkward situation; a mess.

ket·tle·drum, ket′əl·drəm, n. A drum consisting of a hollow hemisphere of brass or copper, with a head of parchment whose pitch may be adjusted.

key, kē, n. An instrument for fastening or opening a lock by moving its bolt; something that secures entrance to a place; something or someone essential; a means of understanding or solving; a book or the like containing solutions of problems; a table, group of notes, etc., interpreting symbols, numbers, lines, etc.; a pin, bolt, wedge, cotter, or other piece to lock or hold parts; a keystone; a contrivance for turning a bolt or nut; one of a set of levers or parts pressed in operating a piano, organ, flute, telegraph, typewriter, or other mechanism; a samara; a scale or system of notes or tones based on a particular note; tone or pitch, as of voice; characteristic style, as of expression or thought.—a. Controlling; of critical importance; pivotal; fundamental.—v.t. To lock with or as with a key; to fasten, secure, or adjust with a key; to regulate the pitch of; to adjust; attune; to make nervous, intense, very eager, etc., usu. followed by up; to provide with a key or keys. —**keyed**, a.

key, kē, n. A reef or islet, esp. one formed of coral. Also **cay.**

key·board, kē′bôrd, n. The series of keys of a piano, typewriter, etc.

key·hole, kē′hōl, n. A hole into which a key is inserted, as in a lock.

key·note, kē′nōt, n. In music, the note on which a key, or system of tones, is founded; the tonic. The determining principle; main idea.—v.t., **-not·ed**, **-not·ing**. To give the keynote address of.

key·note address, n. A speech, as at a political convention, to present the basic issues of the party or its candidates, and to arouse enthusiasm. Also **key·note speech.**

key punch, n. A keyboard-activated machine which, by systematically punching holes in cards, codes information for use in data processing.

key sig·na·ture, n. Mus. The sharps or flats which follow the clef sign and denote the key.

key·stone, kē′stōn, n. The stone at the apex of an arch which locks the whole; a part of something on which the other parts depend.

khak·i, kak′ē, kä′kē, n. pl., **-is**. A stout, twilled cloth of a yellowish-brown color, much used for military uniforms; a dull yellowish-brown color; often pl., clothing, esp. a military uniform, made of khaki.—a. Dull yellowish-brown.

kha·lif, kə·lēf′, kā′lif, kal′if, n. Caliph.

khan, kän, kan, n. The title held by descendants of Genghis Khan, the Mongol conqueror; a term of respect for officials or dignitaries in parts of central Asia.

kib·butz, ki·bûts′, ki·boots′, n. pl., **kib·but·zim**, ki·bût·sēm′. An Israeli collective farm or settlement.

kib·itz·er, kib′it·sər, n. Informal. One who gives unwanted advice, esp. such a person looking on at a card game. —**kib·itz**, v.i.

ki·bosh, kī′bosh, ki·bosh′, n. Informal. That which squelches or stops: to put the kibosh on.

kick, kik, v.t. To give a blow to with the foot; to drive or force by a kick; to score by a kick, as in football.—v.i. To strike out with the foot; to have the habit of striking out; to recoil, as a firearm when fired; in football, to punt, or try for an extra point or field goal. Informal. To object or complain.—n. An act of kicking; a recoil, as of a gun. Informal. An objection or complaint; a stimulating or intoxicating quality; a thrill or exciting sensation; energy; pep; pl., fun; thrills. —**kick in**, Informal. Pay one's share; to contribute, esp. money; to die. —**kick off**, to start play by kicking the football. Informal. To begin; to remove or dismiss. —**kick out**, Informal. To oust, or dismiss forcefully. —**kick the buck·et**, Informal. To die. —**kick up**, to cause to rise. Informal. To provoke (trouble, confusion, etc.); to give evidence, as by pain, of malfunction. —**kick·er**, n.

kick·back, kik′bak, n. Informal. The return of a portion of a commission or payment; a sudden recoil or reaction.

kick·off, kik′ôf, kik′of, n. Kicking the ball to begin play in football; any beginning.

kid, kid, n. A young goat, or its flesh; the skin of a young goat, or leather made from it; pl., gloves or shoes of this leather. Informal. A child or young person. —**kid·dish**, a. —**kid·dish·ness**, n.

kid, kid, v.t., v.i., **kid·ded, kid·ding**. Informal. Tease, jest with, or banter; to deceive or fool; to make goodnatured fun of. —**kid·der**, n.

kid·nap, kid′nap, v.t., **-naped** or **-napped**, **-nap·ing** or **-nap·ping**. To seize and forcibly carry a person away, usu. for ransom. —**kid·nap·er, kid·nap·per**, n.

kid·ney, kid′nē, n. pl., **-neys**. In humans, either of a pair of organs in the back part of the abdominal cavity, which excrete urine; a similar organ in other animals, used as food by humans; constitution, temperament, or type.

kid·ney bean, n. The common bean plant, or its kidney-shaped seed.

kill, kil, v.t. To deprive of life in any manner; cause the death of; slaughter; to destroy; put an end to; defeat or veto; to cancel or delete; to destroy or neutralize the active qualities of; to bring to a stop; spoil the effect of; to while away, as time. Informal. To overcome completely; to consume totally.—v.i. To inflict or cause death; to commit murder.—n. The act of killing; an animal killed. —**kill·er**, n.

kill, kil, n. A creek; a stream.

kill·deer, kil′dēr, n. pl., **-deers** or **-deer**. A common N. American bird of the plover family, noted for its piercing cry. Also **kill·dee.**

kill·ing, kil′ing, n. The act of one who or that which kills; a slaying. Informal. An unusually large profit.—a. Deadly; fatal; overpowering. Informal. Irresistibly amusing.

kill-joy, kil′joy, n. A person who spoils the joy or enjoyment of others.

kiln, kil, kiln, n. A type of oven used to bake, dry, or burn bricks, pottery, etc.

kil·o, kil′lō, kil′ō, n. pl., **kil·os**. A kilogram; a kilometer.

kil·o·cy·cle, kil′ə·sī·kəl, n. A thousand cycles; a thousand cycles per second.

kil·o·gram, kil·o·gramme, kil′ə·gram, n. A measure of mass and weight, equaling 1000 grams or 2.2046 pounds avoirdupois.

kil·o·me·ter, Brit. **kil·o·me·tre**, kil′ə·mē·tər, ki·lom′ə·tər, n. A measure of distance, equaling 1000 meters or .6214 mile.

kil·o·ton, kil′ə·tən, n. A thousand tons; the explosive force of a thousand tons of TNT.

kil·o·watt, kil′ə·wot, n. A unit of electric power equiv-

---

a- hat, fāte, fāre, fäther; **e-** met, mē; **i-** pin, pīne; **o-** not, nōte, ôrb, moove (move), boy, pownd;
u- cūbe, bûll, tûk (took); **ch-** chin; **th-** thick, ŧhen; **zh-** vizhon (vision); **ə-** əgo, takən, pencəl, lemən, bərd (bird).

alent to 1000 watts.

kil·o·watt-hour, kil'ə·wot·owr', *n.* A unit of energy equivalent to the power of one kilowatt working for one hour.

kilt, kilt, *n.* A knee-length pleated skirt, regarded as the national dress of the Scottish Highlander.

kilt·er, kil'tər, *n. Informal.* Good condition; order: to be out of *kilter.*

ki·mo·no, kə·mō'nə, kə·mō'nō, *n.* A loose, robelike garment with wide sleeves and a sash, worn by both Japanese men and women; a woman's dressing gown.

kin, kin, *n.* Relatives collectively; clan; kindred; a relative—*a.* Related; similar. —**next of kin,** one's nearest relative or relatives.

kind, kind, *n.* The nature or determining character; a particular variety or sort. —**in kind,** in the particular or equivalent kind of thing; in goods or produce rather than money. —**kind of,** *Informal.* After a fashion; to some extent; somewhat. —**of a kind,** of the same kind; alike; mediocre or inferior.

kind, kind, *a.* Of a good or benevolent nature or disposition; proceeding from a good-natured readiness to benefit or please others; beneficent; helpful; friendly; considerate; cordial. —**kind·ness,** *n.*

kin·der·gar·ten, kin'dər·gär·tən, *n.* A school or class for young children, usu. between 4 and 6 years old.

kind·heart·ed, kind'här'tid, *a.* Having or showing a kind nature; kindly. —**kind·heart·ed·ness,** *n.*

kin·dle, kin'dəl, *v.t.,* **-dled, -dling.** To set on fire; to light; to rouse or excite, as the passions.—*v.i.* To take fire; to begin burning; to become aglow; to be roused or excited.

kin·dling, kind'ling, *n.* Materials for lighting a fire, as sticks of dry wood.

kind·ly, kind'lē, *adv.* Obligingly; cordially; heartily. —*a.,* **-li·er, -li·est.** Of a kind disposition; sympathetic; congenial; benevolent. —**kind·li·ness,** *n.*

kin·dred, kin'drid, *n.* Relatives by blood, sometimes by marriage; affinity.—*a.* Allied by blood; related; similar.

kin·e·mat·ics, kin·ə·mat'iks, *n. pl. but sing. in constr.* The branch of physics which deals with motion, without reference to the forces producing it. —**kin·e·mat·ic, kin·e·mat·i·cal,** *a.*

kin·e·scope, kin'i·skōp, *n.* A recording on film made from a television program.

ki·net·ic, ki·net'ik, kī·net'ik, *a.* Referring to motion; produced by motion.

ki·net·ics, ki·net'iks, kī·net'iks, *n. pl. but sing. in constr.* The branch of physics which treats of forces causing or changing the motion of masses.

kin·folk, kin'fōk, *n. pl.* Family; relatives; kinsfolk. Also **kin·folks.**

king, king, *n.* The male sovereign of a nation; a monarch; a ruler; one preeminent in his field; a playing card having the picture of a king; the chief piece in the game of chess; a crowned piece in the game of checkers. —**king·ship,** *n.*

king·bird, king'bərd, *n.* Any of various birds of the flycatcher family.

king·bolt, king'bōlt, *n.* A vertical bolt connecting the body of a vehicle with the fore axle, or the body of a railroad car with a truck.

king crab, *n.* The horseshoe crab.

king·dom, king'dəm, *n.* The territory or country subject to a king or queen; domain or realm in a figurative sense; one of the three extensive divisions into which natural objects are classified: the animal, plant, and mineral *kingdoms.*

king·fish, king'fish, *n. pl.,* **-fish** or **-fish·es.** Any of several large American food fishes. *Informal.* One whose leadership or power is unquestioned.

king·fish·er, king'fish·ər, *n.* Any of various usu. crested, bright-colored birds, found worldwide, and feeding on fish and insects.

king·ly, king'lē, *a.,* **-li·er, -li·est.** Belonging or pertaining to a king or kings; royal; monarchical; befitting a king; august; splendid.—*adv.* In a kingly way. —**king·li·ness,** *n.*

king·pin, king'pin, *n.* In bowling, the front or center pin; a kingbolt. *Informal.* The leader or chief person.

king post, *n.* A vertical post between the apex of a triangular roof truss and the tie beam.

King's Eng·lish, *n.* Standard, pure, or correct English. Also **Queen's Eng·lish.**

king's e·vil, *n.* Scrofula.

king-size, king'sīz, *a.* Larger or longer than standard size; exceptionally large. Also **king-sized.**

king snake, *n.* Any of certain large, non-poisonous snakes, found in the southern U.S., that feed on rodents.

kink, kingk, *n.* A twist or tight curl, as in a hair, rope, or thread; a mental whim or quirk; a crotchet; a muscular cramp or spasm; crick.—*v.t.* To cause a kink in.—*v.i.* To form into a kink. —**kink·y,** *a.,* **-i·er, -i·est.**

kins·folk, kinz'fōk, *n. pl.* Kinfolk.

kin·ship, kin'ship, *n.* Relationship; common blood; familial bond.

kins·man, kinz'mən, *n. pl.,* **-men.** A male relative. —**kins·wom·an,** kinz'wûm·ən, *n.*

ki·osk, kē·osk', kē'osk, *n.* A kind of open pavilion or small structure often used as a bandstand or a newsstand.

kip, kip, *n.* The hide of a young or small beast.

kip·per, kip'ər, *n.* A herring or salmon which has been kippered; a male salmon or sea trout during or after the spawning season.—*v.t.* Of fish, to cure by splitting open, cleaning, salting, and smoking or drying.

kirk, kərk, *n. Scot.* A church.

kir·mess, kər'mis, *n.* Kermis.

kis·met, kiz'mit, kis'mit, *n.* Fate; destiny.

kiss, kis, *v.t., v.i.,* To touch with the lips in salutation or as a mark of affection; to make light contact.—*n.* A touch or caress with the lips; a gentle touching or meeting; a kind of confection, usu. bite-size. —**kiss·a·ble,** *a.*

kiss·er, kis'ər, *n.* One who kisses. *Informal.* The face, esp. the mouth.

kit, kit, *n.* A set or collection of tools, supplies, or other objects for a special purpose; the case, bag, box, etc., which contains these objects; a collection of parts to be assembled; equipment for traveling, as by a soldier or hiker.

kitch·en, kich'ən, *n.* A room or place set apart for cooking; the culinary department.

kitch·en·ette, kich·ə·net', *n.* A small area functioning as a kitchen; any small kitchen.

kitch·en po·lice, *n. pl.* Soldiers assigned to assist the cooks of a military unit.

kitch·en·ware, kich'ən·wâr, *n.* Pots, pans, dishes, and other kitchen utensils.

kite, kīt, *n.* A light frame covered with paper or cloth, constructed to fly in the wind at the end of a long string; a hawk with long, pointed wings; any of the highest and lightest sails of a ship; a negotiable paper not representing a genuine transaction, used to obtain money, sustain credit, etc.—*v.i.,* **kit·ed, kit·ing.** To fly like a kite; to obtain money or credit by a kite.—*v.t.* To cause to soar; to use (a kite) to gain money or credit.

kith, kith, *n. Archaic.* Acquaintances or friends collectively.—**kith and kin,** friends and relatives, now usu. only relatives.

kitsch, kich, *n.* Pretentious, crude, mawkish, or gaudy literature or art, intended to appeal to a mass market.

kit·ten, kit'ən, *n.* A young cat.

kit·ten·ish, kit'ə·nish, *a.* Like a kitten; coyly playful. —**kit·ten·ish·ly,** *adv.*

kit·ty, kit'ē, *n. pl.,* **-ties.** An accumulation, usu. small, of money or objects; in card games, a fund into which the players put money for a specific purpose; the stakes.

kit·ty, kit'ē, *n. pl.,* **-ties.** A kitten; a name for a pet cat.

kit·ty-cor·ner, kit'ē·kôr·nər, *a., adv.* Catty-corner.

ki·wi, kē′wē, *n.* The apteryx.

klatch, klatsch, klach, kläch, *n.* An informal social gathering: a coffee *klatch.*

Kleen·ex, klē′neks, *n. Trademark.* A soft paper used as a handkerchief or cleansing tissue.

klep·to·ma·ni·a,   klep·tə·mā′nē·ə,   klep·tə· mān′yə, *n.* A neurotic compulsion to steal, esp. without economic motive. **—klep·to·ma·ni·ac,** *n.*

klieg light, klēg, *n.* A very bright arc lamp used in floodlighting motion picture studios.

knack, nak, *n.* An ability or aptitude; adroitness or dexterity.

knap·sack, nap′sak, *n.* A bag of leather or strong cloth strapped to the back of travelers, used for holding supplies.

knave, nāv, *n.* A rogue; a dishonest or tricky person; the jack in a pack of playing cards. **—knav·er·y,** *n.* **—knav·ish,** *a.* **—knav·ish·ly,** *adv.*

knead, nēd, *v.t.* To work into a mass with pressing and folding movements of the hands; to massage; to make by kneading.

knee, nē, *n.* The joint in man between the thigh and the lower part of the leg; the corresponding joint or region of other vertebrates; something resembling this joint, esp. when bent; the part of a garment covering the knee.—*v.t.,* **kneed, knee·ing.** To strike or touch with the knee.

knee·cap, nē′kap, *n.* The movable bone covering the knee joint in front; the patella.

knee-deep, nē′dēp′, *a.* Deep enough to reach the knees; deeply involved.

kneel, nēl, *v.i.,* **knelt** or **kneeled, kneel·ing.** To genuflect; to fall on the knees; to rest on the knees. **—kneel·er,** *n.*

knee·pan, nē′pan, *n.* The kneecap or patella.

knell, nel, *n.* The sound of a bell rung slowly at a funeral; a bell announcing death or extinction; a doleful sound.—*v.i.* To sound in order to announce a death, disaster, etc.; to sound as an omen or warning. —*v.t.* To summon or proclaim by a knell.

knick·ers, nik′ərz, *n. pl.* Loose breeches reaching just below the knee, where they are gathered in. Also **knick·er·bock·ers,** nik′ər·bok·ərz.

knick·knack, nik′nak, *n.* A trifle or toy; a trinket.

knife, nīf, *n. pl.,* **knives.** A cutting instrument consisting of a thin blade, usu. with a sharp edge, attached to a handle; a knifelike weapon; a blade for cutting, as in a tool or machine.—*v.t.,* **knifed, knif·ing.** To apply a knife to; cut or stab with a knife. *Informal.* To strike at secretly; try to defeat in an underhand way. **—knife·like,** *a.*

knight, nīt, *n.* In the Middle Ages, a man admitted to an honorable military rank after service as page and squire. *Brit.* One holding a nonhereditary dignity conferred by the sovereign and conveying the title *Sir.* A chivalrous person; a champion. A chess piece, usu. the figure of a horse's head.—*v.t.* To dub a knight. **—knight·hood,** *n.* **—knight·ly,** *a., adv.*

knight-er·rant, nīt′er′ənt, *n. pl.,* **knights-er·rant.** In the Middle Ages, a knight who traveled in search of adventures to exhibit his prowess.

knight-er·rant·ry, nīt′er′ən·trē, *n.* The role, character, or practice of a knight-errant; quixotic behavior.

knit, nit, *v.t.,* **knit·ted** or **knit, knit·ting.** To weave or form by looping or knotting a continuous thread by means of needles; to tie together; to join closely; to cause to grow together; to contract into folds or wrinkles, as the brow.—*v.i.* To make a fabric by interlooping yarn or thread by means of needles; to grow together, as broken bones; to become contracted into folds or wrinkles.—*n.* A knitted fabric. **—knit·ter,** *n.* **—knit·ting,** *n.*

knives, nīvz, *n.* Plural of **knife.**

knob, nob, *n.* A rounded protuberance; a rounded handle, as for a door; a domelike mountain or hill. **—knobbed,** *a.* **—knob·by,** *a.,* **-bi·er, -bi·est.**

knock, nok, *v.i.* To strike a blow with the fist, knuckles, or anything hard; to rap; to strike in collision; to make a noise as of striking or pounding.—*v.t.* To give a forcible blow to; hit, strike, or beat; to drive or force by a blow or blows; to strike together; bring into collision. *Informal.* To criticize; disparage.—*n.* The act or the sound of knocking; a rap; a blow or thump. **—knock down,** to take apart; to sell to the highest bidder. *Informal.* To earn; to strike down. **—knock off.** *Informal.* To stop work; to deduct; to do routinely or rapidly; to defeat; to kill. **—knock out,** to render helpless or unconscious, esp. by punching. *Informal.* To exhaust or overwork. **—knock together,** to make or build hastily or crudely. **—knock up.** *Informal.* To make pregnant; to abuse, damage, or hurt.

knock·a·bout, nok′ə·bowt, *a.* Rough, boisterous, noisy; suitable for rough use.—*n.* An aimless wanderer; a small, easily handled yacht with a jib and mainsail but no bowsprit.

knock·down, nok′down, *n.* A striking down or felling; something constructed to be assembled or disassembled easily.

knock·er, nok′ər, *n.* One that knocks; a contrivance fastened to a door to use for knocking.

knock-knee, nok′nē, *n.* Inward curvature of the legs, causing the knees to knock together in walking. **—knock-kneed,** *a.*

knock·out, nok′owt, *n.* The act of knocking out or state of being knocked out; a kayo; blow that knocks someone out. *Informal.* An unusually attractive or striking person or thing, esp. a woman.—*a.*

knoll, nōl, *n.* A small, round hill; mound.

knot, not, *n.* The intertwining of a flexible material, such as rope, to form a knob which fastens or binds; the resulting lump; a bow, usu. of ribbon, for ornamentation; an assemblage of people or objects; a difficult or perplexing situation or problem; a bond or connection, as in marriage; a lump occurring in a tissue; a node or swelling on the stem of a plant; the location on a tree in which a branch grows from the trunk; this section seen in lumber; a unit of speed used on ships: a nautical mile or hourly nautical mile.—*v.t.,* **knot·ted, knot·ting.** To tie in a knot; to form a knot on; to entangle; to unite closely.—*v.i.* To become knotted; to form knots. **—knot·less,** *a.* **—knot·like,** *a.* **—knot·ted,** *a.* **—knot·ty,** *a.*

knot·hole, not′hōl, *n.* A hole in a board, formed by the falling out of a knot.

knout, nowt, *n.* A whip used formerly in Russia to punish criminals.—*v.t.* To flog with the knout.

know, nō, *v.t.,* **knew, known, know·ing.** To understand as fact or truth, or apprehend with clearness and certainty; to have fixed in the mind or memory; to be aware of; be familiar or conversant with; to be skilled in or experienced with; to be acquainted with; to recognize; to be able to distinguish or differentiate.— *v.i.* To have knowledge, or clear and certain perception; to be cognizant or aware; to have information. **—in the know.** *Informal.* Having inside or confidential information. **—know·a·ble,** *a.* **—know·er,** *n.*

know-how, nō′how, *n. Informal.* Ability or experience to do something; technical skill.

know·ing, nō′ing, *a.* Sagacious; astute; suggesting possession of inside information or secret knowledge: a *knowing* expression; conscious; intentional. **—know·ing·ly,** *adv.*

knowl·edge, nol′ij, *n.* Acquaintance with facts, truths, or principles, as from study or investigation; familiarity or conversance; erudition; acquaintance with a thing, place, person; the fact or state of knowing; cognition; clear and certain mental apprehension; range of cognizance; practical understanding of

---

a- hat, fāte, fāre, fäther; **e-** met, mē; **i-** pin, pīne; **o-** not, nōte, ôrb, moove (move), boy, pownd; **u-** cūbe, bûll, tûk (took); **ch-** chin; **th-** thick, +hen; **zh-** vizhon (vision); **ə-** əgo, takən, pencəl, lemən, bərd (bird).

an art or skill; the sum of what is known or may be known.

knowl·edge·a·ble, nol/ə·jə·bəl, *a.* Well-informed; intelligent.

know-noth·ing, nō/nəth·ing, *n.* An ignorant person.

knuck·le, nək/əl, *n.* A joint of a finger, esp. one of the joints at the roots of the fingers; the rounded prominence of such a joint when the finger is bent; a knee or hockjoint of a pig, calf, etc., used as food.—*v.t.* To strike, tap, or touch with the knuckles.—*v.i.* To hold the knuckles on the ground in playing marbles. —**knuck·le down,** to apply oneself vigorously or earnestly. —**knuck·le un·der,** to yield or submit. —**knuck·ly,** *a.*

knurl, nərl, *n.* A knob or protuberance; a ridge, usu. small and one of a series, on the edge of a thumbscrew, coin, etc. —**knurled,** *a.* —**knurl·y,** *a.*

KO or **K.O.** or **k.o.,** *n.* Knockout (in boxing). —*v.t.,* **KO'd, KO'ing.**

ko·a·la, kō·ä/lə, *n.* A marsupial animal of Australia, with gray fur and no tail.

Ko·dak, kō/dak, *n. Trademark.* A small portable camera.

kohl·ra·bi, kōl·rä/bē, kōl/rä·bē, *n. pl.,* **-bies.** A variety of cabbage with an enlarged, turnip-shaped, edible stem.

ko·la, kō/lə, *n.* The kola nut; the tree producing this nut; an extract from the nut. Also **co·la.**

ko·la nut, *n.* The bitter brownish nut or seed of a tropical tree, used as a stimulant and tonic.

ko·lin·sky, kə·lin/skē, *n. pl.,* **-skies.** Any of various Asian minks; their fur.

kook, kook, *n. Informal.* A very odd person; a crazy person. —**kook·y,** *a.,* **-i·er, -i·est.**

Ko·ran, kō·rän/, kō·ran/, *n.* The sacred book of the Moslems, containing the professed revelations of Allah to Mohammed.

ko·sher, kō/shər, *a.* Right, lawful, or clean according to Jewish laws. *Informal.* Proper; authentic.—*v.t.* To make kosher. —**Kosher** food.

kou·mis, koo/mis, *n.* Kumiss.

kow·tow, kow/tow/, *v.i.* To kneel, bend, and touch the ground with the forehead as an act of submission or reverence; to act in a servile manner.—*n.* The performance of kowtowing.

K ra·tion, *n.* An emergency package of food rations developed during W.W. II.

Krem·lin, krem/lin, *n.* The Soviet government; the citadel of Moscow, including within its walls the chief office of the government of the Soviet Union.

Krish·na, krish/nə, *n.* A widely worshiped Hindu god, an incarnation of Vishnu.

Kriss Krin·gle, kris/ kring/gəl, *n.* Santa Claus.

kryp·ton, krip/ton, *n.* A rare inert gaseous element.

ku·dos, koo/dos, kū/dos, *n. pl. but sing. in constr.* Glory; renown; recognition.

ku·miss, koo/mis, *n.* Fermented mare's or camel's milk used as a beverage by Asiatic nomads.

küm·mel, kim/əl, *n.* A liqueur flavored principally with caraway seeds.

kum·quat, kəm/kwot, *n.* A round to oblong, yellow-orange citrus fruit with an acid pulp and a sweet rind used for preserves; the tree bearing this fruit.

L

L, l, el, *n.* The twelfth letter of the English alphabet; the Roman numeral for 50.

la, lä, *n. Mus.* The syllable used for the sixth tone of a major scale.

la, lä, *interj.* An expression of surprise.

lab, lab, *n. Informal.* A laboratory.

la·bel, lā/bəl, *n.* A slip of paper or other printed material which is affixed to an object to indicate its owner, contents, or nature; a word or phrase used to identify or describe persons or ideas; a trademark or brand.—*v.t.,* **-beled, -bel·ing.** To attach a label to; to identify, describe, or classify. —**la·bel·er,** *n.*

la·bi·al, lā/bē·əl, *a.* Pertaining to the lips; of a labium; formed chiefly by the lips, as *b, m, p,* or *ō* and *oo.*—*n.* Any labial sound. —**la·bi·al·ly,** *adv.*

la·bi·ate, lā/bē·āt, *a.* Having a labium or labia; lipped.

la·bi·o·den·tal, lā·bē·ō·den/təl, *a.* Produced by touching the lower lip to the upper teeth, as the *f* or *v* sounds.—*n.* A sound formed in this manner.

la·bi·um, lā/bē·əm, *n. pl.,* **la·bi·a.** A lip or liplike part; any of the outer or inner folds of the vulva.

la·bor, *Brit.* **la·bour,** lā/bər, *n.* Persistent exertion of body or mind; work, esp. physical or manual work, skilled or unskilled, and usu. done for an employer for wages; those engaged in such work, esp. those organized into labor unions; a task done or to be done; the product of toil; the process of childbirth.—*v.i.* To perform labor; work; toil; to move with effort or difficulty; to be burdened, troubled, or distressed; to be in childbirth.—*v.t.* To elaborate laboriously or tediously. —**la·bor·er,** *n.*

lab·o·ra·to·ry, lab/rə·tôr·ē, lab/rə·tōr·ē, *n. pl.,* **-ries.** A building or room equipped for scientific or technical investigation or experimentation; a work-

shop; a place where chemicals or medicines are prepared.

La·bor Day, *n.* In most parts of the U.S. and Canada, the first Monday in September, observed as a legal holiday to honor labor.

la·bored, lā/bərd, *a.* Produced with labor; heavy; forced; constrained; too elaborate.

la·bo·ri·ous, lə·bôr/ē·əs, *a.* Requiring labor; toilsome; not easy; diligent; industrious. —**la·bo·ri·ous·ly,** *adv.* —**la·bo·ri·ous·ness,** *n.*

la·bor-sav·ing, lā/bər·sā·ving, *a.* Adapted to supersede or diminish manual labor.

la·bor un·ion, *n.* A trade union; an organization of wage earners designed to advance the economic interests and general working conditions of its members.

la·bur·num, lə·bər/nəm, *n.* An ornamental small tree, noted for its hanging clusters of yellow flowers.

lab·y·rinth, lab/ə·rinth, *n.* A place with intricate winding passages; a maze; a bewildering arrangement of things or circumstances. —**lab·y·rin·thine,** lab·ə·rin/thin, lab·ə·rin/thēn, *a.* —**lab·y·rin·thi·an,** *a.*

lac, lak, *n.* A resinous substance deposited on trees by an insect of southern Asia, and used as a basis for shellac and varnish.

lace, lās, *n.* A string or cord used for fastening boots, shoes, or a garment; a delicate kind of network or fabric, often in an ornamental pattern; a braid for ornamenting uniforms or hats.—*v.t.* To fasten with lace or string through eyelet holes or hooks; to constrict by drawing laces tightly; to intertwine; to adorn with lace; to add liquor to, as to another liquid; to streak with color. *Informal.* To strike or beat.—*v.i.* To be fastened by a lace. —**laced,** *a.* —**lace·like,** *a.*

—**lac·er**, *n.* —**lac·y**, *a.*

lac·er·ate, las′ə·rāt, *v.t.,* **-at·ed, -at·ing.** To tear; to rend; to make a ragged wound in; to torture; to harrow.—*a.* Rent; torn; tortured; having the appearance of being torn, as a leaf. —**lac·er·a·tion**, las·ə·rā′shən, *n.*

lace·wing, lās′wing, *n.* Any of various insects with four lacelike wings.

lach·es, lach′iz, *n.* Negligence or inexcusable delay in carrying out a duty or claiming a legal right.

lach·ry·mal, lac·ri·mal, lak′rə·məl, *a.* Pertaining to or characterized by tears; of, relating to, or near those organs which produce tears.—*n. pl.* The organs which secrete tears. Also **lach·ry·mal glands.**

lach·ry·mose, lak′rə·mōs, *a.* Given to crying; tearful; tending to provoke tears; mournful. —**lach·ry·mose·ly**, *adv.*

lac·ing, lā′sing, *n.* The act of fastening with a lace; a cord or lace used in drawing tight or fastening together, as in a shoe; a braid or trimming, often of silver or gold. *Informal.* A beating or flogging.

lack, lak, *n.* A deficiency or absence of something necessary, desirable, or customary; that which is wanted or needed.—*v.t.* To be deficient in; to fall short in respect to.—*v.i.* To be absent or deficient. —**lack·ing**, *a., prep.*

lack·a·dai·si·cal, lak·ə·dā′zi·kəl, *a.* Listless; lethargic; lacking in vigor or zest. —**lack·a·dai·si·cal·ly**, *adv.*

lack·ey, lak′ē, *n.* An attending male servant; a footman; any servile follower.—*v.t., v.i.,* **-eyed, -ey·ing.** To act as a lackey; to attend servilely. Also **lac·quey.**

lack·lus·ter, *Brit.* **lack·lus·tre**, lak′ləs·tər, *a.* Without luster, brightness, or vitality; dull.—*n.* Lack of luster.

la·con·ic, lə·kon′ik, *a.* Brief; terse; concise. —**la·con·i·cal·ly**, *adv.*

lac·quer, lak′ər, *n.* A varnish consisting of resins dissolved in a volatile solvent, and used as a protective or decorative coating; a natural varnish from an Asiatic tree, producing a hard, glossy finish, esp. on wood; an article coated with lacquer.—*v.t.* To coat with or as with lacquer. —**lac·quer·er**, *n.*

la·crosse, lə·krôs′, lə·kros′, *n.* A game of North American Indian origin, played with two ten-man teams, each of which tries to advance downfield and score by throwing a small ball into the opponent's goal with a long-handled racket.

lac·tate, lak′tāt, *n.* A salt of lactic acid.—*v.i.,* **-tat·ed, -tat·ing.** To produce or secrete milk.

lac·ta·tion, lak·tā′shən, *n.* In mammals, the production of milk; the time period of milk production; the act of suckling young.

lac·te·al, lak′tē·əl, *a.* Relating to or resembling milk; milky.

lac·tic, lak′tik, *a.* Of or from milk.

lac·tic ac·id, *n.* A syruplike acid, which is present naturally in sour milk.

lac·tose, lak′tōs, *n.* A white, odorless sugar obtained from milk.

la·cu·na, lə·kū′nə, *n. pl.,* **-nas, -nae,** -nē. A gap or hiatus, as in a manuscript; a pit or cavity; one of the numerous minute cavities in the substance of bone.

lad, lad, *n.* A young man or boy; a familiar term applied to any male; fellow; comrade.

lad·der, lad′ər, *n.* A frame of wood, metal, rope, etc., consisting of two long sidepieces connected by crosspieces forming steps for climbing and descending; a means of rising; a series of gradations.

lad·die, lad′ē, *n. Chiefly Sc.* Lad.

lade, lād, *v.t.,* **lad·ed, lad·en** or **lad·ed, lad·ing.** To load, as with a burden or cargo; burden; to lift out or dip, as with a ladle.—*v.i.* To take on cargo; to lade a liquid.

lad·en, lād′ən, *a.* Loaded, weighed down; burdened or oppressed.—*v.t.* To lade.

la·di·da, lä′dē·dä′, *a. Informal.* Affectedly genteel or refined; foppish; pretentious.

la·dies' man, la·dy's man, lā′dēz, *n.* A man who is very fond of or attentive to women.

lad·ing, lā′ding, *n.* The act of one who or that which lades; a load; cargo.

la·dle, lād′əl, *n.* A long-handled utensil with a cuplike bowl for dipping out liquids.—*v.t.,* **la·dled, la·dling.** To dip or convey with or as with a ladle.

la·dy, lā′dē, *n.* A woman of good family or social position, or of good breeding or refinement; a polite term for any woman; the mistress of a household; a woman who is the object of chivalrous devotion; a wife or consort; a noblewoman; (*cap.*) in Great Britain, a title given to women of certain ranks.

la·dy·bug, lā′dē·bəg, *n.* Any of various beneficial beetles, usu. brightly colored, which feed chiefly on plant lice. Also **la·dy bee·tle, la·dy·bird.**

la·dy·fin·ger, lā′dē·fing·gər, *n.* A small sponge cake shaped like a finger. Also **la·dys·fin·ger.**

la·dy·in·wait·ing, lā′dē·in·wā′ting, *n. pl.,* **la·dies-.** A lady who is in attendance upon a queen or princess.

la·dy·kil·ler, lā′dē·kil·ər, *n. Informal.* A man reputed to be very adept at fascinating or seducing women.

la·dy·like, lā′dē·līk, *a.* Like or befitting a lady.

la·dy·love, lā′dē·ləv, *n.* A lady who is loved; a mistress or sweetheart.

la·dy·ship, lā′dē·ship, *n.* The condition or rank of a lady; (*often cap.*) the form used in speaking of or to a woman having the title of *Lady,* used with *her* or *your.*

la·dy's-slip·per, lā′dēz·slip·ər, *n.* A species of orchid whose flower somewhat resembles a slipper. Also **la·dy-slip·per.**

lag, lag, *v.i.,* **lagged, lag·ging.** To fall behind; to hang back; to develop or move comparatively slowly.—*n.* A retardation or falling behind; the amount or interval of time of retardation.

la·ger, lä′gər, *n.* A beer that originated in Germany, which is aged after being brewed. Also **la·ger beer.**

lag·gard, lag′ərd, *a.* Lagging; backward; slow.—*n.* One who lags behind; a backward person; a loiterer.

la·gniappe, la·gnappe, lan·yap′, lan′yap, *n.* In Southern U.S., a small present given by a storekeeper to a customer; an extra; a dividend or tip.

la·goon, lə·goon′, *n.* A shallow body of water, such as a pond, inlet, or small lake, usu. connected with the sea, a lake, or a river; the water within a coral atoll. Also **la·gune.**

la·ic, lā′ik, *a.* Secular; lay. Also **la·i·cal.**—*n.* A layman. —**la·i·cal·ly**, *adv.*

laid, lād, Past tense and past participle of **lay.**

lain, lān, Past participle of **lie** (to be in a recumbent position).

lair, lâr, *n.* The resting place or den of a wild beast.

laird, lârd, *n. Sc.* A landowner or house proprietor.

lais·sez faire, lais·ser faire, les·ə·fer′, *n.* The policy of noninterference or minimal interference by government in industry and private enterprise; noninterference with personal freedom. —**lais·sez-faire**, *a.*

la·i·ty, lā′ə·tē, *n. pl.,* **-ties.** Lay persons collectively, as distinguished from the clergy; people outside of any profession as distinguished from those in it.

lake, lāk, *n.* A sizable inland body of water; a sizable body of any liquid.

lake, lāk, *n.* A red pigment prepared from lac or cochineal by combination with a metallic compound; a red or crimson color; any of various pigments prepared from organic coloring matters and metallic compounds.

lake dwell·ing, *n.* A dwelling, esp. of prehistoric times, built on piles in a lake.

lake trout, *n.* Any of various species of trout, esp. one

---

a- hat, fāte, fâre, fäther; **e-** met, mē; **i-** pin, pīne; **o-** not, nōte, ôrb, moove (move), boy, pownd;
u- cūbe, bŭll, tûk (took); **ch-** chin; **th-** thick, ᵺen; **zh-** vizhon (vision); **ə-** əgo, takən, pencəl, leмən, bərd (bird).

found in northern U.S. and Canadian lakes.

lam, lam, *v.t.,* **lammed, lam•ming.** *Informal.* To beat or thrash.—*v.i. Informal.* To run quickly; run off or away. —*n. Informal.* An escape, esp. from the police. —**on the lam,** running away.

la•ma, lä′mə, *n.* A Lamaist priest or monk.

La•ma•ism, lä′mə•iz•əm, *n.* A variety of Buddhism prevailing in Tibet and Mongolia. —**La•ma•ist,** *n.*

la•ma•ser•y, lä′mə•ser•ē, *n. pl.,* **-ser•ies.** A monastery of lamas.

lamb, lam, *n.* A young sheep, or the meat derived from it; an innocent or very meek person; a gullible person, esp. in financial matters.—*v.i.* To bear or give birth, as a ewe.

lam•baste, lam•bāst′, *v.t.,* **-bast•ed, -bast•ing.** *Informal.* To beat or thrash; to censure; castigate. Also **lam•bast.**

lam•bent, lam′bənt, *a.* Running or moving lightly over a surface, as a flame; playing lightly or brilliantly over a subject; softly bright, as light. —**lam•ben•cy,** *n.* —**lam•bent•ly,** *adv.*

lam•bre•quin, lam′brə•kin, lam′bər•kin, *n.* A protective scarf worn over the helmet in medieval times; a hanging or drapery covering the upper part of a door or window, or suspended from a shelf.

lamb•skin, lam′skin, *n.* The skin of a lamb, usu. dressed with the fleece on; leather made from a lamb's skin.

lame, lām, *a.,* **lam•er, lam•est.** Crippled or physically disabled, esp. in the legs or feet; impaired; sore; painful; unsound; weak.—*v.t.,* **lamed, lam•ing.** To make lame. —**lame•ly,** *adv.* —**lame•ness,** *n.*

la•mé, la•mā′, *n.* A fabric of metallic, esp. gold and silver, threads often interwoven with various other fibers.

lame duck, *n. Informal.* A political official serving out his term until the inauguration of his recently elected successor; a person who is weak or ineffectual.

la•mel•la, lə•mel′ə, *n. pl.,* **-mel•las, -mel•lae,** -mel′ē. A thin plate, scale, or layer, as in bone or in certain mollusk gills. —**la•mel•lar,** *a.* —**lam•el•late,** lam′ə•lāt, lə•mel′it, *a.*

la•ment, lə•ment′, *v.i.* To mourn; to express grief or sorrow; to regret deeply.—*v.t.* To mourn for; to regret; to deplore.—*n.* Lamentation; an elegy. —**lam•en•ta•ble,** lam′ən•tə•bəl, lə•men′tə•bəl, *a.* —**lam•en•ta•bly,** *adv.*

lam•en•ta•tion, lam•ən•tā′shən, *n.* The act of lamenting; a wailing; expression of sorrow.

lam•i•na, lam′ə•nə, *n. pl.,* **-nae,** -nē, **-nas.** A flat, thin plate, sheet, or scale; such a layer or coat lying over another. —**lam•i•nar,** *a.*

lam•i•nate, lam′ə•nāt, *v.t.,* **-nat•ed, -nat•ing.** To form, as metal or wood, into a lamina by compressing or rolling; to divide or separate into thin layers; to cover with laminae; to construct by placing layer upon layer.—*v.i.* To split into thin layers. —lam′ə•nāt, lam′ə•nit, *a.* Laminated; having laminae.—*n.* That which is laminated. —**lam•i•nat•ed,** *a.* —**lam•i•na•tion,** lam•ə•nā′shən, *n.*

lamp, lamp, *n.* A device, often decorative, used to hold light bulbs and direct their light; any contrivance providing light, as by electricity, gas, or inflammable liquid; an apparatus emitting radiation or heat.

lamp•black, lamp′blak, *n.* A fine, black soot of nearly pure carbon, formed by the condensation of the smoke of burning gas, oil, or pitch, and used for pigmentation in paints and printing inks.

lam•poon, lam•poon′, *n.* A keen, often abusive satire in prose, verse, or art which mocks an individual or situation.—*v.t.* To satirize in a lampoon.

lam•prey, lam′prē, *n. pl.,* **-preys.** An eellike animal with a suctorial mouth which preys on fresh- and salt-water fish.

lance, lans, läns, *n.* A long shaft with a sharp-pointed iron or steel head, used by mounted soldiers in a charge; a soldier armed with this weapon; lancer;

some similar weapon or implement; a lancet.—*v.t.,* **lanced, lanc•ing.** To pierce with or as with a lance; to make an incision in with a lancet. —**lance•like,** *a.*

lan•ce•o•late, lan′sē•ə•lāt, lan′sē•ə•lit, *a.* Shaped like the head of a lance; tapering, as certain leaves.

lanc•er, lan′sər, län′sər, *n.* A mounted soldier armed with a lance.

lan•cet, lan′sit, län′sit, *n.* A small surgical instrument, sharp-pointed and generally two-edged.

lance•wood, lans′wûd, läns′wûd, *n.* Any of several trees of the American tropics, esp. one which yields a tough, elastic wood used for archery bows, fishing rods, cabinet wood, etc.

land, land, *n.* The solid substance of the earth's surface, esp. the part not covered by water; ground or soil; rural countryside; a region or country; the people of a country; a realm or domain; landed property or real estate.—*v.t.* To set on or cause to go on land or shore; to bring down upon land or water, as an airplane; to bring into, or cause to arrive in, any place or situation; to pull, as a fish, out of water. *Informal.* To capture, gain, or win.—*v.i.* To come to land or shore, as a vessel; reach; go or come ashore from a ship or boat; to come down upon the surface, as an airplane; alight upon the ground; to come to some place or condition; end up.

lan•dau, lan′dô, lan′dow, *n.* A carriage having four wheels and a divided top, either part of which may be lowered; an automobile with a convertible top over the rear seat.

land•ed, lan′did, *a.* Having an estate in land; consisting of real estate or land.

land•fall, land′fôl, *n.* The first sighting of land on a journey by sea or air; the first land sighted or arrived at after a journey.

land grant, *n.* Public land granted by the government for some special purpose such as railroads, colleges, or roads.

land•hold•er, land′hōl•dər, *n.* A holder, owner, or proprietor of land.

land•ing, lan′ding, *n.* The act of coming ashore or settling on the ground; a place where persons or goods are landed, as from a ship or airplane; a platform between flights of stairs.

land•la•dy, land′lā•dē, *n. pl.,* **-dies.** A mistress of an inn or boarding house; a female landlord.

land•locked, land′lokt, *a.* Enclosed by land; living in water shut off from the sea: *landlocked* salmon.

land•lord, land′lôrd, *n.* The owner of land or of real estate, esp. one who has tenants; the proprietor of an inn or lodginghouse; innkeeper.

land•lub•ber, land′ləb•ər, *n.* A landsman, esp. one who is clumsy or inexperienced aboard a ship.

land•mark, land′märk, *n.* Any fixed, conspicuous object that distinguishes a locality, guides travelers or ships at sea, or defines the boundary of a territory; an event that marks an era; a turning point.

land of•fice, *n.* A government office in which the sales of public lands are recorded.

land-of•fice busi•ness. *Informal.* A very brisk, extensive, or lucrative business.

land•own•er, land′ō′nər, *n.* One who owns land. —**land•own•ing,** *n., a.* —**land•own•er•ship,** *n.*

land•scape, land′skāp, *n.* An extensive natural scene of land forms, viewed from one position; a picture representing such a scene; such pictures in general. —*v.t.* **-scaped, -scap•ing.** To design and develop by landscape gardening.—*v.i.* To work as a landscape gardener. —**land•scap•er,** *n.*

land•scape gar•den•er, *n.* One having special ability or training in the planning and ornamental planting of gardens, parks, and the like. —**land•scape gar•den•ing,** *n.*

land•slide, land′slid, *n.* The slipping or sliding of a considerable portion of soil or rock from a higher to a lower level; the material which slides or slips; a great majority of votes, or overwhelming victory, for a political candidate or party.

lands·man, landz′mən, lăndz′mən, *n. pl.,* **-men.** One who lives on the land; a compatriot; an inexperienced seaman.

land·ward, land′wərd, *a.* Lying, facing, or being in the direction of the land.—*adv.* Toward the land. Also **land·wards.**

lane, lān, *n.* A narrow way or passage between hedges, fences, walls, or houses; any narrow way; a portion of a highway which is intended for one line of vehicles; a fixed route pursued by ships or aircraft; in racing events, each of the parallel paths which mark the courses of competitors; one of the parallel paths in a bowling alley.

lang·syne, lang·zĭn′, lang·sĭn′, *n. Sc.* The time long ago.—*adv.*

lan·guage, lang′gwij, *n.* A system of communication between humans through written and vocal symbols; human speech; speech peculiar to an ethnic, national, or cultural group; words esp. employed in any art, branch of knowledge, or profession; a person's characteristic mode of speech; diction; linguistics; any means of communicating emotions or ideas; body *language,* dolphins' *language.*

lan·guid, lang′gwid, *a.* Flagging; drooping; weak; listless; sluggish; slow; without animation. **—lan·guid·ly,** *adv.*

lan·guish, lang′gwish, *v.i.* To be or become dull, feeble, or spiritless; to pine; to droop or fade; to be no longer vigorous in health; to live through a period of suffering and unhappy circumstances; to adopt a look of wistful tenderness. **—lan·guish·ing,** *a.* **—lan·guish·ing·ly,** *adv.*

lan·guor, lang′gər, *n.* Physical exhaustion or lassitude; feebleness; faintness; listlessness; lack of enthusiasm; apathy; a state of wistful tenderness or sentimental dreaminess. **—lan·guor·ous,** *a.* **—lan·guor·ous·ly,** *adv.*

lank, langk, *a.* Lean, tall, and bony; long and limp, as hair. **—lank·ness,** *n.*

lank·y, lang′kē, *a.,* **-i·er, -i·est.** Awkwardly thin and tall. **—lank·i·ness,** *n.*

lan·o·lin, lan′ə·lin, *n.* An oily or greasy substance obtained from wool, used esp. in ointments. Also **lan·o·line.**

lan·tern, lan′tərn, *n.* A usu. portable case which is transparent or translucent, for enclosing a light and protecting it from wind or rain; the chamber at the top of a lighthouse surrounding the light; an upright structure on a roof or dome to admit light or air, or for decoration.

lan·tern jaw, *n.* A long, thin, projecting lower jaw, in man. **—lan·tern-jawed,** lan′tərn·jôd, *a.*

lan·tha·num, lan′thə·nəm, *n.* A rare, shiny metallic element having a valence of three, and allied to aluminum.

lan·yard, lan·iard, lan′yərd, *n.* A short rope or line for securing or holding something, esp. rigging; a cord or string used for securing or holding objects around the neck or on the belt; a cord with a small hook at one end, used in firing certain kinds of cannon.

lap, lap, *n.* The front part from the waist to the knees when one is in a sitting position; the clothing over this part; an area of influence, responsibility, nurture, or power.

lap, lap, *v.t.,* **lapped, lap·ping.** To wrap or twist around; to enfold; to fold; to double over; to lay partly above; overlap; to cuddle.—*v.i.* To be spread or laid; to be turned over; to lie over something in part, as slates on a roof. *Sports.* To move ahead of someone by one or more laps in a race.—*n.* The portion of an object that lies over another; the folding over of a pliable material; one complete round on a racetrack. **—lap·per,** *n.*

lap, lap, *v.i., v.t.,* **lapped, lap·ping.** To take up liquid or food with the tongue; to feed or drink by lapping; to make a sound like lapping; splash gently.—*n.* The act or sound of lapping. **—lap·per,** *n.*

lap dog, *n.* A small pet dog such as may be held in the lap.

la·pel, lə·pel′, *n.* An outward fold of the front facings of a garment extending from the collar down over the chest.

lap·ful, lap′fûl, *n. pl.,* **lap·fuls, laps·ful.** As much as the lap can contain.

lap·i·dar·y, lap′i·der·ē, *n. pl.,* **-ies.** A craftsman who cuts, polishes, and engraves gems or precious stones.—*a.* Pertaining to the art of cutting, polishing, and engraving precious stones; inscribed on stone.

lap·in, lap′in, *Fr.* lä·pän′, *n.* A rabbit; the fur of a rabbit.

lap·is laz·u·li, lap′is laz′yə·lē, lap′is laz′yə·lī, *n.* A semiprecious stone of a rich blue color, used for jewelry, ornaments, and pigmentation.

lap·pet, lap′it, *n.* A little lap or flap; the lobe of the ear; the wattle of a bird.

lapse, laps, *n.* A slip or error, usu. trivial; an unnoticed passage of time; a slipping or gradual falling downward into disuse, ruin, decay, failure; apostasy; backsliding; a denial or failure due to neglect; forfeiture of a right or privilege, esp. through failure to exercise it within a stipulated time.—*v.i.,* **lapsed, laps·ing.** To err; to deviate from duty, moral integrity, or an established standard; to slip into decay or ruin; to slip gradually; to cease to exist; of time, to pass or elapse; to pass from one person to another through omission or negligence.

lar·board, lär′bōrd, *naut.* lär′bərd, *n. Naut.* Port: opposed to *starboard.*—*a.*

lar·ce·ny, lär′sə·nē, *n. pl.,* **-nies.** The unlawful seizure of any article or articles with the intention of depriving the legal owner; theft. **—lar·ce·nous,** *a.*

larch, lärch, *n.* Any of several deciduous, coniferous trees in the pine family; their wood.

lard, lärd, *n.* The fat of hogs after rendering.—*v.t.* To cover or dress with lard, as meat; to stuff with pieces of bacon, as in cooking fowl; to embellish, as literary works.

lar·der, lär′dər, *n.* A room for storing food; a pantry.

large, lärj, *a.,* **larg·er, larg·est.** Being of great size, extent, or capacity; great in quantity or number; big by comparison with like objects or operations; having wide range or broad scope.—*adv.* In a greater than usual size: to write *large.* **—at large,** without restraint; free; at liberty; fully; with all details; elected by the whole rather than by a part or subdivision. **—large·ness,** *n.*

large·ly, lärj′lē, *adv.* To a great extent; mainly; generally; in great quantity; extensively; much.

large-scale, lärj′skāl′, *a.* Of great size or extent; of great range; in accordance with a scale permitting much detail, as a map.

lar·gess, lar·gesse, lär·jes′, lär′jis, *n.* Charitable or generous giving; a present, gift, or donation given unselfishly.

lar·ghet·to, lär·get′ō, *a., adv. Mus.* Slow, but not as slow as largo.—*n. pl.,* **-tos.**

larg·ish, lärj′ish, *a.* Quite large.

lar·go, lär′gō, *a., adv. Mus.* Slow, with breadth and dignity.—*n. pl.,* **-gos.** A musical movement or passage having a slow tempo.

lar·i·at, lar′ē·ət, *n.* A lasso.

lark, lärk, *n.* Any of various European and Asian singing birds, esp. the skylark; any of various similar birds, as the meadowlark.

lark, lärk, *n.* Merriment; frolic; sport; prank.—*v.i.* To sport; frolic; behave impishly.

lark·spur, lärk′spər, *n.* Any of several annual, herba-

---

a- hat, fāte, fāre, fäther; **e-** met, mē; **i-** pin, pīne; **o-** not, nōte, ôrb, moove (move), boy, pownd; **u-** cūbe, bûll, tûk (took); **ch-** chin; **th-** thick, then; **zh-** vizhon (vision); **ə-** ago, takən, pencəl, lemən, bərd (bird).

ceous plants in the crowfoot family, cultivated for their clusters of blue, pink, or white flowers.

lar·rup, lar′əp, v.t. Informal. To whip or flog.—n. A whipping; a blow.

lar·va, lär′və, n. pl., **-vae,** -vē. The stage which follows the egg and precedes the pupa in the life cycle of an insect; a free-living or detached embryo, usu. strikingly different in appearance from the adult, as a tadpole. —**lar·val,** a.

lar·yn·gi·tis, lar·ən·ji′tis, n. An inflammation of the larynx.

lar·ynx, lar′ingks, n. pl., **lar·ynx·es** or **la·ryn·ges,** lə·rin′jēz. The cartilaginous structure at the upper end of the human trachea which contains and supports the vocal cords and associated structures; a corresponding structure in other vertebrates. —**la·ryn·ge·al,** lə·rin′jē·əl, a.

las·civ·i·ous, lə·siv′ē·əs, a. Lewd; lustful; exciting sensual emotions. —**las·civ·i·ous·ly,** adv. —**las·civ·i·ous·ness,** n.

la·ser, lā′zər, n. A device for amplifying light radiation, in which a beam of light is shot through a crystal causing the crystal to emit an intense, direct light beam.

lash, lash, n. The flexible end of a whip; a whip; a blow with a whip or anything flexible and tough; a sharp, cutting, or ridiculing remark; a violent impact against something, as of rain or wind; an eyelash.—v.t. To whip or beat; to goad or incite; to attack or ridicule severely in words; to strike forcefully against; to switch or flick suddenly.—v.i. To attack or strike with or as with a whip; to censure in sharp terms, followed by out; to wriggle or move suddenly or quickly. —**lash·ing,** n.

lash, lash, v.t. To tie or bind with chain, rope, cord, etc. —**lash·er,** n. —**lash·ing,** n.

lass, las, n. A young woman, usu. unmarried; a girl; a sweetheart.

las·sie, las′ē, n. A young girl; lass.

las·si·tude, las′i·tood, las′i·tūd, n. Weariness or weakness; listlessness.

las·so, las′ō, la·soo′, n. pl., **-sos** or **-soes.** A long rope, usu. woven of hemp or rawhide, with a running noose, used to catch cattle and horses; a lariat.—v.t. To catch with a lasso. —**las·so·er,** n.

last, last, läst, a. Happening or coming after all the others; final; latest; hindmost; remaining; next before the present; conclusive; utmost; extreme; most unlikely; least suitable.—adv. On the last occasion; at the time before the present; after all others; lastly; finally. —n. Someone or something that comes last; the concluding part. —**at last,** finally; after a long time. —**breathe one's last,** die.

last, last, läst, v.i. To continue in time; to endure; to remain in existence; to be sufficient in quantity; to continue unimpaired.

last, last, läst, n. A mold or form of the human foot, on which shoes are formed or repaired.—v.t. To form on or shape by a last.

last·ing, las′ting, lä′sting, a. Enduring; durable; permanent. —**last·ing·ly,** adv.

last·ly, last′lē, läst′lē, adv. Finally; in the last place.

Last Sup·per, n. The last meal shared by Christ and His disciples prior to His crucifixion.

last word, n. The final comment. Informal. Something conclusive or unimprovable; the most recent fashion or trend.

latch, lach, n. A device for securing a door or gate, usu. consisting of a bar which slips into a notch on a doorjamb or gate; any similar device.—v.i., v.t. To secure or fasten by means of a latch. —**latch on·to.** Informal. Get possession of.

latch·key, lach′kē, n. A key used to raise the latch of an outside door.

late, lāt, a., **lat·er** or **lat·ter,** **lat·est** or **last.** Coming or happening after the usual time; slow; tardy; long delayed; far advanced; deceased; departed; last or

recent, as in time or position.—adv. After the usual time, or the time appointed; after delay; not long ago; lately; at an advanced time. —**of late,** lately; recently. —**late·ness,** n.

la·teen sail, la·tēn′ sāl, n. Naut. A triangular sail extended by a long yard.

late·ly, lāt′lē, adv. Recently; not long ago.

la·tent, lāt′ənt, a. Not visible or apparent although present; not manifested; undeveloped or dormant. —**la·ten·cy,** n. —**la·tent·ly,** adv.

la·ter, lā′tər, a. More late. —adv. Late in a greater degree; subsequently; afterward.

lat·er·al, lat′ər·əl, a. Of or pertaining to the side; situated at, proceeding from, or directed toward a side.—n. A lateral part or extension. —**lat·er·al·ly,** adv.

la·tex, lā′teks, n. pl., **la·tex·es** or **lat·i·ces,** lat′i·sēz. A milky juice occurring in special cells of certain plants, as milkweed and plants yielding India rubber, which coagulates on exposure to the air and is the source of natural rubber; any of various thermoplastics produced by emulsion polymerization and used in paints, adhesives, etc.

lath, lath, läth, n. A thin narrow board or slip of wood nailed to the rafters of a building to support roofing material; such wood or other materials used to support plaster, tile, or the like; such materials collectively.—v.t. To cover or line with laths. —**lath·er,** n.

lathe, lāth, n. A machine for shaping wood, metal, or the like by rotating it rapidly against a fixed cutting tool.

lath·er, lath′ər, n. Foam made from water and soap or detergent foam formed in sweating.—v.t. To apply lather to. Informal. To beat or flog.—v.i. To form a lather; to become covered with lather, as a horse. —**lath·er·er,** n. —**lath·er·y,** a.

lath·ing, lath′ing, läth′ing, n. Lath materials; work of putting on lath materials. Also **lath·work.**

Lat·in, lat′ən, lat′in, n. The language of ancient Romans; a native of Latium, a country in ancient Italy; a member of any of the Latin peoples.—a. Referring to those peoples, as the Italians, French, and Spanish, or esp. the Latin Americans, using languages derived from that of ancient Rome; pertaining to the language of the ancient Romans, or its later forms.

Lat·in-A·mer·i·can, lat′ən·ə·mer′i·kən, a. Pertaining to the western hemisphere countries south of the U.S., in which languages derived from Latin are spoken. —**Lat·in A·mer·i·can,** n.

lat·i·tude, lat′ə·tood, lat′ə·tūd, n. The angular distance north or south of the equator measured in degrees; a place or region as marked by its latitude. Freedom from narrow restrictions; permitted freedom of choice or action. —**lat·i·tu·di·nal,** lat·i·tood′i·nəl, lat·ə·tūd′i·nəl, a.

lat·i·tu·di·nar·i·an, lat·ə·tood·i·ner′ē·an, lat·ə·tūd·i·ner′ē·ən, a. Permitting free thought or conduct, esp. in matters of religion.—n. A latitudinarian person.

la·trine, lə·trēn′, n. A public toilet, esp. in a military camp or barracks.

lat·ter, lat′ər, a. More recent; nearer the end; the second of two, as opposed to former.

lat·ter-day, lat′ər·dā′, a. Of a later time; of the present; modern. —**lat·ter·ly,** adv.

Lat·ter-day Saint, n. A Mormon.

lat·tice, lat′is, n. A structure of wood or metal made by crossing laths, rods, or bars, and forming open reticulated work, often in a diagonal pattern; a window or gate made of such laths or strips.—v.t., **-ticed, -tic·ing.** To give the form or appearance of a lattice to; to furnish with a lattice. —**lat·ticed,** a.

lat·tice·work, lat′is·wərk, n. Any lattice or work made of lattices.

laud, lôd, v.t. To praise; to extol; acclaim.—n. A song or hymn of praise. Pl., sing. or pl. in constr., Rom. Cath. Ch. A series of psalms of praise which, when recited with the matins, comprises the first in a series of seven canonical hours.

laud·a·ble, lô′də·bəl, *a.* Praiseworthy; commendable. **—laud·a·bly,** *adv.*

lau·da·num, lôd′ə·nəm, lôd′nəm, *n.* Tincture of opium.

laud·a·to·ry, lô′də·tôr·ē, *a.* Containing or expressing praise. Also **laud·a·tive.**

laugh, laf, läf, *v.i.* To express merriment, amusement, ridicule, nervousness, or the like, with a vocal outburst or chuckling noise and usu. with accompanying facial and bodily manifestations; to be merry, amused, or scornful.—*v.t.* To express by laughing.—*n.* The act or sound of laughing. *Informal.* Something laughable. **—have the last laugh,** to succeed after predicted or apparent defeat.**—laugh at,** to ridicule.**—laugh up one's sleeve,** to laugh to oneself or so as not to be observed.**—laugh off,** to dismiss, reject, or scorn by laughter. **—laugh·er,** *n.* **—laugh·ing·ly,** *adv.*

laugh·a·ble, laf′ə·bəl, *a.* Exciting laughter; comical; ludicrous. **—laugh·a·bly,** *adv.*

laugh·ing gas, laf′ing, *n.* Nitrous oxide.

laugh·ing jack·ass, *n.* An Australian bird, so named for its raucous, braying song.

laugh·ing stock, laf′ing·stok, lä′fing·stok, *n.* An object of ridicule; a butt for laughter or jokes.

laugh·ter, laf′tər, läf′tər, *n.* The act or sound of laughing.

launch, lônch, länch, *v.t.* To propel, drive, or move into the air or the water; to set afloat for the first time; to put into operation; initiate; to throw, as a lance.—*v.i.* To enter into a new field of activity; to rush headlong or plunge with enthusiasm, usu. followed by *into;* to set out or begin, usu. with *out* or *forth.*—*n.* The setting afloat of a ship or boat; a kind of motorboat, long, low, and usu. open; the blast-off of a rocket, missile, or space vehicle. **—launch·er,** *n.*

launch·ing pad, lônch′ing, *n.* The platform upon which a guided missile or rocket rests before firing. Also **launch pad.**

laun·der, lôn′dər, län′dər, *v.t.* To wash, as clothes; to wash and iron. *Informal.* To make something unsavory or illegal, esp. money, appear respectable or legal through surreptitious maneuvers.—*v.i.* To wash and iron; to submit to washing and ironing. **—laun·der·er,** *fem.* **laun·dress,** *n.*

laun·der·ette, lôn·də·ret′, län·də·ret′, *n.* Laundromat.

Laun·dro·mat, lôn′drə·mat, län′drə·mat, *n. Trademark.* A business establishment consisting of coin-operated automatic laundry equipment.

laun·dry, lôn′drē, län′drē, *n. pl.,* **-dries.** A place or establishment where washing and ironing are done; articles to be washed or already washed.

laun·dry·man, lôn′drē·man, län′drē·man, *n. pl.,* **-men.** An employee or manager of a laundry; one who picks up and returns laundry. **—laun·dry·wom·an,** *n. pl.,* **-wom·en.**

lau·re·ate, lôr′ē·it, *a.* Recognized or deserving of distinction; crowned with laurel as an honor; of or pertaining to a poet laureate.—*n.* A poet laureate.

lau·rel, lôr′əl, lor′əl, *n.* A small evergreen tree of southern Europe; any of various trees similar to the true laurel; a branch or wreath of it; the foliage of this tree as an emblem of victory or distinction. *Pl.* Honor won, as by achievement.

la·va, lä′və, lav′ə, *n.* The molten or fluid rock which issues from a volcano or volcanic vent; a variety of this substance caused by hardening of lava under variable conditions.

lav·a·liere, lav·a·lier, lav·ə·lēr′, lä·və·lēr′, *n.* A pendant, usu. of jewels, suspended on a chain that is worn around the neck.

lav·a·to·ry, lav′ə·tôr·ē, *n. pl.,* **-ries.** A room with means for washing the hands and face, and often with toilet conveniences; a place where washing is done; a vessel for washing or bathing purposes.

lave, lāv, *v.t.,* **laved, lav·ing.** To wash or bathe; to wash or flow against.

lav·en·der, lav′ən·dər, *n.* A European mint with spikes of pale purple flowers, and yielding a fragrant oil; the dried flowers or other parts of these plants, used in sachets and as a preservative; a pale purple color.—*a.* Pale, delicate purple.

lav·ish, lav′ish, *a.* Using or bestowing in great abundance; prodigal; exceedingly liberal; extravagant. —*v.t.* To bestow or spend in great abundance or without stint. **—lav·ish·ly,** *adv.* **—lav·ish·ness,** *n.*

law, lô, *n.* The body of rules or principles, prescribed by authority or established by custom, which a state, community, society, or the like recognizes as binding on its members; one of the individual rules; the controlling influence of such rules, or the condition of society brought about by their observance; these rules as a system or institution; the department of knowledge or study concerned with such rules or system of rules; a body of such rules concerned with a particular subject; a body of such laws derived from a particular source; the legal profession; legal action or judicial remedy: to go to *law;* any rule or injunction that must be obeyed; a rule or commandment derived from conscience, reason, or divine will. *Informal.* A policeman. Any governing force in business, art, games, language, or the like; a statement of a relation or sequence of phenomena invariable under the same conditions: the *law* of gravitation. *Math.* A rule on which something depends, as the construction of a curve. **The Law,** the law of Moses; the Torah.**—lay down the law,** to state authoritatively one's wishes, views, or instructions.

law·a·bid·ing, lô′ə·bī·ding, *a.* Observant of the law; obeying the law.

law·break·er, lô′brā·kər, *n.* One who violates the law. **—law·break·ing,** *n., a.*

law·ful, lô′fəl, *a.* Allowed by law; agreeable or conformable to law; legitimate; rightful. **—law·ful·ly,** *adv.* **—law·ful·ness,** *n.*

law·giv·er, lô′giv·ər, *n.* One who gives, makes, or promulgates a law or a code of laws; a legislator. **—law·giv·ing,** *n., a.*

law·less, lô′lis, *a.* Not founded on, governed by, or conforming to law; not controlled by law; illegal; disorderly. **—law·less·ly,** *adv.* **—law·less·ness,** *n.*

law·mak·er, lô′mā·kər, *n.* A legislator or lawgiver. **—law·mak·ing,** *a., n.*

lawn, lôn, län, *n.* A space of ground covered with grass, and kept neatly mown, generally in front of or around an estate or house.

lawn, lôn, län, *n.* A thin or sheer linen or cotton fabric.

lawn mow·er, *n.* A machine for mowing lawns, propelled by hand or by a motor.

lawn ten·nis, *n.* Tennis played outdoors on a prepared court, esp. one of grass.

Law of Mo·ses, mō′zis. *n.* The Pentateuch, or first five books of the Old Testament; Torah.

law·ren·ci·um, lô·ren′sē·əm, lō·ren′sē·əm, *n.* A very short-lived radioactive element.

law·suit, lô′soot, *n.* An action or a prosecution of a claim in a court of justice.

law·yer, lô′yər, loi′ər, *n.* A person trained in the law; one whose profession is to conduct lawsuits in a court or to give legal advice and aid; attorney-at-law.

lax, laks, *a.* Loose or slack; not tense, rigid, or firm; lacking in tone or vigor; loose in morals; lacking in strictness or severity; careless; not precise; vague. **—lax·i·ty,** *n.* **—lax·ly,** *adv.* **—lax·ness,** *n.*

lax·a·tive, lak′sə·tiv, *a.* Having the quality of loosening the intestines and relieving constipation.—*n.* A medicine that acts as a gentle purgative.

---

a- hat, fāte, fāre, fäther; **e-** met, mē; **i-** pin, pīne; **o-** not, nōte, ôrb, moove (move), boy, pownd; **u-** cūbe, bŭll, tûk (took); **ch-** chin; **th-** thick, ŧhen; **zh-** vizhon (vision); **ə-** əgo, takən, pencəl, lemən, bərd (bird).

lay, lā, *v.t.,* **laid, lay·ing.** To put in a position of rest or recumbency; to bring or throw down; to place, set, or cause to be in a particular situation or condition; to dispose in proper position or in an orderly fashion; to bury; devise or arrange; bring forth and deposit, as an egg or eggs; to deposit, as a wager; bet; to make, as a wager or bet; bring to a person's notice; set, as a snare; locate, as a scene; to present, as a claim; impute or ascribe; to impose as a burden, duty, penalty, or the like; set, as a table; place on or over a surface, as paint; cover with something else; to cause to subside; to appease or suppress. *Informal.* Have sexual intercourse with.—*v.i.* To lay eggs; to bet; to deal blows, usu. followed by *on, at, about;* to apply oneself vigorously. *Nonstandard.* Lie: as, to *lay* down.—*n.* The way or position in which a thing is laid or lies. *Informal.* One of, or one's partner in, sexual intercourse.—**lay for,** *Informal.* To await, as in ambush. —**lay into,** to attack vigorously.—**lay low,** *Informal.* To thrash, soundly; prostrate; stay hidden.—**lay off,** to put aside; to dismiss, esp. temporarily, as a workman; stop working; take a rest. *Informal.* To mark off; to stop or cease.—**lay out,** to extend at length; spread out; prepare a body for burial; to plot or plan out; to expend, as money, for a particular purpose. *Informal.* To knock out or kill.—**lay up,** to put away for future use; store up; to cause to remain in bed or indoors through illness or injury; to put a ship in a dock.

lay, lā, *v.* Past tense of **lie.**

lay, lā, *a.* Of the people or laity as distinguished from the clergy, or from some other learned profession.

lay, lā, *n.* A song; a ballad; a narrative poem.

lay·er, lā′ər, *n.* A thickness of some material laid on or spread over a surface; a stratum; one who or that which lays; a shoot or twig attached to the living stock for the purpose of propagation.—*v.t., v.i.* Make a layer of; to propagate by layers.

lay·ette, lā·et′, *n.* Clothing, blankets, any other necessities for a newborn child.

lay·man, lā′mən, *n. pl.,* **-men.** A person who is not a clergyman; a person who is not professionally or specially knowledgeable in a specified area.

lay·off, lā′ôf, lā′of, *n.* Discharge, as of workmen; a period of closing down.

lay·out, lā′owt, *n.* Plan or arrangement, as of a newspaper; the arrangement of equipment and materials, as in an office or shop. *Informal.* A place or establishment.

lay·o·ver, lā′ō·vər, *n.* A postponement; a short halt; a stopover.

laze, lāz, *v.i.,* **lazed, laz·ing.** To be lazy; to idle.—*v.t.* To pass, as time, lazily, used with *away.*

la·zy, lā′zē, *a.,* **-zi·er, -zi·est.** Reluctant to work or exert oneself in any way; indolent; moving slowly; sluggish.—**la·zi·ly,** *adv.* —**la·zi·ness,** *n.*

la·zy·bones, lā′zē·bōnz, *n. pl., sing. or pl. in constr.* *Informal.* A lazy person.

la·zy Su·san, soo′zən, *n.* A large, circular, revolving tray for food or condiments.

lea, lē, lā, *n. Poet.* A meadow or grassy plain.

leach, lēch, *v.t.* To cause, as water, to percolate through something; to rid of solubles by percolation; to draw from a material by percolation; extract.—*v.i.* To undergo the action of percolating water, as ashes. —*n.* A leaching; the material leached; a vessel for use in leaching.

lead, led, *n.* A heavy, soft, malleable, bluish-gray metal, commonly found in combination as galena. A plummet suspended by a line, as for taking soundings; bullets or shot; a thin strip of type metal for increasing the spaces between lines of type; graphite, or a small stick of it used in pencils.—*a.* Made of lead or one of its alloys.—*v.t.* To cover, line, frame, treat, fill, or weight with lead. *Print.* To insert leads between the lines of.

lead, lēd, *v.t.,* **led, lead·ing.** To guide or conduct by showing the way; to command, govern, direct; to be first among; to induce or influence; to initiate and guide; to compel to motion, as with a rein or by the hand; to direct, as the playing of music; to pass or live through; to cause to live through or endure; in cards, to make the first play.—*v.i.* To guide; to have preeminence; to take the first place; to have authority; to be chief, commander, or director; to conduct, bring, draw, induce; to be led or submit to being led; to afford a way or passage; in cards, to make the first play.—*n.* Guidance; direction; precedence; the first or foremost place; position in advance, or the extent of advance; something that leads; a conductor conveying electricity; a guiding indication; in cards, the initiation of play, or first card played; the principal part in a play, or the person who plays it; the first paragraph of a news story.—**lead off,** to begin; open; be the first batter in the line-up in baseball.—**lead on,** to persuade or entice to proceed, esp. in a wrong or unwise course.—**lead up,** to proceed gradually or indirectly toward something; prepare the way (with *to*).

lead·en, led′ən, *a.* Made of lead; heavy; oppressive; sluggish; dull, spiritless, or gloomy; of a dull gray color. —**lead·en·ly,** *adv.* —**lead·en·ness,** *n.*

lead·er, lē′dər, *n.* One who or that which leads; a guide, commander, conductor, etc.; one fitted to lead; a principal or important editorial article, as in a newspaper; a principal article of trade, esp. one offered at a low price to attract customers; in fishing, a length of silkworm, gut, or the like, for attaching a hook or lure to the line; a conductor or director, as of an orchestra, band, or chorus. *Pl., print.* A row of dots or short lines to lead the reader's eye across a space. —**lead·er·less,** *a.* —**lead·er·ship,** *n.*

lead·ing, lē′ding, *a.* Guiding; conducting; chief; principal.—*n.* Guidance; direction.

lead·ing, led′ing, *n.* The act of covering, filling, framing, etc., with lead; a lead border; the spacing between lines of type.

lead·ing ques·tion, lē′ding, *n.* A question which suggests the answer or guides the answerer.

lead pen·cil, led pen′sil, *n.* A pencil with a thin stick of graphite as its writing material.

leaf, lēf, *n. pl.,* **leaves.** One of the lateral outgrowths of a stem, often broad and flat and usu. green, which produces food by photosynthesis; the leaves of some plants, as tobacco or tea, as a commercial product; foliage. Something resembling a leaf; a thin sheet of metal; a lamina or layer; loosely, a petal; a single thickness of paper, comprising two pages; a sliding, hinged, or detachable flat part, as of a door, shutter, or table top.—*v.i.* To produce leaves; to turn over papers or pages.—*v.t.* To flip or turn, as pages. —**turn over a new leaf,** to begin anew, esp. with the intent to improve or reform. —**leaf·less,** *a.*

leaf·age, lē′fij, *n.* Leaves; foliage.

leaf·let, lēf′lit, *n.* A small flat or folded sheet of printed matter; one of the several blades or divisions of a compound leaf; a small or young leaf.

leaf·stalk, lēf′stok, *n.* A petiole.

leaf·y, lē′fē, *a.,* **-i·er, -i·est.** Abounding in or covered with leaves. —**leaf·i·ness,** *n.*

league, lēg, *n.* An association of parties, persons, or states for promotion of their mutual interests and goals; the covenant or compact binding such an association; an association of athletic teams.—*v.t.,* **leagued, lea·guing.** To combine or unite in a league.

league, lēg, *n.* Any of several measures of distance, usu. about three miles.

leak, lēk, *v.i.* To let air, water, etc., enter or escape through a hole, crack, etc.; to pass in or out in this manner; to become known, sometimes unintentionally: Rumors will *leak* out.—*v.t.* To leak in or out; to divulge (information, etc.) without authorization.—*n.* A hole, crack, or opening not meant to be there, by which water, air, etc., enters or escapes; the act of leaking; a means of escape. *Informal.* A means for the escape of a secret, or the escape itself. *Elect.* A point where current escapes from a conductor. —**leak·age**, *n.* —**leak·i·ness**, *n.*, —**leak·y**, *a.*, -**i·er**, -**i·est**.

lean, lēn, *v.i.*, **leaned** or **leant**, lent; **lean·ing**. To slope from a straight or perpendicular position or line; to slant; to incline in feeling or opinion; to tend toward; to rest, as for support; to depend or rely, used with *on.*—*v.t.* To cause to lean; to incline; to support or rest.—*n.* Inclination.

lean, lēn, *a.* Thin; spare; containing little or no fat; meager; poor; marked by scarcity.—*n.* Meat having little or no fat. —**lean·ly**, *adv.* —**lean·ness**, *n.*

lean·ing, lē'ning, *n.* Inclination; bias; tendency.

lean-to, lēn'too, *n. pl.*, -**tos**. A shed or building extension, whose roof slopes away from a support, as a post, wall, or tree.

leap, lēp, *v.i.*, **leaped** or **leapt**, **leap·ing**. To spring from the ground with feet in the air; to move with springs or bounds; to act on impulse; to make a sudden transition.—*v.t.* To pass over by leaping; to cause to leap, as one's riding horse.—*n.* The act of leaping; a place to leap; the space passed over by leaping; a jump; spring; a sudden transition.—**by leaps and bounds**, very swiftly. —**leap·er**, *n.*

leap·frog, lēp'frog, lēp'frôg, *n.* A game in which one player leaps over another player who is in a stooping posture.

leap year, *n.* A year containing 366 days in which a 29th day is added to February. Every year whose number is exactly divisible by 4, as 1968, is a leap year except for centenary years, which must be exactly divisible by 400, as 2000.

learn, lėrn, *v.t.*, **learned** or **learnt**, **learn·ing**. To gain knowledge of, or skill in; to acquire by study or experience; become aware of; to memorize.—*v.i.* To gain knowledge, skill, etc. —**learn·er**, *n.*

learn·ed, lėr'nid, *a.* Having, showing, or containing vast knowledge; erudite; characterized by or devoted to scholarship. —**learn·ed·ly**, *adv.* —**learn·ed·ness**, *n.*

learn·ing, lėr'ning, *n.* Knowledge or skill acquired by study in any field; the process of obtaining skill or knowledge.

lease, lēs, *n.* A contract authorizing the use and possession of land and/or buildings for a fixed time and fee, usu. payable in installments; the specified time for rental.—*v.t.*, **leased**, **leas·ing**. To grant by lease; to hold under a lease.

leash, lēsh, *n.* A thong or line by which a dog or other animal is held; control or restraint.—*v.t.* To hold, as by a leash; to restrain, as anger.

least, lēst, *a.* Smallest in size, amount, degree, or the like; slightest.—*n.* The least amount, quantity, or degree.—*adv.* To the least extent, amount, or degree. —**at least**, at the least or lowest estimate; at any rate; in any case.—**in the least**, in the smallest degree.

least·wize, lēst'wiz, *adv. Informal.* At least; at any rate. Also **least·ways**, lēst'wāz.

leath·er, leth'ėr, *n.* The skin of animals, esp. of cattle, dressed and prepared for use by tanning or similar processes; tanned hide.—*a.* Pertaining to or consisting of leather.—*v.t.* To furnish or cover with leather.

leath·er·neck, leth'ėr·nek, *n. Informal.* A member of the U.S. Marine Corps.

leath·er·y, leth'ə·rē, *a.* Pertaining to or resembling leather; tough.

leave, lēv, *v.t.*, **left**, **leav·ing**. To go away from, depart from, or quit; to allow to remain in the same place or condition; to go away from permanently; separate or withdraw from; to allow to rest or remain for action or decision; to result in or have as an aftermath; to have remaining after death, as: He *leaves* a widow and two children; to bequeath by will; to station to remain

behind; to give for use after one's departure; to stop or cease (with *off*); to omit or exclude (with *out*). *Nonstandard.* To allow, let: *Leave* him stay.—*v.i.* To go away, depart, or set out. —**leav·er**, *n.*

leave, lēv, *n.* Liberty granted to act; permission, esp. to be absent for a period; the duration of the absence granted; a formal parting, usu. preceded by *take.*—**on leave**, absent from duty with permission.

leave, lēv, *v.i.*, **leaved**, **leav·ing**. To put forth leaves; leaf. —**leaved**, *a.*

leav·en, lev'ən, *n.* A substance, as yeast or a mass of fermented dough, used to produce fermentation in dough; an agent which works to produce a gradual change or modification. Also **leav·en·ing**.—*v.t.* To raise, as a dough, by means of leaven; to permeate with a modifying or transforming influence.

leaves, lēvz, *n.* Plural of **leaf**.

leave-tak·ing, lēv'tā·king, *n.* The act of taking leave; a bidding good-bye.

leav·ing, lē'ving, *n.* That which is left; residue; *pl.*, remains or refuse.

lech·er, lech'ėr, *n.* A man immoderately given to sexual indulgence. —**lech·er·ous**, *a.* —**lech·er·ous·ly**, *adv.* —**lech·er·y**, *n. pl.*, -**ies**.

lec·tern, lek'tėrn, *n.* A desk or stand from which parts of a church service are read; a stand upon which a speaker or lecturer may rest notes or books.

lec·ture, lek'chėr, *n.* A discourse read or delivered before an audience or class, usu. for the purpose of instruction; a reprimand or formal reproof.—*v.t.*, -**tured**, -**tur·ing**. To give a lecture to; to reprimand or reprove.—*v.i.* To deliver lectures. —**lec·tur·er**, *n.*

ledge, lej, *n.* Any relatively narrow, projecting shelf; a ridge or shelf of rocks.

ledg·er, lej'ėr, *n.* The principal book of accounts containing the final entries of debits and credits.

lee, lē, *n.* Shelter, esp. the side or part that is sheltered or turned away from the wind.—*a.* Of or pertaining to the lee; in the same direction as the wind is blowing.

leech, lēch, *n.* Any of the bloodsucking, usu. aquatic worms formerly used by physicians for bloodletting; a person who clings to another, esp. with a view to gain.

leek, lēk, *n.* An herb, allied to the onion but with a cylindrical bulb and flat leaves which are used in cooking.

leer, lēr, *n.* A sidelong glance expressive of malignity, lasciviousness, or slyness.—*v.i.* To cast a sly, malicious, or lascivious look. —**leer·ing·ly**, *adv.*

leer·y, lēr'ē, *a. Informal.* Wary (of); suspicious.

lees, lēz, *n. pl.* The sediments of a liquid, esp. liquor or wine; the dregs.

lee·ward, lē'wėrd, *Naut.* loo'ėrd, *a.* Pertaining to the side away from the wind; downwind.—*n.* The sheltered side.—*adv.*

lee·way, lē'wā, *n.* A degree of freedom of thought or action; additional time, space, money, within which to function; the lateral drift of a ship in motion to leeward.

left, left, *a.* Belonging to or situated near the side of a person or thing which is turned toward the west when one faces north. (*Often cap.*) Belonging to or pertaining to the political Left.—*n.* The left side, or what is on the left side. (*Often cap.*) In politics, the complex of groups and individuals having liberal, socialistic, or radical views and policies. In boxing, the left hand or a blow with the left hand.—*adv.* On or to the left side. —**left·ist**, *n., a.* (*Sometimes cap.*)

left-hand, left'hand', *a.* On or to the left; of, for, or with the left hand.

left-hand·ed, left'han'did, *a.* Using the left hand more easily than the right; preferably using the left hand; adapted to or performed by the left hand; moving or rotating from right to left; counter-

---

a- hat, fāte, fāre, fäther; **e-** met, mē; **i-** pin, pīne; **o-** not, nōte, ôrb, moove (move), boy, pownd; **u-** cūbe, bůll, tůk (took); **ch-** chin; **th-** thick, then; **zh-** vizhon (vision); **ə-** əgo, takən, pencəl, lemən, bėrd (bird).

clockwise; clumsy or awkward; ambiguous or insincere.—*adv.* Also **left·hand·ed·ly.** —**left·hand·ed·ness,** *n.*

left·o·ver, left′ō·vər, *n.* Something left over or remaining; an unconsumed remnant of food, as from a meal.—*a.*

left wing, *n.* A political party, faction, or group which advocates leftist principles. —**left-wing,** *a.* —**left-wing·er,** *n.*

leg, leg, *n.* One of the members or limbs which support and move the human or animal body; that part of a garment which covers the leg; something resembling or suggesting a leg, as the supports of a piece of furniture; one of the sides of a triangle other than the base or the hypotenuse; the course or run made by a sailing vessel on one tack; one of the distinct portions or stages of any course or journey.—*v.i.,* **legged, leg·ging.** *Informal.* To walk or run: We'll *leg it* together.—**pull one's leg.** *Informal.* To deceive; to tantalize or tease.—**shake a leg.** *Informal.* To hurry.

leg·a·cy, leg′ə·sē, *n. pl.,* **-cies.** A bequest; a particular thing or sum of money given by the last will or testament; anything handed down by an ancestor or predecessor.

le·gal, lē′gəl, *a.* Of or pertaining to law; characteristic of the profession of the law; determined by or conforming to the law; acknowledged by law rather than by equity; permitted by law, or lawful. —**le·gal·ly,** *adv.*

le·gal·ism, lē′gə·liz·əm, *n.* Strict or very literal adherence to law. —**le·gal·ist,** *n.* —**le·gal·is·tic,** lē·gə·lis′tik, *a.*

le·gal·i·ty, lēgal′ə·tē, *n. pl.,* **-ties.** The state or quality of being legal; lawfulness.

le·gal·ize, lē′gə·līz, *v.t.,* **-ized, -iz·ing.** To make legal; authorize; sanction. —**le·gal·i·za·tion,** lē·gə·lə·zā′shən, *n.*

le·gal ten·der, *n.* A legally approved currency to be given in payment of a debt and which must be accepted by the creditor.

leg·ate, leg′it, *n.* An ecclesiastic delegated by the Pope as his representative; a deputy, envoy, or ambassador.

leg·a·tee, leg·ə·tē′, *n.* One to whom a legacy is bequeathed.

le·ga·tion, lə·gā′shən, *n.* A diplomatic minister and his assistants when the minister is not of the highest, or ambassadorial rank; the official residence of such a minister; the status of a legate.

le·ga·to, lə·gä′tō, *a., adv. Mus.* Smooth and connected, one note gliding into the next.

leg·end, lej′ənd, *n.* A story or account, non-historical or unverifiable, which is handed down by tradition from earlier times and popularly accepted as factual; a body or collection of such stories dealing with a person, a culture, etc.; a caption or inscription, as on a coat of arms or monument; a list which defines or explains, as symbols on a map.

leg·end·ar·y, lej′ən·der·ē, *a.* Pertaining to or of the nature of a legend; celebrated or described in legend.

leg·er·de·main, lej·ər·də·mān′, *n.* Sleight of hand; a deceptive performance which depends on dexterity of hand, usu. magic or juggling; trickery; deception.

leg·ging, leg′ing, *n.* A covering or protection for the leg. *Usu. pl.* Pants worn over trousers, esp. for outdoor winter wear.

leg·gy, leg′ē, *a.,* **-gi·er, -gi·est.** *Informal.* Having long shapely legs; having overly long legs.

leg·horn, leg′hôrn, leg′ərn, *n. (Usu. cap.)* A Mediterranean breed of domestic chickens. —leg′ərn, leg′hôrn. A variety of straw plait; a hat or bonnet made of this straw.

leg·i·ble, lej′ə·bəl, *a.* Capable of being read; consisting of that which can be readily noted. —**leg·i·bil·i·ty,** lej·ə·bil′ə·tē, *n.* —**leg·i·bly,** *adv.*

le·gion, lē′jən, *n.* An ancient Roman infantry unit consisting of 3000 to 6000 troops with a complement of cavalry; a large body of troops; a great number.—*a.*

Innumerable: used predicatively. —**le·gion·ar·y,** *a., n. pl.,* **-ies.** —**le·gion·naire,** lē·jən·âr′, *n.*

leg·is·late, lej′is·lāt, *v.i.,* **-lat·ed, -lat·ing.** To make or enact laws.—*v.t.* To effect by legislation, usu. with *into* or *out.* —**leg·is·la·tive,** *a.* —**leg·is·la·tor,** *n.*

leg·is·la·tion, lej·is·lā′shən, *n.* The making or enacting of laws; laws enacted.

leg·is·la·ture, lej′is·lā·chər, *n.* The officially empowered body of persons who make laws for a nation or state.

le·git, lə·jit′, *a. Informal.* Legitimate.

le·git·i·mate, lə·jit′ə·mit, *a.* According to law; lawful; in accordance with established rules or accepted standards; born of parents legally married; genuine; pertaining to the live theater as opposed to motion pictures, television, etc.; resting on or ruling by the principle of hereditary right; in accordance with reasoning; logical.—lə·jit′ə·māt, *v.t.,* **-mat·ed, -mat·ing.** To make or declare legitimate; to authorize or justify. —**le·git·i·ma·cy,** *n.* —**le·git·i·mate·ly,** *adv.*

le·git·i·mist, lə·jit′ə·mist, *n.* One who supports legitimate authority, esp. that based on hereditary right.

le·git·i·mize, lə·jit′ə·mīz, *v.t.,* **-mized, -miz·ing.** To legitimate.

leg·ume, leg′ūm, lə·gūm′, *n.* A simple, dry, podlike fruit which splits along two seams, as a pea pod; any plant of the legume family, the species of which have such fruits. —**le·gu·mi·nous,** lə·gū′mə·nəs, *a.*

le·i, lā′ē, lā, *n. pl.,* **leis.** In the Hawaiian Islands, a wreath of flowers or leaves for the neck or head.

lei·sure, lē′zhər, lezh′ər, *n.* Opportunity or time afforded by freedom from immediate occupation or duty; free or unoccupied time; ease.—*a.* Free or unoccupied; having leisure.—**at lei·sure,** with free or unrestricted time; without haste; unoccupied.—**at one's lei·sure,** at one's convenience.

lei·sure·ly, lē′zhər·lē, lezh′ər·lē, *a.* Acting without hurrying; suggesting ample leisure; deliberate.—*adv.* —**lei·sure·li·ness,** *n.*

leit·mo·tif, leit·mo·tiv, līt′mō·tēf, *n.* A theme associated throughout an opera or music drama with a particular person, situation, or idea.

lem·ming, lem′ing, *n.* Any of various small, arctic, mouselike rodents which migrate in great numbers in search of food and often perish in the sea.

lem·on, lem′ən, *n.* The yellow, acid fruit of a subtropical tree; the tree itself; a light yellow color. *Informal.* Something disappointing or worthless.—*a.* A light yellow color.

lem·on·ade, lem·ə·nād′, *n.* A drink made of lemon juice, water, and sweetening.

le·mur, lē′mər, *n.* Any of various small, arboreal, nocturnal mammals related to monkeys, found chiefly in Madagascar.

lend, lend, *v.t.,* **lent, lend·ing.** To grant for temporary use on condition of the thing or its equivalent being returned; to grant the use of (money) at a specified rate of interest; to furnish in general, as assistance; to accommodate or adapt (oneself): He *lent* himself to the scheme.—*v.i.* To make a loan or loans.—**lend a hand,** to assist. —**lend·er,** *n.*

length, lengkth, length, *n.* The longest measure of any object, in distinction from thickness or width; linear measure from end to end; extent from start to finish; distance to a place; a portion of space measured lengthwise; some definite long measure; long continuance; extent in conduct or action: to go to great *lengths.*—**at length,** with amplitude of detail; at last; finally.

length·en, lengk′thən, leng′thən, *v.t.* To make or become longer.

length·wise, lengkth′wīz, length′wīz, *adv., a.* In the direction of the length; in a longitudinal direction of the length; in a longitudinal direction. Also **length·ways.**

length·y, lengk′thē, leng′thē, *a.,* **-i·er, -i·est.** Long; protracted: a *lengthy* discourse. —**length·i·ly,** *adv.*

—length·i·ness, n.

le·ni·ent, lē′nē·ənt, lēn′yənt, a. Mild; merciful; clement; gentle. —**le·ni·ence, le·ni·en·cy,** n. —**le·ni·ent·ly,** adv.

len·i·tive, len′ə·tiv, a. Having the quality of softening or mitigating, as medicines.—n. A soothing medicine or application.

len·i·ty, len′ə·tē, n. Lenience.

lens, lenz, n. pl., **lenses.** A piece of transparent substance, usu. glass, having two opposite surfaces, either both curved or one curved and one plane, used for changing the direction of light rays, as in magnifying, or in correcting errors of vision; a combination of such pieces; some analogous device, as for affecting sound waves; that part of the eye which focuses light rays on the retina.

lent, lent, v. Past tense and past participle of **lend.**

Lent, lent, n. A 40-day period, excluding Sundays, of self-denial, fasting, and penitence, continuing until Easter. —**Lent·en,** a. (Sometimes l.c.)

len·til, len′təl, n. An annual plant of the legume family having flattened, biconvex, edible seeds; the seed of the plant.

len·to, len′tō, a. Mus. Slow.—adv. Mus. Slowly.

Le·o, lē′ō, n. The Lion, a constellation in the northern hemisphere; the fifth sign of the zodiac.

le·o·nine, lē′ə·nīn, a. Pertaining to or resembling a lion.

leop·ard, lep′ərd, n. A large, ferocious Asiatic or African mammal of the cat family, characterized by a tawny coat with black markings; any of various related animals, as the jaguar, panther, and cheetah. —**leop·ard·ess,** n. fem.

le·o·tard, lē′ə·tärd, n. A one-piece, stretchable, skin-tight garment worn by dancers, acrobats, or the like.

lep·er, lep′ər, n. A person affected with leprosy.

lep·i·dop·ter·ous, lep·ə·dop′tər·əs, a. Of or pertaining to an order of insects including the butterflies and moths.

lep·re·chaun, lep′rə·kôn, lep′rə·kon, n. Ir. folklore. A mischievous elf, usu. in the form of an old man.

lep·ro·sy, lep′rə·sē, n. An infectious, chronic disease variously characterized by ulcerations, tubercular nodules, loss of fingers and toes, and nerve paralysis. Also **Han·sen's dis·ease.**

lep·rous, lep′rəs, a. Affected with leprosy; of or like leprosy.

les·bi·an, lez′bē·ən, a. (Sometimes cap.) Of or pertaining to female homosexuals.—n. (Sometimes cap.) A female homosexual. —**les·bi·an·ism,** n.

lese maj·es·ty, lēz maj′i·stē, n. Any crime or offense against the sovereign power in a state, or the dignity of the sovereign; treason.

le·sion, lē′zhən, n. An injury; a wound; an abnormal, localized change in the structure of an organ or tissue.

less, les, a. Fewer or smaller in size, amount, or degree; lower in consideration, dignity, or importance, with than.—n. A smaller amount or quantity.—adv. To a smaller extent, amount, or degree.—prep. Lacking; minus; without.

les·see, le·sē′, n. The person to whom a lease is given.

less·en, les′ən, v.t. To make less; to disparage.—v.i. To become less.

less·er, les′ər, a. Less; smaller; the less important or smaller of two.

les·son, les′ən, n. An assignment to be studied or learned by a student; a period or division of instruction: a music lesson; an instructive experience or example; a reprimand or lecture; a portion of Scripture read at religious services.

les·sor, les′ôr, le·sôr′, n. One who leases to a tenant.

lest, lest, conj. For fear that; in case.

let, let, v.t., **let, let·ting.** To permit; to allow; to permit to enter, pass, or go; to rent or lease; to make or cause: Let me hear you sing. Used in the imperative mood as an auxiliary to express a proposal, command, suggestion, or warning: Let me go! Let's accept. Let him try to resist.—v.i. To be or become rented.—**let down,** to disappoint or betray.—**let off,** to excuse; to permit to avoid punishment.—**let on,** to pretend; to reveal.—**let up,** to abate; to cease.

let, let, n. In certain games, as tennis, an interference with the course of the ball on account of which the stroke or point must be played over again.

let·down, let′down, n. Disappointment or dejection; a lessening or decrease.

le·thal, lē′thəl, a. Causing death; deadly; fatal. —**le·thal·ly,** adv.

leth·ar·gy, leth′ər·jē, n. pl., **-gies.** Unnatural sleepiness; dullness; sluggish inactivity; drowsiness; an abnormally deep sleep, from which a person can scarcely be awakened. —**le·thar·gic,** lə·thär′jik, **le·thar·gi·cal,** a.

Le·the, lē′thē, n. Gr. mythol. One of the streams of Hades which contained waters that induced oblivion in the drinker; oblivion; forgetfulness.

let's, lets. Contraction of **let us.**

let·ter, let′ər, n. A symbol or character used to represent a speech sound; a written or printed message; an official document granting certain rights or privileges; exact wording or literal meaning; an award for participation in some school activity, often athletic. Pl. Learning; erudition; literature or the literary profession: a man of letters.—v.t. To write letters on; inscribe.—**to the letter,** in precise accordance with instructions; in accordance with the exact words or literal meaning. —**let·ter·er,** n.

let·tered, let′ərd, a. Learned; versed in literature; educated; marked or designated with letters.

let·ter·head, let′ər·hed, n. A printed heading on a piece of stationery, usu. giving a name and address; a sheet of paper with such a heading.

let·ter·ing, let′ər·ing, n. The process or act of engraving, stamping with, or forming letters; the letters produced by this process.

let·ter of cred·it, n. A bank document entitling the person named therein to a specified amount of money which he may withdraw from that bank or any of its affiliates.

let·ter·per·fect, let′ər·pər′fikt, a. Correct to the smallest detail; verbatim.—adv. Perfectly; precisely.

let·ter·press, let′ər·pres, n. Printing. Words impressed by raised type.

let·tuce, let′əs, n. A common vegetable of the composite family, having edible leaves often used in salads; the leaves.

let·up, let′əp, n. Informal. Stop or pause; lessening; lull.

leu·ke·mi·a, loo·kē′mē·ə, n. A fatal disease of the blood, in which there is an excess of white corpuscles in the blood.

leu·ko·cyte, leu·co·cyte, loo′kə·sīt, n. A white blood corpuscle; a white or colorless blood cell active in the defense against infection and bacteria.

Le·vant, lə·vant′, n. The countries adjoining the eastern Mediterranean, from W. Greece to W. Egypt. —**Le·van·tine,** lə·van′tēn, lev′ən·tin, a., n.

lev·ee, lev′ē, n. An embankment for preventing the overflowing of a river; a landing place for vessels; a quay.

lev·ee, lev′ē, lə·vē′, n. A morning reception held by a prince or great personage; a reception.

lev·el, lev′əl, n. A device for determining the horizontal plane; a measuring of differences in elevation with such an instrument; a horizontal condition; position vertically; elevation; a flat or horizontal surface, esp.

---

a- hat, fāte, fâre, fäther; **e-** met, mē; **i-** pin, pīne; **o-** not, nōte, ôrb, moove (move), boy, pownd; **u-** cūbe, bůll, tůk (took); **ch-** chin; **th-** thick, ᵺen; **zh-** vizhon (vision); **ə-** əgo, takən, pencəl, lemən, bərd (bird).

land; a rating, status, or value: a social *level;* extent or degree: *level* of education.—*a.* Having no part higher than another; having an even surface; horizontal; even or equable; uniform or evenly distributed; calm; steady.—*v.t.,* **-eled, -el•ing.** To make level, smooth, flat, or even, as a surface; to lay low or demolish by bringing to the level of the ground; to raise or lower to a particular level; to bring to a common level; to make even or uniform; to aim, as a weapon; to direct (words, etc.) with emphasis.—*v.i.* To be on a level or plane; to measure with a level; to bring things or persons to a common level; to aim, esp. a weapon. *Informal.* To be truthful; straightforward.—**one's lev•el best.** *Informal.* One's very best; one's utmost.—**on the lev•el,** honest or reliable. —**lev•el•er,** *n.* —**lev•el•ly,** *adv.* —**lev•el•ness,** *n.*

lev•el-head•ed, lev′əl-hed′id, *a.* Characterized by sound judgment; having common sense; sensible. —**lev•el-head•ed•ness,** *n.*

lev•er, lev′ər, lē′vər, *n.* A bar used for lifting or prying; a bar or rigid piece, rotating about a fixed axis or fulcrum, which lifts or sustains weight at one point by means of applied force at a second point.—*v.t., v.i.* To move with or apply a lever.

lev•er•age, lev′ər•ij, *n.* The action of a lever; the mechanical advantage or power gained by using a lever; increased power of acting.

le•vi•a•than, lə•vī′ə•thən, *n.* A sea monster mentioned in the Old Testament; any huge marine animal, as the whale; anything, esp. a ship, of huge size.—*a.*

Le•vis, lē′viz, *n. Trademark.* Heavy, close-fitting denim pants which are strengthened at the strain points with rivets.

lev•i•tate, lev′ə•tāt, *v.i.,* **-tat•ed, -tat•ing.** To rise or float in the air.—*v.t.* To cause to rise or float in the air. —**lev•i•ta•tion,** lev•ə•tā′shən, *n.*

lev•i•ty, lev′ə•tē, *n.* Inappropriate or excessive frivolity; buoyancy; lightness of weight.

lev•y, lev′ē, *n. pl.,* **-ies.** A raising or collecting, as of money or troops, by authority or force; that which is raised.—*v.t.,* **-ied, -y•ing.** To make a levy of; collect, as taxes or contributions; impose, as an assessment; to raise or enlist, as troops, for service; to get going or start, as a war.—*v.i.* To make a levy; to seize property, esp. for unpaid debts.

lewd, lood, *a.* Inclined to, characterized by, or inciting to lust or lechery; lascivious; obscene. —**lewd•ly,** *adv.* —**lewd•ness,** *n.*

lex, leks, *n. pl.,* **le•ges,** lē′jēz. *Latin.* Law.

lex•i•cog•ra•phy, lek•si•kog′rə•fē, *n.* The act of compiling or writing a dictionary; the occupation of composing dictionaries. —**lex•i•cog•ra•pher,** *n.* —**lex•i•co•graph•ic,** lek•si•kō•graf′ik, lek•si•kə•graf′ik, **lex•i•co•graph•i•cal,** *a.*

lex•i•con, lek′si•kon, lek′si•kən, *n.* A dictionary, usu. one of Greek, Hebrew, or Latin; the particular vocabulary associated with a profession, activity, or field of interest.

Ley•den jar, līd′ən jär, *n.* A glass jar coated inside and outside, usu. with tinfoil, to within a third of the top, so that it may be readily charged with static electricity.

li•a•bil•i•ty, lī•ə•bil′ə•tē, *n. pl.,* **-ties.** The state or fact of being legally responsible or under obligation; the extent to which one is liable, as for a debt; the state of being liable or susceptible; a hindrance or drawback. *Usu. pl.* Debts or pecuniary obligations.

li•a•ble, lī′ə•bəl, *a.* Answerable for consequences; under obligation legally to make good a loss; responsible; likely to incur something undesirable.

li•ai•son, lē•ā•zôn′, lē′ə•zon, lē•ā′zon, lē•ā′zən, *Fr.* lye•zôn′, *n.* A connection or intercommunication, esp. between armed forces units; an illicit affair between a man and a woman; the joining in pronunciation of a usu. silent final consonant to a following word that begins with a vowel sound.

li•ar, lī′ər, *n.* One who lies, or purposely makes false

statements.

li•ba•tion, lī•bā′shən, *n.* A pouring out of wine or other liquid in honor of a deity; the liquid poured out; humorously, a drink.

li•bel, lī′bəl, *n.* A defamatory writing or representation. *Law.* A malicious writing or representation which brings its object into contempt or exposes him to public derision; the act of publishing such a writing. —*v.t.,* **-beled, -bel•ing.** To publish a libel against; to defame by libel. —**li•bel•er,** *n.*

li•bel•ous, lī′bə•ləs, *a.* Of a slanderous, defamatory nature; given to libel. —**li•bel•ous•ly,** *adv.*

lib•er•al, lib′ər•əl, lib′rəl, *a.* Generous; ample; not literal or strict, as translation; tolerant or broadminded, esp. in religion or politics; favoring progress and reforms.—*n.* One who is tolerant, broad-minded, or in favor of progress and reforms. (*Often cap.*) A member of a liberal political party. —**lib•er•al•ly,** *adv.* —**lib•er•al•ness,** *n.*

lib•er•al arts, *n. pl.* A general course of study including abstract science and esp. the arts and humanities, as opposed to a practical, technical course of study.

lib•er•al•ism, lib′ər•ə•liz•əm, lib′rə•liz•əm, *n.* Liberal principles or policies, esp. in the social, political, economic, or religious spheres.

lib•er•al•i•ty, lib•ə•ral′ə•tē, *n. pl.,* **-ties.** The quality of being liberal or broadminded; generosity; a generous gift.

lib•er•al•ize, lib′ər•ə•līz, lib′rə•līz, *v.t.,* **-ized, -iz•ing.** To render liberal.—*v.i.* To become liberal. —**lib•er•al•i•za•tion,** lib•ər•ə•lə•zā′shən, *n.*

lib•er•ate, lib′ə•rāt, *v.t.,* **-at•ed, -at•ing.** To set at liberty; to free; to disengage. —**lib•er•a•tion,** lib•ə•rā′shən, *n.* —**lib•er•a•tor,** *n.*

lib•er•tar•i•an, lib•ər•ter′ē•ən, *n.* One who maintains the doctrine of the freedom of the will; one who advocates liberty, esp. with regard to thought or conduct.—*a.*

lib•er•tine, lib′ər•tēn, lib′ər•tin, *n.* One who is lacking in moral or sexual restraint; one who leads a dissolute, licentious life.—*a.* Licentious; dissolute. —**lib•er•tin•ism,** lib′ər•tē•niz•əm, lib′ər•ti•niz•əm, *n.*

lib•er•ty, lib′ər•tē, *n. pl.,* **-ties.** Freedom or release from slavery, captivity, or restraint; freedom from arbitrary or oppressive government or control; independence from external or foreign rule; power or right of doing, thinking, or speaking according to choice; freedom to occupy or use a locale (with *of);* an immunity, privilege, or right enjoyed by grant or prescription; leave granted to a sailor to go ashore; unwarranted or impertinent freedom in action or speech.—**at lib•er•ty,** free; authorized; permitted; unoccupied; unemployed.

li•bid•i•nous, li•bid′i•nəs, *a.* Having a strong sexual desire; lustful. —**li•bid•i•nous•ly,** *adv.* —**li•bid•i•nous•ness,** *n.*

li•bi•do, li•bē′dō, li•bī′dō, *n.* The sexual instinct; those instincts and drives activating human action —**li•bid•in•al,** li•bid′i•nəl, *a.*

Li•bra, lī′brə, lē′brə, *n.* The Balance, a constellation; the seventh sign in the zodiac.

li•brar•i•an, lī•brer′ē•ən, *n.* One qualified by training for library service; one in charge of a library.

li•brar•y, lī′brer•ē, lī′brə•rē, lī′brē, *n. pl.,* **-ies.** A place set apart to contain books and other literary material for reading, study, or reference; a collection of books or the like.

li•bret•to, li•bret′ō, *n. pl.,* **-tos, -ti, -tē.** The words of an opera or other extended musical composition; a book containing the words. —**li•bret•tist,** *n.*

lice, līs, *n.* Plural of **louse.**

li•cense, esp. *Brit.* **li•cence,** lī′səns, *n.* Formal permission from a constituted authority to do something, as to marry; a certificate of such permission; an official permit; freedom of action, speech, thought, permitted or conceded; disregard of legal or moral restraints; laxity; licentiousness.—*v.t.,* **li•censed, li•**

cens·ing; li·cenced, li·cenc·ing. To give permission or license to do something; to authorize. **—li·cen·see,** li·sən·sē′, *n.* **—li·cens·er,** *n.*

li·cen·ti·ate, li·sen′shē·it, li·sen′shē·āt, *n.* One who has received a license, as from a university, to practice an art or profession, a university degree intermediate between bachelor and doctor in some European universities.

li·cen·tious, li·sen′shəs, *a.* Unrestrained by law or morality, esp. in sexual behavior; lascivious; lewd. **—li·cen·tious·ly,** *adv.* **—li·cen·tious·ness,** *n.*

li·chee, lē′chē, *n.* Litchi.

li·chen, lī′kən, *n.* Any of a group of compound plants made up of fungi in symbiotic union with algae, growing in patches on rocks, trees, and the like.—*v.t.* To cover with lichens.

lic·it, lis′it, *a.* Lawful. **—lic·it·ly,** *adv.*

lick, lik, *v.t.* To pass the tongue over the surface of; take with the tongue, usu. with *up, off, from;* render or bring by strokes of the tongue; to pass or play lightly over, as waves or flames. *Informal.* To beat, thrash, or defeat.—*n.* A stroke of the tongue over something; a small quantity; a place to which wild animals resort to lick salt occurring naturally there. *Informal.* A blow; a brief stroke of activity; a spurt; *pl.,* opportunity; turn. **—a lick and a prom·ise,** superficial or hasty work. **—lick in·to shape,** bring into appropriate form or condition. **—lick one's chops,** eagerly anticipate, as food. **—lick·er,** *n.* **—lick·ing,** *n.*

lick·e·ty-split, lik′i·tē·split′, *adv. Informal.* Very quickly; in great haste.

lick·spit·tle, lik′spit·əl, *n.* A flatterer; a toady.

lic·o·rice, li·quo·rice, lik′ə·ris, lik′ər·ish, lik′rish, *n.* A European leguminous plant; the sweet-tasting dried root of this plant, or an extract made from it; candy flavored with this extract.

lid, lid, *n.* A movable piece, whether separate or hinged, for closing the opening of any container; an eyelid. *Informal.* A hat; means of repression or restraint, as on prices. **—lid·ded,** *a.*

lie, lī, *v.i.,* **lay, lain, ly·ing.** To be in a recumbent or prostrate position, as on a bed; to assume such a position; to rest in a horizontal or flat position; to be placed or situated; to be or stay in a specified state or condition; to extend or continue; to be buried, as in a tomb or grave; to be inherent or to exist.—*n.* The manner, relative position, or direction in which something lies.**—lie down,** to rest, usu. in a horizontal position; to neglect or fail in one's duty; to submit abjectly to defeat, insult, etc.**—lie in,** to be confined in childbirth.**—lie low,** to remain hidden.

lie, lī, *v.i.,* **lied, ly·ing.** To speak falsely or utter untruth knowingly, as with intent to deceive; to express what is false or convey a false impression.—*v.t.* To bring or put by lying.—*n.* A false statement made with intent to deceive; an intentional untruth; something intended to convey a false impression.**—give the lie to,** to charge with lying; to show to be false.**—lie in one's throat or teeth,** to lie in blatant contradiction of truth.

lie de·tec·tor, *n.* A device which detects physical evidences of the tension which accompanies lying.

lief, lēf, *adv.* Gladly; willing: She would as *lief* go out.

liege, lēj, *a.* Owing allegiance and service, as a feudal vassal to his lord; entitled to allegiance and service, as a feudal lord.—*n.* A liege lord; a vassal; a subject, as of a ruler.

lien, lēn, lē′ən, *n.* A legal claim; the right to retain or sell the property of another as security, payment, or satisfaction of a claim.

lieu, loo, *n. Archaic.* Place; stead.**—in lieu of,** in place of; instead of.

lieu·ten·an·cy, loo·ten′ən·sē, *n. pl.,* **-cies.** The rank, commission, or authority of a lieutenant.

lieu·ten·ant, loo·ten′ənt, *Brit. except navy,* lef·

ten′ənt, *n.* An officer, civil or military, who takes the place of a superior in his absence; a commissioned officer in the army, ranking next below a captain; a commissioned naval officer, ranking next below lieutenant commander.

lieu·ten·ant colo·nel, *n.* A military officer next in rank below a colonel.

lieu·ten·ant com·mand·er, *n.* A navy officer who ranks immediately below a commander.

lieu·ten·ant gen·er·al, *n.* A military officer next in rank below a general.

lieu·ten·ant gov·er·nor, *n.* An elected state official ranking next below a governor, who assumes the governor's duties in the event of his absence, resignation, or death. *Brit.* Deputy governor.

life, līf, *n. pl.,* **lives,** līvz. The quality that distinguishes animals and plants from dead bodies or inorganic matter, marked by metabolism, growth, reproduction, irritability, etc.; the time during which such quality continues; the period from birth to death; spiritual existence after death; period during which anything continues to exist or be useful; a person's history; a person's condition or circumstances; mode, manner, or course of living; social surroundings and characteristics; one who or that which is necessary to someone; an absorbing or indispensable interest or activity; that which makes alive or lively; a particular aspect or phase of living; animating or inspiring principle; animation or vivacity; energy; a living person; collectively, living beings in any number; narrative of a person's life; a biography or memoir; human affairs; course of things in the world.—*a.* Lifelong; of or relating to vital existence; working from a living model.**—for life,** until death.**—take life,** to kill.

life belt, *n.* A type of life preserver which resembles a belt.

life·blood, līf′blud, *n.* That which is essential to existence.

life·boat, līf′bōt, *n.* A boat constructed, equipped, and stocked for saving persons from drowning; such a boat carried on board a ship for emergency use.

life buoy, *n.* A buoyant device, in various forms, to enable persons in the water to keep afloat until rescued.

life ex·pect·an·cy, *n.* The number of years that a person is likely to live, as projected by statistical probability.

life·guard, līf′gärd, *n.* A skilled swimmer employed at a pool or beach to save bathers from drowning.

life in·sur·ance, *n.* Insurance on the life of an individual, providing payment to a beneficiary or beneficiaries upon the death of the insured, or to the insured upon reaching a specified age.

life·less, līf′lis, *a.* Deprived of life; dead; inanimate; dull; inactive. **—life·less·ly,** *adv.* **—life·less·ness,** *n.*

life·like, līf′līk, *a.* Resembling or simulating life; giving the impression of real life.

life·line, līf′līn, *n.* A rope projected to a foundering ship or to a drowning person; any vital transportation route used to carry vital supplies.

life·long, līf′lông, līf′long, *a.* Lasting or continuing through life.

life pre·serv·er, *n.* A buoyant jacket, belt, or other similar device for saving persons in the water from sinking and drowning.

lif·er, līf′ər, *n. Informal.* One in something, as the army or prison, for life.

life·sav·er, līf′sā·vər, *n.* One who saves another from death, as from drowning. *Informal.* One who or that which aids in time of need; a lifeguard. **—life·sav·ing,** *n., a.*

life-size, līf′sīz′, *a.* Of the size of the original object or living person. Also **life-sized.**

life-style, līf′stīl, *n.* The pattern, attributes, or circum-

---

stances of a person's life. One's life-style could be urban, suburban, or rural, mobile or rooted, married or single, luxurious or Spartan, conventional or unconventional, etc.

life•time, līf′tīm, *n.* The period of time that life continues.

life•work, līf′wərk′, *n.* The entire or chief work of a lifetime.

lift, lift, *v.t.* To move or bring upward into the air or to a higher position; to raise to a higher position; to hold up or display; to raise in rank, dignity, condition, or estimation; to elevate or exalt; to elate, often with *up;* to send up audibly or loudly; to pay off, as a mortgage; to perform surgery on the face, for removing wrinkles and minimizing signs of age; to stop; as artillery fire. *Informal.* To steal; to plagiarize.—*v.i.* To move upward or rise; to rise and disperse; to pull or strain in the effort to lift something; to yield to upward pressure; rise.—*n.* The act of lifting; the distance through which something is lifted; lifting force; the weight or load lifted; a helping upward or onward; a ride in a vehicle, esp. one given to aid a pedestrian; exaltation or uplift; a holding up of the head; a rise of ground; a device or apparatus for lifting; *chiefly Brit.,* an elevator. One of the layers of leather forming the heel of a boot or shoe. —**lift•er,** *n.*

lift-off, lift′ôf, lift′of, *n.* The action of a rocket vehicle as it separates from its launch pad in a vertical ascent.

lift truck, *n.* A motorized or hand-driven truck or dolly designed for unloading, lifting, and moving loads.

lig•a•ment, lig′ə•mənt, *n.* A band of strong, fibrous tissue connecting bones at a joint, or serving to hold in place and support body organs; any tie or bond.

lig•a•ture, lig′ə•chər, lig′ə•choor, *n.* The act of binding; anything that binds, as a cord or band. *Mus.* A slur or the notes connected by it. *Print.* A type consisting of two or more connected letters, as *ae, fi,* or *fl;* a thread, wire, or the like for tying blood vessels.—*v.t.* **-tured, -tur•ing.** To bind or tie up, as with a ligature.

light, līt, *n.* That which makes things visible; the form of radiant energy that stimulates the organs of sight, plus infrared and ultraviolet rays; an illuminating source, as the sun; a lamp; the illumination from a particular source; the illumination from the sun, or daylight; daybreak; illumination; supply of light; clearness; brightness; a particular kind of illumination; the aspect in which a thing appears or is regarded; open view or public knowledge; mental or spiritual illumination or enlightenment; a person who is a shining example; a luminary; a means of kindling; ignition; an opening for illumination, as a window; a particular expression of the eyes; a representation of light, as in a painting; *pl.,* understanding, standards, or philosophy of life: she lived according to her *lights.*—*a.* Having light or illumination: as, pale, whitish, or not deep or dark in color.—*v.i.,* **light•ed** or **lit, light•ing.** To take fire or become kindled; to become bright, as with light or color, used with *up;* to brighten with animation or joy, used with *up:* Their faces *light up* with happiness.—*v.t.* To kindle or ignite; to turn on; to furnish with light or illumination; to make bright or to animate, often with *up.*—**bring to light, come to light,** to reveal or be revealed.—**in light of,** with awareness of; considering: *In light of* the circumstances, his decision appears correct.—**see the light,** to become aware of or understand. —**light•ness,** *n.*

light, līt, *a.* Of little weight; not heavy; of less than usual or average weight; of little density; of small amount, force, or intensity; requiring little mental effort; not profound, serious, or heavy; easy to endure, deal with, or perform; trifling, trivial, or of little moment or importance; free from sorrow or care.—*adv.* Lightly. —**light•ness,** *n.*

light, līt, *v.i.,* **light•ed** or **lit, light•ing.** To descend from a horse, vehicle, etc.; to alight; land; come down from flight; to come by chance; to fall unexpectedly, as a blow.—**light into.** *Informal.* To attack physically or verbally.—**light out.** *Informal.* To leave suddenly; flee quickly.

light•en, līt′ən, *v.i.* To become lighter; grow brighter. —*v.t.* To make light or clear; illuminate.

light•en, līt′ən, *v.t.* To make less heavy; to lessen.—*v.i.* To become lighter; to become more cheerful.

light•er, lī′tər, *n.* One who or that which lights, illuminates, or ignites.

light•er, lī′tər, *n.* A shallow barge used to load and unload ships.

light-fin•gered, līt′fing′gərd, *a.* Dexterous with the fingers, esp. in picking pockets or petty theft.

light-foot•ed, līt′fût′id, *a.* Nimble; springy of step; light of foot; graceful. —**light•foot•ed•ly,** *adv.* —**light•foot•ed•ness,** *n.*

light-head•ed, līt′hed′id, *a.* Dizzy; frivolous. —**light-head•ed•ly,** *adv.* —**light-head•ed•ness,** *n.*

light-heart•ed, light•heart•ed, līt′här′tid, *a.* Cheerful; optimistic. —**light-heart•ed•ly, light• heart•ed•ly,** *adv.* —**light-heart•ed•ness, light• heart•ed•ness,** *n.*

light heav•y•weight, *n.* A boxer weighing between 161 and 175 pounds.

light•house, līt′hows, *n.* A tower with a powerful light to warn of danger to navigators.

light•ing, lī′ting, *n.* Illumination; the device or system which provides illumination.

light•ly, līt′lē, *adv.* In a light manner; with little weight or intensity; gently; easily, or without trouble or effort; nimbly; cheerfully; indifferently; without due consideration or reason.

light-mind•ed, līt′mīn′did, *a.* Frivolous. —**light-mind•ed•ly,** *adv.* —**light-mind•ed•ness,** *n.*

light•ning, līt′ning, *n.* A discharge of atmospheric electricity resulting in a flash of light; the flash of light.—*a.*—*v.i.,* To release a spark or flash of lightning.

light•ning bug, *n.* Firefly.

light•ning rod, *n.* A metallic rod attached to structures to protect them from lightning by conducting the electric charge into the earth or water.

light•weight, līt′wāt, *n.* One of less than average weight; a boxer intermediate in weight between a featherweight and welterweight.

light-year, līt′yēr, *n.* The distance traversed by light in one year, about 5,880,000,000,000 miles.

lig•nite, lig′nīt, *n.* A brownish-black coal, mineralized to a certain degree, but retaining a distinct woody texture. —**lig•nit•ic,** lig•nit′ik, *a.*

like, līk, *a.* Of the same form, appearance, kind, character, or amount; corresponding or agreeing in general or in some noticeable respect; similar.—*n.* A counterpart, match, or equal.—*prep.* In a similar manner with; similarly to; in the manner characteristic of; giving promise or indication of: It looks *like* rain.—*adv.* —*conj. Nonstandard.* Just as or as: It was *like* we thought; as if: *like* he was afraid.

like, līk, *v.t.,* **liked, lik•ing.** To take pleasure in, or find to one's taste; to regard with favor, or have a kindly or friendly feeling for; to want.—*v.i.* To feel inclined, or wish.—*n. Usu. pl.* **A likes.** —**lik•a•ble, like•a•ble,** *a.* —**lik•a•ble•ness, like•a•ble•ness,** *n.*

like•li•hood, līk′lē•hûd, *n.* Probability; something which is probable.

like•ly, līk′lē, *a.,* **-li•er, -li•est.** Credible; probable; suitable, well-adapted, or convenient for some purpose; promising.—*adv.* Probably.

like-mind•ed, līk′mīn′did, *a.* Having the same belief, opinion, or purpose.

lik•en, lī′kən, *v.t.* To compare.

like•ness, līk′nis, *n.* The condition or quality of being like; that which closely resembles or represents something else, esp. a portrait.

like•wise, līk′wīz, *adv.* In like manner; also; too.

lik•ing, lī′king, *n.* Feeling of inclination or attraction; favor or fancy; pleasure or taste.

li•lac, lī′lək, lī′lak, *n.* A shrub with large clusters of fragrant flowers in white or various shades of purple; a light purple color.—*a.* Having a purple color, as that of lilacs.

Lil·li·pu·tian, lil·ə·pū′shən, *a.* Tiny; diminutive; petty.—*n.* A tiny person.

lilt, lilt, *n.* A springing movement or step; a buoyant, sprightly song or tune.—*v.t., v.i.* **—lilt·ing,** *a.*

lil·y, lil′ē, *n. pl.,* **-ies.** Any plant with showy, funnelshaped flowers of various colors.—*a.* Like or suggestive of a white lily; delicately fair.

lil·y-liv·ered, lil′ē-liv·ərd, *a.* Cowardly.

lil·y of the val·ley, *n. pl.,* **lil·ies of the val·ley.** An herb with a raceme of drooping, bell-shaped, fragrant white flowers.

li·ma bean, lī′mə, *n.* A bean with a broad, flat, edible seed; the seed, a common vegetable.

limb, lim, *n.* One of the jointed appendages of the human or animal body, as an arm or leg; a large or main branch of a tree.**—out on a limb.** *Informal.* In a vulnerable position. **—limbed,** limd, *a.*

lim·ber, lim′bər, *a.* Easily bent; flexible; pliant; being able to move or bend one's body with ease; supple. —*v.t., v.i.* To render or become limber, usu. followed by *up.* **—lim·ber·ness,** *n.*

lim·bo, lim′bō, *n. (Often cap.),* A supposed region bordering hell, considered the abode for the souls of unbaptized children and virtuous people who lived before the time of Christ; a place, state, or condition of people and things forgotten or no longer wanted.

Lim·burg·er, lim′bər·gər, *n.* A soft cheese with a pungent odor and sharp flavor.

lime, līm, *n.* Calcium oxide, a white caustic solid prepared by calcining limestone or other calciumcarbonate substances, and used in making mortar and cement.—*v.t.,* **limed, lim·ing.** To treat or spread with lime. **—lim·y,** *a.,* **lim·i·er, lim·i·est.**

lime, līm, *n.* A greenish-yellow acid fruit that grows on a subtropical tree; the tree itself. **—lime·like,** *a.*

lime·light, līm′līt, *n.* A powerful light produced by an oxyhydrogen flame on a piece of lime, formerly used as a stage spotlight; a center of public interest; spotlight.—*v.t.* **—lime·light·er,** *n.*

lim·er·ick, lim′ər·ik, *n.* An amusing verse composed of five lines.

lime·stone, līm′stōn, *n.* A rock consisting chiefly of calcium carbonate.

lim·it, lim′it, *n.* The final or furthest bound or point as to extent, amount, continuance, or procedure; a boundary; *usu. pl.,* a tract or area within boundaries. —*v.t.* To restrict by fixing limits, often with *to.* **—lim·it·a·ble,** *a.* **—lim·i·ta·tive,** lim′i·tā·tiv, *a.* **—lim·it·er,** *n.* **—lim·it·less,** *a.*

lim·i·ta·tion, lim·i·tā′shən, *n.* A limiting condition, circumstance, or restriction; the act of limiting; the state of being limited. *Law.* A period of time within which an action or prosecution must be brought in the courts.

lim·it·ed, lim′i·tid, *a.* Confined within limits; of a train or bus, restricted in number of passengers and stops. **—lim·it·ed·ly,** *adv.* **—lim·it·ed·ness,** *n.*

lim·ou·sine, lim′ə·zēn, lim·ə·zēn′, *n.* A closed automobile, esp. one with the chauffeur partitioned off from the passengers; a large vehicle for shuttling passengers to and from airport terminals.

limp, limp, *v.i.* To walk lamely.—*n.* The act of limping. **—limp·er,** *n.* **—limp·ing·ly,** *adv.*

limp, limp, *a.* Lacking stiffness or firmness, as of substance, fiber structure, or bodily frame. **—limp·ly,** *adv.* **—limp·ness,** *n.*

lim·pet, lim′pit, *n.* A mollusk or shellfish having a conical shell opening widely on the bottom with a flatsoled foot for creeping and clinging to rocks.

lim·pid, lim′pid, *a.* Characterized by clearness or transparency; serene; lucid. **—lim·pid·i·ty,** lim·pid′i·tē, *n.* **—lim·pid·ly,** *adv.* **—lim·pid·ness,** *n.*

lin·age, lī′nij, *n.* The number of printed lines on a page.

lin·den, lin′dən, *n.* A tree with yellowish or creamcolored flowers and heart-shaped leaves.

line, līn, *n.* A mark or stroke long in proportion to its breadth, made with a pen, pencil, or tool on a surface; something resembling a traced line; one of the furrows or marks on the palm of the hand; a row or series; *usu. pl.,* the spoken words of a play or actor's part. A short written message: Drop a *line* to a friend; a course of action, procedure, or thought; a bit of knowledge or information, followed by *on:* to get a *line on* his whereabouts. *Informal.* Ingratiating or persuasive speech: His *line* gained her sympathy; one's field of experience, interest, or taste. A kind of occupation or business and the merchandise peculiar to it; a real or imaginary boundary or limit; a continuous chronological succession of people, plants, or animals, esp. in family descent; a path, usu. straight, between something observed and the observer; a thread, string, cord, or rope; a system of public conveyances; the wire or wires connecting points or stations, as for telegraph, telephone, and television. *Often pl.* A distribution and entrenchment of troops for defense purposes. *Sports.* Ten bowling frames; the seven football players who stand abreast of the line of scrimmage. —*v.t.,* **lined, lin·ing.** To trace by a line or lines; sketch; delineate; to mark with a line or lines; to bring into a line, often followed by *up;* to form or arrange a line along.—*v.i.* To take a position in a line; form a line, often followed by *up.*—**hold the line,** to take a firm position; maintain existing conditions.—**in line,** conforming to standards.—**in line for,** next to receive or achieve.—**on the line,** directly, frankly, or promptly.—**out of line,** not complying with proper practices or standards.—**read be·tween the lines,** to discover a meaning not explicitly expressed.—**toe the line,** to strictly comply with an order or rule.

line, līn, *v.t.,* **lined, lin·ing.** To cover on the inside; to protect by a layer on the inside.—*n.*

lin·e·age, lin′ē·ij, *n.* Line of descent from an ancestor; race; family.

lin·e·al, lin′ē·əl, *a.* Hereditary; transmitted by direct or continuous descent. **—lin·e·al·ly,** *adv.*

lin·e·a·ment, lin′ē·ə·mənt, *n. Usu. pl.* The outline or contour of a body or figure, particularly of the face; distinctive or characteristic features.

lin·e·ar, lin′ē·ər, *a.* Of or pertaining to a line or lines; resembling a line or thread; pertaining to length, or involving measurement in one direction only. **—lin·e·ar·ly,** *adv.*

line·back·er, līn′bak·ər, *n.* A defensive football player positioned behind the linemen. **—line·back·ing,** *n.*

line drive, *n.* A baseball hit sharply along a line approximately parallel to the ground; a liner.

line·man, līn′mən, *n. pl.,* **-men.** A repairman who works on electric power, telephone, or telegraph lines. Also **lines·man.** A railway employee who inspects the tracks; a football player who plays forward, as a guard, tackle, or center.

lin·en, lin′ən, *n.* Cloth, thread, or yarn of flax; *usu. pl.,* articles previously made of linen, but now often made of cotton: table *linens.*—*a.* Made of flax or flax yarn; linen textured.

lin·er, lī′nər, *n.* One of a line of steamships or airplanes; a cosmetic preparation used to accentuate the eyes; in baseball, a line drive.

lin·er, lī′nər, *n.* Something serving as a lining; a coat lining which may be zipped in or out of a coat.

lines·man, līnz·mən, *n.* An official employed to watch the lines which mark out the field, as in tennis, or who marks the distances gained and lost, as in football; a lineman (worker on telephone lines, etc.).

line-up, line·up, līn′əp, *n.* The formation of persons

---

or things into a line, or into position for action; the persons or things themselves, esp. a line of suspects assembled by the police for identification. *Sports.* A schedule of the positions of players.

lin·ger, ling′gər, *v.i.* To remain or stay on in a place longer than is usual or expected, as if from reluctance to leave it; loiter; to die slowly. **—lin·ger·er,** *n.* **—lin·ger·ing·ly,** *adv.*

lin·ge·rie, län′zhə·rā′, län′zhə·rē, *n.* Women's underwear and sleepwear.

lin·go, ling′gō, *n. pl.,* **-goes.** *Informal.* Language; speech; a language one does not understand.

lin·gua fran·ca, ling′gwə frang′kə, *n.* A compound language spoken along the Mediterranean coast, serving as a common medium of communication; any language, often hybrid, serving as a means of communication.

lin·gual, ling′gwəl, *a.* Of or pertaining to the tongue or some tonguelike part; pertaining to the use of the tongue in speaking; pertaining to languages. **—lin·gual·ly,** *adv.*

lin·guist, ling′gwist, *n.* A person skilled in languages; a polyglot.

lin·guis·tics, ling·gwis′tiks, *n. pl., sing.* or *pl.* in *constr.* The science dealing with the origin, structure, history, regional variations, and phonetic attributes of language. **—lin·guis·tic,** *a.* **—lin·guis·ti·cal,** *a.* **—lin·guis·ti·cal·ly,** *adv.*

lin·i·ment, lin′ə·mənt, *n.* A preparation for rubbing on the skin, as for sprains or bruises.

lin·ing, lī′ning, *n.* A layer of material on the inner side of something.

link, lingk, *n.* One of the rings or separate pieces of which a chain is composed; one of the parts of any chainlike arrangement.—*v.t., v.i.* To join; unite. **—linked,** *a.* **—link·er,** *n.*

link, lingk, *n.* A torch usu. made of tow with tar or pitch.

link·age, ling′kij, *n.* The act of linking; a system of links.

links, lingks, *n. pl.* A golf course.

lin·net, lin′it, *n.* A small Old World finch.

li·no·le·um, li·nō′lē·əm, *n.* A floor covering made of oxidized linseed oil and ground cork on a backing of canvas.

lin·seed, lin′sēd, *n.* Flaxseed.

lin·seed oil, *n.* The oil obtained by pressing flaxseed, used for its drying qualities in making paints, printing inks, and the like.

lint, lint, *n.* Fluff or fuzz consisting of yarn or fabric ravelings; a soft substance made by scraping linen, used for dressing wounds. **—lint·y,** *a.,* **-i·er, -i·est.**

lin·tel, lin′təl, *n.* The horizontal structure over a door, window, or similar opening.

li·on, lī′ən, *n.* A large, tawny, meat-eating animal of the cat family, native in Africa and southern Asia, the male of which has a full, flowing mane; a man of great strength or courage; a prominent person. **—li·on·ess,** lī′ə·nis, *n. fem.* **—li·on·like,** *a.*

lion·heart·ed, lī′ən·här′tid, *a.* Brave; courageous.

li·on·ize, lī′ə·nīz, *v.t.,* **-ized, -iz·ing.** To treat as a celebrity. **—li·on·i·za·tion,** lī·ən·ə·zā′shən, *n.* **—li·on·iz·er,** *n.*

li·on's share, *n.* The largest portion.

lip, lip, *n.* Either of two fleshy parts or folds forming the margins of the mouth; a liplike part or structure; the margin or edge of a vessel, esp. a projecting edge as of a pitcher. *Informal.* Impudent talk.—*a.* Applied to the lip or lips; labial; insincere; superficial.—*v.t.,* **lipped, lip·ping.** To touch with the lips; to utter; to use the lips in playing a musical instrument.

lip·py, lip′ē, *a.,* **-pi·er, -pi·est.** *Informal.* Impudent in speech.

lip read·ing, *n.* The reading or understanding, as by a deaf person, of the movements of another's lips forming words. **—lip-read,** lip′rēd, *v.t.,* **-read, -read·ing. —lip-read·er,** *n.*

lip·stick, lip′stik, *n.* A cosmetic, contained in a small

tube, for coloring the lips.

liq·ue·fy, lik′wə·fī, *v.t., v.i.,* **-fied, -fy·ing.** To convert or be converted from a solid form to a liquid. **—liq·ue·fac·tion,** lik·wə·fak′shən, *n.* **—liq·ue·fi·a·ble,** *a.* **—liq·ue·fi·er,** *n.*

li·queur, li·kər′, *n.* Any of a class of alcoholic liquors, usu. strong, sweet, and highly flavored.

liq·uid, lik′wid, *a.* Able to flow like water; neither gaseous nor solid; clear, transparent, or bright; flowing easily and smoothly; of movement, facile; in cash, or easily convertible into cash.—*n.* A fluid substance that is not a gas. **—li·quid·i·ty,** li·kwid′i·tē, **liq·uid·ness,** *n.* **—liq·uid·ly,** *adv.*

liq·ui·date, lik′wi·dāt, *v.t.,* **-dat·ed, -dat·ing.** To settle or pay, as a debt or claim; to reduce, as accounts, to order; to turn into cash; to settle the accounts and distribute the assets of; to do away with.—*v.i.* To liquidate debts or accounts; go into liquidation. **—liq·ui·da·tion,** lik·wi·dā′shən, *n.* **—liq·ui·da·tor,** *n.*

liq·uor, lik′ər, *n.* A distilled alcoholic beverage as distinguished from a fermented beverage; any liquid. —*v.t. Informal.* To ply with liquor, often with *up.*—*v.i.* To drink liquor, often with *up.*

lisle, līl, *n.* A kind of twisted thread made of cotton; material made of this thread.

lisp, lisp, *v.i., v.t.* To pronounce imperfectly, as by giving the sound of *th* or *dh* to the sibilant letters *s* and *z;* to speak imperfectly.—*n.* The habit or act of lisping. **—lisp·ing·ly,** *adv.*

lis·some, lis·som, lis′əm, *a.* Supple; flexible; lithe; agile. **—lis·some·ly,** *adv.* **—lis·some·ness,** *n.*

list, list, *n.* A record consisting of a series of names, words, or the like; a number of names of persons or things set down one after another; a catalog.—*v.t.* To set down together in a list, or make a list of.—*v.i.* To be presented for sale at a specific price, as in a catalog. **—list·ed,** *a.* **—lis·ter,** *n.* **—list·ing.** *n.*

list, list, *v.i.* To careen or incline to one side, as a ship.—*v.t.* To cause to lean to one side.—*n.* A leaning to one side.

lis·ten, lis′ən, *v.i.* To give close attention in order to hear; to give ear; to hear and attend to.—*n.*—**listen in,** to participate in hearing (a broadcast, telephone conversation, etc.); to eavesdrop. **—lis·ten·er,** *n.*

list·less, list′lis, *a.* Characterized by a lack of interest or energy; spiritless. **—list·less·ly,** *adv.* **—list·less·ness,** *n.*

list price, *n.* The published or suggested retail price of a commodity.

lit·a·ny, lit′ə·nē, *n. pl.,* **-nies.** A prayer comprising a series of solemn invocations and their fixed responses.

li·tchi, lē′chē, *n. pl.,* **-tchis.** A sweet, thin-shelled fruit yielded by a tree of China; the litchi tree. Also **li·chee.**

li·ter, lē′tər, *n.* Metric measure of capacity, a cubic decimeter, and equivalent to 1.0567 U.S. liquid quarts.

lit·er·a·cy, lit′ər·ə·sē, *n.* Possessing the skills of reading and writing.

lit·er·al, lit′ər·əl, *a.* According to the letter or verbal expression; following the letter or exact words; tending to interpret statements factually or unimaginatively; consisting of or expressed by letters. **—lit·er·al·i·ty,** lit·ə·ral′i·tē, **lit·er·al·ness,** *n.* **—lit·er·al·ly,** *adv.*

lit·er·ar·y, lit′ə·rer·ē, *a.* Pertaining to or dealing with letters or literature; well-read; engaged in the writing profession. **—lit·er·ar·i·ly,** *adv.* **—lit·er·ar·i·ness,** *n.*

lit·er·ate, lit′ər·it, *a.* Able to read and write; educated; learned.—*n.* **—lit·er·ate·ly,** *adv.*

lit·e·ra·ti, lit·ə·rä′tē, lit·ə·rā′tī, *n. pl.* Literary men; scholars.

lit·er·a·ture, lit′ər·ə·chər, lit′ər·ə·chûr, lit′rə·chər, *n.* The class of writings in which imaginative expression, aesthetic form, universality of ideas, and permanence are characteristic features, as fiction, poetry, romance, and drama; literary productions collectively; the literary productions upon a given subject, or a particular branch of knowledge; the collective writings of a country or period; the occupation of an author or writer. *Informal.* Any printed material.

lithe, līth, *a.* Easily bent; pliant; flexible; limber. Also **lithe·some,** līth'səm, **—lithe·ly,** *adv.* **—lithe·ness,** *n.*

lith·i·um, lith'ē·əm, *n.* A metallic element, soft and silver-white, the lightest metal known.

lith·o·graph, lith'ə·graf, lith'ə·gräf, *n.* A print produced by lithography.—*v.t.* To produce or copy by lithography. **—li·thog·ra·pher,** li·thog'rə·fər, *n.* **—lith·o·graph·ic,** lith·ə·graf'ik, *a.* **—lith·o·graph·i·cal·ly,** *adv.*

li·thog·ra·phy, li·thog'rə·fē, *n.* The art or process of producing a picture, writing, or the like, on a flat, specially prepared stone or metal plate, and of taking ink impressions from this as in ordinary printing.

lit·i·gate, lit'ə·gāt, *v.t.,* **-gat·ed, -gat·ing.** To make the subject of a lawsuit.—*v.i.* **—lit·i·ga·tion,** lit·ə·gā'shən, *n.* **—lit·i·ga·tor,** *n.*

lit·mus, lit'məs, *n.* A blue coloring matter procured from certain lichens, used as a test for acids.

lit·mus pa·per, *n.* Paper colored with litmus that turns red in acids and blue again in alkalies.

lit·ter, lit'ər, *n.* Articles scattered in a slovenly manner; scattered rubbish; the young produced at one birth by a mammal that normally bears multiple young; a stretcher; a portable, often canopied couch or bed carried on a shafted frame; straw, hay, or other soft substance used as a bed for animals or as plant protection.—*v.t.* To make untidy, as a place, with scattered articles; to scatter in a careless manner; to give birth to.—*v.i.* To scatter matter about in a careless or slovenly manner; to bring forth a litter.

lit·ter·bug, lit'ər·bəg, *n. Informal.* One who strews refuse or trash on public property.

lit·tle, lit'əl, *a.,* **lit·tler** or **less** or **less·er; lit·tlest** or **least.** Small or relatively small in size or extent; short in duration; having a small amount of dignity, power, importance, or status; small in mind; petty, mean, or narrow.—*n.* That which is insignificant; a short time or distance; a small quantity, space, degree, or the like. —*adv.,* **less, least.** In a small quantity or degree; infrequently; not at all.—**lit·tle by lit·tle,** by degrees; gradually.—**make lit·tle of,** treat as insignificant.

lit·to·ral, lit'ər·əl, *a.* Of or pertaining to a shore.—*n.* The shore or area along a shore.

lit·ur·gy, lit'ər·jē, *n. pl.,* **-gies.** The ritual or established formulas for public worship. **—lit·ur·gist,** lit'ər·jist, *n.* **—li·tur·gic,** li·tər'jik, **li·tur·gi·cal,** *a.*

liv·a·ble, live·a·ble, liv'ə·bəl, *a.* Endurable; habitable or suitable for living in, as a house. **—liv·a·ble·ness, live·a·ble·ness,** *n.*

live, liv, *v.i.,* **lived, liv·ing.** To have life; to continue; to remain effective; to pass or spend life in a particular manner; to conduct oneself in life; to abide, dwell, reside; to feed or subsist, with *on.*—*v.t.* To pass or spend; to illustrate by example.—**live and let live,** to practice tolerance toward the conduct or beliefs of others.—**live down,** to live so as to atone for an error, scandal, or the like.—**live up to,** to satisfy an aim or standard; to fulfill an obligation. **—liv·er,** *n.*

live, liv, *a.* Being alive; of or pertaining to life or living beings; characterized by or indicating the presence of living creatures; full of life, energy, or activity; of present interest, as a question or issue; burning or glowing; vivid or bright; loaded or unexploded; charged with or carrying a current of electricity; pertaining to a performance or appearance in person.

lived, līvd, *a.* Having life or a life as specified, usu. used in compounds.

live·li·hood, liv'lē·hůd, *n.* Means of maintaining life; support of life.

live·long, liv'lông, liv'long, *a.* Lasting a long time; entire, esp. when seemingly slow in passing.

live·ly, liv'lē, *a.,* **-li·er, -li·est.** Brisk; vivacious; active;

spirited; strong; keen; full of activity; fresh; resilient; bright.—*adv.* In a lively manner. **—live·li·ness,** *n.*

liv·en, lī'vən, *v.t.* To put life into; to cheer, often with *up.*—*v.i.* To brighten, usu. with *up.* **—liv·en·er,** *n.*

liv·er, liv'ər, *n.* A large glandular organ, situated in the abdominal cavity, which secretes bile and performs various metabolic functions; a similar organ in an animal; such an organ, or the flesh of one, used as food.

liv·er·wurst, liv'ər·wərst, *n.* Liver sausage.

liv·er·y, liv'ə·rē, liv'rē, *n. pl.,* **-ies.** The distinctive uniform or attire worn by male servants; the care and feeding of horses at a certain rate; the stable which affords such care. **—liv·er·ied,** *a.* **—liv·er·y·man,** *n. pl.,* **-men.**

live·stock, līv'stok, *n.* Domestic animals, kept on a farm for use and profit.

live' wire, līv, *n.* A wire carrying a current of electricity. *Informal.* An energetic, alert, or enterprising person.

liv·id, liv'id, *a.* Black and blue, as bruised flesh; of a lead or ashen color, as the face; discolored by contusion, as flesh. *Informal.* Enraged; furious. **—li·vid·i·ty,** liv·id'ə·tē, **liv·id·ness,** *n.* **—liv·id·ly,** *adv.*

liv·ing, liv'ing, *n.* The act or condition of one who or that which lives; manner or course of life; means of maintaining life or livelihood; those alive, preceded by *the.*—*a.* Alive; not dead; in actual existence or use; active, vigorous, or strong; burning or glowing; pertaining to or sufficient for living: *living* conditions, a *living* wage. **—liv·ing·ly,** *adv.* **—liv·ing·ness,** *n.*

liv·ing room, *n.* A room for general family use and social activity.

liv·ing wage, *n.* An income sufficient for a wage earner to support himself and his dependents at or above minimum standards.

liz·ard, liz'ərd, *n.* A four-legged reptile with an elongated body, tapering tail, and scaly or granular skin.

lla·ma, lä'mə, *n.* A woolly-haired S. American mammal related to the camel but smaller and used as a beast of burden.

lla·no, lä'nō, *n. pl.,* **-nos.** A treeless plain.

lo, lō, *interj.* Look; see; behold.

load, lōd, *n.* That which is laid on or placed in anything for conveyance; a burden; the quantity that can be or usu. is carried; the charge of a firearm. *Informal.* A sufficient quantity of liquor drunk to intoxicate. *Pl. Informal.* A great quantity or number.—*v.t.* To put a load on or in; to supply abundantly or excessively with something; to burden or oppress; to charge, as a firearm; to place on or in something for conveyance. —*v.i.* To take on a load; load a firearm; become loaded, burdened, or weighted. **—load·ed,** *a.* **—load·er,** *n.*

loaf, lōf, *n. pl.,* **loaves.** Bread baked in a mass of definite form; a shaped or molded mass of other food.

loaf, lōf, *v.i.* To lounge; to idle away one's time.—*v.t.* To pass or spend in idleness, as time.

loaf·er, lō'fər, *n.* A lazy person; a shoe for casual wear.

loam, lōm, *n.* A rich soil compounded of sand, clay, and organic matter. **—loam·y,** *a.*

loan, lōn, *n.* The act of lending or condition of being lent; that which is lent, esp. a sum of money at interest.—*v.t., v.i.* To lend.

loan shark, *n. Informal.* A money lender who charges exorbitant, usu. illegal, rates of interest.

loan word, *n.* A word borrowed or adopted from another language.

loath, loth, lōth, *a.* Very averse; reluctant; unwilling. **—loath·ness,** *n.*

loathe, lōth, *v.t.,* **loathed, loath·ing.** To feel disgust for; to abhor.

loath·ing, lō'thing, *n.* Extreme disgust or aversion; abhorrence. **—loath·ing·ly,** *adv.*

loath·some, lōth'səm, lōth'səm, *a.* Exciting disgust;

odious; detestable. **—loath·some·ly,** adv. **—loath·some·ness,** n.

lob, lob, v.t., **lobbed, lob·bing.** To throw, hit, or toss in a high arc or curve.—v.i. To lob an object, as a ball.

lob·by, lob′ē, n. pl., **-bies.** An entrance hall used as a waiting room in a theater, apartment building, or hotel. A person or group of people, representing special interests, who endeavor by personal persuasion to influence legislators' voting policies and other decision-making.—v.i. To try to influence legislators. —v.t. To back or try to secure passage of. **—lob·by·ist,** n.

lobe, lōb, n. A roundish projection or division, as of an organ or leaf; the soft, pendulous lower part of the external ear. **—lo·bar,** lō′bər, lō′bär, a. **—lo·bate,** lō′bāt, a. **—lobed,** a.

lob·ster, lob′stər, n. An edible, marine, stalk-eyed crustacean having two enormous claws.

lo·cal, lō′kəl, a. Pertaining to a particular place; limited or confined to a spot, place, or definite district; pertaining to a particular segment of an organization; making a stop at every station along the way.—n. One living in a particular place; a local segment of an organization; a bus or train that stops at every station on the route. **—lo·cal·ly,** adv.

lo·cale, lō-kal′, n. A place, esp. with reference to its characteristics or an event related to it.

lo·cal·i·ty, lō-kal′i·tē, n. pl., **-ties.** A position, situation, place, or district; a geographical place or situation.

lo·cal·ize, lō′kə·līz, v.t., v.i., **-ized, -iz·ing.** To fix in or assign to a particular place. **—lo·cal·i·za·tion,** lō·kəl·ə·zā′shən, n.

lo·cate, lō′kāt, lō·kāt′, v.t., **-cat·ed, -cat·ing.** To set in a particular spot or position; to place; to ascertain the whereabouts of; to point out something, as on a map.—v.i. To settle. **—lo·ca·ter, lo·ca·tor,** n.

lo·ca·tion, lō·kā′shən, n. The act of locating; the place where one settles.

loch, lok, n. A lake; an arm of the sea running into the land.

lo·ci, lō′sī, n. Plural of **lo·cus.**

lock, lok, n. A tuft of hair; a tuft of wool, or the like; pl., the hair on one's head.

lock, lok, n. A contrivance for fastening or securing something; the mechanism in a firearm by means of which the charge is exploded; an enclosed portion of a canal or river, with gates at each end, for raising or lowering vessels from one level to another; any of various grapples or holds in wrestling.—v.t. To fasten, as a door or gate, by the operation of a lock; to secure by so fastening doors, gates, or the like; to shut in a place fastened by a lock, often followed by up; to join or unite firmly by interlinking or intertwining; to move, as a vessel, by means of a lock or locks, as in a canal.—v.i. To become locked; to go or pass by means of a lock or locks, as a vessel.**—lock, stock, and barrel,** completely; totally. **—lock·a·ble,** a.

lock·er, lok′ər, n. A chest, drawer, compartment, closet, or the like, that may be locked.

lock·et, lok′it, n. A small case for holding a miniature portrait, a lock of hair, or other keepsake, and worn as an ornament, often on a necklace.

lock·jaw, lok′jô, n. A form of tetanus which causes the jaws to become locked together.

lock·out, lok′owt, n. An employer's closing or partial closing of a place of work until the employees accept the employer's terms.

lock·smith, lok′smith, n. One whose occupation is to make or repair locks.

lock·up, lok′əp, n. A place for the temporary detention of persons under arrest; a jail.

lo·co, lō′kō, a. Informal. Insane; crazy.

lo·co·mo·tion, lō·kə·mō′shən, n. The act or power of moving from place to place. **—lo·co·mo·tor,** a., n.

lo·co·mo·tive, lō·kə·mō′tiv, a. Of or pertaining to movement from place to place; moving from place to

place by its own powers of locomotion, as an animal. —n. A self-propelled engine used for moving trains.

lo·co·weed, lō′kō·wēd, n. A plant found in southwestern U.S., that causes disease in cattle.

lo·cus, lō′kəs, n. pl., **-ci,** -sī. A place; locality. Math. The set of or figure consisting of all points, lines, or surfaces that satisfy a given condition.

lo·cust, lō′kəst, n. A grasshopper which migrates in large numbers, destroying vegetation. A thorny-branched, white-flowered American legume tree.

lo·cu·tion, lō·kū′shən, n. A phrase; a style of speech or verbal expression.

lode, lōd, n. A vein or body of metallic ore.

lode·star, lōd′stär, n. A star that shows the way, esp. the North Star.

lode·stone, lōd′stōn, n. The mineral, magnetite, which possesses magnetic polarity and attracts iron; something that attracts.

lodge, loj, v.t., **lodged, lodg·ing.** To furnish with a room in one's house for payment; to have as a lodger; to serve as a habitation or shelter for; to shelter; to harbor; to bring or send into a particular place or position; to contain or enclose; to vest, as with power; to lay, as information or a complaint, before a court or similar authority.—v.i. To live in hired quarters in another's house or a hotel; to be fixed or implanted in a place or position.—n. A small shelter or habitation, used as a temporary abode, as in the hunting season; a resort inn or hotel; the habitation of an animal, esp. of a beaver or muskrat; the meeting place of a branch of a fraternal or secret society; the members composing the branch; a secret society as a whole. **—lodg·er,** n. **—lodg·ment, lodge·ment,** n.

lodg·ing, loj′ing, n. A place of abode, esp. a temporary one; accommodation in a house, esp. in rooms for hire; pl., a room or rooms hired for residence in another's house.

loft, lôft, loft, n. A floor or room above another, esp. that directly beneath the roof; a hayloft; a gallery in a church or hall, as for a choir; any upper story of a warehouse, mercantile building, or factory.—v.t. To hit upward, as a golf ball; to go over or clear, as an obstacle.—v.i. To hit or propel something into the air.

loft·y, lôf′tē, lof′tē, a., **-i·er, -i·est.** Extremely high; tall; elevated; proud; haughty; stately. **—loft·i·ly,** adv. **—loft·i·ness,** n.

log, lôg, log, n. A bulky piece of unhewed timber either from a branch or tree trunk; a device for measuring the rate of a ship's velocity through the water; a record or account, as of ship and aircraft travel, motion picture shooting, or radio and television transmission.—v.t. To cut into logs; to record or account for.—v.i. To chop down and transport trees.

log, lôg, log, n. Logarithm.

lo·gan·ber·ry, lō′gən·ber·ē, n. pl., **-ries.** The red fruit of the bramble related to the blackberry; the plant itself.

log·a·rithm, lôg′ə·rith·əm, log′ə·rith·əm, n. The exponent or power to which a fixed number, called the base, must be raised in order to produce a given number, called the antilogarithm. Also **log. —log·a·rith·mic,** lôg·ə·rith′mik, log·ə·rith′mik, **log·a·rith·mi·cal,** a. **—log·a·rith·mi·cal, log·a·rith·mi·cal·ly,** adv.

log·book, lôg′bûk, log′bûk, n. A book containing the record of a journey of a ship, aircraft, etc.

loge, lōzh, n. A box in a theater or opera house; the front section of the first balcony.

log·ger, lô′gər, log′ər, n. One engaged in logging, a lumberjack.

log·ger·head, lô′gər·hed, log′ər·hed, n. A large-headed marine turtle of the Atlantic Ocean.

log·ic, loj′ik, n. The science of formal reasoning, using principles of valid inference; a system of reasoning or argumentation; the apparently unavoidable cause and effect relationship of events leading to a particular conclusion. **—lo·gi·cian,** lō·jish′ən, n.

log·i·cal, loj′i·kəl, *a.* Of or pertaining to logic. Reasoning in accordance with the principles of logic. **—log·i·cal·i·ty,** loj′i·kal′i·tē, *n.* **—log·i·cal·ly,** *adv.* **—log·i·cal·ness,** *n.*

lo·gis·tics, lō·jis′tiks, *n. pl. but sing. in constr.* The branch of military science concerned with the procurement, transportation, maintenance, and supply of troops, equipment, and facilities. **—lo·gis·tic, lo·gis·ti·cal,** *a.*

log·jam, lôg′jam, log′jam, *n.* A group of logs which have wedged together in a river; any barrier, impediment, or deadlock.

log·roll·ing, lôg′rō·ling, log′rō·ling, *n.* The practice, esp. among legislators, of trading votes or favors for mutual political profit. **—log·roll,** *v.t., v.i.*

lo·gy, lō′gē, *a.,* **-gi·er, -gi·est.** *Informal.* Heavy; sluggish; dull.

loin, loyn, *n. Usu. pl.* The part or parts of the body of man on either side of the vertebral column between the false ribs and the hipbone; a cut of meat from the loin of an animal, esp. a portion including the vertebrae of such parts.

loin·cloth, loyn′klôth, *n.* A piece of cloth worn about the loins or hips, commonly worn by natives of warm countries.

loi·ter, loy′tər, *v.i.* To linger idly or aimlessly in or about a place or on one's way; to move or go in a slow manner.—*v.t.* To pass, as time, in an idle or aimless manner, usu. followed by *away.* **—loi·ter·er,** *n.*

loll, lol, *v.i.* To recline in a lax, lazy manner; to lounge; to hang extended loosely, as the tongue of a dog.—*v.t.* To let hang or droop.—*n.*

lol·li·pop, lol·ly·pop, lol′ē·pop, *n.* A hard candy that is on a short stick. Also **suck·er.**

lone, lōn, *a.* Solitary; not having others near.

lone·ly, lōn′lē, *a.,* **-li·er, -li·est.** Unfrequented by man; deserted; not having others near; sad from want of companionship; characterized by sadness, desolation, or the feeling of emptiness. **—lone·li·ly,** *adv.* **—lone·li·ness,** *n.*

lon·er, lō′nər, *n.* A person who chooses to be alone.

lone·some, lōn′səm, *a.* Depressed due to a lack of company; lonely; isolated. **—by one's lone·some.** *Informal.* All by oneself. **—lone·some·ly,** *adv.* **—lone·some·ness,** *n.*

long, lông, *a.* Having considerable extent or duration; not short; having many items, as a series, enumeration, or the like; having a specified extension in space, duration, quantity, or the like; beyond the normal or standard quantity, space, or duration; extending to a great distance in space or time; lengthy; tedious; having a long time to run.—*n.* Something that is long; a long time.—*adv.* For or through a great extent of space or time; for a specified period or time; throughout the entire time; at a point of time far distant from the time indicated.—**in the long run,** after a long course or experience; in the final result.—**so long as, as long as,** provided that.

long, lông, long, *v.i.* To desire earnestly or eagerly, usu. followed by an infinitive, or by *for* or *after.*

long dis·tance, *n.* The service handling telephone calls between distant areas. **—long-dis·tance,** lông′dis′təns, long′dis′təns, *a., adv.*

lon·gev·i·ty, lon·jev′i·tē, *n.* Long life; a period of time in a job or position.

long·hair, lông′her, long′her, *n. Informal.* An intellectual; a performer or devotee of the arts, esp. of classical music; a long-haired, unconventional person.—*a.* Also **long-hair, long-haired.**

long·hand, lông′hand, long′hand, *n.* The ordinary written characters used in handwriting, with the words completely written out.—*a.*

long·ing, lông′ing, long′ing, *n.* An earnest desire; a yearning.—*a.* **—long·ing·ly,** *adv.*

lon·gi·tude, lon′ji·tood, lon′ji·tūd, *n.* Distance east or west of the prime meridian, expressed in degrees or in hours and minutes.

lon·gi·tu·di·nal, lon·jə·too′də·nəl, lon·jə·tū′də·nəl, *a.* Lengthwise; pertaining to longitude. **—lon·gi·tu·di·nal·ly,** *adv.*

long-lived, lông′līvd′, long′līvd′, lông′livd′, long′livd′, *a.* Having a long life; lasting long. **—long-lived·ness,** *n.*

long-play·ing, lông′plā′ing, long′plā′ing, *a.* Indicating a phonograph record which plays at 33⅓ revolutions per minute.

long-range, lông′rānj′, long′rānj′, *a.* Relating to extended distances or long periods of future time.

long·shore·man, lông′shôr·mən, long′shôr·mən, *n. pl.,* **-men.** A dock laborer employed at loading and unloading ships.

long shot, *n.* Any undertaking offering little hope of success but great gains if achieved.—**not by a long shot.** *Informal.* Not at all; decidedly out of the question.

long-suf·fer·ing, lông′səf′ər·ing, long′səf′ər·ing, *a.* Bearing injuries or provocation for a long time; patient.—*n.* **—long-suf·fer·ing·ly,** *adv.*

long-term, lông′tərm, long′tərm, *a.* Having a relatively long duration.

long-wind·ed, lông′win′did, long′win′did, *a.* Talking or writing at a tedious length; capable of prolonged exertion without being out of breath. **—long-wind·ed·ly,** *adv.* **—long-wind·ed·ness,** *n.*

long·wise, lông′wīz, long′wīz, *adv.* Lengthwise. Also **long·ways,** lông′wāz.

look, lûk, *v.i.* To employ one's vision; to direct the eyes toward an object; consider; to have or assume a particular air or manner; to seem or appear to the mind or eye; to have a particular indicated direction, outlook, or situation.—*v.t.* To express or show by a look; to seek, followed by *up;* to examine, often followed by *over.*—*n.* Act of looking; usu. pl., outward aspect or appearance.—**look af·ter,** to take care of. **—look back,** to recollect or reflect on.—**look down on,** to regard as inferior. **—look for·ward to,** to expect eagerly.—**look in,** to make a brief visit.—**look out,** to be alert or watchful.—**look the oth·er way,** to ignore or avoid.—**look up to,** to respect or admire. **—look·er,** *n.*

look·er-on, lûk′ər·ôn′, lûk′ər·on′, *n. pl.,* **look·ers-on.** A spectator or onlooker.

look·ing glass, *n.* A mirror.

look·out, lûk′owt, *n.* The act of looking out; a watch kept, as for something that may happen; a person or party stationed or employed to keep such a watch; a station or place from which a watch is kept.

loom, loom, *n.* A machine or apparatus for weaving yarn or thread into a fabric; the art or the process of weaving.

loom, loom, *v.i.* To appear indistinctly or come into view in indistinct and enlarged form; to impend or threaten.

loon, loon, *n.* A diving waterfowl characterized by prolonged underwater swimming, a sharp, pointed bill, and a laughterlike call.

loon, loon, *n.* An idle or worthless man; a crazy person.

loon·y, loo′nē, *a.,* **-i·er, -i·est.** *Informal.* Crazy; insane; extremely foolish.—*n. pl.,* **-ies.** *Informal.* A lunatic. **—loon·i·ness,** *n.*

loop, loop, *n.* A folding or doubling of a portion of a cord, thread, ribbon, or the like, upon itself, so as to leave an opening between the parts; the portion so doubled; anything shaped like a loop.—*v.t.* To form into a loop or loops; to encircle with something arranged in a loop; to fasten by a loop.—*v.i.* To make or form a loop or loops.—**loop the loop,** to execute a loop or series of loops in an airplane; to traverse a looplike course or track, as on a roller coaster.

---

a- hat, fāte, fâre, fäther; e- met, mē; i- pin, pīne; o- not, nōte, ôrb, moove (move), boy, pownd;
u- cūbe, bûll, tûk (took); ch- chin; th- thick, ŧhen; zh- vizhon (vision); ə- ə̄go, takən, pencəl, lemən, bərd (bird).

loop·hole, loop/hōl, *n.* A small aperture in a wall for observation, ventilation, or illumination; an opportunity for escape or evasion, esp. a textual basis in a document or law for escape or evasion of taxes, legal commitments, or obligations.—*v.t.,* **-holed, -hol·ing.**

loose, loos, *a.,* **loos·er, loos·est.** Free from bonds, fetters, or restraint; free or released from fastening or attachment; unpackaged; unemployed or unappropriated; lacking proper control or power of restraint; not tight or constricted; free from moral restraint, or lax in principle or conduct; not firmly fixed in place; slack, relaxed, or lacking tension; not fitting closely, as garments; not close or compact; having freedom while still being associated.—*v.t.,* **loosed, loos·ing.** To let loose or free from bonds or restraint; to release, as from constraint, obligation, or penalty; to slacken, relax, or make less tight.—*v.i.* To let go a hold; to shoot or let fly an arrow.—*adv.* In a loose manner; loosely.—**cut loose, let loose,** to free. *Informal.* To enjoy oneself in an unrestrained way. —**loose·ly,** *adv.* —**loose·ness,** *n.*

loos·en, loo/sən, *v.t.* To render less firm, tight, or compact.—*v.i.* To become loose or looser.

loose end, *n.* A matter left unsettled or unfinished. —at loose ends, in a confused, undecided, or unsettled state.

loot, loot, *n.* Spoils or plunder; anything dishonestly and ruthlessly appropriated. *Informal.* Money.—*v.t.* To plunder or pillage; rob.—*v.i.* To plunder. —**loot·er,** *n.*

lop, lop, *v.t.,* **lopped, lop·ping.** To remove or cut off the top, extreme, or superfluous parts of anything, usu. with *off;* to trim or clip, as a tree.

lop, lop, *v.i.,* **lopped, lop·ping.** To hang loosely or limply.—*v.t.* To allow to hang loosely.—*a.* Drooping: *lop*-eared.

lope, lōp, *v.i.,* **loped, lop·ing.** To move or run with a long, easy stride.—*v.t.*—*n.* The act or the gait of loping. —**lop·er,** *n.*

lop·sid·ed, lop/si/did, *a.* Larger or heavier at one side than the other. —**lop·sid·ed·ly,** *adv.* —**lop·sid·ed·ness,** *n.*

lo·qua·cious, lō·kwā/shəs, *a.* Talkative; verbose. —**lo·qua·cious·ly,** *adv.* —**lo·qua·cious·ness,** *n.* —**lo·quac·i·ty,** lō·kwas/i·tē, *n. pl.,* **-ties.**

lord, lôrd, *n.* A person possessing supreme power and authority, as a ruler, governor, monarch. (*Cap.*) A designation of the Supreme Being; God; Jesus Christ. (*Cap.*) *Brit.* A title given to peers below the rank of duke, as a marquis, earl, viscount, baron.—*v.i.* To domineer; to rule with arbitrary or despotic sway, followed by *it.*

lord·ly, lôrd/lē, *a.,* **-li·er, -li·est.** Befitting or suitable for a lord; grand, dignified, or elegant.—*adv.* —**lord·li·ness,** *n.*

lord·ship, lôrd/ship, *n.* The authority or rank of a lord; the territory over which a lord has jurisdiction; sovereignty; (*cap.*) in Great Britain, the title accorded a lord, usu. used with *his* or *your.*

lore, lōr, lôr, *n.* The store of knowledge which exists regarding a specific subject.

lor·gnette, lôrn·yet/, *n.* Opera glasses or eyeglasses with a handle.

lor·ry, lôr/ē, *n. pl.,* **-ries.** A large, motor-driven truck.

lose, looz, *v.t.,* **lost, los·ing.** To come to be without, by some chance, and have no hope of finding; to mislay; to suffer the loss or deprivation of; to fail to keep, preserve, or maintain; to forfeit or relinquish; to cease to have; to bring to destruction or ruin, now used chiefly in the passive: the ship and crew were *lost.* To have slip from sight, hearing, or attention; to become separated from or ignorant of; to waste; to fail to have, get, or catch; to miss; to fail to win.—*v.i.* To suffer loss; to fail to win; to lessen or depreciate in some way. —**los·a·ble,** *a.* —**los·er,** *n.* —**los·ing,** *a., n.*

loss, lôs, los, *n.* That which is lost; deprivation of, or a state of being without something that one has had; state of grief caused by death, or death itself; the failure to preserve or maintain.—at a loss, in a state of bewilderment or uncertainty.

lost, lôst, lost, *a.* No longer possessed or retained; no longer to be found; having gone astray, or bewildered as to place or direction; not used to good purpose, as opportunities, time, or labor; that which one has failed to win.—**lost cause,** a venture which is unsuccessful or doomed to failure.

lot, lot, *n.* One of a set of specially marked objects used to decide a question, make a decision, or select a winner by random selection; the casting or drawing of such objects as a method of deciding something; the decision or choice so made; allotted share or portion. *Informal.* A number of things or persons collectively. —*v.t.,* **lot·ted, lot·ting.** To cast or draw lots for; allot. —*v.i.* To cast or draw lots.—*adv.*

loth, lōth, *a.* Loath.

Lo·thar·i·o, lō·thār/ē·ō, *n. pl.,* **-os.** A man who seduces women; a rake.

lo·tion, lō/shən, *n.* A liquid for medicinal or cosmetic use which is applied the skin.

lot·ter·y, lot/ə·rē, *n. pl.,* **-ies.** A game or method of fund raising, by sale of numbered tickets which, when drawn by chance, entitle the holders to prizes; any affair that seems determined by chance.

lot·to, lot/ō, *n.* A game played by drawing numbered disks and covering corresponding numbers on cards, the winner being the first player to fill a row.

lo·tus, lō/təs, *n. pl.,* **-tus·es.** A plant which, according to legend, yielded a fruit that induced a state of forgetfulness and indolence in those who ate it; the fruit itself; a water lily. Also **lo·tos.**—**lo·tus-eat·er,** lō/təs-ē/tər, *n.*

loud, lowd, *a.* Strongly heard; of great volume or sound intensity, or carrying far; making very audible sounds. *Informal.* Flashy or showy; vulgar. —**loud·ly,** *adv.* —**loud·ness,** *n.*

loud-mouthed, lowd/mowthd, lowd/mowtht, *a.* Loud of voice to the irritation of others. —**loud-mouth, loud·mouth,** loud/mowth, *n.*

loud·speak·er, lowd/spē·kər, *n.* A device for amplifying sound.

lounge, lownj, *v.i.,* **lounged, loung·ing.** To pass time idly and indolently; loll; to move or go in a leisurely, easy manner.—*v.t.* To pass, as time, in lounging.—*n.* A kind of sofa for reclining; a place for lounging; a room open to the public where liquor is served, as in a hotel. —**loung·er,** *n.* —**loung·ing,** *a.*

louse, lows, *n. pl.,* **lice,** līs. A wingless, flat-bodied insect with biting and sucking mouth parts that is parasitic on man, animals, and plants. *Informal.* A mean or despicable person.—*v.t.*—**louse up.** *Informal.* To botch or mess up.

lous·y, low/zē, *a.,* **-i·er, -i·est.** Infested with lice. *Informal.* Foul or despicable; bad or inferior; well-provided with or having too much of something, followed by *with.* —**lous·i·ly,** *adv.* —**lous·i·ness,** *n.*

lout, lowt, *n.* An awkward person; a clown. —**lout·ish,** *a.* —**lout·ish·ly,** *adv.* —**lout·ish·ness,** *n.*

lou·ver, loo/vər, *n.* An arrangement of slats covering a window or other opening so arranged as to admit air but exclude rain. —**lou·vered,** *a.*

love, ləv, *n.* A feeling of warm personal attachment or deep affection; a strong or passionate affection for a person of the opposite sex; an object of love or affection; sweetheart.—*v.t.,* **loved, lov·ing.** To have deep or passionate affection for; be in love with; to treat with gestures of love; caress; to like very much or take great pleasure in; be fond of.—*v.i.* To have or express love; be in love. —**for love,** without compensation.—**for love or mon·ey,** for any consideration; by any means.—**for the love of,** for the sake of.—**in love,** enamored of someone or something.—**make love to,** to kiss, embrace, etc., as lovers.—**no love lost,** no love wasted, as between persons who care little for each other. —**lov·a·ble, love·a·ble,** ləv/ə·bəl, *a.* —**lov·a·bil·i·ty,** ləv·ə·bil/ə·tē, *a.* —**lov·a·ble·ness,** *n.* —**lov·a·**

bly, *adv.* —**love·less,** *a.*

love·bird, lev/berd, *n.* Any of various small parrots, remarkable for the apparent affection shown between mates.

love·lorn, lev/lôrn, *a.* Forsaken by one's love; pining or suffering because of this.

love·ly, lev/lē, *a.*, **-li·er, -li·est.** Charmingly or exquisitely beautiful; of great moral or spiritual beauty. *Informal.* Delightful or highly pleasing. —*adv.* —**love· li·ness,** *n.*

lov·er, lev/er, *n.* One who loves; one who is enamored of another person; a paramour; *pl.*, two persons in love with each other.

love seat, *n.* A small-sized sofa.

lov·ing, lev/ing, *a.* Affectionate; expressing love or kindness. —**lov·ing·ly,** *adv.* —**lov·ing·ness,** *n.*

lov·ing cup, *n.* A large cup, having two or more handles, given as a trophy.

low, lō, *a.* Of small extent upward; of less than average or normal height or depth; situated or occurring not far above the ground or floor; lying or being below the general level; far down in the scale of rank or estimation; lowly, humble, or meek; coarse or vulgar; dissolute or degraded; cheap; near depletion; lacking in strength or vigor; small in amount, degree, or force; not loud; depressed˙or dejected. —*adv.* In or to a low position, point, or degree; near the ground, floor, or base; not aloft; humbly; cheaply; softly; quietly. —*n.* That which is low; an arrangement of gears, as in an automobile, which yields a low speed; a low or the lowest level, degree, card, etc.; an area of low barometric pressure. —**low·ness,** *n.*

low·born, lō/bôrn, *a.* Of humble birth.

low·boy, lō/boy, *n.* A chest of drawers supported by short legs.

low·brow, lō/brow, *n. Informal.* A person who is uninterested in cultural matters or one who has vulgar tastes. —*a. Informal.* Of or pertaining to those of uncultivated tastes.

low·down, low-down, lō/down/, *a.* Mean; sneaking; contemptible. —lō/down, *n. Informal.* The facts in the case; the truth.

low·er, lō/er, *a.*, *compar. of* **low.** In a position or condition considered inferior to other values or ranks; located beneath something. —*v.t.* To make lower in position; to let down; to take or bring down; to reduce; to humble; to weaken. —*v.i.* To decrease; to become lower. —*n.*

low·er, low/er, *v.i.* To frown; to look sullen; to appear dark or gloomy; to threaten a storm. —*n.* A frown; a gloomy sky.

low·er-case, lō/er·kās/, *a.* Of small letters in printing, as opposed to capital letters. —*n.* —*v.t.* To type, set, or print with small letters.

low·er class, *n.* A class in society below all others in social rank. —**low·er-class,** *a.*

low·er·ing, low/er·ing, *a.* Threatening a storm; sullen. —**low·er·ing·ly,** *adv.*

low·er·y, low/er·ē, *a.* Cloudy; gloomy.

low-key, lō/kē/, *a.* Subdued; restrained; limited in intensity. Also **low-keyed.**

low·land, lō/land, *n.* Land which is lower than the neighboring country. —**low·land·er,** *n.*

low·ly, lō/lē, *a.*, **-li·er, -li·est.** Low or humble in position in life; not lofty or exalted; meek. —*adv.* In a low position, manner, or condition. —**low·li·ness,** *n.*

low-mind·ed, lō/mīn/did, *a.* Having ˙a mean or degraded mind. —**low-mind·ed·ly,** *adv.* —**low-mind· ed·ness,** *n.*

low tide, *n.* The lowest water level of the tide.

lox, loks, *n.* A variety of smoked salmon.

loy·al, loy/el, *a.* Faithful to one's oath, engagements, or obligations; faithful to any person or thing conceived as imposing obligations. —**loy·al·ist,** loy/e·

list, *n.* —**loy·al·ly,** *adv.* —**loy·al·ty,** *n. pl.*, **-ties.**

loz·enge, loz/inj, *n.* A small tablet, usu. medicated and sweetened, originally in the shape of a diamond.

LP, el/pē/, *a. Trademark.* Pertaining to a microgroove phonograph record rotating at the speed of 33¹/₃ revolutions per minute. —*n.* A long-playing record.

LSD, el/es/dē/, *n.* Lysergic acid diethylamide, a hallucinogenic drug, affecting the central nervous system, producing changes in thought, perception, and behavior.

lu·au, loo/ow, *n.* A Hawaiian feast.

lub·ber, lub/er, *n.* An awkward or clumsy individual; one who is unskilled in seamanship. —**lub·ber·li· ness,** *n.* —**lub·ber·ly,** *a.*, *adv.*

lu·bri·cant, loo/bre·kent, *n.* A lubricating material, as grease or oil.

lu·bri·cate, loo/bre·kāt, *v.t.*, **-cat·ed, -cat·ing.** To make slippery or smooth; to apply an oily or greasy substance in order to diminish friction. —*v.i.* To apply or serve as a lubricant to something. —**lu·bri·ca·tion,** loo/bre·kā/shen, *n.* —**lu·bri·ca·tive,** *a.* —**lu·bri·ca· tor,** *n.*

lu·cid, loo/sid, *a.* Easily understood, clear, or intelligible; rational, sane; shining; transparent. —**lu·cid·i·ty,** loo·sid/e·tē, **lu·cid·ness,** *n.* —**lu·cid·ly,** *adv.*

Lu·cite, loo/sīt, *n. Trademark.* A thermoplastic acrylic resin, used esp. as a substitute for glass.

luck, lek, *n.* Whatever happens to a person, as if by chance, in the course of events; fate; good fortune or success. —**luck·i·ly,** *adv.* —**luck·i·ness,** *n.*

luck·y, lek/ē, *a.*, **-i·er, -i·est.** Favored by luck; meeting with or resulting in success; believed capable of bringing success.

lu·cra·tive, loo/kre·tiv, *a.* Yielding profit or gain; profitable. —**lu·cra·tive·ly,** *adv.* —**lu·cra·tive· ness,** *n.*

lu·cre, loo/ker, *n.* Money; monetary profit.

lu·cu·brate, loo/kyū·brāt, *v.i.*, **-brat·ed, -brat·ing.** To write or study arduously, esp. at night. —**lu·cu· bra·tion,** loo/kyū·brā/shen, *n.* —**lu·cu·bra·tor,** *n.*

lu·di·crous, loo/de·kres, *a.* Producing laughter; comical; very ridiculous. —**lu·di·crous·ly,** *adv.* —**lu· di·crous·ness,** *n.*

luff, lef, *n.* The sailing of a ship with its head to the wind; the forward edge of a fore-and-aft sail. —*v.i.* To bring a ship's head close to the wind.

Luft·waf·fe, lûft/väf·e, *n.* The German air force during the Nazi regime.

lug, leg, *v.t.*, **lugged, lug·ging.** To haul; to drag; to pull along or carry. —*v.i.* To pull or tug. —*n.* A projecting part of an object resembling the human ear, as a handle.

lug·gage, lug/ij, *n.* Baggage, esp. hand baggage, such as suitcases, valises, etc.

lug·ger, leg/er, *n.* A small vessel or craft with either two or three lugsails.

lug·sail, leg/sāl, *n.* A sail with four corners fastened to a yard that crosses the mast at a slant.

lu·gu·bri·ous, lû·goo/brē·es, lû·gū/brē·es, *a.* Mournful; doleful, esp. in an exaggerated manner. —**lu·gu·bri·ous·ly,** *adv.* —**lu·gu·bri·ous·ness,** *n.*

luke·warm, look/wôrm/, *a.* Moderately warm; tepid; not ardent or zealous; indifferent. —**luke·warm·ly,** *adv.* —**luke·warm·ness,** *n.*

lull, lel, *v.t.* To cause to rest or sleep by gentle, soothing means; to quiet or calm down by deception. —*v.i.* To subside; to become calm. —*n.* A temporary quiet before or after a storm or great activity.

lull·a·by, lel/e·bī, *n. pl.*, **-bies.** A song to lull or quiet babies.

lum·ba·go, lem·bā/gō, *n.* Rheumatism of the lower back.

lum·bar, lem/ber, lem/bär, *a.* Of or pertaining to the loin or loins.

---

a- hat, fāte, fāre, fäther; **e-** met, mē; **i-** pin, pīne; **o-** not, nōte, ôrb, moove (move), boy, pownd; **u-** cūbe, bûll, tûk (took); **ch-** chin; **th-** thick, ᵺen; **zh-** vizhon (vision); **ə-** ego, taken, pencel, lemen, berd (bird).

lum·ber, ləm′bər, *v.i.* To move clumsily or heavily. —**lum·ber·ing·ly,** *adv.*

lum·ber, ləm′bər, *n.* Timber or logs sawed or split into various sizes for use as boards.—*v.t.* To convert, as logs, into lumber.—*v.i.* To cut or saw into lumber for marketing. —**lum·ber·er,** *n.*

lum·ber·ing, ləm′bər·ing, *n.* Logging.

lum·ber·jack, ləm′bər·jak, *n.* One who cuts or transports timber; a logger.

lum·ber·man, ləm′bər·mən, *n. pl.,* -**men.** A lumberjack; one who sells lumber.

lu·men, loo′mən, *n. pl.,* **lu·mens, lu·mi·na,** loo′mə·nə. A unit for measuring the light that falls on one square centimeter from a candle one centimeter distant.

lu·mi·nar·y, loo′mə·ner·ē, *n. pl.,* -**ies.** A person of eminence in a particular field; a body or thing that gives light, as the sun or moon.—*a.*

lu·mi·nes·cence, loo·mə·nes′əns, *n.* An emission of light not due directly to incandescence and occurring at a temperature below that of incandescent bodies; the light so produced. —**lu·mi·nes·cent,** *a.*

lu·mi·nous, loo′mə·nəs, *a.* Radiating or reflecting light; enlightening; clear or readily intelligible. —**lu·mi·nos·i·ty,** loo·mə·nos′ə·tē, *n.* —**lu·mi·nous·ly,** *adv.* —**lu·mi·nous·ness,** *n.*

lum·mox, ləm′əks, *n.* A dull-witted, awkward person.

lump, ləmp, *n.* A piece or mass of solid matter of no particular shape; a swelling; an aggregation, collection, or mass. *Informal.* A dull, stolid person; a big, sturdy person.—*v.t.* to unite into one aggregation, collection, or mass.—*v.i.* To form a lump or lumps; to move heavily.—**a lump in one's throat,** a tightening of the throat, as from an emotion.

lump, ləmp, *v.t., Informal.* To regard or endure with displeasure; put up with as a disagreeable necessity: Like it or *lump* it.

lump·y, ləm′pē, *a.,* -**i·er,** -**i·est.** Full of lumps; covered with lumps, as a surface; like a lump, as in being heavy or clumsy; rough or choppy, as water. —**lump·i·ly,** *adv.* —**lump·i·ness,** *n.*

lu·na·cy, loo′nə·sē, *n. pl.,* -**cies.** The height of folly or extravagant conduct; insanity.

lu·nar, loo′nər, *a.* Pertaining to or of the moon.

lu·nate, loo′nāt, *a.* Having a crescent shape, like that of the half-moon.

lu·na·tic, loo′nə·tik, *n.* An insane person.—*a.* Insane; mad; extremely irrational or reckless; for use by the insane, as an asylum.

lunch, lənch, *n.* A light meal, esp. one served between breakfast and dinner.—*v.i.* To eat lunch. —**lunch·er,** *n.*

lunch·eon, lən′chən, *n.* A midday meal, usu. a formal one.

lunch·room, lənch′room, lənch′rûm, *n.* A room where lunch may be eaten, in a school or other building; a restaurant where light meals are served.

lung, ləng, *n.* Either of the two saclike respiratory organs in man and other vertebrates that are air-breathing.

lunge, lənj, *n.* A thrust, as in fencing; any sudden forward movement.—*v.i.,* **lunged, lung·ing.** To make a lunge or thrust; move with a lunge.—*v.t.* To thrust; cause to move with a lunge.

lunk·head, ləngk′hed, *n. Informal.* A stupid person; a blockhead. —**lunk·head·ed,** *a.*

lu·pine, loo′pīn, *a.* Like a wolf; wolfish; ravenous.

lu·pine, lu·pin, loo′pin, *n.* A plant with blue, pink, or white flowers common in the eastern U.S.

lurch, lərch, *v.i.* To roll or heave suddenly to one side; to stagger.—*n.* A sudden roll of a ship; a stagger.

lurch, lərch, *n.* A thorough defeat.—**in the lurch,** in a hopeless situation.

lure, lûr, *n.* An enticement through the prospect of pleasure or advantage; an artificial bait or decoy, used in capturing animals or fish.—*v.t.,* **lured, lur·ing.** To entice; to attract.

lu·rid, lûr′id, *a.* Glaringly vivid or sensational; lighted up or shining with an unnatural or fiery glare. —**lu·rid·ly,** *adv.* —**lu·rid·ness,** *n.*

lurk, lərk, *v.i.* To lie in wait; to move furtively; to be concealed. —**lurk·er,** *n.* —**lurk·ing·ly,** *adv.*

lus·cious, ləsh′əs, *a.* Highly pleasing to the taste or smell; pleasurable to the senses. —**lus·cious·ly,** *adv.* —**lus·cious·ness,** *n.*

lush, ləsh, *a.* Having luxuriant foliage; marked by extravagance, opulence, or abundance. —**lush·ly,** *adv.* —**lush·ness,** *n.*

lush, ləsh, *n. Informal.* One who habitually drinks liquor to excess.—*v.t., v.i. Informal.* To drink liquor to excess.

lust, ləst, *n.* Sexual appetite; intense longing or passionate desire.—*v.i.* To have carnal desire; to desire eagerly, with *after* or *for.* —**lust·ful,** ləst′fəl, *a.* —**lust·ful·ly,** *adv.* —**lust·ful·ness,** *n.*

lus·ter, ləs′tər, *n.* Sheen; brightness or brilliance; splendor or distinction, as of achievement; fame; glossy surface of porcelain or pottery; fabric with a sheen.—*v.t.* To furnish with a gloss.—*v.i.* To become glossy. —**lus·ter·less,** *a.*

lus·trous, ləs′trəs, *a.* Characterized by luster or sheen; luminous; bright; shining. —**lus·trous·ly,** *adv.* —**lus·trous·ness,** *n.*

lust·y, ləs′tē, *a.,* -**i·er,** -**i·est.** Characterized by life, spirit, vigor, or health; robust or hearty. —**lust·i·ly,** *adv.* —**lust·i·ness,** *n.*

lute, loot, *n.* A stringed musical instrument, having a pear-shaped body and long, fretted, sharply-angled neck.

lu·te·ti·um, loo·tē′shē·əm, *n.* A metallic element of the rare-earth series.

lut·ist, loo′tist, *n.* A lute player; a lute maker.

lux·u·ri·ant, ləg·zhûr′ē·ənt, lək·shûr′ē·ənt, *a.* Exuberant in growth, as vegetation or foliage; richly abundant, profuse, or superabundant. —**lux·u·ri·ance, lux·u·ri·an·cy,** *n.* —**lux·u·ri·ant·ly,** *adv.*

lux·u·ri·ate, ləg·zhûr′ē·āt, lək·shûr′ē·āt, *v.i.,* -**at·ed,** -**at·ing.** To indulge or revel without restraint, followed by *in;* to live luxuriously. —**lux·u·ri·a·tion,** ləg·zhûr·ē·ā′shən, lək·shûr·ē·ā′shən, *n.*

lux·u·ri·ous, ləg·zhûr′ē·əs, lək·shûr′ē·əs, *a.* Marked by abundance or plentiful supply; opulent; furnished with luxuries; overelaborate. —**lux·u·ri·ous·ly,** *adv.* —**lux·u·ri·ous·ness,** *n.*

lux·u·ry, lək′shə·rē, ləg′zhə·rē, *n. pl.,* -**ries.** Any nonessential, usu. costly or scarce, which is personally gratifying; free or constant indulgence in such nonessentials.

ly·cée, lē·sā′, *n.* In France, a secondary school which prepares students for university study, and which is operated by the state.

ly·ce·um, li·sē′əm, *n.* An organization or a building for popular education through plays, lectures, concerts, and discussions.

lye, lī, *n.* Any strong alkaline solution used chiefly in washing or in making soap.

ly·ing, lī′ing, *n.* Intentional untruthfulness.—*a.* Marked by, or given to lying.

ly·ing-in, lī′ing·in′, *n.* A woman's confinement during and following childbirth.—*a.* Referring to childbirth.

lymph, limf, *n.* A clear, bodily fluid, composed of plasma and white corpuscles, and carried in the lymphatic vessel system. —**lym·phoid,** lim′foyd, *a.*

lym·phat·ic, lim·fat′ik, *a.* Referring to, containing, or conveying lymph; sluggish.

lymph node, *n.* One of the many masses of lymphatic tissue found throughout the lymphatic system.

lynch, linch, *v.t.* To put to death by mob action, esp. by hanging or burning, without authority or due process of law. —**lynch·er,** *n.* —**lynch·ing,** *n.*

lynx, lingks, *n. pl.,* **lynx, lynx·es.** A wildcat of the N. Hemisphere having relatively long legs, a very short tail, tufted ears, and cheek ruffs.

lynx-eyed, lingks′id, *a.* Sharp-sighted.

lyre, līr, *n.* A harplike musical instrument of ancient

Greece.

lyr•ic, lir′ik, *a.* Having the form and musical quality of a song; expressing ardent personal feelings; having a lightness of voice, as a tenor or soprano.—*n.* A lyric poem; *usu. pl.,* the text of a song. **—lyr•i•cal,** *a.* **—lyr•i•cal•ly,** *adv.* **—lyr•i•cal•ness,** *n.* **—lyr•i•cism,**

lir′i•siz•əm, *n.* **—lyr•i•cist,** lir′i•sist, *n.*

ly•ser•gic ac•id, li•sər′jik, li•sər′jik, *n.* An acidic crystalline solid which is the base of LSD.

ly•sine, li′sēn, li′sin, *n.* A basic amino acid, necessary for nutrition.

M

M, m, em, *n. pl.,* **M's, Ms, m's, ms.** The thirteenth letter of the English alphabet.

ma, mä, *n. Informal.* Mamma or mother.

M.A. Abbr. for Master of Arts.

ma'am, mam, mäm, məm, *n. Informal.* Madam.

ma•ca•bre, mə•käb′ər, mə•käb′rə, *a.* Ghastly; hideous; gruesome; suggesting or dwelling on the frightening, ugly aspect of death. **—ma•ca•bre•ly,** *adv.*

mac•ad•am, mə•kad′əm, *n.* Macadamized roadway; the material used for making it.

mac•ad•am•ize, mə•kad′ə•miz, *v.t.,* **-ized, -iz•ing.** To make a road by the laying down and pressing together of layers of small broken stones, often held together with tar or asphalt. **—mac•ad•am•i•za•tion,** mə•kad•ə•mə•zā′shən, *n.*

ma•caque, mə•kak′, *n.* Any of several Asian monkeys, with cheek pouches and a short tail.

mac•a•ro•ni, mak•ə•rō′nē, *n. pl.,* **-nis, -nies.** A dough of fine wheat flour dried in tubular form.

mac•a•roon, mak•ə•roon′, *n.* A small sweet cooky, made of egg white and sugar, and containing almond meal or shredded coconut.

ma•caw, mə•kô′, *n.* A large, long-tailed parrot, inhabiting tropical and subtropical America, notable for its brilliant plumage.

mace, mās, *n.* A medieval weapon of war consisting of a heavy staff or club, often with a spiked metal head; a staff borne before or by certain officials as a symbol of office. **—mace•bear•er,** mās′ber•ər, *n.*

mace, mās, *n.* A spice made from the dried covering of the seed of the nutmeg and usu. ground.

Mace, mās, *n. Trademark.* A chemical spray which will render a person docile on contact. **—mace,** *v.t.,* **maced, mac•ing.** To spray with Mace.

mac•er•ate, mas′ə•rāt, *v.t.,* **-at•ed, -at•ing.** To soften or separate the parts of by steeping in a liquid; to soften or break up, as food, by the digestive process. **—***v.i.* **—mac•er•a•tion,** mas•ə•rā′shən, *n.* **—mac•er•a•tor,** *n.*

Mach, mäk, *n.* The ratio of the speed of a moving body to the speed of sound within the medium in which it moves. Mach 1 is speed equal to that of sound. Also **Mach num•ber.**

ma•chet•e, mə•shet′ē, mə•chet′ē, *n.* A large knife used in Central and South America as a tool or a weapon.

Mach•i•a•vel•li•an, mak•ē•ə•vel′ē•ən, *a.* Pertaining to Niccolò Machiavelli, 1460–1527, an Italian writer and statesman; in conformity with Machiavelli's principles; crafty and deceitful in seeking and maintaining political power; marked by unscrupulous cunning or guile.—*n.* One who adopts the principles of Machiavelli. **—Mach•i•a•vel•li•an•ism,** *n.*

mach•i•nate, mak′ə•nāt, mash′ə•nāt, *v.t., v.i.,* **-nat•ed, -nat•ing.** To contrive or devise with evil purpose; to plot. **—mach•i•na•tion,** mak•ə•nā′shən, mash•ə•nā′shən, *n.* **—mach•i•na•tor,** *n.*

ma•chine, mə•shēn′, *n.* An apparatus used in the performance of some kind of work; a mechanical apparatus or contrivance; something operated by a mechanical apparatus; the body of persons conducting and controlling the activities of a political party or other organization; a device which transmits and modifies force or movement, as the lever, wedge, wheel and axle, pulley, screw, and inclined plane. **—***v.t.,* **-chined, -chin•ing.** To make, prepare, or finish with a machine or mechanical apparatus. **—ma•chin•a•bil•i•ty,** *n.* **—ma•chin•a•ble, ma•chine•a•ble,** *a.* **—ma•chine•like,** *a.*

ma•chine gun, *n.* An automatic weapon capable of delivering a rapid and continuous round of gunfire. **—ma•chine-gun,** *v.t.,* **-gunned, -gun•ning.** To shoot or fire at, employing a machine gun. **—ma•chine gun•ner,** *n.*

ma•chine lan•guage, *n.* Instructions or information expressed in the form of a code which can be directly processed by a computer.

ma•chin•er•y, mə•shē′nə•rē, *n. pl.,* **-ies.** Any collection or functioning unit of machines or mechanical apparatus; the parts of a machine, collectively; any combination or system of agencies by which action is maintained.

ma•chine tool, *n.* A usually automatic power-driven tool that cuts and shapes metal, such as a lathe, drill, or planer.

ma•chin•ist, mə•shē′nist, *n.* One who operates machinery or machine tools; one who makes, assembles, or repairs machines.

mack•er•el, mak′ər•əl, *n. pl.,* **-el, -els.** An edible fish of the N. Atlantic.

mack•i•naw, mak′ə•nô, *n.* A short coat of a thick blanketlike, often plaid, woolen material. Also **Mack•i•naw coat.**

mack•in•tosh, mac•in•tosh, mak′in•tosh, *n.* A cloth coat made waterproof by means of rubber; the cloth itself; any waterproof coat.

mac•ra•mé, mak′rə•mā, *n.* Trimming, fringe, or heavy lace of knotted thread, usu. in geometrical patterns. Also **mac•ra•mé lace.**

mac•ro•cosm, mak′rə•koz•əm, *n.* The great world, or universe; any complex setup. **—mac•ro•cos•mic,** mak•rə•koz′mik, *a.* **—mac•ro•cos•mi•cal•ly,** *adv.*

ma•cron, mā′kron, mak′ron, *n.* A short horizontal line placed over a vowel to indicate the pronunciation is long, as ā in *cave.*

mad, mad, *a.,* **mad•der, mad•dest.** Insane; foolish or imprudent; affected with or characterized by wild excitement; frenzied or frantic; wild with eagerness, fondness, or desire; infatuated; furious with anger; furious in violence; abnormally furious or violent; affected with rabies; rabid.—*n.* A period or interval of bad temper; anger. **—like mad.** *Informal.* Frantically; with much haste or enthusiasm. **—mad as a hat•ter,** quite crazy. **—mad•ly,** *adv.* **—mad•ness,** *n.*

---

a- hat, fāte, fāre, fäther; **e-** met, mē; **i-** pin, pīne; **o-** not, nōte, ôrb, moove (move), boy, pownd; **u-** cūbe, bůll, tûk (took); **cn-** chin; **th-** thick, then; **zh-** vizhon (vision); **ə-** əgo, takən, pencəl, lemən, bərd (bird).

mad·am, mad′əm, *n. pl.*, **mes·dames**, mā·däm′, *Fr.* me·däm′, **mad·ams**. A term of address used orig. to a woman of rank or authority, but now as a conventional courtesy to any woman, *pl.* **mes·dames**. A woman who operates a brothel, *pl.* **mad·ams**.

mad·ame, mad′əm, *Fr.* mä·däm′, *n. pl.*, **mes·dames**, mä·däm′, *Fr.* me·däm′. A French title of respect, used to or of a married woman.

mad·cap, mad′kap, *a.* Rash, impulsive, or reckless; flighty or harebrained.—*n.*

mad·den, mad′ən, *v.t.* To make mad; to craze; to enrage.—*v.i.* To become mad; to act as if mad. —**mad·den·ing**, *a.* —**mad·den·ing·ly**, *adv.*

mad·der, mad′ər, *n.* A European plant once widely cultivated for its roots which yield a scarlet dye; the dye itself.

made, mād, *a.* Fashioned or constructed, not naturally existing; specially prepared from various ingredients; assured of success or fortune. —**have it made**. *Informal.* To be fortunately situated, or certain to be successful.

mad·e·moi·selle, mad·ə·mə·zel′, *Fr.* mäd·mwä·zel′, *n. pl.*, **mad·e·moi·selles**, **mes·de·moi·selles**, *Fr.* mäd·mwä·zel′. The conventional French title of respect for a girl or unmarried woman.

made-up, mād′əp, *a.* Concocted, fabricated, or invented; wearing facial cosmetics or make-up.

mad·house, mad′hows, *n.* A confused or chaotic situation or place; a hospital or asylum for the mentally disturbed.

mad·man, mad′man, mad′mən, *n. pl.*, **-men**. A lunatic; a maniac.

Ma·don·na, mə·don′ə, *n.* The Virgin Mary; a statue or picture of the Virgin Mary.

mad·ras, mad′rəs, mə·dras′, mə·dräs′, *n.* A cotton cloth having woven stripes or patterns and used for garments.

mad·ri·gal, mad′rə·gəl, *n.* A short love or pastoral lyric poem adaptable to musical accompaniment, popular, esp. during the 16th century; a part song without instrumental accompaniment, usu. for five or six voices, and using contrapuntal imitation. —**mad·ri·gal·ist**, *n.*

mael·strom, māl′strəm, *n.* Any great or forceful whirlpool; a turbulent and agitated state or condition.

maes·tro, mä·es′trō, mī′strō, *n.* A master of music, such as a conductor, composer, or performer; a master of any art.

Ma·fi·a, mä′fē·ə, *n.* In Sicily, a secret organization which disregards laws and enforces its own code, often by terrorism; similar and perhaps related organizations in the U.S. and other countries, alleged to be engaged in large-scale criminal activities, as gambling and traffic in narcotics.

mag·a·zine, mag′ə·zēn, mag·ə·zēn′, *n.* A periodical publication, usu. with a paper cover, containing miscellaneous articles, and often illustrations and photographs; a building or room for keeping military stores, as arms, ammunition, and provisions; a room or place for keeping gunpowder and other explosives, as in a fort or on a warship; a chamber in a rifle or shotgun from which cartridges are automatically fed.

ma·gen·ta, mə·jen′tə, *n.* A purplish-red color.

mag·got, mag′ət, *n.* The wormlike larva of many insects, esp. that found in decaying animal matter. —**mag·got·y**, *a.*

Ma·gi, mā′jī, *n. pl., sing.* **Ma·gus**. The three wise men who came to Jerusalem to pay homage to the infant Jesus; the priestly caste in Media and Persia, believed to be magicians.

mag·ic, maj′ik, *n.* The art of producing effects by seemingly superhuman control over the powers of nature; sorcery; enchantment; the use of sleight of hand to create illusions or perform tricks.—*a.* —**mag·i·cal**, *a.* —**mag·i·cal·ly**, *adv.*

ma·gi·cian, mə·jish′ən, *n.* One skilled in magic.

mag·is·te·ri·al, maj·i·stēr′ē·əl, *a.* Belonging to a master or ruler; authoritative. —**mag·is·te·ri·al·ly**, *adv.* —**mag·is·te·ri·al·ness**, *n.*

mag·is·tra·cy, maj′i·strə·sē, *n. pl.*, **-cies**. The office or dignity of a magistrate; the district of a magistrate, a body of magistrates.

mag·is·trate, maj′i·strāt, maj′i·strit, *n.* A civil officer in the executive branch of the government; a low-ranking judicial officer with limited jurisdiction, as a justice of the peace.

mag·ma, mag′mə, *n. pl.*, **-mas**, **-ma·ta**, -mə·tə. Molten material within or beneath the earth's crust, from which igneous rock is formed. —**mag·mat·ic**, mag·mat′ik, *a.*

mag·nan·i·mous, mag·nan′ə·məs, *a.* Exhibiting nobleness of soul and generosity of mind; rising above ignoble motives and resentment. —**mag·nan·i·mous·ly**, *adv.* —**mag·nan·i·mous·ness**, *n.* —**mag·na·nim·i·ty**, mag·nə·nim′ə·tē, *n. pl.*, **-ties**.

mag·nate, mag′nāt, mag′nit, *n.* A person of rank, influence, or power.

mag·ne·sia, mag·nē′zhə, mag·nē′shə, *n.* A white tasteless substance used in manufacturing, and in medicine as an antacid and mild laxative. —**mag·ne·sian**, *a.*

mag·ne·si·um, mag·nē′zē·əm, mag·nē′zhəm, *n.* A light, malleable, ductile, silver-white metallic element that burns with a dazzling light, used in lightweight alloys.

mag·net, mag′nit, *n.* A body, as a piece of iron or steel, which possesses the property of attracting certain substances, esp. iron; lodestone; any person or thing that attracts or draws. —**mag·net·ic**, mag·net′ik, *a.* —**mag·net·i·cal·ly**, *adv.*

mag·net·ic field, *n.* Any space or region in which magnetic forces are present.

mag·net·ic north, *n.* The direction indicated by a magnetic compass as north, generally different from that considered true north.

mag·net·ic tape, *n.* A ribbon of paper, metal, or plastic coated with material which is sensitive to electromagnetic impulses: used in making magnetic recordings.

mag·net·ism, mag′nə·tiz·əm, *n.* The characteristic properties possessed by the magnet; the agency producing magnetic phenomena; magnetic power or charm.

mag·net·ize, mag′nə·tīz, *v.t.*, **-ized**, **-iz·ing**. To communicate magnetic properties to; to exert an attracting or compelling influence upon. —**mag·net·iz·a·ble**, *a.* —**mag·net·i·za·tion**, mag·nə·tə·zā′shən, *n.* —**mag·net·iz·er**, *n.*

mag·ne·to, mag·nē′tō, *n. pl.*, **-tos**. A magnetoelectric machine, esp. a small electric generator with permanent magnets. Also **mag·ne·to·e·lec·tric gen·er·a·tor**, **mag·ne·to·gen·er·a·tor**.

mag·ne·tom·e·ter, mag·nə·tom′ə·tər, *n.* An instrument to measure magnetic forces.—**mag·ne·to·met·ric**, mag·nē·tō·me′trik, *a.*—**mag·ne·tom·e·try**, *n.*

mag·nif·i·cent, mag·nif′ə·sənt, *a.* Making a splendid appearance or show; fine in a way that commands admiration or awe; extraordinarily superb; impressive. —**mag·nif·i·cence**, *n.* —**mag·nif·i·cent·ly**, *adv.*

mag·ni·fy, mag′nə·fī, *v.t.*, **-fied**, **-fy·ing**. To make great or greater; increase the apparent dimensions of, as by use of a lens; represent as greater than reality; exaggerate.—*v.i.* To enlarge the apparent dimensions of objects. —**mag·ni·fi·a·ble**, *a.* —**mag·ni·fi·ca·tion**, mag·nə·fə·kā′shən, *n.* —**mag·ni·fi·er**, *n.*

mag·ni·tude, mag′nə·tood, mag′nə·tūd, *n.* Greatness, or great size, amount, extent, or importance; size, amount, or extent, without reference to greatness or smallness; the brightness of a star expressed according to the numerical system used by astronomers.

mag·no·lia, mag·nōl′yə, mag·nō′lē·ə, *n.* An ornamental tree or shrub native to eastern N. America and Asia, having showy terminal flowers often appearing before the leaves; the blossom of such a tree.

mag·num, mag′nəm, *n.* A wine bottle with a capacity of about 51 liquid ounces.

mag·num o·pus, *n.* A great work; masterpiece.

mag·pie, mag′pī, *n.* A large black-and-white bird native to Europe and N. America, noted for its mischievousness and noisy, harsh voice.

mag·uey, mə·gā′, mag′wā, *n.* A Mexican plant, the juice of which is used in making the Mexican beverages pulque and mescal.

ma·ha·ra·jah, ma·ha·ra·ja, mä·hə·rä′jə, *n.* An Indian prince ruling over a native state or much territory.

ma·ha·ra·ni, mä·hə·rä′nē, *n.* A female Indian ruler; the wife of a maharajah. Also **ma·ha·ra·nee.**

ma·hat·ma, mə·hät′mə, *n.* A highly esteemed, saintly, wise person, esp. in India. *—a.*

mah-jongg, mah-jong, mä′zhông′, mä′zhong′, *n.* A game of Chinese origin, usu. played by 4 persons with 144 dominolike pieces marked in suits.

ma·hog·a·ny, mə·hog′ə·nē, *n. pl.,* **-nies.** A tropical tree having reddish-brown, strong, hard, heavy wood; a reddish-brown color. *—a.* Being mahogany in color.

ma·hout, mə·howt′, *n.* In India and the E. Indies, an elephant driver and keeper.

maid, mād, *n.* A female servant; a young unmarried woman; a virgin.

maid·en, mād′ən, *n.* A young unmarried woman. *—a.* Befitting or pertaining to a maiden; unmarried, as a woman; made, used, or appearing for the first time; virgin; fresh; unused.

maid·en·hair, mād′ən·hār, *n.* A common native N. American fern.

maid·en·head, mād′ən·hed, *n.* The hymen.

maid·en name, *n.* A woman's surname prior to her marriage.

maid of hon·or, *n.* An unmarried woman who is a bride's principal attendant at a wedding.

maid·ser·vant, mād′sər·vənt, *n.* A female servant.

mail, māl, *n.* Letters, papers, and packages which are sent and delivered through the post office; the postal system. *—v.t.* To send through the mail; to put in a mailbox for delivery. **—mail·a·ble,** *a.*

mail, māl, *n.* Armor made of pliable metal plates; any defensive covering. *—v.t.* **—mailed,** *a.*

mail·box, māl′boks, *n.* A box for deposited mail awaiting collection and delivery; a box which receives private mail, as at a residence.

mail·man, māl′man, *n. pl.,* **-men.** One who carries and delivers mail; a postman.

mail or·der, *n.* An order sent by mail for goods to be shipped to the buyer; the goods received. **—mail-order,** *a.*

maim, mām, *v.t.* To mutilate, cripple, or disable. **—maim·er,** *n.*

main, mān, *a.* Principal, chief, or most eminent; foremost in importance, rank, or size. *—n.* All one's strength; violent effort; the chief portion; most important point; a principal gas or water conduit as distinguished from the smaller ones supplied by it; the ocean. **—in the main,** for the most part.

main·land, mān′land, mān′lend, *n.* The principal section of a country or continent as compared with an island near it. **—main·land·er,** *n.*

main·ly, mān′lē, *adv.* In the main; chiefly.

main·mast, mān′mast, mān′mäst, mān′məst, *n.* The principal mast in a ship or other vessel.

main·sail, mān′sāl, mān′səl, *n.* The principal sail of a ship.

main·spring, mān′spring, *n.* The principal spring in a watch; the main cause of any action.

main·stream, mān′strēm, *n.* The main channel of a river that has many tributaries; the principal current or prevailing trend of opinion or activity.

main·tain, mān·tān′, *v.t.* To preserve or keep in any particular state or condition; to support; to keep possession of; to continue; to furnish sustenance for; provide the expenses of; to uphold; to defend; to vindicate or justify; to assert. **—main·tain·a·ble,** *a.*

main·te·nance, mān′tə·nəns, *n.* The act of maintaining or being maintained.

maî·tre d'hô·tel, mā·trə·dō·tel′, *Fr.* met·rə·dō·tel′, *n. pl.,* **maî·tres d'hô·tel.** A hotel steward or headwaiter in a restaurant.

maize, māz, *n.* Indian corn; yellow, esp. a color like that of ripe corn.

maj·es·ty, maj′i·stē, *n. pl.,* **-ties.** Grandeur or dignity of rank, character, or manner. (*Usu. cap.*) A title of emperors, kings, and queens, preceded by *his, her,* or *your.* **—ma·jes·tic,** mə·jes′tik, **ma·jes·ti·cal,** *a.* **—ma·jes·ti·cal·ly,** *adv.*

ma·jol·i·ca, mə·jol′i·kə, mə·yol′i·kə, *n.* Italian pottery coated with enamel and usu. richly decorated.

ma·jor, mā′jər, *a.* Greater, as in size, amount, extent, importance, or rank. *Mus.* Of an interval, being greater by a half step than the corresponding minor interval. *—n.* One of superior rank in a specified area; the subject or course of academic study pursued by a student as his area of specialization; a commissioned officer ranking next below a lieutenant colonel and next above a captain. *—v.i.* To pursue a principal course of study, followed by *in.*

ma·jor-do·mo, mā′jər·dō′mō, *n. pl.,* **-mos.** The chief steward who manages a large household.

ma·jor gen·er·al, *n.* A military officer next in rank below a lieutenant general and above a brigadier general.

ma·jor·i·ty, mə·jôr′ə·tē, mə·jor′ə·tē, *n. pl.,* **-ties.** The greater part or number; the number which is over half of a particular total; a number of voters or votes, jurors, or others in agreement, constituting the greater part or more than half of the total number; a group, as a political party, with the most votes; the state or time of being of full legal age; the military rank or office of a major.

ma·jor league, *n.* One of the two principal leagues in professional baseball; a league of similar importance in other sports, as football, basketball, or hockey.

make, māk, *v.t.,* **made, mak·ing.** To bring into existence by shaping a portion of matter or by combining parts of ingredients; form or fashion; frame or construct; manufacture or produce; be sufficient to constitute; serve for; become by development; to produce by any action or causative agency; give rise to or cause; fix or establish, as rules; enact, as laws; to score, as in games; to form in the mind, as a judgment, an estimate, or a plan; judge or infer as to the truth, nature, or meaning of something; to produce, earn, or get for oneself, as by work or actions; acquire, gain, or win; to bring into a certain form or condition, or convert; prepare for use; assure the success or fortune of; to cause or compel to do something; to do, perform, execute, or effect; put forth or deliver. *—v.i.* To make something; to bring about, effect, or operate, usu. with *for;* to cause something or someone to be as specified; show oneself in action or behavior; start to do, or as if to do, something; to direct or pursue the course, or go; to rise; increase in size, depth or volume. *—n.* Style or manner of being made; form or build; structure; constitution; disposition, character, or nature; the act or process of making. **—make be·lieve,** pretend. **—make do,** manage or carry on with material of poor quality. **—make good,** fulfill, as a promise; succeed. **—make love,** participate in sexual intercourse. **—make off,** to leave, often in haste. **—make out,** succeed. *Informal.* Neck, as in sexual endeavor. **—make o·ver,** remodel. **—make pub·lic,** disclose. **—make sure,** ascertain the truth of. **—make**

---

a- hat, fāte, fāre, fäther; **e-** met, mē; **i-** pin, pīne; **o-** not, nōte, ôrb, moove (move), boy, pownd; **u-** cūbe, bůll, tûk (took); **ch-** chin; **th-** thick, then; **zh-** vizhon (vision); **ə-** ago, takən, pencəl, lemən, bərd (bird).

time, to hurry; flirt. **—make tracks,** move swiftly. **—make up,** become reconciled after quarreling; consist of; put on cosmetics or dress, as for a part; to flatter or make advances to. **—make way,** give room for passing; give place; advance. **—mak·a·ble,** *a.* **—ma·ker,** *n.*

make-be·lieve, māk′bi·lēv, *n.* Pretense; fiction.—*a.* Unreal; pretended.

make·shift, māk′shift, *n.* A temporary substitute or contrivance.—*a.* Having the nature of a substitute.

make-up, māk′əp, *n.* Cosmetics, such as lipstick, which women use on their faces or other areas of the body; physical or mental constitution. *Informal.* A second examination administered to students who are absent from or fail the original test. Also **make·up.**

mak·ing, mā′king, *n.* The act of one who or that which produces, forms, effects, evolves, or makes. **—in the mak·ing,** in the process of being made.

mal·a·dapt·ed, mal·ə·dap′tid, *a.* Not suited to a particular condition or situation.

mal·ad·just·ment, mal·ə·jəst′mənt, *n.* An unsatisfactory adjustment. **—mal·ad·just·ed,** *a.*

mal·ad·min·is·ter, mal·əd·min′i·stər, To administer or conduct inefficiently or dishonestly. **—mal·ad·min·is·tra·tion,** mal·əd·min·i·strā′shən, *n.*

mal·a·droit, mal·ə·droyt′, *a.* Not dexterous; awkward, inept, or tactless. **—mal·a·droit·ly,** *adv.* **—mal·a·droit·ness,** *n.*

mal·a·dy, mal′ə·dē, *n. pl.,* **-dies.** Any disease of the human body; an ailment.

ma·laise, ma·lāz′, ma·lez′, *n.* A condition of generalized bodily uneasiness, weakness, or discomfort; an indefinite feeling of morbid discontent or ill-being.

mal·a·prop, mal′ə·prop, *n.* A malapropism.—*a.* Given to malapropisms.

mal·a·prop·ism, mal′ə·prop·iz·əm, *n.* A ludicrous misuse of words, esp. through incorrect choice of a word with a sound similar to the correct one.

ma·lar·i·a, mə·lār′ē·ə, *n.* A disease, usu. intermittent or remittent, and characterized by attacks of chills, fever, and sweating, caused by parasitic protozoans, transferred to the body by mosquitoes. **—ma·lar·i·al, ma·lar·i·an, ma·lar·i·ous,** *a.*

ma·lar·key, ma·lar·ky, mə·lär′kē, *n. Informal.* Deceptive or nonsensical talk.

mal·con·tent, mal′kən·tent, *a.* Dissatisfied, discontented, or rebellious.—*n.*

male, māl, *a.* Belonging to the sex which produces sperm, fertilizes the female, and begets young; pertaining to or thought to be characteristic of this sex; masculine; consisting of men; designating a part which fits into a corresponding part.—*n.* A male human being or animal. **—male·ness,** *n.*

mal·e·dict, mal′ə·dikt, *v.t.* To curse.

mal·e·dic·tion, mal·ə·dik′shən, *n.* The utterance of a curse against an individual; a curse. **—mal·e·dic·to·ry,** mal·ə·dik′tə·rē, *a.*

mal·e·fac·tion, mal·ə·fak′shən, *n.* An evil deed; an offense; crime.

mal·e·fac·tor, mal′ə·fak·tər, *n.* An evildoer; an offender against the law; a criminal.

ma·lev·o·lent, mə·lev′ə·lənt, *a.* Having an evil disposition toward another or others; malicious. **—ma·lev·o·lence,** *n.* **—ma·lev·o·lent·ly,** *adv.*

mal·fea·sance, mal·fē′zəns, *n.* Illegal, unjustified, or detrimental conduct, esp. in the performance of public or official duties. **—mal·fea·sant,** *a., adv.*

mal·for·ma·tion, mal·fôr·mā′shən, *n.* Abnormal structure, esp. of a bodily part. **—mal·formed,** mal·fôrmd′, *a.*

mal·func·tion, mal·fəngk′shən, *n.* Failure to function partially or totally.—*v.i.*

mal·ice, mal′is, *n.* Desire to inflict injury or suffering on another; active or vindictive ill will. **—ma·li·cious,** mə·lish′əs, *a.* **—ma·li·cious·ly,** *adv.* **—ma·li·cious·ness,** *n.*

ma·lign, mə·līn′, *v.t.* To speak evil of; slander.—*a.*

Malicious; tending to injure or produce evil effects. **—ma·lign·er,** *n.* **—ma·lign·ly,** *adv.*

ma·lig·nant, mə·lig′nənt, *a.* Having extreme malevolence or enmity; malicious; not benign; tending to cause death. **—ma·lig·nan·cy,** mə·lig′nən·sē, *n. pl.,* **-cies.** **—ma·lig·nant·ly,** *adv.*

ma·lin·ger, mə·ling′gər, *v.i.* To feign illness in order to avoid duty. **—ma·lin·ger·er,** *n.*

mall, môl, *n.* A landscaped public area for walking; an area surrounded with shops or other buildings and closed to vehicular traffic; a planted or paved strip separating lanes of traffic.

mal·lard, mal′ərd, *n. pl.,* **-lards, -lard.** A wild duck common in the northern hemisphere.

mal·le·a·ble, mal′ē·ə·bəl, *a.* Capable of being extended or shaped by hammering or by pressure; adaptable. **—mal·le·a·bil·i·ty,** mal·ē·ə·bil′ə·tē, **mal·le·a·ble·ness,** *n.*

mal·let, mal′it, *n.* A hammer, usu. of wood, used chiefly for driving another tool, as a chisel; the wooden implement used to strike the ball in the game of croquet; the long-handled stick used to drive the ball in polo.

mal·low, mal′ō, *n.* An herbaceous plant characterized by round-toothed leaves and white, purple, or rose flowers.

mal·nour·ished, mal·nər′isht, *a.* Poorly or insufficiently nourished.

mal·nu·tri·tion, mal·noo·trish′ən, *n.* Insufficient or faulty nutrition.

mal·oc·clu·sion, mal·ə·kloo′zhən, *n.* Imperfect closing or meeting, as of the opposing teeth of the upper and lower jaws.

mal·o·dor, mal·ō′dər, *n.* An offensive odor; stench. **—mal·o·dor·ous,** mal·ō′dər·əs, *a.* **—mal·o·dor·ous·ly,** *adv.* **—mal·o·dor·ous·ness,** *n.*

mal·prac·tice, mal·prak′tis, *n.* Improper, neglectful, or illegal performance of duty by one in a public or professional position, as a lawyer or physician. **—mal·prac·ti·tion·er,** mal·prak·tish′ən·ər, *n.*

malt, môlt, *n.* Grain, usu. barley, steeped in water, germinated, dried in a kiln, and then used in brewing and distilling; a beverage produced from malt, as beer, ale, or whisky.—*v.t.* To make into malt.—*v.i.* To convert grain into malt. **—malt·y,** môl′tē, *a.,* **-i·er, -i·est.**

malt·ed milk, môl′tid, *n.* A powder made from dried milk and malted cereals; the beverage made from this powder and milk or other liquid, usu. with ice cream and flavoring.

mal·treat, mal·trēt′, *v.t.* To treat roughly or severely; to abuse. **—mal·treat·ment,** *n.*

mam·ma, ma·ma, mä′mə, *n.* Mother: a term of address used chiefly by young persons.

mam·mal, mam′əl, *n.* Any animal or animal group of the highest vertebrate class which is characterized by suckling of the young, the presence of hair, and live births. **—mam·ma·li·an,** mə·mā′lē·ən, *a., n.*

mam·ma·ry, mam·ə·rē, *a.* Referring to the breast glands that secrete milk.—*n., usu. pl.,* **-ries.** The breasts.

mam·mon, mam′ən, *n.* Riches considered as an evil.

mam·moth, mam′əth, *n.* An extinct species of elephant with long tusks covered with dense, shaggy hair.—*a.* Very large; gigantic.

mam·my, mam′ē, *n. pl.,* **-mies.** A black female nurse or family servant in southern U.S. homes.

man, man, *n. pl.,* **men.** A human being, particularly a male adult; the human species; a male servant; a husband; any human individual; a piece with which a game is played.—*v.t.,* **manned, man·ning.** To supply with men; to assume one's position or station at, on, or in.—*interj. Informal.* An exclamation of surprise or enthusiasm.

man·a·cle, man′ə·kəl, *n.* An instrument of iron for fastening the hands. *Often pl.* Handcuffs; shackles. **—v.t., -cled, -cling.** To put handcuffs on; to shackle.

man·age, man′ij, *v.t.,* **-aged, -ag·ing.** To control and direct, as a person or enterprise; to conduct, carry on, guide, administer; to move or use in the manner desired; to treat with caution or judgment.—*v.i.* To direct or conduct affairs. **—man·age·a·ble,** man′ij·ə·bəl, *a.* **—man·age·a·bil·i·ty,** man·ij·ə·bil′ə·tē, **man·age·a·ble·ness,** *n.* **—man·age·a·bly,** *adv.*

man·age·ment, man′ij·mənt, *n.* The act of managing, treating, directing, carrying on, or using for a purpose; administration; directors or managers of any business.

man·ag·er, man′ij·ər, *n.* One who manages; one who is directly at the head of an undertaking. **—man·ag·er·ship,** *n.*

man·a·ge·ri·al, man·ə·jēr′ē·əl, *a.* Of or belonging to a manager. **—man·a·ge·ri·al·ly,** *adv.*

ma·ña·na, mə·nyä′nə, *Sp.* mä·nyä′nä, *n.* Tomorrow; a future time; tomorrow; at some future time.—*adv.*

man·a·tee, man′ə·tē, man·ə·tē′, *n.* An aquatic, seaweed-eating mammal characterized by a large spindle-shaped body, paddlelike fore limbs, absence of hind limbs, and native to tropical waters.

man·da·la, mən′də·lə, *n.* A graphic cosmic symbol shown as a square within a circle bearing representations of deities arranged symmetrically and used as a meditation aid by Buddhists and Hindus.

man·da·rin, man′də·rin, *n.* A member of any of the nine ranks of officials during the Chinese Empire. A small, flattish orange of Chinese origin, or the tree producing it. Also **man·da·rin or·ange.**

man·date, man′dāt, *n.* A command, order, or injunction; a command from a superior court or official to an inferior one; the instruction as to policy given by the electorate to a representative.—*v.t.* **-dat·ed, -dat·ing.** To consign, as a territory, to a particular nation under a mandate.

man·da·to·ry, man′də·tôr·ē, *a.* Pertaining to, of the nature of, or containing a mandate; obligatory by reason of a command.—*n. pl.,* **-ries.** A person or nation that receives a mandate. **—man·da·to·ri·ly,** *adv.*

man·di·ble, man′də·bəl, *n.* The under jaw bone in vertebrates; the upper or lower bill of a bird. **—man·dib·u·lar,** man·dib′yə·lər, *a.* Also **man·dib·u·lar·y. —man·dib·u·late,** man·dib′yə·lit, *a., n.*

man·do·lin, man′də·lin, man·də·lin′, *n.* A musical instrument having a deep, pear-shaped sound box, fretted neck, and usu. four pairs of metal strings. **—man·do·lin·ist,** *n.*

man·drake, man′drāk, *n.* A European herb of the nightshade family.

man·drill, man′dril, *n.* A large, fierce baboon, native to W. Africa, known by its red and blue facial and rump features.

mane, mān, *n.* The long hair growing about the neck of some animals, as the horse and the lion. **—maned,** *a.*

man·eat·er, man′ē·tər, *n.* A cannibal; any animal that devours human beings. **—man·eat·ing,** *a.*

ma·neu·ver, mə·noo′vər, *n.* A regulated movement, particularly in an army or navy; *pl.,* large tactical movements of troops imitating actual combat conditions; adroit management.—*v.i.* To perform military maneuvers; to employ intrigue or stratagem to effect a purpose.—*v.t.* To cause to perform maneuvers; to handle skillfully. **—ma·neu·ver·a·bil·i·ty,** mə·noo·ver·ə·bil′ə·tē, *n.* **—ma·neu·ver·a·ble,** *a.* **—ma·neu·ver·er,** *n.*

man·ful, man′fəl, *a.* Bold; brave; resolute. **—man·ful·ly,** *adv.* **—man·ful·ness,** *n.*

man·ga·nese, mang′gə·nēs, mang′gə·nēz, *n.* A hard grayish-white metallic element used as an alloying agent to give steel toughness.

mange mānj, *n.* A skin disease affecting animals and sometimes man, characterized by loss of hair and by scabby eruptions, and usu. caused by parasitic mites.

man·ger, mān′jər, *n.* A trough or box in which fodder

is laid for horses or cattle.

man·gle, mang′gəl, *v.t.* **-gled, -gling.** To cut or crush by repeated blows; to mutilate; to spoil; to destroy or badly damage.

man·gle, mang′gəl, *n.* A machine used to smooth or iron fabrics by running them through rollers which are heated.—*v.t.* **-gled, -gling.** To press cloth smooth with a mangle.

man·go, mang′gō, *n. pl.,* **-goes, -gos.** An aromatically-flavored edible fruit of the tropical tree; the tree itself.

man·grove, mang′grōv, *n.* A tropical tree growing on the banks of rivers and on the seacoast, remarkable for giving off new roots from the stem and branches.

man·gy, mān′jē, *a.,* **-gi·er, -gi·est.** Having the mange; mean; squalid or shabby. **—man·gi·ly,** *adv.* **—man·gi·ness,** *n.*

man·han·dle, man′han·dəl, *v.t.* **-dled, -dling.** To handle roughly.

man·hole, man′hōl, *n.* A circular, often covered hole through which one can enter an underground structure for cleaning or repairing.

man·hood, man′hūd, *n.* The state of being a man or adult male person; manly qualities; virility; men collectively.

man·hour, man′owr, *n.* An hour of work by one man, used as a time unit in industry.

man·hunt, man′hənt, *n.* An organized, extensive search for a person. **—man·hunt·er,** *n.*

ma·ni·a, mā′nē·ə, mān′yə, *n.* Intense excitement or enthusiasm; a vehement passion or desire; a rage or craze. **—man·ic,** man′ik, *a.*

ma·ni·ac, mā′nē·ak, *n.* A widly insane person.—*a.* Raving with insanity; mad. **—ma·ni·a·cal,** mə·nī′ə·kəl, *a.* **—ma·ni·a·cal·ly,** *adv.*

man·ic-de·pres·sive, man′ik-di·pres′iv, *a.* Referring to a mental disorder characterized by marked emotional shifts from great excitement and high spirits to deep depression.—*n.* One afflicted with this disorder.

man·i·cure, man′ə·kūr, *n.* The care of the nails and the hands.—*v.t.* **-cured, -cur·ing.** To trim or care for, as the fingernails; to give a manicure to. **—man·i·cur·ist,** *n.*

man·i·fest, man′ə·fest, *a.* Clearly visible to the eye or obvious to the understanding; not obscure or difficult to be seen or understood; evident.—*n.* A shipper's document containing such information as the cargo, destination, and passenger list for a vessel or airplane.—*v.t.* To reveal to the understanding; to display; to exhibit. **—man·i·fest·er,** *n.* **—man·i·fest·ly,** *adv.*

man·i·fes·ta·tion, man·ə·fe·stā′shən, *n.* The act of manifesting a making evident to the eye or the understanding; the exhibition of anything by clear evidence; the appearance in bodily form of a spirit.

man·i·fes·to, man·ə·fes′tō, *n. pl.,* **-tos, -toes.** A public declaration of objectives, usu. by a government or political faction.

man·i·fold, man′ə·fōld, *a.* Having many different parts, elements, features, or forms; multifarious; numerous and varied; having or operating many units of one type.—*n.* A pipe with a number of inlets or outlets, as for exhaust.—*v.t.* To make copies of, as with carbon paper. **—man·i·fold·er,** *n.* **—man·i·fold·ly,** *adv.* **—man·i·fold·ness,** *n.*

man·i·kin, man·a·kin, man·ni·kin, man′i·kin, *n.* A mannequin.

ma·nil·a, ma·nil·la, mə·nil′ə, *a.* Composed of abaca plant fibers.

ma·nil·a pa·per, mə·nil′ə, *n.* A strong, buff-colored or light brown paper formerly made exclusively of Manila hemp.

man in the street, *n.* The average man.

ma·nip·u·late, mə·nip′yə·lāt, *v.t.,* **-lat·ed, -lat·ing.**

To handle, manage, or use, esp. with skill, in some process of treatment or performance; to manage or influence by artful skill, often by unfair tactics. —ma·nip·u·la·ble, *a.* —ma·nip·u·la·tion, mə·nip·yə·lā′shən, *n.* —ma·nip·u·la·tive, *a.* —ma·nip·u·la·tor, mə·nip′yə·lā·tər, *n.* —ma·nip·u·la·to·ry, *a.*

man·kind, man·kīnd′, man′kīnd, *n.* The human race collectively; the males of the human race.

man·like, man′līk, *a.* Resembling a man.

man·ly, man′lē, *a.,* **-li·er, -li·est.** Pertaining to or becoming a man.—*adv.* —**man·li·ness,** *n.*

man-made, man′mād, *a.* Formed or manufactured by humans rather than nature: a *man-made* lake.

man·na, man′ə, *n.* The food miraculously supplied to the children of Israel in the wilderness; divine or spiritual food; a sweetish juice from a species of ash, used as a mild laxative.

manned, mand, *a.* Operated by or containing a man or men: a *manned* spacecraft.

man·ne·quin, man′ə·kin, *n.* A life-sized model of the human figure used for dressmaking, tailoring, or displaying clothes; a person employed as a fashion model.

man·ner, man′ər, *n.* The way in which anything is done or occurs; one's way of performing or behaving. *Pl.* Social conduct or behavior currently considered as polite. *Sing. but pl. in constr.* Sorts or kinds: all *manner* of things.

man·nered, man′ərd, *a.* Having manners of a stated kind: well-*mannered*; having a stilted or affected style in writing or art.

man·ner·ism, man′ə·riz·əm, *n.* A characteristic trait, style, or mode of speech or behavior; an affectation or eccentricity.

man·ner·ly, man′ər·lē, *a., adv.* Showing good manners. —**man·ner·li·ness,** *n.*

man·nish, man′ish, *a.* Characteristic of or resembling a man.

man-of-war, man′əv·wôr′, *n. pl.,* **men-of-war.** A boat employed for the purposes of war; warship.

ma·nom·e·ter, mə·nom′ə·tər, *n.* An instrument for measuring the pressure of gases, vapors, or liquids.

man·or, man′ər, *n.* In England, a landed estate or territorial unit; the mansion of a lord with the land belonging to it; a mansion. Also **man·or house.** —**ma·no·ri·al,** mə·nôr′ē·əl, *a.*

man·pow·er, man′pow·ər, *n.* The power of a man; specif. a unit assumed to be equal to the rate at which a man can do mechanical work, commonly taken as one tenth of a horsepower; power in terms of men available or required.

man·sard, man′särd, *n.* A curb roof with the lower slope approaching the vertical and the higher slope nearly horizontal.

man·serv·ant, man′ser·vənt, *n.* A male servant.

man·sion, man′shən, *n.* A dwelling or residence of great size.

man-sized, man′sīzd, *a. Informal.* Large; suitable in size or kind for a man. Also **man-size.**

man·slaugh·ter, man′slô·tər, *n.* The unlawful killing of a person, without malice aforethought; homicide.

man·slay·er, man′slā·ər, *n.* One who kills a human being. —**man·slay·ing,** *n., a.*

man·tel, man·tle, man′təl, *n.* The ornamental work surrounding and above a fireplace; a narrow shelf or slab above a fireplace. Also **man·tel·shelf.**

man·til·la, man·til′ə, man·tē′ə, *n.* A Spanish woman's scarf, often of lace, covering the head and shoulders; a light cloak or cape.

man·tle, man′təl, *n.* A loose, sleeveless cloak; something that covers or conceals; a chemically prepared, incombustible mesh for a gas jet, which glows when the jet is lighted and gives a brilliant light; the outer covering used as a protective device in blast furnaces; a mantel.—*v.t.,* **-tled, -tling.** To cover with or as with a mantle; envelop; conceal.—*v.i.* To spread over the surface.

man-trap, man′trap, *n.* A snare, esp. to catch trespassers.

man·u·al, man′ū·əl, *a.* Of or pertaining to the hand or hands; performed, made, operated, or used by the hand or hands; requiring human energy; of the nature of a manual or handbook.—*n.* A small book, esp. one designed for ready reference; a handbook. —**man·u·al·ly,** *adv.*

man·u·al al·pha·bet, *n.* A form of communication among the deaf in which various positions of the hand and fingers represent letters of the alphabet.

man·u·al train·ing, *n.* A course of instruction emphasizing hand skills and practical arts, as carpentry and metalwork.

man·u·fac·ture, man·yə·fak′chər, *n.* The making of goods or wares by manual labor or by machinery, esp. on a large scale; any article or material which is manufactured.—*v.t.,* **-tured, -tur·ing.** To make or produce by hand or machinery, esp. on a large scale; to produce as if by mere mechanical industry; produce artificially; invent fictitiously. —**man·u·fac·tur·a·ble,** *a.* —**man·u·fac·tur·al,** *a.* —**man·u·fac·tur·er,** *n.*

ma·nure, mə·noor′, mə·nūr′, *v.t.,* **-nured, -nur·ing.** To treat with fertilizing matter.—*n.* Any natural or artificial substance for fertilizing the soil, esp. dung or refuse.

man·u·script, man′yə·skript, *n.* An author's handwritten or typewritten work from which the printed copy is produced; a book or paper written by hand; a writing of any kind.—*a.* Written with the hand; not printed.

man·y, men′ē, *a.,* **more, most.** Making up a large number; numerous; being one of a large number, followed by *a* or *an: many* a day.—*pron., pl. in constr.* A considerable number of people or things.—*n., pl. in constr.* A great or considerable number. —**the man·y,** the multitude.

man·y-sid·ed, men′ē·sī′did, *a.* Having many sides.

map, map, *n.* A graphic representation or charting of the whole or part of the earth's surface; anything which resembles a map in appearance or function. —*v.t.,* **mapped, map·ping.** To delineate in a map; to represent in detail; to program or devise for the future. —**map·per,** *n.*

ma·ple, mā′pəl, *n.* A tree or shrub native to the northern hemisphere, having oppositely arranged leaves and a dry, double-winged fruit, economically important for lumber and syrup, and as an ornamental shade tree.

ma·ple leaf, *n.* A fan-lobed leaf of the maple tree; symbol or emblem of Canada.

ma·ple sug·ar, *n.* Sugar from the sugar maple tree.

ma·ple syr·up, *n.* A syrup prepared from the natural sap in maple trees.

mar, mär, *v.t.,* **marred, mar·ring.** To injure in any way; to spoil.

ma·ra·ca, mə·rä′kə, *n.* A rhythm instrument consisting of a gourd, or a rattle shaped like a gourd, that contains seeds or pebbles.

mar·a·schi·no, mar·ə·skē′nō, mar·ə·shē′nō, *n.* A kind of liqueur made from sour cherries.

mar·a·schi·no cher·ry, *n.* A cherry flavored with, or preserved in, imitation maraschino and used as a garnish.

mar·a·thon, mar′ə·thon, *n.* A long-distance race, esp. a foot race of about 26 miles; any contest requiring great stamina.

ma·raud, mə·rôd′, *v.i.* To rove in quest of plunder. —*v.t.* To raid. —**ma·raud·er,** *n.*

mar·ble, mär′bəl, *n.* A limestone varying in color, whose texture may be granular or compact; a block or piece of sculpture of this material; a little ball of glass, or other hard substance, used by children in play; *pl.,* a game played with such balls of glass.—*a.* Composed of marble; stained or veined like marble; hard or insensible like marble.—*v.t.,* **-bled, -bling.** To stain or vein like marble. Also **mar·ble·ize,** mär′bə·līz, **-ble·**

ized, -ble·iz·ing. —mar·bled, mar·bly, mär′blē, a.

mar·bling, mär′bling, n. Any marking resembling that of veined marble.

mar·cel, mär·sel′, v.t., -celled, -cel·ling. To wave, as the hair, in a particular style by means of special irons.—n. A marcelling.

march, märch, v.i. To walk with a steady and measured pace, often rhythmically, as soldiers in an organized group; to walk in a dignified, often formal, fashion; to advance steadily.—v.t. To cause to march.—n. The measured and uniform walk of a body of people, as soldiers, moving simultaneously and in order; a stately and deliberate walk; a steady or labored progression; the distance passed over; progress: the march of intellect. A composition rhythmically suited to accompany the movement of marching. —march·er, n.

March, märch, n. The third month of the year, having 31 days. Abbr. Mar.

mar·chion·ess, mär′shə·nis, mär·shə·nes′, n. The wife or widow of a marquis; a female having the rank of a marquis.

Mar·co·ni, mär·kō′nē, It. mär·kô′nē, a. (Sometimes l.c.) Pertaining to wireless telegraphy, as developed by Marconi.

Mar·di gras, mär′dē grä, mär·dē grä′, n. Shrove Tuesday; the last day of the carnival, celebrated in Paris, New Orleans, and other cities with parades and special festivities.

mare, mär, n. The female of the horse, donkey, or zebra, esp. when mature.

mare's-tail, märz′tāl, n. A long, thin, and graceful cirrus cloud.

mar·ga·rine, mär′jer·in, mär′jə·rēn, n. A substitute for butter consisting of a mixture of prepared edible fats extracted from vegetable oils. Also o·le·o·mar·ga·rine, and mar·ga·rin, mär′jer·in.

mar·gin, mär′jin, n. A border or edge; the space surrounding the main body of printing on a page; a limit, or a condition, beyond which something ceases to exist or be possible; an amount allowed or available beyond what is actually necessary; the difference between the cost and the selling price; the smallest return necessary for a business enterprise to remain profitable; security, as a percentage in money, deposited with a broker as a provision against loss on transactions on behalf of his principal.—v.t. To provide with a margin or border; to enter in the margin, as of a book.

mar·gi·nal, mär′ji·nəl, a. Pertaining to a margin; situated on the border or edge; close to minimal requirements, value, or quality: marginal talent. Barely showing a profit. —mar·gi·na·li·a, n. pl. Marginal notes. —mar·gin·al·i·ty, mär·jin·al′ə·tē, n. —mar·gin·al·ly, adv.

mar·gin·ate, mär′jə·nāt, v.t., -at·ed, -at·ing. To furnish with a margin; to border.—a. Having a definite margin. Also mar·gin·at·ed. —mar·gin·a·tion, n.

mar·gue·rite, mär·gə·rēt′, n. Any of several cultivated flowers of the composite family.

mar·i·cul·ture, mär·ə·kəl′chər, n. The cultivation of undersea plants and animals.

mar·i·gold, mar′ə·gōld, n. Bot. Any of the various strong-scented, golden-flowered garden plants of the composite family.

ma·ri·jua·na, ma·ri·hua·na, mar·ə·wä′nə, mär·ə·hwä′nə, n. A narcotic, cannabis, obtained from the dried leaves and flower heads of a type of plant, and usu. smoked in cigarettes; the plant itself.

ma·rim·ba, mə·rim′bə, n. A xylophonelike musical instrument of African origin, popularized and perfected in Central America.

ma·ri·na, mə·rē′nə, n. A small boat basin where moorings, supplies, and repair service are available.

mar·i·nade, mar·ə·nād′, n. A pickle or brine, usu. of vinegar or wine seasoned with herbs and spices, in which one steeps meat or fish before cooking to improve the flavor; a dish of meat or fish thus steeped.—mar′ə·nād, v.t., -nad·ed, -nad·ing. To marinate.

mar·i·nate, mar′ə·nāt, v.t., -nat·ed, -nat·ing. To steep or soak in a marinade. —mar·i·na·tion, n.

ma·rine, mə·rēn′, a. Of or pertaining to the sea; pertaining to navigation or shipping; nautical; naval. —n. One of a class of naval troops serving both on shipboard and on land, esp. a member of the U.S. Marine Corps; seagoing vessels collectively, esp. with reference to nationality.

mar·i·ner, mar′ə·nər, n. One whose occupation is to navigate or assist in navigating ships; seaman; sailor. (Cap.) Aeron. One of several unmanned U.S. spacecrafts used for exploratory flights to other planets, specif. Venus and Mars.

mar·i·on·ette, mar·ē·ə·net′, n. A jointed puppet moved by strings.

mar·i·tal, mar′ə·təl, a. Of or pertaining to marriage.

mar·i·time, mar′ə·tim, a. Bordering on the sea; living near the sea; of or pertaining to the sea, navigation, or shipping: maritime law.

mar·jo·ram, mär′jer·əm, n. A sweet and savory herb, or pot marjoram, both used for flavoring in cooking.

mark, märk, n. A visible trace or impression, as a cut, dent, stain, stamp, or bruise; a symbol, letter, or number used to indicate the degree of achievement or conduct, as of pupils in a school; a symbol to indicate origin, ownership, comparative merit, standard of excellence, or distinction: a trademark; a distinctive property, character, or trait: the mark of a gentleman; a badge, brand, or other visible sign assumed or imposed; a recognized standard: below the mark; a symbol used in writing: a punctuation mark; a target; a goal; a notice.—v.t. To make marks on; to set the boundaries of; to establish limits, often with out; to indicate or designate by or as by marks; to be a distinguishing feature of; to single out or be destined: marked for success; to notice or observe; to give attention to.—v.i. To be attentive; to consider. —leave a mark, to make an impression. —mark down, to lower the price. —mark time, to move the feet as in marching, without advancing. To stop action or progress for a time; to bide one's time. —mark up, to raise prices. —on your mark, be ready to start, esp. a race. —wide of the mark, far from the target; inaccurate.

marked, märkt, a. Furnished with a mark or marks; affixed: the marked price of goods; distinguished or singled out: a marked man; strikingly noticeable. —mark·ed·ly, mär′kid·lē, adv.

mark·er, mär′kər, n. One who or that which marks; anything used for marking locations, as a beacon from a radio station.

mar·ket, mär′kit, n. Traffic in certain goods or services: the cigarette market; country or place of sale: the foreign market; those for whom a commodity or service is made available: the teenage market; a public place where goods are exposed for sale; a shop; purchase or sale, or rate of purchase or sale; those formally conducting a sale: the stock market; the field of business; an occasion on which goods are publicly exposed for sale and buyers assemble to purchase; a fair.—v.i. To deal in a market; to purchase provisions for a household.—v.t. To offer for sale in a market; to sell. —mar·ket·er, n.

mar·ket·a·ble, mär′ki·tə·bəl, a. Capable of being sold. —mar·ket·a·bil·i·ty, mär·ki·tə·bil′ə·tē, n.

mar·ket·ing, mär′ki·ting, n. Trading in a market; buying or selling; the entire process of storing, shipping, advertising, and selling.

mar·ket·place, mar·ket place, mär′kit·plās, n. A place, esp. an open space in a town, where a market is held; the sphere of commerce.

mar·ket re·search, *n.* The collection and organization of data concerning the preferences and buying habits of consumers.

mark·ing, mär′king, *n.* The act of making a mark; a mark or series of marks upon something. *Often pl.* Characteristic arrangement of natural coloring: the *markings* on a bird's egg.

marks·man, märks′mən, *n. pl.,* **marks·men.** One who is skillful at hitting a mark; one who shoots well. —**marks·man·ship,** *n.*

mar·lin, mär′lən, *n.* Any one of a number of oceanic game fish, related to the sailfish and spearfish.

mar·ma·lade, mär′mə·lād, mär·mə·lād′, *n.* A preserve containing small pieces of fruit and rind.

mar·mo·set, mär′mə·zet, *n.* Any of the rather small, squirrellike monkeys with long, hairy, non-prehensile tails.

mar·mot, mär′mət, *n.* Any of several species of short-legged, short-tailed rodents native to northern latitudes and hibernating in burrows.

ma·roon, mə·roon′, *v.t.* To put ashore and leave on a desolate island with punitive intent; to leave abandoned and helpless; to strand.

ma·roon, mə·roon′, *n.* A very dark purplish-red or claret color.—*a.*

mar·quee, mär·kē′, *n.* A rooflike projection over an outer doorway, walk, or terrace used for protection and advertising, as of a theater; a signboard.

mar·quis, mär′kwis, mär·kē′, *n. pl.,* **mar·quis·es, mar·quis,** mär·kēz′. A title of dignity in Britain next in rank to that of duke. Also **mar·quess.**

mar·quise, mär·kēz′, *n. pl.,* **mar·quis·es,** mär·kē′ziz. The wife or widow of a marquis, or a lady holding the rank equal to that of a marquis; a gem, oval in shape, with pointed ends; a marquee.

mar·riage, mar′ij, *n.* The social institution by which a man and woman are legally united and establish a new family unit; wedlock; the state of being married; the action or act of marrying; a wedding; any intimate union. —**mar·riage·a·ble,** mar′i·jə·bəl, *a.* —**mar·riage·a·bil·i·ty,** *n.*

mar·ried, mar′ēd, *a.* United in wedlock; wedded; pertaining to marriage or married persons: *married* life; closely united.

mar·row, mar′ō, *n.* The tissue, of soft and vascular structure, present in bone cavities. The essence; pith; vitality. —**mar·row·y,** *a.*

mar·row·bone, mar′ō·bōn, *n.* A bone containing marrow that is eatable.

mar·ry, mar′ē, *v.t.,* **-ried, -ry·ing.** To join as husband or wife; to take in marriage; to unite intimately.—*v.i.* To enter into the married state; take a husband or wife.

Mars, märz, *n.* The major planet next outside the earth, being the fourth in order from the sun; the Roman god of war.

marsh, märsh, *n.* A tract of low and very wet land; swamp.

mar·shal, mär′shəl, *n.* A general officer of high or the highest rank in various European or other armies; a person charged with the arrangement or regulation of ceremonies; an administrative officer of a U.S. judicial district who performs duties similar to those of a sheriff.—*v.t.,* **-shaled, -shal·ing.** To arrange or place in due or proper order; array, draw for battle, or review; to usher or lead.

marsh el·der, *n.* Any of the herbaceous or shrubby composite plants, with thick leaves and greenish flowers; inhabiting salt marshes or wasteland. Also **sump·weed,** sump′wēd.

marsh gas, *n.* Methane, an inflammable gas resulting from decomposition of vegetation, esp. in marshy land.

marsh·mal·low, märsh′mel·ō, märsh′mal·ō, *n.* A sweet confection made from sugar, gelatin, corn syrup, and albumin, coated with powdered sugar.

marsh·y, mär′shē, *a.,* **-i·er, -i·est.** Pertaining to or of the nature of a marsh or swamp; swampy. —**marsh·i·ness,** *n.*

mar·su·pi·al, mär·soo′pē·əl, *a.* Pertaining to, resembling, or having a pouch; of or pertaining to the marsupials.—*n.* Any of an order of nonplacental mammals which includes the kangaroo, opossum and koala.

mart, märt, *n.* A place where buying and selling are carried on; market.

mar·tial, mär′shəl, *a.* Pertaining to war; military.

mar·tial law, *n.* A temporary military rule imposed in times when civil authority is unable to maintain law and order.

Mar·tian, mär′shən, *a.* Pertaining to Mars, god of war, or to the planet Mars.—*n.* An imaginary inhabitant of Mars.

mar·tin, mar′tən, mär′tin, *n.* Any of various species of swallows, esp. the largest of the swallows. Also **pur·ple mar·tin.**

mar·ti·ni, mär·tē′nē, *n. pl.,* **mar·ti·nis.** A cocktail generally mixed in the proportion three parts gin or vodka to one part dry vermouth.

mar·tyr, mär′tər, *n.* A person who chooses death rather than renounce his or her faith or religious beliefs; one who endures intense suffering for adherence to any principle or belief; one who exaggerates his or her suffering to enlist the sympathy of others. —*v.t.* To put to death for adherence to a belief, principle, or loyalty to a cause; to persecute; to torment or torture. Also **mar·tyr·ize, -ized, -iz·ing.** —**mar·tyr·dom,** *n.*

mar·vel, mär′vəl, *n.* A wonder; an object of great astonishment.—*v.i.,* **-veled, -vel·ing.** To be struck with surprise or astonishment; to wonder.—*v.t.* To be filled with wonder at or about.

mar·vel·ous, mär′və·ləs, *a.* Exciting wonder; astonishing. *Informal.* First rate, excellent. —**mar·vel·ous·ly,** *adv.*

Marx·ism, märk′siz·əm, *n.* The economic, social, and political theories formulated by Karl Marx and Friedrich Engels, stressing the doctrines of dialectical materialism, class struggle, the labor theory of value and leading to the goal of a classless society. —**Marx·ist,** märk′sist, *a., n.* —**Marx·i·an,** mark′sē·ən, *a.*

Mar·y, mār′ē, *n.* Jesus' mother. Also **Vir·gin Mar·y.**

mar·zi·pan, mär′zə·pan, *n.* A candy composed of almond paste, sugar, and egg whites. Also **march·pane.**

mas·car·a, ma·skar′ə, *n.* A cosmetic preparation for darkening the eyelashes.

mas·cot, mas′kət, mas′kot, *n.* A thing, animal, or person thought to bring good luck.

mas·cu·line, mas′kyə·lin, *a.* Of or pertaining to the male sex; manly; virile.—*n.* The masculine gender; a word or form of this gender. —**mas·cu·line·ness, mas·cu·lin·i·ty,** mas·kyə·lin′ə·tē, *n.*

mas·cu·lin·ize, mas′kyə·lə·nīz, *v.t.,* **-ized, -iz·ing.** To infuse a male character into.

mash, mash, *n.* A soft, pulpy mass; a pulpy state or condition; crushed malt or meal of grain mixed with hot water to form wort.—*v.t.* To reduce to a soft, pulpy mass, as by beating or pressure; to crush. —**mash·er,** *n.* One who or that which mashes. *Informal.* A man who makes advances to women, esp. to those who are strangers to him.

mask, mask, mäsk, *n.* A covering for the face, worn for disguise, protection, safety, and the like; a false face; a likeness of a person's face, as in marble, or as molded in plaster, wax, or such: a death *mask;* anything that disguises or conceals; a disguise; a pretense; a masquerade or revel.—*v.t.* To cover with a mask; to disguise or conceal. —**mask·like,** *a.*

masked, maskt, mäskt, *a.* Wearing, or provided with, a mask or masks; disguised; concealed: a *masked* intention.

mas·och·ism, mas′ə·kiz·əm, maz′ə·kiz·əm, *n.* *Psychol.* A form of sexual perversion in which the victim takes pleasure in physical abuse; propensity to derive pleasure from emotional or physical pain; pathological self-destruction. **—mas·och·ist,** *n.* **—mas·och·is·tic,** mas·ə·kis′tik, maz·ə·kis′tik, *a.*

ma·son, mā′sən, *n.* A builder or worker in stone; one who builds with brick, artificial stone, or the like.*—v.t.* To construct of, or strengthen with masonry. **—ma·son·ic,** mə·son′ik, *a.* Having to do with masons or masonry.

Ma·son-Dix·on line, mā′sən·dik′sən, *n.* The boundary between Pennsylvania and Maryland, noted before the extinction of slavery as a line of demarcation between the free and the slave-states. Also **Ma·son and Dix·on's line.**

Ma·son·ite, mā′sə·nīt′, *n. Trademark.* A fiberboard made from steam-treated wood fiber pressed into sheets.

Ma·son jar, *n.* A glass jar with a tight-fitting metal top, used for home canning and preserving of foodstuffs.

ma·son·ry, mā′sən·rē, *n. pl.,* **ma·son·ries.** The art or occupation of a mason. (*Cap.*) The mysteries, and practices of Freemasons.

masque, mask, mask, mäsk, *n.* A dramatic performance popular with courtly audiences in 16th and 17th century England; a masquerade.

mas·quer·ade, mas·kə·rād′, *n.* A festive gathering of costumed individuals wearing masks and other disguises; a disguise worn at such a gathering; a disguise, or false outward show.*—v.i.,* **-ad·ed, -ad·ing.** To take part in a masquerade; disguise oneself; to go about under false pretenses. **—mas·quer·ad·er,** *n.*

mass, mas, *n.* A body of coherent matter, usu. of indefinite shape and often of considerable size: a *mass* of dough; a gathering of incoherent particles, parts, or objects regarded as forming one body: a *mass* of flowers; considerable number or quantity: a *mass* of information; the main body, bulk, or greater part of anything; bulk, size, or massiveness. *Phys.* That property of a body to which its inertia is ascribed, being a measure of its acceleration upon application of a given force.*—v.t.* To gather into or arrange in a mass or masses; assemble.*—v.i.* **—the mass·es,** the ordinary people.

Mass, mas, *n.* The celebration or liturgy of the Eucharist in Roman Catholic, Greek, or Anglican churches.

mas·sa·cre, mas′ə·kər, *n.* The indiscriminate killing of human beings; a brutal murder. *Informal.* A resounding defeat, as in sports.*—v.t.,* **-cred, -cring. —mas·sa·crer,** mas′ə·krər, *n.*

mas·sage, mə·säzh′, mə·säj′, *n.* The act or art of treating the body by rubbing or kneading to stimulate circulation or increase suppleness.*—v.t.,* **-saged, -sag·ing.** To treat by massage. **—mas·sag·er, mas·sag·ist,** *n.*

mass-en·er·gy e·qua·tion, *n.* The equation, $E = mc^2$, which expresses the relationship between energy and mass, in which energy is E, mass is m, and the velocity of light is c.

mas·seur, mə·sėr′, *n.* A man who practices massage.

mas·seuse, mə·soos′, mə·sooz′, *n. pl.,* **mas·seuses.** A woman who practices massage.

mas·sive, mas′iv, *a.* Consisting of or forming a large mass; bulky and heavy; large, solid, substantial, or imposing; broad in scope; of great magnitude, as a sensation.

mass-pro·duce, mas′prə·doos′, mas′prə·dūs′, *v.t.,* **-duced, -duc·ing.** To produce, as goods, in great number, usu. by machine. **—mass-pro·duc·er,** *n.* **—mass pro·duc·tion,** *n.*

mass·y, mas′ē, *a.,* **-i·er, -i·est.** Massive. **—mass·i·ness,** *n.*

mast, mast, mäst, *n.* A long, round piece of timber or a hollow pillar of iron or steel standing upright in a vessel, and supporting the yards, sails, ana rigging; any large vertical pole, as one which supports an antenna.*—v.t.* To fix a mast or masts in; to erect the masts of.

mas·tec·to·my, ma·stek′tə·mē, *n. pl.,* **mas·tec·to·mies.** The surgical removal of a breast.

mas·ter, mas′tər, mä′stər, *n.* One who rules, governs, or directs; an employer; a craftsman skilled or experienced enough to train others and to independently pursue his own trade; one who has possession of something and the power of controlling or using it at will; one eminently skilled in any pursuit, accomplishment, art, or science; one who is proficient or adept: a *master* of sarcasm; a degree in colleges and universities: *Master* of Arts.*—v.t.* To become the master of; to overpower; to become adept at or expert in.*—a.* Belonging to a master; chief; principal; controlling; descriptive of a mechanism which controls other similar mechanisms.

mas·ter·ful, mas′tər·fəl, mä′stər·fəl, *a.* Decisive or authoritative in manner; displaying great skill or mastery.

mas·ter key, *n.* A key that will open a number of locks, proper keys of which cannot be interchanged.

mas·ter·mind, mas′tər·mīnd, mä′stər·mīnd, *v.t.* To adeptly plan or execute as a project or undertaking.*—n.*

mas·ter of cer·e·mo·nies, *n.* A person who acts as moderator or host at a formal or public event. Also **em·cee.** *Abbr.* **m.c.**

mas·ter·piece, mas′tər·pēs, mä′stər·pēs, *n.* One's highest achievement; anything extraordinary in kind or quality.

mas·ter ser·geant, *n.* A noncommissioned officer of the next to highest enlisted grade in the Army and Marine Corps; a noncommissioned rank officer in the Air Force who is in one of the three highest enlisted grades.

mas·ter stroke, *n.* A masterly achievement.

mas·ter·y, mas′tə·rē, mä′stə·rē, *n. pl.,* **mas·ter·ies.** The act of mastering.

mast·head, mast′hed, mäst′hed, *n.* The top of a ship's mast; that part of a periodical, appearing in each issue, and listing the name, editors, staff members, etc.

mas·tic, mas′tik, *n.* An aromatic resin exuding from a tree, and used to make varnish and as a flavoring in liquors; the tree which yields this resin; a preparation used as an adhesive or seal.

mas·ti·cate, mas′tə·kāt, *v.t., v.i.,* **-ca·ted, -ca·ting.** To chew; to reduce to a pulp by crushing or kneading, as rubber. **—mas·ti·ca·ble,** mas′tə·kə·bəl, *a.* **—mas·ti·ca·tion,** mas·tə·kā′shən, *n.* **—mas·ti·ca·tor,** *n.*

mas·tiff, mas′tif, mä′stif, *n.* One of a variety of hunting dogs, large and very stoutly built.

mas·to·don, mas′tə·don, *n.* Any of several extinct species of mammals, resembling the elephant but larger.

mas·toid, mas′toyd, *a.* Of or denoting the projection of the temporal bone behind the ear.*—n.*

mas·tur·bate, mas′tər·bāt, *v.t.,* **-bat·ed, -bat·ing.** To engage in the act of masturbation.*—v.t.* To perform masturbation upon.

mas·tur·ba·tion, mas·tər·bā′shən, *n.* The handling or stimulation, usu. by oneself, of the genital organs.

mat, mat, *n.* A piece of fabric made of plaited or woven straw, hemp, or other fiber, often used to lie on, to cover a floor, or to wipe shoes on; a smaller piece of material set upon a table under a dish of food, a lamp, or a vase; a thickly growing or tangled mass, as of hair or weeds.*—v.t.,* **mat·ted, mat·ting.** To cover with or as with mats or matting; to form into a mat.*—v.i.* To become entangled.

mat, matt, matte, mat, *a.* Without luster; dull: *mat*

---

a- hat, fāte, fāre, fäther; **e-** met, mē; **i-** pin, pīne; **o-** not, nōte, ôrb, moove (move), boy, pownd; **u-** cūbe, bûll, tûk (took); **ch-** chin; **th-** thick, ŧhen; **zh-** vizhon (vision); **ə-** əgo, takən, pencəl, lemən, bərd (bird).

gold.—*n.* A dull surface or finish.—*v.t.,* **mat·ted, mat· ting.** To finish with a dull surface.

mat, mat, *n.* A frame-like piece of pasteboard or other material placed around a picture and extending to the outer frame or acting as a frame itself.—*v.t.,* **mat·ted, mat·ting.** To supply, as a picture, with a mat.

mat·a·dor, mat′ə·dôr, *n.* The bullfighter appointed to kill the bull in bullfights.

match, mach, *n.* A person or thing that equals or closely resembles another in some respect; an engagement for a contest or game; the contest or game itself; a matrimonial compact or alliance; a suitable or potential partner in marriage.—*v.t.* To equal or be equal to; to be the match or counterpart of; to correspond to; to adapt or make to correspond; to pair or assort, as persons or things, with a view to equality or correspondence; to fit together, as two things; to place in opposition or conflict; to provide with an adversary or competition of equal power.—*v.i.* To be equal or suitable; to correspond in some respect; to ally oneself in marriage. —**match·er,** *n.*

match, mach, *n.* A short, slender piece of wood or other material tipped with a chemical substance, which produces fire when rubbed on a rough or chemically prepared surface.

match·book, mach′bûk, *n.* A paper folder in which paper matches are fastened.

match·mak·er, mach′mā·kər, *n.* One who makes, or seeks to bring about, matrimonial matches. —**match·mak·ing,** *n., a.*

mate, māt, *n.* One of a pair; a companion; often used in combination: play*mate*; an equal; an officer in a ship whose duty is to assist the master or other officer; a husband or wife; one of a pair of animals which associate for propagation.—*v.t.,* **mat·ed, mat·ing.** To match; to marry; to join or pair.—*v.i.* To marry; pair for breeding; associate; match. —**mate·less,** *a.*

ma·te·ri·al, mə·tēr′ē·əl, *n.* The substance or substances of which a thing is made; anything serving as crude or raw matter for working upon or developing; something, such as a body of facts or ideas, which is utilized as the foundation for a literary work; a textile fabric. *Pl.* Articles of any kind requisite for making or doing something: writing *materials*.—*a.* Formed or consisting of matter; physical: the *material* world; pertaining to the physical rather than the spiritual or intellectual aspect of things: a *material* civilization; important. *Law.* Of evidence, of such significance as to be likely to influence the determination of an issue. —**ma·te·ri·al·ly,** *adv.*

ma·te·ri·al·ism, mə·tēr′ē·ə·liz·əm, *n.* The philosophical theory which regards matter and its motions as constituting the universe, and all phenomena, including those of the mind, as due to material agencies. Any opinion or tendency based on purely material interests. —**ma·te·ri·al·ist,** *n.* —**ma·te·ri·al·is·tic,** *a.* —**ma·te·ri·al·is·ti·cal·ly,** *adv.*

ma·te·ri·al·ize, mə·tēr′ē·ə·līz, *v.t.,* **-ized, -iz·ing.** To give material form to; to render materialistic; to cause to become a reality.—*v.i.* To assume material or bodily form; become an actual fact.

ma·té·ri·el, mə·tēr·ē·el′, *n.* The aggregate of things used or needed in carrying on any undertaking: distinguished from *personnel.*

ma·ter·nal, mə·tər′nəl, *a.* Of, pertaining to, or being a mother; related through a mother. —**ma·ter·nal·ism,** *n.* —**ma·ter·nal·is·tic,** mə·tər·nə·lis′tik, *a.* —**ma·ter·nal·ly,** *adv.*

ma·ter·ni·ty, mə·tər′nə·tē, *n. pl.,* **ma·ter·ni·ties.** The state or character of being a mother; motherhood.—*a.* Fashioned for or pertaining to the period of a woman's pregnancy and the birth of her child: *maternity* clothes.

math, math, *n. Informal.* Mathematics.

math·e·mat·i·cal, math·ə·mat′ə·kəl, *a.* Pertaining to mathematics. Precise. Also **math·e·mat·ic.** —**math·e·mat·i·cal·ly,** *adv.*

math·e·ma·ti·cian, math·ə·mə·tish′ən, *n.* A specialist in mathematics.

math·e·mat·ics, math·ə·mat′iks, *n. pl. but sing. in constr.* The science dealing with quantity, form, measurement, and arrangement, and in particular with the methods for discovering by concepts and symbols the properties and interrelationships of quantities and magnitudes. Abbr. **math.**

ma·tin, mat′ən, mat′in, *a.* Pertaining to the morning. —*n. pl., usu. sing. in constr., eccles.* Morning worship. —**mat·in·al,** *a.*

mat·i·née, mat·i·nee, mat·ə·nā′, *n.* An entertainment, esp. a dramatic or musical performance, held in the daytime, usu. in the afternoon.

ma·tri·arch, mā′trē·ärk, *n.* A woman holding a ruling position analogous to that of a patriarch, as in a family or tribe. —**ma·tri·ar·chal,** *a.,* —**ma·tri·ar·chal·ism,** *n.* —**ma·tri·ar·chy,** mā′trē·är·kē, *n. pl.,* **ma·tri·ar·chies.**

mat·ri·cide, ma′tri·sīd, mā′tri·sīd, *n.* The killing or murder of one's mother; one who murders his mother.

ma·tric·u·lant, mə·trik′yû·lənt, *n.* One who matriculates.

ma·tric·u·late, mə·trik′yû·lāt, *v.t.,* **-lat·ed, -lat·ing.** To admit to membership, as a student in a college or university.—*v.i.* To be entered ‚ or enrolled.—mə·trik′û·lit, *n.* One who is matriculated. —**ma·tric·u·la·tion,** mə·trik·yû·lā′shən, *n.*

ma·tri·lin·e·al, ma·trə·lin′ē·əl, mā·trə·lin′ē·əl, *a.* Pertaining to or based on the maternal line of descent.

mat·ri·mo·ny, ma′trə·mō·nē, *n. pl.,* **-nies.** The ceremony of marriage; the married state. —**mat·ri·mo·ni·al,** *a.*

ma·trix, mā′triks, ma′triks, *n. pl.,* **ma·tri·ces,** mā′tri·sēz, ma′tri·sēz, **ma·trix·es.** That which originates, develops, or encloses anything. An array of elements in rows and columns, as the coefficients of a set of linear equations, treated as a unit using special algebraic laws in facilitating the study of relations between the elements.

ma·tron, mā′trən, *n.* A mature married woman, esp. one who has children; a female nurse, guard, or attendant; a female superintendent of an institution, as a women's prison.

ma·tron·ly, mā′trən·lē, *a.* Of, like, or pertaining to a matron.

ma·tron of hon·or, *n.* A married woman chosen by the bride to serve as her principal attendant at the wedding.

matt, matte, mat, *a., n., v.t.* Mat.

mat·ter, mat′ər, *n.* The substance or substances of which physical objects are composed; material; a particular kind of substance: coloring *matter*; physical or corporeal substance in general, whether solid, liquid, or gaseous, esp. as distinguished from incorporeal substance, as spirit or mind, or from qualities or actions; whatever occupies space; things or something of a specified kind or in a specified connection: a *matter* of record; ground, reason, or cause: a *matter* of complaint; a thing, affair, or business: a *matter* of life and death; an amount or extent reckoned approximately: a *matter* of ten miles; something of consequence or significance; trouble or difficulty, usu. preceded by *the:* What is *the matter?* That out of which anything is made.

mat·ter, mat′ər, *v.i.* To be of significance or importance.

mat·ter-of-course, mat′ər·əv·kôrs′, mat′ər·əv·kôrs′, *a.* Happening as if in the natural sequence of events; taking things in stride.

mat·ter-of-fact, mat′ər·əv·fakt′, *a.* Treating of facts or realities; not fanciful, imaginative, or idealistic. —**mat·ter-of-fact·ly,** *adv.* —**mat·ter-of-fact·ness,** *n.*

mat·ting, mat′ing, *n.* A coarse, woven fabric of rushes, grass, straw, or hemp used for covering floors and for wrapping articles; material for mats; mat weaving.

mat·ting, mat′ing, *n.* A dull finish or surface, as on

metalwork; also **matte**. A mat or border used in picture framing.

mat·tress, ma'tris, *n.* A case, usu. cloth, filled with foam rubber, straw, cotton, or other resilient material, usu. quilted or fastened together at intervals, used as or on a bed.

mat·u·rate, mach'û·rāt, mat'û·rāt, *v.i., v.t.,* **-rat·ed, -rat·ing.** To ripen or bring to ripeness; mature.

mat·u·ra·tion, mach·û·rā'shən, mat·û·rā'shən, *n.* The process of maturing or ripening.

ma·ture, mə·tûr', mə·tūr', mə·chûr', *a.* Ripe; completely developed physically or mentally; of or characteristic of a state of full physical or emotional development: as, *mature* appearance, *mature* judgment; completely elaborated or perfected, as a plan. *Com.* Having reached the time fixed for payment.—*v.t.,* **-tured, -tur·ing.** To make mature.—*v.i.* To become mature.

ma·tu·ri·ty, mə·tûr'i·tē, mə·tūr'i·tē, mə·chûr'i·tē, *n.* The state or quality of being mature.

mat·zo, mät'sə, mät'sō, *n. pl.,* **mat·zoth, mat·zos,** mät'sōt, mät'səz, mät'sōs. A type of unleavened bread, eaten esp. at the Jewish Passover. Also **mat·za, mat·zah, mat·zoh.**

maud·lin, môd'lin, *a.* Tearful; over-emotional; excessively sentimental.

maul, mall, môl, *n.* A kind of large hammer or mallet, used esp. in driving piles.—*v.t.* To beat with a maul; to batter; to maltreat.

mau·so·le·um, mô·sə·lē'əm, mô·zə·lē'əm, *n. pl.,* **-le·ums, -le·a,** -lē·ə. A magnificent tomb or burial monument.

mauve, mōv, *n.* A light bluish-purple.

mav·er·ick, mav'ər·ik, mav'rik, *n.* In cattle raising regions, an animal found without an owner's brand, esp. a calf separated from its mother. *Informal.* One who departs from the customs or beliefs of his or her group.

mawk·ish, mô'kish, *a.* Lacking a pleasing flavor; characterized by sickly sentimentality.

max·im, mak'sim, *n.* An established principle or general truth; a principle embodying a rule of conduct, as a proverb.

max·i·mal, mak'sə·məl, *a.* Pertaining to or being a maximum; most; greatest possible. **—max·i·mal·ly,** *adv.*

max·i·mize, mak'sə·mīz, *v.t.,* **-mized, -miz·ing.** To make as great as possible; to raise to the maximum.

max·i·mum, mak'sə·məm, *n. pl.,* **max·i·mums, max·i·ma.** The greatest quantity or amount possible; the highest amount, value, or degree attained or recorded: opposed to *minimum.—a.*

may, mā, *aux. v.,* pres. sing. **may, may, may;** pres. pl. **may;** past **might.** Used to express permission or opportunity: you *may* enter. Used to express possibility: We *may* be late. Used to express wish or prayer: *May* you live long. Used to express contingency, esp. in clauses expressing condition, concession, purpose, or result: He fought so that others *may* have peace.

May, mā, *n.* The fifth month of the year, having 31 days.

may·be, mā'bē, *adv.* Perhaps; possibly.

May·day, mā'dā, *n.* The international signal word of ships and airplanes in distress, usu. sent by radiotelephone.

may·flow·er, mā'flow·ər, *n.* Any of several flowers that bloom in May. *(Cap.)* The ship which brought the Pilgrims from England to America in 1620.

may·fly, May fly, mā'flī, *n. pl.,* **may·flies.** Any of various insects with transparent wings; an artificial fly resembling a mayfly which is used in sport fishing.

may·hem, mā'hem, mā'əm, *n. Law.* The act of intentionally maiming a person, or inflicting a disabling wound; a situation involving violent or destructive behavior.

may·on·naise, mā·ə·nāz', mā'ə·nāz, *n.* A salad dressing composed of yolks of eggs beaten with vegetable or olive oil until thick.

may·or, mā'ər, mār, *n.* The chief executive of a city, town, or borough. **—may·or·al,** *a.*

may·or·al·ty, mā'ər·əl·tē, mār'əl·tē, *n. pl.,* **may·or·al·ties.** The office of a mayor; the time of his service.

May·time, mā'tīm, *n.* The month of May. Also **May·tide,** mā'tīd.

maze, māz, *n.* A confusing network of paths or passages; a winding and turning; confusion of thought. *—v.t.,* **mazed, maz·ing.**

ma·zy, mā'zē, *a.,* **-zi·er, -zi·est.** Having the character of a maze; confusing. **—ma·zi·ly,** *adv.* **—ma·zi·ness,** *n.*

Mc·Coy, mə·koy', *n.* The genuine article or person, preceded by *the* or *the real.*

me, mē, *pron.* The objective case of I: used as the direct object, or accusative, and as the indirect object, or dative, of a verb, and as the object of a preposition.

mead, mēd, *n.* A fermented liquor made from honey.

mead·ow, med'ō, *n.* A level tract of land under grass, usu. mowed for hay or used for grazing.

mead·ow·lark, med'ō·lärk, *n.* A N. American brownish songbird of the blackbird family, inhabiting fields and meadows and recognized by its bright yellow breast crossed by a black V, and white outer tail feathers.

mea·ger, mē'gər, *a.* Scanty; small; lacking in quality or quantity; wanting richness, fertility, strength; thin; lean. **—mea·ger·ly,** *adv.* **—mea·ger·ness.**

meal, mēl, *n.* A portion of food prepared, served, or taken at one of the regular times for eating; occasion of taking food; a repast.

meal, mēl, *n.* The edible part of any grain, and of certain leguminous plants, coarsely ground and unsifted, as corn meal, oatmeal, peanut meal, soybean meal, and the like; any ground or powdery substance resembling this.

meal·time, mēl'tīm, *n.* The usual time of eating meals.

meal·worm, mēl'wərm, *n.* The beetle larva which infests and contaminates meal, flour, or grain, often raised for fishing bait.

meal·y, mē'lē, *a.,* **-i·er, -i·est.** Having the qualities of meal; containing meal; flecked; powdery, as meal; overspread with something that resembles meal; mealy-mouthed; pale or sallow. **—meal·i·ness,** *n.*

meal·y-mouthed, mē'lē·mowthd, mē'lē·mowtht, *a.* Unwilling or hesitating to tell the truth in plain language; not sincere.

mean, mēn, *v.t.,* **meant, mean·ing.** To have in the mind; to intend: to *mean* to fix something; to purpose or design; to signify or intend to signify; to denote. *—v.i.* To be minded or disposed; to intend: to *mean* well; to be of a stated significance: His wife *means* everything to him.

mean, mēn, *a.* Of little value; inferior; humble; miserly; contemptible; shabby. *Informal.* Selfish; troublesome; ill-tempered, vicious; excellent, skillful. **—mean·ly,** *adv.* **—mean·ness,** *n.*

mean, mēn, *a.* Occupying a middle position; middle; midway between extremes; intermediate.—*n.* What is midway or intermediate between two extremes; moderation; the simple average formed by adding quantities together and dividing by their number. *Pl. but sing. in constr.* The medium or what is used to accomplish or reach an end; measure or measures adopted; agency; instrumentality: by this *means,* a *means* to an end. *Pl.* Income; revenue; resources; estate. **—by all means,** certainly; on every consideration. **—by no means,** not at all; certainly not.

me·an·der, mē·an'dər, *n.* A roundabout journey.

---

a- hat, fāte, fāre, fäther; **e-** met, mē; **i-** pin, pīne; **o-** not, nōte, ôrb, moove (move), boy, pownd; **u-** cūbe, bûll, tūk (took); **ch-** chin; **th-** thick, ŧhen; **zh-** vizhon (vision); **ə-** əgo, takən, pencəl, lemən, bərd (bird).

Usu. pl. A winding course.—*v.i.* To wind or turn; to have an intricate or winding course; roam aimlessly; ramble, as a conversation. —**me·an·der·ing·ly,** *adv.*

mean·ing, mē′ning, *n.* The intention of a verbal expression, a gesture, or an act; aim or purpose; what is to be understood; signification, as of words; significance or import: the *meaning* of a dream.—*a.* Having intention, usu. used in compounds: a well-*meaning* gesture; significant or expressive: a *meaning* look.

mean·ing·ful, mē′ning·fəl, *a.* Of significance; of value, filled with meaning. —**mean·ing·ful·ly,** *adv.*

mean·ing·less, mē′ning·lis, *a.* Without value or purpose; having no meaning. —**mean·ing·less·ly,** *adv.* —**mean·ing·less·ness,** *n.*

meant, ment, *v.* Past tense of **mean.**

mean·time, mēn′tim, *n.* The interval between one specified period and another.—*adv.* During the interval; at the same moment or time.

mean·while, mēn′hwil, mēn′wil, *adv., n.* Meantime.

mea·sles, mē′zəlz, *n. pl., sing. or pl. in constr.* An infectious disease occurring principally in children and characterized by a widespread red rash.

mea·sly, mē′zlē, *a.,* **-sli·er, -sli·est.** Infected with measles; having larval tapeworms, as meat. *Informal.* Very slight or scanty: a *measly* portion; very unsatisfactory: a *measly* production.

meas·ur·a·ble, mezh′ər·ə·bəl, *a.* Referring to that which may be measured; limited. —**meas·ur·a·bil·i·ty,** mezh·ər·ə·bil′ə·tē, *n.* —**meas·ur·a·bly,** *adv.*

meas·ure, mezh′ər, *n.* The extent of a thing in length, breadth, and thickness, in circumference, capacity, or in any other respect; a standard of measurement, as a foot, pound, quart, or the like; a fixed unit of measurement; the instrument by which extent or capacity is ascertained; any criterion or measuring rod for comparing or judging; the act of measurement; a certain definite quantity: a *measure* of wine; that which is allotted to one; moderation; an indefinite quantity or degree; a decree or act of a legislature: a house *measure*; *often pl.,* something done with a view to the accomplishment of a purpose: *measures* taken to avoid punishment. That division by which notes are grouped according to the regular recurrence of primary accents; that section of music marked off by two bar lines; a bar. The arrangement of the syllables in each line with respect to quantity and accents; a metrical foot.—*v.t.,* **-ured, -ur·ing.** To ascertain the extent, dimensions, or capacity of, esp. against some standard; to judge the greatness or import of; to value; to proportion; to allot or distribute by measure, often with *out* or *off;* to serve as a measure; to pass over or traverse; to compare.—*v.i.* To take a measurement or measurements; to result in or have a given measurement. —**meas·ure up,** to be qualified; to be equal to a standard. —**for good meas·ure,** as an addition; as something extra. —**meas·ur·er,** *n.*

meas·ured, mezh′ərd, *a.* Apportioned, often according to size or extent; judged by a standard; deliberate or carefully chosen; slow and uniform; rhythmical.

meas·ure·ment, mezh′ər·mənt, *n.* The act of measuring; the amount or size ascertained by measuring; a system of measuring.

meat, mēt, *n.* Flesh of animals, usu. mammals, used as food; the edible portion of something: coconut *meat;* food in general or anything eaten as nourishment; the gist, essence, or vital points, as of a discourse or written work.

meat-and-po·ta·toes, *n. pl., sing. or pl. in constr. Informal.* The basic part; the essential content or foundation of something; that which accounts for the major source of trade or profit in a business.—*a.* Having a fundamental or pragmatic quality, as contrasted with that which is amusing or artistic.

meat·y, mē′tē, *a.,* **-i·er, -i·est.** Of or like meat; abounding in meat, as a sauce or casserole; full of substance, or pithy. —**meat·i·ness,** *n.*

mec·ca, mek′ə, *n.* A place attracting many pilgrims or visitors; the goal of one's greatest desires or aspirations.

me·chan·ic, mə·kan′ik, *n.* A worker skilled in the construction, operation, and repair of machinery, motors, or tools; a machinist.—*a.* Mechanical.

me·chan·i·cal, mə·kan′ə·kəl, *a.* Referring to or concerned with the use of tools, or the construction of machines or mechanisms; involving machinery; performed as if by machinery, without spontaneity, spirit, or individuality; of or pertaining to the material forces of nature acting on bodies or masses; pertaining to, or controlled or effected by physical forces, that are not chemical; explaining certain phenomena as due to mechanical action or the physical forces of the universe. —**me·chan·i·cal·ly,** *adv.*

me·chan·i·cal ad·van·tage, *n.* The ratio of the force producing work in a mechanism, or output force, to the force applied to a mechanism, or input force.

me·chan·ics, mə·kan′iks, *n. pl.* The functional, mechanical, or routine details of something. *Sing. in constr.* That area of physics concerned with motion and the effect of forces on material bodies, and including kinematics, kinetics, and statics; the application, both practical and theoretical, of this study to the designing, repairing, assembling, and operating of machines.

mech·a·nism, mek′ə·niz·əm, *n.* The structure or arrangement of parts of a machine or similar device; such parts collectively; a piece of machinery; anything like a machine in its structure or operation; the machinery, or the agencies, means, or procedures, by which a particular effect is produced or a purpose is accomplished; machinery or mechanical appliances in general.

mech·a·nis·tic, mek·ə·nis′tik, *a.* Pertaining to mechanism, or to mechanics; determined mechanically: a *mechanistic* society. —**mech·a·nis·ti·cal·ly,** *adv.*

mech·a·nize, mek′ə·niz, *v.t.,* **-nized, -niz·ing.** To render mechanical; to operate or perform by or as if by machinery; introduce machinery into, as an industry or business. —**mech·a·ni·za·tion,** mek·ə·nə·zā′shən, *n.* —**mech·a·niz·er,** *n.*

med·al, med′əl, *n.* A decorative piece of metal, often coin-shaped, issued as an award to honor a person or to mark an event; a similar object bearing a design of religious significance.—*v.t.,* **-aled, -al·ing.** To award or present a medal to. —**me·dal·lic,** mə·dal′ik, *a.*

me·dal·lion, mə·dal′yən, *n.* A large medal; a circular or oval design used as a motif on fabrics, wallpaper, and the like.

med·dle, med′əl, *v.i.,* **-dled, -dling.** To interfere or take part in a matter in an impertinent, or offensive manner. —**med·dler,** *n.*

med·dle·some, med′əl·səm, *a.* Given to meddling.

me·di·a, mē′dē·ə, *n. pl.* of **medium.**

me·di·al, mē′dē·əl, *a.* Situated in or pertaining to the middle; median; intermediate; average; ordinary.

me·di·an, mē′dē·ən, *a.* Situated in or referring to the middle; medial; noting or referring to a plane dividing something into two equal parts; noting or referring to the middle number or value in a given series: 4 is the *median* number in the series 1, 3, 4, 8, 9.

me·di·an strip, *n.* A narrow piece of land separating opposite lanes on a highway. —**me·di·an·ly,** *adv.*

me·di·ate, mē′dē·it, *a.* Being between two extremes; acting as a means or agent; not direct or immediate; effected by the intervention of an agency.—mē′dē·āt, *v.i.,* **-at·ed, -at·ing.** To interpose between parties at variance with a view to effecting agreement or reconciliation; to be in a middle or intermediate place.—*v.t.* To effect by mediation: to *mediate* a peace.

me·di·a·tion, mē·dē·ā′shən, *n.* The act of or an instance of mediating. —**me·di·a·tive,** mē′dē·ə·tiv, mē′dē·ə·tiv, *n.* —**me·di·a·to·ry,** mē′dē·ə·tôr·ē, *a.*

me·di·a·tor, mē′dē·ā·tər, *n.* One who mediates.

med·ic, med′ik, *n.* A medical practitioner, medical

corpsman, or medical student.

med·i·ca·ble, med/i·kə·bəl, *a.* Responsive to medical treatment; curable. **—med·i·ca·bly,** *adv.*

Med·i·caid, med/i·kād, *n.* A medical aid program sponsored jointly by federal, state, and local governments for the disabled or needy of any age who are not eligible for social security benefits.

med·i·cal, med/i·kəl, *a.* Referring to or connected with medicine or physicians; medicinal; tending to cure. **—med·i·cal·ly,** *adv.*

med·i·cal ex·am·in·er, *n.* A medically trained public official appointed to make post-mortem examinations of the bodies of victims of suicide, homicide, or other unnatural circumstances, in order to determine the cause of the death; a physician appointed by a firm or insurance company to examine employees or applicants.

me·dic·a·ment, mə·dik/ə·mənt, med/i·kə·mənt, *n.* Any substance used for healing wounds or treating diseases.

Med·i·care, med/i·ker, *n.* A U.S. government insurance program, financed by social security, that provides hospital and medical care for certain persons, esp. the aged.

med·i·cate, med/i·kāt, *v.t.,* **-cat·ed, -cat·ing.** To treat with medicine or medicaments.

med·i·ca·tion, med·i·kā/shən, *n.* The act or process of medicating; a medicinal preparation used to treat or cure an ailment.

me·dic·i·nal, mə·dis/ən·əl, *a.* Referring to or having the properties of a medicine; curative: as, *medicinal* substances. **—me·dic·i·nal·ly,** *adv.*

med·i·cine, med/ə·sən, *n.* Any substance used in treating disease or relieving pain; medicament; remedy; the art or science of restoring or preserving health or physical condition, often divided into medicine proper, surgery, and obstetrics; the science of treating disease with drugs or curative substances, as distinguished from *surgery* and *obstetrics;* the medical profession.**—***v.t.,* **-cined, -cin·ing.** To administer medicine to. **—take one's med·i·cine,** to accept suffering or punishment, particularly when oneself is the cause.

med·i·cine man, *n.* Among the American Indians, any man whom they suppose to possess supernatural powers of healing or invoking spirits.

med·i·cine show, *n.* In the 19th century, a traveling group of entertainers who drew potential customers for the remedies and medicines that were offered for sale.

med·i·co, med/i·kō, *n. Informal.* A doctor; a medical student.

me·di·e·val, me·di·ae·val, mē/dē·ē·vəl, med/ē·ē·vəl, *a.* Relating to the Middle Ages or the period between the 8th and the middle of the 15th century. **—me·di·e·val·ism, me·di·ae·val·ism,** *n.*

me·di·o·cre, mē·dē·ō/kər, mē/dē·ō·kər, *a.* Of moderate degree or quality; average; ordinary; barely adequate; inferior. **—me·di·oc·ri·ty,** mē·dē·ok/rə·tē, *n. pl.,* **-ties.**

med·i·tate, med/i·tāt, *v.i.,* **-tat·ed, -tat·ing.** To dwell on anything in thought; to cogitate.**—***v.t.* To contemplate doing; to plan or intend. **—med·i·tat·ing·ly,** *adv.* **—med·i·ta·tor,** *n.*

med·i·ta·tion, med·i·tā/shən, *n.* The act of meditating. **—med·i·ta·tive,** med/i·tā·tiv, *a.*

med·i·ter·ra·ne·an, med·i·tə·rā/nē·ən, *a.* Surrounded by or in the midst of land; inland; *(cap.)* pertaining to, situated on, or near the Mediterranean Sea.

me·di·um, mē/dē·əm, *n. pl.,* **me·di·a,** mē/dē·ə, **me·di·ums.** Something placed or ranked between other things; a mean between two extremes; that by or through which anything is accomplished; conveyed, or carried on; an agency or instrumentality: Television is a communications and advertising *medium;* the culture in which organisms grow, or the substances in which they are preserved for study; a person who is said to be capable of communicating with the spirits of the deceased; the form or material used by an artist.**—***a.* Middle; middling.

med·ley, med/lē, *n. pl.,* **-leys.** A mixture, esp. of heterogeneous elements; a jumble; a piece of music combining airs or passages from various sources.

meek, mēk, *a.* Mild of temper; gentle; submissive; lacking courage.

meet, mēt, *v.t.,* **met, meet·ing.** To come upon or encounter; go to the place of arrival of: to *meet* a train; come into personal acquaintance with, as by formal presentation; to come into contact, junction, or connection with; to come before or to; to face directly or without avoidance; to oppose: to *meet* charges with countercharges; cope or deal effectively with, as an objection; satisfy, as obligations; come into comformity with, as expectations; to encounter in experience; receive: to *meet* one's deserts.**—***v.i.* To come together, face to face, or into company; assemble, as for action or conference; become personally acquainted; to come into contact or form a junction, as lines; to be united; concur or agree; to come together in opposition or conflict, as adversaries.**—***n.* A gathering or meeting for a sports event; those assembled at such a meeting; the place of meeting. **—meet with,** to come across; to encounter in experience; to confer with; receive, as praise. **—meet·er,** *n.*

meet·ing, mē/ting, *n.* A coming together; an assembly for some common purpose, or the persons present; junction.

meet·ing·house, mē/ting·hows, *n.* A building or place used for public meetings.

meg·a·city, meg/ə·sit·ē, *n. pl.,* **meg·a·cit·ies.** A city with 1,000,000 or more inhabitants.

meg·a·cy·cle, meg/ə·sī·kəl, *n.* A unit used to measure the frequency of electromagnetic waves, equal to 1,000,000 cycles per second; a million cycles.

meg·a·lo·ma·ni·a, meg·ə·lō·mā/nē·ə, *n.* A form of mental disorder characterized by extreme overestimation of one's abilities or importance; an obsession for grandiose action. **—meg·a·lo·ma·ni·ac,** *a., n.* **—meg·a·lo·ma·ni·a·cal,** meg·ə·lo·mə·nī/ə·kəl, *a.*

meg·a·lop·o·lis, meg·ə·lop/ə·ləs, *n.* A far-reaching metropolitan area in which cities are linked by connecting suburbs. **—meg·a·lo·pol·i·tan,** meg·ə·lə·pol/ə·tən, *a.*

meg·a·phone, meg/ə·fōn, *n.* A large funnel-shaped instrument for magnifying sound, usu. used in addressing a large audience out of doors.**—***v.t., v.i.,* **-phoned, -phon·ing.**

meg·a·ton, meg/ə·tən, *n.* A unit of explosive force equal to 1,000,000 tons of TNT.

meg·a·watt, meg/ə·wot, *n.* One million watts of power.

mei·o·sis, mī·ō/sis, *n.* The process resulting in the formation of the mature reproductive cells. **—mei·ot·ic,** mī·ot/ik, *a.*

mel·a·mine res·in, mel/ə·mēn, *n.* A substance primarily used as a coating for plastics, fabrics, and paper.

mel·an·cho·li·a, mel·ən·kō/lē·ə, mel·ən·kōl/yə, *n.* A mental disease characterized by great depression, brooding, gloomy forebodings without apparent reason, a marked inaccessibility to most external stimuli, and often, real or imagined physical ailments. **—mel·an·cho·li·ac,** *a., n.*

mel·an·chol·y, mel/ən·kol·ē, *n. pl.,* **-ies.** A state of despondency, esp. frequent or lengthy despondency; somber contemplation.**—***a.* Also **mel·an·chol·ic.** **—mel·an·chol·i·cal·ly, mel·an·chol·i·ly,** *adv.* **—mel·an·chol·i·ness,** *n.*

---

a- hat, fāte, fāre, fäther; **e-** met, mē; **i-** pin, pīne; **o-** not, nōte, ôrb, moove (move), boy, pownd; **u-** cūbe, bull, tūk (took); **ch-** chin; **th-** thick, then; **zh-** vizhon (vision); **ə-** əgo, takən, pencəl, lemən, bərd (bird).

mé·lange, mā·länzh′, *n.* A mixture; an assortment.

mel·a·nin, mel′ə·nin, *n.* Any of various dark pigments found in the hair, skin, or eyes of humans and animals.

mel·a·no·ma, mel·ə·nō′mə, *n. pl.,* **-mas, -ma·ta,** -mə·tə. A tumor, usu. malignant, composed of cells containing dark pigment.

Mel·ba toast, mel′bə, *n.* Crisply toasted bread in thin, small slices.

meld, meld, *v.t., v.i.* To announce and display, as a counting combination of cards in one's hand, for a score.

meld, meld, *v.t., v.i.* To blend; to unite.

me·lee, mā′lā, mā·lā′, mel·ā′, *n.* A confused, all-out, hand-to-hand fracas.

mel·io·rate, mel′yə·rāt, *v.t., v.i.,* **-rat·ed, -rat·ing.** To make better; to ameliorate. —**mel·io·ra·ble,** *a.* —**mel·io·ra·tion,** mēl·yə·rā′shən, *n.* —**mel·io·ra·tor,** *n.*

mel·lif·lu·ous, mə·lif′loo·əs, *a.* Sweet-sounding, as the voice; flowing as with honey; sweetly flowing. Also **mel·lif·lu·ent.** —**mel·lif·lu·ous·ly,** *adv.*

mel·low, mel′ō, *a.* Soft with ripeness; rich or delicate to the eye, ear, or palate, as color, sound, or flavor; toned down by the lapse of time; softened or matured by length of years; genial. *Informal.* Made good humored by liquor; somewhat intoxicated.—*v.t., v.i.* To soften by ripeness or age; to render or to become mellow.

me·lo·de·on, mə·lō′dē·ən, *n.* A wind instrument with metallic free reeds and a keyboard similar to the harmonium; a small organ with metal reeds.

mel·o·dra·ma, mel′ə·drä·mə, mel′ə·dram·ə, *n.* An extravagantly sentimental or emotionally exaggerated drama or play. —**mel·o·dra·mat·ic,** mel·ə·drə·mat′ik, *a.* —**mel·o·dra·mat·i·cal·ly,** *adv.* —**melo·dra·mat·ics,** mel·ə·drə·mat′iks, *n.*

mel·o·dy, mel′ə·dē, *n. pl.,* **-dies.** An agreeable succession of sounds; sweetness of sound; sound highly pleasing to the ear; a succession of tones, usu. produced by a single voice or instrument; distinguished from rhythm and harmony; the particular air or tune of a musical piece. —**me·lod·ic,** mə·lod′ik, *a.* —**me·lod·i·cal·ly,** *adv.* —**me·lo·di·ous,** mə·lō′dē·əs, *a.* —**me·lo·di·ous·ness,** *n.*

mel·on, mel′ən, *n.* The fruit of any of various gourd plants, as the muskmelon or the watermelon; the vine itself. *Informal.* An accumulation of profits, exceeding ordinary dividends, for distribution among the stockholders of a company.

melt, melt, *v.t.,* **melt·ed, melt·ed** or **molt·en, melt·ing.** To reduce from a solid to a liquid or flowing state by heat; to liquefy; to cause to fuse or blend; to soften in attitude.—*v.i.* To become liquid; to dissolve; to pass by imperceptible degrees, often followed by *away*; to blend or to shade, often followed by *into*; to become tender, mild, or gentle.—*n.* Something that is melted; a melting process or melted state; the quantity in a single operation of melting. —**melt·a·bil·i·ty,** *n.* —**melt·a·ble,** *a.* —**melt·er,** *n.*

melt·ing point, *n.* The degree of heat at which a solid will melt or fuse.

melt·ing pot, *n.* A crucible; a container in which substances can be melted; a country, city, or society containing many cultures and ethnic groups.

mem·ber, mem′bər, *n.* A part or organ of an animal body, esp. a limb, as a leg; a constituent part of any structural or composite whole; each of the persons composing a society, party, community, or other body. —**mem·bered,** *a.* —**mem·ber·less,** *a.*

mem·ber·ship, mem′bər·ship, *n.* The state of being a member, as of a society or organization; the total number of members belonging to a body.

mem·brane, mem′brān, *n.* A thin tissue of the animal body which covers organs, lines cavities or canals, or joins adjacent parts; similar tissue in plants. —**mem·bra·nous,** *a.*

me·men·to, mə·men′tō, *n. pl.,* **-tos, -toes.** Anything that reminds one of what is past; a souvenir.

mem·o, mem′ō, *n. Informal.* Memorandum.

mem·oir, mem′wär, *n.* A record or written statement of something noteworthy; a biography. *Usu. pl.* An autobiography.

mem·o·ra·bil·i·a, mem·ər·ə·bil′ē·ə, mem·ər·ə·bil′yə, *n. pl.* Things and occasions worthy of remembrance.

mem·o·ra·ble, mem′ər·ə·bəl, *a.* Worthy to be remembered; remarkable. —**mem·o·ra·bly,** *adv.*

mem·o·ran·dum, mem·ə·ran′dəm, *n. pl.,* **-dums, -da,** -də. A note used in aiding the memory; a brief record; an informal communication about office matters sent among the staff of a company.

me·mo·ri·al, mə·môr′ē·əl, *a.* Of or referring to the memory; preserving the memory of a person or thing; commemorative.—*n.* Something designed or adapted to preserve the memory of a person, an event, or anything belonging to the past. —**me·mo·ri·al·ly,** *adv.*

Me·mo·ri·al Day, *n.* A day, usually the last Monday in May, set apart in most of the States of the U.S. to honor the dead of American wars.

me·mo·ri·al·ize, mə·môr′ē·ə·līz, *v.t.,* **-ized, -iz·ing.** To commemorate; to present a memorial to. —**me·mo·ri·al·i·za·tion,** mə·môr·ē·ə·lə·zā′shən, *n.* —**me·mo·ri·al·iz·er,** *n.* —**me·mo·ri·al·ly,** *adv.*

me·mo·ri·al park, *n.* A cemetery.

mem·o·rize, mem′ə·rīz, *v.t.,* **-rized, -riz·ing.** To commit to memory; learn by heart. —**mem·o·riz·a·ble,** *a.* —**mem·o·ri·za·tion,** mem·ə·rə·zā′shən, *n.*

mem·o·ry, mem′ə·rē, *n. pl.,* **-ries.** The mental capacity or faculty of retaining and reviving impressions, or of recalling previous experiences; this capacity as possessed by a particular individual; the totality of things retained by a person; a person or thing remembered; the length of time over which recollection extends; reputation, esp. after death; the state or fact of being remembered: as, to remain in perpetual *memory;* commemoration: as, a monument erected in *memory* of a person.

men, men, *n. pl. of* **man.**

men·ace, men′is, *v.t.,* **-aced, -ac·ing.** To threaten, as with harm, evil, or death.—*v.i.* To behave in a threatening way.—*n.* A threat; a source of worry; a nuisance.

mé·nage, mā·näzh′, mə·näzh′, *n.* A household; housekeeping.

me·nag·er·ie, mə·naj′ə·rē, mə·nazh′ə·rē, *n.* A collection of animals, esp. wild or foreign animals, for exhibition; a place where such a collection is kept.

mend, mend, *v.t.* To make whole or sound by repairing, as something broken, worn, or otherwise damaged; to reform; restore to due condition by any suitable action; to set right: to *mend* matters.—*v.i.* To become better or improve.—*n.* The act or fact of mending. —**mend·a·ble,** *a.*

men·da·cious, men·dā′shəs, *a.* Given to telling lies; false. —**men·da·cious·ly,** *adv.* —**men·da·cious·ness,** *n.*

men·dac·i·ty, men·das′ə·tē, *n.* A lie; quality of being false.

men·de·le·vi·um, men·də·lē′vē·əm, *n.* A synthetic radioactive element obtained from einsteinium.

men·di·cant, men′də·kənt, *a.* Referring to begging or beggars; referring to a priest who begs.—*n.* A beggar; a begging priest.

me·ni·al, mē′nē·əl, *a.* Referring to household or domestic servants; servile; low.—*n.* A domestic servant; one who is servile. —**me·ni·al·ly,** *adv.*

me·nin·ges, mi·nin′jēz, *n. pl., sing.* **me·ninx,** mē′ningks. Three membranes that cover the brain and spinal cord. —**me·nin·ge·al,** mi·nin′jē·əl, *a.*

men·in·gi·tis, men·in·jī′tis, *n.* Inflammation of the membranes of the brain or spinal cord.

me·nis·cus, mi·nis′kəs, *n. pl.,* **me·nis·cus·es, me·nis·ci,** mi·nis′ī. A crescent or crescent-shaped body; the convex or concave upper surface of a column of liquid.

men·o·pause, men′ə·pôz, *n.* The natural and permanent stopping of menstruation, normally between the ages of 45 and 50; woman's change of life. **—men·o·pau·sal,** *a.*

me·nor·ah, mə·nôr′ə, mə·nôr′ə, *n.* A nine-armed candelabrum used in the celebration of the Jewish holiday of Hanukkah.

men·sal, men′səl, *a.* Monthly.

men·ses, men′sēz, *n. pl., sing. or pl. in constr.* Menstruation.

men·stru·al, men′strōo·əl, men′strəl, *a.* Referring to the menstruation of females.

men·stru·a·tion, men·strōo·ā′shən, *n.* The uterine discharge of blood and mucus occurring, on an average, every 28 days from puberty to menopause; the act or time of menstruation. **—men·stru·ate,** men′strōo·āt, *v.i.,* **-at·ed, -at·ing.**

men·sur·a·ble, men′shər·ə·bəl, *a.* Capable of being measured; measurable.

men·tal, men′təl, *a.* Of or referring to the mind; referring to the totality of an individual's intellectual and emotional processes; intellectual rather than emotional or physical; of, pertaining to, or afflicted by a disorder of the mind; for the treatment or care of persons afflicted by such disorders; performed by or existing in the mind, esp. without the use of written figures. **—men·tal·ly,** *adv.*

men·tal age, *n.* The age which corresponds to the level of an individual's mental abilities.

men·tal de·fi·cien·cy, *n.* Failure in the development of intelligence, characterized by an individual's inability to function adequately in society.

men·tal·i·ty, men·tal′ə·tē, *n. pl.,* **-ties.** Mental capacity; mind.

men·thol, men′thôl, men′thol, *n.* A white, crystalline compound, obtained from oil of peppermint or synthesized, and used in medicine, in perfumes, and in confections. **—men·tho·lat·ed,** men′thə·lā·tid, *a.*

men·tion, men′shən, *n.* A brief notice or remark with regard to something; a casual speaking of; a reference to; a recognition for achievement.**—v.t.** To note briefly; to recognize for notable achievement. **—men·tion·a·ble,** *a.* **—men·tion·er,** *n.*

men·tor, men′tər, *n.* A wise and faithful adviser or tutor.

men·u, men′ū, mā′nū, *n.* A bill of fare; a list of meals that can be served; a meal.

me·ow, mi·aou, mi·aow, mē·ow′, my·ow′, *n.* A sound made by a cat.**—v.i.** To make such a sound.

me·pro·ba·mate, mə·prō′bə·māt, *n.* A powder, used as a tranquilizer and antispasmodic.

mer·can·tile, mər′kən·tēl, mər′kən·til, mər′kən·til, *a.* Of or referring to merchants, trade, or commerce.

mer·can·til·ism, mər′kən·ti·liz·əm, *n.* Mercantile system; the mercantile spirit. **—mer·can·til·ist,** *n., a.*

mer·ce·nar·y, mər′sə·ner·ē, *a.* Motivated by reasons of gain; obtained by hire: said of soldiers serving a foreign ruler or state.**—n. pl.,** **-ies.** One who is hired; a soldier hired into foreign service. **—mer·ce·nar·i·ly,** *adv.*

mer·cer·ize, mər′sə·riz, *v.t.,* **-ized, -iz·ing.** To apply, as to cotton fabrics, caustic soda under stress or tension, in order to increase strength and sheen, and improve retention of dyes.

mer·chan·dise, mər′chən·diz, mər′chən·dis, *n.* Goods; wares, esp. manufactured products.**—mər′chən·diz,** *v.i., v.t.,* **-dised, -dis·ing.** To carry on business activity; to buy or sell; to organize and conduct a campaign for the sale of. Also **mer·chan·dize.** **—mer·chan·dis·er, mer·chan·diz·er,** *n.*

mer·chant, mər′chənt, *n.* One who buys and sells commodities for profit; retail dealer; shopkeeper.**—a.** Referring to trade or commerce.

mer·chant·man, mər′chənt·mən, *n. pl.,* **-men.** A

trading ship.

mer·chant ma·rine, *n.* The commercial ships belonging to a nation; the crew and officers on such ships.

mer·cu·ri·al, mər·kyūr′ē·əl, *a.* Lively; sprightly; fickle; containing or consisting of quicksilver or mercury. **—n.** A preparation of mercury used as a drug.

Mer·cu·ro·chrome, mər·kyūr′ə·krōm, *n. Trademark.* A reddish substance used as an antiseptic.

mer·cu·ry, mər′kyū·rē, *n. pl.,* **-ries.** A heavy, silverwhite metallic element remarkable for its liquid state at ordinary temperatures; quicksilver; a column of this substance used in a thermometer to indicate temperature, or in a barometer, to indicate air pressure.

mer·cy, mər′sē, *n. pl.,* **-cies.** Benevolence, mildness, or tenderness of heart; a disposition that tempers justice and leads to the infliction of a lighter punishment than law or justice will warrant; clemency; an act or exercise of benevolence or favor; a blessing; compassion or pity, or the power to display either. **—at one's mer·cy,** completely in one's power. **—mer·ci·ful,** *a.* **—mer·ci·ful·ly,** *adv.* **—mer·ci·less,** *a.*

mere, mēr, *a., superlative,* **mer·est.** This or that and nothing else; simple; absolute; entire; utter: *mere* folly. **—mere·ly,** *adv.*

mer·e·tri·cious, mer·ə·trish′əs, *a.* Having a gaudy, attractive look; showy, but in bad taste; insincere. **—mer·e·tri·cious·ly,** *adv.* **—mer·e·tri·cious·ness,** *n.*

merge, mərj, *v.t.,* **merged, merg·ing.** To cause to unite; to combine; blend so that individuality is obscured.**—v.i.** To be absorbed; to be blended. **—mer·gence,** *n.*

merg·er, mər′jər, *n.* The legal combination of corporations into a successor corporation; any combination of two or more businesses resulting in a single successor corporation or enterprise; a combination; a uniting.

me·rid·i·an, mə·rid′ē·ən, *n.* A great circle of the earth passing through the poles and any given point on the earth's surface; the half of such a circle included between the poles; the great circle of the celestial sphere which passes through its poles and the observer's zenith. A point or period of highest development or greatest prosperity.**—a.** Of or referring to a meridian; of or referring to midday or noon.

me·rid·i·o·nal, mə·rid′ē·ə·nəl, *a.* Referring to a meridian; southern or southerly.**—n.** An inhabitant of the south, esp. of the south of France.

me·ringue, mə·rang′, *n.* A light mixture made of the beaten whites of eggs and sugar, usu. baked or browned.

mer·it, mer′it, *n.* Excellence deserving honor or reward; worth; something that deserves a reward or punishment. *Sometimes pl.* The state or fact of deserving: to treat a person according to his or her *merits. Pl.* The rights or wrongs of a case or question.**—v.t.** To be worthy of; to deserve. **—mer·i·ted,** *a.* **—mer·it·ed·ly,** *adv.* **—mer·it·less,** *a.*

mer·i·to·ri·ous, mer·ə·tôr′ē·əs, *a.* Possessing or having merit.

mer·maid, mər′mād, *n.* A fabled marine creature with the head and upper body of a woman and a fish's tail; a proficient female swimmer. **—mer·man,** *n. masc., pl.,* **-men.**

mer·ri·ment, mer′i·mənt, *n.* Gaiety; laughter; mirth; hilarity.

mer·ry, mer′ē, *a.,* **-ri·er, -ri·est.** Cheery and full of fun; gay and noisy. **—make mer·ry,** to be jovial; to be festive. **—mer·ri·ly,** *adv.* **—mer·ri·ness,** *n.*

mer·ry-go-round, mer′ē·gō·rownd, *n.* A revolving machine, as a circular platform fitted with hobbyhorses and seats; carousel; any whirl or rapid round, as of business or social life.

mer·ry·mak·er, mer′ē·mā·kər, *n.* One who participates in a gay festivity; an entertainer.

mer·ry·mak·ing, mer′ē·mā·king, n. A convivial entertainment; a festival; the participating in a gay celebration.—a.

me·sa, mā′sə, n. A comparatively small, high tableland or plateau with the sides descending steeply to the surrounding land, common in the southwestern United States.

mes·cal, mes·kal′, n. A strong, colorless, alcoholic liquor made from the fermented juice of the agave plant; the agave plant.

mes·dames, mā·däm, n. pl. of **ma·dame** or **ma·dam**.

mes·de·moi·selles, mā·də·mə·zel′, n. pl. of **mad·e·moi·selle**.

mesh, mesh, n. An arrangement of interlaced or interlocked strands of wires uniformly spaced; netted or netlike work; one of the open spaces of network or a net. Pl. The threads that bind such spaces; the means of catching or holding fast: caught in the *meshes* of the law; the entanglement of gear teeth.—v.t. To catch or entangle in or as in the meshes of a net; to engage, as gear teeth.—v.i. To become enmeshed; to interlock or match.

mesh·work, mesh′wərk, n. Meshed work; network.

me·si·al, mē′zē·əl, mē′sē·əl, a. Middle; median.

mes·mer·ism, mez′mər·iz·əm, mes′mər·iz·əm, n. The doctrine of the induction of a hypnotic state through an influence transmitted from the operator to the subject; the induction, influence, or state concerned; in general, hypnotism. —**mes·mer·ic**, mez·mer′ik, mes·mer′ik, a. —**mes·mer·i·cal·ly**, adv. —**mes·mer·ist**, n.

mes·mer·ize, mez′mə·riz, mes′mə·riz, v.t., -ized, -iz·ing. To hypnotize; to subject to spellbinding influence. —**mes·mer·i·za·tion**, mez·mə·rə·zā′shən, mes·mə·rə·zā′shən, n. —**mes·mer·iz·er**, n.

mes·o·morph, mez′ə·môrf, mes′ə·môrf, n. A muscular type of body structure developed by the relative dominance of tissues derived from the middle of the three cell layers of the embryo; a person having this type of body structure. —**mes·o·mor·phic**, mez·ə·môr′fik, mes·ə·môr′fik, a. —**mes·o·mor·phism**, n. —**mes·o·mor·phy**, n.

me·son, mē′zon, mē′son, mez′on, mes′on, n. Any of a group of subatomic particles with variable masses between those of the electron and proton, and all of which being extremely short-lived.

mes·o·sphere, mez′ə·sfēr, mes′ə·sfēr, n. The area from about 20 to 50 miles above the earth's surface, between the stratosphere and the thermosphere; an atmospheric layer located above the ionosphere, about 250 miles above the earth's crust.

mes·quite, mes·kēt′, mes′kēt, n. A thorny tree or shrub of the SW United States and Mexico that bears beanlike pods rich in sugar, and used as fodder.

mess, mes, n. A disorderly mixture; a state of dirt and disorder; a situation of confusion or embarrassment; a muddle; a dish or quantity of food; a number of persons who eat together, esp. in the military; the place where they eat.—v.i. To make a dirty or untidy mess; to bungle; to meddle in; to take meals in common with others, as one of a *mess*.—v.t. To cause to be untidy; to make a mess of, as one's affairs; to meddle in; to serve up or dish out food for; to supply with meals. —**mess·i·ly**, adv. —**mess·i·ness**, n. —**mess·y**, a., -i·er, -i·est.

mes·sage, mes′ij, n. An oral, written, or signaled communication sent from a person or persons to another or others, as information, advice, tidings, direction, or the like; a telegram; the point or significance of an utterance, novel, play, musical work, or the like; an inspired communication to be delivered to the world; in data processing, a word or words taken as a single unit.

mes·sen·ger, mes′ən·jər, n. One who delivers a message or does an errand; an envoy; courier.

Mes·si·ah, mə·si′ə, n. The deliverer and savior promised to the Jewish people; Jesus, regarded in the Christian religion as the savior.

mess jack·et, n. A man's waist-length jacket for semiformal occasions, also worn by waiters and bellhops as part of their uniform.

mess kit, n. A compact set of eating utensils, including plate, cup, knife, fork, and spoon, used esp. by soldiers and campers. Also **mess gear**.

Messrs., mes′ərz, n. pl. of **mis·ter**.

mes·ti·zo, mes·tē′zo, n. A person born to parents of different races, esp. a person of Spanish and American Indian ancestry.

me·tab·o·lism, mə·tab′ə·liz·əm, n. The sum of the chemical changes in living organisms and cells by which food is converted into living protoplasm, and by which protoplasm is used and broken down into simpler compounds and waste by liberation of energy. —**met·a·bol·ic**, met·ə·bol′ik, **met·a·bol·i·cal**, a.

me·tab·o·lize, mə·tab′ə·liz, v.t., -lized, -liz·ing. To subject to or alter by metabolism.

met·al, met′əl, n. Any of a class of elementary substances as gold, silver, copper, and the like, many of which are characterized by opacity, ductility, conductivity, and a particular luster; an alloy or mixture composed wholly or partly of such substances; an object made of such material.—v.t., -aled, -al·ing. To cover or provide with metal.

met·al·ize, met′ə·liz, v.t., -ized, -iz·ing. To form into or unite with metal; to give metallic properties to.

me·tal·lic, mə·tal′ik, a. Referring to, resembling, or consisting of metal; having the qualities of metal. —**me·tal·li·cal·ly**, adv.

met·al·loid, met′ə·loyd, n. Any of certain elements having some but not all of the properties of a metal. —a. Like a metal and a nonmetal; having the form, appearance, or properties of a metalloid.

met·al·lur·gy, met′ə·lər·jē, n. The technical and scientific study of metals; the process of separating them from other materials in the ore; smelting, refining, shaping, and otherwise developing them. —**met·al·lur·gic**, met·ə·lər′jik, **met·al·lur·gi·cal**, a. —**met·al·lur·gi·cal·ly**, adv. —**met·al·lur·gist**, n.

met·al·work, met′əl·wərk, n. Work, esp. artistic work, in metal; anything made of metal; shaping or forming of metal. —**met·al·work·er**, n. —**met·al·work·ing**, n.

met·a·mor·phism, met·ə·môr′fiz·əm, n. Change of form; metamorphosis; a change in the structure or constitution of a rock due to natural agencies, as pressure and heat, esp. when the rock becomes harder and more crystalline. —**met·a·mor·phic**, a.

met·a·mor·phose, met·ə·môr′fōz, met·ə·môr′fōs, v.t., -phosed, -phos·ing. To change into a different form; to change the shape or character of; to transform.—v.i. To be able to be, or to be transformed in character or shape.

met·a·mor·pho·sis, met·ə·môr′fə·sis, n. pl., -ses, -sēz. Change of form, structure, or substance; any complete change in appearance, character, or circumstance; a form resulting from any such change; a marked change in the form, after the embryonic stage, as the transformation of a tadpole into a frog.

met·a·phor, met′ə·fôr, met′ə·fər, n. A figure of speech in which a term or phrase is applied to something to which it is not literally applicable, in order to suggest a resemblance: She is the flower of my life. —**met·a·phor·ic**, met·ə·fôr′ik, **met·a·phor·i·cal**, a.

met·a·phys·ic, met·ə·fiz′ik, n. Metaphysics.

met·a·phys·ics, met·ə·fiz′iks, n. pl. but sing. in constr. That branch of philosophy which treats of first principles, including the science of being, the science of universal order, and the science or theory of knowledge; philosophy, esp. of the most speculative or esoteric nature. —**met·a·phys·i·cal**, a.

met·a·tar·sus, met·ə·tär′səs, n. pl., -tar·si, -tär′sī. The part of a foot of a hind limb, esp. of its bony structure, included between the tarsus and the toes or phalanges. —**met·a·tar·sal,** *a.*

met·a·zo·an, met·ə·zō′ən, *n.* Any of a large zoological division including all the multicellular animals. —**met·a·zo·al, met·a·zo·ic,** *a.*

mete, mēt, *v.t.,* **met·ed, met·ing.** To divide by measure; to allot, usu. followed by *out:* to *mete out* reward.

me·te·or, mē′tē·ər, *n.* A meteoroid white with heat from its terrific velocity upon entering the earth's atmosphere, and seen as a streak of light.

me·te·or·ic, mē·tē·ôr′ik, mē·tē·or′ik, *a.* Referring to a meteor or meteors; relating to phenomena of the atmosphere; meteorological; transiently brilliant.

me·te·or·ite, mē′tē·ə·rīt, *n.* A meteor which has reached the earth's crust without being completely consumed. —**me·te·or·it·ic,** mē·tē·ə·rit′ik, *a.*

me·te·or·oid, mē′tē·ə·royd, *n.* Any of the many small bodies which travel through interplanetary space and enter the earth's atmosphere as meteors or shooting stars.

me·te·or·ol·o·gy, mē·tē·ə·rol′ə·jē, *n.* The science concerned with atmospheric phenomena, esp. in relation to weather and climate; the atmospheric phenomena and weather of a locality. —**me·te·or·o·log·i·cal,** mē·tē·ə·rə·loj′ə·kəl, *a.* —**me·te·or·o·log·i·cal·ly,** *adv.* —**me·te·or·ol·o·gist,** *n.*

me·te·or show·er, *n.* The phenomenon observed when several meteors at once enter the earth's atmosphere, seeming to radiate out of a common point.

me·ter, me·tre, mē′tər, *n.* Poetic measure; arrangement of words in measured or rhythmic lines or verses; a particular form of such arrangement, based on the kind and number of feet constituting the verse; verse or poetry; the rhythmic element as measured by division into parts of equal time value.

me·ter, me·tre, mē′tər, *n.* The fundamental unit of length, intended to be equal to one ten-millionth of the distance from the equator to the pole measured on a meridian, and equal to 39.37 inches.

me·ter, mē′tər, *n.* An instrument that measures, esp. one that automatically measures and records the quantity of gas, water, electricity, or the like, passing through it or actuating it.—*v.t.* To measure by means of a meter.

me·ter-kil·o·gram-sec·ond, mē′tər·kil′ə·gram·sek′ənd, *a.* Of or relating to a measuring system in which the units of mass, length, and the time are the kilogram, the meter, and the second.

me·ter maid, *n.* A woman employed by the traffic division of a police department to issue tickets for parking violations.

meth·a·done, meth′ə·dōn, *n.* A synthetic, habit-forming drug used to induce sleep and dull pain.

meth·ane, meth′ān, *n.* A colorless, odorless, flammable gas, occurring in marshes and the firedamp of coal mines, and obtained from natural gas.

meth·a·nol, meth′ə·nôl, meth′ə·nol, *n.* A flammable water-soluble, volatile, highly toxic, liquid alcohol used in chemical synthesis and as an antifreeze, fuel, solvent, and denaturant for ethyl alcohol.

meth·od, meth′əd, *n.* A manner of procedure, esp. a systematic or clearly defined way of accomplishing an end; plan; system or order in thought or action; the plan of procedure characteristic of a discipline; logical or scientific arrangement.

me·thod·i·cal, mə·thod′ə·kəl, *a.* Marked by systematic behavior; painstaking; in systematic order. —**me·thod·i·cal·ly,** *adv.*

meth·od·ize, meth′ə·dīz, *v.t.,* **-ized, -iz·ing.** To reduce to method; to prepare by following a method. —**meth·od·iz·er,** *n.*

meth·od·ol·o·gy, meth·ə·dol′ə·jē, *n. pl.,* **-gies.** The system of methods or of classification as it is applied by a science or art. —**meth·od·o·log·i·cal,**

meth·ə·də·loj′ə·kəl, *a.* —**meth·od·ol·o·gist,** *n.*

me·tic·u·lous, mə·tik′yə·ləs, *a.* Overly scrupulous concerning small details; exceedingly careful or fastidious. —**me·tic·u·los·i·ty,** mə·tik·yə·los′ə·tē, *n.* —**me·tic·u·lous·ly,** *adv.*

mé·tier, mā′tyā, mā·tyā′, *n.* Profession; occupation; specialty.

mé·tis, mā·tēs′, mā·tē′, *n. pl.,* **mé·tis,** mā·tēs′, mā·tēz′. A person of racially mixed heritage, esp. a person living in Canada, of mixed American Indian and French Canadian parents.

me-too, mē′too′, *a.* Characterized by the attempt to imitate policies or tactics used successfully by rivals, esp. in politics. —**me-too·er,** *n.* —**me-too·ism,** *n.*

met·ric, met′rik, *n.* A standard or method for measuring.—*a.* Pertaining to a measurement system using the meter as a basis.

met·ri·cal, met′rik·əl, *a.* Referring to rhythm or meter; consisting of poetic meter; of or relating to measurement. —**met·ri·cal·ly,** *adv.*

met·ric sys·tem, *n.* A widely used decimal system of weights and measures, employing the gram and the meter as its basic units.

met·ri·fi·ca·tion, met·rə·fə·kā′shən, *n.* The changing to the use of the metric system.

met·ro, met′rō, *n.* In European cities, esp. London and Paris, an underground railway; subway.

met·ro·nome, met′rə·nōm, *n.* An instrument operated either mechanically or electrically for marking exact time, used esp. in music practice. —**met·ro·nom·ic,** met·rə·nom′ik, *a.*

me·trop·o·lis, mə·trop′ə·lis, *n.* The chief city, though not necessarily the capital, of a country, state, or region; a central or principal point of urban activity: a commercial *metropolis.*

met·ro·pol·i·tan, met·rə·pol′ə·tən, *a.* Referring to or constituting a metropolis or chief city: a *metropolitan* city; characteristic of a metropolis or chief city, or of its inhabitants.—*n.* An inhabitant of a metropolis; one having metropolitan manners. —**met·ro·pol·i·tan·ism,** *n.*

met·tle, met′əl, *n.* Characteristic temperament; spirit; courage; ardor.

met·tle·some, met′əl·səm, *a.* Spirited; courageous; ardent. Also **met·tled.**

Mex·i·can, mek′sə·kən, *a.* Of or referring to Mexico or the people of Mexico.—*n.* A native or inhabitant of Mexico.

mez·za·nine, mez′ə·nēn, mez·ə·nēn′, *n.* A story situated between two main ones; the lower theater balcony or the first rows of balcony seats.

mez·zo, met′sō, mez′ō, *a.* Middle; medium; half.

mi, mē, *n.* The syllable used for the third tone of the scale, as E in the major scale of C; the tone E.

mi·as·ma, mī·az′mə, mē·az′mə, *n. pl.,* **-mas, -ma·ta,** -mə·tə. A threatening, poisonous, or morbid element of the atmosphere; foul-smelling emanations from decaying organic matter, formerly believed poisonous. —**mi·as·mal, mi·as·mat·ic,** mī·az·mat′ik, **mi·as·mic,** *a.*

mi·ca, mī′kə, *n.* A silicate of thin flexible scales having a metallic luster.

Mick·ey Finn, mik′ē fin, *n.* A drink of liquor, or other beverage, to which a drug has secretly been added to render the unsuspecting drinker unconscious.

mi·crobe, mī′krōb, *n.* A microscopic organism, as a bacterium, esp. a pathogenic species; microorganism. —**mi·cro·bi·al,** mī·krō′bē·əl, **mi·cro·bi·an, mi·cro·bic,** *a.*

mi·cro·bi·ol·o·gy, mī·krō·bī·ol′ə·jē, *n.* The science and study of microscopic organisms. —**mi·cro·bi·o·log·i·cal,** mī·krō·bī·ə·loj′ə·kəl, *a.* —**mi·cro·bi·ol·o·gist,** *n.*

mi·cro·cop·y, mī′krō·kop·ē, *n. pl.,* **-ies.** A photographic reduction of a printed page, document, or other graphic material.

mi·cro·cosm, mī′krə·koz·əm, *n.* A little world; anything regarded as a world in miniature; often, man viewed as an epitome of the great world or universe. Also **mi·cro·cos·mos,** mī·krə·koz′məs. —**mi·cro·cos·mic, mi·cro·cos·mi·cal,** *a.*

mi·cro·film, mī′krə·film, *n.* Film containing a photographic copy of printed or graphic material, greatly reduced in size, and viewable through a special enlarger, having the advantage of permanency and occupying small space.

mi·cro·gram, mī′krə·gram, *n.* A unit of weight equaling one millionth of one gram.

mi·cro·groove, mī′krə·groov, *n.* A closely spaced groove cut on long-playing phonograph records for the purpose of including more material on a single disk.

mi·crom·e·ter, mī·krom′ə·tər, *n.* An instrument or device fitted to a telescope or microscope for measuring very small distances, diameters, or angles. —**mi·crom·e·try,** *n.*

mi·cro·mi·cron, mī·krō·mī′kron, *n.* A unit of length equal to one millionth part of a micron.

mi·cro·mil·li·me·ter, mī·krō·mil′ə·mē·tər, *n.* A millionth part of a millimeter; a millimicron.

mi·cron, mi·kron, mī′kron, *n., pl.,* **mi·crons, mi·cra.** A unit of length equal to one millionth of a meter, or one thousandth of a millimeter. Sym. mu.

mi·cro·or·gan·ism, mī·krō·ôr′gə·niz·əm, *n.* A microscopic organism, as a protozoan or bacterium.

mi·cro·phone, mī′krə·fōn, *n.* An instrument for converting sound waves into electrical waves for transmitting, recording, or intensifying such sounds as speech or music. —**mi·cro·phon·ic,** mī·krə·fon′ik, *a.*

mi·cro·pho·to·graph, mī·krə·fō′tə·graf, *n.* Microfilm; a photographic representation of microscopic size; a photograph of microscopic objects. —**mi·cro·pho·to·graph·ic,** mī·krō·fō·tə·graf′ik, *a.* —**mi·cro·pho·tog·ra·phy,** mī·krō·fə·tog′rə·fē, *n.*

mi·cro·read·er, mī′krō·rē·dər, *n.* A projective device used to show the enlarged image or close-up of microfilm or a microphotograph.

mi·cro·scope, mī′krə·skōp, *n.* An optical instrument consisting of a lens or combination of lenses which render minute objects distinctly visible.

mi·cro·scop·ic, mī·krə·skop′ik, *a.* Visible only by the aid of a microscope; minute or tiny; referring to or resembling a microscope; made by, or as by, the aid of a microscope. Also **mi·cro·scop·i·cal.** —**mi·cro·scop·i·cal·ly,** *adv.*

mi·cros·co·py, mī·kros′kə·pē, mī′krə·skō·pē, *n.* The use of the microscope; investigation by means of the microscope. —**mi·cros·co·pist,** *n.*

mi·cro·sec·ond, mī′krə·sek·ənd, *n.* One millionth of one second.

mi·cro·wave, mī·krō·wāv, *n.* An extremely short electromagnetic wave having a very high frequency range; an oven or cooking device that employs microwave energy.

mid, mid, *a.* Being at a point about equal in distance from extremes: *mid*winter; having the central position; intervening.—*adv.* In the middle.

mid·day, mid′dā, *n.* The midpoint of the day; noon.

mid·dle, mid′əl, *a.* Equally distant from limits or extremes: the *middle* point of a road; intervening or intermediate: the *middle* distance; medium: a man of *middle* size.—*n.* The point or part equidistant from extremes or limits; the waist, or middle part of the human body; something intermediate; a mean.—*v.t., v.i.,* **-dled, -dling.** To situate in the center.

mid·dle-aged, mid′əl·ājd′, *a.* Intermediate in age between youth, or the earlier period of adult life, and old age: approximately between 45 and 65 years old; characteristic of or suitable for middle-aged people. —**mid·dle age.** *n.*

mid·dle class, *n.* The class of people intermediate

between the classes of higher and lower social rank or standing; that class of people considered to have average social rank, educational background, financial status, and living standards; an intermediate class. —**mid·dle-class,** mid′əl·klas′, mid′əl·kläs′, *a.*

mid·dle ear, *n.* The area between the outer ear and inner ear.

Mid·dle Eng·lish, *n.* The English language in the second major stage of its development, roughly comprising the period from 1150 to 1475.

mid·dle·man, mid′əl·man, *n. pl.,* **-men.** An intermediary between two parties; a person, as a broker, agent, merchant, or retailer, who intervenes between the producer and the consumer of goods.

mid·dle·most, mid′əl·mōst, *a.* Being in or near the middle; midmost.

mid·dle·weight, mid′əl·wāt, *n.* A person having an average weight; a boxer or wrestler weighing more than 147 pounds but less than 160 pounds.—*a.*

mid·dling, mid′ling, *a.* Medium in size, quality, grade, or rank; mediocre; ordinary. *Informal.* In fairly good health.—*adv. Informal.* Moderately; fairly.

mid·dy, mid′ē, *n. pl.,* **-dies.** *Informal.* A midshipman; a loose blouse with a sailor collar, often extending below the waistline to terminate in a broad band or fold. Also **mid·dy blouse.**

midg·et, mij′it, *n.* A person or thing of unusually small size but with normal proportions.—*a.* Very small.

mid·land, mid′lənd, *a.* Being in the interior region of a country; inland.—*n.* The interior of a country.

mid·line, mid′līn, *n.* A line of balance, as a median line.

mid·most, mid′mōst, *a.* Middlemost.—*adv.*

mid·night, mid′nīt, *n.* The middle of the night; twelve o'clock at night.—*a.* Being or occurring in the middle of the night; very dark.

mid·night sun, *n.* The sun visible at midnight in arctic or antarctic regions during summer.

mid·point, mid-point, mid′poynt′, *n.* A point located at the middle or center.

mid·riff, mid′rif, *n.* The diaphragm; the area of the body between the chest and waist; the section of a garment covering this area; a garment that bares the midriff.

mid·sec·tion, mid′sek·shən, *n.* The central or middle part of anything.

mid·ship, mid′ship, *a.* Being in or belonging to the middle of a ship.

mid·ship·man, mid′ship·mən, *n. pl.,* **-men.** A student officer of the U.S. Naval Academy, Coast Guard Academy, or similar officer training institution, holding a rank below a warrant officer and above a master chief petty officer.

midst, midst, *n.* The middle point, part, or stage; the position of anything surrounded by other things or parts, occurring in the middle of a period of time, or during a course of action; middle.—*prep.* Amid; amidst.

mid·sum·mer, mid′səm′ər, *n.* The middle of summer.

mid·term, mid′tərm, *n.* The point halfway through a school term or term of office. *Informal.* An examination or set of examinations given at the halfway point of a school term.

mid·way, mid′wā, *n.* At a fair or amusement park, the area along which side shows and similar exhibitions are located; the middle of the way or distance. —mid′wā′, *adv., a.* Halfway.

mid·wife, mid′wīf, *n. pl.,* **-wives.** A woman who assists a mother in childbirth.

mid·wife·ry, mid′wī·fər·ē, mid′wīf·rē, *n.* The art or practice of a midwife.

mid·year, mid′yēr, *n.* The middle of the year. *Informal.* An examination or set of examinations given at the middle of an academic year.

mien, mēn, *n.* External manner of a person; look; bearing.

miff, mif, *n. Informal.* An unpleasant mood; a petty quarrel.—*v.t.* To offend; cause to be ill-humored or annoyed.

might, mīt, *n.* Ability or power to do or accomplish; effective power or force of any kind: the *might* of intellect, or of public opinion; bodily strength; superior power or strength: the doctrine that *might* makes right.

might, mīt, *v.* Past tense of **may.**

might·y, mī′tē, *a.,* **-i·er, -i·est.** Possessing, characterized by, or showing might or power; having, showing, or requiring great bodily strength; of great size: a *mighty* rock; great in amount, extent, degree, or importance.—*adv. Informal.* To a great extent or degree: a *mighty* long time. —**might·i·ly,** *adv.* —**might·i·ness,** *n.*

mi·graine, mī′grān, *n.* A recurring headache marked by severe pain, usu. limited to a single side of the head, and often with attendant nausea.

mi·grant, mī′grənt, *a.* Migrating; migratory.—*n.* One who or that which migrates, as a migratory worker.

mi·grate, mī′grāt, *v.i.,* **-grat·ed, -grat·ing.** To move from one place to another; to travel from one country, region, or domicile to settle in another; to go to a new habitat. —**mi·gra·tion,** mī·grā′shən, *n.* —**mi·gra·tor,** *n.* —**mi·gra·to·ry,** mī′grə·tôr·ē, *a.*

mike, mīk, *n. Informal.* Microphone.

mil, mil, *n.* A unit of length equal to .001 of an inch; a military unit of angular measurement, 1/6400 of 360 degrees.

mi·la·dy, mi·lā′dē, *n. pl.,* **-dies.** An English noblewoman.

mild, mīld, *a.* Gentle or temperate in feeling or behavior toward others; characterized by or showing such gentleness, as one's manner or words; not harsh, fierce, or stern; soft; pleasant; not cold, severe, or extreme, as air, weather, or climate; not acute, as disease; not sharp, pungent, or strong, as food or perfume; moderate in intensity, degree, or character. —**mild·ly,** *adv.* —**mild·ness,** *n.*

mil·dew, mil′doo, mil′dū, *n.* Any of numerous minute parasitic fungi producing a whitish coating or discoloration on plants; the coating, discoloration, or the disease produced by such fungi; any similar discoloration due to fungi, as on cotton and linen fabrics, paper, or leather, when exposed to dampness.—*v.t.* To affect with mildew.—*v.i.* To become affected with mildew. —**mil·dew·y,** *a.*

mile, mīl, *n.* A unit of linear measure in the U.S. and other English-speaking nations equivalent to 5,280 feet.

mile·age, mil·age, mī′lij, *n.* Distance in miles; the aggregate number of miles made or traveled in a given time; an allowance for traveling expenses at a fixed rate per mile; a fixed charge per mile, as for railroad transportation; the miles a vehicle can travel on a certain amount of fuel. *Informal.* Durability, use, or value: She got a lot of *mileage* out of the dress.

mil·er, mī′lər, *n.* A man or horse trained to run in competitive one-mile races.

mile·stone, mīl′stōn, *n.* A stone or post set up to mark distance by miles, as along a highway or other line of travel; an event worth noting in the development of a lifetime, a career, or an endeavor. Also **mile·post.**

mi·lieu, mēl·yû′, *n. pl.,* **mi·lieus.** Environment; setting.

mil·i·tant, mil′ə·tənt, *a.* Engaged in warfare; combative; aggressive.—*n.* One engaged in warfare or strife; one using vigorous or violent methods to advance his or her cause. —**mil·i·tan·cy, mil·i·tant·ness,** *n.*

mil·i·ta·rism, mil′i·tə·riz·əm, *n.* Military spirit or policy. —**mil·i·ta·rist,** mil′i·tə·rist, *n.* —**mil·i·ta·ris·tic,** mil·i·tə·ris′tik, *a.* —**mil·i·ta·ris·ti·cal·ly,** *adv.*

—**mil·i·ta·rize,** mil′ə·tə·rīz, *v.t.,* **-rized, -riz·ing.** —**mil·i·ta·ri·za·tion,** mil·i·tə·rə·zā′shən, *n.*

mil·i·tar·y, mil′i·ter·ē, *a.* Of or pertaining to soldiers, the army, armed forces, the affairs of war, or the state of war.—*n.* Military personnel; armed forces, esp. officers. —**mil·i·tar·i·ly,** mil·i·tãr′ə·lē, *adv.*

mil·i·tar·y po·lice, *n.* The branch or service of the army which performs police duties. Abbr. **MP.**

mi·li·tia, mi·lish′ə, *n.* An organization of men and women enrolled and trained as military reserves for the defense of a nation in time of emergency.

milk, milk, *n.* A white or bluish-white liquid secreted by the mammary glands of female mammals for the nourishment of their young; this liquid used for food or as a source of dairy products; any liquid resembling this, as the liquid within a coconut, the juice or sap of certain plants.—*v.t.* To press or draw milk from the udder of, as a cow or goat; to extract something from, as if by milking; drain the contents, strength, information, or wealth from; exploit; elicit.—*v.i.* To draw milk, as from a cow; to yield milk, as a cow. —**milk·er,** *n.* —**milk·y,** mil′kē, *a.,* **-i·er, -i·est.**

milk·maid, milk′mād, *n.* A woman or girl who milks cows or is employed in a dairy.

milk·man, milk′man, *n. pl.,* **-men.** A man who sells or delivers milk, eggs, and other dairy products.

milk of mag·ne·sia, *n.* A milky aqueous liquid used as a counteraction for stomach acidity or as a laxative.

milk shake, *n.* A drink consisting of cold milk, flavoring syrup, and usu. ice cream.

milk sug·ar, *n.* Lactose.

milk tooth, *n.* One of the first, or temporary, teeth in young mammals, later replaced by permanent ones.

milk·weed, milk′wēd, *n.* Any of various plants, mostly with milky juice, and downy stems and leaves.

mill, mil, *n.* A building containing machinery which grinds grain into flour; any of various machines for processing materials by cutting, planing, grinding, polishing, or stamping.—*v.t.* To grind in a mill; to pass through a mill; to form grooves, as on the edge of a coin.—*v.i.* To move in a circular fashion, as a herd of cattle. —**milled,** *a.*

mill, mil, *n.* A monetary unit of the U.S., having the value of one thousandth of a dollar; one tenth of a cent.

mill·board, mil′bôrd, *n.* A thick and strong material produced in paper mills, used for making cartons; pasteboard.

mil·len·ni·um, mi·len′ē·əm, *n. pl.,* **-ni·a,** -nē·ə, **-ni·ums.** An aggregate of a thousand years; the thousand years mentioned in the Bible during which it is believed Christ will reign on earth with his saints; a period of perfection, peace, and happiness on earth to occur at some unspecified time. —**mil·len·ni·al,** mi·len′ē·əl, *a.*

mill·er, mil′ər, *n.* One who keeps or operates a mill, esp. a grain mill; a milling machine.

mil·let, mil′it, *n.* Any of various grasses or small cereal grains grown in many parts of Europe, Asia, and Africa as food for humans, and in the United States as cattle fodder.

mil·li·am·pere, mil·ē·am′pēr, *n.* A one-thousandth part of an ampere.

mil·li·bar, mil′ə·bär, *n.* A unit of air pressure, equaling one thousandth of a bar.

mil·li·gram, mil′ə·gram, *n.* The thousandth part of a gram.

mil·li·li·ter, mil′ə·lē·tər, *n.* In the metric system, a unit of capacity equal to one thousandth of a liter, or 0.061 cubic inch.

mil·li·me·ter, mil′ə·mē·tər, *n.* The thousandth part of a meter, 0.03937 of an inch.

mil·li·mi·cron, mil′ə·mī·kron, *n.* The millionth part of a millimeter, or the thousandth part of a micron, a unit of length.

mil·li·ner, mil'ə·nər, *n.* A designer, maker, trimmer, or seller of women's hats.

mil·li·ner·y, mil'ə·ner·ē, mil'ə·nə·rē, *n.* The business or occupation of a milliner; the articles made or sold by milliners.

mill·ing, mil'ing, *n.* The act of subjecting something to the operation of a mill or milling machine; notches or grooves made by milling.

mil·lion, mil'yən, *n.* The number of ten hundred thousand, or a thousand thousand; often, the amount of a thousand thousand monetary units; a very sizeable number. *Pl.* The multitude or the mass of the common people, used with *the.* **—mil·lionth,** mil'yənth, *a., n.*

mil·lion·aire, mil·lion·naire, mil·yə·nãr', *n.* A person worth a million or millions, as of dollars, pounds, or francs.

mil·li·sec·ond, mil'ə·sek'ənd, *n.* One thousandth of a second.

mill·pond, mil'pond, *n.* A pond or reservoir which supplies water to turn a mill wheel.

mill·run, mil'rən, *n.* A sawmill's marketable production; a mill's output or goods of average quality; the common or ordinary, said of persons or things.

mill·stone, mil'stōn, *n.* One of the stones for grinding grain in a mill; personal burden or problem.

mill·stream, mil'strēm, *n.* The stream of water that turns a mill wheel. Also **mill·race.**

mi·lord, mi·lôrd', *n.* An English lord or gentleman.

milt, milt, *n.* The seminal fluid of male fish.

mime, mīm, *n.* A mimic; an actor or comedian specializing in pantomime or mimicry; the art of narration or portrayal of character, idea, or mood by bodily movements; pantomime.—*v.t.,* **mimed, mim·ing.** To mimic.—*v.i.* To play a part by mimicry, esp. without words. **—mim·er,** *n.*

mim·e·o·graph, mim'ē·ə·graf, *v.t.* To duplicate by means of a mimeograph.—*n.* A device for copying, usu. typewritten material, by using an inked stencil.

mim·ic, mim'ik, *v.t.,* **-icked, -ick·ing.** To imitate or copy closely; to imitate in action or speech, esp. in derision; to resemble or copy through biological imitation.—*n.* One who imitates or mimics; a professional imitator, as an actor or performer; an imitation or copy.—*a.* Of or pertaining to mimicry; imitative; simulated or mock. **—mim·i·cal,** *a.* **—mim·ick·er,** *n.*

mim·ic·ry, mim'ik·rē, *n. pl.,* **-ries.** The act, instance, practice, or result of mimicking.

min·a·ble, mine·a·ble, mī'nə·bəl, *a.* Capable of being mined.

min·a·ret, min·ə·ret', *n.* The slender, lofty turret or tower next to a mosque, having one or more balconies, used by a caller to summon Muslims to daily prayer.

mince, mins, *v.t.,* **minced, minc·ing.** To cut or chop into very small pieces; to diminish in speaking; to pronounce with affected elegance.—*v.i.* To walk with short steps; to affect delicacy in manner; to speak with affected elegance. **—minc·er,** *n.* **—minc·ing,** *a.* **—minc·ing·ly,** *adv.*

mince·meat, mins'mēt, *n.* A chopped mixture of raisins, apples, other fruit, spices, suet, and sometimes meat.

mind, mīnd, *n.* The unconscious and conscious processes that perceive, conceive, comprehend, evaluate, and reason; rational or sound mental state; sanity; state of thought and feeling; opinion; viewpoint; attention; intention; inclination; memory; recollection; a person of superior intellectual power.—*v.t.* To pay attention to; to obey; to attend to; to take care of; concerning; to feel concern about; object to; to notice; to remember.—*v.i.*—**give some·one a piece of one's mind,** rebuke.—**have a good mind to,** have a strong inclination.—**on one's mind,** occupied with worrisome thoughts.—**be of two minds,** be in doubt or undecided. **—mind·ful,** *a.* **—mind·ful·ly,** *adv.* **—mind·ful·ness,** *n.*

mind·ed, mīn'did, *a.* Having a mind of a given kind: *weak-minded.*

mind·less, mīnd'lis, *a.* Stupid; unthinking; inattentive; heedless; careless. **—mind·less·ly,** *a.*—**mind·less·ness,** *n.*

mind read·er, *n.* One who professes the power to read another's mind. **—mind read·ing,** *n.*

mind's eye, *n.* Imagination; memory.

mine, mīn, *pron.* Possessive of I; belonging to me: *mine* is a brown hat; my; now generally used similarly to **hers, ours, yours, theirs,** as equivalent to **my** followed by a noun and serving either for a nominative or an objective case.

mine, mīn, *n.* A pit or excavation in the earth, from which coal, metallic ores, or other mineral substances are taken by digging; the location, buildings, and equipment of such an excavation; a device floating on, or near, the surface of the sea to destroy ships by explosion; a similar device used on land against personnel and vehicles; a rich source or store of wealth or of anything highly valued.—*v.i.* To dig a mine; to burrow.—*v.t.* To dig away the foundation from; to undermine; to sap. **—min·er,** *n.*

mine·field, mīn'fēld, *n.* An area of land or water throughout which mines have been laid; the mines in such an area.

min·er·al, min'ər·əl, *a.* Obtained from mines; pertaining to minerals; neither animal nor plant: the *mineral* kingdom; inorganic.—*n.* A substance obtained by mining; any of a class of substances occurring in nature, usually comprising inorganic substances, as quartz or feldspar, of definite chemical composition, but sometimes including aggregations of such substances, as asphalt or coal; ore; any substance neither animal nor plant.

min·er·al·ize, min'ər·ə·līz, *v.t.,* **-ized, -iz·ing.** To change into a mineral; transform into an ore; impregnate. **—min·er·al·i·za·tion,** min·ər·al·ə·zā'shən, *n.*

min·er·al·o·gy, min·ə·ral'ə·jē, *n.* The science concerned with minerals. **—min·er·al·og·i·cal,** min·ər·ə·loj'ə·kəl, *a.* **—min·er·al·o·gist,** *n.*

min·er·al oil, *n.* Any of a class of oils of mineral origin, used as illuminants, fuels, and in certain medicines, as a laxative.

min·er·al pitch, *n.* Asphalt.

min·er·al wa·ter, *n.* Water which is either naturally or artificially impregnated with gases, carbonates, sulfates or iron, often used for medicinal purposes.

min·e·stro·ne, min·ə·strō'nē, *n.* An Italian soup containing vegetables.

mine·sweep·er, mīn'swē·pər, *n.* A small ship used to remove or detonate mines laid by an enemy. **—mine·sweep·ing,** *n.*

min·gle, ming'gəl, *v.t.,* **-gled, -gling.** To mix up together so as to form one whole; to blend; to join in social affairs.—*v.i.* To become mixed; to join: to *mingle* with or in a crowd.

min·i·a·ture, min'ē·ə·chər, min'ə·chər, *n.* A representation or image of anything on a very small scale; a small scale: as, shown in *miniature.*—*a.* On a small scale. **—min·i·a·tur·ize,** min'ē·ə·chə·rīz, min'ə·chə·rīz, *v.t.,* **-ized, -iz·ing.** **—min·i·a·tur·i·za·tion,** min·ē·ə·chə·rə·zā'shən, *n.*

min·im, min'əm, *n.* The smallest liquid measure, equal to one drop, or one-sixtieth of a dram.

min·i·mal, min'ə·məl, *a.* Pertaining to or being a minimum; least possible; smallest; very small. **—min·i·mal·ly,** *adv.*

min·i·mize, min'ə·mīz, *v.t.,* **-mized, -miz·ing.** To reduce to a minimum; to treat as of the least import or of the smallest proportion or part. **—min·i·mi·za·tion,** min·ə·mə·zā'shən, *n.* **—min·i·miz·er,** *n.*

min·i·mum, min'ə·məm, *n. pl.,* **-mums, -ma,** -mə. The smallest amount or degree; least quantity assignable in a given case.—*a.* Made up of or indicating the lowest or least size, degree, or amount possible.

min·ing, mīn′ing, *n.* The act or work of one who mines, esp. the action, process, or industry of extracting ores from mines; the laying of explosive underwater or land mines.

min·ion, min′yən, *n.* A servile or fawning dependent; an unworthy favorite.

min·is·ter, min′i·stər, *n.* One authorized to conduct religious services; one to whom the executive head of a government entrusts the direction of certain affairs of state: *Minister* of War; a diplomatic representative below ambassadorial rank.—*v.t.* To administer, as medicine; to apply.—*v.i.* To act as a religious minister; to perform service; to give things that are needed: to *minister* to one's needs. **—min·is·te·ri·al,** min·i·stēr′ē·əl, *a.*

min·is·trant, min′i·strənt, *a.* Performing service; acting as minister or attendant.—*n.* An individual who ministers.

min·is·tra·tion, min·i·strā′shən, *n.* The act of ministering.

min·is·try, min′i·strē, *n. pl.,* **-tries.** The act of ministering; the office or functions of a minister, civil or religious; the clergy; the body of ministers of a state or the chief officials of a government; a department of government headed by a minister; the building in which this ministry is housed.

mink, mingk, *n. pl.,* **mink, minks.** A semi-aquatic meat-eating mammal, with a slender, weasellike body; the soft, thick, valuable fur of the mink; clothing made of this fur.

min·now, min′ō, *n.* A small fish used for fishing bait.

mi·nor, mī′nər, *a.* Lesser, as in size, extent, or importance, or being the lesser of two; of a less important or secondary class or kind: *minor* poets, *minor* faults or considerations; under legal age.—*n.* One of inferior rank or importance in a specified class; a subject or a course of study subordinate or supplementary to a major or principal subject or course; a person under legal age.—*v.i. U.S.* To pursue a minor subject or course of study, usu. followed by *in.*

mi·nor·i·ty, mi·nôr′ə·tē, mi·nor′i·tē, *n. pl.,* **-ties.** The state or period of being a minor or under legal age; the smaller part or number; a portion of the population differing from the majority in race, religion, national origin, or political affiliation, esp. when subject to discrimination.—*a.*

min·strel, min′strəl, *n.* In the Middle Ages, a roaming musician who subsisted by reciting verse and singing; a singer, musical performer, or poet; a member of the troupe of a minstrel show.

mint, mint, *n.* A place where currency is manufactured by the government; a place where something is made; a very great amount or number of anything, esp. of money.—*v.t.* To make, as coins, by stamping metal; to coin; to make or fabricate as if by coining: to *mint* words.—*a.* In unused or original condition: a car in *mint* condition.

mint, mint, *n.* Any plant of several aromatic herbs with opposite leaves and small vertically arranged flowers, as the spearmint and peppermint; a candy or cooky flavored with mint.

mint·age, min′tij, *n.* The act or process of minting; coinage; fabrication; the product or result of minting. **—mint·er,** *n.*

mint ju·lep, *n.* Julep.

min·u·end, min′yū·end, *n.* The number from which another number is to be subtracted.

min·u·et, min·yū·et′, *n.* A slow, stately dance, dating back to the 17th century; music in minuet rhythm.

mi·nus, mī′nəs, *prep.* Less by the subtraction of, or decreased by: 10 *minus* 3, gross earnings *minus* cost; lacking or without: a book *minus* its title page, to escape *minus* hat and coat.—*n.* The minus sign; a minus quantity; a deficiency or loss.—*a.* Less; involving or denoting subtraction: a *minus* quantity, the *minus* sign; negative.

mi·nus·cule, min′əs·kūl, mi·nəs′kūl, *a.* Very small.

min·ute, min′it, *n.* The sixtieth part of an hour, or sixty seconds; an indefinitely short space of time: wait a *minute;* a point of time, or an instant or moment: Come here this *minute;* the sixtieth part of a degree. *Pl.* The official record of the proceedings at a meeting of a society, board, committee, council, or other body.—*v.t.,* **-ut·ed, -ut·ing.** To time exactly, as movement or speed; note down; to enter in the minutes of a society or other body.

mi·nute, mī·noot′, mī·nūt′, mi·noot′, mi·nūt′, *a.,* **-nut·er, -nut·est.** *a.* Extremely small, as in size, amount, extent, or degree; of very small scope or individual importance; attentive to or concerned with very small details or particulars.

min·ute hand, min′it, *n.* The hand that indicates the minutes on a clock or watch.

min·ute·man, min′it·man, *n. pl.,* **-men.** One of the American militiamen just before and during the Revolutionary War who held themselves in readiness for instant military service.

mi·nu·ti·a, mi·noo′shē·ə, mi·nū′shē·ə, *n. pl.,* **-ti·ae,** shē·ē′. *Usu. pl.* Small or minor details; trifles.

minx, mingks, *n.* An impudent, bold or forward young woman.

mir·a·cle, mir′ə·kəl, *n.* A wonder; a marvelous thing; something which seems to go beyond the known laws of nature and is held to be the act of a supernatural being; a supernatural event; an indication of a very high standard.

mi·rac·u·lous, mi·rak′yə·ləs, *a.* Like a miracle; able to do miracles; done by the power of the supernatural; very surprising.

mi·rage, mi·räzh′, *n.* An optical illusion, due to atmospheric densities, by which reflected images of distant objects are seen, often inverted; any illusion.

mire, mīr, *n.* Wet, swampy soil; mud; a marsh.—*v.t.,* **mired, mir·ing.** To fix or sink in mire, to cause to become fixed in mire; to entangle.—*v.i.* To sink in mud; to be unable to advance.

mir·ror, mir′ər, *n.* Any polished surface that reflects images of objects; a looking glass; something depicting a true image.—*v.t.* To reflect as in a mirror; to provide a true image of.

mirth, mərth, *n.* Merriment; gaiety. **—mirth·ful,** *a.* **—mirth·ful·ly,** *adv.* **—mirth·ful·ness,** *n.* **—mirthless,** *a.*

mis·ad·ven·ture, mis·əd·ven′chər, *n.* An unfortunate event; misfortune or mischance.

mis·ad·vise, mis·əd·vīz′, *v.t.,* **-vised, -vis·ing.** To give bad advice to.

mis·al·li·ance, mis·ə·lī′əns, *n.* Any improper alliance or association.

mis·an·thrope, mis′ən·thrōp, miz′ən·thrōp, *n.* A hater of mankind. Also **mis·an·thro·pist,** mis·an′thrə·pist, miz·an′thrə·pist, **—mis·an·throp·ic,** mis·ən·throp′ik, miz·ən·throp′ik, **mis·an·throp·i·cal,** *a.* **—mis·an·thro·py,** mis·an′thrə·pē, miz·an′thrə·pē, *n.*

mis·ap·ply, mis·ə·plī′, *v.t.,* **-plied, -ply·ing.** To apply incorrectly. **—mis·ap·pli·ca·tion,** mis·ap·lə·kā′shən, *n.*

mis·ap·pre·hend, mis·ap·ri·hend′, *v.t.* To misunderstand. **—mis·ap·pre·hen·sion,** *n.*

mis·ap·pro·pri·ate, mis·ə·prō′prē·āt, *v.t.,* **-at·ed, -at·ing.** To appropriate wrongly; to put to a wrong or dishonest use. **—mis·ap·pro·pri·a·tion,** mis·ə·prō·prē·ā′shən, *n.*

mis·be·have, mis·bi·hāv′, *v.i.,* **-haved, -hav·ing.** To behave poorly.—*v.t.* To act badly or improperly. **—mis·be·hav·er,** *n.* **—mis·be·ha·vior,** *n.*

mis·cal·cu·late, mis·kal′kyə·lāt, *v.t.,* **-lat·ed, -lat-**

ing. To judge erroneously; to make a wrong guess or estimate of. **—mis·cal·cu·la·tion,** mis·kal·kyə·lā′shən, n. **—mis·cal·u·la·tor,** n.

mis·call, mis·kôl′, v.t. To call by a wrong name.

mis·car·riage, mis·kar′ij, mis′kə·ij, n. The premature delivery of a nonviable fetus; failure to achieve a just or proper result; failure to reach a proper destination.

mis·car·ry, mis·kar′ē, v.i., -ried, -ry·ing. To fail to reach its destination; to fail to attain the intended effect; not to succeed: the project miscarried; to abort.

mis·ce·ge·na·tion, mis·ə·jə·nā′shən, mi·sej·ə·nā′shən, n. Mixture of races by sexual union; interbreeding or intermarriage between different races. **—mis·ce·ge·net·ic,** a.

mis·cel·la·ne·ous, mis·ə·lā′nē·əs, a. Consisting of different elements, types, or things; mixed.

mis·cel·la·ny, mis′ə·lā·nē, n. pl., -nies. A mixture of various kinds; a collection of written compositions by several authors on various subjects.

mis·chance, mis·chans′, mis·chäns′, n. Bad luck; misfortune; mishap; misadventure.

mis·chief, mis′chif, n. Behavior, often playful, that vexes or annoys; a tendency to vex, tease, or upset; one who or that which causes trouble, annoyances, harm or damage; injury, trouble, or harm.

mis·chie·vous, mis′chə·vəs, a. Harmful; injurious; fond of mischief; annoying or troublesome; teasing; playful. **—mis·chie·vous·ly,** adv. **—mis·chie·vous·ness,** n.

mis·ci·ble, mis′ə·bəl, a. Capable of being mixed. **—mis·ci·bil·i·ty,** mis·ə·bil′ə·tē, n.

mis·con·ceive, mis·kən·sēv′, v.t., v.i., -ceived, -ceiv·ing. To receive a false notion or opinion of anything; to misunderstand. **—mis·con·ceiv·er,** n. **—mis·con·cep·tion,** mis·kən·sep′shən, n.

mis·con·duct, mis·kon′dəkt, n. Immoral conduct, esp. adultery; wrong or bad conduct; misbehavior; mismanagement.—mis·kən·dəkt′, v.t. To manage improperly or badly; to misbehave.

mis·con·strue, mis·kən·stroo′, v.t., -strued, -stru·ing. To interpret erroneously; to misunderstand. **—mis·con·struc·tion,** mis·kən·strək′shən, n.

mis·count, mis·kownt′, v.t., v.i. To count erroneously.—n. An erroneous counting.

mis·cre·ant, mis′krē·ənt, n. A scoundrel; a villain. —a. Wicked; vicious; degenerate.

mis·cue, mis·kū′, n. A slip of the cue, causing it to strike the ball improperly; an error or mistake.—v.i., -cued, -cu·ing. To make a miscue; to miss a cue or answer an incorrect one.

mis·deal, mis·dēl′, n. An incorrect deal.—v.t., v.i., -dealt, -deal·ing. To deal cards incorrectly.

mis·deed, mis·dēd′, n. An evil or wicked deed; an immoral act.

mis·de·mean·or, mis·də·mē′nər, n. Misbehavior; a misdeed; any offense not amounting to a felony.

mis·di·rect, mis·di·rekt′, v.t. To direct to a wrong person or place. **—mis·di·rec·tion,** mis·di·rek′shən, n.

mis·do, mis′doo′, v.t., v.i., -did, -done, -do·ing. To do wrongly; botch. **—mis·do·er,** n. **—mis·do·ing,** n.

mis·em·ploy, mis·em·ploy′, v.t. To use badly or improperly. **—mis·em·ploy·ment,** n.

mi·ser, mī′zər, n. A greedy hoarder of wealth; a stingy person. **—mi·ser·li·ness,** n. **—mi·ser·ly,** a.

mis·er·a·ble, miz′ər·ə·bəl, miz′rə·bəl, a. Being in a state of misery, or in wretched circumstances; wretchedly poor or unhappy. Informal. Being in poor health, or ailing. Causing misery; manifesting misery; pitiable or deplorable; of bad character; of wretched quality; extremely inadequate. **—mis·er·a·ble·ness,** n. **—mis·er·a·bly,** adv.

mis·er·y, miz′ə·rē, n. pl., -ies. Distress caused by privation or poverty; physical or mental pain; extreme unhappiness; a cause or source of wretchedness.

mis·fea·sance, mis·fē′zəns, n. The wrongful performance of a lawful act.

mis·fire, mis·fīr′, v.i., -fired, -fir·ing. To fail to fire or explode at the proper time or in the proper manner; to fail to ignite properly; to fail to gain or reach an intended or desired end.

mis·fit, mis·fit′, v.t., v.i., -fit·ted, -fit·ting. To fit poorly.—mis·fit′, mis′fit, n. A wrong or bad fit; one who does not or cannot adjust to his situation or surroundings.

mis·for·tune, mis·fôr′chən, n. Ill fortune; ill luck; calamity; mishap.

mis·giv·ing, mis·giv′ing, n. Often pl. A feeling of doubt, distrust, or apprehension.

mis·gov·ern, mis·gəv′ərn, v.t. To govern or manage badly. **—mis·gov·ern·ment,** n.

mis·guide, mis·gīd′, v.t., -guid·ed, -guid·ing. To guide wrongly; mislead. **—mis·guid·ance,** n. **—mis·guid·ed,** a. **—mis·guid·er,** n.

mis·han·dle, mis·han′dəl, v.t., -dled, -dling. To handle or manage badly; to maltreat.

mis·hap, mis′hap, mis·hap′, n. A regrettable accident; misfortune.

mish·mash, mish′mäsh, mish′mash, n. A hodge-podge; a jumble.

mis·in·form, mis·in·fôrm′, v.t. To give incorrect or misleading information to. **—mis·in·form·ant, mis·in·form·er,** n. **—mis·in·for·ma·tion,** mis·in·fər·mā′shən, n.

mis·in·ter·pret, mis·in·tər′prit, v.t. To interpret erroneously; to understand or explain in a wrong sense. **—mis·in·ter·pre·ta·tion,** mis·in·tər·prə·tā′shən, n. **—mis·in·ter·pret·er,** n.

mis·judge, mis·jej′, v.t., v.i., -judged, -judg·ing. To judge wrongly; to form false or unjust opinions or notions. **—mis·judg·ment, mis·judge·ment,** n.

mis·lay, mis·lā′, v.t., -laid, -lay·ing. To lay in a place not recollected; to lay wrongly: He mislaid the tile.

mis·lead, mis·lēd′, v.t., -led, -lead·ing. To lead astray; to guide into error; to deceive. **—mis·lead·er,** n. **—mis·lead·ing,** a.

mis·man·age, mis·man′ij, v.t., -aged, -ag·ing. To manage or administer poorly, improperly, or dishonestly. **—mis·man·age·ment,** n.

mis·match, mis·mach′, v.t. To match badly or unsuitably.—n.

mis·mate, mis·māt′, v.t., -mat·ed, -mat·ing. To mate or match unsuitably.

mis·name, mis·nām′, v.t., -named, -nam·ing. To call by the wrong name.

mis·no·mer, mis·nō′mər, n. A mistaken or inapplicable name or designation; an incorrect naming, esp. on a legal document.

mi·sog·a·my, mi·sog′ə·mē, mī·sog′ə·mē, n. Hatred of marriage.

mi·sog·y·ny, mi·soj′ə·nē, mī·soj′ə·nē, n. Hatred of women. **—mi·sog·y·nist,** n. **—mi·sog·y·nous,** a.

mis·place, mis·plās′, v.t., -placed, -plac·ing. To put in a wrong or unrecollected place; put, as trust or faith, in an improper or unwise idea, person, or thing. **—mis·place·ment,** n.

mis·play, mis·plā′, n. A wrong or inept play.—v.t. To break the rules or make an error on or with.

mis·print, mis·print′, v.t. To print wrongly. —mis′print, mis·print′, n. A mistake in printing.

mis·pri·sion, mis·prizh′ən, n. Malfeasance by a public official; concealment of a crime, esp. of treason or a felony.

mis·prize, mis·prise, mis·prīz′, v.t., -prized or -prised, -priz·ing or -pris·ing. To scorn or undervalue; to despise.

mis·pro·nounce, mis·prə·nowns′, v.t., v.i., -nounced, -nounc·ing. To pronounce erroneously or incorrectly. **—mis·pro·nun·ci·a·tion,** mis·prə·nən·sē·ā′shən, n.

mis·quote, mis·kwōt′, v.t., v.i., -quot·ed, -quot·ing. To quote erroneously; to cite incorrectly. **—mis·quo·ta·tion,** mis·kwō·tā′shən, n.

mis•read, mis•rēd′, *v.t.,* **-read,** -red, **-read•ing.** To read incorrectly; to interpret wrongly.

mis•rep•re•sent, mis•rep•ri•zent′, *v.t.* To give a false or erroneous representation of; to represent badly. **—mis•rep•re•sen•ta′tion,** mis•rep•rə•sən•tā′shən, *n.* **—mis•rep•re•sen•ta•tive,** *a.*

mis•rule, mis•rool′, *n.* Bad rule; unjust government; disorder; lawless confusion.—*v.t.,* **-ruled, -rul•ing.** To rule unjustly; to govern unwisely or oppressively.

miss, mis, *v.t.* To fail to hit or reach; to fail to meet, obtain, find, perceive; to discover the absence of; to feel or perceive the absence or loss of; to omit; to avoid; to fail to be present at; to let slip.—*v.i.* To fail to hit or strike what is aimed at; to be unsuccessful. *Informal.* To misfire.—*n.* A failure to hit, reach, obtain, do, or the like; loss; want.

miss, mis, *n.* An unmarried female; a young lady; a girl. (*Cap.*) A title of address used with the name of an unmarried female. (*Often cap.*) A term of address used in speaking to a young woman.

mis•sal, mis′əl, *n.* The Roman Catholic liturgical book containing the office of the mass; any prayer book.

mis•shape, mis•shāp′, *v.t.,* **-shaped, -shaped** or **-shap•en, -shap•ing.** To shape poorly; to deform. **—mis•shap•en,** mis•shā′pən, *a.*

mis•sile, mis′əl, *a.* Capable of being thrown or projected from the hand or from any instrument or engine; designed for throwing or firing missiles.—*n.* A weapon or projectile thrown or to be thrown, as a lance, arrow, or bullet; a self-propelled unmanned weapon: a guided *missile* or rocket.

miss•ing, mis′ing, *a.* Absent from the place where it was expected to be found; not to be found; wanting; lost.

miss•ing link, *n.* Something lacking to complete a series; a hypothetical form of animal assumed to have constituted a connecting link between the anthropoid apes and man.

mis•sion, mish′ən, *n.* A group of persons acting as an envoy; the tasks or objectives of those acting as envoys; the sending of an individual or group by an authority to perform a specific service: a religious *mission,* diplomatic *mission,* military *mission;* the building, such as embassy, church, or mission house, which houses the operations of an envoy; a religious congregation without a resident clergyman; a special vocation or calling: Medicine was his life's *mission.* —*v.t.* To assign a mission to, as a person or persons; to organize or establish a mission amidst or in.—*a.* Of or relating to a mission.

mis•sion•ar•y, mish′ə•ner•ē, *n. pl.,* **-ies.** Anyone sent to an area to spread religion or carry on educational or charitable activities; one who tries to convert others to a system or belief which he strongly favors; anyone sent on a mission.

mis•sive, mis′iv, *n.* A letter.

mis•spell, mis•spel′, *v.t., v.i.,* **-spelled** or **-spelt, -spel•ling.** To spell incorrectly. **—mis•spell•ing,** *n.*

mis•spend, mis•spend′, *v.t.,* **-spent, -spend•ing.** To spend for wrong uses.

mis•state, mis•stāt′, *v.t.,* **-stat•ed, -stat•ing.** To state wrongly. **—mis•state•ment,** *n.*

mis•step, mis•step′, *n.* An erroneous step; a mistake in behavior.

mist, mist, *n.* Visible watery vapor suspended in the atmosphere at or near the surface of the earth; something which dims or obscures vision; a film in front of the eyes; a cloud of particles, as of dust, resembling a mist.—*v.t.* To cover with mist; to cloud.—*v.i.* To be misty; to become misty; to drizzle. **—mist•i•ly,** *adv.* **—mist•i•ness,** *n.*

mis•tak•a•ble, mi•stā′kə•bəl, *a.* Capable of being mistaken or misconceived.

mis•take, mi•stāk′, *v.t.,* **-took, -tak•en, -tak•ing.** To

err in identifying; to misjudge, misinterpret.—*v.i.* To be in error.—*n.* An error in opinion, judgment, or perception.

mis•tak•en, mi•stā′kən, *a.* Erroneous; incorrect; having made a mistake. **—mis•tak•en•ly,** *adv.* **—mis•tak•en•ness,** *n.* **—mis•tak•er,** *n.*

Mis•ter, mis′tər, *n.* The conventional title of respect for a man, prefixed to the name and to certain official titles of a man. Abbr. **Mr.**

mis•tle•toe, mis′əl•tō, *n.* A parasitic plant on trees with yellowish-green leaves and flowers and, in winter, small white berries: used as a Christmas decoration.

mis•tral, mis′trəl, mi•sträl′, *n.* A violently cold, northerly wind common to southern France.

mis•treat, mis•trēt′, *v.t.* To treat improperly; to maltreat. **—mis•treat•ment,** *n.*

mis•tress, mis′tris, *n.* The female head of a family, household, estate, or school; a woman exercising supremacy over anything; a woman cohabiting unlawfully with a man, esp. when the man supports her financially; a female owner of an animal or formerly a slave; anything regarded as feminine that rules or commands; a female who has attained mastery in a field.

mis•tri•al, mis•trī′əl, *n.* A trial voided by some error; an inconclusive trial, as where the jury cannot agree.

mis•trust, mis•trəst′, *n.* Lack of confidence or trust; suspicion.—*v.t.* To suspect; to doubt.—*v.i.* To be doubtful or suspicious. **—mis•trust•ful,** *a.* **—mis•trust•ful•ly, mis•trust•ing•ly,** *adv.* **—mis•trust•ful•ness,** *n.*

mist•y, mis′tē, *a.,* **-i•er, -i•est.** Clouded or covered with mist; made up of or characterized by mist; indefinite; indistinct.

mis•un•der•stand, mis•ən•dər•stand′, *v.t., v.i.,* **-stood, -stand•ing.** To misconceive or misinterpret; to mistake; to take in a wrong sense.

mis•un•der•stand•ing, mis•ən•dər•stan′ding, *n.* Misconception; mistake of meaning; a disagreement; dissension.

mis•us•age, mis•ū′sij, mis•ū′zij, *n.* Improper or incorrect use or employment, esp. of words; abuse.

mis•use, mis•ūz′, *v.t.,* **-used, -us•ing.** To treat or use improperly; to abuse; to maltreat.—mis•ūs′, *n.* Improper use; abuse. **—mis•us•er,** mis•ū′zər, *n.*

mis•val•ue, mis•val′ū, *v.t.,* **-ued, -u•ing.** To value wrongly.

mite, mīt, *n.* Any of numerous small, minute animals, including many which live as parasites on animals, plants, and foods.

mite, mīt, *n.* A small coin or a small amount of money; a very small particle, quantity, object, or creature.

mi•ter, mi•tre, mī•tər, *n.* The tall, official headdress of popes, bishops, and abbots; the office of bishop; a miter joint.—*v.t.* To bestow a miter upon, or raise to a rank entitled to it.

mi•ter joint, mi•tre joint, *n.* A joint in which the plane of the abutting surfaces bisects the angle formed by the pieces.

mit•i•cide, mit′i•sīd, *n.* A chemical agent that kills mites. **—mit•i•cid•al,** *a.*

mit•i•gate, mit′ə•gāt, *v.t.,* **-gat•ed, -gat•ing.** To become or make less painful, rigorous, intense, or severe; to assuage.—*v.i.* To become milder; diminish in severity. **—mit•i•ga•tion,** mit•ə•gā′shən, *n.* **—mit•i•ga•tive,** *a.* **—mit•i•ga•tor,** *n.* **—mit•i•ga•to•ry,** mit′ə•gə•tôr•ē, *a.*

mi•to•sis, mī•tō′sis, *n.* The usual method of cell division. **—mi•tot•ic,** mī•tot′ik, *a.* **—mi•tot•i•cal•ly,** *adv.*

mi•tral, mī′trəl, *a.* Of, referring to, or resembling a miter; referring to a valve in the heart which prevents the blood in the left ventricle from returning to the left auricle.

mitt, mit, *n.* A mitten; a women's long glove that does

---

a- hat, fāte, fâre, fäther; **e-** met, mē; **i-** pin, pīne; **o-** not, nōte, ôrb, moove (move), boy, pownd; **u-** cūbe, bûll, tûk (took); **ch-** chin; **th-** thick, ŧhen; **zh-** vizhon (vision); **ə-** əgo, takən, pencəl, lemən, bərd (bird).

not cover the fingers; in baseball, a large, rounded, heavily padded glove worn for hand protection. *Informal.* A hand; a boxing glove.

mit·ten, mit′ən, *n.* A covering for the hand, having a separate cover for the thumb and a wide section for the four fingers; a mitt.

mix, miks, *v.t.,* **mixed** or **mixt, mix·ing.** To put together into one mass by blending; to put together haphazardly, often with *up;* to jumble or confuse; to join, associate, or unite with in company; to form by combining ingredients; to crossbreed.—*v.i.* To become mixed; to associate; to get along; to be crossbred.—*n.* The product or result of mixing; a combination of ingredients prepared, packaged, and sold commercially as a time- or work-saving preparation: a cake *mix;* the proportioned ingredients or formula of a mixture: a *mix* of four to one; an often carbonated beverage, as ginger ale, which is added to alcoholic liquors. *Informal.* A muddle or mess.

mixed, mikst, *a.* Put together or formed by mixing; composed of different elements, sexes, races, qualities, religions; mentally confused.—**mixed up,** completely confused.

mixed num·ber, *n.* A number consisting of a whole number and a fraction, as $4\frac{1}{2}$.

mix·er, mik′sər, *n.* One who or that which mixes; a kitchen appliance used to beat, blend, or mix food. *Informal.* A person with a capacity for mixing sociably with others; a gathering held to acquaint people with one another. A system used in combining or blending sounds from more than one source; the technician who operates such a system.

mix·ture, miks′chər, *n.* The act of mixing, or the state of being mixed; a product of mixing; an assemblage of ingredients mixed together but not chemically combined; any combination of differing elements, kinds, or qualities.

mix-up, miks′əp, *n.* A confused state of things; a muddle. *Informal.* A fight.

miz·zen, miz′ən, *n.* The aftermost fore-and-aft sail of a three-masted vessel; the sail on the mizzenmast of a ketch, yawl, or the like; a mizzenmast.

mne·mon·ic, nē-mon′ik, ni-mon′ək, *a.* Referring to mnemonics; assisting or training the memory.

mne·mon·ics, nē-mon′iks, ni-mon′iks, *n. pl. but sing. in constr.* The art or system of memory training.

mo·a, mō′a, *n.* Any of various extinct, large, flightless birds of New Zealand.

moan, mōn, *v.i.* To utter a low, dull sound from grief or pain; to make lamentations.—*v.t.* To mourn or lament; to express mournfully.—*n.* A low, dull sound due to grief or pain; a sound resembling that made by a person moaning.

moat, mōt, *n.* A ditch or deep trench, often filled with water, surrounding the rampart of a castle or other fortified place.—*v.t.* To surround with or as with a ditch for defense.

mob, mob, *n.* A riotous or disorderly crowd, a lawless crowd; rabble; the lower classes or common people; the masses. *Informal.* A group of criminals.—*v.t.,* **mobbed, mob·bing.** To overcrowd; to attack by crowding.—**mob·bish,** *a.*

mo·bile, mō′bəl, mō′bēl, *a.* Capable of being easily moved; moving; fast-flowing; changeable; varying in goal, emotion, or appearance; readily adaptable; responsive; an individual's or group's ability to move from one social level to another; equipped to move easily; of or pertaining to a mobile.—mō′bēl, *n.* A structure made of several balanced parts, often of metal wire, the parts capable of independent motion when in contact with air currents or a mechanical force. —**mo·bil·i·ty,** mō·bil′ə·tē, *n.*

mo·bile home, *n.* Trailer; a large, trailer-like home capable of being readily moved to new locations, now often set up as a permanent dwelling.

mo·bi·lize, mō′bə·līz, *v.t.,* **-lized, -liz·ing.** To put in a state of readiness for active military service; to orga-

nize for use in time of national emergency; to marshal for use or action.—*v.i.* To undergo preparation or organization for use or action. —**mo·bi·li·za·tion,** mō·bə·lə·zā′shən, *n.*

mob·ster, mob′stər, *n. Informal.* One who belongs to a criminal group; a gangster.

moc·ca·sin, mok′ə·sin, *n.* A kind of soft shoe with a low heel and no laces, resembling a slipper; a heelless shoe, made of soft leather, similar to that once worn by American Indians.

moc·ca·sin flow·er, *n.* A lady's slipper.

mo·cha, mō′kə, *n.* A choice variety of coffee; a coffee, or coffee-chocolate flavoring; a very fine, soft, glove leather made from the skin of African sheep.—*a.*

mock, mok, *v.t.* To imitate or mimic, esp. in contempt or derision; to deride; ridicule; treat with scorn; to disappoint; to deceive; to defy.—*v.i.* To use ridicule; scoff; jeer.—*a.* False; imitation.—*n.* An act of derision or scorn; the object of such an act; a copy or imitation. —**mock·er,** *n.* —**mock·ing·ly,** *adv.*

mock·er·y, mok′ə·rē, *n. pl.,* **-ies.** The act of mocking; ridicule; the object of ridicule; a vain or unsuitable effort; fraudulent or contemptible pretense.

mock·ing·bird, mok′ing·bərd, *n.* A N. American bird remarkable for its faculty of imitating the songs of other birds.

mock or·ange, *n.* A shrub with creamy white flowers resembling orange blossoms.

mock-up, mok′əp, *n.* A model, usu. full size, of any object made for purposes of testing, display, or instruction.

mod·al, mōd′əl, *a.* Of or pertaining to mode, manner, or form. —**mo·dal·i·ty,** mō·dal′ə·tē, *n.* —**mod·al·ly,** *adv.*

mode, mōd, *n.* Manner of acting or doing; a customary or conventional usage in manners or dress; the latest style or fashion; the manner, form, state, or existence of a basic substance; any of various arrangements of the diatonic tones of an octave, differing from one another in the order of the whole steps and halfsteps; the value in a frequency distribution which occurs most frequently.

mod·el, mod′əl, *n.* A standard for imitation or comparison; a pattern; a representation in miniature, to show the construction or serve as a copy of something; anything that serves as an artist's pattern; a person who poses for artists; one employed to put on articles of clothing and display them; mode of structure or formation; a typical form or style.—*a.* Serving as a model; worthy to serve as a model.—*v.t.,* **-eled, -el·ing.** To form or plan according to a model; to make a model of; to wear for display.—*v.i.* To make models; to assume an appearance of natural relief; to be employed for displaying apparel. —**mod·el·er,** *n.*

mod·er·ate, mod′ər·it, *a.* Not extreme; temperate in opinions, views, or behavior; inclined toward the average in size, extent, or quality; mediocre; avoiding the more radical extremes of political and social opinion. —*n.* One who holds moderate rather than extreme or radical opinions.—mod′ə·rāt, *v.t.,* **-at·ed, -at·ing.** To reduce in intensity or severity; to restrain from excess; to preside over.—*v.i.* To become less violent or intense; to preside as a moderator. —**mod·er·ate·ly,** *adv.* —**mod·er·ate·ness,** *n.*

mod·er·a·tion, mod·ə·rā′shən, *n.* The state or quality of being moderate; the act of presiding as a moderator.—**in mod·er·a·tion,** temperately; not excessively.

mod·er·a·tor, mod′ə·rā·tər, *n.* One who or that which moderates; a presiding officer; an arbitrator; a moderating substance for a nuclear reactor, used to retard the speed of neutrons. —**mod·er·a·tor·ship,** *n.*

mod·ern, mod′ərn, *a.* Pertaining to the present time; recent; not ancient; pertaining to or characteristic of the current period, esp. of contemporary forms of art, music, literature, and architecture.—*n.* A person of modern times; a person whose tastes, opinions, and styles are characteristic of the present times; a kind of type face distinguished by heavy down-strokes and thin cross-strokes.

mod•ern•ism, mod′ər•niz•əm, *n.* The thought and action characteristic of modern life; sympathy with or the exercise of thought and action characteristically modern; a usage, practice, or quality characteristically modern. (*Often cap.*) A movement in religious thought that reinterprets church teaching in conformity with developments in science and philosophy. **—mod• ern•ist,** *n.* **—mod•ern•ist•ic,** mod•ər•nis′tik, *a.*

mod•ern•ize, mod′ər•nīz, *v.t.,* **-ized, -iz•ing.** To give a modern character to; to adapt to, as modern styles, opinions, and tastes.—*v.i.* To adopt or conform to modern ideas or style. **—mod•ern•iz•er,** *n.* **—mod• ern•i•za•tion,** mod•ər•nə•zā′shən, *n.*

mod•est, mod′ist, *a.* Characterized by a moderate estimation of oneself or one's capabilities; restrained by a sense of propriety; moderate; not excessive. **—mod•est•ly,** *adv.* **—mod•es•ty,** *n. pl.,* **-ties.**

mod•i•cum, mod′i•kəm, *n.* A little; a small quantity.

mod•i•fi•ca•tion, mod•ə•fə•kā′shən, *n.* The act or state of being modified; the altered result; an altera- tion in form, appearance, or character; a change in form or function as in meaning; qualification.

mod•i•fy, mod′ə•fī, *v.t.,* **-fied, -fy•ing.** To partially change external qualities; to vary; to alter in some respect; to moderate; to qualify; to limit or qualify the intention of. **—mod•i•fi•a•ble,** *a.* **—mod•i•fi•er,** *n.*

mod•ish, mō′dish, *a.* According to the newest mode or fashion; fashionable. **—mod•ish•ly,** *adv.* **—mod• ish•ness,** *n.*

mo•diste, mō•dēst′, *n.* A woman who deals in articles of ladies' dress; a milliner; a dressmaker.

mod•u•late, moj′ů•lāt, *v.t.,* **-lat•ed, -lat•ing.** To con- trol, temper, or modify; to vary or inflect the sound or tone; to change the key of in the course of a composi- tion; to alter the frequency, phase, intensity, or ampli- tude of a carrier wave.—*v.i.* To pass from one key into another.

mod•u•la•tion, moj•ů•lā′shən, *n.* The act of modu- lating; the condition of being modulated. *Mus.* The change from one scale to another. An inflection of the voice that gives expression to an utterance. **—mod• u•la•tor,** *n.* **—mod•u•la•to•ry,** *a.*

mod•ule, moj′ool, *n.* A standard or unit for measur- ing, esp. a unit of measurement by which prefabrica- tion of building materials can be standardized. **—mod•u•lar,** *a.*

mo•dus o•pe•ran•di, mō′dəs op•ə•ran′dī, *n.* A way of operating or working.

mo•dus vi•ven•di, mō′dəs vi•ven′dē, *n.* Mode of living; a temporary arrangement pending a final settle- ment.

mo•gul, mō′gəl, mō•gəl′, *n.* Any great personage.

mo•hair, mō′hār, *n.* The hair of the Angora goat; cloth made of this hair, or clothing made from it.

Mo•ham•med•an, mō•ham′ə•dən, *a.* Referring to Mohammed or the Islam religion founded by him.—*n.* A follower of Mohammed; one who professes to be Muslim. **—Mo•ham•med•an•ism,** *n.*

moi•e•ty, moy′ə•tē, *n. pl.,* **-ties.** The half; a portion or a share.

moil, moyl, *v.i.* To work hard; toil; drudge.—*n.* Toil or drudgery; confusion, turmoil, or trouble. **—moil•er,** *n.* **—moil•ing•ly,** *adv.*

moi•ré, mwä•rā′, *n.* A wavelike pattern or finish, as on silk or metal; a rippled or wavy fabric.—*a.* Having a wavelike pattern. Also **moire,** mwär.

moist, moyst, *a.* Moderately wet; damp; humid; tearful.

mois•ten, moi′sən, *v.t.* To make moist or damp.—*v.i.* To become moist. **—moist•en•er,** *n.*

mois•ture, mois′chər, *n.* Diffused wetness or con- densed liquid. **—mois•tur•ize,** mois′chə•rīz, *v.t.,*

-ized, -iz•ing. **—mois•tur•iz•er,** *n.*

mol, mole, mōl, *n.* The molecular weight of a sub- stance expressed in grams; gram molecule.

mo•lar, mō′lər, *n.* A tooth with a broad surface for grinding, located in back of the canines and incisors in mammals.—*a.* Relating to such a tooth; grinding.

mo•las•ses, mə•las′iz, *n.* A dark-colored, thick syrup produced during the refining of sugar or sorghum.

mold, mould, mōld, *n.* Earth rich in organic matter and favorable to the growth of plants.

mold, mould, mōld, *n.* The matrix in which anything is cast and receives its form; something shaped in or by a mold; cast; form; shape; character.—*v.t.* To form into a particular shape; to shape; to fashion; to influ- ence. **—mold•a•ble,** *a.* **—mold•er,** *n.*

mold, mould, mōld, *n.* A growth of minute fungi forming a downy coating on decaying vegetable or animal matter; any of the fungi that produce such a growth.—*v.t., v.i.* To become or make moldy.

mold•board, mould•board, mōld′bôrd, *n.* The curved metal plate of a plow, which turns over the soil.

mold•er, mōl′dər, *v.i.* To turn to dust by natural decay.

mold•ing, mould•ing, mōl′ding, *n.* The act of one who or that which molds; something molded; a deco- rative edging outlining cornices, jambs, or strips of woodwork; a shaped member in a structure to afford such variety or decoration; shaped material in the form of a strip, used for supporting pictures, covering electric wires, or finishing.

mold•y, mould•y, mōl′dē, *a.,* **-i•er, -i•est.** Over- grown with mold; musty, as from age or decay. **—mold•i•ness,** *n.*

mole, mōl, *n.* A spot, or small, discolored, congenital mark on the human body.

mole, mōl, *n.* A small, insect-eating mammal having small eyes, soft fur, and strong forefeet for burrowing under the ground.

mole, mōl, *n.* A breakwater formed to enclose a harbor or anchorage.

mole, mōl, *n.* Mol.

mo•lec•u•lar, mə•lek′yə•lər, *a.* Referring to or con- sisting of molecules.

mol•e•cule, mol′ə•kūl, *n.* The smallest particle of an element or compound that has all the properties of that element or compound; any very small particle.

mole•hill, mōl′hil, *n.* A small mound or ridge of earth raised by a mole; something insignificant.

mole•skin, mōl′skin, *n.* The soft, fragile pelt of a mole; a strong, twilled, cotton cloth, used in making work and hunting clothes; *usu. pl.,* garments made of this fabric.

mo•lest, mə•lest′, *v.t.* To annoy, disturb, or meddle; to attack or interfere with sexually. **—mo•les•ta•tion,** mō•le•stā′shən, mol•e•stā′shən, *n.* **—mo•lest•er,** *n.*

moll, mol, *n. Informal.* The female companion of a thief or gangster; a prostitute.

mol•li•fy, mol′ə•fī, *v.t., v.i.,* **-fied, -fy•ing.** To alleviate, as pain or irritation; to pacify; to appease; to soothe the disposition of. **—mol•li•fi•ca•tion,** mol•ə•fə•kā′shən, *n.* **—mol•li•fi•er,** *n.* **—mol•li•fy•ing•ly,** *adv.*

mol•lusk, mol•lusc, mol′əsk, *n.* Any of a large phy- lum of invertebrate animals having soft, unsegmented bodies usu. covered with a hard shell of one, two, or more pieces, as snails, mussels, oysters, clams, squids, octopuses and the like. **—mol•lus•can,** mə• ləs′kən, *a., n.*

mol•ly•cod•dle, mol′ē•kod•əl, *n.* A man or boy ac- customed to being coddled; an effeminate man.—*v.t.,* **-dled, -dling.** To coddle or pamper.

molt, moult, mōlt, *v.t., v.i.* To shed, as feathers or skin, to be ready for a new growth. **—molt•er,** *n.*

mol•ten, mōl′tən, *a.* Liquefied by heat; produced by melting and casting. **—mol•ten•ly,** *adv.*

mo•lyb•de•num, mə•lib′də•nəm, *n.* A silver-white

---

a- hat, fāte, fāre, fäther; **e-** met, mē; **i-** pin, pīne; **o-** not, nōte, ôrb, moove (move), boy, pownd; **u-** cūbe, bůll, tůk (took); **ch-** chin; **th-** thick, then; **zh-** vizhon (vision); **ə-** əgo, takən, pencəl, lemən, bərd (bird).

metallic element mainly used in alloy steel.

mom, mom, *n. Informal.* Mother.

mo·ment, mō′mənt, *n.* An indefinitely short space of time; an instant; the present or other particular instant or point of time; the present or current brief space of time; a period, usu. brief, of greatness, happiness, distinction; the precise instant of opportunity; weight, importance, or consequence; a definite stage in the course of events, esp. a particular point in logical or historical development; the result of the multiplication of a quantity by its perpendicular distance from a point or axis; a tendency to produce motion, such as rotation about an axis; a quantifying of such a tendency.

mo·men·tar·y, mō′mən·ter·ē, *a.* Lasting but a moment. **—mo·men·tar·i·ly,** mō·mən·tār′ə·lē, *adv.* **—mo·men·tar·i·ness,** *n.*

mo·men·tous, mō·men′təs, *a.* Of great importance or consequence. **—mo·men·tous·ly,** *adv.* **—mo·men·tous·ness,** *n.*

mo·men·tum, mō·men′təm, *n.* Impetus, as of a moving body; the quantity of motion of a moving body, being equivalent to the product of its mass and velocity.

mon·ad, mon′ad, mō′nad, *n.* Unity; an indivisible unit; an absolutely simple metaphysical entity, conceived as the ultimate unit of being; any simple, single-celled organism; an element, atom, or radical having a valence of one. **—mo·nad·ic,** mə·nad′ik, **mo·nad·i·cal, mo·nad·al,** *a.* **—mo·nad·i·cal·ly,** *adv.*

mon·arch, mon′ərk, *n.* The hereditary ruler of a state as an emperor, king, queen; something or someone superior to others of the same kind; a large butterfly, orange and brown in color with black markings. **—mo·nar·chal,** *a.* **—mo·nar·chal·ly,** *adv.*

mo·nar·chi·cal, mə·när′ki·kəl, *a.* Referring to a monarchy or monarch; ruled by or advocating rule by a monarch. Also **mo·nar·chic. —mo·nar·chi·cal·ly,** *adv.*

mon·ar·chism, mon′ər·kiz·əm, *n.* The principles of monarchy; advocacy of a monarchy or a monarch. **—mon·ar·chist,** *n., a.* **—mon·ar·chist·ic,** *a.*

mon·ar·chy, mon′ər·kē, *n. pl.,* **-chies.** The system of government in which power is vested in a monarch.

mon·as·ter·y, mon′ə·ster·ē, *n. pl.,* **-ies.** A building which houses those living under religious vows and in seclusion; the monks living in such an environment. **—mon·as·te·ri·al,** *a.*

mo·nas·tic, mə·nas′tik, *a.* Pertaining to monasteries, monks and the secluded life within a monastery. Also **mon·as·te·ri·al,** mon·ə·stēr′ē·əl.

mo·nas·ti·cal, mə·nas′tik·əl, *n.* A member of a monastery; a monk. **—mo·nas·ti·cal·ly,** *adv.*

mo·nas·ti·cism, mə·nas′ti·siz·əm, *n.* Monastic life; the monastic system or condition.

mon·au·ral, mon·ôr′əl, *a.* Of or pertaining to sound which is perceived through only one ear; pertaining to a type of sound reproduction heard as if it came from a single source or direction. **—mon·au·ral·ly,** *adv.*

Mon·day, mən′dē, mən′dā, *n.* The second day of the week; the day following Sunday.

mon·e·tar·y, mon′ə·ter·ē, mən′ə·ter·ē, *a.* Referring to money or currency; pecuniary. **—mon·e·tar·i·ly,** mon·ə·tār′ə·lē, mən·ə·tār′ə·lē, *adv.*

mon·e·tize, mon′ə·tiz, mən′ə·tiz, *v.t.,* **-tized, -tizing.** To make legal as money; to form into coin or money. **—mon·e·ti·za·tion,** mon·ə·tə·zā′shən, *n.*

mon·ey, mon′ē, *n. pl.,* **-eys, -ies.** Coin; gold, silver, or other metal, stamped by public authority and used as the medium of exchange; any equivalent for commodities, exchangeable for goods or service, as money orders or checks; a circulating medium; wealth; property having pecuniary value.

mon·ey·chang·er, mən′ē·chān·jər, *n.* One whose business it is to change money at fixed rates; a coin dispenser.

mon·eyed, mon·ied, mən′ēd, *a.* Representing wealth; rich.

mon·ey·mak·er, mən′ē·mā·kər, *n.* A person who successfully accumulates money; a business, product, or scheme which is lucrative. **—mon·ey·mak·ing,** *a., n.*

mon·ey or·der, *n.* An order granted upon payment of a sum and a small commission, by one post office, bank, or telegraph company, and payable at another.

mon·ger, məng′gər, mong′gər, *n.* A trader; a dealer; one who occupies himself with contemptible things: scandal*monger.*

Mon·gol·ism, mong′gə·liz·əm, *n.* A congenital mental deficiency in a child characterized by slanting eyes and a broad skull, face, and hands. Also **mon·gol·oid.**

mon·goose, mong′goos, mon′goos, *n. pl.,* **-goos·es.** A small, ferretlike animal noted for its ability to kill poisonous snakes; any animal of the same genus or of related genera.

mon·grel, məng′grəl, mong′grəl, *n.* Any plant or animal resulting from the crossing of different breeds; a dog of no specific breed; the product of any incongruous mixture.**—***a.* Of mixed breed, race, origin, or nature.

mon·i·ker, mon′ə·kər, *n. Informal.* A name, usu. a nickname.

mon·ism, mon′iz·əm, mō′niz·əm, *n.* The theory that one substance or principle is the basis of all reality. **—mon·ist,** *n.* **—mo·nis·tic,** mō·nis′tik, **mo·nis·ti·cal,** *a.* **—mo·nis·ti·cal·ly,** *adv.*

mo·ni·tion, mō·nish′ən, *n.* Admonition or warning; an official or legal notice.

mon·i·tor, mon′ə·tər, *n.* One who maintains discipline and enforces rules of conduct; anything that reminds or cautions; a student chosen to help with classroom duties; any of certain large lizards of Asia, Africa, and Australia; a former class of heavily-armed, iron-clad vessels riding low in the water; an apparatus, as a receiver, used to check transmission or quality of a broadcast.**—***v.t., v.i.* To oversee, as a monitor; to listen to or view, as a broadcast; to check transmission and quality. **—mon·i·to·ri·al,** mon·ə·tôr′ē·əl, *a.*

monk, məngk, *n.* One of a community of males inhabiting a monastery and bound by vows to celibacy, poverty, and religious obedience. **—monk·ish,** *a.* **—monk·ish·ly,** *adv.*

mon·key, məng′kē, *n. pl.,* **-keys.** Any member, except man, lemurs, and apes, of the primates, the highest order of mammals, as baboons, marmosets; a person likened to such an animal, as a mischievous child or a mimic.**—***v.t.,* **-keyed, -key·ing.** To imitate, as a monkey does; to mimic; to mock.**—***v.i.* To play or trifle idly; fool, often with *with.***—make a mon·key out of,** to make, as a person, seem ridiculous.

mon·key bus·i·ness, *n. Informal.* Deceitful behavior; mischievous, high-spirited, or foolish behavior.

mon·key·shines, məng′kē·shīnz, *n. Informal.* A foolish trick or prank; monkey business.

mon·key wrench, *n.* A wrench with an adjustable jaw.

mon·o·chro·mat·ic, mon·ə·krō·mat′ik, *a.* Consisting of one color or one hue. **—mon·o·chro·mat·i·cal·ly,** *adv.*

mon·o·chrome, mon′ə·krōm, *n.* A painting or design in one color or shades of one color. **—mon·o·chro·mic,** mon·ə·krō′mik, **mon·o·chro·mi·cal,** *a.* **—mon·o·chro·mi·cal·ly,** *adv.***—mon·o·chrom·ist,** *n.*

mon·o·cle, mon′ə·kəl, *n.* A single eyeglass. **—mon·o·cled,** *a.*

mon·o·cli·nal, mon·ə·klīn′əl, *a.* Dipping in one direction, as strata; referring to strata which dip in the same direction.**—***n.* A monocline.

mon·o·cline, mon′ə·klīn, *n.* A monoclinal structure or fold. **—mon·o·cli·nal·ly,** *adv.*

mon·o·cli·nous, mon·ə·klī′nəs, *a.* Having both stamens and pistils in one flower.

mon·o·dist, mon′ə·dist, *n.* One who writes or composes monodies.

mon·o·dy, mon′ə·dē, *n. pl.,* **-dies.** A mournful song or dirge; a poem in which one person laments another's death. A song style in which one part predominates; homophony. **—mo·nod·ic,** mə·nod′ik, *a.*

mo·noe·cious, mə·nē′shəs, *a.* Having male and female flowers on the same plant; hermaphroditic. Also **mo·ne·cious, mo·noi·cous. —mo·noe·cious·ly,** *adv.*

mo·nog·a·my, mə·nog′ə·mē, *n.* The practice or principle of being married to only one person at a time. *Zool.* The pairing with only a single mate. **—mo·nog·a·mist,** *n.* **—mo·nog·a·mous,** *a.*

mon·o·gram, mon′ə·gram, *n.* Two or more letters interlaced into a design, as the initials of a person's name.—*v.t.,* **-grammed, -gram·ming.** To mark with a monogram. **—mon·o·gram·mat·ic,** mon·ə·grə·mat′ik, **mon·o·grammed,** *a.*

mon·o·graph, mon′ə·graf, mon′ə·gräf, *n.* A scholarly book or article on a limited subject or field. **—mo·nog·ra·pher,** mə·nog′rə·fər, *n.* **—mon·o·graph·ic,** mon·ə·graf′ik, *a.*

mon·o·lith, mon′ə·lith, *n.* A single stone block, usu. of great size; something characterized by massiveness and homogeneity: a bureaucratic *monolith.* **—mon·o·lith·ic,** mon·ə·lith′ik, *a.*

mon·o·logue, mon·o·log, mon′ə·lôg, mon′ə·log, *n.* A discourse, dramatic sketch, or poem delivered by one performer; soliloquy; a speech by one person; a series of short, funny stories delivered by a lone comedian. **—mon·o·logu·ist, mon·o·log·ist,** *n.*

mon·o·ma·ni·a, mon·ə·mā′nē·ə, *n.* That mental disorder in which the patient is obsessed by one idea or subject only; excessive enthusiasm for one idea, object, or project. **—mon·o·ma·ni·ac,** *n., a.* **—mon·o·ma·ni·a·cal,** mon·ə·mə·nī′ə·kəl, *a.*

mon·o·met·al·lism, mon·ō·met′ə·liz·əm, *n.* The employment of only one metal as a standard in the coinage of a country. **—mon·o·me·tal·lic,** mon·ō·mə·tal′ik, *a.*

mo·no·mi·al, mō·nō′mē·əl, *n.* An algebraic expression composed of a single term.—*a.* Consisting of a single term.

mon·o·nu·cle·o·sis, mon·ō·noo·klē·ō′sis, mon·ō·nū·klē·ō′sis, *n.* A virus disease of the blood, characterized by the existence of too many cells having a single nucleus. Also **in·fec·tious mon·o·nu·cle·o·sis.**

mon·o·phon·ic, mon·ə·fon′ik, *a.* Of or pertaining to sound reproduction through a single channel: opposite of stereophonic. Also **mon·au·ral.** Characterized by only one unaccompanied melodic line.

mon·o·plane, mon′ə·plān, *n.* An airplane having only one wing on either side of the fuselage.

mo·nop·o·lize, mə·nop′ə·līz, *v.t.,* **-lized, -liz·ing.** To acquire or exercise a monopoly of; to obtain exclusive possession or control of. **—mo·nop·o·li·za·tion,** mə·nop·ə·lə·zā′shən, *n.* **—mo·nop·o·liz·er,** *n.*

mo·nop·o·ly, mə·nop′ə·lē, *n. pl.,* **-lies.** Exclusive control of a commodity or service in a particular market; anything that is the subject of a monopoly; a corporation or the like having a monopoly; an exclusive trading or manufacturing privilege; exclusive possession or control of anything.

mon·o·rail, mon′ə·rāl, *n.* A railway whose cars run on or are suspended from a single rail; the rail itself.

mon·o·so·di·um glu·ta·mate, mon·ō·sō′dē·əm gloo′tə·māt, *n.* A sodium salt used as a seasoning to enhance flavor, esp. of meat.

mon·o·syl·lab·ic, mon·ə·si·lab′ik, *a.* Consisting of one syllable; using, uttering, or consisting of words of only one syllable; brief; terse. **—mon·o·syl·lab·i·cal·ly,** *adv.*

mon·o·syl·la·ble, mon·ə·sil′ə·bəl, *n.* A word of one syllable.

mon·o·the·ism, mon′ə·thē·iz·əm, *n.* The doctrine of, or belief in, the existence of one God only. **—mon·**

o·the·ist, *n.* **—mon·o·the·is·tic,** mon·ə·thē·is′tik, *a.* **—mon·o·the·is·ti·cal·ly,** *adv.*

mon·o·tone, mon′ə·tōn, *n.* Speech continuing in the same tone pitch and stress; sameness or monotony as in sound, color, or style; the repeated singing of a single tone; chant.

mo·not·o·nous, mə·not′ə·nəs, *a.* Uttered or continuing in the same tone, or on one note; unvarying in any respect; tiresomely uniform. **—mo·not·o·nous·ly,** *adv.* **—mo·not·o·nous·ness,** *n.*

mo·not·o·ny, mə·not′ə·nē, *n.* Boring repetition of the same pitch, activities, conversation, or other interests.

mon·o·treme, mon′ə·trēm, *n.* Any of the lowest order of egg-laying mammals, including only the duckbills and echidnas.

mon·o·type, mon′ə·tip, *n. Biol.* The sole representative of its group, as a single species constituting a genus. *Print.* A print from a metal plate on which a picture is painted; the method of producing such a print. (*Cap.*) *Trademark.* A device for casting and setting type in separate units, as opposed to Linotype. **—mon·o·typ·er,** *n.* **—mon·o·typ·ic,** mon·ə·tip′ik, *a.*

mon·o·va·lent, mon·ə·vā′lənt, *n. Chem.* Univalent. **—mon·o·va·lence, mon·o·va·len·cy,** *n.*

mon·ox·ide, mon·ok′sīd, mə·nok′sīd, *n.* An oxide containing one oxygen atom to the molecule.

Mon·roe Doc·trine, mən·rō′, *n.* The policy holding that any attempt by a European country to colonize or interfere in the internal affairs of any country of the Americas would be considered an unfriendly act toward the U.S. government.

mon·sei·gneur, mon·sēn′yər, môn·se·nyər′, *n. pl.,* **mes·sei·gneurs,** mā·sen·yər′. (*Often cap.*) A French title of honor given to princes, bishops, and other high dignitaries; a person with such a title.

mon·sieur, mə·syər′, *n. pl.,* **mes·sieurs,** mes′ərz, me·syər′. The common title of courtesy and respect in France, corresponding to the English *sir* and *Mr.* Abbr. **Mons., M.;** *pl.,* **Messrs., MM.**

Mon·si·gnor, mon·sēn′yər, *n. pl.,* **mon·si·gnors, mon·si·gno·ri,** môn·sēn·yôr′ē. (*Sometimes l.c.*) *Rom. Cath. Ch.* A title conferred upon priests who have received certain papal honors; a priest bearing this title. Abbr. **Monsig., Msgr.**

mon·soon, mon·soon′, *n.* A seasonal wind of the Indian Ocean and southern Asia, blowing from the southwest from April to October and from the northeast during the rest of the year; the rainy season during which this wind blows from the southwest; any wind whose direction is reversed periodically.

mon·ster, mon′stər, *n.* A plant or an animal of abnormal or hideous structure or appearance; a person or thing abhorred because of depravity, deformity, or cruelty; an imaginary or mythical creature such as a sphinx, centaur, or griffin; any huge or unnatural person or thing.—*a.* Of inordinate size or numbers; monstrous.

mon·stros·i·ty, mon·stros′i·tē, *n. pl.,* **-ties.** The state of being monstrous; something abnormal or unnatural; a freak.

mon·strous, mon′strəs, *a.* Unnatural in form or character; enormous; huge; extraordinary; shocking; frightful; horrible. **—mon·strous·ly,** *adv.* **—mon·strous·ness,** *n.*

mon·tage, mon·täzh′, *n.* The art or process of combining many pictorial elements in one photographic composition; a composition produced by this process. *Motion Pictures, TV.* A rapid succession of images illustrating a number of related ideas. A similar technique used in writing, music, painting, etc.

month, mənth, *n.* The period from one new moon to the next, equivalent to 29 days, 12 hours, 44 minutes, and 2.7 seconds; a lunar month; the twelfth part of a

---

a- hat, fāte, fāre, fäther; **e-** met, mē; **i-** pin, pīne; **o-** not, nōte, ôrb, moove (move), boy, pownd;
u- cūbe, bûll, tûk (took); **ch-** chin; **th-** thick, ŧhen; **zh-** vizhon (vision); **ə-** əgo, takən, pencəl, lemən, bərd (bird).

solar year, called a 'solar month'; any one of the twelve parts into which the calendar year is divided, called a 'calendar month'; a period of four weeks or of thirty days.

month•ly, mənth/lē, a. Done, happening, or appearing, once a month or every month; continuing or lasting for a month.—n. pl., **-lies.** A periodical published once a month. Pl. Menstruation; the period of menstruating.—adv. Once a month; by the month.

mon•u•ment, mon/yə•mənt, n. Anything by which the memory of a person, period, or event is perpetuated; a memorial, art, literature, and the like, considered to have enduring value; a stone boundary marker; an area of natural beauty or historical significance which is maintained for public use by a government.

mon•u•men•tal, mon•yə•men/təl, a. Of or serving as a monument; massive or imposing; conspicuously great or gross. **—mon•u•men•tal•ly,** adv.

moo, moo, v.i. To bellow, as a cow.—n. pl., **moos.** A mooing sound or utterance.

mooch, mooch, v.i. Informal. To skulk or sneak; to hang about.—v.t. Informal. To steal (a small amount); pilfer. **—mooch•er,** n.

mood, mood, n. A temporary state of mind; pl., fits of depression or sullen behavior.—**in the mood,** favorably disposed.

mood, mood, n. A special form of verbs expressing certainty, contingency, possibility, or command. Logic. Modality. Also **mode.**

mood•y, moo/dē, a., **-i•er, -i•est.** Subject to or indulging in gloomy, melancholy, or sullen moods; expressing or indicating such ill humor: moody looks. **—mood•i•ly,** adv. **—mood•i•ness,** n.

moon, moon, n. The heavenly body which revolves around the earth; a satellite of any planet: the moons of Jupiter; the period of a revolution of the moon; something in the shape of a moon or crescent. Poet. A month.—v.i. Informal. To wander or gaze idly or moodily.—v.t. Informal. To spend idly, as time.

moon•beam, moon/bēm, n. A ray of light from the moon.

moon•light, moon/līt, n. The light afforded by the moon.—a. Illuminated by or occurring during or by moonlight; moonlit. **—moon•lit,** moon/līt, a.

moon•light•er, moon/lī•tər, n. Informal. A person who holds a second job in addition to his normal, full-time occupation. **—moon•light•ing,** n.

moon•scape, moon/skāp, n. The actual appearance of the moon's topography or a description or representation of it.

moon•shine, moon/shīn, n. The light of the moon; foolish or unrealistic talk. Informal. Illicitly distilled or smuggled liquor. **—moon•shin•er,** n.

moon•stone, moon/stōn, n. A translucent variety of feldspar used as a gem.

moon•struck, moon/strək, a. Affected mentally, supposedly by the moon's influence; dazed; lunatic; excessively romantic or sentimental. Also **moon•strick•en,** moon/strik•ən.

moon•y, moo/nē, a., **-i•er, -i•est.** Resembling the moon or moonlight; absent-minded; dreamy.

moor, mûr, n. A tract of rolling wasteland, often covered with heath; a bog.

moor, mûr, v.t. To confine or secure a boat, ship, aircraft, or the like, in a particular station by cables, anchors, chains, or the like; to fix firmly.—v.i. To be anchored or made secure with cables or chains; to secure a ship in such a manner.

Moor, mûr, n. One of the ancient inhabitants of northwestern Africa; a Mohammedan of the mixed Berber and Arab race inhabiting this region, esp. Morocco; one belonging to the group of this race which in the 8th century invaded and conquered Spain. **—Moor•ish,** a.

moor•ing, mûr/ing, n. Usu. pl. Cables, ropes, etc., by which a ship is moored; the place where a ship is moored.

moose, moos, n. pl., **moose.** A large animal of the deer family, the male of which has enormous antlers.

moot, moot, a. Subject to argument or discussion; debatable or doubtful: a moot point; impractical or insignificant; theoretical.—n. An argument or discussion, esp. of a hypothetical legal case.—v.t. To bring forward for discussion. **—moot•ness,** n.

moot court, n. A mock court which tries hypothetical legal cases as practice for law students.

mop, mop, n. A bundle of yarn or other absorbent material fastened to a stick or handle, and used for cleaning floors; something suggesting a mop: a mop of hair.—v.t., **mopped, mop•ping.** To wipe away; to clean with a mop, as a floor.—**mop up,** to finish; to defeat decisively; to clear of remaining troops.

mop, mop, n. A wry mouth; a grimace.—v.i., **mopped, mop•ping.** To make a wry face.

mope, mōp, v.i., **moped, mop•ing.** To act in a listless, dispirited manner.—v.t. To make dispirited or dejected.—n. A mopish person. Pl. Low spirits. **—mop•er,** n. **—mop•ish,** a.

mop•pet, mop/it, n. A small child; youngster.

mo•raine, mə•rān/, n. An accumulation of stones, rocks, gravel, and other debris carried and deposited by a glacier. **—mo•rain•al, mo•rain•ic,** a.

mor•al, môr/əl, mor/əl, a. Of or concerned with the principles of right and wrong in conduct and character; teaching or upholding standards of good behavior; conforming to the rules of right conduct; sexually virtuous; judged by one's conscience to be ethical or approved; capable of distinguishing between right and wrong; not proven, but sufficient for practical purposes: moral certainty; of or affecting the intellect, emotions, and conduct: a moral victory.—n. The lesson taught by a fable, parable, or story. Pl. Ethics; principles and mode of life; behavior with regard to right or wrong, esp. in relation to sexual matters. **—mor•al•ly,** adv.

mo•rale, mə•ral/, n. Mental attitude, as of soldiers, expressing courage, zeal, hope, or confidence.

mor•al•ist, môr/ə•list, mor/ə•list, n. One who teaches morals; one who practices morality. **—mor•al•is•tic,** môr•ə•lis/tik, a.

mo•ral•i•ty, mə•ral/i•tē, mô•ral/i•tē, n. pl., **-ties.** Moral quality or character; the quality of conforming to the principles of good conduct; moral or virtuous conduct; a moral lesson.

mo•ral•i•ty play, n. A kind of allegorical drama of the 15th and 16th centuries, employing personifications of virtues, vices, or other abstractions as characters.

mor•al•ize, môr/ə•līz, mor/ə•līz, v.t., **-ized, -iz•ing.** To explain in a moral sense; to draw a moral from; to improve the morals of.—v.i. To make moral reflections. **—mor•al•i•za•tion,** môr•ə•lə•zā/shən, n. **mor•al•iz•er,** n.

mo•rass, mə•ras/, n. A tract of low, soft, wet ground; a marsh; a swamp; something that entraps or delays.

mor•a•to•ri•um, môr•ə•tôr/ē•əm, môr•ə•tō/rē•əm, n. pl., **-ums, -a.** A special period of delay granted by law to debtors; the period of such a delay; any temporary suspension of activity.

mo•ray, môr/ā, n. Any of numerous voracious eels; a species common in the Mediterranean and valued as a foodfish.

mor•bid, môr/bid, a. Affected by or characteristic of disease; being in or suggesting an unhealthy mental state; unwholesomely gloomy, sensitive, or extreme. **—mor•bid•ly,** adv. **—mor•bid•i•ty,** môr•bid/ə•tē, **mor•bid•ness,** n.

mor•dant, môr/dənt, a. Pungent, caustic, sarcastic, as wit. Having the property of fixing colors, as in dyeing.—n. A substance used in dyeing to fix the coloring matter; an acid or other corrosive substance used in etching to eat out the lines. **—mor•dan•cy,** n. **—mor•dant•ly,** adv.

more, môr, môr, a., compar. of **many** or **much with**

most *as the superl.* In greater quantity, amount, measure, degree, or number; additional or further.—*n.* A greater quantity, amount, or number; something of greater importance.—*adv.* In or to a greater extent or degree; in addition; further; longer; again.—**more or less,** to an indefinite extent or measure.

more·o·ver, môr′ō′vər, môr′ō′vər, *adv.* Beyond what has been said; further; besides; also.

mo·res, môr′āz, môr′ēz, *n. pl.* Customs; manners; ways; customs prevailing among a people or a social group and accepted as right and obligatory.

mor·ga·nat·ic, môr′gə·nat′ik, *a.* A marriage in which a man of high rank takes as wife a woman of lower station, with the stipulation that neither she nor children of the marriage will have any claim to his rank or property. —**mor·ga·nat·i·cal·ly,** *adv.*

morgue, môrg, *n.* A place where the bodies of dead people are kept until identified or buried; the reference files or library in a newspaper or magazine office.

mor·i·bund, môr′ə·bənd, môr′ə·bənd, *a.* Dying; deathlike.

mo·ri·on, môr′ē·on, môr′rē·on, *n.* A kind of metal helmet having a high crest, worn during the 16th and part of the 17th centuries.

Mor·mon, môr′mən, *n.* A member of that religious body properly known as the Church of Jesus Christ of Latter-day Saints; a 4th century prophet who, according to Mormon tradition, was the author of the Book of Mormon which Joseph Smith published in 1830.—*a.* Pertaining to the Mormons or the Mormon religion. —**Mor·mon·ism,** *n.*

morn, môrn, *n. Poet.* The first part of the day; morning.

morn·ing, môr′ning, *n.* The first part of the day; dawn; the part of the day from midnight to noon; the first or early part of anything.

morn·ing-glo·ry, môr′ning·glôr·ē, môr′ning·glō·rē, *n. pl.,* -**glo·ries.** Any of various twining plants with funnel-shaped flowers of various colors.

morn·ing sick·ness, *n.* Nausea occurring in the early part of the day, characteristic of the first months of pregnancy.

morn·ing star, *n.* A bright planet, Venus, seen in the east before sunrise.

mo·roc·co, mə·rok′ō, *n.* A fine, supple, pebbled leather made from goatskins tanned with sumac. Also **mo·roc·co leath·er.**

mo·ron, môr′on, môr′on, *n.* A mentally retarded adult whose intelligence is equal to that of a normal child from 8 to 12 years of age. *Informal.* One who is stupid or foolish. —**mo·ron·ic,** mə·ron′ik, *a.* —**mo·ron·i·cal·ly,** *adv.*

mo·rose, mə·rōs′, *a.* Of a sullen disposition; gloomy. —**mo·rose·ly,** *adv.* —**mo·rose·ness,** *n.*

mor·pheme, môr′fēm, *n. Ling.* The smallest meaningful unit of a language that cannot be divided into smaller meaningful parts.

mor·phine, môr′fēn, *n.* A bitter crystalline drug, derived from opium, used in medicine to dull pain or induce sleep. Also **mor·phi·a,** môr′fē·ə.

mor·phol·o·gy, môr·fol′ə·jē, *n.* The study of the form and structure of plants and animals. The form of words as affected by inflection, derivation, and composition; the study of word formation. —**mor·pho·log·ic,** môr·fə·loj′ik, **mor·pho·log·i·cal,** *a.* —**mor·phol·o·gist,** *n.*

Mor·ris chair, môr′is, mor′is, *n.* A comfortable armchair with an adjustable back and cushions that can be removed.

mor·row, môr′ō, mor′ō, *n.* The next day after the present or after some other specified day.

Morse code, môrs, *n.* A system of dots, dashes, and spaces, or the corresponding sounds or signals, used in telegraphy and signaling to represent letters of the alphabet or numerals.

mor·sel, môr′səl, *n.* A bite; a small piece of food; a fragment; a little piece of anything.

mor·tal, môr′təl, *a.* Subject to death; causing death; fatal; pertaining to death: *mortal* pain; extreme; dire; human. *Theol.* Incurring the penalty of spiritual death or divine condemnations. *Informal.* Tiresome and prolonged; conceivable or imaginable.—*n.* A being subject to death; a human being. —**mor·tal·ly,** *adv.*

mor·tal·i·ty, môr′tal′i·tē, *n. pl.,* -**ties.** The state of being mortal; frequency of death; the number of deaths in proportion to a population; the human race; humanity.

mor·tar, môr′tər, *n.* A sturdy, bowl-shaped vessel in which substances are reduced to powder with a pestle; a cannon for throwing shells at high angles.

mor·tar, môr′tər, *n.* A mixture of quicklime or cement combined with sand and water and used for binding together stones or bricks.—*v.t.* To bind together or fix with mortar.

mor·tar·board, môr′tər·bôrd, *n.* A square board used by masons to hold mortar; an academic cap with a flat, square top and tassel worn at graduation and other ceremonies.

mort·gage, môr′gij, *n.* A transfer of property to a creditor as security for the repayment of money; the deed by which such a transaction is effected.—*v.t.,* -**gaged,** -**gag·ing.** To convey or place under a mortgage: to *mortgage* land; to pledge: to *mortgage* one's future for a present advantage. —**mort·ga·gee,** môr·gə·jē′, *n.* —**mort·ga·ger, mort·ga·gor,** *n.*

mor·ti·cian, môr·tish′ən, *n.* An undertaker.

mor·ti·fy, môr′tə·fī, *v.t.,* -**fied,** -**fy·ing.** To subdue or bring into subjection, as passions, by abstinence or rigorous severities; to humiliate; to chagrin; to affect with gangrene or decay.—*v.i.* To observe rigorous self-discipline; to become gangrenous. —**mor·ti·fi·ca·tion,** môr·tə·fə·kā′shən, *n.*

mor·tise, môr′tis, *n.* A hole or notch cut in a piece of material, as wood, to fit a corresponding projecting piece, called a tenon, on another piece in order to join the two together.—*v.t.,* -**tised,** -**tis·ing.** To cut a mortise in; to join securely. Also **mor·tice.**

mort·main, môrt′mān, *n. Law.* Inalienable possession of lands or buildings by a religious or other corporation.

mor·tu·ar·y, môr′chū·er·ē, *n. pl.,* -**ies.** A place for the temporary reception of the dead; a funeral home. —*a.* Pertaining to the burial of the dead.

mo·sa·ic, mō·zā′ik, *n.* A picture or design, made by inlaying and cementing together small pieces of colored glass, enamel, or stones; the process of making such an object; any arrangement or design similar to a mosaic.—*a.* Like or pertaining to a mosaic.

Mo·sa·ic, mō·zā′ik, *a.* Relating to Moses, the Hebrew lawgiver, or to his writings and institutions.

mo·sey, mō′zē, *v.i.,* -**seyed,** -**sey·ing.** *Informal.* Move, or go along or away; to move leisurely.

Mos·lem, moz′ləm, mos′ləm, *n.* One who adheres to Islam and surrenders to the will of Allah.—*a.* Of or pertaining to the customs, laws, and religion of Islam.

mosque, mosk, *n.* A Moslem temple or place of worship.

mos·qui·to, mə·skē′tō, *n. pl.,* -**toes,** -**tos.** Any of various dipterous insects, the females having a long proboscis with which they puncture the skin of animals, including man, to suck blood.

mos·qui·to net, *n.* A screen, curtain, or canopy of gauze or fine net for keeping out mosquitoes.

moss, môs, mos, *n.* A small, simple, flowerless plant which forms carpets of vegetation on the ground, rocks, or tree bark, and reproduces by spores.—*v.t.* To cover with moss. —**moss·like,** *a.* —**moss·y,** *a.,* -**i·er,** -**i·est.**

moss·back, môs′bak, mos′bak, *n. Informal.* A very

---

a- hat, fāte, fāre, fàther; e- met, mē; i- pin, pīne; o- not, nōte, ôrb, moove (move), boy, pownd; u- cūbe, bŭll, tûk (took); ch- chin; th- thick, then; zh- vizhon (vision); ə- əgo, takən, pencəl, lemən, bərd (bird).

conservative person.

most, mōst, *a., irreg. superl.* of **many** and **much.** Greatest in any way; greatest in number, amount, or extent; amounting to a majority: *most* people.—*adv.* In the greatest or highest degree, quantity, or extent. —*n., pl. in constr.* The greatest number; the majority; the greatest amount, degree, or advantage.—**at most, at the most,** to the utmost extent.—**for the most part,** mostly.—**make the most of,** to use fully.—**the most.** *Informal.* The greatest; the best.

most·ly, mōst/lē, *adv.* For the most part; almost all; chiefly; mainly.

mot, mō, *n.* A pithy or witty saying.

mote, mōt, *n.* A small particle; a speck.

mo·tel, mō·tel/, *n.* A lodging place, esp. designed for motorists, and open directly to parking. Also **mo·tor court, tour·ist court.**

mo·tet, mō·tet/, *n.* A sacred polyphonic song, usu. unaccompanied.

moth, môth, moth, *n. pl.,* **moths,** môthz, môths. Any of the numerous, usu. nocturnal lepidopterous insects distinguished from the butterflies by their stouter bodies, smaller wings, and less colorful appearance.

moth·ball, môth/bôl, moth/bôl, *n.* A ball of camphor or naphthalene used for repelling moths from stored clothing. Also **moth ball.**

moth-ball, môth/bôl, moth/bôl, *a. Milit.* In protective storage or reserve, as naval vessels, airplanes, tanks, and the like.—*v.t.* To put in storage. Also **moth-ball.**

moth-eat·en, môth/ēt·ən, moth/ēt·ən, *a.* Eaten or damaged by or as if by moths; worn out.

moth·er, məth/ər, *n.* The female who gives birth to a child; a female parent or guardian; something that gives rise to, or exercises protective care over something else: necessity, the *mother* of invention. The head or superior of a female religious community; an elderly woman; the qualities characteristic of a mother.—*a.* Bearing a relation like that of a mother: a *mother* plant or cell; pertaining to or characteristic of a mother: *mother* love; derived from one's mother, native: *mother* tongue.—*v.t.* To be the mother of; give origin or rise to; to care for or protect as a mother does; to acknowledge or claim parentage, authorship of; to assume as one's own; to provide with a mother. —**moth·er·less,** *a.*

moth·er, məth/ər, *n.* A thick, slimy substance composed of bacteria that gathers on the surface of fermenting liquids and produces fermentation, esp. in changing wine or cider to vinegar.

moth·er·hood, məth/ər·hůd, *n.* The state of being a mother; maternity; the qualities or spirit of a mother; mothers collectively.

Moth·er Hub·bard, həb/ərd, *n.* A kind of full, loose gown worn by women.

moth·er-in-law, məth/ər·in·lô, *n. pl.,* **moth·ers-in-law.** The mother of one's husband or wife.

moth·er·land, məth/ər·land, *n.* One's native country; the land of one's ancestors.

moth·er·ly, məth/ər·lē, *a.* Pertaining to or befitting a mother; like a mother; tender and affectionate.—*adv.* —**moth·er·li·ness,** *n.*

moth·er-of-pearl, məth/ər·əv·perl/, *n.* A hard, iridescent lining of certain shells, as that of the pearl oyster; nacre.—*a.*

Moth·er's Day, *n.* A day in honor of mothers, observed annually in the U.S. on the second Sunday in May.

moth·er tongue, *n.* One's native language; a language to which other languages owe their origin.

mo·tif, mō·tēf/, *n.* A repeated theme in a musical, artistic, or literary work; a repeated design, as in lace.

mo·tile, mōt/əl, mō/til, *a. Biol.* Moving, or capable of moving, spontaneously. —**mo·til·i·ty,** mō·til/i·tē, *n.*

mo·tion, mō/shən, *n.* The process of moving or changing place or position; a suggestion or proposal formally made to a deliberative assembly: a *motion* to adjourn; an inward prompting, impulse or inclination.

Law. An application made to a court or a judge for an order, ruling, or the like.—*v.t.* To direct by a significant motion or gesture.—*v.i.* To make a significant motion or gesture. —**mo·tion·less,** *a.* —**mo·tion·less·ly,** *adv.* —**mo·tion·less·ness,** *n.*

mo·tion pic·ture, *n.* A series of photographs projected on a screen in rapid succession, giving the illusion of continuous movement; a play, performance, event, or demonstration presented by this method. *Pl.* The business of creating, producing, or marketing a motion picture.

mo·tion sick·ness, *n.* Discomfort, often including dizziness and nausea, which some people suffer while riding in moving vehicles.

mo·ti·vate, mō/tə·vāt, *v.t.,* **-vat·ed, -vat·ing.** To furnish with a motive; to impel; to induce. —**mo·ti·va·tion,** mō·tə·vā/shən, *n.* —**mo·ti·va·tion·al,** *a.*

mo·tive, mō/tiv, *n.* Something, as a reason or emotion, that impels a person to a certain action or behavior; motif.—*a.* Causing motion; inducing action; forming a motive.—*v.t.* To supply a motive to or for; to prompt; to relate to the theme or prevailing idea.

mot·ley, mot/lē, *a.* Consisting of different colors; composed of an assortment of elements or types; dressed in a garment of several colors.—*n.* An unlikely mixture; a many-colored garment worn by a jester.

mo·tor, mō/tər, *n.* That which imparts motion; a prime mover, as a steam engine, which receives and modifies energy from some natural source in order to utilize it in driving machinery; a machine for converting electric energy into rotary motion; an internal-combustion engine in an automobile, motorboat, or the like; a motorcar.—*a.* Causing or imparting motion; pertaining to or operated by a motor. *Physiol.* Conveying an impulse that results or tends to result in motion, as a nerve; of or pertaining to such nerves.—*v.i.* To drive, ride, or travel in an automobile.—*v.t.* To convey in an automobile.

mo·tor·bike, mō/tər·bīk, *n.* A bicycle propelled by a motor; a small, lightweight motorcycle.

mo·tor·boat, mō/tər·bōt, *n.* A boat driven by a motor. Also **pow·er boat.**

mo·tor·bus, mō/tər·bəs, *n.* A public passenger vehicle. Also **mo·tor coach.**

mo·tor·cade, mō/tər·kād, *n.* A public procession of motorcars or other motor vehicles.

mo·tor·car, mō/tər·kär, *n.* Automobile.

mo·tor court, *n.* Motel.

mo·tor·cy·cle, mō/tər·sī·kəl, *n.* A two-wheeled vehicle propelled by an internal-combustion engine. —*v.i.,* **-cled, -cling.** —**mo·tor·cy·clist,** *n.*

mo·tor·ist, mō/tər·ist, *n.* One who drives an automobile.

mo·tor·ize, mō/tər·īz, *v.t.,* **-ized, -iz·ing.** To provide with a motor or with motor-powered equipment. —**mo·tor·i·za·tion,** mō·tər·i·zā/shən, *n.*

mo·tor·man, mō/tər·mən, *n. pl.,* **-men.** One who operates a vehicle, as a streetcar, subway train, or electric locomotive.

mo·tor pool, *n.* A number of cars owned by the military, a single company, or a government agency and made available for necessary staff use.

mo·tor scoot·er, *n.* A scooterlike vehicle usu. having two wheels separated by a low footboard, and equipped with a motor and a seat for the driver.

mo·tor ve·hi·cle, *n.* Any conveyance powered by a motor and equipped with rubber tires to travel on roads.

mot·tle, mot/əl, *v.t.,* **-tled, -tling.** To mark with spots or blotches of a different color or shade.—*n.* A spotted or blotched appearance. —**mot·tled,** *a.* —**mot·tler,** *n.*

mot·to, mot/ō, *n. pl.,* **-toes, -tos.** A sentence, phrase, or word inscribed on anything as indicative of or appropriate to its purpose or character; a maxim adopted as expressing one's guiding idea or principle.

mound, mownd, *n.* A man-made elevation of earth, rocks, gravel, or the like; a natural hillock or knoll; any pile or heap: a *mound* of discarded clothes. *Baseball.* The elevation on which the pitcher stands when delivering the ball.—*v.t.* To fortify or enclose with a mound; to pile up into a mound.

mount, mownt, *n.* A hill; a mountain; now chiefly poetical, or used in proper names: *Mount* Sinai. The cardboard or other material on which a picture is mounted; the setting of a gem; a hinge used by collectors to affix stamps; a slide used to support objects prepared for microscopic examination; an animal, esp. a horse, used for riding; the manner of mounting an animal or an instance of it.—*v.i.* To increase; to place on high; to go up; to ascend; to get on or upon anything, esp. to get on a horse.—*v.t.* To ascend; to climb up to or upon; to place oneself upon; to furnish with a horse; to raise up; to lift onto a horse; to put on a support: to *mount* a map; to prepare for use: to *mount* a specimen on a slide for microscopic examination; to be equipped with; to do guard duty: to *mount* guard; to start. —**mount·a·ble,** *a.* —**mount·er,** *n.*

moun·tain, mown′tən, *n.* A mass of earth rising higher than a hill above the level of the adjacent land; a large pile.—*a.* Characterizing mountains; inhabiting a mountain; similar to a mountain, as in size.

moun·tain·eer, mown·tə·nēr′, *n.* An inhabitant of a mountainous district; a climber of mountains.—*v.i.* To climb mountains.

moun·tain goat, *n.* A goat native to the mountainous regions of the northwestern U.S. and Canada. Also **Rock·y Moun·tain goat.**

moun·tain li·on, *n.* A puma. Also **cou·gar.**

moun·tain·ous, mown′tə·nəs, *a.* Full of mountains; large as a mountain; huge.

moun·te·bank, mown′tə·bangk, *n.* A quack doctor; any boastful and false pretender; a charlatan.

mount·ing, mown′ting, *n.* That with which an article is mounted, set off, or finished for use.

mourn, mōrn, môrn, *v.i.* To express grief or sorrow; to grieve.—*v.t.* To grieve for; to deplore. —**mourn·er,** *n.*

mourn·ful, mōrn′fəl, môrn′fəl, *a.* Expressing sorrow; causing sorrow; feeling grief. —**mourn·ful·ly,** *adv.* —**mourn·ful·ness,** *n.*

mourn·ing, mōr′ning, môr′ning, *n.* The act of expressing grief; the dress or customary habit worn by mourners.—*a.* Employed to express grief: a *mourning* ring. —**mourn·ing·ly,** *adv.*

mouse, mows, *n. pl.,* **mice,** mīs. Any of various small rodents. *Informal.* A timid individual.—*v.i.,* **moused, mous·ing.** To hunt for or catch mice.—*v.t.* To hunt out, as a cat does mice.

mous·er, mow′zər, *n.* A cat or other animal good at catching mice.

mous·tache, məs′tash, mə·stash′, *n.* Mustache.

mous·y, mows′ē, *a.,* **-i·er, -i·est.** Resembling or characteristic of a mouse; timid; quiet; drab; infested with mice. Also **mous·ey.**

mouth, mowth, *n. pl.,* **mouths,** mowthz. The opening through which man or animals take in food; something providing entrance or exit: the *mouth* of a river.—mowth, *v.t.* To speak in a pompous manner; to speak without understanding or sincere feeling; to rub with the mouth or lips. —**mouthed,** mowthd, mowtht, *a.* —**mouth·er,** mow′thər, *n.*

mouth·ful, mowth′fŭl, *n. pl.,* **-fuls.** As much as a mouth can hold; as much as is taken into the mouth at one time; a small quantity. *Informal.* A speech sound or succession of sounds difficult to utter.—**say a mouth·ful.** *Informal.* To make a wise or important observation.

mouth or·gan, *n.* Harmonica; panpipe.

mouth·piece, mowth′pēs, *n.* That part of an apparatus which is held against, close to, or in the mouth, as of a musical instrument; an agency or person express-

ing the sentiments or views of another or a group; a spokesman. *Informal.* A criminal lawyer.

mouth·y, mow′thē, mow′thē, *a.,* **-i·er, -i·est.** Loud-mouthed; garrulous; bombastic. —**mouth·i·ness,** *n.*

mou·ton, moo′ton, *n.* Sheepskin which has been treated to resemble seal or beaver fur.

mov·a·ble, moo′və·bəl, *a.* Capable of being moved. —*n.* Often *pl.* Anything capable of being moved, as goods, wares, commodities, furniture. *Pl. Law.* A piece of personal property. Also **move·a·ble.** —**mov·a·ble·ness, mov·a·bil·i·ty,** moo·və·bil′ə·tē, *n.* —**mov·a·bly,** *adv.*

move, moov, *v.t.,* **moved, mov·ing.** To cause to change place or posture; to set in motion; to rouse or excite the feelings of, esp. tender feelings; to change the position of, as a piece in a board game. *Parl.* To offer, as a formal proposal, for consideration by a deliberative assembly.—*v.i.* To change place or posture; to change residence; to take action; to begin to act; to progress; to initiate action: to *move* on the project.—*n.* Proceeding; action taken; the moving of a piece in playing chess.—**on the move.** *Informal.* To be busy or active. —**mov·er,** *n.* —**mov·ing,** *a.*

move·ment, moov′mənt, *n.* The act of moving; an individual act or manner of motion; a tactical or strategic relocation of troops; a loosely organized body of individuals or groups working toward some general goal; the moving parts of a mechanism; a detached and independent portion of a composition; rhythm; the voiding of the bowels.

mov·ie, moo′vē, *n. Informal.* A motion picture.

mov·ing pic·ture, *n.* Motion picture.

mow, mow, *n.* A pile of hay or sheaves of grain deposited in a barn; the part of a barn where they are stored.

mow, mō, *v.t.,* **mowed; mowed** or **mown; mow·ing.** To cut down with a scythe or mowing machine, as grass; to cut down indiscriminately, or in great numbers or quantity, as men in a battle.—*v.i.* To cut grass; to use the scythe or mowing machine. —**mow·er,** *n.*

mox·ie, mok′sē, *n. Informal.* Courage; vigor; energy; aggressiveness.

Mr., mis′tər, *n. pl.,* **Messrs.,** mes′ərz. Mister: a title of address preceding the name, or certain official titles, of a man.

Mrs., mis′iz, *n. pl.,* **Mmes.,** mad′əmz. A title of address preceding the name of a married woman.

Ms., miz, *n.* A title of address preceding the name of a woman (either married or unmarried).

much, mәch, *a.,* **more, most.** Great in quantity or amount.—*adv.* To a great amount or extent: nearly: *much* as it was.—*n.* A great quantity; a noteworthy or important thing. —**much·ness,** *n.*

mu·ci·lage, mū′sə·lij, *n.* Any preparation of glue or gummy substance used for adhesion; any of several gummy, gelatinous substances secreted by plants. —**mu·ci·lag·i·nous,** mū·sə·laj′ə·nəs, *a.*

muck, mәk, *n.* Farmyard dung, or decaying vegetable matter, in a moist state; manure; filth; dirt; anything foul or disgusting.—*v.t.* To manure; to dirty or soil; to remove muck from. —**muck·y,** *a.*

muck·rake, mәk′rāk, *v.i.,* **muck·raked, muck·rak·ing.** To expose corruption, real or alleged, esp. in politics; defame. —**muck·rak·er,** *n.*

mu·cous, mū′kəs, *a.* Pertaining to or resembling mucus; slimy; secreting a slimy substance. —**mu·cos·i·ty,** mū·kos′i·tē, *n.*

mu·cous mem·brane, *n.* A membrane that lines all the cavities of the body which open externally, and which secretes mucus.

mu·cus, mū′kəs, *n.* A viscid fluid secreted by the mucous membranes.

mud, mәd, *n.* Wet and soft earth. *Informal.* An abusive charge or remark.—*v.t.,* **mud·ded, mud·ding.** To

---

a- hat, fāte, fāre, fäther; **e-** met, mē; **i-** pin, pīne; **o-** not, nōte, ôrb, moove (move), boy, pownd; **u-** cūbe, bŭll, tŭk (took); **ch-** chin; **th-** thick, ŧhen; **zh-** vizhon (vision); **ə-** əgo, takən, pencəl, lemən, bərd (bird).

smear with or as with mud; to stir up the muddy sediment of.

mud·dle, məd′əl, *v.t.*, **mud·dled, mud·dling.** To confuse with drink; to mix up or jumble together in a confused or bungling way.—*v.i.* To think or act in a confused, ineffective way, with *through.*—*n.* A mess; confusion in thought or action. —**mud·dler,** *n.*

mud·dy, məd′ē, *a.*, **-di·er, -di·est.** Abounding in mud; cloudy, as color; confused or vague, as in expression or thought; dull or unclear, as the mind.—*v.t.*, **mud·died, mud·dy·ing.** To soil with mud; to cloud or make dull.—*v.i.* To become soiled with mud. —**mud·di·ly,** *adv.* —**mud·di·ness,** *n.*

mu·ez·zin, mū·ez′in, *n.* An Islamic crier who, from a mosque, summons the faithful to prayer.

muff, məf, *n.* A tubular cover, usu. made of fur, into which both hands are placed to keep them warm; any failure or inept action. *Sports.* A bungled catch.—*v.t.*, *v.i. Informal.* To bungle; to miss a chance.

muf·fin, məf′in, *n.* A quick bread baked in individual cup-shaped molds.

muf·fle, məf′əl, *v.t.*, **muf·fled, muf·fling.** To enfold or wrap so as to conceal from view or protect from the weather; to deaden the sound of: to *muffle* an oar or a drum; to deaden, as sound, by or as by wrappings.

muf·fler, məf′lər, *n.* Anything used for muffling, esp. a scarf or wrapping worn around the neck or throat for warmth; any of various devices for deadening such sound as that of the escaping gases of an internal-combustion engine.

muf·ti, məf′tē, *n.* Civilian dress as opposed to military or other uniform.

mug, məg, *n.* A drinking vessel, usu. cylindrical and commonly with a handle; the quantity it holds; the face.—*v.t.*, **mugged, mug·ging.** *Informal.* To assault, usu. with the intent of robbing.—*v.i. Informal.* To grimace; to overact or assume a funny or exaggerated face. —**mug·ger,** *n.*

mug·gy, məg′ē, *a.*, **-gi·er, -gi·est.** Damp and close, as the weather; warm and humid. —**mug·gi·ness,** *n.*

mu·lat·to, mə·lat′ō, myû·lat′ō, *n. pl.*, **-toes.** The offspring of parents of whom one is Caucasian and the other Negro.—*a.* Like a mulatto in color.

mul·ber·ry, məl′ber·ē, *n. pl.*, **-ries.** The usu. dark red or purple edible fruit or berry of a tree; the tree itself, one variety of which has leaves that are used for silkworm culture; a dark red or purplish color.

mulch, məlch, *n.* A loose covering of an organic material, such as peat moss, straw, or manure, spread on the ground around plantings to improve the soil and to check freezing, erosion, evaporation, and weed growth.—*v.t.* To cover or to protect (herbs or young trees) with mulch.

mulct, məlkt, *n.* A fine or penalty.—*v.t.* To punish by fine or forfeiture; to defraud; to swindle.

mule, mūl, *n.* A hybrid mammal, the offspring of an ass and a mare, or of a horse and a she-ass; a spinning machine combining the drawing rollers of Arkwright and the jenny of Hargreaves. *Informal.* A stubborn person.

mule, mūl, *n.* A backless slipper.

mule skin·ner, *n. Informal.* A driver of mules.

mu·le·teer, mū·lə·tēr′, *n.* One who drives mules.

mul·ish, mū′lish, *a.* Like a mule; stubborn. —**mul·ish·ly,** *adv.* —**mul·ish·ness,** *n.*

mull, məl, *v.i. Informal.* To study or ruminate, often followed by *over.*

mull, məl, *v.t.* To heat, sweeten, and flavor with spices, as wine.

mul·let, məl′it, *n. pl.*, **-let, -lets.** A fish having two long barbels at the mouth and red coloration; various species of fish with a cylindrical body and gray coloration.

mul·li·gan, məl′ə·gən, *n. Informal.* A stew of meat and vegetables. Also **mul·li·gan stew.**

mul·li·ga·taw·ny, məl·i·gə·tô′nē, *n.* An East Indian curry soup.

mul·lion, məl′yən, *n.* A vertical division between the lights of windows, screens, or doors; a division between the panels in wainscoting. —**mul·lioned,** *a.*

mul·ti·far·i·ous, məl·tə·fār′ē·əs, *a.* Having great multiplicity, diversity, or variety; made up of many different parts. —**mul·ti·far·i·ous·ly,** *adv.* —**mul·ti·far·i·ous·ness,** *n.*

mul·ti·lat·er·al, mul·ti·lat′ər·əl, *a.* Having many sides; polygonal; having three or more parties or nations as participants.

mul·ti·mil·lion·aire, məl·ti·mil·yən·ār′, *n.* A very wealthy individual; one whose wealth is measured in the millions.

mul·ti·ple, məl′tə·pəl, *a.* Consisting of, having, or involving many individuals, parts, elements, or relations.—*n.* A number into which another number may be divided without a remainder: 12 is a *multiple* of 3; a common multiple of two or more numbers, as a number that can be divided by each of them without a remainder.

mul·ti·ple scle·ro·sis, *n.* A serious disease in which parts of the brain and spinal cord harden, causing muscle tremors, partial paralysis, etc.

mul·ti·pli·cand, məl·tə·pli·kand′, *n.* The number to be multiplied by another, which is called the multiplier.

mul·ti·pli·ca·tion, məl·tə·plə·kā′shen, *n.* The act or process of multiplying; the operation by which any given number or quantity may be added to itself any number of times.

mul·ti·plic·i·ty, məl·tə·plis′i·tē, *n.* A great number.

mul·ti·pli·er, məl′tə·pli·ər, *n.* One who or that which multiplies; the number in arithmetic by which another is multiplied.

mul·ti·ply, məl′tə·pli, *v.t.*, **-plied, -ply·ing.** To increase in number; to add to itself any given number of times.—*v.i.* To grow or increase in number; to arrive at the product by the process of multiplication. —məl′tə·plē, *adv.* —**mul·ti·pli·a·ble,** *a.*

mul·ti·tude, məl′tə·tood, məl′tə·tūd, *n.* A great number, collectively; a crowd.—**the multitude,** the common people.

mul·ti·tu·di·nous, məl·tə·tū′də·nəs, məl·tə·too′də·nəs, *a.* Pertaining or belonging to a multitude; consisting of a multitude. —**mul·ti·tu·di·nous·ly,** *adv.* —**mul·ti·tu·di·nous·ness,** *n.*

mum, məm, *a.* Silent; not speaking.—**mum's the word,** say nothing about it.

mum, məm, *n.* Chrysanthemum.

mum·ble, məm′bəl, *v.i.*, *v.t.*, **-bled, -bling.** To mutter; to speak unintelligibly or indistinctly.—*n.* A mumbled utterance. —**mum·bler,** *n.* —**mum·bling·ly,** *adv.*

Mum·bo Jum·bo, məm′bō jəm′bō, *n.* A god of certain African tribes; (*l.c.*) any senseless object of popular idolatry; any involved yet meaningless ritual or incantation. (*L.c.*). *Informal.* Contrived, ostentatious, or unintelligible language; gobbledygook.

mum·mer, məm′ər, *n.* A masked celebrant, esp. at holiday festivals; an actor, esp. in a pantomime.

mum·mer·y, məm′ər·ē, *n.* A masking or masquerade; a farcical show; hypocritical ceremony.

mum·mi·fy, məm′ə·fī, *v.t.*, **-fied, -fy·ing.** To make into a mummy; to embalm and dry, as a mummy. —**mum·mi·fi·ca·tion,** məm·ə·fə·kā′shen, *n.*

mum·my, məm′ē, *n. pl.*, **-mies.** A dead human body embalmed and dried after the manner of those found in Egyptian tombs; something which resembles a mummy.—*v.t.*, **-mied, -my·ing.** To embalm; mummify.

mumps, məmps, *n. pl. but sing. in constr.* A disease consisting of an inflammation of the salivary glands, with swelling along the neck.

munch, mənch, *v.t.*, *v.i.* To chew, sometimes audibly. —**munch·er,** *n.*

mun·dane, mən·dān′, mən′dān, *a.* Of or relating to the world; earthly; routine; ordinary; unexalted. —**mun·dane·ly,** *adv.*

mu·nic·i·pal, mū·nis′ə·pəl, *a.* Pertaining to local

self-government; pertaining to the corporation of a town or city, or to the citizens of a municipality. **—mu·nic·i·pal·ly,** *adv.*

mu·nic·i·pal·i·ty, mū·nis·ə·pal′ə·tē, *n.* A town, city, or borough which has local self-government.

mu·nif·i·cent, myū·nif′i·sənt, *a.* Giving with great generosity or liberality. **—mu·nif·i·cence,** *n.* **—mu·nif·i·cent·ly,** *adv.*

mu·ni·tion, myū·nish′ən, *n. Usu. pl.* Materials used in war for defense or attack.—*a.* Pertaining to munitions: a *munition* ship.—*v.t.* To provide with munitions.

mu·ral, myûr′əl, *a.* Pertaining to or resembling a wall; affixed or applied to a wall.—*n.* A painting executed directly on a wall or ceiling. **—mu·ral·ist,** *n.*

mur·der, mər′dər, *n.* The act of unlawfully killing a human being by another human with premeditated malice.—*v.t.* To kill a human being with premeditated malice. *Fig.* To abuse or violate grossly: to *murder* the queen's English.—*v.i.* To commit murder. **—mur·der·er, mur·der·ess,** *n.*

mur·der·ous, mər′dər·əs, *a.* Pertaining to murder; guilty of murder; accompanied or marked by murder; capable of or intending murder; deadly; bloody. **—mur·der·ous·ly,** *adv.* **—mur·der·ous·ness,** *n.*

mu·ri·at·ic ac·id, myûr·ē·at′ik, *n.* A commercial grade of hydrochloric acid.

murk, mirk, mərk, *n.* Darkness or gloom.

murk·y, mər′kē, *a.,* **-i·er, -i·est.** Dark; obscure; gloomy; thick, as a fog. **—murk·i·ly,** *adv.* **—murk·i·ness,** *n.*

mur·mur, mər′mər, *n.* A low, continuous or continually repeated sound, as that of a stream; a low indistinct sound or hum; a complaint uttered in a low, muttering voice; a sound emitted by the heart which is a sign of an abnormality.—*v.i.* To utter or give out a murmur or hum.—*v.t.* To utter indistinctly; mutter. **—mur·mur·er,** *n.* **—mur·mur·ing,** *n.,* *a.* **—mur·mur·ing·ly,** *adv.*

mur·rain, mər′in, *n.* Any of several diseases that affect cattle, as hoof-and-mouth disease.

mus·cat, məs′kat, məs′kat, *n.* Any of several varieties of grape, usually of light color, and having the flavor or odor of musk: grown for making wine and raisins; the wine so made. Also **mus·ca·tel.**

mus·ca·tel, məs·kə·tel′, *n.* A strong, rich, sweet wine made from muscat grapes; the muscat grape. Also **mus·cat, mus·ca·del.**

mus·cle, məs′əl, *n.* A tissue consisting of elongated fibers which contract on stimulation and produce bodily motion; a contractive organ, consisting of muscle tissue; physical strength; effective force: put *muscle* into the orders.—*v.i.* **-cled, -cling.** *Informal.* To gain one's way or encroach using force or threats, usu. followed by *in.*—*v.t. Informal.* To force or threaten.

mus·cle-bound, məs′əl·bownd, *a.* Having the muscles enlarged, overstrained, and inelastic, as by overexercise.

mus·cu·lar, məs′kyə·lər, *a.* Pertaining to or consisting of muscles; performed by or dependent on muscles; having well-developed muscles; strong or brawny; strong or forceful, esp. with the suggestion of a lack of grace or subtlety. **—mus·cu·lar·i·ty,** məs·kyə·lar′i·tē, *n.* **—mus·cu·lar·ly,** *adv.*

mus·cu·lar dys·tro·phy, dis·trə·fē, *n.* A disease which results in progressive degeneration and atrophy of muscle tissue.

mus·cu·la·ture, məs′kyə·lə·chûr, *n.* The system of muscles; the muscle arrangement in an organ.

Muse, mūz, *n. (Sometimes l.c.)* The spirit or power which is said to inspire artistic creation.

muse, mūz, *v.i.,* **mused, mus·ing.** To think or to meditate in silence; to say thoughtfully.—*v.t.* To think or meditate on. **—mus·er,** *n.* **—mus·ing,** *a.,* *n.* **—mus·ing·ly,** *adv.*

mu·se·um, mū·zē′əm, *n.* A building or area used for exhibiting interesting objects connected with literature, art, science, history, or nature.

mush, məsh, *n.* Meal, usu. cornmeal, boiled in water or milk until it becomes thick and soft; any thick, soft matter or mass. *Informal.* Maudlin sentiment or sentimental language. **—mush·y, -i·er, -i·est,** *a.* **—mush·i·ly,** *adv.* **—mush·i·ness,** *n.*

mush, məsh, *Interj.* The call to start a team of dogs.

mush·room, məsh′room, məsh′rûm, *n.* Any of various rapidly growing, fleshy fungi such as toadstools and morels; any of certain edible species typically having a stalk with an umbrella-like cap; anything of similar shape or of correspondingly rapid growth.—*a.* Of, pertaining to, or made of mushrooms; resembling or suggesting a mushroom in shape.—*v.i.* To have or assume the shape of a mushroom; to sprout, multiply, or develop quickly.

mu·sic, mū′zik, *n.* The art of organizing or arranging sounds into meaningful patterns or forms, usu. involving pitch, harmony, and rhythm; a musical piece or composition; the sound of a musical composition when it is performed; the written or printed score of a composition; a pleasing sound or sounds; euphony. **—face the music,** to accept or take the consequences of one's actions or mistakes.

mu·si·cal, mū′zi·kəl, *a.* Of, pertaining to, or producing music; of the nature of or resembling music; set to or accompanied by music: a *musical* comedy; fond of or skilled in music.—*n.* Musical comedy; a musicale. **—mu·si·cal·ly,** *adv.* **—mu·si·cal·i·ty,** mū·zi·kal′i·tē, **mu·si·cal·ness,** *n.*

mu·si·cal com·e·dy, *n.* A humorous play or film with a plot that is interspersed with songs and dances.

mu·si·cale, mū·zə·kal′, *n.* A social entertainment featuring music.

mu·si·cian, mū·zish′ən, *n.* A person skilled in the composition or performance of music. **—mu·si·cian·ship,** *n.*

musk, məsk, *n.* A substance secreted by the male musk deer, having a strong, lasting odor, and much used in perfumery; a similar secretion of other animals; an artificial imitation of the substance; the odor, or some similar odor. **—musk·y, -i·er, -i·est,** *a.* **—musk·i·ness,** *n.*

musk deer, *n.* A small, hornless, Asian deer, the male of which has a gland containing musk.

mus·kel·lunge, məs′kə·lənj, *n. pl.,* **-lunge.** A large variety of pike found in the lakes and rivers of northern U.S. and Canada. Also **mus·kie.**

mus·ket, məs′kit, *n.* A large-caliber, smoothbore firearm, first developed in the 16th century.

mus·ket·eer, məs·ki·tēr′, *n.* A soldier armed with a musket.

mus·ket·ry, məs′ki·trē, *n.* Musketeers collectively; the art or science of firing small arms.

musk·mel·on, məsk′mel·ən, *n.* A cultivated, herbaceous, trailing vine in the gourd family, with a fleshy, edible fruit; the fruit itself, globular or oblong, often furrowed or warty, with a musky-odored rind and sweet, aromatic yellow-to green flesh; cantaloupe.

musk·rat, məsk′rat, *n. pl.,* **-rat, -rats.** A large, essentially aquatic, fur-bearing, N. American rodent with a long, scaly, sparsely-haired tail, partially webbed hind feet, and a musky odor; the brown fur of this animal.

mus·lin, məz′lin, *n.* A thin cotton fabric made in various degrees of sheerness or fineness, and often printed, woven, or embroidered in patterns; a heavier cotton cloth, bleached or unbleached.

muss, məs, *n. Informal.* A state of disorder, or an untidy or dirty mess.—*v.t. Informal.* To put into disorder; make untidy or messy; rumple. **—mus·sy, -si·er, -si·est,** *a.*

mus·sel, məs′əl, *n.* A bivalve mollusk, in particular an

---

edible marine mollusk.

must, məst, *aux. v.* To be obliged, bound, or compelled to by moral principle, law, order, command, threat of physical force, logical necessity or natural law; to be supposed: It *must* be very late; to be certain: Peace *must* follow.—*n. Informal.* Anything necessary; an essential.—*a.* Necessary; essential.

mus·tache, məs′tash, mə·stash′, *n.* The hair growing on the upper lip or on either half of the upper lip of men. Also **mous·tache, mus·ta·chio,** məs·tä′shō.

mus·tang, məs′tang, *n.* The small, wild horse of western N. America, a descendant of horses imported from Spain.

mus·tard, məs′tərd, *n.* Any of several herbaceous plants in the mustard family, the seeds of some of the species yielding the commercial mustard condiment; the paste or powder prepared from the seeds of some species of these plants, used as a food spice and medicinally for poultices and as a counter-irritant.

mus·tard gas, *n.* An agent of chemical warfare causing destruction of tissue, blindness, and death.

mus·ter, məs′tər, *v.t.* To collect, as troops, for service, review, parade, or exercise; to assemble or bring together, as information.—*v.i.* To assemble or meet in one place, as soldiers.—*n.* An assembling of troops for review or for service; the act of assembling; an assemblage. Also **mus·ter roll.—pass mus·ter,** to pass without censure, as one among a number on inspection.—**mus·ter in** or **out,** to join or be released from military service.

mus·ty, məs′tē, *a.,* **-ti·er, -ti·est.** Tasting or smelling moldy; antiquated. —**mus·ti·ly,** *adv.* —**mus·ti·ness,** *n.*

mu·ta·ble, mū′tə·bəl, *a.* Capable of being altered; subject to change; inconstant in mind or feelings; fickle. —**mu·ta·bil·i·ty,** mū·tə·bil′i·tē, **mu·ta·ble·ness,** *n.* —**mu·ta·bly,** *adv.*

mu·tant, mū′tənt, *n.* The new or altered species or organism which results from mutation.

mu·ta·tion, mū·tā′shən, *n.* A change or alteration, as in form, qualities, or nature; a sudden inheritable change appearing in the offspring of a parent organism due to an alteration in a gene or chromosome, or an increase in the number of chromosomes; the process by which this change occurs; the resultant species or individual. —**mu·tate,** mū′tāt, *v.t., v.i.,* **-tat·ed, -tat·ing.** —**mu·ta·tion·al,** mū·tā′shən·əl, *a.*

mute, mūt, *a.* Silent, or refraining from speech or utterance; incapable of speech.—*n.* A person without the power of speech; a device to deaden or muffle the sound of an instrument.—*v.t.,* **mut·ed, mut·ing.** To deaden or muffle the sound, as of a musical instrument; to soften the intensity, as of a color. —**mute·ly,** *adv.* —**mute·ness,** *n.*

mu·ti·late, mū′tə·lāt, *v.t.,* **-lat·ed, -lat·ing.** To cut off a limb or essential part. —**mu·ti·la·tion,** mū·tə·lā′shən, *n.* —**mu·ti·la·tor,** *n.*

mu·ti·neer, mū·tə·nēr′, *n.* One guilty of mutiny.

mu·ti·ny, mū′tə·nē, *n. pl.,* **-nies.** Revolt against constituted authority; resistance of soldiers or seamen against the authority of their commanders.—*v.i.,* **-nied, -ny·ing.** To engage in mutiny; to rise against military or naval officers. —**mu·ti·nous,** *a.*

mutt, mət, *n. Informal.* A mongrel dog.

mut·ter, mət′ər, *v.i.* To utter words with a low voice and compressed lips; to grumble; to murmur.—*v.t.* To utter in a low, indistinct manner.—*n.* Murmur; obscure utterance. —**mut·ter·er,** *n.* —**mut·ter·ing·ly,** *adv.*

mut·ton, mət′ən, *n.* The flesh of mature sheep, raw or cooked for food.

mu·tu·al, mū′chū·əl, *a.* Equally given and received; interchanged; equally relating to, affecting, or proceeding from two or more together; common to two or more combined; shared alike. —**mu·tu·al·i·ty,** mū·

chū·al′i·tē, *n.* —**mu·tu·al·ly,** *adv.*

muz·zle, məz′əl, *n.* The projecting mouth and nose of an animal; the open end of a gun or pistol; a restrictiveharness for an animal's mouth which prevents biting or eating.—*v.t.,* **-zled, -zling.** To put a muzzle on; to restrain, as opinion. —**muz·zler,** *n.*

my, mī, *pronominal a.* The possessive case of **I,** used as an attributive: *my* face.

my·col·o·gy, mī·kol′ə·jē, *n.* The study of fungi. —**my·col·o·gist,** *n.*

my·na, mī′nə, *n.* Any of numerous Asian starlings, certain varieties of which are domesticated and taught to imitate speech. Also **my·nah.**

my·o·pi·a, mī·ō′pē·ə, *n.* Nearsightedness; lack of foresight. —**my·op·ic,** mī·op′ik, *a.*

myr·i·ad, mir′ē·ad, *n.* A multitude of things or people.—*a.* Innumerable; multitudinous but indefinite.

myr·mi·don, mər′mi·don, *n.* A follower or soldier who willingly executes unscrupulous commands.

myrrh, mər, *n.* Valuable gum resin obtained from small, spiny trees native to Arabia and E. Africa, used medicinally as a tonic, in dentifrices, and in making incense and perfume.

myr·tle, mər′təl, *n.* An evergreen, cultivated shrub in the myrtle family, native to the Mediterranean region, having fragrant white flowers and aromatic berries; an evergreen, ornamental, trailing vine having pale blue or white flowers. Also **per·i·win·kle.**

my·self, mī·self′, *pron., pl.,* **our·selves.** Used to intensify *I*: I *myself* am responsible. Used reflexively as a form of *me,* functioning as the direct or indirect object of a verb or as the object of a preposition: I hit *myself* with the rake handle, gave *myself* a gift, thought only of *myself.* My natural or usual state: After a time, I was *myself* again.

mys·te·ri·ous, mi·stēr′ē·əs, *a.* Partaking of or containing mystery. —**mys·te·ri·ous·ly,** *adv.* —**mys·te·ri·ous·ness,** *n.*

mys·ter·y, mis′tə·rē, mis′trē, *n. pl.,* **-ies.** Anything that is kept secret or remains unexplained or unknown; a puzzling or inexplicable matter or occurrence; any affair, thing, or person not fully explained and therefore arousing curiosity or suspense; a story or dramatic representation of such an affair, object, or person; obscurity, as of something unexplained or puzzling.

mys·tic, mis′tik, *a.* Mysterious; occult; pertaining to mystics or mysticism.—*n.* A believer in mysticism.

mys·ti·cal, mis′ti·kəl, *a.* Beyond the scope of human experience; pertaining to a spiritual event, intuition, or insight which defies comprehension; related to a spiritual communication or contact with God. —**mys·ti·cal·ly,** *adv.* —**mys·ti·cal·ness,** *n.*

mys·ti·cism, mis′tə·siz·əm, *n.* Any seeking to solve the mysteries of existence by internal illumination or special revelation.

mys·ti·fy, mis′tə·fī, *v.t.,* **-fied, -fy·ing.** To perplex purposely; to bewilder; to obscure. —**mys·ti·fi·ca·tion,** mis·tə·fə·kā′shən, *n.*

mys·tique, mis·tēk′, *n.* A complex of vaguely mystical or otherwise nonrational ideas or attitudes associated with some person, profession, institution, etc.: the *mystique* of the American Presidency.

myth, mith, *n.* A fable or legend embodying the convictions of a people as to their gods or other divine personages, their own origin and early history and the heroes connected with it, or the origin of the world; in a looser sense, any invented story; something or someone having no existence in fact. —**myth·ic,** **myth·i·cal,** *a.* —**myth·i·cal·ly,** *adv.*

my·thol·o·gy, mi·thol′ə·jē, *n. pl.,* **-gies.** The study of myths; myths collectively. —**myth·o·log·ic,** mith·ə·loj′ik, **myth·o·log·i·cal,** *a.* —**my·thol·o·gist,** *n.*

N

N, n, en, *n.* The fourteenth letter and the eleventh consonant of the English alphabet.

nab, nab, *v.t.,* **nabbed, nab·bing.** *Informal.* To catch or seize suddenly or unexpectedly; to arrest.

na·bob, nā'bob, *n.* A person of great power or wealth.

na·cre, nā'ker, *n.* Mother-of-pearl.

na·cre·ous, nā'krē·əs, *a.* Consisting of or resembling nacre; having a pearly sheen.

na·dir, nā'dər, nā'dĕr, *n.* That point on the imaginary celestial sphere directly opposite to the zenith and directly under a given place or person; the lowest point; the time of greatest depression.

nag, nag, *n.* A small horse, or in informal language, any horse; an inferior race horse; an aged, worthless horse.

nag, nag, *v.i.,* **nagged, nag·ging.** To scold; to find fault constantly; to be the cause of pain or discomfort: a headache that *nags.*—*v.t.* To harass; to discomfort, as a bad conscience.—*n.* The act of nagging. **—nag·ger,** *n.* **—nag·ging·ly,** *adv.*

nail, nāl, *n.* A slender piece of metal, usu. with one end pointed and the other enlarged, for driving into or through wood or other materials to hold separate pieces together; a thin, horny plate, consisting of modified epidermis, growing on the upper side of the end of a finger or toe.—*v.t.* To fix or fasten with a nail or nails; to make fast or keep firmly in one place or position: Surprise *nailed* him to the spot; to settle decisively, as a bargain, usu. followed by *down. Informal.* To arrest or seize; to catch in some difficulty or lie; to detect and expose, as a lie; to hit: to *nail* him with a left hook. **—hit the nail on the head,** to do or say something exactly right; to understand or guess penetratingly. **—nail·er,** *n.*

na·ive, na·ïve, nä·ēv', *a.* Having or displaying a simple or trusting nature; unsophisticated; ingenuous; credulous. **—na·ive·ly,** *adv.* **—na·ive·ness,** *n.*

na·ive·té, na·ïve·te, nä·ēv·tā', nä·ēv'tā, *n.* The state of being naïve; a naïve action, remark, etc.

na·ked, nā'kid, *a.* Bare of clothing or covering; nude; without a sheath or covering, as a sword; undisguised, unadorned, or plain: as facts or *naked* truth. **—na·ked·ly,** *adv.* **—na·ked·ness,** *n.*

nam·by-pam·by, nam'bē·pam'bē, *a.* Affectedly timid; weakly sentimental; insipid; vapid.—*n.* A *namby-pamby* person.

name, nām, *n.* That by which a person or thing is called or designated, in distinction from other persons or things; title or appellation; reputation or character: one's good or bad *name;* renown or fame: to make a *name* in politics; the mere word by which anything is called, as distinguished from *reality.*—*v.t.,* **named, nam·ing.** To give a name to; to mention by name; to nominate; to identify by giving the name of; to specify.—*a.* Famous; known. **—in the name of,** on behalf of.

name·less, nām'lis, *a.* Without a name; anonymous; not known to fame; obscure; without family or legal name; that cannot or ought not to be named. **—name·less·ly,** *adv.* **—name·less·ness,** *n.*

name·ly, nām'lē, *adv.* That is to say.

name·sake, nām'sāk, *n.* An individual with the same name as another, esp. one named for someone in particular.

nan·keen, nan·kin, nan·kēn', *n.* A cloth of natural, yellowish-buff cotton.

nan·ny, nan'ē, *n. pl.,* **-nies.** *Brit.* A child's nurse. *Informal.* A female goat; also **nan·ny goat.**

nap, nap, *v.i.,* **napped, nap·ping.** To have a short sleep; to drowse; to be caught unprepared.—*v.t.* To

sleep through, as a morning.—*n.* A short sleep. **—nap·per,** *n.*

nap, nap, *n.* The woolly substance on the surface of cloth; the pile, as of a rug; a downy substance, as on some plants.—*v.t.,* **napped, nap·ping.** To raise or put a nap on. **—nap·less, napped,** *a.*

na·palm, nā'pām, *n.* A highly flammable, jellylike substance used with gasoline to make incendiary bombs, in flamethrowers, and the like.

nape, nāp, nap, *n.* The back part of the neck.

naph·tha, naf'thə, nap'thə, *n.* A colorless, volatile liquid, a petroleum distillate, esp. a product intermediate between gasoline and benzine, used as a solvent or fuel; any of various similar liquids distilled from other products.

naph·tha·lene, naf'thə·lēn, nap'thə·lēn, *n.* A white, odorous, crystalline hydrocarbon, usu. prepared from coal tar and used in making dyes and moth balls. Also **naph·tha·line, naph·tha·lin.**

nap·kin, nap'kin, *n.* A square piece of linen, cotton, or paper used at meals to wipe the lips and hands, and to protect the clothes.

nar·cis·sism, när'si·siz·əm, *n.* Self-love; excessive admiration of or fascination with oneself. Also **nar·cism. —nar·cis·sist,** *n.* **—nar·cis·sis·tic,** när·si·sis'tik, *a.*

nar·cis·sus, när·sis'əs, *n. pl.,* **-cis·sus·es, -cis·si,** -sis'ī. Popular, ornamental, spring-blooming, bulbous plants in the amaryllis family, having white, yellow, or orange flowers with a cuplike crown, and including the jonquil and daffodil. (*Cap.*) *Mythol.* A handsome youth who died from hopeless love of his own reflection, and was transformed into a narcissus.

nar·co·sis, när·kō'sis, *n.* The production of stupor or insensibility by a narcotic drug; a state of drowsiness or insensibility.

nar·cot·ic, när·kot'ik, *n.* A substance which relieves pain, induces sleep, and in large doses brings on stupor, coma, and even death, as opium or morphine; an addict.—*a.* Having the properties of a narcotic; inducing narcosis; relating to or induced by narcotics; relating to addicts or treatment for addiction. **—nar·cot·i·cal·ly,** *adv.* **—nar·co·tize,** när'kə·tīz, *v.t.,* **-tized, -tiz·ing.**

nar·is, nār'is, *n. pl.,* **nar·es,** nār'ēz. The nostril; the nasal passage or opening.

nark, närk, *n. Informal.* A narcotics agent.

nar·rate, nar'āt, na·rāt', *v.t.,* **-rat·ed, -rat·ing.** To tell; to relate, as a story.—*v.i.* To recount particulars of a happening. **—nar·ra·tor,** *n.*

nar·ra·tion, na·rā'shən, *n.* The act of narrating; that which is related; a narrative; an explanation accompanying a visual presentation. **—nar·ra·tion·al,** *a.*

nar·ra·tive, nar'ə·tiv, *n.* That which is narrated; the technique or act of narration in speech or writing.—*a.* Pertaining to narration; consisting of a narrative. **—nar·ra·tive·ly,** *adv.*

nar·row, nar'ō, *a.* Of little breadth or width; limited in extent or space; limited in range or scope; limited in amount; lacking breadth of view or sympathy; nearly disastrous: a *narrow* escape.—*n.* A narrow part of a valley, passage, or road; *pl.,* a narrow part of a strait, river, or sound.—*v.t.* To make narrower; limit or restrict.—*v.i.* To become narrower; decrease in breadth. **—nar·row·ly,** *adv.* **—nar·row·ness,** *n.*

nar·row-mind·ed, nar'ō·mīn'did, *a.* Having or showing an illiberal mind, as persons, opinions, utterances; devoid of breadth of view or sympathy; intolerant. **—nar·row-mind·ed·ly,** *adv.* **—nar·row-mind·**

---

a- hat, fāte, fãre, fäther; **e-** met, mē; **i-** pin, pīne; **o-** not, nōte, ôrb, moove (move), boy, pownd;
u- cūbe, bûll, tûk (took); **ch-** chin; **th-** thick, ŧhen; **zh-** vizhon (vision); **ə-** əgo, takən, pencəl, ləmən, bərd (bird).

ed•ness, *n.*

nar•y, när′ē, när′ē, *a. Dial.* Never a; not a; not.

na•sal, nā′zəl, *a.* Of or pertaining to the nose. Produced by expelling the air column entirely through the nose, as in *m, n,* and *ng,* or partially, as in the French nasal vowels; accompanied by resonance produced in the nose: a *nasal* voice.—*n.* A nasal speech sound, as *m, n,* or *ng.* —**na•sal•i•ty,** nā•zal′i•tē, *n.* —**na•sal•ize,** *v.t., v.i.,* **-ized, -iz•ing.** —**na•sal•ly,** *adv.*

nas•cent, nas′ənt, nā′sənt, *a.* Beginning to exist or to grow; coming into being; arising. —**nas•cence, nas•cen•cy,** *n.*

na•stur•tium, nə•stėr′shəm, *n.* Pungent garden herbs having peltate-shaped leaves, spurred, funnel-form flowers of yellow, orange, and red, and climbing by means of coiled petioles.

nas•ty, nas′tē, *a.,* **-ti•er, -ti•est.** Filthy; dirty; indecent; disagreeable; mean: a *nasty* disposition; serious, as an accident. —**nas•ti•ly,** *adv.* —**nas•ti•ness,** *n.*

na•tal, nā′təl, *a.* Of or pertaining to one's birth.

na•tion, nā′shən, *n.* A people inhabiting a certain territory and united by common political institutions; the country or territory itself; a group of persons speaking the same or a cognate language and usu. sharing a common ethnic origin. —**na•tion•hood,** *n.*

na•tion•al, nash′ə•nəl, *a.* Of, pertaining to, or characteristic of a nation or people: a *national* language or literature; of, pertaining to, or maintained by a nation as an organized whole or independent political unit: *national* politics.—*n.* In diplomatic use, a citizen or subject of a particular nation. —**na•tion•al•ly,** *adv.*

Na•tion•al Guard, *n.* The militia organized and maintained in part by a state, paid by the federal government, and available to serve the state or to be made a part of the U.S. Army.

na•tion•al•ism, nash′ən•əl•iz•əm, nash′nəl•iz•əm, *n.* Devotion to the interests of one's own nation; desire for national advancement or independence. —**na•tion•al•ist,** *n.* —**na•tion•al•is•tic,** nash•ən•əl•is′tik, *a.*

na•tion•al•i•ty, nash•ə•nal′i•tē, *n. pl.,* **-ties.** National quality or character; the fact or relation of belonging to a particular nation or country, or origin with respect to a nation; a nation or people: the various *nationalities* of the Balkan Peninsula.

na•tion•al•ize, nash′ən•əl•īz, nash′nəl•īz, *v.t.,* **-ized, -iz•ing.** To make national, esp. to bring under the control or ownership of a nation, as industries or land. —**na•tion•al•i•za•tion,** nash•ə•nəl•ə•zā′shən, *n.*

na•tion-wide, na•tion•wide, nā′shən•wīd′, *a.* Extending throughout the nation.

na•tive, nā′tiv, *a.* Pertaining to the place or circumstances of one's birth; conferred by birth; belonging to one's nature or constitution; indigenous to a particular region; occurring in nature pure or unmixed with other substances, as iron or silver when found almost pure.—*n.* One born in a place or country, and not a foreigner or immigrant; something indigenous to a region. —**na•tive•ly,** *adv.* —**na•tive•ness,** *n.*

na•tiv•i•ty, nə•tiv′i•tē, nā•tiv′i•tē, *n. pl.,* **-ties.** Birth; a natal horoscope. (*Cap.*) The birth of Christ.

nat•ty, nat′ē, *a.,* **-ti•er, -ti•est.** Neatly dressed; of tidy appearance; spruce. —**nat•ti•ly,** *adv.* —**nat•ti•ness,** *n.*

nat•u•ral, nach′ər•əl, nach′rəl, *a.* Pertaining to nature; produced by nature, not artificial; in conformity with the laws of nature; consistent with nature; normal; without affectation or artificiality. *Mus.* Neither sharped nor flatted, as a note; without accidentals, as in the scale of C.—*n. Informal.* A person with inherent ability in a certain area. *Mus.* The symbol or sign which, when assigned to a note, cancels the effect of its previous alteration; a note affected by a natural sign. —**nat•u•ral•ly,** *adv.* —**nat•u•ral•ness,** *n.*

nat•u•ral gas, *n.* A combustible gas formed naturally in the earth, consisting typically of methane with varying amounts of other gases.

nat•u•ral his•to•ry, *n.* The study or description of nature in its widest sense, esp. the biological and earth sciences.

nat•u•ral•ism, nach′ər•ə•liz•əm, nach′rəl•iz•əm, *n.* Action arising from or based on natural instincts and desires alone; close adherence to nature or reality; realism.

nat•u•ral•ist, nach′ər•əl•ist, nach′rəl•ist, *n.* One who makes a study of animals and plants; an adherent of naturalism. —**nat•u•ral•is•tic,** nach′ər•əl•is′tik, *a.*

nat•u•ral•ize, nach′ər•əl•īz, nach′rəl•īz, *v.t.,* **-ized, -iz•ing.** To confer the rights and privileges of a native citizen upon. —**nat•u•ral•i•za•tion,** nach•ə•rəl•i•zā′shən, *n.*

nat•u•ral re•source, *n. Usu. pl.* The collective developed or potential physical and biological wealth of any country, such as oil, minerals, forests, and water; native ability.

nat•u•ral sci•ence, *n.* Any science, as biology, geology, or chemistry, dealing with objects and phenomena of nature.

nat•u•ral se•lec•tion, *n.* The theory that nature tends to maintain and perpetuate those species having particular characteristics of genetic origin that best fit them for survival in their environment.

na•ture, nā′chər, *n.* The instincts or inherent tendencies which determine personal conduct; native or inherent character or disposition; kind or sort: a story of that *nature;* the universe with all its phenomena. (*Sometimes cap.*) The sum total of the forces at work throughout the universe, considered collectively. A primitive, wild, or uncultivated condition; a natural, simple state. —**by na•ture,** innately.

naught, nôt, *n.* Nothing; nought. *Arith.* Zero; cipher. —*a., adv.*

naugh•ty, nô′tē, *a.,* **-ti•er, -ti•est.** Bad; mischievous, or ill-behaved: a *naughty* child; not proper; obscene. —**naugh•ti•ly,** *adv.* —**naugh•ti•ness,** *n.*

nau•se•a, nô′zē•ə, nô′zhə, nô′sē•ə, nô′shə, *n.* Stomach sickness or upset, often with an inclination to vomit; loathing; disgust.

nau•se•ate, nô′zē•āt, nô′zhē•āt, nô′sē•āt, nô′shē•āt, *v.i.,* **-at•ed, -at•ing.** To feel nausea or disgust.—*v.t.* To sicken; to affect with disgust. —**nau•se•at•ing,** *a.*

nau•seous, nô′shəs, nô′zē•əs, *a.* Loathsome or disgusting; causing a feeling of nausea. *Informal.* Feeling ill with nausea. —**nau•seous•ly,** *adv.* —**nau•seous•ness,** *n.*

nau•ti•cal, nô′ti•kəl, *a.* Pertaining to seamanship or navigation. —**nau•ti•cal•ly,** *adv.*

nau•ti•lus, nôt′ə•ləs, *n. pl.,* **-lus•es, -li,** -lī. A cephalopod with a pearly chambered spiral shell. Also **chambered nau•ti•lus, pear•ly nau•ti•lus.**

na•val, nā′vəl, *a.* Consisting of ships or of forces fighting in ships; pertaining to a navy or to ships of war; maritime.

nave, nāv, *n.* The middle part, lengthwise, of a church.

na•vel, nā′vəl, *n.* A scar, usu. a pit or depression, in the middle of the surface of the abdomen at the point of detachment of the umbilical cord; any similar depression, as in a navel orange; the central point or middle of anything or place.

nav•i•ga•ble, nav′i•gə•bəl, *a.* Capable of being navigated; affording passage to ships. —**nav•i•ga•bil•i•ty,** nav•i•gə•bil′ə•tē, **nav•i•ga•ble•ness,** *n.* —**nav•i•ga•bly,** *adv.*

nav•i•gate, nav′i•gāt, *v.i.,* **-gat•ed, -gat•ing.** To travel on water in ships or boats; to plan or compute the course of a vessel or vehicle.—*v.t.* To steer or manage the progress of.

nav•i•ga•tion, nav•ə•gā′shən, *n.* The act of navigating; the science or art of managing ships; the science of determining the location, speed, destination, and direction of airplanes and other craft. —**nav•i•ga•tion•al,** *a.*

nav•i•ga•tor, nav′i•gā•tər, *n.* One who navigates, or is trained in the methods of navigation.

na•vy, nā′vē, *n. pl.,* **-vies.** All of a nation's military vessels. (*Often cap.*) The institutions and equipment for the maintenance of sea defenses, such as personnel, ships, navy yards, stores, and naval academies, together with the governmental agency directing them. A dark blue color; also **na·vy blue.**

na·vy bean, *n.* A dried white bean related to the kidney bean.

nay, nā, *adv.* No: used to express negation or refusal; indeed: used to imply that something more is to be added to an expression, as in asking, *nay*, begging for order.—*n.* Denial; refusal; one who casts a negative vote, or the vote itself.

Na·zi, nä′tsē, nat′sē, *n. pl.*, **Na·zis.** A member of the National Socialist party of Germany, which in 1933 obtained political control of the country under Adolf Hitler. (*Often l.c.*) One believed to hold to similar beliefs; fascist.—*a.* Of or pertaining to the Nazis. —**Na·zism,** nä′tsiz·əm, nat′siz·əm, **Na·zi·ism,** nä′tsē·iz·əm, nat′sē·iz·əm, *n.*

neap, nēp, *n.* One of the lowest tides, or the time of one: opposite to *spring* tide. Also **neap tide.**

near, nēr, *a.* Not far distant in place, time, or degree; closely connected by blood: a *near* relation; intimate or familiar; narrow, as an escape; short, or not circuitous; stingy or miserly.—*adv.* Within a short time, distance, or degree; almost: *near* six feet tall; closely. —*prep.* At no great distance from; close to.—*v.i., v.t.* To approach; to come near. —**near·ly,** *adv.* —**near·ness,** *n.*

near·by, nēr′bī′, *a.* Close at hand; near.—*adv.*

near·sight·ed, nēr′sī′tid, *a.* Short-sighted; seeing clearly at a short distance only. —**near·sight·ed·ly,** *adv.* —**near·sight·ed·ness,** *n.*

neat, nēt, *a.* Tidy and clean; being simple and precise in speech, appearance, or form; clever or ingenious: a *neat* solution to the problem. *Informal.* Great; excellent. —**neat·ly,** *adv.* —**neat·ness,** *n.*

neath, nēth, nēth, *prep. Dial., poet.* Beneath. Also **'neath.**

neb·bish, neb′ish, *n. Informal.* A drab, timid, ineffectual person.

neb·u·la, neb′yū·lə, *n. pl.*, **-las, -lae,** -lē. A vast, cloudlike, interstellar mass, either luminous or dark, consisting of gaseous matter and small quantities of dust.

neb·u·lous, neb′yū·ləs, *a.* Vague; cloudy; of, concerning, or similar to a nebula. —**neb·u·lar,** *a.* —**neb·u·lous·ly,** *adv.* —**neb·u·lous·ness,** *n.*

nec·es·sar·y, nes′i·ser·ē, *a.* Inevitable; indispensable; essential; requisite.—*n. pl.*, **-ies.** Something necessary, indispensable, or requisite; a requisite. —**nec·es·sar·i·ly,** nes·i·sãr′ə·lē, *adv.*

ne·ces·si·tate, nə·ses′i·tāt, *v.t.*, **-ta·ted, -ta·ting.** To make necessary; to compel or force.

ne·ces·si·ty, nə·ses′i·tē, *n. pl.*, **-ties.** Need; compulsion of circumstances; that which is requisite; extreme indigence.

neck, nek, *n.* The part of the body connecting the head and trunk; the part of a garment covering or extending about the neck; any narrow connecting or projecting part suggesting the neck of an animal; a narrow strip of land; a strait or narrow body of water; the slender part of a bottle or any similarly shaped object.—*v.i. Informal.* To fondle and kiss amorously. —**neck and neck,** abreast. —**save one's own neck,** disentangle oneself from danger or difficulties, often at another's expense. —**neck·less,** *a.*

neck·er·chief, nek′ər·chif, *n.* A cloth worn round the neck by women or men.

neck·ing, nek′ing, *n. Informal.* Amorous kissing and fondling.

neck·lace, nek′lis, *n.* An ornament of precious stones, beads, or the like, worn round the neck.

neck·tie, nek′tī, *n.* A band of cloth worn around the neck under the shirt collar and knotted in front.

ne·crol·o·gy, ne·krol′ə·jē, *n. pl.*, **-gies.** A death notice; a register of deaths or obituaries.

nec·ro·man·cy, nek′rə·man·sē, *n.* The art of divining or influencing future events through communication with spirits conjured from the dead; witchcraft; sorcery. —**nec·ro·man·cer,** *n.*

ne·cro·sis, ne·krō′sis, *n.* Death of cellular material or of a section of tissue. —**ne·crot·ic,** ne·krot′ik, *a.*

nec·tar, nek′tər, *n.* The drink of the Greek and Roman gods; a refreshing beverage, often a mixture of fruit juices; a sweet fluid in the flower, which serves to attract insects.

nec·tar·ine, nek·tə·rēn′, nek′tə·rēn, *n.* A variety of the common peach, whose fruit at maturity is smooth like a plum.

née, nee, nā, *a.* Born: as Madame de Staël, *née* Necker.

need, nēd, *n.* The lack or sense of the lack of something wanted or required; a pressing occasion for something; necessity; poverty; indigence.—*v.t.* To have necessity or need for; to want, lack, require.—*v.i.* To be in need; to be obliged to, used as an auxiliary verb.

need·ful, nēd′fəl, *a.* Needed; necessary; requisite. —**need·ful·ly,** *adv.* —**need·ful·ness,** *n.*

nee·dle, nē′dəl, *n.* A small, slender, pointed instrument, usu. of polished steel, with an eye or hole for thread, used in sewing; a slender, rodlike implement used in knitting or one hooked at the end, used in crocheting; the slender instrument or stylus in a phonograph, used in the transmission of sound vibrations; a pointer on a compass or gauge; the sharply pointed end of a syringe, as for hypodermic injections; a needleshaped leaf, as of a conifer.—*v.t.*, **-dled, -dling.** *Informal.* To annoy, tease, or embarrass; to incite or goad to action. —**nee·dle·like,** *a.* —**nee·dler,** **nee·dling.** *n.*

nee·dle·point, nē′dəl·poynt, *n.* Embroidery on canvas, using simple stitches of equal length to make a pattern; a lace made on a paper pattern with a needle only and using buttonhole stitch.—*a.*

need·less, nēd′lis, *a.* Not needed. —**need·less·ly,** *adv.* —**need·less·ness,** *n.*

nee·dle·work, nē′dəl·wərk, *n.* Work executed with a needle. —**nee·dle·work·er,** *n.*

need·n't, nēd′ənt. Contraction of need not.

need·y, nē′dē, *a.*, **-i·er, -i·est.** Poverty-stricken; not having enough to live on. —**need·i·ness,** *n.*

ne'er, nãr, *adv. Poet.* Contraction of never.

ne'er-do-well, nãr′doo·wel, *n.* A good-for-nothing; a worthless person.—*a.* Worthless; by-passed by success.

ne·far·i·ous, ne·fār′ē·əs, *a.* Wicked in the extreme. —**ne·far·i·ous·ly,** *adv.* —**ne·far·i·ous·ness,** *n.*

ne·gate, ni·gāt′, nē′gāt, *v.t., v.i.*, **-ga·ted, -ga·ting.** To deny; nullify.

ne·ga·tion, ni·gā′shən, *n.* The act of denying; a denial; the absence or opposite of what is actual, positive, or affirmative.

neg·a·tive, neg′ə·tiv, *a.* Expressing or containing negation or denial; lacking positive attributes. *Math.* Denoting a quantity less than zero; involving or denoting subtraction. *Elect.* Noting or pertaining to the kind of electricity developed as on resin or amber, when rubbed with flannel. *Photog.* Showing light and shade reversed from the conditions in nature.—*n.* A negative statement, proposition, reply, term, or word; that side of a question which denies what the opposite side affirms; the negative plate or element in a voltaic cell. *Photog.* A negative picture.—*v.t.*, **-tived, -tiv·ing.** To deny, as a statement or proposition; to refuse assent or consent to; veto. —**neg·a·tive·ly,** *adv.* **neg·a·tive·ness, neg·a·tiv·i·ty,** neg·ə·tiv′ə·tē, *n.*

---

a- hat, fãte, fãre, fäther; e- met, mē; i- pin, pīne; o- not, nōte, ôrb, moove (move), boy, pownd; u- cūbe, bull, tūk (took); ch- chin; th- thick, then; zh- vizhon (vision); ə- əgo, takən, pencəl, lemən, bərd (bird).

neg·a·tiv·ism, neg′ə·tiv·iz·əm, *n.* A contrary, skeptical, or iconoclastic attitude or philosophy.

ne·glect, ni·glekt′, *v.t.* To pay insufficient attention to; disregard; to fail to perform or to omit through indifference or carelessness.—*n.* The act or fact of neglecting; disregard; the state of being neglected. —**ne·glect·er, ne·glec·tor, ne·glect·ful·ness,** *n.* —**ne·glect·ful,** *a.* —**ne·glect·ful·ly,** *adv.*

neg·li·gee, neg·li·zhā′, neg′li·zhā, *n.* A woman's dressing gown, usu. long and flowing. Also *Fr.* **neg· li·gé.**

neg·li·gent, neg′li·jənt, *a.* Guilty of or characterized by neglect, as of duty: *negligent* officials; casual; nonchalant. —**neg·li·gence,** *n.* —**neg·li·gent·ly,** *adv.*

neg·li·gi·ble, neg′li·jə·bəl, *a.* So unimportant that it may be safely disregarded. —**neg·li·gi·bly,** *adv.* —**neg·li·gi·bil·i·ty,** neg·li·jə·bil′ə·tē, *n.*

ne·go·ti·a·ble, ni·gō′shē·ə·bəl, ni·gō′shə·bəl, *a.* Capable of being negotiated; of bills and securities, transferable by delivery, with or without endorsement, according to the circumstances, the title passing to the transferee. —**ne·go·ti·a·bil·i·ty,** ni·gō·shə· bil′ə·tē, *n.*

ne·go·ti·ate, ni·gō′shē·āt, *v.i.* **-at·ed, -at·ing.** To confer or bargain, one with another, in order to reach an agreement.—*v.t.* To conduct or manage: *negotiate* a merger; to arrange for; to circulate by endorsement; transfer, sell, or assign in exchange for something of similar value. To succeed in moving through, over, or around: to *negotiate* a difficult situation. —**ne·go· ti·a·tion,** ni·gō·shē·ā′shən, **ne·go·ti·a·tor,** *n.*

Ne·gro, nē′grō, *n. pl.,* **Ne·groes.** A person of Negroid ancestry; a member of the black-skinned ethnic group of mankind.—*a.*

Ne·groid, nē′groyd, *a.* Pertaining to or comprising a major racial division of man principally constituted by the black-skinned peoples of Africa.—*n.*

neigh, nā, *v.i.* To utter the cry of a horse; whinny.—*n.*

neigh·bor, nā′bər, *n.* One who lives near another; one in close proximity; one's fellow-man.—*a.* Adjoining.—*v.t.* To adjoin.—*v.i.* To live close at hand. —**neigh·bor·ing, neigh·bor·ly,** *a.* —**neigh·bor·li· ness,** *n.*

neigh·bor·hood, nā′bər·hůd, *n.* A district or locality, often with reference to its character or inhabitants: a run-down or a fashionable *neighborhood;* a number of persons living near one another in a particular locality. —**in the neigh·bor·hood of,** approximately.

nei·ther, nē′thər, nī′thər, *a.* Not either.—*pron.* Not the one or the other.—*conj.* Not either: *neither* you nor I; nor yet.

nem·e·sis, nem′i·sis, *n. pl.,* **-ses,** -sēz. An agent of retribution or punishment.

ne·o·clas·sic, nē·ō·klas′ik, *a.* Of or pertaining to a revival of classic style, as in art or literature. Also **ne·o·clas·si·cal.** —**ne·o·clas·si·cism,** *n.*

ne·o·lith·ic, nē·ə·lith′ik, *a.* (*Sometimes cap.*) Noting or pertaining to the last part of the Stone Age, characterized by the use of highly finished or polished stone implements and by the development of basic agriculture.

ne·ol·o·gism, nē·ol′ə·jiz·əm, *n.* A new word or phrase; the new usage or meaning of old words. Also **ne·ol·o·gy.**

ne·on, nē′on, *n.* A colorless, inert gaseous element comprising 0.0012 per cent of normal air. —*a.* Pertaining to neon.

ne·o·phyte, nē′ə·fīt, *n.* A new convert or proselyte; a novice; a beginner.

ne·pen·the, ni·pen′thē, *n.* Anything capable of bringing forgetfulness of pain or care. —**ne·pen· the·an,** *a.*

neph·ew, nef′ū, *n.* A son of one's brother or sister or a son of one's sister-in-law or brother-in-law.

ne·phri·tis, ni·frī′tis, *n.* Inflammation of the kidneys. —**ne·phrit·ic,** ni·frit′ik, *a.*

nep·o·tism, nep′ə·tiz·əm, *n.* Favoritism shown to relatives, usu. in the form of desirable jobs. —**nep·o· tist,** *n.*

Nep·tune, nep′toon, nep′tūn, *n.* The planet which is eighth in order from the sun. *Rom. mythol.* The god of the sea; the sea. —**Nep·tu·ni·an,** nep·too′nē·ən, nep·tū′nē·ən, *a.*

nep·tu·ni·um, nep·too′nē·əm, nep·tū′nē·əm, *n.* A radioactive element produced artificially by neutron bombardment and decaying of plutonium.

nerve, nərv, *n.* One of the whitish fibers whose function is to convey sensation and originate motion through all parts of the body; courage or steadiness; strength or power. *Informal.* Impudence; arrogance. *Pl.* Emotional stability: *nerves* like iron; nervousness: as, a shaking bundle of *nerves.*—*v.t.,* **nerved, nerv· ing.** To give nerve, strength, or vigor to. —**get on one's nerves,** to make one nervous or irritable.

nerve·less, nərv′lis, *a.* Not nervous under stress; calm, esp. in emergencies; lacking nerve; feeble; lacking firmness or courage; spiritless; without nerves. —**nerve·less·ly,** *adv.* —**nerve·less·ness,** *n.*

nerve-rack·ing, nerve-wrack·ing, nərv′rak·ing. *a.* Extremely annoying or irritating.

nerv·ous, nər′vəs, *a.* Pertaining to or having nerves; originating from or affecting the nerves; easily agitated; tense or anxious. —**nerv·ous·ly,** *adv.* —**nerv· ous·ness,** *n.*

nerv·ous sys·tem, *n.* The elaborate network of nerve cells making up the ganglia, spinal cord, nerves, and brain, esp. of vertebrate animals and man.

nerv·y, nər′vē, *a.,* **-i·er, -i·est.** *Informal.* Arrogant or insolent; bold or courageous. —**nerv·i·ness,** *n.*

nest, nest, *n.* A structure formed or a place used by a bird for the incubation of its eggs and the rearing of its young; a place used by insects, fish, turtles, rabbits, or the like, for depositing their eggs or young; a snug home, retreat, or resting place; a place where something bad is fostered or flourishes: a *nest* of crime; a set or series of boxes, baskets, tables, cups, or other articles, such that the smaller fit within the larger.—*v.i.* To build or have a nest.—*v.t.* To settle or place in or as in a nest.

nest egg, *n.* A sum of money laid away as the beginning of a fund or as a reserve.

nes·tle, nes′əl, *v.i.,* **-tled, -tling.** To lie close and snug; to be sheltered or situated in a pleasant spot.—*v.t.* To house, shelter, or settle as in a nest; to place or press closely. —**nes·tler,** *n.*

nest·ling, nest′ling, nes′ling, *n.* A young bird in the nest.

net, net, *n.* A bag or other contrivance of strong thread or cord made into an open, meshed fabric, for catching fish, birds, or other animals; anything serving to catch or ensnare; a piece of meshed fabric for any purpose.—*v.t.,* **net·ted, net·ting.** To catch or ensnare with or as with a net; to cover, screen, or enclose with a net or netting.

net, net, *a.* Left after all deductions for taxes, charges, expenses, allowances, discounts, and the like have been deducted, as opposed to *gross.*—*n.* Net income, profits, weight, score, or the like.—*v.t.,* **net·ted, net· ting.** To gain or yield as clear profit.

neth·er, neth′ər, *a.* Lower; lying or being beneath or in the lower part.

neth·er·most, neth′ər·mōst, *a.* Lowest.

neth·er world, *n.* The world of the dead; hell; the underworld. Also **neth·er·world,** neth′ər·wərld.

net·ting, net′ing, *n.* Any piece of network.

net·tle, net′əl, *n.* An herb with stinging hairs.—*v.t.,* **-tled, -tling.** To irritate, provoke, or vex.

net·work, net′wərk, *n.* An interlacement of threads, wires, or strings into a fabric or web; a net; a complicated intermingling of lines, passages, or the like: a *network* of railroads. *TV, radio.* A series of broadcasting stations working as a unit.

neu·ral, nûr′əl, nyûr′əl, *a.* Pertaining to the nerves or nervous system. —**neu·ral·ly,** *adv.*

neu·ral·gia, nû·ral′jə, nyû·ral′jə, *n.* Pain that is usu. sharp and paroxysmal, along the course of a nerve. —**neu·ral·gic,** *a.*

neu·ras·the·ni·a, nûr·əs·thē′nē·ə, nyûr·əs·thē′nē·ə, *n.* A condition characterized by excessive mental and physical fatigue and sometimes by obscure physical complaints or phobias. —**neu·ras·then·ic,** nûr·əs·then′ik, *a., n.*

neu·ri·tis, nû·ri′tis, nyû·ri′tis, *n.* Inflammation of a nerve causing impaired reflexes or paralysis. —**neu·rit·ic,** nû·rit′ik, nyû·rit′ik, *a., n.*

neu·rol·o·gy, nû·rol′ə·jē, nyû·rol′ə·jē, *n.* The science of the nerves or the nervous system and its diseases or disorders. —**neu·ro·log·i·cal,** nûr·ə·loj′i·kəl, *a.* —**neu·rol·o·gist,** *n.*

neu·ron, nûr′on, nyûr′on, *n.* A nerve cell with all its processes. Also **neu·rone,** nûr′ōn, nyûr′ōn. —**neu·ron·ic,** nû·ron′ik, nyû·ron′ik, *a.*

neu·ro·sis, nû·rō′sis, nyû·rō′sis, *n. pl.,* **-ses,** -sēz. A functional nervous or emotional disorder marked by severe anxiety, depression, and the like, without any apparent physical origin.

neu·rot·ic, nû·rot′ik, nyû·rot′ik, *a.* Affected by or relating to a neurosis.—*n.* A person who has a neurosis, or whose behavior suggests one. —**neu·rot·i·cal·ly,** *adv.*

neu·ter, noo′tər, nū′tər, *a. Gram.* Neither masculine nor feminine. *Zool.* Without fully developed sexual organs.—*n. Gram.* A word or inflectional form of the neuter gender; the neuter gender itself. *Zool.* An animal incapable of propagation; an animal after castration.

neu·tral, noo′trəl, nū′trəl, *a.* On neither side in a dispute or armed conflict; indefinite; of a color, without a decided hue, or combining well with most other colors.—*n.* A person or nation that remains neutral; the position of gears when force is not being transmitted from the motor to the working parts, usu. preceded by *in* or *at.* —**neu·tral·i·ty,** noo·tral′i·tē, nū·tral′i·tē, *n.* —**neu·tral·ly,** *adv.*

neu·tral·ism, noo′trəl·iz·əm, nū′trəl·iz·əm, *n.* The policy or advocacy of neutrality, esp. nonalignment in foreign affairs. —**neu·tral·ist,** *n.*

neu·tral·ize, noo′trəl·īz, nū′trəl·īz, *v.t.,* **-ized,** **-iz·ing.** To declare neutral, as in time of war, or invest with neutrality; render ineffective or counteract; to make chemically or electrically inert.—*v.i.* To become neutral. —**neu·tral·i·za·tion,** noo·trəl·ə·zā′shən, *n.* —**neu·tral·iz·er,** *n.*

neu·tri·no, noo·trē′nō, nū·trē′nō, *n.* An uncharged elementary particle with a mass nearing zero.

neu·tron, noo′tron, nū′tron, *n.* An uncharged particle in the nucleus of an atom with a mass nearly the same as that of the proton.

nev·er, nev′ər, *adv.* Not ever; at no time; in no degree; absolutely not.

nev·er·more, nev·ər·mōr′, nev·ər·môr′, *adv.* Never again; at no future time.

nev·er·the·less, nev·ər·thə·les′, *adv.* However; in spite of.

new, noo, nū, *a.* Recently made, invented, produced, or come into being; lately discovered or experienced; unfamiliar; recently brought into a particular location, situation, condition, or relationship; not habituated or accustomed; never in existence or use before; novel; starting afresh; different from a former or older condition; replacing something older; fresh; repeated; modern; contemporary; refreshed; strengthened. —*adv.* Newly.—*n.* Something new. —**new·ish,** *a.* —**new·ness,** *n.*

new·born, noo′bôrn′, nū′bôrn′, *a.* Recently or only just born; born anew or reborn: a *newborn* interest.

new·com·er, noo′kəm·ər, nū′kəm·ər, *n.* One who has lately come; new arrival.

New Deal, *n.* The economic recovery measures and the reform legislation advocated by Franklin D. Roosevelt; the period of his administration. —**New Deal·er,** *n.*

new·el, noo′əl, nū′əl, *n.* A central pillar or upright from which the steps of a winding stair radiate; a post at the head or foot of a stair, supporting the handrail. Also **new·el post.**

new·fan·gled, noo′fang′gəld, nū′fang′gəld, *a.* New-fashioned; of the newest design.

new·ly, noo′lē, nū′lē, *adv.* Lately; recently.

new·ly·wed, noo′lē·wed, nū′lē·wed, *n.* A recently married person.

new moon, *n.* The period of time when the moon is in a direct line between the sun and the earth so that its illuminated side is not visible from the earth; the moon shortly after this phase when it is visible as a crescent.

news, nooz, nūz, *n. pl. but sing. in constr.* Current information about something that has taken place, or about something not known before; recent intelligence regarding any event; esp. as presented by news media such as the papers, radio, or television.

news·boy, nooz′boy, nūz′boy, *n.* A boy who sells or delivers newspapers.

news·cast, nooz′kast, nūz′kast, nooz′käst, nūz′käst, *n.* A broadcast of current events on either television or radio. —**news·cast·er,** *n.*

news·pa·per, nooz′pā·pər, nūz′pā·pər, *n.* A publication issued daily or weekly including news, opinions, features, and advertisements; newsprint. —**news·pa·per·man,** *n.*

news·print, nooz′print, nūz′print, *n.* An inexpensive paper used mostly for newspapers.

news·reel, nooz′rēl, nūz′rēl, *n.* A brief motion picture depicting news events.

news·stand, nooz′stand, nūz′stand, *n.* A booth or stand where newspapers and periodicals are sold.

news·y, noo′zē, nū′zē, *a.,* **-i·er,** **-i·est.** *Informal.* Full of news.

newt, noot, nūt, *n.* Any of various small, colorful, semiaquatic salamanders.

New Tes·ta·ment, *n.* Those books of the Bible comprising the four Gospels, 21 Epistles, Acts of the Apostles, and the Apocalypse of St. John the Evangelist.

New World, *n.* The Western Hemisphere including N. America and S. America.

next, nekst, *a.* Nearest in place, time, rank, or degree; directly following; adjacent.—*adv.* At the time or turn nearest or immediately succeeding.—*prep.* Adjoining or nearest to. —**next to,** practically; nearly; almost; nearest to.

next of kin, *n.* A person's nearest blood relative or relatives.

nex·us, nek′səs, *n. pl.,* **nex·us.** Tie; connection; connector; a linked series.

ni·a·cin, ni′ə·sin, *n.* Nicotinic acid.—*a.*

nib, nib, *n.* The bill or beak of a bird; the point of anything, esp. of a pen.

nib·ble, nib′əl, *v.t.,* **-bled,** **-bling.** To bite a little at a time; to eat in small bits.—*v.i.* To bite gently, usu. followed by *at.*—*n.* A little morsel; the act of nibbling. —**nib·bler,** *n.*

nib·lick, nib′lik, *n.* An iron golf club used to lift the ball high into the air. Also **num·ber nine i·ron.**

nice, nīs, *a.,* **nic·er,** **nic·est.** Pleasing or agreeable; kind; respectable; refined; tactful: a *nice* maneuver; subtle or minute: a *nice* distinction; highly accurate or precise: a *nice* measurement; attractive and delicious: a *nice* meal; fastidious or finicky. —**nice·ly,** *adv.* —**nice·ness,** *n.*

ni·ce·ty, ni′si·tē, *n. pl.,* **-ties.** *Usu. pl.* A delicate or precise point; a minute difference or fine distinction: the *niceties* of his book on Shakespeare; excess of

---

a- hat, fāte, fāre, fäther; **e-** met, mē; **i-** pin, pīne; **o-** not, nōte, ôrb, moove (move), boy, pownd; **u-** cūbe, bŭll, tŭk (took); **ch-** chin; **th-** thick, ŧhen; **zh-** vizhon (vision); **ə-** əgo, takən, pencəl, lemən, bərd (bird).

delicacy or fastidiousness. —**to a ni·ce·ty,** precisely.

niche, nich, *n.* A recess or hollow, as in a wall, for a statue or other decorative object; a place or position suitable or appropriate for a person or thing.

nick, nik, *n.* A notch, chip, or concavity in a surface or border.—*v.t.* To make a nick or notch in. *Informal.* To rob or cheat. —**in the nick of time,** at the final critical moment. —**nick·er,** *n.*

nick·el, nik′əl, *n.* A hard silver-white metallic element, malleable and ductile, much used in alloys. The five-cent coin composed of copper and nickel.

nick·el·o·de·on, nik·ə·lō′dē·ən, *n.* An early jukebox; formerly, a theater with an admission charge of a nickel.

nick·name, nik′nām, *n.* A familiar form of a proper name, as *Jim* for *James;* a name added to or substituted for the proper name of a person or place, as in ridicule or familiarity.—*v.t.,* **-named, -nam·ing.** To give a nickname to, or call by a specified nickname.

nic·o·tine, nik′ə·tēn, *n.* A highly poisonous, volatile alkaloid, derived from tobacco. Also **nic·o·tin,** nik′ə·tin. —**nic·o·tin·ic,** nik·ə·tin′ik, *a.*

nic·o·tin·ic ac·id, *n.* One of the vitamins in the B complex.

niece, nēs, *n.* The daughter of a brother or sister or of a brother-in-law or sister-in-law.

nif·ty, nif′tē, *a.,* **-ti·er, -ti·est.** *Informal.* Smart; stylish; fine.—*n.*

nig·gard, nig′ərd, *n.* A miser; one who is very stingy. —**nig·gard·li·ness,** *n.* —**nig·gard·ly,** *a., adv.*

nigh, nī, *v.t., v.i., adv., prep., a.,* **nigh·er, nigh·est.** *Archaic, dial.* Near.

night, nīt, *n.* That part of the natural day when the sun is beneath the horizon, or the time from sunset to sunrise; a state or time of darkness, depression, misfortune, or the like; a time of sadness or sorrow.—*a.*

night·cap, nīt′kap, *n.* A cap worn in bed. *Informal.* An alcoholic drink taken before going to bed.

night club, *n.* A café or restaurant serving liquor and food and presenting entertainment from night until early morning. Also **night·club.**

night·dress, nīt′dres, *n.* Nightgown.

night·fall, nīt′fôl, *n.* The fall of night; the close of the day; evening.

night·gown, nīt′gown, *n.* A loose gown worn in bed. Also **night·dress.**

night·hawk, nīt′hôk, *n.* A N. American species of the goatsucker family, a relative of the whippoorwill. *Informal.* A person up and about during the night.

night·in·gale, nīt′ən·gāl, nī′ting·gāl, *n.* A bird belonging to the thrush family, well known for the sweet singing of the male at night.

night let·ter, *n.* A telegram sent at night for delivery the following morning at a lower rate than a straight telegram.

night·ly, nīt′lē, *a.* Occurring or happening at night; occurring or happening every night.—*adv.* By night; every night.

night·mare, nīt′mer, *n.* A fearful or terrifying dream; an experience producing the terror or anxiety characteristic of a fearful dream. —**night·mar·ish,** *a.*

night owl, *n.* *Informal.* A person given to staying up late at night. See **night·hawk.**

night·shade, nīt′shād, *n.* Any of various plants related to the potato, tomato, and black nightshade.

night·shirt, nīt′shərt, *n.* A long pullover or tailored sleeping shirt worn usu. by men and boys.

night·time, nīt′tīm, *n.* The time between evening and morning.

ni·hil·ism, nī′əl·iz·əm, nī′hil·iz·əm, *n.* An extreme form of skepticism, denying all real existence; total disbelief in religion or moral principles and obligations, or in established laws and institutions. —**ni·hil·ist,** *n., a.* —**ni·hil·is·tic,** nī·əl·is′tik, *a.*

Ni·ke, nī′kē, *n.* A ground-to-air rocket missile, guided electronically, and able to intercept and destroy bombers at high altitudes.

nil, nil, *n.* Nothing.

nim·ble, nim′bəl, *a.,* **-bler, -blest.** Light and quick in motion; moving with ease and agility; quick-witted; clever. —**nim·ble·ness,** *n.* —**nim·bly,** *adv.*

nim·bus, nim′bəs, *n. pl.,* **-bus·es, -bi,** -bī. A luminous aura believed to surround a divine or holy personage, or an artistic representation of it; a dense rain cloud.

nin·com·poop, nin′kəm·poop, *n.* A fool; a blockhead; a simpleton.

nine, nīn, *n.* The cardinal number between eight and ten; a symbol representing it.—*a.* One more than eight in number. —**ninth,** nīnth, *a.*

nine·pins, nīn′pinz, *n. pl. but sing. in constr.* A bowling game similar to tenpins, played with nine large wooden pins.

nine·teen, nīn′tēn′, *n.* The cardinal number which follows 18; a symbol representing this number.—*a.* One more than 18 in number. —**nine·teenth,** nīn′tēnth′, *a., n.*

nine·ty, nīn′tē, *n. pl.,* **-ties.** The cardinal number which follows 89; nine times ten; a symbol representing this number.—*a.* One more than 89 in number. —**nine·ti·eth,**—*a.*

nin·ny, nin′ē, *n. pl.,* **-nies.** A fool; a simpleton.

nip, nip, *v.t.,* **nipped, nip·ping.** Pinch; bite suddenly; to take off by pinching, biting, or snipping, usu. followed by *off:* to *nip off* buds or shoots from a plant; to check in growth as if by taking off buds; to affect sharply and painfully or injuriously, as cold does.—*n.* The act of nipping; a pinch; a biting quality, as in cold or frosty air. —**nip and tuck,** with one competitor equaling the speed or efforts of the other; extremely close: They ran *nip and tuck* for five miles. —**nip in the bud,** to check or stop in the early stages.

nip, nip, *n.* A sip or small amount of anything, esp. of some alcoholic beverage.—*v.t., v.i.,* **nipped, nip·ping.** To drink in sips; to sip.

nip·per, nip′ər, *n.* One who or that which nips. *Usu. pl.* A device for nipping, as pincers or forceps. *Pl. Informal.* Handcuffs. One of the large claws of a crustacean.

nip·ple, nip′əl, *n.* A protuberance on the female breast with an opening through which the milk ducts discharge; anything resembling a nipple in shape or function, as the mouthpiece of a nursing bottle. **nip·py,** nip′ē, *a.,* **-pi·er, -pi·est.** Sharp; biting, as chilly weather.

nir·va·na, nir·vä′nə, nər·van′ə, *n.* (*Often cap.*) *Buddhism.* The emancipation of the soul, achieved through extinction of the self and characterized by cessation of all suffering and pain, and esp. cessation of the successive cycles of transmigration.

nit, nit, *n.* The egg of a louse or similar parasitic insect; a louse in the immature stage. —**nit·ty,** *a.,* **-ti·er, -ti·est.**

ni·ter, nī′tər, *n.* Potassium nitrate or sodium nitrate. Also **salt·pe·ter.**

nit-pick, nit′pik, *v.i. Informal.* To be overly critical or meticulous.

ni·trate, nī′trāt, *n.* A salt or ester of nitric acid.—*v.t.,* **-trat·ed, -trat·ing.** To treat with nitric acid or a nitrate; to convert into a nitrate. —**ni·tra·tion,** nī·trā′shən, *n.* —**ni·tra·tor,** *n.*

ni·tric, nī′trik, *a.* Of or pertaining to nitrogen.

ni·tric ac·id, *n.* A colorless, highly corrosive liquid, with powerful oxidizing properties.

ni·tro·gen, nī′trə·jən, *n.* A gaseous element, possessing neither color, odor, nor taste, that constitutes about four-fifths of the atmosphere and is essential to life. —**ni·trog·e·nous,** nī·troj′ə·nəs, *a.*

ni·tro·glyc·er·in, nī·trə·glis′ər·in, *n.* A highly flammable, explosive liquid used in making dynamites or rocket propellants, and in medicine for relaxing or dilating blood vessels. Also **ni·tro·glyc·er·ine.**

ni·trous ox·ide, nī′trəs, *n.* A combination of nitrogen and oxygen which sometimes produces an exhilarating effect upon inhaling, used as an anesthetic during dental work and surgery. Also **laugh·ing gas.**

nit·ty-grit·ty, nit′ē·grit′ē, *n. Informal.* The unvarnished or crude essence; vexing or tedious details.

nit·wit, nit′wit, *n.* A stupid person.

nix, niks, *n. Informal.* Nothing.—*adv. Informal.* No.—*interj. Informal.* Stop it: an exclamation of warning.—*v.t. Informal.* To differ with; to prevent or prohibit: to *nix* our plans.

no, nō, *adv.* Nay: used to express dissent, denial, or refusal; not in any degree, not at all: used with a comparative: working *no* faster; not: whether or *no.*—*n. pl.,* **noes, nos.** A denial or refusal; a negative vote or voter: 50 *noes.*—*a.* Not any: of *no* use; not at all, very far from being: He is *no* genius. —**no one,** nobody.

no·be·li·um, nō·bē′lē·əm, *n.* A rare, radioactive, synthetic element.

No·bel prize, nō·bel′ *n.* One of five annual awards provided for by the will of the Swedish industrialist, Alfred Nobel, and given for outstanding contributions in the fields of chemistry, physics, medicine, literature, and the advancement of peace.

no·bil·i·ty, nō·bil′i·tē, *n. pl.,* **-ties.** The body of persons forming a class of society with special hereditary titles, ranks, and privileges; the state or quality of being noble; noble birth or rank.

no·ble, nō′bəl, *a.,* **-bler, -blest.** Famous, illustrious, or great, as persons or their achievements; distinguished by birth, rank, or title, or pertaining to persons so distinguished; of an exalted moral character or excellence; stately or magnificent; of an admirably high quality, type, or class.—*n.* A person of noble birth or rank; a nobleman. —**no·ble·man,** *n. pl.,* **-men.** —**no·ble·ness,** *n.* —**no·ble·wom·an,** *n. pl.,* **-wom·en.** —**no·bly,** *adv.*

no·bod·y, nō′bod·ē, nō′bə·dē, *pron.* No person; no one.—*n. pl.,* **-ies.** A person of no standing or position.

noc·tur·nal, nok·tər′nəl, *a.* Pertaining or belonging to the night; done or occurring at night. —**noc·tur·nal·ly,** *adv.*

noc·turne, nok′tərn, *n.* A dreamy or pensive musical composition.

nod, nod, *v.i.,* **nod·ded, nod·ding.** To let the head sink from sleep; to make an inclination of the head, as in assent, command, beckoning, or salutation.—*v.t.* To incline, as the head; to signify by a nod; to beckon by a nod.—*n.* A quick downward motion of the head as a sign of agreement, salutation, or from drowsiness. —**nod·der,** *n.*

node, nōd, *n.* A knot; a knob; a protuberance; a swelling; a joint or knot on a stem where leaves arise. —**nod·al,** *a.*

nod·ule, noj′ool, *n.* A little knot or lump. —**nod·u·lar,** noj′ə·lər, *a.*

no·el, nō·el′, *n.* A Christmas song or carol. (*Cap.*) Christmas day; yuletide.

nog·gin, nog′in, *n.* A small mug or wooden cup; a measure of liquor equivalent to a gill, or one-quarter of a pint. *Informal.* The head.

noise, noyz, *n.* A din; a sound of any kind.—*v.t.,* **noised, nois·ing.** To spread the report or rumor of.—*v.i.* To make a noise, outcry, or clamor; to talk much or publicly.

noise·less, noyz′lis, *a.* Making or attended with no noise; silent; quiet. —**noise·less·ly,** *adv.* —**noise·less·ness,** *n.*

noi·some, noy′səm, *a.* Offensive, esp. to the sense of smell; fetid; noxious; harmful. —**noi·some·ly,** *adv.* —**noi·some·ness,** *n.*

nois·y, noy′zē, *a.,* **-i·er, -i·est.** Making much noise; abounding in or attended with noise. —**nois·i·ly,** *adv.* —**nois·i·ness,** *n.*

no·mad, nō′mad, nom′ad, *n.* One of those people who shift their residence according to the state of the pasture, supply of food, or seasonal factors, and have no permanent abode; a wanderer.—*a.* Nomadic. —**no·mad·ic,** nō·mad′ik, *a.* —**no·mad·i·cal·ly,** *adv.* —**no·mad·ism,** *n.*

no man's land, *n.* Ground between hostile forces.

nom de plume, nom də ploom′, *n. pl.,* **noms de plume,** nomz də ploom′. Pen name.

no·men·cla·ture, nō′mən·klā·chər, nō·men′klə·chər, *n.* A system of names; the vocabulary of names or technical terms which are appropriated to a science, art, or other field.

nom·i·nal, nom′ə·nəl, *a.* Of, pertaining to, or consisting of a name or names; being something in name only; of a price or a consideration, named as a mere matter of form, being trifling in comparison with the actual value. —**nom·i·nal·ly,** *adv.*

nom·i·nate, nom′ə·nāt, *v.t.,* **-nat·ed, -nat·ing.** To designate for an office or duty; to propose or offer the name of, as a candidate for an office or place. —**nom·i·na·tion,** nom·ə·nā′shən, *n.* —**nom·i·na·tor,** *n.*

nom·i·na·tive, nom′ə·nə·tiv, nom′ə·nā·tiv, *a.* A term applied to that form of a noun or pronoun which is used when the noun or pronoun is the subject of a sentence.—*n.* The nominative case; a nominative word.

nom·i·nee, nom·ə·nē′, *n.* A person nominated.

non·age, non′ij, nō′nij, *n.* The time before a person becomes legally of age.

nonce, nons, *n.* Present occasion or purpose: used mainly in the phrase *for the nonce.*

nonce word, *n.* A word coined for a single occasion, and usually not attaining general use.

non·cha·lant, non′shə·länt′, non′shə·lənt, *a.* Indifferent; casual; coolly unconcerned. —**non·cha·lance,** *n.* —**non·cha·lant·ly,** *adv.*

non·com, non′kom, *n. Informal.* A noncommissioned officer.

non·com·bat·ant, non·kom′bə·tənt, non·kəm·bat′ənt, *n.* A member of a military force whose direct responsibility does not involve actual fighting; a civilian during a period of war.

non·com·mis·sioned of·fi·cer, non·kə·mish′ənd, *n.* A subordinate officer who is selected from the ranks of the enlisted men and who may hold one of several grades, as corporal or sergeant.

non·com·mit·tal, non·kə·mit′əl, *a.* Not indicating or involving commitment. —**non·com·mit·tal·ly,** *adv.*

non·con·duc·tor, non·kən·dək′tər, *n.* A substance which resists or conducts with difficulty such forces as electricity, heat, or sound. —**non·con·duc·ting,** *a.*

non·con·form·ist, non·kən·fôr′mist, *n.* One who does not conform to the prevalent norms of thought or behavior. —**non·con·form·i·ty,** *n.*

non·de·script, non′di·skript, *a.* Defying description or classification; amorphous.—*n.* A person or thing not easily classed or described.

none, nən, *pron. sing. or pl. in constr.* No one; not one; not any, as of something indicated; no part.—*adv.* Not at all: The supply is *none* too great.

non·en·ti·ty, non·en′ti·tē, *n. pl.,* **-ties.** A person or thing utterly without consequence or importance.

none·the·less, nən′thə·les′, *adv.* Nevertheless; however. Also **none the less.**

non·in·ter·ven·tion, non·in·tər·ven′shən, *n.* Abstention from intervening; a policy of not interfering in the affairs of another nation or nations. —**non·in·ter·ven·tion·ist,** *n., a.*

non·met·al, non·met′əl, *n.* An element not having the character of a metal, as carbon, nitrogen, or halogens. —**non·me·tal·lic,** non·mə·tal′ik, *a.*

non·pa·reil, non·pə·rel′, *n.* A person or thing of peerless excellence.—*a.* Without equal.

non·par·ti·san, non·pär′ti·zən, *a.* Not bound by ties or obligations to a regular political party; objective. —*n.* —**non·par·ti·san·ship,** *n.*

---

a- hat, fāte, fāre, fäther; e- met, mē; i- pin, pīne; o- not, nōte, ôrb, moove (move), boy, pownd; u- cūbe, bŭll, tûk (took); ch- chin; th- thick, then; zh- vizhon (vision); ə- ego, takən, pencəl, lemən, bərd (bird).

non·plus, non·pləs′, non′pləs, *v.t.,* **-plused, -plus·ing.** To make completely confused; to utterly baffle.

non·prof·it, non·prof′it, *a.* Not for profit.

non·res·i·dent, non·rez′i·dənt, *a.* Not resident in a particular place, esp. not residing where official duties require one to reside.—*n.* One who is nonresident. **—non·res·i·dence,** *n.* **—non·res·i·den·cy,** *n. pl.,* **-cies.**

non·re·stric·tive, non·ri·strik′tiv, *a.* Pertaining to a descriptive word or phrase, as an adjective clause, which does not limit or modify its antecedent and may be omitted without changing the essence of the thought, as the phrase "who wore green" in the sentence, "The Irish, who wore green, won the game."

non·sec·tar·i·an, non·sek·târ′ē·ən, *a.* Not having an affiliation with any particular religious group.

non·sense, non′sens, *n.* Words or ideas that lack meaning or are absurd; foolish or meaningless actions or behavior. **—non·sen·si·cal,** non·sen′si·kəl, *a.* **—non·sen·si·cal·ly,** *adv.*

non se·qui·tur, non sek′wi·tər, *n.* An inference or a conclusion which does not follow from the premises.

non·stop, non′stop′, *a., adv.* With no stops on the way.

non·sup·port, non·sə·pôrt′, *n.* Failure to support a legal dependent.

non·un·ion, non·ūn′yən, *a.* Not belonging to, or not in accordance with the rules of a trade union; not maintained or manufactured by union workers. **—non·un·ion·ism,** non·ūn′yə·niz·əm, **non·un·ion·ist,** *n.*

non·vi·o·lence, non′vī′ə·ləns, *n.* The practice or principle of abstaining from all forms of violence; the use of passive resistance as a technique of protest. **—non·vi·o·lent,** *a.* **—non·vi·o·lent·ly,** *adv.*

noo·dle, noo′dəl, *n.* Dried unleavened egg dough or paste, usu. shaped in flat strips. *Informal.* The head; a dolt or simpleton. Also **noo·dle·head,** noo′dəl·hed′.

nook, nůk, *n.* A corner; a recess; a secluded retreat.

noon, noon, *n.* The middle of the day; twelve o'clock. Also **noon·day,** noon′dā.—*a.* Pertaining to midday. **—noon·tide,** noon′tīd, *n.* **—noon·time,** noon′tīm, *n.*

no one, *pron.* Nobody; no person. Also **no-one,** nō′wən.

noose, noos, *n.* A loop with a running knot, which tightens as the rope is pulled; a tie, bond, or snare. —*v.t.,* **noosed, noos·ing.** To secure by or as by a noose; ensnare with or catch with a noose; to put to death by hanging; to make a noose with or in, as a rope.

nope, nōp, *adv. Informal.* No.

nor, nôr, *unstressed* nər, *conj.* A word used to render negative the second or a subsequent member or a clause or sentence, specif. as a correlative to *neither* and with other negatives for emphasis; equivalent to *and not* and in this case not always corresponding to a foregoing negative: He is happy, *nor* need we be concerned.

norm, nôrm, *n.* A rule; a pattern; a model; an authoritative standard in a test taken from the average achievement of a group.

nor·mal, nôr′məl, *a.* Conforming with a type or standard considered usual; average: of *normal* intelligence.—*n.* The common or usual condition; the standard. **—nor·mal·cy, nor·mal·i·ty,** nôr·mal′i·tē, *n.* **—nor·mal·ly,** *adv.*

nor·mal·ize, nôr′mə·līz, *v.t.,* **-ized, -iz·ing.** To make normal; to reduce to a standard or norm.—*v.i.* To become normal once again. **—nor·mal·i·za·tion,** nôr·mə·lə·zā′shən, *n.*

north, nôrth, *adv.* In the direction which is to the right of a person facing the setting sun or west; toward or in the north, from the north, as with reference to wind. —*n.* A cardinal point of the compass lying to the right of a person facing the setting sun or west; the direction in which this point lies. (*Cap.*) a quarter or territory situated in this direction.—*a.* Lying toward or situated in the north; directed or proceeding toward the north; coming from the north, as a wind.

north·east, nôrth·ēst′, *Naut.* nôr·ēst′, *n.* The point on the mariner's compass or the general direction midway between north and east; a region in this direction.—*a.* Situated in the northeast; directed toward the northeast: to take a *northeast* course; coming from the northeast, as the wind.—*adv.* From, toward, or in the northeast. **—north·east·ern,** *a.*

north·east·er, nôrth·ēs′tər, *Naut.* nôr·ēs′tər, *n.* A blustery wind or gale from the northeast.

north·east·er·ly, nôrth·ēs′tər·lē, *Naut.* nôr·ēs′tər·lē, *a., adv.* Toward, in, or from the northeast.

north·east·ward, nôrth·ēst′wərd, *Naut.* nôr·ēst′wərd, *adv.* In the direction of or toward the northeast. Also **north·east·wards.**—*a.* Toward the northeast; northeast.—*n.* The northeast. **—north·east·ward·ly,** *a., adv.*

north·er, nôr′thər, *n.* A strong wind or storm from the north.

nor·ther·ly, nôr′thər·lē, *a.* Of or pertaining to the north; directed toward or located in the north; proceeding from or in the north, as the wind.—*adv.* In the direction of or from the north. **—north·er·li·ness,** *n.*

north·ern, nôr′thərn, *a.* Toward the north; proceeding from the north; located in the north; (*often cap.*) characteristic of the inhabitants of a region that is situated toward the north. **—north·ern·most,** *a.*

north·ern·er, nôr′thər·nər, *n.* (*Sometimes cap.*) A native or inhabitant of the north, esp. in the U.S.

north·ern lights, *n. pl.* Aurora borealis.

north·ward, nôrth′wərd, *Naut.* nôr′thərd, *adv.* Toward the north.—*a.* Moving toward, in, to, near, or facing the north. **—north·wards,** *adv.* **—north·ward·ly,** *a., adv.*

north·west, nôrth·west′, *Naut.* nôr·west′, *n.* The direction between the north and the west; the compass point midway between north and west; (*cap.*) a region lying in this direction.—*a.* Proceeding from or directed toward the northwest.—*adv.* Toward or from the northwest. **—north·west·ern,** *a.*

north·west·er, nôrth·wes′tər, *Naut.* nôr·wes′tər, *n.* A strong wind or storm from the northwest.

north·west·er·ly, nôrth·wes′tər·lē, *Naut.* nôr·wes′tər·lē, *a., adv.* Toward the northwest; from the northwest, as the wind.

north·west·ward, nôrth·west′wərd, *Naut.* nôr·west′wərd, *adv., a.* Toward the northwest. Also **north·west·ward·ly.**—*n.* The northwest. **—north·west·wards,** *adv.*

nose, nōz, *n.* The human facial feature which contains the nostrils; the organ that includes the nasal cavities, the nostrils, and olfactory nerve endings, and which functions in speech, respiration, and smelling; the sense of smell; the organ of smell found in vertebrates; something regarded as resembling the nose of an animal or person.—*v.t.,* **nosed, nos·ing.** To perceive or detect by or as by the nose or sense of smell; to nudge or push with the nose: The mare *nosed* her colt away from the fence; to defeat in a close contest, followed by *out.*—*v.i.* Pry or meddle, followed by *about, into;* advance. **—on the nose.** *Informal.* Precisely. **—turn up one's nose at,** to scorn.

nose dive, *n.* Of an airplane, a headlong dive with the 'nose' of the machine pointing downward; any sudden, steep drop. **—nose-dive,** nōz′dīv, *v.i.,* **-dived, -div·ing.**

nose·gay, nōz′gā, *n.* A small bunch of flowers; a bouquet; a posy.

nos·tal·gia, nos·tal′jə, nos·tal′jē·ə, *n.* A longing to return to a past time or to irrecoverable circumstances; homesickness. **—nos·tal·gic,** *a.*

nos·tril, nos′trəl, *n.* One of the two apertures of the nose which give passage to air.

nos·trum, nos′trəm, *n.* A quack medicine; a panacea; cure-all.

nos·y, nos·ey, nō′zē, *a., -i·er, -i·est. Informal.* Prying; inquisitive. **—nos·i·ly,** *adv.* **—nos·i·ness,** *n.*

not, not, *adv.* In no way at all; to no extent: used to show negation, denial, refusal, or prohibition, or to express the negative, reverse, or complete lack of something: It is *not* an easy step to take. You may *not* drive.

no·ta·ble, nō′tə·bəl, *a.* Worthy of notice; remarkable; famous or distinguished.—*n.* A person or thing of note or distinction. —**no·ta·ble·ness, no·ta·bil·i·ty,** nō·tə·bil′ə·tē, *n.* —**no·ta·bly,** *adv.*

no·ta·rize, nō′tə·rīz, *v.t.*, **-rized, -riz·ing.** To authenticate or certify, or to cause to be certified, through the services of a notary public. —**no·ta·ri·za·tion,** nō·tə·rə·zā′shən, *n.*

no·ta·ry, nō′tə·rē, *n. pl.*, **-ries.** A person authorized by law to attest documents, administer oaths, and authenticate deeds and contracts. Also **no·ta·ry pub·lic.**

no·ta·tion, nō·tā′shən, *n.* The act of noting, marking, or setting down in writing; a record, note, or jotting; the process of noting or setting down by means of a special system of signs or symbols, or the particular method or the system of signs used: an algebraic *notation,* a chemical *notation.* —**no·ta·tion·al,** *a.*

notch, noch, *n.* A cut, hollow, or V-shaped nick on a surface or edge; a narrow mountain pass or defile. *Informal.* A step, unit, or degree: falling a *notch* behind his class.—*v.t.* To cut a notch or notches in. —**notched,** *a.*

note, nōt, *n. Often pl.* A memorandum or short summary intended to assist the memory, or for reference or further development; a statement of an explanatory or critical nature added to the test of a book or other manuscript; a short statement giving pertinent information; a brief, informal letter; a written promise to pay an acknowledged debt: a promissory *note;* reputation or distinction: a lecturer of *note;* notice or heed: taking *note* of his remarks; a distinguishing mark or indicative sign which makes some element or condition known: the *note* of anxiety in her voice. A written character which represents a sound of particular duration or pitch; a vocal or instrumental tone. A musical sound, as a bird call.—*v.t.,* **not·ed, not·ing.** To heed or attend to; make particular mention of; to set down in writing or make a memorandum of. —**not·er,** *n.*

note·book, nōt′bûk, *n.* A blank book in which notes or memoranda are written.

not·ed, nō′tid, *a.* Much known by reputation or report; notable; celebrated. —**not·ed·ly,** *adv.* —**not·ed·ness,** *n.*

note·wor·thy, nōt′wər·thē, *a.* Significant; worthy of observation or notice. —**note·wor·thi·ness,** *n.*

noth·ing, neth′ing, *n.* No thing, not anything, or naught; that which is nonexistent: to create a world out of *nothing;* a trifling action, matter, circumstance, or thing, a person of no importance; a nobody or nonentity. *Arith.* A zero or naught (0).—*adv.* In no respect or degree; not at all: It was *nothing* like what we expected. —**noth·ing do·ing.** *Informal.* Absolutely no; definitely not.

noth·ing·ness, neth′ing·nis, *n.* Nonexistence or that which is nonexistent; unconsciousness; utter insignificance, emptiness, or worthlessness.

no·tice, nō′tis, *n.* A written announcement; warning; a printed bulletin, a sign, or a poster; attention; a formal statement of the termination of a contract or agreement; a brief critical review.—*v.t.,* **-ticed, -tic·ing.** To take cognizance of; become aware of; to observe; to mention or make observations on. —**no·tice·a·ble,** *a.* —**no·tice·a·bly,** *adv.*

no·ti·fy, nō′tə·fī, *v.t.,* **-fied, -fy·ing.** To give notice to; to inform by words or writing. —**no·ti·fi·ca·tion,** nō·tə·fə·kā′shən, **no·ti·fi·er,** *n.*

no·tion, nō′shən, *n.* A general concept; an opinion, view, or belief; a fanciful or foolish idea or whim. *Pl.*

Small useful articles such as pins, needles, and ribbons, esp. as displayed for sale.

no·to·ri·ous, nō·tōr′ē·əs, nō·tôr′ē·əs, *a.* Publicly or generally known but regarded with disapproval; widely known. —**no·to·ri·ous·ly,** *adv.* —**no·to·ri·ous·ness, no·to·ri·e·ty,** nō·tə·rī′ə·tē, *n.*

no-trump, nō′tremp′, *n.* Bridge. A bid or declaration in which no suit is designated as trump.—*a.*

not·with·stand·ing, not·with·stan′ding, not·with·stan′ding, *prep.* In spite of.—*adv.* Nevertheless.—*conj.* Although.

nought, nôt, *n., a., adv.* Naught.

noun, nown, *n.* A word that denotes a person, place, thing, condition, action, or quality.

nour·ish, nər′ish, *v.t.* To feed and cause to grow; to supply with nutriment; to encourage, foster, or cherish. —**nour·ish·er,** *n.* —**nour·ish·ing,** *a.*

nour·ish·ment, nər′ish·mənt, *n.* Food, sustenance, nutriment; the act of nourishing; that which promotes any kind of growth or development: intellectual *nourishment.*

no·va, nō′və, *n. pl.,* **-vas, -vae,** -vē. A star which explodes, grows thousands of times brighter, then gradually becomes dim again.

nov·el, nov′əl, *n.* A fictitious prose narrative of considerable length, portraying characters, actions, and scenes representative of real life in a plot of more or less intricacy.—*a.* Of a new kind or different from anything seen or known before; unusual or strange, esp. in a notable or interesting way. —**nov·el·ist,** *n.* —**nov·el·is·tic,** nov·ə·lis′tik, *a.*

nov·el·ette, nov·ə·let′, *n.* A short novel.

nov·el·ty, nov′əl·tē, *n. pl.,* **-ties.** Novel character, newness, or strangeness; something novel or new; a new or novel article of trade, esp. comic or decorative, usu. having temporary appeal.

No·vem·ber, nō·vem′bər, *n.* The eleventh month of the year, containing 30 days.

no·ve·na, nō·vē′nə, *n. pl.,* **-nae,** -nē. *Rom. Cath. Ch.* A devotion of prayers or services on nine consecutive days, or one particular day in nine consecutive months: a *novena* of nine first Fridays.

nov·ice, nov′is, *n.* One who is new to the circumstances in which he or she is placed; a beginner. One who has entered a religious house, but has not taken the vow; a probationer.

no·vi·ti·ate, no·vi·ci·ate, nō·vish′ē·it, nō·vish′ē·āt, *n.* The state or time of being a novice; apprenticeship.

No·vo·cain, nō′və·kān, *n. Trademark.* A local anesthetic, used in dentistry.

now, now, *adv.* At the present time or moment; immediately or at once; at the time or moment only just past; at this time or juncture in some period under consideration or in some course of proceedings described: night was *now* approaching; in these present times or nowadays; under the present or existing circumstances or as matters stand.—*conj.* Now that, since, or seeing that.—*n.* —**now and a·gain,** at one time and again at another; now and then.

now·a·days, now′ə·dāz, *adv.* At the present time; in these days.

no·where, nō′hwer, *adv.* In,at, or to no place.—*n.* Also *dial.* **no·wheres,** nō′hwərz.

no·wise, nō′wīz, *adv.* In no way; not at all.

nox·ious, nok′shəs, *a.* Harmful or injurious to health or physical well-being; unwholesome; morally harmful or pernicious. —**nox·ious·ly,** *adv.* —**nox·ious·ness,** *n.*

noz·zle, noz′əl, *n.* The projecting spout of something. *Informal.* The nose.

nth, enth, *a.* The last or most extreme of a series; utmost.

nu·ance, noo′äns, nū′äns, noo·äns′, nū·äns′, *n.* A

---

subtle or delicate degree of meaning, tone, or feeling.

nub, nəb, *n.* A knob or protuberance. *Informal.* The gist or essence.

nub·bin, nəb′in, *n.* A small lump or piece; a small or imperfect ear of corn, or an undeveloped fruit.

nu·bile, noo′bəl, nū′bəl, *a.* Of an age or stage of physical maturity suitable for marriage: said of young women.

nu·cle·ar, noo′klē·ər, nū′klē·ər, *a.* Of, pertaining to, or comprising a nucleus.

nu·cle·ar phys·ics, *n.* The branch of physics which studies the structure and properties of atomic nuclei.

nu·cle·us, noo′klē·əs, nū′klē·əs, *n. pl.,* **-us·es, -i,** -ī. A central part or thing about which other parts or things are grouped; anything constituting a central part, foundation, or beginning; a complex, usu. round mass of protoplasm present in the interior of all living cells and essential to vital cell activities such as growth, metabolism, assimilation, and reproduction; the central, densest part of an atom.

nude, nood, nūd, *a.* Naked; bare.—*n.* A naked figure depicted in an art form. —**nude·ly,** *adv.* —**nude·ness, nu·di·ty,** *n.*

nudge, nəj, *n.* A jog or gentle poke, as with the elbow.—*v.t.,* **nudged, nudg·ing.** To give a hint or signal by a usu. furtive touch with the hand, elbow, or foot. —**nudg·er,** *n.*

nud·ism, noo′diz·əm, nū′diz·əm, *n.* The practice of going naked, usually as a means of healthful living. —**nud·ist,** *n., a.*

nug·get, nəg′it, *n.* A lump of something, esp. a lump of native gold.

nui·sance, noo′səns, nū′səns, *n.* Something or someone annoying or obnoxious; that which is offensive or irritating; a pest.

null, nəl, *a.* Of no legal or binding force; invalid; void; of no effect, consequence, significance, or value. —**null and void,** of no legal or binding force. —**nul·li·ty,** *n. pl.,* **-ties.**

nul·li·fy, nəl′ə·fī, *v.t.,* **-fied, -fy·ing.** To make null; render or declare legally void or inoperative; to make ineffective, futile, or of no consequence. —**nul·li·fi·ca·tion,** nəl·ə·fə·kā′shən, **nul·li·fi·er,** *n.*

numb, nəm, *a.* Without physical sensation or feeling; not able to move.—*v.t.* To make numb. —**numb·ly,** *adv.* —**numb·ness,** *n.* —**numb·ing,** *a.* —**numb·ing·ly,** *adv.*

num·ber, nəm′bər, *n.* A word, symbol, or a combination of words or symbols used in counting or to denote a total; a numeral; a quantity of individuals; quantity as composed of units: *The difference between many and few is a matter of number;* a single issue of a periodical or a serial section of a book; a single performance or routine in a stage presentation. *Informal.* An article or line of merchandise; a person, esp. a young woman: *His girl is a cute number.* Pl. Mathematics as a system of thought. *Sometimes pl.* Numerical strength or superiority. The property of language which serves to indicate whether a word refers to one, two, or more than two, and in English which serves to indicate whether a word refers to one or more than one.—*v.t.* To ascertain the number of; enumerate; to fix, limit, or reduce the number of; to include as one of a group; to be numbered or included, followed by *with* or *among.* —**num·ber one,** (*often cap.*). *Informal.* Oneself. —**one's num·ber is up.** *Informal.* To be without luck or good fortune; to be about to fail or die. —**with·out num·ber, be·yond num·ber,** innumerable. —**num·ber·er,** *n.* —**num·ber·less,** *a.*

num·bers, nəm′bərz, *n. pl. but sing. in constr. Informal.* An illegal lottery in which one bets on the appearance of particular numbers in a daily newspaper, as in a stock market quotation or other statistical list. Also **num·bers game, num·bers pool.**

numb·skull, nəm′skəl, *n.* Numskull.

nu·mer·al, noo′mər·əl, nū′mər·əl, *a.* Pertaining to or consisting of number.—*n.* A figure, character, or group of figures used to express a number; a word or combination of words expressing a number. —**num·er·al·ly,** *adv.*

nu·mer·ate, noo′mər·āt, nū′mər·āt, *v.t.,* **-at·ed, -at·ing.** To count; enumerate; to read in words, as a numerical symbol or expression. —**nu·mer·a·tion,** noo·mə·rā′shən, *n.*

nu·mer·a·tor, noo′mə·rā·tər, nū′mə·rā·tər, *n.* The term or number above the line in a fraction indicating the number of units taken of the denominator.

nu·mer·i·cal, noo·mar′i·kəl, nū·mar′i·kəl, *a.* Pertaining to, denoted by, or denoting a number or numbers; expressed by or consisting of numbers rather than letters. —**nu·mer·i·cal·ly,** *adv.*

nu·mer·ous, noo′mər·əs, nū′mər·əs, *a.* Consisting of a great number of units or individuals; very many. —**nu·mer·ous·ly,** *adv.* —**nu·mer·ous·ness,** *n.*

nu·mis·mat·ics, noo·miz·mat′iks, nū·miz·mat′iks, *n. pl. but sing. in constr.* The study and/or collecting of rare coins, medals, and related objects. —**nu·mis·mat·ic, nu·mis·mat·i·cal,** *a.* —**nu·mis·ma·tist,** noo·miz′mə·tist, nū·miz′mə·tist, *n.*

num·skull, nəm′skəl, *n.* A dunce; a stupid person. Also **numb·skull.**

nun, nən, *n.* A woman devoted to a religious life who lives in a convent or nunnery, under vows of perpetual chastity, obedience, and poverty.

nun·ci·o, nən′shē·ō, *n. pl.,* **-os.** A papal ambassador to a country with which the Vatican has permanent diplomatic relations.

nun·ner·y, nən′ə·rē, *n. pl.,* **-ies.** A convent in which nuns reside.

nup·tial, nəp′shəl, *a.* Pertaining to marriage; describing wedding rituals or customs.—*n. Usu. pl.* A wedding or marriage. —**nup·tial·ly,** *adv.*

nurse, nərs, *n.* One who tends or takes care of the sick or infirm, esp. one who has undergone appropriate training; a female who has the care of another's child or children.—*v.t.,* **nursed, nurs·ing.** To feed and tend in infancy; to suckle; to nurture; to foster; to try to cure: to *nurse* an indisposition; to handle with care. —*v.i.* To suckle; to feed from the breast. —**nurs·er,** *n.*

nurse·maid, nərs′mād, *n.* A maidservant employed in taking care of children.

nurs·er·y, nər′sə·rē, *n. pl.,* **-ies.** An area set apart for children; a place where trees, shrubs, and flowering plants are raised from seed or otherwise in order to be transplanted or sold.

nurs·er·y rhyme, *n.* A tale for children written in rhyming verse.

nurs·er·y school, *n.* A school for children not old enough for kindergarten.

nur·ture, nər′chər, *n.* Education; breeding; nourishes; food.—*v.t.,* **-tured, -tur·ing.** To nourish; to educate; to train or bring up. —**nur·tur·er,** *n.*

nut, nət, *n.* A fruit consisting of an edible kernel enclosed in a woody or leathery shell; the kernel itself; a hard, indehiscent, one-seeded fruit, as the chestnut or the acorn; something suggesting a nut that is hard to crack, as a difficult question. *Informal.* The head; a witless or crazy person; a very enthusiastic person; a testicle; a perforated metal block with an internal thread used to screw on the end of a bolt. *Pl.* Nonsense.—*v.i.,* **nut·ted, nut·ting.** To seek for or gather nuts.

nut·crack·er, nət′krak·ər, *n.* An instrument for cracking hard-shelled nuts; a brown spotted bird of the crow family.

nut·hatch, nət′hach, *n.* Any of several chubby tree-climbing birds with a long bill and a stubby tail, and which habitually goes headfirst down a tree trunk feeding on nuts and insects.

nut·meg, nət′meg, *n.* The hard, aromatic seed of the fruit of an East Indian tree, used as a spice.

nu·tri·ent, noo′trē·ənt, nū′trē·ənt, *a.* Nourishing; nutritious.—*n.* Any substance which nourishes.

nu·tri·ment, noo′trə·mənt, nū′trə·mənt, *n.* That

which nourishes; food.

nu·tri·tion, noo·trish′ən, nū·trish′ən, n. The act or process by which organisms absorb into their systems their proper food; that which nourishes; nutriment. **—nu·tri·tion·al,** a. **—nu·tri·tion·al·ly,** adv. **—nu·tri·tion·ist,** n.

nu·tri·tious, noo·trish′əs, nū·trish′əs, a. Containing or serving as nutriment; nourishing. **—nu·tri·tious·ly,** adv. **—nu·tri·tious·ness,** n.

nu·tri·tive, noo′trə·tiv, nū′trə·tiv, a. Having the quality of nourishing; nutritious; pertaining to nutrition. **—nu·tri·tive·ly,** adv. **—nu·tri·tive·ness,** n.

nuts, nəts, a. Informal. Insane; eccentric; tremendously enthusiastic, followed by about or over.—interj. Informal. An exclamation expressing disgust, annoyance, scorn, despair, or the like, often followed by to.

nut·shell, nət′shel, n. The hard shell of a nut. **—in a nut·shell,** in short, simple form; briefly.

nut·ty, nət′ē, a., **-ti·er, -ti·est.** Producing or containing nuts; tasting of or like nuts. Informal. Silly; eccentric; crazy. **—nut·ti·ness,** n.

nuz·zle, nəz′əl, v.i., **-zled, -zling.** To thrust or push the nose; to nestle, snuggle up to, or cuddle.—v.t. To thrust the nose against or into something; to cuddle, as a person or thing.

ny·lon, nī′lon, n. A synthetic, thermoplastic chemical substance formable into fibers, sheets, bristles, and filaments of extreme toughness, strength, and elasticity; pl., women's sheer hosiery made of nylon.

nymph, nimf, n. One of a numerous class of inferior divinities, conceived as beautiful maidens inhabiting the sea, rivers, woods, trees, mountains, and meadows, and frequently mentioned as attending a superior deity; a beautiful or graceful young woman or maiden; an insect in an intermediate stage of development, between a larva and an imago. **—nym·phal,** a.

nym·pho·ma·ni·a, nim·fə·mā′nē·ə, n. Uncontrollable sexual desire in females. **—nym·pho·ma·ni·ac,** n., a. Also, informal, **nym·pho,** nim′fō.

O

O, o, ō, n. The fifteenth letter of the English alphabet.

O, ō, interj. A word used before the name in address, esp. in solemn or poetic language, to lend earnestness to an appeal: "Praise the Lord, O Jerusalem," (Ps. cxlvii. 12.) An expression of surprise, gladness, longing, pain: O woe is me.—n. The exclamation "O."

oaf, ōf, n. A stupid dolt; a clumsy, dull-witted person. **—oaf·ish,** a. **—oaf·ish·ly,** adv. **—oaf·ish·ness,** n.

oak, ōk, n. Any of many large forest trees with hard, durable wood.—a. **—oak·en,** a.

oa·kum, ō′kəm, n. The substance of old ropes untwisted and pulled into loose fibers, and used for caulking the seams of wooden ships.

oar, ōr, ôr, n. A long shaft with a blade at one end used to row, propel, or steer a boat.—v.t. To propel with or as with oars; to row.—v.i. To row; move or advance as if by rowing. **—oared,** a. **—oars·man,** n. pl., **-men.**

oar·lock, ōr′lok, ôr′lok, n. A U-shaped or other device for holding an oar during rowing or steering. Also **row·lock.**

o·a·sis, ō·ā′sis, n. pl., **o·a·ses,** ō·ā′sēz. A fertile area or verdant tract where there is water located in the midst of a desert; anything providing relief or refuge.

oat, ōt, n. Usu. pl. A cereal grass cultivated for its edible grain; the grain itself. **—oat·en,** a.

oath, ōth, n. pl., **oaths,** ōths, ōthz. A solemn appeal to God or to some revered person or figure, in attestation of the truth of a statement or one's determination to keep a promise; a formally affirmed statement or promise accepted as an equivalent; the form of words in which such a statement or promise is made: the oath of office; a light or blasphemous use of the name of God or anything sacred; a curse.

oat·meal, ōt′mēl, n. A cooked cereal made from rolled oats.

ob·bli·ga·to, ob·lə·gä′tō, n. pl., **-tos.** Mus. An accompaniment of more or less distinct character and independent value.—a. Pertaining to an obbligato; necessary; obligatory. Also **ob·li·ga·to.**

ob·du·rate, ob′də·rit, ob′dyə·rit, a. Indifferent to or unmoved by human feelings; stubborn; inflexible; unyielding. **—ob·du·ra·cy,** n. **—ob·du·rate·ly,** adv. **—ob·du·rate·ness,** n.

o·be·di·ence, ō·bē′dē·əns, n. The act or habit of obeying; compliance. **—o·be·di·ent,** a. **—o·be·di·ent·ly,** adv.

o·bei·sance, ō·bā′səns, ō·bē′səns, n. A bow or curtsy; an act of reverence, or deference. **—o·bei·sant,** a.

ob·e·lisk, ob′ə·lisk, n. A tapering, four-sided shaft of stone, usu. monolithic, having a pyramidal apex and often seen among the monuments of ancient Egypt; something resembling such a shaft.

o·bese, ō·bēs′, a. Excessively corpulent; fat; overweight. **—o·bese·ness,** **o·bes·i·ty,** ō·bē′si·tē, ō·bes′i·tē, n. **—o·bese·ly,** adv.

o·bey, ō·bā′, v.t. To comply with the commands of; to be ruled by; to submit to the direction or control of.—v.i. To submit to commands or authority; to do as one is bid. **—o·bey·er,** n.

ob·fus·cate, ob·fəs′kāt, ob′fə·skāt, v.t., **-cat·ed, -cat·ing.** To darken or obscure; to bewilder, confuse, or muddle. **—ob·fus·ca·tion,** ob·fəs·kā′shən, n.

o·bit, ō′bit, ob/it, n. Informal. An obituary.

o·bit·u·ar·y, ō·bich′ū·er·ē, n. pl., **-ies.** A published death notice, often including a brief biography.—a. Relating to or recording the decease of a person.

ob·ject, ob′jikt, ob′jekt, n. That toward which the mind is directed in any of its states or activities; some visible and tangible thing; that to which efforts are directed; aim; end; ultimate purpose. A noun or noun substitute on which the action expressed by a transitive verb is exercised; a noun or noun substitute which follows a preposition in a prepositional phrase. **—əb·jekt′,** v.t. To state or urge in opposition; to state as an objection.—v.i. To oppose in words or arguments; to be adverse to something or someone; to voice disapproval. **—ob·ject·less,** ob′jikt·lis, a. **—ob·ject·or,** əb·jekt′ter, n.

ob·jec·tion, əb·jek′shən, n. The act of objecting; that which is said or felt in opposition or disagreement; the reason or cause for disapproving, disagreeing, or disputing; an adverse reason, argument, or charge.

ob·jec·tion·a·ble, əb·jek′shən·ə·bəl, a. Provoking protest or disapproval; reprehensible, offensive, or insulting. **—ob·jec·tion·a·ble·ness,** n. **—ob·jec·**

---

a- hat, fāte, fâre, fäther; e- met, mē; i- pin, pīne; o- not, nōte, ôrb, moove (move), boy, pownd; u- cūbe, bůll, tůk (took); ch- chin; th- thick, ŧhen; zh- vizhon (vision); ə- əgo, takən, pencəl, lemən, bərd (bird).

tion·a·bly, *adv.*

ob·jec·tive, əb·jek′tiv, *a.* Being the object of perception or thought; intent upon or dealing with things external to the mind rather than thoughts or feelings, as a person or a book; being the object of one's endeavors or actions. Noting the case in declension in English that indicates the grammatical object; being in or pertaining to this case.—*n.* An end toward which efforts are directed; something aimed at; an objective point; the objective case, or a word in that case. —**ob·jec·tive·ly,** *adv.* —**ob·jec·tive·ness, ob·jec·tiv·i·ty,** ob·jek·tiv′ə·tē, *n.*

ob·ject les·son, *n.* A lesson in which a material object is made the basis of instruction; something that illustrates a principle in a concrete form.

ob·jur·gate, ob′jər·gāt, əb·jər′gāt, *v.t., v.i.,* **-gat·ed, -gat·ing.** To scold, reprove, or censure; to chastise harshly. —**ob·jur·ga·tion,** ob·jər·gā′shən, *n.* —**ob·jur·ga·to·ry,** əb·jər′gə·tôr·ē, *a.*

ob·late, ob′lāt, *a.* Of a sphere, flattened or depressed at the poles. —**ob·late·ly,** *adv.* —**ob·late·ness,** *n.*

ob·li·gate, ob′lə·gāt, *v.t.,* **-gat·ed, -gat·ing.** To bind morally or legally to fulfill certain conditions. —**ob′lə·git,** ob′lə·gāt, *a.* Bound; constrained.

ob·li·ga·tion, ob·lə·gā′shən, *n.* The act of binding oneself by promise or contract; the binding force of a contract or promise; anything imposing a moral or legal duty; the state or fact of being indebted for a benefit or service, as a debt of gratitude.

ob·lig·a·to·ry, əb·lig′ə·tôr·ē, ob′lə·gə·tô·rē, *a.* Binding morally or legally; required as a matter of obligation.

o·blige, ə·blīj′, *v.t.,* **o·bliged, o·blig·ing.** To constrain by any force, physical, moral, or legal; to compel; to bind by any restraint; to bind by some favor done; to lay under obligation of gratitude; to perform a service for. —**o·blig·er,** *n.*

o·blig·ing, ə·blī′jing, *a.* Disposed to oblige, do favors, or perform services; accommodating; willing; kind. —**o·blig·ing·ly,** *adv.* —**o·blig·ing·ness,** *n.*

ob·lique, ə·blēk′, *a.* Neither perpendicular nor parallel; slanting; not straightforward; indirectly expressed; devious; indirectly aimed at or accomplished.—*v.i.,* **-liqued, -liqu·ing.** To slant; have or take an oblique direction. —**ob·lique·ly,** *adv.* —**ob·lique·ness, ob·liq·ui·ty,** ə·blik′wə·tē, *n.*

ob·lique an·gle, *n.* An angle other than a right angle, as an acute or obtuse angle.

ob·lit·er·ate, ə·blit′ə·rāt, *v.t.,* **-at·ed, -at·ing.** To efface, erase, or blot out, as writing; to destroy any indication or sign of. —**ob·lit·er·a·tion,** ə·blit·ə·rā′shən, *n.* —**ob·lit·er·a·tive,** *a.*

ob·liv·i·on, ə·bliv′ē·ən, *n.* The condition or instance of forgetting; the condition or instance of being forgotten.

ob·liv·i·ous, ə·bliv′ē·əs, *a.* Forgetful; without memory of; causing forgetfulness; without consciousness of; unaware, usu. followed by *of* or *to.* —**ob·liv·i·ous·ly,** *adv.* —**ob·liv·i·ous·ness,** *n.*

ob·long, ob′lông, ob′long, *a.* Rectangular, and having the length greater than the breadth; longer than broad.—*n.* An oblong figure.

ob·lo·quy, ob′lə·kwē, *n. pl.,* **-quies.** Censorious, reproachful, or defamatory language; denunciation of a man or his deeds; the odium and disgrace arising from public blame or vilification.

ob·nox·ious, əb·nok′shəs, *a.* Odious; hateful; offensive; unpopular. —**ob·nox·ious·ly,** *adv.* —**ob·nox·ious·ness,** *n.*

o·boe, ō′bō, *n.* A double-reed wooden wind instrument in the form of a slender tapering tube. —**o·bo·ist,** *n.*

ob·scene, əb·sēn′, *a.* Objectionable or repugnant to acceptable standards of decency or morality; indecent; pornographic; offensive in language or action. —**ob·scene·ly,** *adv.* —**ob·scene·ness, ob·scen·i·ty,** əb·sen′i·tē, əb·sē′ni·tē, *n. pl.,* **-ties.**

ob·scure, əb·skyûr′, *a.,* **-scur·er, -scur·est.** Not easily understood; not expressed with clarity; not clear or distinct to any sense; removed or remote from worldly or important activities; unnoticed, or unknown to fame; lacking illumination; gloomy or dim.—*v.t.,* **ob·scured, ob·scur·ing.** To make dark or dim; to make less intelligible, legible, or visible; to prevent from being seen or known.—*n.* —**ob·scure·ly,** *adv.* —**ob·scure·ness,** *n.* —**ob·scu·ri·ty,** *n. pl.,* **-ties.**

ob·se·qui·ous, əb·sē′kwē·əs, *a.* Excessively obedient or submissive to the will of another; servile. —**ob·se·qui·ous·ly,** *adv.* —**ob·se·qui·ous·ness,** *n.*

ob·se·quy, ob′sə·kwē, *n. pl.,* **-quies.** Usu. pl. A funeral rite or ceremony.

ob·serv·a·ble, əb·zər′və·bəl, *a.* Capable of being observed; worthy of observation. —**ob·serv·a·ble·ness,** *n.* —**ob·serv·a·bly,** *adv.*

ob·ser·vance, əb·zər′vəns, *n.* The action of observing, conforming to, following, or keeping: *observance* of laws, rules, customs, or methods; a keeping or celebrating by appropriate procedure, as ceremonies; a procedure, ceremony, or rite, as for a particular occasion or use: patriotic *observances.*

ob·ser·vant, əb·zər′vənt, *a.* Making quick or careful observation; taking notice; attentive to duties or commands; adhering to in practice, often with *of: observant of* duties.—*n.* —**ob·ser·vant·ly,** *adv.*

ob·ser·va·tion, ob·zər·vā′shən, *n.* The act, power, or habit of observing; a taking notice or paying attention; a remark or judgment based on what has been observed. —**ob·ser·va·tion·al,** *a.*

ob·ser·va·to·ry, əb·zər′və·tô·rē, *n. pl.,* **-ries.** A place used for making observations of natural phenomena, esp. a building for astronomical observations.

ob·serve, əb·zərv′, *v.t.,* **-served, -serv·ing.** To regard attentively; to watch; to notice; to perceive; to discover; to remark in words; to mention; to keep, as a holiday, with due ceremonies; to celebrate; to keep or adhere to in practice; to comply with; to obey.—*v.i.* To attend or watch without joining in; to perceive; to remark; to comment. —**ob·serv·ed·ly,** *adv.* —**ob·serv·er,** əb·zər′vər, *n.* —**ob·serv·ing·ly,** *adv.*

ob·sess, əb·ses′, *v.t.* To occupy a person's thoughts to an unusual degree; preoccupy the mind; to harass or vex through a persistent, usu. undesirable or unwanted thought or emotion. —**ob·ses·sive,** *a.* —**ob·ses·sive·ly,** *adv.*

ob·ses·sion, əb·sesh′ən, *n.* An act of obsessing; a thought or emotion which comes strongly to mind with unwanted persistency; the thought itself.

ob·sid·i·an, əb·sid′ē·ən, *n.* A glassy rock of volcanic origin, usu. of a black color.

ob·so·les·cent, ob·sə·les′ənt, *a.* Becoming obsolete; passing out of use; tending to become out of date. —**ob·so·les·cence,** *n.* —**ob·so·les·cent·ly,** *adv.*

ob·so·lete, ob·sə·lēt′, ob′sə·lēt, *a.* Fallen into disuse or no longer in use; of a discarded type; out-of-date. —**ob·so·lete·ness,** *n.*

ob·sta·cle, ob′stə·kəl, *n.* Anything that stands in the way; an obstruction or impediment.

ob·ste·tri·cian, ob·sti·trish′ən, *n.* A physician that specializes in obstetrics.

ob·stet·rics, əb·ste′triks, *n. pl. but sing. in constr.* That branch of medical science which includes prenatal care, childbirth, and the postnatal period. —**ob·stet·ric, ob·stet·ri·cal,** *a.* —**ob·stet·ri·cal·ly,** *adv.*

ob·sti·nate, ob′stə·nit, *a.* Pertinaciously adhering to an opinion or purpose; fixed firmly in resolution; not yielding to reason or argument; stubborn. —**ob·sti·na·cy,** *n. pl.,* **-cies.** —**ob·sti·nate·ly,** *adv.* —**ob·sti·nate·ness,** *n.*

ob·strep·er·ous, əb·strep′ər·əs, *a.* Unruly, noisy, or boisterous; resisting control, direction, or advice in a noisy or willfully unruly way. —**ob·strep·er·ous·ly,** *adv.* —**ob·strep·er·ous·ness,** *n.*

ob·struct, əb·strəkt′, *v.t.* To block or close, as a street or channel, with obstacles that prevent passing; to hinder or impede the passage, progress, or operation of; to stand in the way of, so as to block the view. —**ob·struc·tive,** *a., n.* —**ob·struc·tor,** *n.*

ob·struc·tion, əb·strək′shən, *n.* The act or a case of obstructing; anything that clogs or closes a way, passage, or channel; an obstacle or impediment to passage, progress, or activity. —**ob·struc·tion·ism,** **ob·struc·tion·ist,** *n.*

ob·tain, əb·tān′, *v.t.* To gain possession of; to procure, receive, get, acquire.—*v.i.* To be in customary or common use: The custom still *obtains.* —**ob·tain·a·ble,** *a.* —**ob·tain·er, ob·tain·ment,** *n.*

ob·trude, əb·trood′, *v.t.,* **-trud·ed, -trud·ing.** To thrust forward; to force into any place or state unduly or without solicitation.—*v.i.* To obtrude oneself; to enter when not invited. —**ob·trud·er, ob·tru·sion,** *n.* —**ob·tru·sive,** *a.* —**ob·tru·sive·ness,** *n.*

ob·tuse, əb·toos′, əb·tūs′, *a.* Not pointed or acute; blunt; not having acute sensibility. —**ob·tuse·ly,** *adv.* —**ob·tuse·ness,** *n.*

ob·verse, ob·vərs′, ob′vərs, *a.* Turned toward or facing one; corresponding to something else, as a counterpart. —**ob′vərs,** *n.* That side of a coin, medal, or the like, which bears the principal design, as opposed to *reverse;* the front or principal face of anything; a counterpart. —**ob·verse·ly,** *adv.*

ob·vi·ate, ob′vē·āt, *v.t.,* **-at·ed, -at·ing.** To counter, eliminate, or prevent, as difficulties or objections, by forethought; to overcome; to clear out of the way. —**ob·vi·a·tion,** ob·vē·ā′shən, **ob·vi·a·tor,** *n.*

ob·vi·ous, ob′vē·əs, *a.* Easily discovered, seen, or understood; perfectly plain or evident. —**ob·vi·ous·ly,** *adv.* —**ob·vi·ous·ness,** *n.*

oc·ca·sion, ə·kā′zhən, *n.* The time of an occurrence, incident, or event, or the event itself; an important or significant event or time; an opportune or convenient time: the right *occasion;* the incidental cause, motive, or reason for a particular action; a demand or requirement: having no *occasion* for it.—*v.t.* To cause incidentally; to produce or bring about.

oc·ca·sion·al, ə·kā′zhə·nəl, *a.* Occurring at times, but not regularly or systematically; made or suitable for a specific occasion: *occasional* verse; intended for use, as a chair or table, as the need arises. —**oc·ca·sion·al·ly,** *adv.*

oc·ci·dent, ok′si·dənt, *n.* The west; the western regions; (*cap.*) the western countries; the western hemisphere, as opposed to the *Orient;* Europe, as opposed to Asia. —**oc·ci·den·tal,** ok·si·den′təl, *a., n.*

oc·clude, ə·klood′, *v.t.,* **-clud·ed, -clud·ing.** To close, shut, or stop up, as a passage; to shut in, out, or off.—*v.i. Dentistry.* To meet closely or fit into each other, as opposing teeth in the upper and lower jaw. —**oc·clu·sive,** *a.*

oc·clu·sion, ə·kloo′zhən, *n.* The act of occluding, or the state of being occluded; the meeting closely of opposing teeth in the upper and the lower jaw.

oc·cult, ə·kəlt′, ok′əlt, *a.* Not disclosed; kept secret; communicated only to the initiated; beyond the bounds of ordinary or natural knowledge. Of or pertaining to certain so-called sciences, as magic or astrology, involving the alleged knowledge or employment of secret or mysterious agencies; having to do with such sciences.—*n.* —**oc·cult·ly,** *adv.* —**oc·cult·ness,** *n.*

oc·cult·ism, ə·kəl′tiz·əm, *n.* The doctrine, study of, or belief in the supernatural and communication with it. —**oc·cult·ist,** *n.*

oc·cu·pan·cy, ok′yə·pən·sē, *n. pl.,* **-cies.** The act of occupying; a holding in possession; the term during which one is an occupant. —**oc·cu·pant,** *n.*

oc·cu·pa·tion, ok·yə·pā′shən, *n.* One's principal employment, business, vocation, trade, or other means of livelihood; the act of occupying or taking possession, as of land or buildings. —**oc·cu·pa·tion·al,** *a.* —**oc·cu·pa·tion·al·ly,** *adv.*

oc·cu·pa·tion·al ther·a·py, *n.* A method of treatment of convalescents utilizing light work for diversion, physical exercise, or vocational training.

oc·cu·py, ok′yə·pī, *v.t.,* **-pied, -py·ing.** To take and keep possession of, as by military conquest; to take up, as room or time; to employ or use, as one's time or attention; to fill, as a post or office; to inhabit or be a dweller in. —**oc·cu·pi·er,** *n.*

oc·cur, ə·kər′, *v.i.,* **-curred, -cur·ring.** To suggest or come to the mind, imagination, or memory; to befall; to happen; to take place; to exist so as to be found or seen. —**oc·cur·rence,** *n.* —**oc·cur·rent,** *a.*

o·cean, ō′shən, *n.* The immense body of salt water covering more than 70 per cent of the earth's surface; any of the geographical divisions of this body; a great expanse or amount: the undulating *ocean* of grass. —*a.* —**o·ce·an·ic,** ō·shē·an′ik, *a.*

o·ce·a·nog·ra·phy, ō·shə·nog′rə·fē, ō·shē·ə·nog′rə·fē, *n.* The science and study of oceanic phenomena; the science dealing with undersea space and the conducting of research in such areas as underwater transportation, communication, geography, and engineering. —**o·ce·a·nog·ra·pher,** *n.* —**o·ce·a·no·graph·ic,** ō·shən·ə·graf′ik, **o·ce·a·no·graph·i·cal,** *a.*

o·ce·lot, ō′sə·lot, os′ə·lot, *n.* A spotted, leopardlike cat, ranging from Texas through S. America, being nocturnal and arboreal.

o·cher, o·chre, ō′kər, *n.* Any of various clays containing iron oxide, and varying in color from pale yellow to brownish-red, much used as pigments in paints; the color itself. —**o·cher·ous, o·chre·ous,** ō′krē·əs, **o·cher·y, o·chry,** ō′krē, *a.*

o'clock, ə·klok′, *adv.* Of or by the clock: used in specifying the hour of the day.

oc·ta·gon, ok′tə·gon, *n.* A figure with eight sides and eight angles. —**oc·tag·o·nal,** ok·tag′ə·nəl, *a.* —**oc·tag·o·nal·ly,** *adv.*

oc·ta·he·dron, ok·tə·hē′drən, *n. pl.,* **-drons, -dra.** A solid with eight faces. —**oc·ta·he·dral,** *a.*

oc·tane, ok′tān, *n.* A hydrocarbon of the methane series.

oc·tane num·ber, *n.* A fuel value that increases with antiknock qualities.

oc·tave, ok′tiv, ok′tāv, *n. Mus.* A tone on the eighth degree from a given tone; the interval between such tones; the harmonic combination of such tones; a series of tones, or of keys of an instrument, extending through this interval; in a diatonic scale, the eighth tone from the bottom, with which the repetition of the scale begins; a group or a stanza of eight lines, as the first eight lines of a sonnet.—*a.*

oc·ta·vo, ok·tā′vō, ok·tä′vō, *n.* The size of one leaf of a sheet of paper folded so as to make eight leaves; a book having eight leaves to each sheet; a page usu. 6 × 9½ inches; a book with pages this size.—*a.*

oc·tet, oc·tette, ok·tet′, *n.* A musical composition for eight voices or instruments; a company of eight singers or players; any group of eight.

Oc·to·ber, ok·tō′bər, *n.* The tenth month of the year in the Gregorian calendar, with 31 days.

oc·to·ge·nar·i·an, ok·tə·jə·nār′ē·ən, *n.* A person eighty years of age, or between eighty and ninety.—*a.* —**oc·tog·e·nar·y,** ok·toj′ə·ner·ē, *a., n.*

oc·to·pus, ok′tə·pəs, *n.* Any cephalopod having eight arms provided with suckers, large eyes, and a naked body with a small, internal shell. Also **dev·il·fish.** A far-reaching and powerful organization.

oc·u·lar, ok′yə·lər, *a.* Of or pertaining to the eye; of the nature of an eye; performed by the eye or eyesight;

perceived by the eye or eyesight; derived from actual sight; actually seeing. —*n.* The eyepiece of an optical instrument. —**oc·u·lar·ly,** *adv.*

oc·u·list, ok′yə·list, *n.* One trained and skilled in the examination and treatment of the eye; an ophthalmologist.

odd, od, *a.* Differing in character from what is ordinary or usual; singular, peculiar, or strange; remaining over after a division into pairs, groups, or parts; not forming part of any particular group, set, or class; being part of a pair, set, or series of which the rest is missing; being a surplus, esp. a small one, over a definite quantity or sum; leaving a remainder of one when divided by two, as a number: opposed to *even;* occasional or casual; out-of-the-way or secluded: *odd* corners of the city. —*n.* That which is or appears to be odd. —**odd·ly,** *adv.* —**odd·ness,** *n.*

odd·ball, od′bôl, *n. Informal.* Someone or something which behaves in an eccentric, curious, or nonconforming manner. —*a.* Unusual or eccentric.

odd·i·ty, od′i·tē, *n. pl.,* **-ties.** A singular person, thing, or occurrence, the state or quality of being odd, unusual, or eccentric; a peculiarity.

odds, odz, *n. pl., sing. or pl. in constr.* The probability ratio for or against something occurring or being so; in a contest, the difference in favor of one over another; amount by which one wager exceeds that of another; an allowance awarded the weaker of two opponents to equalize them. —**at odds,** disagreeing; quarreling.

odds and ends, *n. pl.* Miscellaneous matters or articles; remnants; scraps.

odds-on, odz′on′, odz′ôn′, *a.* Considered as having a better than an even chance to win or reach a goal.

ode, ōd, *n.* A poem of irregular metrical structure, usu. expressing the poet's intense personal feelings; a poem meant to be set to music or to be sung. —**od·ic,** ō′dik, *a.*

o·di·ous, ō′dē·əs, *a.* Arousing hatred, repugnance, or extreme dislike. —**o·di·ous·ly,** *adv.* —**o·di·ous·ness,** *n.*

o·di·um, ō′dē·əm, *n.* Intense hatred or dislike, esp. of something despicable; disgrace associated with something hateful; the quality that provokes hatred.

o·dom·e·ter, ō·dom′i·tər, *n.* A device attached to a wheeled vehicle for recording the number of revolutions of a wheel and thus indicating the distance traveled, as on an automobile.

o·dor, *Brit.* **o·dour,** ō′dər, *n.* That quality perceived through the sense of smell; effect of stimulation of the olfactory organ; scent; a suggestive property; reputation. —**o·dored,** *a.* —**o·dor·less,** *a.* —**o·dor·ous,** *a.* —**o·dor·ous·ly,** *adv.* —**o·dor·ous·ness,** *n.*

o·dor·if·er·ous, ō·dər·if′ər·əs, *a.* Giving off odor or scent, esp. an agreeable fragrance. —**o·dor·if·er·ous·ly,** *adv.*

od·ys·sey, od′i·sē, *n.* (*Often cap.*) A long journey marked by wanderings, adventures, and hardships. (*Cap.*) The poem in which Homer recounts the wanderings and return of Odysseus or Ulysses, from Troy to his home in Ithaca.

Oed·i·pus com·plex, ed′i·pəs, ē′di·pəs, *n.* The desire, most readily expressed in sexual terms, of a son for his mother with a consequential rivalry between the son and his father, a complex which may appear later in life as seeking a mother image in relations with other women. —**oed·i·pal,** *a.* (*Often cap.*).

o'er, ōr, ôr, *adv., prep.* Over, usu. poetical.

of, əv, ov, *unstressed* ev, *prep.* At a distance from; produced by or tracing its source to; on the part of; due to or because of; composed of or holding; identified as; with reference to; from the aggregate of; concerning, relating to, or about. Belonging to or over; relating to or indicating; on, in, in the course of, or noting time; before: as, five minutes *of* six; so as to be free of or wanting: as, relieved *of* worry.

off, ôf, of, *adv.* Away: The child scampered *off.* From or away by removal or separation; no longer continuing; absent from duty or work: time *off;* into existence: The wedding did not come *off;* completely: to kill *off* one's chances; to, at, or in relation to time: to put *off* the party; to, at, or in relation to space: to pace *off* a distance; from a fixed price: a dollar *off;* so as to be out of operation: Turn the lights *off.* —*a.* Denoting one's circumstances: well *off;* no longer operating; not true to facts; free from duty; away; of lessened activity: the *off* season; distant; eccentric; odd: a bit *off.* —*prep.* So as to be removed from or separated: Take if *off* the floor; leading away from: *off* the boulevard; away from: *off* the job; below what is taken as normal or standard: a dollar *off* the price; by means of: to live *off* investments; no longer engaged in. —*interj.* Go away; be off. —**off and on,** now and then; intermittently. Also **on and off.**

of·fal, ôf′fəl, of′əl, *n.* The entrails or trimmings of a butchered animal; waste; refuse; garbage; by-products of milling.

off·beat, ôf′bēt′, of′bēt′, *a. Informal.* Unusual; unconventional; unexpected; out-of-step; mistaken or questionable.

off-col·or, ôf′kəl′ər, of′kəl′ər, *a.* Varying from the standard or desired color; varying from normal propriety or decency; risqué; not in proper health.

of·fend, ə·fend′, *v.t.* To displease or annoy; to make angry; to insult; to be disagreeable to; to cause discomfort to; to hurt; to be offensive to, as the sense of taste, smell, or sight. —*v.i.* To offend or be offensive; to commit a sin or crime. —**of·fend·er,** *n.*

of·fense, ə·fens′, *n.* Something that is offending or displeasing; any wrongdoing; a crime or sin; a misdemeanor. Also ô′fens, of′ens. An act of mounting an attack; an assault; in sports, the team possessing the ball, puck, etc. —**take of·fense,** to become angry or feel resentment at something said or done. —**of·fense·less,** ə·fens′lis, *a.*

of·fen·sive, ə·fen′siv, *a.* Causing displeasure, anger, or resentment; giving a disagreeable sensation; disgusting; pertaining to or relating to attack. —*n.* An attack or aggressive movement; the act of attacking. —**of·fen·sive·ly,** *adv.* —**of·fen·sive·ness,** *n.*

of·fer, ôf′ər, of′ər, *v.t.* To present for acceptance or rejection; to propose for consideration, notice, or action; to indicate an intention; to volunteer; to suggest, promise, or give: This plan *offers* the best chance of success; to inflict or make, or to threaten to inflict: to *offer* resistance; to bid, as a price or payment; to put forward for sale; tender; proffer. —*v.i.* To present itself; make an attempt or suggestion; to sacrifice or present an offering in worship. —*n.* The act of offering; that which is proposed or suggested; the act of bidding a price, or the sum bid. —**of·fer·er, of·fer·or,** *n.*

of·fer·ing, ôf′ər·ing, of′ər·ing, *n.* The act of a person who offers; that which is offered, esp. a contribution of money to a church; a sacrificial gift dedicated to a deity.

of·fer·to·ry, ô′fər·tô·rē, of′ər·tô·rē, *n. pl.,* **-ries.** The verses, anthem, or music said, sung, or played while the offerings of the congregation are received at a religious service; that part of a service at which offerings are made; the offerings themselves. —**of·fer·to·ri·al,** ô·fər·tô′rē·əl, *a.*

off·hand, ôf′hand′, of′hand′, *adv.* Without preparation or study; extemporaneously; brusquely. Also **off·hand·ed·ly.** —*a.* Made or done without study or hesitation; casual or curt. Also **off·hand·ed.** —**off·hand·ed·ness,** *n.*

of·fice, ô′fis, of′is, *n.* The place where an individual or organization conducts its business, or those who work there. (*Cap.*) *U.S.* A federal agency beneath a department in rank. A position in a corporate or governmental organization, esp. one entailing authority, responsibility, or trust; the duty or function entrusted to a person; *often pl.,* an act, usu. a favor or service, done for another; a prescribed form of devotion, or a service for a particular occasion, esp. one for the dead.

of•fice-hold•er, ô/fis-hōl-dər, of/is-hōl-dər, *n.* An individual holding a position with the government.

of•fic•er, ô/fi-sər, of/i-sər, *n.* A person holding a title, office, or post of authority in any public or private institution; a policeman; a commissioned individual in the armed forces; the captain or any of the mates in charge of a passenger or merchant ship.

of•fi•cial, ə-fish/əl, *a.* Pertaining to an office of trust or public duty; derived from the proper office, officer, or authority; communicated by virtue of authority.—*n.* One invested with an office of a public nature. —**of•fi•cial•ism,** *n.* —**of•fi•cial•ly,** *adv.*

of•fi•cial•dom, ə-fish/əl-dəm, *n.* Collectively, all officials; officials as a class; the behavior or viewpoints of officials; the concern or responsibility of an official.

of•fi•ci•ate, ə-fish/ē-āt, *v.i.,* **-at•ed, -at•ing.** To perform official duties; to conduct a religious service; to perform the duties of umpire or referee.—*v.t.* To judge, as an event, according to its rules; to act as priest or minister for; to fulfill, as an office. —**of•fi•ci•a•tion,** ə-fish•ē-ā/shən, *n.* —**of•fi•ci•a•tor,** *n.*

of•fi•cious, ə-fish/əs, *a.* Excessively forward in kindness; offering or performing services not wanted; annoyingly eager to oblige or assist; meddling. —**of•fi•cious•ly,** *adv.* —**of•fi•cious•ness,** *n.*

off•ing, ô/fing, of/ing, *n.* The more distant part of the sea as seen from the shore. —**in the off•ing,** near or in sight; likely to occur; happening soon.

off•set, ôf•set/, of•set/, *v.t.,* **-set, -set•ting.** To equalize or counterbalance; to compensate; to print by offset lithography.—*v.i.* To project, as an offshoot or branch; to make an offset. —ôf/set, of/set, *n.* A start or outset; any offshoot; something which counterbalances or compensates; offset printing.—*a.*

off•set print•ing, *n.* A printing process which transfers the inked design or other copy from a lithographic plate, originally a stone, to a rubber surface, usu. a roller which in turn sets the design off onto the sheet or object to be printed.

off•shoot, ôf/shoot, of/shoot, *n.* Anything conceived as springing or proceeding from a main stock or source.

off•shore, ôf/shôr/, ôf/shōr, of/shôr/, of/shōr, *adv.* Off or away from the shore; at a distance from the shore.—*a.*

off•side, ôf/sīd/, of/sīd/, *a.* In sports, esp. football and ice hockey, referring to a player or a play in illegal territory, or ahead of the ball or puck.—*adv.*

off•spring, ôf/spring, of/spring, *n. pl.,* **-spring, -springs.** Children or young born of a particular parent or progenitor; a descendant; descendants collectively. *Fig.* The product, result, or effect of something.

off•stage, ôf/stāj/, of/stāj/, *n.* The area of a stage not seen by the audience; backstage; the wings.—*a., adv.* Away from or out of the audience's view.

off-the-cuff, ôf/the-kəf/, of/the-kəf, *a. Informal.* Not prepared in advance; impromptu; extemporaneous.

off year, *n.* A year in which some aspect of production or activity is below normal; a year in which there is no major election. —**off-year,** ôf/yēr, of/yēr, *a.*

oft, ôft, oft, *adv. Poet.* Often.

of•ten, ôf/ən, of/ən, ôf/tən, of/tən, *adv.* Frequently; many times; repeatedly.

of•ten•times, ô/fən-tīmz, of/ən-tīmz, *adv.* Frequently; often; many times. Also **oft•times,** ôf/tīmz, of/tīmz.

o•gle, ō/gəl, *v.t.,* **o•gled, o•gling.** To look or stare at boldly, amorously, or with the aim of attracting notice; to eye.—*v.i.* To look boldly, amorously, or flirtatiously; to stare.—*n.* A provocative or flirtatious side glance or look. —**o•gler,** *n.*

o•gre, ō/gər, *n.* A hideous and cruel monster of popular legends and fairy tales who devoured human

flesh; an evil, barbarous, or terrifying person. —**o•gre•ish, o•grish,** ō/gər-ish, ō/grish, *a.*

oh, ō, *interj.* An expression of surprise, pain, disapprobation, or desire; in direct address, an expression used to gain someone's attention.—*n. pl.,* **oh's, ohs.**

ohm, ōm, *n.* The unit of resistance equivalent to the resistance of a conductor in which one volt, the unit difference of potential, produces a current of one ampere. —**ohm•age,** *n.* —**ohm•ic,** *a.*

ohm•me•ter, ōm/mē•tər, *n.* An instrument for measuring electrical resistance in ohms.

oil, oyl, *n.* Any of a large class of substances typically unctuous, viscous, combustible, liquid at ordinary temperatures, and soluble in ether or alcohol but not in water, used for food, lubricating, illuminating, heating, and many other purposes; some substance of similar consistency; an oil color; sometimes, an oil painting; petroleum.—*v.t.* Anoint with oil; moisten, smear, or lubricate with oil; to supply with oil; to convert into oil by melting, as butter; to bribe; make oily or smooth, as in speech: to *oil* the tongue.—*a.* Resembling or related to oil; derived from, utilizing, or providing oil.

oil•cloth, oyl/klôth, oyl/kloth, *n.* Cloth waterproofed with oil and coloring agents.

oil col•or, *n.* Paint made by grinding a pigment in oil.

oil•er, oy/lər, *n.* One who oils; any apparatus for lubricating machinery with oil; a ship propelled by oil; oil tanker.

oil field, *n.* An area, usu. under either land or water, rich in petroleum deposits.

oil paint, *n.* Any paint in which a drying oil is the medium.

oil paint•ing, *n.* The art of painting with oil colors; a picture in oil colors.

oil•skin, oyl/skin, *n.* A cotton fabric waterproofed with oil, used for raincoats and hats. *Pl.* A suit or raincoat made of this material.—*a.*

oil slick, *n.* A slick or smooth film on the surface of water, due to the presence of oil.

oil well, *n.* A well drilled to obtain petroleum.

oil•y, oy/lē, *a.,***-i•er, -i•est.** Pertaining to oil; of the nature of or consisting of oil; resembling oil; smeared or covered with oil, or greasy; smooth, as in manner or speech; bland; unctuous. —**oil•i•ness,** *n.*

oint•ment, oynt/mənt, *n.* Any soft, unctuous substance, usu. medicated, applied to the skin for medicinal and cosmetic purposes; an unguent; a salve.

O.K., ō/kā/, *a., adv.* All right; correct: usu. used to express approval. —ō•kā/, *v.t.,* **O.K.'d, O.K.'ing.** To endorse: as, to *O.K.* a bill; agree; approve. —ō/kā/, *n.* Agreement; endorsement; approval. Also **OK, o•kay, o•keh.**

O•kie, ō/kē, *n. Informal.* A migrant farm worker, usu. from Oklahoma; sometimes derogatorily, a native or inhabitant of Oklahoma.

o•kra, ō/krə, *n.* A tall plant, native to Africa, cultivated in the East and West Indies and southern U.S. for its edible, mucilaginous pods, which are used as a vegetable and in soups and stews; the pods of this plant.

old, ōld, *a.,* **old•er** or **eld•er; old•est** or **eldest.** Having lived, existed, been made, or originated long ago; pertaining to persons advanced in years or having characteristics associated with age; stating a specified age, or length of time: a three-year-*old* child; deteriorated through age or long use, stale: *old* jokes; belonging to remote times; familiar or beloved: *old* fellow; skilled and experienced: an *old* hand at intrigue; (*often cap.*) being the earlier or earliest of two or more things of the same kind: the *Old* Testament, the *Old* World. *Informal.* Used as an intensive: any *old* time.—*n.* An earlier time. —**old•en,** *a.* —**old•ish,** *a.* —**old•ness,** *n.*

Old Eng•lish, *n.* The English language in use during

---

a- hat, fāte, fāre, fäther; **e-** met, mē; **i-** pin, pīne; **o-** not, nōte, ôrb, moove (move), boy, pownd; **u-** cūbe, bull, tûk (took); **ch-** chin; **th-** thick, ŧhen; **zh-** vizhon (vision); **ə-** əgo, takən, pencəl, lemən, bərd (bird).

the period 450 to about 1150 A.D.

old-fash·ioned, ōld/fash/ənd, *a.* Characterized by antiquated fashions, ideas, behavior, or methods; out-of-date; related to or derived from a former era; adhering to traditional or conservative ways and customs.—*n.* An alcoholic beverage made with bitters, water, sugar, whiskey, and fruit.

Old Glo·ry, *n.* The flag of the United States.

old guard, *n.* (*Sometimes cap.*) The members of a community, group, or political party who are conservative in thought or action.

old hand, *n.* One who is experienced in or has extensive knowledge of a subject, situation, or procedure; a veteran.

old maid, *n.* An elderly or confirmed spinster; an excessively prudish and fastidious person; a game of cards which ends with the holder of the odd queen being the loser. **—old-maid·ish,** ōld/mā/dish, *a.*

old man, *n. Informal.* Father; husband; a man, such as a boss or employer, who is in an authoritative position; a masculine form of address, implying warm regard: Hello, *old man.*

old school, *n.* Persons having the character, manners, or opinions of a former age. **—old-school,** ōld/skool/, *a.*

old-shoe, ōld/shoo/, *a. Informal.* Comfortably familiar; easy; informal. **—old shoe,** *n.*

old·ster, ōld/stər, *n. Informal.* An old person.

Old Tes·ta·ment, *n.* The books constituting the Hebrew Bible, including the Mosaic Law and histories, the Prophets, and the Hagiographa.

old-time, ōld/tīm/, *a.* Part of or a mark of old or former times; long-lasting: an *old-time* custom.

old-tim·er, ōld/tī/mər, *n. Informal.* One whose residence, membership, or experience dates back a long time; a veteran; one who is old; one who adheres to old-fashioned ideas or ways.

old wives' tale, *n.* A story or a notion often grounded in superstition and passed down from generation to generation.

old-world, ōld/wərld/, *a.* Of the ancient world; belonging to or characteristic of a former period; of or relating to the Old World as contrasted to the New World or the Americas.

o·le·ag·i·nous, ō·lē·aj/ə·nəs, *a.* Having the nature or qualities of oil; containing oil; producing oil; unctuous. **—o·le·ag·i·nous·ly,** *adv.* **—o·le·ag·i·nous·ness,** *n.*

o·le·o, ō/lē·ō, *n.* Oleomargarine.

o·le·o·mar·ga·rine, ō·lē·ō·mär/jə·rin, ō·lē·ō·mär/jə·rēn, *n.* A substitute for butter made from animal fat or vegetable oils, boiled and churned with milk.

ol·fac·tion, ol·fak/shən, *n.* The act of smelling; the sense of smell. **—ol·fac·to·ry,** ol·fak/tə·rē, ol·fak/trē, *a., n. pl.,* **-ries.**

ol·i·gar·chy, ol/ə·gär·kē, *n. pl.,* **-chies.** A form of government in which the power is exercised by or vested in a few; a state so governed; the ruling few or class collectively. **—ol·i·gar·chic,** ol·ə·gär/kik, **ol·i·gar·chi·cal,** *a.* **—ol·i·garch,** ol/ə·gärk, *n.*

ol·i·gop·o·ly, ol·ə·gop/ə·lē, *n.* The state of a market controlled by few producers, sellers, or stock holders, in relation to many buyers.

ol·ive, ol/iv, *n.* An evergreen tree, of the Mediterranean and other warm regions, grown chiefly for its fruit; the fruit, eaten as a relish, and valuable as a source of oil; the wood of this tree, valued for ornamental work; any of various related or similar trees; the foliage of the tree, a wreath of it, or an olive branch used as an emblem of peace; an olive color, tint, or tinge. **—a.** Of the dull, yellowish-green color of the unripe olive fruit.

ol·ive drab, *n.* Any of various shades of an olive-toned mixture of green and brown; a woolen fabric of this color used for U.S. Army uniforms; the uniform itself.

ol·ive-green, ol/iv·grēn/, *n.* Green with a yellowish or brownish tinge.

ol·ive oil, *n.* An oil expressed from the pulp of olives, used with food, in medicine, and for various other purposes.

O·lym·pic games, ō·lim/pik, *n. pl.* An international competition in numerous sports, held every four years, each time in a different country, and named for an ancient Greek festival; the greatest festival of ancient Greece, the celebration of which included many athletic events, held every four years on the plain of Olympia.

om·buds·man, ôm/bûdz·mən, *n. pl.,* **-men.** An appointed official, especially in Scandinavian countries, charged with investigating reports and complaints of malfeasance by government agencies or officials against private citizens.

om·e·let, om·e·lette, om/ə·lit, om/lit, *n.* Beaten eggs cooked and folded, sometimes with cheese, mushrooms, or other foods.

o·men, ō/mən, *n.* A circumstance or occurrence thought to portend future good or evil; a sign or augury.—*v.t.* To foretell or find out, as by omens.

om·i·nous, om/ə·nəs, *a.* Betokening, foreboding, or threatening evil; inauspicious; having the nature of a portent or sign. **—om·i·nous·ly,** *adv.* **—om·i·nous·ness,** *n.*

o·mis·sion, ō·mish/ən, *n.* The act of leaving out, or the condition of being left out; neglect or failure to do something that should have been done; something left out.

o·mit, ō·mit/, *v.t.,* **o·mit·ted, o·mit·ting.** To pass over or neglect; to fail to do or to use; to leave out; not to insert.

om·ni·bus, om/nə·bəs, *n. pl.,* **-bus·es.** A bus; a collection of writings having the same theme, or by the same author.—*a.* Referring to or covering a number of objects or items at once.

om·nip·o·tence, om·nip/ə·təns, *n.* Unlimited or infinite power as an attribute of God; very great power or influence. **—om·nip·o·tent,** om·nip/ə·tənt, *a.* **—om·nip·o·tent·ly,** *adv.*

om·ni·pres·ent, om·nə·prez/ənt, *a.* Present everywhere at the same time. **—om·ni·pres·ence,** *n.* **—om·ni·pres·ent·ly,** *adv.*

om·nis·cience, om·nish/əns, *n.* The faculty of knowing everything; knowledge unbounded or infinite: an attribute of God. **—om·nis·cient,** om·nish/ənt, *a.* **—om·nis·cient·ly,** *adv.*

om·niv·or·ous, om·niv/ər·əs, *a.* Eating both plant and animal foods; eating food of every kind indiscriminately; absorbing everything avidly: an *omnivorous* tourist. **—om·ni·vore,** om/nə·vôr, *n.* **—om·niv·o·rous·ly,** *adv.* **—om·niv·o·rous·ness,** *n.*

on, on, ôn, *prep.* Positioned above and in contact with a supporting surface; in the immediate proximity: to border *on* absurdity; situated or placed; supported by, suspended by, or dependent on: *on* wheels, *on* foot; in a state, condition, course, process: *on* strike; grounded or based: *on* this account, profit *on* sales; at the risk of: *on* pain of death; at the time or occasion of: *on* Sunday; directed or moving toward: to march *on* the capital; encountering: to happen *on* a person or thing; aiming at or directed toward: to gaze *on* a scene; with reference or respect to: a poem *on* spring.—*adv.* On or into a position of support, contact, or attachment: put the coffee *on;* on oneself or itself: to put one's coat *on;* attached to a thing, as for support; forward, onward, or along, as in any course or process: further *on;* with continuous procedure: to work *on;* into or in active operation or performance: turn *on* the gas.—*a.* Being in action or application; situated nearer; near.—*n.* The condition or fact of being on. **—be on to.** *Informal.* Be fully aware of.

o·nan·ism, ō/nə·niz·əm, *n.* Withdrawal during intercourse before ejaculation; masturbation. **—o·nan·ist,** *n.* **—o·nan·is·tic,** ō·nə·nis/tik, *a.*

once, wəns, *adv.* A single time; even a single time, at any time, or ever: if the facts *once* become known; at one time in the past, or formerly; by one degree or step: a cousin *once* removed.—*a.* That once was; former.—*conj.* If or when at any time; if ever; whenever.—*n.* One time; a single occasion. —**once and for all,** finally; definitely. —**once in a while,** occasionally; infrequently. —**once up·on a time,** at an indefinite time, usu. long ago. —**all at once,** simultaneously; suddenly. —**at once,** simultaneously; immediately.

once-o·ver, wəns/ō′vər, *n. Informal.* A single or brief look or appraisal; a hasty, superficial job.

on·com·ing, on′kəm•ing, *n.* The coming on or approaching of something; approach.—*a.* Approaching.

one, wən, *a.* Being but a single object, unit, or individual, in contrast to two or more; being an individual instance of something; indicating an uncertain or indefinite time: he will show up *one* day; single through union or combination: responding with *one* cheer; being in agreement or accord: of *one* opinion; undivided; forming a whole; the same: It was all *one* and the same to them.—*n.* The first cardinal number; the number between zero and two; the figure 1 representing the number; first in a series; a single person or thing; a unit; unity.—*pron.* Any indefinitely indicated person or thing; a single person or thing of a group already indicated; a certain person or being; someone; anyone. —**at one,** in a state of agreement or accord; united. —**one by one,** one after another; singly and in succession. —**one·ness,** *n.*

one an·oth·er, *pron.* Each other.

one-horse, wən/hôrs′, *a. Informal.* Unimportant: a *one-horse* town.

on·er·ous, on′ər•əs, *a.* Burdensome, oppressive, or troublesome. —**on·er·ous·ly,** *adv.* —**on·er·ous·ness,** *n.*

one·self, wən•self′, *pron.* Someone's own self: used for emphasis, as an object of a verb or proposition, or reflexively. One's usual physical or mental condition: not to feel *oneself.* Also **one's self,** wənz•self′.

one-sid·ed, wən/sī′did, *a.* Having but one side; having one side larger than the other; leaning to one side; existing or occurring on one side only; concerned with or considering but one side of a matter or question; partial, unjust: a *one-sided* judgment; with one contestant having an overwhelming decision or victory. —**one-sid·ed·ly,** *adv.* —**one-sid·ed·ness,** *n.*

one-time, wən/tīm, *a., adv.* Having been so at one time; former.

one-track, wən/trak′, *a.* Having but one track. *Informal.* Confined to a single interest, activity, or idea.

one-up·man·ship, wən•əp/mən•ship, *n.* The tendency to compete, by maintaining a constant advantage or margin of superiority.

one-way, wən/wā′, *a.* Moving or permitting movement in only one direction; one-sided.

on·go·ing, on/gō•ing, *a.* Progressing without interruption.

on·ion, ən/yən, *n.* An edible bulb of a garden herb in the lily family, with a strong characteristic pungent odor and taste; the plant itself. —**on·ion·like,** *a.* —**on·ion·y,** *a.*

on·ion·skin, ən/yən•skin, *n.* A strong, thin, translucent, glossy paper.

on-line, on/līn, *a.* Operating under direct control of the central computer.

on·look·er, on/lŭk•ər, ôn/lŭk•ər, *n.* One who looks on; a spectator. —**on·look·ing,** *a.*

on·ly, ōn/lē, *adv.* For one purpose alone; neither more nor less than; merely; simply; just: It is *only* a bruise, alone; solely; exclusively; as short a time ago as: I told him *only* this morning; in the end: You will *only* wish you had never come; certainly, followed by *too:* He was *only too* pleased to go.—*a.* Single; alone in its class; solitary; incomparable.—*conj.* But; excepting that.

on·o·mat·o·poe·ia, on•ə•mat•ə•pē′ə, *n.* The formation of words by imitation of sounds, as buzz, hum, boom, cuckoo; the use of such words to enhance the rhetorical value of speech or writing. —**on·o·mat·o·poe·ic, on·o·mat·o·po·et·ic,** on•ə•mat•ə•pō•et′ik, *a.* —**on·o·mat·o·poe·i·cal·ly, on·o·mat·o·po·et·i·cal·ly,** *adv.*

on·rush, on/rəsh, ôn/rəsh, *n.* A powerful rush or flow onward. —**on·rush·ing,** *a.*

on·set, on/set, ôn/set, *n.* An assault or attack; a beginning; outset.

on·shore, on/shōr′, on/shôr′, *a.* On or close to the shore; happening or done on land.—*adv.* In the direction of, close to, or parallel with the shore; ashore.

on·slaught, on/slôt, ôn/slôt, *n.* An onset, assault, or attack, esp. a vigorous or furious one.

on·to, on/tōō, ôn/tōō, *unstressed* on/tə, ôn/tə, *prep.* To a place or position on; upon the top of; on. *Informal.* Informed about or alert to: I'm *onto* his tactics.

o·nus, ō/nəs, *n.* A burden; an obligation.

on·ward, on/wərd, ôn/wərd, *adv.* Toward a point ahead or in front; forward. Also **on·wards.**—*a.* Directed or moving onward or forward; forward.

on·yx, on/iks, *n.* An agate with layers of chalcedony, sometimes used for cameos; the color black.—*a.* Black or jet black.

oo·dles, oo/dəlz, *n. pl. Informal.* A large quantity.

oomph, ûmf, *n. Informal.* Personal glamour; physical attractiveness; sex appeal.

ooze, ooz, *n.* Soft mud or slime; a marsh or bog; mud, chiefly the shells of small organisms, covering parts of the ocean bottom; the act of oozing; gentle flow; that which oozes.—*v.i.,* **oozed, ooz·ing.** To filter or exude through pores or small openings; to move slowly and almost unnoticed; of a substance, to exude moisture; to leak out or pass away slowly: His courage *oozed* away bit by bit.—*v.t.* To make by oozing; to exude slowly, as a trickle of moisture. —**oo·zi·ness,** *n.* —**oo·zy,** oo/zē, *a.,* **-zi·er, -zi·est.**

o·pac·i·ty, ō·pas/ə•tē, *n. pl.,* **-ties.** The state of being opaque; darkness.

o·pal, ō/pəl, *n.* A hydrous silica of various colors and varieties, the finest characterized by iridescent reflection of light; a gem of such a mineral.

o·pal·es·cence, ō•pə•les/əns, *n.* A play of colors like that of the opal; the reflection of a milky, iridescent light. —**o·pal·es·cent,** *a.*

o·paque, ō·pāk′, *a.* Impermeable to light; not transparent; dull, not bright; not transmitting sound, heat, or electricity; not lucid; obscure; unintelligent, dense, or stupid.—*n.* Something opaque. —**o·paque·ly,** *adv.* —**o·paque·ness,** *n.*

op art, op′ ärt′, *n.* The mid-20th century school of abstract painting which employs geometrical figures and, often, vibrant colors in an attempt to produce such visual effects and illusions as movement and three-dimensional depth.

o·pen, ō/pən, *a.* Not shut, as a door or window; not closed, covered, or shut up, as a house, box, or drawer; exposed; not enclosed by barriers or partitions; that may be entered, used, or competed for by all: an *open* session; accessible or available, often followed by *to;* without prohibition, as a season. *Informal.* Without or not enforcing legal restrictions: an *open* town. Unfilled, as a position; unoccupied, as time; undecided, as a question; liable or subject, followed by *to;* acting without concealment; candid, or frank; extended, or spread out: an *open* newspaper; generous or liberal: giving with an *open* hand; having openings or apertures, or being perforated or porous; unobstructed, as a passage, country, stretch of water, or view; free from frost, fog, or ice, or being mild and moderate; ready and prepared for business.—*v.t.* To make accessible or available; to clear of obstructions; to establish for use; to make accessible to knowledge, sympathy, or ideas; to make an opening in; to expose to view; to disclose or reveal; to spread out; to make less compact; to set in action, begin, start, or commence.—*v.i.* To become open, as a door or building; to afford access, followed by *in* or *into;* to have an opening, passage, or outlet, followed by *into, upon, toward,* or the like; to become receptive to knowledge, sympathy, or ideas, as the mind; to come into view; to become revealed; to reveal one's knowledge, thoughts, or feelings; to spread out; to begin, as a session, season, or tour.—*n.* An open space; the outdoors; an opening; the condition of being exposed to public view: the news is in the *open;* a tournament or contest that may be entered by either professionals or amateurs. **—o·pen·er,** *n.* **—o·pen·ly,** *adv.* **—o·pen·ness,** *n.*

o·pen air, *n.* The unconfined atmosphere; the air out of doors. **—o·pen-air,** *a.*

o·pen-and-shut, ō′pən·ən·shət′, *a.* Obvious; resolved with ease.

o·pen door, *n.* The policy of admission of all nations to a country upon equal terms, esp. for purposes of trade; free admission or access. **—o·pen-door,** *a.*

o·pen-end, ō′pən·end′, *a.* Having no definite limits; allowing for wide interpretation or freedom of action.

o·pen-eyed, ō′pən·īd′, *a.* Having the eyes open; watchful; aware; amazed.

o·pen-hand·ed, ō′pən·han′did, *a.* Generous; liberal; munificent. **—o·pen-hand·ed·ly,** *adv.* **—o·pen-hand·ed·ness,** *n.*

o·pen-hearth, ō′pən·härth′, *a.* Referring to a type of furnace used in making steel; designating or pertaining to the process by which steel is made in such a furnace, or to the steel so produced.

o·pen house, *n.* A time or occasion when a house is thrown open to all friends who may wish to visit or to enjoy its entertainment; a period during which an institution is open to visitors.

o·pen·ing, ō′pə·ning, *n.* A making or becoming open; the act of beginning, starting, or commencing; the first part or initial stage of anything; the beginning or premiere.

o·pen-mind·ed, ō′pən·mīn′did, *a.* Having or showing a mind open to new arguments or ideas; unprejudiced. **—o·pen-mind·ed·ly,** *adv.*

o·pen-mouthed, ō′pən·mowthd′, ō′pən·mowtht′, *a.* Having the mouth open; gaping, as with astonishment.

o·pen ses·a·me, *n.* Any password or charm at which doors fly open; any means that remove obstacles to success.

o·pen shop, *n.* A business establishment where both union and nonunion workers are employed without discrimination.

o·pen·work, ō′pən·wərk, *n.* Any kind of ornamental or decorative work, of such material as wood, stone, or lace, having openings through its substance.

o·per·a, op′ər·ə, op′rə, *n.* A drama or dramatic composition set to music and sung, acted, and sometimes danced, accompanied by an orchestra; the score, words, or a performance of such a musical drama. **—op·er·at·ic,** op·ə·rat′ik, *a.* **—op·er·at·i·cal·ly,** *adv.*

o·per·a, op′ər·ə, *n.* Plural of **o·pus.**

op·er·a·ble, op′ər·ə·bəl, *a.* Workable; practicable; capable of being treated by surgery. **—op·er·a·bil·i·ty,** op·ər·ə·bil′ə·tē, *n.* **—op·er·a·bly,** *adv.*

op·er·a glass·es, *n.* Small binoculars of low magnifying power, as used in theaters.

op·er·a house, *n.* A theater specifically for the performance of operas.

op·er·ate, op′ə·rāt, *v.i.,* **-at·ed, -at·ing.** To work, act, or function; to exert power or influence; to produce a desired effect; to perform a surgical operation.—*v.t.* To put into operation or cause to continue function-

ing; to drive or control, as a machine; to effect or accomplish.

op·er·a·tion, op·ə·rā′shən, *n.* The act, process, or manner of operating; a mode of activity; a process in some form of work or production; a process or method of operating on the body of a patient, usu. with instruments. **—in op·er·a·tion,** in force or action; operational.

op·er·a·tive, op′ə·rā·tiv, op′ər·ə·tiv, op′rə·tiv, *a.* Operating; exerting force; active in the production of effects; efficacious; producing the effect; having to do with manual, surgical, or other operations.—*n.* A skilled worker; detective; a secret agent. **—op·er·a·tive·ly,** *adv.* **—op·er·a·tive·ness,** *n.*

op·er·a·tor, op′ə·rā·tər, *n.* One who manipulates or handles the production operations of a device or machine; an owner or administrator of a business; a broker. *Informal.* A shrewd person who gains unexpected or abnormal profit from his labors.

op·er·et·ta, op·ə·ret′ə, *n.* A short, often humorous opera, usually having spoken dialogue and a light theme; light opera.

oph·thal·mic, of·thal′mik, op·thal′mik, *a.* Belonging or referring to the eye.

oph·thal·mol·o·gist, of·thal·mol′ə·jist, op·thal·mol′ə·jist, *n.* A doctor whose specialty is ophthalmology.

oph·thal·mol·o·gy, of·thal·mol′ə·jē, *n.* The science that deals with the anatomy, functions, and diseases of the eye. **—oph·thal·mo·log·ic,** of·thal·mə·loj′ik, *a.*

o·pi·ate, ō′pē·it, ō′pē·āt, *n.* Any medicine that contains opium or one of its derivatives and can induce sleep or alleviate pain. *Informal.* Any narcotic; anything that dulls sensation, quiets the nerves, or causes relaxation.—*a.* Inducing sleep; containing opium.

o·pine, ō·pīn′, *v.t.,* **o·pined, o·pin·ing.** To think; to suppose; to hold as an impression or opinion.—*v.i.* To state an opinion.

o·pin·ion, ə·pin′yən, *n.* A judgment or belief that is stronger than an impression but less firm than positive knowledge; a judgment or impression of persons or things regarding their character or qualities; a commonly held attitude or sentiment: public *opinion;* official expression of a judgment by a qualified authority.

o·pin·ion·at·ed, ə·pin′yən·ā·tid, *a.* Conceited or obstinate in opinion; dogmatic. **—o·pin·ion·at·ed·ly,** *adv.* **—o·pin·ion·at·ed·ness,** *n.*

o·pi·um, ō′pē·əm, *n.* The dried juice of the unripe fruit of the opium poppy, a poisonous, narcotic, addictive alkaloid from which morphine and codeine are derived.

o·pos·sum, ə·pos′əm, pos′əm, *n.* A nocturnal mammal, native to eastern U.S., having a prehensile tail and carrying its young in an abdominal pouch.

op·po·nent, ə·pō′nənt, *n.* One who supports the opposite side in a controversy, argument, game, or the like; an adversary.—*a.* Opposing; antagonistic; opposite in position.

op·por·tune, op·ər·toon′, op·ər·tūn′, *a.* Particularly suitable or appropriate; well-timed; timely or convenient. **—op·por·tune·ly,** *adv.* **—op·por·tune·ness,** *n.*

op·por·tun·ism, op·ər·too′niz·əm, op·ər·tū′niz·əm, *n.* The practice or policy of turning every opportunity to one's own advantage, with relatively small regard for possible consequences or the moral or ethical principles involved. **—op·por·tun·ist,** *n., a.* **—op·por·tun·is·tic,** op·ər·too·nis′tik, *a.*

op·por·tu·ni·ty, op·ər·too′nə·tē, op·ər·tū′nə·tē, *n. pl.,* **-ties.** An appropriate or convenient time or occasion; a favorable position or chance.

op·pos·a·ble, ə·pō′zə·bəl, *a.* Capable of being opposed or resisted; capable of being opposed or put opposite to something else, as the thumb and forefinger. **—op·pos·a·bil·i·ty,** ə·pō·zə·bil′ə·tē, *n.*

op·pose, ə·pōz′, *v.t.,* **-posed, -pos·ing.** To act against or contend in opposition to; to strive against,

resist, or combat; to set as an opponent or adversary, or as a resisting or combating force; to set as an obstacle or hindrance; to stand in the way of.—*v.i.* To be or act in opposition. —**op·pos·er**, *n.* —**op·pos·ing·ly**, *adv.*

op·po·site, op′ə·zit, *a.* Situated on opposed sides of something; located in a corresponding position but against each other; tending or going away counter to one another: in the *opposite* direction; contrary or diametrically different.—*n.* One who or that which is contrary or opposite.—*adv.* In an opposite direction. —*prep.* Facing; in a part complementary to: to play *opposite* a famous actor. —**op·po·site·ly**, *adv.* —**op·po·site·ness**, *n.*

op·po·si·tion, op·ə·zish′ən, *n.* The act or condition of opposing; the state of being opposed; resistance; that which opposes; the body of opposers; the political party opposed to the administration; a standing against something. —**op·po·si·tion·al**, *a.*

op·press, ə·pres′, *v.t.* To burden with cruel restrictions; to tyrannize; to treat with unjust severity; to subdue; suppress; to weigh down; to lie heavy upon; to depress. —**op·pres·si·ble**, *a.* —**op·pres·sor**, *n.*

op·pres·sion, ə·presh′ən, *n.* The act of oppressing.

op·pres·sive, ə·pres′iv, *a.* Unreasonably burdensome; unjustly severe; given to oppression; tyrannical; overpowering; overwhelming. —**op·pres·sive·ly**, *adv.* —**op·pres·sive·ness**, *n.*

op·pro·bri·ous, ə·prō′brē·əs, *a.* Expressing opprobrium, as language, epithets, or a speaker; imputing disgrace or shame; abusive; disgraceful or shameful. —**op·pro·bri·ous·ly**, *adv.* —**op·pro·bri·ous·ness**, *n.*

op·pro·bri·um, ə·prō′brē·əm, *n.* The disgrace or reproach incurred by conduct considered shameful or wrong; scornful reproach; a cause or object of such reproach.

opt, opt, *v.i.* To make a choice; choose.

op·tic, op′tik, *a.* Referring to sight or vision; referring to or connected with the eye as the organ of sight, or sight as a function of the brain; constructed to assist the sight; acting by means of sight or light; optical.

op·ti·cal, op′ti·kəl, *a.* Referring to sight; visual; constructed to assist the sight, as devices; acting by means of sight or light, as instruments; related to the eye; pertaining to optics; dealing with or skilled in optics. —**op·ti·cal·ly**, *adv.*

op·ti·cal il·lu·sion, *n.* A misleading image or visual impression presented to the vision; something that deceives by presenting a false impression to the eyes.

op·ti·cian, op·tish′ən, *n.* One who makes glasses for remedying defects of vision.

op·tics, op′tiks, *n. pl. but sing. in constr.* The branch of physical science that deals with vision, and the properties and phenomena of light, its origins and effects, and its role as a medium of sight.

op·ti·mal, op′tə·məl, *a.* Optimum.

op·ti·mism, op′tə·miz·əm, *n.* An inclination to emphasize the happy aspect of any happening or circumstance. —**op·ti·mist**, op′tə·mist, *n.* —**op·ti·mis·tic**, *a.* —**op·ti·mis·ti·cal·ly**, *adv.*

op·ti·mize, op′tə·mīz, *v.i.* **-mized, -miz·ing.** To hold or express optimistic views.—*v.t.* To make the best of; to make or arrange something in order to be highly functional or effective. —**op·ti·mi·za·tion**, *n.*

op·ti·mum, op′tə·məm, *n. pl.,* **op·ti·ma**, op′tə·mə, **op·ti·mums.** The best or most favorable point, degree, or amount for the purpose; the best possible result or highest degree which can be obtained given certain conditions.—*a.* Highly favorable; best; most desirable.

op·tion, op′shən, *n.* The power of choice; the thing chosen or elected; the action of making a choice; a buyer's purchased privilege to decide to buy or sell within an agreed period of time on specified terms; the power of buying something at a future date.

op·tion·al, op′shə·nəl, *a.* Left to one's choice or preference. —**op·tion·al·ly**, *adv.*

op·tom·e·trist, op·tom′ə·trist, *n.* One who is skilled in optometry.

op·tom·e·try, op·tom′ə·trē, *n.* The measurement and examination of the visual powers and the prescribing of appropriate corrective lenses. —**op·to·met·ric**, op·tə·met′rik, **op·to·met·ri·cal**, *a.*

op·u·lent, op′yə·lənt, *a.* Endowed with wealth or power; yielding riches; richly or abundantly supplied. —**op·u·lence**, *n.* —**op·u·lent·ly**, *adv.*

o·pus, ō′pəs, *n. pl.,* **o·pe·ra**, op′ər·ə, op′rə, **o·pus·es.** A literary work; a musical composition or collection of a composer's compositions usu. numbered chronologically according to publication. *Informal.* A play on television or radio; a movie.

or, ôr, *unstressed* ər, *conj.* A particle used to connect words, phrases, or clauses representing alternatives: this road *or* that; one used to connect alternative or equivalent terms: the Hawaiian *or* Sandwich Islands; a word often used in correlation, as in *either . . . or, or . . . or,* and *whether . . . or.*

or·a·cle, ôr′ə·kəl, or′ə·kəl, *n.* A place where hidden knowledge is believed to be revealed; the agency that does the revealing, or what is revealed; a revelation or divine utterance for the guidance of man, or the one who does such revealing; a person whose judgments have great weight. —**o·rac·u·lar**, ô·rak′yə·lər, *a.* —**o·rac·u·lar·i·ty**, ô·rak·yə·lar′ə·tē, *n.* —**o·rac·u·lar·ly**, *adv.*

o·ral, ōr′əl, ôr′əl, *a.* Of or pertaining to the mouth; done, taken, or administered by the mouth; uttered by the mouth, or spoken. —**o·ral·ly**, *adv.*

or·ange, ôr′inj, or′inj, *n.* The round, reddish-yellow, edible fruit of a white-flowered, evergreen tree grown in warm countries; the tree itself; a reddish-yellow color.—*a.* Of or pertaining to the orange; of a reddish-yellow color; made with or flavored like the orange.

or·ange·ade, ôr·inj·ād′, or·inj·ād′, *n.* A drink made of orange juice and sweetened water, often carbonated.

or·ange·wood, ôr′inj·wûd, or′inj·wûd, *n.* The hardwood of orange trees used esp. in carvings and lathe work.

o·rang·u·tan, **o·rang·ou·tan**, ō·rang′ə·tan, *n.* A tree-dwelling ape native to Sumatra and Borneo, characterized by extremely long arms for size of body, a mongoloid look, and brownish-red hair. Also **o·rang, o·rang·u·tang, o·rang·ou·tang, o·rang·ou·tang,** ō·rang′ə·tang.

o·rate, ō·rāt′, ōr′āt, *v.i.,* **o·rat·ed, o·rat·ing.** To deliver an oration; to speak in an ostentatious or pompous manner.

o·ra·tion, ō·rā′shən, *n.* A formal discourse carefully prepared and given on a special occasion; a speech, formal in style and delivery.

or·a·tor, ôr′ə·tər, or′ə·tər, *n.* A public speaker; one who delivers an oration; one who is skilled as a speaker. —**or·a·tor·i·cal**, ôr·ə·tôr′ə·kəl, or·ə·tôr′ə·kəl, *a.* —**or·a·tor·i·cal·ly**, *adv.*

or·a·to·ri·o, ôr·ə·tôr′ē·ō, or·ə·tôr′ē·ō, *n. pl.,* **-os.** An extended musical composition for solo voices, chorus, and orchestra.

or·a·to·ry, ôr′ə·tôr·ē, or′ə·tôr·ē, *n.* The art of an orator; the art of public speaking; the exercise of eloquence.

orb, ôrb, *n.* A sphere or globe; any of the heavenly bodies; the eyeball or eye.

or·bic·u·lar, ôr·bik′yə·lər, *a.* Like an orb; circular; ringlike; spherical; rounded; circular or disc-shaped, as the leaf of the lotus. Also **or·bic·u·late**, ôr·bik′yə·lit. —**or·bic·u·lar·i·ty**, ôr·bik·yə·lar′ə·tē, *n.* —**or·**

---

a- hat, fāte, fāre, fäther; **e-** met, mē; **i-** pin, pīne; **o-** not, nōte, ôrb, moove (move), boy, pownd; **u-** cūbe, bŭll, tûk (took); **ch-** chin; **th-** thick, then; **zh-** vizhon (vision); **ə-** əgo, takən, pencəl, lemən, bərd (bird).

bic·u·lar·ly, *adv.*

or·bit, ôr′bit, *n.* The curved path in space along which a planet moves in its periodical revolution around its central body; a sphere of activity, or customary range of activity.—*v.t.* To project into an orbital path, as a man-made satellite; to circle around, as a planet or satellite.—*v.i.* To travel or move in circles. **—or·bit·al,** *a.* **—or·bit·er,** *n.*

or·chard, ôr′chərd, *n.* Land devoted to the raising of fruit trees, usu. enclosed and often near a dwelling; the fruit trees growing on such an area.

or·ches·tra, ôr′kis·trə, *n.* A company of performers on various musical instruments, that plays concert music, as symphonies, operas, and other compositions; the instruments played; the space reserved for the musicians, usually the front part of the main floor. Also **or·ches·tra pit.** The entire main floor space for spectators. **—or·ches·tral,** ôr·kes′trəl, *a.* **—or·ches·tral·ly,** *adv.*

or·ches·trate, ôr′kis·trāt, *v.t.* **-trat·ed, -trat·ing.** To compose or arrange, as music, for performance by an orchestra. **—or·ches·tra·tion,** ôr·kis·trā′shən, *n.*

or·chid, ôr′kid, *n.* Any of certain temperate to tropical plants with showy, irregular, colorful flowers; a plant belonging to the orchid family; a light bluish-red to light purple color. *Usu. pl.* Praise for the work well done.—*a.* Light bluish-red to light purple.

or·dain, ôr·dān′, *v.t.* To invest with priestly functions; to confer holy orders upon; to decree, as an edict; to give orders for.—*v.i.* To decree; to order; to command. **—or·dain·er,** *n.* **—or·dain·ment,** *n.*

or·deal, ôr·dēl′, ôr·dē′əl, ôr′dēl, *n.* Any severe trial, strict test, or trying experience.

or·der, ôr′dər, *n.* A state or condition marked by harmony or arrangement; the proper arrangement of things; a state of established authority and observance of the law; a properly functioning state; the customary mode or established usage; a rank, grade, or class of society; a command; a direction or commission to make or provide something; the furnished object; a society of persons living by common consent under the same religious, moral, or social regulations; a body of persons of the same occupation or pursuits; any class, kind, or sort of people or things having a particular rank in a scale or distinguished from others by nature or character; an institution having as its purpose the rewarding of meritorious service by the conferring of a dignity; the badge or insignia of such an institution. *Usu. pl.* The rank or status of an ordained Christian minister; the rite or sacrament of ordination.—*v.t.* To arrange methodically or in a particular sequence; to regulate, conduct, or manage; to give an order for; to direct or command to be done; prescribe; to direct to be made, supplied, or furnished; to issue orders or instructions, or to give commands; to give an order or commission.—**in or·der to,** as a means to; with a view to. **—or·der·er,** *n.*

or·dered, ôr′dərd, *a.* Marked by order.

or·der·ly, ôr′dər·lē, *a.* Arranged in order; characterized by regular arrangement; exhibiting order, system, or method, as persons or the mind; characterized by rule or discipline; not unruly or disorderly.—*adv.* In regular sequence; with proper arrangement; methodically; according to established order or rule.—*n. pl.,* **-lies.** An army private or noncommissioned officer who performs menial tasks and carries orders or messages for a superior officer; a hospital attendant who performs necessary but nonmedical services. **—or·der·li·ness,** *n.*

or·di·nal, ôr′də·nəl, *a.* Expressing order or succession: the *ordinal* numbers, *first, second, third.*—*n.* A number denoting order or degree, as *second, tenth.* Also **or·di·nal num·ber.**

or·di·nance, ôr′də·nəns, *n.* A law, edict, or decree established by authority; a law or provision enacted by a municipal government for local application.

or·di·nar·i·ly, ôr′də·ner·ə·lē, ôr·də·nār′ə·lē, *adv.*

In the customary or usual way; in ordinary cases; usually.

or·di·nar·y, ôr′də·ner·ē, *a.* Customary, usual, or normal; of the usual kind; not distinguished in any important way from others; often, somewhat inferior or below the average level of quality.—*n.* Something regular, customary, or usual; the commonplace condition or degree. **—or·di·nar·i·ness,** *n.*

or·di·na·tion, ôr·də·nā′shən, *n.* The conferring or the reception of holy orders; the act of settling, arranging or establishing.

ord·nance, ôrd′nəns, *n.* Artillery; weapons, ammunition, vehicles, and other military equipment collectively.

or·dure, ôr′jər, ôr′dyûr, *n.* Dung; excrement; feces.

ore, ôr, ōr, *n.* A metal-bearing mineral or rock, or a native metal, esp. when valuable enough to be mined; a mineral or natural product serving as a source of some non-metallic substance, as sulfur.

o·reg·a·no, ə·reg′ə·nō, *n.* A perennial herb, in the mint family, cultivated for its purple-pink spiked flowers and its aromatic leaves which are used as a spice.

or·gan, ôr′gən, *n.* Any of various musical instruments, consisting of one or more sets of pipes which produce notes by means of compressed air, played by means of keys arranged in one or more keyboards; one of the independent sets of pipes of such an instrument. An instrument or means of performance; a means or medium of communicating thoughts or opinions: a company publication or house *organ;* a part or member of living organisms, as the heart, having some specific function.

or·gan bank, *n.* A place where human or animal organs or tissues are stored for future surgical use as transplants; a supply of such organs and tissues.

or·gan·dy, or·gan·die, ôr′gən·dē, *n.* A fine, translucent, stiff-finished muslin used for dresses, curtains, and other sheer items.

or·gan grind·er, *n.* A street musician who plays a hand organ or hurdy-gurdy.

or·gan·ic, ôr·gan′ik, *a.* Referring to the organs of an animal or plant; having organs; characterized by the systematic arrangement of parts into a whole; systematic; pertaining to the structure of a thing; constitutional. Pertaining to a class of carbon compounds; referring to the use of such nonchemical fertilizers as manure and compost. **—or·gan·i·cal·ly,** *adv.*

or·gan·ism, ôr′gə·niz·əm, *n.* An individual life form composed of a number of mutually dependent parts; any form of animal or plant life; any organized body or system analogous to a living being: the social *organism.* **—or·gan·is·mal,** ôr·gə·niz′məl, **or·gan·is·mic,** ôr·gə·niz′mik, *a.*

or·gan·ist, ôr′gə·nist, *n.* One who plays an organ.

or·gan·i·za·tion, ôr·gə·nə·zā′shən, *n.* The act or process of organizing; the state or the manner of being organized; that which is organized; any organized whole; a body of persons organized for some end or work. **—or·gan·i·za·tion·al,** *a.* **—or·gan·i·za·tion·al·ly,** *adv.*

or·gan·ize, ôr′gə·niz, *v.t.,* **-ized, -iz·ing.** To form as or into a whole consisting of interdependent or coordinated parts, esp. for harmonious or united action; arrange in a systematic whole, or systematize; prepare by arranging for various factors or details involved; to enroll, as employees, in a labor union; to unionize the employees of, as a factory.—*v.i.* To assume organic structure; to combine in an organized company, party, or the like. **—or·gan·iz·a·ble,** *a.* **—or·gan·iz·er,** ôr′gə·nī·zər, *n.*

or·gasm, ôr′gaz·əm, *n.* The climax of emotional and physical excitement of sexual intercourse. **—or·gas·mic,** ôr·gaz′mik, *a.*

or·gi·as·tic, ôr·jē·as′tik, *a.* Marked by unrestrained revelry. **—or·gi·as·ti·cal·ly,** *adv.*

or·gy, ôr′jē, *n. pl.,* **or·gies.** A drunken, licentious revelry; any uncontrolled indulgence.

o·ri·ent, ôr'ē·ənt, ōr'ē·ent, *a.* Fine or precious, as gems, esp. pearls; brilliant; shining.—*n.* The east: contrasted with the occident; the eastern hemisphere; (*cap.*) the countries to the east and southeast of the Mediterranean. The luster or coloring of a pearl.—*v.t.* To place in any definite position with reference to the points of the compass or other points; to direct to a particular object; adjust with relation to or bring into due relation to surroundings, circumstances, facts; to ascertain the position of with reference to the points of the compass or other points; to find the bearings of.—*v.i.* To turn eastward or in any particular direction.

O·ri·en·tal, ôr·ē·en'təl, *a.* Of the orient or east; eastern; of, pertaining to, or characteristic of the Orient or East; belonging to a division comprising southern Asia and the Malay Archipelago as far as and including the Philippines, Borneo, and Java.—*n.* A native or inhabitant of the Orient or East, esp. one belonging to a native race; an Asiatic. —**o·ri·en·tal·ism, o·ri·en·tal·ist,** *n.* —**o·ri·en·tal·ly,** *adv.*

O·ri·en·tal rug, *n.* A rug of Asiatic origin, either handwoven or hand-knotted. Also **O·ri·en·tal car·pet.**

o·ri·en·tate, ôr'ē·ən·tāt, ōr'ē·ən·tāt, *v.t.,* **-tat·ed, -tat·ing.** To orient.—*v.i.* To be oriented.

o·ri·en·ta·tion, ôr·ē·ən·tā'shən, *n.* The act or process of orienting; or the state of being oriented; insight into one's status in a given circumstance; a program designed to introduce one into a new situation.

or·i·fice, ôr'ə·fis, or'ə·fis, *n.* The mouth or aperture of a tube, pipe, or similar object; an opening; a vent.

o·ri·ga·mi, ôr'ə·gä'mē, *n.* The Japanese art of folding paper into various realistic or decorative shapes; a product of this art.

or·i·gin, ôr'ə·jin, or'ə·jin, *n.* The beginning of anything; the commencement; source; that from which anything primarily proceeds.

o·rig·i·nal, ə·rij'ə·nəl, *a.* Belonging to or referring to the origin, source, or beginning of something; created by one's own thought and imagination independent of the ideas and works of others; capable of fresh thoughts and invention.—*n.* That from which a copy, translation, or the like is made; the person upon whom a literary portrait or a stage character is based; an original work as opposed to a copy or imitation; an early form of something; one who is original in his way of thinking; an eccentric person. —**o·rig·i·nal·i·ty,** ə·rij·ə·nal'ə·tē, *n.* —**o·rig·i·nal·ly,** ə·rij'ə·nə·lē, *adv.*

o·rig·i·nal sin, *n.* A conception of some event or action which reduced man from a blissful to a fallen state; a depravity or tendency to evil, held to be innate in mankind and transmitted from Adam to the race in consequence of his sin.

o·rig·i·nate, ə·rij'ə·nāt, *v.t.,* **-nat·ed, -nat·ing.** To initiate; to give existence to; to invent.—*v.i.* To arise; to derive from; to begin at a specified point. —**o·rig·i·na·tion,** ə·rij·ə·nā'shən, **o·rig·i·na·tor,** *n.* —**o·rig·i·na·tive,** *a.* —**o·rig·i·na·tive·ly,** *adv.*

or·i·son, ôr'i·sən, ôr'i·zən, or'i·zən, *n.* A prayer or supplication.

Or·lon, ôr'lon, *n. Trademark.* An acrylic fiber used in the manufacture of clothing, house furnishings, and in industry.

or·na·ment, ôr'nə·mənt, *n.* An article used to beautify, or to enrich or improve the appearance; an adornment, decoration, or embellishment; anything that lends beauty or renders more pleasing; a person who adds luster, as to surroundings, society, a class, profession, place, or time; the act of adorning or the state of being adorned; adornment or means of adornment.—ôr'nə·ment, *v.t.* To furnish with ornaments. —**or·na·men·tal,** ôr·nə·men'təl, *a.* —**or·na·**

men·ta·tion, ôr·nə·mən·tā'shən, *n.*

or·nate, ôr·nāt', *a.* Adorned; decorated; ornamental; richly and artistically finished; much embellished. —**or·nate·ly,** *adv.* —**or·nate·ness,** *n.*

or·ner·y, ôr'nə·rē, *a.* Ugly in disposition or temper; stubborn; ordinary; common; low or vile. —**or·ner·i·ness,** *n.*

or·ni·thol·o·gy, ôr·nə·thol'ə·jē, *n.* Branch of zoology which treats of the form, structure, classification, and habits of birds. —**or·ni·tho·log·ic,** ôr·nə·thə·loj'ik, **or·ni·tho·log·i·cal,** *a.* —**or·ni·tho·log·i·cal·ly,** *adv.* —**or·ni·thol·o·gist,** *n.*

o·ro·tund, ōr'ə·tənd, *a.* Characterized by fullness, richness, and clearness in voice; pompous in speaking. —**o·ro·tun·di·ty,** ōr·ə·tən'di·tē, *n.*

or·phan, ôr'fən, *n.* A child who has lost through death one or both parents; a young animal separated from its mother.—*a.* Being an orphan; for or referring to orphans.—*v.t.* To reduce to the state of an orphan. —**or·phan·hood,** *n.*

or·phan·age, ôr'fə·nij, *n.* The state of orphanhood; a home or institution for the care of orphans.

or·tho·don·tics, ôr·thə·don'tiks, *n. pl. but sing. in constr.* The branch of dentistry which corrects irregularities or abnormalities of the teeth, usu. by mechanical aids such as braces. Also **or·tho·don·tia,** ôr·thə·don'shə, ôr·thə·don'shē·ə. —**or·tho·don·tic,** *a.* —**or·tho·don·tist,** *n.*

or·tho·dox, ôr'thə·doks, *a.* Sound or correct in opinion or doctrine, esp. theological or religious doctrine; conforming to the Christian faith as represented in the early church creeds; approved or conventional. (*Cap.*) Of or pertaining to the Eastern, or Greek, Orthodox Church; relating to or denoting Orthodox Judaism. —**or·tho·dox·ly,** *adv.* —**or·tho·dox·ness,** *n.*

or·tho·dox·y, ôr'thə·dok·sē, *n. pl.,* **-ies.** Orthodox character; orthodox belief or practice.

or·tho·gen·ic, ôr·thə·jen'ik, *a.* Referring to or concerned with treatment of mentally retarded or seriously maladjusted children.

or·thog·o·nal, ôr·thog'ə·nəl, *a.* Referring to or involving right angles; rectangular, as the angles of the axes of some crystals. —**or·thog·o·nal·ly,** *adv.*

or·thog·ra·phy, ôr·thog'rə·fē, *n. pl.,* **-phies.** The art of writing words with the proper letters; standard or correct spelling; the part of grammar which treats of letters and spelling. —**or·thog·ra·pher,** *n.* —**or·tho·graph·ic,** ôr·thə·graf'ik, **or·tho·graph·i·cal,** *a.* —**or·tho·graph·i·cal·ly,** *adv.*

or·tho·pe·dics, or·tho·pae·dics, ôr·thə·pē'diks, *n. pl. but sing. in constr.* A branch of surgery dealing with the correction of skeletal deformities and with the treatment of chronic diseases of bones and muscles, esp. of the joints and spine. —**or·tho·pe·dic, or·tho·pae·dic,** *a.* —**or·tho·pe·dist, or·tho·pae·dist,** *n.*

Os·car, os'kər, *n.* A statuette awarded by the Academy of Motion Picture Arts and Sciences for an outstanding accomplishment in the movie industry.

os·cil·late, os'ə·lāt, *v.i.,* **-lat·ed, -lat·ing.** To swing to and fro, as a pendulum does; move to and fro between two points; vibrate; to waver between attitudes, opinions, or purposes.—*v.t.* To cause to swing or move to and fro. —**os·cil·la·tion,** os·ə·lā'shən, **os·cil·la·tor,** *n.* —**os·cil·la·to·ry,** os'ə·lə·tôr·ē, *a.*

os·cil·lo·scope, ə·sil'ə·skōp, *n.* An electronic optical device which pictures changes in electric current by means of a cathode ray tube.

os·cu·late, os'kyə·lāt, *v.i., v.t.,* **-lat·ed, -lat·ing.** To kiss; to touch. —**os·cu·la·tion,** os·kyə·lā'shən, *n.* —**os·cu·la·to·ry,** os'kyə·lə·tôr·ē, *a.*

os·mi·um, oz'mē·əm, *n.* A very hard, brittle, and extremely heavy metallic element of the platinum group.

os·mose, oz'mōs, os'mōs, *v.t.,* **-mosed, -mos·ing.** To

---

a- hat, fāte, fâre, fäther; **e-** met, mē; **i-** pin, pīne; **o-** not, nōte, ôrb, moove (move), boy, pownd; **u-** cūbe, bûll, tûk (took); **ch-** chin; **th-** thick, ᵺen; **zh-** vizhon (vision); **ə-** ego, taken, pencəl, lemən, bərd (bird).

subject to diffusion through a membrane.—*v.i.* To go through or be subjected to osmosis.

os·mo·sis, oz·mō′sis, os·mō′sis, *n.* The tendency, when two solutions of differing concentrations are separated by a semipermeable membrane, for the solution of higher density to pass through the membrane until the two solutions are equal in concentration; an instance of this passage or diffusion; any gradual absorption of knowledge or ideas. —**os·mot·ic,** oz·mot′ik, os·mot′ik, *a.* —**os·mot·i·cal·ly,** *adv.*

os·prey, os′prē, *n.* A large, eaglelike hawk, brownish-black above and white below, that dives for fish.

os·si·fy, os′ə·fī, *v.t.,* **-fied, -fy·ing.** To form into bone; to change from a soft substance into bone or a substance of the hardness of bones.—*v.i.* To become bone or like bone in hardness and rigidity; to become inflexible in outlook or habits. —**os·si·fi·er,** *n.*

os·ten·si·ble, os·ten′sə·bəl, *a.* Presented as having a certain character, or outwardly appearing as such; professed; apparent. —**os·ten·si·bly,** *adv.*

os·ten·sive, os·ten′siv, *a.* Manifestly or clearly demonstrative; ostensible. —**os·ten·sive·ly,** *adv.*

os·ten·ta·tion, os·ten·tā′shən, *n.* Pretentious display motivated by vanity or the attempt to impress other people. —**os·ten·ta·tious,** *a.* —**os·ten·ta·tious·ly,** *adv.* —**os·ten·ta·tious·ness,** *n.*

os·te·op·a·thy, os·tē·op′ə·thē, *n.* A method of treatment resting upon the theory that most diseases are due to deformation of some part of the body and can be relieved or cured by manipulation of bones and muscles. —**os·te·o·path,** os′tē·ə·path, *n.* —**os·te·o·path·ic,** os·tē·ə·path′ik, *a.* —**os·te·o·path·i·cal·ly,** *adv.*

os·tra·cism, os′trə·siz·əm, *n.* The act of exiling or excluding; the state of being ostracized or exiled; a political measure among the ancient Greeks by which undesirable persons were banished by public vote for a term of years; banishment from the privileges of society by common consent; expulsion.

os·tra·cize, os′trə·siz, *v.t.,* **-cized, -ciz·ing.** To banish from society by popular decision; to exclude from public or private favor; expatriate; to exile by ostracism.

os·trich, ôs′trich, os′trich, *n.* A large, swift-footed bird, two-toed and flightless, of the arid, sandy regions from Arabia to southern Africa; a large, flightless bird of S. America, the rhea; one who wishes to evade danger by refusing to see it, or one who will not recognize an obvious problem.

oth·er, əth′ər, *a.* Being the remaining one of two or more; being the remaining ones of a number; additional or further: he and one *other* person; different or distinct from the ones mentioned or implied; different in nature or kind; former; second or alternate: every *other* year; not long past: the *other* morning.—*pron.* The other one; someone or something else or different: some child or *other;* another person or thing. —*adv.* Otherwise; differently. —**oth·er·ness,** *n.*

oth·er·wise, əth′ər·wiz, *adv.* In a different manner; differently; by other causes; given other circumstances; in other respects.—*a.* Other; different; under different circumstances.

oth·er world, *n.* The world of the dead; the world to come.

oth·er·world·ly, əth′ər·wərld′lē, *a.* Of, referring to, or devoted to another, often ideal, world, as the world of mind or imagination or the spiritual world to come; oblivious to the material realm. —**oth·er·world·li·ness,** *n.*

o·ti·ose, ō′shē·ōs, ō′tē·ōs, *a.* Idle; useless; futile; needless; ineffective. —**o·ti·ose·ly,** *adv.* —**o·ti·os·i·ty,** ō·shē·os′ə·tē, ō·tē·os′ə·tē, *n.*

ot·ter, ot′ər, *n.* A fish-eating, aquatic, playful mammal, having webbed, clawed feet, bristly whiskers, and a slightly flattened, long, pointed tail, and valued commercially for its smooth, dark brown fur; the fur of this animal.

ot·to·man, ot′ə·mən, *n.* A divan or sofa; a low cushioned seat without back or arms; a cushioned footstool; a corded rayon or silk fabric with a large transverse cord.

ouch, owch, *interj.* An exclamation expressing sudden pain.

ought, ôt, *aux. v.* To have a moral obligation: We *ought* to be truthful; to be correct, proper, or advisable: You *ought* to answer invitations; to be assumed as likely, reasonable, or natural: The computer *ought* to give the correct answer.

ounce, owns, *n.* A unit of weight which is one-twelfth of a pound troy and equal to 480 grains; a unit of weight which is one-sixteenth of a pound avoirdupois and equal to 437.5 grains; fluid ounce; a small amount: an *ounce* of sense.

our, owr, *pronominal a.* Possessive case of the personal pronoun **we,** used as an attributive: *our* country, *our* rights.

ours, owrz, *pron.* Pertaining to or belonging to us; possessive form of **we,** used instead of **our** and a noun, as subject, object, or predicate noun: *Ours* is the best, they took their papers and *ours,* this book is *ours.*

our·self, owr·self′, *pron.* **Myself,** as a single individual, used in the regal or formal style.

our·selves, owr·selvz′, *pron. pl.* A reflexive or emphatic form of the first person plural pronoun: We treated *ourselves* to a good dinner, we *ourselves* prefer modern art. A denotation of our usual or customary state: We didn't feel *ourselves* all day.

oust, owst, *v.t.* To eject, as from a position or location; to forcibly remove.

oust·er, ows′tər, *n.* A removal from property or possessions rightfully owned; a person who removes something.

out, owt, *adv.* Forth from, away from, or not in a place, position, or state: *out* of town; away from one's home, country; away from one's work; from a number, stock, or store: to pick *out;* from a source or material, with *of:* made *out of* scraps; so as to project or extend: to stand *out;* from a state of composure, satisfaction, or harmony: to feel put *out;* so as to deprive or be deprived, with *of:* to cheat *out of* money; having used the last, with *of: out of* coal; with completeness or effectiveness: to dig a hole *out;* into or in existence, activity, or outward manifestation: fever breaking *out;* into or in public notice or knowledge: the truth coming *out;* into or in society: a young girl who came *out* last season.—*prep.* Out or forth from: *out* the window; outside of, on the exterior of, or beyond.—*interj.* Begone! Away!—*a.* Left exposed; not within normal bounds or limits; at a specified financial loss; lacking or without; senseless or no longer conscious; removed from or not in effective operation or play, as in a game; no longer employed or in office; at odds; no longer in working order; no longer available; extinguished; headed outward; in baseball, failing to reach the intended base: *out* at first.—*n.* A person or thing that is out; escape valve: to have an *out;* a put-out. *Pl.* Odds or bad terms: on the *outs* with her.—*v.i.* to go or come out: Murder will *out;* to go away from or out of doors; to utter or come out with: *Out* with your speech.—*v.t.* To put out.—**all out,** completely in full force.—**out and a·way,** by far.—**out and out,** thoroughly, completely; undisguised.—**out from un·der,** relieved of a difficulty or burden.—**out of hand,** out of control.

out·bid, owt·bid′, *v.t.,* **-bid, -bid·den, -bid·ding.** To bid more than; to go beyond in the offer of a price. —**out·bid·der,** *n.*

out·board, owt′bôrd, *a.* Situated on the outside of a ship or aircraft; situated away from the centerline of a ship or of a fuselage; having an outboard motor.—*adv.* On the exterior, or farther away from the center.—*n.* A boat having an outboard motor, or the motor itself.

out·board mo·tor, *n.* A portable engine having a tiller and propeller, usu. powered by gasoline and mounted on a small boat.

out·bound, owt'/bownd, *a.* Outward bound.

out·brave, owt·brāv', *v.t.,* **-braved, -brav·ing.** To surpass in bravery; to confront or withstand defiantly.

out·break, owt'/brāk, *n.* A breaking out; a sudden manifestation, as of war, anger, disease; a riot or public disorder.

out·build·ing, owt'/bil·ding, *n.* A detached building subordinate to a main building. Also **out·house.**

out·burst, owt'/bėrst, *n.* A sudden and forceful breaking or bursting out, as of emotion; a spurt, as of energy or growth.

out·cast, owt'/kast, owt'/käst, *n.* One who is cast out or expelled; an exile; one driven from home or country. —*a.* Cast out; characteristic of what is cast out; thrown away; rejected.

out·class, owt·klas', *v.t.* To surpass in class or grade; be of a distinctly higher class.

out·come, owt'/kəm, *n.* That which comes out of or results from something; the issue; the result; the consequence; the conclusion.

out·cry, owt'/krī, *n. pl.,* **-cries.** A vehement or loud cry; cry of distress, righteous anger, or the like; clamor; noisy opposition.

out·dat·ed, owt·dā'/tid, *a.* Put out of date; rendered antiquated or obsolete.

out·dis·tance, owt·dis'/təns, *v.t.,* **-tanced, -tan·cing.** To leave far behind; to surpass in any competition or career.

out·do owt·doo', *v.t.,* **out·did, out·done, out·do·ing.** To excel; to surpass; to perform beyond, as one's normal expectations.

out·door, owt'/dōr, *a.* Being, belonging, or performed in the open air or outside the house.

out·doors, owt·dôrz', *adv.* Out of the house; in the open air.—*n. pl. but sing. in constr.* The world existing beyond house boundaries; open air.

out·er, ow'/tėr, *a.* Being on the outside; external; farther removed from a central point.

out·er·most, ow'/tėr·mōst, *a.* Being the most distant; farthest from the center.

out·er space, *n.* Space beyond earth's atmosphere; interstellar and interplanetary space.

out·face, owt·fās', *v.t.,* **-faced, -fac·ing.** To confront; to defy; to brave; to stare down.

out·field, owt'/fēld, *n.* The part of a baseball field beyond the diamond or infield, or the players stationed in it. **—out·field·er,** *n.*

out·fit, owt'/fit, *n.* The act of fitting out or equipping, as for a voyage, journey, trip, expedition, or for any purpose; an assemblage of articles for fitting out or equipping: an explorer's *outfit;* a set of articles for any purpose: a cooking *outfit;* a complete ensemble of coordinated clothing. *Informal.* A body of persons associated as a unit for any purpose, as an army unit; any party, company, or set.—*v.t.,* **-fit·ted, -fit·ting.** To furnish with an outfit; equip.—*v.i.* To furnish oneself with an outfit. **—out·fit·ter,** *n.*

out·flank, owt·flangk', *v.t.* To go or extend beyond the flank or wing of, as of an opposing regiment or team; to outmaneuver; to get the better of.

out·fox, owt·foks', *v.t.* To get the better of, as by craftiness; to outsmart.

out·go, owt·gō', *v.t.,* **out·went, out·gone, out·go·ing.** To advance beyond; to excel; to surpass.— owt'/gō, *n. pl.,* **out·goes.** A going out; expenditure.

out·go·ing, owt'/gō·ing, *a.* Going out; friendly or responsive—*n.* The act of going out; that which goes out.

out·grow, owt·grō', *v.t.,* **-grew, -grown, -grow·ing.** To surpass in growing; grow too large for; grow out of fitness for or sympathy with: to *outgrow* early surroundings or friends; put off, leave behind, or lose in the changes incident to development or the passage of time: to *outgrow* opinions, habits, or weaknesses.

out·growth, owt'/grōth, *n.* A growing out or forth; that which grows out; an offshoot; a natural development, product, or result.

out·guess, owt·ges', *v.t.* To show oneself smarter than; to anticipate.

out·house, owt'/hows, *n.* A small house or building near the main one; an outside privy.

out·ing, ow'/ting, *n.* An excursion, pleasure trip, or the like; an airing.

out·land·ish, owt·lan'/dish, *a.* Strange in looks or actions; bizarre or extremely ridiculous; foreign; distant or remote. **—out·land·ish·ly,** *adv.* **—out·land·ish·ness,** *n.*

out·last, owt·last', *v.t.* To last longer than; to exceed in duration.

out·law, owt'/lô, *n.* A person excluded from the benefits and protections of the law because of having defied the law; a habitual criminal.—*v.t.* To remove from legal jurisdiction or deprive of legal force; to prohibit; to deprive of the benefits and protection of the law, as a person or group; to condemn as an outlaw. **—out·law·ry,** *n.*

out·lay, owt'/lā, *n.* A laying out or expending, as of money; that which is laid out or expended; disbursement.—owt·lā', *v.t.,* **-laid, -lay·ing.** To spend as money.

out·let, owt'/let, owt'/lit, *n.* The place or opening by which anything is let out, escapes, or is discharged; that part in a wiring system from which current may be taken; a medium of self-expression; a marketplace for products.

out·line, owt'/lin, *n.* The line, real or apparent, by which a figure or object is bounded; the contour; a drawing or a style of drawing showing only lines of contour; *sometimes pl.,* account or sketch of the principal aspects of something being considered, as a project or plan.—*v.t.,* **-lined, -lin·ing.** To draw the outline of, as of a figure or object; to give the main features of; to sketch verbally.

out·live, owt·liv', *v.t.,* **-lived, -liv·ing.** To survive longer than; to endure the results of.

out·look, owt'/lûk, *n.* One's mental view; the prospect of a situation; the place from which an observer sees; the view from a place.

out·ly·ing, owt'/lī·ing, *a.* Lying away from the main body or center; remote; being on the exterior or frontier; beyond the boundary or limit.

out·mod·ed, owt·mō'/did, *a.* No longer in style; obsolete.

out·num·ber, owt·nəm'/bėr, *v.t.* To be greater in number.

out-of-date, owt·əv·dāt', *a.* Not stylish; obsolete. **—out-of-date·ness,** *n.*

out·post, owt'/pōst, *n.* A post or station outside the limits of a camp or at a distance from the main body of an army, protecting the latter against unsuspected attack; the troops placed at such a station; a remote settlement.

out·put, owt'/pût, *n.* The act of turning out; production; the quantity or amount produced, as in a given time; the product or yield, as of an industry; processed data.

out·rage, owt'/rāj, *n.* A terrible act of violence; a wanton transgression of law or decency; a gross violation of morality; an enormous insult.—*v.t.,* **-raged, -rag·ing.** To wantonly abuse; to subject to a gross insult; to rape.

out·ra·geous, owt·rā'/jes, *a.* Characterized by an outrage; atrocious; violent; indecent or lawless; extravagant; excessive. **—out·ra·geous·ly,** *adv.* **—out·ra·geous·ness,** *n.*

---

a- hat, fāte, fāre, fäther; **e-** met, mē; **i-** pin, pīne; **o-** not, nōte, ôrb, moove (move), boy, pownd; **u-** cūbe, bûll, tûk (took); **ch-** chin; **th-** thick, ŧhen; **zh-** vizhon (vision); **ə-** əgo, takən, pencəl, lemən, bėrd (bird).

out·range, owt·rānj′, *v.t.,* **-ranged, -rang·ing.** To possess a longer range than; to move beyond the range of.

out·rank, owt·rangk′, *v.t.* To rank above.

out·reach, owt·rēch′, *v.t.* To reach beyond; exceed. —*v.i.* To reach out.—owt′rēch, *n.* A reaching out; length of reach.

out·rig·ger, owt′rig·ər, *n.* A framework ending in a float, extended outward from the side of a canoe to prevent upsetting; a spar rigged out from a ship's mast to extend a sail or rope; a frame or part placed to project beyond a main structure and act as a support.

out·right, owt′rīt′, owt′rīt, *adv.* Completely, entirely, or altogether: to sell a thing *outright;* without restraint, reserve, or concealment; openly; straight out or ahead, or directly onward; forthwith; at once.—owt′rīt, *a.* Complete or total; downright or unqualified; directed straight out or on.

out·run, owt·rən′, *v.t.,* **-ran, -run, -run·ning.** To exceed in speed or distance in running; to exceed or go beyond.

out·sell, owt·sel′, *v.t.,* **-sold, -sell·ing.** To outdo in selling; sell more than; to be sold in greater number than.

out·set, owt′set, *n.* A setting out; beginning; start; opening.

out·shine, owt·shīn′, *v.t.,* **-shone, -shin·ing.** To shine more brightly than; to surpass in luster; to be superior to in excellence, wit, or the like.—*v.i.* To shine forth.

out·side, owt′sīd′, owt′sīd, *n.* The external, outer, or exposed parts or surface of an object; the external aspect or features; the space immediately without or beyond an enclosure or boundary.—owt′sīd′, owt′sīd′, *a.* Referring to or being on the outside; external; performed beyond a set limit or enclosure; not from or of a designated group; only remotely possible: an *outside* chance.—owt·sīd′, *adv.* On or toward the outside; toward, near, or on the limits; outdoors.—owt′sīd′, out′sīd, *prep.* To, toward, or on the external side of; beyond the boundary or boundaries of. *Informal.* Except.—**at the out·side.** *Informal.* At the greatest limit, or maximum.—**out·side of.** *Informal.* Other than; besides.

out·sid·er, owt·sī′dər, *n.* One who is not connected with or admitted to a particular association, set, or group; someone or something outside a wall, boundary, or the like; a contender regarded as unlikely to win.

out·skirts, owt′skərts, *n. pl.* The part or district near the edge or boundary of a city or other area; border district.

out·smart, owt·smärt′, *v.t.* Outwit.

out·spo·ken, owt·spō′kən, *a.* Free or bold in speech; spoken with candor or boldness. —**out·spo·ken·ly,** *adv.* —**out·spo·ken·ness,** *n.*

out·stand·ing, owt·stan′ding, *a.* Prominent; eminent; excellent; striking; still existing or unpaid, as a debt; projecting or protruding. —**out·stand·ing·ly,** *adv.* —**out·stand·ing·ness,** *n.*

out·strip, owt·strip′, *v.t.,* **-stripped, -strip·ping.** To outrun; to advance beyond; to excel; to surpass.

out·ward, owt′wərd, *a.* Exterior; external; obvious; easily visible; referring to the physical as opposed to the mental or spiritual; superficial; turned or moving away from the inside or center. Also **out·wards.** —**out·ward·ly,** *adv.* —**out·ward·ness,** *n.*

out·wear, owt·wār′, *v.t.,* **-wore, -worn, -wear·ing.** To last longer than; to outgrow; to outlive; to wear out by using.

out·weigh, owt·wā′, *v.t.* To exceed in weight; to exceed or surpass in value, influence, or importance.

out·wit, owt·wit′, *v.t.,* **-wit·ted, -wit·ting.** To defeat by superior ingenuity; to prove too clever for; to outsmart; to trick.

o·va, ō′və, *n.* Plural of **o·vum.**

o·val, ō′vəl, *a.* Of the general shape of the outline of an egg; resembling the longitudinal section of an egg; elliptical.—*n.* An object or figure in the shape of an egg; an elliptical figure. —**o·val·ly,** *adv.* —**o·val·ness,** *n.*

o·va·ry, ō′və·rē, *n. pl.,* **-ries.** One of the pair of female reproductive glands of vertebrates in which ova and sex hormones are formed and developed; a case enclosing ovules or young seeds. —**o·var·i·an,** ō·vâr′ē·ən, *a.*

o·vate, ō′vāt, *a.* Egg-shaped; oval.

o·va·tion, ō·vā′shən, *n.* An enthusiastic public reception of a person; a burst of enthusiastic and prolonged applause.

ov·en, əv′ən, *n.* A chamber or receptacle for baking, heating, or drying.

o·ver, ō′vər, *prep.* Above in position; higher up than; reaching higher than: in water *over* one's head; above in authority, power, or rank; beyond one's ability to understand; above in degree, quality, or amount; in preference to; in excess of; on or upon; upon, thus altering one's disposition or attitude: a vast happiness came *over* him; to and fro, on or in: to travel all *over* Europe; through all parts of: to go *over*; above and to the other side of; from side to side of, or to the other side of, or across; on the other side of; during the duration of; in reference to, concerning, or about: to quarrel *over* a matter.—*adv.* Past the top or edge of something; so as to bring the upper side under: to turn a thing *over;* remaining beyond a certain amount: Five goes into seven once, with two left *over;* once more, or again; in repetition; from an upright to a prone position: He fell *over;* so as to cover or affect the whole surface; through a region or area; past the top level or brim: spilling *over;* from beginning to end, or all through; from side to side, or to the other side; across any intervening space; from one person or party to another; on the other side, as of a sea, river, or any space; at some distance, as in a direction indicated; throughout or beyond a period of time: to stay *over* until Monday.—*a.* Upper; higher up; higher in authority, or power; that which is in excess or addition; remaining; surplus; extra; too great; excessive; completed or past; serving or intended as an outer covering; outer.—*n.* An amount in excess or addition; an extra.—**o·ver and a·bove,** in addition to; besides. —**o·ver and o·ver,** repeatedly.

o·ver·act, ō·vər·akt′, *v.t., v.i.* To act or perform to excess or with exaggeration.

o·ver·age, ō′vər·āj′, *a.* Older than the customary or specified age.

o·ver·all, ō′vər·ôl, *a.* From one extreme limit of a thing to the other; covering or including everything.

o·ver·alls, ō′vər·ôlz, *n. pl.* Loose, stout trousers, usu. with a part extending over the chest and supported by shoulder straps, worn by workmen and others, often over other clothing to protect it.

o·ver·awe, ō·vər·ô′, *v.t.,* **-awed, -aw·ing.** To restrain by awe, fear, or superior influence.

o·ver·bear·ing, ō·vər·bâr′ing, *a.* Domineering; dictatorial; haughtily or rudely arrogant. —**o·ver·bear·ing·ly,** *adv.*

o·ver·blown, ō·vər·blōn′, *a.* More than full-blown, as a flower; excessive; stout, plump, or unusually large; inflated with vanity, pomposity, or conceit; pretentious.

o·ver·board, ō′vər·bôrd, *adv.* Over the side of a ship or boat.—**go o·ver·board,** to be extravagant; to act in an exaggerated manner.

o·ver·build, ō·vər·bild′, *v.t.,* **-built, -build·ing.** To construct more buildings than required, as in an area or town; to erect on too costly or too elaborate a scale.

o·ver·cast, ō·vər·kast′, ō′vər·kast, *v.t.* To darken: clouds that *overcast* the sky; to cover with gloom.—*v.i.* To become dark or overcast.—*a.* Cloudy; gloomy.—*n.* A covering, esp. of clouds.

o·ver·charge, ō·vər·chärj′, *v.t.,* **-charged, -charg·ing.** To charge too high a sum or price; to overload; to exaggerate.—*v.i.* To make too high a charge.—ō′vər·chärj, *n.* A charge that is excessive.

o·ver·coat, ō/vər·kōt, *n.* A coat worn over all other clothing; a topcoat; an extra coat of paint applied to a surface.

o·ver·come, ō·vər·kəm/, *v.t.,* -came, -come, -com·ing. To conquer; get the better of; surmount, as temptations and obstacles; to lay low emotionally or physically, as does illness, liquor, or fatigue. —*v.i.* To gain the superiority; be victorious. —**o·ver·com·er,** *n.*

o·ver·com·pen·sa·tion, ō·vər·kom·pən·sā/shən, *n.* The action of making amends for a handicap or disadvantage with greater effort than is immediately required, resulting in the development of a new capability to supplant or balance the deficiency, or in the appearance of a pathological symptom. —**o·ver·com·pen·sate,** ō·vər·kom/pen·sāt, *v.i., v.t.,* -sat·ed, -sat·ing.

o·ver·con·fi·dence, ō·vər·kon/fə·dəns, *n.* Too great or excessive confidence; foolhardiness. —**o·ver·con·fi·dent,** *a.*

o·ver·do, ō·vər·doo/, *v.t.,* -did, -done, -do·ing. To do to excess; to use excessively; to overact; to overtax the strength of; to exaggerate; to cook too much. —*v.i.* To carry to extremes.

o·ver·dose, ō/vər·dōs, *n.* Too great a dose. Also **o·ver·dos·age,** o·vər·dōs/ij. —ō·vər·dōs/, *v.t.,* -dosed, -dos·ing.

o·ver·draft, ō/vər·draft, *n.* The action of overdrawing an account at a bank; a draft in excess of one's credit; the amount of the excess.

o·ver·draw, ō·vər·drô/, *v.t.,* -drew, -drawn, -draw·ing. To withdraw, as from one's bank account, larger sums than are to one's credit; to depict with exaggeration. —*v.i.* To withdraw from an account beyond the amount of one's balance.

o·ver·drive, ō/vər·drīv, *n.* A gear system by means of which the drive shaft turns faster than the engine, thereby reducing power output.

o·ver·due, ō·vər·doo/, ō·vər·dū/, *a.* Past the time of payment; belated, or past the specified arrival time; delayed or deferred too long.

o·ver·em·pha·sis, ō·vər·em/fə·sis, *n.* Excessive emphasis; undue stress. —**o·ver·em·pha·size,** ō·vər·em/fə·sīz, *v.t.,* -sized, -siz·ing.

o·ver·es·ti·mate, ō·vər·es/tə·māt, *v.t.,* -mat·ed, -mat·ing. To estimate too high; to overvalue. —ō·vər·es/tə·mit, *n.* —**o·ver·es·ti·ma·tion,** ō·vər·es·tə·mā/shən, *n.*

o·ver·flow, ō·vər·flō/, *v.t.,* -flowed, -flown, -flow·ing. To flow or spread over; to inundate; to cause to run over the brim of; to deluge; to overwhelm. —*v.i.* To swell and run over the brim or banks; to be so full that the contents run over; to abound. —ō·vər·flō, *n.* An inundation; a flowing over; superabundance; an opening to carry off surplus liquid.

o·ver·gen·er·ous, ō·vər·jēn/ər·əs, *a.* Unexpectedly magnanimous; liberal to excess. —**o·ver·gen·er·ous·ness,** *n.*

o·ver·grow, ō·vər·grō/, *v.t.,* -grew, -grown, -grow·ing. To cover with growth; to outgrow. —*v.i.* To grow beyond natural or suitable size.

o·ver·growth, ō/vər·grōth, *n.* Excessive growth; growth over or on an object.

o·ver·hand, ō/vər·hand, *adv.* With the hand over the object; with the knuckles upward; with the hand raised above the shoulder, as in pitching a ball. Also **o·ver·hand·ed.** —*a.*

o·ver·hang, ō·vər·hang/, *v.t.,* -hung, -hang·ing. To hang or be suspended over; extend or jut over; to impend or threaten, as danger or evil; hang or rest over, as if ominously. —*v.i.* To hang over; project or jut out over something below. —ō/vər·hang, *n.* An overhanging; a projection; the extent of projection, as of the bow of a vessel.

o·ver·haul, ō·vər·hôl/, *v.t.* To investigate or examine thoroughly, as for repair, revision, or correction; to repair or restore; to gain upon or overtake. —ō·vər·hôl, *n.* An examination and thorough repair. Also **o·ver·haul·ing.**

o·ver·head, ō/vər·hed, *a.* Aloft; in the sky, esp. near the zenith; above one's head. —ō·vər·hed/, *adv.* Over; above. —ō/vər·hed, *n.* Business expenses, as rent, office expenses, taxes, or depreciation, which are not directly chargeable to production.

o·ver·hear, ō·vər·hēr/, *v.t.,* -heard, -hear·ing. To hear, as a speaker or conversation, though not intended or expected to hear.

o·ver·joy, ō·vər·joy/, *v.t.* To give great or excessive joy to.

o·ver·joyed, ō·vər·joyd/, *a.* Enthusiastically delighted.

o·ver·kill, ō/vər·kil, *n.* The capacity for destruction beyond what is necessary for victory by military weapons, chiefly nuclear; an instance of such action.

o·ver·land, ō/vər·land, *a.* By land; made upon or across the land. —*adv.* Across, upon, or by means of land.

o·ver·lap, ō·vər·lap/, *v.t.,* -lapped, -lap·ping. To extend, cover, or fold over; to extend so as to lie or rest upon. —*v.i.* To lap over, upon part of another. —ō·vər·lap, *n.* The lapping of one thing over another; the amount or degree of such overlapping; the place where such overlapping occurs.

o·ver·lay, ō·vər·lā/, *v.t.,* -laid, -lay·ing. To lay or place over or upon another thing; to cover, overspread, or surmount with something; to finish with a layer or applied decoration of something. —ō·vər·lā, *n.* Something laid over something else; a covering; a layer or decoration of something applied.

o·ver·look, ō·vər·lûk/, *v.t.* To fail to notice, perceive, or consider; to disregard or ignore; to look over, as from a higher position; to afford a view down over; to rise above; to look over; to oversee or super vise. —ō/vər·lûk, *n.* Land, as a bluff, commanding a view.

o·ver·lord, ō/vər·lôrd, *n.* One who is lord over another; a person with great authority, influence, or power. —*v.t.* To govern or rule domineeringly. —**o·ver·lord·ship,** *n.*

o·ver·ly, ō/vər·lē, *adv.* Overmuch; excessively too much; too.

o·ver·much, ō·vər·məch/, *a.* Too much; exceeding what is necessary or proper. —*adv.* In too great a degree. —*n.* More than sufficient; an excess.

o·ver·night, ō·vər·nīt/, *adv.* Through or during the night; in the course of the night or evening; for the night; suddenly or more quickly than expected: Cities sprang up *overnight.* —ō/vər·nīt, *a.* Lasting through the night; performed or happening at night; made for nighttime or limited use: an *overnight* bag.

o·ver·pass, ō·vər·pas/, *v.t.* To pass over; to cross; to surpass; to surmount; overlook; transgress. —*v.i.* To pass by or over. —ō/vər·pas, *n.* A section of a highway, railroad, or the like that bridges or crosses over another road or highway.

o·ver·play, ō·vər·plā/, *v.t.* To play, act, or behave to excess or in an exaggerated manner; to surpass or defeat in playing. —*v.i.* To overemphasize a dramatic part or action.

o·ver·pow·er, ō·vər·pow/ər, *v.t.* To vanquish by power or force; to subdue; to affect violently or intensely: His emotions *overpowered* him; to furnish with excessive power. —**o·ver·pow·er·ing,** *a.* —**o·ver·pow·er·ing·ly,** *adv.*

o·ver·rate, ō·vər·rāt/, *v.t.,* -rat·ed, -rat·ing. To rate too favorably; to regard as having more valuable qualities than is really the case.

o·ver·reach, ō·vər·rēch/, *v.t.* To reach or extend over or beyond; to aim at but go beyond: to *overreach*

---

a- hat, fāte, fâre, fäther; **e-** met, mē; **i-** pin, pīne; **o-** not, nōte, ôrb, moove (move), boy, pownd;
u- cūbe, bŭll, tŭk (took); **ch-** chin; **th-** thick, ŧhen; **zh-** vizhon (vision); **ə-** əgo, takən, pencəl, lemən, bərd (bird).

the target; to defeat, as oneself, by excessive eagerness or cunning in promoting one's aims; to overexert by reaching too far; to get the better of; to outwit.—*v.i.* To reach too far; to extend over; to cheat.

o·ver·ride, ō·vər·rīd′, *v.t.,* **-rode, -rid·den, -rid·ing.** To ride over; to trample down; to supersede; to annul.

o·ver·rule, ō·vər·rool′, *v.t.,* **-ruled, -rul·ing.** To exercise rule or influence over; to prevail over so as to change the purpose or action; to rule against, as a plea, argument, or objection; disallow; to rule against or disallow the arguments of.

o·ver·run, ō·vər·rən′, *v.t.,* **-ran, -run, -run·ning.** To swarm over in great numbers so as to injure; to spread or grow rapidly over, as vines or weeds; to spread rapidly throughout, as a new idea or fashion; to run over or overflow; to run beyond; to exceed.—*v.i.* To run over or overflow; to extend beyond the proper or desired limit.

o·ver·seas, ō·vər·sēz′, *adv.* Beyond or across the sea; abroad.—ō′vər·sēz, *a.* Beyond the sea; relating to travel over the sea. Also **o·ver·sea.**

o·ver·see, ō·vər·sē′, *v.t.,* **-saw, -seen, -see·ing.** To superintend; to take charge of; to observe secretly or by accident. **—o·ver·se·er,** ō′vər·sē·ər, *n.*

o·ver·sexed, ō·vər·sekst′, *a.* Having or giving evidence of an overly strong sexual urge.

o·ver·shad·ow, ō·vər·shad′ō, *v.t.* To cast a shadow over; make dark; to shelter; to dominate; to diminish the importance of.

o·ver·shoe, ō′vər·shoo, *n.* A shoe worn over another; an outer waterproof shoe or boot designed for protection.

o·ver·shoot, ō·vər·shoot′, *v.t.,* **-shot, -shoot·ing.** To shoot or go over or beyond, as a point, limit, or target: *overshoot* the mark; to drive or force beyond the proper limit; to overreach.—*v.i.* To shoot beyond or above the target; to proceed beyond.

o·ver·sight, ō′vər·sīt, *n.* A mistake of omission; superintendence; watchful care.

o·ver·sim·pli·fy, ō·vər·sim′plə·fī, *v.t.,* **-fied, -fy·ing.** To simplify in such a manner as to alter, distort, or cloud the meaning of.—*v.i.* To be engaged in too much simplification. **—o·ver·sim·pli·fi·ca·tion,** o·vər·sim·plə·fə·kā′shən, *n.*

o·ver·size, ō′vər·sīz′, *a.* Of excessive size; of a size larger than is necessary or usual. Also **o·ver·sized.**—*n.* An object which is exceptionally large; a large size.

o·ver·sleep, ō·vər·slēp′, *v.i.,* **-slept, -sleep·ing.** To sleep beyond the hour for waking.—*v.t.* To sleep beyond or through; to allow, as oneself, to sleep too late.

o·ver·spread, ō·vər·spred′, *v.t.,* **-spread, -spread·ing.** To extend or spread over; to cover completely.

o·ver·state, ō·vər·stāt′, *v.t.,* **-stat·ed, -stat·ing.** To exaggerate; to state in too strong terms. **—o·ver·state·ment,** *n.*

o·ver·stay, ō·vər·stā′, *v.t.* To stay too long; to stay beyond the limits or duration of; to wear out, as one's welcome.

o·ver·step, ō·vər·step′, *v.t.,* **-stepped, -step·ping.** To step over or beyond; to exceed.

o·ver·strung, ō′vər·strung′, *a.* Too highly strung; hypersensitive.

o·ver·stuff, ō·vər·stəf′, *v.t.* To fill too full; to provide with a complete covering of deep upholstery.

o·vert, ō·vərt′, ō′vərt, *a.* Open to view; public; apparent. **—o·vert·ly,** *adv.*

o·ver·take, ō·vər·tāk′, *v.t.,* **-took, -tak·en, -tak·ing.** To come upon or catch up with in following; to reach or go beyond; to take by surprise.

o·ver·tax, ō·vər·taks′, *v.t.* Oppress with taxes; to make excessive demands on, as one's strength or capabilities.

o·ver-the-coun·ter, ō′vər·thə·kown′tər, *a.* Sold in another way than on an organized securities exchange, as stocks; legally sold without a prescription.

o·ver·throw, ō·vər·thrō′, *v.t.,* **-threw, -thrown, -throw·ing.** To cast down, as from a position of power; to upset or overturn; to throw over and beyond.—*v.i.* To throw over and beyond.—ō′vər·thrō, *n.* An overthrowing; deposition; defeat.

o·ver·time, ō′vər·tīm, *n.* Time beyond a set limit; time during which one works beyond the regular hours; payment for overtime.—*a.,* *adv.* Of, during, or for overtime.

o·ver·tone, ō′vər·tōn, *n.* One of the secondary sounds of a tone, set higher in pitch, which along with the fundamental produces timbre; a harmonic; the color of light produced by its reflection from a painted surface; a second and usu. less important meaning or implication.

o·ver·ture, ō′vər·chər, *n.* An orchestral composition forming the introduction to an opera or oratorio; an opening of negotiations; a proposal or an offer.

o·ver·turn, ō·vər·tərn′, *v.t.* To turn over; throw over with violence; upset; overthrow; destroy the power of; defeat; bring to ruin.—*v.i.* To turn over on its side or face; upset; capsize.—ō′vər·tərn, *n.* The act of overturning or the state of being overturned.

o·ver·view, ō′vər·vyoo, *n.* Any broad, comprehensive view or survey.

o·ver·ween·ing, ō′vər·wē′ning, *a.* Arrogant; conceited; presumptuous; inordinate; extreme. **—o·ver·ween·ing·ly,** *adv.* **—o·ver·ween·ing·ness,** *n.*

o·ver·weight, ō′vər·wāt, *n.* Extra weight above the legal amount, as for shipping; weight beyond the customary or healthful amount; greater weight; preponderance.—*a.* Weighing more than is permitted or considered normal.

o·ver·whelm, ō·vər·hwelm′, ō·vər·welm′, *v.t.* To cover up or bury; submerge; to overcome or crush; to defeat; to overthrow; to overcome totally: grief that *overwhelms.* **—o·ver·whelm·ing,** *a.* **—o·ver·whelm·ing·ly,** *adv.*

o·ver·work, ō·vər·wərk′, *v.t.,* **-worked** or **-wrought, -work·ing.** To cause to work too much; to use to excess; to excite to the point of frenzy; to decorate with, over the entire surface.—*v.i.* To toil excessively; to do more than the required amount of work. —ō′vər·wərk, *n.* Excessive work; work done beyond the stated amount.

o·ver·wrought, ō·vər·rôt′, *a.* Overworked or taxed beyond one's strength; affected or excited to excess; emotionally distressed; overly elaborated.

o·vi·duct, ō′vi·dəkt, *n.* A passage which conducts the ovum or egg from an ovary. Also **Fal·lo·pi·an tube.**

o·vip·a·rous, ō·vip′ər·əs, *a.* Producing eggs that are hatched after being expelled from the body. **—o·vip·ar·ous·ly,** *adv.* **—o·vip·ar·ous·ness,** *n.*

o·void, ō′voyd, *a.* Having a shape like an egg; ovate. Also **o·voi·dal.**—*n.* A body which is egg-shaped.

o·vu·late, ov′yə·lāt, ō′vyə·lāt, *v.i.,* **-lat·ed, -lat·ing.** To produce or release an ovum from an ovary. **—o·vu·la·tion,** ov·yə·lā′shən, *n.*

o·vule, ō′vūl, *n.* A little egg; an ovum, esp. when small, immature, or unfertilized; a rudimentary seed. **—o·vu·lar,** ō′vyə·lər, *a.*

o·vum, ō′vəm, *n. pl.,* **o·va,** ō′və. An egg; the female reproductive cell.

owe, ō, *v.t.,* **owed, ow·ing.** To be under obligation to pay; to be in debt or beholden for; to cherish a certain feeling toward a person.

owl, owl, *n.* Any of various large-headed, nocturnal birds of prey with large, forward-directed talons. **—owl·ish,** or **owl·ish,** *a.*

own, ōn, *a.* Distinctly and emphatically belonging to oneself: *my own* idea.—*v.t.* To hold or possess, esp. property; to acknowledge.—*v.i.* To have; to admit: She *owned* up to it. **—own·er,** *n.*

ox, oks, *n. pl.,* **ox·en,** ok′sən, Any animal of the bovine kind; a bull, castrated and full grown.

ox·al·ic ac·id, ok·sal′ik, *n.* A poisonous, white,

crystalline acid, used for bleaching, cleaning, and dyeing.

ox·bow, oks′bō, *n.* A bow-shaped piece of wood placed around the neck of an ox; a geologic feature, as a bow-shaped bend in a river.

ox·ford, oks′fərd, *n.* A low shoe, usu. laced over the instep.

ox·i·da·tion, ok·sə·dā′shən, *n.* The act or process of uniting with oxygen; the process by which an element in a compound gains or loses electrons in forming the compound. **—ox·i·da·tive,** *a.* **—ox·i·dant,** ok′sə·dənt, *n.*

ox·ide, ok′sīd, ok′sid, *n.* A compound of oxygen with another element or a radical.

ox·i·dize, ok′sə·dīz, *v.t.,* **-diz·ed, -diz·ing.** To convert into an oxide; combine with oxygen; to cover with a coating of oxide, or rust; to take away hydrogen so that the valence of the positive element is higher.—*v.i.* To become oxidized.

ox·y·a·cet·y·lene, ok·sē·ə·set′ə·lēn, *a.* Of, referring to, or using a mixture of oxygen and acetylene:

the *oxyacetylene* torch used in welding.

ox·y·gen, ok′sə·jən, *n.* A colorless, odorless, gaseous element, occurring as O_2, constituting about one-fifth of the volume of the atmosphere, which supports combustion and the respiratory process of animals and plants.

ox·y·gen·ate, ok′sə·jə·nāt, *v.t.,* **-at·ed, -at·ing.** To treat or combine with oxygen. **—ox·y·gen·a·tion,** ok·sə·jə·nā′shən, *n.*

ox·y·gen mask, *n.* A device covering the nose and mouth and supplying oxygen from an adjoining tank.

ox·y·gen tent, *n.* A cover delivering and retaining pure oxygen, placed over the head and shoulders of a patient to aid respiration.

oys·ter, oy′stər, *n.* Any edible marine bivalve mollusk with an irregularly shaped shell, found in shallow water.

o·zone, ō′zōn, *n.* A form of oxygen, O_3, produced esp. when an electric spark is passed through oxygen or air. *Informal.* Bracing air, as in the mountains or at the seaside.

P

P, p, pē, *n.* The sixteenth letter of the English alphabet.

pa, pä, *n. Informal.* Father.

pab·u·lum, pab′yə·ləm, *n.* Food; food for thought.

pace, pās, *n.* A single step, as in walking or running; the distance traversed in a step; a linear measure commonly two and one-half feet; rate of walking or running; rate of movement; tempo; manner of walking or running; gait; any of the various gaits of a horse. —*v.t.,* **paced, pac·ing.** To cover distance in paces; regulate the pace of; set the pace for; train to a certain pace.—*v.i.* To walk with slow, regular steps; to amble at a pace. **—pac·er,** *n.*

paced, pāst, *a.* Having a specific pace; measured or counted by paces; regulated by a pacemaker.

pace·mak·er, pās′mā·kər, *n.* Someone or something that sets the pace, esp. in a race; a person or thing that serves as an example for others; the area in the right atrium that controls the heartbeat.

pa·cif·ic, pə·sif′ik, *a.* Making peace; conciliatory; peaceable, as in disposition or character; calm, or quiet.

pa·cif·i·ca·tion, pas·ə·fə·kā′shən, *n.* The act of pacifying; appeasement; **—pa·cif·i·ca·tor,** pə·sif′ə·kā·tər, *n.* **—pa·cif·i·ca·to·ry,** pə·sif′ə·kə·tôr·ē, *a.*

pac·i·fi·er, pas′ə·fī·ər, *n.* One who pacifies; a device resembling a nipple for a baby to suck.

pac·i·fism, pas′ə·fiz·əm, *n.* The principle or policy of establishing and maintaining universal peace without recourse to war; refusal to bear arms or to kill. **—pac·i·fist,** pas′ə·fist, *n.*

pac·i·fy, pas′ə·fī, *v.t.,* **-fied, -fy·ing.** To make peaceful; to subdue; to appease; to calm.

pack, pak, *n.* Anything wrapped or tied up, as for carrying; a bundle, parcel, or bale; a fixed quantity of something, wrapped for sale: a *pack* of cigarettes; a group of certain animals, as hounds or wolves; a beautifying material: a mud *pack;* a wrapping of the body in wet or dry cloths for therapeutic purposes; a mass of floating pieces of ice driven together; a group of things or persons, said in contempt.—*v.t.* To make into a pack; to put into cans; to press or crowd together; to fill; to make impervious to water, steam,

air; to carry; to send off or dismiss summarily.—*v.i.* To pack goods into compact form; store compactly; become compacted; crowd together.—*a.* Used for transporting: a *pack* animal.

pack, pak, *v.t.* To set up corruptly, as a jury or legislature, so as to further particular interests.

pack·age, pak′ij, *n.* A parcel or bundle; a container; a box, case, or crate; an article of several parts assembled into a unit.—*v.t.* To provide with a container; to bundle. **—pack·ag·er,** *n.*

pack·er, pak′ər, *n.* One who packs; owns a meat packing house; a machine which packs.

pack·et, pak′it, *n.* A small pack; package; a parcel of letters. A vessel carrying goods and passengers on a schedule.

pack·ing, pak′ing, *n.* The act of one who packs; material used for making a tight connection, as in a steam pipe.

pact, pakt, *n.* A contract; an agreement or covenant between persons, groups, or nations.

pad, pad, *n.* A cushion-like mass of soft material; sheets of paper bound together at one edge to form a tablet; a cushion saturated with ink, used to ink a rubber stamp; a wad of gauze or dressing for medical purposes; one of the cushionlike protuberances on the under side of the feet of dogs and other animals; the handle of certain tools; a cushion used as a saddle. *Informal.* Place of residence; a bedroom or bed.—*v.t.,* **pad·ded, pad·ding.** To stuff or fill with padding; to expand falsely: to *pad* an expense account.

pad, pad, *n.* A dull sound, as of footsteps on the ground.—*v.t.,* **pad·ded, pad·ding.** To travel along on foot; to beat down by treading.—*v.i.* To travel on foot; walk softly.

pad·ding, pad′ing, *n.* The act of one who pads; material, as cotton or straw, used to stuff something; matter used to expand a written article, speech, or expense account.

pad·dle, pad′əl, *n.* A short oar for propelling a canoe or similar craft; any of various implements having broad blades, used for stirring, mixing, beating, or the like; a kind of racket used in table tennis; a thin board used in spanking and hazing; one of the broad boards on a paddle wheel; the flipper or limb of certain swimming animals; the act of paddling; swimming with short strokes; the act of spanking.—*v.i.*, **-dled, -dling.** To use a paddle; travel in a canoe; row gently.—*v.t.* To propel with a paddle; to spank. —**pad·dler,** *n.*

pad·dle wheel, *n.* A wheel with paddle boards on its circumference, for propelling a vessel through the water.

pad·dock, pad′ǝk, *n.* An area used for saddling and mounting of horses; a field enclosed for pasture or for exercising animals.

pad·dy, pad′ē, *n. pl.,* **-dies.** Rice in the husk; the flooded land on which rice is grown.

pad·dy wag·on, *n. Informal.* Patrol wagon.

pad·lock, pad′lok, *n.* A portable lock having a hasp or shackle which passes through a ring, or the like, and is then fastened.—*v.t.*

pae·an, pe·an, pē′ǝn, *n.* An ancient Greek hymn in honor of Apollo, who was also called Paean, or Paian; a song of triumph generally; a song of joy or praise.

pa·gan, pā′gǝn, *n.* One who is not a Christian, a Jew, or a Mohammedan; a heathen; an idolater; a person with no religion. —**pa·gan·ism,** pā′gǝ·niz·ǝm, *n.*

page, pāj, *n.* One side of the leaf of a book; a leaf of a book.—*v.t.,* **paged, pag·ing.** To number the pages of; paginate.—*v.i.* To go through a book, page by page.

page, pāj, *n.* A youth appointed to attend and perform errands for members of a legislative body during its sessions, for royalty, or for simulated royalty in plays or pageants, and in such formal functions as a coronation, wedding, or convention.—*v.t.,* **paged, pag·ing.** To act as a page; to summon a person by calling his name continually.

pag·eant, paj′ǝnt, *n.* A spectacle or entertainment; a great display or show; anything showy, without stability or duration. —**pag·ea·t·ry,** paj′ǝn·trē, *n.*

pag·i·nate, paj′ǝ·nāt, *v.t.,* **-nat·ed, -nat·ing.** To number the pages of, as of a book.

pa·go·da, pǝ·gō′dǝ, *n.* A temple of the Far East, in the form of a pyramid or a tower.

pail, pāl, *n.* A cylindrical container with a handle; bucket; amount carried in a pail. Also **pail·ful.**

pain, pān, *n.* Physical ache or distress because of injury or illness; emotional or mental affliction or suffering; grief. *Pl.* The extreme pangs of childbirth; careful effort.—*v.t.* To cause pain to; to distress.—*v.i.* To suffer pain. —**pain·ful, pain·less,** *a.* —**pain·less·ness,** *n.*

pain·kil·ler, pān′kil·ǝr, *n. Informal.* A medicine or narcotic that relieves pain.

pains·tak·ing, pānz′tā·king, *n.* The taking of pains; careful labor.—*a.* —**pains·tak·ing·ly,** *adv.*

paint, pānt, *v.t.* To make, as a picture, by laying on colors; to decorate or protect with a coat of paint; to use facial make-up on; to apply.—*v.i.* To cover something with paint; to make pictures; to use cosmetics.

paint, pānt, *n.* A pigment for use in fine arts or as a protective covering for many surfaces. —**paint·er,** pān′tǝr, *n.*

paint·ing, pān′ting, *n.* A painted surface; the occupation of painting; the art of painting.

pair, pār, *n. pl.,* **pairs, pair.** Two things similar in form; a single thing composed of two pieces which work together; two of a sort; a couple; a brace; a man and his wife; two mated animals.—*v.t.* To arrange in pairs; match.—*v.i.* To join in pairs; be one of a pair; associate oneself with another.

pais·ley, pāz′lē, *a.* Typically made of woolen material, patterned in bright colors; having the pattern characteristic of paisley.—*n.* A paisley fabric or article of clothing.

pa·jam·as, pǝ·jä′mǝz, pǝ·jam′ǝz, *n. pl.* A loose garment, consisting of jacket and trousers, worn for sleeping or lounging.

pal, pal, *n. Informal.* An intimate associate or friend.

pal·ace, pal′is, *n.* The house in which an emperor, a king, or other distinguished person resides; a splendid residence.

pal·at·a·ble, pal′ǝ·tǝ·bǝl, *a.* Agreeable to the palate or taste; savory; agreeable to the mind or feelings. —**pal·at·a·bil·i·ty,** pal·ǝ·tǝ·bil′ǝ·tē, *n.* —**pal·at·a·bly,** *adv.*

pal·ate, pal′it, *n.* The roof of the mouth which separates the nasal and oral cavities and consists of the *hard palate* and the *soft palate;* the sense of taste; intellectual taste.

pa·la·tial, pǝ·lā′shǝl, *a.* Pertaining to or like a palace; becoming or suitable for a palace; magnificent. —**pa·la·tial·ly,** *adv.*

pal·a·tine, pal′ǝ·tīn, pal′ǝ·tin, *a.* Referring to a palace; possessing royal privileges.—*n.* A vassal or lord invested with royal privileges and rights within his province or territory; a high official of a royal palace. —**pal·at·i·nate,** pǝ·lat′ǝ·nit, *n.*

pa·lav·er, pǝ·lav′ǝr, *n.* A lengthy talk or conference; superfluous or idle talk; flattery.—*v.t.* To flatter.—*v.i.* To talk idly.

pale, pāl, *a.* A whitish color; wan; pallid; not bright; dim; feeble.—*v.t., v.i.,* **paled, pal·ing.** To cause to be or become pale. —**pale·ly,** *adv.* —**pale·ness,** *n.*

pale, pāl, *n.* A picket; a barrier which surrounds and encloses an area; a district within a fixed boundary; the bounds within which socially acceptable behavior is confined.

Pa·le·o·lith·ic, pā·lē·ǝ·lith′ik, *a.* Early part of the Stone Age characterized first by the development of primitive stone implements and later by the appearance of cave paintings anb crude sculpture.

pa·le·on·tol·o·gy, pā·lē·on·tol′ǝ·jē, *n.* The science of ancient life which treats of fossil remains. —**pa·le·on·to·log·ic,** pā·lē·on·tǝ·loj′ik, **pa·le·on·to·log·i·cal,** *a.* —**pa·le·on·tol·o·gist,** *n.*

pal·ette, pal′it, *n.* A thin board or tablet used by painters to lay and mix colors on; the set of colors on a palette; a selection of colors, as those used by a particular artist.

pal·imp·sest, pal′imp·sest, *n.* A parchment from which one writing has been erased to make room for another, often leaving the first faintly visible, a process to which many ancient manuscripts were subjected.

pal·in·drome, pal′in·drōm, *n.* A word, verse, or sentence that is the same when read backward or forward, as *radar.*

pal·ing, pā′ling, *n.* A fence formed of pales or pickets; the act of building a fence of pales or pickets; an individual pale; pales collectively.

pal·i·sade, pal·ǝ·sād′, *n.* A fence of pales or stakes set for enclosure or defense; something resembling a fence of stakes; *pl.,* a line of lofty cliffs.—*v.t.* **-sad·ed, -sad·ing.** To fortify with a palisade.

pall, pôl, *n.* A large cloth thrown over a coffin or a tomb; an enveloping covering or cloud; an atmosphere of an oppressive nature.—*v.t.* To cover with a pall.

pall, pôl, *v.i.* To become devoid of interest or attraction; to have a dulling or wearying effect.—*v.t.* To make vapid; to cloy.

pal·la·di·um, pǝ·lā′dē·ǝm, *n.* A silver-white, malleable and ductile, metallic element of the platinum group.

pall·bear·er, pôl′bār·ǝr, *n.* One of those who attend the coffin at a funeral.

pal·let, pal′it, *n.* A small or rude bed; a bed or mattress of straw.

pal·let, pal′it, *n.* A movable platform used for the storage or movement of goods.

pal·li·ate, pal′ē·āt, *v.t.,* **-at·ed, -at·ing.** To try to conceal the significance of by excuses and apologies; to mitigate, lessen, or abate. —**pal·li·a·tion,** pal·ē·ā′shǝn, *n.*

pal·lid, pal′id, *a.* Pale, wan; deficient in color.

pal·lor, pal′ər, *n.* Paleness; wanness.

palm, päm, *n.* Any of the tropical or subtropical trees with a tall, usu. unbranched stem surmounted by a crown of large, palmately cleft, fan-shaped leaves; a representation of such a leaf or branch, as on a decoration of honor, or as an addition of honor to a military decoration; the victor's reward of honor, or the honor of being victorious or of surpassing others; triumph; success. **—pal·ma·ceous,** *a.*

palm, päm, *n.* That part of the inner surface of the hand which extends from the wrist to the bases of the fingers.—*v.t.* To touch or stroke with the palm or hand; to conceal in the palm; to pick up furtively; to impose fraudulently.**—palm off,** to pass off fraudulently or deceptively.

pal·mate, pal′māt, pal′mit, *a.* Shaped like a hand with the fingers extended; webbed. **—pal·mate·ly,** *adv.*

palm·er, pä′mər, *n.* A pilgrim who had returned from the Holy Land, in token of which he bore a palm branch.

palm·is·try, pä′mi·strē, *n.* The art or practice of telling fortunes and interpreting character by the lines and configurations of the palm of the hand. **—palm·ist,** *n.*

Palm Sun·day, *n.* The Sunday next before Easter: so called from the custom of solemnly blessing and distributing palm branches and carrying them in memory of Christ's triumphal entry into Jerusalem.

palm·y, pä′mē, *a.,* **-i·er, -i·est.** Having many palms; flourishing; prosperous.

pal·o·mi·no, pal·ə·mē′nō, *n. pl.,* **-nos.** A golden-coated horse with a white, flaxen, or ivory mane and tail.

pal·pa·ble, pal′pə·bəl, *a.* Perceptible to the touch; tangible; easily perceived and directed; plain; obvious. **—pal·pa·bil·i·ty,** pal·pə·bil′ə·tē, *n.* **—pal·pa·bly,** *adv.*

pal·pate, pal′pāt, *v.t.,* **-pat·ed, -pat·ing.** To examine by the sense of touch. **—pal·pa·tion,** pal·pā′shən, *n.*

pal·pi·tate, pal′pi·tāt, *v.i.,* **-tat·ed, -tat·ing.** To pulsate violently: applied particularly to an abnormally rapid and strong beat of the heart, as from fright or disease; to throb; to tremble; to quiver. **—pal·pi·ta·tion,** pal·pi·tā′shən, *n.*

pal·sy, pôl′zē, *n.* Paralysis; any condition in which energies or powers of resolution are weakened seriously; any palsied or paralyzing influence.—*v.t.,* **-sied, -sy·ing.** To affect with palsy; paralyze.

pal·ter, pôl′tər, *v.i.* To act insincerely; to equivocate; to haggle; to use trickery. **—pal·ter·er,** *n.*

pal·try, pôl′trē, *a.,* **-tri·er, -tri·est.** Petty; trivial; inferior; worthless; mean; despicable. **—pal·tri·ness,** *n.*

pam·pas, pam′pəz, *n. pl.* The immense grassy plains of South America, particularly of Argentina. **—pam·pe·an,** pam·pē′ən, pam′pē·ən, *a.*

pam·per, pam′pər, *v.t.* To indulge, as a child, to the full or to excess; to gratify the tastes or desires of; to coddle. **—pam·per·er,** *n.*

pam·phlet, pam′flit, *n.* A small, unbound publication; a short treatise or essay, usu. on a current or controversial topic, published by itself.

pam·phlet·eer, pam·flə·tēr′, *n.* A writer of pamphlets.

pan, pan, *n.* A vessel used for cooking and other domestic purposes; any of various open or closed vessels; headpan. *Informal.* The face.—*v.t.,* **panned, pan·ning.** To wash, as gravel or sand, in a pan; to separate, as gold, by such washing. *Informal.* To criticize severely.—*v.i.* To wash gravel or sand while searching for gold.

pan, pan, *v.i.,* **panned, pan·ning.** To move a camera in a horizontal or vertical plane in order to follow a person or object in motion.

pan·a·ce·a, pan·ə·sē′ə, *n.* A remedy for all diseases; a cure-all; a solution for any difficulty. **—pan·a·ce·an,** *a.*

pa·nache, pə·nash′, pə·näsh′, *n.* An ornamental plume or tuft of feathers on a helmet or cap; an ornate or showy style; flamboyance.

pan·cake, pan′kāk, *n.* A thin, flat cake of batter cooked in a pan or on a griddle.—*v.i.* **-caked, -cak·ing.** To land an airplane by dropping vertically with less forward glide than usual.

pan·cre·as, pan′krē·əs, pang′krē·əs, *n.* A gland situated near the stomach, secreting an important digestive fluid, pancreatic juice, into the duodenum, and producing insulin. **—pan·cre·at·ic,** pan·krē·at′ik, *a.*

pan·dem·ic, pan·dem′ik, *a.* Of a disease, prevalent throughout an entire country or continent, or the whole world; general; universal.—*n.* A pandemic disease.

pan·de·mo·ni·um, pan·də·mō′nē·əm, *n.* Wild lawlessness or uproar; chaos; a place of riotous disorder or lawless confusion.

pan·der, pan′dər, *n.* A go-between in love affairs; one who solicits clients for prostitutes or furnishes women for prostitution; a pimp; a procurer; one who caters to or takes advantage of another's weaknesses.—*v.i.* To act as a pander.

pane, pān, *n.* A single sheet of glass in a frame; a piece of glass for a compartment; a panel in a door.

pan·el, pan′əl, *n.* A distinct portion or compartment of any surface, sunk below or raised above the general level, or enclosed by a frame or border; the list of persons summoned for service as jurors; the body of persons composing a jury; a mount of instruments or control devices, as in an aircraft's cockpit; a control board.—*v.t.,* **-eled, -el·ing.** To arrange in, or furnish with panels; ornament with a panel or panels.

pan·el·ing, pan′əl·ing, *n.* A wall or other surface consisting of panels; panels collectively.

pan·el·ist, pan′əl·ist, *n.* One who is a member of a panel.

pan·el truck, *n.* A small, enclosed truck commonly used for light deliveries.

pang, pang, *n.* A sudden, brief, sharp pain; a spasm; a sudden feeling of mental distress.

pan·han·dle, pan′han·del, *n.* The handle of a pan; a narrow projecting strip of land that is not a peninsula, esp. part of a state.

pan·han·dle, pan′han·del, *v.i.,* **-died, -dling.** *Informal.* To confront and beg from strangers on the street.

pan·ic, pan′ik, *n.* Acute fear or demoralizing terror, often contagious in a group situation; an outbreak of fear in financial circles. *Informal.* An unusually humorous situation or person.—*a.* Of or caused by panic. —*v.t.,* **-icked, -ick·ing.** To affect with panic.—*v.i.* To be affected by panic.

pan·nier, pan·ier, pan′yər, *n.* A basket for carrying on a person's back; a skirt puffed or draped at the hips.

pan·o·ply, pan′ə·plē, *n. pl.,* **-plies.** A complete suit of armor; any complete equipment of war or defense; a complete covering or array of something. **—pan·o·plied,** *a.*

pan·o·ram·a, pan·ə·ram′ə, pan·ə·rä′mə, *n.* An unobstructed view or prospect over a wide area; a continuously passing or changing scene or series of events. **—pan·o·ram·ic,** *a.* **—pan·o·ram·i·cal·ly,** *adv.*

pan·sy, pan′zē, *n. pl.,* **-sies.** An annual or short-lived perennial flower with variously and richly colored blossoms. *Informal.* A male homosexual.

pant, pant, *v.i.* To breathe quickly or spasmodically; to gasp; to throb or heave rapidly or violently; to yearn or long for.—*v.t.* To breathe or gasp out.—*n.* A quick, short breath; a gasp.

pan·ta·loon, pan·tə·loon′, *n. pl.* A man's closely-

---

a- hat, fāte, fāre, fäther; **e-** met, mē; **i-** pin, pīne; **o-** not, nōte, ôrb, moove (move), boy, pownd; **u-** cūbe, bŭll, tŭk (took); **ch-** chin; **th-** thick, ŧhen; **zh-** vizhon (vision); **ə-** əgo, takən, pencəl, lemən, bərd (bird).

fitting garment covering the hips and legs, varying in form during the 18th and 19th centuries; trousers.

pan•the•ism, pan′thē•iz•əm, *n.* The doctrine that all aspects of the universe are divinely inspired; the Roman worship of all the gods. —**pan•the•ist,** *n.* —**pan•the•is•tic,** pan•thē•is′tik, *a.*

pan•the•on, pan′thē•on, *n.* A temple dedicated to all the gods; a public building containing tombs or memorials of the illustrious dead of a nation; the deities of a people collectively.

pan•ther, pan′thər, *n.* The unspotted puma or cougar; the black phase of the leopard. *Informal.* A fierce or violent person.

pan•ties, pan′tēz, *n. pl.* Brief underpants for women or children.

pan•to•mime, pan′tə•mīm, *n.* The dramatic technique of communicating through mute gestures; gesture without speech; dumb show.—*v.t., v.i.,* **-mimed,** **-mim•ing.** To represent or express by pantomime. —**pan•to•mim•ic,** pan•tə•mim′ik, *a.* —**pan•to•mim•ist,** pan′tə•mi•mist, *n.*

pan•try, pan′trē, *n. pl.,* **-tries.** A room or closet for provisions, silverware, china, glassware, and table linen; a room adjacent to a dining room and kitchen where foods are arranged prior to serving.

pants, pants, *n. pl.* Trousers; underpants, usu. worn by women or children.

pant•suit, pant′soot, *n.* A woman's coordinated suit consisting of a jacket and a pair of slacks.

pant•y•hose, pan′tē•hōz, *n.* A one-piece, skintight garment serving as panties and stockings.

pap, pap, *n.* A nipple of the breast; a teat; something resembling or shaped like a teat.

pap, pap, *n.* Soft food for infants or invalids.

pa•pa, pä′pə, pə•pä′, *n.* Father: used chiefly by children.

pa•pa•cy, pā′pə•sē, *n. pl.,* **-cies.** The office and dignity of the pope; papal authority and jurisdiction; the popedom; the popes collectively; the term of office of a particular pope; (*cap.*) the form of government of the Roman Catholic Church.

pa•pal, pā′pəl, *a.* Belonging to the pope, the papacy, or the Roman Catholic Church.

pa•per, pā′pər, *n.* A substance used for writing, printing, packaging, and wall covering, made chiefly from rag, wood, or other vegetable fiber reduced to a pulp; a piece, leaf, or sheet of paper; material like paper, as papyrus; any written or printed document; such documents as promissory notes, bills of exchange; *pl.,* document that establishes one's identity, a journal; an essay or article on some subject. *Informal.* Free passes to an entertainment; an audience admitted free of charge.—*v.t.* To cover with paper; to enclose or fold in paper; provide with paper.—*a.* Made out of paper; paperlike; having to do with clerical work; existing only on paper. —**pa•per•er,** *n.* —**pa•per•y,** *a.*—**on pa•per,** in written form; in the planning or theoretical stage.

pa•per•back, pā′pər•bak, *n.* A book bound in paper.

pa•per•weight, pā′pər•wāt, *n.* A small weight laid on loose papers to keep them in place.

pa•per•work, pā′pər•wərk, *n.* The handling of correspondence, forms, and written reports necessary to conduct business.

pa•pier-mâ•ché, pä•pər•mə•shā′, *Fr.* pä•pyä′mä•shā′, *n.* A material prepared by pulping different kinds of paper into a mass, which is molded into various articles, dried, and japanned.—*a.* Unreal; pretentious.

pa•pil•la, pə•pil′ə, *n. pl.,* **-lae,** -lē. A nipple; one of certain small protuberances, such as the papillae of the tongue.

pa•poose, pap•poose, pa•poos′, pə•poos′, *n.* An infant or young child of N. American Indian parentage.

pap•ri•ka, pa•prē′kə, pap′rə•kə, *n.* The fruit of a variety of pepper, used in cooking, esp. as a condiment, as in Hungarian goulash.

Pap smear, pap, *n.* An examination of cells for evidence of uterine cancer or of any condition interpreted as precancerous. Also **Pap test.**

pa•py•rus, pə•pī′rəs, *n. pl.,* **-rus•es, -ri,** -rē, -rī. A tall, aquatic, reedlike plant; a paper prepared from the stems of this plant by the ancients; an ancient document or manuscript written on this material.

par, pär, *n.* An equality in value or standing; an average or normal amount, degree, quality, condition, or the like; a commonly accepted standard; in golf, the number of strokes allowed to a hole or course as representing skillful playing.—*a.* Normal; average.

par•a•ble, par′ə•bəl, *n.* An allegorical story from which a moral message or religious truth is taught.

par•a•chute, par′ə•shoot, *n.* An apparatus, used for descending safely through the air, that opens something like an umbrella, catching the air to retard the speed of descent.—*v.i.,* **-chut•ed, -chut•ing.** To jump from an airplane and descend by parachute.—*v.t.* To drop men or supplies by parachute. —**par•a•chut•ist,** par′ə•shoo•tist, *n.*

pa•rade, pə•rād′, *n.* An organized march, sometimes featuring floats and instrumental music; a marshaling of troops for inspection.—*v.t., v.i.,* **-rad•ed, -rad•ing.** To exhibit in a showy manner; to assemble and march in military order.

par•a•digm, par′ə•dim, par′ə•dīm, *n.* An example of a word, as a noun, adjective, or verb, in its various inflections; an example; a model. —**par•a•dig•mat•ic,** par•ə•dig•mat′ik, *a.*

par•a•dise, par′ə•dīs, *n.* The garden of Eden; heaven; a place of bliss. —**par•a•di•si•a•cal,** par•ə•di•sī′ə•kəl, *a.*

par•a•dox, par′ə•doks, *n.* A statement or proposition seemingly self-contradictory or absurd, and yet expressing a truth; a self-contradictory and false proposition; an opinion or statement contrary to received opinion. —**par•a•dox•i•cal,** par•ə•dok′sə•kəl, *a.*

par•af•fin, par′ə•fin, *n.* A white or colorless waxy mixture of hydrocarbons obtained from petroleum: used for candles, preservative coatings, electrical insulation, and in pharmacology and in the manufacture of perfumes and cosmetics.

par•a•gon, par′ə•gon, *n.* A model or pattern of excellence or perfection; a flawless pearl of exceptional size.

par•a•graph, pfir′ə•graf, par′ə•gräf, *n.* A distinct portion of written or printed matter dealing with a particular point or quoting one speaker; a note, item, or brief article, as in a newspaper, usually forming a distinct, undivided whole.—*v.t.* To divide into paragraphs; express in a paragraph; write or publish paragraphs about. —**par•a•graph•er,** *n.*

par•a•keet, par′ə•kēt, *n.* Any of several popular cage birds with a tapering tail and capable of mimicking human speech.

par•al•lax, par′ə•laks, *n.* The apparent displacement of an object due to a change in the position of the observer. —**par•al•lac•tic,** par•ə•lak′tik, *a.*

par•al•lel, par′ə•lel, *a.* Pertaining to lines, to planes, and to curves which are equidistant at all corresponding points; corresponding; analogous.—*n.* Anything parallel in direction, course, or tendency; any of the imaginary circles on the earth's surface, parallel to the equator.—*v.t.,* **-leled, -lel•ing.** To make parallel; furnish a parallel for; compare.

par•al•lel bars, *n. pl.* A pair of horizontal bars on uprights, used in gymnastics.

par•al•lel•o•gram, par•ə•lel′ə•gram, *n.* A quadrilateral having its opposite sides parallel and equal.

pa•ral•y•sis, pə•ral′ə•sis, *n. pl.,* **-ses,** -sēz. Partial or complete loss of the power of voluntary motion, or of sensation, in one or more parts of the body; inability to react or respond. —**par•a•lyt•ic,** par•ə•lit′ik, *a., n.*

par•a•lyze, par′ə•līz, *v.t.,* **-lyzed, -lyz•ing.** To affect with paralysis; to destroy the energy and power of.

par•a•me•ci•um, par•ə•mē′shē•əm, par•ə•mē•sē•əm, *n. pl.,* **-ci•a,** -sē•ə. Any of a group of one-celled, slipper-shaped protozoans having an oblique oral groove and moving by means of cilia.

par·a·med·ic, par/ə·med·ik, *n.* A person trained in basic medical procedures, who assists a physician.

pa·ram·e·ter, pə·ram/ə·tər, *n.* In a mathematical expression, a constant or variable whose value determines the specific form of the expression; any fixed boundary or limit.

par·a·mount, par/ə·mownt, *a.* Foremost in importance; preeminent; superior to all others.—*n.* An overlord. **—par·a·mount·cy,** *n.* **—par·a·mount·ly,** *adv.*

par·a·mour, par/ə·mûr, *n.* An illicit or unlawful lover, esp. of a wedded person; a lover; a loved one.

par·a·noi·a, par·ə·noy/ə, *n.* A mental disorder characterized chiefly by systematic delusions, esp. of persecution or grandeur. **—par·a·noid,** par/ə·noyd, *a., n.*

par·a·pet, par/ə·pit, par/ə·pet, *n.* A wall or rampart to cover soldiers from the attacks oa the enemy in front; a breastwork.

par·a·pher·nal·ia, par·ə·fər·nāl/yə, par·ə·fər·nā/lē·ə, *n. pl., sing. or pl. in constr.* Personal property of any kind; apparatus or equipment; ornaments; the belongings of a wife over and above her dowry.

par·a·phrase, par/ə·frāz, *n.* A restatement of the sense of a text or passage in other words.—*v.t., v.i.,* **-phrased, -phras·ing.** To put in paraphrase. **—par·a·phras·er,** *n.* **—par·a·phras·tic,** par·ə·fras/tik, *a.*

par·a·ple·gi·a, par·ə·plē/jē·ə, par·ə·plē/jə, *n.* Paralysis of both legs and the lower trunk. **—par·a·ple·gic,** par·ə·plē/jik, *a., n.*

par·a·psy·chol·o·gy, par·ə·sī·kol/ə·jē, *n.* The study and investigation of psychic phenomena, including telepathy, clairvoyance, and extrasensory perception.

par·a·site, par/ə·sīt, *n.* An animal or plant which lives on or in a living organism; one who lives on others without making a fitting return. **—par·a·sit·ic,** par·ə·sit/ik, *a.* **—par·a·sit·i·cal·ly,** *adv.* **—par·a·sit·ism,** par/ə·si·tiz·əm, *n.*

par·a·sol, par/ə·sôl, par/ə·sol, *n.* A woman's umbrella used as a protection against the sun.

par·a·sym·pa·thet·ic nerv·ous sys·tem, par·ə·sim·pə·thet/ik, *n.* The section of the autonomic nervous system which slows the heart beat, contracts the pupils, dilates blood vessels, and in general functions in contrast to the sympathetic nervous system.

par·a·thi·on, par·ə·thī/on, *n.* A very poisonous insecticide.

par·a·troop·er, par/ə·troo·pər, *n.* A soldier trained to parachute into battle from an aircraft.

par·a·ty·phoid, par·ə·tī/foyd, *n.* An infectious bacterial disease with symptoms resembling typhoid fever.

par·boil, pär/boyl, *v.t.* To boil in part; precook. *Informal.* To make unpleasantly hot.

par·cel, pär/səl, *n.* One or more items wrapped or otherwise packed up; a package; a collection; a portion of anything.—*v.t.,* **-celed, -cel·ling.** To divide into parts or portions; to make or pack up as a parcel.

par·cel post, *n.* The department of a post office system which conveys and delivers parcels of limited size.

parch, pärch, *v.t.* To dry or shrivel by exposure to heat or extreme cold; to cause thirst; to preserve, as corn or peas, by drying.—*v.i.* To become very dry.

parch·ment, pärch/mənt, *n.* The skin of sheep, goats, lambs, or calves prepared for use as a writing material; a manuscript or document on such material; a diploma.

pard, pärd, *n. Informal.* A partner; a companion.

par·don, pär/dən, *v.t.* To forgive; to exempt from punishment; to make allowances to for a discourtesy. —*n.* Forgiveness; release from the consequences of a wrong act. **—par·don·a·ble,** *a.* **—par·don·ab·ly,** *adv.*

pare, pâr, *v.t.,* **pared, par·ing.** To cut or trim the covering of; to trim or cut; diminish gradually.

par·e·gor·ic, par·ə·gôr/ik, par·ə·gor/ik, *n.* Camphorated tincture of opium, used to relieve diarrhea; a drug used in cough remedies; an anodyne which relieves pain.

par·ent, pâr/ənt, par/ənt, *n.* A father or mother; ancestor; a plant or animal that produces offspring; cause; source. **—pa·ren·tal,** pə·ren/təl, *a.*

par·ent·age, pâr/ən·tij, par/ən·tij, *n.* Ancestry; birth; origin; character or circumstances of parents.

pa·ren·the·sis, pə·ren/thə·sis, *n. pl.,* **-ses,** sēz. An explanatory or qualifying comment inserted into the midst of a passage and usu. marked off by upright curves (), brackets, commas, or dashes; these upright curves. **—par·en·thet·ic,** par·ən·thet/ik, **par·en·thet·i·cal,** *a.*

pa·re·sis, pə·rē/sis, par/ə·sis, *n.* Incomplete paralysis, affecting motion but not sensation. **—pa·ret·ic,** pə·ret/ik, pə·rē/tik, *n., a.*

par ex·cel·lence, pär ek/sə·läns, *adv.* Superbly; preeminently.—*a.*

par·fait, pär·fā/, *n.* A dessert made of beaten eggs and whipped cream and frozen without stirring; a sundae made of layers of ice cream.

pa·ri·ah, pə·rī/ə, *n.* An outcast; one of a low caste of southern India and of Burma; one despised by society.

par·i·mu·tu·el, par/i·mū/choo·əl, *n.* A system of betting on a horse race in which those who bet on the winning horses divide the total money wagered in proportion to their bet.

par·ish, par/ish, *n.* A division of a diocese; the congregation of a church; geographical area assigned to a specific church. **—pa·rish·ion·er,** pə·rish/ə·nər, *n.*

par·i·ty, par/ə·tē, *n.* Equality, as in amount, status, or character; equivalence; correspondence; similarity or analogy.

park, pärk, *n.* An area of land set aside for public recreation or conservation of natural resources, usu. under government control; a stadium or amusement area.—*v.t.* To put temporarily in a place. *Informal.* To lay down, put, or leave.—*v.i.* To leave a vehicle standing or parked. *Informal.* To caress or neck, in a parked car.

par·ka, pär/kə, *n.* A hooded fur coat worn in northeastern Asia and in Alaska; any similarly styled coat worn in areas of extreme cold.

park·ing lot, *n.* An area used for the outdoor parking of automobiles.

Park·in·son's dis·ease, pär/kin·sənz, *n.* A progressive form of paralysis marked by loss of flexibility in the muscles, tremor, and a jerky gait.

park·way, pärk/wā, *n.* A wide thoroughfare landscaped with trees and shrubs; a driveway through a park.

par·lance, pär/ləns, *n.* A way of speaking; idiom; speech.

par·lay, pär/lē, pär·lā/, *v.t., v.i.,* **-layed, -lay·ing.** To place a bet on one race or contest, the winnings, if any, to be wagered on a subsequent contest; to exploit advantageously.

par·ley, pär/lē, *v.i.,* **-leyed, -ley·ing.** To speak with a person on some point of mutual concern; to confer with an enemy.—*n.* Mutual conversation; conference with an enemy.

par·lia·ment, pär/lə·mənt, *n. (Usu. cap.)* The legislature of the United Kingdom, composed of the House of Lords and the House of Commons; a legislative assembly or body, esp. one having different estates.

par·lia·men·tar·i·an, pär·lə·men·târ/ē·ən, *n.* One skilled in parliamentary procedure or debate.

par·lia·men·ta·ry, pär·lə·men/tə·rē, *a.* Of or having to do with a parliament or its members; enacted by a parliament; in accordance with the rules of a parlia-

---

a- hat, fāte, fāre, fäther; **e-** met, mē; **i-** pin, pīne; **o-** not, nōte, ôrb, moove (move), boy, pownd; **u-** cūbe, bûll, tûk (took); **ch-** chin; **th-** thick, ŧhen; **zh-** vizhon (vision); **ə-** əgo, takən, pencəl, lemən, bərd (bird).

ment: *parliamentary* procedures.

par·lor, par·lour, pär′lər, *n.* A room in which guests are received and entertained; a living room.

pa·ro·chi·al, pə·rō′kē·əl, *a.* Belonging to a parish; limited in range or scope; narrow.

pa·ro·chi·al school, *n.* A primary or secondary school maintained by a parish.

par·o·dy, par′ə·dē, *n. pl.,* **-dies.** A literary composition in which the form and expressions of serious writings are closely imitated but adapted to a ridiculous subject or a humorous method of treatment; a burlesque imitation.—*v.t.,* **-died, -dy·ing.** To make an imitation or parody of. —**pa·rod·ic,** pə·rod′ik, *a.* —**par·o·dist,** par′ə·dist, *n.*

pa·role, pə·rōl′, *n.* The release of a prisoner before having served his full sentence on condition of his future good conduct; the period of a parole.—*v.t.,* **pa·roled, pa·rol·ing.** To release on or by parole.

pa·rot·id gland, pə·rot′id, *n.* Either of the two salivary glands on either side of the face, located one in front of each ear.

par·ox·ysm, par′ək·siz·əm, *n.* A sudden and violent access of passion or emotion; a fit; any sudden onset or intensification of a disease or symptom. —**par·ox·ys·mal,** par·ək·siz′məl, *a.*

par·quet, pär·kā′, *n.* A flooring of parquetry; the main floor of a theater extending back from the orchestra pit.—*v.t.,* **-queted,** -kād, **-quet·ing,** -kā·ing. To construct of parquetry, as a floor.

par·quet·ry, pär′ki·trē, *n.* Mosaic work of wood, usu. in geometric pattern, used for floors or wainscoting.

par·rot, par′ət, *n.* Any of certain birds, including the parakeet, lovebird, cockatoo, macaw, and others, characterized by their ability to imitate human speech; a person who repeats what is heard, without any thought of its meaning.—*v.t.* To repeat, without understanding. —**par·rot·like, par·rot·y,** *a.*

par·ry, par′ē, *v.t.,* **-ried, -ry·ing.** To ward off, as a blow or a thrust; to turn aside; evade; avoid.—*v.i.* To ward off a blow.—*n. pl.,* **-ries.** A verbal evasion; a defensive move in fencing.

parse, pärs, *v.t.* To analyze or describe grammatically. —*v.i.* To show the several parts of speech composing a sentence and their relation to each other by agreement.

par·si·mo·ny, pär′sə·mō·nē, *n.* Excessive care in the use or expenditure of money; extreme frugality; stinginess; miserliness. —**par·si·mo·ni·ous,** pär·sə·mō′nē·əs, *a.* —**par·si·mo·ni·ous·ly,** *adv.* —**par·si·mo·ni·ous·ness,** *n.*

par·sley, pärs′lē, *n.* A well-known garden herb widely grown for its leaves which are used as a garnish for foods.

pars·nip, pär′snip, *n.* An herbaceous European biennial having an edible thickened white taproot; the root.

par·son, pär′sən, *n.* One who has the parochial charge of a church parish; a clergyman, minister, or preacher.

par·son·age, pär′sən·ij, *n.* The official dwelling of a parson.

part, pärt, *n.* A portion or division of a whole: a piece, section, or fragment; a constituent; an essential or integral portion or element; a division; an allotted portion; a share; a character sustained in a play or real life; a role.—*v.t.* To divide into parts; break; cleave; to dissolve, as a relationship or a connection; to divide into shares; distribute in parts; to put or hold apart; separate.—*v.i.* —*adv.* In part; partially.—*a.* Partial.—**for one's part,** so far as concerns one.—**for the most part,** as concerns the greatest part; mostly.—**in good part,** without offense; good-naturedly.—**in part,** to some extent.—**part and par·cel,** an essential part: used emphatically.—**take part,** to participate.

par·take, pär·tāk′, *v.i.,* **-took, -tak·en, -tak·ing.** To take a part or share in common with others. —**par·ta·ker,** *n.*

part·ed, pär′tid, *a.* Divided; separated.

par·the·no·gen·e·sis, pär·the·nō·jen′ə·sis, *n.* The development of an egg into a new individual without fertilization by a sperm, occurring usu. in lower plants and invertebrates.

par·tial, pär′shəl, *a.* Affecting one part only; not complete or total; prejudiced in favor of one side. —**par·tial·ly,** *adv.*

par·ti·al·i·ty, pär·shē·al′ə·tē, *n. pl.,* **-ties.** The state of being partial; favoritism; bias; a special fondness.

par·tic·i·pant, pär·tis′ə·pənt, *a.* Sharing; having a share or part.—*n.* One who takes part in or shares in something.

par·tic·i·pate, pär·tis′ə·pāt, *v.i.,* **-pat·ed, -pat·ing.** To partake; to take a part or have a share in common with others. —**par·tic·i·pa·tion,** pär·tis·ə·pā′shən, *n.* —**par·tic·i·pa·tive,** *a.*

par·ti·cip·i·al, pär·tə·sip′ē·əl, *a.* Pertaining to or having the nature and use of a participle; formed from a participle.—*n.* A participle.

par·ti·ci·ple, pär′tə·sip·əl, *n.* A part of speech, so called because it partakes of the character both of a verb and an adjective.

par·ti·cle, pär′ti·kəl, *n.* A minute portion, piece, or degree; a clause or article, as of a document; any tiny component of matter, such as electron, proton, and neutron.

par·ti·col·ored, pär′tē·kəl·ərd, *a.* Colored differently in different parts; diversified. Also **par·ty·col·ored.**

par·tic·u·lar, pər·tik′yə·lər, *a.* Belonging or referring to some one person, thing, group, class, occasion, or other category; special; not general; characteristic; noteworthy, marked, or unusual; detailed, minute, or circumstantial.—*n.* A distinct part of something. *Usu. pl.* Points, details, or circumstances.—**in particular,** especially. —**par·tic·u·lar·ly,** *adv.*

par·tic·u·lar·i·ty, pər·tik·yə·lar′ə·tē, *n. pl.,* **-ties.** The fact of being particular; a peculiar or special character; a detailed statement; attentive to details; a particular trait.

par·tic·u·lar·ize, pər·tik′yə·lə·rīz, *v.t.,* **-ized, -iz·ing.** To make particular; state or treat in detail.—*v.i.*

par·tic·u·late, pər·tik′yə·lit, *a.* Consisting of or referring to minute, separate particles.

part·ing, pär′ting, *a.* Serving to part; dividing; separating; the act of dividing or separating; leave-taking.

par·ti·san, pär′tə·zən, pär′tə·sən, *n.* An adherent, esp. a particularly zealous supporter of a party, faction, or person.—*a.* Biased in favor of a party or interest. —**par·ti·san·ship,** *n.*

par·tite, pär′tīt, *a.* Divided into parts.

par·ti·tion, pär·tish′ən, *n.* The act of parting, or the fact of being parted; separation; something that separates; a part, division, or section.—*v.t.* To divide into parts or portions; distribute.

par·ti·tive, pär′tə·tiv, *a.* Serving to separate into parts.

part·ly, pärt′lē, *adv.* In part; in some measure or degree; not wholly.

part·ner, pärt′nər, *n.* A sharer; an associate in an enterprise; a spouse; one who holds a partnership in a business. —**part·ner·ship,** *n.*

part of speech, *n.* Any of the traditional classes of words differentiated by their meaning and syntactic function in a sentence, as the noun, pronoun, verb, adverb, adjective, conjunction, preposition, and interjection.

par·tridge, pär′trij, *n. pl.,* **-tridg·es, -tridge.** A common name for several game birds, esp. the ruffed grouse and the bobwhite.

part-time, pärt′tīm, *a.* Employed or functioning less than the usual or normal number of hours; distinguished from *full-time.*

par·tu·ri·ent, pär·tûr′ē·ənt, pär·tür′ē·ənt, *a.* Bringing forth or about to bring forth young; about to bring forth an original thought or other creation.

par·tu·ri·tion, pär·tû·rish′ən, pär·chû·rish′ən, *n.*

The act of bearing young.

par·ty, pär′tē, *n. pl.,* **-ties.** A person or a number of persons united in purpose or opinion, taking one side of an issue; a group of persons united by certain political views; a social gathering or entertainment of invited guests; a group of persons gathered for a specific purpose; a person; a certain individual.

par·ty line, *n.* A single telephone line serving several subscribers; a boundary line between adjoining properties; political policies followed by its members.

par·ve·nu, pär′və·noo, pär′və·nū, *n.* One who has suddenly acquired wealth or position above his class, but who lacks the social graces appropriate to his new status.—*a.* Like a parvenu.

pas·chal, pas′kəl, *a.* Of or referring to the Jewish Passover; of or referring to the Christian Easter.

pa·sha, pə·shä′, pash′ə, pä′shə, *n.* A title of courtesy placed after a person's name in Turkey and in Arabic countries, formerly conferred upon military commanders and governors of provinces.

pass, pas, päs, *v.i.* To go, move onward, proceed; to be successful in an examination, test, or inspection; to go away or depart; to die, usu. used with *on;* to move past; to elapse or be spent; to happen or occur; to make one's or its way; to undergo alteration or conversion; to circulate; to be accepted; to be exchanged or conveyed; to go uncensored or unchallenged; to be voided or excreted; to be enacted or ratified; to give judgment; to be conveyed from one to another; to make a pass, as in football or hockey; in cards, to forgo one's opportunity to bid or to play.—*v.t.* To move past; surpass; to undergo successfully: to *pass* an exam; go beyond; spend; circulate: *pass* counterfeit money; omit payment; transfer; to pronounce judgment; transfer ownership; to throw the ball or puck to another player, in football or hockey; in baseball, to walk a batter.—*n.* The act of passing; a road, navigable channel, or defile affording passage through an obstructed area; a written permission to enter, leave, or move about in an area; a free ticket for transportation or admission; the granting of permission for personnel to be absent from duty; passing an examination acceptably but without honors; a motion of the hands along or over an object; a movement of the hand intended to divert, deceive, or cast a spell; manipulation of an object, as by a juggler; a complete process through a machine; the passing of a ball or puck from one player to a teammate.—**pass a·way,** to die.—**pass out,** to distribute. *Informal.* To become unconscious; faint.—**pass over,** not do something about; disregard.—**pass up.** *Informal.* To ignore the advantages of; neglect.

pass·a·ble, pas′ə·bəl, *a.* That may be traveled on, crossed, or traversed; tolerable; capable of being enacted.

pass·a·bly, pas′ə·blē, *adv.* Tolerably; fairly; moderately.

pas·sage, pas′ij, *n.* The act of passing; movement, transit, or transition; a traveling from one place to another; lapse, as of time; progress or course, as of events; the passing into law of a legislative measure; a means of passing; a way or route; an avenue; a channel; a hall, corridor, or the like; an indefinite portion of a writing or speech.

pas·sage·way, pas′ij·wā, *n.* A way for passage, as in a building or among buildings; a passage.

pass·book, pas′bŭk, *n.* A book held by a depositor; bankbook.

pas·sé, pa·sā′, pas′ā, *a.* Past; old-fashioned; past the prime of life.

pas·sen·ger, pas′ən·jər, *n.* One who travels on a plane, ship, railroad, bus, taxi, or other conveyance.

pass·er-by, pas·ər·bī′, pas′ər·bī, *n. pl.,* **pass·ers-by.** One who passes by.

pass·ing, pas′ing, pä′sing, *a.* Going by; fleeting, transitory; superficial, hasty, cursory; current; acceptable; fulfilling requirements.—**in pass·ing,** as one proceeds; incidentally.

pas·sion, pash′ən, *n.* A compelling feeling or emotion; love; ardent affection; lust; violent agitation of mind; violent anger; zeal; a display of deep feeling; a pursuit to which one is devoted. The last suffering and death of Jesus Christ. —**pas·sion·less,** *a.*

pas·sion·ate, pash′ən·it, *a.* Capable of or characterized by passion or intense feeling; readily moved to anger; fiery; moved by sexual desire; vehement. —**pas·sion·ate·ly,** *adv.* —**pas·sion·ate·ness,** *n.*

pas·sive, pas′iv, *a.* Being without response to something normally expected to provoke emotion or feeling; not active; inert; influenced or incited by an outside agency: distinguished from *active;* noting a verbal inflection indicating that the subject experiences the action of the verb.—*n.* The passive voice; the passive form of a verb.

pass·key, pas′kē, *n.* A key that opens several locks; a master key.

Pass·o·ver, pas′ō·vər, *n.* A seven-day festival of the Jews occurring in the spring of the year to commemorate the escape of the Hebrews from slavery in Egypt.

pass·port, pas′pôrt, pas′pōrt, *n.* A warrant issued to a citizen of a country giving him permission to travel, protection while out of the country, and the right of reentry; a document authorizing a vessel to proceed, issued esp. in wartime; something that enables one to pass, or to attain an object.

pass·word, pas′wərd, *n.* A secret word by which one having a right to pass is recognized; a watchword.

past, past, *a.* Gone by; ended; over; belonging to a time previous to this; bygone; preceding.—*prep.* Beyond in time; after; beyond in position; further than; beyond in number; beyond the scope or influence of.—*n.* A former or past time; an earlier time.—*adv.* So as to pass by or beyond.

pas·ta, päs′tə, *n.* An unleavened paste or dough prepared with flour and eggs and used in making spaghetti, noodles, and macaroni.

paste, pāst, *n.* A kind of adhesive made of various compounds; a dough used in cooking, as for pies or pastry; pasta; any of various mashed, whipped, or ground foods.—*v.t.,* **pas·ted, pas·ting.** To fasten or cement with paste; to cover with something applied by means of paste. *Informal.* To strike severely with a blow; to punch, as on the face.

paste·board, pāst′bôrd, *n.* Paper pulp or layers of treated paper rolled into rigid sheets; cardboard.

pas·tel, pa·stel′, *n.* A soft, pale color; a kind of dried paste made of pigments ground with chalk; a chalk crayon made with such paste; a drawing made with such crayons.

pas·teur·ize, pas′chə·rīz, pas′tə·rīz, *v.t.,* **-ized, -iz·ing.** To subject, as milk, wine, beer, fruit juices, or other liquids, to a temperature ranging from 140 to 155° F. in order to kill the bacteria which cause fermentation. —**pas·teur·i·za·tion,** pas·chə·rə·zā′shən, *n.*

pas·tille, pa·stēl′, pa·stil′, *n.* A sweetened lozenge; a troche; a small roll for burning as a fumigant or disinfectant; pastel for making crayons.

pas·time, pas′tīm, *n.* That which amuses and serves to make time pass agreeably; sport; diversion.

pas·tor, pas′tər, *n.* A minister of the gospel having charge of a church and congregation.

pas·to·ral, pas′tər·əl, *a.* Referring to shepherds, or to the care of flocks or herds; living as a shepherd or shepherds; used for pasture; having the simplicity or charm of farm country; pertaining to the country or to life in the country; rustic or rural; portraying the life of shepherds or of the country in an idyllic manner, as a work of literature, art, or music.—*n.* A poem or play

---

a- hat, fāte, fāre, fäther; **e-** met, mē; **i-** pin, pīne; **o-** not, nōte, ôrb, moove (move), boy, pownd; **u-** cūbe, bŭll, tûk (took); **ch-** chin, **th-** thick, **th**en; **zh-** vizhon (vision); **ə-** əgo, takən, pencəl, lemən, bərd (bird).

dealing with the life of shepherds; a pastoral picture or work of art.

pas·tor·ate, pas/tər·it, *n.* The office or jurisdiction of a pastor; a body of pastors; a parsonage.

pas·tra·mi, pə·strä/mē, *n.* Beef, usu. a shoulder cut, smoked or pickled and highly seasoned.

pas·try, pā/strē, *n. pl.,* **-tries.** A sweet, baked food made of flaky dough, or of which the dough constitutes the principal baked ingredient, as the crust of a pie or tart.

past tense, *n.* One of the forms of a verb indicating action or state of being that is past or took place in the past.

pas·ture, pas/chər, *n.* Grass for the food of cattle or other animals; ground covered with grass for the food of animals; a grazing ground.—*v.t.,* **-tured, -tur·ing.** To feed on growing grass, or to supply pasture for. —*v.i.* To graze. —**pas·tur·age,** *n.*

past·y, pā/stē, *a.,* **-i·er, -i·est.** Like paste; of the texture of paste; pale and unhealthy of complexion.

pat, pat, *n.* A light stroke or blow with something; a gentle stroke with the hand or fingers; a small mass of something, as butter.—*v.t.,* **pat·ted, pat·ting.** To strike lightly with something flat; to strike gently with the palm or fingers as an expression of affection, kindness, or approval; to strike the floor with light footsteps.—*v.i.* To strike lightly; to walk or run with light footsteps.

pat, pat, *a.* Apt; opportune; mastered or learned; glib. —*adv.* Aptly; promptly or readily; perfectly.—**stand pat,** to be unyielding; to stand steadfast or firm. —**pat·ly,** *adv.* —**pat·ness,** *n.*

patch, pach, *n.* A piece of cloth sewn on a garment to repair it; a piece of material protecting a wound or injury; a small piece of ground.—*v.t.* To mend with patches or pieces; to smooth over or settle.

patch test, *n.* A test for allergic sensitivity when small pads impregnated with the allergen are applied.

patch·work, pach/wərk, *n.* Work composed of cloth of assorted figures or colors sewn together.

patch·y, pach/ē, *a.,* **-i·er, -i·est.** Full of patches; irregular or uneven in texture or quality.

pate, pāt, *n.* The head of a person; the top of the head; the brain: used disparagingly or humorously.

pâ·té, pä·tā/, *n. pl.,* **pâ·tés,** pä·tāz/, A meat, fowl, or fish paste, often cooked in pastry as an hors d'oeuvre; a small pie or patty.

pat·ent, pat/ənt, *a.* Open to view or knowledge, manifest; open, as a door or a passage; pertaining to a grant by a government of exclusive rights; conferred by a patent, as a right or privilege; of a kind specially protected by a patent; evident, belonging as if by a proprietary claim.—*n.* An official document conferring some right or privilege; a government grant conferring the exclusive rights to the manufacture or sale of a new invention for a certain term of years; an invention or process which has been patented; a tract of land granted by a patent. —**pa·ten·cy,** pāt/ən·sē, *n.* —**pat·ent·ly,** *adv.*

pat·ent·ee, pat·ən·tē/, *n.* One to whom a patent is granted.

pat·ent leath·er, *n.* Leather with a finely varnished glossy surface, used for shoes, boots, purses, and other accessories.

pa·ter·nal, pə·tər/nəl, *a.* Of or pertaining to a father; fatherly; related on the father's side. —**pa·ter·nal·ly,** *adv.*

pa·ter·nal·ism, pə·tər/nə·liz·əm, *n.* The principle of an authority in managing the affairs of a country, community, company, or of individuals, in the manner of a father's relationship with his children.

pa·ter·ni·ty, pə·tər/nə·tē, *n.* Fatherhood; the fact of being a father; derivation from a father: the child's *paternity;* origin; authorship.

path, path, *n. pl.,* **paths,** pathz, paths. A way beaten or trodden by the feet of man or beast; a narrow or unimportant road; a footway; course of life, conduct, or procedure.

pa·thet·ic, pə·thet/ik, *a.* Causing or arousing pity or sorrow; typified by arousing such emotions; affecting the feelings.

path·find·er, path/fīn·dər, *n.* One who finds a path or way, as through a wilderness; one who embarks on new paths, as in art or science.

pa·thol·o·gy, pə·thol/ə·jē, *n. pl.,* **-gies.** The science dealing with the nature of diseases, their causes, symptoms, and effects; circumstances which constitute a diseased condition. —**path·o·log·ic,** path·ə·loj/ik, **path·o·log·ic·al,** *a.* —**path·o·log·i·cal·ly,** *adv.* —**pa·thol·o·gist,** pə·thol/ə·jist, *n.*

pa·thos, pā/thos, *n.* The quality that arouses such emotions as pity, compassion, sorrow, or sympathy; expression of strong or deep feeling.

path·way, path/wā, *n.* A path; a narrow way to be passed on foot.

pa·tience, pā/shəns, *n.* The quality, capacity, or act of being patient.

pa·tient, pā/shənt, *a.* Bearing pain or trial without complaining; sustaining afflivtons with fortitude, calmness, or submission.—*n.* One who or that which is passively affected; a person who is under medical treatment. —**pa·tient·ly,** *adv.*

pat·i·na, pat/ə·nə, *n.* The fine green rust, considered valuable when found on ancient bronzes, copper coins, or medals; a surface change due to age.

pa·ti·o, pat/ē·ō, pä/tē·ō, *n. pl.,* **-os.** A court; an inner court open to the sky; a paved area attached to a house, for outdoor enjoyment.

pat·ois, pat/wä, *n. pl.,* **pat·ois,** pat/wäz. A dialect differing from the standard language of the country; a provincial or illiterate form of speech; the jargon of a social or professional group.

pa·tri·arch, pā/trē·ärk, *n.* The father and ruler of a family; the male head of a family or tribal line; a person regarded as the father or founder of an order or class; one of the elders or leading older members of a community.

pa·tri·ar·chy, pā/trē·är·kē, *n. pl.,* **-chies.** A form of social organization in which the father is head of the group, and in which descent is measured in the male line; a group governed in this way.

pa·tri·cian, pə·trish/ən, *a.* Referring to the senatorial order in ancient Rome; of noble birth; high social status.—*n.* A person of noble birth; high social status.

pat·ri·mo·ny, pa/trə·mō·nē, *n. pl.,* **-nies.** A right or estate inherited from one's father or ancestors; heritage; a church estate or endowment.

pa·tri·ot, pā/trē·ət, pā/trē·ot, *n.* A person who loves his country, and zealously supports and defends it and its interests. —**pa·tri·ot·ic,** pā·trē·ot/ik, *a.* —**pa·tri·ot·i·cal·ly,** *adv.* —**pa·tri·ot·ism,** *n.*

pa·trol, pə·trōl/, *v.i., v.t.,* **pa·trolled, pa·trol·ling.** To walk around or through, for the purpose of protection.—*n.* One or more policemen or soldiers patrolling an area; act of patrolling; a group of Boy Scouts. —**pa·trol·ler,** *n.*

pa·trol·man, pə·trōl/mən, *n. pl.,* **-men.** An individual who patrols a particular district.

pa·trol wag·on, *n.* A vehicle used by the police for the conveyance of prisoners.

pa·tron, pā/trən, *n.* A customer or client, particularly on a regular basis, of a store, restaurant, barbershop, or other establishment; one who supports a person, institution, or cause; a patron saint. —**pa·tron·ess,** pā/trə·nis, *n. fem.*

pa·tron·age, pā/trə·nij, pat/rən·ij, *n.* The trade or business given to a commercial establishment; the support, protection, or encouragement of a patron; the right or power to make political job appointments; condescension when conferring favor.

pa·tron·ize, pā/trə·nīz, pat/rə·nīz, *v.t.,* **-ized, -iz·ing.** To give one's regular trade or patronage to; to show favor in a condescending manner. —**pa·tron·iz·ing,** *a.* —**pa·tron·iz·ing·ly,** *adv.*

pat·ro·nym·ic, pat′rə·nim′ik, *n.* A surname derived from the name of the male parent or paternal ancestor, usu. by adding a suffix or prefix, as in Johnson, son of John, or McHenry, son of Henry.

pat·sy, pat′sē, *n. pl.,* **-sies.** *Informal.* One who gets the blame; scapegoat; sucker.

pat·ter, pat′ər, *v.t.* To repeat or say rapidly or glibly; to recite or repeat in a rapid, mechanical way, as prayers.—*v.i.* To talk rapidly.—*n.* Rapid talk; any group's jargon; light, rapid speech, as that used by comedians.

pat·ter, pat′ər, *v.i.* To strike or move with a succession of slight tapping sounds; to move in a quick manner. —*v.t.* To cause to patter.—*n.* The act of pattering.

pat·tern, pat′ərn, *n.* An original or model proposed for imitation; an ornamental design or decoration; a natural arrangement of parts; distinguishable or perceptible traits or peculiarities of a certain person or persons.—*v.t.* To make, according to a pattern.—*v.i.* To make a pattern. —**pat·terned,** *a.*

pat·ty, pat′ē, *n. pl.,* **-ties.** A small, flat cake of ground meat or chopped fish; a small pie; a thin, circular piece of candy.

pau·ci·ty, pô′si·tē, *n.* Smallness of number; scarcity; scantiness.

paunch, pônch, *n.* The belly and its contents; potbelly; the abdomen. —**paunch·i·ness,** *n.* —**paunch·y,** *a.,* **-i·er, -i·est.**

pau·per, pô′pər, *n.* An extremely poor person; one in a state of poverty. —**pau·per·ism,** *n.*

pause, pôz, *n.* A temporary cessation from action; a short stop; delay; a momentary suspension in speech to clarify meaning.—*v.t.,* **paused, paus·ing.** To make a brief stop; to halt speech or action; wait or linger; hesitate. —**paus·er,** *n.*

pave, pāv′, *v.t.,* **paved, pav·ing.** To cover, surface, or lay with concrete, asphalt, brick, gravel, or other material, as a street or sidewalk.—**pave the way,** to make it easier for; to prepare for. —**pav·er,** *n.*

pave·ment, pāv′mənt, *n.* A paved walk or road; a surface which is covered with paving material; the material with which anything is paved. *Brit.* A sidewalk.

pa·vil·ion, pə·vil′yən, *n.* An open building used for exhibitions and entertainment; a section which projects from the main part of a building.

pav·ing, pā′ving, *n.* Pavement; the material used for a pavement.

paw, pô, *n.* The foot of animals having claws or nails.—*v.i., v.t.* To draw or scrape with the forefoot along the ground. *Informal.* To handle roughly or rudely.

pawl, pôl, *n.* A pivoted bar for catching the teeth of a ratchet wheel to keep the wheel moving in one direction only.

pawn, pôn, *n.* The state of being held as security for borrowed money; some article or chattel deposited as a pledge for borrowed money; a hostage.—*v.t.* To give or deposit as security for a loan; to stake. —**pawn·er, pawn·or,** pôn′ər, pôn·ôr, *n.*

pawn, pôn, *n.* In chess, one of eight men of the lowest rank; a person who is manipulated to serve another's own ends.

pawn·bro·ker, pôn′brō·kər, *n.* A person who lends money at interest on personal property deposited as a pledge.

pawn·shop, pôn′shop, *n.* An establishment where articles are pawned, redeemed, and sold.

pay, pā, *v.t.,* **paid, pay·ing.** To discharge, as a debt or obligation, by giving or doing something; to compensate; to yield a recompense or return to; to requite; to retaliate against or punish; to give or render compliments; to make, as a call or visit.—*v.i.* —*n.* Payment, as of wages; wages, salary, or stipend; payment.

—*a.*—**pay up,** to make full payment; to give payment upon demand. —**pay·ee,** pā·ē′, *n.* —**pay·er,** *n.*

pay·a·ble, pā′ə·bəl, *a.* Justly owed and unpaid; due; suitable for payment.

pay·check, pā′chek, *n.* Wages or salary paid in the form of a check; salary; wages.

pay dirt, *n.* Earth containing a sufficient quantity of metal to be profitably worked by the miner. *Informal.* Any source of profit.

pay·load, pā′lōd, *n.* The portion of a load producing revenue, such as passengers, baggage, or freight; the explosive charge in the warhead of a missile.

pay mas·ter, pā′mas·tər, pā′mä·stər, *n.* One who is authorized to pay out salaries or wages.

pay·ment, pā′mənt, *n.* The act of paying; whatever is paid; reward or punishment.

pay·off, pā′ôf, pā′of, *n.* The act or occasion of payment of wages or debts; the moment of reckoning; the ending of a narrative. *Informal.* A bribe.

pay·roll, pā′rōl, *n.* A roll or list of persons to be paid. Also **pay roll.**

pea, pē, *n. pl.,* **peas, pease.** The round, highly nutritious seed of a hardy leguminous vine in wide cultivation; the plant itself.

peace, pēs, *n.* A state of quiet or tranquility; calm, quietness, or repose; freedom from war or hostility; serenity.—**at peace,** in a tranquil state; in a state of harmony.

peace·a·ble, pēs′ə·bəl, *a.* Tranquil; disposed to peace; keeping peace; peaceful. —**peace·a·bly,** *adv.*

peace·ful, pēs′fəl, *a.* Tranquil; quiet; free from noise or tumult; liking or keeping peace; pertaining to peace. —**peace·ful·ly,** *adv.* —**peace·ful·ness,** *n.*

peace·mak·er, pēs′mā·kər, *n.* An individual, group, or country that reconciles, or attempts to reconcile, parties at variance.

peace of·fic·er, An officer invested with power to preserve civil peace, as a sheriff, policeman, or constable.

peace·time, pēs′tīm, *n.* A period of peace, esp. between nations.—*a.*

peach, pēch, *n.* The fruit of a small tree, native to China and widely cultivated in north temperate regions; the tree itself; a peach color. *Informal.* A person or thing that is greatly admired.

pea·cock, pē′kok, *n. pl.,* **-cocks, -cock.** The male of the peafowl, a bird distinguished for its long, erect tail with rich coloring of green, blue, and gold; a vain, pompous, arrogant person.

pea green, *n.* A light green with a yellowish tinge.

peak, pēk, *n.* The pointed top of a mountain; the pointed top of anything; the highest point or degree of development; a projecting point: the *peak* of a man's beard.—*v.t., v.i.* To make into or assume the form of a peak. —**peaked,** pēkt, *a.*

peak·ed, pēk′id, *a.* Having a pale or wan appearance; thin; sickly.

peal, pēl, *n.* A loud, prolonged sound of bells, thunder, or laughter; a set of bells tuned to each other in the major scale.—*v.i., v.t.* To sound with a peal or peals; ring.

pea·nut, pē′nət, *n.* A widely cultivated subtropical legume with edible oily seeds borne in pods below the ground; the seed itself. *Informal.* An unimportant person or thing; *pl.,* a small or trifling sum of money.—*a.*

pear, pãr, *n.* An edible fruit typically rounded but elongated and tapering toward the stem.

pearl, pėrl, *n.* A smooth body formed around an irritant, usu. produced by oysters and valued as a gem when perfectly colored and lustrous; something similar in shape and luster; what is precious or best; a pale shade of gray with a blue tinge.—*a.*—*v.i.* To hunt or fish for pearls; color or shape like pearls. —**pearl·y,** *a.*

---

a- hat, fāte, fãre, fäther; e- met, mē; i- pin, pīne; o- not, nōte, ôrb, moove (move), boy, pownd; u- cūbe, bûll, tûk (took); ch- chin; th- thick, then; zh- vizhon (vision); ə- ago, takən, pencəl, lemən, bərd (bird).

peas·ant, pez′ənt, n. A countryman who is engaged in working on the land as a small farmer or a farm laborer; a rustic; a simple person. *Informal.* A simple-minded, uncouth person.—a. Rustic; rural. —**peas·ant·ry,** n.

peat, pēt, n. Partially decayed, highly combustible, dry plant material usu. formed in swamps; a piece of this suitable for fuel. —**peat·y,** a.

peb·ble, peb′əl, n. A small stone worn and rounded by the action of water.—v.t. **-bled, -bling.** To treat, as leather, so as to give a rough, granulated texture; to pelt with pebbles. —**peb·bly,** a.

pe·can, pi·kän′, pi·kan′, pē′kan, n. A very productive nut tree related to the hickory; the nut itself.

pec·ca·dil·lo, pek·ə·dil′ō, n. pl., **-loes, -los.** A slight trespass or offense; a petty crime or fault.

peck, pek, n. A fourth of a bushel, a dry measure of eight quarts. *Informal.* A great amount.

peck, pek, v.t. To strike with the beak or with a pointed object or instrument.—v.i. To make holes with a beak or a pointed instrument; to nibble at food; to nag. *Informal.* A perfunctory kiss. —**peck·er,** n.

pec·tin, pek′tin, n. A complex carbohydrate found highly concentrated in certain ripe fruits, forming a viscous solution in water, and, when combined with sugar and acid, yielding fruit jelly.

pec·to·ral, pek′tər·əl, a. Of or pertaining to the breast or chest; thoracic; worn on the breast or chest.

pec·u·late, pek′yə·lāt, v.t., v.i. **-lat·ed, -lat·ing.** To appropriate, as public money or goods entrusted to one's care; to embezzle. —**pec·u·la·tion,** pek·yə·lā′shən, n. —**pec·u·la·tor,** n.

pe·cu·liar, pi·kūl′yər, a. Strange; unusual or uncommon; different in nature from others of the same kind; belonging characteristically or exclusively to a person, thing, or group. —**pe·cu·liar·ly,** adv. —**pe·cu·li·ar·i·ty,** pi·kū·lē·ar′i·tē, n. pl., **-ties.**

pe·cu·ni·ar·y, pi·kū′nē·er·ē, a. Relating to or connected with money; entailing a money penalty.

ped·a·gogue, ped′ə·gog, ped′ə·gôg, n. A school teacher; derogatively, one who is dogmatic or pedantic. —**ped·a·gog·ic,** ped·ə·goj′ik, ped·ə·gō′jik, **ped·a·gog·i·cal,** a. —**ped·a·gog·i·cal·ly,** adv.

ped·a·go·gy, ped′ə·gō·jē, ped′ə·goj·ē, n. The art or science of teaching.

ped·al, ped′əl, n. A lever to be pressed down by the foot, as in playing some musical instruments or operating certain mechanisms; a sort of treadle.—v.t., v.i. **-aled, -al·ing.** To drive by pedaling, as a bicycle.—a.

ped·ant, ped′ənt, n. A person who lays undue stress on rules and details; one who relies on book learning and neglects practical reasoning. —**pe·dan·tic,** pə·dan′tik, a. —**pe·dan·ti·cal·ly,** adv. —**ped·ant·ry,** ped′ən·trē, n.

ped·dle, ped′əl, v.i., v.t. **-dled, -dling.** To travel about and retail small wares; to be engaged in a small business. —**ped·dler,** ped·ler, **ped·lar,** n.

ped·es·tal, ped′i·stəl, n. A support for a column, statue, vase, or table; a foundation or base.—**put on a pedestal,** to esteem as a hero or idol; glorify.

pe·des·tri·an, pə·des′trē·ən, n. One who walks or journeys on foot; a walker.—a. Walking; commonplace, dull, or prosaic. —**pe·des·tri·an·ism,** n.

pe·di·at·rics, pē·dē·a′triks, ped·ē·a′triks, n. pl. but sing. in constr. The science which deals with the medical care and diseases of children. —**pe·di·at·ric,** a. —**pe·di·a·tri·cian,** pē·dē·ə·trish′ən, ped·ē·ə·trish′ən, **pe·di·at·rist,** n.

ped·i·cure, ped′i·kyūr, n. Podiatry; one whose business is the care of the feet. —**ped·i·cur·ist,** n.

ped·i·gree, ped′ə·grē, n. A line of ancestors; lineage; a genealogy; a table or list tracing ancestry, as of domesticated animals. —**ped·i·greed,** a.

ped·i·ment, ped′ə·mənt, n. Arch. A low triangular part resembling a gable, crowning the front of buildings. —**ped·i·men·tal,** ped·ə·men′təl, a. —**ped·i·ment·ed,** a.

pe·dom·e·ter, pi·dom′i·tər, n. An instrument which measures the distance a person walks.

peek, pēk, v.i. To look quickly or furtively; peep.—n. A quick, furtive glance; a peep.

peel, pēl, v.t., v.i. To strip or lose the skin, bark, or rind from. *Informal.* To remove one's clothes.—n. The rind or skin of a fruit or vegetable.—**keep one's eyes peeled,** to keep a close watch; be alert.

peep, pēp, v.i. To utter the shrill little cry of a young bird or a mouse; cheep; squeak; to speak in a thin, weak voice.—n. A peeping cry or sound; any of various small sandpipers. —**peep·er,** n.

peep, pēp, v.i. To look through a small aperture or from a hiding place; look slyly, pryingly, or furtively; peek; begin to appear.—v.t. To show or protrude slightly.—n. A brief or stealthy look; the first appearance; peephole. —**peep·er,** n.

peep·hole, pēp′hōl, n. A hole or gap through which one may peep.

peer, pēr, n. One of the same rank or qualities; an equal; a member of one of the five degrees of British nobility: duke, marquis, earl, viscount, baron.—v.i. To look as in the effort to discern clearly; to peep out or appear slightly. —**peer·age,** n. —**peer·ess,** n. fem.

peer·less, pēr′lis, a. Unequaled. —**peer·less·ly,** adv.

peeve, pēv, v.t., **peeved, peev·ing.** To render peevish; irritate.—n. A source of annoyance.

peev·ish, pē′vish, a. Cross; fretful; querulous. —**pee·vish·ly,** adv. —**pee·vish·ness,** n.

pee·wee, pē′wē, n. *Informal.* An exceptionally small person or thing.—a. Tiny.

peg, peg, n. A pin of wood or other material driven or fitted into something, as to fasten parts together, to hang things on, to make fast a rope or string on, to stop a hole, or to mark some point. *Informal.* A throw, as in baseball.—v.t., **pegged, peg·ging.** To drive or insert a peg into; fasten or mark with or as with pegs.—v.i. To work persistently.—a. Tapered near the bottom, as the legs of pants.

pe·jo·ra·tive, pi·jôr′ə·tiv, pi·jor′ə·tiv, pej·ə·rā′tiv, a. Having or indicating a disparaging meaning; depreciative.—n. A pejorative form or word. —**pe·jo·ra·tive·ly,** adv.

Pe·king·ese, Pe·ki·nese, pē·kə·nēz′, n. pl., **-ese.** A small, short-legged dog having a flat face and a long, silky coat.

pe·koe, pē′kō, n. A fine, black tea native to India, Ceylon, and Java.

pelf, pelf, n. Money, riches: often used disparagingly.

pel·i·can, pel′ə·kən, n. A large, fish-eating, web-footed water bird having a long flat bill with a distensible pouch beneath, for storing food.

pel·la·gra, pə·lā′grə, pə·lag′rə, n. A disease affecting the skin, digestive system, and nervous system, caused by niacin deficiency.

pel·let, pel′it, n. A small, round or spherical body; a bullet.—v.t. To form into pellets; to hit with pellets.

pell-mell, pell·mell, pel′mel′, adv. In a disordered manner; with confused haste.—a.—n.

pel·lu·cid, pə·loo′sid, a. Admitting the passage of light; translucent; limpid or clear; lucid. —**pel·lu·cid·i·ty,** pel·ū·sid′i·tē, **pel·lu·cid·ness,** n. —**pel·lu·cid·ly,** adv.

pelt, pelt, n. The skin of an animal with the hair or wool on it; the untanned hide of an animal. —**pelt·ry,** n.

pelt, pelt, v.t. To strike successively with something thrown or driven; hurl; fling; to assail verbally.—v.i. To continue beating steadily, as with rain or heavy hail. —n. —**pelt·er,** n.

pel·vis, pel′vis, n. pl., **-vis·es, -ves,** -vēz. The basin-like bony cavity in the lower part of the trunk of many vertebrates; the bones forming this cavity. —**pel·vic,** a.

pem·mi·can, pem·i·can, pem′ə·kən, n. A food preparation exhibiting excellent keeping qualities and consisting of dried meat and melted fat, sometimes mixed with dried fruit, and pressed into cakes.

pen, pen, *n.* Any instrument for writing with ink; a small instrument of steel or other metal, with a split point, used, when fitted into a holder, for writing with ink; the pen and penholder together.—*v.t.,* **penned, pen·ning.** To write with a pen; compose and write. —**pen·ner,** *n.*

pen, pen, *n.* A small enclosure for domestic animals; any place of confinement.—*v.t.,* **penned** or **pent, pen·ning.** To confine in or as in a pen.

pen, pen, *n. Informal.* A penitentiary.

pe·nal, pēn·əl, *a.* Of or relating to penalties or punishment.

pe·nal·ize, pēn′ə·līz, pen′ə·līz, *v.t.,* **-ized, -iz·ing.** To impose a penalty on; to declare liable to penalty. —**pe·nal·i·za·tion,** pē·nəl·ə·zā′shən, *n.* —**pe·nal·ly,** *adv.*

pen·al·ty, pen′əl·tē, *n. pl.,* **-ties.** Punishment; the disadvantage or hardship associated with an action or condition.—*a.*

pen·ance, pen′əns, *n.* The suffering to which a person subjects himself as an expression of repentance for sin.

pen·chant, pen′chənt, *n.* Strong inclination, taste, liking, or bias.

pen·cil, pen′səl, *n.* An instrument for marking, drawing, or writing made of a strip of chalk, graphite, or the like encased in wood or metal.—*v.t.,* **-ciled** or **cilled, -cil·ing** or **-cil·ling.** To write or mark with or as with a pencil.

pend, pend, *v.i.* To await a judgment or decision.

pend·ant, pend·ent, pen′dənt, *n.* Anything hanging down, esp. from the neck, used for decoration or ornamentation.

pend·ent, pend·ant, pen′dənt, *a.* Hanging; suspended; overhanging; not yet determined; pending. —**pend·en·cy,** *n.* —**pend·ent·ly,** *a.*

pend·ing, pen′ding, *a.* Remaining undecided; impending; imminent.—*prep.* During; until.

pen·du·lous, pen′jū·ləs, *a.* Hanging so as to swing freely; undecided; vacillating. —**pen·du·lous·ly,** *adv.* —**pen·du·lous·ness,** *n.*

pen·du·lum, pen′jə·ləm, pen′dyə·ləm, *n.* A body so suspended from a fixed point as to swing to and fro by the alternate action of gravity and momentum; the swinging piece in a clock serving as the regulating power.

pen·e·tra·ble, pen′ə·trə·bəl, *a.* That can be penetrated. —**pen·e·tra·bil·i·ty,** pen·ə·trə·bil′ə·tē, **pen·e·tra·ble·ness,** *n.* —**pen·e·tra·bly,** *adv.*

pen·e·trate, pen′ə·trāt, *v.t.,* **-trat·ed, -trat·ing.** To enter or pierce; to affect deeply; to understand; to permeate.—*v.i.* To enter, pass into, or diffuse with; to comprehend the meaning of; to have a profound effect upon. —**pen·e·tra·tive,** *a.*

pen·e·trat·ing, pen′ə·trā·ting, *a.* Having the power of entering or piercing; sharp; acute; discerning. —**pen·e·trat·ing·ly,** *adv.*

pen·e·tra·tion, pen·ə·trā′shən, *n.* The act or power of penetrating; a penetrating attack; the entering of a country and gaining of influence; the depth a projectile penetrates into a target; discernment; mental acuteness; insight.

pen·i·cil·lin, pen·ə·sil′in, *n.* An antibiotic produced from molds, effective in inhibiting the growth of a number of disease-producing bacteria.

pen·in·su·la, pə·nin′sə·lə, pə·nins′ə·lə, *n.* A portion of land almost surrounded by water, connected to the mainland by an isthmus. —**pen·in·su·lar,** *a.*

pe·nis, pē′nis, *n. pl.,* **-nes, -nēz, -nis·es.** The male copulatory organ, also serving as the organ of urination. —**pe·nile,** pēn′əl, pē′nīl, **pe·ni·al,** pē′nē·əl, *a.*

pen·i·tent, pen′i·tənt, *a.* Sorrow for sins or offenses and resolved on amendment; contrite.—*n.* One who is penitent. —**pen·i·tence,** *n.* —**pen·i·ten·tial,** pen·ə·

ten′shəl, *a., n.* —**pen·i·ten·tial·ly,** *adv.* —**pen·i·tent·ly,** *adv.*

pen·i·ten·tia·ry, pen·i·ten′shə·rē, *n. pl.,* **-ries.** A place for imprisonment and reformatory discipline; a federal or state prison.—*a.* Pertaining to or intended for penal confinement and discipline; of an offense, punishable by imprisonment in a penitentiary.

pen·knife, pen′nīf, *n. pl.,* **-knives.** A small pocket-knife.

pen·man·ship, pen′mən·ship, *n.* The art or skill of handwriting; quality or manner of writing.

pen name, *n.* A name an author assumes to sign a work or works; pseudonym.

pen·nant, pen′ənt, *n.* Any long, narrow flag or banner, usu. tapering to a point; a flag serving as an emblem, as of success in an athletic contest.

pen·ni·less, pen′ē·lis, *a.* Impoverished; destitute.

pen·non, pen′ən, *n.* A tapering, triangular, swallow-tailed flag; a pennant.

pen·ny, pen′ē, *n. pl.,* **-nies.** A cent in the U.S. and Canada; a sum of money: He made a pretty *penny* on the deal.

pen·ny an·te, *n.* Poker played for very low stakes, usu. pennies. *Informal.* A trifling transaction.—*a.*

pen·ny pinch·er, *n.* One who spends money reluctantly. —**pen·ny-pinch·ing,** pen′ē·pinch′ing, *n., a.*

pen·ny·weight, pen′ē·wāt, *n.* A troy weight containing 24 grains, one-twentieth of an ounce.

pen·ny-wise, pen′ē·wīz′, *a.* Extremely saving or cautious in trifling matters.

pe·nol·o·gy, pē·nol′ə·jē, *n.* The study of crime prevention, prison and reformatory management, and the correction of criminals. —**pe·no·log·i·cal,** pē·nə·loj′i·kəl, *a.* —**pe·nol·o·gist,** *n.*

pen·sion, pen′shən, *n.* A stated allowance paid regularly to a person on his retirement or injury.—*v.t.* To grant a pension to. —**pen·sion·a·ble,** *a.* —**pen·sion·ar·y,** *a., n. pl.,* **-ies.** —**pen·sion·er,** *n.*

pen·sive, pen′siv, *a.* Engaged in serious or melancholy thought or reflection. —**pen·sive·ly,** *adv.* —**pen·sive·ness,** *n.*

pent, pent, *a.* Pent-up.

pen·ta·gon, pen′tə·gon, *n.* A figure of five sides and five angles; (*cap.*) the central office building of the U.S. Defense Department and military forces. —**pen·tag·o·nal,** pen·tag′ə·nəl, *a.* —**pen·tag·o·nal·ly,** *adv.*

pen·tam·e·ter, pen·tam′i·tər, *n.* A verse of five metrical feet.

Pen·ta·teuch, pen′tə·took, pen′tə·tūk, *n.* The first five books of the Old Testament.

pen·tath·lon, pen·tath′lən, *n.* An athletic contest comprising five track and field events; a contest in the modern Olympic games consisting of five events: fencing, swimming, shooting, riding, and jumping.

Pen·te·cost, pen′tə·kôst, pen′tə·kost, *n.* A Christian festival on the seventh Sunday after Easter, commemorating the descent of the Holy Ghost upon the apostles. —**Pen·te·cos·tal,** pen·tə·kô′stəl, *a.*

pent·house, pent′hows, *n.* A dwelling or apartment situated on the roof of a building.

pent-up, pent′əp′, *a.* Closely confined; shut in; repressed.

pe·nult, pē′nəlt, pi·nəlt′, *n.* That preceding the last of a series, esp. the syllable next to the last in a word. Also **pe·nul·ti·ma,** pi·nəl′tə·mə. —**pe·nul·ti·mate,** pi·nəl′tə·mit, *a., n.*

pe·num·bra, pi·nəm′brə, *n. pl.,* **-bras, -brae,** -brē. An area of partial shadow between the full light and the complete shadow formed by the sun, moon, etc., during an eclipse; the grayish marginal portion of a sunspot. —**pe·num·bral,** *a.*

pe·nu·ri·ous, pi·nûr′ē·əs, pi·nyûr′ē·əs, *a.* Meanly parsimonious or stingy. —**pe·nu·ri·ous·ly,** *adv.* —**pe·nu·ri·ous·ness,** *n.*

---

a- hat, fāte, fâre, fäther; **e-** met, mē; **i-** pin, pīne; **o-** not, nōte, ôrb, moove (move), boy, pownd; **u-** cūbe, bŭll, tŭk (took); **ch-** chin; **th-** thick, ŧhen; **zh-** vizhon (vision); **ə-** əgo, takən, pencəl, lemən, bərd (bird).

pen·u·ry, pen′yə·rē, *n.* Want or destitution; extreme poverty.

pe·on, pē′ən, pē′on, *n.* A day laborer or unskilled worker, esp. in Latin America; a person kept in servitude to work out a debt. —**pe·on·age**, *n.*

pe·o·ny, pē′ə·nē, *n. pl.*, **-nies.** An herb or subshrub widely cultivated and having large flowers of crimson, pink, yellow, or white colors.

peo·ple, pē′pəl, *n. pl.*, **-ple, -ples.** The whole body of persons constituting a community, tribe, race, or nation; the persons of any particular group, company, or number; persons in relation to a superior or leader; one's family or relatives; the populace, usu. with *the;* persons indefinitely, whether men or women: *People may say what they please;* human beings.—*v.t.*, **-pled, -pling.** To populate. —**peo·pler**, *n.*

pep, pep, *n. Informal.* Spirit or animation; vigor, energy, or vim.—*v.t.*, **pepped, pep·ping.** *Informal.* To animate or invigorate, usu. followed by *up.*

pep·per, pep′ər, *n.* A pungent spice derived from the dried unripe fruit of a vine; the fruit ground for black pepper; the green or red pepper fruits of the garden vegetable.—*v.t.* To sprinkle with pepper; to pelt with shot or missiles.

pep·per·corn, pep′ər·kôrn, *n.* The dried unripe berry or fruit of the pepper plant.

pep·per·mint, pep′ər·mint, *n.* A perennial herb of the mint family, grown for its leaves which have a pungent oil; the oil itself; a candy or lozenge flavored with this oil.

pep·per·y, pep′ə·rē, *a.* Noticeably flavored with pepper; having pepperlike qualities, such as sharpness or pungency; having a choleric temper. —**pep·per·i·ness**, *n.*

pep·py, pep′ē, *a.* **-pi·er, -pi·est.** *Informal.* Lively; energetic; animated. —**pep·pi·ness**, *n.*

pep·sin, pep·sine, pep′sin, *n.* An enzyme formed in the stomach that helps digest proteins.

pep·tic, pep′tik, *a.* Promoting or relating to digestion.—*n.* A medicine which promotes digestion.

per, pər, *prep.* Through, by, or by means of; for each: five dollars *per* year.

per·am·bu·late, pər·am′byə·lāt, *v.t.*, **-lat·ed, -lat·ing.** To walk; traverse; to survey the boundaries of while walking.—*v.i.* —**per·am·bu·la·tion**, pər·am·byə·lā′shən, *n.* —**per·am·bu·la·to·ry**, *a.*

per·am·bu·la·tor, pər·am′byə·lā·tər, *n.* One who perambulates. A small carriage for a young child or infant, pushed by hand. Also **ba·by car·riage.**

per an·num, pər·an′əm, *adv.* By the year; for or in each year; annually.

per·cale, pər·kāl′, pər·kal′, *n.* A closely woven, smooth-finished cotton fabric.

per cap·i·ta, pər kap′i·tə, *adv., a.* For or by each person individually.

per·ceive, pər·sēv′, *v.t.*, **-ceived, -ceiv·ing.** To have or obtain awareness of by the senses; to discern, know, or understand. —**per·ceiv·a·ble**, *a.* —**per·ceiv·a·bly**, *adv.*

per·cent, per cent, pər·sent′, *n. pl.*, **per·cent, per·cents.** A rate determined by the hundred; a proportion for or of every hundred. Also **per·cent·age.**—*a.* Pertaining to a whole proportioned into 100 equal parts. Sym. %. Abbr. **p.c., pct.**

per·cent·age, pər·sen′tij, *n.* A rate or proportion per hundred; an allowance, duty, commission, discount, or rate of interest on a hundred; loosely, a proportion in general. *Informal.* Individual gain; advantage or profit. Also **per·cent.**

per·cen·tile, pər·sen′til, pər·sen′til, *n. Statistics.* Any of the points dividing a range of data into 100 equal intervals and indicating the percentage of a distribution falling below it.

per·cep·ti·ble, pər·sep′tə·bəl, *a.* Capable of being perceived; discernible. —**per·cep·ti·bil·i·ty**, pər·sep·tə·bil′ə·tē, *n.* —**per·cep·ti·bly**, *adv.*

per·cep·tion, pər·sep′shən, *n.* The act of perceiving; apprehension with the mind or the senses; an immediate or intuitive recognition, as of a moral or esthetic quality; the faculty of perceiving; the result or product of perceiving. —**per·cep·tion·al, per·cep·tu·al**, pər·sep′choo·al, *a.* —**per·cep·tu·al·ly**, *adv.*

perch, pərch, *n.* A pole or rod fixed horizontally to serve as a roost for birds; an elevated position or station; a linear measure equaling one rod; a square rod.—*v.i.* To alight or rest upon a perch.—*v.t.* To set or place on a perch.

perch, pərch, *n. pl.*, **perch, perch·es.** A spiny-finned, fresh-water game fish used for food.

per·chance, pər·chans′, pər·chäns′, *adv.* Perhaps; maybe; by chance.

per·co·late, pər′kə·lāt, *v.t.*, **-lat·ed, -lat·ing.** To strain or filter; to permeate; to make in a percolator, as coffee.—*v.i.* To pass through small pores; to filter; to ooze. —**per·co·la·tion**, pər·kə·lā′shən, *n.*

per·co·la·tor, pər′kə·lā·tər, *n.* A kind of coffeepot in which boiling water is forced upward and seeps down through the ground coffee.

per·cus·sion, pər·kəsh′ən, *n.* The act of percussing; the striking of one body against another with some violence; the shock or vibration so produced; impact. —**per·cus·sion·ist**, pər·kəsh′ə·nist, *n.* —**per·cus·sive**, pər·kəs′iv, *a.*

per·cus·sion in·stru·ment, *n.* A musical instrument that is played by striking, as a drum or piano.

per di·em, pər dē′əm, pər dī′əm, *adv.* By the day.—*n.* A daily allowance.

per·di·tion, pər·dish′ən, *n.* The place or state of eternal damnation; hell; spiritual death.

per·e·gri·nate, pār′ə·grə·nāt, *v.t., v.i.*, **-nat·ed, -nat·ing.** To travel, esp. by walking. —**per·e·gri·na·tion**, per·ə·grə·nā′shən, *n.* —**per·e·grine**, *a.*

per·e·grine fal·con, per′ə·grin, *n.* A hawk of world-wide distribution noted for its swift flight. Also **per·e·grine.**

per·emp·to·ry, pər·emp′tə·rē, pār′əmp·tôr·ē, *a.* Precluding debate or expostulation; decisive; authoritative; dogmatic. *Law.* Final; determinate. —**per·emp·to·ri·ly**, *adv.* —**per·emp·to·ri·ness**, *n.*

per·en·ni·al, pə·ren′ē·əl, *a.* Lasting or continuing throughout the year; lasting for an indefinitely long time; continuing more than two years, said of plants. —*n.* —**per·en·ni·al·ly**, *adv.*

per·fect, pər′fikt, *a.* Carried through to completion in every detail; complete; in a state of complete excellence; faultless; of supreme moral excellence; completely skilled or versed; exact; correct in every detail; unmitigated or utter. *Gram.* Denoting an action or state completed at the present time.—*n. Gram.* The perfect tense; a verb form in this tense.—pər·fekt′, *v.t.* To bring to completion or finish; to make perfect or faultless; improve. —**per·fect·er**, pər·fek′tər. —**per·fect·ness**, *n.* —**per·fect·i·ble**, pər·fek′tə·bəl. —**per·fect·i·bil·i·ty**, pər·fek·tə·bil′ə·tē, *n.* —**per·fec·tive**, pər·fek′tiv, *a.* —**per·fec·tive·ness**, *n.*

per·fec·tion, pər·fek′shən, *n.* The state or quality of being perfect; flawlessness; the highest degree of proficiency; a perfect embodiment of something; the act of perfecting. —**per·fec·tion·ist**, *n., a.*

per·fect·ly, pər′fikt·lē, *adv.* In a perfect manner or degree; completely; quite.

per·fi·dy, pər′fi·dē, *n.* Breach of faith; treachery; faithlessness. —**per·fid·i·ous**, pər·fid′ē·əs, *a.* —**per·fid·i·ous·ly**, *adv.* —**per·fid·i·ous·ness**, *n.*

per·fo·rate, pər′fə·rāt, *v.t., v.i.*, **-rat·ed, -rat·ing.** To pierce with a pointed instrument; to make a hole through by boring or punching.—pər′fə·rit, pər′fə·rāt, *a.* —**per·fo·ra·tor**, *n.* —**per·fo·ra·tion**, pər·fə·rā′shən, *n.*

per·force, pər·fôrs′, pər·fôrs′, *adv.* Of necessity.

per·form, pər·fôrm′, *v.t.* To do; to fulfill; to act or represent, as on the stage.—*v.i.* To act or exhibit talent, esp. before an audience. —**per·form·a·ble**, *a.* —**per·form·er**, *n.*

per·for·mance, pər·fôr′məns, *n.* An entertainment presented before an audience; the act or manner of exhibiting an art, skill, or capacity; the degree to which anything functions as intended; the act of performing or condition of being performed.

per·fume, per′fūm, pər·fūm′, *n.* A substance that emits a pleasing scent; the fragrant odor emitted by such a substance.—pər·fūm′, *v.t.,* **-fumed, -fum·ing.** Fill with a pleasing odor; to scent. **—per·fum·er,** pər·fū′mər, *n.* **—per·fum·er·y,** pər·fū′mə·rē, *n. pl.,* **-ies.**

per·func·to·ry, pər·fəngk′tə·rē, *a.* Done in a half-hearted or careless manner; careless; indifferent. **—per·func·to·ri·ly,** *adv.* **—per·func·to·ri·ness,** *n.*

per·haps, pər·haps′, *adv.* Possibly; maybe.

per·i·gee, per′i·jē, *n.* That point of the moon's orbit which is nearest the earth. **—per·i·ge·al, per·i·ge·an,** per·i·jē′əl, per·i·jē′ən, *a.*

per·i·he·li·on, per·ə·hē′lē·ən, per·ə·hēl′yən, *n. pl.,* **-a.** That point in the orbit of a planet or comet at which it is nearest the sun.

per·il, pär′əl, *n.* Danger; exposure of person or property to injury, loss, or destruction.—*v.t.,* **-iled** or **-illed, -il·ing** or **-il·ling.** To expose to danger. **—per·il·ous,** *a.* **—per·il·ous·ly,** *adv.* **—per·il·ous·ness,** *n.*

pe·rim·e·ter, pə·rim′i·tər, *n.* The boundary of a figure having two dimensions; the sum of all sides of the boundary. **—per·i·met·ric,** per·ə·me′trik, **per·i·met·ri·cal,** *a.* **—per·i·met·ri·cal·ly,** *adv.*

pe·ri·od, pēr′ē·əd, *n.* An indefinite portion of time characterized by certain features or conditions; any specified division or portion of time; a round of time marked by some recurring process or action; one of the specified portions of time into which a school day or game is divided; the point of completion or conclusion of any course; the time of each month during which a woman menstruates; the point or character (.) used to mark the end of a complete declarative sentence or to indicate an abbreviation.—*a.* Of or pertaining to a particular historical period.

pe·ri·od·ic, pēr·ē·od′ik, *a.* Performed at intermittent intervals; recurring. **—pe·ri·o·dic·i·ty,** pēr·ē·ə·dis′ə·tē, *n.*

pe·ri·od·i·cal, pēr·ē·od′i·kəl, *n.* A publication which appears at regular intervals.—*a.* Regularly published. **—pe·ri·od·i·cal·ly,** *adv.*

pe·ri·od·ic law, *n.* The principle that the properties of elements are periodic functions of their atomic numbers, that is, that the chemical and physical properties recur periodically when the elements are arranged in the order of their atomic numbers.

pe·ri·od·ic ta·ble, *n.* A table illustrating the periodic system, in which the chemical elements, arranged in the order of their atomic numbers, are shown in related groups.

per·i·pa·tet·ic, per·i·pə·tet′ik, *a.* Walking about, perambulating, or itinerant.—*n.* **—per·i·pa·tet·i·cal·ly,** *adv.*

pe·riph·er·y, pə·rif′ə·rē, *n. pl.,* **-ies.** The circumference of a circle or the line forming the boundary of any rounded or closed figure; the external boundary of any surface or area; the relatively minor or secondary aspects of a situation or thing. **—pe·riph·er·al,** *a.* **—pe·riph·er·al·ly,** *adv.*

per·i·phrase, per′ə·frāz, *n.* A roundabout expression or statement.

per·i·scope, per′i·skōp, *n.* A tubular instrument containing a system of mirrors and lenses, used to view objects which are above the line of direct vision, as when submerged in a submarine or a trench. **—per·i·scop·ic,** per·ə·skop′ik, **—per·i·scop·i·cal,** *a.*

per·ish, per′ish, *v.i.* To lose life, esp. in a violent manner; to die untimely.

per·ish·a·ble, per′i·shə·bəl, *a.* Liable to perish.—*n. Usu. pl.* Goods subject to decay, esp. food. **—per·**

ish·a·bil·i·ty, per·i·shə·bil′ə·tē, **per·ish·a·ble·ness,** *n.* **—per·ish·a·bly,** *adv.*

per·i·stal·sis, per·i·stôl′sis, per·i·stal′sis, *n. pl.,* **-ses, -sēz.** The automatic movement of constriction and relaxation of a tubelike muscular organ or system as the intestines, which propels the contents forward. **—per·i·stal·tic,** *a.*

per·i·style, per′ə·stīl, *n.* A series of columns surrounding a courtyard or a building; an open space enclosed by a series of columns.

per·i·to·ne·um, per·i·tə·nē′əm, *n. pl.,* **-ums, -a.** A thin, smooth, serous membrane lining the internal surface of the abdomen. **—per·i·to·ne·al, per·i·to·nae·al,** *a.*

per·i·to·ni·tis, per·i·tə·nī′tis, *n.* An inflammation of the peritoneum.

per·i·wig, per′i·wig, *n.* A small wig.

per·i·win·kle, per′i·wing·kəl, *n.* A creeping, evergreen ground cover, having symmetrical blue or white flowers.

per·i·win·kle, per′i·wing·kəl, *n.* A marine gastropod or sea snail.

per·jure, pər′jər, *v.t.,* **-jured, -jur·ing.** *Usu. refl.* To cause to be guilty of perjury. **—per·jur·er,** *n.*

per·ju·ry, pər′jə·rē, *n. pl.,* **-ries.** The act of willfully making a false oath or violating an oath or promise. *Law.* The act of knowingly making a false statement on a matter material to the issue in question while under oath in a judicial proceeding.

perk, pərk, *v.i.* To hold up the head jauntily; to regain one's liveliness or spirit, usu. with *up*.—*v.t.*—*a.* Jaunty.

perk·y, pər′kē, *a.,* **-i·er, -i·est.** Trim; saucy; jaunty; spirited. Also **perk. —perk·i·ly,** *adv.* **—perk·i·ness,** *n.*

per·ma·nent, pər′mə·nənt, *a.* Continuing in the same state, or without any change; durable; lasting; fixed—**per·ma·nence, per·ma·nen·cy,** *n.* **—per·ma·nent·ly,** *adv.*

per·ma·nent, pər′mə·nənt, *n.* A wave set in the hair by a chemical preparation and lasting for several months. Also **per·ma·nent wave.**

per·ma·nent press, *n.* A fabric finish reputed to possess permanent crease resistance; an article of clothing or a fabric possessing this finish.—*a.*

per·me·a·ble, pər′mē·ə·bəl, *a.* Capable of being permeated. **—per·me·a·bil·i·ty,** pər·mē·ə·bil′i·tē, *n.* **—per·me·a·bly,** *adv.*

per·me·ate, pər′mē·āt, *v.t., v.i.,* **-at·ed, -at·ing.** To pass through the substance or mass of; penetrate; be diffused through; pervade; saturate. **—per·me·a·tion,** per·mē·ā′shən, *n.* **—per·me·a·tive,** *a.*

per·mis·si·ble, pər·mis′ə·bəl, *a.* That may be permitted; allowable. **—per·mis·si·bil·i·ty,** pər·mis·ə·bil′ə·tē, *n.* **—per·mis·si·bly,** *adv.*

per·mis·sion, pər·mish′ən, *n.* The act of permitting; authorization; formal consent.

per·mis·sive, pər·mis′iv, *a.* Permitting or allowing; tolerant of behavior which others would not allow; lenient. **—per·mis·sive·ly,** *adv.* **—per·mis·sive·ness,** *n.*

per·mit, pər·mit′, *v.t.,* **-mit·ted, -mit·ting.** To allow to do something; to allow to be done or occur; to tolerate; to afford opportunity for; to afford opportunity to.—*v.i.* To grant leave or permission; allow liberty to do something; afford opportunity or possibility; allow or admit, usu. followed by *of*.—pər′mit, pər·mit′, *n.* An authoritative or official certificate of permission. **—per·mit·ter,** pər·mit′ər, *n.*

per·mu·ta·tion, pər·myū·tā′shən, *n.* Alteration; a rearranging of the order of a set of things, such as *abc* into *acb, bac, bca,* etc.; any of the resulting arrangements or groups.

per·ni·cious, pər·nish′əs, *a.* Injurious; destructive; fatal; deadly. **—per·ni·cious·ly,** *adv.* **—per·ni·cious·ness,** *n.*

per·o·ra·tion, per·a·rā'shan, *n*. The concluding part of an oration; the summing up of an argument.

per·ox·ide, pa·rok'sīd, *n*. That oxide of a given element or radical which contains the greatest or an unusual amount of oxygen; hydrogen peroxide.—*v.t.*, **-id·ed, -id·ing**. To bleach, as hair, by means of peroxide.

per·pen·dic·u·lar, per·pen·dik'ya·lar, *a*. Being at right angles with the plane of the horizon; vertical; upright.—*n*. A perpendicular line or plane. —**per·pen·dic·u·lar·i·ty**, per·pen·dik·ya·lăr'a·tē, *n*. —**per·pen·dic·u·lar·ly**, *adv*.

per·pe·trate, per'pi·trāt, *v.t.*, **-trat·ed, -trat·ing**. To do; to be guilty of; to commit. —**per·pe·tra·tion**, per·pa·trā'shen, **per·pe·tra·tor**, *n*.

per·pet·u·al, per·pech'oo·el, *a*. Continuing or enduring forever or indefinitely; continuing without interruption; continuous. —**per·pet·u·al·ly**, *adv*.

per·pet·u·ate, per·pech'oo·āt, *v.t.*, **-at·ed, -at·ing**. To make perpetual; to cause to endure or to be continued indefinitely. —**per·pet·u·a·tion**, per·pech·oo·ā'shen, **per·pet·u·a·tor**, *n*.

per·pe·tu·i·ty, per·pi·too'i·tē, per·pi·tū'i·tē, *n. pl.*, **-ties**. The state or character of being perpetual; endless.

per·plex, per·pleks', *v.t.* To confuse; hamper with complications, confusion, or uncertainty. —**per·plexed, per·plex·ing**, *a*. —**per·plex·ing·ly, per·plex·ed·ly**, *adv*. —**per·plex·i·ty**, per·plek'si·tē, *n. pl.*, **-ties**.

per·qui·site, per'kwi·zit, *n*. An incidental fee or profit over and above fixed income, salary, or wages.

per se, per sē', per sā', *adv. Latin*. By itself; inherently or intrinsically.

per·se·cute, per'sa·kūt, *v.t.*, **-cut·ed, -cut·ing**. To harass or afflict with repeated acts of cruelty or annoyance; to afflict or punish because of particular opinions or adherence to a particular creed or mode of worship. —**per·se·cu·tive**, *a*. —**per·se·cu·tor, per·se·cu·tion**, per·sa·ku'shen, *n*.

per·se·vere, per·sa·vēr', *v.i.*, **-vered, -ver·ing**. To continue resolutely despite difficulties encountered. —**per·se·ver·ance**, *n*. —**per·se·ver·ing**, *a*. —**per·se·ver·ing·ly**, *adv*.

per·si·flage, per'sa·fläzh, *n*. Idle, bantering talk; frivolous treatment of any subject.

per·sim·mon, per·sim'en, *n*. A tree with very hard wood and an edible plumlike fruit; the plumlike fruit.

per·sist, per·sist', per·zist', *v.i.* To continue in the pursuit of any course commenced; to continue in the face of some amount of opposition; to be insistent. —**per·sist·ence, per·sis·ten·cy**, *n*.

per·sist·ent, per·sis'tant, per·zis'tant, *a*. Inclined to persist; persevering. —**per·sist·ent·ly**, *adv*.

per·snick·et·y, per·snik'i·tē, *a. Informal*. Finicky; extremely fastidious; overly precise.

per·son, per'sen, *n*. A human being; the self or individual personality of a human being; the living body of a human being; the form or inflection of a pronoun or verb that indicates the speaker (first *person*), one spoken to (second *person*), or a person or thing spoken of (third *person*.)—**in per·son**, in one's own bodily presence.

per·son·a·ble, per'sen·a·bel, *a*. Having a pleasant personality or disposition.

per·son·age, per'sa·nij, *n*. A person of distinction.

per·son·al, per'sa·nel, *a*. Pertaining to a person as distinct from a thing; relating to, characteristic of, or affecting some individual person; private; done in person, not by representative. *Gram*. Denoting or pointing to the person: a *personal* pronoun.—*n*. A news item or advertisement concerning a person or persons.

per·son·al ef·fects, *n*. The private possessions of an individual, as clothing or jewelry.

per·son·al·i·ty, per·sa·nal'i·tē, *n. pl.*, **-ties**. The sum of characteristics that constitute an individual; the state of existing as an intelligent being; a person of

distinction; *usu. pl.*, a remark, usu. disparaging, reflecting on some person.

per·son·al·ize, per'sen·al·īz, *v.t.*, **-ized, -iz·ing**. To make personal; to mark with one's initials or name; to personify.

per·son·al·ly, per'sen·el·ē, *adv*. In a personal manner; in person; as regards one's individuality.

per·so·na non gra·ta, per·sō'ne non grä'te, per·sō'ne non grä'te, *n. Latin*. An unacceptable or unwelcome person.

per·son·ate, per'sa·nāt, *v.t.*, **-at·ed, -at·ing**. To assume the character or appearance of, whether in real life or on the stage; impersonate. —**per·son·a·tion**, per·sa·nā'shen, **per·son·a·tor**, *n*.

per·son·i·fy, per·son'a·fi, *v.t.*, **-fied, -fy·ing**. To represent, as an abstract or inanimate thing, as if endowed with the character of a rational being; typify. —**per·son·i·fi·ca·tion**, per·son·i·fa·kā'shen, **per·son·i·fi·er**, *n*.

per·son·nel, per·sa·nel', *n*. The body of persons engaged or employed in any occupation, service, or work.

per·spec·tive, per·spek'tiv, *n*. The art or science of drawing or otherwise representing objects or scenes on a plane so that they appear to have their natural dimensions and spatial relations; the appearance of an object with regard to dimensions and spatial position; the ability to evaluate information, situations, and the like with respect to their meaningfulness or comparative importance.—*a*. Pertaining to the art of perspective. —**per·spec·tive·ly**, *adv*.

per·spi·ca·cious, per·spa·kā'shes, *a*. Having keen mental perception or discernment. —**per·spi·ca·cious·ly**, *adv*. —**per·spi·ca·cious·ness, per·spi·cac·i·ty**, per·spa·kas'a·tē, *n*.

per·spi·cu·i·ty, per·spa·kū'a·tē, *n*. Clearness in expression or style; lucidity. —**per·spic·u·ous, per·spik'yū·es**, *a*. —**per·spic·u·ous·ly**, *adv*.

per·spi·ra·tion, per'spa·rā'shen, *n*. The act of perspiring; sweat.

per·spire, per·spīr', *v.i.*, *v.t.*, **-spired, -spir·ing**. To excrete perspiration through the pores of the skin; to sweat.

per·suade, per·swād', *v.t.*, **-suad·ed, -suad·ing**. To influence, by argument or advice, to a certain belief or course of action; to convince. —**per·suad·a·ble**, *a*. —**per·suad·er**, *n*.

per·sua·sion, per·swā'zhen, *n*. The act or power of persuading; the state of being persuaded; a conviction or beliefs; a religious creed or system of beliefs; a sect adhering to a system of beliefs.

per·sua·sive, per·swā'siv, *a*. Having the power of persuading; tending to persuade or influence.—*n*. —**per·sua·sive·ly**, *adv*. —**per·sua·sive·ness**, *n*.

pert, pert, *a*. Forward; saucy; lively; smart; chic. —**pert·ly**, *adv*. —**pert·ness**, *n*.

per·tain, per·tān', *v.i.* To have reference or relation; to relate; to belong or be connected as a part, adjunct, possession, or attribute; to be appropriate.

per·ti·na·cious, per·ta·nā'shes, *a*. Holding firmly to any opinion, purpose, or design; stubborn. —**per·ti·na·cious·ly**, *adv*. —**per·ti·na·cious·ness, per·ti·nac·i·ty**, per·ta·nas'a·tē, *n*.

per·ti·nent, per'ta·nent, *a*. Pertaining to the subject or matter in hand; relevant. —**per·ti·nence, per·ti·nen·cy**, *n*. —**per·ti·nent·ly**, *adv*.

per·turb, per·terb', *v.t.* To disturb, esp. in the mind; to agitate; to cause to be disordered or confused. —**per·turb·a·ble**, *a*. —**per·tur·ba·tion**, per·ter·bā'shen, *n*.

pe·ruke, pa·rook', *n*. A wig.

pe·ruse, pa·rooz', *v.t.*, **-rused, -rus·ing**. To read with careful attention; to examine carefully. —**pe·rus·al, pe·rus·er**, *n*.

per·vade, per·vād', *v.t.*, **-vad·ed, -vad·ing**. To extend presence, activity, or influence throughout. —**per·vad·er, per·va·sion**, *n*. —**per·va·sive**, *a*.

—per·va·sive·ly, *adv.* —per·va·sive·ness, *n.*

per·verse, pər·vərs', *a.* Deviating from accepted or expected behavior or opinion; contrary. —per·verse·ly, *adv.* —per·verse·ness, per·ver·si·ty, *n.*

per·ver·sion, pər·vər'zhən, pər·vər'shən, *n.* The act of perverting; abnormal sexual instinct, desire, or activity.

per·vert, pər·vərt', *v.t.* To lead astray morally or to corrupt; to lead into mental error or false judgment; to turn from the proper to an improper use or purpose; to distort; to debase.—pər'vərt, *n.* A sexual deviate; one who has been perverted. —per·vert·ed, pər·vər'tid, *a.* —per·vert·ed·ly, *adv.* —per·vert·er, *n.* —per·vert·i·ble, *a.*

per·vi·ous, pər'vē·əs, *a.* Permeable; allowing an entrance or passage through; open to suggestion or argument. —per·vi·ous·ness, *n.*

pes·ky, pes'kē, *a.,* -ki·er, -ki·est. *Informal.* Troublesome; annoying; vexing. —pesk·i·ly, *adv.* —pesk·i·ness, *n.*

pes·si·mism, pes'ə·miz·əm, *n.* The tendency to take the most unfavorable view of situations or actions. —pes·si·mist, *n.* —pes·si·mis·tic, pes·ə·mis'tik, *a.* —pes·si·mis·ti·cal·ly, *adv.*

pest, pest, *n.* Anything very noxious or destructive; a mischievous, annoying, or destructive person; an epidemic or plague.

pes·ter, pes'tər, *v.t.* To annoy persistently; to bother.

pest·hole, pest'hōl, *n.* An insanitary place open to the outbreak and spread of disease.

pest·i·cide, pes'ti·sīd, *n.* Any substance, used to destroy weeds, insects, rodents, etc.

pes·tif·er·ous, pes·tif'ər·əs, *a.* Pestilential; infectious; noxious or evil in any manner. *Informal.* Irritating or bothersome. —pes·tif·er·ous·ly, *adv.* —pes·tif·er·ous·ness, *n.*

pes·ti·lence, pes'tə·ləns, *n.* Any contagious disease that is epidemic and usu. deadly; anything evil or destructive. —pes·ti·len·tial, pes·tə·len'shəl, *a.*

pes·ti·lent, pes'tə·lənt, *a.* Infectious; noxious to morals or society; pernicious; troublesome. —pes·ti·lent·ly, *adv.*

pes·tle, pes'əl, pes'təl, *n.* An instrument for breaking, grinding, or mixing substances in a mortar.—*v.t.,* -tled, -tling. To pound or pulverize with or as with a pestle.—*v.i.*

pet, pet, *n.* An animal kept for companionship; a favorite pampered or indulged individual.—*a.* Cared for or kept as a pet; favorite; personal or particular. —*v.t.,* -ted, -ting. To fondle; to indulge. *Informal.* To kiss and caress.—*v.i.* —pet·ter, *n.*

pet, pet, *n.* A slight fit of peevishness.—*v.i.,* -ted, -ting. To fret or sulk.

pet·al, pet'əl, *n.* One of the leaflike divisions of the inner floral envelope or corolla of a flower. —pet·aled, pet·alled, *a.*

pet·cock, pet'kok, *n.* A small faucet for draining off water or oil from a cylinder or for releasing excess air pressure from a tank, radiator, or the like. Also pet cock.

pe·ter, pē'tər, *v.i. Informal.* To diminish gradually and then disappear or cease, followed by *out.*

pet·i·ole, pet'ē·ōl, *n.* A leafstalk; the stalk connecting the blade of the leaf with the branch or stem.

pe·tite, pə·tēt', *a.* Little or tiny; small and shapely, esp. a woman. —pe·tite·ness, *n.*

pet·it four, pet'ē·fōr', pet'ē·fôr', *n. pl.,* pet·its fours, pet·it fours. A small, iced and decorated cake or cookie.

pe·ti·tion, pə·tish'ən, *n.* A formal, written request to a superior authority soliciting some favor; an entreaty; something requested or solicited.—*v.t., v.i.* To make a petition, request, or supplication to; to solicit. —pe·ti·tion·ar·y, *a.* —pe·ti·tion·er, *n.*

pet·rel, pet'rəl, *n.* A black sea bird with white rump patches, sometimes found far out at sea.

pet·ri·fy, pet'rə·fī, *v.t.,* -fied, -fy·ing. To convert to stone; to turn into a fossil; to make callous or obdurate; to paralyze or stupefy with fear or amazement. —*v.i.* To become stone; to become paralyzed with fear. —pet·ri·fac·tion, pet·rə·fak'shən, *n.*

pe·tro·chem·is·try, pet·rō·kem'is·trē, *n.* The branch of chemistry concerned with petroleum and the chemical products derived from petroleum and natural gas. —pe·tro·chem·i·cal, *a., n.*

pet·rol, pet'rəl, *n. Brit.* Gasoline.

pet·ro·la·tum, pet·rə·lā'təm, *n.* A substance obtained from petroleum and used in medical dressings and ointments, in explosives as a stabilizer, and as a rust preventive. Also pe·tro·le·um jel·ly.

pe·tro·le·um, pə·trō'lē·əm, *n.* An oily, flammable liquid which is a form of bitumen or a mixture of various hydrocarbons, occurring naturally in the upper strata of the earth in various parts of the world, and commonly obtained by drilling.

pet·ti·coat, pet'ē·kōt, *n.* An underskirt, worn by women.—*a.* Female; influenced by women.

pet·ti·fog, pet'ē·fog, pet'ē·fôg, *v.i.,* -fogged, -fog·ging. To be contentious or argumentative over trivialities; to practice law in a deceitful manner. —pet·ti·fog·ger, pet·ti·fog·ger·y, *n.*

pet·tish, pet'ish, *a.* Unpredivtably irritable; petulant. —pet·tish·ly, *adv.* —pet·tish·ness, *n.*

pet·ty, pet'ē, *a.,* -ti·er, -ti·est. Trivial; of little consequence; having a narrow outlook; small-minded; of secondary rank. —pet·ti·ly, *adv.* —pet·ti·ness, *n.*

pet·ty cash, *n.* Money kept on hand for minor expenses.

pet·ty of·fic·er, *n.* A naval enlisted man whose rank corresponds with that of a noncommissioned officer in the army.

pet·u·lant, pech'ə·lənt, *a.* Showing irritation or impatience, esp. over a trivial matter. —pet·u·lance, pet·u·lan·cy, *n.* —pet·u·lant·ly, *adv.*

pe·tu·ni·a, pə·too'nyə, pə·tū'nyə, *n.* A popular plant with a variety of color patterns to its large funnelform flowers.

pew, pū, *n.* One of the benchlike seats fixed in a church for use by the congregation.

pew·ter, pū'tər, *n.* Any of various alloys in which tin is the chief constituent, usu. one of tin and lead; a vessel or utensil made of such an alloy, used for tableware.

pe·yo·te, pā·ō'tē, *n. pl.,* -tes. A cactus used for its hallucinatory effects. Also mes·cal, pe·yo·tl, pā·ōt'əl.

pha·e·ton, fā'i·tən, *n.* An open four-wheeled carriage drawn by two horses; a touring car.

pha·lanx, fā'langks, fal'angks, *n. pl.,* -lanx·es, -lang·es, -lan'jēz. In ancient Greece, a body of heavily-armed infantry formed in ranks and files close and deep, with shields joined and long spears overlapping; any body of troops in close array; a compact or closely massed body of persons, animals, or things. *Pl.,* -lang·es, -lan'jēz. Any of the digital bones of the hand or foot.

phal·lus, fal'əs, *n. pl.,* phal·li, fal'ī, phal·lus·es. An image of the male reproductive organ, symbolizing in certain ancient religious systems the generative power in nature; the penis or clitoris. —phal·lic, *a.*

phan·tasm, fan'taz·əm, *n.* A creation of the fancy or imagination; an apparition; a deceptive likeness of something. Also phan·tas·ma. —phan·tas·mal, fan·taz'məl, phan·tas·mic, fan·taz'mik, *a.*

phan·tas·ma·go·ri·a, fan·taz·mə·gōr'ē·ə, fan·taz·mə·gôr'ē·ə, *n.* A shifting series of phantasms, illusions, or deceptive appearances, as in a dream or as created by the imagination. —phan·tas·ma·go·ri·al, phan·tas·ma·gor·ic, *a.*

---

a- hat, fāte, fāre, fäther; e- met, mē; i- pin, pīne; o- not, nōte, ôrb, moove (move), boy, pownd; u- cūbe, bûll, tûk (took); ch- chin; th- thick, then; zh- vizhon (vision); ə- əgo, takən, pencəl, lemən, bərd (bird).

phan·ta·sy, fan′tə·sē, fan′tə·zē, *n. pl.,* **-sies.** Fantasy.

phan·tom, fan′təm, *n.* An appearance without material substance; an apparition or specter.—*a.* Illusive; spectral.

phar·aoh, fãr′ō, *n. (Often cap.)* A title of the ancient Egyptian kings.

Phar·i·see, far′i·sē, *n.* One of an ancient Jewish sect noted for strict interpretation and observance of the written and oral law and for pretensions to superior sanctity; *(l.c.)* a sanctimonious and hypocritically censorious person. —**phar·i·sa·ic,** far·i·sā′ik, **phar·i·sa·i·cal,** *a.* —**phar·i·sa·ism, phar·i·see·ism,** far′i·sā·iz·əm, far′i·sē·iz·əm, *n.*

phar·ma·ceu·ti·cal, fär·mə·soo′ti·kəl, *a.* Pertaining to the knowledge or art of pharmacy.—*n.* A medicine or drug product. Also **phar·ma·ceu·tic.** —**phar·ma·ceu·ti·cal·ly,** *adv.*

phar·ma·ceu·tics, fär·mə·soo′tiks, *n. pl. but sing. in constr.* The science of preparing medicines; pharmacy.

phar·ma·cist, fär′mə·sist, *n.* A druggist.

phar·ma·col·o·gy, fär·mə·kol′ə·jē, *n.* The science or knowledge of drugs, or the art of preparing medicines. —**phar·ma·co·log·ic,** fär·mə·kə·loj′ik, **phar·ma·co·log·i·cal,** *a.* —**phar·ma·col·o·gist,** *n.*

phar·ma·co·poe·ia, fär·mə·kə·pē′ə, *n.* A book of directions and requirements for the preparation of medicines. —**phar·ma·co·poe·ial,** *a.*

phar·ma·cy, fär′mə·sē, *n. pl.,* **-cies.** The art of preparing and compounding medicines, and of dispensing them; a drugstore.

phar·ynx, far′ingks, *n. pl.,* **phar·yn·ges,** fə·rin′jēz, **phar·ynx·es.** The muscular tube which connects the cavity of the mouth and the esophagus. —**pha·ryn·ge·al,** fə·rin′jē·əl, far·in·jē′əl, *a.* Also **pha·ryn·gal,** fə·ring′gəl.

phase, fāz, *n.* Any of the appearances or aspects in which a thing of varying modes or conditions manifests itself to the eye or mind; a stage of change or development; the particular appearance presented by a planet or the moon at a given time.—*v.t.,* **phased, phas·ing.** To put in the same phase; synchronize; to conduct by phases. —**phase in,** to introduce or bring into use gradually or by stages. —**phase out,** to withdraw from use gradually. —**pha·sic,** *a.*

Ph.D., *n.* Doctor of Philosophy.

pheas·ant, fez′ənt, *n. pl.,* **-ant, -ants.** A large, long-tailed bird.

phe·no·bar·bi·tal, fē·nō·bär′bi·tal, fē·nō·bär′bi·tôl, *n.* A crystalline barbiturate usu. in white powder form, and used as a hypnotic or sedative.

phe·nol, fē′nōl, fē′nol, *n.* Carbolic acid, a coal tar derivative, or a hydroxyl derivative of benzene. —**phe·nol·ic,** fi·nō′lik, fi·nol′ik, *a.*

phe·nom·e·non, fi·nom′ə·non, *n. pl.,* **-na, -nons.** A visible manifestation or appearance; something extraordinary; an exceedingly remarkable thing or person. —**phe·nom·e·nal,** *a.* —**phe·nom·e·nal·ly,** *adv.*

phew, fū, *interj.* An exclamation of disgust, relief, etc.

phi·al, fī′əl, *n.* Vial.

Phil·a·del·phi·a law·yer, fil·ə·del′fē·ə, *n.* A clever, sharp lawyer.

phi·lan·der, fi·lan′dər, *v.i.* To make love to a woman in a casual, uninvolved way, without having serious intentions. —**phi·lan·der·er,** *n.*

phi·lan·thro·py, fi·lan′thrə·pē, *n. pl.,* **-pies.** Love of mankind, esp. as shown in practical efforts to promote well-being by donating to needy causes; such benevolent activity or a particular instance of it. —**phil·an·throp·ic,** fil·ən·throp′ik, **phil·an·throp·i·cal,** *a.* —**phil·an·throp·i·cal·ly,** *adv.* —**phi·lan·thro·pist,** *n.*

phi·lat·e·ly, fi·lat′ə·lē, *n.* The collection or study of stamps and other stamped or imprinted materials. —**phil·a·tel·ic,** fil·ə·tel′ik, **phil·a·tel·i·cal,** *a.* —**phi·lat·e·list,** *n.*

phil·har·mon·ic, fil·här·mon′ik, fil·ər·mon′ik, *a.*

Fond of harmony or music; relating or pertaining to symphonic and other musical organizations.

Phi·lis·tine, fə·lis′tən, fə·lis′tēn, fil′əs·tēn, *n.* A person deficient in culture and aesthetics; a person of narrow views; a prosaic, practical person. —**Phi·lis·tin·ism,** *n.*

phil·o·den·dron, fil·ə·den′drən, *n. pl.,* **-drons, -dra.** A tree-climbing vine native to the American tropics.

phi·lol·o·gy, fi·lol′ə·jē, *n.* The scientific study of written records of literary, social, and cultural history in order to establish authenticity, accuracy, and meaning; linguistics, esp. historical and comparative. —**phi·lol·o·gist, phi·lol·o·ger, phil·o·lo·gi·an,** fil·ə·lō′jē·ən, *n.* —**phil·o·log·i·cal,** fil·ə·loj′i·kəl, *a.* **phil·o·log·ic,** *a.* —**phil·o·log·i·cal·ly,** *adv.*

phi·los·o·pher, fi·los′ə·fər, *n.* A person who formulates theories on questions of philosophy; a person versed in philosophy; one who governs his life by philosophical principles.

phil·o·soph·i·cal, fil·ə·sof′i·kəl, *a.* Pertaining to or according to philosophy; proceeding from philosophy; temperate, detached, or calm. Also **phil·o·soph·ic.** —**phil·o·soph·i·cal·ly,** *adv.*

phi·los·o·phize, fi·los′ə·fīz, *v.i.* **-phized, -phiz·ing.** To reason or theorize as a philosopher; discourse in a pedantic or moralistic manner.—**phi·los·o·phiz·er,** *n.*

phi·los·o·phy, fi·los′ə·fē, *n. pl.,* **-phies.** The study or science of the truths or principles underlying all knowledge; the study or science of the principles of a particular branch of knowledge; a system of philosophical doctrine; a system of principles for guidance in practical affairs; wise composure in dealing with problems.

phil·ter, fil′tər, *n.* A drug or potion supposed to have the power of exciting love magically; any potion supposed to have magical powers.—*v.t.,* **-tered, -ter·ing.** To charm with a philter.

phle·bi·tis, fli·bī′tis, *n.* Inflammation of the inner membrane of a vein. —**phle·bit·ic,** fli·bit′ik, *a.*

phle·bot·o·my, fli·bot′ə·mē, *n.* The opening of a vein for letting blood; bleeding. —**phle·bot·o·mist,** *n.*

phlegm, flem, *n.* Thick mucus secreted in the respiratory passages; self-possession; sluggishness.

phleg·mat·ic, fleg·mat′ik, *a.* Sluggish in temperament; apathetic. Also **phleg·mat·i·cal.** —**phleg·mat·i·cal·ly,** *adv.*

phlox, floks, *n.* A N. American plant with showy flowers of various colors.

pho·bi·a, fō′bē·ə, *n.* A persistent, exaggerated, and usu. illogical fear or dread. —**pho·bic,** *a.*

phoe·be, fē′bē, *n.* A gray-brown American flycatching bird with an upright posture and a persistent tail-wagging habit.

phoe·nix, phe·nix, fē′niks, *n.* A beautiful bird of ancient Egyptian legend said to be the only one of its kind and to live 500 or 600 years, then burning itself on a funeral pyre and rising youthful from its ashes: an emblem of immortality.

phone, fōn, *n. Informal.* A telephone.—*v.i., v.t.,* **phoned, phon·ing.**

pho·neme, fō′nēm, *n.* One of a set of the basic sounds of speech of a language which provide the changes that differentiate between words. —**pho·ne·mic,** fə·nē′mik, fō·nē′mik, *a.*

pho·net·ics, fə·net′iks, fō·net′iks, *n. pl. but sing. in constr.* The study of how speech sounds are produced, transmitted, received, and transcribed. —**pho·net·ic, pho·net·i·cal,** *a.* —**pho·net·i·cal·ly,** *adv.*

phon·ic, fon′ik, fō′nik, *a.* Pertaining to sound, esp. speech sounds; phonetic; voiced.

phon·ics, fon′iks, fō′niks, *n. pl. but sing. in constr.* A method of teaching beginning reading, spelling, and pronunciation through phonetic interpretation of words; the science of sound; acoustics.

pho·no·graph, fō′nə·graf, fō′nə·gräf, *n.* A record player. —**pho·no·graph·ic,** fō·nə·graf′ik, *a.* —**pho·no·graph·i·cal·ly,** *adv.*

pho·nol·o·gy, fō·nol′ə·jē, *n. pl.,* **-gies.** The study of the sounds of a particular language; the system of sounds used in a language. —**pho·no·log·ic**, fōn·ə·loj′ik, **pho·no·log·i·cal**, *a.* —**pho·no·log·i·cal·ly**, *adv.* —**pho·nol·o·gist**, fō·nol′ə·jist, *n.*

pho·ny, pho·ney, fō′nē, *a.,* **-ni·er, -ni·est, -ney·er, -ney·est.** *Informal.* Not genuine; counterfeit; bogus; fraudulent.—*n. pl.,* **-nies, -neys.** *Informal.* Something fake or counterfeit. —**pho·ni·ness**, *n.*

phos·phate, fos′fāt, *n.* A salt of any of several oxygen acids of phosphorus; a fertilizing material containing such salts; a carbonated drink containing fruit syrup and a little phosphate.

phos·pho·res·cence, fos·fə·res′əns, *n.* The property of being luminous at temperatures below incandescence; the luminous appearance of objects having this property. —**phos·pho·resce**, *v.i.,* **-resced, -resc·ing.** —**phos·pho·res·cent**, *a.* —**phos·pho·res·cent·ly**, *adv.*

phos·pho·rus, fos′fər·əs, *n. pl.,* **-ri,** -rī. A solid nonmetallic element: the white or yellow form is poisonous, very flammable, and luminous in the dark; the red form, used in matches, is less flammable and not poisonous.

pho·to, fō′tō, *n. pl.,* **-tos.** *Informal.* Shortened form of **pho·to·graph.**

pho·to·cop·y, fō′tə·kop·ē, *n. pl.,* **-ies.** A photographic reproduction of graphic material.—*v.t.,* **-ied, -y·ing.** To make a photocopy.

pho·to·e·lec·tric, fō·tō·i·lek′trik, *a.* Pertaining to the electricity or electrical effects produced by light.

pho·to·e·lec·tric cell, *n.* A vacuum tube in which the action of light produces or changes the strength of electric current.

pho·to·en·grav·ing, fō·tō·en·grā′ving, *n.* A process in which the action of light is used to obtain a picture upon a plate or block, in line or halftone, for subsequent reproduction on a printing press. —**pho·to·en·grave**, *v.t.,* **-graved, -grav·ing.** —**pho·to·en·grav·er**, *n.*

pho·to fin·ish, *n.* A finish of a horse race in which the leading horses are so close that a photograph is needed to determine the winner.

pho·to·flash, fō′tə·flash, *n.* An electrical device which produces a momentary flash of brilliant light; a flash bulb.

pho·to·gen·ic, fō·tə·jen′ik, *a.* Constituting a favorable subject for photography; producing phosphorescence.

pho·to·graph, fō′tə·graf, fō′tə·gräf, *n.* A picture obtained by means of photography.—*v.t.* To take a photograph of.—*v.i.* To take photographs; appear in a photograph: She *photographs* well. —**pho·tog·ra·pher**, fə·tog′rə·fər, *n.*

pho·tog·ra·phy, fə·tog′rə·fē, *n.* The art or the process of obtaining accurate representations of objects by means of the chemical action of light or other kinds of radiant energy on specially treated surfaces. —**pho·to·graph·ic**, fō·tə·graf′ik, *a.* Also **pho·to·graph·i·cal.** —**pho·to·graph·i·cal·ly**, *adv.*

pho·to·gra·vure, fō·tə·grə·vyûr′, fō·tə·grā′vyər, *n.* A process for making prints from an intaglio plate prepared by light acting on a sensitive surface; a print so made.

pho·to·off·set, fō·tō·ôf′set, fō·tō·of′set, *n.* Offset lithography.

Pho·to·stat, fō′tə·stat, *n. Trademark.* A special camera for making facsimile copies of drawings or documents, directly as positives on sensitized paper; *(often l.c.)* the copy thus produced.—*v.t., v.i.,* **-stat·ed, -stat·ing.** *(l.c.)* To copy with a Photostat. —**pho·to·stat·ic**, fō·tə·stat′ik, *a.*

pho·to·syn·the·sis, fō·tō·sin′thə·sis, *n.* The process by which green plants manufacture a simple

sugar from carbon dioxide and water in the presence of light and chlorophyll, with oxygen produced as a by-product.

phrase, frāz, *n.* Two or more connected words not including a finite verb with its subject; an idiom, or manner or style of expression; one or more words spoken in a single breath with a pause before and after, and forming a meaningful unit.—*v.t.,* **phrased, phras·ing.** To express in a particular manner. —**phras·al**, *a.* —**phras·ing**, *n.*

phra·se·ol·o·gy, frā·zē·ol′ə·jē, *n.* Manner of expression; choice of words; diction.

phre·net·ic, fri·net′ik, *a.* Frenetic. Also **phre·net·i·cal.**

phre·nol·o·gy, fri·nol′ə·jē, *n.* The theory that the shape of the human skull is indicative of a person's character, degree of mental development, etc. —**phre·nol·o·gist**, *n.*

phy·lac·ter·y, fə·lak′tə·rē, *n. pl.,* **-ies.** Either of two small leather cases containing slips inscribed with certain texts from the Pentateuch, worn on the left arm and forehead by orthodox Jewish men.

phy·log·e·ny, fī·loj′ə·nē, *n.* The origin and evolution of types of species of animal and plant forms; the history of racial origins. Also **phy·lo·gen·e·sis**, fī·lə·jen′i·sis. —**phy·lo·ge·net·ic**, fī·lō·jə·net′ik, **phy·lo·gen·ic**, fī·lə·jen′ik, *a.* —**phy·log·e·nist**, *n.*

phy·lum, fī′ləm, *n. pl.,* **phy·la**, fī′lə. A major division in the classification of animals and plants under which related classes are grouped.

phys·ic, fiz′ik, *n.* Any medicine; a medicine that purges; a cathartic.—*v.t.,* **-icked, -ick·ing.** To purge with a cathartic.

phys·i·cal, fiz′i·kəl, *a.* Pertaining to the body, or bodily; of or pertaining to material nature; pertaining to the properties, processes, laws, or science of nature, or to physics. —**phys·i·cal·ly**, *adv.*

phys·i·cal ed·u·ca·tion, *n.* A course of athletic training and hygiene to develop and care for the body.

phys·i·cal sci·ence, *n.* Any of the sciences which deal primarily with inanimate matter or energy: physics, astronomy, chemistry, geology, etc.

phys·i·cal ther·a·py, *n.* Physiotherapy.

phy·si·cian, fi·zish′ən, *n.* One legally qualified to practice medicine; a doctor engaged in general medical practice.

phys·ics, fiz′iks, *n. pl. but sing. in constr.* That branch of science which treats of the laws, properties, and interactions of matter, motion, and energy. —**phys·i·cist**, fiz′i·sist, *n.*

phys·i·og·no·my, fiz·ē·og′nə·mē, fiz·ē·on′ə·mē, *n. pl.,* **-mies.** The art of discerning character from the features of the body, esp. the face. —**phys·i·og·nom·ic**, fiz·ē·og·nom′ik, fiz·ē·ə·nom′ik, **phys·i·og·nom·i·cal**, *a.* —**phys·i·og·no·mist**, *n.*

phys·i·og·ra·phy, fiz·ē·og′rə·fē, *n.* The description of natural phenomena; physical geography. —**phys·i·og·ra·pher**, *n.* —**phys·i·o·graph·ic**, fiz·ē·ə·graf′ik, **phys·i·o·graph·i·cal**, *a.*

phys·i·ol·o·gy, fiz·ē·ol′ə·jē, *n.* The science dealing with the normal functions of living plant and animal organisms or their organs. —**phys·i·o·log·ic**, fiz·ē·ə·loj′ik, **phys·i·o·log·i·cal**, *a.* —**phys·i·o·log·i·cal·ly**, *adv.* —**phys·i·ol·o·gist**, fiz·ē·ol′ə·jist, *n.*

phys·i·o·ther·a·py, fiz·ē·ō·thār′ə·pē, *n.* The treatment of disease, bodily weaknesses, or defects by physical remedies, such as massage and exercise. Also **phys·i·cal ther·a·py.**

phy·sique, fi·zēk′, *n.* The physical or bodily structure or appearance.

pi, pī, *n.* The sixteenth letter π . π of the Greek alphabet; The Greek letter π. π used as the symbol for the ratio of the circumference of a circle to its diameter; the ratio itself, 3.141592.

---

pi, pie, pī, *n.* Printing types mixed together indiscriminately.—*v.t.,* **pied, pi•ing** or **pie•ing.** To reduce to a state of disorder.

pi•a•nis•si•mo, pē•ə•nis/ə•mō, *a.* Mus. Very soft.—*adv.*—*n.* Mus. A piece or movement so played.

pi•an•ist, pē•an/ist, pē/ə•nist, *n.* A performer on the piano.

pi•an•o, pē•an/ō, *n. pl.,* **-os.** A musical instrument with a keyboard by means of which metal strings are struck by felt-covered hammers to bring forth musical sounds. Also **pi•an•o•for•te.**

pi•an•o, pē•ä/nō, *a., adv.* Mus. Soft; softly.—*n.* A passage performed in this manner.

pi•an•o•for•te, pē•an•ə•fôr/tē, pē•an•ə•fôrt, *n.* A piano (the instrument).

pi•az•za, pē•az/ə, *It.* pyat/tsä, *n.* An open public square in a town or city, esp. in Italy; a veranda of a house.

pi•ca, pī/kə, *n.* A size of printing type, 12-point; a standard printing measure, equalizing the depth of this type size, about one-sixth of an inch; a kind of typewriter type having 10 characters to the linear inch.

pic•a•dor, pik/ə•dôr, *n.* A horseman in a bullfight who prods or weakens the bull by pricking him with a lance.

pic•a•resque, pik•ə•resk/, *a.* Of or characterized by a fictional narrative describing the adventures or fortunes of a vagabond hero in an episodic literary style.

pic•a•yune, pik•ə•yoon/, *a.* Of little value or account; small; petty; mean. Also **pic•a•yun•ish.**—*n.* A coin of little value; any trifling thing or person.

pic•ca•lil•li, pik/ə•lil•ē, *n.* A relish of various chopped vegetables and pungent spices.

pic•co•lo, pik/ə•lō, *n. pl.,* **-los.** A small flute with a pitch an octave higher than that of the ordinary flute. —**pic•co•lo•ist,** *n.*

pick, pik, *v.t.* To choose or select carefully; to detach or remove, esp. with the fingers; to pluck or gather; to use a pointed instrument in order to remove pieces of clinging matter; to eat daintily; to pierce, indent, dig into, or break up with a pointed instrument; to separate or pull apart, as fibers; to open, as a lock, with a pointed instrument; to steal the contents of, as a pocket or purse; to seek and find occasion for: to *pick* a quarrel; to seek or find, as flaws; to pluck, as the strings of an instrument; to play, as a stringed instrument, by plucking with the fingers.—*v.i.* To make careful or fastidious selection; to strike with or use a pick; to pluck or gather something; to eat with small bites or daintily; to pilfer.—*n.* Choice or selection; the right of selection; the choicest or most desirable part or example; an act of picking; a stroke with something pointed; the quantity of a plant crop picked at a particular time. —**pick at,** to touch, pull on, or toy with; to eat only a tiny bit at a time. *Informal.* To nag at. —**pick off,** shoot one at a time; in baseball, catch a runner off base. —**pick on.** *Informal.* Harass; tease; find fault with. —**pick out,** to choose; to distinguish (something) from its surroundings. —**pick over,** to examine carefully, usu. one by one. —**pick up,** to take up, as with the hand; to take up into a group, vehicle, etc.; to make tidy or put into order; to acquire casually, by chance, or without instruction; to accelerate; to take into custody; to bring within range of sight or hearing. *Informal.* To revive, recover, or improve; to make a casual acquaintance with (a stranger, esp. of the opposite sex). —**pick•er,** *n.*

pick, pik, *n.* A tool consisting of a pointed, usu. curved metal head secured to a wooden handle and used for loosening and breaking up soil, rock, and the like; any pointed tool or instrument for picking; a plectrum.

pick•ax, pick•axe, pik/aks, *n. pl.,* **-ax•es.** A pick with a sharp point at one end and a broad blade at the other.

picked, pikt, *a.* Specially selected for a particular purpose; cleaned by picking.

pick•er•el, pik/ər•əl, pik/rəl, *n. pl.,* **-el, -els.** Any of

various smaller species of pike.

pick•et, pik/it, *n.* A stake or post that is sharpened or pointed, used to form a fence or to secure a tent or other object; a person posted before or near a place of business at the time of a strike in order to discourage or prevent entrance by workers or customers; a protester or demonstrator; a detachment of troops stationed ahead of an encampment to guard against a surprise attack.—*v.t.* To fence or fortify with pickets or pointed stakes; to fasten to a picket or stake; to place or post as a guard or picket.—*v.i.* To be stationed as a picket. —**pick•et•er,** *n.*

pick•ing, pik/ing, *n. Usu. pl.* That which is left to be picked or gleaned; profits or benefits not honestly obtained.

pick•le, pik/əl, *n.* An item of food, esp. a cucumber, preserved in brine or a vinegar solution; a solution of salt and water or of vinegar in which meat, fish, or vegetables are preserved or marinated. *Informal.* A state or condition of difficulty or disorder; a plight. —*v.t.,* **-led, -ling.** To preserve in or treat with brine or vinegar.

pick•pock•et, pik/pok•it, *n.* One who steals from people's pockets.

pick•up, pik/əp, *n.* Acceleration; a truck with a small, open body for carrying light loads; a receiving device that converts a sound, scene, or other form of intelligence into corresponding electric signals; a device for reproducing sound by converting mechanical vibrations into electric impulses. *Informal.* A person with whom informal social contact is made, often for sexual purposes; an increase or improvement, esp. in business. *Informal.* Something, as alcohol, that revives or stimulates; also **pick-me-up,** pik/mē•əp.

pick•y, pik/ē, *a.,* **-i•er, -i•est.** Unduly particular or fussy; finicky.

pic•nic, pik/nik, *n.* An outdoor pleasure excursion, usu. one with a meal carried along. *Informal.* A pleasurable or easy experience or undertaking.—*v.i.,* **-nicked, -nick•ing.** To have or take part in a picnic. —**pic•nick•er,** *n.*

pic•to•ri•al, pik•tōr/ē•əl, pik•tôr/ē•əl, *a.* Pertaining to, expressed in, or of the nature of a picture; illustrated by or containing pictures.—*n.* A periodical in which pictures are an important feature. —**pic•to•ri•al•ly,** *adv.*

pic•ture, pik/chər, *n.* A painting, drawing, photograph, or other visual representation; any visual image; a mental image; a motion picture; a graphic or vivid description; the image or counterpart of: He is the *picture* of his father; a representative example of something; an overall view of a situation or event. —*v.t.,* **-tured, -tur•ing.** To represent pictorially; to illustrate; to imagine; to depict in words; to describe graphically.

pic•tur•esque, pik•chə•resk/, *a.* Quaint and charming; suggesting a picture. —**pic•tur•esque•ly,** *adv.* —**pic•tur•esque•ness,** *n.*

pic•ture win•dow, *n.* A large window with a single pane which frames a view.

pid•dle, pid/əl, *v.i.,* **-dled, -dling.** To deal in trifles; to waste time. *Informal.* To urinate.—*v.t.* To dawdle, usu. followed by *away.* —**pid•dling,** *a.*

pidg•in, pij/ən, *n.* A composite language developed as a means of communication between speakers of different languages and resulting in a simplification and combination of pronunciation, grammar, and vocabulary of the two languages.

pie, pī, *n.* A one- or two-layered crust or pastry filled with fruit, meat, or any of a variety of sweets. *Informal.* Anything considered excellent or easily accomplished.

pie•bald, pī/bôld, *a.* Having spots or patches of white and black or other colors.—*n.* A spotted animal, usu. a horse.

piece, pēs, *n.* A fragment or part of anything separated from the whole; a definite quantity or portion or something considered as an entity; one item of a group, set, or the like; a standard amount or length according to which an item is produced or sold; an instance or example; an artistic or literary composition; a small object, as a disk or figure, used in games for counting, moving on a board, or the like.—*v.t.,* **pieced, piec·ing.** To mend or enlarge by the addition of a piece; to unite or join. —**a piece of one's mind.** *Informal.* A bluntly expressed criticism or rebuke. —**of a piece, of one piece,** of the same type; in accord. —**speak one's piece,** voice one's opinions or attitudes. —**piec·er,** *n.*

piece goods, *n. pl.* Goods sold by the piece or by linear measure. Also **yard goods.**

piece·meal, pēs′mēl, *adv.* Piece by piece; in pieces; gradually.—*a.* Done bit by bit.

piece·work, pēs′wərk, *n.* Work paid for by the unit or the quantity of pieces produced. —**piece·work·er,** *n.*

pied, pīd, *a.* Parti-colored; variegated; spotted.

pier, pēr, *n.* A wharf or quay resting on columns or piles, projecting from shore into a body of water, and serving as a docking place for ships or as a recreation area; a support for a bridge, arch, or masonry of any kind.

pierce, pērs, *v.t., v.i.,* **pierced, pierc·ing.** To penetrate or run into or through with a pointed instrument or the like; to make a hole or opening in; tunnel; perforate; to force or make a way into or through; to penetrate with the eye or mind; to penetrate or sound sharply through. —**pierc·ing,** *a.* —**pierc·ing·ly,** *adv.*

pi·e·tism, pī′ə·tiz·əm, *n.* Deep piety; affectation of piety; religiosity. —**pi·e·tis·tic,** pī·ə·tis′tik, **pi·e·tis·ti·cal,** *a.*

pi·e·ty, pī′i·tē, *n. pl.,* **-ties.** The quality of being pious; reverence for God or a Supreme Being; regard for or fidelity to religious obligations; dutiful respect or regard for parents or others; a pious act.

pif·fle, pif′əl, *n. Informal.* Silly talk or written matter; nonsense.

pig, pig, *n.* A young swine; the flesh of swine, used for food. *Informal.* A person or animal of piggish character or habits; an oblong mass of metal that has been run while molten into a mold; one of the molds for such masses of metal.—*v.i.,* **pigged, pig·ging.** To farrow; to lie or huddle together; to live like pigs.

pi·geon, pij′ən, *n.* A bird with a compact body and short legs, and widely distributed throughout the world. *Informal.* A simpleton or dupe.

pi·geon·hole, pij′ən·hōl, *n.* One of a series of small compartments in a desk, open in front, and used for holding letters and papers.—*v.t.,* **-holed, -hol·ing.** To place or file in a pigeonhole; assign to a definite place in some orderly system; put aside, esp. with the intention of ignoring or forgetting.

pi·geon-toed, pij′ən·tōd, *a.* Having the toes or feet turned inward.

pig·gish, pig′ish, *a.* Like a pig; greedy; selfish; filthy. —**pig·gish·ly,** *adv.* —**pig·gish·ness,** *n.*

pig·gy·back, pig′ē·bak, *adv., a.* On the back or shoulders; pertaining to the shipping of one carrier on another; truck trailers or automobiles traveling on railroad flatcars.—*a.*

pig·gy bank, *n.* A savings bank for coins.

pig·head·ed, pig′hed·id, *a.* Stupidly obstinate; perverse; stubborn. —**pig·head·ed·ly,** *adv.* —**pig·head·ed·ness,** *n.*

pig i·ron, *n.* Crude, impure iron cast in the form of oblong ingots; crude iron as a material.

pig·ment, pig′mənt, *n.* A coloring matter or substance which when mixed with a liquid becomes a paint; any substance whose presence in the tissues or cells of animals or plants colors them.—*v.t.* —**pig·men·tar·y,** *a.*

pig·men·ta·tion, pig·mən·tā′shən, *n.* Coloration

with or deposition of pigment, esp. excessive deposition of skin pigment.

pig·pen, pig′pen, *n.* An enclosed area for keeping pigs or hogs; a dirty or untidy place.

pig·skin, pig′skin, *n.* The skin of a pig; leather made from it. *Informal.* A football.

pig·sty, pig′stī, *n. pl.,* **-sties.** A pen for pigs.

pig·tail, pig′tāl, *n.* The hair in a braid. —**pig-tailed,** *a.*

pike, pīk, *n. pl.,* **pikes, pike.** A slender, voracious freshwater fish having a long snout.

pike, pīk, *n.* A turnpike.

pike, pīk, *n.* A long staff having a pointed head of iron or steel, formerly used as a weapon.—*v.t.,* **piked, pik·ing.** To pierce, wound, or kill with a pike.

pike, pīk, *n.* A sharp point; a spike; the pointed end of anything, as of an arrow or a spear.

pik·er, pī′kər, *n. Informal.* One who gambles in a small, cautious way; one who does anything in a contemptibly small or cheap way.

pi·las·ter, pi·las′tər, *n.* A rectangular pillar or column projecting from and constituting part of a wall.

pil·chard, pil′chərd, *n.* A food fish resembling the herring but smaller.

pile, pīl, *n.* A heavy stake or beam of timber, driven into the ground to support a superstructure or form part of a wall.—*v.t.,* **piled, pil·ing.** To furnish, strengthen, or support with piles.

pile, pīl, *n.* An assemblage of things lying one upon another; a mass of any matter, rising to some height; a heap; a funeral or sacrificial pyre; a large structure, building, or mass of buildings. *Informal.* A large number, quantity, or amount of anything.—*v.t.,* **piled, pil·ing.** To lay or dispose in a pile, often with *up;* to accumulate or amass, with *up;* to cover or load with a pile or piles.—*v.i.* To gather or rise in a pile or piles, as snow; to accumulate, or mount up, as money, interest, debts, or evidence; to move in a body and more or less confusedly, with *in, into, out, off,* or *down.*

pile, pīl, *n.* Hair; wool, fur, or pelage; the nap of a fabric; a piled fabric or carpet. —**piled,** *a.*

pile, pīl, *n. Usu. pl.* A hemorrhoid.

pile driv·er, *n.* In construction, a machine for driving in piles, either a steam hammer or a weight which is dropped from a height on the head of a pile.

pil·fer, pil′fər, *v.i., v.t.* To steal in small quantities. —**pil·fer·age, pil·fer·er,** *n.*

pil·grim, pil′grəm, *n.* One who journeys to some sacred place as an act of devotion; a traveler or wanderer, esp. in foreign lands.

pil·grim·age, pil′grə·mij, *n.* A journey made to some sacred place as an act of devotion; a long journey. —*v.i.,* **-aged, -ag·ing.**

pil·ing, pī′ling, *n.* A structure composed of piles.

pill, pil, *n.* A small, rounded mass of medicinal substance, to be swallowed whole; something unpleasant that has to be accepted or endured.—*v.t.* To form into or dose with pills. —**the pill,** an oral contraceptive in pill form.

pil·lage, pil′ij, *v.t.,* **-laged, -lag·ing.** To plunder; to take as plunder.—*v.i.* To take, loot, or plunder.—*n.* The act of plundering. —**pil·lag·er,** *n.*

pil·lar, pil′ər, *n.* An upright shaft or structure used as a support, or standing alone, as for a monument; a person who is a chief supporter of a state, institution, or cause.—*v.t.* To provide or support with pillars. —**from pil·lar to post,** from one situation to another.

pill·box, pil′boks, *n.* A box for holding pills; a small concrete blockhouse.

pil·lion, pil′yən, *n.* A cushion or pad placed behind the saddle on a horse or motorcycle for another rider. —*adv.*

pil·lo·ry, pil′ə·rē, *n. pl.,* **-ries.** A wooden frame with holes for securely holding the head and hands, once used to punish an offender by holding him up to public

---

a- hat, fāte, fâre, fäther; **e-** met, mē; **i-** pin, pīne; **o-** not, nōte, ôrb, moove (move), boy, pownd; **u-** cūbe, bŭll, tûk (took); **ch-** chin; **th-** thick, ŧhen; **zh-** vizhon (vision); **ə-** əgo, takən, pencəl, lemən, bərd (bird).

scorn.—*v.t.*, **-ried, ry·ing.** To place in a pillory; to subject to public ridicule or contempt.

pil·low, pil′ō, *n.* A support for the head during sleep or rest, specif. a bag or case filled with feathers, sponge rubber, or other soft material.—*v.t., v.i.* To rest on or as on a pillow.

pil·low·case, pil′ō·kās, *n.* A removable case for a pillow. Also **pil·low slip.**

pi·lot, pi′lət, *n.* The operator of an aircraft or spacecraft; a person qualified and usu. licensed to conduct ships in and out of harbors or through hazardous waters; the helmsman of a vessel; guide; director. —*v.t.* To act as the pilot of; to guide through dangers or difficulties.—*a.* Pertaining to something that leads or shows the way. —**pi·lot·age,** *n.* —**pi·lot·less,** *a.*

pi·lot·house, pi′lət·hows, *n.* An enclosed place on the deck of a vessel, sheltering the steering gear and the helmsman.

pi·lot light, *n.* A small gas jet kept burning continuously to ignite any of the main gas burners when desired.

pi·men·to, pi·men′tō, *n. pl.*, **-tos.** A tropical American tree from whose small, unripe berries allspice is prepared; sweet pepper. Also **pi·mien·to,** pi·myen′tō.

pimp, pimp, *n.* One who procures customers for a prostitute, in exchange for a percentage of her earnings.—*v.i.* To solicit for prostitutes.

pim·ple, pim′pəl, *n.* A small swelling of the skin, with an inflamed base; pustule. —**pim·pled, pim·ply,** *a.*

pin, pin, *n.* A piece of metal, wood, or the like, used for fastening separate articles together, or used as a support from which a thing may be hung; something like a pin in shape or use; a badge or ornament attached to a pin; a wood club used as a target in bowling and similar games; a fall in wrestling.—*v.t.*, **pinned, pin·ning.** To fasten with a pin; to gain a fall in wrestling. —**on pins and nee·dles.** *Informal.* Nervous, anxious, or uneasy. —**pin down,** to force to decide on or reveal an intention or position. —**pin on,** to accuse, as of a crime.

pin·a·fore, pin′ə·fōr, pin′ə·fôr, *n.* A sleeveless garment which may be worn on top of a blouse.

pi·ña·ta, pēn·yä′tə, *n.* A pot or figure, usu. of pottery and brightly decorated, filled with gifts and candies, hung from ceilings in Mexican and Central American homes, to be broken by children during the Christmas holidays. Also **pi·na·ta.**

pince-nez, pans′nā, pins′nā, *n. pl.*, **pince-nez.** A pair of eyeglasses kept in place by a spring which pinches the bridge of the nose.

pin·cers, pin′sərz, *n. pl. but sing. in constr.* A tool with two handles and jaws for gripping, pulling, or clipping something. Also **pin·chers,** pin′chərz.

pinch, pinch, *v.t.* To squeeze between the fingers, the teeth, claws, or the parts of an instrument; to compress or cramp painfully; to cause to become drawn or thin; to restrict in funds or circumstances. *Informal.* To steal; to arrest.—*v.i.* To squeeze or press painfully; hurt; to be unduly frugal; to be stingy.—*n.* The act of pinching; the quantity of a material that can be held by a finger and thumb; a small quantity; a time of urgent need or emergency; hardship. *Informal.* An arrest; a theft. —**pinch pen·nies,** to be very frugal or stingy. —**pinch·er,** *n.*

pinch·beck, pinch′bek, *n.* An alloy of copper and zinc, resembling gold; anything sham or spurious.—*a.*

pinch hit·ter, *n. Baseball.* A substitute who takes the turn at bat of a weaker or less reliable batsman; one who substitutes for another person, esp. in emergencies. —**pinch-hit,** pinch′hit′, *v.i.*, **-hit, -hit·ting.** —**pinch hit,** *n.*

pin curl, *n.* A curl that is moistened and secured with a clip or bobby pin.

pin·cush·ion, pin′kûsh·ən, *n.* A small cushion or pad in which pins are stuck for keeping.

pine, pīn, *n.* Any of a group of trees or shrubs having evergreen, needle-shaped leaves and woody cones;

the wood of any such tree. —**pine·like,** *a.* —**pin·y, pine·y,** *a.*

pine, pīn, *v.i.*, **pined, pin·ing.** To long intensely and painfully, often with *for*; to lose vigor and health from grief, regret, or longing, often followed by *away*; to languish.

pin·e·al bod·y, pin′ē·əl, *n.* A small, usu. cone-shaped body in the brain of vertebrates having no proven function. Also **pin·e·al gland.**

pine·ap·ple, pīn′ap′əl, *n.* A tropical plant having a large fruit and a crown of spiny leaves. *Informal.* A fragmentation grenade, pineapplelike in shape.

pine nut, *n.* An edible pine seed.

pine tar, *n.* A thick tar derived from pine wood used in roofing, soaps, remedies, disinfectants, etc.

pin·feath·er, pin′feth·ər, *n.* A newly emerging, undeveloped feather. —**pin·feath·ered,** *a.* —**pin·feath·er·y,** *a.*

pin·fold, pin′fōld, *n.* An enclosure for stray animals, esp. cattle; a pound or pen.—*v.t.* To restrain by a barrier, as within a pinfold.

ping, ping, *n.* A brief, high-pitched, metallic ringing sound.—*v.i.*

Ping-Pong, ping′pong, *n. Trademark.* Table tennis.

pin·head, pin′hed, *n.* The head of a pin; something very small or insignificant. *Informal.* A person having little intelligence. —**pin·head·ed,** *a. Informal.* Dull or stupid.

pin·hole, pin′hōl, *n.* A small hole or perforation made by or as by a pin.

pin·ion, pin′yən, *n.* The outer segment of a bird's wing; the wing of a bird, or the flight feathers collectively; a feather; a quill.—*v.t.* To cut one pinion off or bind the wings of, as a bird, so as to prevent it from flying; to bind, as a person's arms or hands; to disable in this way, or shackle; to bind or hold fast, as to a thing.

pin·ion, pin′yən, *n.* A small gearwheel, or cogwheel, engaging with a larger one or with a rack.

pink, pingk, *v.t.* To pierce or stab; to punch, as cloth or leather, with small holes or figures for ornament; to finish the edge of, as fabric, with a scalloped or notched pattern.

pink, pingk, *n.* Pink- to rose-colored showy flowers, as the sweet william, carnation, and garden pink; a pale reddish color of various shades; the highest form or degree: in the *pink* of condition; the highest type or example of excellence. *Informal.* One whose political or economic opinions are regarded as leftist, or moderately radical.—*a.* Pertaining to the color pink. *Informal.* Having somewhat radical political views. —**pink·ish,** *a.*

pink·eye, pingk′ī, *n.* Contagious inflammation of the mucous membranes of the eyelids.

pink·ie, pink·y, ping′kē, *n. Informal.* The smallest finger.

pink·ing shears, *n. pl.* Scissors having serrated blades, used to cut a notched, non-fraying edge on fabrics.

pink·o, ping′kō, *n. pl.*, **-os, -oes.** *Informal.* A person holding leftist but not extremely radical political opinions.

pin mon·ey, *n.* Any small amount of money reserved for minor expenditures.

pin·na, pin′ə, *n. pl.*, **pin·nas, pin·nae,** pin′ē. A leaflet of a pinnate fern leaf; the wing or feather of a bird; the fin of a fish. —**pin·nal,** *a.*

pin·na·cle, pin′ə·kəl, *n.* A high peak; the highest point or apex, as of power or achievement. *Arch.* A small structure which rises above the roof of a building or crowns a buttress or tower.—*v.t.*, **-cled, -cling.** To put a pinnacle or pinnacles on; to put on or as on a pinnacle.

pin·nate, pin′āt, pin′it, *a.* Shaped, formed, or branching like a feather. —**pin·nate·ly,** *adv.* —**pin·na·tion,** pi·nā′shən, *n.*

pi·noch·le, pi·noc·le, pē′nək·əl, pē′nok·əl, *n.* A

card game played by two, three, or four persons, with two decks of 24 cards each; the combination of the queen of spades and the jack of diamonds in this game. Also **pe·nuch·le, pe·nuck·le.**

pin·point, pin′poynt, *n.* The pointed end of a pin; a tiny or insignificant object or matter.—*v.t.* To locate precisely.—*a.* Precise, fine, or exact.

pin·prick, pin′prik, *n.* A puncture made with or as with a pin; a minor nuisance or irritation.—*v.t., v.i.*

pin·set·ter, pin′set·ər, *n. Bowling.* A device which removes fallen pins and resets all pins for a new frame. Also **pin·spot·ter,** pin′spot·ər.

pin stripe, *n.* A very narrow stripe used as a fabric design; a pattern or garment with these stripes. —**pin-striped,** pin′strīpt, *a.*

pint, pīnt, *n.* A measure of capacity containing one half of a quart.

pin·tail, pin′tāl, *n. pl.,* **-tail, -tails.** A duck having a long, needle-pointed tail. —**pin-tailed,** *a.*

pin·tle, pin′təl, *n.* A pin or bolt that serves as an axis.

pin·to, pin′tō, *a.* Piebald; mottled; spotted.—*n. pl.,* **-tos.** A pied or spotted horse. A spotted bean; also **pin·to bean.**

pin·up, pin′əp, *n.* A wall accessory, or something hung on a wall, as a lamp. *Informal.* A picture or photograph of a glamorous girl hung on an admirer's wall; the girl herself; also **pin·up girl.**—*a.* Designed to be hung on or attached to a wall. *Informal.* Pertaining to or having the attributes of a pinup girl. Also **pin-up.**

pin·wheel, pin′hwēl, *n.* A child's toy consisting of paper or plastic spokes fastened by a pin to a stick so as to revolve in the wind or when blown; a wheel-shaped firework which revolves rapidly and shoots off colored fire when ignited.

pin·worm, pin′wərm, *n.* A small nematoid worm infesting the intestine and rectum, esp. of children.

pi·o·neer, pī·ə·nēr′, *n.* One of those who first enter or settle in a region, opening it for occupation and development by others; one of those who are first or earliest in any field of inquiry, enterprise, or progress: *pioneers* in electronics.—*v.t.* To go before and prepare, as a way.—*v.i.* To act as a pioneer; to clear the way.

pi·ous, pī′əs, *a.* Having or showing a dutiful spirit of reverence for God or an earnest regard for religious obligations; devout; religious; godly; practised or used from religious motives, real or pretended, or for some good object: a *pious* fraud, a *pious* deception. —**pi·ous·ly,** *adv.* —**pi·ous·ness,** *n.*

pip, pip, *n.* A disease of fowl, marked by a secretion of thick mucus in the throat and mouth or by a formation of scaly crust on the tongue; any minor human disorder: used humorously.

pip, pip, *n.* The seed of a fleshy fruit, as an orange. *Informal.* Anything or anyone extraordinary or admirable.

pip, pip, *v.i.,* **pipped, pip·ping.** To chirp or peep, as a chicken.—*v.t.* To crack or break through, as an egg-shell, during the process of hatching.

pipe, pīp, *n.* A hollow cylinder of metal, etc., for conveying a fluid; a tube; material formed into a tube or tubes; piping or tubing; a tubular organ or passage in an animal body; *pl.,* the respiratory passages. A tube used as, or to form an essential part of, a musical wind instrument; a wind instrument consisting of a single tube or tubes; *usu. pl.,* a bagpipe. A boatswain's whistle; one of the tubes from which the tones of an organ are produced; *pl.,* the voice, esp. as used in singing. The note or call of a bird; a tube with a small bowl at one end, used for smoking tobacco or some other substance; a quantity, as of tobacco, that fills the bowl and is smoked at one time,—*v.i.,* **piped, pi·ping.** To play on a pipe; to make or utter a shrill sound.—*v.t.* To play, as music, on a pipe; to sing, as a

bird; to attract or lead by playing on a pipe; summon or order by sounding the boatswain's pipe or whistle; to supply with pipes; to convey by means of pipes; to trim or finish, as a garment, with piping. —**pipe down.** *Informal.* To stop making noise; be silent. —**pipe up,** to start to sing or to play, as an instrument; to speak forcefully.

pipe clay, *n.* A white clay used for making tobacco pipes and for cleaning white leather. —**pipe-clay,** pīp′klā, *v.t.* To whiten with pipe clay.

pipe dream, *n. Informal.* Any fantastic notion; an unrealistic goal or desire.

pipe·line, pīp′līn, *n.* A conduit of pipe used to transmit oil, water, gases, etc., to market or refinery; a direct way or means for conveying information.—*v.t., -lined, -lin·ing.* To convey by a pipeline; provide with a pipeline.

pipe or·gan, *n.* An organ constructed of pipes of various lengths with both pedal and manual keyboards.

pip·er, pī′pər, *n.* One who plays on a pipe; a bagpiper.

pip·ing, pī′ping, *n.* The act of one who pipes; the music of pipes; a shrill sound; material formed into a pipe or pipes; pipes collectively; a tubular band of fabric used for trimming garments along the edges and seams; a cordlike ornamentation made of icing, used on pastry.—*a.* Playing on a musical pipe; emitting a shrill sound. —**pip·ing hot,** so hot as to hiss.

pip·it, pip′it, *n.* A bird distinguished by its habit of wagging its tail and walking instead of hopping.

pip·pin, pip′in, *n.* Any of several varieties of apples. *Informal.* Anything or anyone extraordinary or admirable.

pip-squeak, pip′skwēk, *n. Informal.* One who is small or inconsequential.

pi·quant, pē′kənt, pē′känt, *a.* Being agreeably sharp or pungent to the taste; interesting or stimulating; having an intriguing character; lively. —**pi·quan·cy, pi·quant·ness,** *n.* —**pi·quant·ly,** *adv.*

pique, pēk, *n.* An offense taken; a sense of resentment; irritation.—*v.t.,* **piqued, pi·quing.** To nettle; to irritate; to stimulate, as one's interest; to touch with envy, jealousy, or other passion.—*v.i.* To cause irritation.

pi·qué, pi·kā′, pē·kā′, *n.* A cotton, silk, or rayon fabric woven with a quilted effect and crosswise ribs or raised stripes.

pi·ra·cy, pī′rə·sē, *n. pl.,* **-cies.** Robbery on the high seas; the profession of a pirate; literary theft or any infringement of copyright law.

pi·ra·nha, pi·rän′yə, pi·ran′yə, *n.* Any small, voracious S. American fresh-water fish which will attack an animal of any size, including man.

pi·rate, pī′rit, *n.* A robber on the high seas; an armed ship or vessel engaged in piracy; a person who appropriates the literary work or invention of another without compensation or permission.—*v.t.,* **-rat·ed, -rat·ting.** To commit an act of piracy upon; to appropriate by piracy; to publish without right or permission.—*v.i.* To commit piracy. —**pi·rat·i·cal,** pi·rat′i·kəl, *a.* —**pi·rat·i·cal·ly,** *adv.*

pi·rogue, pē′rōg, *n.* A kind of canoe made from a single trunk of a tree hollowed out; a dugout boat.

pir·ou·ette, pēr·ů·et′, *n.* A whirling about on one foot or on the points of the toes, as in dancing; a quick, short turn or whirl of a horse.—*v.i.,* **-et·ted, -et·ting.** To perform a pirouette; whirl, as on the toes; move in pirouettes.

Pis·ces, pī′sēz, pis′ēz, *n. pl.* The Fishes, a zodiacal constellation; the twelfth sign of the zodiac; the class of animals that includes the true fishes.

pis·ci·cul·ture, pis′i·kəl·chər, pī′si·kəl·chər, *n.* The breeding, rearing, preservation, and feeding of fish by artificial means; fish culture.

pis·ta·chi·o, pi·stash′ē·ō, pi·stä′shē·ō, *n. pl.,* **-os.**

---

a- hat, fāte, fâre, fäther; e- met, mē; i- pin, pīne; o- not, nōte, ôrb, moove (move), boy, pownd;
u- cūbe, bůll, tůk (took); ch- chin; th- thick, then; zh- vizhon (vision); ə- əgo, takən, pencəl, lemən, bərd (bird).

One of several species of small trees in the cashew family; the nut itself, used as a confection; a flavoring prepared from this nut; a light green color.

pis·til, pis'til, *n.* The female reproductive organ in a flowering plant comprised of the ovary, the style, and the stigma.

pis·til·late, pis'tə·lit, pis'tə·lāt, *a.* Of a flower, having pistils and no stamens.

pis·tol, pis'təl, *n.* A small firearm designed to be fired with one hand only.—*v.t.,* **-toled, -tol·ing.** To shoot with a pistol.

pis·ton, pis'tən, *n.* A disk or short cylinder that fits closely within a hollow cylinder, and moves back and forth under pressure of a fluid, as in a steam engine, or compresses a fluid as in a pump. *Mus.* A sliding valve used to change the pitch in a cornet or the like.

pit, pit, *n.* A hole or cavity in the ground; a mining excavation; a concealed excavation in the ground that serves as a trap for animals or men; the abode of evil spirits and lost souls; hell; a hollow or indentation in a surface; a natural hollow or depression in the body: the *pit* of the stomach; a small scar such as those left on the skin after smallpox; an enclosure for combats, as of dogs or cocks; a section of a theater, nearest and below the stage, that is occupied by the orchestra; that part of the floor of a commodity exchange devoted to a special kind of trading: the grain *pit*—*v.t.,* **pit·ted, pit·ting.** To match in a conflict or contest; to mark with pits or depressions.—*v.i.* To become marked with pits.

pit, pit, *n.* The stone of a fruit, as of a cherry, peach, or plum.—*v.t.* To remove, as the stones, from: to *pit* prunes.

pitch, pich, *n.* A dark-colored, sticky or viscous substance left after the distillation of coal tar or wood tar, etc.; asphalt; the sap which exudes from the bark of pines.—*v.t.* To smear or cover over with pitch.

pitch, pich, *v.t.* To set up or erect, as a tent or camp; to put in a fixed or definite position; to set at a certain angle, degree, or level; to set at a particular pitch, or determine the key or keynote of, as a tune; to throw, fling, hurl, or toss. *Baseball.* To deliver or serve the ball to the batter. *Mech.* To engage; interlock.—*v.i.* To encamp; to throw or toss; to plunge or fall forward or headlong; to plunge with alternate fall and rise of bow and stern; to lurch; to slope downward, or dip. *Baseball.* To deliver or serve the ball to the batter; fill the position of pitcher.—*pich, n.* The act of pitching; a throw; a plunge forward or headlong, or a lurch; the pitching movement of a ship or plane. *Informal.* An aggressive sales talk; something that is pitched; point, position, or degree, as in a scale: a *pitch* of ecstasy. *Mus.* Degree of highness or lowness of a tone or of sound; downward inclination or slope; a sloping part or place; the slope or steepness of a roof. *Mech.* The distance between two things, esp. in a series; the distance between the centers of two adjacent teeth in a toothed wheel or rack.—**pitch in·to,** to attack; to start with fervor: *pitch into* one's work.

pitch, pich, *n. Aerospace.* The variation in flight from horizontal to vertical: one of the three axes, along with roll and yaw, on which the altitude of a space vehicle may be controlled.

pitch-black, pich'blak', *a.* Utterly black.

pitch·blende, pich'blend, *n.* A black or brown mineral consisting largely of uranium oxide; an ore of uranium and radium.

pitch·er, pich'ər, *n.* A container with a handle and a spout or lip, for holding and pouring liquids.

pitch·er, pich'ər, *n.* One who pitches. *Baseball.* The player who throws the ball to the batter.

pitch·fork, pich'fôrk, *n.* A fork used in lifting or throwing hay or sheaves of grain.—*v.t.* To lift or throw with a pitchfork.

pitch·y, pich'ē, *a.,* **-i·er, -i·est.** Full of or abounding in pitch; smeared with pitch; resembling pitch.

pit·e·ous, pit'ē·əs, *a.* Exciting or deserving pity or

sympathy; pathetic. —**pit·e·ous·ly,** *adv.* —**pit·e·ous·ness,** *n.*

pit·fall, pit'fôl, *n.* A concealed pit prepared as a trap for animals or men. *Fig.* Any hidden trap or danger.

pith, pith, *n.* The soft, spongy cellular tissue in the center of the stems of many plants; the essential part; center, essence, or gist: the *pith* of the matter.—*v.t.* To take the pith from, as from a plant.

pith·y, pith'ē, *a.,* **-i·er, -i·est.** Forceful; having meaning and substance; consisting of pith; of, containing, or abounding in pith. —**pith·i·ly,** *adv.* —**pith·i·ness,** *n.*

pit·i·a·ble, pit'ē·ə·bəl, *a.* Deserving to be pitied; exciting or arousing pity; lamentable; contemptible, miserable, or pitiful. —**pit·i·a·ble·ness,** *n.* —**pit·i·a·bly,** *adv.*

pit·i·ful, pit'i·fəl, *a.* Deserving pity; arousing compassion; miserable; insignificant; contemptible. —**pit·i·ful·ly,** *adv.* —**pit·i·ful·ness,** *n.*

pit·i·less, pit'i·lis, *a.* Without pity; merciless. —**pit·i·less·ly,** *adv.* —**pit·i·less·ness,** *n.*

pit·man, pit'mən, *n. pl.,* **-men.** One who works in a pit, as in coal mining.

pit·tance, pit'əns, *n.* A small allowance; any very small portion allowed or assigned.

pit·ted, pi'tid, *a.* Having pits or indentations, as pockmarks on the face.

pi·tu·i·tar·y, pi·too'i·ter·ē, pi·tū'i·ter·ē, *a.* Of or pertaining to the pituitary gland.—*n. pl.,* **-ies.** The pituitary gland. *Med.* Any of several hormone extracts taken from the pituitary gland.

pi·tu·i·tar·y gland, *n.* A small, oval-shaped endocrine gland situated at the base of the brain and secreting hormones with a broad range of effects on growth, metabolism, maturation, reproduction, and other bodily functions.

pit·y, pit'ē, *n. pl.,* **-ies.** The suffering of one person excited by the distresses of another; compassion; mercy; the ground or subject of pity; cause of grief; a thing to be regretted.—*v.t.,* **-ied, -y·ing.** To feel pity or compassion toward.—*v.i.* To feel compassion or pity. —**pit·y·ing,** *a.* —**pit·y·ing·ly,** *adv.*

piv·ot, piv'ət, *n.* Something upon which a related part rotates or oscillates; that on which something hinges or depends; the person upon whom a line, as of troops, wheels about; a quick turning around on one foot; the act of pivoting.—*v.t.* To mount on, attach by, or provide with a pivot or pivots.—*v.i.* To turn on or as on a pivot. —**piv·ot·al,** *a.* —**piv·ot·al·ly,** *adv.*

pix·i·lat·ed, pik'sə·lā·tid, *a.* Slightly unbalanced mentally; eccentric.

pix·y, pix·ie, pik'sē, *n. pl.,* **-ies.** A fairy, esp. one who is mischievous.

piz·za, pēt'sə, *n.* A spicy Italian dish, consisting of cheese and tomatoes, with sausage, anchovies, or various additions, spread on a layer of bread dough and baked.

piz·ze·ri·a, pēt·sə·rē'ə, *n.* A place where pizzas are baked, sold, and eaten.

piz·zi·ca·to, pit·sə·kä'tō, *a.* Played by plucking the strings with the finger instead of using the bow, as on a violin.—*n. pl.,* **-ti,** -tē. A note or passage so played. —*adv.*

plac·a·ble, plak'ə·bəl, plā'kə·bəl, *a.* Capable of being easily appeased or pacified. —**plac·a·bil·i·ty,** plā·kə·bil'i·tē, plā·kə·bil'i·tē, *n.* —**plac·a·bly,** *adv.*

plac·ard, plak'ärd, *n.* A written or printed notice posted in a public place.—plak'ärd, plə·kärd', *v.t.* To post placards on; to inform by means of a placard.

pla·cate, plā'kāt, plak'āt, *v.t.,* **-cat·ed, -cat·ing.** To appease, pacify, or conciliate. —**pla·cat·er,** *n.* —**pla·ca·tion,** plā·kā'shən, *n.* —**pla·ca·tive, pla·ca·to·ry,** plā'kə·tiv, plāk'ə·tôr·ē, *a.*

place, plās, *n.* An indefinite expanse or region: a faraway *place;* a site or other locality; a broad way or open square in a city; any portion of space marked off by its use or character: an eating or parking *place;* a house, room, or other dwelling; a passage in a book or piece of music; an order of proceedings: in the first *place*; rank; social class or station; order of priority or importance; an office, appointment, or job; a duty or right: it is not his *place* to say; ground or occasion: a party is no *place* for gloom; room or stead; to act in *place* of another; position in a sequence or scale, as of numbers or musical notes; the original or natural position of something: each in its proper *place*; a position won in a race or competition: to win first *place*. *Astron*. The position in the sky of a heavenly body at any time. *Informal*. A state of success or achievement: He will get some *place*. *Sports*. One of the leading positions at the finish line in a race; in U.S. horse racing, the position of second at the finish line.—*v.t.*, **placed, plac·ing**. To locate; arrange in position; to appoint, induct, or establish in an office or job; to put into a particular rank, state, or condition; to fix in a period of time: History *places* him at the time of Plato; entrust or bestow: to *place* confidence in a friend; recognize or identify: to *place* a face or accent.—*v.t.* To be among the first three at the finish line; to come in second at a horse show.

pla·ce·bo, plə·sē′bō, *n. pl.*, **-bos, -boes**. A preparation with little or no healing value given to please a patient, or as a control in testing the effectiveness of a genuine drug; anything intended to gratify or humor.

place kick, *n*. In football, a kick in which the ball is kicked over the opponents′ goal post. —**place-kick**, plǎs′kik, *v.t.* —**place kick·er**, *n*.

place·ment, plǎs′mənt, *n*. The act of placing, or the state of being placed; the placing of a person in suitable employment; the placing of a football in position to kick a goal from the field.

pla·cen·ta, plə·sen′tə, *n. pl.*, **-tas, -tae**, -tē. The organ by which the fetus of most mammals is attached to the wall of the uterus and through which the fetus receives nourishment. —**pla·cen·tal**, *a*.

plac·er, plǎ′sər, *n*. One who places, sets, or arranges; one of the winning contestants in a race, either a person or an animal.

plac·er, plas′ər, *n*. A glacial or alluvial deposit containing particles of gold or other valuable minerals; a place where deposits are washed to obtain such minerals.

place set·ting, *n*. A complete set of the dishes and utensils needed to serve one person at a meal.

plac·id, plas′id, *a*. Gentle; quiet; undisturbed. —**pla·cid·i·ty**, plə·sid′i·tē, **plac·id·ness**, *n*. —**plac·id·ly**, *adv*.

plack·et, plak′it, *n*. The opening or slit in a petticoat or skirt.

pla·gia·rism, plā′jə·riz·əm, plā′jē·ə·riz·əm, *n*. The appropriating and putting forth as one's own the ideas, language, or designs of another; something appropriated and put forth in this manner. —**pla·gia·rist**, *n*. —**pla·gia·ris·tic**, plā·jə·ris′tik, *a*.

pla·gia·rize, plā′jə·rīz, plā′jē·ə·rīz, *v.t.*, **-rized, -riz·ing**. To appropriate by plagiarism; to appropriate ideas or passages from, by plagiarism.—*v.i.* To commit plagiarism. —**pla·gia·riz·er**, *n*.

pla·gia·ry, plā′jə·rē, plā′jē·ə·rē, *n. pl.*, **-ries**. A plagiarist.

plague, plāg, *n*. A widespread disease with a high mortality rate occurring in several forms: bubonic, pneumonic, and septicemic; a great affliction, disaster, or evil; a cause of annoyance or trouble; nuisance.—*v.t.*, **plagued, pla·guing**. To harass or trouble; annoy or vex; to afflict with disease, calamity, or evil. —**pla·guer**, *n*.

pla·guy, **pla·guey**, plā′gē, *a*. *Informal*. Causing vexation; annoying; troublesome.—*adv*. Annoyingly or excessively. —**pla·gui·ly**, *adv*.

plaid, plad, *n*. A large rectangular outer garment or wrap, frequently of tartan, worn by Scottish Highlanders; a fabric woven in a tartan pattern; such a cross-barred pattern.—*a*. Having such a pattern. —**plaid·ed**, *a*. Wearing a plaid.

plain, plān, *a*. Level, flat, even, or smooth; without ornament or embellishment: a *plain* dress; homely; without disguise, cunning, or affectation: *plain* talk; unrefined or unsophisticated: *plain* people; clear or unmistakable; simple: *plain* furnishings; not highly seasoned: *plain* food; sheer, mere, or downright: *plain* foolishness.—*n*. An area of level land. —**plain·ly**, *adv*. —**plain·ness**, *n*.

plain·clothes man, plān′klōz′mən, plān′klōthz′mən, *n. pl.*, **-men**. A police detective who does not wear a uniform while on duty. Also **plain·clothes·man**.

plain·song, plān′sông, plān′song, *n*. The simple, grave, and unadorned chant from the early Christian church.

plain-spo·ken, plān′spō′kən, *a*. Plain or frank in speech; forthright; candid; blunt; outspoken.

plaint, plānt, *n*. Lamentation; complaint.

plain·tiff, plān′tif, *n*. The person who brings a suit before a court of law.

plain·tive, plān′tiv, *a*. Expressive of sorrow; voicing melancholy. —**plain·tive·ly**, *adv*. —**plain·tive·ness**, *n*.

plait, plāt, plat, *n*. A fold or pleat; a braid, as of hair or straw. Also **plat**.—*v.t.* To fold; to double in narrow strips; to braid; to interweave the locks or strands of. —**plait·ing**, *n*.

plan, plan, *n*. A devised scheme; a way of executing an act; a method or arrangement; an aim or project; the representation of anything drawn on a plane and forming a map or chart; the representation of a horizontal section of a building, showing the extent, division, and distribution of its area into apartments and passages.—*v.t.*, **planned, plan·ning**. To invent or contrive for construction; to scheme; to devise; to form in design.—*v.i.* —**plan·less**, *a*. —**plan·ner**, *n*.

plane, plān, *n*. A carpenter's hand tool with an oblique cutting blade, used in trimming, leveling, smoothing, or shaping a piece of wood or wood surface.—*v.t.*, **planed, plan·ing**. To make smooth, esp. by the use of a plane.—*v.i.* To work with a plane; to work as a plane.

plane, plān, *n*. A smooth or level surface; a part of something having a level surface; an airplane; a surface such that if any two points in it be joined by a straight line, the whole of the straight line will be in the surface; a certain position of achievement, development, living, or the like.—*a*. Without elevations or depressions; even; level; flat; concerned with level surfaces: *plane* geometry.—*v.i.*, **planed, plan·ing**. To soar, as a glider; to skim across water, as a speedboat; to go by plane.

plan·er, plā′nər, *n*. A power machine that smoothes or finishes metal or wood surfaces; a thing that or one who planes.

plan·et, plan′it, *n*. Any one of the heavenly bodies revolving about the sun and shining by reflected light: Mercury, Venus, Earth, Mars, Jupiter, Saturn, Uranus, Neptune, and Pluto.

plan·e·tar·i·um, plan·ə·tār′ē·əm, *n. pl.*, **-ums, -a**. An astronomical mechanism which, by the movement of its parts, represents the motions and orbits of the planets and other heavenly bodies on a domed ceiling; the building in which this mechanism is housed.

plan·e·tar·y, plan′i·ter·ē, *a*. Of, pertaining to, or resembling a planet or the planets.

plan·e·toid, plan′i·toyd, *n*. Any of a numerous group of very small planets between the orbits of Mars and Jupiter; an asteroid.

plan·ish, plan′ish, *v.t.* To make smooth, as wood; to condense, smooth, and toughen, as a metallic pilate, by light blows of a hammer; polish. —**plan·ish·er**, *n*.

---

a- hat, fâte, fâre, fäther; e- met, mē; i- pin, pīne; o- not, nōte, ôrb, moove (move), boy, pownd; u- cūbe, bûll, tûk (took); ch- chin; th- thick, ŧhen; zh- vizhon (vision); ə- əgo, takən, pencəl, lemən, bərd (bird).

plank, plangk, *n.* A long, flat piece of timber thicker than a board; timber in such pieces; something to stand on or to cling to for support; an article in a platform of political or other principles.—*v.t.* To lay, cover, or furnish with planks. —**walk the plank,** to be compelled, as prisoners of pirates, to walk off a plank extending over the water from a ship's side.

plank·ing, plang'king, *n.* The act of laying or covering with planks; planks collectively, as in a floor.

plank·ton, plangk'tən, *n.* The mass of small organisms, plant and animal, floating or drifting in a body of water. —**plank·ton·ic,** plangk·ton'ik, *a.*

plant, plant, plänt, *n.* One of the organisms of the vegetable kingdom, as distinct from the animal kingdom, having cellulose cell walls and in green plants able to manufacture food from inorganic materials; a seedling ready for transplanting; a slip or cutting. The fixtures, machinery, tools, and sometimes the buildings, necessary to carry on any trade or business; the buildings and other equipment of any institution; a person who is put into an audience to take an apparently spontaneous part in proceedings. *Informal.* A scheme to trick or swindle; a person or thing placed to trap or mislead.—*v.t.* To put in the ground for growth; to sow with seeds or furnish with plants, as a plot of land; to establish in the mind, as a belief; to stock or furnish with animals; to fix or set in position. *Informal.* To place forcefully, as a punch; to station or place for purposes of observation or discovery: to *plant* a spy in a smuggling ring, to *plant* evidence; to conceal, as stolen articles. —**plant·a·ble,** *a.* —**plant·like,** *a.*

plan·tain, plan'tin, *n.* A common dooryard weed with broad, strongly ribbed, basal leaves and long tight flower heads.

plan·tain, plan'tin, *n.* A tropical plant in the banana family, whose cooked fruit is an important food in the tropics.

plan·ta·tion, plan·tā'shən, *n.* A large estate, esp. in warm climates, planted in various crops and cultivated chiefly by resident workers; the act of planting for growth; the area planted.

plant·er, plan'tər, plän'tər, *n.* One who plants; the owner or occupant of a plantation; an implement or machine for planting seeds; an ornamental container, of various shapes and materials, in which plants can be grown.

plant louse, *n.* An aphid, or any of several related insects which infest plants.

plaque, plak, *n.* A thin flat plate or tablet of metal or porcelain, intended for ornament, as on a wall or set in a piece of furniture; a platelike brooch or ornament, esp. one worn as the badge of an honorary order.

plasm, plaz'əm, *n.* Plasma.

plas·ma, plaz'mə, *n.* A nearly colorless fluid in which the corpuscles of the blood are suspended; a human blood product used for transfusions and prepared by removing all red cells, white cells, and platelets from whole blood; protoplasm. —**plas·mic, plas·mat·ik,** plaz·mat'ik, *a.*

plas·ter, plas'tər, plä'stər, *n.* A pasty composition, as of lime, sand, water, and often hair, used for covering walls and ceilings, where it hardens in drying; a solid or semisolid preparation for spreading upon cloth and applying to the body for some remedial or other purpose; plaster of Paris.—*v.t.* To apply or to cover with plaster; to overspread with anything, esp. thickly or to excess: to *plaster* a wall with photographs; to lay flat like a layer of plaster. —**plas·ter·er,** *n.* —**plas·ter·ing,** *n.* —**plas·ter·work,** *n.*

plas·ter·board, plas'tər·bôrd, pläs'tər·bôrd, *n.* Large boardlike sheets having an inner core of hardened gypsum bonded to outer layers of paper, felt, or other fiber, used for insulating or forming walls.

plas·tered, plas'tərd, plä'stərd, *a. Informal.* Intoxicated; drunk.

plas·ter of Par·is, plas·ter of par·is, par'is, *n.* Calcined gypsum, a white powdery material which sets rapidly when mixed with water, used for making casts and molds.

plas·tic, plas'tik, *a.* Having the power of molding or shaping formless or yielding material: the *plastic* force which molds society; pertaining to molding or modeling, as in sculpture and ceramics: *plastic* figures; pliable; impressionable; concerned with the remedying or restoring of malformed, injured, or lost parts: *plastic* surgery; pertaining to the formation of new tissue in the living body.—*n.* Any of various natural or synthetic, usu. resinous, organic substances, which, when subjected to heat and pressure, can be cast, pressed, extruded, or molded into a variety of shapes; anything that can be molded. —**plas·ti·cal·ly,** *adv.* —**plas·tic·i·ty,** pla·stis'i·tē, *n.* —**plas·ti·ciz·er,** plas'ti·si·zər, *n.*

plat, plat, *v.t.* **plat·ted, plat·ting.** To interweave; to plait.—*n.* Braid; plait.

plate, plāt, *n.* A shallow, usu. circular vessel, from which food is eaten; the contents of such a vessel; a service of food for one person at table; a course served on one plate: a thin, flat sheet or piece of metal or other material, esp. of uniform thickness; metal in such sheets; a flat, polished piece of metal on which something may be or is engraved; such a piece engraved to print from; plated metallic ware; a platelike part, structure, or organ; a piece of metal or other firm substance with artificial teeth attached, worn in the mouth after the loss of natural teeth; a sensitized sheet of glass or metal, on which to take a photograph; one of the interior elements of a vacuum tube; a timber laid horizontally, as in a wall, to receive the ends of other timbers. *Baseball.* Home base. *Mining.* Shale.—*v.t.* **plat·ed, plat·ing.** To cover or overlay with metal plates for protection; coat with a thin film of gold, silver, or nickel by mechanical means. —**plat·er,** *n.*

pla·teau, pla·tō', *n. pl.,* **-teaus, -teaux,** -tōz. A broad, flat area of somewhat elevated land; a tableland; a time or area in the development of something evidenced by neither progress nor decline.—*v.i.* To make stable; to reach a plateau.

plate·ful, plāt'fûl, *n. pl.,* **-fuls.** As much as a plate will hold.

plate glass, *n.* A fine kind of glass, cast in thick plates, used for mirrors and large windowpanes.

plate·let, plāt'lit, *n.* A minute plate or platelike body; a blood platelet.

plat·form, plat'fôrm, *n.* Any flat or horizontal structure raised above an adjoining level; the raised walk at a railroad station for landing passengers and goods; a place raised above the floor of a hall set apart for the speakers at public meetings; the aggregate of principles adopted or avowed by any body of people, such as a political party.

plat·form car, *n.* Flatcar.

plat·ing, plā'ting, *n.* The action of one who or that which plates; a thin coating of gold, silver, or nickel; an external layer of metal plates.

plat·i·num, plat'ə·nəm, *n.* A heavy, grayish-white metallic element, ductile and resistant to most chemicals, used for jewelry and in chemistry, dentistry, electronics, and industry.

plat·i·num blonde, *n.* An extremely light hair color, nearing white, but having a slightly metallic tinge or sheen, usu. artificial; one whose hair is such a color.

plat·i·tude, plat'i·tood, plat'i·tūd, *n.* A trite or dull remark; dullness; repetition of the obvious. —**plat·i·tu·di·nal, plat·i·tu·di·nous,** plat·ə·too'də·nəl, plat·ə·too'də·nəs, *a.*

plat·i·tu·di·nize, plat·ə·too'də·nīz, plat·ə·tū'də·nīz, *v.i.,* **-nized, -niz·ing.** To utter platitudes.

Pla·ton·ic, plə·ton'ik, *a.* Of or pertaining to the Greek philosopher Plato or his doctrines; *(l.c.)* purely spiritual or free from sensual desire, as applied to love or friendship between persons of the opposite sex; of persons, feeling or professing such love. —**pla·ton·i·**

cal·ly, *adv.*

pla·toon, plə·tōōn´, *n.* A unit of a company, troop, or battery, comprised of a headquarters and two or more squads or sections and commanded by a commissioned officer, usu. a second lieutenant; group, body, or unit of people, usu. with something in common: a *platoon* of firemen.

plat·ter, plat´ər, *n.* A plate; a large, shallow, serving dish, esp. one that is oval-shaped.

plat·y·pus, plat´ə·pəs, *n. pl.,* **-pus·es, -pi,** -pī. One of the most primitive mammals, having such birdlike characteristics as webbed feet, a bill similar to a duck's, and the ability to lay eggs.

plau·dit, plô´dit, *n. Usu. pl.* Applause; praise bestowed.

plau·si·ble, plô´zə·bəl, *a.* Apparently right; using arguments that may be open to question; convincingly spoken. **—plau·si·bil·i·ty**, plô·zə·bil´ə·tē, **plau·si·ble·ness**, *n.* **—plau·si·bly**, *adv.*

play, plā, *n.* A dramatic performance, as on the stage; a dramatic composition; amusement or recreation; diversion; sport; fun; the carrying on of a game; manner of playing; an act or performance in playing; turn to play; the state, as of a ball, of being played with or in use: in *play*; gambling; amusement of children; action, conduct, or dealing of a specific kind: fair *play*, foul *play*; light and quick, alternating or irregular, motion: the *play* of lights on a fountain; action, activity, or operation; freedom of movement within a space, as of a part of a mechanism; freedom for action, or scope for activity.—*v.t.* To perform, as a drama, on or as on the stage; act the part of in a drama or in real life; to give performances in: to *play* the larger cities; to do, perform, or execute; to engage in a game or pastime; represent or imitate in sport: to *play* school; to wager; lay a wager or wagers on; to contend against in a game; to employ, as a player, in a game; to move or employ, in playing a game; to use as if in playing a game; to perform, as music, on an instrument; perform on, as a musical instrument; to cause to move or change lightly or quickly: to *play* colored lights on a fountain; to allow, as a hooked fish, to exhaust itself by pulling on the line; to operate or cause to operate, esp. continuously or with repeated action: to *play* a hose on a fire.—*v.i.* To engage in diversion, amusement, or recreation; sport; to do something only in sport, which is not to be taken seriously; to amuse oneself or toy *(with)*: to *play with* the ball; trifle; to take part in a game; to take part in a game for stakes; gamble; to act in a specified way: to *play* fair; to perform on a musical instrument; of the instrument or the music, to sound in performance; to act on or as on the stage; perform; to move freely within a space, as a part of a mechanism; to operate continuously or with repeated action, often on something; to move about lightly or quickly; move lightly or quickly with alternating or irregular motion, as flames, waves, or wind. **—make a play for.** *Informal.* To try to enter into a sexual relationship; to try to profit by making a favorable impression. **—play back**, to run through (a recently recorded disc or tape). **—play down**, to minimize. **—play in·to a per·son's hands**, to act in such a way as to give him or her an advantage. **—play off**, to decide (a tie) by a play-off, to oppose one against another. **—play on** or **up·on**, to work on the feelings or weaknesses of another for one's own purposes. **—play out**, to finish; unwind; be or become exhausted. **—play the game**, to play or behave fairly. **—play up**, to emphasize. **—play up to.** *Informal.* To attempt to curry favor; flatter. **—play·a·ble**, *a.*

play·act, plā´akt, *v.i.* To pretend.—*v.t.* To act out or dramatize. **—play·act·ing**, *n.*

play·back, plā´bak, *n.* The act of translating back into sound, as a tape recording; an apparatus used for the reproduction of sound recordings; the recording so reproduced.

play·bill, plā´bil, *n.* A placard or other notice exhibited as an advertisement of a play.

play·boy, plā´boy, *n.* A man whose time is spent in the type of pleasure-producing activities found at parties, nightclubs, etc.

play·er, plā´ər, *n.* One who plays; an actor; a musician; a gambler; a thing or automatic device that plays.

play·er pi·an·o, *n.* A type of piano which plays automatically by means of a mechanical device contained within the instrument.

play·ful, plā´fəl, *a.* Sportive; full of sprightly humor; amusing. **—play·ful·ly**, *adv.* **—play·ful·ness**, *n.*

play·go·er, plā´gō·ər, *n.* One who frequents the theater.

play·ground, plā´grownd, *n.* A piece of ground set apart for open-air recreation, esp. one connected with a school.

play·house, plā´hows, *n. pl.,* **-hous·es.** A theater; a house to play in: a child's *playhouse*; a toy house.

play·ing card, plā´ing, *n.* One of a set or pack of cards for use in playing games; one of the well-known set of 52 cards in four suits (diamonds, hearts, spades, and clubs).

play·let, plā´lit, *n.* A short, dramatic play.

play·mate, plā´māt, *n.* A companion in play.

play·off, plā´ôf, plā´of, *n.* An additional game or part of a game played in a contest in the event of a tie; a succession of games to determine a championship.

play·pen, plā´pen, *n.* A small, movable enclosure for a very young child to play in.

play·thing, plā´thing, *n.* A toy.

play·time, plā´tīm, *n.* Time for play.

play·wright, plā´rīt, *n.* An author of plays.

pla·za, plä´zə, plaz´ə, *n.* A public square in a city.

plea, plē, *n.* A pleading or appeal; that which is alleged in support, justification, or defense; an excuse.

plead, plēd, *v.i.,* **plead·ed** or **plead, plead·ing.** To argue in support of a claim, or in defense against the claim of another; to urge reasons for or against.—*v.t.* To discuss, defend, and attempt to maintain by arguments or reasons. **—plead·a·ble**, *a.* **—plead·er**, *n.* **—plead·ing**, *a., n.*

pleas·ant, plez´ənt, *a.* Pleasing; agreeable; enjoyable. **—pleas·ant·ly**, *adv.* **—pleas·ant·ness**, *n.*

pleas·ant·ry, plez´ən·trē, *n. pl.,* **-ries.** A humorous remark or action; a jest; banter.

please, plēz, *v.t.,* **pleased, pleas·ing.** To gratify, satisfy, or content; to be the will or desire of: May it *please* the court; to be so obliging or kind as to, used in the imperative with a request: *Please* pass the salt.—*v.i.* To give pleasure; to like or prefer: Do it whenever you *please*.

pleas·ing, plē´zing, *a.* Giving pleasure or satisfaction. **—pleas·ing·ly**, *adv.* **—pleas·ing·ness**, *n.*

pleas·ur·a·ble, plezh´ər·ə·bəl, *a.* Pleasing. **—pleas·ur·a·ble·ness**, *n.* **—pleas·ur·a·bly**, *adv.*

pleas·ure, plezh´ər, *n.* The feeling produced by the enjoyment or expectation of good; delight; a state of agreeable sensations or emotions; a source of gratification or happiness; amusement or entertainment; sensual gratification; will or choice: to go or stay at one's *pleasure*.

pleat, plēt, *n.* A fold of definite, even width made by doubling cloth upon itself, and pressing, stitching, or otherwise fastening in place.—*v.t.* To fold or arrange in pleats. Also **plait.** **—pleat·ed**, *a.* **—pleat·er**, *n.*

pleb, pleb, *n.* A plebeian; a plebe.

plebe, plēb, *n.* A member of the lowest class at the U.S. Military Academy and the U.S. Naval Academy.

ple·be·ian, plə·bē´ən, *a.* Pertaining to the common people; vulgar; common.—*n.* One of the common

---

a- hat, fāte, fāre, fäther; **e-** met, mē; **i-** pin, pīne; **o-** not, nōte, ôrb, moove (move), boy, pownd; **u-** cūbe, bůll, tůk (took); **ch-** chin; **th-** thick, then; **zh-** vizhon (vision); **ə-** əgo, takən, pencəl, lemən, bərd (bird).

people.

pleb·i·scite, pleb′ə·sīt, pleb′ə·sit, *n.* A vote by the qualified voters of a whole community or nation, in order to determine the popular will on some public issue.

pledge, plej, *n.* A promise; a formal agreement to perform or refrain from performing some act; anything given as security for the payment of a debt or for performance of some agreement or obligation; the state of being held as such security: property being held in *pledge;* one who has promised to join a fraternity or other social group, but has not been formally accepted.—*v.t.,* **pledged, pledg·ing.** To promise; to give as a pledge or pawn; to bind or engage solemnly; to drink a toast to. —**pledg·ee,** plej·ē′, *n.* —**pledg·er, pledg·or,** plej′ôr, *n.*

ple·na·ry, plē′nə·rē, plen′ə·rē, *a.* Full; complete; attended by all qualified members, as a meeting.

plen·i·po·ten·ti·ar·y, plen·i·pə·ten′shē·er·ē, plen·i·pə·ten′shə·rē, *n. pl.,* **-ies.** A person invested with full power to transact any business, as an ambassador or envoy.—*a.*

plen·i·tude, plen′i·tood, plen′i·tūd, *n.* The state of being full or complete; plenty.

plen·te·ous, plen′tē·əs, *a.* Abundant. —**plen·te·ous·ly,** *adv.*

plen·ti·ful, plen′ti·fəl, *a.* Existing in great plenty; abundant; ample. —**plen·ti·ful·ly,** *adv.*

plen·ty, plen′tē, *n.* An abundance; a full or adequate supply; an abundance of the necessities and luxuries of life: a time of *plenty.*—*a. Informal.* Plentiful; being in abundance; ample.—*adv. Informal.* Sufficiently.

pleth·o·ra, pleth′ər·ə, *n.* Overfullness; superabundance. —**ple·thor·ic,** ple·thôr′ik, pleth′ə·rik, *a.*

pleu·ra, plûr′ə, *n. pl.,* **pleu·rae,** plûr′ē. A thin membrane which covers the inside of the thorax and also invests the lungs. —**pleu·ral,** *a.*

pleu·ri·sy, plûr′i·sē, *n.* An inflammation of the pleura, often accompanied by fever and respiratory difficulty. —**pleu·rit·ic,** plû·rit′ik, *a.*

plex·us, plek′səs, *n. pl.,* **-us·es, -us.** A network of vessels, nerves, or fibers; any complicated structure forming a network of interlacing parts.

pli·a·ble, plī′ə·bəl, *a.* Bent easily; flexible; flexible in disposition; easily persuaded; adaptable. —**pli·a·bil·i·ty,** plī·ə·bil′i·tē, **pli·a·ble·ness,** *n.* —**pli·a·bly,** *adv.*

pli·ant, plī′ənt, *a.* Easily bent; readily yielding to force or pressure without breaking; flexible; limber; plastic; easily persuaded. —**pli·an·cy, pli·ant·ness,** *n.* —**pli·ant·ly,** *adv.*

pli·ca·tion, plī·kā′shən, *n.* A folding or fold; the folded state. Also **plic·a·ture,** plik′ə·chûr.

pli·ers, plī′ərz, *n. pl., sing. or pl. in constr.* A small pair of pincers with long jaws adapted to holding small articles and to bending and shaping wire.

plight, plīt, *n.* Condition or situation, usu. a bad one: to be in a sorry *plight.*

plight, plīt, *v.t.* To pledge in engagement to marry: to *plight* one's troth; to give in pledge, as one's word of honor.

plink, plingk, *v.i.* To shoot at targets chosen at random; to make a light, sharp, jingling sound.—*v.t.* To shoot at informally or casually: to *plink* old tin cans; to cause to make a light, sharp, jingling sound.—*n.* The sound of plinking.

plod, plod, *v.i.,* **plod·ded, plod·ding.** To walk heavily or trudge; to work with dull perseverance; to drudge. —*v.t.* To walk heavily over or along.—*n.* The act of plodding; a sound of or as of a heavy tread. —**plod·der,** *n.* —**plod·ding,** *a.*

plop, plop, *v.i.,* **plopped, plop·ping.** To make a sound like that of a flat object striking water without a splash; to fall plump: She *plopped* into bed.—*v.t.* To let loose or throw with a heavy drop.—*n.* A plopping sound or fall; the act of plopping.—*adv.* With a plop.

plot, plot, *n.* A small piece of land, esp. one devoted to a special purpose; a plan or chart, as of an estate or building; a secret scheme, esp. one with an evil or illegal purpose; the main story or scheme of a play, poem, or novel.—*v.t.,* **plot·ted, plot·ting.** To make a plan or chart of; to mark on a map or plan, as a course or position; to secretly contrive and plan for; to create or draft the plot of, as a novel.—*v.i.* To form plots; conspire. —**plot·ter,** *n.*

plow, plow, *n.* An agricultural implement for cutting furrows and in turning up the soil, as for sowing or planting; any of various implements resembling or suggesting this, as a kind of tool for cutting grooves or a contrivance for clearing away snow from a road or track.—*v.t.* To make furrows in or turn up, as the soil, with a plow; to make, as a furrow, ridge, or groove, with, or as if with a plow.—*v.i.* To work with a plow; to move through anything in the manner of a plow; plod. Also **plough.** —**plow back,** to put back, as profits, into a business. —**plow un·der,** to obliterate or cause to disappear. —**plow·a·ble,** *a.* —**plow·er,** *n.* —**plow·man,** *n. pl.,* **-men.**

plow·share, plow′sher, *n.* The cutting edge of a plow.

ploy, ploy, *n.* A stratagem designed to disorient or defeat an enemy or rival; a maneuver; a tactic.

pluck, plək, *v.t.* To pick or pull: to *pluck* a blossom; to vibrate the strings of (a musical instrument) by a similar action; to jerk out or remove the feathers of: to *pluck* a chicken; to snatch or drag, with *off, away.*—*v.i.* To twitch; pull sharply.—*n.* The act of picking or plucking; courage and tenacity. —**pluck·er,** *n.*

pluck·y, plək′ē, *a.,* **-i·er, -i·est.** Spirited; courageous. —**pluck·i·ly,** *adv.* —**pluck·i·ness,** *n.*

plug, pləg, *n.* Any piece of wood or other material used to stop a hole; an electrical device fitting like a plug into an opening or openings of an outlet to establish a connected circuit; a spark plug; a fireplug; a cake of tobacco, usu. for chewing. *Informal.* Something worn-out or inferior; favorable publicity; a shot or bullet.—*v.t.,* **plugged, plug·ging.** To insert, as a plug; to make tight by stopping with a plug. *Informal.* To publicize a product favorably; to punch; to shoot.—*v.i. Informal.* To work steadily; to shoot at; to back a cause or individual. —**plug in,** to insert a plug in an outlet to complete an electrical connection. —**plug·ger,** *n.*

plum, pləm, *n.* The edible fruit of a small tree in the rose family, smooth-skinned, and containing an oblong stone; the tree itself; a color varying in shade from light to dark reddish purple. *Informal.* Some desirable thing: the *plums* given out by the party in power. —**plum·like,** *a.*

plum·age, ploo′mij, *n.* Feathers collectively; the entire feathery covering of a bird.

plumb, pləm, *n.* A small weight of lead or other heavy material, esp. one attached to a line and used in testing the perpendicularity of walls or in sounding; a plummet.—*a.* True according to a plumb line; perpendicular; vertical. *Informal.* Downright or absolute. —*adv.* In a perpendicular or vertical direction; exactly, precisely, or directly. *Informal.* Completely or absolutely: He is *plumb* crazy. Also **plum.**—*v.t.* To test or adjust by a plumb line; make vertical; to sound with or as with a plumb line, as the ocean. —**out of plumb, off plumb,** not vertical; out of alignment.

plumb bob, *n.* The bob or weight of a plumb line.

plumb·er, pləm′ər, *n.* One who fits and repairs water and drainage pipes.

plumb·ing, pləm′ing, *n.* Plumber's trade or work; the assemblage of pipes and fixtures used to convey water and waste; the act of using a plumb.

plumb line, *n.* A cord having a metal weight attached to one end, used to determine the true vertical or perpendicular direction, and for sounding; a line of exact vertical direction.

plume, ploom, *n.* The feather of a bird, particularly a large or conspicuous feather; a feather or collection of feathers worn as an ornament, token of honor, or prize; plumage.—*v.t.,* **plumed, plum·ing.** To preen; to

adorn with feathers or plumes. —**plume·like,** *a.*
—**plum·y,** *a.,* **-i·er, -i·est.**

plum·met, pləm′it, *n.* A plumb bob.—*v.i.* To drop or plunge straight down.

plump, pləmp, *v.i.* To fall heavily or suddenly.—*v.t.* To drop or throw heavily or suddenly, often with *down*; to utter or say bluntly, often with *out*; to praise or publicize favorably.—*n.* A heavy or sudden fall; the sound caused by this fall.—*adv.—a.* Direct; downright; blunt. —**plump·er,** *n.*

plump, pləmp, *a.* Well filled out or rounded in form; somewhat fleshy or fat; chubby.—*v.t.* To make plump; to fatten, often with *up* or *out.—v.i.* To become plump, often with *up* or *out.* —**plump·ly,** *adv.* —**plump·ness,** *n.*

plun·der, plən′dər, *v.t.* To rob of goods or valuables forcibly; pillage.—*v.i.* To commit looting.—*n.* The act of plundering; robbing; that which is taken by theft; robbery or fraud. —**plun·der·er,** *n.* —**plun·der·ous,** *a.*

plunge, plənj, *v.t.,* **plunged, plung·ing.** To thrust into water or other fluid substance, or into any easily penetrable substance; to immerse; to thrust; to drive into any state or condition; to place, as a potted plant, into sand or soil.—*v.i.* To thrust or drive oneself into water or a declivity; to drive or to rush in; to fall or rush impulsively into some situation; to descend suddenly, as on a hill or road.—*n.* A dive, rush, or leap into something; a place for diving.

plung·er, plən′jər, *n.* One who plunges; a pistonlike cylinder sometimes used in force pumps; a device consisting of a suction cup at one end of a stick, used in unclogging drains.

plunk, pləngk, *v.t. Informal.* To strum or pluck, as the strings of a stringed instrument; to throw or push heavily or suddenly, usu. followed by *down.—v.i. Informal.* To give forth a twanging sound; to drop down heavily or suddenly.—*n.* The act or sound of plunking.—*adv.* —**plunk·er,** *n.*

plu·ral, plûr′əl, *a.* Containing more than one; consisting of, involving, or designating two or more.—*n.* The plural number; a form of a word expressing more than one. Abbr. **pl.** —**plu·ral·ly,** *adv.* —**plu·ral·ize,** *v.t.,* **-ized, -iz·ing.**

plu·ral·ism, plûr′əl·iz·əm, *n.* The quality of being plural; the nature of a society within which diverse ethnic, social, and cultural interests exist and develop together. —**plu·ral·ist,** *n.* —**plu·ral·is·tic,** plûr·ə·lis′tik, *a.*

plu·ral·i·ty, plû·ral′i·tē, *n. pl.,* **-ties.** The state of being plural; the greater number; a multitude; the majority; the excess of votes for one candidate over those for another, esp. when there are more than two candidates and none receives over half the total votes.

plus, pləs, *a.* More, by a certain amount; involving or denoting addition: a *plus* quantity, or having *plus* values; positive. *Informal.* With something in addition: The new car has power *plus.—n.* The plus sign; a plus quantity; something additional; a surplus or gain. —*prep.* More by the addition of, or increased by: 10 *plus* 3; with the addition of; with.

plush, pləsh, *n.* A fabric with a nap longer than that of velvet.—*a.* Made of plush; luxurious. —**plush·i·ness,** *n.* —**plush·y,** *a.,* **-i·er, -i·est.**

plus sign, *n. Math.* A symbol, +, signifying either addition or a positive quantity.

plu·toc·ra·cy, ploo·tok′rə·sē, *n. pl.,* **-cies.** Government by the wealthy; a ruling class of wealthy people. —**plu·to·crat,** ploo′tə·krat, *n.* —**plu·to·crat·ic,** ploo·tə·krat′ik, *a.*

plu·to·ni·um, ploo·tō′nē·əm, *n.* A synthetic radioactive element produced by bombarding neptunium from uranium 235 indirectly with neutrons.

plu·vi·al, ploo′vē·əl, *a.* Rainy; relating to rain.

ply, plī, *n. pl.,* **plies.** An individual layer or thickness, as

in fabric or plywood; one twist or strand of thread, rope, or yarn. A tendency; a prejudice.—*v.t.,* **plied, ply·ing.** To twist, mold, or bend.

ply, plī, *v.t.,* **plied, ply·ing.** To employ with diligence: to *ply* a needle; to practice or work at: to *ply* the trade of mason; to furnish with or offer insistently: to *ply* a guest with food; to question constantly; to run or travel, as on a schedule.—*v.i.* To work steadily; to offer service; to run regularly between any two places, as a vessel or vehicle.

ply·wood, plī′wûd, *n.* A building material consisting of two or more thin sheets, strips, or layers of wood glued together.

p.m., P.M., pē′em′, *n.* After noon.

pneu·mat·ic, noo·mat′ik, nū·mat′ik, *a.* Consisting of, resembling, or pertaining to air, gas, or wind; moved or played by means of air, as an organ; filled with or fitted to contain air, as a tire; operated by means of the compression or exhaustion of air, as an air hammer. —**pneu·mat·i·cal·ly,** *adv.*

pneu·mat·ics, noo·mat′iks, nū·mat′iks, *n. pl. but sing. in constr.* That branch of physics treating of the mechanical properties of air and other gases.

pneu·mo·nia, nû·mōn′yə, nyû·mōn′yə, *n.* Inflammation of the lungs; an acute infectious disease of the lungs, either viral or bacteriological in origin.

pneu·mon·ic, nû·mon′ik, nyû·mon′ik, *a.* Of or having pneumonia; pulmonary.

poach, pōch, *v.t.* To cook in simmering water or other liquid, as eggs.

poach, pōch, *v.i.* To intrude or trespass on the property of another in order to catch game or fish; to steal game or fish.—*v.t.* —**poach·er,** *n.*

pock, pok, *n.* A pustule raised on the surface of the body in an eruptive disease, as smallpox; a pit or scar left on the skin by such a disease.

pock·et, pok′it, *n.* A small fabric pouch inserted in a garment, for carrying money or small articles; money or financial means; any pouchlike receptacle, hollow, or cavity; a small mass of ore; a small, isolated group or region: a *pocket* of infection; an air pocket.—*a.* Suitable for carrying in the pocket; small enough to go in the pocket; diminutive.—*v.t.* To put into one's pocket; to take possession of as one's own, often dishonestly; to enclose or confine, as in a pocket. —**in one's pock·et,** under one's control.

pock·et bil·liards, *n. pl. but sing. in constr.* See **pool.**

pock·et·book, pok′it·bûk, *n.* A small case or receptacle, as of leather, for papers or money, intended to be carried in the pocket; a woman's handbag; pecuniary resources.

pock·et e·di·tion, *n.* A book published in a size small enough to be fitted in the pocket. Also **pock·et·book** or **pock·et book.**

pock·et·ful, pok′it·fûl, *n.* As much as can be carried in a pocket.

pock·et·knife, pok′it·nīf, *n. pl.,* **-knives.** A knife with blades which fold into the handle, suitable for carrying in the pocket.

pock·et mon·ey, *n.* Money used for minor current expenses; spending money.

pock·et ve·to, *n.* An indirect veto of a bill by an executive through retention of the bill, unsigned, past the adjournment of the legislature.

pock·mark, pok′märk, *n.* A mark or scar on the skin made by smallpox or some other disease.—*v.t.* —**pock·marked,** *a.*

pod, pod, *n.* A more or less elongated, two-valved fruit, as that of the pea or bean; a general term for many dry fruits.—*v.i.,* **pod·ded, pod·ding.** To produce pods; to swell out like a pod. —**pod·like,** *a.*

podg·y, poj′ē, *a.,* **-i·er, -i·est.** Pudgy.

po·di·a·trist, pō·dī′ə·trist, pə·dī′ə·trist, *n.* One who

---

a- hat, fāte, fāre, fäther; **e-** met, mē; **i-** pin, pīne; **o-** not, nōte, ôrb, moove (move), boy, pownd; **u-** cūbe, bûll, tûk (took); **ch-** chin; **th-** thick, ŧhen; **zh-** vizhon (vision); **ə-** əgo, takən, pencəl, lemən, bərd (bird).

diagnoses and treats disorders of the human foot. Also **chi·rop·o·dist. —po·di·a·try,** *n.*

po·di·um, pō′dē·əm, *n. pl.,* **-a, -ums.** A small, raised platform or stand used by conductors and public speakers; a dais.

Po·dunk, pō′dungk, *n. Informal.* Any small town or village considered as backward, dull, and insignificant.

po·em, pō′əm, *n.* A verse composition, esp. one characterized by economy of linguistic expression, vivid imagery, and intense emotional tone; composition not in verse but characterized by beauty of form and emotional intensity: a symphonic *poem*; anything having qualities or effects reminiscent of poetry. **—po·et·ic,** pō·et′ik, **po·et·i·cal,** *a.* **—po·et·i·cal·ly,** *adv.*

po·e·sy, pō′ə·sē, pō′ə·zē, *n. pl.,* **-sies.** The art of or skill in composing poems; poetry.

po·et, pō′it, *n.* A person who writes poetry; one endowed with great imaginative and creative power. **—po·et·ess,** *n.*

po·et·ize, pō′i·tiz, *v.i.,* **-ized, -iz·ing.** To write poetry. *—v.t.* To express poetically; to treat poetically. **—po·et·iz·er,** *n.*

po·et lau·re·ate, *n. pl.,* **po·ets lau·re·ate.** The poet who is appointed a salaried lifetime honorary member of the British royal household; a poet considered the most renowned or most representative of a country or area.

po·et·ry, pō′i·trē, *n.* The art or craft of writing poems; poems collectively; something poetic; the quality, spirit, or effect of a poem or of something poetic.—*a.*

po·go stick, pō′gō *n.* A kind of pole containing a strong spring, with handles at the top and footrests near the bottom, propelled by jumping in a series of hops, and used esp. by children.

po·grom, pō·grom′, pō′grəm, *n.* Any organized massacre, esp. one directed against the Jews; an attack on a minority people.

poign·ant, poyn′yənt, poyn′ənt, *a.* Very painful or acute to the feelings; strong, piercing, or keen; pointed or precise; apt; moving or arousing the emotions; pungent. **—poign·an·cy,** *n.* **—poig·nant·ly,** *adv.*

poin·set·ti·a, poyn·set′ē·ə, *n.* A tropical winter-flowering shrub, native to America, having upper leaves which are red, pink, or white and surround the true, inconspicuous, greenish-yellow flowers, and often grown in greenhouses esp. for the Christmas trade.

point, poynt, *n.* The end of, or the mark made by the end of, a sharp piercing instrument, as a pin or needle; the tip of an extremity, as a fingertip; a tapering or sharp end, as of a pin; a tool or instrument which pricks or pierces; a mark of punctuation, as a period. *Geom.* That which has position but not extension: the *point* at which two lines intersect; a locality or place; a fixed or exactly indicated position; a limit or degree reached; a precise instant or moment; the essential or critical idea or thing: the *point* of the speech; a particular purpose: to gain one's *point*; a suggestion; a single element or fact of something: some good *points* in the book; *pl.,* the extremities of an animal, as of a dog; a unit of scoring; a unit of measurement; a unit of stock prices; a unit for measuring type; a protruding part, as of land; a cape; lace worked by a needle; point lace.—*v.t.* To direct, as the finger, toward an object or place; to aim; to indicate the position of or give attention to, often followed by *out*; to give a point to; to separate or mark with dots; to punctuate; to add to the point or force of, usu. followed by *up.*—*v.i.* To designate an object or direction by use of the finger, usu. followed by *to* or *at*; to direct the thought, attention, or mind; to indicate a tendency toward or probability of something; to face, lie in, or have an indicated direction. **—point·y,** *a.*

point-blank, poynt′blangk′, *a.* Aimed or fired directly at the mark; direct; plain; explicit; blunt.—*adv.*

point·ed, poyn′tid, *a.* Having a sharp point; aimed, as a gun; aimed at or expressly referring to some particular person; marked; pertinent; barbed, as wit or criticism. **—point·ed·ly,** *adv.* **—point·ed·ness,** *n.*

point·er, poyn′tər, *n.* One who or that which points; an indicator, as the needle on a gauge. *Informal.* A piece of beneficial advice or information; tip.

poin·til·lism, pwan′tə·liz·əm, *n.* A method in which paint is applied in points or dots of unmixed color, which are blended by the eye. **—poin·til·list,** *n.*

point lace, *n.* Needlepoint.

point·less, poynt′lis, *a.* Having no point or points; blunt; having no meaning, sense, or effectiveness, as a comment or act.

point of view, *n.* The position from which something is observed or appraised; personal standpoint; attitude; judgment.

poise, poyz, *n.* A balancing; equilibrium; self-possession during stress; composure; dignified bearing or movements; a suspension or wavering between two states, as between rest and motion.—*v.t.,* **poised, pois·ing.** To set or maintain an equilibrium; to hold in suspension between two states: *poised* himself to throw a ball; to remain in place precariously: to *poise* a golf ball at the cup.—*v.i.* To sustain equilibrium; to hover; to be prepared for a change of state: a bird *poised* for flight.

poi·son, poy′zən, *n.* Any agent that chemically destroys life or health upon contact with or absorption by an organism; something that taints, corrupts, or destroys.—*v.t.* To give poison to; to kill or harm with poison; to put poison in or on; to impair; corrupt. **—poi·son·er,** *n.* **—poi·son·ing,** *n.* **—poi·son·ous,** *a.*

poi·son i·vy, *n.* A woody N. American climber or vine with aerial rootlets, trifoliate leaves, and white berries and possessing an oil poisonous to the touch, causing a severe skin rash.

poi·son oak, *n.* An erect sumac, having no aerial rootlets, poisonous to the touch, and native to southeastern U.S.

poi·son·ous, poy′zə·nəs, *a.* Having the qualities or effects of poison.

poi·son-pen, poy′zən·pen′, *a.* Pertaining to malicious writings intended to threaten or destroy another's reputation.

poi·son su·mac, *n.* A highly poisonous shrub or small tree, a species of sumac with milky juice, smooth branches speckled with dark dots, pinnate leaves, and whitish berries, growing in swamps.

poke, pōk, *n.* A pouch; a small bag; a sack.

poke, pōk, *v.t.,* **poked, pok·ing.** To push or thrust something long or pointed against, as the hand, finger, or a stick; to cause by pushing, thrusting, or jabbing: to *poke* an opening; to hit; to push out, in, from, or through: to *poke* out of the snow; to force or rouse, often with *up*: to *poke* a fire *up.*—*v.i.* To push, jab, or thrust with the finger or a stick; to grope, as in the dark; to hit out at something; to search, followed by *about*; to intrude: to *poke* into a neighbor's business; to busy oneself without a definite object, followed by *about*; to push out obtrusively.—*n.* One who dawdles; a sudden push; a punch with the fist: to take a *poke* at. **—poke one's nose in·to,** to meddle. **—poke fun at,** to ridicule.

pok·er, pō′kər, *n.* One who pokes; something which pokes; an iron or steel bar or rod used in poking or stirring a fire.

pok·er, pō′kər, *n.* A gambling game played with cards in which a bet is made by each player on the value of the cards dealt to him.

pok·er face, *n. Informal.* An impassive face, appropriate for concealing the value of a poker hand; one who deliberately or habitually shows such a face.

pok·y, pō′kē, *a.,* **-i·er, -i·est.** Very slow; dull; narrow, cramped, or confined. Also **pok·ey. —pok·i·ly,** *adv.* **—pok·i·ness,** *n.*

pok·y, pok·ey, pō′kē, *n. pl.,* **-ies, -eys.** Jail.

po·lar, pō'lər, *a.* Pertaining to a pole or the poles of a sphere; pertaining to one of the poles of the earth; having direct opposites; being central; pivotal.

po·lar bear, *n.* A large, white bear of the arctic regions.

po·lar cir·cle, *n.* The Arctic or the Antarctic Circle, 23 degrees 27 minutes from the respective poles.

Po·lar·is, pō·lar'is, *n.* A star among the 20 brightest, which is located at the tip of the handle of the Little Dipper, the northernmost star in the constellation Ursa Minor; also **pole·star, North Star;** a two-staged guided missile capable of being fired from a submarine while submerged.

po·lar·i·ty, pō·lar'i·tē, *n. pl.,* **-ties.** The quality of possessing magnetic poles; the possession of an axis with reference to which certain physical properties are determined; a positive or negative polar condition, as in electricity; the possession of two opposite principles or tendencies.

po·lar·i·za·tion, pō·lər·i·zā'shən, *n.* The production or acquisition of polarity; a state, or the production of a state, in which rays of light exhibit different properties in different directions; the existence of two opposing or contrasting tendencies or principles.

po·lar·ize, pō'lə·rīz, *v.t., v.i.,* **-ized, -iz·ing.** To develop polarity or polarization in. **—po·lar·iz·a·ble,** pō·lə·rīz'ə·bəl, *a.* **—po·lar·iz·er,** *n.*

Po·lar·oid, pō'lə·royd, *n. Trademark.* A lens or other device that has been plastic-treated to polarize light passing through it.

pole, pōl, *n.* A long, slender piece of wood, metal, or other material; a perch or square rod equal to 30¼ square yards; a measure of length containing 16½ ft.—*v.t.,* **poled, pol·ing.** To support with poles; to bear or convey on poles.—*v.i.* To move a raft or boat with a pole. **—pole·less,** *a.*

pole, pōl, *n.* Each of the two points at which the axis of the earth cuts the celestial sphere, and about which the stars seem to revolve; each of the extremities of the axis of the earth or of any spherical body; either of two directly opposite opinions, principles, or tendencies; a focal point of interest or attention. *Phys.* Each of the two segments or parts of a magnet, electric battery, or dynamo at which certain opposite forces appear to be concentrated.

pole·cat, pōl'kat, *n.* A European carnivore similar to the weasel, having an offensive odor; a skunk.

po·lem·ic, pə·lem'ik, pō·lem'ik, *n.* Any controversial argument, particularly one attacking a strongly-held belief, principle, or doctrine; one who disputes another over a controversial issue.—*a.* **—po·lem·i·cal,** *a.* **—po·lem·i·cal·ly,** *adv.* **—po·lem·i·cist,** *n.*

po·lem·ics, pə·lem'iks, pō·lem'iks, *n. pl., sing. or pl. in constr.* The practice of arguing or debating subjects that are controversial in nature.

pole·star, pōl'stär, *n.* Polaris or the North Star; that which serves as a guide.

pole vault, *n.* An athletic field event featuring a vault or leap, generally over a horizontal bar, performed with the aid of a long pole. **—pole-vault,** pōl'vôlt, *v.i.* **—pole-vault·er,** *n.*

po·lice, pə·lēs', *n.* An organized civil force for maintaining order, preventing and detecting crime, and enforcing the laws. *Pl. in constr.* The members of such a force; the regulation and control of a community, esp. with reference to the maintenance of public order, safety, health, morals, and the like; any body of men and women officially maintained or employed to keep order and enforce regulations.—*v.t.,* **po·liced, po·lic·ing.** To regulate, control, or keep in order, by or as by use of the police.

po·lice dog, *n.* A dog of any kind used or trained to assist the police. *Informal.* Any dog of the German shepherd breed.

po·lice state, *n.* A country whose citizens are strictly controlled by governmental authority, esp. through a secret police force.

po·lice sta·tion, *n.* The headquarters of the police in a particular area, to which arrested persons are taken.

pol·i·cy, pol'ə·sē, *n. pl.,* **-cies.** The principles on which any measure or course of action is based; prudence or wisdom of governments or individuals in the management of their affairs, public or private.

pol·i·cy, pol'ə·sē, *n. pl.,* **-cies.** A written insurance contract; a lottery for gambling purposes.

pol·i·cy·hold·er, pol'ə·sē·hōl'dər, *n.* One who holds an insurance policy or contract.

po·li·o, pō'lē·ō, *n. Informal.* Poliomyelitis.

pol·i·o·my·e·li·tis, pol·ē·ō·mī·ə·lī'tis, pō·lē·ō·mī·ə·lī'tis, *n.* Inflammation of the gray matter of the spinal cord, esp. an infectious form causing motor paralysis followed by atrophy of the muscles, and sometimes with lasting disability.

pol·ish, pol'ish, *v.t.* To make smooth and glossy, usually by friction; to make elegant or refined; to bring to a finished state; perfect.—*v.i.* To take on a smooth and glossy surface, through being polished.—*n.* A substance used to impart a gloss; a gloss and smoothness of surface produced by friction; the process or act of polishing; elegance of manners; refinement of style. **—pol·ish off.** *Informal.* To finish rapidly; dispose of completely. **—pol·ish up.** *Informal.* To improve. **—pol·ish·er,** *n.*

po·lite, pə·līt', *a.* Showing by speech and behavior a considerate regard for others; polished; cultured: *polite* society; refined; well-bred. **—po·lite·ly,** *adv.* **—po·lite·ness,** *n.*

pol·i·tic, pol'i·tik, *a.* Prudent and sagacious; cunning; artful; political: body *politic.*

po·lit·i·cal, pə·lit'i·kəl, *a.* Pertaining to or involved in politics; pertaining to citizens or government; pertaining to or characteristic of politicians; having a fixed or organized system of government. **—po·lit·i·cal·ly,** *adv.*

po·lit·i·cal sci·ence, *n.* That science which deals with the structure, organization, and principles of government. **—po·lit·i·cal sci·en·tist,** *n.*

pol·i·ti·cian, pol·i·tish'ən, *n.* One versed in the science of government; one skilled in politics; one who occupies himself or herself with politics as a profession; one involved in politics for personal gain.

po·lit·i·cize, pə·lit'i·sīz, *v.i.,* **-cized, -ciz·ing.** To engage in or discuss politics.—*v.t.* To lend a political character to; to make political in nature.

pol·i·tick, pol'ə·tik, *v.i.* To engage in political activity. **—pol·i·tick·er,** *n.*

pol·i·tics, pol'ə·tiks, *n. pl., sing. or pl. in constr.* The science of government; political science; the policies and aims of a government of a nation or state; the conduct and contests of political parties; political affairs; political connections or beliefs of a person; the plotting or scheming of those seeking personal power, glory, position, or the like.

pol·i·ty, pol'ə·tē, *n. pl.,* **-ties.** The form or manner of government of a nation, state, or other institution; administrative control.

pol·ka, pōl'kə, pō'kə, *n.* A lively round dance of Bohemian origin, with music in duple time; a piece of music for such a dance or in its rhythm.—*v.i.,* **polkaed, pol·ka·ing.** To dance the polka.

pol·ka dot, *n.* A dot or round spot repeated to form a pattern on a textile fabric; a pattern of or a fabric with such dots.

poll, pōl, *n.* The head, esp. the part of it on which the hair grows; a person in a number or list; a list of individuals, as for taxing or voting; a survey of public opinion on a given subject; the voting at an election; the number of votes cast, or the numerical results of the voting: a heavy *poll. Usu. pl.* The place where votes are cast.—*v.t.* To cut off or cut short the hair, branches, horns, etc., of; crop; shear; to enroll in a list or register; to take or register the votes of; to receive at the polls, as votes; to cast at the polls, as a vote; to canvass in a survey.—*v.i.* To vote at the polls; give one's vote. **—poll•ee,** pō•lē′, **poll•er,** *n.*

pol•len, pol′ən, *n.* The male element in flowering plants made up of masses of fine, usu. yellow, powdery grains or microspores and produced in the anther of the stamen.

pol•len count, *n.* The average number of pollen grains of specified plants, usu. ragweed, in a cubic yard of air, taken over a 24-hour period at a stated place.

pol•li•nate, pol′ə•nāt, *v.t.,* **-nat•ed, -nat•ing.** To transfer pollen from the anther of a flower to the stigma of (the same or another flower), by wind, water, insect, or human. **—pol•li•na•tion,** pol•ə•nā′shən, **pol•li•na•tor,** *n.*

pol•li•wog, pol′ē•wog, *n.* A tadpole. Also **pol•ly•wog.**

poll•ster, pōl′stər, *n.* A poll taker.

poll tax, *n.* A tax on every person, esp. as a prerequisite for voting.

pol•lu•tant, pə•loot′ənt, *n.* Something that pollutes, esp. chemicals or refuse material released into the atmosphere or water.

pol•lute, pə•loot′, *v.t.,* **-lut•ed, -lut•ing.** To make foul or unclean; soil; taint; to corrupt or defile; make morally unclean. **—pol•lut•er,** *n.* **—pol•lu•tion,** *n.*

Pol•ly•an•na, pol•ē•an′ə, *n.* A blindly or overly optimistic person who tends to discover something good in everything.

po•lo, pō′lō, *n.* A game resembling hockey, played on horseback with long-handled mallets and a wooden ball; any game resembling this, as water polo. **—po•lo•ist,** *n.*

pol•o•naise, pol•ə•nāz′, pō•lə•nāz′, *n.* A slow, marchlike dance of Polish origin; music in three-four time, for or in the manner of such a dance.

po•lo•ni•um, pə•lō′nē•əm, *n.* A radioactive element discovered in pitchblende by M. and Mme. Curie.

pol•ter•geist, pōl′tər•gīst, *n.* A ghost or spirit which is said to manifest its presence by noises and other disturbances.

pol•y•an•dry, pol′ē•an•drē, pol•ē•an′drē, *n.* The practice of having more than one husband at the same time. **—pol•y•an•drous,** *a.*

pol•y•chro•mat•ic, pol•ē•krō•mat′ik, *a.* Exhibiting many colors.

pol•y•chrome, pol′ē•krōm, *a.* Having several or many colors.

pol•y•es•ter, pol′ē•es•tər, *n.* A long-chain ester of high molecular weight produced by polymerization and used chiefly in making fibers, resins, and plastics.

pol•y•eth•yl•ene, pol•ē•eth′ə•lēn, *n.* A polymer of ethylene, which is a plastic film widely used in packaging and electrical insulation.

po•lyg•a•mist, pə•lig′ə•mist, *n.* A person who practices polygamy.

po•lyg•a•my, pə•lig′ə•mē, *n.* The custom or practice of plural marriage; the state of having more than one wife or husband at the same time; the practice of simultaneously having more than one mate. **—po•lyg•a•mous,** *a.*

pol•y•glot, pol′ē•glot, *n.* A book containing many languages; a text made up of several languages; an individual who can speak or write a number of languages; a mixture of languages.—*a.* Versed in several languages; multilingual; composed of several languages.

pol•y•gon, pol′ē•gon, *n.* A closed plane figure with three or more straight sides; a figure on a sphere formed by arcs of great circles. **—po•lyg•o•nal,** pə•lig′ə•nəl, *a.* **—po•lyg•o•nal•ly,** *adv.*

pol•y•graph, pol′ē•graf, pol′ē•gräf, *n.* An instrument for multiplying copies of a writing; a prolific or many-

sided author; an instrument which records such bodily changes as fluctuations in blood pressure or heartbeat, and may be employed in lie detection. **—pol•y•graph•ic,** pol•ē•graf′ik, *a.*

po•lyg•y•ny, pə•lij′ə•nē, *n.* The condition of having more than one wife or female mate at one time. **—po•lyg•y•nous,** *a.*

pol•y•he•dron, pol•ē•hē′drən, *n. pl.,* **-drons, -dra.** A solid bounded by many plane faces. **—pol•y•he•dral,** *a.*

pol•y•mer, pol′i•mər, *n.* Any of two or more polymeric compounds.

pol•y•mer•ize, pə•lim′ə•rīz, pol′i•mə•rīz, *v.i., v.t.,* **-ized, -iz•ing.** To combine into a new compound with the same proportion of elements but with a greater molecular weight and different physical properties. **—po•lym•er•ism,** *n.* **—po•lym•er•i•za•tion,** pə•lim•ər•ə•zā′shən, pol•i•mər•ə•zā′shən, *n.*

pol•y•mor•phism, pol•i•môr′fiz•əm, *n.* The property of having, assuming, or passing through various forms, stages, characters, etc. **—pol•y•mor•phic, pol•y•mor•phous,** *a.*

pol•y•no•mi•al, pol•i•nō′mē•əl, *a.* Consisting of or pertaining to several names or terms.—*n.*

pol•yp, pol′ip, *n.* A sedentary coelenterate animal, either single, as hydras, or part of a colony, as coral, usu. having a hollow cylindrical body with a fixed base at one end and a mouth surrounded by tentacles at the other; a bulging or projecting mass of tissue that may be new growth, a center of infection, a malformation, or degenerative tissue.

pol•y•phon•ic, pol•i•fon′ik, *a.* Having two or more independent yet harmonizing melodic parts. **—po•lyph•o•ny,** pə•lif′ə•nē, *n.*

pol•y•sty•rene, pol•i•stī′rēn, *n.* A colorless transparent plastic, a polymer of styrene, used esp. as an insulator and in packaging and making molded products.

pol•y•syl•lab•ic, pol•i•si•lab′ik, *a.* Consisting of many, or more than three, syllables, as a word; characterized by such words, as a language. **—pol•y•syl•lab•i•cal•ly,** *adv.*

pol•y•syl•la•ble, pol′i•sil•ə•bəl, pol•i•sil′ə•bəl, *n.* A polysyllabic word.

pol•y•tech•nic, pol•i•tek′nik, *a.* Of or designating an educational institution in which instruction is given in many technical arts and applied sciences.—*n.* A school of instruction in applied sciences and technical arts.

pol•y•the•ism, pol′i•thē•iz•əm, *n.* The doctrine or worship of a plurality of gods. **—pol•y•the•ist,** *n.* **—pol•y•the•is•tic,** pol•i•thē•is′tik, **pol•y•the•is•ti•cal,** *a.*

pol•y•un•sat•u•rat•ed, pol•ē•ən•sach′ə•rā•tid, *a.* Of or pertaining to animal or vegetable fats having two or more double bonds per molecule: when consumed by humans, they help lower the cholesterol content in the blood.

pom•ace, pəm′is, *n.* The substance of apples or of similar fruit crushed by grinding; the pulpy matter or substance resulting from crushing or grinding.

po•made, pə•mād′, pə•mäd′, pō•mäd′, pō•mād′, *n.* A perfumed ointment used as a grooming aid for the hair and scalp.—*v.t.,* **po•mad•ed, po•mad•ing.** To groom with pomade.

pome•gran•ate, pom′gran•it, pəm′gran•it, pəm•gran′it, *n.* A globe-shaped, edible fruit as large as an orange, having a reddish, hard rind filled with a tasty, red, many-seeded pulp; the small tree, cultivated in warm climates, which produces this fruit.

pom•mel, pəm′əl, pom′əl, *n.* A knob or ball on the hilt of a sword, dagger, etc.; the protuberant part of the front and top of a saddle.—*v.t.,* **-meled, -mel•ing.** To beat with, or as if with, the fists or a pommel. Also **pum•mel.**

pomp, pomp, *n.* A display distinguished by splendor or magnificence; a pageant; magnificence; splendor;

pretentious display or show.

pom·pa·dour, pom/pə·dôr, pom/pə·dûr, *n.* An arrangement of a woman's hair in which it is raised above the forehead, usu. over a pad; a man's hair style in which the hair is brushed up from the forehead.

pom·pon, pom/pon, *n.* An ornament, as of wool or feathers, shaped into a ball or tuft, for a hat, slippers, or costumes; a type of chrysanthemum or dahlia having a small flower head resembling a pompon.

pomp·ous, pom/pəs, *a.* Exhibiting an exaggerated sense of dignity; high-flown and ornate, as speech; ostentatious; displaying pomp; splendid; showing self-importance. **—pom·pos·i·ty,** pom·pos/ə·tē, *n.* **—pomp·ous·ly,** *adv.* **—pomp·ous·ness,** *n.*

pon·cho, pon/chō, *n. pl.,* **-chos.** A garment, orig. from South America, like a blanket with a slit in the middle for the head to pass through; a raincoat constructed like a poncho.

pond, pond, *n.* A body of still water smaller than a lake, often formed artificially, as by damming a stream.

pon·der, pon/dər, *v.t.* To weigh carefully in the mind; to reflect upon; to examine carefully.*—v.i.* To think; to reflect seriously; to deliberate, often with *on* or *over.* **—pon·der·a·ble,** *a.* **—pon·der·er,** *n.*

pon·der·ous, pon/dər·əs, *a.* Very heavy; massive; unmanageable due to weight or size; stolid or dull. **—pon·der·ous·ly,** *adv.* **—pon·der·ous·ness,** *n.*

pon·iard, pon/yərd, *n.* A dagger.

pon·tiff, pon/tif, *n.* Chief priest; the Pope; a bishop.

pon·tif·i·cal, pon·tif/i·kəl, *a.* Of, pertaining to, or characteristic of a pontiff; papal; ostentatiously dogmatic. **—pon·tif·i·cal·ly,** *adv.*

pon·tif·i·cate, pon·tif/ə·kit, pon·tif/ə·kāt, *n.* The office or term of office of a pontiff.—pon·tif/ə·kāt, *v.i.,* **-cat·ed, -cat·ing.** To perform the function of a pontiff; to speak or behave dogmatically.

pon·toon, pon·toon/, *n.* A flat-bottomed boat or other float, as an airtight drum, used to support a temporary bridge spanning a river; an inflatable device used to raise a submerged vessel; a float on a seaplane.

po·ny, pō/nē, *n. pl.,* **po·nies.** A horse of a small breed, specif. one not over 14 hands high; a small horse, esp. in western U.S.; something small of its kind; a small glass for liquor, or the amount of liquor it will hold. *Informal.* A crib, translation, or other illicit aid.*—v.t., v.i.,* **-nied, -ny·ing.** *Informal.* To prepare lessons, by means of a pony or crib; to pay, as in settling an account, used with *up.*

po·ny ex·press, *n.* A postal system operated through the western U.S. during 1860-61, in which mail was carried by mounted relay riders.

po·ny·tail, pō/nē·tāl, *n.* A long hair style in which the hair is pulled to the back of the crown, gathered with a rubber band or clip, and left to fall free.

pooch, pooch, *n.* A dog.

poo·dle, poo/dəl, *n.* Any of several breeds of intelligent, solid-colored dogs with long, curly or silky hair.

pooh, poo, *interj.* An expression of scorn or contempt.

pooh-pooh, poo·poo/, *v.t.* To express scorn or contempt for; to sneer at.

pool, pool, *n.* A small body of standing, usu. fresh water; a small pond; a puddle; any small collection of liquid standing on a surface: a *pool* of blood; a still, deep place in a stream; a swimming pool.

pool, pool, *n.* A federation of competing parties to reconcile interests, control prices, or the like; a combination formed for speculation as for manipulating the prices of stocks; a combination of interests or funds for common advantage; a service or facility shared by a number of people: a car *pool;* the stakes in certain games; a game played by two or more persons on a billiard table with six pockets, the object of the game being to pocket balls numbered 1-15 by means of cues; also **pock·et bil·liards.**—*v.t.* To put, as interests or money, into a pool, or common stock or fund, as for distribution according to agreement; form a pool of; make a common interest of.*—v.i.* To enter into or form a pool.

pool·room, pool/room, pool/rûm, *n.* A place, usu. public, where pool or billiards is played; also **pool hall, pool·hall,** pool/hôl.

poop, poop, *n.* The stern of a ship; a short deck above the ordinary deck at the stern of a ship: also **poop deck.**—*v.t.* To break over the stern, as waves.

poop, poop, *v.t. Informal.* To exhaust or tire.*—v.i. Informal.* To become fatigued, usu. with *out;* to withdraw, usu. with *out.*

poop, poop, *n. Informal.* Information, possibly but not necessarily official.

poor, pûr, *a.* Having little or nothing in the way of wealth, goods, or means of subsistence; lacking means to procure the comforts or the necessities of life; characterized by or showing poverty; deficient or lacking in something specified: a region *poor* in mineral deposits; humble or insignificant; unfortunate. **—***n.* A poor person; poor persons collectively. **—poor·ish,** *a.* **—poor·ly,** *adv.* **—poor·ness,** *n.*

pop, pop, *n.* A popping; a short, quick, explosive sound; a shot with a firearm; an effervescent beverage, esp. one that is nonalcoholic.*—v.i.,* **popped, pop·ping.** To make a short, quick, explosive sound or report; to burst open with such a sound, as popcorn; to shoot with a firearm; to come or go quickly, suddenly, or unexpectedly, used with *in, into, out, off, down,* or *up;* protrude.*—v.t.* To cause to make a sudden, explosive sound; to put or thrust quickly, suddenly, or unexpectedly, with *in, into, out, up,* or *down.*—*adv.* With a pop or explosive sound; quickly, suddenly, or unexpectedly, as: The engine went *pop.* **—pop off,** to leave or die abruptly; to talk loudly or angrily, and usu. thoughtlessly. **—pop the question.** *Informal.* To propose marriage.

pop, pop, *a. Informal.* Popular.

pop art, *n.* A style of painting and sculpture which employs examples of the popular communications media, as advertisements or comic strips. **—pop art·ist,** *n.*

pop·corn, pop/kôrn, *n.* A variety of Indian corn whose kernels on being heated burst into puffs of starchy material; popped corn.

pope, pōp, *n.* (*Often cap.*) The Bishop of Rome, the head of the Roman Catholic Church.

pop·er·y, pō/pə·rē, *n.* The religion of the Church of Rome: used pejoratively. **—pop·ish,** *a.*

pop-eyed, pop/īd, *a.* Having wide, bulging eyes.

pop·gun, pop/gən, *n.* A toy pellet gun which pops when fired.

pop·in·jay, pop/in·jā, *n.* A fop; a coxcomb.

pop·lar, pop/lər, *n.* Any of various rapidly growing trees yielding a light, soft wood; the wood itself.

pop·lin, pop/lin, *n.* Corded fabric of cotton, rayon, silk, or wool, used for clothing and household goods.

pop·per, pop/ər, *n.* One who or that which pops; a utensil for popping corn.

pop·py, pop/ē, *n. pl.,* **-pies.** A type of plant with showy flowers of various colors, including a variety which is the source of opium; an extract, as opium, from such a plant; a bright, orange-red color; also **pop·py red.** **—pop·pied,** *a.*

pop·py·cock, pop/ē·kok, *n. Informal.* Idle talk; nonsense.

pop·py seed, *n.* The flavorful, gray-black seed obtained from the poppy plant.

pop·u·lace, pop/yə·lis, *n.* The common people; the multitude; population.

pop·u·lar, pop/yə·lər, *a.* Pleasing to or liked by the people in general; well-liked; pertaining to or of the common people; easy to comprehend; plain; familiar.

---

pop·u·lar·i·ty, pop·yə·lar/i·tē, *n.* The state or quality of being popular, or esteemed by the people at large; good will or favor proceeding from the people.

pop·u·lar·ize, pop/yə·lər·īz, *v.t.,* **-ized, -iz·ing.** To make popular; to make understandable to the layman. **—pop·u·lar·i·za·tion,** pop·yə·lər·ə·zā/shən, *n.* **—pop·u·lar·iz·er,** *n.*

pop·u·late, pop/yə·lāt, *v.t.,* **-lat·ed, -lat·ing.** To inhabit; to people.

pop·u·la·tion, pop·yə·lā/shən, *n.* The total number of persons inhabiting a country, city, or any district or area; the body of inhabitants of a place; the number or body of inhabitants of a particular race or class in a place; the act or process of populating; the state of a locality with reference to the number of its inhabitants.

pop·u·la·tion ex·plo·sion, *n.* An extremely rapid rate of population increase.

pop·u·lism, pop/yə·liz·əm, *n.* (*Sometimes cap.*) The political advocacy of the interests of the ordinary citizen, esp. as contrasted with various special interests, privileged groups, etc. **—pop·u·list,** *n.*

pop·u·lous, pop/yə·ləs, *a.* Full of inhabitants; thickly settled with people; crowded. **—pop·u·lous·ly,** *adv.*

por·ce·lain, pôr/sə·lin, pôrs/lin, *n.* A fine, strong, translucent ceramic material, usu. glazed; china; a vessel or object made of this material.

porch, pōrch, pôrch, *n.* An exterior appendage to a building forming a covered approach or vestibule to a doorway; a covered walk or portico; a veranda.

por·cine, pôr/sin, pôr/sin, *a.* Pertaining to swine; hoglike.

por·cu·pine, pôr/kyə·pīn, *n.* Any of several rodents, covered with sharp spines, or quills, which the animal can erect at will for its defense.

pore, pōr, pôr, *v.i.,* **pored, por·ing.** To look with steady, continued attention or application; to ponder; to read or examine anything with steady perseverance, usu. followed by *on, upon,* or *over.*

pore, pōr, pôr, *n.* A minute opening, as in the skin or in plant leaves, through which fluids and other substances are excreted or absorbed; any small interstice of this nature, as in a stone or other solid.

pork, pōrk, pôrk, *n.* The flesh of swine used as food. *Informal.* Appropriations or favors granted by governments for political reasons rather than because of public necessity. Also **pork bar·rel.**

pork·er, pōr/kər, pôr/kər, *n.* A hog or pig, esp. one fattened for pork.

por·nog·ra·phy, pôr·nog/rə·fē, *n.* Literature or art calculated solely to supply sexual excitement; obscene literature or art. **—por·nog·ra·pher,** *n.* **—por·no·graph·ic,** pôr·nə·graf/ik, *a.* **—por·no·graph·i·cal·ly,** *adv.*

po·rous, pōr/əs, pôr/əs, *a.* Having many pores; permeable by liquids, light, or air. **—po·ros·i·ty,** pō·ros/ə·tē, *n.* **—po·rous·ly,** *adv.* **—po·rous·ness,** *n.*

por·poise, pôr/pəs, *n. pl.,* **-pois·es, -poise.** Any of gregarious sea mammals, five to eight feet long, usu. blackish above and paler beneath, and having a blunt, rounded snout.

por·ridge, pôr/ij, por/ij, *n.* A food made by slowly stirring oatmeal, or other meal, into boiling water or milk and cooking until thick.

port, pōrt, pôrt, *n.* A city or town at which ships load or unload; a recess, as of the sea or a lake, where vessels may take refuge from storms; a harbor. *Informal.* An airport; any place where persons and merchandise are allowed to pass, by water or land, into and out of a country and where customs officers are stationed to inspect or appraise imported goods; also **port of en·try.**

port, pōrt, pôrt, *n.* An opening in the side of a ship for loading cargo or for the admission of light and air.

port, pōrt, pôrt, *v.t.* To carry, as a rifle, with both hands, in a slanting direction across the front of the body.

port, pōrt, pôrt, *n.* The left side of a ship or aircraft as one faces forward. Also **lar·board.—a.** Relating to port; on the left. **—v.t., v.i.** To turn or put to the left side.

port, pōrt, pôrt, *n.* A type of sweet wine, usu. of a dark red color.

port·a·ble, pōr/tə·bəl, pôr/tə·bəl, *a.* Capable of being carried or transported from place to place; easily carried.**—n.** An object which is portable. **—port·a·bil·i·ty,** pōr·tə·bil/ə·tē, *n.***—port·a·bly,** *adv.*

por·tage, pōr/tij, pôr/tij, *n.* The act of carrying; carriage; the carrying of boats or goods overland from one navigable water to another; a place or course over which this must be done; cost of carriage or transporting.**—v.t., v.i.,** **-taged, -tag·ing.**

por·tal, pōr/təl, pôr/təl, *n.* A door or gate, esp. a large and impressive one; the entrance to a mine, tunnel, or bridge.

por·tend, pōr·tend/, pôr·tend/, *v.t.* To indicate or warn beforehand; forebode.

por·tent, pōr/tent, pôr/tent, *n.* An indication or omen of something about to happen, esp. something momentous or calamitous; prophetic significance. **—por·ten·tous,** pōr·ten/təs, pôr·ten/təs, *a.*

por·ter, pōr/tər, pôr/tər, *n.* One who has charge of a door or gate; a doorkeeper.

por·ter, pōr/tər, pôr/tər, *n.* A carrier; a person who carries or conveys burdens or luggage for hire, as at a railroad terminal; an attendant in a railroad sleeping car or parlor car.

por·ter·house, pōr/tər·hows, pôr/tər·hows, *n.* A choice cut of beefsteak from between the prime ribs and the sirloin.

port·fo·li·o, pōrt·fō/lē·ō, pôrt·fō/lē·ō, *n. pl.,* **-os.** A portable case in the form of a large book, for holding loose drawings or papers; the itemized securities and investments held by an investor or bank.

port·hole, pōrt/hōl, pôrt/hōl, *n.* An opening like a window in a ship's side, for admitting light and air; an opening in a wall or door through which to shoot.

por·ti·co, pōr/ti·kō, pôr/ti·kō, *n. pl.,* **-coes, -cos.** A kind of porch fronted with columns, often at the entrance of a building.

por·tion, pōr/shən, pôr/shən, *n.* That which is divided off, as a part from a whole; a part considered by itself though not actually divided; an allotment; share; the amount of food usu. served one person.**—v.t.** To divide or distribute into portions or shares, often followed by *out.* **—por·tion·less,** *a.*

port·ly, pōrt/lē, pôrt/lē, *a.,* **-li·er, -li·est.** Rather heavy or corpulent; stout. **—port·li·ness,** *n.*

port of call, *n.* A port where a ship makes a brief stop, for repairs, to pick up or discharge cargo or passengers, or as one of a scheduled series of such stops.

por·trait, pôr/trit, pôr/trāt, *n.* A painted picture or representation of a person, esp. of a face, generally drawn from life; a vivid description or delineation in words. **—por·trait·ist,** *n.*

por·trai·ture, pôr/tri·chər, *n.* A portrait; the art of drawing portraits, or of vividly describing in words.

por·tray, pôr·trā/, *v.t.* To paint or draw the likeness of; enact the part of, as in a play; to describe in words. **—por·tray·er,** *n.*

por·tray·al, pôr·trā/əl, *n.* The act of portraying; a portrait.

pose, pōz, *v.i.,* **posed, pos·ing.** To assume or hold a physical position or attitude for some artistic purpose; to affect a particular character, as with a view to the impression made on others; represent oneself, esp. falsely: He *posed* as an expert on French literature. **—v.t.** To place in a suitable position or attitude for a picture, tableau, or the like; to state or assert.**—n.** An attitude or posture of body; a mental attitude, esp. one assumed for effect; affectation.

pose, pōz, *v.t.,* **posed, pos·ing.** To embarrass or puzzle by a difficult question or problem.

pos·er, pō/zər, *n.* One who poses.

pos·er, pō/zər, *n.* A baffling problem.

po·seur, pō·zər/, *n.* One who poses or is affected,

esp. to impress others.

posh, posh, *a.* Elegant or high-class.

pos·it, poz′it, *v.t.* To set firmly; fix; to lay down as a position or principle; assume as a fact.

po·si·tion, pə·zish′ən, *n.* Situation, place, or location, esp. with reference to other objects; customary or appropriate place; status; a post or job; manner of standing or of being placed: in a prone *position;* mental attitude, that on which one takes a stand; point of view; the act of positing.—*v.t.* To place. **—po·si·tion·al,** *a.* **—po·si·tion·er,** *n.*

pos·i·tive, poz′i·tiv, *a.* Explicitly laid down or expressed: a *positive* declaration; determined by enactment or convention: *positive* law; admitting of no question: *positive* proof; stated; definite; emphatic; overconfident or dogmatic; absolute; real; not speculative or theoretical; constructive; consisting in or characterized by the presence or possession of distinguishing or marked qualities or features: opposed to *negative;* measured or proceeding in a direction assumed as that of increase, progress, or onward motion; pertaining to the kind of electricity developed on glass when rubbed with silk; of a point or part in an electrical circuit, having a higher electric potential than that of another point or part, and away from which the current flows; denoting a quantity greater than zero; indicating the presence of bacteria that cause disease. *Photog.* Showing the lights and shades as seen in the original print, not reversed.—*n.* Something positive. *Photog.* A positive picture. **—pos·i·tive·ly,** *adv.* **—pos·i·tive·ness,** *n.*

pos·i·tiv·ism, poz′i·ti·viz·əm, *n.* The state or quality of being positive; definiteness.

pos·i·tron, poz′i·tron, *n.* A positively charged particle with a mass and ionizing power equal to that of an electron.

pos·se, pos′ē, *n.* A posse comitatus; a body or force armed with legal authority.

pos·se co·mi·ta·tus, pos′ē kom·i·tā′təs, *n.* The body of people that a sheriff is empowered to call into service, usu. in case of emergency.

pos·sess, pə·zes′, *v.t.* To have as property; own; to have a faculty, quality, or attribute: to *possess* patience; maintain control over, as oneself or one's mind; of a spirit, esp. an evil one, to occupy and control, or dominate from within, as a person; to make, as a person, the owner, holder, or master of property or information; to cause to be dominated or influenced, as by a feeling or idea; of a man, to have sexual relations with, as one of the opposite sex. **—pos·ses·sor,** *n.*

pos·sessed, pə·zest′, *a.* Dominated or moved by a passion, madness, or an evil spirit; demented; self-possessed; calm; possessing or having: She is *possessed* of considerable talent.

pos·ses·sion, pə·zesh′ən, *n.* The act or fact of possessing; the state of being possessed; ownership; actual holding or occupancy, as distinct from ownership; a thing possessed; *pl.,* property or wealth.

pos·ses·sive, pə·zes′iv, *a.* Of or pertaining to possession or ownership; having a desire to possess. **—pos·ses·sive·ly,** *adv.* **—pos·ses·sive·ness,** *n.*

pos·si·bil·i·ty, pos·ə·bil′i·tē, *n. pl.,* **-ties.** The state or condition of being possible; something that is possible.

pos·si·ble, pos′ə·bəl, *a.* That may be or may exist; that may be now, or may happen or come to pass.

pos·si·bly, pos′ə·blē, *adv.* Perhaps; in a possible manner.

pos·sum, pos′əm, *n.* Opossum.

post, pōst, *n.* A stout piece of timber, metal, or the like, set upright as a support or a point of attachment: a sign *post.*—*v.t.* To affix, as a notice, to a post or wall; to bring to public notice by or as by a placard: to *post*

a reward.

post, pōst, *n.* A position of duty, employment, or trust, to which one is assigned or appointed; a trading post.—*v.t.* To station at a post or place as a sentry; to appoint to a post of command.

post, pōst, *n.* A single dispatch or delivery of mail, or the mail itself; the letters coming to a single person or recipient; an established service or system for the conveyance of letters, esp. under governmental authority; a post office or a postal letter box.—*v.t.* To place in a post office or a letter box for transmission; mail; to enter, as an item, in due place and form; to supply with information or inform.—*v.i.* To travel with speed; to rise up from the saddle and fall back in rhythm with the horse's gait.—*adv.* **—post·al,** *a.*

post·age, pō′stij, *n.* The charge for the conveyance of a letter or other matter sent by post or mail, ordinarily prepaid by means of a stamp or stamps.

post·age stamp, *n.* An official stamp in the form of a design on an envelope, or a printed adhesive label to be affixed to a letter or other mail, as evidence of prepayment of the required postage.

post·box, pōst′boks, *n.* A mailbox.

post card, *n.* Any card, often with a picture on it, to which a stamp may be affixed for transmittal through the mail; a similar card, on which a stamp has been printed, issued by the government. Also **post·al card.**

post·date, pōst·dāt′, *v.t.,* **-dat·ed, -dat·ing.** To date, as a check, letter, or other document, later than the actual date of execution; to come later in time.

post·er, pō′stər, *n.* A large printed bill or placard posted for advertising or public information; one who posts placards.

pos·te·ri·or, po·stēr′ē·ər, *a.* Situated behind, or hinder, as opposed to *anterior;* coming after in order, as in a series; later.—*n.* The hinder part of the body; the buttocks. **—pos·te·ri·or·i·ty,** po·stēr·ē·ôr′i·tē, po·stēr·ē·or′i·tē, *n.*

pos·ter·i·ty, po·stār′i·tē, *n.* All future or succeeding generations; the descendants that proceed from one progenitor.

post·grad·u·ate, pōst·graj′ū·it, *n.* One who engages in advanced academic studies after graduation, usu. from high school or college.—*a.*

post·haste, pōst′hāst′, *adv.* With great speed; promptly.

post·hu·mous, pos′chū·məs, *a.* Born after the death of the father; published after the death of the author; being or continuing after one's decease. **—post·hu·mous·ly,** *adv.*

post·lude, pōst′lood, *n.* A concluding piece or movement; a voluntary of organ music at the end of a church service.

post·man, pōst′mən, *n. pl.,* **-men.** A letter carrier; mail carrier.

post·mark, pōst′märk, *n.* An official mark stamped on a letter or other mail, to cancel the postage stamp and indicate the place and date of sending or of receipt. —*v.t.* To stamp with a postmark.

post·mas·ter, pōst′mas·ter, pōst′mä·stər, *n.* The official in charge of a post office. **—post·mis·tress,** pōst′mis·tris, *n. fem.*

post me·rid·i·em, pōst mə·rid′ē·əm, *a.* After noon. Abbr. **p.m., P.M.**

post·mor·tem, pōst·môr′təm, *a.* Subsequent to death, as an examination of the body.—*n.* A postmortem examination; an autopsy.

post·na·sal, pōst′nā′zəl, *a.* Pertaining to the posterior cavities of the nose; occurring behind the nose: *postnasal* drip.

post·na·tal, pōst′nāt′əl, *a.* Subsequent to birth. **—post·na·tal·ly,** *adv.*

post of·fice, *n.* The governmental department charged with the conveyance of letters; an office or

---

station of a governmental postal system, for receiving, distributing, and transmitting mail, selling postage stamps, and other services.

post·paid, pōst/pād/, *a., adv.* Having the postage prepaid, as a letter.

post·par·tum, pōst/pär/təm, *a.* After childbirth.

post·pone, pōst/pōn/, *v.t.*, **-poned, -pon·ing.** To put off; to defer to a future or later time; to subordinate. —**post·pon·a·ble,** *a.* —**post·pone·ment,** *n.* —**post·pon·er,** *n.*

post·script, pōst/skript, *n.* An addition to a letter after it is concluded and signed by the writer; something appended. Abbr. **p.s., P.S.**

pos·tu·lant, pos/chə·lənt, *n.* A petitioner or applicant for something; a candidate for admission into a religious order.

pos·tu·late, pos/chə·lāt, *v.t.*, **-lat·ed, -lat·ing.** To ask, demand, or claim; to claim or assume the existence or truth of, esp. as a basis for reasoning; assume without proof, or as self-evident. —pos/chə·lit, *n.* Something postulated; an axiom; a prerequisite. —**pos·tu·la·tion,** pos·chə·lā/shən, *n.* —**pos·tu·la·tor,** *n.*

pos·ture, pos/chər, *n.* The relative disposition of the various parts of anything; the position or carriage of the body and limbs as a whole; an unnatural attitude, pose, or contortion of the body; a mental or spiritual attitude; a position, condition, or state, esp. of affairs. —*v.t.*, **-tured, -tur·ing.** To place in a particular posture or attitude, or dispose in postures.—*v.i.* To assume a particular posture or mental attitude, esp. one that is affected or unnatural. **pos·tur·al,** *a.* —**pos·tur·er,** *n.*

post·war, pōst/wôr/, *a.* Belonging to the period after a war.

po·sy, pō/zē, *n. pl.*, **po·sies.** A single flower; a bunch of flowers.

pot, pot, *n.* An earthen, metallic, or other vessel, usu. rounded and deep, used for domestic or other purposes; a container holding a growing plant; a vessel with its contents; a potful; liquor or drink; a state of gradual ruination. *Informal.* A large sum of money; marijuana. —*v.t.*, **pot·ted, pot·ting.** To put into a pot; put up and preserve in a pot; cook or stew in a pot; plant in a flower pot; to shoot or kill.—*v.i. Informal.* To take a pot shot; shoot. —**pot·ted,** *a.*

po·ta·ble, pō/tə·bəl, *a.* Suitable for drinking.—*n. Often pl.* Something that may be drunk.

pot·ash, pot/ash, *n.* Potassium carbonate; potassium hydroxide.

po·tas·si·um, pə·tas/ē·əm, *n.* A soft, whitish metallic element found combined in nature.

po·tas·si·um car·bon·ate, *n.* A white solid used in the manufacture of glass, soap, and other products.

po·tas·si·um cy·a·nide, *n.* A very poisonous, white, crystalline substance used in metallurgy, photography, etc.

po·tas·si·um hy·drox·ide, *n.* A white, caustic solid used in making soft soap. Also **pot·ash.**

po·tas·si·um ni·trate, *n.* A compound used in preservatives, fertilizers, and gunpowders; niter; saltpeter.

po·ta·to, pə·tā/tō, *n. pl.*, **-toes.** The edible tuber of a cultivated plant; the plant itself.

po·ta·to chip, *n.* A paper-thin potato slice, fried to a crispy state, and salted.

pot·bel·ly, pot/bel·ē, *n.* A protuberant belly. —**pot·bel·lied,** *a.*

pot·boil·er, pot/boy·lər, *n. Informal.* A work of literature or art, usu. inferior in quality, produced merely to provide monetary gain.

po·tent, pōt/ənt, *a.* Possessed of great power or authority; powerful; mighty; capable of sexual intercourse: usu. said of a male; cogent or effective, as reasons or motives; producing powerful physical or chemical effects, as a drug. —**po·ten·cy,** *n.* —**po·tent·ly,** *adv.*

po·ten·tate, pōt/ən·tāt, *n.* A person who possesses great power or sway; a prince; sovereign; emperor.

po·ten·tial, pə·ten/shəl, *a.* Being a possibility, not an actuality; latent; that may be manifested.—*n.* Anything that may be possible; at a given point, the work required to bring a unit of positive electricity from an infinite distance to that point under given conditions of electrification. —**po·ten·ti·al·i·ty,** pə·ten·shē·al/ə·tē, *n. pl.*, **-ties.** —**po·ten·tial·ly,** *adv.*

pot·hole, pot/hōl, *n.* A circular cavity in the rocky bed of a river; a hole or deep pit in the surface of a highway, street, or sidewalk.

po·tion, pō/shən, *n.* A draft or drink; a liquid supposedly having magical or poisonous powers.

pot·luck, pot/lək, *n.* Whatever may be in a pot or provided for a family meal and given to guests; an informal meal where each guest brings a dish to be shared.

pot·pour·ri, pō·pû·rē/, pot/pûr·ē, *n.* Dried flower petals and spices kept in a jar for the fragrance; a musical medley; a collection of miscellaneous literary extracts; any collection of mixed or unrelated parts.

pot·sherd, pot/shərd, *n.* A fragment of earthenware.

pot shot, *n.* A shot fired at game merely to fill the pot, with little regard to the rules of sport; a shot at an animal or person within easy range, as from ambush; a haphazard shot; a casual attempt at something; a censorious remark.

pot·tage, pot/ij, *n.* A thick vegetable soup with or without meat.

pot·ter, pot/ər, *n.* One who makes earthenware vessels or crockery of any kind.

pot·ter's wheel, *n.* A horizontal revolving disk used to hold ceramic clay as it is shaped by the potter.

pot·ter·y, pot/ə·rē, *n. pl.*, **-ies.** Ware made by shaping moist clay and then hardening it with intense heat; the business, the place of business, or art of a potter.

pot·ty, pot/ē, *n. pl.*, **-ties.** A pot for toilet use by small children.

pot·ty-chair, pot/ē·chār, *n.* A small, open-seated chair placed over a pot for a child's use in toilet training.

pouch, powch, *n.* A bag, sack, or similar receptacle, esp. one for small articles; a small moneybag; something shaped like or resembling a bag or pocket.—*v.t.* To put into or enclose in a pouch, bag, or pocket; to pocket; sometimes, of a fish or bird, to swallow; to arrange in pouchlike form.—*v.i.* To form a pouch or a pouchlike cavity. —**pouched,** powcht, *a.* —**pouch·y,** pow/chē, *a.*, **-i·er, -i·est.**

poul·tice, pōl/tis, *n.* A soft dressing composed of meal, bread, or other softening substance, to be applied to sore or inflamed parts of the body.—*v.t.*, **-ticed, -tic·ing.** To cover with a poultice; to apply a poultice to.

poul·try, pōl/trē, *n.* Domestic fowls, as cocks and hens, turkeys, ducks, and geese.

pounce, powns, *n.* The claw or talon of a bird of prey; a pouncing or sudden swoop, as on prey.—*v.t.*, **pounced, pounc·ing.** To seize with the talons, or swoop down upon and seize suddenly, as does a bird of prey.—*v.i.* To swoop down suddenly and lay hold; to spring, dash, or come suddenly: to *pounce* into a room.

pound, pownd, *n.* A unit of avoirdupois weight equal to 16 ounces; a unit of troy weight equal to 12 ounces; a British monetary unit once equivalent to 20 shillings or 240 pence, now equivalent to 100 pennies; a monetary unit of varying value, used in several other countries.

pound, pownd, *v.t.* To crush by beating; to pulverize; to strike repeatedly with great force; to batter, often with *out;* to produce by striking or thumping: to *pound* out a tune on the piano; to force by battering; to make solid or firm by beating.—*v.i.* To strike heavy blows repeatedly or batter; to beat or throb violently; to give forth a thumping sound; to ride heavily; to move along with force or vigor.—*n.* The act of pounding; a heavy blow or its sound.

pound, pownd, *n.* An enclosed place kept by authority for keeping stray cattle, dogs, etc., or for keeping goods until redeemed; an enclosed place for sheltering, keeping, confining, or trapping animals; a place of confinement or imprisonment.—*v.t.* To shut up in a pound; impound; confine within limits.

pound·age, pown'dij, *n.* A tax or rate of so much per pound sterling or per pound weight; weight in pounds.

pound-fool·ish, pownd'fŏo'lish, *a.* Foolish or careless in regard to large sums.

pour, pôr, pōr, *v.t.* To send, as a liquid, fluid, or anything in loose particles, flowing or falling, as from a container, or into, over, or on something: to *pour* water on fire, to *pour* sugar on cereal; to send forth continuously and rapidly; to express freely or without reserve: to *pour* forth one's ideas.—*v.i.* To flow continuously, as a stream; to rain hard: to *pour* all day; to move or proceed in great quantity or number: The crowd *poured* into the streets.—*n.* A pouring; downpour. —**pour·a·ble,** *a.* —**pour·er,** *n.*

pout, powt, *v.i.* To thrust out the lips, as in sullenness, contempt, or displeasure; to look sullen; to swell out, as the lips; to express in a pouting manner.—*v.t.* To push out sulkily, as the lips.—*n.* A pushing out of the lips as in sullenness; a fit of sullenness.

pov·er·ty, pov'ər·tē, *n.* The condition of being poor with respect to money, goods, or means of getting along; deficiency or lack of something specified: *poverty* of ideas.

pov·er·ty-strick·en, pov'ər·tē·strik·ən, *a.* Suffering from poverty; very poor.

POW, *n.* Prisoner of war. Also **P.O.W.**

pow·der, pow'dər, *n.* Any solid substance in the state of fine, loose particles; dust; a preparation in this form for some special purpose, as for medicinal use; a cosmetic: face *powder*; gunpowder.—*v.t.* To sprinkle or cover with powder; to reduce to powder; pulverize. —*v.i.* To use powder as a cosmetic; to become pulverized. —**pow·der·y,** *a.*

pow·der blue, *n.* Pale blue blended with gray. —**pow·der-blue,** *a.*

pow·der keg, *n.* A small cask of metal or wood, containing gunpowder or blasting powder; a potentially violent situation or condition.

pow·der puff, *n.* A soft, fluffy ball or pad, for applying cosmetic powder to the skin.

pow·der room, *n.* A ladies' rest room having washing and toilet facilities.

pow·er, pow'ər, *n.* Ability to do or act; capability of doing something; *often pl.,* a particular faculty of body or mind; great ability to act; strength, might, or force; political or national strength: the balance of *power* in Europe; authority; one who or that which possesses or exercises authority or influence: the great *powers* of the world. *Informal.* A large number or amount. Energy or force available for application to work; the time rate at which energy or force is exerted or converted into work; the product obtained by multiplying a quantity by itself one or more times: Four is the second *power* of two.—*v.t.* To supply with a means or source of power or energy.

pow·er·boat, pow'ər·bōt, *n.* A motorboat.

pow·er·ful, pow'ər·fəl, *a.* Having or exerting great power or force; potent, as a drug; having or showing great intellectual force; mighty. —**pow·er·ful·ly,** *adv.* —**pow·er·ful·ness,** *n.*

pow·er·house, pow'ər·hows, *n.* A station for generating electricity. *Informal.* A person of dynamic energy and power.

pow·er·less, pow'ər·lis, *a.* Lacking power; helpless.

pow·er plant, *n.* The apparatus for supplying power for a particular mechanical process or operation; the building and equipment involved in generating power.

pow·wow, pow'wow, *n.* Among the N. American Indi-ans, a priest or medicine man, or a ceremony, esp. one accompanied by magic, feasting, and dancing; a council or conference of or with Indians. *Informal.* Any conference or meeting.—*v.i.* To hold a powwow. *Informal.* To confer.

pox, poks, *n.* A disease marked by watery blisters on the skin, such as chicken pox; syphilis.

prac·ti·ca·ble, prak'tə·kə·bəl, *a.* Capable of being effected or performed; feasible; usable, useful. —**prac·ti·ca·bil·i·ty,** prak·ti·kə·bil'ə·tē, **prac·ti·ca·ble·ness,** *n.* —**prac·ti·ca·bly,** *adv.*

prac·ti·cal, prak'ti·kəl, *a.* Referring or relating to practice or action: *practical* agriculture; referring to or connected with the ordinary activities of the world: *practical* affairs; suitable for actual use: a *practical* method; engaged in actual practice or work; fitted for actual work or useful activities: a *practical* man; interested in realities; mindful of the results, usefulness, advantages, or disadvantages of action or procedure; matter-of-fact. —**prac·ti·cal·i·ty,** prak·ti·kal'ə·tē, *n.* —**prac·ti·cal·ly,** *adv.*

prac·ti·cal joke, *n.* A joke or jest carried out in action instead of words. —**prac·ti·cal jok·er,** *n.*

prac·ti·cal nurse, *n.* A nurse, lacking a degree as a registered nurse, but with sufficient training and nursing skills to care for the sick professionally.

prac·tice, prak'tis, *v.t.* To carry out in action, esp. to carry out or perform habitually or usually: *Practice* what you preach; to exercise or pursue, as a profession, art, or occupation: to *practice* medicine; to exercise or train, as a person, in order to achieve proficiency.—*v.i.* To do something habitually or as a practice; to pursue a profession, esp. law or medicine; to exercise repeatedly in order to gain proficiency.—*n.* Habitual performance; a habit or custom; the action of doing something; the exercise of a profession or occupation, esp. law or medicine; the business of a professional; repeated performance or systematic exercise for the purpose of acquiring skill or proficiency; a condition of proficiency resulting from frequent exercise: to be in *practice*.

prac·ticed, prak'tist, *a.* Experienced; skilled.

prac·tice teach·er, *n.* Student teacher.

prac·ti·tion·er, prak·tish'ən·ər, *n.* One who is engaged in the exercise of any art or profession.

prae·di·al, pre·di·al, prē'dē·əl, *a.* Consisting of or relating to land.

prag·mat·ic, prag·mat'ik, *a.* Treating historical phenomena with special reference to their causes and results; concerned with practical consequences or values; busy or active; meddlesome; dogmatic.—*n.* A pragmatic sanction; a busybody; a conceited person. —**prag·mat·i·cal,** *a.* —**prag·mat·i·cal·ly,** *adv.* —**prag·mat·i·cal·ness,** *n.*

prag·ma·tism, prag'mə·tiz·əm, *n.* A concern for and emphasis on practical matters; a system of philosophy which regards the practical consequences and useful results of ideas as the test of their truthfulness and which considers truth itself to be a process. —**prag·ma·tist,** *n., a.* —**prag·ma·tis·tic,** prag·mə·tis'tik, *a.*

prai·rie, prār'ē, *n.* An extensive, mostly level tract of grassland, usu. treeless, with fertile soil and flowering plants.

prai·rie dog, *n.* A small, burrowing rodent, found on the N. American prairies.

praise, prāz, *n.* Commendation bestowed on someone or something; homage offered as an act of worship and expressed in words or song.—*v.t.,* **praised, prais·ing.** To commend; to applaud. —**prais·er,** *n.*

praise·wor·thy, prāz'wər·thē, *a.* Worthy or deserving of praise. —**praise·wor·thi·ly,** *adv.* —**praise·wor·thi·ness,** *n.*

pra·line, prä'lēn, prä'lēn, prä·lēn', *n.* Any of various sweets made of almonds, pecans, or other nuts

---

a- hat, fāte, fāre, fäther; e- met, mē; i- pin, pīne; o- not, nōte, ôrb, moove (move), boy, pownd;
u- cūbe, bůll, tůk (took); ch- chin; th- thick, ŧhen; zh- vizhon (vision); ə- əgo, takən, pencəl, lemən, bərd (bird).

cooked in a boiling syrup.

pram, pram, *n. Brit. Informal.* Baby carriage.

prance, prans, *v.i.,* **pranced, pranc·ing.** To spring or bound from the hind legs, as a horse; to ride on a horse moving in this manner; to strut about in a showy or spirited manner.—*v.t.* To cause to prance.—*n.* A prancing act or movement. **—pranc·er,** *n.*

prank, prangk, *n.* A trick of a frolicsome or malicious nature. **—prank·ish,** *a.* **—prank·ster,** *n.*

prate, prāt, *v.i.,* **prat·ed, prat·ing.** To talk a lot without saying very much; to babble; chatter.—*v.t.* To talk foolishly.—*n.* Foolish chatter. **—prat·er,** *n.* **—prat·ing·ly,** *adv.*

prat·fall, prat′fôl, *n. Informal.* A fall on the backside or buttocks; an embarrassing mistake or blunder.

prat·tle, prat′əl, *v.i.,* **-tled, -tling.** To talk much and idly on trifling subjects; to talk like a child.—*v.t.* To speak in a childish or babbling manner.—*n.* Babble. **—prat·tler,** *n.* **—prat·tling·ly,** *adv.*

prawn, prôn, *n.* Any of various shrimplike shellfish, certain of which are used as food.—*v.i.* To fish for prawns. **—prawn·er,** *n.*

pray, prā, *v.i.* To ask for something with earnestness; to beg; to address confession, supplication, or thanks to an object of worship.—*v.t.* To make earnest request to; to entreat; to ask earnestly for.

prayer, prār, *n.* The act of asking for a favor with earnestness; a petition; that which is asked; the words of a supplication; a formula of church service or of worship, public or private.

pray·er, prā′ər, *n.* One who prays. **—prayer·ful,** *a.*

prayer book, prār′bûk, *n.* A book containing prayers used in worship; (*usu. cap.*) The Book of Common Prayer.

preach, prēch, *v.i.* To deliver a sermon; to give earnest advice; to talk in a wearying manner.—*v.t.* To endorse in writing or public speech; to explain, as something, in a sermon; to deliver, as a sermon. **—preach·er,** *n.*

preach·i·fy, prē′chə·fī, *v.i.,* **-fied, -fy·ing.** To give wearying, long-winded moral advice.

preach·ment, prēch′mənt, *n.* The act of giving a sermon; a tedious discourse or sermon.

preach·y, prē′chē, *a.,* **-i·er, -i·est.** *Informal.* Apt to preach or talk long-windedly.

pre·ad·o·les·cence, prē·ad·ə·les′əns, *n.* The years which immediately precede adolescence, usu. from the age of 9 to 12. **—pre·ad·o·les·cent,** *a., n.*

pre·am·ble, prē′am·bəl, *n.* A preliminary statement; a preface.

pre·ar·range, prē·ə·rānj′, *v.t.,* **-ranged, -rang·ing.** To arrange beforehand. **—pre·ar·range·ment,** *n.*

pre·as·signed, prē·ə·sīnd′, *a.* Assigned in advance.

pre·can·cel, prē·kan′səl, *v.t.,* **-celed, -cel·ing.** To cancel, as a postage stamp, before using in the mail. **—pre·can·cel·la·tion,** prē·kan·sə·lā′shən, *n.*

pre·car·i·ous, pri·kār′ē·əs, *a.* Depending on unknown or unforeseen causes or events; risky; having little base or foundation. **—pre·car·i·ous·ly,** *adv.* **—pre·car·i·ous·ness,** *n.*

pre·cau·tion, pri·kô′shən, *n.* Previous caution; a measure taken beforehand to ward off evil or to secure good. **—pre·cau·tion·ar·y,** pri·kô′shə·ner·ē, *a.*

pre·cede, pri·sēd′, *v.t.,* **-ced·ed, -ced·ing.** To go before in the order of time, place, rank, or importance; to begin with introductory material; to preface.—*v.i.* To be or go before or ahead of.

prec·e·dence, pres′i·dəns, pri·sēd′əns, *n.* The act or state of going before; the state of being before in rank or dignity; a being earlier in time; the right to a more honorable place in social formalities; order or adjustment of place according to rank.

prec·e·dent, pres′ə·dənt, *n.* Something done or said that may serve as an example or rule to be followed in a subsequent act of a like kind. **—**pri·sēd′ənt, *a.* Going before in time; anterior; antecedent.

pre·ced·ing, pri·sē′ding, *a.* That precedes; going or coming before; previous.

pre·cept, prē′sept, *n.* A commandment intended as an authoritative rule of action; a maxim or guide respecting moral conduct; an injunction.

pre·cep·tive, pri·sep′tiv, *a.* Giving or containing precepts for the regulation of conduct; admonitive; instructive.

pre·cep·tor, pri·sep′tər, *n.* A teacher; an instructor. **—pre·cep·to·ri·al,** prē·sep·tôr′ē·əl, *a.*

pre·ces·sion, prē·sesh′ən, *n.* The act or fact of preceding; precedence. **—pre·cess·ion·al,** *a.*

pre·cinct, prē′singkt, *n.* Divisions within a city, town, or county for voting purposes; a police district of a city; the police station within such a district.

pre·cious, presh′əs, *a.* Of high price; much esteemed; highly cherished; affectedly refined; flagrant. *Informal.* Great: *a precious* amount of good her frankness did her!—*adv.* Extremely; very.—*n.* A beloved individual. **—pre·ci·os·i·ty,** presh·ē·os′ə·tē, **pre·cious·ness,** *n.*

prec·i·pice, pres′i·pis, *n.* A steep bank, cliff, or extremely steep overhang; a dangerous situation. **—prec·i·pi·tous,** pri·sip′i·təs, *a.*

pre·cip·i·tant, pri·sip′ə·tənt, *a.* Falling or rushing headlong; precipitate.—*n.* A substance which, when added to a solution, induces precipitation. **—pre·cip·i·tant·ly,** *adv.* **—pre·cip·i·tant·ness,** *n.*

pre·cip·i·tate, pri·sip′ə·tāt, *v.t.,* **-tat·ed, -tat·ing.** To hasten the occurrence of; bring about suddenly; to separate out, as a substance, in solid form from a solution; to condense from a state of vapor into the form of rain or dew; to cast, plunge, or send violently or abruptly.—*v.i.* To separate from a solution as a precipitate; to be condensed as rain or dew; to fall headlong.—pri·sip′ə·tit, *a.* Headlong; rushing headlong or rapidly onward; exceedingly sudden or abrupt; overhasty; rash. **—**pri·sip′ə·tit, pri·sip′ə·tāt, *n.* A substance precipitated from a solution; moisture condensed in the form of rain, dew, or snow. **—pre·cip·i·ta·tive,** *a.* **—pre·cip·i·ta·tor,** *n.*

pre·cip·i·ta·tion, pri·sip·ə·tā′shən, *n.* The act of precipitating, or state of being precipitated; the process by which any substance is made to separate from another or others in a solution, and fall to the bottom; the results of atmospheric condensation, i.e., snow, sleet, hail, dew, fog, or rainfall.

pre·cip·i·tous, pri·sip′ə·təs, *a.* Very steep; like a precipice; headlong. **—pre·cip·i·tous·ly,** *adv.* **—pre·cip·i·tous·ness,** *n.*

pré·cis, prā·sē′, prā′sē, *n. pl.,* **-cis,** -sēz. A brief summary or abstract of a book or document.

pre·cise, pri·sīs′, *a.* Sharply or exactly limited or defined as to meaning; exact; exact in conduct; strict; formal. **—pre·cise·ness,** *n.*

pre·ci·sion, pri·sizh′ən, *n.* The state of being precise as to meaning; exactness; accuracy. **—pre·ci·sion·ist,** *n.*

pre·clude, pri·klood′, *v.t.,* **-clud·ed, -clud·ing.** To shut out; to impede; to hinder; to hinder by anticipative action. **—pre·clu·sion,** pri·kloo′zhən, *n.* **—pre·clu·sive,** pri·kloo′siv, *a.*

pre·co·cious, pri·kō′shəs, *a.* Forward in development, esp. mental development, as a child or young person; prematurely developed, as the mind or faculties; pertaining to or showing premature development. **—pre·co·cious·ly,** *adv.* **—pre·co·cious·ness,** *n.* **—pre·coc·i·ty,** pri·kos′ə·tē, *n.*

pre·cog·ni·tion, prē·kog·nish′ən, *n.* Foreknowledge of a situation or of an event. **—pre·cog·ni·tive,** prē·kog′nə·tiv, *a.*

pre·con·ceive, prē·kən·sēv′, *v.t.,* **-ceived, -ceiving.** To form a conception or opinion of beforehand; to form a notion or idea of in advance. **—pre·con·cep·tion,** prē·kən·sep′shən, *n.*

pre·cook, prē·kûk′, *v.t.* To partially or completely cook for quick heating and serving at a later time.

pre·cur·sor, pri·kər′sər, *n.* A forerunner; one who or that which precedes an event and indicates its approach; a predecessor. **—pre·cur·so·ry,** a.

pre·date, prē·dāt′, v.t., **-dat·ed, -dat·ing.** To date by anticipation; to antedate; to come before in time.

pred·a·tor, pred′ə·tər, n. Someone or something that is predatory.

pred·a·to·ry, pred′ə·tôr·ē, a. Plundering; pillaging. **—pred·a·to·ri·ly,** adv.

pre·dawn, prē·dôn′, a. Pertaining to the time immediately preceding sunrise.

pred·e·ces·sor, pred′ə·ses·ər, n. One who precedes or goes before another in some position; a thing which is succeeded by another thing.

pre·des·ti·nate, prē·des′tə·nāt, v.t., **-nat·ed, -nat·ing.** To predetermine or foreordain. **—pre·des′tə·nit,** pri·des′tə·nāt, a. Foreordained.

pre·des·ti·na·tion, prē·des·tə·nā′shən, n. The act of decreeing or foreordaining events; fate; destiny; the doctrine that God has from eternity determined whatever comes to pass.

pre·des·tine, prə·des′tin, v.t., **-tined, -tin·ing.** To decree or determine beforehand.

pre·de·ter·mine, prē·di·tər′min, v.t., **-mined, -min·ing.** To determine or decide beforehand; influence. **—pre·de·ter·mi·na·tion,** prē·di·tər·mə·nā′shən, n.

pred·i·ca·ble, pred′ə·kə·bəl, a. Capable of being affirmed.—n. Anything that may be predicated or affirmed. **—pred·i·ca·bil·i·ty,** pred·ə·kə·bil′ə·tē, n.

pre·dic·a·ment, pri·dik′ə·mənt, n. An unpleasant, trying, or dangerous situation.

pred·i·cate, pred′i·kāt, v.t., **-cat·ed, -cat·ing.** To proclaim or declare; affirm or assert; to connote or imply.—v.i. To make an affirmation or assertion. **—pred′i·kit,** a. Belonging to the predicate. **—pred′i·kit,** n. The word or words expressing what is affirmed or denied of a subject. **—pred·i·ca·tion,** pred·i·kā′shən, n. **—pred·i·ca·tive,** a.

pred·i·cate nom·i·na·tive, n. A noun, pronoun, or adjective, in certain languages, in the nominative case, identifying or modifying the subject of a linking verb.

pre·dict, pri·dikt′, v.t. To foretell.—v.i. To make a prediction. **—pre·dict·a·ble,** a. **—pre·dict·a·bly,** adv. **—pre·dict·a·bil·i·ty,** n.

pre·dic·tion, pri·dik′shən, n. The act of predicting; a foretelling; a prophecy. **—pre·dic·tive,** pri·dik′tiv, a.

pre·di·lec·tion, pred·ə·lek′shən, prē·də·lek′shən, n. A preconceived liking; partiality or preference.

pre·dis·po·si·tion, prē·dis·pə·zish′ən, n. The state of being previously disposed toward something; previous inclination or tendency. **—pre·dis·pose,** prē·dis·pōz′, **-posed, -pos·ing,** v.t.

pre·dom·i·nant, pri·dom′ə·nənt, a. Prevalent over others; superior in strength, influence, or authority; ruling; controlling. **—pre·dom·i·nance, pre·dom·i·nan·cy,** n.

pre·dom·i·nate, pri·dom′ə·nāt, v.i., **-nat·ed, -nat·ing.** To have surpassing power, influence, or authority; to surpass in number, size, or power.—v.t. To rule over; to dominate.—a. **—pre·dom·i·na·tion,** pri·dom·ə·nā′shən, n.

pre·em·i·nent, prē·em′ə·nənt, a. Eminent before or above others; superior to or surpassing others; distinguished beyond others. **—pre·em·i·nence,** n.

pre·empt, prē·empt′, v.t. To take before others. **—pre·emp·tor,** n.

pre·emp·tion, prē·emp′shən, n. The act or the right of purchasing before others; a prior assertion of ownership. **—pre·emp·tive,** prē·emp′tiv, a.

preen, prēn, v.t. To trim or clean with the beak; to make, as oneself, attractive by careful grooming; to show vanity or pride, as in some personal achievement.—v.i. To primp; to gloat. **—preen·er,** n.

pre·ex·ist, pre-ex·ist, prē·ig·zist′, v.t., v.i. To exist beforehand. **—pre·ex·ist·ence,** n. **—pre·ex·ist·**

ent, a.

pre·fab, prē′fab′, n. Something that is prefabricated, as a house.

pre·fab·ri·cate, prē·fab′rə·kāt, v.t., **-cat·ed, -cat·ing.** To fabricate or construct beforehand. **—pre·fab·ri·ca·tion,** prē·fab·rə·kā′shən, n.

pref·ace, pref′is, n. Something spoken as introductory to a discourse, or written as introductory to a book or other composition.—v.t., **-aced, -ac·ing.** To introduce with a preface. **—pref·a·to·ry,** pref′ə·tôr·ē, a.

pre·fer, pri·fər′, v.t., **-ferred, -fer·ring.** To set above something else in estimation; to hold in greater favor or esteem; to choose rather than: to prefer one to another; to offer for one's consideration or decision; to raise; to exalt. **—pre·fer·rer,** n.

pref·er·a·ble, pref′ər·ə·bəl, a. Worthy to be preferred; more eligible; more desirable. **—pref·er·a·ble·ness, pre·fer·a·bil·i·ty,** pref·ər·ə·bil′ə·tē, n. **—pref·er·a·bly,** adv.

pref·er·ence, pref′ər·əns, n. The preferring of one thing before another; the right or condition of having a choice or of being chosen; the thing or person preferred; a special advantage made available to one over another, as in trade between countries.

pref·er·en·tial, pref·ə·ren′shəl, a. Of or relating to preference; showing preference or partiality to; permitting a statement of preference, as the ballot in voting. **—pref·er·en·tial·ly,** adv.

pre·fer·ment, pri·fər′mənt, n. Advancement to a higher office, dignity, or station; promotion; a superior or valuable place or office.

pre·fix, prē·fiks′, v.t. To put or fix before or at the beginning of another thing, as a title preceding a name; to settle, fix, or appoint beforehand: to prefix the hour of meeting. **—prē′fiks,** n. A letter, syllable, or word put to the beginning of a stem, root, or base, usu. varying its meaning.

pre·flight, prē·flīt′, a. Happening before or preparing for an airplane flight.

pre·form, prē·fôrm′, v.t. To form or decide beforehand. **—prē′fôrm,** n. Something formed beforehand or only partly formed.

preg·na·ble, preg′nə·bəl, a. Capable of being taken or won by force; vulnerable. **—preg·na·bil·i·ty,** preg·nə·bil′ə·tē, n.

preg·nan·cy, preg′nən·sē, n. pl., **-cies.** The state, period, or quality of being pregnant.

preg·nant, preg′nənt, a. Carrying a fetus in the body; being with young; full or replete, usu. followed by with: pregnant with significance; showing fertility; full of consequence or significance.

pre·heat, prē·hēt′, v.t. To heat beforehand or before starting a subsequent process.

pre·hen·sile, pri·hen′sil, a. Capable of grasping, esp. by wrapping around something: a prehensile tail of a monkey. **—pre·hen·sil·i·ty,** prē·hen·sil′ə·tē, n.

pre·his·tor·ic, prē′his·tôr′ik, a. Relating to a period before that time when written history begins.

pre·his·to·ry, prē·his′tə·rē, n. The study of humans in the time which precedes written events; a history of the events prior to a situation or crisis.

pre·judge, prē·jej′, v.t., **-judged, -judg·ing.** To judge before hearing; to condemn beforehand or prematurely. **—pre·judg·er, pre·judg·ment, pre·judge·ment,** n.

prej·u·dice, prej′ū·dis, n. An opinion or judgment, favorable or more often unfavorable, conceived without proof or competent evidence; a bias against a race, creed, group, or the like; the holding of such feelings.—v.t., **-diced, -dic·ing.** To implant a prejudice in the mind of; to injure by an act or judgment.

prej·u·di·cial, prej·ū·dish′əl, a. Disposed to prejudice or hurt; injurious; detrimental. **—prej·u·di·cial·ly,** adv. **—prej·u·di·cial·ness,** n.

---

a- hat, fāte, fâre, fäther; **e-** met, mē; **i-** pin, pīne; **o-** not, nōte, ôrb, moove (move), boy, pownd; **u-** cūbe, bŭll, tûk (took); **ch-** chin; **th-** thick, then; **zh-** vizhon (vision); **ə-** əgo, takən, pencəl, lemən, bərd **(bird).**

prel·ate, prel'it, *n.* An ecclesiastic of a high order, as an archbishop, bishop, or patriarch; a dignitary of the church. —**prel·ate·ship,** *n.* —**prel·a·ture,** prel'ə·chər, *n.*

pre·lim, prē'lim, *n. Informal.* Preliminary.

pre·lim·i·nar·y, pri·lim'ə·ner·ē, *a.* Introductory; preceding the main discourse or business; prefatory. —*n. pl.,* **-ies.** Something introductory or preparatory; a preliminary examination, as for a college degree. —**pre·lim·i·nar·i·ly,** pri·lim·ə·nãr'ə·lē, *adv.*

prel·ude, prel'ūd, prāl'ūd, prē'lood, prā'lood, *n.* Something preparatory or leading up to what follows; an introductory happening or performance.—*v.t.,* **-ud·ed, -ud·ing.** To introduce with a prelude.—*v.i.* To serve as a prelude.

pre·ma·ture, prē·mə·tûr', prē·mə·tūr', prē·mə·chūr, *a.* Happening, arriving, existing, or done before the proper time; untimely. —**pre·ma·ture·ness,** pre·ma·tu·ri·ty, *n.*

pre·med·i·cal, prē·med'i·kəl, *a.* Referring to or engaged in studies preparatory to the professional study of medicine.

pre·med·i·tate, prē·med'ə·tāt, *v.t.,* **-tat·ed, -tat·ing.** To plan, consider, or think on beforehand.—*v.i.* To deliberate or think beforehand. —**pre·med·i·ta·tor,** *n.* —**pre·med·i·tat·ed,** *a.* —**pre·med·i·tat·ed·ly,** *adv.* —**pre·med·i·ta·tive,** *a.*

pre·med·i·ta·tion, prē·med·ə·tā'shən, *n.* The act of premeditating.

pre·men·stru·al, prē·men'stroo·əl, *a.* Referring to the period just prior to menstruation.

pre·mier, pri·mêr', prē·mêr', *a.* First; chief; principal; senior.—*n.* The first or chief minister of state; prime minister. —**pre·mier·ship,** *n.*

pre·miere, pri·mêr', pri·myãr', *n.* The initial public performance of a drama, opera, etc.—*v.i.* To be performed or shown publicly for the first time.—*v.t.* To present publicly for the first time.—*a.* First; principal; initial.

prem·ise, prem'is, *v.t.,* **-ised, -is·ing.** To set forth or make known beforehand, as introductory to the main subject; to lay down as a prior proposition.—*v.i.* To make or assume a premise.—*n.* A proposition laid down as a base of argument. *Pl.* Land including houses or tenements.

pre·mi·um, prē'mē·əm, *n.* A reward given for a particular action or as an incentive; a bonus offered as an inducement to purchase a product; the amount paid as the consideration for a contract of insurance; a sum above the nominal value of a thing; a sum, besides the interest, which is paid for the loan of money. —**at a pre·mi·um,** above the usual price; valuable; in demand.

pre·mo·ni·tion, prē·mə·nish'ən, prem·ə·nish'ən, *n.* A sense of fear concerning the future without any reason; previous warning or notice. —**pre·mon·i·to·ry,** pri·mon'ə·tôr·ē, *a.* —**pre·mon·i·to·ri·ly,** *adv.*

pre·na·tal, prē·nāt'əl, *a.* Previous to birth. —**pre·na·tal·ly,** *adv.*

pre·oc·cu·pa·tion, prē·ok·yə·pā'shən, *n.* The state of being mentally occupied with a subject other than the immediate concern.

pre·oc·cu·py, prē·ok'yə·pī, *v.t.,* **-pied, -py·ing.** To occupy the attention of. —**pre·oc·cu·pied,** *a.*

prep, prep, *n. Informal.* Preparatory.

prep·a·ra·tion, prep·ə·rā'shən, *n.* The act of preparing; the state of being prepared; something prepared, manufactured, or compounded: a medicinal *preparation.*

pre·par·a·to·ry, pri·par'ə·tôr·ē, *a.* Serving to prepare the way for something; introductory.—*adv.* —**pre·par·a·to·ri·ly,** *adv.*

pre·par·a·to·ry school, *n.* A private school providing an education which is designed primarily to prepare students for college.

pre·pare, pri·pãr', *v.t.,* **-pared, -par·ing.** To make ready: to *prepare* a manuscript for printing; fit out or

equip; to get ready, manufacture, or compose, as a meal or medicine.—*v.i.* To put things or oneself in readiness; make preparations. —**pre·par·er,** *n.*

pre·par·ed·ness, pri·pãr'id·nis, *n.* The state of being prepared.

pre·pay, prē·pā', *v.t.,* **-paid, -pay·ing.** To pay in advance. —**pre·pay·ment,** *n.*

pre·plan, prē·plan', *v.t.,* **-planned, -plan·ning.** To anticipate an accomplishment by setting forth the steps necessary to a successful conclusion.

pre·pon·der·ant, pri·pon'dər·ənt, *a.* Preponderating; superior in weight, force, influence, or number; predominant. —**pre·pon·der·ance,** pri·pon'der·əns, *n. Also* **pre·pon·der·an·cy.** —**pre·pon·der·ant·ly,** *adv.*

pre·pon·der·ate, pri·pon'də·rāt, *v.i.,* **-at·ed, -at·ing.** To exceed something else in weight; to incline downward because of greater weight; to be superior in power, influence, or amount; predominate. —**pre·pon·der·at·ing·ly,** *adv.* —**pre·pon·der·a·tion,** pri·pon·də·rā'shən, *n.*

prep·o·si·tion, prep·ə·zish'ən, *n.* An indeclinable part of speech, as *by, in, to, for, from,* usu. placed before a noun or its equivalent forming a prepositional phrase, and showing the relation to a substantive, verb, or adjective: a man *from* the city. —**prep·o·si·tion·al,** *a.*

pre·pos·sess, prē·pə·zes', *v.t.* To possess or dominate mentally beforehand, as a prejudice does; prejudice or bias, esp. favorably.

pre·pos·sess·ing, prē·pə·zes'ing, *a.* Making a favorable first impression. —**pre·pos·sess·ing·ly,** *adv.*

pre·pos·ter·ous, pri·pos'tər·əs, *a.* Contrary to nature, reason, or common sense; utterly foolish; absurd.

pre·puce, prē'pūs, *n.* A fold of skin covering the head of the penis or the clitoris; foreskin. —**pre·pu·tial,** pri·pū'shəl, *a.*

pre·re·cord, prē·ri·kôrd', *v.t.* To record, as a television program, before the actual presentation to the public.

pre·req·ui·site, prē·rek'wə·zit, *a.* Necessary to something subsequent.—*n.* Something that is prerequisite.

pre·rog·a·tive, pri·rog'ə·tiv, *n.* An official or hereditary right which may be asserted without question.—*a.* Having or pertaining to a prerogative.

pres·age, pres'ij, *n.* Something which portends or foreshadows a future event; a prognostic; an omen. —pres'ij, pri·sāj', *v.t.,* **-aged, -ag·ing.**—*v.i.* To form or utter a prediction. —**pres·ag·er,** *n.*

pres·by·ter, prez'bə·tər, pres'bə·tər, *n.* In the Presbyterian church, a member of a presbytery.

Pres·by·te·ri·an, prez·bə·têr'ē·ən, pres·bə·têr'ē·ən, *a.* Designating or referring to various churches having this form of government and holding more or less modified forms of Calvinism.—*n.* A member of a Presbyterian church. —**Pres·by·te·ri·an·ism,** prez·bə·têr'ē·ə·niz·əm, *n.*

pres·by·ter·y, prez'bə·ter·ē, pres'bə·ter·ē, *n. pl.,* **pres·by·ter·ies.** A body of presbyters or elders; the district under the jurisdiction of such elders; the part of a church appropriated to the clergy.

pre·school, prē'skool', *a.* Pertaining to the period or to a child in the period from infancy to school age. —prē'skool, *n.* A nursery school.

pre·scribe, pri·skrīb', *v.t.,* **-scribed, -scrib·ing.** To lay down as a rule or a course to be followed; ordain as duties or actions; to order for use, as a remedy or treatment.—*v.i.* To lay down rules, direct, or dictate; to designate remedies or treatment to be used. —**pre·scrib·er,** *n.*

pre·script, pri·skript', prē'skript, *a.* Set down as a rule; prescribed. —prē'skript, *n.* A regulation or precept.

pre·scrip·tion, pri·skrip'shən, *n.* A physician's direction, usually written, for the preparation and use of a medicine; the medicine prescribed; the act of prescribing; that which is prescribed. —**pre·scrip·tive,** pri·skrip′tiv, *a.*

pre·sea·son, prē·sē′zən, *a.* Of or referring to the first games or other events of a regularly scheduled season, as exhibition professional baseball games.

pres·ence, prez′əns, *n.* The state of being present, as with others or in a place; attendance or company: to request one's *presence* at a gathering; immediate vicinity or close proximity: an act done in the *presence* of witnesses; a confident bearing; personal appearance or bearing; a person, esp. of dignified or fine appearance, or an imposing personage; something ghostly felt as present.

pres·ence of mind, *n.* Coolness and self-possession on difficult occasions.

pre·sent, pri·zent′, *v.t.* To bring, as a person, before or into the presence of another, esp. a superior; introduce formally; bring before the public; come to show, as oneself, before a person, in or at a place, etc.; to show or exhibit: to *present* a fine appearance; bring before the mind, or offer for consideration: to *present* facts; to direct, point, or turn to something or in a particular way: to *present* one's face to the foe; to level or aim, as a weapon; to hold out for taking; hand or send in, as a bill or a check, for payment; give, esp. in a formal or ceremonious way; to afford or furnish; to approach with something offered; to furnish or endow with a gift or the like, esp. by formal act: to *present* a man with a gold watch.—*n.* Something presented; a gift. —**pre·sent·er,** *n.*

pres·ent, prez′ənt, *a.* Being with one or others; being here or there, rather than elsewhere; existing in a place, thing, combination, or the like: Copper is *present* in many minerals; being actually or here under consideration; being at hand: a very *present* danger; being, existing, or occurring at this time or now: opposed to *past* and *future;* for the time being: articles for *present* use.—*n.* The present time; the present tense, or a verb form in the present tense.

pre·sent·a·ble, pri·zen′tə·bəl, *a.* Capable of being presented; in such dress or appearance as to be able to present oneself without embarrassment; suitable to be exhibited or offered. —**pre·sent·a·bil·i·ty,** pri·zen·tə·bil′ə·tē, **pre·sent·a·ble·ness,** *n.* —**pre·sent·a·bly,** *adv.*

pre·sent arms, pri·zent′, *n.* The position in which a rifle is held perpendicularly in front of the body, in the manual of arms; the order to take this position.

pres·en·ta·tion, prez·ən·tā′shən, prē·zən·tā′shən, *n.* The act of presenting, or the state of being presented; introduction, as of a person at court; that which is presented, as a gift.

pres·ent-day, prez′ənt·dā′, *a.* Of this day; of the present or recent times; current: *present-day* styles.

pres·ent·ly, prez′ənt·lē, *adv.* In a little time; soon; forthwith; now.

pres·ent par·ti·ci·ple, *n.* A participle having present meaning, formed by adding the suffix *-ing* to a verb.

pres·ent per·fect, *n.* A verb tense, formed from a past participle preceded by the present tense of *have,* and denoting a completed action completed at the present time: The boy *has eaten.*

pre·serv·a·tive, pri·zər′və·tiv, *a.* Having the power to or tending to preserve.—*n.* That which preserves or has the power of preserving.

pre·serve, pri·zərv′, *v.t.,* **-served, -serv·ing.** To keep or save from harm or destruction; to save; to keep in the same state; to uphold, sustain, protect; to cause to remain good and wholesome, as food, by canning, smoking, pickling, or otherwise.—*v.i.* To preserve foods; to protect game for purposes of sport.—*n.* That which preserves or is preserved; *usu. pl.,* fruit which

has been cooked and canned, as in the form of jam; a place set apart for the shelter and protection of game or other natural resources. —**pre·serv·a·ble,** *a.* —**pres·er·va·tion,** prez·ər·vā′shən, **pre·serv·er,** *n.*

pre·side, pri·zīd′, *v.i.,* **-sid·ed, -sid·ing.** To hold a place of authority over others, as a president, judge of a court, or chairman of a meeting; to direct. —**pre·sid·er,** *n.*

pres·i·den·cy, prez′ə·dən·sē, *n. pl.,* **-cies.** The office of a president; *(often cap.)* The office and term of the president of the United States.

pres·i·dent, prez′ə·dənt, *n. (Often cap.)* The chief executive of a republic; the chief officer of a corporation, company, board of trade, governmental unit, or similar organization; the chief officer of a college or university. —**pres·i·den·tial,** prez·ə·den′shəl, *a.*

press, pres, *n.* An instrument or machine by which any body is squeezed, crushed, or forced into a more compact form; a printing press; printed literature in general, esp. newspapers, with *the;* newspaper reporters; a printing, publishing, or broadcasting establishment, and its personnel; a crowd; the act of pressing; the state of being pressed or pressured; a wine vat or cistern; urgency; a wooden or metal frame to prevent warping, as of a tennis racket; the state of smoothness of a pressed garment.—*v.t.* To act on with force or weight; to squeeze; to crush; to squeeze for the purpose of making smooth; to iron, as clothing; to embrace closely; to constrain or compel; to distress: to be *pressed* for money; to urge or solicit with earnestness; to importune; to enforce; to bear hard upon.—*v.i.* To exert pressure; to bear heavily; to strain or strive eagerly; to crowd; to force one's way; to urge; to iron clothes. —**press·er,** pres′ər, *n.*

press a·gent, *n.* A person employed to promote the interests of a person, product, or organization, through advertisements and other notices.

press·board, pres′bôrd, *n.* Pasteboard.

press box, *n.* An area reserved for reporters at a sporting event.

press con·fer·ence, *n.* An interview granted by a celebrity or dignitary to many reporters at the same time.

press·ing, pres′ing, *a.* Urgent.

press re·lease, *n.* A prepared statement or bulletin given to a newspaper for publication.

pres·sure, presh′ər, *n.* The act of pressing; the state of being squeezed or crushed; a constraining force acting on the mind; severity, as of personal circumstances; urgency; demand on one's time or energies: the *pressure* of business; force exerted per unit area of surface; atmospheric pressure; electromotive force.—*v.t.,* **-sured, -sur·ing.** To persuade forcefully, or compel; to pressurize.

pres·sure cook·er, *n.* An apparatus which may be sealed for rapid cooking or sterilizing under high-pressure steam. —**pres·sure-cook,** *v.t.*

pres·sure gauge, *n.* A gauge used to measure the pressure of a gas or fluid.

pres·sure group, *n.* Any special interest group that attempts to influence legislative or public opinion.

pres·su·rize, presh′ə·rīz, *v.t.,* **-rized, -riz·ing.** To fill with air under pressure in order to maintain near-normal levels when outside pressure is low, as in aircraft flying at high altitudes; to fill (a container) with compressed air, gas, or liquid; to cook with steam pressure. —**pres·su·riz·er,** **pres·sur·i·za·tion,** presh·ər·ə·zā′shən, *n.*

press·work, pres′wərk, *n.* The operation of and work done by a printing press.

pres·ti·dig·i·ta·tion, pres·tə·dij·ə·tā′shən, *n.* Sleight of hand; legerdemain; juggling. —**pres·ti·dig·i·ta·tor,** pres·tə·dij′ə·tā·tər, *n.*

pres·tige, pre·stēzh′, pre·stēj′, *n.* Renown or influence derived from previously established personal attributes, achievements, or associations.—*a.* Showing or having the attributes of quality, rank, or distinction.

pres·tig·ious, pre·stij'əs, pre·stē'jəs, *a.* Having an excellent reputation.

pres·to, pres'tō, *n.* A quick, lively, musical passage. —*adv.* Quickly; immediately; in haste.

pre·sum·a·ble, pri·zoom'ə·bəl, *a.* Capable of being presumed; probable. —**pre·sum·a·bly,** *adv.*

pre·sume, pri·zoom', *v.t.,* **-sumed, -sum·ing.** To take for granted; to suppose (something); to dare, used with an infinitive: I do not *presume* to know all.—*v.i.* To suppose or believe without examination; to take the liberty. —**pre·sum·er,** *n.*

pre·sum·ing, pri·zoom'ing, *a.* Presumptuous.

pre·sump·tion, pri·zəmp'shən, *n.* A supposition; a ground for presuming; a strong probability; presumptuousness; arrogance.

pre·sump·tive, pri·zəmp'tiv, *a.* Based on presumption or probability.

pre·sump·tu·ous, pri·zəmp'choo·əs, *a.* Imbued with or characterized by presumption; arrogant; overconfident.

pre·sup·pose, prē·sə·pōz', *v.t.,* **-posed, -pos·ing.** To suppose or assume in advance; to take for granted. —**pre·sup·po·si·tion,** prē·səp·ə·zish'ən, *n.*

pre·tend, pri·tend', *v.t.* To allege falsely; to make false appearance or representation of; to feign or affect: to *pretend* zeal.—*v.i.* To feign or make believe; to put in a claim, usu. with *to.* —**pre·tend·ed,** *a.*

pre·tend·er, pri·ten'dər, *n.* One who pretends.

pre·tense, pri·tens', prē'tens, *n.* The act of pretending; affectation; an excuse.

pre·ten·sion, pri·ten'shən, *n.* A demand or claim to privilege, honor, title, or rank; pretentiousness.

pre·ten·tious, pri·ten'shəs, *a.* Full of pretension; showy. —**pre·ten·tious·ness,** *n.*

pre·test, prē'test, *n.* A preliminary trial or test for exploratory purposes. —prē·test', *v.t.* To administer a pretest to.

pre·text, prē'tekst, *n.* A reason or motive assumed as a cover for the real reason or motive; a pretense.

pret·ti·fy, prit'i·fī, *v.t.,* **-fied, -fy·ing.** To make pretty: often used with a disparaging intent: to *prettify* a work of art. —**pret·ti·fi·ca·tion,** prit·i·fi·kā'shən, *n.*

pret·ty, prit'ē, *a.* Having a pleasing and attractive appearance, without great beauty; affected; nice; good or fine; used ironically: a *pretty* state of affairs; a great deal: the car cost a *pretty* penny.—*adv.* In some degree; moderately: *pretty* often.—*n. pl.,* **-ties.** Someone or something that is pretty.—*v.t.,* **-tied, -ty·ing.** —**pret·ti·ly,** *adv.* —**pret·ti·ness,** *n.* —**pret·ty·ish,** *a.*

pret·zel, pret'səl, *n.* A crisp, glazed, salted, usually knot-shaped cracker.

pre·vail, pri·vāl', *v.i.* To overcome; to gain victory or superiority, used with *over* or *against;* to be in force; to have great power or influence; to succeed; to overcome by persuasion, with *on* or *upon:* They *prevailed on* him to go.

pre·vail·ing, pri·vā'ling, *a.* Predominant.

prev·a·lent, prev'ə·lənt, *a.* Prevailing; widely existing. —**prev·a·lence,** *n.*

pre·vent, pri·vent', *v.t.* To keep from occurring; thwart.—*v.i.* To interpose a hindrance. —**pre·vent·a·bil·i·ty,** *n.* —**pre·vent·a·ble, pre·vent·i·ble,** *a.* —**pre·vent·er,** *n.*

pre·ven·tion, pri·ven'shən, *n.* The act of preventing.

pre·ven·tive, pri·ven'tiv, *a.* Serving to prevent or hinder.—*n.* A precautionary agent or measure; a drug or other substance for preventing disease. Also **pre·vent·a·tive,** pri·ven'tə·tiv.

pre·view, prē'vū, *n.* A previous view or showing; a view in advance, as of a motion picture.—*v.t.* To view or exhibit beforehand or in advance.

pre·vi·ous, prē'vē·əs, *a.* Going before in time; prior.

pre·war, prē'wôr', *a.* Before the war.

prey, prā, *n.* An animal seized or hunted as food by a meat-eating animal; a person or thing that becomes the victim of an attacker, a fraud, or the like; the act or the habit of preying: a beast of *prey.*—*v.i.* To take and devour prey; to victimize, as by fraud; to have a harmful or wasting influence or effect: to *prey* on one's mind; to attack or plunder: usu. followed by *on* or *upon.* —**prey·er,** *n.*

price, prīs, *n.* The sum or amount of money or its equivalent for which anything is bought, sold, or offered for sale; that which must be given, done, or undergone in order to obtain a thing; to gain a victory at a heavy *price;* value or worth.—*v.t.,* **priced, pric·ing.** To fix the price of; to ask the price of. —**pric·er,** *n.*

price·less, prīs'lis, *a.* Having a value beyond all price; invaluable. *Informal.* Very amusing.

prick, prik, *n.* A puncture made by a needle, thorn, or the like; the act of pricking; the sensation of being pricked; any pointed instrument or weapon.—*v.t.* To pierce with a sharp point; puncture; sting, as with remorse or sorrow; to urge on or incite; to cause to stand erect or point upward, as the ears of an animal. —*v.i.* To perform the action of piercing or puncturing something; to have a sensation of being pricked; to rise erect or point upward, as the ears of an animal, followed by *up.* —**prick up one's ears,** to listen carefully; become attentive. —**prick·er,** *n.*

prick·le, prik'əl, *n.* A sharp, small point or pointed projection, esp. one growing from the bark of a plant; a pricking or tingling sensation.—*v.t.,* **-led, -ling.** To prick; to cause a pricking sensation in.—*v.i.* To be affected with a pricking sensation.

prick·ly, prik'lē, *a.* **-li·er, -li·est.** Full of or armed with prickles; full of troublesome points, or difficult to deal with; having the sensation of being pricked; tingling. —**prick·li·ness,** *n.*

prick·ly heat, *n.* An itching sensation and rash, due to an inflammation of the sweat glands.

pride, prīd, *n.* The quality or state of being proud; inordinate self-esteem; a reasonable self-reference based on a consciousness of worth; that which causes one to be proud. A group of lions.—*v.t.,* **prid·ed, prid·ing.** To indulge in pride: used reflexively, with *on* or *upon:* to *pride* oneself on one's accomplishments.

pride·ful, prīd'fəl, *a.* Full of pride; arrogant.

pri·er, prī'ər, *n.* One who looks or searches curiously into something.

priest, prēst, *n.* A clergyman ranking below bishop in the Roman Catholic, Eastern Orthodox, or Episcopalian church; a person consecrated to the ministry; the title of people selected and trained to perform sacred functions. —**priest·ess,** prē'stis, *n. fem.* —**priest·hood,** *n.*

priest·ly, prēst'lē, *a.,* **-li·er, -li·est.** Pertaining to a priest or to priests. —**priest·li·ness,** *n.*

prig, prig, *n.* One who affects great superiority in principles, views, or standards, esp. in a self-righteous way. —**prig·gish,** prig'ish, *a.*

prim, prim, *a.,* **prim·mer, prim·mest.** Affectedly or formally precise or proper, as persons, or behavior; stiffly formal, neat, or regular.—*v.i.,* **primmed, prim·ming.** To draw up the mouth in an affectedly nice or precise way.—*v.t.* To make prim, as in appearance. —**prim·ness,** *n.*

pri·ma·cy, prī'mə·sē, *n. pl.,* **-cies.** The state of being first in rank or importance.

pri·ma don·na, prē'mə don'ə, prim'ə don'ə, *n. pl.,* **pri·ma don·nas.** The first or chief female singer in an opera; a vain, temperamental person.

pri·mal, prī'məl, *a.* Primary; original; primitive; first in importance.

pri·ma·ri·ly, prī·mâr'ə·lē, prī'mâr·ə·lē, *adv.* Chiefly; principally; essentially; at first.

pri·ma·ry, prī'mer·ē, prī'mə·rē, *a.* First in time; earliest; primitive; first in order in any series or sequence; preparatory, or lowest in order: *primary* schools; first or highest in rank or importance; chief; principal;

original, not derived or subordinate; fundamental; basic.—*n. pl.,* **-ries.** That which is first in order, rank, or importance; a meeting or gathering of the voters of a political party in an election district, as for nominating candidates for office; caucus.

pri•mate, prī′māt, prī′mit, *n.* An archbishop or bishop ranking first among the bishops of a province or country.

pri•mate, prī′māt, *n.* Any of the highest order of mammals, including humans, monkeys, apes, and lemurs.

prime, prīm, *a.* First in importance or significance: a *prime* consideration; principal; highest in rank, dignity, or authority: the *prime* minister; chief; first in excellence or value; of the first grade or best quality: *prime* ribs of beef; earliest; primitive; fundamental. —*n.* The most flourishing stage or state; the period or state of greatest perfection or vigor of human life; the choicest or best part of anything; the beginning or earliest stage of any period.—*v.t.,* **primed, prim•ing.** To prepare or make ready for a particular purpose or operation; to pour liquid into, as a pump, so as to keep out the air and establish suction, thus preparing it for operation; to cover, as a surface, with a preparatory coat or color, as in painting; to supply or equip beforehand with information, words, or the like.—*v.i.* Of a boiler or steam engine, to operate so that water is carried over into the cylinder with the steam; to become prime.

prime me•rid•i•an, *n.* A meridian from which longitude east and west is reckoned, as that of Greenwich, England.

prime min•is•ter, *n.* The principal minister of a government; the chief of the cabinet or ministry.

prim•er, prim′ər, *n.* A small, elementary book for teaching children to read; a book of elementary principles.

prim•er, prī′mər, *n.* One who or that which primes.

prime rate, *n.* The minimum bank loan interest.

prime time, *n.* The major hours for watching television, between 8 p.m. and 11 p.m.

pri•me•val, prī•mē′vəl, *a.* Original; primitive.

prim•ing, prī′ming, *n.* The powder used to ignite a charge; the action or means with which something is primed.

prim•i•tive, prim′ə•tiv, *a.* Being the first or earliest of the kind or in existence, esp. in an early age of the world; unaffected or little affected by civilizing influences; rude, or rudely simple; old-fashioned; early; rudimentary, as an organ; primordial.—*n.* Something primitive; an artist, esp. a painter belonging to an early period; a work of art by such an artist; a primitive person.

pri•mo•gen•i•tor, prī•mə•jen′ə•tər, *n.* The first father or earliest forefather; an ancestor.

pri•mo•gen•i•ture, prī•mə•jen′ə•chər, *n.* The state of being the first-born of the same parents; the right of the first-born son to succeed to his father's estate to the exclusion of the younger sons and any daughters.

pri•mor•di•al, prī•môr′dē•əl, *a.* First in order of development; original; existing from the beginning. —**pri•mor•di•al•ly,** *adv.*

primp, primp, *v.t.* To adorn, dispose, or dress in a fussy, exacting manner.—*v.i.* To groom oneself in a finicky, overly careful manner.

prim•rose, prim′rōz, *n.* A type of perennial herb with yellow flowers, grown in flower gardens; a pale yellow color. Also **prim•rose yel•low.**—*a.* Referring to the primrose; of a pale yellow color.

prim•rose path, *n.* The leading of a gay or merry life; indulgence in the sensual pleasures of life; the tempting, easy way.

prince, prins, *n.* A male, nonreigning member of a royal family; the actual or nominal ruler of a small state or territory; a man at the head of any class or profession: a merchant *prince;* a man of admirable, likable personal qualities.

prince con•sort, *n. pl.,* **princ•es con•sort.** A prince who is the husband of a reigning female sovereign.

prince•ly, prins′lē, *a.,* **-li•er, -li•est.** Referring to a prince; resembling a prince; noble; generous; lavish. —**prince•li•ness,** *n.*

prin•cess, prin′sis, prin′ses, *n.* A nonregnant female member of a royal family; the consort of a prince.

prin•ci•pal, prin′sə•pəl, *a.* Chief; highest or first in rank, character, authority, or importance.—*n.* A chief or head; one who has a leading part, as in a play; the chief executive of a public school; the capital of an estate, as distinct from income; a capital sum lent on interest, due as a debt, or used as a fund, as distinct from interest. —**prin•ci•pal•ly,** *adv.*

prin•ci•pal•i•ty, prin•sə•pal′ə•tē, *n. pl.,* **-ties.** The territory of a prince, or the country which gives title to a prince; the position or office of a prince; sovereignty; supreme power.

prin•ci•ple, prin′sə•pəl, *n.* A general truth; a law comprehending many subordinate truths; a method or rule adopted as the basis for action or conduct; uprightness: a man of *principle;* the primary source from which anything proceeds; a basic doctrine or tenet; an underlying cause; a precept seen in natural phenomena or underlying the operation of a machine: the *principle* of gravity.

prin•ci•pled, prin′sə•pəld, *a.* Characterized by, or founded on, ethical principles.

print, print, *n.* An indentation or mark made by the pressure of one body or thing on another; something with which an impression is made; a stamp or die; printed lettering; printed matter; a picture or design printed from an engraved block or plate; a photographic picture made from a negative.—*v.t.* To indent or mark, as a surface; to impress on the mind or memory; to produce, as a book or picture, by applying inked types, plates, or blocks to paper; to write in letters like those commonly used in print; to mark, as cloth, with a pattern or design in color.—*v.i.* To take impressions from type, as in a press; produce by means of a press or other printing process; to follow the vocation of a printer; to write in characters such as are used in print. —**in print,** in printed form; still available for purchase from the publisher. —**out of print,** no longer available for purchase from the publisher. —**print•er,** *n.*

print•a•ble, prin′tə•bəl, *a.* Capable of being printed; fit to print.

print•ed cir•cuit, *n.* A circuit for electronic equipment which uses paths of conductive material printed on an insulating sheet or panel to conduct the current.

print•ing, prin′ting, *n.* The act of one who or that which prints; the process, or business of producing books, newspapers, or periodicals by impression from movable type or plates; typography; printed matter; all the copies of a book printed at one time; writing in which the letters are like those commonly used in print.

print•ing press, *n.* A machine for printing on paper or the like from type or plates.

print-out, print′owt, *n.* The processed data issued in printed form by a computer on continuous strips of paper.

pri•or, prī′ər, *a.* Preceding in time or in order; earlier or former. —**pri•or to,** in advance of; before.

pri•or, prī′ər, *n.* A superior officer in a monastic order or religious house next in rank below an abbot. —**pri•or•ate,** prī′ər•it, *n.*

pri•or•ess, prī′ər•is, *n.* A woman holding a position corresponding to that of a prior, sometimes ranking next below an abbess.

---

a- hat, fāte, fāre, fäther; **e-** met, mē; **i-** pin, pīne; **o-** not, nōte, ôrb, moove (move), boy, pownd; **u-** cūbe, bûll, tûk (took); **ch-** chin; **th-** thick, ŧhen; **zh-** vizhon (vision); **ə-** əgo, takən, pencəl, lemən, bərd (bird).

pri•or•i•ty, prī•ôr′ə•tē, prī•or′ə•tē, *n. pl.,* **-ties.** The state of being earlier in time, or of preceding something else; precedence in order, importance, or rank; the having of certain rights and privileges before another; that which needs or merits attention before others.

pri•or•y, prī′ə•rē, *n. pl.,* **-ries.** A religious house ruled by a prior or prioress.

prism, priz′əm, *n.* A solid whose bases are similar, equivalent, and parallel polygons, and whose sides are parallelograms; a body of this form, made of glass or other transparent substance, used esp. for polarizing or separating light into its spectrum. **—pris•mat•ic,** priz•mat′ik, *a.* **—pris•mat•i•cal•ly,** *adv.*

pris•on, priz′ən, *n.* A place of confinement or restraint; a public building for the confinement or custody of criminals and others committed by process of law; a jail.—*v.t.* To shut up in a prison; to confine.

pris•on•er, priz′ə•nər, priz′nər, *n.* One who is confined in a prison; a person under arrest, whether in prison or not; one whose liberty is restrained.

pris•sy, pris′ē, *a.,* **-si•er, -si•est.** Precise; prim. **—pris•si•ly,** *adv.* **—pris•si•ness,** *n.*

pris•tine, pris′tēn, pris′tin, pris•tēn′, *a.* Belonging to a primitive or early state or period; original; primitive; pure; uncontaminated.

pri•va•cy, prī′və•sē, *n.* A state of being private; seclusion; solitude.

pri•vate, prī′vit, *a.* Belonging to some particular person or persons: *private* property; pertaining to or affecting a particular person or a small group of persons: a *private* wrong; individual; personal; intended only for the person or persons immediately concerned; confidential; not holding public office or employment; not of an official or public character; secluded; intimate; of, pertaining to, or receiving special privileges and services in a hospital; of the rank of private.—*n.* In the U.S. Army and Marine Corps, any enlisted man below the rank of corporal. *Pl.* The external organs of sex. Also **pri•vate parts. —in pri•vate,** in secret; not publicly.

pri•vate first class, *n.* An enlisted man with a rank above private and immediately below that of corporal.

pri•va•tion, prī•vā′shən, *n.* The state of being deprived; destitution; want. **—priv•a•tive,** priv′ə•tiv, *a.*

priv•et, priv′it, *n.* An ornamental shrub with small white flowers, much used for hedges.

priv•i•lege, priv′ə•lij, priv′lij, *n.* A right or immunity enjoyed by a person or persons beyond the common advantages of others; any of the more sacred and vital rights common to all citizens under a modern constitutional government.—*v.t.,* **-leged, -leg•ing.** To grant a privilege to.

priv•i•leged, priv′ə•lijd, priv′lijd, *a.* Relating to a favored person or group; limited to a chosen individual or group: *privileged* documents.

priv•y, priv′ē, *a.* Participating in the knowledge of something private or secret, usu. followed by *to:* Many persons were *privy* to the plot; private, esp. with reference to a sovereign.—*n. pl.,* **-ies.** An outdoor toilet. **—priv•i•ly,** *adv.*

prix fixe, prē fēks′, *n.* A fixed price for a meal at a restaurant.

prize, prīz, *n.* A reward for victory or superiority, as in a contest or competition; that which is won in a lottery or the like; anything much valued; something seized or captured; the act of seizing or capturing.—*a.* That has gained a prize; worthy of a prize; outstanding. —*v.t.,* **prized, priz•ing.** To seize as a prize. **—prize•win•ner,** prīz′win•ər, *n.* **—prize•win•ning,** *a.*

prize, prīz, *v.t.,* **prized, priz•ing.** To value or esteem highly.

prize•fight, prīz′fīt, *n.* An exhibition contest between boxers for a prize, usu. money. **—prize•fight•er, prize•fight•ing,** *n.*

prize ring, *n.* A rope-enclosed platform or other area for prize fighting.

pro, prō, *adv.* In favor of a proposition or opinion: opposed to *con.—n. pl.,* **pros.** A consideration, argument, or vote for something; a person arguing or voting for a proposal.

pro, prō, *a.* Professional: a *pro* golfer.—*n. pl.,* **pros.**

prob•a•bil•i•ty, prob•ə•bil′ə•tē, *n. pl.,* **-ties.** The state or quality of being probable; likelihood; the ratio of the number of chances by which an event may happen to the number by which it may both happen and fail.

prob•a•ble, prob′ə•bəl, *a.* Supported by or based on evidence which inclines the mind to belief, but leaves some room for doubt; likely. **—prob•a•bly,** *adv.*

pro•bate, prō′bāt, *n.* The official proving of a will as genuine; an officially certified copy of a will so proved.—*a.* Of or pertaining to probate.—*v.t.,* **-bat•ed, -bat•ing.** To establish the genuineness of, as a will.

pro•ba•tion, prō•bā′shən, *n.* The act of proving; proof; a preliminary trial or examination; a period of suspension of penalty, as of imprisonment for a crime or of dismissal because of scholastic failure: usu. preceded by *on;* a period of time during which a delinquent must report at regular intervals to a probation officer. **—pro•ba•tion•al, pro•ba•tion•ar•y,** *a.* **—pro•ba•tion•al•ly,** *adv.*

pro•ba•tion•er, prō•bā′shə•nər, *n.* One who is on probation or trial.

pro•ba•tive, prō′bə•tiv, prob′ə•tiv, *a.* Serving or designed for testing or trial; affording proof or evidence.

probe, prōb, *n.* An instrument for examining the depth or other circumstances of a wound, or cavity; an investigation, esp. of an alleged illegal activity; a device used to explore outer space and send back data.—*v.t.,* **probed, prob•ing.** To apply a probe to; to inquire thoroughly into.—*v.i.* **—prob•er,** *n.*

prob•lem, prob′ləm, *n.* A question proposed for solution or decision; a knotty point requiring clarification. —*a.* Not well adjusted in behavior: a *problem* child; dealing with matters arising out of conflicting social values and relationships: a *problem* drama.

prob•lem•at•ic, prob•lə•mat′ik, *a.* Constituting a problem; doubtful. **—prob•lem•at•i•cal,** *a.*

pro•bos•cis, prō•bos′is, *n. pl.,* **-cis•es, -ci•des,** -dēz. The snout or trunk projecting from the head of an elephant or other animal.

pro•ce•dure, prə•sē′jər, *n.* The act or manner of proceeding in any action or process; a particular course or mode of action, esp. a mode of conducting legal, parliamentary, or other business. **—pro•ce•dur•al,** *a.* **—pro•ce•dur•al•ly,** *adv.*

pro•ceed, prə•sēd′, *v.i.* To go onward; to continue or renew motion or progress; to advance; to issue or come from an origin or source, used with *from.*

pro•ceed•ing, prə•sē′ding, *n.* The act of one who or that which proceeds; action; a particular action or course of action; *pl.,* records of the doings of a society; a legal step or measure: to institute *proceedings* against a person.

pro•ceeds, prō′sēdz, *n. pl.* The financial return from a business undertaking.

proc•ess, pros′es, *n.* A succession of actions undertaken to bring about some desired result: a *process* for refining metal; a series of gradual changes moving toward some particular end: the aging *process;* a summons, writ, or judicial order to compel a defendant to appear in court; the proceedings of a court or legal action; a projecting outgrowth; a forward movement.—*v.t.* To treat or prepare by some particular process; to institute a legal action against.—*v.i.* To undergo processing.—*a.* Produced or treated by some artificial or specified means: *process* sugar.

pro•ces•sion, prə•sesh′ən, *n.* The moving along in orderly succession, in a formal manner, of a line of persons, animals, vehicles, or other things; the line of persons or things moving along.—*v.i.* To move in procession.

pro•ces•sion•al, prə•sesh′ə•nəl, *a.* Of, pertaining

to, or characteristic of a procession.—*n.* A book containing hymns or litanies for use in religious processions.

pro·claim, prō·klām′, prə·klām′, *v.t.* To make known by public announcement; to announce officially. —**pro·claim·er,** *n.*

proc·la·ma·tion, prok·lə·mā′shən, *n.* The act of proclaiming; an official public announcement or declaration.

pro·cliv·i·ty, prō·kliv′ə·tē, *n. pl.,* **-ties.** Inclination or propensity; tendency.

pro·cras·ti·nate, prō·kras′tə·nāt, *v.t.,* **-nat·ed, -nat·ing.** To put off from day to day; to delay.—*v.i.* To delay action. —**pro·cras·ti·na·tion,** prō·kras·tə·nā′shən, **pro·cras·ti·na·tor,** *n.*

pro·cre·ate, prō′krē·āt, *v.t.,* **-at·ed, -at·ing.** To beget; to reproduce. —**pro·cre·a·tion,** prō·krē·ā′shən, *n.* —**pro·cre·a·tive,** *a.* —**pro·cre·a·tor,** *n.*

proc·tor, prok′tər, *n.* A person employed to manage another's cause; an individual in a college or university whose function is to see that order is kept and to supervise examinations.—*v.t., v.i.* To supervise. —**proc·to·ri·al,** prok·tôr′ē·əl, *a.*

proc·u·ra·tor, prok′yə·rā·tər, *n.* The manager of another's affairs. —**proc·u·ra·to·ri·al,** prok·yə·rə·tôr′ē·əl, *a.* —**proc·u·ra·tor·ship,** *n.*

pro·cure, prō·kyûr′, *v.t.,* **-cured, -cur·ing.** To obtain, as by effort, labor, or purchase; to get, gain, come into possession of; to obtain for prostitution.—*v.i.* To pimp. —**pro·cur·a·ble,** *a.* —**pro·cur·ance, pro·cure·ment, pro·cur·er,** *n.*

prod, prod, *v.t.,* **prod·ded, prod·ding.** To poke or jab with something pointed; to rouse as if by poking; to urge into action.—*n.* An act of prodding; a poke or jab; any of various pointed instruments, as a goad. —**prod·der,** *n.*

prod·i·gal, prod′ə·gəl, *a.* Given to extravagant expenditure; wasteful; lavishly bountiful.—*n.* One who spends money extravagantly; a waster. —**prod·i·gal·i·ty,** prod·ə·gal′ə·tē, *n.* —**prod·i·gal·ly,** *adv.*

pro·di·gious, prə·dij′əs, *a.* Extraordinary; huge; marvelous. —**pro·di·gious·ness,** *n.*

prod·i·gy, prod′ə·jē, *n. pl.,* **-gies.** A young person of extraordinary talent or ability; a marvel or wonder, as a remarkable deed, occurrence, or accomplishment.

pro·duce, prə·doos′, prə·dūs′, *v.t.,* **-duced, -duc·ing.** To bring forth into existence; to bring about; to give birth to; to bear, furnish, yield; to bring about the performance of, as a movie or play; to extend, as a line.—*v.i.* To bring forth or yield appropriate offspring, products, or consequences. —prod′oos, prod′yoos, prō′dūs, *n.* That which is produced; yield; product, specif. agricultural products collectively.

pro·duc·er, prə·doo′sər, prə·dū′sər, *n.* One who or that which produces; one who finances or supervises the making of motion pictures or plays.

prod·uct, prod′əkt, *n.* A thing produced by nature, as fruit, grain, or vegetables; that which is produced by labor or mental application; a production; something resulting as a consequence; result; the result of, or quantity produced by, the multiplication of two numbers or quantities together.

pro·duc·tion, prə·dək′shən, *n.* The act or process of producing; that which is produced or made; the total amount of something produced: *Production* is low this year. *Informal.* An exaggerated process: He makes a *production* out of combing his hair.

pro·duc·tive, prə·dək′tiv, *a.* Having the power of producing; fertile; producing good crops; bringing into being. —**pro·duc·tive·ness, pro·duc·tiv·i·ty,** prō·dək·tiv′ə·tē, *n.*

prof, prof, *n. Informal.* Professor.

pro·fane, prə·fān′, prō·fān′, *a.* Irreverent toward God or holy things; secular; implying contempt of religious things through speech or action; blasphemous; polluted or vulgar.—*v.t.,* **-faned, -fan·ing.** To treat with irreverence; desecrate; misuse. —**pro·fan·a·to·ry,** prō·fan′ə·tôr·e, *a.* —**pro·fane·ness, pro·fan·er,** *n.*

pro·fan·i·ty, prə·fan′ə·tē, prō·fan′ə·tē, *n. pl.,* **-ties.** The quality of being profane; that which is profane.

pro·fess, prə·fes′, *v.t.* To acknowledge or own publicly to be; to make protestations or a pretense of; to declare one's allegiance to.—*v.i.* To make a declaration. —**pro·fessed,** *a.* —**pro·fess·ed·ly,** *adv.*

pro·fes·sion, prə·fesh′ən, *n.* A vocation requiring specialized training in a field of learning, art, or science; a leading vocation or business; the body of persons engaged in a calling or vocation; an avowal or public acknowledgment of one's beliefs or loyalties.

pro·fes·sion·al, prə·fesh′ə·nəl, *a.* Referring to a profession; engaged in a profession, esp. law, medicine, or the ministry; referring to activities engaged in for pay that are generally thought to be leisure activities: *professional* sports.—*n.* A member of any profession; a person who does something very well. —**pro·fes·sion·al·ism,** *n.*

pro·fes·sion·al·ize, prə·fesh′ə·nə·līz, *v.t., v.i.,* **-ized, -iz·ing.** To make professional.

pro·fes·sor, prə·fes′ər, *n.* The highest ranking teacher of any art, science, or other branch of learning, esp. in a university or college. —**pro·fes·so·ri·al,** prō·fe·sôr′ē·əl, *a.* —**pro·fes·so·ri·al·ly,** *adv.* —**pro·fes·sor·ship,** *n.*

prof·fer, prof′ər, *v.t.* To offer for acceptance.—*n.* An offer made. —**prof·fer·er,** *n.*

pro·fi·cien·cy, prə·fish′ən·sē, *n.* The state of being proficient; skill, knowledge.

pro·fi·cient, prə·fish′ənt, *a.* Well-versed in any business, art, or branch of learning; skilled; competent. —*n.* An expert.

pro·file, prō′fil, *n.* An outline or contour, esp. an outline of the human face seen sideways; the side view of the face; the outline or contour of anything; a numerical or graphic analysis, as of the abilities disclosed by intelligence tests; a short biographical outline.—*v.t.,* **-filed, -fil·ing.** To draw in profile; to give a profile of.

prof·it, prof′it, *n.* Any advantage, benefit, or return; the advantage or gain resulting to the owner of capital from its employment in any undertaking; the excess of income over expenditure, specif. the difference, when an excess, between the original cost and selling price of anything; the ratio in any year of this gain to the sum invested; revenue from investments or property. —*v.i.* To derive profit or benefit; to be of use or advantage.—*v.t.* To benefit; to be of service to; to advance. —**prof·it·less,** *a.*

prof·it·a·ble, prof′it·ə·bəl, *a.* Yielding or bringing profit or gain; useful; advantageous. —**prof·it·a·bil·i·ty,** prof·ə·tə·bil′ə·tē, **prof·it·a·ble·ness,** *n.* —**prof·it·a·bly,** *adv.*

prof·it·eer, prof·ə·tēr′, *n.* An individual who takes advantage of abnormal conditions, such as those of wartime, to make excessive profit.—*v.i.* To make or try to make excess profits.

prof·it shar·ing, *n.* The sharing of profits, as between employer and employee. —**prof·it-shar·ing,** *a.*

prof·li·gate, prof′lə·git, *a.* Very immoral; rash in extravagance.—*n.* One who has forsaken all principles; a spendthrift. —**prof·li·ga·cy,** prof′lə·gə·sē, *n.*

pro·found, prə·fownd′, *a.* Intellectually deep; deep in knowledge or skill; characterized by intensity; far below the surface; low; deep.—*n.* The deep sea; the ocean; an abyss.

pro·fun·di·ty, prə·fən′də·tē, *n. pl.,* **-ties.** The quality or condition of being profound.

pro·fuse, prə·fūs′, *a.* Extravagant; prodigal; poured forth abundantly; copious.

---

a- hat, fāte, fāre, fäther; **e-** met, mē; **i-** pin, pīne; **o-** not, nōte, ôrb, moove (move), boy, pownd; **u-** cūbe, bùll, tûk (took); **ch-** chin; **th-** thick, ᵺen; **zh-** vizhon (vision); **ə-** ago, takən, pencəl, lemən, bərd (bird).

pro·fu·sion, prə·fū′zhən, *n.* Rich abundance; great amount, usu. followed by *of;* prodigality; lavish expenditure.

pro·gen·i·tor, prō·jen′ə·tər, *n.* An ancestor in the direct line; a forefather; an originator.

prog·e·ny, proj′ə·nē, *n. pl.,* -nies. Offspring collectively; children; descendants.

pro·ges·ter·one, prō·jes′tə·rōn, *n.* A female sex hormone, produced in the ovaries, which prepares the uterus for the fertilized ovum. Also **pro·ges·tin**, prō·jes′tin.

prog·no·sis, prog·nō′sis, *n. pl.,* -ses, -sēz. A forecast of the probable course of a disease and the possibility of recovery; any forecast.

prog·nos·tic, prog·nos′tik, *a.* Foretelling; relating to a prognosis.—*n.* A sign by which a future event may be known or foretold; an omen; prediction.

prog·nos·ti·cate, prog·nos′tə·kāt, *v.t.,* -cat·ed, -cat·ing. To foretell by means of present signs; to predict. —**prog·nos·ti·ca·tion**, prog·nos·tə·kā′shən, *n.* —**prog·nos·ti·ca·tive**, *a.* —**prog·nos·ti·ca·tor**, *n.*

pro·gram, prō′gram, prō′grəm, *n.* A schedule or plan to be followed; a list of items, pieces, or performers in a musical, theatrical, or other entertainment; an entertainment with reference to its pieces or numbers; a prospectus or syllabus; a logically related order of actions to be performed by a computer.—*v.t.,* -grammed, -gram·ming, or -gramed, -gram·ing. To arrange or enter in a program; to draw up, as a program for.—*v.i.* To draw up a program. —**pro·gram·mer, pro·gram·er**, *n.*

prog·ress, prog′res, *n.* A going or traveling forward or onward, or a march or journey; a forward course of action, of events, or of time; a proceeding to a further or higher stage, or through such stages successively: the *progress* of a scholar in her studies; advance or advancement in general. —prə·gres′, *v.i.* To go forward or onward; proceed; to make progress.

pro·gres·sion, prə·gresh′ən, *n.* The act of progressing.

pro·gres·sive, prə·gres′iv, *a.* Characterized by progressing or going forward or onward; passing on successively from one member of a series to the next; proceeding step by step; making progress toward higher or better conditions, more enlightened or liberal ideas, or the use of new and advantageous methods: a *progressive* nation or community; a disease, continuously increasing in extent or severity.—*n.* One who is progressive, or who favors progress or reform, esp. in political matters. —**pro·gres·siv·ism**, *n.*

pro·gres·sive jazz, *n.* A modern jazz style characterized by the mixture of jazz and non-jazz elements.

pro·hib·it, prō·hib′it, *v.t.* To forbid, as an action, by authority or interdict; to prevent or debar.

pro·hi·bi·tion, prō·ə·bish′ən, *n.* The act of prohibiting; an order or decree forbidding; the interdiction by law of the manufacture and sale of alcoholic drinks.

pro·hi·bi·tion·ist, prō·ə·bish′ə·nist, *n.* One who advocates the prohibition of the manufacture and sale of alcoholic beverages.

pro·hib·i·tive, prō·hib′ə·tiv, *a.* That prohibits or forbids something; serving to prevent the use or purchase of something: *prohibitive* costs. Also **pro·hib·i·to·ry**, prō·hib′ə·tôr·ē.

pro·ject, prə·jekt′, *v.t.* To propose, contemplate, or plan, as something to be carried out; to throw or cast forward or onward; to cause to stick out; to use, as one's voice or movements, so as to communicate clearly to the entire audience.—*v.i.* To extend or protrude beyond something else; jut out; to make oneself clearly understood by an audience, through proper use of one's voice or movements. —proj′ekt, *n.* Something contemplated or planned; a plan; scheme; a large undertaking: a housing *project;* a specific piece of research.

pro·jec·tile, prə·jek′til, prə·jek′tīl, *n.* A body hurled forward, as through the air: a missile for a gun,

cannon, or other weapon.—*a.* Driving forward, as a force; capable of being projected or impelled forward, as a missile.

pro·jec·tion, prə·jek′shən, *n.* The act of projecting or the state of being projected; the state or fact of sticking out; a part that sticks out; the act of projecting an image from a slide or motion picture onto a screen; the image produced; the calculation of a future possibility.

pro·jec·tion·ist, prə·jek′shə·nist, *n.* One who operates a motion-picture projector.

pro·jec·tive, prə·jek′tiv, *a.* Of or pertaining to projection; produced, or capable of being produced, by projection. —**pro·jec·tive·ly**, *adv.* —**pro·jec·tiv·i·ty**, prō·jek·tiv′ə·tē, *n.*

pro·jec·tor, prə·jek′tər, *n.* An apparatus for throwing an image on a screen: a slide *projector;* a device for projecting a beam of light, as a lens.

pro·le·tar·i·at, prō·lə·tār′ē·ət, *n.* That class of the community which is dependent for support on daily or casual employment; the laboring class, or wage earners in general. —**pro·le·tar·i·an**, *a.*

pro·lif·er·ate, prō·lif′ə·rāt, *v.t., v.i.,* -at·ed, -at·ing. To grow or produce by multiplication of parts, as in budding or cell division. —**pro·lif·er·a·tion**, prō·lif·ə·rā′shən, *n.* —**pro·lif·er·a·tive**, *a.*

pro·lif·ic, prō·lif′ik, *a.* Producing offspring or young; bearing or yielding fruit abundantly; fruitful; producing much: a *prolific* writer; characterized by abundant production: a *prolific* season for fruit. —**pro·lif·i·ca·cy**, prō·lif·i·cə·sē, *n.* —**pro·lif·i·cal·ly**, *adv.*

pro·lix, prō′liks, *a.* Long and wordy; talking at great length. —**pro·lix·i·ty**, prō·lik′sə·tē, *n.* —**pro·lix·ly**, *adv.* —**pro·lix·ness**, *n.*

pro·logue, prō′lôg, prō′log, *n.* A preliminary discourse; a preface or introductory part of a discourse, poem, play, or novel; any introductory proceeding or event.—*v.t.,* -logued, -log·uing. To introduce with or as with a prologue.

pro·long, prə·lông′, prə·long′, *v.t.* To lengthen in time; to extend the duration of; to lengthen. —**pro·lon·ga·tion**, prō·lông·gā′shən, **pro·long·er**, *n.*

prom, prom, *n. Informal.* A college or high school formal dance.

prom·e·nade, prom·ə·nād′, prom·ə·näd′, *n.* A walk, esp. in a public place, as for pleasure or display; the grand march of all guests at the opening of a formal ball; a prom or dance.—*v.i.,* -nad·ed, -nad·ing. To take a promenade.—*v.t.* To take a promenade through or about. —**prom·e·nad·er**, *n.*

prom·i·nence, prom′ə·nəns, *n.* The state of being prominent. Also **prom·i·nen·cy.**

prom·i·nent, prom′ə·nənt, *a.* Standing out beyond the adjacent surface or line; projecting; conspicuous; noticeable; famous, important, or leading: a *prominent* citizen. —**prom·i·nent·ly**, *adv.*

pro·mis·cu·i·ty, prom·ə·skū′ə·tē, prō·mi·skū′i·tē, *n. pl.,* -ties. The state of being promiscuous, esp. in sexual relationships.

pro·mis·cu·ous, prə·mis′kū·əs, *a.* Mingled indiscriminately; forming part of a confused crowd or mass; indiscriminate, esp. in sexual relations; random; haphazard. —**pro·mis·cu·ous·ly**, *adv.*—**pro·mis·cu·ous·ness**, *n.*

prom·ise, prom′is, *n.* A declaration made, as to another person, with respect to the future, giving assurance that one will do or not do something, or that something shall or shall not happen; a pledge; vow; an indication of what may be expected: The clouds give *promise* of rain; an indication of fulfillment or future excellence: a writer or a book that shows *promise;* basis for hope; that which is promised.—*v.t.,* -ised, -is·ing. To make a promise of: to *promise* help; to engage to give in marriage. *Informal.* To assure emphatically.—*v.i.* To make a promise; to afford ground for expectation, usu. followed by *well* or *fair.* —**prom·is·a·ble**, *a.* —**prom·is·er**, *n.* —**prom·ise·ful**, *a.*

Prom•ised Land, *n.* Heaven; a place where hopes are realized and troubles cease.

prom•is•ing, prom/i•sing, *a.* Giving favorable promise of future success.

prom•is•so•ry, prom/ə•sôr•ē, *a.* Containing a promise; referring to a binding declaration of something to be done in the future.

prom•on•to•ry, prom/ən•tôr•ē, *n. pl.,* **-ries.** A high point of land or rock projecting into the sea; a headland.

pro•mote, prə•mōt/, *v.t.* **-mot•ed, -mot•ing.** To contribute to the growth, enlargement, or power of; to forward; to advance to a higher rank; help to organize, as a commercial undertaking; attempt to increase the sale of by advertising. *Informal.* To wangle. **—pro•mot•a•ble,** *a.*

pro•mot•er, prə•mō/tər, *n.* One who or that which promotes.

pro•mo•tion, prə•mō/shən, *n.* Advancement; the state of being raised in status; active encouragement of sales by means of advertising. **—pro•mo•tive,** prə•mō/tiv, *a.*

prompt, prompt, *a.* Ready and quick to act as occasion demands; punctual.—*v.t.* To move or incite to action or exertion; to suggest to the mind.—*v.i.* To give cues to actors from a position off-stage.—*n.* An instance of prompting. **—prompt•er,** *n.*

prom•ul•gate, prom/əl•gāt, *v.t.,* **-gat•ed, -gat•ing.** To make known by public declaration, as laws; proclaim; announce. **—prom•ul•ga•tion,** prom•əl•gā/shən, *n.*

prone, prōn, *a.* Lying with the face downward; sloping downward; inclined.

prong, prông, prong, *n.* A sharp-pointed instrument; the tine of a fork or of a similar instrument; a pointed projection, as the tips of a deer's antlers.—*v.t.* To stab, as with a fork or prong.

pro•noun, prō/nown, *n.* One of a class of words often used instead of a noun or noun phrase already mentioned so that the noun need not be repeated.

pro•nounce, prə•nowns/, *v.t.,* **-nounced, -nounc•ing.** To speak, as phrases or words; to utter, as letters or words, in a specified manner; to utter formally, officially, or solemnly: The court *pronounced* sentence; to declare or affirm: to *pronounce* it a forgery.—*v.i.* To speak with confidence or authority; to utter an opinion; to articulate using a certain pronunciation. **—pro•nounce•a•ble,** *a.* **—pro•nounc•er,** *n.*

pro•nounced, prə•nownst/, *a.* Strongly marked or defined; decided. **—pro•nounc•ed•ly,** *adv.*

pro•nounce•ment, prə•nowns/mənt, *n.* The act of pronouncing; a formal announcement; a decision.

pron•to, pron/tō, *adv. Informal.* Promptly.

pro•nun•ci•a•tion, prə•nən•sē•ā/shən, *n.* The act of pronouncing or uttering; articulation; the mode of uttering words or letters.

proof, proof, *n.* Any effort, process, or operation that ascertains truth or fact; a test; a trial; what serves as evidence; what proves or establishes; the degree of strength of liquor: 80 *proof;* a rough impression of type, in which errors may be detected and marked for correction; a test print taken from a photographic negative.—*a.* Impenetrable; able to resist physically or morally, often used with *against* or in combination: *proof against* heat or temptation, water*proof*, shock*proof*.—*v.t.* To examine for and correct errors or flaws in; to proofread.

proof•read, proof/rēd, *v.t., v.i.,* **-read,** -red, **-read•ing.** To read, as printers' proofs, in order to detect and mark errors. **—proof•read•er,** *n.*

prop, prop, *n.* That which sustains an incumbent weight; a support; a stay.—*v.t.,* **propped, prop•ping.** To support by placing something under or against; to support by standing under or against; to help support or sustain. *Informal.* Theatrical property; an airplane propeller.

prop•a•gan•da, prop•ə•gan/də, *n.* Allegations, facts, opinions, and the like, systematically spread with the intention of helping or harming some individual, group, or movement; the dissemination of such information, often used disparagingly to denote half-truths and biased information, utilized mainly by political factions. **—prop•a•gan•dist,** prop•ə•gan/dist, *n., a.* **—prop•a•gan•dis•tic,** prop•ə•gan•dis/tik, *a.* **—prop•a•gan•dis•ti•cal•ly,** *adv.* **—prop•a•gan•dism,** *n.* **—prop•a•gan•dize,** prop•ə•gan/dīz, *v.t., v.i.,* **-dized, -diz•ing.**

prop•a•gate, prop/ə•gāt, *v.t.,* **-gat•ed, -gat•ing.** To breed; to cause to reproduce (itself), as applied to animals and plants; to pass on by heredity; to spread from person to person or from place to place; to generate, or produce; to originate.—*v.i.* To have young; to be reproduced by generation, or by new shoots or plants; to spread. **—prop•a•ga•tive,** *a.* **—prop•a•ga•tor,** *n.*

prop•a•ga•tion, prop•ə•gā/shən, *n.* The act of propagating. **—prop•a•ga•tion•al,** *a.*

pro•pane, prō/pān, *n.* A gaseous hydrocarbon of the methane series, found in petroleum and used in organic synthesis, for household fuel, and numerous industrial purposes.

pro•pel, prə•pel/, *v.t.,* **-pelled, -pel•ling.** To drive forward; to urge or press onward.

pro•pel•lant, prə•pel/ənt, *n.* Something or someone that propels, as a fuel. **—a.** Also **pro•pel•lent.**

pro•pel•ler, prə•pel/ər, *n.* One who or that which propels; a device consisting of a rotating shaft fitted with blades for propelling a ship or aircraft. Also **pro•pel•lor.**

pro•pen•si•ty, prə•pen/sə•tē, *n. pl.,* **-ties.** Natural inclination, tendency, or disposition.

prop•er, prop/ər, *a.* Strictly belonging or applicable: the *proper* use of a word; accurate; normal or regular; adapted or appropriate to circumstances: the *proper* tool for the job; fit; suitable; decorous or decent; of a name, noun, or adjective, designating a particular person or thing, and written with an initial capital letter, as John, Chicago. **—prop•er•ly,** *adv.* **—prop•er•ness,** *n.*

prop•er•ty, prop/ər•tē, *n. pl.,* **-ties.** That which one owns; goods or lands owned; a piece of land or real estate; something at the disposal of a person, a group of persons, or the community; advantages that are the *property* of every citizen; an essential or distinctive attribute or quality of a thing. **—prop•er•tied, prop•er•ty•less,** *a.*

proph•e•cy, prof/ə•sē, *n. pl.,* **-cies.** A foretelling or declaration of something to come, esp. a prophet's foretelling inspired by God; a book of prophecies.

proph•e•sy, prof/ə•sī, *v.t.,* **-sied, -sy•ing.** To foretell; to predict; to speak as with divine guidance.—*v.i.* To utter predictions. **—proph•e•si•er,** *n.*

proph•et, prof/it, *n.* A person inspired or instructed by God to announce future events; a predictor.

pro•phet•ic, prə•fet/ik, *a.* Referring to a prophet or prophecy; predictive. Also **pro•phet•i•cal. —pro•phet•i•cal•ly,** *adv.*

pro•phy•lac•tic, prō•fə•lak/tik, prof•ə•lak/tik, *a.* Preventive; defending from or warding off disease.—*n.* A medicine which protects or defends against disease; a preventive device, as a contraceptive. **—pro•phy•lac•ti•cal•ly,** *adv.*

pro•phy•lax•is, prō•fə•lak/sis, prof•ə•lak/sis, *n.* Preventive or protective treatment against disease.

pro•pin•qui•ty, prō•ping/kwə•tē, *n.* Nearness in place, or time; kinship.

pro•pi•ti•ate, prō•pish/ē•at, *v.t.,* **-at•ed, -at•ing.** To appease or to conciliate. **—pro•pi•ti•a•tion,** prō•

pish·ē·ā′shən, *n.* —**pro·pi·ti·a·to·ry,** prō·pish′ē·ə·tôr·ē, *a.*

pro·pi·tious, prə·pish′əs, *a.* Favorably disposed. —**pro·pi·tious·ly,** *adv.*

prop·jet en·gine, prop′jet, *n.* Turbo-propeller engine.

pro·po·nent, prə·pō′nənt, *n.* One who makes a proposal, or lays down a proposition; one in favor of a doctrine or cause.

pro·por·tion, prə·pôr′shən, *n.* Comparative relation between things or magnitudes as to size, quantity, number, etc.: the *proportion* of births to deaths; ratio; in general, relation, comparison, or analogy: a large or a small *proportion* of a total amount; a portion or part; *pl.*, dimensions: a rock of gigantic *proportions.*—*v.t.* To adjust in proper proportion or relation; to divide into or distribute in proportionate parts. —**pro·por·tion·a·ble,** *a.* —**pro·por·tion·a·bly,** *adv.*

pro·por·tion·al, prə·pôr′shə·nəl, *a.* Being in or characterized by proportion; corresponding; relative. —*n.* One of the quantities of a proportion. —**pro·por·tion·al·i·ty,** prə·pôr·shə·nal′ə·tē, *n.*

pro·por·tion·ate, prə·pôr′shə·nit, *a.* Proportioned; being in due proportion; proportional. —prə·pôr′shə·nāt, *v.t.,* -at·ed, -at·ing. To make proportionate.

pro·pos·al, prə·pō′zəl, *n.* The act of proposing; a plan; an offer of marriage.

pro·pose, prə·pōz′, *v.t.,* -posed, -pos·ing. To put forward, as a matter, subject, or case, for consideration, discussion, or disposal; to state; to present, as a person, for acceptance for some position; to offer or suggest, as a toast; intend.—*v.i.* To make a proposal, esp. one of marriage; to formulate or entertain a purpose or design. —**pro·pos·er,** *n.*

prop·o·si·tion, prop·ə·zish′ən, *n.* The act of putting forward something for consideration or discussion; an assertion; an offer of terms for a transaction, as in business; a plan or scheme proposed. *Informal.* A thing, matter, or person considered as something to be dealt with, handled, or encountered; an immoral or indecent proposal.—*v.t. Informal.* To propose a project or deal to; to make an immoral suggestion to. —**prop·o·si·tion·al,** *a.*

pro·pound, prə·pownd′, *v.t.* To offer for consideration; to propose. —**pro·pound·er,** *n.*

pro·pri·e·tar·y, prə·prī′ə·ter·ē, *a.* Referring or belonging to a proprietor; denoting exclusive control over property; of manufacture and sale of a product, restricted by patent or copyright: a *proprietary* medicine; pertaining to property or ownership.—*n. pl.,* -ies. An owner or proprietor; a body of proprietors; something owned or held as property.

pro·pri·e·tor, prə·prī′ə·tər, *n.* An owner. —**pro·pri·e·tor·ship,** *n.*

pro·pri·e·ty, prə·prī′ə·tē, *n. pl.,* -ties. Conformity to an acknowledged or correct standard of behavior, principles, rules, or customs; decorum; suitability; justness. —**the pro·pri·e·ties,** the established customs of social life.

pro·pul·sion, prə·pəl′shən, *n.* The act of propelling or driving forward or onward; the state of being propelled; a propulsive force. —**pro·pul·sive,** prə·pəl′siv, *a.*

pro·rate, prō·rāt′, *v.t., v.i.,* -rat·ed, -rat·ing. To assess or distribute proportionately. —**pro·ra·tion,** prō·rā′shən, *n.*

pro·sa·ic, prō·zā′ik, *a.* Commonplace or dull: a *prosaic* life; matter-of-fact or unimaginative; of writing, having the character or spirit of prose as opposed to poetry. —**pro·sa·i·cal·ly,** *adv.* —**pro·sa·ic·ness,** *n.*

pro·scribe, prō·skrib′, *v.t.,* -scribed, -scrib·ing. To prohibit; to exclude from the protection of the law; to outlaw. —**pro·scrib·er,** *n.*

pro·scrip·tion, prō·skrip′shən, *n.* The act of proscribing. —**pro·scrip·tive,** *a.*

prose, prōz, *n.* The ordinary written or spoken language of human beings; language without poetical measure: opposed to *verse.*—*a.*—*v.t., v.i.,* prosed, **pros·ing.** To write in prose; write or speak tediously.

pros·e·cute, pros′ə·kūt, *v.t.* To follow up or out, go on with, or pursue something undertaken or begun; to carry on or practice; to seek to enforce or obtain by legal process, as a claim or right; to institute legal proceedings against.—*v.i.* To institute and carry on a legal prosecution; act as prosecutor. —**pros·e·cut·a·ble,** *a.*

pros·e·cu·tion, pros·ə·kū′shən, *n.* The act or process of prosecuting; the party by whom such proceedings are instituted and carried on.

pros·e·cu·tor, pros·ə·kū′tər, *n.* One who prosecutes; one who institutes and carries on legal proceedings in a court of justice, esp. in a criminal court; a prosecuting attorney.

pros·pect, pros′pekt, *n.* The outlook for the future, or that which appears as an indication of what may be expected. *Pl.* Apparent probabilities of advancement, success, or profit. A looking forward; something in view as a source of profit; a likely or potential candidate; mental view or survey, as of a subject or situation.—*v.t., v.i.* To explore, as a region, as for gold. —**pros·pec·tor,** *n.*

pro·spec·tive, prə·spek′tiv, *a.* Being in the future; expected or potential.

pro·spec·tus, prə·spek′təs, *n.* A brief sketch describing the main features of some proposed enterprise, as the plan of a literary work, or the proposals of a new business.

pros·per, pros′pər, *v.i.* To be successful, esp. to gain in wealth; to turn out successfully, as affairs; to thrive.—*v.t.* To make prosperous.

pros·per·i·ty, pro·sper′ə·tē, *n.* The state of being prosperous; good fortune.

pros·per·ous, pros′pər·əs, *a.* Characterized by good fortune; successful; well-to-do.

pros·tate, pros′tāt, *n.* The prostate gland.

pros·tate gland, *n.* An organ, part muscle and part gland, which is found at the base of the bladder, and secretes a milky fluid ejected with the sperm.

pros·the·sis, pros·thē′sis, *n. pl.,* -ses, -sēz. The addition of an artificial part to supply a missing part; the part thus added. —**pros·thet·ic,** pros·thet′ik, *a.* —**pros·thet·i·cal·ly,** *adv.*

pros·thet·ics, pros·thet′iks, *n. pl., sing.* or *pl. in constr.* The branch of medicine specializing in artificial replacements, as of limbs or teeth. —**pros·the·tist,** pros′thi·tist, *n.*

pros·tho·don·tics, pros·thə·don′tiks, *n. pl., sing.* or *pl. in constr.* The branch of dentistry dealing with the making of artificial teeth and other oral structures. —**pros·tho·don·tist,** *n.*

pros·ti·tute, pros′ti·toot, pros′ti·tūt, *n.* A woman who performs sexual intercourse for gain or hire; a harlot; any person who puts his or her abilities to a base or unworthy use for money or other gain.—*v.t.,* -tut·ed, -tut·ing. To offer, as oneself, for sexual intercourse for gain or hire; to surrender to any unworthy purpose for gain. —**pros·ti·tu·tion,** pros·tə·too′shən, **pros·ti·tu·tor,** *n.*

pros·trate, pros′trāt, *v.t.,* -trat·ed, -trat·ing. To lay flat, as on the ground; to cast down, as oneself, in humility or adoration; to overthrow, overcome, or reduce to helplessness: *prostrating* one's enemy; to reduce to physical weakness or exhaustion: to be *prostrated* by disease.—*a.* Lying flat or at full length, as on the ground; lying with the face to the ground, as in token of submission or humility; overthrown, overcome, or helpless; in a state of physical weakness or exhaustion. —**pros·tra·tion,** pros·trā′shən, **pros·tra·tor,** *n.* —**pros·tra·tive,** *a.*

pros·y, prō′zē, *a.,* -i·er, -i·est. Like prose; tedious. —**pros·i·ly,** *adv.* —**pros·i·ness,** *n.*

pro·tag·o·nist, prō·tag′ə·nist, *n.* The leading character or actor in a literary work; a leading character generally.

pro·te·an, prō′tē·ən, *a.* Readily taking on different shapes, characters, or roles.

pro·tect, prə·tekt′, *v.t.* To cover or shield from danger or injury; to defend; to guard. —**pro·tect·ing,** prə·tek′ting, *a.* —**pro·tec·tive,** *a.* —**pro·tec·tive·ly,** *adv.* —**pro·tec·tive·ness, pro·tec·tor,** *n.*

pro·tec·tion, prə·tek′shən, *n.* The act of protecting or state of being protected; one who or that which protects. *Informal.* Money exacted by racketeers for exemption from injury or violence; bribery of a minor official for exemption from legal action; the coverage afforded by an insurance policy.

pro·tec·tion·ism, prə·tek′shə·niz·əm, *n.* The economic system of protection for commodities produced within one's economy. —**pro·tec·tion·ist,** *a., n.*

pro·tec·tor·ate, prə·tek′tər·it, *n.* The relationship in which a weaker state has protection and some control from a stronger state; the dependent state in such a relationship.

pro·té·gé, prō′tə·zhā, prō·tə·zhā′, *n.* One under the care and protection of another who is interested in his or her career or future.

pro·tein, prō′tēn, prō′tē·in, *n.* One of a class of complex chemical compounds which contain carbon, hydrogen, nitrogen, oxygen, and sulfur, are essential constituents of living matter, and on decomposition yield various amino acids.

pro·test, prə·test′, *v.i.* To make a formal declaration of opposition to something; to object; to affirm with solemnity.—*v.t.* To object to; make or enter a protest against; to assert. —prō′test, *n.* A solemn declaration of opinion against some act; a formal statement, usu. in writing; the act of protesting.

Prot·es·tant, prot′i·stənt, *n.* A Christian not belonging to a Roman Catholic or an Eastern Orthodox church; (*l.c.*) one who protests.—*a.* Belonging or pertaining to the religion of the Protestants. (*L.c.*) Protesting. —**Prot·es·tant·ism,** *n.*

prot·es·ta·tion, prot·i·stā′shən, prō·təs·tā′shən, *n.* A solemn declaration; an act of protesting; a protest.

pro·tist, prō′tist, *n.* Any of a group of organisms, including all the one-celled animals and plants. —**pro·tis·tan,** prō·tis′tən, *a., n.*

pro·to·col, prō′tə·kol, *n.* Rules of etiquette and order in diplomatic or military ceremonies; the minutes or rough draft of some diplomatic document.—*v.i.* To draft a protocol.

pro·ton, prō′ton, *n.* A nuclear particle with a positive charge equal and opposite to that of an electron, the number of nuclear protons being the atomic number of an atom.

pro·to·plasm, prō′tə·plaz·əm, *n.* The living matter of all vegetable and animal cells and tissues. —**pro·to·plas·mic,** prō·tə·plaz′mik, *a.*

pro·to·type, prō′tə·tip, *n.* The original or model on which something is formed; an example displaying typical characteristics of a class. —**pro·to·ty·pal,** prō·tə·ti′pəl, **pro·to·typ·ic,** prō·tə·tip′ik, *a.*

pro·to·zo·an, prō·tə·zō′ən, *n.* Any of the animals in the first or lowest zoological division or phylum, including all single-celled, microscopic organisms. —*a.* Like a protozoan. Also **pro·to·zo·ic.**

pro·tract, prō·trakt′, *v.t.* To draw out or lengthen in time; to prolong; to lengthen out in space; to draw, using a protractor and scale. —**pro·trac·tion,** prō·trak′shən, *n.* —**pro·trac·tive,** *a.*

pro·trac·tile, prō·trak′til, *a.* Capable of being protracted or thrust forward.

pro·trac·tor, prō·trak′tər, *n.* One who or that object which protracts or delays; an instrument for laying down and measuring angles on paper.

pro·trude, prō·trood′, *v.t.,* -**trud·ed,** -**trud·ing.** To thrust forward; to cause to project.—*v.i.* To stand out prominently. —**pro·trud·ent, pro·tru·si·ble,** prō·

troo′sə·bəl, *a.*

pro·tru·sion, prō·troo′zhən, *n.* The act of protruding; something which protrudes. —**pro·tru·sive,** prō·troo′siv, *a.*

pro·tu·ber·ance, prō·too′bər·əns, prō·tū′bər·əns, *n.* Protuberant state or form.

pro·tu·ber·ant, prō·too′bər·ənt, prō·tū′bər·ənt, *a.* Sticking out beyond the surrounding surface.

proud, prowd, *a.* Having a proper self-esteem; self-respecting; feeling satisfaction or elation at some honor; taking pride in something; actuating a feeling of pride; possessing or displaying a high and unreasonable opinion of one's own excellence; arrogant. —**proud·ly,** *adv.* —**proud·ness,** *n.*

prove, proov, *v.t.,* **proved, proved** or **prov·en, prov·ing.** To try by an experiment; to test or make a trial of; to establish the truth or reality of by reasoning or evidence; to demonstrate.—*v.i.* To be found or ascertained by experience or trial; to turn out to be: The report *proved* to be false. —**prov·a·ble,** *a.* —**prov·a·bly,** *adv.* —**prov·er,** *n.*

prov·erb, prov′ərb, *n.* A short, pithy, popular saying, long in use, embodying some familiar truth, often in picturesque language; an adage; a wise saying.—*v.t.* To utter in the form of a proverb; to make (something) the subject of a proverb.

pro·ver·bi·al, prə·vər′bē·əl, *a.* Of, referring to, or characteristic of a proverb: a *proverbial* mode of expression; notorious. —**pro·ver·bi·al·ly,** *adv.*

pro·vide, prə·vid′, *v.t.,* -**vid·ed,** -**vid·ing.** To bring about or ensure by foresight; arrange for beforehand: The contract *provides* that specified materials shall be used; to supply for a purpose: to *provide* food for the needy; to yield: wealth the forests *provide;* to supply something: to *provide* a building with fire escapes. —*v.i.* To take measures with due foresight: to *provide* against accident; to make arrangements for supplying means of support, with *for:* to *provide for* a person in one's will. —**pro·vid·a·ble,** *a.* —**pro·vid·er,** *n.*

pro·vid·ed, prə·vi′did, *conj.* It being stipulated or understood; on the condition or supposition: to consent *provided* or *provided that* all the others agree.

prov·i·dence, prov′ə·dəns, *n.* The care and supervision of God over His creatures; (*cap.*) God. —**prov·i·den·tial,** *a.*

prov·i·dent, prov′ə·dənt, *a.* Foreseeing wants and making provision to supply them; frugal; economical.

pro·vid·ing, prə·vi′ding, *conj.* Making the stipulation that; provided.

prov·ince, prov′ins, *n.* An administrative unit of a country; the proper duty, office, or business of a person; a sphere of action or speculation. *Pl.* Territory at some distance from the metropolis.

pro·vin·cial, prə·vin′shəl, *a.* Referring to a province; simple; of narrow interests or thought; descriptive of certain styles of architecture, furniture, or decor derived from the provinces.—*n.* A person belonging to a province as distinguished from the metropolis; one who displays narrowness of interests or thoughts. —**pro·vin·ci·al·i·ty,** prə·vin·shē·al′ə·tē, *n.* —**pro·vin·cial·ly,** *adv.* —**pro·vin·cial·ist,** *n.* —**pro·vin·cial·ize,** *v.t.,* -**ized,** -**iz·ing.**

pro·vin·cial·ism, prə·vin′shə·liz·əm, *n.* Narrow-mindedness, ignorance, or naiveté which is the result of a provincial life; a peculiarity, particularly of speech, characteristic of a province.

pro·vi·sion, prə·vizh′ən, *n.* The act of providing; a measure taken beforehand; accumulation of stores or materials beforehand; a stipulation. *Pl.* A stock of food provided. —*v.t.* To provide with food. —**pro·vi·sion·er,** *n.*

pro·vi·sion·al, prə·vizh′ə·nəl, *a.* Provided for present need or for the occasion; temporary. Also **pro·vi·sion·ar·y,** prə·vizh′ə·ner·ē.

---

a- hat, fāte, fāre, fäther; e- met, mē; i- pin, pīne; o- not, nōte, ôrb, moove (move), boy, pownd;
u- cūbe, bůll, tůk (took); ch- chin; th- thick, ŧhen; zh- vizhon (vision); ə- əgo, takən, pencəl, lemən, bərd (bird).

prov·o·ca·tion, prov·ə·kā′shən, *n.* The act of provoking.

pro·voc·a·tive, prə·vok′ə·tiv, *a.* Serving or apt to provoke; exciting; stimulating.—*n.* Anything that tends to provoke. **—pro·voc·a·tive·ly,** *adv.* **—pro·voc·a·tive·ness,** *n.*

pro·voke, prə·vōk′, *v.t.,* **-voked, -vok·ing.** To excite to anger; irritate; to excite or arouse, as hunger; to stimulate to action. **—pro·vok·ing·ly,** *adv.*

prov·ost, prō′vŏst, prov′əst, *n.* A superintendent or official directing educational activities; the chief dignitary of a cathedral or collegiate church.

prow, prow, *n.* The forepart of a ship; the bow; a projecting forward part, esp. of an airplane.

prow·ess, prow′is, *n.* Bravery; valor; exceptional ability.

prowl, prowl, *v.i., v.t.* To rove or wander stealthily, as a beast in search of prey.—*n.* The act of prowling. **—prowl·er,** *n.*

prox·i·mal, prok′sə·məl, *a.* Nearest the point of attachment or insertion, as the extremity of a bone or limb.

prox·i·mate, prok′sə·mit, *a.* Next; nearest; closely adjacent; coming next or very near in time; nearly or fairly accurate; approximate. **—prox·i·mate·ly,** *adv.*

prox·im·i·ty, prok·sim′ə·tē, *n.* The state of being proximate.

prox·y, prok′sē, *n. pl.,* **-ies.** The agency of a person who acts as a substitute for another person; authority to act for another; a deputy; a document by which one person authorizes another to vote in his or her place.

prude, prood, *n.* A person who shows excessive propriety and modesty.

pru·dence, prood′əns, *n.* The quality or fact of being prudent; good judgment; discretion; economy or frugality. **—pru·dent,** prood′ənt, *a.*

pru·den·tial, proo·den′shəl, *a.* Of, proceeding from, or characterized by prudence; having discretionary powers, esp. in business dealings.

prud·er·y, proo′də·rē, *n. pl.,* **-ies.** Extreme modesty or propriety.

prud·ish, proo′dish, *a.* Characteristic of or like a prude; priggish.

prune, proon, *n.* A dried plum.

prune, proon, *v.t.,* **pruned, prun·ing.** To lop or cut off, as the superfluous branches or twigs of trees and shrubs; to trim with a knife; to clear, as of anything superfluous.—*v.i.* **—prun·er,** *n.*

pru·ri·ent, prŏŏr′ē·ənt, *a.* Inclined or inclining to erotic thoughts; eagerly desirous. **—pru·ri·ence, pru·ri·en·cy,** *n.*

Prus·sian blue, prəsh′ən, *n.* A deep blue pigment.

pry, prī, *v.i.,* **pried, pry·ing.** To look closely or curiously; peer; peep; to search or inquire inquisitively into something: to *pry* into the affairs of others.—*n. pl.,* **pries.** The act or an act of prying; an inquisitive person. **—pry·er, pri·er,** *n.* **—pry·ing,** *a.*

pry, prī, *n. pl.,* **pries.** Any instrument for raising or moving a thing by force of leverage; leverage.—*v.t.,* **pried, pry·ing.** To raise, move, or force with a pry, or by force of leverage; to extract, open, or obtain with difficulty.

psalm, säm, *n.* A sacred song or hymn.—*v.t.* To praise in psalms.

psalm·book, säm′bŭk, *n.* Psalter; a book containing the psalms or other songs for use in church services.

psalm·ist, sä′mist, *n.* A writer or composer of psalms.

Psal·ter, sôl′tər, *n.* The Book of Psalms of the Bible; a book containing the Psalms alone.

pseu·do, soo′dō, *a.* False; counterfeit.

pseu·do·nym, soo′də·nim, *n.* A false or feigned name, esp. one assumed by a writer; a pen name. **—pseu·don·y·mous,** soo·don′ə·məs, *a.*

pseu·do·preg·nan·cy, soo·dō·preg′nən·sē, *n.* A condition of certain mammals which is similar to, but is not, pregnancy. **—pseu·do·preg·nant,** *a.*

pseu·do·sci·ence, soo·do·sī′əns, *n.* A body of related information, theories, and methods wrongly considered to be scientific. **—pseu·do·sci·en·tif·ic,** soo·dō·sī·ən·tif′ik, *a.*

pshaw, shô, *interj.* An exclamation expressing impatience or contempt.

psil·o·cy·bin, sil·ə·sī′bin, *n.* An alkaloid derived from a Mexican fungus, used as a hallucinogen.

pso·ri·a·sis, sə·rī′ə·sis, *n.* A chronic skin disease characterized by red, scaly patches. **—pso·ri·at·ic,** sôr·ē·at′ik, *a.*

psych, sīk, *v.t.,* **psyched, psych·ing.** *Informal.* To arouse: *psych* a team up; confuse; upset: *psych* out a rival; figure out: *psych* out a problem.

Psy·che, sī′kē, *n.* The soul or spirit personified, usu. represented in art as a fair maiden, often with the wings of a butterfly. (*L.c.*) A person's mental components, both conscious and unconscious.

psych·e·del·ic, sī·kə·del′ik, *a.* Of, referring to, or causing extraordinary changes in consciousness, as the intensification of sense perception and awareness, hallucination, and delusion.

psy·chi·a·trist, si·kī′ə·trist, sī·kī′ə·trist, *n.* A physician specializing in psychiatry.

psy·chi·a·try, si·kī′ə·trē, sī·kī′ə·trē, *n.* The branch of medicine which deals with the diagnosis and treatment of emotional and mental disorders. **—psy·chi·at·ric,** sī·kē·a′trik, *a.* **—psy·chi·at·ri·cal·ly,** *adv.*

psy·chic, sī′kik, *a.* Of or pertaining to the human soul or mind; mental, as opposed to *physical;* of or referring to a supposed nonphysical force assumed to operate in various obscure phenomena, as those of telepathy, clairvoyance, spiritualism; esp. susceptible to supposedly supernatural influences.—*n.* A person unusually sensitive to some nonphysical or spiritual influence; a medium. **—psy·chi·cal,** *a.* **—psy·chi·cal·ly,** *adv.*

psy·cho, sī′kō, *n. Informal.* A mentally sick or neurotic individual.

psy·cho·a·nal·y·sis, sī·kō·ə·nal′ə·sis, *n.* A method of studying and analyzing the subconscious thoughts of an individual, as disclosed by free association or dreams, in order to detect hidden mental conflicts which may produce disorders of mind and body. **—psy·cho·an·a·lyt·ic,** sī·kō·an·ə·lit′ik, **psy·cho·an·a·lyt·i·cal,** *a.*

psy·cho·an·a·lyst, sī·kō·an′ə·list, *n.* One who is qualified to practice psychoanalysis. **—psy·cho·an·a·lyze,** sī·kō·an′ə·līz, *v.t.,* **-lyzed, -lyz·ing.**

psy·cho·bi·ol·o·gy, sī·kō·bī·ol′ə·jē, *n.* The study of the interaction or relationship between mind and body; the biological aspects of psychology. **—psy·cho·bi·o·log·ic,** sī·kō·bī·ə·loj′ik, **psy·cho·bi·o·log·i·cal,** *a.* **—psy·cho·bi·ol·o·gist,** *n.*

psy·cho·dra·ma, sī·kō·drä′mə, *n.* A kind of group therapy that treats patients by helping them to dramatize roles likely to shed light on their problems.

psy·cho·dy·nam·ic, sī·kō·dī·nam′ik, *a.* Referring to the study of behavior in relation to motivation. **—psy·cho·dy·nam·i·cal·ly,** *adv.* **—psy·cho·dy·nam·ics,** *n. pl., sing. or pl. in constr.*

psy·cho·gen·e·sis, sī·kō·jen′ə·sis, *n.* The genesis or origin and development of the soul or mind; origin or development due to psychic or mental, as opposed to bodily, activity. **—psy·cho·ge·net·ic,** sī·kō·jə·net′ik, *a.* **—psy·cho·ge·net·i·cal·ly,** *adv.*

psy·cho·gen·ic, sī·kō·jen′ik, *a.* Of psychic or mental origin. **—psy·cho·gen·i·cal·ly,** *adv.*

psy·cho·log·i·cal, sī·kə·loj′ə·kəl, *a.* Of or pertaining to psychology; mental or subjective: a condition of affairs that is purely *psychological.*—Also **psy·cho·log·ic. —psy·cho·log·i·cal·ly,** *adv.*

psy·chol·o·gist, sī·kol′ə·jist, *n.* One trained in psychology.

psy·chol·o·gy, sī·kol′ə·jē, *n.* That branch of knowledge which deals with the human mind; knowledge derived from a careful examination of consciousness and behavior; the aggregate of mental and behavioral qualities typical of a group or one of its members.

psy·cho·mo·tor, *a.* Pertaining to movement induced by mental action.

psy·cho·neu·ro·sis, sī·kō·nū·rō′sis, sī·kō·nū·rō′sis, *n. pl.,* **-ses,** -sēz. A neurosis in which the patient's anxieties and various physical complaints are emotional, and without physical cause. **—psy·cho·neu·rot·ic,** sī·kō·nū·rot′ik, *a., n.*

psy·cho·path, sī′kō·path, *n.* An individual with a psychopathic personality; a mentally unstable person.

psy·cho·pa·thol·o·gy, sī·kō·pa·thol′ə·jē, *n.* Mental pathology. **—psy·cho·pa·thol·o·gist,** *n.* **—psy·cho·path·o·log·ic,** sī·kō·path·ə·loj′ik, **psy·cho·path·o·log·i·cal,** *a.*

psy·chop·a·thy, sī·kop′ə·thē, *n.* Abnormal mental condition. **—psy·cho·path·ic,** sī·kə·path′ik, *a., n.* **—psy·cho·path·i·cal·ly,** *adv.*

psy·cho·sis, sī·kō′sis, *n. pl.,* **-ses,** -sēz. A major mental disorder, characterized by a disintegration of personality and an inability to relate to others. **—psy·chot·ic,** sī·kot′ik, *a., n.* **—psy·chot·i·cal·ly,** *adv.*

psy·cho·so·mat·ic, sī·kō·sō·mat′ik, *a.* Having bodily symptoms of mental or emotional origin.—*n.* **—psy·cho·so·mat·i·cal·ly,** *adv.*

psy·cho·ther·a·py, sī·kō·ther′ə·pē, *n.* Psychological methods of treatment to correct maladjustments and mental disorders. Also **psy·cho·ther·a·peu·tics,** sī·kō·ther·ə·pū′tiks. **—psy·cho·ther·a·peu·tic,** *a.* **—psy·cho·ther·a·peu·ti·cal·ly,** *adv.* **—psy·cho·ther·a·pist,** *n.*

PT boat, pē′tē′, *n.* A small naval vessel, highly maneuverable and fast, which carries torpedoes and usu. depth charges.

pto·maine, pto·main, tō′mān, tō·mān′, *n.* Any of a class of basic organic compounds, some of them very poisonous, produced in animal and vegetable matter during decay.

pto·maine poi·son·ing, *n.* Food poisoning.

pub, pəb, *n. Informal.* A public house; a tavern.

pu·ber·ty, pū′bər·tē, *n.* The period in both male and female marked by the functional development of the generative system; the age at which persons become capable of reproduction.

pu·bes·cence, pū·bes′əns, *n.* The state of one who is arriving or has arrived at puberty; puberty; short soft hairs, as those covering plants. Also **pu·bes·cen·cy.** **—pu·bes·cent,** pū·bes′ənt, *a.*

pu·bic, pū′bik, *a.* Pertaining to the middle part of the lower abdominal region.

pub·lic, pəb′lik, *a.* Not private; relating to, regarding, or affecting a state, nation, or community: the *public* service; proceeding from many or the many; belonging to people in general: a *public* subscription; general; common; widely known: a *public* hero; regarding not private interest but the good of the community: *public* spirit.—*n.* The general body of humankind or of a nation, state, or community; the people, indefinitely, with *the;* the audience, as those who favor an author or celebrity. **—pub·lic·ly,** *adv.* **—pub·lic·ness,** *n.*

pub·li·ca·tion, pəb·lə·kā′shən, *n.* The act of publishing; that which is offered, as a book, magazine, newspaper, map, or the like, to the public by sale or free distribution; the state of being printed and published.

pub·lic de·fend·er, *n.* An elected or court-appointed attorney who defends, at public expense, persons charged with criminal offenses who cannot afford legal counsel.

pub·li·cist, pəb′lə·sist, *n.* A press agent; a specialist in public relations.

pub·li·ci·ty, pəb·lis′ə·tē, *n.* Public awareness resulting from the spreading of information in the various communications media; the actions involved in bringing information to public notice.

pub·li·cize, pəb′lə·sīz, *v.t.,* **-cized, -ciz·ing.** To give publicity to; bring to public notice; advertise.

pub·lic prop·er·ty, *n.* Anything considered as owned by the public, the state, or community.

pub·lic re·la·tions, *n. pl. but sing. in constr.* Actions taken by an individual or group to promote favorable public opinion.

pub·lic sale, *n.* An auction.

pub·lic school, *n.* An elementary or secondary school established by state law in a district, county, or town, and maintained by taxes as part of a free education system for the children of the community.

pub·lic ser·vant, *n.* An employee of the government.

pub·lic serv·ice, *n.* A business which supplies services and commodities, as electricity or transportation, to the public; a service furnished free to the public; government service, as civil service. **—pub·lic serv·ant,** *n.*

pub·lic speak·ing, *n.* The action or art of effective oral expression in public.

pub·lic u·til·i·ty, *n.* A business, industry, or agency engaged in providing or making available to the public a commodity or service of general importance or need.

pub·lic works, *n. pl.* Anything built or constructed by the government with public funds for the use of the general public.

pub·lish, pəb′lish, *v.t.* To cause to be printed and offered for sale to the public; as a newspaper, book, magazine, or the like; to make public.—*v.i.* **—pub·lish·a·ble,** *a.*

pub·lish·er, pəb·lish·ər, *n.* One who publishes, esp. one who publishes books, newspapers, magazines, maps, or the like.

puce, pūs, *a.* Dark brown; reddish brown.—*n.*

puck, pək, *n.* A rubber disk used in ice hockey.

puck·er, pək′ər, *v.t.* To gather into small folds or wrinkles.—*v.i.* To become wrinkled.—*n.* A fold or collection of folds.

pud·ding, pûd′ing, *n.* A usu. baked or boiled dish made of flour, rice, or other starchy substance, with milk and eggs.

pud·dle, pəd′əl, *n.* A small pool of water or other liquid.—*v.t.,* **-dled, -dling.** To make muddy.

pudg·y, pəj′ē, *a.,* **-i·er, -i·est.** Fat and short. **—pudg·i·ness,** *n.*

pueb·lo, pweb′lō, *n. pl.,* **-los.** A village of certain Indians, built of adobe or stone in the form of a communal house or group of houses.

pu·er·ile, pū′ər·il, pwer′il, pwer′īl, *a.* Of or referring to a child; juvenile; childishly foolish. **—pu·er·il·i·ty,** pū·ər·il′ə·tē, *n.*

puff, pəf, *v.i.* To blow with short, quick blasts, as the wind; breathe quick and hard; to go or move with puffing: to *puff* up the stairs; to emit puffs or whiffs of vapor or smoke; to smoke a cigarette, cigar, or pipe with puffs; to become inflated or distended, usu. followed by *up.*—*v.t.* To send forth, as air or vapor, in short, quick blasts; to smoke, as a cigarette; to inflate or distend with breath or air; to inflate with pride or vanity, often followed by *up;* elate; to arrange in puffs, as the hair.—*n.* A short, quick blast, as of wind or breath; an inflated or distended part of a thing; a swelling; a form of light pastry; a loose cylindrical roll of hair; a portion of material gathered and held down at the edges but left full in the middle, as in a garment; a quilted bed cover, filled with wool, cotton, or down; powder puff; puffball. **—puff·i·ness,** *n.* **—puff·y,** *a.,* **-i·er, -i·est.**

puff ad·der, *n.* A large, venomous African viper.

puff·er, pəf′ər, *n.* One who or that which puffs.

pug, pəg, *n.* One of a breed of dogs resembling a small bulldog. *Informal.* A prizefighter.

---

a- hat, fāte, fâre, fäther; e- met, mē; i- pin, pīne; o- not, nōte, ôrb, moove (move), boy, pownd; u- cūbe, bûll, tûk (took); ch- chin; th- thick, ŧhen; zh- vizhon (vision); ə- əgo, takən, pencəl, lemən, bərd (bird).

pu·gil·ism, pū′jə·liz·əm, *n.* The practice of boxing or fighting with the fists. **—pu·gil·ist,** *n.* **—pu·gil·is·tic,** pū·jə·lis′tik, *a.*

pug·na·cious, pəg·nā′shəs, *a.* Disposed or inclined to fighting; belligerent; quarrelsome. **—pug·na·cious·ness, pug·nac·i·ty,** pug·nas′ə·tē, *n.*

pug nose, *n.* A short, somewhat wide nose turning up at the tip. **—pug-nosed,** pəg′nōzd, *a.*

puke, pūk, *v.i., v.t.,* **puked, puk·ing.** To vomit.

pull, pûl, *v.t.* To draw or tug at with force: to *pull* a person's hair; draw or haul toward oneself or itself, or in a particular direction: to *pull* a trigger, to *pull* a sled up a hill; tear: *pull* it to pieces; to draw or pluck away from a place of growth or attachment: to *pull* a tooth; to strain, as a muscle or ligament. *Informal.* To draw out for use, as a knife or a pistol.—*v.i.* To give a pull; to tug; to inhale; to row.—*n.* An act of pulling or drawing; a tug; force expended in pulling; pulling power. *Informal.* Influence, as with persons able to grant favors. A part or thing to be pulled, as a handle or the like.**—pull a face,** to grimace.**—pull a·part,** to break into pieces; to examine critically.**—pull down,** to destroy. *Informal.* To be paid or to receive, as wages.**—pull for,** to actively support; encourage.**—pull off.** *Informal.* To put through successfully.**—pull one·self to·geth·er,** to quiet down; to recover from a momentary emotional disturbance.**—pull one's leg,** to tease, esp. by humorous and repeated deceit; to kid someone.**—pull out,** to withdraw.**—pull strings,** to seek out and accept the advantage of another's power or influence in order to advance oneself.**—pull through,** to get through a difficult or dangerous situation or condition.**—pull to·geth·er,** to cooperate.**—pull up,** to halt; to move by pulling toward one.

pull·back, pûl′bak, *n.* The process of pulling back or withdrawing; something used for holding or drawing back.

pul·let, pûl′it, *n.* A young hen or chicken.

pul·ley, pûl′ē, *n.* One of the simple machines used for raising weights and consisting of a small wheel which moves around an axle, and has a groove cut in its circumference in which a cord runs; a wheel in a piece of machinery which transmits power or changes the direction of motion by means of a belt or band.

Pull·man, pûl′mən, *n.* A sleeping car with accommodations.

pull·out, pûl′owt, *n.* A leaving or pulling out.

pull·o·ver, pûl′ō·vər, *n.* Clothing, as a shirt or sweater, which is put on by pulling it over the head.

pul·mo·nar·y, pûl′mə·ner·ē, pəl′mə·ner·ē, *a.* Of or referring to the lungs; of the nature of a lung, or lunglike; affecting the lungs; having lungs or lunglike organs.

pulp, pəlp, *n.* Soft, undissolved animal or vegetable matter; the soft, succulent part of fruit; material reduced to a soft uniform mass for making paper; a magazine or other publication, often containing lurid, sensational material.—*v.t.* To make into pulp; to deprive of the pulp.—*v.i.* To become pulp. **—pulp·i·ness,** *n.* **—pulp·y,** pəl′pē, *a.,* **-i·er, -i·est.**

pul·pit, pûl′pit, pəl′pit, *n.* A platform or raised structure in a church, from which the clergyman delivers the sermon or conducts the service.**—the pul·pit,** preachers or the clergy collectively; the work performed by preachers.

pulp·wood, pəlp′wûd, *n.* The soft wood of spruce, pine, and various other trees, used to make paper.

pul·sate, pəl′sāt, *v.i.,* **-sat·ed, -sat·ing.** To beat or throb rhythmically; to vibrate.

pul·sa·tion, pəl·sā′shən, *n.* The process of beating or throbbing; a beat of the pulse; a throb.

pul·sa·tor, pəl′sā·tər, pəl′sā′tər, *n.* That which pulsates, beats, or throbs. **—pul·sa·to·ry,** pəl′sə·tôr·ē, *a.*

pulse, pəls, *n.* The beating or throbbing of the arteries caused by contractions of the heart; a pulsation; any rhythmic, regular throbbing or beat; vibration; public opinion.—*v.i.,* **pulsed, puls·ing.** To beat; vibrate; throb.

pul·ver·ize, pəl′və·rīz, *v.t.,* **-ized, -iz·ing.** To reduce to fine powder, as by beating, grinding, or the like; to crush or demolish.—*v.i.* To become reduced to fine powder. **—pul·ver·iz·a·ble,** *a.* **—pul·ver·i·za·tion,** pəl·vər·ə·zā′shən, **pul·ver·iz·er,** *n.*

pu·ma, pū′mə, *n. pl.,* **-mas, -ma.** A large, slender, tawny cat native to N. and S. America, having a small head and long tail tipped with black.

pum·ice, pəm′is, *n.* A porous, stony substance from volcanoes, lighter than water, used for polishing and smoothing ivory, wood, marble, metals, or glass.—*v.t.* Also **pum·ice stone. —pu·mi·ceous,** pū·mish′əs, *a.*

pum·mel, pəm′əl, *v.t.,* **-meled or -melled, -mel·ing or -mel·ling.** To pommel.—*n.* A pommel.

pump, pəmp, *n.* An instrument or machine, consisting of an arrangement of a piston, cylinder, and valves, employed for raising water or other liquid to a higher level, for moving liquids or gases through a pipe or pipeline, or for exhausting or compressing air or other gases.—*v.i.* To work a pump; to move up and down like a pump handle.—*v.t.* To raise with a pump; to free from water or other fluid by a pump, often with *out:* to *pump out* a ship; to inflate with a pump, usu. with *up;* to put artful questions to for the purpose of extracting information; to discharge, eject, drive, or force by means of a pump or as though by a pump. **—pump·a·ble,** *a.* **—pump·er,** *n.*

pump, pəmp, *n.* A woman's shoe, low-cut and without fastenings; a similarly cut type of dress shoe for men.

pum·per·nick·el, pəm′pər·nik·əl, *n.* A dark, coarse bread made from rye.

pump·kin, pəmp′kin, pəng′kin, *n.* A long, trailing vine in the gourd family; the large, orange, furrowed fruit of this plant.

pun, pən, *n.* The use of a word in such a manner as to bring out different meanings or applications; a play on a word or words.—*v.i.,* **punned, pun·ning.** To make puns.

punch, pənch, *v.t.* To pierce or perforate with a pointed sharp instrument; to give a sharp thrust or blow to, esp. with the fist; to drive, as cattle; to poke or prod, as with a stick.—*v.i.*—*n.* A tool or apparatus for piercing, perforating, or stamping materials; a thrusting blow, esp. with the fist; vigorous effectiveness; vitality: a story or a play that lacks *punch.***—punch in,** to punch the arrival time of an employee, on a clock. **—punch·er,** *n.*

punch, pənch, *n.* In the U.S., a cold beverage made with water, and with or without alcohol, and sweetened and flavored with sugar and fruit juice.

punch card, *n.* A card that includes data, later recorded for retrieval by electronic computers, according to the pattern of the holes in the card.

punch-drunk, pənch′drəngk, *a.* Having cerebral injury resulting from repeated head blows, as received while boxing, and showing grogginess and slowness in speech and muscular movement. *Informal.* Confused; groggy.

punch line, *n.* The last part, phrase, or sentence of an anecdote that contains the major point.

punch press, *n.* A machine for forming metal.

punch·y, pən′chē, *a.,* **-i·er, -i·est.** *Informal.* Punch-drunk.

punc·tu·al, pəngk′choo·əl, *a.* Exact to the time agreed on. **—punc·tu·al·i·ty,** pəngk·choo·əl′ə·tē, *n.* **—punc·tu·al·ly,** *adv.* **—punc·tu·al·ness,** *n.*

punc·tu·ate, pəngk′choo·āt, *v.t.,* **-at·ed, -at·ing.** To mark or divide with punctuation marks; to interrupt at intervals: to *punctuate* a speech by cheers; to give point or emphasis: He *punctuated* his remarks with gestures.—*v.i.* To insert or use marks of punctuation. **—punc·tu·a·tor,** *n.*

punc·tu·a·tion, pəngk·choo·ā′shən, *n.* The act of punctuating; esp. the practice, art, or system of inserting marks or points in writing or printing in order to make the meaning clear.

punc·tu·a·tion mark, *n.* Any of the conventional symbols which organize written language and clarify relations between words.

punc·ture, pəngk′chər, *n.* The action or an act of pricking or perforating, as with a pointed instrument or object; a mark or hole so made.—*v.t.* **-tured, -tur·ing.** To prick, pierce, or perforate: to *puncture* the skin with a pin.—*v.i.* To be pricked or punctured. **—punc·tur·a·ble,** *a.*

pun·dit, pən′dit, *n.* One of great authority and learning.

pun·gent, pən′jənt, *a.* Sharply affecting the sense of smell and taste; biting; affecting the mind in a sharp or piercing manner; caustic; poignant. **—pun·gen·cy,** *n.* **—pun·gent·ly,** *adv.*

pun·ish, pən′ish, *v.t.* To inflict a penalty on, as for an offense, real or imputed: to *punish* a disobedient child; to inflict a penalty for an offense or fault: to *punish* theft; to handle severely or roughly, as in a fight or struggle.—*v.i.* To inflict punishment. **—pun·ish·a·ble,** *a.*

pun·ish·ment, pən′ish·mənt, *n.* The act of punishing.

pu·ni·tive, pū′nə·tiv, *a.* Pertaining to, involving, or inflicting punishment.

punk, pəngk, *n. Informal.* A person or thing of no importance; a hoodlum of limited experience or power; a young, naive boy.—*a. Informal.* Poor in quality; wretched; in poor health.

pun·ster, pən′stər, *n.* One skilled in or fond of making puns.

punt, pənt, *v.i., v.t.,* To drop and kick a football before it touches the ground.—*n.* A kick made in this way. **—punt·er,** *n.*

pu·ny, pū′nē, *a.,* **-ni·er, -ni·est.** Small and weak; underdeveloped in size and strength; petty or insignificant. **—pu·ni·ness,** *n.*

pup, pəp, *n.* A puppy; a young seal.—*v.i.,* **pupped, pup·ping.** To give birth to pups.

pu·pa, pū′pə, *n. pl.,* **pu·pae,** pū′pē, **-pas.** The intermediate form of an insect occurring between the larva and adult stages; an insect in this form. **—pu·pal,** *a.*

pu·pate, pū′pāt, *v.i.,* **-pat·ed, -pat·ing.** To become a pupa. **—pu·pa·tion,** pū·pā′shən, *n.*

pu·pil, pū′pəl, *n.* A young person under the care of an instructor or tutor; a student.

pu·pil, pū′pəl, *n.* The round opening in the middle of the eye's iris through which the rays of light pass to the retina. **—pu·pil·ar, pu·pil·lar·y,** *a.*

pup·pet, pəp′it, *n.* A small figure, human or animal, moved by hand or by cords or rods in a dramatic presentation; a marionette; a person who is a mere tool of another.

pup·pet·eer, pəp·i·tēr′, *n.* One who operates puppets.

pup·pet·ry, pəp′i·trē, *n. pl.,* **-ries.** The art of presenting puppet shows; mummery; mere show; a set of puppets.

pup·py, pəp′ē, *n. pl.,* **-pies.** A young animal, esp. a young dog; a conceited and insignificant young man. **—pup·py·ish,** *a.*

pup·py love, *n.* Adolescent love.

pup tent, *n.* Shelter tent.

pur·chase, pər′chəs, *v.t.,* **-chased, -chas·ing.** To gain; to get by payment of money or its equivalent; to buy; to get by labor, danger, or other means.—*n.* Acquisition in general; buying; that which is purchased. **—pur·chas·a·ble,** *a.* **—pur·chas·er,** *n.*

pure, pūr, *a.* Free from all unnecessary matter, esp. from anything that pollutes; free from anything that contaminates; innocent; spotless; chaste; stainless; genuine; ceremonially clean; unpolluted; mere; sheer; absolute: *pure* agony; theoretical or abstract.

—pure·ly, *adv.* **—pure·ness,** *n.*

pu·rée, pū·rā′, pū·rē′, pyūr′ā, *n.* Meat, fish, or vegetables boiled into a pulp and passed through a sieve. **—v.t., -réed, -rée·ing.**

pur·ga·tive, pər′gə·tiv, *a.* Purging; cleansing; bringing about a bowel movement.—*n.* A medicine that evacuates the bowels.

pur·ga·to·ry, pər′gə·tôr·ē, *n. pl.,* **-ries.** In Roman Catholic belief, a place in which souls after death are purified from venial sins and suffer punishment for all sins not atoned for. *Informal.* Any place or state of temporary suffering. **—pur·ga·to·ri·al,** pər·gə·tôr′ē·əl, *a.*

purge, pərj, *v.t.,* **purged, purg·ing.** To cleanse or purify by carrying off whatever is impure or foreign; to remove by cleansing, usu. followed by *out, away,* or *off;* to clear of moral defilement; to clear of accusation or the charge of a crime; to remove from a position of influence in a political party or nation; to evacuate the bowels.—*v.i.* To produce bowel evacuations; to become purified or clean.—*n.* The act of purging; anything that purges. **—purg·er,** *n.*

pu·ri·fy, pyūr′ə·fī, *v.t.,* **-fied, -fy·ing.** To make pure or clear; to free from unnecessary elements; to free from pollution ceremonially; to cleanse from whatever renders one unclean and unfit for sacred services. **—v.i.** To grow or become pure or clear. **—pu·ri·fi·ca·tion,** pyūr·ə·fə·kā′shən, **pu·ri·fi·er,** *n.*

pur·ism, pyūr′iz·əm, *n.* Insistence on, and observance of, rigid purity in language. **—pur·ist,** *n.* **—pu·ris·tic,** pyūr·is′tik, *a.*

pu·ri·tan, pyūr′ə·tən, *n.* One who affects great purity or strictness of life and religious principles; *(cap.)* one of a class of Protestants that arose in the 16th century within the Church of England.—*a.* Puritanical; *(cap.)* of or referring to the Puritans. **—pu·ri·tan·i·cal,** pyūr·ə·tan′ə·kəl, *a.* **—pu·ri·tan·i·cal·ly,** *adv.*

pu·ri·ty, pyūr′ə·tē, *n.* The condition of being pure; cleanness; innocence; chastity; degree of saturation or intensity, as of a color.

purl, pərl, *v.t., v.i.* To invert, as a stitch, in knitting; to embroider, as a border of fabric.—*n.* An embroidered border; an inversion of the stitches in knitting.

pur·loin, pər·loyn′, *v.t.* To steal; to filch.—*v.i.* To practice theft. **—pur·loin·er,** *n.*

pur·ple, pər′pəl, *n.* A color that is a blend of red and blue in about equal proportions.—*a.* Of a purple color; regal or imperial; of speech or writing that is highly fancy: *purple* prose; colored with profanity.—*v.t., v.i.,* **-pled, -pling.** To turn or to make purple. **—pur·plish,** pər′plish, *a.*

pur·port, pər′pôrt, *n.* Meaning; tenor; import, often as implied or professed rather than directly stated.—pər·pôrt′, pər′pôrt, *v.t.* To convey, as a certain meaning; to signify; imply; to claim, esp. falsely. **—pur·port·ed,** *a.* **—pur·port·ed·ly,** *adv.*

pur·pose, pər′pəs, *n.* That which is set up as an objective to be reached or accomplished; the use for which something is intended, its reason for being; resolution; firm intention.—*v.t.,* **-posed, -pos·ing.** To intend; to resolve; to set as a goal or aim. **—on purpose,** with previous design; intentionally. **—pur·pose·ful,** *a.* **—pur·pose·ful·ly,** *adv.*

pur·pose·ly, pər′pəs·lē, *adv.* By purpose or design; intentionally.

pur·pos·ive, pər′pə·siv, *a.* Pertaining to, showing, or having purpose; adapted to or serving some useful function or end; firm; resolute.

purr, pur, pər, *n.* The soft, murmuring sound uttered by a cat when pleased.—*v.i.* To utter a soft, murmuring sound.—*v.t.* To signify by or as by purring.

purse, pərs, *n.* A small bag, pouch, or case for carrying money; a woman's handbag; a sum of money offered as a prize; any baglike receptacle resembling a purse

---

a- hat, fāte, fāre, fäther; **e-** met, mē; **i-** pin, pīne; **o-** not, nōte, ôrb, moove (move), boy, pownd; **u-** cūbe, bŭll, tŭk (took); **ch-** chin; **th-** thick, then; **zh-** vizhon (vision); **ə-** əgo, takən, pencəl, lemən, bərd (bird).

or pocket; money, resources, or wealth.—*v.t.,* **pursed, purs•ing.** To pucker; to contract into folds or wrinkles as if drawing together the mouth of a purse or bag: She *pursed* her lips.

purs•er, pėr′sėr, *n.* An officer on board a ship, charged with the keeping of accounts and documents, and with the service and care of passengers on a passenger ship.

pur•su•ant, pėr•soo′ėnt, *a.* Done in consequence of anything; agreeable with, conformable to, or according to, used with *to;* pursuing; following.—*adv.* Conformably, used with *to.*

pur•sue, pėr•soo′, *v.t.,* **-sued, -su•ing.** To follow for the purpose of overtaking or capturing; to chase; to haunt: Misfortune *pursues* him; to seek to attain; to continue or proceed in; to carry on; to follow: to *pursue* a course.—*v.i.* To go in pursuit; to proceed. —**pur•su•er,** *n.*

pur•suit, pėr•soot′, *n.* The act of pursuing; a regular pastime or occupation.

pur•sy, pėr′sē, *a.,* **-si•er, -si•est.** Short-winded; fat. —**pur•si•ness,** *n.*

pu•ru•lent, pyûr′ė•lėnt, pyûr′yė•lėnt, *a.* Consisting of pus; full of or resembling pus; discharging pus. —**pu•ru•lence, pu•ru•len•cy,** *n.* —**pu•ru•lent•ly,** *adv.*

pur•vey, pėr•vā′, *v.t.* To provide or furnish, as provisions or other necessities. —**pur•vey•or,** *n.*

pur•vey•ance, pėr•vā′ėns, *n.* Act or business of purveying; provisions.

pur•view, pėr′vū, *n.* The body of a statute, as distinguished from the *preamble;* the limit or scope of a statute: limit of the sphere of authority; the scope of concern or study; one's outlook or scope of vision.

pus, pĕs, *n.* A thick, yellowish-white substance produced by suppuration and found in abscesses and healing sores.

push, pûsh, *v.t.* To press against with force; to drive or move by steady pressure: opposed to *pull;* to press or urge forward; shove; thrust; to advocate; to press for or promote energetically: to *push* a trade or sale.—*v.i.* To make a thrust against something; to press oneself onward, as against obstacles; to project.—*n.* The act of pushing; impetus; a thrust; a vigorous effort.—**push off,** to depart from shore, as in a boat, or raft.—**push on,** to resume one's journey after an interruption; to press on against difficulty or opposition. —**push•er,** *n.*

push•y, pûsh′ē, *a.,* **push•i•er, push•i•est.** Enterprising; annoyingly aggressive. —**push•i•ly,** *adv.* —**push•i•ness,** *n.*

push but•ton, *n.* A button that starts or stops a machine when it is pushed. —**push-but•ton,** *a.*

push•cart, pûsh′kärt, *n.* A light cart to be pushed by hand, used by street venders.

push•o•ver, pûsh′ō•vėr, *n. Informal.* Anyone easily overcome or deceived; anything done easily.

pu•sil•lan•i•mous, pū•sė•lan′ė•mės, *a.* Without strength; cowardly. —**pu•sil•la•nim•i•ty,** pū•sė•lė•nim′ė•tē, *n.* —**pu•sil•lan•i•mous•ly,** *adv.*

puss, pûs, *n.* A cat; an affectionate name for a child.

puss, pûs, *n. Informal.* The face; mouth.

puss•y, pûs′ē, *n. pl.,* **-ies.** A cat; kitten; a silky catkin, as of a willow.

puss•y•foot, pûs′ē•fût, *v.i.* To go with a soft, stealthy tread like that of a cat; proceed or act cautiously, as if afraid to commit oneself on a point at issue.

puss•y wil•low, pûs′ē, *n.* A small tree or shrub, having conspicuous silky flower clusters or catkins opening before the leaves.

pus•tule, pės′chool, *n.* An elevation of the skin, having an inflamed base and containing pus; any small bump on the skin similar to a pimple or blister. —**pus•tu•lar, pus•tu•late,** *a.*

put, pût, *v.t.,* **put, put•ting.** To move, as a thing or person, so as to place it in some place or position; place; lay; to subject to the suffering of something: to *put* a person to expense; to set to a duty, task, or action; to force to some course or action: to *put*

someone to flight; to incite or urge; to translate into another language; to adapt, as words, to music; to express; to assign: to *put* a certain construction upon an action; to set at a particular amount in a scale of estimation: to *put* the distance at three miles; to bet: to *put* a sum on a horse; to apply, as to a use; to propose for answer, consideration, or deliberation: to *put* a question; to impose as a burden, charge, or the like: to *put* a tax on an article; to invest; to lay the blame of, usu. followed by *on* or *to:* to *put* the blame *on* carelessness; to throw or cast, esp. with a forward motion of the hand when raised close to the shoulder: to *put* the shot.—*v.i.* To go, move, or proceed: The ship *put* back to port.—*a. Informal.* Fixed: to stay *put.*—**put a•cross.** *Informal.* To make acceptable, as a point of view; to carry out successfully, esp. through trickery.—**put a•side, a•way,** or **by,** to place in reserve, as money; save; to discard or thrust aside.—**put down,** to write down; to repress or crush; to depose or demote. *Informal.* To humiliate or deflate.—**put forth,** to send out, as buds or leaves; to grow; to publish or issue; to propose or offer; to put into operation; exert; to set out, or start, esp. to sea.—**put for•ward,** to advance for consideration; propose.—**put in,** to interpose, as a remark; to make a request or application; to enter a port or harbor. *Informal.* To pass or spend, as time, in a manner specified.—**put off,** to defer or postpone; to rebuff; to discard or take off, as one's clothes.—**put on,** to assume a manner falsely; to clothe oneself in; to produce. *Informal.* To tease by fooling or exaggeration.—**put out,** to extinguish, as a fire; to irritate; to publish; to produce for sale; to retire a batter or runner in baseball.—**put o•ver.** *Informal.* To carry out successfully; put across; to succeed in carrying out through trickery.—**put through,** to carry to successful completion; to cause to go through. —**put up,** to erect or construct; to can or preserve, as fruit or vegetables; to provide, as capital; to nominate, as a candidate. *Informal.* To accommodate; to wager or stake, as a sum of money.—**put up to,** to incite or prompt.—**put up with,** to bear with patience; tolerate.

pu•ta•tive, pū′tė•tiv, *a.* Supposed. —**pu•ta•tive•ly,** *adv.*

put-on, pût′on′, pût′ôn′, *a.* Assumed; pretended. —pût′on, pût′ôn, *n. Informal.* An affectation; a deception or hoax.

pu•tre•fac•tion, pū•trė•fak′shėn, *n.* The act or process of putrefying; that which is putrefied.

pu•tre•fy, pū′trė•fī, *v.t.,* **-fied, -fy•ing.** To render putrid; to cause to rot with an offensive smell.—*v.i.* To become putrid; to rot.

pu•trid, pū′trid, *a.* In a state of decay or putrefaction; corrupt; rotten; most offensive or vile. —**pu•trid•i•ty,** pū•trid′ė•tē, **pu•trid•ness,** *n.*

putt, pėt, *n.* A gentle stroke made on a golf green.—*v.t., v.i.,* **putt•ed, putt•ing.** To tap, as a golf ball, in the direction of the cup.

put•ter, pėt′ėr, *v.i.* To occupy oneself with useless matters: often followed by *around;* to waste time idly; to dawdle. —**put•ter•er,** *n.*

put•ting green, *n.* Smooth turf surrounding a hole in golf.

put•ty, pėt′ē, *n.* A kind of paste compounded of soft carbonate of lime and linseed oil, used by glaziers for fixing the panes of glass in window frames or filling in crevices in wooden surfaces; any of various compounds similar to this in use or in consistency; a person who is easily influenced: He was *putty* in her hands.—*v.t.,* **-tied, -ty•ing.** To cement with putty; to fill up with putty.

put-up, pût′ėp, *a. Informal.* Planned beforehand in a secret or crafty manner: a *put-up* job.

put-up•on, pût′ė•pon, *a.* Imposed upon.

puz•zle, pėz′ėl, *v.t.,* **-zled, -zling.** To perplex or confuse; to discover or resolve by long cogitation, used with *out.*—*v.i.* To be bewildered or uncertain; to ponder over a problem.—*n.* A toy or contrivance which tries the ingenuity; something which is puzzling; perplexity. **—puz·zler,** *n.*

puz·zle·ment, pez′əl·mənt, *n.* Bewilderment or perplexity; that which puzzles.

Pyg·my, Pig·my, pig′mē, *n. pl.,* **Pyg·mies, Pig·mies.** A member of any of various Negroid peoples of small stature, esp. of Africa; a small or dwarfish person; anything very small of its kind; one who is of small importance, or who has some quality in very small measure.—*a.* (Often *l.c.*) Of or pertaining to the Pygmies; (*l.c.*) of very small stature or size; diminutive or tiny; of very small capacity or power.

py·lon, pī′lon, *n.* A large structure indicating the entrance to a bridge or street; a metal tower supporting electric power lines.

pyr·a·mid, pir′ə·mid, *n.* A solid structure whose base is square and whose sides are triangular and meet at a point; one of the ancient structures of this form built in different parts of the world, often used as tombs, the most famous being those of Egypt; anything pyramidal in form.—*v.i.* To raise or increase something, as costs, by gradual addition.—*v.t.* To arrange in the form of a pyramid; to raise or increase, as costs or wages, by gradual additions. **—py·ram·i·dal,** pi·ram′ə·dəl, *a.*

pyre, pīr, *n.* A heap of combustible materials, specif.

such a heap on which a dead body is laid to be burned; a funeral pile.

Py·rex, pī′reks, *n. Trademark.* A heat-resistant, siliceous glass used for cookware and in various industrial applications.

py·ric, pī′rik, *a.* Relating to or caused by burning.

py·ro·ma·ni·a, pī·rə·mā′nē·ə, pī·rə·mān′yə, *n.* An uncontrollable impulse to set things on fire. **—py·ro·ma·ni·ac,** *n.* **—py·ro·ma·ni·a·cal,** pī·rō·mə·nī′ə·kəl, *a.*

py·rom·e·ter, pī·rom′ə·tər, *n.* An instrument which measures extremely high temperatures. **—py·rom·e·try,** *n.*

py·ro·tech·nics, pī·rə·tek′niks, *n. pl., sing. or pl. in constr.* The art of making fireworks; the making and use of fireworks for display or military purposes; a display of fireworks or something resembling fireworks; a brilliant or sensational display. **—py·ro·tech·nic, py·ro·tech·ni·cal,** *a.*

Pyr·rhic vic·to·ry, pir′ik, *n.* A victory costing the victor more than the loser.

py·thon, pī′thon, pī′thən, *n.* Any of various large, non-poisonous, Old-World tropical snakes, which kill by squeezing; any of various related or similar snakes, as a boa.

Q

Q, q, kū, *n.* The seventeenth letter of the English alphabet, usu. followed by *u.*

quack, kwak, *v.i.* To cry like a duck.—*n.* The cry of a duck or a similar sound.

quack, kwak, *n.* One who pretends to skill or knowledge which he or she does not possess; a charlatan; a pretender, esp. a pretender to medical skill.—*a.* Referring to or characterized by quackery: *quack* medicines, a *quack* doctor.—*v.i.* To make pretensions; to play the quack. **—quack·ish,** *a.*

quack·er·y, kwak′ə·rē, *n. pl.,* **-ies.** The boastful pretensions or fakery of a quack; humbug.

quad, kwod, *n.* A quadrangle or court, as of a college.

quad, kwod, *n. Informal.* Quadruplet.

quad·ran·gle, kwod′rang·gəl, *n.* A plane figure having four sides and four angles; a square or quadrangular court surrounded by buildings; the buildings surrounding such a court. **—quad·ran·gu·lar,** kwod·rang′gyə·lər, *a.*

quad·rant, kwod′rənt, *n.* The quarter of a circle; the arc of a circle containing 90°; something having the shape of a quarter circle, as a machine part; an instrument with a graduated arc of 90°, for measuring angular altitudes. **—quad·ran·tal,** kwod·ran′təl, *a.*

quad·ra·phon·ic, kwod·rə·fon′ik, *a.* Relating to or using an electronic system of sound reproduction that has four channels for transmitting the sound through four speakers.

quad·rate, kwod′rit, kwod′rāt, *a.* Square; rectangular.—*n.* A square; something square or rectangular. —*v.t.,* **-rat·ed, -rat·ing.** To bring into accord with; to adapt.—*v.i.* To agree; conform.

quad·rat·ic, kwod·rat′ik, *a.* Pertaining to, denoting, or containing a square; involving the square or second power of an unknown quantity: a *quadratic* equation. —*n.* A quadratic equation or polynomial. **—quad·rat·i·cal·ly,** *adv.*

quad·rat·ics, kwod·rat′iks, *n. pl. but sing. in constr.*

That branch of algebra which treats of quadratic equations.

quad·ra·ture, kwod′rə·chər, *n.* The act of squaring.

quad·ri·lat·er·al, kwod·rə·lat′ər·əl, *a.* Having four sides.—*n.* A plane figure having four sides and four angles; something so formed.

qua·drille, kwə·dril′, *n.* A dance consisting generally of five figures or movements executed by four couples each forming the side of a square; the music for such a dance.

quad·ril·lion, kwod·ril′yən, *n.* In the U.S. and France, one thousand trillions, represented by a 1 followed by 15 zeros; in Great Britain and Germany, one million trillions, represented by a 1 followed by 24 zeros.—*a.* **—quad·ril·lionth,** *a., n.*

quad·roon, kwod·roon′, *n.* The offspring of a mulatto and a white person; a person having one Negro grandparent.

quad·ru·ped, kwod′rû·ped, *n.* A four-footed animal.—*a.* Having four feet. **—quad·ru·pe·dal,** kwod·roo′pə·dəl, kwod·rû·ped′əl, *a.*

quad·ru·ple, kwod·roo′pəl, kwod′rû·pəl, *a.* Fourfold; consisting of four parts; four times as great.—*n.* A number or amount four times as great as another. —*v.t.,* **-pled, -pling.** To make four times as great.—*v.i.* To become four times as great.

quad·ru·plet, kwod·roo′plit, kwod′rû·plit, *n.* Any group or combination of four; one of four children born at one birth.

quad·ru·pli·cate, kwod·roo′pli·kit, kwod·roo′pli·kāt, *a.* Four times repeated; fourfold.—*n.* One of four things that are identical.—kwod·roo′pli·cāt, *v.t.,* **-cat·ed, -cat·ing.**

quaff, kwäf, kwaf, kwôf, *v.t., v.i.* To drink copiously and with great pleasure.—*n.* The act of drinking in this manner; the beverage consumed. **—quaff·er,** *n.*

quag·mire, kwag′mīr, kwog′mīr, *n.* A piece of soft boggy land that yields under foot; a bog; a problem or

---

a- hat, fāte, fâre, fäther; **e-** met, mē; **i-** pin, pīne; **o-** not, nōte, ôrb, moove (move), boy, pownd; **u-** cūbe, bûll, tûk (took); **ch-** chin; **th-** thick, then; **zh-** vizhon (vision); **ə-** əgo, takən, pencəl, lemən, bərd (bird).

situation not easily resolved. **—quag·mired, quag·mir·y,** a.

quail, kwāl, n. A small, chickenlike bird, the bobwhite, with a white throat, stubby tail, and clearly enunciated whistle; a small, Old-World, brown, partridgelike bird. **—quail·like,** a.

quail, kwāl, v.i. To cower or lose heart, as before danger or difficulty.

quaint, kwānt, a. Antique in appearance; attractive or pleasing in an unusual, old-fashioned, or picturesque way; whimsical; fanciful.

quake, kwāk, v.i., **quaked, quak·ing.** To shake, tremble, or shudder, as from fear; of objects, to vibrate, shake, or tremble from internal convulsions or shock. —n. An act of shaking or trembling; an earthquake.

Quak·er, kwā'kər, n. One of the religious sect called the Society of Friends.

qual·i·fi·ca·tion, kwol·ə·fə·kā'shən, n. The act of qualifying, or the state of being qualified; that which fits a person or thing for any purpose, as for a place, an office, or employment; modification or limitation.

qual·i·fied, kwol'ə·fīd, a. Having the necessary qualifications; competent; modified: a qualified statement. **—qual·i·fied·ly,** adv.

qual·i·fy, kwol'ə·fī, v.t., **-fied, -fy·ing.** To furnish with the knowledge, skill, or other prerequisites necessary for a purpose; to make fit for any place, office, or occupation; to ascribe qualities to; name or characterize; to restrict; to limit by exceptions: to qualify a statement; to modify the quality or strength of; to dilute or otherwise make fit for taste.—v.i. To make oneself capable of holding any office or enjoying any privilege; to establish a right to exercise any function. **—qual·i·fi·a·ble,** a. **—qual·i·fi·er,** n.

qual·i·ta·tive, kwol'ə·tā·tiv, a. Pertaining to quality; estimable according to quality.

qual·i·ty, kwol'ə·tē, n. pl., **-ties.** That which makes or helps to make anything such as it is; a distinguishing property, characteristic, or attribute; the level of excellence of something: a product of high quality; superiority; moral characteristic, good or bad; social position in relation to others: a man of quality.

qualm, kwäm, kwôm, n. A sudden feeling of sickness or nausea; a scruple or twinge of conscience; compunction; a sudden sensation of uneasiness. **—qualm·ish,** a.

quan·da·ry, kwon'də·rē, kwon'drē, n. pl., **-ries.** A state of difficulty, perplexity, or hesitation; a predicament.

quan·ti·fi·er, kwon'tə·fī·ər, n. A word specifying quantity.

quan·ti·fy, kwon'tə·fī, v.t., **-fied, -fy·ing.** To determine the quantity of; measure. **—quan·ti·fi·a·ble,** a. **—quan·ti·fi·ca·tion,** kwon·tə·fə·kā'shən, n.

quan·ti·ta·tive, kwon'tə·tā·tiv, a. Estimable according to quantity; relating or having regard to quantity.

quan·ti·ty, kwon'tə·tē, n. pl., **-ties.** That property by virtue of which a thing is measurable; extent; measure; size; any amount: a quantity of earth; a large or considerable amount: wheat shipped in quantity; anything which can be multiplied, divided, or measured; anything to which mathematical processes are applicable.

quan·tum, kwon'təm, n. pl., **quan·ta,** kwon'tə. Quantity or amount; a particular amount; a share or portion; in the quantum theory, a particle or cell composed of the smallest amount of energy capable of existing independently, or this amount of energy regarded as a unit.

quar·an·tine, kwôr'ən·tēn, kwor'ən·tēn, n. A detention or isolation to prevent the spread of disease; a place of confinement or isolation; a system of measures, as for observation or disinfection, maintained by governmental or public authority at ports or frontiers thus preventing the spread of disease.—v.t., **-tined, -tin·ing.** To detain, isolate, or ostracize by quarantine; to put in or subject to quarantine. **—quar·an·tin·a·ble,** a.

quar·rel, kwôr'əl, kwor'əl, n. An angry dispute; a wrangle; a breach of friendship; the basis or ground of variance, complaint, or objection.—v.i., **-reled, -rel·ing, -relled, -rel·ling.** To dispute violently; to wrangle; to squabble; to fall out; to find fault. **—quar·rel·er, quar·rel·ler,** n.

quar·rel·some, kwôr'əl·səm, kwor'əl·səm, a. Inclined or apt to quarrel.

quar·ri·er, kwôr'ē·ər, kwor'ē·ər, n. One who works in a quarry. Also **quar·ry·man,** pl., **quar·ry·men.**

quar·ry, kwôr'ē, kwor'ē, n. pl., **-ries.** Any animal pursued for prey; game; any object of pursuit.

quar·ry, kwôr'ē, kwor'ē, n. pl., **-ries.** An open pit where stones are dug, cut, or blasted from the earth. —v.t., **-ried, -ry·ing.** To dig or take from a quarry; to form a quarry in. **—quar·ry·ing,** n.

quart, kwôrt, n. Two liquid pints; one-quarter gallon.

quar·ter, kwôr'tər, n. One of four parts into which anything is divided or divisible; a fourth part or portion, as of a pound, yard, mile, or calendar year; one-fourth of a dollar, or 25 cents; a U.S. or Canadian coin having this value; a measure, esp. of grain, equal to a fourth of a ton or eight bushels; in schools and universities, one-fourth of the teaching period of the year; one of the four cardinal points of the compass; any point of the compass; a district or locality, specif. a particular region of a town, city, or country: the Latin quarter of Paris; an unspecified individual, group, locality, or the like: orders from a higher quarter; a fourth part of the carcass of a mammal, including a limb: one-fourth of the playing time of a game, as football or basketball; pl., residence, shelter, or lodging.—a. Equal to or being a quarter of anything.—v.t. To divide into four equal parts; to separate or cut into parts; to furnish, as soldiers, with lodgings or shelter; to pass over, as a region, by crossing back and forth.—v.i. To be stationed; to lodge.

quar·ter·back, kwôr'tər·bak, n. A football player who calls signals and directs the offensive plays of his team from a position behind the center from whom he may receive the ball, then usually handing it off or passing it to another member of the team; the position of such a player.—v.t. To direct, as the offensive plays of a football team.—v.i. To play or execute the position or duties of a quarterback.

quar·ter-deck, kwôr'tər·dek, n. The stern or rear part of the upper deck, usu. reserved for the exclusive use of the ship's officers.

quar·ter horse, n. A sturdy, short-legged horse bred for racing short distances, usu. one quarter mile, and in herding cattle.

quar·ter·ing, kwôr'tər·ing, n. The act of one who or that which divides into quarters; the providing of lodging or the quarters themselves.—a. That quarters; set at right angles.

quar·ter·ly, kwôr'tər·lē, a. Pertaining to or consisting of a quarter, esp. a quarter of a year; occurring or done at the end of every quarter of a year.—n. pl., **-lies.** A periodical issued once every quarter of a year.—adv. In or by quarters; once in a quarter of a year.

quar·ter·mas·ter, kwôr'tər·mas·tər, n. A military officer who has charge of quarters, clothing, food, supplies, and other necessities; a petty officer who attends a ship's compass, signals, and navigational apparatus.

quar·ter sec·tion, n. In Canadian and U.S. government land surveying, a square area of land comprising one quarter of a square mile or 160 acres.

quar·tet, kwôr·tet', n. A piece of music arranged for four voices or four instruments; the persons who execute a quartet; any set of four. Also **quar·tette.**

quartz, kwôrts, n. A common, important mineral, silicon dioxide, appearing in many forms and colors, and occurring in masses or in hexagonal crystals as amethyst and rock crystal.

quash, kwosh, *v.t.* To subdue, put down, or quell; to put an end to: to *quash* a rebellion.

qua·si, kwā′zī, kwā′sī, kwä′sē, kwä′zē, *a.* Resembling or alike in certain characteristics or features.—*adv.* As if; seemingly but not absolutely: a *quasi*-historical account.

qua·ter·nar·y, kwot′ər·ner·ē, kwə·tər′nə·rē, *a.* Consisting of four; arranged in fours.

quat·rain, kwot′rān, *n.* A stanza of four lines, usu. rhyming alternately.

qua·ver, kwā′vər, *v.i.* To shake or tremble; to speak or sing with a tremulous voice; to produce trills on a musical instrument or in singing.—*v.t.* To utter or sing with a tremulous sound.—*n.* A shake or tremble, esp. of the voice. —**quav·er·ing·ly,** *adv.* —**qua·ver·y,** *a.*

quay, kē, *n.* A landing place built along a line of coast or a river bank, or forming the side of a harbor, at which vessels are loaded and unloaded; a wharf.

quea·sy, kwē′zē, *a.*, **-si·er, -si·est.** Sick at the stomach; affected with nausea; apt to cause nausea; uneasy or qualmish, as the conscience. —**quea·si·ly,** *adv.* —**quea·si·ness,** *n.*

queen, kwēn, *n.* The spouse, consort, or widow of a king; a woman who is the sovereign of a kingdom; a woman preeminent among others; the fertile female in a colony of ants or bees; a playing card on which a queen is pictured.—*v.i.* To reign or act as a queen. —**queen·li·ness,** *n.* —**queen·ly,** *adv.*, *a.*

queen con·sort, *n.* A ruling king's wife who has no share in his exercise of sovereignty.

queen dow·a·ger, *n.* The widow of a king.

queen moth·er, *n.* A queen dowager who is also the mother of the reigning sovereign.

queer, kwēr, *a.* Strange or odd; of questionable character; suspicious; faint, or queasy; mentally unbalanced or deranged. *Informal.* Homosexual; bad, worthless, or counterfeit.—*v.t.* To ruin or spoil; jeopardize; to put, as a person, in a hopeless or unfavorable position as to success, favor, or the like.—*n. Informal.* A homosexual; counterfeit money.

quell, kwel, *v.t.* To subdue; to cause to cease by using force; to crush, as in insurrection; to quiet; to allay, as anxieties or fears. —**quell·er,** *n.*

quench, kwench, *v.t.* To extinguish; to put out, as a fire; to slake or satisfy, as thirst; to suppress, stifle, or check; to cool abruptly, as heated steel in the tempering process, by sudden immersion into water.—*v.i.* To be extinguished; to go out; to lose zeal. —**quench·a·ble,** *a.* —**quench·er,** *n.*

quer·u·lous, kwer′ə·ləs, kwer′yə·ləs, *a.* Complaining or of a habitually complaining disposition; fretful; peevish.

que·ry, kwēr′ē, *n. pl.*, **-ries.** A question; an inquiry to be answered or resolved.—*v.i.*, **-ried, -ry·ing.** To ask a question or questions.—*v.t.* To seek by questioning; to examine by questions; to express doubt of; to mark with a query.

quest, kwest, *n.* The act of seeking; search; pursuit; an expedition taken to achieve or to find something; the members of such an expedition.—*v.i.* To make search or inquiry; to pursue game.—*v.t.* To search or seek for. —**quest·er,** *n.* —**quest·ing·ly,** *adv.*

ques·tion, kwes′chən, *n.* An interrogative sentence soliciting an answer; a query; an inquiry; a subject of debate; a point of doubt or difficulty; a controversy; the act of inquiring.—*v.i.* To ask a question or questions; to debate; to doubt.—*v.t.* To interrogate; to inquire of by asking questions; to express doubt of; to challenge. —**ques·tion·er,** *n.*

ques·tion·a·ble, kwes′chə·nə·bəl, *a.* Open to being questioned or inquired into; disputable; suspicious; doubtful as to honesty or morality; uncertain. —**ques·tion·a·ble·ness, ques·tion·a·bil·i·ty,** kwes·chən·ə·bil′ə·tē, *n.* —**ques·tion·a·bly,** *adv.*

ques·tion mark, *n.* A symbol (?) used in writing and printing to indicate a question, and usu., as in English, placed at the end of the question; something unknown; a mystery: The enemy's strategy is still a *question mark.*

ques·tion·naire, kwes·chə·nār′, *n.* A systematic series of questions prepared for distribution in order to gather detailed information for analytical purposes.

queue, kū, *n.* Braided hair hanging behind the head; a line of people or vehicles, esp. those awaiting their turn.—*v.t., v.i.,* **queued, queu·ing.** To line up; to form a queue.

quib·ble, kwib′əl, *n.* A turn of language to evade the point in question; an evasion; a trivial point of disagreement.—*v.i.,* **-bled, -bling.** To evade the point in question by means of trivial objections or misleading questions; to bicker. —**quib·bler,** *n.*

quick, kwik, *a.* Taking place rapidly; immediate; prompt; mentally agile; alert; perceptive; receptive to learning: a *quick* mind; nimble; acting or able to act with rapidity; emotionally sensitive or volatile; easily offended or hurt; impatient: a *quick* temper; twisting or reversing direction abruptly: a *quick* turn in the road.—*adv.* In a quick manner.—*n.* The living flesh, esp. sensitive areas beneath fingernails or toenails: nails trimmed down to the *quick;* the center of sensibility: The insult stung her to the *quick.*

quick·en, kwik′ən, *v.t.* To make quicker; to accelerate; to make alive; to revive or resuscitate; to refresh; to stimulate.—*v.i.* To come alive; to become quicker or more rapid. —**quick·en·er,** *n.*

quick-freeze, kwik′frēz, *v.t.*, **-froze, -fro·zen, -freez·ing.** To preserve, as foods, by rapid freezing that permits lengthy storage and prevents damage to taste and appearance on thawing.

quick·ie, kwik′ē, *n. Informal.* Something produced or accomplished in an extremely short period of time, often trivial in subject or makeshift in execution.

quick·lime, kwik′līm, *n.* Lime in the dry state, before it is slaked with water.

quick·sand, kwik′sand, *n.* An area of soft or loose, wet sand of considerable depth, yielding under weight and hence apt to engulf persons, animals, and objects coming upon it.

quick·sil·ver, kwik′sil·vər, *n.* Mercury, liquid at ordinary temperatures.—*a.*—*v.t.* To cover with an amalgam of mercury.

quick-tem·pered, kwik′tem′pərd, *a.* Easily moved to anger.

quick-wit·ted, kwik′wit′id, *a.* Having a ready wit; mentally quick and alert. —**quick-wit·ted·ly,** *adv.* —**quick-wit·ted·ness,** *n.*

quid, kwid, *n.* A piece of tobacco or other substance chewed and rolled about in the mouth.

qui·es·cent, kwē·es′ənt, kwī·es′ənt, *a.* Being in a state of repose; still; quiet. —**qui·es·cence,** *n.*

qui·et, kwī′ət, *a.* Marked by silence or relative silence: a *quiet* road; secluded; making no objectionable or disturbing noise: *quiet* people for neighbors; silent: Keep *quiet;* not in action or motion; still; tranquil; not turbulent; calm; mild; unobtrusive: a *quiet* warning; subdued, as a sense of humor; not glaring or showy, as colors.—*n.* Stillness; rest; tranquillity; calmness. —*v.t.* To make or cause to be quiet; to calm; to pacify. —*v.i.* To become quiet or still.—*adv.* In a silent or calm manner. —**qui·et·ly,** *adv.* —**qui·et·ness, qui·et·er,** *n.*

qui·e·tude, kwī′ə·tood, kwī′ə·tūd, *n.* A state of rest; quiet; tranquillity.

quill, kwil, *n.* One of the large feathers of the wing or tail of a bird; the hard tubelike part of a feather nearest the body; a feather, as of a goose, formed into a pen for writing; one of the hollow spines of a porcupine or hedgehog.—*v.t.* To flute or pleat, as cloth, in small, regular folds; to pierce with a quill; to remove quills

---

a- hat, fāte, fāre, fäther; e- met, mē; i- pin, pīne; o- not, nōte, ôrb, moove (move), boy, pownd; u- cūbe, bûll, tûk (took); ch- chin; th- thick, ŧhen; zh- vizhon (vision); ə- əgo, takən, pencəl, lemən, bərd (bird).

from.

quilt, kwilt, *n.* A cover or coverlet made by stitching one cloth over another, with some soft substance between; any thick or warm coverlet; any quilted article.—*v.t.* To stitch together, as two pieces of cloth, with some soft substance between; to line in the manner of a quilt.—*v.i.* To make a quilt. **—quilt•er,** *n.*

quilt•ing, kwil/ting, *n.* The act or operation of forming a quilt; the material used for making quilts; quilted work.

quince, kwins, *n.* The acid, yellow, fuzzy pome fruit of a small tree in the rose family, used in making jellies and marmalade; the tree itself, native to western Asia.

qui•nine, kwī/nīn, *n.* A bitter, crystalline alkaloid, obtained from the bark of several species of cinchona trees, and used, esp. in the form of a salt, as a remedy for malaria.

quint, kwint, kint, *n.* A set or sequence of five playing cards. *Informal.* A quintuplet.

quin•tes•sence, kwin•tes/əns, *n.* An extract from anything, containing the most essential part of it; the perfect embodiment of a thing. **—quin•tes•sen•tial,** kwin•tə•sen/shəl, *a.*

quin•tet, quin•tette, kwin•tet/, *n.* A vocal or instrumental composition in five parts; the five people or instruments performing it; a group of five persons or things.

quin•til•lion, kwin•til/yən, *n.* In U.S. and France, a thousand quadrillions, signified by 1 followed by 18 zeros; in Great Britain and Germany, a million quadrillions, signified by 1 followed by 30 zeros.—*a.* **—quin•til•lionth,** *a., n.*

quin•tu•ple, kwin•too/pəl, kwin•tū/pəl, kwin•tū̇/pəl, kwin•təp/əl, *a.* Arranged or divided in five or in fives; five times as large or as many.—*n.* A number that is five times another in amount.—*v.t., v.i.,* **-pled, -pling.** To make or be made five times as great.

quin•tu•plet, kwin•təp/lit, kwin•too/plit, kwin•tū̇/plit, kwin•tū̇/plit, *n.* A collection of five of a kind; any one of five offspring born at the same birth.

quip, kwip, *n.* A smart, sarcastic comment or observation; a clever, impromptu remark; a quibble.—*v.i.,* **quipped, quip•ping.** To make or utter a quip. **—quip•pish,** *a.* **—quip•ster,** kwip/stər, *n.*

quirk, kwərk, *n.* A peculiar characteristic or mannerism; a subterfuge; a shift; a quibble; a sudden or sharp turn; a sweeping or flourish, as in writing. **—quirk•i•ly,** *adv.* **—quirk•i•ness,** *n.* **—quirk•y,** *a.,* **-i•er, -i•est.**

quis•ling, kwiz/ling, *n.* A traitor who works against his own country from within.

quit, kwit, *v.t.,* **quit** or **quit•ted, quit•ting.** To discontinue or cease; to leave; to give up or abandon; to let go of, as something grasped.—*v.i.* To stop doing something; to resign from employment; to go away; to give up a struggle; accept defeat.—*a.* Released or absolved from a debt, penalty, or obligation; free; rid, sometimes followed by *of.*—*n.* Act of quitting.

quit•claim, kwit/klām, *n.* The giving up of a claim. —*v.t.* To give up or release one's claim, as to a right or possession.

quite, kwīt, *adv.* Completely, wholly, entirely, or totally: not *quite* done; really; actually; to a great extent or degree; very: *quite* warm.

quits, kwits, *a.* Even, or on equal terms, by repayment or retaliation.—**call it quits,** to stop an activity.

quit•ter, kwit/ər, *n.* One who quits or gives up.

quiv•er, kwiv/ər, *n.* A case for arrows; the arrows carried in such a case.

quiv•er, kwiv/ər, *v.i.* To shake or tremble; to show a slight tremulous motion.—*n.* The act or state of quivering; a tremor.

quix•ot•ic, kwik•sot/ik, *a.* Romantic to extravagance; visionary; high-flown and impractical. Also **quix•ot•i•cal. —quix•ot•i•cal•ly,** *adv.*

quiz, kwiz, *n. pl.,* **quiz•zes.** A questioning or examining; a brief, informal examination, as of students; a hoax; a jest; an eccentric or odd person or thing.—*v.t.,* **quizzed, quiz•zing.** To test, as a student, by questioning; to question intensively: *quiz* a suspect. **—quiz•zer,** *n.*

quiz•zi•cal, kwiz/ə•kəl, *a.* Comical or odd; confused or questioning; teasing; ridiculing. **—quiz•zi•cal•i•ty,** kwiz•ə•kal/ə•tē, *n.* **—quiz•zi•cal•ly,** *adv.*

quoin, koyn, kwoyn, *n.* An external angle of a wall; one of the stones forming it.

quoit, kwoyt, *n.* A flattened iron ring, or a circle of heavy rope, used in a game in which it is thrown at a fixed peg in the ground; *pl. but sing. in constr.,* the game played with such rings.

quon•dam, kwon/dəm, *a.* Having been formerly.

Quon•set hut, kwon/sit, *n. Trademark.* A compact, serviceable, prefabricated metal shelter or hut resembling a semicircular arch in cross section.

quo•rum, kwôr/əm, *n.* The number of members of any body that must be present to legally transact business.

quo•ta, kwō/tə, *n.* A proportional part or share of a fixed quantity assigned to each or which each person or group has to contribute.

quot•a•ble, kwō/tə•bəl, *a.* Capable of or suitable for being quoted. **—quot•a•bil•i•ty,** kwō•tə•bil/ə•tē, *n.*

quo•ta•tion, kwō•tā/shən, *n.* The act of quoting; the passage quoted or cited; the stated current price of a commodity or stock, or the statement or publishing of this price.

quo•ta•tion mark, *n.* One of the pair of marks (" ") used to indicate the beginning and end of a quotation.

quote, kwōt, *v.t.,* **quot•ed, quot•ing.** To repeat from some author or speaker; to repeat by way of authority or illustration; to cite or cite the words of; to surround with quotation marks; to name, as the price of an article or service; to state the current price of, as of stocks or bonds.—*v.i.* To make quotations.—*n. Informal.* Quotation; quotation mark.

quo•tid•i•an, kwō•tid/ē•ən, *a.* Daily; recurring daily. —*n.* Something, esp. a fever, that recurs daily.

quo•tient, kwō/shənt, *n. Math.* The number resulting from the division of one number by another, and showing how often the lesser quantity is contained in the greater.

R

R, r, är, *n.* The eighteenth letter of the English alphabet.

rab·bet, rab′it, *n.* A cut, groove, or recess on the edge or surface of a board, cut so as to receive the end or edge of another piece shaped to fit it; the joint so made.—*v.t., v.i.,* **-bet·ed, -bet·ing.** To cut, form, or be joined by a rabbet.

rab·bi, rab′ī, *n. pl.,* **-bis.** The ordained leader of a synagogue empowered to perform religious and legal ceremonies; a teacher or master, used as a title.

rab·bin·i·cal, rə·bin′ə·kəl, *a.* Of or pertaining to the rabbis or their learning, opinions, or writings. Also **rab·bin·ic. —rab·bin·i·cal·ly,** *adv.*

rab·bit, rab′it, *n.* A small, long-eared, burrowing rodent of the hare family; any of various other long-eared mammals, as the cottontail; the pelt of a hare or rabbit.

rab·ble, rab′əl, *n.* A disorderly crowd or assemblage of persons, esp. of a low, rough, or turbulent kind; a mob.—*v.t.,* **-bled, -bling.** To mob.—**the rab·ble,** contemptuously, the lower classes; the masses.

rab·id, rab′id, *a.* Furious; raging; mad; affected with rabies; excessively or unreasonably enthusiastic: a *rabid* boxing fan. —**rab·id·ly,** *adv.*

ra·bies, rā′bēz, *n.* Hydrophobia; an infectious disease of small animals, particularly dogs, believed to be caused by a virus, transmitted to man by the bite of an infected animal, and usu. proving fatal unless treatment is instituted early in the incubation period.

race, rās, *n.* A contest of speed, as in running, riding, driving, or the like; any competition; a strong or rapid current of water; a channel leading water to or from a place where its energy is utilized.—*v.i.,* **raced, rac·ing.** To engage in a contest of speed; run a race; to run, move or go swiftly.—*v.t.* To run a race with; try to beat in a contest of speed; to cause to run in a race or races; to cause to run, move, or go swiftly: to *race* an engine.

race, rās, *n.* A group of persons connected by common descent or origin; a family, tribe, or people; a major division of mankind characterized by a combination of certain physical traits which are genetically transmitted: the Mongolian *race;* any group, class, or kind, esp. a class of persons: the *race* of politicians.

race·course, rās′kôrs, *n.* Racetrack.

race horse, rās′hôrs, *n.* A horse bred or kept for racing. Also **race·horse.**

ra·ceme, rā·sēm′, *n.* A flower cluster which bears, at intervals along its length, flowers with equal stalks.

rac·er, rā′sər, *n.* One who or that which races or takes part in a race, as a race horse, a bicycle, a yacht; anything having great speed; an American blacksnake.

race·track, rās′trak, *n.* A course, usu. oval, where races of horses, dogs, automobiles, or the like, are held. Also **race·course.**

ra·chis, rā′kis, *n. pl.,* **ra·chis·es, rach·i·des,** rak′i·dēz, rā′ki·dēz. Any of various axial structures, esp. the axis of an inflorescence when somewhat elongated as in a raceme; the shaft of a feather, esp. the part bearing the web, as distinguished from the quill portion. Also **rha·chis.**

ra·cial, rā′shəl, *a.* Pertaining to or characteristic of race or extraction, a race, or races; stemming from differences between races. —**ra·cial·ly,** *adv.*

rac·ism, rā′siz·əm, *n.* The belief that a particular race is inherently superior; a social or political policy based upon this notion. Also **ra·cial·ism,** rā′shəl·iz·əm. —**rac·ist,** *n.*

rack, rak, *n.* A framework on or in which articles may be placed or displayed; a spreading framework set on a wagon for carrying hay or straw in large loads; an apparatus or instrument used for torturing persons by stretching the body.—*v.t.* To torture, as with a rack; to distress acutely; torment; to strain in mental effort: to *rack* one's brains; to place, as pool balls, in a rack.

rack, rak, *n. Obs.* Wreck.—**go to rack and ru·in,** to decline or decay.—**rack up.** *Informal.* To wreck.

rack·et, rak′it, *n.* A light bat having a network of nylon or catgut stretched in a more or less elliptical frame, used in tennis, badminton, and the like; the paddle used in playing table tennis. Also **rac·quet.**

rack·et, rak′it, *n.* Loud noise. *Informal.* Any scheme, trick, dodge, or special way of proceeding; an organized illegal activity, such as bootlegging or the extortion of money by threat or violence from those engaged in some legitimate business.

rack·et·eer, rak·ə·tēr′, *n. Informal.* One engaged in some dishonest or illegal racket.—*v.i. Informal.* To act as a racketeer; to engage in some racket.

rac·on·teur, rak·on·tər′, *n.* A skilled teller of stories, anecdotes, etc.

rac·y, rā′sē, *a.,* **-i·er, -i·est.** Spirited; sprightly; having a strong, characteristic taste or flavor; slightly indecent or risqué; suggestive: a *racy* anecdote. —**rac·i·ly,** *adv.* —**rac·i·ness,** *n.*

ra·dar, rā′där, *n.* An electronic system or device for determining the presence and location of an object by transmitting radio signals, which are reflected by the object and picked up by a receiving system.

ra·di·al, rā′dē·əl, *a.* Pertaining to a ray or radius; grouped or appearing like radii or rays. —**ra·di·al·ly,** *adv.*

ra·di·ance, rā′dē·əns, *n.* Brightness; brilliant or sparkling luster; quality of being radiant or shining. Also **ra·di·an·cy.**

ra·di·ant, rā′dē·ənt, *a.* Emitting rays of light; bright; shining: the *radiant* sun; bright with joy, hope, or the like: a *radiant* face; emitted or transmitted in rays. —**ra·di·ant·ly,** *adv.*

ra·di·ant en·er·gy, *n.* Energy transmitted through space by an electromagnetic wave.

ra·di·ate, rā′dē·āt, *v.i.,* **-at·ed, -at·ing.** To issue or proceed in rays or straight lines from a point or surface, as heat or light; to emit rays.—*v.t.* To emit or send out in direct lines or rays from a point or surface; to give forth an aura of: She *radiates* joy.—rā′dē·it, rā′dē·āt, *a.* Having rays; having lines proceeding as from a center like radii.

ra·di·a·tion, rā·dē·ā′shən, *n.* The act of radiating or state of being radiated; that which is radiated; radiant energy; the emission of energy as waves or as nuclear particles.

ra·di·a·tor, rā′dē·ā·tər, *n.* That which radiates; an appliance for heating a room by means of water or steam; a mechanism for cooling circulating water in engines.

rad·i·cal, rad′ə·kəl, *a.* Of or pertaining to a root or roots; touching what is fundamental: a *radical* change; thorough; extreme, esp. in the way of reform: *radical* opinions or principles; (*often cap.*) belonging or pertaining to extremists in politics. *Math.* Pertaining to or forming a root; noting or pertaining to the radical sign.—*n.* One who holds or follows extreme principles. (*Often cap.*) An extremist in politics. *Math.* A quantity expressed as a root of another quantity; radical sign; an atom or group of atoms which remains unchanged during certain reactions. The root of a

---

a- hat, fāte, fâre, fäther; **e-** met, mē; **i-** pin, pīne; **o-** not, nōte, ôrb, moove (move), boy, pownd;
u- cūbe, bůll, tûk (took); **ch-** chin; **th-** thick, then; **zh-** vizhon (vision); **ə-** əgo, takən, pencəl, lemən, bərd (bird).

word. —**rad·i·cal·ly,** *adv.*

rad·i·cal·ism, rad′ə·kə·liz·əm, *n.* The holding or following of radical or extreme views or principles; the principles or practices of radicals.

rad·i·cal sign, *n.* The mathematical symbol (√) put in front of a term to indicate the extraction of its root.

ra·di·o, rā′dē·ō, *n. pl.,* **-os.** Wireless telegraphy or telephony; a wireless telegraph, telephone, or other apparatus for transmitting or receiving messages by means of modulated electromagnetic waves; a wireless message or broadcast; the radio communications industry.—*a.* Of, pertaining to, used in, or sent by radio; wireless; pertaining to electromagnetic waves with frequencies exceeding 15,000 cycles per second.—*v.t., v.i.,* **-oed, -o·ing.** To transmit, as a message or a program, or transmit a message to by radio.

ra·di·o·ac·tive, rā·dē·ō·ak′tiv, *a.* Pertaining to or caused by radioactivity.

ra·di·o·ac·tiv·i·ty, rā·dē·ō·ak·tiv′ə·tē, *n.* The emission of alpha rays, beta rays, or gamma rays in elements, as uranium, which undergo spontaneous atomic disintegration.

ra·di·o·fre·quen·cy, rā·dē·ō·frē′kwən·sē, *n. pl.,* **-cies.** A wave frequency above 15,000 cycles per second, used in radio transmission; the frequency of a particular radio transmission. Also **ra·di·o fre·quen·cy.**

ra·di·o·gram, rā′dē·ō·gram, *n.* A message sent by radiotelegraphy; a radiograph.

ra·di·o·graph, rā′dē·ō·graf, *n.* An image or picture produced by the action of x-rays or other rays from radioactive substances.—*v.t.* To make a radiograph of. —**ra·di·og·ra·phy,** rā·dē·og′rə·fē, *n.*

ra·di·ol·o·gy, rā·dē·ol′ə·jē, *n.* The science dealing with rays or rays from radioactive substances, esp. for medical uses. —**ra·di·ol·o·gist,** *n.*

ra·di·o tel·e·scope, *n.* An astronomical instrument that receives, amplifies, and measures radio waves coming from sources in outer space.

rad·ish, rad′ish, *n.* The crisp, pungent, edible root of a garden plant of the mustard family; the plant itself.

ra·di·um, rā′dē·əm, *n.* A radioactive metallic element found in certain minerals, as pitchblende, in the uranium series: used in radiography, in medicine for treating cancer, and in luminous materials, as paints.

ra·di·us, rā′dē·əs, *n. pl.,* **-i, -ī, -us·es.** A straight line extending from the center of a circle or sphere to the circumference or surface; a circular area of an extent indicated by the length of a given radius: every house within a *radius* of 40 miles; that one of the two bones of the forearm which is on the thumb side.

ra·don, rā′don, *n.* A radioactive, heavy, gaseous element, chemically inert, formed as a disintegration product of radium.

raf·fi·a, raf′ē·ə, *n.* A fibrous substance obtained from a palm plant of Madagascar, used for tie bands, hats, mats, baskets, and similar products; the tree itself.

raf·fish, raf′ish, *a.* Flashily vulgar; tawdry; rakish; disreputable.

raf·fle, raf′əl, *n.* A lottery in which persons participate by buying chances for a specific prize.—*v.i.,* **-fled, -fling.** To engage in a raffle.—*v.t.* To dispose of by means of a raffle, usu. followed by *off.*

raft, raft, *n.* A float of logs, planks, or other pieces of timber fastened together.

raft, raft, *n. Informal.* A great quantity or number; a lot: a whole *raft* of children.

raft·er, raf′tər, *n.* One of the sloping timbers of a roof, which supports the outer covering.

rag, rag, *n.* Any piece of useless or discarded cloth; *pl.,* tattered or threadbare garments.

rag, rag, *v.t.,* **ragged, rag·ging.** *Informal.* To torment, scold, or tease.

rag·a·muf·fin, rag′ə·məf·in, *n.* A child in very ragged clothing; any unkempt, raggedly dressed person.

rage, rāj, *n.* Violent anger; fury; violent force or intense activity, as of a storm; intense or violent desire or

feeling; passion; that which is extremely popular or in style; a fad.—*v.i.,* **raged, rag·ing.** To be furious with anger; to act or move furiously: the sea that *rages;* to prevail unchecked, as disease. —**rag·ing,** *a.* —**rag·ing·ly,** *adv.*

rag·ged, rag′id, *a.* Torn, worn to rags, or tattered: *ragged* clothing; clothed in rags of tattered garments; having or characterized by loose or hanging shreds or fragmentary bits: a *ragged* wound; shaggy, as an animal's coat; full of rough or sharp projections, as rocks; in a rough, wild, neglected state: a *ragged* garden; rough, imperfect, or faulty: a *ragged* piece of work. —**rag·ged·ly,** *adv.* —**rag·ged·ness,** *n.*

rag·man, rag′man, rag′mən, *n. pl.,* **-men.** A man who gathers or deals in rags and discarded objects.

rag·time, rag′tīm, *n.* Syncopated music with a regularly accented accompaniment, one of the earliest forms of jazz; the rhythm characteristic of this music.

rag·weed, rag′wēd, *n.* One of two herbs of the composite family, the common ragweed, and the giant ragweed, plants whose pollen is a major cause of hay fever.

raid, rād, *n.* Any sudden attack or foray; an unannounced entry or sudden attack by officers of the law in order to make seizures and arrests.—*v.t.* To make a raid on.—*v.i.* To take part in a raid. —**raid·er,** *n.*

rail, rāl, *n.* A bar of wood or metal extending from one upright post to another, as in a fence; one of the parallel steel bars forming a track for the wheels of a locomotive, railroad car, streetcar, elevated, or subway; a railing, as on the deck of a ship; railroad.—*v.t.* To enclose or provide with rails.

rail, rāl, *n.* Any of several species of marsh birds, having short wings and long toes adapted for running over boggy areas.

rail, rāl, *v.i.* To utter reproaches; to use insolent and reproachful language; to scold: followed by *at* or *against.*—*v.t.* To force or cause as a result of railing.

rail·ing, rā′ling, *n.* A fence or barrier of wood or iron, constructed of posts and rails; balustrade; rails in general; the materials for rails.

rail·ler·y, rā′lə·rē, *n. pl.,* **-ies.** Good-humored teasing; jesting language; banter.

rail·road, rāl′rōd, *n.* A permanent roadway consisting of one or more pairs of parallel steel rails laid several feet apart, making a track over which the wheels of trains, etc., may run; the tracks and all the land, trains, buildings, machinery, etc., used in transportation by rail; the company or owners operating and managing such an organization.—*v.t.* To transport by railroad. *Informal.* Rush through forcefully and without careful consideration, esp. a bill through a legislature; send a person to prison on a false charge.—*v.i.* Work for a railroad. —**rail·road·er,** *n.* —**rail·road·ing,** *n.*

rail·way, rāl′wā, *n.* A railroad.

rai·ment, rā′mənt, *n.* Clothing in general; garments.

rain, rān, *n.* The moisture of the atmosphere condensed and deposited in drops of water; the descent of such watery drops; a rainfall; a heavy continuous quantity of anything falling in the manner of rain.—*v.i.* To fall, as rain, usu. preceded by *it:* It *rained* all night; fall like rain; to send down rain.—*v.t.* To send down or shower, as rain; to cause to fall or send down like rain: to *rain* abuse.—**rain or shine,** under any weather conditions.

rain·bow, rān′bō, *n.* A bow or arc of prismatic colors, formed by the refraction and reflection of rays of light through drops of rain, appearing in the sky opposite the sun; any similar display of color.

rain check, *n.* A ticket stub good for a later performance of an outdoor event which is stopped by rain; an offer deferred for a later time.

rain·coat, rān′kōt, *n.* A coat of waterproof material for wearing as a protection from rain.

rain·drop, rān′drop, *n.* A drop of rain.

rain·fall, rān′fôl, *n.* A fall or shower of rain; the amount of water or other form of moisture falling within a given time and area.

rain•y, rā/nē, *a.,* **-i•er, -i•est.** Characterized by rain; wet with rain; bringing or threatening rain. **—rain•i•ly,** *adv.* **—rain•i•ness,** *n.*

raise, rāz, *v.t.,* **raised, rais•ing.** To set upright; to cause to rise or move upward; elevate; to restore to life: to *raise* the dead; to rouse; to stir up; excite or agitate; give vigor to: as, to *raise* his spirits; to build; produce; set up; to breed, as animals; to rear, as a young person; to promote growth of, as flowers; bring up: to *raise* a question; to lift to a higher position; turn upward, as the eyes; to advance in rank, dignity, or position; promote; to make higher or nobler; to get together or gather together: to *raise* money for charity, to *raise* an army; to bring to an end: *raise* the siege; to increase in height; to cause to become light, as dough or bread; to increase in amount, as rent or prices; in games, to bet or bid more than; to increase in degree; intensity, or force, as temperature or noise; to utter; cause to be heard.—*v.i.* In games, to make a higher bet or bid.—*n.* A raising; a raised place; an increase, as of prices, wages, or a bid; the amount of such an increase. **—rais•er,** *n.*

rai•sin, rā/zən, *n.* A grape of some sweet variety dried in the sun or artificially, and used in cooking or eaten raw; a dark shade of purplish blue.

rake, rāk, *n.* An agricultural implement with teeth or tines for gathering together hay or leaves, or breaking and smoothing the surface of ground; any of various implements of a similar form.—*v.t.,* **raked, rak•ing.** To gather together, draw, or remove with a rake; to clear, smooth, or prepare with a rake; to search through industriously or thoroughly.—*v.i.* To use a rake; to search with or as with a rake; to scrape or sweep, with *over.* **—rak•er,** *n.*

rake, rāk, *n.* One who is lewd; a libertine.

rake-off, rāk/ôf, rāk/of, *n. Informal.* A commission, or percentage taken; a rebate, often illegitimate.

rak•ish, rā/kish, *a.* Stylish; dashing; jaunty; immoral; dissolute; having an inclination which suggests or implies speed: *rakish* masts. **—rak•ish•ly,** *adv.* **—rak•ish•ness,** *n.*

ral•ly, ral/ē, *v.t.,* **-lied, -ly•ing.** To bring together or into order again, as an army or company which has been scattered; to draw or call together, as persons, to give assistance or for common action; to concentrate or revive, as one's strength or spirits.—*v.i.* To come together or into order again, as to renew a conflict; to come together in a body for common action; to come to the assistance of a person, party, or cause; to acquire fresh strength or vigor; revive or recover; recover partially from illness.—*n. pl.,* **-lies.** An act of rallying; a recovery from dispersion or disorder, as of troops; a drawing or coming together of persons for common action; a renewal or partial recovery of strength or activity.

ral•ly, ral/ē, *v.t., v.i.,* **-lied, -ly•ing.** To tease.

ram, ram, *n.* A male sheep; any of various devices for battering, crushing, driving, or forcing something; a battering ram; the heavy weight which strikes the blow in a pile driver or the like.—*v.t.,* **rammed, ram•ming.** To drive or force by heavy blows: to *ram* piles into the earth; to strike against with great force; dash violently against. **—ram•mer,** *n.*

ram•ble, ram/bəl, *v.i.,* **-bled, -bling.** To wander about leisurely or aimlessly; to take an irregular course with turns or windings, as a stream or a path; to grow in an irregular, haphazard way; to talk or write discursively or without sequence of ideas.—*n.* A leisurely, carefree, or aimless stroll. **—ram•bling,** *a.*

ram•bler, ram/blər, *n.* One who or that which rambles; any of various climbing roses, having small flowers in clusters.

ram•bunc•tious, ram•bəngk/shəs, *a.* Boisterous,

turbulent, or noisy; unruly.

ram•i•fi•ca•tion, ram•ə•fə•kā/shən, *n.* A result or outgrowth: to pursue a subject in all its *ramifications*; the act, process, or manner of ramifying; a branch.

ram•i•fy, ram/ə•fī, *v.t., v.i.,* **-fied, -fy•ing.** To divide into branches or parts; to develop new extensions or form new constituent categories.

ramp, ramp, *n.* A sloping passage or surface connecting two different levels, as of a road, stadium, building, or the like.

ram•page, ram•pāj/, *v.i.,* **-paged, -pag•ing.** To rush, rage, or storm about violently.—ram/pāj, *n.* A state of boisterous passion or excitement; violent conduct.

ramp•ant, ram/pənt, *a.* Violent; wild; unchecked; bursting usual limits; standing upon hind legs, as an animal; in heraldry, of a beast, represented in profile, standing upright on the left hind leg with the foreleqs elevated. **—ram•pan•cy,** *n.* **—ram•pant•ly,** *adv.*

ram•part, ram/pärt, *n.* An elevation or mound of earth around a place, on which the parapet is raised; such a structure including the parapet; a bulwark; a defense.

ram•rod, ram/rod, *n.* A rod for ramming down the charge of a muzzle-loading firearm; in general, a rod used to clean the barrels of firearms.—*v.t.* To force upon, esp. by means of authority.

ram•shack•le, ram/shak•əl, *a.* Tumble-down; tumble-down through careless construction; rickety.

ran, ran, *v.* Past tense of **run.**

ranch, ranch, *n.* An establishment and tract of land for raising and grazing livestock, esp. in western U.S.; the buildings and personnel of such an establishment; an extensive farm, as for fruit growing.—*v.i.* To manage, own, or work on a ranch.

ranch•er, ran/chər, *n.* One who owns or is employed on a ranch.

ran•cid, ran/sid, *a.* Having a rank smell or taste; rank or sour-smelling from spoilage, as oils, fats, or butter. **—ran•cid•i•ty,** ran•sid/ə•tē, **ran•cid•ness,** *n.*

ran•cor, rang/kər, *n.* Bitterness, deep resentment, or spite; malice. **—ran•cor•ous,** *a.*

ran•dom, ran/dəm, *n.* A lack of direction, rule, or method.—*a.* Done without aim or purpose; left to chance; fortuitous.—**at ran•dom,** in a haphazard or fortuitous manner; by chance. **—ran•dom•ly,** *adv.* **—ran•dom•ness,** *n.*

range, rānj, *v.t.,* **ranged, rang•ing.** To set in a row or rows; to arrange systematically; to classify; to rank; to rove through or over; to roam; to place, as livestock, on grazing land.—*v.i.* To vary within certain limits; be found; occur; to move over an area thoroughly; to rove or wander; to lie or go in a particular direction; to extend.—*n.* A series of things in a line; a row, as a *range* of mountains; the extent of variations of quantity, degree, or quality: the whole *range* of religion; an expanse of open country used for livestock grazing; the distance from a weapon to its target; the maximum distance a weapon can shoot; an area for shooting or bombing practice; the distance an aircraft, ship, etc., can travel before its fuel is exhausted; the act of wandering around; a stove for cooking and baking.

rang•er, rān/jər, *n.* One who ranges; a member of a mounted, roving troop or police force; a warden patrolling forest areas.

rang•y, rān/jē, *a.,* **-i•er, -i•est.** Slender and long-limbed. **—rang•i•ness,** *n.*

rank, rangk, *n.* A row or line of persons or things; a line of soldiers side by side; official class, place, or standing; degree of eminence; comparative station; high social position; distinction or eminence. *Pl.* An army; the order of common soldiers: reduce an officer to the *ranks.*—*v.t.* To place abreast in a rank or line; to place in a particular class, order, or division; to outrank.—*v.i.* To be ranged, classed, or included, as in a particular class, order, or division; to have a certain rank; to be highest in rank.—**pull rank on.** *Informal.* To use one's superior position in demanding obedience from subordinates.

rank, rangk, *a.* Luxuriant in growth; causing vigorous growth; strong and offensive to the smell or taste; total; utter: *rank* nonsense; gross or coarse; disgusting. —**rank·ness,** *n.*

rank and file, *n.* The common people apart from officers or leaders; the common soldiers, esp. those ranking below sergeant.

ran·kle, rang′kəl, *v.i.,* **-kled, -kling.** To produce bitterness or rancor in the mind; to continue to irritate; to fester.—*v.t.* To irritate; to inflame; to make bitter.

ran·sack, ran′sak, *v.t.* To search thoroughly; to plunder; to strip by plundering.

ran·som, ran′səm, *n.* The payment for the release of an individual from captivity; the price paid for such release or for goods captured by an enemy.—*v.t.* To pay a ransom for; to redeem from captivity; to deliver or release after ransom payment.

rant, rant, *v.i.* To talk or declaim in a loud, agitated, or extravagant manner; rave.—*v.t.* To utter in a wild or immoderate way.—*n.* A ranting speech. —**rant·er,** *n.*

rap, rap, *v.t.,* **rapped, rap·ping.** To strike with a sharp, quick blow.—*v.i.* To strike a quick blow; knock. *Informal.* To converse, chat, or discuss.—*n.* A quick, smart blow; a knock; the sound resulting from such a blow. *Informal.* Blame, responsibility, or punishment; a criminal charge.—**beat the rap.** *Informal.* To escape punishment for a crime.—**bum rap.** *Informal.* Conviction or blame for a crime or misdeed of which one is not guilty.—**take the rap.** *Informal.* To take the punishment or blame for a crime, esp. when not guilty.

ra·pa·cious, rə·pā′shəs, *a.* Given to plunder; accustomed to seizing or taking possession of property by violence; subsisting on living animals seized in predation; avaricious; grasping. —**ra·pa·cious·ly,** *adv.* —**ra·pac·i·ty,** rə·pas′ə·tē, *n.*

rape, rāp, *n.* The offense of sexual intercourse with a woman forcibly and against her will.—*v.t.* To ravish or forcibly have sexual intercourse with; to pillage, as in war.—*v.i.* To ravish or commit rape. —**rap·ist,** *n.*

rape, rāp, *n.* An annual herb of the mustard family, widely cultivated as forage for sheep, hogs, and cattle, and for its oil-yielding seeds.

rap·id, rap′id, *a.* Very swift or quick; moving or advancing with speed; showing speed in progression: *rapid* growth; marked by speed or swiftness: a *rapid* knitter.—*n. Usu. pl.* A swift current in a river, where the channel is descending. —**ra·pid·i·ty,** rə·pid′ə·tē, *n.* —**rap·id·ly,** *adv.* —**rap·id·ness,** *n.*

rap·id-fire, rap′id·fīr, *a.* Firing shots in rapid succession; characterized by rapid procedure, esp. in speech: *rapid-fire* questions and replies.

ra·pi·er, rā′pē·ər, *n.* A sword used in the 16th and 17th centuries mainly for thrusting, and having a straight, two-edged, long blade.

rap·ine, rap′in, *n.* The act of plundering; the seizing and carrying away of things by force.

rap·port, ra·pōr′, ra·pôr′, *n.* Harmony; affinity.

rap·proche·ment, rap·rōsh·män′, *n.* A coming or bringing together or into accord; a reconciling; an establishment or restoration of harmonious relations.

rap·scal·lion, rap·skal′yən, *n.* A good-for-nothing fellow; a rascal.

rapt, rapt, *a.* Entirely absorbed; transported emotionally; enraptured; ecstatic.

rap·ture, rap′chər, *n.* A state of great delight or ecstasy. —**rap·tur·ous,** *a.* —**rap·tur·ous·ly,** *adv.* —**rap·tur·ous·ness,** *n.*

rare, rār, *a.,* **rar·er, rar·est.** Coming or occurring far apart in time; seldom seen or occurring; unusual; uncommon; unusually excellent or fine; thinly distributed over an area, or few and widely separated.

rare, rār, *a.,* **rar·er, rar·est.** Not thoroughly cooked; underdone.

rare·bit, rār′bit, *n.* Welsh rabbit, a dish made with

cheese.

rar·e·fy, rār′ə·fī, *v.t.,* **-fied, -fy·ing.** To make rare or less dense; to refine; make more elevated or abstruse.—*v.i.* To become thin or less dense. —**rar·e·fac·tion,** rār·ə·fak′shən, *n.* —**rar·e·fied,** *a.*

rare·ly, rār′lē, *adv.* Seldom; extremely; with uncommon excellence.

rar·i·ty, rār′ə·tē, *n. pl.,* **-ties.** The state or quality of being rare or uncommon; someone or something that is rare or uncommon; someone or something valued for scarcity or excellence; the state of being thin or less dense.

ras·cal, ras′kəl, *n.* A base or dishonest person; a playful designation for a knavish, roguish person or mischievous animal. —**ras·cal·i·ty,** ras·kal′i·tē, *n.* —**ras·cal·ly,** *a., adv.*

rash, rash, *a.* Acting or speaking without due deliberation and caution; precipitate; uttered, formed, or undertaken hastily or recklessly. —**rash·ly,** *adv.* —**rash·ness,** *n.*

rash, rash, *n.* An eruption on the skin, usu. in the form of red spots or patches; an unusually large number of occurrences within a certain length of time.

rasp, rasp, *v.t.* To scrape or abrade with a rough instrument; scrape or rub roughly; to grate upon or irritate; to remove by scraping; to utter with a grating sound.—*v.i.* To scrape or grate; to make a grating sound.—*n.* A coarse form of file, having separate pointlike teeth; the act of rasping; a rasping or grating sound. —**rasp·ing·ly,** *adv.* —**rasp·y,** *a.,* **-i·er, -i·est.**

rasp·ber·ry, raz′ber·ē, raz′bə·rē, *n. pl.,* **-ries.** The fruit of several shrubs of the rose family, consisting of small, juicy red, black, or pale yellow fruits; a plant bearing such fruit; a pinkish or purplish-red color. *Informal.* A sound of contempt made by vibrating the lips and tongue.

rat, rat, *n.* Any of certain long-tailed rodents, distinguished from the mouse by larger size and by certain dental features; any of various similar animals. *Informal.* One who abandons his associates, esp. in time of trouble; a stool pigeon or informer.—*v.i.,* **rat·ted, rat·ting.** To hunt or catch rats. *Informal.* To desert one's associates, esp. in time of trouble; to act as an informer.—**smell a rat,** to be suspicious that something is amiss. —**rat·ter,** *n.*

rat·a·ble, rate·a·ble, rāt′ə·bəl, *a.* Capable of being rated.

ratch·et, rach′it, *n.* A toothed bar with which a pawl engages; the pawl used with such a device; a mechanism consisting of such a toothed bar or wheel together with the pawl.

rate, rāt, *v.t., v.i.,* **rat·ed, rat·ing.** To chide with vehemence; to scold.

rate, rāt, *n.* A given quantity or value measured with relation to a specific unit value or to a standard: typing at the *rate* of 60 words per minute; the price or amount fixed on anything; degree, as regards speed, performance, or the like; grade, rank, or rating.—*v.t.,* **rat·ed, rat·ing.** To settle or fix the value, rank, or degree of; to estimate; to fix the relative scale, rank, or position of; to deem or consider. *Informal.* To be entitled to.—*v.i.* To have a certain value, rank, or position.—**at an·y rate,** at least; under any conditions.

rath·er, rath′ər, räth′ər, *adv.* More readily or willingly; with preference or choice; with better reason; more properly; more correctly speaking; to the contrary of what has been stated; somewhat: *rather* pretty.

rat·i·fy, rat′ə·fī, *v.t.,* **-fied, -fy·ing.** To confirm; to approve and sanction by formal action. —**rat·i·fi·ca·tion,** rat·ə·fə·kā′shən, *n.* —**rat·i·fi·er,** *n.*

rat·ing, rā′ting, *n.* A grading, as of rank or class; status; the act of estimating or evaluating.

ra·tio, rā′shō, rā′shē·ō, *n. pl.,* **-tios.** The relation between two similar magnitudes in respect to the number of times the first contains the second, integrally or fractionally: the *ratio* of 5 to 2, which may be written 5:2 or $^5/_2$.

ra·ti·oc·i·na·tion, rash·ē·os·ə·nā′shən, *n.* Reasoning; the process of exact thinking.

ra·tion, rash′ən, rā′shən, *n.* A daily allowance or provisions to soldiers and sailors; any fixed amount or quantity allotted; a share or portion.—*v.t.* To supply with rations; to allot in a fixed amount; to issue provisions to; to limit or restrict the use of.

ra·tion·al, rash′ə·nəl, *a.* Having reason or the faculty of reasoning; endowed with reason; agreeable to reason; pertaining to or acting in conformity to reason; sane; judicious. **—ra·tion·al·i·ty,** rash·ə·nal′i·tē, *n.* **—ra·tion·al·ly,** *adv.*

ra·tion·ale, rash·ə·nal′, *n.* A statement of reasons; an account or exposition of the principles of some process, phenomenon, or belief; the basis or reason for something.

ra·tion·al·ism, rash′ə·nə·liz·əm, *n.* The theory that reason should be the supreme criterion of truth and source of knowledge. **—ra·tion·al·ist,** *n.* **—ra·tion·al·is·tic,** rash·ə·nə·lis′tik, *a.* **—ra·tion·al·is·ti·cal·ly,** *adv.*

ra·tion·al·ize, rash′ə·nə·līz, rash′nə·līz, *v.t.,* **-ized, -iz·ing.** To explain or justify; to cause to conform to reason; to attribute logical or creditable motives for actions actually resulting from other, often unrecognized, motives.—*v.i.* To find motives for conduct which are plausible but false. **—ra·tion·al·i·za·tion,** rash·nəl·ə·zā′shən, *n.* **—ra·tion·al·iz·er,** *n.*

rat·line, rat·lin, rat′lin, *n.* One of the small ropes which horizontally traverse the shrouds, forming a rope ladder.

rat race, *n. Informal.* Any hectic, usu. futile, activity or mode of existence.

rat·tan, ra·tan, ra·tan′, *n.* The commercial name for the long trailing stems of several Asiatic species of palm, used for making light furniture, wickerwork, and walking sticks.

rat·tle, rat′əl, *v.i.,* **-tled, -tling.** To make quick, sharp, rapidly repeated noises, as from the collision of hard objects; to clatter; to go or act with clattering noises; to speak eagerly and rapidly; to chatter.—*v.t.* To cause to make a rapid succession of sharp, clattering sounds; to speak, execute, or render rapidly. *Informal.* To upset or confuse.—*n.* A rapid succession of sharp, clattering sounds; an instrument, as an infant's toy, constructed to produce a clattering sound; the horny organ at the extremity of the tail of the rattlesnake.

rat·tle·brain, rat′əl·brān, *n.* A flighty, vacuous, or chattering person.

rat·tler, rat′lər, *n.* One who rattles; a rattlesnake.

rat·tle·snake, rat′əl·snāk, *n.* Any of various venomous American snakes, having several loosely joined horny pieces or rings at the end of the tail, which produce a rattling or whirring sound when shaken.

rat·tle·trap, rat′əl·trap, *n.* A shaky, rickety object, esp. a dilapidated car.

rat·ty, rat′ē, *a.,* **-ti·er, -ti·est.** Pertaining to or full of rats. *Informal.* Shabby; despicable.

rau·cous, rô′kəs, *a.* Hoarse; harsh, as the voice; boisterous and unruly. **—rau·cous·ly,** *adv.*

raun·chy, rôn′chē, rän′chē, *a.,* **-chi·er, -chi·est.** *Informal.* Slovenly; worn out; lewd.

rav·age, rav′ij, *n.* Desolation or destruction by violence; devastation; ruin.—*v.t.,* **-aged, -ag·ing.** To lay waste to; to devastate; to pillage.—*v.i.* To do damage; to be destructive. **—rav·ag·er,** *n.*

rave, rāv, *v.i.,* **raved, rav·ing.** To speak irrationally; to be delirious; to be wild, furious, or raging; to talk with excessive enthusiasm.—*v.t.* To utter wildly and excitedly.—*n.* Frenzy; an extravagantly enthusiastic review. **—rav·er,** *n.*

rav·el, rav′əl, *v.t.,* **-eled, -el·ing.** To untwist; to unwind, as the threads of a knitted fabric; to entangle; to involve.—*v.i.* To become frayed. **—rav·el·er,** *n.*

ra·ven, rā′vən, *n.* A large bird of the crow family, having glossy black iridescent plumage, shaggy throat feathers, and a croaking voice, and inhabiting wild regions of the northern hemisphere.—*a.* Of a shiny black color.

rav·en·ous, rav′ə·nəs, *a.* Rapacious; voracious; starved; eager for gratification. **—rav·en·ous·ly,** *adv.*

ra·vine, rə·vēn′, *n.* A long, deep, hollow or gorge worn by a flowing stream.

ra·vi·o·li, rä·vē·ō′lē, *n. pl., sing. or pl. in constr.* Small squares of dough enclosing meat or cheese, cooked and served in sauce or otherwise.

rav·ish, rav′ish, *v.t.* To seize and carry away, as a woman, by violence; to commit a rape upon; to violate; to plunder, as a city; to transport with joy or ecstasy. **—rav·ish·ment,** *n.*

rav·ish·ing, rav′i·shing, *a.* Delightful; entrancing.

raw, rô, *a.* Not altered from its natural state by cooking; not subjected to some industrial or manufacturing process: *raw* silk; having the flesh exposed; sore; harsh; coarse; lacking refinement; just finished: *raw* work; immature; inexperienced: *raw* soldiers; bleak; chilly; cold and damp: a *raw* day. *Informal.* Harshly unfair: a *raw* deal. **—in the raw,** uncultivated, unrefined. *Informal.* Naked. **—raw·ness,** *n.*

raw·boned, rô′bônd′, *a.* Having little flesh on the bones; gaunt; lean.

raw·hide, rô′hīd, *n.* The untanned skin of cattle; a rope or whip made of this.

ray, rā, *n.* A narrow beam or line of light; radiance; a raylike line or stretch of something, as of color; any of a system of parts radially arranged; a gleam or trace: a *ray* of hope; one of a system of straight lines passing through a point; a stream of material particles as produced by a radioactive element; one of the branches or arms of a starfish; a ray flower; one of the branches of an umbel.—*v.i., v.t.* To emit or send forth in rays; radiate.

ray, rā, *n.* One of a class of cartilaginous fishes, of which the skate is a well-known example, having a flattened body and broadened pectoral fins.

ray·on, rā′on, *n.* A synthetic fiber made by forcing semiliquid cellulose material through a finely perforated metal plate; fabric or yarn made from these fibers.

raze, rase, rāz, *v.t.,* **razed, raz·ing, rased, ras·ing.** To tear down, to demolish, or to level to the ground. **—raz·er,** *n.*

ra·zor, rā′zər, *n.* A sharp-edged instrument used esp. for shaving or cutting hair.

razz, raz, *n. Informal.* A derisive sound made with the lips.—*v.t. Informal.* To tease; to deride.

raz·zle-daz·zle, raz′əl·daz′əl, *n. Informal.* A bewildering, gaudy, or dazzling performance or activity.

re, rā, *n. Mus.* The syllable used for the second tone of a major scale.

re, rē, *prep.* About; concerning.

reach, rēch, *v.t.* To succeed in touching or seizing with the outstretched hand or anything extended or cast: to *reach* a book on a high shelf; to take or bring by a stretching effort with the hand or the like; to interest or impress; to penetrate to and affect: to *reach* one's audience; to stretch or extend so as to touch or meet: the bookcase which *reaches* the ceiling; to get to, or get as far as: The boat *reached* the shore; to come to: Sound *reaches* the ear; to come to or arrive at by motion or progress: to *reach* a conclusion; to attain; to amount to: The cost will *reach* millions.—*v.i.* To make a stretch, as with the hand or arm; to make a movement as if to touch or seize something: to *reach* for a weapon; to make a stretch of a certain length with the hand, arm, or something else; to extend in operation or effect: news *reaching* to the homefront; to extend in space or time: Elizabeth's reign *reached* into the 17th century.—*n.* The act or an act of reaching: to make a *reach* for a weapon; the extent or distance of reaching: the *reach* of the arm, out of *reach*; range of effective action, power, or capacity; mental capacity; a continuous stretch or extent of something: a *reach* of woodland.

re·act, rē·akt′, *v.i.* To act or perform in response to an influence; to act against or in opposition to an influence or force; to move in a reverse manner or way; to act chemically. —**re·ac·tive,** *a.*

re·ac·tion, rē·ak′shən, *n.* Action in return or in response; reversed action or action tending toward a previous condition; a movement toward a previous social or political order; reflex action, as in a muscle or nerve; loosely, one's attitude, impression, etc., in response to something. *Chem.* The reciprocal action of two substances.

re·ac·tion·ar·y, rē·ak′shə·ner·ē, *a.* Pertaining to, proceeding from, or favoring reaction.—*n. pl.,* **-ies.** A person who favors a previous, esp. outmoded, political or social order.

re·ac·ti·vate, rē·ak′tə·vāt, *v.i., v.t.,* **-vat·ed, -vat·ing.** To become or cause to become effective or operative again.

re·ac·tor, rē·ak′tər, *n.* An apparatus that initiates and controls spontaneous disintegration of fissionable material.

read, rēd, *v.t.,* **read, red, read·ing.** To apprehend the meaning of, as something written or printed; to peruse, as a letter or book; to utter aloud, as something written or printed; to make out the significance of, by scrutiny or observation: to *read* the sky; to discover or explain the meaning of, as a dream or riddle; to make out the character or future of, as a person, by the interpretation of outward signs; to attribute, as something not expressed or directly indicated, to what is read or considered: to *read* hostility into a person's remarks; to understand or take, as something read or observed, in a particular way; to learn or discern by or as by perusal: to *read* another's thoughts; to bring or put by reading: to *read* a child to sleep; of a thermometer or other instrument, to register or indicate.—*v.i.* To inspect and apprehend the meaning of written or other signs or characters; to read or peruse writing or printing; to utter aloud or render in speech, written or printed words that one is perusing; to have a certain wording; to admit of being taken or interpreted: a sentence that *reads* two different ways.—read, *a.* Having knowledge gained by reading; well-informed through reading, usu. used in compounds: as, well-*read.*—**read be·tween the lines,** to discover a meaning, implication, or purpose not explicitly expressed. —**read in,** to feed data into a computer.—**read out,** to expel, as a member, from a party or organization by public declaration; to recover data from a computer.

read·a·ble, rē′də·bəl, *a.* Capable of being read; legible; easy or interesting to read. —**read·a·bil·i·ty,** rē·də·bil′i·tē, **read·a·ble·ness,** *n.* —**read·a·bly,** *adv.*

read·er, rē′dər, *n.* One who reads; a schoolbook for instruction and practice in reading; a professional reciter; an evaluator or proofreader of manuscripts.

read·ing, rē′ding, *n.* The action or practice of one who reads; the extent to which one has read; literary knowledge; the utterance or recital of recorded words; a given passage in a particular text; the indication of a dial or a graduated instrument; an interpretation given to anything: her *reading* of the situation; a rendering of a dramatic part or musical composition.

re·ad·just, rē·ə·jəst′, *v.t.* To adjust or settle again; to put in order again. —**re·ad·just·ment,** *n.*

read·y, red′ē, *a.,* **-i·er, -i·est.** Fit for immediate use; willing; inclined; apt; offering itself at once; at hand; convenient; on the point or brink, followed by *to: ready* to begin.—*v.t.,* **-ied, -y·ing.** To prepare, make ready.—*n.* The condition of being ready; the position of a rifle before aiming. —**read·i·ly,** *adv.* —**read·i·ness,** *n.*

read·y-made, red′ē·mād′, *a.* Made or prepared be-

forehand and kept in stock ready for use or sale: *ready-made* clothes.

re·a·gent, rē·ā′jənt, *n.* A substance used to determine the composition of other substances by the chemical reactions it causes.

re·al, rē′əl, rēl, *a.* True; existing or occurring as fact; actual; genuine or not counterfeit; not artificial; not imitation; unfeigned or sincere; noting or pertaining to immovable property, as lands and tenements: opposed to *personal.*—*adv. Informal.* Really; very.

re·al es·tate, *n.* Land and whatever by nature or artificial annexation is a part of it, as trees or buildings; ownership of or property in lands.

re·al·ism, rē′əl·liz·əm, *n.* Attention to or concern with what is real; the tendency to view or represent things as they really are, as opposed to *idealism* or *romanticism;* close resemblance in literature or art to what is real; a style of writing that emphasizes fidelity to the details, often unpleasant, of nature or everyday life. —**re·al·ist,** rē′ə·list, *n.* —**re·al·is·tic,** rē·ə·lis′tik, *a.* —**re·al·is·ti·cal·ly,** *adv.*

re·al·i·ty, rē·al′ə·tē, *n. pl.,* **-ties.** The state or fact of being real, having actual existence, or having actually occurred; a real thing or fact; that which is real as opposed to that which is imagined or merely apparent. —**in re·al·i·ty,** actually; in fact or truth.

re·al·ize, rē′ə·liz, *v.t.,* **-ized, -iz·ing.** To understand clearly; to make real, or give reality to, as dreams or fears; to make realistic or lifelike, as a description or a picture; to conceive or comprehend as real; to convert into cash or money; to gain for oneself by trade or effort; of property, to bring as a return.—*v.i.* To convert property or anything of value into cash or money. —**re·al·iz·a·ble,** *a.* —**re·al·i·za·tion,** rē·əl·ə·zā′shən, *n.*

re·al·ly, rē′ə·lē, rē′lē, *adv.* In reality; actually or truly; indeed.

realm, relm, *n.* A kingdom; a region, sphere, domain, or scope of influence or power.

Re·al·tor, rē′əl·tər, rē′əl·tôr, *n. Trademark.* A broker or other individual in the real estate business who is an active member of the National Association of Real Estate Boards.

re·al·ty, rē′əl·tē, *n.* Real estate.

ream, rēm, *n.* A bundle or package of paper of 480, 500, or 516 sheets. *Pl. Informal.* A voluminous amount: *reams* of information.

ream, rēm, *v.t.* To enlarge or shape (a hole) with a reamer; to remove, as a defect, by reaming; to squeeze juice from with a reamer.

ream·er, rē′mər, *n.* A rotating tool for enlarging or shaping a hole; a utensil for squeezing juice from fruit; someone or something that reams.

re·an·i·mate, rē·an′ə·māt, *v.t.,* **-mat·ed, -mat·ing.** To revive, resuscitate, or restore to life or animation; to infuse new vigor or courage into. —**re·an·i·ma·tion,** rē·an·ə·mā′shən, *n.*

reap, rēp, *v.t.* To cut with a sickle, scythe, or machine, as a grain crop; to gather or harvest; to receive as a recompense or return: to *reap* the benefits.—*v.i.* To perform the act of reaping; to receive the results of one's labor or actions.

reap·er, rē′pər, *n.* One who reaps; a reaping machine.

re·ap·pear, rē·ə·pēr′, *v.i.* To appear again or anew. —**re·ap·pear·ance,** *n.*

re·ap·por·tion·ment, rē·ə·pōr′shən·mənt, rē·ə·pôr′shən·mənt, *n.* The act of changing the allotment of something; a redistribution of representatives in a legislature. —**re·ap·por·tion,** *v.t.*

rear, rēr, *v.t.* To support, bring up, or care for to maturity: to *rear* children; to breed or raise, as animals; to grow, as plants; to erect; build; raise to an upright position; lift up.—*v.i.* To rise on the hind legs; to rise high or tower aloft, as a building.

rear, rēr, *n.* The back or the side opposite the front; backside; the space or position behind, or at the back of anything; background; the rump; the part of a military force farthest from the front.—*a.* Situated at or pertaining to the rear of anything.

rear ad·mi·ral, *n.* A commissioned naval officer ranking higher than captain and lower than vice-admiral.

re·arm, rē·ärm′, *v.t.* To arm again; to furnish with new or better weapons. **—re·ar·ma·ment,** rē·är′mə·mənt, *n.*

re·ar·range, rē·ə·rānj′, *v.t.,* **-ranged, -rang·ing.** To arrange again; to put in proper order again. **—re·ar·range·ment,** *n.*

rear·ward, rēr′wərd, *a.* Last; backward.—*adv.* Toward or in the rear. Also **rear·wards.—***n.* A last or rear position.

rea·son, rē′zən, *n.* A ground or motive; a justification or explanation; the intellectual faculty; normal powers of mind; sanity; sound judgment or good sense; sensible speech or advice.—*v.i.* To exercise the faculty of reason; draw conclusions or inferences from facts or premises; to discuss or argue in a logical manner. —*v.t.* To argue about or discuss; to think out logically, often used with *out:* to *reason out* a problem; to conclude or infer; to persuade by reasoning or argument.—**bring to rea·son,** to direct, as someone, to a reasonable course of thought.—**by rea·son of,** by virtue of.—**in rea·son,** in accordance with reason; justly or properly; within limits prescribed by reason.—**stand to rea·son,** to be obvious or reasonable.—**with rea·son,** with justifiable cause. **—rea·son·er,** *n.*

rea·son·a·ble, rēz′nə·bəl, rē′zən·ə·bəl, *a.* Agreeable to reason or sound judgment: a *reasonable* supposition; rational; having or exercising sound judgment; not exceeding the limit prescribed by reason, or not excessive; moderate, as charges or prices. **—rea·son·a·bil·i·ty,** rēz·nə·bil′ə·tē, **rea·son·a·ble·ness,** *n.* **—rea·son·a·bly,** *adv.*

rea·son·ing, rē′zə·ning, rəz′ning, *n.* The act or process of one who reasons; the process of drawing conclusions or inferences from facts or premises.

re·as·sem·ble, rē·ə·sem′bəl, *v.t.,* **-bled, -bling.** To collect or assemble again.—*v.i.* To come or meet together again. **—re·as·sem·bly,** *n.*

re·as·sume, rē·ə·soom′, *v.t.* To resume; to take up again. **—re·as·sump·tion,** rē·ə·səmp′shən, *n.*

re·as·sure, rē·ə·shûr′, *v.t.,* **-sured, -sur·ing.** To restore courage and self-confidence to; to hearten; to assure anew. **—re·as·sur·ance,** *n.* **—re·as·sur·ing·ly,** *adv.*

re·bate, rē′bāt, ri·bāt′, *v.t.,* **-bat·ed, -bat·ing.** To diminish or reduce; to return; to deduct or make a discount from, as an invoice.—*n.* A refund; abatement in price; deduction. **—re·bat·er,** *n.*

reb·el, reb′əl, *n.* One who revolts from the government to which he owes allegiance; one who defies and seeks to overthrow any authority or control.—*a.* Rebellious; relating to rebels; defiant.—ri·bel′, *v.i.,* **-elled, -el·ling.** To reject or take up arms against one's government; to refuse to obey an authority, tradition, or control; to feel or show disgust or revulsion.

re·bel·lion, ri·bel′yən, *n.* The act of rebelling; an armed rising against an established government; open resistance to, or refusal to obey, lawful authority.

re·bel·lious, ri·bel′yəs, *a.* Engaged in, or characterized by, rebellion; mutinous; resisting control **—re·bel·lious·ly,** *adv.* **—re·bel·lious·ness,** *n.*

re·birth, rē·bərth′, rē′bərth, *n.* Birth anew; renascence; revival.

re·born, rē·bôrn′, *a.* Born anew; regenerated.

re·bound, ri·bownd′, *v.i.* To spring or bound back; to fly back by force after impact with another body.—*v.t.* To cause to bound or spring back.—rē′bownd, ri·bownd′, *n.* A rebounding; recoil; an emotional reaction following frustration, preceded by *on the:* He

married *on the rebound* after his divorce.

re·buff, ri·bəf′, *n.* A forcing or driving back; a sudden check; a repulse; a refusal; a rejection of solicitation. —*v.t.* To beat back; to offer sudden resistance to; to repel the advances of; to snub.

re·build, rē·bild′, *v.t.,* **-built, -build·ing.** To build again; to build after having been demolished; to reconstruct.

re·buke, ri·būk′, *v.t.,* **-buked, -buk·ing.** To reprehend sharply; to reprimand; to reprove.—*n.* A direct and severe reprimand; reproof. **—re·buk·er,** *n.*

re·bus, rē′bəs, *n. pl.,* **re·bus·es.** A set of words represented by figures or pictures of objects whose names resemble in sound those words or the syllables of which they are composed; a kind of puzzle made up of such figures or pictures.

re·but, ri·bət′, *v.t.,* **-but·ted, -but·ting.** To refute, as by counter evidence; to oppose by argument or countervailing proof. **—re·but·ter,** *n.*

re·but·tal, ri·bət′əl, *n.* The act of rebutting; refutation; confutation.

re·cal·ci·trant, ri·kal′sə·trənt, *a.* Exhibiting resistance or opposition to regulation or authority; refractory; difficult to handle or manage.—*n.* **—re·cal·ci·trance, re·cal·ci·tran·cy,** *n.*

re·call, ri·kôl′, *v.t.* To call or bring back; to order to return; to take back or revoke; to revive in memory.—ri·kôl′, rē′kôl, *n.* A calling back; revocation; the power of calling back or revoking; the removal of an official from office by a popular vote.

re·cant, ri·kant′, *v.t., v.i.* To retract; to unsay; to make formal contradiction of something which one had previously asserted. **—re·can·ta·tion,** rē·kan·tā′shən, *n.*

re·ca·pit·u·late, rē·kə·pich′ū·lāt, *v.t.,* **-lat·ed, -lat·ing.** To repeat or summarize, as the principal facts or points mentioned in a preceding discourse.—*v.i.* To repeat in brief what has been said before. **—re·ca·pit·u·la·tion,** rē·kə·pich·ə·lā′shən, *n.*

re·cap·ture, rē·kap′chər, *v.t.,* **-tured, -tur·ing.** To capture again; recover by capture.—*n.* Recovery or retaking by capture.

re·cast, rē·kast′, *v.t.,* **-cast, -cast·ing.** To cast or found again; to mold again or reconstruct, as a speech; to put into a new form.—rē′kast, *n.*

re·cede, ri·sēd′, *v.i.,* **-ced·ed, -ced·ing.** To move back; to retreat; to withdraw; to slope backward.

re·ceipt, ri·sēt′, *n.* The act of receiving; a written acknowledgment of something received, as money or goods; a recipe. *Usu. pl.* That which is received.—*v.t.* To give a receipt for.—*v.i.* To make out a receipt.

re·ceiv·a·ble, ri·sē′və·bəl, *a.* Such as may be received: accounts *receivable;* capable of being received, as payment due.—*n. pl.* Assets listed as outstanding accounts.

re·ceive, ri·sēv′, *v.t.,* **-ceived, -ceiv·ing.** To get or obtain; to take, as a thing given, paid, or communicated; to accept; believe; allow to enter in an official capacity; to welcome as a guest; to hold, admit, contain, or have capacity for: a box to *receive* contributions; to be the object of; to suffer; to experience.

re·ceiv·er, ri·sē′vər, *n.* One who receives; a person appointed to manage the affairs of an enterprise in reorganization or liquidation; an electronic device which converts signs or waves into observable sensory forms.

re·ceiv·er·ship, ri·sē′vər·ship, *n.* The legal status of an enterprise under control of a receiver; the position of being in the hands of a receiver.

re·cent, rē′sənt, *a.* Of late origin, occurrence, or existence; new; not of remote date, antiquated style, or the like; fresh. **—re·cent·ly,** *adv.* **—re·cen·cy, re·cent·ness,** *n.*

re·cep·ta·cle, ri·sep′tə·kəl, *n.* A place or vessel in

which something is received and contained; a repository.

re·cep·tion, ri·sep′shən, *n.* A receiving; a manner of receiving a person or thing: a favorable *reception;* a formal occasion or ceremony of receiving guests or official personages; admission or credence, as of an opinion or doctrine; the act or process of receiving radio or TV programs or signals.

re·cep·tion·ist, ri·sep′shə·nist, *n.* A person employed to greet callers, esp, at a business office.

re·cep·tive, ri·sep′tiv, *a.* Able to receive readily, as impressions, suggestions, or teachings; able to take in, hold, or contain; pertaining to a receptor. **—re·cep·tive·ly,** *adv.* **—re·cep·tive·ness, re·cep·tiv·i·ty,** rē·sep·tiv′ə·tē, *n.*

re·cess, ri·ses′, rē′ses, *n.* The time or period during which normal activity is suspended; a cavity or indentation in an otherwise smooth surface, as a niche, alcove, or sunken space formed in a wall.—ri·ses′, *v.t.* To make a recess in; to put in a recess.—*v.i.* To take a recess.

re·ces·sion, ri·sesh′ən, *n.* The act of receding; a going back; a withdrawal; departure or retirement, as the procession of clergy at the conclusion of a religious service; a temporary business slump, less extreme or prolonged than a depression. **—re·ces·sion·ar·y,** *a.*

re·ces·sion·al, ri·sesh′ə·nəl, *a.* Of or pertaining to recession: a *recessional* hymn; of or pertaining to a recess, as of a legislative body.—*n.* A musical composition played or sung at the end of a religious service or program.

re·ces·sive, ri·ses′iv, *a.* Tending to recede; receding.

re·charge, rē·chärj′, *v.t., v.i.,* **-charged, -charg·ing.** To charge again or anew, as a battery; reload. —rē′chärj, *n.* A second or additional charge.

rec·i·pe, res′ə·pē, *n.* A list of instructions for preparing, mixing, and cooking food to produce a particular dish.

re·cip·i·ent, ri·sip′ē·ənt, *n.* A person or thing that receives; a receiver.—*a.* Receptive or receiving. **—re·cip·i·ence, re·cip·i·en·cy,** *n.*

re·cip·ro·cal, ri·sip′rə·kəl, *a.* Moving alternately backward and forward; given, performed, or felt in return; given or felt by each to or toward the other; mutual: *reciprocal* affection. *Gram.* Expressing mutual relation, as the pronouns "each other," "one another."—*n.* That by which a given quantity is multiplied to produce one. **—re·cip·ro·cal·ly,** *adv.*

re·cip·ro·cate, ri·sip′rə·kāt, *v.t.,* **-cat·ed, -cat·ing.** To cause to move alternately backward and forward; to give or feel in return; to give and receive reciprocally: to *reciprocate* favors; to interchange; to make correspondent.—*v.i.* To move alternately backward and forward; to make return, as for something given; to make interchange; to be correspondent. **—re·cip·ro·ca·tion,** ri·sip·rə·kā′shən, *n.* **—re·cip·ro·ca·tive,** *a.*

rec·i·proc·i·ty, res·ə·pros′ə·tē, *n.* The state or character of being reciprocal; equal commercial or trade rights or privileges enjoyed mutually by two countries.

re·cit·al, ri·sīt′əl, *n.* The act of reciting; a narrative or description; an entertainment usu. given by a single performer or by several soloists: an organ *recital.*

rec·i·ta·tion, res·ə·tā′shən, *n.* The act of reciting, as a composition committed to memory; public performance of a literary reading; classroom response to a teacher after studied preparation; anything recited.

rec·i·ta·tive, res·ə·tə·tēv′, *n.* A vocal form having no definite rhythmic pattern or strictly constructed melody; a musical recitation or declamation.—*a.*

re·cite, ri·sīt′, *v.t.,* **-cit·ed, -cit·ing.** To say over or repeat the words of; to repeat, as a piece of poetry or prose, before an audience; to relate the facts, or give an account of; to enumerate.—*v.i.* To recite or repeat something from memory; to recite a lesson or some

part of a lesson before a teacher.

reck·less, rek′lis, *a.* Heedless, rash, careless, usu. with *of* before an object: *reckless* of consequences. **—reck·less·ly,** *adv.* **—reck·less·ness,** *n.*

reck·on, rek′ən, *v.t.* To count, compute, or calculate as to number or amount; to esteem, regard as, or consider: to be *reckoned* a fool. *Informal.* To think or suppose.—*v.i.* To count; make a computation; to settle accounts; to depend or rely (*on*).**—reck·on with,** to deal with, as something to be taken into account.

reck·on·ing, rek′ə·ning, *n.* The act of reckoning; count, computation, or calculation; the settlement of accounts, as between parties; a statement of an amount due, or a bill; an accounting, as for things received or done: a day of *reckoning.*

re·claim, ri·klām′, *v.t.* To bring waste, as land, into a condition for cultivation or other use; to recover in a pure or usable form from waste or used articles: to *reclaim* rubber.

rec·la·ma·tion, rek·lə·mā′shən, *n.* The act or process of reclaiming; the state of being reclaimed.

re·cline, ri·klīn′, *v.i.,* **-clined, -clin·ing.** To lean or lie back; to rest in a recumbent position.—*v.t.* To cause to lean back on something; to place in a recumbent position. **—re·clin·er,** *n.*

rec·luse, rek′loos, ri·kloos′, *n.* A person who lives in retirement or seclusion; a religious devotee who lives in an isolated cell.—ri·kloos′, *a.* Living shut up or apart from the world; sequestered.

rec·og·ni·tion, rek·əg·nish′ən, *n.* The act of recognizing or the state of being recognized; formal acknowledgment; friendly cognizance or attention.

re·cog·ni·zance, ri·kog′nə·zəns, ri·kon′ə·zəns, *n. Law.* An obligation agreed upon before a magistrate or court, wherein a particular act must be performed; the sum of money liable to forfeiture for nonperformance of such an obligation.

rec·og·nize, rek′əg·nīz, *v.t.,* **-nized, -niz·ing.** To know again, or perceive to be identical with something previously known; to identify from knowledge of appearance or character; to acknowledge or treat as valid; to acknowledge formally as existing or as entitled to consideration; to acknowledge as the person entitled to speak at the particular time; to acknowledge acquaintance with, as by a salute; to show appreciation of, as by some reward or tribute. **—rec·og·niz·a·ble,** *a.* **—rec·og·niz·a·bly,** *adv.*

re·coil, ri·koyl′, *v.i.* To rebound; to fall back; to take a sudden backward motion after an advance; to start or draw back; to shrink back.—rē′koyl, ri·koyl′, *n.* A starting or falling back; rebound; a shrinking back. **—re·coil·less,** ·ri·koyl′lis, rē′koyl·lis, *a.*

re·col·lect, rē·kə·lekt′, *v.t.* To collect or gather again, as something scattered; to compose or rally: to *re-collect* oneself.

rec·ol·lect, rek·ə·lekt′, *v.t.* To recover or recall; to bring back to the mind or memory; to remember.—*v.i.* To remember or recall something. **—rec·ol·lec·tion,** *n.*

rec·om·mend, rek·ə·mend′, *v.t.* To commend to another; to entrust; to commend or give favorable representations of; to make acceptable; to attract favor to; to advise, as an action, practice, measure, or remedy; to set forward as advisable. **—rec·om·mend·a·ble,** *a.* **—rec·om·mend·er,** *n.*

rec·om·men·da·tion, rek·ə·men·dā′shən, *n.* The act of recommending; a favorable representation; that which recommends, procures favor, or obtains a favorable reception; a letter commending another.

rec·om·pense, rek′əm·pens, *v.t.,* **-pensed, -pens·ing.** To give or render an equivalent to, as for services, loss, or the like; to reward; to compensate; to return an equivalent for; repay; to make compensation for. —*n.* An equivalent returned for anything given, done, or suffered; compensation; reward.

rec·on·cile, rek′ən·sīl, *v.t.,* **-ciled, -cil·ing.** To conciliate anew; to restore to union and friendship after estrangement; to adjust or settle, as differences or quarrels; to bring to acquiescence or quiet submission: to *reconcile* oneself to afflictions; to make consistent or congruous, followed by *with* or *to;* to remove apparent discrepancies from; to harmonize, followed by *to* or *with.*—*v.i.* To become reconciled. —**rec•on•cil•a•ble,** *a.* —**rec•on•cil•a•bly,** *adv.* —**rec•on•cil•er, rec•on•cil•i•a•tion,** rek•ən•sil•ē•ā′shən, **rec•on•cile•ment,** *n.*

rec•on•dite, rek′ən•dīt, ri•kon′dīt, *a.* Hidden from understanding; obscure.

re•con•di•tion, rē•kən•dish′ən, *v.t.* To restore to a good or satisfactory condition; put in operating condition again.

re•con•firm, rē•kən•fərm′, *v.t.* To confirm again; to give more strength to: *reconfirm* one's opinions with additional evidence.

re•con•nais•sance, ri•kon′ə•səns, *n.* An examination or observation of territory, esp. enemy territory, by ground troops or aircraft.

re•con•noi•ter, rek•ə•noy′tər, rē•kən•oy′tər, *v.t.,* **-tered, -ter•ing.** To examine or survey, as a tract or region, for military, geologic, or engineering purposes; to make a preliminary survey of.—*v.i.* To carry out a reconnaissance.

re•con•sid•er, rē•kən•sid′ər, *v.t., v.i.* To consider again.—*v.i.* To again take up a settled matter. —**re•con•sid•er•a•tion,** rē•kən•sid•ər•ā′shən, *n.*

re•con•struct, rē•kən•strəkt′, *v.t.* To construct again; to rebuild.

re•con•struc•tion, rē•kən•strək′shən, *n.* The act of constructing again; something reconstructed; (*often cap.*) the governmental reorganization of the seceded states after the Civil War.

re•cord, ri•kôrd′, *v.t.* To note, chart, or inscribe, manually or mechanically, as for the purpose of preserving evidence; to indicate; to set down in some permanent form; to make a tape or phonograph record of.—*v.i.* To record something; to make a record. —rek′ərd, *n.* The state or fact of being recorded, as in writing; an account in writing or mechanical form preserving the memory or knowledge of facts or events; a disc having characteristic grooves for reproducing sound on a phonograph; a report, list, or aggregate of actions or achievements; a notable degree of attainment, esp. the highest degree attained. —rek′ərd, *a.* Making or affording a record; being foremost in degree of attainment: a *record* year for sales.—**off the rec•ord,** unofficial; not intended for quotation publicly.—**on rec•ord,** intended for public knowledge.

re•cord•er, ri•kôr′dər, *n.* One who records official transactions; a registering apparatus; a magistrate with limited jurisdiction in court proceedings; an old, simple flute with eight finger holes; a tape or wire device for recording.

re•cord•ing, ri•kôr′ding, *n.* The process of making a tape recording, or other transcription of sounds; a phonograph record.

rec•ord play•er, *n.* A machine consisting of a turntable, loudspeaker, and other equipment which plays phonograph records; a phonograph.

re•count, rē•kownt′, *v.t.* To count again.—rē′kownt, rē•kownt′, *n.* An additional or second count, as of ballots in an election.

re•count, ri•kownt′, *v.t.* To relate in detail; to narrate or tell in order; to enumerate.

re•coup, ri•koop′, *v.t.* To obtain or regain an equivalent for, as something lost or relinquished; to repay. —*v.i.* To regain or obtain an equivalent of something lost or relinquished.

re•course, rē′kôrs, ri•kôrs′, ri•kôrs′, *n.* A going to, as for help or protection; the person or thing that helps, protects, or supplies.

re•cov•er, ri•kəv′ər, *v.t.* To regain after losing; to restore, as oneself, from sickness, faintness, or the like; to retrieve; to make up for; to reclaim for use, as resources or materials.—*v.i.* To regain health after sickness; to regain a former state or condition, as after misfortune or disturbance of mind.

re•cov•er, rē•kəv′ər, *v.t.* To cover again.

re•cov•er•y, ri•kəv′ə•rē, *n. pl.,* **-ies.** The act or power of regaining; restoration from sickness, faintness, or misfortune.

rec•re•ant, rek′rē•ənt, *a.* Treacherous; yielding to an enemy; cowardly; unfaithful; false.—*n.* One who yields; one who begs for mercy; a deserter.

re•cre•ate, rē•krē•āt′, *v.t.,* **-at•ed, -at•ing.** To create anew, as in one's imagination. —**re•cre•a•tion,** *n.*

rec•re•a•tion, rek•rē•ā′shən, *n.* Amusement or diversion which gives enjoyment; refreshment of the strength and spirits, as after toil; anything providing entertainment or relaxation. —**rec•re•a•tion•al,** *a.*

re•crim•i•nate, ri•krim′ə•nāt, *v.i.,* **-nat•ed, -nat•ing.** To answer one accusation with another; to charge an accuser with the like.—*v.t.* To accuse in return. —**re•crim•i•na•tion,** ri•krim•ə•nā′shən, *n.* —**re•crim•i•na•tive, re•crim•i•na•to•ry,** ri•krim′ə•nə•tôr•ē, *a.*

re•cruit, ri•kroot′, *n.* A newly enlisted soldier; a new member of an organization or group.—*v.t.* To make up by enlistment; to supply with new men; to refresh; to renew, as the health, spirits, or strength.—*v.i.* To enlist new soldiers; to gain health, spirits, or the like; to gain new supplies of anything wasted or needed. —**re•cruit•er, re•cruit•ment,** *n.*

rec•tal, rek′təl, *a.* Near to, involving, or pertaining to the rectum.

rec•tan•gle, rek′tang•gəl, *n.* A right-angled parallelogram; a quadrilateral figure with all its angles being right angles.

rec•tan•gu•lar, rek•tang′gyə•lər, *a.* Right-angled; having an angle or angles of ninety degrees; having the shape of a rectangle.

rec•ti•fi•er, rek′tə•fi•ər, *n.* One who or that which rectifies; a device for obtaining direct electric current from alternating current.

rec•ti•fy, rek′tə•fi, *v.t.,* **-fied, -fy•ing.** To make or put right; to refine by repeated distillation; to make a direct current from an alternating current. —**rec•ti•fi•a•ble,** *a.* —**rec•ti•fi•ca•tion,** rek•tə•fə•kā′shən, *n.*

rec•ti•lin•e•ar, rek•tə•lin′ē•ər, *a.* Bounded by straight lines; consisting of a straight line or lines; straight.

rec•ti•tude, rek′tə•tood, rek′tə•tūd, *n.* Rightness of principle or practice; uprightness; integrity; honesty; correct judgment; correctness.

rec•tor, rek′tər, *n.* A clergyman of the Protestant Episcopal Church or Anglican Church who has charge of a parish. *Rom. Cath. Ch.* A priest who is responsible for a congregation or a religious house. The head of certain schools, colleges, and universities.

rec•to•ry, rek′tə•rē, *n. pl.,* **-ries.** A parish church; a parish held by a rector; a rector's habitat; parsonage.

rec•tum, rek′təm, *n. pl.,* **-tums, -ta.** The lower six to eight inches of the large intestine, ending at the anus.

re•cum•bent, ri•kəm′bənt, *a.* Leaning; reclining; lying down. —**re•cum•ben•cy,** *n.* —**re•cum•bent•ly,** *adv.*

re•cu•per•ate, ri•koo′pə•rāt, *v.i.,* **-at•ed, -at•ing.** To recover from illness or fatigue; to regain financial solvency.—*v.t.* To regain what was lost, as health or finances; to recover. —**re•cu•per•a•tion,** ri•koo•pə•rā′shən, *n.* —**re•cu•per•a•tive,** *a.*

re•cur, ri•kər′, *v.i.,* **-curred, -cur•ring.** To occur again or be repeated at a stated interval; to return to one's thoughts. —**re•cur•rence,** *n.*

re•cur•rent, ri•kər•ənt, *a.* Returning from time to time; recurring.

red, red, *a.,* **red•der, red•dest.** Resembling or pre-

---

a- hat, fāte, fāre, fäther; **e-** met, mē; **i-** pin, pīne; **o-** not, nōte, ôrb, moove (move), boy, pownd; **u-** cūbe, būll, tūk (took); **ch-** chin; **th-** thick, ᵺen; **zh-** vizhon (vision); **ə-** ego, takən, pencəl, lemən, bərd (bird).

dominantly the color of blood; ruddy; (*often cap.*) communistic, or endorsing radical political or social change, esp. by force.—*n.* A primary color at the lower extreme of the visible spectrum; a color like that of blood; a red dye or pigment; (*often cap.*) a Communist, or a far left radical or revolutionary.—**in the red.** *Informal.* In debt.—**see red.** *Informal.* To be very angry. —**red·ness,** *n.*

red·bird, red′bərd, *n.* The cardinal.

red blood cell, *n.* A cell that gives the red color to the blood of vertebrates.

red-blood·ed, red′blud′id, *a.* Having red blood; of healthy strength or vigor; vigorous; virile.

red·breast, red′brest, *n.* The robin.

Red Cross, *n.* The Red Cross Society, an international organization for the care of the sick and wounded in war, and of the victims of floods, epidemics, etc.

red·den, red′ən, *v.t.* To make red.—*v.i.* To become red; to flush or blush.

red·dish, red′ish, *a.* Somewhat red; tending to redness.

re·dec·o·rate, rē·dek′ə·rāt, *v.t., v.i.,* **-rat·ed, -rat·ing.** To decorate again or anew. —**re·dec·o·ra·tion,** rē·dek·ə·rā′shən, *n.*

re·ded·i·cate, rē·ded′ə·kāt, *v.t.,* **-cat·ed, -cat·ing.** To dedicate again. —**re·ded·i·ca·tion,** rē·ded·ə·kā′shən, *n.*

re·deem, ri·dēm′, *v.t.* To buy or pay off, or clear by payment: to *redeem* a mortgage; to buy back; to recover; to discharge or fulfill, as a pledge or promise; to make atonement or amends for; to deliver or rescue; to deliver from sin and its consequences. —**re·deem·a·ble,** *a.*

re·deem·er, ri·dē′mər, *n.* One who redeems; (*cap.*) Jesus Christ.

re·demp·tion, ri·demp′shən, *n.* The act of redeeming, or the state of being redeemed; repurchase, as of something sold; recovery by payment of something pledged or mortgaged; a paying off, as of a mortgage, bond, or note; deliverance from sin and its consequences; salvation. —**re·demp·tive,** *a.*

red-hand·ed, red′han′did, *a.* In the very act: said of a person caught committing a crime; self-incriminating.

red her·ring, *n.* A subterfuge whose object is to distract or divert notice from the relevant problem.

red-hot, red′hot′, *a.* Red with heat; very hot; greatly excited; very enthusiastic; violent or furious: a *red-hot* debate; very new or fresh, as news.

re·di·rect, rē·də·rekt′, rē·di·rekt′, *v.t.* To direct again or anew. —**re·di·rec·tion,** *n.*

red-let·ter, red′let′ər, *a.* Memorable or especially happy: a *red-letter* day in one's life.

red·neck, red′nek, *n. Informal.* A poor, white, rural laborer of southern U.S.

re·do, rē·doo′, *v.t.,* **-did, -done, -do·ing.** To do over; to do again; to redecorate.

red·o·lent, red′ə·lənt, *a.* Having or diffusing a sweet scent; odorous; reminiscent, often with *of.* —**red·o·lence, red·o·len·cy,** *n.*

re·dou·ble, rē·dub′əl, *v.t.,* **-bled, -bling.** To increase; to double; to fold again.—*v.i.* To become twice as much; to become intensified.

re·doubt·a·ble, ri·dowt′ə·bəl, *a.* Formidable; to be dreaded; deserving respect. —**re·doubt·a·bly,** *adv.*

re·dound, ri·downd′, *v.i.* To come back in effect, or have an effect or result, followed by *to.*

re·dress, ri·dres′, *v.t.* To remedy or put right. —rē′dres, ri·dres′, *n.* Relief from wrong, injury, or oppression.

red snap·per, *n.* A reddish, edible, saltwater fish found along the Florida coast and in the Gulf of Mexico.

red·start, red′stärt, *n.* A brightly colored American warbler, the male largely black with orange patches on wing and tail, and constantly spreading its tail like a fan; a small European thrush with red on tail and breast.

red tape, *n.* Rigid or excessive routines and procedures causing delay or inaction, as in a bureaucracy.

re·duce, ri·doos′, ri·dūs′, *v.t.* **-duced, -duc·ing.** To diminish in size, quantity, or value; to make less or lower, as in strength or degree; to bring to an inferior condition; to subdue or subjugate; to bring to an indicated state or condition, with *to: reduce* someone *to* despair.—*v.i.* To become smaller, less, or lower; to lower one's weight. —**re·duc·er,** *n.* —**re·duc·i·ble,** *a.*

re·duc·tion, ri·dək′shən, *n.* The act of reducing; the state of being reduced; subjugation; the act of making a copy, as of a map, on a smaller scale.

re·dun·dant, ri·dən′dənt, *a.* Superfluous; exceeding what is natural or necessary; verbose. —**re·dun·dance,** *n.* —**re·dun·dan·cy,** *n. pl.,* **-cies.** —**re·dun·dant·ly,** *adv.*

re·du·pli·cate, ri·doo′plə·kāt, ri·dū′plə·kāt, *v.t., v.i.,* **-cat·ed, -cat·ing.** To double again; to repeat.—ri·doo′plə·kit, ri·doo′plə·kāt, *a.* Redoubled; repeated. —**re·dup·li·ca·tion,** ri·doo·plə·kā′shən, *n.*

red·wood, red′wůd, *n.* A pine-like tree of northern California, remarkable for its great girth and its height, which ranges from 200 to more than 300 feet.

re·ech·o, rē·ek′ō, *v.t.,* **-oed, -o·ing.** To echo back; to reverberate again.—*v.i.* To resound.—*n. pl.,* **-oes.** The echo of an echo; a repeated echo.

reed, rēd, *n.* The straight stalk of any of various tall grasses growing in marshy places; the plant itself; any of various things made from such a stalk; a musical pipe made from a reed or the hollow stalk of some other plant; a thin piece of wood or metal partially covering the mouthpiece of wind instruments, producing sound when vibrated by a current of air; an instrument with such a device.

reed·y, rē′dē, *a.,* **-i·er, -i·est.** Abounding with reeds; resembling a reed; having the thin, high tone of a reed instrument. —**reed·i·ness,** *n.*

reef, rēf, *n.* A ledge of rocks or coal in the ocean lying at or near the surface of the water.

reef, rēf, *n.* The part of a sail which may be or is rolled or folded up.—*v.t.* To reduce the size of a sail by rolling or folding up a part.

reef·er, rē′fər, *n.* One who reefs; a close-fitting jacket of strong cloth. *Informal.* A marijuana cigarette.

reek, rēk, *v.i., v.t.* To emit a strong and unpleasant odor; to be strongly pervaded with something unpleasant or offensive.—*n.* A strong, unpleasant smell.

reel, rēl, *n.* A revolving frame for winding yarn, film, a fishing line, etc.; a spool; the material wound on a reel; a length of motion-picture film wound on one reel.—*v.t.* To wind upon a reel; to pull by winding around a reel, with *in.*—**reel off,** to produce without effort.

reel, rēl, *v.i.* To whirl; to sway, swing, or rock under a blow, shock, etc.; to sway, stagger, or lurch from giddiness or drunkenness.—*v.t.* To cause to reel.—*n.* A reeling or staggering movement.

reel, rēl, *n.* A lively group dance; the music for this dance.

re·e·lect, rē·i·lekt′, *v.t.* To elect again. —**re·e·lec·tion,** *n.*

re·em·pha·size, rē·em′fə·sīz, *v.t.,* **-sized, -siz·ing.** To stress again; to reiterate.

re·en·force, rē·en·fōrs′, rē·en·fôrs′, *v.t.,* **-forced, -forc·ing.** Reinforce. —**re·en·force·ment,** *n.*

re·en·list, rē·en·list′, *v.t., v.i.* To enlist again. —**re·en·list·ment,** *n.*

re·en·ter, rē·en′tər, *v.t.* To enter again or anew. —**re·en·trance,** rē·en′trəns, *n.*

re·en·try, rē·en′trē, *n. pl.,* **-tries.** A new or second entry; the return of a space vehicle, rocket, or the like from outer space into the earth's atmosphere.

re·es·tab·lish, rē·ə·stab′lish, *v.t.* To establish anew. —**re·es·tab·lish·ment,** *n.*

re·ex·am·ine, rē·ig·zam′ən, *v.t.,* **-ined, -in·ing.** To examine anew. —**re·ex·am·i·na·tion,** rē·ig·zam·ə·nā′shən, *n.*

re·fec·to·ry, ri·fek/tə·rē, *n. pl.,* **-ries.** A room, esp. in convents and colleges, where meals are taken; dining hall.

re·fer, ri·fər/, *v.t.,* **-ferred, -fer·ring.** To send or direct for assistance, information, or decision; to hand over, as to another person, for treatment or decision: to *refer* a matter to a third party; to assign, as to an order, kind, period, or class; to attribute to a cause, source, or motive.—*v.i.* To have relation; to have recourse; to consult: to *refer* to one's notes; to allude; to direct the attention. —**re·fer·a·ble,** ref/ər·ə·bəl, ri·fər/ə·bəl, *a.* —**re·fer·ral,** *n.*

ref·er·ee, ref·ə·rē/, *n.* One to whom a matter in dispute has been referred for settlement or decision; an authoritative official in football or other sports. —*v.t., v.i.,* **-eed, -ee·ing.**

ref·er·ence, ref/ər·əns, *n.* The act of referring; the act of alluding; direct allusion; respect or regard: with *reference* to his letter; a person or thing referred to; a passage or note in a work by which a person is referred to another passage or book; one of whom inquiries may be made in regard to a person's character and ability; a written statement or letter as to one's ability and character.—*v.t.,* **-enced, -enc·ing.** To supply or furnish with references.

ref·er·en·dum, ref·ə·ren/dəm, *n. pl.,* **-dums, -da.** The referral to public vote, for final approval or rejection, of measures proposed or passed by a representative body having legislative powers; the vote so taken.

ref·er·ent, ref/ər·ənt, *n.* Something referred to, as a word, person, or concept.

re·fill, rē·fil/, *v.t.* To fill again.—rē/fil, *n.* A second filling or serving; any product packaged to replace the original contents of a refillable container. —**re·fill·a·ble,** *a.*

re·fine, ri·fīn/, *v.t.,* **-fined, -fin·ing.** To make fine or pure; to free from impurities; to purify from what is coarse, inelegant, or rude; make elegant or cultivated; to make precise or more subtle.—*v.i.* To become fine or pure; to become more elegant or polished; to make fine distinctions.

re·fined, ri·fīnd/, *a.* Having no impurities; polished or elegant in character; characterized by precision or exactness.

re·fine·ment, ri·fīn/mənt, *n.* Elegance of manners or language; fineness of feeling or taste; a fine distinction; subtle reasoning; an improved form of something; the act of refining or state of being refined; process of refining.

re·fin·er·y, ri·fī/nə·rē, *n. pl.,* **-ies.** A place and apparatus for refining sugar, metals, or oil.

re·fin·ish, rē·fin/ish, *v.t.* To put a new surface on, as wood or metal.

re·fit, rē·fit/, *v.t.,* **-fit·ted, -fit·ting.** To restore, repair, or fit out anew, as ships.—*v.i.* To be repaired, supplied, or made ready again.—*n.* The act of so repairing or supplying.

re·flect, ri·flekt/, *v.t.* To cast or direct back from a surface, as light, heat, or sound; to give back an image of; to mirror or imitate: to *reflect* another's attitude or opinion; to cast or direct back as a result: His courtesy *reflects* credit on his upbringing; to make evident or reveal: His act *reflects* his true feelings on the matter. —*v.i.* To throw back rays, beams, or the like; to turn back one's thoughts upon anything; to think at length or consider seriously; to revolve matters in the mind; to bring reproach; to cast censure or blame; to give a certain impression.

re·flec·tion, ri·flek/shən, *n.* The act of reflecting, or the state of being reflected; an image given back from a reflecting surface; attentive or continued consideration or meditation; the conclusion or thought resulting from such meditating; a discrediting remark; reproach.

re·flec·tive, ri·flek/tiv, *a.* Having the capability of throwing back rays, beams, or the like; reflecting; resulting from reflection; given to extended contemplation. —**re·flec·tive·ly,** *adv.* —**re·flec·tive·ness,** *n.*

re·flec·tor, ri·flek/tər, *n.* One who reflects; that which reflects; a polished surface of metal or other suitable material for reflecting light, heat, or sound in any required direction.

re·flex, rē/fleks, *n.* Something reflected; an image; a reflex action or movement.—*a.* Noting or pertaining to an involuntary action or movement in response to a stimulation of sensory nerve cells: Sneezing is a *reflex* action; turned or bent back.—ri·fleks/, *v.t.* To turn or bend back.

re·flex·ive, ri·flek/siv, *a.* Of a verb, having a pronoun object which is the same as its subject, as *cut* in: He *cut himself;* a pronoun, used as an object and identical with the subject, as *himself* in: He *cut himself.*—*n.* A reflexive verb or pronoun.

re·for·est, rē·fôr/ist, *v.t.* To replant with forest trees. —**re·for·est·a·tion,** rē·fôr·əs·tā/shən, *n.*

re·form, ri·fôrm/, *v.t.* To change from worse to better.—*v.i.* To abandon evil and return to good; to amend one's behavior.—*n.* A rearrangement or reconstruction which brings a better order of things; an instance of such; an improvement. —**re·formed,** *a.* —**re·form·er, re·form·ist,** *n.*

re·form, rē·fôrm/, *v.t., v.i.* To form again or anew.

Ref·or·ma·tion, ref·ər·mā/shən, *n.* The religious revolution of the 16th century which divided the Roman Catholic Church, with the dissidents establishing the Protestant churches. (*L.c.*) The act of reforming or the condition of being reformed.

re·form·a·to·ry, ri·fôr/mə·tôr·ē, *n. pl.,* **-ries.** An institution for the reformation of juveniles who have been convicted of lesser criminal offenses. Also **reform school.**—*a.* Tending to reform. Also **re·form·a·tive.**

re·fract, ri·frakt/, *v.t.* To deflect, as a ray of light, at a certain angle on passing from one medium into another of a different density. —**re·frac·tive,** *a.*

re·frac·tion, ri·frak/shən, *n.* The act of refracting or state of being refracted; a deflection or change of direction impressed upon rays of light or heat passing from one transparent medium into another of different density, as from air into water.

re·frac·to·ry, ri·frak/tə·rē, *a.* Perverse or disobedient; stubborn; unmanageable; resisting ordinary treatment, as certain diseases, or as metals that are difficult to fuse. —**re·frac·to·ri·ly,** *adv.* —**re·frac·to·ri·ness,** *n.*

re·frain, ri·frān/, *v.i.* To keep oneself from saying, doing, or feeling something; forbear; abstain, often followed by *from.*

re·frain, ri·frān/, *n.* A verse or phrase repeated at intervals in a poem or song, esp. at the end of every stanza; the musical setting for this verse or phrase.

re·fresh, ri·fresh/, *v.t.* To make fresh or vigorous again; to give new strength or energy to.—*v.i.* To have refreshment; to become fresh anew; revive. —**re·fresh·ing,** *a.*

re·fresh·er, ri·fresh/ər, *a.* Reviewing previously studied material, and often instructing in new developments: a *refresher* course.—*n.* One who or that which refreshes.

re·fresh·ment, ri·fresh/mənt, *n.* The act of refreshing, or the condition of being refreshed; that which refreshes, as food, drink, or rest. *Pl.* Food or drink, as a light meal or snack.

re·frig·er·ant, ri·frij/ər·ənt, *n.* A cooling agent; a gas used in mechanical refrigerators, as ammonia.

re·frig·er·ate, ri·frij/ə·rāt, *v.t.,* **-at·ed, -at·ing.** To cool; keep cool; to chill or freeze, as foods, in order to preserve. —**re·frig·er·a·tion,** ri·frij·ə·rā/shən, *n.*

---

a- hat, fāte, fāre, fäther; e- met, mē; i- pin, pīne; o- not, nōte, ôrb, moove (move), boy, pownd;
u- cūbe, bûll, tûk (took); ch- chin; th- thick, ŧhen; zh- vizhon (vision); ə- əgo, takən, pencəl, lemən, bərd (bird).

re·frig·er·a·tor, ri·frij′ə·rā·tər, *n.* That which refrigerates, cools, or keeps cool; a box or room in which materials, as foods, are kept cool, either by the action of ice or by evaporation of various liquid gases.

re·fu·el, rē·fū′əl, *v.t.* To supply afresh with fuel: to *refuel* an airplane.—*v.i.* To take on a fresh supply of fuel.

ref·uge, ref′ūj, *n.* Shelter or protection from danger or distress; any safe place or asylum.

ref·u·gee, ref·yû·jē′, ref′yû·jē, *n.* One who flees for refuge; one who in times of persecution, political commotion, or the like, flees to a foreign country for safety.

re·ful·gent, ri·fəl′jənt, *a.* Casting a bright light; shining; radiant. —**re·ful·gence,** *n.*

re·fund, ri·fənd′, *v.t.* To return in payment or compensation for what has been taken; to pay back; to restore; to reimburse.—*v.i.* To make compensation. —rē′fənd, *n.* A repayment; the sum repaid.

re·fur·bish, rē·fer′bish, *v.t.* To furbish a second time or anew; to renovate; to clean.

re·fus·al, ri·fū′zəl, *n.* The act of refusing; denial of anything demanded, solicited, or offered for acceptance; option of accepting or rejecting.

re·fuse, ri·fūz′, *v.t.,* **-fused, -fus·ing.** To deny, as a request, demand, invitation, or command; to decline to do or grant, often with an infinitive as object: He *refused* to give me the book; to decline to accept; to reject: to *refuse* an office; to deny the request of; to say no to: I could not *refuse* him.—*v.i.* To decline a request; not to comply.

ref·use, ref′ūs, *n.* That which is discarded as worthless or useless; garbage; trash; rubbish.—*a.* Rejected as worthless; discarded: *refuse* matter.

re·fute, ri·fūt′, *v.t.,* **-fut·ed, -fut·ing.** To disprove and overthrow by argument, evidence, or countervailing proof; to prove to be false; confute. —**re·fu·ta·ble,** ref′yə·tə·bəl, ri·fū′tə·bəl, *a.* —**ref·u·ta·tion,** ref·yû·tā′shən, *n.*

re·gain, ri·gān′, *v.t.* To gain anew; to recover what has been lost; to reach again: He *regained* the shore.

re·gal, rē′gəl, *a.* Of, pertaining to, or befitting a king; royal; stately; magnificent. —**re·gal·ly,** *adv.*

re·gale, ri·gāl′, *v.t.,* **-galed, -gal·ing.** To entertain in a lavish or agreeable manner; to provide a feast for; to delight with something pleasing.—*v.i.* To feast.

re·ga·li·a, ri·gā′lē·ə, ri·gāl′yə, *n. pl.,* The symbols of royalty, as the scepter, crown, or the like; the insignia or decorations of some society or office; fancy clothes.

re·gard, ri·gärd′, *v.t.* To look upon or think of in a particular way; view or consider: to *regard* a person as a friend; to heed; to esteem; to take into consideration; to contemplate or observe; to concern: This scheme *regards* your child's education.—*v.i.* To pay attention; heed; to look or gaze.—*n.* Reference or relation: to err with *regard* to facts; an aspect or particular: quite pleasing in this *regard;* notice or heed; consideration; look or gaze; respect; esteem; kindly feeling: a token of my *regard. Pl.* Sentiments of esteem or affection: Give her my *regards.*

re·gard·ful, ri·gärd′fəl, *a.* Mindful, often followed by *of: regardful* of appearances.

re·gard·ing, ri·gär′ding, *prep.* Respecting; concerning; in reference to: to be at a loss *regarding* something.

re·gard·less, ri·gärd′lis, *a.* Having or showing no regard; careless; negligent.—*adv.* Without regard to advice, expense, or consequence; despite.—**re·gard·less of,** in spite of; notwithstanding. —**re·gard·less·ly,** *adv.*

re·gat·ta, ri·gat′ə, ri·gä′tə, *n.* A boat race or a program of such races.

re·gen·cy, rē·jən·sē, *n. pl.,* **-cies.** The office or function of a regent or body of regents; a body of regents, or a government consisting of regents; a territory under the control of a regent or regents; the term of office of a regent.

re·gen·er·ate, ri·jen′ə·rāt, *v.t.,* **-at·ed, -at·ing.** To generate or produce anew; to bring into existence again, as cells or tissues; to recreate in a better form or condition; to cause to be born again spiritually. —*v.i.* To come into existence or be formed again; to reform; to become regenerate.—ri·jen′ər·it, *a.* Formed again or anew; reconstituted or made over in a better form; reformed; born again spiritually. —**re·gen·er·a·cy, re·gen·er·a·tion,** ri·jen·ə·rā′shən, *n.* —**re·gen·er·a·tive,** *a.*

re·gent, rē′jənt, *n.* One who exercises the ruling power in a kingdom during the minority, absence, or disability of the sovereign; a member of the governing board of certain universities and other institutions.

re·gime, rə·zhēm′, rā·zhēm′, *n.* System of management or rule; administration.

reg·i·men, rej′ə·mən, *n.* A regulated course of diet, exercise, or manner of living, intended to preserve or restore health or to attain some result.

reg·i·ment, rej′ə·mənt, *n.* A unit of organization in an army, being next below a brigade and usu. commanded by a colonel; a large body or number, as of persons.—rej′ə·ment, *v.t.* To form into a regiment or organized group; organize or systematize; organize or control strictly or rigidly; assign to a regiment or group; make uniform. —**reg·i·men·tal,** rej·ə·men′təl, *a.* —**reg·i·men·ta·tion,** rej·ə·men·tā′shən, *n.*

re·gion, rē′jən, *n.* Any more or less extensive, continuous part of a surface or space; a part of the earth's surface; a locality; a part of a space or a body; a domain, realm, or sphere; a place in, or a division of, the body or a part of the body.

re·gion·al, rē′jə·nəl, *a.* Of or pertaining to a particular region. —**re·gion·al·ly,** *adv.*

reg·is·ter, rej′i·stər, *n.* A book in which entries of occurrences, names, or the like are recorded; record; list; a mechanical contrivance by which certain data are recorded: a cash *register;* a contrivance for regulating the passage of heat, air, or the like, usu. placed where a duct opens into a room; the placement, or tone quality of a voice or instrument.—*v.t.* To enter or cause to be entered, in a register; to enroll, as voters or students; to cause to be recorded for security in transmission, as mail at a post office, by payment of a special fee; to indicate or show, as on a scale; to show, as one's emotions, by facial expression or by actions. —*v.i.* To enter one's name, or cause it to be entered, in a register; to indicate something, as by a record or on a scale; to register surprise, joy, or the like; to be registered or indicated; to create an impression. —**reg·is·tered,** *a.* —**reg·is·trant,** *n.*

reg·is·tered nurse, *n.* A nurse licensed by state authority to practice nursing, having completed her training and passed a state examination.

reg·is·trar, rej′i·strär, rej·i·strär′, *n.* One whose business is to write or keep a register; a keeper of records, esp. at a university or college.

reg·is·tra·tion, rej·ə·strā′shən, *n.* The act or an instance of registering or recording; a document indicating this; an entry in a register; the number of those registered; enrollment.

reg·is·try, rej′ə·strē, *n. pl.,* **-tries.** The act of entering in a register; the place where a register is kept; a fact recorded in an official book; the book.

re·gress, ri·gres′, *v.i.* To go back; move in a backward direction.—rē′gres, *n.* Return; retrogression. —**re·gres·sion, re·gres·sor,** *n.*

re·gret, ri·gret′, *v.t.,* **-gret·ted, -gret·ting.** To feel sorrow or be sorry for: to feel sorry about: to *regret* an unfortunate mistake.—*n.* The feeling of one who regrets; sorrowful feeling, disappointment, or dissatisfaction over anything that one wishes might have been otherwise; *pl.,* a polite expression of regretful feeling, as due to an inability to accept an invitation. —**re·gret·ta·ble,** *a.* —**re·gret·ta·bly,** *adv.* —**re·gret·ter,** *n.* —**re·gret·ful,** *a.* —**re·gret·ful·ly,** *adv.* —**re·gret·ful·**

ness, *n.*

reg·u·lar, reg′yə·lər, *a.* Conforming to what is common custom, usual, or normal: a *regular* practice; of uniform or even construction, degree, or arrangement: as *regular* temperature, *regular* features; of an ordered or habitual character: a *regular* patron, a *regular* meeting of the board; periodic, or methodically recurring: a *regular* heartbeat. *Gram.* Having the most common form of inflectional ending. *Geom.* Having equal sides and equal angles.—*n.* One who is habitually steady or loyal, as a customer, political party member, or the like; a soldier belonging to a permanent army; an athletic team member scheduled to play in each game and event. **—reg·u·lar·i·ty,** reg·yə·lar′ə·tē, *n.*

reg·u·late, reg′yə·lāt, *v.t.,* **-lat·ed, -lat·ing.** To adjust by rule or established mode; to govern by or subject to certain rules or restrictions; to direct; to put or keep in good order; to control and cause to act properly. **—reg·u·la·tive,** *a.* **—reg·u·la·tor,** *n.* **—reg·u·la·to·ry,** reg′yə·lə·tô·rē, *a.*

reg·u·la·tion, reg·yə·lā′shən, *n.* The act of regulating; a rule prescribed by a superior as to the actions of those under his control; a governing direction; a precept; a law.—*a.* According to regulation; standard; required; ordinary; usual.

re·gur·gi·tate, ri·gər′jə·tāt, *v.t.,* **-tat·ed, -tat·ing.** To rush or surge back; to pour forth.—*v.t.* To cause to rush or surge back; to pour forth. **—re·gur·gi·ta·tion,** ri·gər·jə·tā′shən, *n.*

re·ha·bil·i·tate, rē·hə·bil′ə·tāt, *v.t.,* **-tat·ed, -tat·ing.** To restore to a former capacity or position; to reinstate; to reestablish in the esteem of others; to restore to a healthy condition or useful capacity. **—re·ha·bil·i·ta·tion,** rē·hə·bil·ə·tā′shən, *n.* **—re·ha·bil·i·ta·tive,** *a.*

re·hash, rē·hash′, *v.t.* To repeat; discuss again; to work up into a new form, as old writings.—rē′hash, *n.* Something made up of materials formerly used.

re·hears·al, ri·hər′səl, *n.* A trial performance or drill for preparing the finished public performance.

re·hearse, ri·hərs′, *v.t.,* **-hearsed, -hears·ing.** To practice repeatedly prior to public performance; to repeat; recite; narrate or recount.—*v.i.* To take part in a rehearsal. **—re·hears·er,** *n.*

reign, rān, *n.* Royal authority; sovereignty; the time during which a monarch reigns; power, sway, or influence.—*v.i.* To possess or exercise sovereign power; to rule; to be predominant; to prevail.

re·im·burse, rē·im·bərs′, *v.t.,* **-bursed, -burs·ing.** To pay back; to refund; to pay back to; to recompense; to pay an equivalent to for expenditure or loss. **—re·im·burse·ment,** *n.*

rein, rān, *n. Usu. pl.* The strap by which the rider restrains and governs a horse or other animal. A means of curbing, restraining, or guiding.—*v.t.* To govern, guide, or restrain, as by reins.—*v.i.* To restrain a horse by use of reins, followed by *up* or *in.*—**draw rein,** slow one's speed; to curtail.—**give rein to,** to allow complete freedom.

re·in·car·na·tion, rē·in·kär·nā′shən, *n.* Belief that the soul returns after death to live in a new body; rebirth of the soul in a new living form; a new embodiment.

rein·deer, rān′dēr, *n. pl.,* **-deer.** Any of various species of deer with branched antlers in both male and female, found in northern or arctic regions of Asia, Europe, and N. America and often domesticated.

re·in·force, rē·in·fôrs′, rē·in·fôrs′, *v.t.,* **-forced, -forc·ing.** To strengthen; to strengthen with more troops, ships, or equipment. Also **re·en·force.**

re·in·force·ment, rē·in·fôrs′mənt, rē·in·fôrs′mənt, *n.* The act of reinforcing; something that strengthens. *Often pl.* Additional troops or forces to augment an army or fleet. Also **re·en·force·ment.**

re·in·state, rē·in·stāt′, *v.t.,* **-stat·ed, -stat·ing.** To place again in possession; to restore to a former state. **—re·in·state·ment.**

re·it·er·ate, rē·it′ə·rāt, *v.t.,* **-at·ed, -at·ing.** To repeat again and again; to do or say repeatedly. **—re·it·er·a·tion,** rē·it·ə·rā′shən, *n.*

re·ject, ri·jekt′, *v.t.* To refuse to receive, recognize, or acknowledge; to throw away as useless or vile; to cast off; to discard; to disgorge or vomit.—rē′jekt, *n.* One who or that which is rejected. **—re·jec·tion,** ri·jek′shən, *n.*

re·joice, ri·joys′, *v.i.,* **-joiced, -joic·ing.** To experience joy and gladness; to be joyful; to exult, usu. followed by *in.*—*v.t.* To make joyful; to gladden. **—re·joic·er,** *n.* **—re·joic·ing,** *n.* **—re·joic·ing·ly,** *adv.*

re·join, rē·joyn′, *v.t., v.i.* To come or join together again; reunite.

re·join, ri·joyn′, *v.t., v.i.* To say in reply; answer; respond.

re·join·der, ri·joyn′dər, *n.* An answer to a reply; a retort.

re·ju·ve·nate, ri·joo′və·nāt, *v.t.,* **-nat·ed, -nat·ing.** To make young again; to restore to youthful vigor or freshness. **—re·ju·ve·na·tion,** ri·joo·və·nā′shən, *n.* **—re·ju·ve·na·tor,** *n.*

re·kin·dle, rē·kin′dəl, *v.t., v.i.,* **-dled, -dling.** To kindle again; to inflame again; to rouse anew.

re·lapse, ri·laps′, *v.i.,* **-lapsed, -laps·ing.** To slip or slide back, esp. from recovery or convalescence to illness; to return to a former bad state or practice; to backslide.—ri·laps′, rē′laps, *n.* A recurrence of illness; a falling back. **—re·laps·er,** *n.*

re·late, ri·lāt′, *v.t.,* **-lat·ed, -lat·ing.** To tell; to narrate the particulars of; to form or show a connection or relationship.—*v.i.* To have reference; to stand in some relation with, followed by *to.* **—re·lat·er, re·lat·or,** *n.*

re·lat·ed, ri·lā′tid, *a.* Allied; connected by blood, alliance, or marriage.

re·la·tion, ri·lā′shən, *n.* Connection perceived or imagined between things; a certain position or connection of one thing with regard to another; relationship by blood or marriage; kinship; a kinsman or kinswoman; the act of recounting that which is related or told; narrative. *Pl.* The state or conditions of being related.—**in re·la·tion to,** with reference, respect, or regard to. **—re·la·tion·al,** *a.*

re·la·tion·ship, ri·lā′shən·ship, *n.* The state of being related by blood, marriage, or other alliance; kinship; connection.

rel·a·tive, rel′ə·tiv, *a.* Having relation to or bearing on something; close in connection; pertinent; relevant; not absolute or existing by itself; depending on or incident to something else; applied to a word which relates to another word or words, called the antecedent.—*n.* Something considered in its relation to something else; a person connected by blood; a kinsman or kinswoman; a word which relates to or represents another word, called its antecedent, esp. the pronouns *who, which,* and *that.* **—rel·a·tive·ly,** *adv.*

rel·a·tiv·i·ty, rel·ə·tiv′ə·tē, *n.* The state or fact of being relative; relativeness; the theory, formulated mathematically by Albert Einstein, asserting the equivalence of mass and energy, the interdependence of space and time, and the relativity to the observer of all motion except the absolute, constant velocity of light.

re·lax, ri·laks′, *v.t.* To slacken; make lax; to make less tense or rigid; to make less severe or rigorous; to lessen in strictness; to slacken or abate in attention, effort, or labor; to relieve from strain, restraint, or worries.—*v.i.* To become loose, lax, or languid; to abate in severity; to become less tense or worried; to slacken in attention or effort; to unbend; to rest or seek recreation.

---

a- hat, fāte, fâre, fäther; e- met, mē; i- pin, pīne; o- not, nōte, ôrb, moove (move), boy, pownd; u- cūbe, bŭll, tûk (took); ch- chin; th- thick, ŧhen; zh- vizhon (vision); ə- ego, takən, pencəl, lemən, bərd (bird).

re·lax·a·tion, rē·lak·sā′shən, *n.* The act of relaxing or state of being relaxed; a lessening of tension, effort, or severity; recreation; entertainment.

re·lay, rē·lā′, *v.t.,* **-laid, -lay·ing.** To lay again, as paving blocks; to lay anew.

re·lay, rē′lā, *n.* A relay race; a fresh supply of food, horses, men, etc.; any device by which telephonic or telegraphic messages are sent to a greater distance or strengthened.—ri·lā′, rē′lā, *v.t.,* **-layed, -lay·ing.** To carry forward by or as by relays; to transmit by means of relay.—v.i. To relay a message.

re·lay race, rē′lā, *n.* A race between teams, each member of which runs part way and is relieved by a teammate. Also **re·lay.**

re·lease, ri·lēs′, *v.t.,* **-leased, -leas·ing.** To set free from restraint or confinement; to liberate; to free from pain, grief, or worry; to free from obligation or penalty; to allow to be published, shown, or sold; to give up or let go, as a claim.—n. A releasing or being released; liberation; relief; discharge from obligation or responsibility; the act of introducing to the public, as news, plays, films, or books; the material released, esp. to the press; the waiving of a claim or right; a document comprising the waiver. **—re·leas·a·ble,** *a.* **—re·leas·er,** *n.*

rel·e·gate, rel′ə·gāt, *v.t.,* **-gat·ed, -gat·ing.** To send away; to banish. **—rel·e·ga·tion,** rel·ə·gā′shən, *n.*

re·lent, ri·lent′, *v.i.* To become less harsh; to become more mild and sympathetic; to yield.

re·lent·less, ri·lent′lis, *a.* Unrelenting; harsh; merciless.

rel·e·vant, rel′ə·vənt, *a.* To the purpose; pertinent; applicable; bearing on the issue in question. **—rel·e·vance, rel·e·van·cy,** *n.* **—rel·e·vant·ly,** *adv.*

re·li·a·ble, ri·lī′ə·bəl, *a.* Such as may be relied on; trustworthy; dependable. **—re·li·a·bil·i·ty,** ri·lī·ə·bil′ə·tē, **re·li·a·ble·ness,** *n.* **—re·li·a·bly,** *adv.*

re·li·ance, ri·lī′əns, *n.* The act of relying; dependence; confidence; trust; a person or thing depended upon.

re·li·ant, ri·lī′ənt, *a.* Having reliance; confident; self-reliant.

rel·ic, rel′ik, *n.* That which is left after the loss, decay, or destruction of the rest; something preserved in remembrance, as a memento, souvenir, or keepsake; bones, garments, or other mementos of saints or martyrs, preserved for veneration; any outmoded custom, institution, or the like.

re·lief, ri·lēf′, *n.* The removal of anything painful or burdensome; ease from pain; that which removes pain, grief, or other evil; help given to the poor in the form of food or money; release from duty by a substitute or substitutes; such a substitute; the projection or prominence of a figure in sculpture, drawing, etc., above or beyond the ground on which it is formed; a piece of artistic work in one or other of these styles; prominence or distinctness given to anything by something presenting a contrast to it; the differences in surface elevations of a country.

re·lief map, *n.* A map portraying by means of contour lines the elevations of a land area.

re·lieve, ri·lēv′, *v.t.,* **-lieved, -liev·ing.** To remove or lessen, as anything that pains or distresses; to free from pain, grief, anxiety, or anything considered to be an evil; to help or aid the poor or the sick; to release from a post or duty by substituting another person or party, or serving as the substitute; to set off by contrast; to give the appearance of projection to.—**re·lieve of,** to rob: to *relieve* one *of* his wallet. **—re·liev·a·ble,** *a.* **—re·liev·er,** *n.*

re·li·gion, ri·lij′ən, *n.* Recognition on the part of man of a controlling superhuman power or powers entitled to obedience, reverence, and worship; a particular system of faith in and worship of a Supreme Being or a god or gods; an object of conscientious or encompassing devotion: his country was his *religion.*

re·li·gi·os·i·ty, ri·lij·ē·os′i·tē, *n.* Pious, sentimen-

tal, or affected religiousness.

re·li·gious, ri·lij′əs, *a.* Of, pertaining to, concerned or connected with religion; pious, devout, or godly; scrupulously faithful or conscientious.—n. pl., **-gious.** A member of a religious order, as a monk, friar, or nun; anyone devoutly religious.

re·lin·quish, ri·ling′kwish, *v.t.* To give up; release.

rel·ish, rel′ish, *v.t.* To like the taste or flavor of; to be pleased with or gratified by.—v.i. To have a pleasing taste.—n. A pleasing taste; liking; a pickled, spiced, or glazed seasoning served with the meat or fish course.

re·live, rē·liv′, *v.t.,* **-lived, -liv·ing.** To live or experience over again.—v.i. To live again.

re·lo·cate, rē·lō′kāt, *v.t., v.i.,* **-cat·ed, -cat·ing.** To locate again; to move to a different place to live. **—re·lo·ca·tion,** rē·lō·kā′shən, *n.*

re·luc·tance, ri·lək′təns, *n.* The state or quality of being reluctant; unwillingness.

re·luc·tant, ri·lək′tənt, *a.* Striving against doing something; unwilling; averse; granted unwillingly: *reluctant* obedience.

re·ly, ri·lī′, *v.i.,* **-lied, -ly·ing.** To have confidence or trust; depend, with *on* or *upon.*

re·main, ri·mān′, *v.i.* To continue in a place; to continue in an unchanged form or condition; to endure; to last; to be left.—n. pl. That which is left; that which is left of a human being after life is gone; a dead body.

re·main·der, ri·mān′dər, *n.* That which remains; the quantity that is left after subtraction or division.

re·mand, ri·mand′, *v.t.* To send, call, or order back; to send back to jail to await trial or resumption of a hearing.—n. The state of being remanded; the act of remanding; one who is remanded.

re·mark, ri·märk′, *n.* A brief statement; an observation; a comment; the act of observing or taking notice.—v.t. To express by way of comment or observation; to observe or to note in the mind.—v.i. To make a remark, with *on* or *upon.*

re·mark·a·ble, ri·mär′kə·bəl, *a.* Worthy of notice; extraordinary; unusual; conspicuous. **—re·mark·a·ble·ness,** *n.* **—re·mark·a·bly,** *adv.*

re·me·di·a·ble, ri·mē′dē·ə·bəl, *a.* Capable of being remedied.

re·me·di·al, ri·mē′dē·əl, *a.* Affording a remedy; intended to remedy: *remedial* measures.

rem·e·dy, rem′ə·dē, *n. pl.,* **-dies.** Something that cures or relieves a disease or bodily disorder; something that corrects or removes an evil of any kind. —v.t., **-died, -dy·ing.** To cure, heal, or relieve; to put right, or restore to the natural or proper condition: to *remedy* a matter.

re·mem·ber, ri·mem′bər, *v.t.* To bring back to the mind or recall from memory; recollect; to hold in the mind; to maintain awareness of: to *remember* an appointment; to have in mind for rewarding with a gift, tip, or bequest: to *remember* the mailman at Christmas; to mention in the sending of greetings: *Remember* me to your sister.—v.i. To have or make use of one's memory; to recollect.

re·mem·brance, ri·mem′brəns, *n.* That which is remembered; something kept in mind; the condition of being remembered; the power of remembering; a keepsake; a gift given as a token of regard. *Often pl.* Warm greetings.

re·mind, ri·mīnd′, *v.t.* To put in mind; to cause to recollect or remember: to *remind* a person of his promise. **—re·mind·er,** *n.*

rem·i·nisce, rem·ə·nis′, *v.i.,* **-nisced, -nisc·ing.** To indulge in reminiscence; recall past experiences.

rem·i·nis·cence, rem·ə·nis′əns, *n.* Recollection; that which is recollected or recalled to mind. *Often pl.* A narration of past incidents within one's personal experience.

rem·i·nis·cent, rem·ə·nis′ənt, *a.* Calling to mind; suggestive, usu. followed by *of;* pertaining to reminiscence; given to reminiscing.

re·miss, ri·mis′, *a.* Careless or negligent in performing duty or business; showing carelessness or negligence.

re·mis·sion, ri·mish′ən, *n.* The act of remitting; diminution; abatement; forgiveness; discharge from penalty; temporary abatement of pain or disease. Also **re·mit·tal,** ri·mit′əl.

re·mit, ri·mit′, *v.t.,* **-mit·ted, -mit·ting.** To transmit or send, as money, in payment; to refrain from exacting, as a payment or punishment; to pardon; to forgive, as sins; to relax; to abate; to allow to slacken: to *remit* vigilance; to send or give back.—*v.i.* To transmit money; to slacken; to become less intense for a time: The fever *remits* at a certain time every day.

re·mit·tance, ri·mit′əns, *n.* The act of transmitting money, vouchers, or the like, in return or payment for goods purchased or services rendered; the amount remitted.

rem·nant, rem′nənt, *n.* The last small part, as of unused cloth; a scrap or fragment.—*a.*

re·mod·el, rē·mod′əl, *v.t.* To model anew; to reconstruct.

re·mon·strance, ri·mon′strəns, *n.* The act of remonstrating; a strong statement of reasons against something.

re·mon·strate, ri·mon′strāt, *v.i.,* **-strat·ed, -strat·ing.** To exhibit or present strong reasons against an act, measure, or any course of proceedings.—*v.t.* To plead or say in opposition or protest.

re·morse, ri·môrs′, *n.* The keen pain or anguish excited by a sense of guilt; painful memory of wrongdoing. **—re·morse·ful,** *a.* **—re·morse·ful·ly,** *adv.* **—re·morse·less,** *a.*

re·mote, ri·mōt′, *a.,* **-mot·er, -mot·est.** Distant in place or time, not directly producing an effect; slight; inconsiderable: a *remote* resemblance; of a person, aloof or abstracted.

re·mount, rē·mownt′, *v.t., v.i.* To mount again. —rē′mownt, rē·mownt′, *n.* A fresh horse or horses to mount.

re·mov·a·ble, ri·moo′və·bəl, *a.* Capable of being removed.

re·mov·al, ri·moo′vəl, *n.* A moving from one place to another; change of place or site; the act of displacing from an office or post; the act of removing; a dismissal.

re·move, ri·moov′, *v.t.,* **-moved, -mov·ing.** To shift from the position occupied; to put in another place in any manner; to take off, as clothing; to displace from an office, post, or position; to cause to leave, as a person or thing; to put an end to; to make away with.—*v.i.* To change place in any manner; to move from one place to another.—*n.* An interval; stage; a step in any scale of gradation.

re·moved, ri·moovd′, *a.* Changed in place; displaced from office; remote; separate from others in time, place, or relationship: a cousin twice *removed.*

re·mu·ner·ate, ri·mū′nə·rāt, *v.t.,* **-at·ed, -at·ing.** To pay an equivalent to for any service, loss, or sacrifice. **—re·mu·ner·a·tion,** ri·mū′nə·rā′shən, *n.* **—re·mu·ner·a·tive,** ri·mū′nə·rā·tiv, ri·mū′nər·ə·tiv, *a.*

ren·ais·sance, ren·ə·säns′, ren′ə·säns, ri·nā′səns, *n.* The revival of anything which has long been in decay or extinct. (*Cap.*) The transitional movement in Europe from the Middle Ages to the modern world; the European revival of letters and arts in the 14th, 15th, and 16th centuries; the time of that revival.—*a.* (*Cap.*) Pertaining to the European Renaissance; of or pertaining to the styles of art and literature prevalent at that time.

re·nas·cence, ri·nas′əns, ri·nā′səns, *n.* Rebirth; renewal; revival.—**the Renascence,** the Renaissance. **—re·nas·cent,** *a.*

rend, rend, *v.t.,* **rent** or **rend·ed, rend·ing.** To tear asunder; to split; to take away with violence; to tear away, used with *from, away,* or *off;* to affect, as the heart, with deep anguish or sorrow.—*v.i.* To be or to become rent or torn; to split something.

ren·der, ren′dər, *v.t.* To give in return; to give or pay back; to give in compliance with a request or duty; to submit consideration; to furnish; to report: to *render* an account; to afford; to perform; to give for use or benefit: to *render* services; to make or cause to be; to invest with qualities: to *render* a fortress more secure; to translate from one language into another; to interpret or bring into full expression to others; to reproduce: to *render* a piece of music; to depict; to yield or surrender; to boil down and clarify: to *render* tallow.

ren·dez·vous, rän′də·voo, rän′dā·voo, *n. pl.,* **-vous,** -vooz. An appointment or engagement to meet at a fixed place and time; a meeting by special appointment or engagement; a place appointed, esp. for the assembling of troops or ships.—*v.i., v.t.,* **-voused,** -vood, **-vous·ing,** -voo·ing. To assemble at a time or place previously appointed.

ren·di·tion, ren·dish′ən, *n.* A rendering; interpretation; translation; the act of reproducing or exhibiting artistically.

ren·e·gade, ren′ə·gād, *n.* An apostate from a religious faith; one who deserts to an enemy or opposing party; a deserter.

re·nege, ri·nig′, *v.i.,* **-neged, -neg·ing.** To play a card of another suit when able and required by the game rules to follow suit. *Informal.* To fail to keep one's word or a promise.

re·new, ri·noo′, ri·nū′, *v.t.* To make new again; to restore to a former or sound condition; to revive; to make again: to *renew* a treaty; to resume; to continue by repeating: to *renew* a subscription; to grant again, as a new loan; to replenish, as supplies.—*v.i.* To become new; to grow afresh; to begin again.

re·new·al, ri·noo′əl, ri·nū′əl, *n.* An act or instance of renewing; the state of being renewed.

ren·net, ren′it, *n.* The inner membrane of the calf's fourth stomach; a derivation from this membrane, used to coagulate milk.

re·nounce, ri·nowns′, *v.t.,* **-nounced, -nounc·ing.** To disown; to repudiate; to cast off or reject.

ren·o·vate, ren′ə·vāt, *v.t.,* **-vat·ed, -vat·ing.** To renew; to restore to freshness or to a good condition. **—ren·o·va·tion,** ren·ə·vā′shən, *n.*

re·nown, ri·nown′, *n.* Fame; exalted reputation; eminence.

re·nowned, ri·nownd′, *a.* Famous.

rent, rent, n. Compensation paid at intervals to the owner of a property by the tenant or user; the amount paid.—*v.t.* To grant the possession and enjoyment of for a certain rent; to let on lease; to take and hold on the payment of rent.—*v.i.* To be leased or let for rent.

rent, rent, *n.* An opening made by tearing; a breach; schism.—*v.* Past tense and past participle of **rend.**

rent·al, ren′təl, *n.* A schedule of rents; a sum paid or received as rent; the act of renting.—*a.*

re·nun·ci·a·tion, ri·nən·sē·ā′shən, *n.* The act of renouncing; an instance of this.

re·or·gan·i·za·tion, rē·ôr′gə·nə·zā′shən, *n.* The act or process of reorganizing, or the state of being reorganized.

re·or·gan·ize, rē·ôr′gə·nīz, *v.t., v.i.,* **-ized, -iz·ing.** To organize anew.

re·pair, ri·pār′, *v.t.* To restore to a sound or good state; to make amends for.—*n. Often pl.* Restoration to a sound or good state; the part that is repaired, or added while repairing. Reparation; condition as regards repairing: a building in good *repair.*

re·pair, ri·pār′, *v.i.* To go; to betake oneself.

re·pair·man, ri·pār′man, ri·pār′mən, *n. pl.,* **-men.** A man whose trade is making repairs.

---

rep·a·ra·ble, rep/ər·ə·bəl, *a.* Capable of being repaired or corrected.

rep·a·ra·tion, rep·ə·rā/shən, *n.* The act of repairing; repair; what is done to repair a wrong. *Pl.* Indemnification for loss or damage, as demanded of a country defeated in war.

rep·ar·tee, rep·ər·tē/, rep·ər·tā/, *n.* A smart, ready, and witty reply; conversation distinguished by witty responses.

re·past, ri·past/, *n.* A meal; food.

re·pa·tri·ate, rē·pā/trē·āt, *v.t.* **-at·ed**, **-at·ing.** To return, as a war prisoner or refugee, to his own country. **—re·pa·tri·a·tion**, rē·pā·trē·ā/shən, *n.*

re·pay, ri·pā/, *v.t.*, **-paid**, **-pay·ing.** To pay back, as money; to make some return to; to make return or requital for: to *repay* kindness with surliness; to return, as a visit.—*v.i.* To make return or repayment. **—re·pay·ment**, *n.*

re·peal, ri·pēl/, *v.t.* To rescind, as a law or statute; to revoke; to abrogate by an authoritative act.—*n.* The act of repealing; revocation.

re·peat, ri·pēt/, *v.t.* To say or utter again; to say or utter in reproducing the words of another: to *repeat* a sentence after the teacher; to do, make, perform, or execute again: to *repeat* an action; to tell, as a secret, to another or others.—*v.i.* To do or say something again.—ri·pēt/, rē/pēt, *n.* The act or an act of repeating; repetition; something repeated; a musical passage to be repeated; a program on radio or TV previously broadcast. **—re·peat·able**, *a.* **—re·peat·ed**, *a.*

re·peat·er, ri·pē/tər, *n.* Person or thing that repeats; a firearm that fires several shots without reloading; a person who illegally votes more than once at the same election; an habitual lawbreaker.

re·pel, ri·pel/, *v.t.*, **-pelled**, **-pel·ling.** To drive back; to force away; discourage; to reject; to repulse; to create aversion or distaste in: That smell *repels* me.—*v.i.* To cause repugnance or aversion; to act with force in opposition.

re·pel·lent, ri·pel/ənt, *a.* Having the effect of repelling; able or tending to repel or drive off; repulsive; deterring.—*n.* That which repels; a substance, as a waterproofing agent, used on fabric; a substance that wards off insects.

re·pent, ri·pent/, *v.i.* To feel sorrow, remorse, or regret for one's past conduct; to be penitent; to have a change of mind about a past action, usu. with *of:* to *repent* of a rash decision.—*v.t.* To remember with compunction or self-reproach; to feel remorse on account of: to *repent* cruel words. **—re·pent·ance**, *n.* **—re·pent·ant**, *a.*

re·per·cus·sion, rē·pər·kəsh/ən, *n.* A rebounding or recoil; reverberation or echo; a reaction; an indirect or unexpected consequence or result.

rep·er·toire, rep/ər·twär, rep/ər·twôr, *n.* A list of dramas, operas, parts, pieces, etc., that a performer or company is prepared to perform; such works collectively.

rep·er·to·ry, rep/ər·tōr·ē, rep/ər·tôr·ē, *n. pl.*, **-ries.** A repertoire; a store or collection of things.

rep·e·ti·tion, rep·ə·tish/ən, *n.* The act of repeating or saying over; something said, done, or experienced a second time; that which is repeated. **—rep·e·ti·tious**, *a.* **—re·pet·i·tive**, ri·pet/ə·tiv, *a.*

re·place, ri·plās/, *v.t.*, **-placed**, **-plac·ing.** To put again in the former place; to restore or return; to fill the place of; to be a substitute for. **—re·place·a·ble**, *a.*

re·place·ment, ri·plās/mənt, *n.* The act of replacing; that which replaces; a substitute.

re·plen·ish, ri·plen/ish, *v.t.* To fill again; to restock.

re·plete, ri·plēt/, *a.* Completely filled; thoroughly supplied, usu. followed by *with:* a scene *replete* with pathos. **—re·ple·tion**, *n.*

rep·li·ca, rep/lə·kə, *n.* A copy of a picture or piece of sculpture made by the original artist; any reproduction

or copy.

re·ply, ri·pli/, *v.i.*, **-plied**, **-ply·ing.** To make answer in words or writing; to respond; to answer by deeds.—*v.t.* To say or return in answer, often followed by a noun clause: He *replied* that he would go.—*n. pl.*, **-plies.** That which is said, written, or performed in answer.

re·port, ri·pōrt/, ri·pôrt/, *v.t.* To bear or bring back, as an answer; to relate, as facts or discoveries; to give an account of; to tell, esp. publicly; to give an official or formal account or statement of; to lay a charge or make a disclosure against: I will *report* you.—*v.i.* To make a statement of facts; to discharge the office of a reporter; to go or present oneself: *Report* to the office in ten minutes.—*n.* An account brought back; a statement of facts given in reply to inquiry; a news account; a story circulated; rumor; fame; repute; public character: a man of good *report*; the sound of an explosion or shot.

re·port card, *n.* A report of a student's scholastic achievement, issued periodically by a school.

re·port·ed·ly, ri·pōr/tid·lē, ri·pôr/tid·lē, *adv.* According to rumor or report.

re·port·er, ri·pōr/tər, ri·pôr/tər, *n.* One who reports; a member of a newspaper staff whose duty is to give an account of public events; one who prepares reports of court proceedings for publication. **—rep·or·to·ri·al**, rep·ər·tōr/ē·əl, *a.*

re·pose, ri·pōz/, *v.t.*, **-posed**, **-pos·ing.** To put, as confidence or trust (in a person or thing).

re·pose, ri·pōz/, *v.i.*, **-posed**, **-pos·ing.** To lie at rest; to rest; to be at peace or tranquil.—*v.t.* To lay to rest; rest.—*n.* The state of reposing or resting; rest; sleep; peace or tranquillity; calmness; composure. **—re·pose·ful**, *a.*

re·pos·i·to·ry, ri·poz/ə·tō·rē, ri·poz/ə·tôr·ē, *n. pl.*, **-ies.** A place where things are, or may be deposited for safety, preservation, or sale.

re·pos·sess, rē·pə·zes/, *v.t.* To possess again, esp. for default of payment; to restore ownership or possession to. **—re·pos·ses·sion**, *n.*

rep·re·hend, rep·ri·hend/, *v.t.* To charge with a fault; to chide sharply; to reprove; to blame; to censure.

rep·re·hen·si·ble, rep·ri·hen/sə·bəl, *a.* Deserving to be reprehended or censured; deserving reproof.

rep·re·sent, rep·ri·zent/, *v.t.* To typify; to portray by pictorial or sculptured art; to act the part of, as in a play; to bring before the mind; to describe; to speak and act with authority on behalf of; to be a substitute or agent for: to *represent* the owners; to serve as a sign or symbol of: Words *represent* ideas or things.

rep·re·sen·ta·tion, rep·ri·zen·tā/shən, *n.* The act of representing; the state, condition, or right of being represented; representatives collectively; that which represents or portrays, as a picture or statue; a dramatic performance; an account or statement.

rep·re·sent·a·tive, rep·ri·zen/tə·tiv, *a.* Fitted to represent, portray, or typify; acting as a substitute for another or others; representing; pertaining to or based on the principle of government by representation; typical of a kind, class, or group.—*n.* One who or that which represents; someone or something that exemplifies a class, kind, or quality; a member of the U.S. House of Representatives or the lower house of a state in the U.S.

re·press, ri·pres/, *v.t.* To crush, quell, or subdue; to check or control, as desires; to restrain. **—re·pres·sion**, *n.*

re·prieve, ri·prēv/, *n.* The suspension of the execution of a sentence; a warrant or authorization for this; respite; temporary ease or relief.—*v.t.*, **-prieved**, **-priev·ing.** To grant a reprieve or respite to; to suspend or delay the execution of; to provide temporary relief to.

rep·ri·mand, rep/rə·mand, *n.* A severe reproof; a sharp or formal rebuke.—*v.t.* To reprove severely.

re·print, rē·print/, *v.t.* To print again; to print a second or new edition of.—**rē′print,** *n.* A reproduction of a printed work.

re·pris·al, ri·prī′zəl, *n.* The resorting to force short of war by one nation against another to procure redress of grievances; any retaliatory act; a recapturing.

re·proach, ri·prōch′, *v.t.* To charge with a fault; to censure; to bring disgrace to.—*n.* An expression of censure or blame; blame; source of discredit; disgrace: He was a *reproach* to his family; object of contempt, scorn, or derision.

re·proach·ful, ri·prōch′fəl, *a.* Containing or expressing reproach or censure: a *reproachful* glance.

rep·ro·bate, rep′rə·bāt, *a.* Unprincipled; morally depraved.—*n.* One who is wicked. **—rep·ro·ba·tion,** rep·rə·bā′shən, *n.*

re·pro·duce, rē·prə·doos′, rē·prə·dūs′, *v.t.,* **-duced, -duc·ing.** To produce again or anew, as music on wire or tape; to produce, as offspring; to make a replica of.—*v.i.* To bear or produce offspring.

re·pro·duc·tion, rē·prə·dək′shən, *n.* The act or process of reproducing; that which is produced or presented anew; a copy; the process by which a plant or animal gives rise to another of its kind.

re·pro·duc·tive, rē·prə·dək′tiv, *a.* Pertaining to reproduction; tending to reproduce.

re·proof, ri·proof′, *n.* The expression of blame or censure.

re·prove, ri·proov′, *v.t.,* **-proved, -prov·ing.** To charge with a fault; to express disapproval of.

rep·tile, rep′til, rep′til, *n.* Any of the airbreathing, cold-blooded vertebrates, as snakes, lizards, and alligators.—*a.* Of or like a reptile. **—rep·til·i·an,** rep·til′ē·ən, rep·til′yən, *a., n.*

re·pub·lic, ri·pəb′lik, *n.* A state or other political unit in which the supreme power is vested in the whole voting community which elects, indirectly or directly, representatives to exercise the power.

re·pub·li·can, ri·pəb′li·kən, *a.* Pertaining to or having the character of a republic. (*Cap.*) Pertaining or relating to the Republican Party.—*n.* One who favors or prefers a republican form of government. (*Cap.*) A member of the Republican Party.

re·pub·li·can·ism, ri·pəb′li·kən·iz·əm, *n.* Republican government or principles; adherence to or advocacy of such principles.

Re·pub·li·can Par·ty, *n.* One of the two main political parties in the U.S.

re·pu·di·ate, ri·pū′dē·āt, *v.t.,* **-at·ed, -at·ing.** To reject; to cast away or disown; to disavow; to refuse to acknowledge or pay, as a debt. **—re·pu·di·a·tion,** ri·pū·dē·ā′shən, *n.*

re·pug·nance, ri·pəg′nəns, *n.* The state of being opposed or of feeling aversion; a feeling of strong dislike or objection. Also **re·pug·nan·cy.**

re·pug·nant, ri·pəg′nənt, *a.* Highly distasteful; offensive; objectionable; contrary, as in character; standing or being in opposition.

re·pulse, ri·pəls′, *v.t.,* **-pulsed, -puls·ing.** To repel; to drive back; to refuse, reject, or rebuff by discourtesy or coldness.—*n.* The condition of being repelled or driven back by force; the act of driving back; a rejection; refusal; denial.

re·pul·sion, ri·pəl′shən, *n.* The act of repulsing or repelling; the condition of being repelled; a feeling of repugnance or aversion.

re·pul·sive, ri·pəl′siv, *a.* Causing aversion, distaste, or disgust; acting so as to repel.

rep·u·ta·ble, rep′yə·tə·bəl, *a.* Being in good repute; held in esteem; honorable. **—rep·u·ta·bly,** *adv.* **—rep·u·ta·bil·i·ty,** rep·yə·tə·bil′ə·tē, *n.*

rep·u·ta·tion, rep·yə·tā′shən, *n.* Character by report; opinion of character generally held; good name; distinction; a specific credit or character attributed to someone or something: a *reputation* for integrity.

re·pute, ri·pūt′, *v.t.,* **-put·ed, -put·ing.** To hold in thought; to regard, account, or consider as indicated, usu. used in the passive: It is *reputed* to be the best.—*n.* Reputation; character attributed by public report; honorable name. **—re·put·ed·ly,** *adv.*

re·quest, ri·kwest′, *n.* The expression of desire to some person for something to be granted or done; a petition; the thing asked for or requested; a state of being esteemed and sought after, or asked for: an article in much *request.*—*v.t.* To make a request for; to solicit or express desire for; to express a request to: to *request* the class to leave; to ask for.

req·ui·em, rek′wē·əm, rē′kwē·əm, *n.* A dirge, service, or hymn for the repose of souls of the dead. (*Usu. cap.*). A funeral mass for the dead; the musical setting of this mass.

re·quire, ri·kwīr′, *v.t.,* **-quired, -quir·ing.** To demand; to order; to insist on having; to have need or necessity for: to *require* a blood transfusion; to need or want. —*v.i.* To demand or force; compel.

re·quire·ment, ri·kwīr′mənt, *n.* The act of requiring; demand; that which requires the doing of something; an essential condition: the *requirements* for a job; something required or necessary.

req·ui·site, rek′wə·zit, *a.* Required by the nature of things or by circumstances; necessary.—*n.* That which is necessary; something indispensable.

req·ui·si·tion, rek·wə·zish′ən, *n.* An authoritative request; a demand; a written application or request, as for supplies; state of being required; a requirement; request.—*v.t.* To make a requisition or demand upon.

re·quit·al, ri·kwīt′əl, *n.* The action or act of requiting; something done or given in return; compensation.

re·quite, ri·kwīt′, *v.t.,* **-quit·ed, -quit·ing.** To repay; to recompense or reward; to do or give in return.

re·run, rē′rən, *n.* An added running, as a later showing of a motion picture or television show after its first run; that which is being reshown; the action of rerunning.—rē·rən′, *v.t.,* **-ran, -run, -run·ning.** To run again.

re·sale, rē′sāl, rē·sāl′, *n.* The action of selling once again.

re·scind, ri·sind′, *v.t.* To repeal; to revoke or annul.

res·cue, res′kū, *v.t.,* **-cued, -cu·ing.** To free from confinement, danger, or evil; save.—*n.* The act or an instance of rescuing. **—res·cu·er,** *n.*

re·search, ri·sərch′, rē′sərch, *n.* Diligent inquiry or examination in seeking facts or principles; an experimental investigation.—*v.i., v.t.* To investigate. **—re·search·er,** *n.*

re·sem·blance, ri·zem′bləns, *n.* The state or quality of resembling; likeness.

re·sem·ble, ri·zem′bəl, *v.t.,* **-bled, -bling.** To be or look like; to have similarity to in form, figure, or qualities.

re·sent, ri·zent′, *v.t.* To be angry, indignant, or provoked at; to show ill or injured feeling for. **—re·sent·ful,** *a.*

re·sent·ment, ri·zent′mənt, *n.* A sense of injury; anger arising from a sense of wrong.

res·er·va·tion, rez·ər·vā′shən, *n.* The act of reserving or keeping back; concealment or withholding from disclosure; a condition, limitation, or qualification; a tract of public land set aside for some special purpose, esp. for the protection of wild life, or for the use of a tribe of Indians; the reserving in advance of accommodations in a hotel, airplane, or the like.

re·serve, ri·zərv′, *v.t.,* **-served, -serv·ing.** To keep in store for future use; to withhold from present use for another purpose; to keep back for a time; to retain: to *reserve* a right; to settle or arrange ahead: to *reserve* a room.—*n.* The act of reserving; that which is reserved; a piece of land set aside; a reservation; something in the mind withheld from disclosure; the habit of re-

---

a- hat, fāte, fāre, fäther; **e-** met, mē; **i-** pin, pīne; **o-** not, nōte, ôrb, moove (move), boy, pownd; **u-** cūbe, bŭll, tûk (took); **ch-** chin; **th-** thick, ᴛHen; **zh-** vizhon (vision); **ə-** ᴀgo, takᴇn, pencᴇl, lemᴏn, bᴇrd (bird).

straining the feelings; a certain formality or reticence toward others; caution in personal behavior; banking capital retained in order to meet liabilities; a branch of the military forces, not included in the regular services but trained and kept for active service in exigencies.

re·served, ri·zėrvd′, *a.* Kept for another or future use; showing reserve in behavior; restrained; reticent.

re·serv·ist, ri·zėr′vist, *n.* A member of the reserve forces of an army, navy, or other military organization.

res·er·voir, rez′ėr·vwär, rez′ėr·voor, *n.* A pond or similar place where water is collected and stored for use; a receptacle or chamber for holding a liquid or fluid, as oil or gas; a great supply, store, or reserve of anything.

re·set, rē·set′, *v.t.,* **-set, -set·ting.** To set again.

re·side, ri·zīd′, *v.i.,* **-sid·ed, -sid·ing.** To dwell permanently or for a length of time; to exist or abide (in): His influence *resides in* his astuteness; of privileges, powers, etc., to be vested (in).

res·i·dence, rez′i·dens, *n.* The act of residing; period of abode; the place where a person resides.

res·i·den·cy, rez′ə·dən·sē, *n. pl.,* **-cies.** A residence; an official residence; a period of advanced training in a medical specialty.

res·i·dent, rez′ə·dənt, *a.* Dwelling in a place to carry out one's duties; residing; inherent.—*n.* One who resides in a place for some time; a doctor during a period of training in a specialized field.

res·i·den·tial, rez·ə·den′shəl, *a.* Relating to residence or to residents; suitable or used for residence.

re·sid·u·al, ri·zij′oo·əl, *a.* Pertaining to or constituting a residue; remaining or left over.

res·i·due, rez′ə·doo, rez′ə·dū, *n.* That which remains after a part is taken, separated, or dealt with in some way; remainder; the rest.

re·sign, ri·zīn′, *v.t.* To give up, as an office or post; to submit (oneself), as to fate.—*v.i.* To relinquish one's position, often with *from.*

res·ig·na·tion, rez·ig·nā′shən, *n.* The act of resigning or giving up; a document stating that one is giving up something, esp. an office; the state of being resigned; patience.

re·signed, ri·zīnd′, *a.* Accepting whatever happens; submissive; fatalistic.

re·sil·ient, ri·zil′yənt, ri·zil′ē·ənt, *a.* Rebounding; springing back to original shape after being bent, stretched, or compressed; quickly regaining spirits or health after misfortune or illness; buoyant. **—re·sil·ience, re·sil·ien·cy,** *n.*

res·in, rez′in, *n.* Any of a class of solid or semisolid substances as rosin and mastic, obtained from the exudations of many plants, and used in making plastics, varnishes, medicines, and printing inks. **—res·in·ous,** *a.*

re·sist, ri·zist′, *v.t.* To withstand; to oppose or act in opposition to; to strive against; defeat.—*v.i.* To offer opposition. **—re·sist·er,** *n.* **—re·sist·i·ble,** *a.*

re·sist·ance, ri·zis′təns, *n.* The act of resisting; a force acting in opposition to another force so as to destroy it or to diminish its effect; the property of a conductor that limits the strength of a current by causing part of the electrical energy to be dissipated in the form of heat or light. (*Often cap.*) A guerrilla or underground force. **—re·sist·ant,** *a., n.*

re·sist·less, ri·zist′lis, *a.* Incapable of being resisted; irresistible.

re·sis·tor, ri·zis′tər, *n.* A conducting body or device put into a circuit to offer resistance for such purposes as the production of light or heat, or the control of current.

res·o·lute, rez′ə·loot, *a.* Having a fixed purpose; determined; steadfast.

res·o·lu·tion, rez·ə·loo′shən, *n.* The state of being resolute; a resolve made; a fixed purpose or determination; the state of acting with fixed purpose; firmness; a formal decision or opinion of a legislative body or other group; the act of resolving or separating into component parts; the answer or solution to a problem.

re·solve, ri·zolv′, *v.t.,* **-solved, -solv·ing.** To reduce to constituent elements or simple parts; to analyze; to separate or change by or through a process; to clear of difficulties: to *resolve* doubts; to explain; to solve; to fix in determination or purpose; to determine; to form, constitute, or express by resolution and vote, as a legislative body.—*v.i.* To form an opinion or decision; to determine; to become separated into component parts or principles.—*n.* That which has been resolved; fixed purpose of mind; a settled determination; a resolution.

re·solved, ri·zolvd′, *a.* Determined; fixed in purpose.

res·o·nance, rez′ə·nəns, *n.* The state or quality of being resonant; the property of a mechanical system enabling it to vibrate sympathetically in response to vibrations of a particular frequency from another body.

res·o·nant, rez′ə·nənt, *a.* Capable of returning sound; resounding; full of resonance; intensified by resonance; echoing back.

res·o·nate, rez′ə·nāt, *v.i.,* **-nat·ed, -nat·ing.** To resound; to exhibit resonance. *Informal.* To feel sympathetic (*to*): She *resonated to* her colleague's idea.

res·o·na·tor, rez′ə·nā·tər, *n.* That which resounds; an apparatus for increasing sound by resonance.

re·sort, ri·zôrt′, *v.i.* To go: to *resort* to a place; to have recourse: to *resort* to force; to betake oneself, esp. frequently.—*n.* Recourse; the act of visiting or frequenting; a place frequented; a vacation or recreation place; a refuge.

re·sound, ri·zownd′, *v.i.* To be filled with sound; to echo; reverberate; sound loudly; to be echoed; to be celebrated or extolled.—*v.t.* To sound loudly; to echo; extol. **—re·sound·ing,** *a.* **—re·sound·ing·ly,** *adv.*

re·source, rē′sōrs, rē′sôrs, ri·sōrs′, ri·sôrs′, *n.* Any source of aid or support, esp. one kept in reserve; an expedient action or measure; means yet untried; resort; *pl.,* funds; available sources, means, or capabilities of any kind; real and potential wealth, as of a country; the ability to deal with any problem or situation. **—re·source·ful,** ri·sōrs′fəl, ri·sôrs′fəl, *a.* **—re·source·ful·ly,** *adv.* **—re·source·ful·ness,** *n.*

re·spect, ri·spekt′, *n.* Regard; a holding in high estimation or honor; the state of being held in high regard; *pl.,* an expression of regard, esteem, or deference: to pay one's *respects.* Consideration or courtesy: *respect* for his privacy; a point or particular: wrong in this *respect;* relation; reference: with *respect* to delivery.—*v.t.* To hold in high estimation or honor; to treat with consideration; to avoid interfering with or intruding upon; to have reference or regard to. **—re·spect·ful,** *a.* **—re·spect·ful·ly,** *adv.* **—re·spect·ful·ness,** *n.*

re·spect·a·ble, ri·spek′tə·bəl, *a.* Worthy of respect; having a good reputation or character; decent; socially acceptable in a conventional way; presentable; moderately excellent; average; moderately large in number or size. **—re·spect·a·bil·i·ty,** ri·spek·tə·bil′ə·tē, *n.*

re·spect·ing, ri·spek′ting, *prep.* Regarding; in regard to; concerning.

re·spec·tive, ri·spek′tiv, *a.* Relating or pertaining severally to each of a number of persons or things.

re·spec·tive·ly, ri·spek′tiv·lē, *adv.* In their respective relations; individually in their given order.

res·pi·ra·tion, res·pə·rā′shən, *n.* The act of respiring; the inhalation and exhalation of air; breathing; in animals and plants, the sum total of the chemical and physical processes involved in oxidation by which oxygen is absorbed into the system and the oxidation products, esp. carbon dioxide, are released. **—res·pi·ra·to·ry,** res′pər·ə·tôr·ē, *a.*

res·pi·ra·tor, res′pə·rā·tər, *n.* A masklike contrivance covering the mouth, or nose and mouth, which serves as protection against the inhalation of cold air or harmful matter; a machine used for providing artificial respiration.

re·spire, ri·spīr′, *v.i.,* **-spired, -spir·ing.** To breathe; to inhale air into the lungs and exhale it.—*v.t.* To breathe in and out, as air.

res·pite, res′pit, *n.* A time of relief or rest; delay; postponement; a reprieve.

re·splend·ent, ri·splen′dənt, *a.* Very bright; shining with brilliant luster; magnificent. **—re·splend·ence,** ri·splen′dəns, *n.*

re·spond, ri·spond′, *v.i.* To answer or reply; to answer by action; to react.—*v.t.* To reply.

re·spond·ent, ri·spon′dənt, *a.* Responding; answering.—*n.* One who responds; a defendant.

re·sponse, ri·spons′, *n.* The act of responding or replying; a reply; an answer; the answer of the choir or congregation to the clergyman during a church service; the activity or behavior of an animal or a plant as a result of stimulation; reaction.

re·spon·si·bil·i·ty, ri·spon·sə·bil′ə·tē, *n. pl.,* **-ties.** The state of being responsible; that for which one is responsible; a trust, obligation, or duty; ability to meet payments or obligations; trustworthiness.

re·spon·si·ble, ri·spon′sə·bəl, *a.* Accountable for performance or discharge of duty or trust; involving responsibility; capable of making decisions; able to answer for one's behavior; reliable; trustworthy.

re·spon·sive, ri·spon′siv, *a.* Answering; responding; sensitive to influences; sympathetic.

rest, rest, *n.* The refreshing quiet or repose of sleep; refreshing ease; relief from anything that wearies, troubles, or disturbs; cessation or absence of motion: a body at *rest,* to bring a machine to *rest*; a piece or thing for something to rest on; a support or supporting device; in music, an interval or silence between tones; a mark or sign indicating it.—*v.i.* To take rest or refresh oneself with rest, as by sleeping, lying down, or relaxing the body or mind; to be at ease; to cease from motion, come to rest, or stop; to be discontinued, or go without further action or notice: to let a matter *rest*; to recline, sit, or lean for rest or ease; lie or be set for support: a ladder *resting* against a wall; to be fixed or directed, as the gaze or the eyes, on something; to be imposed as a duty or burden (*on* or *upon*); to rely (*on* or *upon*); to be based (*on* or *upon*); to lie, be found, or be as indicated: The blame *rests* with them. —*v.t.* To give rest to, or refresh with rest; to bring to rest, or to a halt or stop; to lay or place for rest, ease, or support; to base, or let depend: to *rest* one's hopes on assurances; to direct or fix, as the eyes.—**at rest,** in a motionless state, as in death or sleep; still; immobile; tranquil.

rest, rest, *n.* That which is left; the remainder; the others: The *rest* of the boys have gone.—*v.i.* To remain; to continue to be.

res·tau·rant, res′tər·ənt, res′tə·ränt, *n.* A commercial establishment serving meals or refreshments.

rest·ful, rest′fəl, *a.* Full of rest; giving rest; quiet; being at rest; peaceful.

res·ti·tu·tion, res·tə·too′shən, res·ti·tū′shən, *n.* Restoration to the former or original state or position; the restoration of property or rights previously taken away.

res·tive, res′tiv, *a.* Restless; resisting control; balky; unruly.

rest·less, rest′lis, *a.* Unquiet; continually moving; being without rest; unable to rest or sleep; not satisfied to be at rest; unsettled; discontented.

res·to·ra·tion, res·tə·rā′shən, *n.* The act of restoring; state or condition of being restored; that which has been restored.

re·stor·a·tive, ri·stōr′ə·tiv, ri·stôr′ə·tiv, *a.* Capable of restoring; pertaining to restoration.—*n.* That which restores consciousness or health.

re·store, ri·stōr′, ri·stôr′, *v.t.,* **-stored, -stor·ing.** To

bring back into existence, use, or the like; reestablish: to *restore* peace; to bring back to a former, original, or normal condition; renew: to *restore* a building; to give back or make restitution of, as anything taken away or lost.

re·strain, ri·strān′, *v.t.* To hold back; to check.

re·straint, ri·strānt′, *n.* The act of restraining; a holding back or hindering; that which restrains or hinders; self-restraint; reserve.

re·strict, ri·strikt′, *v.t.* To limit; confine; restrain within bounds. **—re·strict·ed,** *a.* **—re·strict·ed·ly,** *adv.*

re·stric·tion, ri·strik′shən, *n.* The act of restricting, or state of being restricted; that which restricts; a restraint; limitation.

re·stric·tive, ri·strik′tiv, *a.* Limiting; imposing restraint.

re·sult, ri·zəlt′, *v.i.* To proceed, spring, or rise, as a consequence, from facts, arguments, premises, a combination of circumstances, or the like; to terminate, followed by *in*: This measure will *result in* good or evil.—*n.* Consequence; conclusion; outcome; effect; product; that which proceeds naturally or logically from facts, premises, or the state of things.

re·sult·ant, ri·zəl′tənt, *a.* Following as a result or consequence.—*n.* Result; outcome.

re·sume, ri·zoom′, *v.t.,* **-sumed, -sum·ing.** To take up again after interruption; to take again: to *resume* your positions; to take back: to *resume* the car's title.—*v.i.* To begin again.

ré·su·mé, re·su·me, rez′oo·mā, rez·oo·mā′, *n.* A summing up; a summary, as of a job applicant's qualifications and experience.

re·sump·tion, ri·zəmp′shən, *n.* The act of resuming; taking back, or taking again.

re·sur·gent, ri·sər′jənt, *a.* Rising again; reviving; tending to surge back. **—re·sur·gence,** *n.*

res·ur·rect, rez·ə·rekt′, *v.t.* To raise from the dead; to restore to life; to bring back into practice or use.—*v.i.* To be restored from death.

res·ur·rec·tion, rez·ə·rek′shən, *n.* A rising again to life; the state of those who have returned to life; a revival or restoration, esp. after decay or disuse.—**the Res·ur·rec·tion,** the rising of Christ after the Crucifixion; the rising of the dead on the day of judgment.

re·sus·ci·tate, ri·səs′ə·tāt, *v.t.,* **-tat·ed, -tat·ing.** To revive; to recover, esp. from apparent death or unconsciousness.—*v.i.* To revive; to come to life again. **—re·sus·ci·ta·tion,** ri·səs·ə·tā′shən, *n.*

re·sus·ci·ta·tor, ri·səs′ə·tā·tər, *n.* One who resuscitates; a device used to initiate respiration and relieve asphyxiation.

re·tail, rē′tāl, *n.* The sale of goods in small quantities directly to a consumer.—*a.* Engaged in or relating to the sale of merchandise at retail.—rē′tāl, ri·tāl′, *v.t.* To sell in small quantities or by the piece; to sell, as goods, directly to a consumer; to repeat in detail, as a story or gossip, ri·tāl′.—rē′tāl, *v.i.* To cost at retail. —*adv.* **—re·tail·er,** *n.*

re·tain, ri·tān′, *v.t.* To keep possession of; to continue to hold or have: to *retain* heat; to keep in mind; remember; to engage, esp. by the payment of a preliminary fee, as a lawyer.

re·tain·er, ri·tā′nər, *n.* A fee paid to secure services, as of a lawyer.

re·tain·er, ri·tā′nər, *n.* One who or that which retains; a person attached to a noble house and owing it service.

re·take, rē·tāk′, *v.t.,* **-took, -tak·en, -tak·ing.** To take again; to recapture; to photograph, film, or record again.—rē′tāk, *n.* The act of retaking; a retaking: A *retake* was ordered of both the film and sound tracks.

re·tal·i·ate, ri·tal′ē·āt, *v.t.,* **-at·ed, -at·ing.** To repay, as a wrong or injury, with the like.—*v.i.* To return like for like, esp. to do evil in return for evil. **—re·tal·i·a-**

---

a- hat, fāte, fâre, fäther; **e-** met, mē; **i-** pin, pīne; **o-** not, nōte, ôrb, moove (move), boy, pownd; **u-** cūbe, bŭll, tûk (took); **ch-** chin; **th-** thick, ŧhen; **zh-** vizhon (vision); **ə-** əgo, takən, pencəl, lemən, bərd (bird).

tion, ri·tal·ē·ā′shən, *n.* **—re·tai·i·a·to·ry,** ri·tal′ē·ə·tôr·ē, *a.*

re·tard, ri·tärd′, *v.t.* To cause to slow; delay or hinder, as the course, progress, or advance of; to impede. —*v.i.* To be delayed.—*n.* Retardation; delay. **—re·tard·ant,** *a., n.*

re·tar·da·tion, rē·tär·dā′shən, *n.* The act of retarding; the condition of being retarded; that which retards; hindrance.

re·tard·ed, ri·tär′did, *a.* Showing retardation; abnormally slow, esp. in mental development.

retch, rech, *v.i.* To make an effort to vomit; to strain, as in vomiting.

re·ten·tion, ri·ten′shən, *n.* The act of retaining; the state of being retained; the capacity for retaining; the power of memory.

re·ten·tive, ri·ten′tiv, *a.* Characterized by retention; having strong powers of recollection, esp. of learned material.

ret·i·cent, ret′ə·sənt, *a.* Disposed to be silent; not inclined to speak freely; reserved. **—ret·i·cence,** *n.*

ret·i·na, ret′ə·nə, ret′nə, *n. pl.,* **-nas, -nae,** -nē. The innermost coat of the part of the eyeball, consisting of light-sensitive cells connected to the brain by the optic nerve, and serving to receive the image transmitted by the lens. **—ret·i·nal,** *a.*

ret·i·nue, ret′ə·noo, ret′ə·nū, *n.* The attendants of a distinguished personage.

re·tire, ri·tīr′, *v.i.,* **-tired, -tir·ing.** To withdraw; to go back; to draw back; to go from a company or from a public place into privacy; to retreat from action or danger; to withdraw from business or active life; to recede; to go to bed.—*v.t.* To designate as no longer being qualified for active service: to *retire* a military officer; to withdraw from circulation by taking up and paying: to *retire* a bill; to put out, as a player, in baseball.

re·tired, ri·tīrd′, *a.* Secluded apart from public view: a *retired* life, a *retired* locality; withdrawn from business or active life; pertaining to such withdrawal: *retired* pay.

re·tire·ment, ri·tīr′mənt, *n.* The act of retiring; state of living a retired life; seclusion; privacy.

re·tir·ing, ri·tīr′ing, *a.* Withdrawing; retreating; reserved.

re·tool, rē·tool′, *v.t., v.i.* To equip with new tools or machinery, esp. for the manufacture of new or redesigned products; to reorganize, as for the purpose of modernizing.

re·tort, ri·tôrt′, *v.t.* To answer, as an argument or accusation, by another to the contrary; reply quickly, and usu. harshly or incisively; to return in kind, as a deed or statement.—*v.i.* To make a retort or retorts. —*n.* The act of retorting; a severe, incisive, or witty reply.

re·tort, ri·tôrt′, *n.* A vessel, commonly a glass bulb with a long neck bent downward, used for distilling or decomposing substances by heat.

re·touch, rē·tech′, *v.t.* To improve by new touches or the like, as a painting, photographic negative, etc.

re·trace, ri·trās′, *v.t.,* **-traced, -trac·ing.** To trace or track back; to go over again.

re·tract, ri·trakt′, *v.t., v.i.* To draw back or in, as claws; to withdraw or disavow, as a statement, opinion, offer, promise, etc. **—re·trac·tion,** *n.* **—re·trac·tor,** *n.*

re·trac·tile, ri·trak′təl, *a.* Capable of being drawn back or in, as a cat's claws.

re·tread, rē·tred′, *v.t.* To put a new tread on. —rē′tred, *n.* A tire whose tread has been replaced.

re·treat, ri·trēt′, *n.* The act of withdrawing; a military operation by which troops retire in advance of an enemy; the signal for a retreat; on a military post, the signal, as by bugle, for the lowering of the flag at sunset; a place or period of retirement, self-examination, religious meditation, or the like.—*v.i.* To make a retreat; to withdraw.**—beat a retreat,** to retreat quickly or ignominiously.

re·trench, ri·trench′, *v.t.* To cut down or reduce, as expenses.—*v.i.* To economize; reduce expenses. **—re·trench·ment,** *n.*

re·tri·al, rē·trī′əl, *n.* A second or new trial.

ret·ri·bu·tion, re·trə·bū′shən, *n.* Requital, esp. punishment for wrong or evil done.

re·trieve, ri·trēv′, *v.t.,* **-trieved, -triev·ing.** To recover or regain; to rescue or save; to restore or bring back to a former and better state; to make amends for; to make good or repair; of dogs, to find and fetch, as killed or wounded game.—*v.i.* To retrieve game.

re·triev·er, ri·trē′ver, *n.* One who or that which retrieves; a dog bred or trained to retrieve game.

ret·ro·ac·tive, re·trō·ak′tiv, *a.* Referring to a prior time and effective as of that time: a *retroactive* pay raise; retrospective.

ret·ro·grade, re′trə·grād, *a.* Moving backward; tending to fall back toward a worse condition.—*v.i.,* **-grad·ed, -grad·ing.** To move or go backward; to fall back toward a worse condition.

ret·ro·gress, re′trə·gres, re·trə·gres′, *v.i.* To move backward; go back; revert. **—ret·ro·gres·sion,** re·trə·gresh′ən, *n.* **—ret·ro·gres·sive,** re·trə·gres′iv, *a.*

ret·ro·rock·et, re′trō·rok·it, *n.* A decelerating rocket attached to a space vehicle to supply braking action under certain conditions.

ret·ro·spect, re′trə·spekt, *n.* Contemplation of the past; a survey of past time, events, or experiences.**—in ret·ro·spect,** in considering what is past. **—ret·ro·spec·tion,** ret·rə·spek′shən, *n.* **—ret·ro·spec·tive,** ret·rə·spek′tiv, *a.,* .

re·turn, ri·tərn′, *v.t.* To give back; to turn back or in the reverse direction; to put, bring, take, or send back: to *return* a book to its shelf; to restore; to report or announce officially; to render, as a verdict; to reciprocate, repay: to *return* a compliment.—*v.i.* To turn back or away; to go or come back; to make reply, or retort.—*n.* The act or fact of returning; a bringing, sending, or giving back; a going or coming back; that which is returned. *Often pl.* A report, esp. a formal or official report: election *returns;* a yield or profit, as from labor, land, business, or investment.—*a.* Of or pertaining to return or returning: the *return* trip; sent, given, or done in return: a *return* shot or thrust; recurring or taking place a second time: a *return* match in sports.

re·turn·a·ble, ri·tər′nə·bəl, *a.* Able to be returned, as merchandise; legally required to be returned.

re·turn·ee, ri·tər·nē′, ri·tər′nē, *n.* One who has returned, esp. a veteran returning from overseas military service.

re·un·ion, rē·ūn′yən, *n.* The act of coming together again; a gathering of relatives, friends, schoolmates, etc., meeting after separation.

re·u·nite, rē·ū·nīt′, *v.t., v.i.,* **-nit·ed, -nit·ing.** To unite again; to bring together again.

rev, rev, *n. Informal.* Revolution, as of a motor, propeller, wheel, or the like.—*v.t.,* **revved, rev·ving.** *Informal.* To increase the speed of, usu. used with *up.*

re·vamp, rē·vamp′, *v.t.* To patch up again; repair.

re·veal, ri·vēl′, *v.t.* To make known; to lay open to view, display, or exhibit.

rev·eil·le, rev′ə·lē, *n.* The beat of a drum, a bugle call, or some other signal given about daybreak to awaken soldiers.

rev·el, rev′əl, *v.i.* To take great pleasure or delight, usu. followed by *in:* He *reveled in* their astonishment; to make merry; indulge in boisterous festivities.—*n.* Boisterous merrymaking or festivity; revelry. **—rev·el·er,** *n.*

rev·e·la·tion, rev·ə·lā′shən, *n.* The act of revealing; disclosure; something revealed; a disclosure of divine will or presence.

Rev·e·la·tion, rev·ə·lā′shən, *n. Often pl.* The last book of the New Testament; the Apocalypse.

rev·el·ry, rev′əl·rē, *n. pl.,* **-ries.** An act of reveling; boisterous or noisy festivity.

re•venge, ri•venj′, *v.t.*, **-venged, -veng•ing.** To avenge; to inflict injury for or on account of.—*n.* The act of revenging; retaliation; the infliction of pain or injury in return for a wrong.

re•venge•ful, ri•venj′fəl, *a.* Full of revenge; harboring revenge.

rev•e•nue, rev′ə•nū, rev′ə•noo, *n.* Receipts of a government from taxes and duties; income in general.

rev•e•nu•er, rev′ə•noo•ər, rev′ə•nū•ər, *n. Informal.* A U.S. Treasury Department agent.

re•ver•ber•ate, ri•vėr′bə•rāt, *v.t.*, **-at•ed, -at•ing.** To return, as sound; to send back; to reecho; to reflect, as heat or light.—*v.i.* To rebound; to be reflected, as rays of light; to reecho; to resound. **—re•ver•ber•a•tion**, ri•vėr•bə•rā′shən, *n.*

re•vere, ri•vėr′, *v.t.*, **-vered, -ver•ing.** To regard with respect and affection mingled with awe; to venerate.

rev•er•ence, rev′ər•əns, rev′rəns, *n.* An attitude of deep respect, esp. an awed, adoring respect; veneration; a bow; the state of being honored. (*Cap.*) A common title of the clergy, used with *his* and *your.* —*v.t.*, **-enced, -enc•ing.** To regard with reverence.

rev•er•end, rev′ər•ənd, rev′rənd, *a.* Worthy of reverence. (*Often cap.*) A title of respect given to clergymen.—*n. Informal.* A clergyman.

rev•er•ent, rev′ər•ənt, rev′rənt, *a.* Expressing reverence.

rev•er•en•tial, rev•ə•ren′shəl, *a.* Proceeding from reverence, or expressing it.

rev•er•ie, rev•er•y, rev′ə•rē, *n. pl.,* **-ies.** A waking dream; a loose or irregular train of thought occurring in musing or meditation.

re•ver•sal, ri•vėr′səl, *n.* The act of reversing or the condition of being reversed.

re•verse, ri•vėrs′, *v.t.*, **-versed, -vers•ing.** To turn or put in an opposite or contrary direction or position; to turn upside down or inside out; to overturn, set aside, or annul: to *reverse* a judgment or decree; to cause to operate or revolve in a contrary direction, as a mechanism.—*v.i.* To move or change to a contrary direction; to shift a mechanism into reverse direction.—*a.* Of an opposite or contrary condition, arrangement, character, or the like: in *reverse* direction; having the back or opposite side presented to view: the *reverse* side of the question; of a motion or manner of operation opposite to the usual: a mechanism running in *reverse* gear.—*n.* That which is turned about or contrary; the back or opposite side or surface of something; an unfavorable change or turn of affairs: a business *reverse*; a gear or mechanism that reverses something; the state of moving in reverse.

re•vers•i•ble, ri•vėr′sə•bəl, *a.* Capable of being reversed; capable of being turned outside in, as a jacket; having two usable sides.

re•ver•sion, ri•vėr′zhən, *n.* A reverting or returning, as to original form or condition; the act of turning about; a reversal; the returning of an estate to the grantor or his heirs.

re•vert, ri•vėrt′, *v.i.* To return or come back; to turn back; to return to the possession of the donor, or of the former owner or heirs.

re•view, ri•vū′, *v.t.* To view or examine again; to notice or study critically; to write a critical notice of or discuss critically after an examination; to discover merits or defects, as a newly published book; to inspect, esp. to make a formal or official examination of the state of: to *review* troops; to look back on.—*v.i.* To make or write reviews.—*n.* A second or repeated view; a reexamination or revision; renewed study, as for a test; a general survey; a critical examination of a new publication, with remarks; a criticism; a critique; an official inspection of military or naval forces.

re•view•er, ri•vū′ər, *n.* One who reviews; one who critically examines a new publication, movie, play, or the like.

re•vile, ri•vīl′, *v.t.*, **-viled, -vil•ing.** To assail with contemptuous language; to speak evil of.—*v.i.* To use contemptuous language.

re•vise, ri•vīz′, *v.t.*, **-vised, -vis•ing.** To examine or reexamine and make corrections on; to look over with care for corrections; to change and amend.—*n.* A revision; a reexamination and correction; a corrected proof after revision.

re•vi•sion, ri•vizh′ən, *n.* The act of revising; a reexamination for correction; that which is revised.

re•vi•sion•ist, ri•vizh′ən•ist, *n.* One who favors revisions, esp. in an ideology or school of thought. **—re•vi•sion•ism**, *n.*

re•viv•al, ri•vī′vəl, *n.* The act of reviving, or the state of being revived; restoration to life or consciousness, or to vigor, strength, or the like; restoration to use, acceptance, or currency; an awakening, in a church or a community, of interest in religion; a service or a series of services for the purpose of effecting a religious awakening.

re•viv•al•ist, ri•vī′və•list, *n.* One who promotes a religious revival.

re•vive, ri•vīv′, *v.t.*, **-vived, -viv•ing.** To set going or activate again: to *revive* old feuds; to make operative or valid again; to bring back into notice, use, or currency; to present again, as an old play or film; to restore to life or to consciousness.—*v.i.* To return to life or consciousness; to gain fresh strength or vigor; to return to use; to become operative or valid again.

rev•o•ca•ble, rev′ə•kə•bəl, *a.* Capable of being revoked.

rev•o•ca•tion, rev•ə•kā′shən, *n.* The act of recalling, revoking, or annulling.

re•voke, ri•vōk′, *v.t.*, **-voked, -vok•ing.** To annul by recalling or taking back; to make void; to cancel, repeal, or reverse.

re•volt, ri•vōlt′, *v.i.* To rebel against established authority; to be grossly offended or disgusted, followed by *at.*—*v.t.* To repel; to disgust.—*n.* The act of revolting; rebellion.

rev•o•lu•tion, rev•ə•loo′shən, *n.* The act of revolving or rotating; the complete overthrow and replacement of a government or political system by the governed; a radical change of circumstances in a scientific, social, or industrial system; a cycle of time or a succession of events that recurs periodically; a circular motion around an axis; the completed turn so made; one complete orbit made by a heavenly body around another; one full rotation of a planet or body on its axis.

rev•o•lu•tion•ar•y, rev•ə•loo′shə•ner•ē, *a.* Pertaining to a political revolution; tending to produce a revolution; suggesting drastic change.—*n. pl.,* **-ies.** A revolutionist.

rev•o•lu•tion•ist, rev•ə•loo′shə•nist, *n.* A person who advocates or participates in a revolution; a revolutionary.

rev•o•lu•tion•ize, rev•ə•loo′shə•nīz, *v.t.*, **-ized, -iz•ing.** To bring about a revolution in; to effect a complete or fundamental change in. **—rev•o•lu•tion•iz•er**, *n.*

re•volve, ri•volv′, *v.i.*, **-volved, -volv•ing.** To move along a curving path around a center; to travel in an orbit; to rotate on an axis; to recur cyclically: The years *revolve.*—*v.t.* To cause to circle round or rotate; to turn over in the mind; to ponder.

re•volv•er, ri•vol′vər, *n.* A pistol having a revolving breech cylinder so constructed as to discharge several shots in quick succession without being reloaded.

re•vue, ri•vū′, *n.* A loosely constructed and often satirical theatrical exhibition of a topical character, consisting of dances, skits, and songs.

re•vul•sion, ri•vəl′shən, *n.* A sudden and strong

---

a- hat, fāte, fāre, fäther; **e-** met, mē; **i-** pin, pīne; **o-** not, nōte, ôrb, moove (move), boy, pownd; **u-** cūbe, bŭll, tŭk (took); **ch-** chin; **th-** thick, ŧhen; **zh-** vizhon (vision); **ə-** əgo, takən, pencəl, lemən, bərd (bird).

re·ward, ri·wôrd′, *v.t.* To give something to in return; to bestow a recompense, remuneration, or token of favor upon.—*n.* That which is given in return for achievement or service; recompense; a sum of money offered for capturing or detecting a criminal, or for the recovery of anything lost.

re·write, rē·rīt′, *v.t.,* -wrote, -writ·ten, -writ·ing. To write over again, esp. in altered form; to revise.—rē′rīt, *n.* A revision; a news story or other article that has been rewritten.

rhap·sod·ic, rap·sod′ik, *a.* Having the characteristics of a rhapsody in form or feeling; excessively enthusiastic. Also **rhap·sod·i·cal. —rhap·sod·i·cal·ly,** *adv.*

rhap·so·dize, rap′sə·dīz, *v.i., v.t.,* -dized, -diz·ing. To talk, write, or recite rhapsodically.

rhap·so·dy, rap′sə·dē, *n. pl.,* -dies. A spoken or written work depending less on logical structure than on emotional appeal; a musical composition of irregular form, usu. instrumental. —**rhap·so·dist,** *n.*

rhe·a, rē′ə, *n.* Any of the large, flightless S. American birds resembling the African ostrich but smaller and having three toes.

rhe·ni·um, rē′nē·əm, *n.* A rare metallic element resembling manganese, with a high melting point.

rhe·o·stat, rē′ə·stat, *n.* An instrument for regulating the strength of an electric current by means of adjustable resistances.

rhe·sus, rē′səs, *n.* A short-tailed, light brown monkey, native to India, used for research in medicine and biology.

rhet·o·ric, ret′ər·ik, *n.* The art of effective discourse, spoken or written; persuasive oratory; artificial, exaggerated, or bombastic language.

rhe·tor·i·cal, ri·tôr′ə·kəl, *a.* Pertaining to, exhibiting, or involving rhetoric; used for oratorical display; grandiloquent.

rhe·tor·i·cal ques·tion, *n.* A question which is put forward to create an effect, not to receive an answer.

rhet·o·ri·cian, ret·ə·rish′ən, *n.* One well versed in rhetoric; a speaker or writer of elaborate prose.

rheum, room, *n.* A thin watery fluid discharged by the mucous glands, as in catarrh; a cold; any watery matter which collects in the eyes, nose, or mouth.

rheu·mat·ic, roo·mat′ik, *a.* Pertaining to or characteristic of rheumatism; affected with rheumatism.—*n.* One subject to or afflicted with rheumatism. —**rheu·mat·i·cal·ly,** *adv.*

rheu·mat·ic fe·ver, *n.* A severe infectious disease, usu. occurring in young adults or children, characterized by painful swollen joints, fever, and often by inflamed heart lining and valves.

rheu·ma·tism, roo′mə·tiz·əm, *n.* A painful inflammation affecting muscles and joints, attended by swelling and stiffness.

rhine·stone, rīn′stōn, *n.* An artificial gem made of paste or glass, often cut to imitate the diamond.

rhi·no, rī′nō, *n. pl.,* -nos, -no. A rhinoceros.

rhi·noc·er·os, rī·nos′ər·əs, *n. pl.,* -os·es, -os. Any of various large, thick-skinned mammals found in Asia and Africa, and having one or two upright horns on the snout.

rhi·zome, rī′zōm, *n.* A rootlike stem, either lying on or under the ground, which usually produces roots below ground and sends up shoots progressively from the upper surface.

rho·di·um, rō′dē·əm, *n.* A silver-white metallic element found in platinum ores, used in electroplating to inhibit corrosion.

rho·do·den·dron, rō·də·den′drən, *n.* Any of several evergreen shrubs and trees with showy pink, purple, or white flowers and oval or oblong leaves.

rhom·bic, rom′bik, *a.* Being of the form of a rhombus.

rhom·boid, rom′boyd, *n.* A quadrilateral figure whose opposite sides and angles are equal, but which is neither equilateral nor equiangular.—*a.* Shaped like a rhombus or rhomboid. Also **rhom·boi·dal,** rom·boy′dəl.

rhom·bus, rom′bəs, *n. pl.,* -bus·es, -bi, -bī. A quadrilateral figure whose sides are equal and the opposite sides parallel, and whose angles are usually oblique rather than right.

rhu·barb, roo′bärb, *n.* A large garden plant having thick leaf stalks used for making dessert sauces, pies, and tarts. *Informal.* A noisy dispute.

rhyme, rim, *n.* A correspondence of sound in the final portions of two or more syllables; a word having a sound similar to another, as *sound* and *round;* the correspondence in sound of the terminating word or syllable of one line of poetry with that of another line; poetry; meter; a verse or poem with corresponding sounds at the ends of the lines.—*v.i.,* rhymed, rhym·ing. To form a rhyme; to make verses.—*v.t.* To put into rhyme; to use, as sounds or as rhymes.

rhyme·ster, rīm′stər, *n.* A maker of rhymes; an inferior poet.

rhythm, rith′əm, *n.* Measured movement, as in dancing, music, verse, or the like; movement or procedure with regular recurrence of a beat, accent, etc.; a specific arrangement of accented and unaccented beats, and long and short durations: the waltz *rhythm,* limerick *rhythm.* —**rhyth·mic,** rith′mik, *a.* —**rhyth·mi·cal,** rith′mə·kəl, *a.* —**rhyth·mi·cal·ly,** *adv.*

rib, rib, *n.* One of the slender curved bones that attach from each side of the vertebral column in man and most other vertebrates enclosing the thoracic cavity and protecting certain important organs; a cut of beef or other meat that includes one or several ribs; something resembling a rib in form, use, or position, as a spoke of an umbrella; a principal vein in a leaf; a prominent ridge or wale on cloth, such as corduroy. —*v.t.,* ribbed, rib·bing. To form or equip with ribs; to enclose or protect with ribs. *Informal.* To make, as a person, the butt of a joke; to tease.

rib·ald, rib′əld, *a.* Offensive or vulgar in speech; coarsely joking or mocking; abusive or irreverent. —**rib·ald·ry,** *n. pl.,* -ries.

rib·bon, rib′ən, *n.* A narrow band of silk, satin, or other material generally used as an ornament or a fastener; a narrow band of inked cloth, as used in a typewriter; a narrow, thin strip of anything suggestive of a ribbon.

ri·bo·fla·vin, rī′bō·flā·vin, *n.* A growth-producing crystalline compound belonging to the vitamin B complex, occurring naturally in milk, liver, egg yolk, leafy vegetables, and prepared synthetically.

ri·bo·nu·cle·ic ac·id, rī·bō·noo·klē′ik, *n.* A nucleic acid occurring chiefly in cytoplasm.

rice, rīs, *n.* The starchy fruit or grain of a species of grass cultivated in warm climates and constituting an important food; the plant itself.—*v.t.* riced, ric·ing. To reduce to a form resembling that of rice: to *rice* potatoes.

rich, rich, *a.* Having abundant material possessions; wealthy; well supplied; abounding; productive; fertile; composed of valuable ingredients; sumptuous; costly; abounding in nutritive or agreeable qualities: *rich* soil; excessively sweet, luscious, or highly flavored, as food; gratifying to the senses; vivid; bright; sweet, mellow, or full in tone; highly fragrant; containing a high ratio of gasoline to air. *Informal.* Very amusing; absurd. —**rich·ness,** *n.*

rich·es, rich′iz, *n. pl.* That which makes rich; abundant possessions; wealth.

rick, rik, *n.* A stack or pile of corn or hay, the top part rounded and often thatched to protect the pile from rain.—*v.t.* To pile in ricks.

rick·ets, rik′its, *n.* A disease of children in which there is usually some softening and distortion of the bones due to faulty deposition of calcium or a vitamin D deficiency, or both.

rick·et·y, rik′ə·tē, *a.,* -i·er, -i·est. Shaky; ready to collapse; affected with rickets; feeble or imperfect in general; irregular, as in movement. —**rick·et·i·ness,** *n.*

rick·shaw, rik′shô, *n.* A small, two-wheeled vehicle drawn by one or more men, used in the Orient. Also **rick·sha, jin·rik·i·sha.**

ric·o·chet, rik·ə·shā′, *n.* A glancing rebound, as of a projectile off a flat surface.—*v.i.* To skip, as a stone, along the surface of water.

rid, rid, *v.t.,* **rid or rid·ded, rid·ding.** To free; to deliver; to clear; to disencumber: to *rid* a person of a burden.

rid·dance, rid′əns, *n.* The act of ridding; a clearing away.—**good rid·dance,** fortunate relief from something disagreeable.

rid·dle, rid′əl, *n.* A proposition put in obscure or ambiguous terms to puzzle or exercise the ingenuity; a puzzling question; anything or anyone puzzling. —*v.t.,* **-dled, -dling.** To solve; to explain.—*v.i.* To speak ambiguously or in riddles.

rid·dle, rid′əl, *n.* A large sieve with coarse meshes, employed for separating coarser materials from finer. —*v.t.,* **-dled, -dling.** To pass through or separate with a riddle; screen; to perforate with holes.

ride, rid, *v.i.,* **rode, rid·den, rid·ing.** To be carried on the back of an animal; sit on and manage a horse or other animal in motion; to be borne along on or in a vehicle or any kind of conveyance; to be carried on something as if on horseback; to move or float on the water; to depend upon: the future *rides* on this election. *Informal.* To continue without change or interruption: Let the matter *ride.*—*v.t.* To sit on and manage; to sit or be mounted on, as if on horseback; be carried or borne along on; to control, dominate, or tyrannize over. *Informal.* To harass or torment; to cause to ride.—*n.* A journey or excursion on a horse or in a vehicle; a device or conveyance for riding on, as in an amusement park.—**ride out,** to sustain or endure successfully.

rid·er, rī′dər, *n.* One who or that which rides; a passenger on a conveyance; a clause added to a legislative bill, often having nothing to do with the subject of the bill itself.

ridge, rij, *n.* The long and narrow upper part or crest of something, as a hill or a wave; a long, narrow elevation of land, or a chain of hills or mountains; the horizontal line in which the tops of the rafters of a roof meet; any raised narrow strip, as in plowed ground or on cloth. —*v.t.,* **ridged, ridg·ing.** To provide with or form into a ridge or ridges; mark with or as with ridges.—*v.i.* To form ridges.

ridge·pole, rij′pōl, *n.* A horizontal timber at the top of a roof, or pole at the top of a tent.

rid·i·cule, rid′ə·kūl, *n.* Words or actions intended to excite contemptuous laughter at a person or thing; derision.—*v.t.,* **-culed, -cul·ing.** To deride; make fun of.

ri·dic·u·lous, ri·dik′yə·ləs, *a.* Deserving or causing ridicule or derision; absurd; preposterous, or laughable.

rife, rīf, *a.* Prevailing; prevalent; abundant; abounding, followed by *with.*

rif·fle, rif′əl, *n.* An expanse of wavy, ripply water caused by a ridge, shoal, or other obstruction; such an obstruction; a way of shuffling cards.—*v.t.,* **-fled, -fling.** To shuffle (cards) by flipping through each of two parts of the deck with the thumbs so that the cards intermix.—*v.i.* To flip or thumb (through), as a book.

riff·raff, rif′raf, *n.* Worthless or low persons; the disreputable element of society; the rabble.

ri·fle, rī′fəl, *n.* A shoulder gun having spiral grooves cut in the barrel to spin the bullet so as to increase its range and accuracy.—*v.t.,* **-fled, -fling.** To groove, as the inside of a gun barrel.

ri·fle, rī′fəl, *v.t.,* **-fled, -fling.** To ransack and rob; to search and rob; to plunder, pillage, or strip, as a conquered city; to carry off, as booty.

ri·fling, rī′fling, *n.* The act or process of cutting rifles or spiral grooves in a gun barrel; the system of spiral grooves in a rifle.

rift, rift, *n.* A cleft; fissure; geological fault; a disagreement or estrangement.—*v.t., v.i.* To burst open; to split.

rig, rig, *v.t.,* **rigged, rig·ging.** To fit, as a vessel or a mast, with the necessary shrouds, stays, and other equipment; to fit, as shrouds, stays, or braces, to the proper mast, yard, or the like; to furnish with equipment; to fit, usu. with *out* or *up;* to prepare, esp. in a makeshift fashion, often with *up. Informal.* To dress, or adorn with finery; to manipulate, control, or fix, usu. fraudulently, for one's own advantage or profit.—*n.* The arrangement of the masts, spars, and sails on a boat or ship; equipment; apparatus: the *rig* of an oil well. *Informal.* A vehicle with a horse or horses, as for driving; dress, costume, or finery.

rig·ger, rig′ər, *n.* One who rigs; one whose occupation is the fitting of the rigging of ships.

rig·ging, rig′ing, *n.* The ropes and other equipment used to support and work the sails of a ship.

right, rīt, *a.* In accordance with what is just or good, as conduct; in conformity with fact, reason, or some standard; correct: the *right* answer; correct in judgment, opinion, or action; sound or normal, as the mind; in good health or spirits; in a satisfactory state or in good order: the *right* setup; principal, front, or upper: the *right* side of cloth; most advantageous or desirable; fitting or appropriate: to say the *right* thing; real or genuine; belonging, pertaining to, or near the side of a person or thing which is turned toward the east when the face is turned toward the north: opposed to *left;* formed by or with reference to a line or plane that is perpendicular to a base: a *right* angle. —*n. Often pl.* A just claim or title, whether legal, prescriptive, or moral. That which is just or moral: a choice between *right* and wrong; that which accords with fact, reason, or propriety; the condition of being correct; the right hand; the right side or direction; a blow delivered with the right hand; anything intended for use on the right side. (*Cap.*) Politically conservative or reactionary persons, parties, or blocs, usu. preceded by *the.*—*adv.* In a straight line; straight or directly; quite or completely: *right* to the ceiling; immediately: *right* after dinner; exactly, precisely, or just: *right* there; uprightly or righteously; correctly or accurately: to hear *right;* properly or fittingly: to serve one *right;* advantageously, favorably, or well; toward or on the right: to turn *right;* very, used in titles: the *Right* Reverend.—*v.t.* To bring to an upright position; to put in a proper state; to make correct: to *right* errors; to do justice to; to redress, as a wrong.—*v.i.* To resume an upright or the proper position.—**by rights,** in justice or fairness.—**right a·way** or **off,** immediately; without condition or order. —**right·ly,** *adv.* —**right·ness,** *n.*

right an·gle, *n.* An angle of 90 degrees.

right·eous, rī′chəs, *a.* Upright; virtuous; acting in accordance with the dictates of morality; agreeing with right; just; equitable.

right·ful, rīt′fəl, *a.* Having a right or just claim; legitimate; equitable or just, as actions; belonging by just claim; legal; proper.

right-hand, rīt′hand′, *a.* Of, for, or with the right hand; on or to the right; most efficient or useful as a helper.

right-hand·ed, rīt′han′did, *a.* Having the right hand or arm more serviceable than the left; preferring to use the right hand; adapted to or performed by the right hand; situated on the side of the right hand; moving or rotating from left to right, or clockwise: a *right-handed* screw.—*adv.*

a- hat, fāte, fãre, fäther; e- met, mē; i- pin, pīne; o- not, nōte, ôrb, moove (move), boy, pownd; u- cūbe, bŭll, tûk (took); ch- chin; th- thick, ŧhen; zh- vizhon (vision); ə- əgo, takən, pencəl, lemən, bərd (bird).

right·ism, rī′tiz·əm, n. (Sometimes cap.) Advocacy of conservatism or reactionary actions or ideas, as in politics. —**right·ist,** n., a. (Sometimes cap.)

right of way, n. A right of passage, as over another's land; statutory or common law allowing one particular vehicle to proceed before another. Also **right-of-way,** rīt′əv·wā.

right tri·an·gle, n. A triangle which has a right angle.

right wing, n. Persons belonging to a reactionary or conservative political group. —**right-wing,** rīt′wing, a. —**right-wing·er,** n.

rig·id, rij′id, a. Stiff; not pliant; not easily bent: a rigid pole; set; fixed; strict in opinion, practice, or discipline; severely strict; rigorous; inflexible. —**ri·gid·i·ty,** ri·jid′ə·tē, n.

rig·ma·role, rig′mə·rōl, n. Incoherent statements; nonsense; unnecessarily complicated or ritualistic procedure.

rig·or, rig′ər, n. Rigidity; austerity; strictness; inflexible exactness; sternness; harshness.

rig·or·ous, rig′ər·əs, a. Characterized by rigor; severe; stringent; scrupulously accurate or precise.

rile, rīl, v.t., **riled, ril·ing.** Informal. To stir or unsettle, as water; to anger; to irritate.

rill, ril, n. A small brook; a rivulet.

rim, rim, n. The border, edge, or margin of a thing, esp. of an object that is circular.—v.t. **rimmed, rim·ming.** To provide or form with a rim.

rime, rim, n. Hoarfrost.—v.t., v.i., **rimed, rim·ing.** To coat with or congeal into hoarfrost.

rime, rim, n. Rhyme.—v.t., v.i., **rimed, rim·ing.** Rhyme. —**rim·er,** n.

rind, rīnd, n. The outward coat or covering, usu. firm or hard, as of trees, fruits, or cheese.

ring, ring, n. A circular band of metal or other material: a key ring; a small, circular band, as of precious metal, for wearing on the finger; anything having the form of a circular band; one of the concentric layers of wood produced yearly in the trunks of trees; a circular line or mark; a circular course: to dance in a ring; a number of persons or things disposed in a circle; a group of persons cooperating for selfish, sometimes illicit, purposes; an enclosed area for races, games, etc., esp. a square-shaped area for boxing matches. —**the ring,** prize fighting.—v.i. To form a ring or rings; move in a ring.—v.t. To surround with a ring; to draw a ring around; to form into a ring; to provide with a ring or rings; to mark with rings. —**ring·er,** n.

ring, ring, v.i., **rang, rung, ring·ing.** To produce a resonant sound, as a bell which is struck; to resound or reverberate; to cause to sound, as a bell; to express or exhibit a specified quality: his offer rings hollow; to experience buzzing.—v.t. To cause to sound; to sound by striking or ringing; to celebrate or proclaim by ringing: The chimes rang the news; to summon, usher, or signal by a bell ring, followed by in or out: to ring in the New Year.—n. The sound of a bell or other sonorous body; any loud sound continued, repeated, or reverberated; a characteristic sound: the ring of falsehood; a telephone call; a chime of bells; the act of ringing a bell.

ring·er, ring′ər, n. One who or something which rings, as a chime or bell. Informal. One who or that which is remarkably like another person or thing: He is a ringer for my brother.

ring·lead·er, ring′lē·dər, n. One who leads a group, esp. in violation of law or authority.

ring·let, ring′lit, n. A curl, esp. a curl of hair; a small circle or ring.

ring·mas·ter, ring′mas·tər, n. One who has charge of the performances in a circus ring.

ring·side, ring′sīd, n. The area directly around a ring, as the first row around a boxing ring; a place which offers a very close view.—a., adv.

ring·worm, ring′wərm, n. A disease caused by fungi, appearing in the form of rings or patches on different parts of the body, esp. on the scalp.

rink, ringk, n. A smooth, usu. artificial expanse of ice used for ice skating, etc.; a smooth, usu. wooden flooring for roller skating; the building used for ice or roller skating.

rinse, rins, v.t., **rinsed, rins·ing.** To wash lightly, as by running water over or into or by plunging momentarily into water: to rinse a dish; to cleanse in this manner: to rinse one's mouth; to remove, as dirt or soap, in this way.—n. The act or process of rinsing; any product used for rinsing.

ri·ot, rī′ət, n. Any public disturbance of a boisterous and violent nature, usu. caused by a large crowd; a vivid or brilliant display, as of colors; boisterous festivity; revelry; wild or loose activity. Informal. An amusing or hilarious person or thing.—v.i. To participate in a public disorder; to act in an unrestrained or wanton manner.—v.t. To spend in riotous activity, as time or money.—**run ri·ot,** to act without restraint; to grow abundantly, as vines.—**read the ri·ot act to,** to reprimand vehemently and usu. threateningly.

ri·ot·ous, rī′ə·təs, a. Characterized by or of the nature of rioting; inciting to or taking part in a riot; marked by or indulging in unrestrained revelry; boisterous or uproarious: riotous mirth.

rip, rip, v.t., **ripped, rip·ping.** To separate or divide by cutting or tearing, as fabric; to tear or cut open, as a package; to take out by cutting or tearing, as a page; to cut or split wood with the grain.—v.i. To be torn apart. Informal. To move recklessly: He ripped into the fracas.—n. A rent caused by tearing; a tear.—**rip off.** Informal. To steal; swindle; vitiate. —**rip·per,** n.

rip, rip, n. A stretch of choppy water at sea or in a river.

ri·par·i·an, ri·per′ē·ən, a. Referring to or located on the bank of a body of water.

ripe, rīp, a. Ready for reaping and use; resembling a mature fruit; rosy; brought to perfection or to the best state; fit for use, as cheese; fully developed; matured; advanced: of a ripe age; consummate: a ripe scholar; ready for action or effect: ripe for a war.

rip·en, rī′pən, v.t., v.i. To grow or cause to grow ripe; to mature.

rip-off, rip′ôf, rip′of, n. Informal. A swindle.

rip·ple, rip′əl, v.i., **-pled, -pling.** To form small waves on the surface, as water when agitated by a gentle breeze; to flow with a light ruffling of the surface; to form or have small waves.—v.t. To form small waves on; to agitate lightly; to mark, as with ripples; to cause to have ripples.—n. A small wave; any similar movement or appearance; a sound, as of water flowing in ripples.

rip·saw, rip′sô, n. A saw that is coarse-toothed, used for cutting wood along the grain.

rip·tide, rip′tīd, n. The clash of opposing tides or currents causing a violent agitation in the water.

rise, rīz, v.i., **rose, ris·en, ris·ing.** To get up from a lying, sitting, or kneeling posture; to get up from sleep or rest; to come to life again; to become active in opposition or resistance; to come into being; appear: Worries rose in his mind; to originate, issue, or be derived; to have a source; to move from a lower to a higher position; ascend; to come above the horizon, as a heavenly body; to extend directly upward: The tower rises to a height of 60 feet; to have an upward slant or curve: The ground rises behind the house; to attain greater rank, status, or wealth; to prove equal to or worthy of: She rose to the challenge; become animated or cheerful, as the spirits; to increase; to become louder or of higher pitch, as the voice; to swell or puff up, as dough from the action of yeast. —v.t. To cause to rise.—n. The act or an act of rising; appearance above the horizon; elevation in position, fortune, power, or the like; an increase; origin or beginning, as of a stream; a coming into existence or notice; extension upward; the amount of this extension; upward slope, as of ground or a road; a piece of rising or high ground.—**get a rise out of.** Informal. To draw an angry or emotional response from, by deliberate provocation.—**give rise to,** to originate or produce: Her secretive conduct *gave rise to* suspicions.

ris·er, rī′zər, *n.* One who rises, as from bed: an early *riser;* the vertical face of a stair step.

ris·i·ble, riz′ə·bəl, *a.* Of, causing, capable of, or inclined to laughter. —**ris·i·bil·i·ty,** riz·ə·bil′ə·tē, *n. pl.,* **-ties.**

risk, risk, *n.* Exposure to the chance of injury or loss; a hazard or dangerous chance; a person or thing considered with reference to loss, damage, injury, or death.—*v.t.* To expose to the chance of injury or loss; hazard; to take or run the risk of: to *risk* defeat or loss.—**take a risk,** to endanger oneself.

risk·y, ris′kē, *a.,* **-i·er, -i·est.** Dangerous; hazardous; full of or involving risk. —**risk·i·ness,** *n.*

ris·qué, ri·skā′, *a.* Tending toward or verging on impropriety; off-color.

rite, rīt, *n.* A prescribed or formal procedure used in religious or other solemn ceremonies: the baptismal *rite;* any formal or ceremonial practice or custom.

rit·u·al, rich′ū·əl, *a.* Pertaining to, consisting of, or prescribing rites.—*n.* The rites or ceremonies, collectively, of a church or other religious body; the order of any solemn ceremony; a book describing or prescribing such rites.

rit·u·al·ism, rich′ū·ə·liz·əm, *n.* Strict observance of prescribed forms of ritual; the study of rituals; an excessive use of rituals. —**rit·u·al·ist,** *n.* —**rit·u·al·is·tic,** rich·ū·ə·lis′tik, *a.* —**rit·u·al·is·ti·cal·ly,** *adv.*

ritz·y, rit′sē, *a.,* **-i·er, -i·est.** *Informal.* Elegant; ostentatiously fashionable; snobbish.

ri·val, rī′vəl, *n.* One who is in pursuit of the same object as another; a competitor; one who emulates or strives to equal or exceed another in excellence.—*a.* Having the same pretensions or claims; standing in competition for superiority.—*v.t.* To stand in competition with; to strive to equal or excel.

ri·val·ry, rī′vəl·rē, *n. pl.,* **-ries.** The act of rivaling; competition; emulation.

riv·er, riv′ər, *n.* A natural stream of water of considerable size flowing in a definite course or channel; a similar stream of something other than water; any abundant stream or copious flow.—**sell down the riv·er,** to betray or deceive.—**send up the riv·er.** *Informal.* To send or sentence to prison.

riv·er·side, riv′ər·sīd, *n.* The bank of a river.—*a.*

riv·et, riv′it, *n.* A short metallic pin or bolt with a head, used to join pieces, as sheets of metal, by inserting the shaft through aligned holes in the pieces and then hammering the plain end to form a second head.—*v.t.* To fasten with a rivet; clinch; fasten firmly; fix firmly or engross, as the eyes or attention. —**riv·et·er,** *n.*

riv·i·er·a, riv·ē·âr′ə, *n.* A coastal resort area usu. characterized by a temperate climate.

riv·u·let, riv′yə·lit, *n.* A small stream or brook.

RNA, är′en′ā′, *n.* Ribonucleic acid.

roach, rōch, *n. pl.,* **roach, roach·es.** A European freshwater fish of the carp family.

roach, rōch, *n.* Cockroach. *Informal.* The butt of a marijuana cigarette.

road, rōd, *n.* An open way or public passage; a piece of ground between one place and another for travel; a highway or the like; any route or way: the *road* to happiness.—**on the road.** *Informal.* Traveling, as a salesman; on tour, as a circus or a theatrical company.

road·bed, rōd′bed, *n.* The foundation on which the rails, ties, and ballast of a railroad lie; the material or surface of which a road is made.

road·block, rōd′blok, *n.* An obstacle on a road; a barricade to stop lawbreakers or enemy troops.

road hog, *n.* A driver who blocks traffic by straddling lanes with his car.

road·run·ner, rōd′rən·ər, *n.* A long-tailed, swift, largely terrestrial bird of the cuckoo family, found esp.

in S.W. United States. Also **road run·ner.**

road·side, rōd′sīd, *n.* The edge of a road.—*a.* On or close to the edge of a road.

road·ster, rōd′stər, *n.* An open automobile having a single seat and a compartment for luggage or rumble seat in the rear.

road·way, rōd′wā, *n.* A road; the part of a road on which vehicles or people travel.

roam, rōm, *v.i.* To wander; to ramble; to rove.—*v.t.* To range; to wander over.—*n.* The act of roaming; a wandering.

roan, rōn, *a.* Having a bay, sorrel, or dark color, with numerous spots of gray or white: said of horses.—*n.* A roan color; a horse or animal of a roan color.

roar, rōr, rôr, *v.i.* To make a full, loud, continued sound; to howl; to laugh loudly.—*v.t.* To indicate or express with a roar.—*n.* A full, loud sound of some continuance; an outcry of joy or mirth.

roast, rōst, *v.t.* To cook or prepare for the table by exposure to heat, as on a spit, in an oven, or the like; to heat to excess; to dry and parch by exposure to heat. *Informal.* To ridicule or criticize severely.—*v.i.* To become roasted; to cook food by roasting; to feel very hot.—*n.* That which is roasted or intended for roasting, as a piece of beef; an act of roasting.—*a.* Roasted: *roast* beef.

roast·er, rō′stər, *n.* One who or that which roasts; a pan or other contrivance for roasting; something, as a pig or chicken, suitable for roasting.

rob, rob, *v.t.,* **robbed, rob·bing.** To deprive of something by unlawful force, violence, or threat of violence: to *rob* a traveler; to commit robbery upon: to *rob* a home; to deprive of something illegally or unjustly. —*v.i.* To commit robbery. —**rob·ber,** *n.*

rob·ber·y, rob′ə·rē, *n. pl.,* **-ies.** The act or practice of robbing.

robe, rōb, *n.* A long, loose or flowing gown or outer garment worn by men or women, esp. for formal or state occasions; a bathrobe or dressing gown; an official vestment, as of a judge.—*v.t.,* **robed, rob·ing.** To clothe or invest in a robe or robes; dress.—*v.i.* To put on a robe.

rob·in, rob′in, *n.* A large, common N. American thrush with a dull reddish breast; a smaller thrush of Europe, having a yellowish-red breast.

ro·bot, rō′bət, rō′bot, *n.* A mechanical, manlike device capable of performing certain mechanical motions and tasks; an automaton; a person who behaves or works mechanically.

ro·bust, rō·bəst′, rō′bəst, *a.* Possessed of or indicating great strength or health; strong or enduring; vigorous; rude, rough, or boisterous; strong or full-flavored, as coffee.

rock, rok, *n.* A large mass of stone forming a cliff or the like; a large detached mass of stone; a stone of any size; something resembling or suggesting a rock; a firm foundation or support. *Informal.* Any gem; a diamond.—**on the rocks.** *Informal.* Ruined, destitute, or bankrupt; served with ice cubes only, as a beverage.

rock, rok, *v.t.* To move or sway to and fro or from side to side; move to and fro in a cradle, the arms, or the like, esp. soothingly; to shake or sway powerfully with emotion.—*v.i.* To move or sway to and fro or from side to side.—*n.* A rocking movement; an act of rocking. *Informal.* Rock′n′roll.

rock-and-roll, rok′ən·rōl′, *n.* Rock′n′roll.

rock bot·tom, *n.* The lowest point possible. —**rock·bot·tom,** rok′bot′əm, *a.*

rock-bound, rok′bownd, *a.* Hemmed in, covered, or surrounded by rocks.

rock can·dy, *n.* Sugar in hard, cohering crystals of considerable size.

rock·er, rok′ər, *n.* One who or that which rocks; one

---

of the curved pieces on which a cradle or a rocking chair rocks; a rocking chair.—**off one's rock·er.** *Informal.* Crazy.

rock·et, rok'it, *n.* A firework, missile, or other usu. cylindrical device propelled by the upward thrust of escaping gases liberated by combustion; a rocket-propelled bomb, aircraft, or space vehicle.—*v.t.* To transport or convey with rocket propulsion.—*v.i.* To move like a rocket.

rock·et·ry, rok'ə·trē, *n.* The science or study of rocket flight, development, and design.

rock·ing chair, rok'ing, *n.* A chair mounted on rockers.

rock·ing horse, *n.* A toy horse mounted on rockers; a hobbyhorse.

rock 'n' roll, rok'ən·rōl', *n.* A style of popular music derived esp. from hillbilly music and the blues, originally having a strong, repetitious rhythm and melody, but later increasingly amorphous and often psychedelic.

rock-ribbed, rok'ribd, *a.* Having ridges of rock, exceedingly firm or unyielding.

rock salt, *n.* Mineral salt; common salt found in masses or beds.

rock wool, *n.* A material of woollike fibers, made by passing steam through molten rock or slag, and used for insulation.

rock·y, rok'ē, *a.,* **-i·er, -i·est.** Inclined to rock; tottering; unsteady; uncertain. *Informal.* Weak; dizzy, as from drinking.

rock·y, rok'ē, *a.,* **-i·er, -i·est.** Full of rocks; resembling a rock; tough; hazardous; resolute; insensitive. —**rock·i·ness,** *n.*

ro·co·co, rə·kō'kō, rō·kə·kō', A flamboyant style of French decoration and architecture, distinguished by exceptionally elaborate and dainty ornamentation and by curved rather than straight lines.—*a.* Like or in the manner of the rococo; gaudy or overdone.

rod, rod, *n.* A stick, staff, bar, or the like, of various materials, as wood or metal; a shoot or slender stem of any woody plant; a stick or switch used to punish; chastisement or punishment; a staff used for measuring; a linear measurement equal to 5½ yards or 16½ feet; a square measure of 30¼ square yards; a scepter or staff carried to symbolize office or authority; a fishing pole.

ro·dent, rōd'ənt, *n.* Any of an order of mammals, as the squirrel, rat, mouse, or the like, characterized by continually growing incisors adapted for nibbling or gnawing.

ro·de·o, rō'dē·ō, rō·dā'ō, *n. pl.,* **-os.** A public performance of cowboy skills, including bronco riding, steer wrestling, and calf roping; a cattle roundup.

roe, rō, *n.* The milt or eggs of fishes.

roe, rō, *n. pl.,* **roes, roe.** A small, agile Old-World deer.

roe·buck, rō'bək, *n.* A male roe deer; less properly, any roe deer.

roent·gen, rent'gən, *n.* The unit used internationally as a measure of radiation.

roent·gen ray, *n.* (*Often cap.*) X-ray.

rog·er, roj'ər, *interj.* Radio communication code meaning, 'message received and understood.'

rogue, rōg, *n.* A dishonest person; a rascal; a vagrant; a vagabond; a lone animal, as an elephant, displaying a fierce disposition. —**ro·guish,** rō'gish, *a.* —**ro·guish·ly,** *adv.* —**ro·guish·ness,** *n.*

ro·guer·y, rō'gə·rē, *n. pl.,* **-ies.** Conduct characteristic of a rogue; trickery; dishonest practice; playful mischief.

rogue's gal·ler·y, *n.* A collection of portraits of criminals, used by police as a means of identification.

roil, royl, *v.t.* To make turbid by stirring; to annoy or anger.

roist·er, roy'stər, *v.i.* To bluster; to swagger; to be noisy, vaunting, or turbulent.

role, rōl, *n.* A character portrayed by an actor; a customary function.

roll, rōl, *v.i.* To move smoothly along a surface by turning over and over, as a ball or wheel; to move or be moved on wheels, rollers, or the like; to flow or appear to move with the undulations and continuity of waves: hills *rolling* to the sea; to take the shape of a ball or cylinder by curling or turning over on itself one or many times; to pass or elapse, with *on* or *by*; to make a low, deep, rumbling sound, as thunder or drums; to trill, as a canary; to move from side to side in a swaying, rocking motion, as a ship; to become flat or spread out by the use of a roller; to get started or progress: Let's get *rolling.*—*v.t.* To set in motion by causing to turn over and over, as a ball; to convey or move using wheels or rollers; to form into a ball or cylinder by turning over upon itself, or wrapping around itself; to cause to undulate or flow steadily onward; to spread out or make level by pressing with a roller; to give a swaying or rocking motion to: Waves *roll* a ship; to wrap or contain with a substance or covering; to rotate, as the eyes; to sound with a trill, as r's; to give forth in a full, reverberating manner; to beat, as a drum, with such rapidity that the successive beats seem to blend. *Informal.* To rob (someone drunk, asleep, unconscious, etc.).—*n.* A list, register, or catalog containing names; anything rolled up in a cylindrical or rounded form; a small lump of bread dough rolled or doubled on itself and baked; a roller; act of rolling; an undulation of surface: the *roll* of a prairie; a rolling motion; a deep, prolonged sound or rumble; the rapid, continuous beating of a drum. *Informal.* Paper money rolled up. —**roll back,** to push back; to reduce prices, wages, etc., to a previous, lower level, esp. by government direction. —**roll up.** *Informal.* To increase or accumulate, as profits.

roll call, *n.* The calling of a roll or list of names, as of soldiers or students, to find out who is present.

roll·er, rō'lər, *n.* One who or that which rolls; a cylinder, wheel, or caster upon which something is rolled along; a cylinder on which something is rolled up; a cylindrical body for rolling over something to be spread out, leveled, crushed, compacted, impressed, or inked; a long, swelling wave advancing steadily.

roll·er bear·ing, *n.* A bearing in which the shaft turns on steel rollers to reduce friction.

roll·er coast·er, *n.* A railroad, found in amusement parks, which has open cars and operates on a course marked by steep ascents and descents and sharp curves.

roll·er skate, *n.* A form of skate with small wheels or rollers instead of a runner.

roll·er-skate, rō'lər·skāt, *v.i.,* **-skat·ed, -skat·ing.** To move around on roller skates. —**roll·er skat·er,** *n.*

rol·lick, rol'ik, *v.i.* To move in a jolly, swaggering manner; to be jovial in behavior; to frolic. —**rol·lick·ing,** rol'i·king, *a.*

roll·ing mill, *n.* A mill where metal is rolled into sheets, bars, or the like; a machine used for rolling metal.

roll·ing pin, *n.* A cylinder of wood or other material for rolling out dough.

roll·ing stock, *n.* The wheeled vehicles of a railroad, including locomotives and cars.

ro·ly-po·ly, rō'lē·pō'lē, *a.* Rotund; plump.—*n. pl.,* **-lies.** A short, plump person or animal.

ro·maine, rō·mān', *n.* A variety of lettuce with long, comparatively narrow, crisp leaves.

Ro·man, rō'mən, *a.* Pertaining to Rome or the Roman people; pertaining to the Roman Catholic religion. (*Usu. l.c.*) Applied to the common upright letter in printing, as distinguished from *italic.*—*n.* A native or citizen of Rome. (*Usu. l.c.*) Roman lettering in printing.

Ro·man can·dle, *n.* A kind of firework, consisting of a tube which shoots up white or colored balls of fire.

Ro·man Cath·o·lic, *a.* Of or pertaining to the Roman Catholic Church of which the pope, or bishop of Rome, is the visible head; referring to a member of the Roman Catholic Church.—*n.*

ro·mance, rō·mans′, rō′mans, *n.* A tale usu. involving heroic deeds, supernatural events, chivalric love, or unusual adventures; a tale or novel, usu. of imaginary characters in a remote setting, and portraying heroic, adventurous, mysterious, or fanciful events; a love story; romantic character or quality; romantic spirit or sentiment; a love affair; a made-up story; fanciful invention or exaggeration. —rō·mans′, *v.i.,* -manced, -manc·ing. To invent or relate romances; to indulge in fanciful or extravagant stories; to think or talk romantically.—*v.t. Informal.* To court, or seek a romance with.

Ro·mance, rō′mans, rō·mans′, *a.* Pertaining to the group of languages called Romance.—*n.* The dialects and languages of Europe which descended from Latin, including French, Spanish, Portuguese, Italian, and Rumanian.

Ro·man·esque, rō·mə·nesk′, *a.* Noting or pertaining to the style which, developing from that of the later Roman Empire, prevailed in western Europe until the middle of the 12th century, characterized esp. by the round arch and vault and by massive, weighty decorative effects.—*n.* The Romanesque style of architecture.

Ro·man nu·mer·als, *n.* The letters of ancient Rome which were used as numerals and which remain in limited use today. The basic Roman letters and their numeric equivalents are: I = 1, V = 5, X = 10, L = 50, C = 100, D = 500, and M = 1000.

ro·man·tic, rō·man′tik, *a.* Pertaining to romance or romances; partaking of romance; fanciful; imaginative; fictitious; imaginary; amorous; ardent; visionary; impractical; of or pertaining to romanticism.—*n.* A romantic individual; romanticist.

ro·man·ti·cism, rō·man′tə·siz·əm, *n.* A literary and artistic movement of the 19th century marked by lyricism, individualism, and emphasis on the feelings and imagination; romantic spirit, tendency, or doctrine. —**ro·man·ti·cist,** *n.*

ro·man·ti·cize, rō·man′tə·sīz, *v.t.,* -cized, -ciz·ing. To interpret or invest with a romantic character.

romp, romp, *v.i.* To play boisterously; to frolic; to proceed so as to win easily.—*n.* Spirited play or frolic. *Informal.* An easy win.

romp·er, rom′pər, *n.* One who romps. *Usu. pl.* A child's one-piece garment.

rood, rood, *n.* A cross or crucifix; a square measure equal to a quarter of an acre or 40 square rods.

roof, roof, rûf, *n.* The cover of any house or building; the top or highest part of something, as of a carriage or car; a house.—*v.t.* To cover with a roof; to enclose in a house; to shelter.

roof·ing, roo′fing, rûf′ing, *n.* The act of covering with a roof; material used or suitable for roofs; a roof.

roof·tree, roof′trē, rûf′trē, *n.* The ridgepole of a roof; the roof; a shelter or dwelling.

rook, rûk, *n.* In chess, a usu. turret-shaped piece which can move any number of unoccupied squares parallel to the sides of the board. Also **cas·tle.**

rook, rûk, *n.* A metallic-black European crow, nesting in colonies and feeding on insects and seeds; a cheat; a trickster.—*v.t.,v.i.* To cheat; to defraud.

rook·er·y, rûk′ə·rē, *n. pl.,* -ies. A place used by rooks for breeding and nesting; an area used for breeding by flocks of sea birds and seals; an old, neglected building, crowded with tenants.

rook·ie, rûk′ē, *n. Informal.* An inexperienced newcomer, as in professional sports; a beginner; a novice; a new recruit.

room, room, rûm, *n.* One of the partitioned areas inside a building or structure, usu. for occupancy or a specific purpose; a place of lodging that is rented; an amount of space available for use: plenty of *room* in the backyard; latitude, possibility, opportunity: *room* for improvement; the group of people inside a room: a

room becoming hushed.—*v.i.* To have lodgings; to inhabit a rented room.

room·er, roo′mər, rûm′ər, *n.* One who rents a room or group of rooms, esp. without board; a lodger.

room·ful, room′fûl, rûm′fûl, *n.* Enough to fill a room; the objects or people in a room.

room·ing house, *n.* A house where rooms are rented, usu. furnished; lodging house.

room·mate, room′māt, rûm′māt, *n.* One who shares a room or several rooms with another person or persons.

room·y, roo′mē, rûm′ē, *a.,* -i·er, -i·est. Having ample room; spacious. —**room·i·ly,** *adv.* —**room·i·ness,** *n.*

roost, roost, *n.* The pole or support on which fowls rest at night; a place in which birds may roost; any place for resting or the like.—*v.i.* To occupy a roost; to lodge; to settle down or rest. —**rule the roost,** to dominate; control.

roost·er, roo′stər, *n.* The male of the domestic chicken.

root, root, rût, *n.* That part of a plant which fixes itself in the earth and absorbs nutrients; a bulb, tuber, or similar part of a plant; that which resembles a root in position or function: the *root* of a tooth; the foundation or base; the essence or heart of; the origin or cause of something; that part of a word which conveys its essential meaning, as distinguished from the formative or inflectional parts by which this meaning is modified; an ultimate form or element from which words are derived; a number *a* so related to a larger number *b* that, when multiplied by itself a given number of times, it yields exactly number *b:* two is the s ̣̣uare *root* of four and the cube *root* of eight.—*v.i.* To send forth roots; to begin to develop; to be firmly fixed or established; to have a beginning, source, or cause. —*v.t.* To establish by or as if by roots; to plant or impress deeply: principles *rooted* in the mind.

root, root, rût, *v.t., v.i.* To turn up with the snout, as a swine; to unearth or find; to hunt or rummage for something.

root, root, rût, *v.i. Informal.* To cheer, applaud, encourage, or support something, esp. a contestant or team. —**root·er,** *n.*

root beer, *n.* A carbonated beverage made from various root and herb extracts, which are fermented in solution with yeast and sugar.

root hair, *n.* A delicate tubular filament growing from the tip region of a root.

root·stock, root′stok, rût′stok, *n.* Origin or source; a rhizome.

rope, rōp, *n.* A thick, long cord of twisted or braided fibers, as hemp, wire, nylon, or other material; a series of things or quantity of material twisted together: a *rope* of onions; a hangman's noose; a lasso.—*v.t.,* roped, rop·ing. To tie, fasten, or bind with a rope; to enclose with a rope, ropes, or the like, usu. followed by *off;* to lasso.—*v.i.* To be drawn or twisted into a form resembling a rope; to become ropy. —**end of one's rope.** *Informal.* The extremity of one's resources; the lack of further resorts or alternatives. —**give one e·nough rope.** *Informal.* To allow a person the freedom to pursue a mistaken course or deed. —**know the ropes.** *Informal.* To be well-acquainted with the methods and details of any business or operation. —**on the ropes.** *Informal.* To be in a defenseless or hopeless position.

rop·y, rō′pē, *a.,* -i·er, -i·est. Drawing into viscous filaments or threads; stringy; resembling or similar to a rope or ropes. —**rop·i·ly,** *adv.* —**rop·i·ness,** *n.*

ro·sa·ry, rō′zə·rē, *n. pl.,* -ries. A sequence or series of prayers; a string of beads, joined to a crucifix, used to count and separate the sequence of such prayers; a rose garden; a bed of roses.

rose, rōz, *n.* A plant which is cultivated for its attractive

---

a- hat, fāte, fāre, fäther; e- met, mē; i- pin, pīne; o- not, nōte, ôrb, moove (move), boy, pownd;
u- cūbe, bûll, tûk (took); ch- chin; th- thick, then; zh- vizhon (vision); ə- əgo, takən, pencəl, lemən, bərd (bird).

flowers; the flower of such a plant; a deep pinkish color; a design, ornament, or gem in the shape of a rose; various materials; a compass card.—*a.* Like the rose flower in color or scent; abounding in roses, as a garden. —**bed of ros•es,** a condition of ease or contentment.

ro•se•ate, rō/zē•it, rō/zē•āt, *a.* Rose-colored; rosy; happy; favorable; optimistic.

rose•bud, rōz/bəd, *n.* The bud of a rose.

rose-col•ored, rōz/kəl•ərd, *a.* Of rose color; pink or rosy; bright or promising; cheerful or optimistic. —**through rose-colored glasses,** optimistically; in an unduly favorable light.

rose•mar•y, rōz/mər•ē, *n. pl.,* **-ies.** A species of green shrub native to the Mediterranean regions with aromatic leaves used as a seasoning and as the source of a volatile oil used in medicines and perfumes.

ro•sette, rō•zet/, *n.* Any formation, object, part, or arrangement which resembles a rose.

rose wa•ter, *n.* Water tinctured with the essential oil of roses.

rose•wood, rōz/wûd, *n.* Any of several species of tropical S. American trees which yield one of the finest of cabinet woods, having coarse, dense, even grains streaked with red or purple; the tree itself.

Rosh Ha•sha•nah, rōsh hə•shä/nə, *n.* The Jewish New Year.

ros•in, roz/in, *n.* The hard, translucent, yellowish to amber-colored resin formed when oil of turpentine is distilled from crude turpentine: used in making varnish and printing inks, and for rubbing on violin bows.—*v.t.* To rub or cover over with rosin.

ros•ter, ros/tər, *n.* A list of persons or groups, such as military personnel, with their order of duty.

ros•trum, ros/trəm, *n. pl.,* **-tra, -trums.** A platform from which a speaker addresses his audience.

ros•y, rō/zē, *a.,* **-i•er, -i•est.** Pink or pinkish-red, like the color of many roses; bright or promising; cheerful or optimistic; made or consisting of roses. —**ros•i•ly,** *adv.* —**ros•i•ness,** *n.*

rot, rot, *v.i.,* **rot•ted, rot•ting.** To decompose; to decay; to become corrupt morally; to become unsound or weak.—*v.t.* To cause to decompose; to bring to corruption.—*n.* The process of decaying; the condition of being rotten; decay; rotten matter; any of various plant and animal diseases marked by decay.

ro•ta•ry, rō/tə•rē, *a.* Turning, as a wheel on its axis; pertaining to or characterized by a rotating motion; having one or more parts that turn around an axis: a *rotary* printing press.—*n. pl.,* **-ries.** A circular routing of traffic in one direction at the junction of three or more roads.

ro•ta•ry en•gine, *n.* An engine in which torque is produced directly by impulsion of fuel, as a turbine; a radial internal-combustion engine whose cylinders revolve around a fixed crankshaft.

ro•tate, rō/tāt, *v.i., v.t.,* **-tat•ed, -tat•ing.** To revolve or cause to move around a center or on an axis; to succeed or cause to succeed in a regular order.

ro•ta•tion, rō•tā/shən, *n.* The act of rotating or turning on an axis; one complete turn on an axis; the motion of the earth or of other heavenly bodies on an axis; a return or succession in a series; established succession; a recurring series of different crops grown on the same ground.

rote, rōt, *n.* Repetition or routine. —**by rote,** merely by memory with little intelligence or understanding.

ro•tis•ser•ie, rō•tis/ə•rē, *n.* A device with a rotating spit for roasting food, esp. meat.

ro•tor, rō/tər, *n.* The rotating part of a machine or apparatus; an assemblage of revolving airfoils which supports jet planes and helicopters during flight.

rot•ten, rot/ən, *a.* Decaying, or decomposed by the natural process of decay; foul-smelling; corrupt; unsound or weak. *Informal.* Unsatisfactory or worthless.

ro•tund, rō•tənd/, *a.* Round or rounded; spherical; plump; full-toned, resonant, or sonorous, as a voice.

—**ro•tun•di•ty,** *n. pl.,* **-ties.**

ro•tun•da, rō•tən/də, *n.* A round building, esp. one with a dome; a large and high circular hall or room in a building, esp. one surmounted by a dome.

rou•é, roo•ā/, *n.* A sensualist; rake.

rouge, roozh, *n.* A cosmetic used to give an artificial red color to the cheeks or lips; a ferrous oxide powder used for polishing glass, gold, silver, or the like.—*v.i.,* **rouged, roug•ing.** To paint the cheeks or lips with rouge.—*v.t.*

rough, rəf, *a.* Having many irregularities of surface; not smooth: *rough* skin; shaggy or fuzzy: the *rough* coat of an animal; uneven or uncultivated: *rough* terrain; tending toward violence or unruliness: *rough* play; agitated or turbulent, as water; stormy, as weather; harsh or rude: a *rough* reply; out of control or rebellious: a *rough* mob; exhausting or unpleasant: a *rough* day; of coarse texture, as material or food; unrefined or discourteous: a *rough* individual; requiring physical exertion rather than intelligence: a *rough* job; not perfected or polished: a *rough* outline; approximate; not fully thought out: a *rough* idea; crude or unpolished, as a grain.—*n.* Any rough terrain, as on a golf course; something coarse or unrefined.—*v.t.* To make rough; to treat roughly or violently, usu. followed by *up:* to *rough up* an opponent; to make a first draft of, followed by *in:* to *rough in* the characters.—*v.i.* To roughen or become rough.—*adv.* In a rough manner. —**rough it,** to do without comforts or conveniences.

rough•age, rəf/ij, *n.* Rough or coarse material; the coarser kinds of fodder or food, as certain fruits, bran, or straw, which are proportionately high in cellulose.

rough-and-tum•ble, rəf/ən•təm/bəl, *a.* Characterized by disregard of rules; scrambling; boisterous.—*n.* A rough-and-tumble struggle.

rough•en, rəf/ən, *v.t., v.i.* To make or become rough.

rough-hew, rəf/hū/, *v.t.,* **-hewed, -hewed,** or **-hewn, -hew•ing.** To hew coarsely without smoothing; to form or shape crudely. —**rough•hewn,** *a.*

rough•house, rəf/hows, *n. Informal.* Rough play; rowdy conduct.—*v.i., v.t.,* **-housed, -hous•ing.** *Informal.* To act or treat in a rough or rowdy way.

rough•neck, rəf/nek, *n. Informal.* A rough, coarse fellow.

rough•rid•er, rəf/rī•dər, *n.* One who breaks horses; one accustomed to strenuous riding.

rough•shod, rəf/shod/, *a.* Shod, as a horse, with shoes having calks or points. —**ride rough•shod over,** to pursue a violent or selfish course, regardless of the effect on others.

rou•lette, roo•let/, *n.* A game of chance in which a moving ball drops into a numbered compartment of a spinning disk, with bets placed on which compartment the ball will settle in; a tool furnished with a small toothed wheel, used by engravers for producing dotted work.

round, rownd, *a.* Having every part of the surface at an equal distance from the center; spherical; globular; circular; cylindrical; having a curved form; semicircular; swelling; plump; moving in circles; returning: a *round* trip; given in the closest multiple of ten, a hundred, etc.: 397 is 400 in *round* numbers; large; considerable: a good *round* sum; unqualified: a *round* assertion.—*adv.* In a circle, ring, or the like, or so as to surround something: to gather *round* a speaker; on all sides, or about, whether circularly or otherwise; in all directions from a center; in the region about a place: the country *round;* in circumference: a tree 40 inches *round;* through a round, circuit, or series, as of places or persons: enough to go *round;* through a round, or recurring period, of time, esp. to the present or particular time: time rolls *round;* throughout, or from beginning to end of: the year *round.*—*prep.* On every side of; around; about; in a circular course.—*n.* That which is round, as a circle, sphere, or globe; a series of activities, duties, etc., coming back to where it began: a *round* of toasts; the step of a ladder; an interval of play or of a match in sports; a cut of beef from the thigh between the knee and the rump; a dance in a ring; a general discharge of firearms by a body of troops, in which each soldier fires once; ammunition for firing once.—*v.t.* To make round; to make full or complete; to make full, smooth, and flowing; to go in a circular course about.—*v.i.* To grow or become round. —**make the rounds,** to make a series of stops or visits. —**in the round,** surrounded on all sides, as a theatre stage surrounded by audience seats. —**round·ly,** *adv.* —**round·ness,** *n.*

round·a·bout, rownd′ə·bowt, *n.* A circuitous road, line of thought, or the like.—*a.* Indirect; going round; encompassing.

round·ed, rown′did, *a.* Made round; with smooth edges; fully developed, or polished: a *rounded* education.

round·er, rown′dər, *n.* Someone or something that rounds, esp. a tool or machine for rounding surfaces or edges. *Informal.* A person who habitually patronizes places of amusement such as taverns, night clubs, brothels, etc.

round·ish, rown′dish, *a.* Somewhat round.

round rob·in, *n.* A written petition, protest, etc., signed by names in a circle so that it may be impossible to ascertain who headed the list; a letter sent in turn to each member of a group; a sports tournament in which each contestant plays every other contestant.

round-shoul·dered, rownd′shōl·dərd, *a.* Having a rounded back or stooping shoulders.

round·up, rownd′əp, *n.* The driving together of cattle or other animals for inspection, branding, or the like, as in the western U.S.; the men and horses who do this, or the herd so collected; any similar driving or bringing together: a police *roundup* of known hoodlums; a summary or résumé. —**round up,** *v.t.*

rouse, rowz, *v.t.,* **roused, rous·ing.** To wake from sleep; to excite to thought or action from a state of idleness, or inattention; to agitate; startle; surprise. —*v.i.* To wake from sleep or repose; to be excited to thought or action.—*n.* The act of rousing. —**rous·er,** *n.*

rous·ing, row′zing, *a.* Able to awaken or excite; stirring; lively or brisk; vigorous. *Informal.* Extraordinary, astonishing, or outrageous, as an untrue statement.

roust, rowst, *v.t., v.i. Informal.* To arouse, often followed by *up*; to expel, followed by *out*.

roust·a·bout, rows′tə·bowt, *n.* An unskilled or transient laborer, esp. one who works in a circus, on the waterfront, or on ranches or oil fields.

rout, rowt, *n.* A riot or uproar; the breaking or defeat of troops; the disorder and confusion of troops thus defeated; a tumultuous crowd; a rabble or mob.—*v.i.* To turn over or dig up with the snout, as swine; search or rummage.—*v.t.* To bring or get out by poking about or searching, usu. followed by *out;* to break the ranks of and put to flight in disorder; force or drive out, usu. with *out;* cause to get up or out of bed, usu. with *out* or *up;* to hollow out or furrow, as with a scoop, gouge, or machine.

route, root, rowt, *n.* A way or road for passage or travel; a way or course taken, or to be taken: to fix a *route* for a procession; a customary or regular line of passage or travel; the line or direction of a road, railroad, or the like.—*v.t.,* **rout·ed, rout·ing.** To fix the route of; send or forward by a particular route.

rout·er, row′tər, *n.* Any of various tools or machines for routing, hollowing out, or furrowing.

rou·tine, roo·tēn′, *n.* A procedure, daily or frequently pursued, as in business; duties or actions done regularly or at regular intervals: the *routine* of dentist's visits; a practice adhered to by force of habit; all or part of a performer's regular act.—*a.* Commonplace; habitual; of, by, or relating to an established proce-

dure.

rou·tin·ize, roo·tē′nīz, *v.t.,* **-ized, -iz·ing.** To develop into or reduce to an established procedure or routine.

rove, rōv, *v.i.,* **roved, rov·ing.** To wander; to ramble; to go, move, or pass without specific direction or destination.—*v.t.* To wander over or about.—*n.* An act of wandering or roving. —**rov·er,** *n.*

row, rō, *v.i.* To move a boat by means of oars.—*v.t.* To impel along the surface of water by oars, as a boat; to use or be provided with, as a number of oars; to take part in by rowing, as a race; to employ for rowing, as oars or oarsmen.—*n.* An excursion taken in a boat having oars; an act of rowing. —**row·er,** *n.*

row, rō, *n.* A series of persons or things arranged in a continuous line; a line; a rank; a file.—*v.t.* To place or form in a row. —**long** or **hard row to hoe,** a difficult undertaking.

row, row, *n.* A noisy disturbance, dispute, or commotion.—*v.i.* To take part in a quarrel.

row·boat, rō′bōt, *n.* A small boat propelled by rowing.

row·dy, row′dē, *n. pl.,* **-dies.** A rough, disorderly person; one given to quarreling or fighting.—*a.,* **-di·er, -di·est.** Of the nature of or characteristic of a rowdy; rough and disorderly. —**row·di·ly,** *adv.* —**row·di·ness,** *n.*

row house, rō, *n.* One of a group of houses built in a row, usu. alike in design, and joined by a common sidewall to its neighbor.

row·lock, rō′lok, *n.* Oarlock.

roy·al, roy′əl, *a.* Of or pertaining to a king, queen, or sovereign: the *royal* family; established or chartered by, or existing under the patronage of, a sovereign: a *royal* society or academy; befitting or appropriate to a sovereign; magnificent; majestic; noble. *Informal.* Fine, very good: in *royal* spirits; beyond the common or ordinary in size or quality. —**roy·al·ly,** *adv.*

roy·al blue, *n.* A deep, vivid blue.

roy·al·ist, roy′ə·list, *n.* A supporter or adherent of a king or a royal government.

roy·al pur·ple, *n.* A deep purple.

roy·al·ty, roy′əl·tē, *n. pl.,* **-ties.** Royal status, dignity, or power; sovereignty; character or quality proper to or befitting a sovereign; kingliness; nobility; generosity; a royal person; royal persons collectively; a kingdom; a compensation or portion of proceeds paid to the owner of a right, as an oil right or a patent, for the use of it; a fixed portion of the proceeds from his or her work, paid to an author or composer.

rub, rəb, *v.t.,* **rubbed, rub·bing.** To move along the surface of, backwards, forwards, or in a circular motion, with friction or stress; to apply friction to; to wipe; to clean; to scour or scrub; to smear all over; to chafe; to kill or obliterate, usu. followed by *out.*—*v.i.* To move along the surface of a body with pressure; to grate; to chafe; to fret; to have the capacity to be rubbed in some way: Newsprint *rubs* off easily.—*n.* An act of rubbing: a back *rub;* a difficulty, obstruction, etc.; a rough surface, character, etc.; something grating to the feelings; a gibe, sarcasm, etc. —**rub it in.** *Informal.* To repeatedly stress something disagreeable in order to irritate. —**rub the wrong way.** *Informal.* To aggravate; vex.

rub·ber, rəb′ər, *n.* An elastic, resilient, cohesive solid made from the juice of certain tropical trees and shrubs; this substance chemically treated for manufacture into tires and various industrial items; a similar synthetic material; something made of these materials, as an eraser or overshoe; a person who rubs to polish or smooth; a massager; something used to rub with. *Informal.* A condom.—*a.* —**rub·ber·y,** *a.*

rub·ber, rəb′ər, *n.* A series of games, usu. an odd number, of which the majority determines the winning side; the decisive game of such a series.

rub·ber ce·ment, *n.* A liquid adhesive composed of

rubber dispersed in an organic solvent, usu. benzene.

rub·ber·ize, rəb/ə·rīz, v.t., **-ized, -iz·ing.** To coat or impregnate with rubber or rubber preparation, as a fabric.

rub·ber·neck, rəb/ər·nek, n. *Informal.* One who stretches or cranes his or her neck to look at something; a sightseer.—v.i. *Informal.* To look or gape at something by stretching the neck.—a.

rub·ber plant, n. Any of several East Indian plants yielding commercial India rubber; a familiar greenhouse plant with thick, glossy, green, oblong leaves.

rub·ber stamp, n. A small, inked rubber printing plate to which hand pressure is applied to imprint documents, packages, or the like; one who tenders his or her approval without question or careful personal judgment. —**rub·ber-stamp**, rəb·ər·stamp/, v.t.

rub·bish, rəb/ish, n. Debris; waste; trash; nonsense. —**rub·bish·y**, a.

rub·ble, rəb/əl, n. Pieces of solid material irregularly broken, as debris; stones of irregular shapes and dimensions. —**rub·bly**, a., **-bli·er, -bli·est.**

rub·down, rəb/down, n. A brisk massage.

rube, roob, n. *Informal.* An awkward, unsophisticated country person; a hick.

ru·bel·la, roo·bel/ə, n. German measles.

ru·be·o·la, roo·bē/ə·lə, roo·bē·ō/lə, n. Measles; German measles.

Ru·bi·con, roo/bi·kon, n. A river in N. Italy. —**cross the Rubicon**, to make an irrevocable decision.

ru·bi·cund, roo/bə·kənd, a. Red; reddish; ruddy.

ru·bid·i·um, roo·bid/ē·əm, n. A silver-white metallic element resembling, but more active than, potassium.

ru·bric, roo/brik, n. The title of a statute, formerly printed in red letters; a distinctive mark placed after a signature or the like; any formulated, fixed, or authoritative injunction or duty.

ru·by, roo/bē, n. pl., **ru·bies.** A gem of various shades of red corundum; a deep, red color.—a. Deep red in color; resembling a ruby.

ruck·sack, rək/sak, rûk/sak, n. A kind of knapsack carried by tourists, hikers, or other travelers.

ruck·us, rək/əs, n. *Informal.* A disturbance; uproar; tumult.

rud·der, rəd/ər, n. A movable, vertical instrument attached in a submerged position at the helm and used in steering a ship; that which guides or governs a course; the subsidiary airfoil by means of which an aircraft is turned to left or right.

rud·dy, rəd/ē, a., **-di·er, -di·est.** Having a red color; of a lively, fresh, rosy color: a *ruddy* complexion. —**rud·di·ly**, adv. —**rud·di·ness**, n.

rude, rood, a., **rud·er, rud·est.** Unformed by art, taste, or skill; having coarse manners; discourteous; violent or boisterous, as the weather. —**rude·ly**, adv. —**rude·ness**, n.

ru·di·ment, roo/də·mənt, n. That which is in an undeveloped state; an unformed or unfinished beginning. *Usu. pl.* Elements or first principles of any art or science; the elements or elementary notions. —**ru·di·men·tal**, roo·də·men/təl, a. —**ru·di·men·ta·ry**, roo·də·men/tə·rē, roo·də·men/trē, a.

rue, roo, v.t., **rued, ru·ing.** To regret; to repent.—v.i. To have compassion; to become sorrowful.—n.

rue, roo, n. A perennial herb, having clusters of tiny yellow flowers and strongly scented leaves containing aromatic oils used in medicine and for flavoring.

rue·ful, roo/fəl, a. Causing lamentation or sorrow: a *rueful* situation; sorrowful or remorseful: a *rueful* expression on one's face. —**rue·ful·ly**, adv. —**rue·ful·ness**, n.

ruff, rəf, n. A large, stiff, pleated collar; a frill of feathers or hair standing out around the neck of an animal; a ruffle. —**ruffed**, a.

ruf·fi·an, rəf/ē·ən, rəf/yən, n. A boisterous, brutal fellow.—a. Like or belonging to a ruffian; brutal.

ruf·fle, rəf/əl, v.t., **-fled, -fling.** To disturb the surface of; to rumple; to furnish or adorn with ruffles; to erect,

as the feathers of a bird; to agitate; to turn hastily, as the pages of a book; to shuffle, as cards.—v.i. To become disordered or rumpled; to flutter: The banners *ruffled* in the wind; to become agitated or disturbed; to swagger.—n. A surface disturbance; a ripple; a state of agitation.—n. A strip of plaited fabric attached to some border of a garment, as to the wristband; a frill.

ruf·fle, rəf/əl, n. A low, continuous beating of a drum, less loud than the roll.—v.t., **-fled, -fling.** To beat a ruffle on, as a drum.

rug, rəg, n. A floor covering of thick, heavy fabric, often wool, with a nap or pile; a piece of thick material used to cover the legs when traveling, or sitting outdoors.

Rug·by, rəg/bē, n. One of the two principal varieties of football; played esp. in England.

rug·ged, rəg/id, a. Rough with projections or irregularities of surface: *rugged* rocks; of ground, etc., roughly broken, rocky, hilly, or otherwise difficult of passage; of the features or face, roughly irregular, heavy, or hard in form; rough or tempestuous, as weather; severe or trying, as times or life; harsh or stern, as persons; ungentle or rude, as actions; homely or plain, but with a rough force: *rugged* maxims hewn from life; sturdy or strong, rather than elegant. *Informal.* Robust or vigorous. —**rug·ged·ly**, adv. —**rug·ged·ness**, n.

ru·in, roo/in, n. That change of anything which destroys it or entirely unfits it for use; destruction; overthrow; downfall; a building or anything in a state of decay or dilapidation; the state of being destroyed or rendered worthless: to go to *ruin. Often pl.* The remains of a decayed city, house, or fortress.—v.t. To bring to destruction; to defeat; to create a state of insolvency.—v.i. To fall into ruins; to run to ruin.

ru·in·a·tion, roo·in·ā/shən, n. The act of ruinating; ruin; destruction.

ru·in·ous, roo/in·əs, a. Fallen to ruin; bringing or tending to bring ruin: a *ruinous* tornado.

rule, rool, n. Government; control; an established principle, standard, or guide for action; a maxim, canon, or precept to be observed; a point of law settled by authority; custom or habitual practice: As a *rule* I rise late; an instrument by which straight lines are drawn; an instrument for measuring short lengths.—v.t., **ruled, rul·ing.** To govern; to control, conduct, guide; to mark with lines, using a ruler.—v.i. To have power or command; to exercise supreme authority, often followed by *over.* —**rule out**, to exclude; eliminate; prevent.

rule of thumb, n. A rule suggested by practical rather than scientific knowledge; a rough calculation.

rul·er, roo/lər, n. One that rules or governs; an instrument, made of wood, plastic, or metal, with straight edges or sides which by guiding a pen or pencil along the edge draws straight lines; also used for measuring length.

rul·ing, roo/ling, a. Governing; reigning; predominant.—n. A rule, or decision settled by a judge, a court of law, or another authority; the act of controlling or governing; the process of drawing lines or measuring by using a ruler.

rum, rəm, n. Liquor distilled from sugar cane juice or molasses.

rum·ba, rəm/bə, n. A dance of complex rhythm having a Cuban Negro origin; a ballroom version of this dance; music for the rumba.—v.i., **-baed, -ba·ing.** To perform the rumba. Also **rhum·ba.**

rum·ble, rəm/bəl, v.i., **-bled, -bling.** To make a low, heavy, muffled, continued sound; to proceed with or travel with such a sound.—v.t. To cause to emit or to utter with a deep, rolling sound.—n. A low, heavy, continuous sound; a seat or a baggage compartment at the rear portion of a carriage or a roadster: also **rum·ble seat.** *Informal.* A street fight, usu. among rival gangs of youths. —**rum·bler**, n. —**rum·bling**, adv. —**rum·bly**, a.

ru·mi·nant, roo′mə·nənt, *a.* Chewing the cud; characterized by chewing again what has been swallowed, as *ruminant* animals; given to deep thought; contemplative.—*n.* A member of an order of herbivorous hoofed mammals that chew the cud, as the camel, cow, deer, goat, and the like.

ru·mi·nate, roo′mə·nāt, *v.i.,* **-nat·ed, -nat·ing.** To chew the cud; to think again and again; to ponder. —*v.t.* To chew over again; to muse or meditate on. —**ru·mi·na·tion,** roo·mə·nā′shən, *n.* —**ru·mi·na·tive,** *a.* —**ru·mi·na·tor,** *n.*

rum·mage, rəm′ij, *v.t.,* **-maged, -mag·ing.** To search thoroughly or actively through, as a place, turning over or looking through contents; to ransack.—*v.i.* To search actively, as in a place or receptacle.—*n.* Miscellaneous articles; odds and ends; a rummaging search. —**rum·mag·er,** *n.*

rum·my, rəm′ē, *n.* A popular card game.

rum·my, rəm′ē, *n. pl.,* **-mies.** *Informal.* An habitual drunk; an intoxicated person.

ru·mor, roo′mər, *n.* A current story, report, or statement passing from one person to another, without any known authority for the truth of it; hearsay; gossip. —*v.t.* To tell or circulate by an unverified report.

ru·mor·mon·ger, roo′mər·mong·gər, roo′mər·məng·gər, *n.* One who begins and encourages the spread of rumors, esp. malicious ones.

rump, rəmp, *n.* The end of the backbone of an animal, with the parts adjacent; the buttocks; the section of beef from this area; a last, often inferior, remnant.

rum·ple, rəm′pəl, *v.t.,* **-pled, -pling.** To wrinkle or crumple; to ruffle.—*v.i.* To become creased, crumpled, or wrinkled.—*n.* An irregular fold or crease; a wrinkle, esp. untidy.

rum·pus, rəm′pəs, *n.* A riot. *Informal.* Uproar; fracas.

rum·pus room, *n.* A room furnished and used for parties and other recreation.

run, rən, *v.i.,* **ran, run, run·ning.** To move more quickly than in walking, using the legs to lift the feet from the ground for a fraction of time in each step; to move quickly; to flee; to make a short, hasty trip or visit; to move or be propelled: The ball *ran* along the ground; to contend in a race; to enter into a contest; to campaign for public office; to finish a contest in a designated position: to *run* second; to migrate or ascend a river to spawn, as a fish; to move or be moved: the ship *ran* aground; to pass or go back and forth from place to place; to turn as a wheel; to move freely; to unravel; to flow; to leak; to become fluid; to fuse; to melt; to discharge pus or other matter: An ulcer *runs*; to spread and blend: Colors *run* in washing; to continue in operation: The mills are *running*; to pass from one state to another: to *run* into debt; to proceed or pass, as time; to extend, stretch, lie: The street *runs* east and west; to have a certain written form: The story *runs* as follows; to have a tendency; recur: Artistic ability *runs* in the family; to be published or circulated; to continue or be repeated: The play *ran* for a hundred nights; to be carried to a pitch; to rise: Feeling *runs* high; to vary in growth: Apples *run* large this season; to make withdrawals, as from a bank, in quick succession; to continue before it becomes due and payable: A bill has ninety days to *run*; to sail with a following wind.—*v.t.* To cause to run or go quickly: He *ran* his eyes over the page; to go over, as a distance, quickly; to accomplish by running; to contend against, as in a race; to cause, as a horse, to go fast; to enter as a contestant in a race; to bring about a certain condition: She *ran* herself into a state of collapse; to pursue; to force to go: The hounds *ran* the fox to cover; to leave; to transport: He *ran* her there in his car; to break through or evade: to *run* a blockade; smuggle; to maintain in operation: to *run* a machine; to print; to publish; to analyze, treat, or

refine; to cause to be carried in a certain course: to *run* a ship aground; to stand for office: to *run* for mayor; to conduct, as an enterprise; to make a number of strokes, points, etc., without a miss, as in games; to encounter; to incur: to *run* the risk of being killed; to cause, as water, to flow; to pour forth in a stream; to accumulate, as charges, for payment at a later date; to make slide freely, as a rope; to pierce; to stab: to *run* a person through with a rapier; to graze; to melt; to form in a mold by melting; to mark, trace, or draw, as a line.—*n.* The act of running; a running gait; a period of rapid movement; a distance traversed: a ten-mile *run*; a passage from one place to another; a trip; an interval during which a factory or machine operates continuously; that which is produced in a period of continuous operation; a defect in knitted fabric, where stitches have come undone; direction or arrangement; grain; distinctive course; tenor; general tendency; privilege or use: the *run* of the building; a continued course: a *run* of ill luck; an unbroken length of something; a series of playing cards, usu. in a given suit, in rank order; an unusual demand, as on a bank for payment of its notes; a sustained sale or demand as for some commodity; the flow, as of a liquid, during a particular period; a stream; a swift current; a broadly inclusive class or type: the normal *run* of students; a sloping course, as for skiing; a path where animals, as deer, run; a large extent of ground for livestock; the movement of fish migrating to spawn; the fish thus migrating; a unit of scoring in baseball. *Mus.* A rapid succession of notes.—*a.* Liquefied or melted; made from material molten and cast in a mold. —**a run for one's mon·ey,** a satisfactory return for one's effort or expenditure, often in competition. —**in the long run,** in the final result; in the conclusion or end. —**on the run,** hastily; fleeing from: He is *on the run* from prison. —**run a·cross,** to discover or meet accidentally. —**run af·ter,** to chase. —**run down,** to pursue and overtake; to strike down by running against; to disparage; belittle; to cease operating through loss of motive power; to trace the source of; to decrease; decline; to decline in health or vigor. —**run foul of,** to come into collision with; to clash with. —**run in,** to visit informally. *Informal.* To arrest. —**run in·to,** collide with; meet; to blend. —**run off,** to depart hurriedly; to repeat or create quickly; to decide the winner of a dead heat by a subsequent contest; to send away; to produce on a machine such as a printing press or typewriter. —**run on,** to continue; to talk incessantly. —**run out,** to stop after running to the end; to come to an end; to become exhausted; to expire: The lease *runs out* in October; expel. —**run out of,** to use up a quantity of. —**run o·ver,** to ride or drive over: to *run over* a chicken; to overflow; to go over cursorily; rehearse. —**run through,** to stab or pierce; to consume or spend rapidly or recklessly; to rehearse rapidly. —**run up,** to make hastily; to accumulate, as debts.

run·a·bout, rən′ə·bowt, *n.* One who runs about from place to place; a small motorboat.

run·a·round, rən′ə·rownd, *n. Informal.* Evasive action, esp. in answer to a question or request.

run·a·way, rən′ə·wā, *n.* A person, horse, etc., that runs away; that which cannot be controlled or halted; an act of running away; an easily won victory or race.—*a.* Having run away; escaped; of a machine, horse, car, etc., out of control; accomplished by running away or eloping; decisive or easily won, as a race; uncontrolled and usu. rapid: *runaway* inflation.

run·down, rən′down, *n.* A summing-up; a concise review: a *rundown* of expenses.

run-down, rən′down′, *a.* Tired; weak; sick; lacking vigor; dilapidated; shabby; no longer running because unwound, as a timepiece.

rung, rəng, *n.* One of the horizontal crosspieces form-

---

a- hat, fāte, fâre, fäther; **e-** met, mē; **i-** pin, pīne; **o-** not, nōte, ôrb, moove (move), boy, pownd; **u-** cūbe, bŭll, tûk (took); **ch-** chin; **th-** thick, ŧhen; **zh-** vizhon (vision); **ə-** əgo, takən, pencəl, lemən, bərd (bird).

ing the steps of a ladder; a rounded or shaped piece fixed for strengthening purposes, as between the legs of a chair.

run-in, rən′in, *n.* An altercation.

run•ner, rən′ər, *n.* One who runs; a racer; a messenger; one who solicits business; a device which enables an object to move or slide; that on which something runs or slides: the *runner* of a sleigh or skate; narrow carpeting, as for a staircase or hallway; a narrow piece of cloth, usu. decorative, suitable for a dresser or table; smuggler; any of a number of twining plants; a slender stem of such plants.

run•ner-up, rən′ər-əp′, *n.* The player or team that finishes second in a contest.

run•ning, rən′ing, *a.* Moving rapidly; kept for racing: a *running* horse; climbing or creeping, as a plant; moving freely; functioning; linear: ten miles *running*; flowing; fluid; current; sustained; repeated; accomplished or initiated while running; in succession; without any intervening day or year: to visit two days *running*; discharging pus or matter.—*n.* The act of one who runs; a quantity run: the first *running* of a still.—*adv.* —**out of the run•ning,** having no chance to win.

run•ning mate, *n.* A candidate for the subordinate of two related offices, as the vice-president.

run•ny, rən′ē, *a.,* **-ni•er, -ni•est.** Tending to drip or run: a *runny* nose.

run•off, rən′ôf, rən′of, *n.* Something which runs off, as rain which flows off from the land in streams; a deciding final race or contest.

run-of-the-mill, rən′əv-thə-mil′, *a.* Average; ordinary.

run-on, rən′on, rən′ôn, *a.* Of something added.—*n.* Added material.

runt, rənt, *n.* Any animal below the usual size of the breed; the smallest in a litter, esp. puppies or pigs; an undersized person, often used contemptuously. —**runt•y,** *a.,* **-i•er, -i•est.**

run-through, rən′throo, *n.* A rapid rehearsal of a part, play, or speech before public performance; a cursory review.

run•way, rən′wā, *n.* A way along which something runs; a hard-surfaced, clear pathway used by planes for taking off and landing.

rup•ture, rəp′chər, *n.* The act of breaking or bursting; the state of being broken; a hernia; a breach of concord between either individuals or nations.—*v.t.,* **-tured, -tur•ing.** To make a rupture in; to burst.—*v.i.* To suffer a breach or rupture.

ru•ral, rûr′əl, *a.* Pertaining to the country, as distinguished from a city or town; pertaining to agriculture or farming. —**ru•ral•ly,** *adv.*

ru•ral•ize, rûr′ə•līz, *v.i.,* **-ized, -iz•ing.** To go into or dwell in the country.—*v.t.* To render rural. —**ru•ral•i•za•tion,** rûr•ə•li•zā′shən, *n.*

ru•ral route, *n.* A country mail route serviced by U.S. post office carriers.

ruse, rooz, *n.* An artifice or trick.

rush, rəsh, *v.i.* To move, act, or go with speed, impetuosity, or violence; to go, come, or pass rapidly: Tears *rush* to the eyes.—*v.t.* To act, move, or drive with speed or violence: to *rush* the injured to the hospital; to send, push, or force with unusual speed: to *rush* a bill through Congress; to attack suddenly and swiftly. *Informal.* To heap attention on.—*n.* The act of rushing; an eager flocking of people to some place: the California gold *rush*; an unexpected sudden surge or appearance: a *rush* of blood to his face; hurried activity or busy haste: the *rush* of city life; a hurried state, as from pressure of affairs. *Informal.* Concentrated attention paid a women by a suitor, to a prospective member by

a fraternity or sorority, etc.—*a.* Requiring haste: a *rush* order for goods; characterized by rush, press of work, or traffic: the *rush* hours on the subway. —**rush•er,** *n.*

rush, rəsh, *n.* A type of grasslike herb with pithy or hollow stems, found in wet or marshy places; a stem of such a plant, used for making chair bottoms, mats, and baskets.

rus•set, rəs′it, *n.* A yellowish-brown, light-brown, or reddish-brown color; a kind of winter apple with a rough brownish skin.—*a.* Yellowish-brown or reddish-brown in color.

Rus•sian rou•lette, rəsh′ən, *n.* A suicidal game in which the participants spin the cylinder of a revolver loaded with one bullet, place the muzzle against the head, and pull the trigger.

rust, rəst, *n.* The red or orange coating which forms on the surface of iron when exposed to air and moisture; any accretion resembling rust; a reddish or yellowish-brown color.—*v.i.* To contract rust, or grow rusty, as iron; to become rust-colored; to deteriorate or become impaired, as through inaction or disuse.—*v.t.* To affect with rust; to make rust-colored.

rus•tic, rəs′tik, *a.* Of, pertaining to, or living in the country as distinguished from towns or cities; rural; simple or unsophisticated; uncouth; made or built in country fashion or of simple materials.—*n.* A country person, esp. an unsophisticated one.

rus•ti•cate, rəs′ti•kāt, *v.i.,* **-cat•ed, -cat•ing.** To go to the country; stay in the country.—*v.t.* To send to or domicile in the country; to render rustic or countrified; to construct or finish, as masonry, in the rustic manner. —**rus•ti•ca•tion,** rəs•ti•kā′shən, *n.* —**rus•ti•ca•tor,** *n.* —**rus•tic•i•ty,** rə•stis′i•tē, *n. pl.,* **-ties.**

rus•tle, rəs′əl, *v.i.,* **-tled, -tling.** To make a succession of slight, soft sounds, as of parts rubbing gently one on another, as leaves or bushes, silks, or papers; to cause such sounds to be made by moving or stirring something; to move, go, or pass with such sounds. *Informal.* To move or work energetically or vigorously.—*v.t.* To move or stir something so as to cause a rustling sound: The wind *rustles* the leaves. *Informal.* To move or get by energetic action; to steal, esp. cattle.—*n.* The sound made by anything that rustles.

rus•tler, rəs′lər, *n. Informal.* A vigorous, energetic person; a cattle thief.

rust-proof, rəst′proof, *a.* Not subject to rusting.

rust•y, rəs′tē, *a.,* **-i•er, -i•est.** Affected by or covered with rust; consisting of or produced by rust; rust-colored; impaired through disuse or neglect; affected with rust disease, as a plant. —**rust•i•ly,** *adv.* —**rust•i•ness,** *n.*

rut, rət, *n.* The periodical sexual excitement of deer and some other animals; the time during which this occurs.—*v.i.,* **rut•ted, rut•ting.**

rut, rət, *n.* A furrow or track worn into a surface, as by the passage of wheels; a habitual or stereotyped pattern of behavior.—*v.t.,* **rut•ted, rut•ting.** To make ruts in or on.

ru•ta•ba•ga, roo•tə•bā′gə, *n.* A garden vegetable in the mustard family, producing a solid underground tuber with white or yellow flesh; the edible tuber itself.

ru•the•ni•um, roo•thē′nē•əm, *n.* A rare, steel-gray, metallic element of the platinum group.

ruth•less, rooth′lis, *a.* Having no mercy or pity; cruel.

rut•ty, rət′ē, *a.,* **-ti•er, -ti•est.** Full of ruts, as a highway or road.

rye, rī, *n.* A hardy cereal plant allied to wheat, cultivated as food for livestock and for making flour and whiskey; the grain or seeds of this plant; whiskey distilled wholly or partly from rye.

S

S, s, es, *n.* The nineteenth letter of the English alphabet; something having the shape of the letter **S** or **s.**

's. A written ending representing the possessive of most singular nouns, plural nouns that do not end in *s* or *es*, pronouns, and noun phrases, and adding the sound of *s* or *z*: child's, men's, someone's.

's. A contraction of **has**: She's arrived; a contraction of **is**: She's here; a contraction of **us**: Let's go. *Informal.* A contraction of **does**: What's he need? *Informal.* A contraction of **as**: so's to let him know.

Sab·bath, sab'əth, *n.* The seventh day of the week, Saturday, as the day of rest and religious observances among the Jews and certain Christian sects; the first day of the week, Sunday, similarly observed by most Christians.—*a.* Pertaining to or characteristic of the Sabbath.

Sab·bat·i·cal, sə·bat'i·kəl, *a.* Relating to or characteristic of the Sabbath; (*l.c.*) providing time for rest and regeneration. Also **Sab·bat·ic.**—*n.* (*L.c.*) A sabbatical year.

sab·bat·i·cal year, *n.* A year's leave, with remuneration, granted by some educational institutions every seven years to teachers and professors for study, travel, or research.

sa·ber, sā'bər, *n.* A heavy cavalry sword having a broad, thick-backed, and slightly curved blade.—*v.t.* To strike, cut, or kill with a saber.

sa·ber rat·tling, *n.* A verbal threat of war or an aggressive show of military power.

sa·ber-toothed ti·ger, sā'bər·tootht, *n.* Any of the extinct, large, catlike carnivores that had excessively long upper canine teeth of curved, saberlike appearance.

sa·ble, sā'bəl, *n.* A carnivorous mammal found chiefly in the northern regions of Asia, and hunted for its dark, lustrous fur; the fur of the sable; the color black or dark brown.—*a.* Extremely dark; black; consisting of the fur from the sable.

sab·o·tage, sab'ə·täzh, *n.* Malicious injury or destruction to work, tools, or machinery, or any underhanded interference with production or business, as caused by discontented employees or by agents of the enemy during a time of war; any malicious attacking or undermining.—*v.t.,* **-taged, -tag·ing.** To injure, destroy, or attack by sabotage.

sab·o·teur, sab·ə·tər', *n.* One who commits or practices sabotage.

sa·bra, sä'brə, *n.* A native of Israel.

sac, sak, *n.* A bag or cyst in an animal or plant, often a receptacle for a liquid.

sac·cha·rin, sak'ə·rin, *n.* A white, crystalline substance, synthetically produced, and used primarily as a calorie-free sugar substitute.

sac·cha·rine, sak'ə·rin, *a.* Pertaining to sugar; sugary; cloyingly sweet.—*n.* Saccharin.

sac·er·do·tal, sas·ər·dō'təl, *a.* Pertaining to priests or the priesthood; priestly.

sa·chet, sa·shā', *n.* A small bag or case which contains a perfumed powder; the sachet powder itself.

sack, sak, *n.* A large bag of some strong, woven material, as for grain, potatoes, or coal; the amount which a sack will hold; any bag. *Informal.* A bed; dismissal or discharge, as from employment: to give someone the *sack.*—*v.t.* To put into a sack or sacks. *Informal.* To dismiss, as from employment. —**hit the sack.** *Informal.* To go to sleep or to bed. —**sack out.** *Informal.* To fall asleep; to go to bed.

sack, sak, *v.t.* To pillage or loot after capture, as a city; plunder.—*n.* The pillaging of a captured place.

—**sack·er,** *n.*

sack·cloth, sak'klôth, sak'kloth, *n.* Coarse cloth of which sacks are made; coarse cloth worn in mourning or for penance. —**in sack·cloth and ash·es,** in a condition of remorse, sorrow, or repentance.

sack·ful, sak'fûl, *n. pl.,* **-fuls.** The amount or quantity a sack will hold.

sack·ing, sak'ing, *n.* A coarse, woven fabric, as of hemp or flax, used to make sacks.

sac·ra·ment, sak'rə·mənt, *n.* Any of certain solemn religious ceremonies of the Christian church regarded as outward and visible signs of inward and spiritual grace. (*Often cap.*) The Eucharist, or the consecrated elements of the Eucharist. Something regarded as possessing a sacred character or a mysterious significance; a sign, token, or symbol. —**sac·ra·men·tal,** sak·rə·men'təl, *a.*

sa·cred, sā'krid, *a.* Appropriated or dedicated to a deity or to some religious purpose; consecrated; hallowed; holy; pertaining to religion: *sacred* music: opposed to *profane* and *secular*; reverently dedicated to some person or object: a monument *sacred* to the memory of a person; secured against violation by reverence or respect: a *sacred* oath. —**sa·cred·ly,** *adv.* —**sa·cred·ness,** *n.*

sa·cred cow, *n. Informal.* Any person or group considered to be above criticism or censure.

sac·ri·fice, sak'ri·fīs, *n.* An offering to a deity in propitiation or homage; that which is so offered; a giving up of something valued, esp. for the sake of something valued more highly; the thing so surrendered or devoted; a loss of profit incurred in selling something below its value; in baseball, a bunt, fly ball, etc., which advances or scores a runner although the batter is retired.—*v.t.,* **-ficed, -fic·ing.** To make a sacrifice or offering of.—*v.i.* To offer or make a sacrifice. —**sac·ri·fic·er,** *n.* —**sac·ri·fi·cial,** sak·rə·fish'əl, *a.*

sac·ri·lege, sac'rə·lij, *n.* The violation or profanation of anything sacred or held sacred.

sac·ri·le·gious, sak·rə·lij'əs, sak·rə·lē'jəs, *a.* Guilty of or involving sacrilege; impious.

sac·ro·il·i·ac, sak·rō·il'ē·ak, *a.* Pertaining to the sacrum and the ilium, and sometimes to the joints or ligaments connecting them.—*n.*

sac·ro·sanct, sak'rō·sangkt, *a.* Exceptionally sacred and inviolable; holy and venerable. —**sac·ro·sanc·ti·ty,** sak·rō·sang'tə·tē, **sac·ro·sanct·ness,** *n.*

sac·rum, sak'rəm, sā'krəm, *n. pl.,* **-rums, -ra.** A bone resulting from the fusion of two or more vertebrae between the lumbar and the coccygeal regions: in humans forming the posterior wall of the pelvis. —**sa·cral,** *a.*

sad, sad, *a.,* **sad·der, sad·dest.** Full of sorrow; causing sorrow; grieving; distressing; unfortunate; dark; somber; pitifully bad or contemptible: a *sad* showing at the box office. —**sad·ly,** *adv.* —**sad·ness,** *n.*

sad·den, sad'ən, *v.t.* To make sad or sorrowful.—*v.i.* To become sad or sorrowful.

sad·dle, sad'əl, *n.* A contrivance secured on the back of a horse or other animal to serve as a seat for a rider; a similar seat, as on a bicycle; something resembling a saddle in shape or position.—*v.t.,* **-dled, -dling.** To put a saddle upon, as a horse; to load or charge as with a burden: They *saddled* her with responsibilities; to impose as a burden (upon).—*v.i.* To saddle a horse or get into the saddle, often followed by *up.*

sad·dle-backed, sad'əl·bakt, *a.* Having the back or upper surface concavely curved like a saddle, as a

---

a- hat, fāte, fāre, fäther; **e-** met, mē; **i-** pin, pīne; **o-** not, nōte, ôrb, moove (move), boy, pownd;
u- cūbe, bûll, tûk (took); **ch-** chin; **th-** thick, ŧhen; **zh-** vizhon (vision); **ə-** əgo, takən, pəncəl, lemən, bərd (bird).

sway-backed horse.

sad·dle·bag, sad′əl·bag, n. One of a pair of bags hanging from a saddle or laid over the back of an animal, bicycle, or motorcycle.

sad·dle horse, n. A horse used or trained esp. for riding with a saddle.

sad·dle soap, n. A mild castile soap, used to clean and condition leather.

sad·dle sore, n. A sore which develops on a horse's back from the rubbing of a saddle; an irritation on the rider caused by the chafing of a saddle. —**sad·dle·sore**, sad′əl·sôr, a.

sad·ism, sad′iz·əm, sā′diz·əm, n. The pathological derivation of sexual pleasure from inflicting physical or mental pain upon another; the tendency to take pleasure in cruelty. —**sad·ist**, n., a. —**sa·dis·tic**, sə·dis′tik, sā·dis′tik, a. —**sa·dis·ti·cal·ly**, adv.

sad·o·mas·o·chism, sā·dō·mas′ə·kiz·əm, sad·ō·mas′ə·kiz·əm, n. A derivation of pleasure from inflicting pain upon oneself and another. —**sad·o·mas·o·chist**, n.

sad sack, n. Informal. A bumbling, ineffectual person.

sa·fa·ri, sə·fär′ē, n. pl., -**ris**. A journey or expedition, esp. in eastern Africa, as for hunting; a body of such persons.

safe, sāf, a., **saf·er**, **saf·est**. Free from or not liable to danger; having escaped hurt, injury, or damage; not exposing to harm; trustworthy; dependable; involving no danger, risk, or error; without danger of controversy: a safe judgment.—n. A receptacle, usu. a metal box or vault, for keeping valuables secure from damage or theft.

safe-con·duct, sāf′kon′dəkt, n. A document serving as a pass or warrant of security used when traveling in a foreign or hostile country, esp. during war; such a privilege; a convoy or guard providing protection for safe passage.

safe·crack·er, sāf′krak·ər, n. A person who forces open safes with the intent of theft. Also **safe·break·er**, sāf′brā·kər. —**safe·crack·ing**, n.

safe-de·pos·it, sāf′di·poz·it, a. Providing safekeeping for valuables: safe-deposit vaults or boxes.—n. A room or vault where valuables may be stored in safety.

safe·guard, sāf′gärd, n. One who or that which defends or protects; a defense; protection.—v.t. To guard; to defend.

safe·keep·ing, sāf′kē′ping, n. The act of keeping in safety.

safe·ty, sāf′tē, n. pl., -**ties**. The state or quality of being safe; freedom from danger or injury; a device for the prevention of accidents: a safety on a gun.

safe·ty belt, n. A life belt; a strap for fastening a person to a seat or other fixed object to prevent injury; seat belt.

safe·ty glass, n. Glass panes fused with a middle protective agent such as plastic or wire to prevent its shattering on impact.

safe·ty match, n. A match which will light only when rubbed on a specially prepared friction substance.

safe·ty pin, n. A pin bent back on itself to form a spring and having a guard to cover the point.

safe·ty valve, n. A valve, as in a steam boiler, which opens automatically under abnormal pressure and allows excess steam or fluid to escape; any outlet for the release of excess emotion, energy, or anxiety.

safe·ty zone, n. A marked section usu. in the middle of a thoroughfare, reserved for the use of pedestrians to ensure their safety from motorized vehicles. Also **safe·ty is·land**.

saf·flow·er, saf′low·ər, n. A thistlelike herb, bearing large orange-red flowers and seeds abundant with oil; the dried florets, used medicinally or as a red dyestuff.

saf·fron, saf′rən, n. A crocus, with purple flowers; an orange-colored product consisting of the dried stigmas of this crocus, used to color and flavor confectionery and other foods; an orange-yellow color: also **saf·fron yel·low**.—a. Orange-yellow: a saffron moon.

sag, sag, v.i., **sagged**, **sag·ging**. To incline or hang owing to insufficiently supported weight; to sink or curve in the middle; to hang unevenly; to droop; to lose vigor or firmness; to decline in value.—v.t. To cause to bend or give way.—n. The state or act of sagging; a sagging area.

sa·ga, sä′gə, n. A medieval Icelandic or Norse tale of legendary or heroic deeds; any story of heroic exploits.

sa·ga·cious, sə·gā′shəs, a. Wise; quick in apprehension; shrewd. —**sa·gac·i·ty**, sə·gas′ə·tē, n.

sage, sāj, a., **sag·er**, **sag·est**. Wise; judicious.—n. An extremely wise, usually older, person. —**sage·ly**, adv. —**sage·ness**, n.

sage, sāj, n. A shrubby perennial whose grayish-green leaves are used in medicine and for seasoning; the leaves themselves; sagebrush.

sage·brush, sāj′brəsh, n. Any sagelike bushy plants in the composite family common on the dry plains of the western U.S. Also **sage**.

Sag·it·ta·ri·us, saj·i·tār′ē·əs, n. The ninth zodiacal sign; a constellation represented by the figure of a centaur in the act of shooting an arrow.

said, sed, a. Previously referred to or mentioned: the said testimony.

sail, sāl, n. A piece of cloth, usu. canvas, spread to the wind to cause a boat to move through the water; something similar to that in form and function; pl., **sail**. A ship or other vessel. A passage in a vessel, esp. in a sailing vessel.—v.i. To be conveyed in a vessel on water; to begin a voyage; to operate a sailboat; to glide through the air; to pass smoothly along. Informal. To pass quickly; to hurry into action, used with in.—v.t. To pass over, as water, by means of sails; to navigate, as a ship. —**make sail**, to put up a sail or sails; to begin a journey on water. —**sail in·to**, to hurry into action; to attack; castigate. —**set sail**, to embark upon a voyage. —**un·der sail**, having the sails spread; sailing.

sail·boat, sāl′bōt, n. A boat propelled by or fitted for a sail or sails.

sail·cloth, sāl′klôth, sāl′kloth, n. Canvas, cotton, or synthetic materials of strong weave.

sail·er, sā′lər, n. A ship or vessel, esp. in reference to its speed or manner of sailing.

sail·fish, sāl′fish, n. pl., -**fish**, -**fish·es**. A large marine fish with a long, high, dorsal fin resembling a sail.

sail·ing, sā′ling, n. The act of one who or that which sails; the methods and art of navigation; the departure or time of departure of a ship.

sail·or, sā′lər, n. A seaman; a mariner; a member of a ship's crew; a rigid straw hat with a flat, low crown and a circular brim.

saint, sānt, n. A person of exceptional virtue who has died and been canonized; one of the blessed in heaven; an angel; a holy person; an uncommonly patient, unselfish person.—v.t. To canonize. —**saint·hood**, **saint·ship**, n.

Saint Ber·nard, bər·närd′, n. One of a breed of large dogs with a massive head and long hair, used in the Swiss Alps for rescuing travelers from the snow.

saint·ed, sān′tid, a. Canonized; holy; entered into heaven.

saint·ly, sānt′lē, a., -**li·er**, -**li·est**. Resembling or appropriate to a saint. —**saint·li·ness**, n.

Saint Pat·rick's Day, pat′riks dā, n. March 17th, observed by the Irish in honor of St. Patrick.

Saint Val·en·tine's Day, n. February 14th, a day for exchanging valentines and gifts as tokens of affection.

sake, sāk, n. Purpose; benefit; interest; account, used with for: for his sake, for the sake of the community.

sa·ke, sä′ki, sä′kē, n. An alcoholic beverage made in Japan from fermented rice.

sal, sal, n. Salt: used in combination: sal soda.

sal·a·ble, **sale·a·ble**, sāl′ə·bəl, a. Capable of

being sold; in demand. **—sal·a·bil·i·ty,** săl·ə·bil′ə· tē, n. **—sal·a·bly,** adv.

sa·la·cious, sə·lā′shəs, a. Lustful; obscene; lewd.

sal·ad, sal′əd, n. A combination of vegetables or fruits that are cut up and served with a dressing; a similar dish prepared with fruit, meat, seafood, or cheese, usu. served as a main course.

sal·a·man·der, sal′ə·man·dər, n. Any of various lizardlike, scaleless amphibians with a long tail and short limbs, certain of which are aquatic; an imaginary reptile inhabiting fire.

sa·la·mi, sə·lä′mē, n. A spicy beef, or beef and pork sausage.

sal·a·ry, sal′ə·rē, n. pl., **-ries.** The recompense to be paid periodically to a person for regular work, esp. other than manual labor. **—sal·a·ried,** a.

sale, sāl, n. The act of selling; the amount sold; the exchange or transfer of a commodity for an agreed upon price; an offering of goods at reduced prices; auction; opportunity of selling; demand: There is a large sale for this item. Pl. The collective operation of promoting, selling, and distributing goods or services. **—for sale,** available to purchasers. **—on sale,** offered at a reduced price. **—sales,** a.

sales·man, sālz′mən, n. pl., **-men.** A person, esp. a man, whose occupation is selling, either in a store or by canvassing.

sales·man·ship, sālz′mən·ship, n. The work of a salesman; ability or skill at selling.

sales·per·son, sālz′pər·sən, n. pl., **-peo·ple.** One whose occupation is to sell goods or merchandise, esp. in a store. Also **sales·clerk,** sālz′klərk.

sales·room, sālz′room, sālz′rûm, n. A place in which merchandise is displayed and sold.

sales tax, n. A tax placed upon merchandise, usu. a direct percentage of the sale price.

sa·li·ent, sā′lē·ənt, sāl′yənt, a. Conspicuous; prominent; springing; shooting up or out, as a jet of water; projecting outward: a salient angle.—n. A protruding part or angle. **—sa·li·ence, sa·li·en·cy,** n. **—sa·li· ent·ly,** adv. **—sa·li·ent·ness,** n.

sa·line, sā′līn, sā′lēn, a. Consisting of salt; salty.—n. One of the metallic salts; a medicinal solution of salt. **—sa·lin·i·ty,** sə·lin′i·tē, n.

sa·li·va, sə·lī′və, n. The watery, viscid, slightly acid fluid which is secreted by glands of the mouth, serving to moisten the mouth and food, which starts the digesting of starches. **—sal·i·var·y,** sal′ə·ver·ē, a.

sal·i·vate, sal′ə·vāt, v.i., **-vat·ed, -vat·ing.** To secrete saliva.—v.t. To cause to have an abnormal secretion and discharge of saliva in. **—sal·i·va·tion,** sal·ə· vā′shən, n.

sal·low, sal′ō, a. Of a pale, sickly, grayish-yellow color: a sallow complexion.—v.t. To make sallow. **—sal·low·ish,** a.

sal·ly, sal′ē, n. pl., **-lies.** An offensive sortie by besieged troops; a sudden leaping or rushing forth; a brief outburst; an excursion or side trip; a clever remark or flight of wit or fancy.—v.t., **-lied, -ly·ing.** To make a sally.—v.i. To go forth, as besieged troops.

salm·on, sam′ən, n. pl., **-ons, -on.** A marine and freshwater food fish, with yellowish-pink flesh, common in the northern Atlantic Ocean near the mouths of large rivers, which it ascends in order to spawn; a variety of this species confined to lakes, and called 'landlocked salmon'; any of various other fishes of the same family; a pinkish-orange color.

sa·lon, sə·lon′, n. A drawing room or reception room for guests, as in a large, elegant apartment or house; an assembly of guests in such a room; a hall or place used for the exhibition of works of art; a stylish shop or place of business: a Parisian dress salon, a beauty salon.

sa·loon, sə·loon′, n. A bar, taproom, or tavern; a large public room or place: an exhibiting saloon, a dining saloon; a large cabin of a ship.

sal so·da, n. Sodium carbonate.

salt, sôlt, n. Sodium chloride, a crystalline compound used as a seasoning and preservative; a compound produced by the combination of a base, commonly a metallic oxide, with an acid. Pl. Any of several salts used as purgatives. Informal. Wit, piquancy, or sarcasm; an old sailor.—a. Preserved with salt; prepared with or tasting of salt. Informal. Sharp; pungent.—v.t. To season with or as with salt; to preserve with salt; to add, as a mineral, to a mine; to give a false impression of value; to give zest to. **—salt a·way,** to preserve in salt. Informal. To save, as money. **—with a grain of salt,** with an attitude of doubt or disbelief. **—worth one's salt,** worthy of one's reward or wages.

salt·cel·lar, sôlt′sel·ər, n. A small vessel or shaker for holding salt.

salt·ed, sôl′tid, a. Seasoned, cured, or otherwise treated with salt; preserved.

sal·tine, sôl·tēn′, n. A crisp, thin, salted cracker.

salt lick, n. A place where animals lick an exposed natural salt deposit; a salt spring.

salt mine, n. An area where salt is mined; one's place of work when considered as drudgery.

salt·shak·er, sôlt′shā·kər, n. A salt container with a perforated top through which the salt is sprinkled.

salt·wa·ter, sôlt′wô·ter, sôlt′wo·ter, a. Of, containing, or living in salty water, as that of the ocean and of certain lakes.

salt·wort, sôlt′wert, n. Any of various plants of sea beaches, salt marshes, and alkaline regions, used in the production of soda ash.

salt·y, sôl′tē, a., **-i·er, -i·est.** Impregnated with, containing, or tasting of salt; pungent or risqué. **—salt·i· ness,** n.

sa·lu·bri·ous, sə·loo′brē·əs, a. Healthful; wholesome.

sal·u·tar·y, sal′yə·ter·ē, a. Promoting health; beneficial; wholesome.

sal·u·ta·tion, sal·yə·tā′shən, n. The act of greeting; any manner of greeting; the direct address of a letter following the heading, such as 'Dear Sir.'

sa·lu·ta·to·ry, sə·loo′tə·tôr·ē, a. Pertaining to or of the nature of a salutation.—n. pl., **-ries.** A welcoming address, esp. at commencement ceremonies.

sa·lute, sə·loot′, v.t., **-lut·ed, -lut·ing.** To greet with words or a gesture of welcome, courtesy, or homage; to show respect by touching the cap with the right hand; to honor by presenting arms, dipping colors, or the like.—v.i. To perform a salute; to greet.—n. The act or attitude of saluting. **—sa·lut·er,** n.

sal·vage, sal′vij, n. The act of saving a ship or its cargo from wreck or capture by an enemy; the saving of anything from fire or danger; property so saved; payment for saving it.—v.t., **-vaged, -vag·ing.** To make salvage of. **—sal·vage·a·ble,** a. **—sal·vag· er,** n.

sal·va·tion, sal·vā′shən, n. The act of saving; preservation from destruction or danger; the means or cause of saving; his agility was his salvation; the redemption of humanity from the bondage and penalty of sin; redemption.

Sal·va·tion Ar·my, n. A religious society organized along quasi-military lines for purposes of evangelism and care of the poor and degraded.

salve, sav, säv, n. A soothing ointment applied to wounds or sores; a balm; anything that heals, relieves, or placates.—v.t. salved, salv·ing. To ease or soothe by, or as if by, applying salve.

salve, salv, v.t., salved, salv·ing. To salvage, as a ship or goods. **—sal·vor,** n.

sal·vo, sal′vō, n. pl., **-vos, -voes.** A simultaneous discharge of artillery, firearms, or other weapons, often as a salute; a volley; a round of cheers or applause.

Sa·mar·i·tan, sə·mar′i·tən, *a.* Pertaining to ancient Samaria or its people.—*n.* (Often *l.c.*) A benevolent person. Also **good Sa·mar·i·tan.**

sam·ba, sam′bə, säm′bə, *n.* A popular Brazilian dance which originated in Africa; music for a samba. —*v.i.,* **-baed, -ba·ing.** To dance the samba.

same, sām, *a.* Identical; not different or another: the *same* man; of the identical kind; just mentioned or denoted; monotonous.—*pron.* The same thing or person; the thing just denoted.—*adv.* Similarly; in the same manner. —**all the same,** nevertheless; immaterial: It's *all the same* to me. —**just the same,** nevertheless; in like manner. —**same·ness,** *n.*

sam·o·var, sam′ə·vär, sam·ə·vär′, *n.* A tea urn in which the water is heated by a tube containing live coals.

sam·ple, sam′pəl, *n.* A small part or quantity of anything intended to be representative of the whole. —*v.t.,* **-pled, -pling.** To take a sample of; to examine or judge by a sample.—*a.*

sam·pler, sam′plər, *n.* A piece of embroidered work done by beginners for practice.

sam·pler, sam′plər, *n.* One who samples; a collection of samples.

sam·pling, sam′pling, *n.* The act of selecting a sample, as for analyzing; a sample.

Sam·son, sam′sən, *n.* An ancient Hebrew judge of great strength; any extraordinarily strong man.

san·a·to·ri·um, san·ə·tôr′ē·əm, san·ə·tō′rē·əm, *n. pl.,* **-ri·ums, -ri·a,** -rē·ə. An establishment for the treatment of diseases, as tuberculosis, or for invalids or convalescents; a health resort. Also **san·i·tar·i·um.**

sanc·ti·fy, sangk′tə·fī, *v.t.,* **-fied, -fy·ing.** To make holy or sacred; to purify from sin. —**sanc·ti·fi·ca·tion,** sangk·tə·fə·kā′shən, *n.* —**sanc·ti·fi·er,** *n.* —**sanc·ti·fied,** *a.*

sanc·ti·mo·ny, sangk′tə·mō·nē, *n.* The external appearance of sanctity; affected or hypocritical devoutness. —**sanc·ti·mo·ni·ous,** sangk·tə·mō′nē·əs, *a.*

sanc·tion, sangk′shən, *n.* Authoritative permission; an official confirmation or ratification of some specific action. *Usu. pl.* A method often adopted by a group of nations to force another nation to desist in its violation of some particular international law: *sanctions* of boycotting.—*v.t.* To ratify or confirm: to *sanction* a law or a covenant; to authorize or approve. —**sanc·tion·a·ble,** *a.* —**sanc·tion·er,** *n.*

sanc·ti·ty, sangk′ti·tē, *n. pl.,* **-ties.** The state or quality of being sacred or holy; holiness.

sanc·tu·ar·y, sangk′chū·er·ē, *n. pl.,* **-ies.** A sacred or holy place, as a church, a temple, or a sacred grove; an esp. holy place in a temple or church; an asylum; immunity from arrest afforded by refuge in such a place; a refuge for wildlife.

sanc·tum, sangk′təm, *n. pl.,* **-tums, -ta.** A sacred place; a private retreat or room.

sand, sand, *n.* The more or less fine debris of rocks, consisting of small, loose grains. *Usu. pl.* A tract or region, as a desert or a beach, composed principally of sand. *Usu. pl. Fig.* Moments of life or time; a reddish-yellow color.—*v.t.* To sprinkle with or as with sand; bury under sand; to abrade or polish with sand or sandpaper. —**sand·er,** *n.*

san·dal, san′dəl, *n.* A kind of shoe, consisting of a sole fastened to the foot, generally by means of straps; a light slipper; a low-cut rubber overshoe.

san·dal·wood, san′dəl·wûd, *n.* The fragrant wood of any of certain Asiatic trees, used for ornamental carving and burned as incense; any of various other similar trees or their woods.

sand·bag, sand′bag, *n.* A bag filled with sand, used in flood control or fortification, or as ballast.—*v.t.,* **-bagged, -bag·ging.** To furnish with sandbags; hit or stun with a sandbag. *Informal.* Coerce by crude

means. —**sand·bag·ger,** *n.*

sand·bank, sand′bangk, *n.* A bank of sand.

sand bar, *n.* A ridge of sand formed in a river or the sea by the action of tides or currents.

sand·blast, sand′blast, *n.* A blast of air or steam laden with sand, used to clean, grind, cut, or decorate hard surfaces; the apparatus used to apply such a blast.—*v.t., v.i.* To cleanse or engrave with a sandblast.

sand·box, sand′boks, *n.* A box of sand for children's play; a box of sand for any purpose.

sand-cast, sand′kast, *v.t.,* **-cast·ed, -cast·ing.** To prepare, as a casting, by pouring metal into molds made of sand. —**sand cast·ing,** *n.*

sand·lot, sand′lot, *n.* A vacant urban lot used for playing games.

sand·man, sand′man, *n. pl.,* **-men.** An imaginary person who sprinkles sand into children's eyes to make them sleepy.

sand·pa·per, sand′pā·pər, *n.* Strong paper upon which a layer of sand has been fixed with glue, used for smoothing or polishing.—*v.t.* To smooth or polish with sandpaper.

sand pile, *n.* A pile of sand, esp. for children to play in.

sand·pi·per, sand′pī·pər, *n.* Any of various small, shore-inhabiting birds.

sand·stone, sand′stōn, *n.* Stone composed of agglutinated grains of sand.

sand·storm, sand′stôrm, *n.* A windstorm which blows along great clouds of sand.

sand·wich, sand′wich, san′wich, *n.* Two thin slices of bread between which is placed meat, cheese, or the like; anything resembling a sandwich.—*v.t.* To form into or as into a sandwich: to *sandwich* a vacation between two jobs.

sand·y, san′dē, *a.,* **-i·er, -i·est.** Consisting of or abounding with sand; resembling sand; of a yellowish-red color. —**sand·i·ness,** *n.*

sane, sān, *a.,* **san·er, san·est.** Mentally sound; not deranged; having or showing sound judgment. —**sane·ly,** *adv.* —**sane·ness,** *n.*

San·for·ize, san′fə·rīz, *v.t.,* **-ized, -iz·ing.** *Trademark.* To treat, as cloth, so as to prevent shrinkage.

sang, sang, *v.* Past tense of **sing.**

sang-froid, sän·frwä′, *n.* Coolness; composure; imperturbability.

san·gui·nar·y, sang′gwə·ner·ē, *a.* Attended by bloodshed; consisting of blood; bloodthirsty.

san·guine, sang′gwin, *a.* Having the color of blood; ruddy, as a complexion; vigorous; confident; cheerful; optimistic.—*n.* —**san·guine·ly,** *adv.* —**san·guine·ness,** *n.*

san·i·tar·i·um, san·i·tär′ē·əm, *n. pl.,* **-ums, -a.** Sanatorium.

san·i·tar·y, san′i·ter·ē, *a.* Pertaining to or designed to promote health; hygienic. —**san·i·tar·i·ly,** *adv.*

san·i·tar·y nap·kin, *n.* A pad of absorbent material, usu. cotton, used by women during the menstrual period.

san·i·ta·tion, san·i·tā′shən, *n.* The adoption of sanitary measures to eliminate unhealthy elements; hygiene.

san·i·tize, san′ə·tīz, *v.t.,* **-tized, -tiz·ing.** To render sanitary; disinfect.

san·i·ty, san′i·tē, *n.* The state of being sane or of sound mind; rationality; reasonableness.

sans, sanz, *prep.* Without.

San·skrit, San·scrit, san′skrit, *n.* The ancient language of the Hindus, which is the language of religion and classical literature in India.—*a.*

San·ta Claus, san′tə klôz, *n.* A symbolic figure of Christmas: a stout, white-bearded, jovial old gentleman in red clothing, who supposedly distributes presents at Christmas. Also **Saint Nich·o·las.**

sap, sap, *n.* The juice or vital circulating fluid of a plant; any vital fluid, as blood; vigor or vitality; sapwood. *Informal.* Someone foolish or gullible; a saphead.—*v.t.,* **sapped, sap·ping.** To drain the sap from.

sap, sap, *v.t.,* **sapped, sap•ping.** To approach, as an enemy position, with narrow trenches protected by parapets; to weaken or destroy insidiously; to enervate; to undermine.

sap•head, sap′hed, *n. Informal.* A simpleton; a fool. **—sap•head•ed,** *a.*

sa•pi•ent, sā′pē•ənt, *a.* Wise or sagacious: often used ironically. **—sa•pi•ence, sa•pi•en•cy,** *n.*

sap•less, sap′lis, *a.* Destitute of sap; dry; withered; lacking vigor or vitality; dull.

sap•ling, sap′ling, *n.* A young tree; a youth.

sa•pon•i•fy, sə•pon′ə•fī, *v.t.,* **-fied, -fy•ing.** To convert (a fat or oil) into soap by treating with an alkali.

sap•per, sap′ər, *n.* That which or one who saps; a soldier who constructs trenches, fieldworks, etc., or who lays, uncovers, and disarms mines.

sap•phire, saf′īr, *n.* Any of the various kinds of corundum, with the exception of the ruby, used for gems, esp. those of various shades of blue; such a precious gem; a rich blue color.

sap•phism, saf′iz•əm, *n.* Lesbianism.

sap•py, sap′ē, *a.,* **-pi•er, -pi•est.** Abounding with sap; juicy; energetic; young. *Informal.* Stupid; sentimental. **—sap•pi•ness,** *n.*

sap•suck•er, sap′sək•ər, *n.* Any of several small woodpeckers that damage trees by exposing the sapwood to drink the sap.

sap•wood, sap′wûd, *n.* The new, outer, physiologically active wood of a tree.

Sar•a•cen, sar′ə•sən, *n.* Any of the nomadic Arab peoples living between Syria and Arabia; a Moslem, esp. during the Crusades.

sa•ran, sə•ran′, *n.* A thermoplastic which is durable, flexible, waterproof, and chemically resistant.

sar•casm, sär′kaz•əm, *n.* A bitter, cutting expression; a caustic remark; a gibe; a taunt; the employment of ironical or satirical language. **—sar•cas•tic,** sär•kas′tik, *a.* **—sar•cas•ti•cal•ly,** *adv.*

sar•co•ma, sär•kō′mə, *n. pl.,* **-mas, -ma•ta.** Any of various malignant tumors originating in the connective tissue.

sar•coph•a•gus, sär•kof′ə•gəs, *n. pl.,* **-gi, -jī, -gus•es.** A stone coffin, esp. a large ornamental one.

sard, särd, *n.* A compact variety of chalcedony having a translucent, brownish-red color.

sar•dine, sär•dēn′, *n. pl.,* **-dines, -dine.** One of several small edible fish, related to the herring, and preserved in tins with oil.

sar•don•ic, sär•don′ik, *a.* Bitterly ironical; sarcastic; scornful; mocking. **—sar•don•i•cal•ly,** *adv.*

sar•gas•sum, sär•gas′əm, *n.* A species of seaweed widely distributed in the warmer waters of the globe, as the common gulfweed. Also **sar•gas•so.**

sa•ri, sa•ree, sär′ē, *n. pl.,* **sa•ris, sa•rees.** The chief garment of a Hindu woman, consisting of a long piece of cotton or silk cloth wound round the body, with one end thrown over the shoulder and sometimes the head.

sa•rong, sə•rông′, sə•rong′, *n.* The principal garment for both sexes in the Malay Archipelago, consisting of colored silk or cotton enveloping the lower part of the body like a skirt; a kind of cloth for such garments.

sar•sa•pa•ril•la, sas•pə•ril′ə, sär•sə•pə•ril′ə, *n.* The dried root of certain trailing or climbing tropical American plants; a beverage or medicine made from this root.

sar•to•ri•al, sär•tōr′ē•əl, sär•tôr′ē•əl, *a.* Of or pertaining to a tailor or to his work; pertaining to dress, esp. of men.

sash, sash, *n.* A band or scarf worn over the shoulder or around the waist for ornament.

sash, sash, *n.* The framed part of a window in which the glass is fixed.**—v.t.** To furnish with window sashes.

sa•shay, sa•shā′, *n. Informal.* To move in a strutting or gliding way.

sass, sas, *n. Informal.* A pert, discourteous retort; back talk.**—v.t. Informal.** To respond in an impertinent manner; to talk back.

sas•sa•fras, sas′ə•fras, *n.* A N. American tree; the aromatic bark of its root, used medicinally and esp. for flavoring beverages or confectionery.

sas•sy, sas′ē, *a.,* **-si•er, -si•est.** Saucy; pert; impudent.

Sa•tan, sāt′ən, *n.* The chief evil spirit; the great adversary of humanity; the devil.

sa•tan•ic, sā•tan′ik, sə•tan′ik, *a.* Of or characteristic of Satan; extremely wicked. Also **sa•tan•i•cal.**

sa•tan•ism, sāt′ə•niz•əm, *n.* Satanic disposition or practice. (*Cap.*) The worship of Satan, esp. in mockery of Christian ritual. **—sa•tan•ist,** *n.*

satch•el, sach′əl, *n.* A small suitcase or bag which may be carried either by the hand or slung from the shoulder.

sate, sāt, *v.t.,* **sat•ed, sat•ing.** To satisfy completely, as the appetite or desire; to glut or satiate.

sa•teen, sa•tēn′, *n.* Cotton cloth woven and treated to resemble satin.

sat•el•lite, sat′ə•līt, *n.* A small planet revolving around a larger one; a secondary planet or moon; anything dependent on another thing; a subservient follower; a small city or nation which is under the economic, military, or political domination of a larger state; any man-made object orbiting the earth or a celestial body.**—a.**

sa•ti•a•ble, sā′shē•ə•bəl, sā′shə•bəl, *a.* Capable of being satiated or satisfied. **—sa•ti•a•bly,** *adv.* **—sa•ti•a•bil•i•ty,** sā•shə•bil′ə•tē, **sa•ti•a•ble•ness,** *n.*

sa•ti•ate, sā′shē•āt, *v.t.,* **-at•ed, -at•ing.** To satisfy, as the appetite or desire; to fill or gratify to excess. **—sā′shē•it,** sā′shē•āt, *a.* Filled to satiety. **—sa•ti•at•ed,** *a.* **—sa•ti•a•tion,** sā•shē•ā′shən, *n.*

sa•ti•e•ty, sə•tī′ə•tē, *n.* The state of being satiated; surfeit.

sat•in, sat′ən, *n.* A silk fabric so woven and finished as to have a characteristic smoothness and gloss on one surface.**—a.** Of or like satin. **—sat•in•y,** *a.*

sat•ire, sat′īr, *n.* The use of irony, sarcasm, or ridicule in exposing, denouncing, or deriding vice, folly, or the like; a literary composition or branch of literature, in which vices and the like are held up to ridicule.

sa•tir•i•cal, sə•tēr′ə•kəl, *a.* Of, relating to, or marked by satire. Also **sa•tir•ic.** **—sa•tir•i•cal•ly,** *adv.*

sat•i•rist, sat′ər•ist, *n.* A writer of satires; one who indulges in satire.

sat•i•rize, sat′ə•rīz, *v.t.,* **-rized, -riz•ing.** To assail with satire; make the object of satire. **—sat•i•riz•er,** *n.*

sat•is•fac•tion, sat•is•fak′shən, *n.* The act of satisfying, or the state of being satisfied; fulfillment of desires, demands, or needs; the cause of gratification; payment, as for debt; reparation, as of a wrong or injury; release from doubt or conviction.

sat•is•fac•to•ry, sat•is•fak′tə•rē, *a.* Affording satisfaction. **—sat•is•fac•to•ri•ly,** *adv.*

sat•is•fy, sat′is•fī, *v.t.,* **-fied, -fy•ing.** To fulfill the desires, expectations, or demands of, as a person; to supply fully the needs of; to pay, as a creditor; to make reparation to or for; to give assurance to or convince; to answer sufficiently, as an objection.**—v.i.** To give contentment or satisfaction; to make reparation or to atone. **—sat•is•fi•a•ble,** *a.* **—sat•is•fi•er,** *n.* **—sat•is•fy•ing•ly,** *adv.*

sat•u•ra•ble, sach′ər•ə•bəl, *a.* Able to be saturated.

sat•u•rate, sach′ə•rāt, *v.t.,* **-rat•ed, -rat•ing.** To cause to become completely penetrated or soaked; to unite with a substance until no more can be absorbed or added. **—sat•u•ra•tion,** sach•ə•rā′shən, *n.*

sat•u•rat•ed, sach′ə•rā•tid, *a.* Soaked, impregnated, or imbued thoroughly; free from the admixture of

---

a- hat, fāte, fâre, fäther; **e-** met, mē; **i-** pin, pīne; **o-** not, nōte, ôrb, moove (move), boy, pownd; **u-** cūbe, bŭll, tûk (took); **ch-** chin; **th-** thick, <del>th</del>en; **zh-** vizhon (vision); **ə-** ago, takən, pencəl, lemən, bərd (bird).

white, as colors.

Sat·ur·day, sat′ər·dē, sat′ər·dā, n. The seventh or last day of the week; the day following Friday. **—Sat·ur·days,** adv.

Sat·urn, sat′ərn, n. The planet, located between Jupiter and Uranus, encircled by rings thought to be composed of icy particles.

sat·ur·na·li·a, sat·ər·nā′lē·ə, n. pl., sing. or pl. in const. A period of unrestrained revelry and often licentiousness; an orgy.

sat·ur·nine, sat′ər·nīn, a. Gloomy; grave; morose; heavy and forbidding.

sa·tyr, sā′tər, sat′ər, n. A deity or demigod of the Greeks and Romans, half man and half goat; a lecher. **—sa·tyr·ic,** sə·tēr′ik, a.

sauce, sôs, n. Any preparation, usu. liquid or soft, eaten as a relish, dressing, or gravy accompaniment to food; stewed fruit: apple sauce. Informal. Sauciness; alcoholic drink.—v.t., **sauced, sauc·ing.** To dress or prepare with sauce; to season; to give zest to. Informal. To speak impertinently to.

sauce pan, sôs′pan, n. A small pot for boiling or stewing.

sau·cer, sô′sər, n. A shallow piece of china or other ware, small and round in shape, in which a cup is set; any dish, plate, or vessel shaped like a saucer.

sau·cy, sô′sē, a. **-ci·er, -ci·est.** Flippant or impudent; pert; sprightly. **—sau·ci·ly,** adv. **—sau·ci·ness,** n.

sauer·kraut, sow′ər·krowt, n. A traditionally German cabbage cut fine, salted, and allowed to ferment.

sau·na, sow′nə, sô′nə, n. A steam bath taken in the Finnish manner, the steam coming from water being poured over heated stones; a bathhouse or room for taking a sauna.

saun·ter, sôn′tər, sän′tər, v.i. To walk along leisurely; to stroll.—n. A leisurely, aimless walk; a stroll. **—saun·ter·er,** n.

sau·sage, sô′sij, n. Minced pork, beef, or other meats, often combined with various added ingredients and seasonings, either stuffed into a casing or formed into patties. **—sau·sage·like,** a.

sau·té, sô·tā′, sô·tā′, a. Cooked or browned quickly in a pan containing a little fat.—n. A dish of food sautéed.—v.t., **-téed, -tée·ing.** To pan-fry quickly using a little fat.

sav·age, sav′ij, a. Untamed, ferocious, or fierce: savage beasts; barbarous or uncivilized; furious or violent: a savage temper; untaught or rude: savage manners; uncultivated or wild, as the forest or wilderness.—n. A human being in his or her native, uncivilized state; a cruel or brutal person; a barbarian; one who is rude or uncultivated. **—sav·age·ness,** n. **—sav·age·ry,** n. pl., **-ries.**

sa·van·na, sa·van·nah, sə·van′ə, n. An extensive, open, grassy plain of tropical or subtropical regions.

sa·vant, sə·vänt′, sav′ənt, n. A person of learning; scholar.

save, sāv, v.t., **saved, sav·ing.** To rescue from danger; preserve from harm, loss, destruction, etc.; maintain; safeguard; to keep from being lost, as a game or match; to set apart or lay by, as for future use; to avoid the spending or waste of, as money, goods, or time; to treat carefully in order to reduce wear or fatigue; to prevent the occurrence of; to obviate the necessity of: A stitch in time saves nine; deliver from the power and consequences of sin.—v.i. To lay up money as the result of economy; to be economical in expenditure; to keep someone or something from injury or danger; to keep without spoiling, esp. food.—n. An act of saving. **—sav·a·ble, save·a·ble,** a. **—sav·er,** n.

save, sāv, prep. Except or but: All the children save two went to the picnic.—conj. Except; but: used with that.

sav·ing, sā′ving, a. That saves; redeeming or compensating: a saving feature; accustomed to save; economical; making a reservation: a saving clause.—n.

Economy; a reduction in expenditure: a saving of 20 percent; that which is saved. Pl. Money saved.—prep. Except or save: none saving imperfect ones; with all due respect to or for: saving your presence.—conj. Except; but.—sav·ing·ly, adv.

sav·ior, sāv′yər, n. One who saves, rescues, or delivers. (Cap). A title of God and esp. of Christ, often preceded by 'the.'

sa·voir-faire, sav′wär·fâr′, n. The knowledge of just what to do or say; tact.

sa·vor, sā′vər, n. The quality of something that affects the palate, esp. in a favorable way; a specific flavor or smell; the ability to stimulate or excite.—v.i. To have a particular taste or flavor; to have the distinctive quality or appearance, followed by of: His conduct savors of pride.—v.t. To season; to taste or smell with relish; to take delight in. **—sa·vor·er,** n.

sa·vor·y, sā′və·rē, a., **-i·er, -i·est.** Having a pleasant flavor and smell; pleasantly piquant to the taste; respectable. **—sa·vor·i·ly,** adv. **—sa·vor·i·ness,** n.

sa·vor·y, sā′və·rē, n. An herb native in southern Europe and much cultivated as a seasoning. Also **sum·mer sa·vor·y.**

sav·vy, sav′ē, v.t., v.i., **-vied, -vy·ing.** Informal. To know; understand.—n. Informal. Understanding; intelligence; common sense.—a., **-vi·er, -vi·est.** Informal. Characterized by shrewdness or understanding.

saw, sô, n. A hand tool or powered cutting instrument consisting of a blade, band, or disk of thin metal with a dentated or toothed edge.—v.t., **sawed, sawed** or **sawn, saw·ing.** To cut with a saw; to move through as if with a saw: to saw the air.—v.i. To use a saw; to be cut with a saw, as wood. **—saw·er,** n. **—saw·like,** a.

saw, sô, v. Past tense of **see.**

saw, sô, n. A proverb; maxim.

saw·buck, sô′bək, n. A sawhorse with X-shaped end supports. Informal. A ten-dollar bill.

saw·dust, sô′dəst, n. Particles of wood produced by the operation of a saw.

sawed-off, sôd′ôf, sôd′of, a. Cut off with a saw at one end. Informal. Short of or unusually small stature, as a man.

saw·horse, sô′hôrs, n. A frame for holding wood that is being sawed.

saw·mill, sô′mil, n. An establishment where timber is sawed into planks or boards by machinery; a machine for sawing timber.

saw-toothed, sô′tootht, a. Having teeth like a saw; serrated. Also **saw·tooth.**

saw·yer, sô′yər, n. One who saws wood, esp. as an occupation.

sax, saks, n. Informal. A saxophone.

Sax·on, sak′sən, n. An Anglo-Saxon; an Englishman; the language of the Saxons; a native of modern Saxony; one of the people formerly dwelling in northern Germany who invaded and conquered England in the 5th and 6th centuries.—a. English; pertaining to Saxons.

sax·o·phone, sak′sə·fōn, n. A tubular brass or silver wind instrument, with a reed mouthpiece and tonal finger keys. **—sax·o·phon·ist,** n.

say, sā, v.t., **said, say·ing.** To utter or speak; to give as a belief or opinion; to repeat or recite: to say a pledge; to communicate; to allege or report: They say he will be promoted.—v.i. To speak; to declare; to state an opinion.—n. Something said; opportunity or turn to speak; authority: He has the final say.—adv. About; approximately: That will cost, say, ten dollars. **—that is to say,** in other words; otherwise. **—say·a·ble,** a. **—say·er,** n.

say·ing, sā′ing, n. That which is said; a proverb; a maxim; an adage.

say-so, sā′sō, n. Informal. One's personal statement or assertion; the right to decide.

scab, skab, n. A sort of crust formed over a sore in healing. Informal. A nonunion workman, a union worker who does not participate in a strike, or one who takes a striker's place at work; a scoundrel.—*v.i.,* **scabbed, scab·bing.** To form or to have scabs. *Informal.* To work as a scab.

scab·bard, skab′ərd, *n.* The sheath of a sword or other similar weapon.

scab·by, skab′ē, *a.,* **-bi·er, -bi·est.** Covered or coated with scabs. *Informal.* Low or mean; vile. **—scab·bi·ness,** *n.*

sca·bies, skā′bēz, skā′bi·ēz, *n. pl. but sing. in constr.* An easily transmitted skin disease, afflicting cattle and sheep as well as humans.

scad, skad, *n. pl.,* **scad, scads.** The saurel, a popular salt-water food fish.

scad, skad, *n. Usu. pl. Informal.* Large amounts or quantities of, as *scads* of money.

scaf·fold, skaf′əld, skaf′ōld, *n.* A temporary structure for holding workers and materials during the erection, repair, or decoration of a building; an elevated platform on which a criminal is executed; any raised framework.—*v.t.* To furnish or support with a scaffold.

scaf·fold·ing, skaf′əl·ding, *n.* A scaffold or system of scaffolds; materials for scaffolds.

sca·lar, skā′lər, *a.* Resembling a ladder, as numbers and lines on a thermometer; of a quantity, having magnitude but not direction, as temperature.—*n.* An entity representing that which has a magnitude without direction: compare **vec·tor.**

scal·a·wag, skal′ə·wag, *n. Informal.* A worthless person; scamp; rascal.

scald, skôld, *v.t.* To burn with or as with hot liquid or steam; to cleanse with boiling or hot liquid; to heat to a temperature just short of the boiling point: to *scald* milk; to scorch or scathe with burning words.—*v.i.* To be or become scalded.—*n.* A burn caused by hot liquid or steam.—**scald·ing,** *a.*

scale, skāl, *n.* A balance or any other device for weighing; either of the dishes or pans of a balance. —*v.t.,* **scaled, scal·ing.** To weigh in or as in scales; to have a weight of.—**tip the scale,** to weigh, usu. with *at.*—**turn the scales,** to change an expected outcome.

scale, skāl, *n.* One of the thin, flat, horny plates that form the covering of certain animals, as fishes; any thin, platelike layer or flake such as peels from a surface.—*v.t.,* **scaled, scal·ing.** To remove the scales from; to remove in scales; to cover with a scale.—*v.i.* To come off in scales; to become coated with scale. —**scaled,** *a.* —**scale·less,** *a.* —**scale·like,** *a.* —**scal·i·ness,** *n.*

scale, skāl, *n.* A succession or progression of steps or degrees; a graduated series or table, as of prices; a series of marks separated by distances for measurement; an instrument with graduated spaces for measuring; the proportion which the representation of an object bears to the object: a model on a *scale* of one inch to a foot; a certain relative or proportionate size or extent; a system of numerical notation: the decimal *scale. Mus.* A series of tones ascending or descending according to fixed intervals: the major *scale* of C. —*v.t.,* **scaled, scal·ing.** To climb; to climb up or over; to measure by or as if by a scale; to make according to scale; to reduce according to a fixed proportion, usu. with *down.*—*v.i.* To climb, ascend, or mount.

scal·lion, skal′yən, *n.* A kind of onion with a long stalk and small, narrow bulb; a shallot; a leek.

scal·lop, skäl′əp, skal′əp, *n.* A type of bivalve mollusk, with a large muscle valued as seafood; one of the shells or valves of a mollusk, usually having radial ribs and a wavy outer edge; a scallop shell or a dish in which seafood is baked or served; one of a series of semicircular shapes along an edge for ornamentation. Also **scol·lop.**—*v.t.* To mark, cut, or ornament with scallops; to bake, usu. with a milky sauce topped with crumbs. —**scal·lop·er,** *n.*

scalp, skalp, *n.* The skin and hair of the top and back

of the head; a part of this skin and hair cut from a person's head by the N. American Indians as a trophy of victory.—*v.t.* To cut or tear the scalp from. *Informal.* To buy and resell at greatly increased prices, as theater tickets; to buy and sell so as to make small, quick profits, as stocks.—*v.i. Informal.* To scalp tickets, stocks, etc. **—scalp·er,** *n.*

scal·pel, skal′pəl, *n.* A small, sharp-bladed knife used in dissections and surgery.

scal·y, skā′lē, *a.,* **-i·er, -i·est.** Covered with or abounding in scales or scale; characterized by scales. **—scal·i·ness,** *n.*

scamp, skamp, *n.* A worthless fellow; a rascal.—*v.t.* To act or function in a careless manner. **—scamp·er,** *n.*

scamp·er, skam′pər, *v.i.* To run hastily or in a frolicking manner; to hurry away.—*n.* A hurried or quick run.

scan, skan, *v.t.,* **scanned, scan·ning.** To examine minutely; to scrutinize; to pass over quickly with the eyes: to *scan* a newspaper; to examine, as verse, by counting the metrical feet or syllables; to pass over (an object) with an electronic beam so as to pick up and transmit, as a television image.—*v.i.* To scan verse; of verse, to comply with metrical rules.—*n.* A scanning. **—scan·ner,** *n.*

scan·dal, skan′dəl, *n.* A discreditable or disgraceful event, action, or circumstance; an offense resulting from fault or misdeed; public reproach or disgrace; malicious, defamatory talk; one who disgraces or offends: She was a *scandal* to her family.

scan·dal·ize, skan′də·līz, *v.t.,* **-ized, -iz·ing.** To offend by some action considered improper or outrageous; to shock. **—scan·dal·iz·er,** *n.* **—scan·dal·i·za·tion,** skan·dəl·ə·zā′shən, *n.*

scan·dal·mon·ger, skan′dəl·məng·gər, skan′dəl·mong·gər, *n.* One who spreads gossip or scandal.

scan·dal·ous, skan′də·ləs, *a.* Causing, consisting of, or spreading scandal or offense; shameful.

scan·dal sheet, *n.* A publication, as a newspaper, based on gossip and scandal.

Scan·di·na·vi·an, skan·də·nā′vē·ən, *a.* Of or pertaining to Scandinavia, the region comprising Norway, Sweden, and Denmark, and sometimes Iceland, Finland, and the Faroe Islands, or to the inhabitants or languages of Scandinavia.

scan·sion, skan′shən, *n.* The analysis or division of the metrical structure of verse.

scant, skant, *a.* Scarcely sufficient; having a limited supply, usu. followed by *of: scant of* resources; meager; not quite amounting to a specified quantity: a *scant* cup of flour.—*v.t.* To limit; to give out sparingly. **—scant·ness,** *n.*

scan·ties, skan′tēz, *n. pl.* Women's panties.

scant·y, skan′tē, *a.,* **-i·er, -i·est.** Barely adequate; meager; lacking in amplitude or extent. **—scant·i·ly,** *adv.* **—scant·i·ness,** *n.*

scape·goat, skāp′gōt, *n.* One made to bear the blame for the misdeeds of others.

scape·grace, skāp′grās, *n.* An unprincipled or mischievous fellow; a rascal; a rogue.

scap·u·la, skap′yə·lə, *n. pl.,* **-las, -lae,** -lē. Shoulder blade.

scar, skär, *n.* The mark of a wound remaining on the skin after healing; any lasting effect caused by past action, emotional stress, or mental injury.—*v.t.* **scarred, scar·ring.** To mark with a scar; to cause lasting injury to.—*v.i.* To be marked with a scar; to form a scar.

scar, skär, *n.* A cliff; an isolated detached rock; a bare and rocky area on the side of a hill or mountain.

scarce, skärs, *a.* Small in quantity in proportion to the demand; not plentiful or abundant; deficient; rare; uncommon.—*adv.* Scarcely. **—scarce·ness,** *n.* **—scar·ci·ty,** *n.*

scare, skär, *v.t.,* **scared, scar·ing.** To frighten.—*v.i.* To

---

a- hat, fāte, fāre, fäther; **e-** met, mē; **i-** pin, pīne; **o-** not, nōte, ôrb, moove (move), boy, pownd; **u-** cūbe, bûll, tûk (took); **ch-** chin; **th-** thick, ŧhen; **zh-** vizhon (vision); **ə-** əgo, takən, pencəl, lemən, bərd (bird).

scarecrow

become fearful or alarmed.—*n.* A sudden fright or panic, usu. inspired by a trifling cause; a scared condition.—**scare up.** *Informal.* To obtain or collect with some difficulty, or on short notice. —**scar•er,** *n.*

scare•crow, skâr′krō, *n.* An object, usu. a crude figure of a man dressed in old clothes, set up in a field to frighten away birds, esp. crows, from crops; something frightening but harmless; a ragged or skinny person.

scare•mon•ger, skâr′məng•gər, skâr′mong•gər, *n.* An alarmist.

scarf, skärf, *n. pl.,* **scarfs, scarves,** skärvz. A square or long piece of material usu. worn around a person's head, neck, or shoulders, decoratively or for protection or warmth; a sash indicating official rank; a necktie, kerchief, or muffler.—*v.t.* To tie, decorate, wrap, or cover, using or as if using, a scarf. —**scarf•less,** *a.* —**scarf•like,** *a.*

scarf•skin, skärf′skin, *n.* The outermost layer of the skin; the epidermis.

scar•i•fy, skar′ə•fī, *v.t.,* **-fied, -fy•ing.** To scratch, or superficially pierce the skin; to criticize severely; to break or stir up, as soil, without turning over. —**scar•i•fi•ca•tion,** skar•ə•fə•kā′shən, *n.*

scar•let, skär′lit, *n.* A red color brighter than crimson; cloth or apparel of such a color.—*a.* Of the color scarlet; lewd; dissolute.

scar•let fe•ver, *n.* A contagious disease, characterized by fever, inflammation of the throat, and an extensive scarlet rash.

scarp, skärp, *n.* The inner sloping wall of the surrounding ditch of a rampart; an escarp; any steep slope.—*v.t.* To form into a steep slope.

scar•y, skâr′ē, *a.,* **-i•er, -i•est.** Causing fright or alarm; easily frightened.

scat, skat, *v.i.,* **scat•ted, scat•ting.** *Informal.* To go or drive away in haste.—*interj. Informal.* An exclamation used to drive away animals, as a cat.

scathe, skāth, *v.t.,* **scathed, scath•ing.** To assail with harsh criticism; hurt, esp. by scorching or searing.—*n.* Hurt or injury. —**scathe•less,** *a.*

scath•ing, skā′thing, *a.* Bitterly severe, as a remark or reprimand. —**scath•ing•ly,** *adv.*

scat•o•log•i•cal, skat•ə•loj′ə•kəl, *a.* Relating to excrement or to obscenity, esp. in literature.

scat•ter, skat′ər, *v.t.* To throw loosely about; to distribute in various directions at irregular intervals; to sprinkle; to disperse, as a mob.—*v.i.* To disperse and separate.—*n.* The act of scattering. —**scat•ter•a•ble,** *a.* —**scat•ter•er,** *n.*

scat•ter•brain, skat′ər•brān, *n.* A flighty, thoughtless, or forgetful person. —**scat•ter•brained,** *a.*

scat•ter rug, *n.* A rug suitable for placing over a small area on a floor.

scav•enge, skav′inj, *v.t.,* **-enged, -eng•ing.** To cleanse from dirt or filth, as a street; to search out, as useful material, from amid refuse.—*v.i.* To act as a scavenger; to seek or ransack, as for food.

scav•en•ger, skav′in•jər, *n.* One who searches in refuse for usable items; an animal that feeds on dead matter; a street cleaner.

sce•nar•i•o, si•när′ē•ō, si•när′ē•ō, *n. pl.,* **-os.** An outline of the plot of a dramatic work or motion picture.

sce•nar•ist, si•när′ist, si•när′ist, *n.* A writer of the scenario for a motion picture.

scene, sēn, *n.* The surroundings amid which anything happens; location or locale; a landscape or view; a unified series of actions and events connected and exhibited; a part of a play, the division of an act; the imaginary place in which the action of a play is supposed to occur; one of the painted slides, hangings, or other devices serving as background or scenery for a play; a display of strong emotion, esp. in the presence of others: He made a *scene.*—**behind the scenes,** out of sight of the theater audience; privately; covertly.

scen•er•y, sē′nə•rē, *n. pl.,* **-ies.** The general appearance or natural features of a place, as a landscape; the backdrops and accessories representing the setting of a play or other stage production.

sce•nic, sē′nik, sen′ik, *a.* Of or pertaining to natural scenery; affording a beautiful view; pertaining to a scene in art, or to stage scenery; dramatic. Also **sce•ni•cal.**

scent, sent, *n.* A specific smell, esp. when pleasing; an odor left on the ground by an animal enabling it to be followed; perfume; the sense of smell.—*v.t.* To recognize by smelling; to be suspicious of, as trouble; to perfume.—*v.i.* To track by the sense of smell. —**scent•ed,** *a.*

scep•ter, sep′tər, *n.* A rod or wand, borne in the hand as an emblem of regal or imperial power; sovereignty; supremacy.—*v.t.,* **-tered, -ter•ing.** To invest with regal authority.

sched•ule, skej′ûl, skej′əl, *n.* A list, catalog, or table, esp. a timetable; a written or printed statement of details, often in classified or tabular form.—*v.t.,* **-uled, -ul•ing.** To make a schedule of; to plan or arrange for a specified date. —**sched•u•lar,** *a.*

sche•ma, skē′mə, *n. pl.,* **-ma•ta.** A diagram, plan, or scheme. —**sche•mat•ic,** skē•mat′ik, *a., n.* —**sche•mat•i•cal•ly,** *adv.*

sche•ma•tize, skē′mə•tīz, *v.t.,* **-tized, -tiz•ing.** To reduce to or arrange according to a scheme.

scheme, skēm, *n.* A plan of something to be done; a project; a plot, esp. one that is underhanded or crafty; a system or framework of related theories or precepts; an impractical project; a sketch or diagrammatic representation: an astrological *scheme* of the heavens. —*v.t.* To make a plan for; to plot.—*v.i.* To lay plans; to intrigue. —**schem•er,** *n.* —**schem•ing,** *a.*

scher•zo, skär′tsō, *n. pl.,* **-zos, -zi,** -tsē. A playful or satirical movement, as in a symphony or sonata.

Schick test, shik′ test, *n.* An injection used to test immunity to diphtheria.

schism, siz′əm, skiz′əm, *n.* Division in or separation from an organized body, esp. a church; the offense of causing such a division.

schis•mat•ic, siz•mat′ik, skiz•mat′ik, *a.* Of, pertaining to, or promoting schism. Also **schis•mat•i•cal.** —*n.* One who promotes or participates in a schism.

schist, shist, shist, *n.* Any of certain crystalline rocks which readily split into parallel layers.

schiz•o, skit′sō, *n. pl.,* **-os.** *Informal.* A person who is schizophrenic.

schiz•oid, skit′soyd, skiz′oyd, *a.* Pertaining to, resembling, or predisposed to schizophrenia.—*n.* One whose behavior suggests a tendency toward schizophrenia.

schiz•o•phre•ni•a, skit•sə•frē′nē•ə, skiz•ə•frē′nē•ə, *n.* Psychosis characterized by withdrawal from reality, delusions, and progressive deterioration. —**schiz•o•phren•ic,** skit•sə•fren′ik, *a., n.*

schle•miel, shlə•mēl′, *n. Informal.* An unlucky person prone to clumsiness; an inept, bungling clod. Also **schle•mihl.**

schmaltz, shmälts, shmôlts, *n. Informal.* Effusive or mawkish music, art, etc. Also **schmalz.**—**schmaltz•y,** *a.*

schmo, shmō, *n. Informal.* A naive, foolish, or boring person; a jerk. Also **schmoe.**

schnapps, schnaps, shnäps, shnaps, *n.* A dram of Hollands gin or other spirits; liquor generally.

schnau•zer, shnow′zər, *n.* A breed of German terrier with a wiry coat.

schnit•zel, shnit′səl, *n.* A cutlet, esp. of veal.

schnook, shnûk, *n. Informal.* An insignificant or stupid person; a dope.

schnor•kel, shnôr′kəl, *n., v.i.* Snorkel.

schnoz•zle, shnoz′əl, *n. Informal.* The nose.

schol•ar, skol′ər, *n.* A person of great learning or academic accomplishment; such a person who does research, study, writing, and is often a published authority in one particular field: a Shakepeare *scholar;*

a student who holds a scholarship; a student.

schol·ar·ly, skol/ər·lē, *a.* Characteristic of or suitable to a scholar. **—schol·ar·li·ness,** *n.*

schol·ar·ship, skol/ər·ship, *n.* The body of learning and knowledge attained through scholarly study; the quality of scholarly work; aid or award given to a student, usu. financial assistance on the basis of his or her merit or need.

scho·las·tic, skə·las/tik, *a.* Of or pertaining to schools, scholars, or education; pedantic. Also **scho·las·ti·cal.—***n. (Often cap.)* A theologian or philosopher of the Middle Ages.

scho·las·ti·cism, skə·las/tə·siz·əm, *n.* Close adherence to traditional teachings of a school or sect. *(Cap.)* The system of theological and philosophical teaching predominant in the Middle Ages.

school, skool, *n.* A place or establishment where instruction is given; a regular course of meetings of a teacher or teachers and students for instruction: a business *school;* a session of an establishment for instruction: no *school* today; the body of students or pupils attending a school; any place, situation, or experience constituting a source of instruction or training; the body of pupils or followers of a particular master; a body of persons who accept the same teachings or principles; a particular faculty or department of a university: the graduate *school;* a building or room in a university, set apart for some particular purpose.**—***v.t.* To teach or educate, as at an institution or school.

school, skool, *n.* A large number of fish, porpoises, or whales feeding or migrating together.**—***v.i.* To form into or move in a school, as fish.

school age, *n.* Childhood years during which school attendance is required.

school board, *n.* A board in charge of public education.

school·boy, skool/boy, *n.* A boy attending school.

school bus, *n.* A motor vehicle for transporting children to and from school.

school·child, skool/child, *n. pl.,* **-chil·dren.** A child attending school.

school·girl, skool/gərl, *n.* A girl attending school.

school·house, skool/hows, *n.* A building in which school, esp. the elementary grades, is conducted.

school·ing, skool/ing, *n.* Education or instruction received in a school; the act of teaching or the process of being taught in school.

school·marm, skool/märm, *n. Informal.* A woman teacher, esp. one thought to be old-fashioned and prudish.

school·mas·ter, skool/mas·tər, skool/mä·stər, *n.* A man who teaches or directs in a school.

school·mate, skool/māt, *n.* A companion or associate at school.

school·mis·tress, skool/mis·tris, *n.* A woman who presides over or teaches in a school.

school·room, skool/room, skool/rûm, *n.* A room in which school is conducted.

school·teach·er, skool/tē·chər, *n.* One who instructs in a grammar school or high school. **—school·teach·ing,** *n.*

school·work, skool/wərk, *n.* All of the work done for studies at a school.

schoon·er, skoo/nər, *n.* A sailing vessel having at least two masts, fore and aft; a tall beer glass.

schuss, shûs, shoos, *n.* A high-speed, straight, downhill run on skis. **—***v.t., v.i.*

schwa, shwä, *n.* The indeterminate vowel sound of most syllables that are not stressed in English, as the *a* in *scholar,* the *u* in *tetanus,* the *i* and *e* in *prominent,* and the *o* in *piston;* the phonic symbol denoting that sound (ə).

sci·at·ic, sī·at/ik, *a.* Pertaining to the hip, or to the nerve running along the back of each thigh.

sci·at·i·ca, sī·at/i·kə, *n.* Pain in the hip region, or along the course of a sciatic nerve.

sci·ence, sī/əns, *n.* Knowledge, esp. of facts or principles, gained by systematic study; a particular branch of knowledge, esp. one dealing with a body of facts or truths systematically arranged and showing the operation of general laws: the *science* of mathematics; systematized knowledge, esp. of the laws and facts of the physical or material world; skill resulting from training.

sci·ence fic·tion, *n.* Fiction that imaginatively uses scientific fact and speculation.

sci·en·tif·ic, sī·ən·tif/ik, *a.* Pertaining to science: *scientific* experiments. **—sci·en·tif·i·cal·ly,** *adv.*

sci·en·tif·ic meth·od, *n.* A research method characterized by the definition of a problem, the gathering of data, and the drafting and empirical testing of the hypotheses.

sci·en·tist, sī/ən·tist, *n.* A person versed in or devoted to science; a scientific person.

scim·i·tar, sim·i·tar, sim/i·tər, *n.* An oriental sword, the blade of which is single-edged, short, and curved. Also **scim·i·ter.**

scin·til·la, sin·til/ə, *n.* A spark; trace; particle.

scin·til·lant, sin/tə·lənt, *a.* Sparkling.

scin·til·late, sin/tə·lāt, *v.i.,* **-lat·ed, -lat·ing.** To emit sparks; to sparkle or twinkle, as the stars; to flash. **—***v.t.* To send forth, as sparks or flashes. **—scin·til·lat·ing,** *a.* **—scin·til·la·tion,** sin·tə·lā/shən, *n.*

sci·on, sī/ən, *n.* A descendant; an heir; a cutting from a plant, esp. one used for grafting.

scis·sor, siz/ər, *v.t.* To cut, clip, or slash with scissors.

scis·sors, siz/ərz, *n. pl.* A cutting instrument consisting of two blades with handles movable on a pivot in the center, and which cut from opposite sides against an object placed between them: often spoken of as a *pair of scissors.*

scle·ra, sklī/rə, *n.* The fibrous white outer coating of the eyeball which is contiguous with the cornea. Also **scle·rot·i·ca,** sklə·rot/i·kə.

scle·ro·sis, sklī·rō/sis, *n. pl.,* **-ses,** -sēz. A hardening and thickening of a tissue or a part, usu. from excessive growth of fibrous or connective tissue; a disease exhibiting such hardening.

scle·rot·ic, sklī·rot/ik, *a.* Pertaining to the sclera: the *sclerotic* coat of the eye; hard, firm, as the sclera; affected with or pertaining to sclerosis.

scle·rous, sklēr/əs, skler/əs, *a.* Hard; bony.

scoff, skôf, skof, *n.* An expression of mockery, scorn, or contempt; a jeer; an object of derision.**—***v.i.* To mock, often followed by *at.*—*v.t.* To mock; to ridicule. **—scoff·er,** *n.* **—scoff·ing·ly,** *adv.*

scold, skōld, *v.t.* To find fault with in an ill-tempered manner, as a result of impatience, irritation, or anger; to chide or rebuke.**—***v.i.* To find fault; to use nagging or abusive language.**—***n.* One who scolds. **—scold·er,** *n.* **—scold·ing,** *n.*

scol·lop, skol/əp, *n., v.t.* Scallop.

sconce, skons, *n.* An ornamental bracket, as attached to a wall, for holding one or more candles or other lights.

scone, skōn, skon, *n.* A doughy, round pastry; a flat, round cake of wheat flour, barley meal, or the like, cooked on a griddle.

scoop, skoop, *n.* A ladle or ladlelike utensil, for taking up and carrying loose materials, as flour or sugar; a spoon-shaped instrument for dishing up soft food: an ice cream *scoop;* the quantity taken up at one time by any such instrument; a double *scoop* of ice cream; the shovellike bucket attached to heavy construction equipment used to dig and remove such materials as earth in road building; the amount of material taken up; a movement as of scooping. *Informal.* An item or

---

a- hat, fāte, fāre, fäther; **e-** met, mē; **i-** pin, pīne; **o-** not, nōte, ôrb, moove (move), boy, pownd; **u-** cūbe, bûll, tûk (took); **ch-** chin; **th-** thick, ŧhen; **zh-** vizhon (vision); **ə-** ego, takən, pencəl, lemən, bərd (bird).

story released by one newspaper or newscast ahead of the competition; a news beat; information or explanatory details, usu. of recent origin: What's the *scoop* on that deal? *Informal.* A big haul, as of money made in speculation.—*v.t.* To take up or out with or as with a scoop; to gather or appropriate as if with a scoop, usu. followed by *in* or *up. Informal.* To get the better of by a scoop or beat, as a rival newspaper. **—scoop·er,** *n.* **—scoop·ful,** *n.*

scoot, skoot, *v.t. Informal.* To send or impel at high speed.—*v.i. Informal.* To dart, go, or make off swiftly or hastily.—*n.* The act or an act of scooting; a swift, darting movement or course.

scoot·er, skoo′ter, *n.* A child's vehicle with a board set between tandem wheels guided by a vertical handlebar and driven by standing with one foot on the board and pushing against the ground with the other foot; a motor scooter.

scope, skōp, *n.* Extent or range of view, outlook, application, operation, or effectiveness: a mind of limited *scope;* space for movement or activity; extent in space.

scorch, skôrch, *v.t.* To burn superficially or slightly; affect in color, taste, etc., by burning slightly; parch or shrivel with heat; to assault verbally.—*v.i.* To be or become scorched.—*n.* A superficial burn; scorching effect. **—scorched,** *a.* **—scorch·ing,** *a.*

scorch·er, skôr′cher, *n.* One who or that which scorches. *Informal.* A very hot day; a cutting, stinging rebuke.

score, skōr, skôr, *n.* A notch, cut, or scratch, esp. one used for keeping a tally; any account showing indebtedness: to settle an old *score;* a grievance or grudge; account, reason, or motive; the record of points made in a game or match; the aggregate of points made by a side or individual; a grade or rating, as in a test or an examination; a group or set of twenty; *pl.,* an indeterminately large number; the complete notation for a composition, whether for a single voice or instrument or for an entire symphony, choral work, etc.—*v.t.,* **scored, scor·ing.** To make notches or cuts in; to draw a line through in order to cancel, used with *out;* to censure severely; to record, as by notches or marks; to write down as a debt; to gain for addition to one's score in a game; make a score of; to gain as a success; to grade or evaluate, as on an examination or in a test; to orchestrate; write out in musical score.—*v.i.* To make notches, cuts, marks, or lines on something; to keep score, as of a game; to make a point or points in a game or contest; to win an advantage; to achieve a success.**—know the score.** *Informal.* To have complete awareness of the realities of one's situation. **—score·less,** *a.* **—scor·er,** *n.*

score·board, skōr′bôrd, skôr′bôrd, *n.* A large display board in a stadium or other sports arena which shows the score and other facts of the game or event.

score·keep·er, skōr′kē·per, skôr′kē·per, *n.* An official who keeps score at a sports contest or game.

scorn, skôrn, *n.* Extreme and open contempt due to one's opinion of the meanness or unworthiness of an object or person; the expression of this feeling; the object of scornful feeling.—*v.t.* To act or feel toward with disdain. **—scorn·er,** *n.* **—scorn·ful,** *a.* **—scorn·ful·ness,** *n.*

Scor·pi·o, skôr′pē·ō, *n.* A constellation once thought to resemble a scorpion; the eighth sign of the zodiac.

scor·pi·on, skôr′pē·en, *n.* An arachnid, having a pair of large, clawlike pincers and a long, jointed, curled tail terminating in a venomous sting; a whip or scourge.

Scot, skot, *n.* A native of Scotland.

Scotch, skoch, *a.* Scottish. *Informal.* Frugal or miserly.—*n.* Scotch whisky; the people of Scotland.

scotch, skoch, *v.t.* To cut; gash; wound so as to cripple or make harmless; suppress; stamp out; end decisively.

Scotch-I·rish, skoch′ī′rish, *a.* Designating or relating to the Scottish settlers in Northern Ireland.—*n.* One whose ancestors are Scottish and Irish.

Scotch·man, skoch′men, *n. pl.,* **-men.** A Scotsman; a Scot.

Scotch tape, *n. Trademark.* A thin, rolled transparent or translucent adhesive tape, usu. made of cellulose or cellophane.

Scotch ter·ri·er, *n.* Scottish terrier.

Scotch whis·ky, *n.* A whiskey made from malted barley, distilled in Scotland.

scot-free, skot′frē′, *a.* Unhurt or unpunished.

Scot·land Yard, skot′lend, *n.* Metropolitan police headquarters in London, England; the London police force, esp. its department of crime investigation.

Scots, skots, *a.* Scotch or Scottish.—*n.* The dialect of English which is spoken in Scotland.

Scots·man, skots′men, *n. pl.,* **-men.** A Scot. Also **Scotch·man.**

scot·tie, skot′ē, *n. (Often cap.)* A Scottish terrier. *(Cap.)* A Scotsman.

Scot·tish, skot′ish, *a.* Characteristic of or pertaining to Scotland. Also **Scots.**—*n.* The inhabitants of Scotland; the dialect of English spoken in Scotland. Also **Scots.**

Scot·tish ter·ri·er, *n.* A small, wiry-haired terrier with erect ears and short legs. Also **Scotch ter·ri·er, Scot·tie, Scot·ty.**

scoun·drel, skown′drel, *n.* A base, mean, worthless person; a rascal. **—scoun·drel·ly,** *a.,* **-li·er, -li·est.**

scour, skowr, skow′er, *v.t.* To cleanse or polish by hard rubbing with some suitable implement or substance: to *scour* pots and pans; clear out, as a channel or drain, by removing dirt or by flushing with water; to remove by or as by cleansing; get rid of.—*v.i.* To rub a surface in order to cleanse or polish it; to become shiny and bright, as by rubbing.—*n.* A scouring; the place scoured; a material used in scouring. **—scour·er,** *n.*

scour, skowr, skow′er, *v.i.* To move rapidly or energetically; range about, as in search of something.—*v.t.* To run or pass quickly over or along; range over, as in quest of something. **—scour·er,** *n.*

scourge, skerj, skûrj, *n.* A lash or whip for inflicting suffering or punishment; a punishment or vindictive affliction; one who or that which causes universal affliction or disaster: Disease is a *scourge* of humanity.—*v.t.,* **scourged, scourg·ing.** To lash or whip with a scourge; to afflict greatly; to satirize. **—scourg·er,** *n.*

scour·ings, skowr′ingz, *n. pl.* Dirt or refuse material removed by scouring.

scout, skowt, *n.* One sent out to gain and bring in information; the act of reconnoitering; boy scout; girl scout.—*v.i.* To act as a scout.—*v.t.* To observe or watch closely.

scout, skowt, *v.t., v.i.* To reject scornfully; scoff; mock; jeer.

scout·ing, skowt′ing, *n.* The activities of those who scout, esp. of Girl Scouts and Boy Scouts of America.

scout·mas·ter, skowt′mas·ter, skowt′mä·ster, *n.* The leader of a band of scouts.

scow, skow, *n.* A kind of large, flat-bottomed boat.—*v.t.* To carry by scow.

scowl, skowl, *v.i.* To wrinkle the brows, as in frowning or displeasure; to look sullen, angry, or threatening.—*v.t.* To express or affect by scowling.—*n.* A deep, angry frown. **—scowl·er,** *n.*

scrab·ble, skrab′el, *v.i.,* **-bled, -bling.** To scratch about or scrape with the hands or paws; to struggle; to scramble; to make irregular marks; to scrawl; to scribble.—*v.t.* To gather or scrape together hurriedly; to scramble; to scrawl or scribble.—*n.* A scratching, scraping, or clawing; a scribble; a scramble or struggle. **—scrab·bler,** *n.*

scrag, skrag, *n.* A lean or scrawny person or animal; a lean or bony piece of meat. *Informal.* The neck.—*v.t.,* **scragged, scrag·ging.** *Informal.* To wring the neck of; choke; hang.

scrag·gly, skrag′lē, *a.,* **-gli·er, -gli·est.** Rough; ragged; shaggy; unkempt.

scrag·gy, skrag′ē, *a.,* **-gi·er, -gi·est.** Rough; lean; scrawny.

scram, skram, *v.i.,* **scrammed, scram·ming.** *Informal.* To go away at once.

scram·ble, skram′bəl, *v.i.,* **-bled, -bling.** To move or climb quickly by the aid of the hands, or on all fours; to snatch eagerly at or struggle to get, before others. —*v.t.* To throw or mix together; to disorder or confuse: to *scramble* the letters in a word. —**scram·bler,** *n.* —**scram·bling,** *n.*

scrap, skrap, *n.* A small piece or fragment; a portion or particle of leftover food, usu. to be thrown away; material which has been manufactured, used, and discarded as being fit only for reworking: *scraps* of iron; the fragmental excess left after the making or processing of something.—*v.t.,* **scrapped, scrap·ping.** To cause to become scrap; to give up or discard as no longer sufficiently workable.—*a.* Discarded; composed of fragments.

scrap, skrap, *n. Informal.* A fight, scrimmage, or quarrel.—*v.i.,* **scrapped, scrap·ping.** *Informal.* To fight or get into a quarrel. —**scrap·per,** *n.*

scrap·book, skrap′bůk, *n.* A book for the preservation of such mementos as prints, invitations, or extracts from other books; an album.

scrape, skrāp, *v.t.,* **scraped, scrap·ing.** To rub, as with something sharp or rough, so as to smooth, roughen, or remove something from the surface; to remove from (a surface) in this way; to grate or scratch against or across; to mar, scar, or damage in this way; to collect as if by scraping, with difficulty or on short notice, usu. with *together.*—*v.i.* To rub or scrape something; to produce a harsh sound; to drag back a foot in executing a low bow; to barely succeed with great effort; to be excessively frugal.—*n.* The action, act, noise, place, or result of scraping; a predicament or quarrel. —**scrap·able,** *a.* —**scrap·er,** *n.*

scrap·per, skrap′ər, *n. Informal.* One who scraps or fights.

scrap·py, skrap′ē, *a.,* **-pi·er, -pi·est.** Consisting of scraps; disconnected.

scrap·py, skrap′ē, *a.,* **-pi·er, -pi·est.** *Informal.* Tending toward argument or scrapping. —**scrap·pi·ly,** *adv.* —**scrap·pi·ness,** *n.*

scratch, skrach, *v.t.* To rub, tear, or mark the surface of with something sharp or abrasive; to gouge, dig, or peel off with scraping or clawing action; to scrape gently with fingernails, claws, or the like, to ease an itch; to pull or rub along a rough, abrasive surface; to strike out or discard by or as if by crossing off with a line; to scribble, draw, or sketchily write: to *scratch* a note.—*v.i.* To claw, tear, scrape, or the like by using fingernails or claws; to soothe an itch by gently scraping or stroking with fingernails or claws; to make a gritty, screeching sound; to withdraw from competition; to work and expend effort and just get by.—*n.* A slight wound or mark on a surface, made by scratching; the sound of scratching.—*a.* Used for doodling, jotting, or practice: *scratch* paper.—**start from scratch,** to begin with nothing. —**scratch·a·ble,** *a.* —**scratch·er,** *n.*

scratch·y, skrach′ē, *a.,* **-i·er, -i·est.** Causing a harsh, grating noise; consisting of or marked with scratches: a *scratchy* desk; causing itching or other skin irritation: a *scratchy* woolen shirt; rough or ragged. —**scratch·i·ly,** *adv.* —**scratch·i·ness,** *n.*

scrawl, skrôl, *v.t., v.i.* To write or draw poorly, hastily, or illegibly.—*n.* Hasty or illegible writing. —**scrawl·er,** *n.* —**scrawl·y,** *a.,* **-i·er, -i·est.**

scrawn·y, skrô′nē, *a.,* **-i·er, -i·est.** Thin; rawboned. —**scrawn·i·ness,** *n.*

scream, skrēm, *v.i.* To cry out with a loud, shrill voice,

as in anger, fright, or pain; to laugh very loudly, shrilly, or hysterically; to shriek; give out any very sharp, shrill, or loud sound; produce a very vivid or shocking effect, as certain colors.—*v.t.* To say in a loud, shrill voice.—*n.* A shriek or sharp, shrill cry; a sharp, harsh sound. —**scream·er,** *n.*

scream·ing·ly, scrē′ming·lē, *adv.* To a great degree; extraordinarily: *screamingly* funny. —**scream·ing,** *a., n.*

screech, skrēch, *v.i.* To cry out with a sharp, shrill voice; to shriek.—*v.t.* To emit with a screech.—*n.* A sharp, shrill cry; shrill noise. —**screech·er,** *n.*

screen, skrēn, *n.* A framework or curtain used to shut out the sun, rain, or cold, or to conceal something from sight; anything which shelters, protects, or conceals: a *screen* of mist; a surface on which a motion picture is projected; motion pictures collectively; a frame containing mesh, inserted in a window or doorway to shut out insects; an apparatus which prevents interference among various agencies: a magnetic *screen.*—*v.t.* To shelter or protect from inconvenience, injury, or danger; to conceal; to sift by passing through a screen; to supply with a screen to shut out insects; to project, as a picture, on a screen; to select by a process of elimination: The company *screens* all applicants carefully.—*v.i.* To appear on a motion picture screen. —**screen·a·ble,** *a.* —**screen·er,** *n.*

screen·ing, skrē′ning, *n.* The exhibiting of a motion picture; the plastic or metal material used as a mesh in screens.

screen·play, skrēn′plā, *n.* The scenario for a motion picture.

screen test, *n.* A brief film audition. —**screen-test,** skrēn′test, *v.t.*

screw, skroo, *n.* A pointed metal cylinder having a slotted head, driven into a surface by turning with a screwdriver; a similarly headed metal cylinder for fitting into a specific socket; anything spirally formed; one complete turn of a screw; a twisting or rotating movement. *Informal.* Sexual intercourse; a prison guard.—*v.t.* To press, operate, or make firm by means of a screw; to twist; to contort, as features; to extort. *Informal.* To have sexual intercourse with; to cheat —*v.i.* To operate or to be adjusted by turning; to engage in extortion.—**have a screw loose.** *Informal.* To be peculiar, or mentally unbalanced.—**put the screws on,** *to use force.*—**screw a·round.** *Informal.* To loaf. —**screw up.** *Informal.* To ruin, confuse, or bungle. —**screw·er,** *n.*

screw·ball, skroo′bôl, *n. Informal.* A zany or eccentric person.

screw·driv·er, skroo′drī·vər, *n.* A tool for setting or removing screws by turning the slot in the screw head; a vodka and orange juice cocktail.

screw·y, skroo′ē, *a.,* **-i·er, -i·est.** Winding or twisting about like the thread of a screw. *Informal.* Unsound or upsetting; crazy.

scrib·ble, skrib′əl, *v.t.* To write with haste, or without care.—*v.i.* To scrawl.—*n.* Hasty or careless writing; a scrawl. —**scrib·bler,** *n.*

scribe, skrīb, *n.* One who writes; a copyist, esp. one who copied manuscripts in ancient times.—*v.t.,* **scribed, scrib·ing.** To mark wood with a pointed tool; to score or mark for accurate fitting. —**scrib·al,** *a.*

scrim, skrim, *n.* A durable, loosely woven cotton or linen fabric, used for curtains, etc.; a similar fabric used in the theater as a transparent curtain, backdrop, etc.

scrim·mage, skrim′ij, *n.* A skirmish; a rough or vigorous fight or struggle, esp. between a number of persons.—*v.i., v.t.,* **-maged, -mag·ing.** —**scrim·mage line,** line of scrimmage. —**scrim·mag·er,** *n.*

scrimp, skrimp, *v.t.* To be sparing of or in; to stint on the amount of, as food; to make too scanty or small.

äv.i. To use severe economy.—*a.* Scanty; meager.

scrimp•y, skrim′pē, *a.,* **-i•er, -i•est.** Scanty; meager.

scrip, skrip, *n.* A scrap of paper or short writing, as a schedule or list; a certificate or other document, esp. one entitling the holder to a fraction of a share of stock; paper currency, esp. in amounts of less than a dollar, or for use in emergencies or in combat zones.

script, skript, *n.* Handwriting; the characters used in handwriting; a mode of writing; the manuscript of a play or movie.

scrip•tur•al, skrip′chər•əl, *a.* Contained in any religious or sacred writing. (*Cap.*) Contained in or according to the Scriptures.

scrip•ture, skrip′chər, *n.* (*Cap.*) The Bible; the books of the Old or New Testament; a passage or quotation from the Bible. Also **Ho•ly Scrip•tures.** (*L.c.*) Anything written, esp. religious or sacred writings.

script•writ•er, skript′rī•tər, *n.* An author of scripts for radio, television, or motion pictures.

scrod, skrod, *n.* A young codfish.

scroll, skrōl, *n.* A roll of paper, parchment, or the like; a writing formed into a roll; an ornament of a coiled or spiral form.

scroll-work, skrōl′wərk, *n.* Ornamental work prominently decorated with scrolls.

scrooge, skrooj, *n. (Often cap.)* A stingy, miserly person.

scro•tum, skrō′təm, *n. pl.,* **-ta, -tums.** In mammals, the external pouch which contains the testicles. **—scro•tal,** *a.*

scrounge, skrownj, *v.t., v.i.* To search or look around for; to forage; pilfer; to borrow without intent to repay.**—scrounge a•round,** to search at random. **—scroung•er,** *n.*

scrub, skrəb, *v.t.,* **scrubbed, scrub•bing.** To clean by rubbing: He *scrubbed* his hands; to rub hard with a brush, cloth, or the like, as in washing: to *scrub* a floor. *Informal.* To eliminate; cancel; to delay; to postpone: The airline *scrubbed* the flight.—*v.i.* To cleanse things by hard rubbing.—*n.* A scrubbing. **—scrub•ber,** *n.*

scrub, skrəb, *n.* A low or stunted tree; low trees or shrubs collectively; anything undersized or inferior.

scrub•by, skrəb′ē, *a.,* **-bi•er, -bi•est.** Low or stunted, as trees and shrubs; covered with scrub; undersized, inferior, or poor.

scrub•wom•an, skrŭb′wûm•ən, *n. pl.,* **-wom•en.** A woman who is hired to do heavy cleaning work.

scruff, skrəf, *n.* The back of the neck.

scruff•y, skrəf′ē, *a.,* **-i•er, -i•est.** Slovenly; unkempt; threadbare.

scrump•tious, skrəmp′shəs, *a. Informal.* Superlatively fine or nice; splendid.

scrunch, skrənch, *v.t., v.i.* To chew or crunch, as food; to crumple.—*n.* An act or sound of scrunching.

scru•ple, skroo′pəl, *n.* A feeling of uneasiness affecting the conscience or the sense of property, which tends to restrain one's action.—*v.t., v.i.,* **-pled, -pling.** To have scruples; hesitate at.

scru•pu•lous, skroo′pyə•ləs, *a.* Having scruples; showing a strict regard for what is right; very careful or exact. **—scru•pu•los•i•ty,** skroo•pyə•los′i•tē, **scru•pu•lous•ness,** *n.* **—scru•pu•lous•ly,** *adv.*

scru•ta•ble, skroo′tə•bəl, *a.* Capable of being penetrated or understood by investigation.

scru•ti•nize, skroo′tə•nīz, *v.t.,* **-nized, -niz•ing.** To subject to scrutiny.—*v.i.* To conduct a careful investigation. **—scru•ti•niz•er,** *n.* **—scru•ti•niz•ing•ly,** *adv.*

scru•ti•ny, skroo′tə•nē, *n. pl.,* **-nies.** Close examination; a searching look.

scu•ba, skoo′bə, *n.* A compact underwater breathing device worn on the back by free divers.

scud, skəd, *v.i.,* **scud•ded, scud•ding.** To run or move quickly; dart.—*n.* The act of scudding; clouds, spray, etc., driven by the wind.

scuff, skəf, *v.i.* To walk without raising the feet; shuffle.—*v.t.* To scrape with the feet; to mar the surface of

by scraping or hard usage, as shoes or furniture.—*n.* The act, sound, or mark of scuffing; a flat house slipper that covers only the front portion of the foot.

scuf•fle, skəf′əl, *v.i.,* **-fled, -fling.** To struggle or grapple closely; to walk in a shuffling manner.—*n.* A confused, tumultuous fight.

scull, skəl, *n.* An oar worked from side to side over the stern of a boat as a means of propulsion; one of a pair of short, laterally placed oars operated by one person; a boat propelled by sculls.—*v.t.* To propel or convey by means of sculls.—*v.i.* To propel a boat with sculls. **—scull•er,** *n.*

scul•ler•y, skəl′ə•rē, *n. pl.,* **-ies.** A place where culinary utensils are cleaned and kept; a back kitchen.

sculpt, skəlpt, *v.t., v.i. Informal.* To sculpture.

sculp•tor, skəlp′tər, *n.* One who creates three-dimensional artwork usu. by processes such as chiseling and carving. **—sculp•tress,** *n. fem.*

sculp•ture, skəlp′chər, *n.* The art form of a three-dimensional work, created by a sculptor; a statue or other example of such art; such objects of art collectively; the patterned appearance of the surfaces of some shells and leaves that is a result of a contrast in texture and depth.—*v.t.,* **-tured, -tur•ing.** To fashion and produce, as a work of art that is three-dimensional.—*v.i.* To mold or model in the manner of a sculptor. **—sculp•tur•al,** *a.*

scum, skəm, *n.* The extraneous matter which rises to the surface of liquids in boiling or fermentation; refuse; worthless or vile persons; rabble.—*v.t.,* **scummed, scum•ming.** To clear from the surface, as impure matter.—*v.i.* To form scum; to be covered with scum. **—scum•my,** *a.,* **-mi•er, -mi•est.**

scurf, skərf, *n.* Minute scales of outer skin, as dandruff.

scur•ri•lous, skər′ə•ləs, *a.* Obscenely jocular; gross; abusive. **—scur•ril•i•ty,** skər•il′ə•tē, *n. pl.,* **-ties.**

scur•ry, skər′ē, *v.i.,* **-ried, -ry•ing.** To run or move rapidly; to scamper; to hurry.—*n. pl.,* **-ries.** A scurrying; the sound of scurrying.

scur•vy, skər′vē, *n.* A disease characterized in part by swollen and readily bleeding gums, livid skin patches, and exhaustion, affecting persons who are deprived of vitamin C. **—a., -vi•er, -vi•est.** Vile; mean; low. **—scur•vi•ly,** *adv.* **—scur•vi•ness,** *n.*

scut•tle, skət′əl, *n.* A square hole with a lid in the wall or roof of a house; the lid itself; a small hatchway with a cover in the desk, side, or bottom of a ship.—*v.t.,* **-tled, -tling.** To sink (a ship) by making holes through the bottom or by opening the scuttles; to discard, as an idea.

scut•tle, skət′əl, *v.i.,* **-tled, -tling.** To run hastily.—*n.* A quick pace; a short run.

scut•tle•butt, skət′əl•bət, *n. Informal.* Rumor; gossip.

scythe, sīth, *n.* An instrument used in mowing or reaping, consisting of a long curving blade fixed to a handle at an angle.—*v.t.,* **scythed, scyth•ing.** To mow with a scythe.

sea, sē, *n.* The continuous mass of salt water which covers the greater portion of the earth; the ocean; a segment of this that is enclosed to some degree by land: the North *Sea;* a name given to some large landlocked lakes: the Caspian *Sea;* a large wave or surge: A *sea* put the deck awash; large swells or series of waves: A heavy *sea* was running that night; any large quantity: a *sea* of difficulties; a flood; the vocation of a sailor.—*a.***—at sea,** aboard ship on the ocean; bewildered or perplexed.

sea a•nem•o•ne, *n.* Any of several marine polyps, found in rocky crevices and in tide pools, resembling flowers.

sea bass, *n.* A common marine food fish.

sea•bed, sē′bed, *n.* The ocean floor.

Sea•bee, sē′bē, *n.* One who serves with any of the construction battalions established by the U.S. Navy.

sea•board, sē′bôrd, *n.* The seacoast.

sea breeze, *n.* A cool breeze blowing from the sea

toward land.

sea·coast, sē'kōst, *n.* The land immediately adjacent to the sea; the coast.

sea cow, *n.* Any aquatic mammal, as the dugong and the manatee; the walrus.

sea cu·cum·ber, *n.* A type of marine animal shaped somewhat like a cucumber.

sea dog, *n.* The dogfish; the common seal; an old or seasoned sailor.

sea·far·ing, sē'fâr·ing, *a.* Following the occupation of a seaman; traveling by sea.—*n.* Travel by sea; a sailor's calling. —**sea·far·er,** *n.*

sea·food, sē'food, *n.* Any edible fish, shellfish, or other aquatic animal.

sea·go·ing, sē'gō·ing, *a.* Made for oceangoing: a *seagoing* vessel; seafaring. —**sea·go·er,** *n.*

sea·green, sē'grēn', *a.* Having the color of sea water; of a bluish-green color. —**sea green,** *n.*

sea gull, *n.* A gull inhabiting the sea; loosely, any gull.

sea horse, *n.* A small fish, related to the pipefish, with head and neck likened to a horse; a fabled animal, half horse and half fish; a marine walrus.

seal, sēl, *n. pl.,* **seals, seal.** A large, meat-eating marine mammal, having limbs adapted into webbed flippers for propulsion; any seal pelt products, as fur or leather; a very dark, rich, gray-brown color.—*v.i.* To hunt seals. —**seal·like,** *a.*

seal, sēl, *n.* A ring or other hard object engraved with a figure or sign for the purpose of making an impression on a soft substance, as wax or paper; the impression or mark made; the wax, stamp, or other fastening of a letter, envelope, or other piece; that which shuts, fastens, or secures; that which insures secrecy, usu. by preventing opening without breakage of the seal; a mark or sign which authenticates, confirms, or pledges; the symbol of a high office; an ornamental piece of gummed paper sold to raise funds for a cause: an Easter *seal.*—*v.t.* To affix, as a seal, as a mark of authenticity; to make final or binding by or as by fastening a seal to; to place, as a mark or sign, upon to confirm fulfillment of standard specifications; to fasten securely to prevent undetected opening; to close with or as with a seal; to fix, determine, or finalize: to *seal* one's fate; to authorize or give under the power of a seal.—**un·der seal,** affixed with or as with an authoritative seal. —**seal·er,** *n.*

sea lam·prey, *n.* A large lamprey which ascends rivers to spawn.

sea legs, *n. pl.* The ability to walk on a ship's deck while it is pitching or rolling without losing one's balance.

sea lev·el, *n.* The approx. mean level of the ocean surface, esp. as used in determining the elevation of mountains, cities, etc.

seal·ing wax, sē'ling, *n.* A composition of resinous materials which softens when heated and solidifies when cooled, used for fastening folded papers, envelopes, and the like.

sea li·on, *n.* Any of various eared seals of large size.

seal·skin, sēl'skin, *n.* The skin of the fur seal; a coat or other garment made of sealskin.—*a.*

seam, sēm, *n.* A joining line formed by sewing together two pieces of material; the stitches in this joining line; a suture; the line formed by the joining of any two edges; a wrinkle; the line or space between planks joined together; a thin layer or stratum, as of rock. —*v.t.* To unite with a seam; to wrinkle.—*v.i.* To become cracked or cleft. —**seam·er,** *n.* —**seam·like,** *a.*

sea·maid, sē'mād, *n.* A mermaid.

sea·man, sē'mən, *n. pl.,* **-men.** A sailor, esp. one below the rank of officer; an enlisted man whose rank is below that of petty officer.

sea·man·ship, sē'mən·ship, *n.* The art of operating, navigating, and maintaining a ship; skill in this art.

seam·stress, sēm'stris, *n.* A woman whose occupation is sewing; a woman proficient in sewing.

seam·y, sē'mē, *a.,* **-i·er, -i·est.** Lowly; sordid; having seams or showing them, as the underside of a garment. —**seam·i·ness,** *n.*

sé·ance, sā'äns, *n.* A meeting conducted by a spiritualist with the view of evoking communication with spirits of the dead.

sea ot·ter, *n.* A rare marine otter, with a very valuable brown fur.

sea·plane, sē'plān, *n.* An airplane for use over the sea, esp. one provided with floats.

sea·port, sē'pōrt, sē'pôrt, *n.* A port, or a town with a port, on or near the sea.

sea pow·er, *n.* Naval strength of a country.

sea·quake, sē'kwāk, *n.* A submarine eruption or earthquake.

sear, sēr, *v.t.* To wither; to burn the surface of; to scorch; to make callous or insensible; to brand.—*v.i.* To wither or dry up.—*a.* Dry; withered.—*n.* A scar caused by searing.

search, sərch, *v.t.* To go through or look through carefully in seeking to find something; to read attentively or examine for information; to explore thoroughly; probe: to *search* one's own heart; to uncover or learn by a search, usu. followed by *out.*—*v.i.* To make a search.—*n.* The act or an act of searching. —**search·a·ble,** *a.* —**search·er,** *n.*

search·ing, sər'ching, *a.* Examining carefully; keenly observant or penetrating, as the eyes or gaze.

search·light, sərch'līt, *n.* An apparatus pivoted so as to project a strong beam of light in any direction; the beam of light.

search war·rant, *n.* A warrant granted by a judge or magistrate legalizing a police search of private premises.

sea·scape, sē'skāp, *n.* An expanse of sea or seashore within view; a painting or other artistic representation of the sea.

sea ser·pent, *n.* A huge, legendary, sea-dwelling monster discussed by seamen and some scientists, but as yet unverified.

sea·shell, sē'shel, *n.* The shell of any marine mollusk.

sea·shore, sē'shōr, sē'shôr, *n.* The rocky or sandy place where the land meets the edge of the sea.

sea·sick·ness, sē'sik·nis, *n.* Nausea and vomiting produced by the rolling or pitching of a vessel at sea. —**sea·sick,** *a.*

sea·side, sē'sīd, *n.* The land by the sea; the seacoast; the beach.—*a.* Pertaining to the seaside.

sea·son, sē'zən, *n.* One of the four divisions of the year (spring, summer, autumn, winter) characterized by distinctive temperature, rainfall, vegetation, and the like; that period of the year in which something is most obtainable: the peach *season;* that part of the year when a particular activity, profession, or the like is greatest: the hockey *season;* the time surrounding an important occasion: the Christmas *season;* any particular time; a convenient or suitable time.—*v.t.* To enhance or heighten the flavor of, by adding spices or the like; to give relish or zest to; to bring to the best state for use: to *season* timber by drying or hardening; to accustom: to *season* by experience.—*v.i.* To become seasoned. —**in season,** ready for use; at the proper or suitable time; within the prescribed hunting season; of an animal, ready for mating.—**sea·son·er,** *n.*

sea·son·a·ble, sē'zə·nə·bəl, *a.* Suitable to the time or season; opportune.

sea·son·al, sē'zə·nəl, *a.* Pertaining to or accompanying the seasons, or a certain season only. —**sea·son·al·ly,** *adv.*

sea·son·ing, sē'zə·ning, *n.* An ingredient, esp. a spice, salt, or herb, added to food to heighten or

---

a- hat, fāte, fâre, fäther; e- met, mē; i- pin, pīne; o- not, nōte, ôrb, moove (move), boy, pownd; u- cūbe, bûll, tûk (took); ch- chin; th- thick, ᴛhen; zh- vizhon (vision); ə- əgo, takən, pencəl, ləmən, bərd (bird).

enhance the flavor.

seat, sēt, *n.* Something made or used for sitting on, as a chair or bench; the particular part of a chair on which one sits; the buttocks, or that part of a garment which covers them; that on which the base of anything rests; the base itself; site or location: a *seat* of learning; a place to seat one person, as in a theater; a right to sit as a member in a legislative or similar body.—*v.t.* To place on a seat or seats; to accommodate with seats: This theater *seats* four hundred people; to put a seat on, as a chair; to install or settle in a position of authority, or the like; to set firmly or securely on a base. —**seat·er,** *n.*

seat belt, *n.* Safety belt.

seat·ing, sē′ting, *n.* The act of furnishing with a seat or seats; the arrangement of the seats, as in a theater or room; material used to cover seats.

sea ur·chin, *n.* A type of marine animal having a roundish body with many projecting spines.

sea wall, *n.* A strong embankment or wall on the shore to prevent encroachment of the sea.

sea·ward, sē′wərd, *a.* Directed toward the sea; coming from the sea.—*adv.* Toward the sea; also **sea·wards.**—*n.* A course or position away from the shore.

sea·way, sē′wā, *n.* The sea as a route for travel; an ocean traffic lane; an inland waterway deep enough to admit ocean shipping.

sea·weed, sē′wēd, *n.* Any plant or plants growing in the sea, esp. a marine alga.

sea·wor·thy, sē′wer·thē, *a.* Of a ship, in good condition and fit for a voyage. —**sea·wor·thi·ness,** *n.*

se·ba·ceous, si·bā′shəs, *a.* Of, containing, or secreting fat or fatty matter.

sec, sek, *a.* Of wines, dry, not sweet.

se·cant, sē′kənt, sē′kant, *n.* A straight line that intersects a curve at two or more points. *Trig.* The ratio of the hypotenuse to the side adjacent to an acute angle in a right triangle.

se·cede, si·sēd′, *v.i.,* **-ced·ed, -ced·ing.** To withdraw formally from an association. —**se·ced·er,** *n.*

se·ces·sion, si·sesh′ən, *n.* The act or event of seceding. (*Usu. cap.*) *U.S.* The withdrawal of Southern states from the Union which touched off the Civil War. —**se·ces·sion·ist,** *n.*

se·clude, si·klood′, *v.t.,* **-clud·ed, -clud·ing.** To isolate, keep apart, or retire from natural contact with society; separate, or shelter from public observation or influence.

se·clud·ed, si·kloo′did, *a.* Shut off or separated from others; private. —**se·clud·ed·ly,** *adv.* —**se·clud·ed·ness,** *n.*

se·clu·sion, si·kloo′zhən, *n.* The act of secluding; the state of being secluded; retirement; solitude; an isolated, private place. —**se·clu·sive,** *a.*

sec·ond, sek′ənd, *a.* Next after the first; being the ordinal of two; subordinate or inferior to a first; alternate to a first: every *second* month; other or another: a *second* family car; bearing likeness to a prototype: a *second* home; acquired, but deeply ingrained, as a characteristic: *second* nature.—*n.* One who or that which follows the first; one who acts as the aide of a principal, as in a duel. *Pl.* An additional helping of food. *Usu. pl.* Merchandise that is flawed or otherwise substandard in quality; in parliamentary procedure, the expression signifying formal support of another's proposal.—*adv.* In the second place, group, rank, etc. Also **sec·ond·ly.**—*v.t.* To support; assist; promote; advance; to act as second to (a duelist, etc.); to support formally, as a resolution, motion, etc.

sec·ond, sek′ənd, *n.* The sixtieth part of a minute of time; a moment or instant; the sixtieth part of a minute of a degree, often represented by the sign ''.

sec·ond·ar·y, sek′ən·der·ē, *a.* Of less than first rating, place, rank, or importance; subordinate; derivative, rather than original; pertaining to a school between the elementary and collegiate levels, as a high school.—*n.* A person or object that is second in order or position. —**sec·ond·ar·i·ly** sek·ən·dār′ə·lē, *adv.*

sec·ond-best, sek′ənd·best′, *a.* Next to or nearly the best.

sec·ond child·hood, *n.* Senility; dotage.

sec·ond-class, sek′ənd·klas′, *a.* Of or relating to the class next after the first; second-rate; mediocre; inferior; pertaining to the second grade of accommodations for travel; designating a class of mail including newspapers and periodicals.—*adv.* By second-class ticket, conveyance, etc. —**sec·ond class,** *n.*

sec·ond fid·dle, *n. Informal.* One who plays a role subsidiary to another.

sec·ond-guess, sek′ənd·ges′, *v.t.* To speculate on alternatives after a choice has been made or can no longer be made; to attempt to outguess or outsmart. —**sec·ond-guess·er,** *n.*

sec·ond hand, *n.* The hand of a watch or clock that indicates seconds.

sec·ond·hand, sek′ənd·hand′, *a.* Not original or primary; not new; having been used or worn; dealing in used goods: a *secondhand* bookstore.—*adv.* —**sec·ond hand,** *n.* —**at sec·ond hand,** from an intermediary means.

sec·ond lieu·ten·ant, *n.* The lowest rank accorded to commissioned U.S. Army, Air Force, or Marine Corps officers.

sec·ond per·son, *n.* The form of many languages used to signify the one or ones that a speaker or writer is addressing.

sec·ond-rate, sek′ənd·rāt′, *a.* Of the second rank or class; inferior; mediocre.—*adv.* —**sec·ond-rat·er,** *n.*

sec·ond sight, *n.* The power of seeing things future or distant; prophetic vision.

sec·ond-sto·ry man, sek′ənd·stô′rē, *n. Informal.* One who burglarizes, entering a building above the ground floor.

se·cre·cy, sē′kri·sē, *n. pl.,* **-cies.** The state or quality of being secret or hidden; concealment; secretiveness.

se·cret, sē′krit, *a.* Apart from the knowledge of others; known only to one or to few: *secret* password; not made public: *secret* negotiations between Russia and France; secluded: a *secret* hideout; occult: *secret* rites; hidden: a *secret* compartment.—*n.* Something concealed: a thing kept from general knowledge; a thing not discovered or explained; a mystery.

sec·re·tar·i·at, sek·ri·tār′ē·ət, *n.* The position of secretary; the clerical staff of an organization; the place where a secretary transacts business; the administrative department of a governmental organization, as the United Nations.

sec·re·tar·y, sek′ri·ter·ē, *n. pl.,* **-ies.** One who carries on another's correspondence and performs other routine tasks; an officer of an organization or business who keeps records and assists in major decisions; a piece of furniture with facilities for writing. (*Cap.*) A government officer whose business is to superintend and manage the affairs of a particular department of government: *Secretary* of Defense. —**sec·re·tar·i·al,** sek·rə·tār′ē·əl, *a.*

se·crete, si·krēt′, *v.t.,* **-cret·ed, -cret·ing.** To produce, release, or discharge by secretion; to keep secret; conceal.

se·cre·tion, si·krē′shən, *n.* The process, usu. glandular, by which substances are separated from the blood, elaborated into different materials such as bile or urine, and released into or from the body; a secreted substance.

se·cre·tive, si·krē′tiv, *a.* Producing or aiding secretion.—sē′krə·tiv. Inclined to secrecy or privacy.

se·cre·to·ry, si·krē′tə·rē, *a.* Pertaining to secretion.—*n. pl.,* **-ries.** A secreting gland, organ, etc.

se·cret po·lice, *n.* A police group operating in a covert manner, usu. to protect political interests of the government.

se·cret serv·ice, *n.* Intelligence or espionage, as conducted by a government; an agency for espionage. (*Cap.*) A division of the U.S. Treasury Department, charged chiefly with the suppression of counterfeiting and with the protection of certain personages, esp. the President and his family.

sect, sekt, *n.* A body of persons who follow a teacher or leader, or are united by philosophical or religious tenets.

sec·tar·i·an, sek·târ'ē·ən, *a.* Pertaining to a sect or sects; strongly or bigotedly attached to a sect.—*n.* One of a sect; a bigot. **—sec·tar·i·an·ism,** *n.*

sec·tion, sek'shən, *n.* A part cut or separated from the rest; a portion or division; a distinct part of a country or people, community or class: the Italian *section* of the city; the act of cutting or separation by cutting; one square mile of land; a representation of an object as if cut by an intersecting plane; a thin slice of anything for microscopic examination.—*v.t.* To separate or divide into sections; depict sections of by shading.

sec·tion·al, sek'shə·nəl, *a.* Pertaining to a section or sections; of a particular zone or sphere of activity; comprised of sections or parts.—*n.* A couch or sofa consisting of several sections which may be arranged in a variety of ways.

sec·tor, sek'tər, *n.* A separate part; a distinguishable subdivision: the government *sector* of an economy; a mathematical instrument consisting of two legs hinged at one end and marked to fit various radii and scales, used in making diagrams.—*v.t.* To separate into sectors. **—sec·to·ri·al,** sek·tôr'ē·əl, *a.*

sec·u·lar, sek'yə·lər, *a.* Pertaining to this present world or to things not spiritual or sacred; worldly; not devoted to religious use: *secular* music; extending over a very long period of time.—*n.* A layman.

sec·u·lar·ism, sek'yə·lə·riz·əm, *n.* Secular spirit or tendencies; the view that public education and other matters of civil policy should be conducted without the introduction of a religious element.

sec·u·lar·ize, sek'yə·lə·rīz, *v.t.,* **-ized, -iz·ing.** To make secular; to separate from religious or spiritual connections or influences. **—sec·u·lar·i·za·tion,** sek·yə·lər·ə·zā'shən, *n.* **—sec·u·lar·iz·er,** *n.*

se·cure, si·kyûr', *a.* Free from fear; confident of safety; free from danger; not likely to give way or fail; safe; such as to be depended on; capable of resisting assault or attack; stable; sure, or confident.—*v.t.,* **-cured, -cur·ing.** To make secure; to protect; to make certain; to enclose or confine effectually; to make certain of payment, as a creditor; to warrant against loss; to make fast or firm: to *secure* a door; to get possession of.—*v.i.* To become safe. **—se·cur·a·ble,** *a.* **—se·cure·ness,** *n.* **—se·cur·er,** *n.*

se·cu·ri·ty, si·kyûr'i·tē, *n. pl.,* **-ties.** The state of being secure; confidence of safety; that which secures or makes safe; something that secures against financial want or loss; surety; a person who guarantees another's obligations; pledge or deposit of property, as a bond, a certificate of stock, or the like. *Pl.* Certificates of stocks, bonds, or notes.

Se·cu·ri·ty Coun·cil, *n.* The organ of the United Nations which has as its primary function the maintenance of international peace and security.

se·dan, si·dan', *n.* A type of automobile that is enclosed, and has two or four doors.

se·date, si·dāt', *a.* Calm in feelings and manner; serene; staid; dignified. **—se·date·ness,** *n.*

se·date, si·dāt', *v.t.,* **-dat·ed, -dat·ing.** To place under sedation, as a person.

se·da·tion, si·dā'shən, *n.* The practice or act of alleviating pain, distress, or tension through the use of sedatives.

sed·a·tive, sed'ə·tiv, *a.* Tending to calm or tranqui-

lize; allaying irritability, irritation, or pain.—*n.* A medicine which sedates.

sed·en·tar·y, sed'ən·ter·ē, *a.* Accustomed to sit; requiring much sitting; inactive. **—sed·en·tar·i·ness,** *n.*

sedge, sej, *n.* Any of a family of grasslike plants growing mostly in swamps and marshes, and on riverbanks.

sed·i·ment, sed'ə·mənt, *n.* The matter which subsides to the bottom of water or any other liquid; settlings; dregs; matter deposited by wind and water. **—sed·i·men·tal, sed·i·men·ta·ry,** sed·ə·men'təl, sed·ə·men'tə·rē, *a.* **—sed·i·men·ta·tion,** sed·ə·mən·tā'shən, *n.*

se·di·tion, si·dish'ən, *n.* Incitement to rebellion against lawful authority, esp. clandestinely or without overt acts of treason. **—se·di·tion·ar·y,** *a., n.*

se·di·tious, si·dish'əs, *a.* Pertaining to, marked by, aiding in, or guilty of sedition.

se·duce, si·doos', si·dūs', *v.t.,* **-duced, -duc·ing.** To persuade from the path of duty; to lead astray; to tempt; to entice to a surrender of chastity. **—se·duc·er,** *n.* **—se·duc·i·ble, se·duce·a·ble,** *a.* **—se·duc·tion,** si·dək'shən, **se·duce·ment,** *n.*

se·duc·tive, si·dək'tiv, *a.* Tending to seduce; alluring. **—se·duc·tive·ness,** *n.*

sed·u·lous, sej'ə·ləs, *a.* Assiduous; diligent; painstaking and persevering. **—se·du·li·ty, si·doo'lə·tē, sed·u·lous·ness,** *n.*

see, sē, *v.t.,* **saw, seen, see·ing.** To perceive by the eye; to look at or behold; to view, as a play; to visualize; to recognize; to discover; to examine; to experience; to ensure; to meet or associate with; to consult: to *see* an expert; to visit: to go to *see* a friend; to provide for; to help: to *see* her through this difficult period; to attend or escort: to *see* a person home; to find fitting or acceptable; to choose to have: I would *see* him in prison before I gave him money.—*v.i.* To have the sense of sight; to perceive mentally; to discern; to examine or inquire; to be attentive; to take care; to observe.**—see a·bout,** to give attention to. **—see off,** to escort to a place of departure.**—see out,** to stay with, as an undertaking, until it is finished. **—see through,** to penetrate; to comprehend the actual character of; to detect; to persevere. **—see·a·ble,** *a.*

see, sē, *n.* The authority, office, or seat of a bishop.

seed, sēd, *n. pl.,* **seeds, seed.** The impregnated and matured ovule of a plant, which may develop into a new plant; loosely, one of the grains of wheat and other grasses; any plant part capable of reproduction, as a bulb or tuber; semen; that from which anything springs; offspring; descendants.—*v.t.* To scatter or sow, as seeds; to plant seeds in, as a field; to take the seeds out of, as fruit; to sprinkle or scatter chemicals into, as clouds, to cause rainfall; to arrange, as competitive teams or players, so that the most skilled are matched in the later rounds of play; to handle in this way: they *seeded* him fourth.—*v.i.* To bear and drop seeds; to plant or sow seed.**—go to seed,** to bear and shed seed, as a flower; to become shabby or weak; to deteriorate, as a person. **—seed·er,** *n.*

seed·bed, sēd'bed, *n.* Any plot of soil which has been prepared for planting.

seed·case, sēd'kās, *n.* A seed vessel; pod.

seed·ling, sēd'ling, *n.* A plant produced from seed rather than from a graft; any very small or young plant.

seed·pod, sēd'pod, *n.* The capsule or container which holds the seeds of such plants as the lima bean and milkweed; pod.

seed·y, sē'dē, *a.,* **-i·er, -i·est.** Abounding with seeds; producing seeds; gone to seed. *Informal.* Worn-out; shabby; wretched; slightly disreputable. **—seed·i·ly,** *adv.* **—seed·i·ness,** *n.*

see·ing, sē'ing, *conj.* Inasmuch as; since.

---

a- hat, fāte, fāre, fäther; **e-** met, mē; **i-** pin, pīne; **o-** not, nōte, ôrb, moove (move), boy, pownd; **u-** cūbe, bŭll, tûk (took); **ch-** chin; **th-** thick, ŧhen; **zh-** vizhon (vision); **ə-** əgo, takən, pencəl, lemən, bərd (bird).

See·ing Eye dog, *n.* A dog trained to guide a blind person.

seek, sēk, *v.t.,* **sought, seek·ing.** To go in search of; to look for, often followed by *out;* to ask for or request: to *seek* advice; to go to: to *seek* a shady spot; to aim at; to try, usu. followed by an infinitive; to strive after. —*v.i.* To make search or inquiry. —**seek·er,** *n.*

seem, sēm, *v.i.* To appear: The boys *seem* happy; to feel as if: I still *seem* to hear his voice; to give an indication of being present: There *seems* good reason to fear him; to be apparent; to assume an air; to pretend. —**seem·er,** *n.*

seem·ing, sē'ming, *a.* Appearing; having the appearance, whether real or not.—*n.* Appearance, esp. a false appearance; show. —**seem·ing·ness,** *n.*

seem·ly, sēm'lē, *a.,* **-li·er, -li·est.** Becoming; fitting; proper; pleasing in appearance.—*adv.* Becomingly; fittingly. —**seem·li·ness,** *n.*

seep, sēp, *v.i.* To pass gradually, as liquid, through a porous substance; percolate; ooze.—*n.* Moisture that seeps out; seepage. —**seep·y,** *a.,* **-i·er, -i·est.**

seep·age, sē'pij, *n.* The act or process of seeping; leakage.

se·er, sē'ər, *n.* One who sees.—sēr. A prophet, or person said to be gifted with second sight. —**seer·ess,** sēr'is, *n. fem.*

seer·suck·er, sēr'sək·ər, *n.* A fabric of linen, rayon, or cotton, usu. striped, with alternate stripes being crinkled in the weaving.

see·saw, sē'sô, *n.* An amusement in which children move alternately up and down when seated one or more at each end of a plank balanced on some support; a plank adjusted for this sport; an up-and-down or a back-and-forth movement or procedure. —*a.* Moving up and down or back and forth.—*v.i., v.t.* To move or cause to move in a seesaw manner.

seethe, sēth, *v.t.,* **seethed, seeth·ing.** To boil; to soak or steep.—*v.i.* To boil; to surge or foam as if boiling; to be in a state of agitation or excitement.—*n.* The act or the fact of seething; a state of agitation or excitement. —**seeth·ing,** *a.*

seg·ment, seg'mənt, *n.* A piece or part cut or marked off; one of the parts into which anything naturally separates or is naturally divided; a division or section. —seg·ment', *v.t., v.i.* To separate or divide into segments. —**seg·men·tal,** seg·men'təl, *a.* —**seg·men·tar·y,** seg'mən·ter·ē, *a.*

seg·men·ta·tion, seg·mən·tā'shən, *n.* A division into segments.

seg·re·gate, seg'rə·gāt, *v.t.,* **-gat·ed, -gat·ing.** To separate or set apart from the others; isolate; to subject to separation from the main body of society, as for racial reasons.—*v.i.* To separate or go apart; segregation.—seg'rə·git, seg'rə·gāt, *n.* A segregated object, person, or class of persons.

seg·re·gat·ed, seg'rə·gā·tid, *a.* Characterized by racial segregation: *segregated* schools; working against the interests of a particular group: *segregated* housing ordinances.

seg·re·ga·tion, seg·rə·gā'shən, *n.* The act of segregating, or the state of being segregated; isolation; something segregated; the practice of separating from the main body an ethnic or other group, as in education, housing, or employment.

seg·re·ga·tion·ist, seg·rə·gā'shə·nist, *n.* One who advocates or enforces segregation, esp. the segregation of races.

sei·gneur, sēn·yər', sän·yər', *n.* A man of rank or authority; a lord, esp. a feudal lord. Also **seign·ior,** sān·yôr', sēn'yər.

seine, sān, *n.* A fishing net which hangs vertically in the water.—*v.t., v.i.,* **seined, sein·ing.** To fish for or catch with a seine.

seis·mic, sīz'mik, sīs'mik, *a.* Characteristic of, resulting from, or subject to earthquakes. Also **seis·mal,** **seis·mi·cal.** —**seis·mi·cal·ly,** *adv.*

seis·mo·graph, sīz'mə·graf, sīs'mə·graf, *n.* An instrument for recording the intensity, duration, and direction of an earthquake. —**seis·mog·ra·pher,** sīz·mog'rə·fər, *n.* —**seis·mo·graph·ic,** sīz·mə·graf'ik, *a.* —**seis·mog·ra·phy,** sīz·mog'rə·fē, *n.*

seis·mol·o·gy, sīz·mol'ə·jē, sīs·mol'ə·jē, *n.* The scientific study of earthquakes and of artificially produced vibrations of the earth. —**seis·mo·log·ic,** sīz·mə·loj'ik, *a.* —**seis·mo·log·i·cal,** *a.* —**seis·mol·o·gist,** *n.*

seize, sēz, *v.t.,* **seized, seiz·ing.** To lay hold of suddenly or forcibly; clutch or grasp: to *seize* a weapon; grasp with the mind: to *seize* an idea; to take possession of by force or at will: to *seize* enemy ships; to take possession or control of as if by suddenly laying hold: A fever *seized* him; to take possession of by legal authority, or confiscate: to *seize* smuggled goods; to capture; to take prisoner or take into custody; take advantage of promptly: to *seize* an opportunity.—*v.i.* To take possession by force or at will, usu. followed by *on* or *upon;* to have recourse to some expedient, usu. followed by *on* or *upon:* to *seize on* a pretext or excuse. —**seiz·er,** *n.*

sei·zure, sē'zhər, *n.* The act of seizing or taking sudden hold; a taking into possession of an individual or property; a sudden attack, as of some disease; a fit.

sel·dom, sel'dəm, *adv.* Rarely; not often.—*a.* Rare; infrequent.

se·lect, si·lekt', *v.t.* To choose in preference to another or others; pick out from a number.—*v.i.* To make a choice or selection.—*a.* Selected; choice; superior; exclusive. —**se·lect·ed,** *a.* —**se·lec·tor,** *n.*

se·lec·tion, si·lek'shən, *n.* The act of selecting or the fact of being selected; choice; a thing or a number of things selected: a volume of prose *selections.*

se·lec·tive, si·lek'tiv, *a.* Having the function or power of selecting; making selection.

se·lec·tive serv·ice, *n.* Selection of persons from the total manpower of a nation for compulsory service in one of the armed forces.

se·lec·tiv·i·ty, si·lek·tiv'i·tē, *n.* The state or quality of being selective.

se·le·ni·um, si·lē'nē·əm, *n.* A nonmetallic element chemically resembling sulfur and tellurium, and having an electrical resistance that changes under the action of light: used in photoelectric cells.

self, self, *n. pl.,* **selves.** A person or thing, with respect to his, her, or its own person, individuality, or identity: her very *self,* religion's *self;* the individual consciousness, as the seat of subjective thought and action; the nature or character of a person or thing at a particular time or in a particular aspect: his better *self—pron.* Myself; himself; herself.—*a.* Being the same throughout; uniform; being of the same material or kind as the rest: a *self* belt; of, by, to, for, or from oneself or itself: used in combination.

self-a·base·ment, self·ə·bās'mənt, *n.* Degradation of oneself, esp. because of feelings of guilt or inferiority.

self-ab·ne·ga·tion, self'ab·nə·gā'shən, *n.* Self-sacrifice; self-denial.

self-a·buse, self·ə·būs', *n.* Self-reproach; masturbation.

self-ad·dressed, self'ə·drest', *a.* Addressed to oneself: In writing for information, enclose a *self-addressed* envelope.

self-ag·gran·dize·ment, self·ə·gran'diz·mənt, *n.* The increase of one's position, power, or wealth with little or no regard for the rights of others. —**self-ag·gran·diz·ing,** self·ə·gran'dī·zing, *a.*

self-as·sur·ance, self·ə·shûr'əns, *n.* Self-confidence. —**self-as·sured,** *a.*

self-cen·tered, self'sen'tərd, *a.* Centered in oneself; engrossed in oneself; selfish. —**self-cen·tered·ness,** *n.*

self-col·lect·ed, self·kə·lek'tid, *a.* Self-possessed.

self-com·mand, self·kə·mand', *n.* Command of feelings; self-control; poise.

self·com·posed, self·kəm·pōzd′, *a.* In control of one's emotions; calm.

self·con·fessed, self·kən·fest′, *a.* Openly avowed or admitted.

self·con·fi·dence, self·kon′fi·dəns, *n.* The state or quality or being confident or certain of oneself, or one's abilities. **—self·con·fi·dent,** *a.*

self·con·scious, self·kon′shəs, *a.* Conscious of oneself or one's own thoughts or actions; excessively conscious of oneself; given to thinking excessively of oneself as an object of observation to others; exhibiting shyness or embarrassment. **—self·con·scious·ness,** *n.*

self·con·tained, self·kən·tānd′, *a.* Containing in oneself or itself all that is necessary; reserved; self-controlled; of a machine, complete in itself.

self·con·trol, self·kən·trōl′, *n.* Control of oneself or one's actions and feelings; self-restraint. **—self·con·trolled,** *a.*

self·cor·rect·ing, self·kə·rek′ting, *a.* Geared to the automatic correction of errors in operation, as mechanisms.

self·crit·i·cism, self·krit′ə·siz·əm, *n.* The act or capability of viewing one's acts or motives in an objective or depreciatory manner. **—self·crit·i·cal,** *a.*

self·de·cep·tion, self·di·sep′shən, *n.* The act or fact of deceiving oneself. **—self·de·cep·tive,** *a.*

self·de·fense, self′di·fens′, *n.* The defense of one's own person, property, or reputation; the physical art of self-defense, as in boxing or judo.

self·de·ni·al, self′di·nī′əl, *n.* The denial of oneself; the sacrifice of one's own desires. **—self·de·ny·ing,** *a.*

self·de·ter·mi·na·tion, self′di·tər·mə·nā′shən, *n.* Determination by oneself or itself; free will; the determining by a people of the form of government they shall have, without reference to the wishes of any other nation. **—self·de·ter·min·ing,** self·di·tər′mə·ning, *a., n.*

self·dis·ci·pline, self·dis′ə·plin, *n.* Self-imposed regulation or ordering of one's own thoughts or actions, often with a view toward improvement. **—self·dis·ci·plined,** *a.*

self·ed·u·cat·ed, self′ej′ū·kā′tid, *a.* Educated by one's own efforts, without formal instruction. **—self·ed·u·ca·tion,** self·ej·ə·kā′shən, *n.*

self·ef·fac·ing, self′ə·fā′sing, *a.* Modestly keeping oneself in the background; retiring; timid.

self·em·ployed, self′im·ployd′, *a.* Deriving one's income directly from one's profession, skills, or services, without dependence upon employment by others. **—self·em·ploy·ment,** *n.*

self·es·teem, self′əs·tēm′, *n.* Esteem or respect for oneself.

self·ev·i·dent, self·ev′i·dənt, *a.* Evident without proof or reasoning. **—self·ev·i·dence,** *n.*

self·ex·plan·a·to·ry, self·iks·plan′ə·tôr·ē, *a.* Explaining itself; obvious.

self·ex·pres·sion, self′ik·spresh′ən, *n.* Expression of one's own personality, esp. in art. **—self·ex·pres·sive,** *a.*

self·ful·fill·ment, self′fûl·fil′mənt, *n.* The realization of one's ambitions or the full development of one's potentialities through one's own efforts. **—self·ful·fill·ing,** *a.*

self·gov·ern·ment, self′gəv′ərn·mənt, *n.* Government of a state, community, or other body of persons by its members jointly; autonomy. **—self·gov·erned, self·gov·ern·ing,** *a.*

self·help, self′help′, *n.* The act or the faculty of helping oneself, or getting along without assistance from others.

self·hood, self′hûd, *n.* The character of being oneself; personality; selfishness.

self·im·age, self′im′ij, *n.* One's conception or idea of oneself.

self·im·por·tance, self′im·pôr′təns, *n.* High opinion of oneself; conceit. **—self·im·por·tant,** *a.*

self·im·posed, self′im·pōzd′, *a.* Set or thrust upon one by oneself.

self·im·prove·ment, self′im·proov′mənt, *n.* Improvement of oneself, one's mind, abilities, or the like, by one's own efforts.

self·in·duced, self′in·doost′, self′in·dūst′, *a.* Induced by oneself or itself.

self·in·dul·gence, self′in·dəl′jəns, *n.* Free indulgence or gratification of one's appetites or desires. **—self·in·dul·gent,** *a.*

self·in·flict·ed, self′in·flik′tid, *a.* Inflicted on one by oneself, as a wound.

self·in·ter·est, self·in′tər·ist, self·in′trist, *n.* Interest or concern for oneself or one's own advantage; selfishness. **—self·in·ter·est·ed,** *a.*

self·ish, sel′fish, *a.* Caring only or chiefly for oneself; proceeding from love of self. **—self·ish·ness,** *n.*

self·knowl·edge, self′nol′ij, *n.* The knowledge of one's own real character, abilities, or worth.

self·less, self′lis, *a.* Having no regard for or thought for oneself; unselfish. **—self·less·ness,** *n.*

self·love, self′ləv′, *n.* Love of one's own person which serves to direct one's actions; regard for one's own well-being, welfare, advantage, or happiness. **—self·lov·ing,** *a.*

self·made, self′mād′, *a.* Having achieved success by one's personal efforts: a *self-made* man.

self·per·pet·u·at·ing, self·pər·pech′ū·ā·ting, *a.* Denoting a situation in which one manages to remain in a certain position indeterminately; regeneration of oneself. **—self·per·pet·u·a·tion,** self·pər·pech·ū·ā′shən, *n.*

self·pit·y, self′pit′ē, *n.* Pity for oneself. **—self·pit·y·ing,** *a.*

self·pol·li·na·tion, self′pol·ə·nā′shən, *n.* Pollination of a flower by its own pollen or by pollen from another flower on the same plant.

self·pos·sessed, self′pə·zest′, *a.* Composed; cool; not disturbed. **—self·pos·sess·ed·ly,** *adv.* **—self·pos·ses·sion,** *n.*

self·pres·er·va·tion, self′prez·ər·vā′shən, *n.* The preservation of oneself from destruction or injury; an instinct to protect oneself from injury.

self·pro·pelled, self′prə·peld′, *a.* Propelled by itself; of a vehicle, containing an engine, motor, or the like, by which it is propelled. Also **self·pro·pel·ling.**

self·re·al·i·za·tion, self′rē·ə·li·zā′shən, *n.* The development or fulfillment of one's potentialities.

self·re·li·ance, self′ri·lī′əns, *n.* Dependence on one's own powers or abilities. **—self·re·li·ant,** *a.*

self·re·spect, self′ri·spekt′, *n.* Respect for oneself or one's own character. **—self·re·spect·ing,** *a.*

self·re·straint, self′ri·strānt′, *n.* Restraint or control imposed on oneself; self-control. **—self·re·strain·ing,** *a.*

self·right·eous, self·rī′chəs, *a.* Assured of one's own uprightness, morality, and virtue, esp. when intolerant of the beliefs and actions of others. **—self·right·eous·ness,** *n.*

self·sac·ri·fice, self·sak′rə·fīs, *n.* The denial of oneself or of self-interest for the benefit of another. **—self·sac·ri·fic·ing,** *a.*

self·same, self′sām, *a.* The very same; identical.

self·sat·is·fied, self·sat′is·fīd, *a.* Content with oneself. **—self·sat·is·fac·tion,** self′sat·is·fak′shən, *n.* **—self·sat·is·fy·ing,** *a.*

self·serv·ice, self′sər′vis, *n.* Service by oneself; the serving of oneself in a restaurant, shop, or the like, rather than being served by attendants.—*a.*

self·serv·ing, self′sər′ving, *a.* Putting one's own interest first; selfish.

---

self-start·er, self/stär/tər, *n.* A device which starts an internal-combustion engine without the necessity of cranking it by hand; one who applies his or her efforts without instruction or directions from others. —**self-start·ing,** *a.*

self-styled, self/stīld/, *a.* Called or styled by oneself: a *self-styled* expert.

self-suf·fi·cient, self·sə·fish/ənt, *a.* Independent of the aid of others; somewhat conceited. Also **self-suf·fic·ing,** self·sə·fī/sing. —**self-suf·fi·cien·cy,** *n.*

self-sup·port, self/sə·pōrt/, self/sə·pôrt/, *n.* The act or fact of supporting or maintaining oneself or itself without outside aid. —**self-sup·port·ing,** *a.*

self-taught, self/tôt/, *a.* Taught by oneself without formal instruction.

self-will, self/wil/, *n.* Determination to have one's own way; willfulness; obstinacy. —**self-willed,** *a.*

sell, sel, *v.t.,* **sold, sell·ing.** To give possession of, control over, title to, or the services of, to a purchaser for money or other payment; to invite purchase of; to accept a price or reward for, or make profit or gain on, usu. on an object improper for such use, as a friend or one's soul; to give up or sacrifice at some cost to an adversary, as one's life or honor. *Informal.* To cause, though salesmanship, to be accepted, adopted, or purchased by a person or group, used with *to:* To *sell* an idea *to* the public; to cheat, trick, or hoax.—*v.i.* To sell something; to be on sale at a particular price: wool that *sells* for three dollars a yard; to be in demand as an item for purchase: Bathing suits *sell* in hot weather; to win acceptance or adoption when presented by, or as if by salesmanship: a look that will *sell;* to accomplish a sale.—*n. Informal.* An instance of cheating —**sell out,** to completely dispose of by selling; to betray one's integrity, one's cause, one's associates, etc. —**sell short,** to undervalue; to sell without having full possession°of, while expecting to both profit by the sale and eventually fulfill the terms of sale.

sell·er, sel/ər, *n.* One who sells; an item for sale, usu. with regard to the speed or volume in which it is sold: a car which is a poor *seller.*

sell-out, sel/owt, *n.* An event, usu. theatrical or athletic, to which every seat has been sold; the operation of selling out.

Selt·zer, selt/sər, *n.* A natural, effervescent mineral water containing salt and small amounts of sodium, calcium, and magnesium carbonates. *(Often l.c.)* A commercial product of similar composition. Also **Selt·zer wa·ter.**

sel·vage, sel·vedge, sel/vij, *n.* A woven boarder on a fabric, designed to prevent fraying; that portion of a lock which accommodates the bolt; a border of excess material, as on wall paper. —**sel·vaged, sel·vedged,** *a.*

se·man·tics, si·man/tiks, *n. pl. but sing. in constr.* The study of word meanings, esp. as they develop and change; the study of the relationship between signs or symbols and that which they represent.—**se·man·tic, se·man·ti·cal,** *a.* —**se·man·ti·cal·ly,** *adv.*

sem·a·phore, sem/ə·fôr, *n.* An apparatus for conveying visual signals at a distance by moving flags, lights, blades, arms, or the like.—*v.t., v.i.,* **-phored, -phor·ing.** To signal by means of a semaphore.

sem·blance, sem/bləns, *n.* Similarity or resemblance; mere external show; form, figure, image, or likeness; the smallest or flimsiest resemblance.

se·men, sē/mən, *n.* The whitish, viscous substance which carries spermatozoa, and is secreted by the male reproductive organs.

se·mes·ter, si·mes/tər, *n.* A period or term of six months; half an academic year, usu. lasting 15 to 18 weeks.

sem·i·an·nu·al, sem·ē·an/yū·əl, *a.* Occurring or appearing every half-year or twice in a year; lasting for half a year. —**sem·i·an·nu·al·ly,** *adv.*

sem·i·ar·id, sem·ē·ar/id, *a.* Characterized by scant annual rainfall.

sem·i·au·to·mat·ic, sem·ē·ô·tə·mat/ik, *a.* Partly self-operating.

sem·i·cir·cle, sem/ē·sər·kəl, *n.* The half of a circle; the part of a circle comprehended between its diameter and half of its circumference; anything in the form of a half circle. —**sem·i·cir·cu·lar,** sem·ē·sər/kyə·lər, *a.*

sem·i·clas·si·cal, sem·ē·klas/i·kəl, *a.* Inferior in importance or quality to the classical; esp. in music, a classical composition of popular appeal, or one having characteristics of both classical and popular music. —**sem·i·clas·sic,** *n.*

sem·i·co·lon, sem/i·kō·lən, *n.* The punctuation sign (;) indicating a separation less definite than a period and more definite than the comma.

sem·i·con·duc·tor, sem/ē·kən·dək/tər,sem/i·kən·dək/tər, *n.* A material having an electrical conductivity intermediate between that of a metal and an insulator, and used in making electronic components, as transistors or rectifiers. —**sem·i·con·duct·ing,** *a.*

sem·i·con·scious, sem·ē·kon/shəs, sem·i·kon/shəs, *a.* Not completely conscious; half conscious. —**sem·i·con·scious·ness,** *n.*

sem·i·de·tached, sem·ē·di·tacht/, *a.* Partly detached; designating either of two houses joined by one common wall.

sem·i·fi·nal, sem·ē·fīn/əl, *a.* Designating or pertaining to a round, contest, or match which immediately precedes the final and decisive one, as in a tournament.—*n.* Also sem/i·fi·nəl. *Often pl.* A semifinal round, contest, or the like. —**sem·i·fi·nal·ist,** *n.*

sem·i·flu·id, sem·ē·floo/id, *a.* Imperfectly fluid; able to flow, but heavy and viscous.—*n.* Semiliquid.

sem·i·for·mal, sem·ē·fôr/məl, sem·i·fôr/məl, *a.* Partially or moderately formal, esp. in dress.

sem·i·gloss, sem·ē·glos/, sem·ē·glôs/, *a.* Having a low gloss or luster.

sem·i·liq·uid, sem·ē·lik/wid, sem·i·lik/wid, *a.* Imperfectly liquid; semifluid.—*n.* A semiliquid substance.

sem·i·month·ly, sem·ē·mənth/lē, sem·i·mənth/lē, *a.* Occurring or appearing every half month.—*n. pl.,* **-lies.** A semimonthly publication; anything happening every half month or two times a month.—*adv.* Every half month.

sem·i·nal, sem/ə·nəl, *a.* Pertaining to or consisting of seed or semen; germinal; acting as a source; influencing later developments: a *seminal* writer. —**sem·i·nal·ly,** *adv.*

sem·i·nar, sem/ə·när, *n.* A group of students, as in a university, engaged in advanced study and original research under an instructor; a course of study so arranged; a room where such a course is taught.

sem·i·nar·y, sem/ə·ner·ē, *n. pl.,* **-nar·ies.** A school, college, or university in which people are instructed in preparation to be rabbis, priests, or ministers; a place of education, esp. for girls; an area where something originates or grows. —**sem·i·nar·i·an,** sem·ə·när/ē·ən, *n.*

Sem·i·nole, sem/ə·nōl, *n. pl.,* **-nole, -noles.** Any of a tribe of the Muskhogean family, and now residing in Florida and Oklahoma; the language spoken by the tribe.—*a.*

sem·i·of·fi·cial, sem·ē·ə·fish/əl, *a.* Partly official; having some degree of official authority. —**sem·i·of·fi·cial·ly,** *adv.*

sem·i·per·ma·nent, sem·ē·pər/mə·nent, sem·i·pər/mə·nənt, *a.* Permanent in certain ways; lasting indefinitely.

sem·i·per·me·a·ble, sem·ē·pər/mē·ə·bəl, sem·i·pər/mē·ə·bəl, *a.* Permeable only to certain substances.

sem·i·pre·cious, sem/ē·presh/əs, *a.* Of or belonging to a class of gems, as the amethyst and garnet, ranked below such precious gems as the diamond and ruby.

sem·i·pri·vate, sem·ē·prī/vit, sem·i·prī/vit, *a.* Somewhat but not completely private, as a hospital room containing two or three beds.

sem·i·pro·fes·sion·al, sem·ē·prə·fesh′ə·nəl, *a.* Engaged in some sport or other activity for pay but only as a part-time occupation; resembling professional work but demanding less skill, knowledge, and the like.—*n.*

sem·i·pro, sem′ē·prō, sem′i·prō, *a., n. Informal.* Semiprofessional. —**sem·i·pro·fes·sion·al·ly,** *adv.*

sem·i·pub·lic, sem·ē·pub′lik, sem·i·pub′lik, *a.* Partly or to some degree available to the public: a *semipublic* golf course.

sem·i·skilled, sem·ē·skild′, sem·i·skild′, *a.* Having or requiring some degree of skill but not as much as skilled labor.

sem·i·sol·id, sem·ē·sol′id, sem·i·sol′id, *a.* Partially solid; of a somewhat firm consistency; extremely viscous.—*n.* A semisolid substance.

Se·mit·ic, sə·mit′ik, *a.* Of or referring to Caucasian peoples, including Jews and Arabs or their languages.—*n.* The Semitic branch of the Afro-Asian family of languages, including Hebrew, Arabic, and others.

Sem·i·tism, sem′i·tiz·əm, *n.* Semitic character or characteristics, esp. the ways, ideas, or influence of the Jewish people.

sem·i·trail·er, sem′ē·trā·lər, *n.* A freight carrier having only rear wheels and supported in front by its connection to a truck tractor; the entire apparatus, including tractor and trailer. Also **sem·i,** sem′ī.

sem·i·trop·ics, sem·ē·trop′iks, sem·i·trop′iks, *n. pl. but sing. in constr.* Subtropics. —**sem·i·trop·ic,** **sem·i·trop·i·cal,** *a.*

sem·i·vow·el, sem′ē·vow·əl, *n.* A sound having the sonorous quality of a vowel, but lacking the duration, distinction, and central position of a vowel, as *w* in *wish,* *r* in *red,* and *y* in *yellow;* a letter signifying a semivowel.

sem·i·week·ly, sem·ē·wēk′lē, sem·i·wēk′lē, *a.* Occurring or appearing every half week.—*n. pl.,* **-lies.** A semiweekly publication.—*adv.* Every half week.

sem·i·year·ly, sem·ē·yēr′lē, sem·i·yēr′lē, *a.* Occurring half-yearly or twice yearly.—*adv.* Twice yearly; half-yearly.

sen·a·ry, sen′ə·rē, *a.* Of, pertaining to, or containing six.

sen·ate, sen′it, *n.* An assembly or council having the highest deliberative and legislative powers in a government. (*Cap.*) The upper of the two houses in various legislatures, as in France, Canada, the U.S., or individual states of the U.S.

sen·a·tor, sen′ə·tər, *n.* (*Often cap.*) A member of a senate. —**sen·a·tor·ship,** *n.*

sen·a·to·ri·al, sen·ə·tôr′ē·əl, *a.* Composed of, or referring to, a senator or senate. —**sen·a·to·ri·al·ly,** *adv.*

send, send, *v.t.,* **sent, send·ing.** To cause, as a person, to go; to enable to go: They *sent* him to college; to cause to be conveyed or transmitted; to direct, order, or compel to go; to drive, impel, throw, or deliver, as a ball, blow, or the like; to emit or discharge, as light, odor, or sound, usu. followed by *forth* or *out. Informal.* To thrill or excite.—*v.i.* To dispatch a messenger, agent, or message.—**send down,** to expel or suspend.—**send for,** to request by message to come or to be brought.—**send in,** to dispatch to a central destination, as entries in a competition.—**send out,** to put into circulation; distribute.—**send pack·ing,** to dismiss in an abrupt way; to send off in disgrace.—**send up.** *Informal.* To sentence to a term of imprisonment. —**send·er,** *n.*

send-off, send′ôf, send′of, *n. Informal.* A friendly demonstration in honor of a person setting out on a journey, course, career, or the like; a start given to a person or thing.

se·nile, sē′nīl, sen′īl, sen′īl, *a.* Referring to old age;

characterized by the weakness of old age, esp. a decline in mental faculties.

se·nil·i·ty, si·nil′ə·tē, *n.* The state of being senile; old age.

sen·ior, sēn′yər, *a.* Older or elder, often abbreviated and used following the name of a person who is the older of two persons bearing the name: John Smith, *Sr.;* of earlier date; ranking before others by virtue of tenure in office, position, or service; of higher rank or standing; noting or referring to the highest class or the final year of universities, colleges, and high schools.—*n.* A person who is older than another; an aged person; one ranking before others by virtue of tenure; one of higher rank or standing; a member of the highest class in a university, college, or high school.

sen·ior cit·i·zen, *n.* An elderly person, esp. one sixty-five years or older, whose income is derived from a pension.

sen·ior high school, *n.* A high school comprised of grades 10 through 12 or grades 9 through 12.

sen·ior·i·ty, sēn·yôr′ə·tē, sēn·yor′ə·tē, *n.* State of being senior; superior age; priority of birth; priority due to length of service or superiority in rank or office.

sen·na, sen′ə, *n.* Any of various herbs, shrubs, or trees; the dried leaflets of various species of these plants, used as a laxative medicine.

se·ñor, sān·yôr′, sān·yôr′, *n. pl.,* **se·ñors.** A gentleman; sir. (*Cap.*) As a title, Mr.

se·ño·ra, sān·yôr′ə, sān·yôr′ə, *n.* A lady, usu. married or elderly; madam. (*Cap.*) As a title, Mrs.

se·ño·ri·ta, sān·yə·rē′tə, *n.* A young lady, esp. unmarried; miss. (*Cap.*) As a title, Miss.

sen·sate, sen′sāt, *a.* Understood by a sense or the senses.

sen·sa·tion, sen·sā′shən, *n.* An impression made upon the mind through the medium of one of the organs of sense; a conscious experience resulting from sensory stimulation, as seeing, hearing, or kinesthesis. A general feeling arising from intrapsychic sources and not dependent upon bodily stimulation: a *sensation* of awe; a state of excitement or heightened interests; something that produces excited interest or feeling.

sen·sa·tion·al, sen·sā′shə·nəl, *a.* Relating to sensation or the senses; producing excited interest or emotion, esp. when superficial; startling or exciting; exceedingly good or excellent. —**sen·sa·tion·al·ly,** *adv.* —**sen·sa·tion·al·ism,** *n.*

sense, sens, *n.* Any of the special faculties connected with bodily organs by which humans and other animals perceive external objects and their own bodily changes, as sight, hearing, smell, taste, and touch; these faculties collectively; their operation or function; sensation; a feeling or perception produced through the organs of touch, taste, and the like, or resulting from a particular condition of some part of the body: a *sense* of cold; any special capacity for perception, estimation, or appreciation: an esthetic *sense;* any more or less vague perception or impression of something; sound practical intelligence; what is sensible or reasonable; meaning, substance, or signification. Usu. *pl.* Clear or sound mental faculties: He has lost his *senses.*—*v.t.,* **sensed, sensing.** To perceive through the senses; become aware of; to understand.

sense·less, sens′lis, *a.* Lacking or deprived of sensation; in a state of unconsciousness; stupid or foolish. —**sense·less·ness,** *n.*

sense or·gan, *n.* A specialized organ, such as the nose, ear, or eye, that is sensitive to or registers external stimuli; a receptor.

sen·si·bil·i·ty, sen·sə·bil′ə·tē, *n. pl.,* **-ties.** The state or quality of being sensible or capable of sensa-

---

a- hat, fāte, fāre, fäther; **e-** met, mē; **i-** pin, pīne; **o-** not, nōte, ôrb, moove (move), boy, pownd; **u-** cūbe, bŭll, tŭk (took); **ch-** chin; **th-** thick, ŧhen; **zh-** vizhon (vision); **ə-** əgo, takən, pencəl, lemən, bərd (bird).

tion; the capacity to experience emotion or feeling; delicacy or keenness of feeling: an artistic *sensibility*.

sen·si·ble, sen′sə·bəl, *a.* Possessing or containing sense, judgment, or reason: a *sensible* remark; reasonable; capable of perceiving either by the senses or intellect; aware; persuaded, usu. followed by *of*: *sensible of* his problem; of sufficient magnitude or quantity to excite sensation. **—sen·si·ble·ness,** *n.* **—sen·si·bly,** *adv.*

sen·si·tive, sen′si·tiv, *a.* Having the capacity to receive impressions from external influences; having feelings easily excited; of keen sensibility; pertaining to work or operations of a highly delicate, secretive, or precarious nature: He was in a *sensitive* position; readily affected by or responsive to the action of appropriate agents: photographic paper that is *sensitive* to light; easily affected, moved, or liable to change: a *sensitive* balance.

sen·si·tiv·i·ty, sen·si·tiv′ə·tē, *n. pl.,* **-ties.** The state of being sensitive; readiness of muscles or nerves to respond to stimuli.

sen·si·tize, sen′si·tīz, *v.t.,* **-tized, -tiz·ing.** To render sensitive.—*v.i.* To be rendered sensitive. **—sen·si·ti·za·tion,** sen·si·tə·zā′shən, *n.* **—sen·si·tiz·er,** *n.*

sen·sor, sen′sər, *n.* Something which is capable of receiving and responding to a stimulus, esp. a mechanism, as an electric eye.

sen·so·ry, sen′so·rē, *a.* Relating to sensation; conveying sense impulses: *sensory* nerves. Also **sen·so·ri·al,** sen·sôr′ē·əl.

sen·su·al, sen′shoo·əl, *a.* Referring to the body and the physical senses as distinguished from those of the spirit; voluptuous; indulging in lust; grossly luxurious. **—sen·su·al·i·ty,** sen·shoo·al′ə·tē, *n.* **—sen·su·al·ly,** *adv.*

sen·su·al·ism, sen′shoo·ə·liz·əm, *n.* A state of subjection to the sensual appetites; sensuality. **—sen·su·al·ist,** *n.*

sen·su·al·ize, sen′shoo·ə·līz, *v.t.,* **-ized, -iz·ing.** To make sensual. **—sen·su·al·i·za·tion,** sen·shoo·ə·lə·zā′shən, *n.*

sen·su·ous, sen′shoo·əs, *a.* Referring to the senses; appealing to the senses, esthetically as well as physically; readily affected through the senses: a *sensuous* nature.

sen·tence, sen′təns, *n.* A group of interrelated words consisting of a subject and predicate, expressed or implied, with or without modifiers, which conveys or implies a complete thought or emotion and which may be declarative, exclamatory, interrogative, or imperative in construction or mood. A judgment or decision arrived at by a judge or court in a criminal proceeding, formally pronounced upon the defendant following his or her conviction and designating the punishment imposed; the punishment so inflicted.—*v.t.,* **-tenced, -tenc·ing.** To pronounce sentence or judgment on.

sen·tient, sen′shənt, *a.* Capable of perceiving or feeling.—*n.* Something or someone who is sentient; the perceptive or conscious mind.

sen·ti·ment, sen′tə·mənt, *n.* A thought prompted by feeling; a tendency to be swayed by feeling; emotion. *Often pl.* A particular disposition of mind in view of some subject: Those are my *sentiments* on the matter.

sen·ti·men·tal, sen·tə·men′təl, *a.* Having or pertaining to emotion or sentiment; manifesting an excess of sentiment. **—sen·ti·men·tal·ly,** *adv.*

sen·ti·men·tal·i·ty, sen·ti·men·tal′ə·tē, *n. pl.,* **-ties.** A sentimental condition or quality, often to excess; any sentimental expression. **—sen·ti·men·tal·ist,** sen·ti·men′tə·list, *n.*

sen·ti·men·tal·ize, sen·ti·men′tə·līz, *v.i.,* **-ized, -iz·ing.** To indulge in or act with sentiment.—*v.t.* To regard sentimentally; to form into that which is sentimental. **—sen·ti·men·ta·li·za·tion,** sen·ti·men·tə·lə·zā′shən, *n.*

sen·ti·nel, sen′tə·nəl, *n.* One who watches or keeps guard; a sentry.—*v.t.,* **-neled, -nel·ing.** To watch over

as a sentinel.

sen·try, sen′trē, *n. pl.,* **-tries.** A person on guard, as at a gate or other entrance; guard or watch.

sen·try box, *n.* A small shed to shelter a sentry.

se·pal, sē′pəl, *n.* One of the parts of the calyx of a flower. **—se·paled, se·palled,** *a.*

sep·a·ra·ble, sep′ər·ə·bəl, *a.* Capable of being separated or disjoined. **—sep·a·ra·bil·i·ty,** sep·ər·ə·bil′ə·tē, *n.* **—sep·a·ra·bly,** *adv.*

sep·a·rate, sep′ə·rāt, *v.t.,* **-rat·ed, -rat·ing.** To divide, disconnect, or keep apart, as by a barrier: to *separate* two houses by a wall; to sever; to sever relations with, as by legal separation; to divide or scatter into individual parts: to *separate* members of a group; to extract from a mixture or compound.—*v.i.* To withdraw from association: a husband *separated* from his wife; to split or come apart.—sep′ər·it, *a.* Disjoined or disconnected; distinct or individual: many *separate* reasons.—sep′ər·it, *n. Usu. pl.* The matching or contrasting articles of women's clothes which may be worn in various combinations. **—sep·a·rate·ness,** *n.*

sep·a·ra·tion, sep·ə·rā′shən, *n.* The act of separating; the state of being separate or disconnected; a means, line, point, or place of division; a gap, space, or the like.

sep·a·ra·tist, sep′ər·ə·tist, *n.* One who withdraws or separates.—*a.* **—sep·a·ra·tism,** *n.*

sep·a·ra·tive, sep′ər·ə·tiv, *a.* Tending or inclined to separate.

sep·a·ra·tor, sep′ə·rā·tər, *n.* One who or that which separates.

se·pi·a, sē′pē·ə, *n.* The brown pigment prepared from the inky secretion of various cuttlefish and used in drawing; a picture or photograph tinted with this pigment or in this color; the dark brown color of the pigment.—*a.*

sep·sis, sep′sis, *n. pl.,* **-ses,** -sēz. A poisoned state of the system due to a spread of infection through the blood.

Sep·tem·ber, sep·tem′bər, *n.* The ninth month of the year, containing 30 days.

sep·ten·ni·al, sep·ten′ē·əl, *a.* Lasting or continuing seven years; happening once every seven years.

sep·tet, sep·tette, sep·tet′, *n.* A company of seven singers or players; any group of seven persons or things.

sep·tic, sep′tik, *a.* Infective; pus-forming.—*n.* A substance which causes putrefaction or sepsis. **—sep·ti·cal·ly,** *adv.* **—sep·tic·i·ty,** sep·tis′i·tē, *n.*

sep·ti·ce·mi·a, sep·ti·sē′mē·ə, *n.* The presence in the bloodstream of infectious microorganisms or their toxins; blood poisoning. **—sep·ti·ce·mic,** *a.*

sep·tic tank, *n.* A tank into which sewage is conveyed and where organic solids remain until decomposed by the action of anaerobic bacteria.

sep·tu·a·ge·nar·i·an, sep·choo·ə·jə·nâr′ē·ən, *n.* A person seventy years of age, or anywhere in his seventies.—*a.*

sep·tum, sep′təm, *n. pl.,* **-ta,** -tə. A dividing wall, membrane, or the like in a plant or animal structure.

sep·tu·ple, sep′tû·pəl, sep′tū·pəl, sep·too′pəl, sep·tū′pəl, *a.* Composed of seven; sevenfold.—*v.t.,* **-pled, -pling.** To multiply seven times.—*v.i.*—*n.* A sevenfold quantity or number.

sep·ul·cher, sep′əl·kər, *n.* A burial place; a tomb; a small cavity in an altarstone in which the relics of saints are placed.—*v.t.,* **-chered, -cher·ing.** To bury or inter in a sepulcher. **—se·pul·chral,** sə·pəl′krəl, *a.*

se·quel, sē′kwəl, *n.* That which follows and forms a continuation; a succeeding part; consequence; result.

se·quence, sē′kwəns, *n.* The process of following; a particular order or arrangement of succession; a series of things; a consequence or following development.

se·quent, sē′kwənt, *a.* Following; succeeding; resultant.—*n.* That which comes after or follows; a result.

se·quen·tial, si·kwen′shəl, *a.* Following in sequence; succeeding; characterized by regular sequence of parts. **—se·quen·tial·ly,** *adv.*

se·ques·ter, si·kwes′tər, *v.t.* To set apart or separate; to seclude or withdraw. **—se·ques·tered,** *a.* **—se·ques·tra·ble,** *a.*

se·ques·tra·tion, sē·kwes·trā′shən, si·kwes·trā′ shən, *n.* A retirement; withdrawal.

se·quin, sē′kwin, *n.* A small glittering disk or spangle used to ornament a dress, sweater, or the like. **—se· quined, se·quinned,** *a.*

se·quoi·a, si·kwoy′ə, *n.* Either of two gigantic coniferous trees of California, the redwood and the giant sequoia.

se·ra·pe, sa·ra·pe, sə·rä′pē, *n.* A blanket or shawl made of colorful wool or other heavy material, worn as an outer garment in Mexico and other Latin American countries; poncho.

ser·aph, ser′əf, *n. pl.,* **-aphs, -a·phim,** -ə·fim. An angel of the highest order, esp. one of those said to be around the throne of God. **—se·raph·ic,** si·raf′ik, *a.*

ser·e·nade, ser·ə·nād′, *n.* A presentation of vocal or instrumental music traditionally performed at night in the open air, esp. by a gentleman as a complimentary gesture to a lady; any such entertainment performed as a mark of good will toward distinguished persons; a piece of music appropriate to such an occasion; a musical form for instruments consisting of several movements.—*v.t.,* **-nad·ed, -nad·ing.** To entertain with a serenade.—*v.i.* To perform a serenade. **—ser· e·nad·er,** *n.*

ser·en·dip·i·ty, ser·ən·dip′ə·tē, *n.* The faculty of making happy or interesting discoveries unexpectedly or by accident. **—ser·en·dip·i·tous,** *a.*

se·rene, sə·rēn′, *n.* Clear or fair, as the sky; calm; unruffled; undisturbed. (*Usu. cap.*) Exalted: used in titles of the members of some royal families: His *Serene* Highness. **—se·rene·ness,** *a.*

se·ren·i·ty, sə·ren′ə·tē, *n. pl.,* **-ties.** The quality or condition of being serene; tranquility; calmness; quietness; peace.

serf, sərf, *n.* In the Middle Ages, a person bound in the service of a landowner and attached to the land and transferred with it.

serge, sərj, *n.* A kind of twilled fabric woven of wool; twilled fabric of cotton, silk, or rayon, used esp. for linings.

ser·geant, sär′jənt, *n.* A non-commissioned officer in the U.S. Army and Marine Corps of any rank above corporal and in the Air Force above airman first class; a police officer next in rank below a captain or lieutenant; a sergeant at arms.

ser·geant at arms, *n.* An officer of a court, or other formal body, whose duty is to preserve order.

ser·geant ma·jor, *n.* The highest non-commissioned officer in the U.S. Army and Marine Corps.

se·ri·al, sēr′ē·əl, *a.* Referring to a series; successive. *—n.* A story or composition running through a successive number of periodicals or broadcasts; a publication issued in successive numbers. **—se·ri·al·ly,** *adv.* **—se·ri·al·ist,** *n.* **—se·ri·al·i·za·tion,** ser·ē·ə·lə·zā′ shən, *n.* **—se·ri·al·ize,** *v.t.,* **-ized, -iz·ing.**

se·ries, sēr′ēz, *n.* A succession of like or corresponding items, occurrences, or events; a sequence of things having a progressive order, arrangement, or relation.—*a.* **—in se·ries,** having a series arrangement.

se·ri·ous, sēr′ē·əs, *a.* Grave in manner or disposition; solemn; deliberative or thoughtful; being in earnest; important; weighty; attended with danger; giving rise to apprehension. **—se·ri·ous·ly,** *adv.* **—se·ri· ous·ness,** *n.*

se·ri·ous-mind·ed, sēr′ē·əs·mīn′did, *a.* Being in earnest. **—se·ri·ous-mind·ed·ly,** *adv.*

ser·mon, sər′mən, *n.* A discourse delivered in public, esp. by a clergyman during a church service, for religious instruction or the inculcation of morality; any other type of discourse which is similar in intent; any lengthy, tedious harangue; a homily. **—ser·mon·ize,** *v.i.,* **-ized, -iz·ing.** To preach; to discourse.—*v.t.* To deliver a sermon to. **—ser·mon·iz·er,** *n.*

se·rol·o·gy, si·rol′ə·jē, *n.* The scientific study of the nature and actions of blood serum. **—se·ro·log·ic,** sēr·ə·loj′ik, **se·ro·log·i·cal,** *a.* **—se·rol·o·gist,** *n.*

se·rous, sēr′əs, *a.* Resembling serum.

ser·pent, sər′pənt, *n.* A reptile without limbs that is of an extremely elongated form and moves by muscular contractions of the body; a snake; a treacherously subtle, malicious person.

ser·pen·tine, sər′pən·tēn, sər′pən·tin, *a.* Referring to, resembling, or having the qualities of a serpent; treacherously subtle; cunning; curving, winding, or turning like a moving serpent; sinuous; crooked.—*n.* A rock or mineral, often used as a decorative material, usu. colored green with shades and spots resembling a serpent's skin.

ser·rate, ser′it, ser′āt, *a.* Notched like the edge of a saw; toothed. Also **ser·rat·ed.**—ser′āt, *v.t.,* **-rat·ed, -rat·ing.** To render serrate.

ser·ra·tion, se·rā′shən, *n.* Serrated condition or form; a serrated edge or formation.

se·rum, sēr′əm, *n. pl.,* **se·rums, se·ra,** sēr′ə. A clear, pale-yellow liquid which separates from the clot in the coagulation of blood; a fluid obtained from the blood of an animal which has been immunized.

serv·ant, sər′vənt, *n.* One who serves or does services for another; a person who is employed by another for domestic duties; a slave; public or civil servant.

serve, sərv, *v.i.,* **served, serv·ing.** To act as a servant; to wait at table; to offer or hand food or drink to guests; to perform duties for others; to go through a term of service, as a soldier or sailor; to perform official duty, as on a jury; to have a definite use; to suffice: This apartment will *serve* for the moment; in tennis, handball, and certain other games, to put the ball in play.—*v.t.* To be a servant to; to go through, as a term of service or imprisonment; to render active service to, as a king or commander, in the army or navy; to render obedience to, as God; to perform the duties of, as an office; to answer the requirements of: to *serve* one's needs; to contribute to; promote; to provide with a regular or continuous supply of something; to treat in a specified manner; of a male animal, to mate or copulate with; in tennis and the like, to put, as the ball, in play. *Law.* To make legal delivery of, as a process or writ.—*n.* The act, manner, or right of serving, as in tennis or handball.

serv·er, sər′vər, *n.* One who serves; that which serves or is used in serving food or drink; the player who puts the ball in play, as in tennis.

serv·ice, sər′vis, *n.* An act of helpful activity; the rendering of aid; the performance of duties as a servant; the act or manner of waiting at table; employment in any duties or work for others, or for an institution, or the like; a department of public employment; the duty or work of public servants; the armed forces: to be in the *service;* one of the branches of these forces. *Usu. pl.* Work done for others which does not result in products: medical *services.* The supplying of some commodity, as water or gas, required by the public; the organized system of apparatus and employees for supplying a commodity; repair, maintenance, or installation provided for the buyer of an article by the seller; public religious worship; ritual or form prescribed for public worship or for some particular occasion: the marriage *service;* a set of dishes or other tableware required for a particular use: a tea *service;* in tennis and certain other games, the act or manner of putting the ball in play; the ball as put into play.—*a.* Referring to or for use by servants or tradesmen; supplying services: a *service* industry; of or relating to armed services.—*v.t.,* **-iced, -ic·ing.** To make fit for service, or restore to condition for service, as an automobile; to supply a service to.—**at one's serv·ice,** ready to serve one.

serv·ice·a·ble, sər′və·sə·bəl, *a.* Being of service; useful; durable, as materials or clothing. —**serv·ice·a·bil·i·ty,** serv·ice·a·ble·ness, *n.* —serv·ice·a·bly, *adv.*

serv·ice charge, *n.* A sum charged for a service, as an addition to a basic fee.

serv·ice door, *n.* A door primarily for the use of servants and to deliver goods.

serv·ice·man, sər′vis·man, sər′vis·mən, *n. pl.,* **-men.** A man who is a member of any nation's armed forces; a man whose income is derived from maintenance and repair work.

serv·ice med·al, *n.* A medal presented to a member of the armed forces in recognition of honorable participation.

serv·ice sta·tion, *n.* Gas station; an establishment providing a service.

ser·vile, sər′vil, sər′vīl, *a.* Pertaining to or characteristic of a slave or servant; submissive; fawning. —**ser·vil·i·ty,** sər·vil′ə·tē, **ser·vile·ness,** *n.*

serv·ing, sər′ving, *n.* The act of one who or that which serves; an amount of food or drink sufficient for one person; a helping.

ser·vi·tude, sər′və·tood, sər·və·tūd, *n.* The condition of being a slave; slavery, bondage; any condition of subjection: intellectual *servitude;* compulsory service or labor as a punishment for criminals: penal *servitude.*

ser·vo·mech·an·ism, sər′vō·mek·ə·niz·əm, *n.* A low-power device or control system used to actuate and control a more complex or more powerful mechanism. Also **ser·vo.**

ses·a·me, ses′ə·mē, *n.* A tropical plant whose small, oval seeds are edible and yield an oil; the seeds themselves.

ses·qui·cen·ten·ni·al, ses·kwi·sen·ten′ē·əl, *a.* Referring to or marking the end of a period of 150 years.—*n.* A 150th anniversary or its celebration.

ses·sion, sesh′ən, *n.* The sitting together of a court, legislature, or the like, for conference or the transaction of business: Congress is now in *session;* a single continuous sitting, or period of sitting, of persons assembled for conference, business, or the like; a continuous series of sittings or meetings of a court or the like; the period or term during which such a series is held; a single continuous course or period of lessons or study in the work of a day at school: a morning or afternoon *session;* a portion of the year during which instruction is given at a college or the like: a summer *session.*

set, set, *v.t.,* **set, set·ting.** To put in a particular or proper position or a specific condition; put, as a price or value, on something; to fix or appoint as a boundary; to present, as an example; to assign, as a task; to put in proper position or order for use, as a table or a trap; to fix or mount in a frame or setting, as a gem; to shape or curl, as moist hair; to adjust according to a standard, as a clock; to place in thought or estimation: to *set* great store by a thing; put in a fixed, rigid state, as the muscles or the mind; to cause to become firm or hard, as mortar; to arrange, as music, for certain voices or instruments; to put in a position suitable for restoration to the normal condition, as a broken or dislocated bone; to arrange in the order required for printing, as type.—*v.i.* To decline toward or pass below the horizon, as the sun; to sit on eggs, as a hen; to hang or fit in a particular manner, as clothes; to assume a fixed or rigid state, as muscles; to become firm or solid, as mortar; to begin to move or start, usu. followed by *forth, off,* or *out.*—*n.* The act or an act of

setting or the state of being set; a number of things customarily used together or forming a collection, as golf clubs; a number or group of things having in common their nature or function; the assumption of a fixed, rigid, or hard state, as by cement; a radio or television receiver; a construction representing a place in which action occurs in a motion picture, stage, or television production.—*a.* Fixed or appointed beforehand; fixed, rigid, or unvarying; resolved or determined; ready or prepared; formed, built, or made: thick-*set.*—**set a·bout,** to start work upon.—**set a·gainst,** to instigate hostility against; to balance or correlate.—**set a·part,** to place separately.—**set a·side,** to put to one side; dismiss from the mind.—**set back,** to hold up or hinder.—**set down,** to put down in writing or printing; to consider; to place at rest on a flat surface; to make a landing, as with an airplane. —**set forth,** declare.—**set for·ward,** to adjust forward to the correct time, as a watch or clock—**set in,** to begin.—**set off,** to cause ignition or explosion; to offer a contrast to.—**set on,** to attack.—**set out,** to begin a trip; to attempt or try; to plant; to place on display. —**set to,** to make a beginning or start work.—**set up,** to place in an erect position, to erect or construct; to establish or set in active existence; to propose or suggest. *Informal.* To pay for or treat; to exhilarate or elate.

set·back, set′bak, *n.* A halt or interruption of progress.

set-in, set′in, *a.* Formed or constructed separately and attached to another part or unit: a *set-in* sleeve, *set-in* bookcase.

set·off, set′ôf, set′of, *n.* Something that counterbalances or makes up for something else.

set·tee, se·tē′, *n.* A long seat with a back to it.

set·ter, set′ər, *n.* Any of three breeds of long-haired hunting dogs.

set·ting, set′ing, *n.* The act of one who or that which sets; the manner or position in which anything is set; that in which something, as a jewel, is set or mounted; the surroundings of anything; the scenery, costumes, and the like of a play; the items, as silver, china, or glass, needed to set one place at a table or an entire table.

set·tle, set′əl, *v.t.,* **-tled, -tling.** To resolve, determine, or fix conclusively: to *settle* on a selling price; to place in order or a proper state; to pay, satisfy, or close, as an account or claim; to colonize or establish residence in; to establish or fix in any way of life, occupation, dwelling, or the like; to quiet; to place in a fixed or permanent position; to clear, as liquid, of dregs or sediment; to cause to sink to the bottom; to make compact by causing to sink gradually; to bring to a conclusion; to terminate by mutual agreement of the litigants: to *settle* a lawsuit.—*v.i.* To come to an agreement, decision, or resolution, often followed by *on* or *upon;* to pay or adjust an account, bill, or debt; to establish residence in a different country or place; to become calm or free from agitation, often followed by *down;* to sink or fall gradually or subside; to become transparent or clear by the sinking of particles or sediment; to become compact or firm; said of an animal, to conceive.—**set·tle down,** to begin living an orderly, routine life after being independent or irresponsible: to *settle down* after marriage; to become composed or calm; to become absorbed in or apply oneself to one's assignment, work, or the like.

set·tle·ment, set′əl·mənt, *n.* The act of settling or state of being settled; colonization; a tract of land which has been colonized; the adjustment or liquidation of a claim or account; the sinking or settling of a building; a deed by which property is settled; the property settled in such a way. An establishment providing educational and social services to the people of a particular slum area; also **set·tle·ment house.**

set·tler, set′lər, *n.* One who settles; a colonist.

set·tling, set′ling, *n.* The act of one who settles or that which sinks. *Pl.* Dregs; sediment.

set-to, set/too, *n.* A brief but intense argument or fight.

set•up, set/əp, *n.* The way in which something is arranged or organized; makeup; a plan of action. *Informal.* The glassware and ingredients. except liquor, provided to persons mixing their own drinks; a contest, game, or undertaking made easy to win or accomplish; a table setting, esp. in a restaurant.

sev•en, sev/ən, *n.* The cardinal number between six and eight; a symbol representing it; a set of seven persons or things.—*a.* —**sev•enth,** *a., n.*

sev•en seas, *n. pl. (Sometimes cap.)* The oceans of the world.

sev•en•teen, sev-ən-tēn/, *n.* The cardinal number between sixteen and eighteen; a symbol representing it; a set of seventeen persons or things.—*a.* —**sev•en•teenth,** *a., n.*

sev•enth heav•en, *n.* A state of great joy or happiness.

sev•en•ty, sev/ən-tē, *n.* The cardinal number between 69 and 71; a symbol representing it; a set of 70 persons or things.—*a.* —**sev•en•ti•eth,** *a., n.*

sev•er, sev/ər, *v.t.* To part or divide, esp. by force; to separate into parts by cutting or rending; disunite. —*v.i.* To undergo separation; to be divided. —**sev•er•a•bil•i•ty,** *n.* —**sev•er•a•ble,** *a.*

sev•er•al, sev/ər•əl, *a.* More than two but not very many; divers; separate or respective: experts in their *several* areas.—*n.* A small number of persons or things; some. —**sev•er•al•ly,** *adv.*

sev•er•al•fold, sev/ər•əl•fōld, *a.* Several times as great as much; consisting of several parts, ways, or aspects.—*adv.*

sev•er•ance, sev/ər•əns, *n.* The act of severing or state of being severed; separation; partition.

se•vere, si•vēr/, **se•ver•er, se•ver•est.** Very strict or harsh in discipline, government, or judgment: *severe* punishment; stern in disposition, appearance, or manner; critical or serious: a *severe* disease; plain, simple or restrained in manner, decoration, or style; causing hardship or distress: *severe* weather; rigorous, or difficult to undergo or perform: a *severe* test. —**se•vere•ness,** *n.*

se•ver•i•ty, si•ver/ə•tē, *n. pl.,* **-ties.** The quality or state of being severe.

sew, sō, *v.t.* **sewed, sewn,** or **sewn, sew•ing.** To unite or fasten together with stitches; to make or mend with needle and thread.—*v.i.* To practice sewing.—**sew up,** to gain exclusive control of; to finish successfully.

sew•age, soo/ij, *n.* The waste matter carried away by sewers.

sew•er, soo/ər, *n.* An artificial channel or canal, usu. underground, which carries off drainage water and other waste materials.

sew•er, sō/ər, *n.* One who sews or that which sews.

sew•er•age, soo/ər•ij, *n.* The removal of water and other waste materials by sewers; the system of sewers; sewage.

sew•ing, sō/ing, *n.* The act or task of one who sews; something that is to be or has been sewn.

sew•ing ma•chine, *n.* Any of various machines used for making stitches.

sex, seks, *n.* The total physical and behavioral characteristics by which the male and female are distinguished; either of the two groups, male and female, into which organisms are divided according to their distinct functions in the reproductive process; activities relating to or based on sexual attraction, sexual relations, or sexual reproduction; sexual intercourse. —*v.t.* To find out the sex of, as of chicks.

sex ap•peal, *n.* Physical appeal to those of the opposite sex.

sex chro•mo•some, *n.* A chromosome which acts as a determinant of the sex of the offspring.

sexed, sekst, *a.* Belonging to a sex; being sexually appealing.

sex hor•mone, *n.* A hormone affecting the growth or function of the sexual organs and of secondary sex characteristics.

sex•less, seks/lis, *a.* Having or seeming to have no sex; exciting or evidencing no sexual desires. —**sex•less•ness,** *n.*

sex•ol•o•gy, sek•sol/ə•jē, *n.* The science that deals with sexual behavior, esp. of humans. —**sex•o•log•i•cal,** sek•sə•loj/ə•kəl, *a.* —**sex•ol•o•gist,** *n.*

sex•tant, seks/tənt, *n.* An instrument for determining angular distances, chiefly employed by navigators for determining position.

sex•tet, seks•tet/, *n.* Any collection of six items or any group of six.

sex•ton, seks/tən, *n.* An official of a church charged with taking care of the building and its contents and ringing the bell.

sex•tu•ple, seks•too/pəl, seks•tū/pəl, seks/too•pəl, seks/tū•pəl, *a.* Sixfold; consisting of six parts; six times as much or as great.—*n.* An amount or number six times greater than another.—*v.t., v.i.,* **-pled, -pling.** To make or become six times as great.

sex•tu•plet, seks•tup/lit, seks•too/plit, *n.* Six of a kind; one of six offspring born at the same birth to a single mother.

sex•u•al, sek/shoo•əl, *a.* Referring to sex or the sexes; motivated by or exhibiting sex. —**sex•u•al•ly,** *adv.* —**sex•u•al•i•ty,** sek•shoo•al/ə•tē, *n.*

sex•u•al in•ter•course, *n.* Coitus or copulation.

sex•y, sek/sē, *a.,* **sex•i•er, sex•i•est.** Involving excessive sex: a *sexy* story; sexually provocative or exciting. —**sex•i•ness,** *n.*

sh, sh, *interj.* A shortened form of **hush,** used in commanding silence.

shab•by, shab/ē, *a.,* **-bi•er, -bi•est.** Threadbare or much worn; despicable; inferior or slovenly. —**shab•bi•ly,** *adv.* —**shab•bi•ness,** *n.*

shack, shak, *n.* A roughly built hut or shanty.—**shack up,** *Informal.* To cohabit or have illicit sexual relations.

shack•le, shak/əl, *n.* A handcuff, or the like, that restricts the use of either set of limbs. *Usu. pl.* That which obstructs or restrains free action or thought. A fastener or clasp.—*v.t.,* **-led, -ling.** To tie or confine the limbs of, so as to prevent free motion; to bind or confine so as to inhibit or prevent independent action or thought. —**shack•ler,** *n.*

shad, shad, *n. pl.,* **shad, shads.** A type of northern Atlantic fish related to the herring and valued as food.

shade, shād, *n.* Comparative darkness; a state or place of relative obscurity; a place or state of dimness caused by interception of the sun's rays or other source of light; anything used to intercept light: a window *shade;* a cover used to soften the light cast by a lamp; a visor worn to protect the eyes; the dark or darker part of a picture; degree or gradation of light or brightness of color; a small or scarcely perceptible degree or amount: a *shade* of difference. *Pl. Informal.* Sunglasses.—*v.t.,* **shad•ed, shad•ing.** To produce a darkening or a shadowing effect on or in; to shelter or hide from view.—*v.i.* To vary or change by slight degrees, as one color into another. —**shade•less,** *a.*

shad•ing, shā/ding, *n.* The representation of light and shade in a picture; a subtle distinction or variation; shade.

shad•ow, shad/ō, *n.* A figure projected in silhouette on the ground or other surface by means of interception of light; a space from which light has been intercepted; semidarkness; semiobscurity; the merest hint: a *shadow* of doubt; a dark part of a picture; any actuality that seems insubstantial or unreal; a shade; an inseparable companion or follower; a remnant: a *shadow* of his former self. *Pl.* The semidarkness.—*v.t*

---

a- hat, fāte, fâre, fäther; **e-** met, mē; **i-** pin, pīne; **o-** not, nōte, ôrb, moove (move), boy, pownd; **u-** cūbe, bûll, tûk (took); **ch-** chin; **th-** thick, ŧhen; **zh-** vizhon (vision); **ə-** əgo, takən, pencəl, lemən, bərd (bird).

To shade; to darken; to throw a gloom over; to protect; to mark with slight gradations of color; to represent faintly or imperfectly; to follow closely, as a detective. —**shad·ow·er,** n. —**shad·ow·like,** a.

shad·ow box, n. A decorative case or cabinet for display of art objects or personal treasures.

shad·ow·box, shad'ō·boks, v.i. To practice boxing, as for exercise, by pretending an imaginary opponent.

shad·ow·y, shad'ō·ē, a. Full of shade or shadow.

shad·y, shā'dē, a., -i·er, -i·est. Abounding with shade or shades; casting or causing shade. *Informal.* Disreputable. —**shad·i·ly,** adv. —**shad·i·ness,** n.

shaft, shaft, shäft, n. The long and narrow body of a spear or arrow; the spear or arrow itself; a pointed remark; a ray of light; the long handle of certain tools or instruments; the columnar part of anything; a rotating, cylindrical bar used to transmit motive power.—v.t. To fit or push with a shaft.—**get the shaft.** *Informal.* To be cheated or treated unfairly.

shaft, shaft, shäft, n. A narrow, deep passage in the earth for mining; a passageway for light or ventilation; an opening passing between floors in a building.

shaft·ing, shaf'ting, shäf'ting, n. A system of shafts through which motion is communicated; the material used to make shafts.

shag, shag, n. Rough, matted hair, wool, or the like; the long or rough nap of cloth; a cloth with a heavy nap.—v.t., **shagged, shag·ging.** To make rough or shaggy.—v.i. To become or appear shaggy.—a. Shaggy; also **shag·ged.** —**shag·like,** a.

shag·bark, shag'bärk, n. A species of hickory yielding high-grade hickory nuts. Also **shell·bark,** shel'bärk, **shag·bark hick·o·ry.**

shag·gy, shag'ē, a., -gi·er, -gi·est. Long, rough, matted, or tangled; covered with or having long, rough growth; having a long or rough nap; untrimmed or unkempt. —**shag·gi·ly,** adv. —**shag·gi·ness,** n.

shake, shāk, v.i., **shook, shak·en, shak·ing.** To move with jerky vibrations to and fro, up and down, or in different directions; to quiver, tremble, shiver, or vibrate; to react in a certain way to vigorous joggling, followed by *off, out, from,* or *down;* wrinkles that *shake out;* to be unstable or to totter; to clasp each other's hand in making an agreement, greeting, or the like.—v.t. To cause to move with jerky vibrations; to brandish or wave toward, usu. as if in threat or reprimand; to grab and jostle vigorously in order to bring about certain action or reaction; to disturb or make turbulent; to cause to wobble; to cause to tremble; to dislodge or remove by joggling: to *shake* salt; to throw off or make oneself free from: to *shake* a fear.—n. The act or occurrence of shaking, vibrating, jerking, or rocking; a rapid wavering motion from side to side, as a tremor or shiver; a handshake; that which results from shaking, as a crack or fissure; a milk shake. *Pl.* A period of shuddering shivers, as from a chill, usu. preceded by *the. Informal.* A very short amount of time: to be done in a *shake;* a chance, opportunity, or deal: a fair *shake.*—**no great shakes.** *Informal.* Not exceptionally talented, exciting, or interesting.—**shake a leg.** *Informal.* To move faster or hurry.—**shake down.** *Informal.* To bring down by shaking: to *shake down* nuts from a tree; to cause to settle by shaking; to exact money from by compulsion, esp. dishonestly or illicitly; to search, as for contraband.—**shake up,** to stir or loosen by shaking vigorously; to upset by unexpected changes.

shake·down, shāk'down, n. *Informal.* An exaction of money by compulsion, esp. dishonestly or illicitly; an exhaustive search.

shak·er, shā'kər, n. One who or that which shakes; a container, as for salt, with holes through which its contents may be shaken out; any container in which ingredients, usu. liquid, may be mixed by a shaking motion.

Shake·spear·e·an, Shake·spear·i·an, shāk·spēr'ē·ən, a. Relating to Shakespeare.—n. A scholar

of Shakespeare's works.

shake-up, shāk'əp, n. An upsetting change or reorganization.

shak·y, shā'kē, a., -i·er, -i·est. Given to shaking; shaking, trembling, as the voice; weak or feeble; insecure or unreliable; uncertain or not to be depended on, as one's knowledge of a subject. —**shak·i·ly,** adv. —**shak·i·ness,** n.

shale, shāl, n. A rock of laminated structure formed by the consolidation of claylike, fine-grained sediments.

shale oil, n. A crude mineral oil distilled from shale.

shall, shal, *unstressed* shəl, aux. v., **should.** Used in first person to indicate simple futurity: We *shall* ask the waiter. Used in the second and third persons to denote determination or resolve: then you *shall* succeed; to denote pledge or promise: for we *shall* not fail you; to denote obligation or command: then said proprietor *shall* obtain a license; to denote inescapability or inevitability: since each *shall* meet his destiny. Used interrogatively in all persons to ask direction or propriety: *Shall* I pick him up?

shal·lot, shə·lot', n. A plant of the lily family, having mild-flavored, clustered bulbs used in cooking and pickling.

shal·low, shal'ō, a. Not deep, as water or a dish; lacking depth or superficial, as thought, knowledge, or feeling.—n. *Often pl.* A shallow part of a body of water; a shoal.—v.t., v.i. To make or become shallow. —**shal·low·ness,** n.

sham, sham, n. Something that is not what it pretends to be; a cover for giving a thing a different outward appearance: a pillow *sham;* a pretender.—a. Pretended; imitation; counterfeit.—v.t., **shammed, shamming.** To pretend falsely to be; to assume the appearance of: to *sham* illness.—v.i. To pretend to be or do what one is not or does not.

sha·man, shä'mən, shā'mən, sham'ən, n. A priest or sorcerer among various tribes of northern Asia and northwestern N. America, supposed to have the power to deal with and protect against spirits; a medicine man. —**sha·man·ism,** n. —**sha·man·ist,** n., a.

sham·bles, sham'bəlz, n. pl., sing. or pl. in constr. A slaughterhouse; a place or scene of carnage or execution; a place, state, or scene of disorder or destruction.

shame, shām, n. The painful feeling arising from the consciousness of something dishonorable, ridiculous, or the like done by oneself or another, or of being in a situation offensive to decency, self-respect, or pride: to blush with *shame;* susceptibility to this feeling: to be without *shame;* disgrace, or dishonor: to bring *shame* upon one's family; a fact or circumstance bringing disgrace or discredit: It's a *shame* that you can't come.—v.t., **shamed, sham·ing.** To cause to feel shame; to make ashamed: His actions, under the circumstances, *shamed* us all; to drive or force through shame: He *shamed* the child into silence; to disgrace; dishonor.—**for shame!** You ought to feel shame.—**put to shame,** to bring shame upon; to eclipse or outshine: Her cooking skills *put* mine *to* shame.

shame·faced, shām'fāst, a. Modest or bashful; showing shame: *shamefaced* apologies. —**shame·fac·ed·ly,** adv. —**shame·fac·ed·ness,** n.

shame·ful, shām'fəl, a. Bringing shame or disgrace; scandalous; indecent. —**shame·ful·ly,** adv.

shame·less, shām'lis, a. Having no shame or modesty. —**shame·less·ly,** adv. —**shame·less·ness,** n.

sham·mer, sham'ər, n. One who shams.

sham·my, sham'ē, n. A kind of soft leather; chamois.

sham·poo, sham·poo', v.t., -pooed, -poo·ing. To wash, as the hair and scalp, esp. with a special solution; to clean, as a carpet, with a special substance.—n. A cleansing compound used for shampooing; the act or an act of shampooing. —**sham·poo·er,** n.

sham·rock, sham'rok, n. A plant with triple leaves,

usu. a yellow-flowered species of trefoil: the national emblem of Ireland.

shang·hai, shang′hī, shang·hī′, *v.t.,* **-haied, -hai·ing.** To render unconscious with drugs, and ship on a vessel wanting hands; to bring about by deception or force.

Shan·gri-la, shang′grə·lä, shang·grə·lä′, *n.* An earthly paradise; any secluded, idyllic hideaway.

shank, shangk, *n.* In humans, that part of the leg between the knee and the ankle; the corresponding part in certain animals; a cut of meat from this part of an animal; the leglike, stemlike, or shaftlike part of many objects, as a golf club or a smoker's pipe.

shan't, shant, shänt. *Informal.* Contraction of shall not.

shan·tey, shan′tē, *n. pl.,* **-teys.** A sailors' song, esp. one sung in rhythm with their work. Also **chan·tey.**

shan·ty, shan′tē, *n. pl.,* **-ties.** A roughly built hut, cabin, or house, as in frontier districts; any building of flimsy or rough construction.—*a.* Of or relating to a shanty.

shan·ty·town, shan′tē·town, *n.* That part of a town or city, or a town itself, in which most of the dwellings are shanties.

shape, shāp, *n.* The external form, outline, or contour of a thing; the form of a particular thing; an orderly arrangement or form: to put one's room into *shape;* the condition or state of existence, esp. good condition: a man out of *shape;* the form of the human body; a figure or form seen dimly: *shapes* romping in the mist; something used to give form, as a shaped mold.—*v.t.,* **shaped, shap·ing.** To create or give a definite form to: to *shape* a government; to adjust in outline, or form to obtain fit or appropriateness: to *shape* a head of hair; to give definite character or direction to: *shape* the future.—*v.i.* To develop or assume a definite shape, form, or character. —**shap·a·ble, shape·a·ble,** *a.* —**shaped,** shāpt, *a.* —**shap·er,** *n.*

shape·less, shāp′lis, *a.* Without shape.

shape·ly, shāp′lē, *a.,* **-li·er, -li·est.** Having a pleasing shape; well-formed. —**shape·li·ness,** *n.*

share, shār, *n.* The portion or part allotted or belonging to an individual among a number, all of whom receive or contribute; one's just or full portion; each of the equal parts into which the capital stock of a joint-stock company or a corporation is divided.—*v.t.,* **shared, shar·ing.** To divide and distribute in shares; to use or occupy jointly; to participate in, enjoy, or suffer with others.—*v.i.* To have a share or part; participate, often with *in.* —**shar·er,** *n.*

share·crop·per, shār′krop·ər, *n.* A tenant farmer who pays as rent a share of the crop. —**share·crop,** *v.i., v.t.,* **-cropped, -crop·ping.**

share·hold·er, shār′hōl·dər, *n.* One who holds or owns a share or shares, as in a corporation; a stockholder.

shark, shärk, *n.* Any of a group of mostly marine fishes, certain species of which are large and ferocious, destructive to other fish and to humans.

shark, shärk, *n.* One who preys greedily on others by usury, swindling, or other trickery. *Informal.* One who has unusual ability or proficiency in a particular field. —*v.t.* To obtain by trickery; steal.—*v.i.*

shark·skin, shärk′skin, *n.* Shark hide made into leather; a fabric made of any of various yarns, characterized by a smooth, durable finish.

sharp, shärp, *a.* Having a thin cutting edge or a fine point; not blunt or rounded; characterized by sudden change of direction, as a turn; angular, as the features; composed of hard, angular grains, as sand; clear or distinct in outline; strongly marked, as a contrast; keenly affecting the senses; pungent in taste; sour, biting, or acrid; piercing or shrill in sound; keenly cold, as weather; intensely painful or distress-

ing: a *sharp* pain; severe, harsh, or caustic: *sharp* words; quick or eager: *sharp* desire; brisk: a *sharp* run; of keen perception: *sharp* ears; vigilant or attentive: a *sharp* watch; mentally acute or quick: a *sharp* lad; shrewd to the point of dishonesty: *sharp* practice. *Informal.* Stylish: a *sharp* dresser.—*v.t.* In music, to raise the pitch, esp. a half step.—*v.i.* To sound above the true pitch.—*adv.* In a sharp manner; punctually: at one o'clock *sharp;* quickly or briskly; attentively: Look *sharp!*—*n.* Something sharp. *Mus.* A tone one half step above a given tone, the character, or indicates this on the musical staff. —**sharp·ness,** *n.*

sharp·en, shär′pən, *v.t.* To make sharp or sharper. —*v.i.* To grow or become sharp. —**sharp·en·er,** *n.*

sharp·er, shär′pər, *n.* A swindler. Also **sharp·ie.**

sharp-eyed, shärp′īd′, *a.* Having acute vision; observant.

sharp·ie, sharp·y, shär′pē, *n. Informal.* An extremely alert person.

sharp·shoot·er, shärp′shoo·tər, *n.* A person skilled in shooting with exactness; an excellent marksman. —**sharp·shoot·ing,** *n.*

sharp-tongued, shärp·təngd′, *a.* Using or characterized by caustic, harsh language.

sharp-wit·ted, shärp′wit′id, *a.* Having acute mental faculties. —**sharp-wit·ted·ly,** *adv.* —**sharp-wit·ted·ness,** *n.*

shat·ter, shat′ər, *v.t.* To reduce to scattered or loose fragments, or break in pieces, as by a sudden blow; to wreck or ruin, as fortunes, happiness, or lives; to impair, as health or nerves, seriously or completely; to crush in spirit.—*v.i.* To break suddenly into fragments, or fly in pieces, as glass.—*n.* A shattered state, as of the nerves. *Usu. pl.* Fragments due to shattering.

shat·ter·proof, shat′ər·proof, *a.* Designed so as to be proof against shattering: *shatterproof* glass.

shave, shāv, *v.i.,* **shaved, shaved** or **shav·en, shav·ing.** To remove hair or a beard by means of a razor. —*v.t.* To remove hair from, by cutting close to the skin with a razor; to cut or trim closely, or reduce to a smooth or bare surface; to cut or scrape away the surface of, with a sharp-edged tool; to reduce to the form of shavings or thin slices; to scrape.—*n.* An act or process of shaving; a thin piece or slice shaved off; a shaving; a narrow miss or escape: a close *shave.*

shav·er, shā′vər, *n.* One who shaves; a tool used for shaving; an electric razor. *Informal.* A youngster; a boy.

shav·ing, shā′ving, *n.* The act of that which or one who shaves; a thin slice, esp. of metal or wood pared off.

shawl, shôl, *n.* An article of dress, usu. of a square or oblong shape, worn chiefly by females as a loose covering for the shoulders or head.—*v.t.* To cover with a shawl.

she, shē, *pron.* A personal pronoun of the third person, referring to the female in question or last mentioned; the woman or female: *She* who listens learns; anything traditionally considered feminine: *She* was a good ship.—*n. pl.,* **shes.** Any female person; any female animal, often used in combination: a *she*-goat.

sheaf, shēf, *n. pl.,* **sheaves.** A quantity of the stalks of wheat, rye, oats, or other plants, bound together; a bundle of papers or the like tied together; anything comparable in appearance to a sheaf of grain.—*v.t.* To collect and bind; to make sheaves of. —**sheaf·like,** *a.*

shear, shēr, *v.t.,* **sheared, sheared** or **shorn, shear·ing.** To cut off or remove by or as by cutting with a sharp instrument; to cut the wool, fleece, or hair from, as sheep; to strip or deprive, as by cutting, usu. followed by *of;* to cut with a sharp instrument, usu. with some form of shears.—*v.i.* To cut with a sharp instrument; to move by or as if by cutting.—*n.* The act or process of shearing. A deformation in a solid produced by stress and consisting of a displacement of two contacting layers in opposite directions: the stress involved in such a strain.—**shears,** shĕrz, *n. pl.* Any of several cutting tools or machines with two blades resembling those of scissors but generally larger. —**shear•er,** *n.*

sheared, shĕrd, *a.* Formed, shaped, or completed by shearing.

sheath, shĕth, *n. pl.,* **sheaths,** shethz. A case or covering for the blade of a sword; or the like; any similar encasing cover; a dress that is unbelted and usu. closefitted; the covering on a wire or cable. —**sheath•less,** *a.* —**sheath•like,** *a.*

sheathe, shĕth, *v.t.,* **sheathed, sheath•ing.** To put into or supply with a sheath; to protect by covering with sheathing. —**sheath•er,** *n.*

sheath•ing, shē′thing, *n.* The act of one who sheathes; that which sheathes; any material used for such a purpose.

sheave, shĕv, *v.t.,* **sheaved, sheav•ing.** To gather or collect into a sheaf or sheaves.

sheaves, shĕvz, *n. pl.* Plural form of **sheaf.**

she•bang, shə•bang′, *n. Informal.* A thing, a matter, or an affair in its entirety, usu. preceded by *whole:* The *whole shebang* collapsed.

she'd, shĕd. Contraction of she had or she would.

shed, shed, *v.t.,* **shed, shed•ding.** To let flow or fall, as tears; to lose, as blood; throw off, or give out, as a light; to drop or cast off or separate from, seasonally or in a life process, as a seed, feather, or fur; to repel or by other means prevent penetration: a roof or a coat that *sheds* water.—*v.i.* To drop off, as a leaf; to lose, as hair; to cast off in a life process, as feathers or fur.—*n.* Anything that sheds or has been shed.

shed, shed, *n.* A crude structure intended only for storage or shelter.

sheen, shēn, *n.* Brightness, radiance, or light; luster: the *sheen* of satin or of pearls.—*v.i.* Shine. —**sheen•y,** shē′nē, *a.,* **-i•er, -i•est.**

sheep, shēp, *n. pl.,* **sheep.** Any of the ruminant mammals closely allied to the goats, which has many domesticated varieties, valuable for their flesh, wool, and other products; leather made from the skin of these animals; a meek, timid, or stupid person.

sheep•dog, sheep dog, shēp′dôg, shēp′dog, *n.* A dog trained to tend sheep, often a collie.

sheep•herd•er, shēp′hər•dər, *n.* One who herds or tends grazing sheep. —**sheep•herd•ing,** *n.*

sheep•ish, shē′pish, *a.* Foolishly bashful; overmodest; like a sheep in meekness or obedience.

sheep•shear•ing, shēp′shēr•ing, *n.* The act of shearing sheep; the season when sheep are sheared. —**sheep•shear•er,** *n.*

sheep•skin, shēp′skin, *n.* The skin of a sheep, esp. such a skin dressed with the wool on, as for a garment; that which is made from the skin of sheep, as parchment or leather. *Informal.* A diploma, sometimes made of parchment.

sheer, shēr, *a.* Being transparent or nearly so, with little body or substance: a *sheer* fabric; total or complete in the sense of being unrelieved by any other element; total or complete, without reservation or qualification: *sheer* foolishness; of or pertaining to steepness that is extreme: a *sheer* cliff.—*adv.* Totally, completely, or nearly so: a quarrel that split them *sheer* apart; vertically, or extremely steeply: to climb *sheer* up the wall.—*n.* A fabric that is lightweight and transparent. —**sheer•ly,** *adv.* —**sheer•ness,** *n.*

sheet, shĕt, *n.* A large, oblong piece of cotton, linen, or other cloth used as bedding; a piece of paper, usu. rectangular in shape; a newspaper, a periodical, or an infrequent publication; a large, flat, and usu. thin layer, surface, or the like; a broad expanse, surface, or stretch of something: a *sheet* of ice; a flat, thin, metal utensil used for baking: a cookie *sheet.*—*v.t.* To provide with sheets or a sheet; to cover or wrap with a sheet.—*v.i.* To spread or fall in a sheet.

sheet glass, *n.* Glass cut into large, flat sheets.

sheet•ing, shē′ting, *n.* Cloth or other material used for or formed into sheets.

sheet light•ning, *n.* Lightning appearing in sheet form or as wide, expanded, diffused flashes: caused by a distant flash of lightning being reflected, as by clouds.

sheet met•al, *n.* Metal in thin plates.

sheet mu•sic, *n.* Musical compositions usu. printed separately on unbound sheets.

sheik, sheikh, shĕk, *n.* A title of dignity belonging to the chiefs of the Arabic tribes, or to Moslem priests, now used among Moslems as a title of respect. *Informal.* A rake.

shelf, shelf, *n.pl.,* **shelves,** shelvz. A board of wood or a thin narrow slab of another material fixed horizontally to a wall or other frame, for holding articles; that which the shelf contains; any projection similar to this, as a ledge of rock; a shoal; bedrock, as found under soil or gravel deposits.—**on the shelf,** put aside or out of use; laid aside temporarily.

she'll, shĕl. Contraction of she will or she shall.

shell, shel, *n.* A hard outside covering, esp. that of a mollusk; the material of which such a covering is composed; the hard outside casing of a nut; the outside layer of an egg; an object that is concave or hollow like a shell; a hollow projectile containing a bursting charge, as for heavy artillery, small arms, or shotguns; a withdrawn, reserved attitude behind which one's emotions or thoughts are concealed: Her gay charm drew him out of his *shell;* an arena or stage covered with a half dome: a band *shell* in the park. *Fig.* That which is a hollow form or merely an outline of what was or is real: a *shell* of one's former self.—*v.t.* To remove or separate from a natural casing, husk, pod, or the like; to bombard with explosives.—*v.i.* To shed, emerge from, or cast off a casing or shell.—**shell out.** *Informal.* To hand over or give out, as money; contribute. —**shelled, shell-like, shel•ly,** *a.* —**shel•ler,** *n.*

shel•lac, shel•lack, shə•lak′, *n.* Lac which has been purified, used for making varnish; a varnish made by dissolving this material in a solution.—*v.t.,* **-lacked, -lack•ing.** To coat or treat with shellac. *Informal.* To defeat, or throttle.

shel•lack•ing, shə•lak′ing, *n. Informal.* A definite defeat; a whipping or beating.

shell•fire, shel′fir, *n.* The firing of explosive shells or projectiles.

shell•fish, shel′fish, *n. pl.,* **-fish, -fish•es.** An animal that is aquatic and whose external covering consists of a shell, as a crustacean or a mollusk.

shell shock, *n.* Combat fatigue. —**shell•shocked,** *a.*

shel•ter, shel′tər, *n.* That which provides a cover or protection against injury, danger, or discomfort, as from the weather, or the like; a refuge; the protection so provided: The cyclist took *shelter* under an overpass; temporary quarters or refuge: an animal *shelter.*—*v.t.* To provide shelter for.—*v.i.* To take shelter. —**shel•ter•er,** *n.*

shelve, shelv, *v.t.,* **shelved, shelv•ing.** To place on a shelf; to put aside from active use; to dismiss; to furnish with shelves.—*v.i.* To slope or incline gradually. —**shelv•er,** *n.*

shelv•ing, shel′ving, *n.* The shelves, as of a room or shop, collectively; the material used for making shelves; the degree or condition of sloping; the action of placing something on a shelf.

she•nan•i•gan, shə•nan′ə•gən, *n. Usu. pl. Informal.* Mischief or trickery; a deceitful action.

shep•herd, shep′ərd, *n.* A person employed in tending sheep; one who exercises spiritual care over a community; a pastor or minister.—*v.t.* To guard, herd, or watch like a shepherd. —**shep•herd•ess,** shep′ər•dis, *n.* A female shepherd.

sher•bet, shər′bit, *n.* A fruit-flavored water ice.

sher•iff, sher′if, *n.* The chief law enforcement officer of a county, who maintains law and order, maintains the jail, and summons jurors to court sessions.

sher·ry, sher/ē, *n. pl.,* **-ries.** A fortified Spanish wine of amber color; any of a number of similar wines.

she's, shēz. Contraction of she is or she has.

shib·bo·leth, shib/ə·lith, shib/ə·leth, *n.* A peculiarity of speech or custom that distinguishes a particular group or class of people; the watch-word of a party; a pet phrase of a party.

shield, shēld, *n.* A broad piece of defensive armor carried on the arm; any defense or protection.—*v.t.* To cover, as with a shield; to cover or protect from danger or anything harmful or disagreeable, as a rubberized apron worn to shield the clothing; to defend; to protect. **—shield·er,** *n.*

shift, shift, *v.t.* To transfer or change from one place, arrangement, person, direction, or position to another; to remove and exchange for another; to change the arrangement of, as gears while driving an automobile.—*v.i.* To change place, position, or direction; to undergo a change, often a systematic change; to live, get along, or succeed; to change the arrangement of gears in an automobile while driving.—*n.* An instance of shifting; the period of time which comprises a person's working hours, esp. at a concern operating all or most of a twenty-four hour day: an 11 P.M. to 7 A.M. *shift;* the group of people who work during a particular one of such specified periods: an energetic night *shift;* a contrivance or resource, usu. deceptive; gearshift.**—shift for one·self,** to be independent or to make one's own way. **—shift·er,** *n.* **—shift·ing·ness,** *n.*

shift·less, shift/lis, *a.* Lazy; inefficient.

shift·y, shif/tē, *a.,* **-i·er, -i·est.** Full of shifts; changing; suggesting a nature that is tricky. **—shift·i·ly,** *adv.* **—shift·i·ness,** *n.*

shill, shil, *n. Informal.* A person posing as a purchaser or gambler to decoy onlookers into participating.

shil·ly-shal·ly, shil/ē·shal·ē, *v.i.,* **-lied, -ly·ing.** To act in an undecided manner; to hesitate; to be concerned with trifles.

shim·mer, shim/ər, *v.i.* To shine with a tremulous light; to gleam in a subdued manner; to seem to waver or quiver, as in poor light; to glimmer.—*n.* A subdued gleam or glistening. **—shim·mer·y,** shim/ə·rē, *a.,* **-i·er, -i·est.**

shim·my, shim/ē, *n. pl.,* **-mies.** An American jazz dance of the 1920's, characterized by rapid shaking of the hips and shoulders; unusual vibration or wobbling, as of an automobile wheel.—*v.i.,* **-mied, -my·ing.** To dance the shimmy; to vibrate or wobble.

shin, shin, *n.* The forepart of the leg between the ankle and the knee.—*v.i., v.t.,* **shinned, shin·ning.** To climb, as a polelike structure, by means of the hands and legs alone.

shin·bone, shin/bōn, *n.* The bone of the shin; the tibia.

shin·dig, shin/dig, *n. Informal.* A large and often noisy, elaborate party.

shine, shīn, *v.i.,* **shone** or **shined, shin·ing.** To emit light; to be radiant by reflected light; to exhibit brightness or splendor: *shine* in society.—*v.t.* To cause or make to shine; to polish.—*n.* Brightness due to the emission or reflection of light; luster; fair weather; a polish given to shoes. *Informal.* Fancy or liking: He's taken a *shine* to you.**—shine up to.** *Informal.* To try to impress or please.

shin·er, shī/nər, *n.* One who or that which shines. *Informal.* A black eye resulting from a blow.

shin·gle, shing/gəl, *n.* A thin piece of wood or other building material used in overlapping rows as a roof covering; a ladies' short haircut. *Informal.* A small signboard, as displayed outside the office of a doctor or lawyer.—*v.t.,* **-gled, -gling.** To cover with shingles;

to cut, as hair, short and shaped to the head. **—shin·gler,** *n.*

shin·gle, shing/gəl, *n.* A loose sheet or bed of small, water-worn stones or pebbles as on a beach. **—shin·gly,** *a.,* **-i·er, -i·est.**

shin·gles, shing/gəlz, *n. pl., sing.* or *pl. in constr.* A painful viral infection involving the central nervous system and characterized by the eruption of groups of blisters on the skin along the affected nerves.

shin·ing, shī/ning, *a.* Luminous; radiant; gleaming; conspicuously fine: a woman's *shining* talents. **—shin·ing·ly,** *adv.*

shin·ny, shin/ē, *v.i.,* **-nied, -ny·ing.** *Informal.* To climb, as a pole, using shins and arms.

shin·y, shī/nē, *a.,* **-i·er, -i·est.** Characterized by sunshine; bright; glossy; brilliant. **—shin·i·ness,** *n.*

ship, ship, *n.* A seagoing vessel of considerable size; the personnel or crew of a vessel; an airship or airplane.—*v.t.,* **shipped, ship·ping.** To put or take on board a ship for transportation; to send or transport by ship, rail, or other means. *Informal.* To send away or get rid of: to *ship* the kids to camp.—*v.i.* To go on board a ship; embark.**—when one's ship comes in,** when one attains financial success. **—ship·pa·ble,** *a.*

ship bis·cuit, *n.* Hardtack.

ship·board, ship/bôrd, *a.* Happening aboard a ship: a *shipboard* romance.**—on ship·board,** on a ship.

ship·build·er, ship/bil·dər, *n.* One whose business or work is the designing and building of ships. **—ship·build·ing,** *n.*

ship·mate, ship/māt, *n.* One who serves on the same ship with another; a fellow sailor.

ship·ment, ship/mənt, *n.* The act of transporting goods or cargo; the goods shipped.

ship·per, ship/ər, *n.* One who sends goods by any means of transportation, as by railroad, truck, airplane, or ship.

ship·ping, ship/ing, *n.* The collective fleet of ships serving a country or port; tonnage; the business of transporting merchandise.

ship·ping clerk, *n.* A clerk who attends to the details of sending or receiving shipments.

ship·shape, ship/shāp, *a.* Having a seamanlike order; neat and trim; well-arranged.

ship·wreck, ship/rek, *n.* The wreck of a ship; destruction; failure; ruin.—*v.t.* To make to suffer shipwreck; to ruin.

ship·yard, ship/yärd, *n.* A place in which ships are constructed or repaired.

shirk, shərk, *v.t.* To avoid or get out of unfairly.—*v.i.* To avoid an obligation or duty.—*n.* One who seeks to avoid duty. **—shirk·er,** *n.*

shirr, shər, *v.t.* To draw up or gather, as cloth, on several parallel threads; to bake, as eggs removed from the shell, in a shallow dish or individual dishes.

shirt, shərt, *n.* A loose, usu. lightweight garment worn by men or women on the upper part of the body and usu. having a collar, sleeves, and a button-front closing; an undershirt.**—keep one's shirt on.** *Informal.* To be patient; to keep calm.**—lose one's shirt.** *Informal.* To suffer a severe financial loss. **—shirt·less,** *a.*

shirt·tail, shərt/tāl, *n.* The extended part of a shirt, below the waist, which is tucked into the trousers.

shirt·waist, shərt/wāst, *n.* A woman's loosely fitting tailored blouse; a dress with the front opening and bodice details of a man's shirt.

shish ke·bab, shish/kə·bob, *n.* Kabob roasted or broiled on a skewer.

shiv·er, shiv/ər, *v.i.* To shake involuntarily or tremble, as with cold, fear, or excitement.—*v.t.* To make, as a sail, to shake.—*n.* A shivering motion or state. **—shiv·er·y,** shiv/ə·rē, *a.,* **-i·er, -i·est.**

shoal, shōl, *n.* A place where the water of a river, lake, or sea is shallow; a sandbank or bar.—*a.* Shallow.—*v.i.*

---

a- hat, fāte, fâre, fäther; **e-** met, mē; **i-** pin, pīne; **o-** not, nōte, ôrb, moove (move), boy, pownd; **u-** cūbe, bûll, tûk (took); **ch-** chin; **th-** thick, then; **zh-** vizhon (vision); **ə-** ago, takən, pencəl, lemən, bərd (bird).

To become shallow.—*v.t.* To cause or allow to become shallow.

shoal, shōl, *n.* A school of fish; a large number of persons or things gathered together.—*v.i.* To collect or swim in a shoal; to throng.

shock, shok, *n.* A sudden, violent blow or impact; a sudden disturbance or commotion; a sudden and startling effect on the mind or emotions; the reason for such disturbances; a sudden weakening effect on the bodily functions due to some violent impression on the nervous system, as from a severe injury or a violent emotional disturbance; the resulting condition of nervous depression or prostration; the effect produced on the body by the sudden passage of a current of electricity through it.—*v.t.* To strike with intense and painful surprise; to give an electric shock to; to subject to bodily or nervous shock; to startle by outraging the sense of propriety or decency.—*v.i.* To experience a shock.

shock, shok, *n.* A matted, bushy mass, esp. of hair.—*a.* Shaggy.

shock ab·sorb·er, *n.* A device for deadening the shock or concussion of sudden impact or rapid motion: the *shock absorbers* of an automobile.

shock·er, shok'ər, *n.* One who or that which shocks.

shock·ing, shok'ing, *a.* Causing horror, digust, pain, or intense surprise.

shock ther·a·py, *n.* A treatment for mental disorders, based on the coma or other shock effects induced by injections of drugs, such as insulin, or by the application of electrical currents to the brain. Also **shock treat·ment.**

shock wave, *n.* A wave formed by compression in a medium when an object moves violently through the medium at a speed in excess of that sound.

shod, shod, *a.* Equipped with a shoe or shoes.

shod·dy, shod'ē, *n. pl.,* **-dies.** A cloth made of any inferior material; anything inferior made to resemble what is of superior quality.—*a.,* **-di·er, -di·est.** Made of or containing shoddy; inferior but pretentious. —**shod·di·ly,** *adv.* —**shod·di·ness,** *n.*

shoe, shoo, *n. pl.,* **shoes.** An external covering, usu. of leather, for the human foot, consisting of a heavy sole and a lighter upper part, esp. such a covering ending a short distance above, at, or below the ankle, as distinguished from a boot; a horseshoe; a thing or part resembling a shoe in form, position, or use; the part of a brake which acts upon the wheel.—*v.t.,* **shod, shod, shoe·ing.** To provide or fit with a shoe, metal plate, or the like. —**be in some·one's shoes,** to be in someone else's position or situation. —**fill some·one's shoes,** to equal someone's ability or success, or to face the responsibility of some particular person. —**the shoe is on the oth·er foot,** the situation has been reversed.

shoe·horn, shoo'hôrn, *n.* A curved piece of polished horn, metal, or similar material used to aid in putting on shoes.

shoe·lace, shoo'lās, *n.* A shoestring.

shoe·mak·er, shoo'mā·kər, *n.* One who makes or repairs shoes.

sho·er, shoo'ər, *n.* One who puts shoes on horses.

shoe·string, shoo'string. *n.* A string or lace for fastening a shoe. —**on a shoe·string.** *Informal.* With a very small amount of money used to start or carry on an enterprise or business.

shoo, shoo, *interj.* An exclamation used to scare or drive away animals, and the like.—*v.t.* To scare or drive away by calling out 'shoo.'—*v.i.* To call out 'shoo.'

shoo-in, shoo'in, *n. Informal.* A contestant who is favored to be a sure winner.

shoot, shoot, *v.t.,* **shot, shoot·ing.** To fire or discharge: to *shoot* a rifle; to hit, wound, or kill with a missile discharged from a weapon; to propel, emit, thrust, or send forth forcefully, suddenly, or rapidly: to *shoot* a question; to put forth or extend: a plant *shooting* up stems and leaves; to discard or dump; to send down a chute; to pass rapidly through, over, or

down: to *shoot* the rapids; to take a snapshot or picture of; to wear out, exhaust, or squander: to *shoot* a wad of money; to aim and send toward a goal, as a ball or puck.—*v.i.* To take a shot, or to thrust forth missiles from a weapon; to move, dart, or spurt swiftly or suddenly: sparks which *shoot* upward; to come forth from the ground, or put forth buds or shoots, as a plant; to grow rapidly, often with *up;* to project, extend, or jut: a cape which *shoots* into the sea; to take a snapshot or movies with a camera; to propel a ball, puck, marble, dice, or the like in a particular direction, as toward the goal or another player.—*n.* Any growing or sprouting from a main stock; an offshoot; the act of shooting with a weapon; an expedition for shooting game; a swift or sudden movement; a cast or throw; a heavy rush, as of water; a rapid; a sloping trough, upright shaft, or the like, for conveying coal, ore, or grain to a receptacle below. —**shoot at, shoot for,** to aim at or aspire to. —**shoot down,** to fell or destroy with or as with a gun: to *shoot down* a dove. *Informal.* To thwart or betray: to *shoot down* an idea. —**shoot off one's mouth,** to talk too much and indiscreetly. —**shoot the breeze,** to chat casually. —**shoot the bull,** to exaggerate or brag. —**shoot the works,** to expend all of one's effort or resources. —**shoot up,** to grow rapidly. *Informal.* To maim or damage by shooting: to *shoot up* a bar. —**shoot·er,** *n.*

shoot·ing gal·ler·y, *n.* A place for practice in shooting, as at a carnival.

shoot·ing i·ron, *n. Informal.* A firearm.

shoot·ing star, *n.* A meteor.

shop, shop, *n.* A building or room in which articles are made or prepared and sold; a building or room appropriated to the selling of goods. A store or department of a store that sells a particular type of merchandise; also **shoppe.** A workshop; one's place of business or occupation; matters pertaining to one's occupation, as a subject of conversation: to talk *shop;* the instruction in working with machinery, tools, or in a specific trade.—*v.i.,* **shopped, shop·ping.** To visit shops or stores for the purpose of purchasing or examining goods; to hunt for a bargain.—*v.t.* To seek out or inspect something presented for sale by or in.

shop·keep·er, shop'kē·pər, *n.* One who sells goods in a shop; a tradesman.

shop·lift·er, shop'lif·tər, *n.* One who steals goods from a shop. —**shop·lift·ing,** *n.*

shop·per, shop'ər, *n.* One who shops.

shop·ping bag, *n.* A sturdy, large-size bag with handles, used by shoppers to carry their purchases.

shop stew·ard, *n.* A union member chosen to represent his or her fellow workers in dealing with the management. Also **shop chair·man.**

shop·talk, shop'tôk, *n.* Specialized terminology having to do with a particular occupation.

shop·worn, shop'wôrn, *a.* Worn, marred, or damaged from exposure or handling.

shore, shôr, *n.* The land immediately adjacent to an ocean, sea, lake, or river; land, as differentiated from water; land, in the sense of homeland: native *shores.* —*a.* Of or pertaining to land, as differentiated from water. —**shore·line,** shôr'līn, *n.*

shore leave, *n.* A limited period of free time which may be spent ashore, granted to navy personnel stationed aboard ship.

shore pa·trol, *n.* A police detail of the U.S. Navy, Marine Corps, and Coast Guard that is maintained for the purpose of surveillance ashore.

short, shôrt, *a.* Not having great length; not long; not tall; not of long duration; curt; brief; abrupt; sharp; severe; uncivil: a *short* answer; not retentive: a *short* memory; inadequate; scanty; deficient: in *short* supply; scantily supplied or furnished, followed by *on: short on* equipment; not possessed of a reasonable or usual amount: to be *short* of money.—*adv.* Abruptly; curtly; at a point before some specified standard or condition: to fall *short*, to cut *short*.—*n.* Anything short; deficiency. *Pl.* Trousers worn to the knee or above; short pants worn as underwear by men.—*v.t., v.i.* To cheat, as by delivering less than the agreed amount or quantity; to short circuit. —**for short,** for the purpose of briefness. —**in short,** in summary. —**short of,** inferior to; less than; lacking. —**short·ly,** *adv.* —**short·ness,** *n.*

short·age, shôr′tij, *n.* Any deficiency.

short-change, shôrt′chānj′, *v.t.* -changed, -chang·ing. To give less change for money than is properly due; to cheat. —**short-chang·er,** *n.*

short cir·cuit, *n.* A side circuit or shunt of relatively low resistance connecting two points of an electric circuit of greater resistance.

short-cir·cuit, shôrt′sər′kit, *v.t.* To establish a short circuit in; to cut off by the establishment of a short circuit. *Informal.* To by-pass; hinder.—*v.i.* To form a short circuit.

short·com·ing, shôrt′kəm·ing, *n.* A failure to reach a quantity or amount; deficiency; a defect.

short-cut, shôrt′kət, *n.* A route shorter than one usu. used; a timesaving method of accomplishing any work or undertaking.—*a.*

short-cut, *v.t., v.i.,* -cut, -cut·ting. To use a shorter way or method.

short·en, shôrt′ən, *v.t.* To make short or shorter; to lessen; to make, as pastry, crisp with the addition of fat or other shortening.—*v.i.* To become short or shorter. —**short·en·er,** *n.*

short·en·ing, shôrt′ən·ing, shôrt′ning, *n.* The act of abbreviating or becoming abbreviated. Butter, lard, or other edible fat.

short·hand, shôrt′hand, *n.* Any system of quick writing, substituting contractions and symbols for letters and words; stenography; any system of contracted communication.—*a.*

short-hand·ed, shôrt′han′did, *a.* Not having the full or necessary number of workers. —**short-hand·ed·ness,** *n.*

short line, *n.* Any short route operated by a bus company, airline, or the like.

short-lived, shôrt′līvd′, shôrt′livd′, *a.* Not living or lasting long.

short or·der, *n.* Food that can be cooked and served quickly when ordered in a restaurant. —**in short or·der,** quickly.

short shrift, *n.* Slight consideration, mercy, or attention as given people or situations.

short-sight·ed, shôrt′sī′tid, *a.* Unable to see far; near-sighted; myopic; lacking in foresight; characterized by lack of foresight: a *short-sighted* policy. —**short-sight·ed·ly,** *adv.* —**short-sight·ed·ness,** *n.*

short-tem·pered, shôrt′tem′pərd, *a.* Having a short temper; quick-tempered.

short-term, shôrt′tərm′, *a.* Involving or applying to a comparatively short time.

short·wave, shôrt′wāv′, *n.* An electromagnetic wave, shorter than those in the standard broadcast band. —**short·wave,** *a.*

short-wind·ed, shôrt′win′did, *a.* Affected with shortness of breath after physical effort.

shot, shot, *n.* A discharge of a firearm or other missile weapon; the act of shooting. Any of the small globular pieces of lead for use in shotguns or the like; pl., **shot.** The flight of a missile, or its range or distance; one who shoots; a marksman; an aimed throw or stroke, often for scoring, as in certain games; a try, attempt, or guess: taking a *shot* at finding the error. *Informal.* An injection of a drug given hypodermically: a rabies *shot;* a small quantity of liquor, specif. an ounce or jigger, to be drunk in one swallow. A camera exposure or snapshot; small globules of hardened metal in a casting.—*v.t.,* **shot·ted, shot·ting.** To load with shot.

—*v.i.* To manufacture or form shot. —**call one's shots,** to specify in advance what move one will attempt to make. —**call the shots.** *Informal.* To direct or control what will happen: being in a position where he can *call the shots,* quickly; at once. —**like a shot,** quickly; at once. —**not by a long shot.** *Informal.* Decidedly not; never. —**shot in the arm.** *Informal.* Something having a revitalizing or stimulating effect. —**shot in the dark.** *Informal.* A random guess.

shot, shot, *a.* Having a changeable color; variegated; interspersed: brown hair *shot* with silver; permeated, usu. followed by *through with:* a sermon *shot through with* humor. *Informal.* Completely worn out; ruined.

shot·gun, shot′gən, *n.* A light, smooth-bored, often double-barreled gun for firing shot at short range.—*a.* Pertaining to or as with a shotgun; involving the use of force; covering a wide range in an indiscriminate or hit-or-miss fashion: to prescribe a *shotgun* remedy. —*v.t.,* -gunned, -gun·ning. To shoot at with a shotgun; to coerce.

shot·gun wed·ding, *n. Informal.* A marriage necessitated by the bride's pregnancy.

shot put, *n.* An athletic event in which a heavy shot or ball is cast as far as possible. —**shot-put·ter,** shot′pût·ər, *n.*

should, shûd, *aux. v.* The past form of **shall,** used as such only in indirect discourse: He told me I *should* never fail. Used to indicate condition in conjunction with or instead of *if:* She will laugh, *should* I fall, she will laugh *if* I *should* fall. Used to show obligation or duty, often with doubtful fulfillment: I *should* go home now. Used in the present perfect tense of the obligatory sense to indicate failure to do something: I *should* have gone home an hour ago. Used to denote a surprise happening: Who *should* appear, but my father! Used to express probability or expectancy: She *should* arrive tomorrow. Used to soften or temper a command, suggestion, or opinion: I *should* think you had had enough to eat. *Informal.* Used ironically to mean the opposite: With grades like mine, I *should* talk. Used interrogatively to ask direction or inquire as to propriety, used similarly to *shall* but often with more emphasis on duty or obligation: *Should* I apologize?

shoul·der, shōl′dər, *n.* The joint by which the arm of a human or the foreleg of other mammals is connected with the body; the bones and muscles of this part conjointly. *Pl.* Both shoulders and the area below or behind the neck lying between them. A prominent or projecting part: the *shoulder* of a hill; that part of wearing apparel which covers the shoulders; the flat open space bordering either side of a roadway.—*v.t.* To push or thrust with the shoulder; shove; bump; to take upon the shoulder or shoulders, as an obligation.—*v.i.* To force one's way, as through a crowd. —**cry on one's shoul·der,** to tell another person one's troubles. —**rub shoul·ders with,** to join or mix with. —**shoul·der to shoul·der,** with combined effort; cooperating: working *shoulder to shoulder.* —**straight from the shoul·der,** in a straightforward manner; openly; frankly.

shoul·der blade, *n.* Either of the two large, flat, triangle-shaped bones in the upper back on either side and forming the dorsal part of the shoulders in humans and other mammals.

should·n't, shûd′ənt. Contraction of should not.

shout, showt, *n.* A loud cry, as one expressing joy, triumph, fear, or the like.—*v.i.* To utter a sudden and loud cry.—*v.t.* To utter with a shout. —**shout·er,** *n.*

shout·ing dis·tance, *n.* Easy or comfortable reach of the voice, usu. preceded by *within.*

shove, shəv, *v.t.,* shoved, shov·ing. To force or push along; to press against; to jostle.—*v.i.* To push or drive forward.—*n.* An act of shoving; a push. —**shove off,** to push a boat from the shore. *Informal.* To leave.

---

a- hat, fāte, fâre, fäther; **e-** met, mē; **i-** pin, pīne; **o-** not, nōte, ôrb, moove (move), boy, pownd; **u-** cūbe, bûll, tûk (took); **ch-** chin; **th-** thick, ŧhen; **zh-** vizhon (vision); **ə-** ego, takən, pencəl, lemən, bərd (bird).

—**shov·er,** *n.*

shov·el, shəv′əl, *n.* An implement consisting of a broad and slightly hollow blade, or shallow scoop, with a long handle, used for gathering up, throwing, or removing loose matter such as coal, earth, or the like.—*v.t.,* **-eled, -el·ing.** To take up and throw with a shovel; to clear, as a path, with a shovel; to scoop up hastily or in masses using or as if using a shovel.—*v.i.* To work with or as with a shovel. —**shov·el·er,** *n.*

shov·el·ful, shəv′əl·fûl, *n.* A quantity sufficient to fill a shovel.

show, shō, *v.t.,* **showed, shown** or **showed, show·ing.** To cause or allow to be seen; expose to view; to display, as for sale; to guide; to point out or indicate in order to inform; to grant: to *show* favor.—*v.i.* To be seen; to appear or arrange to appear in a certain manner: to *show* to advantage; to give an exhibition or performance.—*n.* An exhibition, display, or performance; the act or an act of exhibiting: a *show* of hands; theater or company providing entertainments; an indication or trace: a *show* of blood; a minimal or token, empty, or half-hearted display or performance made in gesture only. —**show·off,** to display in an arrogant way. —**show·up,** to reveal; to outshine or surpass; be evident or visible. *Informal.* To put in an appearance. —**show·er,** *n.*

show·bill, shō′bil, *n.* A poster advertising a show or another matter for public attention.

show·boat, shō′bōt, *n.* A river steamboat with stage and a troupe of actors.

show·case, shō′kās, *n.* A glass cabinet or case within which articles are placed for sale or exhibition; a setting for exhibiting or displaying something, as a model or idea.—*v.t.,* **-cased, -cas·ing.**

show·down, shō′down, *n.* The laying down of one's cards, face upward, in a card game; confrontation.

show·er, show′ər, *n.* A brief fall of rain, hail, sleet, or snow; a similar fall, as of tears, sparks, bullets, or other objects which are small; a very large supply or quantity given; a gift of presents, usu. of a particular kind, as to a prospective bride; a bath in which water is showered upon the body from above; the room or apparatus for such a bath.—*v.t.* To pour down in or as in a shower; bestow lavishly; to wet or cleanse with or as with a shower.—*v.i.* —**show·er·y,** *a.*

show·ing, shō′ing, *n.* The act of one who or that which shows; exhibition; display; show; a record or performance.

show·man, shō′mən, *n. pl.,* **-men.** One who produces a show; a person who has skill in presenting anything dramatically. —**show·man·ship,** *n.*

show·off, shō′ôf, shō′of, *n.* Pretentious display; a person who shows off.

show·piece, shō′pēs, *n.* That which is exhibited or displayed; that which is an outstanding example of its type or sort.

show·place, shō′plās, *n.* A place recognized as an example of fine taste, as in architecture, furnishings, or overall beauty.

show·room, shō′room, shō′rûm, *n.* A room in which goods are exhibited for the purpose of advertising or sale.

show·y, shō′ē, *a.,* **-i·er, -i·est.** Making a show or imposing display: *showy* flowers; gaudy. —**show·i·ly,** *adv.* —**show·i·ness,** *n.*

shrap·nel, shrap′nəl, *n.* A hollow projectile containing a collection of bullets or the like and a bursting charge; shell fragments.

shred, shred, *n.* An irregular piece torn or cut off; a tatter; a fragment.—*v.t.,* **shred·ded** or **shred, shred·ding.** To tear or cut into small pieces, esp. narrow strips, as paper.—*v.i.* To be torn into shreds. —**shred·der,** *n.*

shrew, shroo, *n.* One of several small, insect-eating mammals with a pointed nose and small eyes; an ill-tempered scold. —**shrew·like,** *a.*

shrewd, shrood, *a.* Astute; sharp in grasp of practical considerations. —**shrewd·ly,** *adv.* —**shrewd·ness,** *n.*

shrew·ish, shroo′ish, *a.* Having the disposition or ways of a shrew; nagging.

shriek, shrēk, *n.* A loud, sharp, shrill cry or other sound.—*v.i.* To utter a loud, sharp, shrill sound.—*v.t.* To utter or cry in a shriek.

shrill, shril, *a.* High-pitched and piercing, as the voice; uttering or producing such sound; lacking in moderation.—*adv.* With or in a shrill sound.—*v.i.* To sound shrilly, as the voice.—*v.t.* To utter or give forth shrilly. —*n.* A shrill sound. —**shril·ly,** *adv.* —**shrill·ness,** *n.*

shrimp, shrimp, *n. pl.,* **shrimps, shrimp.** Any of various small, long-tailed, chiefly marine, ten-footed shellfish, several varieties of which are esteemed as a table delicacy. *Informal.* A diminutive or insignificant person.—*a.* Of or pertaining to the catching and handling of shrimp: a *shrimp* fisherman.—*v.i.* To try to catch shrimp.

shrine, shrin, *n.* A container for holding the remains or fragments of something held sacred; a tomb or other structure, often large, that houses such articles of veneration; a place hallowed because of significant associations: a *shrine* of art.—*v.t.,* **shrined, shrin·ing.** To place in a shrine.

shrink, shringk, *v.i.,* **shrank** or **shrunk, shrunk·en, shrink·ing.** To draw back, as from danger; to recoil; to contract or become reduced in size as a result of subjection to conditions of moisture or temperature or both, as woolen cloth in hot water; to become less: Distances have *shrunk* since the introduction of air travel; to diminish in amount or value.—*v.t.* To cause to contract.—*n.* The act of shrinking. —**shrink·a·ble,** *a.* —**shrink·er,** *n.*

shrink·age, shring′kij, *n.* The process or condition of shrinking; the amount or extent of shrinking.

shrink·ing vi·o·let, *n.* One who tends to make himself or herself as inconspicuous as possible.

shriv·el, shriv′əl, *v.t., v.i.,* **-eled, -el·ing.** To contract or shrink; to draw into wrinkles; to wither; to become or make useless or helpless.

shroud, shrowd, *n.* The garment of the dead; that which cloaks, as a long, loose garment.—*v.t.* To enshroud for burial; to cover or veil: Mystery *shrouded* the incident.

shrub, shrəb, *n.* Any of various low, woody perennial plants, usu. with several permanent woody stems.

shrub·ber·y, shrəb′ə·rē, *n. pl.,* **-ies.** Shrubs collectively.

shrub·by, shrəb′ē, *a.,* **-bi·er, -bi·est.** Full of, consisting of, or resembling shrubs.

shrug, shrəg, *v.t., v.i.,* **shrugged, shrug·ging.** To raise or draw up the shoulders, as in expressing dissatisfaction or uncertainty.—*n.* A drawing up of the shoulders. —**shrug off,** to ignore or take little notice of.

shuck, shək, *n.* A husk or pod, as the outer covering of maize; the shell of an oyster or clam.—*interj. Usu. pl.* An exclamation showing contempt or disgust.—*v.t.* To remove the shucks from. *Informal.* To undress. —**shuck·er,** *n.*

shud·der, shəd′ər, *v.i.* To tremble as with fear or horror.—*n.* A convulsive shaking of the body; tremor. —**shud·der·y,** *a.*

shuf·fle, shəf′əl, *v.t.,* **-fled, -fling.** To move, as the feet, along the ground or floor without lifting them; to move this way and that; to mix, as cards in a pack; to jumble together; to put, thrust, or bring trickily or carelessly, usu. followed by *into, in,* or *out:* to *shuffle* oneself *into* a position of power.—*v.i.* To move the feet without lifting them; to scrape the feet over the floor in dancing; to move in a clumsy manner, usu. with *into;* to act in a shifting or evasive manner.—*n.* A scraping movement of the feet; an evasive trick; a shuffling of cards in a pack; a dance in which the feet are shuffled along the floor. —**shuf·fle off,** to thrust aside or get rid of. —**shuf·fler,** *n.*

shuf·fle·board, shəf′əl·bôrd, *n.* A game played by pushing disks forcefully with a cue so that they will slide the length of the playing area.

shun, shən, *v.t.* **shunned, shun·ning.** To keep clear of; to avoid. **—shun·ner,** *n.*

shunt, shənt, *v.t.* To shove or turn aside or out of the way; to shift; to switch; to sidetrack; to put aside; to get rid of; to divert, as a part of a current, by means of a shunt; place on or furnish with a shunt.—*v.i.* To move or turn aside.—*n.* An act of shunting; a turning aside; a shift. **—shunt·er,** *n.*

shush, shəsh, *interj.* Be quiet; hush.—*v.t.* To hush.

shut, shət, *v.t.,* **shut, shut·ting.** To put in position to close an entrance or aperture, as a door, gate, cover, or lid; to close by folding or bringing together the outward covering parts of, as the eyes or a book; to confine or enclose, usu. followed by *in* or *up;* to bar, exclude, or cut off, usu. followed by *out* or *off.*—*v.i.* To become shut or closed; to close.—*n.* The act, time, or place of shutting or closing.—*a.* Closed. **—shut down,** to close for a time: to *shut down* a factory. **—shut in,** to enclose or confine. **—shut off,** to prevent the passage of; to close. **—shut out,** to bar. **—shut up,** to close tightly, as a house; to confine, or imprison. *Informal.* To stop talking or cause to stop talking.

shut·down, shət′down, *n.* A shutting down or stopping for a time.

shut·eye, shət′ī, *n. Informal.* Sleep.

shut·in, shət′in, *n.* A person who is confined to a place by infirmity or disease.—*a.* Confined by infirmity; lacking in openness and sociability.

shut·off, shət′ôf, shət′of, *n.* The mechanism or device for shutting off something.

shut·out, shət′owt, *n.* The act of shutting out, or the state of being shut out.

shut·ter, shət′ər, *n.* One who or that which shuts; a hinged or sliding cover for a window; a movable cover for closing an opening; a mechanical device for opening and closing the aperture of a camera lens.—*v.t.* To close with or as with a shutter.

shut·tle, shət′əl, *n.* A device in a loom, for passing or shooting the weft thread through the shed from one side of the web to the other; the rotating container that carries the lower thread or bobbin in a sewing machine; a means of transportation which makes short and frequent trips between two points.—*v.t., v.i.,* **-tled, -tling.** To move or cause to move to and fro like a shuttle. **—shut·tle·like,** *a.*

shy, shī, *a.,* **shi·er, shi·est, shy·er, shy·est.** Reserved, retiring, modest, and coy rather than social; self-conscious; timid; hesitant and indecisive; wanting, or short of, usu. used with *on.*—*v.i.,* **shied, shy·ing.** To start away, recoil, or rear in fright, as a horse; to avoid something, usu. used with *from:* to *shy* away *from* political discussion. **—shy·ness,** *n.*

shy·ster, shī′stər, *n. Informal.* A dishonest lawyer; anyone unethical.

Si·a·mese twins, sī·ə·mēz′, sī·ə·mēs′, *n.* Twins congenitally united.

sib·i·lant, sib′ə·lənt, *a.* Hissing; making a hissing sound, as when pronouncing *s, sh, z, zh, ch,* or *j.*—*n.* The hissing sound made when pronouncing *s, sh, z, zh, ch,* or *j.* **—sib·i·lance,** *n.*

sib·ling, sib′ling, *n.* A brother or a sister.—*a.* Having to do with a brother or a sister.

sic, sik, *v.t.,* **sicked, sick·ing.** To pursue; attack, as in a command given to a dog; to rouse to an attack: He *sicked* his dog on the intruder.

sick, sik, *a.* Affected with disease of any kind; not healthy; ill; affected with nausea; inclined to vomit: being *sick* to the stomach; depressed: being heart*sick* or home*sick;* satiated; wearied, usu. with *of:* sick of rainy weather; mentally unsound; deranged; morally corrupt: the *sick* fancies of a *sick* mind; preoccupied with that which is morbid, gruesome, or sadistic: *sick* humor; used by or set apart for the ill: a *sick*bed;

accompanying or suggesting illness: a *sick* smell; repelled: an attitude that makes one *sick.*—*n., pl. in constr.* Those who are sick collectively, usu. preceded by *the.*

sick·bed, sik′bed, *n.* A bed on which a sick person lies, often specially built for the purpose.

sick·en, sik′ən, *v.t.* To make sick; to make squeamish; to disgust.—*v.i.* To become sick. **—sick·en·ing,** *a.*

sick·ish, sik′ish, *a.* Nauseating or sickening; somewhat sick.

sick·le, sik′əl, *n.* A curved blade or hook with a handle, for use in cutting grain or grass.

sickle cell, *n.* A crescent-shaped, red blood cell with abnormal hemoglobin, often causing a fatal anemic disease.

sick·ly, sik′lē, *a.,* **-li·er, -li·est.** Habitually ailing or indisposed; not robust; pertaining to ill health: a *sickly* complexion; causing sickness; nauseating; mawkish: *sickly* sentimentality. **—sick·li·ness,** *n.*

sick·ness, sik′nis, *n.* The state of being sick; disease; ill health; nausea; stomach distress; any disordered state.

sick·room, sik′room, sik′rûm, *n.* A room occupied by a sick person.

side, sīd, *n.* One of the surfaces or lines bounding a thing; either of the two surfaces of paper, cloth, or other thin objects; one of the two surfaces of an object other than the front, back, top, and bottom, usu. specified as right or left; a slope, as of a bank or hill; an aspect or phase: to study all *sides* of a question; one of the two or more parties concerned in a case, contest, or the like; either part, or line of descent, of a family, with reference to the father or the mother; the space adjacent to one.—*a.* Being at or on one side; coming from or directed toward one side; subsidiary or incidental; seen or taken from the side.—*v.t.,* **sid·ed, sid·ing.** To furnish, as a building, with sides; to put aside or away. **—on the side,** as a secondary occupation, interest, or concern; in addition to the main issue. **—side by side,** being one beside the other; together. **—side with,** to support or sympathize with in a dispute. **—take sides,** to support or favor one side or party in a controversy.

side·arm, sīd′ärm, *a.* Referring to a baseball pitching style in which the throwing arm swings nearly horizontally out from the body.

side arms, *n. pl.* Weapons carried at the side of the body, as revolvers.

side·board, sīd′bôrd, *n.* A piece of dining room furniture consisting of a kind of table with drawers in which articles for use on the dining table, esp. silver and linens, may be kept; one of the boards used to form a side, as of a farm wagon.

side·burns, sīd′bərnz, *n. pl.* Whiskers extending down from the hairline on the sides of the face and worn with the chin shaved.

side·car, sīd′kär, *n.* A small car, usu. for a passenger, at the side of a motorcycle.

sid·ed, sī′did, *a.* Characterized by or having sides, usu. preceded by a number: a one-*sided* conversation.

side dish, *n.* A food served in addition to the principal part of a course.

side ef·fect, *n.* An unintended, esp. harmful, secondary reaction to a drug.

side·kick, sīd′kik, *n. Informal.* A constant companion or close associate; a pal.

side·light, sīd′līt, *n.* Light coming from the side; incidental information on a subject.

side·line, sīd′līn, *n.* A line at the side of something; a secondary business or activity followed in addition to a primary occupation; an additional or auxiliary line of goods: a *sideline* of groceries in a drug store; one of the marks or lines which define the limit of play on the side of the field or court in football, basketball, or

---

a- hat, fâte, fãre, fäther; **e-** met, mē; **i-** pin, pīne; **o-** not, nōte, ôrb, moove (move), boy, pownd;
u- cūbe, bûll, tûk (took); **ch-** chin; **th-** thick, ŧhen; **zh-** vizhon (vision); **ə-** əgo, takən, pencəl, lemən, bərd (bird).

the like. *Usu. pl.* The area outside these boundary lines.—*v.t.*, **-lined, -lin·ing.** To remove or prevent from participation, esp. in sports.

side-long, sīd′lông, sīd′long, *a.* Inclined, slanting, or in the direction of the side; not directly in front; indirect or subtle: *side-long* remark.—*adv.*

side·show, sīd′shō, *n.* A small or minor show in connection with a principal one, as with a circus; any subordinate matter.

side·split·ting, sīd′split·ing, *a.* Extremely hearty or uproarious, as laughter.

side·step, sīd′step, *n.* A step or stepping to one side, as to avoid something.—*v.i.*, **-stepped, -step·ping.** To step to one side; to avoid a problem or decision.—*v.t.* To avoid by stepping to one side, as an obstacle or decision.

side·swipe, sīd′swīp, *n.* A sweeping stroke or blow with or along the side of something.—*v.t.*, **-swiped, -swip·ing.** To give a sideswipe to.

side·track, sīd′trak, *v.t.*, *v.i.* To shift to a side track, as a train; to divert, as from a subject.—*n.* A railroad siding.

side·walk, sīd′wôk, *n.* A walk, usu. paved, by the side of a street or road, for use by pedestrians.

side·walk su·per·in·tend·ent, *n. Informal.* A bystander watching work in progress at a construction or demolition site.

side·wall, sīd′wôl, *n.* Any wall forming a side of something, esp. the side surface of a pneumatic tire.

side·ward, sīd′wərd, *adv.*, *a.* Toward one side. —**side·wards,** *adv.*

side·way, sīd′wā, *n.* A byway.—*adv.*, *a.* Sideways.

side·ways, sīd′wāz, *adv.* Toward or from one side; indirectly; facing to the side.—*a.* Facing, moving, or projected toward or away from one side; oblique or evasive.

sid·ing, sī′ding, *n.* Any material, as overlapping boards or metal strips, that covers the outer wall surface of frame buildings; a short additional line of rails laid at the side of a main line.

si·dle, sīd′əl, *v.i.*, **-dled, -dling.** To approach by moving side foremost, as in a cautious or shy manner.—*n.* A sideways movement.

siege, sēj, *n.* The encampment of an army about a fortified place to reduce and capture it by cutting off supplies and other offensive operations; any prolonged or persistent endeavor to overcome resistance; a long period of distress, illness, or trouble.

si·en·na, sē·en′ə, *n.* A rust-colored earth used as a yellowish-brown pigment called 'raw sienna' before roasting in a furnace, and a reddish-brown pigment called 'burnt sienna' after roasting.

si·er·ra, sē·er′ə, *n.* A chain of hills or mountains, the peaks of which suggest the teeth of a saw.

si·es·ta, sē·es′tə, *n.* A nap or rest taken at midday.

sieve, siv, *n.* An instrument with a meshed or perforated bottom, usu. with a circular frame, used for separating the coarser from the finer parts of loose matter, or for straining liquids and the like.—*v.t.*, *v.i.*, **sieved, siev·ing.** To sift.

sift, sift, *v.t.* To separate the coarser from the finer parts of, as meal or ashes, by shaking in a sieve; to let fall through a sieve: to *sift* sugar; to separate by or as by a sieve; to examine with close scrutiny.—*v.i.* To use a sieve; to pass or fall through or as through a sieve. —**sift·er,** *n.*

sift·ings, sif′tingz, *n. pl.* Parts of matter sifted out.

sigh, sī, *v.i.* To emit a prolonged and audible breath, as from sorrow, weariness, relief, or yearning; to yearn or long for; to make a sound resembling or suggesting a sigh, as wind.—*v.t.* To utter or express with a sigh.—*n.* An act or sound of sighing. —**sigh·er,** *n.*

sight, sīt, *n.* The power or faculty of seeing; vision; the act or fact of seeing; the range or field of vision: land being in *sight;* a view or glimpse; mental view, regard, or estimation. *Pl.* Something seen or that merits seeing: the *sights* of the city; something extraordinary or

shocking; a spectacle: He looked a *sight* in that hat; an observation taken with a surveying instrument or the like to determine exact direction or position; an aim with a gun; a device on a firearm, optical instrument, or the like to guide the eye in aiming or viewing.—*v.t.* To get sight of; to see: to *sight* land; to take a sighting or observation of, esp. with an instrument.—*v.i.* To take a sight or aim, as in shooting; to make a careful observation: to *sight* along the hedgerow while trimming it in a straight line.—*a.* Based upon unprepared or unstudied comprehension: a *sight* translation. —**at first sight,** as soon as glimpsed: knowing *at first sight* that he liked her. —**at sight,** immediately upon sight of. —**catch sight of,** to get a brief look at; glimpse: to *catch sight of* the deer. —**know by sight,** to recognize by appearance only; not to be well acquainted with: He's someone I *know* only *by sight.* —**on sight,** as soon as seen: orders to shoot the escaped killer *on sight.* —**out of sight,** too far away to see; unreasonable. —**sight un·seen,** without preliminary viewing: property purchased *sight unseen.* —**sight·a·ble,** *a.* —**sight·ed,** *a.* —**sight·er,** *n.*

sight·ed, sī′tid, *a.* Having sight or vision.

sight·less, sīt′lis, *a.* Without sight; blind; invisible.

sight·ly, sīt′lē, *a.* Pleasing to the eye.

sight-read, sīt′rēd, *v.t.*, **-read,** -red, **-read·ing.** To read or perform without previous acquaintance with the subject matter, as a musical composition.—*v.i.* To perform at first sight, esp. music.

sight·see·ing, sīt′sē·ing, *n.* The act of visiting points or places of general interest, as in a foreign city.—*a.* Pertaining to seeing sights. —**sight·se·er,** *n.*

sign, sīn, *v.t.* To affix a signature: to *sign* one's name to a document; dispose of by affixing one's signature to a document, followed by *away;* engage by written agreement: baseball club *signs* a new player; to mark or impress with a sign; communicate by a sign.—*v.i.* To write one's signature, as in token of agreement, obligation, or receipt of something; to make a sign or signal; enlist, followed by *up.* —**sign off,** to announce the end of a radio or TV program. —**sign·er,** *n.*

sign, sīn, *n.* An indication; a symbol, used instead of the word or words which it represents, as in math or music; a motion or gesture to express an idea; a signal; an inscribed board, plate, space, or the like providing information, or advertisement, as on or in front of a place of business; a trace or vestige; an omen or portent.

sig·nal, sig′nəl, *n.* Something used or serving to give warning, information, direction, or the like, as a gesture, sound, or object; anything agreed upon or understood as the occasion for concerted action; anything that causes, or incites to action; the electrical impulse transmitted or received in telegraphy, telephony, television, radio, or radar.—*a.* Used for signaling or as a signal; outstanding: a *signal* success.—*v.t.*, **-naled, -nal·ing.** To make a signal or signals to; to communicate signals.—*v.i.* —**sig·nal·er,** *n.*

sig·nal·man, sig′nəl·mən, *n. pl.*, **-men.** A person employed in signaling, as in the army, navy, or on a railroad.

sig·na·to·ry, sig′nə·tôr·ē, *a.* Signing a document, esp. a treaty.—*n. pl.*, **-ries.** A person who signs, esp. a representative of a state, who signs a treaty.

sig·na·ture, sig′nə·chər, *n.* A person's name, or a mark representing it, as signed or written by that person, to a letter or other document; the act of signing a document.

sign·board, sīn′bôrd, *n.* A board displaying information, guiding, or advertising.

sig·net, sig′nit, *n.* A small seal, as in a finger ring; a small seal used for certain official documents; the stamp or impression made by a signet.

sig·nif·i·cance, sig·nif′ə·kəns, *n.* The quality of being significant; meaning; that which is intended to be expressed; importance.

sig·nif·i·cant, sig·nif′ə·kənt, *a.* Having meaning;

suggestive of a concealed meaning: a *significant* look; important.

sig·ni·fi·ca·tion, sig·nə·fə·kā′shən, *n*. The act of signifying; that which is expressed by signs or words; meaning.

sig·ni·fy, sig′nə·fī, *v.t.*, **-fied**, **-fy·ing**. To make known by signs, speech, or action; to be a sign or indication of; represent; to betoken or portend.—*v.i.* To be of importance or consequence. —**sig·ni·fi·a·ble**, *a*. —**sig·ni·fi·er**, *n*.

sign lan·guage, *n*. A system of manual signs or gestures used as a substitute for speech by the deaf or between people who do not speak the same language. Also **hand lan·guage**.

sign·post, sīn′pōst, *n*. A post on which a sign hangs, giving guidance or information; an obvious clue.

si·lage, sī′lij, *n*. Fodder preserved in a silo.

si·lence, sī′ləns, *n*. Absence of any sound; stillness; muteness; omission of mention: to pass over a matter in *silence*.—*v.t.*, **-lenced**, **-lenc·ing**. To put or bring to silence; to still; to put to rest, as doubts or scruples.—*interj.* Be quiet.

si·lenc·er, sī′lən·sər, *n*. One who or that which silences; a device for deadening the report of a firearm.

si·lent, sī′lənt, *a*. Refraining from speech; speechless; making no sound of any kind; noiseless, quiet, or still; tacit or unspoken; taking no open or active part in something.

si·lent part·ner, *n*. One sharing finance but not management of a business.

sil·hou·ette, sil·oo·et′, *n*. A flat representation of the profile, external outline, or shape of a person or thing; the dark solid shape or outline of a thing against a light background: the *silhouette* of a tree.—*v.t.*, **-et·ted**, **-et·ting**. To represent or show in or as in a silhouette.

sil·ic·a, sil′ə·kə, *n*. Silicon dioxide, a hard, white or colorless substance occurring in nature as quartz, sand, flint, opal, agate, and other forms: used in glass manufacture.

sil·i·ca gel, *n*. Silica in a highly adsorbent, colloidal form, used as an agent for dehydrating, and deodorizing air and gases.

sil·i·con, sil′ə·kon, sil′ə·kən, *n*. A nonmetallic element having both crystalline and amorphous forms, occurring in a combined state in rocks and minerals, and constituting more than one-fourth of the earth's crust.

sil·i·cone, sil′ə·kōn, *n*. A compound made by substituting silicon for carbon in substances such as oils, greases, synthetic rubber, and resins, to provide greater stability and resistance to water and to temperature extremes.

silk, silk, *n*. The fine, soft, lustrous fiber obtained from the cocoon of the silkworm; thread, cloth, or any material made of this fiber; a garment of such material; similar fibers produced by some other animal, plant, or process, as the hairlike styles on an ear of corn; a parachute.—*v.i.* To be in the course of developing silk, as corn. —**silk·like**, *a*.

silk·en, sil′kən, *a*. Made of silk; having certain qualities of silk, as softness, smoothness to the touch, delicateness, gloss, sheen, or luster; smooth-tongued or ingratiating; luxurious; clothed in silk.

silk hat, *n*. A man's tall, cylindrical dress hat, usu. covered with shiny, black silk plush.

silk·weed, silk′wēd, *n*. A type of milkweed having silky down in the seed pod.

silk·worm, silk′wɜrm, *n*. A hairless, yellow caterpillar which produces a cocoon of valuable silk and emerges as a moth; any larva which spins a silken cocoon.

silk·y, sil′kē, *a.*, **-i·er**, **-i·est**. Similar to or made of silk; soft and smooth to the touch; glossy; delicate; tender.

—**silk·i·ly**, *adv.* —**silk·i·ness**, *n*.

sill, sil, *n*. A horizontal stone or timber on which a structure rests; the horizontal piece at the bottom of a door, window, or similar opening.

sil·ly, sil′ē, *a.*, **-li·er**, **-li·est**. Deficient in strength of intellect or in common sense, or showing such deficiency, as persons, in the mind, actions, or speech; absurdly foolish, stupid, or senseless; absurd or ridiculous. *Informal.* Stunned or dazed. —**sil·li·ly**, *adv.* —**sil·li·ness**, *n*.

si·lo, sī′lō, *n. pl.*, **si·los**. A pit or chamber, usu. an airproof, towerlike structure, in which green fodder and grain are preserved for future use as ensilage; a pit or underground chamber for storing grain; an underground structure for housing and launching ballistic missiles or rockets.—*v.t.*, **-loed**, **-lo·ing**. To put into or preserve in a silo.

silt, silt, *n*. A deposit of mud or fine soil from running water; fine earthy sediment.—*v.i.* To become filled or choked up with silt; to ooze.—*v.t.* To choke or fill up with silt or mud. —**sil·ta·tion**, sil·tā′shən, *n*. —**silt·y**, sil′tē, *a.*, **-i·er**, **-i·est**.

sil·ver, sil′vər, *n*. A white metallic element, ductile and malleable, having the highest electrical and thermal conductivity of any substance: Money, esp. coin; a standard of government currency; dining utensils, such as hollow-ware made of or plated with this metal; flatware, whether made of this metal or another; a color, specif. a shade of gray.—*a*. Of or referring to this metal; having the sheen or brightness of this metal. *Informal.* Having a certain glibness of speech: a *silver* tongue.—*v.t.* To cover, as flatware, with silver or a similar coating; to apply an amalgam to: to *silver* a mirror; to give a silvery sheen or luster to; to tinge with gray.—*v.i.*

sil·ver bro·mide, *n*. A pale yellow compound, used in coatings for photographic plates and films because of its sensitivity to light.

sil·ver chlo·ride, *n*. A white compound, used esp. in photography and silver plating because of its sensitivity to light.

sil·ver·fish, sil′vər·fish, *n. pl.*, **-fish**, **-fish·es**. A white or silvery variety of the goldfish; any of certain small, silvery, wingless insects, which damage paper, cloth, and books by feeding on the starch in them.

sil·ver fox, *n*. A variation of the common red fox having black, silver-tipped fur.

sil·ver lin·ing, *n*. A reason or prospect for hope in an unfavorable situation.

sil·ver ni·trate, *n*. A white, crystalline salt of silver, widely used in photography and industry and as an antiseptic.

sil·ver plate, *n*. Flatware made of silver or of a base metal coated with silver; the coating itself.

sil·ver screen, *n*. The screen upon which moving pictures are shown; collectively, motion pictures, often preceded by *the*.

sil·ver·smith, sil′vər·smith, *n*. A person whose occupation is repairing or making silver articles.

sil·ver spoon, *n*. Riches, esp. wealth which has been inherited: to be born with a *silver spoon* in one's mouth.

sil·ver stand·ard, *n*. A monetary system or standard in which the basic unit is equivalent to a specified amount and quality of silver.

sil·ver-tongued, sil′vər·təngd′, *a*. Eloquent.

sil·ver·ware, sil′vər·wer, *n*. A collective name for various articles, esp. eating utensils, made of silver, silverplate, or other metals.

sil·ver·y, sil′və·rē, *a*. Like silver in appearance or sound; containing or coated with silver. —**sil·ver·i·ness**, *n*.

sim·i·an, sim′ē·ən, *a*. Pertaining to, characteristic of, or like apes and monkeys.—*n*. An ape or monkey.

---

a- hat, fāte, fâre, fäther; **e**- met, mē; **i**- pin, pīne; **o**- not, nōte, ôrb, moove (move), boy, pownd; **u**- cūbe, bŭll, tûk (took); **ch**- chin; **th**- thick, ᵺen; **zh**- vizhon (vision); **ə**- əgo, takən, pencəl, lemən, bɜrd (bird).

sim·i·lar, sim′ə·lər, *a.* Like; resembling but not identical; having a like form or appearance.

sim·i·lar·i·ty, sim·ə·lar′i·tē, *n. pl.*, **-ties**. The state of being similar; close likeness.

sim·i·le, sim′ə·lē, *n.* A figure of speech likening or comparing two dissimilar things by the use of *like* or as: *Her lips are like roses.*

si·mil·i·tude, si·mil′i·tood, si·mil′i·tūd, *n.* Likeness; a counterpart or double; an imaginative likening, as an allegory or parable.

sim·mer, sim′ər, *v.i.* To make a gentle murmuring sound under the action of continued heat, as liquids just below the boiling point; to continue in a state approaching boiling or just at the point of boiling, as liquids; to continue in a state of subdued activity or suppressed excitement.—*v.t.* To keep in a state or cook in a liquid approaching boiling or just at the point of boiling.—*n.* A process or condition of simmering. —**sim·mer down**, to reduce in amount or quantity by simmering. *Informal.* To become quiet or to calm down.

si·mon·ize, sī′mə·nīz, *v.t.*, **-ized**, **-iz·ing.** To polish or make glossy and smooth, esp. with or as with wax.

Si·mon Le·gree, sī′mən li·grē′, *n.* The brutal slave overseer in *Uncle Tom's Cabin* by Harriet Beecher Stowe; any brutal, relentless master.

sim·pa·ti·co, sim·pä′ti·kō, sim·pat′i·kō, *a. Informal.* Congenial; sympathetic.

sim·per, sim′pər, *v.i.* To smile in a self-conscious, silly, or affected manner; to smirk.—*v.t.* To tell with a simper.—*n.* A smile which is silly or shows self-consciousness; an affected smile or smirk. —**sim·per·er**, *n.* —**sim·per·ing·ly**, *adv.*

sim·ple, sim′pəl, *a.*, **-pler**, **-plest.** Easily intelligible; not complicated; not difficult to use or deal with; plain; not elaborate: a *simple* pattern or design; unaffected and artless in manner; fundamental: the *simple* truth; single; not complex or compound: *simple* fracture; sincere: a *simple*, open reply; common; humble: just *simple* folk; not wise or knowledgeable: a foolishly *simple* brand of logic; naive; gullible; weak in intellect; mentally retarded.—*n.* Something not mixed or compounded; a foolish person. —**sim·ple·ness**, *n.*

sim·ple frac·tion, *n.* A fraction which has whole numbers for both denominator and numerator.

sim·ple in·ter·est, *n.* Interest calculated only on the original principal.

sim·ple ma·chine, *n.* Any of a number of elementary mechanical devices, as the lever, wedge, wheel and axle, pulley, screw, and inclined plane.

sim·ple-mind·ed, sim′pəl-mīn′did, *a.* Artless or without sophistication; lacking in keen mental perception; deficient mentally; foolish. —**sim·ple-mind·ed·ness**, *n.*

sim·ple sen·tence, *n.* A sentence having one main and no subordinate clause.

sim·ple·ton, sim′pəl·tən, *n.* A silly or foolish person.

sim·plex, sim′pleks, *a.* Simple; consisting of or characterized by a single element or action: *simplex* telegraphy, in which one message at a time is sent over a single wire.

sim·plic·i·ty, sim·plis′i·tē, *n. pl.*, **-ties**. The state or quality of being simple; plainness or freedom from ornament, luxury, ostentation, or the like; sincerity or unaffectedness; deficiency of mental acuteness, subtlety, or good sense.

sim·pli·fy, sim′plə·fī, *v.t.*, **-fied**, **-fy·ing.** To make simple, less complicated, or easier. —**sim·pli·fi·ca·tion**, sim·plə·fə·kā′shən, *n.* —**sim·pli·fi·er**, *n.*

sim·plism, sim′pliz·əm, *n.* Oversimplification; reducing a situation or problem to a single factor while disregarding the other complicating factors. —**sim·plis·tic**, sim·plis′tik, *a.* —**sim·plis·ti·cal·ly**, *adv.*

sim·ply, sim′plē, *adv.* In a simple manner; clearly; plainly; sincerely; merely or solely; foolishly; absolutely: *simply* beautiful.

sim·u·late, sim′yə·lāt, *v.t.*, **-lat·ed**, **-lat·ing.** To feign; to assume the appearance or character of; counterfeit; imitate. —**sim·u·la·tion**, sim·yə·lā′shən, *n.* —**sim·u·la·tive**, *a.* —**sim·u·la·tor**, *n.*

si·mul·cast, sī′məl·kast, *v.t.*, **-cast** or **-cast·ed**, **-cast·ing.** To broadcast by radio and television simultaneously.—*n.* A program so broadcasted.

si·mul·ta·ne·ous, sī·məl·tā′nē·əs, sim·əl·tā′nē·əs, *a.* Taking place or happening at the same time; done at the same time. —**si·mul·ta·ne·ous·ness**, **si·mul·ta·ne·i·ty**, sī·məl·tə·nē′i·tē, *n.*

sin, sin, *n.* The voluntary or willful departure of an individual from a custom prescribed by divine law or society in general; wickedness; a transgression; an offense against any standard: a *sin* against community standards.—*v.i.*, **sinned**, **sin·ning.** To commit a sin; to violate any known rule of duty; to transgress.

since, sins, *adv.* From then till now; before now; ago; after that time.—*prep.* Continuously from the time of: *since* yesterday; subsequent to; after.—*conj.* In the interval after the time when: I have been ill twice *since* I saw you last; without interruption, from the time when: *since* we saw you last; because; seeing that; inasmuch as.

sin·cere, sin·sēr′, *a.* Being in inward reality or intent the same as in outward appearance; without guile; honest; hiding or withholding nothing; real, genuine, or true.

sin·cer·i·ty, sin·sar′i·tē, *n.* The quality, condition, or state of being sincere; truthfulness; genuineness; earnestness. Also **sin·cere·ness**, sin·sēr′nis.

sine, sīn, *n.* A function of an acute angle in a right triangle, equal to the ratio of the opposite leg to the hypotenuse.

si·ne·cure, sī′nə·kyûr, sin′ə·kyûr, *n.* Any position which requires little or no work yet usu. pays well; a very easy job.

si·ne qua non, sī′nē kwä non′, *n.* Something indispensable.

sin·ew, sin′ū, *n.* A tendon; that which gives strength or vigor.—*v.t.* To strengthen, as by sinews.

sin·ew·y, sin′ū·ē, *a.* Consisting of or resembling sinews; tough; vigorous.

sin·ful, sin′fəl, *a.* Full of sin; wicked. —**sin·ful·ly**, *adv.* —**sin·ful·ness**, *n.*

sing, sing, *v.i.*, **sang** or **sung**, **sung**, **sing·ing.** To utter words or sounds with musical inflections of the voice; to perform a vocal composition; to make musical sounds, as a violin; to give out a small shrill or humming sound: the kettle *sings*. *Informal.* To disclose information or confess to a crime.—*v.t.* To utter with musical modulations of the voice; to act or produce an effect on by singing: to *sing* one to sleep.—*n.* The performance of a vocal composition; a public gathering for singing; a buzzing, humming, or ringing sound. —**sing out**, to call loudly; shout. —**sing·a·ble**, *a.*

singe, sinj, *v.t.*, **singed**, **sing·ing.** To burn slightly; to scorch; to burn the surface, ends, or outside of.—*n.* A superficial burning of the surface; a slight burn.

sing·er, sing′ər, *n.* One who or that which sings, esp. a skilled or professional vocalist.

sin·gle, sing′gəl, *a.* Alone; solitary; unmarried; consisting of one part or member; unique; one only; separate; suitable for one person: a *single* bed; sincere, honest, dedicated: *single* devotion.—*n.* One individual person or thing; a hotel, restaurant, or other accommodation suitable for just one person; in baseball, a hit which allows the batter to reach first base only. *Pl.* A game or match, as tennis, played with only one person on each side.—*v.t.*, **-gled**, **-gling.** To pick or choose out from others: to *single* out a rose.—*v.i.* In baseball, to make a one-base hit. —**sin·gle·ness**, *n.*

sin·gle-breast·ed, sing′gəl·bres′tid, *a.* Having a front center fastening with only one row of loops, buttons, or the like: a *single-breasted* coat.

sin·gle com·bat, *n.* A fight restricted to two persons.

sin·gle file, n. A file or line of persons or things arranged or moving along one behind another.—*adv.*

sin·gle-hand·ed, sing'gəl·han'did, a. Accomplished by one person; unassisted; possessing or using only one hand. **—sin·gle-hand·ed·ly,** adv. **—sin·gle-hand·ed·ness,** n.

sin·gle-mind·ed, sing'gəl·mīn'did, a. Having or showing a single purpose; steadfast. **—sin·gle-mind·ed·ly,** adv. **—sin·gle-mind·ed·ness,** n.

sin·gle-space, sing'gəl·spās', v.t., v.i., -spaced, -spac·ing. To type or print on every successive blank line.

sin·gle·ton, sing'gəl·tən, n. An only card of a suit in a hand; a single person or thing distinct from others in a group.

sin·gle-track, sing'gəl·trak', a. Having only a single track, as a railroad; able to go or act but one way at a time, as the mind. Also **one-track,** wən'trak.

sin·gly, sing'glē, adv. Individually; separately; each alone; without partners or aid; one at a time.

sing·song, sing'sông, sing'song, n. Regular, rhythmical sounds; verse having regular, monotonous rhyme and rhythm.—a.

sin·gu·lar, sing'gyə·lər, a. Extraordinary or remarkable, as in character or extent: a *singular* success; unusual or strange: a *singular* occurrence; being the only one of the kind; unique; separate; noting a word form which signifies one person or thing: a *singular* noun or a *singular* verb form: opposed to *plural.*—n. The singular number; a word form in this number. **—sin·gu·lar·i·ty,** sing·gyə·lar'i·tē, n. pl., -ties.

sin·is·ter, sin'i·stər, a. Foreboding; ominous; threatening evil or disaster; evil; disastrous or unfortunate. **—sin·is·ter·ness,** n.

sink, singk, v.i., **sank** or **sunk, sunk** or **sunk·en, sink·ing.** To go under or to the bottom, as in water; become submerged; to fall gently downward, as a leaf; to fall slowly from weakness or fatigue; settle down into a reclining, sitting, or kneeling posture: *sink* into a chair; to go down toward or below the horizon, as the sun; to have a downward slope, as ground; to assume a hollow appearance, as the cheeks; to enter, usu. with *in* or *into*, as ideas or truth penetrating into the mind; to pass gradually into some state, as silence; pass or fall into some lower state, as of fortune or estimation; fail markedly in physical strength; to decrease in amount or degree, as value, prices, or rates; become lower in tone or pitch, as the voice.—v.t. To cause to sink or become submerged: to *sink* the enemy's ships; to cause to fall, descend, or go down; to make lower; reduce; to invest, esp. unprofitably. —n. A basin or receptacle, as in a kitchen, equipped with a water supply and drain and used for washing; a place of vice or corruption; a low-lying area where waters collect or disappear by sinking downward or by evaporating; a sinkhole. **—sink·a·ble,** a.

sink·er, sing'kər, n. One who or that which sinks; a weight, as on a fish line or net, to sink it.

sink·hole, singk'hōl, n. A hole or funnel-like cavity formed in rock by the action of water; a depression or hollow where drainage collects.

sin·less, sin'lis, a. Free from or without sin.

sin·ner, sin'ər, n. One who sins.

sin·u·ate, sin'yū·it, sin'yū·āt, a. Bent in and out; winding; sinuous. Also **sin·u·at·ed.** —sin'yū·āt, v.i., -at·ed, -at·ing. To curve or bend in and out; to wind.

sin·u·ous, sin'yū·əs, a. Abounding in curves, bends, or turns; winding; indirect; devious. **—sin·u·os·i·ty,** sin·yū·os'ə·tē, **—sin·u·ous·ness,** n.

si·nus, sī'nəs, n. A curve, bend, or fold; a curving part or recess; any of various cavities, recesses, or passages, as a hollow in a bone, or a reservoir or channel for venous blood; a cranial hollow, containing air, which connects with the nasal cavities.

si·nus·i·tis, sī·nə·sī'tis, n. Inflammation of any sinus, as of those in the bones of the face.

sip, sip, v.t., v.i., **sipped, sip·ping.** To drink by drawing through the lips in small quantities; to drink in or absorb, esp. in small quantities.—n. A small draft taken with the lips; the act of sipping. **—sip·per,** n.

si·phon, sy·phon, sī'fən, n. A curved tube used to convey a liquid up over a side or elevation to a lower level by atmospheric pressure; a bottle which dispenses aerated water by means of gas pressure which drives the liquid out through a tube: also **si·phon bot·tle, sy·phon bot·tle.**—v.t. To convey, remove, or empty by means of a siphon.—v.i. To pass or be conveyed through or as if through any siphon.

sir, sər, n. A respectful or formal term of address used to a man. *(Cap.)* The distinctive title of a knight or a baronet, used before the given name: *Sir* Walter Scott.

sire, sīr, n. The male parent of a mammal; a respectful term of address used to a man, formerly to any superior or elder, but now only to a king or other sovereign.—v.t., **sired, sir·ing.** To beget; become the sire of, now used esp. of stallions and other domestic animals.

si·ren, sī'rən, n. Any of several sea nymphs in Greek mythology, who by their sweet singing brought sailors to rocky destruction; a dangerously enticing woman; an instrument which produces musical tones from air or gas passing forcefully through holes in a rapidly rotating disk; a similar instrument which produces a loud, piercing sound, as to sound a warning.—a. Of a siren; alluring.

sir·loin, sər'loyn, n. The upper part of a loin cut of beef, closest to the rump.

sis·sy, sis'ē, n. pl., -sies. *Informal.* An effeminate boy or man; a coward; a little girl.—a. **—sis·si·fied,** a. **—sis·sy·ish,** a.

sis·ter, sis'tər, n. A female born of the same parents with respect to any other offspring of this same family; any female enjoying the intimacy and affection of a sister; a female belonging to a community of nuns; an object thought of as female in relationship to other similar objects: This ship is the *sister* of the other. **—sis·ter·li·ness,** n. **—sis·ter·ly,** a.

sis·ter·hood, sis'tər·hûd, n. The state of being a sister; a society of females united in one faith or one community, as nuns; a group of women bound by common interests.

sis·ter-in-law, sis'tər·in·lô, n. pl., **sis·ters-in-law.** A husband's or wife's sister; a brother's wife.

sit, sit, v.i., **sat, sit·ting.** To rest upon the haunches or buttocks; to repose on a seat; to remain or rest; be situated or located; to lie or weigh on: Grief *sits* heavily on his heart; to have a position theoretically involving sitting: to baby-*sit*; to perch or to roost; to incubate, as a bird covers and warms eggs for hatching; to suit, often followed by *well*; to fit or suit when put on; to have title to the occupancy of a place in a public assemblage or governing body: The senator *sits* for Ohio; to exercise judicial authority: to *sit* in judgment.—v.t. To usher to, or place in a seat, as a waiter; to contain seats for: a theater that *sits* 500 people.—n. The act of one who is sitting; a session of sitting; the hang or fit of a garment. **—sit on one's hands,** to do nothing. **—sit on,** to squelch or quash. **—sit pret·ty,** to be in a favorable position. **—sit tight,** to be patient. **—sit loose.** *Informal.* To relax. **—sit out,** to outwait. **—sit up,** to extend one's bedtime. *Informal.* To become alert, often followed by *and take notice.* **—sit in on,** to join or be party to.

si·tar, si·tär', n. A stringed instrument of India having a pear-shaped body, a long neck, and a varied number of strings.

sit-down strike, sit'down, n. A strike in which the employees stop work but remain in their place of

---

a- hat, fāte, fāre, fäther; **e-** met, mē; **i-** pin, pīne; **o-** not, nōte, ôrb, moove (move), boy, pownd; **u-** cūbe, bûll, tûk (took); **ch-** chin; **th-** thick, ᴛʜen; **zh-** vizhon (vision); **ə-** əgo, takən, pencəl, lemən, bərd (bird).

employment, refusing to quit the premises until their demands are met. Also **sit-down.**

site, sīt, *n.* A place where anything is constructed or planned: the *site* of the new bank; the scene of an event: the *site* of the explosion.

sit-in, sit′in, *n.* The organized, usu. passive, occupying of premises customarily denied to members of a group: a *sit-in* held in a hotel dining room by Blacks protesting racial discrimination.

sit-ter, sit′ər, *n.* One who sits; a hen that is brooding; a baby-sitter.

sit-ting, sit′ing, *a.* Holding a seated position; for the purpose of sitting; incubating; occupying a place in an official capacity. The act of a person who sits or of a thing which sits; a period of time spent seated for a specific purpose, as for a studio photograph; an authorized meeting of a group; space or time given to meal service, as on shipboard.

sit-ting duck, *n. Informal.* One who or that which is very vulnerable; an easy target.

sit-ting room, *n.* A living room; parlor.

sit-u-ate, sich′ū̇-āt, *v.t.,* **-at-ed, -at-ing.** To give a place to; to locate; to position; to fix permanently.

sit-u-at-ed, sich′ū̇-ā-tid, *a.* Having a site; located; placed or permanently fixed with respect to any other object or place; circumstanced.

sit-u-a-tion, sich-ū̇-ā′shən, *n.* Position or location in respect to physical surroundings; locality; state, condition, or position with respect to society or circumstances; temporary state or position; place, post, or permanent employment; job.

six, siks, *n.* The cardinal number between five and seven; a symbol representing it; a set of six persons or things.—*a.* Being one more than five in number.—**at six-es and sev-ens,** in confusion. —**sixth,** *a., n.*

six-pack, siks′pak, *n.* A package, usu. fitted with a handle, which contains six cans or six bottles of a beverage.

six-shoot-er, siks′shoo-tər, *n. Informal.* A revolver that can fire six shots without being reloaded.

six-teen, siks′tēn′, *n.* The cardinal number between 15 and 17; a symbol representing it; a set of 16 persons or things.—*a.* —**six-teenth,** *a., n.*

sixth sense, siksth, *n.* Intuition.

six-ty, siks′tē, *n.* The cardinal number between 59 and 61; a symbol representing it; a set of 60 persons or things.—*a.* —**six-ti-eth,** *a., n.*

siz-a-ble, size-a-ble, sīz′ə-bəl, *a.* Of considerable size; quite large. —**siz-a-ble-ness,** *n.* —**siz-a-bly,** *adv.*

size, sīz, *n.* The volume, bulk, or spatial surface dimensions of anything; a conventional relative measure of dimension, as of shoes, gloves, or the like; the degree, range, extent, or amount; the total number or the count: the *size* of a class; a usu. succinct recapitulation: That's about the *size* of it.—*v.t.,* **sized, siz-ing.** To make, adjust, or arrange according to size. —**size up.** *Informal.* To form or make a judgment or estimate of: He *sized* the applicant *up* from his appearance; to meet certain specifications or be equivalent to.

size, sīz, *n.* A filler for porous material, such as wood, paper, or cloth, that is compounded of glues and varnishes, or of starches, glutens, or gelatins.—*v.t.,* **sized, siz-ing.** To apply or prepare with sizing. —**siz-ing,** *n.*

sized, sīzd, *a.* Having a particular or specified size: a middle-*sized* house; suitable for a certain size: a purse-*sized* mirror.

siz-zle, siz′əl, *v.i.,* **-zled, -zling.** To make a hissing sound, as in frying or burning. *Informal.* To be very hot; to be angry or resentful: She's *sizzling* over the offense.—*n.* A sizzling sound. —**siz-zler,** *n.*

skate, skāt, *n.* A steel runner or blade fixed to a metal frame that is fastened onto the sole of a shoe, and which enables the wearer to glide rapidly over ice. —*v.i.,* **skat-ed, skat-ing.** To glide or move on or as if on skates. —**skat-er,** *n.*

skate, skāt, *n. pl.,* **skate.** Any of several species of the ray fishes.

skate, skāt, *n. Informal.* An inferior or wornout horse; a nag; a person: a good *skate,* a cheap*skate;* a contemptible individual.

ske·dad·dle, ski·dad′əl, *v.i.,* **-dled, -dling.** *Informal.* To scamper off hastily; run away.—*n. Informal.* A hurried departure.

skeet, skēt, *n.* A type of trapshooting in which the shooter fires at clay disks hurled at varying speeds. Also **skeet shoot-ing.**

skein, skān, *n.* A quantity of thread or yarn formed in loose loops or rounds of uniform size by winding upon a reel; something that suggests the coils or twists of the skein; a flight of a flock of wildfowl.

skel·e·ton, skel′ə-tən, *n.* The total bony framework which sustains the softer body parts of vertebrates; the supporting framework of anything; an outline or rough draft. *Informal.* One who is very thin or lean.—*a.* Of or pertaining to the total bony structure; the barest minimum: Only a *skeleton* crew. —**skel·e·tal,** *a.*

skel·e·ton key, *n.* A key which can be used to open several different locks.

skep·tic, scep·tic, skep′tik, *n.* One who doubts the truth of any principle or system of principles; a disbeliever; one who disbelieves religious doctrines; one who doubts the possibility of any certain knowledge. —**skep·ti·cal, scep·ti·cal,** *a.* —**skep·ti·cism, scep·ti·cism,** skep′tə-siz-əm, *n.*

sketch, skech, *n.* A drawing rapidly executed and intended to give only general features; a first rough draft, as of a play, painting, book, or the like; an outline or general delineation of anything; a short essay, story, or dramatic piece.—*v.t.* To draw a sketch of; to make a rough draft of; to give the principal points or ideas of; to delineate.—*v.i.* To do a sketch. —**sketch·er,** *n.*

sketch·book, skech′bŭk, *n.* A drawing book for making sketches. Also **sketch book.**

sketch·y, skech′ē, *a.,* **-i·er, -i·est.** Possessing the character of a sketch; giving rough outlines; unfinished or superficial. —**sketch·i·ly,** *adv.* —**sketch·i·ness,** *n.*

skew, skū, *a.* Having an oblique position; turned or twisted to one side; slanting; sloping.—*adv.*—*v.i.* To move in an oblique course; turn aside; swerve.—*v.t.* To put askew; to distort.—*n.* A sideward or oblique movement; a slant.

skew·er, skū′ər, *n.* A pin of wood or metal for fastening and holding meat in place while cooking; anything similar in appearance or use.—*v.t.* To fasten with skewers; to pierce.

skew·ness, skū′nis, *n.* The state of being skew; asymmetry in the curve of a statistical frequency distribution.

ski, skē, *n. pl.,* **skis, ski.** One of a pair of long, narrow runners curving up in front, made of metal, wood, or plastic, and fastened to the feet for gliding over snow.—*v.i.,* **skied, ski·ing.** To travel on skis. —**ski·er,** *n.*

skid, skid, *n.* An act of skidding; a sideslip; a plank, bar, log, or the like, esp. one of a pair, on which something heavy may be slid or rolled along; one of a number of such logs forming a skidway; a low, small, sometimes wheeled platform upon which materials are piled to facilitate handling; a shoe or some other device for preventing the wheel of a vehicle from rotating, as when descending a hill.—*v.t.,* **skid·ded, skid·ding.** To place on, equip, or check with skids; to send into a skid.—*v.i.* To slide onward without rotating, as the wheels of a speeding car after sudden braking; to slip sidewards while in motion, as the wheels of a vehicle on an icy surface. —**on the skids.** *Informal.* On a downward route to ruin or defeat. —**skid·der,** *n.*

skid row, *n. (Sometimes cap.) Informal.* An urban area which contains cheap hotels, barrooms, etc., frequented esp. by vagrants and derelicts.

skiff, skif, *n.* Any small, light boat that can be rowed or sailed easily by one person.

ski·ing, skē'ing, *n.* The act, art, or sport of racing, gliding, or jumping on skis.

ski jump, *n.* A specially prepared course, from which a skier may jump; a jump from such a takeoff course.

ski lift, *n.* A motor-driven device which conveys skiers up a slope or mountain.

skill, skil, *n.* A developed proficiency or dexterity in some art, craft, or the like; a trade or craft requiring special training. **—skilled,** *a.*

skil·let, skil'it, *n.* A frying pan.

skil·ful, skil'fəl, *a.* Having skill; dexterous; expert. **—skill·ful·ly,** *adv.* **—skill·ful·ness,** *n.*

skim, skim, *v.t.,* **skimmed, skim·ming.** To clear, as liquid, from any substance floating on the top; to lift or remove, as floating substance, from liquid: to *skim* cream from milk; to pass or move lightly and rapidly over; to cause to move or pass lightly and rapidly over: to *skim* a pebble across water; to glance over in a superficial manner: to *skim* a newspaper article.—*v.i.* To pass lightly and rapidly over a surface; to glance over hastily; to become coated or covered with a film.—*n.* An instance of skimming; something skimmed off, as cream.—*a.* Skimmed.

skim·mer, skim'ər, *n.* One who or that which skims; a flat spoon or ladle for skimming liquids; a wide-brimmed, flat-crowned hat, usu. made of hard straw.

skim milk, *n.* Milk from which the cream has been removed. Also **skimmed milk.**

skim·ming, skim'ing, *n.* The act of one who or that which skims. *Usu. pl.* That which is removed by skimming.

skimp, skimp, *v.t.* To scrimp; to stint the amount of; to do carelessly.—*v.i.* To use stingy economy; to scamp work.—*a.* Meager; scanty. **—skimp·i·ly,** *adv.* **—skimp·i·ness,** *n.* **—skimp·ing·ly,** *adv.*

skimp·y, skim'pē, *a.,* **-i·er, -i·est.** Scanty; meager; parsimonious.

skin, skin, *n.* The external covering of an animal body, esp. when soft and flexible; such covering stripped from the body of a small animal, as distinguished from the *hide* of a large animal; a hide or pelt; a vessel made of the skin of an animal, used for holding liquids; any outer coating, as the rind or peel of fruit.—*v.t.,* **skinned, skin·ning.** To furnish or cover with or as with skin; strip or deprive of skin; peel; to strip or pull off, as a covering; to abrade or scrape skin from: to *skin* an elbow. *Informal.* To strip of money or belongings; to fleece, as in gambling or any sharp practice.—*v.i.* To become covered with skin, as a wound. **—by the skin of one's teeth.** *Informal.* By a very narrow margin; barely. **—get un·der one's skin.** *Informal.* To irritate; annoy; impress deeply. **—save one's skin.** *Informal.* To escape or avoid bodily or personal harm. **—skinned,** *a.*

skin-deep, skin'dēp', *a., adv.* Not penetrating beyond the skin; superficial; slight.

skin div·ing, *n.* A water sport in which a swimmer wearing a light mask or goggles, fins, and a device for breathing, is able to explore underwater. **—skin-dive,** skin'dīv, *v.i.,* **-dived** or **-dove, -div·ing. —skin div·er,** *n.*

skin·flint, skin'flint, *n.* A stingy person.

skin graft, *n.* The skin transplanted in skin grafting.

skin graft·ing, *n.* The process whereby pieces of healthy skin are transplanted from a donor's or the patient's body to replace skin which has been destroyed, as by burns.

skin·less, skin'lis, *a.* Having no skin.

skin·ner, skin'ər, *n.* One who skins; one who prepares skins, as for the market; a dealer in skins. *U.S. Informal.* A driver of mules, oxen, or other draft animals.

skin·ny, skin'ē, *a.,* **-ni·er, -ni·est.** Very thin; undesirably slender; emaciated.

skin·tight, skin'tīt', *a.* Fitting nearly as tightly as the skin, as an item of clothing.

skip, skip, *v.i.* To spring, jump, or leap lightly from the ground; to move along with light, springing movements; to ricochet; to pass from one point, thing, or subject to another, disregarding or omitting whatever intervenes. *Informal.* To leave hastily or secretly.—*v.t.* To jump lightly over; to miss, or disregard, as one step in a series; to send, as a missile, ricocheting along a surface. *Informal.* To leave hastily, or flee from.—*n.* A skipping movement.

ski pole, *n.* A pointed metal pole used in pairs as a skiing aid.

skip·per, skip'ər, *n.* The captain of a ship; any captain or leader.—*v.t.* To act as captain of, as a ship.

skir·mish, skər'mish, *n.* A brief fight in war between small parties; a short, minor contest of any kind.—*v.i.* To take part in a skirmish. **—skir·mish·er,** *n.*

skirt, skərt, *n.* The lower and loose part of a coat or other garment from the waist downward; a woman's garment resembling a petticoat; something that resembles a skirt; a border, margin, or extreme part.—*v.t.* To border; to evade: The speaker *skirted* any controversial issues.—*v.i.* To be on or pass along the border of. **—skirt·er,** *n.*

skirt·ing, skər'ting, *n.* Cloth for making skirts; an edging or border; a bordering finish of wood or other material placed along the base of an interior wall of a building.

skit, skit, *n.* A short, comic, theatrical scene.

ski tow, *n.* One of the various types of ski lifts consisting of an endless, motor-driven rope which skiers grasp to be pulled up a slope.

skit·ter, skit'ər, *v.i.* To go, run, or glide lightly or rapidly; skim or skip along a surface.—*v.t.* To cause to skitter.

skit·tish, skit'ish, *a.* Easily frightened, as a horse; shy or timid; restlessly playful or lively; changeable or fickle.

skiv·vy, skiv'ē, *n. pl.,* **-vies.** *Informal.* A man's undershirt. *Pl.* Such a shirt and shorts.

skoal, skōl, *interj.* A toast wishing good health to someone in drinking.

skul·dug·ger·y, skull·dug·ger·y, skəl·dəg'ə·rē, *n. Informal.* Trickery; deviousness.

skulk, skəlk, *v.i.* To lie or wait in hiding, as for a sinister purpose; to lurk or move around in a sneaky manner. —*n.* One who skulks. **—skulk·er,** *n.*

skull, skəl, *n.* The cranium or bony case that forms the framework of the head and encloses the brain; the brain as the seat of intelligence: Can't you get it through your thick *skull?*

skull and cross·bones, *n.* A representation of the face of a human skull, with two bones crossed beneath it, formerly the design on a pirate flag, now a generalized warning of danger to life.

skull·cap, skəl'kap, *n.* A brimless cap fitting closely to the head; the upper, domed part of the skull, covering the brain.

skunk, skəngk, *n.* Any of various small, black-and-white, omnivorous mammals of N. America, provided with glands that eject a fetid fluid when the animal is disturbed. *Informal.* A despicable person.

sky, skī, *n. pl.,* **skies.** The apparent arch of heaven; the firmament. *Pl.* The region of clouds; weather; climate. —*v.t.,* **skied, sky·ing.** To hit or throw, as a ball, high into the air.

sky blue, *n.* A color of blue, as of the sky on a day that is clear. **—sky-blue,** skī'bloo', *a.*

sky·cap, skī'kap, *n.* A person employed to carry passenger luggage at an airport.

---

a- hat, fāte, fâre, fäther; e- met, mē; i- pin, pīne; o- not, nōte, ôrb, moove (move), boy, pownd; u- cūbe, bůll, tůk (took); ch- chin; th- thick, ťhen; zh- vizhon (vision); ə- ego, takən, pencəl, lemən, bərd (bird).

sky·div·ing, skī′dī·ving, *n.* The sport of jumping from an airplane and performing various acrobatic maneuvers before opening the parachute.

sky-high, skī′hī′, *a., adv.* As high as the sky; very high.

sky·lark, skī′lärk, *n.* A European lark, celebrated for the song it sings as it rises in flight.—*v.i.* To frolic; play pranks.

sky·light, skī′līt, *n.* A window admitting daylight, as through the roof of a house.

sky·line, skī′līn, *n.* The horizon that is visible; a silhouette, as of trees or buildings, observed against the sky.

sky·rock·et, skī′rok·it, *n.* A rocket that ascends high in the air, exploding with brilliant sparks and color. —*v.i.* To shoot up rapidly, as prices.

sky·scrap·er, skī′skrā·pər, *n.* A very high building, characteristically American.

sky·ward, skī′wərd, *a., adv.* Directed toward the sky. —**sky·wards,** *adv.*

sky·way, skī′wā, *n.* An elevated highway, usu. over a densely populated area. *Informal.* An air lane.

sky·writ·ing, skī′rī·ting, *n.* The writing in the air, as for advertising purposes, done by means of vapor discharged from an airplane. —**sky·writ·er,** *n.*

slab, slab, *n.* A broad, flat, somewhat thick piece of stone, wood, or other solid material; a thick slice of anything: a *slab* of meat.—*v.t.,* **slabbed, slab·bing.** To make into slabs; to cover with slabs.

slack, slak, *a.* Not drawn tightly, as a rope; not tense or taut; loose; negligent or remiss; slow or sluggish, as the water; not brisk or active, as business or work; soft or limp, as a handclasp.—*adv.* In a slack manner.—*n.* A slack condition.—*v.t.* To neglect or shirk; to cause or allow to become slack or less intense.—*v.i.* To be slack or remiss; to become less vigorous; to become less taut. —**slack·ness,** *n.*

slack·en, slak′ən, *v.t.* To make less active or intense, as efforts or pace; to make looser or less taut.—*v.i.* To become less active; to become less tense or taut.

slack·er, slak′ər, *n.* A person who shirks duties or work.

slack-jawed, slak′jôd′, *a.* Having one's mouth hanging open, as in surprise.

slacks, slaks, *n. pl.* Men's or women's trousers, esp. for casual wear.

slag, slag, *n.* Vitrified mineral waste removed in the reduction of metals from their ores; cinder.

slake, slāk, *v.t.,* **slaked, slak·ing.** To quench, as thirst; to satisfy; to abate; to lessen; to cause crumbling of, as quicklime, by mixing with water.—*v.i.* To become slaked.

sla·lom, slä′ləm, slä′lōm, *n.* In skiing, a descent or race down a wavy or zigzag course marked by upright poles.—*v.i.* To ski over such a course.

slam, slam, *v.t.,* **slammed, slam·ming.** To shut with force and noise, as a door; thrust or cast violently and noisily: He *slammed* the window; dash or throw with a bang: She *slammed* the ball against the wall. *Informal.* To strike or hit violently; to criticize severely.—*v.i.* To close with a bang, as a door; dash or strike with violent and noisy impact: shutters *slamming* in the wind.—*n.* A slamming, as of a door; a violent and noisy closing, dashing, or impact, or the noise made; a bang. *Informal.* A violent blow; severe or captious criticism; in bridge, the winning of all 13 tricks in one deal (**grand slam**), or of all but one (**little** or **small slam**).

slam-bang, slam′bang′, *adv. Informal.* With noisy or headlong violence.—*a. Informal.* Violent and noisy; careless and quick.

slan·der, slan′dər, *n.* A false report maliciously uttered, and tending to injure the reputation of another; the uttering of such reports.—*v.t.* To defame by slander.—*v.i.* To speak slander. —**slan·der·er,** *n.* —**slan·der·ous,** *a.*

slang, slang, *n.* Colloquial words and phrases typically more colorful, inelegant, or short-lived than those in standard usage; vocabulary peculiar to a profession or group; jargon.—*v.i.* To use slang.—*v.t.* To address with slang.—*a.* —**slang·i·ly,** *adv.* —**slang·i·ness,** *n.* —**slang·y,** *a.,* **-i·er, -i·est.**

slant, slant, *v.i.* To have or take an oblique direction or position; to slope; to have bias.—*v.t.* To give an oblique direction or position to; to present, as information, so as to reflect a certain attitude or bias.—*n.* A slanting or oblique direction or position; slope; a bias; viewpoint.—*a.* Slanting; oblique. —**slant·ways,** slant′wāz, *adv.* —**slant·wise,** slant′wīz, *a., adv.*

slap, slap, *n.* A smart blow, esp. with the open hand or with something flat; a smack; a sound like that made by a slap; a direct rebuke.—*v.t.,* **slapped, slap·ping.** To strike smartly, esp. with the open hand or with something flat; slam; to insult.—*v.i.* To strike or beat with a sharp, resounding impact, as waves.—*adv. Informal.* With or as with a slap; suddenly; directly. —**slap·per,** *n.*

slap·dash, slap′dash, *adv.* In a careless, hasty manner.—*a.* Careless; haphazard.

slap·hap·py, slap′hap·ē, *a.,* **-pi·er, -pi·est.** *Informal.* Punch-drunk; giddy.

slap·stick, slap′stik, *n.* A type of broad comedy in which rough play and knockabout methods prevail. —*a.* Using or marked by the use of broad, rough comedy.

slash, slash, *v.t.* To cut or wound with a sweeping stroke, as of an edged instrument; gash; to make slits in, as a garment, in order to show an underlying fabric of different color or kind; to assail sharply, as with criticism.—*v.i.* To deliver a sweeping, cutting stroke, as at something; to make one's way by or as by cutting, as through the waves.—*n.* A sweeping stroke, as with an edged instrument or a whip; a gash. —**slash·er,** *n.*

slash·ing, slash′ing, *a.* Dealing sweeping, cutting strokes; sharp and violent; unsparingly severe, as criticism.—*n.* A slash.

slat, slat, *n.* A long, thin, narrow strip of wood or metal; a lath.—*v.t.,* **slat·ted, slat·ting.** To furnish or make with slats. —**slat·ted,** *a.*

slate, slāt, *n.* A fine-grained rock formed by the compression of clay, shale, or sometimes coal, that tends to split along parallel cleavage planes; a thin piece or plate of this rock or a similar material, used esp. for roofing; tentative list of candidates, officers, or the like to be considered for acceptance by a nominating committee; a dark, dull, bluish or purplish-gray color like that of slate; a record of behavior or deeds: a clean *slate*.—*v.t.,* **slat·ed, slat·ing.** To cover or roof with slates; to set down, designate, or schedule for nomination or action.—*a.* —**slate·like,** *a.* —**slat·y,** *a.,* **-i·er, -i·est.**

slath·er, slath′ər, *v.t. Informal.* To spread thickly or in a lavish manner, as jam on bread.—*n. Usu. pl.* Lavish or wasteful amounts.

slat·tern, slat′ərn, *n.* A slovenly, untidy woman; a slut. —**slat·tern·li·ness,** *n.* —**slat·tern·ly,** *a., adv.*

slaugh·ter, slô′tər, *n.* The killing or butchering of cattle, sheep, or pigs, for food; the brutal killing of a person; a massacre; carnage.—*v.t.* To kill or butcher, as animals, for food; to slay in a violent manner; to slay in great numbers; to massacre. —**slaugh·ter·er,** *n.*

slaugh·ter·house, slô′tər·hows, *n.* A place in which animals are butchered for the market.

Slav, släv, slav, *a.* Of, pertaining to, or characteristic of the Slavs; Slavic.—*n.* One of a race of peoples widely spread over eastern, southeastern, and central Europe. Also **Slav·ic.**

slave, slāv, *n.* One who is the property of another; a bond servant; one entirely under the domination of some influence: a *slave* to a drug; one who labors like a slave; a drudge.—*v.i.,* **slaved, slav·ing.** To work like a slave; to traffic in or hold slaves.

slave driv·er, *n.* An overseer of slaves at their work; a harsh or exacting taskmaster.

slav·er, slav′ər, *v.i.* To allow saliva to issue from the mouth; slobber.—*v.t.* To smear with saliva.—*n.* Saliva driveling from the mouth; drivel or nonsense.

slav·er, slă′vər, *n.* A dealer in or an owner of slaves; a vessel engaged in slave traffic.

slav·er·y, slā′və·rē, slăv′rē, *n.* The state or condition of a slave, bondage; complete subjection; the system of keeping slaves; a condition of subjection resembling that of slaves, as to a habit; drudgery.

slav·ish, slā′vish, *a.* Pertaining to or befitting a slave: *slavish* submission; servilely imitative, or lacking originality. —**sla·vish·ly,** *adv.* —**slav·ish·ness,** *n.*

slaw, slô, *n.* Sliced or chopped cabbage served cold or hot, with dressing; coleslaw.

slay, slā, *v.t.,* **slew, slain, slay·ing.** To put to death in a violent manner. *Informal.* To overwhelm: He *slays* his competition everywhere he goes. —**slay·er,** *n.*

slea·zy, slē′zē, *a.,* **-zi·er, -zi·est.** Lacking firmness of texture; flimsy; cheap in quality. —**slea·zi·ly,** *adv.* —**slea·zi·ness,** *n.*

sled, sled, *n.* A vehicle mounted on runners for conveying loads or people over snow, ice, or rough ground; a sledge; a small vehicle of this kind, as used in coasting; a sleigh.—*v.t.,* **sled·ded, sled·ding.** To convey on a sled.—*v.i.* To ride or to be carried on a sled. —**sled·der,** *n.*

sled·ding, sled′ing, *n.* The act of conveying or riding on a sled; the state or condition of any work or progress: hard *sledding.*

sledge, slej, *n.* A sledge hammer.—*v.t.,* **sledged, sledg·ing.** To pound or strike with a sledge hammer.

sledge, slej, *n.* A vehicle mounted on low runners for the conveyance of loads or passengers over snow, ice, or rough ground; a sled.—*v.t.,* **sledged, sledg·ing.** To convey in a sledge.—*v.i.* To travel with a sledge.

sledge ham·mer, *n.* A large, heavy hammer, usu. wielded with both hands.

sleek, slēk, *a.* Smooth or glossy to the touch or in appearance, as fur, an animal, or the like; having a well-fed or well-groomed appearance; smooth or suave in speech, manners, or the like.—*v.t.* To make smooth or glossy. —**sleek·er,** *n.* —**sleek·ness,** *n.*

sleep, slēp, *v.i.,* **slept, sleep·ing.** To take rest afforded by a voluntary suspension of the bodily functions and the natural suspension of consciousness; slumber; to lie in death; to be quiet or still, as the sea.—*v.t.* To take rest in, as a particular type of sleep: to *sleep* the sleep of the righteous; to spend, as the time, in sleep, usu. used with *away* or *out;* to get rid of, as a headache, by sleeping, usu. used with *off* or *away.*—*n.* The state of a person or an animal that sleeps; a period of sleeping or slumber; the repose of death; quiet or stillness; dormancy or inactivity. —**sleep on,** to postpone a decision upon. —**sleep with,** to engage in sexual intercourse with.

sleep·er, slē′pər, *n.* One who or that which sleeps; a railroad sleeping car. *Often pl.* A sleeping garment with feet, usu. worn by children. *Informal.* An unnoticed or unpromising book, play, racehorse, etc., which achieves striking success.

sleep·ing bag, *n.* A large, front-zippered bag used for sleeping outdoors.

sleep·ing sick·ness, *n.* A disease, generally fatal, which is common in certain parts of Africa, characterized usu. by fever, weight loss, and progressive lethargy, and caused by a parasite.

sleep·less, slēp′lis, *a.* Wakeful; unable to sleep. —**sleep·less·ness,** *n.*

sleep·walk, slēp′wôk, *v.i.* To walk while asleep. —**sleep·walk·er,** *n.* —**sleep·walk·ing,** *n.*

sleep·y, slē′pē, *a.,* **-i·er, -i·est.** Drowsy; characterized by drowsiness: *sleepy* eyes; lethargic or sluggish; quiet: the *sleepy* streets of the village. —**sleep·i·ly,** *adv.* —**sleep·i·ness,** *n.*

sleep·y·head, slē′pē·hed, *n.* A sleepy or drowsy person.

sleet, slēt, *n.* Snow or rain in a half-frozen state; a covering of ice that forms, as on roads or trees, when rain freezes; the combination of rain with either hail or snow.—*v.i.* To fall as sleet. —**sleet·y,** *a.* —**sleet·i·ness,** *n.*

sleeve, slēv, *n.* The part of a garment that is fitted to cover the arm; a tubular part that fits around a cylindrical shaft.—*v.t.,* **sleeved, sleev·ing.** To put in sleeves. —**laugh in** or **up one's sleeve,** to be inwardly amused, often with disdain. —**up one's sleeve,** hidden but readily available: He had several plans *up his sleeve.* —**sleeved,** *a.* —**sleeve·less,** slēv′lis, *a.*

sleigh, slā, *n.* A light, usu. open vehicle on runners generally drawn by a horse or horses, used for carrying passengers or goods over snow and ice.—*v.i.* To travel or ride in a sleigh. —**sleigh·er,** *n.*

sleigh bell, *n.* A small bell, commonly attached to the harness of a horse drawing a sleigh.

sleight, slīt, *n.* Skill; dexterity; craftiness. —**sleight of hand,** dexterity in moving the hands, esp. as a skill of magicians or jugglers; legerdemain; prestidigitation.

slen·der, slen′dər, *a.* Small in proportion to height or length, as persons, animals, or things; slim; thin, as a book; small in size; meager or scanty. —**slen·der·ness,** *n.*

slen·der·ize, slen′də·rīz, *v.t., v.i.,* **-ized, -iz·ing.** To make or to become slender or more slender.

sleuth, slooth, *n. Informal.* A detective.—*v.t., v.i.* To track as a detective.

slew, sloo, *v.* Past tense of **slay.**

slew, sloo, *n.* A swamp or backwater. Also **slough.**

slew, sloo, *n. Informal.* A large amount.

slice, slīs, *n.* A thin, broad, flat piece cut from something: a *slice* of bread; a part, portion, or share of something; a cut or movement as in slicing.—*v.t.,* **sliced, slic·ing.** To cut into slices; divide into parts, or shares; to cut as or like a slice, often used with *off, away, from.*—*v.i.* To cut slices; to cut through something, as with a knife. —**slic·er,** *n.*

slick, slik, *a.* Sleek, smooth, or glossy; craftily smooth of speech, or behavior; sly; clever; slippery, esp. as a roadway or walkway; glib, superficial, as the output of certain authors, or the magazine that features such writing. *Informal.* First rate.—*n.* A slippery or greasily smooth place or spot, as an oil-covered area on water. *Informal.* A magazine featuring glib or superficial writing.—*adv.* In a slick manner.—*v.t.* To make sleek; to make smart or fine, often followed by *up.* —**slick·ness,** *n.*

slick·er, slik′ər, *n.* A long, loose, oilskin or waterproof outer coat; a raincoat. *Informal.* A tricky person; a sophisticated city dweller.

slide, slīd, *v.i.,* **slid, slid** or **slidden, slid·ing.** To move along in continuous contact with a smooth or slippery surface under the impetus of a thrust or initial effort: to *slide* on ice; slip, followed by *down, off;* to slip; to glide, as over ground; go unregarded, or take its own course: to let matters *slide.*—*v.t.* To cause to slip or slide, as over a surface, or with a smooth, gliding motion; slip, as some article, easily or quietly, followed by *in, into.*—*n.* The act or an act of sliding; a smooth surface, esp. of ice, for sliding on; a chute for children's play; a landslide; an avalanche; the mass of matter sliding down; a plate of glass or other material on which objects are placed for microscopic examination; a transparent photographic plate for projection on a screen; a chute; a sliding piece or part; a rail or groove on or in which something slides. —**slid·er,** *n.*

slide rule, *n.* A device used for rapid mathematical calculation, consisting essentially of a rule having a sliding piece moving along it, both parts being marked with graduated logarithmic scales.

slight, slīt, *a.* Small in amount or degree: a *slight* increase; of little importance; slender or slim; frail or flimsy.—*v.t.* To treat as of slight importance; disregard or ignore, as in contempt.—*n.* Slighting indifference or treatment; an instance of slighting treatment. —**slight·er,** *n.* —**slight·ing,** *a.*

slim, slim, *a.,* **slim·mer, slim·mest.** Slender; slight; flimsy; inferior; small.—*v.t., v.i.,* **slimmed, slim·ming.** To make or become slender. —**slim·ness,** *n.*

slime, slīm, *n.* Thin, glutinous mud; any ropy or viscous liquid matter, esp. of a foul or unpleasant kind; a viscous secretion: the trail of *slime* left by a snail.—*v.t.,* **slimed, slim·ing.** To cover or smear with or as with slime.

slim·y, slī′mē, *a.,* **-i·er, -i·est.** Like or consisting of slime; revolting. —**slim·i·ly,** *adv.* —**slim·i·ness,** *n.*

sling, sling, *n.* An instrument for hurling stones and other missiles, consisting of a strap with two strings attached, the impetus being supplied by whirling the whole rapidly before releasing one string, thus discharging the missile; a slingshot; a bandage for holding an injured limb suspended; a shoulder strap by which something is suspended or carried, as a rifle; the act or an instance of slinging.—*v.t.,* **slung, sling·ing.** To throw, cast, hurl, or fling, as from the hand; a slingshot, or other slinging device; to place in or secure with a sling; to raise, lower, or otherwise move by such means; to suspend. —**sling·er,** *n.*

sling·shot, sling′shot, *n.* A forked piece of wood which has an elastic band fastened to the prongs for shooting small stones and pebbles.

slink, slingk, *v.i.,* **slunk, slink·ing.** To go in a furtive manner, as from fear or shame; to creep stealthily.

slink·y, sling′kē, *a.,* **-i·er, -i·est.** Characterized by slow, slinking movements. *Informal.* Delineating the figure and its movements: a *slinky* dress.

slip, slip, *v.i.,* **slipped, slip·ping.** To pass or go smoothly or easily; to glide or slide, followed by *along, away, down, off, over, through:* a scarf that *slips off;* to slide suddenly and involuntarily, as on a smooth surface; to lose one's foothold; to move, slide, or start from place, position, or fastening: an ax *slips* from the handle; to get away, escape, or be lost: to let an opportunity *slip;* to pass insensibly, as from the mind or memory; to pass quickly or imperceptibly, as time, followed by *away, by;* to get easily or quickly into or out of: to *slip* into or out of a garment; to go quietly or steal: She *slipped* in the back door; pass carelessly or without attention, as over a matter; to make an error or mistake.—*v.t.* To pass, put, or draw with a smooth, easy, or sliding motion: to *slip* one's hand into a drawer; to put on or take off easily or quickly, as a garment, followed by *on* or *off;* escape from, as a pursuer; to let pass unheeded; to escape, as one's memory.—*n.* The act of slipping; an error in judgment or conduct; a mistake, often inadvertently made, as in speaking or writing: a *slip* of the tongue; a woman's undergarment of dress or skirt length; a pillowcase; an inclined plane sloping to the water, on which vessels are built or repaired; a pasture in a dock, for vessels to lie in. —**let slip,** to reveal unintentionally. —**slip some·thing ov·er on.** *Informal.* To deceive.

slip, slip, *n.* A piece cut from a plant suitable for propagation; a young, slender person; a cutting; any strip: a *slip* of paper; a paper form used as a record: a sales *slip.*—*v.t.,* **slipped, slip·ping.** To take cuttings: to *slip* a philodendron.

slip·cov·er, slip′kəv·ər, *n.* A fitted, removable covering made of cloth or plastic, used on upholstered furniture.

slip·knot, slip′not, *n.* A knot which may easily be slipped or undone.

slip-on, slip′on, slip′ôn, *a.* Designed to be put on easily over the head: *slip-on* sweater.—*n.* A slip-on garment.

slip·o·ver, slip′ō·vər, *a.* Designed for easily slipping over the head, as a blouse or a sweater; pullover.—*n.* A slipover garment.

slip·page, slip′ij, *n.* The act of slipping, as of gears; the amount of slipping.

slipped disk, *n.* An inflamed or displaced intervertebral disk resulting in pressure on the spinal nerves.

slip·per, slip′ər, *n.* A low-cut, lightweight shoe, easily slipped on and off, worn mainly indoors: bedroom *slippers;* a fancy shoe, designed for formal wear: evening *slippers.*

slip·per·y, slip′ə·rē, slip′rē, *a.,* **-i·er, -i·est.** Allowing or causing anything to slip readily; not to be trusted; tricky. —**slip·per·i·ness,** *n.*

slip·py, slip′ē, *a.,* **-pi·er, -pi·est.** Slippery.

slip·shod, slip′shod, *a.* Wearing slippers, esp. ones worn down at the heel; untidy; slovenly.

slip·stick, slip′stik, *n. Informal.* Slide rule.

slip-up, slip′əp, *n. Informal.* A slip, failure, mistake, error, or oversight. —**slip up,** *v.i.,* **slipped, slip·ping.**

slit, slit, *v.t.,* **slit, slit·ting.** To cut lengthwise; to cut into long pieces or strips; to cut a long fissure or opening in.—*n.* A long, narrow opening; a slash. —**slit·ter,** *n.*

slith·er, slith′ər, *v.i.* To slide down or along a surface, as a snake; slip along.—*v.t.* To cause to slide.—*n.* A slithering movement; a slide. —**slith·er·y,** *a.*

sliv·er, sliv′ər, *n.* A small piece, as of wood, split, broken, or cut off; a slender fragment or piece; a splinter.—*v.t.* To split or cut off, as a sliver; split or cut into slivers.—*v.i.* To split. —**sliv·er·er,** *n.* —**sliv·er·like,** *a.*

slob, slob, *n. Informal.* A person who is untidy, stupid, or boorish.

slob·ber, slob′ər, *v.t.* To let saliva or other liquid run from the mouth; to drool; to gush with excessive sentimentality.—*v.t.* To wet or make foul by slobbering; to utter with slobbering.—*n.* Saliva or liquid dribbling from the mouth; gushing, excessively sentimental talk or actions. Also **slab·ber.** —**slob·ber·er,** *n.* —**slob·ber·ing·ly,** *adv.* —**slob·ber·y,** *a.*

sloe, slō, *n.* A dark purple, plumlike fruit; the thorny shrub it grows on; blackthorn.

sloe-eyed, slō′īd, *a.* Having slanted or soft, dark eyes.

slo·gan, slō′gən, *n.* A catchword or phrase, as of a political party or in advertising. —**slo·gan·eer,** slō·gə·nēr′, *n.*

sloop, sloop, *n.* A vessel with one mast, fore-and-aft sails, and usu. one jib.

slop, slop, *n.* Liquid mud; liquid refuse. *Informal.* Unappetizing liquid or food. *Pl.* Swill.—*v.t.,* **slopped, slop·ping.** To spill or splash, as liquid; to drink or eat messily and noisily; to feed with slops, as livestock. —*v.i.* To walk or go through mud, slush, or water; to spill or splash liquid.

slope, slōp, *n.* Inclination or slant; an inclined surface, extent of land, etc.—*v.i.,* **sloped, slop·ing.** To take or have an inclined or slanting direction downward or upward from the horizontal; to slant.—*v.t.* To direct at a slope or inclination; to form with a slope or slant. —**slop·er,** *n.*

slop·py, slop′ē, *a.,* **-pi·er, -pi·est.** Muddy, slushy, or very wet: The ground is *sloppy* after a heavy rain; splashed or soiled with liquid; watery and unappetizing. *Informal.* Careless; untidy, as in dress. —**slop·pi·ly,** *adv.* —**slop·pi·ness,** *n.*

slosh, slosh, *n.* Slush or watery snow; the splash of any liquid.—*v.i.* To splash in slush, mud, or water.—*v.t.* To splash around in a liquid; to splash with a liquid.

slosh·y, *a.,* **-i·er, -i·est.** Slushy.

slot, slot, *n.* A narrow depression, slit, or groove, esp. one to receive or admit something: a coin *slot;* a position or place in a succession, series, or sequence.—*v.t.,* **slot·ted, slot·ting.** To provide with a slot or slots; to make a slot in.

sloth, slôth, slōth, sloth, *n.* Disinclination to action; laziness; any of several American mammals which live in trees and are characterized by sluggish movements. —**sloth·ful,** *a.* —**sloth·ful·ly,** *adv.* —**sloth·ful·ness,** *n.*

slot ma·chine, *n.* A machine for vending small articles, gambling, or weighing, operated by dropping a coin in a slot.

slouch, slowch, *v.i.* To sit, stand, or move in an awkward, drooping manner; to have a droop or downward bend, as a hat.—*v.t.* To cause to droop or bend down.—*n.* A drooping or bending forward; an awkward, or slovenly person. *Informal.* An awkward, inefficient, or incompetent person, esp. used negatively: He's no *slouch* at this game. **—slouch·er,** *n.* **—slouch·i·ly,** *adv.* **—slouch·i·ness,** *n.* **—slouch·y,** *a.,* **-i·er, -i·est.**

slough, slow, sloo, *n.* A section of soft, muddy ground or bog; a marsh or swamp; a boggy depression in an otherwise dry area such as a prairie. Also **slew, slue.** A condition of degradation or helplessness: mired in a *slough* of ignorance. **—slough·y,** *a.,* **-i·er, -i·est.**

slough, sləf, *n.* The outer skin of a snake which is shed periodically; any part of an animal that is naturally shed or molted; anything that is shed or cast off.—*v.i.* To be shed or cast off, as the slough or skin of a snake.—*v.t.* To shed as or like a slough; to cast, throw off, usu. followed by *off:* to *slough off* responsibility. **—slough·i·ness,** *n.* **—slough·y,** *a.,* **-i·er, -i·est.**

slov·en, sləv'ən, *n.* One who is habitually negligent of personal appearance or habits; one who works or acts in a negligent, slipshod manner.

slov·en·ly, sləv'ən·lē, *a.,* **-li·er, -li·est.** Having the habits of a sloven; careless or slipshod. **—slov·en·li·ness,** *n.*

slow, slō, *a.* Sluggish in nature or function; naturally inactive; dull of understanding; tardy: *slow* in arriving; not readily disposed, used with *to: slow to* wrath; taking a long time for acting or occurring: a *slow* walker; not fast; slack, as trade; running at less than the proper rate of speed; indicating a time earlier than the correct time, as a clock or watch; behind the times: a *slow* old town; dull or tedious: *slow* company.—*adv.*—*v.t.* To make slow or slower; reduce the speed of.—*v.i.* To become slow or slower. **—slow·ish,** *a.* **—slow·ness,** *n.*

slow·down, slō'down, *n.* A slowing of motion or effort, esp. the deliberate reduction of effort by laborers to force concessions from employers.

slow-mo·tion, slō'mō'shən, *a.* Referring to motion pictures in which the action appears much slower than it actually was.

slow·poke, slō'pōk, *n. Informal.* A person whose temperament or pace is slow.

slow-wit·ted, slō'wit'id, *a.* Slow of intelligence.

sludge, sləj, *n.* Mud, mire, or ooze; slush; sediment; broken ice, as on the surface of the sea; sediment resulting from treating waste or sewage; a mixture of any finely powdered substance and water. **—sludg·y,** *a.,* **-i·er, -i·est.**

slue, sloo, *n.* See **slough.**

slug, sləg, *n.* Any of various slimy, elongated land animals related to the land snails, but having no shell or only a rudimentary one; any of several insect larva that resemble these animals.

slug, sləg, *n.* A piece of metal for firing from a gun; bullet; any heavy piece of crude metal; a piece of metal formed like a coin and used illegally as currency, esp. in parking meters and pay telephones.

slug, sləg, *v.t.,* **slugged, slug·ging.** To strike heavily; hit hard, esp. with the fist or with a bat: He *slugged* the baseball out of the park.—*n. Informal.* A heavy blow, esp. with the fist; a single drink of straight liquor. **—slug·ger,** *n.*

slug·gard, sləg'ərd, *n.* One who is habitually inactive or slothful.—*a.* Lazy. **—slug·gard·li·ness,** *n.*

slug·gish, sləg'ish, *a.* Habitually inactive; lazy; slow, as business; having little motion: a *sluggish* stream. **—slug·gish·ness,** *n.*

sluice, sloos, *n.* A canal or channel through which

water is conducted, with the flow regulated by a valve or gate; the body of water so controlled; a floodgate; a drain; a stream of surplus water; a long, sloping trough, into which water is directed to separate gold from gravel or sand; any such trough for washing ore.—*v.t.,* **sluiced, sluic·ing.** To let out, as water; to open a sluice upon.—*v.i.* To flow or pour through or as through a sluice.

slum, sləm, *n. Often pl.* A thickly populated, squalid part of a city, inhabited by the poorest people.—*v.i.,* **slummed, slum·ming.** To visit, esp. out of curiosity, slums or other areas regarded inferior to one's ordinary surroundings. **—slum·mer,** *n.*

slum·ber, sləm'bər, *v.i.* To sleep, usu. lightly; to drowse or doze; to be inert or in a state of inactivity. —*v.t.* To spend sleeping.—*n.* Sleep, usu. light sleep. **—slum·ber·er,** *n.*

slum·ber·ous, sləm'bər·əs, *a.* Pertaining to, resembling, or inducing sleep; drowsy; soporific. Also **slum·brous,** sləm'brəs.

slum·ber par·ty, *n.* A party usu. of young girls who dress in their nightclothes and stay overnight at one of the girls' homes. Also **pa·ja·ma par·ty.**

slump, sləmp, *v.i.* To drop heavily; to decline or fall suddenly and markedly, as prices; to assume a bent, slouching posture; to sink heavily, as the spirits.—*n.* The act or an act of slumping; a drop, fall, or decline; any sustained period of unusually inferior business activity, athletic performance, etc.; a bent, slouching posture.

slur, slər, *v.t.,* **slurred, slur·ring.** To pass over lightly or without due consideration, often followed by *over;* to pronounce indistinctly, as a syllable or word; to slander; belittle. In music, to run notes together smoothly; to mark with a slur.—*v.i.* To go through hurriedly and carelessly, as in speaking or singing.—*n.* A slurred utterance or sound; a disparaging remark; a slight; a smear; a stain, as upon a reputation; the running together of musical notes without a break.

slurp, slərp, *v.t., v.i. Informal.* To eat or drink with sucking sounds.—*n.*

slush, sləsh, *n.* Partly melted, watery snow; liquid mud or watery mire; silly talk or writing.—*v.t.* To splash with slush or mud; to grease, polish, or cover with slush. —*v.i.* To go through slush or mud with a splashing sound; to wash or dash with splashes. **—slush·i·ness,** *n.* **—slush·y,** slush'ē, *a.,* **-i·er, -i·est.**

slush fund, *n.* A fund available for use, as in a political campaign, for bribery or other corrupt purposes.

slut, slət, *n.* A dirty, slovenly woman; a slattern; a female dog. **—slut·tish,** *a.*

sly, slī, *a.,* **sli·er** or **sly·er, sli·est** or **sly·est.** Cunning, crafty, or wily; underhand or secret; mischievous. **—on the sly,** in a secret manner. **—sly·ly, sli·ly,** *adv.* **—sly·ness,** *n.*

smack, smak, *v.i.* To have a taste or flavor: It *smacks* of onions; to have or impart a suggestion or trace.—*n.* A slight taste or flavor; a smattering. *Informal.* Heroin.

smack, smak, *v.t.* To separate forcefully, as the lips, so as to produce a sharp sound, often as a sign of relish, as in eating; to bring, throw, or send with a sharp, resounding blow; to strike smartly, esp. with the open hand or anything flat. *Informal.* To kiss loudly.—*v.i.* To smack the lips; to strike or come together smartly; to make a sharp sound.—*n.* A smacking of the lips; a smart, resounding blow. *Informal.* A loud kiss.—*adv.* Suddenly and sharply; directly; straight.

smack-dab, smak'dab', *adv. Informal.* Precisely; directly: to walk *smack-dab* into a closed door.

smack·er, smak'ər, *n.* One who or that which smacks. *Informal.* A dollar.

smack·ing, smak'ing, *a.* Resounding sharply, as a kiss or a smart blow; brisk, lively, as a breeze.

small, smôl, *a.* Little in size; little in degree, duration, or number; trivial; weak; gentle; soft; narrow-minded; ungenerous; mean; humble; poor; obscure; of letters, not capital.—*adv.* In a small way; in faint tones; into small pieces.—*n.* A small thing, amount, or part. —**small·ish,** *a.*

small arms, *n. pl.* Rifles, pistols, and other firearms designed to be held in the hands when firing.

small change, *n.* Coins of low denomination; a person or thing of little significance.

small fry, *n. pl.* Small creatures collectively, esp. young fish; young children.

small game, *n.* Game animals smaller than big game, as rabbits.

small hours, *n. pl.* The early hours of the morning.

small in·tes·tine, *n.* The long, narrow, upper section of the intestines from the stomach to the large intestine, and which serves, through its secretions, to digest the nutritive substances.

small-mind·ed, smôl/mín/did, *a.* Selfish; petty; narrow-minded. —**small-mind·ed·ness,** *n.*

small po·ta·toes, *n. pl., sing. or pl. in constr. Informal.* Insignificant things or persons.

small·pox, smôl/poks, *n.* An acute virus disease, highly contagious, and marked by fever and pustular eruptions which leave permanent scarring of the skin.

small-scale, smôl/skāl/, *a.* Small in size; limited in extent or output.

small talk, *n.* Light, trivial social conversation.

small-time, smôl/tīm/, *a.* Unimportant; of little or no value or influence. —**small-tim·er,** *n.*

smart, smärt, *v.i.* To be a source of sharp, local pain, as a wound; to wound the feelings, as with sharp words; to feel stinging pain, as from a wound; to suffer from wounded feelings: to *smart* under unjust criticism. —*v.t.* To cause a sharp pain to or in.—*a.* Keen or stinging, as pain; sharply severe, as blows; brisk or vigorous: to set a *smart* pace; having or showing quick intelligence; clever, as in business dealings; advantageous: a *smart* deal; witty, esp. in a superficial way; chic, or trim in appearance, as persons or dress; fashionable: a *smart* restaurant; impertinent or saucy, as remarks.—*adv.*—*n.* A sharp, localized pain; acute mental anguish. —**smart·ness,** *n.*

smart al·eck, smärt/ al·ik, *n. Informal.* A self-assertive, conceited, obnoxious person. —**smart-al·eck·y, smart-al·eck,** *a.*

smart·en, smär/tən, *v.t.* To make smart or trim; to render brisk or lively; to educate, followed by *up:* smarten up his sales approach.

smart·y, smär/tē, *n. pl., -ies. Informal.* A person who shows off; smart aleck. Also **smart·y-pants, smart·ie.**

smash, smash, *v.t.* To break in pieces; to dash to pieces; to crush by a sudden blow; to wreck financially; to strike violently, usu. followed by *into* or *against.* —*v.i.* To be broken into pieces; to be reduced to utter wrack and ruin, often followed by *up.*—*n.* A violent, shattering blow; the sound of such a blow; defeat or total financial ruin. *Informal.* A resounding success: The party was a real *smash.*—*a. Informal.* Strikingly successful: The play was a *smash* hit. —**smash·er,** *n.*

smash·ing, smash/ing, *a.* Violent or crushing: a *smashing* blow. *Informal.* Outstandingly good or successful: They had a simply *smashing* vacation.

smash-up, smash/əp, *n. Informal.* A smashing to pieces; a collision, esp. one involving motor vehicles; a defeat or catastrophe.

smat·ter, smat/ər, *n.* A smattering. —**smat·ter·er,** *n.*

smat·ter·ing, smat/ər·ing, *n.* A superficial or slight knowledge, usu. followed by *of.*

smear, smēr, *v.t.* To overspread with anything oily, greasy, viscous, or sticky; to soil or stain; to soil or defame, as a reputation. *Informal.* To defeat overwhelmingly.—*v.i.* To become or be overspread.—*n.* A substance that smears; a stain; material daubed on a slide for microscopic analysis; a substance to be spread on a surface; slander. —**smear·er,** *n.*

smear·y, smēr/ē, *a., -i·er, -i·est.* Smeared; tending to

smear or soil. —**smear·i·ness,** *n.*

smell, smel, *v.t.,* **smelled** or **smelt, smel·ling.** To perceive through the function of the olfactory nerves in the nose; to detect the odor of; to test by the smell of; to detect, often with *out:* to *smell out* the truth.—*v.i.* To exercise the sense of smell; to have a scent or odor; to suggest something: a deal that *smells* of duplicity; to be suspect: In my opinion, the entire scheme *smells.*—*n.* The sense of perceiving with the nose; that which affects the olfactory organs; an odor. —**smell·er,** *n.* —**smell·y,** smel/ē, *a., -i·er, -i·est.*

smel·ling salts, *n. pl.* A form of ammonia, inhaled for resuscitation and stimulation.

smelt, smelt, *n.* Any of various food fishes having a salmonlike structure but small in size.

smelt, smelt, *v.t.* To melt or fuse, as ore, for the purpose of separating the metal from extraneous substances; to obtain, as a metal, by this process.

smelt·er, smel/tər, *n.* One who smelts ore; a place for smelting ores: also **smelt·er·y,** smel/tə·rē.

smid·gen, smij/ən, *n. Informal.* A small bit or amount. Also **smid·geon, smid·gin.**

smile, smil, *v.i.* To express pleasure, kindness, or amusement by an upward turning of the corners of the mouth; to express slight contempt, sarcasm, or pity by similar mouth movements; to look joyous; to appear favorable.—*v.t.* To express by a smile; to dispel by smiling, followed by *away.*—*n.* The act of smiling; a pleasant or favoring aspect. —**smil·er,** *n.* —**smil·ing·ly,** *adv.*

smirch, smərch, *v.t.* To stain or discolor; to smudge; to disgrace, as one's reputation. Also **be·smirch.**—*n.*

smirk, smərk, *v.i.* To smile in an affected or offensively familiar way.—*v.t.* To utter or say with a smirk.—*n.* The facial expression of one who smirks. —**smirk·er,** *n.* —**smirk·ing·ly,** *adv.*

smite, smit, *v.t.,* **smote, smit·ten** or **smit, smit·ing.** To strike forcibly; to slay; to kill; to afflict; punish; to affect with love or other sudden and powerful feeling. —*v.i.* To strike. —**smit·er,** *n.*

smith, smith, *n.* One who works in metals: silver*smith;* a blacksmith. Also **smith·y.**

smith·er·eens, smith·ər·ēnz/, *n. pl. Informal.* Small pieces or fragments; bits.

smit·ten, smit/ən, *a.* Struck forcibly; seriously affected; enamored.

smock, smok, *n.* A loose outer garment, worn to protect other garments while working.—*v.t.* To gather by smocking; to dress in a smock.

smock·ing, smok/ing, *n.* Decorative stitches of embroidery used to gather cloth into even folds.

smog, smog, smôg, *n.* A mixture of smoke and fog, as seen esp. in highly populated industrial areas. —**smog·gy,** *a., -gi·er, -gi·est.*

smoke, smōk, *n.* The visible, cloudlike, gray, brown, or blackish mixture of gases and suspended carbon particles resulting from combustion, esp. of wood, coal, or other organic matter; anything resembling this; something unsubstantial or without result; an instance of smoking tobacco or the like; that which is smoked, as a cigar or cigarette.—*v.i.,* **smoked, smok·ing.** To give off smoke; to give out smoke improperly, as a stove; to send forth steam or vapor or dust; puff on a pipe, cigar, or cigarette. *Informal.* To be intensely angry.—*v.t.* To suck in and exhale the smoke of, as a cigar or cigarette; to fumigate; to cure, as meat; to color by the action of smoke; to drive from cover, as an animal, with smoke, usu. followed by *out;* to bring into public knowledge, usu. followed by *out.* —**smoke·less,** *a.*

smoke·house, smōk/hows, *n.* A building for curing meat or fish by means of smoke.

smok·er, smō/kər, *n.* One who or that which smokes; a railroad car or compartment, for travelers who wish to smoke; also **smok·ing car.**

smoke screen, *n.* A screen of smoke used to hide a maneuver from an enemy; anything done as a means of concealing the facts of a case.

smoke·stack, smōk′stak, *n.* A chimney through which the smoke and gases of combustion are discharged, as on a locomotive or building.

smok·ing jack·et, *n.* A man's lounging jacket worn in the home.

smok·y, smō′kē, *a.*, -i·er, -i·est. Emitting smoke or much smoke, as a fire or a torch; apt to emit smoke in the wrong way, as a stove; filled with smoke; hazy; darkened with smoke; having the character of smoke; smokelike in color, as dull or brownish gray; cloudy. —**smok·i·ly**, *adv.* —**smok·i·ness**, *n.*

smol·der, smoul·der, smōl′dər, *v.i.* To burn and smoke without flame; to exist in a suppressed state; to display signs of suppressed feelings, as of hate or anger.—*n.* Dense smoke resulting from slow combustion; smoldering matter; an inward, continued heat of feeling.

smooch, smooch, *v.i. Informal.* To kiss; caress; to neck.—*n. Informal.* A kiss.

smooth, smooth, *a.* Free from irregularities as perceived by touching; free from hairy growth: a *smooth* face; free from inequalities of surface: a *smooth* road; even; flat; free from roughness: a *smooth* voyage; being free from lumps, as batter; free from breaks or abrupt bends: *smooth* curves; easy and uniform, as motion; elegant, or polished, as a speaker; tranquil; pleasant; suave; free from harshness of taste, as wine; not harsh to the ear, as sound.—*v.t.* To make smooth, as a surface, by planing, or sanding; make even, flat, or easy, as a way: to *smooth* one's path; remove obstructions in making something smooth, usu. with *away* or *out:* to *smooth away* difficulties; to make more smooth or elegant, as wording; refine, as manners; to calm; to gloss over, as something unpleasant or wrong.—*v.i.* To become smooth.—*n.* An act of smoothing; that which is smooth; a smooth place. —*adv.* Evenly. —**smooth·er**, *n.* —**smooth·ness**, *n.*

smooth·en, smooth′ən, *v.t., v.i.* To make or become smooth.

smooth·ie, smooth·y, smooth′ē, *n. Informal.* One who has polished manners, performs with assurance, and is persuasive; a person who is glib.

smor·gas·bord, smôr′gəs·bôrd, *n.* A buffet consisting of a variety of hot and cold foods; a restaurant serving such a buffet; any hodgepodge.

smoth·er, smuth′ər, *v.* To stifle, as smoke does; to kill by depriving of the air necessary for life; to extinguish, as a fire, by covering; to cover closely or thickly, often followed by *in:* a house *smothered in* vines; to suppress as by covering up; to check or quell; to deaden or muffle, as sound.—*v.i.* To become stifled or suffocated; to be suppressed or hidden.—*n.* Dense, stifling smoke; a smoking or smoldering state; dust, fog, spray, or the like in a dense or enveloping cloud; an overspreading profusion of anything. —**smoth·er·y**, *a.*, -i·er, -i·est.

smudge, smej, *n.* A spot; a smear; a blur; a smoldering fire to repel insects or protect fruit from frost; the smoke from such a fire.—*v.t.* smudged, smudg·ing. To smear or stain; to blur; to protect by a smoldering fire, as against insects or frost.—*v.i.* To cause or make a smudge; to become smudged. —**smudg·i·ly**, *adv.* —**smudg·i·ness**, *n.* —**smudg·y**, *a.*, -i·er, -i·est.

smug, smeg, *a.*, **smug·ger, smug·gest**. Self-important or self-satisfied; neat; trim. —**smug·ly**, *adv.* —**smug·ness**, *n.*

smug·gle, smeg′əl, *v.t.*, -gled, -gling. To import or export secretly and contrary to law, without payment of legally required duties; to manage clandestinely. —*v.i.* To practice smuggling. —**smug·gler**, *n.*

smut, smet, *n.* A particle of soot or sooty matter; a black or dirty mark; a smudge; obscenity; a fungus disease of plants.—*v.t.*, smut·ted, smut·ting. To

smudge or soil with some black or dirty substance —*v.i.* To become smutty.

smutch, smech, *v.t., n.* Smudge.

smut·ty, smat′ē, *a.*, -ti·er, -ti·est. Soiled with smut, soot, or the like; grimy; dirty; obscene; given to obscene talk or writing; affected with the disease smut, as a plant. —**smut·ti·ly**, *adv.* —**smut·ti·ness**, *n.*

snack, snak, *n.* A light portion of food, usu. eaten between meals; a portion or bit of something.—*v.i.* To eat a light portion of food, esp. between meals.

snack bar, *n.* A restaurant which serves snacks.

sna·fu, sna·foo′, snaf′oo, *a. Informal.* Confused; chaotic.—*v.t.*, -fued, -fu·ing. *Informal.* To make chaotic or disordered.—*n. Informal.* Anything in chaos.

snag, snag, *n.* A short, projecting stump, as of a branch broken; any sharp or rough projection; a jagged hole or tear made from or as if from catching and tearing on a projection; any obstacle: to strike a *snag* in carrying out plans.—*v.t.*, snagged, snag·ging. To run, catch upon, or damage by a snag; to impede, as a snag does; to clear of snags.—*v.i.* To become caught in an obstacle. —**snag·gy**, *a.*, -gi·er, -gi·est.

snag·gle·tooth, snag′əl·tooth, *n. pl.*, -teeth. A tooth growing out beyond or apart from others. —**snag·gle·toothed**, *a.*

snail, snāl, *n.* Any of various aquatic and land mollusks, esp. those having a spiral shell, and including the shell-less slug; a slow or lazy person; a sluggard. —**snail·like**, *a.* —**snail·paced**, *a.*

snake, snāk, *n.* Any scaly, limbless, long-bodied reptile; a serpent; a treacherous person.—*v.i.*, snaked, snak·ing. To move in a tortuous manner, as a snake. —*v.t.* To move, twist, or wind in the manner of a snake; to make, as one's way, in a creeping manner. —**snake·like**, *a.* —**snak·i·ly**, *adv.*

snake·bite, snāk′bīt, *n.* The bite of a snake, esp. that of a poisonous species; illness resulting from a snakebite.

snake charm·er, *n.* An entertainer who mesmerizes venomous snakes by music or by rhythmically moving to and fro.

snake dance, *n.* A parade or procession in single file that moves in serpentine fashion.

snake in the grass, *n.* A hidden danger; a treacherous, yet seemingly harmless person.

snake pit, *n. Informal.* A mental hospital, esp. one having inadequate facilities and offering inhumane treatment; any place where there is disorder or maltreatment.

snake·skin, snāk′skin, *n.* The skin of a snake; leather made from such a skin.

snak·y, snā′kē, *a.*, -i·er, -i·est. Of or pertaining to snakes; abounding in snakes; snakelike; twisting, winding, or sinuous; venomous; treacherous. —**snak·i·ly**, *adv.* —**snak·i·ness**, *n.*

snap, snap, *v.i.*, snapped, snap·ping. To make a sudden, sharp sound; to crack, as a whip; crackle; click, as a mechanism; catch, as a lock; to break suddenly, esp. with a sharp, cracking sound; to flash, as the eyes; to act with a sudden movement: He *snapped* into action; to make a quick or sudden bite or snatch, often with *at;* to utter a quick, sharp reproof, often with *at.*—*v.t.* To seize with or as with a quick bite or snatch, usu. followed by *up:* He'll *snap up* their offer; to take with or as with one bite or snatch, usu. followed by *off:* to *snap off* his head; to crack, as a whip; to strike, shut, open, or operate with a sharp sound or movement: to *snap* the jaws together; to utter or say in a quick, sharp manner; to break suddenly, esp. with a cracking sound; to cause, as a rope, to part suddenly; to take a photograph of.—*n.* A sharp cracking or clicking sound, or an action causing such a sound: a *snap* of a whip; a fastener operating with such a sound; a sudden breaking, as of something

---

brittle; briskness or energy, as of persons; a quick, sharp speech or manner of speaking; a quick or sudden bite or snatch; something obtained by or as by biting or snatching; a short spell, as of cold weather; a snapshot. *Informal.* An easy job or piece of work; a small or crisp cake: a ginger*snap*.—*a.* Shutting with a snap; without thought. *Informal.* Easy.—*adv.* Briskly. **—snap one's fin•gers at,** to be indifferent to. **—snap out of it.** *Informal.* To recover. **—snap•per,** *n.*

snap•back, snap′bak, *n.* A sudden or abrupt recovery or rebound.

snap•drag•on, snap′drag•ən, *n.* An herb long cultivated for its spikes of showy flowers of various colors, with corollas suggesting the mouth of a dragon.

snap•per, snap′ər, *n.* Any of various large, edible, marine fish; one who or that which snaps; a snapping turtle.

snap•ping tur•tle, *n.* A large, savage turtle of N. American rivers and lakes, which snaps at its prey with powerful jaws.

snap•pish, snap′ish, *a.* Apt to snap or bite; cross. **—snap•pish•ness,** *n.*

snap•py, snap′ē, *a.,* **-pi•er, -pi•est.** Snappish; snapping or crackling in sound, as a fire; quick or sudden. *Informal.* Lively; stylish. **—make it snap•py.** *Informal.* Hurry up; be quick. **—snap•pi•ly,** *adv.* **—snap•pi•ness,** *n.*

snap•shot, snap′shot, *n.* A photograph, usu. small and informal, taken with a hand-held camera.

snare, snâr, *n.* A contrivance, as a noose, by which a small animal may be entangled; a trap; a lure.—*v.t.,* **snared, snar•ing.** To catch with a snare; to trap. **—snar•er,** *n.*

snare drum, *n.* A small, double-headed drum, having metal or catgut strings stretched across the lower head which produce a rattling effect.

snarl, snärl, *v.t.* To entangle; to form knots in, as string; to create confusion.—*v.i.* To become complicated or entangled.—*n.* A knot; a complication. **—snarl•er,** *n.* **—snarl•y,** *a.,* **-i•er, -i•est.**

snarl, snärl, *v.i.* To growl exposing the teeth, as an angry dog; to speak in surly tones.—*v.t.* To express in an angry and threatening manner: to *snarl* a reply.—*n.* A menacing growl. **—snarl•er,** *n.* **—snarl•ing•ly,** *adv.* **—snarl•y,** *a.,* **-i•er, -i•est.**

snatch, snach, *v.i.* To make a sudden motion or effort to seize something, as with the hand, usu. followed by *at;* to catch or grasp, followed by *at.*—*v.t.* To take by a sudden grasp, often used with *up, from, out of,* or *away;* to take or get suddenly: to *snatch* a kiss; to remove suddenly, often used with *away* or *from;* to rescue by prompt action: to *snatch* from danger. *Informal.* To kidnap.—*n. pl.,* **snatch•es.** An act of snatching; something snatched or taken hastily; a bit or scrap of something; a brief spell of activity: to work in *snatches;* a brief period. *Informal.* A kidnaping. **—snatch•er,** *n.*

snatch•y, snach′ē, *a.,* **-i•er, -i•est.** Characterized by snatches; spasmodic; irregular: *snatchy* reading. **—snatch•i•ly,** *adv.*

snaz•zy, snaz′ē, *a.,* **-zi•er, -zi•est.** *Informal.* Stylish; fancy.

sneak, snēk, *v.i.* To go in a stealthy manner, as if afraid or ashamed to be seen, usu. followed by *about, along, in, off,* or *out;* slink; skulk; to go away quickly and quietly; to act in a furtive, underhand, or mean way. —*v.t.* To move, put; or pass in a stealthy manner: to *sneak* a thing out of the house.—*n.* One who sneaks; a contemptible person; an act of sneaking. *Informal.* A going away quietly or a stealthy departure.—*a.* Stealthy.

sneak•er, snē′kər, *n.* One who sneaks; a sneak. *Informal.* A tennis shoe.

sneak•ing, snē′king, *a.* Acting in a furtive or underhanded way; not generally avowed, as a feeling or suspicion.

sneak pre•view, *n.* The showing of a motion picture prior to its release in order to determine audience reactions.

sneak thief, *n.* One who steals without using force, as by sneaking into houses through unlocked doors or windows.

sneak•y, snē′kē, *a.,* **-i•er, -i•est.** Pertaining to or having something to do with a sneak; deceitful. **—sneak•i•ly,** *adv.* **—sneak•i•ness,** *n.*

sneer, snēr, *v.i.* To show contempt by a particular facial expression; to speak or write derisively.—*v.t.* To utter with a sneer.—*n.* A look or oral expression of contempt. **—sneer•er,** *n.* **—sneer•ing•ly,** *adv.*

sneeze, snēz, *v.i.,* **sneezed, sneez•ing.** To emit breath suddenly and audibly through the nose and mouth by spasmodic action.—*n.* An act or sound of sneezing. **—sneeze at.** *Informal.* To show contempt for; to consider lightly. **—sneez•er,**—*n.* **—sneez•y,** *a.,* **-i•er, -i•est.**

snick•er, snik′ər, *v.i.* To laugh in a partially smothered way, usu. indicating derision; to titter.—*v.t.* To express audibly with a snicker.—*n.* A half-smothered, usu. derisive laugh.

snide, snīd, *a.* Malicious; insinuating; slyly derogatory.

sniff, snif, *v.i.* To draw air audibly through the nose, usu. in a series of quick inhalations; to convey scorn by or as by short, quick breaths, followed by *at.*—*v.t.* To draw in through the nose, as odors or air; to sense: to *sniff* impending danger.—*n.* The act of sniffing; the sound so produced; that which is sniffed: a *sniff* of fresh air.

snif•fle, snif′əl, *v.i.,* **-fled, -fling.** To sniff repeatedly, as from a cold in the head.—*n.* An act or sound of sniffling; *pl.,* a condition, as nasal congestion, marked by sniffling, usu. preceded by *the.* **—snif•fler,** *n.*

snif•fy, snif′ē, *a.,* **-fi•er, -fi•est.** Inclined to sniff, as in disdain; disdainful. **—sniff•i•ly,** *adv.* **—sniff•i•ness,** *n.* **—sniff•ish,** *a., n.*

snif•ter, snif′tər, *n.* A large, bowl-shaped glass, usu. with a short stem. *Informal.* A small drink of liquor.

snip, snip, *v.t.,* **snipped, snip•ping.** To cut with a small, quick stroke, as with scissors; to take off by or as by cutting in this way.—*v.i.*—*n.* An act of snipping; a small cut made by snipping; a small piece snipped off; a small piece, bit, or amount of anything; *pl.,* small, sturdy shears used in cutting sheet metal. *Informal.* A young, small, or insignificant person. **—snip•per,** *n.*

snipe, snīp, *n.* Any of a group of long-billed game birds frequenting marshy places.—*v.i.,* **sniped, snip•ing.** To shoot snipe; to shoot at soldiers or civilians at will from under cover.—*v.t.* To shoot at or shoot by sniping. **—snip•er,** *n.*

snip•py, snip′ē, *a.,* **-pi•er, -pi•est.** *Informal.* Sharp or curt in speech or manner, esp. in a supercilious way; scrappy or fragmentary. Also **snip•pe•ty,** snip′ə•tē. **—snip•pi•ness, snip•pet•i•ness,** *n.* **—snip•pi•ly,** *adv.*

snit, snit, *n.* A state of agitation or vexation.

snitch, snich, *v.t. Informal.* To steal.—*v.i. Informal.* To turn informer; to tattle, usu. followed by *on.* **—snitch•er,** *n.*

sniv•el, sniv′əl, *v.i.,* **-eled, -el•ing.** To weep or cry with sniffling; whine; to sniffle; to draw up mucus audibly through the nose.—*v.t.* To utter with sniveling or sniffing.—*n.* Weak or pretended weeping; a hypocritical show of feeling; mucus running from the nose. **—sniv•el•er,** *n.*

snob, snob, *n.* One who snubs people whom he considers his social or intellectual inferiors, and who cultivates and imitates persons of wealth, social status, or intelligence; a person with a smug, superior air in matters of knowledge or taste. **—snob•ber•y,** *n.* **—snob•bish,** *a.*

snood, snood, *n.* A band for confining the hair; a meshlike cap for holding hair in place.—*v.t.* To bind or confine with a snood.

snoop, snoop, *v.i. Informal.* To prowl or pry.—*n.* An act or instance of snooping; one who snoops. **—snoop•y,** *a.,* **-i•er, -i•est.** **—snoop•er,** *n.*

snoot, snoot, *n. Informal.* The nose; a contemptuous grimace; a snob.

snoot·y, snoo⁄tē, *a.*, **-i·er, -i·est.** Snobbish. **—snoot·i·ly**, *adv.* **—snoot·i·ness**, *n.*

snooze, snooz, *v.i.*, **snoozed, snooz·ing.** *Informal.* To sleep; doze; nap.—*n. Informal.* A doze; a nap. **—snooz·er**, *n.*

snore, snōr, snôr, *v.i.*, **snored, snor·ing.** To breathe during sleep through the mouth and nose, making hoarse sounds.—*v.t.* To pass time in snoring, usu. followed by *away* or *out.*—*n.* A loud, harsh respiration during sleep. **—snor·er**, *n.*

snor·kel, snôr⁄kəl, *n.* A device enabling a submarine to stay submerged for long periods; a mouth-held tube enabling a swimmer to breathe with his face in the water.—*v.i.* To swim underwater, breathing by means of a snorkel.

snort, snôrt, *v.i.* To force the breath violently through the nostrils with a loud, harsh sound, as a horse; to make a similar sound; to express contempt by such a sound. *Informal.* To laugh boisterously.—*v.t.* To utter with a snort.—*n.* An act or sound of snorting. *Informal.* A small drink, usu. of straight liquor. **—snort·er**, *n.*

snot, snot, *n. Informal.* Nasal mucus; a vile or obnoxious person.

snot·ty, snot⁄ē, *a.*, **-ti·er, -ti·est.** *Informal.* Soiled by mucus; mean; contemptible; petty; impudent.

snout, snowt, *n.* A part of an animal's head projecting forward and containing the nose or the nose and jaws; the muzzle; a nozzle or spout. *Informal.* A person's nose, esp. when large. **—snout·ed**, *a.* **—snout·y**, *a.*, **-i·er, -i·est.**

snow, snō, *n.* The water vapor of the atmosphere precipitated in partially frozen, white, crystalline flakes; these flakes as a layer on the ground or elsewhere; a snowfall or snowstorm; something resembling snow, as in color or texture.—*v.i.* To send down snow; to fall or descend like snow.—*v.t.* To let fall, as or like snow; to cover with snow, usu. followed by *over, under,* or *up. Informal.* To impress with glib charm.

snow·ball, snō⁄bôl, *n.* A round mass of snow pressed or rolled together.—*v.t.* To throw or pelt snowballs at; to cause to become larger, multiply, or accumulate at a quickly accelerating speed.—*v.i.* To throw snowballs; to increase at a quickly accelerating speed.

snow blind·ness, *n.* Temporarily reduced sight caused by the glare of sunlight reflected by snow. **—snow-blind**, snō⁄blīnd, *a.*

snow·blow·er, snō⁄blō·ər, *n.* A snowplow that operates by drawing the snow through the machine and blowing it aside.

snow·bound, snō⁄bownd, *a.* Shut in, confined, or brought to a halt by snow.

snow·cap, snō⁄kap, *n.* A covering of snow that forms a cap on the top of anything, as on the peak of a mountain. **—snow-capped**, *a.*

snow·drift, snō⁄drift, *n.* A bank or mass of snow driven together by the wind.

snow·fall, snō⁄fôl, *n.* A fall of snow; the amount of snow fallen.

snow·flake, snō⁄flāk, *n.* One of the small, feathery masses or flakes in which snow falls.

snow job, *n. Informal.* An effort to influence by means of exaggerated or insincere talk.

snow·man, snō⁄man, *n. pl.*, **-men.** A figure made of snow that is packed to suggest a person's form.

snow·mo·bile, snō⁄mō·bēl, *n.* An automotive vehicle for traveling on snow.

snow·plow, snō⁄plow, *n.* An automotive implement for clearing away the snow from roads, railroads, and other surfaces.

snow·shoe, snō⁄shoo, *n.* A light, racket-shaped frame across which is stretched a network of rawhide, at-tached to the foot to enable the wearer to walk on deep snow without sinking in.—*v.i.*, **-shoed, -shoe·ing.** To walk on snowshoes. **—snow·sho·er**, *n.*

snow·suit, snō⁄soot, *n.* An outer garment consisting of a jacket and long trousers, and worn by children in winter weather.

snow tire, *n.* A tire which has a deep tread for added traction on icy and snowy surfaces.

snow-white, snō⁄hwīt⁄, *a.* White as snow.

snow·y, snō⁄ē, *a.*, **-i·er, -i·est.** Abounding with snow; covered with snow; relating to snow; pure. **—snow·i·ly**, *adv.* **—snow·i·ness**, *n.*

snub, snəb, *v.t.*, **snubbed, snub·bing.** To treat with contempt or neglect; to check, or rebuke with a sarcastic remark.—*n.* A rebuke; a rebuff; the abrupt halting of the movement of a line, rope, or the like.—*a.* Turned up, as the nose. **—snubbed**, *a.* **—snub·ber**, *n.*

snub·by, snəb⁄ē, *a.*, **-bi·er, -bi·est.** Short, wide, and turned up, as a nose; snubbing. **—snub·bi·ness**, *n.*

snub-nosed, snəb⁄nōzd, *a.* Having a short, upturned nose.

snuff, snəf, *n.* The charred or partly consumed portion of a candlewick.—*v.t.* To extinguish, followed by *out.* **—snuff out.** *Informal.* Put an end to suddenly, as to kill.

snuff, snəf, *v.t.* To draw in through the nose, as air; to inhale; to smell; to sniff or smell in examination, as animals.—*v.i.* To snort or sniff.—*n.* A sniff.

snuff, snəf, *n.* A powdered preparation of tobacco inhaled through the nose; a small pinch of this used at a time. **—up to snuff.** *Informal.* Meeting the standard.

snuf·fle, snəf⁄əl, *v.i.*, **-fled, -fling.** To breathe noisily through the nose; to sniffle; to speak with a nasal twang; to snivel or whine.—*v.t.* To speak or utter nasally.—*n.* An act of snuffling; the sound produced; an affected nasal twang; *pl.*, nasal congestion, or the sniffles. **—snuf·fler**, *n.* **—snuf·fly**, *a.*, **-fli·er, -fli·est.**

snuff·y, snəf⁄ē, *a.*, **-i·er, -i·est.** Resembling snuff; given to taking snuff; dingy. **—snuff·i·ness**, *n.*

snug, snəg, *a.*, **snug·ger, snug·gest.** Comfortable or cozy, as a place; trim, neat, or compactly arranged; adequately protected from the weather; fitting closely, but not too closely, as a garment; pleasant or agreeable, esp. in a small, exclusive way; well-concealed; secret.—*adv.*—*v.i.*, **snugged, snug·ging.** To snuggle; nestle.—*v.t.* To make snug. **—snug·ly**, *adv.* **—snug·ness**, *n.*

snug·gle, snəg⁄əl, *v.i.*, **-gled, -gling.** To lie or press closely, as for warmth or comfort or from affection; nestle; cuddle.—*v.t.* To draw or press closely to.—*n.* The act of snuggling.

so, sō, *adv.* To an unspecified but understood degree or quantity: Do only *so* much and no more; in a corresponding manner; likewise: She left and *so* did she; in this manner; as demonstrated: It should be done *so*; as was mentioned or stated: I think *so*; very much; greatly: The cruel remark hurt him *so*; the case being such: *So* you came back, did you? most certainly: I did *so* lock the door! as a consequence: He is ill and *so* cannot attend; having the purpose of: a gift *so* honoring the occasion; in a way which results from: As you sow, *so* shall you reap; indeed; assuredly; to emphasize or confirm something stated before: He said he would stay, and *so* he will; thereupon: and *so* they set out on their journey.—*a.* Understood or accepted; very well: *So* be it; true as predicted: She said it would be hot and *so* it turned out.—*conj.* For which reason; therefore: It was late, *so* she went home. **—interj.** *Informal.* Indeed! Well! What about it?: *So* what?—*pron.* Such as previously stated or suggested: He was the only tenant and remained *so*; that which is approximate to something in amount or number: He bought ten or *so* items. **—so as,** in order to: He came along *so as* to provide an escort; used as an antecedent, in a comparative or qualitative sense: *so far as* I

---

a- hat, fāte, fāre, fäther; **e-** met, mē; **i-** pin, pīne; **o-** not, nōte, ôrb, moove (move), boy, pownd;
u- cūbe, bůll, tůk (took); **ch-** chin; **th-** thick, ₮hen; **zh-** vizhon (vision); **ə-** əgo, takən, pencəl, lemən, bərd (bird).

know, *so* new *as* to be questionable. **—so that,** in order that: She started early *so that* she would arrive on time. **—so to speak,** in a manner of speaking: We were all at sea, *so to speak,* until the situation was finally explained to us.

soak, sōk, *v.i.* To lie in and become saturated with water or some other liquid; to be thoroughly wet; to pass, as a liquid, through pores or openings, usu. with *in, through,* or *out;* to permeate; to penetrate the mind, used with *in* or *into.*—*v.t.* To place and keep in liquid in order to saturate thoroughly; to drench; to steep; to draw, remove, or extract by or as by soaking; to take in or up by absorption, often with *up:* Blotting paper *soaks up* ink. *Informal.* To charge or tax exorbitantly.—*n.* The act of soaking or the state of being soaked; the liquid in which anything is soaked. **—soak·age,** *n.* **—soak·er,** *n.* **—soak·ing·ly,** *adv.*

so-and-so, sō′ən·sō, *n. pl.,* **so-and-sos.** *Informal.* An indefinite person or thing; an irritating or annoying person.

soap, sōp, *n.* A chemical compound of an alkali and fat, soluble in water, and used for detergent or cleansing purposes.—*v.t.* To rub or wash over with soap. **—no soap,** rejected, as a proposal or idea.

soap·box, sōp′boks, *n.* A box, esp. a wooden box, in which soap is packed; an empty wooden box of this kind used as a temporary platform by speakers addressing gatherings of persons on public streets. Also **soap box.**—*v.i.* To address or harangue an audience from a soapbox or other informal platform.—*a.* Of or characteristic of impassioned orators or oratories.

soap bub·ble, *n.* A thin film of soap forming a hollow globule; something pleasant but ephemeral.

soap op·er·a, *n.* A daytime, serialized broadcast program dramatizing personal or domestic situations in a highly melodramatic manner.

soap·suds, sōp′sədz, *n. pl.* Foamy, soapy water; the bubbles on such water.

soap·y, sō′pē, *a.,* **-i·er, -i·est.** Containing or resembling soap; having the qualities of soap; smeared with soap. *Informal.* Flattering. **—soap·i·ly,** *adv.* **—soap·i·ness,** *n.*

soar, sōr, sôr, *v.i.* To fly aloft, as a bird or airplane; to rise to a height: a mountain that *soars* above a plain; to rise above what is usual: costs that *soar;* to be transported upward.—*n.* An act of upward flight; the range or height of a soaring flight. **—soar·er,** *n.*

sob, sob, *v.i.,* **sobbed, sob·bing.** To weep with convulsive catching of the breath; to produce such a sound: Wind *sobs* through the trees.—*v.t.* To express with sobs: He *sobbed* out the answer.—*n.* A convulsive catching of the breath; a sound like a sob.

so·ber, sō′bər, *a.* Not intoxicated or drunk; habitually temperate, notably in the use of liquor; serious, grave, or solemn; free from excess or exaggeration; subdued in tone, as color; not gay or showy, as clothes; sane or rational.—*v.t., v.i.* To make or become sober. **—so·ber·ing·ly,** *adv.* **—so·ber·ness,** *n.*

so·bri·e·ty, sə·brī′i·tē, sō·brī′i·tē, *n.* The condition of being sober; temperance, esp. in the use of intoxicating liquors.

so·bri·quet, sou·bri·quet, sō′bri·kā, *n.* A nickname.

sob sto·ry, *n. Informal.* A sentimental tale intended to evoke compassion or sympathy, often used as an alibi.

so-called, sō′kôld′, *a.* Commonly called or designated thus: the *so-called* birthplace of football; incorrectly, or falsely called thus: robbed by his *so-called* honest employee.

soc·cer, sok′ər, *n.* A variation of football in which a ball is moved toward the opposing team's goal by striking or kicking it, using any part of the body but the hands and arms.

so·cia·ble, sō′shə·bəl, *a.* Inclined to associate with or seek friends; companionable; social.—*n.* An informal social gathering. **—so·cia·bil·i·ty,** sō·shə·bil′ə·tē, **so·cia·ble·ness,** *n.* **—so·cia·bly,** *adv.*

so·cial, sō′shəl, *a.* Pertaining to society; relating to humans living in society or to the public as an aggregate body; ready to mix in friendly relationships; relating to fashionable society: a *social* occasion; gregarious; relating to status: a comparable *social* group; pertaining to the welfare and living conditions of people collectively in communities.—*n.* A social gathering. **—so·ci·al·i·ty,** sō·shē·al′ə·tē, *n.* **—so·cial·ly,** *adv.*

so·cial climb·er, *n.* An individual who ingratiates himself or herself with eminent people to attain a higher social position. **—so·cial climb·ing,** *n.*

so·cial de·moc·ra·cy, *n.* A political doctrine based on a Marxist ideology that advocates a gradual transition from a capitalistic to a socialistic society by democratic means and processes. **—so·cial dem·o·crat,** *n.*

so·cial dis·ease, *n.* A venereal disease; any disease usu. related to social and economic conditions, as tuberculosis.

so·cial·ism, sō′shə·liz·əm, *n.* A theory or method of social organization and government whereby the citizenry jointly owns the means of production and distribution, and the power of administrative control is vested in the state.

so·cial·ist, sō′shə·list, *n.* One who advocates socialism. (*Cap.*) A person who belongs to the political party so named.—*a.* **—so·cial·is·tic,** sō·shə·lis′tik, *a.* **—so·cial·is·ti·cal·ly,** *adv.*

so·cial·ite, sō′shə·līt, *n.* A man or woman of socially elite circles.

so·cial·ize, sō′shə·līz, *v.t.,* **-ized, -iz·ing.** To render social, to suit something to the needs of society; to make fit for life in companionship with others.—*v.i.* To participate in friendly interchange. **—so·cial·i·za·tion,** sō·shəl·ə·zā′shən, *n.* **—so·cial·iz·er,** *n.*

so·cial·ized med·i·cine, sō′shə·līzd, *n.* Governmental subsidy of physicians and health care to provide medical care of an entire population.

so·cial sci·ence, *n.* The branch of knowledge dealing with all that relates to the social condition, or to the relations and institutions involved in people's existence as members of an organized community. **—so·cial sci·en·tist,** *n.*

so·cial se·cu·ri·ty, *n.* (*Usu. cap.*) A plan for old-age pensions, survivors' benefits, and health insurance administered by the U.S. government and maintained by federal funds and payments required of employers and their employees.

so·cial stud·ies, *n. pl.* Those courses in a curriculum concerned with humans and their relation to society and its functioning, as history or sociology.

so·cial wel·fare, *n.* Any or all services organized and sponsored by an agency, as a municipality, for the benefit of the disadvantaged.

so·cial work, *n.* Any activity or professional approach directed toward the betterment of social conditions, as by organizations or individuals seeking to improve the condition of the poor. Also **social service.** **—so·cial work·er,** *n.*

so·ci·e·ty, sə·sī′i·tē, *n. pl.,* **-ties.** A group of persons united for the promotion of a common aim, as literary, political, or benevolent; persons from any region or any period of time viewed in regard to manners, customs, or standards of living; human beings collectively, seen as having characteristics in common; those who recognize each other as associates and friends; the wealthy, or fashionable section of any community; the relationship of people to one another; companionship.—*a.* **—so·ci·e·tal,** *a.*

so·ci·o·ec·o·nom·ic, sō·sē·ō·ek·ə·nom′ik, sō·shē·ō·ē·kə·nom′ik, *a.* Of or pertaining to social and economic factors as intertwined in their effect.

so·ci·ol·o·gy, sō·sē·ol′ə·jē, sō·shē·ol′ə·jē, *n.* The science of the evolution, structure, and functioning of human society. **—so·ci·o·log·i·cal,** sō·sē·ə·loj′ə·kəl, *a.* **—so·ci·ol·o·gist,** *n.*

so·ci·o·po·lit·i·cal, sō·sē·ō·pə·lit′i·kəl, sō·shē·ō·pə·lit′i·kəl, *a.* Pertaining to or involving factors that are both social and political.

sock, sok, *n. pl.,* **socks, sox.** A short stocking reaching just above the ankle.

sock, sok, *v.t. Informal.* To strike or hit hard.—*n. Informal.* A hard blow. —**socked in,** prohibited from flying a plane because of adverse weather conditions.

sock·et, sok′it, *n.* A hollow part or piece for receiving and holding some part or thing: an electric light bulb *socket;* the *socket* of the eye.—*v.t.* To place in or fit with a socket.

sod, sod, *n.* The surface layer of the ground with the grass growing on it; a piece lifted from that surface; turf; sward.—*v.t.,* **sod·ded, sod·ding.** To cover with sod.

so·da, sō′də, *n.* A common name for various compounds of sodium, esp. sodium carbonate or washing soda, bicarbonate of soda or baking soda, and sodium hydroxide or caustic soda; a soft drink consisting of soda water, flavoring, and ice cream.

so·da crack·er, *n.* A crisp, light cracker containing baking soda.

so·da foun·tain, *n.* A serving table or counter equipped to prepare and serve ice cream, soft drinks, and the like.

so·da jerk, *n. Informal.* The waiter who makes and serves sodas, ice cream, or the like at a soda fountain.

so·dal·i·ty, sō·dal′ə·tē, *n. pl.,* **-ties.** Fellowship; brotherhood; association; society; a Catholic society for religious or charitable purposes.

so·da pop, *n.* A bottled, carbonated soft drink, usu. flavored artificially.

so·da wa·ter, *n.* An effervescent beverage consisting of water charged with carbon dioxide; soda pop; a mixture of sodium bicarbonate, water, and often an acid, used as a gastric aid.

sod·den, sod′ən, *a.* Soaked with liquid or moisture; heavy, or soggy, as food; bloated, as the face; expressionless or stupid.—*v.t., v.i.* To make or become sodden. —**sod·den·ness,** *n.*

so·di·um, sō′dē·əm, *n.* A soft, silver-white metallic element abundant in nature but always in a combined state, and chemically very active.

so·di·um bi·car·bo·nate, *n.* A white crystalline compound, used in baking powder and medical preparations; baking soda.

so·di·um car·bon·ate, *n.* An alkaline compound of sodium, used as a bleaching agent, and as a water softener.

so·di·um chlo·ride, *n.* Common salt.

so·di·um hy·drox·ide, *n.* A white compound, used in soap, leather, paper, and petroleum products. Also **caus·tic so·da, lye, so·da.**

so·di·um-va·por lamp, sō′dē·əm-vā·pər, *n.* A lamp containing sodium vapor which becomes luminous when an electric current is passed between two electrodes, often used for highway lighting.

Sod·om, sod′əm, *n.* In the Bible, an ancient city destroyed by God for its wickedness; a sinful, wicked place.

sod·om·y, sod′ə·mē, *n.* Unnatural sexual intercourse, esp. of one man with another or of a human being with an animal.

so·ev·er, sō·ev′ər, *adv.* At all; in any case: used with generalizing force, as after *who, what, when, where, how, any,* or *all:* Choose what*soever* person you please.

so·fa, sō′fə, *n.* A long, upholstered seat or couch.

so·fa bed, *n.* A sofa which can be opened to form a full-sized bed.

soft, sôft, soft, *a.* Yielding readily to touch or pressure; easily divided, or altered in shape; not hard or stiff; smooth and agreeable to the touch, as skin or hair;

low or subdued in sound; not glaring, as light or color; not hard or sharp, as outlines; gentle or mild, as wind or rain. *Informal.* Not hard or severe: a *soft* job; gentle, mild, lenient, or compassionate, as persons; characterized by gentleness or tenderness, as the disposition. *Informal.* Easily imposed upon; of delicate constitution; not strong or robust; of money, in paper currency rather than coin; of water, relatively free from mineral salts that interfere with the action of soap. —*adv.*—*n.* That which is soft or yielding; the soft part of anything; softness. —**soft·ness,** *n.*

soft·ball, sôft′bôl, soft′bôl, *n.* A game similar to baseball but requiring a larger, softer ball pitched underhand.

soft-boiled, sôft′boyld′, soft′boyld′, *a.* Of eggs, boiled only until the yolk and white are semicongealed; sentimental; mild-mannered.

soft coal, *n.* Bituminous coal.

soft drink, *n.* A nonalcoholic beverage.

sof·ten, sô′fən, sof′ən, *v.t.* To make soft or more soft; alleviate.—*v.i.* To become soft or less hard. —**sof·ten·er,** *n.*

soft-head·ed, sôft′hed′id, soft′hed′id, *a.* Foolish or silly. —**soft·head,** *n.* —**soft-head·ed·ly,** *adv.*

soft-heart·ed, sôft′här′tid, soft′här′tid, *a.* Sympathetic. —**soft-heart·ed·ness,** *n.*

soft pal·ate, *n.* See palate.

soft ped·al, *n. Informal.* Something that dampens or reduces effect.

soft-ped·al, sôft·ped′əl, soft·ped′əl, *v.i.,* **-aled, -aling.** To use the soft pedal, as in playing the piano.—*v.t. Informal.* To tone down; make less noticeable: to *soft-pedal* an issue in a campaign.

soft sell, *n.* A method of using indirect and subtle suggestion in advertising.

soft-shell, sôft′shel, soft′shel, *a.* Having a fragile or soft shell. Also **soft-shelled.**—*n.* An animal with a soft shell, as the crab.

soft-shoe, sôft′shoo′, soft′shoo′, *a.* Of or pertaining to a type of tap dancing in which the dancer wears shoes that are soft-soled and without metal taps.

soft soap, *n.* A soap in a semifluid or liquid form. *Informal.* Flattery. —**soft-soap,** sôft′sōp′, soft′sōp′, *v.t. Informal.* To flatter; cajole. —**soft-soap·er,** *n.*

soft-spo·ken, sôft′spō′kən, soft′spō′kən, *a.* Speaking softly; having a mild or gentle voice; suave.

soft·ware, sôft′wer, soft′wer, *n.* The programs and programming support necessary to put a computer through its assigned tasks, as distinguished from the actual machine; any aspect of an apparatus not specifically connected with its hardware.

soft·wood, sôft′wûd, soft′wûd, *n.* Any wood which is relatively soft or easily cut; a tree yielding such wood; the wood of any coniferous tree; a coniferous tree.

soft·y, soft·ie, sôf′tē, sof′tē, *n. pl.,* **sof·ties.** *Informal.* One who is easily imposed upon or is extremely sentimental.

sog·gy, sog′ē, *a.,* **-gi·er, -gi·est.** Soaked; soppy; humid, as weather; damp and heavy, as ill-baked bread; sodden; spiritless, dull, or stupid. —**sog·gi·ly,** *adv.* —**sog·gi·ness,** *n.*

soil, soyl, *n.* That portion of the earth's surface in which plants grow, usu. consisting of a mixture of disintegrated rock and decayed organic matter; earth; a particular kind of earth: a sandy *soil;* the ground; a country or region: to set foot on foreign *soil.*

soil, soyl, *v.t.* To make dirty, esp. on the surface: to *soil* a book by handling; smudge, or stain; to tarnish, as with disgrace: to *soil* one's reputation.—*v.i.* To become soiled or smirched.—*n.* A soiling or being soiled: to protect clothes from *soil;* a spot, mark, or stain due to soiling; corruption; filth; sewage.

soil con·ser·va·tion, *n.* Any of various practices, as crop rotation, designed to maintain or improve the resources of the soil.

soi·ree, soi·rée, swä·rā′, *n.* An evening party or social gathering.

so·journ, sō′jėrn, sō·jėrn′, *v.i.* To make a temporary stay. —sō′jėrn, *n.* A temporary stay; a place of temporary stay. —**so·journ·er,** *n.*

sol, sōl, *n.* In music, the fifth tone of the major scale. Also, **so.**

Sol, sol, *n.* The sun.

sol·ace, sol′is, *n.* Comfort in sorrow or trouble; something that gives comfort, or relief.—*v.t.,* **-aced, -ac·ing.** To comfort, or cheer, as a person; relieve, as sorrow. —**sol·ac·er,** *n.*

so·lar, sō′lėr, *a.* Of or pertaining to the sun: the *solar* system; determined by the sun: *solar* day; proceeding from the sun, as light or heat; operating by the light or heat of the sun, as a mechanism; subject to the influence of the sun.

so·lar bat·ter·y, *n.* A device for converting the sun's energy into electricity.

so·lar cell, *n.* A unit that converts radiant energy, as sunlight, into electrical energy.

so·lar flare, *n.* A temporary but violent eruption of energy from some spot on the sun's surface.

so·lar·i·um, sō·lãr′ē·əm, sə·lãr′ē·əm, *n. pl.,* **-ums, -a.** Any glass-enclosed porch, or similar area exposed to the rays of the sun; any enclosed area having overhead sun lamps, as in a resort or health club.

so·lar·ize, sō′lə·rīz, *v.t.,* **-ized, -iz·ing.** To affect or harm by sunlight; to alter by excessive exposure to light.—*v.i.* To become injured by overexposure. —**so·lar·i·za·tion,** sō·lėr·ə·zā′shən, *n.*

so·lar plex·us, *n.* A network of nerves situated at the upper part of the abdomen; the middle part of the abdomen.

so·lar sys·tem, *n.* The sun together with all the planets and other bodies revolving round it.

so·lar wind, *n.* The continuous emanation of charged particles in all directions from the sun, which affects the magnetic fields of planets in the solar system.

sol·der, sod′ėr, *n.* Any of various fusible alloys applied in a melted state to metal surfaces to unite them.—*v.t.* To unite with solder; to join closely and intimately.—*v.i.* To unite things with solder; to become soldered. —**sol·der·er,** *n.*

sol·dier, sōl′jėr, *n.* One who serves in an army for pay; one engaged in military service, esp. an enlisted man as contrasted with a commissioned officer; a man of military skill or experience; one who contends or serves in any cause.—*v.i.* To serve as a soldier.

sol·dier of for·tune, *n.* A military adventurer ready to serve wherever there is promise of profit or adventure.

sol·dier·y, sōl′jə·rē, *n.* Soldiers collectively; military training.

sole, sōl, *n.* The bottom of the foot; the corresponding underpart of a shoe, boot, or the like, exclusive of the heel; the bottom or undersurface of anything.—*v.t.,* **soled, sol·ing.** To furnish with a sole. —**soled,** *a.*

sole, sōl, *n.* Any of various flatfishes with a small mouth, a food fish common along European coasts and the Pacific coast of N. America.

sole, sōl, *a.* Being the only one or ones: the *sole* reason for his conduct; being unique; pertaining to one individual or group to the exclusion of all others: having the *sole* right to something; lonely or solitary.

sol·e·cism, sol′ə·siz·əm, *n.* A mistake in using language, esp. an ungrammatical construction; a breach of etiquette; impropriety; inconsistency.

sole·ly, sōl′lē, *adv.* As the only one or ones: the employers are *solely* responsible; wholly; merely.

sol·emn, sol′əm, *a.* Grave, sober; such as to cause serious thoughts or a grave mood: a *solemn* sight; characterized by dignified or serious formality, as proceedings of a formal ceremonious character; marked by or observed with religious rites. —**sol·emn·ly,** *adv.* —**sol·emn·ness,** *n.*

so·lem·ni·ty, sə·lem′ni·tē, *n. pl.,* **-ties.** The state or character of being solemn, serious, or earnest. *Usu. pl.* A solemn observance, ceremonial proceeding, or special formality: to commemorate an event with all due *solemnities.*

sol·em·nize, sol′əm·nīz, *v.t.,* **-nized, -niz·ing.** To commemorate with rites or ceremonies; to perform the ceremony of, esp. marriage; to render solemn, serious, or grave. —**sol·em·ni·za·tion,** sol·əm·nə·zā′shən, *n.*

sole·ness, sōl′nis, *n.* The state or condition of being sole, alone, or without others.

so·lic·it, sə·lis′it, *v.t.* To seek for by earnest or respectful request, or formal application; urge or importune; to accost or entice with immoral intention.—*v.i.* To make request, as for something desired; solicit business orders or trade; to importune a person with immoral intention. —**so·lic·i·ta·tion,** sə·lis·i·tā′shən, *n.*

so·lic·i·tor, sə·lis′i·tėr, *n.* One who solicits, esp. one who seeks funds for charity; one whose business it is to solicit orders or trade.

so·lic·i·tous, sə·lis′i·təs, *a.* Anxious over something, used with *about* or *for;* anxiously desirous, with *of;* eager, used with infinitive; careful or particular. —**so·lic·i·tous·ness,** *n.*

so·lic·i·tude, sə·lis′i·tood, sə·lis′i·tūd, *n.* The state of being solicitous; concern; anxiety. *Usu. pl.* Causes of concern.

sol·id, sol′id, *a.* Having the interior completely filled up; not hollow; of matter neither liquid nor gaseous; pertaining to or having the dimensions of length, breadth, and thickness, as a geometrical figure; not flimsy; unanimous, as in opinion; sound or valid, as reasons or arguments; reliable or sensible; financially sound; entire or uninterrupted; uniform in tone or shade; real or genuine: *solid* comfort.—*n.* A spatial figure having the three dimensions of length, breadth, and thickness, as a cube; matter exhibiting relative firmness and volume. —**so·lid·i·ty,** sə·lid′ə·tē, **sol·id·ness,** *n.*

sol·i·dar·i·ty, sol·ə·dar′i·tē, *n. pl.,* **-ties.** Union or fellowship arising from common responsibilities and interests, as between members of a class, or between classes or groups; community of interests, purposes, or action.

sol·id ge·om·e·try, *n.* The geometry that deals with three-dimensional figures.

so·lid·i·fy, sə·lid′ə·fī, *v.t.,* **-fied, -fy·ing.** To make solid or into a hard or compact mass; to change from a liquid or gaseous form to a solid; to unite firmly or consolidate.—*v.i.* To become solid or compact. —**so·lid·i·fi·ca·tion,** sə·lid·ə·fə·kā′shən, *n.*

sol·id-state, sol′id·stāt′, *a.* Of any electronic device, having solid material such as transistors substituted for movable parts, filaments, or vacuum tubes.

so·lil·o·quize, sə·lil′ə·kwiz, *v.i.,* **-quized, -quiz·ing.** To talk to oneself; speak a soliloquy. —**so·lil·o·quist,** sə·lil′ə·kwist, *n.*

so·lil·o·quy, sə·lil′ə·kwē, *n. pl.,* **-quies.** The act or an instance of talking to oneself; in drama, a monologue.

sol·i·taire, sol′i·tėr, *n.* Any of numerous card games played by a single individual; also **pa·tience;** a gem, esp. a diamond, set alone, as in a ring.

sol·i·tar·y, sol′i·ter·ē, *a.* Alone; living alone or avoiding the society of others; being the only one or ones: a *solitary* instance; characterized by solitude, as a place; unfrequented, secluded, or lonely.—*n. pl.,* **-ies.** One who lives alone or in solitude, or avoids the society of others. —**sol·i·tar·i·ly,** *adv.* —**sol·i·tar·i·ness,** *n.*

sol·i·tude, sol′i·tood, sol′i·tūd, *n.* The state of being alone; a lonely, deserted place.

so·lo, sō′lō, *n. pl.,* **so·los, so·li,** sō′lē. A musical composition or passage intended for performance by one voice or one instrument, with or without accompaniment; any performance, as a dance, by one person; an airplane pilot's first unaccompanied flight.—*a.* Performing or performed alone; alone; without a companion or partner.—*adv.* Alone; unaccompanied.—*v.i.,* **-loed, -lo·ing.** To perform a solo. —**so·lo·ist,** *n.*

Sol·o·mon, sol′ə·mən, *n.* An extraordinarily wise man.

So·lon, sō′lən, *n.* (*Often l.c.*) A wise lawgiver or legislator; a sage.

so long, interj. *Informal.* Good-by.

sol·stice, sol′stis, *n.* Either of the two times in the year when the sun is at its greatest distance from the celestial equator, reaching the northernmost point on June 21 and the southernmost point on Dec. 22, called respectively, in the northern hemisphere, *summer solstice* and *winter solstice;* a farthest point; a turning point.

sol·u·ble, sol′yə·bəl, *a.* Susceptible of being dissolved in a fluid; capable of being solved or resolved. —**sol·u·bil·i·ty,** sol·yə·bil′ə·tē, **sol·u·ble·ness,** *n.* —**sol·u·bly,** *adv.*

sol·ute, sol′ūt, sō′loot, *n.* A dissolved substance.—*a.* Having passed into solution.

so·lu·tion, sə·loo′shən, *n.* The act of solving, clearing up, or explaining; an explanation or answer; the method of resolving a problem; the act of dissolving or state of being dissolved; the homogeneous combination of a liquid, solid, or gas with another liquid or, more rarely, a gas or solid; the preparation formed by this combination.

solve, solv, *v.t.,* **solved, solv·ing.** To find an answer for; explain; to make clear; find or attain a solution to, as a problem. —**solv·a·ble,** *a.* —**solv·a·bil·i·ty,** sol·və·bil′ə·tē, **solv·a·ble·ness,** *n.* —**solv·er,** *n.*

sol·vent, sol′vent, *a.* Able to pay all just debts; having the power of dissolving.—*n.* Any substance that dissolves other substances; that which explains or solves. —**sol·ven·cy,** *n.*

so·mat·ic, sō·mat′ik, *a.* Of or pertaining to the body; physical.

so·ma·to·type, sō′mə·tə·tīp, sə·mat′ə·tīp, *n.* Physique; body type.

som·ber, som′bər, *a.* Dark; shadowy; dimly lighted; dark and dull, as color; gloomy; depressing; serious or melancholy in appearance. —**som·ber·ly,** *adv.* —**som·ber·ness,** *n.*

som·bre·ro, som·brār′ō, *n. pl.,* **-ros.** A broad-brimmed hat with a high crown, made of felt or straw, worn in Spain and Mexico.

some, səm, *a.* Expressing a certain indeterminate quantity, sometimes a considerable quantity; situated at *some* distance; indicating a person or thing not definitely known or not specific, often followed by *or other;* certain, as distinct from others: *Some* people don't think so. *Informal.* Important; unusual: That was *some* game!—*pron.* Unspecified persons or things, often followed by *of: some of* us; a certain undetermined additional amount: a pound and then *some.* —*adv.* Approximately: *some* 20 people. *Informal.* Considerably: to go *some* to win.

some·bod·y, səm′bod·ē, səm′bəd·ē, *pron.* A person unknown or of uncertain identity.—*n. pl.,* **-ies.** A person of distinction or consequence.

some·day, səm′dā, *adv.* At some unspecified time in the future.

some·how, səm′how, *adv.* In some way not yet known or evident.

some·one, səm′wən, *pron.* Some person; somebody.

some·place, səm′plās, *adv.* In some locality or other.

som·er·sault, səm′ər·sôlt, *n.* A head-over-heels revolution of the body performed either forward or backward, from a standing or a sitting position.—*v.i.* To execute a somersault. Also **sum·mer·sault, som·er·set,** səm′ər·set.

some·thing, səm′thing, *n.* An indeterminate or unknown event or thing; an indefinite quantity or degree; a little; a person or thing of considerable importance. —*adv.* In some degree or measure: It was *something* like that.

some·time, səm′tīm, *adv.* At some vaguely indefinite time in the future; at an unspecified time.—*a.* Having been formerly; former; late.

some·times, səm′tīmz, *adv.* At times; now and then; on occasion.

some·way, səm′wā, *adv.* In some way; somehow. Also **some·ways.**

some·what, səm′hwot, səm′hwət, *adv.* In some degree or measure; rather; slightly.—*pron.* Some indeterminate quantity, degree, portion, or the like; a person or thing having in some measure a nature or quality: She is *somewhat* of a bore.

some·where, səm′hwer, *adv.* In, at, or to some place unspecified or not known; in one place or another; at some location not definitely known or stated.—*n.* A place not known or not specified.

som·nam·bu·late, som·nam′byə·lāt, *v.i.,* **-lat·ed, -lat·ing.** To walk in one's sleep.—*v.t.* To walk through or across while sleeping. —**som·nam·bu·lant,** *a.* —**som·nam·bu·la·tion,** som·nam·bye·lā′shən, **som·nam·bu·lism,** *n.* —**som·nam·bu·list,** *n.*

som·no·lent, som′nə·lənt, *a.* Sleepy; drowsy. —**som·no·lence, som·no·len·cy,** *n.*

son, sən, *n.* A male child or person in relation to his parents; any male descendant; one related as if by ties of sonship; a familiar term of address to a man or boy, as from an older person; a person considered native to a particular place: a *son* of the plains.

so·nar, sō′när, *n.* A device similar to radar for detecting a submerged submarine, mine, or school of fish, for measuring water depths, and for communicating, based on the outward projection of sound waves and the echoes which they send back when they strike a submerged object.

so·na·ta, sə·nä′tə, *n.* A usu. instrumental musical composition of usu. three or four movements having contrasting rhythms but related keys.

song, sông, song, *n.* The act or art of singing; vocal music; that which is sung; a ballad; a piece of music adapted for singing or simulating a piece to be sung: Mendelssohn's *Songs Without Words;* the musical or tuneful sounds produced by certain birds or insects. —**for a song,** for a low price.

song and dance, *n.* A theatrical act which consists of some song and dance, esp. as seen in vaudeville. *Informal.* An alibi or account that is misleading or untrue; nonsense.

song·bird, sông′bərd, song′bərd, *n.* A bird that sings.

song·fest, sông′fest, song′fest, *n. Informal.* A festival at which group singing is the chief entertainment.

song·ster, sông′stər, song′stər, *n.* A singer; a songbird; a writer of songs; a book of songs. —**song·stress,** *n. fem.*

song·writ·er, sông′rī·tər, song′rī·tər, *n.* A composer or lyricist of popular songs.

son·ic, son′ik, *a.* Of or pertaining to sound waves; referring to speeds approximating that of sound, about 740 miles per hour. —**son·i·cal·ly,** *adv.*

son·ic boom, *n.* A loud, explosive report caused by an airplane as it reaches the speed of sound.

son-in-law, sən′in·lô, *n. pl.,* **sons-in-law.** A man married to one's daughter.

son·net, son′it, *n.* A poem, properly expressive of a single complete thought, of 14 lines.

son·net·eer, son·ə·tēr′, *n.* A writer of sonnets; an inferior poet.—*v.i.* To compose sonnets.

son·ny, sən′ē, *n. pl.,* **-nies.** Little son: often used as a familiar term of address to a boy.

so·no·rous, sə·nôr′əs, sə·nōr′əs, son′ər·əs, *a.* Giving out or capable of giving out a sound, esp. a deep or resonant sound; loud, deep, or resonant, as a sound; rich and full in sound, as language or verse; resounding, as in an orator's delivery.—**so·nor·i·ty**, sə·nôr′i·tē, sə·nor′i·tē, **so·no·rous·ness**, n.

soon, soon, adv. Within a short period after this or that time or event: We shall soon know; before long; promptly or quickly; readily or willingly: I would as soon walk as ride.—**soon·er or lat·er**, eventually.

soot, soot, sût, n. A black substance formed from fuel in combustion, rising in fine particles and adhering to the sides of the chimney conveying the smoke.—v.t. To smudge or cover with soot.—v.i. To use soot as a fertilizer or as a slug repellant.

soothe, sooth, v.t., **soothed**, **sooth·ing**. To calm the feelings of; relieve, ease, comfort, or refresh.—v.i. To exert a soothing influence; bring calm or comfort. —**sooth·er**, n. —**sooth·ing**, a.

sooth·say·er, sooth′sā·ər, n. A person who claims to foretell the future; one who makes prophecies. —**sooth·say·ing**, n.

soot·y, sût′ē, soo′tē, a., **-i·er**, **-i·est**. Covered, blackened, or smudged with soot; consisting of or resembling soot; of a black, dark brown, or dusky color. —**soot·i·ly**, adv. —**soot·i·ness**, n.

sop, sop, n. Something dipped in broth or other liquid food, and intended to be eaten; something given to pacify or bribe; a weak-willed person; a wet mass. —v.t., **sopped**, **sop·ping**. To soak in a liquid; to wet through; to absorb, as a liquid, usu. followed by up.—v.i. To be or become completely wet.—**sop·ping**, a.

soph·ist, sof′ist, n. One who reasons ingeniously or subtly, but whose arguments are usu. specious or fallacious. —**soph·ism**, n. —**so·phis·tic**, sə·fis′tik, **so·phis·ti·cal**, a.

so·phis·ti·cate, sə·fis′tə·kāt, v.t., **-cat·ed**, **-cat·ing**. To make less natural or simple; to alter, as a person, by education or experience; disillusion; to increase the complexity of; refine.—v.i. To use sophistry; to quibble. —sə·fis′tə·kit, sə·fis′tə·kāt, n. One who is sophisticated. —**so·phis·ti·ca·tion**, sə·fis·tə·kā′shən, n. —**so·phis·ti·ca·tor**, n.

so·phis·ti·cat·ed, sə·fis′tə·kā·tid, a. Changed from the natural character or original simplicity by education or experience; appreciated by or identified with intellectuals or sophisticates; worldly-wise; subtle; cultivated; intricate or complex: a sophisticated radar alarm system.

soph·ist·ry, sof′i·strē, n. pl., **-ries**. Specious or fallacious reasoning; sophism.

soph·o·more, sof′ə·môr, sof′môr, n. In American high schools, colleges, and universities, a student in the second year of a four-year course; one in the second year of any endeavor.

soph·o·mor·ic, sof·ə·môr′ik, sof·ə·mōr′ik, a. Of, pertaining to, or characteristic of a sophomore; suggestive of or resembling the traditional stereotyped sophomore, as in intellectual conceit, pretensions, or self-assurance. Also **soph·o·mor·i·cal**. —**soph·o·mor·i·cal·ly**, adv.

sop·o·rif·ic, sŏp·ə·rif′ik, sop·ə·rif′ik, a. Causing sleep; tending to cause sleep; marked by lethargy or drowsiness.—n. A drug that causes sleep.

sop·py, sop′ē, a., **-pi·er**, **-pi·est**. Soaked, drenched, or very wet, as ground; rainy, as weather.

so·pran·o, sə·pran′ō, sə·prä′nō, n. pl., **so·pran·os**, sə·pran′ōz, **so·pran·i**, sə·prä′nē. The highest range of female voice; one who sings soprano; an instrument with a soprano range; the music or part for such an instrument or voice.—a. Having a soprano range.

sor·cer·er, sôr′sər·ər, n. A conjuror; one practicing witchcraft or sorcery; a magician. —**sor·cer·ess**, n. fem.

sor·cer·y, sôr′sə·rē, n. pl., **-ies**. Divination through the supposed assistance of evil spirits; black magic; enchantment; witchcraft. —**sor·cer·ous**, a.

sor·did, sôr′did, a. Filthy; neglected or squalid; base or mean in character; meanly avaricious; selfish. —**sor·did·ness**, n.

sore, sōr, sôr, a., **sor·er**, **sor·est**. Painful or tender, as a bruise, or wound; stiff and tender, as from physical exertion; suffering mental anguish or grief. Informal. Angered, irritated, or resentful; severe; distressing; extreme.—n. A place on the body where the skin or flesh is bruised, cut, infected, or painful; any cause of sorrow, pain, misery, or vexation. —**sore·ly**, adv. —**sore·ness**, n.

sore·head, sōr′hed, sôr′hed, n. Informal. One easily offended or angered. —**sore·head·ed**, a.

sor·ghum, sôr′gəm, n. A cereal plant cultivated for fodder, grain, and juice; a syrup or molasses boiled down from the juice.

so·ror·i·ty, sə·rôr′i·tē, sə·ror′i·tē, n. A group of girls or women belonging to a national or local organization, often designed to promote social life, as in colleges, or mutual interests, as in a profession.

sor·rel, sôr′əl, sor′əl, n. A reddish-brown color; a horse of this color.—a. Reddish-brown.

sor·rel, sôr′əl, sor′əl, n. Any of certain perennial plants, esp. a succulent acid herb used in salads.

sor·row, sor′ō, sôr′ō, n. Pain of mind from loss, disappointment, or calamity; grief; regret; sadness; the manifestation of sadness.—v.i. To be affected with sorrow; to grieve; to be sad. —**sor·row·er**, n. —**sor·row·ful**, a.

sor·ry, sor′ē, sôr′ē, a., **-ri·er**, **-ri·est**. Feeling regret, sympathy, pity, or the like: to be sorry for a loss; of a deplorable, pitiable, or miserable kind: a sorry plight; sorrowful, grieved, or sad; poor, mean, or pitiful: a sorry horse.—interj. Pardon; an expression of apology. —**sor·ri·ly**, adv. —**sor·ri·ness**, n.

sort, sôrt, n. A particular kind, species, variety, or class: to have more of that sort in stock; a number of persons or things ranked together as being of the same general character: The cases fall into two sorts; a person or thing as being of a particular character: a good sort of man; a more or less adequate example of something: A unicorn is a sort of mythical horse.—v.t. To arrange according to sort, kind, or class: to sort the laundry; classify; to separate or take from others, followed by out: to sort out clothes needed for the trip; to class, group, or place, followed by with or together. —**af·ter a sort**, in an imperfect manner; after a fashion. —**of sorts, of a sort**, of a mediocre or an undetermined kind: a writer of sorts. —**out of sorts**, not in the normal condition of good health or high spirits. —**sort of**. Informal. To a certain extent: to feel sort of discouraged. —**sort·a·ble**, a. —**sort·er**, n.

sor·tie, sôr′tē, n. A sudden or surprise incursion against the enemy by troops under siege; a flight of a single aircraft into enemy airspace; a sally.—v.i. To go on a sortie.

S O S, es′ō′es′, n. The international radio code signal used by aircraft or ships at sea when in distress; any signal or request for aid.

so-so, sō′sō, sō′sō′, a. Indifferent or mediocre; neither very good nor very bad.—adv. Indifferently; tolerably. Also **so·so**.

sot, sot, n. A person stupefied by excessive consumption of alcohol; a habitual drunkard. —**sot·ted**, a. —**sot·tish**, a. —**sot·tish·ness**, n.

sot·to vo·ce, sot′ō vō′chē, adv. In an undertone; privately; softly.

sou·bri·quet, soo′bri·kā, n. Sobriquet.

souf·flé, soo·flā′, soo′flā, a. Puffed up; made light, as by beating and baking. Also **souf·fléed**.—n. A light and puffy baked entrée.

sough, sŭf, sow, v.i. To emit a rustling, murmuring, or whistling sound, like that of the wind.—n. Such a sound.

sought, sôt, v. Past tense and past participle of **seek**.

soul, sōl, n. The principle of life, feeling, thought, and action in humans, regarded as a distinct entity separate from the body, and commonly held to be separable in existence from the body; the spiritual part of humans as distinct from the physical; an umbrella term with many meanings including the essence of being black; a disembodied spirit of a deceased person; the seat of the feelings or sentiments; the capacity for exalted emotions; a human being: every *soul* aboard the ship; noble warmth of feeling, spirit, or courage; essential element of something; the inspirer of some action, movement, or group; the embodiment of some quality: His brother was the *soul* of honor.—*a.* Characteristic of or relating to blacks or black culture: a *soul* sister. —**souled,** *a.*

soul·ful, sōl′fəl, *a.* Full of soul; of a deeply emotional nature or character. —**soul·ful·ly,** *adv.* —**soul·ful·ness,** *n.*

soul·less, sōl′lis, *a.* Without a soul or spirit; heartless; without emotion.

soul mate, *n.* One for whom a person feels a strong attraction, usu. someone of the opposite sex.

soul·searching, sōl′ser·ching, *n.* A deep self-analysis of one's innermost motives and convictions.

sound, sownd, *n.* The sensation produced in the organs of hearing by certain vibrations or sound waves conveyed by the atmosphere, water, or other medium; the sound wave producing this sensation; the particular auditory effect produced by a given source or medium: the *sound* of bells; any audibly perceptible vibrations or auditory effect: a variety of *sounds;* a noise, vocal utterance, musical tone, or the like: the *sounds* from next door; the import or effect of a communication or event: The offer of peace had a glorious *sound;* mere noise without meaning: His speech was all *sound* and no substance.—*v.i.* To make a sound: The gong *sounds* for lunch; to be heard, as a sound; to impart a certain effect: a story that *sounds* false.—*v.t.* To cause to make a sound: to *sound* a trumpet; to give forth, as a sound: The soprano *sounded* high C; to announce, order, or direct by a sound: to *sound* a retreat; to utter audibly, pronounce, or express: to *sound* each syllable. —**sound off.** *Informal.* To call out, as each member of a group giving in sequence his or her name; to speak out frankly, as in airing a grievance. —**with·in sound of,** not far from; within earshot. —**sound·a·ble,** *a.*

sound, sownd, *a.* In good condition; undamaged or unimpaired; solid: *sound* walls or floors; free from disease, injury or decay: a *sound* body or mind; financially strong: a *sound* investment; sensible: *sound* judgment; of substantial character or worth: a *sound* value; well-founded: *sound* reasoning; unbroken and deep: a *sound* sleep; vigorous and thorough: a *sound* scolding; upright; good; loyal.—*adv.* Deeply: *sound* asleep. —**sound·ly,** *adv.* —**sound·ness,** *n.*

sound, sownd, *v.t.* To measure or try the depth of, as water, a deep hole, or the like, by letting down a lead plummet on the end of a line or by some equivalent means; to investigate; to seek to ascertain: to *sound* the depth of a person's character; to seek to elicit the views of, as a person, through indirect inquiry, often followed by *out:* to *sound out* his feelings on the subject.—*v.i.* To use the lead and line or similar device for measuring depth, as at sea; to explore, esp. by indirect inquiry. —**sound·a·ble,** *a.*

sound, sownd, *n.* A passage or channel of water, as between the mainland and an isle or connecting two seas.

sound·box, sownd′boks, *n.* The hollow chamber of a stringed musical instrument which increases sonority of tone.

sound ef·fects, *n. pl.,* Lifelike imitations of sounds, as of rain, creaking doors, hoofbeats, etc., produced mechanically as called for during production of motion pictures, radio programs, etc.

sound·er, sown′dər, *n.* One who or that which sounds or measures the depth of water; a telegraphic device that sounds or clicks in response to electromagnetic impulses; a surgical probe.

sound·ing, sown′ding, *n. Often pl.* The act or process of measuring depth or examining the bottom of water with or as with a lead and line; *pl.,* depths of water, ascertained by means of a lead and line, as at sea.

sound·ing, sown′ding, *a.* Emitting or producing a sound or sounds.

sound·ing board, *n.* A thin, resonant plate of wood forming part of a musical instrument, enhancing the strength and quality of the tones; a board or reflecting structure placed over or behind and above a speaker, orchestra, or the like, to direct the sound toward the audience; one or more persons toward whom ideas or opinions are directed in order to test their reactions. Also **sound·board.**

sound·less, sownd′lis, *a.* Having no sound; noiseless; silent. —**sound·less·ness,** *n.*

sound·proof, sownd′proof, *a.* Impervious to sound. —*v.t.* To insulate against sound.

sound track, *n.* A sound record made along one edge of a motion-picture film.

sound wave, *n.* A pressure wave, in the air or any other elastic medium, that constitutes audible or ultrasonic sound.

soup, soop, *n.* A liquid food in which meat, fish, or vegetables have been boiled with various added ingredients and seasonings. *Informal.* A heavy fog or overcast; nitroglycerin. —**soup up.** *Informal.* To improve or better the capacity for higher speed, as of an automobile engine.

soup kitch·en, *n.* A place, usu. operated by a charitable organization, which serves food to the poor either free or for a nominal charge.

soup·y, soo′pē, *a.,* **-i·er, -i·est.** Like soup; having the consistency or appearance of soup; dense or thick, as a fog; sentimental.

sour, sowr, sow′ər, *a.* Having an acid taste, such as vinegar or lemon juice; tart; rendered acid by fermentation; affected or spoiled by fermentation; characteristic of what is so affected; distasteful or disagreeable; unpleasant; of persons, harsh in spirit or temper; austere; peevish; rendered impure by compounds of sulfur, as gasoline.—*n.* That which is sour; something sour.—*v.i.* To become sour or acid; to turn sour; to become harsh, morose, or peevish.—*v.t.* To make sour or acid; to render acid or to spoil by fermentation; to make disagreeable or unpleasant; to embitter. —**sour·ish,** *a.* —**sour·ness,** *n.*

sour·ball, sowr′bôl, sow′ər·bôl, *n.* A tart, fruit-flavored, hard candy. *Informal.* One who is constantly ill-tempered and grouchy.

source, sōrs, sôrs, *n.* The place from which anything comes or is obtained; anything from which something proceeds or arises; an origin; that from which news, information, or evidence, esp. of an original character, is obtained.

source book, *n.* A book or compilation of orig. material, as laboratory notes, letters, or official documents.

sour grapes, *n.* False contempt or scorn displayed for something one does not or cannot have.

souse, sows, *v.t.,* **soused, sous·ing.** To plunge into water or other liquid; to drench, immerse, or saturate, as with a liquid; to dash or pour, as water. *Informal.* To intoxicate.—*v.i.* To be plunged into water or a liquid; to fall with a splash; to be soaked or drenched; to be steeping or soaking in something. *Informal.* To drink to intoxication.—*n.* An act of sousing. *Informal.* A drunkard.

south, sowth, *n.* One of the four cardinal points of the compass, directly opposite to the north; the region lying opposite to the north. (*Cap.*) The section of the

---

a- hat, fāte, fâre, fäther; **e-** met, mē; **i-** pin, pīne; **o-** not, nōte, ôrb, moove (move), boy, pownd; **u-** cūbe, bûll, tûk (took); **ch-** chin; **th-** thick, ᵺen; **zh-** vizhon (vision); **ə-** ego, takən, pencəl, lemən, bərd (bird).

U.S. below the Mason-Dixon line and east of the Mississippi River.—*a.* Situated in the south or in a southern direction; pertaining to the south; proceeding from the south.—*adv.* Toward, from, or in the south.

south•bound, sowth/bownd, *a.* Going or traveling south.

south•east, sowth-ēst/, *n.* The direction midway between south and east; a region in this direction; the direction on the compass halfway between the south and east points; a region situated in this direction. (*Cap.*) The region in the southeast part of the U.S.—*a.* Situated in the southeast; proceeding toward the southeast; coming from the southeast.—*adv.* In or toward the southeast.

south•east•er, sowth-ē/stər, *n.* A strong wind, usu. of gale proportions, from the southeast.

south•east•er•ly, sowth-ē/stər-lē, *a., adv.* Toward or from the southeast.

south•east•ern, sowth-ē/stərn, *a.* Situated in, or going toward the southeast; coming from the southeast, as a wind; of or pertaining to the southeast. **—south•east•ern•er,** *n.*

south•east•ward, sowth-ēst/wərd, *adv.* Toward the southeast. Also **south•east•wards.**—*a.* Toward, in, or from the southeast.—*n.* The southeast. **—south•east•ward•ly,** *a., adv.*

south•er, sow/thər, *n.* A wind, gale, or storm from the south.

south•er•ly, səth/ər-lē, *a., adv.* Moving, directed, or situated toward the south; coming from the south, as a wind.

south•ern, səth/ərn, *a.* (*Sometimes cap.*) Belonging to or of the south or South; coming from the south, as a storm. **—south•ern•most,** *a.*

south•ern•er, səth/ər-nər, *n.* A native or inhabitant of the south. (*Usu. cap.*) A native or inhabitant of the southern U.S.

South•ern Hem•i•sphere, *n.* That half of the earth lying south of the equator.

south•ern lights, *n. pl.* The aurora australis.

south•paw, sowth/pô, *n.* A left-handed baseball pitcher. *Informal.* A left-handed person.

South Pole, *n.* The southern end of the earth's axis; (*l.c.*) the pole on a magnet pointing to the south.

south•ward, sowth/wərd, *adv.* Toward the south; south. Also **south•wards.**—*a.* Moving, bearing, facing, or situated toward the south.—*n.* The southward part, direction, or point. **—south•ward•ly,** *adv.*

south•west, sowth-west/, *n.* The point of the compass halfway between the south and west points; (*cap.*) the southwestern area of the U.S.—*a.* Lying in the direction of the southwest; coming from the southwest.—*adv.* From, toward, or in the southwest.

south•west•er, sowth-wes/tər, *n.* A strong wind or storm out of the southwest.

south•west•er•ly, sowth-wes/tər-lē, *a., adv.* Toward or from the southwest.

south•west•ern, sowth-wes/tərn, *a.* Pertaining to, or coming from the southwest; situated in the southwest. **—south•west•ern•er,** *n.*

south•west•ward, sowth-west/wərd, *adv.* Toward the southwest. Also **south•west•wards.**—*a.* Toward or in the southwest.—*n.* The southwest. **—south•west•ward•ly,** *a., adv.*

sou•ve•nir, soo-və-nēr/, soo/və-nēr, *n.* That which calls to mind or revives the memory of anything; a memento; a keepsake.

sov•er•eign, sov/rən, *a.* Supreme in power; possessing supreme dominion or jurisdiction; royal; free of outside influence or control: a *sovereign* nation; having power and importance; excellent.—*n.* A supreme ruler; the person having the highest power or authority in a state, as a king or queen; a monarch.

sov•er•eign•ty, sov/rən-tē, *n. pl.,* **-ties.** The state of being sovereign; the supreme power in a state; an independent government.

so•vi•et, sō/vē•et, sō/vē•ət, sov/ē•ət, *n.* An elected legislative body or council, esp. in the Soviet Union; similar councils in other socialist governments. (*Cap.*), *pl.* The citizens and the leaders of the Soviet Union. —*a.* Pertaining to or of a soviet.

sow, sō, *v.t.,* **sowed, sown** or **sowed, sow•ing.** To scatter, as seed upon the earth, for the purpose of growth; to plant by strewing; to spread abroad; to propagate: to *sow* discord.—*v.i.* To scatter seed for growth and the production of a crop. **—sow•er,** *n.*

sow, sow, *n.* The female of the swine.

soy, soy, *n.* A salty brown sauce, as for fish, made in the Orient from soybeans; a soybean. Also **soy sauce.**

soy•bean, soy/bēn, *n.* A protein-rich leguminous plant, used for forage; its seeds, used as a source of oil, flour, foods, etc.

spa, spä, *n.* A mineral spring; a place, as a resort, which people frequent for its mineral waters.

space, spās, *n.* The unlimited or indefinitely great general area or expanse of three dimensions in which, or in portions of which, all material objects are located; the portion or extent of this in a given instance: the *space* occupied by a body; a reserved seat or room, as on a train; extent or room in three dimensions; a particular extent of surface: forests covering acres of *space;* linear distance: trees set at an equal *space* apart; extent of time: a *space* of two hours; an interval of time or a while; the territory outside the atmosphere of the earth; outer space.—*v.t.,* **spaced, spac•ing.** To divide into spaces; to set some distance apart. **—space•less,** *a.* **—spac•er,** *n.*

Space-Age, *n.* The period ushered in with the successful launching of the first space satellite, Sputnik, on October 4, 1957, and continuing with subsequent space probes.

space•craft, spās/kraft, *n.* Spaceship.

space flight, *n.* A journey by an unmanned or manned vehicle into outer space.

space heat•er, *n.* A small stove or a portable heating device for warming a space that is enclosed, esp. a room. **—space heat•ing,** *n.*

space•man, spās/man, spās/mən, *n. pl.,* **-men.** A person who travels beyond the atmosphere of the earth; astronaut.

space med•i•cine, *n.* That branch of medicine concerned with the effects of flight through the atmosphere and in space upon the human body. Also **aer•o•space med•i•cine.**

space•ship, spās/ship, *n.* Any unmanned or manned vehicle, as a rocket, for travel outside of the earth's atmosphere. Also **space•craft.**

space suit, *n.* A pressurized suit supplied with oxygen and other necessities for human life, work, and movement in outer space or at great heights in the atmosphere.

space•walk, spās/wôk, *n.* Any movement made by an astronaut outside a space vehicle that is orbiting in space.

spac•ing, spā/sing, *n.* The act of one who or that which spaces; the manner in which spaces are arranged.

spa•cious, spā/shəs, *a.* Containing much space, as a house; amply large or roomy; vast: this *spacious* world; broad in scope, range, or inclusiveness. **—spa•cious•ness,** *n.*

Spack•le, spak/əl, *n. Trademark.* A product with the pastelike consistency of plastering material, used to repair cracks in walls or ceilings before decorating. —*v.t.,* **-led, -ling.** To repair or spread with this product.

spade, spād, *n.* A black figure shaped like a heart placed with the point upward, used on playing cards; a card of this suit bearing such figures; *pl.,* the suit of playing cards bearing such markings.

spade, spād, *n.* An instrument for digging, having a broad blade of iron and a stout handle, adapted for use with both hands and one foot; a tool or instrument which resembles a spade.—*v.t.,* **spad•ed, spad•ing.**

To dig with a spade. **—call a spade a spade,** to call things by their proper names; to speak plainly and candidly. **—spade·ful,** *n.* **—spad·er,** *n.*

spade·work, spād/werk, *n.* Preparatory work for a project; any labor in which a spade is used.

spa·ghet·ti, spə·get/ē, *n.* A kind of flour paste of Italian origin cut in long, slender, solid, cordlike pieces, to be boiled and then served with various sauces.

span, span, *n.* The space between the point of a person's thumb to that of the little finger when the hand is spread, usu. taken as nine inches; a short space of time; the total stretch, extent, or reach of anything; the portion contained between limits of space or time.—*v.t.,* **spanned, span·ning.** To measure by the hand with fingers encompassing the object; to measure or extend across; to construct with something that bridges across.

span·gle, span/gəl, *n.* A small, circular ornament of metal or plastic stitched on an article of dress; any small, sparkling object.—*v.t.,* **-gled, -gling.** To set, sprinkle, or adorn with spangles.—*v.i.* To glitter with or as with spangles; to glisten.

Span·iard, span/yərd, *n.* An inhabitant of Spain; a person of Spanish birth.

span·iel, span/yəl, *n.* Any of various breeds of dogs of small or medium size, usu. with a long, silky coat and drooping ears; a submissive, fawning, or cringing person.

Span·ish, span/ish, *a.* Of or relating to Spain, its people, or its language.

Span·ish A·mer·i·ca, *n.* The parts of the Western Hemisphere where the language is Spanish, including Mexico, and most parts of Central America and South America.

Span·ish moss, *n.* A lichen-like plant of the pineapple family, found in the southern U.S., forming long, pendulous gray tufts which drape the branches of trees.

spank, spangk, *v.t.* To slap or smack with the open hand against the buttocks as a punishment.—*n.* **spank·er,** *n.*

spank·ing, spang/king, *a.* Moving with a quick lively pace; brisk. *Informal.* Exceptional; extremely fine.—*adv. Informal.* Unusually or extremely: a *spanking* new car.—*n.* Several slaps against the buttocks for punishment.

spar, spär, *n.* A piece of timber of considerable length in proportion to its thickness.—*v.t.,* **sparred, spar·ring.** To furnish or fit with spars.

spar, spär, *v.i.,* **sparred, spar·ring.** To move the arms in a way suitable for immediate attack or defense; to box; to fight by striking with spurs, as cocks; to argue.—*n.* A preliminary flourish of the fists; a boxing match; a dispute.

spare, spār, *v.t.,* **spared, spar·ing.** To refrain from harming or destroying, or leave uninjured: *spare* an enemy; to save from strain, discomfort, or annoyance; to refrain from employing, as some instrument, means, or aid: to *spare* no pains, time, or expense; to set aside or allow for a particular purpose: to *spare* time for an undertaking; to give, lend, or part with, as from a supply, esp. without inconvenience or loss; to dispense with or do without; to use economically or frugally; to refrain from using up or wasting; to have left in excess or as surplus.—*v.i.* To refrain from inflicting injury or punishment; to exercise leniency or mercy; to use economy, or be frugal or saving.—*a.,* **spar·er, spar·est.** Kept in reserve, as for possible future need: a *spare* tire; being in excess of present need: *spare* time; sparing, or economical, as persons; frugally restricted, as living, as fare; lean or thin, as a person.—*n.* A spare thing or part, as an extra tire carried for emergency use; sparing or economical use of. **—spare·a·ble,** *a.* **—spare·ness,** *n.* **—spar·er,** *n.*

spare·rib, spār/rib, *n.* A cut of pork containing ribs from the upper or fore end of the row, where there is little meat adhering.

spar·ing, spār/ing, *a.* Saving or frugal, often followed by *of* or *in: sparing of* words; meager or limited; merciful or lenient. **—spar·ing·ness,** *n.*

spark, spärk, *n.* An ignited or fiery particle such as is thrown off by burning wood; a small arc at a point where the continuity of an electric circuit is interrupted; a small amount or trace of something; a trace of life or vitality, as in a person; a gleam or flash, as of light.—*v.i.* To emit sparks, as of fire; send forth flashes; issue as or like sparks.—*v.t.* To stimulate, as activity or interest; activate. **—spark·er,** *n.*

spark coil, *n.* An induction coil for producing sparks.

spar·kle, spär/kəl, *v.i.,* **-kled, -kling.** To issue in or as in little sparks, as fire or light; to emit little sparks, as burning matter; to send forth or shine with little flashes of light, as a brilliant gem or star; to glitter; be bright as with flashes, as the eyes; to effervesce with small, glistening bubbles, as wine; to be brilliant, showily clever, or smart, as wit; to be lively or vivacious, as a person.—*v.t.* To cause to sparkle or glisten.—*n.* A little spark or fiery particle; luster, or flashing play of light: the *sparkle* of a diamond; brilliance or vivacity.

spar·kler, spär/klər, *n.* One who or that which sparkles; a firework that emits little sparks; a sparkling gem, esp. a diamond.

spark plug, *n.* A device inserted in the cylinder of an internal-combustion engine, containing the two terminals between which passes the electric spark for igniting the explosive gases.

spar·row, spar/ō, *n.* Any of several small, hardy European birds, introduced into N. America from Europe.

spar·row·grass, spar/ō·gras, *n. Informal.* Asparagus.

spar·row hawk, *n.* Any of several small hawks of N. America.

sparse, spärs, *a.,* **spars·er, spars·est.** Thinly scattered, distributed, or diffused: a *sparse* population; not thick or dense: *sparse* hair; scanty or meager. **—sparse·ness,** *n.*

Spar·tan, spär/tən, *a.* Of or pertaining to Sparta, an ancient city of southern Greece; suggestive of the ancient Spartans in simplicity, austerity, and discipline; brave; stoical.—*n.*

spasm, spaz/əm, *n.* A sudden, abnormal, involuntary muscular contraction; a convulsion; any sudden, brief fit or spell of unusual energy, feeling, or activity.

spas·mod·ic, spaz·mod/ik, *a.* Pertaining to or of the nature of a spasm; characterized by spasms; resembling spasms; convulsive; sudden and violent, but brief; occurring or proceeding intermittently. Also **spas·mod·i·cal. —spas·mod·i·cal·ly,** *adv.*

spas·tic, spas/tik, *a.* Pertaining to, of the nature of, or characterized by spasm, esp. muscular spasm.—*n.* A person given to spasms or convulsions, esp. one suffering from cerebral palsy. **—spas·ti·cal·ly,** *adv.*

spat, spat, *v.* Past tense and past participle of **spit.**

spat, spat, *n.* A petty quarrel; a light blow; a slap; a smack; a splash, esp. of large rain drops.—*v.i.,* **spat·ted, spat·ting.** To engage in a petty quarrel; strike sharply; to spatter.—*v.t.* To strike lightly; to slap.

spa·tial, spā/shəl, *a.* Of or pertaining to space; existing or occurring in space. Also **spa·cial. —spa·ti·al·i·ty,** spā·shē·al/ə·tē, *n.* **—spa·tial·ly,** *adv.*

spat·ter, spat/ər, *v.t.* To scatter or dash in small particles or drops: to *spatter* mud; to splash with something in small particles: to *spatter* the ground with water; to sprinkle or spot with something that soils or stains.—*v.i.* To send out small particles or drops; to fly out or fall in small particles or drops; to

---

a- hat, fāte, fāre, fäther; **e-** met, mē; **i-** pin, pīne; **o-** not, nōte, ôrb, moove (move), boy, pownd; **u-** cūbe, bůll, tûk (took); **ch-** chin; **th-** thick, ŧhen; **zh-** vizhon (vision); **ə-** əgo, takən, pencəl, lemən, bərd (bird).

strike as in a shower, as bullets.—*n.* The act or the sound of spattering; a splash or spot of something spattered.

spat·u·la, spach′ə·lə, *n.* An implement with a thin, broad, flexible blade, used for spreading a variety of substances.

spawn, spôn, *n.* The eggs of fishes, amphibians, mollusks, or crustaceans extruded in masses; a swarming brood or numerous progeny: often used disparagingly; persons regarded as the offspring of some stock; any product or result.—*v.i.* To produce eggs or spawn; to be reproductive; to issue like spawn.—*v.t.* To produce, as spawn; to bring forth, esp. in great numbers; to give rise to, as rumors.

spay, spā, *v.t.* To remove the ovaries, as from female animals.

speak, spēk, *v.i.,* **spoke, spok·en, speak·ing.** To utter words with the ordinary voice; to talk; make oral communication: to *speak* to someone of various matters; to converse: They *speak* for hours on the phone. To deliver an address or discourse: to *speak* at a rally; to make communication or disclosure by any means; to emit a sound, as a musical instrument; to make a report or noise; to bark, as dogs.—*v.t.* To utter orally and articulately: to *speak* words of praise; to express or make known with the voice: to *speak* the truth; to declare by any means of communication; to use, or be able to use, in oral utterance, as a language: to *speak* French. **—so to speak,** in a way of speaking. **—speak for,** to represent or speak in behalf of; to claim for oneself. **—speak out,** to verbalize one's ideas and opinions freely. **—speak·a·ble,** *a.*

speak-eas·y, spēk′ē·zē, *n. pl.,* **-eas·ies.** A place where intoxicating liquors are sold illegally: used esp. when prohibition was in effect in the U.S.

speak·er, spē′kər, *n.* One who speaks; one who speaks formally before an audience; an orator; a loudspeaker. (*Usu. cap.*) The presiding officer of the House of Representatives of the U.S., or some other similar assembly. **—spea·ker·ship,** *n.*

speak·ing, spē′king, *n.* The act, utterance, or discourse of one who speaks.—*a.* That speaks; giving information as if by speech; expressive; lifelike. **—on speak·ing terms,** having an association that allows conversing.

spear, spēr, *n.* A weapon for thrusting or throwing, consisting of a long staff to which a sharp head, as of iron or steel, is fixed; the act of spearing.—*v.t.* To pierce with or as with a spear.—*v.i.* To go or penetrate like a spear. **—spear·er,** *n.*

spear, spēr, *n.* A sprout or shoot of a plant, as a blade of grass.—*v.i.* To sprout; to shoot up.

spear·head, spēr′hed, *n.* The sharp-pointed head of a spear; a leader or a leading force.—*v.t.* To act as leader of.

spear·mint, spēr′mint, *n.* The common mint, an aromatic herb used for flavoring.

spe·cial, spesh′əl, *a.* Of a distinct or particular kind or character: a *special* type of food; particular, individual, or unique: the *special* features of a plan; having a particular function: a *special* messenger; specific or dealing with particulars; different from what is ordinary: a *special* occasion; extra; exceptional: *special* care.—*n.* A special person or thing; a train, newspaper edition, television program, commodity, etc., featured or scheduled for a particular occasion, time, or purpose. **—spe·cial·ly,** *adv.*

spe·cial de·liv·er·y, *n.* The delivering of pieces of mail outside the normal delivery schedule, for an extra fee.

spe·cial in·ter·est, *n.* Any group of persons, as a corporation, seeking special benefits or advantages, esp. from the government, often at a disadvantage to the public's welfare.

spe·cial·ist, spesh′ə·list, *n.* One who devotes himself or herself to one subject or to one particular branch of a subject or pursuit, esp. a medical practitioner.

spe·cial·ize, spesh′ə·līz, *v.i.,* **-ized, -iz·ing.** To pursue a particular line of study, work, or the like; of an organism, to adapt to a particular habitat or function by modification.—*v.t.* To render special or specific; to specify or particularize. **—spe·cial·i·za·tion,** spesh·ə·lə·zā′shən, *n.*

spe·cial·ty, spesh′əl·tē, *n. pl.,* **-ties.** The state or condition of being particular or special; special or particular character; a special subject of study or line of work; an article of trade of special character; a novelty.

spe·cie, spē′shē, spē′sē, *n.* Coin, as opposed to paper money, usu. preceded by *in:* paid *in specie.*

spe·cies, spē′shēz, spē′sēz, *n. pl.,* **spe·cies.** A class of individuals having some common characteristics; distinct kind; a classification next below a genus consisting of animals or plants having certain distinctive characteristics in common and able to interbreed. **—the spe·cies,** the human race.

spec·i·fi·a·ble, spes·ə·fī′ə·bəl, *a.* That may be specified.

spe·cif·ic, spi·sif′ik, *a.* Having a special application or reference; explicit or definite: to be *specific* in one's statements; precise or particular: a *specific* sum of money; specially belonging to and characteristic of a thing or group of things; of a special or particular kind.—*n.* Something specific, as a statement or quality. **—spe·cif·i·cal·ly,** *adv.* **—spec·i·fic·i·ty,** spes·ə·fis′ə·tē, *n.*

spec·i·fi·ca·tion, spes·ə·fə·kā′shən, *n.* The act of specifying; that which is specified. *Usu. pl.* A detailed, itemized description of dimensions, plans, materials, and other requirements, as for something proposed for construction; something specified, as in a bill of particulars; the act of making specific or clarifying.

spe·cif·ic grav·i·ty, *n.* The ratio of the weight of a given volume of any substance to that of the same volume of some other substance taken as a standard.

spec·i·fy, spes′ə·fī, *v.t.,* **-fied, -fy·ing.** To state explicitly; to designate as one condition of a group of specifications; to designate in detail.**—spec·i·fi·er,** *n.*

spec·i·men, spes′ə·mən, *n.* A part or an individual taken as representative or typical of a whole or group; an animal, plant, mineral, or organism preserved as an example of its kind, as for scientific study; a sample of a body substance to be analyzed for diagnostic purposes. *Informal.* A strange sort of person.

spe·cious, spē′shəs, *a.* Apparently good or right but without real merit: *specious* promises; plausible; pleasing to the eye, but deceptive: a *specious* appearance. **—spe·ci·os·i·ty,** spē·shē·os′i·tē, *n. pl.,* **-ties.** **—spe·cious·ness,** *n.*

speck, spek, *n.* A tiny spot; a particle; a fleck: a *speck* of dirt; a small mark; a minute dot.—*v.t.* To spot; to mark, as with specks or spots.

speck·le, spek′əl, *n.* A little spot in anything, of a different color from that of the thing itself; a speck. —*v.t.,* **-led, -ling.** To mark with small specks or spots.

specs, speks, *n. pl.* Spectacles, eyeglasses; abbr. for **spec·i·fi·ca·tions.**

spec·ta·cle, spek′tə·kəl, *n.* Anything presented to the sight or view, esp. something of a striking kind; a public show or display, esp. on a large scale: a dramatic *spectacle;* a person or thing exhibited to public view as an object of wonder or of contempt; *pl.,* a pair of glass lenses, together with frames to hold them on the nose and usu. ears, which aid defective vision or protect the eyes. **—spec·ta·cled,** *a.*

spec·tac·u·lar, spek·tak′yə·lər, *a.* Pertaining to or of the nature of a spectacle or show; marked by a strikingly unusual display.—*n.* That which is spectacular, esp. a lavish television production. **—spec·tac·u·lar·ly,** *adv.*

spec·ta·tor, spek′tā·tər, spek·tā′tər, *n.* One who observes, watches, or looks on; one who is present at and watches a play or spectacle.

spec·ta·tor sport, n. Any sport which many individuals choose to enjoy as spectators rather than by actual participation, as baseball, hockey, or soccer.

spec·ter, spek'tər, n. A disembodied but visible spirit; a ghost; anything that haunts or horrifies.

spec·tral, spek'trəl, a. Pertaining to or characteristic of a specter; ghostly; of or pertaining to a spectrum or spectra.

spec·tro·scope, spek'trə·skōp, n. An optical instrument used to form and analyze spectra. **—spec·tro·scop·ic,** spek·trə·skop'ik, **spec·tro·scop·i·cal,** a. **—spec·tros·co·py,** spek·tros'kə·pē, n.

spec·trum, spek'trəm, n. pl., **-tra, -trums.** A band or broad range of frequencies having a common characteristic, as audibility, visibility, or electromagnetism; a series of images formed when radiant energy undergoes dispersion, esp. a series of colors, usu. described as passing by degrees through red, orange, yellow, green, blue, indigo, and violet, produced when white light is passed through a prism; any continuous sequence or broad range: the ideological *spectrum*.

spec·u·late, spek'yə·lāt, v.i., **-lat·ed, -lat·ing.** To meditate or reflect; to theorize; to purchase stocks or other commodities when there is a large risk, but with the hope of large profit by selling at an opportune time. **—spec·u·la·tion,** spek·yə·lā'shən, n. **—spec·u·la·tor,** n.

spec·u·la·tive, spek'yə·lā·tiv, spek'yə·lə·tiv, a. Contemplative; strictly theoretical; not practical; factually validated; pertaining to financial speculation; risky.

speech, spēch, n. The faculty or power of expressing thoughts and emotions by articulated words; the act of speaking; anything that is spoken; a public address; a particular language or dialect; an individual style of speaking; the study of the theory and various practices of oral communication.

speech·i·fy, spēch'ə·fī, v.i., **-fied, -fy·ing.** To make a speech or harangue: used humorously or derisively.

speech·less, spēch'lis, a. Deprived of the faculty of speech; dumb; mute; silent; incapable of expression in words. **—speech·less·ness,** n.

speed, spēd, n. Rapidity of movement; the rate or swiftness of motion or action; the act of moving swiftly; a drug in the amphetamine group.—v.t., **sped** or **speed·ed, speed·ing.** To accelerate the rate of; to further the progress of; to cause to move or go with haste; to dismiss with good wishes.—v.i. To make haste; to accelerate the rate of motion, usu. followed by *up*; to drive a vehicle beyond the legal limit. **—speed·er, speed·ster,** spēd'stər, n.

speed·boat, spēd'bōt, n. A motorboat designed for speed. **—speed·boat·ing,** n.

speed lim·it, n. The maximum or minimum limit of speed permitted by law.

speed·om·e·ter, spē·dom'i·tər, spi·dom'i·tər, n. An instrument for indicating the speed of a vehicle.

speed read·ing, n. Any of several teaching or learning techniques for increasing flexibility and rate of reading.

speed trap, n. A section of roadway, where hidden police or electronic devices trap unwary drivers exceeding the speed limit.

speed-up, spēd'əp, n. An increase in the rate of speed, as in some process or work.

speed·way, spēd'wā, n. A non-public road or course used for racing automobiles or motorcycles.

speed·y, spē'dē, a., **-i·er, -i·est.** Rapid in motion; swift; quick; fast. **—speed·i·ly,** adv. **—speed·i·ness,** n.

spe·le·ol·o·gy, spē·lē·ol'ə·jē, n. The scientific study and exploration of caves. **—spe·le·ol·o·gist,** n.

spell, spel, v.t., **spelled** or **spelt, spell·ing.** To repeat, point out, write, or print the proper letters of in their regular order; to form by letters; to amount to, or signify: The job *spelled* success for her.—v.i. To form words with the proper letters, either in reading or writing; to read letter by letter. **—spell out,** to explain clearly: objectives that were *spelled out;* to discern or make out; to read with labor or difficulty.

spell, spel, n. A charm consisting of some words of occult power; any magic charm.

spell, spel, n. Any period of time; a particular period or type of weather: a hot *spell;* a period of illness.—v.t. To relieve for a while.—v.i. To take a rest period.

spell·bind, spel'bīnd, v.t., **-bound, -bind·ing.** To hold spellbound, or as by a spell; to entrance. **—spell·bind·er,** n. **—spell·bound,** spel'bownd, a.

spell·er, spel'ər, n. One who spells; a manual or textbook of exercises used for spelling instruction; also **spell·ing book.**

spell·ing, spel'ing, n. The act of one who spells; the way in which a word is spelled; orthography.

spell·ing bee, n. A spelling contest.

spe·lun·ker, spi·ləng'kər, n. A person who likes to explore caves; a speleologist.

spend, spend, v.t., **spent, spend·ing.** To expend or pay out, as funds; to consume or exhaust, as strength; to waste, as resources; to pass, as time; to employ, as time, effort, or thought on some project or activity. —v.i. To make expenditures; to be exhausted, or wasted. **—spend·a·ble,** a. **—spend·er,** n.

spend·thrift, spend'thrift, n. One who spends his or her means lavishly or improvidently.—a.

spent, spent, a. Expended; exhausted; vitiated.

sperm, spərm, n. pl., **sperm, sperms.** The reproductive seminal fluid of males; semen; a spermatozoon; sperm oil; a sperm whale.

sper·ma·cet·i, spər·mə·set'ē, spər·mə·sē'tē, n. A white, waxy material obtained from the oil of the sperm whale and some other marine mammals and used in making ointments, cosmetics, and other commercial products.

sper·mat·ic, spər·mat'ik, a. Pertaining to, resembling, or conveying sperm; seminal; relating to a sperm gland.

sper·mat·ic cord, n. The cord by which the testicle is suspended within the scrotum, and which contains the blood vessels and nerves of the testicle.

sper·ma·to·zo·on, spər·mə·tə·zō'on, spər·mə·tə·zō'ən, n. pl., **-a.** One of the numerous minute, usu. actively motile bodies contained in semen or sperm, which serve to fertilize the ovum of the female; any mature male reproductive cell. **—sper·ma·to·zo·ic,** a.

sperm oil, n. The thin, yellowish oil obtained from the sperm whale's cranial cavity and blubber, used esp. as a lubricant for delicate machinery.

sperm whale, n. An enormous, toothed whale, having spermaceti in the cranial basin of its blunt head.

spew, spū, v.i., v.t. To vomit; cast forth; eject; discharge.—n. That which is spewed; vomit. Also **spue.** **—spew·er,** n.

sphag·num, sfag'nəm, n. Any of various mosses which grow in wet, acid areas and are much used in the potting and shipping of plants.

sphere, sfēr, n. A solid generated by the revolution of a semicircle about its diameter; a round body whose surface is at all points equidistant from the center; a globe; a ball; a heavenly body, as a planet or star; an orbit, as of a planet; the place, region, or environment within which a person or thing exists or has being; a field of activity or operation: the *sphere* of science or of law.—v.t. **sphered, spher·ing.** To enclose in or as in a sphere; to form into a sphere. **—spher·ic,** a. **—sphe·ric·i·ty,** sfi·ris'i·tē, n.

sphere of in·flu·ence, n. Any territory over which the power, interests, and influence of another country or nation are predominant.

---

a- hat, fāte, fāre, fäther; e- met, mē; i- pin, pīne; o- not, nōte, ôrb, moove (move), boy, pownd; u- cūbe, bûll, tûk (took); ch- chin; th- thick, then; zh- vizhon (vision); ə- əgo, takən, pencəl, lemən, bərd (bird).

spher·i·cal, sfēr'i·kəl, *a.* Having the form of a sphere; globular; pertaining or belonging to a sphere or spheres; relating to the celestial bodies, esp. to their astrological influence. —**spher·i·cal·ly**, *adv.*

sphe·roid, sfēr'oyd, *n.* A body formed by rotating an ellipse about one of its axes; a body resembling a sphere, but not perfectly spherical.—*a.* Approximately spherical. —**sphe·roi·dal**, sfi·roy'dəl, *a.*

sphinc·ter, sfingk'tər, *n.* A contractile ringlike muscle surrounding and capable of closing a natural orifice or passage. —**sphinc·ter·al**, *a.* —**sphinc·ter·ic**, sfingk·tär'ik, *a.*

sphinx, sfingks, *n. pl.,* **sphinx·es**, **sphin·ges**, sfin'jēz. (*Sometimes cap.*) In Greek mythology, a monster with the head of a woman on the winged body of a lion or a dog, which proposed a riddle to passersby, killing those unable to guess it; an enigmatic or inscrutable person; an Egyptian figure having the head of a man, a ram, or a hawk, and the body of a lion. (*Usu. cap.*) The colossal stone figure of this kind near Cairo, Egypt.

spice, spīs, *n.* Any of a class of pungent or aromatic substances of plant origin, as pepper, cinnamon, cloves, and the like, used as seasoning or preservatives; such substances as a material or collectively; a spicy or aromatic odor or fragrance; something that gives zest.—*v.t.,* **spiced**, **spic·ing**. To prepare or season with a spice or spices; to give zest or interest to by something added.

spice box, *n.* A receptacle for holding jars or other containers of spices.

spick-and-span, **spic-and-span**, spik'ən·span', *a.* Perfectly new; fresh; neat and clean.

spi·cule, spik'ūl, *n.* A small or minute, slender, sharp-pointed body or part; a small, needle-like crystal, process, or the like; a floral spikelet. Also **spic·u·la**, —**spic·u·lar**, **spic·u·late**, *a.*

spic·y, spī'sē, *a.,* **-i·er**, **-i·est**. Seasoned with or containing spice; of the nature of or resembling spice; abounding in or yielding spices; aromatic or fragrant; piquant or pungent: a *spicy* speech; of a somewhat improper or scandalous nature: a *spicy* story. —**spic·i·ly**, *adv.* —**spic·i·ness**, *n.*

spi·der, spī'dər, *n.* Any of the eight-legged, wingless arachnids, known for the spinning of webs which serve as nests and as traps for prey; any of various things resembling or suggesting a spider.

spi·der·y, spī'də·rē, *a.* Like or suggesting a spider; delicate, suggesting a spider's web; full of or infested with spiders.

spiel, spēl, shpēl, *n. Informal.* A talk or speech used as a lure; a pitch.—*v.i. Informal.* To talk or speak with extravagance. —**spiel·er**, *n.*

spi·er, spī'ər, *n.* One who spies.

spiff·y, spif'ē, *a.,* **-i·er**, **-i·est**. *Informal.* Spruce; smart; fine. —**spiff·i·ness**, *n.*

spig·ot, spig'ət, *n.* A faucet; a plug or peg that is turned to open or stop a faucet, or that plugs the small hole in a cask of liquid.

spike, spīk, *n.* A large, strong nail or pin, esp. of iron, as for fastening rails; that which resembles a spike; a stiff, sharp-pointed piece or part; a sharp metal projection on the sole or the heel of a shoe, as of a golfer, to prevent slipping; *pl.,* shoes with such projections; high heels, as on shoes for women, that are very narrow.—*v.t.,* **-spiked**, **spik·ing**. To fasten or provide with a spike or spikes; to pierce with or impale on a spike; to injure, as another player or a competitor, with the spikes of one's shoe, as in baseball. *Informal.* To add liquor or alcohol to, as a drink.

spike, spīk, *n.* An ear, as of wheat or other grain. —**spiked**, *a.*

spik·y, spī'kē, *a.,* **-i·er**, **-i·est**. In the shape of a spike; set with spikes.

spill, spil, *v.t.,* **spilled** or **spilt**, **spill·ing**. To cause or allow, as liquid, or any matter in grains or loose pieces, to run or fall from a container, esp. accidentally or wastefully; to shed, esp. blood, as in killing or

wounding; to scatter; to cause to fall from a horse, vehicle, or the like. *Informal.* To disclose or tell, as secret.—*v.i.* To run or escape from a container, esp. by accident or in careless handling, as liquid, loose particles, or the like.—*n.* A spilling, as of liquid, or a quantity spilled or the mark made. *Informal.* A throw or fall from a horse, vehicle, or the like; spillway. —**spill the beans**. *Informal.* To reveal information inadvertently, as a secret.

spil·lage, spil'ij, *n.* The action of spilling something; the amount spilled.

spill·way, spil'wā, *n.* A channel or passage for the overflow water of a lake, reservoir, dam, or river.

spin, spin, *v.t.,* **spun**, **spun**, **spin·ning**. To draw out and twist, as a fiber of wool, flax, cotton, etc., either by hand or by machinery, into thread or yarn; to form, as any material into thread: to *spin* glass; to produce, as a thread, cobweb, or silk, by pushing out from the body a long, slender filament of a natural sticky matter that hardens in the air, as of spiders or silkworms; to cause to turn around rapidly, as on an axis: to *spin* a top; whirl; to produce or evolve in a manner suggestive of spinning thread; to tell, as a yarn or story; to draw out or prolong, often used with *out:* to *spin out* a story.—*v.i.* To turn round rapidly, as on an axis, as the earth or a top; to produce a thread from the body, as spiders; to draw out and twist wool or the like into thread or yarn; to move, go, run, ride, or travel rapidly; to be affected with a sensation of whirling, as the head.—*n.* The act of causing a spinning or whirling motion; a spinning or whirling motion of anything; a rapid run, ride, drive, or the like, as for exercise; a moving or going rapidly along.

spin·ach, spin'ich, *n.* An annual plant, with hollow stems and edible, fleshy leaves: its leaves used as a vegetable.

spi·nal, spī'nəl, *a.* Pertaining to or resembling the spine or backbone.—*n.* An anesthetic injected into the spinal cord. —**spi·nal·ly**, *adv.*

spi·nal col·umn, *n.* In an animal with a backbone, the series of small bones or vertebrae forming the axis of the skeleton and protecting the spinal cord; the spine; the backbone.

spi·nal cord, *n.* The cord of nervous tissue enclosed within the spinal column.

spin·dle, spin'dəl, *n.* The rod or pin on a spinning wheel by which the thread is twisted and on which it is wound; one of the rods of a spinning machine or shuttle holding the bobbins on which the thread is wound as it is spun; any rod or pin which turns around or on which something turns, as an axle, axis, or shaft; a needlelike spike secured on a wider and heavier base, used to hold bills, notes, and other papers.—*v.i.,* **-dled**, **-dling**. To shoot up or grow into a long, slender stalk or stem, as a plant; to grow long and slender. —*v.t.* To form into the shape of a spindle; to furnish with a spindle; to impale, as papers, on the needlelike rod of a spindle.

spin·dle·legs, spin'dəl·legz, *n. pl.* Long, slender legs. *Sing. in constr. Informal.* A person having long, slender legs. Also **spin·dle·shanks**, spin'dəl·shangks. —**spin·dle·leg·ged**, *a.* —**spin·dle·shanked**, *a.*

spin·dling, spind'ling, *a.* Long, or tall and slender, often disproportionately so.—*n.* That which is spindling.

spin·dly, spind'lē, *a.,* **-dli·er**, **-dli·est**. Of a slender, weak form.

spine, spīn, *n.* The backbone of a vertebrate animal which provides the main support for its body; any rigid, pointed outgrowth on the body of an animal, as the quills of a porcupine; a thornlike, slightly woody structure, as on a plant or tree; a long, narrow projection or outcropping, as of rock; an inner quality of strength of character.

spine·less, spīn'lis, *a.* Without spines or sharp-pointed processes; having no spine or backbone;

having a weak spine or backbone; lacking the natural strength of a spine; limp; without moral force or courage; feeble.

spin·et, spin′it, *n.* A small musical instrument of the harpsichord family; a small, compact, upright piano.

spin·na·ker, spin′ə·kər, *n.* A triangular racing sail, used when running before the wind.

spin·ner, spin′ər, *n.* One who or that which spins; a fishing lure consisting of a blade or spoon, used in trolling or casting.

spin·ning wheel, *n.* A small device operated by foot or hand for spinning wool, cotton, or flax into thread or yarn.

spin-off, spin′ôf, spin′of, *n.* A parent corporation's distribution to its own stockholders of the stock of a subsidiary corporation.

spi·nose, spī′nōs, spī·nōs′, *a.* Full of spines; spiny; spinous.

spi·nous, spī′nəs *a.* Covered with or having spines; thorny, as a plant.

spin·ster, spin′stər, *n.* An unmarried woman past the usual or conventional age for marrying; an old maid.

spin·y, spī′nē, *a.* Full of spines, as a gooseberry shrub; having spines, as a porcupine; like a spine; perplexing; troublesome. **—spin·i·ness,** *n.*

spi·ra·cle, spī′rə·kəl, spir′ə·kəl, *n.* In animals, an opening for air or water to enter in the process of breathing: Insects breathe through *spiracles* along their sides.

spi·ral, spī′rəl, *n.* A curve traced in a plane by a point moving around a fixed point while continually approaching it or continually going away from it; a helix; one of the turns or coils of a spiral or helix; an object or form in the shape of a spiral or helix.—*a.* Curving around a fixed point in the form of a spiral; winding about an axis in continually advancing planes; helical; of or resembling a spire or spiral.—*v.i.,* **-raled, -ral·ing.** To take the form of a spiral; to move in a spiral path.—*v.t.* To make into the form of a spiral; to cause to spiral. **—spi·ral·ly,** *adv.*

spire, spīr, *n.* A slender, tapering formation narrowing upward to a point; a pyramidal or conical structure upon a tower or roof; the terminal upper part of a steeple; a blade, sprout, shoot, or stalk of a plant. —*v.i.,* **spired, spir·ing.** To taper upwards; to pyramid; to shoot up, as a blade of grass. **—spired,** *a.*

spir·it, spir′it, *n.* That which is believed to be the principle of conscious life and the vital principle in humans; the incorporeal part of humans: to be present in *spirit* if not in body; the soul, regarded as separable from the body at death; conscious incorporeal being, as opposed to matter: the world of *spirit;* a supernatural, incorporeal being or presence inhabiting a place or thing: *spirits* of the air or water; a fairy, sprite, or elf; an angel or demon; the soul or heart as the seat of feelings or sentiments, or of animation of the body: to break a person's *spirit;* mettle or courage: a man of *spirit;* vigor or liveliness, as in action, words, or music: attitude: something done in the right *spirit;* character or disposition: meek in *spirit;* an inspiring or animating person or influence: the leading *spirit* in an undertaking; an inspiring or animating principle that pervades and tempers thought, feeling, or action: the *spirit* of love, or *spirit* of reform; the dominant tendency of anything: the *spirit* of the age; the general meaning or intent of a regulation, statement, or the like, as opposed to its literal interpretation: the *spirit,* not the letter, of the law; the essence or active principle of a substance as extracted in liquid form, esp. by distillation; a solution in alcohol of an essential or volatile principle; also **es·sence.** *Often pl.* A liquor obtained by distillation, esp. a strong distilled alcoholic liquor; alcohol; any of certain subtle fluids formerly supposed to permeate the body: natural or animal

spirits. Pl. Feelings with respect to exaltation or depression: to be in high or low *spirits.* (*Cap.*) The divine influence as an agency working on humans; the third person of the Trinity, the Holy Spirit.—*v.t.* To carry off mysteriously or secretly, usu. followed by *away:* The witnesses were *spirited away;* to animate with fresh ardor or courage; encourage; to urge on or stir up, as to action.—*a.* Referring to that which operates by burning a volatile liquid such as alcohol: a *spirit* lamp or *spirit* stove.

spir·it·ed, spir′i·tid, *a.* Animated; lively; full of spirit, courage, energy, or the like; having a spirit or disposition of a certain character, used in compounds: high-*spirited.*

spir·it gum, *n.* A special kind of glue which is used to fix artificial hair to a person's skin.

spir·it·ism, spir′i·tiz·əm, *n.* The doctrine or practices of spiritualism. **—spir·it·ist,** *n.*

spir·it·less, spir′it·lis, *a.* Without spirit, vigor, or enthusiasm; depressed or listless. **—spir·it·less·ness,** *n.*

spir·i·tous, spir′i·təs, *a.* Spirituous.

spir·it·u·al, spir′i·chů·əl, *a.* Of, referring to, or consisting of spirit; referring to incorporeal or disembodied spirits, esp. the spirits of the dead; of or referring to the spirit or soul as distinguished from the physical nature; symbolic or mystical, with reference to the spirit or to things having acquired a religious nature; religious; sacred; referring or belonging to the church or things ecclesiastical.—*n.* A spiritual or religious song. *Usu. pl.* Spiritual things or matters, esp. of the church. **—spir·it·u·al·ly,** *adv.*

spir·it·u·al·ism, spir′i·chů·ə·liz·əm, *n.* The belief or doctrine that the spirits of the dead survive after mortal life and communicate with the living, esp. through the intercession of a medium; the practices or phenomena associated with this belief; spiritual quality or tendency. **—spir·it·u·al·ist,** *n.* **—spir·it·u·al·is·tic,** spir·i·chů·ə·lis′tik, *a.*

spir·it·u·al·i·ty, spir·i·chů·al′ə·tē, *n. pl.,* **-ties.** The quality or fact of being spiritual. *Often pl.* Property or revenue of the church or of an ecclesiastic in his official capacity.

spir·it·u·al·ize, spir′i·chů·ə·līz, *v.t.,* **-ized, -iz·ing.** To make spiritual, esp. to free from corrupting secular influences. **—spir·it·u·al·i·za·tion,** spir·i·chů·ə·lə·zā′shən, *n.*

spir·it·u·ous, spir′i·chů·əs, *a.* Containing alcohol as the characteristic ingredient; alcoholic; of beverages, distilled. **—spir·it·u·os·i·ty,** spir·i·chů·os′ə·tē, *n.*

spi·ro·chete, spī′rə·kēt, *n.* Any of the slender, threadlike bacteria having a spiral shape, some species of which cause syphilis and yaws.

spirt, spert, *n.* Spurt.—*v.t., v.i.*

spit, spit, *v.i.,* **spit** or **spat, spit·ting.** To eject saliva from the mouth; to do this at or on a person to express hatred, contempt, or the like; to sputter; to fall in scattered drops or flakes, as rain or snow; to produce a hissing noise.—*v.t.* To eject, as saliva, from the mouth; to throw out or emit like saliva; to utter angrily or spitefully, often used with *out;* to say or speak without hesitation or reserve, often used with *out;* to light or set: *spit* a fuse.—*n.* Saliva, esp. when ejected; spittle; the act or an act of spitting. **—spit and im·age.** *Informal.* Perfect image or likeness. Also **spit·ting im·age. —spit·ter,** *n.*

spit, spit, *n.* A sharply pointed, slender rod for thrusting into or through and holding meat to be roasted over heat; any of various rods, pins, or the like used for particular purposes; a narrow point of land projecting into the water; a long, narrow shoal extending from the shore.—*v.t.,* **spit·ted, spit·ting.** To pierce, stab, or transfix, as with a spit.

spit and pol·ish, *n.* Great attention, possibly to the

---

extreme, given to neatness and appearance, esp. in military affairs.

spit curl, *n.* A ringlet of hair, usu. moistened and flattened against the cheek or forehead.

spite, spīt, *n.* Malicious ill will; a desire to frustrate, annoy, or thwart another; malevolent bitterness. —*v.t.,* **spit·ed, spit·ing.** To show malice toward; to thwart. —**in spite of,** despite; notwithstanding.

spite·ful, spīt′fəl, *a.* Filled with spite.

spit·fire, spīt′fīr, *n.* A person, usu. feminine, of fiery disposition.

spit·tle, spit′əl, *n.* The secretion of the salivary glands; spit.

spit·toon, spi·tōon′, *n.* A container for spit; a cuspidor.

spitz, spits, *n.* A small, solidly built dog, usu. white, with long, thick hair, a forward-curving tail, and pointed ears.

splash, splash, *v.t.* To wet or soil by dashing masses or particles of water, mud, or other liquid or semiliquid substance; spatter; to mark as if with splashes; to dash, as water, about in scattered masses or particles; to make, as one's way, with splashing. —*v.i.* To dash a liquid or semiliquid substance about; fall, move, or go with a splash or splashes. —*n.* An act of splashing; the sound of splashing; a quantity splashed upon a thing; a spot caused by something splashed; a patch, as of color or light. *Informal.* A striking show, or an ostentatious display. —**splash·er,** *n.* —**splash·y,** *a.,* **-i·er, -i·est.** —**splash·i·ly,** *adv.* —**splash·i·ness,** *n.*

splash·board, splash′bôrd, *n.* A board, guard, or screen to protect from splashing.

splash·down, splash′down, *n.* The landing at sea of a spacecraft. —**splash down,** *v.i.*

splash guard, *n.* Heavy material, usu. rubber, hung from the back of a motorcycle or other motor vehicle to cover the rear wheels and keep water and mud from being thrown onto cars behind.

splat·ter, splat′ər, *v.t., v.i.* To splash; spatter; sputter.

splay, splā, *v.t.* To spread out, expand, or extend; to make slanting; bevel; to dislocate, as a bone. —*v.i.* To have an oblique or slanting direction; to flare or spread out. —*n.* A spread or flare. —*a.* Spread out; clumsy or awkward; oblique or awry.

splay·foot, splā′fût, *n. pl.,* **-feet.** A broad, flat foot, esp. one turned more or less outward; such a condition. —*a.* —**splay·foot·ed,** *a.*

spleen, splēn, *n.* A spongy glandular organ situated in the upper part of the abdomen, forming one of the ductless glands; ill humor, latent spite, depression, or peevish outburst. —**spleen·ful,** *a.*

splen·did, splen′did, *a.* Gorgeous; magnificent; luxuriously elegant; grand; strikingly admirable or fine: a *splendid* idea; shining or brilliant.

splen·dif·er·ous, splen·dif′ər·əs, *a. Informal.* Quite splendid; fine.

splen·dor, splen′dər, *n.* Brilliancy; resplendence; magnificence; pomp; glory; grandeur; eminence. —**splen·dor·ous,** *a.*

sple·net·ic, spli·net′ik, *a.* Of or relating to the spleen; ill-humored; irritable.

splice, splīs, *v.t.,* **spliced, splic·ing.** To unite, as two ropes, by interweaving the strands of the ends; to join, as wires, by twisting and soldering; to overlap and fasten, as rails or pieces of timber; to butt and bind, as film or recording tapes; to insert, as new sound track, into film; to graft; to piece. —*n.* The act or result of splicing: the *splice* in a rope. —**splic·er,** *n.*

splint, splint, *n.* A thin piece of wood or other stiff material used to hold a fractured or dislocated bone in position when set, or to maintain any part of the body in a fixed position; one of a number of thin strips of wood to be woven together to make a chair seat, basket, or the like. —*v.t.* To secure, hold in position, or support by means of a splint or splints.

splin·ter, splin′tər, *n.* A rough piece of wood, bone, or the like, usu. long, thin, and sharp, split or broken off from a main body; a splint; a sliver. —*v.t.* To split or break into splinters. —*v.i.* To be split or broken into splinters; to break off in splinters. —*a.* Independent of or separated from a larger or main body or organization: a *splinter* group. —**splin·ter·y,** *a.*

split, split, *v.t.,* **split, split·ting.** To separate or part from end to end or between layers, often forcibly or by cutting; to separate off by cleaving lengthwise: to *split* a piece from a block; to break or tear apart; to divide into distinct parts or portions; to divide, as persons, into different groups, as by discord; to divide between two or more persons: to *split* a bottle of wine with a friend; to separate into parts by interposing something: to *split* an infinitive. —*v.i.* To break or part lengthwise; to part, divide, or separate in any way; to divide something, usu. in equal parts, with another or others. —*n.* The act or an act of splitting; a crack, rent, or fissure caused by splitting; a rupture in a party, or between persons; a schism; a faction or party, formed by a rupture or schism. *Informal.* A drink containing only half the usual quantity; a bottle, as of champagne, half the usual size; a confection made from a sliced banana, ice cream, syrup, whipped cream, and nuts. *Often pl.* The feat of separating the legs, while sinking to the floor, until they extend at right angles to the body. —*a.* That has undergone splitting; parted lengthwise; divided: a *split* vote. —**split hairs,** to make very fine distinctions in argument. —**split the difference,** to divide the difference between two parties equally. —**split·ta·ble,** *a.* —**split·ter,** *n.*

split-lev·el, split′lev′əl, *a.* Having reference to the layout of a house in which the distance between adjacent levels is about half a story.

split sec·ond, *n.* A portion of a second; a brief instant.

split-sec·ond, *a.* Accurate: *split-second* timing.

splotch, sploch, *n.* A spot or stain, esp. of large and irregular shape; a daub; a smear; a blot; a splash, as of paint. —*v.t.* To mark with a splotch or splotches. —**splotch·y,** *a.,* **-i·er, -i·est.**

splurge, splərj, *n. Informal.* A showing off; an exorbitant expenditure. —*v.i., v.t.,* **splurged, splurg·ing.** To show off by spending a lot.

splut·ter, splət′ər, *n.* A stammering utterance; a confused sound; a bustle; a stir. —*v.i.* To speak hastily and confusedly, as when bewildered or frightened; to sputter, as fireworks, esp. a sparkler; sizzle, as frying fat. —*v.t.* To utter in a hasty and confused manner; stammer. —**splut·ter·er,** *n.*

spoil, spoyl, *v.t.,* **spoiled** or **spoilt, spoil·ing.** To damage permanently as to excellence, value, or usefulness: to *spoil* a cake in the making; to impair in character or disposition by unwise treatment, esp. by excessive indulgence. —*v.i.* To plunder, pillage, or rob; to become spoiled, bad, or unfit for use, as food. —*n.* Waste material, as that cast up in mining, excavating, or quarrying. *Often pl.* Booty, loot, or plunder taken in war or robbery. *Usu. pl.* Public offices with their advantages viewed as won by a victorious political party: the *spoils* of office. —**spoil·ing for.** *Informal.* To crave.

spoil·age, spoy′lij, *n.* The act of spoiling; that which is spoiled; decay; the loss due to spoilage.

spoil·er, spoy′lər, *n.* One who or that which spoils; a plunderer or despoiler.

spoil·sport, spoyl′spôrt, *n.* One who, by his or her unsociable actions, spoils the sport or enjoyment of others.

spoke, spōk, *n.* One of the bars or rods radiating from the hub of a wheel and supporting the rim. —*v.t.,* **spoked, spok·ing.** To fit or furnish with or as with spokes.

spo·ken, spō′kən, *a.* Oral, as opposed to *written;* equivalent to *speaking,* used in compounds: civil-*spoken.*

spokes·man, spōks′mən, *n. pl.,* **-men.** One who speaks for another or others. —**spokes·wom·an,**

spōks/wûm•ən, *n. fem. pl.,* -wom•en.

sponge, spenj, *n.* Any water-dwelling animal having a porous shell-like skeleton and living in attached colonies; the framework or skeleton of these animals, which is composed of horny elastic fibers, easily compressible, readily absorbing fluids, and as readily giving them out again upon compression, and used for bathing and general cleaning; a sterile dressing used in surgery; a kind of mop for cleaning cannon after a discharge; a sponge bath. *Informal.* One intentionally dependent upon others; a parasite.—*v.t.,* **sponged, spong•ing.** To cleanse or wipe with a sponge; to destroy all traces of. *Informal.* To gain by underhanded methods.—*v.i.* To imbibe, as a sponge; to dive for or gather sponges. *Informal.* To live parasitically. —**throw in the sponge.** *Informal.* To yield or admit defeat.

spong•er, *n.* A person who or a boat which gathers sponges. *Informal.* One who lives at the expense of others.

sponge rub•ber, *n.* A kind of rubber having the texture or structure of that of a sea sponge and used for padding and insulating purposes.

spon•gy, spen/jē, *a.,* -gi•er, -gi•est. Resembling a sponge; soft and full of cavities; of an open, loose, easily compressible texture; highly absorbent. —**spon•gi•ness,** *n.*

spon•sor, spon/sər, *n.* One who answers for another; one who is responsible for another's default; a firm which finances the broadcasting of a television or radio program and receives in return the advertisement of its service or product; one who is patron for an infant at baptism; a godfather or godmother.—*v.t.* To be or act as sponsor for. —**spon•sor•ship,** *n.*

spon•ta•ne•i•ty, spon•tə•nē/ə•tē, *n. pl.,* -ties. The fact, state, or quality of being spontaneous.

spon•ta•ne•ous, spon•tā/nē•əs, *a.* Arising from one's own tendencies or impulses, without forethought; caused by inborn qualities. —**spon•ta•ne•ous•ly,** *adv.* —**spon•ta•ne•ous•ness,** *n.*

spon•ta•ne•ous com•bus•tion, *n.* The ignition of a substance or body from the rapid oxidation of its own constituents, without the application of heat from an external source.

spoof, spoof, *n. Informal.* A playful hoax; an act of good-natured teasing; deception.—*v.t., v.i. Informal.* To hoax; deceive; tease.

spook, spook, *n. Informal.* A ghost or apparition; a specter.—*v.t. Informal.* To haunt; to startle, frighten, or cause to stampede, esp. as animals. —**spook•ish,** *a.*

spook•y, spoo/kē, *a.,* i•er, i•est. Pertaining to or resembling spooks; ghostly; haunted; uncanny; uneasy or skittish, as animals, esp. horses. —**spook•i•ly,** *adv.* —**spook•i•ness,** *n.*

spool, spool, *n.* A small cylinder of wood or other material, typically expanded with a collar at each end and having a hole lengthwise through the center and on which wire, yarn, tape, or thread, is wound; any cylindrical piece or contrivance on which something is wound; the amount of material upon it.—*v.t.* To wind on a spool.

spoon, spoon, *n.* A utensil used for eating, measuring, taking up, or stirring, consisting of a small, usu. oval, shallow bowl with a handle; any of various implements, objects, or parts resembling or suggesting this.—*v.t.* To take up or transfer in a spoon; to hollow out or shape like a spoon.

spoon•er•ism, spoo/nə•riz•əm, *n.* A phrase in which the initial or other sounds are accidentally transposed, as in *dats and cogs* for *cats and dogs.* —**spoon•er•is•tic,** spoo•nə•ris/tik, *a.*

spoon-fed, spoon/fed, *a.* Fed with a spoon; treated with excessive care and concern; coddled; pampered; not allowed to develop self-reliance or independence.

spoon-feed, spoon/fēd/, spoon/fēd, *v.t.* **-fed, -feed•ing.** To feed as with a spoon; to supply with facts or information, with the effect of inhibiting independent inquiry.

spoon•ful, spoon/fûl, *n. pl.,* -fuls. As much as a spoon can contain.

spo•rad•ic, spə•rad/ik, *a.* Occurring at irregular intervals; occasional; scattered. Also **spo•rad•i•cal.** —**spo•rad•i•cal•ly,** *adv.*

spo•ran•gi•um, spə•ran/jē•əm, *n. pl.,* -gi•a, -jē•ə. In plants, a case or covering in which the asexual spores of algae, mosses, and ferns are produced.

spore, spôr, *n.* An asexual reproductive cell of algae, fungi, mosses, and ferns, as distinguished from a true seed; a thick-walled bacterium in a dormant or resting stage.—*v.i.,* **spored, spor•ing.** To develop spores, as in plants.

sport, spôrt, *n.* Diversion, amusement, or recreation; a pleasant pastime; a pastime pursued in the open air or having an athletic character, as hunting, fishing, racing, baseball, bowling, or wrestling; mere jest or pleasantry: to do or say a thing in *sport;* derisive jesting or ridicule; something tossed about like a plaything; a laughingstock; one who is interested in sports. *Informal.* A person of sportsmanlike or admirable qualities, or considered with reference to such qualities: a good *sport;* one who is interested in pursuits involving betting or gambling; a flashy or vulgarly showy person.—*a.* Of or pertaining to sport or sports, esp. of the outdoor or athletic kind. Also **sports.**—*v.t.* To pass, as time, in amusement or sport; spend or squander lightly or recklessly, often followed by *away. Informal.* To display freely in public: to *sport* ⸱ ⸱oll of money.—*v.i.* To amuse oneself with some pleasant pastime or recreation; engage in some outdoor or athletic pastime or sport; to deal lightly, or too lightly, or to trifle, as with something serious. —**sport•er,** *n.* —**sport•ful,** *a.* —**sport•ful•ly,** *adv.* —**sport•ful•ness,** *n.*

sport•ing, spôr/ting, *a.* Engaging in, given to, or interested in open-air or athletic sports; pertaining to, or suitable for such sports: *sporting* goods; sportsmanlike, as qualities or conduct. *Informal.* Involving or inducing the taking of risk: a *sporting* proposition. —**sport•ing•ly,** *adv.*

spor•tive, spôr/tiv, *a.* Inclined toward or characterized by sport.

sports car, *n.* A small, high-powered, low-lined, two-seated automobile. Also **sport car.**

sports•cast, spôrts/kast, *n.* A program on radio or television in which a sporting event is broadcast or sports news is reported. —**sports•cast•er,** *n.*

sport shirt, *n.* A soft, short- or long-sleeved shirt for informal wear, usu. squared-off around the bottom so that it may be worn outside or inside slacks. Also **sports shirt.**

sports•man, spôrts/mən, *n. pl.,* -men. A man who engages in sports, esp. in some open-air sport as hunting, fishing, racing, or yachting; one who exhibits qualities, esp. esteemed in those who engage in sports, such as fairness, self-control, and courtesy. —**sports•wom•an,** spôrts/wûm•ən, *n. fem. pl.,* -wom•en. —**sports•man•like, sports•man•ly,** *a.* —**sports•man•ship,** *n.*

sports•wear, spôrts/wār, *n.* Clothes worn for outdoor or informal activities.

sports•writ•er, spôrts/rī•tər, *n.* One who writes news stories about sporting events.

sport•y, spôr/tē, *a.,* -i•er, -i•est. *Informal.* Flashy or vulgarly showy; smart in dress, appearance, manners, or the like; stylish; like or befitting a sport or sportsman; sportsmanlike or sporting. —**sport•i•ly,** *adv.* —**sport•i•ness,** *n.*

spot, spot, *n.* A mark made by foreign matter, as mud

---

a- hat, fāte, fāre, fäther; e- met, mē; i- pin, pīne; o- not, nōte, ôrb, moove (move), boy, pownd; u- cūbe, bûll, tûk (took); ch- chin; th- thick, then; zh- vizhon (vision); ə- əgo, takən, pencəl, lemən, bərd (bird).

or ink; a stain, blot, splotch, blotch, or fleck; a blemish or flaw; a part of a surface, as a patch of color or light; a place or locality, as where a house stood or a ship sank; a place of specific interest: a *spot* for sightseeing, a night *spot;* a position in sequence or in order, as in a narrative or on a program.—*v.t.,* **spot•ted, spot• ting.** To mark, as with foreign matter such as mud, blood, paint, or ink; to stain, blot, splotch, blotch, speck, fleck, dot, or stud.—*v.i.* To cause a stain; to become marked: silk *spotted* by water.—*a.* Made, paid, or delivered at once: a *spot* sale; made at random: a *spot* check; broadcast locally: a *spot* news announcement, a *spot* commercial message. **—in spots,** at times or by snatches. **—in a spot,** in a difficult situation. **—on the spot.** *Informal.* At the very place; at once; where or when needed. **—high spot.** *Informal.* Something memorable. **—hit the spot.** *Informal.* To satisfy a craving or need. **—spot•ta•ble,** *a.* **—spot• less,** *a.* **—spot•less•ly,** *adv.* **—spot•less•ness,** *n.*

spot•light, spot′līt, *n.* A strong light thrown upon a particular spot in order to render some object, person, or group esp. conspicuous, as on a stage; an extra light mounted on a vehicle and capable of casting a strong beam; intense or unusual prominence resulting in wide public interest.—*v.t.* To cast a beam of light upon; to focus attention on.

spot•ted, spot′id, *a.* Marked with or characterized by a spot or spots; blemished.

spot•ted fe•ver, *n.* Any of various fevers characterized by spots on the skin; tick fever carried by the wood tick.

spot•ter, spot′ər, *n.* One who volunteers to watch for enemy aircraft, as in time of war; an employee designated by his or her superiors to watch for and report any evidence of dishonesty among his fellow employees.

spot•ty, spot′ē, *a.,* **-ti•er, -ti•est.** Full of or having spots; spotted; lacking in uniformity or harmony. **—spot•ti•ly,** *adv.* **—spot•ti•ness,** *n.*

spouse, spows, spowz, *n.* A married person; husband or wife.

spout, spowt, *n.* A nozzle or projecting mouth of a vessel, as a pitcher, used in directing the stream of liquid poured out; a pipe or conduit.—*v.t.* To pour out in a jet and with some force; to throw out through a spout or pipe; to utter in a pompous manner.—*v.i.* To issue in a strong jet; to run, as from a spout; to spurt; to make a speech, esp. in a pompous manner. **—spout•er,** *n.*

sprain, sprān, *v.t.* To overstrain or wrench, as the ankle, wrist, or other part of the body at a joint, so as to injure without producing dislocation.—*n.* An act of spraining; the condition of being sprained.

sprat, sprat, *n.* A small food fish, of the herring family.

sprawl, sprôl, *v.i.* To spread and stretch the body carelessly in an ungraceful position; to lie or sit with the limbs stretched out or straggling; to spread irregularly or ungracefully, as flowers, vines, or handwriting.—*v.t.* To cause to straggle or spread out.—*n.* An awkward, sprawling position.

spray, sprā, *n.* Water or other liquid broken up into small particles and blown or falling through the air; a jet of fine particles of liquid squirted from an atomizer or other appliance, as for medicinal treatment; a liquid to be discharged in such a jet, or an appliance for discharging it; a quantity of particles of matter, flying through the air: *spray* of sand.—*v.t.* To scatter in the form of fine particles; to apply as a spray: to *spray* an insecticide on plants.—*v.i.* To scatter spray; to issue forth as spray. **—spray•er,** *n.*

spray, sprā, *n.* A small branch, twig, or shoot of some plant with its leaves, flowers, or berries, either growing or detached: a *spray* of holly or roses.

spray gun, *n.* A mechanical device using air pressure to squirt out a liquid, as a spray of pesticide or paint, and looking like a gun.

spread, spred, *v.t.,* **spread, spread•ing.** To draw or stretch out to the full width or extent, as a cloth, a rolled or folded map, or wings; to extend over a greater area, or period, often followed by *out:* to *spread out* a group of papers; to display or set forth in full, as on a record; to distribute in a sheet or layer: to *spread* hay to dry; to apply in a thin layer or coating on something: to *spread* plaster on walls; to set or prepare, as a dining table; to extend or distribute over a region; to send out in various directions, as light or sound.—*v.i.* To become stretched out or extended, as a flag in the wind; to extend over a greater or a considerable area or period; to be or lie fully displayed, as a landscape; to be able to be spread or applied in a thin layer, as a soft substance; to become shed abroad, diffused, or disseminated, as light, influences, rumors, ideas, or infections; to be forced apart or separate, as rails.—*n.* The act of spreading, or the state of being spread; the extent of spreading: to measure the *spread* of the branches of a tree; capacity for spreading; a stretch, expanse, or extent of something; a covering for a bed, table, or the like, esp. a bedspread. *Informal.* A repast set out, esp. a choice repast or feast; any food preparation used for spreading on bread or crackers, as jam or peanut butter; a ranch or farm, esp. in the west. **—spread one•self thin,** to dissipate one's energies and interests at the expense of thoroughness in any one project or even of one's health.

spread-ea•gle, spred′ē•gəl, *a.* Having or suggesting the form of a spread eagle; having the arms and legs stretched away from the body.—*v.t.,* **-gled, -gling.** To stretch out in the manner of a spread eagle, as a person or thing.—*v.i.* To affect the position of a spread eagle.

spread•er, spred′ər, *n.* One who or that which spreads; a blunt-edged knife for applying food preparations to crackers or bread.

spree, sprē, *n.* A merry frolic; excessive indulgence in a particular activity: a shopping *spree.*

sprig, sprig, *n.* A shoot, twig, or small branch; a small spray of some plant with its leaves or flowers; an ornament or a decorative figure having the form of such a spray.—*v.t.,* **sprigged, sprig•ging.** To decorate, as fabrics or pottery, with a design of sprigs or small floral sprays.

spright•ly, sprīt′lē, *a.,* **-li•er, -li•est.** Vivacious, or cheerfully gay; spirited.—*adv.* Lively; briskly. **—spright•li•ness,** *n.*

spring, spring, *v.i.,* **sprang** or **sprung, sprung, spring•ing.** To rise or move suddenly and lightly: to *spring* into the air; leap, jump, or bound; to fly back or away in escaping from a forced position, as by elastic force or from the action of a spring; split, crack, or become warped, as boards; to issue suddenly, as water or fire, often with *forth, out,* or *up;* spout or gush; come into being, often with *up:* towns *spring up;* to arise by growth, as from a seed; proceed or originate, as from a source or cause; to rise or extend upward, as a spire.—*v.t.* To cause to spring; to cause to fly back, move, or act by elastic force or a spring: to *spring* a trap or a lock; to cause to start out of place or work loose; to bring out, produce, or make suddenly: to *spring* a surprise on a person; to leap over.—*n.* The act of springing; a leap, jump, or bound; a flying back from a forced position; elasticity or springiness; an elastic device or body, as a strip or wire of steel coiled spirally, which, when compressed, bent, or otherwise forced from its normal shape, has the power of recovering this because of its elasticity; an issue of water from the earth, flowing away as a small stream or standing as a pool or small lake; the place of such an issue: hot *springs;* a source of something; the first season of the year in N. America including March, April, and May, following winter and preceding summer; the time beginning after the vernal equinox and lasting until the summer solstice.—*a.* Of, referring to, or suitable for the season of spring.

spring·board, spring′bôrd, n. A flexible board used by gymnasts and acrobats in vaulting, tumbling, or leaping; a similar board, projected over water, used for diving; a point of departure toward a new beginning or change.

spring-clean·ing, spring′klē′ning, n. A thorough cleaning of a place, traditionally the complete, painstaking housecleaning done each spring.

spring·er span·iel, n. A hunting dog used for flushing or retrieving game birds.

spring fe·ver, n. The lazy, restless, or listless feeling usu. accompanying the arrival of spring.

spring·time, spring′tīm, n. The spring season; the earliest stage: the *springtime* of life.

spring·y, spring′ē, a., **-i·er, -i·est.** Having springlike action or elasticity; light and lively: a *springy* step; containing many springs of water; spongy, as turf underfoot. **—spring·i·ly,** adv. **—spring·i·ness,** n.

sprin·kle, spring′kəl, v.t., **-kled, -kling.** To scatter, as a liquid or powder, in drops or particles; to let fall in minute quantities here and there; to overspread, as with drops or particles of water or powder; to diversify or intersperse with objects scattered here and there. **—v.i.** To be sprinkled; to issue in drops or particles; to rain slightly.**—n.** The act or an act of sprinkling; that which is sprinkled; a light rain; a small quantity or number. **—sprink·ler,** n.

sprink·ler sys·tem, n. An overhead arrangement of pipes and sprinklers which turn on automatically at a specified temperature showering water or extinguishing chemicals in a room, area, or building on fire; an underground pipeline connected to sprinklers used to water lawns.

sprin·kling, spring′kling, n. A small quantity falling in drops or particles; a small number or quantity scattered as if sprinkled; the act of scattering in small drops or particles.

sprint, sprint, v.i. To race, move, or run at high speed, esp. at short intervals or over a short distance.**—n.** A short run or race at high speed; a spurt of speed. **—sprint·er,** n.

sprite, sprit, n. A kind of elf or goblin.

sprock·et wheel, n. A wheel with cogs or sprockets to engage with the links of a power chain.

sprout, sprowt, v.i. To begin growth; to shoot forth, as a plant from a seed; to bud; to grow rapidly, as a beard.**—v.t.** To remove shoots, as from a potato.**—n.** The shoot or bud of a plant; a fresh outgrowth from a plant or tree; anything similar to or like a sprout.

spruce, sproos, n. Any member of the pine family, consisting of cone-bearing evergreen trees, as the Norway spruce, the white spruce; the wood of any such tree.

spruce, sproos, a., **spruc·er, spruc·est.** Neat or smart in dress; trim; smug.**—v.t., spruced, spruc·ing.** To trim or dress in a spruce manner.**—v.i.**

spry, sprī, a., **spry·er, spry·est** or **spri·er, spri·est.** Nimble; active; vigorous; lively. **—spry·ly,** adv. **—spry·ness,** n.

spud, spəd, n. A straight, narrow spade for digging up weeds or cutting roots. *Informal.* A potato.

spue, spū, v.i., v.t., **spued, spu·ing.** Spew.**—n.**

spume, spūm, n. Froth; foam; scum; frothy matter on turbulent water or on liquors.**—v.i., spumed, spum·ing.** To froth; to foam.**—v.t.** To spew forth, eject, or discharge. **—spum·ous,** a. **—spum·y,** a., **-i·er, -i·est.**

spunk, spəngk, n. *Informal.* A quick, ardent temper; mettle or pluck.

spunk·y, spəng′kē, a., **-i·er, -i·est.** *Informal.* Full of pluck or spirit. **—spunk·i·ly,** adv. **—spunk·i·ness,** n.

spur, spər, n. An instrument having a little wheel with sharp points, worn on a horse rider's heel for pricking the horse to hasten its pace; an incitement or stimulus; the hard pointed projection on certain birds' or insects' legs which serves as an instrument of offense and defense; something that projects; a snag; a short branch or root of a tree that projects.**—v.t.,** **spurred, spur·ring.** To prick with or as with spurs; to urge or encourage to action; to gash or strike with spurs; to furnish with spurs.**—v.i.** To spur one's horse to make it go fast; to ride fast; to hurry. **—on the spur of the mo·ment,** impulsively; without thought.

spu·ri·ous, spyûr′ē·əs, a. Not legitimate; bastard; not genuine. **—spu·ri·ous·ness,** n.

spurn, spərn, v.t. To reject with disdain; to kick.**—v.i.** To reject anything with disdain or contempt.**—n.** Disdainful rejection; contemptuous treatment; a kick. **—spurn·er,** n.

spurred, spərd, a. Wearing spurs; having prolongations or shoots like spurs, as on the leg of a rooster.

spurt, spərt, v.i. To gush or issue suddenly in a stream or jet, as a liquid; to show marked, increased activity, energy, or effort for a short period. Also **spirt.—v.t.** To force out suddenly in a stream or jet, as a liquid; to squirt. Also **spirt.—n.** A sudden jet or gush of water or other liquid; a marked increase of effort for a short period or distance, as in running or rowing; a sudden outburst, as of feeling. Also **spirt. —spurt·er,** n. **—spur·tive,** a.

sput·nik, spət′nik, spût′nik, n. Any of a series of artificial earth satellites placed into orbit by the Soviet Union, the first of which was launched in October of 1957.

sput·ter, spət′ər, v.i. To speak excitedly, in a rapid or confused manner; to give off particles or drops of moisture explosively with snapping or popping sounds, as a candle does when burning; to involuntarily spit saliva or particles of food from the mouth when speaking.**—v.t.** To jabber; to give out in particles explosively or forcibly.**—n.** The sound or act of sputtering. **—sput·ter·er,** n.

spu·tum, spū′təm, n. pl., **spu·ta,** spū′tə. Spittle or any matter mixed with saliva which is spat out.

spy, spī, n. pl., **spies.** One who keeps a person or place under close or secret surveillance; one employed by a government to obtain secret information by hidden means, or on false pretenses, usu. pertaining to diplomatic, military, or naval affairs of other countries, esp. a belligerent in time of war; the act of spying or watching secretly.**—v.i., spied, spy·ing.** To make secret observations; to act as a spy; to examine or search for something closely or carefully.**—v.t.** To watch or make secret observations, as of a place, person, or actions, usu. with hostile intent; to find out by observation or scrutiny; to catch sight of, or see.

spy·glass, spī′glas, n. A telescope, esp. a small telescope.

squab, skwob, n. pl., **squabs, squab.** A young, unfledged pigeon; a short, fat person.**—a.** Fat; short and stout; unfeathered.

squab·ble, skwob′əl, v.i., **-bled, -bling.** To engage in a noisy quarrel; to have a petty dispute.**—n.** A scuffle; a petty quarrel. **—squab·bler,** n.

squad, skwod, n. A small unit of soldiers organized for drill, inspection, or duty; the smallest tactical unit of the U.S. Army, esp. of the infantry; any small group of persons engaged in a common enterprise: a police *squad.***—v.t., squad·ded, squad·ding.** To form into squads; assign to a squad.

squad car, n. An automobile used for patrol duty by police.

squad·ron, skwod′rən, n. A flight formation of airplanes, usu. of the same type; a basic tactical unit; one or more Naval divisions of vessels or aircraft; an Army unit composed of a headquarters and two or more troops of cavalry; an organized group formed for a particular purpose.**—v.t.** To put into squadrons.

squal·id, skwol′id, a. Foul or filthy due to neglect;

---

wretched; morally debased or disgusting; sordid. **—squal·id·ly,** adv. **—squal·id·ness,** n.

squall, skwôl, n. A sudden, violent gust of wind, often accompanied by rain, snow, or sleet; any disturbance or commotion.—v.i. To blow like a squall. **—squall·y,** a., **-i·er, -i·est.**

squall, skwôl, v.i. To cry out or scream loudly, discordantly, and violently.—v.t. To utter in a harsh, screaming tone.—n. The act or sound of squalling; a loud, discordant cry. **—squall·er,** n.

squal·or, skwol'ər, n. The state or condition of being squalid; wretchedness and filth.

squan·der, skwon'dər, v.t. To spend extravagantly or wastefully: to *squander* an entire inheritance.—n. The act of squandering; extravagant or wasteful expenditure. **—squan·der·er,** n.

square, skwâr, n. A four-sided plane figure having all its sides equal and all its angles right angles; any space or area, or any flat object or piece, having this form or a form approximating it; a square, rectangular, or quadrilateral area in a city or town, marked off by neighboring and intersecting streets; the distance along one side of such an area: a house two *squares* from here; an open area of this or other form, in a city or town, usually planted with grass and trees; an L-shaped or T-shaped instrument for determining or testing right angles; squared form or condition; the second power of a number or quantity, that is the product of the number or quantity multiplied by itself: The *square* of 4, 4 × 4, is 16.—a. Having four equal sides and four right angles, as a figure or area; of a specified length on each side of a square: an area 2 feet *square,* which contains 4 *square* feet; designating a unit representing an area in the form of a square of the length of a specified linear unit along each edge, used in expressing surface measurement: a *square* inch, *square* foot, *square* mile, an area of 4 *square* feet, which is equivalent to an area 2 feet *square;* pertaining to such units, or to surface measurement: *square* measure; having four sides and four right angles, but not equilateral; cubical or approximately so, or rectangular and of three dimensions: a *square* box; having a square section, or one that is merely rectangular: a *square* file; having a solid, sturdy form with rectilinear and angular outlines: a man of *square* build; of the form of a right angle, or having some part or parts rectangular: a *square* corner; at right angles, or perpendicular: one line *square* to another; straight, level, or even, as one surface with another; leaving no balance of debt on either side, or having all accounts settled: to make accounts *square,* to get *square* with a person; just, fair, or equitable: *square* dealing; honest, honorable, or upright. *Informal.* Substantial or satisfying: a *square* meal; disdainful or ignorant of the latest customs, fashions, or fads; conservative; old-fashioned.—adv. So as to be square; at right angles. *Informal.* Fairly or honestly.—v.t., **squared, squar·ing.** To reduce to square or rectangular form; to make cubical, or approximately so; to mark out in one or more squares or rectangles; make straight, level, or even; to regulate, as by a standard; conform to or harmonize with; adjust harmoniously or satisfactorily; to balance, as accounts; settle, as a debt, often with *up;* to find the equivalent of in square measure; to multiply, as a number or quantity, by itself.—v.i. To accord or agree, often with *with.* **—on the square,** at right angles. **—square a·way,** to straighten things up or to make something ready. **—square·ly,** adv. **—square·ness,** n.

square dance, n. A group dance, as a quadrille, performed by several couples arranged in a square or other set pattern. **—square-dance,** v.i., **-danced, -danc·ing. —square danc·ing,** n.

square meas·ure, n. A unit for measuring surface area; a system of such units.

square root, n. A quantity whose square equals a given quantity: 3 is the *square root* of 9.

squar·ish, skwâr'ish, a. Approximately square. **—squar·ish·ly,** adv.

squash, skwosh, v.t. To press into a flat mass or pulp; to crush; to suppress or put down; to quash. *Informal.* To silence, as with a crushing retort.—v.i. To be pressed into a flat mass or pulp; to make a splashing sound; splash.—n. The act of squashing, the impact of a soft, heavy body falling on a surface, or the sound produced by this; something crushed; something soft and easily crushed; a game resembling rackets. **—squash·er,** n.

squash, skwosh, n. pl., **squash·es, squash.** A plant cultivated in the Americas for food; the flesh of this fruit boiled and mashed, or baked.

squash·y, skwosh'ē, a., **-i·er, -i·est.** Soft or pulpy, as overripe food; soft and wet; muddy. **—squash·i·ly,** adv. **—squash·i·ness,** n.

squat, skwot, v.i., **squat·ted** or **squat, squat·ting.** To sit down in a low or crouching position with the legs drawn up closely beneath or in front of the body; to crouch down, as an animal; to settle on land, esp. public or new land, without any title or right, or under government regulation for the purpose of acquiring title.—v.t. To put in a squatting attitude or posture.—a. Short and thickset or thick, as persons or animals; low and thick or broad; seated or being in a squatting position; crouching.—n. The act or fact of squatting or crouching. **—squat·ly,** adv. **—squat·ness,** n.

squat·ter, skwot'ər, n. One who or that which squats; one who settles on land, esp. public or new land, without any title or permission; one who settles on land under government regulation, for the purpose of acquiring title.

squat·ty, skwot'ē, a., **-ti·er, -ti·est.** Squat; short and thick; low and broad: a *squatty* house.

squaw, skwô, n. A N. American Indian woman, esp. a wife: a derogatory term.

squawk, skwôk, v.i. To utter a loud, harsh cry, as a duck or other fowl when frightened. *Informal.* To complain, esp. vehemently or loudly.—v.t. To give forth with a squawk.—n. A loud, harsh cry or sound. *Informal.* A complaint which is loud or vehement. **—squawk·er,** n. **—squawk·y,** skwô'kē, a., **-i·er, -i·est.**

squeak, skwēk, v.i. To utter a sharp, shrill cry, as a pig or mouse; to make a sharp noise, as an ungreased wheel or door.—v.t.—n. A sharp, shrill cry or noise. *Informal.* A close escape, usu. preceded by *close* or *narrow.* **—squeak·er,** n. **—squeak·ing·ly,** adv. **—squeak·y,** skwē'kē, a., **-i·er, -i·est.**

squeal, skwēl, n. A more or less prolonged, sharp, shrill cry or sound. *Informal.* An act of informing on a person.—v.i. To utter a more or less prolonged, sharp, shrill cry, as in pain, fear, or the like, as persons or animals; to emit a shrill sound. *Informal.* To turn informer.—v.t. To utter or produce with a squeal. **—squeal·er,** n.

squeam·ish, skwē'mish, a. Easily shocked or offended; prudish; dainty in taste or requirements; easily nauseated; qualmish. **—squeam·ish·ly,** adv. **—squeam·ish·ness,** n.

squee·gee, skwē'jē, n. An implement edged with rubber or leather, for sweeping water from wet decks, scraping water off windows after washing, or the like; any of various similar devices.—v.t., **-geed, -gee·ing.** To sweep, scrape, or press with or as with a squeegee.

squeeze, skwēz, v.t., **squeezed, squeez·ing.** To press forcibly together; compress; to apply pressure upon in order to extract: to *squeeze* a lemon; to thrust forcibly or force by pressure: to *squeeze* one's hand into a tight glove; to hug; to press in one's hand: She *squeezed* his hand when she said good night; to oppress, as with abhorrent duties.—v.i. To exert a compressing force; to force a way through some narrow or crowded place: to *squeeze* between the two cars; to yield to pressure.—n. The act of squeezing; a hug; a small quantity or amount of anything obtained by squeezing. *Informal.* Exertion of pressure to extort favors or money. **—squeez·er,** *n.*

squelch, skwelch, *v.t.* To strike or press with crushing force; squash. *Informal.* To put down or suppress completely; to silence, as with a crushing retort.—*v.i.* To make a splashing sound, as of something wet under impact; to become squelched or squashed.—*n.* A squelched or crushed mass of anything; a squelching sound. *Informal.* A crushing argument or retort. **—squelch·er,** *n.*

squib, skwib, *n.* A short, witty or sarcastic saying or writing; a lampoon; a news story which is short and sometimes used to fill space.

squid, skwid, *n. pl.,* **squids, squid.** Any of several ten-armed small marine animals, having slender bodies and caudal fins and much used for bait.

squig·gle, skwig′əl, *v.i.,* **-gled, -gling.** To make hasty and illegible twisting marks, as in writing; to move restlessly.—*v.t.* To mark or write in squiggles.—*n.* A short, twisting mark, usu. illegible.

squint, skwint, *v.i.* To look with partially closed eyes, as toward a brilliant light; to suffer from cross-eye; to peer or look quickly sideways.—*v.t.* To cause to look sideways or with partially closed eyes; to cause, as the eyes, to be half-shut.—*n.* Strabismus, or cross-eye. *Informal.* A cursory look: I took a *squint* at the report; a side glance.—*a.* Peering obliquely, as with distrust; suffering from cross-eye. **—squint·er,** *n.* **—squint· ing·ly,** *adv.* **—squint·y,** *a.,* **-i·er, -i·est.**

squint-eyed, skwint′īd, *a.* Having eyes that squint; glancing sideways; displaying a malicious attitude.

squire, skwīr, *n.* A young man of aristocratic birth who, seeking knighthood, waited or attended upon a knight; a title used by a justice of the peace, local judge, or other dignitary, esp. in country districts and small towns; a man who escorts a lady in public.—*v.t.,* **squired, squir·ing.** To attend as or in the manner of a squire; to accompany or escort, as a girl or woman.

squirm, skwərm, *v.i.* To move like a worm, with writhing; wriggle; to display or feel suffering or distress, as from humiliation, embarrassment, or pain.—*n.* A wriggling motion. **—squirm·y,** *a.,* **-i·er, -i·est.**

squir·rel, skwər′əl, skwerl, *n.* Any of the tree-dwelling, bushy-tailed rodents, common in Europe and N. America; the pelt of a squirrel.

squirt, skwərt, *v.i.* To eject liquid in a jet or stream from a narrow opening; to issue in a jetlike stream.—*v.t.* To cause, as a liquid, to issue in a jet from a narrow opening; eject in a jetlike stream; to wet with a liquid so ejected.—*n.* An act of squirting; a jet, as of water; an instrument for squirting, as a syringe. *Informal.* An insignificant, self-assertive person, a young or small person. **—squirt·er,** *n.*

squish, skwish, *v.t., v.i.* To squash or squeeze.—*n.* A squashing sound. **—squish·y,** *a.,* **-i·er, -i·est.**

stab, stab, *v.t.,* **stabbed, stab·bing.** To pierce, wound, or kill with a pointed weapon; to inflict keen or severe pain on; to pierce.—*v.i.* To aim a blow with a pointed weapon; to be extremely cutting.—*n.* The thrust of a pointed weapon; keen, poignant pain. *Informal.* A brief effort or attempt: He took a *stab* at writing. **—stab· ber,** *n.*

sta·bil·i·ty, stə·bil′ə·tē, *n. pl.,* **-ties.** The state or quality of being stable; fixedness or firmness in position; continuance in the same state or without change; endurance or permanence; steadfastness, as of character or purpose.

sta·bi·lize, stā′bə·līz, *v.t.,* **-lized, -liz·ing.** To make or keep firm, stable, or constant.—*v.i.* **—sta·bi·li·za· tion,** stā·bə·lə·zā′shən, *n.*

sta·bi·liz·er, stā′bə·lī·zər, *n.* A person or thing which produces stabilization.

sta·ble, stā′bəl, *n.* A building fitted for the lodging and feeding of horses and cattle, esp. of horses; a collection of animals belonging in such a building; an establishment where race horses are kept and trained; the horses belonging to, or the persons connected with, such an establishment.—*v.t., v.i.* **-bled, -bling.** To put or lodge in or as in a stable.

sta·ble, stā′bəl, *a.* Able to stand firm, or not likely to fall or give way, as a structure, support, or foundation; firm; steady; stationary; able or likely to continue or last, or firmly established: a *stable* government; enduring or permanent; reliable; level-headed; not readily decomposing, as a chemical. **—sta·bly,** *adv.* **—sta·ble·ness,** *n.*

sta·bling, stā′bling, *n.* The act of one who stables horses or other animals; accommodation for animals; stables collectively.

stac·ca·to, stə·kä′tō, *a.* Characterized by performing the notes of a musical passage in a crisp manner; consisting of short, sharp, or distinct sounds: a *staccato* burst of machine-gun fire.—*adv.*

stack, stak, *n.* A large, usu. circular or rectangular pile of hay, straw, or the like; any more or less orderly pile or heap; a set of bookshelves ranged one above another, as in a library. *Pl.* The section in any library where books are kept; a number of chimneys or flues grouped together; smokestack; a vertical exhaust or vent pipe. *Informal.* A great quantity or number.—*v.t.* To pile or arrange in the form of a stack: to *stack* hay; to cover or load with something in stacks or piles; to arrange, as aircraft, at various altitudes while awaiting landing instructions. **—blow one's stack.** *Informal.* To blow one's top. **—stack the cards** or **deck,** to arrange the playing cards in the pack in a particular manner, so as to secure an unfair advantage; to arrange circumstances to secure an advantage, usu. unfairly. **—stack·er,** *n.*

sta·di·um, stā′dē·əm, *n. pl.,* **-di·ums, -di·a,** -dē·ə. A structure for athletic games, usu. having an oval shape and tiers of seats for spectators.

staff, staf, *n. pl.,* **staves, staffs.** A stick or club carried for support or combat; a rod used as a symbol of office, as a baton or mace; a supporting pole: a flag*staff;* the five parallel lines and four spaces between them on which notes and other musical characters are written; also **stave.** A group of people assisting a supervisor in carrying out an undertaking: a hospital *staff;* a body of military officers who help the commander plan, administer, or coordinate operations; that which provides support or sustenance: bread, the *staff* of life.—*v.t.* To provide with personnel: to *staff* an office with clerks.—*a.*

staff·er, staf′ər, *n.* One of a staff of workers, esp. a newspaper writer.

stag, stag, *n.* The male red deer; the male of other members of the deer family, as the caribou; a hart, sometimes applied particularly to a hart in its fifth year; a man at a dance unaccompanied by a woman; a social gathering of men only.—*v.i.,* **stagged, stag· ging.** To attend a social event without a companion of the opposite sex.—*a.* For men only.—*adv.*

stage, stāj, *n.* A single step or degree in a process; a particular period in a course of progress, action, or development; a level in a series of levels; a raised platform or floor for any purpose, esp. a platform or raised floor for theatrical performances; the theater; the dramatic profession; the scene of any action or career; a stopping point or station on a journey; the distance between such stations; any portion of a journey; a stagecoach; one of the propulsion elements of a rocket vehicle, usu. separated and dropped off when its fuel is exhausted.—*v.t.,* **staged, stag·ing.** To present on the theatrical stage; to furnish with a stage or staging.—*v.i.* To go by stages; to travel by stagecoach.

stage·coach, stāj′kōch, *n.* A coach drawn by horses,

formerly used on regular runs between scheduled places for the conveyance of passengers, freight, or mail.

stage fright, *n.* Nervousness experienced on facing an audience.

stage-hand, stāj'hand, *n.* A worker in a theater who handles props and scenery.

stage man·a·ger, *n.* One who supervises the technical aspects of production and performance of a play, regulating all matters behind the scenes including lights, props, costumes, and other details.

stage-struck, stāj'strøck, *a.* Having a great love for the theater; seized by a passionate desire to become an actor; referring to an immature or unrealistic idea or feeling about the theater.

stage whis·per, *n.* A loud whisper by an actor on stage, intended to be heard by the audience but not by the other actors; an aside.

stag·ger, stag'ər, *v.i.* To sway from one side to the other while standing or walking; to reel; to walk or stand unsteadily; to hesitate; to become less confident or determined.—*v.t.* To cause to doubt and waver; to make to hesitate; to make less confident; to strike as incredible; to amaze.—*n.* A sudden swing or reel of the body, as if about to fall. —**stag·ger·er,** *n.* —**stag·ger·ing,** *a.*

stag·ing, stā'jing, *n.* The act or process of putting a play on the stage; a temporary platform or structure of posts and boards for support, as in building; scaffolding; the separation of a stage of a rocket following blast-off.

stag·nant, stag'nent, *a.* Not flowing, as a stream; impure from lack of motion, as water; not brisk: Trade is *stagnant*. —**stag·nan·cy,** *n.*

stag·nate, stag'nāt, *v.i.,* -**nat·ed,** -**nat·ing.** To cease to run or flow; to have no current, as water; to become impure from lack of current; to become dull or inactive, as trade. —**stag·na·tion,** stag·nā'shen, *n.*

stag·y, stage·y, stā'jē, *a.,* -**i·er,** -**i·est.** Suggestive of the theater; displaying theatrical artificiality or pomposity. —**stag·i·ly,** *adv.* —**stag·i·ness,** *n.*

staid, stād, *a.* Sober; steady; sedate. —**staid·ness,** *n.*

stain, stān, *v.t.* To discolor with spots or streaks of dirt, blood, or other foreign matter; to bring shame upon; to blemish; to color in a particular way, esp. to color with something which penetrates the substance.—*v.i.* To produce a stain or to become stained.—*n.* A discoloration produced by foreign matter; a spot, esp. one penetrating beneath the surface and not easily removable; a cause of shame; a blemish; coloration produced by staining anything; a dye or pigment used in staining. —**stain·a·ble,** *a.* —**stained,** *a.* —**stain·er,** *n.*

stained glass, *n.* Any glass that is colored by having metallic oxides or other pigments fused, baked, or burned into its surface: used mostly in church windows. —**stained-glass,** *a.*

stain·less steel, *n.* An alloy of steel highly resistant to rust or corrosion.

stair, stār, *n.* A succession of steps rising one above the other arranged as a way between two points at different heights in a building. *Pl.* A stairway.

stair·case, stār'kās, *n.* Any structure of stairs with the supporting devices needed for safety and support.

stair·way, stār'wā, *n.* A passageway which allows movement from one level or floor of a building to another by a series of stairs; a staircase.

stair·well, stār'wel, *n.* A vertical shaft, opening, or enclosed area within which are stairs or a stairway.

stake, stāk, *n.* A piece of wood sharpened at one end and set in the ground as a support to something, or as part of a fence; the post to which one condemned to die by fire was fastened; that which is pledged or wagered; something hazarded; the state of being pledged or put at hazard, preceded by *at:* His honor is *at stake.*—*v.t.,* **staked, stak·ing.** To set and plant like a stake; to mark the limits of by stakes, followed by *out:* to *stake out* land; to pledge; to lay down as a stake; to

hazard upon the issue of a competition.

stake·hold·er, stāk'hōl·dər, *n.* One who holds the money when a wager is laid.

sta·lac·tite, sta·lak'tīt, stal'ak·tīt, *n.* A mass of stony matter, usu. in a conical form, originating from the roof of a cavern: opposed to *stalagmite.*

sta·lag·mite, sta·lag'mīt, stal'ag·mīt, *n.* A deposit of stony matter on the floor of a cavern, often rising into columns which meet and unite with the stalactites above.

stale, stāl, *a.,* **stal·er, stal·est.** Tasteless from age; having lost its spirit or flavor from being long kept; being worn out or valueless from use or long familiarity; trite.—*v.t., v.i.,* **staled, stal·ing.** To make or be useless or stale. —**stale·ness,** *n.*

stale·mate, stāl'māt, *n.* A position of the pieces in chess when no move can be made without putting the king in check; any position in which no action can be taken; a deadlock.—*v.t.,* -**mat·ed,** -**mat·ing.** To subject or bring to a stalemate.

Sta·lin·ism, stä'li·niz·əm, *n.* The principles by which Joseph Stalin controlled the Soviet Union, esp. referring to his repressive and dictatorial methods. —**Sta·lin·ist,** *n., a.*

stalk, stôk, *n.* The stem or main axis of a plant; the connecting or supporting part of a flower, leaf, or plant; a supporting part or stem of anything. —**stalked,** *a.* —**stalk·y,** *a.,* -**i·er,** -**i·est.**

stalk, stôk, *v.i.* To pursue or approach game stealthily, as behind a cover; to walk with slow, stiff, or haughty strides; to proceed in a sinister or deliberate manner. —*v.t.* To pursue, as game, stealthily, as behind a cover.—*n.* An act or course of stalking game or the like; a slow, stiff stride or striding gait. —**stalk·er,** *n.*

stall, stôl, *n.* A compartment in a stable or shed for the accommodation of one animal; a stable or shed for horses or cattle; a booth in which merchandise is displayed for sale or in which some business is carried on: a butcher's *stall;* a stand or table on which goods are displayed for sale: a book*stall;* one of a number of fixed enclosed seats, as in the choir of a church, esp. for the use of the clergy; a compartment or chamber for any of various purposes: a shower *stall;* the condition of being stalled.—*v.t.* To put or keep in a stall or stalls, as animals or automobiles; to furnish with stalls; to bring to a standstill; to cause, as an engine, to stop, usu. unintentionally; to cause to stick fast, as in snow.—*v.i.* To occupy a stall, as an animal; to come to a standstill; to stick fast, as in mire. —**stalled,** *a.*

stall, stôl, *n. Informal.* Anything used as a pretense, or trick.—*v.t. Informal.* To put off, evade, or deceive, often followed by *off;* to divert attention from, as a thief at work.—*v.i. Informal.* To act evasively or deceptively.

stal·lion, stal'yen, *n.* An uncastrated male horse, esp. an adult used for breeding purposes.

stal·wart, stôl'wert, *a.* Large and strong in frame; muscular; sturdy; brave; bold; resolute.—*n.* A person having such qualities; a partisan who is uncompromising. —**stal·wart·ness,** *n.*

sta·men, stā'men, *n. pl.,* **sta·mens, stam·i·na,** stam'ə·nə. The pollen-bearing organ, and the so-called male organ, of a flower, consisting of the filament and the anther.

stam·i·na, stam'ə·nə, *n.* Strength of physical constitution; power to endure conditions of difficulty or hardship, as disease or fatigue.

stam·mer, stam'ər, *v.i.* To pause or falter involuntarily while speaking.—*v.t.* To utter with hesitations, repetitions, or stops.—*n.* A stammering manner of speaking. —**stam·mer,** *n.* —**stam·mer·ing·ly,** *adv.*

stamp, stamp, *v.t.* To strike or press forcibly by thrusting the foot downward; to mark with an impression; to imprint; to fix deeply: *stamp* in memory; to coin or mint; to affix a stamp to, as a postage stamp; to crush by the downward action of a kind of pestle.—*v.i.* To strike the foot forcibly downward, or to walk in such a manner, esp. in rage.—*n.* The act of stamping; an instrument for making impressions on other bodies; a mark imprinted; a postage stamp; an instrument for cutting materials into various forms by a downward pressure; general character fixed on anything: the *stamp* of genius. **—stamp out,** to extinguish, as fire, by stamping on with the foot; to eradicate; to suppress or quell by strong measures, as a revolution.

stam•pede, stam•pēd′, *n.* A sudden rush or headlong flight of a body of animals in fright, as cattle or horses; any headlong general flight, as of troops in panic; an unconcerted general rush or movement, as of persons actuated by a common impulse.—*v.i.,* **-ped•ed, -ped• ing.** To scatter or flee in a stampede, as cattle or persons; make an unconcerted general rush, as persons actuated by a common impulse.—*v.t.* To produce a stampede among; cause to stampede. **—stam•ped• er,** *n.* **—stam•ped•ing•ly,** *adv.*

stamp•er, stam′per, *n.* One who or that which stamps; an instrument, tool, or machine for stamping.

stamp•ing ground, *n.* A person's or animal's most familiar surroundings or usual place of activity.

stance, stans, *n.* A style of standing or positioning the body; a particular attitude, emotional or mental, toward something.

stanch, stanch, stänch, *v.t.* To stop the flow of, as a liquid, esp. blood. Also **staunch. —stanch•er,** *n.*

stanch, stänch, stanch, *a.* Staunch.

stand, stand, *v.i.,* **stood, stand•ing.** To take or keep an upright position on the feet; to have a specified height when in this position: He *stands* six feet in his socks; to cease walking or moving; to stop; to take a position or stand as indicated: to *stand* aside; to remain firm or steadfast, as in a cause; to adopt a certain course, as of adherence or support; to be in an upright position, as things; to be set, placed, or fixed; to be located or situated; to show a specified position of the parties concerned: The score *stands* 14 to 12 at the quarter; to remain valid: That rule still *stands;* to remain motionless; to be or become stagnant, as water; to be or remain in a specified state, condition, relation, or situation, as persons or things: He *stood* alone in that opinion.—*v.t.* To cause to stand; to set upright; set; to undergo, or submit to: to *stand* trial; to endure without hurt or damage, or without giving way: Material that will *stand* wear; to put up with or tolerate.—*n.* The act of standing; a halt or a stop; a determined effort against or for something; a position taken or maintained with respect to others or to some question; the place where a person or thing stands, as a position or station; the place where a witness stands to testify in court; also **wit•ness stand.** *Usu. pl.* A raised platform or other structure, as for spectators at a race course or an athletic field, or along the route of a parade, or for a speaker. A framework on or in which articles are placed for support or exhibition; a piece of furniture of various forms, on or in which to put articles: a wash-*stand;* a small, light table; a stall, booth, table, or the like, where articles are exposed for sale or some business is carried on: a fruit *stand* or news*stand;* a site or location for business; a place or station occupied by vehicles which are available for hire; the growing trees or those of a particular species or grade, in a given area; a standing growth, as of grass or wheat; a halt of a theatrical company on tour: a one-night *stand.* **—stand a chance** or **a show,** to have a chance or possibility, esp. to have a chance of winning, surviving, or the like. **—stand by,** to side with or aid; to affirm; to be ready. **—stand for,** to be a symbol of; represent; to put up with or tolerate. **—stand in,** to act as a substitute; to be in partnership with. **—stand off,** to put off; to deny; to remain at some distance away. **—stand on,** to base one's position on; to rest or depend on; to be based on; to be punctilious

about; to assert or claim respect for, as one's rights. *Naut.* To continue on the same course or tack. **—stand out,** to stick out; to be distinct; to excel; to continue. **—stand o•ver,** to postpone for consideration, treatment, or settlement. **—stand to rea•son,** to be in accordance with reason. **—stand up,** to remain whole; hold up under pressure. *Informal.* To fail to keep an appointment with. **—stand•er,** *n.*

stand•ard, stan′dərd, *n.* By general consent, a basis of comparison, or established criterion; an authorized unit of weight or measure; the legal rate of intrinsic value in coins; the prescribed degree of fineness for gold or silver; a certain commodity treated as being of invariable value and serving as a measure of value for all other commodities; something which stands upright, as a tall candlestick, a timber, or a rod; a flag, emblematic figure, or other object raised on a pole to indicate a rallying point of an army or fleet.—*a.* Serving as a standard of weight, measure, or value, or of comparison or judgment; conformed or conforming to any such standard; of recognized excellence or established authority.

stand•ard•ize, stan′dər•dīz, *v.t.,* **-ized, -iz•ing.** To conform to or regulate by a standard; bring to or make of an established standard size, shape, weight, quality, or strength. **—stand•ard•i•za•tion,** stan•dər•də•zā′ shən, *n.*

stand•ard time, *n.* The mean solar time based on the passage of the sun over a specific meridian and adopted for use over a considerable area or time zone.

stand•by, stand′bī, *n. pl.,* **-bys.** One who stands by another to help out; a supporter; anything that takes the place of something else.

stand•ee, stan•dē′, *n. Informal.* One who stands when there are no seats available.

stand-in, stand′in, *n.* A person employed to substitute for a movie star during dangerous action or while cameras and lights are being adjusted; a substitute. **—stand in,** *v.i.*

stand•ing, stan′ding, *n.* Position or status as to social, professional, or personal reputation; good reputation, position, or credit; length of existence, continuance, or experience; the act of one who or that which stands. *Sports.* A ranking of teams or individual contestants according to their competitive performances during a given season.—*a.* In an upright position; motionless; lasting; continuing in operation: a *standing* rule.

stand-off•ish, stand′ôf′ish, *a.* Somewhat reserved and unfriendly. **—stand-off•ish•ness,** *n.*

stand•out, stand′owt, *n.* Something that is notable or prominent because of excellence.

stand•pipe, stand′pīp, *n.* A vertical pipe or tower into which water is pumped in order to obtain a required level for adequate pressure.

stand•point, stand′poynt, *n.* The point at which one stands to view something; a mental point of view; viewpoint.

stand•still, stand′stil, *n.* A state of cessation of movement or action; a halt; a stop.

sta•nine, stā′nīn, *n.* A standard aptitude or performance test score of units from the lowest, or one, to nine, and having a median of five.

stan•za, stan′zə, *n.* A group of lines of verse, arranged in pattern as regards length, rhyme scheme, and meter, and forming a division of a poem. **—stan•za•ic,** stan•zā′ik, *a.*

sta•pes, stā′pēz, *n. pl.,* **sta•pes, sta•ped•es,** stə• pē′dēz. The innermost of the three small bones in the middle ear of mammals. **—sta•pe•di•al,** stə•pē′dē• əl, *a.*

staph•y•lo•coc•cus, staf•ə•lō•kok′əs, *n. pl.,* **-ci,** -sī. Any of certain bacteria in which the individual organisms form irregular clusters which cause inflammation and the formation of pus.

sta·ple, stā'pəl, *n.* A loop of metal with pointed ends for driving into a surface to hold a hasp, hook, pin, bolt, or the like; a bent piece of wire used to bind papers, magazines, or sections of a book together. —*v.t.,* **-pled, -pling.** To fasten with a staple or staples. —**sta·pler,** *n.*

sta·ple, stā'pəl, *n. Usu. pl.* A necessary or basic article, esp. a food, as sugar; the principal commodity grown or manufactured in a country, district, or town; the principal element or ingredient in anything; raw or unmanufactured material; the thread or pile of wool, cotton, or flax.—*a.* Established in business: a *staple* trade; chief.—*v.t.,* **-pled, -pling.** To grade or sort fibers, as of wool.

sta·pler, *n.* A dealer in staple commodities; one employed in assorting wool according to its staple.

star, stär, *n.* Any luminous body seen in the heavens at night, except the moon, the planets, comets, meteors, and nebulae; any of the celestial bodies that shine by their own light, as the sun; any of the celestial bodies which are said to influence man and his destiny; anything which resembles a star; a figure with points radiating like the spokes of a wheel; an asterisk; a distinguished, celebrated, or prominent person; a brilliant theatrical or operatic performer; a movie star. —*v.t.,* **starred, star·ring.** To set or adorn with stars; to bespangle; to set apart for special attention with an asterisk; to feature as the leading performer.—*v.i.* To shine as a star; to be celebrated; to perform a leading role in a theatrical production. —**star·less,** *a.* —**star·like,** *a.*

star·board, stär'bərd, *n.* The right-hand side of a ship looking toward the prow: opposed to **port.**—*a.* Referring to the right-hand side of a ship.—*adv.* In the direction of starboard.—*v.t., v.i.* To steer to the right.

starch, stärch, *n.* A white, tasteless carbohydrate, occurring in plants, and forming an important constituent of rice, corn, wheat, beans, potatoes, and many other vegetable foods; a commercial preparation of the substance used to stiffen fabrics in laundering, and for many industrial purposes; stiffness or formality, as of manner. *Informal.* Stamina, vigor, or vitality.

star·dom, stär'dəm, *n.* The world or class of professional stars of the performing arts or sports; status of a star.

stare, stär, *v.i.,* **stared, star·ing.** To look with eyes fixed wide open; to gaze intently, as in admiration, surprise, horror, or impudence.—*v.t.* To affect by staring at; gaze steadily at.—*n.* The act of gazing steadily. —**star·er,** *n.*

star·fish, stär'fish, *n. pl.,* **-fish, -fish·es.** Any of a class of marine animals having the body radially arranged, usu. in the form of a star, with five or more rays or arms radiating from a central disk.

star·gaze, stär'gāz, *v.i.,* **-gazed, -gaz·ing.** To gaze at the stars; to engage in daydreaming. —**star·gaz·ing,** *n.*

stark, stärk, *a.* Mere, pure, or downright; harsh or desolate; very severe or grim, stiff; rigid, as in death. —*adv.* Wholly; entirely.

star·let, stär'lit, *n.* Any young actress being groomed to eventual stardom, esp. in the movies.

star·light, stär'līt, *n.* The light proceeding from the stars.—*a.*

star·ling, stär'ling, *n.* Any of numerous birds with a dark, iridescent plumage, native to Europe and introduced into N. America.

star·ry, stär'ē, *a.,* **-ri·er, -ri·est.** Abounding with or lighted by stars: a *starry* sky; of, pertaining to, or proceeding from the stars: *starry* light; of the nature of or consisting of stars: *starry* worlds; resembling a star; star-shaped or stellate; shining like stars: *starry* eyes; studded with starlike figures or markings. —**star·ri·ly,** *adv.* —**star·ri·ness,** *n.*

star·ry-eyed, stär'ē-īd, *a.* Tending to be idealistic or fanciful.

Stars and Stripes, *n.* An informal name for the flag of the United States.

star-span·gled, stär'spang·gəld, *a.* Decorated or spangled with stars. —**The Star-Span·gled Ban·ner,** the national anthem of the U.S.; the flag of the U.S.

start, stärt, *v.i.* To move suddenly and spasmodically, caused by surprise, pain, or any sudden feeling; to set out; to commence a course, as a race or a journey. —*v.t.* To rouse suddenly from concealment; to set going; to originate, establish, or introduce.—*n.* A sudden involuntary twitch, spring, or motion, caused by surprise, fear, or pain; a sudden change of pace; a quick movement; a bursting forth; a spasmodic effort; the beginning of a crack or opening in a structure; a beginning of motion; the setting of something going; a first motion from a place or in a race; the outset. —**start·er,** *n.*

star·tle, stär'təl, *v.t.,* **-tled, -tling.** To excite by sudden alarm, surprise, or apprehension; to alarm.—*v.i.* To be alarmed; to start.—*n.* A sudden surprise or shock.

star·tling, stärt'ling, *a.* Causing sudden alarm or surprise. —**star·tling·ly,** *adv.*

star·va·tion, stär·vā'shən, *n.* The state of starving or being starved, extreme suffering from want of food. —*a.* Liable to cause starvation; insufficient to maintain the ordinary level of subsistence: *starvation* wages.

starve, stärv, *v.i.,* **starved, starv·ing.** To perish or suffer extremely from hunger; to suffer from poverty or want.—*v.t.* To kill with hunger.

stash, stash, *v.t. Informal.* To hide or store in a secret place for safekeeping or future use.

sta·sis, stā'sis, stas'is, *n. pl.,* **-ses,** -sēz. The state of inactivity caused by the opposition of equal forces.

state, stāt, *n.* Condition of a person or thing; condition of circumstances; a condition of certain time, phase, or stage; a condition connoting riches, rank, dignity, and pomp; the body politic of a nation; the sovereign political entity of a fixed territory; the civil rule of government, as distinguished from *church* or *military.* (*Sometimes cap.*) One of the commonwealths or bodies politic which together make up a federal union.—*a.* Of, for, or pertaining to a state or nation; of or denoting a government agency or authority.—*v.t.,* **stat·ed, stat·ing.** To express in writing or words; to narrate; to recite; to aver, allege, or declare; to settle. —**stat·a·ble,** *a.*

state·craft, stāt'kraft, *n.* The art of conducting state affairs; statesmanship.

stat·ed, stā'tid, *a.* Determined or fixed: *stated* rules.

state·hood, stāt'hŭd, *n.* The condition or status of a state, esp. a state of the U.S.

state·less, stāt'lis, *a.* Being without a state or nationality. —**state·less·ness,** *n.*

state·ly, stāt'lē, *a.,* **-li·er, -li·est.** Dignified; imposing; lofty; majestic; magnificent.

state·ment, stāt'mənt, *n.* The act of stating something; something stated; in business, an abstract of an account, as one rendered periodically to show the balance due.

state·room, stāt'room, stāt'rûm, *n.* A private room on a ship or train.

state·side, stāt'sid, *a.* Toward, leaving, or being in the U.S.

states·man, stāts'mən, *n. pl.,* **-men.** A man who is versed in government and in the management of government affairs; a political leader showing an unselfish interest in the common good. —**states·man·like,** *a.* —**states·man·ship,** *n.*

States' rights, *n. pl., sing. or pl. in constr.* All powers that the Constitution neither gives the Federal Government nor denies the state; an interpretation of the Constitution marked by an extremely broad conception of these state privileges and opposing Federal claims to these powers through liberal interpretation; belief in the right of the state to nullify an action of the Federal government that it deems unconstitutional. Also **State rights.**

stat·ic, stat′ik, *a.* Pertaining to a fixed or stationary condition; pertaining to bodies at rest or forces in equilibrium; noting or pertaining to atmospheric electricity that interferes with radar, radio reception, or television reception.—*n.* A disturbance in radio or television reception due to electrical interference in the atmosphere. *Informal.* Difficulty; back talk.

stat·ics, stat′iks, *n. pl. but sing. in constr.* That branch of mechanics which treats of the relations of forces in equilibrium, the body upon which they act being in a state of rest.

sta·tion, stā′shən, *n.* The act or manner of standing; the place in which anything stands; position; the headquarters of the police force or other public service in a municipality; a place or building equipped for particular work, research, or the like: a postal *station;* a studio equipped for radio and television broadcasting; standing, as of persons or things; relative position in the social scale; a regular stopping place: a railroad *station;* a bus *station.*—*v.t.* To assign a station to; post at a station.

sta·tion·ar·y, stā′shə·ner·ē, *a.* Remaining in the same station or place; not moving; fixed; remaining in the same condition.

sta·tion·er, stā′shə·nər, *n.* One who sells paper, pens, pencils, ink, and various other materials connected with writing.

sta·tion·er·y, stā′shə·ner·ē, *n.* Paper and envelopes used in letter writing; various materials employed in writing, as pencils, pens, and paper.

sta·tion wag·on, *n.* An automobile without a trunk but with a large area for packages and suitcases loaded through a tailgate.

stat·ism, stā′tiz·əm, *n.* A system in which the state regulates the economy. —**stat·ist,** *n., a.*

sta·tis·tic, stə·tis′tik, *n.* An element or datum of statistics; a statistical fact, as the mean, median, or standard deviation. —**sta·tis·ti·cal,** *a.* —**sta·tis·ti·cal·ly,** *adv.*

stat·is·ti·cian, stat·ə·stish′ən, *n.* A person knowledgeable in statistics; a person skilled in the use or practices of statistics.

sta·tis·tics, stə·tis′tiks, *n. pl. but sing. in constr.* The science of the systematic collection of data so as to present descriptive information about a larger population of which the data is construed as representative, or to infer the significance of underlying factors whose effects are reflected in the data. *Pl. in constr.* The numerical data of statistics.

sta·tor, stā′tər, *n.* The stationary part of an electric generator or motor: opposed to *rotor.*

stat·u·ar·y, stach′oo·er·ē, *n. pl.,* **-ies.** Statues collectively.

stat·ue, stach′oo, *n.* A representation of a person or an animal carved in stone or wood, molded in some plastic material, or cast in bronze or the like, properly one of considerable size and in the round.

stat·u·esque, stach·oo·esk′, *a.* Like or suggesting a statue, as in formal dignity, studied grace, or classic beauty.

stat·u·ette, stach·oo·et′, *n.* A small statue.

stat·ure, stach′ər, *n.* The natural height of an animal body; growth, maturity, development: professional *stature.*

sta·tus, stā′təs, stat′əs, *n.* Standing or position in regard to rank or condition; prestige; position or state of affairs.

sta·tus quo, stā′təs kwō′, stat′əs kwō′, *n.* The state in which anything was or is; the existing state of affairs.

stat·ute, stach′oot, *n.* An enactment that is formally expressed and documented as a law; written law, as opposed to *common law;* a permanent rule or law enacted by the governing body of a corporation or institution.

stat·ute mile, *n.* A mile.

staunch, stônch, stänch, *a.* Watertight; sound or firm in structure or substance; strong; substantial; firm or steadfast in principle.

stave, stāv, *n.* One of the thin, narrow, shaped pieces of wood which form the sides of a cask or similar vessel; a stick, rod, pole, or the like; a verse or stanza of a poem or song; the staff on which musical notes are written.—*v.t.,* **staved** or **stove, stav·ing.** To break the staves of; to break or crush inward.

stay, stā, *v.i.,* **stayed, stay·ing.** To remain, as in a place, situation, or company, instead of departing; to dwell or reside; to continue to be as specified, as to condition; to keep up, to hold out or endure, as in a race or other contest, often followed by *with;* to stop or halt; to pause or wait before proceeding or continuing.—*v.t.* To bring to a stop or halt; to hold back, detain, or restrain, as from going or proceeding further; to suspend or delay, as proceedings; to suppress or quell, as violence, strife, or emotions; to temporarily appease or satisfy, as the cravings of the stomach or appetite; to check, arrest, or stop, as movement, action, or processes; to remain through or during, as a period of time; to remain to the end of, remain beyond, or outstay, usu. followed by *out.*—*n.* The act of staying or stopping; a stop, halt, or pause; a standstill; continuance in a place; a sojourn or temporary residence. *Informal.* Staying power, or endurance. —**stay put.** *Informal.* To remain where or as placed; remain fixed. —**stay·er,** *n.*

stay, stā, *n.* A strong rope or wire, used to support a funnel or mast; a guy.—*v.t.,* **stayed, stay·ing.** To support or secure, as a mast, with a stay or stays.

stay, stā, *n.* Something that supports or steadies; a flat piece of plastic, bone, or metal used to stiffen collars, corsets, and other clothing.—*v.t.,* **stayed, stay·ing.** To support or hold up; to strengthen or sustain; fix on for support.

stead, sted, *n.* The place of a person or thing for which someone or something is substituted. —**stand in good stead,** to be helpful or of use to.

stead·fast, sted·fast, sted′fast, sted′fəst, *a.* Fixed; firm; constant or firm in resolution. —**stead·fast·ly,** *adv.* —**stead·fast·ness,** *n.*

stead·y, sted′ē, *a.,* **-i·er, -i·est.** Firmly placed or fixed; stable in position or equilibrium; even or regular in movement; uniform; continuous; free from excitement or agitation; settled, staid, or sober, as a person; an exclamation ordering one to control his temper or emotions. An order to the helmsman to keep the ship on its present course.—*n. pl.,* **-ies.** *Informal.* A person's regular date or sweetheart.—*v.t.,* **-ied, -y·ing.** To make steady.—*v.i.* To become steady.—*adv.* In a steady manner. —**stead·i·er,** *n.* —**stead·i·ly,** *adv.* —**stead·i·ness,** *n.*

steak, stāk, *n.* A cut of beef, pork, fish, or the like, suitable for broiling or frying.

steal, stēl, *v.t.,* **stole, stol·en, steal·ing.** To take dishonestly or wrongfully; to appropriate, as ideas, credit, or words, without right or acknowledgment; to take by surprise or without permission: to *steal* a kiss; to move, bring, or put secretly or quietly. *Baseball,* Of a runner, to reach, as a base, while the pitcher delivers tha ball to the plate.—*v.i.* To commit theft; to move or go secretly; to pass, come, spread, or the like, imperceptibly, gently, or gradually: the years *steal* by.—*n. Informal.* An act of stealing; a theft; the thing stolen; a bargain. The act or instance of stealing, as a base. —**steal·er,** *n.*

stealth, stelth, *n.* A secret or clandestine method of procedure; a proceeding by secrecy. —**stealth·y,** *a.,* **-i·er, -i·est.** —**stealth·i·ly,** *adv.* —**stealth·i·ness,** *n.*

steam, stēm, *n.* A gaseous substance into which water

---

is converted under heat and pressure; the visible moist vapor which rises from water when subjected to heat; an exhalation of vapor. *Informal.* Energy.—*v.i.* To give out or be covered by steam or vapor; to rise in a vaporous form. *Informal.* To exhibit anger.—*v.t.* To expose to steam; to apply steam to.

steam•boat, stēm′bōt, *n.* A ship powered by a steam engine.

steam en•gine, *n.* An engine in which steam pressure is directed against a piston or turbine to produce power.

steam•er, stē′mər, *n.* A steamship; a container in which articles are subjected to the action of steam.

steam•fit•ter, stēm′fit•ər, *n.* One who installs and repairs steam pipes and their accessories for ventilating, heating or refrigerating systems. —**steam•fit•ting,** *n.*

steam i•ron, *n.* An iron designed with a water container for emitting steam onto the material being ironed.

steam•roll•er, stēm′rō•lər, *n.* A heavy machine for crushing, compacting, or leveling materials in road construction; an agency for crushing opposition, esp. with ruthless disregard of rights.—*v.t.* To go over or crush, as with a steamroller.

steam•ship, stēm′ship, *n.* A ship propelled by steam.

steam shov•el, *n.* A machine for digging or excavating, operated by its own engine.

steam tur•bine, *n.* A turbine powered by steam discharged under high pressure.

steam•y, stē′mē, *a.,* **-i•er, -i•est.** Consisting of or abounding in steam; vaporous; misty. —**steam•i•ly,** *adv.* —**steam•i•ness,** *n.*

ste•a•tite, stē′ə•tīt, *n.* A soft stone form with a soapy or greasy feel. Also **soap•stone.**

sted•fast, sted′fast, *a.* Steadfast.

steed, stēd, *n.* A horse, esp. a spirited one; a horse for state or war.

steel, stēl, *n.* An alloy of iron and carbon with various other constituents which can be alloyed with other metals to produce variations in hardness, strength, elasticity, and malleability; a condition of extreme hardness, sternness, or rigor.—*a.*—*v.t.* To make hard or stubborn; to render insensible or obdurate.

steel band, *n.* A type of percussion band common in the West Indian islands, esp. Trinidad, using drums made from steel oil barrels whose sides have been cut to different heights to give certain tones.

steel blue, *n.* A lustrous blue-gray color, resembling steel-tempered blue.

steel•head, stēl′hed, *n. pl.,* **-heads, -head.** A rainbow trout, having a silver luster, much sought after by sportsmen.

steel wool, *n.* A mass of fine steel filaments matted or woven together for use in polishing or scouring.

steel•works, stēl′wərks, *n. pl., sing. or pl. in constr.* An establishment where steel is made and often manufactured into girders, rails, parts of machinery, and the like. —**steel•work•er,** *n.*

steel•y, stē′lē, *a.,* **-i•er, -i•est.** Made of steel; resembling or suggestive of steel, as in color or hardness. —**steel•i•ness,** *n.*

steel•yard, stēl′yärd, *n.* A weighing instrument consisting of a balance with unequal arms, the longer being graduated and having a weight which is moved to counterbalance any object hung from a hook on the short arm.

steep, stēp, *a.* Ascending or descending sharply; sloping sharply. *Informal.* Very high in price.—*n.* A very steep place. —**steep•ly,** *adv.* —**steep•ness,** *n.*

steep, stēp, *v.t.* To soak in a liquid; to immerse and saturate; to macerate; to extract the essence of by soaking.—*v.i.* To be soaked in a liquid.—*n.* A liquid in which things are steeped.

steep•en, stē′pən, *v.i., v.t.* To become or cause to become steeper.

stee•ple, stē′pəl, *n.* A tall, tapering structure, usu. culminating in a spire, surmounting the roof or tower of a building, esp. a church.

stee•ple•chase, stē′pəl•chās, *n.* A race in which horses jump over a course of artificial obstacles. —**stee•ple•chas•er,** *n.*

stee•ple•jack, stē′pəl•jak, *n.* A person whose job is to climb steeples and towers to inspect or make repairs.

steer, stēr, *v.t.* To guide the course of a vessel by means of a rudder or helm; to guide, pilot, or lead; to direct the course of, to govern or rule; to restrain or control.—*v.i.* To guide a vehicle, etc., by a rudder, steering wheel, etc.; to pursue a course; to be steered or guided in a particular direction.—*n. Informal.* Information intended as guidance; a tip. —**steer clear of,** to avoid. —**steer•a•ble,** *a.* —**steer•er,** *n.*

steer, stēr, *n.* A young, castrated bovine, esp. one raised for beef.

steer•age, stēr′ij, *n.* A part or division of a ship with minimal accommodations allotted to passengers traveling at the cheapest rate; the act or method of steering a vessel.

steer•ing gear, *n.* The apparatus or mechanism for steering something, as a vessel, automobile, or airplane.

steer•ing wheel, *n.* A wheel which is turned by hand to operate the steering of a vehicle, as an automobile.

stein, stīn, *n.* A mug, esp. for beer; the quantity of beer this mug holds.

stel•lar, stel′ər, *a.* Referring to or resembling stars; referring to a renowned film, stage, or sports personality.

stem, stem, *n.* The main body of a tree, shrub, or other plant which supports the branches; a trunk; a stalk; the stock or line of descent of a family; ancestry or pedigree; something resembling or suggesting the stem of a plant, flower, or the like; a long, slender part of an object, as the tube of a tobacco pipe; the slender part of a goblet; a part of a word, usu. a derivative of a root, which serves as the base of inflectional forms. —*v.t.,* **stemmed, stem•ming.** To remove the stem from.—*v.i.* To be derived or descended; to originate. —**stem•less,** *a.*

stem, stem, *v.t.,* **stemmed, stem•ming.** To dam up; to stop; as the flow of a stream or other force; to stanch; to make progress against.

stemmed, stemd, *a.* Having a stem: long-*stemmed*; with the stem taken off: *stemmed* stringbeans.

stem•ware, stem′wār, *n.* Vessels, as of glass, having a stem uniting the body to the foot or base, as goblets or wineglasses.

stem•wind•er, stem′wīn•dər, *n.* A watch wound by turning a knob at the stem; something very outstanding in its class. —**stem•wind•ing,** *a.*

stench, stench, *n.* A foul smell; a stink. —**stench•y,** *a.,* **-i•er, -i•est.**

sten•cil, sten′səl, *n.* A thin sheet of metal, paper, or other material, pierced with letters or designs, which, when brushed with ink or color, are reproduced on the surface beneath.—*v.t.,* **-ciled, -cil•ing.** To mark or paint by means of a stencil.

sten•o, sten′ō, *n. Informal.* Stenographer.

ste•nog•ra•pher, stə•nog′rə•fər, *n.* One who uses stenography to record letters, memoranda, or other spoken material and then transcribes and types the notes.

ste•nog•ra•phy, stə•nog′rə•fē, *n.* Any system of shorthand writing. —**sten•o•graph•ic,** sten•ə•graf′ik. —**sten•o•graph•i•cal•ly,** *adv.*

sten•to•ri•an, sten•tôr′ē•ən, *a.* Very loud or powerful in sound.

step, step, *n.* A movement made by lifting the foot and setting it down again as in walking, running, or dancing; the space passed over or measured by one movement of the foot in such stepping; the sound made by the foot in stepping; footprint; a manner of walking; gait; a pace uniform with that of others or in time with music. *Pl.* Movements or course in walking or running. A move or proceeding, as toward some course of action; a measure; a stage in a process; degree or rank; a support for the foot as on a ladder or stair; a pattern of movement in a dance; an offset part of an object; a socket, frame, or platform for supporting the lower end of a mast.—*v.i.*, **stepped, step·ping.** To move by lifting the foot and setting it down again; to walk or go on foot; to move with measured steps, as in a dance; to go briskly or fast, as a horse; to come or happen with ease: to *step* into a fortune; to tread by intention or accident; to press with the foot, in order to operate some mechanism.—*v.t.* To perform the steps of, as a dance; to measure, as ground or distance, by steps, followed by *off* or *out.* —**in step,** moving in rhythm, as in dancing, or in cadence, as in marching; in harmony or agreement. —**step down,** to give up one's position; to reduce by degrees. —**step in,** to come into a situation. —**step on it.** *Informal.* To hurry or move faster. —**step out,** to go out for a brief time; to walk in quick step. *Informal.* To go out socially. —**step up,** to increase by stages; to be increased; to come to the front. —**take steps,** to begin action on a problem. —**watch one's step,** to be careful.

step·broth·er, step/brŭth·ər, *n.* One's stepfather's or stepmother's son by a former marriage.

step·child, step/child, *n. pl.,* **-child·ren.** A child of one's husband or wife by a former marriage.

step·daugh·ter, step/dô·tər, *n.* A daughter of one's husband or wife by a former marriage.

step·fa·ther, step/fä·thər, *n.* The husband of one's mother in a second or subsequent marriage.

step·lad·der, step/lad·ər, *n.* A portable ladder having four legs and flat steps, hinged at the top, and opening to form its own support.

step·moth·er, step/mŭth·ər, *n.* The wife of one's father in a second or subsequent marriage.

step·par·ent, step/pâr·ənt, *n.* A stepfather or stepmother.

steppe, step, *n.* One of the vast, level, treeless plains of southeastern Europe and of Asia; an extensive plain.

stepped-up, stept·əp/, *a. Informal.* Speeded up; increased.

step·ping·stone, step/ing·stōn, *n.* A raised stone used to step on in crossing; an aid by which an end may be accomplished; an assistance to progress.

step·sis·ter, step/sis·tər, *n.* A stepfather's or stepmother's daughter by a former spouse.

step·son, step/sən, *n.* The son of a husband or wife by a former spouse.

stere, stēr, *n.* A French unit of solid measure, equal to a cubic meter.

ster·e·o, ster/ē·ō, stēr/ē·ō, *n. pl.,* **-e·os.** A stereophonic sound system; stereophonic sound; stereotype.—*a.* Stereophonic; referring to a stereoscope.

ster·e·o·phon·ic, ster·ē·ə·fon/ik, stēr·ē·ə·fon/ik, *a.* Referring to a sound system in which acoustical elements are arranged so as to reproduce the spatial distribution of the original sound for the listener. —**ster·e·o·phon·ic·al·ly,** adv.

ster·e·o·scope, ster/ē·ə·skōp, stēr/ē·ə·skōp, *n.* An optical instrument which enables the viewer to look upon two pictures taken with a small difference in angular view, each eye looking upon one picture only, so that two images are conveyed to the brain as one, and the objects thus appear solid and real as in nature. —**ster·e·o·scop·ic,** ster·ē·ə·skop/ik, *a.*

ster·e·o·type, ster/ē·ə·tīp, stēr/ē·ə·tīp, *n.* A process of making metal plates for printing by taking a mold of composed type and then taking a cast from this mold in type metal; a set image; a standardized or typical image or conception held by or applied to members of a certain group.—*v.t.,* **-typed, -typ·ing.** To make a stereotype of; give a fixed form to.

ster·e·o·typed, ster/ē·ə·tīpt, stēr/ē·ə·tīpt, *a.* Reproduced in stereotype plates; fixed or settled in form; conventional.

ster·ile, ster/il, *a.* Free from living germs or microorganisms; incapable of producing offspring; barren; unproductive of vegetation, as soil; infertile; unfruitful. —**ster·il·i·ty,** ste·ril/ə·tē, *n.*

ster·i·lize, ster/ə·līz, *v.t.,* **-lized, -liz·ing.** To render sterile. —**ster·i·li·za·tion,** ster·ə·lə·zā/shən, —**ster·i·liz·er,** *n.*

ster·ling, stər/ling, *a.* Referring to English money; of silver; made of silver of this quality; conforming to the highest standard or thoroughly excellent.

stern, stərn, *a.* Severe, as regards facial expression; gloomy; severe of manner; harsh; rigidly steadfast; immovable. —**stern·ly,** adv. —**stern·ness,** *n.*

stern, stərn, *n.* The hinder part of a ship or boat.

ster·num, stər/nəm, *n. pl.,* **ster·na,** stər/nə, **ster·nums.** A bone or series of bones extending along the ventral portion of the body, connected with the clavicles and the true ribs; the breastbone.

stern-wheel·er, stərn/hwē·lər, stərn/wē·lər, *n.* A boat propelled at the stern by an engine-powered paddle wheel.

ster·oid, stoo/oyd, stēr/oyd, *n.* A class of fat-soluble organic compounds including sterols, bile acids, sex hormones, and certain digitalis compounds.

steth·o·scope, steth/ə·skōp, *n.* An instrument used to convey sounds in the body to the ear of the examiner. —**steth·o·scop·ic,** steth·ə·skop/ik, *a.*

ste·ve·dore, stē/və·dôr, *n.* One whose occupation is to stow goods and packages in a ship's hold; one who loads or unloads vessels.—*v.t., v.i.,* **-dored, dor·ing.** To load or unload freight.

stew, stoo, stū, *n.* A preparation of food cooked by stewing. *Informal.* A state of uneasiness, agitation, or perturbation.—*v.t.* To cook, as food, by simmering or slow boiling.—*v.i.* To be cooked by slow boiling. *Informal.* To fret, worry, or fuss.

ste·ward, stoo/ərd, stū/ərd, *n.* A manager of a large estate or who takes care of financial or other affairs for another person; an executive of a club, hotel, passenger ship, or restaurant who buys food and liquor and superintends their preparation and serving; a man on a passenger ship who waits on table.

stew·ard·ess, stoo/ər·dis, stū/ər·dis, *n.* A woman who attends to passengers, esp. on an airplane.

stick, stik, *n.* A relatively long and slender piece of wood; a branch or shoot of a tree or shrub cut or broken off; an elongated piece of wood; a rod or wand; a club or cudgel; any of various elongated articles or pieces resembling sticks. *Informal.* A stiff, dull person; a golf club; baseball bat.—*v.t.,* **stuck, stick·ing.** To pierce or stab; to fasten onto by piercing; to secure with something inserted; to thrust into, out, or through; to attach by causing to adhere to the surface; to put or set in a specified place; to fix or impale on a pointed instrument; to obstruct or bring to a halt, usu. in the passive: to be *stuck* in a traffic jam. *Informal.* To baffle or confound, usu. in the passive: to be *stuck* for an answer; to cheat or swindle. —*v.i.* To cleave or cling to the surface; to adhere; to stay or remain in place; to hold firm or cling resolutely, as to an idea or promise; stay close, as when shadowing or chasing someone; to project, protrude, or be conspicuous; to be hindered from making progress. —**stick by,** to remain loyal or faithful to. —**stick it out.** *Informal.* To endure or see something through to the end. —**stick up.** *Informal.* To hold up and rob, esp. with a gun. —**stick up for.** *Informal.* To support or defend.

stick·er, stik/ər, *n.* One who or that which sticks; an adhesive label; one who causes something to adhere.

stick-in-the-mud, stik/in·thə·məd, *n. Informal.* A

slow, dull, or backward person.

stick·le·back, stik′əl·bak, *n.* Any of certain very small fishes found in ponds and streams, having spines on their backs, and remarkable for building nests.

stick·ler, stik′lər, *n.* One who insists on perfection. *Informal.* Anything puzzling; a sticker.

stick·pin, stik′pin, *n.* A decorative pin, often bejeweled, to be worn on a man's tie.

stick-up, stick·up, stik′əp, *n. Informal.* A sticking up; a holdup; a robbery.

stick·y, stik′ē, *a.* **-i·er, -i·est.** Having the quality of adhering; viscous; humid or damp, as the weather. *Informal.* Awkward; difficult: a *sticky* situation or problem. **—stick·i·ly,** *adv.* **—stick·i·ness,** *n.*

stiff, stif, *a.* Rigid; not easily bent; not working or moving smoothly or easily; not supple, pliant; constrained; ungraceful; thick or dense in consistency; not liquid or fluid; haughty or excessively formal in manner; tense, or drawn very tight; maintained in a stubborn, tenacious manner; potent; having strength, power, or force of movement. *Informal.* Unusually severe or harsh; exceedingly difficult or arduous; intoxicated or drunk; expensive or very high in price. **—n.** *Informal.* A corpse; a clumsy, rough, or boring person. **—stiff·ly,** *adv.* **—stiff·ness,** *n.*

stiff·en, stif′ən, *v.t., v.i.* To make or become stiff; to make or to become less flexible. **—stiff·en·er,** *n.*

stiff-necked, stif′nekt′, *a.* Stubborn; obstinate; haughty.

sti·fle, stī′fəl, *v.t.,* **-fled, -fling.** To kill by impeding respiration; to suffocate; to smother; to deaden, as flame or sound; to suppress or conceal; to keep from being known. **—v.i. —sti·fler,** *n.* **—sti·fling,** *a.* **—sti·fling·ly,** *adv.*

stig·ma, stig′mə, *n. pl.,* **-mas, -ma·ta,** -mä′tə. Any mark of infamy; a blemish or stain, as on one's character; a natural mark on the skin. *Bot.* The upper extremity of the style, and the part which receives the pollen. **—stig·ma·ta,** *n. pl.* Marks like the wounds on the crucified body of Christ supernaturally impressed upon the bodies of certain persons, as St. Francis. **—stig·ma·tic,** sitg·mat′ik, *a.* **—stig·mat·i·cal·ly,** *adv.*

stig·ma·tize, stig′mə·tīz, *v.t.,* **-tized, -tiz·ing.** To mark with a stigma; to call or characterize by some opprobrious epithet; to produce marks or spots on. **—stig·ma·ti·za·tion,** stig·mə·tə·zā′shən, *n.*

stile, stīl, *n.* A series of steps or a frame of bars for getting over a fence; a turnstile.

sti·let·to, sti·let′ō, *n. pl.,* **-tos, -toes.** A small dagger having a slender blade.

still, stil, *a.* Motionless; silent; soft or low; without agitation; of or indicating a fixed or motionless picture. **—v.t.** To silence or quiet; to appease or allay; to quiet or restrain. **—v.i.** To grow silent or calm. **—n.** Noiselessness; quiet; a photograph showing no motion. **—adv.** Continuously: The boys are *still* here; despite; nonetheless; however; motionlessly; to a greater extent. **—still·ness,** *n.*

still, stil, *n.* A distilling apparatus, esp. an illegal one. **—v.t., v.i.** To distill.

still·birth, stil′bərth, *n.* The birth of any fetus or offspring which is dead; a fetus or offspring which is stillborn. **—still·born,** stil′bôrn′, *a.*

still life, *n. pl.,* **still lifes.** A portrayal, painting, or photograph of inanimate objects. **—still-life,** *a.*

stilt, stilt, *n.* A long piece of wood or like material used in pairs for walking with the feet raised above the ground; one of several pillars used to support a structure above water or land. **—v.t.**

stilt·ed, stil′tid, *a.* Elevated; pompous; stiff and bombastic. **—stilt·ed·ly,** *adv.*

stim·u·lant, stim′yə·lənt, *n.* That which stimulates; a stimulus.

stim·u·late, stim′yə·lāt, *v.t.,* **-lat·ed, -lat·ing.** To excite or arouse to action by some strong motive or by persuasion; to spur on. **—stim·u·la·tion,** stim·yə·lā′shən, *n.* **—stim·u·la·tive,** *a.*

stim·u·lus, stim′yə·ləs, *n. pl.,* **-li,** -lē, -lī. Something that incites to action or exertion; an incitement; a stimulant.

sting, sting, *v.t.,* **stung, sting·ing.** To prick or wound with some sharp-pointed organ; to affect painfully or irritatingly: to be *stung* by nettles; to pain sharply, hurt, or wound; to affect with acute mental pain: to be *stung* with remorse; to goad or drive as by sharp irritation. **—v.i.** To use or have a sting, as bees; to cause mental pain or irritation, as by criticism; to feel a smarting pain, as from the sting of an insect or from a blow; to feel acute mental pain or irritation. **—n.** The act of stinging; a wound inflicted by stinging; the pain or smart caused by stinging; any sharp or smarting wound, hurt, or physical or mental pain; any of various sharp-pointed, often venom-bearing organs of insects and other animals capable of inflicting painful or dangerous wounds; a glandular hair on certain plants, as nettles, which emits an irritating fluid; anything or an element in anything that wounds, pains, or irritates; the capacity to wound or pain; something that goads to action by causing sharp irritation; a sharp stimulus or incitement: to be driven by the *sting* of jealousy. **—sting·er,** *n.* **—sting·ing·ly,** *adv.*

sting ray, *n.* Any of the ray family of marine fish whose dorsal spines at the base of a whiplike tail are able to inflict severe, sometimes poisonous wounds.

stin·gy, stin′jē, *a.,* **-i·er, -i·est.** Extremely close-fisted and miserly; lacking generosity; niggardly; scanty. **—stin·gi·ly,** *adv.* **—stin·gi·ness,** *n.*

stink, stingk, *v.i.,* **stank** or **stunk, stunk, stink·ing.** To emit a strong offensive smell; to be odious or loathsome; to have a bad reputation. *Informal.* To be of distastefully low quality; to possess an offensively large amount of something: to *stink* of money, to *stink* with culture. **—v.t.** To cause to have an offensive smell: Burning cabbage *stunk* up the kitchen. **—n.** A strong, offensive smell; stench. *Informal.* A violent disagreement. **—stink·er,** *n.* **—stink·y,** *a..* **-i·er, -i·est.**

stint, stint, *v.t.* To limit to a particular amount or quantity; to restrict. **—v.i.** To exert restraint; to set limits. **—n.** Limit or restraint exerted; a specific amount of work assigned to be completed: one's *stint* for the day. **—stint·er,** *n.*

sti·pend, stī′pend, *n.* Any periodical payment or compensation for services rendered; periodic payment for defraying expenses.

stip·ple, stip′əl, *v.t.,* **-pled, -pling.** To paint, draw, or engrave by means of dots, as distinct from lines. **—n.** A painting done by stippling.

stip·u·late, stip′yə·lāt, *v.i.,* **-lat·ed, -lat·ing.** To make an agreement or covenant to do or forbear anything; to specify or arrange as a condition for an agreement; to promise. **—stip·u·la·tion,** stip·yə·lā′shən, *n.* **—stip·u·la·to·ry,** stip′yə·lə·tôr′ē, *a.*

stir, stər, *v.t.,* **stirred, stir·ring.** To mix in order to blend, dissolve, or agitate the ingredients; to move or disturb the arrangement of; to bestir or arouse, as from sleep; to excite or incite to action: to *stir up* dissension; to evoke, as an emotion: to *stir* one's anger. **—v.i.** To move slightly: No one *stirred* when the bell rang; to be in brisk motion; to be deeply moved or aroused. **—n.** The act of stirring; hustle; general excitement.

stir·ring, stər′ing, *a.* Active or busy, as in business; rousing; exciting. **—stir·ring·ly,** *adv.*

stir·rup, stər′əp, stir′əp, *n.* A strap hanging from a saddle used to assist one in mounting a horse, posting, and retaining one's seat.

stitch, stich, *v.t.* To sew; to unite together by sewing. **—v.i.** To practice needlework; to sew. **—n.** A single pass of the needle in sewing; a single turn of the thread around a needle in knitting; a sharp pain in the side; a furrow or ridge. *Informal.* A small part: not willing to do a *stitch* of work; clothing: not a *stitch* to wear. **—stitch•er,** *n.*

stoat, stōt, *n.* The ermine, esp. in summer when its coat is brown.

stock, stok, *n.* Money or property serving as capital; the subscribed capital of a company or corporation, divided into transferable shares of uniform amount; the shares of a particular company or corporation; a quantity of something accumulated, as for future use; goods kept on hand by a merchant or a commercial house for sale to customers; implements or animals used, kept, or employed in operating an establishment; the horses, cattle, sheep, and other useful animals kept or raised on a farm or ranch; a part of an object or instrument in which other parts are inserted or to which they are attached, as a body or handle supporting working parts; the wooden piece to which the barrel and lock of a rifle or other firearm are attached; the support upon which the bow of a crossbow is mounted; the beam of a plow to which the blades and handles are attached; the hub of a wheel; the block of wood from which a bell is hung; the block of wood or piece of metal which constitutes the body of a carpenter's plane; the shorter and thicker piece of a T-square; the handle or brace by which a boring bit is held and rotated; an adjustable handle for holding and turning the dies used in cutting screw threads; the handle of a whip; the person from whom a given line of descent is derived; lineal descent or lineage; the orig. type from which a race or other group of animals or plants has been derived; a race or other related group of animals or plants; a related group of languages; the main upright part of anything, as the vertical beam of a cross; a supporting structure of various kinds; the support of the block on which an anvil is fitted, or of the anvil itself; the frame of a spinning wheel; a frame in which a horse or other animal is secured for shoeing or for a veterinary operation; the material from which anything is made; the broth, used as a foundation for soups and sauces; the repertoire of a theatrical company or the company itself; the main stem or trunk of a tree or other plant; a rhizome or rootstock; a stem in which a graft is inserted and which is its support; a plant that furnishes slips or cuttings. *Pl.* The timbers or frame on which a ship or boat rests while in course of construction; an old instrument of punishment consisting of a framework between two posts with holes for confining the ankles and sometimes the wrists of an offender placed in a sitting position and exposed to public derision. *—v.t.* To furnish with a store of something; to fasten or to provide with a stock, as a rifle.*—v.i.* To accumulate a store of supplies; to sprout.*—a.* Of or pertaining to stock; kept regularly in stock or on hand, as for use or sale; staple; standard; of the common or ordinary type; in common use; commonplace; forming part of a repertoire, as a play or piece; appearing together in repertoire, as a company; pertaining to stock plays or pieces, or to a stock company.*—adv.* Completely, used in compounds: *stock-still.* **—in stock,** in store or on hand as for use or sale; actually present in the stock of goods of a dealer. **—out of stock,** lacking, esp. temporarily, from the stock of goods of a dealer. **—stock up,** to lay up a stock or supply of something. **—take stock,** to make an appraisal or estimate of resources or prospects; to make an examination or inspection for the purpose of forming an opinion. **—take stock in,** take an interest in. *Informal.* To believe in; attach importance to.

stock•ade, sto•kād′, *n.* A defensive barrier consisting of strong posts or timbers fixed upright in the ground; an enclosure or pen made with posts and stakes.*—v.t.,* **-ad•ed, -ad•ing.** To protect or fortify with a stockade.

stock•brok•er, stok′brō•kər, *n.* A broker who purchases and sells stocks or shares for his customers.

stock car, *n.* A standard assembly line model car modified for racing; a wooden-slatted boxcar for transporting livestock.

stock ex•change, *n.* The building where corporate stocks or securities are bought and sold; an association of brokers or dealers in stocks and bonds.

stock•hold•er, stok′hōl•dər, *n.* One who is owner of shares of stock in a corporation.

stock•ing, stok′ing, *n.* A close-fitting covering for the foot and leg.

stock mar•ket, *n.* A market where stocks or shares are bought and sold; the purchase and sale of stocks or shares: The *stock market* was dull today.

stock•pile, stok′pīl, *n.* An accumulation of supplies or goods for future use; a stock or store, as of war materials.*—v.t., v.i.,* **-piled, -pil•ing.** To store and put away for future use; hoard.

stock•y, stok′ē, *a.,* **-i•er, -i•est.** Of solid and sturdy form or build; thickset. **—stock•i•ly,** *adv.* **—stock•i•ness,** *n.*

stock•yard, stok′yärd, *n.* A yard connected with a slaughterhouse, railroad, or market, for temporarily keeping cattle, sheep, swine, or horses.

stodg•y, stoj′ē, *a.,* **-i•er, -i•est.** Of a thick, semisolid consistency; heavy, as food; heavy, dull, or uninteresting; stupidly or tediously commonplace; lacking style and interest; dowdy. **—stodg•i•ly,** *adv.* **—stodg•i•ness,** *n.*

sto•ic, stō′ik, *n.* A person who is indifferent to both pleasure and pain. (*Cap.*) A disciple of the Greek philosopher Zeno teaching that men should strive to be free from passion, unmoved by joy or grief, and able to submit without complaint to the unavoidable necessity by which all things are governed.

sto•i•cal, stō′i•kəl, *a.* Impassive; manifesting or maintaining indifference to pleasure or pain. (*Cap.*) Stoic.

stoke, stōk, *v.t., v.i.,* **stoked, stok•ing.** To poke, stir up, and feed, as a fire; to tend the fire of, as a furnace. **—stok•er,** stō′kər, *n.*

stole, stōl, *n.* A narrow strip of decorated silk or other material worn over the shoulders by priests or clergymen; a scarf of fur, marabou, or fabric worn around the shoulders by women. **—stoled,** *a.*

stol•id, stol′id, *a.* Slow to feel or show emotion; dull; unexcitable. **—sto•lid•i•ty,** stə•lid′ə•tē, *n.* **—stol•id•ly,** *adv.*

sto•ma, stō′mə, *n. pl.,* **-ma•ta, -mə•tə, -mas.** A tiny pore in leaves through which gaseous exchange takes place; a breathing pore or similar mouthlike opening common in certain worms and insects.

stom•ach, stəm′ək, *n.* The pouchlike enlargement in the alimentary canal which is the main organ of digestion where food is acted upon to yield nutrients to the body; the desire for food caused by hunger; appetite; inclination; liking.*—v.t.* To be able to eat, retain, or digest; to bear, as without open resentment or without opposition; to brook: to *stomach* an affront.

stom•ach•er, stəm′ə•kər, *n.* An ornamental covering for the chest and stomach worn by women.

stomp, stomp, *v.t., v.i. Informal.* Stamp, esp. with intent to harm, often followed by *on.*

stone, stōn, *n.* A hard concretion of earth or mineral matter, as lime, silica, or clay; a generally movable mass of such material; products utilizing this material: paving *stone;* a calculous concretion in the kidneys or bladder; the disease arising therefrom; the surface on which pages are composed by setting type from galleys into page forms. *Brit.* A common measure of weight.*—v.t.,* **stoned, ston•ing.** To throw stones at; to remove the seed from.

stoned, stōnd, *a. Informal.* Intoxicated or drugged.

Stone Age, *n.* The age in the history of mankind marked by the use of stone implements.

---

a- hat, fāte, fāre, fäther; **e-** met, mē; **i-** pin, pīne; **o-** not, nōte, ôrb, moove (move), boy, pownd; **u-** cūbe, bull, tûk (took); **ch-** chin; **th-** thick, ŧhen; **zh-** vizhon (vision); **ə-** ago, takən, pencəl, lemən, bərd (bird).

stone-deaf, stōn′def′, *a.* Totally deaf.

stone·ma·son, stōn′mā·sən, *n.* One who prepares stones for building, or builds with them. —**stone·ma·son·ry,** *n.*

stone·wall, *v.i.* To use delaying acts or tactics in discussion or politics; to filibuster.

ston·y, ston·ey, stō′nē, *a.,* **-i·er, -i·est.** Referring to or resembling stone or rock; pitiless or insensitive; rigid or without motion; expressionless; petrifying. —**ston·i·ly,** *adv.* —**ston·i·ness,** *n.*

stooge, stooj, *n.* One who acts as a foil, as for a comedian. *Informal.* An underling or stool pigeon.

stool, stool, *n.* A seat with three or four legs but without arms or back, intended as a seat for one person; a toilet seat; a discharge from the bowels.

stool pi·geon, *n.* A pigeon used as a decoy. *Informal.* One who acts as a spy or informer for the police; a person employed as a decoy or secret confederate.

stoop, stoop, *v.i.* To bend, bow or lean from an erect position; to condescend or deign; to demean, degrade, or lower oneself.—*v.t.* To bend, bow, lean, or collapse, as the top part of something: to *stoop* the head; to bring down from an accustomed or proper level of dignity; to let down or lower, as a sail or flag.—*n.* An act of stooping; a stooping movement; a stooping attitude or carriage of body, as a slouch; a descent from dignity or superiority; a condescension; the downward swoop of a bird of prey.

stoop, stoop, *n.* The steps rising into a platform at the entrance of a house; a small porch entranceway to a house.

stop, stop, *v.t.,* **stopped, stop·ping.** To halt, arrest, check, bring to a standstill; to restrain or hold back from proceeding or completing; to cut off, intercept, or withhold; to cease, desist, or to put an end to; to discontinue; to close, as a door; to stanch, as a flow of blood. *Sports.* To knock out, as in boxing; to keep, as an opponent, from making a score; to defeat, as an opponent.—*v.i.* To come to a halt, as in a journey; to stay, remain, or sojourn.—*n.* The act of stopping or halting; a closing or filling up, as of a hole; the state of being at a standstill; an arrest of movement, action, or operation; a check; an end put to anything; a stay or sojourn made at a place, as in the course of a journey; a plug or other stopper for an opening; a save or play that stops an opponent from scoring; a hole in a wind instrument; the act of closing a hole in a wind instrument or pressing the string in a stringed instrument to produce a particular note.

stop·gap, stop′gap, *n.* That which fills up a gap; a temporary expedient or substitute; makeshift.

stop·light, stop′līt, *n.* A traffic signal which directs the pedestrian or motorist to stop; a red taillight on a vehicle which lights up to indicate when the driver is slowing down or stopping.

stop·o·ver, stop′ō·vər, *n.* A short stop at a point in a journey; a stop with the privilege of continuing the journey later without extra fare.

stop·page, stop′ij, *n.* The act of stopping or state of being stopped; a halt.

stop·per, stop′ər, *n.* One who or that which stops; a plug or piece for closing a bottle, tube, drain, or the like; a stopple.

stop·watch, stop′woch, *n.* A watch, marked in fractions of seconds, which can be instantaneously stopped or started, used for timing races or test runs.

stor·age, stôr′ij, *n.* The act of storing or being stored; a certain place or space in which to keep something.

stor·age cell, *n.* A cell or connection of cells capable of being recharged by a reverse flow of current through the electrolyte. Also **stor·age bat·ter·y.**

store, stôr, stōr, *n.* A place where goods are kept for sale; a shop; *pl.,* supplies of food, clothing, or other requirements; a supply or stock, as for future use; a stock of anything accumulated or possessed: a *store* of information.—*v.t.,* **stored, stor·ing.** To supply or stock with something, as for future use; deposit in a storehouse, warehouse, or other place, for keeping.

store·house, stôr′hows, *n.* A house or building in which things are stored; any repository or source of abundant supplies.

store·keep·er, stôr′kē·pər, *n.* An owner or manager of a retail shop.

store·room, stôr′room, *n.* A room in which supplies, household articles, or odds and ends may be stored.

sto·ried, stôr′ēd, *a.* Recorded or celebrated in history or story.

sto·ried, sto·reyed, stôr′ēd, *a.* Having stories or floors, usu. used in compounds: two-*storied* houses.

stork, stôrk, *n.* A tall wading bird, mostly of the Old World.

storm, stôrm, *n.* A disturbance of the normal condition of the atmosphere, manifesting itself by winds of unusual force or direction, often accompanied by rain, snow, hail, thunder and lightning; a tempest; a heavy fall of rain, snow, or hail; a heavy descent or discharge of missiles or blows; any violent disturbance of the social, political, or domestic order; any violent outburst.—*v.i.* To blow with unusual force, or to rain, snow, or hail, esp. with violence; to rage with violence or angry fury; to complain or scold violently; to rush with violence: to *storm* out of a room; to go or travel with furious speed; to deliver a violent attack or fire, as with artillery; to rush to an assault or attack.—*v.t.* To subject to or as to a storm; to utter or say with angry vehemence; to make a violent assault on, as a fortified position, or take by assault.

storm cel·lar, *n.* A cellar or underground chamber for refuge during violent storms.

storm door, *n.* An outer or additional door for protection against stormy weather and winter cold.

storm win·dow, *n.* An additional window used outside another window to provide insulation and protection from weather.

storm·y, stôr′mē, *a.,* **-i·er, -i·est.** Marked by storm or storms; tempestuous; passionate; angry. —**storm·i·ly,** *adv.* —**storm·i·ness,** *n.*

sto·ry, stôr′ē, *n. pl.,* **-ries.** A narrative, either true or fictitious, in prose or verse, designed to interest or amuse the hearer or reader; a tale; a fictitious tale; such narratives or tales as a branch of literature; the plot, or incidents, of a novel, poem, or drama; an anecdote; a report, account, or rumor of some matter; a legend or romance. *Informal.* A falsehood or lie. —*v.t.,* **-ried, -ry·ing.** To ornament with scenes from history or legend.

sto·ry, stôr′ē, *n. pl.,* **-ries.** A complete horizontal section of a building, having one continuous or approximately continuous floor; each of a series of divisions or stages of anything, placed horizontally one above another.

sto·ry·book, stôr′ē·bûk, *n.* A book containing one or more stories, often illustrated in color, usu. for children.

sto·ry·tell·er, stôr′ē·tel·ər, *n.* One who tells stories, true or fictitious; a writer of stories. *Informal.* A liar or fibber. —**sto·ry·tell·ing,** *a., n.*

stoup, stoop, *n.* A basin for holy water in Roman Catholic churches.

stout, stowt, *a.* Bulky in figure, solidly built, or thickset, as persons; bold, hardy, or dauntless; firm, determined, stubborn or uncompromising; strong of body, stalwart, or sturdy.—*n.* Strong dark ale, beer, or porter. —**stout·ly,** *adv.* —**stout·ness,** *n.*

stout-heart·ed, stowt′här′tid, *a.* Brave and resolute; courageous.

stove, stōv, *n.* An apparatus which provides heat for cooking or for heating a room or house by means of electricity or by burning fuel.—*v.t.,* **stoved, stov·ing.** To heat in or as if in a stove.

stove·pipe, stōv′pīp, *n.* A pipe, as of sheet metal, serving as the chimney of a stove or connecting a stove with a chimney flue. *Informal.* A man's hat, which is very tall and made of silk.

stow, stō, *v.t.* To place, as cargo, in proper order in the hold of a ship; to place or arrange compactly, or pack. —**stow away,** to conceal oneself aboard a ship or other conveyance; put something in a safe, concealed place.

stow·age, stō′ij, *n.* The act or operation of stowing; the state or manner of being stowed; room or accommodation for stowing something; a place in which something is or may be stowed; that which is stowed or to be stowed; a charge for stowing something.

stow·a·way, stō′ə·wā, *n.* One who conceals himself aboard a ship or other conveyance in order to obtain free passage or to escape by stealth from a place.

stra·bis·mus, strə·biz′məs, *n.* A disorder of vision due to the turning of one eye or both eyes from the normal position so that both cannot be directed at the same point or object at the same time.

strad·dle, strad′əl, *v.t.,* -dled, -dling. To spread wide apart; to walk, stand, or sit with one leg on each side of; to take up or occupy an equivocal position, or appear to favor both sides of a touchy question.—*v.i.* To walk, stand, or sit with the legs wide apart; to be spread wide apart.—*n.* The act of straddling; the distance that is straddled. *Informal.* The taking or holding of an equivocal position. —**strad·dler,** *n.*

strafe, strāf, străf, *v.t.,* strafed, straf·ing. To bombard heavily; assail with machine guns fired from attack planes.

strag·gle, strag′əl, *v.i.,* -gled, -gling. To wander about in a scattered fashion; to extend irregularly in various directions, or without orderly and compact arrangement. —**strag·gler,** *n.*

strag·gly, strag′lē, *a.,* -gli·er, -gli·est. Disorganized; rambling; spreading irregularly about.

straight, strāt, *a.* Without crooks, bends, or curvature; evenly formed or set: *straight* shoulders; direct, or leading or going directly to some point; candid, plain, or without circumlocution; honest, honorable, as conduct or dealings; unmodified or unaltered: *straight* comedy. *Informal.* Undiluted or unblended, as whiskey; reliable, as reports.—*n.* The condition of being straight; a straight form or position; a straight section, as of an auto racing course; in cards, a sequence of five cards of various suits.—*adv.* In a straight line; without crookedness, bends, or curves: to walk *straight;* in a straight or even form or position: to sit *straight;* in a straight or direct course to some point, or directly: to go *straight* to a place; without circumlocution; straightforwardly, honestly, honorably, or virtuously: to go *straight;* in a continuous course: to keep *straight* on; without delay; immediately, followed by *off;* without qualification of any kind. —**straight·ly,** *adv.* —**straight·ness,** *n.*

straight·a·way, strāt′ə·wā, *a.* Straight onward, without turn or curve, as a course in horse racing or yacht racing.—*n.* A straightaway course for racing; a race ver such a course; a straight section of a race course.

straight·edge, strāt′ej, *n.* A piece or bar made perfectly straight on the edge, and used to test surfaces or to draw straight lines.

straight·en, strāt′ən, *v.t., v.i.* To make straight; to become straight. —**straight·en·er,** *n.*

straight·for·ward, strāt·fôr′wərd, *a.* Proceeding ahead in a straight course; honest; open; absent of deceit.—*adv.* —**straight·for·ward·ly, straight·for·wards,** *adv.*

straight·way, strāt′wā, *adv.* Immediately.

strain, strān, *n.* Ancestry or descent; the group of descendants of a common ancestor; hereditary or natural character or disposition; a streak or trace; a kind or sort; a group of animals or plants equivalent to, or forming a part of a race, breed, or variety.

strain, strān, *v.t.* To draw tight or taut, as a line; stretch; stretch to the utmost tension or exert to the utmost; to impair or weaken by stretching or overexertion, as a muscle or tendon; imperil the strength of by subjecting to too great stress; to make excessive demands upon, or tax severely, as resources or credit; to press or pass through a colander, cloth, or other filter, to separate the clear liquid from denser or solid constituents.—*v.i.* To exert a stretching force; pull forcibly against; to balk; to work very hard; to suffer stress.—*n.* A forcible straining or stretching of something; stress; the condition of being strained or stretched; an injury to a muscle, tendon, or other ligament, due to excessive tension or use; a distortion of any body or structure resulting from stress; the deformation of a body, resulting from mechanical stress; strong muscular or physical effort; great effort of any kind; a severe demand or tax, or something that makes such a demand, on powers, resources, feelings, or character traits: a *strain* on one's pocketbook, credulity, or good nature; a melody, tune, or song; a passage or piece of poetry; a flow or burst of language; eloquence; tone, style, or spirit in expression.

strain·er, strā′nər, *n.* One who or that which strains, esp. a filter, colander, or cloth for straining liquids.

strait, strāt, *n.* A narrow passage of water connecting two larger bodies of water. *Often pl.* A position of difficulty, distress, or need: in desperate *straits.*

strait·en, strāt′ən, *v.t.* To make strait; to contract, confine, hem in, narrow; to put in financial difficulties.

strait·jack·et, strāt′jak·ət, *n.* A kind of jacket or coat of strong material for confining violent patients or other persons.

strait-laced, strāt′lāst′, *a.* Constrained; strict in manners or morals.

strand, strand, *n.* The land bordering a sea or other body of water; shore.—*v.t.* To drive or leave aground on a shoreline; to leave in a position of helplessness or isolation.—*v.i.* To be driven ashore; to bog down in difficulties.

strand, strand, *n.* A number of yarns or threads which are twisted together to form a rope or cord; a string of pearls or beads.—*v.t.* To break a strand or strands of.

strange, strānj, *a.,* strang·er, strang·est. Unfamiliar, unknown, or outside of one's previous experience; out of one's natural environment or locality; singular, extraordinary, or curious; queer, odd, surprising, or unaccountable. —**strange·ly,** *adv.* —**strange·ness,** *n.*

stran·ger, strān′jər, *n.* A foreigner or alien; a newcomer in a place or locality; a person with whom one has had no personal acquaintance; an outsider, as with reference to a family, society, or other associated body; a person or thing that is unfamiliar: *a stranger* to hard work.

stran·gle, strang′gəl, *v.t.,* -gled, -gling. To destroy the life of by compressing the windpipe; to choke; to suppress or stifle.—*v.i.* To die from strangulation or choking. —**stran·gler,** *n.*

stran·gu·la·tion, strang·gyə·lā′shən, *n.* The act of strangling; the state of being strangled. —**stran·gu·late,** strang′gū·lāt, *v.t., v.i.,* -lat·ed, -lat·ing.

strap, strap, *n.* A flexible, narrow strip of leather or other substance having various uses, as binding, fastening, or holding; a loop which may be used to hold onto.—*v.t.,* strapped, strap·ping. To beat with a strap; to sharpen on a strap; to cause to suffer a shortage: *strapped* for cash. —**strap·less,** *a.*

strap·ping, strap′ing, *a. Informal.* Of imposing build; muscular.

strat·a·gem, strat′ə·jəm, *n.* A maneuver in war; a plan for deceiving an enemy; an instance of clever generalship; any clever plan to gain an advantage.

stra·te·gic, strə·tē′gik, *a.* Referring to, marked by, or like strategy: *strategic* maneuvers. —**stra·te·gi·cal·ly,** *adv.*

strat·e·gy, strat′ə·jē, *n. pl.,* -gies. The science of

forming and carrying out military operations; generalship, distinguished from *tactics;* The use of artifice or finesse in carrying out any project. —**strat·e·gist,** strat/i·jist, *n.*

strat·i·fi·ca·tion, strat·ə·fə·kā/shən, *n.* The process by which strata are formed; an arrangement in strata or layers; any hierarchical division of society according to income, culture, or other characteristics; the act of stratifying or the state of being stratified.

strat·i·fy, strat/ə·fī, *v.t.,* -**fied,** -**fy·ing.** To form into strata or layers, as substances in the earth; put in layers; divide society according to layers.—*v.i.* To be divided into layers.

stra·to·cu·mu·lus, strā·tō·kū/myə·ləs, *n. pl.,* -**li,** -lī. A cloud consisting of large, dark, rounded masses and often fully covering the sky.

strat·o·sphere, strat/ə·sfēr, *n.* A layer of the atmosphere about seven miles above the surface of the earth within which the temperature remains approximately constant. —**strat·o·spher·ic,** strat·ə·sfēr/ik, *a.*

stra·tum, strā/təm, strat/əm, *n. pl.,* **stra·ta,** strā/tə, **stra·tums.** A layer of material, often one of a number of parallel layers placed one upon another; one of a number of portions of some body likened to layers or levels; a level or grade of a people or population with reference to social position or education; a bed of one kind of sedimentary rock or earth, usu. consisting of a series of layers representing continuous periods of deposition.

stra·tus, strā/təs, *n. pl.,* **stra·ti,** strā/tī. A low, dense, horizontal cloud.

straw, strô, *n.* The stalk or stem of certain species of grain when cut, and after being thrashed; a tube of any material, used to draw up a beverage to one's mouth. —*a.* Referring to, or made of straw; worthless.

straw·ber·ry, strô/ber·ē, strô/bə·rē, *n. pl.,* -**ries.** A fruit and plant, the fruit being edible and succulent.

straw boss, *n. Informal.* An assistant foreman or overseer of a work gang who has no real status or authority, but who assists in supervision.

straw man, *n.* A figure of a man shaped of straw; a puppet; a person, as a perjured witness, used to disguise another man's activities; a weak opponent or argument set up so as to be readily defeated.

straw vote, *n.* An unofficial vote or poll.

stray, strā, *v.i.* To wander from a direct course; to roam, meander or go astray; to deviate or to err, as to wander from the path of duty or rectitude; to digress while thoughts wander.—*n.* Any domestic animal that wanders at large or is lost.

streak, strēk, *n.* A relatively long, narrow, usu. irregular mark, smear, band, or stripe; a vein, strain, or admixture of anything. *Informal.* A period or run: a *streak* of hard luck. —**streak·y,** strē/kē, *a.,* -**i·er,** -**i·est.**

stream, strēm, *n.* Any river, brook, or course of running water; a flow of air or gas, or of light; a steady current in the sea or in a river; anything issuing as if in a flow: a *stream* of words; the dominant opinion of a group: the *stream* of public opinion.—*v.i.* To flow in a stream; to move continuously; stretch out in a long line; float at full length.—*v.t.* To send forth in a current or stream; cause to stretch out or float at full length.

stream·er, strē/mər, *n.* Anything which streams; a long narrow flag; a pennon; a banner.

stream·line, strēm/līn, *n.* In a fast-moving body, a shape or contour that decreases air or liquid resistance.—*v.t.,* -**lined,** -**lin·ing.** To shape in a way that decreases air or liquid resistance; to simplify; to modernize.

stream·lined, strēm/līnd, *a.* Having characteristics of a streamline; possessing a smooth flow.

street, strēt, *n.* A way, road, or thoroughfare in a city, chiefly a main way, as distinguished from a lane or alley; the people living on a street.

street·car, strēt/kär, *n.* A public passenger car running on rails set in the street.

street·walk·er, strēt/wô·kər, *n.* A prostitute who solicits on the street. —**street·walk·ing,** *n.*

strength, strengkth, strength, *n.* The state or inherent capacity of being strong; toughness: the *strength* of bone and muscle; power or vigor of any kind; capacity for exertion: *strength* of mind, memory; power of resisting, as stress, strain, or attacks; that on which confidence or reliance is placed; support; force or power in expressing meaning, as in vehemence of speech; vividness; intensity; potency; force as measured or stated in figures.

strength·en, strengk/thən, streng/thən, *v.t.* To make strong or stronger; add strength to; confirm; establish; make greater.—*v.i.* To grow strong. —**strength·en·er,** *n.*

stren·u·ous, stren/ū·əs, *a.* Zealous, vigorous, or energetic; requiring great exertion. —**stren·u·os·i·ty,** stren·ū·os/ə·tē, *n.* —**stren·u·ous·ly,** *adv.*

strep·to·coc·cus, strep·tə·kok/əs, *n. pl.,* -**coc·ci,** kok/sī. Any of several spherical or oval bacteria found in long chains or pairs and are usu. pathogenic to human beings. —**strep·to·coc·cal, strep·to·coc·cic,** strep·tə·kok/sik, *a.*

strep·to·my·cin, strep·tō·mī/sin, *n.* An antibiotic derived from a soil fungus and esp. effective against tuberculosis.

stress, stres, *n.* A constraining, urging, or impelling physical force; strain; a force tending to produce strain or tension and to change the form or dimensions of a solid; a factor causing mental or emotional strain or tension; importance or weight ascribed to something; emphasis provided by the relative loudness of a word.—*v.t.* To put emphasis on; cause to undergo some form of stress. —**stress·ful,** *a.* —**stress·ful·ly,** *adv.* —**stress·less,** *a.* —**stress·less·ness,** *n.*

stretch, strech, *v.t.* To extend or distend forcibly; to draw tight; to make tense; to extend beyond normal dimensions or bounds: to *stretch* one's patience; to reach or extend across, as a line from one pole to another; to augment the quantity of through dilution; to strain or exert extra effort: to *stretch* oneself to win; to make a limited amount cover a larger need.—*v.i.* To attain greater length or width; to bear extension without breaking; to reach across an area; stretch one's body at full length; to extend one's limbs and muscles to their limit, as for relief from a cramped position.—*n.* A stretching or the state of being stretched; elasticity; an extended portion or expanse, as of time, road, water, or the like; the utmost extent or reach of something; a straight portion of the racetrack. *Informal.* A period of confinement in prison; a period of limbering up or relaxing. —**stretch·a·bil·i·ty,** *n.* —**stretch·a·ble,** *a.*

stretch·er, strech/ər, *n.* One who or that which stretches; type of litter, as a frame of stretched canvas for carrying the disabled or dead.

strew, stroo, *v.t.,* **strewed, strewed** or **strewn, strewing.** To scatter or sprinkle: always applied to dry substances separable into parts or particles; to throw loosely apart; to spread abroad; to disseminate.

stri·a, strī/ə, *n. pl.,* **stri·ae,** strī/ē. A slight furrow or ridge; a narrow stripe or streak, as of color or texture.

stri·ate, strī/āt, *v.t.,* -**at·ed,** -**at·ing.** To mark with striae; to furrow, stripe, or streak.

strick·en, strik/ən, *a.* Afflicted, as with disease, trouble, or sorrow; deeply affected; a mental blow, or the like: a *stricken* look; struck, as hit or wounded by a weapon, missile, or the like.

strict, strikt, *a.* Narrowly or carefully limited or restricted; exact or precise: the *strict* meaning of a word; close; careful; absolute, perfect, or complete; characterized by or acting in close conformity to requirements or principles; severe in rule, discipline, or management; rigorously scrupulous, strait-laced, or austere; closely or rigorously enforced or maintained, as discipline, guard, or imprisonment. —**strict·ly,** *adv.*

—**strict·ness,** *n.*

stric·ture, strik´chər, *n.* A sharp criticism or censorious remark; censure; a restriction; a morbid contraction of any canal or duct of the body.

stride, strīd, *v.i.,* **strode, strid·den, strid·ing.** To walk with long steps; to take a long step; to pass, as over or across, by a long step; to straddle: an arch *striding* over a temple entrance.—*v.t.* To walk with long steps. —*n.* A progressing by long steps or a striding gait: his natural *stride;* a long step in walking; a single movement or step in running; advancement or rapid progress.

stri·dent, strīd´ənt, *a.* Loud and harsh; shrill.

strid·u·la·tion, strĭj·ə·lā´shən, *n.* The shrill, grating sound made by rubbing together certain parts of the body, as a cricket or katydid.

strife, strīf, *n.* The striving or contending of opposing parties; contention, quarreling, fighting, or conflict; a quarrel, struggle, clash, or dispute. —**strife·ful,** *a.* —**strife·less,** *a.*

strike, strīk, *v.i.,* **struck, struck** or **strick·en, strik·ing.** To hit or dash on or against something; impinge; to deal or aim a blow or stroke; to deal blows; to launch an attack; to quit work together, as a group of employees; to sound a percussion: The clock *strikes;* to ignite or be ignited by friction, as a match; to come suddenly or unexpectedly upon; to make an impression on the mind; to fall upon, as light; to proceed on a path or trail, esp. in a new direction.—*v.t.* To give a blow to someone or something; to come into sharp contact with something: The ship *struck* a rock; to stamp or impress, as a coin; to print from type or the like; to pierce or stab with a sharp weapon; to draw, as an arc; to cancel, as a name from a list; to hook, as a fish, by a jerking motion; to knock, rap, or tap; to play upon, as a harp or the like; to afflict suddenly, as with disease or misfortune; to affect deeply or overwhelm, as with terror; to cause a feeling; to enter suddenly; to assume, as an attitude or posture; to cause to penetrate quickly, as a chill; to put forth or send down, as roots; to impinge upon; to fall upon, as light; to enter the mind of or occur to, as a person; to impress strongly, as a beautiful scene; to come upon or encounter suddenly; to find or discover, as an ore deposit; to make or conclude, as an agreement or bargain; to fix or establish, as a price; to estimate or determine, as a mean or average; to lower or take down, as a sail or flag; to quit in a body, as work.—*n.* An act of striking; concerted quitting of work by a body of employees to coerce their employer in some way, usu. to obtain higher wages; the part of a lock which holds a bolt; an unsuccessful attempt on the part of the batter to hit a pitched ball, or anything ruled to be equivalent to this; the knocking down of all the pins with the first ball in bowling; sudden success or good fortune; the discovery of petroleum or of a rich vein of ore; a bombing or strafing attack by airplanes; the quantity or number struck off at any one time; the action of a fish as it rises to seize the bait. —**strike out,** to make three strikes in baseball and be out; put a batter out on three strikes. —**strike·less,** *a.*

strike zone, *n.* In baseball, the area directly over home plate, between the batter's knees and shoulders when in batting stance.

strik·ing, strī´king, *a.* Having an impact of surprise or admiration; remarkable; forcible; dramatic or impressive, esp. in appearance. —**strik·ing·ly,** *adv.*

string, string, *n.* A slender cord or thick thread; something resembling this, as tape, ribbon, leather, or the like used for binding, tying, lacing, or drawing together; a strand or necklace of beads or other objects threaded or strung on a cord; a number or series of objects, events, or utterances in a row; the tightly stretched cord or wire of musical instruments which produces a tone when caused to vibrate; a bowstring; a set or number of: to own a *string* of race horses; in sports, a group of players rated according to their skill: to make first *string* on the team; one of the sloping sides of a stair supporting the treads and risers; the stroke made to determine who opens the game in billiards; the line from behind which the cue ball is played after having been out of play.—*v.t.,* **strung, strung** or **stringed, string·ing.** To thread on or as on a line; to extend, as a cord, from one point to another; to furnish with or as with a string or strings; to arrange in a string or series, as: to *string* phrases. —*v.i.* To form into a string or strings, as a glutinous substance does when pulled. —**on a string.** *Informal.* Under another's control or influence. —**pull strings,** to gain an objective, often, surreptitiously, through the use of one's influence or power. —**string a·long.** *Informal.* To keep someone available or waiting through promises or deceit; to falsely encourage. —**string a·long with.** *Informal.* To go along with, esp. as in agreement or trust. —**string out,** to lengthen, extend, or prolong.

string bean, *n.* Any of several kinds of beans, the unripe pod of which is used for food; the pod itself. *Informal.* A tall, slim person.

strin·gent, strin´jənt, *a.* Compelling, constraining, or urgent; rigorously exacting, binding, strict, or severe: *stringent* regulations or obligations. —**strin·gen·cy,** *n.* —**strin·gent·ly,** *adv.*

string quar·tet, *n.* A composition written normally for the four stringed instrument parts of first and second violin, viola, and cello; four musicians constituting a group to perform string quartets and other chamber music.

string tie, *n.* A narrow bow tie with long, loose-hanging ends.

string·y, string´ē, *a.,* **-i·er, -i·est.** Consisting of or resembling strings; fibrous: *stringy* meat; ropy; sinewy; wiry. —**string·i·ness,** *n.*

strip, strip, *v.t.,* **stripped, strip·ping.** To rob, plunder, or disposses: to *strip* a man of his possessions; remove, as a covering, from; to divest; deprive of covering or clothing; undress; deprive of insignia or honors: *strip* a soldier of his rank; dismantle or divest of equipment; remove color from, as cloth or one's hair, as for redyeing.—*v.i.* To become stripped; to divest oneself of clothes; to execute a striptease.

strip, strip, *n.* A narrow piece, comparatively long and usu. of uniform width, as of cloth, paper, metal, or the like; a long, narrow tract of land or forest; a landing strip; a connected series of pictures or cartoons: comic *strip.*—*v.t.,* **stripped, strip·ping.** To cut into strips.

stripe, strīp, *n.* A relatively long, narrow band: the *stripes* of a zebra; a long narrow piece of anything, as a strip of braid; a streak or layer of a different nature within a substance; style, variety, or distinctive quality; a badge of rank, service, good conduct, wounds, or the like; a striped uniform.—*v.t.,* **striped, strip·ing.** To mark or alter with a stripe or stripes. —**striped,** *a.*

strip·ling, strip´ling, *n.* A youth in adolescence; a boy.

strip·per, strip´ər, *n.* One who strips; that which strips, as an appliance or machine for stripping. *Informal.* A stripteaser.

strip·tease, strip´tēz, *n.* An act, formerly associated with burlesque, in which a woman performer disrobes gradually, usu. accompanied by music, body gyrations, and the audience's vocal encouragement. —**strip·teas·er,** strip´tē·zər, *n.*

strive, strīv, *v.i.,* **strove, striv·en, striv·ing.** To make efforts; to endeavor with earnestness; to contend or vie.

stro·bo·scope, strō´bə·skōp, strob´ə·skōp, *n.* An instrument used in studying the rapid revolution or vibration of a body by illuminating it intermittently with a flash of light or by viewing it through openings in a revolving disk. —**stro·bo·scop·ic,** strō·bə·skop′ik, *a.* —**stro·bo·scop·ic·al·ly,** *adv.*

stroke, strōk, *n.* An act of striking, a blow dealt or aimed; a hitting of or upon anything; a striking of a clapper or hammer, as on a bell; a throb or pulsation, as of the heart; an act of divine chastisement; an attack of apoplexy or of paralysis; a discharge of lightning; a piece of luck befalling one: a *stroke* of bad or good luck; a single complete movement, esp. each of the succession of movements of the arms and legs in swimming; a vigorous attempt to attain some object; a measure adopted for a particular purpose; a feat or achievement: a *stroke* of genius; mark traced by or as if by a pen, pencil, or brush; a distinctive or effective touch in a literary composition; a single pull of the oar; a manner or style of moving the oars.—*v.t.,* **stroked, strok·ing.** To rub lightly or caress; to row as stroke or oarsman of, as a boat or crew; to mark with a stroke or strokes, as of a pen; to cancel, as by a mark of a pen.

stroll, strōl, *v.i.* To walk leisurely as inclination directs; take an unhurried walk; to wander, rove, or roam from place to place, as a vagrant or an itinerant: Gypsies *strolling,* a player *strolling.*—*v.t.* To wander idly along or through.—*n.* A leisurely walk.

stroll·er, strō′lər, *n.* A saunterer; a wanderer; a vagrant; a strolling or itinerant player or performer; a carriage resembling a chair, designed for young children.

strong, strông, strong, *a.* Having physical power; able or powerful mentally or morally; naturally sound or healthy; not easily broken; firm; having great wealth or resources; having a particular quality or qualities in a great degree: *strong* tea; having great force or expressiveness; amounting to an indicated number: an army 10,000 *strong.*—*adv.* In a strong manner. —**strong·ish,** *a.* —**strong·ly,** *adv.* —**strong·ness,** *n.*

strong-arm, strông′ärm, strong′ärm, *a. Informal.* Having, using, or involving the use of muscular or physical force, as: *strong-arm* methods.—*v.t. Informal.* To use force against; to rob using violent methods.

strong·box, strông′boks, strong′boks, *n.* A strong, lockable box or chest for the storage of valuables, as jewels or documents.

strong·hold, strông′hōld, strong′hōld, *n.* A fortified place; a place of security; a center or place where any particular group exerts a dominating influence.

strong-mind·ed, strông′mīn′did, strong′mīn′did, *a.* Having a strong, determined, or vigorous mind; showing independent thinking. —**strong-mind·ed·ly,** *adv.* —**strong-mind·ed·ness,** *n.*

stron·ti·um, stron′shē·əm, stron′shəm, stron′tē·əm, *n.* A pale yellow metallic element having compounds used in making medicines, flares, fireworks, and electronic tubes, and in refining beet sugar. —**stron·tic,** stron′tik, *a.*

stron·ti·um 90, *n.* A radioactive isotope of strontium present in the fallout from certain nuclear reactions, constituting a hazard due to its assimilability by plants and animals.

strop, strop, *n.* A strip of leather used for sharpening straight razors; a razor strop.—*v.t.,* **stropped, strop·ping.** To sharpen with a strop.

struc·tur·al, strək′chər·əl, *a.* Of or referring to structure; essential to a structure; referring to the structure of rock; referring to or showing the arrangement or mode of attachment of the atoms which constitute a molecule of a substance: a *structural* formula. —**struc·tur·al·ly,** *adv.*

struc·ture, strək′chər, *n.* Arrangement of parts, elements, or constituents; something built or constructed; a building; an edifice; a bridge, dam, or framework; any construction; anything composed of parts arranged together in some way.—*v.t.,* **-tured, -tur·ing.** To provide with a structure; to construct. —**struc·tured,** *a.* —**struc·ture·less,** *a.*

strug·gle, strəg′əl, *v.i.,* **-gled, -gling.** To put forth violent bodily effort against any opposing force; to make strenuous efforts toward an end; do something that is difficult.—*n.* A strong effort, or series of efforts, against any adverse agencies or conditions, as in order to maintain one's existence or to attain some end. —**strug·gler,** *n.* —**strug·gling,** *a.* —**strug·gling·ly,** *adv.*

strum, strəm, *v.i.* To play by brushing the fingers lightly across the strings of a musical instrument.—*v.t.* To brush the fingers across the strings of, as a musical instrument: *strum* a guitar. —**strum·mer,** *n.*

strum·pet, strəm′pit, *n.* A prostitute.

strut, strət, *v.i.,* **strut·ted, strut·ting.** To walk with a lofty, proud gait and erect head; to walk with affected dignity or pompousness.—*v.t.* To exhibit or show off; support or brace with a strut or struts.—*n.* A proud, exaggerated step or walk; a supporting structural piece designed to relieve weight or stress lengthwise; a brace.

strych·nine, strik′nin, strik′nēn, strik′nīn, *n.* A colorless, crystalline, poisonous alkaloid obtained from the seeds of an E. Indian tree and used as an antidote for poisoning by depressant drugs; the tree itself; a poison for rodents. Also **strych·ni·a,** strik′nē·ə. —**strych·nic,** strik′nik, *a.*

stub, stəb, *n.* The stump of a tree; any remaining part after use or wear, as of a cigarette or pencil; the portion detached from a ticket or check.—*v.t.,* **stubbed, stub·bing.** To strike, as one's foot, against a projecting obstruction. —**stub·by,** stəb′ē, *a.,* **-i·er, -i·est.**

stub·ble, stəb′əl, *n.* The stumps of corn or other grain left in the ground by the scythe or sickle; any rough growth, as a beard. —**stub·bled,** —**stub·bly,** **-i·er, -i·est,** *a.*

stub·born, stəb′ərn, *a.* Unreasonably or perversely obstinate; not moved or persuaded by reason; maintained in an obstinate or inflexible manner; hard to control or manage. —**stub·born·ly,** *adv.* —**stub·born·ness,** *n.*

stuc·co, stək′ō, *n. pl.,* **-coes, -cos.** A cement or concrete in imitation of stone, for coating exterior walls of houses; any of various plasters, cements, and finishes used for cornices and moldings of rooms and other decorations.—*a.*—*v.t.,* **-coed, -co·ing.** To cover or ornament with stucco.

stuck-up, stək′əp′, *a. Informal.* Having great conceit; arrogant.

stud, stəd, *n.* An establishment in which horses are kept for breeding; a stallion kept for breeding purposes. —**at stud,** available or used for breeding: said of male animals.

stud, stəd, *n.* A post or upright prop, as in the wall of a building to which laths or boards are nailed in forming partitions or walls in houses; a boss, knob, nail head, or other protuberance projecting from a surface or part, esp. as an ornament; an ornamental button or fastener for holding together parts of a dress or shirt.—*v.t.,* **stud·ded, stud·ding.** To furnish with or support by studs or upright props; to set with or as with studs, bosses, or the like; to scatter over with things set at intervals. —**stud·ding,** *n.*

stu·dent, stood′ənt, stūd′ənt, *n.* A person attending an educational institution; one studying anything. —**stu·dent·ship,** *n.*

stud·ied, stəd′ēd, *a.* Well-considered; deliberate: a *studied* insult. —**stud·ied·ly,** *adv.* —**stud·ied·ness,** *n.*

stu·di·o, stoo′dē·ō, *n. pl.,* **-os.** The working room of a creative person; a place used for the filming of motion pictures; a place from which television or radio programs are broadcast.

stu·di·ous, stoo′dē·əs, stū′dē·əs, *a.* Given to study; intent and diligent in scholastic effort. —**stu·di·ous·ly,** *adv.* —**stu·di·ous·ness,** *n.*

stud·y, stəd′ē, *n. pl.,* **-ies.** Application of the mind to books, to arts or science, or to any subject for the purpose of learning; earnest endeavor; a branch of learning studied; an object of study; a building, apartment, or room devoted to study; a period of deep thought.—*v.i.,* **-ied, -y-ing.** To apply one's mind to learning; to dwell in thought; to ponder.—*v.t.* To apply the mind to, as a subject, for the purpose of learning; to consider attentively; to examine closely.

stuff, stəf, *n.* Substance or matter indefinitely; the matter of which anything is formed; refuse or worthless matter; trash; personal property or equipment; a general name for woven fabrics, as wool or silk. *Informal.* One's field or ability: to know your *stuff.*—*v.t.* To fill by packing or crowding material into; to cram; to crowd in together; to fill the skin of, as a dead animal, for presenting and preserving its form; to fill with seasoning: to *stuff* a leg of veal.—*v.i.* To feed gluttonously. —**stuff-er,** *n.*

stuffed shirt, *n. Informal.* A pompous or pretentious person.

stuff-ing, stəf′ing, *n.* That with which anything is or may be stuffed; seasoned bread crumbs or other filling used to stuff a fowl, roast, or other meat before cooking.

stuff-y, stəf′ē, *a.,* **-i-er, -i-est.** Difficult to breathe in, or close, as the air of a room; obstructing respiration. *Informal.* Stodgy or old-fashioned. —**stuff-i-ly,** *adv.* —**stuff-i-ness,** *n.*

stul-ti-fy, stəl′tə-fī, *v.t.,* **-fied. -fy-ing.** To make or cause to appear foolish or ridiculous; to render wholly futile or ineffectual, as efforts. —**stul-ti-fi-ca-tion,** stəl·tə·fə·kā′shən, *n.* —**stul-ti-fi-er,** *n.*

stum-ble, stəm′bəl, *v.i.,* **-bled, -bling.** To trip in walking; to walk unsteadily; to speak falteringly; to discover by chance, usu. followed by *on* or *upon.*—*n.* The act of stumbling; a blunder. —**stum-bler,** *n.* —**stum-bling-ly,** *adv.*

stum-bling block, *n.* Any obstacle.

stump, stəmp, *n.* The lower end of a tree or plant left after the main part falls or is cut off; any basal portion remaining after the main part has been removed in some way, as after the amputation of a limb of the body; a short remainder, as of a pencil or cigar; the platform or place of political speechmaking.—*v.t.* To clear of stumps, as land. *Informal.* To nonplus, embarrass, or render completely at a loss.—*v.i.* To walk heavily or clumsily, as if with a wooden leg; to make stump speeches. —**stump-er,** *n.* —**stump-y,** *a.,* **-i-er, -i-est.**

stun, stən, *v.t.,* **stunned, stun-ning.** To render insensible or dizzy by force or violence; to render senseless by a blow; to surprise completely; to confound by a loud or distracting noise.—*n.* The action of stunning or the state of being stunned.

stun-ning, stən′ing, *a.* Of striking excellence, beauty, style, or attractiveness. —**stun-ning-ly,** *adv.*

stunt, stənt, *v.t.* To hinder from normal or free growth or progress; to check in development or growth; dwarf. —**stunt-ed,** *a.* —**stunt-ed-ness,** *n.*

stunt, stənt, *n.* A performance serving as a display of strength, skill, or the like, as in athletics; an unusual or daring feat, done esp. to attract publicity or attention. —*v.i.* To do a stunt or stunts.

stu-pe-fy, stoo′pə-fī, stū′pə-fī, *v.t.,* **-fied, -fy-ing.** To make stupid, as with a narcotic, shock, or strong emotion; stun; to overwhelm with amazement; astound. —**stu-pe-fac-tion,** stoo·pə·fak′shən, *n.* —**stu-pe-fi-er,** *n.* —**stu-pe-fy-ing-ly,** *adv.*

stu-pen-dous, stoo·pen′dəs, stū·pen′dəs, *a.* Great and wonderful; of astonishing magnitude or elevation; grand. —**stu-pen-dous-ly,** *adv.* —**stu-pen-dous-ness,** *n.*

stu-pid, stoo′pid, stū′pid, *a.* Extremely dull of perception or understanding; mentally slow; senseless; stupefied; boring or dull: a *stupid* movie; in a state of

stupor. —**stu-pid-i-ty,** stoo·pid′ə·tē, *n.* —**stu-pid-ly,** *adv.* —**stu-pid-ness,** *n.*

stu-por, stoo′pər, stū′pər, *n.* Suspension or great diminution of sensibility, as in disease or as caused by narcotics, intoxicants, or the like; a state of suspended or deadened sensibility. —**stu-por-ous,** *a.*

stur-dy, stər′dē, *a.,* **-di-er, -di-est.** Strong, as in substance, construction, texture, build, or the like: *sturdy* walls; firm, stout, or indomitable: *sturdy* resistance; of strong or hardy growth, as a plant. —**stur-di-ly,** *adv.* —**stur-di-ness,** *n.*

stur-geon, stər′jən, *n. pl.,* **stur-geon, stur-geons.** Any of various large fishes found in fresh and salt waters of northern regions, valued for their flesh and as a source of caviar.

stut-ter, stət′ər, *v.t., v.i.* Stammer.—*n.* A stuttering mode of utterance; a stuttered utterance. —**stut-ter-er,** *n.* —**stut-ter-ing-ly,** *adv.*

sty, stī, *n. pl.,* **sties.** A pen or enclosure for swine; any filthy hovel or place.

sty, stī, *n. pl.,* **sties.** A small inflamed bump or enlargement of a sebaceous gland on the edge of the eyelid.

style, stīl, *n.* Manner of writing or speaking with regard to language; distinctive way of writing of an author; a characteristic mode of presentation in any of the fine arts; fashion: a person dressed in *style;* a stylus; slender structure in plants through which pollen tubes grow.—*v.t.,* **styled, styl-ing.** To name or call; to give a particular form to: to *style* a dress. —**styl-er,** *n.*

styl-ish, stī′lish, *a.* Pertaining to current fashion standards; chic. —**styl-ish-ly,** *adv.* —**styl-ish-ness,** *n.*

styl-ist, stī′list, *n.* One who maintains, creates, or is master of a particular style, esp. a writer or speaker; a designer of fashions, as clothing. —**sty-lis-tic,** stī-lis′tik, **sty-lis-ti-cal,** *a.* —**sty-lis-ti-cal-ly,** *adv.*

styl-ize, stī′līz, *v.t.,* **-ized, -iz-ing.** To conform or cause to conform to a particular style, as of representation or treatment in art; conventionalize. —**styl-i-za-tion,** stī·lə·zā′shən, *n.* —**styl-iz-er,** *n.*

sty-lus, stī′ləs, *n. pl.,* **sty-lus-es, sty-li,** stī′lī. The pointed piece which produces the indentations or incisions in making a phonograph record; a similar device in a phonograph, for reproducing sounds from such a record; a pointed instrument used in art, drawing, or engraving.

sty-mie, stī′mē, *n. pl.,* **-mies.** An opponent's ball on a putting green when it is directly between the player's ball and the hole for which he is playing.—*v.t.,* **-mied, -mie-ing.** To hinder with a stymie, or as a stymie does.

styp-tic, stip′tik, *a.* Having the quality of stopping the bleeding of a wound; astringent. Also **styp-ti-cal.**—*n.* —**styp-tic-i-ty,** stip·tis′i·tē, *n.*

Sty-ro-foam, stī′rə·fōm, *n. Trademark.* A lightweight polystyrene plastic, usu. used as insulating material or in decorations.

suave, swäv, *a.* Gracious or agreeable in manner; polished or sophisticated. —**suave-ly,** *adv.* —**suave-ness,** *n.* —**suav-i-ty,** *n.*

sub, səb, *a.* Secondary in rank or importance, used in combination: a *sub*plot.

sub, səb, *v.i.,* **subbed, sub-bing.** *Informal.* To substitute, or act as substitute, for another.—*n. Informal.* A substitute.

sub, səb, *n. Informal.* Submarine.

sub-al-tern, səb·ôl′tərn, *a.* Having a lower or subordinate position.—*n.* A subordinate.

sub-arc-tic, səb·ärk′tik, səb·är′tik, *a.* Referring to a region or climate next to the Arctic Circle; anything approximating conditions or life in areas near the Arctic.

sub-as-sem-bly, səb·ə·sem′blē, *n. pl.,* **-blies.** Any assembled unit which forms part of a more extensive assembly. —**sub-as-sem-bler,** *n.*

sub-base-ment, səb′bās·mənt, *n.* A basement, or

one of a series of levels, below the main basement of a building.

sub·chas·er, səb/chā·sər, *n.* Submarine chaser.

sub·class, səb/klas, səb/kläs, *n.* A fundamental subgroup of a class; a subdivision of a class, consisting of related orders.

sub·com·mit·tee, səb/kə·mit·ē, *n.* A part or division of a committee, usu. doing a specific task.

sub·con·scious, səb·kon/shəs, *a.* Existing or operating beneath or beyond consciousness; not wholly conscious.—*n.* That part of the mental processes which is not in the realm of consciousness. **—sub·con·scious·ly,** *adv.* **—sub·con·scious·ness,** *n.*

sub·con·ti·nent, səb·kon/tə·nənt, *n.* A large, independent subdivision of a continent: the Indian *subcontinent;* large land form, smaller than a continent, such as Greenland. **—sub·con·ti·nen·tal,** səb·kon·tə·nen/təl, *a.*

sub·con·tract, səb·kon/trakt, səb/kon·trakt, *n.* A contract under another contract for carrying out the previous contract or a part of it.—səb·kən·trakt/, *v.t.* To make a subcontract for.—*v.i.* To make a subcontract. **—sub·con·trac·tor,** *n.*

sub·cul·ture, səb/kəl·chər, *n.* A portion of an ethnic group which has enough distinctive characteristics to be distinguished from the overall group. **—sub·cul·tur·al,** *a.*

sub·cu·ta·ne·ous, səb·kū·tā/nē·əs, *a.* Situated, used, lying, or made immediately under the skin. **—sub·cu·ta·ne·ous·ly,** *adv.*

sub·deb·u·tante, səb/deb/ū·tänt, *n.* A young girl in the years before her debut into society; a girl in her middle teens. Also **sub·deb,** səb/deb.

sub·di·vide, səb·di·vid/, səb/di·vid, *v.t.,* **-vid·ed, -vid·ing.** To divide parts into more parts; to divide into lots, as in land.—*v.i.* To be subdivided. **—sub·di·vid·a·ble,** *a.* **—sub·di·vid·er,** *n.*

sub·di·vi·sion, səb/di·vizh·ən, *n.* A tract of land which has been subdivided for the purpose of a housing development. **—sub·di·vi·sion·al,** *a.*

sub·due, səb·doo/, səb·dū/, *v.t.,* **-dued, -du·ing.** To conquer and bring into permanent subjection; to overcome by discipline; to melt or soften, as the heart; to tone down or make less intense. **—sub·du·a·ble,** *a.* **—sub·du·al,** *n.* **—sub·du·er,** *n.*

sub·en·try, səb/en·trē, *n. pl.,* **-tries.** An entry listed under a main entry.

sub·freez·ing, səb/frē/zing, *a.* Lower than the temperature needed to solidify a liquid.

sub·group, səb/groop, *n.* One of the parts of a group; a secondary grouping or division; a component group of elements within one of the larger vertical groupings in the periodic table; a group, all of whose elements are elements of another group.

sub·head, səb/hed, *n.* A subordinate head or title, under which is treated one of the divisions of a subject treated under a larger heading; a subordinate division of a heading or title; a subordinate to the head of a school.

sub·hu·man, səb·hū/mən, səb·ū/mən, *a.* Below the human race or type; less than or not quite human; almost human.

sub·ject, səb/jikt, *n.* One who or that which is under the control or influence of another; a person as an object of medical or surgical treatment, as a psychological experiment; something that forms a matter of thought or discourse: a *subject* of conversation; the theme of a sermon, book, or story; a motive or cause; the word or words in a sentence, denoting that of which something is predicated.—*a.* Being under domination, control, or influence, often used with *to: subject to* laws; liable, or having a tendency, usu. followed by *to: subject to* headaches; open or exposed, used with *to: subject to* attack or ridicule; being dependent or conditional upon something, usu. followed by *to:* His consent is *subject to* your approval.—səb·jekt/, *v.t.* To bring under domination,

control, or influence, usu. followed by *to;* cause to undergo or experience something, usu. followed by *to:* to *subject* metal *to* heat; make liable, lay open, or expose, usu. followed by *to:* to *subject* oneself *to* unpleasant comment. **—sub·jec·tion,** səb·jek/shən, *n.*

sub·jec·tive, səb·jek/tiv, *a.* Belonging to the thinking subject rather than to the object of thought; referring to a thinking subject; personal; individual; relating to conditions of the mind rather than from experience; referring to or designating the subject of a sentence; expressing the thoughts or emotions of an author or artist; illusory; imaginary. **—sub·jec·tive·ly,** *adv.* **—sub·jec·tive·ness, sub·jec·tiv·i·ty,** səb·jek·tiv/ə·tē, *n.*

sub·join, səb·joyn/, *v.t.* To add at the end.

sub·ju·gate, səb/jə·gāt, *v.t.,* **-gat·ed, -gat·ing.** To conquer; to compel to submit; to enslave. **—sub·ju·ga·tion,** səb·jə·gā/shən, *n.* **—sub·ju·ga·tor,** *n.*

sub·junc·tive, səb·jəngk/tiv, *a.* Designating a mood or form of verbs expressing condition, hypothesis, or contingency.

sub·lease, səb/lēs, *n.* A lease granted by one who is himself a lessee of the property. **—səb·lēs/,** *v.t.,* **-leased, -leas·ing.** To grant a sublease of; sublet; to take or hold a sublease of.

sub·let, səb/let/, *v.t.,* **-let, -let·ting.** To sublease; of a contractor, to let under a subcontract.—*n.*

sub·li·mate, səb/lə·māt, *v.t.,* **-mat·ed, -mat·ing.** To transfer the energy of, as a basic drive, into a higher, nobler, or more ethical goal; to sublime, as a solid substance. **—sub·li·ma·tion,** səb·lə·mā/shən, *n.*

sub·lime, sə·blīm/, *a.,* **-lim·er, -lim·est.** Elevated or lofty in thought, sentiment, language, or style; striking the mind with a sense of grandeur or power, or awakening awe, veneration, or exalted feeling by reason of grandeur, beauty, or the like, as scenes in nature or works of art.—*v.t.,* **-limed, lim·ing.** To convert, as a solid substance, by heat into a vapor, which on cooling condenses again to solid form without apparent liquefaction. **—sub·lime·ly,** *adv.* **—sub·lime·ness,** *n.* **—sub·lim·er,** *n.*

sub·lim·i·nal, səb·lim/ə·nəl, *a.* Beneath the conscious level. **—sub·lim·i·nal·ly,** *adv.*

sub·lim·i·ty, sə·blim/ə·tē, *n. pl.,* **-ties.** The state or quality of being sublime; the emotion produced by what is sublime.

sub·ma·chine gun, səb·mə·shēn/, *n.* A lightweight, portable, automatic or semiautomatic gun.

sub·mar·gin·al, səb·mär/jə·nəl, *a.* Below the margin; unproductive: *submarginal* cropland.

sub·ma·rine, səb·mə·rēn/, *a.* Situated, occurring, or living under the surface of the sea; built, operating, or intended for use beneath the surface of the sea; of or referring to a submarine or submarines. **—səb/mə·rēn,** səb·mə·rēn/, *n.* A vessel so designed that it can be submerged and navigated under water.

sub·merge, səb·mərj/, *v.t.,* **-merged, -merg·ing.** To put or sink below the surface of water or other liquid.—*v.i.* To sink or plunge under water, or beneath the surface of any enveloping medium. Also **sub·merse. —sub·mer·gence,** *n.* **—sub·mer·gi·ble,** *a.*

sub·merse, səb·mərs/, *v.t., v.i.,* **-mersed, -mers·ing.** Submerge. **—sub·mer·sion,** *n.*

sub·mers·i·ble, səb·mər/sə·bəl, *a.* Operating under water.—*n.* A ship that can operate under water.

sub·mi·cro·scop·ic, səb·mī·krə·skop/ik, *a.* Smaller than visible with an ordinary light microscope.

sub·mis·sion, səb·mish/ən, *n.* The act of submitting; submissive conduct or attitude.

sub·mis·sive, səb·mis/iv, *a.* Ready to submit; humbly obedient; indicating submission. **—sub·miss·ive·ly,** *adv.* **—sub·miss·ive·ness,** *n.*

sub·mit, səb·mit/, *v.t.,* **-mit·ted, -mit·ting.** To yield, as something, in surrender, compliance, or obedience; to refer or present for the decision or approval of another or others: to *submit* a plan; to declare or suggest with

519 **suburb**

deference, as one's opinion.—*v.i.* To yield in surrender, compliance, or obedience.

sub·nor·mal, səb·nôr′məl, *a.* Below the normal; less than the normal intelligence.—*n.* —**sub·nor·mal·i·ty,** səb·nôr′mal′ə·tē, *n.*

sub·or·di·nate, sə·bôr′də·nit, *a.* Placed in or belonging to a lower order or rank; subject to or under the authority of a superior; dependent; modifying: a *subordinate* clause or *subordinate* conjunction.—*n.* A subordinate person or thing. —sə·bôr′də·nāt, *v.t.,* -nat·ed, -nat·ing. To place in a lower order or rank. —**sub·or·di·nate·ly,** *adv.* —**sub·or·di·nate·ness, sub·or·di·na·tion,** sə·bôr·də·nā′shən, *n.* —**sub·or·di·na·tive,** *a.*

sub·orn, sə·bôrn′, *v.t.* To bribe or induce someone to commit an illegal act; to bribe or induce, as a witness, to give false evidence. —**sub·or·na·tion,** səb·ôr·nā′shən, *n.* —**sub·orn·er,** *n.*

sub·poe·na, sub·pe·na, sə·pē′nə, *n.* A judicial writ or process commanding, under threat of penalty, the attendance in court of the witness on whom it is served.—*v.t.,* -naed, -na·ing. To serve with a writ of subpoena.

sub ro·sa, səb rō′zə, *adv.* Secretly or confidentially.

sub·scribe, səb·skrīb′, *v.t.,* -scribed, -scrib·ing. To give or pay, as a sum of money, whether as a contribution toward some object or as in payment for something; to write, inscribe, or sign, as one's name, to a document, letter, or other paper.—*v.i.* To give or pay money as a contribution or in payment; to agree to pay for the future delivery of a specified number of magazines, newspapers, or periodicals, usu. for a reduced rate; to sign one's name to something. —**sub·scrib·er,** *n.*

sub·scrip·tion, səb·skrip′shən, *n.* The act of subscribing; the subscribing of money as a contribution toward some object or in payment for shares, a book, a periodical, or service; a sum subscribed.

sub·se·quent, səb′sə·kwənt, *a.* Following, coming, or being after something else in time; following in the order of place or succession. —**sub·se·quence,** *n.* —**sub·se·quent·ly,** *adv.* —**sub·se·quent·ness,** *n.*

sub·ser·vi·ent, səb·sʉr′vē·ənt, *a.* Servile, submissive, or obsequious; useful as an instrument to promote a purpose; acting as a subordinate. —**sub·ser·vi·ence, sub·ser·vi·en·cy,** *n.* —**sub·ser·vi·ent·ly,** *adv.*

sub·side, səb·sīd′, *v.i.,* -sid·ed, -sid·ing. To sink or settle to a lower level; to fall into a state of quiet; to become tranquil; to abate. —**sub·sid·ence,** səb·sīd′əns, səb′sə·dəns, *n.*

sub·sid·i·ar·y, səb·sid′ē·er·ē, *a.* Lending some aid or assistance; subordinate.—*n. pl.,* -ar·ies. One who or that which is subsidiary; a company controlled by another company by virtue of ownership of the controlling stock. Also **sub·sid·i·ar·y com·pa·ny.**

sub·si·dize, səb′sə·dīz, *v.t.,* -dized, -diz·ing. To furnish with a subsidy; to purchase the assistance of by a subsidy. —**sub·si·di·za·tion,** səb·sə·də·zā′shən, *n.* —**sub·si·diz·er,** *n.*

sub·si·dy, səb′sə·dē, *n. pl.,* -dies. A sum of money granted by a government to an organization, institution, or industry, esp. one benefiting the health and welfare of the country, as a charity, hospital, or public service; a gift of money; grant.

sub·sist, səb·sist′, *v.i.* To exist; to have continued existence.

sub·sist·ence, səb·sis′təns, *n.* Existence; means of support; the state of maintaining one's existence.

sub·soil, səb′soyl, *n.* The bed or stratum of earth or earthy matter which lies immediately under the surface soil.

sub·son·ic, səb·son′ik, *a.* Referring to or possessing a speed which is less than the speed of sound, as in air

or some other medium; operable at such speeds; referring to sound waves having a frequency lower than the auditory capacity of the human ear.

sub·stance, səb′stəns, *n.* That of which a thing consists or is made up; matter; material; a body; that which is real; the essential or material part; firmness; substantiality; material means and resources; goods.

sub·stand·ard, səb·stan′dərd, *a.* Less than or deviating from the norm or requirement.

sub·stan·tial, səb·stan′shəl, *a.* Of considerable size or amount; having considerable worth or value; real; strong; solid; possessed of considerable wealth. —**sub·stan·ti·al·i·ty,** səb·stan·shē·al′ə·tē, *n.* —**sub·stan·tial·ly,** *adv.* —**sub·stan·tial·ness,** *n.*

sub·stan·ti·ate, səb·stan′shē·āt, *v.t.,* -at·ed, -at·ing. To establish by proof or competent evidence. —**sub·stan·ti·a·tion,** səb·stan·shē·ā′shən, *n.* —**sub·stan·ti·a·tive,** *a.*

sub·stan·tive, səb′stən·tiv, *n.* A noun; a word or a phrase which is used like a noun.—*a.* Denoting a substance; used as a substantive; having independent existence; belonging to the real nature of a thing; actual; permanent. —**sub·stan·ti·val,** *a.* —**sub·stan·ti·val·ly, sub·stan·tive·ly,** *adv.* —**sub·stan·tive·ness,** *n.*

sub·sti·tute, səb′sti·toot, səb′sti·tūt, *v.t.,* -tut·ed, -tut·ing. To put in the place of another.—*v.i.* To act as one who or that which substitutes.—*n.* A person or thing acting for or serving the purpose of another.—*a.* —**sub·sti·tut·a·ble,** *a.* —**sub·sti·tu·tion,** səb·sti·too′shən, *n.* —**sub·sti·tu·tion·al,** *a.* —**sub·sti·tu·tion·al·ly,** *adv.* —**sub·sti·tu·tion·ar·y,** *a.*

sub·stra·tum, səb′strā·təm, səb′strat·əm, *n. pl.,* -ta, -tums. That which is laid or spread under something; a foundation.

sub·struc·ture, səb′strək·chər, *n.* Foundation.

sub·sume, səb·soom′, *v.t.,* -sumed, -sum·ing. To include, as a specific idea, term, or proposition, under another more general one; bring under a rule, as a case or instance; include in a larger, higher, or more inclusive class. —**sub·sum·a·ble, sub·sump·tive,** *a.* —**sub·sump·tion,** *n.*

sub·teen, səb′tēn′, *n.* A person near adolescence.

sub·tend, səb·tend′, *v.t.* To extend under or be opposite to, as the side of a triangle opposite an angle.

sub·ter·fuge, səb′tər·fūj, *n.* Deception or other artifice to conceal something or to escape difficulty or unpleasantness.

sub·ter·ra·ne·an, səb·tə·rā′nē·ən, *a.* Underground; being hidden or secret. Also **sub·ter·ra·ne·ous.** —**sub·ter·ra·ne·an·ly, sub·ter·ra·ne·ous·ly,** *adv.*

sub·ti·tle, səb′tī·təl, *n.* A secondary or subordinate title of a literary work, usually of explanatory character; the written translation of the dialogue of a foreign film, usu. projected on the bottom of the screen; the captions and titles used between scenes of a silent film.

sub·tle, sət′əl, *a.* Sly in design; artful; cunning; cunningly devised; ingenious; thin or tenuous in substance; delicate in texture of workmanship; acute or penetrating in intellect; difficult to understand. —**sub·tle·ness,** *n.* —**sub·tle·ty,** *n.* —**sub·tly,** *adv.*

sub·tract, səb·trakt′, *v.t.* To withdraw or take away, as a part from a whole.—*v.i.* To take away something or a part, as from a whole. —**sub·tract·er,** *n.* —**sub·trac·tion,** *n.* —**sub·trac·tive,** *a.*

sub·tra·hend, səb′trə·hend, *n.* The sum or number to be subtracted from another, as opposed to *minuend.*

sub·trop·i·cal, səb·trop′ə·kəl, *a.* Adjoining the tropics; indigenous to or characteristic of the regions lying near the tropics. Also **sub·trop·ic.** —**sub·trop·ics,** *n. pl.*

sub·urb, səb′ʉrb, *n. Often pl.* A district lying immedi-

a- hat, fāte, fāre, fäther; e- met, mē; i- pin, pīne; o- not, nōte, ôrb, moove (move), boy, pownd; u- cūbe, bůll, tůk (took); ch- chin; th- thick, ŧhen; zh- vizhon (vision); ə- əgo, takən, pencəl, lemən, bərd (bird).

ately outside a city or town. **—sub·ur·ban,** sə·bər′bən, *a., n.* **—sub·ur·ban·ite,** *n.*

sub·ur·bi·a, sə·bər′bē·ə, *n.* Suburbs as a group; suburbanites as a group; activities, standards, and outlooks considered as typical of suburbanites.

sub·ver·sion, səb·var′zhən, səb·var′shən, *n.* The act of subverting or overthrowing. **—sub·ver·sion·ar·y,** *a.* **—sub·ver·sive,** *a., n.* **—sub·ver·sive·ly,** *adv.* **—sub·ver·sive·ness,** *n.*

sub·vert, səb·vart′, *v.t.* To destroy; to overthrow: to *subvert* a government. **—sub·vert·er,** *n.*

sub·way, səb′wā, *n.* An electric railway beneath the surface of the streets in a large city; any underground passage for utilities or pedestrians.

suc·ceed, sək·sēd′, *v.i.* To accomplish what is attempted or intended; to come after or take the place of another by descent, election, appointment, or the like, often followed by *to;* to come next after something else in an order or series.**—***v.t.* To come after and take the place of, as in an office or estate; to come next after in an order or series, or in the course of events; follow. **—suc·ceed·er,** *n.*

suc·cess, sək·ses′, *n.* The favorable or prosperous termination of attempts or endeavors; the attainment of wealth, position, or the like; a thing or a person that is successful.

suc·cess·ful, sək·ses′fəl, *a.* Resulting in or attended with success; achieving or having achieved success; having succeeded in obtaining wealth, position, recognition, or the like. **—suc·cess·ful·ly,** *adv.* **—suc·cess·ful·ness,** *n.*

suc·ces·sion, sək·sesh′ən, *n.* The coming of one thing or person after another in order, sequence, or the course of events: five sunny days in *succession;* a number of persons or things following one another in order or sequence; the process, right, or act by which one person succeeds to the office, rank, estate, or the like of another. **—suc·ces·sion·al,** *a.* **—suc·ces·sion·al·ly,** *adv.*

suc·ces·sive, sək·ses′iv, *a.* Following in order or in uninterrupted course. **—suc·ces·sive·ly,** *adv.* **—suc·ces·sive·ness,** *n.*

suc·ces·sor, sək·ses′ər, *n.* A person or thing that succeeds or follows; a person who takes the place which another has left.

suc·cinct, sək·singkt′, *a.* Compressed into few words; concise. **—suc·cinct·ly,** *adv.* **—suc·cinct·ness,** *n.*

suc·cor, sək′ər, *n.* Aid; help; assistance in difficulty or distress; the person or thing that brings relief.**—***v.t.* To help in difficulty or distress. **—suc·cor·er,** *n.*

suc·co·tash, sək′ə·tash, *n.* A dish consisting of corn cooked together with lima or other beans.

suc·cu·bus, sək′yə·bəs, *n. pl.,* **-bi, -bī,** -bī, -bē. A female demon believed to have sexual intercourse with men during sleep.

suc·cu·lent, sək′yə·lənt, *a.* Full of juice; juicy; rich in desirable qualities. **—suc·cu·lence, suc·cu·len·cy,** *n.* **—suc·cu·lent·ly,** *adv.*

suc·cumb, sə·kəm′, *v.i.* To give way to superior force; yield; die.

such, səch, *a.* Of the kind, character, degree, or extent of that or those indicated or implied: *Such* a woman is dangerous; being similar or the same as that last stated or indicated: *Such* nonsense is the case; of so extreme a degree or kind: *such* honor.**—***pron.* Such a person or thing or persons or things; the person or thing or persons or things indicated: once a friend but no longer *such.***—***adv.* So, very, in such a manner, or to such a degree: *such* terrible deeds. **—as such,** as being what is indicated or implied: The leader, *as such,* is entitled to respect; in itself: Vice, *as such,* does not appeal to him. **—such as,** for example.

suck, sək, *v.t.* To draw into the mouth by the action of the lips and tongue; to draw, as something, from with the mouth; to draw in or imbibe by suction.**—***v.i.* To draw fluid into the mouth; to draw milk from the

breast; to draw in a substance by suction.**—***n.* The act of drawing with the mouth. **—suck in.** *Informal.* To deceive or take advantage of.

suck·er, sək′ər, *n.* One who or that which sucks; an organ in animals for sucking; a fish of the carp family; a shoot or branch which proceeds from the roots or lower part of a stem. *Informal.* A person easily duped, deceived, or cheated; a lollipop.

suck·le, sək′əl, *v.t.,* **-led, -ling.** To nurse at the breast; to nurture.**—***v.i.* To nurse from the breast.

suck·ling, sək′ling, *n.* An unweaned young child or other mammal.

su·crose, soo′krōs, *n.* The ordinary sugar obtained from sugar cane, sugar beets, and sorghum.

suc·tion, sək′shən, *n.* The act, process, or condition of sucking; the force which sucks or draws a substance into an interior space or causes the parts surrounding an interior space to adhere more firmly together when a partial vacuum is produced; the production of this force.

sud·den, səd′ən, *a.* Occurring without notice; coming unexpectedly; hastily put in use, employed, or prepared; quick; rapid; hasty; rash. **—all of** or **on a sudden,** unexpectedly; without warning. **sud·den·ly,** *adv.* **—sud·den·ness,** *n.*

suds, sədz, *n. pl., sing.* or *pl. in constr.* Water impregnated with soap and forming a froth or lather; soapy water.**—***v.t.* To wash with suds.**—***v.i.* To produce suds. **—suds·y,** səd′zē, *a.,* **-i·er, -i·est.**

sue, soo, *v.t.,* **sued, su·ing.** To seek justice or right from by legal process; to institute a process in law against.**—***v.i.* To prosecute; to make legal claim; to seek by request; to petition; to plead. **—su·er,** *n.*

suede, swād, *n.* Kid or leather finished on the wrong or flesh side with a soft nap, or on the outer side after removal of a thin outer layer; a woolen fabric with a similar finish or appearance. Also **suède.**

su·et, soo′it, *n.* The fatty tissue found around the loins and kidneys of the ox, sheep, deer, and other animals, which is harder than the fat from other parts and yields tallow when processed. **—su·et·y,** *a.*

suf·fer, səf′ər, *v.t.* To feel or bear with painful, disagreeable, or distressing effects; to undergo, as pain; to be affected by; to allow.**—***v.i.* To feel or undergo pain of body or mind; to sustain loss or damage. **—suf·fer·a·ble,** *a.* **—suf·fer·a·ble·ness,** *n.* **—suf·fer·a·bly,** *adv.* **—suf·fer·er,** *n.* **—suf·fer·ing,** *n.* **—suf·fer·ing·ly,** *adv.*

suf·fer·ance, səf′ər·əns, səf′rəns, *n.* Passive consent by not forbidding or hindering; tolerance; endurance.

suf·fice, sə·fīs′, sə·fīz′, *v.i.,* **-ficed, -fic·ing.** To be enough or sufficient.**—***v.t.* To satisfy; to be equal to the wants or demands of. **—suf·fic·er,** *n.*

suf·fi·cien·cy, sə·fish′ən·sē, *n. pl.,* **-cies.** The state of being sufficient; adequacy; capacity; self-confidence.

suf·fi·cient, sə·fish′ənt, *a.* Equal to the end proposed; enough. **—suf·fi·cient·ly,** *adv.*

suf·fix, səf′iks, *n.* A letter or syllable or a number of letters or syllables affixed to the end of a word or to a verbal stem or root to qualify the meaning or form a derivative word; a terminal formative element of a word, as *-th* in *warmth, -ly* in *godly,* or *-ation* in *flirtation.*

suf·fo·cate, səf′ə·kāt, *v.t.,* **-cat·ed, -cat·ing.** To choke or kill by stopping respiration; stifle, as by depriving of air; smother.**—***v.i.* To become choked, stifled, or smothered. **—suf·fo·cat·ing·ly,** *adv.* **—suf·fo·ca·tion,** səf·ə·kā′shən, *n.* **—suf·fo·ca·tive,** *a.*

suf·frage, səf′rij, *n.* The right to vote; a vote given in deciding a question or choosing a person or measure.

suf·fra·gette, səf·rə·jet′, *n.* A woman who favors giving women the right to vote.

suf·fuse, sə·fūz′, *v.t.,* **-fused, -fus·ing.** To overspread, as with color, light, or fluid. **—suf·fu·sion,**

sə·fū′zhən, n. —suf·fu·sive, sə·fū′siv, a.

sug·ar, shŏŏg′ər, n. A sweet, white, crystalline substance, obtained chiefly from the juice of the sugar cane and sugar beet; sucrose; any of the class of carbohydrates to which this substance belongs, as glucose, levulose, and lactose.—v.t. To cover, sprinkle, mix, or sweeten with sugar; to sweeten, as if with sugar; to make agreeable.—v.i. To form sugar; to make maple sugar. —sug·ar·less, a. —sug·ar·like, a. —sug·ar·y, a., -i·er, -i·est.

sug·ar beet, n. A species of beet whose thick, white root is a major source of sugar.

sug·ar cane, n. A tall grass constituting the chief source of the commercial sugar, sucrose.

sug·ar-coat, shŏŏg′ər-kōt, v.t. To put a coating of sugar on; to surround with a deceptive aura of attractiveness or acceptability.

sug·ar ma·ple, n. A tree of northern N. America from the sap of which maple syrup and maple sugar are made; the hardwood from this tree, much used for furniture.

sug·ar·plum, shŏŏg′ər·pləm, n. A small sweetmeat made of sugar with various flavoring and coloring ingredients; a bonbon.

sug·gest, səg·jest′, sə·jest′, v.t. To place or bring, as an idea, proposition, or plan, before a person's mind for consideration or possible action; to propose, as a person or thing, as suitable or possible; hint; to call up in the mind, as a thing, through association or natural connection of ideas: said of a thing. —sug·gest·er, n. —sug·gest·i·ble, a. —sug·gest·i·bil·i·ty, n.

sug·ges·tion, səg·jes′chən, sə·jes′chən, n. The act of suggesting or the state of being suggested; indirect conveyance of an idea, or intimation; a hint.

sug·ges·tive, səg·jes′tiv, sə·jes′tiv, a. That suggests; tending to suggest thoughts or ideas, or conveying a suggestion or intimation; giving a seeming indication of something, such as something improper or indecent. —sug·ges·tive·ly, adv. —sug·ges·tive·ness, n.

su·i·cide, soo′ə·sīd, n. One who intentionally takes one's own life; the intentional taking of one's own life.—v.i., -cid·ed, -cid·ing. To commit suicide.—v.t. To kill (oneself). —su·i·cid·al, soo·ə·sīd′əl, a.

suit, soot, n. A set of garments, vestments, or armor, intended to be worn together, esp. a set of outer garments, as jacket, vest, and trousers; a livery, uniform, or garb; the act or process of suing in a court of law; a process instituted in a court of justice for the enforcement or protection of a right or claim, or for the redress of a wrong; one of the four sets or classes, spades, clubs, hearts, and diamonds, into which playing cards are divided.—v.t. To make appropriate, adapt, or accommodate, as one thing to another; be adapted or suitable for; to satisfy or please.—v.i. To be suitable or satisfactory. —fol·low suit, to follow example.

suit·a·ble, soo′tə·bəl, a. Suiting or being in accordance; fitting; proper; becoming. —suit·a·bil·i·ty, suit·a·ble·ness, n. —suit·a·bly, adv.

suit·case, soot′kās, n. A kind of flat, oblong valise used to carry clothing and other articles, esp. when traveling.

suite, swēt, soot, n. A connected series of rooms to be used together by one person or a number of persons; a company of followers or attendants; a matched set of furniture designed for a given room.

suit·ing, soo′ting, n. Cloth for making suits of clothes.

suit·or, soo′tər, n. One who courts a woman; a wooer; one who institutes a lawsuit; a petitioner.

sul·fa, sul·pha, sel′fə, a. Chemically related to sulfanilamide; pertaining to, containing, or consisting of any of a family of drugs chemically related to sulfanilamide.—n. A sulfa drug.

sul·fa·nil·a·mide, sul·pha·nil·a·mide, sel·fə·nil′ə·mīd, sel·fə·nil′ə·mid, n. A colorless, crystalline compound, used for its therapeutic action in numerous bacterial infections, as in pneumonia and gonorrhea.

sul·fate, sul·phate, sel′fāt, n. A salt of sulfuric acid.

sul·fide, sul·phide, sel′fīd, n. A compound of sulfur with a more electropositive element or radical.

sul·fur, sul·phur, sel′fər, n. A nonmetallic element, ordinarily a yellow crystalline solid which burns with a blue flame and a suffocating odor, and is used in medicine, in vulcanizing rubber, and in making matches and gunpowder.

sul·fu·ric, sul·phu·ric, sel·fyŏŏr′ik, a. Of, pertaining to, or containing sulfur.

sul·fu·ric ac·id, n. A colorless, oily, and strongly corrosive compound used in manufacturing explosives, fertilizers, and chemicals. Also sul·phu·ric ac·id, oil of vit·ri·ol, vit·ri·ol.

sul·fur·ous, sul·phur·ous, sel′fər·əs, sel·fyŏŏr′əs, a. Full of sulfur; pertaining to or resembling sulfur; like the suffocating fumes or the heat of burning sulfur; fiery; hellish; blasphemous; containing sulfur. —sul·fur·ous·ly, sul·phur·ous·ly, adv. —sul·fur·ous·ness, sul·phur·ous·ness, n.

sulk, sŏlk, v.i. To be sulky.—n. A state or fit of sulking.

sulk·y, sel′kē, a., -i·er, -i·est. Sulking; sullenly ill-humored or resentful; marked by ill-humored aloofness or reserve.—n. pl., -ies. A light, two-wheeled, one-horse carriage carrying one person. —sulk·i·ly, adv. —sulk·i·ness, n.

sul·len, sel′ən, a. Showing ill humor by a gloomy silence or reserve; silently and persistently ill-humored; morose; indicative of gloomy ill humor; gloomy or dismal, as weather, places, or sounds. —sul·len·ly, adv. —sul·len·ness, n.

sul·ly, sel′ē, v.t., -lied, -ly·ing. To soil, spot, or tarnish; defile; to impair the purity or brilliance of.—v.i. To be soiled or tarnished.

sul·tan, sel′tən, n. The sovereign of a Mohammedan country. —sul·tan·ic, sel·tan′ik, a.

sul·tan·a, sel·tan′ə, sel·tä′nə, n. The wife, mother, sister, or daughter of a sultan; also sul·tan·ess, sel′tən·is. A variety of seedless grape used esp. to make raisins or wine.

sul·tan·ate, sel′tə·nāt, n. The rule or territory of a sultan. Also sul·tan·ship.

sul·try, sel′trē, a., -tri·er, -tri·est. Very hot and moist, or hot, close, and heavy; hot or burning, as with anger or passion. —sul·tri·ly, adv. —sul·tri·ness, n.

sum, sem, n. The aggregate of two or more numbers, magnitudes, quantities, or particulars as determined by the mathematical process of addition; an arithmetical problem to be solved or such a problem worked out; an indefinite quantity or amount, esp. of money: to lend small sums; the substance, gist, or essence of a matter.—v.t., summed, sum·ming. To combine into an aggregate; summarize.

su·mac, su·mach, soo′mak, shoo′mak, n. A shrub or tree, the powdered leaves of certain species being used for tanning.

sum·ma·rize, sem′ə·rīz, v.t., -rized, -riz·ing. To make a summary of; to constitute a summary of. —sum·ma·ri·za·tion, sem·ər·ə·zā′shən, n. —sum·ma·riz·er, sum·mar·ist, n.

sum·ma·ry, sem′ə·rē, a. Reduced into few words; concise; quickly executed without ceremony.—n. pl., -ries. An abridged or condensed statement or account. —sum·mar·i·ly, sem′ə·rə·lē, sə·mār′ə·lē, adv. —sum·mar·i·ness, n.

sum·ma·tion, sə·mā′shən, n. The process of summing; a recapitulation or reviewing of previous arguments or facts, usu. expressing one or more final conclusions, as in any debate or court trial. —sum·

a- hat, fāte, fāre, fäther; e- met, mē; i- pin, pīne; o- not, nōte, ôrb, moove (move), boy, pownd; u- cūbe, bŭll, tŭk (took); ch- chin; th- thick, then; zh- vizhon (vision); ə- əgo, takən, pencəl, lemən, bərd (bird).

ma·tion·al, a.

sum·mer, səm′ər, n. The second and warmest season of the year, between spring and autumn; a year of life; a period of ripeness, brightness, or prosperity.—a. Of or occurring in summer.—v.i. To spend or pass the summer. **—sum·mer·y,** a.

sum·mer·house, səm′ər·hows, n. A structure in a park or garden intended to provide a shady and cool place in the heat of summer.

sum·mit, səm′it, n. The highest point or part, as of a hill, line of travel, or any object; the top or apex; the highest stage or degree.—a. Of or pertaining to diplomacy between chiefs of state or the highest ranking government officials: a summit meeting.

sum·mon, səm′ən, v.t. To call or cite by authority to appear at a specified place, esp. before a court of justice; to call or order together: to summon congress; to call up, muster, or excite into action, usu. followed by up, as: Summon up your courage. **—sum·mon·er,** n.

sum·mons, səm′ənz, n. pl., **sum·mons·es.** A call or command by authority to appear at a specific place or to attend to some public duty; a call by authority to appear in a court; the written or printed document by which such a call is given.—v.t.

sump, səmp, n. A pit, well, or cesspool in which water or other liquid is collected.

sump·tu·ar·y, səmp′chū·er·ē, a. Relating to expense; regulating expense or expenditure: sumptuary laws.

sump·tu·ous, səmp′chū·əs, a. Costly; having an impressively expensive appearance; luxurious; magnificent. **—sump·tu·ous·ly,** adv. **—sump·tu·ous·ness,** n.

sun, sən, n. The central body of the solar system, a star around which the earth and other planets revolve and from which they receive light and heat; some similar celestial body; sunlight; the sun's warmth; a day; a year; sunrise; anything brilliant or glorious.—v.t., **sunned, sun·ning.** To expose to the heat or light of the sun or of a sun lamp.—v.i. To expose oneself to the rays of the sun or a sun lamp.

sun·bathe, sən′bāth, v.i., **-bathed, -bath·ing.** To lie exposed to the sun. **—sun·bath·er,** n.

sun·beam, sən′bēm, n. A ray of the sun perceived as a beam of visible light.

sun·bon·net, sən′bon·it, n. A large bonnet shading the face and projecting down over the neck.

sun·burn, sən′bərn, n. Inflammation of the skin, caused by prolonged exposure to the sun's rays; the discoloration or tan so produced.—v.t., v.i., **-burned** or **-burnt, -burn·ing.** To affect or be affected with sunburn.

sun·dae, sən′dē, sən′dā, n. An individual portion of ice cream with fruit or other syrup poured over it, and often with whipped cream, minced nuts, or other additions.

Sun·day, sən′dē, sən′dā, n. The first day of the week; the Christian Sabbath; the Lord's day.

Sun·day School, n. A school for religious instruction held on Sundays; its pupils and teachers collectively.

sun·der, sən′dər, v.t., v.i. To part; to divide; to disunite in almost any manner, as by rending, cutting, or breaking. **—sun·der·ance,** n.

sun·di·al, sən′di·əl, sən′dīl, n. An instrument that shows the time of day by means of a shadow cast by the sun onto a dial.

sun·down, sən′down, n. Sunset.

sun·dries, sən′drēz, n. pl. Various small things, too minute or numerous to be individually specified.

sun·dry, sən′drē, a. Several; various; miscellaneous.

sun·fish, sən′fish, n. pl., **-fish, -fish·es.** Any of various small fresh-water fishes of N. America, with a deep, compressed body.

sun·flow·er, sən′flow·ər, n. Any of several tall herbs with large leaves and yellow-rayed flowers.

sung, səng, v. Past participle and sometimes past tense of **sing.**

sun·glass·es, sən′glas·iz, n. pl. Eyeglasses which have tinted or colored lenses for protecting the eyes from strong, glaring sunlight.

sunk, səngk, v. A past tense and past participle of **sink.**

sunk·en, səng′kən, a. Submerged; lying on the bottom of the sea or other water; hollow or recessed; lying below the normal level; constructed or located at a lower level.

sun lamp, n. An electric lamp which emits ultraviolet rays and is used mainly therapeutically or as an indoor source of sun tan.

sun·light, sən′līt, n. The light of the sun.

sun·lit, sən′lit, a. Lighted by the sun.

sun·ny, sən′ē, a., **-ni·er, -ni·est.** Like the sun; lighted up or warmed by the direct rays of the sun; cheery or pleasant, as: a sunny disposition. **—sun·ni·ly,** adv. **—sun·ni·ness,** n.

sun·rise, sən′rīz, n. The ascent or appearance of the sun above the horizon; the time when this takes place.

sun·set, sən′set, n. The disappearance or seeming descent of the sun below the horizon; the time when the sun sets.

sun·shine, sən′shīn, n. The light of the sun; brightness or happiness. **—sun·shin·y,** a.

sun·spot, sən′spot, n. One of the relatively dark patches which appear periodically on the surface of the sun.

sun·stroke, sən′strōk, n. A type of heatstroke resulting from exposure to the direct rays of the sun.

sun tan, n. A browning or darkening of the skin due to exposure to the sun or a sun lamp. Also **sun·tan,** sən′tan.

sun·up, sən′əp, n. Sunrise.

sup, səp, v.i., **supped, sup·ping.** To eat the evening meal; to take supper.

su·per, soo′pər, n. Informal. A superintendent or supernumerary.—a. Informal. Very fine; first-rate; extremely good; of the greatest or an excessive degree.

su·per·a·bun·dant, soo·pər·ə·bən′dənt, a. Abounding far above or beyond necessity. **—su·per·a·bun·dance,** n. **—su·per·a·bun·dant·ly,** adv.

su·per·an·nu·ate, soo·pər·an′yū·āt, v.t., **-at·ed, -at·ing.** To allow to retire from service on a pension, on account of old age or infirmity; to discard or set aside as too old.—v.i. To become retired. **—su·per·an·nu·at·ed,** a. **—su·per·an·nu·a·tion,** soo·pər·an·yū·ā′shən, n.

su·perb, sû·pərb′, a. Grand; august; stately; splendid; rich; sumptuous; showy; very fine; first-rate. **—su·perb·ly,** adv. **—su·perb·ness,** n.

su·per·car·go, soo·pər·kär·gō, n. pl., **-goes, -gos.** A person on a merchant ship whose business is to manage sales and superintend all the commercial concerns of the voyage.

su·per·charge, soo′pər·chärj, v.t., **-charged, -charg·ing.** To overload or charge excessively; to apply a supercharger to an engine.

su·per·charg·er, soo′pər·chärj·ər, n. A device by which an increased quantity of air is supplied to the cylinders of an internal-combustion engine, producing greater power.

su·per·cil·i·ous, soo·pər·sil′ē·əs, a. Having a haughty air or manner; disdainful; acting as if others were inferior; haughty; overbearing; arrogant. **—su·per·cil·i·ous·ly,** adv. **—su·per·cil·i·ous·ness,** n.

su·per·e·go, soo·pər·ē′gō, soo·pər·eg′ō, n. A system within the mind which brings perceived parental, social, or moral standards to bear upon the actions and decisions of the ego.

su·per·e·rog·a·to·ry, soo·pər·ə·rog′ə·tôr·ē, a. Exceeding one's duty; beyond necessity; superfluous.

su·per·fi·cial, soo·pər·fish′əl, a. Lying on or pertaining to the surface; not penetrating the substance of a thing; not deep or profound as regards knowledge; not learned or thorough; not going to the heart of things; not genuine. **—su·per·fi·ci·al·i·ty,** soo·par·fish·ē·al′ə·tē, *n. pl.,* **-ties. —super·fi·cial·ly,** *adv.* **—su·per·fi·cial·ness,** *n.*

su·per·fine, soo·par·fīn′, *a.* Very fine; surpassing others in fineness; excessively or faultily subtle.

su·per·flu·ous, sū·par·flū·əs, *a.* Being more than is wanted; more than sufficient or necessary; redundant. **—su·per·flu·i·ty,** soo·par·floo′ə·tē, *n. pl.,* **-ties. —su·per·flu·ous·ly,** *adv.* **—su·per·flu·ous·ness,** *n.*

su·per·high·way, soo′par·hī·wā, soo·par·hī′wā, *n.* A high-speed, multilane highway often with safety medians and limited access interchanges.

su·per·hu·man, soo·par·hū′mən, *a.* Above or beyond what is human; divine. **—su·per·hu·man·i·ty,** soo·par·hū·man′ə·tē, *n.* **—su·per·hu·man·ly,** *adv.* **—su·per·hu·man·ness,** *n.*

su·per·im·pose, soo·par·im·pōz′, *v.t.,* **-posed, -pos·ing.** To lay or impose on something else; to add (something) over something else. **—su·per·im·po·si·tion,** soo·par·im·pə·zish′ən, *n.*

su·per·in·tend, soo·par·in·tend′, *v.t.* To have the charge and oversight of; to take care of with authority. **—su·per·in·tend·ence, su·per·in·tend·en·cy,** *n.*

su·per·in·tend·ent, soo·par·in·ten′dənt, *n.* One who superintends or has the oversight and charge of something; a manager; a maintenance supervisor in an apartment building who acts as the agent of the owner.

su·pe·ri·or, sū·pēr′ē·ər, sə·pēr′ē·ər, *a.* Higher in rank, office, or quality; excellent; supercilious: putting on *superior* airs.*—n.* One who is superior to another or others in social station, rank, power, excellence, or qualities of any kind; the chief of a monastery, convent, or abbey. **—su·pe·ri·or·i·ty,** sə·pēr·ē·ôr′i·tē, sə·pēr·ē·or′i·tē, *n.* **—su·pe·ri·or·ly,** *adv.*

su·per·la·tive, sə·par′lə·tiv, sū·par′lə·tiv, *a.* Of the highest rank or degree; surpassing all others; referring to that form of an adjective or adverb which expresses the highest or utmost degree of comparison.*—n.* That which is of the highest rank or degree; the superlative degree of adjectives or adverbs; a word in the superlative degree. **—su·per·la·tive·ly,** *adv.* **—su·per·la·tive·ness,** *n.*

su·per·man, soo′par·man, *n. pl.,* **-men.** A man of seemingly more than human powers.

su·per·mar·ket, soo′par·mär·kit, *n.* A large retail market selling food and other household items and usu. operating on a self-service, cash-and-carry basis, esp. one of a chain of such markets.

su·per·nal, sū·par′nəl, *a.* Being or coming from above; lofty; relating to things above the world and worldly concerns; celestial; heavenly; ethereal; divine. **—su·per·nal·ly,** *adv.*

su·per·nat·u·ral, soo·par·nach′ər·əl, *a.* Referring to divine, ghostly, or infernal transcendence or violation of what are assumed to be natural laws; miraculous; eerie.*—n.* Anything supernatural; supernatural beings, actions, or happenings, preceded by *the;* existence or forces above the natural, preceded by *the.* **—su·per·nat·u·ral·ism,** *n.* **—su·per·nat·u·ral·ly,** *adv.* **—su·per·nat·u·ral·ness,** *n.*

su·per·nu·mer·ar·y, soo·par·noo′mə·rer·ē, soo·par·nū′mə·rer·ē, *n. pl.,* **-ies.** A person or thing beyond what is necessary or usual; an actor who appears briefly on stage, usu. in a nonspeaking role. *—a.* Exceeding a designated, necessary, or usual number; extra; superfluous.

su·per·pow·er, soo′par·pow·ər, *n.* Power on an extraordinary or extensive scale; an extremely powerful nation, as the United States or the Soviet Union, whose policies and actions greatly affect those of smaller, less powerful nations.

su·per·scribe, soo·par·skrīb′, *v.t.,* **-scribed, -scrib·ing.** To write on the top, outside, or surface of, as a name or address; to put an inscription on. **—su·per·scrip·tion,** soo·par·skrip′shən, *n.*

su·per·script, soo′par·skript, *n.* A sign, letter, or numeral positioned high on a line of writing, as the 2 in x^2.*—a.*

su·per·sede, soo·par·sēd′, *v.t.,* **-sed·ed, -sed·ing.** To set aside as void, useless, or obsolete, usu. in favor of something mentioned; to succeed to the position, function, or office of; to supplant. **—su·per·sed·er,** *n.*

su·per·son·ic, soo·par·son′ik, *a.* Pertaining to or attaining speeds greater than that of sound: a *supersonic* aircraft; of or pertaining to frequencies above those that can be heard by the human ear. **—su·per·son·i·cal·ly,** *adv.*

su·per·star, soo′par·stär, *n. Informal.* A person of great celebrity or great distinction, esp. in athletics or the entertainment arts.

su·per·sti·tion, soo·par·stish′ən, *n.* A belief or notion entertained, either popularly or by an individual, regardless of reason or knowledge, of the significance of a particular thing, circumstance, occurrence, proceedings, or the like: the *superstitions* about Friday, the number 13, a black cat, a four-leaf clover.

su·per·sti·tious, soo·par·stish′əs, *a.* Full of or inclined to superstition; pertaining to or caused by superstition. **—su·per·sti·tious·ly,** *adv.* **—su·per·sti·tious·ness,** *n.*

su·per·struc·ture, soo′par·strək·chər, *n.* Any structure built on something else, esp. all of a building above the basement or foundation; anything erected on some foundation or basis, as a concept.

su·per·vene, soo·par·vēn′, *v.i.,* **-vened, -ven·ing.** To take place or happen as something supplementary, extraneous, or unforeseen. **—su·per·ven·tion,** soo·par·ven′shən, *n.*

su·per·vise, soo′par·viz, *v.t.,* **-vised, -vis·ing.** To oversee in order to direct, as employees; to superintend. **—su·per·vi·sion,** soo·par·vizh′ən, *n.* **—su·per·vi·sor,** *n.* **—su·per·vi·so·ry,** soo·par·vī′zə·rē, *a.*

su·pine, soo·pīn′, *a.* Lying on the back, or with the face or front upward; inactive; passive; inert; esp. inactive or passive from indolence or indifference. **—su·pine·ly,** *adv.* **—su·pine·ness,** *n.*

sup·per, sap′ər, *n.* The evening meal; the last meal of the day, taken in the evening.

sup·plant, sə·plant′, *v.t.* To displace or take the place of, as a person, esp. by treacherous or underhand means; to displace; supersede; replace, as a thing, by something else. **—sup·plan·ta·tion,** səp·lan·tā′shən, *n.* **—sup·plant·er,** *n.*

sup·ple, səp′əl, *a.,* **-pler, -plest.** Bending readily without breaking or deformation, as: *supple* leather; flexible; limber; lithe; characterized by ease and adaptability in mental action: a *supple* mind; conforming readily to circumstances or to the will or humor of others. **—sup·ple·ly, sup·ply,** *adv.* **—sup·ple·ness,** *n.*

sup·ple·ment, səp′lə·mənt, *n.* An addition to anything, esp. a book, magazine, or other publication, by which it is made fuller, more correct, up-to-date, or complete; that which adds or supplies what is lacking or insufficient. *—*səp′lə·ment *v.t.—*To increase or complete by a supplement; to furnish what is lacking. **—sup·ple·men·tal, sup·ple·men·ta·ry,** səp·lə·men′təl, səp·lə·men′tə·rē, *a.* **—sup·ple·men·ta·tion,** səp·lə·men·tā′shən, *n.*

sup·pli·ant, səp′lē·ənt, *a.* Entreating or begging earnestly; asking earnestly and humbly.*—n.* A humble petitioner. **—sup·pli·ant·ly,** *adv.*

sup·pli·cant, səp′lə·kənt, *n., a.* Suppliant.

sup·pli·cate, səp′lə·kāt, *v.t.,* **-cat·ed, -cat·ing.** To entreat or beg humbly for.*—v.i.* To petition with earnestness; to implore. **—sup·pli·ca·tion,** səp·lə·kā′shən, *n.* **—sup·pli·ca·to·ry,** səp′lə·kə·tôr·ē, *a.*

sup·ply, sə·plī′, *v.t.,* **-plied, -ply·ing.** To furnish or

---

a- hat, fāte, fāre, fäther; **e-** met, mē; **i-** pin, pīne; **o-** not, nōte, ôrb, moove (move), boy, pownd; **u-** cūbe, bŭll, tŭk (took); **ch-** chin; **th-** thick, then; **zh-** vizhon (vision); **ə-** əgo, takən, pencəl, lemən, bərd (bird).

provide, followed by *with:* to *supply with* money; to make up for or compensate for, as a loss, lack, or absence; to satisfy, as a want, need, or demand.—*n. pl.,* **-plies.** The act of supplying, furnishing, providing, or satisfying; a quantity of something provided or on hand, as for use; a stock or store; *usu. pl.,* a provision, stock, or store of food or other things necessary for maintenance: *supplies* for an army. **—sup•pli•er,** *n.*

sup•port, sə•pōrt′, sə•pôrt′, *v.t.* To bear or hold up, as a load, mass, part, or structure; to bear with fortitude, or submission; tolerate; to sustain, as a person, the mind, spirits, or courage; to maintain, as a person, family, or institution, by supplying with things necessary to existence; provide for; to uphold, as a person, cause, or policy; to maintain or advocate, as a theory or cause; to corroborate; to act with or second a leading actor; to assist in any performance.—*n.* The act of supporting; the state of being supported; maintenance, as of a person or family, with necessities, means, or funds; a thing or a person that supports. **—sup•port•a•ble,** *a.* **—sup•port•a•ble•ness,** *n.* **—sup•port•a•bly,** *adv.* **—sup•port•er,** *n.* **—sup•port•ive,** *a.*

sup•pose, sə•pōz′, *v.t.,* **-posed, -pos•ing.** To lay down or regard as fact for the sake of argument or illustration: *Suppose* the shipment is delayed; to suggest or propose: *Suppose* we postpone our decision until next week; to assume or take for granted: I *suppose* he will go; to imagine: I *suppose* you want a definite answer; to demand or expect, used in the passive: Aren't you *supposed* to be at work? To imply or presuppose: Creation *supposes* a creator.—*v.i.* To make or form a supposition; to think. **—sup•pos•a•ble,** *a.* **—sup•pos•a•bly,** *adv.* **—sup•posed,** *a.* **—sup•pos•ed•ly,** *adv.*

sup•pos•ing, sə•pō′zing, *conj.* In the event that; provided that.

sup•po•si•tion, səp•ə•zish′ən, *n.* The act of supposing; what is assumed hypothetically; an assumption; a conjecture; hypothesis. **—sup•po•si•tion•al,** *a.* **—sup•po•si•tion•al•ly,** *adv.*

sup•pos•i•to•ry, sə•poz′ə•tôr•ē, *n. pl.,* **-ries.** A mass of some prepared substance, usu. in the form of a cone or cylinder, for introduction into the rectum, vagina, or urethra.

sup•press, sə•pres′, *v.t.* To overpower and crush; to put down; to quell, as a revolt, mutiny, or riot; to restrain from utterance; to conceal, as one's feelings; not to tell or reveal, as news; to retain without making public. **—sup•press•i•ble,** *a.* **—sup•pres•sion,** *n.* **—sup•pres•sor,** *n.*

sup•pu•rate, səp′yə•rāt, *v.i.,* **-rat•ed, -rat•ing.** To generate pus or matter; fester. **—sup•pu•ra•tion,** səp•yə•rā′shən, *n.* **—sup•pu•ra•tive,** *a., n.*

su•pra•re•nal gland, soo•prə•rē′nəl, *n.* Adrenal gland.

su•prem•a•cy, sə•prem′ə•sē, sû•prem′ə•sē, *n. pl.,* **-cies.** Highest or supreme authority or power. **—su•prem•a•cist,** *n.*

su•preme, sə•prēm′, sû•prēm′, *a.* Highest in authority; holding the highest place in government or power; highest as to quality or degree; greatest possible; last or ultimate; final. **—su•preme•ly,** *adv.* **—su•preme•ness,** *n.*

Su•preme Be•ing, *n.* God.

Su•preme Court, *n.* The Federal court which is highest in the judicial system of the United States; the highest appellate court in most states.

sur•cease, sər′sēs, *n. Archaic.* End; a cessation.

sur•charge, sər′chärj, *n.* An extra tax, charge, or cost; an overcharge; an addition overprinted on a stamp which in some way differentiates it or changes its denomination.—*v.t.,* **-charged, -charg•ing.** To add on an extra charge, cost, or tax; to mark with a surcharge or new denomination.

sur•cin•gle, sər′sing•gəl, *n.* A belt or girth encircling a horse's body and fastening a saddle, pack, or the like

on a horse's back.

sure, shûr, *a.,* **sur•er, sur•est.** Perfectly confident; knowing and believing; certain; fully persuaded; certain to find or retain; to be depended on; unfailing; firm; stable; secure; infallible; inevitable; destined. —*adv.* Certainly; without doubt. **—be sure,** be or do as designated. **—for sure,** a certainty. **—sure enough.** *Informal.* Might have been supposed or expected. **—to be sure,** without doubt; admittedly; certainly. **—sure•ly,** *adv.* **—sure•ness,** *n.*

sure-fire, shûr′fīr, *a. Informal.* Sure to succeed or to meet expectations; dependable; unfailing.

sure-foot•ed, shûr′fût′id, *a.* Not liable to stumble, slip, or fall; not liable to err. **—sure-foot•ed•ly,** *adv.*

sure•ty, shûr′i•tē, shûr′tē, *n. pl.,* **-ties.** One responsible for another, called the principal, who is primarily liable; one who binds himself to stand good for another; security against loss, damage, or default of payment; certainty; security; ground of security or safety; guarantee; a bail. **—sure•ty•ship,** *n.*

surf, sərf, *n.* The swell of the sea which breaks upon a shore or upon sandbanks or rocks.—*v.i.* To float one's body or to ride a surfboard toward shore on cresting waves. **—surf•y,** *a.,* **-i•er, -i•est.**

sur•face, sər′fis, *n.* An exterior layer or boundary of anything that has length and breadth: the *surface* of a solid or liquid; any face of an object: the *surface* of a coin; outward or external appearance: Beneath the *surface* the company is in turmoil.—*a.* External; superficial, as appearances; denoting movement by land or sea, as opposed to underground or air travel.—*v.t.,* **-faced, -fac•ing.** To apply a particular surface to.—*v.i.* To come to the surface: The diver *surfaced* far from shore. **—sur•face-less,** *a.* **—sur•fac•er,** *n.*

surf•board, sərf′bôrd, *n.* An oblong, buoyant board used to ride incoming waves in the sport of surfboarding.—*v.i.* To ride a surfboard. **—surf•board•er,** *n.*

sur•feit, sər′fit, *n.* An excessive amount or supply; intemperance or overindulgence, esp. in eating or drinking; physical discomfort from overeating or too much drink; a reaction of disgust to gluttony or intemperance.—*v.i.* To do anything excessively; to suffer from overindulgence. **—sur•feit•er,** *n.*

surge, sərj, *n.* A sudden or powerful flow; a large wave or billow.—*v.i.,* **surged, surg•ing.** To swell; to flow suddenly or powerfully; to rise high and roll, as waves.

sur•geon, sər′jən, *n.* A medical man who specializes in the practice of surgery.

sur•ger•y, sər′jə•rē, *n. pl.,* **-ies.** The practice which involves the performance of operations on the human subject to cure diseases or injuries of the body; the operative branch of medicine; a room where surgical operations are performed. **—sur•gi•cal,** sər′ji•kəl, *a.* **—sur•gi•cal•ly,** *adv.*

sur•ly, sər′lē, *a.,* **-li•er, -li•est.** Sternly sour; cross and rude; churlish; rough or tempestuous.—*adv.* **—sur•li•ly,** *adv.* **—sur•li•ness,** *n.*

sur•mise, sər•mīz′, sər′mīz, *n.* A thought or supposition with little or no ground to go upon; a guess or conjecture. **—**sər•mīz′, *v.t.,* **-mised, -mis•ing.** To guess; to conjecture.

sur•mount, sər•mownt′, *v.t.* To mount or rise above; to overcome, to surpass; to be located over, above, or on top of; to position on top of or above. **—sur•mount•a•ble,** *a.*

sur•name, sər′nām, *n.* A name held in common by a family; family name; last name.—sər′nām, sər•nām′, *v.t.* To give a surname to.

sur•pass, sər•pas′, *v.t.* To exceed; to be more than; to outdo: to *surpass* expectation; to excel, as in a profession; to go beyond, as in distance, limit, degree, amount, or the like. **—sur•pass•a•ble,** *a.* **—sur•pass•ing,** *a.* **—sur•pass•ing•ly,** *adv.*

sur•plice, sər′plis, *n.* A white garment worn by priests, deacons, and choristers, as in the Roman Catholic Church, over their other dress at religious services.

sur·plus, sėr′pləs, *n.* That which remains when use or need is satisfied; that which more than suffices.—*a.* —**sur·plus·age,** *n.*

sur·prise, sėr·priz′, *n.* The act of coming upon unawares, or of taking suddenly and without preparation; an emotion excited by something happening suddenly and unexpectedly.—*v.t.,* **-prised, -pris·ing.** To fall upon suddenly and unexpectedly; to attack or take unawares; to strike with wonder or astonishment; to astonish. —**sur·pris·al,** *n.* —**sur·pris·er,** *n.* —**sur·pris·ing,** *a.* —**sur·pris·ing·ly,** *adv.*

sur·re·al·ism, sə·rē′ə·liz·əm, *n.* (*Sometimes cap.*) An early 20th century movement in literature and art based on the expression of nonrational thought, and seeking to suggest what takes place in dreams and in the subconscious mind. —**sur·re·al·ist,** *n., a.* —**sur·re·al·is·tic,** sə·rē·ə·lis′tik, *a.* —**sur·re·al·is·ti·cal·ly,** *adv.*

sur·ren·der, sə·ren′dər, *v.t.* To yield to the power of another or relinquish possession of; to abandon; to give or deliver up upon compulsion or demand: to *surrender* stolen money; to yield to some influence or emotion, said esp. of the self.—*v.i.* To give up or yield to another's supremacy or power.—*n.* A yielding or giving up.

sur·rep·ti·tious, sėr·əp·tish′əs, *a.* Done or acquired by stealth or without proper authority; secretive or clandestine, as actions. —**sur·rep·ti·tious·ly,** *adv.* —**sur·rep·ti·tious·ness,** *n.*

sur·rey, sėr′ē, *n. pl.,* **-reys.** A light, four-wheeled, two-seated carriage with or without a top, seating four persons.

sur·ro·gate, sėr′ə·gāt, sėr′ə·git, *n.* Someone acting in place of another, as a deputy; a substitute; in some states, a judicial officer of probate court. —sėr′ə·gāt, *v.t.,* **-gat·ed, -gat·ing.** To put in the place of another; to appoint as successor or substitute for oneself.

sur·round, sə·rownd′, *v.t.* To encompass or enclose on all sides. —**sur·round·er,** *n.*

sur·round·ing, sə·rown′ding, *n.* An act or movement of encompassing; *usu. pl.,* those things which surround; an environment.—*a.*

sur·tax, sėr′taks, *n.* A heightened or extra tax in addition to the usual levy.—*v.t.* To charge with such a tax.

sur·veil·lance, sėr·vā′ləns, sėr·vāl′yəns, *n.* Watch kept over some person or thing, esp. in the case of spying or guarding. —**sur·veil·lant,** *a., n.*

sur·vey, sėr·vā′, *v.t.* To view with a scrutinizing eye; to determine the boundaries, extent, position, or natural features of, as any portion of the earth's surface, by means of measurements and the application of geometry and trigonometry.—*v.i.* To practice the surveying of land. —sėr′vā, sėr·vā′, *n.* A close examination or inspection to ascertain condition, quantity, or quality; a random sampling of facts and figures; the determination of dimensions and other topographical particulars of any part of the earth's surface; the plan or account drawn up of such particulars. —**sur·vey·ing,** *n.* —**sur·vey·or,** *n.*

sur·viv·al, sėr·vi′vəl, *n.* The act of surviving; a living beyond the life of another person or beyond any event; any habit, usage, or belief remaining from ancient times and existing merely from custom.

sur·vive, sėr·viv′, *v.t.,* **-vived, -viv·ing.** To outlive; to live beyond the life of; to live beyond: to *survive* one's usefulness.—*v.i.* To remain alive; to live after the death of another or after anything else. —**sur·vi·vor,** *n.*

sus·cep·ti·ble, sə·sep′tə·bəl, *a.* Capable of being acted on or affected in any way; capable of emotional impression. —**sus·cep·ti·bil·i·ty,** sə·sep·tə·bil′ə·tē, **sus·cep·ti·ble·ness,** *n.* —**sus·cep·ti·bly,** *adv.*

sus·pect, sə·spekt′, *v.t.* To mistrust; to imagine to be guilty upon slight evidence or without proof; to doubt.—*v.i.* To have suspicions. —sės′pekt, *n.* One suspected, esp. of a crime. —sės·pekt′, sə·spekt′, *a.* Suspected; open to suspicion.

sus·pend, sə·spend′, *v.t.* To hang; to debar for a time from any privilege; to cause to cease for a time from operation or effect; to postpone or defer, as in sentencing.—*v.i.* To cease for a while.

sus·pend·er, sə·spen′dər, *n.* One that suspends. *Usu. pl.* A pair of braces for trousers.

sus·pense, sə·spens′, *n.* A state of uncertainty, with more or less apprehension or anxiety; a sense of insecurity. —**sus·pense·ful,** *a.*

sus·pen·sion, sə·spen′shən, *n.* The act of suspending or hanging up; a delaying, deferment, or temporary cessation; the parts of an automobile or railway car by which the chassis is connected to the axles in such a way as to cushion the movements of the chassis; the state of being in the form of particles floating undissolved in a fluid; a support for something suspended.

sus·pen·sion bridge, *n.* A bridge having its roadway suspended from ropes, chains, or wire cables usu. hung between towers of masonry or steel.

sus·pi·cion, sə·spish′ən, *n.* The act of suspecting; the feeling of one who suspects; condition of being suspected; a very small amount; slight trace.

sus·pi·cious, sės·pish′əs, *a.* Tending to arouse suspicion; showing suspicion: *suspicious* glares. —**sus·pi·cious·ly,** *adv.* —**sus·pi·cious·ness,** *n.*

sus·tain, sə·stān′, *v.t.* To support or bear up, esp. from underneath; to bear up against; to suffer, undergo, or endure without failing or yielding; to nourish or furnish sustenance for; to aid or keep from ruin; to hold valid in law or to establish by evidence; to confirm or corroborate. —**sus·tain·a·ble,** *a.* —**sus·tain·er,** *n.* —**sus·tain·ment,** *n.*

sus·te·nance, sės′tə·nəns, *n.* That which supports life, as food or provisions; subsistence; the act of sustaining; the state of being supported or maintained.

su·ture, soo′chər, *n.* The line along which two things or parts are joined; the uniting of the lips or edges of a wound or incision by stitching; one of the seams uniting the bones of the skull.—*v.t.,* **-tured, -tur·ing.** To join with or as with a suture. —**su·tur·al,** *a.* —**su·tur·al·ly,** *adv.*

su·ze·rain, soo′zə·rin, soo′zə·rān, *n.* Formerly, a feudal lord or baron; a ruler or state which exercises political control over the foreign relations of a locally autonomous vassal state. —**su·ze·rain·ty,** *n.*

svelte, svelt, *a.* Slender, esp. gracefully slender in figure. —**svelte·ly,** *adv.* —**svelte·ness,** *n.*

swab, swäb, *n.* A mop for cleaning floors, ships' decks, and the like; a small bit of cotton or other material attached to a stick used in cleansing or in medicine as an applicator.—*v.t.,* **swabbed, swab·bing.** To clean with a swab or mop. —**swab·ber,** *n.*

swad·dle, swäd′əl, *v.t.,* **-dled, -dling.** To swathe, or wrap with strips of various kinds of cloth, as an infant.—*n.* A cloth band or strip used for the purpose of swaddling.

swad·dling clothes, *n. pl.* Cloth strips or bands wrapped about an infant, esp. a newborn.

swag, swag, *n. Informal.* Booty or plunder.

swag·ger, swag′ər, *v.i.* To strut with a proud, defiant, or insolent air; to boast noisily; to bluster; to brag.—*n.* An arrogant strut. —**swag·ger·er,** *n.* —**swag·ger·ing,** *a.* —**swag·ger·ing·ly,** *adv.*

swain, swān, *n.* A lover; a young man dwelling in the country; a peasant or rustic; a country gallant. —**swain·ish,** *a.* —**swain·ish·ness,** *n.*

swale, swāl, *n.* A low place in the surface of the ground; a slight depression in a tract of land, usu. more moist and often with ranker vegetation than the

---

a- hat, fāte, fâre, fäther; **e-** met, mē; **i-** pin, pīne; **o-** not, nōte, ôrb, moove (move), boy, pownd;
u- cūbe, bůll, tûk (took); **ch-** chin; **th-** thick, ŧhen; **zh-** vizhon (vision); **ə-** ₐgo, takₐn, pencₐl, lemₐn, bėrd (bird).

adjacent higher land.

swal·low, swäl′ō, *n.* Any of certain birds usu. having forked tails and long slim wings, and noted for their swift flight and rigid migratory habits.

swal·low, swäl′ō, *v.t.* To receive, as food or liquid, through the throat into the stomach by muscular contractions in the throat; to draw into or absorb, often followed by *up: The stampede swallowed them up. Informal.* To accept gullibly as true, as a falsehood or deception; to put up with: to *swallow* an affront; to forbear or conceal, as one's wrath; to revoke or withdraw, as something said.—*v.i.* To go through the action of swallowing.—*n.* The action of swallowing; an amount or quantity swallowed in one gulp. —**swal·low·er,** *n.*

swal·low·tail, swäl′ō·tāl, *n.* A swallow's tail or something resembling it; a type of man's formal dress coat: also **swal·low-tailed coat.**

swam, swam, *v.* Past tense of **swim.**

swa·mi, swa·my, swä′mē, *n. pl.,* -**mis.** A Hindu religious teacher; a Hindu title of great respect; a pundit.

swamp, swämp, *n.* A piece of spongy land, or low ground saturated with water; a bog, fen, marsh, or morass. Also **swamp·land,** swämp′land.—*v.t.* To plunge or sink in a swamp, or as in a swamp; to plunge into inextricable difficulties; to overwhelm; to sink or cause to become filled, as a boat, with water.—*v.i.* To sink or become submerged; to be overwhelmed. —**swamp·y,** *a.,* -**i·er,** -**i·est.** —**swamp·i·ness,** *n.*

swan, swän, *n.* A long-necked, webfooted bird similar to but larger than the goose, and noted for its grace and its usu. snowy white plumage.

swank, swangk, *v.i.* To swagger; show off.—*n. Informal.* Swagger; ostentatious behavior; dashing smartness.—*a. Informal.* Ostentatious; fashionable. —**swank·i·ly,** *adv.* —**swank·i·ness,** *n.* —**swank·y,** *a.,* -**i·er,** -**i·est.**

swan's-down, swans·down, swänz′down, *n.* The down or under feathers of the swan; a fine, soft, thick woolen cloth; a thick cotton with a soft nap on one side.

swan song, *n.* The final work, as of a composer or poet, based upon the ancient belief that a swan sings a song just before death.

swap, swop, *n., v.t.,* **swapped, swap·ping.** *Informal.* Barter; exchange; trade.

sward, swôrd, *n.* The grassy surface of land; turf; greensward.—*v.t.* To cover, as the ground, with sward.

swarm, swôrm, *n.* A body of honeybees which emigrate from a hive and fly off together, with a queen, to start a new colony; a body of bees settled together, as in a hive; a great number of things or persons, esp. in motion.—*v.i.* To fly off together in a body from a hive to start a new colony, as bees; to move about, along, or forth in great numbers, as things or persons; to congregate or occur in masses or multitudes; be exceedingly numerous; abound or teem, followed by *with.*—*v.t.* To swarm about, over, or in; to throng; overrun.

swarth·y, swôr′thē, swôr′thē, *a.,* -**i·er,** -**i·est.** Being of a dark hue or dusky complexion; dark-colored. —**swarth·i·ness,** *n.*

swash, swäsh, swôsh, *v.i.* To splash water; to dash or strike; to swagger.—*v.t.* To dash or strike with extreme force.—*n.* A dashing blow or the sound it makes.

swash·buck·ler, swäsh′bek·ler, swôsh′bek·ler, *n.* A swaggering fellow. —**swash·buck·ling,** *a.*

swas·ti·ka, swäs′ti·ka, *n.* A figure consisting of a cross with arms of equal length, each arm having a continuation at right angles, and all four continuations turning the same way; the Nazi party's official emblem.

swat, swät, *v.t.,* **swat·ted, swat·ting.** To hit with a smart or violent blow.—*n.* A smart or violent blow. —**swat·ter,** *n.*

swatch, swäch, *n.* A sample of cloth or other material.

swath, swäth, swôth, *n.* The space covered by the stroke of a scythe or the cut of a mowing machine; a long and relatively narrow extent of anything. Also **swathe.** —**cut a swath,** to make a pretentious display.

swathe, swäth, *v.t.,* **swathed, swath·ing.** To bind or wrap with a band or bandage.—*n.* A bandage, band, or wrapping.

sway, swä, *v.i.* To swing backward and forward; to incline or hang; to have the judgment or feelings inclining one way; to govern.—*v.t.* To move backward and forward; to bias; to rule.—*n.* Power exerted in governing; rule; influence. —**sway·a·ble,** *a.* —**sway·er,** *n.*

sway·back, swä′bak, *n.* An unnatural downward curving or sagging of the back, esp. of a horse. —**sway-backed,** *a.* Also **sway-back.**

swear, swār, *v.i.,* **swore, sworn, swear·ing.** To utter a solemn declaration, with an appeal to God for the truth of what is affirmed; to promise upon oath; to give evidence on oath; to use profane language.—*v.t.* To utter on oath; to promise solemnly; to vow; to utter in a profane manner. —**swear by,** to name someone as one's witness, as a god; to have faith or confidence in. —**swear in,** to induct into service or office by administering an oath. —**swear off,** to renounce or abstain from, as liquor. —**swear out,** to obtain, as a warrant for arrest, by making a charge or accusation under oath. —**swear·er,** *n.*

swear·word, swār′werd, *n.* A profane word or oath used in swearing.

sweat, swet, *v.i.,* **sweat** or **sweat·ed, sweat·ing.** To excrete watery fluid through the pores of the skin; to perspire, esp. profusely; to exude moisture; to gather moisture on the surface due to condensation; of liquids, to ooze out or be exuded like sweat; to ferment. *Informal.* To toil; to feel anxiety, impatience, or vexation; to suffer punishment.—*v.t.* To emit, as moisture, through the pores of the skin; to exude in drops or small particles; to send forth or get rid of like or with sweat, often with *off* or *out;* to wet or stain with sweat; to cause to sweat. *Informal.* To cause to work hard, esp. at low wages under unfavorable conditions; to extort money from; to subject to severe questioning or brutal treatment, in order to extract information. —*n.* The moisture excreted through the pores of the skin; perspiration; moisture exuded from something or collected on a surface due to condensation; a period or condition of sweating; a state of perturbation, anxiety, or impatience. —**no sweat.** *Informal.* Causing no difficulty; easily handled. —**sweat blood.** *Informal.* To be in a state of acute anxiety; to exert oneself to the utmost, esp. mentally. —**sweat out.** *Informal.* To endure something through to the end; wait helplessly. —**sweat·i·ly,** *adv.* —**sweat·i·ness,** *n.* —**sweat·less,** *a.* —**sweat·y,** *a.,* -**i·er,** -**i·est.**

sweat·er, swet′er, *n.* A knitted or crocheted blouse-like garment usu. for informal wear.

sweat gland, *n.* One of the minute glands of the skin that secrete sweat.

sweat shirt, *n.* A loose fitting, usu. collarless, heavy cotton jersey pullover, often worn by athletes when exercising.

sweat·shop, swet′shop, *n.* A usu. small factory or shop in which the workers are subjected to adverse conditions as to hours, wages, and environment.

sweep, swēp, *v.t.,* **swept, sweep·ing.** To clear or clean, as a floor, of dirt or litter by or as by means of a broom; to make, as a path, by clearing a space; to clear, as a surface, of something on or in it; to brush or rub against: garments that *sweep* the ground; to pass over with a steady, driving movement or with an unimpeded course, as winds.—*v.i.* To sweep an area with a broom, or as a broom does; to move steadily and strongly or swiftly; to move, pass, or extend in a continuous or curving stretch.—*n.* A moving, removing, or clearing by or as by a broom: to make a clean *sweep* of incompetence; the steady driving motion or swift onward course of something: the *sweep* of the wind or waves; the range or compass, as of something sweeping about; a continuous extent or stretch, as of road, shore, etc.; a curving, esp. a curving, line, form, part, or mass; one who sweeps, esp. a chimney sweeper; a leverlike device for raising or lowering a bucket in a well; a large oar used in small vessels; a winning of all the games in a series, match, etc.; complete victory. *Pl. Informal.* Sweepstakes. **—sweep•er,** *n.*

sweep•ing, swē′ping, *a.* Including a large number in a single act or assertion: a *sweeping* accusation; comprehensive.**—n. pl.** Things collected by sweeping; rubbish. **—sweep•ing•ly,** *adv.* **—sweep•ing•ness,** *n.*

sweep•stakes, swēp′stāks, *n. pl. but sing. in constr.* Any gaming transaction, as a lottery or horserace, in which a number of persons contribute a certain stake or entry fee, the total amount becoming the property of one or several of the contributors under certain conditions. Also **sweep•stake.**

sweet, swēt, *a.* Having a pleasant taste or flavor like that of sugar or honey; pleasing to the nose, ear, eye or mind; gentle; kind; obliging; not salt or salted; not stale; fresh: *sweet* milk.**—n.** That which is sweet; a sweet food or drink; a pleasure; a sweetheart; *pl.,* candy or other sweetmeat.**—adv. —sweet on.** *Informal.* Extremely fond of, or in love with. **—sweet•ish,** *a.* **—sweet•ly,** *adv.* **—sweet•ness,** *n.*

sweet•bread, swēt′bred, *n.* The pancreas or thymus of an animal used as food.

sweet•bri•er, sweet•bri•ar, swēt′brī•ər, *n.* A native European species of wild rose having hooked, bristly prickles, pink flowers which are single, and fragrant leaves.

sweet corn, *n.* A variation of corn which has translucent kernels and a sweet taste.

sweet•en, swēt′ən, *v.t.* To make sweet to the taste; to make pleasing to the mind or senses; to increase the agreeable qualities of.**—v.i.** To become sweet. **—sweet•en•er, sweet•en•ing,** *n.*

sweet•heart, swēt′härt, *n.* A lover, either male or female; one who is a beloved person.

sweet•meat, swēt′mēt, *n. Often pl.* A delicate confection, candy, or preserve.

sweet pea, *n.* An annual climbing plant, popular for its various-colored, sweet-scented flowers.

sweet potato, *n.* A tropical plant of the morning glory family, largely cultivated for its edible tuberous roots; the root, eaten as a vegetable.

sweet-talk, swēt′tôk, *v.i. Informal.* To use words that are cajoling or flattering.**—v.t.** *Informal.* To cajole; to coax.

sweet tooth, *n. Informal.* A great liking for sweet things or sweetmeats.

sweet wil•liam, wil′yəm, *n.* A flower of the pink family, bearing small flowers of various colors in dense clusters. Also **sweet Wil•liam.**

swell, swel, *v.i.,* **swelled, swelled** or **swoll•en, swell•ing.** To increase in size or extent; to bulge out, as sails; to be puffed up with some feeling; to increase in intensity or volume, as sound.**—v.t.** To increase the size of; to inflate.**—n.** The act of swelling; gradual increase; a succession of long unbroken waves setting in one direction, as after a storm; a surge; a crescendo and diminuendo in musical sound.**—a.** *Informal.* Excellent or wonderful.

swelled head, *n. Informal.* A conceited attitude about oneself.

swell•head, swel′hed, *n. Informal.* A person who is vain or conceited.

swell•ing, swel′ing, *n.* That which is swollen; a protuberance or enlargement.

swel•ter, swel′tər, *v.i.* To be overcome and faint with heat.**—n.** A condition of intense heat. **—swel•ter•ing,** *a.* **—swel•ter•ing•ly,** *adv.*

swept, swept, *v.* Past tense and past participle of **sweep.**

swerve, swərv, *v.i.,* **swerved, swerv•ing.** To wander from any line prescribed, as a fast-moving car; to turn aside from a rule or duty; to deviate; to turn to one side.**—v.t.** To cause to swerve.**—n.** A swerving.

swift, swift, *a.* Moving with great speed or rapidity; coming suddenly or without delay.**—n.** Any of several small, plain, long-winged, rapid-flying birds resembling the swallow. **—swift•ly,** *adv.* **—swift•ness,** *n.*

swig, swig, *n. Informal.* A large draft, esp. of an alcoholic drink.**—v.t., v.i.,** **swigged, swig•ging.** *Informal.* To drink rapidly, greedily, or in large drafts. **—swig•ger,** *n.*

swill, swil, *n.* Liquid or partly liquid food for animals, esp. kitchen refuse given to swine; kitchen refuse in general.**—v.i.** To drink greedily or excessively.**—v.t.** To guzzle or drink greedily or to excess. **—swill•er,** *n.*

swim, swim, *v.i.,* **swam, swum, swim•ming.** To move through water by the motion of the hands, feet, or fins; to be supported on water or other fluid; to float; to glide with a smooth motion; to overflow; to be dizzy or giddy; to seem to float or whirl.**—v.t.** To pass or cross, as water, by swimming; to cause to swim or float.**—n.** The act of swimming; a dizziness or giddiness. **—in the swim.** *Informal.* In the main stream or current of society, activity, or the like. **—swim•mer,** *n.*

swim•ming•ly, swim′ing•lē, *adv.* Very easily or successfully.

swin•dle, swin′dəl, *v.t.,* **-dled, -dling.** To cheat and defraud or with deliberate artifice.**—v.i.** To practice deception in order to acquire illegally the assets of another.**—n.** A fraudulent scheme intended to dupe people out of money or property. **—swin•dler,** *n.*

swine, swin, *n. pl.,* **swine.** The domesticated hog or pig; a coarse, greedy, or brutish person. **—swin•ish,** *a.*

swing, swing, *v.t.,* **swung, swing•ing.** To cause to move to and fro, sway, or oscillate, as something suspended from above; to cause to move in alternate directions about a fixed point or line of support, as a door on its hinges; to move, as the fist or something held, with a sweeping or rotational movement. *Informal.* To sway or influence as desired: to *swing* a district in an election; bring off: to *swing* a business deal.**—v.i.** To move to and fro or from side to side, as a pendulum; to ride in a swing; to move in alternate directions about a point or line of support, as a gate on its hinges; to move with a free, swaying motion, as soldiers on the march.**—n.** The act or manner of swinging; the swinging, or a swinging movement, of something held; a curving movement or course; a moving of the body or a part of the body with a free, swaying motion, as in walking; a steady marked rhythm, as of verse or music; insistently rhythmic jazz music, often played by dance bands and marked by free improvisation; freedom of action; something that swings, esp. a seat suspended from above.**—a.** Pertaining to a swing, or to swing music. **—in full swing,** fully in progress. **—swing•a•ble,** *a.* **—swing•ing,** *a.* **—swing•er,** *n.*

swing shift, *n.* An evening work shift, usu. from 4 p.m. until midnight.

swipe, swip, *v.t., v.i.,* **swiped, swip•ing.** To strike with a sweeping blow. *Informal.* To steal.**—n.** A strong, sweeping, or glancing blow.

swirl, swərl, *v.i.* To whirl in eddies.**—v.t.** To cause to twist or curve.**—n.** A whirling motion; an eddy, as of water; a twist or curl, as in a grain of wood. **—swirl•ing•ly,** *adv.* **—swirl•y,** *a.,* **-i•er, -i•est.**

swish, swish, *v.i.* To move with or make a sibilant sound, as a slender rod or a bullet cutting sharply through the air; to rustle, as silk.**—v.t.** To cause to swish.**—n.** A swishing movement or sound.**—a.** Making a swishing sound. **—swish•er,** *n.* **—swish•ing•ly,**

---

a- hat, fāte, fāre, fäther; **e-** met, mē; **i-** pin, pīne; **o-** not, nōte, ôrb, moove (move), boy, pownd; **u-** cūbe, bûll, tûk (took); **ch-** chin; **th-** thick, then; **zh-** vizhon (vision); **ə-** əgo, takən, pencəl, lemən, bərd (bird).

adv. **—swish•y,** swish/ē, *a.,* **-i•er, -i•est.**

switch, swich, *n.* A small flexible twig or rod, esp. one used for whipping; an instance of whipping or lashing with a switch; a sudden shift or changing: a *switch* of opinion; a device for connecting or breaking an electric circuit or changing direction of current; a device for moving a short section of rail and turning a railroad train from one set of tracks to another.—*v.t.* To strike with a switch; to change over or shift, as votes, support, conversation, or the like; to turn on or off or into a new electrical circuit by means of a switch; to transfer or shunt, as a train, from one line of tracks to another.—*v.i.* To shift or divert; to be turned or diverted. **—switch•er,** *n.*

switch•blade knife, swich/blād, *n.* A pocketknife with a blade which snaps open and locks when a button is pressed.

switch•board, swich/bôrd, *n.* An apparatus consisting of a frame or panel on which are mounted switches for making electric circuit connections, as for a series of lights in a building or for telephone wires in an exchange.

switch-hit•ter, swich/hit/ər, *n.* A baseball player who is able to bat from either side of the plate. *Informal.* A person who can do something well in more than one way.

swiv•el, swiv/əl, *n.* A fastening device which allows the thing fastened to turn around freely.—*v.t., v.i.,* **-eled, -el•ing.** To turn on or as on a swivel.

swiv•el chair, *n.* A chair whose seat rotates horizontally on a swivel base.

swiz•zle stick, swiz/əl, *n.* A small slender rod or stick, usu. made of glass or plastic, and used for mixing or stirring drinks.

swoon, swoon, *v.i.* To faint.—*n.* A fainting fit. **—swoon•er,** *n.* **—swoon•ing•ly,** *adv.*

swoop, swoop, *v.i.* To descend upon prey from above; to descend upon suddenly.—*v.t.* To snatch; seize.—*n.* A falling on and seizing in the manner of a bird of prey. **—swoop•er,** *n.*

swop, swop, *v.t., v.i.,* **swopped, swop•ping.** Swap.—*n.*

sword, sôrd, sōrd, *n.* A weapon having various forms but consisting typically of a long, straight, or slightly curved blade, sharp-edged on one side or both sides, with one end pointed and the other fixed in a hilt or handle. **—at swords' points,** in the position or relation of active enemies. **—sword•like,** *a.*

sword•fish, sôrd/fish, sōrd/fish, *n. pl.,* **-fish, -fish•es.** A large marine food fish having the upper jaw elongated into a swordlike process.

sword•play, sôrd/plā, sōrd/plā, *n.* The action or skill involved in handling a sword, esp. that of fencers in a match. **—sword•play•er,** *n.*

swords•man, sôrdz/mən, sōrdz/mən, *n. pl.,* **-men.** A man armed with or skilled in the use of the sword, as one who fences with sabers. Also **sword•man.** **—swords•man•ship,** *n.*

swore, swôr, swōr, *v.* Past tense of **swear.**

sworn, swôrn, swōrn, *v.* Past participle of **swear.**

swum, swəm, *v.* Past participle of **swim.**

swung, swəng, *v.* Past tense and past participle of **swing.**

syc•a•more, sik/ə•môr, *n.* The plane tree or buttonwood; the sycamore maple, a common shade tree of Europe and Asia, with ornate yellow flowers.

syc•o•phant, sik/ə•fənt, *n.* A fawning, self-seeking flatterer; a servile parasite. **—syc•o•phan•cy,** *n.* **—syc•o•phan•tic,** sik•ə•fan/tik, **syc•o•phan•ti•cal,** *a.* **—syc•o•phan•ti•cal•ly,** *adv.*

syl•lab•ic, si•lab/ik, *a.* Pertaining to, consisting of, or representing a syllable; pronounced syllable by syllable; forming a separate syllable, as the *l* sound in *bottle.*

syl•lab•i•cate, si•lab/ə•kāt, *v.t.,* **-cat•ed, -cat•ing.** To form into syllables; syllabify. **—syl•lab•i•ca•tion,** si•lab•ə•kā/shən, *n.*

syl•lab•i•fy, si•lab/ə•fī, *v.t.,* **-fied, -fy•ing.** To form

into syllables. **—syl•lab•i•fi•ca•tion,** si•lab•ə•fə•kā/shən, *n.*

syl•la•ble, sil/ə•bəl, *n.* A sound or combination of sounds uttered together or at a single impulse of the voice, and constituting a word or part of a word; the closest representation in phonetics for such an utterance.—*v.t.,* **-bled, -bling.** To utter distinctly; to articulate; to pronounce in syllables.—*v.i.* To utter syllables.

syl•la•bus, sil/ə•bəs, *n. pl.,* **-bus•es, -bi,** -bī. A brief summary or outlined statement of the principal points of a discourse, legal brief, or course of lectures.

syl•lo•gism, sil/ə•jiz•əm, *n.* A form of reasoning or argument, consisting of a *major premise,* a *minor premise,* and a *conclusion* drawn from them, as: All insects have six legs; a bee is an insect; therefore, a bee has six legs. **—syl•lo•gis•tic,** sil•ə•jis/tik, *a.*

sylph, silf, *n.* An elemental spirit of the air; a woman of graceful and slender proportions. **—sylph•like,** *a.*

syl•van, sil•van, sil/vən, *a.* Of, pertaining to, or inhabiting the woods; wooded.

sym•bi•o•sis, sim•bī•ō/sis, sim•bē•ō/sis, *n.* The state of two dissimilar organisms living in close relationship, each benefiting from such an association, as the algae and fungi in lichens. **—sym•bi•ot•ic,** sim•bī•ot/ik, sim•bē•ot/ik, *a.* **—sym•bi•ot•i•cal•ly,** *adv.*

sym•bol, sim/bəl, *n.* Something standing for or calling up something else, esp. a concrete object which stands for an intangible object or idea; a character, letter, or cipher which by convention or arbitrary usage has come to represent something else, as the name of a chemical element.—*v.t.* Symbolize. **—sym•bol•ic,** sim•bol/ik, **sym•bol•i•cal,** *a.*

sym•bol•ism, sim/bə•liz•əm, *n.* The practice of representing things by symbols, or of investing things with a symbolic meaning or character; a set or system of symbols; symbolic meaning or character. **—sym•bol•ist,** *n.*

sym•bol•ize, sim/bə•līz, *v.t.,* **-ized, -iz•ing.** To serve as a symbol of; to represent by a symbol or symbols. —*v.i.* To express or represent in symbols. **—sym•bol•i•za•tion,** sim•bəl•ə•zā/shən, *n.* **—sym•bol•iz•er,** *n.*

sym•me•try, sim/i•trē, *n. pl.,* **-tries.** The correspondence in size, form, and arrangement of parts on opposite sides of a plane, line, or point, each part on one side having its counterpart on the other side; excellence of proportion. **—sym•met•ric,** si•met/rik, **sym•met•ri•cal,** *a.*

sym•pa•thet•ic, sim•pə•thet/ik, *a.* Expressive of, produced by, or exhibiting sympathy; having sympathy or common feeling with another. **—sym•pa•thet•i•cal•ly,** *adv.*

sym•pa•thize, sim/pə•thīz, *v.i.,* **-thized, -thiz•ing.** To be in sympathy or agreement of feeling, as one person with another; to express sympathy or condole, usu. followed by *with;* to be in approving accord, as with a person, party, cause, or policy. **—sym•pa•thiz•er,** *n.* **—sym•pa•thiz•ing•ly,** *adv.*

sym•pa•thy, sim/pə•thē, *n. pl.,* **-thies.** Feeling corresponding to that which another feels; a feeling that enables a person to enter into and in part share another's feelings; fellow feeling; compassion; commiseration.

sym•pho•ny, sim/fə•nē, *n. pl.,* **-nies.** An elaborate composition for a full orchestra, consisting usu. of three or four contrasted but intimately related movements; a concert by a symphony orchestra; a consonance or harmony of sounds; any harmonious blending or agreeable combination. **—sym•phon•ic,** sim•fon/ik, *a.*

sym•po•si•um, sim•pō/zē•əm, *n. pl.,* **-si•a,** -zē•ə, **-si•ums.** A meeting or conference for discussion of some subject; a collection of opinions expressed, or a series of articles contributed, by several persons on a given subject or topic.

symp•tom, simp/təm, *n.* Any circumstance or condition which serves as evidence of something not seen; a circumstance or condition which results from or accompanies a disease, and by which the existence and the nature of a disease may be diagnosed.

symp·to·mat·ic, simp·tə·mat′ik, *a.* Pertaining to a symptom or symptoms; indicative (*of*): *symptomatic* of cancer; according to symptoms: a *symptomatic* diagnosis of disease. Also **symp·to·mat·i·cal.** —**symp·to·mat·i·cal·ly,** *adv.*

syn·a·gogue, syn·a·gog, sin′ə·gog, sin′ə·gôg, *n.* A congregation of Jews assembled for the purpose of worship; a Jewish place of worship. —**syn·a·gog·al, syn·a·gog·i·cal,** sin′ə·gog·əl, sin·ə·goj′i·kəl, *a.*

syn·apse, sin′aps, si·naps′, *n.* The area in which contact takes place and where a neuron transmits nerve impulses to another neuron.

sync, singk, *n.* Synchronism; synchronization.—*a.* —*v.i., v.t.,* **synced, sync·ing.** Synchronize.

syn·chro·nism, sing′krə·niz·əm, *n.* Concurrence of two or more events or facts in time; simultaneousness; arrangement of contemporaneous events or persons in tabular form. —**syn·chro·nis·tic,** sing·krə·nis′tik, **syn·chro·nis·ti·cal,** *a.* —**syn·chro·nis·ti·cal·ly,** *adv.*

syn·chro·nize, sing′krə·nīz, *v.i.,* **-nized, -niz·ing.** To concur or agree in time; to proceed or operate at exactly the same rate.—*v.t.* To make to agree in time; to cause to proceed or operate at exactly the same rate. —**syn·chro·ni·za·tion,** sing·krə·ni·zā′shən, *n.* —**syn·chro·niz·er,** *n.*

syn·chro·nous, sing′krə·nəs, *a.* Happening at the same time or rate; simultaneous. Also **syn·chro·nal.** —**syn·chro·nous·ly,** *adv.* —**syn·chro·nous·ness,** *n.*

syn·co·pate, sing′kə·pāt, sin′kə·pāt, *v.t.,* **-pat·ed, -pat·ing.** To modify, as a piece of music, by displacing normal accents to create rhythmic contradiction; to contract, as a word, by taking one or more letters or syllables from the middle, as in reducing *Gloucester* to *Gloster.* —**syn·co·pa·tion,** sing·kə·pā′shən, *n.* —**syn·co·pa·tor,** *n.*

syn·di·cate, sin′də·kit, *n.* A combination of bankers or capitalists formed for the purpose of carrying out some project requiring large resources of capital; any combination of persons, companies, or the like resembling this, esp. an association of publishers of newspapers or other periodicals in different places, for purchasing articles or stories and publishing them simultaneously. *Informal.* An association of criminals in organized crime. —sin′də·kāt, *v.t.,* **-cat·ed, -cat·ing.** To combine into a syndicate; to manage through a syndicate; to publish simultaneously in a number of periodicals in different places. —**syn·di·ca·tion,** sin·də·kā′shən, *n.* —**syn·di·ca·tor,** *n.*

syn·drome, sin′drōm, *n.* The combination of symptoms characteristic of a disease. *Informal.* The set of circumstances characteristic of a certain social condition. —**syn·drom·ic,** sin·drom′ik, *a.*

syn·od, sin′əd, *n.* An assembly of ecclesiastics or other church delegates for the discussion and decision of ecclesiastical affairs; an assembly, convention, or council of any kind. —**syn·od·al,** *a.*

syn·o·nym, sin′ə·nim, *n.* A word that has the same meaning, or the same general meaning, as a particular word in the same language. —**syn·o·nym·ic,** sin·ə·nim′ik, **syn·o·nym·i·cal,** *a.* —**syn·o·nym·i·ty,** sin·ə·nim′i·tē, *n.*

syn·on·y·mous, si·non′ə·məs, *a.* Having the same meaning, as words; equivalent in meaning. —**syn·on·y·mous·ly,** *adv.*

syn·on·y·my, si·non′ə·mē, *n. pl.,* **-mies.** The character of being synonymous; equivalence in meaning; the use or coupling of synonyms in discourse; the study of synonyms; a set, list, or system of synonyms.

syn·op·sis, si·nop′sis, *n. pl.,* **-ses,** -sēz. A brief or condensed statement giving a general view of some

subject, as a novel, play, or movie; a summary. —**syn·op·tic,** sin·op′tik, **syn·op·ti·cal,** *a.*

syn·tac·tic, sin·tak′tik, *a.* Of or pertaining to syntax; in accordance with the rules of syntax. Also **syn·tac·ti·cal.** —**syn·tac·ti·cal·ly,** *adv.*

syn·tax, sin′taks, *n.* The structure of sentences; the established rules of usage for arrangement of the words of sentences into their proper forms and relations.

syn·the·sis, sin′thə·sis, *n. pl.,* **-ses,** -sēz. The combination of parts or elements, as material substances or objects of thought, into a complex whole: opposed to *analysis;* a complex whole made up of parts or elements combined; the forming or building up of a complex substance or compound by the union of elements or the combination of simpler compounds or radicals. —**syn·the·sist,** *n.*

syn·the·size, sin′thə·sīz, *v.t.,* **-sized, -siz·ing.** To combine into a complex whole; treat synthetically; to make up by combining parts or elements.

syn·thet·ic, sin·thet′ik, *a.* Of, pertaining to, proceeding by, or involving synthesis; noting or pertaining to compounds produced artificially by chemical reaction in a laboratory as opposed to those of natural origin; not authentic or genuine; man-made.—*n.* Any product of synthesis. —**syn·thet·i·cal,** *a.* —**syn·thet·i·cal·ly,** *adv.*

syph·i·lis, sif′ə·lis, *n.* A chronic, infectious venereal disease. —**syph·i·lit·ic,** sif·ə·lit′ik, *a., n.*

sy·ringe, sə·rinj′, sēr′inj, *n.* A small, portable device for drawing in a quantity of a fluid and ejecting it in a stream, used for cleansing wounds or injecting fluids into the body, and commonly consisting of a tube, narrowed at its outlet, fitted with a piston or a rubber bulb.—*v.t.,* **-ringed, -ring·ing.** To cleanse, wash, or inject by means of a syringe.

syr·up, sir·up, sēr′əp, sər′əp, *n.* Any of various sweet, usu. viscous liquids; a preparation of water or fruit juice boiled down with sugar. —**syr·up·y, sir·up·y,** *a.* **-i·er, -i·est.**

sys·tem, sis′təm, *n.* A combination of things or parts forming a whole; an ordered and comprehensive assemblage of facts, phenomena, or doctrines in a particular field of knowledge: the solar *system,* a *system* of philosophy; a coordinated body of methods, or a complex scheme or plan of procedure: a *system* of government or taxation, a *system* of numbering; government, business, politics, or society in general: He rebelled against the *system;* due method, or orderly manner of arrangement or procedure: work that shows *system;* an assemblage of parts or organs of the same or similar tissues, or concerned with the same function: the nervous *system;* the body as a whole: to expel poison from the *system.*

sys·tem·at·ic, sis·tə·mat′ik, *a.* Having or involving a system, method, or plan; characterized by system or method; methodical; arranged in or comprising an ordered system; pertaining to or in accordance with a system of classification. Also **sys·tem·at·i·cal.** —**sys·tem·at·i·cal·ly,** *adv.* —**sys·tem·at·ic·ness,** *n.*

sys·tem·a·tize, sis′tə·mə·tīz, *v.t.,* **-tized, -tiz·ing.** To arrange in or according to a system; to make systematic. Also **sys·tem·ize,** sis′tə·mīz. **-ized, -iz·ing.** —**sys·tem·a·ti·za·tion,** sis·tə·mə·tə·zā′shən, *n.* —**sys·tem·a·tiz·er,** *n.*

sys·tem·ic, si·stem′ik, *a.* Pertaining to or affecting a bodily system or the body as a whole: a *systemic* disease. —**sys·tem·i·cal·ly,** *adv.*

sys·to·le, sis′tə·lē, *n.* The regularly repeated contraction of the heart that forces the blood through the circulatory system: opposed to *diastole.* —**sys·tol·ic,** si·stol′ik, *a.*

---

a- hat, fãte, fãre, fäther; **e-** met, mē; **i-** pin, pine; **o-** not, nōte, ôrb, moove (move), boy, pownd; **u-** cūbe, bûll, tûk (took); **ch-** chin; **th-** thick, then; **zh-** vizhon (vision); **ə-** əgo, takən, pencəl, lemən, bərd (bird).

T

T, t, tē, *n.* The twentieth letter of the English alphabet. —**to a T,** to perfection; exactly.

't, t. A contracted form of the pronoun 'it,' usu. used before a verb, as: '*t*is, '*t*will, '*t*was.

tab, tab, *n.* A small flap, strap, loop, or similar appendage, as on a garment; a tag or label; a small piece projecting from a card or folder to aid in filing.—*v.t.,* **tabbed, tab·bing.** To furnish or ornament with a tab or tabs; to single out or name. —**keep tab** or **tabs on.** *Informal.* To keep track of; watch carefully.

tab·by, tab′ē, *n. pl.,* **-bies.** A cat with a striped or brindled coat; a domestic cat, esp. female.—*a.* Made of or resembling tabby; striped or brindled.

tab·er·nac·le, tab′ər·nak·əl, *n.* A tent used by the Israelites as a portable sanctuary in the wilderness during the Exodus; any place or house of worship, esp. one designed for a large audience; a canopied niche or recess, as for an image or statue; formerly, the human body as the temporary abode of the soul. —**tab·er·nac·u·lar,** tab·ər·nak′yə·lər, *a.*

ta·ble, tā′bəl, *n.* An article of furniture consisting of a flat top resting on legs or on a pillar, on which to serve meals, play games, perform work, or set ornaments; the board at or around which persons sit at meals; the food placed on a table to be eaten; a company of persons at a table, as for a meal, game, or business transaction; a flat or plane surface; an arrangement of words, numbers, signs, etc., exhibiting a set of facts or relations, often in parallel columns; a list of items or particulars; a synopsis or scheme.—*v.t.,* **-bled, -bling.** To place, as money or a card, upon a table; to postpone, as a proposal or resolution, for discussion at some future, frequently unspecified time. —**turn the tables,** to bring about a complete reversal of circumstances or relations between two persons or parties.

tab·leau, tab′lō, ta·blō′, *n. pl.,* **-leaux,** -lōz, **-leaus.** A striking representation; a picture; a picturelike representation of a scene by performers, often in costume, striking appropriate poses and remaining motionless. Also **ta·bleau vi·vant,** vē·vän′.

ta·ble·cloth, tā′bəl·klôth, tā′bəl·kloth, *n.* A cloth for covering a table.

ta·ble d'hôte, tä′bəl·dōt′, tab′əl·dōt′, *n.* A meal of prearranged courses served at a fixed price for guests at a hotel or restaurant.

ta·ble·land, tā′bəl·land, *n.* A plateau.

ta·ble·spoon, tā′bəl·spoon, *n.* A spoon larger than a teaspoon or a dessertspoon, used in serving food; a standard unit of measurement in cooking, equivalent to three teaspoons, or 1/2 fluid ounce. —**ta·ble·spoon·ful,** *n. pl.,* **-fuls.**

tab·let, tab′lit, *n.* A pad of sheets of paper, as for notes or letters; a thin, flat piece or sheet, as of wood, ivory, or slate, used for writing or drawing; a small disk or lozenge of medicine, as of aspirin.

table tennis, *n.* A game very similar to tennis, played by two or teams of two players on a rectangular table using wood paddles and a small plastic ball. Also **Ping-Pong.**

ta·ble·ware, tā′bəl·wer, *n.* Dishes and utensils used at the table or at meals.

tab·loid, tab′loyd, *n.* A newspaper with pages half the standard size, containing condensed stories and articles and numerous pictures.—*a.* Compressed; condensed; in small form.

ta·boo, ta·bu, tə·boo′, ta·boo′, *a.* Forbidden, as by social usage; interdicted.—*n.* Among the Polynesians and related races, the system whereby things are set apart as sacred or placed under interdiction; a prohibition or interdiction of something; exclusion from use or practice.—*v.t.,* **-booed, -boo·ing; -bued, -bu·ing.** To put under a taboo; to prohibit or forbid.

ta·bor, ta·bour, tā′bər, *n.* A small kind of drum, used esp. by a pipe or fife player to accompany himself.

tab·u·lar, tab′yə·lər, *a.* Pertaining to or of the nature of a table or tabulated arrangement; ascertained from or computed by the use of tables; having the form of a table, tablet, or tablature. —**ta·bu·lar·ly,** *adv.*

tab·u·late, tab′yə·lāt, *v.t.,* **-lat·ed, -lat·ing.** To put or form into a table, scheme, list, or synopsis. —**tab·u·la·tion,** tab·yə·lā′shən, *n.* —**tab·u·la·tor,** *n.*

ta·chom·e·ter, ta·kom′i·tər, tə·kom′i·tər, *n.* An instrument for measuring velocity; a device for indicating the revolutions per minute of an engine, esp. an automobile engine.

tac·it, tas′it, *a.* Silent; unspoken; implied but not expressed in words. —**tac·it·ly,** *adv.* —**tac·it·ness,** *n.*

tac·i·turn, tas′i·tərn, *a.* Speaking little or infrequently; habitually silent. —**tac·i·tur·ni·ty,** tas·i·tər′ni·tē, *n.*

tack, tak, *n.* A stubby, usu. tapered, sharp-pointed nail having a broad head; a loosely sewed stitch; a procedure or course of action; the heading of a sailing ship in reference to the position or trim of the sails; a shift in direction; a back and forth or zigzag course.—*v.t.,* **tacked, tack·ing.** To fasten; to attach, as with tacks; to add on as a supplement or addition.—*v.i.* To alter a ship's course by tacking; to change abruptly one's ideas, conduct, or attitude; shift; veer. —**tack·er,** *n.*

tack·le, tak′əl, *n.* Apparatus, appliances, or equipment for various kinds of work or sport; gear, as football suits; an arrangement of one or more pulleys with rope or cable in a block, used for hoisting and lowering large, heavy weights; the act of grabbing and bringing to the ground, as in football; a football player usu. positioned between a guard and an end.—*v.t.,* **-led, -ling.** To take upon, as something difficult; to try to do, master, or resolve: He *tackled* the problem vigorously; in football, to throw to the ground, as an opposing ball carrier.—*v.i.* In football, to tackle the opposing ball carrier. —**tack·ler,** *n.* —**tack·ling,** *n.*

tack·y, tak′ē, *a.,* **-i·er, -i·est.** Adhesive; sticky. *Informal.* Shabby or dowdy. —**tack·i·ness,** *n.*

ta·co, tä′kō, *n. pl.,* **-cos.** A food of Mexican-Spanish origin, made by folding a fried tortilla over a spiced filling.

tact, takt, *n.* Skill or adroitness in doing or saying exactly what is required; a highly developed perception of what is tasteful, proper, or aesthetically pleasing. —**tact·ful,** *a.* —**tact·ful·ly,** *adv.* —**tact·ful·ness,** *n.* —**tact·less,** *a.*

tac·ti·cal, tak′ti·kəl, *a.* Pertaining to tactics; characterized by skillful tactics or adroit maneuvering.

tac·tics, tak′tiks, *n. pl., sing.* or *pl. in constr.* The branch of military science that deals with the positioning and maneuvering of forces in a battle area or for immediate objectives: distinguished from *strategy;* any methods employed to gain an objective. —**tac·ti·cian,** tak·tish′ən, *n.*

tac·tile, tak′til, *a.* Pertaining to or possessing the sense of touch; capable of being touched or felt; tangible. —**tac·til·i·ty,** tak·til′i·tē, *n.*

tad·pole, tad′pōl, *n.* The young or aquatic larva of the frog or similar amphibian prior to the loss of its tail and gills and to the development of legs.

taf·fe·ta, taf′ə·tə, *n.* A closely woven, stiff fabric of silk or synthetic fibers, esp. rayon or acetate, having a lustrous finish.—*a.*

taf·fy, taf′ē, *n.* A candy made of molasses or brown sugar and butter. Also **tof·fee, tof·fy.** *Informal.* Flattery; cajolery.

tag, tag, *n.* A piece or strip, as of paper, leather, or plastic, used as a mark or label: a price or luggage *tag;* a loose end or tatter; a point or binding, as of metal or plastic, as at the tip of a shoelace; the last line or lines of a song, actor's speech, etc.; an addition to a speech or other writing, as the moral of a fable; a children's game in which one player chases the others until he touches one of them, who then takes his place as pursuer.—*v.t.*, **tagged, tag·ging.** To furnish or label with a tag or tags; to touch, as in the game of tag. *Informal.* To follow closely; to hit solidly.—*v.i.* To follow closely, used with *after* and *along.* —**tag·like,** *a.*

tail, tāl, *n.* The extreme rear part of an animal or organism that forms a distinct and usu. flexible appendage to the body; something resembling or suggesting this in shape or position: the *tail* of a kite; the bottom or concluding part of anything; the after portion of a rear part of an airplane. *Informal.* Someone who keeps close undercover surveillance of another; a shadow; the posterior or rump. *Pl. Informal.* The reverse of a coin; men's formal attire.—*v.t. Informal.* To follow, as someone under surveillance.—*v.i. Informal.* To follow after.—*a.* Coming from, or being in, the rear. —**tailed,** *a.* —**tail·er,** *n.* —**tail·less,** *a.* —**tail·like,** *a.*

tail·gate, tāl′gāt, *n.* A rear mounted board or gate on a truck or station wagon, hinged or sliding in a frame to allow easy access for loading or unloading.—*v.i., v.t.,* **-gat·ed, -gat·ing.** To drive hazardously close behind (another vehicle).

tail·light, tāl′līt, *n.* A light at the rear of a train, automobile, or truck. Also **tail lamp.**

tai·lor, tā′lər, *n.* One whose business is to make or alter outer garments, as coats or suits.—*v.i.* To do the work of a tailor.*v.t.* To make by tailor's work; to adjust or adapt to a particular need or use. —**tai·lored,** *a.* —**tai·lor·ing,** *n.*

tai·lor-made, tā′lər·mād′, *a.* Made by or as by a tailor; made or adjusted to a particular need or purpose.

tail·piece, tāl′pēs, *n.* A piece forming a tail; an end piece; an appendage; a small picture or ornamental design at the end of a chapter or section in a book.

tail·spin, tāl′spin, *n.* A downward movement of an aircraft with the nose foremost and the tail whirling in circles above; a sudden collapse into confusion, depression, failure, or the like. Also **tail spin.**

tail·wind, tāl′wind, *n.* A wind coming from the rear.

taint, tānt, *v.t.* To imbue with something noxious or offensive; to infect; to corrupt; disgrace.—*v.i.* To become infected, corrupted, or contaminated.—*n.* Any trace of that which is bad, harmful, or offensive; corruption; a blemish on one's reputation. —**taint·less,** *a.*

take, tāk, *v.t.,* **took, tak·en, tak·ing.** To grasp; to lay hold of; to seize; to get into one's hand; to obtain; to lay hold of and remove; to catch suddenly; to entrap; to surprise; to capture, as by force of arms; to rent or lease; to win, as a prize; to choose and make one's own; to select; to receive or accept, as an offer; to assume, as a position; to submit to; to put up with; to subject oneself to, as an oath; to understand; to receive with good or ill will: to *take* an act amiss; to look upon as; to suppose or consider: to *take* something to be right; to experience or feel, as pride; to carry off; to put an end to, as one's life; to subtract; to attract or allure: to *take* one's fancy; to be infected with: to *take* a cold; fasten on or assail, as by a blast, a disease, etc.; to convey; to use for conveyance: to *take* a train; to conduct or lead: the path *takes* him home; to guide; to negotiate: to *take* the stairs two at a time; to clear; to avail oneself of, as an opportunity; to employ for advantage or pleasure, as a nap or vacation; to have recourse to, as shelter; to form or adopt, as a plan; to use, as precaution; to place oneself in; to occupy, as space or time; to consume; to require: This job *takes* patience; to receive and swallow, as medicine; to copy; to draw, as a sketch; to photograph; to

put in writing. *Baseball.* To refrain from swinging at, as a pitch. *Informal.* To cheat.—*v.i.* To direct one's course; to betake oneself; to turn in some direction; to suit the public taste; to please; to have the intended effect, as medicine; to catch hold, as a mechanical device; to become: to *take* sick.—*n.* The quantity of anything taken. *Motion pictures.* An uninterrupted span of filming. *Informal.* Receipts from a sport event, play, or the like. —**take after,** to imitate; to resemble. —**take back,** to retract, as a statement. —**take down,** to write down or record. *Informal.* To cheat. —**take in,** to admit; to comprehend. *Informal.* To cheat. —**take off,** to remove or lift from the surface. *Informal.* To mimic. *Informal.* To leave. —**take on,** to assume, as new duties, to undertake; to acquire; to hire. —**take over,** to assume control or ownership of. —**take to,** to become fond of; to resort to. —**take to heart,** to be deeply affected by. —**take up,** to tighten or shorten; to adopt, as a trade. —**take up with,** to associate with. —**tak·er,** *n.*

take-home pay, tāk′hōm, *n. Informal.* Wages or salary after all deductions, esp. of taxes, have been made.

take·off, tāk′ôf, tāk′of, *n.* The leaving of the ground in leaping or in beginning a flight in an airplane; the place at which this occurs; departure. *Informal.* An imitation or caricature.

tak·ing, tā′king, *n.* The act of one who or that which takes. *Pl. Informal.* Receipts.—*a.* Captivating; winning; charming. *Informal.* Infectious. —**tak·ing·ly,** *adv.* —**tak·ing·ness,** *n.*

talc, talk, *n.* A soft mineral which is smooth to the touch, and may be of a white, gray, or greenish color. Also **tal·cum,** tal′kəm.—*v.t.,* **talced** or **talcked, talc·ing** or **talck·ing.** To coat or treat with talc.

tal·cum pow·der, *n.* Talc in a refined, powdered form, often perfumed for cosmetic use.

tale, tāl, *n.* A narrative of events that have happened or are imagined to have happened; a short story, true or fictitious; a piece of information, esp. gossip; a rumor; a falsehood; a lie.

tale·bear·er, tāl′ber·ər, *n.* A person who tells tales or spreads rumors likely to breed trouble; a gossip. —**tale·bear·ing,** *a., n.*

tal·ent, tal′ənt, *n.* A special natural ability or aptitude; a capacity for achievement or success; natural ability; cleverness; a person or a group of persons of ability; any of various ancient units of weight or money. —**tal·ent·ed,** *a.*

tales·man, tālz′mən, tā′lēz·mən, *n. pl.,* **-men.** A person selected, usu. from a group of bystanders in a court, to serve on a jury in order to make up a deficiency in the number of jurors.

tal·is·man, tal′is·mən, tal′iz·mən, *n. pl.,* **-mans.** An object having an engraved figure or symbol which is thought to preserve the bearer from harm and bring good luck; something that produces extraordinary effects on human behavior; any charm or amulet. —**tal·is·man·ic,** tal·is·man′ik, tal·iz·man′ik, **tal·is·man·i·cal,** *a.* —**tal·is·man·i·cal·ly,** *adv.*

talk, tôk, *v.i.* To utter words in exchanging or expressing thoughts; speak; to confer; to gossip; to communicate in any way, as by signs or signals. *Informal.* To give secret information, as to the police.—*v.t.* To use as a means of conversation or communication: to *talk* French; speak; to use as the subject of a conversation: to *talk* politics; to utter: to *talk* nonsense; to have a certain effect on by talking.—*n.* The act of talking; informal conversation, discourse, or lecture; report; rumor; gossip; a subject of discourse; a conference or discussion: peace *talks*; empty or pointless conversation. —**talk back,** *Informal.* To reply rudely or impertinently. —**talk big.** *Informal.* To brag or boast. —**talk down to,** to patronize by speaking condescendingly. —**talk o·ver,** to discuss orally; consider; weigh; to win over; persuade by talking. —**talk·er,** *n.*

talk·a·tive, tô/kə·tiv, *a.* Tending to talk excessively. —**talk·a·tive·ly,** *adv.* —**talk·a·tive·ness,** *n.*

talk·ie, tô/kē, *n. Informal.* A motion picture with sound. Also **talk·ing pic·ture.**

talk·ing-to, tôk/ing·too, *n. pl.,* **-tos.** *Informal.* A scolding.

talk·y, tô/kē, *a.,* **-i·er, -i·est.** Talkative; disposed to talk; loquacious.

tall, tôl, *a.* High in stature; having the height indicated: *two feet tall. Informal.* Fanciful; extravagant: a *tall* story; considerable in difficulty, extent, or amount: a *tall* order to fill.—*adv.* Straight; proudly: to stand or walk *tall.* —**tall·ish,** *a.* —**tall·ness,** *n.*

tal·low, tal/ō, *n.* The harder and less fusible fat of cattle and sheep, used in candles, soap, and the like. —**tal·low·y,** *a.,* **-i·er, -i·est.**

tal·ly, tal/ē, *n. pl.,* **-lies.** An account or reckoning; a record of debit and credit or of the score of a game; a mark made to register a certain number of objects in keeping account, as four verticals and a diagonal for a group of five; a ticket, label, or mark used as a means of identification, as when attached to a plant or tree.—*v.t.* **-lied, -ly·ing.** To mark on a tally; to count or reckon up.—*v.i.* To correspond, as one part of a tally with the other; to accord or agree.

tal·ly·ho, tal·ē·hō/, *interj.* The huntsman's cry to urge on his hounds. —tal/ē·hō, *n. pl.,* **-hos.** The cry of 'tallyho'; a four-in-hand coach.

Tal·mud, täl/mûd, tal/məd, *n.* The body of Jewish civil and canonical laws, traditions, and explanations, or the book that contains them. —**Tal·mud·ic,** täl·mû/dik, tal·mĕd/ik, **Tal·mud·i·cal,** *a.* —**Tal·mud·ism,** *n.* —**Tal·mud·ist,** *n.*

tal·on, tal/ən, *n.* A claw, esp. of a bird of prey. —**tal·oned,** *a.*

tam, tam, *n.* A tam-o'-shanter.

ta·ma·le, tə·mä/lē, *n.* A highly seasoned Mexican dish made by combining ground meat and peppers, then rolling the mixture in a coating of cornmeal dough, wrapping it in cornhusks and steaming it.

tam·a·rack, tam/ə·rak, *n.* The American larch or any of various related larches; wood from any of these tamaracks.

tam·a·rind, tam/ə·rind, *n.* A tropical leguminous tree having yellow flowers with red stripes; the fruit of this tree containing an acid pulp used in medicines and foods.

tam·bou·rine, tam·bə·rēn/, *n.* A musical instrument formed of a hoop over which parchment is stretched, and having small metal jingles inserted in the rim.

tame, tām, *a.,* **tam·er, tam·est.** Domesticated; submissive; spiritless; dull.—*v.t.,* **tamed, tam·ing.** To make tame; to render obedient or spiritless; subdue; tone down.—*v.i.* To become tame. —**tam·a·ble, tame·a·ble,** *a.* —**tame·ly,** *adv.* —**tame·ness,** *n.* —**tam·er,** *n.*

tam-o'-shan·ter, tam/ə·shan·tər, *n.* A Scottish cap, usu. having a tight, often decorative headband and a round, flat crown with a pompon at the center. Also **tam.**

tamp, tamp, *v.t.* To force or drive down by successive light blows; to ram tight with tough clay or other substance, as a hole bored for blasting.

tam·per, tam/pər, *v.i.* To meddle or interfere; to make alterations by corruption or adulteration, usu. followed by *with:* to *tamper with* a document.—*v.t.* —**tam·per·er,** *n.*

tan, tan, *v.t.,* **tanned, tan·ning.** To convert into leather, as animal skins, by steeping in an infusion of oak or other tanbark; to make brown by exposure to the rays of the sun. *Informal.* To beat, flog, or thrash.—*v.i.* To become tanned; to become tan-colored or sunburned.—*n.* The bark of the oak, willow, or other trees, used for tanning; tanbark; a yellowish-brown color; a brown skin color resulting from exposure to the rays of the sun.—*a.* —**tan·nish,** *a.*

tan·a·ger, tan/ə·jər, *n.* Any of a group of American birds of the finch family, remarkable for their bright colors, as the scarlet tanager.

tan·bark, tan/bärk, *n.* Tree bark, esp. hemlock or oak, which is rich in tannin and is used in the tanning of hides.

tan·dem, tan/dəm, *adv.* One before the other.—*a.* Arranged one before the other.—*n.* A vehicle drawn by two horses harnessed one before the other; the horses themselves; a bicycle having two seats, one behind the other: also **tan·dem bi·cy·cle.**

tang, tang, *n.* A strong taste or flavor; a pungent or distinctive odor; a long and slender projecting strip, tongue, or prong forming part of a chisel, file, knife, etc., for inserting or fixing into a handle or stock. —**tanged,** *a.* —**tang·y,** *a.,* **-i·er, -i·est.**

tan·gent, tan/jənt, *a.* Touching; touching at one point only and not intersecting, as a straight line in relation to a curve or a plane in relation to a sphere.—*n.* A tangent line, plane, curve, or surface; a function of an acute angle in a right triangle, equal to the ratio of the opposite leg to the adjacent leg. —**fly,** or **go, off on,** or **at, a tan·gent,** to go suddenly from one course of action or train of thought to another. —**tan·gen·cy,** *n.*

tan·gen·tial, tan·jen/shəl, *a.* Of or related to a tangent; touching; slightly connected; digressive.

tan·ge·rine, tan·jə·rēn/, *n.* A small, shiny orange, easily skinned and segmented; the tree producing this fruit: also **man·da·rin;** a reddish-orange color.

tan·gi·ble, tan/jə·bəl, *a.* Capable of being touched or grasped; perceptible by the touch; material; capable of being possessed or realized by the mind; real; actual.—*n. Usu. pl.* Material or tangible assets. —**tan·gi·bil·i·ty,** tan·jə·bil/ə·tē, **tan·gi·ble·ness,** *n.* —**tan·gi·bly,** *adv.*

tan·gle, tang/gəl, *v.t.,* **-gled, -gling.** To interweave or interlace so as to be difficult to unravel; to entangle or entrap.—*v.i.* To become or be tangled. *Informal.* To quarrel.—*n.* A knot of threads or other things confusedly interwoven; a state of complication. *Informal.* A quarrel. —**tan·gled,** *a.* —**tan·gle·ment,** *n.* —**tan·gly,** *a.,* **-gli·er, -gli·est.**

tan·go, tang/gō, *n. pl.,* **-gos.** A ballroom dance originated in Argentina and performed by couples gliding and dipping in slow tempo to an accented rhythm; the music to which it is danced.—*v.i.,* **-goed, -go·ing.** To perform the tango.

tank, tangk, *n.* A large receptacle or structure for holding water or other liquid or a gas; an armored vehicle having caterpillar treads and containing cannon or machine guns fired from inside.—*v.t.* To put or store in a tank. —**tank·age,** *n.*

tank·ard, tang/kərd, *n.* A large drinking vessel with a hinged lid and a handle, usu. of silver or pewter.

tank car, *n.* A railroad car equipped to carry gases or liquids.

tank·er, tang/kər, *n.* A vehicle designed to transport liquids, esp. gasoline or oil, as a ship, railroad car, or truck.

tan·ner, tan/ər, *n.* One whose occupation is to tan hides.

tan·ner·y, tan/ə·rē, *n. pl.,* **-ies.** A business establishment where hides are tanned.

tan·nin, tan/in, *n.* Any of a group of astringent vegetable compounds having tanning properties, used commercially in manufacturing leather, inks, and dyes. Also **tan·nic acid,** tan/ik.

tan·ta·lize, tan/tə·līz, *v.t.,* **-lized, -liz·ing.** To tease or torment by presenting something desirable to the view, but continually frustrating the expectations by keeping it out of reach; to excite by expectations or hopes which will not be realized. —**tan·ta·liz·er,** *n.* —**tan·ta·liz·ing,** *a.* —**tan·ta·liz·ing·ly,** *adv.*

tan·ta·lum, tan/tə·ləm, *n.* A rare, gray-white, metallic element which is hard, ductile, and resistant to single acids.

tan·ta·mount, tan/tə·mownt, *a.* Equivalent, followed by *to.*

tan·trum, tan/trəm, *n.* An outburst of anger or rage; a violent display of temper.

Tao·ism, dow/iz·əm, tow/iz·əm, *n.* A nontheistic Chinese religion teaching simplicity and conformity to the Tao or Way. **—Tao·ist,** *a., n.*

tap, tap, *n.* A spigot; a faucet; a plug to stop a hole in a cask.—*v.t.,* **tapped, tap·ping.** To pierce or open, as a cask, so as to let out fluid from; to penetrate or open up: to *tap* a telephone, to *tap* a water main; to call upon, as a reserve: to *tap* a resource. *Informal.* To borrow money from. **—on tap,** available for tapping, as ale or beer; having a tap. *Informal.* Handy or readily available.

tap, tap, *v.t.,* **tapped, tap·ping.** To strike lightly, as with something small.—*v.i.* To strike a gentle, audible blow.—*n.* A gentle blow; the sound of such a blow; a leather or metal plate, etc., affixed to a shoe sole or heel.

tap dance, *n.* A dance in which the dancer's special shoes cause the steps to be audible. **—tap-dance,** tap/dans, *v.i.,* **-danced, -danc·ing.**

tape, tāp, *n.* A narrow woven band of cotton or linen, used for tying or fastening; a long strip or ribbon of paper, plastic, or metal: ticker *tape,* friction *tape,* magnetic *tape;* a string stretched across the finishing line of a race.—*v.t., v.i.,* **taped, tap·ing.** To tie or secure with tape; to record on magnetic tape. **—tap·er,** *n.* One who or that which tapes. **—tape·like,** *a.*

tape meas·ure, *n.* A long cloth, metal, or paper tape marked with inches or centimeters and used in measuring. Also **tape·line,** tāp/līn.

ta·per, tā/pər, *v.i.* To become gradually slenderer or less in diameter: an awl *tapers* off to a point; to diminish; to grow gradually less.—*v.t.* To make smaller, esp. toward one particular end; to reduce gradually; to lessen.—*n.* Gradual diminution of thickness in an elongated object; a small candle, esp. one which is very slender. **—ta·per·er,** *n.* **—ta·per·ing·ly,** *adv.*

tape-re·cord, tāp/ri·kôrd, *v.t.* To record, as music, on magnetic tape. **—tape re·cord·er,** *n.* **—tape re·cord·ing,** *n.*

tap·es·try, tap/i·strē, *n. pl.,* **-tries.** A colorful, handwoven, patterned or pictorial cloth usu. used as a wall hanging but occasionally as a furniture covering or a throw.—*v.t.,* **-tried, -try·ing.** To decorate or furnish with, or as with, tapestry; to weave in the manner of tapestry.

tape·worm, tāp/wərm, *n.* Any of various flat or tapelike worms, parasitic when adult in the alimentary canal of man and other vertebrates.

tap·i·o·ca, tap·ē·ō/kə, *n.* A nutritious substance prepared from dried cassava starch, usu. in granular form, and used in making puddings or for thickening liquids.

ta·pir, tā/pər, *n.* Any of several Central and South American or Malayan nocturnal mammals with a flexible snout.

tap·room, tap/room, tap/rŭm, *n.* A barroom.

tap·root, tap/root, tap/rŭt, *n.* The main root of a plant which penetrates the earth downward.

taps, taps, *n. pl. but sing. in constr.* A bugle call or drum beat used esp. in the military to signal the putting out of lights at night; a bugle sounded at military funerals.

tar, tär, *n.* A thick, dark-colored viscid product obtained by the destructive distillation of organic substances and bituminous minerals, as certain woods and coal.—*v.t.,* **tarred, tar·ring.** To smear with tar.

tar, tär, *n. Informal.* A sailor.

tar·an·tel·la, tar·ən·tel/ə, *n.* A swift, whirling Italian dance in 6/8 time; music for this dance.

ta·ran·tu·la, tə·ran/chə·lə, *n. pl.,* **-las, -lae,** -lē. Any of various spiders, usu. large and hairy, which have a painful although not very poisonous bite and are common in the southwestern U.S.

tar·dy, tär/dē, *a.,* **-di·er, -di·est.** Late; not punctual; moving at a slow pace; dilatory. **—tar·di·ly,** *adv.* **—tar·di·ness,** *n.*

tare, târ, *n.* Any of several species of vetch or any seed of a vetch; a weed pest of grainfields.

tare, târ, *n.* A deduction made from the gross weight of goods as an allowance for the weight of the container or conveyance.

tar·get, tär/git, *n.* A disk, board, or other object, usu. marked with concentric circles, to be aimed at in shooting practice or contests; any object used for this purpose; anything fired at; anything aimed at; a goal; an object of abuse, scorn, derision, or the like.—*v.t.* To designate or use as a goal; to cause to become the object of an attack.

tar·iff, tar/if, *n.* A list or schedule of goods with the legal duties imposed on them when imported or exported; a duty as given in such a schedule; any table or scale of charges or prices.—*v.t.* To set a tax, duty, or charge on.

tarn, tärn, *n.* A small mountain lake or pool.

tar·nish, tär/nish, *v.t.* To diminish or destroy the luster of; to soil or sully; to disgrace.—*v.i.* To lose luster; become dull or discolored; to become soiled or sullied.—*n.* A discoloration, esp. on metal; a blot; a tarnished state. **—tar·nish·a·ble,** *a.*

ta·ro, tär/ō, *n. pl.,* **-ros.** A plant cultivated in the tropics for its edible tuberous roots; the root of this plant.

tarp, tärp, *n. Informal.* Tarpaulin.

tar·pau·lin, tär·pô/lin, tär/pə·lin, *n.* A covering or sheet of canvas or other material, waterproofed with tar or paint and used to protect something exposed to weather or moisture; canvas or other material so waterproofed.

tar·pon, tär/pən, *n. pl.,* **-pons, -pon.** A large, silver-scaled sport fish inhabiting the warm waters off the Florida coast and the Gulf of Mexico.

tar·ry, tar/ē, *v.i.,* **-ried, -ry·ing.** To delay or be tardy; to linger or loiter; wait; remain; sojourn.—*n. pl.,* **-ries.** A stay or sojourn.

tar·ry, tär/ē, *a.,* **-ri·er, -ri·est.** Of, like, or coated with tar.

tar·sal, tär/səl, *a.* Pertaining to the tarsus.—*n.* A tarsal part, as a bone or joint.

tar·sus, tär/səs, *n. pl.,* **tar·si,** tär/sī. The ankle; the collection of bones composing the ankle.

tart, tärt, *a.* Sharp to the taste; sour; cutting; caustic: a *tart* rejoinder. **—tart·ly,** *adv.* **—tart·ness,** *n.*

tart, tärt, *n.* A small pastry shell filled with cooked fruit or other sweetened preparation, usu. without a top crust. *Informal.* A prostitute.

tar·tan, tär/tən, *n.* A kind of woolen cloth, having stripes and crossbars in various colors, traditionally worn by Scottish Highlanders, each clan having its own pattern and colors; the pattern itself; a plaid; a garment of any such design or material.—*a.*

tar·tar, tär/tər, *n.* An acid substance deposited from the juice of grapes in winemaking; a yellowish, hard substance deposited on the teeth. **—tar·tar·ic,** tär·tar/ik, tär·tär/ik, *a.* **—tar·tar·ous,** *a.*

task, task, *n.* A piece of work to be done; a burdensome, difficult, or unpleasant chore or duty.—*v.t.* To impose a task upon; to oppress with severe labor. **—take to task,** to reprimand; to reprove.

task force, *n.* A temporary merging of units or individuals under one command with the purpose of accomplishing one specific mission or objective.

task·mas·ter, task/mas·tər, *n.* One who assigns or imposes tasks, esp. taxing, burdensome ones; one who rigorously oversees the work of others.

tas·sel, tas/əl, *n.* A hanging bunch of threads, small cords, or strands fastened to a roundish knob or head; something resembling this: a corn *tassel.*—*v.t., v.i.,* **-seled, -sel·ing.** To provide with, form into, remove, or

---

a- hat, fāte, fâre, fäther; **e-** met, mē; **i-** pin, pīne; **o-** not, nōte, ôrb, moove (move), boy, pownd;
u- cūbe, bŭll, tŭk (took); **ch-** chin; **th-** thick, then; **zh-** vizhon (vision); **ə-** ego, taken, pencəl, lemən, bərd (bird).

534

produce tassels.

taste, tāst, *v.t.,* **tast·ed, tast·ing.** To try the flavor or quality of, as food, by taking into the mouth; to eat or drink a little of; to perceive the flavor of by the sense of taste; to have or get experience: to *taste* freedom.—*v.i.* To eat or drink a small amount (*of*); to have a particular flavor or taste.—*n.* The sense by which the flavor of things is perceived; the flavor or quality of a thing as perceived by the sense of taste; a small quantity of something tasted, eaten, or drunk; a morsel, bit, or sip; a liking for something: a *taste* for music; the sense of what is harmonious, beautiful, or socially proper; the perception and appreciation of what constitutes excellence in the fine arts.

taste bud, *n.* One of the many tiny end organs of the sense of taste located in the epithelium of the tongue.

taste·ful, tāst'fəl, *a.* Having, displaying, or being in accordance with good taste. **—taste·ful·ly,** *adv.* **—taste·ful·ness,** *n.*

taste·less, tāst'lis, *a.* Having no taste or flavor; insipid; dull or uninteresting; lacking in aesthetic taste. **—taste·less·ly,** *adv.* **—taste·less·ness,** *n.*

tast·er, tā'stər, *n.* One who tastes; one who tests food, provisions, or liquors by tasting samples.

tast·y, tā'stē, *a.,* **-i·er, -i·est.** Pleasing to the taste. **—tast·i·ly,** *adv.* **—tast·i·ness,** *n.*

tat, tat, *v.i., v.t.,* **tat·ted, tat·ting.** To make tatting or make by tatting. **—tat·ter,** tat'ər, *n.*

tat·ter, tat'ər, *n.* A torn piece hanging loose from the main part, as of a garment; *pl.,* torn or ragged clothing.—*v.t.* To tear or wear into tatters.—*v.i.* To become ragged. **—tat·tered,** *a.*

tat·ting, tat'ing, *n.* A kind of looped and knotted lace made by hand on a small shuttle; the act of making such lace.

tat·tle, tat'əl, *v.i.,* **-tled, -tling.** To chatter, prate, or talk idly; to gossip or let out secrets.—*v.t.* To disclose by tattling.—*n.* Idle or frivolous talk; gossip.

tat·tle·tale, tat'əl·tāl, *n.* A talebearer.—*a.* Indicating or revealing; telltale.

tat·too, ta·too', *n. pl.,* **-toos.** A signal on a drum or bugle at night, for soldiers or sailors to repair to their quarters; a beating of a drum; any beating or pulsation like the beating of a drum.—*v.i.,* **-tooed, -too·ing.** To beat rhythmically.—*v.t.* To beat or tap on.

tat·too, ta·too', *n. pl.,* **-toos.** The act or practice of marking the skin with indelible patterns, pictures, or legends by making punctures in it and inserting pigments; a pattern, legend, or picture so made.—*v.t.,* **-tooed, -too·ing.** To mark, as skin, with tattoos; to put, as tattoos, on the skin. **—tat·too·er, tat·too·ist,** *n.*

taught, tôt, *v.* Past tense and past participle of **teach.**

taunt, tônt, tänt, *v.t.* To reproach with jeers or sarcasm; to provoke with scornful or insulting words.—*n.* A bitter or sarcastic challenge or reproach; insulting invective. **—taunt·er,** *n.* **—taunt·ing·ly,** *adv.*

taupe, tōp, *n.* A medium to dark brownish-gray color, sometimes with a pinkish or yellowish cast.

Tau·rus, tôr'əs, *n.* The Bull, a constellation; the second sign of the zodiac.

taut, tôt, *a.* Tight; not slack; tense; high-strung; unrelaxed: *taut* nerves or muscles; correctly or neatly arranged; tidy. **—taut·ly,** *adv.* **—taut·ness,** *n.*

tau·tol·o·gy, tô·tol'ə·jē, *n.* A useless repetition of the same idea or meaning in different words; needless redundancy; an example of this. **—tau·to·log·i·cal,** tô·tə·loj'ə·kəl, *a.* **—tau·to·log·i·cal·ly,** *adv.*

tav·ern, tav'ərn, *n.* A place where alcoholic beverages are sold by the drink; an inn.

taw, tô, *n.* A choice or fancy playing marble with which to shoot; the line from which the players shoot in playing marbles.—*v.i.* To shoot a marble.

taw·dry, tô'drē, *a.,* **-dri·er, -dri·est.** Showy, without taste or elegance; cheap; gaudy. **—taw·dri·ly,** *adv.* **—taw·dri·ness,** *n.*

taw·ny, tô'nē, *a.,* **-ni·er, -ni·est.** Of a yellowish-brown color.—*n.* A yellowish-brown color. **—taw·ni·ness,** *n.*

tax, taks, *n.* A charge imposed by governmental authority upon property, individuals, or transactions to raise money for public purposes; a similar assessment on members of any organization; a strain, serious burden, or heavy demand.—*v.t.* To impose a tax upon; to subject to a strain or make heavy demands upon: to *tax* one's patience; to accuse or impute to: to *tax* a man with rudeness. **—tax·a·bil·i·ty,** tak·sə·bil'ə·tē, *n.* **—tax·a·ble,** *a.* **—tax·er,** *n.*

tax·a·tion, tak·sā'shən, *n.* The act of laying or imposing a tax or taxes; the state of being taxed; the money raised by taxes.

tax·i, tak'sē, *n. pl.,* **-is, -ies.** A taxicab.—*v.i.,* **-ied, -i·ing** or **-y·ing.** To ride or travel in a taxicab; to move over the surface of the ground or water under its own power, as an airplane preparing for takeoff.—*v.t.* To cause, as an airplane, to taxi.

tax·i·cab, tak'sē·kab, *n.* A public vehicle for hire, esp. an automobile, fitted with a taximeter.

tax·i·der·my, tak'sə·dər·mē, *n.* The art of preparing, stuffing, and mounting the skins of animals so that they retain their natural appearance. **—tax·i·der·mic,** tak·sə·dər'mik, *a.* **—tax·i·der·mist,** *n.*

tax·i·me·ter, tak'sē·mē·tər, *n.* A device fitted to a public cab or other vehicle for automatically computing and indicating the fare due at any moment.

tax·on·o·my, tak·son'ə·mē, *n.* Classification, esp. in relation to its principles or laws; the classification of plants and animals into established groups or categories on the basis of their natural relationships. **—tax·o·nom·ic,** tak·sə·nom'ik, **tax·o·nom·i·cal,** *a.* **—tax·o·nom·i·cal·ly,** *adv.* **—tax·on·o·mist,** *n.*

tax·pay·er, taks'pā·ər, *n.* One who pays a tax or is subject to a tax.

T-bone, tē'bōn, *n.* A beefsteak taken from the loin and containing a T-shaped bone and some tenderloin. Also **T-bone steak.**

tea, tē, *n.* The dried and prepared leaves of a shrub from which a somewhat bitter, aromatic beverage is prepared by infusion in hot water; the beverage so prepared; the shrub itself; a service of tea, with or without other food, in the later afternoon; an afternoon reception at which tea is served. *Informal.* Marijuana.

tea bag, *n.* A porous container of cloth or paper which holds enough tea leaves for one serving of tea.

teach, tēch, *v.t.,* **taught, teach·ing.** To give instruction to; to guide the studies of: to *teach* a class; to impart the knowledge of: to *teach* history; to train; to give skill in the use of; to instruct by implying: an experience that *teaches* a lesson.—*v.i.* To give instruction; to work as a teacher. **—teach·a·ble,** *a.* **—teach·a·ble·ness, teach·a·bil·i·ty,** tēch·ə·bil'ə·tē, *n.* **—teach·ing,** *n.*

teach·er, tē'chər, *n.* One who teaches, esp. one whose profession or occupation is teaching; a tutor; an instructor.

teach·ing ma·chine, *n.* An automatic device that allows a student to learn at his or her own rate by presenting a unit of information and questions as part of a planned sequence of such units, and requiring a satisfactory response from the student before the next unit is presented.

tea·cup, tē'kəp, *n.* A cup in which tea is served. **—tea·cup·ful,** *n. pl.,* **-fuls.**

teak, tēk, *n.* A tree growing in different parts of the East Indies, yielding a strong, durable, and valuable timber; the wood obtained from this tree: also **teak·wood,** tēk'wûd.

tea·ket·tle, tē'ket·əl, *n.* A portable kettle with a cover, spout, and handle, in which to boil water.

teal, tēl, *n. pl.,* **teals, teal.** Any of several short-necked freshwater ducks; a dull, darkish color of a greenish-blue hue: also **teal blue.**

team, tēm, *n.* A number of persons associated in a joint action or endeavor; one of the sides in a contest: a football *team;* two or more horses or other draft animals harnessed together to draw a vehicle or implement.—*v.t.* To harness or join together in a team.—*v.i.* To form a team, usu. followed by *up* or *together*.—*a.*

team·mate, tēm′māt, *n.* A fellow team member.

team·ster, tēm′stər, *n.* One who drives a team or other vehicle, as a truck, esp. as an occupation.

team·work, tēm′wərk, *n.* The work of a team or number of persons acting together.

tea·pot, tē′pot, *n.* A vessel with a lid, spout, and handle, in which tea is made and from which it is poured and served.

tear, tēr, *n.* A limpid, droplike liquid secretion of the lacrimal gland which moistens the surface of the eye and cleanses it of foreign particles; this liquid appearing in the eyes or flowing from them, esp. through grief or joy; *pl.,* weeping; sorrow or misery.—*v.i.* To shed or emit tears. —**tear·y,** *a.,* **-i·er, -i·est.**

tear, tār, *v.t.,* **tore, torn, tear·ing.** To pull apart or in pieces by force; rend: a nation *torn* by civil war; effect by rending: to *tear* a hole in one's coat; to lacerate; distress greatly: to *tear* the heart with anguish; to remove by force: to *tear* oneself from a place.—*v.i.* To become torn; to move with violence or haste: He *tore* out of the house.—*n.* The act or an act of tearing; a rent or fissure; a violent outburst, as of rage or enthusiasm. *Informal.* A spree. —**tear down,** to take down or apart; to disassemble; to cast aspersions upon. —**tear in·to.** *Informal.* To attack unrestrainedly, esp. verbally. —**tear·er,** *n.*

tear·drop, tēr′drop, *n.* A tear.

tear·ful, tēr′fəl, *a.* Weeping; causing or provoking tears. —**tear·ful·ly,** *adv.* —**tear·ful·ness,** *n.*

tear·gas, tēr′gas, *n.* A substance causing excessive tearing and therefore temporary partial blindness: used primarily by police in dispersing mobs.

tea·room, tē′room, tē′rûm, *n.* A room or shop where tea and other refreshments are served to customers. Also **tea·shop,** tē′shop.

tease, tēz, *v.t.,* **teased, teas·ing.** To comb or card, as wool; to raise a nap on, as cloth, with teasels; to worry or irritate by persistent petty requests, trifling raillery, or other annoyance; to excite sexually without the intention of satisfying.—*v.i.* To worry or disturb a person by importunity or persistent petty annoyance. —*n.* The act of teasing, or the state of being teased; one who or that which teases or annoys. —**teas·er,** *n.* —**teas·ing·ly,** *adv.*

tea·sel, tē′zəl, *n.* A plant with prickly leaves and flower heads; the bur or dried flower head of these plants, covered with stiff, hooked bracts, used for teasing or teaseling cloth; any mechanical contrivance used for the same purpose.—*v.t.,* **-seled, -sel·ing.** To raise a nap on with teazels.

tea·spoon, tē′spoon, *n.* The small spoon commonly used to stir tea, coffee, or the like; a teaspoonful; a unit of measurement in cooking, equivalent to one-third of a tablespoon. —**tea·spoon·ful,** *n. pl.,* **-fuls.**

teat, tēt, tit, *n.* A nipple.

tech·ne·ti·um, tek·nē′shē·əm, *n.* A silver-gray, metallic element produced artificially.

tech·ni·cal, tek′ni·kəl, *a.* Belonging or pertaining to an art or arts; characteristic of a particular art, science, profession, or trade: a *technical* term; pertaining to or connected with the mechanical or industrial arts and the applied sciences: a *technical* school. —**tech·ni·cal·ly,** *adv.* —**tech·ni·cal·ness,** *n.*

tech·ni·cal·i·ty, tek·ni·kal′ə·tē, *n. pl.,* **-ties.** A technical character; the use of technical methods or terms; a technical point or detail, esp. one significant only to an expert; a technical term or expression.

tech·ni·cian, tek·nish′ən, *n.* One highly trained in the technicalities of a subject, profession, or occupation; one skilled in the technique of an art, as sculpture, painting, ballet, or music.

Tech·ni·col·or, tek′nə·kəl·ər, *n. Trademark.* A process for making color motion pictures by superposing the three primary colors to produce the finished print.

tech·nique, tek·nēk′, *n.* Method of performance: the *technique* of the poet; technical skill.

tech·noc·ra·cy, tek·nok′rə·sē, *n. pl.,* **-cies.** A theory of government, advocating control and management of industrial resources and reorganization of society by technologists and engineers. —**tech·no·crat,** tek′nə·krat, *n.* —**tech·no·crat·ic,** tek·nə·krat′ik, *a.*

tech·nol·o·gy, tek·nol′ə·jē, *n.* The branch of knowledge that deals with the industrial arts and sciences; utilization of such knowledge. —**tech·no·log·i·cal,** tek·nə·loj′i·kəl, *a.* Also **tech·no·log·ic.** —**tech·nol·o·gist,** *n.*

ted·dy bear, ted′ē bər, *n.* A stuffed figure of a bear, used as a toy.

te·di·ous, tē′dē·əs, tē′jəs, *a.* Involving or causing tedium; tiresome; wearisome; monotonous. —**te·di·ous·ly,** *adv.* —**te·di·ous·ness,** *n.*

te·di·um, tē′dē·əm, *n.* Irksomeness; wearisomeness.

tee, tē, *n.* The starting place, orig. a small heap of earth, from which a golf ball is driven at the beginning of play for each hole; a small peg of wood, plastic, rubber, or metal from which the ball is hit at the beginning of play for each hole.—*v.t.,* **teed, tee·ing.** To place on a tee, as a golf ball. —**teed off.** *Informal.* Indignant or disgusted.

teem, tēm, *v.i.* To be stocked to overflowing; to be prolific or abundantly fertile.—*v.t.* To produce; to bring forth.

teen·ag·er, tēn′ā·jər, *n.* A person from the age of 13 through 19. —**teen-age,** *a.*

teens, tēnz, *n. pl.* The years from 13 through 19, esp. as a person's age.

tee·ny, tē′nē, *a.,* **-ni·er, -ni·est.** *Informal.* Tiny.

tee·pee, tē′pē, *n.* Tepee.

tee·ter, tē′tər, *v.i.* To seesaw; move unsteadily.—*v.t.* To cause to teeter.—*n.* A seesaw; a seesaw motion.

tee·ter·board, tē′tər·bôrd, *n.* A seesaw. Also **tee·ter-tot·ter,** tē′tər·tot·ər.

teethe, tēth, *v.i.,* **teethed, teeth·ing.** To grow teeth; to cut one's teeth. —**teeth·ing,** *n.*

tee·to·tal, tē·tōt′əl, *a.* Of or pertaining to, advocating, or pledged to total abstinence from intoxicating drink; absolute, complete, or entire. —**tee·to·tal·er, tee·to·tal·ist,** *n.* —**tee·to·tal·ism,** *n.* —**tee·to·tal·ly,** *adv.*

teg·u·ment, teg′yə·mənt, *n.* A cover or covering; an integument.

tel·e·cast, tel′ə·kast, *v.t., v.i.,* **-cast** or **-cast·ed, -cast·ing.** To broadcast by television.—*n.* A televised broadcast. —**tel·e·cast·er,** *n.*

tel·e·com·mu·ni·ca·tion, tel·ə·kə·mū·nə·kā′shən, *n. Often pl. but sing. in constr.* The science of communication by electronically transmitted waves, as by radio, television, radar, telephone, telegraph, and the like; any communication transmitted in this manner.

tel·e·gram, tel′ə·gram, *n.* A communication sent by telegraph.

tel·e·graph, tel′ə·graf, *n.* An apparatus, system, or process for transmitting messages or signals over a distance.—*v.t.* To transmit, as a message, by telegraph; to send a message to by telegraph.—*v.i.* To send a message by telegraph. —**te·leg·ra·pher,** tə·leg′rə·fər, *n.* —**tel·e·graph·ic,** tel·e·graph·i·cal, *a.*

te·leg·ra·phy, tə·leg′rə·fē, *n.* The art or practice of constructing or operating telegraphs.

te·lep·a·thy, tə·lep′ə·thē, *n.* Communication of one mind with another by some means beyond normal sensory perception. —**tel·e·path·ic,** tel·ə·path′ik, *a.* —**tel·e·path·i·cal·ly,** *adv.* —**te·lep·a·thist,** tə·

ep/ə•thist, *n.*

tel•e•phone, tel/ə•fōn, *n.* An apparatus, system, or process for the transmission of sound or speech to a distant point.—*v.t.,* **-phoned, -phon•ing.** To speak to by means of a telephone.—*v.i.* To communicate or send a message by telephone. —**tel•e•phon•er,** *n.* —**tel•e•phon•ic,** tel•ə•fon/ik, *a.*

te•leph•o•ny, tə•lef/ə•nē, *n.* The construction and operation of telephones and telephonic systems.

tel•e•pho•to, tel/ə•fō•tō, *a.* Denoting a lens structure in a camera which permits large photographs to be taken of far-off objects.

tel•e•pho•tog•ra•phy, tel•ə•fə•tog/rə•fē, *n.* The art of photographing objects too distant for the ordinary camera, by the use of a telephoto lens; the art of electrically reproducing photographs or pictures at a distance by a special telegraphic process. —**tel•e•pho•to•graph•ic,** tel•ə•fō•tə•graf/ik, *a.*

tel•e•scope, tel/ə•skōp, *n.* An optical instrument used for making distant objects appear nearer and larger.—*v.t., v.i.,* **-scoped, -scop•ing.** To slide together, or into something else, after the manner of the tubes of a jointed telescope; to be driven one into another, as railroad cars in collision; to shorten; condense.

tel•e•scop•ic, tel•ə•skop/ik, *a.* Pertaining to or seen by means of a telescope; visible only through a telescope; far-seeing; having sections that slide one inside another like the tubes of some telescopes. Also **tel•e•scop•i•cal.**

tel•e•thon, tel/ə•thon, *n.* A lengthy television program, usu. to raise funds.

Tel•e•type, tel/ə•tip, *n. Trademark.* A teletypewriter. —*v.t.,* **-typed, -typ•ing.** (*L.c.*) To transmit, as a message, by Teletype.—*v.i.* (*L.c.*) To operate or use a Teletype. —**tel•e•typ•ist,** *n.*

tel•e•type•writ•er, tel•ə•tīp/rī•tər, *n.* A telegraphic apparatus resembling a typewriter, used for sending, receiving, and automatically printing out messages.

tel•e•vise, tel/ə•vīz, *v.t., v.i.,* **-vised, -vis•ing.** To transmit by television.

tel•e•vi•sion, tel/ə•vizh•ən, *n.* The transmission of scenes or moving pictures by conversion of light rays to electrical waves, which are reconverted to reproduce the original image; a set which receives television broadcasts; the industry of television broadcasting; television broadcasts collectively.—*a.*

tell, tel, *v.t.,* **told, tell•ing.** To give an account or narrative of; to narrate; to relate; to make known by speech or writing; to announce or proclaim; to utter; to express in words; to reveal or divulge, as something secret or private; to say plainly or positively; to decide; discern; to bid or command.—*v.i.* To give an account; to make a report; to give evidence or be an indication, usu. followed by *of;* to disclose something secret or private; to produce a marked or severe effect. —**tell off.** *Informal.* To scold severely.

tell•er, tel/ər, *n.* One who or that which tells, relates, or communicates; one employed in a bank to receive or pay out money over the counter.

tell•ing, tel/ing, *a.* Operating with great effect; forceful or striking. —**tell•ing•ly,** *adv.*

tell•tale, tel/tāl, *n.* One who heedlessly or maliciously reveals private, secret, or confidential matters; a tattler; a talebearer; a thing serving to reveal or disclose something.—*a.* Pertaining to anything that reveals what is not intended to be known.

tel•lu•ri•um, te•lūr/ē•əm, *n.* A rare, silver-white element resembling sulphur in its chemical properties, and usu. occurring in nature combined with gold, silver, or other metals.

Tel•star, tel/stär, *n.* The first artificial communications satellite, launched July 10, 1962, from Cape Canaveral (Kennedy).

tem•blor, tem/blər, tem/blôr, *n.* An earthquake.

te•mer•i•ty, tə•mār/i•tē, *n.* Extreme recklessness; rashness.

tem•per, tem/pər, *v.t.* To bring to a proper or desirable state by or as by mingling with something else; to modify by or as by blending or admixture; to soften or tone down; to prepare, as colors, by mixing with oil or another solvent; to keep within bounds; to curb.—*v.i.* To be or become tempered.—*n.* Mental balance, equanimity, or calmness: The provocation made him lose his *temper;* constitution or natural disposition; a particular frame of mind, feeling, or humor; heat of mind or passion, shown in outbursts of anger or resentment; the degree of hardness or flexibility of a substance given by tempering; a substance added to something to modify its properties. —**tem•per•a•bil•i•ty,** tem•pər•ə•bil/ə•tē, *n.* —**tem•per•a•ble,** *a.* —**tem•per•er,** *n.*

tem•per•a, tem/pər•ə, *n.* A method of painting in which the colors are mixed with some water-soluble binding, esp. egg yolk or an egg and oil mixture, to achieve a quick-drying mat finish; a painting done by this method; the pigment so prepared.

tem•per•a•ment, tem/pər•ə•mənt, tem/prə•mənt, *n.* The mixture of elements or qualities which make up a personality; nature; disposition; a sensitive, irritable, or rebellious disposition.

tem•per•a•ment•al, tem•pər•ə•men/təl, tem•prə•men/təl, *a.* Moody; whimsical; irritable; sensitive; high-strung; impulsive; showing a strongly marked individual temperament; arising from temperament; constitutional.

tem•per•ance, tem/pər•əns, tem/prəns, *n.* The observance of moderation in one's emotions, thoughts, or acts; restrained indulgence in, or abstinence from intoxicating beverages.

tem•per•ate, tem/pər•it, tem/prit, *a.* Showing self-restraint or moderation; moderate as regards the indulgence of the appetites or desires, esp. in using intoxicating liquors; not violent, excessive, or extreme; calm; not liable to excessive heat or cold: a *temperate* climate. —**tem•per•ate•ly,** *adv.* —**tem•per•ate•ness,** *n.*

Tem•per•ate Zone, *n.* Either of two latitudinal belts or zones on the earth between the tropics and the polar circles.

tem•per•a•ture, tem/pər•ə•chər, tem/prə•chər, *n.* The degree or intensity of heat or cold as measured on a thermometric scale; the body heat in animals, esp. man; any amount of body heat above a normal level, as above approx. 99° Fahrenheit in man.

tem•pered, tem/pərd, *a.* Having a certain disposition or temper; treated by tempering to the desired degree of hardness or elasticity.

tem•pest, tem/pist, *n.* An extensive current of wind rushing with great velocity and violence, often accompanied by hail, rain, or snow; a violent tumult or commotion.—*v.t.* To disturb or stir up violently.

tem•pes•tu•ous, tem•pes/chū•əs, *a.* Belonging to, resembling, characterized by, or having something to do with a tempest; violent. —**tem•pes•tu•ous•ly,** *adv.* —**tem•pes•tu•ous•ness,** *n.*

tem•plate, tem/plit, *n.* A flat, thin board or piece of sheet iron whose edge is shaped in some particular way, so that it may serve as a guide or test in making an article with a corresponding contour.

tem•ple, tem/pəl, *n.* An edifice dedicated to the service or worship of a deity or deities; a building, usu. large or pretentious, devoted to some public use. —**tem•pled,** *a.* —**tem•ple•like,** *a.*

tem•ple, tem/pəl, *n.* The flattened region on either side of the forehead.

tem•po, tem/pō, *n. pl.,* **-pos, -pi,** -pē. The speed or pace at which a musical piece, passage, or movement is to be played or sung; characteristic pace; rate of activity in general.

tem•po•ral, tem/pər•əl, tem/prəl, *a.* Pertaining to this life or this world; secular, civil, or lay; pertaining to measured or limited time; having limited existence. —**tem•por•al•i•ty,** tem•pə•ral/ə•tē, *n.* —**tem•po•**

ral·ly, *adv.* —**tem·po·ral·ness,** *n.*

tem·po·ral, tem′pər·əl, tem′prəl, *a.* Of or pertaining to the temple or temples of the head.

tem·po·rar·y, tem′pə·rer·ē, *a.* Existing or continuing for a limited time; transient. —**tem·po·rar·i·ly,** tem·pə·râr′ə·lē, *adv.* —**tem·po·rar·i·ness,** *n.*

tem·po·rize, tem′pə·rīz, *v.i.,* **-rized, -riz·ing.** To comply with the time or occasion, or yield temporarily or ostensibly to the current of opinion or circumstances; to act indecisively or use evasive means in order to gain time or delay matters. —**tem·po·ri·za·tion,** tem·pər·ə·zā′shen, *n.* —**tem·po·riz·er,** *n.* —**tem·po·riz·ing·ly,** *adv.*

tempt, tempt, *v.t.* To entice to an act which is evil, immoral, or unwise; to entice to something wrong by some specious argument or inducement; to invite or allure; to try to entice or persuade. —**tempt·a·ble,** *a.* —**temp·ta·tion,** temp·tā′shen, *n.* —**tempt·er,** *n.* —**tempt·ing,** *a.* —**tempt·ress,** *n.*

ten, ten, *n.* The cardinal number between nine and eleven; a playing card with ten spots.

ten·a·ble, ten′ə·bəl, *a.* Capable of being held, maintained, or defended. —**ten·a·bil·i·ty,** ten·ə·bil′ə·tē, **ten·a·ble·ness,** *n.* —**ten·a·bly,** *adv.*

te·na·cious, ti·nā′shəs, *a.* Holding fast, or characterized by keeping a firm hold; clinging or adhering persistently to something, often followed by *of;* highly retentive; persistent, stubborn, or obstinate; holding together; cohesive; tough. —**te·na·cious·ly,** *adv.* —**te·na·cious·ness,** *n.* —**te·nac·i·ty,** ti·nas′i·tē, *n.*

ten·ant, ten′ənt, *n.* One who occupies lands or houses for which he pays rent; a dweller; an occupant.—*v.t.* To hold or possess as a tenant.—*v.i.* To live as a tenant; to dwell. —**ten·an·cy,** *n. pl.,* **-cies.** —**ten·ant·a·ble,** *a.* —**ten·ant·less,** *a.*

ten·ant farm·er, *n.* One who farms land not his own and who pays rent with a portion of the crops or in cash.

tend, tend, *v.i.* To be directed or lead to or toward; to be naturally disposed or impelled to move in a particular direction; to incline or have a bent or drift in a particular direction.

tend, tend, *v.t.* To attend to by work, services, or care; to look after.—*v.i.* To attend by action or care, usu. followed by *to.*

ten·den·cy, ten′dən·sē, *n. pl.,* **-cies.** A natural or prevailing disposition to move, proceed, or act in some direction or toward some point, end, or result; an inclination, bent, or predisposition to something.

ten·den·tious, ten·den·cious, ten·den′shəs, *a.* Having a definite tendency, aim, or bias. —**ten·den·tious·ly, ten·den·cious·ly,** *adv.* —**ten·den·tious·ness, ten·den·cious·ness,** *n.*

ten·der, ten′dər, *a.* Soft or delicate in substance; yielding readily to force or pressure; easily broken; fragile; unable to endure fatigue, hardship, or rough treatment; young or immature; delicate, soft, or gentle; sympathetic; kind; compassionate; affectionate or loving; acutely or painfully sensitive; of a delicate or ticklish nature, or requiring careful or tactful handling.—*v.t.* To make tender. —**ten·der·ly,** *adv.* —**ten·der·ness,** *n.*

tend·er, ten′dər, *n.* One who attends to or takes charge of something; a vessel employed to attend one or more larger vessels, as for supplying provisions.

ten·der, ten′dər, *v.t.* To present formally for acceptance; to offer or proffer; to offer, as money or goods, in payment of a debt or other obligation.—*v.i.* To make a tender or offer.—*n.* An offer of something for acceptance; that which is offered; an offer, as of money or goods, in payment or satisfaction of a debt or other obligation. —**ten·der·er,** *n.*

ten·der·foot, ten′dər·fût, *n. pl.,* **-foots, -feet.** A novice or newcomer; one inexperienced in the rigors of the outdoor life in the ranching areas of the western states.

ten·der·ize, ten′də·rīz, *v.t.,* **-ized, -iz·ing.** To make tender or palatable. —**ten·der·iz·er,** *n.*

ten·der·loin, ten′dər·loyn, *n.* A strip of tender meat forming part of the loin of beef or pork.

ten·don, ten′dən, *n.* A hard, tough cord or bundle of fibers by which a muscle is attached to a bone or other part which it serves to move.

ten·dril, ten′drəl, *n.* A threadlike part of a climbing plant, serving to attach a plant to its support; something similar: curly *tendrils* of hair.

ten·e·ment, ten′ə·mənt, *n.* Any house or building to live in, or a dwelling house; a portion of a house or building occupied by a tenant as a separate dwelling; a tenement house. —**ten·e·men·ta·ry,** ten·ə·men′tə·rē, *a.*

ten·e·ment house, *n.* A house or building divided into sets of rooms tenanted by separate families or individuals, esp. a badly maintained building occupied by families in crowded parts of large cities.

ten·et, ten′it, *n.* Any opinion, principle, dogma, or doctrine believed or maintained as true by an organized group.

ten·nis, ten′is, *n.* A game with rackets in which the ball must pass back and forth over a net and land within a marked court.

ten·nis shoe, *n.* A lightweight sports shoe, usu. with a canvas upper and a flat, soft rubber sole. Also **sneak·er.**

ten·on, ten′ən, *n.* A projecting part on the end of a piece of wood for insertion into a corresponding hole or mortise to form a joint.—*v.t.* To join or fit with a tenon.

ten·or, ten′ər, *n.* The prevailing course or progression; the general direction or drift of thought in written or spoken discourse; the highest of the adult male natural voices; one who sings a tenor part; a musical instrument normally played in the range between alto and bass.—*a.* In music, of or for the tenor.

ten·pins, ten′pinz, *n. pl. but sing. in constr.* A game in which players bowl a ball down a bowling alley at ten wooden pins placed in a triangle and attempt to knock them down. Also **bowl·ing.** —**ten·pin,** *n.* A pin used in such a game.

tense, tens, *a.,* **tens·er, tens·est.** Stretched tight; taut or rigid; in a strained nervous or emotional condition. —*v.t., v.i.,* **tensed, tens·ing.** To make or become tense; stiffen. —**tense·ly,** *adv.* —**tense·ness,** *n.* —**ten·si·ty,** *n.*

tense, tens, *n.* One of the forms which verbs take in order to express the time or length of the action or condition referred to, such as past, present, or future; a set of such forms for the various persons.

ten·sile, ten′səl, *a.* Capable of tension or being extended; ductile. —**ten·sil·i·ty,** ten·sil′i·tē, *n.*

ten·sion, ten′shən, *n.* The act of stretching or straining; stiffness or tightness; mental or emotional strain; an intense or uncomfortable feeling between people or groups of people; stress on a material caused by a stretching or pulling force.—*v.t.* —**ten·sion·al,** *a.* —**ten·sion·less,** *a.* —**ten·sive,** *a.*

tent, tent, *n.* A portable shelter consisting of some flexible covering, stretched and sustained by poles. —*v.t.* To lodge in or furnish with tents.—*v.i.* To lodge or camp out in tents. —**tent·ed,** *a.*

ten·ta·cle, ten′tə·kəl, *n.* An elongated appendage on the head of many of the lower forms of animals, used as an instrument of prehension or as a feeler. —**ten·ta·cled,** *a.* —**ten·tac·u·lar,** ten·tak′yə·lər, *a.*

ten·ta·tive, ten′tə·tiv, *a.* Temporary, provisional, or unsure; based on trial or experiment. —**ten·ta·tive·ly,** *adv.* —**ten·ta·tive·ness,** *n.*

ten·ter·hook, ten′tər·hûk, *n.* A hook for stretching

cloth on a drying frame. **—on ten·ter·hooks,** in suspense; anxious.

tenth, tenth, *a.* Following the ninth; being the ordinal of ten; being one of ten equal parts into which anything is divided.—*n.* One of ten equal parts; that which follows the ninth in a series. **—tenth·ly,** *adv.*

ten·u·ous, ten′yů·əs, *a.* Thin or slender; of little density; rare; weak, unsure, or vague. **—ten·u·ous·ly,** *adv.* **—ten·u·ous·ness,** *n.*

ten·ure, ten′yər, *n.* The act, manner, or right of holding property; the terms or conditions upon which anything is held or possessed; length of time of holding or possessing; a status granted to one after serving a period of time in a particular position which assures permanency in that position. **—ten·u·ri·al,** ten·yûr′ē·əl, *a.* **—ten·u·ri·al·ly,** *adv.*

te·pee, tē′pē, *n.* The American Indian cone-shaped tent. Also **tee·pee.**

tep·id, tep′id, *a.* Lukewarm. **—te·pid·i·ty,** te·pid′i·tē, **tep·id·ness,** *n.* **—tep·id·ly,** *adv.*

te·qui·la, tə·kē′lə, *n.* An alcoholic liquor distilled from the Mexican agave plant.

ter·cen·te·nar·y, tər·sen·ten′ə·rē, tər·sen′tə·ner·ē, *n. pl.,* **-ies.** The 300th anniversary of any event. —*a.* Also **ter·cen·ten·ni·al,** tər·sen·ten′ē·əl.

ter·cet, tər′sit, tər·set′, *n.* A group of three rhyming lines.

term, tərm, *n.* A word or phrase by which something fixed and definite is expressed; a limit; the time for which anything lasts; a time or period fixed in some way; a day on which rent or interest is regularly payable; one of the periods into which a school year is divided; *pl.,* words or language used in a general way; conditions or propositions stated and offered for acceptance; relative position or footing.—*v.t.* To name; to denominate. **—bring to terms,** to reduce to submission or to conditions. **—come to terms,** to agree. **—in terms of,** with regard to.

ter·ma·gant, tər′mə·gənt, *n.* A brawling, turbulent woman; a shrew.—*a.* Abusive; querulous; vixenish. **—ter·ma·gant·ly,** *adv.*

ter·mi·na·ble, tər′mə·nə·bəl, *a.* That may be terminated, as a contract, etc.; limitable; coming to an end after a certain time: a loan *terminable* in 5 years.

ter·mi·nal, tər′mə·nəl, *n.* That which terminates; an extremity; a terminus or station.—*a.* Relating to or forming the end or extremity; pertaining to or occurring in a fixed time period; causing death, as a disease. **—ter·mi·nal·ly,** *adv.*

ter·mi·nate, tər′mə·nāt, *v.t.,* **-nated, -nat·ing.** To bound; to limit; to form the extreme point or side of; to put an end to; to complete.—*v.i.* To come to an end. **—ter·mi·na·tion,** tər·mə·nā′shən, *n.* **—ter·mi·na·tive,** *a.* **—ter·mi·na·tive·ly,** *adv.* **—ter·mi·na·tor,** *n.*

ter·mi·nol·o·gy, tər·mə·nol′ə·jē, *n. pl.,* **-gies.** A set of terms used in a particular field of knowledge. **—ter·mi·no·log·i·cal,** tər·mə·nə·loj′ə·kəl, *a.* **—ter·mi·no·log·i·cal·ly,** *adv.*

term in·sur·ance, *n.* A type of insurance designed to pay benefits for losses incurred during a specific period of time only.

ter·mi·nus, tər′mə·nəs, *n. pl.,* **-nus·es, -ni,** -nī. The end or limit; the finishing point or goal; extremity; either termination point of a travel line.

ter·mite, tər′mīt, *n.* A pale-colored, soft-bodied, wood-eating, social insect, often very destructive to furniture and wooden structures.

tern, tərn, *n.* A bird allied to the gull, but which usu. has a slenderer body and bill.

ter·race, tār′is, *n.* A raised level with a vertical or sloping front or sides; one of a series of levels with vertical or sloping front, rising one above another; an open platform, promenade, or porch; balcony; an open, usu. paved area adjoining a house or building; patio; a row of houses running along the face or top of a slope, or a street with such a row or rows.—*v.t.,* **-raced, -rac·ing.** To form into or furnish with a terrace or terraces.

ter·ra cot·ta, tār′ə kot′ə, *n.* A type of earthenware or clay, usu. unglazed, baked in a kiln to a durable hardness; an object made of such clay; its brownish or dull orange color, or a similar color. **—ter·ra-cot·ta,** *a.*

ter·ra fir·ma, tār′ə fər′mə, *n.* Firm or solid earth.

ter·rain, tə·rān′, tār′ān, *n.* A tract of land, esp. as considered with reference to its suitability for a certain purpose.

ter·ra·pin, tār′ə·pin, *n.* A N. American tidewater or fresh-water turtle.

ter·rar·i·um, tə·rār′ē·əm, *n. pl.,* **-a, -ums.** An enclosure usu. having glass sides for growing plants or keeping small land animals.

ter·res·tri·al, tə·res′trē·əl, *a.* Pertaining to or existing on the earth; pertaining to land, as opposed to water or air; pertaining to the world; mundane or worldly.—*n.* **—ter·res·tri·al·ly,** *adv.*

ter·ri·ble, tār′ə·bəl, *a.* Exciting fear or terror; dreadful; appalling; extreme; difficult. *Informal.* Disagreeable or very bad; of inferior quality. **—ter·ri·ble·ness,** *n.* **—ter·ri·bly,** *adv.*

ter·ri·er, tār′ē·ər, *n.* Any of various breeds of energetic dogs orig. used to hunt small burrowing animals, as rabbits.

ter·rif·ic, tə·rif′ik, *a.* Terrifying; dreadful. *Informal.* Extraordinary, extreme, or splendid. **—ter·rif·i·cal·ly,** *adv.*

ter·ri·fy, tār′ə·fī, *v.t.,* **-fied, -fy·ing.** To cause or pervade with terror; frighten; to alarm or shock; to menace; intimidate. **—ter·ri·fy·ing·ly,** *adv.*

ter·ri·to·ry, tār′ə·tôr·ē, *n. pl.,* **-ries.** Any tract of land, region, or district; the land and waters belonging to or under the jurisdiction of a state, sovereign, or other body. (*Cap.*) In the government of the U.S., a region or district not admitted to the Union as a state but with an organized government; some similar district elsewhere; domain or province; the region assigned to a salesman, agent, or the like. **—ter·ri·to·ri·al,** tār·ə·tôr′ē·əl, ter·ə·tō′rē·əl, *a.*

ter·ror, tār′ər, *n.* Intense, sharp, overmastering fear, or a feeling or instance of this; a cause of intense fear. *Informal.* A person or thing that is esp. dreadful or unpleasant. **—ter·ror·less,** *a.*

ter·ror·ism, tār′ər·iz·əm, *n.* A terrorizing; state of being terrorized; the systematic use of terror, esp. through unlawful violence, to intimidate or coerce, or to overthrow a government. **—ter·ror·ist,** *n.* **—ter·ror·is·tic,** tər·ər·is′tik, *a.* **—ter·ror·less,** *a.*

ter·ror·ize, tār′ə·rīz, *v.t.,* **-ized, -iz·ing.** To fill or overcome with terror; to dominate, coerce, or subdue by intimidation. **—ter·ror·i·za·tion,** ter·ər·ə·zā′shən, *n.* **—ter·ror·iz·er,** *n.*

ter·ry, tār′ē, *n. pl.,* **-ries.** A fabric with uncut pile loops, esp. a cotton one used for towels. Also **ter·ry cloth.**

terse, tərs, *a.,* **ters·er, ters·est.** Free from superfluity; neat and concise; to the point. **—terse·ly,** *adv.* **—terse·ness,** *n.*

ter·ti·ar·y, tār′shē·er·ē, tər′shə·rē, *a.* Of the third order, rank, or formation; third.

tes·sel·lat·ed, tes′ə·lā·tid, *a.* Formed by inlaying materials of different colors in little squares, triangles, or other geometrical figures, or by mosaic work. **—tes·sel·late,** *v.t.,* **-lat·ed, -lat·ing.** **—tes·sel·la·tion,** tes·ə·lā′shən, *n.*

test, test, *n.* Any trial or examination; means of trial; a criterion; a standard; means of discrimination; a group of questions or problems to be answered or solved as a gauge of ability, knowledge, or aptitude. —*v.t.* To try; to subject to trial and examination.—*v.i.* To make, give, or achieve a certain rating or score from an examination. **—test·a·ble,** *a.* **—test·er,** *n.*

tes·ta·ment, tes′tə·mənt, *n.* A will. (*Cap.*) Either of the two general divisions of the Bible: the Old Testament or the New Testament. **—tes·ta·men·ta·ry,** tes·tə·men′tə·rē, *a.*

tes·tate, tes′tāt, *a.* Having made and left a valid will.

tes·ta·tor, tes′tā·tər, te·stā′tər, *n.* One who makes a will; one leaving a will at death. **—tes·ta·trix,** te·stā′triks, *n. fem. pl.,* **tes·ta·tri·ces,** te·stā′tri·sēz.

tes·ti·cle, tes′tə·kəl, *n.* One of the two reproductive glands in the male. Also **tes·tis.** **—tes·tic·u·lar,** te·stik′yə·lər, *a.*

tes·ti·fy, tes′tə·fī, *v.i.,* **-fied, -fy·ing.** To make a solemn declaration; to indicate; to give evidence under oath.—*v.t.* To affirm or declare solemnly; to state in support of; to bear witness to; to affirm under oath. **—tes·ti·fi·er,** *n.*

tes·ti·mo·ni·al, tes·tə·mō′nē·əl, *n.* A writing certifying to the character, conduct, or qualifications of a person, or to the value or excellence of a thing; a letter of recommendation; something given or done as an expression of appreciation.—*a.* Relating to or serving as testimony or a testimonial.

tes·ti·mo·ny, tes′tə·mō·nē, *n. pl.,* **-nies.** Evidence given by a witness under oath or affirmation; evidence given in support of a fact or statement; proof; open declaration or profession, as of faith.

tes·tis, tes′tis, *n. pl.,* **-tes, -tēz.** A testicle.

tes·tos·ter·one, te·stos′tə·rōn, *n.* A male testicular hormone that promotes male secondary sex characteristics.

test tube, *n.* A hollow cylinder of thin glass with one end closed, used in scientific experiments. **—test-tube,** test′toob′, test′tūb′, *a.*

tes·ty, tes′tē, *a.,* **-ti·er, -ti·est.** Touchy; easily irritated or annoyed. **—tes·ti·ly,** *adv.* **—tes·ti·ness,** *n.*

tet·a·nus, tet′ə·nəs, *n.* An infectious, often fatal disease, which gains entrance to the body through wounds, characterized by more or less violent tonic spasm and rigidity of many muscles. Tetanus of the jaw muscles is called lockjaw. **—te·tan·ic,** ti·tan′ik, **te·tan·i·cal,** *a.*

tête-à-tête, tāt′ə·tāt′, *a.* Private; between or for two persons exclusively.—*n.* A private talk between two people.—*adv.*

teth·er, teth′ər, *n.* A rope or chain by which an animal is confined within certain limits; the limit of one's powers, capabilities, or resources.—*v.t.* To confine with a tether.

tet·ra·eth·yl lead, tet·rə·eth′əl led, *n.* A heavy liquid which is oily, colorless, and poisonous, used to prevent knocking in engines.

tet·ra·he·dron, te·trə·hē′drən, *n. pl.,* **-drons, -dra.** A triangular pyramid having four plane faces. **—tet·ra·he·dral,** *a.*

te·tral·o·gy, te·tral′ə·jē, *n. pl.,* **-gies.** A series of four interrelated works, as of literature, music, art, and the like.

text, tekst, *n.* The main part of a printed or written work, as distinguished from index, pictures, notes, and the like; the exact or original wording of a printed or written work; a subject or a theme; the words of a musical composition; a textbook; a passage of Scripture, esp. one selected as the theme of a sermon or discussion. **—tex·tu·al,** tex′chū·əl, *a.*

text·book, tekst′bûk, *n.* A book used by students for a particular branch of study; a manual of instruction.

tex·tile, teks′til, teks′tīl, *a.* Woven or capable of being woven; formed by weaving.—*n.* A fabric made by weaving; any material, as a yarn or thread, which may be used for weaving.

tex·ture, teks′chər, *n.* The characteristic disposition of the interwoven or intertwined threads, strands, or the like which make up a textile fabric; the characteristic disposition of the constituent parts of anything. **—tex·tur·al,** *a.* **—tex·tur·al·ly,** *adv.* **—tex·tured,** *a.*

thal·a·mus, thal′ə·məs, *n. pl.,* **-mi, -mī.** A part of the forebrain composed of gray matter which relays sensory impulses to the cortex of the brain. **—tha·lam·ic,** thə·lam′ik, *a.* **—tha·lam·i·cal·ly,** *adv.*

thal·li·um, thal′ē·əm, *n.* A rare metallic element, soft and malleable, resembling lead, and having poisonous compounds.

thal·lo·phyte, thal′ə·fīt, *n.* Any one of the lowest phylum of plants, comprising the algae bacteria, lichens, fungi, and some minor groups. **—thal·lo·phyt·ic,** thal·ə·fit′ik, *a.*

thal·lus, thal′əs, *n. pl.,* **thal·li,** thal′ī, **thal·lus·es.** A vegetative body undifferentiated into true leaves, stem, and root as the plant body of typical thallophytes.

than, than, *unstressed* thən, *conj.* A particle used after certain adjectives and adverbs which express comparison or diversity, such as *more, better, other, otherwise, rather,* or *else,* for the purpose of introducing the second member of the comparison.—*prep.* Compared with.

thank, thangk, *v.t.* To give thanks or express gratitude to; to blame or hold accountable for, usu. used ironically. **—thank·er,** *n.*

thank·ful, thangk′fəl, *a.* Expressive of gratitude; grateful; appreciative. **—thank·ful·ly,** *adv.* **—thank·ful·ness,** *n.*

thank·less, thangk′lis, *a.* Not feeling or expressing gratitude; ungrateful; not appreciated. **—thank·less·ly,** *adv.* **—thank·less·ness,** *n.*

thanks, thangks, *n. pl.* An expression of gratitude. **—interj.** I thank you. **—thanks to,** due to; because of.

thanks·giv·ing, thangks·giv′ing, *n.* The act of expressing thanks. (*Cap.*) A national U.S. holiday celebrated on the fourth Thursday of November: also **Thanks·giv·ing Day.**

that, that, *unstressed* thət, *a. pl.,* **those.** Being previously mentioned or otherwise understood: *that* man; being more remote, as in place, time, or consideration, as opposed to *this:* I was talking about this year, but you were thinking about *that* year.—*pron. pl.,* **those.** One or something previously mentioned or otherwise understood: We talked about *that* yesterday; one or something more remote, as opposed to *this:* When this happens, *that* will surely follow; something; an unspecified or unknown quality or object: *That* is the thing I don't like about him; who, whom, or which: the subject *that* we were talking about.—*adv.* To such an extent, degree, or amount; so: He shouldn't pay *that* much.—*conj.* Used chiefly to connect a subordinate to a principal clause, as to introduce a reason, purpose, consequence, or to supply any subject or object of the principal verb: We knew *that* he was gone; used to introduce a wish: Would *that* I were there!

thatch, thach, *n.* Any of various natural materials, as straw, reeds, or palm leaves, used as roofing for a dwelling; also **thatch·ing.**—*v.t.* To cover with thatch. **—thatch·er,** *n.*

thaw, thô, *v.i.* To be reduced from a frozen to a semiliquid or liquid state; to melt; to become sufficiently warm to melt ice or snow; to become less reserved, formal, or tense.—*v.t.* To cause to thaw; to make less cold or reserved.—*n.* The process of thawing; a period of warmer weather that causes ice and snow to melt.

the, *stressed* thē, *unstressed before a consonant* thə, *unstressed before a vowel* thē, *def. art.* Used, esp. before nouns, with a specifying or particularizing effect, as opposed to the indefinite or generalizing force of the indefinite article, *a* or *an:* the book you borrowed; used to mark a noun as denoting something well-known or unique: *the* Alps; used with, or as part of, a title: *the* President of the U.S.; used to mark a noun as denoting a superlative example of its kind: *the* man for the job; used before a noun generically: *the* cat is a mammal; used before adjectives used as nouns: to heal *the* sick, *the* sublime. *Informal.* Used in place of a possessive pronoun: *the* wife.

---

the, *t̶h̶ə, t̶h̶ē, adv.* In or by that; on that account; in some degree: used to modify an adjective or adverb in the comparative degree: His shirt is none *the* worse for wear; by how much; by so much; in what degree; in that degree: used correlatively, in one instance with relative force and in the other with demonstrative force: *the* more *the* merrier, *the* sooner *the* better.

the·a·ter, the·a·tre, *t̶h̶ē/ə·tər, n.* A building or place for the presentation of plays, operas, or movies; a playhouse; a room with seats rising stepwise for lectures or the like; dramatic representation as a division of the performing arts; dramatic quality or impact: wonderful *theater;* the locality where important events take place.

the·at·ri·cal, *t̶h̶ē·at/ri·kəl, a.* Pertaining to a theater or to scenic representations; calculated for display; artificial. Also **the·at·ric.**—*n. pl.* Dramatic presentations, esp. when given by amateurs. **—the·at·ri·cal·ism,** *t̶h̶ē·at·ri·kal/ə·tē,* **the·at·ri·cal·i·ty,** *n.* **—the·at·ri·cal·ly,** *adv.*

thee, *t̶h̶ē, pron.* The objective and dative case of *thou.*

theft, *theft, n.* The act of stealing; larceny.

their, *t̶h̶ār, unstressed t̶h̶ər, a.* Pertaining or belonging to them: the possessive case of the third person plural pronoun, **they.**

theirs, *t̶h̶ārz, pron.* That which pertains or belongs to a particular group; the possessive case of **they,** used predicatively.

the·ism, *t̶h̶ē/iz·əm, n.* A religious or philosophical doctrine utilizing the concept of deity to explain man's existence; the doctrine that all things originate in a unitary God; monotheism. **—the·ist,** *n., a.* **—the·is·tic,** *t̶h̶ē·is/tik,* **the·is·ti·cal,** *a.* **—the·is·ti·cal·ly,** *adv.*

them, *t̶h̶em, unstressed t̶h̶əm, pron.* The objective case of **they.**

theme, *t̶h̶ēm, n.* A subject of discourse or discussion; a short dissertation composed by a student on a given subject; the leading subject in a composition or movement; a melody identifying a dance band, radio program, etc.: also **theme song.** **—the·mat·ic,** *t̶h̶ē·mat/ik, a.* **—the·mat·i·cal·ly,** *adv.*

them·selves, *t̶h̶em·selvz/, t̶h̶əm·selvz/, pron. pl.* A reflexive or emphatic form of the third person plural pronoun, **they.**

then, *t̶h̶en, adv.* At that time; immediately or soon afterward; next in order of time; next in place; in addition; besides; in that case; in those circumstances.—*a.* Being or existing at that time.—*n.* That time. **—then and there,** immediately; at that time and place.

thence, *t̶h̶ens, adv.* From that place; from that time; for that reason; from this; out of this.

thence·forth, *t̶h̶ens·fôrth/, t̶h̶ens·fôrth/, adv.* From that time or place forward. Also **thence·for·ward, thence·for·wards,** *t̶h̶ens·fôr/wərd.*

the·oc·ra·cy, *t̶h̶ē·ok/rə·sē, n. pl.,* **-cies.** Government by priests or by an ecclesiastical institution claiming to be divinely directed; a state thus governed. **—the·o·crat,** *t̶h̶ē/ə·krat, n.* **—the·o·crat·ic, the·o·crat·i·cal,** *a.* **—the·o·crat·i·cal·ly, adv.*

the·ol·o·gy, *t̶h̶ē·ol/ə·jē, n. pl.,* **-gies.** The philosophical discipline dealing with the question of God in relation to other philosophical questions; a branch of Christian systematics dealing with man's creatural state; an historical analysis of the doctrines and beliefs of a religion. **—the·o·lo·gian,** *t̶h̶ē·ə·lō/jən, t̶h̶ē·ə·lō/jē·ən, n.* **—the·o·log·ic, the·o·log·i·cal,** *t̶h̶ē·ə·loj/i·kəl, a.* **—the·o·log·i·cal·ly, adv.*

the·o·rem, *t̶h̶ē/ə·rəm, t̶h̶ēr/əm, n.* A position to be proved as a logical development of other positions; a position accepted as an acknowledged truth or established principle. **—the·o·re·mat·ic,** *t̶h̶ē·ər·ə·mat/ik, t̶h̶ēr·ə·mat/ik, a.* **—the·o·re·mat·i·cal·ly, adv.*

the·o·ret·i·cal, *t̶h̶ē·ə·ret/i·kəl, a.* Pertaining to or depending on theory or speculation; hypothetical; speculative; visionary; not practical. Also **the·o·ret·ic.** **—the·o·ret·i·cal·ly, adv.*

the·o·rize, *t̶h̶ē/ə·rīz, v.i.,* **-rized, -riz·ing.** To form one or more theories; to speculate. **—the·o·re·ti·cian, the·o·rist,** *t̶h̶ē·ər·ə·tish/ən, t̶h̶ē/ə·rist, n.* **—the·o·ri·za·tion,** *t̶h̶ē·ər·ə·zā/shən, n.* **—the·o·riz·er, n.*

the·o·ry, *t̶h̶ē/ə·rē, t̶h̶ēr/ē, n. pl.,* **-ries.** A systematic arrangement of facts with respect to some real or hypothetical laws; a hypothetical explanation of phenomena; a hypothesis not yet empirically verified as law but accepted as the basis of experimentation; a plan or system suggested as a method of action; an ideal arrangement of events, usu. preceded by *in;* abstract knowledge; speculation; conjecture.

the·os·o·phy, *t̶h̶ē·os/ə·fē, n. pl.,* **-phies.** A form of philosophical or religious thought characterized by the belief in a transcendent reality which can be perceived or experienced mystically. **—the·o·soph·ic,** *t̶h̶ē·ə·sof/ik,* **the·o·soph·i·cal,** *a.* **—the·o·soph·i·cal·ly, adv.* **—the·os·o·phist, n.*

ther·a·peu·tic, *ther·ə·pū/tik, a.* Curative. Also **ther·a·peu·ti·cal.** **—ther·a·peu·ti·cal·ly, adv.*

ther·a·peu·tics, *ther·ə·pū/tiks, n. pl. but sing. in constr.* That branch of medicine dealing with the treatment of diseases. **—ther·a·peu·tist, n.*

ther·a·py, *thār/ə·pē, n. pl.,* **-pies.** The treatment of disability or disease, as by some remedial or curative process; curative or therapeutic quality or ability. **—ther·a·pist, n.*

there, *t̶h̶ār, t̶h̶ər, adv.* In that place; at that place; to that place; at that point; in that particular instance or respect.—*interj.* Used with an expression of greeting: Hello, *there!* An expression of consolation: *There, there;* an expression of defiance, usu. preceded by *so;* an expression of relief, as at a task completed; an expression of satisfaction or approval.—*pron.* Used to begin clauses or sentences before a verb when there is an inversion of the subject: *There* came a day of reckoning; that place, as previously designated: She lives near *there.*—*n.* That state, position, or point.

there·a·bout, *t̶h̶ār/ə·bowt, adv.* Near that place; about that time; near that number, degree, or quantity; approximately. Also **there·a·bouts.**

there·af·ter, *t̶h̶er·af/tər, adv.* After that; afterward.

there·at, *t̶h̶er·at/, adv.* At that place; at that time; on that account.

there·by, *t̶h̶er·bī/, t̶h̶ār/bī, adv.* By that means; in connection with that.

there·for, *t̶h̶er·fôr/, adv.* For that, this, or it.

there·fore, *t̶h̶ār/fôr, adv., conj.* For that or this reason; consequently.

there·from, *t̶h̶er·frəm/, t̶h̶er·from/, adv.* From that; from this; from it.

there·in, *t̶h̶er·in/, adv.* Into or in that or this place, time, or thing; in that or this particular point or respect.

there·of, *t̶h̶er·ov/, t̶h̶er·əv/, adv.* Of that, this, or it; because of that reason or cause.

there·on, *t̶h̶er·on/, t̶h̶er·ôn/, adv.* On that or this; thereupon.

there·to, *t̶h̶er·too/, adv.* To that or this, as thing or place.

there·to·fore, *t̶h̶er·tə·fôr/, t̶h̶er·tə·fôr/, adv.* Up to or before that time; prior to that.

there·up·on, *t̶h̶er·ə·pon/, t̶h̶er·ə·pôn/, adv.* Upon that or this; in consequence of that; therefore; at once.

there·with, *t̶h̶er·with/, t̶h̶er·with/, adv.* With that or this; moreover or besides that; thereupon or immediately following.

ther·mal, *t̶h̶ər/məl, a.* Of, caused by, or pertaining to heat. **—ther·mal·ly, adv.*

ther·mo·dy·nam·ics, *t̶h̶ər·mō·dī·nam/iks, t̶h̶ər·mō·dī·nam/iks, n. pl. but sing. in constr.* That area of physics which deals with heat and its relationship with various other forms of energy, esp. mechanical energy. **—ther·mo·dy·nam·ic, ther·mo·dy·nam·i·cal, a.*

ther·mo·e·lec·tric·i·ty, *t̶h̶ər·mō·ē·lek·tris/ə·tē, t̶h̶ər·mō·i·lek·tris/ə·tē, n.* Electricity produced directly from heat. **—ther·mo·e·lec·tric,** *t̶h̶ər·mō·ē·*

lek′trik, thər·mō·i·lek′trik, **ther·mo·e·lec·tri·cal,** *a.*

ther·mom·e·ter, thər·mom′i·tər, *n.* An instrument by which temperatures are measured, consisting usu. of a closed glass tube containing some liquid, most often mercury or alcohol, which expands or contracts with variations of temperature. —ther·mo·met′ric, thər·mə·me′trik, **ther·mo·met·ri·cal,** *a.* —ther·mo·met·ri·cal·ly, *adv.*

ther·mo·nu·cle·ar, thər·mō·noo′klē·ər, thər·mō·nū′klē·ər, *a.* Of or pertaining to nuclear reactions or processes, esp. nuclear fusion, which in their inception require extremely high temperatures.

ther·mo·plas·tic, thər·mə·plas′tik, *a.* Becoming soft and supple when heated, as of various plastics. —*n.* Any material or substance of this kind.

ther·mos bot·tle, thər′məs, *n.* Vacuum bottle. Also **ther·mos.**

ther·mo·stat, thər′mə·stat, *n.* An automatic device for regulating temperature, as one in which the expansion of a piece of metal by heat closes an electric circuit, which in turn causes a ventilator or the like to open. —ther·mo·stat·ic, thər·mə·stat′ik, *a.* —ther·mo·stat·i·cal·ly, *adv.*

the·sau·rus, thi·sôr′əs, *n. pl.,* -sau·ri, sôr′ī, -sau·rus·es. A book containing synonyms and antonyms.

the·sis, thē′sis, *n. pl.,* -ses, -sēz. A proposition, statement, or assertion laid down or stated, esp. one to be discussed and proved or to be maintained against objections; a dissertation, as one presented by a candidate for a diploma or degree.

Thes·pi·an, thes′pē·ən, *a.* Pertaining to tragedy or to the dramatic art in general; tragic; dramatic.—*n.* A tragedian; an actor or actress.

thew, thū, *n. Usu. pl.* Well-developed muscles or strong sinews; *pl.,* strength or power, esp. muscular.

they, ṯhā, *pron.*—sing. nom. *he, she,* or *it,* poss. *his, her,* or *its,* obj. *him, her,* or *it;* pl. nom. *they,* poss. *their* or *theirs,* obj. *them;* intens. and refl. *themselves.* Nominative plural of *he, she,* and *it* used in designating two or more persons, creatures, or things whose identity is already established; often used to denote persons indefinitely or people in general: *They* say he beats his wife.

thi·a·mine, thī′ə·mēn, thī′ə·min, *n.* A B-complex vitamin necessary for proper activity of the nervous system and carbohydrate metabolism. Also Vitamin B_1, **thi·a·min,** thī′ə·min.

thick, thik, *a.* Having relatively great extent from one surface or side to its opposite; not thin; having a specified measurement in depth or in a direction perpendicular to that of length and breadth; placed close together, dense, or compact; numerous, abundant, or plentiful; filled, covered, or abounding, usu. followed by *with;* having great consistency or density; containing much solid matter in suspension or solution; dense with mist, smoke, or haze, as the weather or atmosphere; muffled, husky, hoarse, or indistinct; dull; stupid. *Informal.* Close in friendship or intimate.—*adv.*—*n.* That which is thick; the thickest, most crowded, or most active part, as of a fight. —**lay it on thick.** *Informal.* To exaggerate or overstate; to praise or flatter excessively. —**through thick and thin,** through good and bad circumstances; loyally. —thick·ish, *a.* —thick·ly, *adv.* —thick·ness, *n.*

thick·en, thik′ən, *v.i., v.t.* To become or make thick or thicker; to become or make more involved, intense, or complicated. —thick·en·er, *n.* —thick·en·ing, *n., a.*

thick·et, thik′it, *n.* A thick or dense growth of shrubs, bushes, or small trees. —thick·et·ed, *a.*

thick-head·ed, thik′hed′id, *a.* Stupid; dull. —thick·head·ed·ness, *n.*

thick·set, thik′set′, *a.* Of thick form or build; stocky; stout; set or growing thickly, or in close arrangement; dense.—*n.* A thicket.

thick-skinned, thik′skind′, *a.* Having a thick skin; not easily irritated, as by criticism or ridicule; callous or insensitive.

thief, thēf, *n. pl.,* **thieves.** One who steals secretly or without open force; a person who commits or is guilty of theft.

thieve, thēv, *v.t., v.i.,* **thieved, thiev·ing.** To rob or steal. —thiev·ish, *a.* —thiev·ish·ly, *adv.* —thiev·ish·ness, *n.*

thiev·er·y, thē′və·rē, *n. pl.,* -ies. The practice or the act of stealing.

thigh, thī, *n.* That part of the leg between the hip and the knee.

thigh·bone, thī′bōn, *n.* Femur.

thim·ble, thim′bəl, *n.* A usu. metal or plastic bell-shaped cap worn on the finger to push the needle in sewing.

thin, thin, *a.,* **thin·ner, thin·nest.** Having relatively little extent from one surface or side to its opposite, or not thick; of small cross section in comparison with the length, or slender; having little flesh, spare, or lean; easily seen through, transparent, flimsy, or inadequate; not dense; sparse; having relatively slight consistency, as a liquid; fluid; without solidity or substance, or unsubstantial; faint, slight, poor, or feeble; lacking body, richness, or strength.—*adv.* In a thin manner; thinly.—*v.t.,* **thinned, thin·ning.** To make thin or thinner.—*v.i.* To become thin or thinner; become reduced or diminished, or go: used with *down, off,* or *away.* —thin·ly, *adv.* —thin·ness, *n.* —thin·nish, *a.*

thine, ṯhin, *pron.* The possessive form of **thou** used predicatively or without a noun following, or attributively before a noun beginning with a vowel or *h;* thy.

thing, thing, *n.* That which is or may become an object of thought, whether animate or inanimate; that which exists individually, whether in fact or in idea; an entity; that which cannot be specifically designated or precisely described; that which is signified, as distinguished from a word, symbol, or idea representing it; an inanimate object; a living being or creature, regarded with pity, affection, or contempt; a matter or affair; an occurrence; performance; deed; *pl.,* personal possessions or belongings. *Informal.* A phobia or obsession. —**make a good thing of,** to gain or benefit by, as an experience or situation. —**see things,** to have hallucinations. —**the thing,** the advisable, proper, or important result or act; that which is fashionable.

think, thingk, *v.t.,* **thought, think·ing.** To form or conceive mentally, as a thought; to speculate upon or ponder, usu. followed by *over* or *through;* to examine or solve rationally, usu. followed by *out;* to concentrate on or be preoccupied with, as a particular subject; recollect or remember; to plan or contrive, used with *up;* intend; to believe or suppose; to consider or suppose as specified; to suspect; to anticipate or expect.—*v.i.* To exercise the intellectual faculties in forming ideas, judgments, etc.; to reason; meditate; to form or have an idea or mental image, used with *of* or *about;* to reflect upon; to remember, usu. with *of;* to have consideration, usu. with *of;* to make mental discovery or plan, usu. with *of;* to have a notion or plan, usu. with *of;* to have a belief or opinion as indicated: to *think* well of someone; expect: She didn't *think* to find him there.—*a.* —**think bet·ter of,** to reconsider or alter, as an intended action; to hold a higher opinion of. —**think fit,** to regard as desirable or appropriate. —think·a·ble, *a.* —think·er, *n.* —think·ing, *a., n.*

think tank, *n.* A group of specialists working together for the solution of problems.

thin·ner, thin′ər, *n.* A volatile liquid used to thin paint.

thin-skinned, thin′skind′, *a.* Unduly sensitive to abuse; easily offended or irritated.

third, thərd, *a.* Following the second; being the ordinal

---

a- hat, fāte, fāre, fäther; **e-** met, mē; **i-** pin, pīne; **o-** not, nōte, ôrb, moove (move), boy, pownd; **u-** cūbe, bûll, tûk (took); **ch-** chin; **th-** thick, ṯhen; **zh-** vizhon (vision); **ə-** ego, takən, pencəl, lemən, bərd (bird).

of 3; being one of three equal parts into which anything is divided.—*n.* One of three equal parts; that which follows the second in series. —**third·ly**, *adv.*

third class, *n.* The rank, class, or grade classified under second class; the cheapest accommodations, as on trains and ships; the U.S. postal classification which consists of printed matter as circulars and books, excluding regular periodicals and newspapers. —**third-class**, *thərd′klas′, a.*

third de·gree, *n. Informal.* The use of severe measures in examining a person in order to get information or a confession.

third di·men·sion, *n.* Thickness or depth; the dimension that distinguishes a solid object from a two-dimensional object; a quality or something that enhances reality. —**third-di·men·sion·al**, thərd·di·men′shən·əl, *a.*

third per·son, *n.* A form of a pronoun or verb that is used by a writer or speaker in referring to the person or thing spoken about, as *he, she, it,* or *they.*

third-rate, thərd′rāt′, *a.* Quite inferior; far below average. —**third-rat·er**, *n.*

thirst, thərst, *n.* The distressing sensation of dryness in the mouth and throat caused by need of fluids; the physical condition resulting from this want; strong or eager desire; a craving.—*v.i.* To feel thirst; be thirsty; to have a strong desire.

thirst·y, thər′stē, *a.*, -**i·er**, -**i·est.** Having thirst; craving drink; lacking moisture, as land or plants; dry, parched, or arid; eagerly desirous, or eager. —**thirst·i·ly**, *adv.* —**thirst·i·ness**, *n.*

thir·teen, thər′tēn′, *n.* The cardinal number between twelve and fourteen; a symbol representing it.—*a.*

thir·teenth, thər′tēnth′, *a.* Following the twelfth; being the ordinal of 13; being one of 13 equal parts into which anything is divided.—*n.*

thir·ti·eth, thər′tē·ith, *a.* Following the twenty-ninth; being the ordinal of 30; being one of 30 equal parts into which anything is divided.—*n.*

thir·ty, thər′tē, *n. pl.*, -**ties.** The cardinal number between 29 and 31; a symbol representing it.—*a.*

this, ŧhis, *pron. pl.,* **these.** A demonstrative term indicating a person, thing, idea, or condition as being present, near, mentioned, understood, or referred to now; the person or thing emphasized: contrasted with *that.*—*a.* To the indicated extent or degree: *this* much, *this* far, or *this* early.

this·tle, this′əl, *n.* A prickly plant with small purple or white flower heads. —**this·tly**, *a.*, -**i·er**, -**i·est.**

this·tle·down, this′əl·down, *n.* The silky down of the fruit of a thistle.

thith·er, ŧhith′ər, ŧhith′ər, *adv.* To that place; toward, or in that direction.—*a.* On the other side; farther.

thong, thông, thong, *n.* A strap of leather used for fastening anything.

tho·rax, thōr′aks, thôr′aks, *n. pl.*, -**rax·es**, -**ra·ces**, -rə·sēz. The cavity of the body formed by the spine, ribs, and breastbone, and containing the lungs and heart; the chest; the portion of an insect between the head and abdomen. —**tho·rac·ic**, thô·ras′ik, *a.*

tho·ri·um, thōr′ē·əm, thôr′ē·əm, *n.* A heavy, grayish, radioactive metallic element used in alloys and for generating atomic energy.

thorn, thôrn, *n.* A sharp-pointed growth from a branch; a spine; a prickle; a similar process on an animal; any of various thorny shrubs or trees; something that wounds, or causes discomfort or annoyance. —**thorn in the side**, the origin or cause of worry or annoyance. —**thorn·less**, *a.* —**thorn·like**, *a.*

thorn·y, thôr′nē, *a.*, -**i·er**, -**i·est.** Full of thorns, spines, or prickles; vexatious; full of problems or difficulties. —**thorn·i·ness**, *n.*

thor·ough, thər′ō, *a.* Carried completely through to the end; complete or perfect; marked by detailed and accurate attention; characterized as being very careful and accurate. —**thor·ough·ly**, *adv.* —**thor·ough·ness**, *n.*

thor·ough·bred, thər′ō·bred, *a.* Of pure or unmixed breed, stock, or race, as a horse or other animal; well-bred; thoroughly educated, trained, or accomplished.—*n.* A thoroughbred person or animal.

thor·ough·fare, thər′ō·fer, *n.* An unobstructed road or street for public traffic; passage or the right of passing.

thor·ough·go·ing, thər′ō·gō·ing, *a.* Going to all lengths; zealous; absolute or unmitigated.

those, ŧhōz, *a., pron.* Plural of **that.**

thou, ŧhow, *pron.*—sing. nom. *thou,* poss. *thy* or *thine,* obj. *thee;* pl. nom. *you* or *ye,* poss. *your* or *yours,* obj. *you* or *ye;* intens. and refl. *thyself.* The nominative second person singular personal pronoun; you: now restricted to poetic, Biblical, or ecclesiastic style.

though, ŧhō, *conj.* Notwithstanding that; while; although; granting or allowing it to be the fact that, often preceded by *even.*—*adv.* However; for all that. —**as though**, as if.

thought, thôt, *n.* The act or power of thinking; an idea; a conception; a judgment; a fancy; deliberation or reflection; purpose; expectation; opinion.

thought, thôt, *v.* Past tense and past participle of **think.**

thought·ful, thôt′fəl, *a.* Full of thought; meditative; attentive; considerate. —**thought·ful·ly**, *adv.* —**thought·ful·ness**, *n.*

thought·less, thôt′lis, *a.* Exhibiting a lack of thought; heedless; inconsiderate. —**thought·less·ly**, *adv.* —**thought·less·ness**, *n.*

thou·sand, thow′zənd, *n. pl.*, -**sand**, -**sands.** The cardinal number between 999 and 1,001; a symbol representing this number.—*a.* —**thou·sandth**, *a., n.*

thrall, thrôl, *n.* One in bondage; slave; serf. —**thrall·dom, thral·dom**, *n.*

thrash, thrash, *v.t.* To beat soundly with a stick or whip; to defeat completely; thresh.—*v.i.* To toss about or move violently; thresh.—*n.* An instance or act of thrashing. —**thrash o·ver** or **out**, to go or talk over again and again in order to reach a conclusion or solution. —**thrash·er**, *n.* —**thrash·ing**, *n.*

thrash·er, thrash′ər, *n.* A long-tailed thrushlike American song bird commonly found in shrubbery.

thread, thred, *n.* A fine cord, esp. such as is used for sewing; a cord consisting of the twisted filaments of a fibrous substance, spun out into a slender line; anything resembling this; the main thought that connects the parts of a speech, story, etc.; any slender filament; the prominent spiral part of a screw.—*v.t.* To pass a thread through the eye or aperture of; to pass or go through, as a narrow way.—*v.i.* To form into a thread, as syrup; go on a careful or winding course. —**thread·er**, *n.* —**thread·less**, *a.* —**thread·like**, *n.*

thread·bare, thred′ber, *a.* Having the nap worn off so as to show the separate threads; poor; shabby. —**thread·bare·ness**, *n.*

thread·y, thred′ē, *a.*, -**i·er**, -**i·est.** Like thread; filamentous; containing thread; stringy; feeble, as a pulse; without fullness, as a voice. —**thread·i·ness**, *n.*

threat, thret, *n.* A menace, as a thing or person; a declaration of an intention to inflict punishment, loss, or pain on another; a warning or sign of impending danger or damage.

threat·en, thret′ən, *v.t.* To use threats toward; to menace; to exhibit the appearance of bringing something evil or unpleasant on; to show to be impending. —*v.i.* To utter or employ threats. —**threat·en·er**, *n.* —**threat·en·ing·ly**, *adv.*

three, thrē, *n.* The cardinal number between two and four; the symbol representing it.—*a.*

three-deck·er, thrē′dek′ər, *n.* Anything having three decks, tiers, or layers.

three-di·men·sion·al, thrē′di·men′shə·nəl, *a.* Referring to something which lies or seems to lie in all three planes of height, width, and depth.

three·fold, thrē′fōld, *a.* Consisting of three in one; triple.—*adv.*

three-ring cir·cus, thrē′ring, *n.* A circus in which simultaneous acts occur in three rings; any occasion characterized by a confusion of simultaneously occurring activities. Also **three-ringed cir·cus.**

three·score, thrē′skōr′, thrē′skôr′, *a.* Of or having three times twenty; sixty.

three·some, thrē′səm, *a.* Consisting of or performed by three.—*n.* Group of three persons; a game played by three persons; the players.

thren·o·dy, thren′ə·dē, *n. pl.,* **-dies.** A song of lamentation; a funeral song. **—thre·no·di·al,** thri·nō′dē·əl, **thre·nod·ic,** thri·nod′ik, *a.* **—thren·o·dist,** *n.*

thresh, thresh, *v.t.* To beat out, as grain, by striking the stalks with a flail or by passing them through a threshing machine; to beat or whip; to thrash.—*v.i.* To thresh or beat grain; to thrash or toss about.

thresh·er, thresh′ər, *n.* One who or that which threshes; one who separates seeds from wheat or other grain by beating with a flail; a device or machine for this purpose; a warm seas shark with an elongated upper lobe of the tail: also **thrash·er,** thrash′ər.

thresh·old, thresh′ōld, thresh′hōld, *n.* A doorsill; the stone or piece of timber which lies under a door; beginning; outset.

threw, throo, *v.* Past tense of **throw.**

thrice, thrīs, *adv.* Three times; threefold.

thrift, thrift, *n.* Economical management, conservation of resources, economy, or frugality. **—thrift·less,** *a.*

thrift·shop, thrift′shop, *n.* A store selling secondhand merchandise usu. for charity.

thrift·y, thrift′ē, *a.,* **-i·er, -i·est.** Economical; saving; frugal; thriving; flourishing. **—thrift·i·ly,** *adv.* **—thrift·i·ness,** *n.*

thrill, thril, *v.t.* To affect with a keen emotion, as of delight or excitement; to cause to tremble or quiver. —*v.i.* To produce a tingling sensation; to vibrate; to shiver; to quiver or move with a tremulous movement. —*n.* A thrilling sensation; that which causes a thrilling sensation. **—thrill·ful, thrill·ing,** *a.* **—thrill·ing·ly,** *adv.*

thril·ler, thril′ər, *n.* Person or thing that thrills. *Informal.* A sensational or suspenseful motion picture, play, or story, esp. a murder mystery.

thrive, thrīv, *v.i.,* **thrived** or **throve, thrived** or **thriv·en, thriv·ing.** To prosper or succeed; to increase; to be marked by prosperity; to go on or turn out well; to grow vigorously; to flourish. **—thriv·er,** *n.* **—thriv·ing,** *a.* **—thriv·ing·ly,** *adv.*

throat, thrōt, *n.* The passage that leads from the nose and mouth to the lungs and stomach; the front part of the neck; any of various narrow channels or parts. —*v.t.* To express gutturally, or from one's throat. **—cut one's own throat.** *Informal.* To be the cause of one's own downfall. **—jump down some·one's throat.** *Informal.* To be suddenly and vehemently critical; to berate. **—lump in one's throat,** a sensation of inability to swallow, esp. due to emotion. **—ram some·thing down one's throat.** *Informal.* To coerce another into agreement with or acceptance of something. **—stick in one's throat,** to resist expression, as words one hesitates to utter. **—throat·ed,** *a.*

throat·y, thrō′tē, *a.* **-i·er, -i·est.** Of utterances, having a husky or guttural sound. **—throat·i·ly,** *adv.* **—throat·i·ness,** *n.*

throb, throb, *v.i.,* **throbbed, throb·bing.** To beat, as the heart or pulse, with more than usual force or rapidity; to show, exhibit, or feel emotion; to palpitate, quiver, or vibrate.—*n.* A beat or strong pulsation; palpitation. **—throb·ber,** *n.*

throe, thrō, *n.* A violent spasm or pang; *pl.,* the pains of childbirth; the agony of death; any violent convulsion or struggle.

throm·bo·sis, throm·bō′sis, *n. pl.,* **-ses,** -sēz. A coagulation of the blood in a blood vessel or in the heart during life. **—throm·bot·ic,** throm·bot′ik, *a.*

throne, thrōn, *n.* The chair or seat occupied by a sovereign; the office or dignity of a sovereign; the occupant of a throne; a sovereign.—*v.t., v.i.,* **throned, thron·ing.** To place or sit on or as on a throne. **—throne·less,** *a.*

throng, thrông, throng, *n.* A crowd; a great number; a number of things crowded together.—*v.i.* To crowd together; to come in multitudes.—*v.t.* To crowd or press; to fill with a crowd.

throt·tle, throt′əl, *v.t.,* **-tled, -tling.** To stop the breath of by compressing the throat; to strangle; to choke or suffocate in any way; to silence or check as if by choking; to obstruct the flow of, as steam, by means of a valve; to decrease the speed of, as an engine, by diminishing the fuel supply in this way.—*v.i.* To undergo suffocation; to choke.—*n.* A lever for volume control of fuel or steam in an internal-combustion or steam engine. Also **throt·tle valve.** The lever that controls this handle or valve. **—throt·tler,** *n.*

through, thru, throo, *prep.* In at one end, side, or surface, and out at the other; from one end or side to the other; here and there, or everywhere, over the surface or within the limits of; during the whole period of; from the beginning to the end of; having reached the end of: to be *through* one's work; having finished successfully; by reason of or in consequence of; by means of.—*adv.* In at one end, side, or surface and out at the other; from one end or side of a thing to the other; all the way, or along the whole distance; completely; throughout: She was wet *through;* from the beginning to the end; to the end; to a favorable or successful conclusion; having completed an action or process.—*a.* Extending the whole distance from one end, side, or surface to the other, esp. with little or no interruption; finished. **—through and through,** thoroughly.

through·out, throo·owt′, *prep.* In, or to every part of; everywhere in; from the beginning to the end of.—*adv.* In or to every part; at every moment or point; through the whole time or action.

through·way, throo′wā, *n.* Thruway.

throw, thrō, *v.t.,* **threw, thrown, throw·ing.** To project or propel forcibly through the air by a sudden jerk or straightening of the arm; to fling or toss; to propel or cast in any way; to hurl, project, or cast; to exert or use; to direct, as a glance; to cause to go or come into some place, position, or condition, as if by throwing; to put on hastily; to move, as a lever, in order to connect or disconnect parts of an apparatus or mechanism; to connect, or disconnect by such a procedure; to shape, as clay, on a potter's wheel. *Informal.* To permit an opponent to win, as a game, unnecessarily or in accordance with a previous agreement; to cast, as dice; to cause to fall off. *Informal.* To upset: Don't let the bad news *throw* you; to give or act as host for: to *throw* a party.—*v.i.* To cast, fling, or hurl something.—*n.* An act of throwing or casting; a cast or a fling; distance a thing is or may be thrown; a lightweight cover or spread. **—throw cold water on,** to raise objections to the point of discouragement. **—throw in,** to add as a gift; contribute. **—throw in the sponge** or **towel,** to admit defeat. **—throw off,** to discard; reject; elude by deception; produce effortlessly or offhandedly. **—throw oneself at,** to make obvious attempts to win the romantic attentions of. **—throw oneself into,** to attack enthusiastically. **—throw oneself on** or **upon,** to seek the consideration or mercy of another. **—throw open,** to waive any restriction. **—throw over,** to cast off relations with. **—throw together,** to assemble or put together haphazardly. **—throw up,** to abandon; to build hastily. *Informal.* To vomit. **—throw·er,** *n.*

throw·a·way, thrō′ə·wā, *n.* A handbill containing advertising matter, which is distributed door-to-door,

---

or handed out on the street.

throw•back, thrō′bak, *n.* A reversion to an ancestral type; a throwing back; a setback.

throw rug, *n.* Scatter rug.

thru, throo, *prep., adv., a.* Through.

thrum, thrəm, *v.i., v.t.,* **thrummed, thrum•ming.** To play on a stringed instrument by plucking the strings, esp. in an idle manner; to sound when thrummed on, as a guitar; to drum or tap idly with the fingers.—*n.* The act or sound of thrumming; any dull, monotonous sound. —**thrum•mer,** *n.*

thrush, thrəsh, *n.* A passerine bird of various species, esp. the wood thrush, robin, and hermit thrush, celebrated as a songbird.

thrust, thrəst, *v.t.,* **thrust, thrust•ing.** To push forcibly, shove, or drive; to impel; to put or drive with force; to put forth or extend in some direction; to put forcibly, as a person, into some position or condition; to interpose; to stab or pierce.—*v.i.* To push forcefully or suddenly against something; to push or force one's way, with *against, through,* etc.—*n.* A forcible push or drive; a lunge or stab; an outward or sidewise stress or strain, as of an arch upon an abutment; the push exerted by the rotation of a propeller; the rearward discharge of burning fuels, etc., which propels a rocket or jet engine forward; the tenor or gist, as of remarks. —**thrust•er,** *n.*

thru•way, throo′wā, *n.* A divided, highspeed highway uninterrupted by grade crossings and with limited access and exit facilities. Also **through•way.**

thud, thəd, *v.i., v.t.,* **thud•ded, thud•ding.** To beat or strike with a dull sound of heavy impact.—*n.* A dull sound, as of a heavy blow or fall; a blow causing such a sound.

thug, thəg, *n.* A cutthroat; a ruffian. —**thug•ger•y, thug•gism,** *n.* —**thug•gish,** *a.*

thu•li•um, thoo′lē•əm, *n.* A metallic element of the rare-earth series.

thumb, thəm, *n.* The short, thick, opposable inner digit of the human hand, next to the forefinger; the part of a mitten or glove that covers the thumb.—*v.t.* To soil or wear with the thumbs in handling, as the pages of a book; to leaf through quickly, as the pages of a book; to handle clumsily. *Informal.* To signal, as a request for a ride in a passing car, by gesturing with the thumb. —*v.i. Informal.* To hitchhike. —**all thumbs.** *Informal.* Clumsy or awkward with the hands. —**thumbs down.** *Informal.* An expression of denial or disapproval. —**thumbs up.** *Informal.* An expression of acceptance or approval. —**under one's thumb, under the thumb of,** subject to the persuasion or power of. —**thumb one's nose,** to signal, as defiance or scorn, by putting the thumb to the nose and extending the fingers. —**thumb•less,** *a.* —**thumb•like,** *a.*

thumb•nail, thəm′nāl, *n.* The nail of the thumb; something very small or short.—*a.* Brief; concise: a *thumbnail* sketch.

thumb•screw, thəm′skroo, *n.* A screw that may be turned by the finger and thumb. Formerly, an instrument of torture for squeezing or pressing the thumb.

thumb•tack, thəm′tak, *n.* A tack with a large, flat head, designed to be thrust into an object by the thumb or a finger.

thump, thəmp, *n.* The sound made by the sudden fall of a heavy body; a heavy blow given with anything that is thick.—*v.t.* To beat with something thick or heavy. *Informal.* To beat severely.—*v.i.* To strike or fall with a heavy blow.

thump•ing, thəm′ping, *a.* Like thumps, beating, or throbbing. *Informal.* Of exceptional size, extent, or the like.

thun•der, thən′dər, *n.* The sound which follows a flash of lightning; any loud resounding noise; a threat or denunciation.—*v.i.* To emit thunder, usu. impersonal: It *thundered* yesterday; to emit a loud echoing noise; to utter loud or angry threats or denunciations. —*v.t.* To utter loudly or vehemently, as a threat or

denunciation. —**steal some•one's thun•der,** to appropriate without permission, as someone's creation, idea, or argument. —**thun•der•er,** *n.*

thun•der•bolt, thən′dər•bōlt, *n.* An electrically produced discharge in the form of lightning followed by thunder; someone or something which is a dreadful threat, denunciation, or censure.

thun•der•clap, thən′dər•klap, *n.* A clap or burst of thunder.

thun•der•cloud, thən′dər•klowd, *n.* A dark and dense cloud that produces lightning and thunder.

thun•der•head, thən′dər•hed, *n.* A round, swelling mass of cumulus clouds appearing when conditions are right for thunderstorms.

thun•der•ous, thən′dər•əs, *a.* Producing thunder or a noise like thunder: *thunderous* applause. —**thun•der•ous•ly,** *adv.*

thun•der•show•er, thən′dər•show•ər, *n.* A shower of rain in conjunction with thunder and lightning.

thun•der•storm, thən′dər•stôrm, *n.* A storm of thunder and lightning, and usu. precipitation and wind.

thun•der•struck, thən′dər•strək, *a.* Struck by, or as if by lightning; amazed; confounded; stupefied. Also **thun•der•strick•en,** thən′dər•strik•ən.

Thurs•day, thərz′dē, thərz′dā, *n.* The fifth day of the week; the day following Wednesday.

thus, thəs, *adv.* In this or that way, manner, or state; accordingly; to this degree or extent; so; therefore; hence.

thwack, thwak, *v.t.* To strike, bang, beat, or thrash with a flat object.—*n.* A heavy blow with something flat or heavy. —**thwack•er,** *n.*

thwart, thwôrt, *v.t.* To oppose successfully, or prevent from accomplishing a purpose; to frustrate, as a purpose; to baffle.—*a.* Passing or lying crosswise or across.

thy, t͟hī, *pronominal a. Archaic.* Your: *thy* trust comforts me.

thyme, tīm, *n.* A small, aromatic plant whose leaves are used as a seasoning in cooking. —**thym•ic,** *a.*

thy•mus, thī′məs, *n.* A ductless gland situated in the upper thoracic cavity. Also **thy•mus gland.**—*a.* —**thy•mic,** *a.*

thy•roid, thī′royd, *a.* Pertaining to the principal cartilage of the larynx; pertaining to the thyroid gland.—*n.* The thyroid cartilage; the thyroid gland; a preparation made from the thyroid glands of certain domesticated animals and used for treating disorders of the thyroid. —**thy•roid•less,** *a.*

thy•roid gland, *n.* A ductless, two-lobed gland, adjacent to the larynx and upper trachea, which affects growth and metabolism.

thy•self, t͟hī•self′, *pron. Archaic.* Yourself.

ti, tē, *n.* The syllable representing the seventh or highest tone in a diatonic scale.

ti•ar•a, tē•ar′ə, tē•är′ə, tē•ār′ə, *n.* A woman's ornamental crown or coronet; the Pope's triple crown.

tib•i•a, tib′ē•ə, *n. pl.,* **-as, -ae,** -ē. The large bone of the lower leg; the shinbone. —**tib•i•al,** *a.*

tic, tik, *n.* A habitual spasmodic contraction of certain muscles, esp. of the face.

tick, tik, *n.* A light, quick touch or tap: a *tick* of a clock; a recurring click or beat; a small mark serving as a check or the like.—*v.i.* To emit or produce a tick.—*v.t.* To mark with ticks; check: She *ticked* off the items one by one.

tick, tik, *n.* Any of various mites, parasitic on animals, which bury the head in the skin of the host and suck the blood.

tick, tik, *n.* The cover or case of a mattress or pillow.

tick•er, tik′ər, *n.* One who or that which ticks; a telegraphic instrument which automatically prints stock market reports or the like, on a narrow tape. *Informal.* A watch; the heart.

tick•er tape, *n.* A paper ribbon on which information is printed by a ticker.

tick•et, tik′it, *n.* A slip, usu. of paper or cardboard, entitling its holder to some service or right; a written or printed card affixed to something to indicate its nature or price; a label or tag; a list of candidates of a political party to be voted on. *Informal.* A summons given out to the violator of a traffic or parking law. —*v.t.* To attach a ticket to; to distinguish by means of a ticket; to furnish with a ticket.

tick•ing, tik′ing, *n.* A strong fabric used for the ticks of pillows or mattresses.

tick•le, tik′əl, *v.t.,* -**led,** -**ling.** To touch or stroke lightly so as to excite a tingling or itching sensation; to titillate; to excite agreeably or gratify.—*v.i.* To have or cause to have a tingling or itching sensation.—*n.* A tickling sensation.

tick•ler, tik′lər, *n.* One who or that which tickles; a memorandum book or the like kept to tickle or jog the memory.

tick•lish, tik′lish, *a.* Sensitive to tickling; unsteady; unsettled; easily offended; touchy; requiring careful handling; delicate; risky; difficult. —**tick•lish•ly,** *adv.* —**tick•lish•ness,** *n.*

tick-tack-toe, tik•tak•tō′, *n.* A game in which two persons alternately mark crosses and ciphers in a figure of nine squares, the object being to place three marks of one kind in a row. Also **tic-tac-toe.**

ti•dal, tīd′əl, *a.* Of or pertaining to tides. —**tid•al•ly,** *adv.*

ti•dal wave, *n.* A dangerously large ocean wave produced by an earthquake, windstorm, or extraordinarily high tide; any overwhelming occurrence.

tid•bit, tid′bit, *n.* A delicious morsel of food; any pleasing item, as of gossip.

tid•dly•winks, tid′lē•wingks, *n. pl. but sing. in constr.* A game in which participants press plastic disks against the edges of smaller ones lying on a flat surface in an attempt to flick them into a cup. Also **tid•dle•dy•winks,** tid′əl•dē•wingks.

tide, tīd, *n.* The periodical rise and fall of the waters of the ocean and its estuaries about every 12 hours, due to the gravitational attraction of the moon and sun; a stream or current; any rising or falling tendency; an extent of time.—*v.i.,* **tid•ed, tid•ing.** To flow to and fro as the tide; to float or drift with the tide.—*v.t.* To carry or buoy up as the tide does. —**tide o•ver,** to help along for a time, esp. through a period of difficulty.

tide•land, tīd′land, *n.* Land inundated at high tide and dry at ebb tide.

tide•wa•ter, tīd′wô•tər, tīd′wä•tər, *n.* Water affected by the ordinary flow and ebb of the tide; an area where the waters are acted upon by tides.—*a.*

ti•dings, tī′dingz, *n. pl., sing. or pl. in constr.* News; information; intelligence.

ti•dy, tī′dē, *a.,* **ti•di•er, ti•di•est.** In neat condition, orderly, or trim; given to keeping things neat and in order. *Informal.* Considerable: a *tidy* sum; moderately or fairly satisfactory: a *tidy* agreement.—*v.t., v.i.,* **ti•died, ti•dy•ing.** To make tidy, orderly, or neat, often followed by *up.*—*n. pl.,* **ti•dies.** A covering for the backs or arms of upholstered furniture. —**ti•di•ly,** *adv.* —**ti•di•ness,** *n.*

tie, tī, *v.t.,* **tied, ty•ing.** To bind or make fast with a cord, string, or the like; to draw together the parts of with a knotted string or the like; to fasten by tightening and knotting the string or strings of; to draw together into a knot, as a cord or lace; to form by looping and interlacing, as a knot; to fasten, join, or connect in any way; to confine, restrict, or limit; to equal or make the same score in a contest.—*v.i.* To make a bond or connection; to become tied; to make the same score or be equal in a contest.—*n.* A cord, string, or the like with which something is tied; a necktie; an ornamental knot or bow; anything that makes fast or secures; a link or connection; a restraint or constraint; an equality achieved in points, votes, and the like; a contest in

which this occurs; one of the transverse beams to which the rails that form a railroad track are fastened. —**tie down,** to hinder or limit. —**tie up,** to tie firmly; wrap up; hinder; stop; invest or dispose of so as to make unavailable for other uses; have a full schedule or be very busy: usu. passive.

tie-in, tī′in, *n.* Relation; connection.

tie•pin, tī′pin, *n.* A decorative straight pin with a clasp used to hold a necktie in place.

tier, tēr, *n.* One of a series of rows or ranks rising one behind or above another.—*v.t.* To arrange in tiers. —*v.i.* To rise in tiers.

tie-up, tī′əp, *n.* A slowing or stoppage of business, transportation, telephone service, or the like. *Informal.* An association or connection.

tiff, tif, *n.* A slight or petty quarrel; a slight fit of ill humor.—*v.i.* To have a petty quarrel; to be in a tiff.

ti•ger, tī′gər, *n.* A large, carnivorous, Asiatic feline mammal, having a tawny-colored coat with vertical black stripes; a person with fierce or aggressive traits. —**ti•ger•ish, ti•grish,** *a.* —**ti•ger•like,** *a.*

ti•ger lil•y, *n.* A lily with flowers of an orange color spotted with black.

tight, tīt, *a.* Securely or closely fixed in place; drawn or stretched so as to be tense or taut; fitting closely, esp. too closely; difficult to deal with or manage; compressed or packed full; impervious to water, steam, air, and the like; concise or succinct; firm or strict. *Informal.* Nearly even or close; stingy or parsimonious; drunk.—*adv.* Closely, firmly, or securely. —**tight•ly,** *adv.*— —**tight•ness,** *n.*

tight•en, tīt′ən, *v.t., v.i.* To make or become tight or tighter. —**tight•en•er,** *n.*

tight-fist•ed, tīt′fis′tid, *a.* Stingy.

tight-lipped, tīt′lipt′, *a.* Saying very little; taciturn.

tight•rope, tīt′rōp, *n.* A rope tautly stretched above the ground, used by acrobats.

tights, tīts, *n. pl.* A garment of close-fitting, stretchable material covering the lower part of the body and the legs, worn esp. by dancers, acrobats, or gymnasts.

tight•wad, tīt′wäd, *n. Informal.* A stingy person.

ti•gress, tī′gris, *n.* A female tiger.

tike, tīk, *n.* Tyke.

til•de, til′də, *n.* A diacritical mark (~) used esp. in Spanish over *n* to represent the *ny* sound, as in *señora.*

tile, tīl, *n.* A thin slab, plate, or shaped piece of baked clay, often glazed and ornamented, used for covering roofs, lining walls, paving floors, draining land, or in ornamental work; tiles collectively.—*v.t.,* **tiled, til•ing.** To cover with tiles.

til•ing, tī′ling, *n.* The operation of covering with tiles; tiles collectively.

till, til, *prep.* To the time of; up to the time of; until. —*conj.* To the time that or when; until.

till, til, *v.t.* To do labor on, as by plowing, harrowing, and sowing upon, as the soil, for the raising of crops; to cultivate.—*v.i.* To cultivate the soil. —**till•a•ble,** *a.* —**till•er,** *n.*

till, til, *n.* A drawer or tray in which cash is kept.

till•age, til′ij, *n.* The operation or art of tilling land; the land under cultivation.

till•er, til′ər, *n.* The bar or lever fitted to the rudder of a boat for steering.

tilt, tilt, *v.t.* To cause to lean or incline from the vertical or horizontal; to slope or slant; to rush at or charge, as in a joust.—*v.i.* To move into or assume a sloping position or direction; to engage in a joust, tournament, or similar contest.—*n.* The act of tilting, or the state of being tilted; a sloping position; a joust or some similar contest; the exercise of riding with a lance or the like at a mark; any encounter, combat, or contest. —**at full tilt,** with full speed. —**tilt•er,** *n.*

tilth, tilth, *n.* The act or operation of tilling; tillage;

---

cultivation; the state of being tilled: land in good or bad *tilth;* tilled land; land under cultivation.

tim·ber, tim′bər, *n.* Wood suitable for building or for use in carpentry; the wood of growing trees suitable for structural uses; growing trees themselves; a single beam or piece of wood forming, or capable of forming, part of a structure. Personal character or quality. —*v.t.*—*interj.* A warning call when a tree is cut and ready to fall.

tim·bered, tim′bərd, *a.* Made of or furnished with timber; covered with growing trees, or wooded: the *timbered* slopes.

tim·ber line, *n.* The elevation at which timber ceases to grow. Also **tree line.** —**tim·ber-line,** *a.*

tim·ber wolf, *n.* A gray wolf of northern U.S. and Canada.

tim·bre, tam′bər, tim′bər, *n.* That distinctive quality in a sound which sets it apart from another sound of the same pitch and volume.

time, tim, *n.* The system of those relations which any event has to any other as past, present, or future; indefinite continuous duration regarded as that in which events succeed one another; a system or method of measuring or reckoning the passage of time; limited extent of time, as between two successive events; a particular period considered as distinct from other periods: for the *time* being; a prescribed or allotted term or period, as of one's life, of apprenticeship, of pregnancy, or the like; a period with reference to personal experience of a specified kind; a period allowed, as for payment; a period of work of an employee, or the pay for it; the period necessary for or occupied by something; leisure or spare time; a particular or definite point during the day; a particular part of a year, day, or the like; an appointed, fit, due, or proper moment; the right moment or opportunity; each occasion of a recurring action; the arrangement of the successive beats or measures, each kind of measure employed in music containing a certain number of these beats. *Often pl.* A period in the history of the world, or contemporary with the life or activities of a notable person; the period or era now or then present; a period considered with reference to its events or prevailing conditions, tendencies, or ideas. *Pl. Math.* A multiplicative word in phrasal combinations expressing how many instances of a quantity or factor are taken together. *Informal.* A term of imprisonment: to do *time.*—*v.t.,* timed, tim·ing. To appoint the time of or choose the moment or occasion for; to regulate as to time, as a train or a clock; to mark the rhythm or measure of; to fix the duration of; to ascertain or record the time, duration, or rate of.—*v.i.* To keep time; to sound or move in unison or harmony.—*a.* Related or pertaining to time; planned to occur or happen within or at a desired time; payable or redeemable on or any time after some designated date or after some specified amount of time following purchase; pertaining to installment payments. —**be·hind the times,** outmoded; passe; old-fashioned. —**keep time,** to indicate or record time correctly, as a timepiece or watch; to conduct, play, or sing some composition while strictly adhering to the rhythm or tempo. —**time of one's life.** *Informal.* An experience or event of great enjoyment.

time cap·sule, *n.* A receptacle which holds typical records and objects from the current culture set into a cornerstone or in the earth to be uncovered in a future age.

time·card, tim′kärd, *n.* A sheet for recording, usu. mechanically, an employee's attendance and hours worked.

time clock, *n.* A clock with an attachment by which a record may be made of the time of the arrival and departure of employees.

time-hon·ored, tim′on·ərd, *a.* Venerable and worthy of honor by reason of antiquity and long continuance.

time·keep·er, tim′kē·pər, *n.* One who or that which

keeps time; one who records and announces time of occurrence or time occupied, as in certain athletic events. —**time·keep·ing,** *n.*

time·less, tim′lis, *a.* Eternal; referring to no particular time. —**time·less·ly,** *adv.* —**time·less·ness,** *n.*

time·ly, tim′lē, *a.,* -li·er, -li·est. Seasonable; opportune; well-timed.—*adv.* —**time·li·ness,** *n.*

time-out, tim′owt′, *n.* A temporary cessation of action, esp. in a sports contest; a rest break. Also **time out.**

time·piece, tim′pēs, *n.* A clock or watch.

tim·er, ti′mər, *n.* One who measures or records time; a device for recording time or intervals of time; a mechanism which allows a machine or appliance to operate automatically and then shut off at some predetermined time.

time·serv·er, tim′sər·vər, *n.* One who for his own ends adapts his opinions and manners to the times or complies with the ruling power. —**time·serv·ing,** *a., n.*

time-share, tim′shār, *v.i.,* -shared, -shar·ing. To allocate or assign parts of the complete operating time, as of a computer, to at least two functions.—*v.t.*

time sheet, *n.* A record of employees' hours at work.

time·ta·ble, tim′tā·bəl, *n.* A schedule of times of the arrival and departure of railroad trains or the like.

time·worn, tim′wôrn, *a.* Worn or impaired by time; ancient or showing the effects of time.

time zone, *n.* Any of 24 longitudinal segments of the globe, roughly divided by meridians 15° apart beginning at Greenwich, England, and differing by one hour before or after each adjoining segment.

tim·id, tim′id, *a.* Fearful; lacking courage to meet danger; not bold. —**ti·mid·ly,** *adv.* —**tim·id·i·ty,** ti·mid′ə·tē, **tim·id·ness,** *n.*

tim·ing, ti′ming, *n.* The adjusting of an action, phrase, or sound to occur at the instant of maximum effect, or to coordinate with other motions, sounds, or effects; the act of measuring the time passed in a performance or contest.

tim·or·ous, tim′ər·əs, *a.* Fearful of danger; timid; indicating or marked by fear. —**tim·or·ous·ly,** *adv.* —**tim·or·ous·ness,** *n.*

tim·o·thy, tim′ə·thē, *n.* A coarse grass with cylindrical spikes, valuable as fodder.

tim·pa·ni, tim′pə·nē, *n. pl., sing. or pl. in constr.* A set of orchestral kettledrums. —**tim·pa·nist,** *n.*

tin, tin, *n.* A silver-white, malleable, ductile metallic element, used as a protective coating and in alloys; a container, box, can, or vessel fashioned from tin or tin plate.—*v.t.,* tinned, tin·ning. To cover or plate with tin.—*a.* Made of tin; counterfeit; cheap.

tin can, *n.* A sealed metal container, usu. constructed from tin-plated sheet steel, used to preserve food.

tinc·ture, tingk′chər, *n.* A tinge or shade of color; a slight taste added to any substance; slight quality added to anything; an extract or solution of the active principles of some substance in a solvent, usu. alcohol.—*v.t.,* -tured, -tur·ing. To tinge; to impart a slight color to.

tin·der, tin′dər, *n.* An inflammable substance used for kindling fire; any highly combustible material. —**tin·der·y,** *a.,* -i·er, -i·est.

tin·der·box, tin′dər·boks, *n.* A box in which tinder is kept; anything extremely combustible; a potential source of contagious violence.

tine, tin, *n.* The spike of a fork; a prong. —**tined,** *a.*

tin·foil, tin′foyl, *n.* Tin, aluminum, or a tin-lead alloy, beaten and rolled into thin sheets, used for wrapping products. Also **tin foil. —tin-foil,** *a.*

tinge, tinj, *v.t.,* tinged, tinge·ing or ting·ing. To give a certain shade, flavor, or quality to; to color.—*n.* A slight degree of color, taste, flavor, or quality infused or added to something; touch; tint; trace.

tin·gle, ting′gəl, *v.i.,* -gled, -gling. To have a sensation of slight stings, quivers, or prickles, as from a sharp blow or cold; to cause such a sensation.—*v.t.* To cause to tingle.—*n.* A tingling sensation. —**tin·gler,** *n.*

—tin•gling•ly, *adv.* —tin•gly, *a.*, -gli•er, -gli•est.

tink•er, ting/kər, *n.* A mender of pots, kettles, pans, and other metal household articles; a bungler; a jack-of-all-trades. Also **tink•er•er.** An act or instance of tinkering.—*v.i.* To do the work of a tinker; to work unskillfully or clumsily at anything.—*v.t.* To repair in a clumsy or makeshift way.

tin•kle, ting/kəl, *v.i.*, -kled, -kling. To make small, quick, sharp sounds, as a little bell; to jingle.—*v.t.* To cause to make sharp, quick, ringing sounds.—*n.* A small, quick, sharp, ringing noise or sound. —**tin•kling,** *n.* —tin•kly, *a.*, -kli•er, -kli•est.

tin•ny, tin/ē, *a.*, -ni•er, -ni•est. Pertaining to or resembling tin; lacking in resonance; tasting like tin. —**tin•ni•ly,** *adv.* —tin•ni•ness, *n.*

tin plate, *n.* Thin sheet steel or iron coated with tin. Also **tin•plate.** —tin-plate, tin/plāt, *v.t.*, **tin-plat•ed, tin-plat•ing.** —tin-plat•er, *n.*

tin•sel, tin/səl, *n.* Thin strips, pieces, or sheets of glittering metallic material used for ornamentation. —*a.*—*v.t.*, -seled, -sel•ing. To adorn with tinsel or anything showy and superficial. —**tin•sel•ly,** *a.*, -i•er, -i•est.

tint, tint, *n.* A slight coloring or tincture; a hue; a tinge; degree of intensity of a color; hair dye.—*v.t.* To give a slight coloring to. —**tint•er,** *n.* —tint•ing, *n.* —tint•less, tint/lis, *a.*

tin•tin•nab•u•lar, tin•ti•nab/yə•lər, *a.* Of or relating to bells or their sound. —**tin•tin•nab•u•la•tion,** tin•ti•nab•yə•lā/shən, *n.*

tin•type, tin/tīp, *n.* A photograph in the form of a positive taken on a sensitized sheet of enameled tin or iron.

ti•ny, tī/nē, *a.*, -ni•er, -ni•est. Very small; little; minute. —**ti•ni•ly,** *adv.* —ti•ni•ness, *n.*

tip, tip, *n.* A slender, pointed extremity or end; the top, summit, or apex.—*v.t.*, **tipped, tip•ping.** To furnish with a tip; to serve as or form the tip of. —**tip•less,** *a.*

tip, tip, *v.t.*, **tipped, tip•ping.** To cause to assume a slanting or sloping position; incline; tilt; to upset, followed by *over.*—*v.i.* To assume a slanting or sloping position; incline; to be overturned or upset; to tumble or topple, followed by *over.*—*n.* The act of tipping; the state of being tipped. —**tip•pa•ble,** *a.* —tip•per, *n.*

tip, tip, *n.* A small present of money bestowed for services; a gratuity. *Informal.* A piece of private or secret information, often used with *off;* a useful hint, suggestion, or idea.—*v.t.*, **tipped, tip•ping.** To give a gratuity to. *Informal.* To give private or secret information to, often followed by *off.*—*v.i.* To give a gratuity. —**tip•less,** *a.* —tip•pa•ble, *a.* —tip•per, *n.*

tip, tip, *v.t.*, **tipped, tip•ping.** To strike or hit with a light, smart blow; tap.—*n.* A light, smart blow; a tap.

tip-off, tip/ôf, tip/of, *n. Informal.* The act of disclosing confidential information; a tip or hint; a caution or warning.

tip•ple, tip/əl, *v.i.*, -pled, -pling. To drink intoxicating liquors habitually.—*v.t.*—*n.* —tip•pler, *n.*

tip•ster, tip/stər, *n. Informal.* One who is paid for supplying tips.

tip•sy, tip/sē, *a.*, -si•er, -si•est. Intoxicated, but not to complete drunkenness; characterized by or due to intoxication; unsteady as if from intoxication. —**tip•si•ly,** *adv.* —tip•si•ness, *n.*

tip•toe, tip/tō, *n.* The tips of the toes collectively.—*v.i.*, -toed, -to•ing. To move or go about on tiptoe.—*a.* Characterized by standing or walking on tiptoe; eagerly expectant; cautious or stealthy.—*adv.* On the tips of one's toes. —**on tip•toe,** expectant; cautious or stealthy.

tip•top, tip/top, *n.* The summit. *Informal.* The best.—*a. Informal.* Excellent.—*adv.* Very well.

ti•rade, tī/rād, tī•rād/, *n.* A long, violent speech; a harangue.

tire, tīr, *v.t.*, **tired, tir•ing.** To exhaust the strength of; to fatigue; to exhaust the attention or patience of.—*v.i.* To become weary; to have the attention or patience exhausted. —**tire•less,** *a.* —tire•less•ly, *adv.* —tire•less•ness, *n.*

tire, tīr, *n.* A pneumatic structure that encircles the wheels of a vehicle; a band or hoop, as of steel or hard rubber, forming the tread of a vehicle wheel.

tired, tīrd, *a.* Exhausted; fatigued; weary; hackneyed; trite. *Informal.* Impatient or disgusted. —**tired•ly,** *adv.* —tired•ness, *n.*

tire•some, tīr/səm, *a.* Tending to tire; boring; tedious. —**tire•some•ly,** *adv.* —tire•some•ness, *n.*

tis•sue, tish/oo, *n.* In plants and animals, an aggregate of cells usu. of similar structure which perform the same or related functions; any of various woven fabrics of light texture; an interwoven or interconnected series; thin, soft paper.

tis•sue pa•per, *n.* A semitransparent, soft paper used for wrapping things.

tit, tit, *n.* A titmouse.

tit, tit, *n.* A teat; a breast.

ti•tan, tīt/ən, *n.* A person or thing of enormous size or strength.—*a.* Titanic; gigantic.

ti•tan•ic, tī•tan/ik, *a.* Enormous in size or strength; colossal. —**ti•tan•i•cal•ly,** *adv.*

ti•ta•ni•um, tī•tā/nē•əm, *n.* A very hard, silver to dark gray metallic element occurring in many rocks, mainly ilmenite and rutile, used chiefly in metallurgy.

tit for tat, *n.* An equivalent given in return, as in retaliation; blow for blow.

tithe, tīth, *n.* The tenth part of the annual income paid as a tax for the support of religious institutions.—*v.t.*, **tithed, tith•ing.** To pay a tithe, as for the support of the church.—*v.i.* To give or pay a tithe. —**tith•a•ble,** *a.* —tithe•less, *a.*

ti•tian, tish/ən, *n.* A reddish-brown or auburn color.—*a.*

tit•il•late, tit/ə•lāt, *v.t.*, -lat•ed, -lat•ing. To tickle; to excite agreeably. —**tit•il•la•tion,** tit•ə•lā/shən, *n.* —tit•il•la•tive, *a.*

ti•tle, tīt/əl, *n.* The distinguishing name of a book, poem, piece of music, picture, or other work; any descriptive or distinctive appellation; a distinguishing appellation belonging to a person by right of rank, office, or attainment, or assigned as a mark of respect or courtesy; established or recognized right to something; anything affording ground for a claim; legal right to the possession of property, esp. real property; the championship in sports.—*v.t.*, **ti•tled, ti•tling.** To furnish with a title. —**ti•tled,** *a.*

tit•mouse, tit/mows, *n. pl.,* -mice. A bird distinguished by its crest and rusty flanks.

tit•ter, tit/ər, *v.i.* To laugh with a stifled sound or with restraint; to laugh nervously.—*n.* —tit•ter•er, *n.* —tit•ter•ing•ly, *adv.*

tit•tle, tit/əl, *n.* A particle; a jot; an iota.

tit•u•lar, tich/ə•lər, tit/yə•lər, *a.* Having the title or name only; nominal; of, pertaining to, or constituting a title.—*n.* One who holds a title. —**tit•u•lar•ly,** *adv.*

tiz•zy, tiz/ē, *n. pl.,* -zies. *Informal.* An agitated state of mind; a dither.

TNT, T.N.T., tē/en/tē/, *n.* Trinitrotoluene. *Informal.* Anything likened to an explosive.

to, too, *unstressed* tŭ, *a.*, *prep.* Toward, specifying a point or person to be approached and reached; in the direction of, expressing motion toward; to the degree that; in contact or contiguity with; until, regarding a point in time; designated for; for the purpose of; toward, concerning a destined or appointed end; in direct contact with; to the limit of; in addition to; in adherence to; by comparison with; in agreement or accordance with; in reference or relation to. Used to supply the place of the dative in other languages, connecting transitive verbs with their indirect or direct objects, and adjectives, nouns, and intransitive or passive verbs with a following noun which limits their action or application; used as the ordinary sign or accompaniment of the infinitive expressing orig. motion, direction, purpose, and the like, as in the ordinary uses with a substantive object, but now appearing in many cases as a mere meaningless sign.—*adv.* Toward a person, thing, or point implied or understood. *Informal.* To a point of contact, of a closed position; to a matter, or to action or work; to one's senses: after he came *to.* —**to and fro,** to and from some place or thing; in opposite or different directions alternately.

toad, tōd, *n.* A tailless, warty-skinned, terrestrial amphibian.

toad·stool, tōd'stool, *n.* Any of various fungi having a stalk with an umbrellalike cap, esp. those that are poisonous.

toad·y, tō'dē, *n. pl.,* **-ies.** A sycophant; a flatterer. —*v.t.,* **-ied, -y·ing.** To fawn upon in a servile manner; to play the sycophant to.—*v.i.* To act as a toady. —**toad·y·ism,** *n.*

toast, tōst, *v.t.* To brown, as bread, by exposure to heat; to heat or warm thoroughly at a fire.—*v.i.* To become toasted.—*n.* Bread in slices superficially browned by heat.

toast, tōst, *n.* A person whose health is proposed; an event, sentiment, person, or the like, to which one drinks; a call on another or others to drink to some person or thing, or the act of thus drinking.—*v.t.* To propose as a toast; drink to the health of or in honor of.—*v.i.* To propose or drink a toast.

toast·er, tōst'ər, *n.* One who toasts; an instrument for toasting bread, etc.

toast·mas·ter, tōst'mas·tər, *n.* One who is appointed to propose or announce the toasts at a public dinner and introduces the after-dinner speakers. —**toast·mis·tress,** tōst'mis·tris, *n. fem.*

to·bac·co, tə·bak'ō, *n. pl.,* **-cos, -coes.** A plant whose leaves are prepared for smoking or chewing or as snuff; the leaves so prepared.

to·bac·co·nist, tə·bak'ə·nist, *n.* A dealer in tobacco and smoking supplies.

to·bog·gan, tə·bog'ən, *n.* A flat-bottomed sled turned up in front, used for sliding down snow-covered slopes.—*v.i.* To use such a sled; to fall rapidly, as stock prices. —**to·bog·gan·er, to·bog·gan·ist,** *n.*

toc·sin, tok'sin, *n.* An alarm bell.

to·day, to-day, tə·dā', *adv.* On this present day; at the present time; in these days.—*n.* This present day or age.

tod·dle, tod'əl, *v.i.,* **-dled, -dling.** To walk with short steps in a tottering way, as a child or an old person. —*n.* The act of walking in this manner; an unsteady gait. —**tod·dler,** *n.*

tod·dy, tod'ē, *n. pl.,* **-dies.** A drink made of a liquor, hot water, and sugar, often spiced with bitters, clove, or lemon peel.

to-do, tə·doo', *n. pl.,* **to-dos.** *Informal.* Bustle; hurry, commotion; fuss.

toe, tō, *n.* One of the terminal digits of the foot; the forepart of the foot or hoof of a horse or the like; a part, as of a stocking or shoe, to cover the toes; a part resembling a toe or the toes in shape or position.—*v.t.,* **toed, toe·ing.** To furnish with a toe or toes; to touch or reach with the toes; to kick with the toe.—*v.i.* To place or move the toes in a manner specified. —**toe the mark** or **line.** *Informal.* To conform to a certain standard, as of duty or conduct. —**toe·less,** *a.*

toed, tōd, *a.* Having a toe or toes; fastened by nails driven in an oblique manner.

toe·hold, tō'hōld, *n.* A small place or ledge used to support one's toes while climbing; a way of progress, an advantage, or a footing.

toe·nail, tō'nāl, *n.* The nail growing on a toe; a nail driven obliquely.—*v.t.* To fasten or secure by nails obliquely driven.

tof·fee, tof·fy, tô'fē, tof'ē, *n.* A hard sweetmeat or candy.

to·ga, tō'gə, *n. pl.,* **-gas, -gae,** -jē. The loose outer garment of the citizens of ancient Rome when appearing in public. —**to·gaed,** *a.,* tō'gəd.

to·geth·er, tû·geth'ər, tə·geth'ər, *adv.* Into or in one gathering, company, mass, or body; into or in union, closeness, contact, or collision, as two or more things; into or in relationship or association, as two or more persons; taken or considered collectively or conjointly; into or in a condition of unity or compactness, or so as to form a connected whole or compact body, as at the same time or simultaneously; without intermission or interruption; in cooperation or conjointly; with one another, mutually, or reciprocally. —**to·geth·er·ness,** *n.*

tog·gle, tog'əl, *n.* A transverse pin, bolt, or rod placed through an eye of a rope or link of a chain for various purposes, as to fit into a bight, loop, or ring in another rope or chain, thus fastening the two ropes or chains together, or to serve as a hold for the fingers; a toggle joint, or a device furnished with one.—*v.t.,* **-gled, -gling.** To furnish with a toggle or toggles; to secure or fasten with a toggle or toggles.

tog·gle switch, *n.* A switch composed of a lever which moves to open or close an electrical circuit.

toil, toyl, *v.i.* To engage in severe and continuous work or exertion; to labor arduously.—*v.t.* To bring, effect, or produce by toil.—*n.* Hard and continuous work or exertion. —**toil·er,** *n.*

toi·let, toy'lit, *n.* A bathroom or water closet; a fixture in the bathroom with a seat and bowl containing water for feces and urine which are then flushed away; the act or process of dressing, including bathing and arranging the hair.—*a.*

toi·let pa·per, *n.* A light, soft paper for bathroom use. Also **bath·room tis·sue, toi·let tis·sue.**

toi·let·ry, toi'li·trē, *n. pl.,* **-ries.** Any article, as soap, cologne, or a comb, used in grooming oneself.

toi·let wa·ter, *n.* A lightly perfumed liquid containing alcohol.

toil·some, toyl'səm, *a.* Laborious; fatiguing. —**toil·some·ly,** *adv.* —**toil·some·ness,** *n.*

to·ken, tō'kən, *n.* Something intended or supposed to represent or indicate another thing or an event; a memento of friendship or affection; something that serves by way of pledge of authenticity, good faith, or the like; a stamped metal disk or the like, used for payment of fares or similar purposes.—*a.*—*v.t.* To be a symbol of; to serve as a token of.

tol·er·a·ble, tol'ər·ə·bəl, *a.* Capable of being borne or endured; moderately good or agreeable; passable. —**tol·er·a·ble·ness, tol·er·a·bil·i·ty,** tol·ər·ə·bil'ə·tē, *n.* —**tol·er·a·bly,** *adv.*

tol·er·ance, tol'ər·əns, *n.* The state or fact of being tolerant; the act of, or capacity to endure; endurance; the capacity to endure or resist the action of a drug or poison.

tol·er·ant, tol'ər·ənt, *a.* Inclined or disposed to tolerate; forbearing. —**tol·er·ant·ly,** *adv.*

tol·er·ate, tol'ə·rāt, *v.t.,* **-at·ed, -at·ing.** To put up with; to suffer to be, or to be practiced or done, without prohibition or hindrance; to endure or resist the action of, as a drug or poison. —**tol·er·a·tion,** tol·ə·rā'shen, *n.* —**tol·er·a·tive,** *a.* —**tol·er·a·tor,** *n.*

toll, tōl, *n.* A payment exacted for some right or privilege, esp. for the right of passage along a road or over a bridge; a compensation for services rendered; the cost, as in damage or loss, incurred in any undertaking or happenstance.—*v.t., v.i.* To exact or collect as toll.

toll, tōl, *v.t.* To cause, as esp. a large bell, to sound slowly and regularly; to lure or decoy, as game.—*v.i.* To sound slowly and regularly, as a bell.—*n.* The sound made by a tolling bell; the act of tolling a bell.

toll·booth, tōl'booth, *n. pl.,* **-booths.** A booth or stall, as by a road or bridge, where tolls are collected.

toll·gate, tōl′gāt, *n.* A gate, as across a road or at the approach to a bridge, where toll is taken.

toll·house, tōl′hows, *n.* A booth or house near a tollgate, where the toll collector is stationed; toll-booth.

toll road, *n.* A road, esp. a highway, on which toll is charged. Also **toll·way.**

tol·u·ene, tol′ū·ēn, *n.* A colorless, flammable, mobile liquid hydrocarbon obtained from coal tar and petroleum, used in making explosives, dyes, and as a solvent. Also **meth·yl·ben·zene.**

tom, tom, *n.* The male of certain animals, often used in compounds: *tom*cat.

tom·a·hawk, tom′ə·hôk, *n.* A light ax used by the N. American Indians as a weapon and tool.—*v.t.* To strike, cut, or kill with a tomahawk.

to·ma·to, tə·mā′tō, tə·mä′tō, *n. pl.,* **-toes.** A widely cultivated plant bearing a slightly acid, pulpy fruit, commonly red, sometimes yellow, used as a vegetable; the fruit itself.

tomb, toom, *n.* An excavation in earth or rock for a dead body; a grave, chamber, or vault; a mausoleum. —*v.t.* To place in or as in a tomb; bury. —**tomb·less,** *a.* —**tomb·like,** *a.*

tom·boy, tom′boy, *n.* A boisterous, wild girl. —**tom·boy·ish,** *a.* —**tom·boy·ish·ness,** *n.*

tomb·stone, toom′stōn, *n.* A marker erected over a grave, usu. bearing an inscription.

tom·cat, tom′kat, *n.* A male cat.

tome, tōm, *n.* A book, usu. a large one.

tom·fool·er·y, tom·foo′lə·rē, *n. pl.,* **-ies.** Senseless; a silly or foolish performance, matter, or thing; nonsense.

to·mor·row, to-mor·row, tə·môr′ō, tə·mor′ō, *n.* The day after this day; a future time.—*adv.*

tom·tit, tom′tit, *n.* A name sometimes given to the chickadee and wren in the U.S.

tom-tom, tom′tom, *n.* A native Indian or African small-headed drum, usu. played with the hands.

ton, tən, *n.* A unit of weight equivalent to 2,000 pounds avoirdupois, a 'short ton' in the U.S., and 2,240 pounds avoirdupois, a 'long ton' in Great Britain. *Often pl. Informal.* A great number or quantity; a lot.

to·nal·i·ty, tō·nal′ə·tē, *n. pl.,* **-ties.** A system of composition in which the tones and chords are related to a central keynote; the tone values of dark and light in a work as distinguished from, although often affected by, color values.

tone, tōn, *n.* Any sound that impresses the ear with its individual character, esp. pitch; quality of sound or timbre; strength or volume of sound; a modulation of the voice, as expressive of an emotion; a stress, accent, or inflection of voice; the distinctive sound of any voice or instrument; a pure or fundamental note without overtones or harmonics; timbre; state of mind or disposition; mood; the general or prevailing character, as of morals, manners, or sentiments; a harmonious relationship of colors or their gradations of light and dark; that condition of a vital body in which the parts have tension, the organs function normally, and the tissues are firm, sound, and resilient.—*v.t.,* **toned, ton·ing.** To give certain tone to; to utter in an affected voice.—*v.i.* To adopt a certain tone. —**tone down,** to subdue or moderate; to become softer. —**tone up,** to raise the strength or quality of; to gain in strength. —**ton·al,** *a.* —**ton·al·ly,** *adv.* —**tone·less,** *a.* —**tone·less·ly,** *adv.* —**tone·less·ness,** *n.*

tone arm, *n.* The pivoted pickup bar of a record player with a head consisting of a needle set into a cartridge.

tone-deaf, tōn′def, *a.* Lacking the capability to discriminate distinctions in musical pitch.

tong, tông, tong, *n.* A secret Chinese society in the U.S.

tongs, tôngz, tongz, *n. pl., sing. or pl. in constr.* An instrument of metal with two hinged or pivoted arms, used for handling or grasping things.

tongue, təng, *n.* The freely moving organ within the mouth, with the power to shape itself for different purposes, as tasting, swallowing, and in human beings, articulation or speech; the power or act of speech; the whole sum of words used by a particular linguistic group or their dialect; a point or strip of land, rock, or ice extruding from its surroundings; the pole with which a wagon is pulled; the sealing flap in back of the laced or buckled facing of a shoe; the enclosed member of a tongue-and-groove joint. —**hold one's tongue,** to maintain silence. —**on the tip of one's tongue,** almost, but not quite, recollected. —**slip of the tongue,** the wrong word used.

tongue-and-groove joint, təng·ə·groov′, *n.* A means of joining two boards by inserting a ridge or tongue on the edge of one board into a groove in the other.

tongue-in-cheek, təng′ən·chēk′, *a.* With obvious insincerity for the purpose of sarcasm or humor, usu. preceded by *with.*

tongue-lash, təng′lash′, *v.t., v.i. Informal.* To rebuke harshly. —**tongue-lash·ing,** *n.*

tongue-tied, təng′tīd, *a.* Unable to speak freely, as from surprise.

tongue twist·er, *n.* A phrase, word, or sentence which is difficult to utter rapidly due to the repetition of similar sounds or alliteration of the consonants, as 'rubber baby buggy bumpers.'

ton·ic, ton′ik, *a.* Referring to, maintaining, increasing, or restoring the tone or healthy condition of the system or organs, as a medicine; invigorating or bracing to the physical system, or to the mind or moral nature.—*n.* A tonic agent or remedy; anything invigorating or bracing, physically, mentally, or morally; quinine water. —**ton·i·cal·ly,** *adv.*

to·night, to-night, tə·nīt′ *n.* The present night; the night after the present day.—*adv.* On or in the present night, or the night after the present day.

ton·nage, tən′ij, *n.* The carrying capacity of a merchant ship expressed in tons of 100 cubic feet; ships collectively considered with reference to carrying capacity or together with their cargoes.

ton·sil, ton′səl, *n.* One of two oblong masses of soft tissue, located on each side of the throat. —**ton·sil·lar, ton·sil·ar,** *a.*

ton·sil·lec·to·my, ton·sə·lek′tə·mē, *n. pl.,* **-mies.** An operation for the removal of the tonsils.

ton·sil·li·tis, ton·sə·lī′tis, *n.* Inflammation of the tonsils. —**ton·sil·lit·ic, ton·sə·lit′ik,** *a.*

ton·so·ri·al, ton·sôr′ē·əl, *a.* Of or referring to barbering or a barber.

ton·sure, ton′shər, *n.* The act of removing the hair of the head by clipping or shaving, as from the crown of the heads of those entering the priesthood or a monastic order; that area of the head bared by such shaving.—*v.t.,* **-sured, -sur·ing.** To shave or clip the head of.

too, too, *adv.* Likewise; also; in addition; more than enough, excessively; very; exceedingly; over and above.

tool, tool, *n.* Any implement used by a craftsman or laborer at his work; an instrument employed in manual labor for facilitating mechanical operations; the cutting part on various machines driven by power; a machine tool; the entire machine; a decoration or ornamentation stamped on a book cover; a person used by another as an instrument to accomplish certain ends.—*v.t.* To shape with a tool; to ornament, as a book cover.—*v.i.* To use or employ tools.

tool·box, tool′boks, *n.* A box for storing tools.

tool·house, tool′hows, *n.* A building used for tool storage. Also **tool·shed,** tool′shed.

tool·mak·er, tool′mā·kər, *n.* A workman who makes

---

and repairs tools and related items. —**tool·mak·ing,** n.

tool·room, tool′room, tool′rûm, n. A room in which implements and tools are kept, fixed, or made, esp. in a machine shop.

toot, toot, v.i. To make a noise like that of a pipe or horn, esp. in brief blasts.—v.t. To sound, as a horn.—n. A sound blown on a horn; a similar noise. —**toot·er,** n.

tooth, tooth, n. pl., **teeth.** One of the hard bodies or processes, usu. attached in a row to each jaw, serving for the seizing and mastication of food or as weapons of attack or defense; any projection resembling or suggesting a tooth; one of a series of projections, as on a comb, rake, or saw; one of a series of projections on the edge of a wheel or gear which engage with corresponding parts of another wheel or body.—v.t., **toothed, tooth·ing.** To furnish with teeth; to bite or gnaw; to fix into (something) by means of or in the manner of teeth.—v.i. To interlock, as cogwheels. —**by the skin of one's teeth,** by a small margin. —**cut one's teeth on,** to begin an activity or career by doing. —**in one's teeth, in the teeth,** in direct opposition or conflict; to one's face or openly. —**in the teeth of,** so as to face or confront, or straight against; in defiance of or in spite of. —**put teeth in,** to make effective. —**set one's teeth,** to resolve to do; to prepare for adversity. —**show one's teeth,** to show hostility or act in a threatening manner. —**to the teeth,** so as to be fully equipped. —**tooth·like,** a.

tooth·ache, tooth′āk, n. Pain in a tooth arising from decay. —**tooth·ach·y,** a.

tooth·brush, tooth′brəsh, n. A small brush for cleaning the teeth.

tooth·less, tooth′lis, a. Being without or showing absence of teeth; lacking effectiveness or power. —**tooth·less·ly,** adv. —**tooth·less·ness,** n.

tooth·paste, tooth′pāst, n. A dentifrice in paste form.

tooth·pick, tooth′pik, n. A small instrument, usu. pointed, for picking substances from between the teeth.

tooth pow·der, n. A powdered dentifrice.

tooth·some, tooth′səm, a. Palatable; agreeable to the taste; desirable or attractive. —**tooth·some·ly,** adv. —**tooth·some·ness,** n.

tooth·y, too′thē, a., **-i·er, -i·est.** Having or exhibiting conspicuous teeth. —**tooth·i·ly,** adv. —**tooth·i·ness,** n.

top, top, n. The highest or uppermost point, part, or surface of anything; a part considered as higher; part serving as a cover or lid; the head, esp. the crown of the head; that part of anything which is first or foremost; the beginning; the highest or leading place, position, or rank; one who or that which occupies the highest or leading position; the highest pitch or degree; the choicest part.—a. Referring to, situated at, or forming the top; highest; uppermost; upper; highest in degree; greatest; foremost; chief; principal.—v.t., **topped, top·ping.** To remove, as the top of; to put on, as a top; to be at or constitute, as the top of; to reach, as the top of; to rise above; to exceed in height, amount, or number; to surpass, excel, or outdo.—v.i. —**blow one's top.** Informal. To become very angry; to lose one's sanity. —**on top,** successful; victorious; dominant. —**on top of,** above and resting upon; upon; in addition to; close upon; following upon. —**o·ver the top,** in excess of a predetermined goal. —**top off,** to complete by or as by putting a top on; to finish. —**top out,** to complete a building, as the framework of the top story.

top, top, n. A child's toy, usu. cone-shaped, made to spin on a point.

to·paz, tō′paz, n. A mineral, fluosilicate of aluminum, usu. occurring in prismatic crystals of various colors, and used as a gem; a yellow variety of sapphire; a yellow variety of quartz.

top·coat, top′kōt, n. A lightweight overcoat.

top draw·er, n. Informal. High quality; highest rank, priority, or authority.—a.

tope, tōp, v.i., **toped, top·ing.** To drink alcoholic beverages immoderately and frequently. —**top·er,** n.

top·flight, top′flit′, a. Informal. Superior; first-rate.

top hat, n. A man's tall, cylindrical, dress hat, usu. covered with silk.

top·heav·y, top′hev·ē, a., **-heav·i·er, -heav·i·est.** Having the top part too heavy for the lower; badly balanced or proportioned. —**top·heav·i·ly,** adv. —**top·heav·i·ness,** n.

to·pi, tō′pē, n. pl., **-pis.** An antelope native to central Africa with a purplish-brown coat.

to·pi·ar·y, tō′pē·er·ē, a. Shaped, esp. ornamentally, by clipping, pruning, or training, as trees or shrubs. —n. pl., **-ies.** Any work or art of this kind; a garden which contains topiary work.

top·ic, top′ik, n. The subject of a discourse, argument, or literary composition; a subject of speech or writing.

top·i·cal, top′i·kəl, a. Referring to or dealing with matters of current or local interest; of or referring to any topic of speech or writing; of or referring to a place; local. —**top·i·cal·i·ty,** top·ə·kal′ə·tē, n. pl., **top·i·cal·i·ties.**

top·knot, top′not, n. An ornamental knot of hair or bow of ribbon worn on the top of the head; the crest of a bird.

top·less, top′lis, a. Without a top, esp. without a part covering the breasts.

top·most, top′mōst, a. Highest; uppermost.

top·notch, top′noch′, a. Informal. First-rate; excellent. —**top·notch·er,** n.

to·pog·ra·phy, tə·pog′rə·fē, n. pl., **-phies.** The accurate and detailed description of any region; the features of a locality or region collectively. —**to·pog·ra·pher,** n. —**top·o·graph·i·cal,** top·ə·graf′ə·kəl, a. —**top·o·graph·i·cal·ly,** adv.

top·ping, top′ing, n. Something put on a thing at the top to complete it, as any sauce or garnish.—a. Rising above something else; surpassing; very high in degree.

top·ple, top′əl, v.i., **-pled, -pling.** To fall forward, as from top-heaviness; to tumble down; to totter.—v.t. To overturn or cause to fall; overthrow.

top-se·cret, top′sē′krit, a. Classified as most highly secret and accessible only to specially authorized personnel.

top·soil, top′soyl, n. The uppermost layer or surface of the soil.—v.t. To remove the topsoil from, as an area of land.

top·sy·tur·vy, top′sē·tər′vē, adv. Upside down; in or into a state of confusion or disorder.—a. Turned upside down; confused or disorderly.—n. pl., **-vies.** Inversion of the natural order; a state of confusion or disorder. —**top·sy·tur·vi·ly,** adv. —**top·sy·tur·vi·ness,** n.

toque, tōk, n. A woman's close-fitting hat of soft material, brimless or with a narrow brim.

To·rah, Tor·a, tōr′ə, tôr′ə, n. The Pentateuch; Mosaic law; broadly, instruction, doctrine, or law contained in the Old Testament.

torch, tôrch, n. A light to be carried in the hand, formed of some combustible substance; fig., a guiding light from which inspiration emanates; any readily carried device for the emission of an esp. hot flame, as for use in working with solder. Brit. Flashlight. —**car·ry a or the torch for.** Informal. To be intensely in love with, usu. without the possibility of reciprocation. —**torch·like,** a.

torch·bear·er, tôrch′bār·ər, n. One who carries a lighted torch; a person in the vanguard of supporters of a cause.

torch·light, tôrch′līt, n. The light of a torch or of torches.—a. Illuminated by torches: a torchlight parade.

tor·e·a·dor, tôr′ē·ə·dôr, n. A bullfighter.

to·re·ro, tə·rār′ō, n. pl., **-ros.** A matador; a bullfighter.

to·ri·i, tōr′ē·ē, n. pl., **to·ri·i.** A form of decorative gateway or portal in Japan, consisting of two upright wooden posts connected at the top by two horizontal crosspieces, and commonly found at the entrance to Shinto temples.

tor·ment, tôr′ment, *n.* Extreme pain; anguish of body or mind; torture; that which causes such pain. —tôr·ment′, *v.t.* To put to extreme pain or anguish; to torture; to afflict; to tease, vex, or harass. —**tor·ment·ing·ly,** *adv.* —**tor·men·tor, tor·ment·er,** *n.*

tor·na·do, tôr·nā′dō, *n. pl.,* **-does, -dos.** A destructive rotatory storm appearing as a whirling, advancing funnel extending downward from a black cloud. —**tor·nad·ic,** tôr·nād′ik, *a.*

tor·pe·do, tôr·pē′dō, *n. pl.,* **-does.** A submarine explosive device for destroying hostile ships, esp. a self-propelled, cigar-shaped missile containing explosives which is launched from a tube in a submarine and explodes upon impact with the ship fired at; any of various other explosive devices.—*v.t.,* **-doed, -do·ing.** To attack, hit, damage, or destroy with a torpedo or torpedoes.—*v.i.* To use, discharge, or explode torpedoes.

tor·pid, tôr′pid, *a.* Having lost motion or the power of motion and feeling; numb; dull; sluggish; inactive; listless. —**tor·pid·i·ty,** tôr·pid′ə·tē, *n.* —**tor·pid·ly,** *adv.*

tor·por, tôr·pər, *n.* A state of suspended physical powers and activities; dormancy, as of a hibernating animal; sluggish inactivity or inertia; apathy.

torque, tôrk, *n.* That which produces or tends to produce torsion or rotation.

tor·rent, tôr′ənt, tor′ənt, *n.* A stream of water flowing with great rapidity and violence; a rushing, violent, or abundant and unceasing stream of anything; a violent downpour of rain. —**tor·ren·tial,** tə·ren′shəl, to·ren′shəl, *a.* —**tor·ren·tial·ly,** *adv.*

tor·rid, tôr′id, tor′id, *a.* Subject to parching or burning heat, esp. of the sun; parching or burning; oppressively hot; characterized by great heat of feeling; passionate. —**tor·rid·i·ty,** tə·rid′ə·tē, tor·rid·ness, *n.* —**tor·rid·ly,** *adv.*

tor·sion, tôr′shən, *n.* The act of twisting or the resulting state; the twisting of a body by two equal and opposite forces. —**tor·sion·al,** *a.* —**tor·sion·al·ly,** *adv.*

tor·so, tôr′sō, *n. pl.,* **-sos, -si,** -sē. The trunk of the human body.

tort, tôrt, *n.* A wrong, other than a breach of contract, such as the law requires compensation for in damages.

torte, tôrt, *Ger.* tôr′tə, *n. pl.,* **tortes,** *Ger.* tor·ten. Any rich cake consisting of eggs, sugar, butter, and often nuts, fruit, and bread crumbs, usu. containing little flour.

tor·til·la, tôr·tē′ə, *n. pl.,* **-las,** tôr·tē′əz. A thin, round, cornmeal cake.

tor·toise, tôr′təs, *n.* A turtle, esp. a terrestrial one.

tor·toise shell, *n.* The shell, or outer shell, of a tortoise; the horny shell of some turtles, with mottled or clouded yellow and brown coloration, used for making combs, inlaying, or the like. —**tor·toise-shell,** *n., a.*

tor·to·ni, tôr·tō′nē, *n.* An ice cream of rich, heavy cream and eggs, usu. containing cherries, minced almonds, crushed macaroons, or the like.

tor·tu·ous, tôr′choo·əs, *a.* Full of twists, turns, or bends; twisting, winding, or crooked; not direct or straightforward; pursuing an indirect or devious course or policy, as persons. —**tor·tu·ous·ly,** *adv.* —**tor·tu·ous·ness,** *n.*

tor·ture, tôr′chər, *n.* The act of inflicting excruciating pain from sheer cruelty or in hatred or revenge; a method of inflicting such pain; subjection to any excruciating or severe pain, physical or mental; the pain or suffering caused or undergone; extreme an-

guish of body or mind.—*v.t.,* **-tured, -tur·ing.** To subject to torture; to afflict with severe pain of body or mind. —**tor·tur·a·ble,** *a.* —**tor·tured·ly,** *adv.* —**tor·tur·er,** *n.* —**tor·ture·some,** *a.* —**tor·tur·ing·ly,** *adv.*

toss, tôs, tos, *v.t.* To throw, pitch, or fling, esp. lightly or carelessly; to throw or send, as a ball, from one to another; to throw, pitch, heave, or jerk about with irregular motions; to agitate, disturb, or disquiet; to raise or jerk upward suddenly; to discuss freely and casually; to throw, as a coin, into the air to decide something by the side turned up when it falls, often used with *up;* to mix gently, as a salad.—*v.i.* To pitch, rock, sway, or move irregularly, as a ship on a rough sea; to fling or jerk oneself or move restlessly about, esp. on a bed or couch; to throw something; to throw a coin into the air in order to decide something by the way it falls, often used with *up.*—*n.* An act of tossing; the state of being tossed; a throw or pitch, or the distance to which something is or may be thrown; a tossup, as of a coin. —**toss off,** to do or accomplish casually and quickly; to drink rapidly, esp. in one draft. —**toss·er,** *n.*

toss·up, tôs′əp, tos′əp, *n. Informal.* The tossing up of a coin in order to decide something by its fall; an even or fifty-fifty chance.

tot, tot, *n.* A young child; a small quantity.

to·tal, tōt′əl, *a.* Of or referring to the whole of something; constituting or comprising the whole; entire; complete in extent or degree; absolute, unqualified, or utter.—*n.* The total amount, sum, or aggregate; the whole.—*v.t.,* **-taled** or **-talled, -tal·ing** or **-tal·ling.** To bring to a total; add up; to reach a total of; amount to.—*v.i.* To amount, often followed by *to.*

to·tal·i·tar·i·an, tō·tal·ə·tār′ē·ən, *a.* Of or pertaining to a centralized form of government in which those in control grant neither recognition nor tolerance to parties of differing opinion.—*n.* An adherent of totalitarian principles. —**to·tal·i·tar·i·an·ism,** tō·tal·ə·tār′ē·ən·iz·əm, *n.*

to·tal·i·ty, tō·tal′ə·tē, *n. pl.,* **-ties.** The state of being total; a total or whole.

to·tal·i·za·tor, tō·tal′ə·zā·tər, *n.* An apparatus for registering and indicating the total of operations, measurements, and the like; a pari-mutuel machine.

to·tal·ly, tōt′ə·lē, *adv.* In a total manner or degree; wholly; entirely; completely.

tote, tōt, *v.t.,* **tot·ed, tot·ing.** *Informal.* To carry or bear, as a burden or load.—*n.* A woman's large handbag: also **tote bag.** *Informal.* An act of toting. —**tot·er,** *n.*

to·tem, tō′təm, *n.* Among primitive cultures, an object or thing in nature, often an animal, assumed as the token or emblem of a clan, family, or related group; a representation of such an object serving as the distinctive mark of the clan or group. —**to·tem·ic,** tō·tem′ik, *a.* —**to·tem·ism,** tō′tə·miz·əm, *n.* —**to·tem·ist,** *n.* —**to·tem·is·tic,** tō·tə·mis′tik, *a.*

to·tem pole, *n.* A pole or post carved and painted with totemic figures by Indians of the northwest coast of N. America.

tot·ter, tot′ər, *v.i.* To walk or go with faltering steps; to sway or rock on the base or ground; to shake or tremble.—*n.* An unsteady movement or gait. —**tot·ter·er,** *n.* —**tot·ter·y,** *a.* —**i·er, -i·est.**

tot·ter·ing, tot′ər·ing, *a.* Walking falteringly or shakily; unstable; precarious. —**tot·ter·ing·ly,** *adv.*

tou·can, too′kan, too·kän′, *n.* A bird in tropical America with a very large beak and striking coloration.

touch, təch, *v.t.* To put the hand, finger, or the like on or into contact with; to come into contact with so as to feel or perceive; to strike or hit gently; to be adjacent to; adjoin or border on; to come up to; to compare with; to modify or improve, as a painting; to mark or relieve slightly, as with color; to treat or affect in some way by contact; tinge or imbue; to affect with some

---

feeling or emotion, as tenderness, pity, or gratitude; to allude, pertain, or relate to. *Informal.* To succeed in getting money from.—*v.i.* To place the hand, finger, or part of the body on or in contact with something; to come into or be in contact.—*n.* The act of touching; the state or fact of being touched; that sense by which anything material is perceived by means of the contact with it of some part of the body; the sensation or effect imparted or experienced by touching something; coming into or being in contact; mental sensitivity; a close relation of communication, agreement, or sympathy; a slight attack, as of illness; a slight added action or effort in doing or completing any piece of work; the manner of execution in artistic work; a detail in any artistic work; a slight amount of some quality or attribute; a slight quantity or degree; a distinguishing characteristic or trait; the act of testing anything. *Informal.* The act of soliciting money, as a loan or gift; the money so obtained; a person easily victimized for a loan. **—touch off,** to cause to explode; to ignite; to cause to happen. **—touch on,** to mention briefly or in passing. **—touch•a•ble,** *a.* **—touch•a•ble•ness,** *n.* **—touch•er,** *n.*

touch and go, *n.* An uncertain, precarious, delicate state of affairs. **—touch-and-go,** *a.* Hasty, sketchy, or desultory; risky; precarious.

touch•down, tech′down, *n.* The act or play of possessing a football or behind the opponent's goal line, thereby scoring six points; the moment when an aircraft's landing gear touches the landing surface.

tou•ché, too-shā′, *interj.* An exclamation indicating that an opponent has been touched by the tip of the foil; an expression acknowledging that an opponent has been successful, as in an argument.

touched, techt, *a.* Emotionally stirred or moved; unbalanced; mentally ill.

touch•ing, tech′ing, *a.* Affecting; moving; pathetic. **—prep.** In reference or relation to. **—touch•ing•ly,** *adv.* **—touch•ing•ness,** *n.*

touch•stone, tech′stōn, *n.* A stone, formerly used to test the purity of gold and silver; any test or criterion by which the qualities of a thing are tried.

touch sys•tem, *n.* A typewriting system in which each finger is trained by touch to locate and use certain keys.

touch-tone tel•e•phone, tech′tōn, *n.* A push-button operated telephone.

touch-type, tech′tīp, *v.t.,* **-typed, -typ•ing.** To type without having to look at the keyboard, as in the touch system. **—touch-typ•ist,** *n.*

touch•y, tech′ē, *a.,* **-i•er, -i•est.** Apt to take offense on slight provocation; irritable; precarious, risky, or ticklish. **—touch•i•ly,** *adv.* **—touch•i•ness,** *n.*

tough, tef, *a.* Strong; durable; yielding to force without breaking; difficult to cut or chew, as food; physically or mentally able to endure hardship; stubborn; hard to manage or deal with; difficult to achieve or perform; demanding or rigorous; strict, harsh, or severe. *Informal.* Rowdy; rough; belligerent; vicious; unfortunate, as bad luck.—*n.* *Informal.* A rough or rowdy person. **—tough•ly,** *adv.* **—tough•ness,** *n.*

tough•en, tef′en, *v.i.* To grow tough.—*v.t.* To make tough. **—tough•en•er,** *n.*

tou•pee, too-pā′, too-pē′, *n.* A patch of false hair or a partial wig worn to cover a bald spot.

tour, tûr, A lengthy trip or excursion, as for sightseeing or business; a journey in a circuit; a turn or period of service at one place.—*v.i.* To make a tour.—*v.t.* To make a tour of; to take or present on a tour, as a ballet or play.

tour de force, tûr de fôrs′, *n. pl.,* **tours de force,** tûr. An achievement which requires ingenuity, great ability, or strength; an artistic work which cannot be equaled or surpassed.

tour•ism, tûr′iz-em, *n.* The custom or practice of traveling for pleasure; the business or occupation of providing various services for tourists.

tour•ist, tûr′ist, *n.* One who makes a tour; one who travels for pleasure.—*a.*

tour•ma•line, tûr′me-lin, tûr′me-lēn, *n.* A complex silicate mineral occurring in black and various colors, the clear varieties used as gemstones.

tour•na•ment, tûr′ne-ment, *n.* A contest of skill in which players compete in a series of games; a series of games or athletic events in which teams or individuals compete against one another; a type of combat in the Middle Ages performed by opposing armored knights on horseback.

tour•ni•quet, ter′ne-kit, *n.* A bandage which is tightened by twisting with a stick to arrest hemorrhage.

tou•sle, tow′zel, *v.t.,* **-sled, -sling.** To put into disorder; to dishevel; to rumple.—*n.*

tout, towt, *v.i., v.t. Informal.* To solicit employment, votes, or business importunately; to spy on a race horse to obtain information for betting purposes.—*n.* **—tout•er,** tow′ter, *n.*

tow, tō, *v.t.* To drag or pull by means of a rope, chain, or hitch; to haul.—*n.* The act of towing, or the state of being towed; a rope, chain, or hitch for towing; something towed; that which tows; a ski tow. **—in tow,** under guidance or in charge; accompanying or following.

tow•age, tō′ij, *n.* A charge for towing.

to•ward, tōrd, tôrd, te-wôrd′, *prep.* In the direction of; facing; in expectation of or for; close to or near in time; aiding or contributing to; in regard or with respect to. Also **to•wards.**

tow•el, tow′el, *n.* A cloth or soft paper for drying or wiping anything.—*v.t., v.i.,* **-eled, -el•ing.** To wipe or dry with a cloth or towel.

tow•el•ing, tow′e-ling, *n.* Cloth or other material used for making towels.

tow•er, tow′er, *n.* A structure or building, relatively tall and narrow, either standing alone or forming part of another edifice; any tall, thin structure; a tall, movable wooden structure used in ancient warfare in storming a fortified place; a citadel; a fortress.—*v.i.* To rise or fly high; to soar; to be lofty; to stand sublime; to surpass all others. **—tow•ered,** *a.*

tow•er•ing, tow′er-ing, *a.* Very high or lofty; outstanding; extreme; excessive.

tow•head, tō′hed, *n.* A head of flaxen or light-colored hair, or a person with such hair. **—tow-head•ed,** *a.*

tow-line, tō′līn, *n.* A line by which anything is or may be towed.

town, town, *n.* A collection of inhabited houses larger than a village; a city or borough; the central area of a city; a municipal corporation, in New England, with less elaborate organization and powers than a city; a township, in states excluding New England; the townspeople.—*a.* Characteristic of a town. **—go to town.** *Informal.* To achieve rapidly; to advance. **—on the town.** *Informal.* Enjoying entertainment, esp. in nightclubs and the like. **—paint the town red.** *Informal.* To celebrate boisterously.

town cri•er, *n.* A public official who formerly issued proclamations in a town, usu. by loud, verbal announcement.

town hall, *n.* A building belonging to a town, usu. containing offices of town officials.

town house, *n.* A house in town, as distinguished from a country residence belonging to the same individual; a house occupied by a single family, usu. two-storied and connected by a common wall to the side of a similar house.

town meet•ing, *n.* A general meeting of the inhabitants or voters of a town.

town•ship, town′ship, *n.* An administrative division of a county with varying corporate powers; a region or district, in surveys of public land, usu. six miles square.

towns•man, townz′men, *n. pl.,* **-men.** An inhabitant of a town; an inhabitant of one's own or the same town.

towns•peo•ple, townz′pē-pel, *n. pl.* The inhabitants

of a town. Also **towns·folk.**

tow·path, tō′path, tō′päth, n. A path along the bank of a canal or river for use, as by animals or men, in towing boats.

tow·rope, tō′rōp, n. A rope used in towing. Also **tow·line.**

tow truck, n. A vehicle used for towing stalled or wrecked automobiles.

tox·e·mi·a, tok·sē′mē·ə, n. A form of blood poisoning, esp. one in which the toxins produced by certain microorganisms enter the blood. —**tox·e·mic,** tok·sē′mik, tok·sem′ik, a.

tox·ic, tok′sik, a. Of, pertaining to, or caused by a toxin or poison; poisonous. Also **tox·i·cal.** —**tox·i·cal·ly,** adv.

tox·ic·i·ty, tok·sis′ə·tē, n. pl., **-ties.** Poisonous or toxic quality, or the degree or state of being toxic; poisonousness.

tox·i·col·o·gy, tok·sə·kol′ə·jē, n. The science of poisons, their effects, antidotes, detection, and the like. —**tox·i·co·log·ic,** tok·sə·kə·loj′ik, **tox·i·co·log·i·cal,** a. —**tox·i·co·log·i·cal·ly,** adv. —**tox·i·col·o·gist,** n.

tox·in, tok′sin, n. A poison produced in living or dead organisms or their products; any of the specific poisonous products generated by pathogenic microorganisms, and constituting the causative agents in various diseases.

tox·oid, tok′soyd, n. A toxin whose toxic property has been eliminated, usu. by a chemical agent, but retaining its antigenic qualities that produce immunity on injection into the body by initiating antibody production.

toy, toy, n. A plaything; a thing or matter of little or no value or importance, or a trifle; a trinket; a small variety of dog.—a. Designed as a toy, as for children or others to play with; of petty character or diminutive size.—v.i. To act idly or without seriousness; to trifle; flirt. —**toy·like,** a.

trace, trās, n. Any mark, impression, or appearance left when the thing itself no longer exists; a minute quantity or insignificant particle; a nearly immeasurable amount of a chemical ingredient or element; a track, path, or trail, as left by an object or a person.—v.t., **traced, trac·ing.** To follow by traces left; to track out; to discover or find by investigation; to draw in outline; to decorate or embellish; to imprint, as designs; to copy, as a drawing or engraving, by following the lines and marking them on a sheet superimposed through which they appear.—v.i. To walk; to trace back in origin, time, or history. —**trace·a·ble,** a. —**trace·a·ble·ness,** n. —**trace·a·bly,** adv. —**trace·less,** a. —**trac·er,** n.

trace, trās, n. Either of the two straps, ropes, or chains by which a carriage, wagon, or the like is drawn by a harnessed horse or other draft animal. —**kick o·ver the trac·es,** to cast aside control.

trace el·e·ment, n. An element which is utilized by plants and animals in extremely small amounts and which is necessary to their physiological functioning.

trac·er·y, trā′sə·rē, n. pl., **-ies.** Ornamental work consisting of intersecting or ramified ribs, bars, or the like.

tra·che·a, trā′kē·ə, n. pl., **-ae, -ē, -as.** The tube extending from the larynx to the bronchi, serving as the passage for conveying air to and from the lungs; the windpipe. —**tra·che·al,** trā′kē·əl, a.

tra·che·ot·o·my, trā·kē·ot′ə·mē, n. pl., **-mies.** The operation of cutting into the trachea.

tra·cho·ma, trə·kō′mə, n. An inflammation of the lining of the eyelids.

trac·ing, trā′sing, n. That which is produced by tracing, marking, or drawing; a traced copy of a drawing or the like, made on a transparent material.

track, trak, n. One or more pairs of parallel lines of rails with their ties for railroad vehicles; a wheel rut; the mark or series of marks left by something that has passed; a way made or beaten by the feet of men or animals; a course of action or conduct or a method of proceeding; a path or course made or laid out for some particular purpose; a train or succession of ideas, occurrences, or events; a course laid out for running or racing; the collective sports taking place on a track. Usu. pl. A series of footprints or other marks left by an animal or a person.—v.t. To trace or pursue by or as by the track, traces, or footprints left; to follow, as a track or course; to make one's way through or traverse; to make a track of footprints on; to make a track with, as dirt, mud, snow, or tar, carried on the feet while walking; to furnish with a track or tracks, as for railroad vehicles; to observe or follow the progress of, as an aircraft or rocket, by sighting and watching.—v.i. To follow up a track or trail; to run in the same track, as the wheels of a vehicle. —**in one's tracks.** Informal. In the position where someone is. —**keep track of,** to follow the course of. —**lose track of,** to neglect to keep advised of. —**make tracks.** Informal. To leave or go quickly. —**off the track,** going off from the subject or objective. —**on the track of,** in close pursuit of. —**on the wrong side of the tracks,** in a poor neighborhood. —**track·a·ble,** a. —**track·er,** n.

track·age, trak′ij, n. The collective tracks of a railroad or railway; the right of one railroad company to use the tracks of another company; the amount charged for this privilege or right.

track and field, n. A category of athletics including various running, jumping, and throwing events performed on a circular track and the field adjoining it.

track meet, n. An athletic competition involving track and field events.

tract, trakt, n. A stretch or extent of land or water; a region; a particular area of the body, esp. a system of related organs.

tract, trakt, n. A brief treatise usu. dealing with a religious, moral, or political topic.

trac·ta·ble, trak′tə·bəl, a. Capable of being easily trained or managed; docile; governable; pliable. —**trac·ta·bil·i·ty,** trak·tə·bil′ə·tē, **trac·ta·ble·ness,** n. —**trac·ta·bly,** adv.

trac·tion, trak′shən, n. The act of drawing or pulling; a body's friction on a surface; the action of pulling on an organ or muscle to relieve or lessen pressure, or repair a dislocation. —**trac·tion·al, trac·tive,** trak′tiv, a.

trac·tor, trak′tər, n. A strong, heavy-treaded, motorized vehicle used for pulling or drawing heavy equipment and farm machinery; a truck which hitches to and hauls a trailer and consists of an engine and a cab.

trade, trād, n. A business or calling, esp. some line of skilled mechanical work; anything practiced as a means of getting a living or money; a line of mercantile or commercial business or the traffic in a particular commodity or class of commodities; those engaged in a particular line of business; the buying and selling or exchanging of commodities either by wholesale or by retail; business, patronage, or custom; a particular commercial or business transaction; a purchase, sale, or exchange; a bargain or deal.—v.t., **trad·ed, trad·ing.** To buy, sell, barter, or traffic in; to exchange.—v.i. To carry on trade; to traffic, followed by in; to make an exchange; to make purchases or to shop.—a. —**trade in,** to exchange, as a used item, for credit toward the purchase of a similar one. —**trade on** or **up·on,** to use for personal gain.

trade-in, trād′in, n. A used article, as a car or radio, given in trade as part payment for a new article; an instance of business transacted in this manner.

trade·mark, trād/märk, *n.* A distinctive mark, wording, or device adopted by a manufacturer, business, or dealer, usu. registered with a government agency, to distinguish his goods from those of others.—*v.t.* To stamp, as a trademark, on.

trad·er, trā/dər, *n.* One engaged in trade or commerce; a vessel employed regularly in any particular trade.

trades·man, trādz/mən, *n. pl.*, **-men.** A skilled laborer; craftsman; mechanic.

trade un·ion, *n.* A labor union, comprised of workers in related fields or crafts. **—trade un·ion·ism,** *n.* **—trade un·ion·ist,** *n.*

trade wind, *n.* One of the winds prevailing over the oceans from about 30° north latitude to about 30° south latitude, and blowing toward the equator.

trad·ing post, *n.* A station established for carrying on trade in a thinly settled region.

trad·ing stamp, *n.* A printed stamp given by the dealer to the customer, a quantity of which may be redeemed for merchandise.

tra·di·tion, trə·dish/ən, *n.* The handing down of opinions, doctrines, practices, rites, and customs from generation to generation by oral communication; that which is handed down from age to age by oral communication. **—tra·di·tion·less,** *a.*

tra·di·tion·al, trə·dish/ə·nəl, *a.* Pertaining to or derived from tradition; communicated from ancestors to descendants. **—tra·di·tion·al·ism,** *n.* **—tra·di·tion·al·ist,** *n., a.* **—tra·di·tion·al·ly,** *adv.*

tra·duce, trə·doos/, trə·dūs/, *v.t.*, **-duced, -duc·ing.** To misrepresent willfully; to defame. **—tra·duce·ment,** *n.* **—tra·duc·er,** *n.*

traf·fic, traf/ik, *n.* Goods or persons collectively passing along a road, railroad, boat route, or airway; the movement of these goods or persons; dealings; the transportation business; an interchange of goods or merchandise; a heavy exchange or buying and selling of anything, as goods; the business flow of a system of communication; illegal trade.—*v.i.*, **-ficked, -fick·ing.** To do business, esp. illegally; to have business or dealings, usu. followed by *with.* **—traf·fick·er,** *n.*

traf·fic court, *n.* A court whose jurisdiction is usu. limited to decisions on charges of violation of traffic ordinances or statutes.

traf·fic light, *n.* Color-coded lights that caution, stop, and start traffic. Also **traf·fic sig·nal.**

tra·ge·di·an, trə·jē/dē·ən, *n.* A writer, or esp. an actor of tragedy.

trag·e·dy, traj/ə·dē, *n. pl.*, **-dies.** A drama portraying the struggle of a strong-willed hero against fate, culminating in disaster and usu. death; any disaster, misfortune, death, or sequence of interrelated disastrous events.

trag·ic, traj/ik, *a.* Pertaining to tragedy; lamentable; dreadful. Also **trag·i·cal. —trag·i·cal·ly,** *adv.* **—trag·i·cal·ness,** *n.*

trail, trāl, *v.t.* To draw behind or along the ground; to drag; to cause to float after itself; to mark or track out; to follow, as a detective.—*v.i.* To sweep over a surface by being pulled or dragged; to grow with long, slender, and creeping stems, as a plant; to lag; to grow ineffectual or dwindle, usu. followed by *off.*—*n.* A path or route created by the usu. repeated passage of men or animals; anything drawn out behind; evidence of passage left behind by a moving object or body.

trail·blaz·er, trāl/blā/zər, *n.* One who blazes a trail through a wilderness; any innovator in his field. **—trail·blaz·ing,** *a.*

trail·er, trā/lər, *n.* One who or that which trails; any vehicle attached to, and drawn by a car, tractor, or truck; a house on wheels, attachable to an automobile and fitted with conveniences, as for camping.

trail·er camp, *n.* A parking area equipped with utility outlets for temporary or permanent use by house trailers, mobile campers, and similar vehicles. Also **trail·er court, trail·er park.**

train, trān, *n.* A connected series of railway cars; a line or procession of persons, vehicles, animals, or the like traveling together; a succession or series of proceedings, events, ideas, or circumstances; a body of followers or attendants; aftermath or consequence; a series or row of objects or parts; an elongated part of a garment trailing behind on the ground; a trail or stream of something from a moving object.—*v.t.* To form, as behavior, habits, and mental attitude, by discipline and instruction; to make proficient by instruction and practice; to discipline and instruct, as an animal, in the performance of tasks; to make fit, as a person, for some athletic feat or contest; to bring to bear on some object, or to point, aim, or direct, as a firearm, camera, telescope, or eye; to bring, as a plant, into a particular shape or position by bending, pruning, or other means.—*v.i.* To give the discipline and instruction, drill, or practice designed to impart proficiency; to undergo such discipline, instruction, or drill; to get oneself into condition, as for a contest or athletic event. **—train·a·ble,** *a.* **—train·er,** *n.* **—train·ing,** *n., a.*

train·man, trān/mən, *n. pl.*, **-men.** A man employed on a railroad train.

traipse, trāps, *v.i.*, **traipsed, traips·ing.** *Informal.* To walk about, esp. without definite purpose.—*v.t., n.*

trait, trāt, *n.* A distinguishing or peculiar feature or quality; a characteristic.

trai·tor, trā/tər, *n.* One who violates his allegiance and betrays his country; one guilty of treason. **—trai·tor·ous,** *a.* **—trai·tor·ous·ly,** *adv.*

tra·jec·to·ry, trə·jek/tə·rē, *n. pl.*, **-ries.** The curve in the vertical plane traced by an object moving through space.

tram, tram, *n.* A silk thread of two strands twisted loosely together, and used for cross threads in weaving of silk and velvet fabrics.

tram, tram, *n.* A wheeled truck or car on which loads are transported in mines. *Brit.* A streetcar.

tram·mel, tram/əl, *n.* Usu. *pl.* Anything that hinders, confines, or impedes activity, freedom, or progress. —*v.t.*, **-meled** or **-melled, -mel·ing** or **-mel·ling.** To confine; to hamper; to shackle. **—tram·mel·er,** *n.*

tramp, tramp, *v.i.* To walk with a heavy step; to walk heavily or steadily; to go on a walking excursion or expedition; to go about as a vagabond.—*v.t.* To walk heavily or steadily through or over; to traverse on foot.—*n.* A person who travels about on foot from place to place; a hobo; a firm, heavy, resounding tread; the sound made by a continuing heavy tread; a walking excursion or expedition; a freight vessel which does not run regularly between fixed ports, but takes a cargo wherever shippers desire. *Informal.* Any sexually promiscuous female. **—tramp·er,** *n.*

tram·ple, tram/pəl, *v.i.*, **-pled, -pling.** To tread or step heavily.—*v.t.* To tread heavily, roughly, or carelessly on or over; to trample on, domineer harshly over, or crush; to put out, force, or reduce by trampling.—*n.* **—tram·pler,** *n.*

tram·po·line, tram·pə·lēn/, tram/pə·lin, *n.* A heavy canvas or net fastened by springs or elastic rope inside a horizontal rectangular frame and used in acrobatic tumbling. **—tram·po·lin·er, tram·po·lin·ist,** *n.*

trance, trans, *n.* A half-conscious state, as between sleeping and waking; a dazed or bewildered condition; a condition of complete mental absorption or deep musing.

tran·quil, trang/kwil, *a.* Quiet; calm; undisturbed; peaceful; not easily agitated. **tran·quil·li·ty, tran·quil·i·ty,** trang·kwil/ə·tē, *n.* **—tran·quil·ly,** *adv.* **—tran·quil·ness,** *n.*

tran·quil·ize, tran·quil·lize, trang/kwə·līz, *v.t.*, **-ized** or **-lized, -iz·ing** or **-liz·ing.** To render tranquil, esp. by administering drugs; to compose; to calm. —*v.i.* To become tranquil or composed.

tran·quil·iz·er, tran·quil·liz·er, trang/kwə·lī·

zər, *n.* That which tranquilizes; a drug capable of relieving tension.

trans·act, tran·sakt′, tran·zakt′, *v.t.* To conduct or carry through, as affairs or business.—*v.i.* To carry through affairs or negotiations. **—trans·ac·tor,** *n.*

trans·ac·tion, tran·sak/shən, tran·zak/shən, *n.* The act of transacting; an instance or process of transacting something, or that which is transacted; *pl.*, records, often published, of the doings of a learned society. **—trans·ac·tion·al,** *a.*

trans·al·pine, tranz·al/pïn, *a.* Across or beyond the Alps, esp. as viewed from Italy.—*n.* A native or inhabitant of a country beyond the Alps.

trans·at·lan·tic, trans·et·lan/tik, tranz·et·lan/tik, *a.* Extending across the Atlantic; on the other side of the Atlantic.

trans·ceiv·er, tran·sē/vər, *n.* A combined transmitter and receiver in one radio device.

tran·scend, tran·send′, *v.t.* To go above or beyond, or exceed, as a limit; surpass, excel, or exceed.—*v.i.* To be transcendent. **—tran·scend·ent,** tran·sen/dənt, *a.*

tran·scen·den·tal, tran·sen·den/tǝl, *a.* Supernatural; abstract or metaphysical; idealistic, lofty, or extravagant. **—tran·scen·den·tal·ly,** *adv.* **—tran·scen·den·tal·ism,** tran·sen·den/tǝ·liz·əm, *n.*

trans·con·ti·nen·tal, trans·kon·tə·nen/təl, *a.* Passing or extending across a continent; on the far or other side of a continent.

tran·scribe, tran·skrib′, *v.t.,* -scribed, -scrib·ing. To make a handwritten or typed copy of, as the text of a document, shorthand notes, or lecture notes; to record for later radio broadcasting, as a performance or announcement. **—tran·scrib·er,** *n.*

tran·script, tran/skript, *n.* A written or typed copy; an official school report which includes a student's courses, grades, and credits.

tran·scrip·tion, tran·skrip/shən, *n.* The act of transcribing; a transcript or copy; the arrangement of a musical composition for a voice or instrument other than that for which it was originally written; a composition so arranged; a recording of a musical, dramatic, or other performance made for radio broadcasting. **—tran·scrip·tion·al, tran·scrip·tive,** *a.*

tran·sept, tran/sept, *n.* That portion of a church built in the form of a cross, which is between the nave and choir and projects externally on each side. **—tran·sep·tal,** tran·sep/təl, *a.* **—tran·sep·tal·ly,** *adv.*

trans·fer, trans·fər′, trans/fər, *v.t.,* -ferred, -fer·ring. To convey or remove from one place or person to another; to make over the possession or control of; to sell or give; to convey, as a drawing, design, or pattern, from one surface to another.—*v.i.* To transfer oneself; to be transferred; to change from one conveyance to another. —trans/fər, *n.* The act of transferring. Also **trans·fer·al, trans·fer·ral,** trans·fər/əl. That which is transferred, as a drawing, pattern, or the like; a point or place for transferring; a means or system of transferring; a ticket entitling a passenger to continue his journey on another conveyance. **—trans·fer·a·ble,** *a.* **—trans·fer·ence,** *n.*

trans·fig·ure, trans·fig/yər, *v.t.,* -ured, -ur·ing. To change the outward form or appearance of; to elevate and glorify; to idealize. **—trans·fig·ure·ment,** *n.* **—trans·fig·u·ra·tion,** trans·fig·yə·rā/shən, *n.*

trans·fix, trans·fiks′, *v.t.,* -fixed, -fix·ing. To pierce through as with a pointed weapon; to hold or make immovable, as with awe or terror. **—trans·fix·ion,** trans·fik/shən, *n.*

trans·form, trans·fôrm′, *v.t.* To change in form or appearance; metamorphose; to change in condition, nature, or character.—*v.i.* To change in form, appearance, or character; to become transformed. **—trans·form·a·ble,** *a.* **—trans·for·ma·tion,** trans·fər·mā/shən, *n.* **—trans·form·a·tive,** *a.*

trans·form·er, trans·fôr/mər, *n.* An appliance in alternating current circuits for changing current to a lower or higher voltage.

trans·fuse, trans·fūz′, *v.t.,* -fused, -fus·ing. To cause to be instilled or imbibed; to instill or impart; to transfer, as blood, from the veins or arteries of one person or animal to those of another. **—trans·fus·i·ble, trans·fus·a·ble,** *a.* **—trans·fu·sion,** trans·fū/zhən, *n.*

trans·gress, trans·gres′, tranz·gres′, *v.t.* To overpass, as some law or rule prescribed; to break or violate; infringe.—*v.i.* To offend by violating a law; to sin. **—trans·gres·sive,** *a.* **—trans·gres·sor,** *n.* **—trans·gres·sion,** trans·gresh/ən, tranz·gresh/ən, *n.*

tran·sient, tran/shənt, tran/zhənt, *a.* Passing quickly away; not permanent, lasting, or durable; momentary; passing.—*n.* A transient or temporary person or thing. **—tran·sient·ly,** *adv.*

tran·sis·tor, tran·zis/tər, *n.* A device using a semiconductor that performs many of the functions of an electron tube but without having its requirements for space or power.

tran·sis·tor·ize, tran·zis/tə·rīz, *v.t.,* -ized, -iz·ing. To furnish or design with transistors.

trans·it, tran/sit, tran/zit, *n.* The passing over or through; the process of conveying.

tran·si·tion, tran·zish/ən, tran·sish/ən, *n.* Passage from one place or state to another; change or process of change. **—tran·si·tion·al,** *a.* **—tran·si·tion·al·ly,** *adv.*

tran·si·tive, tran/si·tiv, tran/zi·tiv, *a.* Denoting a verb whose action passes directly to a complement from its subject and requires this direct object to express the full meaning of the predicate. Having the power of passing or making transition. **—tran·si·tive·ly,** *adv.* **—tran·si·tive·ness, tran·si·tiv·i·ty,** *n.*

tran·si·to·ry, tran/si·tôr·ē, *a.* Unstable; fleeting; temporary. **—tran·si·to·ri·ly,** *adv.* **—tran·si·to·ri·ness,** *n.*

trans·late, trans·lāt′, tranz·lāt′, trans/lāt, tranz/lāt, *v.t.,* -lat·ed, -lat·ing. To render into another language; to express in other terms or words; to transform, as one medium or condition into another.—*v.i.* To practice translation; to be able to be translated. **—trans·lat·a·bil·i·ty,** *n.* **—trans·lat·a·ble,** *a.* **—trans·lat·or,** *n.*

trans·la·tion, trans·lā/shən, tranz·lā/shən, *n.* The act of translating, esp. the act or process of turning into another language; that which is produced by turning into another language. **—trans·la·tion·al, trans·la·tive,** *a.*

trans·lit·er·ate, trans·lit/ə·rāt, tranz·lit/ə·rāt, *v.t.,* -at·ed, -at·ing. To express or represent in the alphabetic characters of another language. **—trans·lit·er·a·tion,** tranz·lit·ə·rā/shən, *n.*

trans·lu·cent, trans·loo/sənt, tranz·loo/sənt, *a.* Allowing light to pass through, but not transparent. **—trans·lu·cence, trans·lu·cen·cy,** *n.* **—trans·lu·cent·ly,** *adv.*

trans·mi·grate, trans·mī/grāt, tranz·mī/grāt, *v.i.,* -grat·ed, -grat·ing. To pass from one country or region to another; to pass from one body into another, as the soul after death. **—trans·mi·gra·tion,** trans·mi·grā/shən, tranz·mi·grā/shən, *n.* **—trans·mi·gra·tor,** *n.* **—trans·mi·gra·to·ry,** *a.*

trans·mis·sion, trans·mish/ən, tranz·mish/ən, *n.* The act of transmitting, or the state of being transmitted; a device or unit that transmits power from an engine to a driven component, as in an automobile. **—trans·mis·si·bil·i·ty,** tranz·mis·ə·bil/ə·tē, *n.* **—trans·mis·si·ble,** tranz·mis·iv/ə·tē, *n.* **—trans·mis·si·ble, trans·mis·sive,** *a.*

trans·mit, trans·mit′, tranz·mit′, *v.t.,* -mit·ted, -mit·ting. To cause to pass or be conveyed from one point to another, as by post, wire, rail, conduit, or air; to communicate by sending; to send from one person or place to another; to hand down, as by heredity; to spread, as disease; to allow, as light, sound, heat, or the like, to pass through.—*v.i.* To send out electrical energy in a signal, as radio, radar, television, or any other electromagnetic broadcast wave; to transfer movement from one part of a machine to another, as in automobile transmission systems. —**trans·mit·ta·ble**, *a.* —**trans·mit·tal**, *n.*

trans·mit·ter, trans·mit′ər, tranz·mit′ər, *n.* One who or that which transmits; the sending or transmittal equipment.

trans·mute, trans·mūt′, tranz·mūt′, *v.t.*, **-mut·ed**, **-mut·ing**. To change from one nature, form, or substance into another; to metamorphose.—*v.i.* —**trans·mut·er**, *n.* —**trans·mut·a·ble·ness**, **trans·mut·a·bil·i·ty**, *n.* —**trans·mut·a·bly**, *adv.* —**trans·mu·ta·tion**, trans·mū·tā′shən, tranz·mū·tā′shən, *n.* —**trans·mut·a·ble**, *a.*

trans·na·tion·al, trans·nash′ə·nəl, tranz·nash′ə·nəl, *a.* Transcending national boundaries or narrow national interests.

trans·o·ce·an·ic, trans·ō·shē·an′ik, tranz·ō·shē·an′ik, *a.* Across the ocean.

tran·som, tran′səm, *n.* A small window above a door or larger window; the crossbar separating a window or door from such a window. —**tran·somed**, *a.*

trans·pa·cif·ic, trans·pə·sif′ik, *a.* Extending across the Pacific; on the other side of the Pacific.

trans·par·ent, trans·pār′ənt, trans·par′ənt, *a.* Having the property of transmitting rays of light through a material so that bodies behind or beyond can be distinctly seen; easily seen through; guileless or frank; unable to hide feelings. —**trans·par·en·cy**, trans·pār′ən·sē, trans·par′ən·sē, *n. pl.*, **-cies.** —**trans·par·ent·ly**, *adv.* —**trans·par·ent·ness**, *n.*

tran·spire, tran·spir′, *v.t.*, **-spired**, **-spir·ing**. To excrete, as waste matter, in the form of perspiration, through the pores of the skin; to emit, as water vapor, from the stomata of plants.—*v.i.* To be emitted through the pores of the skin or through the stomata of plants; to become public gradually; to come to light; to take place; to happen.

trans·plant, trans·plant′, *v.t.* To remove, as a plant, from one place and plant in another; to remove from one place to another; to transfer, as an organ or a portion of tissue, from one part of the body to another or from one person or animal to another.—*v.i.* —trans′plant, trans·plänt, *n.* The act of transplanting; something that has been transplanted. —**trans·plant·a·ble**, *a.* —**trans·plan·ta·tion**, trans·plan·tā′shən, *n.* —**trans·plant·er**, *n.*

tran·spon·der, tran·spon′dər, *n.* A radio or radar device that, on receiving a pulse emitted by an interrogator, automatically emits a signal in response.

trans·port, trans·pōrt′, trans·pôrt′, *v.t.* To carry or convey from one place to another; to carry away with pleasurable emotion; to send away in banishment. —trans′pōrt, trans′pôrt, *n.* A vessel engaged in transporting goods and passengers; transportation; conveyance; a vehement emotion; passion; rapture; ecstasy. —**trans·port·a·bil·i·ty**, *n.* —**trans·port·a·ble**, *a.* —**trans·port·er**, *n.*

trans·por·ta·tion, trans·pər·tā′shən, *n.* The act of transporting; the means of conveyance from one place to another; a ticket purchased to travel on some public carrier.

trans·pose, trans·pōz′, *v.t.*, **-posed**, **-pos·ing**. To change the place or order of, as words or phrases, by putting each in the place of the other; to cause to change places; to change the musical key of, either higher or lower than the original.—*v.i.* —**trans·pos·a·ble**, *a.* —**trans·po·si·tion**, trans·pə·zish′ən, *n.*

trans·verse, trans·vərs′, tranz·vərs′, trans′vərs, tranz′vərs, *a.* Being in a cross direction; being across. —**trans·verse·ly**, *adv.*

trans·ves·tism, trans·ves′tiz·əm, tranz·ves′tiz·əm, *n.* The practice of wearing or compulsion to wear clothes appropriate to the other sex. Also **trans·ves·ti·tism.** —**trans·ves·tite**, trans·ves′tīt, tranz·ves′tīt, *a., n.*

trap, trap, *n.* A contrivance used for taking game; a mechanical device that shuts suddenly by means of a spring, or a snare; any device for catching one unawares; any of various contrivances for preventing the passage of steam, water, and the like; a device for suddenly releasing or tossing into the air objects to be shot at, as pigeons or clay targets; a golf course hazard, as a depression filled with sand; a light, two-wheeled carriage; any trap door. *Informal.* Mouth; a night club.—*v.t.*, **trapped**, **trap·ping.** To catch in a trap; to take by stratagem; to furnish or set with traps; to stop and hold by or as by a trap.—*v.i.* To set traps for game; to catch animals in traps for their furs. —**trap·per**, trap′ər, *n.*

trap, trap, *v.t.*, **trapped**, **trap·ping.** To adorn; to dress with ornaments.

trap, trap, *n.* An igneous rock, dark in color and often columnar in structure, as basalt.

trap door, *n.* A door flush, or nearly so, with the surface of a floor, ceiling, or roof.

tra·peze, tra·pēz′, *n.* A sort of swing suspended by two cords on which various acrobatic feats are performed. —**tra·pez·ist**, *n.*

tra·pe·zi·um, trə·pē′zē·əm, *n. pl.*, **-zi·ums**, **-zi·a**, **-zē·ə.** A plane figure bounded by four straight lines, no two of which are parallel.

trap·e·zoid, trap′ə·zoyd, *n.* A four-sided plane figure having two of its opposite sides parallel. —**trap·e·zoi·dal**, trap·ə·zoy′dəl, *a.*

trap·pings, trap′ingz, *n. pl.* Ornamental accessories, esp. as put on horses; general ornaments of dress; finery.

trap·shoot·ing, trap′shoo·ting, *n.* The sport of shooting at clay targets thrown into the air by a machine called a trap. —**trap·shoot·er**, *n.*

trash, trash, *n.* Waste or worthless matter; rubbish; pointless or vulgar writing or ideas; worthless art; a worthless person or persons.—*v.t.* —**trash·i·ly**, *adv.* —**trash·i·ness**, *n.* —**trash·y**, trash′ē, *a.*, **-i·er**, **-i·est.**

trau·ma, trow′mə, trô′mə, *n. pl.*, **-mas**, **-ma·ta**, **-mə·tə.** A wound; a bodily injury produced by violence or some kind of shock; a disordered or disturbed state, either mental or behavioral, which is an effect of some kind of stress or injury, and which sometimes has a lifelong effect; a shock. —**trau·mat·ic**, trə·mat′ik, trô·mat′ik, trow·mat′ik, *a.* —**trau·mat·i·cal·ly**, *adv.*

tra·vail, trə·vāl′, trav′āl, trav′əl, *n.* Extremely difficult, strenuous work; physical or mental hardship; pain and suffering.—*v.i.*

trav·el, trav′əl, *v.i.*, **-eled** or **-elled**, **-el·ing** or **-el·ling.** To go from place to place or make a journey; to proceed or advance in any way; to keep company. *Informal.* To go swiftly; in basketball, to walk.—*v.t.* To journey over or pass through, as a city or a street; to journey a certain distance.—*n.* The act of traveling or journeying; *pl.*, journeys or trips. —**trav·el·er**, *Brit.* **trav·el·ler**, trav′ə·lər, trav′lər, *n.*

trav·e·logue, **trav·e·log**, trav′ə·lôg, trav′ə·log, *n.* A lecture describing travel, usu. illustrated.

trav·erse, trav′ərs, trə·vərs′, *v.t.*, **-ersed**, **-ers·ing.** To go across, over, through, or along; to deny, resist, or thwart; to contradict.—*v.i.* To go across, over, or up and down.—*n.* The process of moving over, across, or through; a thing that crosses or blocks; something which forms a barrier, as a curtain, railing, or screen. —*a.* Going or reaching across; relating to the hanging or operating of draperies that can be pulled apart or together with a cord. —**tra·vers·a·ble**, *a.* —**tra·vers·al**, *n.* —**tra·vers·er**, *n.*

trav·es·ty, trav′is·tē, *n. pl.*, **-ties.** A literary composition or artistic work characterized by burlesque of a serious work or subject; a composition so bad that it seems to be of this kind; any grotesque or debased likeness or imitation.—*v.t.*, **-tied, -ty·ing.** To make a travesty on.

trawl, trôl, *n.* A long line from which short lines with baited hooks are suspended, used in sea fishing; also **trawl line.** A fishing net which a boat drags along the bottom of the sea; also **trawl net.**—*v.i.* To fish with a trawl net.—*v.t.* To catch, as fish, with a trawl.

trawl·er, trô/lər, *n.* A fishing vessel which uses a trawl net.

tray, trā, *n.* A shallow receptacle with rimmed edge on which objects may be carried.

treach·er·ous, trech/ər·əs, *a.* Characterized by treason; faithless; deceptive; uncertain or unreliable; risky. **—treach·er·ous·ly,** *adv.* **—treach·er·ous· ness,** *n.*

treach·er·y, trech/ə·rē, *n. pl.,* **-ies.** Violation of allegiance, or of faith and confidence; treason.

trea·cle, trē/kəl, *n. Brit.* Molasses; excessive sentiment and sweetness. **—trea·cly,** *a.,* **-cli·er, -cli·est.**

tread, tred, *v.t.,* **trod, trod·den** or **trod, tread·ing.** To step or walk on, along, in, or over; to crush under the feet; to form by stepping or tramping upon; to treat with contempt or brutality.—*v.i.* To set the feet down in stepping; to walk; to press or trample with the feet, usu. followed by *on* or *upon.*—*n.* The act, sound, or way of stepping or walking; a step; one of several objects on which a person walks or an object moves; the design or pattern made on a tire; the horizontal part of a stair step. **—tread on some·one's toes,** to irritate, insult, or affront someone. **—tread wa·ter,** to hold oneself upright in the water and one's head above water by making motions with the legs and the arms. **—tread·er,** *n.*

trea·dle, tred/əl, *n.* A foot lever of a loom or other machine used to produce motion.—*v.i.,* **-dled, -dling.**

tread·mill, tred/mil, *n.* An endless belt moved by a beast of burden to operate a mill; a monotonous and futile routine.

trea·son, trē/zən, *n.* Disloyalty or treachery to one's country; the illegal act of giving aid and comfort to the enemies of one's country. **—trea·son·a·ble, trea· son·ous,** *a.* **—trea·son·a·bly,** *adv.*

treas·ure, trezh/ər, *n.* Any form of accumulated wealth; something or someone very much valued. —*v.t.,* **-ured, -ur·ing.** To hoard; to collect or store for future use; to cherish; to prize. **—treas·ur·a·ble,** *a.*

treas·ur·er, trezh/ər·ər, *n.* One who has the care of a treasure or treasury. **—treas·ur·er·ship,** *n.*

treas·ure-trove, trezh/ər·trōv, *n.* Money or the like found hidden, the owner of which is not known; any valuable discovery.

treas·ur·y, trezh/ə·rē, *n. pl.,* **-ies.** A place where the revenues of a government or group are deposited and debts discharged; (*often cap.*) that department of a government, corporation, or the like which has charge of the finances; (*cap.*) a department of the U.S. federal government which has charge of collection and disbursement of funds; (*l.c.*) a place where valuable articles are kept; a collection of treasures or things of value.

treat, trēt, *v.t.* To act or behave toward; to look upon or view in a particular way; to deal with by applying remedies; to handle in writing, speaking, or any medium of art; to subject to the action of a substance or agent in order to alter or improve; to entertain without expense to the guest.—*v.i.* To handle a topic in writing or speaking, usu. followed by *of;* to provide or pay for entertainment; to discuss settlement terms; to negotiate.—*n.* An entertainment given as a compliment or expression of regard; anything that affords much pleasure; the process of treating; one person's turn to entertain. **—treat·a·ble,** *a.* **—treat·er,** *n.*

trea·tise, trē/tis, *n.* A written formal composition on some subject.

treat·ment, trēt/mənt, *n.* The act or the manner of treating; characteristic style or method in art, music, or literature; conduct or behavior toward a person; manner of proceeding in applying medicinal remedies or surgery to cure an illness.

trea·ty, trē/tē, *n. pl.,* **-ties.** A formally negotiated agreement between nations.

tre·ble, treb/əl, *a.* Threefold; triple; pertaining to the highest or most acute sounds; playing or singing the highest part or most acute sounds; having shrillness or high pitch.—*n.* The highest vocal or instrumental part in a piece of music; soprano; a shrill or high-pitched sound or voice; the upper range of musical pitch.—*v.t., v.t.,* **-bled, -bling.** To make thrice as much; to triple. **—tre·bly,** treb/lē, *adv.*

tree, trē, *n.* A perennial plant having a woody trunk of considerable size, from which spring branches, or, in the palms, fronds; something resembling a tree: a genealogical tree.—*v.t.,* **treed, tree·ing.** To drive to a tree.—*v.i.* To take refuge in a tree. **—up a tree.** *Informal.* Cornered; in a difficult situation. **—tree·less,** *a.* **—tree·less·ness,** *n.* **—tree·like,** *a.*

tree frog, *n.* Any of various small, brightly colored, tree-dwelling frogs, usu. having adhesive suckers on the ends of the toes.

tre·foil, trē/foyl, *n.* An herb having leaves of three leaflets, and reddish, purple, yellow, or white flower heads; an ornamental figure or structure resembling a trifoliate leaf. **—tre·foiled,** *a.*

trek, trek, *v.t.,* **trekked, trek·king.** To pull or haul by a draft animal.—*v.i.* To travel slowly.—*n.* The act of trekking; a migration; a journey, as a slow or difficult one. **—trek·ker,** *n.*

trel·lis, trel/is, *n.* A frame or structure of latticework for the support of growing vines.—*v.t.* To furnish with a trellis; enclose with a trellis; train on a trellis.

trem·ble, trem/bəl, *v.i.,* **-bled, -bling.** To shake involuntarily with quick, short movements, as from fear, excitement, weakness, or cold; to quake, quiver, or shiver; to be agitated with fear or apprehension.—*n.* The act of trembling; a state or fit of trembling. **—trem·bles,** *n. pl. but sing. in constr.* **—trem·bler,** *n.* **—trem·bly,** *a.,* **-bli·er, -bli·est.** **—trem·bling·ly,** *adv.*

tre·men·dous, tri·men/dəs, *a. Informal.* Such as may astonish by magnitude, force, greatness, or superiority; exceptional; sufficient to excite fear or terror; terrible; awful; dreadful. **—tre·men·dous·ly,** *adv.* **—tre·men·dous·ness,** *n.*

trem·o·lo, trem/ə·lō, *n. pl.,* **-los.** A tremulous or vibrating effect produced on certain instruments and in the human voice, as to express emotion.

trem·or, trem/ər, *n.* Involuntary shaking of the body or limbs, as from fear, weakness, or fever; a vibration; a trembling or quivering effect. **—trem·or·ous,** *a.*

trem·u·lous, trem/yə·ləs, trem/ū·ləs, *a.* Characterized by trembling; fearful or timorous; vibratory or quivering. **—trem·u·lous·ly,** *adv.* **—trem·u·lous· ness,** *n.*

trench, trench, *n.* A narrow excavation of considerable length cut into the ground; a ditch; a long, narrow excavation, the earth from which is thrown up in front to serve as a shelter.—*v.t.* To cut; to divide by cutting. —*v.i.* To dig a trench; to encroach or infringe, used with *on* or *upon.*

trench·ant, tren/chənt, *a.* Incisive or keen, as language, or a person speaking or writing; vigorous, or effective; clearly or sharply defined, as an outline. **—trench·an·cy,** *n.* **—trench·ant·ly,** *adv.*

trench coat, *n.* A double-breasted, belted, waterproof outer coat.

trench·er·man, tren/chər·mən, *n. pl.,* **-men.** An eater, esp. one who has a hearty appetite.

trench foot, *n.* A condition of the feet resembling

---

a- hat, fāte, fāre, fäther; **e-** met, mē; **i-** pin, pīne; **o-** not, nōte, ôrb, moove (move), boy, pownd; **u-** cūbe, bůll, tûk (took); **ch-** chin; **th-** thick, ŧhen; **zh-** vizhon (vision); **ə-** əgo, takən, pencəl, lemən, bərd (bird).

frostbite, frequently terminating in gangrene, and caused by exposure to wet and cold.

trench mouth, *n.* Acute inflammation of the tonsils, mouth, and gums, with ulcers of the affected tissue, swelling, and fever, often resulting in the loss of teeth.

trend, trend, *n.* A general course, drift, or tendency; the direction of such a course, drift, or tendency.—*v.i.* To have a general tendency, as events; to tend to take a particular direction.

trend•y, tren′dē, *a.,* **-i•er, -i•est.** Stylish; keeping up with a current fashion or trend.

tre•pan, tri•pan′, *n.* A boring tool in the form of a rotary saw, used in cutting shafts in rock; a similar tool for cutting disks from metal plate or the like.—*v.t.,* **-panned, -pan•ning.** To cut with a trepan. —**trep•an•a•tion,** trep•ə•nā′shən, *n.*

tre•phine, tri•fīn′, tri•fēn′, *n.* A surgical trepan for removing disks of bone from the skull.—*v.t.,* **-phined, -phin•ing.** To operate upon with a trephine. —**treph•i•na•tion,** tref•ə•nā′shən, *n.*

trep•i•da•tion, trep•ə•dā′shən, *n.* Tremulous alarm, agitation, or perturbation; utter dread; trembling of the limbs, as in paralytic affections; a vibratory movement.

tres•pass, tres′pəs, *v.i.* To commit a transgression or offense; to sin; to make an improper inroad on a person's presence, time, or privacy; to encroach or infringe, followed by *on.*—*v.t.* To commit, as a transgression; to transgress or violate.—*n.* A transgression; an offense, sin, or wrong; an encroachment or intrusion. —**tres•pass•er,** *n.*

tress, tres, *n.* A lock of hair. *Usu. pl.* Long locks or curls of hair, esp. of a woman. —**tressed,** trest, *a.*

tres•tle, tres′əl, *n.* A frame used as a support, consisting typically of a horizontal beam or bar fixed at each end to a pair of spreading legs; a supporting framework composed chiefly of vertical or inclined pieces used for various purposes, as for carrying railroad tracks across a gap.

trey, trā, *n.* The three in a deck of playing cards or the face of any die or domino having three dots.

tri•ad, trī′ad, *n.* A group of three. —**tri•ad•ic,** *a.* —**tri•ad•i•cal•ly,** *adv.*

tri•al, trī′əl, tril, *n.* The examination of a cause in controversy between parties before a proper tribunal and the determination thereof; the act of trying or testing; an attempt; an experiment; proof through experience; that which tests strength of character, faith, fact, or principle; temptation; an examination. —*a.* Of, relating to, or used by way of trial, proof, experiment, or sample.

tri•al and er•ror, *n.* That form of experimentation in which a variety of methods are tried before arriving at the desired result.

tri•an•gle, trī′ang•gəl, *n.* A polygon bounded by three sides and containing three angles; anything shaped or arranged in such a manner; a triad or group of three; an emotional situation involving three people. —*a.* **tri•an•gu•lar,** trī•ang′gyə•lər, *a.* —**tri•an•gu•lar•i•ty,** trī•ang•gyə•lar′ə•tē, *n.* —**tri•an•gu•lar•ly,** *adv.*

tri•an•gu•late, trī•ang′gyə•lāt, *v.t.,* **-lat•ed, -lat•ing.** To make triangular; to divide into triangles.—*a.* Triangular; composed of or marked with triangles. —**tri•an•gu•la•tion,** trī•ang•gyə•lā′shən, *n.*

tribe, trīb, *n.* A division, class, or distinct portion of a people or nation; a family or race descending from the same progenitor; a division of animals or plants of various ranks. —**trib•al,** *a.* —**tribes•man,** trībz′mən, *n. pl.,* **-men.**

trib•u•la•tion, trib•yə•lā′shən, *n.* That which occasions affliction or distress; distress; trouble.

tri•bu•nal, trī•būn′əl, tri•bōōn′əl, *n.* A court of justice; the seat occupied by a judge or magistrate when presiding in a court.

trib•une, trib′ūn, *n.* A person who champions the rights of the people; a title of several types of officials in ancient Rome, esp. the magistrates chosen by the

plebeians to represent their interests in opposition to those of the patricians. **trib•une•ship, trib•u•nate,** *n.*

trib•u•tar•y, trib′yə•ter•ē, *a.* Flowing into a larger stream or other body of water; furnishing subsidiary aid; paying or required to pay tribute.—*n. pl.,* **-ies.** A stream contributing its flow to a larger stream or other body of water; one who pays tribute. —**trib•u•tar•i•ly,** *adv.*

trib•ute, trib′ūt, *n.* Anything said or done in commemoration of a person or event, given as a token of gratitude or esteem; an annual or stated sum paid by one head of state to another, either as acknowledgment of submission or by virtue of some treaty; a rent or tax: any exorbitant payment obtained by coercion.

trice, trīs, *n.* A moment: now used chiefly in *in a trice.*

tri•ceps, trī′seps, *n. pl.,* **-cep•ses,** -sep•sēz, **-ceps.** A muscle having three heads or points of origin, esp. one extending along the back of the upper arm.

trich•i•no•sis, trik•ə•nō′sis, *n.* A disease due to the presence of the trichina worm in the intestines and muscular tissues.

trick, trik, *n.* A crafty or fraudulent device; an artifice, stratagem, ruse, or wile; a deceptive or illusory appearance; a roguish or mischievous performance or prank; a practical joke; a hoax; a foolish, disgraceful, or mean performance or action; the art or knack of doing something; a clever or dexterous feat, as for exhibition or entertainment; a peculiar habit, practice, or way of acting; a peculiar quality, feature, trait, or characteristic; the cards collectively which are played and won in one round in a game.—*v.t.* To deceive by trickery; to cheat or swindle, used with *out of;* to beguile by trickery, used with *into.*—*v.i.* To practice trickery or deception; to cheat; to play tricks; to trifle.—*a.* —**trick•er,** *n.*

trick•er•y, trik′ə•rē, *n. pl.,* **-ies.** The practice of tricks; cheating.

trick•le, trik′əl, *v.i.,* **-led, -ling.** To flow or fall by drops or in a small, broken stream; to come, go, pass, or proceed as if by drops or in a small stream.—*v.t.* To let or cause to flow by drops or in a gentle stream.—*n.* A trickling flow or stream; a quantity of anything proceeding as if by drops or in a small stream.

trick•ster, trik′stər, *n.* A person who plays tricks on others; a deceiver; a cheat.

trick•y, trik′ē, *a.,* **-i•er, -i•est.** Given to or characterized by deceitful tricks; crafty; deceptive; uncertain. —**trick•i•ly,** *adv.* —**trick•i•ness,** *n.*

tri•col•or, trī′kəl•ər, *n.* A flag having three colors, usu. arranged in equal stripes, as in the flag of France. —**tri•col•ored,** *a.*

tri•cus•pid, trī•kəs′pid, *a.* Having three cusps or points, as a tooth.—*n.* A tricuspid tooth.

tri•cy•cle, trī′sik•əl, *n.* A three-wheeled vehicle, propelled by two pedals and designed for a child.

tri•dent, trīd′ənt, *n.* An instrument having the form of a fork with three prongs.—*a.* —**tri•den•tate,** trī•den′tāt, *a.* —**tri•den•tal,** trī•den′təl, *a.*

tri•di•men•sion•al, trī•də•men′shə•nəl, *a.* Having the three dimensions of length, width, and depth.—**tri•di•men•sion•al•i•ty,** trī•də•men•shə•nal′ə•tē, *n.*

tried, trīd, *a.* Tested; proved; dependable; having withstood hardship or distress.

tri•en•ni•al, trī•en′ē•əl, *a.* Occurring every three years; lasting three years.—*n.* —**tri•en•ni•al•ly,** *adv.*

tri•en•ni•um, trī•en′ē•əm, *n. pl.,* **-ni•ums,** -ni•a, -nē•ə. A period of three years.

tri•fle, trī′fəl, *n.* A matter of slight importance, or a trivial or insignificant affair or circumstance; a toy, trinket, or knickknack; a literary work, or musical composition of light or trivial character; a small quantity or amount of anything; a dish consisting of whipped cream or some substitute, as beaten whites of eggs, and usu. containing cake soaked in wine or liqueur, and jam or fruit.—*v.i.,* **-fled, -fling.** To deal lightly, followed by *with;* amuse oneself, followed by *with;* to act or talk in an idle or frivolous way.—*v.t.* To utter lightly or idly; to pass, as time, idly or frivolously, followed by *away.* —**trif•ler,** *n.*

tri•fling, trī′fling, *a.* Frivolous; shallow; of slight importance; trivial. —**tri•fling•ly,** *adv.* —**tri•fling•ness,** *n.*

tri•fo•cals, trī•fō′kəlz, *n. pl.* Eyeglasses having a segmented lens for adjustment to three distances.

tri•fo•li•ate, trī•fō′le•it, trī•fō′le•āt, *a.* Having three leaves.

trig•ger, trig′ər, *n.* A small, fingerlike projection actuating a weapon's firing mechanism when pulled or depressed by a finger; a device, as a lever, the pulling or pressing of which releases a pin or spring; an act or happening which incites, stimulates, or influences action or emotion.—*v.t.* To shoot, as a gun; to start or set off; initiate. —**quick on the trig•ger.** *Informal.* Quick to respond, understand, or act; alert. —**trig•ger•less,** *a.*

trig•ger-hap•py, trig′ər•hap•ē, *a. Informal.* Having a tendency to fire a gun heedlessly; heedless and irresponsible in advocating situations and actions that might lead to war; bellicose in attitude.

trig•ger•man, trig′ər•mən, trig′ər•man, *n. pl.,* **-men.** *Informal.* A professional killer, esp. of the underworld; a gangster's bodyguard.

trig•o•nom•e•try, trig•ə•nom′ə•trē, *n.* The branch of mathematics that deals with the relations between the sides and angles of triangles and the calculations based on these relations. —**trig•o•no•met•ric,** trig•ə•nə•met′rik, *a.* —**trig•o•no•met•ri•cal,** *a.* —**trig•o•no•met•ri•cal•ly,** *adv.*

trill, tril, *v.t.* To sing or play with a vibratory effect; to articulate with a rapid vibration of one vocal organ against another.—*v.i.* To resound tremulously or vibrantly; to execute a trill.—*n.* The sound of trilling or a succession of such sounds.

tril•lion, tril′yən, *n.* In the U.S. and France, a million times a million; a digit followed by twelve zeros as 1,000,000,000,000. In Great Britain or Germany, a million billions or a digit followed by eighteen zeros. —**tril•lionth,** *n., a.*

tri•lo•bite, trī′lə•bīt, *n.* Any of a group of extinct sea-dwelling anthropods of the Paleozoic era, varying in length from an inch or less to two feet.

tril•o•gy, tril′ə•jē, *n. pl.,* **-gies.** A series of three related dramas, operas, or novels forming one connected whole.

trim, trim, *v.t.,* **trimmed, trim•ming.** To reduce to a neat or orderly state by clipping, paring, pruning, lopping, or otherwise removing superfluous waste or used parts; to modify, as opinions, according to expediency; to adjust the controls of some vehicle, as an airplane, so that the craft is in horizontal movement; to adjust, as sails or yards, with reference to the direction of the wind and the course of the ship; to deck with ornaments. *Informal.* To rebuke or reprove; to beat or thrash; to defeat, as in a game.—*v.i.* to assume a particular position or trim in the water, as a vessel; to adapt one's course of action in order to get on under conflicting conditions or to stand well with both or all parties.—*n.* Proper conditions or order; the set of a ship in the water, the condition of a ship when properly balanced; the adjustment of the sails, with reference to the direction of the wind and the course of the ship; decorative trimming; the decorative merchandise in a store window; trimming by cutting or clipping, as a type of haircut; the position or attitude of any aircraft relative to the proper horizontal plane necessary for balanced flight; the visible woodwork on the interior of a building; decorations of furnishings on the exterior and interior of some vehicle, as a car.—*a.,* **trim•mer, trim•mest.** Pleasingly neat or smart in appearance; in good condition. —**trim•ly,** *adv.* —**trim•ness,** *n.*

tri•mes•ter, trī•mes′tər, *n.* One of three equal periods or terms into which some colleges and universities divide the year. —**tri•mes•tral, tri•mes•tri•al,** *a.*

trim•mer, trim′ər, *n.* One who or that which trims; a tool or machine for trimming or clipping, paring, or pruning; a machine for trimming lumber; an apparatus for stowing, arranging, or shifting cargo, coal, or the like; a person who trims in his course of action, as in politics; one who pursues a cautious policy between parties, accommodating himself to one side or another as expediency may dictate.

trim•ming, trim′ing, *n.* Anything used or serving to trim or decorate; a decorative fitting or finish. *Informal.* A reproving, a beating or thrashing, or a defeat. *Pl.* Accompaniments to plain dishes or food; pieces cut off in clipping, paring, or pruning.

tri•month•ly, trī•mənth′lē, *a.* Taking place or performed every three months, as a payment on a loan.

tri•ni•tro•tol•u•ene, trī•nī•trō•tol′ū•ēn, *n.* A high explosive made of toluene treated with nitric acid; TNT.

Trin•i•ty, trin′ə•tē, *n.* The union of three distinct persons, Father, Son, and Holy Spirit, in one Godhead; (*l.c.*) a group of three; triad; *pl.,* **-ties.**

trin•ket, tring′kit, *n.* A small ornament, as a jewel, a ring, and the like; a thing of no great value; a trifle.

tri•o, trē′ō, *n. pl.,* **-os.** A musical composition for three voices or instruments; a company of three singers or players; any group of three persons or things.

trip, trip, *n.* A journey or voyage; jaunt or excursion for pleasure or health; a tripping, stumbling, or loss of footing; a sudden impeding or catching of a person's foot so as to throw him down; the act of tripping or stepping lightly; a light, quick tread; a slip, mistake, or blunder; a projecting part or catch for starting or checking some movement. *Informal.* An experience resulting from the use of psychedelic drugs.—*v.i.,* **tripped, trip•ping.** To make a journey, excursion, or trip; to strike the foot against something or have the foot suddenly impeded or caught, so as to stagger or fall; to stumble; to step lightly or nimbly, skip, or dance; to tip or tilt; to make a slip or a mistake, as in a statement; to behave improperly; to commit a fault or moral error.—*v.t.* To cause to trip, stumble, or fall by suddenly impeding or catching the foot; to cause to lose the footing or to upset; to tip or tilt; to overthrow or bring into confusion; to cause to make a slip or error, followed by *up;* to release or operate suddenly, as a catch or a clutch. —**trip•ping•ly,** *adv.*

tri•par•tite, trī•pär′tīt, *a.* Divided into three parts; made between or including three parties. —**tri•par•tite•ly,** *adv.* —**tri•par•ti•tion,** trī•pär•tish′ən, *n.*

tripe, trīp, *n.* The first and second divisions of the stomach of a ruminant, esp. of oxen or goats, prepared for use as food. *Informal.* Anything poor or worthless.

trip•ham•mer, trip′ham•ər, *n.* A power-operated heavy hammer with a massive head that is repeatedly raised and then let fall by a tripping device. Also **trip ham•mer.**

tri•ple, trip′əl, *a.* Threefold; consisting of three parts; of three kinds; three times as great.—*n.* A triad; something triple or threefold; a hit in baseball which allows the batter to get to third base.—*v.t.,* **-pled, -pling.** To make triple.—*v.i.* To become triple. —**tri•ply,** trip′lē, *adv.*

tri•plet, trip′lit, *n.* One of three offspring born at the same birth.

trip•li•cate, trip′lə•kāt, *v.t.,* **-cat•ed, -cat•ing.** To make threefold; triple; make or produce a third time or in units of three.—trip′lə•kit, trip′lə•kāt, *a.* Threefold; triple; tripartite. —**trip•li•ca•tion,** trip•lə•kā′shən, *n.*

tri•pod, trī′pod, *n.* A vessel, as a pot, caldron, or vase, with three feet or legs; a three-legged frame or stand

---

a- hat, fãte, fâre, fâther; **e-** met, mē; **i-** pin, pīne; **o-** not, nōte, ôrb, moove (move), boy, pownd; **u-** cūbe, bûll, tûk (took); **ch-** chin; **th-** thick, ŧhen; **zh-** vizhon (vision); **ə-** əgo, takən, pencəl, lemən, bərd (bird).

of any kind, as one for supporting a camera.—*a.* —**trip·o·dal,** trip′ə·dəl, *a.* —**tri·pod·ic,** trī·pod′ik, *a.*

trip·tych, trip′tik, *n.* A painting or carving on three adjacent panels, often used for an altarpiece.

tri·sect, trī·sekt′, *v.t.* To cut or divide into three usu. equal parts. —**tri·sec·tion,** trī·sek′shən, *n.* —**tri·sec·tor,** *n.*

trite, trīt, *a.* Used so commonly as to have lost its novelty and interest; commonplace; stale. —**trite·ly,** *adv.* —**trite·ness,** *n.*

trit·u·rate, trich′ə·rāt, *v.t.,* -**rat·ed,** -**rat·ing.** To reduce to fine particles or powder by rubbing, grinding, bruising, or the like; pulverize.—*n.* A triturated substance; a trituration. —**trit·u·ra·ble,** trich′ər·ə·bəl, *a.* —**trit·u·ra·tor,** *n.*

tri·umph, trī′əmf, *n.* A victory; a conquest; a distinguished success or achievement; the exultation of victory; joy over success; elation or exultant gladness.—*v.i.* To gain a victory or be victorious; to rejoice over success. —**tri·um·phal,** trī·əm′fəl, *a.* —**tri·um·phal·ly,** *adv.* —**tri·um·phant,** trī·əm′fənt, *a.* —**tri·um·phant·ly,** *adv.*

tri·um·vir, trī·əm′vər, *n. pl.,* -**virs,** -**vi·ri,** -və·rī. One of three persons associated in an office, esp. in a triumvirate of ancient Rome. —**tri·um·vi·ral,** *a.*

tri·um·vi·rate, trī·əm′vər·it, trī·əm′və·rāt, *n.* The joint government of three officers or magistrates; any association of three in office or authority.

triv·et, triv′it, *n.* A three-legged stand; a short-footed metal stand on which to place hot dishes at the table.

triv·i·a, triv′ē·ə, *n. pl.* Insignificant matters; trifles; unimportant things.

triv·i·al, triv′ē·əl, *a.* Commonplace; trifling; insignificant; of little worth or importance; inconsiderable. —**triv·i·al·i·ty,** triv·ē·al′ə·tē, *n. pl.,* -**ties.** —**triv·i·al·i·za·tion,** triv·e·əl·ə·zā′shən, *n.* —**triv·i·al·ly,** *adv.*

tri·week·ly, trī·wēk′lē, *a.* Occurring or appearing once every three weeks; happening or appearing three times each week.—*n. pl.,* -**lies.** A publication issued three times a week.

tro·che, trō′kē, *n.* A small medicinal lozenge.

trog·lo·dyte, trog′lə·dīt, *n.* A cave dweller, esp. a prehistoric or primitive man; a hermit. —**trog·lo·dyt·ic,** trog·lə·dit′ik, *a.*

troi·ka, troy′kə, *n.* A team of three horses abreast; the vehicle drawn by them; the vehicle and horses together; any group of three related or acting together.

Tro·jan Horse, *n.* A wooden horse presented to the city of Troy by the Greeks and used as a means of getting Greek soldiers inside the gates; any person, process, or device which is intended to weaken, subvert, or destroy from within.

troll, trōl, *v.t., v.i.* To sing or utter in a full, rolling voice; to sing in the manner of a round or catch; to fish for or in, by moving or dragging the hook and line; to cause to turn round and round.—*n.* A song whose parts are sung in succession; a round; the method of trolling for fish. —**troll·er,** *n.*

troll, trōl, *n.* One of a race of supernatural beings conceived as giants or dwarfs, inhabiting caves.

trol·ley, trol′ē, *n. pl.,* -**leys.** A streetcar; a pulley or a truck traveling on an overhead track and serving to support and move a suspended object; a grooved metallic wheel or pulley carried on the end of a pole by an electric car and held in contact with an overhead conductor, usu. a suspended wire, from which it collects the current for the propulsion of the car; a low truck that runs on a track. Also **trol·ly.**—*v.t., v.i.,* -**leyed,** -**ley·ing.** To convey or go by trolley.

trol·ley car, *n.* A street railway car propelled electrically by current taken from a conductor by means of a trolley.

trol·lop, trol′əp, *n.* A sloppily dressed woman; a prostitute; a lascivious woman.

trom·bone, trom·bōn′, trom′bōn, *n.* A large brass musical instrument having a sliding piece for varying the length of the tube in order to produce a desired note. —**trom·bon·ist,** trom′bō·nist, trom·bō′nist, *n.*

troop, troop, *n.* A body of soldiers; *pl.,* soldiers collectively; a cavalry unit corresponding in organization to an infantry; an assemblage of persons or things.—*v.i.* To gather or move in a company; to go or come in great numbers.

troop·er, troo′pər, *n.* A cavalryman; a member of the mounted police; a highway patrolman.

tro·phy, trō′fē, *n. pl.,* -**phies.** Anything taken in war, hunting, or the like; anything serving as a token or evidence of victory, valor, or skill; a prize. esp. in sports; any memento or memorial.

trop·ic, trop′ik, *n.* Either of two corresponding parallels of latitude, each 23°27′ from the equator, the northern one being called the tropic of Cancer, and the southern, the tropic of Capricorn; *pl.,* the regions lying between these parallels or near them on either side.—*a.* Characteristic of, pertaining to, or taking place in the tropics.

trop·i·cal, trop′i·kəl, *a.* Pertaining to the tropics; being within the tropics; incident to the tropics. —**trop·i·cal·ly,** *adv.*

tro·pism, trō′piz·əm, *n.* The natural tendency of an organism to respond to an external stimulus, as light or gravity. —**tro·pis·tic,** trō·pis′tik, *a.*

trop·o·sphere, trop′ə·sfēr, trōp′ə·sfēr, *n.* The layer of the atmosphere nearest the earth, varying in depth from seven to twelve miles. —**trop·o·spher·ic,** trop·ə·sfēr′ik, *a.*

trot, trot, *v.i.,* **trot·ted, trot·ting.** To go at a gait between a walk and a canter, in which the legs of a mammal, esp. a horse, move in diagonal pairs; to go at a quick, steady gait; to move briskly.—*v.t.* To cause to trot. *Informal.* To bring forward for, or as for inspection, followed by *out.*—*n.* The gait of a horse or the like when trotting; a trotting sound.

trot·ter, trot′ər, *n.* A horse bred and gaited to trot, esp. in harness races.

trou·ba·dour, troo′bə·dôr, *n.* A writer or singer of love songs.

trou·ble, trəb′əl, *v.t.,* -**bled,** -**bling.** To disturb or distress; to put to some slight labor or pains; to annoy.—*v.i.* To worry; to bother.—*n.* Distress of mind; grief; worry; anxiety; annoyance; labor, or exertion: Don't go to a lot of *trouble* in preparing dinner; a distressing physical condition or ailment: foot *trouble;* a difficulty or unfortunate state or condition. —**in trou·ble,** in difficulties. —**trou·bler,** *n.*

trou·ble·mak·er, trəb′əl·mā·kər, *n.* A person causing difficulties for others, either intentionally or unintentionally.

trou·ble·shoot·er, trəb′əl·shoo·tər, *n.* One who is skillful in locating and repairing malfunctions in machines and mechanical equipment; one who resolves or eliminates business or political disputes or problems.

trou·ble·some, trəb′əl·səm, *a.* Giving or causing trouble; annoying.

trough, trôf, trof, *n.* A vessel, generally rather long and not very deep, for holding water, food for animals, or the like; a channel or spout for conveying water; anything resembling a trough in shape, as a depression between two ridges or between two waves. —**trough-like,** *a.*

trounce, trowns, *v.t.,* **trounced, trounc·ing.** To beat or punish severely. *Informal.* To defeat by a wide margin.

troupe, troop, *n.* A troop; a company, particularly a touring band of players, dancers, acrobats, or the like.—*v.i.,* **trouped, troup·ing.** To tour as a member of a traveling company.

troup·er, troo′pər, *n.* A member of a troupe; an experienced actor. *Informal.* A person faithful to a cause or duty, as a conscientious worker.

trou·sers, trow′zərz, *n. pl.* An outer garment worn usu. by men and boys, extending from the waist to the ankles and covering each leg separately; pants.

trous·seau, troo′sō, troo·so′, *n. pl.,* -**seaux,** -**seaus,**

-sōz. The collection of clothes, other items of personal attire, and linens for the houshold, which a bride assembles in anticipation of her marriage.

trout, trowt, *n. pl.,* **trout, trouts.** A food and game fish found in cold fresh waters of Europe and the Americas.

trow·el, trow′əl, *n.* A tool resembling a small, flat spade, used for spreading and dressing mortar and plaster; a scooplike gardener's tool, used in taking up plants and turning over dirt.—*v.t.* To dress or form with a trowel. **—trow·el·er, trow·el·ler,** *n.*

troy weight, *n.* A weight used chiefly in weighing gold and silver.

tru·an·cy, troo′ən·sē, *n. pl.,* **-cies.** The act or an act of playing truant; truant conduct or habit. Also **tru·ant·ry.**

tru·ant, troo′ənt, *n.* One who shirks or neglects his or her duty; a child who stays away from school without leave.—*a.* Staying away from school without leave, as a child; pertaining to or characteristic of a truant.—*v.i.* To be truant.

tru·ant of·fic·er, *n.* An employee of the public schools who officially investigates absences of pupils.

truce, troos, *n.* A suspension of hostilities, as between armies, for a specified period, by agreement; an armistice; an agreement or treaty establishing this; respite, intermission, or freedom, as from trouble or pain.

truck, trək, *n.* Any of a class of self-propelled vehicles of various sizes and designs for transporting goods; a barrow with two very low front wheels, on which sacks or luggage are moved; a low, rectangular frame on which heavy loads are moved.—*v.t.* To put on a truck; to transport by a truck or trucks.—*v.i.* To convey articles or goods on a truck; to drive a truck.

truck, trək, *n. U.S.* Vegetables raised for the market; barter; a bargain or deal; the payment of wages in goods instead of money.—*v.t.* To exchange, trade, or barter; to peddle or hawk.—*v.i.* To exchange commodities; to barter; to traffic or have dealings.

truck·age, trək′ij, *n.* Conveyance by a truck or trucks; the charge for this.

truck·er, trək′ər, *n.* One, as a person or company, that is in the business of conveying articles or goods on a truck or trucks. One who drives a truck: also **truck·driv·er.**

truck farm, *n. U.S.* A farm devoted to the growing of vegetables for market. **—truck farm·er,** *n.* **—truck farm·ing,** *n.*

truck·ing, trək′ing, *n.* The act or business of conveying articles or goods on trucks.

truck·load, trək′lōd, *n.* A load filling a truck.

truck sys·tem, *n.* The method of making wage payments in goods rather than in money.

truc·u·lent, trək′yə·lənt, *a.* Fierce; savage; inspiring terror; quarrelsome in manner or tone; defiantly rude. **—truc·u·lence,** *n.* **—truc·u·lent·ly,** *adv.*

trudge, trəj, *v.i.,* **trudged, trudg·ing.** To make one's way on foot; walk, esp. to walk wearily.—*v.t.* To walk wearily along.—*n.* An act of trudging. **—trudg·er,** *n.*

true, troo, *a.,* **tru·er, tru·est.** Steadfast, as to a friend, a cause, or a promise; loyal; faithful; trusty; honest, honorable, or upright; sincere: *true* interest in a person's welfare; truthful; being consistent with the actual state of things: a *true* story; not false; correct, or accurate: a *true* balance; reliable, unfailing, or sure: a *true* sign; of the right kind, such as it should be, or proper; real or genuine: *true* gold; correctly called or answering to a description.—*n.* Exact or accurate information, position, or adjustment; that which is true, used with *the.*—*v.t.,* **trued, true·ing** or **tru·ing.** To make true; shape, adjust, or place exactly or accurately; make perfectly straight, level, square, or the like. —*adv.* In a true manner. **—true·ness,** *n.*

true-blue, troo′bloo′, *a.* Loyal; unwavering.

true-false, troo′fôls′, *a.* Designating a statement or series of statements, as an examination, to be answered as true or false.

true·love, troo′ləv, *n.* One truly loving or loved; a sweetheart.

truf·fle, traf′əl, troo′fəl, *n.* Any of various subterranean edible fungi, commonly with a brown or black, warty exterior.

tru·ism, troo′iz·əm, *n.* An undoubted or self-evident truth. **—tru·is·tic,** *a.*

tru·ly, troo′lē, *adv.* In a true manner.

trump, trəmp, *n.* One of the suit of cards which temporarily ranks above the other suits; *often pl.,* such a suit of cards; a powerful asset or resource.—*v.t.* To take, as a trick, with a trump; to surpass; outdo; beat.—*v.i.* To play a trump. **—trump up,** to invent or concoct in order to deceive; fabricate.

trum·pet, trəm′pit, *n.* Any of a class of musical wind instruments with a penetrating, powerful tone, consisting of a long, metallic tube, commonly once or twice curved round upon itself, having a cup-shaped mouthpiece at one end and a flaring bell at the other; an organ stop having a tone resembling that of a trumpet; a trumpeter; a sound like that of a trumpet; any article or device shaped like a trumpet.—*v.i.* To blow or sound a trumpet.—*v.t.* To sound on a trumpet; to utter with a sound like that of a trumpet; to proclaim loudly or widely. **—trum·pet·like,** *a.*

trum·pet·er, trəm′pə·tər, *n.* One who sounds or plays a trumpet; one who proclaims or announces something loudly or widely.

trun·cate, trəng′kāt, *v.t.,* **-cat·ed, -cat·ing.** To shorten by cutting abruptly; to cut short.—*a.* Truncated. **—trun·ca·tion,** trəng·kā′shən, *n.*

trun·cat·ed, trəng′kā·tid, *a.* Shortened by the cutting off of a part.

trun·cheon, trən′chən, *n.* A club; a heavy short stick; a baton, esp. one symbolizing authority; a tree whose branches have been lopped off to produce rapid growth.—*v.t.* **—trun·cheoned,** *a.*

trun·dle, trən′dəl, *v.t.,* **-dled, -dling.** To cause to roll: to *trundle* a hoop; to move in a wheeled vehicle.—*v.i.* To roll on.—*n.* A little wheel, as a caster; a small carriage or truck with low wheels. **—trun·dler,** *n.*

trun·dle bed, *n.* A low bed, usu. on trundles or casters, which can be pushed under a high bed when not in use. Also **truck·le bed.**

trunk, trəngk, *n.* The main stem of a tree, as distinct from the branches and roots; a large box, chest, or case for holding clothes and other articles, as for use on a journey; a large automobile compartment for the storage of a spare tire, tools, luggage, or the like; the body of a human being or other animal, considered apart from the head and limbs; the torso; the long, flexible, cylindrical nasal appendage of the elephant, having the nostrils at the extremity. The main line of a river, railroad, or canal; the main line of a telephone or telegraph line; also **trunk line.** *Pl.* Short, tight-fitting breeches or shorts, as worn by athletes, swimmers, or the like.—*a.* Noting or referring to the main line, as of a railroad.

truss, trəs, *v.t.* To tie, bind, or fasten, as with a rope; to secure; to furnish or support, as a bridge, with a truss or trusses; to bolster; to make fast with skewers or string, as wings of a turkey, prior to roasting; to confine or enclose, as the body, with snug clothes.—*n.* A combination of beams, bars, or ties arranged in a triangle or series of triangles to form a rigid framework, and used in bridges and roofs to give support and rigidity to part or all of the structure. **—truss·er,** *n.*

trust, trəst, *n.* Reliance on the integrity or justice of a person or confidence in some quality, feature, or attribute of a thing; confident expectation or hope: a *trust* in tomorrow; credit or confidence in the ability or

---

a- hat, fāte, fāre, fäther; **e-** met, mē; **i-** pin, pīne; **o-** not, nōte, ôrb, moove (move), boy, pownd; **u-** cūbe, bull, tûk (took); **ch-** chin; **th-** thick, then; **zh-** vizhon (vision); **ə-** ago, takən, pencəl, lemən, bərd (bird).

intention of a person to pay at some future time for goods, property, or services received: buying on *trust;* a person or thing that one relies on; the state of one to whom something is entrusted; the obligation or responsibility imposed on one in whom confidence or authority is placed; care, safekeeping, or custody.—*a.* Of or referring to trust or a trust; held in trust: a *trust* fund.—*v.i.* To have faith or confidence in something or someone; to hope; to sell goods on credit.—*v.t.* To have trust or confidence in; to rely on; to believe; to allow to be somewhere or do something without fear of consequences; to give credit to, as a person, for goods or services supplied; to expect confidently or to hope, usu. followed by a clause or infinitive: *Trusting* to complete the first job, he began another. **—trust•er,** *n.* **—trust•less,** *a.*

trus•tee, trə•stē′, *n.* One to whom property or funds have been legally entrusted to be administered for the benefit of another; a person, usu. one of a body of persons, appointed to administer the affairs of a company, institution, or the like.—*v.t.,* **-teed, -tee•ing.** To place in the hands of a trustee or trustees. **—trus•tee•ship,** *n.*

trust•ful, trəst′fəl, *a.* Full of trust; trusting; confiding. **—trust•ful•ly,** *adv.*

trust fund, *n.* Any estate, esp. stock, securities, or money, which is held in trust.

trust•wor•thy, trəst′wər•thē, *a.* Worthy of trust or confidence; reliable. **—trust•wor•thi•ly,** *adv.* **—trust•wor•thi•ness,** *n.*

trust•y, trəs′tē, *a.,* **-i•er, -i•est.** Deserving confidence or trust; reliable. **—trust•i•ness,** *n.*

truth, trooth, *n. pl.,* **truths,** trooᵗhz. Conformity to fact or reality; honesty; a true statement; the state or quality of being true; (*often cap.*) a spiritual or philosophical verity. **—in truth,** actually; in fact.

truth•ful, trooth′fəl, *a.* Speaking the truth; in accordance with reality or the facts. **—truth•ful•ly,** *adv.* **—truth•ful•ness,** *n.*

truth se•rum, *n.* A drug, as scopolamine or one of certain barbiturates, used to induce a state in which a subject will talk freely when questioned, as about criminal involvement or about repressed memories in psychotherapy.

try, trī, *v.t.,* **tried, try•ing.** To attempt to do or accomplish: easy until you *try* it; to test the effect or result of: to *try* an experiment; to put to the test in order to determine the quality, value, or accuracy of; to attempt to open, as a door or window, in order to find out whether it is locked or fastened; to strain the endurance or patience of; to examine and determine judicially, as a cause; to determine judicially the guilt or innocence of, as of a person.—*v.i.* To make an attempt or effort. **—try on,** to put on in order to test fit or appearance. **—try out,** to test the effect of. **—try out for,** to engage in competition for, as for a position or a part in a play.

try•ing, trī′ing, *a.* That tests severely; hard to endure; annoying.

try•out, trī′owt, *n. Informal.* A trial or test made to determine the fitness of a person or thing for a particular purpose: *tryouts* for football.

try square, *n.* A carpenter's square, used to test the squareness of something built.

tryst, trist, trīst, *n.* An appointment to meet; an appointed meeting place.

tset•se, tset′sē, tsēt′sē, *n. pl.,* **-se, -ses.** A fly of southern Africa, which is the intermediate host or transmitter of sleeping sickness and other diseases in humans and domestic animals. Also **tset•se fly.**

T-shirt, tē′shərt, *n.* A collarless, lightweight, short-sleeved pullover shirt of cotton, worn by men as an undershirt; a similar outer shirt. Also **tee shirt.**

T-square, tē′skwär, *n.* A T-shaped ruler for making parallel lines, the crosspiece acting as a guide as it slides along the edge of a table or drawing board.

tsu•na•mi, tsoo•nä′mē, *n.* A huge sea wave resulting from a seaquake or submarine volcanic eruption; a tidal wave.

tub, təb, *n.* A round, open, wooden vessel, broad in proportion to height, usu. made of staves held together by hoops and fitted around a flat bottom; any similar container; a receptacle for bathing in; a bathtub. *Informal.* A slow, clumsy ship or boat.—*v.t.,* **tubbed, tub•bing.** To put or set in a tub.

tu•ba, too′bə, tū′bə, *n. pl.,* **-bas, -bae,** -bē. A brass musical instrument of very large size and low pitch.

tu•bal, too′bəl, *a.* Of or pertaining to a tube or tubes.

tub•by, təb′ē, *a.,* **-bi•er, -bi•est.** Tub-shaped; round like a tub; corpulent; having a sound like that of an empty tub when struck; having a dull sound; without resonance. **—tub•bi•ness,** *n.*

tube, toob, tūb, *n.* A hollow, usu. cylindrical body, as of metal, glass, rubber, or plastic, used for fluids; material of tubular form; any tubelike instrument; a small collapsible metal or plastic cylinder closed at one end with the other end open and being provided with a cap and used for holding and dispensing material, as toothpaste, or other semiliquids; any hollow cylindrical vessel or organ.—*v.t.,* **tubed, tub•ing.** To furnish or fit with a tube or tubes; to cause to pass through or enclose in a tube.

tube•less, toob′lis, tūb′lis, *a.* Pertaining to a tire without an inner tube.

tu•ber, too′bər, tū′bər, *n.* A fleshy, usu. oblong or rounded thickening or outgrowth of a subterranean stem, bearing minute scalelike leaves with buds or eyes in their axils, from which new plants may arise, as the potato.

tu•ber•cle, too′bər•kəl, tū′bər•kəl, *n.* A small, rounded projection, as on a bone; a small, firm, rounded nodule or swelling; the characteristic lesion of tuberculosis.

tu•ber•cu•lar, too•bər′kyə•lər, tū•bər′kyə•lər, *a.* Of, referring to, a tubercle or tubercles; pertaining to tuberculosis.—*n.* A person afflicted with tuberculosis. **—tu•ber•cu•lar•ly,** *adv.*

tu•ber•cu•lin, too•bər′kyə•lin, tū•bər′kyə•lin, *n.* A liquid made from cultures of the tubercle bacillus, used in the diagnosis and treatment of tuberculosis.

tu•ber•cu•lin test, *n.* A test for a hypersensitive reaction to tuberculin indicating a present or past tubercular disease.

tu•ber•cu•lo•sis, too•bər•kyə•lō′sis, tū•bər•kyə•lō′sis, *n.* An infectious disease affecting any of various tissues of the body, due to the tubercle bacillus, and characterized by the production of tubercles; this disease when affecting the lungs; consumption.

tu•ber•cu•lous, too•bər′kyə•ləs, tū•bər′kyə•ləs, *a.* Tubercular; pertaining to or of the nature of tuberculosis.

tu•ber•ous, too′bər•əs, tū′bər•əs, *a.* Covered with or characterized by rounded or wartlike prominences or tubers.

tub•ing, too′bing, tū′bing, *n.* The act of making, or providing with, tubes; a series of tubes; a piece of tube or tubing.

tu•bu•lar, too′byə•lər, tū′byə•lər, *a.* Of or referring to a tube or tubes.

tu•bule, too′būl, tū′būl, *n.* A small tube; a minute tubular structure.

tuck, tək, *v.t.* To pull up into a fold or a folded arrangement; to thrust the edge or end of, as a covering, closely into place between retaining parts or things, followed by *in* or *up:* to *tuck in* one's shirt; to cover snugly; to thrust into a close, concealing, or safe place: to *tuck* money into a purse; to sew tucks in. *Informal.* To eat or drink, followed by *in* or *away:* to *tuck away* a whole pie.—*v.i.* To draw together; contract; to make tucks.—*n.* A tucked piece or part; a fold stitched in fabric or a garment to decorate or to control the fit.

tuck•er, tək′ər, *n.* One who or that which tucks; a device in a sewing machine for making tucks.

tuck•er, tək′ər, *v.t. Informal.* To weary, tire, or exhaust, often with *out.*

tuck-point, tək′poynt, *v.t.* To fill or finish, as mortar joints in masonry work, with a fillet of mortar or putty. —**tuck-point•er,** *n.* —**tuck point•ing,** *n.*

Tues•day, tooz′dē, tooz′dā, tūz′dē, tūz′dā, *n.* The third day of the week; the day following Monday. —**Tues•days,** *adv.*

tuf•fet, təf′it, *n.* A tuft, as of grass; a low stool.

tuft, təft, *n.* A bunch or clump of small, usu. soft and flexible things, as feathers, hair, and the like, fixed at the base and with the upper ends loose; any like cluster.—*v.t.* To furnish or decorate with or arrange in a tuft or tufts.—*v.i.* To form a tuft or tufts; to grow in tufts. —**tuft•er,** *n.* —**tuft•y,** *a.,* -i•er, -i•est.

tug, təg, *v.t.* To pull at with force or effort; to move by pulling forcibly; drag or haul.—*v.i.* To pull with force or effort: to *tug* at a heavy carton; to strive hard.—*n.* The act of tugging; a strong pull; a struggle; a tugboat. —**tug•ger,** *n.*

tug•boat, təg′bōt, *n.* A small, strongly built, and powerful boat designed for pulling or pushing other craft, as ocean-going vessels or barges.

tug of war, *n.* An athletic contest between two teams pulling at the opposite ends of a rope; a severe or critical struggle, as between contending forces.

tu•i•tion, too•ish′ən, tū•ish′ən, *n.* The amount charged for instruction at an educational institution; instruction. —**tu•i•tion•al,** *a.*

tu•lip, too′lip, tū′lip, *n.* Any of the liliaceous plants cultivated in many varieties, and having large, showy, usu. erect, cup-shaped or bell-shaped flowers of various colors; a flower or bulb of such a plant. —**tu•lip•like,** *a.*

tulle, tool, *n.* A thin, delicate net of silk, nylon, or rayon.

tum•ble, təm′bəl, *v.i.,* -bled, -bling. To perform leaps, somersaults, or other feats of bodily agility; to roll about; to toss; to fall headlong; to stumble or fall over; to fall or collapse, as a structure, government, or the like; to fall suddenly or rapidly, as prices or stocks; to lose a position of authority: to *tumble* from power. —*v.t.* To disorder by or as by tossing about; to throw, cast, put or send in a hasty, or rough manner; to subject to the action of a tumbling barrel.—*n.* An act of tumbling; a tumbled condition; a confused heap.

tum•ble-down, təm′bəl•down, *a.* In a tumbling or falling condition; rickety.

tum•bler, təm′blər, *n.* One who or that which tumbles; one who performs leaps, somersaults, and other bodily feats; a glass with a flat bottom and without a stem or handle; the revolving drum in a clothes dryer; in a lock, any locking or checking part which, when in the proper position, prevents the movement of the bolt; a device in a selective transmission which moves a gear into place; a cam.

tum•ble•weed, təm′bəl•wēd, *n.* Any of various plants, having a branching upper part which in autumn becomes detached from the roots and is driven about by the wind.

tum•bling, təm′bling, *n.* Acrobatics; leaps, springs, somersaults and other feats of bodily agility performed as a skill in sports competition or for exercise.

tum•bling bar•rel, *n.* A revolving drum in which articles or substances are tumbled, as for the purpose of polishing or mixing.

tu•mid, too′mid, tū′mid, *a.* Swollen, enlarged, or distended, as a body organ or part; pompous or bombastic in language or style. —**tu•mid•i•ty,** too•mid′ə•tē, **tu•mid•ness,** *n.*

tum•my, təm′ē, *n. pl.,* -mies. *Informal.* Stomach.

tu•mor, too′mər, tū′mər, *n.* An abnormal or morbid swelling in any part of the body; a swollen part. —**tu•mor•ous,** *a.* —**tu•mor•like,** *a.*

tu•mult, too′məlt, tū′məlt, *n.* The commotion, disturbance, or agitation of a multitude; an uproar; irregular or confused motion; an uprising or riot; emotional or mental agitation.

tu•mul•tu•ous, too•məl′choo•əs, tū•məl′choo•əs, *a.* Full of or marked by tumult or uproar; loud and confused, as sounds; rough, as waters; agitated, as the mind or feelings. —**tu•mul•tu•ous•ly,** *adv.* —**tu•mul•tu•ous•ness,** *n.*

tu•na, too′nə, *n. pl.,* **tu•na, tu•nas.** Any of various large game and food fishes, belonging to the mackerel family and found in warm waters of the Atlantic Ocean, Pacific Ocean, and the Mediterranean Sea; the processed flesh of these fish, used as food; also **tu•na fish.**

tun•a•ble, tune•a•ble, too′nə•bəl, tū′nə•bəl, *a.* Capable of being tuned; in tune.

tun•dra, tən′drə, *n.* One of the vast level or rolling treeless plains of the arctic regions of Europe, Asia, and N. America, having the ground frozen beneath the surface even in summer.

tune, toon, tūn, *n.* A pleasing, rhythmical succession of musical sounds; a melody, with or without the harmony accompanying it; agreement in pitch, unison, or harmony: many voices or instruments sounding in *tune;* accord or harmony in relationships; correct adjustment, as of circuits with respect to frequency. —*v.t.,* **tuned, tun•ing.** To adjust the tones of, as of a musical instrument, to a correct or given standard of pitch; to bring into harmony; to adjust mechanisms or motors into proper condition; to adjust, as a circuit, so as to bring into resonance with another circuit; to establish contact with, as a source of transmission, with *in.*—*v.i.* To put a musical instrument in tune; to sound or be in harmony; to give forth a musical sound. —**call the tune,** to make final decisions or to control. —**change one's tune,** to change one's stated opinions or actions. —**sing a dif•fer•ent tune,** to alter behavior or ideas. —**to the tune of.** *Informal.* At the cost of: He wrecked his car *to the tune of* a thousand dollars. —**tune in,** to adjust a receiving apparatus so as to accord in frequency with a sending apparatus whose signals are to be received. —**tune out,** to shut out the signals of a sending station by altering the frequency of the circuits of a receiving apparatus. —**tune up,** to bring a musical instrument to the proper pitch; to put in tune; to put a machine or motor into proper working condition.

tune•ful, toon′fəl, tūn′fəl, *a.* Full of tune or melody.

tune•less, toon′lis, tūn′lis, *a.* Without tune or melody; silent.

tun•er, too′nər, tū′nər, *n.* A person or thing that tunes; one whose occupation is the tuning of musical instruments; a receiver part which can be adjusted to pick up a particular signal or frequency.

tune-up, toon′əp, tūn′əp, *n.* The process of putting a machine or motor in working order.

tung•sten, təng′stən, *n.* A rare, metallic element having a bright-gray color, a metallic luster, and a high melting point, used in the manufacture of highspeed steel tools, electric lamp filaments, and other products.

tu•nic, too′nik, tū′nik, *n.* A garment like a shirt or gown, worn by both sexes among the ancient Greeks and Romans; a woman's garment, either loose or close-fitting, extending below the waist and over the skirt.

tun•ing fork, *n.* A steel instrument with two prongs producing a musical sound of a certain fixed pitch when set in vibration, and serving as a guide to tune musical instruments.

tun•nel, tən′əl, *n.* A subterranean passage; a roadway beneath the ground, as through a hill or mountain, esp. one for automobiles or trains; an approximately horizontal passage, as in a mine; the burrow of an animal.—*v.t.,* -neled, -nel•ing. To make or form like a

---

a- hat, fāte, fāre, fäther; **e-** met, mē; **i-** pin, pīne; **o-** not, nōte, ôrb, moove (move), boy, pownd; **u-** cūbe, bûll, tûk (took); **ch-** chin; **th-** thick, ᵺhen; **zh-** vizhon (vision); **ə-** əgo, takən, pencəl, lemən, bərd (bird).

tunnel: to *tunnel* a passage under a river; to make or form a tunnel through or under; to perforate, as with tunnels: wood *tunneled* by shipworms.—*v.i.* To make a tunnel or tunnels: to *tunnel* through the Alps. —**tun·nel·er**, *Brit.* **tun·nel·ler**, *n.* —**tun·nel·like**, *a.*

tur·ban, tər/bən, *n.* A headdress of Mohammedan origin worn by men of eastern Mediterranean and Oriental countries, consisting of a long scarf of silk, linen, or cotton, wound directly around the head or around a cap; a headdress resembling this; a small hat, either brimless or with the brim turned up close against the crown. —**tur·baned**, *a.*

tur·bid, tər/bid, *a.* Having the lees or sediment disturbed; muddy; foul with extraneous matter; not clear; muddled or confused. —**tur·bid·i·ty**, tər·bid/ə·tē, **tur·bid·ness**, *n.*

tur·bine, tər/bin, tər/bīn, *n.* Any of a class of engines which deliver power created by a continuous flow or jets of steam, air, water, or other liquids, against the curved blades or vanes of a rotor or series of rotors.

tur·bo, tər/bō, *n. pl.,* **tur·bos.** A turbine, as in a turbojet airplane; a turbosupercharger.

tur·bo·car, tər/bō·kär, *n.* An automotive vehicle, esp. a racing car, powered by a gas turbine.

tur·bo·charg·er, tər·bo·chär/jər, *n.* A turbosupercharger.

tur·bo·fan, tər/bō·fan, *n.* The fan or fans driven by a turbine in a ducted fan jet engine; a turbofan engine.

tur·bo·jet en·gine, tər/bō·jet, *n.* An airplane engine consisting of an air intake, a compressor driven by a turbine, a combustion chamber, and a cone-shaped exhaust from which the blast of a jet of hot gases produced in the combustion chamber causes a thrust. Also **tur·bo·jet.**

tur·bo·pro·pel·ler en·gine, tər·bō·prə·pel/ər, *n.* A jet engine which provides power chiefly by a turbine-driven propeller; an airplane with such an engine. Also **tur·bo·prop.**

tur·bo·su·per·charg·er, tər·bō·soo/pər·chär·jər, *n.* A supercharger operated by a turbine which is powered by the exhaust gases of the engine.

tur·bot, tər/bət, *n. pl.,* **tur·bot, tur·bots.** A large European flatfish, much esteemed as food.

tur·bu·lence, tər/byə·ləns, *n.* A turbulent state or condition; an irregular condition of the atmosphere, characterized by updrafts, downdrafts, and gusts. Also **tur·bu·len·cy.**

tur·bu·lent, tər/byə·lənt, *a.* Disposed or given to violent disturbances, disorder, or agitation; tumultuous.

tu·reen, tů·rēn/, tū·rēn/, *n.* A rather large, deep, covered vessel for holding and serving soup or other food.

turf, tərf, *n. pl.,* **turfs.** The covering of grass and other plants with their matted roots forming the upper or surface layer of certain land; a piece cut from this; sod; a grass course or dirt track used for racing horses, usu. preceded by *the. Informal.* The territory ruled by gangsters or youthful street gangs.—*v.t.* To cover, as barren ground, with turf or sod.

tur·gid, tər/jid, *a.* Swollen; distended beyond its natural state; inflated. —**tur·gid·i·ty**, tər·jid/ə·tē, **tur·gid·ness**, *n.*

tur·key, tər/kē, *n. pl.,* **tur·keys. tur·key.** A large bird, native to N. America and domesticated in much of the world, having a bare head and red, yellow, and brown plumage; the bird's flesh, eaten as food. —**talk tur·key.** *Informal.* To discuss a situation bluntly.

Turk·ish, tər/kish, *a.* Of, pertaining to, or derived from the Turks or Turkey; of or pertaining to the Turkic language.—*n.*

Turk·ish bath, *n.* A kind of bath in which, after a copious perspiration in a heated room, the body is soaped, washed, massaged, and the like.

Turk·ish tow·el, turk·ish tow·el, *n.* A kind of thick cotton towel or toweling with a long nap.

tur·mer·ic, tər/mər·ik, *n.* An East Indian plant of the ginger family, whose rhizomes are used as a condiment, a yellow dye, and as a chemical test for the presence of alkalis; the powder from this rhizome; one of several similar plants or substances.

tur·moil, tər/moyl, *n.* A state or condition of extreme commotion, upset, tumult, or confusion.

turn, tərn, *v.t.* To cause to move around on an axis or about a center; to rotate: to *turn* a wheel; to cause to move around or partly around, as for opening, closing, or tightening: to *turn* a key; to change the position of by or as if by rotating: to *turn* a box on its side; to reverse the position of: to *turn* a page; to reverse, as a garment, so that the inner side becomes the outer; to ponder, often with *over;* to twist or sprain: to *turn* an ankle while going downstairs; to cause, as the stomach, to feel upset; to shape, as a piece of wood, into rounded form, as on a lathe; to form or express gracefully: to *turn* a sentence; to change or alter the nature, character, or appearance of, usu. followed by *in* or *into:* to *turn* stocks *into* cash; to apply to some use or purpose: to *turn* something to good use; to direct, avert, aim, or set going toward or away from something specified: to *turn* one's eyes from an accident, to *turn* a hose on a burning house; to change the color of, as leaves; to cause to ferment or become sour: milk *turned* by warm weather; to change or reverse the course of; to go around, as a corner; to get past: to *turn* twenty-one; to cause to go away; send; drive: to *turn* a stranger from one's door; to alienate: to *turn* children against their parents; distract; infatuate: to *turn* someone's head.—*v.i.* To move around on an axis or about a center; rotate; revolve; to shift about: to toss and *turn;* to change direction: to *turn* to the right; to direct one's thought, attention, or desire toward or away from something; to hinge or depend, usu. followed by *on* or *upon:* The question *turns on* a crucial point; to have a sensation of whirling; to take an attitude or policy of hostility or opposition: to *turn* against one's friends; to change position in order to resist or attack: The animal *turned* on its owner; to change or alter in nature, character, or appearance, followed by *to* or *into;* to change so as to be or become: to *turn* pale; to undergo a change of color, as leaves; to become sour or fermented, as milk or wine; to shape material into rounded form on a lathe; to assume a curved form; bend.—*n.* A total or partial rotation; revolution; something that revolves or rotates, as a lathe; the act or an act of changing or reversing course or direction; a place or point where such a change occurs; an opportunity or time for one of a number of persons acting in rotation or succession: a *turn* at bat; round; spell; rounded or curved form; natural inclination, bent, tendency, or aptitude: of a philosophical *turn* of mind; change in nature, condition, circumstance, or character: a *turn* for the better in the weather; direction, or trend: a rightward *turn* in his politics; an act of service or disservice; a single round, as of a wound or coiled rope. —**at eve·ry turn,** everywhere; every time; constantly. —**by turns,** one after another; alternately or in rotation. —**in turn,** in due order of succession. —**out of turn,** out of due order of succession. —**take turns,** to follow one another, alternately or in rotation. —**to a turn,** to perfection. —**turn back,** to make return the same way; drive back; fold back; return. —**turn down,** to fold down; decrease the force or volume of. *Informal.* To reject. —**turn in,** to fold inward; to inform on; to submit; bend inward. *Informal.* To go to bed. —**turn off,** to shut off the flow of; to put out, as an electric light. *Informal.* To bore or arouse boredom or dislike in. —**turn on,** to cause a flow of, as water; to switch on. *Informal.* Cause to become excited or interested; to begin taking a narcotic or psychedelic drug. —**turn out,** to send away; produce, esp. quickly; to empty by turning inside out. —**turn over,** to turn an object so that another side faces up; to hand over; capsize; to start, as a motor. —**turn to,** to apply oneself to a task.

—**turn up,** to fold over or up; give an upward direction to; dig up; place with the face upward; increase the force or volume of; to make one's appearance; to happen.

turn·a·bout, tərn′ə·bowt, *n.* The act or an act of facing another direction or turning about, as in opinion or direction.

turn·a·round, tərn′ə·rownd, *n.* A complete or round trip, as of a ship, and the time consumed in such a trip; an area large enough to allow a vehicle to completely turn around; a turnabout.

turn·coat, tərn′kōt, *n.* One who changes his or her party or principles, usu. to opposing positions; a renegade; a traitor.

turn·down, tərn′down, *n. Informal.* A refusal.—*a.* That is or may be turned down; folded or doubled down: a *turndown* collar.

turn·er, tər′nər, *n.* One who or that which turns; one who fashions objects on a lathe.

turn·ing, tər′ning, *n.* The act of someone or something which turns; the point of bending or reversal, as in a road; the art or operation of shaping something, as on a lathe.

turn·ing point, *n.* A point at which a decisive change takes place; a critical point; a crisis.

tur·nip, tər′nip, *n.* The thick, fleshy, edible root of various cultivated plants; any one of these plants.

turn·key, tərn′kē, *n.* A person who has charge of the keys of a prison; a jailer.

turn·off, tərn′ôf, tərn′of, *n.* A road or ramp curving off from a main road.

turn·out, tərn′owt, *n.* An instance or act of turning out; the number of persons present at an event; an amount produced; output.

turn·o·ver, tərn′ō·vər, *n.* The act or result of turning over; an overthrow; the flow of people through a checkpoint; the replacement rate of employees in a firm or the total number of workers replaced; business volume in a given period; a reversal of position or belief; a triangular pastry.

turn·pike, tərn′pīk, *n.* A road designed for high-speed travel on which a toll for maintenance is collected at regular intervals.

turn·stile, tərn′stīl, *n.* A device consisting of a post surmounted by four horizontal arms which revolve as a person pushes by them, placed in a gateway to control passage through it.

turn·ta·ble, tərn′tā·bəl, *n.* The circular revolving platform of a record player; any rotating stand, such as used in pottery making or for displaying objects.

turn·up, tərn′əp, *n.* The act or fact of turning up; that which is turned up.—*a.* That is or may be turned up.

tur·pen·tine, tər′pən·tin, *n.* Any of various oily resins derived from various coniferous trees and yielding a volatile oil, as oil of turpentine, and a resin when distilled.—*v.t.,* **-tined, -tin·ing.** To treat with turpentine; to apply turpentine.

tur·pi·tude, tər′pə·tood, tər′pə·tūd, *n.* Inherent baseness or vileness; moral depravity.

tur·quoise, tur·quois, tər′koyz, tər′kwoyz, *n.* A sky-blue or greenish-blue mineral, containing a little copper and iron, valuable as a gemstone; a light blue color with a greenish tinge: also **tur·quoise blue.**

tur·ret, tər′it, *n.* A small tower, usu. one forming part of a larger structure; an attachment on a lathe or similar machine for holding a number of tools: also **tur·ret·head.**

tur·tle, tər′təl, *n.* Any of an order of reptiles having the body enclosed in a shell from between which the head, tail, and four legs protrude, as aquatic species, as distinguished from a tortoise, or terrestrial species. —**turn tur·tle,** to capsize.

tur·tle·dove, tər′təl·dəv, *n.* An Old-World bird of the dove family, smaller than the ordinary domestic pi-geon, celebrated in poetry for its cooing and the constancy of its affection.

tur·tle·neck, tər′təl·nek, *n.* A high, rolled-over, tight-fitting collar, found esp. on a sweater; a sweater or shirt having this type of collar.

tush, təsh, *interj.* An exclamation indicating rebuke, impatience, or contempt.

tusk, təsk, *n.* The long, pointed, and often protruding tooth on each side of the jaw of certain animals, as in the elephant; the canine tooth of various animals, as the bear or walrus; any sharp, tusklike projection.—*v.t.* To dig, tear, or gore with the tusks; to furnish with tusks or tusklike projections. —**tusked,** *a.* —**tusk·er,** *n.* —**tusk·like,** *a.*

tus·sive, təs′iv, *a.* Of or relating to a cough. Also **tus·sal.** —**tus·sis,** *n.*

tus·sle, təs′əl, *v.i.,* **-sled, -sling.** To struggle; to scuffle; to wrestle.—*n.* A scuffle.

tut, tət, *interj.* An exclamation used to check or rebuke or to express impatience or contempt. Also **tut-tut,** tət′tət′.

tu·te·lage, toot′ə·lij, tūt′ə·lij, *n.* Guardianship; protection bestowed; instruction; guidance.

tu·tor, too′tər, tū′tər, *n.* One employed to instruct another privately in some branch of learning; a private instructor; a teacher subordinate to a professor in some American universities and colleges.—*v.t.* To act as a tutor to; to teach or instruct, esp. privately; to train, school, or discipline.—*v.i.* To act as a tutor or private instructor; to study under a tutor. —**tu·tor·ship,** *n.*

tu·tor·age, too′tər·ij, tū′tər·ij, *n.* A tutor's position or authority; a tutoring fee.

tu·to·ri·al, too·tôr′ē·əl, tū·tôr′ē·əl, *a.* Belonging to a tutor or instructor.—*n.* A class given by an instructor or tutor.

tut·ti-frut·ti, too′tē·froo′tē, *n.* A preserve of mixed fruits; ice cream or some other confection containing a variety of fruit flavorings or fruits, usu. candied and minced.

tu·tu, too′too, *n.* A full, very short skirt, usu. of layers of tulle or other thin fabric, worn by a ballet dancer.

tux·e·do, tək·sē′dō, *n.* (*Often cap.*) A dress coat for evening wear; an entire suit of semi-formal clothing.

TV, tē′vē′, *n. pl.,* **TVs, TV's.** Television; television set.

TV din·ner, *n.* A commercially packaged, frozen meal, usu. placed on an aluminum, partitioned tray, that is ready to be served when heated.

twad·dle, twod′əl, *n.* Empty, trivial, or silly talk or writing.

twain, twān, *n.* The two-fathom or twelve-foot mark on a riverboat sounding line.

twang, twang, *v.i.* To sound with a quick, sharp, vibrating noise; to be released with such a sound; to speak with a harsh, nasal tone.—*v.t.* To cause to sound with a quick, vibrating noise; to utter with a harsh, nasal tone; to cause to emit a vibrating sound by pulling and suddenly releasing, as a bowstring.—*n.* A sharp, quick, vibrating sound, as of a plucked banjo string; a plucking action; a harsh, nasal tone of voice; a sound similar to this; the speech typical of a region or people, esp. when characterized by nasal intonations. —**twang·y,** twang′ē, *a.,* **-i·er, -i·est.**

tweak, twēk, *v.t.* To pinch and pull with a sudden twist and jerk.—*n.* An abrupt, twisting pinch.

tweed, twēd, *n.* A coarse, twilled woolen fabric, used esp. for coats, jackets, and suits; *pl.,* clothing made of tweed. —**tweed·y,** *a.,* **-i·er, -i·est.** —**tweed·i·ness,** *n.*

'tween, tween, twēn, *prep.* Contraction of **between.**

tweet, twēt, *n.* A weak, chirping note of a young bird.—*v.i.* To utter weak chirps.

tweet·er, twē′tər, *n.* A small loudspeaker that reproduces high-frequency sounds in high-fidelity audio equipment.

---

a- hat, fāte, fāre, fäther; **e-** met, mē; **i-** pin, pine; **o-** not, nōte, ôrb, moove (move), boy, pownd; **u-** cūbe, bŭll, tŭk (took); **ch-** chin; **th-** thick, ŧhen; **zh-** vizhon (vision); **ə-** əgo, takən, pencəl, lemən, bərd (bird).

tweez·ers, twē′zərz, *n. pl.* Small pincers used to pluck out hairs and to pick up or hold small objects. **—tweeze,** *v.t.,* **tweezed, tweez·ing.**

twelve, twelv, *n.* The cardinal number between 11 and 13; a symbol representing it; a set of 12 persons or things; a dozen.—*a.* **—twelfth,** *a.*

twelve·month, twelv′mənth, *n.* A year.

twen·ty, twen′tē, *n. pl.,* **-ties.** The cardinal number between 19 and 21; a symbol representing it; a set of 20 persons or things. **—twen·ti·eth,** *a.*

twen·ty-one, twen′tē-wən′, *n.* The cardinal number between 20 and 22; a symbol representing it; a set of 21 persons or things.

twerp, twərp, *n. Informal.* A contemptible person, esp. an insignificant or obnoxious boy or man; a jerk.

twice, twis, *adv.* Two times, as in succession: to write *twice* a week; on two occasions; in two instances: *twice* as much.

twid·dle, twid′əl, *v.t.,* **-dled, -dling.** To twirl or turn round and round, esp. with the fingers; to play with idly.—*v.i.* To play with something idly, as by touching or handling; to twirl.—*n.* The act of twiddling; a twirl.—**twid·dle one's thumbs,** to keep turning one's thumbs or fingers idly about each other; to do nothing; to be idle. **—twid·dler,** *n.*

twig, twig, *n.* A slender shoot of a tree or other plant; a small offshoot from a branch or stem; a small, dry, woody piece fallen from a branch. **—twig·gy,** *a.,* **-gi·er, -gi·est.**

twi·light, twi′līt, *n.* The light from the sky when the sun is below the horizon in the morning and esp. in the evening; the time during which this light prevails; any dim light; a condition or period following full development or glory.—*a.* Of, referring to, or resembling twilight.

twill, twil, *n.* A fabric woven with the weft threads so crossing the warp as to produce an effect of parallel diagonal lines, as in serge; the characteristic weave of such fabrics.—*v.t.* To weave in the manner of a twill. **—twilled,** *a.*

twin, twin, *n.* One of two young brought forth at a birth; either of two persons or things closely related, or resembling each other.—*a.* Being two, or one of two young born at the same birth: *twin* sisters; being two persons or things closely related or much alike, or forming a pair; being one of two such persons or things; consisting of two similar parts or elements joined or connected: a *twin* vase.—*v.t.,* **twinned, twin·ning.** To conceive or bring forth as twins; to pair; to combine.—*v.i.* To bring forth twins.

twine, twin, *n.* Strong thread or string composed of two or more strands twisted together; the act of twining; the state of being twined; a twisted thing or part; a coil; a twist or turn; a knot or tangle.—*v.t.,* **twined, twin·ing.** To twist together to form a thread, string, or the like; interwind; twist, as one strand with that of another; put, encircle, or wreathe, about or around by winding: to *twine* ivy about the head.—*v.i.* To become twined or twisted together; to wind itself about or around something; grow in convolutions about a support, as in plants. **—twin·er,** *n.*

twinge, twinj, *n.* A sudden, sharp pain: a *twinge* of rheumatism; a pain or pang in the mind: a *twinge* of remorse.—*v.t.,* **twinged, twing·ing.** To affect with sudden, sharp pain, as in body or mind.—*v.i.* To have or feel a twinge or twinges.

twin·kle, twing′kəl, *v.i.,* **-kled, -kling.** To open and shut the eyes rapidly; to gleam; to sparkle.—*v.t.* To give off, as light, in intermittent flashes.—*n.* A wink or quick motion of the eye; a gleam or sparkle of the eye or of a star. **—twin·kler,** *n.*

twin·kling, twing′kling, *n.* The act of that which twinkles; an instant.

twirl, twərl, *v.t.* To cause to rotate rapidly; spin; whirl. —*v.i.* To rotate rapidly; spin; whirl.—*n.* A twirling action or motion; twist; curl; coil; whorl. **—twirl·er,** *n.* **—twirl·y,** *a.,* **-i·er, -i·est.**

twist, twist, *v.t.* To combine, as two or more strands or threads, by winding together; intertwine; entangle; to form by or as by winding strands together; to encircle with something wound about; to wring out of shape or place, or sprain: to *twist* one's ankle; to distort; to force down, into, off, or out, by a turning movement; to pervert; to perplex; to form into a coil, knot, or the like, by winding or rolling: to *twist* the hair into a knot; to bend tortuously; to cause to move with a rotary motion; to turn so as to face in another direction; to turn, as on an axis.—*v.i.* To be or become intertwined; to wind or twine about something; writhe or squirm; to wind, curve, or bend; to turn or rotate as on an axis; to turn so as to face in another direction; to change shape with a spiral movement; to meander, as a stream.—*n.* Any deviation, curve, turn, or bend; spin; anything formed by or as by twisting or twining parts together, as in rope; a twisting awry; a peculiar turn, bent, bias, or the like, as in mind or nature; a twisting action, force, or stress; thread, cord, or the like.

twist·er, twis′tər, *n.* One who or that which twists; a whirlwind or tornado.

twit, twit, *v.t.,* **twit·ted, twit·ting.** To vex or annoy by bringing to remembrance a fault, or the like; to taunt. —*n.* A reproach.

twitch, twich, *v.t.* To pull with an abrupt motion; to jerk.—*v.i.* To be suddenly contracted, as a muscle.—*n.* A brief involuntary contraction of the muscles; a jerk. **—twitch·er,** *n.*

twit·ter, twit′ər, *v.i.* To utter a succession of small, tremulous, intermittent notes, as certain birds; to chatter; to tremble from eagerness or excitement. —*v.t.* To say, as with a twitter.—*n.* A small, intermittent noise or series of chirpings; an excited state. **—twit·ter·er,** *n.* **—twit·ter·y,** *a.,* **-i·er, -i·est.**

'twixt, twikst, *prep.* Contraction of **betwixt.**

two, too, *n.* The cardinal number between one and three; a symbol representing it; a set of two persons or things.—*a.*—**in two,** into two parts.—**put two and two to·geth·er,** to come to the obviously correct conclusion.

two-bit, too′bit, *a. Informal.* Worth 25 cents; petty; small-time; cheap.

two bits, *n. pl. but sing. in constr. Informal.* 25 cents.

two-by-four, too′bi·fôr′, too′bə·fôr′, *a.* Indicating a thickness of two units and a width of four units, usu. in inches. *Informal.* Small; cramped.—*n.* A cut piece of timber or lumber widely used in building.

two-di·men·sion·al, too-də-men′shə·nəl, *a.* Having only two dimensions.

two-faced, too′fāst, *a.* Having two faces; deceitful; hypocritical.—**two-fac·ed·ly,** *adv.* **—two-fac·ed·ness,** *n.*

two-fist·ed, too′fis′tid, *a. Informal.* Strong; vigorous; aggressive.

two·fold, too′fōld, *a.* Double; multiplied by two.—*adv.*

two-hand·ed, too′han′did, *a.* Requiring the use of both hands; requiring or needing two persons for use: a *two-handed* saw.

two-sid·ed, too′si′did, *a.* Having or consisting of two sides or aspects. **—two-sid·ed·ness,** *n.*

two·some, too′səm, *n.* Two together or in company.

two-step, too′step, *n.* A round dance in duple rhythm, characterized by sliding steps; a piece of music for, or in the rhythm of, this dance.—*v.i.,* **-stepped, -step·ping.**

two-time, too′tim, *v.t.,* **-timed, -tim·ing.** To be secretly unfaithful to, as a spouse or lover; to double-cross.

two-way, too′wā′, *a.* Allowing traffic to simultaneously move in opposite directions: a *two-way* street; allowing or involving a reciprocal arrangement or exchange: a *two-way* communication; usable in two ways.

ty·coon, ti′koon′, *n. Informal.* An exceptionally wealthy and powerful businessman; a shogun.

tyke, tike, tīk, *n. Informal.* Any small or young child; a dog; a cur.

tym·bal, tim′bəl, *n. Informal.* Timbal.

tym·pan·ic mem·brane, *n.* A membrane separating the middle ear from the passage of the external ear. Also **ear·drum.**

type, tip, *n.* A kind, class, or group as distinguished by a particular character; a person or thing embodying the characteristic qualities of a kind, class, or group: the athletic *type*; the standard or model; a rectangular piece or block, usu. of metal, having on its upper surface a letter or character in relief for use in printing; such pieces or blocks collectively; a printed character or, esp., printed characters.—*v.t.,* **typed, typ·ing.** To typewrite; to reproduce in type or print; to designate the particular type of, as a blood sample; to identify.—*v.i.* To typewrite. —**typ·a·ble, type·a·ble,** *a.*

type·cast, tip′kast, *v.t.* To cast, as an entertainer, in the part of a character similar to himself in personality, or the like.

type·face, tip′fās, *n.* A printing face of type.

type·script, tip′skript, *n.* Matter produced by a typewriter.

type·set·ter, tip′set·ər, *n.* One who sets type; a compositor; a typesetting machine. —**type·set,** *v.t.,* **-set, -set·ting.**—*n., a.*

type·write, tip′rīt, *v.t., v.i.,* **-wrote, -writ·ten, -writ·ing.** To print by a typewriter. Also **type.**

type·writ·er, tip′rī·tər, *n.* A keyboard machine for producing writing resembling type impressions.

type·writ·ing, tip′rī·ting, *n.* The act or art of using a typewriter; work done on a typewriter.

ty·phoid, tī′foyd, *n.* An infectious, often fatal, febrile disease, characterized by intestinal inflammation and ulceration, due to a specific bacillus which is usu. introduced with food or drink. Also **ty·phoid fe·ver.**—*a.*

ty·phoon, tī·foon′, *n.* A hurricane occurring in the China Sea and western Pacific.

ty·phus, tī′fəs, *n.* An acute infectious disease transmitted by fleas and lice. Also **ty·phus fe·ver.** —**ty·phous,** *a.*

typ·i·cal, tip′ə·kəl, *a.* Symbolic; of the nature of or serving as a representative specimen; conforming to some type; characteristic. Also **typ·ic.** —**typ·i·cal·ly,** *adv.* —**typ·i·cal·ness, typ·i·cal·i·ty,** *n.*

typ·i·fy, tip′ə·fī, *v.t.,* **-fied, -fy·ing.** To represent by a type; signify; symbolize; to constitute or serve as the typical specimen of. —**typ·i·fi·ca·tion,** tip·ə·fə·kā′shən, *n.*

typ·ist, tī′pist, *n.* A typewriter operator.

ty·po, tī′pō, *n. Informal.* A typographical error.

ty·pog·ra·phy, tī·pog′rə·fē, *n.* The work of setting and arranging types and of printing from them; the general character or appearance of printed matter. —**ty·pog·ra·pher,** *n.* —**ty·po·graph·ic,** tī·pə·graf′ik, *a.* —**ty·po·graph·i·cal,** *a.* —**ty·po·graph·i·cal·ly,** *adv.*

ty·ran·ni·cal, ti·ran′ə·kəl, tī·ran′ə·kəl, *a.* Of, referring to, or befitting a tyrant; arbitrary; despotic; severely oppressive. Also **ty·ran·nic.** —**ty·ran·ni·cal·ly,** *adv.* —**ty·ran·ni·cal·ness,** *n.*

tyr·an·nize, tir′ə·nīz, *v.i.,* **-nized, -niz·ing.** To exercise power or control cruelly or oppressively, often followed by *over;* to reign as a tyrant.—*v.t.* To rule or treat tyrannically. —**tyr·an·niz·er,** *n.*

tyr·an·ny, tir′ə·nē, *n. pl.,* **-nies.** The government or rule of a tyrant or absolute ruler; a state ruled by a tyrant; oppressive or unjust government by any ruler; despotic abuse or authority; undue severity or harshness.

ty·rant, tī′rənt, *n.* An absolute ruler owing his office to usurpation; a king or ruler who uses his power oppressively or unjustly.

ty·ro, ti·ro, tī′rō, *n.* A beginner in learning; any novice.

U

U, u, ū, *n.* The twenty-first letter of the English alphabet.

u·biq·ui·tous, ū·bik′wə·təs, *a.* Existing or being everywhere simultaneously. Also **u·biq·ui·tar·y.** —**u·biq·ui·tous·ly,** *adv.* —**u·biq·ui·tous·ness,** *n.*

u·biq·ui·ty, ū·bik′wə·tē, *n.* The state of being present everywhere; omnipresent.

U-boat, ū′bōt, *n.* A German submarine.

ud·der, əd′ər, *n.* A mamma or mammary gland, esp. when large and baggy with more than one teat, as in cows.

UFO, ū·ef·ō′, *n.* An unidentified flying object.

ugh, əkh, ûkh, û, əg, *interj.* An exclamation of horror, recoil, disgust, or the like.

ug·ly, əg′lē, *a.,* **-li·er, -li·est.** Repulsive or displeasing in appearance; disagreeable, unpleasant, or objectionable; morally revolting; base; vile; discreditable or disgraceful; troublesome; threatening disadvantage or danger. *Informal.* Ill-natured, quarrelsome, or vicious. —**ug·li·ly,** *adv.* —**ug·li·ness,** *n.*

u·kase, ū′kās, ū·kāz′, *n.* Any decree or order issued by an authority.

u·ku·le·le, ū·kə·lā′lē, *Hawaiian* oo·kû·lā′lā, *n.* A musical instrument, usu. four-stringed, similar to a guitar but smaller. Also **uke.**

ul·cer, əl′sər, *n.* A sore open either to the surface of the body or to a natural cavity, and accompanied by the disintegration of tissue and usu. the formation of pus; a corrupting condition or influence. —**ul·cer·ous,** *a.*

ul·cer·ate, əl′sə·rāt, *v.t., v.i.,* **-at·ed, -at·ing.** To make or to become ulcerous. —**ul·cer·a·tion,** *n.*

ul·na, əl′nə, *n. pl.,* **ul·nae,** -nē, **ul·nas.** In human beings, that one of the two long bones of the forearm which is on the side opposite to the thumb. —**ul·nar,** *a.*

ul·ster, əl′stər, *n.* A heavy, long, loose overcoat, often having a belt.

ul·te·ri·or, əl·tēr′ē·ər, *a.* Being beyond what is seen or avowed, or intentionally kept concealed; being beyond what is immediate or present, or coming at a subsequent time or stage; being or situated beyond, or on the farther side. —**ul·te·ri·or·ly,** *adv.*

ul·ti·mate, əl′tə·mit, *a.* Farthest or most remote; extreme; last, as in a series; coming as a final result; final and decisive; forming the final aim or object; beyond which it is impossible to proceed, as by investigation or analysis; fundamental; elemental.—*n.* The final point; the final result; the conclusion; a fundamental fact or principle. —**ul·ti·mate·ly,** *adv.* —**ul·ti·mate·ness,** *n.*

ul·ti·ma·tum, əl·tə·mā′təm, əl·tə·mä′təm, *n. pl.,*

---

a- hat, fāte, fâre, fäther; **e-** met, mē; **i-** pin, pīne; **o-** not, nōte, ôrb, moove (move), boy, pownd; **u-** cūbe, bŭll, tûk (took); **ch-** chin; **th-** thick, ŧhen; **zh-** vizhon (vision); **ə-** əgo, takən, pencəl, lemən, bərd (bird).

-tums, -ta, -tə. In any dispute, the final proposal or statement of terms or conditions for settlement.

ul·tra, əl′trə, *a.* Going beyond what is usual or ordinary; excessive; extreme.—*n.* An extremist.

ul·tra·con·serv·a·tive, əl·trə·kən·sər′və·tiv, *a.* Very or overly conservative.

ul·tra·high fre·quen·cy, əl·trə·hī, *n.* Any radio frequency in the range of 300 to 3000 megacycles per second.

ul·tra·ma·rine, əl·trə·mə·rēn′, *a.* Of a deep blue color called ultramarine.—*n.* A deep blue color.

ul·tra·son·ic, əl·trə·son′ik, *a.* Of or referring to frequencies above the range of human audibility, or above 20,000 vibrations per second. —**ul·tra·son·ics**, *n. pl. but sing. in constr.*

ul·tra·vi·o·let, əl·trə·vī′ō·lit, *a.* Beyond the end that is violet in the visible spectrum, as of light rays with very short wavelengths.—*n.* Radiation that is ultraviolet.

ul·u·late, ūl′yə·lāt, əl′yə·lāt, *v.i.,* -lat·ed, -lat·ing. To howl; to hoot; to wail loudly. —**ul·u·lant**, *a.* —**ul·u·lation**, ūl·yə·lā′shən, *n.*

um·bel, əm′bəl, *n.* An inflorescence, which consists of a number of flower stalks nearly equal in length and spreading from a common center. —**um·bel·lar**, **um·bel·late**, **um·bel·lat·ed**, *a.* —**um·bel·late·ly**, *adv.*

um·ber, əm′bər, *n.* An earth used in its natural state as a brown pigment or, after heating, as a reddish-brown pigment; the color of such a pigment.—*a.* Of the color of umber.—*v.t.* To color with or as with umber.

um·bil·i·cal, əm·bil′ə·kəl, *a.* Referring to the navel or umbilicus; formed or located in the middle, like a navel.

um·bil·i·cal cord, *n.* A cordlike structure which passes from the navel of the fetus or embryo to the mother's placenta, supplying nourishment for and carrying wastes from the fetus.

um·bra, əm′brə, *n. pl.,* -bras, -brae, -brē. Any area of total shadow; shade; the conical portion of a shadow cast by a celestial body that cuts off all light from a particular source.

um·brage, əm′brij, *n.* Resentment; offense; suspicion or doubt; shade caused by foliage. —**um·bra·geous**, əm·brā′jəs, *a.* —**um·bra·geous·ly**, *adv.* —**um·bra·geous·ness**, *n.*

um·brel·la, əm·brel′ə, *n.* A portable fabric screen or canopy extended on an expandable or collapsible radial frame fastened to a rod or stick and used for shelter from sun or rain. —**um·brel·la·like**, *a.*

u·mi·ak, oo′mē·ak, *n.* An open, flat-bottomed Eskimo boat consisting of hides stretched over a wooden framework.

um·laut, ûm′lowt, *n.* In Germanic languages, the change of a vowel in one syllable through the influence of a vowel in the syllable immediately following; a vowel so changed by an umlaut; a mark (··) over a vowel, as ä, ö, ü, used to mark a vowel sound.

um·pire, əm′pīr, *n.* An official who enforces the rules of play in baseball and other games; any person to whose sole decision a controversy or question between parties is referred.—*v.t., v.i.,* -pired, -pir·ing. To act or serve as an umpire.

ump·teen, əmp′tēn′, *a. Informal.* Numerous, but of an indeterminate number; many. —**ump·teenth**, əmp′tēnth′, *a.*

un·a·bashed, ən·ə·basht′, *a.* Not embarrassed or put to shame. —**un·a·bash·ed·ly**, *adv.*

un·a·ble, ən·ā′bəl, *a.* Not having sufficient ability or knowledge; incompetent; not able.

un·a·bridged, ən·ə·brijd′, *a.* Not shortened; complete; comprehensive.

un·ac·cep·ta·ble, ən·ak·sep′tə·bəl, *a.* Not acceptable, pleasing, or adequate; not welcome. —**un·ac·cept·ed**, *a.*

un·ac·com·pa·nied, ən·ə·kəm′pə·nēd, *a.* Having no attendants or companions; alone; performed without an accompaniment.

un·ac·count·a·ble, ən·ə·kown′tə·bəl, *a.* Not explicable; such that no reason or explanation can be given; strange; not responsible or accountable for. —**un·ac·count·a·ble·ness**, *n.* —**un·ac·count·a·bly**, *adv.*

un·ac·cus·tomed, ən·ə·kəs′təmd, *a.* Uncommon; not usual or familiar.

un·ac·quaint·ed, ən·ə·kwān′tid, *a.* Unfamiliar; not having knowledge, usu. followed by *with.*

un·a·dorned, ən·ə·dôrnd′, *a.* Not decorated or embellished.

un·a·dul·ter·at·ed, ən·ə·dəl′tə·rā·tid, *a.* Genuine; pure. —**un·a·dul·ter·at·ed·ly**, *adv.*

un·ad·vised, ən·əd·vizd′, *a.* Without advice or due consideration; rash; imprudent. —**un·ad·vis·ed·ly**, *adv.* —**un·ad·vis·ed·ness**, *n.*

un·af·fect·ed, ən·ə·fek′tid, *a.* Natural; not artificial; simple; sincere; unchanged. —**un·af·fect·ed·ly**, *adv.* —**un·af·fect·ed·ness**, *n.*

un·a·fraid, ən·ə·frād′, *a.* Not afraid; fearless or without reluctance.

un·A·mer·i·can, ən·ə·mer′ə·kən, *a.* Not American; considered disregardful of or antagonistic toward American customs, ideals, or institutions; unpatriotic.

u·nan·i·mous, ū·nan′ə·məs, *a.* Agreeing in opinion or determination; showing or formed by complete accord. —**u·na·nim·i·ty**, ū·nə·nim′ə·tē, *n.* —**u·nan·i·mous·ly**, *adv.* —**u·nan·i·mous·ness**, *n.*

un·an·swer·a·ble, ən·an′sər·ə·bəl, *a.* Having no known answer; not capable of refutation. —**un·an·swer·a·bly**, *adv.* —**un·an·swered**, *a.*

un·ap·pe·tiz·ing, ən·ap′ə·tī′zing, *a.* Not appetizing; without appeal.

un·ap·pre·ci·at·ed, ən·ə·prē′shē·ā·tid, *a.* Not appreciated; not properly valued or esteemed. —**un·ap·pre·ci·a·tive**, *a.*

un·ap·proach·a·ble, ən·ə·prō′chə·bəl, *a.* That cannot be approached; inaccessible; difficult to know or get acquainted with; aloof; unmatched. —**un·ap·proach·a·ble·ness**, *n.* —**un·ap·proach·a·bly**, *adv.* —**un·ap·proached**, *a.*

un·armed, ən·ärmd′, *a.* Not having armor or weapons. —**un·arm**, ən·ärm′, *v.t.*

un·a·shamed, ən·ə·shāmd′, *a.* Not ashamed; devoid of shame; unabashed.

un·asked, ən·askt′, *a.* Not invited.

un·a·spir·ing, ən·ə·spir′ing, *a.* Not aspiring; unambitious.

un·as·sail·a·ble, ən·ə·sā′lə·bəl, *a.* Not open to question, disapproval, or attack. —**un·as·sail·a·ble·ness**, *n.* —**un·as·sail·a·bly**, *adv.* —**un·as·sailed**, *a.*

un·as·sist·ed, ən·ə·sis′tid, *a.* Unaided.

un·as·sum·ing, ən·ə·soo′ming, *a.* Not bold, forward, or arrogant; modest; unpretentious. —**un·as·sum·ing·ly**, *adv.* —**un·as·sum·ing·ness**, *n.*

un·at·tached, ən·ə·tacht′, *a.* Not attached; unmarried or unengaged; not associated with or committed to a certain person, organization, or task.

un·at·tain·a·ble, ən·ə·tā′nə·bəl, *a.* Not able to be gained, obtained, or arrived at. —**un·at·tained**, *a.*

un·at·tend·ed, ən·ə·ten′did, *a.* Having no attendance; not escorted or accompanied; not carried out or attended, often followed by *to;* neglected.

un·au·thor·ized, ən·ô′thə·rīzd, *a.* Not warranted by proper authority; not formally sanctioned, or justified.

un·a·vail·a·ble, ən·ə·vā′lə·bəl, *a.* Not available or accessible; not suitable or ready for use. —**un·a·vail·a·bil·i·ty**, ən·ə·vā·lə·bil′ə·tē, *n.* —**un·a·vail·a·bly**, *adv.*

un·a·void·a·ble, ən·ə·voy′də·bəl, *a.* Not to be shunned; inevitable. —**un·a·void·a·bil·i·ty**, ən·ə·voy·də·bil′ə·tē, **un·a·void·a·ble·ness**, *n.* —**un·a·void·a·bly**, *adv.*

un·a·ware, ən·ə·wâr′, *a.* Not aware; not knowing; not cognizant. —**un·a·ware·ness**, *n.*

un·a·wares, ən·ə·wârz′, *adv.* Without being aware,

or unknowingly; inadvertently; unexpectedly.

un·backed, ən·bakt′, *a.* Without backing or support; not endorsed or wagered on.

un·bal·anced, ən·bal′ənst, *a.* Not balanced or not properly balanced; lacking mental balance, or steadiness and soundness of judgment; mentally disordered or deranged.

un·bar, ən·bär′, *v.t.,* -barred, -bar·ring. To unfasten; to unlock or open.

un·bear·a·ble, ən·bār′ə·bəl, *a.* Unable to be endured; intolerable. —**un·bear·a·ble·ness**, *n.* —**un·bear·a·bly**, *adv.*

un·beat·en, ən·bēt′ən, *a.* Not beaten; not struck or pounded; not mixed by beating; not defeated or surpassed. —**un·beat·a·ble**, *a.*

un·be·com·ing, ən·bi·kəm′ing, *a.* Unattractive; not suitable, esp. to a place or person; improper; indecorous. —**un·be·com·ing·ly**, *adv.* —**un·be·com·ing·ness**, *n.*

un·be·lief, ən·bi·lēf′, *n.* Incredulity; skepticism; the absence of belief, esp. in religious doctrines.

un·be·liev·a·ble, ən·bi·lē′və·bəl, *a.* Unable to be believed; incredible. —**un·be·liev·a·bly**, *adv.*

un·be·liev·er, ən·bi·lē′vər, *n.* A person who does not believe; a doubter or skeptic; one who lacks religious faith. —**un·be·liev·ing**, *a.* —**un·be·liev·ing·ly**, *adv.* —**un·be·liev·ing·ness**, *n.*

un·bend, ən·bend′, *v.t.,* -bent or -bend·ed, -bend·ing. To relax, set at ease, or release, as from strain, exertion, or formality; to straighten out or up from a bent condition; to free from tension or flexure, as a bow.—*v.i.* To become relaxed or to act with freedom; to give up stiffness or austerity of manner; unwind.

un·bend·ing, ən·ben′ding, *a.* Unyielding; stiff; resolute, as in character; rigid; inflexible.—*n.* Ease; relaxation. —**un·bend·ing·ly**, *adv.* —**un·bend·ing·ness**, *n.*

un·bi·ased, ən·bī′əst, *a.* Free from prejudice; impartial. —**un·bi·ased·ly**, *adv.*

un·bid·den, ən·bid′ən, *a.* Not commanded; spontaneous; uninvited; not requested or summoned. Also **un·bid.**

un·bind, ən·bīnd′, *v.t.,* -bound, -bind·ing. To release or free from shackles or restraints; to untie; to unfasten; to loose.

un·blem·ished, ən·blem′isht, *a.* Not blemished or marred; untarnished; pure; spotless.

un·bolt, ən·bōlt′, *v.t.* To unfasten or unlock; to open. —**un·bolt·ed**, *a.*

un·born, ən·bôrn′, *a.* Not yet born; future; not yet brought into existence or life.

un·bos·om, ən·bûz′əm, ən·boo′zəm, *v.t.* To reveal, esp. in confidence; to disclose, as one's personal opinions or feelings, often used with reflexive pronouns.—*v.i.* To disclose or reveal one's opinions or feelings, esp. in confidence. —**un·bos·om·er**, *n.*

un·bound, ən·bownd′, *a.* Not bound, as pages in a book; untied; freed, as from shackles or bonds; unconfined.

un·bound·ed, ən·bown′did, *a.* Having no bounds; unlimited in extent; without restraint. —**un·bound·ed·ly**, *adv.* —**un·bound·ed·ness**, *n.*

un·bowed, ən·bowd′, *a.* Not bowed or bent; not forced to yield or submit; unsubdued.

un·break·a·ble, ən·brāk′ə·bəl, *a.* Not breakable.

un·bri·dled, ən·brid′əld, *a.* Not harnessed with a bridle; unrestrained; ungoverned; unruly. —**un·bri·dle**, *v.t.,* un·bri·dled, un·bri·dling.

un·bro·ken, ən·brō′kən, *a.* Not broken; intact or whole; not interrupted; continuous; not tamed and rendered tractable; not impaired or disordered. —**un·bro·ken·ly**, *adv.*

un·buck·le, ən·bək′əl, *v.t.,* -buck·led, -buck·ling. To unfasten the buckle or buckles of.

un·bur·den, ən·bər′dən, *v.t.* To rid of or free from a load or burden; to relieve the mind, heart, or the like of, as by making a confession or disclosure.

un·but·ton, ən·bət′ən, *v.t., v.i.* To unfasten one or more buttons of. —**un·but·toned**, *a.*

un·called-for, ən·kôld′fôr, *a.* Not called for or required; unnecessary and improper; unwarranted; gratuitous.

un·can·ny, ən·kan′ē, *a.,* -ni·er, -ni·est. Suggesting the intervention of inexplicable or supernatural influences; eerie; mysterious; strange in an uncomfortable way. —**un·can·ni·ly**, *adv.* —**un·can·ni·ness**, *n.*

un·cap, ən·kap′, *v.t., v.i.,* -capped, -cap·ping. To remove the cap or cover from, as a jar or bottle.

un·ceas·ing, ən·sēs′ing, *a.* Not ceasing; perpetual; continual. —**un·ceas·ing·ly**, *adv.* —**un·ceas·ing·ness**, *n.*

un·cer·e·mo·ni·ous, ən·ser·ə·mō′nē·əs, *a.* Not using ceremony; informal; abrupt or curt; rude or discourteous. —**un·cer·e·mo·ni·ous·ly**, *adv.* —**un·cer·e·mo·ni·ous·ness**, *n.*

un·cer·tain, ən·sər′tən, *a.* Not sure or certain; doubtful; not certainly known; unreliable; not to be depended on; undecided; vague; not steady; variable; inconstant; capricious. —**un·cer·tain·ly**, *adv.* —**un·cer·tain·ness**, *n.* —**un·cer·tain·ty**, *n. pl.,* -ties.

un·chal·lenged, ən·chal′injd, *a.* Not challenged or objected to; not called in question.

un·change·a·ble, ən·chān′jə·bəl, *a.* Not capable of change; not subject to variation; immutable. —**un·change·a·bly**, *adv.* —**un·changed**, *a.* —**un·chang·ing**, *a.*

un·char·i·ta·ble, ən·char′ə·tə·bəl, *a.* Ungenerous; unforgiving; harsh; censorious; severe in judging. —**un·char·i·ta·ble·ness**, *n.* —**un·char·i·ta·bly**, *adv.*

un·chart·ed, ən·chär′tid, *a.* Not indicated or recorded, as on a map or chart; unknown.

un·chris·tian, ən·kris′chən, *a.* Contrary to Christian principles or spirit; uncharitable.

un·cir·cum·cised, ən·sər′kəm·sīzd, *a.* Not circumcised; non-Jewish.

un·civ·il, ən·siv′əl, *a.* Not courteous; ill-mannered; rude. —**un·civ·il·ly**, *adv.*

un·civ·i·lized, ən·siv′ə·līzd, *a.* Not civilized; wild; barbarous; savage.

un·class·i·fi·a·ble, ən·klas′ə·fī·ə·bəl, *a.* Not classifiable. —**un·clas·si·fied**, *a.*

un·cle, əng′kəl, *n.* The brother of one's father or mother; the husband of one's aunt.—*say* **un·cle.** *Informal.* To admit defeat; submit.

un·clean, ən·klēn′, *a.* Not clean; foul or dirty; filthy; unchaste; spiritually or morally impure. —**un·cleaned**, *a.* —**un·clean·ly**, *adv.* —**un·clean·ness**, *n.*

un·clear, ən·klēr′, *a.* Clouded; obscure; indistinct; uncertain. —**un·clear·ed**, *a.*

Un·cle Sam, əng′kəl, *n.* A personification of the government or the people of the United States, as a tall, thin man having white whiskers.

Un·cle Tom·ism, tom′iz·əm, *n.* A submissive or subservient attitude of some blacks toward a patronizing or paternalistic position held by some whites.

un·cloak, ən·klōk′, *v.t.* To remove the cloak from; to reveal or unmask.—*v.i.* To divest oneself of a cloak or similar garments.

un·clothe, ən·klōth′, *v.t.,* -clothed or -clad, -cloth·ing. To strip of clothes; undress; uncover. —**un·clothed**, *a.*

un·clut·tered, ən·klət′ərd, *a.* Neat; orderly; without litter.

un·coil, ən·koyl′, *v.t., v.i.* To unwind.

un·com·fort·a·ble, ən·kəm′fər·tə·bəl, ən·kəmf′tə·bəl, *a.* Affording no comfort; causing bodily discomfort; uneasy; ill at ease; disquieting. —**un·com·fort·a·ble·ness**, *n.* —**un·com·fort·a·bly**, *adv.*

un·com·mit·ted, ən·kə·mit′id, *a.* Not committed;

---

not obligated by any pledge to hold to any course of action.

un·com·mon, ən·kom'ən, *a.* Not common; not usual; rare; remarkable; extraordinary. —**un·com·mon·ly,** *adv.* —**un·com·mon·ness,** *n.*

un·com·mu·ni·ca·tive, ən·kə·mū'nə·kā·tiv, ən·kə·mū'nə·kə·tiv, *a.* Not inclined to communicate with others; reserved. —**un·com·mu·ni·ca·tive·ly,** *adv.* —**un·com·mu·ni·ca·tive·ness,** *n.*

un·com·pre·hend·ing, ən·kom·pri·hen'ding, *a.* Not comprehending; not perceiving.

un·com·pro·mis·ing, ən·kom'prə·mī·zing, *a.* Not accepting or making of any compromise; inflexible; unyielding; making no exceptions. —**un·com·pro·mised,** *a.* —**un·com·pro·mis·ing·ly,** *adv.* —**un·com·pro·mis·ing·ness,** *n.*

un·con·cern, ən·kən·sərn', *n.* Want of concern; indifference; freedom from solicitude; cool and undisturbed state of mind.

un·con·cerned, ən·kən·sərnd', *a.* Feeling no concern or solicitude; having or taking no interest; indifferent. —**un·con·cern·ed·ly,** *adv.* —**un·con·cern·ed·ness,** *n.*

un·con·di·tion·al, ən·kən·dish'ə·nəl, *a.* Not limited by any conditions; absolute. —**un·con·di·tion·al·ly,** *adv.*

un·con·firmed, ən·kən·fərmd', *a.* Not firmly established; not ratified; unverified.

un·con·nect·ed, ən·kə·nek'tid, *a.* Not connected; separate; not coherent. —**un·con·nect·ed·ly,** *adv.* —**un·con·nect·ed·ness,** *n.*

un·con·quer·a·ble, ən·kong'kər·ə·bəl, *a.* Not conquerable; incapable of being subdued or brought under control. —**un·con·quered,** *a.*

un·con·scion·a·ble, ən·kon'shə·nə·bəl, *a.* Contrary to the dictates of conscience; unscrupulous or unprincipled; exceeding that which is reasonable or customary. —**un·con·scion·a·ble·ness,** *n.* —**un·con·scion·a·bly,** *adv.*

un·con·scious, ən·kon'shəs, *a.* Not conscious or aware, often used with *of;* temporarily devoid of consciousness or not having the mental faculties awake; not known to or perceived by oneself; unintentional. —*n.* a general name for the mental processes which are not conscious. —**un·con·scious·ly,** *adv.* —**un·con·scious·ness,** *n.*

un·con·sti·tu·tion·al, ən·kon·stə·too'shə·nəl, ən·kon·stə·tū'shə·nəl, *a.* Not consistent or in accordance with the basic laws or constitution. —**un·con·sti·tu·tion·al·i·ty,** *n.* —**un·con·sti·tu·tion·al·ly,** *adv.*

un·con·strained, ən·kən·strānd', *a.* Voluntary; having no feeling that checks one's words or actions; natural.

un·con·test·ed, ən·kən·tes'tid, *a.* Not disputed or contended; unchallenged.

un·con·trol·la·ble, ən·kən·trō'lə·bəl, *a.* That cannot be controlled, ruled, or restrained; ungovernable. —**un·con·trol·la·bly,** *adv.* —**un·con·trolled,** *a.*

un·con·ven·tion·al, ən·kən·ven'shə·nəl, *a.* Not bound by or conforming to convention, rule, or precedent; out of the ordinary; nonconformist. —**un·con·ven·tion·al·i·ty,** ən·kən·ven·shə·nal'ə·tē, *n.* —**un·con·ven·tion·al·ly,** *adv.*

un·count·ed, ən·kown'tid, *a.* Not counted; innumerable.

un·cou·ple, ən·kəp'əl, *v.t.,* **-pled, -pling.** To unfasten or release, as anything coupled.—*v.i.* To become loose or unfastened.

un·couth, ən·kooth', *a.* Lacking in manners or social graces; crude; awkward or ungainly; unusual. —**un·couth·ly,** *adv.* —**un·couth·ness,** *n.*

un·cov·er, ən·kəv'ər, *v.t.* To disclose; to remove a cover or covering from; to remove a head covering from, esp. a hat as in showing respect.—*v.i.* To take off a cover or covering; to take off one's hat, as in showing respect. —**un·cov·ered,** *a.*

unc·tion, əngk'shən, *n.* The act of anointing, esp. for medical purposes or as a religious rite; that which is applied or used in anointing; an unguent or ointment; something soothing or comforting.

unc·tu·ous, əngk'choo·əs, *a.* Of the nature of, resembling, or characteristic of an unguent or ointment; oily; greasy; characterized by religious unction or fervor, esp. of an affected kind; excessively smooth or suave. —**unc·tu·os·i·ty,** əngk·choo·os'ə·tē, *n.* —**unc·tu·ous·ness,** *n.* —**unc·tu·ous·ly,** *adv.*

un·curl, ən·kərl', *v.t.* To straighten out, as something curled.—*v.i.*

un·cut, ən·kət', *a.* Not cut; unabridged; not shortened; not cut to shape, or not ground.

un·daunt·ed, ən·dôn'tid, *a.* Not discouraged or dismayed; fearless; intrepid. —**un·daunt·ed·ly,** *adv.* —**un·daunt·ed·ness,** *n.*

un·de·ceive, ən·di·sēv', *v.t.,* **-ceived, -ceiv·ing.** To free from deception, misunderstanding, illusion, or mistake. —**un·de·ceiv·a·ble,** *n.*

un·de·cid·ed, ən·di·sī'did, *a.* Not decided; not settled; not having the mind made up; irresolute. —**un·de·cid·ed·ly,** *adv.* —**un·de·cid·ed·ness,** *n.*

un·de·fined, ən·di·find', *a.* Not having fixed limits; indefinite; not defined or explained. —**un·de·fin·a·ble,** *a.*

un·de·mon·stra·tive, ən·də·mon'strə·tiv, *a.* Not demonstrative; not inclined to outwardly express the feelings; reserved. —**un·de·mon·stra·tive·ly,** *adv.* —**un·de·mon·stra·tive·ness,** *n.*

un·de·ni·a·ble, ən·di·nī'ə·bəl, *a.* Incapable of being denied; indisputable; unquestionably good. —**un·de·ni·a·ble·ness,** *n.* —**un·de·ni·a·bly,** *adv.* —**un·de·nied,** *a.*

un·de·pend·a·ble, ən·di·pen'də·bəl, *a.* Unreliable; untrustworthy. —**un·de·pend·a·bil·i·ty,** ən·di·pen·də·bil'ə·tē, —**un·de·pend·a·ble·ness,** *n.*

un·der, ən'dər, *prep.* Beneath and covered by; below the surface of; at a point or position lower than; in the position or state of bearing, supporting, sustaining, or undergoing; beneath, or included in, as a classification; as designated, indicated, or represented by; below in degree, amount, price, or the like; less than; below in rank, dignity, or the like; subject to the rule, direction, guidance, or instruction of; subject to the influence or conditioning force of; with the favor or aid of; authorized, warranted, or attested by; in accordance with; during the regime, government, or political system of.—*adv.* Below or beneath something; beneath the surface; in a lower place; in a lower degree or amount, esp. than is required; in a subordinate position or condition; in or into subjection or submission.—*a.* Situated beneath; lower in position; lower in degree or amount, esp. than is required or desired; subordinate; inferior. —**go un·der,** to be drowning; to fail, esp. in business.

un·der·a·chiev·er, ən·dər·ə·chē'vər, *n.* One whose performance is low compared to his potential. —**un·der·a·chiev·ment,** *n.*

un·der·act, ən·dər·akt', *v.t., v.i.* To act or perform inadequately, or without sufficient energy or force; underplay.

un·der·age, ən·dər·āj', *a.* Not having reached a requisite or legal age. —ən·dər·ij', *n.* Shortage.

un·der·arm, ən'dər·ärm, *a.* Under the arm; executed or delivered with the hand below the shoulder, or underhand.—*adv.* Underhand.—*n.* The armpit.

un·der·bel·ly, ən'dər·bel·ē, *n. pl.,* **-lies.** The lower area of the abdomen; any area that is vulnerable to attack.

un·der·brush, ən'dər·brəsh, *n.* Shrubs and small trees in a wood; undergrowth.

un·der·car·riage, ən'dər·kar·ij, *n.* The supporting framework beneath the body of an automobile or other vehicle.

un·der·charge, ən·dər·chärj', *v.t.,* **-charged, -charg·ing.** To charge less than a fair or usual price for; to put into or load with an inadequate charge, esp.

a gun.—ən′dər•chärj, *n.* Too low a charge or price; any load or charge that is insufficient or inadequate.

un•der•class•man, ən•dər•klas′mən, *n. pl.,* **-men.** A student belonging to the class of freshmen or sophomores, as in a college or secondary school.

un•der•clothes, ən′dər•klōz, ən′dər•klo̡thz, *n. pl.* Underwear. Also **un•der•cloth•ing,** ən′dər•klō′thing.

un•der•coat, ən′dər•kōt, *n.* A coat that is worn under another; a coat or layer of varnish, paint, or another surface-sealing compound over which a finishing coat may be applied: also **un•der•coat•ing,** ən′dər•kō′ting.—*v.t.* To apply any undercoating or undercoat to.

un•der•cov•er, ən•dər•kəv′ər, *a.* Done or acting in secret, esp. working as a spy or secret investigator.

un•der•cur•rent, ən′dər•kər•ənt, *n.* A current below the upper or surface currents, or below the surface; an underlying tendency more or less different from what is visible or apparent.

un•der•cut, ən′dər•kət, *v.t.,* **-cut, -cut•ting.** To cut under or beneath; to undersell, or to work for wages or payment lower than, as some competitor.—*v.i.* To undercut any person or thing.—*n.* A cut, or a cutting away, underneath.—*a.* Cut away underneath or resulting from such a cut.

un•der•de•vel•oped, ən•dər•di•vel′əpt, *a.* Insufficiently or incompletely developed; insufficiently or incompletely industrialized. —**un•der•de•vel•op,** *v.t.,* **-oped, -op•ing.**

un•der•dog, ən′dər•dog, *n.* One who is pitted against a presumably superior opponent in any struggle or conflict; any predicted loser; a victim of neglect or oppression, esp. by society.

un•der•done, ən•dər•dən′, *a.* Not sufficiently or fully cooked; rare.

un•der•es•ti•mate, ən•dər•es′tə•māt, *v.t., v.i.,* **-mat•ed, -mat•ing.** To estimate at too low a rate.—ən•dər•es′tə•mit, *n.* An estimate at too low a rate. —**un•der•es•ti•ma•tion,** ən•dər•es•tə•mā′shən, *n.*

un•der•foot, ən•dər•fŭt′, *adv., a.* Under the foot or feet; in the way.

un•der•gar•ment, ən′dər•gär•mənt, *n.* A garment worn under another garment, esp. under an outer garment.

un•der•go, ən•dər•gō′, *v.t.,* **-went, -gone, -go•ing.** To experience; to pass through; to endure; to suffer.

un•der•grad•u•ate, ən•dər•graj′ŏo•it, *n.* A student of a university or college who has not received his first degree.

un•der•ground, ən•dər•grownd′, *adv.* Beneath the surface of the ground; in concealment or secrecy; not openly.—ən′dər•grownd. *a.* Existing, situated, operating, or taking place beneath the surface of the ground; hidden; secret; clandestine.—ən′dər•grownd, *n.* The place or region beneath the surface of the ground; any underground space or passage; a clandestine organization or movement engaged in subversive or disruptive activity against the established governmental authority, esp. in an occupied country.

un•der•growth, ən′dər•grōth, *n.* Vegetation growing under large trees in forests; also **un•der•brush.**

un•der•hand, ən′dər•hand, *a.* Secret or covert; sly; not open, esp. secret and crafty or dishonorable.—*adv.* Secretly; stealthily; slyly; not openly or aboveboard.

un•der•hand•ed, ən•dər•han′did, *a.* Underhand. —**un•der•hand•ed•ly,** *adv.* —**un•der•hand•ed•ness,** *n.*

un•der•lie, ən•dər•lī′, *v.t.,* **-lay, -lain, -ly•ing.** To lie beneath; to be situated under; to be at the basis of; to form the foundation of; to be subject or liable to.

un•der•line, ən′dər•līn, *v.t.,* **-lined, -lin•ing.** To mark underneath or below with a line; to underscore; to emphasize; to stress.—*n.*

un•der•ling, ən′dər•ling, *n.* A subordinate, used esp. in disparagement; an inferior.

un•der•ly•ing, ən′dər•lī•ing, *a.* Lying under or beneath; basic or fundamental.

un•der•mine, ən•dər•mīn′, ən′dər•mīn, *v.t.,* **-mined, -min•ing.** To form a mine or passage or make an excavation under, as in military operations; to wear away and weaken the foundations or base of; to affect injuriously or weaken by secret or underhand means; to weaken or destroy insidiously or gradually. —**un•der•min•er,** *n.*

un•der•most, ən′dər•mōst, *a., adv.* Lowest in position, place, rank, or condition.

un•der•neath, ən•dər•nēth′, *prep.* Under; beneath or below; under the appearance, form, or disguise of.—*adv.* Beneath; below; in or at a lower place or level.—*a.* Lower; positioned under or below.—*n.* Underside; the lower part.

un•der•pants, ən′dər•pants, *n. pl.* An undergarment for the lower part of the body.

un•der•pass, ən′dər•pas, *n.* A passage running underneath, esp. a passage for crossing under a railway or road.

un•der•pin•ning, ən′dər•pin•ing, *n.* A support or prop. *Pl. Informal.* Legs.

un•der•priv•i•leged, ən•dər•priv′ə•lijd, ən′dər•priv•lijd, *a.* Denied access by restrictive economic or social conditions to the fundamental privileges or rights to which all members of a society are entitled.

un•der•rate, ən•dər•rāt′, *v.t.,* **-rat•ed, -rat•ing.** To undervalue; to underestimate.

un•der•score, ən•dər•skōr′, *v.t.,* **-scored, -scor•ing.** To underline or draw a line or lines under; to accentuate or emphasize.—ən′dər•skōr, *n.* An underline.

un•der•sea, ən′dər•sē, *a.* Located, adapted for use, or carried on beneath the sea's surface; submarine.—*adv.* Beneath the sea's surface.

un•der•sec•re•tar•y, ən•dər•sek′rə•ter•ē, *n. pl.,* **-ies.** A secretary subordinate to the principal secretary.

un•der•sell, ən•dər•sel′, *v.t.,* **-sold, -sell•ing.** To sell merchandise at a lower price than, as a competitor; to sell for less than the actual price or value. —**un•der•sell•er,** *n.*

un•der•shirt, ən′dər•shərt, *n.* A collarless inner shirt worn beneath another shirt.

un•der•shot, ən′dər•shot, *a.* Having the lower incisor teeth projecting beyond the upper ones when the mouth is closed; driven by water passing beneath, as a water wheel.

un•der•side, ən′dər•sid, *n.* The lower side or surface underneath.

un•der•signed, ən•dər•sīnd′, *a.* Having one's name signed at the bottom or end of any document or letter; signed or subscribed at the bottom or end.—**the un•der•signed,** the person or persons signing any document.

un•der•stand, ən•dər•stand′, *v.t.,* **-stood, -stand•ing.** To perceive the meaning of, grasp the idea of, or comprehend; to be thoroughly acquainted or familiar with, as a subject; to apprehend clearly the character or nature of, as a person; to comprehend, as by knowing the symbols or words employed; to interpret; to take as a fact or as settled; to gain knowledge of, come to know, or learn by hearing; to accept as truth or to believe; to conceive the meaning of in a particular way; to supply mentally, as an unexpressed word, phrase, or idea necessary to the complete meaning.—*v.i.* To perceive what is meant; to have information or knowledge about something; to be informed; to believe; to accept with tolerance or sympathy. —**un•der•stand•a•bil•i•ty,** ən•dər•stan•də•bil′ə•tē, *n.* —**un•der•stand•a•ble,** ən•dər•stan′də•bəl, *a.* —**un•der•stand•a•bly,** *adv.*

---

a- hat, fāte, fāre, fäther; **e-** met, mē; **i-** pin, pīne; **o-** not, nōte, ôrb, moove (move), boy, pownd; **u-** cūbe, bŭll, tûk (took); **ch-** chin; **th-** thick, ̡then; **zh-** vizhon (vision); **ə-** əgo, takən, pencəl, lemən, bərd (bird).

un·der·stand·ing, ən·dər·stan'ding, n. The act of one who understands; the ability or power to acquire and interpret knowledge; comprehension; intelligence, mental faculties, or power of discernment; personal interpretation; knowledge of a particular field; ability to cope or deal with something; a state of mutually friendly relations between persons; a mutual agreement, usu. of a private or unannounced kind; an agreement involving a joint action or settling differences.—a. Possessing or showing intelligence, comprehension, or discernment; tolerant. —**un·der·stand·ing·ly,** adv.

un·der·state, ən·dər·stāt', v.t., -stat·ed, -stat·ing. To state or represent less strongly than the truth will bear; to state in a deliberately restrained manner. —**un·der·state·ment,** n.

un·der·stood, ən·dər·stůd', a. Agreed upon or consented to; assumed; unexpressed but implied or supplied mentally.

un·der·stud·y, ən'dər·stəd·ē, v.t., -ied, -y·ing. To study, as a part, in order to replace the regular actor or actress when necessary.—v.i. To act as an understudy to an actor or actress.—n. pl., -ies. One trained and retained to act as a substitute for an actor or actress.

un·der·take, ən·dər·tāk', v.t., -took, -tak·en, -tak·ing. To take on oneself, as a task or performance; to attempt; guarantee.

un·der·tak·er, ən'dər·tā·kər, n. One whose business it is to prepare the dead for burial and to take charge of funerals. Also **mor·ti·cian.**

un·der·tak·ing, ən'dər·tāk·ing, n. The act of one who undertakes any task or responsibility; a task, enterprise, or something undertaken; a promise, pledge, or guarantee.

un·der-the-coun·ter, ən'dər·thə·kown'tər, a. Sold or transacted surreptitiously; illegal; illicit.

un·der·tone, ən'dər·tōn, n. A low or subdued tone, as of speech or sound; an underlying quality or element; a subdued tone or color.

un·der·tow, ən'dər·tō, n. The forceful current of water below the surface in a direction different from that at the surface.

un·der·wa·ter, ən'dər·wôt·ər, ən'dər·wot·ər, a. Being or occurring under water; designed to be used under water.—adv.—n.

un·der·wear, ən'dər·wār, n. Garments or clothing worn under the outer clothing, esp. those nearest the skin.

un·der·weight, ən'dər·wāt, n. Weight deficiency; weight below average.—a. Having a weight deficiency.

un·der·world, ən'dər·werld, n. A social stratum of persons engaged in vice or crime; organized criminals; racketeers; the region inhabited by the dead; Hades.

un·der·write, ən'dər·rit, v.t., -wrote, -writ·ten, -writ·ing. To write below or under; to subscribe; to set one's name to, as a statement with which one agrees; to guarantee to assume financial responsibility for, as a business enterprise; to sign, as an insurance policy, thereby becoming answerable for specific losses stated in the policy; to insure; to assume liability for, by insurance, as losses to a certain amount; to guarantee the sale of, as a new issue of stock or other financial securities to be presented for public subscription.—v.i. To engage in the business of underwriting. —**un·der·writ·er,** n.

un·de·sir·a·ble, ən·di·zīr'ə·bəl, a. Not desirable; not to be wished; objectionable.—n. —**un·de·sir·a·bil·i·ty,** ən·di·zīr·ə·bil'ə·tē, —**un·de·sir·a·ble·ness,** n. —**un·de·sir·a·bly,** adv.

un·de·ter·mined, ən·di·tər'mind, a. Not determined; not decided, fixed, or settled.

un·dies, ən'dēz, n. pl. Informal. Underwear, esp. women's or children's.

un·dip·lo·mat·ic, ən·dip·lə·mat'ik, a. Tactless. —**un·dip·lo·mat·i·cal·ly,** adv.

un·dis·ci·plined, ən·dis'ə·plind, a. Not disciplined;

not properly trained.

un·dis·closed, ən·di·sklōzd', a. Not exposed; not revealed.

un·dis·posed, ən·di·spōzd', a. Not sold, allocated, or otherwise settled, usu. followed by of.

un·dis·tin·guished, ən·di·sting'gwisht, a. Not having any distinguishing mark or characteristic; mediocre.

un·di·vid·ed, ən·di·vīd'id, a. Not divided; unbroken; whole.

un·do, ən·doo', v.t., -did, -done, -do·ing. To reverse, as something which has been done; to annul; to untie or unfasten; to open up; to bring ruin or distress upon; to destroy.—v.i. —**un·do·er,** n.

un·do·ing, ən·doo'ing, n. The reversal of what has been done; ruin; destruction; the process of opening or unfastening.

un·doubt·ed, ən·dow'tid, a. Not doubted; not called in question; indisputable. —**un·doubt·ed·ly,** adv. —**un·doubt·ing,** a.

un·dress, ən·dres', v.t., -dressed or -drest, -dress·ing. To divest of clothes; to remove the bandages from.—v.i. To take off one's clothes.

un·due, ən·doo', ən·dū', a. Not due; not yet demandable by right; not right; not lawful; improper; excessive.

un·du·lant, ən'dyə·lənt, ən'jə·lənt, a. Waving; wavy.

un·du·late, ən'dyə·lāt, ən'jə·lāt, v.i., -lat·ed, -lat·ing. To have a wavy motion; to rise and fall in waves; to move in curving or bending lines; to wave.—v.t. To cause to wave, or move with a wavy motion.—ən'jə·lit, ən'jə·lāt, ən'də·lit, ən'dyə·lit, ən'dyə·lāt, a. Wavy or having a wavy edge. Also **un·du·lat·ed.** —**un·du·la·tion,** ən·dyə·lā'shən, ən·jə·lā'shən, n.

un·du·ly, ən·doo'lē, ən·dū'lē, adv. Excessively; unjustifiably; improperly.

un·dy·ing, ən·dī'ing, a. Not ending or dying; not subject to death; immortal.

un·earth, ən·erth', v.t. To dig up or bring forth from the earth; to bring to light; to discover or find out.

un·earth·ly, ən·erth'lē, a. Not earthly; supernatural or weird; unreal; absurd or ridiculous. —**un·earth·li·ness,** n.

un·eas·y, ən·ē'zē, a., -i·er, -i·est. Not easy in body or mind; uncomfortable; restless; disturbed; not easy in manner; embarrassed; constrained. —**un·ease,** n. —**un·eas·i·ly,** adv. —**un·eas·i·ness,** n.

un·em·ployed, ən·em·ployd', a. Not employed; not in use; out of work.—**the un·em·ployed,** persons without jobs.

un·em·ploy·ment, ən·em·ploy'mənt, n. Lack of employment; an unemployed condition.

un·e·qual, ən·ē'kwəl, a. Not equal; not of the same type, size, quantity, quality, or the like; inadequate; insufficient; not uniform; unbalanced or unevenly distributed. —**un·e·qual·ly,** adv.

un·e·qualed, ən·ē'kwəld, a. Not to be equaled; unparalleled; unrivaled.

un·e·quiv·o·cal, ən·i·kwiv'ə·kəl, a. Not doubtful; clear; not ambiguous. —**un·e·quiv·o·cal·ly,** adv.

un·err·ing, ən·ər'ing, ən·er'ing, a. Committing no mistake; incapable of error; certain or exact. —**un·err·ing·ly,** adv.

un·eth·i·cal, ən·eth'ə·kəl, a. Not ethical; not in accordance with the rules for right conduct or practice. —**un·eth·i·cal·ly,** adv.

un·e·ven, ən·ē'vən, a. Not level, smooth, or flat; rough; not straight, parallel, or equally balanced; odd; not divisible by two without a remainder. —**un·e·ven·ly,** adv. —**un·e·ven·ness,** n.

un·ex·cep·tion·a·ble, ən·ik·sep'shə·nə·bəl, a. Not liable to any exception or objection; unobjectionable; faultless. —**un·ex·cep·tion·a·ble·ness,** n. —**un·ex·cep·tion·a·bly,** adv.

un·ex·pect·ed, ən·ik·spek'tid, a. Not expected; unforeseen. —**un·ex·pect·ed·ly,** adv. —**un·ex·pect·ed·ness,** n.

un·fail·ing, ən·fāʹling, *a.* Not failing or liable to fail; always fulfilling a hope, promise, or want; inexhaustible or never ending; sure, certain, or infallible. **—un·fail·ing·ly,** *adv.* **—un·fail·ing·ness,** *n.*

un·faith·ful, ən·fāthʹfəl, *a.* Not faithful; not observant of promises, vows, allegiance, or duty; disloyal; violating the marriage vow; inexact, incomplete, or inaccurate. **—un·faith·ful·ly,** *adv.* **—un·faith·ful·ness,** *n.*

un·fa·mil·iar, ən·fə·milʹyər, *a.* Not well known; having an element of strangeness. **—un·fa·mil·i·ar·i·ty,** ən·fə·mil·ē·arʹə·tē, *n.* **—un·fa·mil·iar·ly,** *adv.*

un·fast·en, ən·fasʹən, *v.t.* To loosen; to detach; to unbind; to untie.—*v.i.* To become loosened, detached, or untied. **—un·fas·ten·a·ble,** *a.* **—un·fas·ten·er,** *n.*

un·fath·om·a·ble, ən·fathʹə·mə·bəl, *a.* Too deep to be measured; incapable of being interpreted.

un·fa·vor·a·ble, ən·fāʹvər·ə·bəl, *a.* Not favorable; discouraging; giving an adverse judgment or opinion; somewhat prejudicial. **—un·fa·vor·a·ble·ness,** *n.* **—un·fa·vor·a·bly,** *adv.*

un·feel·ing, ən·fēʹling, *a.* Devoid of feeling; insensible; devoid of sympathy for others; hard-hearted. **—un·feel·ing·ly,** *adv.* **—un·feel·ing·ness,** *n.*

un·feigned, ən·fānd', *a.* Not feigned; not counterfeit; not hypocritical; real; sincere. **—un·feign·ed·ly,** *adv.*

un·fet·ter, ən·fetʹər, *v.t.* To free from restraint; to set at liberty. **—un·fet·tered,** *a.*

un·fin·ished, ən·finʹisht, *a.* Not finished; incomplete; imperfect.

un·fit, ən·fit', *a.* Not fit; improper; unsuitable; not suited or adapted; not competent.—*v.t.* To render unfit; to make unsuitable; to disqualify. **—un·fit·ly,** *adv.* **—un·fit·ness,** *n.* **—un·fit·ting,** *a.*

un·flat·ter·ing, ən·flatʹər·ing, *a.* Not flattering; not affording a favorable prospect.

un·flinch·ing, ən·flinʹching, *a.* Not flinching; not shrinking. **—un·flinch·ing·ly,** *adv.*

un·fold, ən·fōld', *v.t.* To open; to expand; to spread out; to lay open, as for viewing; to disclose; to reveal. —*v.i.* To become gradually expanded; to open out; to become disclosed.

un·for·get·ta·ble, ən·fər·getʹə·bəl, *a.* Never to be forgotten. **—un·for·get·ta·bly,** *adv.*

un·for·giv·a·ble, ən·fər·givʹə·bəl, *a.* Incapable of being forgiven; unpardonable.

un·for·tu·nate, ən·fôrʹchə·nit, *a.* Not fortunate; unlucky or unhappy; ill-fated; sad; deplorable.—*n.* An unfortunate person. **—un·for·tu·nate·ly,** *adv.* **—un·for·tu·nate·ness,** *n.*

un·found·ed, ən·fownʹdid, *a.* Having no real foundation; groundless; baseless; not confirmed. **—un·found·ed·ly,** *adv.* **—un·found·ed·ness,** *n.*

un·friend·ly, ən·frendʹlē, *a.,* **-li·er, -li·est.** Not friendly; not kind; hostile; not favorable.—*adv.* In an unkind manner. **—un·friend·li·ness,** *n.*

un·frock, ən·frok', *v.t.* To deprive of the function and privileges of a priest or clergyman.

un·furl, ən·fərl', *v.t.* To spread or shake out from a furled state, as a sail or a flag; unfold.—*v.i.* To become unfurled.

un·gain·ly, ən·gānʹlē, *a.* Clumsy; awkward; uncouth.—*adv.* In a clumsy, ungainly manner. **—un·gain·li·ness,** *n.*

un·gird, ən·gərd', *v.t.,* **un·gir·ded** or **un·girt, un·gird·ing.** To loosen, or free from a girdle; to unbind.

un·glazed, ən·glāzd', *a.* Not furnished with glass; lacking windows; not covered with vitreous matter: *unglazed* pottery.

un·god·ly, ən·godʹlē, *a.,* **-li·er, -li·est.** Godless; wicked; impious; sinful. *Informal.* Preposterous; outrageous. **—un·god·li·ness,** *n.*

un·gov·ern·a·ble, ən·gəvʹər·nə·bəl, *a.* Incapable of being governed, ruled, or restrained; unruly; wild. **—un·gov·ern·a·ble·ness,** *n.* **—un·gov·ern·a·bly,** *adv.*

un·gra·cious, ən·grāʹshəs, *a.* Unmannerly; not pleasing; rude; offensive; disagreeable. **—un·gra·cious·ly,** *adv.* **—un·gra·cious·ness,** *n.*

un·gram·mat·i·cal, ən·grə·matʹə·kəl, *a.* Not according to the rules of grammar; grammatically awkward; contrary to accepted usage. **—un·gram·mat·i·cal·ly,** *adv.*

un·grate·ful, ən·grātʹfəl, *a.* Not grateful; making poor or no returns for kindness; unpleasing; disagreeable. **—un·grate·ful·ly,** *adv.* **—un·grate·ful·ness,** *n.*

un·guard·ed, ən·gärʹdid, *a.* Unprotected or undefended; imprudent; having no guard. **—un·guard·ed·ly,** *adv.* **—un·guard·ed·ness,** *n.*

un·guent, angʹgwənt, *n.* A salve applied to sores and wounds; an ointment.

un·gu·late, angʹgyə·lit, angʹgyə·lāt, *a.* Of the nature of a hoof; hooflike; having hoofs.—*n.* An ungulate mammal.

un·ham·pered, ən·hamʹpərd, *a.* Not hindered or restricted; unimpeded.

un·hand, ən·hand', *v.t.* To take the hands from; to release from a grasp; to let go.

un·hand·y, ən·hanʹdē, *a.,* **-i·er, -i·est.** Not handy; inconvenient; not skillful in the use of the hands; awkward.

un·hap·py, ən·hapʹē, *a.,* **-pi·er, -pi·est.** Not happy, cheerful, or gay; miserable or wretched; inappropriate or unsuitable. **—un·hap·pi·ly,** *adv.* **—un·hap·pi·ness,** *n.*

un·harmed, ən·härmd', *a.* Not harmed or injured; unscathed; sound.

un·health·y, ən·helʹthē, *a.,* **-i·er, -i·est.** Not healthy; habitually weak or indisposed; sickly; unfavorable to the preservation of health; likely to generate disease; unwholesome; risky. **—un·health·i·ly,** *adv.* **—un·health·i·ness,** *n.*

un·heard, ən·hərd', *a.* Not perceived by the ear; not granted an audience; unknown.

un·heard-of, ən·hərdʹov, ən·hərdʹəv, *a.* Never known before; unprecedented; not known to fame; unknown.

un·heed·ed, ən·hēʹdid, *a.* Disregarded; unnoticed. **—un·heed·ful,** *a.* **—un·heed·ing,** *a.*

un·hinge, ən·hinj', *v.t.,* **-hinged, -hing·ing.** To take from the hinges; to take off the hinges of; to disturb the calm of; to unsettle; to render unstable or wavering; to discompose or disorder, as the mind or opinions.

un·hitch, ən·hich', *v.t.* To untie or unloosen, as a dog from a chain; unfasten.

un·ho·ly, ən·hōʹlē, *a.,* **-li·er, -li·est.** Not sacred; not hallowed or consecrated; wicked; evil. *Informal.* Dreadful; outrageous. **—un·ho·li·ly,** *adv.* **—un·ho·li·ness,** *n.*

un·hook, ən·hůk', *v.t.* To undo the hook or hooks of.—*v.i.* To become or be unhooked.

un·horse, ən·hôrs', *v.t.,* **-horsed, -hors·ing.** To throw from, or as if from, a horse.

un·hur·ried, ən·hərʹēd, *a.* Not hurried; without haste; leisurely.

un·hurt, ən·hərt', *a.* Not hurt; not harmed; free from wound or injury. **—un·hurt·ful,** *a.*

u·ni·cam·er·al, ū·nə·kamʹər·əl, *a.* Consisting of a single legislative chamber. **—u·ni·cam·er·al·ly,** *adv.*

u·ni·cel·lu·lar, ū·nə·selʹyə·lər, *a.* Consisting of one cell only, as an amoeba.

u·ni·corn, ūʹnə·kôrn, *n.* A legendary horselike animal having a long spiral horn growing out of the forehead.

u·ni·fi·ca·tion, ū·nə·fə·kāʹshən, *n.* The act of uniting; the state of being united.

u·ni·form, ūʹnə·fôrm, *a.* Having always the same form; not changing in shape, appearance, or character; not varying in degree or rate; invariable; consis-

---

a- hat, fāte, fāre, fāther; **e-** met, mē; **i-** pin, pīne; **o-** not, nōte, ôrb, moove (move), boy, pownd; **u-** cūbe, bůll, tůk (took); **ch-** chin; **th-** thick, then; **zh-** vizhon (vision); **ə-** əgo, takən, pencəl, lemən, bərd (bird).

tent at all times; conformi. j to one rule or mode.—*n.* A style of clothing of the same general appearance as that worn by other members of the same body.—*v.t.* To bring about uniformity in; to equip with or array in a uniform. —**u·ni·formed,** *a.* —**u·ni·form·i·ty,** ū·nə·fôr′mə·tē, *n.* —**u·ni·form·ly,** *adv.* —**u·ni·form·ness,** *n.*

u·ni·fy, ū′nə·fī, *v.t.,* **-fied, -fy·ing.** To form into one; to reduce to unity by resolving differences; to consolidate. —**u·ni·fi·er,** *n.*

un·i·lat·er·al, ū·nə·lat′ər·əl, *a.* One-sided; pertaining to one side; showing or containing one side only; not reciprocal. —**u·ni·lat·er·al·ism,** *n.* —**u·ni·lat·er·al·ly,** *adv.*

un·im·ag·i·na·ble, ən·i·maj′ə·nə·bəl, *a.* Not capable of being imagined, conceived, or thought of; inconceivable.

un·im·paired, ən·im·pārd′, *a.* Not diminished; not enfeebled by time or injury.

un·im·peach·a·ble, ən·im·pēch′ə·bəl, *a.* Not to be called in question; blameless; irreproachable. —**un·im·peach·a·bly,** *adv.*

un·im·por·tance, ən·im·pôr′təns, *n.* Lack of importance, consequence, or significance. —**un·im·por·tant,** *a.*

un·im·proved, ən·im·proovd′, *a.* Not brought to a more desirable condition; lacking development leading to full potentialities and profits, as real estate; not put in a better condition for ease of travel; not made better by instruction or study; not bred selectively to enhance the species.

un·in·hib·it·ed, ən·in·hib′i·tid, *a.* Heedless of conventional proscriptions or constraints in personal conduct; open. —**un·in·hib·it·ed·ly,** *adv.*

un·in·ter·est·ed, ən·in′tər·ə·stid, ən·in′tris·tid, *a.* Not interested; indifferent; not personally concerned. —**un·in·ter·est·ing,** *a.*

un·ion, ūn′yən, *n.* The act of uniting or the state of being united; junction; combination; something formed by uniting, as of persons, societies, states, or nations, joined or associated together for a common purpose; a labor union; a combination of states or nations into one political body; (*cap.*) the United States of America, preceded by *the*; marriage; sexual intercourse.—*a.* Of or pertaining to a union, esp. a labor union; (*cap.*) of or pertaining to the U.S., esp. during the Civil War.

un·ion·ism, ūn′yə·niz·əm, *n.* The principle of union; trade unionism; (*cap.*) loyalty to the federal union of the United States of America at the time of the American Civil War. —**un·ion·ist,** *n.*

un·ion·ize, ūn′yə·nīz, *v.t.,* **-ized, -iz·ing.** To form into or cause to join a union, esp. a labor union. —**un·ion·i·za·tion,** *n.*

un·ion jack, *n.* A marine flag consisting of the union of a national flag or ensign; (*often cap.*) the national flag of Great Britain.

u·nique, ū·nēk′, *a.* Without a like or equal; unmatched; unequaled; uncommon or rare. —**u·nique·ly,** *adv.* —**u·nique·ness,** *n.*

u·ni·son, ū′ni·sən, ū′ni·zən, *n.* Coincidence in pitch of two or more tones or voices, as in speaking; a sounding together at the same pitch or in octaves, as of different voices or instruments performing the same part.—**in u·ni·son,** in accord or agreement; simultaneity of like actions or sounds.

u·nit, ū′nit, *n.* A single thing or person; any group of things or persons regarded as one; one of the individuals or groups making up a whole; any standard quantity or amount for use in measurement; a piece of machinery or group of machines with a specified function; the smallest whole number; one; a portion of a course organized around a specific theme and often crossing traditional course divisions; a specific quantity of hours of work used to determine student credits.

u·nite, ūnīt′, *v.t.,* **u·nit·ed, u·nit·ing.** To join, combine, or incorporate so as to form one connected whole; to cause to hold together or adhere; to join in marriage; to associate by some bond or tie; to join in action, interest, opinion, or feeling; to have or exhibit in union or combination.—*v.i.* To become joined together so as to form a connected whole in action, opinion, or feeling. —**u·nit·er,** *n.*

u·nit·ed, ū·nī′tid, *a.* Joined together; combined; made one; of or produced by two or more; in accord or agreement. —**u·nit·ed·ly,** *adv.*

u·ni·ty, ū′ni·tē, *n. pl.,* **-ties.** The state or fact of being one; oneness; one single thing; something complete in itself; the oneness of a complex whole; concord, harmony, or agreement; the number one; the arrangement of elements, as in a picture, book, musical, work, etc., to secure a single effect or harmonious whole.

u·ni·valve, ū′nə·valv, *a.* Having one valve only, as a snail shell; also **u·ni·valved, u·ni·val·vu·lar,** ū·nə·val′vyə·lər.—*n.* A shell having one valve only; a mollusk with a shell composed of a single piece.

u·ni·ver·sal, ū·nə·vər′səl, *a.* Of, pertaining to, or characteristic of all or the whole; affecting, concerning, or involving all; used or understood by all; existing or prevailing in all parts; embracing all subjects or fields; of, or pertaining to the universe, all nature, or all existing things.—*n.* A widely applicable principle, judgment, or idea. —**u·ni·ver·sal·ly,** *adv.* **u·ni·ver·sal·i·ty,** ū·nə·vər·sal′i·tē, *n.* —**u·ni·ver·sal·ness,** *n.*

u·ni·ver·sal·ize, ū·nə·vər′sə·līz, *v.t.,* **-ized, -iz·ing.** To make universal.

u·ni·verse, ū′nə·vərs, *n.* The totality of existing or created things, including all matter and all space; the cosmos; the whole world; mankind; a world or sphere in which something exists or prevails.

u·ni·ver·si·ty, ū·nə·vər′sə·tē, *n. pl.,* **-ties.** An institution concerned with the higher branches of learning, having various undergraduate schools and also graduate and professional schools; the faculty and students of a university collectively; the grounds, equipment, and buildings of a university.

un·just, ən·jəst′, *a.* Contrary to justice and right; unfair. —**un·just·ly,** *adv.* —**un·just·ness,** *n.*

un·kempt, ən·kempt′, *a.* Uncombed; untidy, as in dress; disheveled.

un·kind, ən·kīnd′, *a.* Wanting in kindness; without consideration; cruel. —**un·kind·ness,** *n.*

un·kind·ly, ən·kīnd′lē, *a.,* **-li·er, -li·est.** Unkind; ungracious.—*adv.* —**un·kind·li·ness,** *n.*

un·known, ən·nōn′, *a.* Not known; unfamiliar; strange; not ascertained, discovered, or identified.—*n.* One who or that which is unknown.

un·law·ful, ən·lô′fəl, *a.* Contrary to law; illegal; not born in wedlock; illegitimate. —**un·law·ful·ly,** *adv.* —**un·law·ful·ness,** *n.*

un·learn, ən·lərn′, *v.t.,* **-learned** or **-learnt, -learn·ing.** To forget the knowledge of.

un·learn·ed, ən·lər′nid, ən·lərnd′, *a.* Not learned or erudite; ignorant; illiterate. Not gained through instruction, ən·lərnd′. —**un·learn·ed·ly,** *adv.*

un·leash, ən·lēsh′, *v.t.* To free from, as a leash; to let go of.

un·less, ən·les′, *conj.* If it were not that; if not: He will speak *unless* you object.—*prep.* Except.

un·let·tered, ən·let′ərd, *a.* Without education; untaught; ignorant; without letters.

un·like, ən·līk′, *a.* Not like; different or dissimilar; having no resemblance.—*prep.* Different from; not like or typical of. —**un·like·ness,** *n.*

un·like·ly, ən·līk′lē, *a.,* **-li·er, -li·est.** Not likely; improbable; holding little prospect of success; unpromising.—*adv.* —**un·like·li·ness,** *n.*

un·lim·ber, ən·lim′bər, *v.t.* To prepare for action or use.—*v.i.* To work at a task which prepares something for action.

un·lim·it·ed, ən·lim′i·tid, *a.* Not limited; boundless; infinite; vast; not restrained.

un·load, ən·lōd′, *v.t.* To take the load from; to remove the burden, cargo, or freight from; to get rid or dispose of; to relieve of anything burdensome; to withdraw the charge from, as a firearm.—*v.i.* To unload something. —**un·load·er,** *n.*

un·lock, ən·lok′, *v.t.* To unfasten, as something which has been locked; to open; to lay open or disclose.—*v.i.*

un·looked-for, ən·lûkt′fôr, *a.* Not looked for or expected; unforeseen.

un·loose, ən·loos′, *v.t.*, **-loosed, -loos·ing.** To loosen; to untie; to set free; to release. Also **un·loos·en.**

un·luck·y, ən·lək′ē, *a.*, **-i·er, -i·est.** Not lucky or fortunate; not successful in one's undertakings; illomened or inauspicious. —**un·luck·i·ly,** *adv.* —**un·luck·i·ness,** *n.*

un·make, ən·māk′, *v.t.*, **-made, -mak·ing.** To reduce to the original matter or state; to destroy; ruin; undo; to depose from office or authority. —**un·mak·er,** *n.*

un·man, ən·man′, *v.t.*, **-manned, -man·ning.** To deprive of the qualities of a man; to deprive of manly courage and fortitude; emasculate.

un·manned, ən·mand′, *a.* Having no men aboard: an *unmanned* satellite.

un·mask, ən·mask′, *v.t.* To strip of a mask or disguise; to expose in the true character.—*v.i.* To put off a mask or disguise.

un·mean·ing, ən·mē′ning, *a.* Having no meaning or signification; mindless; senseless. —**un·mean·ing·ly,** *adv.* —**un·mean·ing·ness,** *n.*

un·men·tion·a·ble, ən·men′shən·ə·bəl, *a.* Unfit to be mentioned or noticed.—*n.* A thing unfit to be mentioned or noticed; *pl.*, articles of dress not to be mentioned in polite circles; underwear.

un·mer·ci·ful, ən·mər′si·fəl, *a.* Relentless; cruel; merciless; extreme or excessive. —**un·mer·ci·ful·ly,** *adv.*

un·mis·tak·a·ble, ən·mis·tā′kə·bəl, *a.* Not capable of being mistaken or misunderstood; clear. —**un·mis·tak·a·bly,** *adv.*

un·mit·i·gat·ed, ən·mit′ə·gā·tid, *a.* Not softened or toned down; having no redeeming feature or qualification; unmodified. —**un·mit·i·gat·ed·ly,** *adv.*

un·nat·u·ral, ən·nach′ər·əl, *a.* Not natural; contrary to the laws of nature; contrary to normal behavior; perverse; cruel in the extreme; forced; affected; artificial. —**un·nat·u·ral·ly,** *adv.* —**un·nat·u·ral·ness,** *n.*

un·nec·es·sar·y, ən·nes′i·ser·ē, *a.* Not necessary; needless. —**un·nec·es·sar·i·ly,** *adv.*

un·nerve, ən·nərv′, *v.t.*, **-nerved, -nerv·ing.** To deprive of nerve; to deprive of composure, as with shock.

un·num·bered, ən·nəm′bərd, *a.* Not numbered; innumerable or countless; not counted.

un·ob·jec·tion·a·ble, ən·əb·jek′shən·ə·bəl, *a.* Not liable to objection; not likely to be condemned as faulty, false, or improper.

un·or·gan·ized, ən·ôr′gə·nīzd, *a.* Not organized; not unionized.

un·pack, ən·pak′, *v.t.* To take from a package; to remove a wrapper from; to remove the contents from; to unload.—*v.i.* To unpack a suitcase.

un·par·al·leled, ən·par′ə·leld, *a.* Having no parallel or equal; unequaled; matchless.

un·par·don·a·ble, ən·pär′dən·ə·bəl, *a.* Not to be forgiven; incapable of being pardoned.

un·pleas·ant, ən·plez′ənt, *a.* Not pleasing; disagreeable. —**un·pleas·ant·ly,** *adv.* —**un·pleas·ant·ness,** *n.*

un·plumbed, ən·pləmd′, *a.* Not measured by a plumb line; unfathomed; not investigated.

un·pop·u·lar, ən·pop′yə·lər, *a.* Not popular; generally disapproved; not having the public favor. —**un·pop·u·lar·i·ty,** ən·pop·yə·lar′i·tē, *n.* —**un·pop·u·lar·ly,** *adv.*

un·prec·e·dent·ed, ən·pres′ə·den·tid, *a.* Having no precedent; not matched by any previous instance;

unheard of. —**un·prec·e·dent·ed·ly,** *adv.*

un·prin·ci·pled, ən·prin′sə·pəld, *a.* Not having moral principles; unscrupulous.

un·print·a·ble, ən·prin′tə·bəl, *a.* Unacceptable for printed publication, usu. due to obscenity; offensive.

un·pro·fes·sion·al, ən·prə·fesh′ə·nəl, *a.* Contrary to the rules or standards of a profession; lacking professional qualifications or competence. —**un·pro·fes·sion·al·ly,** *adv.*

un·qual·i·fied, ən·kwol′ə·fid, *a.* Not having the requisite qualifications; without sufficient education, abilities, or accomplishments; not legally competent to act; unlimited; unrestricted; absolute. —**un·qual·i·fied·ly,** *adv.*

un·ques·tion·a·ble, ən·kwes′chən·ə·bəl, *a.* Not open to question; beyond dispute or doubt; certain; indisputable; beyond criticism. —**un·ques·tion·a·bly,** *adv.*

un·ques·tioned, ən·kwes′chənd, *a.* Not questioned; not interrogated; not inquired into; not called in question; undisputed.

un·quote, ən·kwōt′, *v.i.*, **-quot·ed, -quot·ing.** To end a quotation.—*v.t.*

un·rav·el, ən·rav′əl, *v.t.*, **-eled, -el·ing.** To free from a tangled state; disengage the threads or fibers of; to free from complication or difficulty; to solve.—*v.i.* To become unraveled. —**un·rav·el·ment,** *n.*

un·read, ən·red′, *a.* Not read or perused; not having gained knowledge by reading.

un·re·al, ən·rē′əl, *a.* Not real; imaginary; artificial; impractical or visionary.

un·rea·son·a·ble, ən·rē′zən·ə·bəl, *a.* Not reasonable; immoderate or exorbitant. —**un·rea·son·a·ble·ness,** *n.* —**un·rea·son·a·bly,** *adv.*

un·rea·son·ing, ən·rē′zə·ning, *a.* Not exercising reason; thoughtless; hasty. —**un·rea·son·ing·ly,** *adv.*

un·re·fined, ən·ri·find′, *a.* Not purified; not converted into a finished product; not polished in language, taste, or behavior.

un·re·gen·er·ate, ən·ri·jen′ər·it, *a.* Not regenerated in heart or spirit; not having reformed; sinful. —**un·re·gen·er·a·cy,** *n.* —**un·re·gen·er·ate·ly,** *adv.*

un·re·lat·ed, ən·ri·lā′tid, *a.* Not connected by blood or affinity; having no connection of any kind.

un·re·lent·ing, ən·ri·len′ting, *a.* Not becoming lenient, gentle, or merciful; pitiless; not slackening; unflagging. —**un·re·lent·ing·ly,** *adv.*

un·re·mit·ting, ən·ri·mit′ing, *a.* Not relaxing or slackening; incessant; continuous.

un·re·serve, ən·ri·zərv′, *n.* Absence of reserve; frankness. —**un·re·served,** *a.* —**un·re·serv·ed·ly,** *adv.* —**un·re·serv·ed·ness,** *n.*

un·rest, ən·rest′, *n.* Mental restlessness; disquiet; uneasiness; anxiety; turmoil.

un·ri·valed, ən·rī′vəld, *a.* Having no rival, competitor, or equal; peerless; incomparable.

un·roll, ən·rōl′, *v.t.* To open out, as something rolled; to lay open or display.—*v.i.* To unfold; to uncoil; to become unrolled.

un·ruf·fled, ən·rəf′əld, *a.* Calm; tranquil; not agitated; smooth; not disturbed.

un·ru·ly, ən·roo′lē, *a.*, **-li·er, -li·est.** Disregarding restraint; disposed to violate laws; lawless; turbulent; ungovernable; disorderly. —**un·ru·li·ness,** *n.*

un·sad·dle, ən·sad′əl, *v.t.*, **-dled, -dling.** To take the saddle from; to unhorse; unseat.—*v.i.* To remove a saddle from an animal.

un·said, ən·sed′, *a.* Not spoken.

un·sa·vor·y, ən·sā′və·rē, *a.* Unappealing; disagreeable to the taste or sense of smell; unpleasing; offensive; morally objectionable.

un·say, ən·sā′, *v.t.*, **un·said, un·say·ing.** To take back (something said).

un·scathed, ən·skāthd′, *a.* Uninjured.

---

a- hat, fāte, fâre, fäther; **e-** met, mē; **i-** pin, pīne; **o-** not, nōte, ôrb, moove (move), boy, pownd;
u- cūbe, bûll, tûk (took); **ch-** chin; **th-** thick, ŧhen; **zh-** vizhon (vision); **ə-** əgo, takən, pencəl, lemən, bərd (bird).

un·schooled, ən·skoold′, *a.* Not taught; untrained; natural; not artificial.

un·scram·ble, ən·skram′bəl, *v.t.,* **-bled, -bling.** To bring out of a scrambled condition; to reduce from confusion to order; to make intelligible.

un·screw, ən·skroo′, *v.t.* To draw the screws from; to unfasten by removing screws; to undo, as a jar cap, by rotating or turning.—*v.i.* To become unscrewed.

un·scru·pu·lous, ən·skroo′pyə·ləs, *a.* Having no scruples; having no principles. **—un·scru·pu·lous·ly,** *adv.* **—un·scru·pu·lous·ness,** *n.*

un·seal, ən·sēl′, *v.t.* To break a seal of; to open after having been sealed.

un·sea·son·a·ble, ən·sē′zən·ə·bəl, ən·sēz′nə·bəl, *a.* Not agreeable to the time of the year; not seasonal; not suited to the time or occasion; inappropriate. **—un·sea·son·a·ble·ness,** *n.* **—un·sea·son·a·bly,** *adv.*

un·seat, ən·sēt′, *v.t.* To remove from a seat; to depose from a political position.

un·seem·ly, ən·sēm′lē, *a.* Not becoming; not conforming to accepted behavior modes; indecent; inappropriate.—*adv.* **—un·seem·li·ness,** *n.*

un·set·tle, ən·set′əl, *v.t.,* **-tled, -tling.** To make uncertain or unstable; disrupt, disturb, or upset.—*v.i.* To become disordered or unsettled.

un·sheathe, ən·shēth′, *v.t.,* **-sheathed, -sheath·ing.** To draw from a sheath, as a sword, knife, or the like.

un·shod, ən·shod′, *a.* Without shoes.

un·sight·ly, ən·sīt′lē, *a.,* **-li·er, -li·est.** Disagreeable to the eye; repulsive; ugly. **—un·sight·li·ness,** *n.*

un·skilled, ən·skild′, *a.* Not skilled; untrained; not demanding skill.

un·skill·ful, ən·skil′fəl, *a.* Not skillful; inexpert; inept. **—un·skill·ful·ly,** *adv.* **—un·skill·ful·ness.**

un·snap, ən·snap′, *v.t.,* **-snapped, -snap·ping.** To loosen or undo by, or as if by, unfastening snap closings.

un·snarl, ən·snärl′, *v.t.* Disentangle.

un·so·phis·ti·cat·ed, ən·sə·fis′tə·kā·tid, *a.* Not sophisticated, not adept in or restrained by social conventions; naïve; uncomplicated; plain. **—un·so·phis·ti·cat·ed·ly,** *adv.* **—un·so·phis·ti·cat·ed·ness, un·so·phis·ti·ca·tion,** ən·sə·fis·tə·kā′shən, *n.*

un·sound, ən·sownd′, *a.* Not strong or reliable; defective; not solid or firm; not well-founded or valid; fallacious. **—un·sound·ly,** *adv.* **—un·sound·ness,** *n.*

un·spar·ing, ən·spār′ing, *a.* Not sparing; liberal; profuse; unmerciful; ruthless. **—un·spar·ing·ly,** *adv.* **—un·spar·ing·ness,** *n.*

un·speak·a·ble, ən·spē′kə·bəl, *a.* Incapable of being spoken; so bad as to preclude description. **—un·speak·a·bly,** *adv.*

un·sta·ble, ən·stā′bəl, *a.* Not stable; irresolute; lacking in emotional control; subject to easy decomposition. **—un·sta·ble·ness,** *n.* **—un·sta·bly,** *adv.*

un·stead·y, ən·sted′ē, *a.,* **-i·er, -i·est.** Not steady; shaky; wavering; not constant in mind; fickle; unsettled; not regular, equable, or uniform; varying. **—un·stead·i·ly,** *adv.*

un·stop, ən·stop′, *v.t.,* **-stopped, -stop·ping.** To free from obstruction, as a drain; to open, as a bottle, by drawing out its stopper or cork.

un·strung, ən·strəng′, *a.* With strings removed or relaxed; nervous; disordered; unstable; upset; weak.

un·stud·ied, ən·stəd′ēd, *a.* Not premeditated; not labored; natural; not learned through study; unversed, followed by *in.*

un·sung, ən·səng′, *a.* Not sung; not celebrated in song or poem; unacclaimed.

un·tan·gle, ən·tang′gəl, *v.t.,* **-gled, -gling.** Disentangle; unsnarl, straighten out or clear up, as anything confused or perplexing.

un·taught, ən·tôt′, *a.* Not instructed, educated, or schooled; ignorant.

un·think·a·ble, ən·thingk′ə·bəl, *a.* Inconceivable; not to be made an object of thought or consideration.

un·think·ing, ən·thing′king, *a.* Not heedful; inconsiderate; not indicating thought or reflection; having no power to think. **—un·think·ing·ly,** *adv.*

un·ti·dy, ən·tī′dē, *a.,* **-di·er, -di·est.** Not tidy or neat; slovenly or disordered. **—un·ti·di·ly,** *adv.* **—un·ti·di·ness,** *n.*

un·tie, ən·tī′, *v.t.,* **-tied, -ty·ing.** To loose or unfasten, as anything tied; to let or set loose by undoing a knot; to undo, as a cord or a knot.—*v.i.* To become untied.

un·til, ən·til′, *conj.* Up to the time that or when; till; before.—*prep.* Onward to or till, as a specified time; before, usu. with negatives.

un·time·ly, ən·tīm′lē, *a.* Not done or happening in the right season; inopportune; premature.—*adv.* Before the natural time; unseasonably. **—un·time·li·ness,** *n.*

un·to, ən·too′, ən′tû, *prep.* Archaic. To: in all uses except the infinitive; until.

un·told, ən·tōld′, *a.* Not told, related, or revealed; too many to be numbered or counted; very great: *untold* wealth.

un·touch·a·ble, ən·təch′ə·bəl, *a.* Not near enough to be touched; inaccessible; unpleasant or dangerous to touch; not subject to bribery, interference, control, or criticism.—*n.* A member of the lowest caste in India. **—un·touch·a·bly,** *adv.*

un·to·ward, ən·tōrd′, ən·tôrd′, *a.* Unlucky; adverse, not easily guided or taught; unruly; stubborn; intractable. **—un·to·ward·ly,** *adv.* **—un·to·ward·ness,** *n.*

un·truth, ən·trooth′, *n.* The state or quality of being untrue; a false assertion; a lie. **—un·truth·ful,** *a.*

un·tu·tored, ən·too′tərd, ən·tū′tərd, *a.* Untaught; uninstructed; rude; naive.

un·used, ən·ūzd′, ən·ûst′, *a.* Not used; not put to use; never having been used, ən·ūzd′. Not accustomed or habituated, followed by *to*, ən·ûst′.

un·u·su·al, ən·ū′zhû·al, *a.* Not usual; not common; rare. **—un·u·su·al·ly,** *adv.* **—un·u·su·al·ness,** *n.*

un·ut·ter·a·ble, ən·ət′ər·ə·bəl, *a.* Incapable of being uttered or expressed; ineffable; inexpressible; unspeakable. **—un·ut·ter·a·bly,** *adv.*

un·var·nished, ən·vär′nisht, *a.* Not overlaid with varnish; plain; straightforward.

un·veil, ən·vāl′, *v.t.* To remove a veil from; to disclose to view.—*v.i.* To remove one's veil; to reveal or disclose oneself.

un·war·y, ən·wār′ē, *a.* Not wary; not cautious; careless; unguarded. **—un·war·i·ly,** *adv.* **—un·war·i·ness,** *n.*

un·well, ən·wel′, *a.* Indisposed; ailing.

un·whole·some, ən·hōl′səm, *a.* Unhealthful; not sound in health; unhealthy. **—un·whole·some·ly,** *adv.* **—un·whole·some·ness,** *n.*

un·wield·y, ən·wēl′dē, *a.* Movable with difficulty; too bulky and awkward to move or be moved easily; cumbersome; clumsy; ponderous. **—un·wield·i·ness,** *n.*

un·will·ing, ən·wil′ing, *a.* Not willing; loath; reluctant. **—un·will·ing·ly,** *adv.* **—un·will·ing·ness,** *n.*

un·wind, ən·wīnd′, *v.t.,* **-wound, -wind·ing.** To undo or uncoil, as something wound; wind off; loosen or untwist, as what is wound; to lessen the tension of.—*v.i.* To become unwound; to become less tense.

un·wise, ən·wīz′, *a.* Not wise; foolish; imprudent; indiscreet. **—un·wise·ly,** *adv.*

un·wit·ting, ən·wit′ing, *a.* Not knowing; unconscious; unaware; accidental. **—un·wit·ting·ly,** *adv.*

un·wont·ed, ən·wŏn′tid, ən·wôn′tid, ən·wən′tid, *a.* Not customary, habitual, or usual. **—un·wont·ed·ly,** *adv.* **—un·wont·ed·ness,** *n.*

un·wor·thy, ən·wər′thē, *a.* Not worthy; lacking worth or excellence; undeserving; a kind not worthy (*of*); beneath the dignity (*of*); undeserving. **—un·wor·thi·ly,** *adv.* **—un·wor·thi·ness,** *n.*

un·wrap, ən·rap′, *v.t.,* **-wrapped, -wrap·ping.** To take off a wrapper from; to open or undo.—*v.i.* To become unwrapped.

un·yield·ing, ən-yēl′ding, *a.* Unbending; not pliant; stiff; firm; obstinate.

up, əp, *adv.* To, toward, or in a more elevated position; to or in an erect position; out of bed; above the horizon; to or at any point that is considered higher; to or at a source, origin, center, or the like; to or at a higher point or degree in a scale, as of rank, size, value, or pitch; to or at a point of equal advance or extent; in continuous awareness; into or in activity or operation; into existence; into view, prominence, or consideration; into or in a place of safekeeping, storage, or retirement; into or in a state of union or contraction; to the required or final point; to or at an end. *Baseball.* At bat.—*a.* Relatively high; going or directed up or higher; tending or inclining upward. *Informal.* Informed or aware; abreast; finished or over; happening: What's *up?* In any higher state or position; erect; out of bed; above a surface, the ground, or the horizon; being above the normal or former degree, amount, or the like, as water nearing flood level; in an agitated, excited, or active state; prepared or ready for operation, use, or the like; being considered, or presented for consideration; on trial or charged; in sports and games, equal, used in combination with a numeral: The score was *6-up;* in baseball, at bat; at stake, wagered, or bet in gambling.— *prep.* To, toward, or at a higher place or rank on or in; to, toward, or at a point of considered as higher; toward the source or origin of; toward or in the interior of, as a region or country; in an opposite direction to, used in compounds.—*n.* An upward movement; an ascent; a rise of fortune. —*v.t.,* **upped, up·ping.** *Informal.* To put or take higher; to make better; increase.—*v.i. Informal.* To get or start up; to begin something quickly, usu. followed by *and* and a *verb.*—**up a·gainst.** *Informal.* Faced with.—**up a·gainst it.** *Informal.* In a troublesome situation, esp. regarding finances.—**up on** or **in.** *Informal.* Well supplied with information on, aware of.—**up to,** equal to or capable of. *Informal.* Scheming or doing; incumbent or dependent upon.

up-and-com·ing, əp′ən-kəm′ing, *a.* Promising; enterprising; on the way to success or eminence.

up-and-down, əp′ən-down′, *a.* Moving successively upward and downward; pertaining to a surface which is not level; likely to change; vertical.

up·beat, əp′bēt, *n.* The last beat in a musical measure; any unaccented beat.—*a. Informal.* Optimistic; cheerful; lively.

up·braid, əp·brād′, *v.t.* To criticize or scold; to reprove; to chide; to be a reproach to. —**up·braid·er,** *n.* —**up·braid·ing,** *n.* —**up·braid·ing·ly,** *adv.*

up·bring·ing, əp′bring·ing, *n.* The process of bringing up; training; education; care.

up·com·ing, əp′kəm·ing, *a.* Forthcoming.

up·coun·try, əp′kən′trē, *a.* Being or living far away from the coast or border; interior.—əp′kən·trē, *n.* The interior of a country.—əp·kən′trē, *adv.* Toward or in the interior of a country.

up·date, əp·dāt′, *v.t.,* **-dat·ed, -dat·ing.** To make modern or up-to-date.

up·end, əp·end′, *v.t.* To set on end, as a barrel; to upset, defeat, or overthrow.—*v.i.* To stand or turn on end.

up·grade, əp′grād, *n.* An ascending slope or road; an increase, as of status, rank, or quality, usu. preceded by *on the.*—əp·grād′, *v.t.,* **-grad·ed, -grad·ing.** To elevate the rank or status of.—əp′grād′, *a.* Uphill; upward; pertaining to or along an upgrade.—*adv.* Uphill.

up·heav·al, əp·hē′vəl, *n.* The act of upheaving; the condition of being upheaved; an abrupt change or violent disturbance.

up·heave, əp·hēv′, *v.t.,* **up·heaved** or **up·hove, up·heav·ing.** To heave or lift up.—*v.i.* To rise or be lifted.

up·hill, əp′hil′, *adv.* Upward, as on an ascending slope or incline; against obstacles.—*a.* Going up, as on a rising slope; situated on high ground.—*n.* A rising incline.

up·hold, əp·hōld′, *v.t.,* **-held, -hold·ing.** To raise or hold up; to keep elevated or prevent from sinking; to sustain. —**up·hold·er,** *n.*

up·hol·ster, əp·hōl′stər, *v.t.* To provide, as chairs or sofas, with coverings, cushions, stuffings, and springs. —**up·hol·ster·er,** *n.*

up·hol·ster·y, əp·hōl′stə·rē, *n. pl.,* **-ies.** The fabrics, fittings, or decorations supplied by an upholsterer; the business or craft of an upholsterer.

up·keep, əp′kēp, *n.* The process of maintaining; the maintenance of an establishment, a machine, or the like; the cost of this.

up·land, əp′lənd, əp′land, *n.* The higher ground of a region; ground elevated above meadows, valleys, and rivers.—*a.*

up·lift, əp·lift′, *v.t.* To lift up; to raise or elevate; to exalt emotionally or spiritually.—*v.i.*—əp′lift, *n.* The act of lifting up or raising; elevation; emotional or spiritual exaltation. —**up·lift·er,** *n.*

up·most, əp′mōst, *a.* Uppermost.

up·on, ə·pon′, ə·pən′, *prep.* On: used synonymously with *on* in all its meanings, primarily to achieve a desired rhythm or euphony.—*adv.* On.

up·per, əp′ər, *a.* Higher, as in place or position, or in a scale; superior, as in rank, dignity, or station.—*n.* The upper part of a shoe or boot, above the sole. *Informal.* A berth or bunk above another; a drug, esp. a pill, that stimulates.

up·per case, *n.* Capital-letter type used in printing. —**up·per-case,** əp·ər·kās′, *a.*

up·per-class, əp·ər·klas′, *a.* Pertaining to the highest social class.

up·per·class·man, əp·ər·klas′mən, *n. pl.,* **-men.** A junior or senior in high school or college.

up·per·cut, əp′ər·kət, *n.* An upward swinging blow, as in boxing.—*v.t., v.i.,* **-cut, -cut·ting.** To strike with, or use, an uppercut.

up·per hand, *n.* The superior position; the advantage.

up·per·most, əp′ər·mōst, *a.* Highest in place, position, power, or authority.—*adv.* In the topmost place, position, or power; first.

up·pish, əp′ish, *a. Informal.* Proud; arrogant; self-assertive; snobbish. —**up·pish·ly,** *adv.* —**up·pish·ness,** *n.*

up·pi·ty, əp′i·tē, *a. Informal.* Uppish.

up·raise, əp·rāz′, *v.t., Informal.,* **-raised, -rais·ing.** To raise or lift up.

up·rear, əp·rēr′, *v.t.* To rear up; to raise; to construct or erect.—*v.i.* To rise.

up·right, əp′rīt, əp·rīt′, *a.* Vertical; perpendicular; erect on one's feet; of inflexible honesty and moral rectitude.—*n.* Something standing erect as an upright piano; the state of being vertical or upright.—*adv.* —**up·right·ly,** *adv.* —**up·right·ness,** *n.*

up·right pi·an·o, *n.* A piano having a rectangular, upright body.

up·ris·ing, əp′rī·zing, əp·rī′zing, *n.* The act of rising up; a riot; a rebellion; a rise; an ascent.

up·roar, əp′rôr, *n.* A violent disturbance and noise; commotion; clamor; tumult; a state of such disturbance.

up·roar·i·ous, əp·rōr′ē·əs, əp·rôr′ē·əs, *a.* Making an uproar or tumult; noisy; very humorous or comical. —**up·roar·i·ous·ly,** *adv.* —**up·roar·i·ous·ness,** *n.*

up·root, əp·root′, əp·rût′, *v.t.* To tear up by the roots; to eradicate; to tear away, as from a homeland or tradition. —**up·root·er,** *n.*

up·set, əp·set′, *v.t.,* **-set, -set·ting.** To overturn, to perturb or mentally, physically, or emotionally disturb;

---

to disturb or derange completely; to put out of order, or to throw into disorder; to overthrow or defeat unexpectedly, as an opponent in sports, contests, or elections.—*v.i.* To become upset or overturned. —əp′set, *n.* An upsetting or the condition of being upset; an overturn; an overthrow, esp. the defeat of a contestant favored to win; a state of mental, physical, or emotional agitation or disturbance; a disturbance, derangement, or disorder.—əp•set′, *a.* Overturned; disturbed or disordered; mentally, physically, or emotionally agitated or disturbed.—**up•set•ter,** *n.*

up•shot, əp′shot, *n.* Conclusion.

up•side, əp′sīd, *n.* The upper side or part.

up•side down, *adv.* With the upper part undermost; in complete disorder.—**up•side-down,** əp′sīd•down′, *a.*

up•stage, əp′stāj′, *adv.* On, near, or toward the rear of a stage.—*a.* Of or relating to the rear section of a stage.—əp•stāj′, *v.t.,* **-staged, -stag•ing.** To steal the scene or the show from another actor or actress.

up•stairs, əp′stārz′, *a.* Pertaining or relating to an upper story or floor.—*adv.* In, toward, or on an upper story or floor.—*n. pl., usu. sing. in constr.* An upper story or floor.—**kick up•stairs,** to promote to a seemingly better position so as to get rid of.

up•stand•ing, əp•stan′ding, *a.* Standing erect; erect and tall; of a fine, vigorous type; upright or honorable. —**up•stand•ing•ness,** *n.*

up•start, əp′stärt, *n.* One that suddenly rises from a humble position to wealth, power, or consequence.

up•state, əp′stāt′, *a.* Of, denoting, or from the northern part of a state, esp. an area lying north of a major city.—*n.* The northern part of a state. —**up•stat•er,** *n.*

up•stream, əp′strēm′, *adv.* Toward the higher or upper part of a stream, or at its source; against the current.—*a.*

up•swing, əp′swing, *n.* An upward swing or swinging movement, as of a pendulum; an increase, rise, or improvement.

up•take, əp′tāk, *n.* The act of taking up; a lifting; perception or understanding: quick on the *uptake.*

up-to-date, əp′tə•dāt′, *a.* Extending to the present time, or including the latest facts; in accordance with the latest standards, ideas, or style; abreast of the times. —**up-to-date•ness,** *n.*

up•town, əp′town′, *adv.* To or in the upper part of a city or town.—*a.* Moving toward, situated in, or pertaining to the upper part of a city or town.—*n.* The uptown part of a city or town.

up•trend, əp′trend, *n.* An improvement or upward tendency, esp. in economic matters.

up•turn, əp•tərn′, *v.t.* To turn up or over; to turn or direct upward.—*v.i.* To turn upward.—əp′tərn, *n.* An increase or rise, esp. in prices or economic conditions.

up•ward, əp′wərd, *adv.* Toward a higher position or place; toward a higher amount, degree, or rank; with respect to the upper or higher part; toward the source or origin; more. Also **up•wards.**—*a.* Tending or directed upward. —**up•ward** or **up•wards of,** more or higher than.—**up•ward•ly,** *adv.*—**up•ward•ness,** *n.*

u•ra•ni•um, yû•rā′nē•əm, *n.* A heavy, radioactive metallic element, silvery in appearance, ductile and malleable.

U•ra•nus, yûr′ə•nəs, yû•rā′nəs, *n.* The seventh major planet from the sun which has an orbit between Saturn and Neptune and five satellites.

ur•ban, ər′bən, *a.* Belonging to or included in a town or city; characteristic of cities; citified.

ur•bane, ər•bān′, *a.* Possessing or characterized by worldliness, sophistication, and refinement; polished. —**ur•bane•ly,** *adv.*—**ur•bane•ness,** *n.*—**ur•ban•i•ty,** ər•ban′ə•tē, *n.*

ur•ban•ize, ər′bən•īz, *v.t.,* **-ized, -iz•ing.** To render urban, as in character: to *urbanize* a district or its people. —**ur•ban•i•za•tion,** ər•bən•ə•zā′shən, *n.*

ur•chin, ər′chin, *n.* A mischievous, roguish boy or child; a sea urchin.

u•re•a, yû•rē′ə, yûr′ē•ə, *n.* A colorless, soluble, crystalline substance present in the urine of mammals, and produced synthetically for medicine and industry. —**u•re•al, u•re•ic,** *a.*

u•re•mi•a, u•rae•mi•a, yû•rē′mē•ə, *n.* A condition resulting from the retention in the blood of waste products that should normally be eliminated in the urine. —**u•re•mic, u•rae•mic,** *a.*

u•re•ter, yû•rē′tər, *n.* The duct or tube that conveys the urine from the kidney to the bladder.

u•re•thra, yû•rē′thrə, *n. pl.,* **-thrae,** -thrē, **-thras.** A tube extending from the bladder that serves to convey and discharge urine and that, in the male, discharges semen also. —**u•re•thral,** *a.*

urge, ərj, *v.t.,* **urged, urg•ing.** To push or force along; impel with force or vigor; to drive with incitement to speed or effort; to impel, constrain or move to some action; stimulate; to endeavor to induce or persuade, as by entreaties or earnest recommendations; to press by persuasion or recommendation; advocate earnestly.—*v.i.* To exert a driving or impelling force; to press arguments or allegations; to make entreaties or earnest recommendations.—*n.* An involuntary, natural, or instinctive impulse. —**urg•er,** *n.* —**urg•ing•ly,** *adv.*

ur•gent, ər′jənt, *a.* Pressing; necessitating or calling for immediate action; earnestly insistent. —**ur•gen•cy,** *n. pl.,* **-cies.** —**ur•gent•ly,** *adv.*

u•ric, yûr′ik, *a.* Pertaining to or obtained from urine.

u•ri•nal, yûr′ə•nəl, *n.* A wall fixture with flushing facilities used for urination; a room or other structure equipped with one or more such fixtures; a vessel used as a receptacle for urine.

u•ri•nal•y•sis, yûr•ə•nal′ə•sis, *n. pl.,* **-ses,** -sēz. The chemical analysis of urine.

u•ri•nar•y, yûr′ə•ner•ē, *a.* Of or pertaining to urine or to the organs connected with its secretion and discharge.—*n. pl.,* **-ies.** Urinal.

u•ri•nate, yûr′ə•nāt, *v.i.,* **-nat•ed, -nat•ing.** To discharge or pass urine. —**u•ri•na•tion,** yûr•ə•nā′shən, *n.*

u•rine, yûr′ən, *n.* The liquid secretion of the kidneys, which in most mammals is conducted to the bladder by the ureters, and discharged through the urethra.

urn, ərn, *n.* A large, footed vase or vessel of various shapes, in which the ashes of the dead are preserved; a closed container with a spigot for brewing and serving hot beverages.

u•rol•o•gy, yû•rol′ə•jē, *n.* The field of medicine devoted to the study, diagnosis and treatment of any malfunction or disease of the urinary tract. —**u•ro•log•ic,** yûr•ə•loj′ik, **u•ro•log•i•cal,** *a.* —**u•rol•o•gist,** *n.*

us, əs, *pron.* The objective case of **we.**

us•a•ble, use•a•ble, ū′zə•bəl, *a.* In suitable condition or convenient for use. —**us•a•ble•ness, use•a•ble•ness,** *n.* —**us•a•bly, use•a•bly,** *adv.* —**us•a•bil•i•ty, use•a•bil•i•ty,** ū•zə•bil′ə•tē, *n.*

us•age, ūs′ij, ū′zij, *n.* Habitual or customary use or practice; a custom or practice; the customary or established mode of using the sounds, words, and phrases of a language; a way of using a person or thing.

use, ūz, *v.t.,* **used, us•ing.** To employ for some purpose; put into service; utilize; to avail oneself of; employ; to make a practice of; to act or behave toward; treat; to practice habitually or customarily; accustom; inure, now used only in the past participle; to consume; to partake of, as drugs, regularly or habitually.—*v.i.* Formerly did, or was accustomed (*to*): He *used* to go everyday.—ūs, *n.* The act of using or putting into service; the state of being used; an instance or way of using something; a purpose for which something is used; object; function; the power, right, or privilege of using something; service or advantage in or for being used; occasion or need; continual, habitual, or customary employment or practice; custom.—**have no use for.** *Informal.* To have no liking or tolerance for.—**make use of,** to employ; to use for one's own purposes or advantage.—**of no use,** of no service, advantage, or help.—**use up,** to consume entirely by using; to exhaust of strength or energy. —**us·er,** *n.*

used, ūzd, *a.* Utilized in or employed for some accomplishment or function; having undergone use; secondhand.

use·ful, ūs′fəl, *a.* Valuable for use or service; helpful or of practical use; utilitarian. —**use·ful·ly,** *adv.* —**use·ful·ness,** *n.*

use·less, ūs′lis, *a.* Of no use; not serving the purpose; of no practical good; unavailing or futile. —**use·less·ly,** *adv.* —**use·less·ness,** *n.*

ush·er, əsh′ər, *n.* One who guides people to seats, as in a theater; a male who attends a groom at the marriage ceremony.—*v.t.* To act as an usher toward; to escort; to introduce, as a forerunner or harbinger, usu. followed by *in* or *forth.*

u·su·al, ū′zhû·əl, *a.* In common or general use; commonly occurring; customary; ordinary. —**u·su·al·ly,** *adv.* —**u·su·al·ness,** *n.*

u·surp, ū·sərp′, ū·zərp′, *v.t.* To seize and hold possession of, as an office or rights, by force or without lawful right.—*v.i.* To commit an act of unlawful seizure and possession; to encroach. —**u·sur·pa·tion,** ū·zər·pā′shən, *n.* —**u·surp·er,** *n.*

u·su·ry, ū′zhə·rē, *n. pl.,* **-ries.** An excessive or inordinate interest for the use of money borrowed; the practice of taking exorbitant or unlawful interest. —**u·su·rer,** *n.* —**u·su·ri·ous,** ū·zhûr′ē·əs, *a.*

u·ten·sil, ū·ten′səl, *n.* An implement or receptacle for domestic use; an instrument or tool designed for a particular purpose.

u·ter·us, ū′tər·əs, *n. pl.,* **u·ter·i,** ū′tər·ī. The organ in female mammals which serves as a protective place for the ovum while it develops into an embryo or fetus; the womb.

u·til·i·tar·i·an, ū·til·ə·tār′ē·ən, *a.* Consisting in or pertaining to utility; holding forth utility as a standard, esp. as more important than luxury or beauty.

u·til·i·ty, ū·til′i·tē, *n. pl.,* **-ties.** The state or quality of being useful; usefulness; something of use; something providing a beneficial service, esp. to the public, as a telephone or electric power system; *pl.,* stock issued by a utility company, as a telephone company. —*a.* Intended for general rather than limited use; planned to be functional rather than esthetic.

u·ti·lize, ūt′ə·līz, *v.t.,* **-lized, -liz·ing.** To make useful; to adapt to some useful purpose; to turn to profitable account. —**u·ti·liz·a·ble,** *a.* —**u·ti·li·za·tion,** ū·təl·ə·zā′shən, *n.* —**u·ti·liz·er,** *n.*

ut·most, ət′mōst, *a.* Of or in the greatest or highest degree, number, or quantity; being at the farthest point or extremity.—*n.* The extreme extent or farthest possible point; the most of one's power or effort.

U·to·pi·a, ū·tō′pē·ə, *n.* An imaginary island, the setting for Sir Thomas More's *Utopia,* where the highest degree of social and political organization is experienced; (*l.c.*) an ideally perfect situation or place; an idealistic or impracticable plan for improving society. —**U·to·pi·an,** *a.*

ut·ter, ət′ər, *a.* Complete, total, or entire; absolute.

ut·ter, ət′ər, *v.t.* To give expression to with the voice; to pronounce. —**ut·ter·a·ble,** *a.* —**ut·ter·er,** *n.*

ut·ter·ance, ət′ər·əns, *n.* The act of uttering; expression with the voice; manner or power of speaking; something spoken, uttered, or written.

ut·ter·most, ət′ər·mōst, *a., n.* Utmost.

u·vu·la, ū′vyə·lə, *n. pl.,* **-las, -lae,** -lē. A small, conical, fleshy projection suspended from the soft palate over the root of the tongue. —**u·vu·lar,** *a.*

ux·o·ri·ous, ək·sōr′ē·əs, əg·zōr′ē·əs, *a.* Foolishly-fond of one's wife; doting on one's wife. —**ux·o·ri·ous·ly,** *adv.* —**ux·o·ri·ous·ness,** *n.*

V

V, v, vē, *n.* The twenty-second letter of the English alphabet; the Roman numeral representing 5.

va·can·cy, vā′kən·sē, *n. pl.,* **-cies.** The state or condition of being vacant; an unoccupied place or vacant quarters; an unoccupied post, position, or office; an empty space, gap, break, or other opening.

va·cant, vā′kənt, *a.* Having no contents; empty or void; devoid or destitute, usu. followed by *of*; unoccupied, empty, or unfilled; untenanted, as a house or apartment; not filled or occupied by an incumbent or official; free from work, business, or other employment; unoccupied with thought or reflection; characterized by, showing, or proceeding from lack of thought or intelligence. —**va·cant·ly,** *adv.* —**va·cant·ness,** *n.*

va·cate, vā′kāt, *v.t.,* **-cat·ed, -cat·ing.** To make vacant or unoccupied; to give up or quit, as a position; to relinquish the occupancy or possession of; to make void or annul.—*v.i.* To make a position or post vacant; to give up occupancy of a place or residence. *Informal.* To leave; to go away.

va·ca·tion, vā·kā′shən, və·kā′shən, *n.* Freedom or release from some regular activity; a period of suspension of study, work, or other regular duty; a recess, intermission, or holiday.—*v.i.* To take a vacation. —**va·ca·tion·less,** *a.*

vac·ci·nate, vak′sə·nāt, *v.t.,* **-nat·ed, -nat·ing.** To inoculate with the vaccine to produce immunity from smallpox; to inoculate with microorganisms of any other disease.—*v.i.* To practice or perform vaccination, as a preventive action. —**vac·ci·na·tion,** vak·sə·nā′shən, *n.*

vac·cine, vak·sēn′, vak′sēn, vak′sin, *n.* The virus of cowpox used in vaccination; modified microorganisms of any of various other diseases, used for preventive inoculation.—*a.* Pertaining to vaccinia or vaccination; of, pertaining to, or derived from cows.

vac·il·late, vas′ə·lāt, *v.i.,* **-lat·ed, -lat·ing.** To sway unsteadily; waver; fluctuate; to be irresolute, indecisive, or inconstant. —**vac·il·lat·ing,** *a.* —**vac·il·la·tion,** vas·ə·lā′shən, *n.* —**vac·il·la·tor,** *n.*

va·cu·i·ty, va·kū′ə·tē, *n. pl.,* **-ties.** The state of being empty or unfilled; emptiness; a space unfilled or unoccupied; a vacuum; absence of thought; an inane or stupid thing.

vac·u·ous, vak′yû·əs, *a.* Empty; stupid; unintelligent; inane; showing mental vacancy; purposeless; unoccupied or idle. —**vac·u·ous·ly,** *adv.* —**vac·u·ous·ness,** *n.*

vac·u·um, vak′yû·əm, vak′ûm, *n. pl.,* **-ums, -a.** Space devoid of molecules and atoms; an enclosed space from which matter, esp. air has been more or less removed; the condition of being isolated from outside environmental factors; a vacuum cleaner.—a. Pertaining to, using, or causing a vacuum; partly emptied of air; referring to a packaging process in which some of the air is removed from a container before it is sealed. —v.t. Informal. Clean with a vacuum cleaner.

vac·u·um bot·tle, n. A bottle or flask protected by a vacuum jacket which prevents the escape of heat from hot contents or the entrance of heat to cold contents. Also **ther·mos.**

vac·u·um clean·er, n. An apparatus for cleaning by suction.

vac·u·um-packed, vak′yû·əm·pakt′, vak′yûm· pakt′, a. Pertaining to a sealed container from which the air has been removed.

vac·u·um tube, n. A sealed, partially evacuated, glass envelope used to generate, amplify, rectify, or detect oscillations.

vag·a·bond, vag′ə·bond, a. Wandering from place to place without settled habitation; nomadic; good-for-nothing, worthless, or disreputable; of or pertaining to a vagabond or vagrant; aimlessly moving about without certain direction.—n. One who is without a fixed habitation and wanders from place to place; a tramp or vagrant; an idle, worthless fellow. —**vag·a· bond·age,** n. —**vag·a·bond·ish,** a. —**vag·a·bond· ism,** n.

va·gar·y, və·gār′ē, vā′gə·rē, n. pl., **-ies.** A wild, unpredictable, or odd notion or action; a whim; a whimsical idea. —**va·gar·i·ous,** və·gār′ē·əs, a. —**va·gar·i·ous·ly,** adv.

va·gi·na, və·jī′nə, n. pl., **-nas, -nae,** -nē. The canal in female mammals leading from the exterior genital orifice to the uterus. —**vag·i·nal,** vaj′ə·nəl, və·jī′ nəl, a.

va·grant, vā′grənt, n. One without a settled home or habitation; an idle wanderer or stroller.—a. Wandering without any settled habitation; pertaining to one who wanders; moving at random. —**va·gran·cy,** n. pl., **-cies.** —**va·grant·ly,** adv.

vague, vāg, a. Unclear as regards meaning, scope, or the like; indefinite; hazy; uncertain; doubtful. —**vague·ly,** adv. —**vague·ness,** n.

vain, vān, a. Displaying excessive admiration for one's own personal appearance, possessions, qualities, or attainments; unduly proud or conceited; having no real value, worth, or importance; ineffectual, fruitless, or unsuccessful.—**in vain,** without success or effect; in a light, irreverent, or profane way. —**vain·ly,** adv. —**vain·ness,** n.

vain·glo·ry, vān·glôr′ē, vān·glôr′ē, n. pl., **-ries.** Glory, pride, or boastfulness that unduly exalts oneself or one's own performances; vain or empty pomp or show. —**vain·glo·ri·ous,** a. —**vain·glo·ri·ous·ly,** adv. —**vain·glo·ri·ous·ness,** n.

val·ance, val′əns, vā′ləns, n. A short, decorative drapery covering curtain fixtures along the top of a window. —**val·anced,** a.

vale, vāl, n. A valley; earthly life and its afflictions.

val·e·dic·tion, val·ə·dik′shən, n. A bidding farewell.

val·e·dic·to·ri·an, val·ə·dik·tôr′ē·ən, val·ə·dik· tôr′ē·ən, n. A student who delivers the valedictory or farewell oration at a graduating or commencement exercise.

val·e·dic·to·ry, val·ə·dik′tə·rē, a. Bidding farewell; pertaining to an occasion of leave-taking.—n. pl., **-ries.** A farewell or valedictory address or oration.

va·lence, vā′ləns, n. The quality which determines the number of atoms or radicals with which any single atom or radical will unite chemically. Also **va·len·cy.**

val·en·tine, val′ən·tīn, n. A printed card or gift sent by one person to another on St. Valentine's Day; a sweetheart chosen on St. Valentine's Day.

val·et, val′it, val′ā, n. A manservant who is his master's personal attendant; one employed, as by a hotel,

to perform various personal services for the guests.

val·iant, val′yənt, a. Brave; courageous; heroic. —**val·iant·ly,** adv. —**val·iant·ness,** n.

val·id, val′id, a. Sufficiently supported by actual fact; well grounded, sound, or just; having sufficient legal strength or force; good or sufficient in point of law. —**val·id·ly,** adv. —**val·id·ness,** n.

val·i·date, val′ə·dāt, v.t., **-dat·ed, -dat·ing.** To make valid; to confirm; to give legal force to. —**val·i·da· tion,** val·ə·dā′shən, n.

va·lid·i·ty, və·lid′ə·tē, n. pl., **-ties.** The state or quality of being valid; legal strength or force; soundness.

va·lise, və·lēs′, n. A small case for holding a traveler's clothes and related articles.

val·ley, val′ē, n. pl., **-leys.** Any hollow or surface depression of the earth bounded by hills or mountains; the great extent of land drained by a river.

val·or, val′ər, n. That quality which enables a man to encounter danger with firmness; personal bravery; intrepidity; prowess. —**val·or·ous,** a. —**val·or·ous· ly,** adv. —**val·or·ous·ness,** n.

val·u·a·ble, val′yû·ə·bəl, val′yə·bəl, a. Having great value or monetary worth; expensive; having estimable or worthy qualities; of considerable use, service, or importance.—n. Usu. pl. Valuable articles. —**val·u·a· ble·ness,** n. —**val·u·a·bly,** adv.

val·u·a·tion, val·yû·ā′shən, n. The act of estimating or fixing the value of a thing; a value estimated or fixed; the estimation or appreciation of the worth or qualities of a person or thing. —**val·u·a·tion·al,** a.

val·ue, val′ū, n. The worth, merit, usefulness, or importance of a thing; equivalent worth or adequate return; estimated or assigned worth; valuation; force; import, or significance; esteem or regard; the relative effect of color, esp. with reference to the degree of lightness and darkness; pl., the qualities, customs, standards, and principles of a people regarded as desirable.—v.t., **-ued, -u·ing.** To estimate the value of; appraise; to place a certain value or price on; to regard or esteem highly. —**val·ue·less,** a. —**val·ue· less·ness,** n. —**val·u·er,** n.

val·ued, val′ūd, a. Highly regarded or esteemed; having a specified value.

valve, valv, n. Any apparatus or device used to regulate the admission or escape of water, gas, or steam; a movable lid or partition formed in such an apparatus as to open a passage in one direction and to close it in the other; a structure within a hollow organ that opens to allow the passage of a fluid in one direction or shuts to prevent its return; an apparatus in some brass instruments that changes the length of the air column and alters the pitch; one of the separable portions of the shell of a mollusk. —**valve·less,** a. —**val·vu·lar,** a.

va·moose, va·moos′, v.i., v.t., **-moosed, -moos·ing.** Informal. To depart hastily; to quit.

vamp, vamp, n. The section of a boot or shoe that overlays the instep and sometimes the toes. Mus. An improvised accompaniment.—v.t. To supply with a vamp. Mus. To improvise.—v.i. To improvise tunes, accompaniments, and the like. —**vamp·er,** n.

vamp, vamp, n. Informal. A seductive woman who beguiles and exploits men.—v.t. To beguile and seduce.—v.i. To act the part of a vamp.

vam·pire, vam′pīr, n. A reanimated corpse, supposed to suck the blood of sleeping persons at night; one who preys ruthlessly on others; any of various South and Central American bats which suck blood. —**vam· pir·ic,** vam·pēr′ik, a. —**vam·pir·ism,** n.

van, van, n. Vanguard.

van, van, n. A large, covered vehicle, usu. a truck or wagon.

va·na·di·um, və·nā′dē·əm, n. A silvery white hard metallic element, used in certain steels to add toughness and tensile strength, and to form many compounds used in chemical manufacturing.

Van Al·len belt, van al′ən n. Either of two high-intensity radiation zones surrounding the earth. Also **Van Al·len ra·di·a·tion belt.**

van·dal, van′dəl, *n.* One who willfully or ignorantly damages or destroys property.—*a.* Willfully destructive.

van·dal·ism, van′də·liz·əm, *n.* Willful or ignorant destruction of property. —**van·dal·ize,**van′də·liz, *v.t.,* **-ized, -iz·ing.**

Van·dyke beard, van dīk′, *n.* A small, pointed beard.

vane, vān, *n.* A contrivance placed on a spindle at the top of a spire for the purpose of showing the direction of the wind; any of several bladelike surfaces radially connected to a central shaft moved by air or by a fluid. —**vaned,** *a.* —**vane·less,** *a.*

van·guard, van′gärd, *n.* The troops who march in the van or front division of an army; the advance guard; the group at the forefront of any field, movement, or activity.

va·nil·la, və·nil′ə, *n.* A climbing orchid native to tropical regions, and having a podlike fruit which yields a fragrant extract used in flavoring foods and making medicines and perfumes; the bean or podlike fruit of this plant: also **va·nil·la bean;** the flavorful extract made from the podlike fruit.

van·ish, van′ish, *v.i.* To disappear; to pass from a visible to an invisible state; to pass beyond the limit of vision; to be no more. —**van·ish·er,** *n.*

van·i·ty, van′ə·tē, *n. pl.,* **-ties.** The quality or condition of being vain; excessive pride in one's personal appearance, possessions, qualities, or attainments; lack of worth, usefulness, or true value; something that is worthless, useless, or without value; a small piece of luggage, or cosmetic case; a dressing table.

van·quish, vang′kwish, van′kwish, *v.t.* To conquer, overcome, or subdue in battle; to defeat in any contest or struggle. —**van·quish·a·ble,** *a.* —**van·quish·er,** *n.*

van·tage, van′tij, *n.* A position or condition affording superiority; an opportunity likely to give superiority; an advantage.

vap·id, vap′id, *a.* Having lost life, spirit, or flavor; insipid or flat; dull, unanimated, or spiritless. —**va·pid·i·ty,** və·pid′ə·tē, **vap·id·ness,** *n.* —**vap·id·ly,** *adv.*

va·por, vā′pər, *n.* Any visible, diffused substance or hazy matter floating in the atmosphere; an exhalation or fume, as of steam or a gas; a substance which has been vaporized for use in industry, or as an inhalant in medicine; the gaseous form which any solid or liquid assumes when heated.—*v.t.* To vaporize.—*v.i.* To emit vapor; to brag or boast. —**va·por·er,** *n.* —**va·por·ish,** *a.* —**va·por·ish·ness,** *n.*

va·por·ize, vā′pə·rīz, *v.t.,* **-ized, -iz·ing.** To convert into vapor; to cause to evaporate.—*v.i.* To be changed into vapor. —**va·por·i·za·tion,** vā·pər·ə·zā′shən, *n.* —**va·por·iz·er,** *n.*

va·por·ous, vā′pər·əs, *a.* Being in the form of or having the characteristics of vapor; full of vapors; ethereal; fanciful; cloudlike; evanescent; worthless. —**va·por·ous·ly,** *adv.*

va·por trail, *n.* Condensation trail.

va·que·ro, vä·kār′ō, *n. pl.,* **-ros.** A cattle herdsman or a cowboy in the Southwest.

var·i·a·ble, vār′ē·ə·bəl, *a.* Apt or liable to vary or change; changeable; inconstant or fickle, as a person; capable of being varied or changed; alterable; diverse.—*n.* Something variable. *Math.* A quantity or symbol which has no fixed value and is considered with reference to its different possible values. —**var·i·a·bil·i·ty,** ver·ē·ə·bil′ə·tē, **var·i·a·ble·ness,** *n.* —**var·i·a·bly,** *adv.*

var·i·ance, vār′ē·əns, *n.* The state or fact of varying; difference or discrepancy; disagreement, discord, or dissension.—**at var·i·ance,** not in agreement or harmony.

var·i·ant, vār′ē·ənt, *a.* Exhibiting or characterized by variation; varying; tending to change or alter; variable; being an altered or different form of something.—*n.* A variant form, esp. in the pronunciation or spelling of a word.

var·i·a·tion, vār′ē·ā′shən, *n.* The act, process, or result of varying in condition, character, or degree; diversity, alteration, or modification; amount or rate of change; deviation or divergence; a different form of something; the repetition of a melody or theme with changes or elaborations, usu. as one of a series of such changes. —**var·i·a·tion·al,** *a.* —**var·i·a·tion·al·ly,** *adv.*

var·i·col·ored, vār′i·kəl·ərd, *a.* Having various colors; variegated; motley.

var·i·cose, var′ə·kōs, vār′ə·kōs, *a.* Abnormally dilated, as a vein; pertaining to or affected with varicose veins.

var·ied, vār′ēd, *a.* Diversified or characterized by variety: a *varied* assortment; changed or altered: a *varied* form of a word. —**var·ied·ness,** *n.*

var·i·e·gate, vār′ē·ə·gāt, *v.t.,* **-gat·ed, -gat·ing.** To render varied in appearance, esp. by differences in color or texture; to give variety to. —**var·i·e·gat·ed,** *a.* —**var·i·e·ga·tion,** ver·ē·ə·gā′shən, *n.* —**var·i·e·ga·tor,** *n.*

va·ri·e·tal, və·rī′ə·təl, *a.* Of, pertaining to, or characteristic of a variety. —**va·ri·e·tal·ly,** *adv.*

va·ri·e·ty, və·rī′ə·tē, *n. pl.,* **-ties.** The state or character of being various or varied; diversity; difference or discrepancy; a number of things of different kinds; a varied assortment of something; a different form, condition, or phase of something; a kind or sort; entertainment of a mixed character, consisting of a number of individual performances, as of singing or dancing: also **va·ri·e·ty show.**

var·i·ous, vār′ē·əs, *a.* Differing one from another or being of different kinds; exhibiting or marked by variety or diversity; separate or individual: approval by the *various* offices; several or many. —**var·i·ous·ness,** *n.*

var·mint, var·ment, vär′mənt, *n. Informal.* Vermin; an obnoxious animal or person.

var·nish, vär′nish, *n.* A preparation consisting of resinous matter, dissolved in oil, alcohol, or other volatile liquid, which when applied to the surface of wood or metal dries and leaves a hard, glossy, usu. transparent coating; any of various other preparations similarly used; a coating of varnish; a gloss; superficial embellishment or external show, esp. to cover a defect.—*v.t.* To lay varnish on; to invest with a glossy appearance; to adorn; to cover with a deceptive appearance. —**var·nish·er,** *n.*

var·si·ty, vär′sə·tē, *n. pl.,* **-ties.** The principal or first team, esp. in athletics, representing a college, university, school, or the like, in competition.

var·y, vār′ē, *v.t.,* **-ied, -y·ing.** To alter in form, appearance, substance, or position; to make different by a partial change; to diversify.—*v.i.* To alter or be altered in any manner; to deviate. —**var·i·er,** *n.* —**var·y·ing·ly,** *adv.*

vas·cu·lar, vas′kyə·lər, *a.* Pertaining to or containing the system of vessels or ducts which convey fluid, as blood in animals and water and food materials in plants. —**vas·cu·lar·i·ty,** vas·kyə·lar′ə·tē, *n.*

vase, vās, vāz, väz, *n.* A hollow vessel, generally high in proportion to its horizontal diameter, used as a holder for flowers or as a decoration.

vas·ec·to·my, va·sek′tə·mē, *n. pl.,* **-mies.** Excision of the duct that transfers sperm from the testis for ejaculation.

Vas·e·line, vas′ə·lēn, *n. Trademark.* A translucent, yellow or whitish, semisolid petroleum product, used in various preparations for medicinal and other pur-

---

a- hat, fāte, fâre, fäther; **e-** met, mē; **i-** pin, pine; **o-** not, nōte, ôrb, moove (move), boy, pownd; **u-** cūbe, bŭll, tûk (took); **ch-** chin; **th-** thick, ŧhen; **zh-** vizhon (vision); **ə-** əgo, takən, pencəl, lemən, bərd (bird).

poses. Also **vas•e•line.**

vas•o•mo•tor, vas•ō•mō′tər, *a.* Applied to the system of nerves distributed over the muscular coats of the blood vessels, which regulates their size.

vas•sal, vas′əl, *n.* In the feudal system, a person holding lands under the obligation to render military service or its equivalent to his superior; a subject, follower, or retainer; a servant or serf. **—vas•sal•age,** *n.*

vast, vast, *a.* Of great extent; boundless; huge in bulk and size; immense. **—vast•ness,** *n.*

vat, vat, *n.* A large vessel for holding liquids, as a tank, tub, or cistern.—*v.t.,* **vat•ted, vat•ting.** To put in a vat.

Vat•i•can, vat′i•kən, *a.* Of or pertaining to the palace of the popes of papal government.—*n.* The palace of the popes, situated on the Vatican Hill in Rome; papal power.

vaude•ville, vōd′vil, vô′də•vil, *n.* A stage entertainment consisting of a number of individual acts, as singing, dancing, comic sketches, and performances by animals, most popular in the U.S. from about 1890 to about 1930; sometimes, a light play or sketch with musical interludes.

vault, vôlt, *v.i.* To leap or spring, as over something; to leap with the aid of the hands supported on something, as a brace or pole.—*v.t.* To leap over, or clear by jumping, as an obstacle.—*n.* The act or an act of bounding with the aid of the hands supported or something. **—vault•er,** *n.*

vault, vôlt, *n.* An arched structure, commonly made of stones or bricks, usu. forming a ceiling or roof; something resembling an arched roof: the *vault* of heaven; an arched space, chamber, or passage, esp. one underground; any room specially constructed for the safekeeping of things.—*v.t.* To construct or cover with a vault; to arch. **—vault•ed,** *a.*

vault•ing, vôl′ting, *n.* Vaulted work, or vaults collectively.

vault•ing, vôl′ting, *a.* That vaults; of or used in vaulting, as in gymnastics; reaching highly; overreaching; overly aggressive; presumptuous.

vaunt, vônt, vänt, *v.i.* To boast; to brag; to glory.—*v.t.* To boast of.—*n.* A boastful display; a brag. **—vaunt•er,** *n.* **—vaunt•ing•ly,** *adv.*

veal, vēl, *n.* The flesh of the calf as used for food.

vec•tor, vek′tər, *n.* An entity which has direction as well as magnitude, such as a force or velocity; a line segment that represents an entity. **—vec•to•ri•al,** vek•tōr′ē•əl, vek•tôr′ē•əl, *a.*

veep, vēp, *n. Informal.* Any vice-president.

veer, vēr, *v.i.* To shift or change direction, as the wind; to change the direction of its course by turning, as a ship; to turn around, vary, be otherwise minded: said in regard to persons, feelings, or intentions.—*v.t.* To direct, as a ship, as into a different course.—*n.* A change in direction. **—veer•ing•ly,** *adv.*

veg•e•ta•ble, vej′tə•bəl, vej′ə•tə•bəl, *n.* An herb whose fruit, stems, leaves, roots, or other parts are used for food, as the beet, potato, and onion; the edible part of such a plant; loosely, any member of the plant kingdom; a stupid or passive person.—*a.* Of, consisting of, or made from vegetables: a *vegetable* diet; pertaining to or characteristic of plants: *vegetable* growth; of the nature of a plant: a *vegetable* organism; passive or dull. **—veg•e•ta•bly,** *adv.*

veg•e•ta•ble oil, *n.* An oil derived from fruit or plant seeds, having various uses in medicine, cooking, and as a lubricant.

veg•e•tal, vej′ə•təl, *a.* Having the characteristics or nature of a plant or vegetable.

veg•e•tar•i•an, vej•ə•tãr′ē•ən, *n.* One who, for moral or nutritional reasons, abstains from eating meat, fowl, or fish, or in some instances any animal product, and instead lives solely on vegetables, grain, fruit, and nuts.—*a.* Of, characteristic of, or relating to the

veg•e•tar•i•an•ism, vej•ə•tãr′ē•ən•iz•əm, *n.* The

theory, practices, and beliefs of a vegetarian.

veg•e•tate, vej′ə•tāt, *v.i.,* **-tat•ed, -tat•ing.** To grow in the manner of plants; to live in an inactive, passive, or unthinking way.

veg•e•ta•tion, vej•ə•tā′shən, *n.* The act or process of vegetating; plant life collectively, esp. the plant life of an area or region: the *vegetation* of the mountaintops; an inactive, passive, or unthinking existence. **—veg•e•ta•tion•al,** *a.* **—veg•e•ta•tion•less,** *a.*

veg•e•ta•tive, vej′ə•tā•tiv, *a.* Growing or developing as or like plants; pertaining to vegetation; inactive, or unthinking: a *vegetative* way of life.

ve•he•ment, vē′ə•mənt, *a.* Characterized by impetuosity of feeling; fervent or passionate; energetic; violent. **—ve•he•mence, ve•he•men•cy,** *n.*

ve•hi•cle, vē′ə•kəl, *n.* Any means of transporting something from one place to another, as on wheels, tracks, or runners; a conveyance; an instrument of transmission or communication: Language is a *vehicle* for conveying ideas. **—ve•hic•u•lar,** vē•hik′yə•lər, *a.*

veil, vāl, *n.* A piece of light and usu. transparent material worn over the head to protect, conceal, or decorate the face; a piece of material worn so as to fall over the head and shoulders on each side of the face, as the outer head part of the headdress of a nun; something that covers or conceals: a *veil* of smoke.—*v.t.* To cover or conceal with or as with a veil; to hide the real nature of.—*v.i.* To wear a veil.—**take the veil,** to become a nun. **—veiled,** *a.*

veil•ing, vā′ling, *n.* The act of covering or concealing with a veil; a veil.

vein, vān, *n.* One of the system of branching vessels or tubes conveying blood from various parts of the body to the heart; loosely, any blood vessel; one of the strands or bundles of vascular tissue forming the principal framework of a leaf; a body of ore or coal with definite boundaries: a *vein* of gold; a lode; a streak or marking, as of a different shade or color, running through marble, wood, or other natural material; a particular state of mind, humor, or mood.—*v.t.* To furnish with veins; to mark with lines or streaks suggesting veins. **—vein•y,** *a.,* **-i•er, -i•est.**

veined, vānd, *a.* Having or showing veins; streaked.

vein•ing, vā′ning, *n.* An arrangement of veins or veinlike markings.

veld, veldt, velt, felt, *n.* The open country, bearing grass, bushes, or shrubs, or thinly forested, characteristic of southern Africa.

vel•lum, vel′əm, *n.* A fine parchment, usu. of treated kidskin or calfskin, used for writing, printing, painting, and binding; a manuscript on such parchment; a kind of paper resembling such parchment.—*a.*

ve•loc•i•ty, və•los′i•tē, *n. pl.,* **-ties.** Rapidity of motion or operation; quickness; rate of motion; the rate of motion in which direction as well as speed is considered.

vel•ours, vel•our, və•lūr′, *n. pl.,* **ve•lours,** və•lūrz′. A velvety fabric with a nap or pile.

ve•lum, vē′ləm, *n. pl.,* **ve•la,** vē′lə. Any of various veillike membranous coverings or partitions; the soft palate.

vel•vet, vel′vit, *n.* A fabric of silk, cotton, nylon, or rayon, having a thick, soft pile formed of warp thread loops either cut at the outer end or left uncut, and a plain backing; something likened to the fabric velvet, as in softness.—*a.* Made of or covered with velvet: also **vel•vet•ed.** Resembling velvet: also **vel•vet•like.**

vel•vet•een, vel•və•tēn′, *n.* A cloth made of cotton having a short pile in imitation of velvet.—*a.* Made or fashioned of velveteen: a *velveteen* dress.

vel•vet•y, vel′vi•tē, *a.,* **-i•er, -i•est.** Resembling velvet; smooth, soft, or delicate in texture; smooth and mellow tasting, usu. said of liquors: *velvety* bourbon.

ve•nal, vēn′əl, *a.* Purchasable like merchandise, as things not properly bought and sold: *venal* votes; ready to sell one's services or influence basely or unscrupulously; accessible to bribery. **—ve·nal·i·ty,** vi·nal′ə·tē, *n.* **—ve·nal·ly,** *adv.*

ve·na·tion, vē·nā′shən, *n.* The manner in which veins are arranged, as in leaves or insect wings. **—ve·na·tion·al,** *a.*

vend, vend, *v.t.* To sell, often by peddling; to express publicly, as ideas or opinions.—*v.i.* To be bought or sold.

vend·er, vend·or, ven′dər, *n.* One who or that which vends or sells; a seller; any vending machine.

ven·det·ta, ven·det′ə, *n.* Any prolonged and vehement dispute, rivalry, or feud; a blood feud.

vend·i·ble, ven′də·bəl, *a.* Salable; marketable.—*n. Usu. pl.* A vendible article. **—vend·i·bil·i·ty,** ven·də·bil′ə·tē, *n.*

vend·ing ma·chine, *n.* A coin-operated, mechanical device which sells gum, candy, or other small articles.

ve·neer, və·nēr′, *n.* A thin piece of wood or other substance laid upon a less valuable surface; a superficial appearance or show: to hide one's shortcomings under a *veneer* of self-confidence: a facing of some substance, as stone or brick, superimposed on a less durable surface, as wood.—*v.t.* To overlay or face, as a surface, with veneer; to cover, as something unattractive or displeasing, with a more desirable surface. **—ve·neer·er,** *n.* **—ve·neer·ing,** *n.*

ven·er·a·ble, ven′ər·ə·bəl, *a.* Worthy of veneration or reverence, because of high character or office; commanding respect by reason of age and dignity of appearance; hallowed by religious, historic, or other lofty associations; old or ancient: used ironically. **—ven·er·a·bil·i·ty,** ven·ər·ə·bil′ə·tē, **ven·er·a·ble·ness,** *n.* **—ven·er·a·bly,** *adv.*

ven·er·ate, ven′ə·rāt, *v.t.* To regard with respect and reverence; to revere. **—ven·er·a·tion,** ven·ər·ā′shən, *n.* **—ven·er·a·tor,** *n.*

ve·ne·re·al, və·nēr′ē·əl, *a.* Arising from or connected with sexual intercourse with an infected person: *venereal* diseases; pertaining to diseases so arising; adapted to the cure of such diseases: a *venereal* remedy; infected with or suffering from venereal disease.

Ve·ne·tian blind, və·nē′shən, *n.* A window blind made of transverse slips of wood, metal, or the like, which overlap each other when closed, and show open spaces for the admission of light when open.

venge·ance, ven′jəns, *n.* The avenging of a wrong or injury; retribution; revenge.**—with a venge·ance,** with extreme force or violence.

venge·ful, venj′fəl, *a.* Showing vindictiveness; revengeful. **—venge·ful·ness,** *n.*

ve·ni·al, vē′nē·əl, vēn′yəl, *a.* Excusable; trivial. **—ve·ni·al·i·ty,** vē·nē·al′ə·tē, **ve·ni·al·ness,** *n.* **—ve·ni·al·ly,** *adv.*

ven·i·son, ven′ə·sən, ven′ə·zən, *n.* Deer flesh as it is used as human food.

ven·om, ven′əm, *n.* The poisonous fluid secreted by certain animals and introduced into the bodies of other animals by biting, as in the case of snakes, and stinging, as in the case of wasps, or bees; spite; malice.

ven·om·ous, ven′ə·məs, *a.* Provided with venom-producing glands: a *venomous* insect; poisonous; full of venom; malignant, malicious, or spiteful: a *venomous* denunciation. **—ven·om·ous·ness,** *n.*

ve·nous, vē′nəs, *a.* Of, pertaining to, or full of veins; pertaining to the blood that is traveling back to the heart through veins. **—ve·nous·ly,** *adv.* **—ve·nous·ness,** *n.*

vent, vent, *n.* A small outlet or opening for the release of something; exhaust passage, or pipe; a slit, as in a back seam in a piece of clothing; a means of expression: giving *vent* to anger.—*v.t.,* **vent·ed, vent·ing.** To let out; to release, as a repressed feeling; to pour forth.

ven·ti·late, ven′tə·lāt, *v.t.,* **-lat·ed, -lat·ing.** To supply with fresh air for and remove air from, as an office building; to combine with oxygen, as blood in the lungs in breathing; to expose to the free passage of air or wind; to open up for mutual or public consideration; to let be freely discussed; to provide with a small opening or vent, as for the removal of noxious gases. **—ven·ti·la·tion,** ven·tə·lā′shən, *n.* **—ven·ti·la·tor,** *n.*

ven·tral, ven′trəl, *a.* Belonging or pertaining to the belly or the abdomen, or to the surface of the body opposite to the dorsal or back side. **—ven·tral·ly,** *adv.*

ven·tri·cle, ven′trə·kəl, *n.* Any of various hollow organs or parts in an animal body, esp. one of the two cavities of the heart which receive the blood from the auricles and propel it into the arteries.

ven·tril·o·quism, ven·tril′ə·kwiz·əm, *n.* The act, art, or practice of speaking or uttering sounds with barely visible lip movement. Also **ven·tril·o·quy,** ven·tril′ə·kwē. **—ven·tri·lo·qui·al,** ven·trə·lō′kwē·əl, *a.*

ven·tril·o·quist, ven·tril′ə·kwist, *n.* One who practices or is skilled in ventriloquism.

ven·tril·o·quize, ven·tril′ə·kwiz, *v.i., v.t.,* **-quized, -quiz·ing.** To speak as a ventriloquist.

ven·ture, ven′chər, *n.* An undertaking of chance, danger, or hazard, esp. a commercial speculation; a risk; that which is risked or exposed to hazard, as funds or property.—*v.t.* To expose to hazard; to risk; to undertake or run the risk and danger of; to brave; to offer or express, risking denial, objection, or censure. —*v.i.* To dare; to undertake or run a risk.

ven·ture·some, ven′chər·səm, *a.* Inclined to undertake or court hazard or risk; daring. **—ven·ture·some·ness,** *n.*

ven·tur·ous, ven′chər·əs, *a.* Daring; bold; risky; dangerous. **—ven·tur·ous·ness,** *n.*

Ve·nus, vē′nəs, *n.* The second planet from the sun and sixth largest in the solar system; in Roman mythology, the goddess of love and beauty; a beautiful woman.

ve·ra·cious, və·rā′shəs, *a.* Habitually disposed to speak truth; true; exact; accurate. **—ve·ra·cious·ness,** *n.*

ve·rac·i·ty, və·ras′ə·tē, *n. pl.,* **-ties.** Habitual regard to or observance of truth; truthfulness; exactness or precision; a truth.

ve·ran·da, ve·ran·dah, və·ran′də, *n.* A kind of open portico, usu. having a roof, and attached to the outside of a building; a porch.

verb, vərb, *n.* That part of speech whose essential function is to express existence, action, or occurrence; a particular word or phrase that functions as a verb, as *be, eat up, perceive.*

ver·bal, vər′bəl, *a.* Of, pertaining to, or consisting of words; pertaining to or concerned with words only, rather than ideas, facts, or realities; expressed in spoken words; oral: a *verbal* agreement; corresponding word for word; verbatim: a *verbal* translation; of, pertaining to, or derived from a verb: a *verbal* noun or *verbal* auxiliary.—*n.* A part of speech derived from a verb, that functions as a noun, as a gerund or infinitive, or as an adjective, as a present or past participle, but retains some of its original characteristics. **—ver·bal·ly,** *adv.*

ver·bal·ize, vər′bə·līz, *v.t.,* **-ized, -iz·ing.** To express in spoken or written language; to articulate.—*v.i.* To use words in excess; to be verbose; to express something in spoken or written language. **—ver·bal·i·za·tion,** vər·bəl·ə·zā′shən, *n.* **—ver·bal·iz·er,** *n.*

ver·ba·tim, vər·bā′tim, *adv., a.* Word for word; in the same words.

ver·bi·age, vər'bē·ij, *n.* The use of excessive or unnecessary words; verbosity.

ver·bose, vər·bōs', *a.* Abounding in words; using or containing more words than are necessary; wordy. —**ver·bose·ness, ver·bos·i·ty,** vər·bos'ə·tē, *n.*

ver·bo·ten, fər·bō'tən, *a.* Forbidden.

ver·dant, vər'dant, *a.* Green with foliage; covered with growing plants or grass; green in color or hue. —**ver·dan·cy,** *n.*

ver·dict, vər'dikt, *n.* The answer of a jury given to the court concerning any matter committed to their examination and judgment; a decision, judgment, or opinion.

ver·di·gris, vər'də·grēs, vər'də·gris, *n.* A green or bluish-green poisonous compound, used as a pigment, drug, or the like; a green or bluish coating formed on copper, brass, or bronze surfaces exposed to the air for a long time.

ver·dure, vər'jər, *n.* Greenness or freshness of vegetation; green plants or foliage; a flourishing condition; vigor. —**ver·dured,** *a.* —**ver·dur·ous,** *a.*

verge, vərj, *n.* The edge, rim, or margin of something; the limit or point beyond which something begins or occurs: on the *verge* of total collapse.—*v.i.,* **verged, verg·ing.** To be on the verge or border; to border on or approach.

verge, vərj, *v.i.,* **verged, verg·ing.** To incline, slope, turn, or extend in course or direction; to tend, used with *to* or *toward.*

ver·i·fi·ca·tion, ver·ə·fə·kā'shən, *n.* The act of verifying or the state of being verified; a formal assertion of the truth of something; ascertainment of correctness, as by examination or comparison.

ver·i·fy, vār'ə·fī, *v.t.,* **-fied, -fy·ing.** To prove to be true; to confirm; to examine or test the correctness or authenticity of. —**ver·i·fi·a·bil·i·ty,** vər·ə·fī·ə·bil'ə·tē, **ver·i·fi·a·ble·ness,** *n.* —**ver·i·fi·a·ble,** *a.* —**ver·i·fi·er,** *n.*

ver·i·si·mil·i·tude, ver·ə·sə·mil'ə·tood, ver·ə·sə·mil'ə·tūd, *n.* The appearance of truth; anything having only the semblance of truth; probability; likelihood.

ver·i·ta·ble, vār'ə·tə·bəl, *a.* True; agreeable to truth or fact; real; actual. —**ver·i·ta·ble·ness,** *n.* —**ver·i·ta·bly,** *adv.*

ver·i·ty, vār'ə·tē, *n. pl.,* **-ties.** The quality of being true or real; reality; truth.

ver·meil, vər'mil, *n.* A bright red, as the color of vermilion; gilded metal, as silver, copper, or bronze. —*a.*

ver·mic·u·lar, vər·mik'yə·lər, *a.* Pertaining to worms; having wormlike, wavy tracks.

ver·mic·u·late, vər·mik'yə·lit, *a.* Wormlike in shape, markings, movement, or appearance; squirming; winding; worm-eaten. Also **ver·mic·u·lat·ed,** vər·mik'yə·lā·tid.

ver·mi·fuge, vər'mə·fūj, *n.* A medicine or agent that expels parasitic intestinal worms.

ver·mil·ion, ver·mil·lion, vər·mil'yən, *n.* The bright red pigment composed of mercuric sulfide; such a color.—*a.* Of the bright red color of vermilion.

ver·min, vər'mən, *n. pl.,* **ver·min.** Any of certain undesirable, noxious small mammals, as rats or mice, and various parasitic insects, which are destructive to humans and difficult to control; any obnoxious human being. —**ver·min·ous,** *a.*

ver·mouth, ver·muth, vər·mooth', *n.* A white wine spiced with aromatic herbs and used as an ingredient in cocktails and as an aperitif.

ver·nac·u·lar, vər·nak'yə·lər, *a.* Native or originating in the place of its occurrence or use, as language or words, as opposed to *literary* or *learned* language; expressed or written in the native language of a place, as literary works; using such a language, as a speaker or a writer; pertaining to such a language; native or peculiar to a place or to fashionable taste, as a style of architecture.—*n.* The native speech or language of a place; the common language people use every day; the language or phraseology peculiar to a class or profession.

ver·nac·u·lar·ism, vər·nak'yə·lər·iz·əm, *n.* A vernacular word or expression; the use of the vernacular.

ver·nal, vər'nəl, *a.* Belonging to spring; suggestive of spring: *vernal* temperatures; belonging to youth. —**ver·nal·ly,** *adv.*

ver·sa·tile, vər'sə·təl, *a.* Capable of or adapted for turning with ease from one to another of various tasks or subjects; variable or changeable, esp. in feeling, purpose, or policy; capable of being used in many ways. —**ver·sa·tile·ness, ver·sa·til·i·ty,** vər·sə·til'ə·tē, *n.*

verse, vərs, *n.* A stanza or associated group of metrical lines; a succession of metrical feet written or printed as one line; a particular type of metrical composition: iambic *verse,* twentieth-century *verse;* a piece of poetry; poem.

versed, vərst, *a.* Thoroughly acquainted; experienced; proficient (*in*): The lawyer was well *versed* in the penal code.

ver·si·fy, vər'sə·fī, *v.i.,* **-fied, -fy·ing.** To make verses.—*v.t.* To relate in verse; turn into verse. —**ver·si·fi·er,** *n.* —**ver·si·fi·ca·tion,** vər·sə·fə·kā'shən, *n.*

ver·sion, vər'zhən, vər'shən, *n.* A translation; a particular account or description, esp. as contrasted with another or others; a form or variant: an earlier *version* of an invention, the movie *version* of a novel. —**ver·sion·al,** *a.*

ver·sus, vər'səs, *prep.* Against, used to indicate an action brought by one party against another; against, used to denote a contest between two teams or players; contrasted with or considered as one of two alternatives: peace *versus* war.

ver·te·bra, vər'tə·brə, *n. pl.,* **-brae,** -brē, -brā. Any of the bones or segments composing the spinal column in human and other vertebrates, consisting typically of a cylindrical body and an arch with various processes, forming a passage for the spinal cord.

ver·te·bral, vər'tə·brəl, *a.* Of or referring to a vertebra or the vertebrae; spinal. —**ver·te·bral·ly,** *adv.*

ver·te·bral col·umn, *n.* Spinal column.

ver·te·brate, vər'tə·brāt, vər'tə·brit, *a.* Having vertebrae, a backbone, a spinal column; belonging to a division of animals, comprising fishes, amphibians, reptiles, birds, and mammals, all of which have a segmented spinal column.—*n.* A vertebrate animal.

ver·tex, vər'teks, *n. pl.,* **-tex·es, -ti·ces,** -tə·sēz. The highest point of something; the apex; the top; the summit; the crown or top of the head; the point of the heavens toward which a group of stars is oriented.

ver·ti·cal, vər'ti·kəl, *a.* Of, referring to, or situated at the vertex; being in a position or direction perpendicular to the plane of the horizon; upright; plumb; pertaining or related to the top of the head.—*n.* A vertical line or plane; a vertical or upright position; a vertical element in any truss. —**ver·ti·cal·i·ty,** vər·ti·kal'ə·tē, **ver·ti·cal·ness,** *n.* —**ver·ti·cal·ly,** *adv.*

ver·ti·go, vər'tə·gō, *n. pl.,* **-ti·goes, -tig·i·nes,** -tij'ə·nēz. A disordered condition in which individuals feel that their immediate environment is whirling about; dizziness.

verve, vərv, *n.* Poetical or artistic vitality or enthusiasm; energy; rapture.

ver·y, ver'ē, *adv.* Extremely, or exceedingly: *very* soon, *very* tired; actually or truly, used as an intensive emphasizing superlatives or stressing identity or oppositeness: the *very* best thing to be done, in the *very* same place.—*a.,* **-i·er, -i·est.** Precise or identical: the *very* thing you should not have done; mere: The *very* thought is distressing; sheer: to weep for *very* joy; actual: caught in the *very* act; true, genuine, or real: the *very* God; with emphatic or intensive force, being such in the true or full sense of the term, or absolute: the *very* heart of the matter; used as an intensive for emphasis of what is specified: The *very* ground trembled.

ves·i·cant, ves/i·kənt, *n.* A blistering substance or agent; any chemical agent that burns and blisters the skin and other tissue. Also **ves·i·ca·to·ry,** ves/i·kə·tôr·ē, *n. pl.,* **-ries.**

ves·i·cate, ves/i·kāt, *v.t.* **-cat·ed, -cat·ing.** To raise vesicles or blisters on; to blister. **—ves·i·ca·tion,** ves·i·kā/shən, *n.*

ves·i·cle, ves/i·kəl, *n.* A small, bladderlike structure or cavity; a little sac or cyst. **—ve·sic·u·lar,** və·sik/yə·lər, *a.*

ves·per, ves/pər, *a.* Of or relating to evening.—*n.* (*Cap.*) The evening star.

ves·pers, ves/pərz, *n.* (*Often cap.*) The sixth of the seven canonical hours, or the service for it, occurring in the late afternoon or the evening; a religious service held in the late afternoon or the evening.

ves·sel, ves/əl, *n.* Any craft designed to move through water carrying persons or goods, esp. one larger than an ordinary rowboat; ship; airship; boat; a hollow or concave article, as a cup or tub, esp. for holding liquid: a drinking *vessel*; receptacle; container; tube or duct containing or conveying blood or some other bodily fluid.

vest, vest, *n.* A waistcoat, or short sleeveless garment worn under a suit coat reaching from the base of the neck down to or below the waistline; a similar garment, or a part of trimming simulating the front of such a garment.—*v.t.* To clothe, dress, or robe; to dress, as in ecclesiastical vestments; to invest formally, as with a garment or dress; to cover or drape, as an altar; to cover or surround, as if with, or like, a garment; to invest or endow, as a person, with something, esp. with powers or functions.—*v.i.* To put on vestments; to become vested in a person or persons, as a right; to pass into possession; to devolve upon a person as possessor. **—vest·like,** *a.* **—vest·less,** *a.*

ves·tal vir·gin, ves/təl, *n.* One of the virgins consecrated to Vesta, a Roman goddess, and to the service of watching the sacred fire on her altar and keeping it burning; a chaste woman.

vest·ed in·ter·est, ves/tid, *n.* A special interest in the continued existence of systems or institutions that confer or protect personal benefits or privileges; *usu. pl.,* those whose favorable economic, political, or social positions depend on the continued existence of current systems or institutions.

ves·ti·bule, ves/tə·būl, *n.* A hall or antechamber between the outer door and the interior of a building; lobby; an enclosed passage between railroad passenger cars.—*v.t.,* **-buled, -bul·ing.** To provide with a vestibule or vestibules. **—ves·tib·u·lar,** ve·stib/yə·lər, *a.*

ves·tige, ves/tij, *n.* A mark, trace, or visible evidence of something which is no longer present or in existence: the *vestiges* of a fire; a surviving evidence or memorial of some condition, practice, or the like: *vestiges* of a custom; a very slight trace or amount of something. **—ves·tig·i·al,** ve·stij/ē·əl, *a.* **—ves·tig·i·al·ly,** *adv.*

vest·ment, vest/mənt, *n.* A garment, esp. an outer garment, robe, or gown; an official or ceremonial robe; something that clothes or covers like a garment; a garment worn by a clergyman. **—vest·ment·al,** vest·men/təl, *a.*

vest-pock·et, vest/pok·it, *a.* Of a size that fits in a vest pocket; tiny; miniature.

ves·try, ves/trē, *n. pl.,* **-tries.** A room in a church building where vestments are kept; a room in a church building used as a chapel, for meetings, and for Sunday School.

vet, vet, *n. Informal.* Veterinarian.—*v.t.,* **vet·ted, vet·ting.** *Informal.* To examine, treat, or provide care for as

any veterinarian does.—*v.i. Informal.* To practice veterinary medicine or surgery.

vet, vet, *n., a. Informal.* Veteran; veterinarian.

vetch, vech, *n.* Any of a genus of climbing plants of the legume family, grown as feed for cattle.

vet·er·an, vet/ər·ən, vet/rən, *n.* One who has become thoroughly experienced in a profession, occupation, or position through long service; one who has served his or her country in the armed forces, esp. in time of war.—*a.* Experienced through length of participation in a profession or activity; of or pertaining to former members of the armed forces.

vet·er·i·nar·i·an, vet·ər·ə·nār/ē·ən, vet·rə·nār/ē·ən, *n.* One who practices veterinary medicine or surgery.

vet·er·i·nar·y, vet/ər·ə·ner·ē, vet/rə·ner·ē, *n. pl.,* **-ies.** Veterinarian.—*a.* Of or referring to the medical or surgical treatment of cattle, horses, and other, esp. tamed, animals.

vet·er·i·nar·y med·i·cine, *n.* The branch or division of medical science concerned with the prevention, diagnosis, treatment, and general study of the diseases of animals, esp. tamed ones.

ve·to, vē/tō, *n.* The executive power of governors and of the President of the U.S. to refuse a measure passed by their legislatures; a message or official paper stating the reasons of the President of the U.S. or other executive for refusing or vetoing a bill; any prohibition by an authority.—*v.t.,* **-toed, -to·ing.** To forbid; to interdict: to *veto* an act of legislature. **—ve·to·er,** *n.*

vex, veks, *v.t.* To irritate, annoy, provoke, or make angry, esp. with trivial or petty irritations: His awkwardness *vexes* his friends; to torment, plague, or worry; to disturb by motion. **—vex·er,** *n.* **—vex·ing·ly,** *adv.*

vex·a·tion, vek·sā/shən, *n.* The act of vexing or state of being vexed; irritation; annoyance.

vex·a·tious, vek·sā/shəs, *a.* Full of or causing vexation; annoying.

vexed, vekst, *a.* Disturbed; irritated.

vi·a, vi/ə, vē/ə, *prep.* By way of: to drive to California *via* the Grand Canyon in Arizona; by means of: to travel *via* airplane.

vi·a·ble, vi/ə·bəl, *a.* Capable of sustaining independent life, as of a normal newborn child; possessing the ability to grow and develop: *viable* spores, seeds, or eggs; productive or workable: a *viable* plan. **—vi·a·bil·i·ty,** vi·ə·bil/ə·tē, *n.* **—vi·a·bly,** *adv.*

vi·a·duct, vi/ə·dəkt, *n.* A long bridge or series of arches conducting a railroad or road over a valley or other area of low level.

vi·al, vi/əl, *n.* A small glass vessel or bottle which holds liquids.

vi·and, vi/ənd, *n.* An item of food; *usu. pl.,* stocks of food; food of high quality.

vibes, vibz, *n. pl. Informal.* Vibrations, esp. one's reaction to a person or situation.

vi·brant, vi/brənt, *a.* Vibrating; moving to and fro rapidly; vibrating so as to produce sound, as a string; of sounds, characterized by perceptible vibration; resonant; throbbing or pulsating with energy, vitality, or vigor. **—vi·bran·cy,** *n.*

vi·brate, vi/brāt, *v.i.* **-brat·ed, -brat·ing.** To move to and fro, as a pendulum; to oscillate; to move to and fro or up and down quickly and repeatedly; to quiver; to tremble; of sounds, to produce or have a quivering effect; to fluctuate, vacillate.—*v.t.* To cause to move to and fro, to swing, or to oscillate; to cause to quiver; to give forth or emit, as sound, by or as by vibratory motion.

vi·bra·tion, vi·brā/shən, *n.* The act or state of vibrating or being vibrated; a single vibrating motion; an oscillation; a quiver or tremor. *Informal.* One's emotional reaction to a person or situation.

---

a- hat, fāte, fāre, fäther; **e-** met, mē; **i-** pin, pīne; **o-** not, nōte, ôrb, moove (move), boy, pownd; **u-** cūbe, bûll, tûk (took); **ch-** chin; **th-** thick, ŧhen; **zh-** vizhon (vision); **ə-** ego, takən, pencəl, lemən, bərd (bird).

vi·bra·to, vĭ·brä′tō, vē·brä′tō, *n. pl.,* **-tos.** A pulsating effect, produced in singing by the rapid repetition of emphasis on a tone, and on bowed instruments by a rapid change of pitch corresponding to the vocal tremolo.

vi·bra·tor, vĭ′brā·tər, *n.* That which vibrates; any of various instruments or devices causing or having a vibratory motion or action; an electrical device which vibrates and is used for massage.

vi·bra·to·ry, vĭ′brə·tôr·ē, vĭ′brə·tōr′ē, *a.* Consisting in or belonging to vibration.

vi·bur·num, vĭ·bər′nəm, *n.* Any of several shrubs or small trees of the honeysuckle family, grown as ornamentation.

vic·ar, vik′ər, *n.* The priest of a parish who receives only a small salary or stipend, while a layman or church corporation receives the main portion of tithes collected; a parish clergyman not holding the office of rector; a clergyman who usu. has charge of a chapel but not the church proper; a bishop's deputy, usu. in charge of a mission or church; any substitute in office. **—vic·ar·ship,** *n.*

vic·ar·age, vik′ər·ij, *n.* The position, duties, or benefice of a vicar; the house or residence of a vicar.

vi·car·i·ous, vī·kâr′ē·əs, vi·kâr′ē·əs, *a.* Performed or suffered for, or instead of, another; filling the place of another; serving as a substitute or deputy; delegated; felt or realized, as sensations or emotions, by imagining one is taking part in someone else's experiences. **—vi·car·i·ous·ly,** *adv.* **—vi·car·i·ous·ness,** *n.*

vice, vīs, *n.* Any specific immoral or evil habit or practice; an inconsequential personal fault; foible; a defect or blemish.

vice, vīs, *prep.* In the place of; instead of; succeeding.—*a.* Acting in place of.—*n.*

vice ad·mi·ral, *n.* An officer next in rank and command to the admiral.

vice con·sul, vice-con·sul, vīs′kon′səl, *n.* One who acts as substitute for a consul; a consul of subordinate rank. **—vice-con·su·lar,** *a.* **—vice-con·su·late,** *n.* **—vice-con·sul·ship,** *n.*

vice pres·i·dent, *n.* An officer next in rank to a president and assuming his or her duties in the event of the president's absence or incapacity; an officer, as in a large corporation, ranking below the president, and in charge of a specific department, function, or location; (*cap.*) the officer next in rank to, and elected at the same time as the President, succeeding to the presidential office on the resignation, removal, death, or disability of the President. **—vice-pres·i·den·cy,** vīs′prez′ə·dən·sē, *n. pl.,* **-cies. —vice-pres·i·den·tial,** vīs′prez·ə·den′shəl, *a.*

vice·roy, vīs′roy, *n.* One appointed to rule a country or province as the deputy of the sovereign: the *viceroy* of India. **—vice·roy·al,** *a.*

vice squad, *n.* A police unit charged with enforcement of laws dealing with public morality.

vice ver·sa, vī′sə·vər′sə, vī′sē vər′sə, vīs′ vər′sə, *adv.* Conversely; in reverse; with the terms or the case being reversed.

vi·cin·i·ty, vi·sin′ə·tē, *n. pl.,* **-ties.** The adjoining district, space, or country; nearness in place; neighborhood; the quality of being near; propinquity; proximity.

vi·cious, vish′əs, *a.* Addicted to or characterized by vice or immorality; depraved; given or disposed to evil; blameworthy, or wrong: a *vicious* practice; spiteful or malignant: *vicious* lies; having an ugly disposition; savage: a *vicious* temper. **—vi·cious·ly,** *adv.* **—vi·cious·ness,** *n.*

vi·cious cir·cle, *n.* A situation in which a solution to a problem begins a chain of progressively more difficult problems, each created by a solution to a previous problem.

vi·cis·si·tude, vi·sis′ə·tood, vi·sis′ə·tūd, *n.* A passing from one state or condition to another; *pl.,* changes, esp. in regard to the affairs of life or the world;

mutation; an alternating or successive change, as from winter to spring and summer to fall.

vic·tim, vik′tim, *n.* A person destroyed, sacrificed, or injured by another, or by some condition or agency; one who is cheated or duped.

vic·tim·ize, vik′tim·īz, *v.t.,* **-ized, -iz·ing.** To make a victim of; to expose or subject to swindle or deception; to sacrifice. **—vic·tim·i·za·tion,** vik·tim·ə·zā′shən, *n.* **—vic·tim·iz·er,** *n.*

vic·tor, vik′tər, *n.* One who wins or gains the advantage in a contest, struggle, or battle.

Vic·to·ri·an, vik·tôr′ē·ən, *a.* Of or referring to the time of Queen Victoria's reign over Great Britain, 1837-1901; prudish; narrow; pompous; hypocritical. *—n.* One who lived during Queen Victoria's reign, esp. an author. **—Vic·to·ri·an·ism,** vik·tôr′ē·ə·niz·əm, *n.*

vic·to·ri·ous, vik·tôr′ē·əs, *a.* Having conquered or won victory in battle or contest; characterized by or indicating victory. **—vic·to·ri·ous·ly,** *adv.* **—vic·to·ri·ous·ness,** *n.*

vic·to·ry, vik′tə·rē, *n. pl.,* **-ries.** The defeat of an enemy in battle, or of an antagonist in a contest; the superiority or state of triumph gained in any contest or endeavor.

Vic·tro·la, vik·trō′lə, *n. Trademark.* A phonograph.

vict·ual, vit′əl, *n.* (*Usu. pl.*) Provisions of any kind; food for human beings, prepared for eating.—*v.t.,* **-ualed, -ual·ing.** To supply or store with victuals; to provide with stores of food.—*v.i.* To store food or provisions.

vi·cu·ña, vi·koo′nə, vi·kū′nə, vi·koo′nə, vi·kū′nə, vi·koo′nyə, *n.* A S. American cud-chewing animal related to the llama, with soft, silken wool used for making fabrics; cloth made from vicuña wool. Also **vi·cu·na.**

vid·e·o, vid′ē·ō, *a.* Of or referring to the conversion of certain electronic impulses into wave lengths that can be seen on a TV screen.—*n.* The visual component of TV, as distinguished from *audio.*

vid·e·o·tape, vid′ē·ō·tāp′, *n.* Magnetic tape that records the complete TV signal, both video impulses and audio impulses, and is available for instant replay.—*v.t.,* **-taped, -tap·ing.** To record on video tape.

vie, vī, *v.i.,* **vied, vy·ing.** To strive for superiority or to contend, used with *for* or *with.* **—vi·er,** *n.*

Vi·et·nam·ese, vē·et·nə·mēz′, vē·et·nə·mēs′, vyet·nə·mēz′, vyet·nə·mēs′, *a.* Of or referring to the countries of North or South Vietnam or their inhabitants.—*n. pl.,* **-ese.** A native or an inhabitant of North or South Vietnam; the predominant language of Vietnam.

view, vū, *n.* The act of looking or seeing; a visual survey; power of seeing; sight; range of vision; that which is viewed, seen, or beheld, as a sight or picture; particular manner of looking at things; judgment, opinion, or way of thinking; something looked toward or forming the subject of consideration; intention; purpose.—*v.t.* To see; to look on; to examine or inspect; to consider.**—in view,** in the scope of vision; under consideration, as an object or goal.**—in view of,** in consideration of; because of.**—on view,** openly presented for inspection or examination, as by the public.**—with a view to,** with the purpose or intention of; with the hope of: to act *with a view to* happiness.

view·er, vū′ər, *n.* A person who views or watches anything, esp. television programs; an optical device for viewing photographic transparencies.

view·less, vū′lis, *a.* Furnishing no view; having no opinion or point of view.

view·point, vū′poynt, *n.* An opinion, attitude, or point of view.

vig·il, vij′əl, *n.* A keeping awake for any purpose during the natural hours of sleep; a watch kept by night or at other times; a course or period of watchful attention; the eve, or day and night, before a church festival, esp. an eve which is a fast; *usu. pl.,* a nocturnal devotional exercise or service, esp. on the eve of, or before, a church festival.

vig·i·lance, vij/ə·ləns, *n.* The state or quality of being vigilant; watchfulness; circumspection.

vig·i·lant, vij/ə·lənt, *a.* Watchful; on the alert for danger; wary.

vig·i·lan·te, vij·ə·lan/tē, *n.* One of the members of a body of volunteers organized to maintain order by the summary punishment of an offense or crime.

vi·gnette, vin·yet/, *n.* A small running design, as one representing vine leaves, tendrils, and grapes, used on title pages in books; a short literary sketch or description.

vig·or, vig/ər, *n.* Active strength or force of body; physical strength; strength of mind; energy; vitality.

vig·or·ous, vig/ər·əs, *a.* Possessing vigor or physical strength; strong; exhibiting or resulting from vigor, energy, or strength of either body or mind; powerful; energetic; forceful. **—vig·or·ous·ly,** *adv.*

vi·king, vī/king, *n.* (*Cap.*) One of the Scandinavian warriors whose seaborne raiding parties ravaged the European coasts from the 8th to the 10th centuries. (*L.c.*) Any sea rover.

vile, vīl, *a.,* **vil·er, vil·est.** Wretchedly bad: *vile* weather; highly offensive or objectionable; repulsive or disgusting, as to the senses or feelings; morally base, depraved, or despicable: *vile* thoughts; foul, as language; poor, wretched, or sorry, as in quality or state; mean or menial, as tasks; low, degraded, or ignominious, as a condition: *vile* servitude.

vil·i·fy, vil/ə·fi, *v.t.,* **-fied, -fy·ing.** To attempt to degrade by slander; to defame; to malign. **—vil·i·fi·ca·tion,** vil·ə·fə·kā/shən, *n.*

vil·la, vil/ə, *n.* A country residence, usu. of some size and pretension.

vil·lage, vil/ij, *n.* A small assemblage of houses in a country district, being larger than a hamlet and smaller than a town; a sometimes incorporated municipality, as in parts of the U.S.; the village inhabitants collectively.

vil·lain, vil/ən, *n.* A malevolent or harmful person; scoundrel; a character who functions as an evil antagonist in the plot of a literary work; a villein.

vil·lain·ous, vil/ə·nəs, *a.* Having the character of, pertaining to, or befitting a villain; wicked; depraved; unpleasant: *villainous* weather. **—vil·lain·ous·ly,** *adv.* **—vil·lain·ous·ness,** *n.*

vil·lain·y, vil/ə·nē, *n. pl.,* **-ies.** The conduct or actions of a villain; the quality of being villainous; depravity; wickedness.

vil·lein, vil/ən, *n.* One of a feudal class of persons who served as serfs to their lords but who possessed the rights of free men with respect to all other persons.

vil·lous, vil/əs, *a.* Having villi; having the surface covered with fine hairs or woolly substance.

vil·lus, vil/əs, *n. pl.,* **-li,** -lī. One of the minute, hairlike, vascular processes on certain animal membranes, esp. on the mucous membrane of the small intestine, where they help to absorb nutriment; one of the long, soft, straight hairs covering the fruit and other parts of certain plants.

vim, vim, *n.* Vigor; vitality; forceful enthusiasm.

vin·ci·ble, vin/sə·bəl, *a.* Capable of being conquered. **—vin·ci·bil·i·ty,** vin·sə·bil/ə·tē, *n.*

vin·di·cate, vin/də·kāt, *v.t.,* **-cat·ed, -cat·ing.** To clear completely from charges or free from suspicions or guilt; to justify or support, as a legal action; to prove to be just or valid, as a claim; to support, maintain, or defend against denial, censure, or objections. **—vin·di·ca·tion,** vin·də·kā/shən, *n.* **—vin·di·ca·tor,** *n.*

vin·dic·tive, vin·dik/tiv, *a.* Revengeful; given to revenge. **—vin·dic·tive·ly,** *adv.* **—vin·dic·tive·ness,** *n.*

vine, vīn, *n.* Any plant with a long, slender stem that trails or creeps on the ground or climbs by winding itself about a support; the grapevine.

vin·e·gar, vin/ə·gər, *n.* Dilute and impure acetic acid, usu. obtained by the souring of fermented fruit juices, used as a preservative or condiment.

vin·e·gar·y, vin/ə·gə·rē, *a.* Of the nature of or resembling vinegar.

vine·yard, vin/yərd, *n.* A plantation of vines producing grapes, esp. wine grapes.

vi·no, vē/no, *n. Informal.* Wine.

vi·nous, vī/nəs, *a.* Of the nature of or resembling wine; referring to or characteristic of wine.

vin·tage, vin/tij, *n.* The crop of grapes or wine produced from one season; a high quality wine from a superior crop; the gathering of a crop of grapes; a type of person or thing well-known during a past era: a dance of jazz-age *vintage.—a.* Referring to wine, esp. a particular wine, or to a season of wine making; outmoded; referring to a period, age, make, or the like: *vintage* automobile.

vint·ner, vint/nər, *n.* One who deals in wine; wine merchant.

vi·nyl, vīn/əl, *n.* A type of plastic.

vi·ol, vī/əl, *n.* A five- to seven-stringed musical instrument of various sizes and shapes, and ancestor of the modern violin.

vi·o·la, vē·ō/lə, vī·ō/lə, *n.* A musical instrument similar to the violin, but somewhat larger and with the strings tuned a fifth lower, producing a more sonorous tone. **—vi·o·list,** vē·ō/list, vī·ō/list, *n.*

vi·o·la·ble, vī/ə·lə·bəl, *a.* Capable of being violated. **—vi·o·la·bil·i·ty,** vī·ə·lə·bil/ə·tē, *n.*

vi·o·late, vī/ə·lāt, *v.t.,* **-lat·ed, -lat·ing.** To infringe or transgress; to break in upon; to disturb; to desecrate; to treat with irreverence; to profane or profanely meddle with; to ravish or rape; to do injury to; to outrage.—*a.* **—vi·o·la·tor,** *n.*

vi·o·la·tion, vī·ə·lā/shən, *n.* The act of violating; the condition of being violated; desecration or profanation; an infringement or transgression; rape.

vi·o·lence, vī/ə·ləns, *n.* Intense or severe force; severe or injurious treatment or action; an unfair exercise of power or force; an act of violence; an inordinate vehemence of expression or feeling.

vi·o·lent, vī/ə·lənt, *a.* Characterized by or acting with extremely rough physical force; characterized or caused by harsh, destructive force; marked by intensity of force or effect: a *violent* cough; exhibiting or caused by intense emotional or mental force; sudden, intense energy: a *violent* rush.

vi·o·let, vī/ə·lit, *n.* A small plant with purple, blue, yellow, white, or variegated flowers; a bluish purple color.—*a.* Of the color called violet; bluish-purple.

vi·o·lin, vī·ə·lin/, *n.* A treble instrument of wood, having four strings stretched by means of a bridge over a hollow body, held under the chin resting horizontally on the shoulder, and played with a bow; a violinist. **—vi·o·lin·ist,** *n.*

vi·o·lon·cel·lo, vē·ə·lən·chel/ō, *n.* A cello. **—vi·o·lon·cel·list,** vē·ə·lən·chel/ist, *n.*

VIP, V.I.P., vē/ī/pē/, *n. Informal.* Very important person.

vi·per, vī/pər, *n.* Any of a family of poisonous Old-World snakes; any poisonous or reputedly poisonous snake; a malevolent or spiteful person.

vi·ra·go, və·rā/gō, *n. pl.,* **-goes, -gos.** A bold, turbulent, loud, bad-tempered woman; a shrew.

vi·ral, vī/rəl, *a.* Of, relating to, or as a result of a virus.

vir·e·o, vir/ē·ō, *n. pl.,* **-os.** A small American insect-eating bird, having plumage tinted with olive and green.

vir·gin, vər/jən, *n.* A person, esp. a girl or young woman, who has not had sexual intercourse; a chaste woman; a maiden.—*a.* Being or referring to a virgin; chaste; untouched, unsullied; in a pure or natural state; unused or uncultivated; unprocessed; occur-

---

a- hat, fāte, fâre, fäther; **e-** met, mē; **i-** pin, pine; **o-** not, nōte, ôrb, moove (move), boy, pownd; **u-** cūbe, bûll, tûk (took); **ch-** chin; **th-** thick, ŧhen; **zh-** vizhon (vision); **ə-** əgo, takən, pencəl, lemən, bərd (bird).

ring for the first time: *virgin* speech. **—vir·gin·al,** vər′jə·nəl, *a.* **—vir·gin·al·ly,** *adv.*

vir·gin·al, vər′jə·nəl, *n.* Often *pl.* A spinet or small harpsichord, usu. without legs, set on a table, popular in the 16th and 17th centuries.

Vir·gin·ia creep·er, vər·jin′yə krē′pər, *n.* A climbing plant of N. America, having palmate leaves with five leaflets, and bluish-black berries.

Vir·gin·ia reel, vər·jin′yə rēl′, *n.* An American country dance in which the partners begin by facing each other in two lines, and dance a series of figures, called out by the caller.

vir·gin·i·ty, vər·jin′ə·tē, *n.* The state of being a virgin.

Vir·gin Mar·y, *n.* Mary, the mother of Jesus Christ, usu. preceded by *the.*

vir·gin wool, *n.* Wool that has yet to be processed.

vir·gule, vər′gūl, *n.* A slanted line (/) used to denote two alternatives (as in and/or) to replace the word 'per' (50 cents/lb), to divide fractions or dates and to separate lines of poetry.

vir·ile, vir′əl, *a.* Of, pertaining to, or characteristic of a man; masculine or manly; having or exhibiting in a marked degree masculine strength, vigor, or forcefulness. **—vi·ril·i·ty,** və·ril′ə·tē, *n.*

vi·rol·o·gy, vī·rol′ə·jē, və·rol′ə·jē, *n.* The science which deals with viruses and the diseases they cause. **—vi·rol·o·gist,** *n.*

vir·tu·al, vər′choo·əl, *a.* Being in essence or effect, not in fact; not actual but equivalent, so far as result is concerned: a *virtual* denial of a statement.

vir·tu·al·ly, vər′choo·ə·lē, *adv.* In effect if not in actuality; mostly or almost entirely: The movie was *virtually* successful.

vir·tue, vər′choo, *n.* Moral excellence or goodness; chastity, esp. in women; a particular moral excellence: one of the cardinal or theological *virtues;* any praiseworthy quality or trait; merit; inherent power to produce effects.**—by vir·tue of** or **in vir·tue of,** by the power, force, or authority of.

vir·tu·os·i·ty, vər·choo·os′ə·tē, *n. pl.,* **-ties.** The technique or skill of a virtuoso; an interest in the fine arts.

vir·tu·o·so, vər·choo·ō′sō, *n. pl.,* **-sos, -si,** -sē. One who has special knowledge or skill in any field, as in music; one who excels in musical technique or execution; one who has a cultivated appreciation of artistic excellence; a connoisseur of works or objects of art, or a collector of objects of art, curios, antiquities, or the like.**—a. —vir·tu·o·sic,** vər·choo·os′ik, vər·choo·ō′sik, *a.*

vir·tu·ous, vər′choo·əs, *a.* Conforming to moral laws; upright; righteous; moral; chaste. **—vir·tu·ous·ly,** *adv.* **—vir·tu·ous·ness,** *n.*

vir·u·lence, vir′yə·ləns, vir′ə·ləns, *n.* The quality of being virulent; venomous hostility. Also **vir·u·len·cy.**

vir·u·lent, vir′yə·lənt, vir′ə·lənt, *a.* Extremely poisonous, venomous, noxious, or baneful: a *virulent* snake bite; very actively or spitefully injurious to life; very bitter in enmity.

vi·rus, vī′rəs, *n. pl.,* **-rus·es.** Any of a class of submicroscopic, filterable, disease-producing organisms which are dependent upon the host's living cells for their growth and reproduction; a virus disease; a poisoning of the mind by some evil influence.

vi·sa, vē′zə, *n.* An endorsement made upon a passport by an authorized official representing a country which the bearer wishes to visit and denoting that it has been examined, found correct, and permission for entry has been granted.

vis·age, viz′ij, *n.* The face, esp. of a human being; the countenance; aspect; appearance.

vis-à-vis, ve·zə·vē′, *adv., a.* Face to face.**—prep.** In relation to, or compared with; face to face with; opposite to.

vis·cer·a, vis′ər·ə, *n. pl.* The soft interior organs of the body, including the lungs, heart, stomach, and intestines; the intestines.

vis·cer·al, vis′ər·əl, *a.* Of or referring to the viscera; affecting or located within the viscera; having the character of viscera; proceeding from feeling or intuition that is intense or deep.

vis·cid, vis′id, *a.* Sticking or adhering, and having a glutinous consistency. **—vis·cid·i·ty,** vi·sid′ə·tē, *n.* **—vis·cid·ly,** *adv.* **—vis·cid·ness,** *n.*

vis·cos·i·ty, vi·skos′ə·tē, *n. pl.,* **-ties.** The state or quality of being viscous.

vis·count, vī′kownt, *n.* A nobleman ranking next below an earl or count and next above a baron. **—vis·count·cy, vis·count·ship,** *n.*

vis·count·ess, vī′kown·tis, *n.* A viscount's widow or wife; a woman having a corresponding or similar title to a viscount.

vis·cous, vis′kəs, *a.* Sticky, adhesive, thick, or glutinous.

vise, vis, *n.* Any of various devices having two jaws which may be brought together or separated by means of a screw or lever, used to hold an object firmly while work is being done upon it.

vis·i·bil·i·ty, viz·ə·bil′ə·tē, *n. pl.,* **-ties.** The state or quality of being visible; the relative ease with which objects can be seen through the atmosphere under various conditions; the capability of giving an unobstructed range of vision.

vis·i·ble, viz′ə·bəl, *a.* Capable of being seen or perceived by the eye; constructed so as to be open to sight or view; able to be perceived by the mind; apparent, manifest, or obvious; conspicuous.

vi·sion, vizh′ən, *n.* The act, power, or faculty of seeing; sight; the ability to imagine and prepare for the future: He had a *vision* of things to come; foresight; the act or power of perceiving abstract or invisible subjects as clearly as if they were visible objects; a sight such as might be seen in a dream or vision, esp. when conceived of as revelation or prophecy; a vivid imaginative conception or anticipation: *visions* of wealth or glory; a sight, esp. when beautiful or satisfying.

vi·sion·ar·y, vizh′ə·ner·ē, *a.* Given to or characterized by fanciful or impracticable ideas or plans; purely idealistic; utopian; given to or characterized by imagining or dreaming; given to or concerned with seeing visions; unreal; imaginary.**—n. pl.,** **-ies.** One who sees visions; an impractical theorist or enthusiast; a dreamer.

vis·it, viz′it, *v.t.* To come or go to see, as a person or place, in the way of friendship, ceremony, duty, business, or the like; to stay with as a guest; to go to for the purpose of official inspection or examination; to come in order to comfort or aid; to come upon; to inflict punishment for or upon.**—v.i.** To make a visit or visits. *Informal.* To talk casually.**—n.** An act of visiting; the act of going to see a person or place; a stay or sojourn as a guest; the action of going to a place to make an official inspection or examination. *Informal.* A friendly talk.

vis·i·tant, viz′ə·tənt, *n.* A visitor or guest.

vis·i·ta·tion, viz·ə·tā′shən, *n.* A visit; a formal visit by a superior or superintendent in order to inspect; a special dispensation or judgment from heaven; a communication of divine favor or of divine indignation and retribution.

vis·it·ing, viz′i·ting, *a.* Giving specialized or professional assistance in the home for brief periods of time: as, a *visiting* nurse.

vis·it·ing card, *n.* A calling card.

vis·it·ing fire·man, *n. Informal.* An influential, official, or big-spending visitor, as to a city or organization, who is usu. given special tours, or impressively entertained.

vis·i·tor, viz′ə·tər, *n.* One who visits for business, social, or other reasons; a caller.

vi·sor, vī′zər, *n.* The movable face guard of a helmet; a shield, usu. projecting from a cap, worn above the eyes to protect them from glare; a movable part over the inside of a car windshield which can be pulled down to shield the driver's eyes from glare.

vis•ta, vis/tə, *n.* A view or prospect through an avenue, as between rows of trees; the trees that form the avenue; a mental view stretching over an extensive range of time or sequence of events.

vis•u•al, vizh/ōō•əl, *a.* Of or referring to vision; used in sight; perceptible by sight; visible; perceptible by the mind, or of the nature of a mental vision. **—vis•u•al•ly,** *adv.*

vis•ual aid, *n.* Often *pl.* Any of a variety of devices and materials which rely on the sense of sight to inform, as maps, motion pictures, and filmstrips.

vis•u•al•ize, vizh/ōō•ə•līz, *v.t.,* **-ized, -iz•ing.** To make perceptible to the mind or imagination; to form a mental image of.—*v.i.* To call up or form mental images. **—vis•u•al•i•za•tion,** vizh•ōō•əl•ə•zā/shən, *n.*

vi•tal, vīt/əl, *a.* Of or referring to life: *vital* functions or processes; filled with life; being the seat or source of life: the *vital* parts or organs; necessary to life: *vital* air; necessary to the existence, continuance, or well-being of something: a *vital* necessity; indispensable; essential; affecting the existence, well-being, truth, or the like, of something: a *vital* error; of critical importance: *vital problems,* a *vital* contribution to modern thought; imparting life or vigor; vitalizing or invigorating: the *vital* sunlight; affecting life; destructive to life: a *vital* wound.

vi•tal•i•ty, vī•tal/ə•tē, *n. pl.,* **-ties.** The state of showing vital force; energy: full of *vitality;* vigor; the principle of life; animation; the ability to live or a capacity for lasting; continuance.

vi•tal•ize, vīt/ə•līz, *v.t.,* **-ized, -iz•ing.** To give life to; to furnish with vital force; to invigorate. **—vi•tal•i•za•tion,** vī•təl•ə•zā/shən, *n.*

vi•tals, vī/təlz, *n. pl.* Internal parts or organs of animal bodies essential to life, as the heart and lungs; the part of a complex whole essential to its life, existence, or to a sound state.

vi•ta•min, vī•tə•mən, *n.* One of several organic substances occurring in minute quantities in natural foods and necessary for proper metabolism in man and other animals, the lack of which causes various diseases.

vi•ta•min A, *n.* A vitamin obtained from egg yolk and certain other animal products, administered for the condition of night blindness.

vi•ta•min B com•plex, *n.* An important group of B vitamins containing vitamin B₁, vitamin B₂, and others which are water-soluble.

vi•ta•min B₁, *n.* Thiamine.

vi•ta•min B₂, *n.* Riboflavin.

vi•ta•min B₁₂, *n.* A water-soluble, crystalline vitamin, obtained from milk, eggs, liver, fish, and meat, which treats anemia and is used as a nutriment, esp. for animals.

vi•ta•min C, *n.* Ascorbic acid.

vi•ta•min D, *n.* Any of a group of fat-soluble vitamins often prescribed for treatment of rickets and whose common sources are oil from the livers of fish, milk products, and eggs.

vi•ta•min E, *n.* A vitamin found in wheat germ and other grains.

vi•ta•min G, *n.* Riboflavin.

vi•ta•min H, *n.* Biotin.

vi•ta•min K, *n.* A vitamin which occurs in many green vegetables and is necessary for normal blood clotting.

vi•ta•min P, *n.* A vitamin found in paprika and citrus fruits which helps to maintain capillary and cell wall permeability.

vi•ti•ate, vish/ē•āt, *v.t.,* **-at•ed, -at•ing.** To injure the quality of; to impair; to spoil or pollute; to render legally invalid or of no effect; to invalidate. **—vi•ti•a•tion,** vish•ē•ā/shən, *n.*

vit•re•ous, vi•trē•əs, *a.* Referring to or obtained from glass; consisting of glass; resembling glass. **—vit•re•os•i•ty,** vi•trē•os/ə•tē, *n.*

vit•re•ous hu•mor, *n.* The transparent gelatinous substance filling the eyeball behind the lens.

vit•ri•fy, vi/tra•fī, *v.t.,* **-fied, -fy•ing.** To convert into glass by fusion or the action of heat.—*v.i.* To be converted into glass. **—vit•ri•fi•a•ble,** *a.* **—vit•ri•fi•ca•tion,** vi•trə•fə•kā/shən, *n.*

vit•ri•ol, vi/trē•ōl, vit/rē•əl, *n.* Any of certain metallic sulfates of glassy appearance, as of copper, iron, or zinc; sulfuric acid; something highly caustic or severe in its effects, as criticism. **—vit•ri•ol•ic,** vi•trē•ol/ik, *a.*

vi•tu•per•ate, vi•too/pə•rāt, vī•tū/pə•rāt, *v.t.,* **-at•ed, -at•ing.** To censure with abusive language; to abuse; to berate.

vi•tu•per•a•tion, vī•too•pə•rā/shən, vī•tū•pə•rā/shən, *n.* The act of vituperating; abusive railing.

vi•va, vē/və, *interj.* Long live, usu. used with a specified someone in compounds: *Viva Romeo!*

vi•va•cious, vi•vā/shəs, vī•vā/shəs, *a.* Lively; active; sprightly in temper or conduct.

vi•vac•i•ty, vi•vas/ə•tē, vī•vas/ə•tē, *n. pl.,* **-ties.** The quality or condition of being vivacious; liveliness of manner or character; sprightliness of temper or behavior; animation; briskness; cheerfulness; spirit.

vive, vēv, *interj.* Long live, usu. used with a specified person or thing in compounds: *Vive Molière!*

viv•id, viv/id, *a.* Extremely bright, distinct, or intense: a dress of *vivid* red; lively; vigorous; spirited; exhibiting the appearance of life or freshness; realistic; perceived intensely and clearly by the senses; forming clear, strong mental images: his *vivid* description of the accident.

viv•i•fy, viv/ə•fī, *v.t.,* **-fied, -fy•ing.** To endue with life; to animate; to make, as a story, more exciting, vivid, or lively. **—viv•i•fi•ca•tion,** viv•ə•fə•kā/shən, *n.*

vi•vip•ar•ous, vi•vip/ər•əs, *a.* Producing young in a living state, as most mammals.

viv•i•sec•tion, viv•ə•sek/shən, *n.* The dissection of, or otherwise experimenting on, a living animal, esp. for the purpose of ascertaining or demonstrating some fact in physiology or pathology.

vix•en, vik/sən, *n.* A quarrelsome woman; a female fox.

vi•zier, vi•zir, vi•zēr/, *n.* The title of high political officers in the former Turkish Empire and in Moslem countries; a minister of state.

vi•zor, vī/zər, *n.* Visor.

vo•cab•u•lar•y, vō•kab/yə•ler•ē, *n. pl.,* **-ies.** The stock of words used by a people, or by a particular group or person; a list or collection of the words of a language, book, author, branch of science, or the like, usu. in alphabetical order and defined.

vo•cal, vō/kəl, *a.* Of or referring to the voice; uttered with the voice, or oral; rendered by or intended for singing, as music; having a voice; expressing oneself in a free manner of speech; giving forth sound with or as with a voice; voiced; referring to or having the character of a vowel.—*n.* A vocal sound.

vo•cal cords, *n. pl.* Either of two pairs of membranous ligaments projecting into the cavity of the larynx, the edges of which can be drawn together and made to vibrate by the passage of air from the lungs, thus producing vocal sound.

vo•cal•ic, vō•kal/ik, *a.* Of, pertaining to, or of the nature of a vowel; containing or constructed of vowels.

vo•cal•ist, vō/kə•list, *n.* A singer, esp. a trained one.

vo•cal•ize, vō/kə•līz, *v.t.,* **-ized, -iz•ing.** To make vocal; to utter or articulate; to utter, as speech sounds, with the voice, and not merely with the breath; to use

---

a- hat, fāte, fāre, fäther; e- met, mē; i- pin, pīne; o- not, nōte, ôrb, moove (move), boy, pownd; u- cūbe, bull, tûk (took); ch- chin; th- thick, ᵺen; zh- vizhon (vision); ə- əgo, takən, pencəl, lemən, bərd (bird).

as a vowel.—*v.i.* To use the voice, as in speech or song; to become altered to a vowel. —**vo•cai•i•za•tion,** vō•kəl•ə•zā′shən, *n.*

vo•ca•tion, vō•kā′shən, *n.* A particular occupation, business, profession, trade, or calling; a summons to, or fitness for, a particular activity or career.

vo•ca•tion•al, vō•kā′shə•nəl, *a.* Referring to a vocation or occupation: *vocational* schools; pertaining to guidance or training in the development of skills required by different trades: a *vocational* guidance counselor.

vo•cif•er•ous, vō•sif′ər•əs, *a.* Making a loud outcry; clamorous; noisy.

vod•ka, vod′kə, *n.* An intoxicating liquor distilled from potatoes or various cereals, orig. made and much used in Russia.

vogue, vōg, *n.* The prevalent mode or fashion, often preceded by *in;* popular favor; acceptance.

voice, voys, *n.* The sound or sounds uttered by the mouth of living creatures, esp. of human beings in speaking, shouting, or singing; the condition of the voice for speaking or singing: She was in poor *voice;* any sound likened to vocal utterance: the *voice* of the wind; anything likened to speech: the *voice* of nature; the faculty of uttering sounds with the mouth, esp. articulate sounds; speech; expression in spoken or written words, or by other means: to give *voice* to one's disapproval by a letter; expressed opinion or choice: His *voice* was for compromise; the right to express an opinion or choice: to have no *voice* in the matter; expressed wish or injunction: obedient to the *voice* of God; the person or other agency by which something is expressed or revealed; a singer; a voice part; a musical sound caused by vocal cord vibration and throat and oral resonance; sound uttered with the resonance of the vocal cords and not by mere emission of breath; distinctive form of a verb indicating the relation of the subject to the action expressed by the verb, or any of the groups of forms of a verb serving to indicate this: the active or passive *voice.*—*v.t.,* **voiced, voic•ing.** To give voice, utterance, or expression to; to declare or proclaim; to utter with voice or vocal sound.—**in voice,** in good or fit condition as for speaking or singing.—**with one voice,** unanimously.

voice box, *n.* The larynx.

voiced, voyst, *a.* Having a voice or type of voice: low-*voiced;* expressed or stated with the voice; spoken with voice or vocal vibration, as the consonants, *b, d,* and *g.*

voice•less, voys′lis, *a.* Having no voice; mute; uttering no speech or words; silent; uttered without voice or vocal sound, as the consonants, *p, t,* and *k.*

voice•print, voys′print, *n.* A spectographic record of modulation, amplitude, and duration of human speech sounds, used chiefly in criminological identification.

void, voyd, *a.* Having no legal or binding force; null; empty or not containing matter; having no holder or possessor; vacant; unoccupied; devoid; destitute: *void* of learning; not producing any effect; ineffectual; in vain.—*n.* An empty space; a vacuum.—*v.t.* To make or leave vacant; to nullify; to emit or discharge. —**void•a•ble,** *a.*

voile, voyl, *n.* A fabric of rayon, silk, cotton, or wool, which is sheer and used for curtains, women's dresses, or the like.

vol•a•tile, vol′ə•təl, *a.* Having the quality of passing off quickly by evaporation; able to vaporize freely in the air; fickle; apt to change; lively; explosive. —**vol•a•til•i•ty,** vol•ə•til′ə•tē, *n.*

vol•can•ic, vol•kan′ik, *a.* Referring to or characteristic of volcanoes; emitted or discharged from volcanoes. —**vol•can•i•cal•ly,** *adv.*

vol•ca•no, vol•kā′nō, *n. pl.,* **-noes, -nos.** A vent in the earth's crust through which molten rock, steam, ashes, and the like are violently forced from within, gradually forming a conical heap or mountain, commonly with a cup-shaped hollow or crater around the

vent; a mountain or hill having an opening or vent through which heated matter is thrust out violently from the interior of the earth.

vole, vōl, *n.* Any of several small rodents resembling mice.

vo•li•tion, və•lish′ən, *n.* The act of willing; the exercise of the will; the power of willing; will; that which has been decided or chosen by will.

vol•ley, vol′ē, *n. pl.,* **-leys.** A flight of missiles, as of shot or arrows; a simultaneous discharge of a number of missile weapons, as small arms; a return of the ball before it touches the ground, as in tennis or soccer. —*v.t.,* **-leyed, -ley•ing.** To discharge with a volley, or as if with a volley; to return, as a ball, before it touches the ground.—*v.i.* To be discharged at once or with a volley; to return a ball before it touches the ground, as in tennis or soccer.

vol•ley•ball, vol′ē•bôl, *n.* A game, usu. played by two teams in a gymnasium, the object of which is to keep a large ball in motion, from side to side over a high net, by striking it with the hands before it touches the ground; the ball so used.

volt, vōlt, *n.* The unit of electromotive force which has one ampere as a constant or steady current against a resistance of one ohm.

volt•age, vōl′tij, *n.* Electromotive force as expressed and measured in volts.

vol•ta•ic, vol•tā′ik, *a.* Referring to or denoting electricity created by chemical activity, as in an automobile battery; galvanic.

vol•ta•ic cell, *n.* A primary cell.

volt•me•ter, vōlt′mē•tər, *n.* An instrument for measuring electrical force, or difference of potential, in volts between two different points.

vol•u•ble, vol′yə•bəl, *a.* Having a great flow of words; speaking with great fluency; overly fluent. —**vol•u•bly,** *adv.* —**vol•u•bil•i•ty,** vol•yə•bil′ə•tē, *n.*

vol•ume, vol′ūm, vol′yəm, *n.* A book; a book forming one of a related set or series; the size, measure, or amount of anything in three dimensions: the *volume* of a gas; bulk; amount: the *volume* of travel on a railroad; a mass or quantity, esp. a large quantity, of anything; intensity or loudness of tone or sound.

vo•lu•mi•nous, və•loo′mə•nəs, *a.* Forming, filling, or writing a large volume or volumes: a *voluminous* literary work; sufficient to fill a volume or volumes: a *voluminous* correspondence; of great volume, size, or extent: a *voluminous* flow of lava; of ample size, extent, or fullness: a *voluminous* robe. —**vo•lu•mi•nous•ly,** *adv.* —**vo•lu•mi•nous•ness,** *n.*

vol•un•tar•y, vol′ən•ter•ē, *a.* Done, made, brought about, or undertaken of one's own accord or by free choice; having the power of willing or choosing: a *voluntary* agent; exercising one's own will or choice: a *voluntary* substitute; pertaining to or depending on voluntary action: *voluntary* schools; proceeding from a natural impulse; spontaneous: a *voluntary* burst of song; subject to or controlled by the will: *voluntary* muscles; acting or done without compulsion or obligation; done by intention and not by accident; made without valuable consideration: a *voluntary* conveyance or settlement. —**vol•un•tar•i•ly,** vol•ən•ter•ə•lē, *adv.*

vol•un•teer, vol•ən•tēr′, *n.* One who enters into any service or undertakes anything of his own free will; one who enters the military service voluntarily rather than through conscription or draft.—*a.* Being or consisting of volunteers; referring to voluntary entrance into any service.—*v.i.* To offer oneself for some service or undertaking; to enter into a service or enlist as a volunteer.—*v.t.* To offer, as one's services or self, for some duty or purpose; to offer to give, show, or share voluntarily; to offer in speech or communication: to *volunteer* an explanation.

vo•lup•tu•ar•y, və•ləp′choo•er•ē, *n. pl.,* **-ies.** One primarily interested in sensual pleasure and luxury; a sensualist.—*a.*

vo·lup·tu·ous, və·ləp/choo·əs, *a.* Pertaining to, characterized by, exciting, or producing sensual pleasure; gratifying to the senses; concerned with or indulging in sensuous pleasures and luxuries.

vom·it, vom/it, *v.i.* To eject the contents of the stomach through the mouth; to throw up; to be ejected or come out with force or violence.—*v.t.* To eject from the stomach through the mouth; to spew; to cast out or eject as if in vomiting; to send out copiously with force.—*n.* The matter ejected in vomiting.

voo·doo, voo/doo, *n. pl.,* **-doos.** A religion of African origin characterized by mysterious rites or practices of the nature of sorcery, witchcraft, or conjuration, practiced in the West Indies; one who practices such rites.

voo·doo·ism, voo/doo·iz·əm, *n.* The voodoo rites or practices. **—voo·doo·ist,** *n.* **—voo·doo·is·tic,** voo·doo·is/tik, *a.*

vo·ra·cious, və·rā/shəs, vôr·ā/shəs, *a.* Greedy for eating; eating food in large quantities; rapacious; ready to devour or swallow up. **—vo·rac·i·ty,** və·ras/ə·tē, vôr·as/ə·tē, *n.*

vor·tex, vôr/teks, *n. pl.,* **-tex·es, -ti·ces,** -tə·sēz. A whirling mass of water or air, as a whirlpool or whirlwind.

vo·ta·ry, vō/tə·rē, *n. pl.,* **-ries.** One who is bound by vows to a religious life; a monk or a nun; one devoted to any pursuit or study; a devoted follower or admirer, as of some person.

vote, vōt, *n.* A formal expression of will, wish, or choice in some matter, whether of a single individual or of a body of individuals; the means by which such an expression is made, as a ballot or ticket; the right to such expression; the decision reached by voting, as by a majority of ballots cast; a number of votes collectively: the labor *vote.*—*v.i.,* **vot·ed, vot·ing.** To cast a vote or votes.—*v.t.* To enact, establish, or determine by vote; to support or advocate by one's vote: to *vote* Republican. *Informal.* To declare by general consent: to *vote* the rummage sale a great success.

vot·er, vō/tər, *n.* One who votes; one who has a right to vote; an elector.

vot·ing ma·chine, *n.* A machine whose operation by a succession of voters in an election furnishes a record and tally of votes cast.

vo·tive, vō/tiv, *a.* Offered, given, or dedicated in accordance with a vow: a *votive* offering; performed or undertaken in consequence of a vow; of the nature of or expressive of a wish or desire.

vouch, vowch, *v.i.* To support as being true, certain, reliable, or justly asserted, usu. used with *for:* His grades *vouch for* his capabilities; to give warrant or attestation; to give one's own assurance, as surety or sponsor, usu. used with *for:* The judge would *vouch for* his character.

vouch·er, vow/chər, *n.* One who or that which vouches, as for something; a book, document, stamp, or the like which serves to prove the truth of something; a receipt or other written evidence, as of the payment of money.

vouch·safe, vowch·sāf/, *v.t.,* **-safed, -saf·ing.** To grant, often condescendingly; to permit.—*v.i.* To condescend; to deign.

vow, vow, *n.* A solemn promise; an engagement solemnly entered into; an oath made to God or to some deity to perform some act on the fulfillment of certain conditions; a promise to follow out some line of conduct, or to devote oneself to some act or service.

—*v.t.* To promise solemnly; to give, consecrate, or dedicate by a solemn promise, as to a divine power; to threaten solemnly or upon oath: I *vow* vengeance. —*v.i.* To make a promise or vow.**—take vows,** to enter a religious order.

vow·el, vow/əl, vowl, *n.* One of the more or less open and resonant speech sounds, used alone or in combination with consonants to form syllables: distinguished from *consonant;* a letter or character representing such a sound, as in English, *a, e, i, o, u,* and sometimes *y.*—*a.*

voy·age, voy/ij, *n.* A journey by sea from one place, port, or country to another, esp. a journey by water to a distant place or country; formerly, a journey by sea or by land; a journey in a space vehicle or airplane; an account written about a voyage.—*v.i.,* **-aged, -ag·ing.** To take a journey or voyage; to sail or pass by water.—*v.t.* To travel; to pass over. **—voy·ag·er,** *n.*

vo·ya·geur, vwä·yä·zhər/, voy·ə·zhər/, *n.* One of a class of men in Canada hired by some fur company to travel through unsettled regions, esp. by canoe, to transport men and goods and to maintain communications with various stations.

vo·yeur, vwä·yər/, voy·yər/, *n.* One who obtains sexual satisfaction from the sight of sexual actions or objects. **—voy·eur·ism,** *n.* **—voy·eur·is·tic,** vwä·yə·ris/tik, voy·ə·ris/tik, *a.*

vul·can·ite, vəl/kə·nīt, *n.* A form of hard rubber, vulcanized at a high temperature and containing a large proportion of sulfur, used for making combs, electrical insulating equipment, and the like.

vul·can·ize, vəl/kə·nīz, *v.t.,* **-ized, -iz·ing.** To treat, as rubber, with sulfur, and subject to heat, in order to give greater elasticity or durability. **—vul·can·i·za·tion,** vəl·kə·nə·zā/shən, *n.*

vul·gar, vəl/gər, *a.* Lacking in good taste, cultivation, or refinement; somewhat coarse; boorish; crude; indecent or obscene; referring to the common people; popular or current; expressed in the language of the common people, or vernacular: the *vulgar* tongue; ordinary, or deficient in distinction.

vul·gar·ism, vəl/gə·riz·əm, *n.* Vulgarity; a vulgar phrase or expression used in informal speech.

vul·gar·i·ty, vəl·gar/ə·tē, *n. pl.,* **-ties.** The quality of being vulgar; coarseness; a vulgar expression, habit, or action.

vul·gar·ize, vəl/gə·rīz, *v.t.,* **-ized, -iz·ing.** To make vulgar; coarsen; to debase; to make generally acceptable; to popularize. **—vul·gar·i·za·tion,** vəl·gər·ə·zā/shən, *n.*

vul·gate, vəl/gāt, *n. (Cap.)* The Latin version of the Scriptures prepared by Jerome about the close of the 4th century, accepted as the authorized version of the Roman Catholic Church.

vul·ner·a·ble, vəl/nər·ə·bəl, *a.* Capable of being wounded; liable to injury or criticism; subject to being affected injuriously or attacked: a *vulnerable* nation. **—vul·ner·a·bil·i·ty,** vəl·nər·ə·bil/ə·tē, *n.* **—vul·ner·a·bly,** *adv.*

vul·pine, vəl/pīn, vəl/pin, *a.* Referring to the fox; resembling the fox; cunning.

vul·ture, vəl/chər, *n.* Any of certain large birds related to the eagles, hawks, and falcons, which feed chiefly or wholly on dead flesh; a person or thing that preys ravenously and ruthlessly.

vul·va, vəl/və, *n. pl.,* **-vae,** -vē, **-vas.** The female external genital organs.

W

W, w, dəb′əl•ŭ, *n.* The twenty-third letter of the English alphabet.

wab•ble, wob′əl, *v.i., v.t.,* **-bled, -bling.** Wobble.—*n.* A wobble.

WAC, Wac, wak, *n.* A member of the Women's Army Corps; the corps itself.

wack•y, wak′ē, *a.,* **-i•er, -i•est.** *Informal.* Very erratic or eccentric; quite irrational; crazy. **—wack•i•ly,** *adv.* **—wack•i•ness,** *n.*

wad, wod, *n.* A soft mass of fibrous material, as cotton, used for stuffing, stopping an aperture, and the like; a lump, mass, or ball of something; a plug used to hold powder or shot in place in a gun, cartridge, or cannon.—*v.t.,* **wad•ded, wad•ding.** To mold into a wad by rolling, crumpling, compressing, and the like; to plug with a wad; to stuff or line with wadding.—*v.i.* To form into a wad.

wad•dle, wod′əl, *v.i.,* **-dled, -dling.** To sway or rock from side to side in walking; to walk in a tottering manner.—*n.* A characteristic walk: the *waddle* of a duck. **—wad•dler,** *n.* **—wad•dly,** *a.,* **-dli•er, -dli•est.**

wade, wād, *v.i.,* **wad•ed, wad•ing.** To walk through any substance that impedes or hinders the free motion of the legs, as water, snow, or high grass; to move or proceed with difficulty: to *wade* through the required reading assignment.—*v.t.* To pass or cross by wading; to ford. **—wade in** or **wade into.** *Informal.* To attack, esp. verbally, or begin aggressively.

wad•er, wā′dər, *n.* One who wades; any long-legged bird, as the stork, heron, snipe, or rail, that wades in water searching for food; *pl.,* high, waterproof boots used by hunters and fishermen for wading.

WAF, Waf, waf, *n.* A member of the Women in the Air Force; the service itself.

wa•fer, wā′fər, *n.* A small, crisp, sweet cake, biscuit, or cracker; a circular piece of unleavened bread, as used in the Roman Catholic Church in the celebration and administration of the Eucharist; a small thin disk of an adhesive substance, used in the sealing of letters and documents; a thin coating of dried paste or the like covering a powdered drug to be swallowed.

waf•fle, wof′əl, *n.* A crisp batter cake, having deep, latticelike indentations on both sides, baked in a waffle iron.

waf•fle i•ron, *n.* A metal utensil with two indented or studded hinged parts which, when shut together, impress a pattern on the baking batter.

waft, waft, wȧft, *v.t.* To convey or carry lightly through, or as if through, water or air, as objects or odors; to make to sail or float.—*v.i.* To sail or float, as through air.—*n.* The act of one who or that which wafts; any wafting movement or motion; anything, as a sound or odor, conveyed gently through the air; a breath or current, as of wind.

wag, wag, *v.t.,* **wagged, wag•ging.** To move from side to side, forward and backward, or up and down, esp. rapidly and repeatedly, as a dog's tail; to move, as the head, in agreement or denial; to move, as the tongue, in talk or gossip.—*v.i.* To be moved from side to side or one way and the other, esp. rapidly and repeatedly, as the head, the tail, or the tongue.—*n.* An act of wagging. **—wag•ger,** *n.*

wag, wag, *n.* A person who is full of mischievous humor; a wit; a joker. **—wag•gish,** wag′ish, *a.* **—wag•gish•ly,** *adv.* **—wag•gish•ness,** *n.*

wage, wāj, *n.* Often *pl.* Money paid for labor or services, usu. according to specified intervals of work, as by the hour, day, or week. *Pl., sing.* or *pl. in constr.* Recompense; requital: The *wages* of sin is death. —*v.t.,* **waged, wag•ing.** To carry on, as a battle, conflict, or argument: to *wage* war against a nation.

wage earn•er, *n.* One who is paid wages for working.

wa•ger, wā′jər, *n.* A bet; something staked or hazarded on an uncertain event.—*v.t.* To hazard, as money or property, on the issue of a contest or any uncertain event or matter; to stake; to bet.—*v.i.* To make or offer a wager; to bet.

wag•ger•y, wag′ə•rē, *n. pl.,* **-ies.** The manner, action, or attitude of a wag; jocular, mischievous pleasantry; a prank or joke.

wag•gle, wag′əl, *v.i.,* **-gled, -gling.** To move with a wagging motion.—*v.t.* To cause to wag or move rapidly and with short motions.—*n.* A waggling movement.

wag•on, wag′ən, *n.* A four-wheeled vehicle for the transport of heavy loads; a small, four-wheeled cart used as a child's toy vehicle; a station wagon.

wag•on•er, wag′ə•nər, *n.* One who drives a wagon.

wag•on train, *n.* A group or train of wagons traveling together for a common purpose or for transporting supplies.

waif, wāf, *n.* A neglected, homeless person, esp. a young child; a wanderer; any stray or abandoned animal.

wail, wāl, *v.i.* To utter a prolonged, inarticulate, mournful cry, usu. high-pitched or clear-sounding, as in grief or suffering; to give forth a mournful or plaintive sound suggesting a cry, as musical instruments or the wind.—*v.t.* To wail over, bewail, or lament.—*n.* The act or sound of wailing; a wailing cry.

wain•scot, wān′skŏt, wān′skət, *n.* A wooden lining for the walls of rooms, usu. made in panels; the wood-paneled lower portion of a wall, the upper portion of which is finished in some other material. **—wain•scot•ing,** wān′skō•ting, wān′skət•ing, *n.*

wain•wright, wān′rīt, *n.* A wagon maker.

waist, wāst, *n.* The part of the human body between the ribs and the hips; the part of a garment covering the waist; a garment or a part of a garment covering the body from the neck or shoulders to the waistline, that part, often the narrowest, of an object, esp. a central or middle part, which bears some analogy to the human waist: the *waist* of a violin; the central part of a ship; that part of the deck between the forecastle and the quarter-deck; the middle section of an airplane's fuselage.

waist•band, wāst′band, *n.* A band for encircling the waist, esp. such a band forming part of a skirt or trousers.

waist•coat, wes′kət, wāst′kōt, *n. Chiefly Brit.* A vest.

waist•line, wāst′līn, *n.* The line of the waist, between the chest and hip portions of the human body; the measurement of this line; the narrow part on clothing to which the skirt or lower portion attaches.

wait, wāt, *v.i.* To stay or rest in expectation, often followed by *for, till,* or *until;* to be in readiness; to remain neglected or be postponed for a time: a matter that can *wait;* to perform the duties of an attendant, esp. as a waiter or waitress.—*v.t.* To remain stationary or inactive in expectation of; to await: to *wait* one's turn; to postpone in expectation of; to defer: to *wait* dinner for someone.—*n.* An act or interval of waiting; delay. **—lie in wait,** to watch for from a place of concealment, esp. with hostile intent. **—wait on** or **wait up•on,** to act as attendant or servant to; to make a formal, usu. deferential, call upon: to *wait on* the King.

wait•er, wā′tər, *n.* A male attendant who waits upon the guests in a hotel, restaurant, or similar place; one who waits or awaits something or someone.

wait•ing, wāt′ing, *n.* The act of a person who waits. —*a.* Expecting; attending. **—in wait•ing,** in attendance, esp. on a person of royalty.

wait•ing room, *n.* A room provided for the use of persons waiting, as in a railroad station or a physician's office.

wait·ress, wā′tris, *n.* A girl or woman who waits on tables, esp. in a restaurant.

waive, wāv, *v.t.,* **waived, waiv·ing.** To refrain from claim or insistence upon; to relinquish; to forgo; to put aside, postpone, or dismiss.

waiv·er, wā′vər, *n.* An intentional relinquishment of a known right, interest, or advantage; an express or written statement of such relinquishment.

wake, wāk, *v.i.,* **waked** or **woke, waked** or **wok·en, wak·ing.** To become roused from sleep, often followed by *up:* He *woke up* suddenly; to awake; to be or continue to be awake: *waking* or sleeping; to become roused from a quiescent or inactive state; to become aware, as of something perceived: to *wake* to the truth; to remain awake for some purpose or duty. *Informal.* To hold a wake.—*v.t.* To rouse from sleep, often followed by *up:* Wake me *up* for breakfast; to awaken; to rouse from inactivity; to stir up or excite, as feelings. *Informal.* To hold a wake over.—*n.* A watching or a watch kept, esp. for some solemn or ceremonial purpose; an all-night watch over the body of a dead person before burial; the state of being awake: between sleep and *wake.*

wake, wāk, *n.* The track left by a ship or other object moving in the water; the path, track, or course of anything that has passed or preceded. **—in the wake of,** following closely; as a consequence or result of: Arrests increased *in the wake of* the robbery.

wake·ful, wāk′fəl, *a.* Unable to sleep; characterized by absence of sleep: a *wakeful* night; sleeplessly alert, watchful, or vigilant: a *wakeful* enemy. **—wake·ful·ly,** *adv.* **—wake·ful·ness,** *n.*

wak·en, wā′kən, *v.t.* To awake, or rouse from sleep; to awaken; to excite to action; to rouse; to stir; to call forth: to *waken* love or fear.—*v.i.* To wake; to cease to sleep; to awaken.

wale, wāl, *n.* A stripe or ridge produced on the skin, as by the stroke of a whip; a welt; a ridge or rib in the weave of cloth.—*v.t.,* **waled, wal·ing.** To raise wales on; to weave wales into.

walk, wôk, *v.i.* To go or travel on foot at a moderate pace; to proceed by steps; to go on foot for enjoyment or exercise; in baseball, to be advanced to first base after four balls are pitched.—*v.t.* To proceed through, over, or upon, on foot at a moderate pace: to *walk* the streets; to lead, drive, or ride at a walk, as an animal; to conduct on a walk: to *walk* the neighbors around the street; in baseball, to advance to first base by pitching four balls; to inspect, as property, on foot.—*n.* An act of walking or going on foot; a time or interval of walking for exercise or pleasure; a distance walked or to be walked, often in terms of the time required: a ten minutes′ *walk* to school; a manner of walking; a particular profession, activity, or position: various *walks* of life; a place prepared or set apart for walking, as a path; in baseball, advancement to first base after four pitched balls.

walk·a·way, wôk′ə·wā, *n. Informal.* A very easily won competition: to win in a *walkaway.*

walk·er, wô′kər, *n.* A device moving on casters designed to enclose and support a child during his early attempts at walking; a similar framework which may be rigid or movable, with arm supports, to aid an invalid or elderly person in walking; one who walks, esp. one fond of walking.

walk·ie-talk·ie, wô′kē·tô′kē, *n.* A mobile or portable two-way radio-telephone system with a receiver and microphone, which is operated by a battery and compact enough for one person to carry, usu. on his back.

walk·ing pa·pers, *n. pl. Informal.* Official notification that one has been dismissed or discharged.

walk·out, wôk′owt, *n.* A workers′ strike; an expression of disapproval by departure or absence, as from a meeting.

walk·o·ver, wôk′ō·vər, *n. Informal.* Any easy victory.

walk-up, wok′əp, *n. Informal.* An apartment on the second floor or above in a building in which there is no elevator; such a building.—*a.*

walk·way, wôk′wā, *n.* Any passage used by one walking.

wall, wôl, *n.* A vertical structure of stone, brick, wood, or other materials which serves to enclose a space, form a division, support weight, retain earth or water, or perform similar functions; the side of a building or room; something similar to a wall.—*v.t.* To enclose or separate with a wall; to fortify or protect by walls; to fill up with a wall, as an opening. **—go to the wall,** to get the worst of a contest; to be overpowered. **—push to the wall,** to crush; to humiliate or force into a desperate state.

wal·la·by, wol′ə·bē, *n. pl.,* **-bies, -by.** Any of various small and medium-sized kangaroos, some of which are no larger than rabbits.

wall·board, wôl′bōrd, wôl′bôrd, *n.* An artificially prepared board or sheet material for use in making or covering walls and ceilings, as a substitute for wooden boards or plaster.

wal·let, wol′it, wô′lit, *n.* A small case carried in a pocket or handbag for holding money, identification and credit cards, pictures, or the like.

wall·eye, wôl′ī, *n. pl.,* **-eye, -eyes.** Any of various game fishes with large, staring eyes.

wall-eyed, wôl′īd, *a.* Having an eye or the eyes presenting little or no color, as the result of a light-colored or white iris or of white opacity of the cornea; having eyes in which there is an abnormal amount of the white showing, because they are turned away from the center; having large, staring eyes, as some fishes.

wall·flow·er, wôl′flow·ər, *n.* A European perennial plant, growing wild on old walls, cliffs, and similar places, and also cultivated in several varieties, bearing sweet-scented yellow, red, or purple flowers. *Informal.* A person who is left stranded at the side in a social situation, as at a dance, either from shyness or failure to obtain a partner.

wal·lop, wol′əp, *v.t. Informal.* To beat soundly; thrash; to strike with a vigorous blow; to defeat thoroughly, as in a game.—*n. Informal.* A forceful blow; an ability to deliver such blows, as in boxing.

wal·low, wol′ō, *v.i.* To roll the body about, or lie in water, snow, mud, dust, or the like, as for refreshment, as a pig in mud; to live self-indulgently or luxuriously, as in some form of pleasure, manner of life, or the like: to *wallow* in wealth; to flounder about or along clumsily or with difficulty, as a vessel on the waves.—*n.* The act of wallowing; a place where an animal wallows.

wall·pa·per, wôl′pā·pər, *n.* Paper, usu. colored and decorated, for covering the walls of rooms.—*v.t.* To put wallpaper on the walls of.

Wall Street, *n.* A street in the city of New York, famous as the chief financial center of the U.S.; the center for the financiers and financial interests of the U.S.

wall-to-wall, wôl′tə·wôl′, *a.* Covering a floor completely, from wall to wall.

wal·nut, wôl′nət, *n.* One of several trees bearing fruit containing an edible kernel; the nut of these trees; the timber from such a tree, esp. the black walnut.

wal·rus, wôl′rəs, wol′rəs, *n. pl.,* **-rus·es, -rus.** Either of two large, marine, meat-eating mammals of the arctic regions, related to the seals and hunted for the tough hide, the ivory of the tusks, and the oil derived from the blubber.

waltz, wôlts, *n.* A ballroom dance in which the couples glide in a revolving motion around the floor to music in three-quarter time; the music for such a dance.—*v.i.* To dance to waltz time. *Informal.* To perform a task effortlessly, followed by *through:* to *waltz through* a

---

a- hat, fāte, fāre, fäther; **e-** met, mē; **i-** pin, pīne; **o-** not, nōte, ôrb, moove (move), boy, pownd; **u-** cūbe, bûll, tûk (took); **ch-** chin; **th-** thick, ᵺen; **zh-** vizhon (vision); **ə-** ego, takən, pencəl, lemən, bərd (bird).

math assignment.—*v.t.* To lead, as a partner, in a waltz. *Informal.* To move or propel briskly: to *waltz* a misbehaving child out of the classroom.

wam·pum, wom′pəm, wôm′pəm, *n.* Small beads made of shells strung together, formerly used by the N. American Indians as a medium of exchange or for ornamentation.

wan, won, *a.,* **wan·ner, wan·nest.** Having a pale or sickly color; pallid; indicative of or showing fatigue, emotional distress, illness, or the like. —**wan·ness,** *n.*

wand, wond, *n.* A long, slender stick or rod.

wan·der, won′dər, *v.i.* To travel here and there without a specific destination; roam; to go casually; stroll; to go or extend in an irregular direction or course; meander; to deviate or stray morally; err; to stray in one's thoughts; to be irrational or incoherent in speech or thought.—*v.t.* To travel over.—*n.* A ramble or stroll.

wan·der·lust, wän′dər·ləst, *n.* Desire to wander.

wane, wān, *v.i.,* **waned, wan·ing.** To diminish; to decrease or grow less; particularly applied to the illuminated part of the moon, as opposed to *wax*; to decline, as in importance or power; to approach its end: The autumn *wanes.*—*n.* A waning period; the decrease of the illuminated part of the moon to the eye of the spectator; a decline. —**on the wane,** in a decreasing period; waning.

wan·gle, wang′gəl, *v.t.,* **-gled, -gling.** *Informal.* To accomplish or obtain by irregular or devious methods or means: to *wangle* an extra ticket.—*v.i. Informal.* To gain one's ends by devious methods.—*n. Informal.* An act of wangling. —**wan·gler,** *n.*

want, wont, wônt, *v.t.* To feel a desire for; long, wish, need, or crave, often followed by an infinitive: I *want* to sleep; to be without; to lack: to *want* experience; to require or need: The lawn *wants* cutting; to be short of, as a specified extent or amount.—*v.i.* To be needy or impoverished; to have need, usu. followed by *for;* to be inclined, often followed by *to:* Stay home if you *want to.*—*n.* Absence or scarcity of something needed or desired; lack; the state of being in need; poverty; a desire for something.

want ad, *n.* Classified ad.

want·ing, won′ting, wôn′ting, *a.* Lacking or absent: an apparatus with some of the parts *wanting;* deficient in some part, thing, or respect, usu. used with *in:* to be *wanting in* courtesy.—*prep.* Lacking or without; less; minus: a century, *wanting* three years.

wan·ton, won′tən, *a.* Licentious or lustful; indulging unrestrainedly in natural impulses or appetites; unprovoked or unjustified; arising from recklessness or disregard of right or consequences; excessive or immoderate; playful or fun loving.—*n.* A lustful person; a person or other animal inclined to excess frolic or play.—*v.t.* To waste or expend wantonly.—*v.i.* To frolic unrestrainedly or carouse; to indulge in lewdness.

wap·i·ti, wop′ə·tē, *n. pl.,* **-ties, -ti.** A N. American species of deer with long slender antlers; elk.

war, wôr, *n.* An armed clash between nations, or factions in the same nation; a state of hostility or military conflict; an act of enmity or contention; the profession, science, or art of military operations.—*v.i.,* **warred, war·ring.** To make or carry on war; to carry on hostilities; to be in a state of forceful opposition.—*a.* Of, relating to, used in, or caused by war.

war·ble, wôr′bəl, *v.t.,* **-bled, -bling.** To sing melodiously in a trilling, quavering, or vibrating manner.—*v.i.* To have a trilling, quavering, or vibrating sound; to carol or sing with melodious turns or variations.—*n.* A flow of melodious sounds, or a trilling, flexible melody; the act or sound of warbling.

war·bler, wôr′blər, *n.* One who or that which warbles; any of the vividly colored, small, chiefly insectivorous birds of N. and S. America, as the yellow warbler, water thrushes, and the redstart.

war bon·net, *n.* A ceremonial headdress made of feathers attached to a headband or cap and to an extension trailing down the back, worn by the N. American Plains Indians.

war cry, *n.* A battle cry or phrase shouted by fighters in charging an enemy; a slogan or phrase used to unite or rally people in any contest or campaign.

ward, wôrd, *v.t.* To fend off; to turn aside, as a blow, often followed by *off.*—*n.* The act of guarding; a minor, or a mental incompetent who is under guardianship; a certain division or section of a town or city, formed for the convenient transaction of civic business and for political purposes; one of the divisions in a prison or hospital.

war·den, wôr′dən, *n.* One who guards, protects, or defends; one charged with the care or custody of something, as a keeper; the chief official of a prison; a public official charged with superintendence, as over a forest or wild game; a person in charge of enforcing regulations for public safety, as for fire or air raids; the head of certain colleges or schools in Great Britain; a churchwarden. —**war·den·ship,** *n.*

ward·er, wôr′dər, *n.* One who wards or guards something; a keeper or watchman; in Great Britain, a warden in a jail.

ward heeler, *n. Informal.* A worker in a political ward who canvasses votes and solicits contributions in return for a job when his party is in office.

ward·robe, wôrd′rōb, *n.* A place in which clothes are kept, often a piece of furniture resembling a cupboard or cabinet; wearing apparel in general belonging to any one person.

ware, wâr, *n. Usu. pl.* Articles of merchandise; goods; a special type of manufactured item, usu. used in a compound word: as, china*ware;* pottery, or a special type of pottery.

ware·house, wâr′hows, *n.* A building in which wares or goods are kept or stored.

war·fare, wôr′fâr, *n.* The act of military hostilities between nations, political units, or the like; war; any struggle or conflict.

war·head, wôr′hed, *n.* That part of a bomb, guided missile, ballistic missile, torpedo, or other missile containing an explosive, chemical, or atomic charge intended to damage the enemy.

war-horse, wôr′hôrs, *n.* A horse used in war; a charger. *Informal.* A veteran of numerous campaigns and battles, as a politician or soldier.

war·like, wôr′līk, *a.* Fit or prepared for war; disposed or inclined to war; military; pertaining to or suggestive of war; openly antagonistic or hostile.

war·lock, wôr′lok, *n.* A male witch; a magician; a wizard or sorcerer.

warm, wôrm, *a.,* **warm·er, warm·est.** Having or communicating a moderate degree of heat; having a sensation of bodily heat, as from exercise or exertion; producing such a sensation: *warm* clothes; characterized by or showing lively feelings, passions, emotions, or sympathies: a *warm* heart; strongly attached or intimate: *warm* friends; heated, irritated, or angry: to become *warm* when criticized; animated, lively, brisk, or vigorous: a *warm* contest; strong or fresh: a *warm* scent; suggestive of warmth, as the colors red or yellow. *Informal.* Close to a concealed object or fact, as in various games; uncomfortable or unpleasant: a debate too *warm* for comfort.—*v.t.* To make warm; to excite ardor, enthusiasm, or animation in; to affect with kindly feelings.—*v.i.* To become warm; to become ardent, enthusiastic, or animated, followed by *up* or *to:* to *warm to* a task; to grow kindly disposed, followed by *to* or *toward:* My heart *warmed* toward her.

warm-blood·ed, wôrm′blcd′id, *a.* Having warm blood; noting or pertaining to mammals and birds, whose blood temperatures remain relatively constant regardless of the temperature of their surroundings; having an ardent, impetuous, or passionate nature.

warm front, *n.* The irregular forward edge separating an advancing mass of warm air from the cold air it will replace.

warm·heart·ed, warm·heart·ed, wôrm/härt'tid, *a.* Having or showing a genuine interest in or affectionate concern for others; cordial; hearty.

warm·ing pan, *n.* A long-handled, covered, flat vessel, usu. of brass, for holding hot coals or the like, formerly in common use for warming beds.

war·mong·er, wôr/mong·gər, wôr/mong·gər, *n.* One who advocates or seeks to bring about war.

warmth, wôrmth, *n.* The quality or state of being warm; the sensation of heat; gentle heat; hearty kindness or affection; ardor; zeal; fervor; earnestness; slight anger or irritation.

warn, wôrn, *v.t.* To give notice of approaching or probable danger or evil; to inform previously.—*v.i.* To give caution or warning: A storm usu. *warns* before it hits.

warn·ing, wôr/ning, *n.* The act of giving notice or intimation of danger or of cautioning, admonishing, or notifying; notice of this kind given or received; something serving to warn, caution, or admonish.—*a.* Serving as a caution.

warp, wôrp, *v.t.* To change the shape, as of something; to turn or twist out of shape; to turn aside from the true direction; to pervert, as the mind or judgment; to tow or move, as a ship into a required position.—*v.i.* To twist, or be twisted from straightness; to turn from a straight, true, or proper course; to deviate; to swerve; to work forward by means of a rope.—*n.* A twist or distortion, as of wood in drying; a mental quirk, aberration, twist, or bias; the threads which are extended lengthwise in a loom and crossed by the woof; a rope used in moving a ship by attachment to an anchor or post; a towline.

war paint, *n.* Paint applied to the face and parts of the body by American Indians upon going to war.

war·path, wôr/path, *n.* The path or course taken by American Indians on a warlike expedition. —**on the war·path,** looking for, preparing for, or on a warlike or hostile expedition; in an aggressive, angry, or hostile state of mind.

war·rant, wôr/ənt, wor/ənt, *n.* Authorization, sanction, or justification; that which serves to give reliable or formal assurance of something; a security, promise, or guarantee; something having the force of a guarantee or positive assurance of a thing; a writing or document certifying or authorizing something.—*v.t.* To give authority to or authorize; to justify or afford warrant or sanction for: circumstances which do not *warrant* such measures; to give a formal assurance, guarantee, or promise to: to *warrant* proper care; to guarantee the reliability, quality, or other claims of, as an appliance or product; to guarantee compensation against loss; to vouch for or give one's word for, often used with a clause to assert emphatically: I'll *warrant* he did.

war·ran·ty, wôr/ən·tē, wor/ən·tē, *n. pl.,* **-ties.** The act of warranting; warrant; assurance; authorization; a written statement or guarantee made by the manufacturer of a product, assuring the purchaser that repairs or replacement of defective parts will be done without charge for a specified period of time.

war·ren, wôr/ən, wor/ən, *n.* A place where rabbits breed in burrows; a building or collection of buildings containing many tenants in limited quarters.

war·ri·or, wôr/ē·ər, wor/ē·ər, *n.* A man engaged or experienced in warfare; a soldier, esp. a brave or veteran soldier.

war·ship, wôr/ship, *n.* A ship built or armed for war.

wart, wôrt, *n.* A small, dry, hard, nonmalignant lesion of the skin.

wart hog, *n.* Any of several species of African wild swine, notable for the warty growths on the face and the large, curving tusks.

war·time, wôr/tīm, *n.* A time when a nation is at war.—*a.* As a result of or occurring in a time of war: *wartime* experiences.

war·y, wār/ē, *a.,* **-i·er, -i·est.** Carefully watching to detect and avoid deception or danger; on one's guard; careful; marked by prudence or caution: a *wary* glance. —**war·i·ly,** wār/ə·lē, *adv.* —**war·i·ness,** wār/ē·nis, *n.*

was, wəz, woz. The past tense of the first and third person singular of the verb *to be:* I *was,* he *was.*

wash, wosh, wôsh, *v.t.* To immerse in or apply water or other liquid to, for the purpose of cleansing; to scour, scrub, or the like, with water or other liquid; to cleanse from guilt or sin; to wet or bathe with water or another liquid; to cover with water; to flow against or through: The sea *washed* the sand; to carry away in a rush of water; to transport, remove, or deposit by the flow of water or other liquid, usu. followed by *away* or *off;* to separate, as ore, from earth by the action of water: to *wash* gold; to cover with a watery or thin coat of color.—*v.i.* To wash oneself; to wash clothes or other items in water; to withstand washing without being injured, spoiled, or destroyed: a dress that *washes;* to stand being put to the proof: His tale won't *wash;* to be driven or transported by water; to move in waves or beat against: water *washing* against the shore.—*n.* The act of washing; the clothes or other items washed on one occasion; a liquid used for washing or wetting; a thin coat of color spread over surfaces, as water color; the rush, flow, or sweep of water; the sound caused by this: the *wash* of the ocean or tide; the broken, choppy water following a boat; a wake; the air turbulence caused by an airplane; a liquid or lotion used for cosmetic purposes: hair *wash;* mineral with valuable materials extractable by washing; alluvial material; waste liquid containing food refuse, often fed to pigs.—*a.* Washable; capable of being undamaged in washing: *wash* materials. —**wash down,** to clean thoroughly by washing: to *wash down* a window. —**wash out,** to wash; to cleanse; to destroy by force of water: The flood *washed* out the road. *Informal.* To fail; to be eliminated: to *wash out* of school. —**wash up,** to wash the hands or face; to wash the dishes. —**wash·a·ble,** wosh/ə·bəl, wô/shə·bəl, *a.*

wash and wear, *a.* Denoting a fabric or article of clothing which, after washing, requires hardly any or no ironing.

wash·ba·sin, wosh/bā·sin, wôsh/bā·sin, *n.* Washbowl.

wash·board, wosh/bōrd, wosh/bôrd, wôsh/bōrd, wôsh/bôrd, *n.* A board with a ribbed surface, usu. metallic, on which to rub clothes in the washing process.

wash·bowl, wosh/bōl, wôsh/bōl, *n.* A sink or basin for washing the face and hands. Also **wash·ba·sin.**

wash·cloth, wosh/klôth, wosh/kloth, wôsh/klôth, wôsh/kloth, *n.* A square, small cloth which is used to wash one's body.

wash·er, wosh/ər, wô/shər, *n.* One who or that which washes; a washing machine; a flat ring or perforated piece of leather, rubber, or metal, used to give tightness to a joint, to prevent leakage, or to distribute pressure, as under the head of a bolt or nut.

wash·ing, wosh/ing, wô/shing, *n.* The act of cleansing with water, usu. with soap or a detergent; articles, as clothes, washed at one time; a material, as gold, obtained after washing soil; *often pl.,* liquid which has been used for washing something.

wash·ing ma·chine, *n.* A machine for washing clothes.

wash·out, wosh/owt, wôsh/owt, *n.* The washing out or away of earth, esp. from a roadbed by heavy rains or a flood. *Informal.* A failure.

wash·room, wosh/room, wosh/rūm, wôsh/room,

wôsh'rûm, *n.* A room containing one or more wash-bowls and various other toilet facilities, esp. found in public places; a rest room.

wash•stand, wosh'stand, wôsh'stand, *n.* A piece of furniture which holds a basin, pitcher, and other articles for use in washing the face and hands; a permanent fixture having faucets with running water, for use in washing the face and hands.

wash•tub, wosh'təb, wôsh'təb, *n.* A tub for use in washing clothes.

was•n't, wez'ent, woz'ent. Contraction of was not.

wasp, wosp, *n.* Any of various stinging insects, usu. having the waist or base portion of the abdomen narrowly constricted, and many of which live in socie-ties. **—wasp•ish,** wos'pish, *a.* **—wasp•ish•ly,** *adv.* **—wasp•ish•ness,** *n.*

was•sail, wos'əl, *n.* An ancient English drinking toast; a festive occasion where drinking and pledging of healths are indulged in; the liquor used on such occasions, esp. wine or spiced ale on Christmas or New Year's.—*v.i.* To hold a merry drinking meeting; to carouse.—*v.t.* To toast or pledge in drinking.

Was•ser•mann test, wä'sər•mən, *n.* A test used for the detection of syphilis.

wast•age, wā'stij, *n.* The act of wasting; loss by use, wear, decay, or leakage; that which is lost.

waste, wāst, *v.i.,* **wast•ed, wast•ing.** To consume, spend, or employ uselessly or without adequate re-turn: to *waste* money; to use to no avail; to fail or neglect to use: to *waste* an opportunity; to destroy or consume gradually; to wear down or reduce in bodily substance, health, or strength; to lay waste, devastate, or ruin.—*v.i.* To become gradually consumed, used up, or worn away; to diminish gradually or dwindle; to become physically wasted, lose flesh or strength; to pass gradually, as time.—*n.* The act of wasting or the state of being wasted; useless consumption or ex-penditure; neglect, instead of use: *waste* of opportuni-ty; devastation or ruin, as from war or fire; a region or place laid waste or in ruins; anything unused, unpro-ductive, or not properly utilized; a tract of uninhabited, desolate country or desert; anything left over or super-fluous, as excess material or by-products; anything rejected as useless or worthless: refuse; *pl.,* excre-ment.—*a.* Not used or in use: *waste* energy; of land or regions, uninhabited, desolate, barren, or desert; of regions, towns, or habitations, in a state of desolation and ruin; left over or superfluous: *waste* materials; rejected as useless, worthless, or refuse: *waste* paper; used for carrying off or holding waste materi-al. **—waste•ful,** wāst'fəl, *a.* **—waste•ful•ly,** *adv.* **—waste•ful•ness,** *n.*

waste•bas•ket, wāst'bas•kit, *n.* A basket or other container used for wastepaper and other small waste items.

waste•land, wāst'land, *n.* An area of uncultivated or devastated land; any locality, period of history, or institution considered barren of intellectual or imagi-native vigor.

waste•pa•per, waste pa•per, wāst'pā•pər, *n.* Spoiled or used paper which is thrown away.

wast•er, wā'stər, *n.* One who wastes; a squanderer.

wast•rel, wā'strəl, *n.* A wasteful person or spendthrift; an idler or good-for-nothing.

watch, woch, *v.i.* To keep vigil; to be attentive or vigilant; to be closely observant; to give heed; to act as a watchman, guard, or sentinel; to look forward with expectation, often followed by *for;* to wait.—*v.t.* To look with close attention at or on; to keep under close examination or observation; to keep a sharp lookout for; to regard with vigilance and care; to tend; to guard; to look for; to wait for.—*n.* A keeping awake for the purpose of attending, guarding, or preserving a vigil; a guard or number of guards; the time during which a person or body of persons is on guard; a small timepiece, either worn or carried in the pocket; the period of time occupied by each part of a ship's crew

alternately while on duty; a certain part of the officers and crew who together attend to working the ship for an allotted time. **—on the watch,** alert; cautious. **—watch out,** to be cautious or on guard. **—watch o•ver,** to oversee for protection.

watch•dog, woch'dôg, woch'dog, *n.* A dog kept to watch or guard premises and property; a person acting as a guardian, as against illegal activities.

watch•ful, woch'fəl, *a.* Closely or intently observant; giving wary attention; alert; vigilant.

watch•man, woch'mən, *n. pl.,* **-men.** Anyone em-ployed to keep watch or guard, as over an estate or building, esp. during the night.

watch•tow•er, woch'tow•ər, *n.* A tower upon which a sentinel is placed or posted to watch or keep guard, as over prisoners, or for enemies, fires in a forest, or the like.

watch•word, woch'wərd, *n.* A word, phrase, or signal given to a guard or the like, used to ascertain whether an unknown person is friendly or hostile; a password; a motto or slogan.

wa•ter, wô'tər, wot'ər, *n.* The liquid which in a more or less impure state constitutes rain, oceans, lakes, and rivers, and which in a pure state is a transparent, odorless, tasteless liquid, a compound of hydrogen and oxygen, H_2O, freezing at 32° F. or 0° C. and boiling at 212° F. or 100° C.; a special form or variety of this liquid, as rain; a particular body of water; any liquid or aqueous organic secretion, as tears, perspiration, or saliva; a liquid solution or preparation: toilet *water;* the degree of transparency and brilliancy of a precious stone: a diamond of the first *water;* a kind of wavy, lustrous pattern or marking, as on silk fabrics.—*v.t.* To sprinkle, moisten, or drench with water: to *water* a road; to supply with water, as by irrigation; to furnish water to, as a region, as with streams; to supply with water for drinking; to dilute or adulterate with water, often with *down:* to *water down* soup.—*v.i.* To dis-charge, fill with, or secrete water or liquid, as the eyes with tears, or as the mouth at the sight or thought of tempting food. **—a•bove wa•ter,** out of embarrass-ment or trouble, esp. financial trouble. **—hold wa•ter,** to prove sound, tenable, or valid, as a theory. **—in hot wa•ter,** in trouble; in difficulty. **—like wa•ter,** abun-dantly; freely: The beer flowed *like water.*

wa•ter bird, *n.* A swimming or wading bird; a water-fowl.

wa•ter•buck, wô'tər•bək, wot'ər•bək, *n.* Any of vari-ous African antelopes frequenting marshes and reedy places.

wa•ter buf•fa•lo, *n.* An Asiatic buffalo, frequently domesticated for draft use.

wa•ter chest•nut, *n.* Any of various aquatic plants bearing an edible, nutlike fruit; the fruit of these plants.

wa•ter clock, *n.* One of various devices for measur-ing time by the flow of water.

wa•ter clos•et, *n.* A room or enclosed compartment having a toilet that flushes with water; the toilet itself.

wa•ter•col•or, wô'tər•kəl'ər, wot'ər•kəl'ər, *n.* A paint in which the pigment is dissolved in water instead of oil; the art of painting with water colors; a painting done in water colors.

wa•ter cool•er, *n.* An apparatus or vessel which holds and cools drinking water and dispenses it.

wa•ter•course, wô'tər•kōrs, wô'tər•kôrs, wot'ər•kōrs, wot'ər•kôrs, *n.* A stream of water; a river; a brook; a natural channel conveying water, as a stream bed; a channel or canal made for the conveyance of water.

wa•ter•cress, wô'tər•kres, wot'ər•kres, *n.* A peren-nial cress of the mustard family, usu. growing in clear, running water, and bearing pungent leaves which are used for salad and as a garnish.

wa•ter•fall, wô'tər•fôl, wot'ər•fôl, *n.* A fall or perpen-dicular descent of the water of a river or stream; a cascade; a cataract.

wa·ter·fowl, wô′tər·fowl, wot′ər·fowl, *n. pl.,* **-fowls, -fowl.** A water bird, esp. a swimming bird; such birds collectively, esp. swimming game birds.

wa·ter·front, wô′tər·frənt, wot′ər·frənt, *n.* Land abutting on a body of water; a section of a city or town, as a dock, abutting on a harbor.

wa·ter hole, *n.* A hole or hollow in the ground in which water collects; a natural pool or small pond of water, as one used by animals for drinking.

wa·ter·ing place, *n.* A place where water is available, as for cattle; a resort where people go for therapeutic mineral waters or waterside recreational facilities.

wa·ter·less, wô′tər·lis, wot′ər·lis, *a.* Destitute of water, or dry; requiring no water, esp. in cooking.

wa·ter lev·el, *n.* Still water's surface height or water line.

wa·ter lil·y, *n. pl.,* **lil·ies.** Any of various aquatic plants, characterized by large, disklike floating leaves and showy, fragrant flowers; the flower of any such plant.

wa·ter line, *n.* Any of several lines marked or indicated on the hull of a ship, showing the depth to which it sinks when unloaded and when partially or fully loaded.

wa·ter·logged, wô′tər·lôgd, wot′ər·lôgd, *a.* So filled with water as to be heavy or unmanageable, as a ship; excessively saturated with water, as a log, field, or the like.

Wa·ter·loo, wô′tər·loo, wot′ər·loo, *n.* A decisive or crushing defeat.

wa·ter main, *n.* A main or principal pipe or conduit in a system for conveying water, as one that is installed underground.

wa·ter·man, wô′tər·mən, wot′ər·mən, *n. pl.,* **-men.** One who works on boats; a boatman; a ferryman.

wa·ter·mark, wô′tər·märk, wot′ər·märk, *n.* A mark indicating the height to which water rises or has risen, as in a river; a faint letter, design, or the like, often marked in the fabric of paper during the process of manufacture by pressure on the moist pulp, usu. visible only when the sheet is held against strong light.—*v.t.* To mark, as paper, with a watermark; to impress as a watermark, esp. a design.

wa·ter·mel·on, wô′tər·mel·ən, wot′ər·mel·ən, *n.* The large, roundish or elongated, edible fruit of a trailing vine, having a hard, green rind and a sweet, watery, usu. pink or red pulp; the plant or vine.

wa·ter moc·ca·sin, *n.* A large, venomous viper, allied to the copperhead, having a dark crossband pattern and found in swampy areas in the southern part of the U.S.

wa·ter pis·tol, *n.* A toy pistol, usu. made of plastic, that shoots a jet of water.

wa·ter po·lo, *n.* A game played in the water by two teams, each having seven swimmers, the object of which is to propel an inflated ball into a defended goal.

wa·ter pow·er, *n.* The power of water used, or capable of being used, as to drive machinery.

wa·ter·proof, wô′tər·proof, wot′ər·proof, *a.* Impervious to water; rendered impervious to water by some special process, as coating or treating with rubber or the like.—*n.* A waterproof material; a fabric which has been specially treated to render it impervious to water.—*v.t.* To render waterproof.

wa·ter rat, *n.* The American muskrat; any of various aquatic rodents.

wa·ter·re·pel·lent, wô′tər·ri·pel·ənt, wot′ər·ri·pel·ənt, *a.* Consisting of a finish which resists water, but is not entirely impermeable to it.

wa·ter·shed, wô′tər·shed, wot′ər·shed, *n.* An elevated line that forms the division between two areas drained by separate streams, systems, or bodies of water; an area drained by a particular stream, system, or body of water.

wa·ter·side, wô′tər·sīd, wot′ər·sīd, *n.* The bank or margin of a river, ocean, stream, or lake; the shore.

wa·ter·ski, wô′tər·skē, wot′ər·skē, *v.i.,* **-skied, -ski·ing.** To ski on water, achieving and maintaining motion by holding on to a towline pulled by a motorboat.—*n.* A ski used in water-skiing.

wa·ter sof·ten·er, *n.* Any of several chemical substances used in the treatment of hard water to counteract the soap-precipitating property of the metals, magnesium and calcium, present in it, in order to facilitate the formation of suds.

wa·ter·spout, wô′tər·spowt, wot′ər·spowt, *n.* A tornadolike storm over the sea that forms a spinning funnel of air laden with mist and spray, presenting the appearance of a solid column of water reaching upward to the clouds; a pipe or spout from which water is discharged, esp. a drainpipe on the side of a house descending from a gutter.

wa·ter ta·ble, *n.* The level below which the ground is saturated with water.

wa·ter·tight, wô′tər·tīt, wot′ər·tīt, *a.* So tight as to retain or not to admit water; staunch or foolproof.

wa·ter va·por, *n.* Water in a gaseous condition, esp. below the point of boiling, and present in varying quantities in the atmosphere.

wa·ter·way, wô′tər·wā, wot′ər·wā, *n.* A way or channel for water; a river, canal, or other body of water as a way of travel or transport.

wa·ter wheel, *n.* A wheel turned by the action of water and used to perform mechanical work.

wa·ter·works, wô′tər·wərks, wot′ər·wərks, *n. pl.* An aggregate of apparatus and structures by which water is obtained, preserved, purified, and distributed for the use of a city or town.

wa·ter·y, wô′tə·rē, wot′ə·rē, *a.* Full of water; consisting of water: a *watery* grave; of the nature of water: *watery* vapor; referring to or connected with water; resembling water: a *watery* fluid; containing too much water, as liquid food; containing a large proportion of moisture, as fruits; weak, thin, washy, vapid, or poor: a *watery* smile; discharging, filled with, or secreting some aqueous organic liquid; tearful, as the eyes. —**wa·ter·i·ness,** *n.*

watt, wot, *n.* The unit of electric power equal to one joule per second, or a current of one ampere under an electrical pressure of one volt.

watt·age, wot′ij, *n.* An amount of power reckoned in watts.

watt-hour, wot′owr, *n.* A unit of energy or work equal to one watt operating for one hour.

wat·tle, wot′əl, *n.* A hurdle or fence made of interwoven rods, branches, or reeds; the poles, branches, or other such materials used to build such a fence; *pl.,* rods to support thatch on a roof; the fleshy lobe that grows under the throat of certain reptiles and some birds, as the turkey.—*v.t.,* **-tled, -tling.** To twist, interweave, or interlace, as twigs or branches, to form a fence.—*a.* Made from or covered with wattles.

wave, wāv, *n.* A moving swell or ridge on the surface of water or other liquid; a billow; a widespread surge of emotion or opinion; one of a series of curves on a surface; an undulation; a swelling outline; a spell of extremely hot or cold weather; a signal made by waving the hand, flag, or the like, back and forth; a curved or wavelike condition of the hair; a vibration propagated from one set of particles of an elastic medium to the adjoining set, as in heat or light transmission; a graphic representation of such a vibration.—*v.i.,* **waved, wav·ing.** To move loosely up and down, or backward and forward; to float or flutter; to undulate; to be moved as a signal; to beckon.—*v.t.* To move one way and the other; to brandish, as a flag;

---

to signal to, by waving the hand or the like; to beckon; to give a wave to, as hair.

Wave, wāv, *n.* A member of the WAVES, the corps of the U.S. Navy open to women enlistees.

wave·length, wave length, wāv′length, *n.* The least distance between particles moving in the same phase of oscillation in a wave disturbance.

wave·let, wāv′lit, *n.* A small wave.

wa·ver, wā′vər, *v.i.* To sway or move to and fro; to flutter; to be in danger of failing or collapsing; to be unsettled in opinion; to hesitate; to fluctuate; to totter; to reel.—*n.* An act of wavering.

wav·y, wā′vē, *a.,* **-i·er, -i·est.** Rising or swelling in waves; characteristic of or full of waves; undulating on the border or on the surface, as hair or a leaf. **—wav·i·ly,** *adv.* **—wav·i·ness,** *n.*

wax, waks, *n. pl.,* **wax·es.** A solid, yellowish secretion discharged by bees, with which they construct their honeycombs: also **bees·wax;** any of numerous wax-like substances as paraffin or sealing wax.—*v.t.,* **waxed, wax·ing.** To coat, rub, or polish with wax.

wax, waks, *v.i.* To increase in size or strength; to grow in any manner; to become larger or to develop toward fullness, esp. the moon, as opposed to *wane.*—*n.*

wax bean, *n.* A variety of the string bean, having waxy, pale yellow pods.

wax·en, wak′sən, *a.* Made of, or covered with wax; pallid or pale, as one's complexion.

wax myr·tle, *n.* A shrub or tree that bears small berries coated with a waxy substance that may be used for making candles.

wax pa·per, *n.* A paper treated or coated with wax or paraffin to make it waterproof.

wax·wing, waks′wing, *n.* Any of several crested birds of America and Eurasia, having sleek brown plumage, with tiny, horny appendages on their wings the color of red sealing wax.

wax·work, waks′wərk, *n.* Work in wax; figures formed of wax in imitation of real beings. *Pl., sing.* or *pl. in constr.* A place where a collection of such figures is exhibited, or the exhibition itself.

wax·y, wak′sē, *a.,* **-i·er, -i·est.** Resembling wax, as in substance or appearance; pertaining to, abounding in, covered with, or made of wax. **—wax·i·ness,** *n.*

way, wā, *n.* Manner, mode, or fashion: a new *way* of looking at a matter; characteristic or habitual manner: That is only his *way;* a course, plan, or means for attaining an end: to find a *way* to reduce friction; respect or particular: a plan defective in several *ways;* direction: Look this *way;* passage or progress on a course: to lead the *way;* distance: a long *way* off; a path or course leading from one place to another; a road, route, passage, or channel: a high*way;* any line of passage or travel used or available; space for passing or advancing: to make *way;* one's preferred course or mode of procedure: to have one's own *way;* condition, as to health or prosperity: to be in a bad *way;* range of experience or notice: the best device that ever came my *way;* course of life, action, or experience. *Often pl.* A habit or custom: I don't like his *ways.* **—by way of,** by the route of; via; through; as a way, method, or means of: to number articles *by way of* distinguishing them. **—in a way,** in a manner; after a fashion; to some extent. **—make way,** to give room for passing; to stand aside. **—out of the way,** out of the road or path; so as not to obstruct or hinder; off one's hands; apart from what is usual or proper; unusual, improper, or amiss. **—un·der way,** in motion, or moving along, as a ship that has weighed anchor; in progress, as an enterprise.

way·far·er, wā′fâr·ər, *n.* One who journeys or travels; a traveler. **—way·far·ing,** wā′fâr·ing, *a.*

way·lay, wā·lā′, *v.t.,* **-laid, -lay·ing.** To await or intercept in order to seize, rob, or slay; to beset in ambush.

ways and means, *n. pl.* Methods and means, as in legislation, of raising revenue for the use of the government.

way·side, wā′sīd, *n.* The side, border, or edge of a road or highway.—*a.* Growing, situated, or being by or near the side of the way: *wayside* flowers. **—go by the way·side, let go by the way·side,** to put aside or postpone due to a more urgent matter.

way sta·tion, *n.* A station situated between principal stations, as on a railroad.

way·ward, wā′wərd, *a.* Turned or turning away from what is right or proper; forward; disobedient; turning or changing irregularly, or irregular: a *wayward* stream, path, or breeze.

we, wē, *pron., pl. nom.* we, *poss.* our or ours, *obj.* us; *intens. and refl.* ourself or ourselves. The nominative pl. of 'I'; used to refer to the speaker and one or more other persons; used to refer to people in general: *We* are all mortal beings. Used by sovereigns and high officials or by editors and writers in place of 'I'.

weak, wēk, *a.* Not strong; liable to yield, break, or collapse under pressure or strain: a *weak* fortress; deficient in bodily strength or vigor; feeble; infirm; deficient in political strength, governing power, or authority: a *weak* nation; wanting in force, potency, or efficacy; impotent; ineffectual or inadequate: a *weak* battery; deficient in mental power, intelligence, or judgment: a *weak* intellect; deficient in moral strength or firmness, resolution, or force of character: to prove *weak* under temptation; deficient in amount, volume or intensity: *weak* tones or vibrations; deficient, wanting, or poor in something specified: *weak* in punctuation; deficient in the essential or desirable properties or ingredients: *weak* broth.

weak·en, wē′kən, *v.t.* To make weak or weaker.—*v.i.* To become weak or weaker.

weak-kneed, wēk′nēd′, *a.* Yielding readily to opposition or intimidation; showing lack of moral firmness or resolution.

weak·ling, wēk′ling, *n.* One without physical or moral strength.—*a.* Weak; lacking strength or character.

weak·ly, wēk′lē, *a.,* **-li·er, -li·est.** Feeble or sickly; of a frail or delicate constitution.—*adv.* In a weak manner. **—weak·li·ness,** *n.*

weak-mind·ed, wēk′mīn′did, *a.* Irresolute; having or showing mental vacillation; having or showing a feeble intellect.

weak·ness, wēk′nis, *n.* The state or quality of being weak; feebleness; a defect; a failing; a particular fondness, followed by *for;* the object of such fondness.

weal, wēl, *n.* Wheal, welt, or wale.

wealth, welth, *n.* A collective term for riches; material possessions in all their variety; affluence; profusion or abundance of something; all objects which have both utility and the ability of being appropriated and therefore exchanged.

wealth·y, wel′thē, *a.,* **-i·er, -i·est.** Having wealth; affluent; rich; opulent; ample. **—wealth·i·ly,** *adv.* **—wealth·i·ness,** *n.*

wean, wēn, *v.t.* To accustom to do without the mother's milk as food, as a young child or animal; to detach or alienate, as a person, from any object of desire, affection, or habit.

weap·on, wep′ən, *n.* Any instrument of offense or defense in combat; an instrument or means for combating enemies or an opponent; the sting, horns, claws, or the like which animals employ for attack or defense.

weap·on·ry, wep′ən·rē, *n.* An aggregation of assorted weapons; the origination, design, and manufacture of weapons.

wear, wār, *v.t.,* **wore, worn, wear·ing.** To carry or have on the body: to *wear* a coat, badge, or ring; to have or use on the person habitually: to *wear* a beard; to bear or have the aspect or appearance of: to *wear* a smile; to waste or diminish gradually by rubbing, scraping, or washing: The waves *wear* the rocks away; to bring, reduce, or render, as specified, by wear, use, or rubbing: to *wear* clothes to rags; to weary or exhaust, as one's patience or strength; to pass, as time, gradually or tediously, used with *away* or *out*: to *wear away* the hours.—*v.i.* To undergo gradual impairment, diminution, or reduction from wear, use, attrition, or other causes, followed by *away*, *down*, *out*, or *off*; to withstand or last under wear, use, or any continued strain: The rug *wore* well for many years; to become or react, as specified, from use or strain: patience *worn* thin; to pass, as time, slowly or tediously, often with *away*, *down*, *out*, or *off*.—*n.* The act of wearing or the state of being worn, as garments; use; clothing, garments, or other articles for wearing, esp. that which is fashionable or for a particular use, often used in compounds: sports*wear* or beach*wear;* gradual impairment, wasting, or diminution, as from use: cuffs showing *wear;* the ability to endure use; durability. —**wear down,** to reduce or deteriorate by heavy use; to exhaust; to overcome by persistence. —**wear off,** to lessen gradually; disappear. —**wear out,** to become or cause to become unstable through constant wear or use; to use up; to exhaust.

wear and tear, *n.* Loss or deterioration by wearing or ordinary use.

wear·ing, wâr/ing, *a.* Wearying; fatiguing.

wea·ri·some, wēr/ē·səm, *a.* Causing weariness; tiresome; irksome; monotonous.

wea·ry, wēr/ē, *a.*, **-ri·er, -ri·est.** Tired; fatigued; caused by or indicating weariness: a *weary* droop to his shoulders; impatient, disgusted, or unhappy with the continuance of something painful, irksome, or boring.—*v.t.*, **-ried, -ry·ing.** To make weary; to exhaust or harass.—*v.i.* To become weary; to tire. —**wea·ri·ly,** *a.* —**wea·ri·ness,** *n.*

wea·sel, wē/zəl, *n. pl.,* **-sels, -sel.** Any of certain small, carnivorous mammals having a long, slender body, feeding on rodents and small birds, and noted for cunning and ferocity; a cunning, sneaky person. —*v.i.* To be deceptive or evasive in actions or speech; to renege on or escape from a commitment or duty, followed by *out.*

weath·er, weth/ər, *n.* The state of the atmosphere at any particular time with respect to conditions of temperature, pressure, humidity, or other meteorological phenomena; a storm or period of intense heat, high winds, or other disagreeable conditions.—*v.t.* To expose to the effects of the weather; to change, as a result of exposure to the weather; to bear up against and come through, as danger or difficulty.—*v.i.* To undergo change, as disintegration or discoloration, by exposure to the weather; to show resistance to weathering. —**un·der the weath·er.** *Informal.* Ailing, or ill; slightly drunk; having a hangover. —**weath·er·a·bil·i·ty,** weth·ər·ə·bil/ə·tē, *n.*

weath·er·beat·en, weth/ər·bēt·ən, *a.* Beaten, damaged, or worn by the weather; toughened or seasoned by exposure to every kind of weather: a *weather-beaten* complexion.

weath·er·cock, weth/ər·kok, *n.* A vane, often in the figure of a cock, which turns with and shows the direction of the wind.

weath·er·glass, weth/ər·glas, *n.* An instrument to indicate the current state or impending changes of the atmosphere; a barometer.

weath·er·ing, weth/ər·ing, *n.* The action of the natural elements which alter the shape, color, or texture of rocks or earth surfaces.

weath·er·man, weth/ər·man, *n. pl.,* **-men.** A person forecasting and reporting weather conditions.

weath·er·proof, weth/ər·proof, *a.* Able to withstand exposure to all kinds of weather.—*v.t.* To make weatherproof.

weath·er strip, *n.* A narrow strip of material inserted between a door or window and the jamb or casing to exclude wind, rain, and the like.

weath·er·vane, weth/ər·vān, *n.* A vane for indicating the direction of the wind; a weathercock.

weave, wēv, *v.t.,* **wove** or **weaved, wov·en** or **wove, weav·ing.** To form by interlacing threads, yarns, strands, or strips of some materials: to *weave* cloth; to interlace, as threads, yarns, strips, or fibrous material, so as to form a fabric or texture; to form by combining various elements or details into a connected whole: to *weave* a tale; to introduce as an element or detail into a connected whole, followed by *in* or *into:* to *weave* an incident *into* a story; to move, as the body or a vehicle, in a zigzag or winding fashion.—*v.i.* To make cloth; to become woven or interwoven; to move in a zigzag fashion or from side to side.—*n.* The manner of weaving; a particular style of weaving.

weav·er, wē/vər, *n.* One who or that which weaves; one whose occupation is weaving.

web, web, *n.* That which is formed by or as by weaving; a woven fabric, esp. a whole piece of cloth in the course of being woven or after it comes from the loom; something resembling or suggesting a woven fabric; webbing; the structure of delicate threads or filaments spun by a spider and by the larvae of certain insects; a cobweb; a membrane which connects the toes of aquatic birds and mammals; something formed as by weaving or interweaving: the *web* of life; a network.—*v.t.,* **webbed, web·bing.** To envelop or surround with a web; to ensnare.—*v.i.* To form or build a web.

web·bing, web/ing, *n.* Woven material of hemp or cotton, in bands of various widths, for use where strength is required, as for supporting the seats of upholstered chairs or sofas, for brake lining, seat belts, and the like; something forming a web or webs.

web·foot, web/fut, *n. pl.,* **-feet.** A foot in which the toes are joined by a web; an animal that has webbed feet. —**web·foot·ed,** *a.*

wed, wed, *v.t.,* **wed·ded** or **wed, wed·ding.** To marry; to take for husband or for wife; to join in marriage, as a couple; to unite closely or inseparably.—*v.i.* To marry; to contract matrimony.

we'd, wēd. Contraction of we should, we had, or we would.

wed·ding, wed/ing, *n.* The act or ceremony of marrying; marriage; nuptials; a celebration of an anniversary of a marriage; the action or an example of uniting closely.

wedge, wej, *n.* A piece of wood or metal, thick at one end and tapering to a thin edge at the other, used for splitting wood or rocks, for tightening or securing objects, or for raising or levering weights; anything in the form of a wedge: a *wedge* of apple pie; an idea, action, policy, or procedure resulting in change, disruption, or breach.—*v.t.,* **wedged, wedg·ing.** To split with or as with a wedge; to fasten or fix with a wedge; to crowd or compress into a confined space.—*v.i.* To jam in like a wedge; to become wedged.

Wedg·wood ware, wej/wud, *n.* A superior, hard pottery displaying delicate, classical motifs orig. in white cameo relief on an unglazed background tinted blue or black.

wed·lock, wed/lok, *n.* Matrimony; marriage. —**out of wed·lock,** born of natural parents who have not married one another.

Wednes·day, wenz/dē, wenz/dā, *n.* The fourth day of the week; the next day after Tuesday.

wee, wē, *a.,* **we·er, we·est.** Tiny; small; extremely early, as the hours of early morning.

weed, wēd, *n.* Any plant that is useless, troublesome, or injurious to any cultivated plant or crop.—*v.t.* To free from weeds: *weed* the roses; to remove, as weeds, followed by *out:* to *weed out* the clover in the lawn; to remove as undesirable, used with *out:* to *weed out* one's wardrobe.—*v.i.* To remove weeds.

---

weeds, wēdz, *n. pl.* Mourning garments.

weed·y, wē'dē, *a.,* **-i·er, -i·est.** Consisting of weeds; abounding with weeds; pertaining to or resembling weeds, as in growth that is rank or rapid. *Informal.* Lanky, scrawny, or ungainly, esp. of an animal or person: a **weedy** horse.

week, wēk, *n.* A period of seven consecutive days, esp. one beginning with Sunday; the portion of a week devoted to work, school, or business; work-week; a seven-day period before or after a specified day: a *week* from Saturday.

week·day, wēk'dā, *n.* Any day of the week except Saturday and Sunday.

week·end, wēk'end, *n.* The end of the week; the period from Friday night or Saturday to Monday morning.—*v.i.* To pass the weekend, as at a place.

week·ly, wēk'lē, *a.* Pertaining to a week or weekdays; happening or done once a week; determined or reckoned according to intervals of any week: the *weekly* rate.—*adv.* Once a week.

weep, wēp, *v.i.,* **wept, weep·ing.** To manifest grief or other strong passion by shedding tears; to drop or flow like tears; to drip; to give out moisture.—*v.t.* To lament, bewail, or bemoan; to shed tears for; to shed or let fall drop by drop; to ooze; to pour forth in drops, as if tears.

weep·ing, wē'ping, *a.* Expressive of sorrow or grief; tearful; exuding moisture; having slim, drooping branches, as trees.

wee·vil, wē'vəl, *n.* Any of various beetles, destructive to field and garden crops, fruit and shade trees, and to stored products, and whose larvae burrow into and infest nuts, twigs, and grain.

weft, weft, *n.* The threads that are carried in the shuttle across the warp; the woof.

weigh, wā, *v.t.* To measure the weight of or gravitational pull on, as an article, with a balance or scale; to raise or bear up in balancing or estimating the weight of, as with the shoulder or hand; to pay, allot, or measure by weight, usu. followed by *out:* to *weigh out* a pound of nuts; to consider, compare, or evaluate: to *weigh* the alternatives; to oppress or burden with weight or heaviness, followed by *down;* to lift or hoist: to *weigh* anchor.—*v.i.* To have weight; to be equal in weight to: to *weigh* a pound; to be considered important; to rest or press upon as a burden, duties, or worries, usu. followed by *on* or *upon;* to consider or evaluate; to hoist anchor. —**weigh in,** to weigh one's baggage before a flight; to have one's weight recorded preceding a boxing match or race; to be of the weight measured. —**weigh one's words,** to speak with deliberation.

weight, wāt, *n.* An amount of heaviness; a unit for measuring weight or mass; a system of such units: avoirdupois *weight;* a quantity of a substance determined by weighing: a small *weight* of sugar; any heavy mass or object, esp. an object used because of its heaviness, as for holding something down, to drive a mechanism, or as a counterpoise; a burden, as of responsibility; pressure; importance, consequence, or effective influence.—*v.t.* To add weight to; to load with additional weight; to attach a weight or weights to; to burden with or as with weight. —**by weight,** measure according to weight. —**car·ry weight,** to have importance, influence, or authority. —**pull one's weight,** to do one's fair share of any work. —**throw one's weight a·round,** to make unnecessary use of one's power, authority, or influence.

weight·y, wā'tē, *a.,* **-i·er, -i·est.** Having great weight; heavy; ponderous; oppressive, troublesome, or burdensome: a *weighty* problem; important or momentous: *weighty* decisions; forcible or convincing; grave or serious. —**weight·i·ly,** *adv.* —**weight·i·ness,** *n.*

weir, wēr, *n.* A dam across a stream; a fence of twigs or stakes set in a stream to catch or retain fish.

weird, wērd, *a.,* **weird·er, weird·est.** Referring to the supernatural or unearthly; uncanny; eerie; relating to

or resulting from magic or witchcraft; mysterious; fantastic or bizarre: a *weird* theory; odd or strange.

wel·come, wel'kəm, *a.* Received with gladness; producing gladness or pleasure; pleasing; made free to have, use, or enjoy; pertaining to phrases of courtesy. —*n.* A warm salutation to a newcomer or guest.—*v.t.,* **-comed, -com·ing.** To receive hospitably and cheerfully; to accept or receive with gladness.—*interj.* An expression of cordial greeting. —**wear out one's welcome,** to visit so frequently or stay so long that it becomes unpleasant to the host.

weld, weld, *v.t.* To unite or join into firm union, as pieces of metal, by heating the edges and applying pressure, hammering, or with the addition of a fusible filler; to unite closely or bring into harmony.—*v.i.* To be welded.—*n.* The union of metals by welding; the section or joint formed.

wel·fare, wel'fār, *n.* A state or condition of well-being, as of health, happiness, or prosperity; welfare work. —*a.* Of or pertaining to welfare work. —**on wel·fare,** relying or depending on government relief.

wel·fare state, *n.* A state whose government is responsible for the welfare of its citizens through such measures as social security, free medical care, old-age pensions, and providing education, housing, and the like; the social system characteristic of such a state.

wel·fare work, *n.* A program devoted to the betterment of underprivileged people, undertaken by government or private organizations, and providing funds, better housing, hospitalization, jobs, or the like.

well, wel, *n.* A spring or natural source of water; a hole, pit, or shaft sunk in the ground by digging or boring to obtain a supply of water, brine, petroleum, or natural gas; any sunken or deep, enclosed space, as a shaft for air or light, or for stairs, an elevator, or the like, extending vertically through the floors of a building; a vessel, receptacle, or reservoir for a liquid: an ink*well;* a reservoir or source, as of emotions, vigor, knowledge, and the like.—*v.i.* To rise, spring, or gush from the earth or some source, as water, often followed by *up, out,* or *forth:* Tears *welled up* in his eyes.

well, wel, *adv.,* **bet·ter, best.** In a satisfactory, favorable, or advantageous manner: Affairs are going *well;* with propriety, justice or reason: I could not *well* refuse; adequately, or sufficiently: to think *well* before acting; personally or intimately: He knows her *well;* considerably; thoroughly.—*a.* Satisfactory or good: All is *well* with us; right; proper, or fitting; advisable: Is it *well* to act so hastily? In good health, or sound in body and mind: a *well* man.—*interj.* An expression indicating surprise, expectation, doubt, or the like; an expression used as an introduction to or in resuming a conversation. —**as well,** also; in addition; with equal consequence or effect. —**as well as,** moreover; in addition to; as satisfactorily as.

we'll, wel. Contraction of we will or we shall.

well-be·ing, wel'bē'ing, *n.* Welfare; the condition of happiness and good health.

well·born, wel'bôrn', *a.* Born of a noble or respectable family.

well-bred, wel'bred', *a.* Showing or being of good breeding; polite, as in conduct or manners.

well-dis·posed, wel'di·spōzd', *a.* Favorably, benevolently, or sympathetically inclined or disposed, as toward some person or to a certain idea; having a pleasant or good disposition.

well-done, wel'dən', *a.* Accomplished with diligence and skill; completely cooked, esp. as meats.

well-found·ed, wel'fown'did, *a.* Founded on good and valid reasons, facts, or evidence.

well-groomed, wel'groomd', *a.* Neat; trim; tidy and carefully tended, as a lawn.

well-ground·ed, wel'grown'did, *a.* Based on good grounds or reasons; well-founded; well or thoroughly instructed in the fundamental principles of a subject.

well-known, wel'nōn', *a.* Fully known; generally

known or acknowledged; familiar; famous.

well-mean·ing, wel/mē/ning, a. Well-intentioned; stemming from good intentions.

well-nigh, wel/nī/, adv. Very nearly; almost.

well-off, wel/ôf/, wel/of/, a. In a fortunate position; in comfortable circumstances; financially secure.

well-read, wel/red/, a. Having read a great deal; conversant and knowledgeable.

well-spo·ken, wel/spō/kən, a. Said well, fittingly, or with propriety; spoken courteously or in a pleasant manner.

well·spring, wel/spring, n. A stream's source; fountainhead; an unflagging source of supply: a wellspring of knowledge.

well-thought-of, wel/thôt/ov, wel/thôt/ov, a. Highly regarded; held in high esteem.

well-timed, wel/tīmd/, a. Fittingly timed; opportune; timely.

well-to-do, wel/tə·doo/, a. Well-off; prosperous; wealthy.

well-wish·er, wel/wish/ər, n. One who wishes well to a person, a cause, or the like.

well-worn, wel/wôrn/, wel/wôrn/, a. Much worn or affected by wear or use: well-worn garments; trite, hackneyed, or stale: a well-worn saying or theme.

Welsh rab·bit, n. A preparation of melted cheese, usu. seasoned and mixed with ale or beer and milk or cream, poured over toast or sometimes crackers while still hot. Also **Welsh rare·bit.**

welt, welt, n. A decorative or reinforcing seam or edging; a strip of leather sewed around the edge of the upper part of the sole of a boot or shoe; an inflamed stripe raised on the skin by a blow.—v.t. To furnish or decorate with a welt; to strike or thrash as to raise welts on the skin.

wel·ter, wel/tər, v.i. To roll or toss, as waves; to wallow or tumble about; to be doused in or covered with a liquid, esp. blood; to become deeply absorbed. —n. A disordered mass; a state of confusion or turmoil; a rolling and tossing motion, as by waves.

wel·ter·weight, wel/tər·wāt, n. A boxer or wrestler who competes at a weight between 136 and 147 pounds.

wench, wench, n. A woman, esp. a young woman.

wend, wend, v.t. To direct: to wend one's way.

were, wər. The past indicative plural and second person singular, and past subjunctive singular and plural of **be.**

we're, wēr. Contraction of we are.

weren't, wərnt. Contraction of were not.

were·wolf, wer·wolf, wēr/wŭlf, n. pl., **-wolves,** wŭlves. A man transformed into a wolf or having the power to assume a wolf's form.

west, west, n. The cardinal point of the compass directly opposite to east; the point where the sun is seen to set at the equinox; the general direction in which this point lies, or the direction to one's left when facing north; (usu. cap.) a region west of a specified or implied point of reference, as the part of the U.S. west of the Mississippi River; (cap.) those nations west of Asia, more or less united by common traditions and institutions of European origin.—a. Lying toward or situated in the west; western; coming from the west, as the wind.—adv. Toward or in the west; westward.

west·bound, west/bownd, a. Directed or traveling westward.

west·er·ly, wes/tər·lē, a. Of or toward the west; situated in the western region; coming from the west, as a breeze.—adv. Tending, going, or moving toward the west; from the west.—n. pl., **-lies.** A wind from the west.

west·ern, wes/tərn, a. Being in the west, or in the direction of west: a western state; moving or directed to the west; proceeding from the west: a western breeze; (often cap.) referring to or being of the west: a Western pine tree.—n. A westerner; a novel, movie, or play of the western U.S., esp. relating to Indians, pioneers, and cowboys.

west·ern·er, wes/tər·nər, n. A native or inhabitant of the West, esp. of the U.S.

West·ern Hem·i·sphere, n. The part of the earth which includes the continents of North and South America, the surrounding islands, and the adjacent waters.

west·ern·ize, wes/tər·nīz, v.t., **-ized, -iz·ing.** To render western in character, ideas, or ways.—v.i. **—west·ern·i·za·tion,** wes·tər·nə·zā/shən, n.

west·ern·most, wes/tərn·mōst, a. Farthest west.

west·ward, west/wərd, adv. Toward the west. Also **west·wards.**—n. A westward region or direction.—a.

wet, wet, a., **wet·ter, wet·test.** Containing water; soaked with water; rainy; very damp; not totally dry: The paint is still wet. Informal. Permitting the manufacturing and selling of alcoholic drinks.—n. Water or wetness; moisture or humidity in considerable degree; rainy weather; rain.—v.t., **wet** or **wet·ted, wet·ting.** To make wet; to moisten; drench, or soak with water or other liquid; to make wet, as by urinating.—v.i. To become wet. **—wet be·hind the ears,** inexperienced or immature.

wet·back, wet/bak, n. Informal. A Mexican citizen who illegally enters the U.S., often by swimming the Rio Grande.

wet blan·ket, n. Informal. A person or thing that dampens enthusiasm or has a discouraging or depressing effect.

wet nurse, n. A woman who suckles and nurses a child not her own.

we've, wēv. Contraction of we have.

whack, hwak, v.t. Informal. To give a hearty or resounding blow to.—v.i. Informal. To strike or continue striking anything with smart blows.—n. Informal. A hearty or resounding blow.

whale, hwāl, n. Any of various very large mammals of fishlike form; something extraordinarily big, great, or fine of its kind, followed by of: a whale of a finish. —v.t., **whaled, whal·ing.** To carry on the work of taking whales.

whale, hwāl, v.t., **whaled, whal·ing.** To whip, thrash, or beat soundly.—v.i. To strike vigorous blows, often with away: to whale away at a person.

whale·boat, hwāl/bōt, n. A long, narrow boat, sharp at both ends, formerly much used in whaling, and presently carried by sea vessels for a lifeboat.

whale·bone, hwāl/bōn, n. An elastic horny substance growing in place of teeth in the upper jaw of certain whales, and forming a series of thin, parallel plates on each side of the palate; a thin strip of this material, used for stiffening corsets or other garments.

whal·er, hwā/lər, n. A person or ship employed in the whaling industry.

whal·ing, hwā/ling, wā/ling, n. The work or industry of taking whales and processing them; whale fishing.

wharf, hwôrf, n. pl., **wharves,** hwôrvz, **wharfs.** A structure built on the shore of, or projecting out into, a harbor, stream, or the like, so that vessels may be moored alongside.

what, hwət, hwot, pron. pl., **what.** Used in asking for the specifying of something: What did he do? Used to inquire as to the nature, character, class, origin, or the like, of a thing or person: What is he by birth? Used to inquire as to the worth, usefulness, force, or importance of something: What is wealth without health? Used in asking, often elliptically, for repetition or explanation of some word or words: Five what? That which, as many or as much as: Send what was promised. The kind of thing or person that, or such as: just what it professes to be; anything that, or whatev-

---

er: Come *what* may. How much: *What* do you want for your car? Used in parenthetic clauses meaning something that: He went, and *what* is more surprising, gained a hearing. Used with intensive force in exclamatory or interrogative phrases: *What*, two more?—a. Asking for specification between persons or things: *What* book does he mean? Whatever: Take what time you need. How much: *What* money can you borrow? Used with intensive force in exclamatory phrases: *What* luck!—*adv*. To what extent or degree, or how much: *What* does it matter? For what reason or purpose, or why, usu. followed by *for;* in what or some manner or measure, or partly, usu. followed by *with: What* with accidents, his return was delayed.—*conj*. That, as used incorrectly in the phrase *but what:* I don't know *but what* I will.—*interj*. Used to express surprise, disbelief, indignation, and the like: *What!* You shot him? —**and what not,** any other similar things which do not have to be enumerated; and the like. —**what for.** *Informal*. Bodily punishment or chastisement; a severe scolding; any painful lesson or experience: to give one *what for*. —**what have you.** *Informal*. Any other similar things, and the like: an assortment of candies, nuts, and *what have you*. —**what if,** what would the final result or outcome be if; supposing. —**what it takes.** *Informal*. That which is needed or a prerequisite for success or for the achievement of one's goal. —**what's what,** the true or actual nature of things or situation.

what·ev·er, hwɑt·ev'ər, hwot·ev'ər, *pron*. Anything that, usu. found in relative clauses: Do *whatever* you like; what not: pins, needles, and *whatever;* any amount or measure, as of something, or that, used relatively: Keep *whatever* pleases you; no matter what: Do it, *whatever* happens; what ever, or what, used interrogatively: *Whatever* do you mean?—*a*. Any that: Ask *whatever* person you like; no matter what; being what or who it may be: He is unwilling, for no reason *whatever*.

what·not, hwɑt'not, hwot'not, *n*. A stand with shelves, as for bric-à-brac or books; a trivial or unspecified article or object.

what·so·ev·er, hwɑt·sō·ev'ər, hwot·sō·ev'ər, *pron., a*. Whatever, used emphatically: anything, *whatsoever* it be, in any place *whatsoever*.

wheal, hwēl, *n*. A small burning or itching swelling on the skin; a ridge raised on the skin by a stroke, as of a rod or whip.

wheat, hwēt, *n*. The grain of a widely distributed cereal grass used extensively in the form of flour for making bread and other foods; the plant, which bears the grain in dense spikes.

wheat·en, hwēt'ən, *a*. Made of, or relating to, wheat.

wheat germ, *n*. The embryo or germ of a grain of wheat, used particularly as a vitamin source.

whee·dle, hwēd'əl, *v.t.,* -**dled, -dling.** To influence by smooth, flattering words; to coax; to cajole; to get from a person by artful persuasion.—*v.i*. To use beguiling or artful persuasion. —**whee·dler,** *n*.

wheel, hwēl, *n*. A circular frame or solid disk arranged to turn on an axis, as in vehicles or machinery; any instrument, machine, or apparatus shaped like this or having such a frame or disk as an essential feature: a potter's *wheel;* anything resembling or suggesting a wheel in shape or movement; a circular or revolving movement; *pl*., moving, propelling, or animating agencies. *Informal*. A person who is important or influential, esp. in politics or business.—*v.t*. To cause to turn, rotate, or revolve; to move or roll, as a vehicle or piece of furniture, on wheels or casters.—*v.i*. To turn on or as on an axis or about a center; to rotate; to revolve; to turn or change in direction or in procedure or opinion, used with *about* or *around;* to roll along on wheels; to travel along smoothly. —**at the wheel,** steering or driving, as a boat or car. —**wheel and deal.** *Informal*. To act or transact independently and without restraints, esp. in business.

wheel and ax·le, *n*. A simple machine consisting typically of a cylindrical axle on which a wheel, concentric with the axle, is firmly fastened, as to lift a weight attached to a rope by causing the rope to wind up on the axle as the wheel is turned.

wheel·bar·row, hwēl'bar·ō, *n*. A frame or box for conveying a load, supported at one end on a wheel on which to run, and having at the other end two legs on which to rest and two shafts by which a person may lift the legs from the ground and push or pull it along.

wheel·chair, hwēl'chār, *n*. A chair mounted on wheels and used by invalids.

wheeled, hwēld, *a*. Having a wheel or wheels.

wheel·house, hwēl'hows, *n. pl.,* -**hous·es.** The pilot-house of a vessel, which shelters the steering wheel.

wheel·wright, hwēl'rīt, *n*. A man whose occupation is to repair or make wheels.

wheeze, hwēz, *v.i.,* **wheezed, wheez·ing.** To breathe with difficulty and with a whistling sound; to make a similar sound.—*v.t*. To utter with a sound of wheezing.—*n*. A wheezing breath or sound.

wheez·y, hwē'zē, *a.,* -**i·er, -i·est.** Affected with or characterized by wheezing. —**wheez·i·ly,** *adv*. —**wheez·i·ness,** *n*.

whelk, hwelk, *n*. Any of various large sea mollusks having a spiral shell.

whelm, hwelm, *v.t*. To overwhelm.

whelp, hwelp, *n*. The young of the dog, wolf, bear, lion, tiger, or seal; a puppy; a youth: used contemptuously. —*v.i., v.t*. To bring forth, as young, as a dog or lioness.

when, hwen, *adv*. At what time: used interrogatively: *When* are you coming? *When*, did you say? On or at what occasion: used interrogatively.—*conj*. At what time: to know *when* to be silent; at the time that: to rise *when* one's name is called, *when* we were young; at any time that, if, or whenever: He is impatient *when* he is kept waiting. Upon or after which: They had just left *when* company arrived. While on the contrary, although, or whereas.—*pron*. What time: Since *when* have you known this? Which time: They left on Monday, since *when* we have heard nothing.—*n*. The time of anything: the *when* and the where of an act.

whence, hwens, *adv*. From what place; from what source or origin; from what cause.—*conj*. From what place, source, or cause: He told me *whence* he came. From which place, source, or cause, or wherefrom.

whence·so·ev·er, hwens·sō·ev'ər, *conj., adv*. From whatsoever place, source, or cause.

when·ev·er, hwen·ev'ər, *conj*. At whatever time; at any time when: Come *whenever* you like.—*adv. Informal*. When: used emphatically: *Whenever* did he tell you that?

when·so·ev·er, hwen·sō·ev'ər, *adv., conj*. At whatsoever time; whenever.

where, hwār, *adv*. In or at what place: *Where* is he? In what part, or at what point: *Where* is the pain? In what position or circumstances: *Where* do you stand on this question? In what particular, respect, or way: *Where* does this affect us? To what place, point, or end: *Where* are you going? From what source or whence: *Where* did you get such a notion?—*conj*. In or at what place, part, or point: Find *where* he is. In or at the place, part, point, at which: The book is *where* you left it. In a position or case in which; in any place, position, or case, in which, or wherever: Use the lotion *where* pain is felt. To what or whatever place, or to the or any place to which: Go *where* you will. In or at which place or there: They came to the town *where* they lodged for the night.—*n*. The place of something: the *where* of this occurrence.

where·a·bouts, hwār'ə·bowts, *adv*. About where; where.—*conj*. Near or in what place.—*n. pl., sing. or pl. in constr*. The place where a person or thing is; the locality of a person or thing.

where·as, hwār·az', *conj*. The fact or case really being that; when in fact; considering that things are such that.

where•by, hwār•bī′, *adv., conj.* By or by way of which: the door *whereby* she left; by what.

where•fore, hwār′fōr, hwār′fôr, *n.* The cause, reason, or purpose.

where•in, hwār•in′, *adv.* In what; how: *Wherein* did he fail?—*conj.* In what or which: the place *wherein* he works.

where•on, hwār•on′, hwār•ôn′, *adv.* On what; where-upon.—*conj.* On what or which.

where•so•ev•er, hwār•sō•ev′ər, *adv., conj.* Wher-ever.

where•to, hwār•too′, *adv.* To what; whither.—*conj.* To what or which.

where•up•on, hwār•ə•pon′, hwār•ə•pôn′, *adv.* Upon what; whereon.—*conj.* Upon what or which; at or after which.

wher•ev•er, hwār•ev′ər, *adv.* Where: *Wherever* did you find that?—*conj.* In, at, or to whatever place.

where•with, hwār•with′, hwār•with′, *adv.* With what. —*conj.* With what or which; by which.

where•with•al, hwār′with•ôl, *n.* Resources, esp. fi-nancial, needed to accomplish some purpose, preced-ed by *the:* to have the *wherewithal* to go around the world.

wher•ry, hwer′ē, *n. pl.,* **-ries.** A kind of light rowboat used for carrying passengers and goods on rivers.

whet, hwet, *v.t.,* **whet•ted, whet•ting.** To sharpen, as a knife or tool, by grinding or friction; to make keen or eager: to *whet* the appetite; to stimulate.—*n.* The act of whetting.

wheth•er, hweth′ər, *conj.* A term introducing the first of two or more alternatives, and sometimes repeated before the second or later alternative, usu. used in correlation with *or:* It matters *whether* we go *or* stay. Used to introduce a single alternative, the other being implied or understood, or a clause or element not involving alternatives: See *whether* he has come.

whet•stone, hwet′stōn, *n.* A stone for sharpening cutlery or tools by friction.

whew, *interj.* A whistling exclamation or sound ex-pressing astonishment, dismay, or relief.

whey, hwā, *n.* The watery part of milk separated from the more coagulable part, particularly in the process of making cheese.

which, hwich, *pron.* What one, as of a certain number mentioned or implied: *Which* do you want? That or which, referring to things or animals, formerly to per-sons; used relatively with an antecedent expressed, in clauses conveying an additional idea: I read the book, *which* was short. Used in clauses defining or restricting the antecedent, regularly after *that: That which* must be, will be. Used after a preposition: the horse *on which* I rode; the one or thing that: the book *which* I gave you; the fact or occurrence that: She cooked the dinner and *which* was unusual for her, cleaned the house.—*a.* What one: *which* house is yours? Whichever: Take *which* book you want.

which•ev•er, hwich•ev′ər, *a.* No matter which. —*pron.* Anyone. Also **which•so•ev•er,** hwich•sō•ev′ər.

whiff, hwif, *n.* A puff; an inhaling or exhaling.—*v.t.* To puff.—*v.i.* To emit puffs or inhale puffs.

Whig, hwig, *n.* A native supporter of the American Revolution; a member of a political party formed in 1834 in opposition to the Democratic Party, succeed-ed in 1855 by the Republican Party; a member of a relatively liberal political party in the 1700's and 1800's, more recently known as the Liberal Party.

while, hwil, *n.* A space of time: all the *while,* a long *while,* a *while* ago; one's time, as well-spent on some-thing: worth one's *while;* a particular time or occa-sion.—*conj.* During or in the time that; as long as; at the same time, as implying opposition or contrast: *While* he appreciated the honor conferred, he could not accept the position.—*v.t.,* **whiled, whil•ing.** To cause time to pass, esp. in some easy or pleasant manner, usu. used with *away.*—*prep.*

whim, hwim, *n.* A sudden turn of the mind; a freakish or capricious notion.

whim•per, hwim′pər, *v.i.* To cry with a low, whining, broken voice, as a dog.—*v.t.* To utter in a low, whining, or crying tone.—*n.* A low, peevish, broken cry.

whim•si•cal, hwim′zə•kəl, *a.* Full of whims; freakish; capricious; odd; fantastic; changing rapidly and with-out warning.

whim•sy, hwim′zē, *n. pl.,* **-sies.** An odd or fanciful notion; anything odd or fanciful; a product of a quirk or playful fancy, as a humorous literary work.

whine, hwin, *v.i.,* **whined, whin•ing.** To express dis-tress or complaint by a plaintive drawling cry; to complain in an infantile, petty, or ill-humored way. —*v.t.* To express with a whine.—*n.* A drawling, plain-tive tone or cry; a petty, ill-humored complaint.

whin•ny, hwin′ē, *v.i.,* **-nied, -ny•ing.** To neigh.—*v.t.* To utter with a neigh.—*n. pl.,* **-nies.** The neigh or cry of a horse; a horse-like sound.

whip, hwip, *v.t.,* **whipped** or **whipt, whip•ping.** To strike with a lash or with anything thin and flexible; to lash or flog, esp. as punishment; to tongue-lash or treat with cutting severity; to drive on, as with lashes of a whip, followed by *up, on;* to hit or strike in a whiplike fashion: The wind *whipped* the young saplings. *Infor-mal.* To defeat, as in a competition. To take, seize, or move with a sudden, rapid motion, followed by *away, in, out, off;* to beat into a froth or thick foam, as eggs or cream; to overlay or wrap, as the end of a rope, with a cord, twine, or thread; to wrap, as thread, about something, as to reinforce or prevent excessive wear; to sew loosely or overcast, as in hemming or seam-ing.—*v.i.* To turn or start suddenly and rapidly, fol-lowed by *away, around, off, out;* to thrash about violently: girl's hair *whipping* in the wind.—*n.* An instrument for driving animals, as horses, or for cor-rection or punishment, usu. consisting of a rod to which is attached a thong of leather or the like; anything having the flexibility or form of a whip; a dessert of whipped egg whites or cream combined with fruit; a member of a parliament or other legisla-tive body who disciplines and secures the attendance of as many members of his party as possible at important proceedings. **—whip up,** to stir or arouse, as the emotions of a crowd. *Informal.* To put together quickly, or prepare, as a meal.

whip hand, *n.* The hand that holds the whip in riding or driving; advantage; mastery of a situation.

whip•lash, hwip′lash, *n.* An injury to the neck, caused by the head being suddenly jerked forward or back.

whip•per•snap•per, hwip′ər•snap•ər, *n.* An imper-tinent, insignificant person, esp. a young person.

whip•pet, whip′it, *n.* A breed of dog resembling the greyhound but smaller and used chiefly for coursing and racing.

whip•poor•will, hwip′ər•wil, hwip•ər•wil′, *n.* A N. American bird of the goatsucker family, having a brown patterned body, a black throat, tiny feet, a wide bill, and, in the male, white tail feathers: named for its cry.

whir, whirr, hwər, *v.t., v.i.,* **whirred, whir•ring.** To whiz; to fly, dart, revolve, or otherwise move quickly with a whizzing or buzzing sound.—*n.* The buzzing sound made by a quickly revolving wheel, or the like.

whirl, hwərl, *v.i.* To turn round, spin, or rotate rapidly; to turn about or aside quickly; to move, travel, or be carried rapidly along on wheels or similar means; to have the sensation of turning round rapidly.—*v.t.* To cause to turn round, spin, or rotate rapidly: to *whirl* a wheel or a top; to send, drive, or carry in a circular or curving course; to send or carry along with great or

---

a- hat, fāte, fāre, fäther; e- met, mē; i- pin, pīne; o- not, nōte, ôrb, moove (move), boy, pownd; u- cūbe, bûll, tûk (took); ch- chin; th- thick, then; zh- vizhon (vision); ə- əgo, takən, pencəl, lemən, bərd (bird).

dizzying rapidity.—*n.* The act of whirling; rapid rotation or gyration; a whirling movement; a quick turn or swing.

whirl·i·gig, hwər/lə·gig, *n.* Something that whirls, revolves, or goes around; a circling motion; a continuous round or succession; a toy for whirling or spinning, as a top; a merry-go-round or carousel.

whirl·pool, hwərl/pool, *n.* A circular eddy or current in a river or sea; a vortex.

whirl·wind, hwərl/wind, *n.* A mass of air spiraling upward around a more or less vertical axis, as a dust devil, tornado, or water spout; anything resembling a whirlwind, as in violent activity or effect.

whisk, hwisk, *v.t.* To sweep from (a surface) with a whisk broom or brush: to *whisk* crumbs from the table; to whip to a froth with a whisk or beating implement: to *whisk* eggs; to move with a rapid, sweeping stroke; to draw, snatch, or carry lightly and rapidly.—*v.i.* To sweep, pass, or go lightly and rapidly. —*n.* An implement composed of a bunch of loops of wire held together in a handle and used for beating or whipping eggs or cream; an act of whisking; a rapid, sweeping stroke; a light, rapid movement.

whisk broom, *n.* A short-handled, small broom used esp. for brushing clothes.

whisk·er, hwis/kər, *n. pl.* The hair growing on the side of a man's face; the beard; a single hair of the beard; one of the long, stiff, bristly hairs growing about the mouth of certain animals, as the cat or the rat.

whis·key, whis·ky, hwis/kē, *n. pl.,* **-keys, -kies.** A distilled alcoholic liquor made from grain, as barley, malt, rye, or corn, commonly having 40 to 50 percent of alcohol; a single drink of whiskey.—*a.* Made of, related to, or resembling whiskey.

whis·per, hwis/pər, *v.i.* To speak with soft, low sounds, using the breath and lips; to talk softly and privately, often with implication of gossip, slander, or plotting; to make a soft, rustling sound, esp. of trees, water, breezes, and the like.—*v.t.* To utter with soft, low sounds, using the breath and lips; to speak or tell privately: to tell a person in a *whisper.*—*n.* The mode of utterance, or the voice, of one who whispers: to speak in a *whisper;* a sound, word, or remark uttered by whispering; low *whispers;* something said or repeated privately; a soft, rustling sound, as of leaves moving in the wind.

whist, hwist, *n.* A card game played by four players, two against two, with a pack of 52 cards, resembling bridge, which it preceded.

whis·tle, hwis/əl, *v.i.,* **-tled, -tling.** To make a clear musical sound, or a series of such sounds, by forcing the breath through a small opening formed by contracting the lips, or through the teeth; to make such a sound or series of sounds otherwise, as by blowing on a device; to produce a similar sound through a device operated by steam or the like: a noisy factory *whistle;* to move, go, or pass with a whizzing or whistling sound, as a bullet, strong winds, or a missile.—*v.t.* To produce by whistling: to *whistle* a happy tune; to call, direct, or signal by or as by whistling: to *whistle* a cab to the curb.—*n.* An instrument for producing whistling sounds, as by the force of breath, steam, or the like; a sound produced by or as by whistling. **—wet one's whis·tle.** *Informal.* To quench one's thirst.

whis·tler, hwis/lər, *n.* A person or a thing that whistles.

whis·tle stop, *n. Informal.* A town too small for inclusion in a schedule of train stops, but where a train may stop on signal; one of a series of brief appearances at small towns by a campaigning political candidate, esp. to give a speech from the rear platform of his train.

whit, hwit, *n.* The smallest part; an iota: used generally with a negative: not a *whit* better.

white, hwit, *a.,* **whit·er, whit·est.** Of the color of pure snow; reflecting the rays of sunlight or similar light: The *white* beaches were dazzling in the sunlight; light or comparatively light in color; having a light-colored skin, as a Caucasian; pale, as from fear or other strong emotion: *white* with suppressed anger; silvery, gray, or hoary, as hair; accompanied by or covered with snow; wearing white clothing: a *white* friar; free from spot or stain; pure or innocent; not intending harm: a *white* lie; light-colored or yellowish, as wine.—*n.* A luminous achromatic color, devoid of intensity of hue: opposite to *black;* a Caucasian; something white, as a material or substance; a white part of something, as the viscous albumen which surrounds an egg yolk, or the white part of the eyeball; *pl.,* white articles of clothing, esp. as a uniform. **—whit·ish,** hwī/tish, *a.*

white ant, *n.* Termite.

white blood cell, *n.* A colorless blood cell, formed in bone marrow, that destroys germs.

white·cap, hwit/kap, *n.* A wave with a broken, foamy crest.

white-col·lar, hwit/kol/ər, *a.* Of, pertaining to, or designating the class of salaried employees, as clerks or salesmen, whose jobs do not usu. include manual labor, and whose mode of dress therefore is more or less formal.

white cor·pus·cle, *n.* A white blood cell.

white el·e·phant, *n.* A possession of great value but entailing great expense to maintain; anything ostensibly desirable but burdensome to have.

white feath·er, *n.* A symbol of cowardice. **—show the white feath·er,** to behave in a cowardly manner.

white·fish, hwit/fish, *n. pl.,* **-fish·es, -fish.** An edible fish of the Great Lakes region of the U.S., having a bluish back and silvery-white sides.

white flag, *n.* A white banner or piece of cloth raised to indicate surrender, esp. in battle, or as a token of truce.

white gold, *n.* One of various gold alloys, given a white color by its platinum or nickel content.

White House, *n.* The official residence of the President of the U.S. in Washington, D.C., a large two-story freestone building painted white, usu. preceded by *the;* the executive branch of the U.S. government.

white lie, *n.* A lie told with a kind or polite intention; a harmless or non-malicious falsehood concerning something trivial.

whit·en, hwit/ən, *v.t.* To make white; to bleach; to blanch.—*v.i.* To turn or become white or whiter.

white oak, *n.* A large oak tree of eastern N. America, having a light gray bark and a hard, durable wood; the wood of this tree.

white pine, *n.* A tall pine of eastern N. America, yielding a white, soft wood of great commercial importance; the wood itself.

white·wash, hwit/wosh, hwit/wôsh, *n.* A wash or liquid composition, as of lime and water or of whiting, size, and water, used for whitening walls, woodwork, or the like. *Informal.* Anything used as a means of covering up defects, glossing over faults or errors, etc.; a defeat in a game in which the loser fails to score.—*v.t.* To whiten with whitewash. *Informal.* To cover up or gloss over the defects, faults, or errors of by some special means; to subject to a whitewash.

white wa·ter, *n.* Frothy, foamy water, as the water in rapids or breakers.

whith·er, hwith/ər, *adv.* To what place; where.—*conj.* To which place.

whit·ing, hwi/ting, *n. pl.,* **-ings, -ing.** A common European food fish, abundant off the coast of Great Britain; any of various food fishes abundant in the Atlantic waters of N. America.

whit·ing, hwi/ting, *n.* A material made from naturally occurring chalk, used in making putty, whitewash, pigments, detergents, and polishes.

Whit·sun·day, hwit/sən/dē, hwit/sən/dā, *n.* The seventh Sunday after Easter, observed as a church festival in commemoration of the descent of the Holy Spirit on the day of Pentecost.

Whit·sun·tide, hwit/sən·tīd, *n.* The week, esp. the first three days, following Whitsunday or Pentecost.

whit·tle, hwit′əl, *v.t.,* **-tled, -tling.** To cut, dress, or shape, as a block or stick of wood, by removing small chips with a knife; to cut down the amount of or gradually eliminate as if by removing small bits with a knife, usu. followed by *away, down,* or *off.—v.i.* To cut or shape wood by removing small chips with a knife, esp. as a diversion or a pastime. **—whit·tler,** *n.*

whiz, whizz, hwiz, *v.i.,* **whizzed, whiz·zing.** To make a humming or hissing sound; to rush, speed by, or move quickly with a similar sound.—*v.t.* To cause or induce to whiz.—*n. pl.,* **whiz·zes.** A sound between hissing and humming; quick movement causing a similar sound. *Informal.* One who or that which is regarded as very able, attractive, proficient, or excellent: Where math is concerned, she is a real *whiz.*

who, hoo, *pron., nom.* **who,** *poss.* **whose,** *obj.* **whom.** What person: *Who* told you so? Of a person, what as to character, origin, position, or importance: *Who* do they think they are? Used as a simple relative with an expressed antecedent, as a person, sometimes an animal, or a personified thing, in clauses conveying an additional idea: We saw several men *who* were at work. Any person that, used as a simple relative in clauses defining or restricting the antecedent: Release all *who* have served their term. The or any person that, used as a compound relative (with an antecedent not expressed): *Who* procrastinates may suffer later.

whoa, hwō, *interj.* Stop! stand still! used as a command, esp. to horses.

who·ev·er, hoo·ev′ər, *pron., nom.* **who·ev·er,** *poss.* **who·so·ev·er,** *obj.* **whom·ev·er.** Anyone who; whatever person: *Whoever* comes will be welcome; no matter who: *Whoever* she may be, the president will not see her; what person.

whole, hōl, *a.* In a healthy state; sound; well; uninjured; not broken; not defective or imperfect; entire; complete; intact; comprising all parts or units that make up an aggregate; all; total: the *whole* city; not a fraction: a *whole* number.—*n.* An entire thing; a thing complete in itself; the entire or total assemblage of parts making a complete system; unity. **—as a whole,** altogether; all things considered. **—on the whole,** as a rule; all things considered.

whole·heart·ed, hōl′här′tid, *a.* Hearty; enthusiastic; earnest; sincere.

whole num·ber, *n.* A number consisting of one or more units, as 30, as distinguished from a fraction or a mixed number; an integer.

whole·sale, hōl′sāl, *n.* The sale of commodities in large quantities, and esp. for the purpose of resale. —*a.* Of, pertaining to, or engaged in sale by wholesale; extensive and indiscriminate: *wholesale* discharge of workers.—*adv.* In bulk or large quantities; on a large scale and without discrimination.—*v.t., v.i.,* **-saled, -sal·ing.** To sell at or by wholesale. **—whole·sal·er,** *n.*

whole·some, hōl′səm, *a.* Healthful; favorable to morals, religion, or prosperity.

whole step, *n.* An interval equal to the sum of two semitones; two half steps. Also **whole tone.**

whole-wheat, hōl′hwēt′, *a.* Made with the entire wheat grain, as flour; prepared with such flour: *whole-wheat* bread.

whol·ly, hō′lē, *adv.* To the whole amount or extent; so as to comprise or involve all; entirely; totally; altogether; quite.

whom, hoom, *pron.* The objective case of **who.**

whom·ev·er, hoom·ev′ər, *pron.* The objective case of **whoever.**

whom·so·ev·er, hoom′sō·ev·ər, *pron.* Objective case of **whosoever.**

whoop, hoop, hwoop, *n.* A cry or shout, as of a hunter, warrior, or the like; the cry of an owl, crane, or other bird; the whooping or gasping sound characteristic of whooping cough.—*v.i.* To utter a loud cry or shout; to cry, as an owl or certain other birds; to make the characteristic sound accompanying the deep inspiration after a series of coughs in whooping cough.

whoop·ing cough, hoo′ping kôf, hûp′ing, *n.* An infectious disease of the respiratory mucous membrane, esp. of children, characterized by a series of short, convulsive coughs followed by a deep inspiration accompanied by a whooping sound.

whop·per, hwop′ər, *n. Informal.* Something uncommonly large of its kind; a big lie.

whop·ping, hwop′ing, *a. Informal.* Very large of its kind; thumping; huge.

whore, hōr, hôr, *n.* A prostitute; a promiscuous woman.

whorl, hwərl, hwôrl, *n.* A set of leaves or other organs of a plant, all on the same plane, disposed in a circle; a single turn of a univalve shell; any of the circular ridges of a fingerprint; anything having the shape or appearance of a coil. **—whorled,** *a.*

whose, hooz, *pron.* The possessive case of **who,** and sometimes of **which.**

whose·so·ev·er, hooz·sō·ev′ər, *pron.* The possessive case of **whosoever.**

who·so·ev·er, hoo·sō·ev′ər, *pron., nom.* **who·so·ev·er,** *poss.* **whose·so·ev·er,** *obj.* **whom·so·ev·er.** Whoever; any person whatever.

why, hwī, *adv.* For what cause, reason, or purpose; wherefore.—*interj.* Used emphatically or to denote surprise or hesitation.—*n. pl.,* **whys.** The reason: the how and the *why.*—*conj.* The reason for which: His outgoing personality is *why* he is so popular.

wick, wik, *n.* A band or piece of fabric, tape, cord, or loosely twisted threads, as in an oil lamp, candle, cigarette lighter, or the like, which serves to absorb and convey the oil, tallow, or other fuel to the flame. **—wick·ing,** wik′ing, *n.*

wick·ed, wik′id, *a.* Evil; sinful; vicious; disposed to mischief; malicious; unpleasant or offensive: a *wicked* stench; painful or harmful: a *wicked* blow. *Informal.* Excellent: a *wicked* tennis player.

wick·er, wik′ər, *n.* A small, pliant twig or shoot; wickerwork.—*a.* Made of plaited or woven twigs or osiers; covered with such woven work.

wick·er·work, wik′ər·wərk, *n.* Wicker woven together, as used in furniture or baskets; articles made of such material.

wick·et, wik′it, *n.* A small gate or door; a small window; in cricket, the object at which the bowler aims, consisting of two sets of three upright rods, having two small pieces lying in grooves along their tops; in croquet, a wire hoop.

wide, wīd, *a.,* **wid·er, wid·est.** Having a great or considerable distance or extent between the sides; broad; having the extent from side to side limited to a certain degree: three feet *wide;* having a great extent every way; vast; extensive: the *wide* skies of the West; pertaining to a great scope or variety: a *wide* choice of job offers; open to the fullest extent; loose, comfortable, or non-binding: *wide*-leg trousers; failing to hit a mark; remote or distant from anything, as truth or propriety.—*adv.* Over a considerable distance, or expanse: to broadcast far and *wide;* over a specified or limited distance, used in compounds: to campaign state-*wide;* to the full extent: to open a door *wide;* apart from or to one side of a mark: The shot went *wide.*

wide-a·wake, wīd′ə·wāk′, *a.* Fully or totally awake; alert; knowing.

wide-eyed, wīd′īd, *a.* With one's eyes opened fully or widely, as in astonishment or wonder; naive or innocent.

wid·en, wīd′ən, *v.t.* To make wide or wider; to extend the breadth of.—*v.i.* To grow wide or wider; to extend

---

a- hat, fāte, fâre, fäther; **e-** met, mē; **i-** pin, pīne; **o-** not, nōte, ôrb, moove (move), boy, pownd; **u-** cūbe, bŭll, tûk (took); **ch-** chin; **th-** thick, then; **zh-** vizhon (vision); **ə-** əgo, takən, pencəl, lemən, bərd (bird).

in breadth.

wide·spread, wīd′spred′, *a.* Spread to a great distance; extending far and wide; covering a vast area; broadly accepted: *widespread* reforms; comprehensive.

widg·eon, wij′ən, *n. pl.,* **-eons, -eon.** A medium-sized N. American freshwater duck having a short bill.

wid·ow, wid′ō, *n.* A woman who has lost her husband by death and who remains unmarried; a woman whose husband is often away from home, usu. preceded by a word indicating the absence: golf or baseball *widow;* a hand dealt to the table in certain card games.—*v.t.* To reduce, as one, to the state of a widow.

wid·ow·er, wid′ō·ər, *n.* A man who has lost his wife by death and has not remarried.

wid·ow·hood, wid′ō·hûd, *n.* The state or time of being a widow.

width, width, *n.* A measure taken from one side to the other of an object; a portion of the full breadth of something: a *width* of material.

wield, wēld, *v.t.* To exert or exercise, as influence, power, or authority; to use in the hand or hands, as a weapon or tool, with full command and power.

wie·ner, wē′nər, *n.* Frankfurter.

wife, wīf, *n. pl.,* **wives.** A woman who is united to a man in wedlock.

wig, wig, *n.* An artificial covering of hair for the head.

wig·gle, wig′əl, *v.i.,* **-gled, -gling.** To move or go with short, quick, irregular movements from side to side; wriggle.—*v.t.* To cause to wiggle; to move quickly and irregularly from side to side.—*n.* A wiggling movement or course. —**wig·gly,** wig′lē, *a.,* **-gli·er, -gli·est.**

wig·gler, wig′lər, *n.* One who or that which wiggles; the larva of a mosquito, or a wriggler.

wig·wag, wig′wag, *v.t., v.i.,* **-wagged, -wag·ging.** To move to and fro; to signal by movements of flags or lights waved by the signaler according to a code.—*n.* The act of signaling by movements of flags or lights; a message so signaled.

wig·wam, wig′wom, wig′wôm, *n.* An American Indian hut or lodge, usu. of rounded or conical shape, formed of poles overlaid with bark, mats, or skins.

wild, wīld, *a.* Living in a state of nature, as animals that have not been tamed or domesticated: *wild* beasts; growing or produced without cultivation, as plants or flowers; uninhabited, or waste, as land; uncivilized or barbarous, as tribes or savages; undisciplined, unruly: a *wild* gang; of unrestrained violence, fury, or intensity: *wild* storms; unrestrained by reason or prudence: a *wild* venture; extravagant or fantastic: *wild* fancies; disorderly or disheveled: *wild* locks; violently excited: *wild* with rage; wide of the mark: a *wild* throw. *Informal.* Intensely eager or enthusiastic: *wild* about baseball; having a value determined by the holder, as a card.—*adv.* In a wild or unruly manner; wildly.—*n. Often pl.* An uninhabited region or place; wilderness or desert. —**run wild,** to live as a wild animal or as an animal escaped from domestication; to grow unchecked, as a wild plant; to go about freely without discipline or restraint. —**the wild,** an uncultivated, uninhabited, or desolate region or tract; a waste; a wilderness; a desert.

wild boar, *n.* An Old-World hog thought to be the ancestor of the domesticated swine.

wild·cat, wīld′kat, *n. pl.,* **-cat, -cats.** Any of various wild cats resembling the common domestic cat but larger; a violent or quick-tempered person; an oil well which is drilled as an exploratory one; an unsound or unsafe business undertaking.—*a.* Wild, reckless, or irresponsible; running without control or regulation. —*v.t., v.i.,* **-cat·ted, -cat·ting.** To prospect, as for oil or ore, as an independent prospector, esp. in an area of uncertain resources.

wild·cat strike, *n.* An unauthorized violation of an agreement with a labor union by striking workers.

wil·der·ness, wil′dər·nis, *n.* A wild region, as of forest or desert, inhabited only by wild animals.

wild·fire, wīld′fīr, *n.* A highly inflammable composition formerly used in warfare; something that runs or spreads with extraordinary rapidity: The news spread like *wildfire.*

wild flow·er, *n.* The flower of a plant that grows in the wild without cultivation; the plant itself.

wild·fowl, wīld′fowl, *n.* A game bird, esp. a waterfowl, as a duck or a goose.

wild-goose chase, wīld′goos′ chās, *n.* The earnest pursuit of a non-existent or unattainable object.

wild·life, wīld′līf, *n.* Animals or plants that exist in a wild, undomesticated state.

wild rice, *n.* An aquatic, tall grass found in N. America and having a grain which is edible.

Wild West, *n.* The western U.S., esp. when it was unruly frontier territory.

wild·wood, wīld′wûd, *n.* Natural or wild woods or forest land.

wile, wīl, *n.* A trick for deceiving; an enticing artifice; guile or cunning.—*v.t.,* **wiled, wil·ing.** To draw or turn away, as by diverting the mind; to pass leisurely or divertingly, as time, followed by *away.* —**wil·i·ly,** *adv.* —**wil·i·ness,** *n.* —**wil·y,** *a.,* **-i·er, -i·est.**

will, wil, *aux. v., past* **would.** Used before the infinitive or with the infinitive understood. Used to express futurity: We *will* arrive tomorrow. Used to express inevitability: People *will* talk. Used to express disposition or willingness: I *will* go if you do. Used to express determination or insistence: You *will* go, if I have to drag you by the ears. Used to express customary or frequent activity: He *will* write for hours at a time. Used to express capability: This car *will* go eighty miles an hour. Used to express probability: I think this *will* be my brother at the door.—*v.t., v.i.* To wish or desire; to like: Go where you *will.*

will, wil, *n.* The faculty or power of conscious and esp. of deliberate action; the act, experience, or process of exercising this power or faculty; choice; wish; desire; self-control; determination; disposition toward another or others; a legal declaration of a person's wishes as to the disposition of his property after his death; the document containing such a declaration; a testament.—*v.t.* To purpose, determine on, or elect by act of will; to choose; to decide upon or ordain; to influence by exerting will power; to give by will or testament; to bequeath.—*v.i.* To exercise the will; to determine, decide, or ordain, as by act of will; to choose. —**at will,** as one wishes or desires; at one's command.

willed, wild, *a.* Having a will, usu. used in compounds: strong-*willed.*

will·ful, wil·ful, wil′fəl, *a.* Obstinate, unyielding, or stubborn; done by design, or intentional: *willful* murder.

wil·lies, wil′ēz, *n. pl. Informal.* Uneasiness; nervousness; the jitters or creeps, usu. preceded by *the.*

will·ing, wil′ing, *a.* Having the mind inclined, or consenting: *willing* to go home; not averse; desirous or ready: a *willing* employee; compliant; gladly or readily borne, done, or accepted.

will-o'-the-wisp, wil′ə·thə·wisp′, *n.* A light that can be seen flickering over marshes at night, caused by marsh gas; anything that deludes or misleads.

wil·low, wil′ō, *n.* Any of various shrubs or trees, typically having pliable branches used for a variety of purposes, as basketmaking; the wood of a willow.

wil·low·y, wil′ō·ē, *a.* Abounding with willows; resembling a willow; slender and graceful; pliant.

will pow·er, *n.* Strength of mind; determination; resoluteness; self-control.

wil·ly-nil·ly, wil′ē·nil′ē, *adv.* Willingly or unwillingly: She'll have to go *willy-nilly.*

wilt, wilt, *v.i.* To become limp and drooping, as a fading flower; to wither; to lose strength, vigor, assurance, or courage.—*v.t.* To cause to wilt.—*n.* Any of a number of plant diseases, often caused by a fungus, characterized by a wilting of the leaves.

wim·ble, wim′bəl, *n.* An instrument used for boring holes.

wim·ple, wim′pəl, *n.* A woman's cloth headdress laid in plaits over the head and around the chin, sides of the face, and neck, orig. used as outdoor wear and commonly worn by nuns.

win, win, *v.i.,* **won, win·ning.** To gain the victory: to *win* in a context; to succeed in attaining some specified end or state by striving or effort, sometimes followed by *out;* to get, often used with *in, out, through, to,* or the like.—*v.t.* To get by effort, as through labor, competition, or conquest; to gain; to be successful in, as a game or battle; to make, as one's way, as by effort, ability, or the like; to attain or reach, as a point or goal: to *win* the summit of a mountain; to bring to favor or consent, often followed by *over:* to *win over* persons opposed to a plan; persuade; to persuade to love or marriage, or gain in marriage.—*n.* An act of winning; a success; a victory, as in a game.

wince, wins, *v.i.,* **winced, winc·ing.** To recoil or flinch, as in pain; to shrink or start back, esp. suddenly.—*n.* The act of one who winces; a sudden start.

winch, winch, *n.* A hoisting machine in which a cylinder, as a drum or barrel, is turned by a crank so that a rope or chain winding around it raises a weight; a crank having a handle and used for turning an axle, as to operate a grindstone.—*v.t.* To move or hoist with or as with a winch.

wind, wind, *n.* Air naturally or artificially put in motion; a fast-moving, damaging flow of air, as a tornado or gale; a current of air conveying a scent, as of some animal or person; the power of respiration; breath; empty or idle utterance; conceit; intestinal gas; *pl.,* the wind instruments in an orchestra; the players of these instruments.—*v.t.* To detect and follow the scent of; to make short of breath; to allow recovery of breath, as by resting. **—get wind of.** *Informal.* To hear or learn of. **—have** or **get the wind up.** *Informal.* To become alarmed, excited, or upset. **—how the wind blows.** *Informal.* Public tendencies or opinion. **—in the wind.** *Informal.* Afoot, or about to happen. **—sail close to the wind,** to sail directly into the wind; to be frugal or economical; to take a foolish risk.

wind, wīnd, *v.i.,* **wound, wind·ing.** To change direction; to bend or turn; to take a frequently bending course; to meander; to have a circular or spiral course or direction; to coil or twine about something: A vine *winds* around a pole; undergo winding, or winding up, as a clock.—*v.t.* To encircle or wreathe, as with something twined, wrapped, or placed about; to roll or coil, as thread onto a spool; to bring out of a rolled or coiled state, usu. followed by *off* or *from;* to twine, fold, wrap, or place about something; to adjust, as a mechanism, for operation by some turning or coiling process, often followed by *up:* to *wind up* a clock; to make one's or its way in a winding course.—*n.* A winding; a bend or turn.

wind, wīnd, *v.t.,* **wind·ed** or **wound, wind·ing.** To blow, as a horn; to sound by blowing.

wind·bag, wind′bag, *n. Informal.* A voluble, pretentious talker who communicates little of real worth or interest.

wind·break, wind′brāk, *n.* A growth of trees, a fence, or a similar protective structure serving as a shelter from the wind.

wind·ed, win′did, *a.* Out of breath.

wind·fall, wind′fôl, *n.* Fruit or timber, blown down by the wind; an unexpected legacy or piece of good fortune.

wind·flow·er, wind′flow·ər, *n.* An anemone.

wind·ing, wīn′ding, *n.* A turn, curve, or bend, as of a path or road; a coiling of some material around an object; one such complete turn; the action of one who or that which winds.—*a.* Having curves or bends; twisting.

wind in·stru·ment, wind′in·strə·mənt, *n.* An instrument played by breath or air, as the flute, horn, or organ.

wind·jam·mer, wind′jam·ər, *n.* A sailing ship or one of its crew.

wind·lass, wind′ləs, *n.* A hoisting or hauling apparatus, operated mechanically or by hand, consisting of a horizontal barrel or drum on which is wound the rope or chain attached to the object to be raised or moved.

wind·mill, wind′mil, *n.* A mill or similar machine for grinding or pumping, operated by the wind acting on a set of arms, vanes, sails, or slats attached to a horizontal axis so as to form a revolving wheel.

win·dow, win′dō, *n.* An opening in the wall of a building, the cabin of a boat, or the like, for the admission of air or light.

win·dow box, *n.* A box for growing plants, placed at or in a window.

win·dow·pane, win′dō·pān, *n.* One of the plates of glass used in a window.

win·dow shade, *n.* A covering for a window, usu. made of sturdy, treated paper or cloth attached to a spring roller.

win·dow-shop, win′dō·shop, *v.i.,* **-shopped, -shop·ping.** To gaze at articles in the windows of shops, instead of going in to do actual shopping. **—win·dow-shop·per,** *n.*

win·dow sill, *n.* The sill beneath a window.

wind·pipe, wind′pīp, *n.* The trachea.

wind·row, wind′rō, *n.* A row or line of hay raked together to dry before being made into heaps.

wind·shield, wind′shēld, *n.* A framed shield of glass, in one or more sections, projecting above the dashboard of an automobile.

wind·storm, wind′stôrm, *n.* A storm with strong wind, but little or no precipitation.

wind tun·nel, wind, *n.* A long chamber through which air may be forced at selected velocities to test the aerodynamic properties of objects, as airplane parts, models, or the like.

wind·up, wīnd′əp, *n.* The act of bringing to a conclusion or end; a final or concluding part or act.

wind·ward, wind′wərd, *n.* The point or direction from which the wind blows.—*a.* Being on the side toward which the wind blows.—*adv.* Toward the wind. **—to wind·ward,** in a favorable position.

wind·y, win′dē, *a.,* **-i·er, -i·est.** Abounding in wind; windswept; empty or with little substance; verbose. **—wind·i·ly,** *adv.* **—wind·i·ness,** *n.*

wine, wīn, *n.* The fermented juice of the grape, containing up to 15 per cent alcohol by volume, used as a beverage and in cooking; the juice, fermented or unfermented, of various other fruits or plants, used as a beverage; a dark red color, as of some red wines. —*v.t.,* **wined, win·ing.** To supply or entertain with wine, usu. in the phrase *wine and dine:* He *wined and dined* his visiting relatives.

wine cel·lar, *n.* A cellar or other storage place for wine; wines, stored or stocked.

wine press, *n.* A machine in which the juice is pressed out of grapes.

win·er·y, wī′nə·rē, *n. pl.,* **-ies.** An establishment for making wine.

wine·skin, wīn′skin, *n.* A vessel made of the nearly complete skin of a goat, hog, or the like, and used, esp. in the East, for holding wine.

wing, wing, *n.* Either of the two appendages of most birds and of bats, which constitute the forelimbs and correspond to the human arms, but are adapted for flight; either of two corresponding but functionless parts in certain other birds; any of various analogous but structurally different appendages, by means of which insects fly; something resembling or likened to

---

a wing, as a vane or sail of a windmill; a means or instrument of flight, travel, or progress; the act or manner of flying; a faction or group within a political party or other organized body; a part of a building projecting on one side of, or subordinate to, a central or main part; that portion of a main supporting surface confined to one side of an airplane; the platform or space on either side of a stage.—*v.t.* To equip with wings; to enable to fly; to transport on or as on wings; to traverse in flight; to wound or disable the wing of; to wound superficially.—*v.i.* To travel on or as on wings; to fly. —**on the wing,** in flight or motion. —**take wing,** to fly; depart hurriedly. —**under one's wing,** under one's care or protection.

winged, wingd, wing′id, *a.* Having wings; swift; rapid.

wing•span, wing′span, *n.* The overall distance from wing tip to wing tip, as of an airplane.

wing•spread, wing′spred, *n.* The distance between the outermost extremities of the wings, when fully extended, of a bird, other winged creature, or airplane; wingspan.

wink, wingk, *v.i.* To close and open one eyelid rapidly, as in a signal or hint; to close and open the eyelids quickly and involuntarily; to blink; to gleam or twinkle.—*v.t.* To close and open rapidly, as an eye or the eyes; to convey or signify by winking; to move or force by winking, followed by *away* or *back:* to *wink away* the tears.—*n.* The act of winking; the time necessary for winking; an instant; a hint or signal conveyed by winking. *Informal.* A brief nap. —**wink at,** to ignore deliberately, as corruption or connivance.

win•ner, win′ər, *n.* One who wins; a champion or victor.

win•ning, win′ing, *n.* The act of one who wins. *Usu. pl.* The sum won by success in a contest or competition: golf tournament *winnings.*—*a.* Successful in competition with others: a *winning* season; charming or engaging: a *winning* manner.

win•now, win′ō, *v.t.* To free, as grain, from chaff or refuse by means of wind or driven air; to analyze critically; sift: to *winnow* a mass of statements.—*v.i.* To free grain from chaff by wind or driven air.

win•some, win′səm, *a.* Attractive; agreeable; engaging.

win•ter, win′tər, *n.* The cold season of the year.—*a.* Relating to, or occurring in the winter; of a type that is planted in autumn: *winter* wheat.—*v.i.* To spend the winter: to *winter* in the South.—*v.t.* To care for or feed during the winter, esp. plants and cattle.

win•ter•green, win′tər•grēn, *n.* A N. American evergreen shrub of the heath family, having scarlet berries, and yielding a fragrant oil used in confections and medicines.

win•ter•ize, win′tə•rīz, *v.t.,* **-ized, -iz•ing.** To equip or put in readiness for cold winter weather, as a car, by adding an antifreeze to the contents of the radiator. —**win•ter•i•za•tion,** win•tə•rə•zā′shən, *n.*

win•try, win′trē, *a.,* **-tri•er, -tri•est.** Characteristic of winter; cold; stormy; bleak or cheerless. Also **win•ter•y,** win′tə•rē. —**win•tri•ly,** *adv.* —**win•tri•ness,** *n.*

wipe, wīp, *v.t.,* **wiped, wip•ing.** To rub lightly, as a surface, with a cloth, towel, paper, or the hand, in order to clean or dry; to remove by rubbing with or on something, usu. followed by *away* or *off:* to *wipe away* tears; to blot out, as from existence or memory; to rub or draw, as something, over a surface, as in cleaning or drying.—*n.* The act or an act of wiping; a rub, as of one thing over another. —**wipe out,** to completely destroy. —**wip•er,** *n.*

wire, wīr, *n.* A flexible thread of metal; such metal threads collectively; a cable; a telegraph or telephone wire; the wire or cable used to transmit electricity. *Informal.* A telegram.—*a.* Of or resembling wire.—*v.t.,* **wired, wir•ing.** To bind or fasten with wire; to equip with wire. *Informal.* To send by telegraph; to send a telegram to.—*v.i. Informal.* To telegraph. —**pull wires.** *Informal.* To use devious and secret means to influ-

ence or control others. —**un•der the wire.** *Informal.* At the very last moment.

wire-haired, wīr′hārd, *a.* Having coarse, stiff, wirelike hair: a *wire-haired* terrier.

wire•less, wīr′lis, *a.* Operated without a wire or wires, esp. pertaining to telegraph or telephone systems, in which signals are transmitted through space by electromagnetic waves. *Brit.* Radio.—*n.* Wireless telegraphy or telephony; a wireless telegraph or telephone; a wireless message. *Brit.* A radio set.

wire•tap, wīr′tap, *v.t.,* **-tapped, -tap•ping.** To connect a monitoring device to, as a telephone or telegraph wire; to monitor, as a telephone conversation, by means of such a device.—*n.* A concealed device connected, as to a telephone or telegraph wire, to intercept information; the act or practice of using a wiretap. —**wire•tap•per,** wīr′tap•ər, *n.* —**wire•tap•ping,** *n.*

wir•ing, wīr′ing, *n.* The act of one who wires; an arrangement, system, or aggregate of wires.

wir•y, wīr′ē, *a.,* **-i•er, -i•est.** Made of wire; like wire, as in form, texture, or flexibility; tough; lean and sinewy. —**wir•i•ly,** *adv.* —**wir•i•ness,** *n.*

wis•dom, wiz′dəm, *n.* The quality of being wise; the faculty to discern right and truth and to judge or act accordingly; sound judgment; sagacity; discretion; common sense; extensive knowledge.

wis•dom tooth, *n.* A large back molar, so named because it usu. appears when a person is nearing or has reached adulthood.

wise, wīz, *a.,* **wis•er, wis•est.** Having the power of discerning and judging correctly; possessed of discernment, judgment, and discretion; prudent; sensible; judicious; sage; having extensive knowledge; learned; shrewd.

wise, wīz, *n.* Manner; method or way: used in phrases: in any *wise,* in no *wise.*

wise•a•cre, wīz′ā•kər, *n.* One who makes pretensions to great wisdom.

wise•crack, wīz′krak, *n. Informal.* A smart or facetious remark.—*v.i. Informal.* To make wisecracks.

wish, wish, *v.t.* To desire or to long for: often used with an infinitive or a clause: *wish to be* free; to frame or express desires concerning; to desire, as someone or something, to be as stated: to *wish* one well; to invoke upon: to *wish* them good luck; to order or command: I never *wish* to see you again.—*v.i.* To have a desire, usu. used with *for;* to formulate or make a wish.—*n.* A desire; a longing; an expression of desire; a request; a petition; the thing desired. —**wish on,** to impose upon, as something undesirable.

wish•bone, wish′bōn, *n.* The forked bone, which is in front of the breastbone in most birds.

wish•ful, wish′fəl, *a.* Having a desire; desirous; showing desire; longing.

wish•ful think•ing, *n.* Interpreting statements, actions, or the like as being what one desires them to be, not as they are in actuality.

wish•y-wash•y, wish′ē•wosh′ē, wish′ē•wô•shē, *a.* Very thin and weak; diluted; feeble; wanting in substantial qualities or character.

wisp, wisp, *n.* A small bundle of straw or like substance; a thin bunch, tuft, or mass; someone or something delicate or tiny. —**wisp•y,** wis′pē, *a.,* **-i•er, -i•est.**

wis•te•ri•a, wi•stēr′ē•ə, *n.* Any of various climbing shrubs, of the legume family, with pendent racemes of purple, blue, or white flowers and pinnate leaves. Also **wis•tar•i•a,** wi•stēr′ē•ə, wi•stār′ē•ə.

wist•ful, wist′fəl, *a.* Longing; pensive because of absence or lack of something.

wit, wit, *n.* Intelligence; understanding; sagacity; the keen perception and apt expression of surprising, incongruous, or subtle ideas; speech or writing showing such perception and expression; a person endowed with or noted for such perception and expression, esp. one having a talent for witty conversation;

pl., the combined abilities of observation, perception, and comprehension; the proper balance of such abilities: to lose one's *wits.* **—at one's wits' end,** having exhausted or lost one's powers of perceiving or thinking; befuddled.

witch, wich, *n. pl.,* **witch·es.** A woman who professes or is supposed to practice magic; a sorceress; an ugly old woman; a hag; a bewitching or fascinating woman or girl.—*v.t.* To affect by or as by witchcraft; to bewitch; to bring about by or as by witchcraft; to fascinate; to enchant.

witch·craft, wich′kraft, *n.* The practices of witches; sorcery; black magic; enchantment; fascination.

witch doc·tor, *n.* A medicine man, esp. among primitive groups or tribes, who tries to heal others by practicing sorcery.

witch·er·y, wich′ə·rē, *n. pl.,* **-ies.** Witchcraft; sorcery; fascination; entrancing influence.

witch ha·zel, *n.* A N. American shrub, with yellow flowers; an alcoholic solution of an extract obtained from the bark of this shrub, used on bruises and sprains and as an astringent.

witch·ing, wich′ing, *a.* Bewitching.

with, with, with, *prep.* Accompanying: I will go *with* you. In some particular relation to, esp. implying interaction, company, combination, association, or connection: to talk *with,* to blend the milk *with* the eggs; characterized by or having: a man *with* initiative; by means or use of: to cut *with* a knife; using or showing: to work *with* diligence; in correspondence or proportion to: Their power increased *with* their number. In regard to: to be pleased *with* a thing; because of or owing to: to die *with* pneumonia; in the course of: *with* time; in the same direction as: *with* the current; in spite of: *With* all his misfortunes, he seemed happy. From: to part *with* a thing; against, as in opposition or competition: to fight or vie *with;* in the keeping or charge of: Leave it *with* me. Immediately after: *With* that, he left. Of the same belief or opinion as: Is he *with* us in our conclusion? On the side of: She voted *with* the majority. Equal to: He golfs *with* the pros.

with·draw, with·drô′, with·drô′, *v.t., past,* **-drew,** *pp.* **-drawn,** *ppr.* **-draw·ing.** To draw back; to pull out; to remove: He *withdrew* his watch from his pocket; to lead, bring, or take back: to *withdraw* troops; to recall; to retract: *withdrawing* an offer.—*v.i.* To move from or quit a place; to retire; to go away; to retreat. **—with· drawn,** *a.*

with·draw·al, with·drô′əl, with·drô′əl, *n.* Act of withdrawing or taking back; a retraction.

withe, with, with, *n.* A willow or osier twig; a flexible twig used to bind something.

with·er, with′ər, *v.i.* To dry and shrivel up, as a plant, from loss of moisture; to fade or decline; to lose freshness and vigor.—*v.t.* To cause to fade and shrivel; to embarrass or disconcert, as with a contemptuous glance. **—with·ered,** *a.* **—with·er·ing,** *a.*

with·ers, with′ərz, *n. pl.* The junction of the shoulder bones of a horse or other mammal, the highest part of the back.

with·hold, with·hōld′, with·hōld′, *v.t.,* **-held, -hold· ing.** To hold back; to restrain; to keep from action; to keep back; not to grant.—*v.i.* To forbear; to refrain.

with·hold·ing tax, *n.* An installment of an income tax levy deducted from an employee's wages or salary by his employer, and sent to a government department of revenue.

with·in, with·in′, with·in′, *prep.* In the inner or interior part or parts of: *within* this room; inside of: opposed to *without;* in the limits, range, reach, or compass of; not beyond; inside or comprehended by the scope, limits, reach, or influence of: *within* his grasp; not exceeding, not overstepping.—*adv.* In the interior or center; inwardly; internally; in the mind, heart, or soul; in the house or dwelling; indoors; inside; at home.—*n.* The inside part of a building, place, space, or the like.

with·out, with·owt′, with·owt′, *prep.* On or at the outside or exterior of; out of: opposed to *within;* out of the limits, compass, range, or reach of: *without* being heard; beyond; not having or not being with; in absence, with avoidance, or in destitution of; deprived of; not having: *without* enough money.—*adv.* On the outside; outwardly; externally; out of doors; lacking or not having something: can do *without.*—*n.* An outer room, area, place, or the like.

with·stand, with·stand′, with·stand′, *v.t., v.i.,* **-stood, -stand·ing.** To resist, as a physical or moral force; to oppose.

wit·less, wit′lis, *a.* Being without sense or understanding; silly; foolish.

wit·ness, wit′nis, *n.* One who personally sees or observes anything; that which furnishes evidence or proof; attestation of a fact or event; testimony; a person who gives testimony or evidence in a judicial proceeding; one who sees the execution of an instrument, as a will, and subscribes to it for confirmation of its authenticity.—*v.t.* To see or know by personal presence: to *witness* a burglary; to formally attest or testify; to give or serve as evidence of; to subscribe as witness; to be the scene of an action: The gymnasium has *witnessed* many games.—*v.i.* To give evidence; to testify.

wit·ted, wit′id, *a.* Having wit or understanding, usu. used in combination: a quick-*witted* boy.

wit·ti·cism, wit′ə·siz·əm, *n.* A witty sentence, phrase, or remark.

wit·ting, wit′ing, *a.* Having knowledge about something; aware; conscious.—*n.* **—wit·ting·ly,** *adv.*

wit·ty, wit′ē, *a.,* **-ti·er, -ti·est.** Possessed of wit; smartly or cleverly facetious; bright and amusing. **—wit·ti· ly,** *adv.* **—wit·ti·ness,** *n.*

wive, wiv, *v.t.,* **wived, wiv·ing.** To take for a wife.—*v.i.* To marry or take a wife.

wiz·ard, wiz′ərd, *n.* A person who is adept in or practices magic; a magician; an enchanter; a conjurer; an accomplished person: a *wizard* at mathematics. **—wi·zard·ly,** *a.* **—wiz·ard·ry,** wiz′ər·drē, *n.*

wiz·en, wiz′ən, *a.* Dried our and shriveled; withered; shrunken.—*v.t., v.i.* To shrivel, shrink, or wither. **—wiz·ened,** *a.*

wob·ble, wob′əl, *v.i.,* **-bled, -bling.** To move unsteadily in rotating or spinning; to rock from side to side; to vacillate; to tremble or falter.—*v.t.—n.* A wavering; a rocking motion. **—wob·bly,** *a.,* **-bli·er, -bli·est.**

woe, wō, *n.* Grief; sorrow; misery; heavy calamity. *—interj.* An expression of distress or sorrow.

woe·be·gone, wo·be·gone, wō′bi·gôn, wō′bi· gon, *a.* Having a mournful, dejected, or doleful appearance.

woe·ful, wo·ful, wō′fəl, *a.* Full of woe; afflicted with or expressing woe; doleful; piteous; miserable; wretched.

wold, wōld, *n.* A region of unforested, hilly, open country; a moor.

wolf, wulf, *n. pl.,* **wolves,** wulvz. Any of several wild, carnivorous mammals belonging to the dog family; the fur of any such animal; a cruelly rapacious person.—*v.t.* To gulp down, as food; to devour or swallow ravenously. **—cry wolf,** to give a false alarm. **—keep the wolf from the door,** to keep out hunger or want. **—wolf in sheep's cloth·ing,** a hypocrite.

wolf·hound, wulf′hownd, *n.* A hound of any of various breeds, formerly used in hunting wolves.

wolf·ram, wul′frəm, *n.* Tungsten.

wol·ver·ine, wol·ver·ene, wul′və·rēn′, *n.* A carnivorous mammal of the weasel family noted for its strength, ferocity, cunning, and voracity, living in

---

northern forests of N. America.

wom·an, wûm′ən, *n. pl.*, **-en.** The female of the human race; an adult or grownup female, as distinguished from a man; a female servant. **—wom·an·like**, **wom·an·ly**, wûm′ən·lĭk, wûm′ən·lē, *a.* **—wom·an·ly**, *adv.* **—wom·an·li·ness**, *n.*

wom·an·hood, wûm′ən·hûd, *n.* The state, character, or collective qualities of a woman; women in general.

wom·an·ish, wûm′ə·nish, *a.* Suitable to a woman; feminine; effeminate.

wom·an·kind, wûm′ən·kĭnd, *n.* Women in general; the female sex.

wom·an suf·frage, *n.* The political right of women to vote; female suffrage. **—wom·an suf·fra·gist**, *n.*

womb, woom, *n.* The uterus.

wom·bat, wom′bat, *n.* A marsupial mammal of Australia and Tasmania, resembling a small bear, inhabiting a burrow, and feeding on vegetation.

wom·en·folk, wim′in·fōk, *n. pl.* Women. Also **wom·en·folks.**

wom·en's rights, *n. pl.* The rights of women to the same legal protections, privileges, and occupational opportunities as men. Also **wom·an's rights.**

won·der, wən′dər, *v.i.* To think or speculate with curiosity: to *wonder* about a thing; to marvel; to be surprised; to entertain some doubt.—*v.t.* To speculate about, with a clause: to *wonder* what happened; to feel wonder at, with a clause: I *wonder* that you went.—*n.* Something strange and surprising; a cause of surprise, astonishment, or admiration: to see the *wonders* of a city; the emotion excited by something strange and surprising; a feeling of surprised or puzzled interest, sometimes tinged with admiration; a marvel; a prodigy; a miracle or a miraculous deed or event.

won·der·ful, wən′dər·fəl, *a.* Capable of exciting wonder; astonishing; marvelous.

won·der·land, wən′dər·land, *n.* An enchanted or imaginary land; any comparable region or setting: a water *wonderland.*

won·der·ment, wən′dər·mənt, *n.* Wonder; surprise; astonishment; something causing surprise or wonder.

won·drous, wən′drəs, *a.* Wonderful.

wont, wônt, wənt, *a.* Accustomed.—*n.* Custom; habit; use.

won't, wônt, wənt. Contraction of **will not.**

wont·ed, wôn′tid, wən′tid, *a.* Customary or familiar from use or habit.

woo, woo, *v.t.*, **wood, woo·ing.** To court; to solicit in love; to invite, as a circumstance: to *woo* destruction; to seek to gain or bring about.—*v.i.* To make love.

wood, wûd, *n.* The hard fibrous substance composing most of the stem and branches of a tree or shrub, and lying beneath the bark; the trunks or main stems of trees as suitable for architectural and other purposes; timber or lumber; firewood. *Usu. pl.* A large and thick collection of growing trees; a grove or forest.—*a.* Consisting of or produced from wood. **—out of the woods.** *Informal.* Free of danger or difficulties; safe.

wood·bine, wûd′bĭn, *n.* The common honeysuckle; the N. American woodbine having five palmately arranged leaves. Also **Vir·gin·ia Creep·er.**

wood·chuck, wûd′chək, *n.* A burrowing, hibernating marmot common in N. America, having a reddish-brown coat. Also **ground hog.**

wood·cock, wûd′kok, *n. pl.*, **-cocks, -cock.** A popular game bird found throughout Europe, distinguished by its long bill and short legs; a related bird inhabiting eastern N. America.

wood·craft, wûd′kraft, *n.* Skill in anything which pertains to woods or forests; skill in hunting, trapping, or camping, esp. as related to woods: the ability to make or construct objects out of wood; woodworking.

wood·cut, wûd′kət, *n.* A block of wood engraved for use in making prints; a print from such engraving.

wood·cut·ter, wûd′kət·ər, *n.* A person who cuts

wood; one who engraves on wood to make woodcuts.

wood·ed, wûd′id, *a.* Covered with living trees, as hillside.

wood·en, wûd′ən, *a.* Made of wood; consisting of wood; without spirit or expression; ungainly; awkward.

wood·land, wûd′land, wûd′lənd, *n.* Land covered with an abundance of trees and shrubs. **—wûd′lənd**, *a.* Pertaining to or dwelling in the woods.

wood louse, *n. pl.*, **lice.** Any of certain small terrestrial crustaceans, found in decaying wood and other damp places, and having a flattened, elliptical body.

wood·man, wûd′mən, *n. pl.*, **-men.** Woodsman.

wood nymph, *n.* A goddess of the woods.

wood·peck·er, wûd′pek·ər, *n.* Any of numerous birds having a hard, chisellike bill adapted for boring into wood in search of grubs and the like, rigid and sharply pointed tail feathers to assist in climbing, and usu. a striking patterned plumage.

wood·pile, wûd′pīl, *n.* A stack of piled-up wood, esp. that which has been cut for fuel.

wood pulp, *n.* Pulp from wood widely used in making paper.

wood·shed, wûd′shed, *n.* A shed for storing wood, esp. firewood.

woods·man, wûdz′mən, *n. pl.*, **-men.** One accustomed to life in the woods and skilled in the arts connected with it, as woodcraft, hunting, and trapping.

woods·y, wûd′zē, *a.*, **-i·er, -i·est.** Of, like, suggestive of, or associated with the woods: a *woodsy* fragrance.

wood tar, *n.* A tar obtained from wood by distillation or burning slowly without flame; used in its natural state to preserve timber, rope, and the like, or subjected to further destructive distillation, when it yields creosote, various oils, and, finally, wood pitch.

wood thrush, *n.* A large thrush noted for its sweet songs, common in forests of eastern N. America.

wood·wind, wûd′wind, *n.* One of the wind instruments that are blown directly or through a reed and constitute a group comprising the flutes, oboes, clarinets, bassoons, and saxophones; *pl.*, a section or group of woodwind instruments in an orchestra or band.—*a.*

wood·work, wûd′wərk, *n.* Work formed of wood; the part of any structure that is made of wood, as the doors of a house.

wood·y, wûd′ē, *a.*, **-i·er, -i·est.** Abounding with wood; consisting of wood; resembling or pertaining to woods. **—wood·i·ness**, *n.*

woof, wûf, *n.* The threads that cross the warp in weaving; the weft; texture.

wool, wûl, *n.* The fine, soft, curly hair that forms the fleece of sheep and certain other animals; cloth or garments made of wool; woolen yarn; any coating of short, fine hairs or hairlike processes, as on a caterpillar or a plant. **—pull the wool o·ver one's eyes**, to deceive or delude one.

wool·en, **wooll·en**, wûl′ən, *a.* Made of wool; consisting of wool; pertaining to wool.—*n. Usu. pl.* Cloth or clothing made of wool, such as blankets, serges, flannels, and the like.

wool·gath·er·ing, wûl′gath·ər·ing, *n.* Indulgence in idle fancies; wandering of the mind resulting in lack of attention.—*a.* **—wool·gath·er·ing**, *v.i.* **—wool·gath·er·er**, *n.*

wool·ly, wûl′ē, *a.*, **-li·er, -li·est.** Consisting of or containing wool; similar to wool; fleecelike; clothed or covered with wool; wool-bearing; growth covered with a resembling wool. Also **wool·y. —wool·li·ness**, *n.*

wool·ly-head·ed, wûl′ē-hed′id, *a.* Characterized by disorderly or jumbled thinking.

wooz·y, woo′zē, wûz′ē, *a.*, **-i·er, -i·est.** Muddled or confused. **—wooz·i·ly**, *adv.* **—wooz·i·ness**, *n.*

Worces·ter·shire sauce, wûs′tər·shēr, wûs′tər·shər, *n.* A sharp, tangy sauce which originated in

Worcester, England, consisting of vinegar, soy, and various other ingredients.

word, wėrd, *n.* A speech sound or combination of speech sounds, or its representation, used as the smallest unit of meaningful communication by language; something said; a short talk or conversation: to have a *word* with someone; an expression or utterance: a *word* of praise; an authoritative utterance; command: the father's *word* was law; assurance; promise: to give one's *word*; news; information: to send *word* of an occurrence; rumor; a verbal signal; watchword; password. (*Cap.*) The Scriptures, preceded by the. *Pl.* Speech; talk; discourse; conversation; the text of a song or other vocal musical composition; contentious or angry speech: to have *words* with someone.—*v.t.* To express in words; to phrase. **—be as good as one's word,** to act in accord with what one has promised or said. **—by word of mouth,** orally. **—in a word,** in a brief statement; in short. **—take one at his word,** to take seriously another's words as spoken and act accordingly. **—the last word.** *Informal.* The latest thing.

word·book, wėrd/bůk, *n.* A vocabulary; a dictionary; a lexicon.

word for word, *adv.* In the exact words or terms; verbatim; exactly; literally. **—word-for-word,** wėrd/fėr-wėrd/, *a.*

word·ing, wėr/ding, *n.* Expression in words; form of expression; phraseology.

word·less, wėrd/lis, *a.* Not speaking; silent; unexpressed. **—word·less·ly,** *adv.* **—word·less·ness,** *n.*

word-of-mouth, wėrd/ev-mowth/, *a.* Made known or disclosed by oral communication.

word·y, wėr/dē, *a.*, **-i·er, -i·est.** Using many more words than are necessary; verbose. **—word·i·ly,** *adv.* **—word·i·ness,** *n.*

work, wėrk, *n.* Exertion directed to produce or accomplish something; labor; toil; productive or operative activity: to make a machine do *work*; employment; a job; a place where one is employed: not at home but at *work*; that on which exertion or labor is expended: a product of activity or labor: a literary *work*; an engineering structure, as a bridge or dock; workmanship: to do good *work*; a task or undertaking: one's life's *work*; a deed or act; *pl.*, righteous deeds or acts; *pl. but usu. sing. in constr.*, a place or establishment for carrying on some form of labor or industry: an iron *works*; the working parts of a mechanical apparatus: the *works* of a clock.—*v.i.* To do work; to labor; to toil; to be employed, as a person; to be in operation, as a machine; to act or operate effectively; to have an effect or influence: to *work* on one's conscience; to become as specified by or as by continuous effort: to *work* loose.—*v.t.* To bring about by or as by work or effort; to cause; to effect; to operate, as a mine or farm; to adjust, repair, or be in the process of producing, followed by *on:* to *work on* an engine; to use or manage, as a machine, in operation; to put into effective operation; to keep, as a person or animal, at work; to achieve by work or effort: to *work* one's way through college; to find the solution to, as an arithmetic problem; to move, stir, or excite, usu. followed by *up;* to seek to influence or persuade, usu. followed by *on.* **—at work,** working. **—out of work,** having no employment. **—the works.** *Informal.* Everything possible. **—work off,** to rid oneself of by work or effort, as a debt. **—work up,** to develop or concoct.

work·a·ble, wėr/ke-bel, *a.* Able to be worked; achievable, feasible, or possible, as a project. **—work·a·bil·i·ty,** wėr·ke-bil/e-tē, *n.*

work·a·day, wėr/ke-dā, *a.* Relating or pertaining to a working day; everyday; commonplace.

work·bench, wėrk/bench, *n.* A solidly built table at which a carpenter or other artisan works.

work·book, wėrk/bůk, *n.* A book used by students which includes exercises and questions to be worked on directly in the book.

work·day, wėrk/dā, *n.* A day on which work is accomplished; the part of, or hours in, one day during which work is accomplished.

worked-up, wėrkt/ep/, *a.* Excited.

work·er, wėr/ker, *n.* One who works; a laborer; a toiler; a member of the working class; a sterile female working member of an insect colony, as that of bees or termites.

work·horse, wėrk/hôrs, *n.* A horse used for heavy work; a person who derives satisfaction from hard work.

work·house, wėrk/hows, *n.* A house of correction where petty offenders are incarcerated and put to work. *Brit.* A poorhouse or almshouse which houses the poor and supplies them with work.

work·ing, wėr/king, *a.* Engaged in work; concerning or used in work; of a sufficient size or quality for action or use: having a *working* knowledge of mathematics; performing a facilitating function: a *working* diagram; twitching or moving jerkily, as facial muscles under emotional strain.—*n.* The act of working; operation; movement; *pl.*, the part of a quarry, mine, or tunnel where digging has been done or is being done.

work·ing class, *n. pl.*, **class·es.** A class of people whose social status is determined by the economic dependence of its members on manual or industrial employment; the proletariat. **—work·ing-class,** wėr/king-klas, *a.*

work·ing·man, wėr/king·man, *n. pl.*, **-men.** A male member of the working class; a man who earns wages for work, as a manual laborer or a worker in a plant or factory.

work·man, wėrk/men, *n. pl.*, **-men.** A man engaged in manual or mechanical work, as in labor and industry, often used in reference to his work: a skilled *workman.*

work·man·like, wėrk/men·līk, *a.* Like or worthy of a workman; skillful; well-performed.

work·man·ship, wėrk/men·ship, *n.* The art or skill of a workman; the quality or character of work performed; the result or objects produced by a workman or artisan.

work·out, wėrk/owt, *n. Informal.* An exercise or practice session for the development of skills in or in preparation for an athletic activity or event; any rigorous or tiring activity.

work·room, wėrk/room, wėrk/rům, *n.* A room in which work is carried on.

work·shop, wėrk/shop, *n.* A shop or building where any work or handicraft is carried on; a discussion or seminar held for the purpose of intensive study, discussion, and application of some subject or topic.

work·ta·ble, wėrk/tā·bel, *n.* A table at which one works, often with drawers or receptacles for materials, as for sewing.

world, wėrld, *n.* The planet earth; any period, state, or sphere of existence: the next *world*; (*often cap.*) a particular division of the earth: the New *World*. The earth, with its inhabitants, affairs, and characteristic form of existence during a particular period: the prehistoric *world*; mankind; the public generally: The whole *world* knows it. A particular class or association of people having common interests and aims: the sports *world*; any sphere, realm, or domain, with all that pertains to it: the *world* of dreams, the insect *world*; the course of affairs or experience: How goes the *world* with you? *Often pl.* A great quantity or extent: *worlds* of difference. Any celestial body, esp. a planet. **—for all the world,** in every respect. **—in the world,** anywhere; at all; ever: used to add emphasis: What *in the world* is that?

world·ly, wėrld/lē, *a.*, **-li·er, -li·est.** Belonging to the world or present state of man's existence; secular; desirous of temporal benefit or enjoyment; earthly, as opposed to *heavenly* or *spiritual.* —**world·li·ness,** *n.*

world·ly-wise, wərld′lē-wīz′, *a.* Wise as to the affairs of this world.

World Se·ries, *n. pl.* In baseball, a post-season series of games played every October in the U.S. by the pennant winners in each major league until one team wins four games and is declared world champion. Also **World's Se·ries.**

World War I, *n.* A war carried on from 1914 to 1918 with the chief contestants being on the one side the Central Powers of Germany, Austria-Hungary, Turkey, and Bulgaria, and on the other side Great Britain, France, Belgium, Russia, and the U.S., and fought mainly in Europe. Abbr. **W.W.I.**

World War II, *n.* A war carried on from 1939 to 1945 with the chief contestants being on the one side the Axis made up of Germany, Italy, and Japan, and on the other side the Allies made up of Great Britain, France, the Soviet Union, and the U.S., culminating in the surrender of Germany and Japan. Abbr. **W.W.II.**

world-wea·ry, wərld′wēr′ē, *a.* Weary of the world, existence, or material pleasures. —**world-wea·ri·ness,** *n.*

world-wide, wərld′wīd′, *a.* Extending or spread throughout the world.

worm, wərm, *n.* Any of various small invertebrates with more or less slender, elongated bodies and without limbs; any of various small, creeping or boring animals, as an insect larva; something resembling or suggesting a worm in appearance or movement; a groveling, abject, or contemptible person; wretch; the thread of a screw.—*v.t.* To make, as one's way, by creeping or crawling; to insinuate, followed by *in* or *into:* to *worm* oneself *into* someone's good graces; to get by persistent, insidious efforts, followed by *out of* or *from.*—*v.i.* To move or advance slowly or stealthily; to get by insidious means, followed by *in* or *into;* to avoid or escape by insidious means, followed by *out of.*

worm-eat·en, wərm′ēt′ən, *a.* Eaten into or gnawed by worms: *worm-eaten* timbers; impaired by time or decayed; antiquated.

worm·wood, wərm′wûd′, *n.* A bitter, aromatic European herb, chiefly used in making absinthe; something bitter, grievous, or extremely unpleasant; bitterness.

worm·y, wər′mē, *a.,* **-i·er, -i·est.** Containing a worm or worms; infested with worms; worm-eaten; wormlike; groveling; low.

worn, wōrn, *a.* Impaired by wear or use: *worn* clothing; wearied or exhausted; showing the wearing effects of toil, care, suffering, or the like.

worn-out, wōrn′owt′, wôrn′owt′, *a.* Destroyed or much injured by wear; wearied; exhausted with toil.

wor·ri·some, wər′ē-səm, *a.* Worrying, annoying, or disturbing; causing worry; inclined to worry or be anxious.

wor·ry, wər′ē, *v.i.,* **-ried, -ry·ing.** To torment oneself with or suffer from disturbing thoughts; to fret. *Informal.* To move by constant effort, in spite of difficulties or troubles, used with *along* or *through.*—*v.t.* To cause to feel uneasy or anxious; to trouble; to torment with annoyances, cares, or anxieties; to seize, as by the throat, with the teeth and shake or mangle, as one animal does another; to harass by repeated biting or snapping.—*n. pl.,* **-ries.** A worried condition or feeling; harassing care, uneasiness, or anxiety; a cause of uneasiness or anxiety; a trouble; the act of worrying. —**wor·ri·er,** *n.*

wor·ry·wart, wər′ē-wôrt, *n.* One who worries constantly and often without good reason.

worse, wərs, *a., irreg. compar. of* **bad** and **ill.** Bad or ill in a greater or higher degree; inferior in excellence, quality, or character; more faulty, unsatisfactory, or objectionable; more unfavorable or injurious; in less

good condition; in poorer health.—*n.* That which is worse; a worse thing or state.—*adv.* In a worse manner or one which is more evil or wicked; with greater violence or intensity: It is raining *worse* than ever.

wors·en, wər′sən, *v.t., v.i.* To become or cause to become worse.

wor·ship, wər′ship, *n.* The performance of devotional acts in honor of a deity, as a church service; the act of paying divine honors to the Supreme Being or other divine power; religious exercises; reverence; submissive respect; loving or admiring devotion.—*v.t.* To pay divine honors to; to reverence with supreme respect and veneration; to perform religious service to; to adore; to idolize.—*v.i.* To perform acts of adoration; to perform religious service.

wor·ship·ful, wər′ship-fəl, *a.* Worthy of honor; honorable; of or pertaining to a reverent feeling, as to a person.

worst, wərst, *a., irreg. superl. of* **bad** and **ill.** Bad or ill in the greatest or highest degree; most faulty, unsatisfactory, or objectionable; most evil or wicked; most unfavorable or injurious; in the poorest condition.—*n.* That which is worst; the worst thing or state.—*adv.* In the worst manner: to fare *worst;* with the greatest violence or intensity: to hate one *worst* of all.—*v.t.* To give, as a person, the worst of a contest or struggle; defeat; beat. —**at worst,** under the most unfavorable conditions. —**get the worst of some·thing,** to be the loser; undergo defeat. —**if worst comes to worst,** if the very worst happens.

wor·sted, wûs′tid, wər′stid, *n.* Firmly twisted yarn or thread spun from combed long-staple wool, used for weaving, knitting, crocheting, and the like; any kind of cloth woven of such yarn.—*a.*

worth, wərth, *n.* That quality of a thing which renders it valuable or useful; value; wealth or riches of any sort; a certain amount or number of something which may be acquired for a particular sum: a nickel's *worth* of jelly beans.—*a.* Equal in value or price to; deserving of: a cause *worth* defending; possessing specified value: He is *worth* at least two million. —**for all one is worth.** *Informal.* To the utmost; to the limits of one's capabilities. —**put in one's two cents worth.** *Informal.* To contribute one's opinion or views to a discussion or argument.

worth·less, wərth′lis, *a.* Having no value; having no dignity or excellence; not deserving.

worth·while, wərth′hwīl′, *a.* Such as to repay one's time, attention, interest, work, or trouble.

wor·thy, wər′thē, *a.,* **-thi·er, -thi·est.** Having worth; valuable; deserving praise; having merit; deserving, usu. followed by *of,* or an infinitive: *worthy* of love or hatred.—*n. pl.,* **-thies.** A person of high position, great influence, or distinction: Doctors and lawyers are usually town *worthies.* —**wor·thi·ly,** *adv.* —**wor·thi·ness,** *n.*

would, wûd, *unstressed* wəd, *aux. v.* The past and pp. of **will.** Used in conveying a mood, as to express a desire or wish: *Would* it were true! Used to express intent: those who *would* wage war; used to express customary action: She *would* go there daily. Used to express condition: He *would* if asked. Used to express uncertainty: *Would* that be all right? Used in expressing preference: He *would* rather win than lose. Used in expressing the future: They said they *would* come tomorrow. Used to make a statement or question less direct and blunt: *Would* you be so kind?

would-be, wûd′bē, *a.* Wishing, aspiring, or pretending to be: a *would-be* wit; intended to be: *would-be* kindness.

would·n't, wûd′nt. Contraction of would not.

wound, woond, *n.* A cut, breach, or rupture in the skin and flesh of a person or an animal caused by violence; a similar injury to a plant; any injury, hurt, or pain, as to the feelings.—*v.t.* To inflict a wound on; to cut, slash, or lacerate; to hurt the feelings of; to pain.—*v.i.* To inflict hurt or injury.

wow, wow, *interj. Informal.* An exclamation of surprise, wonder, pleasure, or dismay.—*v.t. Informal.* To raise great enthusiasm; to please greatly: to *wow* an audience.

wrack, rak, *n.* Seaweed, esp. when thrown ashore by the waves; a wreck, esp. of a ship; a piece of wreckage; ruin.

wraith, rāth, *n.* An apparition in the exact likeness of a person, seen before or soon after the person's death; a ghost.

wran•gle, rang′gəl, *v.i.,* **-gled, -gling.** To dispute angrily; to brawl; to altercate; to engage in discussion and disputation.—*v.t.* To argue; to debate; to round up or herd, as cattle.—*n.* An angry dispute; a noisy quarrel.

wran•gler, rang′glər, *n.* One who wrangles; a cowboy or herdsman.

wrap, rap, *v.t.,* **wrapped, wrap•ping.** To enclose, envelop, or muffle in something wound or folded about, often with *up:* to *wrap up* an injured hand; to enclose and fasten, as an article or package, within a covering of paper or the like, often with *up:* to *wrap up* a dress for delivery; to wind, fold, or bind, as something, about as a covering; to protect with coverings or outer garments, often with *up;* to surround, envelop, shroud, or hide; to involve.—*v.i.* To wrap oneself, used with *up;* to become wrapped, as about something; to fold.—*n.* Something to be wrapped about the person, as a shawl, scarf, cloak, or robe; *pl.,* outdoor garments or coverings. **—wrapped up in.** *Informal.* Involved, engrossed, or absorbed in, as work, a project, or situation; bound up with, as children or family. **—keep un•der wraps.** *Informal.* To keep concealed or secret.

wrap•per, rap′ər, *n.* One who wraps; that in which anything is wrapped; an outer covering; a loose outer garment; a lady's dressing gown.

wrap•ping, rap′ing, *n. Often pl.* That in which something is wrapped.

wrath, rath, *n.* Violent anger; vehement exasperation; indignation; rage.

wrath•ful, rath′fəl, *a.* Full of wrath; greatly incensed; raging; furious; indicating wrath.

wreak, rēk, *v.t.* To inflict or cause to take effect: to *wreak* vengeance; to carry out the free expression of, as rage or rancor, on an object or person.

wreath, rēth, *n. pl.,* **wreaths,** rēthz. Something twisted or curled; a garland, as of flowers for a grave.

wreathe, rēth, *v.t.,* **wreathed, wreath•ing.** To form into a wreath; to surround with a wreath; to encircle or envelop.—*v.i.* To move or twine circularly; to be interwoven or entwined as a wreath.

wreck, rek, *n.* Any building, structure, or thing reduced to a state of ruin; that which remains of a ruined vessel or of its cargo; the ruin or destruction of a vessel in the course of navigation; shipwreck; the ruin or destruction of anything; someone of poor mental or physical health.—*v.t.* To cause the wreck of, as a vessel, as in the course of navigation; to shipwreck; to involve in a wreck; to cause the ruin or destruction of: to *wreck* a bank.—*v.i.* To suffer wreckage; to act as a wrecker; to engage in wrecking.

wreck•age, rek′ij, *n.* The act of wrecking; the condition of being wrecked; the materials or parts remaining from anything demolished.

wreck•er, rek′ər, *n.* A machine or person which wrecks; one engaged in the business of tearing down buildings to clear the sites; one who removes wreckage, as damaged automobiles or trains, from a right of way; a specially equipped automobile or truck used in removing such wreckage; a person or ship employed to recover cargo or goods from wrecked vessels, as well as the wrecked vessels; one who causes shipwrecks in order to plunder the wrecked ships; a plunderer of any kind.

wren, ren, *n.* Any of various small birds, as the N. American house wren and the European wren.

wrench, rench, *n.* A violent twist, or a pull with twisting; a sprain; an injury by twisting, as in a joint; an emotional shock; any of various tools having jaws or a socket adapted to grip the head of a bolt or a nut to turn it.—*v.t.* To pull with a sudden, sharp, violent jerk; to twist, jerk, or tear from the normal position, as a ligament of the body.—*v.i.* To twist or give a turn or twist.

wrest, rest, *v.t.* To twist; to wrench; to apply a violent twisting force to; to extort or bring out, as by a twisting, painful force; to force, as by torture; to turn from truth or twist from the natural meaning by violence; to pervert.

wres•tle, res′əl, *v.i.,* **-tled, -tling.** To contend by grappling and trying to throw down an adversary; to struggle, strive, or contend, followed by *with:* to *wrestle with* rising costs.—*v.t.* To contend with in wrestling; to strive for control over, as if by force: to *wrestle* a problem to its conclusion.—*n.* A wrestling match. **—wres•tler,** *n.*

wrest•ling, res′ling, *n.* A contact sport in which each of two opponents attempts to force the shoulders of the other to the mat or ground.

wretch, rech, *n.* A miserable person; one who is supremely unhappy; a mean, base, or vile person.

wretch•ed, rech′id, *a.* Miserable or unhappy; causing unhappiness or misery; very poor or mean in quality; despicable.

wrig•gle, rig′əl, *v.i.,* **-gled, -gling.** To move the body to and fro with short motions like a worm or an eel; to move with writhing or twisting of the body; to work by paltry shifts or schemes: to *wriggle* into one's confidence.—*v.t.* To cause, as a person, to wriggle.—*n.* The motion of one who wriggles; a quick, twisting motion like that of a worm or an eel. **—wrig•gly,** rig′lē, *a.,* **-gli•er, -gli•est.**

wrig•gler, rig′lər, *n.* One who or that which wriggles; the larva of a mosquito.

wring, ring, *v.t.,* **wrung, wring•ing.** To twist and squeeze or compress; to forcibly twist out of shape or into an awkward position; to pain, as if by twisting or squeezing; to torture or distress: to *wring* one's heart; to squeeze or press out, as a liquid, esp. by twisting; to extort or force as if by twisting: to *wring* a confession or money from a person; to grip tightly with or without twisting, as the hands.—*n.* A twisting or wringing.

wring•er, ring′ər, *n.* One who wrings; an apparatus for forcing water from clothes, after they have been washed, by compression between rollers.

wrin•kle, ring′kəl, *n.* A small ridge or a furrow, formed by the folding, shrinking, or contraction of any smooth substance; a small crease or fold in the skin, as caused by age.—*v.t.,* **-kled, -kling.** To contract into wrinkles or furrows; to furrow or crease.—*v.i.* To become contracted into wrinkles. **—wrin•kly,** ringk′lē, *a.,* **-kli•er, -kli•est.**

wrin•kle, ring′kəl, *n. Informal.* An innovative or ingenious method, device, or idea.

wrist, rist, *n.* The joint by which the hand is united to the arm, and by means of which the hand moves on the forearm; the section on a glove or other garment which is a covering for the wrist.

wrist•band, rist′band, *n.* The band or part of a sleeve, esp. of a shirt sleeve, which covers the wrist.

wrist watch, *n.* A watch which is attached to a band and fastened on the wrist.

writ, rit, *n.* A written order commanding a person to perform or cease the performance of a specified act.

write, rit, *v.t.,* past **wrote,** *pp.* **writ•ten,** *ppr.* **writ•ing.** To form or trace: to *write* the alphabet on the blackboard; to communicate or describe in writing: to *write* a report on the meeting; to fill out the blank places of: to

---

a- hat, fāte, fāre, fäther; **e-** met, mē; **i-** pin, pīne; **o-** not, nōte, ôrb, moove (move), boy, pownd; **u-** cūbe, bûll, tûk (took); **ch-** chin; **th-** thick, ŧhen; **zh-** vizhon (vision); **ə-** əgo, takən, pencəl, lemən, bərd (bird).

write a money order; to set down as letters, words, numbers, or the like: to *write* several copies of the math assignment; to communicate with, by writing a letter; to create by writing; to create, as by an author or composer; to cover with writing: to *write* several full sheets of paper.—*v.i.* To trace or form characters with a pen, pencil, or the like; to work as an author or writer; to set forth ideas or facts in writing; to produce or communicate by a letter or letters; to produce a certain kind of writing.

write-in, rĭt'in, *a.* Of, pertaining to, or designating votes written in: a *write-in* candidate.—*n.* A vote for a candidate whose name is not printed on the ballot.

writ•er, rĭ'tẽr, *n.* A person who writes, esp. one who has written a particular item: the *writer* of the letter; one who writes as an occupation; an author.

writhe, rĭth, *v.i.,* **writhed, with•ing.** To twist the body about, as in pain; to suffer mental distress, as from acute anguish.—*v.t.* To twist with violence: to *writhe* the body; to distort.—*n.* A writhing action; a twisted shape or contortion.

writ•ing, rī'tĭng, *n.* The act of one who or that which writes; the state of being written, or written form: to obtain a statement in *writing;* that which is written; characters or matter written with a pen or similar instrument: paper bearing *writing;* such characters or matter with respect to style, kind, or quality: childish *writing;* an inscription; a letter; any written or printed paper or document; literary work with respect to style, kind, or quality: allegorical *writing;* a literary composition or production: novels, poems, and miscellaneous *writings;* the occupation or profession of a writer or author.

wrong, rŏng, rong, *a.* Not right; not according to rule, wish, design, or the like; not what ought to be; not according to moral law or right; not according to facts or truth; inaccurate; erroneous; being in error; mistaken; designed to be worn inward: That is the *wrong* side of the dress.—*n.* What is not right, esp. morally; a wrong, unfair, or unjust act; any injury, hurt, pain, or damage.—*adv.* In a wrong direction or manner.—*v.t.* To treat with injustice; to deal harshly or unfairly with; to do injustice to by imputation; to think ill of unfairly. —**go wrong,** to fail or go awry.

wrong•do•er, rŏng'doo•ẽr, rong'doo•ẽr, *n.* One who does wrong or evil. —**wrong•do•ing,** *n.*

wronged, rŏngd, rongd, *a.* Suffering from an injustice; harmed.

wrong•ful, rŏng'fẽl, rong'fẽl, *a.* Injurious; unjust; unfair; contrary to law or justice.

wrong-head•ed, wrong•head•ed, rŏng'hed'id, rong'hed'id, *a.* Stubbornly holding to misguided views or opinions; perversely wrong.

wroth, rŏth, roth, *a.* Very angry.

wrought, rôt, *a.* Worked; elaborated; not rough or crude; beaten and shaped with a hammer or other tool, as metal articles.

wrought-up, rôt'ẽp, *a.* Excited: to be *wrought-up* over a trifle.

wrought i•ron, *n.* A comparatively pure form of iron, as that produced from pig iron, which contains almost no carbon, and which is easily forged and welded. —**wrought-i•ron,** rôt'ī•ẽrn, *a.*

wry, rī, *a.,* **wri•er, wri•est.** Abnormally bent or turned to one side; twisted; ironically humorous: *wry* wit.

X

X, x, eks, *n.* The twenty-fourth letter of the English alphabet and eighteenth consonant; something designated by or having the shape of the letter X or x.

X, eks, *n.* Christ; Christian; (*sometimes l.c.*) the Roman numeral representing 10; an indication of a location on maps or diagrams, as: *X* marks the spot; a movie rating denoting a film for adult viewing only.

x, eks, *n.* A term often used to designate a person, thing, agency, factor, or the like whose true name is unknown or withheld; in mathematics, an unknown quantity; a sign of multiplication: 5 *x* 5 = 25; a sign used between numbers in dimensions: a room 8 feet *x* 12 feet; (*often cap.*) the signature of an illiterate; an indication of choice, as on a ballot; often an indication of error, as in test scoring.

X-chro•mo•some, eks'krō•mə•sōm, *n.* The sex chromosome carrying or associated with female characteristics, which occurs in a paired state in the female cell, and with one Y-chromosome in the male cell.

xe•bec, ze•bec, zẽ'bek, *n.* A small, three-masted vessel having both square and lateen sails, in limited use in Mediterranean commercial traffic.

xe•non, zē'non, *n.* A colorless, odorless, gaseous element in the atmosphere, very rare and chemically inactive.

xen•o•pho•bi•a, zen•ə•fō'bē•ə, *n.* Hatred, distrust, or contempt of foreigners, esp. as reflected in foreign policy or political opinion.

Xmas, kris'məs, *n.* Christmas.

X-rays, x-rays, eks'rāz, *n. pl.* High frequency electromagnetic rays of short wavelength, generated by the impact of high speed electrons on a metal target, capable of penetrating solid masses, destroying living tissue, and affecting a photographic plate; *sing.,* an X-ray photograph, esp. one used in medical diagnosis.

X-ray, x-ray, eks'rā, *v.t.* To examine or treat, as a person, with X-rays; to photograph with X-rays.

xy•lem, zī'ləm, *n.* That part of a plant which forms the woody tissue, and functions in conducting water and minerals.

xy•lo•phone, zī'lə•fōn, *n.* A musical instrument consisting of a graduated series of wooden bars, usu. sounded by striking with small wooden hammers. —**xy•lo•phon•ist,** zī'lə•fō•nist, *n.*

Y

Y, y, wī, *n.* The twenty-fifth letter of the English alphabet; a semivowel; something designated by or having the shape of the letter Y or y.

y, wī. In mathematics, an unknown, used esp. following *x* to form a set; an ordinate.

yacht, yot, *n.* A boat propelled by sail or motor, and used for pleasure trips, private cruising, racing, or the like.—*v.i.* To sail, voyage, or race in a yacht.

yacht•ing, yot′ing, *n.* The practice or sport of navigating, sailing, or voyaging in a yacht.

yachts•man, yots′mǝn, *n. pl.,* **-men.** One who owns or sails a yacht.

yak, yak, *n. pl.,* **yaks, yak.** A large, stocky ox with long, silky hair, living in the mountain regions of Tibet, in both the wild and the domesticated state.

yam, yam, *n.* The starchy, tuberous root of any of various vines much cultivated for food in the warmer regions of both hemispheres; any of these plants; a large sweet potato.

yank, yangk, *v.t., v.i.* To pull with a sudden, vigorous, jerking motion; to jerk.—*n.* A sudden jerking pull; a jerk.

Yan•kee, yang′kē, *n.* A native or inhabitant of any of the northern states of the U.S.; a northern soldier in the American Civil War; any native or inhabitant of the U.S.—*a.* Of, pertaining to, or characteristic of the Yankees.

Yan•kee Doo•dle, *n.* A famous tune, popular in the time of the American Revolution, now regarded as American and national.

yap, yap, *v.i.,* **yapped, yap•ping.** To yelp; to bark snappishly. *Informal.* To talk snappishly, noisily, or foolishly.—*v.t.* To utter by yapping.—*n.* A yelp; a snappish bark. *Informal.* Snappish, noisy, or foolish talk; the mouth.

yard, yärd, *n.* The British and American standard measure of length, equal to 3 feet or 36 inches, or 0.9144 meter; a long cylindrical piece of timber in a ship, slung crosswise to a mast, and supporting and extending a sail.

yard, yärd, *n.* The ground adjoining or surrounding a house or other buildings; an enclosed area outdoors, designed for use by residents, students, and the like; a space with tracks adjacent to a railroad terminal used for the switching or making up of trains.

yard•age, yär′dij, *n.* Measurement or the amount measured in yards.

yard•arm, yärd′ärm, *n.* Either end of a yard of a square sail.

yard goods, *n.* Fabrics or other goods for sale by the yard.

yard•mas•ter, yärd′mas•ter, *n.* One in charge of a railroad yard.

yard•stick, yärd′stik, *n.* A stick a yard long, commonly marked with subdivisions, used for measuring; any standard of measurement.

yarn, yärn, *n.* Thread spun from wool or other fibrous material, esp. that prepared for weaving or for knitting. *Informal.* A story or tale of adventure, extraordinary occurrences, or the like, esp. a tale that is highly improbable.—*v.i. Informal.* To spin a yarn; to tell stories.

yar•row, yar′ō, *n.* A common perennial plant of Europe and N. America, with finely divided leaves, white flowers, and a strong scent.

yaw, yô, *v.i.* To deviate from course, as a ship; to swerve from course by rotating about the vertical axis, as an aircraft, rocket, or the like.—*n.* A sudden deviation of a ship from its course; the rotational movement of an aircraft, rocket, or the like about a vertical axis.

yawn, yôn, *v.i.* To have the mouth open involuntarily with a long inhalation of air, through drowsiness or dullness; to open wide; to stand open, as a chasm, gulf, or the like.—*v.t.* To say or express with a yawn. —*n.* An involuntary opening of the mouth from drowsiness; a gaping or opening wide.

Y-chro•mo•some, wī′krō•mǝ•sōm, *n.* The sex chromosome carrying or associated with male characteristics, occurring with one X-chromosome in males.

ye, thē, *spelling pronunciation* yē, *def. art.* An old written or printed form of 'the': as, *Ye* Olde Pub.

yea, yā, *adv.* Yes: used in affirmation or assent only in oral voting.

year, yēr, *n.* The period of the earth's revolution around the sun, a period of 365 or 366 days, divided into 12 calendar months and now considered as beginning January 1 and ending December 31; a space of 12 calendar months considered from any point: to be gone a *year;* a period out of every 12 months devoted to a certain activity: an academic *year; pl.,* age: big for one's *years.* **—year by year,** during or with each succeeding year. **—year in, year out,** from the beginning to the end of each succeeding year; always.

year•book, yēr′bûk, *n.* A book giving facts about the year, its seasons, festivals, dates, or the like: a high school *yearbook;* a book published annually, each issue containing new or additional information, of general or special nature, in regard to matters pertaining to the year preceding or the year following publication.

year•ling, yēr′ling, *n.* An animal one year old or in the second year of its age.—*a.* A year old.

year•long, yēr′lông′, yēr′long′, *a.* Lasting for a year.

year•ly, yēr′lē, *a.* Pertaining to a year, or to each year; done, made, happening, appearing, or coming once a year, or every year: a *yearly* trip; annual; continuing for a year; lasting but a year.—*adv.* Once a year; annually; every year.

yearn, yern, *v.i.* To feel a deep desire; to be filled with longing; to have a wistful feeling. **—yearn•ing,** *n.*

year-round, yēr′rownd′, *a.* Continuing, lasting, or operating the entire year: a resort open *year-round.*

yeast, yēst, *n.* A yellowish, semifluid substance consisting of the cells of certain minute fungi, which appears in liquids containing sugar, used to induce fermentation in the manufacture of alcoholic liquors, esp. beer, and as a leaven to render bread light and spongy.

yeast•y, yē′stē, *a.,* **-i•er, -i•est.** Of, containing, or resembling yeast; spumy, frothy, or foamy: *yeasty* waves; light, trifling, or frivolous.

yell, yel, *v.i.* To cry out with a strong, loud, clear sound; to scream with pain, fright, rage, or the like; to cheer.—*v.t.* To utter or tell by yelling.—*n.* A cry uttered by yelling; a chant or shout of fixed words or sounds, adopted by a college, group, or the like.

yel•low, yel′ō, *a.* Of a bright color like that of gold, butter, or lemons; having the yellowish skin characteristic of Mongolians; noting or pertaining to the Mongolian race; jaundiced. *Informal.* Cowardly: a man with a *yellow* streak; sensational, esp. morbidly or offensively sensational: said of newspapers and the like: *yellow* journalism; envious.—*n.* A yellow color, between orange and green on the spectrum; a yellow pigment or dye; the yolk of an egg.—*v.t., v.i.* To make or become yellow. **—yel•low•ish,** yel′ō•ish, *a.*

yel•low•bird, yel′ō•bǝrd, *n.* The yellow warbler; the

ǎ- hat, fāte, fāre, fäther; e- met, mē; i- pin, pīne; o- not, nōte, ôrb, moove (move), boy, pownd;
u- cūbe, bûll, tük (took); ch- chin; th- thick, then; zh- vizhon (vision); ǝ- ǝgo, takǝn, pencǝl, lemǝn, bǝrd (bird).

goldfinch.

yel·low fe·ver, *n.* An acute, dangerous, often fatal infectious disease of warm climates, transmitted by the bite of a mosquito, and characterized by jaundice, vomiting, hemorrhages, and fever. Also **yel·low jack.**

yel·low·ham·mer, yel/ō·ham·ər, *n.* A European bunting, the male of which is marked with bright yellow. *Informal.* The flicker of N. America.

yel·low jack, *n.* Yellow fever; a flag flown by ships that are under quarantine.

yel·low jack·et, yel/ō jak·it, *n.* A small, social wasp having bright yellow stripes or markings, and usu. nesting in the ground.

yel·low war·bler, *n.* A small American warbler, the male of which has a bright yellow plumage streaked with brown on the under parts.

yelp, yelp, *v.i.* To give a quick, sharp, shrill cry, as dogs, foxes, or the like; to call or cry out sharply, as from surprise, pain, or excitement.—*v.t.* To utter or express by or as by yelps.—*n.* A quick, sharp bark or cry.

yen, yen, *n. Informal.* An intense desire or longing; a craving or want.—*v.i.,* **yenned, yen·ning.** *Informal.* To crave; to long; to yearn.

yeo·man, yō/mən, *n. pl.,* **-men.** A petty officer in the Navy; formerly, one of a class of lesser freeholders, ranking below the gentry, who cultivated their own land and were early admitted in England to political rights.

yeo·man·ry, yō/mən·rē, *n.* Yeomen collectively.

yes, yes, *adv.* Used for expressing agreement or consent: opposed to *no: Yes,* I will go. Used in contradicting a preceding negative request or assertion: He didn't go there. Oh, *yes* he did! Used, usu. interrogatively, to express doubt, hesitation, or inquisitiveness: *Yes?* Who's there? What is more; moreover: The painting is good, *yes,* very good.—*n. pl.,* **yes·es.** An affirmative approval; aye.

ye·shi·va, ye·shi·vah, yə·shē/və, *n. pl.,* **-vas, -vahs, -voth,** yə·shē/vōt. A Jewish educational institution, as an orthodox seminary, a school for studying the Talmud, or a day school in which both secular and religious subjects are studied.

yes man, *n. Informal.* A subordinate who ingratiatingly agrees with or supports all suggestions or proposals of his superior.

yes·ter·day, yes/tər·dē, yes/tər·dā, *n.* The day next before the present; time not long gone by.—*a., adv.*

yes·ter·year, yes/tər·yēr, *n.* Last year; some time just recently past.—*adv.*

yet, yet, *adv.* At this time or now: while *yet* young; thus far; hitherto, often accompanied by *as:* I have not met him *as yet.* At or before some future time; before all is done: He'll suffer *yet.* Still, used esp. with comparatives: *yet* more surprising; in addition; over and above; further; though the case be such; nevertheless.—*conj.* Nevertheless; notwithstanding; however: He looks fine, *yet* he is not well.

yet·i, yet/ē, *n.* Abominable snowman.

yew, ū, *n.* An evergreen tree of moderate height, a native of the Old World, having a thick, dark foliage.

Yid·dish, yid/ish, *a.* Of or pertaining to the Yiddish language; expressed in Yiddish.—*n.* A language of High German derivation containing vocabulary additions from the Hebrew and Slavic languages, written in Hebrew characters, and spoken by Jews of eastern Europe, their descendants in other countries, and by Jewish emigrants.

yield, yēld, *v.t.* To give forth or produce; to produce or furnish as payment, profit, or interest: an investment *yielding* six per cent; to give up, as to superior power or authority: to *yield* a military position to the enemy; to give up or surrender, as oneself: to *yield* oneself to the temptation to sleep late; to give up or over; relinquish: to *yield* one's place in line.—*v.i.* To give a return, as for labor expended; produce or bear; to surrender or submit, as to superior power: The enemy *yielded* in surrender. To give way to influence, en-

treaty, argument, or the like: He *yielded* to the arguments of the other jurors. To give place or precedence, followed by *to:* to *yield* to a rival; to give way to force or pressure, so as to move, bend, collapse, or the like.—*n.* The act of yielding or producing; that which is yielded; the quantity or amount yielded; the return or profit from a financial transaction or investment.

yield·ing, yēl/ding, *a.* Ready to submit, comply, or yield; compliant; unresisting; flexible; productive.

yip, yip, *v.i.,* **yipped, yip·ping.** To yelp or bark sharply, as a puppy.—*n.* The sound made by young dogs.

Y.M.C.A., YMCA, *n.* Abbreviation for Young Men's Christian Association.

yo·del, yo·dle, yōd/əl, *v.t., v.i.,* **-deled, -del·ing, -dled, -dling.** To sing like the Swiss and Tyrolese mountaineers, by suddenly changing from the natural voice to the falsetto, and vice versa; to yell or call in the same manner.—*n.* **—yo·del·er, yo·dler,** *n.*

yo·ga, yō/gə, *n.* (*Sometimes cap.*) The mystical union of the human soul with the universal spirit; a system of physical and mental exercises devised to effect such a union or to develop physical and spiritual health through the withdrawal of the senses from all external objects and the unbroken meditation upon some principle or esp. significant object. **—yo·gic,** yō/gik, *a.*

yo·gi, yō/gē, *n. pl.,* **-gis.** One who practices or teaches yoga.

yo·gurt, yō/gərt, *n.* A thickened, fermented milk product made by treatment with bacteria cultures and usu. eaten as a health or diet food.

yoke, yōk, *n.* A contrivance for joining together a pair of draft animals, esp. oxen, usu. consisting of a crosspiece with two bow-shaped pieces beneath, one at each end, each bow enclosing the head of an animal; a pair of draft animals fastened together by a yoke; something resembling a yoke or a bow of a yoke in form or use; the part of a horse's double harness supporting a wagon tongue; a shaped piece in a garment, fitted about or below the neck, or about the hips, from which the rest of the garment hangs; an emblem or token of subjection; something that couples or binds together, or a bond or tie: the *yoke* of matrimony.—*v.t.,* **yoked, yok·ing.** To put a yoke on; to join or couple by means of a yoke; to attach, as a draft animal, to a plow or vehicle; to join, couple, link, or unite.—*v.i.* To be or become joined, linked, or united.

yo·kel, yō/kəl, *n.* A rustic or countryman; a country bumpkin.

yolk, yōk, *n.* The yellow part of an egg suspended in the white portion or albumen; an oily secretion from the skin of sheep which renders the pile soft and pliable.

Yom Kip·pur, yom kip/ər, *n.* Day of Atonement.

yon, yon, *a., adv.* yonder.

yon·der, yon/dər, *a.* Being at a distance within view or indicated.—*adv.* At or in that place, as one relatively distant or indicated; there.

yore, yōr, yôr, *n.* Many years ago; the distant past, usu. preceded by *of:* castles *of yore.*

York·shire pud·ding, yôrk/shər, *n.* A pudding made of unsweetened batter, baked under meat, so as to catch the drippings.

you, ū, *unstressed* yû, *pron.*—*poss.* **your** or **yours.** The pronoun of the second person, orig. the objective plural of *ye,* but now used regularly as either objective or nominative and with either plural or singular meaning but always, when used as subject, taking a plural verb; one, or persons generally: *You* can get there by bus.

you'd, ūd. Contraction of you had or you would.

you'll, ūl, *unstressed* yûl. Contraction of you will or you shall.

young, yung, *a.* Being in the first or early stage of life or growth; not old; having the appearance of early life; fresh or vigorous; pertaining to or characteristic of early life or youth; having little experience; raw; green; being younger or junior to another having the same name; being in the early part of existence; the *young* corporation; new.—*n.* Young people or youth, collectively; the offspring of animals. —**with young**, pregnant.

young•ling, yəng′ling, *n.* A young person; an animal in the first part of life; a novice; one with little or no experience.—*a.* Young.

young•ster, yəng′stər, *n.* A young person; a lad.

your, yûr, *unstressed* yər, *pronominal a.* Pertaining or belonging to you; a possessive of **you**.

you're, ûr, *unstressed* yər. Contraction of you are.

yours, yûrz, *pron.* That or those which belong to you; a possessive of **you**: used predicatively, with or without direct reference to a preceding noun: That coat is *yours;* which is *yours?*

your•self, yûr•self′, yər•self′, *pron. pl.,* -**selves**, yûr•selvz′, yər•selvz′. You, not another or others; you, in your own person or individually: used reflexively: Did you make that *yourself?* Used for distinctiveness or emphasis: Only you *yourself* can find the right answer.

youth, ûth, *n. pl.,* **youth, youths**, ûths, ûᵗhz. The state or quality of being young; youthfulness; the part of life between childhood and manhood; a young individual, esp. a young man; young persons collectively.

youth•ful, ûth′fəl, *a.* Being in the early stage of life; young; characteristic of or pertaining to youth; fresh or vigorous, as in youth.

you've, ûv, *unstressed* yûv. Contraction of you have.

yowl, yowl, *v.i.* To give a long distressful or mournful cry, as a dog. —*n.* A long distressful or mournful cry, as that of a dog; a howl.

Yo-Yo, yō′yō, *n. pl.,* -**Yos**. *Trademark.* A toy made of two wheellike disks joined by a center piece holding a string which winds and unwinds while the player holds an end of the string.

yt•ter•bi•um, i•tər′bē•əm, *n.* A metallic element occurring in either bivalent or trivalent form.

yt•tri•um, i′trē•əm, *n.* A rare, grayish, metallic element, found in trivalent form in combination with rare earth elements, and used in nuclear technology, metallurgy, and other industrial applications.

yuc•ca, yək′ə, *n.* A large plant of the lily family, native to N. America, with white flowers in large panicles, and long rigid pointed leaves.

yule, ûl, *n.* Christmas, or the festival of Christmas.

yule log, *n.* Traditionally, a large log of wood forming the basis of a Christmas Eve fire.

yule•tide, ûl′tīd, *n. (Often cap.)* The time or season of Yule or Christmas.

yum•my, yəm′ē, *a.,* -**mi•er**, -**mi•est**. *Informal.* Delicious; delectable; appealing to the various senses.

Y.W.C.A., YWCA, *n.* Abbreviation for Young Women's Christian Association.

Z

Z, z, zē, *n.* The twenty-sixth and final letter of the English alphabet and the nineteenth consonant; something designated by or having the shape of the letter Z or z.

z, zē, *n.* An unknown.

za•ny, zā′nē, *n. pl.,* -**nies**. Any apish buffoon; a clown; a silly person or simpleton.—*a.,* -**ni•er**, -**ni•est**. Characteristic of or pertaining to a zany; humorous in a slapstick or outlandish manner. —**za•ni•ly**, *adv.* —**za•ni•ness**, *n.*

zeal, zēl, *n.* Passionate ardor in the pursuit of anything; eagerness in any cause or behalf; earnestness; enthusiasm.

zeal•ot, zel′ət, *n.* One who is zealous or full of zeal; one carried away by excess of zeal; a fanatical partisan.

zeal•ous, zel′əs, *a.* Inspired with zeal; ardent in the pursuit of a goal or cause; fervent; eager; earnest.

ze•bra, zē′brə, *n. pl.,* -**bras, -bra**. An African mammal, related to the horse and ass, and having a whitish body striped with numerous brownish-black or black bands.

ze•bu, zē′bū, *n.* A bovine animal having a large hump over the shoulders and a very large dewlap, widely domesticated in Asia and Africa.

zed, zed, *n.* The British name for the letter Z.

Zen, zen, *n.* A form of Mahayana Buddhism practiced in China and Japan which asserts that enlightenment can be reached directly through self-discipline, meditation, and intuition rather than through the study of the scriptures.

ze•nith, zē′nith, *n.* The vertical point of the heavens at any place, or the point right above a spectator's head; the highest point, as of a person's career; the culminating point.

zeph•yr, zef′ər, *n.* The west wind; any soft, mild breeze; a light, fine fabric or yarn for knitting; any of various things of fine, light quality.

zep•pe•lin, zep′ə•lən, *n. (Often cap.)* A rigid dirigible with internal gas cells supporting the long, cylindrical body.

ze•ro, zēr′ō, *n. pl.,* -**ros, -roes**. The symbol 0; a cipher; the number that indicates the absence of quantity; the origin of any kind of measurement; the point from which all divisions of a scale are measured in either a positive or negative direction, as on a thermometer; a temperature registering zero on a thermometer; a person or thing of no importance; nonentity; the lowest point or degree; nadir; nothing; nil.—*a.* Of, pertaining to, or being zero; nonexistent; absent, lacking; having limited or no visibility, as an atmospheric ceiling.

ze•ro hour, *n.* The time set for the beginning of an attack or any planned maneuver. *Informal.* The time or moment at which anything critical or decisive takes place.

zest, zest, *n.* That which serves to enhance enjoyment or to add flavor; relish; keen enjoyment; gusto, usu. followed by *for.* —**zest•y**, *a.,* -**i•er**, -**i•est**.

zig•zag, zig′zag, *n.* A line, course, or progression characterized by sharp turns first to one side and then to the other; one of a series of such turns, as in a line or a path.—*a.* Proceeding or formed in a zigzag.—*adv.* In a zigzag manner.—*v.i.,* **zagged, zag•ging**. To proceed in a zigzag line or course.

zinc, zingk, *n.* A bluish-white, metallic element occurring in combination, used as a protective covering or coating, as a component in alloys, as a reducing agent, and as an electrode in a voltaic battery.

zinc ox•ide, *n.* An amorphous white powder, primarily used in paint pigments, cosmetics, and as an antiseptic or astringent in medicine.

---

a- hat, fāte, fāre, fäther; **e-** met, mē; **i-** pin, pīne; **o-** not, nōte, ôrb, moove (move), boy, pownd; **u-** cūbe, bŭll, tûk (took); **ch-** chin; **th-** thick, ᵗhen; **zh-** vizhon (vision); **ə-** əgo, takən, pencəl, lemən, bərd (bird).

zing, zing, *n.* A sharp, high-pitched, whining sound, as of an object moving swiftly through the air; vitality; enthusiasm.—*v.i.* To make a sharp, high-pitched sound.

zin·ni·a, zin′ē·ə, zin′yə, *n.* A plant cultivated in many varieties for its showy flowers in a wide range of color.

Zi·on, zī′ən, *n.* A hill in Jerusalem, site of David's palace and temple, and the center of ancient Hebrew worship; the Israelites; heaven as the final gathering place of true believers.

Zi·on·ism, zī′ə·niz·əm, *n.* A modern plan or movement to colonize Hebrews in Palestine, the land of Zion; a movement to secure for such Jews as cannot or will not be assimilated in the country of their adoption a national homeland in Palestine, part of which now forms the state of Israel. —**Zi·on·ist,** *n.*

zip, zip, *n.* A sudden, brief, hissing sound, as of a flying bullet. *Informal.* Energy or vim.—*v.i.,* **zipped, zip·ping.** To make or move with a zipping or hissing sound. *Informal.* To proceed or act with energy and rapidity: to *zip* to the store and back.

zip, zip, *v.t.,* **zipped, zip·ping.** To fasten or unfasten with a zipper; to enclose or release by opening or closing a zipper: to *zip* papers into a briefcase.—*v.i.* To become fastened or unfastened through the use of a zipper.

ZIP Code, Zip Code, *n.* The system to simplify mail sorting and delivery, consisting of a number of five digits for identification of the state, the city or district, and the postal zone in U.S. delivery areas.

zip·per, zip′ər, *n.* A fastener consisting of metal or plastic toothed tracks set along each of two facing edges and interlocked or separated when an attached piece which slides between them is pulled.

zip·py, zip′ē, *a.,* **-pi·er, -pi·est.** Energetic; peppy; lively; full of vim; brisk.

zir·con, zər′kon, *n.* A common mineral which occurs in small, opaque or transparent prismatic crystals: translucent specimens are classified and used as gems.

zir·co·ni·um, zər·kō′nē·əm, *n.* A hard, grayish, metallic element obtained from the mineral zircon, used in the metallurgic, ceramic, and chemical industries, as an abrasive, and as structural material for nuclear reactors.

zith·er, zith′ər, *n.* A flat, stringed musical instrument consisting of a sounding box with 30 to 40 strings, played with the fingertips and a small pick.

zo·di·ac, zō′dē·ak, *n.* An imaginary belt encircling the heavens, and containing twelve constellations and their twelve astrological signs; a circular or elliptical diagram representing this belt, and usu. containing pictures of the animals and other symbols associated with the constellations and signs. —**zo·di·a·cal,** zō·dī′ə·kəl, *a.*

zom·bie, zom·bi, zom′bē, *n.* A snake deity of West African, Haitian, and southern U.S. voodoo cults; according to voodoo belief, the supernatural power of reanimating a corpse; a human body made an automaton by such a power or by having its soul stolen by sorcery; a person who looks or behaves like a zombie.

zon·al, zōn′əl, *a.* Having the character of or pertaining to a zone.

zone, zōn, *n.* Any continuous tract or area, usu. forming a belt about an object or extending about a point, which differs in some respect or is distinguished for some purpose from adjoining tracts or areas, or within which certain distinguishing circumstances exist or are established: a wheat *zone;* a numbered division of a metropolitan area, so designated to aid in the sorting and distribution of mail; an area or district in a city or town under special restrictions as to buildings; any of five great divisions of the earth's surface, bounded by lines parallel to the equator and named according to the prevailing temperature.—*v.t.,* **-zoned, zon·ing.** To encircle with or surround as with a zone, girdle, or belt; to mark with zones or bands; to divide into zones, tracts, or areas.—*v.i.* To be formed into a zone or zones.

zoo, zoo, *n. pl.,* **zoos.** A park or other area, usu. with both an indoor and outdoor display of various living animals.

zo·ol·o·gy, zō·ol′ə·jē, *n.* That science which treats of the natural history of animals or their structure, physiology, classification, habits, and distribution. —**zo·o·log·i·cal,** zō·ə·loj′ə·kəl, *a.* —**zo·o·log·i·cal·ly,** *adv.* —**zo·ol·o·gist,** zō·ol′ə·jist, *n.*

zoom, zoom, *v.i.* To make a continuous humming sound; to drive an airplane suddenly and very sharply upward at great speed for a short distance; to go rapidly away from or toward a subject with a camera, keeping the subject in focus, giving the effect of greater or lesser distance.—*n.* An act or sound of zooming.

zuc·chi·ni, zoo·kē′nē, *n. pl.,* **-ni, -nis.** A variety or kind of cylindrical, slender, summer squash, the skin of which is dark green and smooth.

zwie·back, zwī′bak, swī′bak, *n.* A kind of bread or biscuit, baked, cut into slices, and toasted.

zy·gote, zī′gōt, zig′ōt, *n.* A cell formed by the union of two gametes; the organism produced from this type of cell.

METRIC SYSTEM

Linear Measure

Unit	Number of meters	U.S. equivalent
micron (μ)	0.000001	0.00003937 inch, 0.03937 mil
millimeter (mm)	0.001	0.03937 inch, 39.37 mils
centimeter (cm)	0.01	0.3937 inch
decimeter (dm)	0.1	3.937 inches
meter (m)	1	39.37 inches
dekameter (dkm)	10	10.93 yards, 32.81 feet
hectometer (hm)	100	109.36 yards, 328.1 feet
kilometer (km)	1000	0.6214 mile

Area

Unit	Number of centares	U.S. equivalent
square millimeter (mm²)	0.000001	0.00155 square inch
square centimeter (cm²)	0.0001	0.155 square inch
centare (ca) or square meter (m²)	1	10.76 square feet
deciare (da)	10	11.96 square yards
aretare (a) or square dekameter (dkm²)	100	119.60 square yards
dekare (dka)	1,000	0.247 acre
hectare (ha) or square hectometer (hm²)	10,000	2.471 acres
square kilometer (km²)	1,000,000	0.386 square mile

Capacity

Unit	Number of liters	Metric equivalent cubic centimeters	U.S. equivalent cubic	U.S. equivalent dry	U.S. equivalent liquid
milliliter (ml)	0.001	1	0.061 cubic inch	0.0018 pint	0.034 fluidounce
centiliter (cl)	0.01	10	0.61 cubic inch	0.018 pint	0.338 fluidounce
deciliter (dl)	0.1	100	6.10 cubic inch	0.18 pint	3.381 fluidounces
liter (l)	1	1,000	61.02 cubic inch	0.908 quart	1.057 quarts
dekaliter (dkl)	10	10,000	0.35 cubic foot	1.14 pecks	2.643 gallons
hectoliter (hl)	100	100,000	3.53 cubic feet	2.84 bushels	26.425 gallons
kiloliter (kl)	1,000	1,000,000	1.31 cubic yards	28.38 bushels	264.25 gallons

Volume

Unit	Number of steres	U.S. equivalent
cubic millimeter (mm³)	0.000000001	0.000061 cubic inch, 0.016 minim
cubic centimeter (cm³ or cc)	0.000001	0.061 cubic inch
cubic decimeter (dm³)	0.001	61.02 cubic inches
decistere (ds)	0.1	3.53 cubic feet
stere (s) or cubic meter (m³)	1	1.308 cubic yards, 35.31 cubic feet
dekastere (dks)	10	13.079 cubic yards
cubic dekameter (dkm³)	1,000	1,307.943 cubic yards

Mass and Weight

Unit	Number of grams	U.S. equivalent (Avoirdupois weight)
milligram (mg)	0.001	0.0154 grain
centigram (cg)	0.01	0.154 grain
decigram (dg)	0.1	1.543 grains
gram (g or gm)	1	0.0353 ounce, 15.43 grains
dekagram (dkg)	10	0.353 ounce
hectogram (hg)	100	3.527 ounces
kilogram (kg)	1,000	2.205 pounds
metric ton (MT or t)	1,000,000	1.102 tons, 2,204.6 pounds

PERIODIC TABLE OF THE ELEMENTS

Group numbers appear above columns in Roman numerals.
Atomic number in the upper left corner of each box.
Element and its symbol in the center of each box.
Atomic weight based on carbon-12, 12.01115, in the lower center of each box.
Numbers in the table in parentheses are mass numbers of the most stable isotopes.

I A	II A	III B	IV B	V B	VI B	VII B	VIII			I B	II B	III A	IV A	V A	VI A	VII A	Noble gases
1 Hydrogen H 1.00797																	2 Helium He 4.0026
3 Lithium Li 6.939	4 Beryllium Be 9.0122											5 Boron B 10.811	6 Carbon C 12.01115	7 Nitrogen N 14.0067	8 Oxygen O 15.9994	9 Fluorine F 18.9984	10 Neon Ne 20.183
11 Sodium Na 22.9898	12 Magnesium Mg 24.312											13 Aluminum Al 26.9815	14 Silicon Si 28.086	15 Phosphorus P 30.9738	16 Sulfur S 32.064	17 Chlorine Cl 35.453	18 Argon Ar 39.948
19 Potassium K 39.102	20 Calcium Ca 40.08	21 Scandium Sc 44.956	22 Titanium Ti 47.90	23 Vanadium V 50.942	24 Chromium Cr 51.996	25 Manganese Mn 54.9380	26 Iron Fe 55.847	27 Cobalt Co 58.9332	28 Nickel Ni 58.71	29 Copper Cu 63.56	30 Zinc Zn 65.37	31 Gallium Ga 69.72	32 Germanium Ge 72.59	33 Arsenic As 74.922	34 Selenium Se 78.96	35 Bromine Br 79.904	36 Krypton Kr 83.80
37 Rubidium Rb 85.47	38 Strontium Sr 87.62	39 Yttrium Y 88.905	40 Zirconium Zr 91.22	41 Niobium Nb 92.906	42 Molybdenum Mo 95.94	43 Technetium Tc (97)	44 Ruthenium Ru 101.07	45 Rhodium Rh 102.905	46 Palladium Pd 106.4	47 Silver Ag 107.87	48 Cadmium Cd 112.40	49 Indium In 114.82	50 Tin Sn 118.69	51 Antimony Sb 121.75	52 Tellurium Te 127.60	53 Iodine I 126.9044	54 Xenon Xe 131.30
55 Cesium Cs 132.905	56 Barium Ba 137.34	57–71 Lanthanide Series (see below)	72 Hafnium Hf 178.49	73 Tantalum Ta 180.948	74 Tungsten W 183.85	75 Rhenium Re 186.2	76 Osmium Os 190.2	77 Iridium Ir 192.20	78 Platinum Pt 195.09	79 Gold Au 196.967	80 Mercury Hg 200.59	81 Thallium Tl 204.37	82 Lead Pb 207.19	83 Bismuth Bi 208.980	84 Polonium Po (209)	85 Astatine At (210)	86 Radon Rn (222)
87 Francium Fr (223)	88 Radium Ra (226)	89–103 Actinide Series (see below)															

Lanthanide Series														
57 Lanthanum La 138.91	58 Cerium Ce 140.12	59 Praseodymium Pr 140.907	60 Neodymium Nd 144.24	61 Promethium Pm (145)	62 Samarium Sm 150.35	63 Europium Eu 151.96	64 Gadolinium Gd 157.25	65 Terbium Tb 158.924	66 Dysprosium Dy 162.50	67 Holmium Ho 164.930	68 Erbium Er 167.26	69 Thulium Tm 168.934	70 Ytterbium Yb 173.04	71 Lutecium Lu 174.97

Actinide Series														
89 Actinium Ac (227)	90 Thorium Th 232.038	91 Protactinium Pa (231)	92 Uranium U 238.04	93 Neptunium Np (237)	94 Plutonium Pu (239)	95 Americium Am (243)	96 Curium Cm (247)	97 Berkelium Bk (247)	98 Californium Cf (251)	99 Einsteinium Es (254)	100 Fermium Fm (253)	101 Mendelevium Md (252)	102 Nobelium No (253)	103 Lawrencium Lw (257)

Atomic weights corrected to correspond with values of the Commission on Atomic Weights as of 1963.

PUNCTUATION

Introduction

Punctuation in written material is often as important as the correct placement of signs and symbols in mathematical calculations. The proper placement of commas, periods, and other punctuation makes the difference between a clear, well-constructed statement and a muddled one. Following are the basic rules for proper punctuation.

PERIOD

1. A period (.) is placed at the end of declarative and imperative sentences and after abbreviations and initials:

Send a letter to Mr. D. M. Green.
Hand me a 1½ in. nail.

2. No period is used at the end of a sentence contained within a longer sentence:

The defendant's reply, "I never saw this man before," surprised everyone.

3. A period is placed after numbers or letters which precede items in a list:

1. the early period before 1800
b. parrots and their allies

QUESTION MARK

4. A question mark (?) is placed after a direct question:

Where will you be this summer?

5. A question mark follows an interrogative sentence even when part of a larger sentence:

How can this be done? I wondered.

6. If intended interrogatively, a declarative or imperative sentence ends with a question mark:

This is what we've been waiting for?

7. A question mark is not used after an indirect question:

He asked how long we'd be staying.

8. A question mark enclosed in parentheses is used to indicate uncertainty:

He said he'll be back on May 5 (?).

EXCLAMATION POINT

9. An exclamation point (!) is used after interjections and at the end of a sentence for emphasis or to indicate strong emotion:

Aha! I caught you!
That's incredible!

APOSTROPHE

10. An apostrophe (') is used in contractions to indicate omitted letters or words, and in dates to indicate omitted numerals.

I've never heard of him.
Come at eight o'clock.
He graduated in '46.

11. An apostrophe with an *s* ('s) is added to form the possessive case of most singular nouns; exceptions are such words as *conscience, righteousness,* etc., and certain ancient or Biblical names, which take an apostrophe without *s.*

man's hat
horse's stable
Marx's theories
Strauss's waltz
appearance' sake
Moses' tablet

12. An apostrophe only is added to form the possessive case of plural nouns ending in *s;* plural nouns not ending in *s* take an apostrophe with *s:*

boys' fathers
men's ties
geese's grain
the Joneses' estates

13. An apostrophe with *s* is added to form the possessive case of indefinite pronouns not ending in *s;* indefinite pronouns ending in *s* take an apostrophe only:

somebody's scarf
others' rights

14. An apostrophe with *s* is used to form the plural of letters, signs, symbols, and numbers; plurals of years, however, are commonly formed with *s* alone:

"Occurred" is spelled with two "r's."
The number is followed by four "8's."
the 1890s (or 1890's)

QUOTATION MARKS

15. Quotation marks (" ") are used to enclose direct quotations, ironic and slang expressions, nicknames, titles of short works, and sections of longer works:

Peter cried, "Let's go!"
"When," the children asked, "are we going to the circus?"
Our "leader," it seems, had vanished.
William H. Bonney was known as "Billy the Kid."
Chapter 2 is titled "Ancient Music."
He sang "The Wanderer," by Schubert.

16. Quotation marks enclose words, phrases, etc., referred to in a sentence:

The words "once upon a time" are used to begin many children's stories.

17. Single quotation marks (' ') enclose quotations within quotations:

"I think," Steve replied, "that George

said, 'No, I am not going.'"

"Spell 'leisure,'" he ordered.

18. Single quotation marks are often used to enclose philosophical and theological terms that have a special meaning:

'beatific vision'

ELLIPSIS POINTS

19. Ellipsis points (. . .) are used to indicate material which has been omitted from a quoted passage. Use three dots to indicate an omission within a sentence; punctuation marks may be retained on either side of the ellipsis, but this is optional:

Samuel Johnson said, "Praise . . . owes its value only to its scarcity."

20. Use four dots—a period followed by three dots—if the omitted material is (1) the end of a sentence, (2) the beginning of the next sentence, (3) the whole next sentence, or (4) the next paragraph or more. If the sentence ends with a question mark or exclamation point, use this punctuation followed by three dots. If the beginning of a sentence is omitted, the sentence will usually begin with a lower-case letter:

In *Walden* Thoreau observed: "Public opinion is a weak tyrant. . . . What a man thinks of himself . . . determines his fate."

As Shaw remarked, "Liberty means responsibility. . . . most men dread it."

COMMA

21. Use commas (,) to set off a series of three or more items joined by *and, or,* or *nor. Etc.,* when used, should be set off by commas:

Marcia, Tony, and Judy went downtown.

Pins, earrings, lockets, etc., are on sale this month.

22. Do not use commas if the items are joined by conjunctions and are relatively simple:

I don't know whether to divide by 2 or 3 or 6.

23. Use a comma to set off a direct quotation:

"It's a terrible book," he said.

John asked, "How much does it cost?"

24. A quotation which is the subject or predicate nominative of a sentence is not set off by a comma:

"We shall overcome" was his motto.

His motto was "We shall overcome."

25. Titles following a proper name are set off by commas:

James Horton, president of Acme Corporation, is on the committee.

26. Appositives are set off by commas:

The janitor, Mr. Brown, is sick today.

27. Words of direct address and interjections are set off by commas:

Charles, go to the back door.

Well, we must try another method.

28. Two or more adjectives preceding a noun are separated by commas, except when the adjective and noun are a unit:

We had a short, rainy spring last year.

All the large electric lights were out.

29. Two or more phrases referring to a single following word are separated by commas:

These shocking, though not unexpected, events could lead to panic.

30. Use commas before conjunctions joining two independent clauses in compound sentences, except when the clauses are short and closely related:

That is an interesting city, but it's too crowded to appeal to me.

Tom walked down the road and his brother followed him.

31. Dependent clauses or participial phrases at the beginning of a sentence are set off by commas, unless a part of the verb:

Although we advised her not to, she went to California.

Walking beside the road was an old man.

32. Dependent clauses at the end of a sentence are set off by commas if not essential to the basic meaning of the sentence:

She went to California, although we advised her not to.

We finally agreed to return if we could meet again next week.

33. Introductory adverbial phrases, unless quite brief, are followed by a comma except when they immediately precede the verb:

While closing the curtains, she noticed a man walking past.

After dinner we went for a walk.

Into the room rushed several dogs.

34. Adverbial clauses or phrases between subject and verb are set off by commas:

Barton, after consulting with several authorities, proposed changes.

35. An adjectival clause or phrase is set off by commas if dropping it would not change the meaning of the noun:

The winning bicycle, which weighed only 12 pounds, was made in France.

36. A parenthetical clause, phrase, or word is set off by commas:

This month there have been, as far as we know, two accidents.

37. Expressions such as "however," "therefore," "after all," etc., are set off by commas if they break the continuity of thought. If they do not break the continuity or require a pause, commas should not be used:

The answer, perhaps, is to send out a questionnaire.

I therefore demand that you remain.

COMMA (Special Uses)

38. Inverted names, as in a list, have a comma between the last and first name:

Whitman, Walt

Whittier, John Greenleaf

39. Words which together might be misunderstood or awkward to read are separated by commas:

Where he is, is not known.

To Frank, Jones was most polite.

40. Expressions such as *i.e., namely,* and *that is* are set off by commas; sometimes a semicolon or other punctuation precedes:

The discussion centered on the ancient Greek tragic playwrights, i.e., Aeschylus, Sophocles, and Euripides.

The ruling applies only to part-time employees; that is, employees working less than thirty hours weekly.

41. Interrelated contrasting clauses should be separated by a comma:

The bigger they are, the harder they fall.

42. Words which are omitted but understood in context are indicated by the use of a comma:

He had a thousand friends when he was rich; when poor, none.

43. A comma is used to separate an interrogative clause from a declarative clause that it follows:

You'll be here tomorrow night, won't you?

44. The parts of addresses are separated by commas:

He lives at 1414 Whitehall Drive, Brighton, Maryland.

45. Commas are used in dates as follows:

On September 12, 1959, the . . .

Thursday, April 25, is . . .

June 1947 (*no comma*)

12 September 1959 (*no comma*)

46. In numbers of four or more digits, use commas to separate thousands, millions, etc. Commas are not used in ZIP codes, phone numbers, page or serial numbers.

3,421 miles

a population of 20,590,120

page 2189

Chicago, Ill. 60602

47. A comma is used to separate two sets of figures:

In 1940, 159 people died of that disease.

COLON

48. A colon (:) is used to introduce series or lists:

Questionnaires were mailed to three states: Maine, Iowa, and Florida.

The steps are as follows:

1. Construct a triangle. . . .
2. Connect points. . . .

49. A complete sentence, question, or long quotation is introduced by a colon:

One rule is paramount: Do not fire until the order is given.

I quote from his recent speech: "In times such as ours . . . caution is our best policy. . . ."

50. A colon is used to introduce speech in a dialog, and following the introductory address of a speaker:

Father: Has he asked you to marry him?

Julie: Oh no, he . . .

Ladies and Gentlemen:

51. Colons are used to punctuate time indications, Bible references, volume and page references, and ratios as follows; many Catholic Bibles, however, now have a comma in place of a colon:

at exactly 3:48 in the afternoon

I Kings 1:20 (or I Kings 1,20)

American Psychologist 10:17-25

in the ratio of 7:5

SEMICOLON

52. Items in a series are separated by a semicolon (;) when the items contain a comma or other internal punctuation:

The number of games played this season is: team A, 3; team B, 5; team C, 2.

53. Two independent clauses which are not joined by a conjunction are separated by a semicolon:

The old buildings I liked; the new ones were atrocious.

54. If the clauses of a compound sentence are long or internally punctuated, a semicolon is used between them, before the conjunction:

The girls, who had been waiting hours for a chance to see their idol, pressed eagerly forward when he appeared; but their disappointment was great when he swiftly darted into the nearest cab without even acknowledging their presence.

55. A semicolon is used between the independent parts of a sentence that contain commas indicating omitted words:

In Illinois we have thirteen delegates; in Indiana, nine; in Iowa, eight.

DASH

56. A dash (—) is used to indicate a sudden break in thought:

He said—to everyone's amazement—that the Chinese were crossing the border.

57. Dashes may be used to set off a phrase or word repeated for emphasis:

That is the price for one volume—one volume only—not for the set.

58. An unfinished word or sentence is indicated by the use of a dash:

"I'm going to snee—," she cried.

59. A phrase which introduces a series and is understood to be repeated before each item is followed by a dash:

The committee decided—
1. to change the date of meeting;
2. to increase the dues;
3. to hold new elections.

60. Dashes may be used in place of commas to clarify the meaning of a sentence:

The basic ingredients of a cake—flour, sugar, milk, and eggs—were ready.

61. A final clause summarizing a series of ideas in a sentence, or which is an expansion of something in the main clause, is set off by a dash:

I always use the dictionary, the thesaurus, and a grammar—three indispensable aids when writing.

After lunch we toured the caves—the same caves where three men had died.

62. A short dash (–) is used to indicate inclusive or continuing numbers, dates, etc. Do not use with such words as *from* and *between:*

the period 1952–59
11:A.M.–9:00 P.M.
pp. 197–210
Sept. 25, 1962–June 6, 1963
from 1952 to 1959 (*not* from 1952–59)

PARENTHESES

63. An independent part of a sentence or paragraph not directly related to the main statement is enclosed in parentheses [( )]:

Three people (all in the last row) were snoring loudly.

The pool will be open until Labor Day. (Last year it closed August 20.)

64. Parentheses are used to enclose letters or numbers enumerating items in a series, or with numerals or other symbols used appositively:

He traced the development of the symphony by using examples from the works of (1) Haydn, (2) Mozart, and (3) Beethoven.

With each order of twelve (12), enclose a check for two dollars ($2.00).

65. A place name which is not part of an official name but is necessary in a sentence is enclosed in parentheses:

The Pittsburg (Kansas) Historical Society should not be confused with the Pittsburgh (Pennsylvania) Historical Society.

BRACKETS

66. Editorial comments or corrections are set off with brackets ([ ]):

He said, "All those left [mostly women and children] should move back."

D[j]akarta was our last stop.

67. Parenthetical material within parentheses is enclosed in brackets:

After writing several novels (mostly about war experiences [such stories were quite popular]), he began writing plays.

HYPHEN

The dictionary is an invaluable aid in all questions concerning hyphenation, and each specific use of a hyphen should be verified in the dictionary. This guide gives only general rules.

68. A hyphen (-) is used to divide a word at the end of a line when the word continues to the next line. Correct syllabication should always be observed:

Joan worked the problems but had considerable difficulty.

69. A hyphen is used to form most compound words containing the following elements:

cross-eyed	single-pace
great-grandmother	double-edged
light-handed	ill-suited
heavy-laden	well-prepared

70. Hyphens are used between the words of a compound modifier when it precedes the noun but are usually omitted when the modifier follows the noun. Do not hyphenate a compound modifier with an adverb ending in *ly.*

He is a well-known author.
He is well known.
a word-for-word translation
The translation was word for word.
a tight-fitting sweater
a tightly fitting sweater

71. A hyphen is used to form compound nouns that show a combination of qualities or functions. Do not hyphenate chemical compounds:

secretary-treasurer
hydrogen peroxide